West's Law School Advisory Board

CONSTITUTIONAL RIGHTS AND LIBERTIES

CASES—COMMENTS—QUESTIONS

Eighth Edition

By

William B. Lockhart

Late Professor of Law, University of California, Hastings
Dean and Professor of Law Emeritus, University of Minnesota

Yale Kamisar

Clarence Darrow Distinguished University Professor of Law,
University of Michigan

Jesse H. Choper

Earl Warren Professor of Public Law,
University of California, Berkeley

Steven H. Shiffrin

Professor of Law,
Cornell University

Richard H. Fallon, Jr.

Professor of Law
Harvard University

This book is an abridgment of Lockhart, Kamisar, Choper, Shiffrin & Fallon's
"Constitutional Law, Cases—Comments—Questions, Eighth Edition".

AMERICAN CASEBOOK SERIES®

WEST PUBLISHING CO.
ST. PAUL, MINN., 1996

This book is an abridgment of Lockhart, Kamisar, Choper, Shiffrin & Fallon's "Constitutional Law, Cases—Comments—Questions, Eighth Edition", West Publishing Co., 1996.

American Casebook Series, the key symbol appearing on the front cover and the WP symbol are registered trademarks of West Publishing Co. Registered in the U.S. Patent and Trademark Office.

ISBN 0–314–20472–5

TEXT IS PRINTED ON 10% POST CONSUMER RECYCLED PAPER

In memory of

WILLIAM B. LOCKHART

who showed us the way

*

Preface

Casebooks are teaching tools, and this is no exception. What distinguishes this book is its commitment to the proposition that a student's understanding of constitutional law is greatly enriched by exposure to a variety of competing perspectives drawn from the best of legal scholarship. To that end, we have reproduced many selections from the literature or woven them into notes and questions that follow almost every main case.

In the five years since the seventh edition of this book was published, a number of significant decisions have been handed down and a wealth of scholarly commentary has been generated. Accordingly, this new edition represents a complete revision and a fresh reevaluation, for purposes of reediting and reorganizing, of all existing materials. It also constitutes the product of an extensive examination of the recent literature—in an effort to further enrich the notes, comments and questions. In addition to full updating, restructuring has been undertaken where called for by recent developments and to make the materials more effectively teachable.

The most significant change is the addition of a new Chapter 4 on constitutional-criminal procedure with substantial sections on arrest, search and seizure; right to counsel; police interrogation and confessions; and lineups. Other revisions appear in parts of Chapter 11 (Equal Protection) dealing with Affirmative Action (Sec. 2, VI), Discriminations Based on Gender (Sec. 3), and Special Scrutiny for Other Classifications (Sec. 4), for which our newest collaborator has primary responsibility.

The cut-off date for this book is March 1, 1996. Significant cases handed down during the last three months of the 1995–96 Supreme Court Term will appear in a supplement that will be published in August 1996. Important developments thereafter will appear in annual supplements.

Case and statute citations, as well as footnotes, of Court and commentators have been omitted without so specifying; other omissions are indicated by asterisks or by brackets. Numbered footnotes are from the original materials; lettered footnotes are ours. The composition of the Court on any date may be obtained by consulting the Table of Justices in Appendix A, originally prepared by Professor John J. Cound, a compilation of basic biographical data on all the individuals who have ever served on the Court.

Over the years, in the course of preparing eight editions, we have become indebted to many teachers (and students) of constitutional law for their valuable suggestions and insights. The contributions to the first edition by Carl A. Auerbach, John C. Cound and Terrance Sandalow persist to date. The book reviews of Ira C. Lupu, Robert B. McKay, Lester J. Mazor, Charles W. Quick, Norman Redlich, Christopher D. Stone, William W. Van Alstyne and Lawrence G. Wallace have all been very helpful, as have the criticisms and suggestions of Vincent A. Blasi, Arthur E. Bonfield, Robert H. Cole, Mary I. Coombs, Frank

I. Goodman, Kenneth Karst, Michael E. Smith, Laurence H. Tribe, and Jonathan Varat.

Just a few weeks before the completed manuscript went to the printer, our senior colleague, William B. Lockhart, who actively participated in all eight editions of the casebook, died at the age of 89. We were fortunate to have him for so long. He and his new contributions to future editions will be missed.

YALE KAMISAR
JESSE H. CHOPER
STEVEN H. SHIFFRIN
RICHARD H. FALLON, JR.

July, 1996

A Photograph of the Nine Justices of the U.S. Supreme Court, 1995–1996

From left to right, Justice Sandra Day O'Connor, Justice Anthony M. Kennedy, Justice Antonin Scalia, Chief Justice William H. Rehnquist, Justice David H. Souter, Justice Ruth Bader Ginsburg, Justice Clarence Thomas, Justice Stephen G. Breyer and Justice John Paul Stevens.

This photograph is reprinted with the permission of National Geographic Society/Supreme Court Historical Society.

Summary of Contents

*

Table of Contents

*

Table of Cases

The principal cases are in bold type. Cases cited or discussed in the text are roman type. References are to pages. Cases cited in principal cases and within other quoted materials are not included.

CONSTITUTIONAL RIGHTS AND LIBERTIES

CASES—COMMENTS—QUESTIONS

Eighth Edition

*

Chapter 1
NATURE AND SCOPE OF JUDICIAL REVIEW

SECTION 1. ORIGINS, EARLY CHALLENGES, AND CONTINUING CONTROVERSY

"Whoever hath an absolute authority to interpret any written or spoken laws, it is he who is truly the lawgiver, to all intents and purposes, and not the person who first spoke or wrote them."

> —Bishop Hoadly's Sermon, preached
> before the King, 1717.

MARBURY v. MADISON
5 U.S.(1 Cranch) 137, 2 L.Ed. 60 (1803).

[Thomas Jefferson, an Anti-Federalist (or Republican), who defeated John Adams, a Federalist, in the presidential election of 1800, was to take office on March 4, 1801. On January 20, 1801, Adams, the defeated incumbent, nominated John Marshall, Adams' Secretary of State, as fourth Chief Justice of the United States. Marshall assumed office on February 4 but continued to serve as Secretary of State until the end of the Adams administration. During February, the Federalist Congress passed (1) the Circuit Court Act, which, inter alia, doubled the number of federal judges and (2) the Organic Act which authorized appointment of 42 justices-of-the-peace in the District of Columbia. Senate confirmation of Adams' "midnight" appointees, virtually all Federalists, was completed on March 3. Their commissions were signed by Adams and sealed by Acting Secretary of State Marshall, but due to time pressures, several for the justices-of-the-peace (including that of William Marbury) remained undelivered when Jefferson assumed the presidency the next day. Jefferson ordered his new Secretary of State, James Madison, to withhold delivery.

[Late in 1801, Marbury and several others sought a writ of mandamus in the Supreme Court to compel Madison to deliver the commissions. The Court ordered Madison "to show cause why a mandamus should not issue" and the case was set for argument in the 1802 Term.

[While the case was pending, the new Republican Congress—incensed at Adams' efforts to entrench a Federalist judiciary and at the "Federalist" Court's order against a Republican cabinet officer—moved to repeal the Circuit Court Act. Federalist congressmen argued that repeal would be unconstitutional as violative

1

of Art. III's assurance of judicial tenure "during good behavior" and of the Constitution's plan for separation of powers assuring the independence of the Judiciary. It "was in this debate that for the first time since the initiation of the new Government under the Constitution there occurred a serious challenge of the power of the Judiciary to pass upon the constitutionality of Acts of Congress. Hitherto, [it had been the Republicans] who had sustained this power as a desirable curb on Congressional aggression and encroachment on the rights of the States, and they had been loud in their complaints at the failure of the Court to hold the Alien and Sedition laws unconstitutional. Now, however, in 1802, in order to counteract the Federalist argument that the Repeal Bill was unconstitutional and would be so held by the Court, [Republicans] advanced the proposition that the Court did not possess the power." [a]

[The Repeal Law passed early in 1802. To forestall its constitutional challenge in the Supreme Court until the political power of the new administration had been strengthened, Congress also eliminated the 1802 Supreme Court Term. Thus, the Court did not meet between December, 1801 and February, 1803.]

[On] 24th February, the following opinion of the court was delivered by CHIEF JUSTICE MARSHALL: * * *

No cause has been shown, and the present motion is for a mandamus. The peculiar delicacy of this case, the novelty of some of its circumstances, and the real difficulty attending the points which occur in it require a complete exposition of the principles on which the opinion to be given by the court is founded. * * *

1st. Has the applicant a right to the commission he demands? * * *

Mr. Marbury, [since] his commission was signed by the President and sealed by the Secretary of State, was appointed; and as the law creating the office gave the officer a right to hold for five years, independent of the executive, the appointment was not revocable, but vested in the officer legal rights, which are protected by the laws of his country.

To withhold his commission, therefore, is an act deemed by the court not warranted by law, but violative of a vested legal right.[b] * * *

2dly. If he has a right, and that right has been violated, do the laws of his country afford him a remedy?

The very essence of civil liberty certainly consists in the right of every individual to claim the protection of the laws, whenever he receives an injury. One of the first duties of government is to afford that protection. * * *

The government of the United States has been emphatically termed a government of laws, and not of men. It will certainly cease to deserve this high appellation, if the laws furnish no remedy for the violation of a vested legal right. * * *

[W]here the heads of departments are the political or confidential agents of the executive, merely to execute the will of the president, or rather to act in cases

a. 1 Charles Warren, *The Supreme Court in United States History* 215 (1922).

b. Consider William Van Alstyne, *A Critical Guide to Marbury v. Madison,* 1969 Duke L.J. 1, 8: "[T]here is clearly an 'issue' of sorts which preceded any of those touched upon in the opinion. Specifically, it would appear that Marshall should have recused himself in view of his substantial involvement in the background of this controversy. * * * Proof of the status of Marbury's commission not only involved circumstances within the Chief Justice's personal knowledge, it was furnished in the Supreme Court by Marshall's own younger brother who had been with him in his office when, as Secretary of State, he had made out the commissions."

in which the executive possesses a constitutional or legal discretion, nothing can be more perfectly clear than that their acts are only politically examinable. But where a specific duty is assigned by law, and individual rights depend upon the performance of that duty, it seems equally clear that the individual who considers himself injured, has a right to resort to the laws of his country for a remedy.[c]
* * *

It remains to be inquired whether,

3dly. He is entitled to the remedy for which he applies? This depends on,

1st. The nature of the writ applied for; and,

2dly. The power of this court.

1st. The nature of the writ. * * *

This writ, if awarded, would be directed to an officer of government, and its mandate to him would be, to use the words of Blackstone, "to do a particular thing therein specified, which appertains to his office and duty, and which the court has previously determined, or at least supposes, to be consonant to right and justice." Or, in the words of Lord Mansfield, the applicant, in this case, has a right to execute an office of public concern, and is kept out of possession of that right.

These circumstances certainly concur in this case.

Still, to render the mandamus a proper remedy, the officer to whom it is to be directed, must be one to whom, on legal principles, such writ may be directed; and the person applying for it must be without any other specific and legal remedy.

1st. With respect to the officer to whom it would be directed. The intimate political relation subsisting between the President of the United States and the heads of departments, necessarily renders any legal investigation of the acts of one of those high officers peculiarly irksome, as well as delicate; and excites some hesitation with respect to the propriety of entering into such investigation. Impressions are often received without much reflection or examination, and it is not wonderful that in such a case as this the assertion, by an individual, of his legal claims in a court of justice, to which claims it is the duty of that court to attend, should at first view be considered by some, as an attempt to intrude into the cabinet, and to intermeddle with the prerogatives of the executive.

It is scarcely necessary for the court to disclaim all pretensions to such a jurisdiction. An extravagance, so absurd and excessive, could not have been entertained for a moment. The province of the court is, solely, to decide on the rights of individuals, not to inquire how the executive, or executive officers, perform duties in which they have a discretion. Questions in their nature political, or which are, by the constitution and laws, submitted to the executive, can never be made in this court.

But [what] is there in the exalted station of the officer, which shall bar a citizen from asserting, in a court of justice, his legal rights, or shall forbid a court to listen to the claim, or to issue a mandamus, directing the performance of a duty, not depending on executive discretion, but on particular acts of congress, and the general principles of law? * * *

c. Consider Norman Redlich, *The Supreme Court—1833 Term,* 40 N.Y.U.L.Rev. 1, 4 (1965): "[T]he Court could have ruled that, since the President had the power to appoint the judges, he also had the power to deliver the commissions which was in a sense the final act of appointment. Viewed as a component of the act of appointment, the delivery of the commissions could have simply been considered as lying within the discretion of the President."

This, then, is a plain case for a mandamus, either to deliver the commission, or a copy of it from the record; and it only remains to be inquired,

Whether it can issue from this court.

The act to establish the judicial courts of the United States authorizes the supreme court "to issue writs of mandamus, in cases warranted by the principles and usages of law, to any courts appointed, or persons holding office, under the authority of the United States." [d]

The secretary of state, being a person holding an office under the authority of the United States, is precisely within the letter of the description; and if this court is not authorized to issue a writ of mandamus to such an officer, it must be because the law is unconstitutional, and therefore absolutely incapable of conferring the authority, and assigning the duties which its words purport to confer and assign. * * *

In the distribution of [the judicial power of the United States] it is declared that "the supreme court shall have original jurisdiction in all cases affecting ambassadors, other public ministers and consuls, and those in which a state shall be a party. In all other cases, the supreme court shall have appellate jurisdiction."

It has been insisted, at the bar, that as the original grant of jurisdiction, to the supreme and inferior courts, is general, and the clause, assigning original jurisdiction to the supreme court, contains no negative or restrictive words, the power remains to the legislature, to assign original jurisdiction to that court in other cases than those specified in the article which has been recited; provided those cases belong to the judicial power of the United States.

If it had been intended to leave it in the discretion of the legislature to apportion the judicial power between the supreme and inferior courts according to the will of that body, it would certainly have been useless to have proceeded further than to have defined the judicial power, and the tribunals in which it should be vested. The subsequent part of the section is mere surplusage, is

---

d. § 13 of the Judiciary Act of 1789 provided: "That the Supreme Court shall have exclusive jurisdiction of all controversies of a civil nature, where a state is a party, except between a state and its citizens; and except also between a state and citizens of other states, or aliens, in which latter case it shall have original but not exclusive jurisdiction. And shall have exclusively all such jurisdiction of suits or proceedings against ambassadors or other public ministers, or their domestics, or domestic servants, as a court of law can have or exercise consistently with the law of nations; and original, but not exclusive jurisdiction of all suits brought by ambassadors or other public ministers, or in which a consul, or vice consul, shall be a party. And the trial of issues of fact in the Supreme Court in all actions at law against citizens of the United States shall be by jury. The Supreme Court shall also have appellate jurisdiction from the circuit courts and courts of the several states, in the cases hereinafter specially provided for; and shall have power to issue writs of prohibition to the district courts, when proceeding as courts of admiralty and maritime jurisdiction, and writs of mandamus, in cases warranted by the principles and usages of law, to any courts appointed, or persons holding office under the authority of the United States."

Consider Van Alstyne, supra, at 15: "Textually, the provision regarding mandamus says nothing expressly as to whether it is part of original or appellate jurisdiction or both, and the clause itself does not speak at all of 'conferring jurisdiction' on the court. The grant of 'power' to issue the writ, however, is juxtaposed with the section of appellate jurisdiction and, in fact, follows the general description of appellate jurisdiction in the same sentence, being separated only by a semicolon. No textual mangling is required to confine it to appellate jurisdiction. Moreover, no mangling is required even if it attaches both to original and to appellate jurisdiction, not as an enlargement of either, but simply as a specification of power which the Court is authorized to use in cases which are *otherwise* appropriately under consideration. Since this case is not otherwise within the specified type of original jurisdiction (e.g., it is not a case in which a state is a party or a case against an ambassador), it should be dismissed."

entirely without meaning, if such is to be the construction. If congress remains at liberty to give this court appellate jurisdiction, where the constitution has declared their jurisdiction shall be original; and original jurisdiction where the constitution has declared it shall be appellate; the distribution of jurisdiction, made in the constitution, is form without substance.

Affirmative words are often, in their operation, negative of other objects than those affirmed; and in this case, a negative or exclusive sense must be given to them, or they have no operation at all.

It cannot be presumed that any clause in the constitution is intended to be without effect; and, therefore, such a construction is inadmissible, unless the words require it. * * *

The authority, therefore, given to the Supreme Court, by the Act establishing the judicial courts of the United States, to issue writs of mandamus to public officers, appears not to be warranted by the Constitution;[e] and it becomes necessary to inquire whether a jurisdiction so conferred can be exercised.

The question whether an Act repugnant to the Constitution can become the law of the land, is a question deeply interesting to the United States; but, happily, not of an intricacy proportioned to its interest. It seems only necessary to recognize certain principles, supposed to have been long and well established, to decide it.

That the people have an original right to establish, for their future government, such principles as, in their opinion, shall most conduce to their own happiness, is the basis on which the whole American fabric has been erected. The exercise of this original right is a very great exertion; nor can it nor ought it to be frequently repeated. The principles, therefore, so established, are deemed fundamental. And as the authority from which they proceed is supreme, and can seldom act, they are designed to be permanent.

This original and supreme will organizes the government, and assigns to different departments their respective powers. It may either stop here, or establish certain limits not to be transcended by those departments.

The government of the United States is of the latter description. The powers of the legislature are defined and limited; and that those limits may not be mistaken, or forgotten, the constitution is written. To what purpose are powers limited, and to what purpose is that limitation committed to writing, if these limits may, at any time, be passed by those intended to be restrained? The distinction between a government with limited and unlimited powers is abolished, if those limits do not confine the persons on whom they are imposed, and if acts prohibited and acts allowed, are of equal obligation. It is a proposition too plain to be contested, that the constitution controls any legislative act repugnant to it; or, that the legislature may alter the constitution by an ordinary act.

Between these alternatives there is no middle ground. The constitution is either a superior paramount law, unchangeable by ordinary means, or it is on a

e. Consider Van Alstyne, supra, at 31: "It can be plausibly argued, however, that the Article III division of judicial power between appellate and original jurisdiction served a useful purpose other than that insisted upon by Marshall. Had Congress *not* adopted the Judiciary Act of 1789 or taken any other action describing Supreme Court jurisdiction, the division itself would have provided a guideline for the Court to follow until Congress was inclined to act." See also id. at 30–33.

By Marshall's interpretation of Art. III, may Congress authorize the Court to exercise appellate jurisdiction in cases involving foreign consuls? See *Bors v. Preston*, 111 U.S. 252, 4 S.Ct. 407, 28 L.Ed. 419 (1884).

level with ordinary legislative acts, and, like other acts, is alterable when the legislature shall please to alter it.

If the former part of the alternative be true, then a legislative act contrary to the constitution is not law: if the latter part be true, then written constitutions are absurd attempts, on the part of the people, to limit a power in its own nature illimitable.

Certainly all those who have framed written constitutions contemplate them as forming the fundamental and paramount law of the nation, and consequently, the theory of every such government must be, that an act of the legislature, repugnant to the constitution, is void.

This theory is essentially attached to a written constitution, and is, consequently, to be considered, by this court, as one of the fundamental principles of our society. It is not therefore to be lost sight of in the further consideration of this subject.

If an act of the legislature, repugnant to the Constitution, is void, does it, notwithstanding its invalidity, bind the courts, and oblige them to give it effect? Or, in other words, though it be not law, does it constitute a rule as operative as if it was a law? This would be to overthrow in fact what was established in theory; and would seem, at first view, an absurdity too gross to be insisted on. It shall, however, receive a more attentive consideration.

It is emphatically the province and duty of the judicial department to say what the law is. Those who apply the rule to particular cases, must of necessity expound and interpret that rule. If two laws conflict with each other, the courts must decide on the operation of each.

So if a law be in opposition to the constitution; if both the law and the constitution apply to a particular case, so that the court must either decide that case conformably to the law, disregarding the constitution; or conformably to the constitution, disregarding the law; the court must determine which of these conflicting rules governs the case. This is of the very essence of judicial duty.

If, then, the courts are to regard the constitution, and the constitution is superior to any ordinary act of the legislature, the constitution, and not such ordinary act, must govern the case to which they both apply.

Those then who controvert the principle that the constitution is to be considered in court, as a paramount law, are reduced to the necessity of maintaining that courts must close their eyes on the constitution, and see only the law.

This doctrine would subvert the very foundation of all written constitutions. It would declare that an Act which, according to the principles and theory of our government, is entirely void, is yet, in practice, completely obligatory. It would declare that if the legislature shall do what is expressly forbidden, such Act, notwithstanding the express prohibition, is in reality effectual. It would be giving to the legislature a practical and real omnipotence, with the same breath which professes to restrict their powers within narrow limits. It is prescribing limits, and declaring that those limits may be passed at pleasure.

That it thus reduces to nothing what we have deemed the greatest improvement on political institutions, a written constitution, would of itself be sufficient, in America, where written constitutions have been viewed with so much reverence, for rejecting the construction. But the peculiar expressions of the Constitution of the United States furnish additional arguments in favor of its rejection.

The judicial power of the United States is extended to all cases arising under the Constitution.

Could it be the intention of those who gave this power, to say that in using it the Constitution should not be looked into? That a case arising under the Constitution should be decided without examining the instrument under which it arises?

This is too extravagant to be maintained.

In some cases, then, the Constitution must be looked into by the judges. And if they can open it at all, what part of it are they forbidden to read or to obey?

There are many other parts of the Constitution which serve to illustrate this subject.

It is declared that "no tax or duty shall be laid on articles exported from any State." Suppose a duty on the export of cotton, of tobacco, or of flour; and a suit instituted to recover it. Ought judgment to be rendered in such a case? Ought the judges to close their eyes on the Constitution, and only see the law?

The Constitution declares "that no bill of attainder or ex post facto law shall be passed."

If, however, such a bill should be passed, and a person should be prosecuted under it, must the court condemn to death those victims whom the Constitution endeavors to preserve?

"No person," says the Constitution, "shall be convicted of treason unless on the testimony of two witnesses to the same overt act, or on confession in open court."

Here the language of the Constitution is addressed especially to the courts. It prescribes, directly for them, a rule of evidence not to be departed from. If the legislature should change that rule, and declare one witness, or a confession out of court, sufficient for conviction, must the constitutional principle yield to the legislative act?

From these, and many other selections which might be made, it is apparent, that the framers of the constitution contemplated that instrument as a rule for the government of courts, as well as of the legislature.

Why otherwise does it direct the judges to take an oath to support it? This oath certainly applies in an especial manner, to their conduct in their official character. How immoral to impose it on them, if they were to be used as the instruments, and the knowing instruments, for violating what they swear to support!

The oath of office, too, imposed by the legislature, is completely demonstrative of the legislative opinion on this subject. It is in these words: "I do solemnly swear that I will administer justice without respect to persons, and do equal right to the poor and to the rich; and that I will faithfully and impartially discharge all the duties incumbent on me as _____, according to the best of my abilities and understanding agreeably to the constitution and laws of the United States."

Why does a judge swear to discharge his duties agreeably to the constitution of the United States, if that constitution forms no rule for his government? If it is closed upon him, and cannot be inspected by him?

If such be the real state of things, this is worse than solemn mockery. To prescribe, or to take this oath, becomes equally a crime.

It is also not entirely unworthy of observation, that in declaring what shall be the supreme law of the land, the constitution itself is first mentioned; and not the laws of the United States generally, but those only which shall be made in pursuance of the constitution, have that rank.

Thus, the particular phraseology of the Constitution of the United States confirms and strengthens the principle, supposed to be essential to all written constitutions, that a law repugnant to the constitution is void; and that courts, as well as other departments, are bound by that instrument.

The rule must be discharged.[f]

––––––––

"We are under a Constitution, but the Constitution is what the judges say it is."

—Charles Evans Hughes, Speech, 1907.

Comments and Questions

Further Historical Context

CHARLES WARREN, 1 *The Supreme Court in United States History,* 232, 242–43 (1922): "Contemporary writings make it very clear that the Republicans attacked the decision, not so much because it sustained the power of the Court to determine the validity of Congressional legislation, as because it enounced the doctrine that the Court might issue mandamus to a Cabinet official who was acting by direction of the President. In other words, Jefferson's antagonism to Marshall and the Court at that time was due more to his resentment at the alleged invasion of his Executive prerogative than to any so-called 'judicial usurpation' of the field of Congressional authority. [It] seems plain [that Marshall might] have construed the language of the section of the Judiciary Act [to escape the necessity] to pass upon its constitutionality. Marshall naturally felt that in view of the recent attacks on judicial power it was important to have the great principle firmly established, and undoubtedly he welcomed the opportunity of fixing the precedent in a case in which his action would necessitate a decision in favor of his political opponents."

––––––––

MORRIS COHEN, *The Faith of a Liberal* 178–80 (1946) (written in 1938): "The section of [the] Act of 1789 which Marshall declared unconstitutional had been drawn up by Ellsworth, his predecessor as Chief Justice, and by others who a short time before had been the very members of the constitutional convention that had drafted its judicial provisions. It was signed by George Washington who had presided over the deliberations of that Convention. Fourteen years later, John Marshall by implication accused his predecessor on the bench, the members of Congress such as James Madison, the Father of the Constitution, and President Washington, of either not understanding the Constitution (which some of them

---

f. Six days later, the Circuit Court Repeal Law was held to be constitutional. *Stuart v. Laird,* 5 U.S. (1 Cranch) 299, 2 L.Ed. 115 (1803). After *Marbury,* the Court did not hold an act of Congress unconstitutional until *Dred Scott v. Sandford,* 60 U.S. (19 How.) 393, 15 L.Ed. 691 (1857).

had drawn up), or else wilfully disregarding it. [To] a secular historian, it is obvious that John Marshall was motivated by the fear of impeachment if he granted the mandamus or dared to declare the Republican Judiciary Repeal Act of 1802 unconstitutional. Having thus refused aid to his fellow Federalists ousted from offices created for them by a 'lame duck' congress, he resorted to a line of sophistical dicta to get even with his political enemy, as indeed he did also in the *Aaron Burr* case. In his letter to his colleague Chase, Marshall offered to abandon judicial supremacy in the interpretation of the Constitution in return for security against impeachment." [g]

Text of the Constitution

Is the doctrine of "judicial review," which gives the Court power to declare an act of a coordinate branch of the government unconstitutional, compelled because a contrary rule "would subvert the very foundation of all written constitutions"?

WILLIAM VAN ALSTYNE, *A Critical Guide to Marbury v. Madison*, 1969 Duke L.J. 1, 17: "[E]ven in Marshall's time (and to a great extent today), a number of nations maintained written constitutions and yet gave national legislative acts the full force of positive law without providing any constitutional check to guarantee the compatibility of those acts with their constitutions [e.g.,] France, Switzerland, and Belgium (and to some extent Great Britain where Magna Carta and other written instruments are roughly described as the constitution but where acts of Parliament are not reviewable)." [h]

Does the "judges' oath" provision (Art. VI, cl. 3) furnish the necessary textual support for the doctrine of judicial review?

JUSTICE GIBSON, dissenting in *Eakin v. Raub*, 12 S. & R. 330 (Pa.1825): [i] "The oath to support the Constitution is not peculiar to the judges, but is taken indiscriminately by every officer of the government, and is designed rather as a test of the political principles of the man, than to bind the officer in the discharge of his duty: otherwise, it were difficult to determine, what operation it is to have in the case of a recorder of deeds, for instance, who, in execution of his office, has nothing to do with the Constitution. But granting it to relate to the official conduct of the judge, as well as every other officer, and not to his political principles, still, it must be understood in reference to supporting the Constitution, only as far as that may be involved in his official duty; and consequently, if his official duty does not comprehend an inquiry into the authority of the legislature, neither does his oath. * * *

g. In 1804, the House impeached Justice Chase due, inter alia, to what the Republicans believed to be Chase's partisan Federalist activities and statements both on and off the Bench. After a lengthy trial in the Senate, the constitutional majority to convict was not obtained. It was generally assumed that, if the effort had been successful, Marshall and other Federalist judges would suffer the same fate. See generally 1 Warren, supra, ch. 6. For a further account of *Marbury*, see 3 Albert Beveridge, *The Life of John Marshall* 105–156 (1919).

h. Consider Cohen, supra, at 185: "Nor is it necessary to consider in detail the argument that this power is necessary for a federal system. The Swiss constitution is a perfect example of a federal system without the judiciary having such power. The late Justice Holmes said, 'I do not think the United States would come to an end if we lost our power to declare an Act of Congress void. I do think the Union would be imperiled if we could not make that declaration as to the laws of the several states.'"

For discussion of the modern growth of various forms of judicial review in other countries—Australia, Austria, Canada, Cyprus, Denmark, Germany, India, Italy, Japan, Norway, Sweden, Turkey, Yugoslavia—see Mauro Cappelletti, *Judicial Review in Comparative Perspective*, 58 Calif.L.Rev. 1017 (1970).

i. This opinion is widely regarded as the most effective answer of the era to Marshall's reasoning supporting judicial review.

"But do not the judges do a positive act in violation of the Constitution, when they give effect to an unconstitutional law? Not if the law has been passed according to the forms established in the Constitution. The fallacy of the question is, in supposing that the judiciary adopts the acts of the legislature as its own; whereas, the enactment of a law and the interpretation of it are not concurrent acts, and as the judiciary is not required to concur in the enactment, neither is it in the breach of the constitution which may be the consequence of the enactment; the fault is imputable to the legislature, and on it the responsibility exclusively rests."

What of Art. III, § 2, cl. 1, extending "the judicial Power" "to *all* cases * * * arising under this Constitution"?

ALEXANDER BICKEL, *The Least Dangerous Branch* 5–6 (1962): "[W]hat the Constitution extends to cases arising under it is 'the judicial Power.' Whether this power reaches as far as Marshall wanted it to go—namely, to reviewing acts of the legislature—is the question to be decided. What are the nature and extent of the function of the Court—the judicial power? Is the Court empowered, when it decided a case, to declare that a duly enacted statute violates the Constitution, and to invalidate the statute? Article III does not purport to describe the function of the Court; it subsumes whatever questions may exist as to that in the phrase 'the judicial Power.' It does not purport to tell the Court how to decide cases; it only specifies which kinds of case the Court shall have jurisdiction to deal with at all. Thus, in giving jurisdiction in cases 'arising under * * * the Laws' or 'under * * * Treaties,' the clause is not read as prescribing the process of decision to be followed. The process varies. I cases 'under * * * the Laws' courts often leave determination of issues of fact and even issues that may be thought to be 'of law' to administrative agencies. And under both 'the Laws * * * and Treaties,' much of the decision concerning meaning and applicability may be received ready-made from the Congress and the President. In some cases of all three descriptions, judicial decision may be withheld altogether [j]—and it is for this reason that it will not do to place reliance on the word 'all' in the phrase 'all cases * * * arising * * *.' To the extent that the Constitution speaks to such matters, it does so in the tightly packed phrase 'judicial Power.'

"Nevertheless, if it were impossible to conceive a case 'arising under the Constitution' which would not require the Court to pass on the constitutionality of congressional legislation, then the analysis of the text of Article III made above might be found unsatisfactory, for it would render this clause quite senseless. But there are such cases which may call into question the constitutional validity of judicial, administrative, or military actions without attacking legislative or even presidential acts as well, or which call upon the Court, under appropriate statutory authorization, to apply the Constitution to acts of the states."

––––––––

What of the supremacy clause (Art. VI, cl. 2)?

HERBERT WECHSLER, *Toward Neutral Principles of Constitutional Law*, 73 Harv.L.Rev. 1, 3–5 (1959): "Judge Hand [*The Bill of Rights* 28 (1958)] concedes that under this clause 'state courts would at times have to decide whether state laws and constitutions, or even a federal statute, were in conflict with the federal constitution' but he adds that 'the fact that this jurisdiction was confined to such occasions, and that it was thought necessary specifically to

––––––––

j. See Sec. 2 infra, "Political Questions."

provide such a limited jurisdiction, looks rather against than in favor of a general jurisdiction.'

"Are you satisfied, however, to view the supremacy clause in this way, as a grant of jurisdiction to state courts, implying a denial of the power and the duty to all others? This certainly is not its necessary meaning; it may be construed as a mandate to all of officialdom including courts, with a special and emphatic admonition that in binds the judges of the previously independent states. That the latter is the proper reading seems to me persuasive when the other relevant provisions of the Constitution are brought into view.

"Article III, section 1 [represented] one of the major compromises of the Constitutional Convention and relegated the establishment vel non of lower federal courts to the discretion of the Congress. None might have been established, with the consequence that, as in other federalisms, judicial work of first instance would all have been remitted to state courts. Article III, section 2 goes on, however, to delineate the scope of the federal judicial power, providing that it 'shall extend [inter alia] to all Cases, in Law and Equity, arising under this Constitution * * *' and further, that the Supreme Court 'shall have appellate jurisdiction' in such cases 'with such Exceptions, and under such Regulations as the Congress shall make.' Surely this means, as section 25 of the Judiciary Act of 1789 took it to mean, that if a court passes on a constitutional issue, as the supremacy clause provides that it should, its judgment is reviewable, subject to congressional exceptions, by the Supreme Court, in which event that Court must have no less authority and duty to accord priority to constitutional provisions that the court that it review. And such state cases might have encompassed every case in which a constitutional issue could possibly arise, since, as I have said, Congress need not and might not have exerted its authority to establish 'inferior' federal courts.

"If you abide with me thus far, I doubt that you will hesitate upon the final step. Is it a possible construction of the Constitution, measured strictly as Judge Hand admonishes by the test of 'general purpose,' that if Congress opts, as it has opted, to create a set of lower courts, those courts in cases falling within their respective jurisdictions and the Supreme Court when it passes on their judgments are less or differently constrained by the supremacy clause than are the state courts, and the Supreme Court when it reviews their judgments? Yet I cannot escape, what is for me the most astonishing conclusion, that this is the precise result of Judge Hand's reading of the text."

Did Judge Hand concede too much in reading the text of the supremacy clause to empower state courts to decide the constitutionality of *federal* statutes? If so, is Chief Justice Marshall's reference to Art. VI persuasive? [k]

k. Consider Charles Black, *The People and The Court* 23–25 (1960): '[T]he most impressive thing in firming the claims of judicial review is the operation of our history since its beginning. And the most striking thing about this history is that the other departments of government, preeminently Congress, have operated under the assumption (and not through mere oversight, for the assumption has in several epochs been passionately challenged) that judicial review is an authentic part of our system of government. One of the most decisive Congressional expressions of this assumption, of special interest because it was passed by the First Congress, is the 25th Section of the first federal Judiciary Act [which] explicitly recognizes and provides for review of state court decisions by the Supreme Court, and lays it down with certainty that the Supreme Court may, by reversing a state judgment that has upheld a state law as against constitutional attack, hold state laws unconstitutional. But it says more than that. It clearly recognizes, first, that the validity of a 'treaty or statute of * * * the United States' may be drawn in question in a state court and that the decision of the state court may be 'against their validity.' It then goes on to say, not only that the Supreme Court may review such a judgment,

WILLIAM VAN ALSTYNE, supra, at 20–22: "The phrase 'in pursuance thereof' might as easily mean *'in the manner prescribed by this Constitution,'* in which case acts of Congress might be judicially reviewable as to their procedural integrity, but not as to their substance. An example of this more limited, procedural, judicial review is found in *Field v. Clark* [143 U.S. 649, 12 S.Ct. 495, 36 L.Ed. 294 (1892)], It is, moreover, far more common in other countries than is substantive constitutional review. * * *

"The phrase might also mean merely that only those statutes adopted by Congress *after* the re-establishment and reconstitution of Congress pursuant to the Constitution itself shall be the supreme law of the land, whereas acts of the earlier Continental Congress, constituted merely under the Articles of Confederation, would not necessarily be supreme and binding upon the several states. Under this view, acts of Congress, like acts of Parliament, *are* the supreme law and not to be second-guessed by any court, state or federal, so long as they postdate ratification of the Constitution.[36]

"* * * *Assuming that an act repugnant to the Constitution is not a law 'in pursuance thereof' and thus must not be given effect as the supreme law of the land, who, according to the Constitution, is to make the determination as to whether any given law is in fact repugnant to the Constitution itself?* [T]he supremacy clause itself cannot be the clear textual basis for a claim by the judiciary that this prerogative to determine repugnancy belongs to it.

"[The phrase] could mean merely that the people should regard the Constitution with deep concern and that *they* should act to prevent Congress from overstepping the Constitution. It might even imply, moreover, a right of civil disobedience or serve as a written reminder to government of the natural right of revolution against tyrannical government which oversteps the terms of the social compact. Such a construction would be consistent with philosophical writings of the period, consistent with the Declaration of Independence, and consistent also with the view of some antifederalists of the period."[l]

but that it may be 'reversed or affirmed' in that Court. If the Supreme Court may 'affirm' a state judgment holding a federal law invalid, then the Supreme Court obviously may, in such a case at least, hold a federal law invalid. So much is beyond cavil on the face of the statute. [But] does it not seem likely that it was also assumed that the federal courts were empowered to pass and would pass, in all cases within their jurisdiction, on the validity of the state laws? Actually, the absurdity of the contrary assumption, in the context of the Judiciary Act of 1789, is even greater than this bare statement makes it appear. For that Act provided (as the law still provides) that parties from different state could sue and be sued in the federal courts. So the hypothesis that the state courts might, while the federal courts might not, pass on the validity of federal statutes, would necessarily imply that parties who were citizens of the same state could appeal to the federal Constitution in court, while those who were citizens of different states could not. This is sheer lunacy—but to clear the members of the First Congress (as they deserve to be cleared) of this charge of lunacy, we have to assume that they took it for granted that the federal constitutional validity of state and fed-

eral laws could be passed on by all courts, state and federal."

36. For a careful elaboration of this point, see 2 William Crosskey, *Politics and the Constitution* 990–1007 (1953).

As distinguished from acts of Congress, treaties were binding upon the several states according to this view merely by having been entered into "under the Authority of the United States," and irrespective of whether they were approved by the Senate as it was proposed to be established pursuant to the new Constitution.

l. Much has been written on the matter of "historical original intent" in respect to judicial review—generally examining pre-Convention judicial precedents in England and the colonies, statements of the framers both within and outside the Constitutional Convention (see especially Alexander Hamilton in Nos. 78 and 80 of *The Federalist* (1788)), and debate during the ratification period—arriving at conflicting conclusions. See, e.g., Louis Boudin, *Government by Judiciary* (1932); Edward Corwin, *The Doctrine of Judicial Review* (1914); William Crosskey, *Politics and the Constitution in the*

The Court as "Final" Arbiter

THOMAS JEFFERSON, writing in 1804, 8 *The Writings of Thomas Jefferson* 310 (1897): "The Judges, believing the [Sedition Law] constitutional, had a right to pass a sentence of fine and imprisonment; because that power was placed in their hands by the Constitution. But the Executive, believing the law to be unconstitutional, was bound to remit the execution of it; because that power has been confided to him by the Constitution. The instrument meant that its co-ordinate branches should be checks on each other. But the opinion which gives to the Judges the right to decide what laws are constitutional, and what not, not only for themselves in their own sphere of action, but for the Legislative and Executive also in their spheres, would make the Judiciary a despotic branch."

———

ANDREW JACKSON, veto message in 1832 on act to recharter Bank of United States (the constitutionality of which had earlier been upheld by the Court), 2 Richardson, *Messages and Papers of the Presidents* 576, 581–82 (1900): "It is as much the duty of the House of Representatives, of the Senate, and of the President to decide upon the constitutionality of any bill or resolution which may be presented to them for passage or approval as it is of the supreme judges when it may be brought before them for judicial decision. The opinion of the judges has no more authority over Congress than the opinion of Congress has over the judges, and on that point the President is independent of both. The authority of the Supreme Court must not, therefore, be permitted to control the Congress or the Executive when acting in their legislative capacities, but to have only such influence as the force of their reasoning may deserve."

———

ABRAHAM LINCOLN, inaugural address in 1861, 2 Richardson, supra, at 5, 9–10: "I do not forget the position assumed by some that constitutional questions are to be decided by the Supreme Court, nor do I deny that such decisions must be binding in any case upon the parties to a suit as to the object of that suit, while they are also entitled to very high respect and consideration in all parallel cases by all other departments of the Government. And while it is obviously possible that such decision may be erroneous in any given case, still the evil effect following it, being limited to that particular case, with the chance that it may be overruled and never become a precedent for other cases, can better be borne than could the evils of a different practice. At the same time, the candid citizen must confess that if the policy of the Government upon vital questions affecting the whole people is to be irrevocably fixed by decisions of the Supreme Court, the instant they are made in ordinary litigation between parties in personal actions the people will have ceased to be their own rulers, having to that extent practically resigned their

History of the United States (1953); William Nelson, *Changing Conceptions of Judicial Review: The Evolution of Constitutional Theory in the States, 1790–1860,* 120 U.Pa.L.Rev. 1166 (1972); Charles Warren, *Congress, the Constitution, and the Supreme Court* (1925). For brief discussion see Levy, *Judicial Review, History, and Democracy: An Introduction,* in Judicial Review and the Supreme Court 1–12 (1967). For the view that "strict intentional-ism" is not a "tenable approach to constitutional decisionmaking," see Paul Brest, *The Misconceived Quest for the Original Understanding,* 60 B.U.L.Rev. 204 (1980).

For review of the broader historical setting, see Bernard Bailyn, *The Ideological Origins of the American Revolution* (1967); Gordon Wood, *The Creation of the American Republic, 1776–1787* (1969).

Government into the hands of that eminent tribunal. Nor is there in this view any assault upon the court or the judges. It is a duty from which they may not shrink to decide cases properly brought before them, and it is no fault of theirs if others seek to turn their decisions to political purposes."

Are these views inconsistent with *Marbury?* Does *Marbury* decide anything more than that *"the Court may refuse to give effect to an act of Congress where the act pertains to the judicial power itself"?* Van Alstyne, supra, at 34. Than that the Court claimed the power of judicial review "only in the defensive sense of safeguarding the Court's original jurisdiction from congressional enlargement"? Frank Strong, *Judicial Review: A Tri-Dimensional Concept of Administrative-Constitutional Law,* 69 W.Va.L.Rev. 111, 249 (1967).

If the Court upholds the constitutionality of a federal statute, may the President refuse to enforce it because be believes it to be unconstitutional May he refuse to enforce it on this ground after Congress has enacted it but before it comes before the Court? May he refuse to enforce it on this ground if Congress overrides his veto? May the President continue to enforce a statute (e.g., by pressing charges for its violation) after the Court has held it unconstitutional? May he refuse to return property that the Court has held was unconstitutionally seized? If Congress forbids the President from taking certain action, may he do so on the ground that Congress' restriction is unconstitutional? Even after the Court has upheld its constitutionality?

———

LEARNED HAND, *The Bill of Rights* 11–15 (1958): "[L]et us try to imagine what would have been the result if the power [of judicial review] did not exist. There were two alternatives, each prohibitive, I submit. One was that the decision of the first 'Department' before which an issue arose should be conclusive whenever it arose later. That doctrine, coupled with its conceded power over the purse, would have made Congress substantially omnipotent, for by far the greater number of issues that could arise would depend upon its prior action. * * *

"As Hamilton intimated, every legislator is under constant pressure from groups of constituents whom it does not satisfy to say, 'Although I think what you want is right and that you ought to have it, I cannot bring myself to believe that it is within my constitutional powers.' Such scruples are not convincing to those whose interests are at stake; and the voters at large will not usually care enough about preserving 'the balance of the Constitution' to offset the votes of those whose interests will be disappointed. [But] the second alternative would have been even worse, for under it each 'Department' would have been free to decide constitutional issues as it thought right, regardless of any earlier decision of the others. Thus it would have been the President's privilege, and indeed his duty, to execute only those statutes that seemed to him to be constitutional, regardless even of a decision of the Supreme Court. The courts would have entered such judgments as seemed to them consonant with the Constitution; but neither the President, nor Congress, would have been bound to enforce them if he or it disagreed, and without their help the judgments would have been waste paper.

"For centuries it has been an accepted canon in interpretation of documents to interpolate into the text such provisions, though not expressed, as are essential to prevent the defeat of the venture at hand; and this applies with especial force to the interpretation of constitutions, which, since they are designed to cover a great multitude of necessarily unforeseen occasions, must be cast in general language, unless they are constantly amended. If so, it was altogether in keeping with established practice for the Supreme Court to assume an authority to keep the states, Congress, and the President within their prescribed powers. Otherwise the government could not proceed as planned; and indeed would almost certainly have foundered, as in fact it almost did over that very issue.

"However, since this power is not a logical deduction from the structure of the Constitution but only a practical condition upon its successful operation, it need not be exercised whenever a court sees, or thinks that it sees, an invasion of the Constitution."

May a Congressman vote against a bill because he believes it to be unconstitutional even though the Court has held to the contrary? May the President veto such a bill on this ground? If the Court has upheld the constitutionality of a federal criminal statute, may a subsequent President grant pardons to all persons convicted under it (see Art. II, § 2, cl. 1)? If the President altogether refuses to "receive Ambassadors and other public Ministers" (see Art. II, § 3), may the Court order him to do so? Or should the "supremacy" of judicial review at least be limited to those decisions that do not "interfere with the procedural machinery of Congress or the federal executive"? Sidney Buchanan, *Judicial Supremacy Reexamined: A Proposed Alternative*, 70 Mich.L.Rev. 1279, 1304 (1972). See Sec. 2 infra—"Political Questions." Is there a distinction between *state* and federal officials in respect to the binding nature of the Court's decisions?

———

COOPER v. AARON (1958), set forth more fully, Ch. 10, Sec. 2, IV: "Article VI of the Constitution makes the Constitution the 'supreme Law of the Land.' In 1803, [*Marbury*] declared the basic principle that the federal judiciary is supreme in the exposition of the law of the Constitution, and that principle has ever since been respected by this Court and the Country as a permanent and indispensable feature of our constitutional system. [Every] state legislator and executive and judicial officer is solemnly committed by oath taken pursuant to Art. VI, ¶ 3 'to support this Constitution.' * * * Chief Justice Marshall spoke for a unanimous Court in saying that: 'if the legislatures of the several states may, at will, annul the judgments of the courts of the United States, and destroy the rights acquired under those judgments, the constitution itself becomes a solemn mockery * * *.' *United States v. Peters,* 9 U.S. (5 Cranch) 115, 136, 3 L.Ed. 53. A Governor who asserts a power to nullify a federal court order is similarly restrained." [m]

Cooper involved the refusal of Arkansas officials to abide by federal court decrees requiring school desegregation. In contrast, if the Court *upholds* the constitutionality of a state law, may that state's supreme court subsequently rule that the state law violates the Constitution? Would the state court's ruling "annul the judgment" of the Supreme Court? See Laurence Tribe, *American Constitutional Law,* 32–42 (2d ed.1988) (hereinafter called Tribe *Treatise*).

Judicial Review and Democracy

ALEXANDER BICKEL, supra, at 16–20: "The root difficulty is that judicial review is a counter-majoritarian force in our system. [W]hen the Supreme Court declares unconstitutional a legislative act or the action of an elected executive, it thwarts the will of representatives of the actual people of the here and now; it

m. For criticism and defense of this "judicial supremacy" analysis, see Daniel Farber, *The Supreme Court and the Rule of Law: Cooper v. Aaron Revisited,* 1982 U.Ill.L.Rev. 387.

exercises control, not in behalf of the prevailing majority, but against it. That [is] the reason the charge can be made that judicial review is undemocratic.

"Most assuredly, no democracy operates by taking continuous nose counts on the broad range of daily governmental activities. * * * Nevertheless, although democracy does not mean constant reconsideration of decisions once made, it does mean that a representative majority has the power to accomplish a reversal. This power is of the essence, and no less so because it is often merely held in reserve.

"It is true, of course, that the process of reflecting the will of a popular majority in the legislature is deflected by various inequalities of representation and by all sorts of institutional habits and characteristics, which perhaps tend most often in favor of inertia.[n] Yet, impurities and imperfections, if such they be, in one part of the system are no argument for total departure from the desired norm in another part. * * *

"No doubt ['interest' or 'pressure groups'] operate forcefully on the electoral process, and no doubt they seek and gain access to and an effective share in the legislative and executive decisional process. Perhaps they constitute also, in some measure, an impurity or imperfection. But no one has claimed that they have been able to capture the governmental process except by combining in some fashion, and thus capturing or constituting (are not the two verbs synonymous?) a majority. They often tend themselves to be majoritarian in composition and to be subject to broader majoritarian influences. And the price of what they sell or buy in the legislature is determined in the biennial or quadrennial electoral marketplace. * * * Judicial review works counter to this characteristic.

"It therefore does not follow from the complex nature of a democratic system that, because admirals and generals and the members, say, of the Federal Reserve Board or of this or that administrative agency are not electorally responsible, judges who exercise the power of judicial review need not be responsible either, and in neither case is there a serious conflict with democratic theory. For admirals and generals and the like are most often responsible to officials who are themselves elected and through whom the line runs directly to a majority. What is more significant, the policies they make are or should be interstitial or technical only and are reversible by legislative majorities * * *—a fact of great consequence. Nor will it do to liken judicial review to the general lawmaking function of judges. In the latter aspect, judges are indeed something like administrative officials, for their decisions are also reversible by any legislative majority—and not infrequently they are reversed.[o] Judicial review, however, is the power to apply and construe the Constitution in matters of the greatest moment, against the

---

n. For a forceful position "that there can be no automatic and blanket equation of Congress or the Executive branch with the voice of the people," see Martin Shapiro, *Freedom of Speech*, 17–25 (1966). Consider Samuel Krislov, *The Supreme Court and Political Freedom* 20 (1968): "If one analyzes the actual rules of behavior in the so-called democratic units of government, we find that they also have mixed aspects, with the possibility—sometimes the actuality—of minority control. The power of the Rules Committee, the filibuster, and the Senate are obvious shortcomings; [the] operational consequences of seniority, and the population base of districts likely to maintain continuity in representation are more veiled aspects." See also Donald Kom-

mers, *Professor Kurland, The Supreme Court, and Political Science,* 15 J.Pub.L. 230 (1966).

o. Compare William Bishin, *Judicial Review in Democratic Theory,* 50 So.Cal.L.Rev. 1099, 1110 (1977): "Closer examination suggests [that] not all of the decisions that such officeholders make can, in fact or theory, be reversed by majoritarian action. [It] must be remembered [that] Congress—especially the Senate—is so structured that representatives of only a minority of the people can prevent the passage of legislation which would overturn prior decisions * * *. Wherever the position of such a minority coincides with the [judge's or administrative officer's] position, therefore, the Constitution gives the principle of reversibility no effect at all."

wishes of a legislative majority, which is, in turn, powerless to affect the judicial decision.''

———

JESSE CHOPER, *The Supreme Court and the Political Branches: Democratic Theory and Practice,* 122 U.Pa.L.Rev. 810, 830–32 (1974): "In the main, the effect of judicial review in ruling legislation unconstitutional is to nullify the finished product of the lawmaking process. It is the very rare Supreme Court decision on constitutionality that affirmatively mandates the undertaking of government action. To make the point in another way, when the Supreme Court finds legislative acts unconstitutional it holds invalid only those enactments that have survived the many hurdles fixed between incipient proposals and standing law.

"The significance of this [is] that most of the antimajoritarian elements that have been found in the American legislative process [are] negative ones. They work to *prevent* the translation of popular wishes into governing rules rather than to *produce* laws that are contrary to majority sentiment. [S]enators representing only fifteen percent of the population may hold sway in the upper house; but their real impact (as is obviously the case with the filibuster as well) is to halt ultimate action rather than facilitate it. For the enactment of law also requires the concurrence of the lower [house]. Furthermore, within each legislative chamber, the ability of the committees and their chairmen and minority members—and frequently of the lobbies and other interest groups as well—to circumvent the majority will of the assembly is most saliently manifested in obstructing the process rather than in making laws. The more formidable task usually is not to stall or defeat a proposal but to organize the requisite support among the dispersed powers so as to form a coalition for its passage. * * *

"Thus, although exceptions exist, '[a] distinguishing feature of our system, perhaps impelled by heritage of sectional division and heterogeneity, is that our governmental structure, institutional habits, and political parties with their internal factional divisions, have combined to produce a system in which major programs and major new directions cannot be undertaken unless supported by a fairly broad popular consensus. This normally has been far broader than 51 percent and often bipartisan as well.' [Consequently,] when the Supreme Court, itself without conventional political responsibility, says 'thou shalt not' to acts of Congress, it usually cuts sharply against the grain of majority rule. The relatively few laws that finally overcome the congressional obstacle course generally illustrate the national political branches operating at their majoritarian best while the process of judicial review depicts that element of the Court's work and that exertion of federal authority with the most brittle democratic roots.[59]"

"The Most Celebrated Footnote in Constitutional Law": Footnote 4 of the *Carolene Products* Case

UNITED STATES v. CAROLENE PRODUCTS CO., 304 U.S. 144, 58 S.Ct. 778, 82 L.Ed. 1234 (1938), upheld the constitutionality of a federal statute that prohibited the shipment in interstate commerce of "filled milk," a product compounded with fat or oil so as to resemble milk or cream. Appellee argued that

---

59. Although no detailed examination of the legislative systems in the states and their political subdivisions has been ventured here, the same conclusion appears to have substantially similar merit in respect to the Court's overturning the laws they produce.

the legislation violated both the commerce and due process clauses. The government countered that appellee's product was an impure, adulterated substance that posed a danger to the public. Writing for the court, Justice Stone took the position that economic regulatory legislation, such as the statute at issue, was entitled to a presumption of constitutionality and should be upheld if supported by any rational basis. Under this approach, the challenged legislation easily passed constitutional muster.[a] In the course of writing his opinion, Justice Stone dropped a footnote (fn. 4) that has been called "the most celebrated footnote in constitutional law" [b] and "the great and modern charter for ordering the relations between judges and other agencies of government."[c] That footnote (case citations omitted) reads as follows:

"There may be narrower scope for operation of the presumption of constitutionality when legislation appears on its face to be within a specific prohibition of the Constitution, such as those of the first ten amendments, which are deemed equally specific when held to be embraced within the Fourteenth.

"It is unnecessary to consider now whether legislation which restricts those political processes which can obviously be expected to bring about repeal of undesirable legislation, is to be subjected to more exacting judicial scrutiny under the general prohibitions of the Fourteenth than are most other types of legislation [referring to cases dealing with restrictions on voting rights and freedom of expression and political association].

"Nor need we enquire whether similar considerations enter into the review of statutes directed at particular religions or national or racial minorities[:] whether prejudice against discrete and insular minorities may be a special condition, which tends seriously to curtail the operation of those political processes ordinarily to be relied upon to protect minorities, and which may call for a correspondingly more searching judicial inquiry."[d]

---

a. "The plaudits accorded [footnote 4] are matched by the disregard of the case itself." Geoffrey Miller, *The True Story of Carolene Products,* 1987 Sup.Ct.Rev. 397, 398. This is unfortunate, points out Professor Miller, id. at 398–99, "because [the case] is interesting in its own right and because its facts shed light on the meaning of the footnote. The statute upheld in the case was an utterly unprincipled example of special interest legislation. The purported 'public interest' justifications so credulously reported by Justice Stone were patently bogus. [It] is difficult to believe that members of the Court were unaware of the true motivation behind this legislation. That they should nevertheless vote to uphold the statute strongly suggested that all bets were off as far as economic regulation was concerned. Footnote four, in this light, can be seen as indicating that the Court intended to keep its hands off economic regulation, no matter how egregious the discrimination or patent the special interests motivation. Rational basis scrutiny of [this sort] could not be taken

seriously if it precluded judicial protection of individual liberties. By separating economic and personal liberties, Justice Stone suggested that the Court might really mean what it said about deference to the legislative will in economic cases."

See also, Neil Komesar, *Taking Institutions Seriously,* 51 U.Chi.L.Rev. 366, 416 (1984): "It does not take much scrutiny to see the dairy lobby at work behind the passage [of] the 'filled milk' act. Indeed, [it] is not too uncharitable [to] suggest that concern for the dairies' pocketbooks rather than for the consumer's health best explains the dairy lobby's efforts."

b. Justice Lewis Powell, *Carolene Products Revisited,* 82 Colum.L.Rev. 1087 (1982).

c. Owen Fiss, *The Forms of Justice,* 93 Harv.L.Rev. 1, 6 (1979).

d. Has the first paragraph of footnote 4 been undervalued in recent years? For an affirmative answer see Peter Linzer, *The Carolene Products Footnote and the Preferred Posi-*

1. *Removing "impurities" in the democratic process.* *Carolene Products* was concerned about the impurity of appellee's product and the need to exclude it from interstate commerce, but, observes, JACK BALKIN, *The Footnote,* 83 Nw.U.L.Rev. 275, 283 (1989), "*Carolene Products* is also about another type of purity and impurity, another type of inclusion and exclusion—that which affects the democratic process. *Carolene Products,* especially in its famous footnote, is concerned with impurities in the democratic process caused by adulteration of the means of political deliberation (the subject of the footnote's second paragraph) or by the exclusion of discrete and insular minorities from full political participation (the footnote's third paragraph). According to the logic of the footnote, certain groups are shut out of the democratic process, relegated to the periphery. They are, to use, Professor Birmayer's expression, 'insider-outsiders'—persons subject to the power of the political community yet excluded from participation within it.[25] The goal of *Carolene Products* is to restore them to their rightful place within the polity through judicial supervision of the results of the democratic process. The role of the judiciary is to exclude legislation which is the result of impurities in the process, and by this exclusion, include those persons previously excluded, or prevent their future exclusion."

2. *"Revers[ing] the spin of the countermajoritarian difficulty."* Bruce Ackerman, *Beyond Carolene Products,* 98 Harv.L.Rev. 713, 714–15 (1985), sees the case and footnote 4 as a "brilliant" effort "to turn the Old Court's recent defeat into a judicial victory": "*Carolene* promises relief from the problem of legitimacy raised whenever nine elderly lawyers invalidate the legislative decisions of our elected representatives. The *Carolene* solution is to seize the high ground of democratic theory and establish that the challenged legislation was produced by a profoundly defective process. By demonstrating that the legislative solution itself resulted from an undemocratic procedure, a *Carolene* court hopes to reverse the spin of the countermajoritarian difficulty. For it now may seem that the original legislative decision, not the judicial invalidation, suffers the greater legitimacy deficit."

3. *Did footnote 4 replace one kind of "judicial activism" with another? Does it cause us to return to another kind of substantive due process?* Consider the remarks of JUSTICE LEWIS POWELL, fn. b supra, at 1089–91 (1982): "Unlike Holmes, Stone lived to see—and indeed helped to preside over—the passing of the *Lochner* era. [But] Footnote 4, as interpreted by many commentators, represented a radical departure of its own. Far from initiating a jurisprudence of judicial deference to political judgments by the legislature, Footnote 4—on this view— undertook to substitute one activist judicial mission for another. Where once the Court had championed rights of property, now—according to some—it should view

tion of Individual Rights: Louis Lusky and John Hart Ely vs. Harlan Fiske Stone, 12 Const.Comm. 277 (1995). Observes Professor Linzer, id. at 278:

"Early on, [footnote 4] was interpreted to mean that 'personal' rights were to be preferred to economic rights, but in recent years, largely through the efforts of Louis Lusky [who was Stone's law clerk when the famous footnote was written and who wrote the first draft of the footnote] and John Hart Ely, it has been interpreted more narrowly, justifying judicial activism only when the majoritarian democracy does not work: Ely describes it as 'representation-reinforcement,' a process-based notion that the courts should use judicial review aggressively only when the electoral process has

broken down or is tampered with or when litigants are deemed not to have a fair chance to achieve change at the ballot box, either because of hostile laws or because of prejudice against them * * *. In rereading Stone's contemporaneous opinions and those of his colleagues, however, I have become convinced that the process-based orientation underestimates the substantive content of the footnote, and that the revisionist attack on the 'preferred position' of non-economic rights needs to be refuted."

25. Lea Brilmayer, *Carolene, Conflicts and the Fate of the "Insider-Outsider,"* 134 U.Pa. L.Rev. 1291, 1294 (1986).

its special function as the identification and protection of 'discrete and insular minorities.' Where the Court before had used the substantive due process clause to protect property rights, now it should use the equal protection clause—a generally forgotten provision that Holmes once dismissed as 'the usual last resort of constitutional arguments'—as a sword with which to promote the liberty interests of groups disadvantaged by political decisions.

"The difference—or so runs the argument—is that protection of minority rights occurs in the name of correcting defects of *process,* defects that may have prevented minorities from gaining for themselves a fair bargain in the political arena. The theory is that the Court—in so protecting minority interests—does not risk imposing its own substantive values and distributive preferences on the Constitution and on the people of the United States.

"* * * Stone referred to discrete and insular minorities in a sentence, divided by a colon, in which he had referred earlier to racial, ethnic, and religious groups. Examining the textual evidence only, I think it would be a plausible reading that these are the only kinds of groups to which the term 'discrete and insular' was intended to refer. In the normal operation of the political process, the term then would suggest that *some* racial, religious, and ethnic groups are not treated fairly and equally. Courts therefore should apply strict scrutiny to laws 'directed at' these disadvantaged groups.

"This idea has intuitive appeal, and it has been widely accepted. But it too may require some form of limitation in its application. In our uniquely heterogeneous society there are countless groups with some claim to being racial, ethnic, or religious. Over our history many have been minorities, ineffective in politics, and often discriminated against. But these conditions do not remain static. Immigrant groups that once were neglected have become influential participants in the political process. One reasonably may doubt the capacity of courts to distinguish wisely among them or determine which groups—at a given time and place—operate effectively within our politics. One also must inquire how far a court may go in determining when a law, nondiscriminatory on its face, fairly may be considered as 'directed at' a particular group.[e]

"The problem is this: in a democratic society there inevitably are both winners and losers. The fact that one group is disadvantaged by a particular piece of legislation, or action of government, therefore does not prove that the process has failed to function properly. To infer otherwise—that the process has been corrupted by invidious discrimination—a judge must have some *substantive* vision of what results the process should have yielded. Otherwise he has no way to know that the process was unfair.

"Here I must pause to wonder. If I am correct about the implicit link between a substantive judgment and a malfunction of process, then one may inquire whether we have not returned in some cases to a kind of substantive due process. And one also may wonder what Stone—who had fought so vigorously against substantive due process—would have had to say about this."

e. Does *Carolene* require that "neutral rules" be strictly scrutinized? Would such scrutiny be contrary to its reasoning? See Brilmayer, fn. 25 supra, at 1307–09. Professor Brilmayer concludes, id. at 1334: "*Carolene*'s cruelest hoax is its suggestion that, once the discriminatory rules are invalidated, our political process problems are over. But, as any excluded person surely realizes, after putting the illusion of *Carolene* to one side, discriminatory rules are only a small part of a very large problem. They are only the first hurdle in a long road to political participation and equality. *Carolene*'s approach has led us seriously astray. It suggests that only discriminatory rules have process defects."

4. *Is Carolene's conception of the impact of prejudice "underinclusive"?* Should courts protect groups that are "anonymous and diffuse" rather than "discrete and insular"? Is "discreteness and insularity" likely to be a source of important bargaining advantage, not disadvantage, for a group involved in pluralist American politics? Consider BRUCE ACKERMAN, supra, at 731–32, 745: "*Carolene*'s empirical inadequacy stems from its underinclusive conception of the impact of prejudice upon American society. It is easy to identify groups in the population that are not discrete and insular but that are nonetheless the victims of prejudice as that term is commonly understood. Thus, the fact that homosexuals are a relatively anonymous minority has not saved the group from severe prejudice.[f] Nor is sexism a nonproblem merely because women are a diffuse, if discrete, majority. Prejudice is generated by a bewildering variety of social conditions. Although some *Carolene* minorities are seriously victimized, they are not the only ones stigmatized; nor is it obvious that all *Carolene* minorities are stigmatized more grievously than any other non-*Carolene* group. Why should the concern with 'prejudice' justify *Carolene*'s narrow fixation upon 'discrete and insular' minorities?

"The answer seemed easy in a world in which members of the paradigmatic *Carolene* minority group—blacks—were effectively barred from voting and political participation. [As] we move beyond the pariah model, however, anonymous or diffuse minorities will increasingly emerge as the groups that can raise the most serious complaints of pluralist disempowerment.

"* * * [A]s long as we use *Carolene* rhetoric to express our constitutional concerns with racial equality and religious freedom, we will find ourselves saying things that are increasingly belied by political reality. While constitutional lawyers decry the political powerlessness of discrete and insular groups, representatives of these interests will be wheeling and dealing in the ongoing pluralistic exchange—winning some battles, losing others, but plainly numbering among the organized interests whose electoral power must be treated with respect by their bargaining partners and competitors. * * *

"* * * [I]f we are to remain faithful to *Carolene*'s concern with the fairness of pluralist politics, we must repudiate the bad political science that allows us to ignore those citizens who have the most serious complaints: the anonymous and diffuse victims of poverty and sexual discrimination who find it most difficult to protect their fundamental interests through effective political organization."[g]

MARTIN v. HUNTER'S LESSEE

14 U.S. (1 Wheat.) 304, 4 L.Ed. 97 (1816).

[Lord Fairfax, a Virginia citizen, willed his Virginia land known as the Northern Neck of Virginia to his nephew, Martin, a British subject resident in England. In 1789, Virginia, acting pursuant to state laws confiscating lands

f. Earlier in his article, id. at 729, Professor Ackerman notes that he "propose[s] to define a minority as 'discrete' when its members are marked out in ways that make it relatively easy for others to identify them. [In] contrast, other minorities are socially defined in ways that give individual members the chance to avoid easy identification. A homosexual, for example, can keep her sexual preference a very private affair and thereby avoid much of the public opprobrium attached to her minority status. It is for this reason that I shall call homosexuals, and groups like them, 'anonymous' minorities and contrast them with 'discrete' minorities of the kind paradigmatically exemplified by blacks."

g. The impact of the *Carolene Products* footnote is further discussed at many points in the materials, especially Chs. 7 and 10.

owned by British subjects, granted land in the Northern Neck to Hunter. The latter brought an action of ejectment against Martin. The Virginia district court ruled for Martin, whose claim was fortified by the anti-confiscation clauses of the treaties of 1783 and 1794 with Great Britain. But the Virginia Court of Appeals reversed, holding that (1) the state's title to the Northern Neck had been perfected before any treaty and (2) in any event, a 1796 Act of Compromise between the Fairfax claimants and the state claimants, formally adopted by the Virginia legislature, had settled the matter against Martin.

[Acting for the purchasers of the Fairfax estate, John Marshall, then a member of the Virginia legislature, had negotiated the compromise. Since he and his brother had organized a syndicate which purchased 160,000 acres of Northern Neck from Martin in 1793, Marshall had a great interest in the case's outcome.

[In *Fairfax's Devisee v. Hunter's Lessee,* 11 U.S. (7 Cranch) 603, 3 L.Ed. 453 (1813), the Supreme Court (Marshall, C.J., not participating) reversed the Virginia Court of Appeals, ruling that Virginia had not perfected title to Northern Neck prior to the grant to Hunter and that therefore the Treaty of 1794 confirmed the title remaining in Martin. Neither Story, J.'s majority opinion nor Johnson, J.'s dissent mentioned the Act of Compromise.

[The cause was remanded to the Virginia Court of Appeals with instructions to enter judgment for appellant, but that court refused to obey the Supreme Court's mandate. All four judges then sitting maintained that in so far as it extended the appellate jurisdiction of the Supreme Court to "this court," § 25 of the Judiciary Act was unconstitutional. Judge Roane—Marshall's arch political enemy—and Judge Fleming (the two judges sitting when the court had decided the case against Martin on the merits) contended further that even if the Judiciary Act were valid the case had not properly been before the Supreme Court since the Virginia decision turned not upon a treaty, but "upon another and ordinary ground of jurisdiction—the act of compromise."

[The case again came to the Supreme Court, Marshall again not sitting.[a]]

STORY, J., delivered the opinion of the court.   * * *

The third article of the constitution is that which must principally attract our attention. [A]ppellate jurisdiction is given by the constitution to the supreme court, in all cases [within "the judicial power of the United States"] where it has not original jurisdiction; subject, however, to such exceptions and regulations as congress may prescribe. [W]hat is there to restrain its exercise over state tribunals, in the enumerated cases? [If] the judicial power extends to the case, it will be in vain to search in the letter of the constitution for any qualification as to the tribunal where it depends. It [is] plain, that the framers of the constitution did contemplate that cases within the judicial cognizance of the United States, not only might, but would, arise in the state courts, in the exercise of their ordinary jurisdiction [pointing to the supremacy clause]. Suppose, an indictment for a crime, in a state court, and the defendant should allege in his defence, that the crime was created by an ex post facto act of the state, must not the state court [have] a right to pronounce on the validity and sufficiency of the defence? [It] was foreseen, that in the exercise of their ordinary jurisdiction, state courts would incidentally take cognizance of cases arising under the constitution, the laws and treaties of the United States. Yet, to all these cases, the judicial power, by the very terms of the constitution, is to extend. It cannot extend, by original

a. For further exploration of the historical background, see 4 Albert Beveridge, *The Life of John Marshall* 144–61 (1919); 2 William Crosskey, *Politics and the Constitution* 785–817 (1953); 1 Charles Warren, *The Supreme Court in United States History* 442–53 (1922).

jurisdiction, if that was already rightfully and exclusively attached in the state courts, which (as has been already shown) may occur; it must, therefore, extend by appellate jurisdiction, or not at all. It would seem to follow, that the appellate power of the United States must, in such cases, extend to state tribunals * * *

It has been argued, that such an appellate jurisdiction over state courts is inconsistent with the genius of our governments, and the spirit of the constitution. That the latter was never designed to act upon state sovereignties, but only upon the people, and that if the power exists it will materially impair the sovereignty of the states, and the independence of their courts. [But the Constitution] is crowded with provisions which restrain or annul the sovereignty of the states, in some of the highest branches of their prerogatives. The tenth section of the first article contains a long list of disabilities and prohibitions imposed upon the states. [The] language of the constitution is also imperative upon the states, as to the performance of many duties. It is imperative upon the state legislatures, to make laws prescribing the time, places and manner of holding elections for senators and representatives, and for electors of president and vice-president. And in these, as well as some other cases, congress have a right to revise, amend or supersede the laws which may be passed by state legislatures. When, therefore, the states are stripped of some of the highest attributes of sovereignty, and the same are given to the United States; when the legislatures of the states are, in some respects, under the control of congress, and in every case are, under the constitution, bound by the paramount authority of the United States; it is certainly difficult to support the argument, that the appellate power over the decisions of state courts is contrary to the genius of our institutions. The courts of the United States can, without question, revise the proceedings of the executive and legislative authorities of the states, and if they are found to be contrary to the constitution, may declare them to be of no legal validity. Surely, the exercise of the same right over judicial tribunals is not a higher or more dangerous act of sovereign power.

Nor can such a right be deemed to impair the independence of state judges. It is assuming the very ground in controversy, to assert that they possess an absolute independence of the United States. In respect to the powers granted to the United States, they are not independent; they are expressly bound to obedience, by the letter of the constitution * * *.

The argument urged from the possibility of the abuse of the revising power, is equally unsatisfactory. [From] the very nature of things, the absolute right of decision, in the last resort, must rest somewhere—wherever it may be vested, it is susceptible of abuse. [A]dmitting that the judges of the state courts are, and always will be, of as much learning, integrity and wisdom, as those of the courts of the United States (which we very cheerfully admit), it does not aid the argument. It is manifest, that the constitution has proceeded upon a theory of its own, and given or withheld powers according to the judgment of the American people, by whom it was adopted. We can only construe its powers, and cannot inquire into the policy or principles which induced the grant of them. The constitution has presumed (whether rightly or wrongly, we do not inquire), that state attachments, state prejudices, state jealousies, and state interests, might sometimes obstruct, or control, or be supposed to obstruct or control, the regular administration of justice. * * *

This is not all. A motive of another kind, perfectly compatible with the most sincere respect for state tribunals, might induce the grant of appellate power over their decisions. * * * Judges of equal learning and integrity, in different states, might differently interpret the statute, or a treaty of the United States, or even the constitution itself: if there were no revising authority to control these jarring and discordant judgments, and harmonize them into uniformity, the laws, the treaties and the constitution of the United States would be different, in different states, and might, perhaps, never have precisely the same construction, obligation or efficiency, in any two states. The public mischiefs that would attend such a state of things would be truly deplorable * * *.

On the whole, the court are of opinion, that the appellate power of the United States does extend to cases pending in the state courts; and that the 25th section of the judiciary act, which authorizes the exercise of this jurisdiction in the specified cases, by a writ of error, is supported by the letter and spirit of the constitution. [It] is an historical fact, that this exposition of the constitution, extending its appellate power to state courts, was, previous to its adoption, uniformly and publicly avowed by its friends, and admitted by its enemies, as the basis of their respective reasonings, both in and out of the state conventions. It is an historical fact, that at the time when the judiciary act was submitted to the deliberations of the first congress, composed, as it was not only of men of great learning and ability, but of men who acted a principal part in framing, supporting or opposing that constitution, the same exposition was explicitly declared and admitted by the friends and by the opponents of that system. It is an historical fact, that the supreme court of the United States have, from time to time, sustained this appellate jurisdiction, in a great variety of cases, brought from the tribunals of many of the most important states in the Union,[b] and that no state tribunal has ever breathed a judicial doubt on the subject or declined to obey the mandate of the supreme court, until the present occasion. * * *

[The Court next rejected the contention that the case was not properly before it because the Virginia decision turned on the Act of Compromise.]

We have not thought it incumbent on us to give any opinion upon the question, whether this court have authority to issue a writ of mandamus to the court of appeals, to enforce the former judgments, as we did not think it necessarily involved in the decision of this cause.

It is the opinion of the whole court, that the judgment of the court of appeals of Virginia, rendered on the mandate in this cause, be reversed, and the judgment of the district court [be] affirmed.

JOHNSON, J. It will be observed, in this case, that the court disavows all intention to decide on the right to issue compulsory process to the state courts; thus leaving us, in my opinion, where the constitution and laws place us— supreme over persons and cases, so far as our judicial powers extend, but not asserting any compulsory control over the state tribunals. In this view, I acquiesce in their opinion, but not altogether in the reasoning or opinion of my brother who delivered it. * * *

Notes and Questions

1. *Was the judgment executed?* Charles Warren reports that the Court "decided to avoid the chance of further friction" with the Virginia Court of Appeals "and accordingly, instead of issuing a second mandate to that Court, it issued its process directly to the District Court [in] which the suit had been

---

b. See, e.g., *Clerke v. Harwood,* 3 U.S. (3 Dall.) 342, 1 L.Ed. 628 (1797) (state law in conflict with treaty). The first Supreme Court decision holding a state law unconstitutional was *Fletcher v. Peck,* 10 U.S. (6 Cranch) 87, 3 L.Ed. 162 (1810) but the case arose in a lower federal court.

originally instituted," 1 Warren, supra, at 450.[c] See also Walter Dodd, *Chief Justice Marshall and Virginia 1813–21,* 12 Am.Hist.Rev. 776, 779 (1907), claiming that the United States marshal was eventually ordered to execute the judgment of the Supreme Court. But William Crosskey insists that execution of judgment was neither issued nor required. Under the Virginia practice, he contends, the proceeding under which the case was brought "served much the same purpose in settling points of law in dispute in land-title controversies, as does a modern action for a declaratory judgment," 2 Crosskey, supra, at 786. Moreover, he adds, "upon the peculiar facts of the case, execution of the judgment would have been a completely vain proceeding; for Hunter could at once have brought a successful action to recover possession again, based on the compromise. There was not a word in the Supreme Court's decision that forbade it." Id. at 806 n.[d]

2. Cohens v. Virginia, 19 U.S. (6 Wheat.) 264, 5 L.Ed. 257 (1821)—which sustained the Court's appellate jurisdiction under § 25 of the Judiciary Act to review state criminal proceedings, and is generally viewed as reaffirming and "supplementing" *Martin,* see 2 Warren, supra, at 10—has stronger historical links with *McCulloch v. Maryland* (set forth, p. 60 infra), see 4 Beveridge, *The Life of John Marshall* 343 (1919).

Appellants were found guilty in a Virginia court of selling lottery tickets in violation of state law. Their defense was that the lottery was organized by the City of Washington, under a congressional statute authorizing the lottery. On appeal to the Supreme Court, they were met with the contentions that the Court had no jurisdiction to review a state criminal case and, in any event, Congress had no power to permit the sale of lottery tickets in a state which prohibited such sale. On the jurisdictional point, Virginia argued that (1) if when the state is a party the Supreme Court has original jurisdiction, this grant excludes appellate jurisdiction; (2) federal courts cannot take original jurisdiction over criminal cases, since that rightfully belongs to the courts of the state whose laws have been violated; (3) consequently, the Supreme Court has no jurisdiction at all. As in *Marbury,* MARSHALL, C.J., used the occasion to express a broad view of the Court's powers, but decided the case on a narrow ground in favor of the Jeffersonians—the federal statute authorizing a lottery had no effect outside the City of Washington.

SECTION 2.　POLITICAL QUESTIONS

Does the principle of judicial review comprehend the Court's acting as "final arbiter" on *all* constitutional questions presented by a case properly within its jurisdiction? Or are some constitutional issues inappropriate for judicial resolution and thus "nonjusticiable"?

c. In respect to its appellate jurisdiction, 28 U.S.C.A. § 2106 presently empowers the Court to "remand the cause and direct the entry of such appropriate judgment, decree or order, or require such further proceedings to be had as may be just under the circumstances."

d. For post-*Martin* instances of state court resistance to Supreme Court orders and various efforts to secure compliance see Walter Murphy, *Lower Court Checks on Supreme Court Power,* 53 Am.Pol.Sci.Rev. 1017 (1959); Charles Warren, *Federal and State Court Interference,* 43 Harv.L.Rev. 345 (1930); Jerry Beatty, *State Court Evasion of United States Supreme Court Mandates During the Last Decade of the Warren Court,* 6 Val.L.Rev. 260 (1972); Notes, 67 Harv.L.Rev. 1251 (1954), 56 Yale L.J. 574 (1947). On the theory of "interposition," see Note, 1 Race Rel.L.Rep. 465 (1956).

NIXON v. UNITED STATES
506 U.S. 224, 113 S.Ct. 732, 122 L.Ed.2d 1 (1993).

CHIEF JUSTICE REHNQUIST delivered the opinion of the Court.

Petitioner Walter L. Nixon, Jr., [a] former Chief Judge of the United States District Court for the Southern District of Mississippi, was convicted by a jury of two counts of making false statements before a federal grand jury and sentenced to prison. The grand jury investigation stemmed from reports that Nixon had accepted a gratuity from a Mississippi businessman in exchange for asking a local district attorney to halt the prosecution of the businessman's son. Because Nixon refused to resign from his office as a United States District Judge, he continued to collect his judicial salary while serving out his prison sentence.

On May 10, 1989, the House of Representatives adopted three articles of impeachment for high crimes and misdemeanors. The first two articles charged Nixon with giving false testimony before the grand jury and the third article charged him with bringing disrepute on the Federal Judiciary.

After the House presented the articles to the Senate, the Senate voted to invoke its own Impeachment Rule XI, under which the presiding officer appoints a committee of Senators to "receive evidence and take testimony." The Senate committee held four days of hearings, during which 10 witnesses, including Nixon, testified. Pursuant to Rule XI, the committee presented the full Senate with a complete transcript of the proceeding and a report stating the uncontested facts and summarizing the evidence on the contested facts. Nixon and the House impeachment managers submitted extensive final briefs to the full Senate and delivered arguments from the Senate floor during the three hours set aside for oral argument in front of that body. Nixon himself gave a personal appeal, and several Senators posed questions directly to both parties. The Senate voted by more than the constitutionally required two-thirds majority to convict Nixon on the first two articles. The presiding officer then entered judgment removing Nixon from his office as United States District Judge.

Nixon thereafter commenced the present suit, arguing that Senate Rule XI violates the constitutional grant of authority to the Senate to "try" all impeachments because it prohibits the whole Senate from taking part in the evidentiary hearings. [The] District Court held that his claim was nonjusticiable and the Court of Appeals for the District of Columbia Circuit agreed.

A controversy is nonjusticiable—i.e., involves a political question—where there is "a textually demonstrable constitutional commitment of the issue to a coordinate political department; or a lack of judicially discoverable and manageable standards for resolving it." *Baker v. Carr,* 369 U.S. 186, 217, 82 S.Ct. 691, 7 L.Ed.2d 663 (1962). But [the] lack of judicially manageable standards may strengthen the conclusion that there is a textually demonstrable commitment to a coordinate branch.

In this case, we must examine Art. I, § 3, cl. 6, to determine the scope of authority conferred upon the Senate by the Framers regarding impeachment. It provides: "The Senate shall have the sole Power to try all Impeachments. When sitting for that Purpose, they shall be on Oath or Affirmation. When the President of the United States is tried, the Chief Justice shall preside: And no Person shall be convicted without the Concurrence of two thirds of the Members present." * * *

Petitioner argues that the word "try" in the first sentence imposes by implication an additional requirement on the Senate in that the proceedings must be in the nature of a judicial trial. From there petitioner goes on to argue that this limitation precludes the Senate from delegating to a select committee the task of hearing the testimony of witnesses * * *.

There are several difficulties with this position which lead us ultimately to reject it. The word "try," both in 1787 and later, has considerably broader meanings than those to which petitioner would limit it. [Thus], we cannot say that the Framers used the word "try" as an implied limitation on the method by which the Senate might proceed in trying impeachments. * * *

The conclusion that the use of the word "try" in the first sentence of the Impeachment Trial Clause lacks sufficient precision to afford any judicially manageable standard of review of the Senate's actions is fortified by the existence of the three very specific requirements that the Constitution does impose on the Senate when trying impeachments: the members must be under oath, a two-thirds vote is required to convict, and the Chief Justice presides when the President is tried. These limitations are quite precise, and their nature suggests that the Framers did not intend to impose additional limitations on the form of the Senate proceedings by the use of the word "try" in the first sentence.

Petitioner devotes only two pages in his brief to negating the significance of the word "sole" in the first sentence of Clause 6. [We] think that the word "sole" is of considerable significance. Indeed, the word "sole" appears only one other time in the Constitution—with respect to the House of Representatives' "sole Power of Impeachment." Art. I, § 2, cl. 5 (emphasis added). The common sense meaning of the word "sole" is that the Senate alone shall have authority to determine whether an individual should be acquitted or convicted. The dictionary definition bears this out. "Sole" is defined as "having no companion," "solitary," "being the only one," and "functioning ... independently and without assistance or interference." If the courts may review the actions of the Senate in order to determine whether that body "tried" an impeached official, it is difficult to see how the Senate would be "functioning ... independently and without assistance or interference."

Nixon [argues] that even if significance be attributed to the word "sole" in the first sentence of the clause, the authority granted is to the Senate, and this means that "the Senate—not the courts, not a lay jury, not a Senate Committee—shall try impeachments." Brief for Petitioner 42. It would be possible to read the first sentence of the Clause this way, but it is not a natural reading. Petitioner's interpretation would bring into judicial purview not merely the sort of claim made by petitioner, but other similar claims based on the conclusion that the word "Senate" has imposed by implication limitations on procedures which the Senate might adopt. Such limitations would be inconsistent with the construction of the Clause as a whole, which, as we have noted, sets out three express limitations in separate sentences.

The history and contemporary understanding of the impeachment provisions support our reading of the constitutional language. The parties do not offer evidence of a single word in the history of the Constitutional Convention or in contemporary commentary that even alludes to the possibility of judicial review in the context of the impeachment powers. This silence is quite meaningful in light of the several explicit references to the availability of judicial review as a check on the Legislature's power with respect to bills of attainder, ex post facto laws, and statutes. See *The Federalist* No. 78.

The Framers labored over the question of where the impeachment power should lie. Significantly, in at least two considered scenarios the power was placed with the Federal Judiciary. [See] *The Federalist* No. 65. The Supreme

Court was not the proper body because the Framers "doubted whether [it] would possess the degree of credit and authority" to carry out its judgment if it conflicted with the accusation brought by the Legislature—the people's representative. In addition, the Framers believed the Court was too small in number: "The awful discretion, which a court of impeachments must necessarily have, to doom to honor or to infamy the most confidential and the most distinguished characters of the community, forbids the commitment of the trust to a small number of persons." Id.

There are two additional reasons why the Judiciary, and the Supreme Court in particular, were not chosen to have any role in impeachments. First, the Framers recognized that most likely there would be two sets of proceedings for individuals who commit impeachable offenses—the impeachment trial and a separate criminal trial. In fact, the Constitution explicitly provides for two separate proceedings. See Art. I, § 3, cl. 7. The Framers deliberately separated the two forums to avoid raising the specter of bias and to ensure independent judgments. [Certainly] judicial review of the Senate's "trial" would introduce the same risk of bias as would participation in the trial itself.

Second, judicial review would be inconsistent with the Framers' insistence that our system be one of checks and balances. In our constitutional system, impeachment was designed to be the *only* check on the Judicial Branch by the Legislature. * * * Judicial involvement in impeachment proceedings, even if only for purposes of judicial review, is counterintuitive because it would eviscerate the "important constitutional check" placed on the Judiciary by the Framers. * * *

Nevertheless, Nixon argues [that] if the Senate is given unreviewable authority to interpret the Impeachment Trial Clause, there is a grave risk that the Senate will usurp judicial power. The Framers anticipated this objection and created two constitutional safeguards to keep the Senate in check. The first safeguard is that the whole of the impeachment power is divided between the two legislative bodies [which] "avoids the inconvenience of making the same persons both accusers and judges; and guards against the danger of persecution from the prevalency of a factious spirit in either of those branches." The second safeguard is the two-thirds supermajority vote requirement. * * *

In addition to the textual commitment argument, we are persuaded that the lack of finality and the difficulty of fashioning relief counsel against justiciability. See *Baker.* We agree with the Court of Appeals that opening the door of judicial review to the procedures used by the Senate in trying impeachments would "expose the political life of the country to months, or perhaps years, of chaos." This lack of finality would manifest itself most dramatically if the President were impeached. The legitimacy of any successor, and hence his effectiveness, would be impaired severely, not merely while the judicial process was running its course, but during any retrial that a differently constituted Senate might conduct if its first judgment of conviction were invalidated. Equally uncertain is the question of what relief a court may give other than simply setting aside the judgment of conviction. Could it order the reinstatement of a convicted federal judge, or order Congress to create an additional judgeship if the seat had been filled in the interim?

Petitioner finally contends that a holding of nonjusticiability cannot be reconciled with our opinion in *Powell v. McCormack,* 395 U.S. 486, 89 S.Ct. 1944, 23 L.Ed.2d 491 (1969). The relevant issue in *Powell* was whether courts could review the House of Representatives' conclusion that Powell was "unqualified" to sit as a Member because he had been accused of misappropriating public funds and abusing the process of the New York courts. We stated that the question of justiciability turned on whether the Constitution committed authority to the House to judge its members' qualifications, and if so, the extent of that commitment. Article I, § 5 provides that "Each House shall be the Judge of the Elections, Returns and Qualifications of its own Members." In turn, Art. I, § 2 specifies three requirements for membership in the House: The candidate must be at least 25 years of age, a citizen of the United States for no less than seven years, and an inhabitant of the State he is chosen to represent. We held that, in light of the three requirements specified in the Constitution, the word "qualifications"—of which the House was to be the Judge—was of a precise, limited nature. [The] claim by the House that its power to "be the Judge of the Elections, Returns and Qualifications of its own Members" was a textual commitment of unreviewable authority was defeated by the existence of this separate provision specifying the only qualifications which might be imposed for House membership. The decision as to whether a member satisfied these qualifications was placed with the House, but the decision as to what these qualifications consisted of was not.[a]

In the case before us, there is no separate provision of the Constitution which could be defeated by allowing the Senate final authority to determine the meaning of the word "try" in the Impeachment Trial Clause. We agree with Nixon that courts possess power to review either legislative or executive action that transgresses identifiable textual limits. [But] we conclude, after exercising that delicate responsibility, that the word "try" in the Impeachment Clause does not provide an identifiable textual limit on the authority which is committed to the Senate.

Affirmed.

JUSTICE STEVENS, concurring.

* * * Respect for a coordinate Branch of the Government forecloses any assumption that improbable hypotheticals like those mentioned by Justice White and Justice Souter will ever occur. * * *

JUSTICE WHITE, with whom JUSTICE BLACKMUN joins, concurring in the judgment.

[The] Court is of the view that the Constitution forbids us even to consider [petitioner's constitutional] contention. I find no such prohibition and would therefore reach the merits of the claim. I concur in the judgment because the Senate fulfilled its constitutional obligation to "try" petitioner.

I. It should be said at the outset that, as a practical matter, it will likely make little difference whether the Court's or my view controls this case.[b] This is so because the Senate has very wide discretion in specifying impeachment trial

---

a. The *Powell* Court felt "compelled to resolve any ambiguity in favor of a narrow construction of the scope of Congress' power to exclude members-elect. A fundamental principle of our representative democracy is, in Hamilton's words, 'that the people should choose whom they please to govern them.' * * * Unquestionably, Congress has an interest in preserving its institutional integrity, but in most cases that interest can be sufficiently safeguarded by the exercise of its power to punish its members for disorderly behavior and, in extreme cases, to expel a member with the concurrence of two-thirds."

On *Powell,* see generally *Symposium,* 17 U.C.L.A.Rev. 1 (1969).

b. Compare Michael J. Gerhardt, *Rediscovering Nonjusticiability: Judicial Review of Impeachments After Nixon,* 44 Duke L.J. 231, 245–46 (1994): "[A] finding of nonjusticiability [is] different from a court's deciding that a wide realm of governmental behavior is constitutional in that a determination of nonjusticiability forecloses a range of potential litigation and signals once and for all that there is no judicial remedy available for any official misconduct within a certain area."

procedures and because it is extremely unlikely that the Senate would abuse its discretion and insist on a procedure that could not be deemed a trial by reasonable judges. Even taking a wholly practical approach, I would prefer not to announce an unreviewable discretion in the Senate to ignore completely the constitutional direction to "try" impeachment cases. When asked at oral argument whether that direction would be satisfied if, after a House vote to impeach, the Senate, without any procedure whatsoever, unanimously found the accused guilty of being "a bad guy," counsel for the United States answered that the Government's theory "leads me to answer that question yes." Especially in light of this advice from the Solicitor General, I would not issue an invitation to the Senate to find an excuse, in the name of other pressing business, to be dismissive of its critical role in the impeachment process.

Practicalities aside, however, since the meaning of a constitutional provision is at issue, my disagreement with the Court should be stated.

II. [T]he issue in the political question doctrine is not whether the Constitutional text commits exclusive responsibility for a particular governmental function to one of the political branches. There are numerous instances of this sort of textual commitment, e.g., Art. I, § 8, and it is not thought that disputes implicating these provisions are nonjusticiable. Rather, the issue is whether the Constitution has given one of the political branches final responsibility for interpreting the scope and nature of such a power.

[T]here are few, if any, explicit and unequivocal instances in the Constitution of this sort of textual commitment. [In] drawing the inference that the Constitution has committed final interpretive authority to one of the political branches, courts are sometimes aided by textual evidence that the judiciary was not meant to exercise judicial review—a coordinate inquiry expressed in *Baker's* "lack of judicially discoverable and manageable standards" criterion. See, e.g., *Coleman v. Miller,* 307 U.S. 433, 452–454, 59 S.Ct. 972, 83 L.Ed. 1385 (1939), where the Court refused to determine the life span of a proposed constitutional amendment given Art. V's placement of the amendment process with Congress and the lack of any judicial standard for resolving the question.

A. [That] the word "sole" is found only in the House and Senate Impeachment Clauses demonstrates that its purpose is to emphasize the distinct role of each in the impeachment process. As the majority notes, the Framers, following English practice, were very much concerned to separate the prosecutorial from the adjudicative aspects of impeachment. Giving each House "sole" power with respect to its role in impeachments effected this division of labor. While the majority is thus right to interpret the term "sole" to indicate that the Senate ought to " 'function independently and without assistance or interference,' " it wrongly identifies the judiciary, rather than the House, as the source of potential interference with which the Framers were concerned when they employed the term "sole."

Even if the Impeachment Trial Clause is read without regard to its companion clause, the Court's willingness to abandon its obligation to review the constitutionality of legislative acts merely on the strength of the word "sole" is perplexing. Consider, by comparison, the treatment of Art. I, § 1, which grants "All legislative powers" to the House and Senate. As used in that context "all" is nearly synonymous with "sole"—both connote entire and exclusive authority. Yet the Court has never thought it would unduly interfere with the operation of the Legislative Branch to entertain difficult and important questions as to the extent of the legislative power. * * *

The historical evidence reveals above all else that the Framers were deeply concerned about placing in any branch the "awful discretion, which a court of impeachments must necessarily have." *The Federalist* No. 65. Viewed against this history, the discord between the majority's position and the basic principles of checks and balances underlying the Constitution's separation of powers is clear. In essence, the majority suggests that the Framers conferred upon Congress a potential tool of legislative dominance yet at the same time rendered Congress' exercise of that power one of the very few areas of legislative authority immune from any judicial review. [In] a truly balanced system, impeachments tried by the Senate would serve as a means of controlling the largely unaccountable judiciary, even as judicial review would ensure that the Senate adhered to a minimal set of procedural standards in conducting impeachment trials.

B. [The] majority finds this case different from *Powell* only on the grounds that, whereas the qualifications of Art. I, § 2 are readily susceptible to judicial interpretation, the term "try" does not provide an "identifiable textual limit on the authority which is committed to the Senate."

This argument comes in two variants. The first, which asserts that one simply cannot ascertain the sense of "try" which the Framers employed and hence cannot undertake judicial review, is clearly untenable. To begin with, one would intuitively expect that, in defining the power of a political body to conduct an inquiry into official wrongdoing, the Framers used "try" in its legal sense. * * *

The other variant of the majority position focuses not on which sense of "try" is employed in the Impeachment Trial Clause, but on whether the legal sense of that term creates a judicially manageable standard. The majority concludes that the term provides no "identifiable textual limit." Yet, [the] term "try" is hardly so elusive as the majority would have it. Were the Senate, for example, to adopt the practice of automatically entering a judgment of conviction whenever articles of impeachment were delivered from the House, it is quite clear that the Senate will have failed to "try" impeachments. Indeed in this respect, "try" presents no greater, and perhaps fewer, interpretive difficulties than some other constitutional standards that have been found amenable to familiar techniques of judicial construction, including, for example, "Commerce . . . among the several States," Art. I, § 8, cl. 3, and "due process of law." Amdt. 5.[c] [3]

III. [T]extual and historical evidence reveals that the Impeachment Trial Clause was not meant to bind the hands of the Senate beyond establishing a set of

---

c. See also Martin H. Redish, *Judicial Review and the "Political Question,"* 79 Nw. U.L.Rev. 1031, 1047 (1985): "Ultimately, *any* constitutional provision can be supplied with working standards of interpretation. To be sure, those standards often will not clearly flow from either the language or history of the provision, but that fact does not distinguish them from many judicial standards invoked every day."

3. The majority's in terrorem argument against justiciability—that judicial review of impeachments might cause national disruption and that the courts would be unable to fashion effective relief—merits only brief attention. In the typical instance, court review of impeachments would no more render the political system dysfunctional than has this litigation.

Moreover, the same capacity for disruption was noted and rejected as a basis for not hearing *Powell*. The relief granted for unconstitutional impeachment trials would presumably be similar to the relief granted to other unfairly tried public employee-litigants. Finally, as applied to the special case of the President, the majority's argument merely points out that, were the Senate to convict the President without any kind of a trial, a constitutional crisis might well result. It hardly follows that the Court ought to refrain from upholding the Constitution in all impeachment cases. Nor does it follow that, in cases of Presidential impeachment, the Justices ought to abandon their Constitutional responsibilities because the Senate has precipitated a crisis.

minimal procedures. Without identifying the exact contours of these procedures, it is sufficient to say that the Senate's use of a factfinding committee under Rule XI is entirely compatible with the Constitution's command that the Senate "try all impeachments." * * *

JUSTICE SOUTER, concurring in the judgment. * * *

As we cautioned in *Baker,* "the 'political question' label" tends "to obscure the need for case-by-case inquiry." The need for such close examination is nevertheless clear from our precedents, which demonstrate that the functional nature of the political question doctrine requires analysis of "the precise facts and posture of the particular case," and precludes "resolution by any semantic cataloguing": "Prominent on the surface of any case held to involve a political question is found a textually demonstrable constitutional commitment of the issue to a coordinate political department; or a lack of judicially discoverable and manageable standards for resolving it; or the impossibility of deciding without an initial policy determination of a kind clearly for nonjudicial discretion; or the impossibility of a court's undertaking independent resolution without expressing lack of the respect due coordinate branches of government; or an unusual need for unquestioning adherence to a political decision already made; or the potentiality of embarrassment from multifarious pronouncements by various departments on one question." Ibid.[d]

Whatever considerations feature most prominently in a particular case, the political question doctrine is "essentially a function of the separation of powers," ibid., existing to restrain courts "from inappropriate interference in the business of the other branches of [the Federal] Government," and deriving in large part from prudential concerns about the respect we owe the political departments. Not all interference is inappropriate or disrespectful, however, and application of the doctrine ultimately turns, as Learned Hand put it, on "how importunately the occasion demands an answer." Learned Hand, *The Bill of Rights* 15 (1958).

This occasion does not demand an answer. The Impeachment Trial Clause * * * contemplates that the Senate may determine, within broad boundaries, such subsidiary issues as the procedures for receipt and consideration of evidence necessary to satisfy its duty to "try" impeachments. Other significant considerations confirm a conclusion that this case presents a nonjusticiable political question: the "unusual need for unquestioning adherence to a political decision already made," as well as "the potentiality of embarrassment from multifarious pronouncements by various departments on one question." * * *

One can, nevertheless, envision different and unusual circumstances that might justify a more searching review of impeachment proceedings. If the Senate were to act in a manner seriously threatening the integrity of its results, convicting, say, upon a coin-toss, or upon a summary determination that an officer of the United States was simply " 'a bad guy,' " judicial interference might well be appropriate. In such circumstances, the Senate's action might be so far beyond the scope of its constitutional authority, and the consequent impact on the Republic so great, as to merit a judicial response despite the prudential concerns that would ordinarily counsel silence. "The political question doctrine, a tool for

---

d. Consider Rebecca L. Brown, *When Political Questions Affect Individual Rights: The Other Nixon v. United States,* 1993 Sup.Ct.Rev. 125, 143, 153: "The six formulations from *Baker* take no account of the need—also mandated by the separation of powers—to ensure that individual rights are not swept up in the passions of the political branches without recourse to an independent judiciary. [Yet the Court] persists in applying the [political question] doctrine in such a way as, most of the time, to do the least violence to those rights."

maintenance of governmental order, will not be so applied as to promote only disorder." *Baker.*[f]

Notes and Questions

1. *Republican form of government.* (a) *Initiative process.* IN PACIFIC STATES TEL. & T. CO. v. OREGON, 223 U.S. 118, 32 S.Ct. 224, 56 L.Ed. 377 (1912), four years after Oregon amended its constitution to allow the people to enact laws through an initiative process, petitioner challenged a tax enacted by an initiative on the ground that the process violated Art. IV, § 4: "The United States shall guarantee to every State in this Union a Republican Form of Government * * *." In essence, the company argued that the initiative process is democratic, not republican. The Court, per WHITE, J., held that the case presented a political question, quoting from *Luther v. Borden,* an action arising out of the Dorr Rebellion in Rhode Island, in which the question of whether the defendant's arrest of the plaintiff was a trespass turned on which of two groups was the lawful government of the state: "[Under Art. IV, § 4], it rests with Congress to decide what government is the established one in a State. For, as the United States guarantee to each State a republican government, Congress must necessarily decide what government is established in the State before it can determine whether it is republican or not. And when the senators and representatives of a State are admitted into the councils of the Union, the authority of the government under which they are appointed, as well as its republican character, is recognized by the proper constitutional authority. And its decision is binding on every other department of the government, and could not be questioned in a judicial tribunal. It is true that the contest in this case did not last long enough to bring the matter to this issue; and as no senators or representatives were elected under the authority of the government of which Mr. Dorr was the head, Congress was not called upon to decide the controversy. Yet the right to decide is placed there, and not in the courts."

Turning from *Luther,* the Court noted that the telephone company's argument proceeds "upon the theory that the adoption of the initiative and referendum destroyed all government republican in form in Oregon. This being so, the contention, if held to be sound, would necessarily affect the validity, not only of the particular statute which is before us, but of every other statute passed in Oregon since the adoption of the initiative and referendum. And indeed the propositions go further than this, since in their essence they assert that there is no governmental function, legislative or judicial, in Oregon, because it cannot be assumed, if the proposition be well founded, that there is at one and the same time one and the same government which is republican in form and not of that character.[a] * * *

---

f. White, J., disagreed with "the prudential version of political question doctrine presented by Justice Souter": "The Constitution requires the courts to determine the validity of statutes passed by Congress when they are challenged, even though such laws are passed with the firm belief that they are constitutional. The exercise of judicial review of this kind, with all of its attendant risk of interference and disrespect, is not conditioned upon a showing in each case that without it the Republic would be at risk. Some account is therefore needed as to why prudence does not counsel against judicial review in the typical case, yet does so in this case."

a. Consider Tribe, *Treatise* 99: "[I]f a court found that a particular feature of state government rendered the government unrepublican, why could not the Court simply declare that feature invalid?" See also Erwin Chemerinsky, *Cases Under the Guarantee Clause Should Be Justiciable,* 65 U.Colo.L.Rev. 849, 872 (1994): "There would be no need to invalidate prior state government actions or to leave the state without a government until the flaws were remedied. For example, when the Supreme Court held that the federal bankrupt-

"Do the provisions of § 4, Art. IV, bring about these strange, far-reaching and injurious results? [D]o they authorize the judiciary to substitute its judgment as to a matter purely political for the judgment of Congress on a subject committed to it and thus overthrow the Constitution upon the ground that thereby the guarantee to the States of a government republican in form may be secured, a conception which after all rests upon the assumption that the States are to be guaranteed a government republican in form by destroying the very existence of a government republican in form in the Nation?

"[The] defendant company does not contend here that it could not have been required to pay a license tax. It does not assert that it was denied an opportunity to be heard as to the amount for which it was taxed, or that there was anything inhering in the tax or involved intrinsically in the law which violated any of its constitutional rights. If such questions had been raised they would have been justiciable, and therefore would have required the calling into operation of judicial power. Instead, however, of doing any of these things, the attack on the statute here made is of a wholly different character. Its essentially political nature is at once made manifest by understanding that the assault which the contention here advanced makes is not on the tax as a tax, but on the State as a State. It is addressed to the framework and political character of the government by which the statute levying the tax was passed. It is the government, the political entity, which (reducing the case to its essence) is called to the bar of this court, not for the purpose of testing judicially some exercise of power assailed, on the ground that its exertion has injuriously affected the rights of an individual because of repugnancy to some constitutional limitation, but to demand of the State that it establish its right to exist as a State, republican in form." [b]

(b) *Malapportionment.* BAKER v. CARR, per BRENNAN, J., held that Tennessee's apportionment of legislative districts with greatly differing populations violated the equal protection clause of the fourteenth amendment: "The question here is the consistency of state action with the Federal Constitution. We have no question decided, or to be decided, by a political branch of government coequal with this Court. Nor do we risk embarrassment of our government abroad, or grave disturbance at home if we take issue with Tennessee as to the constitutionality of her action here challenged. Nor need the appellants, in order to succeed in this action, ask the Court to enter upon policy determinations for which judicially manageable standards are lacking. Judicial standards under the Equal Protection Clause are well developed. [This] case does, in one sense, involve the allocation of political power within a State, and the appellants might conceivably have added a claim under the Guaranty Clause. [Although it] could not have succeeded it does not follow that appellants may not be heard on the equal protection claim which in fact they tender."

FRANKFURTER, J., joined by Harlan, J., dissented: "The present case [is], in effect, a Guarantee Clause claim masquerading under a different label. But it cannot make the case more fit for judicial action that appellants invoke the Fourteenth Amendment rather than Art. IV, § 4, where, in fact, the gist of their complaint is the same. * * *

cy courts were unconstitutional, the Court did not invalidate all of the decisions previously made or immediately banish the courts from existence. The Supreme Court delayed the remedy to provide Congress time to recreate the courts in a manner consistent with the Constitution. In fact, the Court even extended the time period when Congress did not act in a timely fashion."

b. See also *Highland Farms Dairy, Inc. v. Agnew,* 300 U.S. 608, 57 S.Ct. 549, 81 L.Ed. 835 (1937) (rejecting claim that delegation to agency of power to control milk prices violated republican government).

"At first blush, this charge of discrimination based on legislative under-representation is given the appearance of a more private, less impersonal claim, than the assertion that the frame of government is askew. Appellants appear as representatives of a class that is prejudiced as a class, in contradistinction to the polity in its entirety. However, the discrimination relied on is the deprivation of what appellants conceive to be their proportionate share of political influence. * * * Hardly any distribution of political authority that could be assailed as rendering government nonrepublican would fail similarly to operate to the prejudice of some groups, and to the advantage of others, within the body politic. [T]he real battle over the initiative and referendum, or over a delegation of power to local rather than statewide authority, is the battle between forces whose influence is disparate among the various organs of government to whom power may be given. [What] Tennessee illustrates is an old and still widespread method of representation—representation by local geographical division, only in part respective of population—in preference to others, forsooth, more appealing. Appellants contest this choice and seek to make this Court the arbiter of the disagreement. * * * Certainly, 'equal protection' is no more secure a foundation for judicial judgment of the permissibility of varying forms of representative government than is 'Republican Form.' "

(c) If a state's governor dissolved the legislature and suspended all election laws, would (should) the Supreme Court decide whether this violates the guarantee clause? If Congress, legislating under the guarantee clause, permitted a state to establish its government as a monarchy, would (should) a dissenting citizen be barred from Supreme Court review on the ground that this was a "political question"? Suppose Congress mandated that all states have unicameral legislatures? Should the Court hold that the initiative process violates the guarantee clause? Suppose that a city provided all citizens with a technology that made legislative debates on all issues fully available and then allowed citizens to enact legislation on certain issues by popular vote from their own homes? Consider Chemerinsky, supra, at 868: "Madison was particularly concerned that states might be controlled by stable majority coalitions that would systematically impede minority rights.[78] He saw that an integral part of solving the dangers of democracy is having a republican government where people elect representatives and representatives make laws that must comply with state and federal constitutional provisions. [Recently,] historians such as Bernard Bailyn and Gordon Wood, and law professors such as Cass Sunstein and Frank Michelman have argued that the core of a republican government is citizen participation in important public deliberations.[80] Perspectives from both the republican revival and the founders' debates indicate that the Guarantee Clause is not primarily about guaranteeing a particular structure of government in states or even about protecting state governments from federal encroachments. Instead, it is meant to protect the basic individual right of political participation, most notably the right to vote and the right to choose public officeholders."

2. *"Judicially manageable standards."* COLEMAN v. MILLER stated: "[T]he question of a reasonable time [for the pendency of a constitutional amendment before the states involves] an appraisal of a great variety of relevant conditions, political, social and economic, which can hardly be said to be within the appropriate range of evidence receivable in a court of justice and as to which it

---

78. *The Federalist* No. 10.

80. See, e.g., Cass R. Sunstein, *Beyond the Republican Revival,* 97 Yale L.J. 1539 (1988); Frank I. Michelman, *Foreword: Traces of Self-* *Government,* 100 Harv.L.Rev. 4 (1986). But see Richard H. Fallon, Jr., *What is Republicanism, and Is It Worth Reviving?,* 102 Harv. L.Rev. 1695 (1989).

would be an extravagant extension of judicial authority to assert judicial notice. [T]hese conditions are appropriate for the consideration of the political departments of the Government. The questions they involve are essentially political and not justiciable." If the *Coleman* question was "political" for this reason, what of the questions in *Baker*? What of the questions in the *School Segregation Cases,* p. 1173 infra? Is this a helpful test by which to determine justiciability?

3. *Foreign relations.* GOLDWATER v. CARTER, 444 U.S. 996, 100 S.Ct. 533, 62 L.Ed.2d 428 (1979), summarily reversed a court of appeals decision that the President had power to terminate a treaty with Taiwan without congressional approval. REHNQUIST, J., joined by Burger, C.J., and Stewart and Stevens, JJ., believed "that the controversy [is] a nonjusticiable political dispute. [W]hile the Constitution is express as to the manner in which the Senate shall participate in the ratification of a Treaty, it is silent as to that body's participation in the abrogation of a Treaty. In this respect the case is directly analogous to *Coleman.* [In] light of [the] fact that different termination procedures may be appropriate for different treaties, the [case] 'must surely be controlled by political standards.' [T]he justifications for concluding that the question here is political [are] even more compelling than in *Coleman* because it involves foreign relations—specifically a treaty commitment to use military force in the defense of a foreign government if attacked. [W]e are asked to settle a dispute between coequal branches of our government, each of which has resources available to protect and assert its interests, resources not available to private litigants outside the judicial forum."

POWELL, J., concurred because of "prudential considerations": "[A] dispute between Congress and the President is not ready for judicial review unless and until each branch has taken action asserting its constitutional authority. [Since] Congress has taken no official [action], we do not know whether there ever will be an actual confrontation between the Legislative and Executive Branches."

But "reliance upon the political-question doctrine is inconsistent with our precedents. [First,] the text of the Constitution does not unquestionably commit the power to terminate treaties to the President alone. Second, there is no 'lack of judicially discoverable and manageable [standards.]' Resolution of the question may not be easy, but it only requires us to apply normal principles of interpretation to the constitutional provisions at issue. [This] case 'touches' foreign relations, but the question presented to us concerns only the constitutional division of power between Congress and the President. [Finally,] [i]nterpretation of the Constitution does not imply lack of respect for a coordinate branch. *Powell.* * * * 2" a

BRENNAN, J., who would have affirmed on the merits, dissented: "[T]he political question doctrine restrains courts from reviewing an exercise of foreign policy judgment by the coordinate political branch [but] the doctrine does not pertain when a court is faced with the *antecedent* question whether a particular branch has been constitutionally designated as the repository of political decisionmaking power.[b] Cf. *Powell.* The issue of decisionmaking authority must be

2. *Coleman* is not relevant here. [The] proposed constitutional amendment at issue in *Coleman* would have overruled decisions of this Court. Thus, judicial review of the legitimacy of a State's ratification would have compelled this Court to oversee the very constitutional process used to reverse Supreme Court decisions. In such circumstances it may be entire-

ly appropriate for the Judicial Branch of government to step aside. * * *

a. Marshall, J., concurred in the result.

b. *Baker,* per Brennan, J., noted that "it is error to suppose that every case or controversy which touches foreign relations lies beyond judicial cognizance. Our cases in this field seem invariably to show a discriminating analysis of the particular question posed, in terms of the

resolved as a matter of constitutional law, not political discretion; accordingly, it falls within the competence of the courts." [c]

4. *Controversial nature of subject matter.* Should this be an important criterion for determining "political questions"? In *Baker*, Frankfurter, J., argued that "in effect, today's decision empowers the courts of the country to devise what should constitute the proper composition of the legislatures of the fifty States. [The] Court's authority—possessed of neither the purse nor the sword—ultimately rests on sustained public confidence in its moral sanction. Such feeling must be nourished by the Court's complete detachment, in fact and in appearance, from political entanglements and by abstention from injecting itself into the clash of political forces in political settlements." See generally Alexander M. Bickel, *The Least Dangerous Branch* 183–98 (1962).

5. *"Textually demonstrable constitutional commitment."* (a) *Amending process.* (i) Concurring in *Coleman v. Miller*, Black, J., joined by Roberts, Frankfurter and Douglas, JJ., stated that Art. V "grants Congress exclusive power [over] the amending process" and that Congress "is under no duty to accept the pronouncements upon that exclusive power by this Court." Does the language of Art. V support Black, J.? Suppose Congress submitted a proposed constitutional amendment to the states and provided that no African–American could participate in the state ratification process? See generally Laurence H. Tribe, *A Constitution We Are Amending: In Defense of a Restrained Judicial Role,* 97 Harv.L.Rev. 433 (1983); Walter E. Dellinger, *The Legitimacy of Constitutional Change: Rethinking the Amendment Process,* 97 Harv.L.Rev. 386 (1983).

(ii) In *Coleman,* the Court held that "the question of the efficacy of ratifications by state legislatures, in the light of previous rejection or attempted withdrawal, should be regarded as a political question pertaining to the political departments, with the ultimate authority in the Congress in the exercise of its control over the promulgation of the adoption of the Amendment." Does this also apply to the question of whether a state legislature, which has already ratified a proposed amendment, may subsequently rescind that ratification?

(iii) If, pursuant to Art. V, "the legislatures of two-thirds of the several states" apply to Congress to "call a convention for proposing amendments" and Congress ignores the application, is an action for a mandatory injunction "nonjusticiable"? See Arthur E. Bonfield, *The Dirksen Amendment and the Article V Convention Process,* 66 Mich.L.Rev. 949, 976–85 (1968).

history of its management by the political branches, of its susceptibility to judicial handling in the light of its nature and posture in the specific case, and of the possible consequences of judicial action. For example, [w]hile recognition of foreign governments so strongly defies judicial treatment that without executive recognition a foreign state has been called 'a republic of whose existence we know nothing,' and the judiciary ordinarily follows the executive as to which nation has sovereignty over disputed territory, once sovereignty over an area is politically determined and declared, courts may examine the resulting status and decide independently whether a statute applies to that area. [Also, in respect to dates of duration of hostilities,] analysis reveals isolable reasons for the presence of political questions, underlying this Court's refusal to review the political departments' determination of when or whether a war has ended. Dominant is the need for finality in the political determination, for emergency's nature demands 'A prompt and unhesitating obedience,' *Martin v. Mott,* 25 U.S. (12 Wheat.) 19, 30, 6 L.Ed. 537 (calling up of militia). [But] deference rests on reason, not habit. The question in a particular case may not seriously implicate considerations of finality—e.g., a public program of importance (rent control) yet not central to the emergency effort. Further, clearly definable criteria for decision may be available. In such case the political question barrier falls away."

c. Blackmun, J., joined by White, J., dissented. They "would set the case for oral argument and give it the plenary consideration it so obviously deserves."

(b) *Impeachment.* Does *Nixon* preclude all judicial review of the impeachment process? Suppose an impeached federal judge claims that the Senate's conviction was by less than a ⅔ vote? That he was never charged with either "treason, bribery, or other high crimes and misdemeanors" (see Art. II, § 4)? Consider Raoul Berger, *Impeachment: The Constitutional Problems* 117–18, 120 (1973): "Although impeachment was chiefly designed to check Executive abuses and oppressions, there was no thought of delivering either the President or the Judiciary to the unbounded discretion of Congress. This is attested by the Framers' rejection of the unfettered removal by Address [formal request of Congress], by their rejection of 'maladministration' because that was 'so vague' as to leave tenure, 'at the pleasure' of the Senate, and by the substitution of 'high crimes and misdemeanors' with knowledge that it had a 'limited' and 'technical meaning.' "

Suppose a federal judge seeks judicial review of his impeachment and conviction on the ground that he was denied the right to counsel in the proceeding? That many Senators were personally prejudiced against him? That he was impeached because of his race? Because of his political affiliation? Consider Redish, fn. c, p. 31 supra at 1042–43: "I fail to understand a logic that suggests that an appeal to the due process clause of either the fifth or fourteenth amendments can be precluded by a constitutional provision's vesting of power in one of the political branches of government. If the particular exercise of power violates the due process clause, then the fact that a provision in the body of the Constitution authorizes the practice is wholly irrelevant. [It] may well be subject to control through protections contained in the constitutional amendments." Suppose a disappointed candidate for judicial appointment seeks judicial review of the President's failure to nominate him, alleging the foregoing reasons?

(c) *Regulating the militia.* In GILLIGAN v. MORGAN, 413 U.S. 1, 93 S.Ct. 2440, 37 L.Ed.2d 407 (1973), students at Kent State University sought various relief against government officials to prevent repetition of events that had occurred on that campus in May 1970. The court of appeals instructed the federal district court to evaluate the "pattern of training, weaponry and orders in the Ohio National Guard" so as to determine whether it made "inevitable the use of fatal force in suppressing civilian disorders." The Court, per BURGER, C.J., reversed, relying heavily on Art. I, § 8, cl. 16—which grants to Congress "the responsibility for organizing, arming and disciplining the Militia (now the National Guard), with certain responsibilities being reserved to the respective States"— and on federal legislation enacted pursuant thereto: "[T]he nature of the questions to be resolved on remand are subjects committed expressly to the political branches of government. [It] would be difficult to think of a clearer example of the type of governmental action that was intended by the Constitution to be left to the political branches [or] of an area of governmental activity in which the courts have less competence. The complex, subtle, and professional decisions as to the composition, training, equipping, and control of a military force are essentially professional military judgments, subject *always* to civilian control of the Legislative and Executive Branches [which] are periodically subject to electoral accountability." [e]

e. Blackmun, J., joined by Powell, J., concurred: "This case relates to prospective relief in the form of judicial surveillance of highly subjective and technical matters involving military training and command. As such, it presents an '[inappropriate] subject matter for judicial consideration,' for respondents are asking the District Court, in fashioning that prospective relief, 'to enter upon policy determinations for which judicially manageable standards are lacking.' *Baker.* [On] the un-

(d) Do *Nixon, Baker, Powell, Coleman* and *Gilligan* establish that the "political question" doctrine is "a function of the separation of powers"—presently confined exclusively to "the relationship between the judiciary and the coordinate branches of the Federal Government"? That the other *Baker* criteria—including "judicially manageable standards" (note 1 supra) and "the difficulty of fashioning relief" (note 6 infra)—are all subsumed within this specific principle? See R. Brooke Jackson, *The Political Question Doctrine: Where Does It Stand After Powell v. McCormack, O'Brien v. Brown and Gilligan v. Morgan,* 44 U.Colo.L.Rev. 477 (1973). If so, and if the political branches specifically authorize the Court to decide the question, may (should) the Court do so? See Jesse H. Choper, *Judicial Review and the National Political Process* 405–15 (1980). See also note 5, p. 1548 infra.[f]

6. *"Judicial restraint" and the political process.* Consider John P. Frank, *Political Questions,* in Supreme Court & Supreme Law 36, 46 (Cahn ed. 1954): "[T]he basic objective of a plan of government ought to be to put the responsibility for the decision of questions some place, and [the] political question doctrine is useful when it operates to put responsibility at the best place, and is harmful when it puts the decision no place. [W]hat happens in the redistricting cases is that the responsibility, if not taken by the court, is transferred to a body which has a completely vested interest in the maldistricting."[a] Does this adequately respond to Frankfurter, J.'s argument in *Baker* that "appeal must be to an informed, civically militant electorate"; that "in a democratic society like ours, relief must come through an aroused popular conscience that sears the conscience of the people's representatives"? Compare Carl A. Auerbach, *The Reapportionment Cases: One Person, One Vote—One Vote, One Value,* 1964 Sup.Ct.Rev. 1, 2: "It is paradoxical [for] the advocates of judicial self-limitation to criticize the Court for helping to make majority rule effective, because the case for self-restraint rests on the assumption that the Court is reviewing the legislative acts of representatives who are put in office and can be turned out of office by a majority of the people. Since malapportionment destroys this assumption, judicial intervention to remove this obstacle to majority rule may be less intolerable than the self-perpetuation of minority rule."

---

derstanding that this is what the Court's opinion holds, I join that opinion."

Douglas, Brennan, Stewart and Marshall, JJ., dissented because "this case is now moot."

f. For the pre-*Nixon* view that the leading political question cases have *not* "involved abstention from judicial review, or other extraordinary deference" to the political branches—i.e., that the Court has *not* held that the other branches' "determinations were binding on the courts 'right or wrong,' constitutional or unconstitutional"—but rather involved the Court's either "accept[ing] decisions by the political branches [as being] within their constitutional authority," or "refus[ing] some (or all) remedies for want of equity," see Louis Henkin, *Is There a Political Question Doctrine?* 85 Yale L.J. 597 (1976). See also Note, *A Dialogue on the Political Question Doctrine,* 1978 Utah L.Rev. 523.

a. In *Baker,* Clark, J., concurring "would not consider intervention by this Court into so delicate a field if there were any other relief available to the people of Tennessee. But the majority of the people of Tennessee have no 'practical opportunities for exerting their political weight at the polls' to correct the existing 'invidious discrimination.' Tennessee has no initiative and referendum. [T]he legislative policy has riveted the present seats in the Assembly to their respective constituencies, and by the votes of their incumbents a reapportionment of any kind is prevented. The people have been rebuffed at the hands of the Assembly; they have tried the constitutional convention route, but since the call must originate in the Assembly, it, too, has been fruitless. They have tried Tennessee courts with the same result, and Governors have fought the tide only to flounder. It is said that there is recourse in Congress and perhaps that may be, but from a practical standpoint this is without substance. To date Congress has never undertaken such a task in any State."

7. *Presidential war-making power.* (a) If a draftee seeks a federal declaratory judgment that American participation in a particular armed conflict is "unconstitutional in that it was not initially authorized or subsequently ratified by Congressional declaration," is the question "justiciable"? See opinions of Marshall and Douglas, JJ., in *Holtzman v. Schlesinger,* 414 U.S. 1304, 1316, 94 S.Ct. 1, 8, 38 L.Ed.2d 18, 28 (1973)—and lower court decisions and opinions of Supreme Court justices dissenting from denials of certiorari cited therein.[b] Consider Lawrence Velvel, *The War in Viet Nam: Unconstitutional, Justiciable, and Jurisdictionally Attackable,* 16 Kan.L.Rev. 449, 480 (1968): "The proposition that a court may not rule on the issue [because] the question is 'political' [is] at best very dubious, since it denies the court the power to delineate the authority of the various branches of government. Since *Marbury,* it has been clear that this power is a major part of the courts' role in the constitutional scheme." Does this satisfy the *Baker* criteria? Are there "judicially manageable standards"? Consider Archibald Cox, *The Role of Congress in Constitutional Determinations,* 40 U.Cinc.L.Rev. 199, 204 (1971): "[O]ne might formulate a workable principle for delimiting the President's power to engage in military activities overseas, but the task is far from easy. Should the rule permit the use of troops to protect the lives of United States citizens in a foreign country until they can be safely evacuated? Should it permit sending arms with which another nation may defend itself against foreign aggression? Sending 'technicians' to give battlefield instructions in the use of sophisticated weapons? Sending instructors? Sending support troops to protect the bases where logistic support is delivered but to fight only when themselves attacked? If, through gross miscalculation, measures that the rule permits result in armed combat on a sizeable scale, what then may the Executive do, without a declaration of war, to protect the lives of United States soldiers and the national interest during a process of disengagement? May the adverse effects of declaring war upon international relations be taken into account in determining whether the declaration is essential? These are only a few of the pertinent questions." Are there "effective judicial remedies"? Would the Court inevitably be drawn into directing and supervising the conclusion of the war (cf. *Gilligan*)?

(b) Even if there are "political question" considerations lurking, what of the *Baker* "inadequate political redress" factor (note 7 supra)? Consider Warren F. Schwartz & Wayne McCormack, *The Justiciability of Legal Objections to the American Military Effort in Vietnam,* 46 Tex.L.Rev. 1033, 1047 (1968): "It is about as unlikely that a President will, absent judicial intervention, dilute his power by acknowledging the authority of Congress to control the commitment of troops to combat as it was that the state legislators would have weakened their power base through reapportionment. Thus, as in *Baker,* since the political process is itself impaired by the challenged action, there is compelling practical need to restore the effectiveness of the responsible political branch." Is this situation distinguishable from *Baker* because here, if the Court does not intervene, the responsibility is left "to a body (Congress) which has a completely vested interest in" preserving the constitutionally *proper* political authority? Consider John N. Moore, *The Justiciability of Challenges to the Use of Military Forces Abroad,* 10 Va.J.Int'l L. 85, 95–96 (1969): "[S]ince these constitutional claims are intended to resolve a dispute about the relative role of Congress and the Executive and not to apply some constitutional prohibition limiting total governmental power to act, such as the Bill of Rights, if there are institutional checks other than

---

b. See also *Dellums v. Bush,* 752 F.Supp. 1141 (D.D.C.1990)(dictum)(issue of whether Persian Gulf War required congressional authorization *is* justiciable).

judicial determination which each branch exercises on the other it is certainly relevant to the abstention decision. [O]nce a major commitment of troops abroad has been made, Congress could refuse to appropriate funds or to conscript the necessary troops, could censure the President as the House did President Polk for his Mexican War activities, or could even institute impeachment proceedings against the President. And short of these checks, Congress can hold public hearings and mobilize public opinion in a manner which can have a major impact on Executive discretion."

Compare Graham Hughes, *Civil Disobedience and the Political Question Doctrine,* 43 N.Y.U.L.Rev. 1, 16 (1968): "Congress of course might assert that the President has usurped [the power to declare war], but if the courts refused to resolve the dispute we [might] then be presented with a political choice about taking sides but not with a legal question for resolution. If the Constitution reserves powers to Congress in such a way that disputes can be envisaged between Congress and the President, and if the courts tell us that they have no power to resolve such disputes, we can only conclude that such provisions in the Constitution are of no more than hortatory significance." If the President rejects Congress' assertion of authority, what is the likelihood that he will abide by the Court's "resolution of the dispute"? Are the Court's decisions—at least on issues of this nature—of "more than hortatory significance"? See Choper, note 5(d) supra, at 305–08. Compare Leonard G. Ratner, *The Coordinated Warmaking Power—Legislative, Executive and Judicial Roles,* 44 So.Cal.L.Rev. 461, 483 (1971): "Judicial jurisdiction [may] be appropriate to ameliorate the impeachment confrontation that would probably result from presidential defiance of a congressional directive to limit or terminate hostilities. Though a president who defies Congress may also defy the Court, he is more likely to acknowledge the jurisdiction of an impartial and respected tribunal or yield to the pressure of combined legislative and judicial opposition." [c]

(c) If a person is prosecuted for draft evasion—or if a draftee is court martialed for refusing an order to engage in combat and seeks federal habeas corpus—may he obtain an adjudication of the war's constitutionality? Consider Michael E. Tigar, *Judicial Power, The "Political Question Doctrine," and Foreign Relations,* 17 U.C.L.A.L.Rev. 1135, 1177–78 (1970): "[It is] the duty of the Court to consider the legality of a detention by consideration of all the legal rules which are conceded to be operative under the Constitution, laws and treaties of the United States. This determination does not necessarily involve the Executive in litigating the validity of its claim to possess lawfully the power it exercises in conducting a war: it says only that so long as the Executive stays out of the federal courts, its 'right to be let alone' is perhaps arguable, but when it comes into court it must be bound by the rules fashioned by the judiciary and the Congress for the protection of litigants' rights." See also John H. Ely, *War and Responsibility: Constitutional Lessons of Vietnam and Its Aftermath* 55–58 (1993).

SECTION 3. DISCRETIONARY REVIEW

The Supreme Court's original jurisdiction, which typically comprises only a handful of cases each year (mainly concerning "controversies between two or more states"), is presently governed by 28 U.S.C.A. § 1251. The most important

---

c. See also Powell, J., concurring in *Goldwater v. Carter,* note 3 supra: "The spectre of the Federal Government brought to a halt because of the mutual intransigence of the President and the Congress would require this Court to provide a resolution pursuant to our duty 'to say what the law is.' *Marbury.*"

current provisions respecting the Court's appellate jurisdiction, 28 U.S.C.A. §§ 1254 (federal courts of appeals) and 1257 (state courts), both provide for discretionary decisions by the Court itself as to whether to grant the "writ of certiorari."

---

§ 1254. Cases in the courts of appeals may be reviewed by the Supreme Court by the following methods: (1) By writ of certiorari granted upon the petition of any party to any civil or criminal case, before or after rendition of judgment or decree; (2) By certification at any time by a court of appeals of any question of law in any civil or criminal case as to which instructions are desired, and upon such certification the Supreme Court may give binding instructions or require the entire record to be sent up for decision of the entire matter in controversy.

§ 1257. (a) Final judgments or decrees rendered by the highest court of a State in which a decision could be had, may be reviewed by the Supreme Court by writ of certiorari where the validity of a treaty or statute of the United States is drawn in question or where the validity of a statute of any State is drawn in question, on the ground of its being repugnant to the Constitution, treaties, or laws of the United States, or where any title, right, privilege, or immunity is specially set up or claimed under the Constitution or the treaties or statutes of, or any commission held or authority exercised under, the United States.   * * *

Sections 1254 and 1257 previously provided for a form of appeal that required the Court to determine some classes of cases on their merits. Congress removed this form of jurisdiction in 1988 to permit the Court to decide for itself which cases most deserved its attention.

In determining which cases to review, the Supreme Court, in the words of Vinson, C.J., 69 S.Ct. vi (1949), is not "primarily concerned with the correction of errors in lower court decisions. In almost all cases within the Court's appellate jurisdiction, the petitioner has already received one appellate review. [If] we took every case in which an interesting legal question is raised, or our *prima facie* impression is that the decision below is erroneous, we could not fulfill the Constitutional and statutory responsibilities placed upon the Court. To remain effective, the Supreme Court must continue to decide only those cases which present questions whose resolution will have immediate importance far beyond the particular facts and parties involved."

UNITED STATES SUPREME COURT RULES

Rule 10.   Considerations Governing Review on Writ of Certiorari

1. A review on writ of certiorari is not a matter of right, but of judicial discretion. A petition for a writ of certiorari will be granted only when there are special and important reasons therefor. The following, while neither controlling nor fully measuring the Court's discretion, indicate the character of reasons that will be considered: (a) When a United States court of appeals has rendered a decision in conflict with the decision of another United States court of appeals on the same matter; or has decided a federal question in a way in conflict with a

state court of last resort; or has so far departed from the accepted and usual course of judicial proceedings, or sanctioned such a departure by a lower court, as to call for an exercise of this Court's power of supervision. (b) When a state court of last resort has decided a federal question in a way that conflicts with the decision of another state court of last resort or of a United States court of appeals. (c) When a state court or a United States court of appeals has decided an important question of federal law which has not been, but should be, settled by this Court, or has decided a federal question in a way that conflicts with applicable decisions of this Court. * * *

MARYLAND v. BALTIMORE RADIO SHOW, INC.

338 U.S. 912, 70 S.Ct. 252, 94 L.Ed. 562 (1950).

Opinion of JUSTICE FRANKFURTER respecting the denial of the petition for writ of certiorari. * * *

A variety of considerations underlie denials of the writ, and as to the same petition different reasons may lead different Justices to the same result. This is especially true of petitions for review on writ of certiorari to a State court. Narrowly technical reasons may lead to denials. [For detail, see Sec. 5 infra.] A decision may satisfy all these technical requirements and yet may commend itself for review to fewer than four members of the Court. Pertinent considerations of judicial policy here come into play. A case may raise an important question but the record may be cloudy. It may be desirable to have different aspects of an issue further illumined by the lower courts. Wise adjudication has its own time for ripening.

Since there are these conflicting and, to the uninformed, even confusing reasons for denying petitions for certiorari, it has been suggested from time to time that the Court indicate its reasons for denial. Practical considerations preclude. [The] time that would be required is prohibitive, apart from the fact as already indicated that different reasons not infrequently move different members of the Court * * *. It becomes relevant here to note that failure to record a dissent from a denial of a petition for writ of certiorari in nowise implies that only the member of the Court who notes his dissent thought the petition should be granted. * * *

Notes and Questions

1. *The volume of business.* In recent years, roughly 7,000 cases have been filed annually in the Supreme Court. Only a few come within the Court's original jurisdiction or its now-shrunken mandatory appellate jurisdiction; virtually all are petitions for certiorari, which the Court may, but need not, choose to hear. Out of the 7,000 or so cases put before it, the Court will typically accept no more than 150 per Term for full briefing on the merits, oral argument, and plenary decision. In recent years the Court has granted review in even fewer cases; it decided only 95 cases with written opinions in the 1994–95 Term, down from an average of 172 cases each year for the five Terms spanning 1984–88. See the annual November issue, No. 1, of the Harv.L.Rev. for each Term's statistics.

2. *The screening process.* To assist them in screening the petitions, the justices rely heavily on law clerks to summarize the petitions and recommend dispositions. According to recent reports, as many as eight justices now share "pool memos," which are prepared by law clerks and distributed to all justices participating in the pool. See H. W. Perry, Jr., *Deciding to Decide: Agenda*

Setting in the United States Supreme Court 51–64 (1991); John P. Stevens, *The Life Span of a Judge–Made Rule,* 58 N.Y.U.L.Rev. 1, 13–14 (1983). The justices then meet in conference to decide which cases to accept. The Chief Justice prepares a list of cases potentially worthy of consideration, and any other justice may add a case to the "discuss" list. Cases not put on the list are automatically denied review. At conference, there reportedly is relatively little discussion of which cases to grant and which to deny.

Despite the "cert. pool" and a streamlined process of consideration, the screening process makes heavy demands on the justices' time and energy. From time to time, proposals have surfaced to transfer responsibility for management of the Court's docket to some other tribunal.[a] Among the objections to such proposals is that deciding which cases to review is crucial to the Supreme Court's function of overseeing the coherent development and evolution of a uniform body of federal law.[b]

3. *The "rule of four."* (a) By long tradition, it takes the votes of four justices to put a case on the Court's plenary docket. Does the vote of four justices to hear a case oblige the other five to render a decision on the merits, even if some or all believe that argument and decision would squander the Court's time or otherwise be ill-advised?

(b) When the Court feels on oral argument, upon further study, or due to intervening factors, that the basis upon which certiorari was granted no longer exists, the Court may "dismiss the writ as improvidently granted." See Robert L. Stern, Eugene Gressman, Stephen M. Shapiro, & Kenneth S. Geller, *Supreme Court Practice* 231–32, 258–62 (7th ed. 1993). Suppose, however, that the four justices who voted to grant certiorari continue to want the case to be heard. Is a vote to dismiss at that point inconsistent with the "rule of four"? Compare *Triangle Improvement Council v. Ritchie,* 402 U.S. 497, 91 S.Ct. 1650, 29 L.Ed.2d 61 (1971) with *Burrell v. McCray,* 426 U.S. 471, 96 S.Ct. 2640, 48 L.Ed.2d 788 (1976). Consider Stevens, J., concurring in *New York v. Uplinger,* 467 U.S. 246, 251, 104 S.Ct. 2332, 2335, 81 L.Ed.2d 201, 206 (1984): "The Rule of Four is [a] device for deciding when a case must be argued, but its force is largely spent once the case has been heard. At that point, a more fully informed majority of the Court must decide whether some countervailing principle outweighs the interest in judicial economy in deciding the case."[c]

(c) Suppose that four justices vote to grant certiorari in a capital case, and the successful petitioner then applies to the Court for a stay of execution, which would ordinarily require the votes of five justices. Are the five justices who would have denied certiorari obliged by the "rule of four" to attempt to protect the Court's jurisdiction? Compare *Darden v. Wainwright,* 473 U.S. 927, 928, 106 S.Ct. 20, 21, 87 L.Ed.2d 698, 699 (1985)(granting stay of execution by 8–1 vote upon treating the petitioner's request as a petition for certiorari) with *Herrera v. Collins,* 502 U.S. 1085, 112 S.Ct. 1074, 117 L.Ed.2d 279 (1992)(denying stay by

---

a. The most prominent was advanced by a committee chaired by Professor Paul Freund, Report of the Study Group on the Caseload of the Supreme Court (Federal Judicial Center 1972); see Paul A. Freund, *Why We Need the National Court of Appeals,* 59 A.B.A.J. 247 (1973).

b. See, e.g., Earl Warren, *Let's Not Weaken the Supreme Court,* 60 A.B.A.J. 677 (1974).

c. For consideration of the view "that the Rule of Four must inevitably enlarge the size of the Court's argument docket and cause it to hear a substantial number of cases that a majority of the Court deems unworthy of review," see Stevens, supra, at 20.

vote of 5–4). For discussion, see Richard L. Revesz & Pamela S. Karlan, *Nonmajority Rules and the Supreme Court*, 136 U.Pa.L.Rev. 1067, 1074–81 (1988).

4. *Criteria for granting the writ.* How satisfactory are the standards for grants of certiorari that are articulated in Rule 10?[d] Although each of the subparagraphs of Rule 10 refers to a "conflict" of authorities as a basis for certiorari, studies indicate that the Court does not invariably grant certiorari in such cases,[e] and commentators are divided about how to identify "conflicts"[f] and about the importance of resolving conflicts at an early stage before issues have been fully explored in the lower courts.[g]

In recent years, the Court has reversed the judgment below in 60 to 70 percent of the cases in which certiorari is granted[h]—a statistic that seems to confirm the commonsense view that the justices are more likely to vote to hear a case when they believe that it was wrongly decided. See generally Arthur D. Hellman, *Error Correction, Lawmaking, and the Supreme Court's Exercise of Discretionary Review*, 44 U.Pitt.L.Rev. 795 (1983). Nonetheless, other studies indicate that "strategic" voting on whether to grant the writ, including "defensive" votes to deny certiorari based on the fear that a majority of the Court would reverse if review were granted, are relatively rare. See, e.g., Perry, supra, at 198–207.

5. *Significance of denials of certiorari.* The Court has often asserted that the denial of certiorari carries no precedential significance; the Court does not approve the judgment of the lower court, but merely—for unexplained reasons—allows it to stand. But see *United States v. Kras*, 409 U.S. 434, 93 S.Ct. 631, 34 L.Ed.2d 626 (1973).

Consider Peter Linzer, *The Meaning of Certiorari Denials*, 79 Colum.L.Rev. 1227, 1304–05 (1979): "[A] certiorari denial is often not based on the merits and never should bind anyone. [Yet] it seems time to stop pretending that denial of certiorari means nothing. Many times it gives us a glimpse, imperfect to be sure, into the Justices' preliminary attitudes on a given issue."

d. For criticisms and reform suggestions, see Samuel Estreicher & Jonathan Sexton, *Redefining the Supreme Court's Role: A Theory of Managing the Federal Judicial Process* (1986).

e. See, e.g., Floyd Feeney, *Conflicts Involving Federal Law: A Review of Cases Presented to the Supreme Court*, 67 F.R.D. 301 (1975).

f. Compare Feeney, supra, with Note, 59 N.Y.U.L.Rev. 1007 (1984).

g. Compare Richard D. Posner, *The Federal Courts: Crisis and Reform* 163 (1985)(urg-ing that the Court should often allow difficult issues to "simmer" in the lower courts to permit informed and thoughtful decision) with Thomas E. Baker & Douglas D. McFarland, *The Need for a New National Court*, 100 Harv. L.Rev. 1400, 1408–09 (1987)(asserting the importance of uniform national law).

h. See Stern et al., supra, § 4.17, at 195 n. 59.

Chapter 2
SUBSTANTIVE PROTECTION OF ECONOMIC INTERESTS

PREFATORY NOTE

Most of the remaining chapters are concerned with constitutional limitations on government power, independent of limitations arising out of the distribution of powers within the federal system. Some of the limitations are identical, or nearly so, whether applied to the state or federal governments, but are based on different sources. The major limitations on the federal government are found in the Bill of Rights and in Art. I, § 9, while those on state government are based largely on the thirteenth, fourteenth, and fifteenth amendments and on Art. I, § 10. But the fourteenth amendment has now been held to impose on the states most of the limitations the Bill of Rights imposes on the federal government.

These materials do not deal with all the federal constitutional limitations but only those of major significance and difficulty. State constitutions include additional limitations on state government, some similar to federal limitations though occasionally interpreted differently, and some quite dissimilar in terms and purposes. Study of the federal limitations should provide adequate background for handling many of the state-imposed limitations.

SECTION 1. ORIGINS OF SUBSTANTIVE DUE PROCESS

INTRODUCTION

One important concern of this and later chapters is the extent to which the due process clauses of the fifth and fourteenth amendments may be invoked to impose limits on the *substance* of governmental regulations and other activities, as well as to govern the *procedures*, by which government affects "life, liberty and property." That these clauses embody *any* limits on the substance of legislation requires some initial explanation, since their terms refer only to "process."

Professor Edward S. Corwin traced the origin and evolution of due process as a substantive limitation on governmental power in a series of articles,[a] later

a. *The Doctrine of Due Process of Law Before the Civil War*, 24 Harv.L.Rev. 366, 460 (1911); *The Basic Doctrine of American Con-* *stitutional Law*, 12 Mich.L.Rev. 247 (1914); *The "Higher Law" Background of American*

revised in his *Liberty Against Government* (1948).[b] This book, concerned primarily with judicial evolution of concepts designed to limit government regulation of property and economic interests, provides a valuable background for understanding, as well, some of the underpinnings for the later use of the due process clause and first amendment to limit governmental interference with basic personal liberties.

Space limits preclude detailed study here of the judicial search for tools by which to limit governmental power, culminating in the "substantive due process" concept. Here we only sketch some of the more significant steps.

I. JUDICIAL RESPONSE TO PHILOSOPHICAL LIMITS ON GOVERNMENTAL POWER

CALDER v. BULL, 3 U.S. (3 Dall.) 386, 1 L.Ed. 648 (1798), is remembered not for its refusal to interfere when a state legislature set aside a court ruling, but for two opinions that expressed opposing views on the nature and source of limits on government power:

CHASE, J.: "I cannot subscribe to the omnipotence of a State legislature, or that it is absolute and without control; although its authority should not be expressly restrained by the constitution, or fundamental law of the state. The people of the United States erected their constitutions, or forms of government, to establish justice, to promote the general welfare, to secure the blessings of liberty, and to protect their persons and property from violence. The purposes for which men enter into society will determine the nature and terms of the social compact; and as they are the foundation of the legislative power, they will decide what are the proper objects of it. The nature and ends of legislative power will limit the exercise of it. This fundamental principle flows from the very nature of our free republican governments, that no man should be compelled to do what the laws do not require; nor to refrain from acts which the laws permit. There are acts which the federal, or state, legislature cannot do, without exceeding their authority. There are certain vital principles in our free republican governments, which will determine and overrule an apparent and flagrant abuse of legislative power; as to authorize manifest injustice by positive law; to take away that security for personal liberty, or private property, for the protection whereof the government was established. An act of the legislature (for I cannot call it a law), contrary to the great first principles of the social compact, cannot be considered a rightful exercise of legislative authority. The obligation of a law in governments established on express compact, and on republican principles, must be determined by the nature of the power on which it is founded. A few instances will suffice to explain what I mean. A law that punished a citizen for an innocent action or, in other words, for an act, which, when done, was in violation of no existing law; a law that destroys, or impairs, the lawful private contracts of citizens; a law that makes a man a judge in his own cause; or a law that takes property from A and gives it to B: It is against all reason and justice, for a people to intrust a legislature with SUCH powers; and therefore, it cannot be presumed that they have done it. The genius, the nature, and the spirit, of our State governments, amount to a prohibition of such acts of legislation; and the general principles of law and reason forbid them. [To] maintain that our Federal, or State legislature possesses such powers, if they had not been expressly restrained, would, in my

Constitutional Law, 42 Harv.L.Rev. 149, 365 (1928–1929).

b. Republished in *Corwin on the Constitution, Vol. III,* on *Liberty against Government,* edited by Richard Loss (1988).

opinion, be a political heresy, altogether inadmissible in our free republican governments." [a]

IREDELL, J.: "[If] a government, composed of legislative, executive and judicial departments, were established, by a constitution which imposed no limits on the legislative power, the consequence would inevitably be, that whatever the legislative power chose to enact, would be lawfully enacted, and the judicial power could never interpose to pronounce it void. It is true, that some speculative jurists have held, that a legislative act against natural justice must, in itself, be void; but I cannot think that, under such a government any court of justice would possess a power to declare it so.

"[I]t has been the policy of all the American states, which have, individually, framed their state constitutions, since the revolution, and of the people of the United States, when they framed the federal constitution, to define with precision the objects of the legislative power, and to restrain its exercise within marked and settled boundaries. If any act of Congress, or of the legislature of a state, violates those constitutional provisions, it is unquestionably void. [If], on the other hand, the legislature of the Union, or the legislature of any member of the Union, shall pass a law, within the general scope of their constitutional power, the court cannot pronounce it to be void, merely because it is, in their judgment, contrary to the principles of natural justice. The ideals of natural justice are regulated by no fixed standard: the ablest and the purest men have differed upon the subject; and all that the court could properly say, in such an event, would be that the legislature (possessed of an equal right of opinion) had passed an act which, in the opinion of the judges, was inconsistent with the abstract principles of natural justice."

Notes and Questions

1. Compare Lord Coke in *Dr. Bonham's Case*, 8 Co. 113b, 118a, 77 Eng.Rep. 646, 652 (1610): "And it appears in our books, that in many cases, the common law will controul Acts of Parliament, and sometimes adjudge them to be utterly void: for when an Act of Parliament is against common right and reason, or repugnant, or impossible to be performed, the common law will controul it, and adjudge such Act to be void." For commentary on the influence of the Coke dictum, see Corwin, *Liberty Against Government* 34–40 (1948). For philosophical origins of the Chase viewpoint, see Edward S. Corwin, *The "Higher Law" Background of American Constitutional Law*, 42 Harv.L.Rev. 149, 365 (1928–1929). For the extent to which similar viewpoints crept into judicial opinions and decisions between the revolution and 1830, see *Liberty Against Government* 58–67: "The truth is that Iredell's tenet that courts were not to appeal to natural rights and the social compact as furnishing a basis for constitutional decisions was disregarded at one time or another by all of the leading judges and advocates of the initial period of our constitutional history, an era which closes about 1830."

2. *Other early reflections of natural law.* Some early decisions combined the Chase philosophy in *Calder* with broad interpretations of the contract clause, which barred state laws impairing the obligation of contracts. Fletcher v. Peck, 10 U.S. (6 Cranch.) 87, 3 L.Ed. 162 (1810), held that the contract clause prevented legislative annulment of the title of purchasers in good faith, who bought land from grantors who had obtained it by a corruptly-secured legislative grant. To reach this result, the Court construed "contract" to include an "executed con-

---

a. For the view that Chase, J.'s opinion is a philosophical, not a constitutional, argument, see John H. Ely, *On Discovering Fundamental Values*, 92 Harv.L.Rev. 5, 26–27 n. 95 (1978).

tract" or grant of land. MARSHALL, C. J.'s, concluding paragraph revealed the role played by the Chase philosophy: "It is, then, the unanimous opinion of the court, that, in this case, the estate having passed into the hands of a purchaser for a valuable consideration, without notice, the state of Georgia was restrained, either by general principles which are common to our free institutions, or by the particular provisions of the Constitution of the United States, from passing a law whereby the estate of the plaintiff in the premises so purchased could be constitutionally and legally impaired and rendered null and void." JOHNSON, J., concurring, invoked natural justice reasoning: "I do not hesitate to declare that a state does not possess the power of revoking its own grants. But I do it on a general principle, on the reason and nature of things: a principle which will impose laws even on the deity."

Similarly, Terrett v. Taylor, 13 U.S. (9 Cranch.) 43, 3 L.Ed. 650 (1815), per STORY, J., invoked natural justice philosophy and unnamed constitutional provisions to bar Virginia from claiming title to church property under a statute authorizing its sale and the use of the proceeds for the poor of the parish: "[T]hat the legislature can repeal statutes creating private corporations, or confirming to them property already acquired under the faith of previous laws, and by such repeal can vest the property of such corporations exclusively in the state, or dispose of the same to such purposes as they may please, without the consent or default of the corporators, we are not prepared to admit; and we think ourselves standing upon the principles of natural justice, upon the fundamental laws of every free government, upon the spirit and the letter of the constitution of the United States, and upon the decisions of most respectable judicial tribunals in resisting such a doctrine."

During this same period the state courts were protecting vested property rights against legislative interference through a variety of rationales similar to that in *Calder*. See *Liberty Against Government* 65–82 (1948).

II. THE SEARCH FOR A CONSTITUTIONAL BASIS

The philosophical grounds asserted in those early cases for protecting economic interests from legislative power could not long prevail in the face of the growing acceptance of the federal and state constitutions as the only sources of judicially enforceable limitations on legislative power. See *Liberty Against Government* 173: "The doctrine of vested rights attained its meridian in the early thirties, when it came under attack from two sources. The first [was] the notion that the written constitution, being an expression of popular will, was the supreme law of the State and that judicial review could validly operate only on that basis; the second was the related idea, which is connoted by the term 'police power'—that legislation which was not specifically forbidden by the written constitution must be presumed to have been enacted in the *public interest*. Confronted with these doctrines, the champions of the doctrine of vested rights were compelled to find some clause of the written constitution which could be thrown about the doctrine or else to abandon it."

Before the adoption of the fourteenth amendment in 1868, the federal constitution provided little basis for challenging state regulation of economic interests. The Bill of Rights applied only to the federal government,[a] and the

a. *Barron v. Mayor & City Council,* 32 U.S.
(7 Pet.) 243, 8 L.Ed. 672 (1833).

Court soon narrowed the scope of the contract clause,[b] considered Sec. 3 infra. *Charles River Bridge* seemed designed to discourage resort to the federal constitution to escape regulation of economic interests: "It is well settled by the decisions of this court, that a state law may be retrospective in its character, and may divest vested rights; and yet not violate the constitution of the United States, unless it also impairs the obligation of a contract." "Thus it *became more and more evident that the doctrine of vested rights must, to survive, find anchorage in some clause or other of the various State constitutions.*" Liberty Against Government 89.

With federal constitutional grounds not available to protect against most encroachments on economic interests, state judges resorted to the "due process" and "law of the land" clauses of state constitutions. These provisions originally referred to proceeding in accordance with the law and accepted legal procedure. Consider *Liberty Against Government* 90–91: "The 'law of the land' clause of the early State constitutions was usually a nearly literal translation of the famous chapter 29 of the Magna Carta of 1225, the Magna Carta of history.[c] [The] phrase 'due process of law' comes from chapter 3 of the statute of 28 Edward III (1355) which [reads]: 'No man of what state or condition he be, shall be put out of his lands or tenements, nor taken, nor imprisoned, nor disinherited, nor put to death, without he be brought to answer by due process of law.'

"In his Institutes Coke asserts the complete identity in meaning of the two expressions, which he explains as signifying 'due process of the common law,' that is, 'indictment or presentment of good and lawful men [or] writ original of the common law.' Both phrases, in short, were intended to consecrate certain methods of trial; and neither bore any reference to those principles of 'common right and reason' which Coke had invoked in *Dr. Bonham's Case.*"[d]

Professor Corwin pointed out how the state courts began to evolve out of these clauses a substantive limitation on legislative power, aimed first at special legislation designed to affect the rights of specific individuals, and then applied to general legislation interfering with vested rights. See *The Doctrine of Due Process of Law Before the Civil War,* 24 Harv.L.Rev. 366, 460 (1911); *Liberty Against Government* 89–115, 173–74: "Again the ingenuity of Bench and Bar were equal to the exigency. Most State constitutions contained from the outset a paraphrase of chapter 29 of Magna Carta, which declared that no person should be deprived of his 'estate' 'except by the law of the land or a judgment of his peers'; and following the usage of the Fifth Amendment of the United States Constitution, more and more State constitutions came after 1791 to contain a clause which, paraphrasing a statute of Plantagenet times, declared that 'no person shall be deprived of life, liberty or property without due process of law.' By the outbreak of the Civil War a more or less complete transference of the doctrine of vested

---

b. *Proprietors of Charles River Bridge v. Proprietors of Warren Bridge,* 36 U.S. (11 Pet.) 420, 9 L.Ed. 773 (1837) (state grant of right to operate toll bridge did not imply obligation not to authorize competing bridge); *West River Bridge Co. v. Dix,* 47 U.S. (6 How.) 507, 12 L.Ed. 535 (1848) (state grant of exclusive right to operate toll bridge does not bar state from acquiring it by eminent domain); *Stone v. Mississippi,* 101 U.S. (11 Otto) 814, 25 L.Ed. 1079 (1880) (vital public interest permits state to ban lottery business 3 years after it granted 25 year charter).

c. Corwin quoted "its rendition" in the 1780 Massachusetts constitution: "No subject shall be arrested, imprisoned, [or] deprived of his property, [his] life, liberty, or estate, but by the judgment of his peers or the law of the land."

d. The earliest state cases involving a "law of the land" clause found in it no substantive limitation on legislative power. One interpreted it as meaning simply an act of the state legislature, and the other held it to require a jury trial in serious cases. *State v. _____,* 2 Haywood (N.C.) 29, 38 (1794); *Zylstra v. Charleston,* 1 Bay (S.C.) 382 (1794).

rights and most of its Kentian corollaries had been effected in the vast majority of the State jurisdictions. One exception was Kent's distinction between the power of 'regulation,' which he conceded the State, and that of 'destruction,' which he denied it unless it was prepared to compensate disadvantaged owners. The division of judicial opinion on this point was signalized in the middle fifties, when the New York Court of Appeals, in the great *Wynehamer* case, stigmatized a State-wide prohibition statute as an act of destruction, in its application to existing stocks of liquor, which was beyond the power of the State legislature to authorize *even by the procedures of due process of law.* In several other States similar statutes were sustained in the name of the 'police power.' " [e]

WYNEHAMER v. PEOPLE, 13 N.Y. 378 (1856) held by a divided court that a New York prohibition statute violated the state due process clause by forbidding the sale of liquor owned at the time of the enactment of the statute. See *Liberty Against Government* 103, 114–15:

"In *Wynehamer,* [the] court was confronted with a frankly penal statute which provided a procedure, for the most part unexceptionable, for its enforcement. That statute was nonetheless overturned under the due 'process of law' clause, which was [plainly] made to prohibit, regardless of the matter of procedure, a certain kind or degree of exertion of legislative power altogether. The result serves to throw into strong light once more the dependence of the derived notion of due process of law on extra constitutional principles; for it is nothing less *than the elimination of the very phrase under construction from the constitutional clause in which it occurs.* The main proposition of [*Wynehamer*] is that the legislature cannot destroy by any method whatever what by previous law was property. But why not? To all intents and purposes the answer of the court is simply that 'no person shall be *deprived* of life, liberty or *property.'* * * *

"In less than twenty years from the time of its rendition the crucial ruling in *Wynehamer* was far on the way to being assimilated into the accepted constitutional law of the country.[f] The 'due process' clause, which had been intended originally to consecrate a *mode of procedure,* had become a constitutional test of ever increasing reach of *the substantive content of legislation.* Thus was the doctrine of vested rights brought within the constitutional fold, although without dominating it. For confronting it was the still-expanding concept of the police power."

III. FOURTEENTH AMENDMENT

Historical background. The history of the Civil War amendments, particularly the fourteenth, insofar as that history relates to the problems considered in this and later chapters, is thoroughly treated elsewhere. See, e.g., Charles Fairman, *Does the Fourteenth Amendment Incorporate the Bill of Rights? The Original Understanding,* 2 Stan.L.Rev. 5 (1949); Alexander M. Bickel, *The Original Understanding and the Segregation Decision,* 69 Harv.L.Rev. 1 (1955); John P. Frank & Robert F. Munro, *The Original Understanding of "Equal Protection of*

---

e. All extracts from *Liberty Against Government* are reprinted with permission of the publisher, copyright © 1948, Louisiana State University Press.

f. Corwin was referring here to the broad principle exemplified by *Wynehamer*; its actual ruling on state liquor prohibition was rejected by all states but one. See id. at 107.

the Laws" 1972 Wash.U.L.Q. 421 (where other historical studies are cited). Only the barest outline is feasible here.

The thirteenth amendment forbidding involuntary servitude was ratified in 1865, but freeing the slaves did not produce the fruits of freedom, due to the "Black Codes" and other repressive measures.[a] The plight of the blacks and their need at the time was reflected in the Civil Rights Act of 1866, which recognized "all persons born in United States" as United States citizens,[b] and gave to "such citizens, of every race or color, without regard to any previous condition of slavery [the] same right, in every State and Territory in the United States, to make and enforce contracts, to sue, be parties, and give evidence, to inherit, purchase, lease, sell, hold, and convey real and personal property, and to full and equal benefit of all laws and proceedings for the security of person and property, as is enjoyed by white citizens."[c]

Even while that 1866 Civil Rights Act was awaiting enactment, action was under way designed, in part at least, to remove existing doubts as to the power of Congress to enact such legislation. One week after the Senate passed the Civil Rights Act,[d] the Congressional Joint Committee on Reconstruction submitted to both houses of Congress its early version of a fourteenth amendment authorizing Congress to enact laws to protect equal rights.[e] After Congress passed the Civil Rights Act in April[f] over a presidential veto based in part on the view that Congress lacked power to enact the law,[g] the Joint Commission on Reconstruction hammered out a revised proposal that added privileges and immunities, due process, and equal protection provisions as limitations on the states, and authorized Congress to enact legislation to "enforce this article."[h] After further modifications, the most important being the addition of the first sentence relating to citizenship,[i] Congress approved the fourteenth amendment in June, 1866[j] and sent it to the states for ratification.

Ratification was completed in 1868 after bludgeoning the southern states to ratify as a condition for their representation in Congress.[k] Two years later the fifteenth amendment was ratified. Five years later the Court rejected 5 to 4 an attempt to invoke its privileges and immunities, due process, and equal protections clauses to protect economic interests.

SLAUGHTER–HOUSE CASES, 83 U.S. (16 Wall.) 36, 21 L.Ed. 394 (1873), per MILLER, J., upheld a state legislatively-granted monopoly to operate slaughterhouses in the New Orleans area, subject to letting others use the facilities at state-regulated fees. The Court viewed this as an "appropriate, stringent, and effectual" means to "remove from the more densely populated part of the city, the

a. See Gilbert T. Stephenson, *Race Distinctions in American Law* 35–66 (1969 ed.); Gunnar Myrdal, *An American Dilemma* (1962); Frank & Munro, supra, at 444–46.

b. With two exceptions not relevant here.

c. 14 Stat. 27 (1866), 42 U.S.C.A. §§ 1981–1983.

d. Cong.Globe, 39th Cong., 1st Sess. 606 (1866).

e. Fairman, supra, at 21.

f. Cong.Globe, 39th Cong., 1st Sess. 1809, 1861 (1866).

g. Id. at 1860.

h. Fairman, supra, at 41–43.

i. For commentary on this addition see Howard J. Graham, *Our "Declaratory" Fourteenth Amendment,* 7 Stan.L.Rev. 3 (1954).

j. Cong.Globe, 39th Cong., 1st Sess. 2545, 3042, 3149 (1866).

k. 14 Stat. 428, 429 (1867); Walter J. Suthon, *The Dubious Origin of the Fourteenth Amendment,* 28 Tul.L.Rev. 22, 32 (1953).

noxious slaughterhouses and large and offensive collections of animals, [and] to locate them where the convenience, health and comfort of the people require.[a]
* * *

"The first section of the fourteenth article, to which our attention is more specially invited, opens with a definition of citizenship—not only citizenship of the United States, but citizenship of the states. * * * 'All persons born or naturalized in the United States, and subject to the jurisdiction thereof, are citizens of the United States and of the state wherein they reside.' [T]he distinction between citizenship of the United States and citizenship of a state is clearly recognized and established. Not only may a man be a citizen of the United States without being a citizen of a state, but an important element is necessary to convert the former into the latter. He must reside within the state to make him a citizen of it, but it is only necessary that he should be born or naturalized in the United States to be a citizen of the Union. * * *

"The language is, 'No state shall make or enforce any law which shall abridge the privileges or immunities of citizens of the United States.' It is a little remarkable, if this clause was intended as a protection to the citizen of a state against the legislative power of his own state, that the word citizen of the state should be left out when it is so carefully used, and used in contradistinction to citizens of the United States, in the very sentence which precedes it. It is too clear for argument that the change in phraseology was adopted understandingly and with a purpose.

"Of the privileges and immunities of the citizen of the United States, and, of the privileges and immunities of the citizen of the state, and what they respectively are, we will presently consider; but we wish to state here that it is only the former which are placed by this clause under the protection of the federal Constitution, and that the latter, whatever they may be, are not intended to have any additional protection by this paragraph of the amendment."

The opinion distinguished Article IV privileges and immunities mandating equal treatment to citizens of other states. It noted that apart from a few express limitations, such as the prohibition on ex post facto laws, bills of attainder, and laws impairing the obligation of contracts, "the entire domain of the privileges and immunities of citizens of the states [lay] within the constitutional and legislative power of the states, and without that of the federal government. Was it the purpose of the Fourteenth Amendment by the simple declaration that no state should make or enforce any law which shall abridge the privileges and immunities of *Citizens of the United States,* to transfer the security and protection of all the civil rights [from] the states to the federal government? And where it is declared that Congress shall have the power to enforce that article, was it intended to bring within the power of Congress the entire domain of civil rights heretofore belonging exclusively to the states?

"[Such] a construction [would] constitute this court a perpetual censor upon all legislation of the states, on the civil rights of their own citizens * * *.

"We are convinced that no such results were intended by the Congress which proposed these amendments, nor by the legislatures of the states which ratified

---

a. See Herbert Hovenkamp, *Technology, Politics and Regulated Monopoly: An American Historical Perspective,* 62 Tex.L.Rev. 1263, 1295–1308 (1984), for a dramatic historical account of the legislative conversion of the fragmented, unhealthful, mislocated New Orleans slaughtering industry into a well-placed, price-regulated public utility monopoly open to every butcher to use, which solved the health problem and drastically reduced the price of beef.

them.[b]

"The argument has not been much pressed in these cases that the defendant's charter deprives the plaintiffs of their property without due process of law, or that it denies to them the equal protection of the law. The first of these paragraphs has been in the Constitution since the adoption of the Fifth Amendment, as a restraint upon the federal power. It is also to be found in some form of expression in the constitutions of nearly all the states, as a restraint upon the power of the States.

"[U]nder no construction of that provision that we have ever seen, or any that we deem admissible, can the restraint imposed by the state of Louisiana upon the exercise of their trade by the butchers of New Orleans be held to be a deprivation of property within the meaning of that provision.

"[In] the light of the history of these amendments, and the pervading purpose of them, which we have already discussed, [it] is not difficult to give a meaning to [the equal protection] clause. [We] doubt very much whether any action of a state not directed by way of discrimination against the negroes as a class, or on account of their race, will ever be held to come within the purview of this provision. It is so clearly a provision for that race and that emergency, that a strong case would be necessary for its application to any other."

FIELD, J., dissented:[c] "The amendment * * * assumes that there are such privileges and immunities which belong of right to citizens as such, and ordains that they shall not be abridged by State legislation. If this inhibition * * * only refers, as held by the majority of the court, [to] such privileges and immunities as were before its adoption specially designated in the Constitution or necessarily implied as belonging to citizens of the United States, it was a vain and idle enactment, which accomplished nothing, and most unnecessarily excited Congress and the people on its passage. With privileges and immunities thus designated or implied no State could ever have interfered by its laws, and no new constitutional provision was required to inhibit such interference. The supremacy of the Constitution and the laws of the United States always controlled any State legislation of that character. But if the amendment refers to the natural and inalienable rights which belong to all citizens, the inhibition has a profound significance and consequence. * * *

"The terms, privileges and immunities, are not new in the amendment; they were in the Constitution before the amendment was adopted. They are found in [Art. IV, § 2.] In *Corfield v. Coryell*, Mr. Justice Washington said he had 'no

b. Here the opinion added:

"[L]est it should be said that no such privileges and immunities are to be found if those we have been considering are excluded, we venture to suggest some which owe their existence to the federal government, its national character, its Constitution, or its laws.

"One of these is well described in *Crandall v. Nevada,* 73 U.S. (6 Wall.) 35, 18 L.Ed. 745 [1867]. It is said to be the right of the citizen of this great country, protected by implied guarantees of its Constitution, 'to come to the seat of government to assert any claim he may have upon that government, to transact any business he may have with it, to seek its protection, to share its offices, to engage in administering its functions.' * * *

"The right to peaceably assemble and petition for redress of grievances, the privilege of the writ of habeas corpus, are rights of the citizen guaranteed by the federal Constitution. The right to use the navigable waters of the United States, however they may penetrate the territory of the several states, all rights secured to our citizens by treaties with foreign nations, are dependent upon citizenship of the United States, and not citizenship of a state. [To] these may be added the rights secured by the thirteenth and fifteenth articles of amendment, and by the other clause of the fourteenth."

c. Chase, C.J., and Swayne and Bradley, J., joined this dissent. Bradley, J., joined by Swayne, J., also dissented, asserting violation of due process and equal protection.

hesitation in confining these expressions to those privileges and immunities which were, in their nature, fundamental; which belong of right to the citizens of all free governments.' [Field, J., continued with the *Corfield* quotation, supra, p. 281, n.d. In the discussions in Congress upon the passage of the Civil Rights Act repeated reference was made to this language of Mr. Justice Washington. It was cited by Senator Trumbull with the observation that it enumerated the very rights belonging to a citizen of the United States set forth in the first section of the [act].

"The privileges and immunities designated in [Art. IV, § 2] are, then, according to the decision cited, those which of right belong to the citizens of all free governments. [What] the clause in question did for the protection of the citizens of one State against hostile and discriminating legislation of other States, the fourteenth amendment does for the protection of every citizen of the United States against hostile and discriminating legislation against him in favor of others, whether they reside in the same or in different [States].

"This equality of right, with exemption from all disparaging and partial enactments, in the lawful pursuits of life, throughout the whole country, is the distinguishing privilege of citizens of the United States. To them, everywhere, all pursuits, all professions, all avocations are open without other restrictions than such as are imposed equally upon all others of the same age, sex, and condition. The State may prescribe such regulations for every pursuit and calling of life as will promote the public health, secure the good order and advance the general prosperity of society, but when once prescribed, the pursuit or calling must be free to be followed by every citizen who is within the conditions designated, and will conform to the regulations. This is the fundamental idea upon which our institutions rest, and unless adhered to in the legislation of the country our government will be a republic only in name."

Notes and Questions

1. *Objectives of privileges and immunities and citizenship provisions.* An historical study protests that the *Slaughter-House* opinion flies in the face of the congressional purpose for inserting the citizenship sentence. Howard J. Graham, *Our "Declaratory" Fourteenth Amendment,* 7 Stan.L.Rev. 3, 23–26 (1954). "[E]ver since Birney's day, opponents of slavery had regarded all important 'natural' and constitutional rights as being privileges and immunities of *citizens of the United States.* This had been the cardinal premise of antislavery theory from the beginning, and this had been the underlying theory and purpose of Section One from the beginning. The real purpose of adding this citizenship definition was to remove any possible or lingering doubt about the freedman's citizenship."

2. *Resulting scope of privileges and immunities.* Professor McGovney para-phrased the clause as interpreted: "No State shall make or enforce any law which shall abridge any privilege or immunity conferred *by this Constitution, the statutes or treaties of the United States* upon any person who is a citizen of the United States." He then commented, "This narrower construction [renders] it an idle provision, in that it only declares a principle already more amply and more simply expressed in the constitution." Dudley McGovney, *Privileges or Immunities Clause, Fourteenth Amendment,* 4 Iowa Law Bull. (now Iowa L.Rev.) 219, 220, 221 (1918).

3. *The "idle provision."* The restrictive interpretation given the privileges and immunities clause in *Slaughter-House* has been consistently followed. Except

for one quickly-overruled case,[d] the Court has never invalidated state legislation under the fourteenth amendment privileges and immunities clause. On a few occasions a minority of the Court invoked the clause. For details and analysis see Tribe, *American Constitutional Law* 418–26 (1978).

4. *Echoes of Calder and natural justice.* One year after resisting the Field philosophy in *Slaughter-House*, Miller, J., writing for eight justices, echoed *Calder*. Without referring to the Constitution, *Citizens' Savings & Loan Ass'n v. Topeka*, 87 U.S. (20 Wall.) 655, 22 L.Ed. 455 (1875) struck down a tax designed to finance a bonus to attract a private manufacturer to Topeka, as "purely in aid of private or personal [objects] beyond the legislative power and [an] unauthorized invasion of private right: [The] theory of our governments, state and national, is opposed to the deposit of unlimited power anywhere. [There] are limitations on such power which grow out of the essential nature of all free governments. Implied reservations of individual rights, without which the social compact could not exist, and which are respected by all governments entitled to the name. No court, for instance, would hesitate to declare void a statute [which] should enact that the homestead now owned by A should no longer be his, but should henceforth be the property of B." Clifford, J., dissented on much the same basis as did Iredell, J., in *Calder*.[e]

5. *Creative dicta.* Two closely related factors played important roles in the emergence of substantive due process. (1) Lawyers in speeches, treatises, articles and briefs strongly advanced the *laissez faire* concept of government, often urging the due process clause as a constitutional limitation on governmental regulation of business. See the remarkable study of the influence of lawyers in this respect in Benjamin R. Twiss, *Lawyers and the Constitution* 18–173 (1942). (2) Supreme Court justices in dissenting opinions, and state courts, strongly reflected these views, until majority opinions sustaining state regulation began also to recognize that the due process clause imposes some limits on the regulatory power of government. See Edward S. Corwin, *Liberty Against Government* 129–152 (1948).

The Court held fairly firm on its strong position against interference with legislative policy issues as it sustained regulation of the rates of grain elevators in *Munn v. Illinois*, 94 U.S. (4 Otto) 113, 24 L.Ed. 77 (1876), and of railroads in *Railroad Com'n Cases*, 116 U.S. 307, 6 S.Ct. 1191, 29 L.Ed. 636 (1886). Similarly *Mugler v. Kansas*, 123 U.S. 623, 8 S.Ct. 273, 31 L.Ed. 205 (1887), and *Holden v. Hardy*, 169 U.S. 366, 18 S.Ct. 383, 42 L.Ed. 780 (1898), upheld state laws putting liquor dealers out of business and imposing maximum eight-hour days for underground mines and smelters, but in dicta intimated availability of due process protection from laws having "no real or substantial relation" to the public health, morals or safety, or invading "rights secured by the fundamental law," or "not in conformity with natural and inherent principles of justice."

ALLGEYER v. LOUISIANA, 165 U.S. 578, 17 S.Ct. 427, 41 L.Ed. 832 (1897) was the first reasoned decision[a] actually to hold that the substance of economic

---

d. *Colgate v. Harvey*, 296 U.S. 404, 56 S.Ct. 252, 80 L.Ed. 299 (1935), overruled by *Madden v. Kentucky*, 309 U.S. 83, 60 S.Ct. 406, 84 L.Ed. 590 (1940).

e. Because *Topeka's* federal jurisdiction rested on diversity the Court was able to achieve this result on non-constitutional grounds. See *Liberty Against Government* 129; Tribe *Treatise* 563–64.

a. One year earlier *Missouri Pac. Ry. Co. v. Nebraska*, 164 U.S. 403, 17 S.Ct. 130, 41 L.Ed. 489 (1896), held, without further reasons, that a state requirement that a railroad permit con-

legislation violated the federal due process clause. It struck down a Louisiana law forbidding effectuation in Louisiana of an insurance policy entered into outside the state with an unapproved insurance company on property located within the state. While the ruling related to jurisdiction to regulate,[b] the opinion by PECKHAM, J., contained much broader dicta, often repeated later: "The 'liberty' mentioned in that amendment [is] deemed to embrace the right of the citizen to be free in the enjoyment of all his faculties, to be free to use them in all lawful ways; to live and work where he will; to earn his livelihood by any lawful calling; to pursue any livelihood or avocation; and for that purpose to enter into all contracts which may be proper, necessary, and essential to his carrying out to a successful conclusion the purposes above mentioned."

LOCHNER v. NEW YORK

198 U.S. 45, 25 S.Ct. 539, 49 L.Ed. 937 (1905).

JUSTICE PECKHAM delivered the opinion of the Court.

[The Court held invalid a New York statute forbidding employment in a bakery for more than 60 hours a week or 10 hours a day.]

The statute necessarily interferes with the right of contract between the employer and employees. [The] general right to make a contract in relation to his business is part of the liberty of the individual protected by the 14th Amendment. [*Allgeyer.*] The right to purchase or to sell labor is part of the liberty protected by this amendment. * * *

It must, of course, be conceded that there is a limit to the valid exercise of the police power by the state. [Otherwise] the 14th Amendment would have no efficacy and the legislatures of the states would have unbounded power. [In] every case that comes before this court, therefore, where legislation of this character is concerned, and where the protection of the Federal Constitution is sought, the question necessarily arises: Is this a fair, reasonable, and appropriate exercise of the police power of the state, or is it an unreasonable, unnecessary, and arbitrary interference with the right of the individual to his personal liberty, or to enter into those contracts in relation to labor which may seem to him appropriate or necessary for the support of himself and his family? Of course the liberty of contract relating to labor includes both parties to it. The one has as much right to purchase as the other to sell labor.

This is not a question of substituting the judgment of the court for that of the legislature. If the act be within the power of the state it is valid, although the judgment of the court might be totally opposed to the enactment of such a law. But the question would still remain: Is it within the police power of the state? and that question must be answered by the court.

The question whether this act is valid as a labor law, pure and simple, may be dismissed in a few words. There is no reasonable ground for interfering with the liberty of person or the right of free contract, by determining the hours of labor, in the occupation of a baker. There is no contention that bakers as a class are not

struction on its right of way of a private grain elevator not intended to serve the public violated due process by "taking [private property] for the private use of another." Cf. Introduction, Sec. 4 infra.

b. Later cases cut back substantially on the *Allgeyer* jurisdiction ruling. See, e.g., *Alaska* *Packers Ass'n v. Industrial Acc. Com'n,* 294 U.S. 532, 55 S.Ct. 518, 79 L.Ed. 1044 (1935); *Osborn v. Ozlin,* 310 U.S. 53, 60 S.Ct. 758, 84 L.Ed. 1074 (1940); *Watson v. Employers Liab. Assur. Corp.,* 348 U.S. 66, 75 S.Ct. 166, 99 L.Ed. 74 (1954).

equal in intelligence and capacity to men in other trades or manual occupations, or that they are not able to assert their rights and care for themselves without the protecting arm of the state. [They] are in no sense wards of the state. Viewed in the light of a purely labor law, with no reference whatever to the question of health, we think that a law like the one before us involves neither the safety, the morals, nor the welfare, of the public, and that the interest of the public is not in the slightest degree affected by such an act. The law must be upheld, if at all, as a law pertaining to the health of the individual engaged in the occupation of a baker. It does not affect any other portion of the public than those who are engaged in that occupation. Clean and wholesome bread does not depend upon whether the baker works but ten hours per day or only sixty hours a week. [There] is, in our judgment, no reasonable foundation for holding this to be necessary or appropriate as a health law to safeguard the public health, or the health of the individuals who are following the trade of a baker. * * *

We think that there can be no fair doubt that the trade of a baker, in and of itself, is not an unhealthy one to that degree which would authorize the legislature to interfere with the right to labor, and with the right of free contract on the part of the individual, either as employer or employee. In looking through statistics regarding all trades and occupations, it may be true that the trade of a baker does not appear to be as healthy as some other trades, and is also vastly more healthy than still others. To the common understanding the trade of a baker has never been regarded as an unhealthy one. [Some] occupations are more healthy than others, but we think there are none which might not come under the power of the legislature to supervise and control the hours of working therein, if the mere fact that the occupation is not absolutely and perfectly healthy is to confer that right upon the legislative department of the government. [It] is unfortunately true that labor, even in any department, may possibly carry with it the seeds of unhealthiness. But are we all, on that account, at the mercy of legislative majorities? A printer, a tinsmith, a locksmith, a carpenter, a cabinet maker, a dry goods clerk, a bank's, a lawyer's, or a physician's clerk, or a clerk in almost any kind of business, would all come under the power of the legislature, on this assumption. No trade, no occupation, no mode of earning one's living, could escape this all-pervading power, and the acts of the legislature in limiting the hours of labor in all employments would be valid, although such limitation might seriously cripple the ability of the laborer to support himself and his family. In our large cities there are many buildings into which the sun penetrates for but a short time in each day, and these buildings are occupied by people carrying on the business of bankers, brokers, lawyers, real estate, and many other kinds of business, aided by many clerks, messengers, and other employees. Upon the assumption of the validity of this act under review, it is not possible to say that an act, prohibiting lawyers' or bank clerks, or others, from contracting to labor for their employers more than eight hours a day would be invalid. * * *

It is also urged, pursuing the same line of argument, that it is to the interest of the state that its population should be strong and robust, and therefore any legislation which may be said to tend to make people healthy must be valid as health laws, enacted under the police power. If this be a valid argument and a justification for this kind of legislation, it follows that the protection of the Federal Constitution from undue interference with liberty of person and freedom of contract is visionary, wherever the law is sought to be justified as a valid exercise of the police power. Scarcely any law but might find shelter under such assumptions. [Not] only the hours of employees, but the hours of employers, could be regulated, and doctors, lawyers, scientists, all professional men, as well as

athletes and artisans, could be forbidden to fatigue their brains and bodies by prolonged hours of exercise, lest the fighting strength of the state be impaired. We mention these extreme cases because the contention is extreme. We do not believe in the soundness of the views which uphold this law. [The] act is not, within any fair meaning of the term, a health law, but is an illegal interference with the rights of individuals, both employers and employees, to make contracts regarding labor upon such terms as they may think best, or which they may agree upon with the other parties to such contracts. Statutes of the nature of that under review, limiting the hours in which grown and intelligent men may labor to earn their living, are mere meddlesome interferences with the rights of the individual, and they are not saved from condemnation by the claim that they are passed in the exercise of the police power and upon the subject of the health of the individual whose rights are interfered with, unless there be some fair ground, reasonable in and of itself, to say that there is material danger to the public health, or to the health of the employees, if the hours of labor are not curtailed.
* * *

This interference on the part of the legislatures of the several states with the ordinary trades and occupations of the people seems to be on the increase. [It] is impossible for us to shut our eyes to the fact that many of the laws of this character, while passed under what is claimed to be the police power for the purpose of protecting the public health or welfare, are, in reality, passed from other motives. We are justified in saying so when, from the character of the law and the subject upon which it legislates, it is apparent that the public health or welfare bears but the most remote relation to the [law].

JUSTICE HOLMES dissenting: * * *

This case is decided upon an economic theory which a large part of the country does not entertain. If it were a question whether I agree with that theory, I should desire to study it further and long before making up my mind. But I do not conceive that to be my duty, because I strongly believe that my agreement or disagreement has nothing to do with the right of a majority to embody their opinions in law. It is settled by various decisions of this court that state constitutions and state laws may regulate life in many ways which we as legislators might think as injudicious, or if you like as tyrannical, as this, and which, equally with this, interfere with the liberty to contract. Sunday laws and usury laws are ancient examples. A more modern one is the prohibition of lotteries. The liberty of the citizen to do as he likes so long as he does not interfere with the liberty of others to do the same, which has been a shibboleth for some well-known writers, is interfered with by school laws, by the Postoffice, by every state or municipal institution which takes his money for purposes thought desirable, whether he likes it or not. The 14th Amendment does not enact Mr. Herbert Spencer's *Social Statics*. [A] Constitution is not intended to embody a particular economic theory, whether of paternalism and the organic relation of the citizen to the state or of laissez faire. It is made for people of fundamentally differing views, and the accident of our finding certain opinions natural and familiar, or novel, and even shocking, ought not to conclude our judgment upon the question whether statutes embodying them conflict with the Constitution of the United States.

[I] think that the word "liberty," in the 14th Amendment, is perverted when it is held to prevent the natural outcome of a dominant opinion, unless it can be said that a rational and fair man necessarily would admit that the statute proposed would infringe fundamental principles as they have been understood by the traditions of our people and our law. It does not need research to show that no such sweeping condemnation can be passed upon the statute before us. * * *

JUSTICE HARLAN (with whom JUSTICE WHITE and JUSTICE DAY concurred) dissenting:

[Whether] or not this be wise legislation it is not the province of the court to inquire. Under our systems of government the courts are not concerned with the wisdom or policy of legislation.

[The opinion quoted from writers on health problems of workers, pointing out that long hours, night hours, and difficult working conditions, such as excessive heat and exposure to flour dust, were injurious to the health of bakers, who "seldom live over their fiftieth year."]

We judicially know that the question of the number of hours during which a workman should continuously labor has been, for a long period, and is yet, a subject of serious consideration among civilized peoples, and by those having special knowledge of the laws of health.

We also judicially know that the number of hours that should constitute a day's labor in particular occupations involving the physical strength and safety of workmen has been the subject of enactments by Congress and by nearly all of the states. Many, if not most, of those enactments fix eight hours as the proper basis of a day's labor.

I do not stop to consider whether any particular view of this economic question presents the sounder theory. [It] is enough for the determination of this case, and it is enough for this court to know, that the question is one about which there is room for debate and for an honest difference of opinion. There are many reasons of a weighty, substantial character, based upon the experience of mankind, in support of the theory that, all things considered, more than ten hours' steady work each day, from week to week, in a bakery or confectionery establishment, may endanger the health and shorten the lives of the workmen, thereby diminishing their physical and mental capacity to serve the state and to provide for those dependent upon them.

If such reasons exist that ought to be the end of this case, for the state is not amenable to the judiciary, in respect of its legislative enactments, unless such enactments are plainly, palpably, beyond all question, inconsistent with the Constitution of the United States. * * *

SECTION 2. THREE DECADES OF CONTROL OVER LEGISLATIVE POLICY

From *Lochner* in 1905 to *Nebbia* in 1934, infra, the Court frequently substituted its judgment for that of Congress and state legislatures on the wisdom of economic regulation interfering with contract and property interests.[a] It relied mainly upon the due process clauses of the fifth and fourteenth amendments, with occasional resort to the equal protection clause. Between 1899 and 1937, after excluding the civil rights cases, 159 Supreme Court decisions held state statutes unconstitutional under the due process and equal protection clauses and 25 more statutes were struck down under the due process clause coupled with some other provision of the Constitution. Benjamin F. Wright, *The Growth of American Constitutional Law* 154 (1942).

a. See Roscoe Pound, *Liberty of Contract*, 18 Yale L.J. 454 (1909); Ray A. Brown, *Due Process of Law, Police Power, and the Supreme Court*, 40 Harv.L.Rev. 943 (1927).

The Court most freely substituted its judgment for that of the legislature in labor legislation, regulation of prices, and limitations on entry into business. It was most tolerant in the regulation of trade and business practices.[b] A few examples will suffice to show the extent to which the Court interfered with legislative policymaking in economic regulation. With regularity Holmes, J., dissented from this use of the due process clause, joined later by Brandeis and Stone, JJ., and Hughes, C.J.

1. *Control over hours of labor.* We have already seen how the Court barred control over the hours of labor, even in an industry where long hours threatened health. *Lochner* (1905). But in 1908 the Court sustained regulation of work hours for women in *Muller v. Oregon,* 208 U.S. 412, 28 S.Ct. 324, 52 L.Ed. 551 (1908), basing the decision on special considerations relating to women, and in 1917 the Court overruled *Lochner* 5 to 3 in sustaining a regulation of work hours for men in manufacturing establishments. *Bunting v. Oregon,* 243 U.S. 426, 37 S.Ct. 435, 61 L.Ed. 830 (1917). In *Muller* the majority was influenced by the so-called "Brandeis brief," which furnished the Court with overwhelming documentation justifying regulation of hours of labor for women. Felix Frankfurter, Esq., successfully followed the same technique in *Bunting.* See 208 U.S. at 419–20, and 243 U.S. at 433; Henry W. Bikle, *Judicial Determination of Questions of Fact Affecting the Constitutional Validity of Legislative Action,* 38 Harv.L.Rev. 6, 13 (1924).

2. *Control over anti-union discrimination.* At an early date the Court struck down labor legislation forbidding discrimination by employers for union activity and requiring employees to sign "yellow dog" agreements not to join a union. *Adair v. United States,* 208 U.S. 161, 28 S.Ct. 277, 52 L.Ed. 436 (1908) (5th amendment); *Coppage v. Kansas,* 236 U.S. 1, 35 S.Ct. 240, 59 L.Ed. 441 (1915) (14th amendment).

Adair held that for Congress to forbid an interstate railroad to discharge an employee for union membership denied due process. For the Court, Harlan, J., who had dissented in *Lochner,* relied upon the liberty of contract approach in *Lochner* and equated the right of an employee to quit his employment with "the right of the employer, for whatever reason, to dispense with the services of the employee." McKenna and Holmes, JJ., dissented. *Coppage,* per Pitney, J., rejected the claim that the legislature could protect employees from being required to sign yellow dog contracts to obtain or keep needed employment.

These restrictive decisions were distinguished away in *Texas & N.O.R.R. v. Brotherhood of Ry. & S.S. Clerks,* 281 U.S. 548, 50 S.Ct. 427, 74 L.Ed. 1034 (1930) and *NLRB v. Jones & Laughlin Steel Corp.* (1937). They were finally expressly overruled in *Phelps Dodge Corp. v. NLRB,* 313 U.S. 177, 61 S.Ct. 845, 85 L.Ed. 1271 (1941) and *Lincoln Fed. Labor Union v. Northwestern Iron & Met. Co.* (1949), Sec. 3 infra.

3. *Regulation of wages.* Six years after the Court had upheld regulation of hours of labor, it held 5 to 3 that regulation of wages violated due process. *Adkins v. Children's Hosp.,* 261 U.S. 525, 43 S.Ct. 394, 67 L.Ed. 785 (1923) (fifth amendment); *Murphy v. Sardell,* 269 U.S. 530, 46 S.Ct. 22, 70 L.Ed. 396 (1925) (14th amendment); *Morehead v. People of New York ex rel. Tipaldo,* 298 U.S. 587, 56 S.Ct. 918, 80 L.Ed. 1347 (1936) (same). Not until 1937 were these decisions overruled in *West Coast Hotel Co. v. Parrish,* Sec. 3 infra, where the Court

---

b. See summary of such cases in *Nebbia v. New York, infra.*

expressly recognized the unequal bargaining position of workers, and that the wisdom of debatable policy is for the legislature.

4. *Regulation of prices.* The Court also held that regulation of prices for commodities and services violated due process except for a limited class labeled "business affected with a public interest." [c] *Tyson & Bro.—United Theatre Ticket Offices v. Banton,* 273 U.S. 418, 47 S.Ct. 426, 71 L.Ed. 718 (1927) (theatre tickets); *Ribnik v. McBride,* 277 U.S. 350, 48 S.Ct. 545, 72 L.Ed. 913 (1928) (fees of employment agency); *Williams v. Standard Oil Co.,* 278 U.S. 235, 49 S.Ct. 115, 73 L.Ed. 287 (1929) (gasoline prices); cf. *Chas. Wolff Packing Co. v. Court of Industrial Relations,* 262 U.S. 522, 43 S.Ct. 630, 67 L.Ed. 1103 (1923) (compulsory arbitration of wages). *Nebbia v. New York* (1934) severely limited these rulings and they were expressly overruled in *Olsen v. Nebraska ex rel. Western Ref. & Bond Ass'n* (1941), both in Sec. 3 infra.

5. *Limitations on entry into business.* The Court also relied on the "liberty of contract" concept to strike down legislation limiting entry into a business, despite strong demonstrations of need for such limitations. *New State Ice Co. v. Liebmann,* 285 U.S. 262, 52 S.Ct. 371, 76 L.Ed. 747 (1932) (invalid to deny entry into ice business without a finding of "necessity" and that existing facilities are not "sufficient to meet the public needs"); *Louis K. Liggett Co. v. Baldridge,* 278 U.S. 105, 49 S.Ct. 57, 73 L.Ed. 204 (1928) (invalid to limit new entrants into pharmacy business to pharmacists; *Adams v. Tanner,* 244 U.S. 590, 37 S.Ct. 662, 61 L.Ed. 1336 (1917) (invalid to ban private employment agencies that charge fees paid by employees).

In 1973, *North Dakota State Board v. Snyder's Drug Stores,* Sec. 3 infra, overruled *Liggett.* While no cases precisely like *Adams* or *New State Ice* have arisen, the Court in 1963 asserted in effect that *Adams* had been overruled when it unanimously sustained a state prohibition on engaging in the debt adjusting business. See *Ferguson v. Skrupa,* Sec. 3 infra.

SECTION 3. DECLINE OF CONTROL OVER LEGISLATIVE POLICY

NEBBIA v. NEW YORK

291 U.S. 502, 54 S.Ct. 505, 78 L.Ed. 940 (1934).

JUSTICE ROBERTS delivered the opinion of the Court.

[After a year's legislative study of the New York dairy industry, in 1933 New York enacted a law that regulated minimum and maximum retail milk prices, which the Court sustained.]

[Under] our form of government the use of property and the making of contracts are normally matters of private and not of public concern. The general rule is that both shall be free of governmental interference. But neither property rights nor contract rights are absolute; for government cannot exist if the citizen may at will use his property to the detriment of his fellows, or exercise his freedom of contract to work them harm. Equally fundamental with the private right is that of the public to regulate it in the common interest.

c. See Breck P. McAllister, *Lord Hale and Business Affected with a Public Interest,* 43 Harv.L.Rev. 759 (1930); Walton H. Hamilton, *Affectation with Public Interest,* 39 Yale L.J. 1089 (1930); Maurice Finkelstein, *From Munn v. Illinois to Tyson v. Banton: A Study in the Judicial Process,* 27 Colum.L.Rev. 769 (1927).

[T]he guaranty of due process, [demands] only that the law shall not be unreasonable, arbitrary, or capricious, and that the means selected shall have a real and substantial relation to the object sought to be attained. [A] regulation valid for one sort of business, or in given circumstances, may be invalid for another sort, or for the same business under other circumstances, because the reasonableness of each regulation depends upon the relevant facts.

[The opinion here summarized many different kinds of business and property regulations and controls previously sustained against due process attacks.]

The legislative investigation of 1932 was persuasive of the fact [that] unrestricted competition aggravated existing evils and the normal law of supply and demand was insufficient to correct maladjustments detrimental to the community. The inquiry disclosed destructive and demoralizing competitive conditions and unfair trade practices which resulted in retail price cutting and reduced the income of the farmer below the cost of production. [The Legislature] believed conditions could be improved by preventing destructive price-cutting by stores which, due to the flood of surplus milk, were able to buy at much lower prices than the larger distributors and to sell without incurring the delivery costs of the latter. In the order of which complaint is made the Milk Control Board fixed a price of 10 cents per quart for sales by a distributor to a consumer, and 9 cents by a store to a consumer, thus recognizing the lower costs of the store, and endeavoring to establish a differential which would be just to both. In the light of the facts the order appears not to be unreasonable or arbitrary, or without relation to the purpose to prevent ruthless competition from destroying the wholesale price structure on which the farmer depends for his livelihood, and the community for an assured supply of milk.

But we are told that because the law essays to control prices it denies due process. Notwithstanding the admitted power to correct existing economic ills by appropriate regulation of business, [the] appellant urges that direct fixation of prices is a type of regulation absolutely forbidden. [The] argument runs that the public control of rates or prices is per se unreasonable and unconstitutional, save as applied to businesses affected with a public interest * * *.

[W]hat constitutional principle bars the state from correcting existing maladjustments by legislation touching prices? We think there is no such principle. The due process clause makes no mention of sales or of prices any more than it speaks of business or contracts or buildings or other incidents of property. The thought seems nevertheless to have persisted that there is something peculiarly sacrosanct about the price one may charge for what he makes or sells, and that, however able to regulate other elements of manufacture or trade, with incidental effect upon price, the state is incapable of directly controlling the price itself. This view was negatived many years ago. *Munn v. Illinois,* [Sec. 1 supra].

[T]here is no closed class or category of businesses affected with a public interest, and the function of courts in the application of the Fifth and Fourteenth Amendments is to determine in each case whether circumstances vindicate the challenged regulation as a reasonable exertion of governmental authority or condemn it as arbitrary or discriminatory. The phrase "affected with a public interest" can, in the nature of things, mean no more than that an industry, for adequate reason, is subject to control for the public good. [There] can be no doubt that upon proper occasion and by appropriate measures the state may regulate a business in any of its aspects, including the prices to be charged for the products or commodities it sells.

So far as the requirement of due process is concerned, and in the absence of other constitutional restriction, a state is free to adopt whatever economic policy may reasonably be deemed to promote public welfare, and to enforce that policy by legislation adapted to its purpose. The courts are without authority either to declare such policy, or, when it is declared by the legislature, to override it. If the laws passed are seen to have a reasonable relation to a proper legislative purpose, and are neither arbitrary nor discriminatory, the requirements of due process are satisfied. [If] the legislative policy be to curb unrestrained and harmful competition by measures which are not arbitrary or discriminatory it does not lie with the courts to determine that the rule is unwise. With the wisdom of the policy adopted, with the adequacy or practicability of the law enacted to forward it, the courts are both incompetent and unauthorized to deal.

[If] the lawmaking body within its sphere of government concludes that the conditions or practices in an industry make unrestricted competition an inadequate safeguard of the consumer's interests, produce waste harmful to the public, threaten ultimately to cut off the supply of a commodity needed by the public, or portend the destruction of the industry itself, appropriate statutes passed in an honest effort to correct the threatened consequences may not be set aside because the regulation adopted fixes prices reasonably deemed by the Legislature to be fair to those engaged in the industry and to the consuming public. And this is especially so where, as here, the economic maladjustment is one of price, which threatens harm to the producer at one end of the series and the consumer at the other. * * *

Justice McReynolds [dissented, joined by Van Devanter, Sutherland, and Butler, JJ.]:

[P]lainly, I think, this Court must have regard to the wisdom of the enactment. At least, we must inquire concerning its purpose and decide whether the means proposed have reasonable relation to something within legislative power—whether the end is legitimate, and the means appropriate. * * *

The court below [has] not attempted to indicate how higher charges at stores to impoverished customers when the output is excessive and sale prices by producers are unrestrained, can possibly increase receipts at the farm. * * *

Not only does the statute interfere arbitrarily with the rights of the little grocer to conduct his business according to standards long accepted—complete destruction may follow; but it takes away the liberty of 12,000,000 consumers to buy a necessity of life in an open market. [To] him with less than 9 cents it says: You cannot procure a quart of milk from the grocer although he is anxious to accept what you can pay and the demands of your household are urgent! [Grave] concern for embarrassed farmers is everywhere; but this should neither obscure the rights of others nor obstruct judicial appraisement of measures proposed for relief. The ultimate welfare of the producer, like that of every other class, requires dominance of the Constitution.

Notes and Questions

1. *The Nebbia rationale.* Did *Nebbia* appear to retain any degree of judicial review over legislative policy in state economic regulation? What standards of judgment did *Nebbia* suggest the Court would apply? Do you see any significance in the type of interests the Court found sufficient to justify price controls in *Nebbia?* In the sources relied upon by the Court to establish the factual basis for justifying price regulation?

2. *A standard in transition.* (a) WEST COAST HOTEL CO. v. PARRISH, 300 U.S. 379, 57 S.Ct. 578, 81 L.Ed. 703 (1937), sustained 5 to 4 a state regulation of women's wages, overruling earlier decisions. The opinion, per HUGHES, C.J., devoted substantial space to the reasons for regulation of women's wages: "What can be closer to the public interest than the health of women and their protection from unscrupulous and overreaching employers? [The] Legislature of the state was clearly entitled to consider [the] fact that [women] are in the class receiving the least pay, that their bargaining power is relatively weak, and that they are the ready victims of those who would take advantage of their necessitous circumstances. The Legislature was entitled to adopt measures to reduce the evils of the 'sweating system,' the exploiting of workers at wages so low as to be insufficient to meet the bare cost of living, thus making their very helplessness the occasion of a most injurious competition. [Even] if the wisdom of the policy be regarded as debatable and its effects uncertain, still the Legislature is entitled to its judgment."

(b) Compare UNITED STATES v. CAROLENE PRODUCTS CO., 304 U.S. 144, 58 S.Ct. 778, 82 L.Ed. 1234 (1938), per STONE, J., finding due process not violated by a federal statute excluding "filled milk" (non-milk fats added) from interstate commerce: "[R]egulatory legislation affecting ordinary commercial transactions is not to be pronounced unconstitutional unless in the light of the facts made known or generally assumed it is of such a character as to preclude the assumption that it rests upon some rational basis within the knowledge and experience of the legislators. * * *

"Where the existence of a rational basis for legislation whose constitutionality is attacked depends upon facts beyond the sphere of judicial notice, such facts may properly be made the subject of judicial inquiry, and the constitutionality of a statute predicated upon the existence of a particular state of facts may be challenged by showing to the court that those facts have ceased to exist. [B]y their very nature such inquiries, where the legislative judgment is drawn in question, must be restricted to the issue whether any state of facts either known or which could reasonably be assumed affords support for it." Black, J., withheld concurrence in the foregoing portion of the opinion.

(c) Did *Carolene Products* indicate an intention in 1938 to retain the Court's power to strike down economic legislation in appropriate cases? See Robert McCloskey, *Economic Due Process and the Supreme Court: An Exhumation and Reburial,* 1962 Sup.Ct.Rev. 34, 37. What kind of a test of validity would the Court apply?

(d) *United States v. Darby* (1941), Ch. 2, Sec. 3, II, unanimously held FLSA's minimum wage and overtime rate regulations valid under due process on the authority of *West Coast Hotel* without further discussion or justification. Were the reasons for sustaining regulation of women's wages in *West Coast Hotel* so clearly applicable to men's wages as to call for no further justification? Or had the standard for judicial review of interference with "freedom of contract" so changed as to require no justification?

3. *Renunciation of former due process philosophy.* (a) OLSEN v. NEBRASKA, 313 U.S. 236, 61 S.Ct. 862, 85 L.Ed. 1305 (1941), upheld a Nebraska statute fixing maximum fees for employment agencies. DOUGLAS, J.'s, unanimous opinion [a] bluntly rejected the state court's reliance on *Ribnik v. McBride,* 277 U.S. 350, 48 S.Ct. 545, 72 L.Ed. 913 (1928), which had held a similar statute violated due

---

a. McReynolds, J., the last of the four *Nebbia* and *West Coast Hotel* dissenters, retired two days before *Darby* and two months before *Olsen.*

process: "The drift away from *Ribnik* has been so great that it can no longer be deemed a controlling authority. [The Court summarized several cases overruling earlier due process rulings.] These cases represent more than scattered examples of constitutionally permissible price-fixing schemes. They represent in large measure a basic departure from the philosophy and approach of the majority in *Ribnik*. The standard there employed [was] that the constitutional validity of price-fixing legislation, at least in absence of a so-called emergency, was dependent on whether or not the business in question was 'affected with a public interest'. [That] test, labelled by Mr. Justice Holmes in his dissent in [*Tyson*] as 'little more than a fiction', was discarded in *Nebbia*.

"The *Ribnik* case, freed from the test which it employed, can no longer survive. But respondents maintain that the statute here in question is invalid for other reasons. They insist that special circumstances must be shown to support the validity of such drastic legislation as price-fixing, that the executive technical and professional workers which respondents serve have not been shown to be in need of special protection from exploitation, that legislative limitation of maximum fees for employment agencies is certain to react unfavorably upon those members of the community for whom it is most difficult to obtain jobs, that the increasing competition of public employment agencies and of charitable, labor union and employer association employment agencies have curbed excessive fees by private agencies, and [that] there are no conditions which the legislature might reasonably believe would redound to the public injury unless corrected by such legislation.

"We are not concerned, however, with the wisdom, need, or appropriateness of the legislation. Differences of opinion on that score suggest a choice which 'should be left where [it] was left by the Constitution—to the states and to Congress.' *Ribnik,* dissenting opinion. There is no necessity for the state to demonstrate before us that evils persist despite the competition which attends the bargaining in this field. In final analysis, the only constitutional prohibitions or restraints which respondents have suggested for the invalidation of this legislation are those notions of public policy embedded in earlier decisions of this Court but which, as Mr. Justice Holmes long ago admonished, should not be read into the Constitution. [Since] they do not find expression in the Constitution, we cannot give them continuing vitality as standards by which the constitutionality of the economic and social programs of the states is to be determined."

(b) Is the absence in *Olsen* of any judicial explanation of the need to regulate employment agency rates significant? Were there reasons in 1941 to be less skeptical of the *Olsen* expression of no concern over "the wisdom, the need, or appropriateness of the legislation" than of the similar statement in *Nebbia* in 1934? After *Olsen* the Court consistently repudiated *Lochner*-type reasoning in rejecting substantive due process challenges to economic regulation.[b]

b. *Lincoln Fed. Labor Union v. Northwestern Iron & Met. Co.,* 335 U.S. 525, 69 S.Ct. 251, 93 L.Ed. 212 (1949), per Black, J., sustained a state right-to-work law that barred employers' pro-union discrimination: "This Court beginning at least as early as 1934, when [*Nebbia*] was decided, has steadily rejected the due process philosophy enunciated in the *Adair-Coppage* line of cases. [Just] as we have held that the due process clause erects no obstacle to block legislative protection of union members [see Sec. 2, note 2, par. 3 supra], we now hold that legislative protection can be afforded non-union workers."

Day-Brite Lighting v. Missouri, 342 U.S. 421, 72 S.Ct. 405, 96 L.Ed. 469 (1952), per Douglas, J., sustained a requirement that employees have four hours off work with full pay in order to vote: "The liberty of contract argument pressed on us is reminiscent of the philosophy of [*Lochner, Coppage, Adkins v. Children's Hospital*] and others of that vintage. Our recent decisions make plain that we do not sit as a super-legislature to weigh the wisdom of

4. *Social, as distinct from economic, regulation.* WHALEN v. ROE, 429 U.S. 589, 97 S.Ct. 869, 51 L.Ed.2d 64 (1977), per STEVENS, J., upheld a New York law requiring those who fill prescriptions for specified harmful drugs to send copies to the New York Department of Health, where the information, including the patient's name, was to be retained on computers for five years under strict non-disclosure regulations: "There was a time when [the state's inability to demonstrate the need for patient identification] would have provided a basis for invalidating the statute. *Lochner.* [The] holding in *Lochner* has been implicitly rejected many times. State legislation which has some effect on individual liberty or privacy may not be held unconstitutional simply because a court finds it unnecessary, in whole or in part. For we have frequently recognized that individual States have broad latitude in experimenting with possible solutions to problems of vital local concern.

"The New York statute challenged in this [case] is manifestly the product of an orderly and rational legislative decision. It was recommended by a specially appointed commission which held extensive hearings on the proposed [legislation]. There surely was nothing unreasonable in the assumption that the patient identification requirement might aid in the enforcement of laws designed to minimize the misuse of dangerous drugs. For the requirement could reasonably be expected to have a deterrent effect on potential violators as well as to aid in the detection or investigation of specific instances of apparent abuse. At the very least, it would seem clear that the State's vital interest in controlling the distribution of dangerous drugs would support a decision to experiment with new techniques for control. For if an experiment fails [the] legislative process remains available to terminate the unwise experiment." [c]

ABSTENTION EXCEEDING HALF A CENTURY

When faced with substantive due process challenges to economic legislation after 1940, the Court's actual decisions gave full effect to its strong opinions repeatedly asserting that on such matters legislative policy is for the legislature, not the courts. Not since 1937 has the Court struck down economic legislation as violating substantive due process;[a] and only in rare instances have individual

---

legislation nor to decide whether the policy it expresses offends the public welfare. [The] judgment of the legislature that time out for voting should cost the employee nothing may be a debatable one. [But] if our recent cases mean anything, they leave debatable issues as respects business, economic and social affairs to legislative decisions." Jackson, J., dissented and Frankfurter, J., concurred in the result without opinion.

Similarly, *Ferguson v. Skrupa*, 372 U.S. 726, 83 S.Ct. 1028, 10 L.Ed.2d 93 (1963), per Black, J., unanimously spurned a due process challenge to a state law that barred all but lawyers from the business of debt adjusting: "Under the system of government created by our Constitution, it is up to the legislatures, not the courts, to decide on the wisdom and utility of legislation. [The] doctrine that prevailed in *Lochner, Coppage, Adkins* and like cases [has] long since been discarded. We have returned to the original constitutional proposition that courts do not substitute their social and eco-nomic beliefs for the judgment of legislative bodies, who are elected to pass [laws]. [Arguments that] the business of debt adjusting has social utility [are] properly addressed to the legislature, not to us." Harlan, J., concurred in the judgment on the ground that "[this] measure bears a rational relation to a constitutionally permissible objective."

For similar rulings and opinions see *Williamson v. Lee Optical of Okl.*, 348 U.S. 483, 75 S.Ct. 461, 99 L.Ed. 563 (1955); *North Dakota State Bd. v. Snyder's Drug Stores Inc.*, 414 U.S. 156, 94 S.Ct. 407, 38 L.Ed.2d 379 (1973).

c. For cases applying stricter scrutiny to legislation impinging on a limited category of "fundamental" personal rights, see Ch. 7, Sec. 2. However, *Whalen* ruled that the New York law did not unduly impinge on the right to privacy.

a. The last substantive due process decision invalidating economic legislation was *Thompson v. Consolidated Gas Utilities Corp.*, 300

justices withheld their approval of opinions renouncing power under the due process clause to review the wisdom, need, or soundness of such legislation.[b]

Referring to the foregoing due process decisions, and to a similar line of equal protection decisions,[c] Professor McCloskey, p. 334 supra at 38, concluded in 1962: "[T]here could be little doubt as to the practical result: no claim of substantive economic rights would now be sustained by the Supreme Court. The judiciary has abdicated the field." Has the Court "abdicated?" Has it renounced all substantive due process review power over economic legislation? Or has the Court hedged its opinions sufficiently to enable it, without recanting, to reassert substantive due process if it ever concludes that a legislative economic enactment is devoid of any arguable justification? [d]

With such questions in mind, consider DUKE POWER CO. v. CAROLINA ENVIRONMENTAL STUDY GROUP, INC., 438 U.S. 59, 98 S.Ct. 2620, 57 L.Ed.2d 595 (1978). *Duke Power,* per BURGER, C.J., upheld the Price-Anderson Act's limit on the aggregate liability for a single nuclear incident in the atomic energy industry to the amount available through private insurance ($60 million) plus the $500 million indemnification undertaken by the federal government: [e] "[I]t is clear that Congress' purpose was to remove the economic impediments in order to stimulate the private development of electric energy by nuclear power while simultaneously providing the public compensation in the event of a catastrophic nuclear incident. The liability limitation provision thus emerges as a classic example of an economic regulation—a legislative effort to structure and accommodate 'the burdens and benefits of economic life.' *Usery v. Turner Elkhorn Mining Co.,* 428 U.S. 1, 96 S.Ct. 2882, 49 L.Ed.2d 752 (1976). 'It is by now well established that [such] legislative Acts [come] to the Court with a presumption of constitutionality, and that the burden is on one complaining of a due process violation to establish that the legislature has acted in an arbitrary and irrational way.' Ibid. That the accommodation struck may have profound and far-reaching consequences, contrary to appellees' suggestion, provides all the more reason for this Court to defer to the congressional judgment unless it is demonstrably arbitrary or irrational.

"When examined in light of this standard of review, the Price-Anderson Act, in our view, passes constitutional muster. The record before us fully supports the need for the imposition of a statutory limit on liability to encourage private industry participation and hence bears a rational relationship to Congress' concern for stimulating the involvement of private enterprise in the production of electric energy through the use of atomic power; nor do we understand appellees or the District Court to be of a different view. Rather, their challenge is to the alleged arbitrariness of the *particular figure* of $560 million, which is the statutory ceiling on liability. The District Court aptly summarized its position: 'The amount of recovery is not rationally related to the potential losses, [which] could well be many, many times [that] limit.'

U.S. 55, 57 S.Ct. 364, 81 L.Ed. 510 (1937), where the regulation was viewed as taking property for a private purpose.

b. See the Harlan concurrence in *Ferguson v. Skrupa,* and the Jackson dissent and Frankfurter concurrence "in the result" in *Day-Brite Lighting.*

c. For the equal protection cases relating to economic regulation see Ch. 10, Sec. 1.

d. Cf. Christopher T. Wonnell, *Economic Due Process and the Preservation of Competi-*

tion, 11 Hast. Const.L.Q. 91 (1983) (a strongly reasoned argument that substantive due process should be extended to protect "free and open competition for society's lawful occupations [as] a constitutional value" that could invalidate legislation enforcing monopoly conditions, absent a sufficiently strong state interest).

e. Stewart, Rehnquist and Stevens, JJ., concurred in the result without reaching the merits.

"Assuming, arguendo, that the $560 million fund would not insure full recovery in all conceivable circumstances,—and the hard truth is that no one can ever know—it does not by any means follow that the liability limitation is therefore irrational and violative of due process. The legislative history clearly indicates that the $560 million figure was not arrived at on the supposition that it alone would necessarily be sufficient to guarantee full compensation in the event of a nuclear incident. Instead, it was conceived of as a 'starting point' or a working hypothesis. The reasonableness of the statute's assumed ceiling on liability was predicated on two corollary considerations—expert appraisals of the exceedingly small risk of a nuclear incident involving claims in excess of $560 million, and the recognition that in the event of such an incident, Congress would likely enact extraordinary relief provisions to provide additional relief, in accord with prior practice."

Notes and Questions

1. *The standard of review.* (a) Was the standard of review that *Turner Elkhorn* and *Duke Power* asserted with no dissenting voices—"demonstrably arbitrary or irrational"—consistent with the opinions from *Olsen* (1941) to *Snyder* (1973)? In forecasting future decisions on such issues, is it significant that *Duke Power* used four pages to explain why Price-Anderson was not "arbitrary or irrational" and hence "passes constitutional muster?"

(b) Did "arbitrary or irrational" mean something different in 1978 than from 1905 (*Lochner*) to 1934 (*Nebbia*)? *North Dakota State Bd.* (1973), supra, per Douglas, J., in overruling *Liggett Co. v. Baldridge* (1928) [Sec. 2, note 5 supra] to uphold a requirement that pharmacies be owned by pharmacists, noted that " 'a pronounced shift in emphasis since [*Liggett*]' had deprived the words 'unreasonable' and 'arbitrary' of the meaning which *Liggett* ascribed to them." Realistically, what appears to be the standard after *Duke Power?* Does *Duke Power* portend a difference in the results of due process challenges to economic regulation, or does it reflect only a different pattern of opinion writing?

2. *Protection of "personal" rights.* The Court gives far stricter scrutiny and greater constitutional protection to some *personal* rights, often viewed as "fundamental," than to *economic* or *social welfare* interests. This development is considered primarily in Ch. 7, Sec. 2, and Ch. 10, Sec. 4.

3. *Equal protection.* The rise and fall of judicial protection of economic and social welfare interests under the equal protection clause is similar to that under due process, though equal protection issues involve somewhat different concerns and values. See Ch. 10, Sec. 1.

4. *Substantive due process under state constitutions.* Most state constitutions include due process clauses identical or similar to that in the fourteenth amendment. Not all state courts, whose interpretations and applications of their own state constitutions are not ordinarily subject to Supreme Court review, have followed the Court's lead in leaving economic policy decisions to the legislature. A few have continued to follow the Court's 1905–1934 approach, invalidating under state due process clauses economic legislation that the Supreme Court would have upheld.[f]

f. The cases to 1958 are found in Monrad Paulsen, *The Persistence of Substantive Due Process in the States,* 34 Minn.L.Rev. 91 (1950); John A.C. Hetherington, *State Economic Regulation and Substantive Due Process* *of Law,* 53 Nw.U.L.Rev. 13, 226 (1958). A few such decisions continue. See, e.g., *Gillette Dairy, Inc. v. Nebraska Dairy Products Bd.,* 192 Neb. 89, 219 N.W.2d 214 (1974) (milk price control); *Condemarin v. University Hos-*

SECTION 4. "TAKING" OF PROPERTY INTERESTS

INTRODUCTION

The fifth amendment limits the federal government's power of eminent domain: "nor shall private property be taken for a public use without just compensation." Similarly the due process clause has long been held to require a state to compensate the owner when it takes property for a public use,[a] and to forbid taking property for a private use, even with compensation.[b] Space limits do not permit consideration of the extensive body of law relating to eminent domain. Two aspects only are considered here: (1) What are the limits, if any, on the purposes for which property may be taken, even with compensation? (2) Under what circumstances may, or should, a regulation be considered a "taking" that requires compensation?

I. PURPOSE OF "TAKING"

BERMAN v. PARKER, 348 U.S. 26, 75 S.Ct. 98, 99 L.Ed. 27 (1954), per DOUGLAS, J., unanimously upheld the District of Columbia Redevelopment Act, which authorized the Redevelopment Agency to acquire and assemble, by eminent domain or otherwise, real property "for the redevelopment of blighted territory (and) the prevention, reduction, or elimination of blighting factors." The Agency was empowered to transfer such property to public agencies for streets, utilities, recreational facilities and schools; and to lease or sell the remainder, preferably to a private redevelopment company, under terms that required the lessee or purchaser to conform to the redevelopment plan adopted by the National Capital Planning Commission. The Court found no fifth amendment violation in the Agency's taking by eminent domain a well-maintained department store posing no blight or health problem itself, located in a redevelopment area where roughly two-thirds of the dwellings were beyond repair or otherwise blighted:

"The power of Congress over the District of Columbia includes all the legislative powers which a state may exercise over its affairs. We deal, in other words, with what traditionally has been known as the police power. [Subject] to specific constitutional limitations, when the legislature has spoken, the public interest has been declared in terms well-nigh conclusive. In such cases the legislature, not the judiciary, is the main guardian of the public needs to be served by social legislation. [This] principle admits of no exception merely because the power of eminent domain is involved. The role of the judiciary in determining whether that power is being exercised for a public purpose is an extremely narrow one.

"Public safety, public health, morality, peace and quiet, law and order—these are some of the more conspicuous examples of the traditional application of the police power to municipal affairs. Yet they merely illustrate the scope of the power and do not delimit it. Miserable and disreputable housing conditions may do more than spread disease and crime and immorality. They may also suffocate

---

pital, 775 P.2d 348 (Utah 1989)(limitation on state liability).

    a. See *Chicago, B. & Q.R.R. v. Chicago,* 166 U.S. 226, 241, 17 S.Ct. 581, 586, 41 L.Ed. 979, 986 (1897).

    b. *Missouri Pac. Ry. v. Nebraska,* 164 U.S. 403, 17 S.Ct. 130, 41 L.Ed. 489 (1896).

the spirit * * *; make living an almost insufferable burden. They may [be] a blight on the community which robs it of charm, which makes it a place from which men turn. * * *

"We do not sit to determine whether a particular housing project is or is not desirable. The concept of the public welfare is broad and inclusive. The values it represents are spiritual as well as physical, aesthetic as well as monetary. It is within the power of the legislature to determine that the community should be beautiful as well as healthy, spacious as well as clean, well-balanced as well as carefully patrolled. In the present case, the Congress and its authorized agencies have made determinations that take into account a wide variety of values. It is not for us to reappraise them. If those who govern the District of Columbia decide that the Nation's Capital should be beautiful as well as sanitary, there is nothing in the Fifth Amendment that stands in the way.

"Once the object is within the authority of Congress, the right to realize it through the exercise of eminent domain is clear. For the power of eminent domain is merely the means to the end. [Here] one of the means chosen is the use of private enterprise for redevelopment of the area. Appellants argue that this makes the project a taking from one businessman for the benefit of another businessman. But the means of executing the project are for Congress and Congress alone to determine, once the public purpose has been established. The public end may be as well or better served through an agency of private enterprise than through a department of government—or so the Congress might conclude. We cannot say that public ownership is the sole method of promoting the public purposes of community redevelopment projects. * * *

"In the present case, Congress and its authorized agencies attack the problem of the blighted parts of the community on an area rather than on a structure-by-structure basis. That, too, is opposed by appellants. They maintain that since their building does not imperil health or safety nor contribute to the making of a slum or a blighted area, it cannot be swept into a redevelopment plan by the mere dictum of the Planning Commission or the Commissioners. The particular uses to be made of the land in the project were determined with regard to the needs of the particular community. The experts concluded that if the community were to be healthy, if it were not to revert again to a blighted or slum area, as though possessed of a congenital disease, the area must be planned as a whole. It was not enough, they believed, to remove existing buildings that were insanitary or unsightly. It was important to redesign the whole area so as to eliminate the conditions that cause slums—the overcrowding of dwellings, the lack of parks, the lack of adequate streets and alleys, the absence of recreational areas, the lack of light and air, the presence of outmoded street patterns. It was believed that the piecemeal approach, the removal of individual structures that were offensive, would be only a palliative. The entire area needed redesigning so that a balanced, integrated plan could be developed for the region, including not only new homes but also schools, churches, parks, streets, and shopping centers. [Such] diversification in future use is plainly relevant to the maintenance of the desired housing standards and therefore within congressional power."

Notes and Questions

1. *Historical development.* For a study of the rise and fall of limitations on the exercise of the power of eminent domain see Note, *The Public Use Limitation on Eminent Domain: An Advance Requiem,* 58 Yale L.J. 599 (1949). The Court found a "public use" or "public purpose" limitation on the taking of private property, even for compensation, in the fifth amendment and in the due process

clause of the fourteenth amendment. Id.; Allison Dunham, *Griggs v. Allegheny County in Perspective: Thirty Years of Supreme Court Expropriation Law,* 1962 Sup.Ct.Rev. 63, 65. Prior to 1946 the condemnation of private land normally was justified on one of two grounds: (1) "public use" of the property in the sense of actual subjection of the property to use by a segment of the public, or (2) the purchase of the land to eliminate a public evil and thus for a "public purpose." Id. at 66–67.

2. *"Taking" to lessen concentrated land ownership.* HAWAII HOUSING AUTH. v. MIDKIFF, 467 U.S. 229, 104 S.Ct. 2321, 81 L.Ed.2d 186 (1984), per O'CONNOR, J., upheld the use of eminent domain to lessen the concentration of fee simple land ownership, inherited from Hawaii's early feudal land tenure system. In the 1960's the Hawaii legislature found that 72 private owners owned 47% of Hawaiian land, and the state and federal government 49%, leaving only 4% for all other private owners. On Oahu, the most urbanized island, 22 landowners owned 72.5% of the fee simple titles. The legislature found, as summarized by the Court, that such concentrated land ownership was "responsible for skewing the State's residential fee simple market, inflating land prices, and injuring public tranquillity and welfare." The resulting Land Reform Act authorized "eligible tenants" from residential tracts of at least five acres to invoke the Hawaii Housing Authority's (HHA) power to acquire the fee owners "right, title and interest" at a "fair market value" set by negotiation between the lessee and the lessor or by condemnation trial, and then to sell that fee title interest to the tenant-lessee.[a]

In upholding the Act over the challenge that such taking was not for a public use, the Court relied heavily on *Berman* from which it concluded, "The 'public use' requirement is thus coterminus with the scope of a sovereign's police powers. There is, of course, a role for courts to play in reviewing a legislature's judgment of what constitutes a public use, even when the eminent domain power is equated with the police power. But the Court in *Berman* made clear that it is 'an extremely narrow' one. [Where] the exercise of the eminent domain power is rationally related to a conceivable public purpose, the Court has never held a compensated taking to be proscribed by the Public Use Clause.

"On this basis, we have no trouble concluding that the Hawaii Act is constitutional. The people of Hawaii have attempted, much as the settlers of the original 13 Colonies did, to reduce the perceived social and economic evils of a land oligopoly traceable to their monarchs. The land oligopoly has, according to the Hawaii Legislature, created artificial deterrents to the normal functioning of the State's residential land market and forced thousands of individual homeowners to lease, rather than buy, the land underneath their homes. Regulating oligopoly and the evils associated with it is a classic exercise of a State's police powers. We cannot disapprove of Hawaii's exercise of this power.

"Nor can we condemn as irrational the Act's approach to correcting the land oligopoly problem. The Act presumes that when a sufficiently large number of persons declare that they are willing but unable to buy lots at fair prices the land market is malfunctioning. When such a malfunction is signalled, the Act authorizes HHA to condemn lots in the relevant tract.

a. An "eligible tenant" was one who "owns a house on the lot, has a bona fide intent to live on the lot or be a resident of the State, shows proof of ability to pay for a fee interest in it, and does not own residential land elsewhere nearby." The HHA was authorized to proceed under the Act only when 25 such eligible tenants from the tract, or those from half the lots in the tract, whichever is less, filed applications with HHA for the remedy provided by the Act.

"[When] the legislature's purpose is legitimate and its means are not irrational, our cases make clear that empirical debates over the wisdom of takings—no less than debates over the wisdom of other kinds of socioeconomic legislation—are not to be carried out in the federal courts. Redistribution of fees simple to correct deficiencies in the market determined by the state legislature to be attributable to land oligopoly is a rational exercise of the eminent domain power. Therefore, the Hawaii statute must pass the scrutiny of the Public Use Clause." Marshall, J., did not participate.

II. "TAKING" THROUGH REGULATION

PENN CENTRAL TRANSP. CO. v. NEW YORK CITY

438 U.S. 104, 98 S.Ct. 2646, 57 L.Ed.2d 631 (1978).

JUSTICE BRENNAN delivered the opinion of the Court.

[Pursuant to New York City's Landmarks Preservation Law, the Preservation Commission designated Grand Central Terminal, owned by Penn Central, as a "landmark." It denied approval for Penn Central to construct a 55 story office building resting on the roof of the Terminal, cantilevered to preserve the existing Terminal facade. The Commission emphasized the harmful effect of the proposed construction on the dramatic view of the Terminal from Park Avenue South.[a] Choosing not to modify its proposal, or to use its right under New York laws to transfer its unused landmark site development rights to one or more of its eight nearby lots, Penn Central unsuccessfully challenged in the New York courts the constitutionality of this application of the Landmarks Law. The Court upheld the Law as applied.]

[The issue is] whether the restrictions [upon] appellants' exploitation of the Terminal site effect a "taking" of appellants' property for a public use within the meaning of the Fifth Amendment, [made] applicable to the States through the Fourteenth.[25]

A. [W]hat constitutes a "taking" for purposes of the Fifth Amendment has proved to be a problem of considerable difficulty. While this Court has recognized that the "Fifth Amendment's guarantee [is] designed to bar Government from forcing some people alone to bear public burdens which, in all fairness and justice, should be borne by the public as a whole," *Armstrong v. United States,*[b] this Court, quite simply, has been unable to develop any "set formula" for determining when "justice and fairness" require that economic injuries caused by public action be compensated by the government, rather than remain disproportionately concentrated on a few persons. See *Goldblatt v. Hempstead,* 369 U.S. 590, 594, 82 S.Ct. 987, 8 L.Ed.2d 130 (1962). Indeed, we have frequently observed that whether a particular restriction will be rendered invalid by the government's failure to pay for any losses proximately caused by it depends largely "upon the

a. "[To] balance a 55-story office tower above a flamboyant Beaux-Arts facade seems nothing more than an aesthetic joke. Quite simply, the tower would overwhelm the Terminal by its sheer mass. The 'addition' would be four times as high as the existing structure and would reduce the Landmark itself to the status of a curiosity."

25. As is implicit in our opinion, we do not embrace the proposition that a "taking" can never occur unless government has transferred physical control over a portion of a parcel.

b. 364 U.S. 40, 49, 80 S.Ct. 1563, 4 L.Ed.2d 1554 (1960). *Armstrong* found a "taking" in the destruction of a materialman's lien when, on default of the builder, the government took possession of boats he was building for the United States.

particular circumstances [in that] case." *United States v. Central Eureka Mining Co.,* 357 U.S. 155, 168, 78 S.Ct. 1097, 2 L.Ed.2d 1228 (1958), see *United States v. Caltex, Inc.,* 344 U.S. 149, 156, 73 S.Ct. 200, 97 L.Ed. 157 (1952).

In engaging in these essentially ad hoc, factual inquiries, the Court's decisions have identified several factors that have particular significance. The economic impact of the regulation on the claimant and, particularly, the extent to which the regulation has interfered with distinct investment-backed expectations are, of course, relevant considerations. See *Goldblatt.* So, too, is the character of the governmental action. A "taking" may more readily be found when the interference with property can be characterized as a physical invasion by government, see, e.g., *United States v. Causby,* 328 U.S. 256, 66 S.Ct. 1062, 90 L.Ed. 1206 (1946), than when interference arises from some public program adjusting the benefits and burdens of economic life to promote the common good.

"Government hardly could go on if to some extent values incident to property could not be diminished without paying for every such change in the general law," *Pennsylvania Coal Co. v. Mahon,* 260 U.S. 393, 413, 43 S.Ct. 158, 67 L.Ed. 322 (1922), and this Court has accordingly recognized, in a wide variety of contexts, that government may execute laws or programs that adversely affect recognized economic values. * * *

[I]n instances in which a state tribunal reasonably concluded that "the health, safety, morals, or general welfare" would be promoted by prohibiting particular contemplated uses of land, this Court has upheld land-use regulations that destroyed or adversely affected recognized real property interests. See *Nectow v. Cambridge,* 277 U.S. 183, 188, 48 S.Ct. 447, 72 L.Ed. 842 (1928). Zoning laws are, of course, the classic example, see *Euclid v. Ambler Realty Co.,* 272 U.S. 365, 47 S.Ct. 114, 71 L.Ed. 303 (1926) (prohibition of industrial use); *Gorieb v. Fox,* 274 U.S. 603, 608, 47 S.Ct. 675, 71 L.Ed. 1228 (1927) (requirement that portions of parcels be left unbuilt); *Welch v. Swasey,* 214 U.S. 91, 29 S.Ct. 567, 53 L.Ed. 923 (1909) (height restriction), which have been viewed as permissible governmental action even when prohibiting the most beneficial use of the property. See *Goldblatt.*

Zoning laws generally do not affect existing uses of real property, but "taking" challenges have also been held to be without merit in a wide variety of situations when the challenged governmental actions prohibited a beneficial use to which individual parcels had previously been devoted and thus caused substantial individualized harm. *Miller v. Schoene,* 276 U.S. 272, 48 S.Ct. 246, 72 L.Ed. 568 (1928), is illustrative. In that case, a state entomologist, acting pursuant to a state statute, ordered the claimants to cut down a large number of ornamental red cedar trees because they produced cedar rust fatal to apple trees cultivated nearby. Although the statute provided for recovery of any expense incurred in removing the cedars, and permitted claimants to use the felled trees, it did not provide compensation for the value of the standing trees or for the resulting decrease in market value of the properties as a whole. A unanimous Court held that this latter omission did not render the statute invalid. The Court held that the State might properly make "a choice between the preservation of one class of property and that of the other" and since the apple industry was important in the State involved, concluded that the State had not exceeded "its constitutional powers by deciding upon the destruction of one class of property [without compensation] in order to save another which, in the judgment of the legislature, is of greater value to the public."

Again, *Hadacheck v. Sebastian*, 239 U.S. 394, 36 S.Ct. 143, 60 L.Ed. 348 (1915), upheld a law prohibiting the claimant from continuing his otherwise lawful business of operating a brickyard in a particular physical community on the ground that the legislature had reasonably concluded that the presence of the brickyard was inconsistent with neighboring uses. * * *

Goldblatt is a recent example. There, a 1958 city safety ordinance banned any excavations below the water table and effectively prohibited the claimant from continuing a sand and gravel mining business that had been operated on the particular parcel since 1927. The Court upheld the ordinance against a "taking" challenge, although the ordinance prohibited the present and presumably most beneficial use of the property and had, like the regulations in *Miller* and *Hadacheck*, severely affected a particular owner. The Court assumed that the ordinance did not prevent the owner's reasonable use of the property since the owner made no showing of an adverse effect on the value of the land. Because the restriction served a substantial public purpose, the Court thus held no taking had occurred. It is, of course, implicit in *Goldblatt* that a use restriction on real property may constitute a "taking" if not reasonably necessary to the effectuation of a substantial public purpose, see *Nectow;* or perhaps if it has an unduly harsh impact upon the owner's use of the property.

Pennsylvania Coal is the leading case for the proposition that a state statute that substantially furthers important public policies may so frustrate distinct investment-backed expectations as to amount to a "taking." There the claimant had sold the surface rights to particular parcels of property, but expressly reserved the right to remove the coal thereunder. A Pennsylvania statute, enacted after the transactions, forbade any mining of coal that caused the subsidence of any house, unless the house was the property of the owner of the underlying coal and was more than 150 feet from the improved property of another. Because the statute made it commercially impracticable to mine the coal, and thus had nearly the same effect as the complete destruction of rights claimant had reserved from the owners of the surface land, the Court held that the statute was invalid as effecting a "taking" without just compensation. [See] generally Frank I. Michelman, *Property, Utility, and Fairness: Comments on the Ethical Foundations of "Just Compensation" Law,* 80 Harv.L.Rev. 1165, 1229–1234 (1967).

Finally, government actions that may be characterized as acquisitions of resources to permit or facilitate uniquely public functions have often been held to constitute "takings." *Causby* is illustrative. In holding that direct overflights above the claimant's land, that destroyed the present use of the land as a chicken farm, constituted a "taking," *Causby* emphasized that Government had not "merely destroyed property [but was] using a part of it for the flight of its planes." See [also] *United States v. Cress,* 243 U.S. 316, 37 S.Ct. 380, 61 L.Ed. 746 (1917) (repeated floodings of land caused by water project is taking). See generally Michelman, [supra at 1226–1229]; Joseph L. Sax, *Takings and the Police Power,* 74 Yale L.J. 36 (1964).

B. [A]ppellants do not contest that New York City's objective of preserving structures and areas with special historic, architectural, or cultural significance is an entirely permissible governmental goal. [They] do not challenge any of the specific factual premises of the decision below. They accept for present purposes both that the parcel of land occupied by Grand Central Terminal must, in its present state, be regarded as capable of earning a reasonable return, and that the transferable development rights afforded appellants by virtue of the Terminal's designation as a landmark are valuable, even if not as valuable as the rights to construct above the Terminal. In appellants' view none of these factors derogate from their claim that New York City's law has effected a "taking."

[First, they] urge that the Landmarks Law has deprived them of any gainful use of their "air rights" above the Terminal, [entitling] them to "just compensation" measured by the fair market value of these air rights.

[T]he submission that appellants may establish a "taking" simply by showing that they have been denied the ability to exploit a property interest that they heretofore had believed was available for development is quite simply untenable. Were this the rule, this Court would have erred not only in upholding laws restricting the development of air rights, see *Welch*, but also in approving those prohibiting both the subjacent, see *Goldblatt*, and the lateral, see *Gorieb*, development of particular parcels. "Taking" jurisprudence does not divide a single parcel into discrete segments and attempt to determine whether rights in a particular segment have been entirely abrogated. In deciding whether a particular governmental action has effected a taking, this Court focuses rather both on the character of the action and on the nature and extent of the interference with rights in the parcel as a whole—here, the city tax block designated as the "landmark site."

Secondly, appellants [argue that the New York law] effects a "taking" because its operation has significantly diminished the value of the Terminal site. Appellants concede that the decisions sustaining other land use-regulations, which, like the New York City law, are reasonably related to the promotion of the general welfare, uniformly reject the proposition that diminution in property value, standing alone, can establish a "taking," see *Euclid* (75% diminution in value caused by zoning law); *Hadacheck* (87½% diminution in value). [But] appellants argue that New York City's regulation of individual landmarks is fundamentally different from zoning or from historic-district legislation because the controls imposed by New York City's law apply only to individuals who own selected properties.

Stated baldly, appellants' position appears to be that the only means of ensuring that selected owners are not singled out to endure financial hardship for no reason is to hold that any restriction imposed on individual landmarks pursuant to the New York City scheme is a "taking" requiring the payment of "just compensation." [C]ontrary to appellants' suggestions, landmark laws are not like discriminatory, or "reverse spot," zoning: that is, a land-use decision which arbitrarily singles out a particular parcel for different, less favorable treatment than the neighboring ones. In contrast to discriminatory zoning, which is the antithesis of land-use control as part of some comprehensive plan, the New York City law embodies a comprehensive plan to preserve structures of historic or aesthetic interest wherever they might be found in the [city].

Next, appellants observe that New York City's law differs from zoning laws and historic-district ordinances in that the Landmarks Law does not impose identical or similar restrictions on all structures located in particular physical communities. It follows, they argue, that New York City's law is inherently incapable of producing the fair and equitable distribution of benefits and burdens of governmental action which is characteristic of zoning laws and historic-district [legislation]. It is, of course, true that the Landmarks Law has a more severe impact on some landowners than on others, but that in itself does not mean that the law effects a "taking." Legislation designed to promote the general welfare commonly burdens some more than others. The owners of the brickyard in *Hadacheck*, of the cedar trees in *Miller*, and of the gravel and sand mine in

Goldblatt, were uniquely burdened by the legislation sustained in those cases.[30] Similarly, zoning laws often affect some property owners more severely than others but have not been held to be invalid on that account. * * *

[T]he New York City law applies to vast numbers of structures in the city in addition to the Terminal—all the structures contained in the 31 historic districts and over 400 individual landmarks, many of which are close to the Terminal. Unless we are to reject the judgment of the New York City Council that the preservation of landmarks benefits all New York citizens and all structures, both economically and by improving the quality of life in the city as a whole—which we are unwilling to do—we cannot conclude that the owners of the Terminal have in no sense been benefited by the Landmarks Law. Doubtless appellants believe they are more burdened than benefited by the law, but that must have been true, too, of the property owners in *Miller, Hadacheck, Euclid,* and *Goldblatt.* * * *

C. [A]ll we thus far have established is that the [law] is not rendered invalid by its failure to provide "just compensation" whenever a landmark owner is restricted in the exploitation of property [interests], to a greater extent than provided for under applicable zoning laws. We now must consider whether the interference with appellants' property is of such a magnitude that "there must be an exercise of eminent domain and compensation to sustain [it]." *Pennsylvania Coal.* That inquiry may be narrowed to the question of the severity of the impact of the law on appellants' parcel, and its resolution in turn requires a careful assessment of the impact of the regulation on the Terminal site.

Unlike the governmental acts in *Goldblatt, Miller, Causby, Griggs,* and *Hadacheck,* the [law] does not interfere in any way with the present uses of the Terminal. Its designation as a landmark not only permits but contemplates that appellants may continue to use the property precisely as it has been used for the past 65 years: as a railroad terminal containing office space and concessions. So the law does not interfere with what must be regarded as Penn Central's primary expectation concerning the use of the parcel. More importantly, on this record, we must regard the [law] as permitting Penn Central not only to profit from the Terminal but also to obtain a "reasonable return" on its investment.

Appellants, moreover, exaggerate the effect of the law on their ability to make use of the air rights above the Terminal in two respects. First, it simply cannot be maintained, on this record, that appellants have been prohibited from occupying *any* portion of the airspace above the Terminal. [Nothing] the Commission has said or done suggests an intention to prohibit *any* construction above the Terminal. The Commission's report emphasized that whether any construction would be allowed depended upon whether the proposed addition "would harmonize in scale, material and character with [the Terminal]." Since appellants have not sought approval for the construction of a smaller structure, we do not know

---

30. Appellants attempt to distinguish these cases on the ground that, in each, government was prohibiting a "noxious" use of land and that in the present case, in contrast, appellants' proposed construction above the Terminal would be beneficial. We observe that the uses in issue in *Hadacheck, Miller,* and *Goldblatt* were perfectly lawful in themselves. They involve no "blameworthiness, [moral] wrongdoing or conscious act of dangerous risk-taking which induce[d society] to shift the cost

to a pa[rt]icular individual." Joseph L. Sax, *Takings and the Police Power,* 74 Yale L.J. 36, 50 (1964). These cases are better understood as resting not on any supposed "noxious" quality of the prohibited uses but rather on the ground that the restrictions were reasonably related to the implementation of a policy—not unlike historic preservation—expected to produce a widespread public benefit and applicable to all similarly situated property.

that appellants will be denied any use of any portion of the airspace above the Terminal.[34]

Second, to the extent appellants have been denied the right to build above the Terminal, it is not literally accurate to say that they have been denied *all* use of even those pre-existing air rights. Their ability to use these rights has not been abrogated; they are made transferable to at least eight parcels in the vicinity of the Terminal, one or two of which have been found suitable for the construction of new office buildings. Although appellants and others have argued that New York City's transferable development-rights program is far from ideal, the New York courts here supportably found that, at least in the case of the Terminal, the rights afforded are valuable. While these rights may well not have constituted "just compensation" if a "taking" had occurred, the rights nevertheless undoubtedly mitigate whatever financial burdens the law has imposed on appellants and, for that reason, are to be taken into account in considering the impact of regulation.

On this record we conclude that the application of New York City's [law] has not effected a "taking" of appellants' property. The restrictions imposed are substantially related to the promotion of the general welfare and not only permit reasonable beneficial use of the landmark site but afford appellants opportunities further to enhance not only the Terminal site proper but also other properties.[36]
* * *

JUSTICE REHNQUIST, with whom THE CHIEF JUSTICE and JUSTICE STEVENS join, dissenting.

[The] question in this case is whether the cost associated with the city of New York's desire to preserve a limited number of "landmarks" within its borders must be borne by all of its taxpayers or whether it can instead be imposed entirely on the owners of the individual properties.

[While] neighboring landowners are free to use their land and "air rights" in any way consistent with the broad boundaries of New York zoning, Penn Central, absent the permission of appellees, must forever maintain its property in its present state. The property has been thus subjected to a nonconsensual servitude not borne by any neighboring or similar properties.

Appellees have thus destroyed—in a literal sense, "taken"—substantial property rights of Penn Central. While the term "taken" might have been narrowly interpreted to include only physical seizures of property rights, "the construction of the phrase has not been so narrow. The courts have held that the deprivation of the former owner rather than the accretion of a right or interest to the sovereign constitutes the taking." *United States v. General Motors Corp.*, 323 U.S. 373, 378, 65 S.Ct. 357, 89 L.Ed. 311 (1945). [An] examination of the two exceptions where the destruction of property does *not* constitute a taking demonstrates that a compensable taking has occurred here.

1. As early as 1887, the Court recognized that the government can prevent a property owner from using his property to injure others without having to compensate the owner for the value of the forbidden use. *Mugler v. Kansas*, 123

34. Counsel for appellants admitted at oral argument that the Commission has not suggested that it would not, for example, approve a 20-story office tower along the lines of that which was part of the original plan for the Terminal.

36. We emphasize that our holding today is on the present record which in turn is based on

Penn Central's present ability to use the Terminal for its intended purposes and in a gainful fashion. The city conceded at oral argument that if appellants can demonstrate at some point in the future that circumstances have changed such that the Terminal ceases to be, in the city's counsel's words, "economically viable," appellants may obtain relief.

U.S. 623, 8 S.Ct. 273, 31 L.Ed. 205 (1887). [Thus], there is no "taking" where a city prohibits the operation of a brickyard within a residential city, see *Hadacheck*, or forbids excavation for sand and gravel below the water line, see *Goldblatt*. Nor is it relevant, where the government is merely prohibiting a noxious use of property, that the government would seem to be singling out a particular property owner. *Hadacheck*.[8] * * * Appellees are not prohibiting a nuisance. [Instead], Penn Central is prevented from further developing its property basically because *too good* a job was done in designing and building [it].

2. Even where the government prohibits a noninjurious use, the Court has ruled that a taking does not take place if the prohibition applies over a broad cross section of land and thereby "secure[s] an average reciprocity of advantage." *Pennsylvania Coal*. It is for this reason that zoning does not constitute a "taking." While zoning at times reduces *individual* property values, the burden is shared relatively evenly and it is reasonable to conclude that on the whole an individual who is harmed by one aspect of the zoning will be benefited by another.

Here, however, a multimillion dollar loss has been imposed on appellants; it is uniquely felt and is not offset by any benefits flowing from the preservation of some 400 other "landmarks" in New York City. Appellees have imposed a substantial cost on less than one one-tenth of one percent of the buildings in New York City for the general benefit of all its people. It is exactly this imposition of general costs on a few individuals at which the "taking" protection is [directed.] *Armstrong*.

[The] benefits that appellees believe will flow from preservation of the Grand Central Terminal will accrue to all the citizens of New York City. There is no reason to believe that appellants will enjoy a substantially greater share of these benefits. If the cost of preserving Grand Central Terminal were spread evenly across the entire population of the city of New York, the burden per person would be in cents per year—a minor cost appellees would surely concede for the benefit accrued. Instead, however, appellees would impose the entire cost of several million dollars per year on Penn Central. But it is precisely this sort of discrimination that the Fifth Amendment prohibits.

[A] taking does not become a noncompensable exercise of police power simply because the government in its grace allows the owner to make some "reasonable" use of his property. "[I]t is the character of the invasion, not the amount of damage resulting from it, so long as the damage is substantial, that determines the question whether it is a taking." *Cress*,[c] 243 U.S. 316, 328, 37 S.Ct. 380, 61 L.Ed. 746 (1917). *Causby*. * * *[d]

Notes and Questions

1. *Balancing judgments?* (a) Earlier decisions led thoughtful commentators to conclude that in determining whether a regulation constituted a "taking" the

---

8. Each of the cases cited by the Court for the proposition that legislation which severely affects some landowners but not others does not effect a "taking" involved noxious uses of property. See *Hadacheck; Miller; Goldblatt*.

c. Compensation required for damage to property when a federal dam raised water level in tributary stream, causing frequent overflows in one case and loss of water power for mill in the other.

d. On the "taking" issue, see generally—in addition to articles cited in *Penn Central*—Robert Kratovil & Frank J. Harrison, *Eminent*

Domain—Policy and Concept, 42 Calif.L.Rev. 596 (1954); Allison Dunham, *Griggs v. Allegheny County in Perspective: Thirty Years of Supreme Court Expropriation Law,* 1962 Sup. Ct.Rev. 63; Joseph L. Sax, *Takings, Private Property and Public Right,* 81 Yale L.J. 149 (1971); Note, *Zoning,* 91 Harv.L.Rev. 1427, 1462–86 (1978); 92 Harv.L.Rev. 222–32 (1977). For later scholarly commentaries on taking issues, kindled by the more recent takings decisions, see note 3 following *Nollan v. California Coastal Com'n*, infra.

"extent of the diminution of the owner's rights must be weighed against the importance of that diminution to the public," [a] and that "[c]ourts have never been able to develop [a] standard more meaningful than balancing the public need against the private cost." [b] For a helpful critique of such a balancing approach, see Michelman, supra, 80 Harv.L.Rev. at 1193–96, 1234–35.

(b) Is such balancing consistent with *Penn Central?* Did *Penn Central* "demonstrat[e] a method by which competing social and individual interests might be weighed"? Did it "balance public necessity and legitimacy of the regulation against the degree of physical invasion and economic harm"? See Note, 11 Conn.L.Rev. 273, 290 (1979). Or did *Penn Central* reflect "a belief that given the validity of the governmental interest asserted, the nature of the interest plays no further role in determining whether a taking has occurred," and that "[a]ny nondiscriminatory enactment reasonably related to a goal within the police power will be subjected only to a test of economic impact"? See 92 Harv.L.Rev. at 229.

(c) What *ought* the standard to be? *Should* the extent of economic harm that can be imposed without compensation depend on the degree of importance of an admittedly valid governmental interest?

2. *Economic impact on claimant.* What factors appear relevant to deciding whether the "economic impact of the regulation on the claimant" suffices to support a judgment of "taking?" Does *Penn Central* mean that, absent the use of private property for "uniquely public functions," an economic impact will not suffice if the regulation permits continuation of the property's pre-regulation uses and a "reasonable return" on the investment? What kinds of problems are likely to arise from basing such decisions on factors like "reasonable return on investment, "investment-backed expectations," and "primary expectation concerning use?" Cf. 92 Harv.L.Rev. at 231.

3. *The "bundle of rights."* (a) The Eagle Protection Act [16 USCA § 668(a)] forbad the taking, sale, possession or transportation of bald or golden eagles, or parts thereof, except for possession or transportation of eagles or parts obtained prior to the Act. ANDRUS v. ALLARD, 444 U.S. 51, 100 S.Ct. 318, 62 L.Ed.2d 210 (1979), per Brennan, J., unanimously ruled application of the ban to sales of commercially traded Indian artifacts containing eagle parts taken before the Act did not violate the taking clause: "[Where] an owner possesses a full 'bundle' of property rights, the destruction of one 'strand' of the bundle is not a taking, because the aggregate must be viewed in its entirety. Compare *Penn Central.* [In] this case, it is crucial that appellees retain the rights to possess and transport their property, and to donate or devise the protected birds.

"[In] the instant case, it is not clear that appellees will be unable to derive economic benefit from the artifacts; for example, they might exhibit the artifacts for an admissions charge. At any rate, loss of future profits—unaccompanied by any physical property restriction—provides a slender reed upon which to rest a takings claim. Prediction of profitability is essentially a matter of reasoned speculation that courts are not especially competent to perform." [a]

(b) Might the contraband nature of eagle parts in 1979 have influenced the result? Consider the Court's closing comment: "Regulations that bar trade in certain goods have been upheld against" taking claims, citing the decisions ruling

---

a. Kratovil & Harrison, fn. d supra, at 609.

b. Dunham, fn. d supra, at 76.

a. Burger, C.J., concurred only in the judgment.

that the prohibition-day ban was not a taking when applied to the sale of pre-prohibition liquor.[b]

4. *Permanent physical occupation.* LORETTO v. TELEPROMPTER MANHATTAN CATV CORP., 458 U.S. 419, 102 S.Ct. 3164, 73 L.Ed.2d 868 (1982), per MARSHALL, J., found a "taking" in a New York law that, as applied, authorized cable TV installations for tenants of privately-owned apartment houses. The cables, permanently attached to the roofs and outside walls by bolts, screws and other means, were subject to a one-time $1 payment to the landlord: "When faced with a constitutional challenge to a permanent physical occupation of real property, this Court has invariably found a taking.[5] [To] the extent that the government permanently occupies physical property it effectively destroys" the rights to possess, use and dispose of it. "The owner has no right to possess the occupied space himself [or] to exclude the occupier." It "denies the owner any power to control the use of the property [or] to dispose of [it] by sale, [since] the purchaser will be unable to make any use of" it.

"Our holding today is very narrow. We affirm the traditional rule that a permanent physical occupation of property is a taking. In such a case, the property owner entertains an historically-rooted expectation of compensation, and the character of the invasion is qualitatively more intrusive than perhaps any other category of property regulation. We do not, however, question the equally substantial authority upholding a State's broad power to impose appropriate restrictions upon an owner's *use* of his property."

BLACKMUN, J., joined by Brennan and White, JJ., dissented: "In sum, history, teaches that takings claims are properly evaluated under a multifactor balancing test. By directing that all 'permanent physical occupations' automatically are compensable, 'without regard to whether the action achieves an important public benefit or has only minimal economic impact on the owner,' the Court does not further equity so much as it encourages litigants to manipulate their factual allegations to gain the benefit of its per se rule. I do not relish the prospect of distinguishing the inevitable flow of certiorari petitions attempting to shoehorn insubstantial takings claims into today's 'set formula.'"

5. *Regulating harmful activities: Pennsylvania Mining revisited.* KEYSTONE BITUMINOUS COAL ASS'N v. DeBENEDICTIS, 480 U.S. 470, 107 S.Ct. 1232, 94 L.Ed.2d 472 (1987), per STEVENS, J., upheld Pennsylvania's Subsidence Act (§ 4) that forbade mining bituminous coal "so as to cause damage as a result of the caving in, collapse or subsidence of" public buildings, human dwellings, cemeteries, perennial streams, impoundments of water, aquifers supplying public water systems, and coal refuse disposal areas, unless the current owner of the structure consents and the resulting damage is fully repaired or compensated. Pennsylvania required 50% of the coal under protected structures to be kept in place. The Court upheld enforcement of the Act: "Unlike the Kohler Act [in]

---

b. See *Jacob Ruppert, Inc. v. Caffey*, 251 U.S. 264, 40 S.Ct. 141, 64 L.Ed. 260 (1920); *James Everard's Breweries v. Day*, 265 U.S. 545, 44 S.Ct. 628, 68 L.Ed. 1174 (1924).

5. Professor Michelman has accurately summarized the case [law]: "[The] modern significance of physical occupation is that courts, while they sometimes do hold nontrespassory injuries compensable, *never* deny compensation for a physical takeover. The one incontestable case for compensation (short of formal expropriation) seems to occur when the government [or] the public at large, 'regularly' use, or 'permanently' occupy, space or a thing [theretofore] under private ownership." Frank I. Michelman, *Property, Utility, and Fairness: Comments on the Ethical Foundations of "Just Compensation" Law*, 80 Harv. L.Rev. 1165, 1184 (1967) (emphasis original). See also Julius L. Sackman, *Nichols' Law of Eminent Domain* 6–50, 6–51 (rev. 3d ed. 1980); Laurence H. Tribe, *American Constitutional Law* 460 (1978).

Pennsylvania Coal, the Subsidence Act does not merely involve a balancing of the private economic interests of coal companies against the private interests of the surface owners. The Pennsylvania Legislature specifically found that important public interests are served [by] 'providing for the conservation of surface land areas which may be affected in the mining of bituminous [coal], to aid in the protection of the safety of the public, to enhance the value of such lands for taxation, to aid in the preservation of surface water drainage and public water supplies and generally to improve the use and enjoyment of such [lands].'

"[With] regard to the Kohler Act, the Court believed that the Commonwealth had acted only to ensure against damage to some private landowners' homes. Justice Holmes stated that if the private individuals needed support for their structures, they should not have 'take[n] the risk of acquiring only surface rights.' [d] Here, by contrast, the Commonwealth is acting to protect the public interest in health, the environment, and the fiscal integrity of the area. That private individuals erred in taking a risk cannot estop the State from exercising its police power to abate activity akin to a public [nuisance].

"[The] public interest in preventing activities similar to public nuisances is a substantial one, which in many instances has not required compensation. The Subsidence Act, unlike the Kohler Act, plainly seeks to further such an interest. Nonetheless, we need not rest our decision on this factor alone, because petitioners have also failed to make a showing of diminution of value sufficient to satisfy the test set forth in *Pennsylvania Coal* and our other regulatory takings cases.

"The second factor that distinguishes this case from *Pennsylvania Coal* is the finding in that case that the Kohler Act made mining of 'certain coal' commercially impracticable. [The] test to be applied in considering this facial challenge [to the Subsidence Act] is fairly straightforward. A statute regulating the uses that can be made of property effects a taking if it 'denies an owner economically viable use of his land * * *.' Petitioners thus face an uphill battle in making a facial attack on the Act as a taking.

"The hill is made especially steep because petitioners have not claimed, at this stage, that the Act makes it commercially impracticable for them to continue mining their bituminous coal interests in western Pennsylvania. Indeed, petitioners have not even pointed to a single mine that can no longer be mined for profit. [The] total coal in [petitioners'] 13 mines amounts to over 1.46 billion tons. [Section] 4 requires them to leave less than 2% of their coal in place. [But] nowhere near all of the underground coal is extractable even aside from the Subsidence Act. The categories of coal that must be left for § 4 purposes and other purposes are not necessarily distinct sets, and there is no information in the record as to how much coal is actually left in the ground *solely* because of § 4. * * *

"The parties have stipulated that enforcement of [the] 50% rule will require petitioners to leave approximately 27 million tons of coal in place. Because they own that coal but cannot mine it, they contend that Pennsylvania has appropriated it for the public purposes described in the Subsidence Act.

"This argument fails for the reason explained in *Penn Central* and *Andrus.* The 27 million tons of coal do not constitute a separate segment of property for takings law purposes. [When] the coal that must remain beneath the ground is viewed in the context of any reasonable unit of petitioners' coal mining operations

d. As in *Kohler,* the surface owners in *Keystone* had acquired only surface rights and had waived any claims for damages caused by removal of the coal.

and financial-backed expectations, it is plain that the petitioners have not come close to satisfying their burden of proving that they have been denied the economically viable use of that property. The record indicates that only about 75% of petitioners' underground coal can be profitably mined in any event, and there is no showing that petitioners' reasonable 'investment-backed expectations' have been materially affected by the additional duty to retain the small percentage that must be used to support the structures protected by § 4." [e]

REHNQUIST, C.J., dissented, joined by Powell, O'Connor, and Scalia, JJ.: "[The] Subsidence Act [is] much more than a nuisance statute. The central purposes of the Act, though including public safety, reflect a concern for preservation of buildings, economic development, and maintenance of property values to sustain the Commonwealth's tax base. We should hesitate to allow a regulation based on essentially economic concerns to be insulated from the dictates of the Fifth Amendment by labeling it nuisance regulation.

"[More] significantly, our cases have never applied the nuisance exception to allow complete extinction of the value of a parcel of property. Though nuisance regulations have been sustained despite a substantial reduction in value, we have not accepted the proposition that the State may completely extinguish a property interest or prohibit all use without providing [compensation.]

"[The] Court's refusal to recognize the coal in the ground as a separate segment of property for takings purposes is based on the fact that the alleged taking is 'regulatory,' rather than a physical intrusion. On the facts of this case, I cannot see how the label placed on the government's action is relevant to consideration of its impact on property rights."

6. *Conditions on property development permits.* (a)(i) NOLLAN v. CALIFORNIA COASTAL COM'N, 483 U.S. 825, 107 S.Ct. 3141, 97 L.Ed.2d 677 (1987), per SCALIA, J., held an uncompensated taking the Commission's condition that for a permit to replace their small beachfront cottage with a home nearly five times larger, the Nollans must grant a public easement to pass across an eight foot strip of beach between their sea wall and the ocean high tide line. The area seaward from the high tide line was a public beach accessible from a larger public beach one-fourth mile away: "[T]he Commission's assumed power to forbid construction of the house in order to protect the public's view of the beach must surely include the power to condition construction upon some concession by the owner, even a concession of property rights, that serves the same end. If a prohibition designed to accomplish that purpose would be a legitimate exercise of the police power rather than a taking, it would be strange to conclude that providing the owner an alternative to that prohibition which accomplishes the same purpose is not.

"The evident constitutional propriety disappears, however, if the condition substituted for the prohibition utterly fails to further the end advanced as the justification for the prohibition. [The] lack of nexus between the condition and the original purpose of the building restriction converts that purpose to something other than what it was. The purpose then becomes, quite simply, the obtaining of an easement to serve some valid governmental purpose, but without payment of compensation. [In] short, unless the permit condition serves the same govern-

---

e. The Court rejected the contention that the Subsidence Act violated the contract clause by not allowing the owners of the mining interest to hold the surface owners to their contractual waiver of liability for surface damage. The Court invoked the "strong public interest in preventing this type of harm, the environmental effect of which transcends any private agreement between private parties." See Sec. 5 infra.

mental purpose as the development ban, the building restriction is not a valid regulation of land use but 'an out-and-out plan of extortion.'

"The Commission claims [that] we may sustain the condition at issue here by finding that it is reasonably related to the public need or burden that the Nollans' new house creates or to which it contributes. The Nollans' new house, the Commission found, will interfere with 'visual access' to the beach. That in turn (along with other shorefront development) will interfere with the desire of people who drive past the Nollans' house to use the beach, thus creating a 'psychological barrier' to 'access.' [These] burdens on 'access' would be alleviated by a requirement that the Nollans provide 'lateral access' to the beach.

"[It] is quite impossible to understand how a requirement that people already on the public beaches be able to walk across the Nollans' property reduces any obstacles to viewing the beach created by the new house. It is also impossible to understand how it lowers any 'psychological barrier' to using the public beaches. [We] therefore find that the Commission's imposition of the permit condition cannot be treated as an exercise of its land use power for any of these purposes.
* * *

"Justice Brennan argues that imposition of the access requirement is not irrational. In his version of the Commission's argument, the reason for the requirement is that in its absence, a person looking toward the beach from the road will see a street of residential structures including the Nollans' new home and conclude that there is no public beach nearby. If, however, that person sees people passing and repassing along the dry sand behind the Nollans' home, he will realize that there is a public beach somewhere in the vicinity. The Commission's action, however, was based on the opposite factual finding that the wall of houses completely blocked the view of the beach and that a person looking from the road would not be able to see it at all.

"Even if the Commission had made the finding that Justice Brennan proposes, however, it is not certain that it would suffice. [Our] cases describe the condition for abridgement of property rights through the police power as a '*substantial* advanc[ing]' of a legitimate State interest. We are inclined to be particularly careful about the adjective where the actual conveyance of property is made a condition to the lifting of a land use restriction, since in that context there is heightened risk that the purpose is avoidance of the compensation requirement, rather than the stated police power objective."

BRENNAN, J., joined by Marshall, J., dissented: "The Court imposes a standard of precision for the exercise of a State's police power that has been discredited for the better part of this century. [Even] under the Court's cramped standard, the permit condition imposed in this case directly responds to the specific type of burden on access created by appellants' development.

"[The] Commission has sought [to] balance private and public interests and to accept tradeoffs: to permit development that reduces access in some ways as long as other means of access are enhanced. In this case, it has determined that the Nollans' burden on access would be offset by a deed restriction that formalizes the public's right to pass along the shore. In its informed judgment, such a tradeoff would preserve the net amount of public access to the coastline. The Court's insistence on a precise fit between the forms of burden and condition on each individual parcel along the California coast would penalize the Commission for its flexibility, hampering the ability to fulfill its public trust mandate.

"Even if we accept the Court's unusual demand for a precise match between the condition imposed and the specific type of burden on access created by the appellants, the State's action easily satisfies this requirement. [Those] persons who go down to the public beach a quarter-mile away will be able to look down the coastline and see that persons have continuous access to the tidelands, and will observe signs that proclaim the public's right of access over the dry sand. The burden produced by the diminution in visual access—the impression that the beach is not open to the public—is thus directly alleviated by the provision for public access over the dry sand. * * *

"In reviewing a Takings Clause claim, we have regarded as particularly significant the nature of the governmental action and the economic impact of regulation, especially the extent to which regulation interferes with investment-backed expectations. *Penn Central.* The character of the government action in this case is the imposition of a condition on permit approval, which allows the public to continue to have access to the coast. The physical intrusion permitted by the deed restriction is minimal. The public is permitted the right to pass and re-pass along the coast in an area from the seawall to the mean high tide mark. This area is at its *widest* 10 feet, which means that *even without the permit condition,* the public's right of access permits it to pass on average within a few feet of the seawall. [The] intrusiveness of such passage is even less than the intrusion resulting from the required dedication of a sidewalk in front of private residences, exactions which are commonplace conditions on approval of development." [a]

(ii) *Heightened scrutiny.* Might the majority's heightened scrutiny of the relationship between the easement condition and the impact of the proposed building on "public access" be explained by the nature of the taking—permanent physical occupancy? Cf. Frank I. Michelman, *Takings 1987,* 88 Colum.L.Rev. 1600, 1607–1613 (1988); Note, 102 Harv.L.Rev. 992, 997–99 (1989). Or might it portend requirement of tighter means-end relationships when conditions on land development raise taking issues? Cf. Note, *Taking a Step Back: A Reconsideration of the Taking Test of Nollan,* 102 Harv.L.Rev. 448 (1988).

(iii) For consideration of the germaneness approach in the light of similar issues see Kathleen M. Sullivan, *Unconstitutional Conditions,* 102 Harv.L.Rev. 1415 (1989).

(b)(i) DOLAN v. CITY OF TIGARD, ___ U.S. ___, 114 S.Ct. 2309, 129 L.Ed.2d 304 (1994), per REHNQUIST C.J., tightened the nexus standard asserted in *Nollan.* Dolan sought a permit to double the size of her plumbing and electrical supply store in Tigard's central business district. It was to remain located on the eastern portion of her 1.67 acre lot, well beyond the 100 year flood plain of Fanno Creek, which flowed outside the southwest corner of her lot and along its western boundary. The city's long range plan called for use of the Fanno Creek flood plain as a greenway system. The Court ruled the following conditions imposed on granting Dolan's permit were takings: that she dedicate to the city (1) the flood plain portion of her lot to enable the city to improve the drainage system along the creek, and (2) a 15 foot strip adjoining the flood plain for a public pedestrian/bicycle path: "[W]e must first determine whether the 'essential nexus' exists between the 'legitimate state interest' and the permit condition exacted by the city. *Nollan.* If we find that a nexus exists, we must then decide the required degree of connection between the exactions and the projected impact of the proposed

a. Blackmun, J., dissenting, protested the "close nexus" for permit conditions and could find no taking under "traditional taking analysis." Stevens, J. also filed a dissent.

development. We were not required to reach this question in *Nollan,* because we concluded that the connection did not meet even the loosest standard. [It seems obvious] that a nexus exists between preventing flooding along Fanno Creek and limiting development within the creek's 100–year flood plain. [The] same may be said for the city's attempt to reduce traffic congestion by providing for alternative means of transportation.

"The second part of our analysis requires us to determine whether the degree of the exactions demanded by the city's permit conditions bear the required relationship to the projected impact of petitioner's proposed development."

In making this determination the Court first called attention to the city's findings that (1) the increased stormwater flow from petitioner's property "can only add to the public need to manage the [flood plain] for drainage purposes." and (2) that "expanded use of the site is anticipated to generate additional vehicular traffic" and that "a safe pedestrian/bicycle pathway [could] offset some of the traffic demand [and] lessen the increase in traffic congestion."

The Court then examined how state courts had dealt with such issues, since "they have been dealing with [them] a good deal longer than we have." It noted that a number of state courts require the municipality to show a "reasonable relationship between the required dedication and the proposed development."

"[W]e think the 'reasonable relationship' test adopted by a majority of the state courts is closer to the federal constitutional norm than either of those previously discussed. But we do not adopt it as such, partly because the term 'reasonable relationship' seems confusingly similar to the term 'rational basis' which describes the minimal level of scrutiny under the Equal Protection Clause of the Fourteenth Amendment. We think a term such as 'rough proportionality' best encapsulates what we hold to be the requirement of the Fifth Amendment. No precise mathematical calculation is required, but the city must make some sort of individualized determination that the required dedication is related both in nature and extent to the impact of the proposed development.

"[We] turn now to analysis of whether the findings relied upon by the city [here] satisfied these requirements.

"It is axiomatic that increasing the amount of impervious surface will increase the quantity and rate of storm-water flow from petitioner's property. Therefore, keeping the flood plain open and free from development would likely confine the pressures on Fanno Creek created by petitioner's development. [But] the city demanded more—it not only wanted petitioner not to build in the flood plain, but it also wanted petitioner's property along Fanno Creek for its Greenway system. The city has never said why a public greenway, as opposed to a private one, was required in the interest of flood control.

"The difference to petitioner, of course, is the loss of her ability to exclude others. [It] is difficult to see why recreational visitors trampling along petitioner's flood plain easement are sufficiently related to the city's legitimate interest in reducing flooding problems along Fanno Creek, and the city has not attempted to make any individualized determination to support this part of its request. * * *

"If petitioner's proposed development had somehow encroached on existing greenway space in the city, it would have been reasonable to require petitioner to provide some alternative greenway space for the public either on her property or elsewhere. [But] that is not the case here. We conclude that the findings upon which the city relies do not show the required reasonable relationship between the flood plain easement and the petitioner's proposed new building.

"With respect to the pedestrian/bicycle pathway, we have no doubt that the city was correct in finding that the larger retail sales facility proposed by petitioner will increase traffic on the streets of the Central Business District. The city estimates that the proposed development would generate roughly 435 additional trips per day. Dedications for streets, sidewalks, and other public ways are generally reasonable exactions to avoid excessive congestion from a proposed property use. But on the record before us, the city has not met its burden of demonstrating that the additional number of vehicle and bicycle trips generated by the petitioner's development reasonably relate to the city's requirement for a dedication of the pedestrian/bicycle pathway easement. The city simply found that the creation of the pathway 'could offset some of the traffic demand [and] lessen the increase in traffic congestion.'

"As Justice Peterson of the Supreme Court of Oregon explained in his dissenting opinion, however, '[t]he findings of fact that the bicycle pathway system "*could* offset some of the traffic demand" is a far cry from a finding that the bicycle pathway system *will*, or is *likely to,* offset some of the traffic demand.' 317 Ore., at 127, 854 P.2d, at 447 (emphasis in original). No precise mathematical calculation is required, but the city must make some effort to quantify its findings in support of the dedication for the pedestrian/bicycle pathway beyond the conclusory statement that it could offset some of the traffic demand generated."

STEVENS, J., joined by Blackmun and Ginsburg, JJ., dissented. "[In contrast to] the Court's approach, [t]he correct inquiry should instead concentrate on whether the required nexus is present and venture beyond considerations of a condition's nature or germaneness only if the developer establishes that a concededly germane condition is so grossly disproportionate to the proposed development's adverse effects that it manifests motives other than land use regulation on the part of the city.

"[In] our changing world one thing is certain: uncertainty will characterize predictions about the impact of new urban developments on the risks of floods, earthquakes, traffic congestion, or environmental harms. When there is doubt concerning the magnitude of those impacts, the public interest in averting them must outweigh the private interest of the commercial entrepreneur. If the government can demonstrate that the conditions it has imposed in a land-use permit are rational, impartial and conducive to fulfilling the aims of a valid land-use plan, a strong presumption of validity should attach to those conditions. The burden of demonstrating that those conditions have unreasonably impaired the economic value of the proposed improvement belongs squarely on the shoulders of the party challenging the state action's constitutionality. That allocation of burdens has served us well in the past. The Court has stumbled badly today by reversing it." [a]

(ii) Did the justifications advanced to support the "rough proportionality" requirement provide a stable doctrinal or principled foundation for future rough proportionality decisions? Cf. Note, 109 Harv.L.Rev., 290, 205–99 (1995). For extensive information on similar issues in state courts, see Note, 73 N.C.L.Rev. 1677 (1995).

7. *Regulations that leave land without beneficial use.* LUCAS v. SOUTH CAROLINA COASTAL COUNCIL, 505 U.S. 1003, 112 S.Ct. 2886, 120 L.Ed.2d 798 (1992), considered, for the first time in detail, whether denying all economical-

---

a. Souter J., also filed a short dissent.

ly beneficial or productive use of land constituted a taking. In 1986, Lucas bought two lots, then zoned for single family dwellings, 300 feet from a South Carolina beach, intending to build such dwelling on them. Before any construction, an anti-erosion law barred any more "occupiable" improvements that near the seashore. Lucas claimed that this deprived him of any "reasonable economic use of his land." The state supreme court ruled that since the regulation was designed to preserve South Carolina's beaches and thus prevent "serious public harm," the taking clause required no compensation. The Court per SCALIA, J., reversed: "[In] 70–odd years [of] 'regulatory taking' jurisprudence we [have] described at least two discrete categories of regulatory action as compensable without case-specific inquiry into the public interest advanced in support of the restraint. The first encompasses regulations that compel the property owner to suffer a physical 'invasion' of his property. In general (at least with regard to permanent invasions), no matter how minute the intrusion, and no matter how weighty the public purpose behind it, we have required compensation. *Loretto* * * *.

"The second situation in which we have found categorical treatment appropriate is where regulation denies all economically beneficial or productive use of land. See *Agins v. Tiburon,* 447 U.S. 255, 260, 100 S.Ct. 2138, 2141, 65 L.Ed.2d 106 (1980); see also *Nollan; Keystone Bituminous.* * * *

"We have never set forth the justification for this rule. Perhaps it is simply, as Justice Brennan suggested, that total deprivation of beneficial use is, from the landowner's point of view, the equivalent of a physical appropriation. See *San Diego Gas & Electric Co. v. San Diego,* 450 U.S. 621, 652, 101 S.Ct. 1287, 1304, 67 L.Ed.2d 551 (1981) (Brennan, J., dissenting). [Surely,] at least, in the extraordinary circumstance when no productive or economically beneficial use of land is permitted, it is less realistic to indulge our usual assumption that the legislature is simply 'adjusting the benefits and burdens of economic life,' *Penn Central,* in a manner that secures an 'average reciprocity of advantage' to everyone concerned, *Mahon.* And the functional basis for permitting the government, by regulation, to affect property values without compensation—that 'Government hardly could go on if to some extent values incident to property could not be diminished without paying for every such change in the general law,' ibid.—does not apply to the relatively rare situations where the government has deprived a landowner of all economically beneficial uses.

"On the other side of the balance, affirmatively supporting a compensation requirement, is the fact that regulations that leave the owner of land without economically beneficial or productive options for its use—typically, as here, by requiring land to be left substantially in its natural state—carry with them a heightened risk that private property is being pressed into some form of public service under the guise of mitigating serious public harm. [The] many statutes on the books, both state and federal, that provide for the use of eminent domain to impose servitudes on private scenic lands preventing developmental uses, or to acquire such lands altogether, suggest the practical equivalence in this setting of negative regulation and [appropriation].

"It is correct that many of our prior opinions have suggested that 'harmful or noxious uses' of property may be proscribed by government regulation without the requirement of compensation. [The] 'harmful or noxious uses' principle was the Court's early attempt to describe in theoretical terms why government may, consistent with the Takings Clause, affect property values by regulation without incurring an obligation to compensate * * *. 'Harmful or noxious use' analysis was, in other words, simply the progenitor of our more contemporary statements that 'land-use regulation does not effect a taking if it "substantially advance[s] legitimate state interests" ' *Nollan* (quoting *Agins*). * * *

"When it is understood that 'prevention of harmful use' was merely our early formulation of the police power justification necessary to sustain (without compensation) any regulatory diminution in value; and that the distinction between regulation that 'prevents harmful use' and that which 'confers benefits' is difficult, if not impossible, to discern on an objective, value-free basis; it becomes self-evident that noxious-use logic cannot serve as a touchstone to distinguish regulatory 'takings'—which require compensation—from regulatory deprivations that do not require compensation. A fortiori, the legislature's recitation of a noxious-use justification cannot be the basis for departing from our categorical rule that total regulatory takings must be compensated. If it were, departure would virtually always be allowed. * * *

"Where the State seeks to sustain regulation that deprives land of all economically beneficial use, we think it may resist compensation only if the logically antecedent inquiry into the nature of the owner's estate shows that the proscribed use interests were not part of his title to begin with. This accords, we think, with our 'takings' jurisprudence, which has traditionally been guided by the understandings of our citizens regarding the content of, and the State's power over, the 'bundle of rights' that they acquire when they obtain title to property. It seems to us that the property owner necessarily expects the uses of his property to be restricted, from time to time, by various measures newly enacted by the State in legitimate exercise of its police powers; '[a]s long recognized, some values are enjoyed under an implied limitation and must yield to the police power.' *Mahon.* And in the case of personal property, by reason of the State's traditionally high degree of control over commercial dealings, he ought to be aware of the possibility that new regulation might even render his property economically worthless (at least if the property's only economically productive use is sale or manufacture for sale), see *Andrus v. Allard.* In the case of land, however, we think the notion pressed by the Council that title is somehow held subject to the 'implied limitation' that the State may subsequently eliminate all economically valuable use is inconsistent with the historical compact recorded in the Takings Clause that has become part of our constitutional culture.

"Where 'permanent physical occupation' of land is concerned, we have refused to allow the government to decree it anew (without compensation), no matter how weighty the asserted 'public interests' involved, *Loretto,* though we assuredly would permit the government to assert a permanent easement that was a pre-existing limitation upon the landowner's title. We believe similar treatment must be accorded confiscatory regulations, i.e., regulations that prohibit all economically beneficial use of land: Any limitation so severe cannot be newly legislated or decreed (without compensation), but must inhere in the title itself, in the restrictions that background principles of the State's law of property and nuisance already place upon land ownership. A law or decree with such an effect must, in other words, do no more than duplicate the result that could have been achieved in the courts—by adjacent landowners (or other uniquely affected persons) under the State's law of private nuisance, or by the State under its complementary power to abate nuisances that affect the public generally, or otherwise.

"On this analysis, the owner of a lake bed, for example, would not be entitled to compensation when he is denied the requisite permit to engage in a landfilling operation that would have the effect of flooding others' land. [Such] regulatory action may well have the effect of eliminating the land's only economically productive use, but it does not proscribe a productive use that was previously permissible under relevant property and nuisance principles. The use of these properties for what are now expressly prohibited purposes was always unlawful, and (subject to other constitutional limitations) it was open to the State at any point to make the implication of those background principles of nuisance and property law explicit. See Frank I. Michelman, *Property, Utility, and Fairness, Comments on the Ethical Foundations of 'Just Compensation' Law,* 80 Harv. L.Rev. 1165, 1239–1241 (1967). [When,] however, a regulation that declares 'off-limits' all economically productive or beneficial uses of land goes beyond what the relevant background principles would dictate, compensation must be paid to sustain it.

"The 'total taking' inquiry we require today will ordinarily entail (as the application of state nuisance law ordinarily entails) analysis of, among other things, the degree of harm to public lands and resources, or adjacent private property, posed by the claimant's proposed activities, see, e.g., *Restatement (Second) of Torts* §§ 826, 827, the social value of the claimant's activities and their suitability to the locality in question, see, e.g., id., §§ 828(a) and (b), 831, and the relative ease with which the alleged harm can be avoided through measures taken by the claimant and the government (or adjacent private landowners) alike, see, e.g., id., §§ 827(e), 828(c), 830. The fact that a particular use has long been engaged in by similarly situated owners ordinarily imports a lack of any common-law prohibition (though changed circumstances or new knowledge may make what was previously permissible no longer so, see id., § 827, comment g.) So also does the fact that other landowners, similarly situated, are permitted to continue the use denied to the claimant.

"It seems unlikely that common-law principles would have prevented the erection of any habitable or productive improvements on petitioner's land; they rarely support prohibition of the 'essential use' of land, *Curtin v. Benson,* 222 U.S. 78, 86, 32 S.Ct. 31, 33, 56 L.Ed. 102 (1911). The question, however, is one of state law to be dealt with on remand. We emphasize that to win its case South Carolina must do more than proffer the legislature's declaration that the uses Lucas desires are inconsistent with the public interest, or the conclusory assertion that they violate a common-law maxim such as sic utere tuo ut alienum non laedas."

KENNEDY, J., concurred in the judgment: "The common law of nuisance is too narrow a confine for the exercise of regulatory power in a complex and interdependent society. *Goldblatt v. Hempstead.* The State should not be prevented from enacting new regulatory initiatives in response to changing conditions, and courts must consider all reasonable expectations whatever their source. * * * Coastal property may present such unique concerns for a fragile land system that the State can go further in regulating its development and use than the common law of nuisance might otherwise permit."

BLACKMUN, J., dissented: "If one fact about the Court's taking jurisprudence can be stated without contradiction, it is that 'the particular circumstances of each case' determine whether a specific restriction will be rendered invalid by the government's failure to pay compensation. *United States v. Central Eureka Mining Co.,* 357 U.S. 155, 168, 78 S.Ct. 1097, 1104, 2 L.Ed.2d 1228 (1958). This is so because although we have articulated certain factors to be considered, including the economic impact on the property owner, the ultimate conclusion 'necessarily requires a weighing of private and public interests.' *Agins.* When the government regulation prevents the owner from any economically valuable use of his property, the private interest is unquestionably substantial, but we have never before held that no public interest can outweigh it. Instead the Court's prior decisions 'uniformly reject the proposition that diminution in property value, standing alone, can establish a "taking."' *Penn Central.* * * *

"Even more perplexing, however, is the Court's reliance on common-law principles of nuisance in its quest for a value-free taking jurisprudence. In determining what is a nuisance at common law, state courts make exactly the decision that the Court finds so troubling when made by the South Carolina General Assembly today: they determine whether the use is harmful. Common-law public and private nuisance law is simply a determination whether a particular use causes harm. [If] judges in the 18th and 19th centuries can distinguish a harm from a benefit, why not judges in the 20th century, and if judges can, why not legislators? There simply is no reason to believe that new interpretations of the hoary common law nuisance doctrine will be particularly 'objective' or 'value-free.' Once one abandons the level of generality of sic utere tuo ut alienum non laedas, one searches in vain, I think, for anything resembling a principle in the common law of nuisance."

STEVENS, J., also dissented: "The Court's holding today effectively freezes the State's common law, denying the legislature much of its traditional power to revise the law governing the rights and uses of property. Until today, I had thought that we had long abandoned this approach to constitutional law. More than a century ago we recognized that 'the great office of statutes is to remedy defects in the common law as they are developed, and to adapt it to the changes of time and circumstances.' *Munn v. Illinois,* 94 U.S. 113, 134, 24 L.Ed. 77 (1877). As Justice Marshall observed about a position similar to that adopted by the Court today: 'If accepted, that claim would represent a return to the era of *Lochner,* when common-law rights were also found immune from revision by State or Federal Government. Such an approach would freeze the common law as it has been constructed by the courts, perhaps at its 19th–century state of development. It would allow no room for change in response to changes in circumstance. The Due Process Clause does not require such a result.' *PruneYard Shopping Center v. Robins,* 447 U.S. 74, 93, 100 S.Ct. 2035, 2047, 64 L.Ed.2d 741 (1980) (concurring opinion)." [a]

a. Souter, J., expressed no views on the merits, stating that he would dismiss the writ of certiorari as improvidently granted because, after briefing and arguments, the "assumption that [the] state had deprived the owner of his entire economic interest in the subject property [was] highly questionable," yet unreviewable on the record.

The South Carolina supreme court ruled that common law principles of nuisance and property would not forbid the planned construction; hence, Lucas was entitled to compensation for the temporary taking of his property. 309 S.C. 424, 424 S.E.2d 484 (1992).

See generally Robert M. Washburn, *Land Use Control, the Individual and Society: Lucas v. South Carolina Coastal Council,* 52 Md. L.Rev. 162 (1993); Glenn P. Sugameli, *Takings Issues in the Light of Lucas v. South*

Carolina Coastal Council, A Decision Full of Sound and Fury, Signifying Nothing, 12 Envtl. L.J. 439 (1993); Richard A. Epstein, *Lucas v. South Carolina, A Tangled Web of Expectations,* 45 Stan.L.Rev. 1369 (1993); William W. Fisher, *The Trouble with Lucas,* 45 Stan.L.Rev. 1393 (1993); Richard Lazarus, *Putting the Correct Spin on Lucas,* 45 Stan.L.Rev. 1411 (1993); Hope M. Babcock, *Has the U.S. Supreme Court Finally Drained the Swamp of Takings Jurisprudence?: The Impact of Lucas v. South Carolina Coastal Council on Wetlands and Coastal Barrier Beaches,* 19 Harv.Envtl.L.Rev. 1 (1995) (stressing the repeated uses and malleability of the common law of nuisance as it adapts to changing circumstances, needs and values, and making much the same point with respect to other property law concepts, such as the common law of custom and public trust).

8. *Commentaries.* For wide-ranging analyses of developments in the law of takings, see *The Jurisprudence of Taking,* 88 Colum.L.Rev. 1581–1794 (1988), a collection of articles by nine leading scholars. For a thoughtful consideration of the relationship of the public trust concept to the *Nollan* situation, see Gilbert L. Finnell, *Public Access to Coastal Public Property: Judicial Theories and the Taking Issue,* 67 N.C.L.Rev. 627, 660–66 (1989).

9. *Remedies for regulatory taking: inverse condemnation.* (a) In FIRST ENGLISH EVANGELICAL LUTHERAN CHURCH v. LOS ANGELES COUNTY, 482 U.S. 304, 107 S.Ct. 2378, 96 L.Ed.2d 250 (1987), per REHNQUIST, C.J., the state court had "held that a landowner who claims that his property has been 'taken' by a land-use regulation may not recover damages for the time before it is finally determined that the regulation constitutes a 'taking' of his property. * * *

"[The] Court has recognized in more than one case that the government may elect to abandon its intrusion or discontinue regulations. [The] landowner has no right under the Just Compensation Clause to insist that a 'temporary' taking be deemed a permanent taking. But we have not resolved whether abandonment by the government requires payment of compensation for the period of time during which regulations deny a landowner all use of his land.

"[C]ases where the government has only temporarily exercised its right to use private property [reflect] the fact that 'temporary' takings which, as here, deny a landowner all use of his property, are not different in kind from permanent takings, for which the Constitution clearly requires compensation. [In] the present case the interim ordinance was adopted by the county of Los Angeles in January 1979, and became effective immediately. Appellant filed suit within a month after the effective date of the ordinance and yet when the Supreme Court of California denied a hearing in the case on October 17, 1985, the merits of appellant's claim had yet to be determined. The United States has been required to pay compensation for leasehold interests of shorter duration than this. The value of a leasehold interest in property for a period of years may be substantial, and the burden on the property owner in extinguishing such an interest for a period of years may be great indeed. Where this burden results from governmental action that amounted to a taking, the Just Compensation Clause of the Fifth Amendment requires that the government pay the landowner for the value of the use of the land during this period. Cf. *United States v. Causby* ('It is the owner's loss, not the taker's gain, which is the measure of the value of the property taken'). Invalidation of the ordinance or its successor ordinance after this period of time, though converting the taking into a 'temporary' one, is not a sufficient remedy to meet the demands of the Just Compensation Clause."

STEVENS, J., dissented: "[While] virtually all physical invasions are deemed takings, see e.g., *Loretto; Causby,* a regulatory program that adversely affects property values does not constitute a taking unless it destroys a major portion of the property's value. This diminution of value inquiry is unique to regulatory takings. [I] am willing to assume that some cases may arise in which a property owner can show that prospective invalidation of the regulation cannot cure the taking—that the temporary operation of a regulation has caused such a significant diminution in the property's value that compensation must be afforded for the taking that has already occurred. For this ever to happen, the restriction on the use of the property would not only have to be a substantial one, but it would have to remain in effect for a significant percentage of the property's useful life. In such a case an application of our test for regulatory takings would obviously require an inquiry into the duration of the restriction, as well as its scope and severity.

"[The] policy implications of today's decision are obvious and, I fear, far reaching. Cautious local officials and land-use planners may avoid taking any action that might later be challenged and thus give rise to a damage action. Much important regulation will never be enacted, even perhaps in the health and safety area." [a]

(b) Should *First English* be viewed as leaving unresolved whether compensation is required if "a local government [enacts] an expressly temporary, say three-year building moratorium to allow time for study of a problematic situation, and then actually [lifts] the moratorium at the expiration of three years?" Consider Professor Michelman's analysis in *Takings 1987,* supra, at 1614–1621.

SECTION 5. CONTRACT CLAUSE

ALLIED STRUCTURAL STEEL CO. v. SPANNAUS

438 U.S. 234, 98 S.Ct. 2716, 57 L.Ed.2d 727 (1978).

JUSTICE STEWART delivered the opinion of the Court.

[In 1963 Allied adopted a pension plan that vested pension rights only when an employee had worked to age 65, or 15 years to age 60 or 20 years to age 55. Those who quit or were terminated before vesting had no pensions rights. Pensions were payable only from Allied's pension fund to which it made yearly payments based on actuarial predictions. Allied informed its employees that the plan implied no assurance against dismissal and that it retained the right to terminate the pension plan at any time for any reason, subject to use of the fund's assets to pay vested pensions in a specified order of priorities.

[A 1974 Minnesota Act required employers with pension plans, who went out of business in Minnesota, to provide full pensions to all its Minnesota employees who had worked 10 years or more, and to pay a "pension funding charge" sufficient to buy deferred annuities for any pension fund deficiency. As a first step in closing its 30 employee Minnesota operation, Allied terminated 11 employees, 9 of whom had worked for Allied over 10 years, but not long enough to have vested pension rights. Under the Act, Allied's "pension funding charge" was $185,000.]

The Act substantially altered [the company's contractual relationships with its employees] by superimposing pension obligations upon the company conspicuously beyond those that it had voluntarily agreed to undertake. But it does not inexorably follow that the Act, as applied to the company, violates the Contract Clause. * * *

Although it was perhaps the strongest single constitutional check on state legislation during our early years as a Nation, the Contract Clause receded into comparative desuetude [with] the development of the large body of jurisprudence

a. While not joining the foregoing portions of the Stevens dissent, Blackmun and O'Connor, JJ., joined Parts I and III of the dissent, which argued (I) that the complaint did not sufficiently allege an unconstitutional taking, and (III) that the church should have been required to exhaust its remedies in the state courts by "demanding invalidation of the ordinance prior to seeking this Court's review of California procedures."

under the Due Process Clause.[12]   Nonetheless, the Contract Clause remains part of the Constitution.   It is not a dead letter.

[The] Contract Clause does [not] "prevent the State from exercising such powers as are vested in it for the promotion of the common weal, or are necessary for the general good of the public, though contracts previously entered into between individuals may thereby be affected.   This [police power] is paramount to any rights under contracts between individuals." *Manigault v. Springs,* 199 U.S. 473, 480, 26 S.Ct. 127, 50 L.Ed. 274 (1905).[a]   As Mr. Justice Holmes succinctly put the matter [in] *Hudson Water Co. v. McCarter,* 209 U.S. 349, 357, 28 S.Ct. 529, 52 L.Ed. 828: "One whose rights, such as they are, are subject to state restriction, cannot remove them from the power of the State by making a contract about them.   The contract will carry with it the infirmity of the subject matter."

If the Contract Clause is to retain any meaning at all, however, it must be understood to impose *some* limits upon the power of a State to abridge existing contractual relationships, even in the exercise of its otherwise legitimate police power.   The existence and nature of those limits were clearly indicated in a series of cases in this Court arising from the efforts of the States to deal with the unprecedented emergencies brought on by the severe economic depression of the early 1930's.

In *Home Building & Loan Assn. v. Blaisdell,* 290 U.S. 398, 54 S.Ct. 231, 78 L.Ed. 413 (1934), the Court upheld [a] mortgage moratorium law that Minnesota had enacted to provide relief for homeowners threatened with foreclosure.   Although the legislation conflicted directly with lenders' contractual foreclosure rights, the Court there acknowledged that, despite the Contract Clause, the States retain residual authority to enact laws "to safeguard the vital interests of [their] people."   In upholding the state mortgage moratorium law, the Court found five factors significant.   First, the state legislature had declared in the Act itself that an emergency need for the protection of homeowners existed.   Second, the state law was enacted to protect a basic societal interest, not a favored group.   Third, the relief was appropriately tailored to the emergency that it was designed to meet.   Fourth, the imposed conditions were reasonable.[b]   And, finally, the legislation was limited to the duration of the emergency.

The *Blaisdell* opinion thus clearly implied that if the Minnesota moratorium legislation had not possessed the characteristics attributed to it by the Court, it would have been invalid under the Contract Clause of the Constitution.   These implications were given concrete force in [cases] that followed closely in *Blaisdell's* wake.[c]   * * *

---

12.   Indeed, at least one commentator has suggested that "the results might be the same if the contract clause were dropped out of the Constitution, and the challenged statutes all judged as reasonable or unreasonable deprivations of property."   Robert L. Hale, *The Supreme Court and the Contract Clause,* 57 Harv. L.Rev. 852, 890–91 (1944).

a.   *Manigault* held the contract clause did not bar legislation that authorized a riparian owner to dam a creek to facilitate reclamation of lowlands, in violation of his contract with another riparian owner.   Cf.   *Union Dry Goods Co. v. Georgia Pub. Service Corp.,* 248 U.S. 372, 39 S.Ct. 117, 63 L.Ed. 309 (1919) (contract clause not violated by statute autho-

rizing utility to charge rates fixed by commission higher than pre-existing contract rate).

b.   *Blaisdell* stressed that the law did not impair the mortgage indebtedness, that the ultimate right to foreclosure and a deficiency judgment remained, that interest continued to accrue, and that the mortgagor must pay the rental value to be applied to taxes, insurance, and interest.

c.   The Court briefly stated the rulings in three cases that found contract clause violations shortly after *Blaisdell*: *W.B. Worthen Co. v. Thomas,* 292 U.S. 426, 54 S.Ct. 816, 78 L.Ed. 1344 (1934); *W.B. Worthen v. Kavanaugh,* 295 U.S. 56, 55 S.Ct. 555, 79 L.Ed. 1298 (1935); *Treigle v. Acme Homestead Ass'n,* 297 U.S. 189, 56 S.Ct. 408, 80 L.Ed. 575 (1936).

The most recent Contract Clause case in this Court was *United States Trust Co. v. New Jersey,* [infra]. In that case the Court again recognized that although the absolute language of the Clause must leave room for "the 'essential attributes of sovereign power,' necessarily reserved by the States to safeguard the welfare of their citizens," that power has limits when its exercise effects substantial modifications of private contracts. Despite the customary deference courts give to state laws directed to social and economic problems, "[l]egislation adjusting the rights and responsibilities of contracting parties must be upon reasonable conditions and of a character appropriate to the public purpose justifying its adoption." Evaluating with particular scrutiny a modification of a contract to which the State itself was a party, the Court in that case held that legislative alteration of the rights and remedies of Port Authority bondholders violated the Contract Clause because the legislation was neither necessary nor reasonable.

In applying these principles, the first inquiry must be whether the state law has, in fact, operated as a substantial impairment of a contractual relationship.[16] [Minimal] alteration of contractual obligations may end the inquiry at its first stage. Severe impairment, on the other hand, will push the inquiry to a careful examination of the nature and purpose of the state legislation.

The severity of an impairment of contractual obligations can be measured by the factors that reflect the high value the Framers placed on the protection of private contracts. Contracts enable individuals to order their personal and business affairs according to their particular needs and interests. Once arranged, those rights and obligations are binding under the law, and the parties are entitled to rely on them.

Here, the company's contracts of employment [included] the pension plan. The company's maximum obligation was to set aside each year an amount based on the plan's requirements for vesting. * * *

The effect of Minnesota's [Act] on this contractual obligation was severe. The company was required in 1974 to have made its contributions throughout the pre-1974 life of its plan as if employees' pension rights had vested after 10 years, instead of vesting in accord with the terms of the plan. Thus a basic term of the pension contract—one on which the company had relied for 10 years—was substantially modified. The result was that although the company's past contributions were adequate when made, they were not adequate when computed under the 10-year statutory vesting requirement. The Act thus forced a current recalculation of the past 10 years' contributions based on the new, unanticipated 10-year vesting requirement.

Not only did the state law thus retroactively modify the compensation that the company had agreed to pay its employees from 1963 to 1974, but it did so by changing the company's obligations in an area where the element of reliance was vital—the funding of a pension [plan].[18] [The company was] forced to make all the retroactive changes in its contractual obligations at one [time].

16. [The] narrow view that the Clause forbids only state laws that diminish the duties of a contractual obligor and not laws that increase them, a view arguably suggested by *Satterlee v. Matthewson,* 2 Pet. 380, 7 L.Ed. 458, has since been expressly repudiated. *Detroit United Ry. v. Michigan,* 242 U.S. 238, 37 S.Ct. 87, 61 L.Ed. 268; *Georgia Ry. & Power Co. v. Decatur,* 262 U.S. 432, 43 S.Ct. 613, 67 L.Ed. 1065. Moreover, in any bilateral contract the diminution of duties on one side effectively increases the duties on the other. * * *

18. In some situations the element of reliance may cut both ways. Here, the company had relied upon the funding obligation of the pension plan for more than a decade. There was no showing of reliance to the contrary by its employees. Indeed, Minnesota did not act to protect any employee reliance interest dem-

Thus, the [statute] nullifies express terms of the company's contractual obligations and imposes a completely unexpected liability in potentially disabling amounts. [Yet] there is no showing in the record before us that this severe disruption of contractual expectations was necessary to meet an important general social problem. The presumption favoring "legislative judgment as to the necessity and reasonableness of a particular measure," *United States Trust Co.,* simply cannot stand in this case.

[The legislation] clearly has an extremely narrow focus. It applies only to private employers [who] have established voluntary private pension plans, [and] only when such an employer closes his Minnesota office or terminates his pension plan. Thus, this law can hardly be characterized, like the law at issue in the *Blaisdell* case, as one enacted to protect a broad societal interest rather than a narrow class.

Moreover, [this] legislation [was] not enacted to deal with a situation remotely approaching the broad and desperate emergency economic conditions of the early 1930's—conditions of which the Court in *Blaisdell* took judicial notice.[24]
* * *

This Minnesota law simply does not possess the attributes of those state laws that in the past have survived challenge under the Contract Clause of the Constitution. The law was not even purportedly enacted to deal with a broad, generalized economic or social problem. Cf. *Blaisdell.* It did not operate in an area already subject to state regulation at the time the company's contractual obligations were originally undertaken, but invaded an area never before subject to regulation by the State. It did not effect simply a temporary alteration of the contractual relationships of those within its coverage, but worked a severe, permanent, and immediate change in those relationships—irrevocably and retroactively. And its narrow aim was leveled, not at every Minnesota employer, not even at every Minnesota employer who left the State, but only at those who had in the past been sufficiently enlightened as voluntarily to agree to establish pension plans for their employees. * * *

JUSTICE BRENNAN, with whom JUSTICE WHITE and JUSTICE MARSHALL join, dissenting.[e]

[The Minnesota Act] does not abrogate or dilute any obligation due a party to a private contract; rather, like all positive social legislation, the Act imposes new, additional obligations on a particular class of persons. In my view, any constitutional infirmity in the law must therefore derive, not from the Contract Clause, but from the Due Process Clause of the Fourteenth Amendment.

[The Act was] designed to remedy a serious social problem arising from the operation of private pension plans. [B]ecause employers often failed to make contributions to the pension funds large enough adequately to fund their plans, employees often ultimately received only a small amount of those benefits they reasonably anticipated. [Denial] of all pension benefits not because of job related failings but only because the employees are unfortunate enough to be employed at

---

onstrated on the record. Instead, it compelled the employer to exceed bargained-for expectations and nullified an express term of the pension plan.

24. This is not to suggest that only an emergency of great magnitude can constitutionally justify a state law impairing the obligations of contracts. See, e.g., *Veix v. Sixth*

Ward Building & Loan Assn., 310 U.S. at 39–40, 60 S.Ct. 792, 84 L.Ed. 1061 [1945]; *East New York Savings Bank v. Hahn,* 326 U.S. 230, 66 S.Ct. 69, 90 L.Ed. 34; *El Paso v. Simmons,* 379 U.S. 497, 85 S.Ct. 577, 13 L.Ed.2d 446 (1965).

e. Blackmun, J., did not participate.

a plant that closes for purely economic reasons is harsh indeed. [The] closing of a plant is a contingency outside the range of normal expectations of both the employer and the employee. [Although] the Court glides over this fact, it should be apparent that the Act will impose only minor economic burdens on employers whose pension plans have been adequately funded. [An] adequate pension plan fund would include contributions on behalf of terminated employees of 10 or more years service whose rights had not vested. Indeed, without the Act, the closing of the plant would create a windfall for the employer, because, due to the resulting surplus in the fund, his future contributions would be reduced.

[It] is nothing less than an abuse of the English language to interpret, as does the Court, the term "impairing" as including laws which create new duties. While such laws may be conceptualized as "enlarging" the obligation of a contract when they add to the burdens that had previously been imposed by a private agreement, such laws cannot be prohibited by the Clause because they do not dilute or nullify a duty a person had previously obligated himself to perform.[7]

* * *

[More] fundamentally, the Court's distortion of the meaning of the Contract Clause [threatens] to undermine the jurisprudence of property rights developed over the last 40 years. The Contract Clause, of course, is but one of several clauses in the Constitution that protect existing economic values from governmental interference. The Fifth Amendment's command that "private property [shall not] be taken for public use, without just compensation" is such a clause. A second is the Due Process Clause, which during the heyday of substantive due process, see *Lochner,* largely supplanted the Contract Clause in importance and operated as a potent limitation on Government's ability to interfere with economic expectations. Decisions over the past 50 years have developed a coherent, unified interpretation of all the constitutional provisions that may protect economic expectations and these decisions have recognized a broad latitude in States to effect even severe interference with existing economic values when reasonably necessary to promote the general welfare. At the same time the prohibition of the Contract Clause, consistently with its wording and historic purposes, has been limited in application to state laws that diluted, with utter indifference to the legitimate interests of the beneficiary of a contract duty, the existing contract obligation.

Today's conversion of the Contract Clause into a limitation on the power of States to enact laws that impose duties additional to obligations assumed under private contracts must inevitably produce results difficult to square with any rational conception of a constitutional order. [The] validity of such a law will turn upon whether judges see it as a law that deals with a generalized social problem, whether it is temporary (as few will be) or permanent, whether it operates in an area previously subject to regulation, and, finally, whether its duties apply to a broad class of persons. The necessary consequence of the extreme malleability of these rather vague criteria is to vest judges with broad subjective discretion to protect property interests that happen to appeal to them.

---

7. In *Georgia Ry. & Power Co. v. Decatur, Detroit United Ry. v. Michigan,* [fn. 16 supra], and in dictum in other cases, this Court embraced, without any careful analysis and without giving any consideration to *Satterlee v. Matthewson,* [fn. 16, supra], the contrary view that the impairment of a contract may consist in "adding to its burdens" as well as in diminishing its efficacy. These opinions reflect the then-prevailing philosophy of economic due process which has since been repudiated. See *Ferguson v. Skrupa.* In my view, the reasoning of *Georgia Ry.* and *Detroit United Ry.* is simply wrong.

[There] is nothing sancrosanct about expectations rooted in contract that justify according them a constitutional immunity denied other property rights. Laws that interfere with settled expectations created by state property law (and which impose severe economic burdens) are uniformly held constitutional where reasonably related to the promotion of the general welfare.   * * *

Notes and Questions

1. *Contract vs. other property rights.* (a) In what respects, if any, is there a significant difference in the Court's review of economic legislation when challenged under the contract clause as compared to due process? Consider particularly (1) the professed standard of review, (2) the degree of deference to the legislature or strictness of judicial scrutiny, (3) the Court's willingness to hypothesize state purposes to justify the legislation. Cf. 92 Harv.L.Rev. 94–99 (1978).

(b) Ought the degree of constitutional protection from legislative interference differ as between preexisting contract interests and preexisting noncontractual property interests?

2. *Legislatively-added burdens.* Did *Allied Steel* soundly interpret the contract clause to protect against "impairment" by legislatively-added burdens that increase those stated in the contract? Would it have made a difference in the law's validity if it had added a burden of sounder *funding* of the contractual pension benefits without adding to the *benefits*? Cf. *Connolly v. Pension Benefit Guaranty Corp.*, 475 U.S. 211, 106 S.Ct. 1018, 89 L.Ed.2d 166 (1986) (a taking clause decision).

3. *Impairment of government contractual obligations.* One year before *Allied Steel,* UNITED STATES TRUST CO. v. NEW JERSEY, 431 U.S. 1, 97 S.Ct. 1505, 52 L.Ed.2d 92 (1977), per BLACKMUN, J., applied the contract clause to invalidate, 4 to 3,[a] New Jersey and New York laws repealing earlier statutory commitments with Port Authority bond holders not to use revenues pledged as security for the bonds for any railroad facility that was not self-supporting: The purpose of the repeal was to enable the Port Authority to lessen traffic problems by increasing use of mass transit through subsidizing commuter service with revenues from higher bridge and tunnel tolls:

"[The] Contract Clause is not an absolute bar to subsequent modification of a State's own financial obligations. As with laws impairing the obligations of private contracts, an impairment may be constitutional if it is reasonable and necessary to serve an important public purpose. In applying this standard, however, complete deference to a legislative assessment of reasonableness and necessity is not appropriate because the State's self-interest is at stake. [If] a State could reduce its financial obligations whenever it wanted to spend the money for what it regarded as an important public purpose, the Contract Clause would provide no protection at all.[25]"

a. Blackmun J., did not participate in *Spannaus,* but Powell and Stevens, JJ., who had not participated in *U.S. Trust Co.,* joined the *Spannaus* majority, making a majority of six justices voting in the 1970s to revitalize the contract clause.

25. For similar reasons, a dual standard of review was applied under the Fifth Amendment to federal legislation abrogating contractual gold clauses. "There is a clear distinction between the power of the Congress to control or interdict the contracts of private parties when they interfere with the exercise of its constitutional authority, and the power of the Congress to alter or repudiate the substance of its own engagements when it has borrowed money under the authority which the Constitution confers." *Perry v. United States,* 294 U.S. 330, 55 S.Ct. 432, 79 L.Ed. 912 (1935).

The Court considered the repeal "unnecessary" because the need could have been satisfied by a "less drastic modification", such as to "exclude the additional bridge and tunnel tolls from the revenue use limitation," or to encourage use of mass transit by changes in the tax and toll structures for autos. It viewed the repeal also as "unreasonable" because the need for increased mass transit had long been recognized, and the repealed 1962 commitment "was specifically intended to protect the pledged revenues and reserves against the possibility that such concerns would lead the Port Authority into greater involvement in deficit mass transit."

BRENNAN, J., joined by White and Marshall, JJ., dissented: "[Today's decision] remolds the Contract Clause into a potent instrument for overseeing important policy determinations of the state legislature. At the same time, by creating a constitutional safe haven for property rights embodied in a contract, the decision substantially distorts modern constitutional jurisprudence governing regulation of private economic interests."

4. *Generally applicable rule of conduct.* EXXON CORP. v. EAGERTON, 462 U.S. 176, 103 S.Ct. 2296, 76 L.Ed.2d 497 (1983), per MARSHALL, J., unanimously held that a ban on oil and gas producers passing a severance tax increase on to consumers did not violate the contract clause even though pre-existing contracts required consumers to reimburse producers for all severance taxes:

"[T]he pass-through prohibition did not prescribe a rule limited in effect to contractual obligations or remedies, but instead imposed a generally applicable rule of conduct designed to advance 'a broad societal interest,' *Allied Steel,* protecting consumers from excessive prices. The prohibition applied to all oil and gas producers, regardless of whether they happened to be parties to sale contracts that contained a provision permitting them to pass tax increases through to their purchasers. The effect of the pass-through prohibition on existing contracts that did contain such a provision was incidental to its main effect of shielding consumers from the burden of the tax increase.

"Because the pass-through prohibition imposed a generally applicable rule of conduct, it is sharply distinguishable from the measures struck down in *United States Trust* and *Allied Steel. United States Trust* involved New York and New Jersey statutes whose sole effect was to repeal a covenant that the two States had entered into with the holders of bonds issued by The Port Authority of New York and New Jersey. Similarly, the statute at issue in *Allied Steel* directly 'adjust[ed] the rights and responsibilities of contracting parties,' quoting *United States Trust.* * * *

"Alabama's power to prohibit oil and gas producers from passing the increase in the severance tax on to their purchasers is confirmed by several decisions of this Court rejecting Contract Clause challenges to state rate-setting schemes that displaced any rates previously established by contract. * * * And if the Contract Clause does not prevent a State from dictating the price that sellers may charge their customers, plainly it does not prevent a State from requiring that sellers absorb a tax increase themselves rather than pass it through to their customers."

5. *Federal legislation.* PENSION BENEFIT GUARANTY CORP. v. R.A. GRAY & CO., 467 U.S. 717, 104 S.Ct. 2709, 81 L.Ed.2d 601 (1984), involved the federal Multiemployer Pension Plan Amendments Act of 1980 (MPPAA), which implemented the objective of the Employees' Retirement Income Security Act of 1978 (ERISA) to protect employees' retirement benefits from multiemployer pension plans. Among other things, MPPAA required employers withdrawing from a plan to pay a designated sum (beyond their contractual obligation)

amounting to the employer's proportionate share of the plan's "unfunded vested benefits." The Court, per BRENNAN, J., unanimously ruled that it had never held "that the principles embodied in the Fifth Amendment's Due Process Clause are coextensive with prohibitions existing against state impairments of preexisting contracts. Indeed, to the extent that recent decisions of the Court have addressed the issue, we have contrasted the limitations imposed on States by the Contract Clause with the less searching standards imposed on economic legislation by the Due Process Clauses. And, although we have noted that retrospective civil legislation may offend due process if it is 'particularly harsh and oppressive,' that standard does not differ from the prohibition against arbitrary and irrational legislation [under the due process clause. The] strong deference accorded legislation in the field of national economic policy is no less applicable when that legislation is applied retroactively. [R]etroactive legislation does have to meet a burden not faced by legislation that has only future effects. [But] that burden is met simply by showing that the retroactive application of the legislation is itself justified by a rational legislative purpose."

Chapter 3
NATURE AND SCOPE OF FOURTEENTH AMENDMENT DUE PROCESS; APPLICABILITY OF THE BILL OF RIGHTS TO THE STATES

SECTION 1. THE "ORDERED LIBERTY—FUNDAMENTAL FAIRNESS," "TOTAL INCORPORATION" AND "SELECTIVE INCORPORATION" THEORIES

Twining v. New Jersey, 211 U.S. 78, 29 S.Ct. 14, 53 L.Ed. 97 (1908); *Palko v. Connecticut,* 302 U.S. 319, 58 S.Ct. 149, 82 L.Ed. 288 (1937); and *Adamson v. California,* 332 U.S. 46, 67 S.Ct. 1672, 91 L.Ed. 1903 (1947), rejected the "total incorporation" view of the history of the fourteenth amendment, the view—which has never commanded a majority—that the fourteenth amendment made all of the provisions of the Bill of Rights fully applicable to the states.[a] But *Twining* recognized that "it is possible that some of the personal rights safeguarded by the first eight Amendments against National action may also be safeguarded against state action, because a denial of them would be a denial of due process" or because "the specific pledge of particular amendments have been found to be implicit in the concept of ordered liberty and thus through the Fourteenth Amendment, become valid as against the states" (*Palko*). And the Court early found among the procedural requirements of fourteenth amendment due process certain rules paralleling provisions of the first eight amendments. For example, *Powell v. Alabama,* 287 U.S. 45, 53 S.Ct. 55, 77 L.Ed. 158 (1932), held that defendants in a capital case were denied due process when a state refused them the aid of counsel. "The logically critical thing, however," pointed out Harlan, J., years later, "was not that the rights had been found in the Bill of Rights, but that they were deemed * * * fundamental." [b]

a. *Palko,* which held that the fourteenth amendment did not encompass at least certain aspects of the double jeopardy prohibition of the fifth amendment, was overruled in *Benton v. Maryland* (1969), discussed below. The *Twining-Adamson* view that the fifth amendment privilege against self-incrimination is not incorporated in the fourteenth was rejected in *Malloy v. Hogan* (1964), discussed below. *Griffin v. California,* 380 U.S. 609, 5 Ohio Misc. 127, 85 S.Ct. 1229, 14 L.Ed.2d 106 (1965), subsequently applied *Malloy* to overrule the specific holdings of *Twining* and *Adamson,* which had permitted comment on a defendant's failure to take the stand at his criminal trial. These later decisions, however, were still consistent with the rejection of the "total incorporation" interpretation.

b. *Duncan v. Louisiana* (dissent joined by Stewart, J.), discussed below.

Under the "ordered liberty"—"fundamental fairness" test, which procedural safeguards included in the Bill of Rights were applicable to the states and which were not? Consider Cardozo, J., speaking for the *Palko* Court: "[On reflection and analysis there] emerges the perception of a rationalizing principle which gives to discrete instances a proper order and coherence. The right to trial by jury and the immunity from prosecution except as the result of an indictment [are] not of the very essence of a scheme of ordered liberty. To abolish them is not to violate a 'principle of justice so rooted in the traditions and conscience of our people as to be ranked as fundamental.' [What] is true of jury trials and indictments is true also, as the cases show, of the immunity from compulsory self-incrimination. This too might be lost, and justice still be [done.]" [c]

"We reach a different plane of social and moral values when we pass [to those provisions of the Bill of Rights] brought within the Fourteenth Amendment by a process of absorption. These in their origin were effective against the federal government alone. If the Fourteenth Amendment has absorbed them, the process of absorption has had its course in the belief that neither liberty nor justice would exist if they were sacrificed. This is true, for illustration, of freedom of thought and speech. Of that freedom one may say that it is the matrix, the indispensable condition, of nearly every other form of freedom. * * * Fundamental too in the concept of due process, and so in that of liberty, is the thought that condemnation shall be rendered only after trial. The hearing, moreover, must be a real one, not a sham or pretense [discussing *Powell* which] did not turn upon the fact that the benefit of counsel would have been guaranteed to the defendants by [the] Sixth Amendment if they had been prosecuted in a federal court [but on] the fact that in the particular situation laid before us [the aid of counsel] was essential to the substance of a hearing."

The "total incorporation" position received its strongest support in the *Adamson* dissents. In the principal dissent, Black, J., joined by Douglas, J., observed: "I cannot consider the Bill of Rights to be an outworn 18th Century 'strait jacket' as the *Twining* opinion did. Its provisions may be thought outdated abstractions by some. And it is true that they were designed to meet ancient evils. But they are the same kind of human evils that have emerged from century to century wherever excessive power is sought by the few at the expense of the many. In my judgment the people of no nation can lose their liberty so long as a Bill of Rights like ours survives and its basic purposes are conscientiously interpreted, enforced and respected so as to afford continuous protection against

---

c. As pointed out in fn. a supra, the fifth amendment privilege against self-incrimination was subsequently held to be fully applicable to the states via the fourteenth amendment. So was the sixth amendment right to jury trial in criminal cases. *Duncan v. Louisiana* (1968), discussed below.

The above language in *Palko* and language in *Adamson,* infra, and other cases are susceptible of the interpretation that when the Court held that a particular Bill of Rights guarantee was not "incorporated into," or implicit in, fourteenth amendment due process it was *completely* "out." But such a reading of these cases seems unsound. Typically the Court dealt with state procedures transgressing the "outer edges," rather than the basic concept, of a particular Bill of Rights guarantee. It seems most doubtful that in sustaining such challenged procedures the Court was authorizing the states to abolish completely—or to violate the "hardcore" of—e.g., the protection against double jeopardy, or the privilege against self-incrimination, or the right to trial by jury in criminal cases. Rather the Court probably meant that the state rules did not violate the fourteenth amendment because the Bill of Rights guarantee invoked by defendant did not apply to the states *to the full extent* it applied to the federal government. To hold that a particular provision of the Bill of Rights is not *totally* "incorporated," i.e., not binding on the states *in its entirety,* is not to say it is *completely "out"* of the fourteenth amendment. See generally Louis Henkin, *"Selective Incorporation" in the Fourteenth Amendment,* 73 Yale L.J. 74, 79 & n. 18, 80–81 (1963).

old, as well as new, devices and practices which might thwart those purposes. I fear to see the consequences of the Court's practice of substituting its own concepts of decency and fundamental justice for the language of the Bill of Rights as its point of departure in interpreting and enforcing that Bill of Rights. If the choice must be between the selective process of the *Palko* decision applying some of the Bill of Rights to the States, or the *Twining* rule applying none of them, I would choose the *Palko* selective process. But rather than accept either of these choices, I would follow what I believe was the original purpose of the Fourteenth Amendment—to extend to all the people of the nation the complete protection of the Bill of Rights.

"[T]o pass upon the constitutionality of statutes by looking to the particular standards enumerated in the Bill of Rights and other parts of the Constitution is one thing; to invalidate statutes because of application of 'natural law' deemed to be above and undefined by the Constitution is another. 'In the one instance, courts proceeding within clearly marked constitutional boundaries seek to execute policies written into the Constitution; in the other they roam at will in the limitless area of their own beliefs as to reasonableness and actually select policies, a responsibility which the Constitution entrusts to the legislative representatives of the people.' " [d]

Responding, Frankfurter, J.'s concurrence in *Adamson* stressed the "independent potency" of the fourteenth amendment due process clause, maintaining that it "neither comprehends the specific provisions by which the founders deemed it appropriate to restrict the federal government nor is confined to them": [e] "Between the incorporation of the Fourteenth Amendment into the Constitution and the beginning of the present membership of the Court—a period of 70 years—the scope of that Amendment was passed upon by 43 judges. Of all these judges only one, who may respectfully be called an eccentric exception, ever indicated the belief that the Fourteenth Amendment was a shorthand summary of the first eight Amendments theretofore limiting only the Federal Government, and that due process incorporated those eight Amendments as restrictions upon the powers of the States. [To] suggest that it is inconsistent with a truly free society to begin prosecutions without an indictment, to try petty civil cases without the paraphernalia of a common law jury, to take into consideration that one who has full opportunity to make a defense remains silent is, in de Tocqueville's phrase, to confound the familiar with the necessary.

"[Those] reading the English language with the meaning which it ordinarily conveys, those conversant with the political and legal history of the concept of due process, those sensitive to the relations of the States to the central government as well as the relation of some of the provisions of the Bill of Rights to the process of justice, would hardly recognize the Fourteenth Amendment as a cover for the

d. Dissenting separately in *Adamson*, Murphy, J., joined by Rutledge, J., "agree[d] that the specific guarantees of the Bill of Rights should be carried over intact into [the fourteenth amendment but was] not prepared to say that the latter is entirely and necessarily limited by the Bill of Rights. Occasions may arise where a proceeding falls so far short of conforming to fundamental standards of procedure as to warrant constitutional condemnation in terms of a lack of due process despite the absence of a specific provision of the Bill of Rights." In this connection, consider fn. e infra.

e. See also Henry Friendly, *The Bill of Rights as a Code of Criminal Procedure,* 53 Calif.L.Rev. 929, 937 (1965): "[N]o facile formula will enable the Court to escape its assigned task of deciding just what the Constitution protects from state action, as *Estes v. Texas,* 381 U.S. 532, 85 S.Ct. 1628, 14 L.Ed.2d 543 (1965), where no 'specific' could be invoked, showed [for] procedural due process, and *Griswold v. Connecticut* [p. 299 infra] demonstrated for substantive due process."

various explicit provisions of the first eight Amendments. Some of these are enduring reflections of experience with human nature, while some express the restricted views of Eighteenth-Century England regarding the best methods for the ascertainment of facts. The notion that the Fourteenth Amendment was a covert way of imposing upon the States all the rules which it seemed important to Eighteenth Century statesmen to write into the Federal Amendments, was rejected by judges who were themselves witnesses of the process by which the Fourteenth Amendment became part of the Constitution. * * *

"Indeed, the suggestion that the Fourteenth Amendment incorporates the first eight Amendments as such is not unambiguously urged. [There] is suggested merely a selective incorporation of the first eight Amendments into the Fourteenth Amendment. Some are in and some are out, but we are left in the dark as to which are in and which are out. [If] the basis of selection is merely that those provisions of the first eight Amendments are incorporated which commend themselves to individual justices as indispensable to the dignity and happiness of a free man, we are thrown back to a merely subjective test. [In] the history of thought 'natural law' has a much longer and much better founded meaning and justification than such subjective selection of the first eight Amendments for incorporation into the Fourteenth. If all that is meant is that due process contains within itself certain minimal standards which are 'of the very essence of a scheme of ordered liberty,' *Palko,* putting upon this Court the duty of applying these standards from time to time, then we have merely arrived at the insight which our predecessors long ago expressed.

"[A] construction which gives to due process no independent function but turns it into a summary of the specific provisions of the Bill of Rights [would] deprive the States of opportunity for reforms in legal process designed for extending the area of freedom. It would assume that no other abuses would reveal themselves in the course of time than those which had become manifest in 1791. Such a view not only disregards the historic meaning of 'due process.' It leads inevitably to a warped construction of specific provisions of the Bill of Rights to bring within their scope conduct clearly condemned by due process but not easily fitting into the pigeonholes of the specific provisions.

" * * * Judicial review of [the Due Process Clause] of the Fourteenth Amendment inescapably imposes upon this Court an exercise of judgment upon the whole course of the proceedings in order to ascertain whether they offend those canons of decency and fairness which express the notions of justice of English-speaking peoples even toward those charged with the most heinous offenses. These standards of justice are not authoritatively formulated anywhere as though they were prescriptions in a pharmacopoeia. But neither does the application of the Due Process Clause imply that judges are wholly at large. The judicial judgment in applying the Due Process Clause must move within the limits of accepted notions of justice and is not to be based upon the idiosyncracies of a merely personal judgment."

Notes and Questions

1. Are Frankfurter and Black, JJ., each more persuasive in demonstrating why the *other's* test is subjective, ill-defined and unilluminating than in explaining why his own is *not?*

2. *Escape from the "idiosyncrasy of a personal judgment".* If, as Frankfurter, J., insists, the *Palko-Adamson* test is not based upon "the idiosyncrasies of a merely personal judgment," *whose* moral judgments furnish the answer? And

where and *how* are they discoverable? The opinions of the progenitors and architects of our institutions? The opinions of the policy-making organs of state governments? Of state courts? The opinions of other countries? Of other countries in the Anglo-Saxon tradition? See Sanford Kadish, *Methodology and Criteria in Due Process Adjudication—A Survey and Criticism,* 66 Yale L.J. 319, 328–333 (1957). What judgments were relied on in *Palko* and *Adamson?* In *Rochin v. California,* Sec. 3 infra?

3. *History.* Historical research has produced ample support—and ample skepticism—for the "incorporation" theory. Is further historical search likely to do more than "further obscure the judicial value-choosing inherent in due process adjudication which can proceed with greater expectation of success if pursued openly and deliberately rather than under disguise"? Is due process more a moral command than a jural or historical concept? Ought it be? See Kadish, supra, at 340–41.

———

Although the Court continued to apply the *"Palko* selective process" approach to the Bill of Rights, DUNCAN v. LOUISIANA, 391 U.S. 145, 88 S.Ct. 1444, 20 L.Ed.2d 491 (1968) (holding the sixth amendment right to jury trial applicable to the states via the fourteenth amendment), no longer employed the Cardozo-Frankfurter terminology (e.g., whether a particular guarantee was "implicit in the concept of ordered liberty" or required by "the 'immutable principles of justice' as conceived by a civilized society") but instead inquired whether the procedural safeguard included in the Bill of Rights was "fundamental to the *American scheme of justice"* (emphasis added) or "fundamental *in the context of the criminal processes maintained by the American states"* (emphasis added). As WHITE, J., noted for the *Duncan* majority (fn. 14), the different phraseology is significant:

"Earlier the Court can be seen as having asked, when inquiring into whether some particular procedural safeguard was required of a State, if a civilized system could be imagined that would not accord the particular protection [quoting from *Palko*]. The recent cases, on the other hand, have proceeded upon the valid assumption that state criminal processes are not imaginary and theoretical schemes but actual systems bearing virtually every characteristic of the common-law system that has been developing contemporaneously in England and this country. The question thus is whether given this kind of system a particular procedure is fundamental—whether, that is, a procedure is necessary to an Anglo-American regime of ordered liberty. It is this sort of inquiry that can justify the conclusions that state courts must exclude evidence seized in violation of the Fourth Amendment, *Mapp v. Ohio* [p. 125 infra] [and] that state prosecutors may not comment on a defendant's failure to testify, *Griffin v. California* [fn. a supra]. [Of] each of these determinations that a constitutional provision originally written to bind the Federal Government should bind the States as well it might be said that the limitation in question is not necessarily fundamental to fairness in every criminal system that might be imagined but is fundamental in the context of the criminal processes maintained by the American States.

"When the inquiry is approached in this way the question whether the States can impose criminal punishment without granting a jury trial appears quite different from the way it appeared in the older cases opining that States might abolish jury trial. A criminal process which was fair and equitable but used no juries is easy to imagine. It would make use of alternative guarantees and protections which would serve the purposes that the jury serves in the English and American systems. Yet no American State has undertaken to construct such a system. Instead, every American State, including Louisiana, uses the jury extensively, and imposes very serious punishments only after a trial at which the defendant has a right to a jury's verdict. In every State, including Louisiana, the structure and style of the criminal process—the supporting framework and the subsidiary procedures—are of the sort that naturally complement jury trial, and have developed in connection with and in reliance upon jury trial." [f]

Because the *Duncan* Court believed that "trial by jury in criminal cases is fundamental to the American scheme of justice," it held that it was guaranteed by the fourteenth amendment: "The guarantees of jury trial in the Federal and State Constitutions reflect a profound judgment about the way in which law should be enforced and justice administered. A right to jury trial is granted to criminal defendants in order to prevent oppression by the Government. Those who wrote our constitutions knew from history and experience that it was necessary to protect against unfounded criminal charges brought to eliminate enemies and against judges too responsive to the voice of higher authority. The framers of the constitutions strove to create an independent judiciary but insisted upon further protection against arbitrary action. Providing an accused with the right to be tried by a jury of his peers gave him an inestimable safeguard against the corrupt or overzealous prosecutor and against the compliant, biased, or eccentric judge. If the defendant preferred the common-sense judgment of a jury to the more tutored but perhaps less sympathetic reaction of the single judge, he was to have it. Beyond this, the jury trial provisions in the Federal and State Constitutions reflect a fundamental decision about the exercise of official power— a reluctance to entrust plenary powers over the life and liberty of the citizen to one judge or to a group of judges. Fear of unchecked power, so typical of our State and Federal Governments in other respects, found expression in the criminal law in this insistence upon community participation in the determination of guilt or innocence. The deep commitment of the Nation to the right of jury trial in serious criminal cases as a defense against arbitrary law enforcement qualifies for protection under the Due Process Clause of the Fourteenth Amendment, and must therefore be respected by the States."

HARLAN, J., joined by Stewart, J., dissented: "Even if I could agree that the question before us is whether Sixth Amendment jury trial is totally ['incorporated into' the fourteenth amendment] or totally 'out' [see Sec. II infra], I can find in the Court's opinion no real reasons for concluding that it should be 'in.' The basis for distinguishing among clauses in the Bill of Rights cannot be that [only] some are old and much praised, or that only some have played an important role in the development of federal law. These things are true of all. The Court says that some clauses are more 'fundamental' than others, but [uses] this word in a sense that would have astonished Mr. Justice Cardozo and which, in addition, is of no help. The word does not mean 'analytically critical to procedural fairness' for no real analysis of the role of the jury in making procedures fair is even

---

f. See also Powell, J., concurring in the companion 1972 "jury unanimity" cases of *Johnson v. Louisiana* and *Apodaca v. Oregon*, discussed below: "I agree with Mr. Justice White's analysis in *Duncan* that the departure from earlier decisions was, in large measure, a product of a change in focus in the Court's approach to due process. No longer are questions regarding the constitutionality of particular criminal procedures resolved by focusing alone on the element in question and ascertaining whether a system of criminal justice might be imagined in which a fair trial could be afforded in the absence of that particular element. Rather, the focus is, as it should be, on the fundamentality of that element viewed in the context of the basic Anglo-American jurisprudential system common to the States. That approach to due process readily accounts both for the conclusion that jury trial *is* fundamental and that unanimity *is not*."

attempted. Instead, the word turns out to mean 'old,' 'much praised,' and 'found in the Bill of Rights.' The definition of 'fundamental' thus turns out to be circular.

"[Jury trial] is of course not without virtues [but its] principal original virtue—[the limitations it] imposes on a tyrannous judiciary—has largely disappeared. [The] jury system can also be said to have some inherent defects, which are multiplied by the emergence of the criminal law from the relative simplicity that existed when the jury system was devised. It is a cumbersome process, not only imposing great cost in time and money on both the State and the jurors themselves, but also contributing to delay in the machinery of justice. [That] trial by jury is not the only fair way of adjudicating criminal guilt is well attested by the fact that it is not the prevailing way, either in England or in this country.

"[The majority recognizes that not every, or any particular, criminal trial before a judge alone is unfair, or less fair than one held before a jury.] I agree. I therefore see no reason why this Court should reverse the conviction of appellant absent any suggestion that his particular trial was in fact unfair, or compel the State of Louisiana to afford jury trial in an as yet unbounded category of cases that can, without unfairness, be tried to a court.

"[In] sum, there is a wide range of views on the desirability of trial by jury, and on the ways to make it most effective when it is used; there is also considerable variation from State to State in local conditions such as the size of the criminal caseload, the ease or difficulty of summoning jurors, and other trial conditions bearing on fairness. We have before us, therefore, an almost perfect example of a situation in which [the states should serve as laboratories.] [Instead,] the Court has chosen to impose upon every State one means of trying criminal cases; it is a good means, but it is not the only fair means, and it is not demonstrably better than the alternatives States might devise."

Although the Court has remained unwilling to accept the total incorporationists' reading of the fourteenth amendment, in the 1960s it "selectively" "incorporated" or "absorbed" more and more of the specifics of the Bill of Rights into the fourteenth amendment. As White, J., observed in *Duncan*:

"In resolving conflicting claims concerning the meaning of this spacious [fourteenth amendment] language, the Court has looked increasingly to the Bill of Rights for guidance; many of the rights guaranteed by the first eight Amendments to the Constitution have been held to be protected against state action by the Due Process Clause of the Fourteenth Amendment.[g] That clause now protects [the] Fourth Amendment rights to be free from unreasonable searches and seizures and to have excluded from criminal trials any evidence illegally seized; the right guaranteed by the Fifth Amendment to be free of compelled self-incrimination; and the Sixth Amendment rights to counsel, to a speedy and public trial [*Klopfer v. North Carolina*, 386 U.S. 213, 87 S.Ct. 988, 18 L.Ed.2d 1 (1967);

g. See also Black, J., joined by Douglas, J., concurring in *Duncan*: "[I] believe as strongly as ever that the Fourteenth Amendment was intended to make the Bill of Rights applicable to the States. I have been willing to support the selective incorporation doctrine, however, as an alternative, although perhaps less historically supportable than complete incorporation attempted—[because it] keeps judges from roaming at will in their own notions of what policies outside the Bill of Rights are desirable and what are not. And, most importantly for me, the selective incorporation process has the virtue of having already worked to make most of the Bill of Rights' protections applicable to the States."

In re Oliver, 333 U.S. 257, 68 S.Ct. 499, 92 L.Ed. 682 (1948)], to confrontation of opposing witnesses [*Pointer v. Texas,* 380 U.S. 400, 85 S.Ct. 1065, 13 L.Ed.2d 923 (1965)] and to compulsory process for obtaining witnesses [*Washington v. Texas,* 388 U.S. 14, 87 S.Ct. 1920, 18 L.Ed.2d 1019 (1967)]." [h]

―――――

　　　In Pacific Mut. Life Ins. Co. v. Haslip, 499 U.S. 1, 111 S.Ct. 1032, 113 L.Ed.2d 1 (1991) the Court, per Blackmun, J., held that an award of punitive damages against an insurer, for fraud perpetuated by its agent (an award more than four times the amount of compensatory damages and far in excess of the fine that could be imposed for insurance fraud under Alabama law), did not—considering the constraints imposed by Alabama's procedures—violate the Fourteenth Amendment's Due Process Clause. The Court "concede[d] that unlimited jury discretion—or unlimited judicial discretion for that matter—in the fixing of punitive damages may invite extreme results that jar one's constitutional sensibilities," but concluded, after examining Alabama procedures, that "the award here did not lack objective criteria" and thus "did not cross the line into the area of constitutional impropriety."

　　　"The case prompted Justice Scalia, who concurred in the judgment, to make some general comments about "due process of law," " 'fundamental fairness' under the Fourteenth Amendment," the proper role of history in a due process analysis, "incorporation" within the Fourteenth Amendment of the Bill of Rights guarantees, and the difference between the denial of due process and the denial of equal protection. As for the role of history:

　　　"To say that unbroken historical usage cannot save a procedure that violates one of the explicit procedural guarantees of the Bill of Rights (applicable through the Fourteenth Amendment) is not necessarily to say that such usage cannot demonstrate the procedure's compliance with the more general guarantee of 'due process.' In principle, what is important enough to have been included within the Bill of Rights has good claim to being an element of 'fundamental fairness,' whatever history might say; and as a practical matter, the invalidation of traditional state practices achievable through the Bill of rights is at least limited to enumerated subjects. But disregard of 'the procedure of the ages' for incorporation purposes has led to its disregard more generally."

　　　Two years later, without a majority opinion, the Court upheld a 10 million dollar punitive damage award in *TXO Production Corp. v. Alliance Resources Corp.,* 509 U.S. 443, 113 S.Ct. 2711, 125 L.Ed.2d 366 (1993). But then, in *Honda Motor Co., Ltd. v. Oberg,* ＿ U.S. ＿, 114 S.Ct. 2331, 129 L.Ed.2d 336 (1994), the Court, per Stevens, J., ruled that an amendment to the Oregon Constitution, severely limiting judicial review of punitive damage awards, violated due process:

　　　"[There] is a dramatic difference between the judicial review of punitive damage awards under the common law and the scope of review available in Oregon. [A state's] abrogation of a well-established common law protection against arbitrary deprivations of property raises a presumption that its procedures violate the Due Process Clause. [Punitive] damages pose an acute danger of

h. In the area of criminal procedure, the Court has come very close to incorporating all of the relevant Bill of Rights guarantees. But still on the books, is a lonely exception. *Hurtado v. California,* 110 U.S. 516, 4 S.Ct. 111, 28 L.Ed. 232 (1884), refusing to apply to the states the fifth amendment requirement that prosecution be initiated by grand jury indictment. For an overview of the development and application of the selective incorporation doctrine see Jerold Israel, *Selective Incorporation Revisited,* 71 Geo.L.J. 253 (1982).

arbitrary deprivation of property. * * * Judicial review of the amount awarded was one of the few procedural safeguards which the common law provided against that danger. Oregon has removed that safeguard without providing any substitute procedure."

Justice Stevens' majority opinion, observe John Nowak & Ronald Rotunda, *Constitutional Law* 357 (5th ed. 1995), "did not explain the type of standards that would be used for evaluating the adequacy of judicial procedures for the review of punitive damages." Nor did it "set forth standards for determining when a punitive damage award was so excessive that it should be held to violate substantive due process even if the trial and appellate courts had provided the defendant with fair procedures."

SECTION 2. SHOULD THE "SELECTED" PROVISION APPLY TO THE STATES "JOT–FOR–JOT"? "BAG AND BAGGAGE"?

In the 1960s, the Court seemed to be "incorporating" not only the basic notion or general concept of the "selected" provision of the Bill of Rights, but applying the provision to the states *to the same extent* it applied to the federal government. Thus, Brennan, J., observed for a majority in *Malloy v. Hogan,* 378 U.S. 1, 84 S.Ct. 1489, 12 L.Ed.2d 653 (1964): "We have held that the guarantees of the First Amendment, the prohibition of unreasonable searches and seizures of the Fourth Amendment, and the right to counsel guaranteed by the Sixth Amendment, are all to be enforced against the States under the Fourteenth Amendment *according to the same standards that protect those personal rights against federal encroachment.* [The] Court thus has rejected the notion that the Fourteenth Amendment applies to the States only a 'watered-down, subjective version of the individual guarantees of the Bill of Rights.' " (Emphasis added.) And White, J., put it for a majority in *Duncan:* "Because we believe that trial by jury in criminal cases is fundamental to the American scheme of justice, we hold that the Fourteenth Amendment guarantees a right of jury trial in all criminal cases which—*were they to be tried in a federal court*—would come within the Sixth Amendment's guarantee." (Emphasis added.)[i]

The federal guarantees, protested some justices, were being incorporated into the fourteenth amendment "freighted with their entire accompanying body of federal doctrine" (Harlan, J., joined by Clark, J., dissenting in *Malloy v. Hogan*); "jot-for-jot and case-for-case (Harlan, J., joined by Stewart, J., dissenting in *Duncan*); "bag and baggage, however securely or insecurely affixed they may be by law and precedent to federal proceedings" (Fortas, J., concurring in *Duncan*).

Justice Harlan was the most persistent and powerful critic of the *Malloy–Duncan* approach to fourteenth amendment due process. "The consequence," he maintained in his *Malloy* dissent, "is inevitably disregard of all relevant differences which may exist between state and federal criminal law and its enforcement. The ultimate result is compelled uniformity, which is inconsistent with the purpose of our federal system and which is achieved either by encroachment on the State's sovereign powers or by dilution in federal law enforcement of the specific protections found in the Bill of Rights."

i. See also Justice Marshall's opinion for the Court in *Benton v. Maryland,* 395 U.S. 784, 89 S.Ct. 2056, 23 L.Ed.2d 707 (1969) (the validity of the state conviction "must be judged not by the watered-down standard enumerated in *Palko,* but *under this Court's interpretations of the Fifth Amendment double jeopardy provision* "). (Emphasis added.)

Concurring in the result in *Pointer v. Texas,* 380 U.S. 400, 85 S.Ct. 1065, 13 L.Ed.2d 923 (1965) (holding that the Sixth Amendment right of an accused to confront the witnesses against him applies in its entirety to the states via the Fourteenth), Justice Harlan observed that " 'selective' incorporation or 'absorption' amounts to little more than a diluted form of the full incorporation theory. Whereas it rejects full incorporation because of recognition that not all of the guarantees of the Bill of Rights should be deemed 'fundamental,' it at the same time ignores the possibility that not all phases of any given guaranty are necessarily fundamental."

Dissenting in *Duncan,* HARLAN, J., joined by Stewart, J., protested: "Today's Court still remains unwilling to accept the total incorporationists' view of the history of the Fourteenth Amendment. This, if accepted, would afford a cogent reason for applying the Sixth Amendment to the States. The Court is also, apparently, unwilling to face the task of determining whether denial of trial by jury in the situation before us, or in other situations, is fundamentally unfair. Consequently, the Court has compromised on the ease of the incorporationist position, without its internal logic. It has simply assumed that the question before us is whether the Jury Trial Clause of the Sixth Amendment should be incorporated into the Fourteenth, jot-for-jot and case-for-case, or ignored. Then the Court merely declares that the clause in question is 'in' rather than 'out.'

"The Court has justified neither its starting place nor its conclusion. If the problem is to discover and articulate the rules of fundamental fairness in criminal proceedings, there is no reason to assume that the whole body of rules developed in this Court constituting Sixth Amendment jury trial must be regarded as a unit. The requirement of trial by jury in federal criminal cases has given rise to numerous subsidiary questions respecting the exact scope and content of the right. It surely cannot be that every answer the Court has given, or will give, to such a question is attributable to the Founders; or even that every rule announced carries equal conviction of this Court; still less can it be that every such subprinciple is equally fundamental to ordered liberty."

———

In the 1970s matters were brought to a head by the "right to jury trial" cases: *Baldwin v. New York,* 399 U.S. 66, 90 S.Ct. 1886, 26 L.Ed.2d 437 (1970) (no offense can be deemed "petty," thus dispensing with the fourteenth and sixth amendment rights to jury trial, where more than six months incarceration is authorized); *Williams v. Florida,* 399 U.S. 78, 90 S.Ct. 1893, 26 L.Ed.2d 446 (1970) ("that jury at common law was composed of precisely 12 is an historical accident, unnecessary to effect the purposes of the jury system"; thus 6-person jury in criminal cases does not violate sixth amendment, as applied to the states via fourteenth);[a] and the 1972 *Apodaca* and *Johnson* cases, discussed below, dealing with whether unanimous jury verdicts are required in criminal cases.

Dissenting in *Baldwin* and concurring in *Williams,* HARLAN, J., maintained: "[*Williams*] evinces [a] recognition that the 'incorporationist' view of the Due Process Clause of the Fourteenth Amendment, which underlay *Duncan* and is now carried forward into *Baldwin,* must be tempered to allow the States more elbow room in ordering their own criminal systems. With that much I agree. But to

---

a. But *Ballew v. Georgia,* 435 U.S. 223, 98 S.Ct. 1029, 55 L.Ed.2d 234 (1978), subsequently held that a state trial in a non-petty criminal case to a jury of only five persons did deprive a defendant of the right to trial by jury guaranteed by the sixth and fourteenth amendments.

accomplish this by diluting constitutional protections within the federal system itself is something to which I cannot possibly subscribe. Tempering the rigor of *Duncan* should be done forthrightly, by facing up to the fact that at least in this area the 'incorporation' doctrine does not fit well with our federal structure, and by the same token that *Duncan* was wrongly decided.

"[Rather] than bind the States by the hitherto undeviating and unquestioned federal practice of 12-member juries, the Court holds, based on a poll of state practice, that a six-man jury satisfies the guarantee of a trial by jury in a federal criminal system and consequently carries over to the States. This is a constitutional *renvoi*. With all respect, I consider that before today it would have been unthinkable to suggest that the Sixth Amendment's right to a trial by jury is satisfied by a jury of six, or less, as is left open by the Court's opinion in *Williams,* or by less than a unanimous verdict, a question also reserved in today's decision.[b]

"[These decisions] demonstrate that the difference between a 'due process' approach, that considers each particular case on its own bottom to see whether the right alleged is one 'implicit in the concept of ordered liberty,' and 'selective incorporation' is not an abstract one whereby different verbal formulae achieve the same results. The internal logic of the selective incorporation doctrine cannot be respected if the Court is both committed to interpreting faithfully the meaning of the federal Bill of Rights and recognizing the governmental diversity that exists in this country. The 'backlash' in *Williams* exposes the malaise, for there the Court dilutes a federal guarantee in order to reconcile the logic of 'incorporation,' the 'jot-for-jot and case-for-case' application of the federal right to the States, with the reality of federalism. Can one doubt that had Congress tried to undermine the common law right to trial by jury before *Duncan* came on the books the history today recited would have barred such action? Can we expect repeated performances when this Court is called upon to give definition and meaning to other federal guarantees that have been 'incorporated'?

"[I]t is time [for] for this Court to face up to the reality implicit in today's holdings and reconsider the 'incorporation' doctrine before its leveling tendencies further retard development in the field of criminal procedure by stifling flexibility in the States and by discarding the possibility of federal leadership by example."

In the companion cases of *Apodaca v. Oregon,* 406 U.S. 404, 92 S.Ct. 1628, 32 L.Ed.2d 184 (1972) and *Johnson v. Louisiana,* 406 U.S. 356, 92 S.Ct. 1620, 32 L.Ed.2d 152 (1972), upholding the constitutionality of less-than-unanimous jury verdicts in state criminal cases, eight justices adhered to the *Duncan* position that each element of the sixth amendment right to jury trial applies to the states to the same extent it applies to the federal government, but split 4–4 over whether the federal guarantee *did require* jury unanimity in criminal cases. State convictions by less than unanimous votes were sustained only because the ninth member of the Court, newly appointed POWELL, J., read the sixth amendment as requiring jury unanimity, but—taking a Harlan-type approach—concluded that *this feature* of the federal right is not "so fundamental to the essentials of jury trial" as to require unanimity in state criminal cases as a matter of fourteenth amendment

---

b. Cf. Frankfurter, J., for the Court in *Rochin v. California* (1952) (discussed in Sec. 3 infra): "Words being symbols do not speak without a gloss. [T]he gloss may be the deposit of history, whereby a term gains technical content. Thus the requirements of the Sixth and Seventh Amendments for trial by jury in the federal courts have a rigid meaning. No changes or chances can alter the content of the verbal symbol of 'jury'—a body of twelve men who must reach a unanimous conclusion if the verdict is to go against the defendant."

due process: [c]

"[I]n holding that the Fourteenth Amendment has incorporated 'jot-for-jot and case-for-case' every element of the Sixth Amendment, the Court derogates principles of federalism that are basic to our system. In the name of uniform application of high standards of due process, the Court has embarked upon a course of constitutional interpretation that deprives the States of freedom to experiment with adjudicatory processes different from the federal model. At the same time, the Court's understandable unwillingness to impose requirements that it finds unnecessarily rigid (e.g., *Williams*), has culminated in the dilution of federal rights that were, until these decisions, never seriously questioned. The doubly undesirable consequence of this reasoning process, labeled by Mr. Justice Harlan as 'constitutional schizophrenia,' may well be detrimental both to the state and federal criminal justice systems." [d]

BRENNAN, J., joined by Marshall, J., dissented: "Readers of today's opinions may be understandably puzzled why convictions by 11–1 and 10–2 jury votes are affirmed [when] a majority of the Court agrees that the Sixth Amendment requires a unanimous verdict in federal criminal jury trials, and a majority also agrees that the right to jury trial guaranteed by the Sixth Amendment is to be enforced against the States according to the same standards that protect that right against federal encroachment. The reason is that while my Brother Powell agrees that a unanimous verdict is required in federal criminal trials, he does not agree that the Sixth Amendment right to a jury trial is to be applied in the same way to State and Federal Governments. In that circumstance, it is arguable that the affirmance of the convictions [is] not inconsistent with a view that today's decision is a holding that only a unanimous verdict will afford the accused in a state criminal prosecution the jury trial guaranteed him by the Sixth Amendment. In any event, the affirmance must not obscure that the majority of the Court remains of the view that, as in the case of every specific of the Bill of Rights that extends to the States, the Sixth Amendment's jury trial guarantee, however it is to be construed, has identical application against both State and Federal Governments." [e]

SECTION 3. BODILY EXTRACTIONS: ANOTHER LOOK AT THE "DUE PROCESS" AND "SELECTIVE INCORPORATION" APPROACHES

As noted earlier, Justice Harlan maintained that "the difference between a 'due process' approach [and] 'selective incorporation' is not an abstract one

c. But *Burch v. Louisiana,* 441 U.S. 130, 99 S.Ct. 1623, 60 L.Ed.2d 96 (1979), subsequently held, without a dissent on this issue, that conviction by a nonunanimous *six-person* jury in a state criminal trial for a nonpetty offense did violate the sixth and fourteenth amendment rights to trial by jury.

d. See also Powell, J., joined by Burger, C.J., and Rehnquist, J., dissenting in *Crist v. Bretz,* 437 U.S. 28, 98 S.Ct. 2156, 57 L.Ed.2d 24 (1978) (holding that federal rule as to when jeopardy "attaches" in jury trials applies to state cases). Consider, too, Burger, C.J.'s separate opinion in *Crist v. Bretz* and Rehnquist, J.'s separate opinion in *Buckley v. Valeo,* p. 918

infra, maintaining that "not all of the strictures which the First Amendment imposes upon Congress are carried over against the States by the Fourteenth Amendment, [but] only the 'general principle' of free speech."

e. In a separate dissent, Stewart, J., joined by Brennan and Marshall, JJ., protested that "unless *Duncan* is to be overruled," "the only relevant question here is whether the Sixth Amendment's guarantee of trial by jury embraces a guarantee that the verdict of the jury must be unanimous. The answer to that question is clearly 'yes,' as my Brother Powell has cogently demonstrated."

whereby different formulae achieve the same results." But he made this observation in the context of the applicability to the states of the sixth amendment right to trial by jury, which had, or was thought to have, a relatively rigid meaning. Most language in the Bill of Rights, however, is rather vague and general, at least when specific problems arise under a particular phrase. In such cases, does dwelling on the literal language simply *shift the focus of broad judicial inquiry* from "due process" to e.g., "freedom of speech," "establishment of religion," "unreasonable searches and seizures," "excessive bail," "cruel and unusual punishments," and "the assistance of counsel"? See Henry Friendly, *The Bill of Rights as a Code of Criminal Procedure,* 53 Calif.L.Rev. 929, 937 (1965); Jerold Israel, fn. h supra, at 336–38; Sanford Kadish, *Methodology and Criteria in Due Process Adjudication—A Survey and Criticism,* 66 Yale L.J. 319, 337–39 (1957); Herbert Wechsler, *Toward Neutral Principles of Constitutional Law,* 73 Harv. L.Rev. 1, 17–18 (1959). Cf. John Nowak, *Due Process Methodology in the Postincorporation World,* 70 J.Crim.L. & C. 397, 400–01 (1979) (arguing that decisions based on specific guarantees tend to rely on definitional analysis and fail to explore the interests at stake).

In considering whether the right to counsel "begins" at the time of arrest, preliminary hearing, arraignment, or not until the trial itself, or includes probation and parole revocation hearings or applies to juvenile delinquency proceedings, deportation hearings or civil commitments, or, where the defendant is indigent, includes the right to *assigned* counsel or an assigned psychiatrist at state expense, how helpful is the sixth amendment language entitling an accused to "the assistance of counsel for his defense"? Is the specificity or direction of this language significantly greater than the "due process" clause?

To turn to another cluster of problems—which form the basis for this section—in considering whether, and under what conditions, the police may direct the "pumping" of a person's stomach to uncover incriminating evidence, or the taking of a blood sample from him, without his consent, do the "specific guarantees" in the Bill of Rights against "unreasonable searches and seizures" and against compelling a person to be "a witness against himself" free the Court from the demands of appraising and judging involved in answering these questions by interpreting the "due process" clause?

ROCHIN v. CALIFORNIA, 342 U.S. 165, 72 S.Ct. 205, 96 L.Ed. 183 (1952) arose as follows: Having "some information" that Rochin was selling narcotics, three deputy sheriffs "forced upon the door of [his] room and found him sitting partly dressed on the side of the bed, upon which his wife was lying. On a 'night stand' beside the bed the deputies spied two capsules. When asked 'Whose stuff is this?' Rochin seized the capsules and put them in his mouth. A struggle ensued, in the course of which the three officers 'jumped upon him' and [unsuccessfully] attempted to extract the capsules. [Rochin] was handcuffed and taken to a hospital. At the direction of one of the officers a doctor forced an emetic solution through a tube into Rochin's stomach against his will. This 'stomach pumping' produced vomiting. In the vomited matter were found two capsules which proved to contain morphine. [Rochin was convicted of possessing morphine] and sentenced to sixty days' imprisonment. The chief evidence against him was the two capsules."

The Court, per FRANKFURTER, J., concluded that the officers' conduct violated fourteenth amendment due process: "This is conduct that shocks the conscience. Illegally breaking into the privacy of the petitioner, the struggle to open his mouth and remove what was there, the forcible extraction of his stomach's contents—this course of proceeding by agents of government to obtain evidence is bound to offend even hardened sensibilities. They are methods too close to the rack and the screw to permit of constitutional differentiation.

* * * "Due process of law, as a historic and generative principle, precludes defining, and thereby confining, [civilized] standards of conduct more precisely than to say that convictions cannot be brought about by methods that offend 'a sense of justice.' It would be a stultification of the responsibility which the course of constitutional history has cast upon this Court to hold that in order to convict a man the police cannot extract by force what is in his mind but can extract what is in his stomach.

"[E]ven though statements contained in them may be independently established as true[,] [c]oerced confessions offend the community's sense of fair play and decency. So here, to sanction the brutal conduct which naturally enough was condemned by the court whose judgment is before us, would be to afford brutality the cloak of law. Nothing would be more calculated to discredit law and thereby to brutalize the temper of a society."

Concurring, BLACK, J., reasoned that the fifth amendment's protection against compelled self-incrimination applied to the states and that "a person is compelled to be a witness against himself not only when he is compelled to testify, but also when as here, incriminating evidence is forcibly taken from him by a contrivance of modern science." He maintained that "faithful adherence to the specific guarantees in the Bill of Rights insures a more permanent protection of individual liberty than that which can be afforded by the nebulous [fourteenth amendment due process] standards stated by the majority."

DOUGLAS, J., concurring, also criticized the majority's approach. He contended that the privilege against self-incrimination applied to the states as well as the federal government and because of the privilege "words taken from [an accused's] lips, capsules taken from his stomach, blood taken from his veins are all inadmissible provided they are taken from him without his consent. [This] is an unequivocal, definite and workable rule of evidence for state and federal courts. But we cannot in fairness free the state courts from the [restraints of the fifth amendment privilege against self-incrimination] and yet excoriate them for flouting the 'decencies of civilized conduct' when they admit the evidence. This is to make the rule turn not on the Constitution but on the idiosyncracies of the judges who sit here." [a]

---

a. *Irvine v. California,* 347 U.S. 128, 74 S.Ct. 381, 98 L.Ed. 561 (1954), limited *Rochin* to situations involving coercion, violence or brutality to the person. In *Irvine* the police made repeated illegal entries into petitioner's home, first to install a secret microphone and then to move it to the bedroom, in order to listen to the conversations of the occupants— for over a month. Jackson, J., who announced the judgment of the Court and wrote the principal opinion, recognized that "few police measures have come to our attention that more flagrantly, deliberately, and persistently violated the fundamental principle declared by the Fourth Amendment as a restriction on the Federal Government," but adhered to the holding in *Wolf v. Colorado* (1949) (Part IV infra)

that the exclusionary rule in federal search and seizure cases is not binding on the states. (*Wolf* was overruled in *Mapp v. Ohio* (1961) (Part IV infra)). Nor did Jackson, J., deem *Rochin* applicable: "However obnoxious are the facts in the case before us, they do not involve coercion, violence or brutality to the person [as did *Rochin*], but rather a trespass to property, plus eavesdropping."

Because of the "aggravating" and "repulsive" police misconduct in *Irvine,* Frankfurter, J., joined by Burton, J., dissenting, maintained that *Rochin* was controlling, not *Wolf.* (He had written the majority opinions in both cases.) Black, J., joined by Douglas, J., dissented separately, arguing that petitioner had

Breithaupt v. Abram, 352 U.S. 432, 77 S.Ct. 408, 1 L.Ed.2d 448 (1957), illustrated that under the *Rochin* test state police had considerable leeway even when the body of the accused was "invaded." In *Breithaupt,* the police took a blood sample from an unconscious person who had been involved in a fatal automobile collision. A majority, per Clark, J., affirmed a manslaughter conviction based on the blood sample (which showed intoxication), stressing that the sample was "taken under the protective eye of a physician" and that "the blood test procedure has become routine in our everyday life." The "interests of society in the scientific determination of intoxication, one of the great causes of the mortal hazards of the road," outweighed "so slight an intrusion" of a person's body.

Dissenting, Warren, C.J., joined by Black and Douglas, JJ., deemed *Rochin* controlling and argued that police efforts to curb the narcotics traffic, involved in *Rochin,* "is surely a state interest of at least as great magnitude as the interest in highway law enforcement. [Only] personal reaction to the stomach pump and the blood test can distinguish the [two cases]."

Douglas, J., joined by Black, J., dissented, maintaining that "if the decencies of a civilized state are the test, it is repulsive to me for the police to insert needles into an unconscious person in order to get the evidence necessary to convict him, whether they find the person unconscious, give him a pill which puts him to sleep, or use force to subdue him."

Nine years later, even though in the meantime the Court had held in *Mapp v. Ohio,* Part IV infra, that the federal exclusionary rule in search and seizure cases was binding on the states and in *Malloy v. Hogan,* supra, that the fifth amendment's protection against compelled self-incrimination was likewise applicable to the states, the Court still upheld the taking by a physician, at police direction, of a blood sample from an injured person, over his objection. SCHMERBER v. CALIFORNIA, 384 U.S. 757, 86 S.Ct. 1826, 16 L.Ed.2d 908 (1966). In affirming the conviction for operating a vehicle while under the influence of intoxicating liquor, a 5–4 majority, per BRENNAN, J., ruled: (1) that the extraction of blood from petitioner under the aforementioned circumstances "did not offend 'that "sense of justice" ' of which we spoke in *Rochin,*" thus reaffirming *Breithaupt;* (2) that the privilege against self-incrimination, now binding on the states, "protects an accused only from being compelled to testify against himself, or otherwise provide the State with evidence of a testimonial or communicative nature and that the withdrawal of blood and use of the analysis in question did not involve compulsion to these ends"; and (3) that the protection against unreasonable search and seizure, now binding on the states, was satisfied because (a) "there was plainly probable cause" to arrest and charge petitioner and to suggest "the required relevance and likely success of a test of petitioner's blood for alcohol"; (b) the officer "might reasonably have believed that he was confronted with an emergency, in which the delay necessary to obtain a warrant, under the circumstances, threatened 'the destruction of evidence' "; and (c) "the test chosen to measure petitioner's blood-alcohol level was [reasonable and] performed in a reasonable manner."

Dissenting, Black, J., joined by Douglas, J., expressed amazement at the majority's "conclusion that compelling a person to give his blood to help the State

been convicted on the basis of evidence "extorted" from him in violation of the self-incrimination clause, which he considered applicable to the states. Douglas, J., dissenting separately, protested against the use in state prosecutions of evidence seized in violation of the fourth amendment.

to convict him is not equivalent to compelling him to be a witness against himself." "It is a strange hierarchy of values that allows the State to extract a human being's blood to convict him of a crime because of the blood's content but proscribes compelled production of his lifeless papers." [a]

Notes and Questions

1. In light of *Rochin, Breithaupt* and *Schmerber,* when courts decide constitutional questions by "looking to" the Bill of Rights, to what extent do they proceed, as Black, J., said in *Adamson,* "within clearly marked constitutional boundaries"? To what extent does resort to these "particular standards" enable courts to avoid substituting their "own concepts of decency and fundamental justice" for the language of the Constitution?

2. Did *Mapp* and *Malloy,* decided in the interim between *Breithaupt* and *Schmerber,* affect any justice's vote? Did the applicability of the "particular standards" of the fourth and fifth amendments inhibit Black, Douglas or Brennan, JJ., from employing their own concepts of "decency" and "justice" in *Schmerber?* After *Schmerber,* how much force is there in Black, J.'s view, concurring in *Rochin,* that "faithful adherence to the specific guarantees in the Bill of Rights assures a more permanent protection of individual liberty than that which can be afforded by the nebulous standards stated by the majority"?

3. For other recent illustrations of standards and methodology in due process adjudication, see the "death penalty" cases (although nominally "cruel and unusual punishment" cases), Ch. 7 infra. See also the "right of privacy" cases, Ch. 5 infra.

SECTION 4. THE RETROACTIVE EFFECT OF A HOLDING OF UNCONSTITUTIONALITY

In recent years, the Court has considered the retroactive effect of a holding that a law or practice is unconstitutional primarily in the context of criminal procedure decisions.[a] Rejecting what it called the Blackstonian Theory that a new ruling merely sets forth the law as it always existed, *Linkletter v. Walker,* 381 U.S. 618, 5 Ohio Misc. 49, 85 S.Ct. 1731, 14 L.Ed.2d 601 (1965), took the position that "the Constitution neither prohibits nor requires retrospective effect," [b] and that a

---

a. Warren, C.J., and Douglas, J., dissented in separate opinions, each adhering to his dissenting views in *Breithaupt.* In a third dissent, Fortas, J., maintained that "petitioner's privilege against self-incrimination applies" and, moreover, "under the Due Process Clause, the State, in its role as prosecutor, has no right to extract blood from [anyone] over his protest."

a. In none of these cases, apparently, did the Court seriously consider applying the new constitutional ruling "purely prospectively," i.e., not even giving the litigant in the very case the benefit of the decision. "Pure prospectivity" raises "difficult problems concerning the nature of a court's functions; persuasive arguments can be made that courts are badly suited for the general determination and proclamation of future rules and, indeed, that for them to do so violates the Constitution's grant to the judiciary only of power over 'cases' and

'controversies.'" 80 Harv.L.Rev. 140 (1966). Another frequently made point, although it may carry less weight in the criminal procedure area, is that "if the Supreme Court begins regularly to announce new rules prospectively only, petitioners, knowing they will be unlikely to benefit personally, will be deterred from pressing for the new rules." Id.

b. "If an unconstitutional statute or practice effectively never existed as a lawful justification for state action [perhaps the dominant view in the era between the Civil War and the Depression], individuals convicted under the statute or in trials which tolerated the practice were convicted unlawfully even if their trials took place before the declaration of unconstitutionality; such a declaration should have a fully retroactive effect, and previously convicted individuals should be able to win their freedom through the writ of habeas corpus. Alternatively, if a judgment of unconstitutionality

determination of the effect of a judgment of unconstitutionality should turn on "the prior history of the rule in question, its purpose and effect," "whether retrospective operation of the rule will further or retard its operation" and what adverse impact on the administration of justice retroactivity would be likely to have.

The prime purpose of *Mapp v. Ohio,* 367 U.S. 643, 81 S.Ct. 1684, 6 L.Ed.2d 1081 (1961) (imposing the exclusionary rule on the states), emphasized the *Linkletter* Court, was to deter future police misconduct and this purpose would not be advanced by applying the rule to cases which had become "final" (i.e., direct appellate review had been exhausted) prior to the overturning of *Mapp.* The Court recognized that it had given full retroactive effect to some recent law-changing decisions—such as *Gideon v. Wainwright,* 372 U.S. 335, 83 S.Ct. 792, 9 L.Ed.2d 799 (1963) (establishing an absolute right to appointed counsel at least in all serious criminal cases) and the coerced confession cases—but, unlike *Mapp,* the principles in those cases "went to the fairness of the trial—the very integrity of the fact-finding process. [Here] the fairness of the trial is not under attack."

Relying upon the *Linkletter* analysis, STOVALL v. DENNO, 388 U.S. 293, 87 S.Ct. 1967, 18 L.Ed.2d 1199 (1967), set forth a framework for determining whether a new ruling should be given retroactive effect. The "criteria guiding the resolution of the question," observed the *Stovall* Court, "implicate (a) the purpose to be served by the new standards, (b) the extent of the reliance by law enforcement authorities on the old standards, [and] (c) the effect on the administration of justice of a retroactive application of the new standards."

Prior to *Linkletter, Mapp* had already been applied to cases still pending on direct appeal, so the only issue considered by *Linkletter* was whether *Mapp* should be applied to a collateral attack upon a conviction. In applying the *Linkletter* standard, however, *Stovall* and subsequent cases did not draw a distinction between final convictions attacked collaterally and those challenged at various stages of direct review.

Moreover, in limiting the retroactive effect of new rulings, cases applying the *Linkletter–Stovall* standard selected different "starting points." Because *Miranda v. Arizona,* 384 U.S. 436, 10 Ohio Misc. 9, 86 S.Ct. 1602, 16 L.Ed.2d 694 (1966), was viewed as not primarily designed to protect the innocent from wrongful conviction, *Johnson v. New Jersey,* 384 U.S. 719, 8 Ohio Misc. 324, 86 S.Ct. 1772, 16 L.Ed.2d 882 (1966) held that the new rule in *Miranda* affected only cases in which *the trial began* after the date of that landmark decision. Because the use of improper lineups could be challenged on due process grounds even if the new ruling on lineups were not applied retroactively, *Stovall,* supra, declined to give retroactive effect to *United States v. Wade,* 388 U.S. 218, 87 S.Ct. 1926, 18 L.Ed.2d 1149 (1967), the case that established a right to counsel at certain pretrial lineups. But this time the Court selected a different "starting point": the new lineup ruling affected only those pretrial identification procedures *conducted* in the absence of counsel *after the date* of the decisions.[c]

affects only the case at hand [a view which also had support], the legality of the convictions of individuals previously tried is not affected. In *Linkletter,* the Court rejected both extremes." Laurence Tribe, *American Constitutional Law* 29–30 (2d ed. 1988).

c. Although "at first glance the prospectivity rule appears to be an act of judicial self-abnegation," "in reality," observes Francis Al-

len, *The Judicial Quest for Penal Justice: The Warren Court and the Criminal Cases,* 1975 U.Ill.L.F. 518, 530, such a rule "encourages the making of new law by reducing some of the social costs." See also James Haddad, *Retroactivity Should Be Rethought: A Call for the End of the Linkletter Doctrine:* 60 J.Crim.L.C. & P.S. 417, 439 (1969): "The alternative to the prospective-only technique is a more conserva-

Selection of the date of the challenged *police conduct* as the starting point indicated that *police reliance* on the overturned rule was a major factor in retroactivity disputes. In this respect, DESIST v. UNITED STATES, 394 U.S. 244, 89 S.Ct. 1030, 22 L.Ed.2d 248 (1969) is hardly surprising. *Desist* held that *Katz v. United States,* 389 U.S. 347, 88 S.Ct. 507, 19 L.Ed.2d 576 (1967) (overruling *Olmstead v. United States,* 277 U.S. 438, 48 S.Ct. 564, 72 L.Ed. 944 (1928) and holding that wiretapping and other forms of electronic surveillance are subject to Fourth Amendment restraints) should be given what the Court called "wholly prospective application," i.e., applied only to *police activity* occurring *after* the date of the *Katz* decision.[d]

The *Desist* Court saw no significant distinction for retroactive purpose between direct review and collateral attack. All of the reasons for making *Katz* prospective only "also undercut any distinction between final convictions and those still pending on direct review. Both the deterrent purpose of the exclusionary rule and the reliance of law enforcement officers focus upon *the time of the search,* not any subsequent point in the prosecution as the relevant date." (Emphasis added.)

JUSTICE HARLAN wrote a powerful dissent. Two decades later, this dissent seems a good deal more significant than the opinion of the Court in that case. "[A]ll 'new rules' of constitutional law," maintained Harlan, "must, at a minimum, be applied to all those cases which are still subject to direct review by this Court at the time the 'new' decision is handed down." He continued:

"[We release a prisoner] only because the Government has offended constitutional principle in the conduct of his case. And when another similarly situated defendant comes before us, we must grant the same relief or give a principled reason for acting differently. We depart from this basic judicial tradition when we simply pick and choose from among similarly situated defendants those who alone will receive the benefit of a 'new' rule of constitutional law.

"[If] a 'new' constitutional doctrine is truly right, we should not reverse lower courts which have accepted it; nor should we affirm those which have rejected the very arguments we have embraced. Anything else would belie the truism that it is the task of this Court, like that of any other, to do justice to each litigant on the merits of his own case. It is only if each of our decisions can be justified in terms of this fundamental premise that they may properly be considered the legitimate products of a court of law, rather than the commands of a super-legislature."

RETHINKING RETROACTIVITY: HARLAN'S VIEWS COME TO THE FORE

Relying heavily on Justice Harlan's reasoning in *Desist,* a 5–4 majority found the distinction between final convictions and those still pending on direct review persuasive for retroactivity purposes and applied it in SHEA v. LOUISIANA, 470 U.S. 51, 105 S.Ct. 1065, 84 L.Ed.2d 38 (1985). The case arose as follows: When read his *Miranda* rights, Shea asserted his right to counsel. The questioning session was terminated, but the next day, before Shea had communicated with a

tive approach to constitutional criminal procedure. [Detailed requirements] such as those laid down in *Miranda* would no longer be possible."

d. The Court recognized that "[o]f course, Katz himself benefited from the new principle announced [on the date of the *Katz* decision], and [to] that extent the decision has not technically been given wholly prospective application. But [this] is an 'unavoidable consequence of the necessity that constitutional adjudications not stand as mere diction.'"

lawyer, the police again read him his rights. This time he agreed to talk and confessed. The confession was admitted into evidence and Shea was convicted. While his appeal was pending, the Court handed down *Edwards v. Arizona*, 451 U.S. 477, 101 S.Ct. 1880, 68 L.Ed.2d 378 (1981), holding that a custodial suspect's rights are violated when the government uses a confession obtained by police-instigated interrogation—without counsel present—after the suspect has requested a lawyer. The Court, per BLACKMUN, J., held that Shea was entitled to the benefit of the *Edwards* ruling:

"[It is argued] that drawing a distinction between a case pending on direct review and a case on collateral attack produces inequities and injustices that are not any different from those [we purport] to cure. The argument is that the litigant whose *Edwards* claim will not be considered because it is presented on direct-review will be just as unfairly treated as the direct-review litigant whose claim would be bypassed were *Edwards* not the law. The distinction, however, properly rests on considerations of finality in the judicial process. The one litigant already has taken his case through the primary system. The other has not. For the latter, the curtain of finality has not been drawn. Somewhere, the closing must come.

"[It is also argued] that in every case, *Edwards* alone excepted, reliance on existing law justifies the nonapplication of *Edwards*. [But] there is no difference between the petitioner in *Edwards* and the petitioner in the present case. If the *Edwards* principle is not to be applied retroactively, the only way to dispense equal justice to Edwards and to Shea would be a rule that confined the *Edwards* principle to prospective application unavailable even to Edwards himself."

Dissenting JUSTICE WHITE, joined by the Chief Justice and Rehnquist and O'Connor, JJ., maintained that "the attempt to distinguish between direct and collateral challenges for purposes of retroactivity is misguided":

"Under the majority's rule, otherwise identically situated defendants may be subject to different constitutional rules, depending on just how long ago now-unconstitutional conduct occurred and how quickly cases proceed through the criminal justice system. The disparity is no different in kind from that which occurs when the benefit of a new constitutional rule is retroactively afforded to the defendant in whose case it is announced but to no others; the Court's new approach equalizes nothing except the numbers of defendants within the disparately treated classes.

"The majority recognizes that the distinction between direct review and habeas is problematic, but justifies its differential treatment by appealing to the need to draw 'the curtain of finality' on those who were unfortunate enough to have exhausted their last direct appeal at the time *Edwards* was decided. Yet the majority offers no reasons for its conclusion that finality should be the decisive factor. When a conviction is overturned on direct appeal on the basis of an *Edwards* violation, the remedy offered the defendant is a new trial at which any inculpatory statements obtained in violation of *Edwards* will be excluded. It is not clear to me why the majority finds such a burdensome remedy more acceptable when it is imposed on the state on direct review than when it is the result of a collateral attack."

Notes and Questions

1. *Rejection of the "clear break" exception.* Answering a question left open in the *Shea* case, *Griffith v. Kentucky*, 479 U.S. 314, 107 S.Ct. 708, 93 L.Ed.2d 649 (1987), applied *Batson v. Kentucky* (p. 1184 infra) to all convictions not final at the

time of the ruling even though *Batson,* which held that a defendant may establish a prima facie case of racial discrimination in the selection of a petit jury on the basis of the prosecution's use of peremptory challenges, was "an explicit and substantial break with prior precedent." "The fact that the new rule may constitute a clear break with the past," observed a 6–3 majority, "has no bearing on the 'actual inequity that results' when only one of many similarly situated defendants receives the benefit of the new rule."

2. *Adoption of the other part of Harlan's approach to retroactivity. What constitutes a "new rule"?* There were two parts to Justice Harlan's approach to retroactivity. He believed that new rulings should always be applied retroactively to cases on *direct* review (a view adopted in *Shea*), but that generally new rulings should not be applied retroactively to cases on *collateral* review. In *Teague v. Lane,* 489 U.S. 288, 109 S.Ct. 1060, 103 L.Ed.2d 334 (1989), seven justices adopted Harlan's basic position with respect to retroactivity on collateral attack. However, there was no clear majority as to what the exceptions to this general approach should be.

A four-justice plurality, per O'Connor, J. (joined by Rehnquist, C.J., and Scalia and Kennedy, JJ.), identified two exceptions: A new ruling should be applied retroactively to cases on collateral review only (1) if it "places 'certain kinds of primary, private individual conduct beyond the power of the criminal lawmaking authority to proscribe' " or (2) if it mandates "new procedures without which the likelihood of an accurate conviction is seriously diminished." As to what constitutes a "new rule," Justice O'Connor noted for four justices that generally "a case announces a new rule when it breaks new ground or imposes a new obligation" on government or "if the result was not *dictated* by precedent existing at the time the defendant's conviction became final."

3. *Questions about Teague.* Is *Teague's* definition of the claims that will be deemed to rest on new law—and thus be barred from relitigation on habeas unless they fall within a narrow exception—far too expansive? By disabling federal habeas corpus from granting relief whenever reasonable disagreement is possible about the scope or application of an existing rule, does *Teague* "reduce the incentives for state courts, and state law enforcement officials, to take account of the evolving direction of the law?" Should a "new rule" be defined more narrowly, "to exclude rules and decisions that are clearly foreshadowed, not just those that are 'dictated by precedents' "? See Richard Fallon & Daniel Meltzer, *New Law, Non–Retroactivity, and Constitutional Remedies,* 104 Harv.L.Rev. 1731, 1816–17 (1991).

Chapter 4
CONSTITUTIONAL–CRIMINAL
PROCEDURE

Introduction

A general book on constitutional law must necessarily give limited attention to many recent striking developments in this field, worthy of—and increasingly being treated in—casebooks devoted to this subject alone.[a] The materials in this chapter, however, are valuable for a general course in constitutional law not only because the subject matter is so significant but because the Supreme Court's treatment of the problems in this area provides important insights about the Court as an institution.

To what extent do the materials on right to counsel and confessions support the observation, Herbert Packer, *The Courts, the Police and the Rest of Us*, 57 J. Crim.L.C. & P.S. 238, 239 (1966), that "typically the Court's intervention in any given phase of the criminal process has started with a highly particularistic decision dealing on a narrow basis with the facts of a particularly flagrant or shocking case" and then moved toward "increasingly generalized statement, sparked by the Court's despair over the prospect of significantly affecting police practices through its more traditional activity"?

To what extent was the Burger Court's attack on the search and seizure exclusionary rule in the 1970s and 80s and the same Court's apparent retreat from the original lineup cases in the 1970s a product of the dramatic change in Court personnel? Consider J. Harvie Wilkinson, *Serving Justice* 146 (1974): "Criminal rights is probably the area of the Supreme Court's work that is most prone to emotional reaction, either one of sympathy for a disadvantaged suspect or of outrage at the perpetrator of a violent crime. As such it may also be the part of the Court's work most susceptible to swings of the pendulum after a change of personnel."

To what extent would the Court's "revolution in criminal procedure" have ended anyway-or a counter-revolution set in anyway-without any change in personnel, because of the reaction in the late 1960s against assassinations, civil disorders and alarming crime statistics? Consider, in this connection, the Warren Court's decision, and the tone of its opinion, in the famous "stop-and-frisk" case, *Terry v. Ohio*.

---

a. See, e.g., Ronald Allen, Richard Kuhns & William Stuntz, *Constitutional Criminal Procedure* (3d ed. 1995); Yale Kamisar, Wayne LaFave & Jerold Israel, *Modern Criminal Pro-* *cedure* (8th ed. 1994); Stephen Saltzburg & Daniel Capra, *American Criminal Procedure* (5th ed. 1996).

How much truth is there in the observation, Fred Graham, *The Self-inflicted Wound* 4 (1970): "History has played cruel jokes before, but few can compare with the coincidence in timing between the rise in crime, violence and racial tension in the United States and the Supreme Court's campaign to strengthen the rights of criminal suspects against the state. [T]he Court's reform effort could have come at almost any time in the recent past [and] taken root before crime became the problem that it has become." Does Graham's observation miss a larger truth? Has there *never* been a time when the Warren Court's landmark decisions in criminal procedure could have "taken root before crime became [a major] problem" because—judging from the mass media and the claims of law enforcement spokesmen-we have always been in a "crime crisis"? See Yale Kamisar, *On the Tactics of Police–Prosecution Oriented Critics of the Courts*, 49 Corn.L.Q. 436 (1964). See also Kamisar, *When the Cops Were Not "Handcuffed,"* N.Y. Times (Mag.), Nov. 7, 1965, reprinted in Crime and Criminal Justice 46 (Cressey ed. 1971).

Does Miranda (p. 223, infra) and its aftermath underscore the severe limitations upon what the Supreme Court can accomplish in the "police practices" phases of criminal procedure? How significant is it that the Court lacks supervisory power over police practices? That, because it can only hear a handful of cases a year involving police treatment of criminal suspects, the Court is uniquely unable to take a comprehensive view of the subject? That virtually the only law relating to police practices on suspects' rights has been the law that the Court itself has made by judicial decisions? That when and if the Court announces some constitutional right of a suspect, that "right" filters down to the level of flesh and blood suspects "only through the refracting layers of lower courts, trial judges, magistrates and police officials"? That "the entire system of criminal justice below the level of the Supreme Court [is] solidly massed against the criminal suspect"? Can we continue to rely on the Supreme Court to provide adequate definition and protection of the rights of suspects? Or, as was said shortly after the Warren Court era came to an end, is that job "beyond the power of the Court in the best of times, and present times are not the best"? See generally Anthony Amsterdam, *The Supreme Court and the Rights of Suspects in Criminal Cases*, 45 N.Y.U.L.Rev. 785–94, 810–14 (1970). See also Yale Kamisar, *The Warren Court and Criminal Justice: A Quarter- Century Retrospective*, 31 Tulsa L.J. 1 (1995).

SECTION 1.   ARREST, SEARCH AND SEIZURE

I.   THE EXCLUSIONARY RULE

Introduction

Although *Wolf v. Colorado* marked the first time the Supreme Court addressed the question whether the Fourth Amendment exclusionary rule should be imposed on state courts via Fourteenth Amendment Due Process, the federal courts had regularly excluded evidence obtained in violation of the Fourth Amendment's protection against unreasonable searches and seizures since 1914 when the Court promulgated that rule in *Weeks v. United States* (discussed at p. 189, infra). The "federal" exclusionary rule rested not on the empirical proposition that exclusion of the illegally obtained evidence actually deterred illegal arrests and searches, but on what might be called a "principled basis": to avoid "sanctioning" or "ratifying" the police lawlessness that produced the proffered evidence, to keep the judicial process from being contaminated by partnership in police misconduct and, ultimately, to remind the police and assure the public that the Court took constitutional rights seriously.

A dozen years after *Wolf* was handed down, it was overruled in *Mapp v. Ohio*, which many commentators view as the case that launched the Warren Court's "revolution in American criminal procedure." Although, in an effort to maximize approval for its overruling of *Wolf*, the *Mapp* Court advanced as many reasons for the exclusionary rule as it could think of, the dominant theme seems to be that the rule rests on a principled basis rather than an empirical preposition.

But in the post-Warren Court Era, ways of thinking about the exclusionary rule changed. The "deterrence" rationale, and its concomitant "interest balancing," bloomed. Thus, whether the exclusionary rule should be applied was said to present a question "not of rights but of remedies"—a question to be answered by weighing the "likely 'costs' of the rule against its 'likely benefits.'" *United States v. Calandra*, 414 U.S. 338, 94 S.Ct. 613, 38 L.Ed.2d 561 (1974). By "deconstitutionalizing" the rule—by shifting the nature of the debate from arguments about constitutional law and judicial integrity to arguments about "deterrence" and empirical data—the critics of the exclusionary rule won some important victories. See *Calandra*, supra (holding that a grand jury witness may not refuse to answer questions on ground that they are based on fruits of an unlawful search); *Stone v. Powell*, 428 U.S. 465, 96 S.Ct. 3037, 49 L.Ed.2d 1067 (1976) (greatly limiting a state prisoner's ability to obtain federal habeas corpus relief on search-and-seizure grounds); *United States v. Janis*, 428 U.S. 433, 96 S.Ct. 3021, 49 L.Ed.2d 1046 (1976) (explaining that the rule's deterrent purpose would not be furthered by barring evidence obtained illegally by state police from federal civil tax proceedings).

The deterrence rationale and its concomitant "cost benefit" or "balancing approach" to the exclusionary rule reached a high point in *United States v. Leon*, the last case set forth in this chapter. *Leon* adopted a so-called "good faith" (actually a "reasonable mistake") exception to the exclusionary rule. Although the Court gave the impression that *Leon* was little more than a routine application of the "cost-benefit" approach utilized in some of the earlier Burger Court cases, the case is more significant than that. The earlier Burger Court decisions seemed to be based on the assumption that the exclusionary rule, fully applicable in its central setting (a prosecution against the direct victim of a Fourth Amendment violation) need not also be applied in certain *collateral* or *peripheral* contexts (such as grand jury proceedings) because no significant *additional* increment of deterrence would be achieved. Leon, however, dashed hopes that at least in its central application the exclusionary rule would be spared the ordeal of being subjected to "cost-benefit" analysis—of having to "pay its way."

WOLF v. COLORADO

338 U.S. 25, 69 S.Ct. 1359, 93 L.Ed. 1782 (1949).

JUSTICE FRANKFURTER delivered the opinion of the Court.

The precise question for consideration is this: Does a conviction by a State court for a State offense deny the "due process of law" required by the Fourteenth Amendment, solely because evidence that was admitted at the trial was obtained under circumstances which would have rendered it inadmissible in a prosecution for violation of a federal law in a court of the United States because there deemed to be an infraction of the Fourth Amendment? * * *

The security of one's privacy against arbitrary intrusion by the police—which is at the core of the Fourth Amendment—is basic to a free society. It is therefore implicit in "the concept of ordered liberty" and as such enforceable against the States through the Due Process Clause. * * *

Accordingly, we have no hesitation in saying that were a State affirmatively to sanction such police incursion into privacy it would run counter to the guaranty of the Fourteenth Amendment. But the ways of enforcing such a basic right raise questions of a different order. How such arbitrary conduct should be checked, what remedies against it should be afforded, the means by which the right should be made effective, are all questions that are not to be so dogmatically answered as to preclude the varying solutions which spring from an allowable range of judgment on issues not susceptible of quantitative solution.

In *Weeks v. United States,* 232 U.S. 383, 34 S.Ct.341, 58 L.Ed. 652 (1914), this Court held that in a federal prosecution the Fourth Amendment barred the use of evidence secured through an illegal search and seizure. This ruling * * * was not derived from the explicit requirements of the Fourth Amendment; it was not based on legislation expressing Congressional policy in the enforcement of the Constitution. The decision was a matter of judicial implication. Since then it has been frequently applied and we stoutly adhere to it. But the immediate question is whether the basic right to protection against arbitrary intrusion by the police demands the exclusion of logically relevant evidence obtained by an unreasonable search and seizure because, in a federal prosecution for a federal crime, it would be excluded. As a matter of inherent reason, one would suppose this to be an issue as to which men with complete devotion to the protection of the right of privacy might give different answers. When we find that in fact most of the English-speaking world does not regard as vital to such protection the exclusion of evidence thus obtained, we must hesitate to treat this remedy as an essential ingredient of the right. The contrariety of views of the States is particularly impressive in view of the careful reconsideration which they have given the problem in the light of the *Weeks* decision.

[As] of today 30 States reject the *Weeks* doctrine, 17 States are in agreement with it. [Of] 10 jurisdictions within the United Kingdom and the British Commonwealth of Nations which have passed on the question, none has held evidence obtained by illegal search and seizure inadmissible. * * *

The jurisdictions which have rejected the *Weeks* doctrine have not left the right to privacy without other means of protection. Indeed, the exclusion of evidence is a remedy which directly serves only to protect those upon whose person or premises something incriminating has been found. We cannot, therefore, regard it as a departure from basic standards to remand such persons, together with those who emerge scatheless from a search, to the remedies of private action and such protection as the internal discipline of the police, under the eyes of an alert public opinion, may afford. Granting that in practice the exclusion of evidence may be an effective way of deterring unreasonable searches, it is not for this Court to condemn as falling below the minimal standards assured by the Due Process Clause a State's reliance upon other methods which, if consistently enforced, would be equally effective. * * * There are, moreover, reasons for excluding evidence unreasonably obtained by the federal police which are less compelling in the case of police under State or local authority. The public opinion of a community can far more effectively be exerted against oppressive conduct on the part of police directly responsible to the community itself than can local opinion, sporadically aroused, be brought to bear upon remote authority pervasively exerted throughout the country.

We hold, therefore, that in a prosecution in a State court for a State crime the Fourteenth Amendment does not forbid the admission of evidence obtained by an unreasonable search and seizure.   * * *

JUSTICE BLACK, concurring.

* * * I agree with what appears to be a plain implication of the Court's opinion that the federal exclusionary rule is not a command of the Fourth Amendment but is a judicially created rule of evidence which Congress might negate. * * *

JUSTICE MURPHY, with whom JUSTICE RUTLEDGE joins, dissenting.

[T]here is but one alternative to the rule of exclusion. That is no sanction at all.

* * * Little need be said concerning the possibilities of criminal prosecution. Self-scrutiny is a lofty ideal, but its exaltation reaches new heights if we expect a District Attorney to prosecute himself or his associates for well-meaning violations of the search and seizure clause during a raid the District Attorney or his associates have ordered. But there is an appealing ring in another alternative. A trespass action for damages is a venerable means of securing reparation for unauthorized invasion of the home. Why not put the old writ to a new use? When the Court cites cases permitting the action, the remedy seems complete.

But what an illusory remedy this is, if by "remedy" we mean a positive deterrent to police and prosecutors tempted to violate the Fourth Amendment. The appealing ring softens when we recall that in a trespass action the measure of damages is simply the extent of the injury to physical property. If the officer searches with care, he can avoid all but nominal damages—a penny, or a dollar. Are punitive damages possible? Perhaps. But a few states permit none, whatever the circumstances. In those that do, the plaintiff must show the real ill will or malice of the defendant, and surely it is not unreasonable to assume that one in honest pursuit of crime bears no malice toward the search victim. If that burden is carried, recovery may yet be defeated by the rule that there must be physical damages before punitive damages may be awarded. In addition, some states limit punitive damages to the actual expenses of litigation. [Even] assuming the ill will of the officer, his reasonable grounds for belief that the home he searched harbored evidence of crime is admissible in mitigation of punitive damages. [The] bad reputation of the plaintiff is likewise admissible. [If] the evidence seized was actually used at a trial, that fact has been held a complete justification of the search, and a defense against the trespass action. [And] even if the plaintiff hurdles all these obstacles, and gains a substantial verdict, the individual officer's finances may well make the judgment useless—for the municipality, of course, is not liable without its consent. Is it surprising that there is so little in the books concerning trespass actions for violation of the search and seizure clause? * * *

JUSTICE DOUGLAS, dissenting.

* * * I agree with Justice Murphy that [in] absence of [an exclusionary] rule of evidence the Amendment would have no effective sanction. * * *

MAPP v. OHIO

367 U.S. 643, 81 S.Ct. 1684, 6 L.Ed.2d 1081 (1961).

JUSTICE CLARK delivered the opinion of the Court.   * * *

On May 23, 1957, three Cleveland police officers arrived at appellant's residence in that city pursuant to information that "a person [was] hiding out in the home who was wanted for questioning in connection with a recent bombing, and that there was a large amount of policy paraphernalia being hidden in the home." Miss Mapp and her daughter by a former marriage lived on the top floor of the two-family dwelling. Upon their arrival at that house, the officers knocked on the door and demanded entrance but appellant, after telephoning her attorney, refused to admit them without a search warrant.

[The] officers again sought entrance some three hours later when four or more additional officers arrived on the scene. When Miss Mapp did not come to the door immediately, at least one of the several doors to the house was forcibly opened and the policemen gained admittance. Meanwhile Miss Mapp's attorney arrived, but the officers, having secured their own entry, and continuing in their defiance of the law, would permit him neither to see Miss Mapp nor to enter the house. [When the officers broke into the hall, Miss Mapp] demanded to see the search warrant. A paper, claimed to be a warrant, was held up by one of the officers. She grabbed the "warrant" and placed it in her bosom. A struggle ensued in which the officers recovered the piece of paper and as a result of which they handcuffed appellant because she had been "belligerent" in resisting their official rescue of the "warrant" from her person. * * * Appellant, in handcuffs, was then forcibly taken upstairs to her bedroom where the officers searched a dresser, a chest of drawers, a closet and some suitcases. [The] search spread to the rest of the second floor. [The] basement of the building and a trunk found therein were also searched. The obscene materials for possession of which she was ultimately convicted were discovered in the course of that widespread search.

At the trial no search warrant was produced by the prosecution, nor was the failure to produce one explained or accounted for. At best [as the Ohio Supreme Court, which affirmed the conviction, expressed it], "there is, in the record, considerable doubt as to whether there ever was any warrant for the search of defendant's home." * * *

The State says that even if the search were made without authority, or otherwise unreasonably, it is not prevented from using the unconstitutionally seized evidence at trial, citing *Wolf v. Colorado*. [On] this appeal, [it] is urged once again that we review that holding.

[The] Court in *Wolf* first stated that "[t]he contrariety of views of the States" on the adoption of the exclusionary rule of *Weeks* was "particularly impressive". [While] in 1949, prior to the *Wolf* case, almost two-thirds of the States were opposed to the use of the exclusionary rule, now, despite the *Wolf* case, more than half of those since passing upon it, by their own legislative or judicial decision, have wholly or partly adopted or adhered to the *Weeks* rule. * * * Significantly, among those now following the rule is California which, according to its highest court, was "compelled to reach that conclusion because other remedies have completely failed to secure compliance with the constitutional provisions * * *." In connection with this California case, we note that the second basis elaborated in *Wolf* in support of its failure to enforce the exclusionary doctrine against the States was that "other means of protection" have been afforded "the right to privacy." The experience of California that such other remedies have been worthless and futile is buttressed by the experience of other States.

Likewise, time has set its face against what *Wolf* called the "weighty testimony" of *People v. Defore*, 1926, 242 N.Y. 13, 150 N.E. 585. There Justice (then Judge) Cardozo, rejecting adoption of the *Weeks* exclusionary rule in New York, had said that "[t]he Federal rule as it stands is either too strict or too lax." However the force of that reasoning has been largely vitiated by later decisions of this Court. These include the recent discarding of the "silver platter" doctrine, *Elkins v. United States;* [a] * * *.

It, therefore, plainly appears that the factual considerations supporting the failure of the *Wolf* Court to include the *Weeks* exclusionary rule when it recognized the enforceability of the right to privacy against the States in 1949, while not basically relevant to the constitutional consideration, could not, in any analysis, now be deemed controlling.

* * * Today we once again examine *Wolf's* constitutional documentation of the right to privacy free from unreasonable state intrusion, and, after its dozen years on our books, are led by it to close the only courtroom door remaining open to evidence secured by official lawlessness in flagrant abuse of that basic right, reserved to all persons as a specific guarantee against that very same unlawful conduct. We hold that all evidence obtained by searches and seizures in violation of the Constitution is, by that same authority, inadmissible in a state court.[b]

Since the Fourth Amendment's right of privacy has been declared enforceable against the States through the Due Process Clause of the Fourteenth, it is enforceable against them by the same sanction of exclusion as is used against the Federal Government. Were it otherwise then just as without the *Weeks* rule the assurance against unreasonable federal searches and seizures would be "a form of words," valueless and undeserving of mention in a perpetual charter of inestimable human liberties, so too, without that rule the freedom from state invasions of privacy would be so ephemeral and so neatly severed from its conceptual nexus with the freedom from all brutish means of coercing evidence as not to merit this Court's high regard as a freedom "implicit in 'the concept of ordered liberty.'"

[In] extending the substantive protections of due process to all constitutionally unreasonable searches—state or federal—it was logically and constitutionally necessary that the exclusion doctrine—an essential part of the right to privacy— be also insisted upon as an essential ingredient of the right newly recognized by the *Wolf* case. In short, the admission of the new constitutional right by *Wolf* could not consistently tolerate denial of its most important constitutional privi-

a. 364 U.S. 206, 80 S.Ct. 1437, 4 L.Ed.2d 1669 (1960). Under the "silver platter" doctrine, evidence of a federal crime seized by state police in the course of an illegal search while investigating a state crime could be turned over to federal authorities and used in a federal prosecution so long as federal agents had not participated in the illegal search but had simply received the evidence on a "silver platter." In rejecting the doctrine, the Court pointed out that the determination in *Wolf* that Fourteenth Amendment Due Process prohibited illegal searches and seizures by state officers, marked the "removal of the doctrinal underpinning" for the admissibility of state-seized evidence in federal prosecutions.

b. Although an illegal arrest or other unreasonable seizure of the person is itself a violation of the Fourth and Fourteenth Amendments, the *Mapp* exclusionary sanction comes into play only when the police have obtained evidence as a result of the unconstitutional seizure. Such is the case when, for example, the police make an illegal arrest and then conduct a fruitful search which is "incident to" that arrest and thus dependent upon the lawfulness of the arrest for its legality. Such may also be the case when the connection between the illegality and the evidence is less apparent, and even when the evidence is verbal, such as a confession obtained from a defendant some time after his illegal arrest. As explained in *Wong Sun v. United States,* 371 U.S. 471, 83 S.Ct. 407, 9 L.Ed.2d 441 (1963), not "all evidence is 'fruit of the poisonous tree' simply because it would not have come to light but for the illegal actions of the police. Rather, the more apt question in such a case is 'whether, granting establishment of the primary illegality [the evidence] has been come at by exploitation of that illegality or instead by means sufficiently distinguishable to be purged of the primary taint.'" In making that judgment, the "temporal proximity of the arrest and the confession, the presence of intervening circumstances and, particularly, the purpose and flagrancy of the official misconduct, are all relevant. The voluntariness of the statement is a threshold requirement." *Brown v. Illinois,* 422 U.S. 590, 95 S.Ct. 2254, 45 L.Ed.2d 416 (1975).

lege, namely, the exclusion of the evidence which an accused had been forced to give by reason of the unlawful seizure. To hold otherwise is to grant the right but in reality to withhold its privilege and enjoyment. Only last year the Court itself recognized that the purpose of the exclusionary rule "is to deter—to compel respect for the constitutional guaranty in the only effectively available way—by removing the incentive to disregard it."

Indeed, we are aware of no restraint, similar to that rejected today, conditioning the enforcement of any other basic constitutional right. The right to privacy, no less important than any other right carefully and particularly reserved to the people, would stand in marked contrast to all other rights declared as "basic to a free society." * * * [N]othing could be more certain than that when a coerced confession is involved, "the relevant rules of evidence" are overridden without regard to "the incidence of such conduct by the police," slight or frequent. Why should not the same rule apply to what is tantamount to coerced testimony by way of unconstitutional seizure of goods, papers, effects, documents, etc.? We find that, as to the Federal Government the Fourth and Fifth Amendments and, as to the States, the freedom from unconscionable invasions of privacy and the freedom from convictions based upon coerced confessions do enjoy an "intimate relation" in their perpetuation of "principles of humanity and civil liberty * * *." They express "supplementing phases of the same constitutional purpose—to maintain inviolate large areas of personal privacy." The philosophy of each Amendment and of each freedom is complementary to, although not dependent upon, that of the other in its sphere of influence—the very least that together they assure in either sphere is that no man is to be convicted on unconstitutional evidence.

Moreover, our holding * * * is not only the logical dictate of prior cases, but it also makes very good sense. There is no war between the Constitution and common sense. Presently, a federal prosecutor may make no use of evidence illegally seized, but a State's attorney across the street may, although he supposedly is operating under the enforceable prohibitions of the same Amendment. Thus the State, by admitting evidence unlawfully seized, serves to encourage disobedience to the Federal Constitution which it is bound to uphold.

[There] are those who say, as did Justice (then Judge) Cardozo, that under our constitutional exclusionary doctrine "[t]he criminal is to go free because the constable has blundered." *People v. Defore.* In some cases this will undoubtedly be the result. But, as was said in *Elkins,* "there is another consideration—the imperative of judicial integrity." The criminal goes free, if he must, but it is the law that sets him free. Nothing can destroy a government more quickly than its failure to observe its own laws, or worse, its disregard of the charter of its own existence. As Mr. Justice Brandeis, dissenting, said in *Olmstead v. United States,* 277 U.S. 438, 48 S.Ct. 564, 72 L.Ed. 944 (1928): "Our government is the potent, the omnipresent teacher. For good or for ill, it teaches the whole people by its example. [If] the government becomes a lawbreaker, it breeds contempt for law; it invites every man to become a law unto himself; it invites anarchy." Nor can it lightly be assumed that, as a practical matter, adoption of the exclusionary rule fetters law enforcement. Only last year this Court expressly considered that contention and found that "pragmatic evidence of a sort" to the contrary was not wanting. [The] Court noted that:

> "The federal courts themselves have operated under the exclusionary rule of *Weeks* for almost half a century; yet it has not been suggested either that the Federal Bureau of Investigation has thereby been rendered ineffective, or that the administration of criminal justice in the federal courts has

thereby been disrupted.   Moreover, the experience of the states is impressive.
[The] movement toward the rule of exclusion has been halting but seemingly
inexorable."

The ignoble shortcut to conviction left open to the State tends to destroy the
entire system of constitutional restraints on which the liberties of the people rest.
Having once recognized that the right to privacy embodied in the Fourth Amendment is enforceable against the States, and that the right to be secure against
rude invasions of privacy by state officers is, therefore, constitutional in origin, we
can no longer permit that right to remain an empty promise.   Because it is
enforceable in the same manner and to like effect as other basic rights secured by
the Due Process Clause, we can no longer permit it to be revocable at the whim of
any police officer who, in the name of law enforcement itself, chooses to suspend
its enjoyment.   Our decision, founded on reason and truth, gives to the individual
no more than that which the Constitution guarantees him, to the police officer no
less than that to which honest law enforcement is entitled, and, to the courts, that
judicial integrity so necessary in the true administration of justice.   * * *

Reversed and remanded.

JUSTICE BLACK, concurring.   * * *

I am still not persuaded that the Fourth Amendment, standing alone, would
be enough to bar the introduction into evidence against an accused of papers and
effects seized from him in violation of its commands.   For the Fourth Amendment
does not itself contain any provision expressly precluding the use of such evidence,
and I am extremely doubtful that such a provision could properly be inferred from
nothing more than the basic command against unreasonable searches and seizures.   Reflection on the problem, however, in the light of cases coming before the
Court since *Wolf,* has led me to conclude that when the Fourth Amendment's ban
against unreasonable searches and seizures is considered together with the Fifth
Amendment's ban against compelled self-incrimination, a constitutional basis
emerges which not only justifies but actually requires the exclusionary rule.
* * *

JUSTICE DOUGLAS, concurring.

* * *   I believe that this is an appropriate case in which to put an end to the
asymmetry which *Wolf* imported into the law.   * * *

Memorandum of JUSTICE STEWART.

* * *   I express no view as to the merits of the constitutional issue which the
Court today decides.   * * *

JUSTICE HARLAN, whom JUSTICE FRANKFURTER and JUSTICE WHITTAKER join, dissenting.

* * *   I would not impose upon the States this federal exclusionary remedy.
The reasons given by the majority for now suddenly turning its back on *Wolf* seem
to me notably unconvincing.

First, it is said that "the factual grounds upon which *Wolf* was based" have
since changed, in that more States now follow the *Weeks* exclusionary rule than
was so at the time *Wolf* was decided.   While that is true, a recent survey indicates
that at present one half of the States still adhere to the common-law non-
exclusionary rule, and one, Maryland, retains the rule as to felonies.   * * *   But
in any case surely all this is beside the point, as the majority itself indeed seems to
recognize.   Our concern here, as it was in *Wolf,* is not with the desirability of that
rule but only with the question whether the States are Constitutionally free to

follow it or not as they may themselves determine, and the relevance of the disparity of views among the States on this point lies simply in the fact that the judgment involved is a debatable one. Moreover, the very fact on which the majority relies, instead of lending support to what is now being done, points away from the need of replacing voluntary state action with federal compulsion.

The preservation of a proper balance between state and federal responsibility in the administration of criminal justice demands patience on the part of those who might like to see things move faster among the States in this respect. Problems of criminal law enforcement vary widely from State to State. One State, in considering the totality of its legal picture, may conclude that the need for embracing the *Weeks* rule is pressing because other remedies are unavailable or inadequate to secure compliance with the substantive Constitutional principle involved. Another, though equally solicitous of Constitutional rights, may choose to pursue one purpose at a time, allowing all evidence relevant to guilt to be brought into a criminal trial, and dealing with Constitutional infractions by other means. Still another may consider the exclusionary rule too rough and ready a remedy, in that it reaches only unconstitutional intrusions which eventuate in criminal prosecution of the victims. Further, a State after experimenting with the *Weeks* rule for a time may, because of unsatisfactory experience with it, decide to revert to a non-exclusionary rule. And so on. * * * For us the question remains, as it has always been, one of state power, not one of passing judgment on the wisdom of one state course or another. In my view this Court should continue to forbear from fettering the States with an adamant rule which may embarrass them in coping with their own peculiar problems in criminal law enforcement. * * *

* * * Our role in promulgating the *Weeks* rule and its extensions * * * was quite a different one than it is here. There, in implementing the Fourth Amendment, we occupied the position of a tribunal having the ultimate responsibility for developing the standards and procedures of judicial administration within the judicial system over which it presides. Here we review State procedures whose measure is to be taken not against the specific substantive commands of the Fourth Amendment but under the flexible contours of the Due Process Clause. I do not believe that the Fourteenth Amendment empowers this Court to mould state remedies effectuating the right to freedom from "arbitrary intrusion by the police" to suit its own notions of how things should be done * * *.

Finally, it is said that the overruling of *Wolf* is supported by the established doctrine that the admission in evidence of an involuntary confession renders a state conviction constitutionally invalid. Since such a confession may often be entirely reliable, and therefore of the greatest relevance to the issue of the trial, the argument continues, this doctrine is ample warrant in precedent that the way evidence was obtained and not just its relevance, is constitutionally significant to the fairness of a trial. I believe this analogy is not a true one. The "coerced confession" rule is certainly not a rule that any illegally obtained statements may not be used in evidence. I would suppose that a statement which is procured during a period of illegal detention is, as much as unlawfully seized evidence, illegally obtained, but this Court has consistently refused to reverse state convictions resting on the use of such statements. * * *

The point, then, must be that in requiring exclusion of an involuntary statement of an accused, we are concerned not with an appropriate remedy for what the police have done, but with something which is regarded as going to the heart of our concepts of fairness in judicial procedure. The operative assumption of our procedural system is that "ours is the accusatorial as opposed to the inquisitorial system. * * *." [The] pressures brought to bear against an accused leading to a confession, unlike an unconstitutional violation of privacy, do not, apart from the use of the confession at trial, necessarily involve independent Constitutional violations. What is crucial is that the trial defense to which an accused is entitled should not be rendered an empty formality by reason of statements wrung from him, for then "a prisoner [has been] made the deluded instrument of his own conviction." That this is a *procedural right,* and that its violation occurs at the time his improperly obtained statement is admitted at trial, is manifest.

[This], and not the disciplining of the police, as with illegally seized evidence, is surely the true basis for excluding a statement of the accused which was unconstitutionally obtained. In sum, I think the coerced confession analogy works strongly *against* what the Court does today. * * *

UNITED STATES v. LEON

468 U.S. 897, 104 S.Ct. 3405, 82 L.Ed.2d 677 (1984).

JUSTICE WHITE delivered the opinion of the Court. * * *

This case presents the question whether the Fourth Amendment exclusionary rule should be modified so as not to bar the use in the prosecution's case-in-chief of evidence obtained by officers acting in reasonable reliance on a search warrant issued by a detached and neutral magistrate but ultimately found to be unsupported by probable cause. * * *

The Fourth Amendment contains no provision expressly precluding the use of evidence obtained in violation of its commands, and an examination of its origin and purposes makes clear that the use of fruits of a past unlawful search or seizure "work[s] no new Fourth Amendment wrong." The wrong condemned by the Amendment is "fully accomplished" by the unlawful search or seizure itself, and the exclusionary rule is neither intended nor able to "cure the invasion of the defendant's rights which he has already suffered." The rule thus operates as "a judicially created remedy designed to safeguard Fourth Amendment rights generally through its deterrent effect, rather than a personal constitutional right of the person aggrieved."

Whether the exclusionary sanction is appropriately imposed in a particular case, our decisions make clear, is "an issue separate from the question whether the Fourth Amendment rights of the party seeking to invoke the rule were violated by police conduct." Only the former question is currently before us,[a] and it must be resolved by weighing the costs and benefits of preventing the use in the prosecution's case-in-chief of inherently trustworthy tangible evidence obtained in reliance on a search warrant issued by a detached and neutral magistrate that ultimately is found to be defective.

The substantial social costs exacted by the exclusionary rule for the vindication of Fourth Amendment rights have long been a source of concern. "Our cases have consistently recognized that unbending application of the exclusionary sanc-

a. A large quantity of drugs were suppressed on the ground the warrant had not issued on probable cause, in that the affidavit reported only the allegations of an untested informant and limited corroboration by police surveillance of events themselves "as consistent with innocence as * * * with guilt." The Court earlier noted that whether this warrant would pass muster under the intervening and less demanding test of *Illinois v. Gates,* § 3 infra, "has not been briefed or argued," and thus chose "to take the case as it comes to us."

tion to enforce ideals of governmental rectitude would impede unacceptably the truth-finding functions of judge and jury." An objectionable collateral consequence of this interference with the criminal justice system's truth-finding function is that some guilty defendants may go free or receive reduced sentences as a result of favorable plea bargains.[6] Particularly when law enforcement officers have acted in objective good faith or their transgressions have been minor, the magnitude of the benefit conferred on such guilty defendants offends basic concepts of the criminal justice system. Indiscriminate application of the exclusionary rule, therefore, may well "generat[e] disrespect for the law and the administration of justice." Accordingly, "[a]s with any remedial device, the application of the rule has been restricted to those areas where its remedial objectives are thought most efficaciously served."

Close attention to those remedial objectives has characterized our recent decisions concerning the scope of the Fourth Amendment exclusionary rule. The Court has, to be sure, not seriously questioned, "in the absence of a more efficacious sanction, the continued application of the rule to suppress evidence from the [prosecution's] case where a Fourth Amendment violation has been substantial and deliberate * * *." Nevertheless, the balancing approach that has evolved in various contexts—including criminal trials—"forcefully suggest[s] that the exclusionary rule be more generally modified to permit the introduction of evidence obtained in the reasonable good-faith belief that a search or seizure was in accord with the Fourth Amendment." * * *

Only [when a warrant is grounded upon an affidavit knowingly or recklessly false] has the Court set forth a rationale for suppressing evidence obtained pursuant to a search warrant;[b] in the other areas, it has simply excluded such evidence without considering whether Fourth Amendment interests will be advanced. To the extent that proponents of exclusion rely on its behavioral effects on judges and magistrates in these areas, their reliance is misplaced. First, the exclusionary rule is designed to deter police misconduct rather than to punish the errors of judges and magistrates. Second, there exists no evidence suggesting that judges and magistrates are inclined to ignore or subvert the Fourth Amendment

---

6. Researchers have only recently begun to study extensively the effects of the exclusionary rule on the disposition of felony arrests. One study suggests that the rule results in the non-prosecution or nonconviction of between 0.6% and 2.35% of individuals arrested for felonies. Davies, *A Hard Look at What We Know (and Still Need to Learn) About the "Costs" of the Exclusionary Rule: The NIJ Study and Other Studies of "Lost" Arrests,* 1983 A.B.F.Res.J. 611, 621. The estimates are higher for particular crimes the prosecution of which depends heavily on physical evidence. Thus, the cumulative loss due to nonprosecution or nonconviction of individuals arrested on felony drug charges is probably in the range of 2.8% to 7.1%. Davies' analysis of California data suggests that screening by police and prosecutors results in the release because of illegal searches or seizures of as many as 1.4% of all felony arrestees, id., at 650, that 0.9% of felony arrestees are released because of illegal searches or seizures at the preliminary hearing or after trial, id., at 653, and that roughly 0.5%

of all felony arrestees benefit from reversals on appeal because of illegal searches. * * *

Many of these researchers have concluded that the impact of the exclusionary rule is insubstantial, but the small percentages with which they deal mask a large absolute number of felons who are released because the cases against them were based in part on illegal searches or seizures. * * * Because we find that the rule can have no substantial deterrent effect in the sorts of situations under consideration in this case, we conclude that it cannot pay its way in those situations.

b. The reference is to *Franks v. Delaware,* 438 U.S. 154, 98 S.Ct. 2674, 57 L.Ed.2d 667 (1978), where the Court declared "it would be an unthinkable imposition upon [the magistrate's] authority if a warrant affidavit, revealed after the fact to contain a deliberately or recklessly false statement, were to stand beyond impeachment."

or that lawlessness among these actors requires application of the extreme sanction of exclusion.[14]

Third, and most important, we discern no basis, and are offered none, for believing that exclusion of evidence seized pursuant to a warrant will have a significant deterrent effect on the issuing judge or magistrate. Many of the factors that indicate that the exclusionary rule cannot provide an effective "special" or "general" deterrent for individual offending law enforcement officers apply as well to judges or magistrates. And, to the extent that the rule is thought to operate as a "systemic" deterrent on a wider audience, it clearly can have no such effect on individuals empowered to issue warrants. Judges and magistrates are not adjuncts to the law enforcement team; as neutral judicial officers, they have no stake in the outcome of particular criminal prosecutions. The threat of exclusion thus cannot be expected significantly to deter them. Imposition of the exclusionary sanction is not necessary meaningfully to inform judicial officers of their errors, and we cannot conclude that admitting evidence obtained pursuant to a warrant while at the same time declaring that the warrant was somehow defective will in any way reduce judicial officers' professional incentives to comply with the Fourth Amendment, encourage them to repeat their mistakes, or lead to the granting of all colorable warrant requests.[18]

If exclusion of evidence obtained pursuant to a subsequently invalidated warrant is to have any deterrent effect, therefor, it must alter the behavior of individual law enforcement officers or the policies of their departments. One could argue that applying the exclusionary rule in cases where the police failed to demonstrate probable cause in the warrant application deters future inadequate presentations or "magistrate shopping" and thus promotes the ends of the Fourth Amendment. Suppressing evidence obtained pursuant to a technically defective warrant supported by probable cause also might encourage officers to scrutinize more closely the form of the warrant and to point out suspected judicial errors. We find such arguments speculative and conclude that suppression of evidence obtained pursuant to a warrant should be ordered only on a case-by-case basis and only in those unusual cases in which exclusion will further the purposes of the exclusionary rule.[19]

We have frequently questioned whether the exclusionary rule can have any deterrent effect when the offending officers acted in the objectively reasonable belief that their conduct did not violate the Fourth Amendment. "No empirical researcher, proponent or opponent of the rule, has yet been able to establish with any assurance whether the rule has a deterrent effect * * *." But even assuming that the rule effectively deters some police misconduct and provides incentives for

---

14. Although there are assertions that some magistrates become rubber stamps for the police and others may be unable effectively to screen police conduct, we are not convinced that this is a problem of major proportions.

18. Limiting the application of the exclusionary sanction may well increase the care with which magistrates scrutinize warrant applications. We doubt that magistrates are more desirous of avoiding the exclusion of evidence obtained pursuant to warrants they have issued than of avoiding invasions of privacy.

Federal magistrates, moreover, are subject to the direct supervision of district courts. They may be removed for "incompetency, misconduct, neglect of duty, or physical or mental disability." 28 U.S.C. § 631(i). If a magistrate serves merely as a "rubber stamp" for the police or is unable to exercise mature judgment, closer supervision or removal provides a more effective remedy than the exclusionary rule.

19. Our discussion of the deterrent effect of excluding evidence obtained in reasonable reliance on a subsequently invalidated warrant assumes, of course, that the officers properly executed the warrant and searched only those places and for those objects that it was reasonable to believe were covered by the warrant. * * *

the law enforcement profession as a whole to conduct itself in accord with the Fourth Amendment, it cannot be expected, and should not be applied, to deter objectively reasonable law enforcement activity. * * * [20]

This is particularly true, we believe, when an officer acting with objective good faith has obtained a search warrant from a judge or magistrate and acted within its scope. In most such cases, there is no police illegality and thus nothing to deter. It is the magistrate's responsibility to determine whether the officer's allegations establish probable cause and, if so, to issue a warrant comporting in form with the requirements of the Fourth Amendment. In the ordinary case, an officer cannot be expected to question the magistrate's probable-cause determination or his judgment that the form of the warrant is technically sufficient. "[O]nce the warrant issues, there is literally nothing more the policeman can do in seeking to comply with the law." Penalizing the officer for the magistrate's error, rather than his own, cannot logically contribute to the deterrence of Fourth Amendment violations.[22]

We conclude that the marginal or nonexistent benefits produced by suppressing evidence obtained in objectively reasonable reliance on a subsequently invalidated search warrant cannot justify the substantial costs of exclusion. We do not suggest, however, that exclusion is always inappropriate in cases where an officer has obtained a warrant and abided by its terms. [T]he officer's reliance on the magistrate's probable-cause determination and on the technical sufficiency of the warrant he issues must be objectively reasonable,[23] and it is clear that in some circumstances the officer [24] will have no reasonable grounds for believing that the warrant was properly issued.

20. We emphasize that the standard of reasonableness we adopt is an objective one. Many objections to a good-faith exception assume that the exception will turn on the subjective good faith of individual officers. "Grounding the modification in objective reasonableness, however, retains the value of the exclusionary rule as an incentive for the law enforcement profession as a whole to conduct themselves in accord with the Fourth Amendment." The objective standard we adopt, moreover, requires officers to have a reasonable knowledge of what the law prohibits. As Professor Jerold Israel has observed:

"The key to the [exclusionary] rule's effectiveness as a deterrent lies, I believe, in the impetus it has provided to police training programs that make officers aware of the limits imposed by the fourth amendment and emphasize the need to operate within those limits. [An objective good-faith exception] is not likely to result in the elimination of such programs, which are now viewed as an important aspect of police professionalism. Neither is it likely to alter the tenor of those programs; the possibility that illegally obtained evidence may be admitted in borderline cases is unlikely to encourage police instructors to pay less attention to fourth amendment limitations. Finally, [it] should not encourage officers to pay less attention to what they are taught, as the requirement that the officer act in 'good faith' is inconsistent with closing one's mind to the possibility of illegality."

22. * * * Our cases establish that the question whether the use of illegally obtained evidence in judicial proceedings represents judicial participation in a Fourth Amendment violation and offends the integrity of the courts "is essentially the same as the inquiry into whether exclusion would serve a deterrent purpose." * * * Absent unusual circumstances, when a Fourth Amendment violation has occurred because the police have reasonably relied on a warrant issued by a detached and neutral magistrate but ultimately found to be defective, "the integrity of the courts is not implicated."

23. [O]ur good-faith inquiry is confined to the objectively ascertainable question whether a reasonably well-trained officer would have known that the search was illegal despite the magistrate's authorization. In making this determination, all of the circumstances—including whether the warrant application had previously been rejected by a different magistrate—may be considered.

24. References to "officer" throughout this opinion should not be read too narrowly. It is necessary to consider the objective reasonableness, not only of the officers who eventually executed a warrant, but also of the officers who originally obtained it or who provided information material to the probable-cause determination. Nothing in our opinion suggests, for example, that an officer could obtain a warrant on the basis of a "bare bones" affidavit and

Suppression therefore remains an appropriate remedy if the magistrate or judge in issuing a warrant was misled by information in an affidavit that the affiant knew was false or would have known was false except for his reckless disregard of the truth. The exception we recognize today will also not apply in cases where the issuing magistrate wholly abandoned his judicial role in the manner condemned in *Lo–Ji Sales, Inc. v. New York,* 442 U.S. 319, 99 S.Ct. 2319, 60 L.Ed.2d 920 (1979); [c] in such circumstances, no reasonably well-trained officer should rely on the warrant. Nor would an officer manifest objective good faith in relying on a warrant based on an affidavit "so lacking in indicia of probable cause as to render official belief in its existence entirely unreasonable." Finally, depending on the circumstances of the particular case, a warrant may be so facially deficient—i.e., in failing to particularize the place to be searched or the things to be seized—that the executing officers cannot reasonably presume it to be valid.[d]

[The] good-faith exception for searches conducted pursuant to warrants is not intended to signal our unwillingness strictly to enforce the requirements of the Fourth Amendment, and we do not believe that it will have this effect. As we have already suggested, the good-faith exception, turning as it does on objective reasonableness, should not be difficult to apply in practice. When officers have acted pursuant to a warrant, the prosecution should ordinarily be able to establish objective good faith without a substantial expenditure of judicial time.

Nor are we persuaded that application of a good-faith exception to searches conducted pursuant to warrants will preclude review of the constitutionality of the search or seizure, deny needed guidance from the courts, or freeze Fourth Amendment law in its present state.[25] There is no need for courts to adopt the inflexible practice of always deciding whether the officers' conduct manifested

then rely on colleagues who are ignorant of the circumstances under which the warrant was obtained to conduct the search.

c. There the magistrate was held not to have "manifest[ed] that neutrality and detachment demanded of a judicial officer when presented with a warrant application," where he went to the scene and made judgments there about what should be seized as obscene, as he "allowed himself to become a member, if not the leader of the search party which was essentially a police operation."

d. Compare the companion case of *Massachusetts v. Sheppard,* 468 U.S. 981, 104 S.Ct. 3424, 82 L.Ed.2d 737 (1984), where a detective prepared an affidavit for a search warrant to search for various specified items of evidence of a homicide but, because it was Sunday, could only find a warrant form for controlled substances. He presented his affidavit and that form to a judge at his home and pointed out the problem to him, and the judge, unable to locate a more suitable form, told the detective that he would make the necessary changes to make it a proper warrant. He made some changes, but failed to change that part of the warrant which authorized a search only for controlled substances and related paraphernalia. The detective took the two documents and he and other officers then executed the war-

rant, seizing evidence of the homicide. That evidence was suppressed in the state court because the warrant failed to particularly describe the items to be seized, as required by the Fourth Amendment. The Supreme Court, per White, J., held this situation fell within *Leon* because "there was an objectively reasonable basis for the officers' mistaken belief" that "the warrant authorized the search that they conducted." As for defendant's objection that the detective knew when he went to the judge that the warrant was defective, the Court stated: "Whatever an officer may be required to do when he executes a warrant without knowing beforehand what items are to be seized, we refuse to rule that an officer is required to disbelieve a judge who has just advised him, by word and by action, that the warrant he possesses authorizes him to conduct the search he has requested."

25. The argument that defendants will lose their incentive to litigate meritorious Fourth Amendment claims as a result of the good-faith exception we adopt today is unpersuasive. Although the exception might discourage presentation of insubstantial suppression motions, the magnitude of the benefit conferred on defendants by a successful motion makes it unlikely that litigation of colorable claims will be substantially diminished.

objective good faith before turning to the question whether the Fourth Amendment has been violated. * * *

If the resolution of a particular Fourth Amendment question is necessary to guide future action by law enforcement officers and magistrates, nothing will prevent reviewing courts from deciding that question before turning to the good-faith issue.[26] Indeed, it frequently will be difficult to determine whether the officers acted reasonably without resolving the Fourth Amendment issue. Even if the Fourth Amendment question is not one of broad import, reviewing courts could decide in particular cases that magistrates under their supervision need to be informed of their errors and so evaluate the officers' good faith only after finding a violation. In other circumstances, those courts could reject suppression motions posing no important Fourth Amendment questions by turning immediately to a consideration of the officers' good faith. We have no reason to believe that our Fourth Amendment jurisprudence would suffer by allowing reviewing courts to exercise an informed discretion in making this choice. * * *

In the absence of an allegation that the magistrate abandoned his detached and neutral role, suppression is appropriate only if the officers were dishonest or reckless in preparing their affidavit or could not have harbored an objectively reasonable belief in the existence of probable cause. Only respondent Leon has contended that no reasonably well-trained police officer could have believed that there existed probable cause to search his house; significantly, the other respondents advance no comparable argument. Officer Rombach's application for a warrant clearly was supported by much more than a "bare bones" affidavit. The affidavit related the results of an extensive investigation and, as the opinions of the divided panel of the Court of Appeals make clear, provided evidence sufficient to create disagreement among thoughtful and competent judges as to the existence of probable cause. Under these circumstances, the officers' reliance on the magistrate's determination of probable cause was objectively reasonable, and application of the extreme sanction of exclusion is inappropriate.[e]

26. It has been suggested, in fact, that "the recognition of a 'penumbral zone,' within which an inadvertent mistake would not call for exclusion, * * * will make it less tempting for judges to bend fourth amendment standards to avoid releasing a possibly dangerous criminal because of a minor and unintentional miscalculation by the police."

e. Prior to *Leon*, the Supreme Court had often applied the exclusionary rule even when the police acted in reliance upon a subsequently invalidated statute conferring authority to search. But when confronted with such a situation once again in *Illinois v. Krull*, 480 U.S. 340, 107 S.Ct. 1160, 94 L.Ed.2d 364 (1987), the Court, 5–4, ruled otherwise. Blackmun, J., reasoned for the majority: "The approach used in *Leon* is equally applicable to the present case. The application of the exclusionary rule to suppress evidence obtained by an officer acting in objectively reasonable reliance on a statute would have as little deterrent effect on the officer's actions as would the exclusion of evidence when an officer acts in objectively reasonable reliance on a warrant. Unless a statute is clearly unconstitutional, an officer cannot be expected to question the judgment of the legislature that passed the law." The

Court in *Krull* further reasoned that there was no "evidence to suggest that legislators 'are inclined to ignore or subvert the Fourth Amendment' " or "to indicate that applying the exclusionary rule to evidence seized pursuant to the statute prior to the declaration of its invalidity will act as a significant additional deterrent" of legislators.

O'Connor, J., for the dissenters, emphasized: (1) "The distinction drawn between the legislator and the judicial officer is sound" because "a legislature's unreasonable authorization of searches may affect thousands or millions" and thus "poses a greater threat to liberty." (2) "[L]egislators by virtue of their political role are more often subjected to the political pressures that may threaten Fourth Amendment values than are judicial officers." (3) "Providing legislatures a grace period during which the police may freely perform unreasonable searches in order to convict those who might have otherwise escaped creates a positive incentive to promulgate unconstitutional laws."

Yet another *Leon*-style opinion is *Arizona v. Evans*, ___ U.S. ___, 115 S.Ct. 1185, 131 L.Ed.2d 34 (1995), where the defendant was arrested on the basis of an erroneous computer

Accordingly, the judgment of the Court of Appeals is reversed.

JUSTICE BLACKMUN, concurring.

[A]ny empirical judgment about the effect of the exclusionary rule in a particular class of cases necessarily is a provisional one. * * * If it should emerge from experience that, contrary to our expectations, the good faith exception to the exclusionary rule results in a material change in police compliance with the Fourth Amendment, we shall have to reconsider what we have undertaken here. The logic of a decision that rests on untested predictions about police conduct demands no less. * * *

JUSTICE BRENNAN, with whom JUSTICE MARSHALL joins, dissenting. * * *

[The majority's reading of the Fourth Amendment] appears plausible, because, as critics of the exclusionary rule never tire of repeating, the Fourth Amendment makes no express provision for the exclusion of evidence secured in violation of its commands. A short answer to this claim, of course, is that many of the Constitution's most vital imperatives are stated in general terms and the task of giving meaning to these precepts is therefore left to subsequent judicial decision-making in the context of concrete cases. The nature of our Constitution, as Chief Justice Marshall long ago explained, "requires that only its great outlines should be marked, its important objects designated, and the minor ingredients which compose those objects be deduced from the nature of the objects themselves."

A more direct answer may be supplied by recognizing that the Amendment, like other provisions of the Bill of Rights, restrains the power of the government as a whole; it does not specify only a particular agency and exempt all others. The judiciary is responsible, no less than the executive, for ensuring that constitutional rights are respected.

When that fact is kept in mind, the role of the courts and their possible involvement in the concerns of the Fourth Amendment comes into sharper focus. Because seizures are executed principally to secure evidence, and because such evidence generally has utility in our legal system only in the context of a trial supervised by a judge, it is apparent that the admission of illegally obtained evidence implicates the same constitutional concerns as the initial seizure of that evidence. Indeed, by admitting unlawfully seized evidence, the judiciary becomes a part of what is in fact a single governmental action prohibited by the terms of the Amendment. Once that connection between the evidence-gathering role of the police and the evidence-admitting function of the courts is acknowledged, the plausibility of the Court's interpretation becomes more suspect. Certainly nothing in the language or history of the Fourth Amendment suggests that a recognition of this evidentiary link between the police and the courts was meant to be foreclosed. It is difficult to give any meaning at all to the limitations imposed by the Amendment if they are read to proscribe only certain conduct by the police but to allow other agents of the same government to take advantage of evidence secured by the police in violation of its requirements. The Amendment therefore must be read to condemn not only the initial unconstitutional invasion

indication of an outstanding warrant attributable to a court clerk's failure to advise the police that the warrant had been quashed. In concluding the exclusionary rule should not apply to this type of Fourth Amendment violation, the Court reasoned (i) that the arresting officer acted reasonably in relying on the computer record and thus was not in need of deterrence; and (ii) that exclusion would not deter such errors by court clerks, who "have no stake in the outcome of particular criminal prosecutions."

of privacy—which is done, after all, for the purpose of securing evidence—but also the subsequent use of any evidence so obtained.   * * *

Such a conception of the rights secured by the Fourth Amendment was unquestionably the original basis of what has come to be called the exclusionary rule when it was first formulated in *Weeks v. United States.* [The] question whether the exclusion of evidence would deter future police misconduct was never considered a relevant concern in the early cases. [In] those formative decisions, the Court plainly understood that the exclusion of illegally obtained evidence was compelled not by judicially fashioned remedial purposes, but rather by a direct constitutional command.

* * * Indeed, no other explanation suffices to account for the Court's holding in *Mapp,* since the only possible predicate for the Court's conclusion that the States were bound by the Fourteenth Amendment to honor the *Weeks* doctrine is that the exclusionary rule was "part and parcel of the Fourth Amendment's limitation upon [governmental] encroachment of individual privacy."

Despite this clear pronouncement, however, the Court * * * has gradually pressed the deterrence rationale for the rule back to center stage. The various arguments advanced by the Court in this campaign have only strengthened my conviction that the deterrence theory is both misguided and unworkable. First, the Court has frequently bewailed the "cost" of excluding reliable evidence. In large part, this criticism rests upon a refusal to acknowledge the function of the Fourth Amendment itself. If nothing else, the Amendment plainly operates to disable the government from gathering information and securing evidence in certain ways. In practical terms, of course, this restriction of official power means that some incriminating evidence inevitably will go undetected if the government obeys these constitutional restraints. It is the loss of that evidence that is the "price" our society pays for enjoying the freedom and privacy safeguarded by the Fourth Amendment. Thus, some criminals will go free *not,* in Justice (then Judge) Cardozo's misleading epigram, "because the constable has blundered," but rather because official compliance with Fourth Amendment requirements makes it more difficult to catch criminals. Understood in this way, the Amendment directly contemplates that some reliable and incriminating evidence will be lost to the government; therefore, it is not the exclusionary rule, but the Amendment itself that has imposed this cost.

In addition, the Court's decisions over the past decade have made plain that the entire enterprise of attempting to assess the benefits and costs of the exclusionary rule in various contexts is a virtually impossible task for the judiciary to perform honestly or accurately. Although the Court's language in those cases suggests that some specific empirical basis may support its analyses, the reality is that the Court's opinions represent inherently unstable compounds of intuition, hunches, and occasional pieces of partial and often inconclusive data. * * * To the extent empirical data is available regarding the general costs and benefits of the exclusionary rule, it has shown, on the one hand, as the Court acknowledges today, that the costs are not as substantial as critics have asserted in the past, and, on the other hand, that while the exclusionary rule may well have certain deterrent effects, it is extremely difficult to determine with any degree of precision whether the incidence of unlawful conduct by police is now lower than it was prior to *Mapp.* The Court has sought to turn this uncertainty to its advantage by casting the burden of proof upon proponents of the rule. "Obviously," however, "the assignment of the burden of proof on an issue where evidence does not exist and cannot be obtained is outcome determinative. [The] assignment of the burden is merely a way of announcing a predetermined conclusion."

By remaining within its redoubt of empiricism and by basing the rule solely on the deterrence rationale, the Court has robbed the rule of legitimacy. A doctrine that is explained as if it were an empirical proposition but for which there is only limited empirical support is both inherently unstable and an easy mark for critics. The extent of this Court's fidelity to Fourth Amendment requirements, however, should not turn on such statistical uncertainties.   * * *

Even if I were to accept the Court's general approach to the exclusionary rule, I could not agree with today's result.   * * *

At the outset, the Court suggests that society has been asked to pay a high price—in terms either of setting guilty persons free or of impeding the proper functioning of trials—as a result of excluding relevant physical evidence in cases where the police, in conducting searches and seizing evidence, have made only an "objectively reasonable" mistake concerning the constitutionality of their actions. But what evidence is there to support such a claim?

Significantly, the Court points to none, and, indeed, as the Court acknowledges, recent studies have demonstrated that the "costs" of the exclusionary rule—calculated in terms of dropped prosecutions and lost convictions—are quite low. Contrary to the claims of the rule's critics that exclusion leads to "the release of countless guilty criminals," these studies have demonstrated that federal and state prosecutors very rarely drop cases because of potential search and seizure problems. For example, a 1979 study prepared at the request of Congress by the General Accounting Office reported that only 0.4% of all cases actually declined for prosecution by federal prosecutors were declined primarily because of illegal search problems. If the GAO data are restated as a percentage of *all* arrests, the study shows that only 0.2% of all felony arrests are declined for prosecution because of potential exclusionary rule problems.[11] Of course, these data describe only the costs attributable to the exclusion of evidence in all cases; the costs due to the exclusion of evidence in the narrower category of cases where police have made objectively reasonable mistakes must necessarily be even smaller. The Court, however, ignores this distinction and mistakenly weighs the aggregated costs of exclusion in *all* cases, irrespective of the circumstances that led to exclusion, against the potential benefits associated with only those cases in which evidence is excluded because police reasonably but mistakenly believe that

---

11. In a series of recent studies, researchers have attempted to quantify the actual costs of the rule. A recent National Institute of Justice study based on data for the four year period 1976–1979 gathered by the California Bureau of Criminal Statistics showed that 4.8% of all cases that were declined for prosecution by California prosecutors were rejected because of illegally seized evidence. However, if these data are calculated as a percentage of all arrests that were declined for prosecution, they show that only 0.8% of all arrests were rejected for prosecution because of illegally seized evidence.

In another measure of the rule's impact—the number of prosecutions that are dismissed or result in acquittals in cases where evidence has been excluded—the available data again show that the Court's past assessment of the rule's costs has generally been exaggerated. For ex-

ample, a study based on data from 9 mid-sized counties in Illinois, Michigan and Pennsylvania reveals that motions to suppress physical evidence were filed in approximately 5% of the 7,500 cases studied, but that such motions were successful in only 0.7% of all these cases. The study also shows that only 0.6% of all cases resulted in acquittals because evidence had been excluded. In the GAO study, suppression motions were filed in 10.5% of all federal criminal cases surveyed, but of the motions filed, approximately 80–90% were denied. Evidence was actually excluded in only 1.3% of the cases studied, and only 0.7% of all cases resulted in acquittals or dismissals after evidence was excluded. And in another study based on data from cases during 1978 and 1979 in San Diego and Jacksonville, it was shown that only 1% of all cases resulting in nonconviction were caused by illegal searches.

their conduct does not violate the Fourth Amendment. When such faulty scales are used, it is little wonder that the balance tips in favor of restricting the application of the rule.

What then supports the Court's insistence that this evidence be admitted? Apparently, the Court's only answer is that even though the costs of exclusion are not very substantial, the potential deterrent effect in these circumstances is so marginal that exclusion cannot be justified. The key to the Court's conclusion in this respect is its belief that the prospective deterrent effect of the exclusionary rule operates only in those situations in which police officers, when deciding whether to go forward with some particular search, have reason to know that their planned conduct will violate the requirements of the Fourth Amendment.

* * * But what the Court overlooks is that the deterrence rationale for the rule is not designed to be, nor should it be thought of as, a form of "punishment" of individual police officers for their failures to obey the restraints imposed by the Fourth Amendment. Instead, the chief deterrent function of the rule is its tendency to promote institutional compliance with Fourth Amendment requirements on the part of law enforcement agencies generally. Thus, as the Court has previously recognized, "over the long term, [the] demonstration [provided by the exclusionary rule] that our society attaches serious consequences to violation of constitutional rights is thought to encourage those who formulate law enforcement policies, and the officers who implement them, to incorporate Fourth Amendment ideals into their value system." It is only through such an institution-wide mechanism that information concerning Fourth Amendment standards can be effectively communicated to rank and file officers.[13]

If the overall educational effect of the exclusionary rule is considered, application of the rule to even those situations in which individual police officers have acted on the basis of a reasonable but mistaken belief that their conduct was authorized can still be expected to have a considerable long-term deterrent effect. If evidence is consistently excluded in these circumstances, police departments will surely be prompted to instruct their officers to devote greater care and attention to providing sufficient information to establish probable cause when applying for a warrant, and to review with some attention the form of the warrant that they have been issued, rather than automatically assuming that whatever document the magistrate has signed will necessarily comport with Fourth Amendment requirements.

After today's decision, however, that institutional incentive will be lost. Indeed, the Court's "reasonable mistake" exception to the exclusionary rule will tend to put a premium on police ignorance of the law. Armed with the assurance provided by today's decision that evidence will always be admissible whenever an officer has "reasonably" relied upon a warrant, police departments will be encouraged to train officers that if a warrant has simply been signed, it is reasonable, without more, to rely on it. Since in close cases there will no longer be any incentive to err on the side of constitutional behavior, police would have every reason to adopt a "let's-wait-until-its-decided" approach in situations in

---

13. * * * A former United States Attorney and now Attorney General of Maryland, Stephen Sachs, has described the impact of the rule on police practices in similar terms: "I have watched the rule deter, routinely, throughout my years as a prosecutor * * *. [P]olice-prosecutor consultation is customary in all our cases when Fourth Amendment concerns arise * * *. In at least three Maryland jurisdictions, for example, prosecutors are on twenty-four hour call to field search and seizure questions presented by police officers."

which there is a question about a warrant's validity or the basis for its issuance.[14]

Although the Court brushes these concerns aside, a host of grave consequences can be expected to result from its decision to carve this new exception out of the exclusionary rule. A chief consequence of today's decision will be to convey a clear and unambiguous message to magistrates that their decisions to issue warrants are now insulated from subsequent judicial review. Creation of this new exception for good faith reliance upon a warrant implicitly tells magistrates that they need not take much care in reviewing warrant applications, since their mistakes will from now on have virtually no consequence: If their decision to issue a warrant was correct, the evidence will be admitted; if their decision was incorrect but the police relied in good faith on the warrant, the evidence will also be admitted. Inevitably, the care and attention devoted to such an inconsequential chore will dwindle. Although the Court is correct to note that magistrates do not share the same stake in the outcome of a criminal case as the police, they nevertheless need to appreciate that their role is of some moment in order to continue performing the important task of carefully reviewing warrant applications. Today's decision effectively removes that incentive.

Moreover, the good faith exception will encourage police to provide only the bare minimum of information in future warrant applications. The police will now know that if they can secure a warrant, so long as the circumstances of its issuance are not "entirely unreasonable," all police conduct pursuant to that warrant will be protected from further judicial review. The clear incentive that operated in the past to establish probable cause adequately because reviewing courts would examine the magistrate's judgment carefully, has now been so completely vitiated that the police need only show that it was not "entirely unreasonable" under the circumstances of a particular case for them to believe that the warrant they were issued was valid. The long-run effect unquestionably will be to undermine the integrity of the warrant process. * * *

JUSTICE STEVENS, * * * dissenting * * *.

* * * It is probable, though admittedly not certain, that the Court of Appeals would now conclude that the warrant in *Leon* satisfied the Fourth Amendment if it were given the opportunity to reconsider the issue in the light of *Gates*. Adherence to our normal practice following the announcement of a new rule would therefore postpone, and probably obviate, the need for the promulgation of the broad new rule the Court announces today.

[W]hen the Court goes beyond what is necessary to decide the case before it, it can only encourage the perception that it is pursuing its own notions of wise social policy, rather than adhering to its judicial role. I do not believe the Court should reach out to decide what is undoubtedly a profound question concerning the administration of criminal justice before assuring itself that this question is actually and of necessity presented by the concrete facts before the Court. * * *[f]

---

14. The authors of a recent study of the warrant process in seven cities concluded that application of a good faith exception where an officer relies upon a warrant "would further encourage police officers to seek out the less inquisitive magistrates and to rely on boilerplate formulae, thereby lessening the value of search warrants overall. * * *

f. Justice Stevens' separate dissenting opinion is omitted.

II. PROTECTED AREAS
AND INTERESTS

Introduction

If certain police activity is neither a "search" nor a "seizure" in the Fourth Amendment sense, then quite obviously the protections of the Amendment are inapplicable. Deciding just what constitutes a "search" has been especially troublesome. In the leading case (and the first case in this section) of *Katz v. United States,* holding electronic eavesdropping is governed by the Fourth Amendment, the Court decided a search could occur without a physical intrusion into a constitutionally protected area. By requiring instead an infringement upon a justified expectation of privacy, *Katz* unquestionably broadened the scope of the Fourth Amendment. But the Court has since taken a rather narrow view of what privacy expectations are in fact "justified," as is illustrated by the next two cases, *California v. Greenwood* and *Florida v. Riley,* dealing, respectively, with examination of garbage and aerial surveillance. The fourth case in this section, *United States v. Karo,* involving use of an electronic tracking device, concerns the Fourth Amendment's application to sense-enhancing devices. The meaning of *Katz* is also explored in *United States v. White,* concerning the troublesome question of whether it is a search or seizure for an undercover agent secretly to record or transmit the conversations he has with others.

KATZ v. UNITED STATES
389 U.S. 347, 88 S.Ct. 507, 19 L.Ed.2d 576 (1967).

JUSTICE STEWART delivered the opinion of the Court.

The petitioner was convicted [of] transmitting wagering information by telephone from Los Angeles to Miami and Boston in violation of a federal statute. At trial the Government was permitted, over the petitioner's objection, to introduce evidence of the petitioner's end of telephone conversations, overheard by FBI agents who had attached an electronic listening and recording device to the outside of the public telephone booth from which he had placed his calls. In affirming his conviction, the Court of Appeals rejected the contention that the recordings had been obtained in violation of the Fourth Amendment, because "[t]here was no physical entrance into the area occupied by [the petitioner]." We granted certiorari in order to consider the constitutional questions thus presented.

The petitioner has phrased those questions as follows:

"A. Whether a public telephone booth is a constitutionally protected area so that evidence obtained by attaching an electronic listening recording device to the top of such a booth is obtained in violation of the right to privacy of the user of the booth.

"B. Whether physical penetration of a constitutionally protected area is necessary before a search and seizure can be said to be violative of the Fourth Amendment to the United States Constitution."

We decline to adopt this formulation of the issues. In the first place the correct solution of Fourth Amendment problems is not necessarily promoted by incantation of the phrase "constitutionally protected area." Secondly, the Fourth Amendment cannot be translated into a general constitutional "right to privacy." That Amendment protects individual privacy against certain kinds of governmental intrusion, but its protections go further, and often have nothing to do with privacy at all. Other provisions of the Constitution protect personal privacy from other forms of governmental invasion. But the protection of a person's *general* right to privacy—his right to be let alone by other people—is, like the protection of his property and of his very life, left largely to the law of the individual States.

Because of the misleading way the issues have been formulated, the parties have attached great significance to the characterization of the telephone booth from which the petitioner placed his calls. The petitioner has strenuously argued that the booth was a "constitutionally protected area." The Government has maintained with equal vigor that it was not. But this effort to decide whether or not a given "area," viewed in the abstract, is "constitutionally protected" deflects attention from the problem presented by this case. For the Fourth Amendment protects people, not places. What a person knowingly exposes to the public, even in his own home or office, is not a subject of Fourth Amendment protection. [But] what he seeks to preserve as private, even in an area accessible to the public, may be constitutionally protected. * * *

The Government stresses the fact that the telephone booth from which the petitioner made his calls was constructed partly of glass, so that he was as visible after he entered it as he would have been if he had remained outside. But what he sought to exclude when he entered the booth was not the intruding eye—it was the uninvited ear. He did not shed his right to do so simply because he made his calls from a place where he might be seen. No less than an individual in a business office, in a friend's apartment, or in a taxicab, a person in a telephone booth may rely upon the protection of the Fourth Amendment. One who occupies it, shuts the door behind him, and pays the toll that permits him to place a call, is surely entitled to assume that the words he utters into the mouthpiece will not be broadcast to the world. To read the Constitution more narrowly is to ignore the vital role that the public telephone has come to play in private communication.

The Government contends, however, that the activities of its agents in this case should not be tested by Fourth Amendment requirements, for the surveillance technique they employed involved no physical penetration of the telephone booth from which the petitioner placed his calls.

[Although] a closely divided Court supposed in *Olmstead v. United States,* [p. 128 supra] that surveillance without any trespass and without the seizure of any material object fell outside the ambit of the Constitution, we have since departed from the narrow view on which that decision rested. Indeed, we have expressly held that the Fourth Amendment governs not only the seizure of tangible items, but extends as well to the recording of oral statements overheard without any "technical trespass [under] local property law." Once this much is acknowledged, and once it is recognized that the Fourth Amendment protects people—and not simply "areas"—against unreasonable searches and seizures it becomes clear that the reach of that Amendment cannot turn upon the presence or absence of a physical intrusion into any given enclosure.

We conclude that the underpinnings of *Olmstead* have been so eroded by our subsequent decisions that the "trespass" doctrine there enunciated can no longer be regarded as controlling. The Government's activities in electronically listening to and recording the petitioner's words violated the privacy upon which he justifiably relied while using the telephone booth and thus constituted a "search and seizure" [a] within the meaning of the Fourth Amendment.[b] The fact that the

a. This does not mean that privacy is the *only* interest protected by the Fourth Amendment, or that the Amendment comes into play *only* if there is both a "search" and a "seizure." The Fourth Amendment also protects the interests in possession of property and liberty of person, as in *United States v. Place,* p. 155 infra (detention of traveler's luggage 90 minutes was an unreasonable seizure in two respects, as it constituted a deprivation of defendant's "possessory interest in his luggage" and his "liberty interest in proceeding with his itinerary"). In *Soldal v. Cook County,* 506 U.S. 56, 113 S.Ct. 538, 121 L.Ed.2d 450 (1992), where sheriff's deputies knowingly participated in an unlawful eviction which involved hauling

b. See note b on page 144.

electronic device employed to achieve that end did not happen to penetrate the wall of the booth can have no constitutional significance.

The question remaining for decision, then, is whether the search and seizure conducted in this case complied with constitutional standards. In that regard, the Government's position is that its agents acted in an entirely defensible manner: They did not begin their electronic surveillance until investigation of the petitioner's activities had established a strong probability that he was using the telephone in question to transmit gambling information to persons in other States, in violation of federal law. Moreover, the surveillance was limited, both in scope and in duration to the specific purpose of establishing the contents of the petitioner's unlawful telephonic communications. The agents confined their surveillance to the brief periods during which he used the telephone booth, and they took great care to overhear only the conversations of the petitioner himself.

Accepting this account of the Government's actions as accurate, it is clear that this surveillance was so narrowly circumscribed that a duly authorized magistrate, properly notified of the need for such investigation, specifically informed of the basis on which it was to proceed, and clearly apprised of the precise intrusion it would entail, could constitutionally have authorized, with appropriate safeguards, the very limited search and seizure that the Government asserts in fact took place.[c]

the plaintiff's trailer home off the landlord's property, the court of appeals ruled that the Fourth Amendment offers no protection where, as here, the intrusion upon a possessory interest was unaccompanied by an intrusion upon a privacy interest. A unanimous Supreme Court reversed, holding "that seizures of property are subject to Fourth Amendment scrutiny even though no search within the meaning of the Amendment has taken place."

b. More precisely, it could be said that if the government's activities have violated *anyone's* justified expectation of privacy, then that activity constitutes a Fourth Amendment search. However, it has long been established that a defendant in a criminal case who is seeking the suppression of evidence on Fourth Amendment grounds may invoke the violation of his own rights but not the rights of third parties; this concept has traditionally been referred to as "standing." In more recent years the *Katz* analysis has been utilized on that issue: a defendant has standing only if the government violated the privacy on which *he* (as opposed to some other person) justifiably relied. Illustrative is *Rakas v. Illinois*, 439 U.S. 128 (1978), holding that passengers in a car who did not challenge the stopping of the vehicle in which they were riding but only the subsequent search under the seat and in the glove compartment lacked standing to challenge that search; because they asserted no property or possessory interest in the automobile searched or in the property seized, they had not shown they had a legitimate expectation of privacy in the places searched.

c. The Court went on to distinguish the present situation from the kind of electronic surveillance possible under a New York statute which was invalidated in *Berger v. New York*, 388 U.S. 41, 87 S.Ct. 1873, 18 L.Ed.2d 1040 (1967), as a "blanket grant of permission to eavesdrop [without] adequate supervision or protective procedures." That statute, the Court explained in *Berger*, (1) permitted a court order to issue merely on reasonable grounds to believe that evidence of crime may be obtained, without specifying what crime has been or is being committed and without describing what conversations are to be overheard, thus failing to "particularly [describe] the place to be searched, and the person or things to be seized," as required by the Fourth Amendment; (2) permitted installation and operation of surveillance equipment for 60 days, "the equivalent of a series of intrusions, searches and seizures pursuant to a single showing of probable cause"; (3) permitted renewal of the order on the basis of the original grounds on which the initial order was issued, deemed "insufficient without a showing of present probable cause for continuance of the eavesdrop"; (4) placed no termination on the eavesdrop once the conversation sought is seized, as "this is left entirely to the discretion of the officer"; and (5) did not provide for a return on the warrant, "thereby leaving full discretion in the officer as to the use of seized conversations of innocent as well as guilty parties."

Nonconsensual electronic surveillance is authorized in limited circumstances by Title III of the Omnibus Crime Control and Safe Streets Act of 1968, 18 U.S.C.A. §§ 2510–2520. Although the Supreme Court has never passed upon the Act, it has been consistently upheld by the lower courts. Consequently, the focus

[The] Government * * * urges the creation of a new exception to cover this case. It argues that surveillance of a telephone booth should be exempted from the usual requirement of advance authorization by a magistrate upon a showing of probable cause. We cannot agree. Omission of such authorization "bypasses the safeguards provided by an objective predetermination of probable cause, and substitutes instead the far less reliable procedure of an after-the-event justification for [the] search, too likely to be subtly influenced by the familiar shortcomings of hindsight judgment." And bypassing a neutral predetermination of the *scope* of a search leaves individuals secure from Fourth Amendment violations "only in the discretion of the police."

These considerations do not vanish when the search in question is transferred from the setting of a home, an office, or a hotel room, to that of a telephone booth. Wherever a man may be, he is entitled to know that he will remain free from unreasonable searches and seizures. The government agents here ignored "the procedure of antecedent justification [that] is central to the Fourth Amendment," procedure that we hold to be a constitutional precondition of the kind of electronic surveillance involved in this case. * * *

Judgment reversed.[d]

JUSTICE HARLAN, concurring.

* * * As the Court's opinion states, "The Fourth Amendment protects people, not places." The question, however, is what protection it affords to those people. Generally, as here, the answer to that question requires reference to a "place." My understanding of the rule that has emerged from prior decisions is that there is a twofold requirement, first that a person have exhibited an actual (subjective) expectation of privacy and, second, that the expectation be one that society is prepared to recognize as "reasonable." Thus a man's home is, for most purposes, a place where he expects privacy, but objects, activities, or statements that he exposes to the "plain view" of outsiders are not "protected" because no intention to keep them to himself has been exhibited. On the other hand, conversations in the open would not be protected against being overheard, for the expectation of privacy under the circumstances would be unreasonable. * * *

The critical fact in this case is that "[o]ne who occupies it, [a telephone booth] shuts the door behind him, and pays the toll that permits him to place a call, is surely entitled to assume" that his conversation is not being intercepted. The point is not that the booth is "accessible to the public" at other times, but that it is a temporarily private place whose momentary occupants' expectations of freedom from intrusion are recognized as reasonable. * * *

JUSTICE BLACK, dissenting.

* * * Tapping telephone wires, of course, was an unknown possibility at the time the Fourth Amendment was adopted. But eavesdropping (and wiretapping is nothing more than eavesdropping by telephone) was "an ancient practice which at common law was condemned as a nuisance. In those days the eavesdropper listened by naked ear under the eaves of houses or their windows, or beyond their walls seeking out private discourse." There can be no doubt that the Framers were aware of this practice, and if they had desired to outlaw or restrict the use of evidence obtained by eavesdropping, I believe that they would have used the

---

of litigation in recent years has been upon whether particular wiretapping and electronic eavesdropping activities conform to the requirements of the Act.

d. The concurring opinions of Justice Douglas and Justice White are omitted. Justice Marshall did not participate.

appropriate language to do so in the Fourth Amendment. They certainly would not have left such a task to the ingenuity of language-stretching judges.

[By] clever word juggling the Court finds it plausible to argue that language aimed specifically at searches and seizures of things that can be searched and seized may, to protect privacy, be applied to eavesdropped evidence of conversations that can neither be searched nor seized. Few things happen to an individual that do not affect his privacy in one way or another. Thus, by arbitrarily substituting the Court's language, designed to protect privacy, for the Constitution's language, designed to protect against unreasonable searches and seizures, the Court has made the Fourth Amendment its vehicle for holding all laws violative of the Constitution which offend the Court's broadest concept of privacy. * * *

The Fourth Amendment protects privacy only to the extent that it prohibits unreasonable searches and seizures of "persons, houses, papers and effects." No general right is created by the Amendment so as to give this Court the unlimited power to hold unconstitutional everything which affects privacy. Certainly the Framers, well acquainted as they were with the excesses of governmental power, did not intend to grant this Court such omnipotent lawmaking authority as that. The history of governments proves that it is dangerous to freedom to repose such powers in courts. * * *

CALIFORNIA v. GREENWOOD

486 U.S. 35, 108 S.Ct. 1625, 100 L.Ed.2d 30 (1988).

JUSTICE WHITE delivered the opinion of the Court. * * *

In early 1984, Investigator Jenny Stracner of the Laguna Beach Police Department received information indicating that respondent Greenwood might be engaged in narcotics trafficking. * * *

On April 6, 1984, Stracner asked the neighborhood's regular trash collector to pick up the plastic garbage bags that Greenwood had left on the curb in front of his house and to turn the bags over to her without mixing their contents with garbage from other houses. The trash collector cleaned his truck bin of other refuse, collected the garbage bags from the street in front of Greenwood's house, and turned the bags over to Stracner. The officer searched through the rubbish and found items indicative of narcotics use. She recited the information that she had gleaned from the trash search in an affidavit in support of a warrant to search Greenwood's home.

Police officers encountered both respondents at the house later that day when they arrived to execute the warrant. The police discovered quantities of cocaine and hashish during their search of the house. Respondents were arrested on felony narcotics charges. They subsequently posted bail.

The police continued to receive reports of many late-night visitors to the Greenwood house. On May 4, Investigator Robert Rahaeuser obtained Greenwood's garbage from the regular trash collector in the same manner as had Stracner. The garbage again contained evidence of narcotics use.

Rahaeuser secured another search warrant for Greenwood's home based on the information from the second trash search. The police found more narcotics and evidence of narcotics trafficking when they executed the warrant. Greenwood was again arrested.

The Superior Court dismissed the charges against respondents on the authority of *People v. Krivda,* 5 Cal.3d 357, 96 Cal.Rptr. 62, 486 P.2d 1262 (1971), which held that warrantless trash searches violate the Fourth Amendment and the California Constitution. The court found that the police would not have had probable cause to search the Greenwood home without the evidence obtained from the trash searches.

The Court of Appeal affirmed. * * *

The California Supreme Court denied the State's petition for review of the Court of Appeal's decision. We granted certiorari, and now reverse.

The warrantless search and seizure of the garbage bags left at the curb outside the Greenwood house would violate the Fourth Amendment only if respondents manifested a subjective expectation of privacy in their garbage that society accepts as objectively reasonable. Respondents do not disagree with this standard.

They assert, however, that they had, and exhibited, an expectation of privacy with respect to the trash that was searched by the police: The trash, which was placed on the street for collection at a fixed time, was contained in opaque plastic bags, which the garbage collector was expected to pick up, mingle with the trash of others, and deposit at the garbage dump. The trash was only temporarily on the street, and there was little likelihood that it would be inspected by anyone.

It may well be that respondents did not expect that the contents of their garbage bags would become known to the police or other members of the public. An expectation of privacy does not give rise to Fourth Amendment protection, however, unless society is prepared to accept that expectation as objectively reasonable.

Here, we conclude that respondents exposed their garbage to the public sufficiently to defeat their claim to Fourth Amendment protection. It is common knowledge that plastic garbage bags left on or at the side of a public street are readily accessible to animals, children, scavengers, snoops,[4] and other members of the public. Moreover, respondents placed their refuse at the curb for the express purpose of conveying it to a third party, the trash collector, who might himself have sorted through respondents' trash or permitted others, such as the police, to do so. Accordingly, having deposited their garbage "in an area particularly suited for public inspection and, in a manner of speaking, public consumption, for the express purpose of having strangers take it," respondents could have had no reasonable expectation of privacy in the inculpatory items that they discarded.

Furthermore, as we have held, the police cannot reasonably be expected to avert their eyes from evidence of criminal activity that could have been observed by any member of the public. Hence, "[w]hat a person knowingly exposes to the public, even in his own home or office, is not a subject of Fourth Amendment protection." *Katz v. United States.* We held in *Smith v. Maryland,* 442 U.S. 735, 99 S.Ct. 2577, 61 L.Ed.2d 220 (1979), for example, that the police did not violate the Fourth Amendment by causing a pen register to be installed at the telephone company's offices to record the telephone numbers dialed by a criminal suspect.

4. Even the refuse of prominent Americans has not been invulnerable. In 1975, for example, a reporter for a weekly tabloid seized five bags of garbage from the sidewalk outside the home of Secretary of State Henry Kissinger. Washington Post, July 9, 1975, p. A1, col. 8. A newspaper editorial criticizing this journalistic "trashpicking" observed that "[e]vidently ... 'everybody does it.'" Washington Post, July 10, 1975, p. A18, col. 1. We of course do not, as the dissent implies, "bas[e] [our] conclusion" that individuals have no reasonable expectation of privacy in their garbage on this "sole incident."

An individual has no legitimate expectation of privacy in the numbers dialed on his telephone, we reasoned, because he voluntarily conveys those numbers to the telephone company when he uses the telephone. Again, we observed that "a person has no legitimate expectation of privacy in information he voluntarily turns over to third parties." * * *

Our conclusion that society would not accept as reasonable respondents' claim to an expectation of privacy in trash left for collection in an area accessible to the public is reinforced by the unanimous rejection of similar claims by the Federal Courts of Appeals. In addition, of those state appellate courts that have considered the issue, the vast majority have held that the police may conduct warrantless searches and seizures of garbage discarded in public areas. * * *a

JUSTICE BRENNAN, with whom JUSTICE MARSHALL joins, dissenting.

[The] Framers of the Fourth Amendment understood that "unreasonable searches" of "paper[s] and effects"—no less than "unreasonable searches" of "person[s] and houses"—infringe privacy. [In] short, so long as a package is "closed against inspection," the Fourth Amendment protects its contents, "wherever they may be," and the police must obtain a warrant to search it just "as is required when papers are subjected to search in one's own household." * * *

Our precedent, therefore, leaves no room to doubt that had respondents been carrying their personal effects in opaque, sealed plastic bags—identical to the ones they placed on the curb—their privacy would have been protected from warrantless police intrusion. * * *

Respondents deserve no less protection just because Greenwood used the bags to discard rather than to transport his personal effects. Their contents are not inherently any less private, and Greenwood's decision to discard them, at least in the manner in which he did, does not diminish his expectation of privacy.[2]

A trash bag, like any of the above-mentioned containers, "is a common repository for one's personal effects" and, even more than many of them, is "therefore * * * inevitably associated with the expectation of privacy." [A] single bag of trash testifies eloquently to the eating, reading, and recreational habits of the person who produced it. A search of trash, like a search of the bedroom, can relate intimate details about sexual practices, health, and personal hygiene. Like rifling through desk drawers or intercepting phone calls, rummaging through trash can divulge the target's financial and professional status, political affiliations and inclinations, private thoughts, personal relationships, and romantic interests. It cannot be doubted that a sealed trash bag harbors telling evidence of the "intimate activity associated with the 'sanctity of a man's home and the privacies of life,' " which the Fourth Amendment is designed to protect.

The Court properly rejects the State's attempt to distinguish trash searches from other searches on the theory that trash is abandoned and therefore not entitled to an expectation of privacy. As the author of the Court's opinion

a. Justice Kennedy took no part in the consideration or decision of this case.

2. Both to support its position that society recognizes no reasonable privacy interest in sealed, opaque trash bags and to refute the prediction that "society will be shocked to learn" of that conclusion, the Court relies heavily upon a collection of lower court cases finding no Fourth Amendment bar to trash searches. But the authority that leads the Court to be "distinctively unimpressed" with our position, is itself impressively undistinguished. Of 11 Federal Court of Appeals cases cited by the Court, at least two are factually or legally distinguishable, and seven rely entirely or almost entirely on an abandonment theory that the Court has discredited. A reading of the Court's collection of state-court cases reveals an equally unimpressive pattern.

observed last Term, a defendant's "property interest [in trash] does not settle the matter for Fourth Amendment purposes, for the reach of the Fourth Amendment is not determined by state property law." In evaluating the reasonableness of Greenwood's expectation that his sealed trash bags would not be invaded, the Court has held that we must look to "understandings that are recognized and permitted by society." Most of us, I believe, would be incensed to discover a meddler—whether a neighbor, a reporter, or a detective—scrutinizing our sealed trash containers to discover some detail of our personal lives. That was, quite naturally, the reaction to the sole incident on which the Court bases its conclusion that "snoops" and the like defeat the expectation of privacy in trash. When a tabloid reporter examined then-Secretary of State Henry Kissinger's trash and published his findings, Kissinger was "really revolted" by the intrusion and his wife suffered "grave anguish." N.Y. Times, July 9, 1975, p. A1, col. 8. The public response roundly condemning the reporter demonstrates that society not only recognized those reactions as reasonable, but shared them as well. Commentators variously characterized his conduct as "a disgusting invasion of personal privacy," Flieger, Investigative Trash, U.S. News & World Report, July 28, 1975, p. 72 (editor's page); "indefensible [as] civilized behavior," Washington Post, July 10, 1975, p. A18, col. 1 (editorial); and contrary to "the way decent people behave in relation to each other," ibid. * * *

That is not to deny that isolated intrusions into opaque, sealed trash containers occur. When, acting on their own, "animals, children, scavengers, snoops, [or] other members of the general public," *actually* rummage through a bag of trash and expose its contents to plain view, "police cannot reasonably be expected to avert their eyes from evidence of criminal activity that could have been observed by any member of the public."

Had Greenwood flaunted his intimate activity by strewing his trash all over the curb for all to see, or had some nongovernmental intruder invaded his privacy and done the same, I could accept the Court's conclusion that an expectation of privacy would have been unreasonable. Similarly, had police searching the city dump run across incriminating evidence that, despite commingling with the trash of others, still retained its identity as Greenwood's, we would have a different case. But all that Greenwood "exposed [to] the public" were the exteriors of several opaque, sealed containers.

The mere *possibility* that unwelcome meddlers *might* open and rummage through the containers does not negate the expectation of privacy in its contents any more than the possibility of a burglary negates an expectation of privacy in the home; or the possibility of a private intrusion negates an expectation of privacy in an unopened package; or the possibility that an operator will listen in on a telephone conversation negates an expectation of privacy in the words spoken on the telephone. "What a person * * * seeks to preserve as private, *even in an area accessible to the public,* may be constitutionally protected." *Katz.* We have therefore repeatedly rejected attempts to justify a State's invasion of privacy on the ground that the privacy is not absolute. See *Chapman v. United States,* 365 U.S. 610, 81 S.Ct. 776, 5 L.Ed.2d 828 (1961) (search of a house invaded tenant's Fourth Amendment rights even though landlord had authority to enter house for some purposes); *Stoner v. California,* 376 U.S. 483, 84 S.Ct. 889, 11 L.Ed.2d 856 (1964) (implicit consent to janitorial personnel to enter motel room does not amount to consent to police search of room); *O'Connor v. Ortega,* 480 U.S. 709, 107 S.Ct. 1492, 94 L.Ed.2d 714 (1987) (a government employee has a reasonable expectation of privacy in his office, even though "it is the nature of government offices that others—such as fellow employees, supervisors, consensual visitors, and the general public—may have frequent access to an individual's office"). * * *

Nor is it dispositive that "respondents placed their refuse at the curb for the express purpose of conveying it to a third party, [who] might himself have sorted through respondents' trash or permitted others, such as police, to do so." In the first place, Greenwood can hardly be faulted for leaving trash on his curb when a county ordinance commanded him to do so and prohibited him from disposing of it in any other way. * * * More importantly, even the voluntary relinquishment of possession or control over an effect does not necessarily amount to a relinquishment of a privacy expectation in it. Were it otherwise, a letter or package would lose all Fourth Amendment protection when placed in a mail box or other depository with the "express purpose" of entrusting it to the postal officer or a private carrier; those bailees are just as likely as trash collectors (and certainly have greater incentive) to "sor[t] through" the personal effects entrusted to them, "or permi[t] others, such as police to do so." Yet, it has been clear for at least 110 years that the possibility of such an intrusion does not justify a warrantless search by police in the first instance. * * *

FLORIDA v. RILEY

488 U.S. 445, 109 S.Ct. 693, 102 L.Ed.2d 835 (1989).

Justice White announced the judgment of the Court and delivered an opinion, in which The Chief Justice, Justice Scalia and Justice Kennedy join.

On certification to it by a lower state court, the Florida Supreme Court addressed the following question: "Whether surveillance of the interior of a partially covered greenhouse in a residential backyard from the vantage point of a helicopter located 400 feet above the greenhouse constitutes a 'search' for which a warrant is required under the Fourth Amendment and Article I, Section 12 of the Florida Constitution." The court answered the question in the affirmative, and we granted the State's petition for certiorari challenging that conclusion. * * *

We agree with the State's submission that our decision in *California v. Ciraolo*, 476 U.S. 207, 106 S.Ct. 1809, 90 L.Ed.2d 210 (1986), controls this case. There, acting on a tip, the police inspected the back yard of a particular house while flying in a fixed-wing aircraft at 1,000 feet. With the naked-eye the officers saw what they concluded was marijuana growing in the yard. A search warrant was obtained on the strength of this airborne inspection, and marijuana plants were found. The trial court refused to suppress this evidence, but a state appellate court held that the inspection violated the Fourth and Fourteenth Amendments of the United States Constitution and that the warrant was therefore invalid. We in turn reversed, holding that the inspection was not a search subject to the Fourth Amendment. We recognized that the yard was within the curtilage of the house, that a fence shielded the yard from observation from the street and that the occupant had a subjective expectation of privacy. We held, however, that such an expectation was not reasonable and not one "that society is prepared to honor." * * * "In an age where private and commercial flight in the public airways is routine, it is unreasonable for respondent to expect that his marijuana plants were constitutionally protected from being observed with the naked eye from an altitude of 1,000 feet. The Fourth Amendment simply does not require the police traveling in the public airways at this altitude to obtain a warrant in order to observe what is visible to the naked eye."

We arrive at the same conclusion in the present case. * * *

Nor on the facts before us, does it make a difference for Fourth Amendment purposes that the helicopter was flying at 400 feet when the officer saw what was growing in the greenhouse through the partially open roof and sides of the structure. We would have a different case if flying at that altitude had been contrary to law or regulation. But helicopters are not bound by the lower limits of the navigable airspace allowed to other aircraft. Any member of the public could legally have been flying over Riley's property in a helicopter at the altitude of 400 feet and could have observed Riley's greenhouse. The police officer did no more. This is not to say that an inspection of the curtilage of a house from an aircraft will always pass muster under the Fourth Amendment simply because the plane is within the navigable airspace specified by law. But it is of obvious importance that the helicopter in this case was *not* violating the law, and there is nothing in the record or before us to suggest that helicopters flying at 400 feet are sufficiently rare in this country to lend substance to respondent's claim that he reasonably anticipated that his greenhouse would not be subject to observation from that altitude. Neither is there any intimation here that the helicopter interfered with respondent's normal use of the greenhouse or of other parts of the curtilage. As far as this record reveals, no intimate details connected with the use of the home or curtilage were observed, and there was no undue noise, no wind, dust, or threat of injury. In these circumstances, there was no violation of the Fourth Amendment. * * *

JUSTICE O'CONNOR, concurring in the judgment. * * *

In determining whether Riley had a reasonable expectation of privacy from aerial observation, the relevant inquiry after *Ciraolo* is not whether the helicopter was where it had a right to be under FAA regulations. Rather, consistent with *Katz*, we must ask whether the helicopter was in the public airways at an altitude at which members of the public travel with sufficient regularity that Riley's expectation of privacy from aerial observation was not "one that society is prepared to recognize as 'reasonable.' " * * *

Because there is reason to believe that there is considerable public use of airspace at altitudes of 400 feet and above, and because Riley introduced no evidence to the contrary before the Florida courts, I conclude that Riley's expectation that his curtilage was protected from naked-eye aerial observation from that altitude was not a reasonable one. However, public use of altitudes lower than that—particularly public observations from helicopters circling over the curtilage of a home—may be sufficiently rare that police surveillance from such altitudes would violate reasonable expectations of privacy, despite compliance with FAA air safety regulations.

JUSTICE BRENNAN, with whom JUSTICE MARSHALL and JUSTICE STEVENS, join, dissenting.

[Under] the plurality's exceedingly grudging Fourth Amendment theory, the expectation of privacy is defeated if a single member of the public could conceivably position herself to see into the area in question without doing anything illegal. It is defeated whatever the difficulty a person would have in so positioning herself, and however infrequently anyone would in fact do so. In taking this view the plurality ignores the very essence of *Katz*. * * *

It is a curious notion that the reach of the Fourth Amendment can be so largely defined by administrative regulations issued for purposes of flight safety. It is more curious still that the plurality relies to such an extent on the legality of the officer's act, when we have consistently refused to equate police violation of the law with infringement of the Fourth Amendment.[3] But the plurality's willingness to end its inquiry when it finds that the officer was in a position he had a right to be in is misguided for an even more fundamental reason. Finding determinative the fact that the officer was where he had a right to be is, at bottom, an attempt to analogize surveillance from a helicopter to surveillance by a police officer standing on a public road and viewing evidence of crime through an open window or a gap in a fence. In such a situation, the occupant of the home may be said to lack any reasonable expectation of privacy in what can be seen from that road—even if, in fact, people rarely pass that way.

The police officer positioned 400 feet above Riley's backyard was not, however, standing on a public road. The vantage point he enjoyed was not one any citizen could readily share. His ability to see over Riley's fence depended on his use of a very expensive and sophisticated piece of machinery to which few ordinary citizens have access. In such circumstances it makes no more sense to rely on the legality of the officer's position in the skies than it would to judge the constitutionality of the wiretap in *Katz* by the legality of the officer's position outside the telephone booth. The simply inquiry whether the police officer had the legal right to be in the position from which he made his observations cannot suffice, for we cannot assume that Riley's curtilage was so open to the observations of passersby in the skies that he retained little privacy or personal security to be lost to police surveillance. The question before us must be not whether the police were where they had a right to be, but whether public observation of Riley's curtilage was so commonplace that Riley's expectation of privacy in his backyard could not be considered reasonable. * * *

What separates me from Justice O'Connor is essentially an empirical matter concerning the extent of public use of the airspace at that altitude, together with the question of how to resolve that issue. I do not think the constitutional claims should fail simply because "there is reason to believe" that there is "considerable" public flying this close to earth or because Riley "introduced no evidence to the contrary before the Florida courts." * * * I think we could take judicial notice that, while there may be an occasional privately owned helicopter that flies over populated areas at an altitude of 400 feet, such flights are a rarity and are almost entirely limited to approaching or leaving airports or to reporting traffic congestion near major roadways. And, as the concurring opinion agrees, the extent of police surveillance traffic cannot serve as a bootstrap to demonstrate public use of the airspace.

If, however, we are to resolve the issue by considering whether the appropriate party carried its burden of proof, I again think that Riley must prevail. Because the State has greater access to information concerning customary flight patterns and because the coercive power of the State ought not be brought to bear in cases in which it is unclear whether the prosecution is a product of an unconstitutional, warrantless search, the burden of proof properly rests with the State and not with the individual defendant. The State quite clearly has not carried this burden. * * *

Justice Blackmun, dissenting.

3. In *Oliver v. United States*, 466 U.S. 170, 104 S.Ct. 1735, 80 L.Ed.2d 214 (1984), for example, we held that police officers who trespassed upon posted and fenced private land did not violate the Fourth Amendment, despite the fact that their action was subject to criminal sanctions. We noted that the interests vindicated by the Fourth Amendment were not identical with those served by the common law of trespass.

[B]ecause I believe that private helicopters rarely fly over curtilages at an altitude of 400 feet, I would impose upon the prosecution the burden or proving contrary facts necessary to show that Riley lacked a reasonable expectation of privacy. Indeed, I would establish this burden of proof for any helicopter surveillance case in which the flight occurred below 1000 feet—in other words, for any aerial surveillance case not governed by the Court's decision in *California v. Ciraolo.*

In this case, the prosecution did not meet this burden of proof, as Justice Brennan notes. This failure should compel a finding that a Fourth Amendment search occurred. But because our prior cases gave the parties little guidance on the burden of proof issue, I would remand this case to allow the prosecution an opportunity to meet this burden. * * *

UNITED STATES v. KARO

468 U.S. 705, 104 S.Ct. 3296, 82 L.Ed.2d 530 (1984).

JUSTICE WHITE delivered the opinion of the Court.

In *United States v. Knotts,* 460 U.S. 276, 103 S.Ct. 1081, 75 L.Ed.2d 55 (1983), we held that the warrantless monitoring of an electronic tracking device ("beeper")[1] inside a container of chemicals did not violate the Fourth Amendment when it revealed no information that could not have been obtained through visual surveillance. In this case, we are called upon to address two questions left unresolved in *Knotts:* (1) whether installation of a beeper in a container of chemicals with the consent of the original owner constitutes a search or seizure within the meaning of the Fourth Amendment when the container is delivered to a buyer having no knowledge of the presence of the beeper, and (2) whether monitoring of a beeper falls within the ambit of the Fourth Amendment when it reveals information that could not have been obtained through visual surveillance.

In August 1980 Agent Rottinger of the Drug Enforcement Administration (DEA) learned that respondents James Karo, Richard Horton, and William Harley had ordered 50 gallons of ether from government informant Carl Muehlenweg of Graphic Photo Design in Albuquerque, New Mexico. Muehlenweg told Rottinger that the ether was to be used to extract cocaine from clothing that had been imported into the United States. The Government obtained a court order authorizing the installation and monitoring of a beeper in one of the cans of ether. * * *

At about 6:00 p.m. on February 6, * * * two vehicles were under both physical and electronic surveillance. When the vehicles arrived at a house in Taos rented by Horton, Harley, and Michael Steele, the agents did not maintain tight surveillance for fear of detection. When the vehicles left the Taos residence, agents determined using the beeper monitor that the beeper can was still inside the house. Again on February 7, the beeper revealed that the ether can was still on the premises. * * * On February 8, the agents applied for and obtained a warrant to search the Taos residence based in part on information derived through use of the beeper. The warrant was executed on February 10, 1981, and Horton, Harley, Steele, and Evan Roth were arrested, and cocaine and laboratory equipment were seized.

---

1. "A beeper is a radio transmitter, usually battery operated, which emits periodic signals   that can be picked up by a radio receiver."

[The] District Court granted respondents' pre-trial motion to suppress the evidence seized from the Taos residence on the grounds that the initial warrant to install the beeper was invalid and that the Taos seizure was the tainted fruit of an unauthorized installation and monitoring of that beeper. The United States appealed but did not challenge the invalidation of the initial warrant. The Court of Appeals affirmed, holding that a warrant was required to install the beeper in one of the 10 cans of ether and to monitor it in private dwellings and storage lockers. The warrant for the search in Taos and the resulting seizure were tainted by the prior illegal conduct of the Government.

[Because] the judgment below in favor of Karo rested in major part on the conclusion that the installation violated his Fourth Amendment rights and that any information obtained from monitoring the beeper was tainted by the initial illegality, we must deal with the legality of the warrantless installation. It is clear that the actual placement of the beeper into the can violated no one's Fourth Amendment rights. The can into which the beeper was placed belonged at the time to the DEA, and by no stretch of the imagination could it be said that respondents then had any legitimate expectation of privacy in it. The ether and the original 10 cans, on the other hand, belonged to, and were in the possession of, Muehlenweg, who had given his consent to any invasion of those items that occurred. Thus, even if there had been no substitution of cans and the agents had placed the beeper into one of the original 10 cans, Muehlenweg's consent was sufficient to validate the placement of the beeper in the can.

[The] mere transfer to Karo of a can containing an unmonitored beeper infringed no privacy interest. It conveyed no information that Karo wished to keep private, for it conveyed no information at all. To be sure, it created a *potential* for an invasion of privacy, but we have never held that potential, as opposed to actual, invasions of privacy constitute searches for purposes of the Fourth Amendment.   * * *

We likewise do not believe that the transfer of the container constituted a seizure. A "seizure" of property occurs when "there is some meaningful interference with an individual's possessory interests in that property." Although the can may have contained an unknown and unwanted foreign object, it cannot be said that anyone's possessory interest was interfered with in a meaningful way. At most, there was a technical trespass on the space occupied by the beeper. The existence of a physical trespass is only marginally relevant to the question of whether the Fourth Amendment has been violated, however, for an actual trespass is neither necessary nor sufficient to establish a constitutional violation.

[In] *Knotts* law enforcement officials, with the consent of the seller, installed a beeper in a five-gallon can of chloroform and monitored the beeper after delivery of the can to the buyer in Minneapolis, Minnesota. Although there was partial visual surveillance as the automobile containing the can moved along the public highways, the beeper enabled the officers to locate the can in the area of a cabin near Shell Lake, Wisconsin, and it was this information that provided the basis for the issuance of a search warrant. As the case came to us, the installation of the beeper was not challenged; only the monitoring was at issue. The Court held that since the movements of the automobile and the arrival of the can containing the beeper in the area of the cabin could have been observed by the naked eye, no Fourth Amendment violation was committed by monitoring the beeper during the trip to the cabin. In *Knotts,* the record did not show that the beeper was monitored while the can containing it was inside the cabin, and we therefore had no occasion to consider whether a constitutional violation would have occurred had the fact been otherwise.

Here, there is no gainsaying that the beeper was used to locate the ether in a specific house in Taos, New Mexico, and that that information was in turn used to secure a warrant for the search of the house.

[At] the risk of belaboring the obvious, private residences are places in which the individual normally expects privacy free of governmental intrusion not authorized by a warrant, and that expectation is plainly one that society is prepared to recognize as justifiable. Our cases have not deviated from this basic Fourth Amendment principle. Searches and seizures inside a home without a warrant are presumptively unreasonable absent exigent circumstances. In this case, had a DEA agent thought it useful to enter the Taos residence to verify that the ether was actually in the house and had he done so surreptitiously and without a warrant, there is little doubt that he would have engaged in an unreasonable search within the meaning of the Fourth Amendment. For purposes of the Amendment, the result is the same where, without a warrant, the Government surreptitiously employs an electronic device to obtain information that it could not have obtained by observation from outside the curtilage of the house. The beeper tells the agent that a particular article is actually located at a particular time in the private residence and is in the possession of the person or persons whose residence is being surveilled.[a] Even if visual surveillance has revealed that the article to which the beeper is attached has entered the house, the later monitoring not only verifies the officers' observations but also establishes that the article remains on the premises. Here, for example, the beeper was monitored for a significant period after the arrival of the ether in Taos and before the application for a warrant to search. * * *

We cannot accept the Government's contention that it should be completely free from the constraints of the Fourth Amendment to determine by means of an electronic device, without a warrant and without probable cause or reasonable suspicion, whether a particular article—or a person, for that matter—is in an individual's home at a particular time. Indiscriminate monitoring of property that has been withdrawn from public view would present far too serious a threat to privacy interests in the home to escape entirely some sort of Fourth Amendment oversight.

---

a. Compare *United States v. Place*, 462 U.S. 696, 103 S.Ct. 2637, 77 L.Ed.2D 110 (1983), dealing with a temporary seizure of luggage at an airport so that it could be brought into contact with a drug detection dog. The majority declared "that a person possesses a privacy interest in the contents of personal luggage that is protected by the Fourth Amendment. A 'canine sniff' by a well-trained narcotics detection dog, however, does not require opening the luggage. It does not expose noncontraband items that otherwise would remain hidden from public view, as does, for example, an officer's rummaging through the contents of the luggage. Thus, the manner in which information is obtained through this investigative technique is much less intrusive than a typical search. Moreover, the sniff discloses only the presence or absence of narcotics, a contraband item. Thus, despite the fact that the sniff tells the authorities something about the contents of the luggage, the information obtained is limited. This limited disclosure also ensures that the owner of the property is not subjected to the embarrassment and inconvenience entailed in less discriminate and more intrusive investigative methods.

"In these respects, the canine sniff is *sui generis*. We are aware of no other investigative procedure that is so limited both in the manner in which the information is obtained and in the content of the information revealed by the procedure. Therefore, we conclude that the particular course of investigation that the agents intended to pursue here—exposure of respondent's luggage, which was located in a public place, to a trained canine—did not constitute a 'search' within the meaning of the Fourth Amendment."

We also reject the Government's contention that it should be able to monitor beepers in private residences without a warrant if there is the requisite justification in the facts for believing that a crime is being or will be committed and that monitoring the beeper wherever it goes is likely to produce evidence of criminal activity. Warrantless searches are presumptively unreasonable, though the Court has recognized a few limited exceptions to this general rule.

[If] agents are required to obtain warrants prior to monitoring a beeper when it has been withdrawn from public view, the Government argues, for all practical purposes they will be forced to obtain warrants in every case in which they seek to use a beeper, because they have no way of knowing in advance whether the beeper will be transmitting its signals from inside private premises. The argument that a warrant requirement would oblige the Government to obtain warrants in a large number of cases is hardly a compelling argument against the requirement. It is worthy of note that, in any event, this is not a particularly attractive case in which to argue that it is impractical to obtain a warrant, since a warrant was in fact obtained in this case, seemingly on probable cause.

We are also unpersuaded by the argument that a warrant should not be required because of the difficulty in satisfying the particularity requirement of the Fourth Amendment. The Government contends that it would be impossible to describe the "place" to be searched, because the location of the place is precisely what is sought to be discovered through the search. However true that may be, it will still be possible to describe the object into which the beeper is to be placed, the circumstances that led agents to wish to install the beeper, and the length of time for which beeper surveillance is requested. In our view, this information will suffice to permit issuance of a warrant authorizing beeper installation and surveillance.

In sum, we discern no reason for deviating from the general rule that a search of a house should be conducted pursuant to a warrant.[5]

[But] it is clear that the warrant affidavit, after striking the facts about monitoring the beeper while it was in the Taos residence, contained sufficient untainted information to furnish probable cause for the issuance of the search warrant. The evidence seized in the house should not have been suppressed with respect to any of the respondents. * * *

JUSTICE O'CONNOR, with whom JUSTICE REHNQUIST joins, concurring in part and concurring in the judgment. * * *

[A] privacy interest in the location of a closed container that enters a home with the homeowner's permission cannot be inferred mechanically by reference to the more general privacy interests in the home itself. The homeowner's privacy interests are often narrower than those of the owner of the container. A defendant should be allowed to challenge evidence obtained by monitoring a beeper installed in a closed container only if (1) the beeper was monitored when visual tracking of the container was not possible, so that the defendant had a reasonable expectation that the container's movements would remain private, and (2) the defendant had an interest in the container itself sufficient to empower him

---

5. The United States insists that if beeper monitoring is deemed a search, a showing of reasonable suspicion rather than probable cause should suffice for its execution. That issue, however, is not before us. The initial warrant was not invalidated for want of probable cause, which plainly existed, but for mis-leading statements in the affidavit. The Government did not appeal the invalidation of the warrant and as the case has turned out, the Government prevails without a warrant authorizing installation. It will be time enough to resolve the probable cause-reasonable suspicion issue in a case that requires it.

to give effective consent to a search of the container. A person's right not to have a container tracked by means of a beeper depends both on his power to prevent visual observation of the container and on his power to control its location, a power that can usually be inferred from a privacy interest in the container itself. One who lacks either power has no legitimate expectation of privacy in the movements of the container. * * *

JUSTICE STEVENS, with whom JUSTICE BRENNAN and JUSTICE MARSHALL join, concurring in part and dissenting in part. * * *

The attachment of the beeper, in my judgment, constituted a "seizure." The owner of property, of course, has a right to exclude from it all the world, including the Government, and a concomitant right to use it exclusively for his own purposes. When the Government attaches an electronic monitoring device to that property, it infringes that exclusionary right; in a fundamental sense it has converted the property to its own use. Surely such an invasion is an "interference" with possessory rights; the right to exclude, which attached as soon as the can respondents purchased was delivered, had been infringed.[2] That interference is also "meaningful"; the character of the property is profoundly different when infected with an electronic bug than when it is entirely germ free. * * *

The Court recognizes that concealment of personal property from public view gives rise to Fourth Amendment protection when it writes: "Indiscriminate monitoring of property that has been withdrawn from public view would present far too serious a threat to privacy interests in the home to escape entirely some sort of Fourth Amendment oversight." This protection is not limited to times when the beeper was in a home. The beeper also revealed when the can of ether had been moved. When a person drives down a public thoroughfare in a car with a can of ether concealed in the trunk, he is not exposing to public view the fact that he is in possession of a can of ether; the can is still "withdrawn from public view" and hence its location is entitled to constitutional protection. * * *

UNITED STATES v. WHITE

401 U.S. 745, 91 S.Ct. 1122, 28 L.Ed.2d 453 (1971).

[On numerous occasions a government informer, carrying a concealed radio transmitter, engaged defendant in conversations which were electronically overheard by federal narcotics agents. The conversations in a restaurant, defendant's home and in the informer's car were overheard by the use of radio equipment. A number of conversations in the informer's home were not only electronically overheard by an agent stationed outside the house but by another agent who, with the informer's consent, concealed himself in the latter's kitchen closet. At no time did the agents obtain a warrant or court order. The informer was not produced at the trial, but the testimony of the "eavesdropping" agents was admitted and led to defendant's conviction of narcotics violations. The Court of Appeals Circuit read *Katz* as prohibiting testimony about the electronically overheard statements.]

JUSTICE WHITE announced the judgment of the Court and an opinion in which THE CHIEF JUSTICE, JUSTICE STEWART, and JUSTICE BLACKMUN join. * * *

---

2. It makes no difference in this case that when the beeper was initially attached, the can had not yet been delivered to respondents. Once the delivery had been effected, the container was respondents' property from which they had the right to exclude all the world. It was at that point that the infringement of this constitutionally protected interest began.

Hoffa v. United States, 385 U.S. 293, 87 S.Ct. 408, 17 L.Ed.2d 374 (1966), which was left undisturbed by *Katz,* held that however strongly a defendant may trust an apparent colleague, his expectations in this respect are not protected by the Fourth Amendment when it turns out that the colleague is a government agent regularly communicating with the authorities. In these circumstances, "no interest legitimately protected by the Fourth Amendment is involved," for that amendment affords no protection to "a wrongdoer's misplaced belief that a person to whom he voluntarily confides his wrongdoing will not reveal it."   * * *

Concededly a police agent who conceals his police connections may write down for official use his conversations with a defendant and testify concerning them, without a warrant authorizing his encounters with the defendant and without otherwise violating the latter's Fourth Amendment rights. For constitutional purposes, no different result is required if the agent instead of immediately reporting and transcribing his conversations with defendant, either (1) simultaneously records them with electronic equipment which he is carrying on his person, (2) or carries radio equipment which simultaneously transmits the conversations either to recording equipment located elsewhere or to other agents monitoring the transmitting frequency. If the conduct and revelations of an agent operating without electronic equipment do not invade the defendant's constitutionally justifiable expectations of privacy, neither does a simultaneous recording of the same conversations made by the agent or by others from transmissions received from the agent to whom the defendant is talking and whose trustworthiness the defendant necessarily risks.

Our problem is not what the privacy expectations of particular defendants in particular situations may be or the extent to which they may in fact have relied on the discretion of their companions. Very probably, individual defendants neither know nor suspect that their colleagues have gone or will go to the police or are carrying recorders or transmitters. Otherwise, conversation would cease and our problem with these encounters would be nonexistent or far different from those now before us. Our problem, in terms of the principles announced in *Katz,* is what expectations of privacy are constitutionally "justifiable"—what expectations the Fourth Amendment will protect in the absence of a warrant. * * * If the law gives no protection to the wrongdoer whose trusted accomplice is or becomes a police agent, neither should it protect him when that same agent has recorded or transmitted the conversations which are later offered in evidence to prove the State's case.

Inescapably, one contemplating illegal activities must realize and risk that his companions may be reporting to the police. If he sufficiently doubts their trustworthiness, the association will very probably end or never materialize. But if he has no doubts, or allays them, or risks what doubt he has, the risk is his. In terms of what his course will be, what he will or will not do or say, we are unpersuaded that he would distinguish between probable informers on the one hand and probable informers with transmitters on the other. Given the possibility or probability that one of his colleagues is cooperating with the police, it is only speculation to assert that the defendant's utterances would be substantially different or his sense of security any less if he also thought it possible that the suspected colleague is wired for sound. At least there is no persuasive evidence that the difference in this respect between the electronically equipped and the unequipped agent is substantial enough to require discrete constitutional recognition, particularly under the Fourth Amendment which is ruled by fluid concepts of "reasonableness."

Nor should we be too ready to erect constitutional barriers to relevant and probative evidence which is also accurate and reliable. An electronic recording will many times produce a more reliable rendition of what a defendant has said than will the unaided memory of a police agent. It may also be that with the recording in existence it is less likely that the informant will change his mind, less chance that threat or injury will suppress unfavorable evidence and less chance that cross-examination will confound the testimony. Considerations like these obviously do not favor the defendant, but we are not prepared to hold that a defendant who has no constitutional right to exclude the informer's unaided testimony nevertheless has a Fourth Amendment privilege against a more accurate version of the events in question.

It is thus untenable to consider the activities and reports of the police agent himself, though acting without a warrant, to be a "reasonable" investigative effort and lawful under the Fourth Amendment but to view the same agent with a recorder or transmitter as conducting an "unreasonable" and unconstitutional search and seizure. * * *

No different result should obtain where, as in the instant case, the informer disappears and is unavailable at trial; for the issue of whether specified events on a certain day violate the Fourth Amendment should not be determined by what later happens to the informer. His unavailability at trial and proffering the testimony of other agents may raise evidentiary problems or pose issues of prosecutorial misconduct with respect to the informer's disappearance, but they do not appear critical to deciding whether prior events invaded the defendant's Fourth Amendment rights.

The Court of Appeals was in error for another reason. In *Desist v. United States*, 394 U.S. 244, 89 S.Ct. 1030, 22 L.Ed.2d 248 (1969), we held that our decision in *Katz v. United States* applied only to those electronic surveillances that occurred subsequent to the date of that decision. Here the events in question took place in late 1965 and early 1966, long prior to *Katz*. * * *

The judgment of the Court of Appeals is reversed.

JUSTICE BLACK * * * concurs in the judgment of the Court for the reasons set forth in his dissent in *Katz v. United States*.

JUSTICE BRENNAN, concurring in the result.

I agree that *Desist* requires reversal of the judgment of the Court of Appeals. [It] is my view that current Fourth Amendment jurisprudence interposes a warrant requirement not only in cases of third-party electronic monitoring (the situation in this case) but also in cases of electronic recording by a government agent of a face-to-face conversation with a criminal suspect. * * *

JUSTICE DOUGLAS, dissenting.

* * * Monitoring, if prevalent, certainly kills free discourse and spontaneous utterances. Free discourse—a First Amendment value—may be frivolous or serious, humble or defiant, reactionary or revolutionary, profane or in good taste; but it is not free if there is surveillance. Free discourse liberates the spirit, though it may produce only froth. The individual must keep some facts concerning his thoughts within a small zone of people. At the same time he must be free to pour out his woes or inspirations or dreams to others. He remains the sole judge as to what must be said and what must remain unspoken. This is the essence of the idea of privacy implicit in the First and Fifth Amendments as well as in the Fourth. * * *

JUSTICE HARLAN, dissenting.

[Since] it is the task of the law to form and project, as well as mirror and reflect, we should not, as judges, merely recite the expectations and risks without examining the desirability of saddling them upon society. The critical question, therefore, is whether under our system of government, as reflected in the Constitution, we should impose on our citizens the risks of the electronic listener or observer without at least the protection of a warrant requirement.

This question must, in my view, be answered by assessing the nature of a particular practice and the likely extent of its impact on the individual's sense of security balanced against the utility of the conduct as a technique of law enforcement. For those more extensive intrusions that significantly jeopardize the sense of security which is the paramount concern of Fourth Amendment liberties, I am of the view that more than self-restraint by law enforcement officials is required and at the least warrants should be necessary.

The impact of the practice of third-party bugging, must, I think, be considered such as to undermine that confidence and sense of security in dealing with one another that is characteristic of individual relationships between citizens in a free society. [The] argument of the plurality opinion, to the effect that it is irrelevant whether secrets are revealed by the mere tattletale or the transistor, ignores the differences occasioned by third-party monitoring and recording which insures full and accurate disclosure of all that is said, free of the possibility of error and oversight that inheres in human reporting.

Authority is hardly required to support the proposition that words would be measured a good deal more carefully and communication inhibited if one suspected his conversations were being transmitted and transcribed. Were third-party bugging a prevalent practice, it might well smother that spontaneity—reflected in frivolous, impetuous, sacrilegious, and defiant discourse—that liberates daily life. Much offhand exchange is easily forgotten and one may count on the obscurity of his remarks, protected by the very fact of a limited audience, and the likelihood that the listener will either overlook or forget what is said, as well as the listener's inability to reformulate a conversation without having to contend with a documented record. All these values are sacrificed by a rule of law that permits official monitoring of private discourse limited only by the need to locate a willing assistant.

[The] interest [the plurality] fails to protect is the expectation of the ordinary citizen, who has never engaged in illegal conduct in his life, that he may carry on his private discourse freely, openly, and spontaneously without measuring his every word against the connotations it might carry when instantaneously heard by others unknown to him and unfamiliar with his situation or analyzed in a cold, formal record played days, months, or years after the conversation. Interposition of a warrant requirement is designed not to shield "wrongdoers," but to secure a measure of privacy and a sense of personal security throughout our society. * * *

JUSTICE MARSHALL, dissenting.

I am convinced that the correct view of the Fourth Amendment in the area of electronic surveillance is one that brings the safeguards of the warrant requirement to bear on the investigatory activity involved in this case. In this regard I agree with the dissents of Justice Douglas and Justice Harlan.

III. LESSER INTRUSIONS:
STOP AND FRISK

Introduction

Under the monolithic approach to the Fourth Amendment which once obtained, the assumption was that every form of activity which constituted either a search or a seizure had to be grounded in the same quantum of evidence suggested by the Amendment's "probable cause" requirement. But this changed when the Supreme Court recognized in *Camara v. Municipal Court*, 387 U.S. 523, 87 S.Ct. 1727, 18 L.Ed.2d 930 (1967), that at least some Fourth Amendment activity should be judged under a balancing test, that is, by "balancing the need to search against the invasion which the search entails." Doubtless the most significant application of this new balancing test came a year later when, in *Terry v. Ohio*, the first case in this section, the Court applied it to the common police practice of detaining suspicious persons briefly on the street for purposes of investigation.

If there is to be a discrete form of police activity, typically called stop-and-frisk, which is subject to a lesser evidentiary standard, then it is necessary to distinguish such activity from full-fledged arrests requiring probable cause on the one hand and no-seizure police encounters requiring no justification whatsoever on the other. The problems raised by the need to draw such lines are illustrated by *Florida v. Bostich*, the second case in this section.

TERRY v. OHIO
392 U.S. 1, 88 S.Ct. 1868, 20 L.Ed.2d 889 (1968).

CHIEF JUSTICE WARREN delivered the opinion of the court.

[Officer McFadden, a Cleveland plainclothes detective, became suspicious of two men standing on a street corner in the downtown area at about 2:30 in the afternoon. One of the suspects walked up the street, peered into a store, walked on, started back, looked into the same store, and then joined and conferred with his companion. The other suspect repeated this ritual, and between them the two men went through this performance about a dozen times. They also talked with a third man, and then followed him up the street about ten minutes after his departure. The officer, thinking that the suspects were "casing" a stickup and might be armed, followed and confronted the three men as they were again conversing. He identified himself and asked the suspects for their names. The men only mumbled something, and the officer spun Terry around and patted his breast pocket. He felt a pistol, which he removed. A frisk of Terry's companion also uncovered a pistol; a frisk of the third man did not disclose that he was armed, and he was not searched further. Terry was charged with carrying a concealed weapon, and he moved to suppress the weapon as evidence. The motion was denied by the trial judge, who upheld the officer's actions on a stop-and-frisk theory. The Ohio court of appeals affirmed, and the state supreme court dismissed Terry's appeal.]

[The] question is whether in all the circumstances of this on-the-street encounter, [Terry's] right to personal security was violated by an unreasonable search and seizure.

We would be less than candid if we did not acknowledge that this question thrusts to the fore difficult and troublesome issues regarding a sensitive area of police activity—issues which have never before been squarely presented to this Court.

[On] the one hand, it is frequently argued that in dealing with the rapidly unfolding and often dangerous situations on city streets the police are in need of an escalating set of flexible responses, graduated in relation to the amount of information they possess. For this purpose it is urged that distinctions should be made between a "stop" and an "arrest" (or a "seizure" of a person), and between a "frisk" and a "search." Thus, it is argued, the police should be allowed to "stop" a person and detain him briefly for questioning upon suspicion that he may be connected with criminal activity. Upon suspicion that the person may be armed, the police should have the power to "frisk" him for weapons. If the "stop" and the "frisk" give rise to probable cause to believe that the suspect has committed a crime, then the police should be empowered to make a formal "arrest," and a full incident "search" of the person. This scheme is justified in part upon the notion that a "stop" and a "frisk" amount to a mere "minor inconvenience and petty indignity," which can properly be imposed upon the citizen in the interest of effective law enforcement on the basis of a police officer's suspicion.

On the other side the argument is made that the authority of the police must be strictly circumscribed by the law of arrest and search as it has developed to date in the traditional jurisprudence of the Fourth Amendment. It is contended with some force that there is not—and cannot be—a variety of police activity which does not depend solely upon the voluntary cooperation of the citizen and yet which stops short of an arrest based upon probable cause to make such an arrest. The heart of the Fourth Amendment, the argument runs, is a severe requirement of specific justification for any intrusion upon protected personal security, coupled with a highly developed system of judicial controls to enforce upon the agents of the State the commands of the Constitution.

[The] State has characterized the issue here as "the right of a police officer [to] make an on-the-street stop, interrogate and pat down for weapons (known in the street vernacular as 'stop and frisk')." But this is only partly accurate. For the issue is not the abstract propriety of the police conduct, but the admissibility against petitioner of the evidence uncovered by the search and seizure. [In] our system evidentiary rulings provide the context in which the judicial process of inclusion and exclusion approves some conduct as comporting with constitutional guarantees and disapproves other actions by state agents. A ruling admitting evidence in a criminal trial, we recognize, has the necessary effect of legitimizing the conduct which produced the evidence, while an application of the exclusionary rule withholds the constitutional imprimatur.

The exclusionary rule has its limitations, however, as a tool of judicial control. It cannot properly be invoked to exclude the products of legitimate police investigative techniques on the ground that much conduct which is closely similar involves unwarranted intrusions upon constitutional protections. Moreover, in some contexts the rule is ineffective as a deterrent. Street encounters between citizens and police officers are incredibly rich in diversity. They range from wholly friendly exchanges of pleasantries or mutually useful information to hostile confrontations of armed men involving arrests, or injuries, or loss of life. Moreover, hostile confrontations are not all of a piece. Some of them begin in a friendly enough manner, only to take a different turn upon the injection of some unexpected element into the conversation. Encounters are initiated by the police for a wide variety of purposes, some of which are wholly unrelated to a desire to prosecute for crime. Doubtless some police "field interrogation" conduct violates the Fourth Amendment. But a stern refusal by this Court to condone such activity does not necessarily render it responsive to the exclusionary rule. Regardless of how effective the rule may be where obtaining convictions is an important objective of the police, it is powerless to deter invasions of constitutionally guaranteed rights where the police either have no interest in prosecuting or are willing to forego successful prosecution in the interest of serving some other goal.

Proper adjudication of cases in which the exclusionary rule is invoked demands a constant awareness of these limitations. The wholesale harassment by certain elements of the police community, of which minority groups, particularly Negroes, frequently complain, will not be stopped by the exclusion of any evidence from any criminal trial. Yet a rigid and unthinking application of the exclusionary rule, in futile protest against practices which it can never be used effectively to control, may exact a high toll in human injury and frustration of efforts to prevent crime. No judicial opinion can comprehend the protean variety of the street encounter, and we can only judge the facts of the case before us. * * *

[W]e turn our attention to the quite narrow question posed by the facts before us: whether it is always unreasonable for a policeman to seize a person and subject him to a limited search for weapons unless there is probable cause for an arrest.

[It] is quite plain that the Fourth Amendment governs "seizures" of the person which do not eventuate in a trip to the station house and prosecution for crime—"arrests" in traditional terminology. It must be recognized that whenever a police officer accosts an individual and restrains his freedom to walk away, he has "seized" that person. And it is nothing less than sheer torture of the English language to suggest that a careful exploration of the outer surfaces of a person's clothing all over his or her body in an attempt to find weapons is not a "search." Moreover, it is simply fantastic to urge that such a procedure performed in public by a policeman while the citizen stands helpless, perhaps facing a wall with his hands raised, is a "petty indignity." [13] It is a serious intrusion upon the sanctity of the person, which may inflict great indignity and arouse strong resentment, and it is not to be undertaken lightly.

* * * We therefore reject the notions that the Fourth Amendment does not come into play at all as a limitation upon police conduct if the officers stop short of something called a "technical arrest" or a "full-blown search."

In this case there can be no question, then, that Officer McFadden "seized" petitioner and subjected him to a "search" when he took hold of him and patted down the outer surfaces of his clothing. We must decide whether at that point it was reasonable for Officer McFadden to have interfered with petitioner's personal security as he did.[16] And in determining whether the seizure and search were

---

13. Consider the following apt description:

"[T]he officer must feel with sensitive fingers every portion of the prisoner's body. A thorough search must be made of the prisoner's arms and armpits, waistline and back, the groin and area about the testicles, and entire surface of the legs down to the feet." Priar & Martin, *Searching and Disarming Criminals,* 45 J.Crim.L.C. & P.S. 481 (1954).

16. We thus decide nothing today concerning the constitutional propriety of an investiga-

tive "seizure" upon less than probable cause for purposes of "detention" and/or interrogation. Obviously, not all personal intercourse between policemen and citizens involves "seizures" of persons. Only when the officer, by means of physical force or show of authority, has in some way restrained the liberty of a citizen may we conclude that a "seizure" has occurred. We cannot tell with any certainty upon this record whether any such "seizure" took place here prior to Officer McFadden's

"unreasonable" our inquiry is a dual one—whether the officer's action was justified at its inception, and whether it was reasonably related in scope to the circumstances which justified the interference in the first place.

If this case involved police conduct subject to the Warrant Clause of the Fourth Amendment, we would have to ascertain whether "probable cause" existed to justify the search and seizure which took place. However, that is not the case. We do not retreat from our holdings that the police must, whenever practicable, obtain advance judicial approval of searches and seizures through the warrant procedure, * * * or that in most instances failure to comply with the warrant requirement can only be excused by exigent circumstances. [But] we deal here with an entire rubric of police conduct—necessarily swift action predicated upon the on-the-spot observations of the officer on the beat—which historically has not been, and as a practical matter could not be, subjected to the warrant procedure. Instead, the conduct involved in this case must be tested by the Fourth Amendment's general proscription against unreasonable searches and seizures.

Nonetheless, the notions which underlie both the warrant procedure and the requirement of probable cause remain fully relevant in this context. In order to assess the reasonableness of Officer McFadden's conduct as a general proposition, it is necessary "first to focus upon the governmental interest which allegedly justifies official intrusion upon the constitutionally protected interests of the private citizen," for there is "no ready test for determining reasonableness other than by balancing the need to search [or seize] against the invasion which the search [or seizure] entails." And in justifying the particular intrusion the police officer must be able to point to specific and articulable facts which, taken together with rational inferences from those facts, reasonably warrant that intrusion. The scheme of the Fourth Amendment becomes meaningful only when it is assured that at some point the conduct of those charged with enforcing the laws can be subjected to the more detached, neutral scrutiny of a judge who must evaluate the reasonableness of a particular search or seizure in light of the particular circumstances. And in making that assessment it is imperative that the facts be judged against an objective standard: would the facts available to the officer at the moment of the seizure or the search "warrant a man of reasonable caution in the belief" that the action taken was appropriate? * * * Anything less would invite intrusions upon constitutionally guaranteed rights based on nothing more substantial than inarticulate hunches, a result this Court has consistently refused to sanction. * * *

Applying these principles to this case, we consider first the nature and extent of the governmental interests involved. One general interest is of course that of effective crime prevention and detection; it is this interest which underlies the recognition that a police officer may in appropriate circumstances and in an appropriate manner approach a person for purposes of investigating possibly criminal behavior even though there is no probable cause to make an arrest. It was this legitimate investigative function Officer McFadden was discharging when he decided to approach petitioner and his companions. He had observed Terry, Chilton, and Katz go through a series of acts, each of them perhaps innocent in itself, but which taken together warranted further investigation. There is nothing unusual in two men standing together on a street corner, perhaps waiting for someone. Nor is there anything suspicious about people in such circumstances strolling up and down the street, singly or in pairs. Store windows, moreover, are

initiation of physical contact for purposes of searching Terry for weapons, and we thus may assume that up to that point no intrusion upon constitutionally protected rights had occurred.

made to be looked in. But the story is quite different where, as here, two men hover about a street corner for an extended period of time, at the end of which it becomes apparent that they are not waiting for anyone or anything; where these men pace alternately along an identical route, pausing to stare in the same store window roughly 24 times; where each completion of this route is followed immediately by a conference between the two men on the corner; where they are joined in one of these conferences by a third man who leaves swiftly; and where the two men finally follow the third and rejoin him a couple of blocks away. It would have been poor police work indeed for an officer of 30 years' experience in the detection of thievery from stores in this same neighborhood to have failed to investigate this behavior further.

The crux of this case, however, is not the propriety of Officer McFadden's taking steps to investigate petitioner's suspicious behavior, but rather, whether there was justification for McFadden's invasion of Terry's personal security by searching him for weapons in the course of that investigation. We are now concerned with more than the governmental interest in investigating crime; in addition, there is the more immediate interest of the police officer in taking steps to assure himself that the person with whom he is dealing is not armed with a weapon that could unexpectedly and fatally be used against him. Certainly it would be unreasonable to require that police officers take unnecessary risks in the performance of their duties. American criminals have a long tradition of armed violence, and every year in this country many law enforcement officers are killed in the line of duty, and thousands more are wounded. Virtually all of these deaths and a substantial portion of the injuries are inflicted with guns and knives.

In view of these facts, we cannot blind ourselves to the need for law enforcement officers to protect themselves and other prospective victims of violence in situations where they may lack probable cause for an arrest. When an officer is justified in believing that the individual whose suspicious behavior he is investigating at close range is armed and presently dangerous to the officer or to others, it would appear to be clearly unreasonable to deny the officer the power to take necessary measures to determine whether the person is in fact carrying a weapon and to neutralize the threat of physical harm.

[Petitioner] does not say that an officer is always unjustified in searching a suspect to discover weapons. Rather, he says it is unreasonable for the policeman to take that step until such time as the situation evolves to a point where there is probable cause to make an arrest.

[There] are two weaknesses in this line of reasoning however. First, it fails to take account of traditional limitations upon the scope of searches, and thus recognizes no distinction in purpose, character, and extent between a search incident to an arrest and a limited search for weapons. The former, although justified in part by the acknowledged necessity to protect the arresting officer from assault with a concealed weapon, is also justified on other grounds, and can therefore involve a relatively extensive exploration of the person. A search for weapons in the absence of probable cause to arrest, however, must, like any other search, be strictly circumscribed by the exigencies which justify its initiation. Thus it must be limited to that which is necessary for the discovery of weapons which might be used to harm the officer or others nearby, and may realistically be characterized as something less than a "full" search, even though it remains a serious intrusion.

A second, and related, objection to petitioner's argument is that it assumes that the law of arrest has already worked out the balance between the particular

interests involved here—the neutralization of danger to the policeman in the investigative circumstance and the sanctity of the individual. But this is not so. An arrest is a wholly different kind of intrusion upon individual freedom from a limited search for weapons, and the interests each is designed to serve are likewise quite different. An arrest is the initial stage of a criminal prosecution. It is intended to vindicate society's interest in having its laws obeyed, and it is inevitably accompanied by future interference with the individual's freedom of movement, whether or not trial or conviction ultimately follows. The protective search for weapons, on the other hand, constitutes a brief, though far from inconsiderable intrusion upon the sanctity of the person. It does not follow that because an officer may lawfully arrest a person only when he is apprised of facts sufficient to warrant a belief that the person has committed or is committing a crime, the officer is equally unjustified, absent that kind of evidence, in making any intrusions short of an arrest. Moreover, a perfectly reasonable apprehension of danger may arise long before the officer is possessed of adequate information to justify taking a person into custody for the purpose of prosecuting him for a crime.
* * *

Our evaluation of the proper balance that has to be struck in this type of case leads us to conclude that there must be a narrowly drawn authority to permit a reasonable search for weapons for the protection of the police officer, where he has reason to believe that he is dealing with an armed and dangerous individual, regardless of whether he has probable cause to arrest the individual for a crime. The officer need not be absolutely certain that the individual is armed; the issue is whether a reasonably prudent man in the circumstances would be warranted in the belief that his safety or that of others was in danger. * * * And in determining whether the officer acted reasonably in such circumstances, due weight must be given, not to his inchoate and unparticularized suspicion or "hunch", but to the specific reasonable inferences which he is entitled to draw from the facts in light of his experience.

We must now examine the conduct of Officer McFadden in this case to determine whether his search and seizure of petitioner were reasonable, both at their inception and as conducted. He had observed Terry, together with Chilton and another man, acting in a manner he took to be preface to a "stick-up." We think on the facts and circumstances Officer McFadden detailed before the trial judge a reasonably prudent man would have been warranted in believing petitioner was armed and thus presented a threat to the officer's safety while he was investigating his suspicious behavior. The actions of Terry and Chilton were consistent with McFadden's hypothesis that these men were contemplating a daylight robbery—which, it is reasonable to assume, would be likely to involve the use of weapons—and nothing in their conduct from the time he first noticed them until the time he confronted them and identified himself as a police officer gave him sufficient reason to negate that hypothesis. Although the trio had departed the original scene, there was nothing to indicate abandonment of an intent to commit a robbery at some point. Thus, when Officer McFadden approached the three men gathered before the display window at Zucker's store he had observed enough to make it quite reasonable to fear that they were armed; and nothing in their response to his hailing them, identifying himself as a police officer, and asking their names served to dispel that reasonable belief. We cannot say his decision at that point to seize Terry and pat his clothing for weapons was the product of a volatile or inventive imagination, or was undertaken simply as an act of harassment; the record evidences the tempered act of a policeman who in the course of an investigation had to make a quick decision as to how to protect himself and others from possible danger, and took limited steps to do so.

The manner in which the seizure and search were conducted is, of course, as vital a part of the inquiry as whether they were warranted at all. The Fourth Amendment proceeds as much by limitations upon the scope of governmental action as by imposing preconditions upon its initiation. The entire deterrent purpose of the rule excluding evidence seized in violation of the Fourth Amendment rests on the assumption that "limitations upon the fruit to be gathered tend to limit the quest itself." [Thus,] evidence may not be introduced if it was discovered by means of a seizure and search which were not reasonably related in scope to the justification for their initiation.

[A protective search for weapons,] unlike a search without a warrant incident to a lawful arrest, is not justified by any need to prevent the disappearance or destruction of evidence of crime. The sole justification of the search in the present situation is the protection of the police officer and others nearby, and it must therefore be confined in scope to an intrusion reasonably designed to discover guns, knives, clubs, or other hidden instruments for the assault of the police officer.

The scope of the search in this case presents no serious problem in light of these standards. Officer McFadden patted down the outer clothing of petitioner and his two companions. He did not place his hands in their pockets or under the outer surface of their garments until he had felt weapons, and then he merely reached for and removed the guns. He never did invade Katz's person beyond the outer surfaces of his clothes, since he discovered nothing in his pat down which might have been a weapon. Officer McFadden confined his search strictly to what was minimally necessary to learn whether the men were armed and to disarm them once he discovered the weapons. He did not conduct a general exploratory search for whatever evidence of criminal activity he might find.

We conclude that the revolver seized from Terry was properly admitted in evidence against him. At the time he seized petitioner and searched him for weapons, Officer McFadden had reasonable grounds to believe that petitioner was armed and dangerous, and it was necessary for the protection of himself and others to take swift measures to discover the true facts and neutralize the threat of harm if it materialized. The policeman carefully restricted his search to what was appropriate to the discovery of the particular items which he sought. Each case of this sort will, of course, have to be decided on its own facts. We merely hold today that where a police officer observes unusual conduct which leads him reasonably to conclude in light of his experience that criminal activity may be afoot and that the persons with whom he is dealing may be armed and presently dangerous; where in the course of investigating this behavior he identifies himself as a policeman and makes reasonable inquiries; and where nothing in the initial stages of the encounter serves to dispel his reasonable fear for his own or others' safety, he is entitled for the protection of himself and others in the area to conduct a carefully limited search of the outer clothing of such persons in an attempt to discover weapons which might be used to assault him. Such a search is a reasonable search under the Fourth Amendment, and any weapons seized may properly be introduced in evidence against the person from whom they were taken.

Affirmed.

JUSTICE HARLAN, concurring.

[The] holding [has] two logical corollaries that I do not think the Court has fully expressed.

In the first place, if the frisk is justified in order to protect the officer during an encounter with a citizen, the officer must first have constitutional grounds to insist on an encounter, to make a *forcible* stop. Any person, including a policeman, is at liberty to avoid a person he considers dangerous. If and when a policeman has a right instead to disarm such a person for his own protection, he must first have a right not to avoid him but to be in his presence. That right must be more than the liberty (again, possessed by every citizen) to address questions to other persons, for ordinarily the person addressed has an equal right to ignore his interrogator and walk away; he certainly need not submit to a frisk for the questioner's protection. I would make it perfectly clear that the right to frisk in this case depends upon the reasonableness of a forcible stop to investigate a suspected crime.

Where such a stop is reasonable, however, the right to frisk must be immediate and automatic if the reason for the stop is, as here, an articulable suspicion of a crime of violence. Just as a full search incident to a lawful arrest requires no additional justification, a limited frisk incident to a lawful stop must often be rapid and routine. There is no reason why an officer, rightfully but forcibly confronting a person suspected of a serious crime, should have to ask one question and take the risk that the answer might be a bullet. * * *

JUSTICE WHITE, concurring.

* * * I think an additional word is in order concerning the matter of interrogation during an investigative stop. There is nothing in the Constitution which prevents a policeman from addressing questions to anyone on the streets. Absent special circumstances, the person approached may not be detained or frisked but may refuse to cooperate and go on his way. However, given the proper circumstances, such as those in this case, it seems to me the person may be briefly detained against his will while pertinent questions are directed to him. Of course, the person stopped is not obliged to answer, answers may not be compelled, and refusal to answer furnishes no basis for an arrest, although it may alert the officer to the need for continued observation. * * *

JUSTICE DOUGLAS, dissenting.

[Had] a warrant been sought, a magistrate would, therefore, have been unauthorized to issue one, for he can act only if there is a showing of "probable cause." We hold today that the police have greater authority to make a "seizure" and conduct a "search" than a judge has to authorize such action. We have said precisely the opposite over and over again.

[The] infringement on personal liberty of any "seizure" of a person can only be "reasonable" under the Fourth Amendment if we require the police to possess "probable cause" before they seize him. Only that line draws a meaningful distinction between an officer's mere inkling and the presence of facts within the officer's personal knowledge which would convince a reasonable man that the person seized has committed, is committing, or is about to commit a particular crime. * * *

FLORIDA v. BOSTICK

501 U.S. 429, 111 S.Ct. 2382, 115 L.Ed.2d 389 (1991).

JUSTICE O'CONNOR delivered the opinion of the Court. * * *

Drug interdiction efforts have led to the use of police surveillance at airports, train stations, and bus depots. Law enforcement officers stationed at such locations routinely approach individuals, either randomly or because they suspect in some vague way that the individuals may be engaged in criminal activity, and ask them potentially incriminating questions. Broward County has adopted such a program. County Sheriff's Department officers routinely board buses at scheduled stops and ask passengers for permission to search their luggage.

In this case, two officers discovered cocaine when they searched a suitcase belonging to Terrance Bostick. The underlying facts of the search are in dispute, but the Florida Supreme Court, whose decision we review here, stated explicitly the factual premise for its decision:

" 'Two officers, complete with badges, insignia and one of them holding a recognizable zipper pouch, containing a pistol, boarded a bus bound from Miami to Atlanta during a stopover in Fort Lauderdale. Eyeing the passengers, the officers admittedly without articulable suspicion, picked out the defendant passenger and asked to inspect his ticket and identification. The ticket, from Miami to Atlanta, matched the defendant's identification and both were immediately returned to him as unremarkable. However, the two police officers persisted and explained their presence as narcotics agents on the lookout for illegal drugs. In pursuit of that aim, they then requested the defendant's consent to search his luggage. Needless to say, there is a conflict in the evidence about whether the defendant consented to the search of the second bag in which the contraband was found and as to whether he was informed of his right to refuse consent. However, any conflict must be resolved in favor of the state, it being a question of fact decided by the trial judge.' "

Two facts are particularly worth noting. First, the police specifically advised Bostick that he had the right to refuse consent. Bostick appears to have disputed the point, but, as the Florida Supreme Court noted explicitly, the trial court resolved this evidentiary conflict in the State's favor. Second, at no time did the officers threaten Bostick with a gun. The Florida Supreme Court indicated that one officer carried a zipper pouch containing a pistol—the equivalent of carrying a gun in a holster—but the court did not suggest that the gun was ever removed from its pouch, pointed at Bostick, or otherwise used in a threatening manner. The dissent's characterization of the officers as "gun-wielding inquisitor[s]" is colorful, but lacks any basis in fact.

Bostick was arrested and charged with trafficking in cocaine. He moved to suppress the cocaine on the grounds that it had been seized in violation of his Fourth Amendment rights. The trial court denied the motion but made no factual findings. Bostick subsequently entered a plea of guilty, but reserved the right to appeal the denial of the motion to suppress.

The Florida District Court of Appeal affirmed, but considered the issue sufficiently important that it certified a question to the Florida Supreme Court. The Supreme Court reasoned that Bostick had been seized because a reasonable passenger in his situation would not have felt free to leave the bus to avoid questioning by the police. It rephrased and answered the certified question so as to make the bus setting dispositive in every case. It ruled categorically that " 'an impermissible seizure result[s] when police mount a drug search on buses during scheduled stops and question boarded passengers without articulable reasons for doing so, thereby obtaining consent to search the passengers' luggage.' " The Florida Supreme Court thus adopted a *per se* rule that the Broward County Sheriff's practice of "working the buses" is unconstitutional.* The result of this decision is that police in Florida, as elsewhere, may approach persons at random in most public places, ask them questions and seek consent to a search, but they may not engage in the same behavior on a bus. We granted certiorari to determine whether the Florida Supreme Court's *per se* rule is consistent with our Fourth Amendment jurisprudence.

The sole issue presented for our review is whether a police encounter on a bus of the type described above necessarily constitutes a "seizure" within the meaning of the Fourth Amendment. The State concedes, and we accept for purposes of this decision, that the officers lacked the reasonable suspicion required to justify a seizure and that, if a seizure took place, the drugs found in Bostick's suitcase must be suppressed as tainted fruit.

Our cases make it clear that a seizure does not occur simply because a police officer approaches an individual and asks a few questions. So long as a reasonable person would feel free "to disregard the police and go about his business," *California v. Hodari D.,* 499 U.S. 621 (1991), the encounter is consensual and no reasonable suspicion is required. The encounter will not trigger Fourth Amendment scrutiny unless it loses its consensual nature.

[There] is no doubt that if this same encounter had taken place before Bostick boarded the bus or in the lobby of the bus terminal, it would not rise to the level of a seizure. The Court has dealt with similar encounters in airports and has found them to be "the sort of consensual encounter[s] that implicat[e] no Fourth Amendment interest." We have stated that even when officers have no basis for suspecting a particular individual, they may generally ask questions of that individual, ask to examine the individual's identification, and request consent to search his or her luggage—as long as the police do not convey a message that compliance with their requests is required.

Bostick insists that this case is different because it took place in the cramped confines of a bus. A police encounter is much more intimidating in this setting, he argues, because police tower over a seated passenger and there is little room to move around. Bostick claims to find support in cases indicating that a seizure occurs when a reasonable person would believe that he or she is not "free to leave." Bostick maintains that a reasonable bus passenger would not have felt free to leave under the circumstances of this case because there is nowhere to go on a bus. Also, the bus was about to depart. Had Bostick disembarked, he would have risked being stranded and losing whatever baggage he had locked away in the luggage compartment.

The Florida Supreme Court found this argument persuasive, so much so that it adopted a *per se* rule prohibiting the police from randomly boarding buses as a means of drug interdiction. The state court erred, however, in focusing on

---

* The dissent acknowledges that the Florida Supreme Court's answer to the certified question reads like a *per se* rule, but dismisses as "implausible" the notion that the court would actually apply this rule to "trump" a careful analysis of all the relevant facts. Implausible as it may seem, that is precisely what the Florida Supreme Court does. It routinely grants review in bus search cases and quashes denials of motions to suppress *expressly on the basis of its answer to the certified question in this case.*

whether Bostick was "free to leave" rather than on the principle that those words were intended to capture. When police attempt to question a person who is walking down the street or through an airport lobby, it makes sense to inquire whether a reasonable person would feel free to continue walking. But when the person is seated on a bus and has no desire to leave, the degree to which a reasonable person would feel that he or she could leave is not an accurate measure of the coercive effect of the encounter.

Here, for example, the mere fact that Bostick did not feel free to leave the bus does not mean that the police seized him. Bostick was a passenger on a bus that was scheduled to depart. He would not have felt free to leave the bus even if the police had not been present. Bostick's movements were "confined" in a sense, but this was the natural result of his decision to take the bus; it says nothing about whether or not the police conduct at issue was coercive.

In this respect, the Court's decision in *INS v. Delgado,* [466 U.S. 210 (1984)], is dispositive. At issue there was the INS' practice of visiting factories at random and questioning employees to determine whether any were illegal aliens. Several INS agents would stand near the building's exits, while other agents walked through the factory questioning workers. The Court acknowledged that the workers may not have been free to leave their worksite, but explained that this was not the result of police activity: "Ordinarily, when people are at work their freedom to move about has been meaningfully restricted, not by the actions of law enforcement officials, but by the workers' voluntary obligations to their employers." We concluded that there was no seizure because, even though the workers were not free to leave the building without being questioned, the agents' conduct should have given employees "no reason to believe that they would be detained if they gave truthful answers to the questions put to them or if they simply refused to answer."

The present case is analytically indistinguishable from *Delgado.* Like the workers in that case, Bostick's freedom of movement was restricted by a factor independent of police conduct—*i.e.,* by his being a passenger on a bus. Accordingly, the "free to leave" analysis on which Bostick relies is inapplicable. In such a situation, the appropriate inquiry is whether a reasonable person would feel free to decline the officers' requests or otherwise terminate the encounter. This formulation follows logically from prior cases and breaks no new ground. We have said before that the crucial test is whether, taking into account all of the circumstances surrounding the encounter, the police conduct would "have communicated to a reasonable person that he was not at liberty to ignore the police presence and go about his business."[a] Where the encounter takes place is one

---

a. But, in one of the cases cited by the Court as supporting this "test," *California v. Hodari D.,* supra, the Court concluded such communication does not inevitably constitute a seizure. The defendant ran upon seeing a police car, only to be pursued on foot by police, after which the defendant threw away cocaine and the police retrieved it. The state court suppressed the cocaine as the fruit of a seizure made without reasonable suspicion. The Supreme Court, 7–2, stated:

"The narrow question before us is whether, with respect to a show of authority as with respect to application of physical force, a seizure occurs even though the subject does not yield. We hold that it does not.

"The language of the Fourth Amendment, of course, cannot sustain respondent's contention. The word 'seizure' readily bears the meaning of a laying on of hands or application of physical force to restrain movement, even when it is ultimately unsuccessful. ('She seized the purse-snatcher, but he broke out of her grasp.') It does not remotely apply, however, to the prospect of a policeman yelling 'Stop, in the name of the law!' at a fleeing form that continues to flee. That is no seizure. Nor can the result respondent wishes to achieve be produced—indirectly, as it were—by suggesting that Pertoso's uncomplied-with show of authority was a common-law arrest, and then appealing to the principle that all

factor, but it is not the only one. And, as the Solicitor General correctly observes, an individual may decline an officer's request without fearing prosecution. We have consistently held that a refusal to cooperate, without more, does not furnish the minimal level of objective justification needed for a detention or seizure.

The facts of this case, as described by the Florida Supreme Court, leave some doubt whether a seizure occurred. Two officers walked up to Bostick on the bus, asked him a few questions, and asked if they could search his bags. As we have explained, no seizure occurs when police ask questions of an individual, ask to examine the individual's identification, and request consent to search his or her luggage—so long as the officers do not convey a message that compliance with their requests is required. Here, the facts recited by the Florida Supreme Court indicate that the officers did not point guns at Bostick or otherwise threaten him and that they specifically advised Bostick that he could refuse consent.

Nevertheless, we refrain from deciding whether or not a seizure occurred in this case. The trial court made no express findings of fact, and the Florida Supreme Court rested its decision on a single fact—that the encounter took place on a bus—rather than on the totality of the circumstances. We remand so that the Florida courts may evaluate the seizure question under the correct legal standard. We do reject, however, Bostick's argument that he must have been seized because no reasonable person would freely consent to a search of luggage that he or she knows contains drugs. This argument cannot prevail because the "reasonable person" test presupposes an *innocent* person.

The dissent characterizes our decision as holding that police may board buses and by an "*intimidating* show of authority" demand of passengers their "voluntary" cooperation. That characterization is incorrect. Clearly, a bus passenger's decision to cooperate with law enforcement officers authorizes the police to conduct a search without first obtaining a warrant *only* if the cooperation is voluntary. "Consent" that is the product of official intimidation or harassment is not consent at all. Citizens do not forfeit their constitutional rights when they are coerced to comply with a request that they would prefer to refuse. The question to be decided by the Florida courts on remand is whether Bostick chose to permit the search of his luggage.

The dissent also attempts to characterize our decision as applying a lesser degree of constitutional protection to those individuals who travel by bus, rather than by other forms of transportation. This, too, is an erroneous characterization. Our Fourth Amendment inquiry in this case—whether a reasonable person would have felt free to decline the officers' requests or otherwise terminate the encounter—applies equally to police encounters that take place on trains, planes, and city streets. It is the dissent that would single out this particular mode of travel for differential treatment by adopting a *per se* rule that random bus searches are unconstitutional.

common-law arrests are seizures. An arrest requires *either* physical force (as described above) *or,* where that is absent, *submission* to the assertion of authority. * * *

"We do not think it desirable, even as a policy matter, to stretch the Fourth Amendment beyond its words and beyond the meaning of arrest, as respondent urges. Street pursuits always place the public at some risk, and compliance with police orders to stop should therefore be encouraged. Only a few of those orders, we must presume, will be without adequate basis, and since the addressee has no ready means of identifying the deficient ones it almost invariably is the responsible course to comply. Unlawful orders will not be deterred, moreover, by sanctioning through the exclusionary rule those of them that are *not* obeyed. Since policemen do not command 'Stop!' expecting to be ignored, or give chase hoping to be outrun, it fully suffices to apply the deterrent to their genuine, successful seizures."

The dissent reserves its strongest criticism for the proposition that police officers can approach individuals as to whom they have no reasonable suspicion and ask them potentially incriminating questions. But this proposition is by no means novel; it has been endorsed by the Court any number of times. As we have explained, today's decision follows logically from those decisions and breaks no new ground. Unless the dissent advocates overruling a long, unbroken line of decisions dating back more than 20 years, its criticism is not well taken. * * *

JUSTICE MARSHALL, with whom JUSTICE BLACKMUN and JUSTICE STEVENS join, dissenting. * * *

I have no objection to the manner in which the majority frames the test for determining whether a suspicionless bus sweep amounts to a Fourth Amendment "seizure." I agree that the appropriate question is whether a passenger who is approached during such a sweep "would feel free to decline the officers' request or otherwise terminate the encounter." What I cannot understand is how the majority can possibly suggest an affirmative answer to this question.

The majority reverses what it characterizes as the Florida Supreme Court's "*per se* rule" against suspicionless encounters between the police and bus passengers, suggesting only in dictum its "doubt" that a seizure occurred on the facts of this case. However, the notion that the Florida Supreme Court decided this case on the basis of any "*per se* rule" *independent* of the facts of this case is wholly a product of the majority's imagination. As the majority acknowledges, the Florida Supreme Court "stated explicitly the factual premise for its decision." This factual premise contained *all* of the details of the encounter between respondent and the police. The lower court's analysis of whether respondent was seized drew heavily on these facts, and the court repeatedly emphasized that its conclusion was based on "*all the circumstances*" of this case.

The majority's conclusion that the Florida Supreme Court, contrary to all appearances, *ignored* these facts is based solely on the failure of the lower court to expressly incorporate all of the facts into its reformulation of the certified question on which respondent took his appeal. The majority never explains the basis of its implausible assumption that the Florida Supreme Court intended its phrasing of the certified question to trump its opinion's careful treatment of the facts in this case. Certainly, when *this* Court issues an opinion, it does not intend lower courts and parties to treat as irrelevant the analysis of facts that the parties neglected to cram into the question presented in the petition for certiorari. But in any case, because the issue whether a seizure has occurred in any given factual setting is a question of law, nothing prevents this Court from deciding on its own whether a seizure occurred based on *all* of the facts of this case as they appear in the opinion of the Florida Supreme Court.

These facts exhibit all of the elements of coercion associated with a typical bus sweep. Two officers boarded the Greyhound bus on which respondent was a passenger while the bus, en route from Miami to Atlanta, was on a brief stop to pick up passengers in Fort Lauderdale. The officers made a visible display of their badges and wore bright green "raid" jackets bearing the insignia of the Broward County Sheriff's Department; one held a gun in a recognizable weapons pouch. These facts alone constitute an intimidating "show of authority." Once on board, the officers approached respondent, who was sitting in the back of the bus, identified themselves as narcotics officers and began to question him. One officer stood in front of respondent's seat, partially blocking the narrow aisle through which respondent would have been required to pass to reach the exit of the bus.

As far as is revealed by facts on which the Florida Supreme Court premised its decision, the officers did not advise respondent that he was free to break off this "interview." Inexplicably, the majority repeatedly stresses the trial court's implicit finding that the police officers advised respondent that he was free to refuse permission to search his travel bag. This aspect of the exchange between respondent and the police is completely irrelevant to the issue before us. For as the State concedes, and as the majority purports to "accept," *if* respondent was unlawfully seized when the officers approached him and initiated questioning, the resulting search was likewise unlawful no matter how well advised respondent was of his right to refuse it. Consequently, the issue is not whether a passenger in respondent's position would have felt free to deny consent to the search of his bag, but whether such a passenger—without being apprised of his rights—would have felt free to terminate the antecedent encounter with the police.

Unlike the majority, I have no doubt that the answer to this question is no. Apart from trying to accommodate the officers, respondent had only two options. First, he could have remained seated while obstinately refusing to respond to the officers' questioning. But in light of the intimidating show of authority that the officers made upon boarding the bus, respondent reasonably could have believed that such behavior would only arouse the officers' suspicions and intensify their interrogation. Indeed, officers who carry out bus sweeps like the one at issue here frequently admit that this is the effect of a passenger's refusal to cooperate. The majority's observation that a mere refusal to answer questions, "without more," does not give rise to a reasonable basis for seizing a passenger, is utterly beside the point, because a passenger unadvised of his rights and otherwise unversed in constitutional law *has no reason to know* that the police cannot hold his refusal to cooperate against him.

Second, respondent could have tried to escape the officers' presence by leaving the bus altogether. But because doing so would have required respondent to squeeze past the gun-wielding inquisitor who was blocking the aisle of the bus, this hardly seems like a course that respondent reasonably would have viewed as available to him. The majority lamely protests that nothing in the stipulated facts shows that the questioning officer "*point[ed]* [his] gu[n] at [respondent] or otherwise *threatened* him" with the weapon. Our decisions recognize the obvious point, however, that the choice of the police to "display" their weapons during an encounter exerts significant coercive pressure on the confronted citizen. We have never suggested that the police must go so far as to put a citizen in immediate apprehension of *being shot* before a court can take account of the intimidating effect of being questioned by an officer with weapon in hand.

Even if respondent had perceived that the officers would *let* him leave the bus, moreover, he could not reasonably have been expected to resort to this means of evading their intrusive questioning. For so far as respondent knew, the bus' departure from the terminal was imminent. Unlike a person approached by the police on the street or at a bus or airport terminal after reaching his destination, a passenger approached by the police at an intermediate point in a long bus journey cannot simply leave the scene and repair to a safe haven to avoid unwanted probing by law enforcement officials. The vulnerability that an intrastate or interstate traveler experiences when confronted by the police outside of his "own familiar territory" surely aggravates the coercive quality of such an encounter.

The case on which the majority primarily relies, *INS v. Delgado,* is distinguishable in every relevant respect. In *Delgado,* this Court held that workers approached by law-enforcement officials inside of a factory were not "seized" for purposes of the Fourth Amendment. The Court was careful to point out, however, that the presence of the agents did not furnish the workers with a reasonable basis for believing that they were not free to leave the factory, as at least some of them did. Unlike passengers confronted by law-enforcement officials on a bus stopped temporarily at an intermediate point in its journey, workers approached by law-enforcement officials at their workplace need not abandon personal belongings and venture into unfamiliar environs in order to avoid unwanted questioning. Moreover, the workers who did not leave the building in *Delgado* remained free to move about the entire factory, a considerably less confining environment than a bus. Finally, contrary to the officer who confronted respondent, the law-enforcement officials in *Delgado* did not conduct their interviews with guns in hand.

Rather than requiring the police to justify the coercive tactics employed here, the majority blames respondent for his own sensation of constraint. The majority concedes that respondent "did not feel free to leave the bus" as a means of breaking off the interrogation by the Broward County officers. But this experience of confinement, the majority explains, "was the natural result of *his* decision to take the bus." Thus, in the majority's view, because respondent's "freedom of movement was restricted by a factor independent of police conduct—*i.e.*, by his being a passenger on a bus," respondent was not seized for purposes of the Fourth Amendment.

This reasoning borders on sophism and trivializes the values that underlie the Fourth Amendment. Obviously, a person's "voluntary decision" to place himself in a room with only one exit does not authorize the police to force an encounter upon him by placing themselves in front of the exit. It is no more acceptable for the police to force an encounter on a person by exploiting his "voluntary decision" to expose himself to perfectly legitimate personal or social constraints. By consciously deciding to single out persons who have undertaken interstate or intrastate travel, officers who conduct suspicionless, dragnet-style sweeps put passengers to the choice of cooperating or of exiting their buses and possibly being stranded in unfamiliar locations. It is exactly because this "choice" is no "choice" at all that police engage this technique.

In my view, the Fourth Amendment clearly condemns the suspicionless, dragnet-style sweep of intrastate or interstate buses. Withdrawing this particular weapon from the government's drug-war arsenal would hardly leave the police without any means of combatting the use of buses as instrumentalities of the drug trade. The police would remain free, for example, to approach passengers whom they have a reasonable, articulable basis to suspect of criminal wrongdoing. Alternatively, they could continue to confront passengers without suspicion so long as they took simple steps, like advising the passengers confronted of their right to decline to be questioned, to dispel the aura of coercion and intimidation that pervades such encounters. There is no reason to expect that such requirements would render the Nation's buses law-enforcement-free zones. * * *

IV. LESSER INTRUSIONS: INSPECTIONS AND REGULATORY SEARCHES

Introduction

The Supreme Court and the lower courts have upheld a rather broad range of administrative inspections and so-called regulatory searches even when conducted without a warrant and without the traditional quantum of probable cause. These decisions manifest further application of the *Camara* balancing test, previously considered as utilized in *Terry* to assay the discrete police practice of stop-and-frisk. But *Camara* itself was an administrative inspection type of case, involving inspection of dwellings for housing code violations, and thus it is not surprising that this balancing process has since been utilized in various other administrative inspection or regulatory search contexts.

One difficult question presented in such cases is that of what *kind* of departure from the traditional probable cause requirement is permissible. One kind of departure, which we have already confronted in *Terry* and which is also sometimes used in the present context as well, is to require individualized suspicion (typically referred to as reasonable suspicion) less compelling than is needed for the usual law enforcement search. Illustrative are *O'Connor v. Ortega*, 480 U.S. 709, 107 S.Ct. 1492, 94 L.Ed.2d 714 (1987), authorizing search of a government employee's workplace for work-related reasons on reasonable suspicion; and *New Jersey v. T.L.O.*, 469 U.S. 325, 105 S.Ct. 733, 83 L.Ed.2d 720 (1985), upholding search of a public school student on reasonable suspicion of a violation of school rules. Another kind of departure is to require no individualized suspicion whatsoever, but instead to require that the inspections or searches be conducted pursuant to some neutral criteria which guard against arbitrary selection of those subjected to such procedures. Illustrative are court decisions upholding airport security checks, driver's license check roadblocks, and sobriety checkpoints. The Court's latest foray into this area, while not a criminal case, provides an excellent vehicle for considering the respective merits of the reasonable suspicion and standardized procedures approaches:

VERNONIA SCHOOL DISTRICT 47J v. ACTON

__ U.S. __, 115 S.Ct. 2386, 132 L.Ed.2d 564 (1995).

Justice Scalia delivered the opinion of the Court.

The Student Athlete Drug Policy adopted by School District 47J in the town of Vernonia, Oregon, authorizes random urinalysis drug testing of students who participate in the District's school athletics programs. We granted certiorari to decide whether this violates the Fourth and Fourteenth Amendments to the United States Constitution.

Petitioner Vernonia School District 47J (District) operates one high school and three grade schools in the logging community of Vernonia, Oregon. As elsewhere in small-town America, school sports play a prominent role in the town's life, and student athletes are admired in their schools and in the community.

Drugs had not been a major problem in Vernonia schools. In the mid-to-late 1980's, however, teachers and administrators observed a sharp increase in drug use. Students began to speak out about their attraction to the drug culture, and to boast that there was nothing the school could do about it. Along with more drugs came more disciplinary problems. Between 1988 and 1989 the number of disciplinary referrals in Vernonia schools rose to more than twice the number reported in the early 1980's, and several students were suspended. Students became increasingly rude during class; outbursts of profane language became common.

Not only were student athletes included among the drug users but, as the District Court found, athletes were the leaders of the drug culture. This caused the District's administrators particular concern, since drug use increases the risk of sports-related injury. Expert testimony at the trial confirmed the deleterious effects of drugs on motivation, memory, judgment, reaction, coordination, and performance. The high school football and wrestling coach witnessed a severe sternum injury suffered by a wrestler, and various omissions of safety procedures and misexecutions by football players, all attributable in his belief to the effects of drug use.

Initially, the District responded to the drug problem by offering special classes, speakers, and presentations designed to deter drug use. It even brought in a specially trained dog to detect drugs, but the drug problem persisted. According to the District Court:

"[T]he administration was at its wits end and [a] large segment of the student body, particularly those involved in interscholastic athletics, was in a state of rebellion. Disciplinary problems had reached 'epidemic proportions.' The coincidence of an almost three-fold increase in classroom disruptions and disciplinary reports along with the staff's direct observations of students using drugs or glamorizing drug and alcohol use led the administration to the inescapable conclusion that the rebellion was being fueled by alcohol and drug abuse as well as the student's misperceptions about the drug culture."

At that point, District officials began considering a drug-testing program. They held a parent "input night" to discuss the proposed Student Athlete Drug Policy (Policy), and the parents in attendance gave their unanimous approval. The school board approved the Policy for implementation in the fall of 1989. Its expressed purpose is to prevent student athletes from using drugs, to protect their health and safety, and to provide drug users with assistance programs.

The Policy applies to all students participating in interscholastic athletics. Students wishing to play sports must sign a form consenting to the testing and must obtain the written consent of their parents. Athletes are tested at the beginning of the season for their sport. In addition, once each week of the season the names of the athletes are placed in a "pool" from which a student, with the supervision of two adults, blindly draws the names of 10% of the athletes for random testing. Those selected are notified and tested that same day, if possible.

The student to be tested completes a specimen control form which bears an assigned number. Prescription medications that the student is taking must be identified by providing a copy of the prescription or a doctor's authorization. The student then enters an empty locker room accompanied by an adult monitor of the same sex. Each boy selected produces a sample at a urinal, remaining fully clothed with his back to the monitor, who stands approximately 12 to 15 feet behind the student. Monitors may (though do not always) watch the student while he produces the sample, and they listen for normal sounds of urination. Girls produce samples in an enclosed bathroom stall, so that they can be heard but not observed. After the sample is produced, it is given to the monitor, who checks it for temperature and tampering and then transfers it to a vial.

The samples are sent to an independent laboratory, which routinely tests them for amphetamines, cocaine, and marijuana. Other drugs, such as LSD, may be screened at the request of the District, but the identity of a particular student does not determine which drugs will be tested. The laboratory's procedures are 99.94% accurate. The District follows strict procedures regarding the chain of custody and access to test results. The laboratory does not know the identity of the students whose samples it tests. It is authorized to mail written test reports only to the superintendent and to provide test results to District personnel by telephone only after the requesting official recites a code confirming his authority.

Only the superintendent, principals, vice-principals, and athletic directors have access to test results, and the results are not kept for more than one year.

If a sample tests positive, a second test is administered as soon as possible to confirm the result. If the second test is negative, no further action is taken. If the second test is positive, the athlete's parents are notified, and the school principal convenes a meeting with the student and his parents, at which the student is given the option of (1) participating for six weeks in an assistance program that includes weekly urinalysis, or (2) suffering suspension from athletics for the remainder of the current season and the next athletic season. The student is then retested prior to the start of the next athletic season for which he or she is eligible. The Policy states that a second offense results in automatic imposition of option (2); a third offense in suspension for the remainder of the current season and the next two athletic seasons.

In the fall of 1991, respondent James Acton, then a seventh-grader, signed up to play football at one of the District's grade schools. He was denied participation, however, because he and his parents refused to sign the testing consent forms. The Actons filed suit, seeking declaratory and injunctive relief from enforcement of the Policy on the grounds that it violated the Fourth and Fourteenth Amendments. [After] a bench trial, the District Court entered an order denying the claims on the merits and dismissing the action. The United States Court of Appeals for the Ninth Circuit reversed, holding that the Policy violated both the Fourth and Fourteenth Amendments * * *. We granted certiorari.

The Fourth Amendment to the United States Constitution provides that the Federal Government shall not violate "[t]he right of the people to be secure in their persons, houses, papers, and effects, against unreasonable searches and seizures...." We have held that the Fourteenth Amendment extends this constitutional guarantee to searches and seizures by state officers, including public school officials, *New Jersey v. T.L.O.*, supra. In *Skinner v. Railway Labor Executives' Assn.*, 489 U.S. 602, 109 S.Ct. 1402, 103 L.Ed.2d 639 (1989), we held that state-compelled collection and testing of urine, such as that required by the Student Athlete Drug Policy, constitutes a "search" subject to the demands of the Fourth Amendment. See also *National Treasury Employees v. Von Raab*, 489 U.S. 656, 109 S.Ct. 1384, 103 L.Ed.2d 685 (1989).

As the text of the Fourth Amendment indicates, the ultimate measure of the constitutionality of a governmental search is "reasonableness." At least in a case such as this, where there was no clear practice, either approving or disapproving the type of search at issue, at the time the constitutional provision was enacted, whether a particular search meets the reasonableness standard " 'is judged by balancing its intrusion on the individual's Fourth Amendment interests against its promotion of legitimate governmental interests.' " Where a search is undertaken by law enforcement officials to discover evidence of criminal wrongdoing, this Court has said that reasonableness generally requires the obtaining of a judicial warrant. Warrants cannot be issued, of course, without the showing of probable cause required by the Warrant Clause. But a warrant is not required to establish the reasonableness of all government searches; and when a warrant is not required (and the Warrant Clause therefore not applicable), probable cause is not invariably required either. A search unsupported by probable cause can be constitutional, we have said, "when special needs, beyond the normal need for law enforcement, make the warrant and probable-cause requirement impracticable."

We have found such "special needs" to exist in the public-school context. There, the warrant requirement "would unduly interfere with the maintenance of the swift and informal disciplinary procedures [that are] needed," and "strict adherence to the requirement that searches be based upon probable cause" would undercut "the substantial need of teachers and administrators for freedom to maintain order in the schools." *T.L.O.* The school search we approved in *T.L.O.,* while not based on probable cause, was based on individualized suspicion of wrongdoing. As we explicitly acknowledged, however, " 'the Fourth Amendment imposes no irreducible requirement of such suspicion.' " We have upheld suspicionless searches and seizures to conduct drug testing of railroad personnel involved in train accidents, see *Skinner;* to conduct random drug testing of federal customs officers who carry arms or are involved in drug interdiction, see *Von Raab;* and to maintain automobile checkpoints looking for illegal immigrants and contraband and drunk drivers.

The first factor to be considered is the nature of the privacy interest upon which the search here at issue intrudes. The Fourth Amendment does not protect all subjective expectations of privacy, but only those that society recognizes as "legitimate." What expectations are legitimate varies, of course, with context, depending, for example, upon whether the individual asserting the privacy interest is at home, at work, in a car, or in a public park. In addition, the legitimacy of certain privacy expectations vis-vis the State may depend upon the individual's legal relationship with the State. For example, in *Griffin v. Wisconsin*, 483 U.S. 868, 107 S.Ct. 3164, 97 L.Ed.2d 709 (1987), we held that, although a "probationer's home, like anyone else's, is protected by the Fourth Amendmen[t]," the supervisory relationship between probationer and State justifies "a degree of impingement upon [a probationer's] privacy that would not be constitutional if applied to the public at large." Central, in our view, to the present case is the fact that the subjects of the Policy are (1) children, who (2) have been committed to the temporary custody of the State as schoolmaster.

Traditionally at common law, and still today, unemancipated minors lack some of the most fundamental rights of self-determination—including even the right of liberty in its narrow sense, i.e., the right to come and go at will. They are subject, even as to their physical freedom, to the control of their parents or guardians. When parents place minor children in private schools for their education, the teachers and administrators of those schools stand in loco parentis over the children entrusted to them.

[In] *T.L.O.* we rejected the notion that public schools, like private schools, exercise only parental power over their students, which of course is not subject to constitutional constraints. Such a view of things, we said, "is not entirely 'consonant with compulsory education laws.' " [But] while denying that the State's power over schoolchildren is formally no more than the delegated power of their parents, *T.L.O.* did not deny, but indeed emphasized, that the nature of that power is custodial and tutelary, permitting a degree of supervision and control that could not be exercised over free adults. "[A] proper educational environment requires close supervision of schoolchildren, as well as the enforcement of rules against conduct that would be perfectly permissible if undertaken by an adult." [Thus,] while children assuredly do not "shed their constitutional rights [at] the schoolhouse gate," the nature of those rights is what is appropriate for children in school. * * *

Fourth Amendment rights [are] different in public schools than elsewhere; the "reasonableness" inquiry cannot disregard the schools' custodial and tutelary responsibility for children. For their own good and that of their classmates, public school children are routinely required to submit to various physical examinations, and to be vaccinated against various diseases. * * * Particularly with regard to medical examinations and procedures, therefore, "students within the school environment have a lesser expectation of privacy than members of the population generally."

Legitimate privacy expectations are even less with regard to student athletes. School sports are not for the bashful. They require "suiting up" before each practice or event, and showering and changing afterwards. Public school locker rooms, the usual sites for these activities, are not notable for the privacy they afford. The locker rooms in Vernonia are typical: no individual dressing rooms are provided; shower heads are lined up along a wall, unseparated by any sort of partition or curtain; not even all the toilet stalls have doors.

There is an additional respect in which school athletes have a reduced expectation of privacy. By choosing to "go out for the team," they voluntarily subject themselves to a degree of regulation even higher than that imposed on students generally. In Vernonia's public schools, they must submit to a preseason physical exam (James testified that his included the giving of a urine sample), they must acquire adequate insurance coverage or sign an insurance waiver, maintain a minimum grade point average, and comply with any "rules of conduct, dress, training hours and related matters as may be established for each sport by the head coach and athletic director with the principal's approval." Somewhat like adults who choose to participate in a "closely regulated industry," students who voluntarily participate in school athletics have reason to expect intrusions upon normal rights and privileges, including privacy.

Having considered the scope of the legitimate expectation of privacy at issue here, we turn next to the character of the intrusion that is complained of. We recognized in *Skinner* that collecting the samples for urinalysis intrudes upon "an excretory function traditionally shielded by great privacy." We noted, however, that the degree of intrusion depends upon the manner in which production of the urine sample is monitored. Under the District's Policy, male students produce samples at a urinal along a wall. They remain fully clothed and are only observed from behind, if at all. Female students produce samples in an enclosed stall, with a female monitor standing outside listening only for sounds of tampering. These conditions are nearly identical to those typically encountered in public restrooms, which men, women, and especially school children use daily. Under such conditions, the privacy interests compromised by the process of obtaining the urine sample are in our view negligible.

The other privacy-invasive aspect of urinalysis is, of course, the information it discloses concerning the state of the subject's body, and the materials he has ingested. In this regard it is significant that the tests at issue here look only for drugs, and not for whether the student is, for example, epileptic, pregnant, or diabetic. Moreover, the drugs for which the samples are screened are standard, and do not vary according to the identity of the student. And finally, the results of the tests are disclosed only to a limited class of school personnel who have a need to know; and they are not turned over to law enforcement authorities or used for any internal disciplinary function. * * *

Finally, we turn to consider the nature and immediacy of the governmental concern at issue here, and the efficacy of this means for meeting it. In both *Skinner* and *Von Raab*, we characterized the government interest motivating the search as "compelling." *Skinner* (interest in preventing railway accidents); *Von Raab* (interest in insuring fitness of customs officials to interdict drugs and handle firearms). [It] is a mistake, however, to think that the phrase "compelling state interest," in the Fourth Amendment context, describes a fixed, minimum quantum of governmental concern, so that one can dispose of a case by answering in isolation the question: Is there a compelling state interest here? Rather, the phrase describes an interest which appears important enough to justify the particular search at hand, in light of other factors which show the search to be relatively intrusive upon a genuine expectation of privacy. Whether that relatively high degree of government concern is necessary in this case or not, we think it is met.

That the nature of the concern is important—indeed, perhaps compelling— can hardly be doubted. Deterring drug use by our Nation's schoolchildren is at least as important as enhancing efficient enforcement of the Nation's laws against the importation of drugs, which was the governmental concern in *Von Raab,* or deterring drug use by engineers and trainmen, which was the governmental concern in *Skinner.* School years are the time when the physical, psychological, and addictive effects of drugs are most severe. [And] of course the effects of a drug-infested school are visited not just upon the users, but upon the entire student body and faculty, as the educational process is disrupted. In the present case, moreover, the necessity for the State to act is magnified by the fact that this evil is being visited not just upon individuals at large, but upon children for whom it has undertaken a special responsibility of care and direction. Finally, it must not be lost sight of that this program is directed more narrowly to drug use by school athletes, where the risk of immediate physical harm to the drug user or those with whom he is playing his sport is particularly high. Apart from psychological effects, which include impairment of judgment, slow reaction time, and a lessening of the perception of pain, the particular drugs screened by the District's Policy have been demonstrated to pose substantial physical risks to athletes.

[As] for the immediacy of the District's concerns: We are not inclined to question—indeed, we could not possibly find clearly erroneous—the District Court's conclusion that "a large segment of the student body, particularly those involved in interscholastic athletics, was in a state of rebellion," that "[d]isciplinary actions had reached 'epidemic proportions,'" and that "the rebellion was being fueled by alcohol and drug abuse as well as by the student's misperceptions about the drug culture." That is an immediate crisis of greater proportions than existed in *Skinner,* where we upheld the Government's drug testing program based on findings of drug use by railroad employees nationwide, without proof that a problem existed on the particular railroads whose employees were subject to the test. And of much greater proportions than existed in *Von Raab,* where there was no documented history of drug use by any customs officials.

As to the efficacy of this means for addressing the problem: It seems to us self-evident that a drug problem largely fueled by the "role model" effect of athletes' drug use, and of particular danger to athletes, is effectively addressed by making sure that athletes do not use drugs. Respondents argue that a "less intrusive means to the same end" was available, namely, "drug testing on suspicion of drug use." We have repeatedly refused to declare that only the "least intrusive" search practicable can be reasonable under the Fourth Amendment. Respondents' alternative entails substantial difficulties—if it is indeed practicable at all. It may be impracticable, for one thing, simply because the parents who are willing to accept random drug testing for athletes are not willing to accept accusatory drug testing for all students, which transforms the process into a badge of shame. Respondents' proposal brings the risk that teachers will impose testing arbitrarily upon troublesome but not drug-likely students. It generates the expense of defending lawsuits that charge such arbitrary imposition, or that simply demand greater process before accusatory drug testing is imposed. And not least of all, it adds to the ever-expanding diversionary duties of schoolteachers the new function of spotting and bringing to account drug abuse, a task for which they are ill prepared, and which is not readily compatible with their vocation. In many respects, we think, testing based on "suspicion" of drug use would not be better, but worse.

Taking into account all the factors we have considered above—the decreased expectation of privacy, the relative unobtrusiveness of the search, and the severity of the need met by the search—we conclude Vernonia's Policy is reasonable and hence constitutional.

We caution against the assumption that suspicionless drug testing will readily pass constitutional muster in other contexts. The most significant element in this case is the first we discussed: that the Policy was undertaken in furtherance of the government's responsibilities, under a public school system, as guardian and tutor of children entrusted to its care. Just as when the government conducts a search in its capacity as employer (a warrantless search of an absent employee's desk to obtain an urgently needed file, for example), the relevant question is whether that intrusion upon privacy is one that a reasonable employer might engage in, so also when the government acts as guardian and tutor the relevant question is whether the search is one that a reasonable guardian and tutor might undertake. Given the findings of need made by the District Court, we conclude that in the present case it is.

We may note that the primary guardians of Vernonia's schoolchildren appear to agree. The record shows no objection to this districtwide program by any parents other than the couple before us here—even though, as we have described, a public meeting was held to obtain parents' views. We find insufficient basis to contradict the judgment of Vernonia's parents, its school board, and the District Court, as to what was reasonably in the interest of these children under the circumstances. * * *

Justice Ginsburg, concurring. * * * I comprehend the Court's opinion as reserving the question whether the District, on no more than the showing made here, constitutionally could impose routine drug testing not only on those seeking to engage with others in team sports, but on all students required to attend school.

Justice O'Connor, with whom Justice Stevens and Justice Souter join, dissenting.

The population of our Nation's public schools, grades 7 through 12, numbers around 18 million. By the reasoning of today's decision, the millions of these students who participate in interscholastic sports, an overwhelming majority of whom have given school officials no reason whatsoever to suspect they use drugs at school, are open to an intrusive bodily search.

In justifying this result, the Court dispenses with a requirement of individualized suspicion on considered policy grounds. [In] making these policy arguments, of course, the Court sidesteps powerful, countervailing privacy concerns. Blanket searches, because they can involve "thousands or millions" of searches, "pos[e] a greater threat to liberty" than do suspicion-based ones, which "affec[t] one person at a time." Searches based on individualized suspicion also afford potential targets considerable control over whether they will, in fact, be searched because a person can avoid such a search by not acting in an objectively suspicious way. And given that the surest way to avoid acting suspiciously is to avoid the underlying wrongdoing, the costs of such a regime, one would think, are minimal.

But whether a blanket search is "better" than a regime based on individualized suspicion is not a debate in which we should engage. In my view, it is not open to judges or government officials to decide on policy grounds which is better and which is worse. For most of our constitutional history, mass, suspicionless searches have been generally considered per se unreasonable within the meaning of the Fourth Amendment. And we have allowed exceptions in recent years only where it has been clear that a suspicion-based regime would be ineffectual. Because that is not the case here, I dissent.

[The view expressed in *Carroll v. United States*, 267 U.S. 132, 45 S.Ct. 280, 69 L.Ed. 543 (1925)] that blanket searches are "intolerable and unreasonable" is well-grounded in history. As recently confirmed in one of the most exhaustive analyses of the original meaning of the Fourth Amendment ever undertaken, what the Framers of the Fourth Amendment most strongly opposed, with limited exceptions wholly inapplicable here, were general searches—that is, searches by general warrant, by writ of assistance, by broad statute, or by any other similar authority. * * *

More important, there is no indication in the historical materials that the Framers' opposition to general searches stemmed solely from the fact that they allowed officials to single out individuals for arbitrary reasons, and thus that officials could render them reasonable simply by making sure to extend their search to every house in a given area or to every person in a given group. * * *

Perhaps most telling of all, as reflected in the text of the Warrant Clause, the particular way the Framers chose to curb the abuses of general warrants—and by implication, all general searches—was not to impose a novel "evenhandedness" requirement; it was to retain the individualized suspicion requirement contained in the typical general warrant, but to make that requirement meaningful and enforceable, for instance, by raising the required level of individualized suspicion to objective probable cause.

[The] view that mass, suspicionless searches, however evenhanded, are generally unreasonable remains inviolate in the criminal law enforcement context. * * *

Thus, it remains the law that the police cannot, say, subject to drug testing every person entering or leaving a certain drug-ridden neighborhood in order to find evidence of crime. And this is true even though it is hard to think of a more compelling government interest than the need to fight the scourge of drugs on our streets and in our neighborhoods. Nor could it be otherwise, for if being evenhanded were enough to justify evaluating a search regime under an open-ended balancing test, the Warrant Clause, which presupposes that there is some category of searches for which individualized suspicion is non-negotiable, would be a dead letter.

Outside the criminal context, however, in response to the exigencies of modern life, our cases have upheld several evenhanded blanket searches, including some that are more than minimally intrusive, after balancing the invasion of privacy against the government's strong need. Most of these cases, of course, are distinguishable insofar as they involved searches either not of a personally intrusive nature, such as searches of closely regulated businesses, or arising in unique contexts such as prisons.

[In] any event, in many of the cases that can be distinguished on the grounds suggested above and, more important, in all of the cases that cannot, see, e.g., *Skinner* (blanket drug testing scheme); *Von Raab* (same); cf. *Camara v. Municipal Court,* supra (area-wide searches of private residences), we upheld the suspicionless search only after first recognizing the Fourth Amendment's longstanding preference for a suspicion-based search regime, and then pointing to sound reasons why such a regime would likely be ineffectual under the unusual circumstances presented. In *Skinner,* for example, we stated outright that " 'some quantum of individualized suspicion' " is "usually required" under the Fourth Amendment, and we built the requirement into the test we announced: "In limited circumstances, where the privacy interests implicated by the search are minimal, and where an important governmental interest furthered by the intrusion would be placed in jeopardy by a requirement of individualized suspicion, a search may be reasonable despite the absence of such suspicion." The obvious negative implication of this reasoning is that, if such an individualized suspicion requirement would not place the government's objectives in jeopardy, the requirement should not be forsaken.

Accordingly, we upheld the suspicionless regime at issue in *Skinner* on the firm understanding that a requirement of individualized suspicion for testing train operators for drug or alcohol impairment following serious train accidents would be unworkable because "the scene of a serious rail accident is chaotic." (Of course, it could be plausibly argued that the fact that testing occurred only after train operators were involved in serious train accidents amounted to an individualized suspicion requirement in all but name, in light of the record evidence of a strong link between serious train accidents and drug and alcohol use.) We have performed a similar inquiry in the other cases as well. * * *

Moreover, an individualized suspicion requirement was often impractical in these cases because they involved situations in which even one undetected instance of wrongdoing could have injurious consequences for a great number of people. See, e.g., *Camara* (even one safety code violation can cause "fires and epidemics [that] ravage large urban areas"); *Skinner,* supra (even one drug- or alcohol-impaired train operator can lead to the "disastrous consequences" of a train wreck, such as "great human loss"); *Von Raab* (even one customs official caught up in drugs can, by virtue of impairment, susceptibility to bribes, or indifference, result in the noninterdiction of a "sizable drug shipmen[t]," which eventually injures the lives of thousands, or to a breach of "national security").

The instant case stands in marked contrast. One searches today's majority opinion in vain for recognition that history and precedent establish that individualized suspicion is "usually required" under the Fourth Amendment (regardless of whether a warrant and probable cause are also required) and that, in the area of intrusive personal searches, the only recognized exception is for situations in which a suspicion-based scheme would be likely ineffectual.

[But] having misconstrued the fundamental role of the individualized suspicion requirement in Fourth Amendment analysis, the Court never seriously engages the practicality of such a requirement in the instant case. And that failure is crucial because nowhere is it less clear that an individualized suspicion requirement would be ineffectual than in the school context. In most schools, the entire pool of potential search targets—students—is under constant supervision by teachers and administrators and coaches, be it in classrooms, hallways, or locker rooms.

The record here indicates that the Vernonia schools are no exception. The great irony of this case is that most (though not all) of the evidence the District introduced to justify its suspicionless drug-testing program consisted of first- or second-hand stories of particular, identifiable students acting in ways that plainly gave rise to reasonable suspicion of in-school drug use—and thus that would have justified a drug-related search under our *T.L.O.* decision. Small groups of students, for example, were observed by a teacher "passing joints back and forth" across the street at a restaurant before school and during school hours. Another group was caught skipping school and using drugs at one of the students' houses. Several students actually admitted their drug use to school officials (some of them being caught with marijuana pipes). One student presented himself to his teacher as "clearly obviously inebriated" and had to be sent home. Still another was observed dancing and singing at the top of his voice in the back of the classroom; when the teacher asked what was going on, he replied, "Well, I'm just high on life." To take a final example, on a certain road trip, the school wrestling coach smelled marijuana smoke in a hotel room occupied by four wrestlers, an observation that (after some questioning) would probably have given him reasonable suspicion to test one or all of them.

In light of all this evidence of drug use by particular students, there is a substantial basis for concluding that a vigorous regime of suspicion-based testing (for which the District appears already to have rules in place) would have gone a long way toward solving Vernonia's school drug problem while preserving the Fourth Amendment rights of James Acton and others like him. And were there any doubt about such a conclusion, it is removed by indications in the record that suspicion-based testing could have been supplemented by an equally vigorous campaign to have Vernonia's parents encourage their children to submit to the District's voluntary drug testing program. In these circumstances, the Fourth Amendment dictates that a mass, suspicionless search regime is categorically unreasonable.

[The] principal counterargument to all this, central to the Court's opinion, is that the Fourth Amendment is more lenient with respect to school searches. That is no doubt correct, for, as the Court explains, schools have traditionally had special guardian-like responsibilities for children that necessitate a degree of constitutional leeway. This principle explains the considerable Fourth Amendment leeway we gave school officials in *T.L.O.* In that case, we held that children at school do not enjoy two of the Fourth Amendment's traditional categorical protections against unreasonable searches and seizures: the warrant requirement and the probable cause requirement.

[The] instant case, however, asks whether the Fourth Amendment is even more lenient than that, i.e., whether it is so lenient that students may be deprived of the Fourth Amendment's only remaining, and most basic, categorical protection: its strong preference for an individualized suspicion requirement, with its accompanying antipathy toward personally intrusive, blanket searches of mostly innocent people. [T]he answer must plainly be no.

I find unpersuasive the Court's reliance on the widespread practice of physical examinations and vaccinations, which are both blanket searches of a sort. [A] suspicion requirement for vaccinations is not merely impractical; it is nonsensical, for vaccinations are not searches for anything in particular and so there is nothing about which to be suspicious. [As] for physical examinations, the practicability of a suspicion requirement is highly doubtful because the conditions for which these physical exams ordinarily search, such as latent heart conditions, do not manifest themselves in observable behavior the way school drug use does.

I do not believe that suspicionless drug testing is justified on these facts. But even if I agreed that some such testing were reasonable here, I see two other Fourth Amendment flaws in the District's program. First, and most serious, there is virtually no evidence in the record of a drug problem at the Washington Grade School, which includes the 7th and 8th grades, and which Acton attended when this litigation began. * * *

Second, even as to the high school, I find unreasonable the school's choice of student athletes as the class to subject to suspicionless testing—a choice that appears to have been driven more by a belief in what would pass constitutional muster, than by a belief in what was required to meet the District's principal disciplinary concern. Reading the full record in this case, it seems quite obvious that the true driving force behind the District's adoption of its drug testing program was the need to combat the rise in drug-related disorder and disruption in its classrooms and around campus. [And] the record in this case surely demonstrates there was a drug-related discipline problem in Vernonia of " 'epidemic proportions.' " The evidence of a drug-related sports injury problem at Vernonia, by contrast, was considerably weaker.

On this record, then, it seems to me that the far more reasonable choice would have been to focus on the class of students found to have violated published school rules against severe disruption in class and around campus, disruption that had a strong nexus to drug use, as the District established at trial. Such a choice would share two of the virtues of a suspicion-based regime: testing dramatically fewer students, tens as against hundreds, and giving students control, through their behavior, over the likelihood that they would be tested. Moreover, there would be a reduced concern for the accusatory nature of the search, because the Court's feared "badge of shame," would already exist, due to the antecedent accusation and finding of severe disruption. In a lesser known aspect of *Skinner,* we upheld an analogous testing scheme with little hesitation. See *Skinner* (describing " 'Authorization to Test for Cause' " scheme, according to which train operators would be tested "in the event of certain specific rule violations, including noncompliance with a signal and excessive speeding").

It cannot be too often stated that the greatest threats to our constitutional freedoms come in times of crisis. But we must also stay mindful that not all government responses to such times are hysterical overreactions; some crises are quite real, and when they are, they serve precisely as the compelling state interest that we have said may justify a measured intrusion on constitutional rights. The only way for judges to mediate these conflicting impulses is to do what they should do anyway: stay close to the record in each case that appears before them, and make their judgments based on that alone. Having reviewed the record here, I cannot avoid the conclusion that the District's suspicionless policy of testing all student-athletes sweeps too broadly, and too imprecisely, to be reasonable under the Fourth Amendment.

SECTION 2. THE RIGHT TO COUNSEL, TRANSCRIPTS AND OTHER AIDS; POVERTY, EQUALITY AND THE ADVERSARY SYSTEM

I. THE RIGHT TO APPOINTED COUNSEL[a]

When the Court, per Sutherland, J., spoke eloquently of the importance of the right to counsel and the essential relationship between "the right to be heard" and "the right to be heard by counsel" in the landmark case of *Powell v. Alabama,* 287 U.S. 45, 53 S.Ct. 55, 77 L.Ed. 158 (1932), which has been called the first "modern" procedural due process case, it was talking about a person's right to be heard by counsel "employed by and appearing for him." Although Justice Black's analysis for the Court thirty years later in *Gideon v. Wainwright* appears to ignore this fact, *Powell* dealt primarily not with the right to appointed counsel, but the historically separate right of the individual to employ her own counsel.

The *Powell* opinion spelled out at some length why the defendants were not afforded "a fair opportunity to secure counsel of [their] own choice" and why, under the circumstances, this constituted a denial of due process. The *Powell* Court went on to say however, and it did this only in the last few pages of a lengthy opinion, that "assuming the inability, even if opportunity had been given, to employ counsel," the failure of the trial court "to make an effective appointment of counsel was likewise a denial of due process." Continued the Court, using very measured language:

> "Whether this would be so in other criminal prosecutions, or under other circumstances, we need not determine. All that is necessary now to decide, as we do decide, is that in a capital case, where the defendant is unable to employ counsel, and is incapable adequately of making his own defense because of ignorance, feeblemindedness, illiteracy, or the like, it is the duty of the court, whether requested or not, to assign counsel for him as a necessary requisite of due process of law; and that duty is not discharged by an assignment at such a time or under such circumstances as to preclude the giving of effective aid in the preparation and trial of the case."

Despite the *Powell* Court's carefully limited statement about the right to appointed counsel in state criminal cases, when the Court held, six years later, in *Johnson v. Zerbst,* 304 U.S. 458, 58 S.Ct. 1019, 82 L.Ed. 1461 (1938), that the Sixth Amendment required *federal* courts to provide indigent defendants with appointed counsel in all serious criminal cases (at least all felony cases), many thought the same rule would soon be applied to state prosecutions. For Justice Black, who wrote the opinion for the *Johnson* Court, painted with a broad brush, giving the impression that the Court was prepared to say that the right to counsel, appointed or retained, was a "fundamental" right made obligatory upon the states by the Fourteenth Amendment.

Thus, Justice Black called the right to counsel "one of the safeguards * * * deemed necessary to insure fundamental human rights of life and liberty" and the Sixth Amendment "a constant admonition that if the constitutional safeguards it provides be lost, justice will not 'still be done.'" Relying heavily on *Powell* 's discussion of the general need for, and importance of, the right to counsel,

a. *Douglas v. California* also deals with the right to appointed counsel—on the first appeal, granted by the state as a matter of right—but because it is based primarily on the Equal Protection Clause it is set forth in the next subsection.

Johnson concluded that the Sixth Amendment embodies "the obvious truth that the average defendant does not have the professional legal skill to protect himself when brought before a tribunal" and that the Amendment "withholds from federal courts, in all criminal proceedings, the power and authority to deprive an accused of his life or liberty unless he has or waives the assistance of counsel."

However, in *Betts v. Brady*, the first case set forth in this section, the Court refused to read *Powell* broadly or to apply *Johnson* to the states via the Fourteenth Amendment's due process clause. Instead, the Court formulated a "prejudice" or "special circumstances" rule: an indigent defendant in a non-capital case [b] had to show specifically that he had been "prejudiced" by the absence of a lawyer or that "special circumstances" (e.g., the defendant's lack of education or intelligence or the gravity and complexity of the offense charged) rendered criminal proceedings without the assistance of defense counsel "fundamentally unfair." [c]

One of the troubles with the *Betts v. Brady* doctrine was that its application was inherently speculative and problematic. A record produced by a layperson defending himself often makes the person *look* overwhelmingly guilty and the case *look* exceedingly simple. Such a record does not reflect what defenses or mitigating circumstances a trained advocate would have seen or what lines of inquiry she would have pursued. This point was made very forcefully by Justice Black (joined by Douglas and Murphy, JJ.), dissenting in *Betts*. Twenty-one years later, Justice Black wrote the opinion for the Court in *Gideon v. Wainwright,* overruling *Betts*.

The opinion in *Gideon,* the second case set forth in this section, might have been written differently. It might, to use concurring Justice Harlan's phrase, have accorded *Betts* "a more respectful burial." For example, Justice Black might have pointed out that in the two decades since *Betts* the assumption that a lawyerless defendant would usually be able to defend himself had fared poorly as the Court repeatedly found "special circumstances" requiring the services of counsel and constantly expanded the concept of "special circumstances." [d] Justice Black might also have noted that the assumption that a "special circumstances" test was more consistent with the "obligations of federalism" than an "absolute rule" had collapsed in the face of the proliferation of federal habeas corpus cases produced by the *Betts* rule and the resulting friction between state and federal courts.

But Justice Black made no attempt to show that developments in the two decades since *Betts* militated in favor of its demise. Perhaps he was reluctant to admit even the *original validity* of a decision that exemplified the evils (to him) of

---

b. Soon after *Betts,* the Court indicated that an indigent person had a "flat" or unqualified right to appointed counsel when (but only when) charged with a crime punishable by death.

c. When the Court reviewed Betts' case, he had appellate counsel, but his lawyer was confident—too confident—that the Court would apply the full measure of the Sixth Amendment right to counsel to the states. Thus, he did not make any analysis of the trial and present any specific examples of how Betts was, or might have been, prejudiced by the absence of counsel. Commentators, upon review of the *Betts* record, have maintained that a number of such examples could have been shown.

d. In *Chewning v. Cunningham,* 368 U.S. 443, 82 S.Ct. 498, 7 L.Ed.2d 442 (1962), the last of the *Betts* rule cases, the Court not only found "special circumstances" requiring the services of counsel, as it had in every case after 1950, but indicated that these circumstances would be made out whenever issues existed that "may well be considered by an *imaginative lawyer* " (emphasis added) without regard to "whether *any would have merit* " (emphasis added). As concurring Justice Harlan protested on that occasion, "the bare possibility that any of these improbable claims could have been asserted does not amount [to] 'exceptional circumstances' " as the *Betts* rule had long been understood.

the "fundamental rights" interpretation of Fourteenth Amendment Due Process.[e] Perhaps he was determined to vindicate his own dissenting opinion in *Betts*.

Although *Gideon* was one of the most popular cases ever decided by the Supreme Court, it came fairly late in the day. Indeed, it is quite surprising that the Court did not establish the constitutional right to appointed counsel in all serious criminal cases until *two years after* it imposed the Fourth Amendment exclusionary rule on state courts as a matter of due process.

It is helpful to view criminal procedural due process as containing two major values or objectives. The first and the more obvious one is insuring the reliability of the guilt-determining process. The second and more elusive one is insuring respect for the dignity or liberty of the individual without regard to the reliability of the criminal process. The search and seizure exclusionary rule implements the second goal; the right to counsel (sometimes called "the most pervasive right" of the accused or "the master key" to all rights) effectuates the first—and the most basic goal. Yet the Court moved ahead on the search and seizure front before it overruled the *Betts* rule.

Moreover, a major criticism of *Weeks* and *Mapp* (Sec. 1, supra) was that because they addressed problems beyond the direct control of the courts these cases could not accomplish their goal—deterring illegal searches and seizures. But this criticism was not applicable to enlargement of the indigent defendant's right to counsel. For the *Betts–Gideon* line of cases dealt with the right to appointed counsel at arraignment, trial and sentencing, matters within the immediate and continuing control of the courts. Assuming arguendo that police officers and sheriffs are insensitive to acquittals and reversals, trial judges and prosecutors are not—and they would be entrusted with the task of carrying out the requirements of an enlarged right to appointed counsel.

Note, too, that when the Court in *Mapp* imposed the exclusionary rule on the states in 1961, the states were evenly split on the question. But when the Court in *Gideon* reconsidered the *Betts* doctrine in 1963, some thirty-seven states—about a three to one margin—provided counsel for all indigent felony defendants regardless of special circumstances. Moreover, as Mr. Gideon's lawyers pointed out to the Supreme Court, of the thirteen states whose laws or rules did not require the appointment of counsel in all felony cases, eight usually did so as a matter of practice. Only five southern states made no regular provision for counsel in noncapital cases.

Of course, three years after *Gideon,* when the Court applied the right to assigned counsel to the proceedings in the police station (see *Miranda*, Ch. 6, § 3), *no* state had chosen to go nearly that far on its own and, unlike *Gideon* (when twenty-two states asked the Court to overrule *Betts*), no state urged the Court to go that far. That is one reason (but hardly the only reason) that *Miranda* had a much colder reception than *Gideon*.

How early in the criminal process the right to counsel should "begin" was not the only question left open by *Gideon*. Another was: At what stage in the criminal process does the right to counsel "end"? The first appeal as of right? Discretionary review in the state supreme court? Discretionary review in the U.S. Supreme Court? (See the next section, infra.) Still another question left open by *Gideon* was: What *kinds* of criminal cases are covered by *Gideon*?

Some thought *Gideon* should be limited to felony cases. Others thought it should include any crime *punishable* by a term of imprisonment. Still others

e. See also, Black, J., dissenting in *Adamson v. California*, p. 102 supra.

thought a line should be drawn, as it had been in cases dealing with the right to jury, between serious misdemeanors and "petty offenses" (those punishable by six months imprisonment or less). As demonstrated by the last two cases in this section, *Argersinger v. Hamlin* and *Scott v. Illinois,* the Court adopted none of the aforementioned approaches.

BETTS v. BRADY

316 U.S. 455, 62 S.Ct. 1252, 86 L.Ed. 1595 (1942).

JUSTICE ROBERTS delivered the opinion of the Court.

Petitioner, an indigent, was indicted for robbery. His request for counsel was denied because local practice permitted appointment only in rape and murder prosecutions. Petitioner then pled not guilty and elected to be tried without a jury. At the trial he chose not to take the stand. He was convicted and sentenced to eight years imprisonment.

[The] due process clause of the Fourteenth Amendment does not incorporate, as such, the specific guarantees found in the Sixth Amendment although a denial by a state of rights or privileges specifically embodied in that and others of the first eight amendments may, in certain circumstances, or in connection with other elements, operate, in a given case, to deprive a litigant of due process of law in violation of the Fourteenth. [Due process] formulates a concept less rigid and more fluid than those envisaged in other specific and particular provisions of the Bill of Rights. Its application is less a matter of rule. Asserted denial is to be tested by an appraisal of the totality of facts in a given case.

[Petitioner] says the rule to be deduced from our former decisions is that, in every case, whatever the circumstances, one charged with crime, who is unable to obtain counsel, must be furnished counsel by the state. Expressions in the opinions of this court lend color to the argument, but, as the petitioner admits, none of our decisions squarely adjudicates the question now presented.

In *Powell v. Alabama,* supra, ignorant and friendless negro youths, strangers in the community, without friends or means to obtain counsel, were hurried to trial for a capital offense without effective appointment of counsel [and] without adequate opportunity to consult even the counsel casually appointed to represent them. This occurred in a State whose statute law required the appointment of counsel for indigent defendants prosecuted for the offense charged. Thus the trial was conducted in disregard of every principle of fairness and in disregard of that which was declared by the law of the State a requisite of a fair trial. This court [stated] further that "under the circumstances [the] necessity of counsel was so vital and imperative that the failure of the trial court to make an effective appointment of counsel was likewise a denial of due process," but added: "whether this would be so in other criminal prosecutions, or under other circumstances, we need not determine. All that it is necessary now to decide, as we do decide, is that in a capital case, where the defendant is unable to employ counsel, and is incapable adequately of making his own defense because of ignorance, feeble-mindedness, illiteracy, or the like, it is the duty of the court, whether requested or not, to assign counsel for him as a necessary requisite of due process of law * * *"

* * * We have construed the [Sixth Amendment] to require appointment of counsel in all [federal] cases where a defendant is unable to procure the services of an attorney, and where the right has not been intentionally and competently waived. [*Johnson v. Zerbst,* supra]. Though [the] amendment lays down no rule

for the conduct of the states, the question recurs whether the constraint laid by the amendment upon the national courts expresses a rule so fundamental and essential to a fair trial, and so, to due process of law, that it is made obligatory upon the states by the Fourteenth Amendment. Relevant data on the subject are afforded by constitutional and statutory provisions subsisting in the colonies and the states prior to the inclusion of the Bill of Rights in the national Constitution, and in the constitutional, legislative, and judicial history of the states to the present date.

[I]n the great majority of the states, it has been the considered judgment of the people, their representatives and their courts that appointment of counsel is not a fundamental right, essential to a fair trial. On the contrary, the matter has generally been deemed one of legislative policy. In the light of this evidence we are unable to say that the concept of due process incorporated in the Fourteenth Amendment obligates the states, whatever may be their own views, to furnish counsel in every such case. Every court has power, if it deems proper, to appoint counsel where that course seems to be required in the interest of fairness.

The practice of the courts of Maryland gives point to the principle that the states should not be straight-jacketed in this respect, by a construction of the Fourteenth Amendment. Judge Bond's opinion states, and counsel at the bar confirmed the fact, that in Maryland the usual practice is for the defendant to waive a trial by jury. This the petitioner did in the present case. Such trials, as Judge Bond remarks, are much more informal than jury trials and it is obvious that the judge can much better control the course of the trial and is in a better position to see impartial justice done than when the formalities of a jury trial are involved.

In this case there was no question of the commission of a robbery. The State's case consisted of evidence identifying the petitioner as the perpetrator. The defense was an alibi. Petitioner called and examined witnesses to prove that he was at another place at the time of the commission of the offense. The simple issue was the veracity of the testimony for the State and that for the defendant. As Judge Bond says, the accused was not helpless, but was a man forty-three years old, of ordinary intelligence and ability to take care of his own interests on the trial of that narrow issue. He had once before been in a criminal court, pleaded guilty to larceny and served a sentence and was not wholly unfamiliar with criminal procedure. It is quite clear that in Maryland, if the situation had been otherwise and it had appeared that the petitioner was, for any reason, at a serious disadvantage by reason of the lack of counsel, a refusal to appoint would have resulted in the reversal of a judgment of conviction.

[To] deduce from the due process clause a rule binding upon the states in this matter would be to impose upon them, as Judge Bond points out, a requirement without distinction between criminal charges of different magnitude or in respect of courts of varying jurisdiction. As he says: "Charges of small crimes tried before justices of the peace and capital charges tried in the higher courts would equally require the appointment of counsel. Presumably it would be argued that trials in the Traffic Court would require it."

As we have said, the Fourteenth Amendment prohibits the conviction and incarceration of one whose trial is offensive to the common and fundamental ideas of fairness and right, and while want of counsel in a particular case may result in a conviction lacking in such fundamental fairness, we cannot say that the amendment embodies an inexorable command that no trial for any offense, or in any court, can be fairly conducted and justice accorded a defendant who is not represented by counsel.

The judgment is affirmed.

JUSTICE BLACK, dissenting, with whom JUSTICE DOUGLAS and JUSTICE MURPHY concur.

To hold that the petitioner had a constitutional right to counsel in this case does not require us to say that "no trial for any offense, or in any court, can be fairly conducted and justice accorded a defendant who is not represented by counsel." This case can be determined by resolution of a narrower question: whether in view of the nature of the offense and the circumstances of his trial and conviction, this petitioner was denied the procedural protection which is his right under the federal constitution. I think he was.

The petitioner [was] a farm hand, out of a job and on relief. [The] court below found that [he] had "at least an ordinary amount of intelligence." It is clear from his examination of witnesses that he was a man of little education.

If this case had come to us from a federal court, it is clear we should have to reverse it, because the Sixth Amendment makes the right to counsel in criminal cases inviolable by the federal government. I believe that the Fourteenth Amendment made the sixth applicable to the states. But this view [has] never been accepted by a majority of this Court and is not accepted today. * * * I believe, however, that under the prevailing view of due process, as reflected in the opinion just announced, a view which gives this Court such vast supervisory powers that I am not prepared to accept it without grave doubts, the judgment below should be reversed.

[The] right to counsel in a criminal proceeding is "fundamental." *Powell v. Alabama.* [A] practice cannot be reconciled with "common and fundamental ideas of fairness and right" which subjects innocent men to increased dangers of conviction merely because of their poverty. Whether a man is innocent cannot be determined from a trial in which as here, denial of counsel has made it impossible to conclude, with any satisfactory degree of certainty, that the defendant's case was adequately presented. * * *

Denial to the poor of the request for counsel in proceedings based on charges of serious crime has long been regarded as shocking to the "universal sense of justice" throughout this country. In 1854, for example, the Supreme Court of Indiana said: "It is not to be thought of, in a civilized community, for a moment, that any citizen put in jeopardy of life or liberty should be debarred of counsel because he was too poor to employ such aid. No Court could be respected, or respect itself, to sit and hear such a trial. The defence of the poor, in such cases, is a duty resting somewhere, which will be at once conceded as essential to the accused, to the Court, and to the public." And most of the other states have shown their agreement by constitutional provisions, statutes, or established practice judicially approved which assure that no man shall be deprived of counsel merely because of his poverty. Any other practice seems to me to defeat the promise of our democratic society to provide equal justice under the law.

GIDEON v. WAINWRIGHT
372 U.S. 335, 83 S.Ct. 792, 9 L.Ed.2d 799 (1963).

JUSTICE BLACK delivered the opinion of the Court.

Petitioner was charged in a Florida state court with having broken and entered a poolroom with intent to commit a misdemeanor. This offense is a felony under Florida law.   Appearing in court without funds and without a lawyer, petitioner asked the court to appoint counsel for him, whereupon the following colloquy took place:

> "The Court: Mr. Gideon, I am sorry, but I cannot appoint Counsel to represent you in this case.   Under the laws of the State of Florida, the only time the Court can appoint Counsel to represent a Defendant is when that person is charged with a capital offense.   * * *

> "The Defendant: The United States Supreme Court says I am entitled to be represented by Counsel."

Put to trial before a jury, Gideon conducted his defense about as well as could be expected from a layman.   He made an opening statement to the jury, cross-examined the State's witnesses, presented witnesses in his own defense, declined to testify himself, and made a short argument "emphasizing his innocence to the charge contained in the Information filed in this case."   The jury returned a verdict of guilty, and petitioner was sentenced to serve five years in the state prison.   Later, petitioner [unsuccessfully attacked his conviction and sentence in the state supreme court on the ground that the trial court's refusal to appoint counsel for him violated his constitutional rights].   Since 1942, when *Betts v. Brady* was decided by a divided Court, the problem of a defendant's federal constitutional right to counsel in a state court has been a continuing source of controversy and litigation in both state and federal courts.   To give this problem another review here, we granted certiorari [and] appointed counsel to represent [petitioner].

We accept *Betts*'s assumption, based as it was on our prior cases, that a provision of the Bill of Rights which is "fundamental and essential to a fair trial" is made obligatory upon the States by the Fourteenth Amendment.   We think the Court in *Betts* was wrong, however, in concluding that the Sixth Amendment's guarantee of counsel is not one of these fundamental rights.   Ten years before *Betts,* this Court, after full consideration of all the historical data examined in *Betts,* had unequivocally declared that "the right to the aid of counsel is of this fundamental character."   *Powell.*   While the Court at the close of its *Powell* opinion did by its language, as this Court frequently does, limit its holding to the particular facts and circumstances of that case, its conclusions about the fundamental nature of the right to counsel are unmistakable.   [The] fact is that in deciding as it did—that "appointment of counsel is not a fundamental right, essential to a fair trial"—the [*Betts* Court] made an abrupt break with its own well-considered precedents.   In returning to these old precedents, sounder we believe than the new, we but restore constitutional principles established to achieve a fair system of justice.   Not only these precedents but also reason and reflection require us to recognize that in our adversary system of criminal justice, any person haled into court, who is too poor to hire a lawyer, cannot be assured a fair trial unless counsel is provided for him.   This seems to us to be an obvious truth.   Governments, both state and federal, quite properly spend vast sums of money to establish machinery to try defendants accused of crime.   Lawyers to prosecute are everywhere deemed essential to protect the public's interest in an orderly society.   Similarly, there are few defendants charged with crime, few indeed, who fail to hire the best lawyers they can get to prepare and present their defenses.   That government hires lawyers to prosecute and defendants who have the money hire lawyers to defend are the strongest indications of the widespread belief that lawyers in criminal courts are necessities, not luxuries.   The right of one charged with crime to counsel may not be deemed fundamental and essential to fair trials in some countries, but it is in ours. From the very beginning, our state and national constitutions and laws have laid great emphasis on procedural and substantive safeguards designed to assure fair trials before impartial tribunals in which every defendant stands equal before the law. This noble ideal cannot be realized if the poor man charged with crime has to face his accusers without a lawyer to assist him. * * *

The Court in *Betts* departed from the sound wisdom upon which the Court's holding in *Powell* rested. Florida, supported by two other States, has asked that *Betts v. Brady* be left intact. Twenty-two States, as friends of the Court, argue that *Betts* was "an anachronism when handed down" and that it should now be overruled. We agree. * * * Reversed.[a]

JUSTICE CLARK, concurring in the result. * * *

[T]he Constitution makes no distinction between capital and noncapital cases. The Fourteenth Amendment requires due process of law for the deprivation of "liberty" just as for deprival of "life," and there cannot constitutionally be a difference in the quality of the process based merely upon a supposed difference in the sanction involved. How can the Fourteenth Amendment tolerate a procedure which it condemns in capital cases on the ground that deprival of liberty may be less onerous than deprival of life—a value judgment not universally accepted—or that only the latter deprival is irrevocable? * * *

JUSTICE HARLAN, concurring.

I agree that *Betts* should be overruled, but consider it entitled to a more respectful burial than has been accorded, at least on the part of those of us who were not on the Court when that case was decided.

I cannot subscribe to the view that *Betts* represented "an abrupt break with its own well-considered precedents." [In *Powell*] this Court declared that under the particular facts there presented—"the ignorance and illiteracy of the defendants, their youth, the circumstances of public hostility [and] above all that they stood in deadly peril of their lives"—the state court had a duty to assign counsel for the trial as a necessary requisite of due process of law. It is evident that these limiting facts were not added to the opinion as an afterthought; they were repeatedly emphasized [and] were clearly regarded as important to the result.

Thus when this Court, a decade later, decided *Betts,* it did no more than to admit of the possible existence of special circumstances in noncapital as well as capital trials, while at the same time to insist that such circumstances be shown in order to establish a denial of due process. The right to appointed counsel had been recognized as being considerably broader in federal prosecutions, see *Johnson v. Zerbst,* but to have imposed these requirements on the States would indeed have been "an abrupt break" with the almost immediate past. The declaration that the right to appointed counsel in state prosecutions, as established in *Powell,* was not limited to capital cases was in truth not a departure from, but an extension of, existing precedent.

The principles declared in *Powell* and in *Betts,* however, had a troubled journey throughout the years that have followed first the one case and then the other. Even by the time of the *Betts* decision, dictum in at least one of the Court's opinions had indicated that there was an absolute right to the services of counsel in the trial of state capital cases.

---

a. Gideon was retried, this time with appointed counsel, and acquitted. See Anthony   Lewis, *Gideon's Trumpet* 223–38 (1964).

[In] noncapital cases, the "special circumstances" rule has continued to exist in form while its substance has been substantially and steadily eroded. In the first decade after *Betts,* there were cases in which the Court found special circumstances to be lacking, but usually by a sharply divided vote. However, no such decision has been cited to us, and I have found none, [after] 1950. At the same time, there have been not a few cases in which special circumstances were found in little or nothing more than the "complexity" of the legal questions presented, although those questions were often of only routine difficulty. The Court has come to recognize, in other words, that the mere existence of a serious criminal charge constituted in itself special circumstances requiring the services of counsel at trial. In truth the *Betts* rule is no longer a reality.

This evolution, however, appears not to have been fully recognized by many state courts, in this instance charged with the front-line responsibility for the enforcement of constitutional rights. To continue a rule which is honored by this Court only with lip service is not a healthy thing and in the long run will do disservice to the federal system.

The special circumstances rule has been formally abandoned in capital cases, and the time has now come when it should be similarly abandoned in noncapital cases, at least as to offenses which, as the one involved here, carry the possibility of a substantial prison sentence. (Whether the rule should extend to *all* criminal cases need not now be decided.)

* * * In what is done today I do not understand the Court to depart from the principles laid down in *Palko* [or] to embrace the concept that the Fourteenth Amendment "incorporates" the Sixth Amendment as such. On these premises I join in the judgment of the Court.

ARGERSINGER v. HAMLIN

407 U.S. 25, 92 S.Ct. 2006, 32 L.Ed.2d 530 (1972).

Justice Douglas delivered the opinion of the Court.

Petitioner, an indigent, was charged in Florida with carrying a concealed weapon, an offense punishable by imprisonment up to six months, a $1,000 fine, or both. The trial was to a judge, and petitioner was unrepresented by counsel. [He was convicted and sentenced to 90 days in jail. The Florida Supreme Court affirmed. Following the line marked out in the jury trial cases, the state court] held that the right to court-appointed counsel extends only to trials "for non-petty offenses punishable by more than six months imprisonment."

[While] there is historical support for limiting the [right] to trial by jury [to] "serious criminal cases," there is no such support for a similar limitation on the right to assistance of counsel. [Thus,] we reject [the] premise that since prosecutions for crimes punishable by imprisonment for less than six months may be tried without a jury, they may always be tried without a lawyer. [The] requirement of counsel may well be necessary for a fair trial even in a petty offense prosecution. We are by no means convinced that legal and constitutional questions involved in a case that actually leads to imprisonment even for a brief period are any less complex than when a person can be sent off for six months or more. * * *

Beyond the problem of trials and appeals is that of the guilty plea, a problem which looms large in misdemeanor as well as in felony cases. Counsel is needed so that the accused may know precisely what he is doing, so that he is fully aware of the prospect of going to jail or prison, and so that he is treated fairly by the prosecution.

In addition, the volume of misdemeanor cases, far greater in number than felony prosecutions, may create an obsession for speedy dispositions, regardless of the fairness of the result. * * *

We must conclude, therefore, that the problems associated with misdemeanor and petty offenses often require the presence of counsel to insure the accused a fair trial. [In his concurring opinion,] Mr. Justice Powell suggests that these problems are raised even in situations where there is no prospect of imprisonment. We need not consider the requirements of the Sixth Amendment as regards the right to counsel where loss of liberty is not involved, however, for here, petitioner was in fact sentenced to jail.

[Under] the rule we announce today, every judge will know when the trial of a misdemeanor starts that no imprisonment may be imposed, even though local law permits it, unless the accused is represented by counsel. He will have a measure of the seriousness and gravity of the offense and therefore know when to name a lawyer to represent the accused before the trial starts.[a]

Justice Powell, with whom Justice Rehnquist joins, concurring with the result. * * *

I am unable to agree with the Supreme Court of Florida that an indigent defendant, charged with a petty offense, may in every case be afforded a fair trial without the assistance of counsel. Nor can I agree with [the Court's] new rule of due process [that] "absent a [valid] waiver, no person may be imprisoned [unless] he was represented by counsel at his trial." It seems to me that the line should not be drawn with such rigidity.

There is a middle course, between the extremes of Florida's six-month rule and the Court's rule, which comports with the requirements of the Fourteenth Amendment. I would adhere to the principle of due process that requires fundamental fairness in criminal trials, a principle which I believe encompasses the right to counsel in petty cases whenever the assistance of counsel is necessary to assure a fair trial.

Due process, perhaps the most fundamental concept in our law, embodies principles of fairness rather than immutable line-drawing as to every aspect of a criminal trial. While counsel is often essential to a fair trial, this is by no means a universal fact. Some petty offense cases are complex; others are exceedingly simple. [The] government often does not hire lawyers to prosecute petty offenses; instead the arresting police officer presents the case. Nor does every defendant who can afford to do so hire lawyers to defend petty charges. Where the possibility of a jail sentence is remote and the probable fine seems small, or where the evidence of guilt is overwhelming, the costs of assistance of counsel may exceed the benefits. It is anomalous that the Court's opinion today will extend the right of appointed counsel to indigent defendants in cases where the right to counsel would rarely be exercised by nonindigent defendants.

Indeed, one of the effects of this ruling will be to favor defendants classified as indigents over those not so classified yet who are in low income groups where engaging counsel in a minor petty offense case would be a luxury the family could not afford. The line between indigency and assumed capacity to pay for counsel is necessarily somewhat arbitrary, drawn differently from State to State and often

---

a. Burger, C.J., concurred in the result. Brennan, J., joined by Douglas and Stewart, JJ., joined the Court's opinion and added a brief concurring opinion.

resulting in serious inequities to accused persons.   The Court's new rule will accent the disadvantage of being barely self-sufficient economically.

[The] rule adopted today [is] limited to petty offense cases in which the sentence is some imprisonment.   The thrust of the Court's position indicates, however, that when the decision must be made, the rule will be extended to all petty offense cases except perhaps the most minor traffic violations.   If the Court rejects on constitutional grounds, as it has today, the exercise of any judicial discretion as to need for counsel if a jail sentence is imposed, one must assume a similar rejection of discretion in other petty offense cases.   It would be illogical— and without discernible support in the Constitution—to hold that no discretion may ever be exercised where a nominal jail sentence is contemplated and at the same time endorse the legitimacy of discretion in "non-jail" petty offense cases which may result in far more serious consequences than a few hours or days of incarceration.

[The] Court's opinion foreshadows the adoption of a broad prophylactic rule applicable to all petty offenses [whether or not the defendant is actually incarcerated].   No one can foresee the consequences of such a drastic enlargement of the constitutional right to free counsel.   But even today's decision could have a seriously adverse impact upon the day to day functioning of the criminal justice system.   * * *

I would hold that the right to counsel in petty offense cases is not absolute but is one to be determined by the trial courts exercising a judicial discretion on a case-by-case basis.   * * *

[T]hree general factors should be weighed.   First, the court should consider the complexity of the offense charged.   For example, charges of traffic law infractions would rarely present complex legal or factual questions, but charges that contain difficult intent elements or which raise collateral legal questions, such as search and seizure problems, would usually be too complex for an unassisted layman.   If the offense were one where the State is represented by counsel and where most defendants who can afford to do so obtain counsel, there would be a strong indication that the indigent also needs the assistance of counsel.

Second, the court should consider the probable sentence that will follow if a conviction is obtained.   The more serious the likely consequences, the greater is the probability that a lawyer should be appointed.   [I]mprisonment is not the only serious consequence the court should consider.

Third, the court should consider the individual factors peculiar to each case.   These, of course, would be the most difficult to anticipate.   One relevant factor would be the competency of the individual defendant to present his own case.   The attitude of the community toward a particular defendant or particular incident would be another consideration.   But there might be other reasons why a defendant would have a peculiar need for a lawyer which would compel the appointment of counsel in a case where the court would normally think this unnecessary.

Such a rule is similar in certain respects to the special circumstances rule applied to felony cases in *Betts,* which this Court overruled in *Gideon.*   One of the reasons for seeking a more definitive standard in felony cases was the failure of many state courts to live up to their responsibilities in determining on a case-by-case basis whether counsel should be appointed.   But this Court should not assume that the past insensitivity of some state courts to the rights of defendants will continue.   Certainly if the Court follows the course of reading rigid rules into the Constitution, so that the state courts will be unable to exercise judicial discretion within the limits of fundamental fairness, there is little reason to think that insensitivity will abate.

* * * We are all strongly drawn to the ideal of extending the right to counsel, but I differ as to two fundamentals: (i) what the Constitution *requires,* and (ii) the effect upon the criminal justice system, especially in the smaller cities and the thousands of police, municipal and justice of the peace courts across the country.

SCOTT v. ILLINOIS

440 U.S. 367, 99 S.Ct. 1158, 59 L.Ed.2d 383 (1979).

JUSTICE REHNQUIST delivered the opinion of the Court. * * *

[Petitioner, an indigent, was charged with shoplifting merchandise valued at less than $150, punishable by as much as a $500 fine, or one year in jail, or both. He was not provided counsel. After a bench trial he was convicted of the offense and fined $50. The Supreme Court of Illinois declined to "extend *Argersinger*" to a case where one is charged with an offense for which imprisonment upon conviction is authorized but not actually imposed.]

In *Argersinger* the Court rejected arguments that social cost or a lack of available lawyers militated against its holding, in some part because it thought these arguments were factually incorrect. But they were rejected in much larger part because of the Court's conclusion that incarceration was so severe a sanction that it should not be imposed as a result of a criminal trial unless an indigent defendant has been offered appointed counsel to assist in his defense, regardless of the cost to the States implicit in such a rule. * * *

Although the intentions of the *Argersinger* Court are not unmistakably clear from its opinion, we conclude today that *Argersinger* did indeed delimit the constitutional right to appointed counsel in state criminal proceedings. Even were the matter *res nova,* we believe that the central premise of *Argersinger*—that actual imprisonment is a penalty different in kind from fines or the mere threat of imprisonment—is eminently sound and warrants adoption of actual imprisonment as the line defining the constitutional right to appointment of counsel. *Argersinger* has proved reasonably workable, whereas any extension would create confusion and impose unpredictable, but necessarily substantial, costs on 50 quite diverse States. We therefore hold that the Sixth and Fourteenth Amendments * * * require only that no indigent criminal defendant be sentenced to a term of imprisonment unless the State has afforded him the right to assistance of appointed counsel in his defense. The judgment [below] is accordingly [affirmed.] [a]

---

a. Concurring Justice Powell noted that "the drawing of a line based on whether there is imprisonment (even for overnight) can have the practical effect of precluding provision of counsel in other types of cases in which conviction can have more serious consequences." He also thought that an "actual imprisonment" rule "tends to impair the proper functioning of the criminal justice system in that trial judges, in advance of hearing any evidence and before knowing anything about the case except the charge, all too often will be compelled to forego the legislatively granted option to impose a sentence of imprisonment upon conviction." Despite his "continuing reservations about the *Argersinger* rule," however, Justice Powell joined the opinion of the Court because "[i]t is important that this Court provide clear guidance to the hundreds of courts across the country that confront this problem daily." He hoped, however, "that in due time a majority will recognize that a more flexible rule is consistent with due process and will better serve the cause of justice."

JUSTICE BRENNAN, with whom JUSTICE MARSHALL and JUSTICE STEVENS join, dissenting.

In my view petitioner could prevail in this case without extending the right to counsel beyond what was assumed to exist in *Argersinger*. Neither party in that case questioned the existence of the right to counsel in trials involving "non-petty" offenses punishable by more than six months in jail. The question the Court addressed was whether the right applied to some "petty" offenses to which the right to jury trial did not extend. The Court's reasoning in applying the right to counsel in the case before it—that the right to counsel is more fundamental to a fair proceeding than the right to jury trial and that the historical limitations on the jury trial right are irrelevant to the right to counsel—certainly cannot support a standard for the right to counsel that is more restrictive than the standard for granting a right to a jury trial. [Argersinger] thus established a "two-dimensional" test for the right to counsel: the right attaches to any "non-petty" offense punishable by more than six months in jail and in addition to any offense where actual incarceration is likely regardless of the maximum authorized penalty.

The offense of "theft" with which Scott was charged is certainly not a "petty" one. It is punishable by a sentence of up to one year in jail. Unlike many traffic or other "regulatory" offenses, it carries the moral stigma associated with common-law crimes traditionally recognized as indicative of moral depravity. The State indicated at oral argument that the services of a professional prosecutor were considered essential to the prosecution of this offense. Likewise, nonindigent defendants charged with this offense would be well advised to hire the "best lawyers they can get." Scott's right to the assistance of appointed counsel is thus plainly mandated by the logic of the Court's prior cases, including *Argersinger* itself.

* * * Not only is the "actual imprisonment" standard unprecedented as the exclusive test, but the problems inherent in its application demonstrate the superiority of an "authorized imprisonment" standard that would require the appointment of counsel for indigents accused of any offense for which imprisonment for any time is authorized. * * *

Perhaps the strongest refutation of respondent's alarmist prophecies that an authorized imprisonment standard would wreak havoc on the States is that the standard has not produced that result in the substantial number of States that already provide counsel in all cases where imprisonment is authorized—States that include a large majority of the country's population and a great diversity of urban and rural environments. Moreover, of those States that do not yet provide counsel in all cases where *any* imprisonment is authorized, many provide counsel when periods of imprisonment longer than 30 days, 3 months, or 6 months are authorized. In fact, Scott would be entitled to appointed counsel under the current laws of at least 33 States.

It may well be that adoption by this Court of an authorized imprisonment standard would lead state and local governments to re-examine their criminal statutes. A state legislature or local government might determine that it no longer desired to authorize incarceration for certain minor offenses in light of the expense of meeting the requirements of the Constitution. In my view this re-examination is long overdue. In any event, the Courts actual imprisonment standard must inevitably lead the courts to make this re-examination, which plainly should more properly be a legislative responsibility.

The Court's opinion turns the reasoning of *Argersinger* on its head. It restricts the right to counsel, perhaps the most fundamental Sixth Amendment right, more narrowly than the admittedly less fundamental right to jury trial. * * * b

II. THE *GRIFFIN–DOUGLAS* "EQUALITY" PRINCIPLE

Introduction

Many commentators believe that the Warren Court's "revolution" in criminal procedure got underway when it handed down *Mapp v. Ohio* (p. 125) in 1961. But arguably the revolution began five years earlier, with *Griffin v. Illinois,* 351 U.S. 12, 76 S.Ct. 585, 100 L.Ed. 891 (1956).

In holding that indigent defendants must be furnished trial transcripts at state expense if such transcripts were necessary to effectuate appellate review, *Griffin* departed from then traditional equal protection doctrine. It viewed the "equality" principle as not only prohibiting the creation of inequalities by a state but imposing an "affirmative duty" to eliminate at least some inequalities not of the state's own doing. Illinois had simply ignored private inequalities of wealth and offered trial transcripts to every appellant on "equal terms," i.e., at a price which amounted to the cost of preparing them. But this was not enough.

There was no opinion of the Court in *Griffin*. Justice Black announced the judgment in a forceful and oft-quoted four-Justice opinion. He called the denial of a transcript for those who need but are unable to pay for one "a misfit in a country dedicated to affording equal justice to all and special privileges to none in the administration of its criminal law." Continued Black: "There can be no equal justice where the kind of trial a man gets depends on the amount of money he has. Destitute defendants must be afforded as adequate appellate review as defendants who have money enough to buy transcripts."

Dissenting Justice Harlan voiced sharp disagreement with Justice Black's approach. Harlan maintained that the Court's resolution of the equal protection claim in effect *required state discrimination*—in favor of indigents. It forced Illinois to give free to indigents "what it requires others to pay for."

But for *Douglas v. California,* the first case set forth in this section, *Griffin* and its early progeny,[a] could be narrowly interpreted as not affecting the right to counsel at all. Rather, the *Griffin* principle could be viewed as concerned merely with the *availability* of direct and collateral review, not the *quality* of such review. But for the *Douglas* case, *Griffin* could be read as requiring only that an indigent be allowed *access* to the courts, not that he be furnished with counsel as well. For the presence of counsel is not a *sine qua non* to access to the courts, as was the

---

b. In a separate dissent, Blackmun, J., maintained that the right to appointed counsel "extends at least as far as the right to jury trial" and thus that "an indigent defendant in a state criminal case must be afforded appointed counsel whenever [he] is prosecuted for a nonpetty criminal offense, that is, one punishable by more than six months' imprisonment *or* whenever the defendant is actually subjected to a term of imprisonment."

a. In the decade and a half following *Griffin*, its underlying principle was broadly applied. *Mayer v. Chicago,* 404 U.S. 189, 92 S.Ct. 410, 30 L.Ed.2d 372 (1971) carried the *Griffin* principle further than the Court ever carried the *Gideon* principle by holding that an indigent appellant cannot be denied a record of

sufficient completeness to permit proper consideration of his claims even though he was convicted of ordinary violations punishable by fine only. More generally, a number of cases seemed to read *Griffin* for the proposition that an indigent defendant must be furnished any valuable or useful "tool" or instrument available for a price to others. See, e.g., *Roberts v. LaVallee,* 389 U.S. 40, 88 S.Ct. 194, 19 L.Ed.2d 41 (1967) (indigent defendant entitled to free transcript of preliminary hearing for use at trial, even though both defendant and his lawyer attended preliminary hearing and no indication of use to which preliminary hearing transcript could be put—points stressed by dissenting Justice Harlan).

availability of the transcript in *Griffin* or the payment of filing fees in other cases applying *Griffin.*

Under this analysis, *Griffin* and the pre-*Gideon* doctrine of *Betts v. Brady* were reconcilable: The state need only provide a road, not guarantee that every person have equally as good a car to drive down it. After *Douglas,* however, the "access to the courts" interpretation of *Griffin* seemed untenable. For the *Douglas* Court considered denying counsel to an indigent appellant "a discrimination at least as invidious as that condemned in *Griffin.*"

Although it was careful to note that it was "dealing only with the *first appeal* granted as a matter of right to [all]" (emphasis in the original), the *Douglas* opinion contains language suggesting that *whenever* an indigent is permitted access to the courts he is *entitled to counsel* as well—that the state must do more than simply place a defendant "on the road," it must see that he has some vehicle—counsel—to use in travelling that "road." Nor is that all. *Griffin* and *Douglas,* at least if read generously, also suggest that the government must furnish an indigent defendant with *any* and *every* legal tool or legal service that a wealthy defendant is able to purchase.

In short not a few people thought that the *Griffin–Douglas* "equality" principle—the view that the administration of criminal justice cannot turn on the amount of money a defendant has—had no "stopping point," at least no obvious one. But the Court found a stopping point in *Ross v. Moffitt,* the second case set forth in this section.

DOUGLAS v. CALIFORNIA

372 U.S. 353, 83 S.Ct. 814, 9 L.Ed.2d 811 (1963).

JUSTICE DOUGLAS delivered the opinion of the Court.

[The] record shows that petitioners requested, and were denied, the assistance of counsel on appeal, even though it plainly appeared they were indigents. In denying petitioners' requests, the California District Court of Appeal stated that it had "gone through" the record and had come to the conclusion that "no good whatever could be served by appointment of counsel." [The court] was acting in accordance with a California rule of criminal procedure which provides that state appellate courts, upon the request of an indigent for counsel, may make "an independent investigation of the record and determine whether it would be of advantage to the defendant or helpful to the appellate court to have counsel appointed. [After] such investigation, appellate courts should appoint counsel if in their opinion it would be helpful to the defendant or the court, and should deny the appointment of counsel only if in their judgment such appointment would be of no value to either the defendant or the court." * * *

We agree, however, with Justice Traynor of the California Supreme Court, who said that the "[d]enial of counsel on appeal [to an indigent] would seem to be a discrimination at least as invidious as that condemned in [*Griffin,*" where] we held that a State may not grant appellate review in such a way as to discriminate against some convicted defendants on account of their poverty. [Whether the issue is a transcript on appeal or the assistance of counsel on appeal] the evil is the same: discrimination against the indigent. For there can be no equal justice where the kind of an appeal a man enjoys "depends on the amount of money he has."

[Under California's] present practice the type of an appeal [one is afforded] hinges upon whether or not he can pay for the assistance of counsel. If he can the appellate court passes on the merits of his case only after having the full benefit of written briefs and oral argument by counsel. If he cannot the appellate court is forced to prejudge the merits before it can even determine whether counsel should be provided. At this stage in the proceedings only the barren record speaks for the indigent, and, unless the printed pages show that an injustice has been committed, he is forced to go without a champion on appeal. Any real chance he may have had of showing that his appeal has hidden merit is deprived him when the court decides on an *ex parte* examination of the record that the assistance of counsel is not required.

* * * We are dealing only with the first appeal, granted as a matter of right to rich and poor alike, from a criminal conviction. We need not now decide whether California would have to provide counsel for an indigent seeking [discretionary review or] whether counsel must be appointed for an indigent seeking review of an appellate affirmance of his conviction in this Court. [But] it is appropriate to observe that a State can, consistently with the Fourteenth Amendment, provide for differences so long as the result does not amount to a denial of due process or an "invidious discrimination." Absolute equality is not required; lines can be and are drawn and we often sustain them. [But] where the merits of the one and only appeal an indigent has as of right are decided without benefit of counsel, we think an unconstitutional line has been drawn between rich and poor.

When an indigent is forced to run this gantlet of a preliminary showing of merit, the right to appeal does not comport with fair procedure. [T]he discrimination is not between "possibly good and obviously bad cases," but between cases where the rich man can require the court to listen to argument of counsel before deciding on the merits, but a poor man cannot. There is lacking that equality demanded by the Fourteenth Amendment where the rich man, who appeals as of right, enjoys the benefit of counsel's examination into the record, research of the law, and marshalling of arguments on his behalf, while the indigent, already burdened by a preliminary determination that his case is without merit, is forced to shift for himself. The indigent, where the record is unclear or the errors are hidden, has only the right to a meaningless ritual, while the rich man has a meaningful appeal. * * *

Judgment of the District Court of Appeals vacated and case remanded.

JUSTICE CLARK, dissenting.

* * * We all know that the overwhelming percentage of *in forma pauperis* appeals are frivolous. Statistics of this Court show that over 96% of the petitions filed here are of this variety. [California's courts] after examining the record certified that [an] appointment [of counsel] would be neither advantageous to the petitioners nor helpful to the court. It, therefore, refused to go through the useless gesture of appointing an attorney. In my view neither the Equal Protection Clause nor the Due Process Clause requires more. I cannot understand why the Court says that this procedure afforded petitioners "a meaningless ritual." To appoint an attorney would not only have been utter extravagance and a waste of the State's funds but as surely "meaningless" to petitioners.

JUSTICE HARLAN, whom JUSTICE STEWART joins, dissenting.

[T]he Court appears to rely both on the Equal Protection Clause and on the guarantees of fair procedure inherent in the Due Process Clause of the Fourteenth Amendment, with obvious emphasis on "equal protection." In my view the Equal Protection Clause is not apposite, and its application to cases like the present one can lead only to mischievous results. This case should be judged solely under the

Due Process Clause, and I do not believe that the California procedure violates that provision.

EQUAL PROTECTION

To approach the present problem in terms of the Equal Protection Clause is, I submit, but to substitute resounding phrases for analysis. I dissented from this approach in [*Griffin*] and I am constrained to dissent from the implicit extension of the equal protection approach here—to a case in which the State denies no one an appeal, but seeks only to keep within reasonable bounds the instances in which appellate counsel will be assigned to indigents.

The States, of course, are prohibited by the Equal Protection Clause from discriminating between "rich" and "poor" *as such* in the formulation and application of their laws. But it is a far different thing to suggest that this provision prevents the State from adopting a law of general applicability that may affect the poor more harshly than it does the rich, or, on the other hand, from making some effort to redress economic imbalances while not eliminating them entirely.

Every financial exaction which the State imposes on a uniform basis is more easily satisfied by the well-to-do than by the indigent. Yet I take it that no one would dispute the constitutional power of the State to levy a uniform sales tax, to charge tuition at a state university, to fix rates for the purchase of water from a municipal corporation, to impose a standard fine for criminal violations, or to establish minimum bail for various categories of offenses. Nor could it be contended that the State may not classify as crimes acts which the poor are more likely to commit than are the rich. And surely, there would be no basis for attacking a state law which provided benefits for the needy simply because those benefits fell short of the goods or services that others could purchase for themselves.

Laws such as these do not deny equal protection to the less fortunate for one essential reason: the Equal Protection Clause does not impose on the States "an affirmative duty to lift the handicaps flowing from differences in economic circumstances." To so construe it would be to read into the Constitution a philosophy of leveling that would be foreign to many of our basic concepts of the proper relations between government and society. The State may have a moral obligation to eliminate the evils of poverty, but it is not required by the Equal Protection Clause to give to some whatever others can afford.

[It] should be noted that if the present problem may be viewed as one of equal protection, so may the question of the right to appointed counsel at trial, and the Court's analysis of that right in *Gideon* [is] wholly unnecessary. The short way to dispose of *Gideon,* in other words, would be simply to say that the State deprives the indigent of equal protection whenever it fails to furnish him with legal services, and perhaps with other services as well, equivalent to those that the affluent defendant can obtain.[a]

The real question in this case, I submit, and the only one that permits of satisfactory analysis, is whether or not the state rule, as applied in this case, is consistent with the requirements of fair procedure guaranteed by the Due Process

---

a. One may ask, too, why the Court failed even to discuss the applicability of the *Griffin–Douglas* "equality" principle to the issue raised in *Scott v. Illinois* (p. 198 supra). Since it is plain that one charged with an offense *punishable* by incarceration may *retain* counsel for his defense, does not the "equality" princi-ple—especially in light of its application in *Mayer v. Chicago,* note a supra—suggest that the "actual imprisonment" standard, even if it defensibly defines the Sixth Amendment right to appointed counsel, is unsatisfactory under the equal protection clause?

Clause. Of course, in considering this question, it must not be lost sight of that the State's responsibility under the Due Process Clause is to provide justice for all. Refusal to furnish criminal indigents with some things that others can afford may fall short of constitutional standards of fairness. The problem before us is whether this is such a case.

DUE PROCESS * * *

We have today held that in a case such as the one before us, there is an absolute right to the services of counsel at trial. *Gideon.* [But] the appellate procedures involved here stand on an entirely different constitutional footing. *First,* appellate review is in itself not required by the Fourteenth Amendment, *McKane v. Durston,* 153 U.S. 684, 14 S.Ct. 913, 38 L.Ed. 867 (1894); see *Griffin,* and thus the question presented is the narrow one whether the State's rules with respect to the appointment of counsel are so arbitrary or unreasonable, *in the context of the particular appellate procedure that it has established,* as to require their invalidation. *Second,* the kinds of questions that may arise on appeal are circumscribed by the record of the proceedings that led to the conviction; they do not encompass the large variety of tactical and strategic problems that must be resolved at the trial. *Third,* as California applies its rule, the indigent appellant receives the benefit of expert and conscientious legal appraisal of the merits of his case on the basis of the trial record, and whether or not he is assigned counsel, is guaranteed full consideration of his appeal. It would be painting with too broad a brush to conclude that under these circumstances an appeal is just like a trial.

What the Court finds constitutionally offensive in California's procedure bears a striking resemblance to the rules of this Court and many state courts of last resort on petitions for certiorari or for leave to appeal filed by indigent defendants *pro se.* Under the practice of this Court, only if it appears from the petition for certiorari that a case merits review is leave to proceed *in forma pauperis* granted, the case transferred to the Appellate Docket, and counsel appointed. Since our review is generally discretionary, and since we are often not even given the benefit of a record in the proceedings below, the disadvantages to the indigent petitioner might be regarded as more substantial than in California. But as conscientiously committed as this Court is to the great principle of "Equal Justice Under Law," it has never deemed itself constitutionally required to appoint counsel to assist in the preparation of each of the more than 1,000 *pro se* petitions for certiorari currently being filed each Term. We should know from our own experience that appellate courts generally go out of their way to give fair consideration to those who are unrepresented.

The Court distinguishes our review from the present case on the grounds that the California rule relates to "the first appeal, granted as a matter of right." [But] I fail to see the significance of this difference. Surely, it cannot be contended that the requirements of fair procedure are exhausted once an indigent has been given one appellate review. Nor can it well be suggested that having appointed counsel is more necessary to the fair administration of justice in an initial appeal taken as a matter of right, which the reviewing court on the full record has already determined to be frivolous, than in a petition asking a higher appellate court to exercise its discretion to consider what may be a substantial constitutional claim.

I cannot agree that the Constitution prohibits a State in seeking to redress economic imbalances at its bar of justice and to provide indigents with full review, from taking reasonable steps to guard against needless expense. This is all that California has done. * * *

ROSS v. MOFFITT

417 U.S. 600, 94 S.Ct. 2437, 41 L.Ed.2d 341 (1974).

[Like many other states, the North Carolina appellate system is multitiered, providing for both an intermediate Court of Appeals and a Supreme Court. North Carolina authorizes appointment of counsel for a convicted defendant appealing to the intermediate court of appeals, but not for a defendant who seeks either discretionary review in the state supreme court or a writ of certiorari in the U.S. Supreme Court. In one case, the Mecklenburg County forgery conviction, respondent sought appointed counsel for discretionary review in the state supreme court. In another case, the Guilford County forgery conviction, respondent was represented by the public defender in the state supreme court, but sought court-appointed counsel to prepare a writ of certiorari to the U.S. Supreme Court. On federal habeas corpus, a unanimous panel of the U.S. Court of Appeals for the Fourth Circuit, per Haynsworth, C.J., held that the *Douglas* rationale required appointment of counsel in both instances.]

JUSTICE REHNQUIST delivered the opinion of the Court.

[In *Griffin,* the Court struck down] an Illinois rule allowing a convicted criminal defendant to present claims of trial error to the [state supreme court] only if he procured a transcript of the testimony adduced at his trial. No exception was made for the indigent defendant, and thus one who was unable to pay the cost of obtaining such a transcript was precluded from obtaining appellate review of asserted trial error.

[*Griffin* and succeeding cases] stand for the proposition that a State cannot arbitrarily cut off appeal rights for indigents while leaving open avenues of appeal for more affluent persons. In *Douglas,* however, [the] Court departed somewhat from the limited doctrine of [these] cases and undertook an examination of whether an indigent's access to the appellate system was adequate. [The *Douglas* Court] concluded that a State does not fulfill its responsibility toward indigent defendants merely by waiving its own requirements that a convicted defendant procure a transcript or pay a fee in order to appeal, and held that the State must go further and provide counsel for the indigent on his first appeal as of right. It is this decision we are asked to extend today. * * *

The precise rationale for the *Griffin* and *Douglas* lines of cases has never been explicitly stated, some support being derived from the Equal Protection Clause of the Fourteenth Amendment, and some from the Due Process Clause of that Amendment. Neither clause by itself provides an entirely satisfactory basis for the result reached, each depending on a different inquiry which emphasizes different factors. "Due process" emphasizes fairness between the State and the individual dealing with the State, regardless of how other individuals in the same situation may be treated. "Equal protection," on the other hand, emphasizes disparity in treatment by a State between classes of individuals whose situations are arguably indistinguishable. We will address these issues separately in the succeeding sections.

Recognition of the due process rationale in *Douglas* is found both in the Court's opinion and in the dissenting opinion of Mr. Justice Harlan. The Court in *Douglas* stated that "[w]hen an individual is forced to run this gantlet of a preliminary showing of merit, the right to appeal does not comport with fair procedure." Mr. Justice Harlan thought that the due process issue in *Douglas* was the only one worthy of extended consideration. * * *

We do not believe that the Due Process Clause requires North Carolina to provide respondent with counsel on his discretionary appeal to the State Supreme Court. At the trial stage of a criminal proceeding, the right of an indigent defendant to counsel [is] fundamental and binding upon the States by virtue of the Sixth and Fourteenth Amendments. But there are significant differences between the trial and appellate stages of a criminal proceeding. The purpose of the trial stage from the State's point of view is to convert a criminal defendant from a person presumed innocent to one found guilty beyond a reasonable doubt. To accomplish this purpose, the State employs a prosecuting attorney who presents evidence to the court, challenges any witnesses offered by the defendant, argues rulings of the court, and makes direct arguments to the court or jury seeking to persuade them of the defendant's guilt. Under these circumstances " * * * reason and reflection require us to recognize that in our adversary system of criminal justice, any person haled into court, who is too poor to hire a lawyer, cannot be assured a fair trial unless counsel is provided for him." *Gideon.*

By contrast, it is ordinarily the defendant, rather than the State, who initiates the appellate process, seeking not to fend off the efforts of the State's prosecutor but rather to overturn a finding of guilt made by a judge or jury below. The defendant needs an attorney on appeal not as a shield to protect him against being "haled into court" by the State and stripped of his presumption of innocence, but rather as a sword to upset the prior determination of guilt. This difference is significant for, while no one would agree that the State may simply dispense with the trial stage of proceedings without a criminal defendant's consent, it is clear that the State need not provide any appeal at all. *McKane v. Durston.* The fact that an appeal *has* been provided does not automatically mean that a State then acts unfairly by refusing to provide counsel to indigent defendants at every stage of the way. Unfairness results only if indigents are singled out by the State and denied meaningful access to that system because of their poverty. That question is more profitably considered under an equal protection analysis.

Language invoking equal protection notions is prominent both in *Douglas* and in other cases treating the rights of indigents on appeal. * * * Despite the tendency of all rights "to declare themselves absolute to their logical extreme," there are obviously limits beyond which the equal protection analysis may not be pressed without doing violence to principles recognized in other decisions of this Court. The Fourteenth Amendment "does not require absolute equality or precisely equal advantages," nor does it require the State to "equalize economic conditions." *Griffin* (Frankfurter, J., concurring). It does require [that] indigents have an adequate opportunity to present their claims fairly within the adversarial system. The State cannot adopt procedures which leave an indigent defendant "entirely cut off from any appeal at all," by virtue of his indigency, *Lane,* or extend to such indigent defendants merely a "meaningless ritual" while others in better economic circumstances have a "meaningful appeal." *Douglas.* The question is not one of absolutes, but one of degrees. In this case we do not believe that the Equal Protection Clause when interpreted in the context of these cases, requires North Carolina to provide free counsel for indigent defendants seeking to take discretionary appeals to the North Carolina Supreme Court, or to file petitions for certiorari in this Court.

[The] facts show that respondent, in connection with his Mecklenburg County conviction, received the benefit of counsel in examining the record of his trial and in preparing an appellate brief on his behalf for the state Court of Appeals. Thus, prior to his seeking discretionary review in the State Supreme Court, his claims "had once been presented by a lawyer and passed upon by an appellate court."

Douglas. We do not believe that it can be said, therefore, that a defendant in respondent's circumstances is denied meaningful access to the North Carolina Supreme Court simply because the State does not appoint counsel to aid him in seeking review in that court. At that stage he will have, at the very least, a transcript or other record of trial proceedings, a brief on his behalf in the Court of Appeals setting forth his claims of error, and in many cases an opinion by the Court of Appeals disposing of his case. These materials, supplemented by whatever submission respondent may make *pro se,* would appear to provide the Supreme Court of North Carolina with an adequate basis on which to base its decision to grant or deny review.

We are fortified in this conclusion by our understanding of the function served by discretionary review in the North Carolina Supreme Court. The critical issue in that court, as we perceive it, is not whether there has been "a correct adjudication of guilt" in every individual case, but rather whether "the subject matter of the appeal has significant public interest," whether "the cause involves legal principles of major significance to the jurisprudence of the state," or whether the decision below is in probable conflict with a decision of the Supreme Court. The Supreme Court may deny certiorari even though it believes that the decision of the Court of Appeals was incorrect, since a decision which appears incorrect may nevertheless fail to satisfy any of the criteria discussed above. Once a defendant's claims of error are organized and presented in a lawyer-like fashion to the Court of Appeals, the justices of the Supreme Court of North Carolina who make the decision to grant or deny discretionary review should be able to ascertain whether his case satisfies the standards established by the legislature for such review.

This is not to say, of course, that a skilled lawyer, particularly one trained in the somewhat arcane art of preparing petitions for discretionary review, would not prove helpful to any litigant able to employ him. An indigent defendant seeking review in the Supreme Court of North Carolina is therefore somewhat handicapped in comparison with a wealthy defendant who has counsel assisting him in every conceivable manner at every stage in the proceeding. But both the opportunity to have counsel prepare an initial brief in the Court of Appeals and the nature of discretionary review in the Supreme Court of North Carolina make this relative handicap far less than the handicap borne by the indigent defendant denied counsel on his initial appeal as of right in *Douglas.* And the fact that a particular service might be of benefit to an indigent defendant does not mean that the service is constitutionally required. The duty of the State under our cases is not to duplicate the legal arsenal that may be privately retained by a criminal defendant in a continuing effort to reverse his conviction, but only to assure the indigent defendant an adequate opportunity to present his claims fairly in the context of the State's appellate process. We think respondent was given that opportunity under the existing North Carolina system.

Much of the discussion in the preceding section is equally relevant to the question of whether a State must provide counsel for a defendant seeking review of his conviction in this Court. North Carolina will have provided counsel for a convicted defendant's only appeal as of right, and the brief prepared by that counsel together with one and perhaps two North Carolina appellate opinions will be available to this Court in order that it may decide whether or not to grant certiorari. This Court's review, much like that of the Supreme Court of North Carolina, is discretionary and depends on numerous factors other than the perceived correctness of the judgment we are asked to review.

There is also a significant difference between the source of the right to seek discretionary review in the Supreme Court of North Carolina and the source of the right to seek discretionary review in this Court. The former is conferred by the statutes of the State of North Carolina, but the latter is granted by statutes enacted by Congress. Thus the argument relied upon in the *Griffin* and *Douglas* cases, that the State having once created a right of appeal must give all persons an equal opportunity to enjoy the right, is by its terms inapplicable. The right to seek certiorari in this Court is not granted by any State, and exists by virtue of federal statute with or without the consent of the State whose judgment is sought to be reviewed.

The suggestion that a State is responsible for providing counsel to one petitioning this Court simply because it initiated the prosecution which led to the judgment sought to be reviewed is unsupported by either reason or authority. It would be quite as logical under the rationale of *Douglas* and *Griffin,* and indeed perhaps more so, to require that the Federal Government or this Court furnish and compensate counsel for petitioners who seek certiorari here to review state judgments of conviction. Yet this Court has followed a consistent policy of denying applications for appointment of counsel by persons seeking to file jurisdictional statements or petitions for certiorari in this Court. In the light of these authorities, it would be odd, indeed, to read the Fourteenth Amendment to impose such a requirement on the States, and we decline to do so.

We do not mean by this opinion to in any way discourage those States which have, as a matter of legislative choice, made counsel available to convicted defendants at all stages of judicial review. Some States which might well choose to do so as a matter of legislative policy may conceivably find that other claims for public funds within or without the criminal justice system preclude the implementation of such a policy at the present time. [T]he Fourteenth Amendment leaves these choices to the State * * *.[a]

JUSTICE DOUGLAS, with whom JUSTICE BRENNAN and JUSTICE MARSHALL concur, dissenting.

[In his opinion below] Chief Judge Haynsworth could find "no logical basis for differentiation between appeals of right and permissive review procedures in the context of the Constitution and the right to counsel." More familiar with the functioning of the North Carolina criminal justice system than are we, he concluded that "in the context of constitutional questions arising in criminal prosecutions, permissive review in the state's highest court may be predictably the most meaningful review the conviction will receive." The North Carolina Court of Appeals, for example, will be constrained in diverging from an earlier opinion of the State Supreme Court, even if subsequent developments have rendered the earlier Supreme Court decision suspect. "[T]he state's highest court remains the ultimate arbiter of the rights of its citizens."

a. A decade after *Ross v. Moffitt,* the Court broke its many years of silence on the issue of an indigent defendant's right to a psychiatrist and other expert assistance and held that, at least when an indigent defendant has made a preliminary showing that his sanity at the time of the offense is likely to be a significant factor at the trial, the state must provide the assistance of a psychiatrist for his defense. *Ake v. Oklahoma,* 470 U.S. 68, 105 S.Ct. 1087, 84 L.Ed.2d 53 (1985).

Ake confirms the tendency of the post-*Ross* cases to rely on due process rather than equal protection analysis in determining the constitutional rights of indigent criminal defendants. Thus the *Ake* Court reaffirmed the need for the state to take steps to assure that an indigent defendant had "a fair opportunity" or "an adequate opportunity" to present his defense. The Court also noted that in implementing the *Griffin* "equality" principle it had "focused on identifying the 'basic tools of an adequate defense or appeal' [and] required that such tools be provided to [those] who cannot afford to pay for them."

Chief Judge Haynsworth also correctly observed that the indigent defendant proceeding without counsel is at a substantial disadvantage relative to wealthy defendants represented by counsel when he is forced to fend for himself in seeking discretionary review from the State Supreme Court or from this Court. It may well not be enough to allege error in the courts below in layman's terms; a more sophisticated approach may be demanded:

"An indigent defendant is as much in need of the assistance of a lawyer in preparing and filing a petition for certiorari as he is in the handling of an appeal as of right. In many appeals, an articulate defendant could file an effective brief by telling his story in simple language without legalisms, but the technical requirement for applications for writs of certiorari are hazards which one untrained in the law could hardly be expected to negotiate.

" 'Certiorari proceedings constitute a highly specialized aspect of appellate work. The factors which [a court] deems important in connection with deciding whether to grant certiorari are certainly not within the normal knowledge of an indigent appellant.' Boskey, *The Right to Counsel in Appellate Proceedings,* 45 Minn.L.Rev. 783, 797 (1961)."

[The] right to discretionary review is a substantial one, and one where a lawyer can be of significant assistance to an indigent defendant. It was correctly perceived below that the "same concepts of fairness and equality which require counsel in a first appeal of right, require counsel in other and subsequent discretionary appeals."

SECTION 3. POLICE INTERROGATION AND CON-FESSIONS

Note on the Due Process "Voluntariness" Test for Admitting Confessions

Whatever the meaning of the elusive terms "involuntary" and "coerced" confessions in the 1950's and 1960's, for centuries the rule that a confession was admissible so long as it was "voluntary" was more or less an alternative statement of the rule that a confession was admissible so long as it was free of influences which made it "untrustworthy" or "probably untrue." Thus, Wigmore, the leading authority on evidence, reflected the law prevailing at the time when in 1940 he pointed out that a confession was not inadmissible because of "any *illegality* in the method of obtaining it" or "because of any connection with the *privilege against self-incrimination.*" (The Court did not apply the privilege against compulsory self-incrimination to the proceedings in the police station and other "in-custody questioning" until its 1966 decision in *Miranda.*)

The "untrustworthiness" rationale, the view that the rules governing the admissibility of confessions were merely a system of safeguards against false confessions, could explain the exclusion of the confession in *Brown v. Mississippi,* 297 U.S. 278, 56 S.Ct. 461, 80 L.Ed. 682 (1936), the first Fourteenth Amendment Due Process confession case, where the deputy sheriff who had presided over the beatings of the defendants conceded that one had been whipped, "but not too much for a Negro." And the same rationale was also adequate to explain the exclusion of confessions in the cases that immediately followed the *Brown* case, such as *Chambers v. Florida,* 309 U.S. 227, 60 S.Ct. 472, 84 L.Ed. 716 (1940) and *Ward v. Texas,* 316 U.S. 547, 62 S.Ct. 1139, 86 L.Ed. 1663 (1942), for they too, involved actual or threatened physical violence. But as the crude practices of the early cases grew outmoded and cases involving more subtle pressures began to appear, it became more difficult to assume that the resulting confessions were untrustworthy.

The first case in this section, *Ashcraft v. Tennessee,* 322 U.S. 143, 64 S.Ct. 921, 88 L.Ed. 1192 (1944), illustrates how the rationale for excluding confessions was changing. There was good reason to think that the defendant had indeed been involved in his wife's murder. Nevertheless, calling the extended police questioning to which Ashcraft had been subjected "inherently coercive," the Court ruled that the defendant's confession should not have been allowed into evidence. Under the circumstances, *Ashcraft* seems to reflect less concern with the reliability of the confession than disapproval of police methods which the Court considered to be dangerous and subject to abuse.

Although he joined Justice Jackson's dissent in *Ashcraft,* Justice Frankfurter soon became the leading exponent of the "police misconduct" or "police methods" rationale for barring the use of confessions. According to this rationale, in order to condemn, and deter, offensive or otherwise objectionable police interrogation methods, it was necessary to exclude confessions produced by such methods regardless of how trustworthy they might be.

Thus in *Watts v. Indiana,* 338 U.S. 49, 69 S.Ct. 1347, 93 L.Ed. 1801 (1949), the second case set forth in this section, and two companion cases, the Court reversed three convictions resting on coerced confessions without disputing the accuracy of Justice Jackson's observation (concurring in *Watts* and dissenting in the other cases) that "checked with external evidence [the confessions in each case] are inherently believable and were not shaken as to truth by anything that occurred at the trial." Justice Frankfurter, who wrote the principal opinion in *Watts,* commented: "In holding that the Due Process Clause *bars police procedure* which violates the basic notions of our accusatorial mode of prosecuting crime and vitiates a conviction based on the fruits of such procedure, we apply the Due Process Clause to its historic function of *assuring appropriate procedure* before liberty is curtailed or life is taken." (Emphasis added.)

Three years later, speaking for the Court in the famous "stomach-pumping" case of *Rochin v. California,* discussed in Ch. 3, Sec. 3, Justice Frankfurter viewed the coerced confession cases as "only instances of the general requirement that states in their prosecution respect certain decencies of civilized conduct." Involuntary confessions, he pointed out, "are inadmissible under the Due Process Clause even though statements contained in them may be independently established as true" because they "offend the community's sense of fair play and decency."

Perhaps the most emphatic statement of the "police methods" rationale appears in *Rogers v. Richmond,* 365 U.S. 534, 81 S.Ct. 735, 5 L.Ed.2d 760 (1961), one of Justice Frankfurter's last opinions on confessions. After more conventional methods had failed to produce any incriminating statements, a police chief pretended to order petitioner's ailing wife brought down to headquarters for questioning. Petitioner promptly confessed to the murder for which he was later convicted. The trial judge found that the police chief's pretense had "no tendency to produce a confession that was not in accord with the truth" and in his charge to the jury he indicated that the admissibility of the confession should turn on its probable reliability. But the Court, speaking through Justice Frankfurter, disagreed:

> "[Convictions based on involuntary confessions must fall] not so much because such confessions are unlikely to be true but because the methods used to extract them offend an underlying principle in the enforcement of our

criminal law; that ours is an accusatorial and not an inquisitional system. * * * Indeed, in many of the cases [reversing] state convictions involving the use of confessions obtained by impermissible methods, independent corroborating evidence left little doubt of the truth of what the defendant had confessed. * * * The attention of the trial judge should have been focused [on] whether the [police behavior] was such as to overbear petitioner's will to resist and bring about confessions not freely self determined—a question to be answered with complete disregard of whether or not petitioner in fact spoke the truth." [a]

Justice Jackson strongly resisted the expansion of the grounds for excluding confessions. *Ashcraft* is a great case only because Jackson's dissent made it so. No piece of writing better illustrates his famed powers of advocacy and extraordinary directness of approach. The crucial question, maintained Jackson, was not whether other suspects might have been overcome by the prolonged questioning, but whether *this particular defendant* had been. Jackson insisted that he had not; Ashcraft "was in possession of his own will and self-control at the time of confession." Ashcraft had decided to match wits with the police and after accusing another who in turn accused him "he knew he had lost the battle of wits." What was wrong with that? If the state is denied the right to apply any pressure to get someone to confess which is "inherently coercive," what pressure *could* it apply? And if it could not apply any "pressure," how could it be expected to get any suspect to confess?

Concurring in *Watts* and dissenting in the two companion cases, Justice Jackson again manifested his resistance to the expansion of the rights of suspects. He articulated concerns that many critics of the Warren Court's "revolution" in criminal procedure would repeat decades later. He underscored the "dilemma" facing a free society: To subject one without counsel to police interrogation "is a real peril to individual freedom," but bringing in a lawyer "means a real peril to solution of the crime."

Jackson voiced strong doubts that prohibiting the police from taking a suspect into custody and questioning him about an unwitnessed murder without advising

a. At least in its advanced stage (the early 1960's), some commentators thought that the "due process" or "voluntariness" test had *three* underlying values or goals, barring the use of confessions (a) which were of doubtful reliability because of the police methods used to obtain them; (b) which were produced by offensive police methods even though the reliability of the confession was not in question; and (c) which were obtained from a person whose volitional power was seriously impaired (e.g., a drugged, extremely intoxicated or "insane" person), even though the confession was neither untrustworthy (because impressively corroborated) nor the product of any conscious police wrongdoing. However, in *Colorado v. Connelly*, 479 U.S. 157, 107 S.Ct. 515, 93 L.Ed.2d 473 (1986), upholding the confession of a mentally ill person (according to expert testimony, "God's voice" told defendant he had only two options: confess his murder or commit suicide), the Court, per Rehnquist, C.J., rejected the third value or goal:

"[All the 'involuntary' confession cases] have contained a substantial element of coercive police conduct. Absent police conduct causally related to the confession, there is simply no basis for concluding that any state action has deprived a criminal defendant of due process of law.

"[The] flaw in respondent's argument is that it would expand our previous line of 'voluntariness' cases into a far-ranging requirement that courts must divine a defendant's motivation for speaking or acting as he did even though there be no claim that governmental conduct coerced his decision.

" * * * We think the Constitution rightly leaves [inquiries into the state of mind of one who has confessed quite apart from any state coercion] to be resolved by state laws governing the admission of evidence and erects no standard of its own in this area. A statement rendered by one in the condition of respondent might be proved to be quite unreliable, but this is a matter to be governed by the evidentiary laws of the forum and not by the Due Process Clause * * *."

him of his rights was "a necessary price to pay for the fairness which we know as 'due process of law.'" He recognized that the Bill of Rights, "even if construed as these provisions traditionally have been, * * * contain an aggregate of restrictions which seriously limit the power of society to solve such crimes as confront us in these cases," but he considered that "good reason for indulging in no unnecessary expansion of them."

A majority of the Court, however, was unpersuaded. As perhaps he knew, Jackson was swimming against the tide.

I. *MASSIAH* AND *ESCOBEDO*: THE COURT GROWS DISENCHANTED WITH THE "VOLUNTARINESS" TEST AND TURNS TO THE RIGHT TO COUNSEL

Introduction

As the rationales for the Court's coerced confession cases evolved, it became increasingly doubtful that terms such as "voluntariness," "coercion" and "breaking the will" were very helpful in deciding the admissibility of confessions. It appeared that such terms were not being used as tools of analysis, but as mere conclusions. When a court concluded that the police had resorted to unacceptable interrogation techniques, it called the resulting confession "involuntary." On the other hand, it seemed, when a court decided the methods the police had employed were permissible or tolerable, it called the resulting confession "voluntary." Moreover, such terms as "voluntariness," "coercion" and "overbearing the will" focused directly on neither of the two underlying reasons that led the courts to bar the use of confessions—the offensiveness of police interrogation methods or the risk that these methods had produced an untrue confession. Thus, as the Court, per O'Connor, J., noted in *Miller v. Fenton,* 474 U.S. 104, 106 S.Ct. 445, 88 L.Ed.2d 405 (1985), "[t]he voluntariness rubric has been variously condemned as 'useless,' 'perplexing,' and 'legal "doubletalk." ' "

Almost everything was relevant under the due process "totality of the circumstances"—"voluntariness" test, e.g., the suspect's age, intelligence, education and prior criminal record; whether he was advised of his rights, held incommunicado or given meals at regular intervals. But with a very few exceptions, e.g. the use or threatened use of physical violence, no single factor was decisive. Because there were so many variables in the voluntariness equation that one determination seldom served as a useful precedent for another, the test offered neither the police nor the courts much guidance. Trial courts were almost invited to give weight to their subjective preferences and appellate courts were discouraged from active review.

Understandably, some members of the Court looked for an alternative approach. In the 1959 *Crooker* case, discussed below, the four dissenters turned to the right to counsel. Five years later, as illustrated by the two cases in this section, *Massiah v. United States* and *Escobedo v. Illinois,* the right to counsel approach to confessions had gained ascendancy.

Crooker v. California, 357 U.S. 433, 78 S.Ct. 1287, 2 L.Ed.2d 1448 (1958), involved a petitioner who had attended one year of law school, during which time he studied criminal law, and who indicated that he was fully aware of his right to remain silent. On the basis of a challenged confession, he was convicted of the murder of his paramour and sentenced to death. A 5–4 majority rejected his argument that by persisting in interrogating him after denying his specific request to contact his lawyer the police had violated his due process right to legal representation and advice and that therefore the use of any confession obtained from him under these circumstances should be barred, even though "voluntarily" made under traditional standards. Such a rule, retorted the Court, per Clark, J., "would have [a] devastating effect on enforcement of criminal law, for it would effectively preclude police questioning—fair as well as unfair—until the accused was afforded opportunity to call his lawyer. Due process * * * demands no such rule." But four dissenting Justices, Douglas, J., joined by Warren, C.J., and Black and Brennan, JJ., maintained that "[t]he demands of our civilization, expressed in the Due Process Clause require that the accused who wants a counsel should have one at any time after the moment of arrest."

The following year, by virtue of *Spano v. New York,* 360 U.S. 315, 79 S.Ct. 1202, 3 L.Ed.2d 1265 (1959), it appeared that a majority of the Court may have arrived at the view that once a person is *formally charged* by indictment or information her constitutional right to counsel has "begun"—at least the right to the assistance of counsel she herself has retained. Four concurring Justices took this position in *Spano*: Justices Black, Douglas and Brennan, all of whom had dissented in *Crooker,* and newly appointed Justice Stewart, who had replaced Justice Burton. In two separate opinions, the concurring Justices emphasized that *Spano* was not a case where the police were questioning a suspect in the course of investigating an unsolved crime, but one where the person interrogated was already under indictment for murder when he surrendered to the authorities.

A majority of the *Spano* Court did not decide the case on the grounds suggested by the concurring Justices because it found the confession inadmissible under the traditional due process "voluntariness" test. But Chief Justice Warren, who wrote the majority opinion, had taken the position a year earlier in *Crooker* that the right to counsel should "begin" even earlier than at the point of indictment. Thus, counting heads, it appeared that by 1959 the views of the concurring Justices in *Spano* commanded a majority of the Court. Any doubts were dispelled by *Massiah v. United States,* the first case in this section.

When, a short five weeks after it had decided *Massiah,* the Court threw out the confession in *Escobedo v. Illinois,* the second case in this section, even though Escobedo had been interrogated *before* "judicial" or "adversary" proceedings had commenced against him, many members of the bench and bar grew alarmed. As they saw it, the "right to counsel" approach to the confession problem threatened the admissibility of even *"volunteered"* statements. They feared that the Court might be in the process of shaping a novel right not to confess except knowingly and with the tactical assistance of counsel.

Perhaps the enthusiastic public reaction to the *Gideon* decision a year earlier had led some members of the Court to believe that *Massiah* and *Escobedo* would also be well-received. But many members of the bench and bar, and the general public as well, soon left little doubt that they were much more enthusiastic about a lawyer for a defendant in the courtroom than they were about a lawyer for a suspect in the police station.

MASSIAH v. UNITED STATES

377 U.S. 201, 84 S.Ct. 1199, 12 L.Ed.2d 246 (1964).

JUSTICE STEWART delivered the opinion of the Court. * * *

[After he had been indicted for conspiracy to possess narcotics aboard a United States vessel and other federal narcotics violations, Massiah retained a lawyer, pled not guilty, and was released on bail. Colson, a codefendant, also retained a lawyer, pled not guilty, and was released on bail. Colson then invited Massiah to discuss the pending case in Colson's car, parked on a city street. Unknown to Massiah, Colson had decided to cooperate with federal agents in their continuing investigation of the case. A radio transmitter was installed under the front seat of Colson's car, enabling a nearby federal agent (Murphy), who was equipped with a recording device, to overhear the Massiah–Colson conversation. As expected, Massiah made several damaging admissions. On the basis of these admissions, Massiah was convicted of several narcotics offenses. The convictions were affirmed by the U.S. Court of Appeals for the Second Circuit.]

In *Spano v. New York,* this Court reversed a state criminal conviction because a confession had been wrongly admitted into evidence against the defendant at his trial. In that case the defendant had already been indicted for first-degree murder at the time he confessed. The Court held that the defendant's conviction could not stand under the Fourteenth Amendment. While the Court's opinion relied upon the totality of the circumstances under which the confession had been obtained, four concurring Justices pointed out that the Constitution required reversal of the conviction upon the sole and specific ground that the confession had been deliberately elicited by the police after the defendant had been indicted, and therefore at a time when he was clearly entitled to a lawyer's help. It was pointed out that under our system of justice the most elemental concepts of due process of law contemplate that an indictment be followed by a trial, "in an orderly courtroom, presided over by a judge, open to the public, and protected by all the procedural safeguards of the law." (Stewart, J., concurring). It was said that a Constitution which guarantees a defendant the aid of counsel at such a trial could surely vouchsafe no less to an indicted defendant under interrogation by the police in a completely extrajudicial proceeding. Anything less, it was said, might deny a defendant "effective representation by counsel at the only stage when legal aid and advice would help him." (Douglas, J., concurring).

[The view taken by the *Spano* concurring Justices] no more than reflects a constitutional principle established as long ago as *Powell v. Alabama,* where the Court noted that "during perhaps the most critical period of the proceedings, [that] is to say, from the time of their arraignment until the beginning of their trial, when consultation, thoroughgoing investigation and preparation [are] vitally important, the defendants [are] as much entitled to such aid [of counsel] during that period as at the trial itself." * * *

Here we deal not with a state court conviction, but with a federal case, where the specific guarantee of the Sixth Amendment directly applies. We hold that the petitioner was denied the basic protections of that guarantee when there was used against him at his trial evidence of his own incriminating words, which federal agents had deliberately elicited from him after he had been indicted and in the absence of his counsel. It is true that in the Spano case the defendant was interrogated in a police station, while here the damaging testimony was elicited from the defendant without his knowledge while he was free on bail. But, as Judge Hays pointed out in his dissent in the Court of Appeals, "if such a rule is to have any efficacy it must apply to indirect and surreptitious interrogations as well as those conducted in the jailhouse. In this case, Massiah was more seriously imposed upon [because] he did not even know that he was under interrogation by a government agent."

The Solicitor General [has] strenuously contended that the federal law enforcement agents had the right, if not indeed the duty, to continue their investigation of the petitioner and his alleged criminal associates even though the petitioner had been indicted. [He] says that the quantity of narcotics involved was such as to suggest that the petitioner was part of a large and well-organized ring, and indeed that the continuing investigation confirmed this suspicion, since it resulted in criminal charges against many defendants. Under these circumstances the Solicitor General concludes that the government agents were completely "justified in making use of Colson's cooperation by having Colson continue his normal associations and by surveilling them."

* * * We do not question that in this case, as in many cases, it was entirely proper to continue an investigation of the suspected criminal activities of the defendant and his alleged confederates, even though the defendant had already been indicted. All that we hold is that the defendant's own incriminating statements, obtained by federal agents under the circumstances here disclosed, could not constitutionally be used by the prosecution as evidence against *him* at his trial. * * *

JUSTICE WHITE, with whom JUSTICE CLARK and JUSTICE HARLAN join, dissenting.

[It is] a rather portentous occasion when a constitutional rule is established barring the use of evidence which is relevant, reliable and highly probative of the issue which the trial court has before it—whether the accused committed the act with which he is charged. Without the evidence, the quest for truth may be seriously impeded and in many cases the trial court, although aware of proof showing defendant's guilt, must nevertheless release him because the crucial evidence is deemed inadmissible. This result is entirely justified in some circumstances because exclusion serves other policies of overriding importance, as where evidence seized in an illegal search is excluded, not because of the quality of the proof, but to secure meaningful enforcement of the Fourth Amendment. But this only emphasizes that the soundest of reasons is necessary to warrant the exclusion of evidence otherwise admissible and the creation of another area of privileged testimony. With all due deference, I am not at all convinced that the additional barriers to the pursuit of truth which the Court today erects rest on anything like the solid foundations which decisions of this gravity should require.

The importance of the matter should not be underestimated, for today's rule promises to have wide application well beyond the facts of this case. The reason given for the result here—the admissions were obtained in the absence of counsel—would seem equally pertinent to statements obtained at any time after the right to counsel attaches, whether there has been an indictment or not; to admissions made prior to arraignment, at least where the defendant has counsel or asks for it; to the fruits of admissions improperly obtained under the new rule; to criminal proceedings in state courts; and to defendants long since convicted upon evidence including such admissions. The new rule will immediately do service in a great many cases.

Whatever the content or scope of the rule may prove to be, I am unable to see how this case presents an unconstitutional interference with Massiah's right to counsel. Massiah was not prevented from consulting with counsel as often as he wished. No meetings with counsel were disturbed or spied upon. Preparation for trial was in no way obstructed. It is only a sterile syllogism—an unsound one, besides—to say that because Massiah had a right to counsel's aid before and during the trial, his out-of-court conversations and admissions must be excluded if obtained without counsel's consent or presence. The right to counsel has never meant as much before and its extension in this case requires some further explanation, so far unarticulated by the Court.

Since the new rule would exclude all admissions made to the police, no matter how voluntary and reliable, the requirement of counsel's presence or approval would seem to rest upon the probability that counsel would foreclose any admissions at all. This is nothing more than a thinly disguised constitutional policy of minimizing or entirely prohibiting the use in evidence of voluntary out-of-court admissions and confessions made by the accused. Carried as far as blind logic may compel some to go, the notion that statements from the mouth of the defendant should not be used in evidence would have a severe and unfortunate impact upon the great bulk of criminal cases.

Viewed in this light, the Court's newly fashioned exclusionary principle goes far beyond the constitutional privilege against self-incrimination, which neither requires nor suggests the barring of voluntary pretrial admissions.

[Whether] as a matter of self-incrimination or of due process, the proscription is against compulsion—coerced incrimination. Under the prior law, announced in countless cases in this Court, the defendant's pretrial statements were admissible evidence if voluntarily made; inadmissible if not the product of his free will. Hardly any constitutional area has been more carefully patrolled by this Court, and until now the Court has expressly rejected the argument that admissions are to be deemed involuntary if made outside the presence of counsel.

The Court presents no facts, no objective evidence, no reasons to warrant scrapping the voluntary-involuntary test for admissibility in this area. Without such evidence I would retain it in its present form.

This case cannot be analogized to the American Bar Association's rule forbidding an attorney to talk to the opposing party litigant outside the presence of his counsel. Aside from the fact that the Association's canons are not of constitutional dimensions, the specific canon argued is inapposite because it deals with the conduct of lawyers and not with the conduct of investigators. Lawyers are forbidden to interview the opposing party because of the supposed imbalance of legal skill and acumen between the lawyer and the party litigant; the reason for the rule does not apply to nonlawyers and certainly not to Colson, Massiah's codefendant.

Applying the new exclusionary rule is peculiarly inappropriate in this case. At the time of the conversation in question, petitioner was not in custody but free on bail. He was not questioned in what anyone could call an atmosphere of official coercion. What he said was said to his partner in crime who had also been indicted. There was no suggestion or any possibility of coercion. What petitioner did not know was that Colson had decided to report the conversation to the police. Had there been no prior arrangements between Colson and the police, had Colson simply gone to the police after the conversation had occurred, his testimony relating Massiah's statements would be readily admissible at the trial, as would a recording which he might have made of the conversation. In such event, it would simply be said that Massiah risked talking to a friend who decided to disclose what he knew of Massiah's criminal activities. But if, as occurred here, Colson had been cooperating with the police prior to his meeting with Massiah, both his evidence and the recorded conversation are somehow transformed into inadmissible evidence despite the fact that the hazard to Massiah remains precisely the same—the defection of a confederate in crime.

[The question presented] is this: when the police have arrested and released on bail one member of a criminal ring and another member, a confederate, is cooperating with the police, can the confederate be allowed to continue his association with the ring or must he somehow be withdrawn to avoid challenge to trial evidence on the ground that it was acquired after rather than before the arrest, after rather than before the indictment?

Defendants who are out on bail have been known to continue their illicit operations. That an attorney is advising them should not constitutionally immunize their statements made in furtherance of these operations and relevant to the question of their guilt at the pending prosecution. * * * Undoubtedly, the evidence excluded in this case would not have been available but for the conduct of Colson in cooperation with Agent Murphy, but is it this kind of conduct which should be forbidden to those charged with law enforcement? It is one thing to establish safeguards against procedures fraught with the potentiality of coercion and to outlaw "easy but self-defeating ways in which brutality is substituted for brains as an instrument of crime detection." But here there was no substitution of brutality for brains, no inherent danger of police coercion justifying the prophylactic effect of another exclusionary rule. Massiah was not being interrogated in a police station, was not surrounded by numerous officers or questioned in relays, and was not forbidden access to others. Law enforcement may have the elements of a contest about it, but it is not a game. Massiah and those like him receive ample protection from the long line of precedents in this Court holding that confessions may not be introduced unless they are voluntary. In making these determinations the courts must consider the absence of counsel as one of several factors by which voluntariness is to be judged. This is a wiser rule than the automatic rule announced by the Court, which requires courts and juries to disregard voluntary admissions which they might well find to be the best possible evidence in discharging their responsibility for ascertaining truth.

ESCOBEDO v. ILLINOIS

378 U.S. 478, 4 Ohio Misc. 197, 84 S.Ct. 1758, 12 L.Ed.2d 977 (1964).

JUSTICE GOLDBERG delivered the opinion of the Court.

[On the night of January 19, petitioner's brother-in-law was fatally shot. A few hours later petitioner was taken into custody for questioning, but he made no statement and was released the following afternoon pursuant to a writ of habeas corpus obtained by his retained counsel. On January 30, one DiGerlando, who was then in police custody and who was later indicted for the murder along with petitioner, stated that petitioner had fired the shots which killed his brother-in-law. That evening petitioner was again arrested and taken to police headquarters. En route to the police station he was told that DiGerlando had named him as the one who fired the fatal shots and that he might as well admit it, but petitioner replied (probably because his attorney had obtained his release from police custody only 11 days earlier or because he had consulted with his attorney in the meantime): "I am sorry but I would like to have advice from my lawyer."

[Shortly after petitioner reached police headquarters, his retained lawyer arrived and spent the next three or four hours trying unsuccessfully to speak to his client. He talked to every officer he could find, but was repeatedly told that he could not see his client and that he would have to get a writ of habeas corpus. In the meantime, petitioner repeatedly but unsuccessfully asked to speak to his lawyer. At one point, petitioner and his attorney came into each other's view for a few moments, but the attorney was quickly ushered away. Petitioner testified that he heard a detective tell his attorney that the latter could not see him until the police "were done."

[Instead of allowing petitioner to meet with his lawyer, the police arranged a confrontation between petitioner and DiGerlando. Petitioner denied that he had fired the fatal shots. He maintained that DiGerlando was lying and, in the presence of the police, told him: "I didn't shoot Manuel, you did it." In this way, petitioner admitted to some knowledge of the crime. After that, he made other statements further implicating himself in the murder plot. At this point, an assistant prosecutor arrived "to take" a statement. The statement, made in response to carefully framed questions, was admitted into evidence. Petitioner was convicted of murder. The Supreme Court of Illinois affirmed.]

The critical question in this case is whether, under the circumstances, the refusal by the police to honor petitioner's request to consult with his lawyer during the course of an interrogation constitutes a denial of "the Assistance of Counsel" in violation of the Sixth Amendment to the Constitution as "made obligatory upon the States by the Fourteenth Amendment," *Gideon*, and thereby renders inadmissible in a state criminal trial any incriminating statement elicited by the police during the interrogation. * * *

In *Massiah* this Court observed that "a Constitution which guarantees a defendant the aid of counsel [at] trial could surely vouchsafe no less to an indicted defendant under interrogation by the police in a completely extrajudicial proceeding. Anything less [might] deny a defendant 'effective representation by counsel at the only stage when legal aid and advice would help him.'"

The interrogation here was conducted before petitioner was formally indicted. But in the context of this case, that fact should make no difference. When petitioner requested, and was denied, an opportunity to consult with his lawyer, the investigation had ceased to be a general investigation of "an unsolved crime." Petitioner had become the accused, and the purpose of the interrogation was to "get him" to confess his guilt despite his constitutional right not to do so. At the time of his arrest and throughout the course of the interrogation, the police told petitioner that they had convincing evidence that he had fired the fatal shots. Without informing him of his absolute right to remain silent in the face of this accusation, the police urged him to make a statement.[5] * * *

Petitioner, a layman, was undoubtedly unaware that under Illinois law an admission of "mere" complicity in the murder plot was legally as damaging as an admission of firing of the fatal shots. The "guiding hand of counsel" was essential to advise petitioner of his rights in this delicate situation. This was the "stage when legal aid and advice" were most critical to petitioner. *Massiah.* * * * It would exalt form over substance to make the right to counsel, under these circumstances, depend on whether at the time of the interrogation, the authorities had secured a formal indictment. Petitioner had, for all practical purposes, already been charged with murder. * * *

In *Gideon* we held that every person accused of a crime, whether state or federal, is entitled to a lawyer at trial. The rule sought by the State here, however, would make the trial no more than an appeal from the interrogation; and the "right to use counsel at the formal trial [would be] a very hollow thing [if], for all practical purposes, the conviction is already assured by pretrial examination." *In re Groban*, 352 U.S. 330 (1957) (Black, J., dissenting). "One can imagine a cynical prosecutor saying: 'Let them have the most illustrious

---

5. Although there is testimony in the record that petitioner and his lawyer had previously discussed what petitioner should do in the event of interrogation, there is no evidence that they discussed what petitioner should, or could, do in the face of a false accusation that he had fired the fatal bullets.

counsel, now. They can't escape the noose. There is nothing that counsel can do for them at the trial.' "

It is argued that if the right to counsel is afforded prior to indictment, the number of confessions obtained by the police will diminish significantly, because most confessions are obtained during the period between arrest and indictment, and "any lawyer worth his salt will tell the suspect in no uncertain terms to make no statement to police under any circumstances." This argument, of course, cuts two ways. The fact that many confessions are obtained during this period points up its critical nature as a "stage when legal aid and advice" are surely needed. *Massiah*. The right to counsel would indeed be hollow if it began at a period when few confessions were obtained. There is necessarily a direct relationship between the importance of a stage to the police in their quest for a confession and the criticalness of that stage to the accused in his need for legal advice. Our Constitution, unlike some others, strikes the balance in favor of the right of the accused to be advised by his lawyer of his privilege against self-incrimination.

We have learned the lesson of history, ancient and modern, that a system of criminal law enforcement which comes to depend on the "confession" will, in the long run, be less reliable and more subject to abuses than a system which depends on extrinsic evidence independently secured through skillful investigation. * * *

We have also learned the companion lesson of history that no system of criminal justice can, or should, survive if it comes to depend for its continued effectiveness on the citizens' abdication through unawareness of their constitutional rights. No system worth preserving should have to *fear* that if an accused is permitted to consult with a lawyer, he will become aware of, and exercise, these rights. If the exercise of constitutional rights will thwart the effectiveness of a system of law enforcement, then there is something very wrong with that system.[14]

We hold, therefore, that where, as here, the investigation is no longer a general inquiry into an unsolved crime but has begun to focus on a particular suspect, the suspect has been taken into police custody, the police carry out a process of interrogations that lends itself to eliciting incriminating statements, the suspect has requested and been denied an opportunity to consult with his lawyer, and the police have not effectively warned him of his absolute constitutional right to remain silent, the accused has been denied "the Assistance of Counsel" in violation of the Sixth Amendment to the Constitution as "made obligatory upon the States by the Fourteenth Amendment," *Gideon,* and that no statement elicited by the police during the interrogation may be used against him at a criminal trial. * * *

Nothing we have said today affects the powers of the police to investigate "an unsolved crime" by gathering information from witnesses and by other "proper investigative efforts." We hold only that when the process shifts from investigatory to accusatory—when its focus is on the accused and its purpose is to elicit a confession—our adversary system begins to operate, and, under the circumstances here, the accused must be permitted to consult with his lawyer.

The judgment of the Illinois Supreme Court is reversed and the case remanded for proceedings not inconsistent with this opinion. * * *

14. The accused may, of course, intelligently and knowingly waive his privilege against self-incrimination and his right to counsel either at a pretrial stage or at the trial. But no knowing and intelligent waiver of any constitutional right can be said to have occurred under the circumstances of this case.

JUSTICE HARLAN, dissenting.

* * * Like my Brother White, I think the rule announced today is most ill-conceived and that it seriously and unjustifiably fetters perfectly legitimate methods of criminal law enforcement.

JUSTICE STEWART, dissenting.   * * *

Massiah is not in point here.   * * * Putting to one side the fact that the case now before us is not a federal case, the vital fact remains that this case does not involve the deliberate interrogation of a defendant after the initiation of judicial proceedings against him.   The Court disregards this basic difference between the present case and Massiah's, with the bland assertion that "that fact should make no difference."

It is "that fact," I submit, which makes all the difference.   Under our system of criminal justice the institution of formal, meaningful judicial proceedings, by way of indictment, information, or arraignment, marks the point at which a criminal investigation has ended and adversary proceedings have commenced.   It is at this point that the constitutional guarantees attach which pertain to a criminal trial.   Among those guarantees are the right to a speedy trial, the right of confrontation, and the right to trial by jury.   Another is the guarantee of the assistance of counsel.

The confession which the Court today holds inadmissible was a voluntary one. It was given during the course of a perfectly legitimate police investigation of an unsolved murder.   The Court says that what happened during this investigation "affected" the trial.   I had always supposed that the whole purpose of a police investigation of a murder was to "affect" the trial of the murderer, and that it would be only an incompetent, unsuccessful, or corrupt investigation which would not do so.   The Court further says that the Illinois police officers did not advise the petitioner of his "constitutional rights" before he confessed to the murder. This Court has never held that the Constitution requires the police to give any "advice" under circumstances such as these.

Supported by no stronger authority than its own rhetoric, the Court today converts a routine police investigation of an unsolved murder into a distorted analogue of a judicial trial.   It imports into this investigation constitutional concepts historically applicable only after the onset of formal prosecutorial pro-ceedings.   By doing so, I think the Court perverts those precious constitutional guarantees, and frustrates the vital interests of society in preserving the legiti-mate and proper function of honest and purposeful police investigation.   * * *

JUSTICE WHITE, whom JUSTICE CLARK and JUSTICE STEWART join, dissenting.

In *Massiah* the Court held that as of the date of the indictment the prosecution is disentitled to secure admissions from the accused.   The Court now moves that date back to the time when the prosecution begins to "focus" on the accused.   Although the opinion purports to be limited to the facts of this case, it would be naive to think that the new constitutional right announced will depend upon whether the accused has retained his own counsel, or has asked to consult with counsel in the course of interrogation.   At the very least the Court holds that once the accused becomes a suspect and, presumably, is arrested, any admission made to the police thereafter is inadmissible in evidence unless the accused has waived his right to counsel.   The decision is thus another major step in the direction of the goal which the Court seemingly has in mind—to bar from evidence all admissions obtained from an individual suspected of crime, whether involun-tarily made or not.   It does of course put us one step "ahead" of the English judges who have had the good sense to leave the matter a discretionary one with the trial court.   I reject this step and the invitation to go farther which the court has now issued.

By abandoning the voluntary-involuntary test for admissibility of confessions, the Court seems driven by the notion that it is uncivilized law enforcement to use an accused's own admissions against him at his trial.   It attempts to find a home for this new and nebulous rule of due process by attaching it to the right to counsel guaranteed in the federal system by the Sixth Amendment and binding upon the States by virtue of the due process guarantee of the Fourteenth Amendment.   The right to counsel now not only entitles the accused to counsel's advice and aid in preparing for trial but stands as an impenetrable barrier to any interrogation once the accused has become a suspect.   From that very moment apparently his right to counsel attaches, a rule wholly unworkable and impossible to administer unless police cars are equipped with public defenders and undercover agents and police informants have defense counsel at their side.   I would not abandon the Court's prior cases defining with some care and analysis the circumstances requiring the presence or aid of counsel and substitute the amorphous and wholly unworkable principle that counsel is constitutionally required whenever he would or could be helpful.   [Under the Court's] new approach one might just as well argue that a potential defendant is constitutionally entitled to a lawyer before, not after, he commits a crime, since it is then that crucial incriminating evidence is put within the reach of the Government by the would-be accused.   Until now there simply has been no right guaranteed by the Federal Constitution to be free from the use at trial of a voluntary admission made prior to indictment.

It is incongruous to assume that the provision for counsel in the Sixth Amendment was meant to amend or supersede the self-incrimination provision of the Fifth Amendment, which is now applicable to the States.   That amendment addresses itself to the very issue of incriminating admissions of an accused and resolves it by proscribing only compelled statements.   Neither the Framers, the constitutional language, a century of decisions of this Court nor Professor Wigmore provides an iota of support for the idea that an accused has an absolute constitutional right not to answer even in the absence of compulsion—the constitutional right not to incriminate himself by making voluntary disclosures.   * * *

The Court chooses [to] rely on the virtues and morality of a system of criminal law enforcement which does not depend on the "confession."   No such judgment is to be found in the Constitution.   It might be appropriate for a legislature to provide that a suspect should not be consulted during a criminal investigation;   that an accused should never be called before a grand jury to answer, even if he wants to, what may well be incriminating questions;   and that no person, whether he be a suspect, guilty criminal or innocent bystander, should be put to the ordeal of responding to orderly noncompulsory inquiry by the State. But this is not the system our Constitution requires.   The only "inquisitions" the Constitution forbids are those which compel incrimination.   Escobedo's statements were not compelled and the Court does not hold that they were.

This new American judges' rule, which is to be applied in both federal and state courts, is perhaps thought to be a necessary safeguard against the possibility of extorted confessions.   To this extent it reflects a deep-seated distrust of law enforcement officers everywhere, unsupported by relevant data or current material based upon our own experience.   Obviously law enforcement officers can make mistakes and exceed their authority, as today's decision shows that even judges can do, but I have somewhat more faith than the Court evidently has in the ability and desire of prosecutors and of the power of the appellate courts to discern and correct such violations of the law.

The Court may be concerned with a narrower matter: the unknowing defendant who responds to police questioning because he mistakenly believes that he must and that his admissions will not be used against him. But this worry hardly calls for the broadside the Court has now fired. The failure to inform an accused that he need not answer and that his answers may be used against him is very relevant indeed to whether the disclosures are compelled. Cases in this Court, to say the least, have never placed a premium on ignorance of constitutional rights. If an accused is told he must answer and does not know better, it would be very doubtful that the resulting admissions could be used against him. When the accused has not been informed of his rights at all the Court characteristically and properly looks very closely at the surrounding circumstances. I would continue to do so. But in this case Danny Escobedo knew full well that he did not have to answer and knew full well that his lawyer had advised him not to answer.

I do not suggest for a moment that law enforcement will be destroyed by the rule announced today. The need for peace and order is too insistent for that. But it will be crippled and its task made a great deal more difficult, all in my opinion, for unsound, unstated reasons, which can find no home in any of the provisions of the Constitution.

II. *MIRANDA*: THE COURT BUILDS A CONFESSION DOCTRINE ON THE PRIVILEGE AGAINST COMPELLED SELF–INCRIMINATION

Introduction

Recall that dissenting in the 1944 *Ashcraft* case, Justice Jackson agreed that the detention and questioning of a suspect for thirty-six hours is "inherently coercive," but quickly added: "[S]o is custody and examination for one hour. Arrest itself is inherently coercive and so is detention. * * * But does the Constitution prohibit use of all confessions made after arrest because questioning, while one is deprived of freedom, is 'inherently coercive'?" Both Jackson and Justice Black, who wrote the majority opinion in *Ashcraft,* knew that in 1944 the Court was not ready for an affirmative answer to Jackson's question. But by 1966 the Court had grown ready.

Yes, answered a 5–4 majority in *Miranda v. Arizona,* the Constitution does prohibit use of all confessions obtained by "in-custody questioning" unless "adequate protective devices" are used to dispel the coercion inherent in such questioning. The protective devices deemed necessary to neutralize the compulsion inherent in the interrogation environment (unless the government adopts other equally effective means, and what they may be remains unclear) are the now familiar "*Miranda* warnings."

The *Miranda* Court's reasoning, if not its result, surprised the late John J. Flynn, Miranda's lawyer in the U.S. Supreme Court. As Flynn later recalled, he and others working on the case had "agreed that the briefs should be written with the entire focus on the Sixth Amendment [right to counsel] because that is where the Court was headed after *Escobedo,*" but "in the very first paragraph [of the *Miranda* opinion] Chief Justice Warren said [in effect], 'It is the Fifth Amendment [privilege against compulsory self-incrimination] that is at issue today.' That was Miranda's effective use of counsel."

Although not happy with the continued momentum of the Warren Court in favor of the rights of suspects, those alarmed by *Massiah* and *Escobedo* must have found some comfort in the *Miranda* Court's switch in emphasis from the right to counsel to the privilege against compelled self-incrimination. Recall that the *Escobedo* dissenters expressed a preference for a self-incrimination approach, rather than a right to counsel approach, because the self-incrimination clause proscribes only *compelled* statements. Of course, the four *Escobedo* dissenters (all of whom also dissented in *Miranda*) were not pleased with the way the *Miranda* majority defined "compulsion" within the meaning of the privilege.

Why, in the thirty years between *Brown v. Mississippi* (1936), the first Fourteenth Amendment Due Process case, and *Miranda,* had the Fifth Amendment's ban against compelling a person in any criminal case "to be a witness against himself" been so neglected in the confession cases? For one thing, this prohibition had not been deemed applicable to the states until 1964, and by that time a large body of law pertaining to "involuntary" or "coerced" confessions had developed. Moreover, and more important, the prevailing pre-*Miranda* view was that compulsion to testify meant *legal* compulsion.

Since a suspect is threatened neither with perjury for testifying falsely nor contempt for refusing to testify at all, it cannot be said, ran the argument, that a person undergoing police interrogation is being "compelled" to be "a witness against himself" within the meaning of the privilege—even though under such circumstances a person may assume or be led to believe that there *are* legal (or extralegal) sanctions for "refusing to cooperate." Since the police have no *legal right* to make a suspect answer (although, prior to *Miranda,* the police did not have to *tell* a person that), there was no legal obligation to answer, ran the argument, to which a privilege in the technical sense could apply.

Although the right to counsel had dominated the confessions scene in the years immediately preceding *Miranda,* there was some reason to think that, at long last, the self-incrimination clause might move to centerstage. In *Malloy v. Hogan,* 378 U.S. 1, 84 S.Ct. 1489, 12 L.Ed.2d 653 (1964) (which did not involve a confession), the Court, per Brennan, J., performed what some called a "shotgun wedding" of the privilege against self-incrimination to the confession rule. *Malloy* not only held the self-incrimination clause applicable to the states, but declared that whenever a question arises in a state *or* federal court "whether a confession is incompetent because not voluntary, the issue is controlled by [the self-incrimination] portion of the Fifth Amendment."

Whether or not this view made good sense, it constituted very questionable recent history. In none of the dozens of state *or* federal confession cases decided in the 1930's, 40's or 50's had the self-incrimination clause been the basis for judgment (although it had occasionally been mentioned in an opinion). But how the *Malloy* opinion looked back was not as important as how it looked forward. The confession rules and the privilege against self-incrimination had become intertwined in *Malloy*—and they would be fused in *Miranda.*

MIRANDA v. ARIZONA (No. 759) *

384 U.S. 436, 10 Ohio Misc. 9, 86 S.Ct. 1602, 16 L.Ed.2d 694 (1966).

CHIEF JUSTICE WARREN delivered the opinion of the Court.

* Together with No. 760, *Vignera v. New York [and] No. 761,* Westover v. United States   *[and] No. 584,* California v. Stewart * * *.

The cases before us raise questions which go to the roots of American criminal jurisprudence: the restraints society must observe consistent with the Federal Constitution in prosecuting individuals for crime. More specifically, we deal with the admissibility of statements obtained from an individual who is subjected to custodial police interrogation and the necessity for procedures which assure that the individual is accorded his privilege under the Fifth Amendment to the Constitution not to be compelled to incriminate himself. * * *

We start here, as we did in *Escobedo* with the premise that our holding is not an innovation in our jurisprudence, but is an application of principles long recognized and applied in other settings. We have undertaken a thorough re-examination of the *Escobedo* decision and the principles it announced, and we reaffirm it. That case was but an explication of basic rights that are enshrined in our Constitution—that "No person * * * shall be compelled in any criminal case to be a witness against himself," and that "the accused [shall] have the Assistance of Counsel"—rights which were put in jeopardy in that case through official overbearing. * * *

Our holding will be spelled out with some specificity in the pages which follow but briefly stated it is this: the prosecution may not use statements, whether exculpatory or inculpatory, stemming from custodial interrogation of the defendant unless it demonstrates the use of procedural safeguards effective to secure the privilege against self-incrimination. By custodial interrogation, we mean questioning initiated by law enforcement officers after a person has been taken into custody or otherwise deprived of his freedom of action in any significant way.[4] As for the procedural safeguards to be employed, unless other fully effective means are devised to inform accused persons of their right of silence and to assure a continuous opportunity to exercise it, the following measures are required. Prior to any questioning, the person must be warned that he has a right to remain silent, that any statement he does make may be used as evidence against him, and that he has a right to the presence of an attorney, either retained or appointed. The defendant may waive effectuation of these rights, provided the waiver is made voluntarily, knowingly and intelligently. If, however, he indicates in any manner and at any stage of the process that he wishes to consult with an attorney before speaking there can be no questioning. Likewise, if the individual is alone and indicates in any manner that he does not wish to be interrogated, the police may not question him. The mere fact that he may have answered some questions or volunteered some statements on his own does not deprive him of the right to refrain from answering any further inquiries until he has consulted with an attorney and thereafter consents to be questioned.

The constitutional issue we decide in each of these cases is the admissibility of statements obtained from a defendant questioned while in custody and deprived of his freedom of action in any significant way. In each, the defendant was questioned by police officers, detectives, or a prosecuting attorney in a room in which he was cut off from the outside world. In none of these cases was the defendant given a full and effective warning of his rights at the outset of the interrogation process. In all the cases, the questioning elicited oral admissions, and in three of them, signed statements as well which were admitted at their trials. They all thus share silent features—incommunicado interrogation of

---

4. This is what we meant in *Escobedo* when we spoke of an investigation which had focused   on an accused.

individuals in a police-dominated atmosphere, resulting in self-incriminating statements without full warnings of constitutional rights. * * *

Again we stress that the modern practice of in-custody interrogation is psychologically rather than physically oriented. * * * Interrogation still takes place in privacy. Privacy results in secrecy and this in turn results in a gap in our knowledge as to what in fact goes on in the interrogation rooms. A valuable source of information about present police practices, however, may be found in various police manuals and texts which document procedures employed with success in the past, and which recommend various other effective tactics. These texts are used by law enforcement agencies themselves as guides.[9] It should be noted that these texts professedly present the most enlightened and effective means presently used to obtain statements through custodial interrogation. By considering these texts and other data, it is possible to describe procedures observed and noted around the country.

[To] highlight the isolation and unfamiliar surroundings, the manuals instruct the police to display an air of confidence in the suspect's guilt and from outward appearance to maintain only an interest in confirming certain details. The guilt of the subject is to be posited as a fact. The interrogator should direct his comments toward the reasons why the subject committed the act, rather than court failure by asking the subject whether he did it. Like other men, perhaps the subject has had a bad family life, had an unhappy childhood, had too much to drink, had an unrequited desire for women. The officers are instructed to minimize the moral seriousness of the offense, to cast blame on the victim or on society. These tactics are designed to put the subject in a psychological state where his story is but an elaboration of what the police purport to know already—that he is guilty. Explanations to the contrary are dismissed and discouraged.

The texts thus stress that the major qualities an interrogator should possess are patience and perseverance.

[When other techniques] prove unavailing, the texts recommend they be alternated with a show of some hostility. One ploy often used has been termed the "friendly-unfriendly" or the "Mutt and Jeff" act:

> "[In] this technique, two agents are employed. Mutt, the relentless investigator, who knows the subject is guilty and is not going to waste any time. He's sent a dozen men away for this crime and he's going to send the subject away for the full term. Jeff, on the other hand, is obviously a kindhearted man. He has a family himself. He has a brother who was involved in a little scrape like this. He disapproves of Mutt and his tactics and will arrange to get him off the case if the subject will cooperate. He can't hold Mutt off for very long. The subject would be wise to make a quick decision. The technique is applied by having both investigators present while Mutt acts out his role. Jeff may stand by quietly and demur at some of

9. The methods described in Inbau and Reid, *Criminal Interrogation and Confessions* (1962), are a revision and enlargement of material presented in three prior editions of a predecessor text, *Lie Detection and Criminal Interrogation* (3d ed. 1953). The authors and their associates are officers of the Chicago Police Scientific Crime–Detection Laboratory and have had extensive experience in writing, lecturing and speaking to law enforcement authorities over a 20–year period. They say that the techniques portrayed in their manuals reflect their experiences and are the most effective psychological strategems to employ during interrogations. Similarly, the techniques described in O'Hara, *Fundamentals of Criminal Investigation* (1959), were gleaned from long service as observer, lecturer in police science, and work as a federal criminal investigator. All these texts have had rather extensive use among law enforcement agencies and among students of police science, with total sales and circulation of over 44,000.

Mutt's tactics. When Jeff makes his plea for cooperation, Mutt is not present in the room."

The interrogators sometimes are instructed to induce a confession out of trickery. The technique here is quite effective in crimes which require identification or which run in series. In the identification situation, the interrogator may take a break in his questioning to place the subject among a group of men in a line-up. "The witness or complainant (previously coached, if necessary) studies the line-up and confidently points out the subject as the guilty party." Then the questioning resumes "as though there were now no doubt about the guilt of the subject." A variation on this technique is called the "reverse line-up":

> "The accused is placed in a line-up, but this time he is identified by several fictitious witnesses or victims who associated him with different offenses. It is expected that the subject will become desperate and confess to the offense under investigation in order to escape from the false accusations."

The manuals also contain instructions for police on how to handle the individual who refuses to discuss the matter entirely, or who asks for an attorney or relatives. The examiner is to concede him the right to remain silent. "This usually has a very undermining effect. First of all, he is disappointed in his expectation of an unfavorable reaction on the part of the interrogator. Secondly, a concession of this right to remain silent impresses the subject with the apparent fairness of his interrogator." After this psychological conditioning, however, the officer is told to point out the incriminating significance of the suspect's refusal to talk:

> "Joe, you have a right to remain silent. That's your privilege and I'm the last person in the world who'll try to take it away from you. If that's the way you want to leave this, O.K. But let me ask you this. Suppose you were in my shoes and I were in yours and you called me in to ask me about this and I told you, 'I don't want to answer any of your questions.' You'd think I had something to hide, and you'd probably be right in thinking that. That's exactly what I'll have to think about you, and so will everybody else. So let's sit here and talk this whole thing over."

Few will persist in their initial refusal to talk, it is said, if this monologue is employed correctly.

In the event that the subject wishes to speak to a relative or an attorney, the following advice is tendered:

> "[T]he interrogator should respond by suggesting that the subject first tell the truth to the interrogator himself rather than get anyone else involved in the matter. If the request is for an attorney, the interrogator may suggest that the subject save himself or his family the expense of any such professional service, particularly if he is innocent of the offense under investigation. The interrogator may also add, 'Joe, I'm only looking for the truth, and if you're telling the truth, that's it. You can handle this by yourself.' "

From these representative samples of interrogation techniques, the setting prescribed by the manuals and observed in practice becomes clear. In essence, it is this: To be alone with the subject is essential to prevent distraction and to deprive him of any outside support. The aura of confidence in his guilt undermines his will to resist. He merely confirms the preconceived story the police seek to have him describe. Patience and persistence, at times relentless questioning, are employed. To obtain a confession, the interrogator must "patiently maneuver himself or his quarry into a position from which the desired object may be obtained." When normal procedures fail to produce the needed result, the police may resort to deceptive strategems such as giving false legal advice. It is important to keep the subject off balance, for example, by trading on his insecurity about himself or his surroundings. The police then persuade, trick, or cajole him out of exercising his constitutional rights.

Even without employing brutality, the "third degree" or the specific strategems described above, the very fact of custodial interrogation exacts a heavy toll on individual liberty and trades on the weakness of individuals.

[In] the cases before us today, given this background, we concern ourselves primarily with this interrogation atmosphere and the evils it can bring. In *Miranda v. Arizona,* the police arrested the defendant and took him to a special interrogation room where they secured a confession. In *Vignera v. New York,* the defendant made oral admissions to the police after interrogation in the afternoon, and then signed an inculpatory statement upon being questioned by an assistant district attorney later the same evening. In *Westover v. United States,* the defendant was handed over to the Federal Bureau of Investigation by local authorities after they had detained and interrogated him for a lengthy period, both at night and the following morning. After some two hours of questioning, the federal officers had obtained signed statements from the defendant. Lastly, in *California v. Stewart,* the local police held the defendant five days in the station and interrogated him on nine separate occasions before they secured his inculpatory statement.

In these cases, we might not find the defendants' statements to have been involuntary in traditional terms. Our concern for adequate safeguards to protect precious Fifth Amendment rights is, of course, not lessened in the slightest. In each of the cases, the defendant was thrust into an unfamiliar atmosphere and run through menacing police interrogation procedures. The potentiality for compulsion is forcefully apparent, for example, in *Miranda,* where the indigent Mexican defendant was a seriously disturbed individual with pronounced sexual fantasies, and in *Stewart,* in which the defendant was an indigent Los Angeles Negro who had dropped out of school in the sixth grade. To be sure, the records do not evince overt physical coercion or patented psychological ploys. The fact remains that in none of these cases did the officers undertake to afford appropriate safeguards at the outset of the interrogation to insure that the statements were truly the product of free choice.

It is obvious that such an interrogation environment is created for no purpose other than to subjugate the individual to the will of his examiner. This atmosphere carries its own badge of intimidation. To be sure, this is not physical intimidation, but it is equally destructive of human dignity. The current practice of incommunicado interrogation is at odds with one of our Nation's most cherished principles—that the individual may not be compelled to incriminate himself. Unless adequate protective devices are employed to dispel the compulsion inherent in custodial surroundings, no statement obtained from the defendant can truly be the product of his free choice.

From the foregoing, we can readily perceive an intimate connection between the privilege against self-incrimination and police custodial questioning. It is fitting to turn to history and precedent underlying the Self–Incrimination Clause to determine its applicability in this situation.

[W]e may view the historical development of the privilege as one which groped for the proper scope of governmental power over the citizen. As a "noble principle often transcends its origins," the privilege has come rightfully to be recognized in part as an individual's substantive right, a "right to a private enclave where he may lead a private life. That right is the hallmark of our democracy." We have recently noted that the privilege against self-incrimination—the essential mainstay of our adversary system—is founded on a complex of values. All these policies point to one overriding thought: the constitutional foundation underlying the privilege is the respect a government—state or federal—must accord to the dignity and integrity of its citizens. To maintain a "fair state-individual balance," to require the government "to shoulder the entire load," 8 Wigmore, *Evidence* (McNaughton rev., 1961), 317, to respect the inviolability of the human personality, our accusatory system of criminal justice demands that the government seeking to punish an individual produce the evidence against him by its own independent labors, rather than by the cruel, simple expedient of compelling it from his own mouth. In sum, the privilege is fulfilled only when the person is guaranteed the right "to remain silent unless he chooses to speak in the unfettered exercise of his own will." *Malloy v. Hogan.*

* * * We are satisfied that all the principles embodied in the privilege apply to informal compulsion exerted by law-enforcement officers during in-custody questioning. An individual swept from familiar surroundings into police custody, surrounded by antagonistic forces, and subjected to the techniques of persuasion described above cannot be otherwise than under compulsion to speak. As a practical matter, the compulsion to speak in the isolated setting of the police station may well be greater than in courts or other official investigations, where there are often impartial observers to guard against intimidation or trickery. * * *

Because of the adoption by Congress of Rule 5(a) of the Federal Rules of Criminal Procedure, and this Court's effectuation of that Rule in *McNabb v. United States,* 318 U.S. 332, 63 S.Ct. 608, 87 L.Ed. 819, (1943) and *Mallory v. United States,* 354 U.S. 449, 77 S.Ct. 1356, 1 L.Ed.2d 1479 (1957), we have had little occasion in the past quarter century to reach the constitutional issues in dealing with federal interrogations. These supervisory rules, requiring production of an arrested person before a commissioner "without unnecessary delay" and excluding evidence obtained in default of that statutory obligation, were nonetheless responsive to the same considerations of Fifth Amendment policy that unavoidably face us now as to the States. In [the *McNabb* and *Mallory* cases] we recognized both the dangers of interrogation and the appropriateness of prophylaxis stemming from the very fact of interrogation itself.[32]

Our decision in *Malloy v. Hogan* necessitates an examination of the scope of the privilege in state cases as well. In *Malloy,* we squarely held the privilege applicable to the States, and held that the substantive standards underlying the privilege applied with full force to state court proceedings. [T]he reasoning in *Malloy* made clear what had already become apparent—that the substantive and procedural safeguards surrounding admissibility of confessions in state cases had become exceedingly exacting, reflecting all the policies embedded in the privilege. The voluntariness doctrine in the state cases, as *Malloy* indicates, encompasses all interrogation practices which are likely to exert such pressure upon an individual as to disable him from making a free and rational choice. The implications of this proposition were elaborated in our decision in *Escobedo,* decided one week after *Malloy* applied the privilege to the States.

---

32. Our decision today does not indicate in any manner, of course, that these rules can be disregarded. When federal officials arrest an individual, they must as always comply with the dictates of the congressional legislation and cases thereunder. * * *

[In *Escobedo*], as in the cases today, we sought a protective device to dispel the compelling atmosphere of the interrogation. In *Escobedo,* however, the police did not relieve the defendant of the anxieties which they had created in the interrogation rooms. Rather, they denied his request for the assistance of counsel.[35] This heightened his dilemma, and made his later statements the product of this compulsion. [The] denial of the defendant's request for his attorney thus undermined his ability to exercise the privilege—to remain silent if he chose or to speak without any intimidation, blatant or subtle. The presence of counsel, in all the cases before us today, would be the adequate protective device necessary to make the process of police interrogation conform to the dictates of the privilege. His presence would insure that statements made in the government-established atmosphere are not the product of compulsion.

It was in this manner that *Escobedo* explicated another facet of the pre-trial privilege, noted in many of the Court's prior decisions: the protection of rights at trial. That counsel is present when statements are taken from an individual during interrogation obviously enhances the integrity of the fact-finding processes in court. The presence of an attorney, and the warnings delivered to the individual, enable the defendant under otherwise compelling circumstances to tell his story without fear, effectively, and in a way that eliminates the evils in the interrogation process. Without the protections flowing from adequate warnings and the rights of counsel, "all the careful safeguards erected around the giving of testimony, whether by an accused or any other witness, would become empty formalities in a procedure where the most compelling possible evidence of guilt, a confession, would have already been obtained at the unsupervised pleasure of the police." *Mapp v. Ohio* (Harlan, J., dissenting).

Today, then, there can be no doubt that the Fifth Amendment privilege is available outside of criminal court proceedings and serves to protect persons in all settings in which their freedom of action is curtailed from being compelled to incriminate themselves. We have concluded that without proper safeguards the process of in-custody interrogation of persons suspected or accused of crime contains inherently compelling pressures which work to undermine the individual's will to resist and to compel him to speak where he would not otherwise do so freely. In order to combat these pressures and to permit a full opportunity to exercise the privilege against self-incrimination, the accused must be adequately and effectively apprised of his rights and the exercise of those rights must be fully honored.

It is impossible for us to foresee the potential alternatives for protecting the privilege which might be devised by Congress or the States in the exercise of their creative rule-making capacities. Therefore we cannot say that the Constitution necessarily requires adherence to any particular solution for the inherent compulsions of the interrogation process as it is presently conducted. Our decision in no way creates a constitutional straitjacket which will handicap sound efforts at reform, nor is it intended to have this effect. We encourage Congress and the States to continue their laudable search for increasingly effective ways of protecting the rights of the individual while promoting efficient enforcement of our criminal laws. However, unless we are shown other procedures which are at least as effective in apprising accused persons of their right of silence and in assuring a continuous opportunity to exercise it, the following safeguards must be observed.

---

35. The police also prevented the attorney from consulting with his client. Independent of any other constitutional proscription, this action constitutes a violation of the Sixth Amendment right to the assistance of counsel and excludes any statement obtained in its wake. See *People v. Donovan,* 193 N.E.2d 628 (N.Y.1963) (Fuld, J.).

At the outset, if a person in custody is to be subjected to interrogation, he must first be informed in clear and unequivocal terms that he has the right to remain silent. For those unaware of the privilege, the warning is needed simply to make them aware of it—the threshold requirement for an intelligent decision as to its exercise. More important, such a warning is an absolute prerequisite in overcoming the inherent pressures of the interrogation atmosphere. It is not just the subnormal or woefully ignorant who succumb to an interrogator's imprecations, whether implied or expressly stated, that the interrogation will continue until a confession is obtained or that silence in the face of accusation is itself damning and will bode ill when presented to a jury.[37] Further, the warning will show the individual that his interrogators are prepared to recognize his privilege should he choose to exercise it.

The Fifth Amendment privilege is so fundamental to our system of constitutional rule and the expedient of giving an adequate warning as to the availability of the privilege so simple, we will not pause to inquire in individual cases whether the defendant was aware of his rights without a warning being given. Assessments of the knowledge the defendant possessed, based on information as to his age, education, intelligence, or prior contact with authorities, can never be more than speculation;[38] a warning is a clearcut fact. More important, whatever the background of the person interrogated, a warning at the time of the interrogation is indispensable to overcome its pressures and to insure that the individual knows he is free to exercise the privilege at that point in time.

The warning of the right to remain silent must be accompanied by the explanation that anything said can and will be used against the individual in court. This warning is needed in order to make him aware not only of the privilege, but also of the consequences of forgoing it. It is only through an awareness of these consequences that there can be any assurance of real understanding and intelligent exercise of the privilege. Moreover, this warning may serve to make the individual more acutely aware that he is faced with a phase of the adversary system—that he is not in the presence of persons acting solely in his interest.

The circumstances surrounding in-custody interrogation can operate very quickly to overbear the will of one merely made aware of his privilege by his interrogators. Therefore, the right to have counsel present at the interrogation is indispensable to the protection of the Fifth Amendment privilege under the system we delineate today. Our aim is to assure that the individual's right to choose between silence and speech remains unfettered throughout the interrogation process. A once-stated warning, delivered by those who will conduct the interrogation, cannot itself suffice to that end among those who must require knowledge of their rights. A mere warning given by the interrogators is not alone sufficient to accomplish that end. Prosecutors themselves claim that the admonishment of the right to remain silent without more "will benefit only the recidivist and the professional." Brief for the National District Attorneys Association as *amicus curiae.* Even preliminary advice given to the accused by his own attorney can be swiftly overcome by the secret interrogation process. Thus, the need for counsel to protect the Fifth Amendment privilege comprehends not merely a right

37. [In] accord with this decision, it is impermissible to penalize an individual for exercising his Fifth Amendment privilege when he is under police custodial interrogation. The prosecution may not, therefore, use at trial the fact that he stood mute or claimed his privilege in the face of accusation.

38. Cf. *Betts v. Brady* [p. 190 supra], and the recurrent inquiry into special circumstances it necessitated. * * *

to consult with counsel prior to questioning but also to have counsel present during any questioning if the defendant so desires.

The presence of counsel at the interrogation may serve several significant subsidiary functions as well. If the accused decides to talk to his interrogators, the assistance of counsel can mitigate the dangers of untrustworthiness. With a lawyer present the likelihood that the police will practice coercion is reduced, and if coercion is nevertheless exercised the lawyer can testify to it in court. The presence of a lawyer can also help to guarantee that the accused gives a fully accurate statement to the police and that the statement is rightly reported by the prosecution at trial. See *Crooker v. California* (Douglas, J., dissenting).

An individual need not make a preinterrogation request for a lawyer. While such request affirmatively secures his right to have one, his failure to ask for a lawyer does not constitute a waiver. No effective waiver of the right to counsel during interrogation can be recognized unless specifically made after the warnings we here delineate have been given. The accused who does not know his rights and therefore does not make a request may be the person who most needs counsel. * * *

Accordingly we hold that an individual held for interrogation must be clearly informed that he has the right to consult with a lawyer and to have the lawyer with him during interrogation under the system for protecting the privilege we delineate today. As with the warnings of the right to remain silent and that anything stated can be used in evidence against him, this warning is an absolute prerequisite to interrogation. No amount of circumstantial evidence that the person may have been aware of this right will suffice to stand in its stead. Only through such a warning is there ascertainable assurance that the accused was aware of this right.

If an individual indicates that he wishes the assistance of counsel before any interrogation occurs, the authorities cannot rationally ignore or deny his request on the basis that the individual does not have or cannot afford a retained attorney. The financial ability of the individual has no relationship to the scope of the rights involved here. The privilege against self-incrimination secured by the Constitution applies to all individuals. The need for counsel in order to protect the privilege exists for the indigent as well as the affluent. In fact, were we to limit these constitutional rights to those who can retain an attorney, our decisions today would be of little significance. The cases before us as well as the vast majority of confession cases with which we have dealt in the past involve those unable to retain counsel. While authorities are not required to relieve the accused of his poverty, they have the obligation not to take advantage of indigence in the administration of justice.[41] Denial of counsel to the indigent at the time of interrogation while allowing an attorney to those who can afford one would be no more supportable by reason or logic than the similar situation at trial and on appeal struck down in *Gideon* and *Douglas v. California*.

In order fully to apprise a person interrogated of the extent of his rights under this system then, it is necessary to warn him not only that he has the right to consult with an attorney, but also that if he is indigent a lawyer will be appointed to represent him. Without this additional warning, the admonition of the right to consult with counsel would often be understood as meaning only that

41. See Kamisar, *Equal Justice in the Gatehouses and Mansions of American Criminal Procedure,* in Criminal Justice in Our Time (1965), 64–81; * * * Report of the Attorney General's Committee on *Poverty and the Administration of Federal Criminal Justice (1963), p. 9* * * *.

he can consult with a lawyer if he has one or has the funds to obtain one. The warning of a right to counsel would be hollow if not couched in terms that would convey to the indigent—the person most often subjected to interrogation—the knowledge that he too has a right to have counsel present. As with the warnings of the right to remain silent and of the general right to counsel, only by effective and express explanation to the indigent of this right can there be assurance that he was truly in a position to exercise it.[43]

Once warnings have been given, the subsequent procedure is clear. If the individual indicates in any manner, at any time prior to or during questioning, that he wishes to remain silent, the interrogation must cease.[44] At this point he has shown that he intends to exercise his Fifth Amendment privilege; any statement taken after the person invokes his privilege cannot be other than the product of compulsion, subtle or otherwise. Without the right to cut off questioning, the setting of in-custody interrogation operates on the individual to overcome free choice in producing a statement after the privilege has been once invoked. If the individual states that he wants an attorney, the interrogation must cease until an attorney is present. At that time, the individual must have an opportunity to confer with the attorney and to have him present during any subsequent questioning. If the individual cannot obtain an attorney and he indicates that he wants one before speaking to police, they must respect his decision to remain silent.

This does not mean, as some have suggested, that each police station must have a "station house lawyer" present at all times to advise prisoners. It does mean, however, that if police propose to interrogate a person they must make known to him that he is entitled to a lawyer and that if he cannot afford one, a lawyer will be provided for him prior to any interrogation. If authorities conclude that they will not provide counsel during a reasonable period of time in which investigation in the field is carried out, they may do so without violating the person's Fifth Amendment privilege so long as they do not question him during that time.

If the interrogation continues without the presence of an attorney and a statement is taken, a heavy burden rests on the Government to demonstrate that the defendant knowingly and intelligently waived his privilege against self-incrimination and his right to retained or appointed counsel. This Court has always set high standards of proof for the waiver of constitutional rights, *Johnson v. Zerbst,* and we reassert these standards as applied to in-custody interrogation. Since the State is responsible for establishing the isolated circumstances under which the interrogation takes place and has the only means of making available corroborated evidence of warnings given during incommunicado interrogation, the burden is rightly on its shoulders.

An express statement that the individual is willing to make a statement and does not want an attorney followed closely by a statement could constitute a waiver. But a valid waiver will not be presumed simply from the silence of the accused after warnings are given or simply from the fact that a confession was in

43. While a warning that the indigent may have counsel appointed need not be given to the person who is known to have an attorney or is known to have ample funds to secure one, the expedient of giving a warning is too simple and the rights involved too important to engage in *ex post facto* inquiries into financial ability when there is any doubt at all on that score.

44. If an individual indicates his desire to remain silent, but has an attorney present, there may be some circumstances in which further questioning would be permissible. In the absence of evidence of overbearing, statements then made in the presence of counsel might be free of the compelling influence of the interrogation process and might fairly be construed as a waiver of the privilege for purposes of these statements.

fact eventually obtained. A statement we made in *Carnley v. Cochran,* 369 U.S. 506 (1962), is applicable here:

> "Presuming waiver from a silent record is impermissible. The record must show, or there must be an allegation and evidence which show, that an accused was offered counsel but intelligently and understandably rejected the offer. Anything less is not waiver."

* * * Moreover, where in-custody interrogation is involved, there is no room for the contention that the privilege is waived if the individual answers some questions or gives some information on his own prior to invoking his right to remain silent when interrogated.[45]

Whatever the testimony of the authorities as to waiver of rights by an accused, the fact of lengthy interrogation or incommunicado incarceration before a statement is made is strong evidence that the accused did not validly waive his rights. In these circumstances the fact that the individual eventually made a statement is consistent with the conclusion that the compelling influence of the interrogation finally forced him to do so. It is inconsistent with any notion of a voluntary relinquishment of the privilege. Moreover, any evidence that the accused was threatened, tricked, or cajoled into a waiver will, of course, show that the defendant did not voluntarily waive his privilege. The requirement of warnings and waiver of rights is a fundamental with respect to the Fifth Amendment privilege and not simply a preliminary ritual to existing methods of interrogation.

The warnings required and the waiver necessary in accordance with our opinion today are, in the absence of a fully effective equivalent, prerequisites to the admissibility of any statement made by a defendant. No distinction can be drawn between statements which are direct confessions and statements which amount to "admissions" of part or all of an offense. The privilege against self-incrimination protects the individual from being compelled to incriminate himself in any manner; it does not distinguish degrees of incrimination. Similarly, for precisely the same reason, no distinction may be drawn between inculpatory statements and statements alleged to be merely "exculpatory." If a statement made were in fact truly exculpatory it would, of course, never be used by the prosecution. In fact, statements merely intended to be exculpatory by the defendant are often used to impeach his testimony at trial or to demonstrate untruths in the statement given under interrogation and thus to prove guilt by implication. These statements are incriminating in any meaningful sense of the word and may not be used without the full warnings and effective waiver required for any other statement. In *Escobedo* itself, the defendant fully intended his accusation of another as the slayer to be exculpatory as to himself.

The principles announced today deal with the protection which must be given to the privilege against self-incrimination when the individual is first subjected to police interrogation while in custody at the station or otherwise deprived of his freedom of action in any significant way. It is at this point that our adversary system of criminal proceedings commences, distinguishing itself at the outset from the inquisitorial system recognized in some countries. Under the system of

---

45. Although this Court held in *Rogers v. United States,* 340 U.S. 367, 71 S.Ct. 438, 95 L.Ed. 344 (1951), over strong dissent, that a witness before a grand jury may not in certain circumstances decide to answer some questions and then refuse to answer others that decision has no application to the interrogation situation we deal with today. No legislative or judicial fact-finding authority is involved here, nor is there a possibility that the individual might make self-serving statements of which he could make use at trial while refusing to answer incriminating statements.

warnings we delineate today or under any other system which may be devised and found effective, the safeguards to be erected about the privilege must come into play at this point.

Our decision is not intended to hamper the traditional function of police officers in investigating crime. When an individual is in custody on probable cause, the police may, of course, seek out evidence in the field to be used at trial against him. Such investigation may include inquiry of persons not under restraint. General on-the-scene questioning as to facts surrounding a crime or other general questioning of citizens in the fact-finding process is not affected by our holding. It is an act of responsible citizenship for individuals to give whatever information they may have to aid in law enforcement. In such situations the compelling atmosphere inherent in the process of in-custody interrogation is not necessarily present.[46]

In dealing with statements obtained through interrogation, we do not purport to find all confessions inadmissible. Confessions remain a proper element in law enforcement. Any statement given freely and voluntarily without any compelling influences is, of course, admissible in evidence. The fundamental import of the privilege while an individual is in custody is not whether he is allowed to talk to the police without the benefit of warnings and counsel, but whether he can be interrogated. There is no requirement that police stop a person who enters a police station and states that he wishes to confess to a crime, or a person who calls the police to offer a confession or any other statement he desires to make. Volunteered statements of any kind are not barred by the Fifth Amendment and their admissibility is not affected by our holding today.

To summarize, we hold that when an individual is taken into custody or otherwise deprived of his freedom by the authorities in any significant way and is subjected to questioning, the privilege against self-incrimination is jeopardized. Procedural safeguards must be employed to protect the privilege, and unless other fully effective means are adopted to notify the person of his right of silence and to assure that the exercise of the right will be scrupulously honored, the following measures are required. He must be warned prior to any questioning that he has the right to remain silent, that anything he says can be used against him in a court of law, that he has the right to the presence of an attorney, and that if he cannot afford an attorney one will be appointed for him prior to any questioning if he so desires. Opportunity to exercise these rights must be afforded to him throughout the interrogation. After such warnings have been given, and such opportunity afforded him, the individual may knowingly and intelligently waive these rights and agree to answer questions or make a statement. But unless and until such warnings and waiver are demonstrated by the prosecution at trial, no evidence obtained as a result of interrogation can be used against him. * * *

If the individual desires to exercise his privilege, he has the right to do so. This is not for the authorities to decide. An attorney may advise his client not to talk to police until he has had an opportunity to investigate the case, or he may wish to be present with his client during any police questioning. In doing so an attorney is merely exercising the good professional judgment he has been taught.

---

46. The distinction and its significance has been aptly described in the opinion of a Scottish court:

"In former times such questioning, if undertaken, would be conducted by police officers visiting the house or place of business of the suspect and there questioning him, probably in the presence of a relation or friend. However convenient the modern practice may be, it must normally create a situation very unfavorable to the suspect." *Chalmers v. H.M. Advocate,* [1954] Sess.Cas. 66, 78 (J.C.).

This is not cause for considering the attorney a menace to law enforcement. He is merely carrying out what he is sworn to do under his oath—to protect to the extent of his ability the rights of his client. In fulfilling this responsibility the attorney plays a vital role in the administration of criminal justice under our Constitution.

In announcing these principles, we are not unmindful of the burdens which law enforcement officials must bear, often under trying circumstances. We also fully recognize the obligation of all citizens to aid in enforcing the criminal law. This Court, while protecting individual rights, has always given ample latitude to law enforcement agencies in the legitimate exercise of their duties. The limits we have placed on the interrogation process should not constitute an undue interference with a proper system of law enforcement. As we have noted, our decision does not in any way preclude police from carrying out their traditional investigatory functions. Although confessions may play an important role in some convictions, the cases before us present graphic examples of the overstatement of the "need" for confessions. In each case authorities conducted interrogations ranging up to five days in duration despite the presence, through standard investigating practices, of considerable evidence against each defendant.[51] Further examples are chronicled in our prior cases.[52]

It is also urged that an unfettered right to detention for interrogation should be allowed because it will often redound to the benefit of the person questioned. When police inquiry determines that there is no reason to believe that the person has committed any crime, it is said, he will be released without need for further formal procedures. The person who has committed no offense, however, will be better able to clear himself after warnings, with counsel present than without. It can be assumed that in such circumstances a lawyer would advise his client to talk freely to police in order to clear himself.

Custodial interrogation, by contrast, does not necessarily afford the innocent an opportunity to clear themselves. A serious consequence of the present practice of the interrogation alleged to be beneficial for the innocent is that many arrests "for investigation" subject large numbers of innocent persons to detention and interrogation. In one of the cases before us, *California v. Stewart,* police held four persons, who were in the defendant's house at the time of the arrest, in jail for five days until defendant confessed. At that time they were finally released. Police stated that there was "no evidence to connect them with any crime." Available statistics on the extent of this practice where it is condoned indicate that these four are far from alone in being subjected to arrest, prolonged detention, and interrogation without the requisite probable cause.

[The] experience in some other countries * * * suggests that the danger to law enforcement in curbs on interrogation is overplayed. The English procedure since 1912 under the Judge's Rules is significant. As recently strengthened, the Rules require that a cautionary warning be given an accused by a police officer as soon as he has evidence that affords reasonable grounds for suspicion; they also require that any statement made be given by the accused without questioning by

---

51. Miranda, Vignera, and Westover were identified by eyewitnesses. Marked bills from the bank robbed were found in Westover's car. Articles stolen from the victim as well as from several other robbery victims were found in Stewart's home at the outset of the investigation.

52. Dealing as we do here with constitutional standards in relation to statements made, the existence of independent corroborating evidence produced at trial is, of course, irrelevant to our decisions. * * *

police.[57] The right of the individual to consult with an attorney during this period is expressly recognized. * * *

Because of the nature of the problem and because of its recurrent significance in numerous cases, we have to this point discussed the relationship of the Fifth Amendment privilege to police interrogation without specific concentration on the facts of the cases before us. We turn now to these facts to consider the application to these cases of the constitutional principles discussed above. In each instance, we have concluded that statements were obtained from the defendant under circumstances that did not meet constitutional standards for protection of the privilege.

No. 759. *Miranda v. Arizona.*

On March 13, 1963, petitioner, Ernesto Miranda, was arrested at his home and taken in custody to a Phoenix police station. He was there identified by the complaining witness. The police then took him to "Interrogation Room No. 2" of the detective bureau. There he was questioned by two police officers. The officers admitted at trial that Miranda was not advised that he had a right to have an attorney present. Two hours later, the officers emerged from the interrogation room with a written confession signed by Miranda. At the top of the statement was a typed paragraph stating that the confession was made voluntarily, without threats or promises of immunity and "with full knowledge of my legal rights, understanding any statement I make may be used against me." [67]

---

57. [1964] Crim.L.Rev. 166–170. These Rules provide in part:

"II. As soon as a police officer has evidence which would afford reasonable grounds for suspecting that a person has committed an offence, he shall caution that person or cause him to be cautioned before putting to him any questions, or further questions, relating to that offence.

"The caution shall be in the following terms:

" 'You are not obliged to say anything unless you wish to do so but what you say may be put into writing and given in evidence.'

"When after being cautioned a person is being questioned, or elects to make a statement, a record shall be kept of the time and place at which any such questioning or statement began and ended and of the persons present.

* * *

"(b) It is only in exceptional cases that questions relating to the offence should be put to the accused person after he has been charged or informed that he may be prosecuted.

* * *

"IV. All written statements made after caution shall be taken in the following manner:

"(a) If a person says that he wants to make a statement he shall be told that it is intended to make a written record of what he says.

"He shall always be asked whether he wishes to write down himself what he wants to say; if he says that he cannot write or that he

would like someone to write it for him, a police officer may offer to write the statement for him. * * *

"(b) Any person writing his own statement shall be allowed to do so without any prompting as distinct from indicating to him what matters are material.

* * *

"(d) Whenever a police officer writes the statement, he shall take down the exact words spoken by the person making the statement, without putting any questions other than such as may be needed to make the statement coherent, intelligible and relevant to the material matters: he shall not prompt him." * * *

[Ed. Note—*The Police and Criminal Evidence 1984* grants British police new powers. E.g., the police are permitted to detain a person without charge for questioning for 24 hours and under certain circumstances to detain a person arrested for a "serious arrestable offense" (e.g., treason, terrorism, murder and kidnapping) up to 36 hours when authorized by a police officer of at least superintendent rank. To counterbalance these additional police powers, the Act contains new safeguards. E.g., a person detained in custody has a right to have this fact notified to a friend or relative and a person detained for an offense other than a "serious arrestable offense" has an absolute right to consult a solicitor at any time.]

67. One of the officers testified that he read this paragraph to Miranda. Apparently, however, he did not do so until after Miranda had confessed orally.

[Miranda] was found guilty of kidnapping and rape. [On] appeal, the Supreme Court of Arizona held that Miranda's constitutional rights were not violated in obtaining the confession and affirmed the conviction. In reaching its decision, the court emphasized heavily the fact that Miranda did not specifically request counsel.

We reverse. From the testimony of the officers and by the admission of respondent, it is clear that Miranda was not in any way apprised of his right to consult with an attorney and to have one present during the interrogation, nor was his right not to be compelled to incriminate himself effectively protected in any other manner. Without these warnings the statements were inadmissible. The mere fact that he signed a statement which contained a typed-in clause stating that he had "full knowledge" of his legal rights does not approach the knowing and intelligent waiver required to relinquish constitutional rights. * * *

No. 760. *Vignera v. New York.*

Petitioner, Michael Vignera, was picked up by New York police on October 14, 1960, in connection with the robbery three days earlier of a Brooklyn dress shop. They took him to the 17th Detective Squad headquarters in Manhattan. Sometime thereafter he was taken to the 66th Detective Squad. There a detective questioned Vignera with respect to the robbery. Vignera orally admitted the robbery to the detective. [T]he defense was precluded from making any showing that warnings had not been given. While at the 66th Detective Squad, Vignera was identified by the store owner and a saleslady as the man who robbed the dress shop. At about 3:00 p.m. he was formally arrested. The police then transported him to still another station, the 70th Precinct in Brooklyn, "for detention". At 11:00 p.m. Vignera was questioned by an assistant district attorney in the presence of a hearing reporter who transcribed the questions and Vignera's answers. This verbatim account of these proceedings contains no statement of any warnings given by the assistant district attorney. * * *

Vignera was [convicted of first degree robbery]. We reverse. The foregoing indicates that Vignera was not warned of any of his rights before the questioning by the detective and by the assistant district attorney. No other steps were taken to protect these rights. Thus he was not effectively apprised of his Fifth Amendment privilege or of his right to have counsel present and his statements are inadmissible.

No. 761. *Westover v. United States.*

At approximately 9:45 p.m. on March 20, 1963, petitioner, Carl Calvin Westover, was arrested by local police in Kansas City as a suspect in two Kansas City robberies. A report was also received from the FBI that he was wanted on a felony charge in California. The local authorities took him to a police station and placed him in a line-up on the local charges, and at about 11:45 p.m. he was booked. Kansas City police interrogated Westover on the night of his arrest. He denied any knowledge of criminal activities. The next day local officers interrogated him again throughout the morning. Shortly before noon they informed the FBI that they were through interrogating Westover and that the FBI could proceed to interrogate him. There is nothing in the record to indicate that Westover was ever given any warning as to his rights by local police. At noon, three special agents of the FBI continued the interrogation in a private interview room of the Kansas City Police Department, this time with respect to the robbery of a savings and loan association and a bank in Sacramento, California. After two or two and one-half hours, Westover signed separate confessions to each of these two robberies which had been prepared by one of the agents during the interrogation. At trial one of the agents testified, and a paragraph on each of the statements states, that the agents advised Westover that he did not have to make a statement, that any statement he made could be used against him, and that he had the right to see an attorney.

Westover was tried by a jury in federal court and convicted of the California robberies. * * *

We reverse. On the facts of this case we cannot find that Westover knowingly and intelligently waived his right to remain silent and his right to consult with counsel prior to the time he made the statement. At the time the FBI agents began questioning Westover, he had been in custody for over 14 hours and had been interrogated at length during that period. The FBI interrogation began immediately upon the conclusion of the interrogation by Kansas City police and was conducted in local police headquarters. Although the two law enforcement authorities are legally distinct and the crimes for which they interrogated Westover were different, the impact on him was that of a continuous period of questioning. There is no evidence of any warning given prior to the FBI interrogation nor is there any evidence of an articulated waiver of rights after the FBI commenced their interrogation. The record simply shows that the defendant did in fact confess a short time after being turned over to the FBI following interrogation by local police. Despite the fact that the FBI agents gave warnings at the outset of their interview, from Westover's point of view the warnings came at the end of the interrogation process. In these circumstances an intelligent waiver of constitutional rights cannot be assumed.

We do not suggest that law enforcement authorities are precluded from questioning any individual who has been held for a period of time by other authorities and interrogated by them without appropriate warnings. A different case would be presented if an accused were taken into custody by the second authority, removed both in time and place from his original surroundings, and then adequately advised of his rights and given an opportunity to exercise them. But here the FBI interrogation was conducted immediately following the state interrogation in the same police station—in the same compelling surroundings. Thus, in obtaining a confession from Westover the federal authorities were the beneficiaries of the pressure applied by the local in-custody interrogation. In these circumstances the giving of warnings alone was not sufficient to protect the privilege.

No. 584. *California v. Stewart.*

In the course of investigating a series of purse-snatch robberies in which one of the victims had died of injuries inflicted by her assailant, respondent, Roy Allen Stewart, was pointed out to Los Angeles police as the endorser of dividend checks taken in one of the robberies. At about 7:15 p.m., January 31, 1963, police officers went to Stewart's house and arrested him. One of the officers asked Stewart if they could search the house, to which he replied, "Go ahead." The search turned up various items taken from the five robbery victims. At the time of Stewart's arrest, police also arrested Stewart's wife and three other persons who were visiting him. These four were jailed along with Stewart and were interrogated. Stewart was taken to the University Station of the Los Angeles Police Department where he was placed in a cell. During the next five days, police interrogated Stewart on nine different occasions. Except during the first interrogation session, when he was confronted with an accusing witness, Stewart was isolated with his interrogators.

During the ninth interrogation session, Stewart admitted that he had robbed the deceased and stated that he had not meant to hurt her. Police then brought Stewart before a magistrate for the first time. Since there was no evidence to connect them with any crime, the police then released the other four persons arrested with him.

Nothing in the record specifically indicates whether Stewart was or was not advised of his right to remain silent or his right to counsel. In a number of instances, however, the interrogating officers were asked to recount everything that was said during the interrogations. None indicated that Stewart was ever advised of his rights.

[The] jury found Stewart guilty of robbery and first degree murder and fixed the penalty as death. On appeal, the Supreme Court of California reversed. It held that under this Court's decision in *Escobedo,* Stewart should have been advised of his right to remain silent and of his right to counsel and that it would not presume in the face of a silent record that the police advised Stewart of his rights.

We affirm. In dealing with custodial interrogation, we will not presume that a defendant has been effectively apprised of his rights and that his privilege against self-incrimination has been adequately safe-guarded on a record that does not show that any warnings have been given or that any effective alternative has been employed. Nor can a knowing and intelligent waiver of these rights be assumed on a silent record. Furthermore, Stewart's steadfast denial of the alleged offenses through eight of the nine interrogations over a period of five days is subject to no other construction than that he was compelled by persistent interrogation to forgo his Fifth Amendment privilege.

Therefore, in accordance with the foregoing, [*Miranda,*[a] *Vignera,* and *Westover* are reversed and *Stewart* is affirmed].[b]

JUSTICE CLARK, dissenting in [*Miranda, Vignera,* and *Westover,* and concurring in the result in *Stewart.*]

[I cannot] agree with the Court's characterization of the present practices of police and investigatory agencies as to custodial interrogation. The materials referred to as "police manuals" are not shown by the record here to be the official manuals of any police department, much less in universal use in crime detection. Moreover, the examples of police brutality mentioned by the Court are rare exceptions to the thousands of cases that appear every year in the law reports.

[The Court's] strict constitutional specific inserted at the nerve center of crime detection may well kill the patient. Since there is at this time a paucity of information and an almost total lack of empirical knowledge on the practical operation of requirements truly comparable to those announced by the majority, I would be more restrained lest we go too far too fast.   * * *

Rather than employing the arbitrary Fifth Amendment rule which the Court lays down I would follow the more pliable dictates of Due Process Clauses of the Fifth and Fourteenth Amendments which we are accustomed to administering and which we know from our cases are effective instruments in protecting persons in police custody. In this way we would not be acting in the dark nor in one full sweep changing the traditional rules of custodial interrogation which this Court

a. On retrial, *Miranda* was again convicted of kidnapping and rape. The conviction was affirmed in *State v. Miranda,* 450 P.2d 364 (Ariz.1969).

b. A week later, the Court ruled that *Escobedo* and *Miranda* applied only to trials begun after the decisions were announced.

has for so long recognized as a justifiable and proper tool in balancing individual rights against the rights of society. It will be soon enough to go further when we are able to appraise with somewhat better accuracy the effect of such a holding. * * *

JUSTICE HARLAN, whom JUSTICE STEWART and JUSTICE WHITE join, dissenting. * * *

While the fine points of [the Court's new constitutional code of rules for confessions] are far less clear than the Court admits, the tenor is quite apparent. The new rules are not designed to guard against police brutality or other unmistakably banned forms of coercion. Those who use third-degree tactics and deny them in court are equally able and destined to lie as skillfully about warnings and waivers. Rather, the thrust of the new rules is to negate all pressures, to reinforce the nervous or ignorant suspect, and ultimately to discourage any confession at all. The aim in short is toward "voluntariness" in a utopian sense, or to view it from a different angle, voluntariness with a vengeance.

To incorporate this notion into the Constitution requires a strained reading of history and precedent and a disregard of the very pragmatic concerns that alone may on occasion justify such strains. I believe that reasoned examination will show that the Due Process Clauses provide an adequate tool for coping with confessions and that, even if the Fifth Amendment privilege against self-incrimination be invoked, its precedents taken as a whole do not sustain the present rules. Viewed as a choice based on pure policy, these new rules prove to be a highly debatable if not one-sided appraisal of the competing interests, imposed over wide-spread objection, at the very time when judicial restraint is most called for by the circumstances.

[The] Court's asserted reliance on the Fifth Amendment [is] an approach which I frankly regard as a *trompe l'oeil.* The Court's opinion in my view reveals no adequate basis for extending the Fifth Amendment's privilege against self-incrimination to the police station. Far more important, it fails to show that the Court's new rules are well supported, let alone compelled, by Fifth Amendment precedents. Instead, the new rules actually derive from quotation and analogy drawn from precedents under the Sixth Amendment, which should properly have no bearing on police interrogation. * * *

Having decided that the Fifth Amendment privilege does apply in the police station, the Court reveals that the privilege imposes more exacting restrictions than does the Fourteenth Amendment's voluntariness test. It then emerges from a discussion of *Escobedo* that the Fifth Amendment requires for an admissible confession that it be given by one distinctly aware of his right not to speak and shielded from "the compelling atmosphere" of interrogation. From these key premises, the Court finally develops the safeguards of warning, counsel, and so forth. I do not believe these premises are sustained by precedents under the Fifth Amendment.[9]

The more important premise is that pressure on the suspect must be eliminated though it be only the subtle influence of the atmosphere and surroundings. The Fifth Amendment, however, has never been thought to forbid *all* pressure to incriminate one's self in the situations covered by it.

9. I lay aside *Escobedo* itself; it contains no reasoning or even general conclusions addressed to the Fifth Amendment and indeed its citation in this regard seems surprising in view of *Escobedo's* primary reliance on the Sixth Amendment.

[A] closing word must be said about the Assistance of Counsel Clause of the Sixth Amendment, which is never expressly relied on by the Court but whose judicial precedents turn out to be linchpins of the confession rules announced today.

[The] only attempt in this Court to carry the right to counsel into the station house occurred in *Escobedo,* the Court repeating several times that that stage was no less "critical" than trial itself. * * * This is hardly persuasive when we consider that a grand jury inquiry, the filing of a certiorari petition, and certainly the purchase of narcotics by an undercover agent from a prospective defendant may all be equally "critical" yet provision of counsel and advice on that score have never been thought compelled by the Constitution in such cases. The sound reason why this right is so freely extended for a criminal trial is the severe injustice risked by confronting an untrained defendant with a range of technical points of law, evidence, and tactics familiar to the prosecutor but not to himself. This danger shrinks markedly in the police station where indeed the lawyer in fulfilling his professional responsibilities of necessity may become an obstacle to truthfinding. See infra, n. 12.

[The] Court's new rules aim to offset [the] minor pressures and disadvantages intrinsic to any kind of police interrogation. The rules do not serve due process interests in preventing blatant coercion since, as I noted earlier, they do nothing to contain the policeman who is prepared to lie from the start. The rules work for reliability in confessions almost only in the Pickwickian sense that they can prevent some from being given at all.[12] * * *

What the Court largely ignores is that its rules impair, if they will not eventually serve wholly to frustrate, an instrument of law enforcement that has long and quite reasonably been thought worth the price paid for it. There can be little doubt that the Court's new code would markedly decrease the number of confessions. To warn the suspect that he may remain silent and remind him that his confession may be used in court are minor obstructions. To require also an express waiver by the suspect and an end to questioning whenever he demurs must heavily handicap questioning. And to suggest or provide counsel for the suspect simply invites the end of the interrogation. See supra, n. 12.

[While] passing over the costs and risks of its experiment, the Court portrays the evils of normal police questioning in terms which I think are exaggerated. Albeit stringently confined by the due process standards interrogation is no doubt often inconvenient and unpleasant for the suspect. However, it is no less so for a man to be arrested and jailed, to have his house searched, or to stand trial in court, yet all this may properly happen to the most innocent given probable cause, a warrant, or an indictment. Society has always paid a stiff price for law and order, and peaceful interrogation is not one of the dark moments of the law.

This brief statement of the competing considerations seems to me ample proof that the Court's preference is highly debatable at best and therefore not to be read into the Constitution. However, it may make the analysis more graphic to consider the actual facts of one of the four cases reversed by the Court. *Miranda*

---

12. The Court's vision of a lawyer "mitigat[ing] the dangers of untrustworthiness" by witnessing coercion and assisting accuracy in the confession is largely a fancy; for if counsel arrives, there is rarely going to be a police station confession. *Watts v. Indiana* (separate opinion of Jackson, J.): "[A]ny lawyer worth his salt will tell the suspect in no uncertain terms to make no statement to police under any circumstances."

serves best, being neither the hardest nor easiest of the four under the Court's standards.[15]

On March 3, 1963, an 18–year–old girl was kidnapped and forcibly raped near Phoenix, Arizona. Ten days later, on the morning of March 13, petitioner Miranda was arrested and taken to the police station. At this time Miranda was 23 years old, indigent, and educated to the extent of completing half the ninth grade. He had "an emotional illness" of the schizophrenic type, according to the doctor who eventually examined him; the doctor's report also stated that Miranda was "alert and oriented as to time, place, and person", intelligent within normal limits, competent to stand trial, and sane within the legal definition. At the police station, the victim picked Miranda out of a lineup, and two officers then took him into a separate room to interrogate him, starting about 11:30 a.m. Though at first denying his guilt, within a short time Miranda gave a detailed oral confession and then wrote out in his own hand and signed a brief statement admitting and describing the crime. All this was accomplished in two hours or less without any force, threats or promises and—I will assume this though the record is uncertain * * *—without any effective warnings at all.

Miranda's oral and written confessions are now held inadmissible under the Court's new rules. One is entitled to feel astonished that the Constitution can be read to produce this result. These confessions were obtained during brief, daytime questioning conducted by two officers and unmarked by any of the traditional indicia of coercion. They assured a conviction for a brutal and unsettling crime, for which the police had and quite possibly could obtain little evidence other than the victim's identifications, evidence which is frequently unreliable. There was, in sum, a legitimate purpose, no perceptible unfairness, and certainly little risk of injustice in the interrogation. Yet the resulting confessions, and the responsible course of police practice they represent, are to be sacrificed to the Court's own finespun conception of fairness which I seriously doubt is shared by many thinking citizens in this country.

[It is] instructive to compare the attitude in this case of those responsible for law enforcement with the official views that existed when the Court undertook three major revisions of prosecutorial practice prior to this case, *Johnson v. Zerbst, Mapp,* and *Gideon.* In *Johnson,* which established that appointed counsel must be offered the indigent in federal criminal trials, the Federal Government all but conceded the basic issue, which had in fact been recently fixed as Department of Justice policy. In *Mapp,* which imposed the exclusionary rule on the States for Fourth Amendment violations, more than half of the States had themselves already adopted some such rule. In *Gideon,* which extended *Johnson v. Zerbst* to the States, an *amicus* brief was filed by 22 States and Commonwealths urging that course; only two States beside the respondent came forward to protest. By contrast, in this case new restrictions on police questioning have been opposed by the United States and in an *amicus* brief signed by 27 States and Commonwealths, not including the three other States who are parties. No State in the country has urged this Court to impose the newly announced rules, nor has any State chosen to go nearly so far on its own.

[The] law of the foreign countries described by the Court * * * reflects a more moderate conception of the rights of the accused as against those of society

---

15. In *Westover,* a seasoned criminal was practically given the Court's full complement of warnings and did not heed them. The *Stewart* case, on the other hand, involves long de- tention and successive questioning. In *Vignera,* the facts are complicated and the record somewhat incomplete.

when other data is considered. Concededly, the English experience is most relevant. In that country, a caution as to silence but not counsel has long been mandated by the "Judges' Rules," which also place other somewhat imprecise limits on police cross-examination of suspects. However, in the court's discretion confessions can be and apparently quite frequently are admitted in evidence despite disregard of the Judges' Rules, so long as they are found voluntary under the common-law test. Moreover, the check that exists on the use of pretrial statements is counter-balanced by the evident admissibility of fruits of an illegal confession and by the judge's often-used authority to comment adversely on the defendant's failure to testify. * * *

[S]ome reference must be made to [the] ironic untimeliness [of these confession rules]. There is now in progress in this country a massive re-examination of criminal law enforcement procedures on a scale never before witnessed. Participants in this undertaking include a Special Committee of the American Bar Association, under the chairmanship of Chief Judge Lumbard of the Court of Appeals for the Second Circuit; a distinguished study group of the American Law Institute, headed by Professor Vorenberg of the Harvard Law School; and the President's Commission on Law Enforcement and Administration of Justice, under the leadership of the Attorney General of the United States. Studies are also being conducted by [other groups] equipped to do practical research.

[It] is no secret that concern has been expressed lest long-range and lasting reforms be frustrated by this Court's too rapid departure from existing constitutional standards. Despite the Court's disclaimer, the practical effect of the decision made today must inevitably be to handicap seriously sound efforts at reform, not least by removing options necessary to a just compromise of competing interests. [T]he legislative reforms when they came would have the vast advantage of empirical data and comprehensive study, they would allow experimentation and use of solutions not open to the courts, and they would restore the initiative in criminal law reform to those forums where it truly belongs. * * *

JUSTICE WHITE, with whom JUSTICE HARLAN and JUSTICE STEWART join, dissenting.

The proposition that the privilege against self-incrimination forbids in-custody interrogation without the warnings specified in the majority opinion and without a clear waiver of counsel has no significant support in the history of the privilege or in the language of the Fifth Amendment. As for the English authorities and the common-law history, the privilege, firmly established in the second half of the seventeenth century, was never applied except to prohibit compelled judicial interrogations. The rule excluding coerced confessions matured about 100 years later, "[b]ut there is nothing in the reports to suggest that the theory has its roots in the privilege against self-incrimination. And so far as the cases reveal, the privilege, as such, seems to have been given effect only in judicial proceedings, including the preliminary examinations by authorized magistrates." Morgan, *The Privilege Against Self–Incrimination*, 34 Minn.L.Rev. 1, 18 (1949).

[That] the Court's holding today is neither compelled nor even strongly suggested by the language of the Fifth Amendment, is at odds with American and English legal history, and involves a departure from a long line of precedent does not prove either that the Court has exceeded its powers or that the Court is wrong or unwise in its present reinterpretation of the Fifth Amendment. It does, however, underscore the obvious—that the Court has not discovered or found the law in making today's decision, nor has it derived it from some irrefutable sources; what it has done is to make new law and new public policy in much the same way that it has in the course of interpreting other great clauses of the

Constitution. This is what the Court historically has done. Indeed, it is what it must do and will continue to do until and unless there is some fundamental change in the constitutional distribution of governmental powers.

But if the Court is here and now to announce new and fundamental policy to govern certain aspects of our affairs, it is wholly legitimate to examine the mode of this or any other constitutional decision in this Court and to inquire into the advisability of its end product in terms of the long-range interest of the country. At the very least the Court's text and reasoning should withstand analysis and be a fair exposition of the constitutional provision which its opinion interprets. Decisions like these cannot rest alone on syllogism, metaphysics or some ill-defined notions of natural justice, although each will perhaps play its part.

[The Court] extrapolates a picture of what it conceives to be the norm from police investigatorial manuals, published in 1959 and 1962 or earlier, without any attempt to allow for adjustments in police practices that may have occurred in the wake of more recent decisions of state appellate tribunals or this Court. But even if the relentless application of the described procedures could lead to involuntary confessions, it most assuredly does not follow that each and every case will disclose this kind of interrogation or this kind of consequence.[2] Insofar as it appears from the Court's opinion, it has not examined a single transcript of any police interrogation, let alone the interrogation that took place in any one of these cases which it decides today. Judged by any of the standards for empirical investigation utilized in the social sciences the factual basis for the Court's premises is patently inadequate.

Although in the Court's view in-custody interrogation is inherently coercive, it says that the spontaneous product of the coercion of arrest and detention is still to be deemed voluntary. An accused, arrested on probable cause, may blurt out a confession which will be admissible despite the fact that he is alone and in custody, without any showing that he had any notion of his right to remain silent or of the consequences of his admission. Yet, under the Court's rule, if the police ask him a single question such as "Do you have anything to say?" or "Did you kill your wife?" his response, if there is one, has somehow been compelled, even if the accused has been clearly warned of his right to remain silent. Common sense informs us to the contrary. While one may say that the response was "involuntary" in the sense the question provoked or was the occasion for the response and thus the defendant was induced to speak out when he might have remained silent if not arrested and not questioned, it is patently unsound to say the response is compelled.

[If] the rule announced today were truly based on a conclusion that all confessions resulting from custodial interrogation are coerced, then it would simply have no rational foundation. * * * Even if one were to postulate that the Court's concern is not that all confessions induced by police interrogation are coerced but rather that some such confessions are coerced and present judicial procedures are believed to be inadequate to identify the confessions that are

2. In fact, the type of sustained interrogation described by the Court appears to be the exception rather than the rule. A survey of 399 cases in one city found that in almost half of the cases the interrogation lasted less than 30 minutes. Barrett, *Police Practices and the Law—From Arrest to Release or Charge*, 50 Calif.L.Rev. 11, 41–45 (1962). Questioning tends to be confused and sporadic and is usual-ly concentrated on confrontations with witnesses or new items of evidence, as these are obtained by officers conducting the investigation. See generally LaFave, *Arrest: The Decision to Take a Suspect into Custody* 386 (1965); ALI, Model Pre–Arraignment Procedure Code, *Commentary § 5.01, at 170, n. 4 (Tent.Draft No. 1, 1966).*

coerced and those that are not, it would still not be essential to impose the rule that the Court has now fashioned. Transcripts or observers could be required, specific time limits, tailored to fit the cause, could be imposed, or other devices could be utilized to reduce the chances that otherwise indiscernible coercion will produce an inadmissible confession.

On the other hand, even if one assumed that there was an adequate factual basis for the conclusion that all confessions obtained during in-custody interrogation are the product of compulsion, the rule propounded by the Court would still be irrational, for, apparently, it is only if the accused is also warned of his right to counsel and waives both that right and the right against self-incrimination that the inherent compulsiveness of interrogation disappears. But if the defendant may not answer without a warning a question such as "Where were you last night?" without having his answer be a compelled one, how can the court ever accept his negative answer to the question of whether he wants to consult his retained counsel or counsel whom the court will appoint? And why if counsel is present and the accused nevertheless confesses, or counsel tells the accused to tell the truth, and that is what the accused does, is the situation any less coercive insofar as the accused is concerned? The court apparently realizes its dilemma of foreclosing questioning without the necessary warnings but at the same time permitting the accused, sitting in the same chair in front of the same policemen, to waive his right to consult an attorney. It expects, however, that not too many will waive the right; and if it is claimed that he has, the State faces a severe, if not impossible burden of proof.

All of this makes very little sense in terms of the compulsion which the Fifth Amendment proscribes. That amendment deals with compelling the accused himself. It is his free will that is involved. Confessions and incriminating admissions, as such, are not forbidden evidence; only those which are compelled are banned. I doubt that the Court observes these distinctions today. By considering any answers to any interrogation to be compelled regardless of the content and course of examination and by escalating the requirements to prove waiver, the Court not only prevents the use of compelled confessions but for all practical purposes forbids interrogation except in the presence of counsel. That is, instead of confining itself to protection of the right against compelled self-incrimination the Court has created a limited Fifth Amendment right to counsel—or, as the Court expresses it, a "right to counsel to protect the Fifth Amendment privilege * * *." The focus then is not on the will of the accused but on the will of counsel and how much influence he can have on the accused. Obviously there is no warrant in the Fifth Amendment for thus installing counsel as the arbiter of the privilege.

In sum, for all the Court's expounding on the menacing atmosphere of police interrogation procedures it has failed to supply any foundation for the conclusions it draws or the measures it adopts.

Criticism of the Court's opinion, however, cannot stop at a demonstration that the factual and textual bases for the rule it propounds are, at best, less than compelling. Equally relevant is an assessment of the rule's consequences measured against community values. The Court's duty to assess the consequences of its action is not satisfied by the utterance of the truth that a value of our system of criminal justice is "to respect the inviolability of the human personality" and to require government to produce the evidence against the accused by its own independent labors. More than the human dignity of the accused is involved; the human personality of others in the society must also be preserved. Thus the values reflected by the privilege are not the sole desideratum; society's interest in the general security is of equal weight.

The obvious underpinning of the Court's decision is a deep-seated distrust of all confessions. As the Court declares that the accused may not be interrogated without counsel present, absent a waiver of the right to counsel, and as the Court all but admonishes the lawyer to advise the accused to remain silent, the result adds up to a judicial judgment that evidence from the accused should not be used against him in any way, whether compelled or not. This is the not so subtle overtone of the opinion—that it is inherently wrong for the police to gather evidence from the accused himself. And this is precisely the nub of this dissent. I see nothing wrong or immoral, and certainly nothing unconstitutional, with the police asking a suspect whom they have reasonable cause to arrest whether or not he killed his wife or with confronting him with the evidence on which the arrest was based, at least where he has been plainly advised that he may remain completely silent. * * * Particularly when corroborated, as where the police have confirmed the accused's disclosure of the hiding place of implements or fruits of the crime, such confessions have the highest reliability and significantly contribute to the certitude with which we may believe the accused is guilty.

[The] rule announced today [is] a deliberate calculus to prevent interrogations, to reduce the incidence of confessions and pleas of guilty and to increase the number of trials. [Under] the present law, the prosecution fails to prove its case in about 30% of the criminal cases actually tried in the federal courts. But it is something else again to remove from the ordinary criminal case all those confessions which heretofore have been held to be free and voluntary acts of the accused and to thus establish a new constitutional barrier to the ascertainment of truth by the judicial process. There is, in my view, every reason to believe that a good many criminal defendants, who otherwise would have been convicted on what this Court has previously thought to be the most satisfactory kind of evidence, will now, under this new version of the Fifth Amendment, either not be tried at all or acquitted if the State's evidence, minus the confession, is put to the test of litigation.

I have no desire whatsoever to share the responsibility for any such impact on the present criminal process.

[There] is another aspect to the effect of the Court's rule on the person whom the police have arrested on probable cause. The fact is that he may not be guilty at all and may be able to extricate himself quickly and simply if he were told the circumstances of his arrest and were asked to explain. This effort, and his release, must now await the hiring of a lawyer or his appointment by the court, consultation with counsel and then a session with the police or the prosecutor. Similarly, where probable cause exists to arrest several suspects as where the body of the victim is discovered in a house having several residents, it will often be true that a suspect may be cleared only through the results of interrogation of other suspects. Here too the release of the innocent may be delayed by the Court's rule.

Much of the trouble with the Court's new rule is that it will operate indiscriminately in all criminal cases, regardless of the severity of the crime or the circumstances involved. It applies to every defendant whether the professional criminal or one committing a crime of momentary passion who is not part and parcel of organized crime. It will slow down the investigation and the apprehension of confederates in those cases where time is of the essence, such as kidnapping, [those] involving the national security, [and] some organized crime situations. In the latter context the lawyer who arrives may also be the lawyer for the defendants' colleagues and can be relied upon to insure that no breach of the organization's security takes place even though the accused may feel that the best thing he can do is to cooperate.

At the same time, the Court's *per se* approach may not be justified on the ground that it provides a "bright line" permitting the authorities to judge in advance whether interrogation may safely be pursued without jeopardizing the admissibility of any information obtained as a consequence. Nor can it be claimed that judicial time and effort, assuming that is a relevant consideration, will be conserved because of the ease of application of the new rule. Today's decision leaves open such questions as whether the accused was in custody, whether his statements were spontaneous or the product of interrogation, whether the accused has effectively waived his rights, and whether nontestimonial evidence introduced at trial is the fruit of statements made during a prohibited interrogation, all of which are certain to prove productive of uncertainty during investigation and litigation during prosecution. For all these reasons, if further restrictions on police interrogation are desirable at this time, a more flexible approach makes much more sense than the Court's constitutional strait-jacket which forecloses more discriminating treatment by legislative or rule-making pronouncements.
* * *

Note: Can Congress "Repeal" Miranda?

Title II of the Crime Control Act of 1968, which purports to repeal *Miranda* in federal prosecutions, amends Chapter 223, title 18, United States Code, by adding the following new sections:

"§ 3501. Admissibility of confessions

"(a) In any criminal prosecution brought by the United States or by the District of Columbia, a confession, as defined in subsection (e) hereof, shall be admissible in evidence if it is voluntarily given. Before such confession is received in evidence, the trial judge shall, out of the presence of the jury, determine any issue as to voluntariness. If the trial judge determines that the confession was voluntarily made it shall be admitted in evidence and the trial judge shall permit the jury to hear relevant evidence on the issue of voluntariness and shall instruct the jury to give such weight to the confession as the jury feels it deserves under all the circumstances.

"(b) The trial judge in determining the issue of voluntariness shall take into consideration all the circumstances surrounding the giving of the confession, including (1) the time elapsing between arrest and arraignment of the defendant making the confession, if it was made after arrest and before arraignment, (2) whether such defendant knew the nature of the offense with which he was charged or of which he was suspected at the time of making the confession, (3) whether or not such defendant was advised or knew that he was not required to make any statement and that any such statement could be used against him, (4) whether or not such defendant had been advised prior to questioning of his right to the assistance of counsel; and (5) whether or not such defendant was without the assistance of counsel when questioned and when giving such confession.

"The presence or absence of any of the above-mentioned factors to be taken into consideration by the judge need not be conclusive on the issue of voluntariness of the confession.

"(c) In any criminal prosecution by the United States or by the District of Columbia, a confession made or given by a person who is a defendant therein, while such person was under arrest or other detention in the custody of any law-enforcement officer or law-enforcement agency, shall not be inadmissible solely because of delay in bringing such person before a commissioner or other officer empowered to commit persons charged with offenses against the laws of the United States or of the District of Columbia if such confession is found by the trial judge to have been made voluntarily and if the weight to be given the confession is left to the jury and if such confession was made or given by such person within six hours immediately following his arrest or other detention: *Provided,* That the time limitation contained in this subsection shall not apply in any case in which the delay in bringing such person before such commissioner or other officer beyond such six-hour period is found by the trial judge to be reasonable considering the means of transportation and the distance to be traveled to the nearest available such commissioner or other officer.

"(d) Nothing contained in this section shall bar the admission in evidence of any confession made or given voluntarily by any person to any other person without interrogation by anyone, or at any time at which the person who made or gave such confession was not under arrest or other detention.

"(e) As used in this section, the term 'confession' means any confession of guilt of any criminal offense or any self-incriminating statement made or given orally or in writing."

Although § 3501 purports to overrule *Miranda,* to date it has not provoked the head-on collision that might have been predicted. The Attorney General in office when the statute was passed instructed his subordinates not to rely on it where it differed from *Miranda,* and, although a later Attorney General changed this as official policy, most U.S. Attorneys appear to have continued to adhere to the restrained position initially taken. According to a 1986 report to the Attorney General by Assistant Attorney General Stephen Markman, head of the Office of Legal Policy (the "Markman report"), at some point the Department of Justice "attempted to establish the validity of [§ 3501] in litigation for several years with inconclusive results," but then "terminated this litigative effort." However, the Markman report urges the Department of Justice "to persuade the Supreme Court to abrogate or overrule the decision in *Miranda* " and views "reliance on [the 1968 statute] designed to achieve that end" as "the most promising line of attack."

When § 3501 was first enacted, most commentators thought it was invalid. Even those who conceded that *Miranda* was subject to congressional revision, i.e., could be displaced by a statute that provides an adequate alternative to the now-familiar warnings, maintained that Title II still fell short because it did little more than "turn the clock back" to the "voluntariness" test espoused by the *Miranda* dissents.

But the case for upholding § 3501 has grown stronger with the passage of years. For the Supreme Court has repeatedly called the *Miranda* rules "not themselves rights protected by the Constitution" but only "procedural safeguards" or "prophylactic rules" designed to "provide practical reinforcement" for the privilege against compelled self-incrimination.

This language first appeared in *Michigan v. Tucker,* 417 U.S. 433, 94 S.Ct. 2357, 41 L.Ed.2d 182 (1974). *Tucker* allowed the testimony of a prosecution witness whose identity had been discovered by questioning defendant in violation of *Miranda.* Although the case involved various factors that arguably limited its implications (e.g., the deviation between the warnings given and the *Miranda* requirements was not substantial and, although the defendant's trial took place after *Miranda,* the police questioning occurred before that case was decided), the *Tucker* Court, per Rehnquist, J., spoke in general terms of the difference between a *Miranda* violation and a constitutional violation:

> "[T]he Court in *Miranda,* for the first time, expressly declared that the Self–Incrimination Clause was applicable to state interrogations at a police station, and that a defendant's statements might be excluded at trial despite their voluntary character under traditional principles.

> "To supplement this new doctrine, and to help police officers conduct interrogations without facing a continued risk that valuable evidence would be lost, the [*Miranda* Court] established a set of specific guidelines, now commonly known as the *Miranda* rules. * * *

> "The [*Miranda* Court] recognized that these procedural safeguards were not themselves rights protected by the Constitution but were instead measures to insure that the right against compulsory self-incrimination was protected. As [it] remarked: '[W]e cannot say that the Constitution necessarily requires adherence to any particular solution for the inherent compulsions of the interrogation process as it is presently conducted.' The suggested safeguards were not intended to 'create a constitutional straitjacket,' *Miranda,* but rather to provide practical reinforcement for the right against compulsory self-incrimination.[d]

> "A comparison of the facts in this case with the historical circumstances underlying the privilege against compulsory self-incrimination strongly indicates that the police conduct here did not deprive [Tucker] of his privilege against self-incrimination as such, but rather failed to make available to him the full measure of procedural safeguards associated with that right since *Miranda.* Certainly no one could contend that the interrogation faced by [Tucker] bore any resemblance to the historical practices at which the right against compulsory self-incrimination was aimed. [H]is statements could hardly be termed involuntary as that term has been defined in the decisions of this Court. * * *

> "Our determination that the interrogation in this case involved no compulsion sufficient to breach the right against compulsory self-incrimination does not mean there was not a disregard, albeit an inadvertent disregard, of the procedural rules later established in *Miranda.* The question for decision is how sweeping the judicially imposed consequences of this disregard shall be."

d. But as Justice Douglas observed in his *Tucker* dissent, the Court, per Rehnquist, J., overlooked other language in the *Miranda* opinion. For example, in the same paragraph from *Miranda* quoted by Justice Rehnquist in *Tucker,* the *Miranda* Court added: "However, unless we are shown other procedures which are at least as effective in apprising accused persons of their right of silence and in assuring a continuous opportunity to exercise it, the following safeguards [the *Miranda* warnings] must be observed." Moreover, later in the opinion, the *Miranda* Court reiterated: "The warnings required and the waiver necessary in accordance with our opinion today are, in the absence of a fully effective equivalent, prerequisites to the admissibility of any statements made by a defendant. * * * Procedural safeguards must be employed to protect the privilege, and unless other fully effective means are adopted to notify the person of his right of silence and to assure that the exercise of the right will be scrupulously honored, the following measures [the *Miranda* warnings] are required."

A decade later, first in *New York v. Quarles,* 467 U.S. 649, 104 S.Ct. 2626, 81 L.Ed.2d 550 (1984) and then in *Oregon v. Elstad,* 470 U.S. 298, 105 S.Ct. 1285, 84 L.Ed.2d 222 (1985), the Court reiterated *Tucker*'s way of looking at, and thinking about, *Miranda.* In both *Quarles* and *Elstad* the Court underscored the distinction between incriminating statements that are *actually* "coerced" or "compelled" and those obtained *merely* in violation of *Miranda*'s "procedural safeguards" or "prophylactic rules."

Does the language in *Tucker, Quarles* and *Elstad* imply that the Court would now uphold the validity of § 3501, which purports to "overrule" *Miranda?* Since the Court has no "supervisory power" over *state* criminal justice, if the *Miranda* rules are not constitutional requirements (but only "second-class" prophylactic safeguards) and *Miranda* violations not constitutional violations (but only "second-class" wrongs), where did the Court get the authority to impose *Miranda* on the states in the first place?

III. APPLYING AND EXPLAINING *MIRANDA*

Introduction

Because *Miranda* was the centerpiece of the Warren Court's "revolution in American criminal procedure" and the prime target of those who thought the courts were "soft" on criminals, almost everyone expected the so-called Burger Court to treat *Miranda* unkindly. And it did—at first. But it must also be said that the Burger Court interpreted *Miranda* fairly generously in some important respects.

The first blows the Burger Court dealt *Miranda* were the impeachment cases, *Harris v. New York,* 401 U.S. 222, 91 S.Ct. 643, 28 L.Ed.2d 1 (1971) and *Oregon v. Hass,* 420 U.S. 714, 95 S.Ct. 1215, 43 L.Ed.2d 570 (1975). *Harris* held that statements preceded by defective warnings, and thus inadmissible to establish the prosecution's case-in-chief, could nevertheless be used to impeach the defendant's credibility if he chose to take the stand in his own defense.[a] The Court noted, but seemed unperturbed by the fact, that some language in the *Miranda* opinion could be read as barring the use of statements obtained in violation of *Miranda* for *any* purpose.

The Court went a step beyond *Harris* in the *Hass* case. In this case, after being advised of his rights, the defendant *asserted* them. Nevertheless, the police refused to honor the defendant's request for a lawyer and continued to question him. The Court ruled that here, too, the resulting incriminating statements could be used for impeachment purposes. Since many suspects make incriminating statements even after the receipt of complete *Miranda* warnings, *Harris* might have been explained—and contained—on the ground that permitting impeachment use of statements acquired without complete warnings would not greatly encourage the police to violate *Miranda.* But in light of the *Hass* ruling, when a suspect asserts his rights, the police arguably have very little to lose and everything to gain by continuing to question him.[b]

a. However, as the Court suggested in *Harris* and subsequently made clear in *Mincey v. Arizona,* 437 U.S. 385, 98 S.Ct. 2408, 57 L.Ed.2d 290 (1978), "involuntary" or "coerced" statements, as opposed to those obtained only in violation of *Miranda,* cannot be used for impeachment purposes.

b. The Court subsequently held that a defendant's prior silence could be used to impeach him when he testified in his own defense, *Jenkins v. Anderson,* 447 U.S. 231, 100 S.Ct. 2124, 65 L.Ed.2d 86 (1980), and that even a defendant's *post*arrest silence (so long as he was not given the *Miranda* warnings) could be

Although language in *Miranda* could be read as establishing a *per se* rule against any further questioning of one who has asserted his "right to silence" (as opposed to his *right to counsel*, discussed below), *Michigan v. Mosley,* 423 U.S. 96, 96 S.Ct. 321, 46 L.Ed.2d 313 (1975) held that under certain circumstances (and what they are is unclear), if they cease questioning on the spot, the police may "try again," and succeed at a later interrogation session. At the very least, it seems, the police must promptly terminate the original interrogation, resume questioning after the passage of a significant period of time, and give the suspect a fresh set of warnings at the outset of the second session. Whether *Mosley* requires more is a matter of dispute.

Perhaps the most frequently litigated *Miranda* question is what constitutes "custody" or "custodial interrogation"? In the first case in this section, *Berkemer v. McCarty,* the Court, per Marshall, J. one of *Miranda*'s strongest defenders, explains at considerable length why the "roadside questioning" of a motorist detained pursuant to a traffic stop is quite different from stationhouse interrogation and thus should not be deemed "custodial interrogation." The *McCarty* Court reached its conclusion without a dissent. More controversial are *Oregon v. Mathiason,* 429 U.S. 492, 97 S.Ct. 711, 50 L.Ed.2d 714 (1977) and *California v. Beheler,* 463 U.S. 1121, 103 S.Ct. 3517, 77 L.Ed.2d 1275 (1983), which demonstrate that if the suspect goes to the stationhouse on his own or "voluntarily" agrees to accompany the police to that site, even *police station* questioning designed to produce incriminating statements may not be "custodial interrogation." Both cases are discussed in *McCarty.*

Another frequently litigated question is what constitutes "interrogation" or "questioning" within the meaning of *Miranda*? This question is addressed by the next two cases in the section: *Rhode Island v. Innis* (1980) and *Illinois v. Perkins* (1990). Considering the alternatives (e.g., limiting "interrogation" to instances where the police directly address a suspect or to situations where the record establishes that the police *intended* to elicit a response), *Innis* gave the key term "interrogation" a fairly generous reading. *Perkins* holds that the coercive atmosphere calling for the *Miranda* warnings is not present when a suspect is *unaware* that he is speaking to a law enforcement officer (in this instance an undercover agent posing as a fellow-prisoner).

In *Edwards v. Arizona,* 451 U.S. 477, 101 S.Ct. 1880, 68 L.Ed.2d 378 (1981) (whose holding is read broadly in *Minnick v. Mississippi,* the fourth case in this section), the Court gladdened the hearts of *Miranda* supporters by invigorating that case in an important respect. Sharply distinguishing the *Mosley* case, supra, the *Edwards* Court held that when a suspect asserts his right to counsel (as opposed to his right to remain silent), the police *cannot* "try again." Once a suspect "expresse[s] his desire to deal with the police only through counsel," *Edwards* instructs us, the suspect may not be subjected to further interrogation by the authorities "until counsel has been made available to him unless [he]

---

used for impeachment purposes, *Fletcher v. Weir,* 455 U.S. 603, 102 S.Ct. 1309, 71 L.Ed.2d 490 (1982). Both *Jenkins* and *Weir* distinguished *Doyle v. Ohio,* 426 U.S. 610, 96 S.Ct. 2240, 49 L.Ed.2d 91 (1976), which deemed it a violation of due process to use a defendant's silence for impeachment purposes when the defendant remained silent *after* being given *Miranda* warnings.

But the Court balked at further expansion of the "impeachment exception" to the ban against illegally seized evidence in *James v. Illinois,* 493 U.S. 307, 110 S.Ct. 648, 107 L.Ed.2d 676 (1990). *James* refused to expand the class of impeachable witnesses from the defendant alone to *all* defense witnesses, maintaining such an expansion "would not promote the truthseeking function to the same extent as did creation of the original exception, and yet it would significantly undermine the deterrent effect of the general exclusionary rule."

himself initiates further communication, exchanges, or conversations with the police." [c]

But then, as discussed earlier, Justice Rehnquist's way of thinking about *Miranda,* which had first surfaced in *Michigan v. Tucker* [see Note on Congressional Overruling, p. 247 supra], reappeared in *New York v. Quarles* and *Oregon v. Elstad. Quarles* recognized a "public safety" exception to *Miranda. Elstad* held that a second confession, immediately preceded by the *Miranda* warnings, was admissible although an earlier statement from the defendant had been obtained in violation of *Miranda.* More generally, both cases viewed *Miranda* warnings as only second-class prophylactic safeguards and *Miranda* violations as only second-class wrongs.

Some of *Miranda*'s defenders found further cause for concern in *Moran v. Burbine,* the last case in this section. That case held that a confession preceded by an otherwise valid waiver of *Miranda* rights should not be excluded either because the police misled an inquiring attorney (asked by defendant's sister to represent him) or because the police failed to inform the defendant that an attorney was trying to reach him. But other commentators noted that the *Burbine* Court had viewed *Miranda* as a serious effort to strike a "proper balance" between, or to "reconcile," law enforcement needs and a suspect's rights and pointed out that this is the way many of *Miranda*'s defenders—not its critics—have talked about the case for the past twenty years.

A. WHAT CONSTITUTES "CUSTODY" OR "CUSTODIAL INTERROGATION?"

BERKEMER v. McCARTY

468 U.S. 420, 104 S.Ct. 3138, 82 L.Ed.2d 317 (1984).

JUSTICE MARSHALL delivered the opinion of the Court.

[After observing McCarty's car weaving in and out of a highway lane, Trooper Williams forced him to stop and asked him to get out of the car. Noticing that McCarty had difficulty standing, the officer concluded that he would be charged with a traffic offense and not allowed to leave the scene. But the officer did not tell McCarty this. When asked to perform a field sobriety test, commonly known as a "balancing test," McCarty could not do so without falling. The officer then asked McCarty whether he had been using intoxicants. McCarty replied that he had consumed two beers and smoked marijuana a short time before. Moreover, his speech was slurred. The officer then formally arrested McCarty and drove him to a county jail where questioning resumed and McCarty made more incriminating statements. At no point in this sequence of events did Williams or anyone else give McCarty the *Miranda* warnings. McCarty's statements were admitted into evidence and he was convicted of operating a motor vehicle while under the influence of alcohol and/or drugs, a first-degree misdemeanor under Ohio law.

[The Court rejected the argument that *Miranda* does not apply to misdemeanor traffic offenses and held that one subjected to custodial interrogation is entitled to the *Miranda* warnings "regardless of the nature or severity of the offense of

---

c. The *Edwards* rule applies even when the police want to question a suspect about an offense *unrelated* to the subject of their initial interrogation. See *Arizona v. Roberson,* 486 U.S. 675, 108 S.Ct. 2093, 100 L.Ed.2d 704 (1988). Moreover, as the Court recently held in *Minnick,* the fourth case in this section, once a suspect invokes his right to counsel, the police may not reinitiate interrogation in the absence of counsel even if the suspect has consulted with an attorney in the interim.

which he is suspected or for which he was arrested." Thus, since "[t]here can be no question that respondent was 'in custody' at least as of the moment he was formally placed under arrest and instructed to get into the police car," and he was not informed of his rights at that juncture, his subsequent admissions should not have been used against him. The Court then addressed the question whether respondent had been in custody at an earlier point, i.e., "whether the roadside questioning of a motorist detained pursuant to a routine traffic stop should be considered 'custodial interrogation.' "]

Two features of an ordinary traffic stop mitigate the danger that a person questioned will be induced "to speak where he would not otherwise do so freely," *Miranda*. First, detention of a motorist pursuant to a traffic stop is presumptively temporary and brief. The vast majority of roadside detentions last only a few minutes. A motorist's expectations, when he sees a policeman's light flashing behind him, are that he will be obliged to spend a short period of time answering questions and waiting while the officer checks his license and registration, that he may then be given a citation, but that in the end he most likely will be allowed to continue on his way. In this respect, questioning incident to an ordinary traffic stop is quite different from stationhouse interrogation, which frequently is prolonged, and in which the detainee often is aware that questioning will continue until he provides his interrogators the answers they seek.

Second, circumstances associated with the typical traffic stop are not such that the motorist feels completely at the mercy of the police. To be sure, the aura of authority surrounding an armed, uniformed officer and the knowledge that the officer has some discretion in deciding whether to issue a citation, in combination, exert some pressure on the detainee to respond to questions. But other aspects of the situation substantially offset these forces. Perhaps most importantly, the typical traffic stop is public, at least to some degree. [This] exposure to public view both reduces the ability of an unscrupulous policeman to use illegitimate means to elicit self-incriminating statements and diminishes the motorist's fear that, if he does not cooperate, he will be subjected to abuse. The fact that the detained motorist typically is confronted by only one or at most two policemen further mutes his sense of vulnerability. In short, the atmosphere surrounding an ordinary traffic stop is substantially less "police dominated" than that surrounding the kinds of interrogation at issue in *Miranda* itself and in the subsequent cases in which we have applied *Miranda*.

In both of these respects, the usual traffic stop is more analogous to a so-called "*Terry* stop" than to a formal arrest. Under the Fourth Amendment, we have held, a policeman who lacks probable cause but whose "observations lead him reasonably to suspect" that a particular person has committed, is committing, or is about to commit a crime, may detain that person briefly in order to "investigate the circumstances that provoke suspicion." * * * Typically, this means that the officer may ask the detainee a moderate number of questions to determine his identity and to try to obtain information confirming or dispelling the officer's suspicions. But the detainee is not obliged to respond. And, unless the detainee's answers provide the officer with probable cause to arrest him, he must then be released. The comparatively nonthreatening character of detentions of this sort explains the absence of any suggestion in our opinions that *Terry* stops are subject to the dictates of *Miranda*.

Respondent contends that to "exempt" traffic stops from the coverage of *Miranda* will open the way to widespread abuse. Policemen will simply delay formally arresting detained motorists, and will subject them to sustained and intimidating interrogation at the scene of their initial detention. * * *

We are confident that the state of affairs projected by respondent will not come to pass. It is settled that the safeguards prescribed by *Miranda* become applicable as soon as a suspect's freedom of action is curtailed to a "degree associated with formal arrest." *California v. Beheler,* 463 U.S. 1121, 103 S.Ct. 3517, 77 L.Ed.2d 1275 (1983) (per curiam). If a motorist who has been detained pursuant to a traffic stop thereafter is subjected to treatment that renders him "in custody" for practical purposes, he will be entitled to the full panoply of protections prescribed by *Miranda.* See *Oregon v. Mathiason,* 429 U.S. 492, 97 S.Ct. 711, 50 L.Ed.2d 714 (1977) (per curiam).[a] * * *

Turning to the case before us, we find nothing in the record that indicates that respondent should have been given *Miranda* warnings at any point prior to the time Trooper Williams placed him under arrest. At no point [during the short period of time between the stop and the formal arrest] was respondent informed that his detention would not be temporary. Although Trooper Williams apparently decided as soon as respondent stepped out of his car that respondent would be taken into custody and charged with a traffic offense, Williams never communicated his intention to respondent. A policeman's unarticulated plan has no bearing on the question whether a suspect was "in custody" at a particular time; the only relevant inquiry is how a reasonable man in the suspect's position would have understood his situation. Nor do other aspects of the interaction of Williams and respondent support the contention that respondent was exposed to "custodial interrogation" at the scene of the stop. From aught that appears in the stipulation of facts, a single police officer asked respondent a modest number of questions and requested him to perform a simple balancing test at a location visible to passing motorists. Treatment of this sort cannot fairly be characterized as the functional equivalent of formal arrest.

We conclude, in short, that respondent was not taken into custody for the purposes of *Miranda* until Williams arrested him. Consequently, the statements respondent made prior to that point were admissible against him. * * *

B. WHAT CONSTITUTES "INTERROGATION" WITHIN THE MEANING OF MIRANDA?

RHODE ISLAND v. INNIS

446 U.S. 291, 100 S.Ct. 1682, 64 L.Ed.2d 297 (1980).

JUSTICE STEWART delivered the opinion of the Court.

a. *Mathiason* makes plain that *Miranda* warnings are not required "simply because the questioning takes place in the station house." *Mathiason,* a suspect in a burglary, agreed over the phone to meet with a police officer at a convenient time and place (the state patrol office, only two blocks from defendant's apartment). *Mathiason* went to the patrol office on his own. When he arrived the officer told him he was not under arrest. The officer then said he wanted to talk to defendant about a burglary. When Mathiason confessed a few moments later he was not, held the Court, being subjected to "custodial interrogation."

There was some reason to think that *Mathiason* might be limited to situations where suspects go to the station house *unaccompanied* by police officers. But *Beheler* made it clear that *Mathiason* could not be read that narrowly. Some hours after the murder weapon (which defendant claimed others had hidden) was found in his backyard, Beheler, as the Court described it, "voluntarily agreed to accompany police to the station house, although the police specifically told [him] that he was not under arrest." At the station house, Beheler agreed to talk about the murder, but the police did not advise him of his *Miranda* rights. The incriminating statements made at the police station, ruled the Court, were not the product of "custodial interrogation."

[*Miranda*] held that, once a defendant in custody asks to speak with a lawyer, all interrogation must cease until a lawyer is present. The issue in this case is whether the respondent was "interrogated" in violation [of *Miranda*].

[At approximately 4:30 a.m., a patrolman arrested respondent, suspected of robbing a taxicab driver and murdering him with a shotgun blast to the back of the head. Respondent was unarmed. He was advised of his rights. Within minutes a sergeant (who advised respondent of his rights) and then a captain arrived at the scene of the arrest. The captain also gave respondent the *Miranda* warnings, whereupon respondent asked to speak with a lawyer. The captain then directed that respondent be placed in a police vehicle with a wire screen mesh between the front and rear seats and be driven to the police station. Three officers were assigned to accompany the arrestee. Although the record is somewhat unclear, it appears that Patrolman Williams was in the back seat with respondent and that Patrolmen Gleckman and McKenna were in front.]

While enroute to the central station, Patrolman Gleckman initiated a conversation with Patrolman McKenna concerning the missing shotgun.[1] As Patrolman Gleckman later testified:

"A. At this point, I was talking back and forth with Patrolman McKenna stating that I frequent this area while on patrol and [that because a school for handicapped children is located nearby,] there's a lot of handicapped children running around in this area, and God forbid one of them might find a weapon with shells and they might hurt themselves."

Patrolman McKenna apparently shared his fellow officer's concern:

"A. I more or less concurred with him [Gleckman] that it was a safety factor and that we should, you know, continue to search for the weapon and try to find it."

[Respondent then interrupted the conversation, stating that he would show the officers where the gun was located. The police vehicle then returned to the scene of the arrest where a search for the shotgun was in progress. There, the captain again advised respondent of his rights. He replied that he understood his rights, but "wanted to get the gun out of the way because of the kids in the area in the school." He then led the police to a nearby field, where he pointed out the shotgun under some rocks.

[Respondent was convicted of murder. The trial judge admitted the shotgun and testimony related to its discovery. On appeal, the Rhode Island Supreme Court concluded that the police had "interrogated" respondent without a valid waiver of his right to counsel; the conversation in the police vehicle had constituted "subtle coercion" that was the equivalent of *Miranda* "interrogation."]

[Since the parties agree that respondent was fully informed of his *Miranda* rights, that he asserted his right to counsel, and that he was "in custody" while being driven to the police station, the issue is whether he was "interrogated" in violation of *Miranda*.] In resolving this issue, we first define the term "interrogation" under *Miranda* before turning to a consideration of the facts of this case.

[Various references throughout the *Miranda* opinion] to "questioning" might suggest that the *Miranda* rules were to apply only to those police interrogation practices that involve express questioning of a defendant while in custody.

---

1. Although there was conflicting testimony about the exact seating arrangements, it is clear that everyone in the vehicle heard the conversation.

We do not, however, construe the *Miranda* opinion so narrowly. The concern of the Court in *Miranda* was that the "interrogation environment" created by the interplay of interrogation and custody would "subjugate the individual to the will of his examiner" and thereby undermine the privilege against compulsory self-incrimination. The police practices that evoked this concern included several that did not involve express questioning [such as] the so-called "reverse lineup" in which a defendant would be identified by coached witnesses as the perpetrator of a fictitious crime, [to induce] him to confess to the actual crime of which he was suspected in order to escape the false prosecution. [It] is clear that these techniques of persuasion, no less than express questioning, were thought, in a custodial setting, to amount to interrogation.

This is not to say, however, that all statements obtained by the police after a person has been taken into custody are to be considered the product of interrogation. [It] is clear [that the *Miranda* warnings] are required not where a suspect is simply taken into custody, but rather where a suspect in custody is subjected to interrogation. "Interrogation," as conceptualized [in *Miranda*], must reflect a measure of compulsion above and beyond that inherent in custody itself.[4]

We conclude that the *Miranda* safeguards come into play whenever a person in custody is subjected to either express questioning or its functional equivalent. That is to say, the term "interrogation" under *Miranda* refers not only to express questioning, but also to any words or actions on the part of the police (other than those normally attendant to arrest and custody) that the police should know are reasonably likely to elicit an incriminating response from the suspect. The latter portion of this definition focuses primarily upon the perceptions of the suspect, rather than the intent of the police. This focus reflects the fact that the *Miranda* safeguards were designed to vest a suspect in custody with an added measure of protection against coercive police practices, without regard to objective proof of the underlying intent of the police. A practice that the police should know is reasonably likely to evoke an incriminating response from a suspect thus amounts to interrogation.[7] But, since the police surely cannot be held accountable for the unforeseeable results of their words or actions, the definition of interrogation can extend only to words or actions on the part of police officers that they *should have known* were reasonably likely to elicit an incriminating response.[8]

4. There is language in the opinion of the Rhode Island Supreme Court in this case suggesting that the definition of "interrogation" under *Miranda* is informed by this Court's decision in *Brewer v. Williams,* [discussed at p. 279 infra, a case that reaffirmed and expansively interpreted *Massiah*]. This suggestion is erroneous. Our decision in *Brewer* rested solely on the Sixth and Fourteenth Amendment right to counsel. That right, as we held in *Massiah,* prohibits law enforcement officers from "deliberately elicit[ing]" incriminating information from a defendant in the absence of counsel after a formal charge against the defendant has been filed. Custody in such a case is not controlling; indeed, the petitioner in *Massiah* was not in custody. By contrast, the right to counsel at issue in the present case is based not on the Sixth and Fourteenth Amendments, but rather on the Fifth and Fourteenth Amendments as interpreted in the *Miranda* opinion. The definitions of "interrogation" under the Fifth and Sixth Amendments, if

indeed the term "interrogation" is even apt in the Sixth Amendment context, are not necessarily interchangeable, since the policies underlying the two constitutional protections are quite distinct.

7. This is not to say that the intent of the police is irrelevant, for it may well have a bearing on whether the police should have known that their words or actions were reasonably likely to evoke an incriminating response. In particular, where a police practice is designed to elicit an incriminating response from the accused, it is unlikely that the practice will not also be one which the police should have known was reasonably likely to have that effect.

8. Any knowledge the police may have had concerning the unusual susceptibility of a defendant to a particular form of persuasion might be an important factor in determining whether the police should have known that their words or actions were reasonably likely to

Turning to the facts of the present case, we conclude that the respondent was not "interrogated" within the meaning of *Miranda*. It is undisputed that the first prong of the definition of "interrogation" was not satisfied, for the [Gleckman–McKenna conversation] included no express questioning of the respondent. Rather, that conversation was, at least in form, nothing more than a dialogue between the two officers to which no response from the respondent was invited.

Moreover, it cannot be fairly concluded that the respondent was subjected to the "functional equivalent" of questioning. It cannot be said, in short, that [the officers should have known that their conversation was reasonably likely to elicit an incriminating response from the respondent]. There is nothing in the record to suggest that the officers were aware that the respondent was peculiarly susceptible to an appeal to his conscience concerning the safety of handicapped children [or that] the police knew that the respondent was unusually disoriented or upset at the time of his arrest.[9]

The case thus boils down to whether, in the context of a brief conversation, the officers should have known that the respondent would suddenly be moved to make a self-incriminating response. Given the fact that the entire conversation appears to have consisted of no more than a few off-hand remarks, we cannot say that the officers should have known that it was reasonably likely that Innis would so respond. This is not a case where the police carried on a lengthy harangue in the presence of the suspect. Nor does the record support the respondent's contention that, under the circumstances, the officers' comments were particularly "evocative." * * *

The Rhode Island Supreme Court erred, in short, in equating "subtle compulsion" with interrogation. That the officers' comments struck a responsive cord is readily apparent. Thus, it may be said, as the Rhode Island Supreme Court did say, that one respondent was subjected to "subtle compulsion." But that is not the end of the inquiry. It must also be established that a suspect's incriminating response was the product of words or actions on the part of the police that they should have known were reasonably likely to elicit an incriminating response.[10] This was not established in the present case. * * *[a]

elicit an incriminating response from the suspect.

9. The record in no way suggests that the officers' remarks were *designed* to elicit a response. It is significant that the trial judge, after hearing the officers' testimony, concluded that it was "entirely understandable that [the officers] would voice their concern [for the safety of the handicapped children] to each other."

10. By way of example, if the police had done no more than to drive past the site of the concealed weapon while taking the most direct route to the police station, and if the respondent, upon noticing for the first time the proximity of the school for handicapped children, had blurted out that he would show the officers where the gun was located, it could not seriously be argued that this "subtle compulsion" would have constituted "interrogation" within the meaning of the *Miranda* opinion.

a. Notwithstanding language in *Innis*, as *Arizona v. Mauro*, 481 U.S. 520, 107 S.Ct. 1931, 95 L.Ed.2d 458 (1987) illustrates, it is not inevitably "interrogation" within the meaning of *Miranda* for the police to allow a scenario to occur which they know may prompt the defendant to incriminate himself. In *Mauro*, a 5–4 majority, per Powell, J., held that it was not interrogation for the police to accede to the request of defendant's wife, also a suspect in the murder of their son, to speak with defendant (who had been given the *Miranda* warnings and had asserted his right to counsel) in the presence of a police officer, who placed a tape recorder in plain sight on a desk. Observed the Court:

"The tape recording of the conversation between Mauro and his wife shows that [the detective who attended their meeting] asked Mauro no questions about the crime or his conduct. Nor is it suggested [that the police decision] to allow Mauro's wife to see him was the kind of psychological ploy that properly could be treated as the functional equivalent of interrogation.

"* * * Mauro was not subjected to compelling influences, psychological ploys, or direct questioning. Thus, his volunteered

CHIEF JUSTICE BURGER, concurring in the judgment. * * *

The meaning of *Miranda* has become reasonably clear and law enforcement practices have adjusted to its strictures; I would neither overrule *Miranda,* disparage it, nor extend it at this late date. I fear, however, that [the Court's opinion] may introduce new elements of uncertainty; under the Court's test, a police officer, in the brief time available, apparently must evaluate the suggestibility and susceptibility of an accused. Few, if any, police officers are competent to make the kind of evaluation seemingly contemplated; even a psychiatrist asked to express an expert opinion on these aspects of a suspect in custody would very likely employ extensive questioning and observation to make the judgment now charged to police officers. * * *

JUSTICE MARSHALL, with whom JUSTICE BRENNAN joins, dissenting.

I am substantially in agreement with the Court's definition of "interrogation" within the meaning of *Miranda.* In my view, the *Miranda* safeguards apply whenever police conduct is intended or likely to produce a response from a suspect in custody. As I read the Court's opinion, its definition of "interrogation" for *Miranda* purposes is equivalent, for practical purposes, to my formulation, since it contemplates that "where a police practice is designed to elicit an incriminating response from the accused, it is unlikely that the practice will not also be one which the police should have known was reasonably likely to have that effect" [fn. 7]. Thus, the Court requires an objective inquiry into the likely effect of police conduct on a typical individual, taking into account any special susceptibility of the suspect to certain kinds of pressure of which the police know or have reason to know.

I am utterly at a loss, however, to understand how this objective standard as applied to the facts before us can rationally lead to the conclusion that there was no interrogation. * * *

One can scarcely imagine a stronger appeal to the conscience of a suspect— *any* suspect—than the assertion that if the weapon is not found an innocent person will be hurt or killed. And not just any innocent person, but an innocent child—a little girl—a helpless, handicapped little girl on her way to school. The notion that such an appeal could not be expected to have any effect unless the suspect were known to have some special interest in handicapped children verges on the ludicrous. As a matter of fact, the appeal to a suspect to confess for the sake of others, to "display some evidence of decency and honor," is a classic interrogation technique.

Gleckman's remarks would obviously have constituted interrogation if they had been explicitly directed to petitioner, and the result should not be different because they were nominally addressed to McKenna. This is not a case where police officers speaking among themselves are accidentally overheard by a suspect. These officers were "talking back and forth" in close quarters with the hand-cuffed suspect, traveling past the very place where they believed the weapon was

statements cannot properly be considered the result of police interrogation.

"In deciding whether particular police conduct is interrogation, we must remember the purpose behind [*Miranda*]: preventing government officials from using the coercive nature of confinement to extract confessions that would not be given in an unrestrained environment. The government actions in this case do not implicate this purpose in any way. Police departments need not adopt inflexible rules barring suspects from speaking with their spouses, nor must they ignore legitimate security concerns by allowing spouses to meet in private. In short, the officers in this case acted reasonably and lawfully by allowing Mrs. Mauro to speak with her husband."

located. They knew petitioner would hear and attend to their conversation, and they are chargeable with knowledge of and responsibility for the pressures to speak which they created.

I firmly believe that this case is simply an aberration, and that in future cases the Court will apply the standard adopted today in accordance with its plain meaning.

Justice Stevens, dissenting.

[In] my view any statement that would normally be understood by the average listener as calling for a response is the functional equivalent of a direct question, whether or not it is punctuated by a question mark. The Court, however, takes a much narrower view. It holds that police conduct is not the "functional equivalent" of direct questioning unless the police should have known that what they were saying or doing was likely to elicit an incriminating response from the suspect. This holding represents a plain departure from the principles set forth in *Miranda*.

From the suspect's point of view, the effectiveness of the warnings depends on whether it appears that the police are scrupulously honoring his rights. Apparent attempts to elicit information from a suspect after he has invoked his right to cut off questioning necessarily demean that right and tend to reinstate the imbalance between police and suspect that the *Miranda* warnings are designed to correct. Thus, if the rationale for requiring those warnings in the first place is to be respected, any police conduct or statements that would appear to a reasonable person in the suspect's position to call for a response must be considered "interrogation."

In short, in order to give full protection to a suspect's right to be free from any interrogation at all, the definition of "interrogation" must include any police statement or conduct that has the same purpose or effect as a direct question. Statements that appear to call for a response from the suspect, as well as those that are designed to do so, should be considered interrogation. By prohibiting only those relatively few statements or actions that a police officer should know are likely to elicit an incriminating response, the Court today accords a suspect considerably less protection. Indeed, since I suppose most suspects are unlikely to incriminate themselves even when questioned directly, this new definition will almost certainly exclude every statement that is not punctuated with a question mark from the concept of "interrogation."

Under my view of the correct standard, the judgment of the Rhode Island Supreme Court should be affirmed because the statements made within Innis' hearing were as likely to elicit a response as a direct question. However, even if I were to agree with the Court's much narrower standard, I would disagree with its disposition of this particular case because the Rhode Island courts should be given an opportunity to apply the new standard to the facts of this case.

ILLINOIS v. PERKINS

496 U.S. 292, 110 S.Ct. 2394, 110 L.Ed.2d 243 (1990).

Justice Kennedy delivered the opinion of the Court.

* * * We hold [that] *Miranda* warnings are not required when the suspect is unaware that he is speaking to a law enforcement officer and gives a voluntary statement.

[When Charlton, who had been a fellow inmate of respondent Perkins in another prison, told police that Perkins had implicated himself in the Stephenson murder, the police placed Charlton and Parisi, an undercover agent, in the same cellblock with Perkins, who was incarcerated on charges unrelated to the Stephenson murder. Parisi and Charlton posed as escapees from a work release program who had been arrested in the course of a burglary. They were instructed to engage Perkins in casual conversation and to report anything he said about the Stephenson murder.

[The cellblock consisted of 12 separate cells that opened onto a common room. Perkins greeted Charlton, who introduced Parisi by his alias. Parisi suggested that the three of them escape. There was further conversation. After telling Charlton that he would be responsible for any killing that might occur during a prison break, Parisi asked Perkins if he had ever "done" anybody. Perkins replied that he had, and proceeded to describe the Stephenson murder in detail.

[The trial court suppressed the statements made to Parisi in the jail. The Appellate Court of Illinois affirmed, reading *Miranda* as prohibiting all undercover contacts with incarcerated suspects which are reasonably likely to elicit an incriminating response.]

Conversations between suspects and undercover agents do not implicate the concerns underlying *Miranda*. The essential ingredients of a "police-dominated atmosphere" and compulsion are not present when an incarcerated person speaks freely to someone that he believes to be a fellow inmate. Coercion is determined from the perspective of the suspect. When a suspect considers himself in the company of cellmates and not officers, the coercive atmosphere is lacking. * * * There is no empirical basis for the assumption that a suspect speaking to those whom he assumes are not officers will feel compelled to speak by the fear of reprisal for remaining silent or in the hope of more lenient treatment should he confess.

It is the premise of *Miranda* that the danger of coercion results from the interaction of custody and official interrogation. We reject the argument that *Miranda* warnings are required whenever a suspect is in custody in a technical sense and converses with someone who happens to be a government agent. Questioning by captors, who appear to control the suspect's fate, may create mutually reinforcing pressures that the Court has assumed will weaken the suspect's will, but where a suspect does not know that he is conversing with a government agent, these pressures do not exist. The State Court here mistakenly assumed that because the suspect was in custody, no undercover questioning could take place. When the suspect has no reason to think that the listeners have official power over him, it should not be assumed that his words are motivated by the reaction he expects from his listeners. "[W]hen the agent carries neither badge nor gun and wears not 'police blue,' but the same prison gray" as the suspect, there is no "*interplay* between police interrogation and police custody." Kamisar, *Brewer v. Williams, Massiah and Miranda: What is "Interrogation"? When Does it Matter?*, 67 Geo.L.J. 1, 67, 63 (1978). * * *

The tactic employed here to elicit a voluntary confession from a suspect does not violate the Self–Incrimination Clause. We held in *Hoffa v. United States*, p. 158 supra, that placing an undercover agent near a suspect in order to gather incriminating information was permissible under the Fifth Amendment. In *Hoffa*, while petitioner Hoffa was on trial, he met often with one Partin, who, unbeknownst to Hoffa, was cooperating with law enforcement officials. Partin reported to officials that Hoffa had divulged his attempts to bribe jury members. We approved using Hoffa's statements at his subsequent trial for jury tampering, on the rationale that "no claim ha[d] been or could [have been] made that

[Hoffa's] incriminating statements were the product of any sort of coercion, legal or factual." [The] only difference between this case and *Hoffa* is that the suspect here was incarcerated, but detention, whether or not for the crime in question, does not warrant a presumption that the use of an undercover agent to speak with an incarcerated suspect makes any confession thus obtained involuntary.

[The Sixth Amendment decisions in *Messiah* and its progeny do not help respondent.] We held in those cases that the government may not use an undercover agent to circumvent the Sixth Amendment right to counsel once a suspect has been charged with the crime. After charges have been filed, the Sixth Amendment prevents the government from interfering with the accused's right to counsel. In the instant case no charges had been filed on the subject of the interrogation, and our Sixth Amendment precedents are not applicable.   * * *

JUSTICE BRENNAN, concurring in the judgment.

Although I do not subscribe to the majority's characterization of *Miranda* in its entirety, I do agree that when a suspect does not know that his questioner is a police agent, such questioning does not amount to "interrogation" in an "inherently coercive" environment so as to require application of *Miranda*. Since the only issue raised at this stage of the litigation is the applicability of *Miranda*, I concur in the judgment of the Court.

This is not to say that I believe the Constitution condones the method by which the police extracted the confession in this case. To the contrary, the deception and manipulation practiced on respondent raise a substantial claim that the confession was obtained in violation of the Due Process Clause.

[The] deliberate use of deception and manipulation by the police appears to be incompatible "with a system that presumes innocence and assures that a conviction will not be secured by inquisitorial means," and raises serious concerns that respondent's will was overborne. It is open to the lower court on remand to determine whether, under the totality of the circumstances, respondent's confession was elicited in a manner that violated the Due Process Clause.   * * *

JUSTICE MARSHALL, dissenting.

The conditions that require the police to apprise a defendant of his constitutional rights—custodial interrogation conducted by an agent of the police—were present in this case. [Because] Perkins received no *Miranda* warnings before he was subjected to custodial interrogation, his confession was not admissible.   * * *

Because Perkins was interrogated by police while he was in custody, *Miranda* required that the officer inform him of his rights. In rejecting that conclusion, the Court finds that "conversations" between undercover agents and suspects are devoid of the coercion inherent in stationhouse interrogations conducted by law enforcement officials who openly represent the State. *Miranda* was not, however, concerned solely with police *coercion*. It dealt with *any* police tactics that may operate to compel a suspect in custody to make incriminating statements without full awareness of his constitutional rights. [Thus,] when a law enforcement agent structures a custodial interrogation so that a suspect feels compelled to reveal incriminating information, he must inform the suspect of his constitutional rights and give him an opportunity to decide whether or not to talk.

[The] pressures unique to custody allow the police to use deceptive interrogation tactics to compel a suspect to make an incriminating statement. The compulsion is not eliminated by the suspect's ignorance of his interrogator's true identity. The Court therefore need not inquire past the bare facts of custody and interrogation to determine whether *Miranda* warnings are required.

[The] exception carved out of the *Miranda* doctrine today may well result in a proliferation of departmental policies to encourage police officers to conduct interrogations of confined suspects through undercover agents, thereby circumventing the need to administer *Miranda* warnings. Indeed, if *Miranda* now requires a police officer to issue warnings only in those situations in which the suspect might feel compelled "to speak by the fear of reprisal for remaining silent or in the hope of more lenient treatment should he confess," presumably it allows custodial interrogation by an undercover officer posing as a member of the clergy or a suspect's defense attorney. Although such abhorrent tricks would play on a suspect's need to confide in a trusted adviser, neither would cause the suspect to "think that the listeners have official power over him." The Court's adoption of the "undercover agent" exception to the *Miranda* rule thus is necessarily also the adoption of a substantial loophole in our jurisprudence protecting suspects' Fifth Amendment rights. * * *

C. **IF A SUSPECT ASSERTS HIS RIGHT TO COUNSEL, MAY THE POLICE "TRY AGAIN"? IF A SUSPECT WHO HAS ASSERTED HIS RIGHT TO COUNSEL IS ALLOWED TO CONSULT WITH AN ATTORNEY, MAY THE POLICE REINITIATE INTERROGATION IN THE ABSENCE OF COUNSEL?**

MINNICK v. MISSISSIPPI

498 U.S. 146, 111 S.Ct. 486, 112 L.Ed.2d 489 (1990).

JUSTICE KENNEDY delivered the opinion of the Court.

To protect the privilege against self-incrimination guaranteed by the Fifth Amendment, we have held that the police must terminate interrogation of an accused in custody if the accused requests the assistance of counsel. *Miranda.* We reinforced the protections of *Miranda* in *Edwards v. Arizona*, 451 U.S. 477 (1981), which held that once the accused requests counsel, officials may not reinitiate questioning "until counsel has been made available" to him.[a] The issue

---

a. But what constitutes a request for counsel within the meaning of the *Edwards* rule? For example, how should the police respond if a suspect makes an ambiguous or equivocal reference to an attorney? Consider *Davis v. United States*, 114 S.Ct. 2350 (1994), which arose as follows:

Defendant, a member of the U.S. Navy, initially waived his rights when interviewed by naval investigative agents in connection with a murder. About an hour and a half into the interview, he said, "Maybe I should talk to a lawyer." However, when asked whether he was requesting a lawyer, defendant replied: "No, I'm not asking for a lawyer." And then he continued on, and said: "No, I don't want a lawyer." After a short break, the interview continued for another hour, until defendant asked to have a lawyer present before saying anything more. The military judge admitted the statements made during the interview and defendant was convicted of murder.

The Supreme Court, per O'Connor, J., upheld the admissibility of the statements, declining to adopt a rule requiring law enforcement officers to cease questioning immediately or to ask clarifying questions when a suspect makes an ambiguous or equivocal reference to an attorney:

"[A] suspect must unambiguously request counsel. [He] must articulate his desire to have counsel present sufficiently clearly that a reasonable police officer in the circumstances would understand the statement to be a request for an attorney. If the statement fails to meet the requisite level of clarity, *Edwards* does not require that the officer stop questioning the suspect. * * *

"The *Edwards* rule—questioning must cease if the suspect asks for a lawyer—provides a bright line that can be applied by officers in the real world of investigation and interrogation without unduly hampering the gathering of information. But if we were to require questioning to cease if a suspect makes a statement that *might* be a request for an attorney, this clarity and ease of application would be lost. Police officers would be forced to make difficult judgment calls about whether the suspect in fact wants a lawyer even though he hasn't said so, with

in the case before us is whether *Edwards'* protection ceases once the suspect has consulted with an attorney.

[Petitioner Minnick and fellow prisoner Dykes escaped from a Mississippi jail and broke into a trailer in search of weapons. In the course of the burglary, they killed two people. Minnick and Dykes fled to Mexico, where they fought, and Minnick then proceeded alone to California where, some four months after the murders, he was arrested by local police and placed in a San Diego jail. The day following his arrest, Saturday, two FBI agents came to the jail to interview him. After being advised of his rights and acknowledging that he understood them, Minnick refused to sign a rights waiver form, but agreed to answer some questions. He maintained that Dykes had killed one victim and forced him to shoot the other, but otherwise he hesitated to discuss what happened at the trailer.]

[At this point] the [FBI] agents reminded him he did not have to answer questions without a lawyer present. According to the [FBI] report, "Minnick stated that he would make a more complete statement then with his lawyer present." The FBI interview ended.

After the FBI interview, an appointed attorney met with petitioner. [He] spoke with the lawyer on two or three occasions, though it is not clear from the record whether all of these conferences were in person.

On Monday [Denham, a Mississippi deputy sheriff,] came to the San Diego jail to question Minnick. Minnick testified that his jailers * * * told him he would "have to talk" to Denham and that he "could not refuse." Denham advised petitioner of his rights, and petitioner again declined to sign a rights waiver form. [However, Minnick agreed to answer some questions and made a number of incriminating statements].

Minnick was tried for murder in Mississippi. He moved to suppress all statements given to the FBI or other police officers, including Denham. The trial court denied the motion with respect to petitioner's statements to Denham, but suppressed his other statements. Petitioner was convicted on two counts of capital murder and sentenced to death. [The state supreme court affirmed.]

Edwards is "designed to prevent police from badgering a defendant into waiving his previously asserted *Miranda* rights." The rule ensures that any statement made in subsequent interrogation is not the result of coercive pressures. *Edwards* conserves judicial resources which would otherwise be expended in making difficult determinations of voluntariness, and implements the protections of *Miranda* in practical and straightforward terms.

the threat of suppression if they guess wrong. We therefore hold that, after a knowing and voluntary waiver of the *Miranda* rights, law enforcement officers may continue questioning until and unless the suspect clearly requests an attorney.

"Of course, when a suspect makes an ambiguous or equivocal statement it will often be good police practice to clarify whether or not he actually wants an attorney. That was the procedure followed [in] this case. [But] we decline to adopt a rule requiring officers to ask clarifying questions. If the suspect's statement is not an unambiguous or unequivocal request for counsel, the officer have no obligation to stop questioning him."

Souter, J., joined by Blackmun, Stevens and Ginsburg, JJ., concurred in the judgment, but could not join in the majority's "further conclusion that if the investigators here had been so inclined, they were at liberty to disregard Davis's reference to a lawyer entirely, in accordance with a general rule that interrogators have no legal obligation to discover what a custodial subject meant by an ambiguous statement that could reasonably be understood to express a desire to consult a lawyer."

The merit of the *Edwards* decision lies in the clarity of its command and the certainty of its application. We have confirmed that the *Edwards* rule provides " 'clear and unequivocal' guidelines to the law enforcement profession." * * *

Our cases following *Edwards* have interpreted the decision to mean that the authorities may not initiate questioning of the accused in counsel's absence. Writing for a plurality of the Court, for instance, then Justice Rehnquist described the holding of *Edwards* to be "that subsequent incriminating statements made *without [Edwards'] attorney present* violated the rights secured to the defendant by the Fifth and Fourteenth Amendments to the United States Constitution." *Oregon v. Bradshaw,* 462 U.S. 1039, 103 S.Ct. 2830, 77 L.Ed.2d 405 (1983) [b] (emphasis added). [In] our view, a fair reading of *Edwards* and subsequent cases demonstrates that we have interpreted the rule to bar police-initiated interrogation unless the accused has counsel with him at the time of questioning. Whatever the ambiguities of our earlier cases on this point, we now hold that when counsel is requested, interrogation must cease, and officials may not reinitiate interrogation without counsel present, whether or not the accused has consulted with his attorney.

We consider our ruling to be an appropriate and necessary application of the *Edwards* rule. A single consultation with an attorney does not remove the suspect from persistent attempts by officials to persuade him to waive his rights, or from the coercive pressures that accompany custody and that may increase as custody is prolonged. The case before us well illustrates the pressures, and abuses, that may be concomitants of custody. Petitioner testified that though he resisted, he was required to submit to both the FBI and the Denham interviews. In the latter instance, the compulsion to submit to interrogation followed petitioner's unequivocal request during the FBI interview that questioning cease until counsel was present. The case illustrates also that consultation is not always effective in instructing the suspect of his rights. One plausible interpretation of the record is that petitioner thought he could keep his admissions out of evidence by refusing to sign a formal waiver of rights. If the authorities had complied with Minnick's request to have counsel present during interrogation, the attorney could have corrected Minnick's misunderstanding, or indeed counseled him that he need not make a statement at all. We decline to remove protection from

b. The *Bradshaw* case indicates that it may not be too difficult to establish that a suspect "initiated" further communication with the police. In *Bradshaw,* defendant asserted his right to counsel but a few moments later, either while still at the police station or enroute to jail, asked the officer: "Well, what is going to happen to me now?" The officer responded: "You do not have to talk to me. * * * I don't want you talking to me unless you so desire * * *." Defendant said he understood and general conversation followed. A 5–4 majority held that the incriminating statements obtained as a result of the general conversation were admissible.

The plurality opinion, written by Justice Rehnquist, joined by Burger, C.J., and White and O'Connor, JJ., observed:

"There are some inquiries such as a request for a drink of water or a request to use a telephone that are so routine that they cannot be fairly said to represent a desire on the part of an accused to open up a more generalized discussion relating directly or in-

directly to the investigation. Such [statements] relating to routine incidents of the custodial relationship, will not generally 'initiate' a conversation in the sense in which that word was used in *Edwards*. [But Bradshaw's question] as to what was going to happen to him evinced a willingness and a desire for a generalized discussion about the investigation; it was not merely a necessary inquiry arising out of the incidents of the custodial relationship. It could reasonably have been interpreted by the officer as relating generally to the investigation."

Dissenting Justice Marshall, joined by Brennan, Blackmun and Stevens, JJ., "agree[d] with the plurality that in order to constitute 'initiation' under *Edwards*, an accused's inquiry must demonstrate a desire to discuss the subject matter of the criminal investigation," but was "baffled [at] the plurality's application of that standard to the facts of this case. [It] is plain that [Bradshaw's] only 'desire' was to find out where the police were going to take him."

police-initiated questioning based on isolated consultations with counsel who is absent when the interrogation resumes.

The exception to *Edwards* here proposed is inconsistent with *Edwards'* purpose to protect the suspect's right to have counsel present at custodial interrogation. It is inconsistent as well with *Miranda,* where we specifically rejected respondent's theory that the opportunity to consult with one's attorney would substantially counteract the compulsion created by custodial interrogation. We noted in *Miranda* that "[e]ven preliminary advice given to the accused by his own attorney can be swiftly overcome by the secret interrogation process. Thus the need for counsel to protect the Fifth Amendment privilege comprehends not merely a right to consult with counsel prior to questioning, but also to have counsel present during any questioning if the defendant so desires."

The exception proposed, furthermore, would undermine the advantages flowing from *Edwards'* "clear and unequivocal" character. Respondent concedes that even after consultation with counsel, a second request for counsel should reinstate the *Edwards* protection. We are invited by this formulation to adopt a regime in which *Edwards'* protection could pass in and out of existence multiple times prior to arraignment, at which point the same protection might reattach by virtue of our Sixth Amendment jurisprudence, see *Michigan v. Jackson,* 475 U.S. 625 (1986). Vagaries of this sort spread confusion through the justice system and lead to a consequent loss of respect for the underlying constitutional principle.

In addition, adopting the rule proposed would leave far from certain the sort of consultation required to displace *Edwards.* Consultation is not a precise concept, for it may encompass variations from a telephone call to say that the attorney is in route, to a hurried interchange between the attorney and client in a detention facility corridor, to a lengthy in-person conference in which the attorney gives full and adequate advice respecting all matters that might be covered in further interrogations. And even with the necessary scope of consultation settled, the officials in charge of the case would have to confirm the occurrence and, possibly, the extent of consultation to determine whether further interrogation is permissible. The necessary inquiries could interfere with the attorney-client privilege.

Added to these difficulties in definition and application of the proposed rule is our concern over its consequence that the suspect whose counsel is prompt would lose the protection of *Edwards,* while the one whose counsel is dilatory would not. There is more than irony to this result. There is a strong possibility that it would distort the proper conception of the attorney's duty to the client and set us on a course at odds with what ought to be effective representation.

Both waiver of rights and admission of guilt are consistent with the affirmation of individual responsibility that is a principle of the criminal justice system. It does not detract from this principle, however, to insist that neither admissions nor waivers are effective unless there are both particular and systemic assurances that the coercive pressures of custody were not the inducing cause. The *Edwards* rule sets forth a specific standard to fulfill these purposes, and we have declined to confine it in other instances. See *Arizona v. Roberson,* [p. 252 supra]. [*Edwards* applies even when the police want to question a suspect about an offense unrelated to the subject of their initial interrogation]. It would detract from the efficacy of the rule to remove its protections based on consultation with counsel.

Edwards does not foreclose finding a waiver of Fifth Amendment protections after counsel has been requested, provided the accused has initiated the conversation or discussions with the authorities; but that is not the case before us. There can be no doubt that the interrogation in question was initiated by the police; it was a formal interview which petitioner was compelled to attend. Since petitioner made a specific request for counsel before the interview, the police-initiated interrogation was impermissible. Petitioner's statement to Denham was not admissible at trial. * * * c

JUSTICE SCALIA, with whom THE CHIEF JUSTICE joins, dissenting.

The Court today establishes an irrebuttable presumption that a criminal suspect, after invoking his *Miranda* right to counsel, can *never* validly waive that right during any police-initiated encounter, even after the suspect has been provided multiple *Miranda* warnings and has actually consulted his attorney. This holding builds on foundations already established in *Edwards,* but "the rule of *Edwards* is our rule, not a constitutional command; and it is our obligation to justify its expansion." *Arizona v. Roberson* (Kennedy, J., dissenting). Because I see no justification for applying the *Edwards* irrebuttable presumption when a criminal suspect has actually consulted with his attorney, I respectfully dissent.

[The] Court [holds that,] because Minnick had asked for counsel during the interview with the FBI agents, he could not—as a matter of law—validly waive the right to have counsel present during the conversation initiated by Denham. That Minnick's original request to see an attorney had been honored, that Minnick had consulted with his attorney on several occasions, and that the attorney had specifically warned Minnick not to speak to the authorities, are irrelevant. That Minnick was familiar with the criminal justice system in general or *Miranda* warnings in particular (he had previously been convicted of robbery in Mississippi and assault with a deadly weapon in California) is also beside the point. The confession must be suppressed, not because it was "compelled," nor even because it was obtained from an individual who could realistically be assumed to be unaware of his rights, but simply because this Court sees fit to prescribe as a "systemic assuranc[e]" that a person in custody who has once asked for counsel cannot thereafter be approached by the police unless counsel is present. Of course the Constitution's proscription of compelled testimony does not remotely authorize this incursion upon state practices; and even our recent precedents are not a valid excuse.

[The *Miranda* Court] expressly adopted the "high standar[d] of proof for the waiver of constitutional rights" set forth in *Johnson v. Zerbst* [p. 187 supra].

Notwithstanding our acknowledgment that *Miranda* rights are "not themselves rights protected by the Constitution [but] instead measures to insure that the right against compulsory self-incrimination [is] protected," *Michigan v. Tucker,* we have adhered to the principle that nothing less than the *Zerbst* standard for the waiver of constitutional rights applies to the waiver of *Miranda* rights. * * *

Edwards, however, broke with this approach * * *. The case stands as a solitary exception to our waiver jurisprudence. It does, to be sure, have the desirable consequences described in today's opinion. In the narrow context in which it applies, it provides 100% assurance against confessions that are "the result of coercive pressures"; it " 'prevent[s] police from badgering a defendant' "; it "conserves judicial resources which would otherwise be expended in making difficult determinations of voluntariness"; and it provides " ' "clear and unequivocal" guidelines to the law enforcement profession.' " But so would a rule that simply excludes all confessions by all persons in police custody. The value of any prophylactic rule (assuming the authority to adopt a prophylactic

c. Justice Souter took no part in the consideration or decision of this case.

rule) must be assessed not only on the basis of what is gained, but also on the basis of what is lost. In all other contexts we have thought the above-described consequences of abandoning *Zerbst* outweighed by " 'the need for police questioning as a tool for effective enforcement of criminal laws,' " *Moran v. Burbine,* [the last case set forth in this section].

In this case, of course, we have not been called upon to reconsider *Edwards,* but simply to determine whether its irrebuttable presumption should continue after a suspect has actually consulted with his attorney. Whatever justifications might support *Edwards* are even less convincing in this context.

Most of the Court's discussion of *Edwards*—which stresses repeatedly, in various formulations, the case's emphasis upon "the 'right to have counsel *present* during custodial interrogation' " (emphasis added by the Court)—is beside the point. The existence and the importance of the *Miranda*-created right "to have counsel *present*" are unquestioned here. What *is* questioned is why a State should not be given the opportunity to prove (under *Zerbst*) that the right was *voluntarily waived* by a suspect who, after having been read his *Miranda* rights twice and having consulted with counsel at least twice, chose to speak to a police officer (and to admit his involvement in two murders) without counsel present.

[One] should not underestimate the extent to which the Court's expansion of *Edwards* constricts law enforcement. Today's ruling, that the invocation of a right to counsel permanently prevents a police-initiated waiver, makes it largely impossible for the police to urge a prisoner who has initially declined to confess to change his mind—or indeed, even to ask whether he has changed his mind. Many persons in custody will invoke the *Miranda* right to counsel during the first interrogation, so that the permanent prohibition will attach at once. Those who do not do so will almost certainly request or obtain counsel at arraignment. We have held that a general request for counsel, after the Sixth Amendment right has attached, also triggers the *Edwards* prohibition of police-solicited confessions, see *Michigan v. Jackson,* 475 U.S. 625 (1986), and I presume that the perpetuality of prohibition announced in today's opinion applies in that context as well. "Perpetuality" is not too strong a term, since although the Court rejects one logical moment at which the *Edwards* presumption might end, it suggests no alternative. In this case Minnick was reapproached by the police three days after he requested counsel, but the result would presumably be the same if it had been three months, or three years, or even three decades. This perpetual irrebuttable presumption will apply, I might add, not merely to interrogations involving the original crime but to those involving other subjects as well. See *Arizona v. Roberson.*

* * * Clear and simple rules are desirable, but only in pursuance of authority that we possess. We are authorized by the Fifth Amendment to exclude confessions that are "compelled," which we have interpreted to include confessions that the police obtain from a suspect in custody without a knowing and voluntary waiver of his right to remain silent. Undoubtedly some bright-line rules can be adopted to implement that principle, marking out the situations in which knowledge or voluntariness cannot possibly be established—for example, a rule excluding confessions obtained after five hours of continuous interrogation. But a rule excluding all confessions that follow upon even the slightest police inquiry cannot conceivably be justified on this basis. It does not rest upon a reasonable prediction that all such confessions, or even most such confessions, will be unaccompanied by a knowing and voluntary waiver.

It can be argued that the same is true of the category of confessions excluded by the *Edwards* rule itself. I think that is so, but, as I have discussed above, the presumption of involuntariness is at least more plausible for that category. There is, in any event, a clear and rational line between that category and the present one, and I see nothing to be said for expanding upon a past mistake. Drawing a distinction between police-initiated inquiry before consultation with counsel and police-initiated inquiry after consultation with counsel is assuredly more reasonable than other distinctions *Edwards* has already led us into—such as the distinction between police-initiated inquiry after assertion of the *Miranda* right to remain silent, and police-initiated inquiry after assertion of the *Miranda* right to counsel or the distinction between what is needed to prove waiver of the *Miranda* right to have counsel present and what is needed to prove waiver of rights found in the Constitution. * * *

Today's extension of the *Edwards* prohibition is the latest stage of prophylaxis built upon prophylaxis, producing a veritable fairyland castle of imagined constitutional restriction upon law enforcement. This newest tower, according to the Court, is needed to avoid "inconsisten[cy] with [the] purpose" of *Edwards'* prophylactic rule, which was needed to protect *Miranda*'s prophylactic right to have counsel present, which was needed to protect the right against *compelled self-incrimination* found (at last!) in the Constitution.

It seems obvious to me that, even in *Edwards* itself but surely in today's decision, we have gone far beyond any genuine concern about suspects who do not *know* their right to remain silent, or who have been *coerced* to abandon it. Both holdings are explicable, in my view, only as an effort to protect suspects against what is regarded as their own folly. The sharp-witted criminal would know better than to confess; why should the dull-witted suffer for his lack of mental endowment? Providing him an attorney at every stage where he might be induced or persuaded (though not coerced) to incriminate himself will even the odds. Apart from the fact that this protective enterprise is beyond our authority under the Fifth Amendment or any other provision of the Constitution, it is unwise. The procedural protections of the Constitution protect the guilty as well as the innocent, but it is not their objective to set the guilty free. That some clever criminals may employ those protections to their advantage is poor reason to allow criminals who have not done so to escape justice.

Thus, even if I were to concede that an honest confession is a foolish mistake, I would welcome rather than reject it; a rule that foolish mistakes do not count would leave most offenders not only unconvicted but undetected. More fundamentally, however, it is wrong, and subtly corrosive of our criminal justice system, to regard an honest confession as a "mistake." While every person is entitled to stand silent, it is more virtuous for the wrongdoer to admit his offense and accept the punishment he deserves. [A] confession is rightly regarded by the sentencing guidelines as warranting a reduction of sentence, because it "demonstrates a recognition and affirmative acceptance of personal responsibility [for] criminal conduct," which is the beginning of reform. We should, then, rejoice at an honest confession, rather than pity the "poor fool" who has made it; and we should regret the attempted retraction of that good act, rather than seek to facilitate and encourage it. To design our laws on premises contrary to these is to abandon belief in either personal responsibility or the moral claim of just government to obedience.

D. IF A SUSPECT DOES NOT REQUEST A LAWYER BUT, UNBE-
KNOWNST TO HIM, A RELATIVE OR FRIEND RETAINS A
LAWYER FOR HIM, DOES THE FAILURE OF THE POLICE TO
ALLOW THE LAWYER TO SEE THE SUSPECT OR THE FAIL-
URE TO INFORM THE SUSPECT THAT AN ATTORNEY IS
TRYING TO REACH HIM VITIATE AN OTHERWISE VALID
WAIVER OF MIRANDA RIGHTS

MORAN v. BURBINE

475 U.S. 412, 106 S.Ct. 1135, 89 L.Ed.2d 410 (1986).

JUSTICE O'CONNOR delivered the opinion of the Court.

After being informed of his rights pursuant to *Miranda* and after executing a
series of written waivers, respondent confessed to the murder of a young woman.
At no point during the course of the interrogation, which occurred prior to
arraignment, did he request an attorney. While he was in police custody, his
sister attempted to retain a lawyer to represent him. The attorney telephoned
the police station and received assurances that respondent would not be questioned further until the next day. In fact, the interrogation session that yielded
the inculpatory statements began later that evening. The question presented is
whether either the conduct of the police or respondent's ignorance of the attorney's efforts to reach him taints the validity of the waivers and therefore requires
exclusion of the confessions.

On the morning of March 3, 1977, Mary Jo Hickey was found unconscious in
a factory parking lot in Providence, Rhode Island. Suffering from injuries to her
skull apparently inflicted by a metal pipe found at the scene, she was rushed to a
nearby hospital. Three weeks later she died from her wounds.

Several months after her death, the Cranston, Rhode Island police arrested
respondent and two others in connection with a local burglary. Shortly before the
arrest, Detective Ferranti of the Cranston police force had learned from a
confidential informant that the man responsible for Ms. Hickey's death lived at a
certain address and went by the name of "Butch." Upon discovering that
respondent lived at that address and was known by that name, Detective Ferranti
informed respondent of his *Miranda* rights. When respondent refused to execute
a written waiver, Detective Ferranti spoke separately with the two other suspects
arrested on the breaking and entering charge and obtained statements further
implicating respondent in Ms. Hickey's murder. At approximately 6:00 p.m.,
Detective Ferranti telephoned the police in Providence to convey the information
he had uncovered. An hour later, three officers from that department arrived at
the Cranston headquarters for the purpose of questioning respondent about the
murder.

That same evening, at about 7:45 p.m., respondent's sister telephoned the
Public Defender's Office to obtain legal assistance for her brother. Her sole
concern was the breaking and entering charge, as she was unaware that respondent was then under suspicion for murder. She asked for Richard Casparian, who
had been scheduled to meet with respondent earlier that afternoon to discuss
another charge unrelated to either the break-in or the murder. As soon as the
conversation ended, the attorney who took the call attempted to reach Mr.
Casparian. When those efforts were unsuccessful, she telephoned Allegra Munson, another Assistant Public Defender, and told her about respondent's arrest
and his sister's subsequent request that the office represent him.

At 8:15 p.m., Ms. Munson telephoned the Cranston police station and asked that her call be transferred to the detective division. In the words of the Supreme Court of Rhode Island, whose factual findings we treat as presumptively correct, 28 U.S.C. § 2254(d), the conversation proceeded as follows:

"A male voice responded with the word 'Detectives.' Ms. Munson identified herself and asked if Brian Burbine was being held; the person responded affirmatively. Ms. Munson explained to the person that Burbine was represented by attorney Casparian who was not available; she further stated that she would act as Burbine's legal counsel in the event that the police intended to place him in a lineup or question him. The unidentified person told Ms. Munson that the police would not be questioning Burbine or putting him in a lineup and that they were through with him for the night. Ms. Munson was not informed that the Providence Police were at the Cranston police station or that Burbine was a suspect in Mary's murder."

At all relevant times, respondent was unaware of his sister's efforts to retain counsel and of the fact and contents of Ms. Munson's telephone conversation.

Less than an hour later, the police brought respondent to an interrogation room and conducted the first of a series of interviews concerning the murder. Prior to each session, respondent was informed of his *Miranda* rights, and on three separate occasions he signed a written form acknowledging that he understood his right to the presence of an attorney and explicitly indicating that he "[did] not want an attorney called or appointed for [him]" before he gave a statement. Uncontradicted evidence at the suppression hearing indicated that at least twice during the course of the evening, respondent was left in a room where he had access to a telephone, which he apparently declined to use. Eventually, respondent signed three written statements fully admitting to the murder.

Prior to trial, respondent moved to suppress the statements. The court denied the motion, finding that respondent had received the *Miranda* warnings and had "knowingly, intelligently, and voluntarily waived his privilege against self-incrimination [and] his right to counsel." Rejecting the contrary testimony of the police, the court found that Ms. Munson did telephone the detective bureau on the evening in question, but concluded that "there was no * * * conspiracy or collusion on the part of the Cranston Police Department to secrete this defendant from his attorney." In any event, the court held, the constitutional right to request the presence of an attorney belongs solely to the defendant and may not be asserted by his lawyer. Because the evidence was clear that respondent never asked for the services of an attorney, the telephone call had no relevance to the validity of the waiver or the admissibility of the statements.

The jury found respondent guilty of murder in the first degree, and he appealed to the Supreme Court of Rhode Island. A divided court rejected his contention that the Fifth and Fourteenth Amendments to the Constitution required the suppression of the inculpatory statements and affirmed the conviction. Failure to inform respondent of Ms. Munson's efforts to represent him, the court held, did not undermine the validity of the waivers. "It hardly seems conceivable that the additional information that an attorney whom he did not know had called the police station would have added significantly to the quantum of information necessary for the accused to make an informed decision as to waiver." Nor, the court concluded, did *Miranda* or any other decision of this Court independently require the police to honor Ms. Munson's request that interrogation not proceed in her absence. In reaching that conclusion, the court noted that because two different police departments were operating in the

Cranston station house on the evening in question, the record supported the trial court's finding that there was no "conspiracy or collusion" to prevent Ms. Munson from seeing respondent. In any case, the court held, the right to the presence of counsel belongs solely to the accused and may not be asserted by "benign third parties, whether or not they happen to be attorneys."

[On federal habeas corpus, the U.S. Court of Appeals for the First Circuit] held that the police's conduct had fatally tainted respondent's "otherwise valid" waiver of his Fifth Amendment privilege against self incrimination and right to counsel. The court reasoned that by failing to inform respondent that an attorney had called and that she had been assured that no questioning would take place until the next day, the police had deprived respondent of information crucial to his ability to waive his rights knowingly and intelligently. The court also found that the record would support "no other explanation for the refusal to tell Burbine of Attorney Munson's call [than] deliberate or reckless irresponsibility." This kind of "blameworthy action by the police," the court concluded, together with respondent's ignorance of the telephone call, "vitiate[d] any claim that [the] waiver of counsel was knowing and voluntary."

We granted certiorari to decide whether a pre-arraignment confession preceded by an otherwise valid waiver must be suppressed either because the police misinformed an inquiring attorney about their plans concerning the suspect or because they failed to inform the suspect of the attorney's efforts to reach him. We now reverse. * * *

Respondent does not dispute that the Providence police followed [the *Miranda* procedures] with precision. [Nor does he contest the state] courts' determination that he at no point requested the presence of a lawyer. He contends instead that the confessions must be suppressed because the police's failure to inform him of the attorney's telephone call deprived him of information essential to his ability to knowingly waive his Fifth Amendment rights. In the alternative, he suggests that to fully protect the Fifth Amendment values served by *Miranda,* we should extend that decision to condemn the conduct of the Providence police. We address each contention in turn.

Echoing the standard first articulated in *Johnson v. Zerbst, Miranda* holds that "[t]he defendant may waive effectuation" of the rights conveyed in the warnings "provided the waiver is made voluntarily, knowingly and intelligently." The inquiry has two distinct dimensions. First the relinquishment of the right must have been voluntary in the sense that it was the product of a free and deliberate choice rather than intimidation, coercion or deception. Second, the waiver must have been made with a full awareness both of the nature of the right being abandoned and the consequences of the decision to abandon it. Only if the "totality of the circumstances surrounding the interrogation" reveal both an uncoerced choice and the requisite level of comprehension may a court properly conclude that the *Miranda* rights have been waived.

Under this standard, we have no doubt that respondent validly waived his right to remain silent and to the presence of counsel. The voluntariness of the waiver is not at issue. [Nor] is there any question about respondent's comprehension of the full panoply of rights set out in the *Miranda* warnings and of the potential consequences of a decision to relinquish them. Nonetheless, the Court of Appeals believed that the "[d]eliberate or reckless" conduct of the police, in particular their failure to inform respondent of the telephone call, fatally undermined the validity of the otherwise proper waiver. We find this conclusion untenable as a matter of both logic and precedent.

Events occurring outside of the presence of the suspect and entirely unknown to him surely can have no bearing on the capacity to comprehend and knowingly relinquish a constitutional right. Under the analysis of the Court of Appeals, the same defendant, armed with the same information and confronted with precisely the same police conduct, would have knowingly waived his *Miranda* rights had a lawyer not telephoned the police station to inquire about his status. Nothing in any of our waiver decisions or in our understanding of the essential components of a valid waiver requires so incongruous a result. No doubt the additional information would have been useful to respondent; perhaps even it might have affected his decision to confess. But we have never read the Constitution to require that the police supply a suspect with a flow of information to help him calibrate his self interest in deciding whether to speak or stand by his rights.[a] Once it is determined that a suspect's decision not to rely on his rights was uncoerced, that he at all times knew he could stand mute and request a lawyer, and that he was aware of the state's intention to use his statements to secure a conviction, the analysis is complete and the waiver is valid as a matter of law.[1] The Court of Appeals' conclusion to the contrary was in error.

Nor do we believe that the level of the police's culpability in failing to inform respondent of the telephone call has any bearing on the validity of the waiver. In light of the state-court findings that there was no "conspiracy or collusion" on the part of the police, we have serious doubts about whether the Court of Appeals was free to conclude that their conduct constituted "deliberate or reckless irresponsibility." But whether intentional or inadvertent, the state of mind of the police is irrelevant to the question of the intelligence and voluntariness of respondent's election to abandon his rights. Although highly inappropriate, even deliberate deception of an attorney could not possibly affect a suspect's decision to waive his *Miranda* rights unless he were at least aware of the incident. Compare *Escobedo* (excluding confession where police incorrectly told the *suspect* that his lawyer " 'didn't want to see' him"). Nor was the failure to inform respondent of the telephone call the kind of "trick[ery]" that can vitiate the validity of a waiver. *Miranda.* Granting that the "deliberate or reckless" withholding of information is objectionable as a matter of ethics, such conduct is only relevant to the constitutional validity of a waiver if it deprives a defendant of knowledge essential to his ability to understand the nature of his rights and the consequences of abandoning them. Because respondent's voluntary decision to speak was made with full awareness and comprehension of all the information *Miranda* requires the police to convey, the waivers were valid.

At oral argument respondent acknowledged that a constitutional rule requiring the police to inform a suspect of an attorney's efforts to reach him would represent a significant extension of our precedents. He contends, however, that the conduct of the Providence police was so inimical to the Fifth Amendment values *Miranda* seeks to protect that we should read that decision to condemn their behavior. Regardless of any issue of waiver, he urges, the Fifth Amendment

---

a. A year later, this language was quoted with approval in *Colorado v. Spring,* 479 U.S. 564, 107 S.Ct. 851, 93 L.Ed.2d 954 (1987), holding that the police need not advise a suspect of the crimes they wish to question him about even though the subject matter of the interrogation is likely to be quite different from what the suspect expects.

1. The dissent incorrectly reads our analysis of the components of a valid waiver to be inconsistent [with] *Edwards.* [But] the dissent never comes to grips with the crucial distinguishing feature of this case—that Burbine at no point requested the presence of counsel, as was his right under *Miranda* to do. [We reject] the dissent's entirely undefended suggestion that the Fifth Amendment "right to counsel" requires anything more than that the police inform the suspect of his right to representation and honor his request that the interrogation cease until his attorney is present.

requires the reversal of a conviction if the police are less than forthright in their dealings with an attorney or if they fail to tell a suspect of a lawyer's unilateral efforts to contact him. Because the proposed modification ignores the underlying purposes of the *Miranda* rules and because we think that the decision as written strikes the proper balance between society's legitimate law enforcement interests and the protection of the defendant's Fifth Amendment rights, we decline the invitation to further extend *Miranda's* reach.

At the outset, while we share respondent's distaste for the deliberate misleading of an officer of the court, reading *Miranda* to forbid police deception of an *attorney* "would cut [the decision] completely loose from its own explicitly stated rationale." As is now well established, "[the] *Miranda* warnings are 'not themselves rights protected by the Constitution but [are] instead measures to insure that the [suspect's] right against compulsory self-incrimination [is] protected.'" *Quarles.* Their objective is not to mold police conduct for its own sake. Nothing in the Constitution vests in us the authority to mandate a code of behavior for state officials wholly unconnected to any federal right or privilege. The purpose of the *Miranda* warnings instead is to dissipate the compulsion inherent in custodial interrogation and, in so doing, guard against abridgement of the suspect's Fifth Amendment rights. Clearly, a rule that focuses on how the police treat an attorney—conduct that has no relevance at all to the degree of compulsion experienced by the defendant during interrogation—would ignore both *Miranda's* mission and its only source of legitimacy.

Nor are we prepared to adopt a rule requiring that the police inform a suspect of an attorney's efforts to reach him. While such a rule might add marginally to *Miranda's* goal of dispelling the compulsion inherent in custodial interrogation, overriding practical considerations counsel against its adoption. As we have stressed on numerous occasions, "[o]ne of the principal advantages" of *Miranda* is the ease and clarity of its application. *Berkemer v. McCarty.* We have little doubt that the approach urged by respondent and endorsed by the Court of Appeals would have the inevitable consequence of muddying *Miranda's* otherwise relatively clear waters. The legal questions it would spawn are legion: To what extent should the police be held accountable for knowing that the accused has counsel? Is it enough that someone in the station house knows, or must the interrogating officer himself know of counsel's efforts to contact the suspect? Do counsel's efforts to talk to the suspect concerning one criminal investigation trigger the obligation to inform the defendant before interrogation may proceed on a wholly separate matter? We are unwilling to modify *Miranda* in a manner that would so clearly undermine the decision's central "virtue of informing police and prosecutors with specificity [what] they may do in conducting [a] custodial interrogation, and of informing courts under what circumstances statements obtained during such interrogation are not admissible."

Moreover, problems of clarity to one side, reading *Miranda* to require the police in each instance to inform a suspect of an attorney's efforts to reach him would work a substantial and, we think, inappropriate shift in the subtle balance struck in that decision. Custodial interrogations implicate two competing concerns. On the one hand, "the need for police questioning as a tool for effective enforcement of criminal laws" cannot be doubted. Admissions of guilt [are] essential to society's compelling interest in finding, convicting and punishing those who violate the law. On the other hand, the Court has recognized that the interrogation process is "inherently coercive" and that, as a consequence, there exists a substantial risk that the police will inadvertently traverse the fine line between legitimate efforts to elicit admissions and constitutionally impermissible compulsion. *Miranda* attempted to reconcile these opposing concerns by giving the *defendant* the power to exert some control over the course of the interrogation. Declining to adopt the more extreme position that the actual presence of a lawyer was necessary to dispel the coercion inherent in custodial interrogation, the Court found that the suspect's Fifth Amendment rights could be adequately protected by less intrusive means. Police questioning, often an essential part of the investigatory process, could continue in its traditional form, the Court held, but only if the suspect clearly understood that, at any time, he could bring the proceeding to a halt or, short of that, call in an attorney to give advice and monitor the conduct of his interrogators.

The position urged by respondent would upset this carefully drawn approach in a manner that is both unnecessary for the protection of the Fifth Amendment privilege and injurious to legitimate law enforcement. Because, as *Miranda* holds, full comprehension of the rights to remain silent and request an attorney are sufficient to dispel whatever coercion is inherent in the interrogation process, a rule requiring the police to inform the suspect of an attorney's efforts to contact him would contribute to the protection of the Fifth Amendment privilege only incidentally, if at all. This minimal benefit, however, would come at a substantial cost to society's legitimate and substantial interest in securing admissions of guilt. Indeed, the very premise of the Court of Appeals was not that awareness of Ms. Munson's phone call would have dissipated the coercion of the interrogation room, but that it might have convinced respondent not to speak at all. Because neither the letter nor purposes of *Miranda* require this additional handicap on otherwise permissible investigatory efforts, we are unwilling to expand the *Miranda* rules to require the police to keep the suspect abreast of the status of his legal representation.

[Respondent] also contends that the Sixth Amendment requires exclusion of his three confessions. [We agree] that once the right *has* attached, it follows that the police may not interfere with the efforts of a defendant's attorney to act as a " 'medium' between [the suspect] and the State" during the interrogation. The difficulty for respondent is that the interrogation sessions that yielded the inculpatory statements took place *before* the initiation of "adversary judicial proceedings." He contends, however, that this circumstance is not fatal to his Sixth Amendment claim. At least in some situations, he argues, the Sixth Amendment protects the integrity of the attorney-client relationship regardless of whether the prosecution has in fact commenced "by way of formal charge, preliminary hearing, indictment, information or arraignment."

We are not persuaded. At the outset, subsequent decisions foreclose any reliance on *Escobedo* and *Miranda* for the proposition that the Sixth Amendment right, in any of its manifestations, applies prior to the initiation of adversary judicial proceedings. * * *

Questions of precedent to one side, we find respondent's understanding of the Sixth Amendment both practically and theoretically unsound. As a practical matter, it makes little sense to say that the Sixth Amendment right to counsel attaches at different times depending on the fortuity of whether the suspect or his family happens to have retained counsel prior to interrogation. More importantly, the suggestion that the existence of an attorney-client relationship itself triggers the protections of the Sixth Amendment misconceives the underlying purposes of the right to counsel. The Sixth Amendment's intended function is not to wrap a protective cloak around the attorney-client relationship for its own sake any more than it is to protect a suspect from the consequences of his own candor. [By] its very terms, [the Sixth Amendment] becomes applicable only when the government's role shifts from investigation to accusation. * * *

Finally, respondent contends that the conduct of the police was so offensive as to deprive him of the fundamental fairness guaranteed by the Due Process Clause of the Fourteenth Amendment. Focusing primarily on the impropriety of conveying false information to an attorney, he invites us to declare that such behavior should be condemned as violative of canons fundamental to the " 'traditions and conscience of our people.' " *Rochin*. We do not question that on facts more egregious than those presented here police deception might rise to a level of a due process violation. Accordingly, Justice Stevens' apocalyptic suggestion that we have approved any and all forms of police misconduct is demonstrably incorrect.[4] We hold only that, on these facts, the challenged conduct falls short of the kind of misbehavior that so shocks the sensibilities of civilized society as to warrant a federal intrusion into the criminal processes of the States. * * *

JUSTICE STEVENS, with whom JUSTICE BRENNAN and JUSTICE MARSHALL join, dissenting.

This case poses fundamental questions about our system of justice. As this Court has long recognized, * * * "ours is an accusatorial and not an inquisitorial system." The Court's opinion today represents a startling departure from that basic insight.

[The] Court's holding focuses on the period after a suspect has been taken into custody and before he has been charged with an offense. The core of the Court's holding is that police interference with an attorney's access to her client during that period is not unconstitutional. The Court reasons that a State has a compelling interest, not simply in custodial interrogation, but in lawyer-free, incommunicado custodial interrogation. Such incommunicado interrogation is so important that a lawyer may be given false information that prevents her presence and representation; it is so important that police may refuse to inform a suspect of his attorney's communications and immediate availability.[8] This conclusion flies in the face of this Court's repeated expressions of deep concern

---

4. [The] dissent's misreading of *Miranda* itself is breathtaking in its scope. For example, it reads *Miranda* as creating an undifferentiated right to the presence of an attorney that is triggered automatically by the initiation of the interrogation itself. Yet, as both *Miranda* and subsequent decisions construing *Miranda* make clear beyond refute, " 'the interrogation must cease until an attorney is present' *only* '[i]f the individual states that he wants an attorney.' " *Michigan v. Mosley* (emphasis added). The dissent condemns us for embracing "incommunicado questioning [as] a societal goal of the highest order that justifies police deception of the shabbiest kind." We, of course, do nothing of the kind. As any reading of *Miranda* reveals, the decision, rather than proceeding from the premise that the rights and needs of the defendant are paramount to all others, embodies a carefully crafted balance designed to fully protect *both* the defendant's and society's interests. The dissent may not share our view that the Fifth Amendment rights of the defendant are amply protected by application of *Miranda as written*. But the dissent is "simply wrong" in suggesting that exclusion of Burbine's three confessions fol-

lows perfunctorily from *Miranda's* mandate. Y. Kamisar, *Police Interrogation and Confessions* 217–218, n. 94 (1980).

Quite understandably, the dissent is outraged by the very idea of police deception of a lawyer. Significantly less understandable is its willingness to misconstrue this Court's constitutional holdings in order to implement its subjective notions of sound policy.

8. This kind of police-maintained incommunicado questioning becomes, in the Court's rendition, "an essential part of the investigatory process." Police interference in communications between a lawyer and her client are justified because "[a]dmissions of guilt [are] essential to society's compelling interest in finding, convicting, and punishing those who violate the law." It is this overriding interest in obtaining self-incriminatory statements in the lawyer-free privacy of the police interrogation room that motivates the Court's willingness to swallow its admitted "distaste for the deliberate misleading of an officer of the court."

about incommunicado questioning. Until today, incommunicado questioning has been viewed with the strictest scrutiny by this Court; today, incommunicado questioning is embraced as a societal goal of the highest order that justifies police deception of the shabbiest kind. * * *

Police interference with communications between an attorney and his client is a recurrent problem. The factual variations in the many state court opinions condemning this interference as a violation of the federal Constitution suggest the variety of contexts in which the problem emerges. In Oklahoma, police led a lawyer to several different locations while they interrogated the suspect; in Oregon, police moved a suspect to a new location when they learned that his lawyer was on his way; in Illinois, authorities failed to tell a suspect that his lawyer had arrived at the jail and asked to see him; in Massachusetts, police did not tell suspects that their lawyers were at or near the police station. In all these cases, the police not only failed to inform the suspect, but also misled the attorneys. The scenarios vary, but the core problem of police interference remains.

[The] near-consensus of state courts and the legal profession's Standards about this recurrent problem lends powerful support to the conclusion that police may not interfere with communications between an attorney and the client whom they are questioning. Indeed, at least two opinions from this Court seemed to express precisely that view. The Court today flatly rejects that widely held view and responds to this recurrent problem by adopting the most restrictive interpretation of the federal constitutional restraints on police deception, misinformation, and interference in attorney-client communications. * * *

Well-settled principles of law lead inexorably to the conclusion that the failure to inform Burbine of the call from his attorney makes the subsequent waiver of his constitutional rights invalid. Analysis should begin with an acknowledgment that the burden of proving the validity of a waiver of constitutional rights is always on the *government.* When such a waiver occurs in a custodial setting, that burden is an especially heavy one because custodial interrogation is inherently coercive, because disinterested witnesses are seldom available to describe what actually happened, and because history has taught us that the danger of over-reaching during incommunicado interrogation is so real.

In applying this heavy presumption against the validity of waivers, this Court has sometimes relied on a case-by-case totality of the circumstances analysis. We have found, however, that some custodial interrogation situations require strict presumptions against the validity of a waiver. *Miranda* established that a waiver is not valid in the absence of certain warnings. *Edwards* similarly established that a waiver is not valid if police initiate questioning after the defendant has invoked his right to counsel. In these circumstances, the waiver is invalid as a matter of law even if the evidence overwhelmingly establishes, as a matter of fact, that "a suspect's decision not to rely on his rights was uncoerced, that he at all times knew that he could stand mute and request a lawyer, and that he was aware of the state's intention to use his statement to secure a conviction." In light of our decision in *Edwards,* the Court is simply wrong in stating that "the analysis is complete and the waiver is valid as a matter of law" when these facts have been established. Like the failure to give warnings and like police initiation of interrogation after a request for counsel, police deception of a suspect through omission of information regarding attorney communications greatly exacerbates the inherent problems of incommunicado interrogation and requires a clear principle to safeguard the presumption against the waiver of constitutional rights.

As in those situations, the police deception should render a subsequent waiver invalid.

Indeed, as *Miranda* itself makes clear, proof that the required warnings have been given is a necessary, but by no means sufficient, condition for establishing a valid waiver. As the Court plainly stated in *Miranda,* "any evidence that the accused was threatened, tricked, or cajoled into a waiver will, of course, show that the defendant did not voluntarily waive his privilege. The requirement of warnings and waiver of rights is a fundamental with respect to the Fifth Amendment privilege and not simply a preliminary ritual to existing methods of interrogation."

In this case it would be perfectly clear that Burbine's waiver was invalid if, for example, Detective Ferranti had "threatened, tricked, or cajoled" Burbine in their private pre-confession meeting—perhaps by misdescribing the statements obtained from DiOrio and Sparks—even though, under the Court's truncated analysis of the issue, Burbine fully understood his rights. For *Miranda* clearly condemns threats or trickery that cause a suspect to make an unwise waiver of his rights even though he fully understands those rights. In my opinion there can be no constitutional distinction—as the Court appears to draw—between a deceptive misstatement and the concealment by the police of the critical fact that an attorney retained by the accused or his family has offered assistance, either by telephone or in person.

Thus, the Court's truncated analysis, which relies in part on a distinction between deception accomplished by means of an omission of a critically important fact and deception by means of a misleading statement, is simply untenable. If, as the Court asserts, "the analysis is at an end" as soon as the suspect is provided with enough information to have the *capacity* to understand and exercise his rights, I see no reason why the police should not be permitted to make the same kind of misstatements to the suspect that they are apparently allowed to make to his lawyer. *Miranda,* however, clearly establishes that both kinds of deception vitiate the suspect's waiver of his right to counsel.

[The] Court makes the alternative argument that requiring police to inform a suspect of his attorney's communications to and about him is not required because it would upset the careful "balance" of *Miranda.* Despite its earlier notion that the attorney's call is an "outside event" that has "no bearing" on a knowing and intelligent waiver, the majority does acknowledge that information of attorney Munson's call "would have been useful to respondent" and "might have affected his decision to confess." Thus, a rule requiring the police to inform a suspect of an attorney's call would have two predictable effects. It would serve *"Miranda's* goal of dispelling the compulsion inherent in custodial interrogation" and it would disserve the goal of custodial interrogation because it would result in fewer confessions. By a process of balancing these two concerns, the Court finds the benefit to the individual outweighed by the "substantial cost to society's legitimate and substantial interest in securing admissions of guilt."

The Court's balancing approach is profoundly misguided. The cost of suppressing evidence of guilt will always make the value of a procedural safeguard appear "minimal," "marginal," or "incremental." Indeed, the value of any trial at all seems like a "procedural technicality" when balanced against the interest in administering prompt justice to a murderer or a rapist caught redhanded. The individual interest in procedural safeguards that minimize the risk of error is easily discounted when the fact of guilt appears certain beyond doubt.

What is the cost of requiring the police to inform a suspect of his attorney's call? It would decrease the likelihood that custodial interrogation will enable the police to obtain a confession. This is certainly a real cost, but it is the same cost that this Court has repeatedly found necessary to preserve the character of our free society and our rejection of an inquisitorial system. * * *

Just as the "cost" does not justify taking a suspect into custody or interrogating him without giving him warnings simply because police desire to question him, so too the "cost" does not justify permitting police to withhold from a suspect knowledge of an attorney's communication, even though that communication would have an unquestionable effect on the suspect's exercise of his rights. The "cost" that concerns the Court amounts to nothing more than an acknowledgment that the law enforcement interest in obtaining convictions suffers whenever a suspect exercises the rights that are afforded by our system of criminal justice. In other words, it is the fear that an individual may exercise his rights that tips the scales of justice for the Court today. The principle that ours is an accusatorial, not an inquisitorial, system, however, has repeatedly led the Court to reject that fear as a valid reason for inhibiting the invocation of rights.

[At] the time attorney Munson made her call to the Cranston Police Station, she was acting as Burbine's attorney. Under ordinary principles of agency law the deliberate deception of Munson was tantamount to deliberate deception of her client. If an attorney makes a mistake in the course of her representation of her client, the client must accept the consequences of that mistake. It is equally clear that when an attorney makes an inquiry on behalf of her client, the client is entitled to a truthful answer. Surely the client must have the same remedy for a false representation to his lawyer that he would have if he were acting *pro se* and had propounded the question himself.

The majority brushes aside the police deception involved in the misinformation of attorney Munson. It is irrelevant to the Fifth Amendment analysis, concludes the majority, because that right is personal; it is irrelevant to the Sixth Amendment analysis, continues the majority, because the Sixth Amendment does not apply until formal adversary proceedings have begun.

In my view, as a matter of law, the police deception of Munson was tantamount to deception of Burbine himself. It constituted a violation of Burbine's right to have an attorney present during the questioning that began shortly thereafter. The existence of that right is undisputed. Whether the source of that right is the Sixth Amendment, the Fifth Amendment, or a combination of the two is of no special importance, for I do not understand the Court to deny the existence of the right.

The pertinent question is whether police deception of the attorney is utterly irrelevant to that right. In my judgment, it blinks at reality to suggest that misinformation which prevented the presence of an attorney has no bearing on the protection and effectuation of the right to counsel in custodial interrogation. The majority parses the role of attorney and suspect so narrowly that the deception of the attorney is of no constitutional significance. [The] character of the attorney-client relationship requires rejection of the Court's notion that the attorney is some entirely distinct, completely severable entity and that deception of the attorney is irrelevant to the right of counsel in custodial interrogation.[53]

53. Prevailing norms of legal practice prevent a lawyer from communicating with a party, rather than a lawyer. See Disciplinary Rule 7–104(A)(1), ABA Code of Professional Responsibility ("During the course of his representation of a client a lawyer shall not: Com-

[In] sharp contrast to the majority, I firmly believe that the right to counsel at custodial interrogation is infringed by police treatment of an attorney that prevents or impedes the attorney's representation of the suspect at that interrogation.

[In] my judgment, police interference in the attorney-client relationship is the type of governmental misconduct on a matter of central importance to the administration of justice that the Due Process Clause prohibits. Just as the police cannot impliedly promise a suspect that his silence will not be used against him and then proceed to break that promise, so too police cannot tell a suspect's attorney that they will not question the suspect and then proceed to question him. Just as the government cannot conceal from a suspect material and exculpatory evidence, so too the government cannot conceal from a suspect the material fact of his attorney's communication.

Police interference with communications between an attorney and his client violates the due process requirement of fundamental fairness. Burbine's attorney was given completely false information about the lack of questioning; moreover, she was not told that her client would be questioned regarding a murder charge about which she was unaware. Burbine, in turn, was not told that his attorney had phoned and that she had been informed that he would not be questioned. Quite simply, the Rhode Island police effectively drove a wedge between an attorney and a suspect through misinformation and omissions.

The majority does not "question that on facts more egregious than those presented here police deception might rise to the level of a due process violation." In my view, the police deception disclosed by this record plainly does rise to that level.

This case turns on a proper appraisal of the role of the lawyer in our society. If a lawyer is seen as a nettlesome obstacle to the pursuit of wrongdoers—as in an inquisitorial society—then the Court's decision today makes a good deal of sense. If a lawyer is seen as an aid to the understanding and protection of constitutional rights—as in an accusatorial society—then today's decision makes no sense at all.
* * *

Note: **Massiah *Revisited*; Massiah *and* Miranda *Compared and Contrasted***

Until the Court handed down its decision in *Brewer v. Williams*, 430 U.S. 387, 97 S.Ct. 1232, 51 L.Ed.2d 424 (1977), often called the "Christian burial speech" case,[a] lasting fame had eluded *Massiah v. United States*, p. 213, supra. Many

municate or cause another to communicate on the subject of the representation with a party he knows to be represented by a lawyer in that matter unless he has the prior consent of the lawyer representing such other party or is authorized by law to do so"). * * *

a. On the day before Christmas, a 10-year-old girl disappeared while with her family in Des Moines, Iowa. Defendant Williams, an escapee from a mental institution and a deeply religious person who considered himself a preacher, was suspected of murdering the young girl, and a warrant was issued for his arrest. The day after Christmas, on the advice of his lawyer, Williams surrendered himself to the Davenport, Iowa, police. Captain Leaming and another Des Moines detective went to Davenport to pick up Williams and drive him back to Des Moines (some 160 miles away). By the time the two Des Moines detective arrived in

Davenport, adversary judicial proceedings had already against Williams and he had already retained local counsel. On the return trip, admittedly in an effort to induce Williams to reveal the location of the girl's body, Leaming made his "Christian burial" remarks—and even called Williams "Reverend." Leaming told Williams:

"They are predicting several inches of snow for tonight, and I feel that you yourself are the only person that knows where this little girl's body is, * * * and if you get a snow on top of it, you yourself may be unable to find it. * * * I feel that we could stop and locate the body, that the parents of this little girl should be entitled to a Christian burial for the little girl who was snatched away from them on Christmas Eve and murdered. And I feel we should stop and locate it on the way in rather than waiting until morning and trying to come back

thought that *Massiah* had only been a stepping stone to *Escobedo*, decided a scant five weeks later, and both cases had been displaced by *Miranda*. But *Brewer v. Williams* made plain that despite the Court's shift from a "right to counsel" base in *Escobedo* to a "compelled self-incrimination base" in *Miranda*, the *Massiah* doctrine was alive and well. Indeed, although few, if any, would have predicted it, during the Burger Court era, the *Massiah* doctrine emerged as a much more potent force than it had ever been in the Warren Court era.

In the process of reviving *Massiah*, however, *Brewer v. Williams* blurred the *Massiah* and *Miranda* rationales. Although this is not clear from the *Williams* opinion, application of *Massiah* turns on neither "custody" nor "interrogation," the key *Miranda* concepts. Rather, the *Massiah* doctrine represents a pure right to counsel approach.

Once adversary proceedings have commenced against an individual (e.g., he has been indicted or arraigned) he is entitled to the assistance of counsel and the government may not "deliberately elicit" incriminating statements from him, neither openly by uniformed police officers nor surreptitiously by "secret agents." This prohibition applies regardless of whether the individual is in "custody" or being subjected to "interrogation" in the *Miranda* sense. There need not be any compelling influences at work, inherent, informal or otherwise. (There certainly were not any in the *Massiah* case itself.)

Nevertheless, perhaps because the lower courts had treated *Williams* as a *Miranda* case, a majority of the *Williams* Court thought it important, if not crucial, to establish that the "Christian burial speech" delivered by Captain Leaming did constitute "interrogation"—and all four dissenters insisted it was not. Considering the Court's subsequent discussion of "interrogation" in *Rhode Island v. Innis* [p. 254 supra], the captain's "speech" does appear to have been a form of "*Miranda* interrogation," but *it did not have to be,* in order for the *Massiah* doctrine to have protected Williams.

United States v. Henry, 447 U.S. 264, 100 S.Ct. 2183, 65 L.Ed.2d 115 (1980), not only reaffirmed the *Massiah–Williams* doctrine, but expanded it by applying it to a situation where the FBI had instructed its paid government informant, ostensibly defendant's "cellmate," not to question defendant about the crime, and there was no showing that he had. Nevertheless, the Court, per Burger, C.J., rejected the government's argument that the incriminating statements were not the result of any "affirmative conduct" on the part of government agents to elicit evidence. The informant "was not a passive listener; rather he had 'some conversations with Mr. Henry' while he was in jail and Henry's incriminatory statements were 'the product of this conversation.'"

Moreover, and more generally, observed the Court: Even if the FBI agent's statement is accepted that "he did not intend that [the informant] would take affirmative steps to secure incriminating information, he must have known that such propinquity likely would lead to that result. [By] intentionally creating a situation likely to induce Henry to make incriminating statements without the assistance of counsel [after Henry had been indicted and counsel had been

out after a snow storm and possibly not being able to find it at all."

Several hours after Captain Leaming made these remarks, and before Leaming's car had reached Des Moines, Williams directed the detectives to the body of the missing girl. The trial court admitted Williams' incriminating statements and he was convicted of murder.

On federal habeas corpus, a 5–4 majority of the Court, per Stewart, J. (author of the *Massiah* opinion), reversed the conviction, viewing the circumstances of the case "constitutionally indistinguishable from those presented in *Massiah*. That the incriminating statements were elicited surreptitiously in [*Massiah*], and otherwise here, is constitutionally irrelevant."

appointed for him], the government violated Henry's Sixth Amendment right to counsel."

This broad—some would say, loose—language would seem to prohibit the government from "planting" even a completely "passive" secret agent in a person's cell once adversary proceedings have commenced against him. But the *Henry* Court cautioned that it was not "called upon to pass on the situation where an informant is placed in [close] proximity [to a prisoner] but makes no effort to stimulate conversations about the crime charged." Moreover, concurring Justice Powell made it plain that he could not join the majority opinion if it held that "the mere presence or incidental conversation of an informant in a jail cell would violate *Massiah*." The *Massiah* doctrine, emphasized Powell, "does not prohibit the introduction of spontaneous conversations that are not elicited by governmental action."

May the government employ a "passive informant" without violating the *Massiah* doctrine? Must the informant be—is it possible for him to be—completely "passive"? Six years after its ruling in *Henry*, the Court shed some light on these questions in another "jail plant" case, *Kuhlmann v. Wilson*, 477 U.S. 436, 106 S.Ct. 2616, 91 L.Ed.2d 364 (1986). The facts seemed quite similar to the situation in *Henry*, but this time a 6–3 majority, per Powell, J., agreed with the district court that the police informant posing as respondent's fellow-prisoner had made "no affirmative effort" of any kind to elicit information from respondent and thus the latter's "spontaneous" and "unsolicited" remarks were admissible. As *Kuhlmann* well illustrates, the line between "active" and "passive" secret agents—between "*stimulating*" conversations with a defendant in order to "elicit" incriminating statements from him and taking no action "beyond *merely listening*"—is an exceedingly difficult one to draw.

SECTION 4. LINEUPS AND OTHER PRE-TRIAL IDENTIFICATION PROCEDURES

Introduction

Although mistaken identification has probably been the single greatest cause of conviction of the innocent, the Supreme Court did not come to grips with this problem until surprisingly late in the day. When it finally did, in 1967, the Court seemed bent on making up for lost time. Although it might have undertaken a case-by-case analysis of various identification situations, as had been done in the confession area in the thirty years prior to *Escobedo* and *Miranda*, only throwing out convictions based on unreliable identifications, the Court leapfrogged the fairness stage and applied the right to counsel to pretrial identifications in one swoop.

As explained in *United States v. Wade*, the first case set forth in this section, the right to counsel in the lineup context is supportive of another right—in this instance, the right to confrontation—in much the same manner that the *Miranda* counsel requirement rests upon the privilege against self-incrimination. (But see *Kirby v. Illinois*, the second case in this chapter.) For various reasons spelled out in the *Wade* opinion, under past lineup practices the defense was often unable "meaningfully to attack the credibility of the witness' courtroom identification." Moreover, pointed out the Court, the need to learn what occurred at the lineup is great, the risk of improper suggestion is substantial, and once the witness has picked out the accused in a pretrial identification proceeding, she is unlikely to go back on her word in court.[a]

Absent circumstances that presented "substantial countervailing policy considerations * * * against the requirement of the presence of counsel" (the Court may have had in mind "alley confrontations," i.e., prompt confrontations with the victim or an eyewitness at the scene of the crime),[b] the 1967 cases seemed to require the presence of counsel at *all* pretrial identifications. The pretrial identifications in *Wade* and *Gilbert* did take place after the defendants had been indicted, and the Court did mention this fact. But such references seemed—and most lower courts considered them to be—merely descriptive of the facts before the Court in those cases, not meant to restrict the operation of the new rule. For nothing in the *Wade* Court's reasoning suggested that a lineup or showup held before formal judicial proceedings begin—which is usually the case—is less riddled with dangers or less difficult for a suspect to reconstruct then one occurring after that point.

Nevertheless, in *Kirby v. Illinois* (1972), the second case in this chapter, the Court did announce a "post-indictment" rule—over the dissent of Justice Brennan, author of the *Wade* and *Gilbert* opinions. Following *Kirby* it became the common practice of law enforcement agencies to avoid the applicability of the right to counsel by conducting identification proceedings before the filing of formal charges.

A year after *Kirby,* the Burger Court struck the *Wade–Gilbert* rule another blow. This time, however, the Court's ruling confirmed the great weight of lower court authority. Unmoved by the argument that the availability of the photographs at trial provides no protection against the suggestive manner in which they may have been originally displayed to the witness or the comments or gestures that may have accompanied the display, the Court ruled in *United States v. Ash* (1973) (discussed infra, in a footnote to *Kirby*) that photographic identification may take place without defense counsel's participation, whether conducted before or after the filing of formal charges, and even though the suspect could have appeared in person at a lineup. Throughout the expansion of the constitutional right to counsel to certain pretrial proceedings, observed the Court, "the function of the lawyer has remained essentially the same as his function at trial"—to assist the accused "in meeting his adversary." But at a photo-identification, unlike a lineup, there is no "trial-like confrontation" involving the "presence of the accused." Again the author of *Wade* and *Gilbert,* Justice Brennan, was among those who dissented.[c]

---

a. *Wade* and *Gilbert* also raised a self-incrimination issue. Relying on *Schmerber v. California,* 384 U.S. 757, 86 S.Ct. 1826, 16 L.Ed.2d 908 (1966), a 5–4 majority ruled that requiring a person to appear in a lineup and to speak for identification (*Wade*) or to provide handwriting exemplars (*Gilbert*) did not violate the privilege. In *Schmerber,* which involved the taking of a blood sample, over his objection, from a person arrested for drunken driving, the Court rejected the contention that the defendant had been "compelled [to] be a witness against himself" in violation of the Fifth Amendment. The self-incrimination clause, observed the Court, "protects an accused only [from] provid[ing] the State with evidence of a testimonial or communicative nature."

b. Even prior to *Kirby v. Illinois,* which limited the 1967 cases to post-indictment identifications, the great majority of lower courts had exempted alley confrontations from the right to counsel requirement.

c. The Warren Court had carved out an exception to the *Wade–Gilbert* rule for pretrial photographic identifications, but apparently a narrow one. In concluding that there was no right to have counsel present at the photo-identification in *Simmons v. United States,* 390 U.S. 377, 88 S.Ct. 967, 19 L.Ed.2d 1247 (1968) and, alternatively, that the procedures utilized in that case were not "impermissively suggestive," the Court stressed, first, that at the time the witnesses viewed the photographs for identification purposes "the perpetrators were still at large" and "it was essential for the FBI

I. *WADE* AND *GILBERT*: CONSTITUTIONAL CONCERN ABOUT THE DANGERS INVOLVED IN EYEWITNESS IDENTIFICATIONS

UNITED STATES v. WADE

388 U.S. 218, 87 S.Ct. 1926, 18 L.Ed.2d 1149 (1967).

JUSTICE BRENNAN delivered the opinion of the Court.

The question here is whether courtroom identifications of an accused at trial are to be excluded from evidence because the accused was exhibited to the witnesses before trial at a post-indictment lineup conducted for identification purposes without notice to and in the absence of the accused's appointed counsel.

The federally insured bank in Eustace, Texas, was robbed on September 21, 1964. A man with a small strip of tape on each side of his face entered the bank, pointed a pistol at the female cashier and the vice president, the only persons in the bank at the time, and forced them to fill a pillowcase with the bank's money. The man then drove away with an accomplice who had been waiting in a stolen car outside the bank. On March 23, 1965, an indictment was returned against respondent, Wade, and two others for conspiring to rob the bank, and against Wade and the accomplice for the robbery itself. Wade was arrested on April 2, and counsel was appointed to represent him on April 26. Fifteen days later [after counsel was appointed] an FBI agent, without notice to Wade's lawyer, arranged to have the two bank employees observe a lineup made up of Wade and five or six other prisoners and conducted in a courtroom of the local county courthouse. Each person in the line wore strips of tape such as allegedly worn by the robber and upon direction each said something like "put the money in the bag," the words allegedly uttered by the robber. Both bank employees identified Wade in the lineup as the bank robber.

At trial the two employees, when asked on direct examination if the robber was in the courtroom, pointed to Wade. The prior lineup identification was then elicited from both employees on cross-examination. At the close of testimony, Wade's counsel moved [to] strike the bank officials' courtroom identifications on [self-incrimination and right to counsel grounds]. The motion was denied, and Wade was convicted. The Court of Appeals for the Fifth Circuit reversed the conviction and ordered a new trial at which the in-court identification evidence was to be excluded, holding that [conducting the lineup in the absence of Wade's appointed counsel violated his Sixth Amendment rights].

[T]he principle of *Powell v. Alabama* and succeeding cases requires that we scrutinize *any* pretrial confrontation of the accused to determine whether the presence of his counsel is necessary to preserve the defendant's basic right to a fair trial as affected by his right meaningfully to cross-examine the witnesses against him and to have effective assistance of counsel at the trial itself. It calls upon us to analyze whether potential substantial prejudice to defendant's rights

agents swiftly to determine whether they were on the right track"; and second, that the witnesses were shown the photographs "only a day [after the bank robbery] while their memories were still fresh."

In *Ash*, although the defendant had been indicted, had been appointed counsel, and had been in detention for more than two years prior to trial, a photo-identification was conducted in the absence of counsel a day before the trial began. It was a photo display that seemed designed more to prompt the witness than to secure an identification.

inheres in the particular confrontation and the ability of counsel to help avoid that prejudice.

The Government characterizes the lineup as a mere preparatory step in the gathering of the prosecution's evidence, not different—for Sixth Amendment purposes—from various other preparatory steps, such as systematized or scientific analyzing of the accused's fingerprints, blood sample, clothing, hair, and the like. We think there are differences which preclude such stages being characterized as critical stages at which the accused has the right to the presence of his counsel. Knowledge of the techniques of science and technology is sufficiently available, and the variables in techniques few enough, that the accused has the opportunity for a meaningful confrontation of the Government's case at trial through the ordinary processes of cross-examination of the Government's expert witnesses and the presentation of the evidence of his own experts. The denial of a right to have his counsel present at such analyses does not therefore violate the Sixth Amendment; they are not critical stages since there is minimal risk that his counsel's absence at such stages might derogate from his right to a fair trial.[a]

But the confrontation compelled by the State between the accused and the victim or witnesses to a crime to elicit identification evidence is peculiarly riddled with innumerable dangers and variable factors which might seriously, even crucially, derogate from a fair trial. The vagaries of eyewitness identification are well-known; the annals of criminal law are rife with instances of mistaken identification. [A] major factor contributing to the high incidence of miscarriage of justice from mistaken identification has been the degree of suggestion inherent in the manner in which the prosecution presents the suspect to witnesses for pretrial identification. A commentator has observed that "[t]he influence of improper suggestion upon identifying witnesses probably accounts for more miscarriages of justice than any other single factor—perhaps it is responsible for more such errors than all other factors combined." Wall, *Eye–Witness Identification in Criminal Cases* 26 [1965]. Suggestion can be created intentionally or unintentionally in many subtle ways. And the dangers for the suspect are particularly grave when the witness' opportunity for observation was insubstantial, and thus his susceptibility to suggestion the greatest.

Moreover, "[i]t is a matter of common experience that, once a witness has picked out the accused at the line-up, he is not likely to go back on his word later on, so that in practice the issue of identity may (in the absence of other relevant evidence) for all practical purposes be determined there and then, before the trial."

The pretrial confrontation for purpose of identification may take the form of a lineup, also known as an "identification parade" or "showup," as in the present case, or presentation of the suspect alone to the witness, as in *Stovall v. Denno*.[b]

---

a. Consider, too, the companion case of *Gilbert v. California,* where the Court held, 5–4 on this issue, that the taking of handwriting exemplars from petitioner "was not a 'critical' stage of the criminal proceedings entitling petitioner to the assistance of counsel" for "there is minimal risk that the absence of counsel might derogate from his right to a fair trial. [If,] for some reason, an unrepresentative exemplar is taken, this can be brought out and corrected through the adversary process at trial since the accused can make an unlimited number of additional exemplars for analysis and comparison by government and defense handwriting experts."

b. In *Stovall v. Denno,* 388 U.S. 293, 87 S.Ct. 1967, 18 L.Ed.2d 1199 (1967), the Court noted the practice of showing suspects singly to potential witnesses "has been widely condemned," but held that under the extraordinary circumstances of the case ("an immediate hospital confrontation was imperative" because it appeared that the sole eye witness was near death) the one-person showing was justified.

It is obvious that risks of suggestion attend either form of confrontation and increase the dangers inhering in eyewitness identification. But as is the case with secret interrogations, there is serious difficulty in depicting what transpires at lineups and other forms of identification confrontations. [For] the same reasons, the defense can seldom reconstruct the manner and mode of lineup identification for judge or jury at trial. [The] impediments to an objective observation are increased when the victim is the witness. Lineups are prevalent in rape and robbery prosecutions and present a particular hazard that a victim's understandable outrage may excite vengeful or spiteful motives. In any event, neither witnesses nor lineup participants are apt to be alert for conditions prejudicial to the suspect. And if they were, it would likely be of scant benefit to the suspect since neither witnesses nor lineup participants are likely to be schooled in the detection of suggestive influences.[13] Improper influences may go undetected by a suspect, guilty or not, who experiences the emotional tension which we might expect in one being confronted with potential accusers. Even when he does observe abuse, if he has a criminal record he may be reluctant to take the stand and open up the admission of prior convictions. Moreover any protestations by the suspect of the fairness of the lineup made at trial are likely to be in vain; the jury's choice is between the accused's unsupported version and that of the police officers present. In short, the accused's inability effectively to reconstruct at trial any unfairness that occurred at the lineup may deprive him of his only opportunity meaningfully to attack the credibility of the witness' courtroom identification.

[The] potential for improper influence is illustrated by the circumstances, insofar as they appear, surrounding the prior identifications in the three cases we decide today. In the present case, the testimony of the identifying witnesses elicited on cross-examination revealed that those witnesses were taken to the courthouse and seated in the courtroom to await assembly of the lineup. The courtroom faced on a hallway observable to the witnesses through an open door. The cashier testified that she saw Wade "standing in the hall" within sight of an FBI agent. Five or six other prisoners later appeared in the hall. The vice president testified that he saw a person in the hall in the custody of the agent who "resembled the person that we identified as the one that had entered the bank."

The lineup in *Gilbert* was conducted in an auditorium in which some 100 witnesses to several alleged state and federal robberies charged to Gilbert made wholesale identifications of Gilbert as the robber in each other's presence, a procedure said to be fraught with dangers of suggestion. And the vice of suggestion created by the identification in *Stovall* was the presentation to the witness of the suspect alone handcuffed to police officers. It is hard to imagine a situation more clearly conveying the suggestion to the witness that the one presented is believed guilty by the police.

The few cases that have surfaced therefore reveal the existence of a process attended with hazards of serious unfairness to the criminal accused and strongly suggest the plight of the more numerous defendants who are unable to ferret out suggestive influences in the secrecy of the confrontation. We do not assume that these risks are the result of police procedures intentionally designed to prejudice an accused. Rather we assume they derive from the dangers inherent in eyewitness identification and the suggestibility inherent in the context of the pretrial identification. * * *

---

13. An additional impediment to the detection of such influences by participants, including the suspect, is the physical conditions often surrounding the conduct of the lineup. In many, lights shine on the stage in such a way that the suspect cannot see the witness. [In] some a one-way mirror is used and what is said on the witness' side cannot be heard. * * *

Insofar as the accused's conviction may rest on a courtroom identification in fact the fruit of a suspect pretrial identification which the accused is helpless to subject to effective scrutiny at trial, the accused is deprived of that right of cross-examination which is an essential safeguard to his right to confront the witnesses against him. And even though cross-examination is a precious safeguard to a fair trial, it cannot be viewed as an absolute assurance of accuracy and reliability. Thus in the present context, where so many variables and pitfalls exist, the first line of defense must be the prevention of unfairness and the lessening of the hazards of eyewitness identification at the lineup itself. The trial which might determine the accused's fate may well not be that in the courtroom but that at the pretrial confrontation, with the State aligned against the accused, the witness the sole jury, and the accused unprotected against the overreaching, intentional or unintentional, and with little or no effective appeal from the judgment there rendered by the witness—"that's the man."

Since it appears that there is grave potential for prejudice, intentional or not, in the pretrial lineup, which may not be capable of reconstruction at trial, and since presence of counsel itself can often avert prejudice and assure a meaningful confrontation at trial, there can be little doubt that for Wade the post-indictment lineup was a critical stage of the prosecution at which he was "as much entitled to such aid [of counsel as] at the trial itself." *Powell v. Alabama.* Thus both Wade and his counsel should have been notified of the impending lineup, and counsel's presence should have been a requisite to conduct of the lineup, absent an "intelligent waiver." No substantial countervailing policy considerations have been advanced against the requirement of the presence of counsel. Concern is expressed that the requirement will forestall prompt identifications and result in obstruction of the confrontations. As for the first, we note that in the two cases in which the right to counsel is today held to apply, counsel had already been appointed and no argument is made in either case that notice to counsel would have prejudicially delayed the confrontations. Moreover, we leave open the question whether the presence of substitute counsel might not suffice where notification and presence of the suspect's own counsel would result in prejudicial delay. And to refuse to recognize the right to counsel for fear that counsel will obstruct the course of justice is contrary to the basic assumptions upon which this Court has operated in Sixth Amendment cases. [In] our view counsel can hardly impede legitimate law enforcement; on the contrary, for the reasons expressed, law enforcement may be assisted by preventing the infiltration of taint in the prosecution's identification evidence. That result cannot help the guilty avoid conviction but can only help assure that the right many has been brought to justice.

Legislative or other regulations, such as those of local police departments, which eliminate the risks of abuse and unintentional suggestion at lineup proceedings and the impediments to meaningful confrontation at trial may also remove the basis for regarding the stage as "critical." But neither Congress nor the federal authorities have seen fit to provide a solution.[c]

We come now to the question whether the denial of Wade's motion to strike the courtroom identification by the bank witnesses at trial because of the absence

c. Nor, it seems, is a solution provided by 18 U.S.C. § 3502, a part of the Omnibus Crime Control and Safe Streets Act of 1968, which states that "the testimony of a witness that he saw the accused commit [the] crime" is admissible in a federal court. This appears to be an unconstitutional attempt to "repeal" *Wade.* According to several commentators, the lower federal courts have ignored this statute and it exists on the books more as an expression of legislative hope than as a binding rule.

of his counsel at the lineup required, as the Court of Appeals held, the grant of a new trial at which such evidence is to be excluded. We do not think this disposition can be justified without first giving the Government the opportunity to establish by clear and convincing evidence that the in-court identifications were based upon observations of the suspect other than the lineup identification. * * * Where, as here, the admissibility of evidence of the lineup identification itself is not involved, a *per se* rule of exclusion of courtroom identification would be unjustified.[d] [A] rule limited solely to the exclusion of testimony concerning identification at the lineup itself, without regard to admissibility of the courtroom identification, would render the right to counsel an empty one. The lineup is most often used, as in the present case, to crystallize the witnesses' identification of the defendant for future reference. We have already noted that the lineup identification will have that effect. The State may then rest upon the witnesses' unequivocal courtroom identification, and not mention the pretrial identification as part of the State's case at trial. Counsel is then in the predicament in which Wade's counsel found himself—realizing that possible unfairness at the lineup may be the sole means of attack upon the unequivocal courtroom identification, and having to probe in the dark in an attempt to discover and reveal unfairness, while bolstering the government witness' courtroom identification by bringing out and dwelling upon his prior identification. Since counsel's presence at the lineup would equip him to attack not only the lineup identification but the courtroom identification as well, limiting the impact of violation of the right to counsel to exclusion of evidence only of identification at the lineup itself disregards a critical element of that right.

We think it follows that the proper test to be applied in these situations is that quoted in *Wong Sun v. United States,* 371 U.S. 471, 83 S.Ct. 407, 9 L.Ed.2d 441 (1963), " '[W]hether, granting establishment of the primary illegality the evidence to which instant objection is made has been come at by exploitation of that illegality or instead by means sufficiently distinguishable to be purged of the primary taint.' " Application of this test in the present context requires consideration of various factors; for example, the prior opportunity to observe the alleged criminal act, the existence of any discrepancy between any pre-lineup description and the defendant's actual description, any identification prior to lineup of another person, the identification by picture of the defendant prior to the lineup, failure to identify the defendant on a prior occasion, and the lapse of time between the alleged act and the lineup identification. It is also relevant to consider those facts which, despite the absence of counsel, are disclosed concerning the conduct of the lineup.

[On] the record now before us we cannot make the determination whether the in-court identifications had an independent origin. [T]he appropriate procedure to be followed is to vacate the conviction pending a hearing to determine whether the in-court identifications had an independent source, or whether, in any event, the introduction of the evidence was harmless error, *Chapman v. California,* 386 U.S. 18, 87 S.Ct. 824, 17 L.Ed.2d 705 (1967), and for the District Court to reinstate the conviction or order a new trial, as may be proper.[e] * * *

d. In *Gilbert,* however, the Court did apply a *per se* exclusionary rule to the testimony of various prosecution witnesses that they had also identified petitioner at a pretrial lineup. See note e infra.

e. Compare *Gilbert,* where various witnesses who identified petitioner in the court-

room also testified, on direct examination by the prosecution, that they had identified petitioner at a prior lineup. "That [pretrial lineup] testimony," ruled the Court, "is the direct result of the illegal lineup 'come at by exploitation of [the primary] illegality.' *Wong Sun.* The State is therefore not entitled to an oppor-

Judgment of Court of Appeals vacated and case remanded with direction.[f]

JUSTICE WHITE whom JUSTICE HARLAN and JUSTICE STEWART join, dissenting in part and concurring in part.

The Court has again propounded a broad constitutional rule barring the use of a wide spectrum of relevant and probative evidence, solely because a step in its ascertainment or discovery occurs outside the presence of defense counsel.

[The] Court's opinion is far-reaching. It proceeds first by creating a new *per se* rule of constitutional law: a criminal suspect cannot be subjected to a pretrial identification process in the absence of his counsel without violating the Sixth Amendment. If he is, the State may not buttress a later courtroom identification of the witness by any reference to the previous identification. Furthermore, the courtroom identification is not admissible at all unless the State can establish by clear and convincing proof that the testimony is not the fruit of the earlier identification made in the absence of defendant's counsel—admittedly a heavy burden for the State and probably an impossible one. To all intents and purposes, courtroom identifications are barred if pretrial identifications have occurred without counsel being present.

The rule applies to any lineup, to any other techniques employed to produce an identification and *a fortiori* to a face-to-face encounter between the witness and the suspect alone, regardless of when the identification occurs, in time or place, and whether before or after indictment or information.[g]

[The] premise for the Court's rule is not the general unreliability of eyewitness identifications nor the difficulties inherent in observation, recall, and recognition. The Court assumes a narrower evil as the basis for its rule—improper police suggestion which contributes to erroneous identifications. The Court apparently believes that improper police procedures are so widespread that a broad prophylactic rule must be laid down, requiring the presence of counsel at all pretrial identifications, in order to detect recurring instances of police misconduct. I do not share this pervasive distrust of all official investigations. None of the materials the Court relies upon supports it. Certainly, I would bow to solid fact, but the Court quite obviously does not have before it any reliable, comprehensive survey of current police practices on which to base its new rule. Until it does, the Court should avoid excluding relevant evidence from state criminal trials.

[The] Court goes beyond assuming that a great majority of the country's police departments are following improper practices at pretrial identifications. To find the lineup a "critical" stage of the proceeding and to exclude identifications made in the absence of counsel the Court must also assume that police "suggestion," if it occurs at all, leads to erroneous rather than accurate identifications and that reprehensible police conduct will have an unavoidable and largely undiscoverable impact on the trial. This in turn assumes that there is now no adequate source from which defense counsel can learn about the circumstances of

tunity to show that that testimony had an independent source. Only a *per se* exclusionary rule as to such testimony can be an effective sanction to assure that law enforcement authorities will respect the accused's constitutional right to the presence of his counsel at the critical lineup. [That] conclusion is buttressed by the consideration that the witness' testimony of his lineup identification will enhance the impact of his in-court identification on the jury and seriously aggravate whatever derogation exists of the accused's right to a fair trial. Therefore, unless the [state supreme court] is 'able to declare a belief that it was harmless beyond a reasonable doubt,' *Chapman*, Gilbert will be entitled on remand to a new trial * * *."

f. Justice Black's opinion, dissenting in part and concurring in part, is omitted.

g. But see *Kirby v. Illinois*, infra.

the pretrial identification in order to place before the jury all of the considerations which should enter into an appraisal of courtroom identification evidence. But these are treacherous and unsupported assumptions [3] resting as they do on the notion that the defendant will not be aware, that the police and the witnesses will forget or prevaricate, that defense counsel will be unable to bring out the truth and that neither jury, judge, nor appellate court is a sufficient safeguard against unacceptable police conduct occurring at a pretrial identification procedure. I am unable to share the Court's view of the willingness of the police and the ordinary citizen-witness to dissemble, either with respect to the identification of the defendant or with respect to the circumstances surrounding a pretrial identification.

There are several striking aspects to the Court's holding. First, the rule does not bar courtroom identifications where there have been no previous identifications in the presence of the police, although when identified in the courtroom, the defendant is known to be in custody and charged with the commission of a crime.[h] Second, the Court seems to say that if suitable legislative standards were adopted for the conduct of pretrial identifications, thereby lessening the hazards in such confrontations, it would not insist on the presence of counsel. But if this is true, why does not the Court simply fashion what it deems to be constitutionally acceptable procedures for the authorities to follow? Certainly the Court is correct in suggesting that the new rule will be wholly inapplicable where police departments themselves have established suitable safeguards.

Third, courtroom identification may be barred, absent counsel at a prior identification, regardless of the extent of counsel's information concerning the circumstances of the previous confrontation between witness and defendant—apparently even if there were recordings or sound-movies of the events as they occurred. But if the rule is premised on the defendant's right to have his counsel know, there seems little basis for not accepting other means to inform. A disinterested observer, recordings, photographs—any one of them would seem adequate to furnish the basis for a meaningful cross-examination of the eyewitness who identifies the defendant in the courtroom. * * *

Finally, I think the Court's new rule is vulnerable in terms of its own unimpeachable purpose of increasing the reliability of identification testimony.

Law enforcement officers have the obligation to convict the guilty and to make sure they do not convict the innocent. They must be dedicated to making the criminal trial a procedure for the ascertainment of the true facts surrounding the commission of the crime. To this extent, our so-called adversary system is not adversary at all; nor should it be. But defense counsel has no comparable

---

3. The instant case and its companions, *Gilbert* and *Stovall* certainly lend no support to the Court's assumptions. The police conduct deemed improper by the Court in the three cases seems to have come to light at trial in the ordinary course of events. One can ask what more counsel would have learned at the pretrial identifications that would have been relevant for truth determination at trial. * * *

h. These identifications are, in effect, one-person showups, albeit in the courtroom. They probably give the witness even a stronger impression that the authorities are convinced they have the right person than do pretrial one-person showups.

In *Moore v. Illinois,* 434 U.S. 220, 98 S.Ct. 458, 54 L.Ed.2d 424 (1977), where "a one-on-one confrontation" occurred at a preliminary hearing, the Court stated that if defendant had been represented by counsel at this hearing, counsel might have avoided the suggestive identification by asking that the defendant be seated in the audience before the identifying witness was called or by seeking to have the hearing postponed until a lineup was conducted. Although such requests are occasionally granted, trial judges, in their discretion, often deny them.

obligation to ascertain or present the truth. Our system assigns him a different mission. He must be and is interested in preventing the conviction of the innocent, but, absent a voluntary plea of guilty, we also insist that he defend his client whether he is innocent or guilty. The State has the obligation to present the evidence. Defense counsel need present nothing, even if he knows what the truth is. [If] he can confuse a witness, even a truthful one, or make him appear at a disadvantage, unsure or indecisive, that will be his normal course.   * * *

I would not extend this system, at least as it presently operates, to police investigations and would not require counsel's presence at pretrial identification procedures. Counsel's interest is in not having his client placed at the scene of the crime, regardless of his whereabouts. Some counsel may advise their clients to refuse to make any movements or to speak any words in a lineup or even to appear in one.[j] [Others] will hover over witnesses and begin their cross-examination then, menacing truthful factfinding as thoroughly as the Court fears the police now do. Certainly there is an implicit invitation to counsel to suggest rules for the lineup and to manage and produce it as best he can.[k] I therefore doubt that the Court's new rule, at least absent some clearly defined limits on counsel's role, will measurably contribute to more reliable pretrial identifications. My fears are that it will have precisely the opposite result. [In] my view, the State is entitled to investigate and develop its case outside the presence of defense counsel. This includes the right to have private conversations with identification witnesses, just as defense counsel may have his own consultations with these and other witnesses without having the prosecutor present.   * * *

II.   THE COURT RETREATS: *KIRBY* AND *ASH*

KIRBY v. ILLINOIS

406 U.S. 682, 92 S.Ct. 1877, 32 L.Ed.2d 411 (1972).

JUSTICE STEWART announced the judgment of the Court in an opinion in which THE CHIEF JUSTICE, JUSTICE BLACKMUN, and JUSTICE REHNQUIST join.

* * * In the present case we are asked to extend the *Wade–Gilbert* per se exclusionary rule to identification testimony based upon a police station show-up that took place *before* the defendant had been indicted or otherwise formally charged with any criminal offense.

On February 21, 1968, [one] Willie Shard reported to the Chicago police that the previous day two men had robbed him on a Chicago street of a wallet containing, among other things, travellers checks and a Social Security card. On February 22, two police officers [investigating an unrelated crime] stopped petitioner and a companion, [Bean], [on a Chicago street]. When asked for identifica-

---

j. Since requiring a person to appear in a lineup or to use his voice as an identifying physical characteristic or to provide handwriting exemplars is not prohibited by the privilege against self-incrimination, the prosecution may comment on the suspect's refusal to cooperate. On occasion, courts have utilized civil or criminal contempt to coerce or punish the suspect who refuses to comply with a court order to participate in some identification proceeding.

k. The cases and commentaries indicate that the prevailing practice has been for counsel to attend the lineup merely as an observer

to assure against abuse and bad faith by law enforcement officers, and to provide the basis for any attack she might wish to make on the identification at trial. Any attempt to give counsel at identification a more active role is fraught with difficulties not only for the police but for counsel herself. If she is entitled to make objections at the lineup procedure, she would be held to have waived these objections if she does not make them at the procedure. If such a possibility of waiver exists, will counsel be under an obligation to raise every conceivable objection?

tion, the petitioner produced a wallet that contained three travellers checks and a Social Security card, all bearing the name of Willie Shard. * * *

Only after arriving at the police station, and checking the records there, did the arresting officers learn of the Shard robbery. [A police car] picked up Shard and brought him to the police station. Immediately upon entering the room [where petitioner and Bean were seated], Shard positively identified them as [his robbers].[a] No lawyer was present [and neither suspect had asked for] or been advised of any right to the presence of counsel. [At the trial Shard] described his identification of the two men at the police station [and] identified them again in the courtroom as the men who had robbed him.

[In] a line of constitutional cases in this Court stemming back to the Court's landmark opinion in *Powell v. Alabama,* it has been firmly established that a person's Sixth and Fourteenth Amendment right to counsel attaches only at or after the time that adversary judicial proceedings have been initiated against him.

This is not to say that a defendant in a criminal case has a constitutional right to counsel only at the trial itself. [But] the point is [that] *all* of [the right to counsel cases] have involved points of time at or after the initiation of adversary judicial criminal proceedings—whether by way of formal charge, preliminary hearing, indictment, information, or arraignment.

The only seeming deviation from this long line of constitutional decisions was *Escobedo* [which] is not apposite here for two distinct reasons. First, the Court in retrospect perceived that the "prime purpose" of *Escobedo* was not to vindicate the constitutional right to counsel as such, but, like *Miranda,* "to guarantee full effectuation of the privilege against self-incrimination. * * * " Secondly, and perhaps even more important for purely practical purposes, the Court has limited the holding of *Escobedo* to its own facts, and those facts are not remotely akin to the facts of the case before us.

The initiation of judicial criminal proceedings is far from a mere formalism. It is the starting point of our whole system of adversary criminal justice. For it is only then that the Government has committed itself to prosecute, and only then that the adverse positions of Government and defendant have solidified. It is then that a defendant finds himself faced with the prosecutorial forces of organized society, and immersed in the intricacies of substantive and procedural criminal law. It is this point, therefore, that marks the commencement of the "criminal prosecutions" to which alone the explicit guarantees of the Sixth Amendment are applicable.[b]

In this case we are asked to import into a routine police investigation an absolute constitutional guarantee historically and rationally applicable only after the onset of formal prosecutorial proceedings. We decline to do so. * * * We decline to [impose] a *per se* exclusionary rule upon testimony concerning an identification that took place long before the commencement of any prosecution whatever.

a. According to dissenting Justice Brennan, Shard testified that he identified petitioner and Bean only after the officers who brought him to the room asked him if they were the robbers.

b. Except for the language in this paragraph, *Kirby* does not explore what constitutes the "initiation" of adversary judicial criminal proceedings. But this language was subsequently relied upon in holding it sufficed that

defendant appeared at a preliminary hearing to determine whether he should be bound over to the grand jury and to set bail. *Moore v. Illinois,* supra. It is generally agreed that a warrantless arrest is not sufficient, but courts differ as to whether adversary proceedings are initiated by the issuance of an arrest warrant upon information and oath.

What has been said is not to suggest that there may not be occasions during the course of a criminal investigation when the police do abuse identification procedures. Such abuses are not beyond the reach of the Constitution. [The] Due Process Clause of the Fifth and Fourteenth Amendments forbids a lineup that is unnecessarily suggestive and conducive to irreparable mistaken identification.[8] When a person has not been formally charged with a criminal offense, *Stovall* strikes the appropriate constitutional balance between the right of a suspect to be protected from prejudicial procedures and the interest of society in the prompt and purposeful investigation of an unsolved crime.

The judgment is affirmed.[c]

JUSTICE BRENNAN, with whom JUSTICE DOUGLAS and JUSTICE MARSHALL join, dissenting. * * *

While it should go without saying, it appears necessary, in view of the plurality opinion today, to re-emphasize that *Wade* did not require the presence of counsel at pretrial confrontations for identification purposes simply on the basis of an abstract consideration of the words "criminal prosecutions" in the Sixth Amendment, [but] in order to safeguard the accused's constitutional rights to confrontation and the effective assistance of counsel at his trial.

In view of *Wade,* it is plain, and the plurality today does not attempt to dispute it, that there inhere in a confrontation for identification conducted after arrest the identical hazards to a fair trial that inhere in such a confrontation conducted "after the onset of formal prosecutorial proceedings." The plurality apparently considers an arrest, which for present purposes we must assume to be based upon probable cause, to be nothing more than part of "a routine police investigation," and thus not "the starting point of our whole system of adversary criminal justice." [The] plurality offers no reason, and I can think of none, for concluding that a post-arrest confrontation for identification, unlike a post-charge confrontation, is not among those "critical confrontations of the accused by the prosecution at pretrial proceedings where the results might well settle the accused's fate and reduce the trial itself to a mere formality."

The highly suggestive form of confrontation employed in this case underscores the point. This showup was particularly fraught with the peril of mistaken identification. In the setting of a police station squad room where all present except petitioner and Bean were police officers, the danger was quite real that Shard's understandable resentment might lead him too readily to agree with the police that the pair under arrest, and the only persons exhibited to him, were indeed the robbers. [On] direct examination, Shard identified petitioner and Bean not as the alleged robbers on trial in the courtroom, but as the pair he saw at the police station. * * *

Wade and *Gilbert,* of course, happened to involve post-indictment confrontations. Yet even a cursory perusal of the opinions in those cases reveals that nothing at all turned upon that particular circumstance. In short, it is fair to conclude that rather than "declin[ing] to depart from [the] rationale" of *Wade* and

8. In view of our limited grant of certiorari, we do not consider whether there might have been a deprivation of due process in the particularized circumstances of this case. That question remains open for inquiry in a federal habeas corpus proceeding.

[Following the U.S. Supreme Court's decision, the denial of Kirby's petition for federal habeas corpus relief was affirmed by the Seventh Circuit in *United States ex rel. Kirby v. Sturges,* 510 F.2d 397 (1975).]

c. As he "would not extend the *Wade–Gilbert* exclusionary rule," Powell, J., concurred in the result.

Gilbert, the plurality today, albeit purporting to be engaged in "principled constitutional adjudication," refuses even to recognize that "rationale." * * * Because Shard testified at trial about his identification of petitioner at the police station showup, the exclusionary rule of *Gilbert* requires reversal.

JUSTICE WHITE, dissenting.

Wade and *Gilbert* govern this case and compel reversal of the judgment below.[d]

d. A year later, in a decision the dissenters there maintained "mark[ed] simply another step towards the complete evisceration of the fundamental constitutional principles" established in the 1967 lineup cases, the Court held that a defendant has no right to have his counsel present while witnesses view pictures of him for identification purposes at a post-indictment photographic display. *United States v. Ash,* 413 U.S. 300, 93, S.Ct. 2568, 37 L.Ed.2d 619 (1973). Shortly before trial, almost three years after the crime, and long after defendant had been incarcerated and appointed counsel, the prosecutor showed five color photographs to a number of witnesses who previously had tentatively identified the black-and-white photograph of defendant. Three witnesses selected defendant's photo. In holding that the right to counsel did not extend to post-indictment photo-identifications, the Court, per Blackmun, J., observed:

"[Although the right to counsel guarantee has been expanded beyond the formal trial itself], the function of the lawyer has remained essentially the same as his function at trial. In all cases considered by the Court, counsel has continued to act as a spokesman for, or advisor to, the accused. * * *

"The function of counsel in rendering 'assistance' continued at the lineup under consideration in *Wade* and its companion cases. Although the accused was not confronted there with legal questions, the lineup offered opportunities for prosecuting authorities to take advantage of the accused. * * *

"Even if we were willing to view the counsel guarantee in broad terms as a generalized protection of the adversary process, we would be unwilling to go so far as to extend the right to a portion of the prosecutor's trial-preparation interviews with witnesses. [The] traditional counterbalance in the American adversary system for these interviews arises from the equal ability of defense counsel to seek and interview witnesses himself.

"That adversary mechanism remains as effective for a photographic display as for other parts of pretrial interviews. No greater limitations are placed on defense counsel in constructing displays, seeking witnesses, and conducting photographic identifications than those applicable to the prosecution. * * *

"Pretrial [photo-identifications] are hardly unique in offering possibilities for the actions of the prosecutor unfairly to prejudice the accused. [In] many ways the prosecutor, by accident or by design, may improperly subvert the trial. The primary safeguard against abuses of this kind is the ethical responsibility of the prosecutor. * * * If that safeguard fails, review remains available under due process standards. These same safeguards apply to misuse of photographs.

"We are not persuaded that the risks inherent in the use of photographic displays are so pernicious that an extraordinary system of safeguards is required."

Dissenting Justice Brennan, joined by Douglas and Marshall, JJ., observed:

"[A]lthough retention of the photographs may mitigate the dangers of misidentification due to the suggestiveness of the photographs themselves, it cannot in any sense reveal to defense counsel the more subtle, and therefore more dangerous, suggestiveness that might derive from the manner in which the photographs were displayed or any accompanying comments or gestures.

"[Moreover] and unlike the lineup situation, the accused himself is not even present at the photographic identification, thereby reducing the likelihood that irregularities in the procedures will ever come to light. * * *

"[A]lthough apparently conceding that the right to counsel attached, not only at the trial itself, but at all 'critical stages' of the prosecution, the Court holds today that, in order to be deemed 'critical,' the particular 'stage of the prosecution' under consideration must, at the very least, involve the physical 'presence of the accused,' at a 'trial-like confrontation' with the Government, at which the accused requires the 'guiding hand of counsel.' A pretrial photographic identification does not, of course, meet these criteria. * * *

"[But the] fundamental premise underlying *all* of this Court's decisions holding the right to counsel applicable at 'critical' pretrial proceedings, is that a 'stage' of the prosecution must be deemed 'critical' for the purposes of the Sixth Amendment if it is one at which the presence of counsel is necessary 'to protect the fairness of *trial itself.*'

"[This] established conception of the Sixth Amendment guarantee is, of course, in no sense dependent upon the physical 'presence of the accused,' at a 'trial-like confrontation' with the Government, at which the accused requires the 'guiding hand of counsel.' * * *

Although *Kirby* and *Ash* severely weakened the original lineup decisions, abuses in photographic displays and in preindictment lineups are not—in theory at least—beyond the reach on the Constitution. A defendant may still convince a court that the circumstances surrounding his identification present so "substantial" a "likelihood of misidentification" as to violate due process. *Neil v. Biggers*, 409 U.S. 188, 93 S.Ct. 375, 34 L.Ed.2d 401 (1972). But it is quite difficult for a defendant to establish this. Although a forceful argument can be made that it ought to be sufficient to vitiate an identification procedure, an "unnecessarily suggestive" identification is not enough—the "totality of circumstances" may still allow identification evidence if, despite the unnecessary "suggestiveness," the out-of-court identification possesses "certain features of reliability." *Manson v. Brathwaite*, 432 U.S. 98, 97 S.Ct. 2243, 53 L.Ed.2d 140 (1977). This approach has been criticized by a number of commentators as an elusive, unpredictable case-by-case standard that is unlikely to be any more illuminating for law enforcement officers or any more manageable for appellate courts than the "totality of circumstances" test for admitting confessions that proved so unsuccessful in the thirty years before *Miranda*.

"[C]ontrary to the suggestion of the Court, the conclusion in *Wade* that a pretrial lineup is a 'critical stage' of the prosecution did not in any sense turn on the fact that a lineup involves the physical 'presence of the accused' at a 'trial-like confrontation' with the Government. And that conclusion most certainly did not turn on the notion that presence of counsel was necessary so that counsel could offer legal advice or 'guidance' to the accused at the lineup. On the contrary, *Wade* envisioned counsel's function at the lineup to be primarily that of a trained observer, able to detect the existence of any suggestive influences and capable of understanding the legal implications of the events that transpire. Having witnessed the proceedings, counsel would then be in a position effectively to reconstruct at trial any unfairness that occurred at the lineup, thereby preserving the accused's fundamental right to a fair trial on the issue of identification."

Chapter 5
THE RIGHT OF "PRIVACY" (OR "AUTONOMY" OR "PERSONHOOD")

Introductory Note

"Whether as substantive due process or as Privacy, 'fundamentality' needs elaboration, especially with respect to the weight particular rights are to enjoy in the balance against public good. Justices Stone and Cardozo suggested that the freedoms of speech, press and religion required extraordinary judicial protection against invasions even for the public good, because of their place at the foundations of democracy and because of the unreliability of the political process in regard to them. If other rights—those to be described as within the Rights of Privacy—are also to be specially guarded against the democratic political process, similar or other justifications must be found—if there are any. Perhaps unusual respect for autonomy and idiosyncrasy as regards some 'personal' matters is intuitively felt by all of us, including Justices; that such deference is 'self-evident' is not self-evident."

—Louis Henkin, *Privacy and Autonomy,* 74 Colum.L.Rev. 1410, 1428–29 (1974).

As noted in Ira Lupu, *Untangling the Strands of the Fourteenth Amendment,* 77 Mich.L.Rev. 981, 1029–30 (1979), "unlike the all-inclusive theory of the *Lochner* era that held all liberties equally inviolable, and unlike the procedural due process theory that assesses the weight of any protected interest in a refined way for purposes of 'balancing,' [what might be called] modern substantive due process theory has a distinct all-or-nothing quality to it. Most liberties lacking textual support are of the garden variety—like liberty of contract—and thus their deprivation is constitutional if rationally necessary to the achievement of a public good. [See, e.g., *Williamson v. Lee Optical Co.,* 348 U.S. 483, 75 S.Ct. 461, 99 L.Ed. 563 (1965)]. Several select liberties, on the other hand, have attained the status of 'fundamental' or 'preferred,' with the consequence that the Constitution permits a state to abridge them only if it can demonstrate an extraordinary justification." A notable example is *Roe v. Wade,* infra, where the Court held that the "right of privacy" encompassed "a woman's decision whether or not to terminate her pregnancy" and thus certain restrictions on abortion could be justified "only by a 'compelling state interest.'" See also *Shapiro v. Thompson,* 394 U.S. 618, 89 S.Ct. 1322, 22 L.Ed.2d 600 (1969), which can be viewed as a "right to travel" case, which, in the course of invalidating a one-year durational residence requirement for welfare, rejected the argument that "a mere showing of a rational relationship between the waiting period and [administrative governmental] objectives will suffice [for] in moving from state to state [appellees] were exercising a constitutional right, and any classification which serves to penalize the exercise of that right, unless shown to be necessary to promote a *compelling* governmental interest, is unconstitutional." As Lupu observes, ibid., "[b]ecause the review standard for ordinary liberties is so deferential, and the standard for preferred liberties so rigid, outcomes are ordained by the designation of 'preferred' [or 'fundamental'] or not."

Regulations dealing with "fundamental rights" call for "strict scrutiny" review just as government classifications based upon what have come to be known as "suspect" criteria trigger "strict" equal protection review. "[T]here is a case to be made for a significant degree of judicial deference to legislative and administrative choices in some spheres. Yet the idea of strict scrutiny acknowledges that other political choices—those burdening fundamental rights, or suggesting prejudice against racial or other minorities—must be subjected to close analysis in order to preserve substantive values of equality and liberty. Although strict scrutiny in this form ordinarily appears as a standard for judicial review, it may also be understood as admonishing lawmakers and regulators as well to be particularly cautious of their *own* purposes and premises and of the effects of their choices." Laurence Tribe, *American Constitutional Law* 1451 (2d ed. 1988) (hereinafter referred to as Tribe, *Treatise*).

Not infrequently, as in *Skinner v. Oklahoma* (discussed immediately below), which is an "equal protection" case in form, and which never mentioned any "right of privacy," but to which "the development of the contemporary concept of a constitutionally protected 'right of privacy' in sexual matters can be traced," (John Nowak & Ronald Rotunda, Constitutional Law 797 5th ed. 1995) (hereinafter referred to as Nowak & Rotunda), a decision can be viewed as either an "equal protection" or a "fundamental rights" (or "substantive due process") case.

Indeed, observes Lupu, at 983–84, "the tangling [of 'liberty' and 'equality'] is most apparent and most serious when viewed in its relationship to the so-called 'fundamental rights' developments in both equal protection and due process clause interpretation. In the sense used here, fundamental rights include all the claims of individual rights, drawn from sources outside of the first eight amendments, that the Supreme Court has elevated to preferred status (that is, rights which the government may infringe only when it demonstrates extraordinary justification). [Which] new rights properly derive from the liberty strand, and which from the equality strand?[6] Sometimes the Court tells us; other times it does not. Often, members of the Court agree upon the preferred status of an interest but disagree about its textual source.[7] On occasion, members of the Court concede that an interest has no textual source, yet battle still over which strand of the fourteenth amendment protects it from state interference."[8]

---

6. Compare *Roe v. Wade* [infra] (due process) with *Eisenstadt v. Baird* [infra] (analogous interests protected by the equal protection clause), and *Loving v. Virginia* [p. 1086 infra] (analogous interests protected by the due process clause) (alternative ground).

7. The reference is to *Griswold v. Connecticut* [infra], in which Bill of Rights' penumbras, the ninth amendment, and "pure" substantive due process compete for attention.

8. In *Shapiro v. Thompson*, the majority held that the equal protection clause protected the right to travel, while Justice Harlan in dissent believed that the due process clause was the relevant shield. A similar doctrinal dispute split the Court in *Zablocki v. Redhail*

SKINNER v. OKLAHOMA, 316 U.S. 535, 62 S.Ct. 1110, 86 L.Ed. 1655 (1942), per DOUGLAS, J., held violative of equal protection Oklahoma's Habitual Criminal Sterilization Act, which authorized the sterilization of persons previously convicted and imprisoned two or more times of crimes "amounting to felonies involving moral turpitude" and thereafter convicted of such a felony and sentenced to prison. (Petitioner, previously convicted of "chicken-stealing" and robbery, had again been convicted of robbery.) Expressly exempted were embezzlement, political offenses and revenue act violations. Thus a person convicted three times of larceny could be subjected to sterilization, but the embezzler could not—although "the nature of the two crimes is intrinsically the same" and they are otherwise punishable in the same manner. The Court recognized that "if we had here only a question as to a State's classification of crimes, such as embezzlement or larceny," no substantial federal question would be presented. "But the instant legislation runs afoul of the equal protection clause" because—

"We are dealing here with legislation which involves one of the basic civil rights of man. Marriage and procreation are fundamental to the very existence and survival of the race. [In] evil or reckless hands [the power to sterilize] can cause races or types which are inimical to the dominant group to wither and disappear. There is no redemption for the individual whom the law touches. [He] is forever deprived of a basic liberty.[a] We mention these matters [in] emphasis of our view that strict scrutiny of the classification which a State makes in a sterilization law is essential, lest unwittingly, or otherwise, invidious discriminations are made against groups or types of individuals in violation of the constitutional guaranty of just and equal laws. [When] the law lays an unequal hand on those who have committed intrinsically the same quality of offense and sterilizes one and not the other, it has made as invidious a discrimination, as if it had selected a particular race or nationality for oppressive treatment."[b]

STONE, C.J., concurred in the result: "[I]f we must presume that the legislature knows—what science has been unable to ascertain—that the criminal tendencies of any class of habitual offenders are transmissible regardless of the varying mental characteristics of its individuals, I should suppose that we must likewise presume that the legislature, in its wisdom, knows that the criminal tendencies of some classes of offenders are more likely to be transmitted than those of others. And so I think the real question [is] not one of equal protection, but whether the wholesale condemnation of a class to such an invasion of personal liberty, without opportunity to any individual to show that his is not the type of case which would justify resort to it, satisfies the demands of due process.

"There are limits to the extent to which the presumption of constitutionality can be pressed, especially where the liberty of the person is concerned [referring to his famous *Carolene Products* footnote, Ch. 1, Sec. 1] and where the presumption is resorted to only to dispense with a procedure which the ordinary dictates of prudence would seem to demand for the protection of the individual from

[infra], where the majority held that the equal protection clause protected the right to marry. Justice Powell, in a concurring opinion, felt the right found its source in the due process clause.

a. The Court began its opinion by observing: "This case touches a sensitive and important area of human rights. Oklahoma deprives certain individuals of a right which is basic to the perpetuation of a race—the right to have offspring."

b. As for *Buck v. Bell,* 274 U.S. 200, 47 S.Ct. 584, 71 L.Ed. 1000 (1927), upholding a sterilization law applicable only to mental defectives in state institutions, "it was pointed out that 'so far as the operations enable those who otherwise must be kept confined to be returned to the world, and thus open the asylum to others, the equality aimed at will be more nearly reached.' Here there is no such saving feature."

arbitrary action. Although petitioner here was given a hearing to ascertain whether sterilization would be detrimental to his health, he was given none to discover whether his criminal tendencies are of an inheritable type.   * * *

"Science has found and the law has recognized that there are certain types of mental deficiency associated with delinquency which are inheritable. But the State does not contend—nor can there be any pretense—that either common knowledge or experience, or scientific investigation, has given assurance that the criminal tendencies of any class of habitual offenders are universally or even generally inheritable. In such circumstances, inquiry whether such is the fact in the case of any particular individual cannot rightly be dispensed with. [A] law which condemns, without hearing, all the individuals of a class to so harsh a measure as the present because some or even many merit condemnation, is lacking in the first principles of due process." [c]

Notes and Questions

1. *Did the Lochner era haunt the Skinner Court?* Why was *Skinner* "unrestrained in its vigorous protection of a nontextual liberty, yet cautious in its grounds that went no farther than the particular case at hand"? To what extent does *Skinner's* "1942 vintage" explain why the Court preferred "a relatively narrow equal protection ground of decision to a broader preferred liberty theory that would have impugned all involuntary sterilization schemes"? No matter how serious the issue, was the Court unwilling to reinstate "substantive activism" a short five years after its repudiation? See Lupu, supra, at 1019.

2. *To what extent was Skinner colored by the Court's concern that the statute invited prejudiced action against powerless minorities?* Consider Tribe, supra, at 1465–66: "Clearly prominent [in] *Skinner* was [the Court's] concern to protect within the realm of personal autonomy 'one of the basic civil rights of man,' the right to reproduce. Yet the Court's opinion makes evident an even greater preoccupation with the notion that the state's classifications had been promulgated with their harshest effect against a relatively powerless minority, that of lower-class, as opposed to white-collar, criminals. [Although] not willing to characterize the group discriminated against as automatically deserving the protection of special judicial scrutiny, the Court combined allusion to the invidiousness of discrimination against the class with discussion of the fundamental right involved. Indeed, since that right—personal autonomy in reproductive matters—had not previously been held fundamental, it seems likely that the *Skinner* Court was moved to give the right such a status, and thereby to assure the most rigorous scrutiny of future governmental intrusions into the reproductive realm, in large part *because* of fear about the invidiously selective and ultimately genocidal way in which governmental control over that realm might tend to be exercised—a fear illustrated by the facts of *Skinner* itself.

"[*Skinner*] is the leading instance in which a new star appears to have been added to the firmament of preferred freedoms primarily because of concerns about invidious discrimination and majoritarian domination. Such concerns of course move to center stage once we are prepared to treat the classification employed by government as so plainly invidious or prejudiced that, quite without regard to the nature of the choice burdened or the interest unequally distributed, strict scrutiny seems required if any semblance of equal justice under law is to be preserved.

c. In a separate concurrence, Jackson, J., agreed that the hearings provided are "too limited [to] afford due process" and also agreed with the Court that the classification denies equal protection.

The theory of invidious or suspect classification [Ch. 11, Secs. 2–3,] thus takes us beyond *Skinner* to a realm in which, even without finding a fundamental right, our tolerance will be at low ebb."

———

"[In *Griswold*, Douglas, J.,] skipped through the Bill of Rights like a cheer-leader—'Give me a P . . . give me an R . . . an I . . . ,' and so on, and found P–R–I–V–A–C–Y as a derivative or penumbral right."

—Robert Dixon, *The "New" Substantive Due Process and the Democratic Ethic: A Prolegomenon,* 1976 B.Y.U.L.Rev. 43, 84.

GRISWOLD v. CONNECTICUT

381 U.S. 479, 85 S.Ct. 1678, 14 L.Ed.2d 510 (1965).

Justice Douglas delivered the opinion of the Court.

Appellant Griswold is Executive Director of the Planned Parenthood League of Connecticut. Appellant Buxton [is] Medical Director for the League at its Center in New Haven—a center open [from] November 1 to November 10, 1961, when appellants were arrested.

They gave information, instruction, and medical advice to *married persons* as to the means of preventing conception. * * * Fees were usually charged, although some couples were serviced free.

The statutes whose constitutionality is involved [are] §§ 53–32 and 54–196 of the General Statutes of Connecticut (1958 rev.). The former provides: "Any person who uses any drug, medicinal article or instrument for the purpose of preventing conception shall be fined not less than fifty dollars or imprisoned not less than sixty days nor more than one year or be both fined and imprisoned." Section 54–196 provides: "Any person who assists, abets, counsels, causes, hires or commands another to commit any offense may be prosecuted and punished as if he were the principal offender." The appellants were found guilty as accessories and fined $100 [each].

Coming to the merits,[a] we are met with a wide range of questions that implicate the Due Process Clause * * *. Overtones of some arguments suggest that *Lochner* should be our guide. But we decline that invitation * * *. We do not sit as a super-legislature to determine the wisdom, need, and propriety of laws that touch economic problems, business affairs, or social conditions. This law, however, operates directly on an intimate relation of husband and wife and their physician's role in one aspect of that relation.

The association of people is not mentioned in the Constitution nor in the Bill of Rights. The right to educate a child in a school of the parents' choice—whether public or private or parochial—is also not mentioned. Nor is the right to study any particular subject or any foreign language. Yet the First Amendment has been construed to include certain of those rights. [See] *Pierce v. Society of Sisters,* 268 U.S. 510 45 S.Ct. 571, 69 L.Ed. 1070 (1925) [and] *Meyer v. Nebraska,* 262 U.S.

a. The Court held that appellants had standing to assert the constitutional rights of   the married persons they advised.

390, 43 S.Ct. 625, 67 L.Ed. 1042 (1923).[b] [T]he State may not, consistently with the spirit of the First Amendment, contract the spectrum of available knowledge. The right of freedom of speech and press includes not only the right to utter or to print, but the right to distribute, the right to receive, the right to read and freedom of inquiry, freedom of thought, and freedom to teach—indeed the freedom of the entire university community. Without those peripheral rights the specific rights would be less secure. And so we reaffirm the principle [of] *Pierce* [and] *Meyer.*

In *NAACP v. Alabama* [p. 870 infra], we protected the "freedom to associate and privacy in one's associations," noting that freedom of association was a peripheral First Amendment right. [In] other words, the First Amendment has a penumbra where privacy is protected from governmental intrusion. In like context, we have protected forms of "association" that are not political in the customary sense but pertain to the social, legal, and economic benefit of the members. *NAACP v. Button*, 371 U.S. 415, 83 S.Ct. 328, 9 L.Ed.2d 405 (1963). [W]hile [association] is not expressly included in the First Amendment its existence is necessary in making the express guarantees fully meaningful.

The foregoing cases suggest that specific guarantees in the Bill of Rights have penumbras, formed by emanations from those guarantees that help give them life and substance. Various guarantees create zones of privacy. The right of association contained in the penumbra of the First Amendment is one, as we have seen. The Third Amendment in its prohibition against the quartering of soldiers "in any house" in time of peace without the consent of the owner is another facet of that privacy. The Fourth Amendment [is another]. The Fifth Amendment in its Self-Incrimination Clause enables the citizen to create a zone of privacy which government may not force him to surrender to his detriment. The Ninth Amendment provides: "The enumeration in the Constitution, of certain rights, shall not be construed to deny or disparage others retained by the people."

The Fourth and Fifth Amendments were described in *Boyd v. United States,* 116 U.S. 616, 630, 6 S.Ct. 524, 532, 29 L.Ed. 746 (1886), as protection against all governmental invasions "of the sanctity of a man's home and the privacies of life." We recently referred in *Mapp v. Ohio* to the Fourth Amendment as creating a "right to privacy, no less important than any other right carefully and particularly reserved to the people."

---

b. Consider Nowak & Rotunda 796: In both *Meyer,* invalidating a state law forbidding all grade schools from teaching subjects in any language other than English, and in *Pierce,* holding a state law requiring students to attend public schools violative of due process, "the majority [per McReynolds, J.] found that the law restricted individual freedom without any relation to a valid public interest. Freedom of choice regarding an individual's personal life was recognized as constitutionally protected. These decisions may only have reflected the attitude of the Court towards government regulation during the apex of 'substantive due process.' While these decisions might today be grounded on the First Amendment, their existence is important to the growth of the right to privacy. If nothing else,

they show a historical recognition of a right to private decision-making regarding family matters as inherent in the concept of liberty."

See also Dennis Hutchinson, *Unanimity and Desegregation: Decisionmaking in the Supreme Court, 1948–58,* 68 Geo.L.J. 1, 49–51 (1979) (Frankfurter, J., long an outspoken critic of the McReynolds opinions in *Meyer* and *Pierce,* warned that the method used in these cases could just as easily produce "another *Lochner* "); Richard Posner, *The Uncertain Protection of Privacy by the Supreme Court,* 1979 Sup.Ct.Rev. 173, 195–96 ("under ostensible modern test of substantive due process," *Meyer* was "incorrectly decided"; its citation in "privacy" cases shows "survival of substantive due process despite frequent disclaimers.")

We have had many controversies over these penumbral rights of "privacy and repose." [*Skinner* and other cases] bear witness that the right of privacy which presses for recognition here is a legitimate one.

The present case, then, concerns a relationship lying within the zone of privacy created by several fundamental constitutional guarantees.[c] And it concerns a law which, in forbidding the *use* of contraceptives rather than regulating their manufacture or sale, seeks to achieve its goals by means having a maximum destructive impact upon that relationship. Such a law cannot stand in light of the familiar principle [that] a "governmental purpose to control or prevent activities constitutionally subject to state regulation may not be achieved by means which sweep unnecessarily broadly and thereby invade the area of protected freedoms." *NAACP v. Alabama.* Would we allow the police to search the sacred precincts of marital bedrooms for telltale signs of the use of contraceptives? The very idea is repulsive to the notions of privacy surrounding the marriage relationship.[d]

We deal with a right of privacy older than the Bill of Rights * * *. Marriage is a coming together for better or for worse, hopefully enduring, and intimate to the degree of being sacred. It is an association that promotes a way of life, not causes; a harmony in living, not political faiths; a bilateral loyalty, not commercial or social projects. Yet it is an association for as noble a purpose as any involved in our prior decisions.

Reversed.

JUSTICE GOLDBERG, whom THE CHIEF JUSTICE and JUSTICE BRENNAN join, concurring.

I [join the Court's opinion]. Although I have not accepted the view that "due process" as used in the Fourteenth Amendment includes all of the first eight Amendments, I do agree that the concept of liberty protects those personal rights that are fundamental, and is not confined to the specific terms of the Bill of Rights. My conclusion [that] it embraces the right of marital privacy though that right is not mentioned explicitly in the Constitution [1] is supported both by numerous decisions [and] by the language and history of the Ninth Amendment [which] reveal that the Framers of the Constitution believed that there are additional fundamental rights, protected from governmental infringement. [The] Ninth Amendment [was] proffered to quiet expressed fears that a bill of specifically enumerated rights could not be sufficiently broad to cover all essential rights and that the specific mention of certain rights would be interpreted as a denial that others were protected.

---

c. Did the Court omit the free exercise clause of the first amendment? Like religious beliefs, are beliefs in the areas of marriage, procreation and child rearing "often deeply held, involving loyalties fully as powerful as those that bind the citizen to the state"? Will the choice of whom to marry or whether or not to have a child, once taken, "have as strong an impact on the life patterns of the individuals involved [as] any adoption of a religious belief or viewpoint"? See Philip Heymann & Douglas Barzelay, *The Forest and the Trees: Roe v. Wade and Its Critics,* 53 B.U.L.Rev. 765, 773–74 (1973).

d. But consider Posner, fn. b supra, at 194: "Such a search would indeed be an invasion of privacy in a conventional sense. But it would be a justifiable invasion if the statute were not otherwise constitutionally objectionable. This case can be seen by imagining that the statute in question forbade not contraception but murder and that the police had probable cause to believe that the suspected murderer had secreted the weapon to his mattress. Furthermore, even if some methods of enforcing the Connecticut statute [violated the Fourth Amendment], that would mean only that the statute was difficult to enforce. [As] the facts of *Griswold* show, the State could enforce the statute without invading anyone's privacy, simply by prosecuting, as accessories, the employees of birth-control clinics."

1. [This Court] has never held that the Bill of Rights or the Fourteenth Amendment protects only those rights that the Constitution specifically mentions by name. * * *

[While] this Court has had little occasion to interpret the Ninth Amendment,[6] "[i]t cannot be presumed that any clause in the constitution is intended to be without effect." [To] hold that a right so basic and fundamental and so deep-rooted in our society as the right of privacy in marriage may be infringed because that right is not guaranteed in so many words by the first eight amendments to the Constitution is to ignore the Ninth Amendment and to give it no effect whatsoever. * * * I do not mean to imply that the Ninth Amendment is applied against the States by the Fourteenth [nor] to state that the Ninth Amendment constitutes an independent source of rights protected from infringement by either the States or the Federal Government. Rather, the Ninth Amendment shows a belief of the Constitution's authors that fundamental rights exist that are not expressly enumerated in the first eight amendments and an intent that the list of rights included there not be deemed exhaustive.

[While] the Ninth Amendment—and indeed the entire Bill of Rights—originally concerned restrictions upon *federal* power, the subsequently enacted Fourteenth Amendment prohibits the States as well from abridging fundamental personal liberties. [In] sum, the Ninth Amendment simply lends strong support to the view that the "liberty" protected by the Fifth and Fourteenth Amendments from infringement by the Federal Government or the States is not restricted to rights specifically mentioned in the first eight amendments.

[The] entire fabric of the Constitution and the purposes that clearly underlie its specific guarantees demonstrate that the rights to marital privacy and to marry and raise a family are of similar order and magnitude as the fundamental rights specifically protected.

[Surely] the Government, absent a showing of a compelling subordinating state interest, could not decree that all husbands and wives must be sterilized after two children have been born to them. Yet by [the dissenters'] reasoning such an invasion of marital privacy would not be subject to constitutional challenge because, while it might be "silly," no provision of the Constitution specifically prevents the Government from curtailing the marital right to bear children and raise a family. [I]f upon a showing of a slender basis of rationality, a law outlawing voluntary birth control by married persons is valid, then, by the same reasoning, a law requiring compulsory birth control also would seem to be valid. In my view, however, both types of law would unjustifiably intrude upon rights of marital privacy which are constitutionally protected.

In a long series of cases this Court has held that where fundamental personal liberties are involved, they may not be abridged by the States simply on a showing that a regulatory statute has some rational relationship to the effectuation of a proper state purpose. [The] State, at most, argues that there is some rational relation between this statute and what is admittedly a legitimate subject of state concern—the discouraging of extra-marital relations. It says that preventing the use of birth-control devices by married persons helps prevent the indulgence by some in such extra-marital relations. The rationality of this justification is dubious, particularly in light of the admitted widespread availability to all persons [in] Connecticut, unmarried as well as married, of birth-control devices for the prevention of disease, as distinguished from the prevention of conception. But in any event, it is clear that the state interest in safeguarding marital fidelity can be served by a more discriminately tailored statute, which does not, like the present

---

6. [It] has been referred to as *"The Forgotten Ninth Amendment,"* in a book with that title by Bennett B. Patterson (1955). * * *

one, sweep unnecessarily broadly, reaching far beyond the evil sought to be dealt with and intruding upon the privacy of all married couples. * * *

JUSTICE HARLAN, concurring in the judgment.

I [cannot] join the Court's opinion [as] it seems to me to evince an approach [that] the Due Process Clause of the Fourteenth Amendment does not touch this Connecticut statute unless the enactment is found to violate some right assured by the letter or penumbra of the Bill of Rights. [W]hat I find implicit in the Court's opinion is that the "incorporation" doctrine may be used to *restrict* the reach of Fourteenth Amendment Due Process. For me this is just as unacceptable constitutional doctrine as is the use of the "incorporation" approach to *impose* upon the States all the requirements of the Bill of Rights. * * *

[T]he proper constitutional inquiry in this case is whether this Connecticut statute infringes the Due Process Clause of the Fourteenth Amendment because the enactment violates basic values "implicit in the concept of ordered liberty." For reasons stated at length in my dissenting opinion in *Poe v. Ullman* [discussed below], I believe that it does. While the relevant inquiry may be aided by resort to one or more of the provisions of the Bill of Rights, it is not dependent on them or any of their radiations. The Due Process Clause of the Fourteenth Amendment stands, in my opinion, on its own bottom.

[While] I could not more heartily agree that judicial "self restraint" is an indispensable ingredient of sound constitutional adjudication, I do submit that the formula suggested [by the dissenters] for achieving it is more hollow than real. "Specific" provisions of the Constitution, no less than "due process," lend themselves as readily to "personal" interpretations by judges whose constitutional outlook is simply to keep the Constitution in supposed "tune with the times".

[Judicial self-restraint will] be achieved in this area, as in other[s], only by continual insistence upon respect for the teachings of history, solid recognition of the basic values that underlie our society, and wise appreciation of the great roles that the doctrines of federalism and separation of powers have played in establishing and preserving American freedoms. Adherence to these principles will not, of course, obviate all constitutional differences of opinion among judges, nor should it. Their continued recognition will, however, go farther toward keeping most judges from roaming at large in the constitutional field than will the interpolation into the Constitution of an artificial and largely illusory restriction on the content of the Due Process Clause.

[Dissenting in POE v. ULLMAN, 367 U.S. 497, 523, 81 S.Ct. 1752, 6 L.Ed.2d 989 (1961), which failed to reach the merits of the constitutional challenge to the Connecticut anti-birth control statute, Harlan, J., had maintained that the statute, "as construed to apply to these appellants, violates the Fourteenth Amendment" because "a statute making it a criminal offense for *married couples* to use contraceptives is an intolerable and unjustifiable invasion of privacy in the conduct of the most intimate concerns of an individual's personal life." Harlan, J., "would not suggest that adultery, homosexuality, fornication and incest are immune from criminal enquiry, however privately practiced," but "the intimacy of husband and wife is necessarily an essential and accepted feature of the institution of marriage, an institution which the State not only must allow, but which always and every age it has fostered and protected. It is one thing when the State exerts its power either to forbid extra-marital sexuality altogether, or to say who may marry, but it is quite another when, having acknowledged a marriage and the intimacies inherent in it, it undertakes to regulate by means of the criminal law the details of that intimacy."

[Although the state had argued the constitutional permissibility of the moral judgment underlying the challenged statute, Harlan, J., could not find anything that "even remotely suggests a justification for the obnoxiously intrusive means it has chosen to effectuate that policy." He deemed "the utter novelty" of the statute "conclusive." "Although the Federal Government and many States have at one time or another [prohibited or regulated] the distribution of contraceptives, none [has] made the *use* of contraceptives a crime. Indeed, a diligent search has revealed that no nation, including several which quite evidently share Connecticut's moral policy, had seen fit to effectuate that policy by the means presented here."

[Because the constitutional challenges to the Connecticut statute "draw their basis from no explicit language of the Constitution, and have yet to find expression in any decision of this Court," Harlan, J., deemed it "desirable at the outset to state the framework of Constitutional principles in which I think the issue must be judged":

["[Were] due process merely a procedural safeguard it would fail to reach those situations where the deprivation of life, liberty or property was accomplished by legislation which by operating in the future could, given even the fairest possible procedure in application to individuals, nevertheless destroy the enjoyment of all three. [I]t is not the particular enumeration of rights in the first eight Amendments which spells out the reach of Fourteenth Amendment due process, but rather [those concepts embracing] rights 'which [are] *fundamental;* which belong [to] the citizens of all free governments.'

["[T]hrough the course of this Court's decisions [due process] has represented the balance which our Nation, built upon postulates of respect for the liberty of the individual, has struck between that liberty and the demands of organized society. [The] balance of which I speak is the balance struck by this country, having regard to what history teaches are the traditions from which it developed as well as the traditions from which it broke. That tradition is a living thing. A decision of this Court which radically departs from it could not long survive, while a decision which builds on what has survived is likely to be sound. No formula could serve as a substitute, in this area, for judgment and restraint.

["[The] full scope of the liberty guaranteed by the Due Process Clause cannot be found in or limited by the precise terms of the specific guarantees elsewhere provided in the Constitution. This 'liberty' is not a series of isolated points pricked out in terms of [the] freedom of speech, press, and religion; [the] freedom from unreasonable searches and seizures; and so on. It is a rational continuum which, broadly speaking, includes a freedom from all substantial arbitrary impositions and purposeless restraints [and] which also recognizes, what a reasonable and sensitive judgment must, that certain interests require particularly careful scrutiny of the state needs asserted to justify their abridgment. Cf. *Skinner.*"] [e]

Justice White, concurring in the judgment.

In my view this Connecticut law as applied to married couples deprives them of "liberty" without [due process] guaranteed by the Fourteenth Amendment against arbitrary or capricious [denials]. Surely the right [to] be free of regulation of the intimacies of the marriage relationship, "come[s] to this Court with a momentum for respect lacking when appeal is made to liberties which derive merely from shifting economic arrangements." *Kovacs v. Cooper,* 336 U.S. 77, 69 S.Ct. 448, 93 L.Ed. 513 (1949) (opinion of Frankfurter, J.).

e. See also the extracts from this dissent in *Planned Parenthood v. Casey,* p. 363 infra.

The Connecticut anti-contraceptive statute deals rather substantially with this relationship. [And] the clear effect of these statutes, as enforced, is to deny disadvantaged citizens of Connecticut, those without either adequate knowledge or resources to obtain private counseling, access to medical assistance and up-to-date information in respect to proper methods of birth control. In my view, a statute with these effects bears a substantial burden of justification when attacked under the Fourteenth Amendment.

An examination of the justification offered, however, cannot be avoided by saying that the Connecticut anti-use statute invades a protected area of privacy and association or that it demeans the marriage relationship. The nature of the right invaded is pertinent, to be sure, for statutes regulating sensitive areas of liberty do, under the cases of this Court, require "strict scrutiny," *Skinner*, and "must be viewed in the light of less drastic means for achieving the same basic purpose." But such statutes, if reasonably necessary for the effectuation of a legitimate and substantial state interest, and not arbitrary or capricious in application, are not invalid under the Due Process Clause. [There] is no serious contention that Connecticut thinks the use of artificial or external methods of contraception immoral or unwise in itself, or that the anti-use statute is founded upon any policy of promoting population expansion. Rather, the statute is said to serve the State's policy against all forms of promiscuous or illicit sexual relationships, be they premarital or extramarital, concededly a permissible and legitimate legislative goal.

[But] I wholly fail to see how the ban on the use of contraceptives by married couples in any way reinforces the State's ban on illicit sexual relationships. [Perhaps] the theory is that the flat ban on use prevents married people from possessing contraceptives and without the ready availability of such devices for use in the marital relationship, there will be no or less temptation to use them in extramarital ones. This reasoning rests on the premise that married people will comply with the ban in regard to their marital relationship, notwithstanding total nonenforcement in this context and apparent nonenforcibility, but will not comply with criminal statutes prohibiting extramarital affairs and the anti-use statute in respect to illicit sexual relationships, a premise whose validity has not been demonstrated and whose intrinsic validity is not very evident. At most the broad ban is of marginal utility to the declared objective. A statute limiting its prohibition on use to persons engaging in the prohibited relationship would serve the end posited by Connecticut in the same way, and with the same effectiveness, or ineffectiveness, as the broad anti-use statute under attack in this case. I find nothing in this record justifying the sweeping scope of this [statute].

JUSTICE BLACK, with whom JUSTICE STEWART joins, dissenting.

[There are] guarantees in certain specific constitutional provisions which are designed in part to protect privacy at certain times and places with respect to certain activities. [But] I think it belittles [the Fourth] Amendment to talk about it as though it protects nothing but "privacy." [The] average man would very likely not have his feelings soothed any more by having his property seized openly than by having it seized privately and by stealth. [And] a person can be just as much, if not more, irritated, annoyed and injured by an unceremonious public arrest by a policeman as he is by a seizure in the privacy of his office or home.

One of the most effective ways of diluting or expanding a constitutionally guaranteed right is to substitute for the crucial word or words of a constitutional guarantee another word or words, more or less flexible and more or less restricted in meaning. This fact is well illustrated by the use of the term "right of privacy" as a comprehensive substitute for the Fourth Amendment's guarantee against "unreasonable searches and seizures." * * * [1] I like my privacy as well as the next one, but I am nevertheless compelled to admit that government has a right to invade it unless prohibited by some specific constitutional provision.

[This] brings me to the arguments made by [the concurring justices]. I discuss the due process and Ninth Amendment arguments together because on analysis they turn out to be the same thing—merely using different words to claim for this Court and the federal judiciary power to invalidate any legislative act [that] it considers to be arbitrary, capricious, unreasonable, or oppressive, or this Court's belief that a particular state law under scrutiny has no "rational or justifying" purpose, or is offensive to a "sense of fairness and justice." If these formulas based on "natural justice" [are] to prevail, they require judges to determine what is or is not constitutional on the basis of their own appraisal of what laws are unwise or unnecessary. [I] do not believe that we are granted power by the Due Process Clause or any [other] provisions to measure constitutionality by our belief that legislation is arbitrary, capricious or unreasonable, or accomplishes no justifiable purpose, or is offensive to our own notions of "civilized standards of conduct." Such an appraisal of the wisdom of legislation is an attribute of the power to make laws, [a] power which was specifically denied to federal courts by the [Framers].

Of the cases on which my [Brothers] rely so heavily, undoubtedly the reasoning of two of them supports their result here—[*Meyer* and *Pierce*]. *Meyer* [relying on *Lochner*,] held unconstitutional, as an "arbitrary" and unreasonable interference with the right of a teacher to carry on his occupation and of parents to hire him, a state law forbidding the teaching of modern foreign languages to young children in the schools.[7] [*Pierce*, per McReynolds, J.] said that a state law requiring that all children attend public schools interfered unconstitutionally with the property rights of private school corporations because it was an "arbitrary, unreasonable, and unlawful interference" which threatened "destruction of their business and property." Without expressing an opinion as to whether either of those cases reached a correct result in light of our later decisions applying the First Amendment to the States through the Fourteenth, I merely point out that the reasoning stated in *Meyer* and *Pierce* was the same natural law due process philosophy which many later opinions repudiated, and which I cannot accept. Brothers White and Goldberg also cite other cases [which] held that States [could not] pass unnecessarily broad laws which might indirectly infringe on First Amendment [freedoms.] Brothers White and Goldberg now apparently would start from this requirement [and] extend it limitlessly to require States to justify any law restricting "liberty" as my Brethren define "liberty." This would mean at the very least, I suppose, that every state criminal statute—since it must inevitably curtail "liberty" to some extent—would be suspect, and would have to be justified to this Court.

1. The phrase "right to privacy" appears first to have gained currency from an article written by Messrs. Warren and (later Mr. Justice) Brandeis in 1890 which urged that States should give some form of tort relief to persons whose private affairs were exploited by others. *The Right to Privacy*, 4 Harv.L.Rev. 193. * * * Observing that "the right of privacy presses for recognition here," today this Court, which I did not understand to have power to sit as a court of common law, now appears to be exalting a phrase which Warren and Brandeis use in discussing grounds for tort relief, to the level of a constitutional [rule].

7. In *Meyer*, in the very same sentence quoted in part by my Brethren in which he asserted that the Due Process Clause gave an abstract and inviolable right "to marry, establish a home and bring up children," Justice McReynolds asserted also that the Due Process Clause prevented States from interfering with "the right of the individual to contract."

My Brother Goldberg has adopted the recent discovery [12] that the Ninth Amendment as well as the Due Process Clause can be used by this Court as authority to strike down all state legislation which this Court thinks violates "fundamental principles of liberty and justice," or is contrary to the "traditions and collective conscience of our people." [One] would certainly have to look far beyond the language of the Ninth Amendment to find that the Framers vested in this Court any such awesome veto powers over lawmaking. [The Ninth] Amendment was passed [to] limit the Federal Government to the powers granted expressly or by necessary implication. [This] fact is perhaps responsible for the peculiar phenomenon that for a period of a century and a half no serious suggestion was ever made that [that] Amendment, enacted to protect state powers against federal invasion, could be used as a weapon of federal power to prevent state legislatures from passing laws they consider appropriate to govern local affairs. * * *

I realize that many good and able men have eloquently spoken and written [of] the duty of this Court to keep the Constitution in tune with the times [but I] reject that philosophy. The Constitution makers knew the need for change and provided for it. [The] Due Process Clause with an "arbitrary and capricious" or "shocking to the conscience" formula was liberally used by this Court to strike down economic legislation in the early decades of this century, threatening, many people thought, the tranquility and stability of the Nation. See, e.g., *Lochner*. That formula, based on subjective considerations of "natural justice," is no less dangerous when used to enforce this Court's views about personal rights than those about economic rights. [So] far as I am concerned, Connecticut's law as applied here is not forbidden by any provision of the Federal Constitution as that Constitution was written, and I would therefore affirm.

JUSTICE STEWART, whom JUSTICE BLACK joins, dissenting.

[T]his is an uncommonly silly law. As a practical matter, the law is obviously unenforceable, except in the oblique context of the present case. As a philosophical matter, I believe the use of contraceptives in the relationship of marriage should be left to personal and private [choice]. As a matter of social policy, I think professional counsel about methods of birth control should be available to all, so that each individual's choice can be meaningfully made. But we are not [asked] whether we think this law is unwise, or even asinine. We are asked to hold that it violates the United States Constitution. And that I cannot do.

In the course of its opinion the Court refers to no less than six Amendments [but] does not say which of these Amendments, if any, it thinks is infringed by this Connecticut law. [As] to the First, Third, Fourth, and Fifth Amendments, I can find nothing in any of them to invalidate this Connecticut law, even assuming that all those amendments are fully applicable against the States. [The] Ninth Amendment, like its companion the Tenth [was] simply to make clear that the adoption of the Bill of Rights did not alter the plan that the *Federal* Government was to be a government of express and limited powers, and that all rights and powers not delegated to it were retained by the people and the individual States. Until today no member of this Court has ever suggested that the Ninth Amendment meant anything [else].

12. See Patterson, *The Forgotten Ninth Amendment* (1955). Mr. Patterson urges that the Ninth Amendment be used to protect unspecified "natural and inalienable rights." The Introduction by Roscoe Pound states that "there is a marked revival of natural law ideas throughout the world. Interest in the Ninth Amendment is a symptom of that revival."

* * *

What provision of the Constitution, then, does make this state law invalid? The Court says it is the right of privacy "created by several fundamental constitutional guarantees." [I] can find no such general right of privacy in the Bill of Rights, in any other part of the Constitution, or in any case ever before decided by this Court.

At the oral argument [we] were told that the Connecticut law does not "conform to current community standards." But it is not the function of this Court to decide cases on the basis of community standards. [If], as I should surely hope, the law before us does not reflect the standards of the people of Connecticut, the people of Connecticut can freely exercise their true Ninth and Tenth Amendment rights to persuade their elected representatives to repeal it. That is the constitutional way to take this law off the books.

Notes and Questions

1. *Is Douglas, J.'s argument logical?* Consider Louis Henkin, *Privacy and Autonomy,* 74 Colum.L.Rev. 1410, 1421–22 (1974): "Although it is not wholly clear, Justice Douglas's argument seems to go something like this: since the Constitution, in various 'specifics' of the Bill of Rights and in their penumbra, protects rights which partake of privacy, it protects other aspects of privacy as well, indeed it recognizes a general, complete right of privacy. And since the right emanates from specific fundamental rights, it too is 'fundamental,' its infringement is suspect and calls for strict scrutiny, and it can be justified only by a high level of public good. A logician, I suppose, might have trouble with that argument. A legal draftsman, indeed, might suggest the opposite: when the Constitution sought to protect private rights it specified them; that it explicitly protects some elements of privacy, but not others, suggests that it did not mean to protect those not mentioned."

2. *Did Griswold successfully avoid "renewing the romance" with "substantive due process"?* *Griswold,* observes Lupu, at 994, "provided the severest test for a Court determined to advance chosen values [without] renewing the romance with the dreaded demon of substantive due process. [Douglas, J.,] drew upon the incorporation legacy, rather than a doctrine of 'naked' substantive due process, and tortured the Bill of Rights into yielding a protected zone of privacy that would not tolerate a law banning contraceptive use by married couples. Justice Goldberg's reliance upon the ninth amendment [was] equally disingenuous in its attempt to avoid the jaws of substantive due process. Only Justices White and Harlan were willing to grapple directly with the fearful creature, and concluded that a law invading marital choice about contraception violated the due process clause itself, independent of links with the Bill of Rights. Shocking though that analysis may have been at the time, subsequent developments seem to have confirmed the White-Harlan view, and not the magical mystery tour of the zones of privacy, as the prevailing doctrine of *Griswold* [referring to *Moore v. East Cleveland* (1977), infra]."

3. *Emanations-and-penumbras theory and "economic" vs. "personal" rights.* Do any of the Justices analytically distinguish between "economic" and "personal" rights? Or is the distinction "only self-imposed"? Consider Paul Kauper, *Penumbras, Peripheries, Emanations, Things Fundamental and Things Forgotten: The Griswold Case,* 64 Mich.L.Rev. 235, 253 (1965).

4. *Are the courts authorized to plug glaring gaps in the Constitution?* Consider Richard Posner, *Sex and Reason* 328 (1992). Judge Posner is not interested in "joining the snipe hunt for a convincing legal-doctrinal ground for

the *Griswold* decision" and "doubt[s] that one exists." "But," he asks, "should that be the end of the legal analysis?" He continues:

"A constitution that did not invalidate so offensive, oppressive, probably undemocratic, and sectarian a law would stand revealed as containing major gaps. Maybe that is the nature of our, as perhaps any, written Constitution; but yet, perhaps the courts are authorized to plug at least the more glaring gaps. Does anyone really believe, in his heart of hearts, that the Constitution should be interpreted so literally as to authorize every conceivable law that would not violate a specific constitutional clause? This would mean that a state could require everyone to marry, or to have sexual intercourse at least once a month, or that it could take away every couple's second child and place it in a foster home. Of course, no state is likely to do such things; and if it were likely, that would argue such a change of moral outlook in this nation as to make our present institutions a poor guide. Yet we do find it reassuring to think that the courts stand between us and legislative tyranny even if a particular form of tyranny was not foreseen and expressly forbidden by the framers of the Constitution."

5. *The "freedom" of a "talented textualist judge."* Although he recognizes that Justice Douglas's *Griswold* opinion "is widely regarded among law professors as fatally flawed," Mark Tushnet, *Two Notes on the Jurisprudence of Privacy,* 8 Const. Comm. 75, 79 (1991), emphasizes that "Justice Douglas's construct is purely textualist; that is, it pays close attention to the language of the Constitution and to the relations among its specific provisions." [a] Adds Tushnet:

"Textualism is ordinarily regarded as the most confining technique of constitutional interpretation, the one that places the most severe limits on a judge's ability to enact personal preferences into constitutional law. Justice Douglas's construct shows that this common perception is erroneous. A talented textualist judge has as much freedom as a talented nontextualist, whether the nontextualist is an originalist, an ethicist, or a process theorist. [By] showing that the purportedly most confining technique of constitutional interpretation can be turned to quite unexpected ends, Justice Douglas's opinion in *Griswold* supports the argument that controversies over methods of constitutional interpretation are unlikely to yield fruitful results of any sort."

6. *"Privacy" or "equality"?* "Seen in the context of the Warren Court's general jurisprudence," observes Martin Shapiro, *Fathers and Sons: The Court, the Commentators, and the Search for Values,* in The Burger Court 218, 228 (V. Blasi ed. 1983), "the fact situation in [*Griswold*] was crucial. The living law of Connecticut was that middle-class women received birth control information and purchased birth control supplies, and the Connecticut statute was enforced only to block the operation of birth control clinics that would bring these services to the poor. *Griswold* was an equality not a privacy decision * * *."

7. *Skinner and Griswold taken together.* Consider Tribe *Treatise* 1340: "Taken together with *Griswold,* which recognized as equally protected the individual's decision *not* to bear a child, the meaning of *Skinner* is that *whether one person's body shall be the source of another's life must be left to that person and that person alone to decide.* That principle seems to collide in the abortion cases

---

a. But cf. Henry Greely, *A Footnote to "Penumbra" in Griswold v. Connecticut,* 6 Const. Comm. 251, 262–65 (1989).

[infra] with a command that is no less fundamental: *an innocent life may not be taken except to save the life of another.*"

————

Griswold invalidated a ban on the *use* of contraceptives by *married* couples. EISENSTADT v. BAIRD, 405 U.S. 438, 92 S.Ct. 1029, 31 L.Ed.2d 349 (1972), overturned a conviction for violating a Massachusetts law making it a felony to *distribute* contraceptive materials, *except* in the case of registered physicians and pharmacists furnishing the materials to *married* persons. Baird had given a woman a package of vaginal foam at the end of his lecture on contraception. He was not charged with distributing to an unmarried person. No proof was offered as to the recipient's marital status. The crime charged was that Baird had no license, and thus no authority, to distribute to anyone. The Court, per BRENNAN, J., concluded that, since the statute is riddled with exceptions making contraceptives freely available and since, if protection of health were the rationale, the statute would be both discriminatory and overbroad, "the goals of deterring premarital sex and regulating the distribution of potentially harmful articles cannot reasonably be regarded as legislative aims." "[V]iewed as a prohibition on contraception per se" the statute "violates the rights of single persons under the Equal Protection Clause." For, "whatever the rights of the individual to access to contraceptives may be, the rights must be the same for the unmarried and the married alike":

"If under *Griswold* the distribution of contraceptives to married persons cannot be prohibited, a ban on distribution to unmarried persons would be equally impermissible. It is true that in *Griswold* the right of privacy in question inhered in the marital relationship. Yet the marital couple is not an independent entity with a mind and heart of its own, but an association of two individuals each with a separate intellectual and emotional make-up. If the right of privacy means anything, it is the right of the *individual,* married or single, to be free from unwarranted governmental intrusion into matters so fundamentally affecting a person as the decision whether to bear or beget a child. On the other hand, if *Griswold* is no bar to a prohibition on the distribution of contraceptives, the State could not, consistently with [equal protection,] outlaw distribution to unmarried but not to married persons. In each case the evil, as perceived by the State, would be identical, and the underinclusion would be invidious."

WHITE, J., joined by Blackmun, J., concurred, emphasizing that "the State did [not] convict Baird for distributing to an unmarried person [but because] Baird had no license and therefore no authority to distribute to anyone." "Given *Griswold,* and absent proof of the possible hazards of using vaginal foam, we could not sustain [Baird's] conviction had it been for selling or giving away foam to a married person. Just as in *Griswold,* where the right of married persons to use contraceptives was 'diluted or adversely affected' by permitting a conviction for giving advice as to its exercise, so here to sanction a medical restriction upon distribution of a contraceptive not proved hazardous to health would impair the exercise of the constitutional right. That Baird could not be convicted for distributing [foam] to a married person disposes of this case. Assuming arguendo that the result would be otherwise had the recipient been unmarried, nothing has been placed in the record to indicate her marital status." [a]

a. Douglas, J., who joined the Court's opinion, also concurred on free speech grounds. Powell and Rehnquist, JJ., did not participate.

Burger, C.J., dissented, "see[ing] nothing in the Fourteenth Amendment or any other part of the Constitution that even vaguely suggests that these medicinal forms of contraceptives must be available in the open market. [By] relying on *Griswold* in the present context, the Court has passed beyond the penumbras of the specific guarantees into the uncircumscribed area of personal predilections."

Notes and Questions

1. *Does Eisenstadt offer a new rationale for Griswold?* Did *Eisenstadt* decide one of *Griswold*'s open issues—the constitutionality of a ban on the use or distribution of contraceptive devices that excluded from its reach the married couple—"by assertion, without a pretext of reasoning"? Harry Wellington, *Common Law Rules and Constitutional Double Standards*, 83 Yale L.J. 221, 296 (1973), so charges: "[W]hether the 'different classes' (married, not married) are [as *Eisenstadt* states] 'wholly unrelated to the objective of the statute,' depends on whether, as *Griswold* insists, the marriage relationship is important to that aspect of liberty that the Court calls privacy. How, then, [could the Court write *Eisenstadt* the way it did] without offering a new rationale for *Griswold*[?]" *Cf.* Thomas Gerety, *Doing Without Privacy*, 42 Ohio St.L.J. 143–44 (1981).

2. *Griswold "unmasked"?* Consider Richard Posner, *The Uncertain Protection of Privacy by the Supreme Court*, 1979 Sup.Ct.Rev. 173, 198: "*Griswold* had at least attempted to relate the right to use contraceptives to familiar notions of privacy by speculating on the intrusive methods by which a statute banning the use of contraceptives might be enforced. This ground was unavailable in [*Eisenstadt*] because the statute there forbade not the use, but only the distribution, of contraceptives. [*Eisenstadt*] is thus a pure essay in substantive due process. It unmasks *Griswold* as based on the idea of sexual liberty rather than privacy." Cf. Michael Perry, *Abortion, the Public Morals, and the Police Power*, 23 U.C.L.A.L.Rev. 689, 705–06 (1976).

3. *The real objection to the statute at issue in Eisenstadt.* The real objection, observes Richard Posner, *Sex and Reason* 330 (1992), "is not that it cannot deter fornication. It will deter some. Indeed, it will deter a good deal more than a statute, unenforceable as a practical matter, making fornication a misdemeanor—the statute whose constitutionality was not questioned." Continues Posner:

"The real objection to the statute is that there is no good reason to deter premarital sex, a generally harmless source of pleasure and for some people an important stage of marital search. (Yet this is an equal objection to a statute forbidding fornication, and the Court has never questioned the constitutionality of such statutes.) There are good reasons for wanting to deter unwanted pregnancies, but that aim is more likely to be achieved by encouraging than by discouraging the use of contraceptives. [An implication of the Court's opinion] is that notwithstanding the unchallenged misdemeanor fornication law (easily overlooked because totally unenforced), unmarried persons have a constitutional right to engage in sexual intercourse. For if they do not, it is an illegal activity; and how can the Constitution be violated by a state's prohibiting the sale of an input (contraception) into that activity?"

4. *The seed from which Roe grew.* According to former Solicitor General Charles Fried, *Order and Law* 77 (1991), when Justice Brennan made the "passing remark" in *Eisenstadt* about the right of the individual to be free from unwarranted governmental intrusion into such matters "as the decision whether to bear or beget a child" he "planted" the "seed [from] which *Roe* grew, so that later [in *Carey* (1977), discussed in the next Note], [he] could say that what

Griswold stood for all along was the proposition that there is a 'constitutional protection of individual autonomy in matters of childbearing.' [When] Justice Brennan, in [*Eisenstadt*], a contraception case, slipped in the irrelevant term 'childbearing,' he was digging a kind of surreptitious doctrinal tunnel to get from *Poe* to *Roe,* a tunnel that a year later would allow Justice Blackmun to get past the critical barrier between contraception and abortion, between what undoubtedly is a matter of privacy and what to some is murder."

5. *From Griswold to Eisenstadt to Carey.* The effect of *Eisenstadt,* notes Tribe *Treatise* 1339, was to "single out as decisive in *Griswold* the element of reproductive autonomy, something the Court made clear in 1977, when it extended *Griswold* and *Baird* " in CAREY v. POPULATION SERVICES INTERN., 431 U.S. 678, 97 S.Ct. 2010, 52 L.Ed.2d 675 (1977), to invalidate a New York law which allowed only pharmacists to sell non-medical contraceptive devices to persons over 16 and prohibited the sale of such items to those under 16. (The Court relied in part on the 1973 *Abortion Cases,* infra.) In striking down the restriction on sales to adults, BRENNAN, J., spoke for six justices; in invalidating the ban on sales to those under 16, he spoke for a four-justice plurality.

As for the restriction on distribution to adults, "where a decision as fundamental as that whether to bear or beget a child is involved, regulations imposing a burden on it may be justified only by compelling interests, and must be narrowly drawn to express only those interests"—and the Court found none of the state interests advanced (e.g., protecting health, facilitating enforcement of other laws) to be "compelling." [a] The state argued that *Griswold* dealt only with the *use* of contraceptives, not their manufacture or sale, but read "in light of its progeny, the teaching of *Griswold* is that the Constitution protects individual decisions in matters of childbearing from unjustified intrusion by the State."

As for the ban on sales to those under 16, Brennan, J., joined by Stewart, Marshall, and Blackmun, JJ., applied a test "apparently less rigorous than the 'compelling state interest' test applied to restrictions on the privacy rights of adults"—restrictions inhibiting privacy rights of minors are valid "only if they serve 'any significant state interest [that] is not present in the case of an adult.' *Planned Parenthood v. Danforth,* infra]." The plurality then rejected what it called "the argument [that] minors' sexual activity may be deterred by increasing the hazards attendant on it," pointing out that that argument had already been rejected by the Court in related areas.[b]

Powell, J., concurred in the judgment, observing that by restricting not only the kinds of retail outlets that may distribute contraceptives, "but even prohibit[ing] distribution by mail to adults"—"thus requiring individuals to buy contraceptives over the counter"—the New York provision "heavily burdens constitutionally protected freedom." He saw "no justification for subjecting restrictions on the sexual activity of the young to heightened judicial review"—"a standard that for all practical purposes approaches the 'compelling interest' standard"—but

a. The Court recognized, however, that "other restrictions may well be reasonably related to the objective of quality control," and thus "express[ed] no opinion on, for example, restrictions on the distribution of contraceptives through vending machines."

b. Nor was the restriction on the privacy rights of minors "saved" by another provision authorizing physicians to supply minors with contraceptives. As with limitations on distribution to adults, "less than total restrictions on access to contraceptives that significantly burden the right to decide whether to bear children must also pass constitutional muster. [This provision] delegates the State's authority to disapprove of minors' sexual behavior to physicians, who may exercise it arbitrarily * * *.''

concurred in the invalidation of the "distribution to minors" restriction on narrow grounds.[c]

ORAL ARGUMENTS IN THE ABORTION CASES [*]

* * *

THE COURT: [I]s it critical to your case that the fetus not be a person under the due process clause? [W]ould you lose your case if the fetus was a person?

SARAH WEDDINGTON [on behalf of appellant Roe]: Then you would have a balancing of interests.

THE COURT: Well you say you have [that] anyway, don't you? * * *

THE COURT: [If] it were established that an unborn fetus is a person, [protected by] the Fourteenth Amendment, you would have almost an impossible case here, would you not?

WEDDINGTON: I would have a very difficult case. * * *

THE COURT: Could Texas constitutionally, in your view, declare [by] statute [that] the fetus is a person, for all constitutional purposes, after the third month of gestation?

WEDDINGTON: I do not believe that the State legislature can determine the meaning of the Federal Constitution. It is up to this Court to make that determination. * * *

ROBERT FLOWERS [on behalf of appellee]: [I]t is the position of the State of Texas that, upon conception, we have a human being; a person, within the concept of the Constitution of the United States, and that of Texas, also.

THE COURT: Now how should that question be decided? Is it a legal question? A constitutional question? A medical question? A philosophical question? Or, a religious question? Or what is it?

FLOWERS: [W]e feel that it could be best decided by a legislature, in view of the fact that they can bring before it the medical testimony * * *.

THE COURT: So then it's basically a medical question?

FLOWERS: From a constitutional standpoint, no, sir. * * *

THE COURT: Of course, if you're right about [the fetus being a person within the meaning of the Constitution], you can sit down, you've won your case. * * * Except insofar as, maybe, the Texas abortion law presently goes too far in allowing abortions.

FLOWERS: Yes, sir. That's exactly right. * * *

THE COURT: Do you think [you have] lost your case, then, if the fetus or the embryo is not a person? Is that it?

FLOWERS: Yes sir, I would say so. * * *

c. White and Stevens, JJ., concurred only in the judgment with respect to the restriction on minors. Rehnquist, J., dissented, observing that if those responsible for the Bill of Rights and Civil War Amendments could have lived to know what their efforts had wrought "it is not difficult to imagine their reaction." Burger, C.J., dissented without opinion.

* These extracts are taken from 75 *Landmark Briefs and Arguments of the Supreme Court of the United States: Constitutional Law* 807–33 (Kurland & Casper ed.).

THE COURT: Under State law [there] are some rights given to the fetus?

FLOWERS: Yes, sir.

THE COURT: And you are asserting these rights against the right of the mother. [And] that's wholly aside from whether the fetus is a person under the Federal Constitution. * * *

FLOWERS: Yes, sir. * * *

THE COURT: I want you to give me [a] medical writing of any kind that says that at the time of conception the fetus is a person. * * *

FLOWERS: [I] find no way [that] any court or any legislature or any doctor anywhere can say that here is the dividing line. Here is not a life; and here is a life, after conception. Perhaps it would be better left to that legislature. * * *

THE COURT: Well, if you're right that an unborn fetus is a person, then you can't leave it to the legislature to play fast and loose dealing with that person. [I]f you're correct, in your basic submission that an unborn fetus is a person, then abortion laws such as that which New York has are grossly unconstitutional, isn't it?

FLOWERS: That's right, yes.

THE COURT: Allowing the killing of people.

FLOWERS: Yes, sir. * * *

[Rebuttal argument of Weddington]

THE COURT: [I] gather your argument is that a state may not protect the life of the fetus or prevent an abortion [at] any time during pregnancy? Right up until the moment of birth? * * *

WEDDINGTON: [T]here is no indication [that] the Constitution would give any protection prior to birth. That is not before the Court. * * *

THE COURT: Well, I don't know whether it is or isn't. * * *

ROE v. WADE

410 U.S. 113, 93 S.Ct. 705, 35 L.Ed.2d 147 (1973).

JUSTICE BLACKMUN delivered the opinion of the Court.

This Texas federal appeal and its Georgia companion, *Doe v. Bolton,* [infra,] present constitutional challenges to state criminal abortion legislation. The Texas statutes [are] typical of those that have been in effect in many States for approximately a century. The Georgia statutes, in contrast, have a modern cast and are a legislative product that, to an extent at least, obviously reflects the influences of recent attitudinal change, of advancing medical knowledge and techniques, and of new [thinking]. The Texas statutes [make procuring an abortion a crime except] "by medical advice for the purpose of saving the life of the mother."

[Jane] Roe alleged that she was unmarried and pregnant [and] that she was unable to get a "legal" abortion in Texas because her life did not appear to be threatened by the continuation of her pregnancy.[a] [The district court held the

---

a. Who was "Jane Roe"? Her real name was Norma McCorvey. Shortly after *Roe* was decided, she revealed who she really was. She explained then that she was an unmarried

Texas abortion statutes unconstitutional, but denied the injunctive relief requested. Roe appealed.]

[R]estrictive criminal abortion laws [like Texas'] in effect in a majority of States [today] derive from statutory changes effected, for the most part, in the latter half of the 19th century. [The Court then reviewed, in some detail, "ancient attitudes," "the Hippocratic Oath" which forbids abortion, "the common law," "the English statutory law," and "the American law." Subsequently, it described the positions of the American Medical Association, the American Public Health Association, and the American Bar Association. Thus,] at common law, at the time of the adoption of our Constitution, and throughout the major portion of the 19th century, [a] woman enjoyed a substantially broader right to terminate a pregnancy than she does in most States today. * * *

Three reasons have been advanced to explain historically the enactment of criminal abortion laws in the 19th century and to justify their [continuance].

It has been argued occasionally that these laws were the product of a Victorian social concern to discourage illicit sexual conduct. Texas, however, does not advance this justification [and] it appears that no court or commentator has taken the argument seriously.

[A] second reason is [that when] most criminal abortion laws were first enacted, the procedure was a hazardous one for the woman. [But] medical data indicat[es] that abortion in early pregnancy, that is, prior to the end of first trimester, although not without its risk, is now relatively safe.

[The] third reason is the State's interest—some phrase it in terms of duty—in protecting prenatal life. Some of the argument for this justification rests on the theory that a new human life is present from the moment of conception. [Only] when the life of the pregnant mother herself is at stake, balanced against the life she carries within her, should the interest of the embryo or fetus not prevail. [In] assessing the State's interest, recognition may be given to the less rigid claim that as long as at least *potential* life is involved, the State may assert interests beyond the protection of the pregnant woman alone. [It] is with these interests, and the weight to be attached to them, that this case is concerned.

The Constitution does not explicitly mention any right of privacy. [But] the Court has recognized that a right of personal privacy, or a guarantee of certain areas or zones of privacy, does exist under the Constitution. In varying contexts the Court or individual Justices have indeed found at least the roots of that right in the First Amendment, *Stanley v. Georgia* [p. 703 infra]; in the Fourth and

woman who had become pregnant as a result of a gang rape. She had tried to get an abortion, but had been unable to pay the price ($650) demanded by a doctor she finally found who was willing to perform an abortion. Because she did not want to subject to "public ridicule" a young child she had from a previous marriage, Ms. McCorvey's one condition for going ahead with the legal challenge was that she remain anonymous. See Philip Bobbitt, *Constitutional Fate* 165 (1982); Fred Friendly & Martha Elliott, *The Constitution: That Delicate Balance* 202–04 (1984). But, as noted in Laurence Tribe, *Abortion: The Clash of Absolutes* 5 (1990), a decade and a half after *Roe* was decided "McCorvey explained, with embar-

rassment, that she had not been raped after all; she had made up the story to hide the fact that she had gotten 'in trouble' in the more usual way. Many reacted with dismay. How could the heroine of the most important abortion rights case have deceived the advocates of such rights?" Comments Tribe: "Few asked why [McCorvey] had felt a *need* to deceive them. In a different sort of society the life she would have faced as an unwed mother might not have been nearly so lonely. In such a society she might not have made up a story about how she became pregnant. In such a society she might not even have chosen an abortion."

Fifth Amendments; in the penumbras of the Bill of Rights, *Griswold;* in the Ninth Amendment, id. (Goldberg, J., concurring); or in the concept of liberty guaranteed by the first section of the Fourteenth Amendment, see *Meyer.* These decisions make it clear that only personal rights that can be deemed "fundamental" or "implicit in the concept of ordered liberty," are included in this guarantee of personal privacy. They also make it clear that the right has some extension to activities relating to marriage, *Loving;* procreation, *Skinner;* contraception, *Eisenstadt;* family relationships, *Prince v. Massachusetts* [discussed at p. 1021 infra]; and child rearing and education, *Pierce.*[b]

This right of privacy, whether it be founded in the Fourteenth Amendment's concept of personal liberty [as] we feel it is, [or] in the [Ninth Amendment], is broad enough to encompass a woman's decision whether or not to terminate her pregnancy. The detriment that the State would impose upon the pregnant woman by denying this choice altogether is apparent. Specific and direct harm medically diagnosable even in early pregnancy may be [involved]. Psychological harm may be imminent. Mental and physical health may be taxed by child care. There is also the distress, for all concerned, associated with the unwanted child, and there is the problem of bringing a child into a family already unable, psychologically and otherwise, to care for it. In other cases, as in this one, the additional difficulties and continuing stigma of unwed motherhood may be involved. All these are factors the woman and her responsible physician necessarily will consider in consultation.

On the basis of elements such as these, appellants and some amici argue that the woman's right is absolute and that she is entitled to terminate her pregnancy at whatever time, in whatever way, and for whatever reason she alone chooses. With this we do not agree. [The] Court's decisions recognizing a right of privacy also acknowledge that some state regulation in areas protected by that right is appropriate. [A] state may properly assert important interests in safeguarding health, in maintaining medical standards, and in protecting potential life. At some point in pregnancy, these respective interests become sufficiently compelling to sustain regulation of the factors that govern the abortion decision.

[Where] certain "fundamental rights" are involved, the Court has held that regulation limiting these rights may be justified only by a "compelling state interest," and that legislative enactments must be narrowly drawn to express only the legitimate state interests at stake.

[Appellee argues] that the fetus is a "person" within the language and meaning of the Fourteenth Amendment. [If so,] appellant's case, of course, collapses, for the fetus' right to life is then guaranteed specifically by the Amendment.

[The] Constitution does not define "person" in so many words. [The Court then listed each provision in which the word appears.] But in nearly all these instances, the use of the word is such that it has application only postnatally. None indicates, with any assurance, that it has any possible pre-natal application. All this, together with our observation that throughout the major portion of the 19th century prevailing legal abortion practices were far freer [than] today, persuades us that the word "person," as used in the Fourteenth Amendment, does not include the unborn. [Thus,] we pass on to other considerations.

b. Do these parental rights permit parents to forbid public school teachers from imposing corporal punishment on their children? See *Ingraham v. Wright* (1977) (p. 606 infra).

The pregnant woman cannot be isolated in her privacy. She carries an embryo and, later, a fetus. [The] situation therefore is inherently different from marital intimacy, or bedroom possession of obscene material, or marriage, or procreation, or education, with which *Eisenstadt, Griswold, Stanley, Loving, Skinner, Pierce,* and *Meyer* [were] concerned.

[Texas] urges that, apart from the Fourteenth Amendment, life begins at conception and is present throughout pregnancy, and that, therefore, the State has a compelling interest in protecting that life from and after conception. We need not resolve the difficult question of when life begins. When those trained [in] medicine, philosophy, and theology are unable to arrive at any consensus, the judiciary, at this point in the development of man's knowledge, is not in a position to speculate as to the answer.

[W]e do not agree that, by adopting one theory of life, Texas may override the rights of the pregnant woman that are at stake. We repeat, however, that the State does have an important and legitimate interest in preserving and protecting the health of the pregnant woman [and] that it has still *another* important and legitimate interest in protecting the potentiality of human life. These interests are separate and distinct. Each grows in substantiality as the woman approaches term and, at a point during pregnancy, each becomes "compelling."

With respect to [the] interest in the health of the mother, the "compelling" point, in the light of present medical knowledge, is at approximately the end of the first trimester. This is so because of the now established medical fact that until the end of the first trimester mortality in abortion is less than mortality in normal childbirth. It follows that, from and after this point, a State may regulate the abortion procedure to the extent that the regulation reasonably relates to the preservation and protection of maternal health. Examples of permissible state regulation in this area are requirements as to the qualifications of the person who is to perform the abortion; [as] to the facility in which the procedure is to be performed, [and] the like. This means, on the other hand, that, for the period of pregnancy prior to this "compelling" point, the attending physician, in consultation with his patient, is free to determine, without regulation by the State, that in his medical judgment the patient's pregnancy should be terminated. If that decision is reached, the judgment may be effectuated by an abortion free of interference by the State.

With respect to [the] interest in potential life, the "compelling" point is at viability [which "is usually placed at about seven months (28 weeks) but may occur earlier, even at 24 weeks."] This is so because the fetus then presumably has the capability of meaningful life outside the mother's womb.[c] State regula-

c. Earlier in its opinion, 410 U.S. at 160, the Court described the point "at which the fetus becomes 'viable' " as the point that the fetus is "potentially able to live outside the mother's womb, albeit with artificial aid." *Planned Parenthood v. Danforth* (1976) (other aspects of which are discussed infra), per Blackmun, J., upheld a Missouri abortion statute defining "viability" as "that stage of fetal development when the life of the unborn child may be continued indefinitely outside the womb by natural or artificial life-supportive systems." In rejecting contentions that the Missouri statute unduly expanded the *Roe* Court's definition of "viability," failed to contain any reference to a gestational time period, and failed to incorporate and reflect the three stages of pregnancy, the Court observed: "[W]e recognized in *Roe* that viability was a matter of medical judgment, skill, and technical ability, and we preserved the flexibility of the term. [The Missouri statute] does the same. [I]t is not the proper function of the legislature or the courts to place viability, which essentially is a medical concept, at a specific point in the gestation period. The time when viability is achieved may vary with each pregnancy, and the determination of whether a particular fetus is viable is, and must be, a matter for the judgment of the

tion protective of fetal life after viability thus has both logical and biological justifications. If the State is interested in protecting fetal life after viability, it may go as far as to proscribe abortion during that period except when it is necessary to preserve the life or health of the mother.

Measured against these standards, [the Texas statute] sweeps too broadly [and] therefore, cannot survive the constitutional attack made upon it here.

[In] *Doe* [infra], procedural requirements contained in one of the modern abortion statutes are considered. That opinion and this one [are] to be read together.[67]

This holding, we feel, is consistent with the relative weights of the respective interests involved, with the lessons and examples of medical and legal history, with the lenity of the common law, and with the demands of the profound problems of the present day. The decision leaves the State free to place increasing restrictions on abortion as the period of pregnancy lengthens, so long as those restrictions are tailored to the recognized state interests. The decision vindicates the right of the physician to administer medical treatment according to his professional judgment up to the points where important state interests provide compelling justifications for intervention. Up to those points, the abortion decision in all its aspects is inherently, and primarily, a medical decision, and basic responsibility for it must rest with the physician. If an individual practitioner abuses the privilege of exercising proper medical judgment, the usual remedies, judicial and intra-professional, are available. * * *

JUSTICE STEWART, concurring.

In 1963, this Court, in *Ferguson v. Skrupa* [372 U.S. 726, 83 S.Ct. 1028, 10 L.Ed.2d 93 (1963)], purported to sound the death knell for the doctrine of substantive due process, [but] [b]arely two years later, in *Griswold,* the Court held a Connecticut birth control law unconstitutional. In view of what had been so recently said in *Skrupa,* the Court's opinion in *Griswold* understandably did its best to avoid reliance on the Due Process Clause of the Fourteenth Amendment as

responsible attending physician. [The statutory definition] merely reflects this fact."

Consider, too, *Colautti v. Franklin,* 439 U.S. 379, 99 S.Ct. 675, 58 L.Ed.2d 596 (1979), per Blackmun, J., striking down on "void for vagueness" grounds a Pennsylvania provision requiring use of a statutorily prescribed technique when the fetus is "viable" or when there is "sufficient reason to believe that the fetus may be viable": "[The provision] subjects the physician to potential criminal liability without regard to fault. [I]t is not unlikely that experts will disagree over whether a particular fetus in the second trimester has advanced to the stage of viability. The prospect of such disagreement, in conjunction with a statute imposing liability for an erroneous determination of viability, could have a profound chilling effect on the willingness of physicians to perform abortions near the point of viability in the manner indicated by their best medical judgment." (White, J., joined by Burger, C.J. and Rehnquist, J., dissented, disagreeing with the Court's interpretation of the statute).

On similar analysis, the *Colautti* majority held "void for vagueness" a provision requir-

ing that "the abortion technique employed shall be that which would provide the best opportunity for the fetus to be aborted alive so long as a different technique would not be necessary to preserve the life or health of the mother."

Colautti reaffirmed that the determination of "viability" is "a matter for medical judgment" and that that point is reached "when, in the judgment of the attending physician on the particular facts of the case before him, there is a reasonable likelihood of the fetus' sustained survival outside the womb, with or without artificial support. Because this point may differ with each pregnancy, neither the legislature nor the courts may proclaim one of the elements entering into the ascertainment of viability—be it weeks of gestation or fetal weight or any other single factor—as the determinant of when the State has a compelling interest in the life or health of the fetus."

67. Neither in this opinion nor in *Doe* do we discuss the father's rights, if any exist in the constitutional context, in the abortion decision. No paternal right has been asserted in either of the [cases].

the ground for decision, [but] it was clear to me then, and it is equally clear to me now, that the *Griswold* decision can be rationally understood only as a holding that the Connecticut statute substantively invaded the "liberty" that is protected by the Due Process Clause of the Fourteenth Amendment. As so understood, *Griswold* stands as one in a long line of pre-*Skrupa* cases decided under the doctrine of substantive due process, and I now accept it as such.

[The] Constitution nowhere mentions a specific right of personal choice in matters of marriage and family life, but the "liberty" protected by the Due Process Clause of the Fourteenth Amendment covers more than those freedoms explicitly named in the Bill of Rights. [As] recently as last Term, in *Eisenstadt,* we recognized "the right of the *individual,* married or single, to be free from unwarranted governmental intrusion into matters so fundamentally affecting a person as the decision whether to bear or beget a child." That right necessarily includes the right of a woman to decide whether or not to terminate her pregnancy. [It] is evident that the Texas abortion statute infringes that right directly. [The] question then becomes whether the state interests advanced to justify this abridgment can survive the "particularly careful scrutiny" that the Fourteenth Amendment here requires.

The asserted state interests are protection of the health and safety of the pregnant woman, and protection of the potential future human life within her. These are legitimate objectives, amply sufficient to permit a State to regulate abortions as it does other surgical procedures, and perhaps sufficient to permit a State to regulate abortions more stringently or even to prohibit them in the late stages of pregnancy. But such legislation is not before us, and I think the Court today has thoroughly demonstrated that these state interests cannot constitutionally support the broad abridgment of personal liberty worked by the existing Texas law. * * *

Justice Douglas, concurring [in *Doe* as well as in *Roe*].

While I join the opinion of the Court, I add a few words.

[The] Ninth Amendment obviously does not create federally enforceable rights. [But] a catalogue of [the rights "retained by the people"] includes customary, traditional, and time-honored rights, amenities, privileges, and immunities that come within the sweep of "the Blessings of Liberty" mentioned in the preamble to the Constitution. Many of them in my view come within the meaning of the term "liberty" as used in the Fourteenth Amendment.

First is the autonomous control over the development and expression of one's intellect, interests, tastes, and personality. These are rights protected by the First Amendment and in my view they are absolute * * *.

Second is freedom of choice in the basic decisions of one's life respecting marriage, divorce, procreation, contraception, and the education and upbringing of children. These rights, unlike those protected by the First Amendment, are subject to some control by the police power. [They] are "fundamental" and we have held that in order to support legislative action the statute must be narrowly and precisely drawn and that a "compelling state interest" must be shown in support of the limitation. * * *[4]

4. My Brother Stewart, writing in the present cases, says that our decision in *Griswold* reintroduced substantive due process that had been rejected in [*Skrupa*]. There is nothing specific in the Bill of Rights that covers [the marital relation]. Nor is there anything in the Bill of Rights that in terms protects the right of association or the privacy in one's association. [Other] peripheral rights are the right to educate one's children as one chooses, and the

[Third] is the freedom to care for one's health and person, freedom from bodily restraint or compulsion, freedom to walk, stroll, or loaf. These rights, though fundamental, are likewise subject to regulation on a showing of "compelling state interest." * * * Elaborate argument is hardly necessary to demonstrate that childbirth may deprive a woman of her preferred life style and force upon her a radically different and undesired future.

[Such reasoning] is, however, only the beginning of the problem. [V]oluntary abortion at any time and place regardless of medical standards would impinge on a rightful concern of society. The woman's health is part of that concern; as is the life of the fetus after quickening. These concerns justify the State in treating the procedure as a medical one.

[T]he Georgia statute outlaws virtually all such operations—even in the earliest stages of pregnancy. In light of modern medical evidence [it] cannot be seriously urged that so comprehensive a ban is aimed at protecting the woman's health. Rather, [this ban] can rest only on a public goal of preserving both embryonic and fetal life.

The present statute has struck the balance between the woman and the State's interests wholly in favor of the latter. [We] held in *Griswold* that the States may not preclude spouses from attempting to avoid the joinder of sperm and egg. [I]t is difficult to perceive any overriding public necessity which might attach precisely at the moment of conception.

[The] protection of the fetus when it has acquired life is a legitimate concern of the State. Georgia's law makes no rational, discernible decision on that score. For under the Act the developmental stage of the fetus is irrelevant when pregnancy is the result of rape or when the fetus will very likely be born with a permanent defect or when a continuation of the pregnancy will endanger the life of the mother or permanently injure her health. When life is present is a question we do not try to resolve. While basically a question for medical experts, [it is], of course, caught up in matters of religion and morality. * * *

JUSTICE WHITE, with whom JUSTICE REHNQUIST joins, dissenting [in *Doe* as well as in *Roe*].

At the heart of the controversy in these cases are those recurring pregnancies that pose no danger whatsoever to the life or health of the mother but are nevertheless unwanted for any one or more of a variety of reasons—convenience, family planning, economics, dislike of children, the embarrassment of illegitimacy, etc. The common claim before us is that for any one of such reasons, or for no reason at all, and without asserting or claiming any threat to life or health, any woman is entitled to an abortion at her request if she is able to find a medical advisor willing to [perform it].

The Court for the most part sustains this position [and] simply fashions and announces a new constitutional right [and], with scarcely any reason or authority for its action, invests that right with sufficient substance to override most existing state abortion statutes. The upshot is that the people and the legislatures of the 50 States are constitutionally disentitled to weigh the relative importance of the continued existence and development of the fetus on the one hand against a spectrum of possible impacts on the mother on the other hand. As an exercise of

right to study the German language. These decisions with all respect, have nothing to do with substantive due process. One may think they are not peripheral rights to other rights that are expressed in the Bill of Rights. But that is not enough to bring into play the protection of substantive due process. * * *

raw judicial power, the Court perhaps has authority [but] in my view its judgment is an improvident and extravagant exercise of the power of judicial review * * *.

JUSTICE REHNQUIST, dissenting.   * * *

I have difficulty in concluding [that] the right of "privacy" is involved in this case. [Texas] bars the performance of a medical abortion by a licensed physician on a plaintiff such as Roe. A transaction resulting in an operation such as this is not "private" in the ordinary usage of that word. Nor is the "privacy" which the Court finds here even a distant relative of the freedom from searches and seizures protected by the Fourth Amendment.

[If] the Court means by the term "privacy" no more than that the claim of a person to be free from unwanted state regulation of consensual transactions may be a form of "liberty" * * * I agree [with] Mr. Justice Stewart [that that "liberty"] embraces more than the rights found in the Bill of Rights. But that liberty is not guaranteed absolutely against deprivation, but only against deprivation without due process of law. The test traditionally applied in the area of social and economic legislation is whether or not a law such as that challenged has a rational relation to a valid state objective. [If] the Texas statute were to prohibit an abortion even where the mother's life is in jeopardy, I have little doubt that such a statute would lack a rational relation to a valid state [objective].[d] But the Court's sweeping invalidation of any restrictions on abortion during the first trimester is impossible to justify under that [standard]. As in *Lochner* and similar cases applying substantive due process standards to economic and social welfare legislation, the adoption of the compelling state interest standard will inevitably require this Court to examine the legislative policies and pass on the wisdom of these policies in the very process of deciding whether a particular state interest put forward may or may not be "compelling." The decision here to break the term of pregnancy into three distinct terms and to outline the permissible restrictions the State may impose in each one, for example, partakes more of judicial legislation than it does of a determination of the intent of the drafters of the Fourteenth Amendment.

The fact that a majority of the States, reflecting after all the majority sentiment in those States, have had restrictions on abortions for at least a century seems to me as strong an indication there is that the asserted right to an abortion is not "so rooted in the traditions and conscience of our people as to be ranked as fundamental." Even today, when society's views on abortion are changing, the very existence of the debate is evidence that the "right" to an abortion is not so universally accepted as the appellants would have us believe.

[By] the time of the adoption of the Fourteenth Amendment in 1868 there were at least 36 laws enacted by state or territorial legislatures limiting abortion. [The] only conclusion possible from this history is that the drafters did not intend to have the Fourteenth Amendment withdraw from the States the power to legislate with respect to this matter. * * *

DOE v. BOLTON, 410 U.S. 179, 93 S.Ct. 739, 35 L.Ed.2d 201 (1973), the companion case to *Roe v. Wade*, sustained, against the contention that it had been rendered unconstitutionally vague by a three-judge district court's interpretation,

d. Is it "irrational" or "invalid" for a state to weigh the *possibility* (or even *probability*) that the mother will die without an abortion against the *certainty* that the fetus will not survive with one and then to legislate against abortions in such situations?

a Georgia provision that permitted a physician to perform an abortion when "based upon his best clinical judgment that an abortion is necessary." (The district court had struck down the statutorily specified reasons: because continued pregnancy would endanger a pregnant woman's life or injure her health; the fetus would likely be born with a serious defect; or the pregnancy resulted from rape.) "The net result of the District Court's decision," observed the Court, "is that the abortion determination, so far as the physician is concerned, is made in the exercise of his professional, that is, his 'best clinical,' judgment in the light of all the attendant circumstances. He is not now restricted to the three situations originally specified. Instead, [the] medical judgment may be exercised in light of all factors—physical, emotional, psychological, familial, and the woman's age— relevant to the well-being of the patient. All these factors may relate to health. This allows the attending physician the room he needs to make his best medical judgment. And it is room that operates for the benefit, not the disadvantage, of the pregnant woman."

However, despite the fact that the Georgia statute was patterned after the American Law Institute's Model Penal Code (1962), which had served as the model for recent legislation in about one-fourth of the states, the Court, per Blackmun, J., invalidated substantial portions of the statute. Struck down were requirements (1) that the abortion be performed in a hospital accredited by the Joint Commission on Accreditation of Hospitals (JCAH); (2) that the procedure be approved by a hospital staff abortion committee; and (3) that the performing physician's judgment be confirmed by independent examinations of the patient by two other physicians.

As for (1): There is no restriction of the performance of nonabortion surgery in a hospital not accredited by the JCAH. This requirement is also invalid "because it fails to exclude the first trimester of pregnancy, see *Roe*. [As] for (2), [we] see no constitutionally justifiable pertinence [for] the advance approval by the abortion committee. We are not cited to any other surgical procedure made subject to committee approval as a matter of state criminal law. The woman's right to receive medical care in accordance with the licensed physician's best judgment and the physician's right to administer it are substantially limited by this statutorily imposed overview." As for (3), the two-doctor concurrence, "the statute's emphasis [is] on the attending physician's 'best clinical judgment that an abortion is necessary.' That should be sufficient. [No] other voluntary medical or surgical procedure for which Georgia requires confirmation by two other physicians has been cited to us."

COMMENTARY ON THE *ABORTION CASES:* (A) WHETHER AND WHY THE CASES WERE WRONGLY DECIDED; (B) HOW A BETTER OPINION REACHING THE SAME RESULT MIGHT HAVE BEEN WRITTEN; AND (C) WHAT LIGHT THE CASES SHED ON THE NATURE OF THE BURGER COURT'S ACTIVISM

1. *The linkage between the abortion decision and the privacy cases.* Consider SUSAN ESTRICH & KATHLEEN SULLIVAN, *Abortion Politics: Writing for an Audience of One*, 138 U.Pa.L.Rev. 119, 125–27 (1989): "The privacy cases rest, as Justice Stevens recognized, [concurring in *Thornburgh*, p. 348 infra], centrally on 'the moral fact that a person belongs to himself [or herself] and not others nor to

society as a whole.' Extending this principle to the abortion decision follows from the fact that '[f]ew decisions [are] more basic to individual dignity and autonomy' or more appropriate to the 'private sphere of individual liberty' than the uniquely personal, intimate, and self-defining decision whether or not to continue a pregnancy [quoting from Blackmun, J., for the Court, in *Thornburgh.*].

"In two senses, abortion restrictions keep a woman from 'belonging to herself.' First and most obviously, they deprive her of bodily self-possession. [P]regnancy increases a woman's uterine size 500–1,000 times, her pulse rate by ten to fifteen beats a minute, and her body weight by 25 pounds or more. Even the healthiest pregnancy can entail nausea, vomiting, more frequent urination, fatigue, back pain, labored breathing, or water retention. There are also numerous medical risks involved in carrying pregnancy to term. [In] addition, labor and delivery impose extraordinary physical demands, whether over the six to twelve hour or longer course of vaginal delivery, or during the highly invasive surgery involved in a cesarean section, which accounts for one out of four deliveries.

"By compelling pregnancy to term and delivery even where they are unwanted, abortion restrictions thus exert far more profound intrusions into bodily integrity than the stomach pumping the Court invalidated in *Rochin* [p. 113 supra] or the surgical removal of a bullet from a shoulder [invalidated] in *Winston v. Lee* [470 U.S. 753, 105 S.Ct. 1611, 84 L.Ed.2d 662 (1985)]. 'The integrity of an individual's person is a cherished value of our society' [*Winston*] because it is so essential to identity; as former Solicitor General Charles Fried, who argued for the United States in *Webster* [p. 348 infra], recognized in another context: '[to say] that my body can be used is [to say] that I can be used.' "

2. *The precedents relied on by Roe.* Taken together, maintain Philip Heymann & Douglas Barzelay, *The Forest and the Trees: Roe v. Wade and Its Critics,* 53 B.U.L.Rev. 765, 772 (1973), the *Meyer–Pierce–Skinner–Griswold–Eisenstadt* line of cases "clearly delineate a sphere of interests—which the Court now groups and denominates 'privacy'—implicit in the 'liberty' protected by the fourteenth amendment. At the core of this sphere is the right of the individual to make for himself—except where a very good reason exists for placing the decision in society's hands—the fundamental decisions that shape family life: whom to many; whether and when to have children; and with what values to rear these children." But see Donald Regan, *Rewriting Roe v. Wade,* 77 Mich.L.Rev. 1569, 1639 (1979): "[The *Meyer–Eisenstadt* line of cases which Heymann & Barzelay say] establish a 'realm of private decision as to matters of marriage, procreation and child rearing' [are] a rag-tag lot. Most of them either claim to be or are best understood as being primarily about something other than marriage, procreation and child-rearing." Moreover, continues Regan, supra, at 1641–42: "Whether or not the cases from *Meyer* to *Eisenstadt* establish a right of family-related freedom-of-choice, none of these cases involves a state interest remotely like the interest in protecting 'potential' but *already conceived* human life. Accordingly none of those cases establishes or even suggests that the right of family-related freedom-of-choice is weighty enough to overcome the state's interest in forbidding abortion."

Consider, too, Richard Epstein, *Substantive Due Process by Any Other Name: The Abortion Cases,* 1973 Sup.Ct.Rev. 159, 170–72: "If we must hazard an attempt to find the common thread which runs through [the *Meyer–Eisenstadt* line of cases], it might well be the principle of classic liberalism: the state is entitled to restrict the liberty of any individual within its jurisdiction only where necessary to protect other persons from harm. [But] the general principle will have only an empty exception if 'harm to another' does not cover the death of another person. Let it be accepted that the unborn child is a person (or even is to be treated like one), and it is clear beyond all question that the abortion cases fall not within the general rule that protects the liberty of each person to do as he pleases but within the exception that governs the infliction of harm to others. And the case, moreover, becomes instantly distinguishable from that posed by the state regulation of contraception, because no one claims that there is a person before conception."

3. *Does Roe reflect the same circular reasoning of the earlier substantive due process cases?* JOSEPH GRANO, *Judicial Review and a Written Constitution in a Democratic Society*, 28 Wayne L.Rev. 1, 24 (1981) maintains that it does: The right to terminate a pregnancy can be deemed fundamental only if the fetus is not regarded as a form of life entitled to protection. No a priori moral principle can resolve the question of the fetus' status. By declaring the woman's right 'fundamental,' however, the Court necessarily rejected the legislative judgment that fetal life deserves protection. At this point, some might object that the Court merely concluded that public opinion was too divided to justify such a restraint on the woman's choice, but this conclusion went to the weight of the state's interest. The Court's test required that it first decide whether a fundamental right was implicated, and it could not do this, any more than it could in *Allgeyer* or *Lochner*, or any more than Justice Harlan could in *Poe v. Ullman*, without making its own moral assessment of the activity in question, an assessment not subject to demonstration by analytic reasoning."

4. *"Privacy" or "autonomy"—or "fundamentality"?* Consider LOUIS HENKIN, *Privacy and Autonomy*, 74 Colum.L.Rev. 1410, 1427 (1974): "Most aspects of an individual's life are not 'fundamental,' and in these his liberty is subject to the police power of federal and state governments, with presumptions of statutory validity, and a heavy, generally hopeless, burden on a resisting individual to show that a regulation has no conceivable public purpose, or that there is no rational relation between means and ends. Some, fewer, aspects of individual life are 'fundamental,' constitute a zone of prima facie autonomy (called Privacy), are presumed sacrosanct, and will bow only to a compelling public good clearly established. We are not told the basis—in language, history, or whatever else may be relevant to constitutional interpretation—for concluding that 'liberty' includes some individual autonomy that is 'fundamental' and much that is not. We are not told what is the touchstone for determining 'fundamentality.' We are not told why Privacy satisfies that test (unless Privacy is a tautology for fundamentality). [What] is it that makes my right to use contraceptives a right of Privacy, and fundamental, but my right to contract to work 16 hours a day or to pay more for milk than the law fixes, not a right of Privacy and not fundamental? Is it, as some suspect, that the game is being played backwards: that the private right which intuitively commends itself as valuable in our society in our time, or at least to a majority of our Justices at this time, is called fundamental, and if it cannot fit comfortably into specific constitutional provisions it is included in Privacy?"[a]

5. *Did the Court decide the question without admitting it?* Consider Michael McConnell, *How Not to Promote Serious Deliberation about Abortion*, 58 U.Chi. L.Rev. 1181, 1198 (1991): "Society has no choice but to decide to whom it will extend protection. It is not helpful to call this decision 'private' for there is no

---

a. See also Ira Lupu, *Untangling the Strands of the Fourteenth Amendment*, 77 Mich.L.Rev. 981, 1032–33 (1979); Michael Perry, *Substantive Due Process Revisited*, 71 Nw. U.L.Rev. 417, 440–41 (1976); Richard Posner, *The Uncertain Protection of Privacy in the Supreme Court*, 1979 Sup.Ct.Rev. 173, 199.

more inherently political question than the definition of the political community. When the *Roe* Court stated, '[w]e need not resolve the difficult question of when life begins,' it was deciding the question without admitting it, and thus without having to support its decision with reasons. Worse yet, it was suggesting that the question of human life was irrelevant to the decision. *Any* conscientious determination of when the developing fetus attains a moral-legal status worthy of protection, supported by reasons, would be preferable to that.''

6. *Is there no reality in the womb, only theories? Is personhood a biological fact or a legal status?* In one passage, protests John Noonan, *The Root and Branch of Roe v. Wade*, 63 Neb.L.Rev. 668, 672–73 (1984), "[*Roe*] spoke of the unborn before viability as 'a theory of life,' as though there were competing views as to whether life in fact existed before viability. The implication could also be found that there was no reality there in the womb but merely theories about what was there. [To] judge from the weight the Court gave the being in the womb—found to be protectible in any degree only in the last two months of pregnancy—the Court itself must have viewed the unborn as pure potentiality or a mere theory before viability. The Court's opinion appeared to rest on the assumption that the biological reality could be subordinated or ignored by the sovereign speaking through the Court.''

But consider Catharine MacKinnon, *Reflections on Sex Equality Under Law*, 100 Yale L.J. 1281, 1315 (1991): "[T]he only point of recognizing fetal personhood, or a separate fetal entity, is to assert the interests of the fetus *against* the pregnant woman. * * * Personhood is a legal and social status, not a biological fact. [In] my opinion and in the experience of many pregnant women, the fetus is a human form of life. It is alive. But the existence of sex inequality in society requires that completed live birth mark the personhood line. If sex equality existed socially—if women were recognized as persons, sexual aggression were truly deviant, and childrearing were shared and consistent with a full life rather than at odds with it—the fetus still might not be considered a person but the question of its political status would be a very different one.''[b]

7. *Is the question of when human life begins "nonjusticiable"?* Consider Scalia, J., concurring in *Ohio v. Akron Center for Reproductive Health* (1990) (p. 361 infra): "I continue to believe [that] the Constitution contains no right to abortion. It is not to be found in the longstanding traditions of our society, nor can it be logically deduced from the text of the Constitution—not, that is, without volunteering a judicial answer to the nonjusticiable question of when human life begins. Leaving this matter to the political process is not only legally correct, it is pragmatically so.'' Compare JED RUBENFELD, *On the Legal Status of the Proposition that "Life Begins at Conception,"* 43 Stan.L.Rev. 599, 615–16 (1991): "Justice Scalia has it exactly backward * * *. [G]iven the contraception cases, a right to abortion *cannot be denied* without volunteering a judicial answer to the question of when human life begins. To see why this is so, * * * suppose an overpopulated state embarked on a campaign of infanticide, supporting its measures with the determination that human life did not begin until age five. Personhood is not and cannot be a 'political question.' It is a question, indeed *the* question, of who holds legal rights. When the rights at stake are *constitutional*, state legislatures plainly are not entitled to the last word. [For] this reason,

b. See also Frances Olsen, *Unravelling Compromise*, 103 Harv.L.Rev. 105, 128 (1989); Jed Rubenfeld, *On the Legal Status of the Proposition that "Life Begins at Conception,"* 43 Stan.L.Rev. 599, 617–20, 627–35 (1991); Mark Tushnet, *Two Notes on the Jurisprudence of Privacy*, 8 Const.Comm. 75, 84–85 (1991). But cf. Laurence Tribe, *Abortion: The Clash of Absolutes* 119 (1990).

deference to a state's determination that life begins at conception *is* a judicial answer to Justice Scalia's 'nonjusticiable' question of when life begins. * * * Abortion cannot be flatly prohibited unless the judiciary either (1) abdicates its constitutional responsibility to oversee state determinations of personhood, or (2) concurs that fetuses may be regarded as persons from the moment of conception."

8. *Why must legislation assume that a nonviable fetus is* not *a person?* Consider CHARLES FRIED, *Order and Law* 78 (1991): "If the Constitution implied that a nonviable fetus is a person entitled to equal protection of the laws, then laws restricting abortion would be constitutionally compelled. I know of no argument forcing that inference, but I also know of no argument that the nonviable fetus is *not* such a person. On this question the Constitution is silent. It is in that space that legislators must choose. It is an utter non sequitur to pass from the premise that the Constitution is silent on this point to the conclusion that legislation must assume that the fetus is *not* a person. Nor is it sensible or even logical to argue that the very importance of the question forces us to fill up society's answer in constitutional rather than legislative terms. Matters of war and peace, the choice between socialism and capitalism, whether there shall be race and gender discrimination in private employment, are just some of the questions of equal importance; they too are decided not in constitutional but in legislative terms."

See also RICHARD POSNER, *Legal Reasoning from the Bottom Up: The Question of Unenumerated Constitutional Rights,* 59 U.Chi.L.Rev. 433, 444 (1992): "[Professor Ronald Dworkin] is able to make abortion a matter of the varying opinions that Americans hold about the sanctity of life, rather than an issue of life or death,[c] only because he will not allow states to define the fetus as a person and therefore abortion as murder. (If he did allow this, he would not be able to distinguish abortion from infanticide.) Yet the states are allowed to decide what is property and (in the case of prisoners for example) what is liberty, for purposes of the Due Process Clause; why not what is a person? Can't a state decide that death means brain death rather than a stopped heart? And if it can decide when life ends why can't it decide when life begins? [An] Illinois statute makes abortion murder, and on the civil side wrongful death. The Supremacy Clause prevents its application to abortions privileged by *Roe,* but with that qualification the constitutionality of the statute cannot be doubted. It shows that the states are already in the business of defining human life."

If the Constitution leaves a state free to decide that a fetus is a constitutional person whose rights may be competitive with the rights of a pregnant woman, responds RONALD DWORKIN, *Unenumerated Rights: Whether and How Roe Should be Overruled,* 59 U.Chi.L.Rev. 381, 399–402 (1992), "then *Roe* could safely be reversed without the politically impossible implication that states were required to prohibit abortion. The Supreme Court could then say that while some states have chosen to declare fetuses persons within their jurisdiction, other states need not make the same decision." Continues Dworkin:

"There is no doubt that a state can protect the life of a fetus in a variety of ways. A state can make it murder for a third-party intentionally to kill a fetus, as Illinois has done, for example. [Such] laws violate no constitutional rights, because no one has a constitutional right to injure with impunity. [The] suggestion that states are free to declare a fetus a person, and thereby justify outlawing abortion, is a very different matter, however. That suggestion assumes that a state can curtail some persons' constitutional rights by adding new persons to the

---

c. See the extracts from Dworkin's article in note 11 infra.

constitutional population. The constitutional rights of one citizen are of course very much affected by who or what else also has constitutional rights, because the rights of others may compete or conflict with his. So any power to increase the constitutional population by unilateral decision would be, in effect, a power to decrease rights the national Constitution grants to others. * * *

"[Judge Posner] says that states can decide whether 'death means brain death' or 'a stopped heart' and that it follows that they can 'decide when life begins.' A state can certainly decide when life begins and ends for any number of reasons. [It] can fix the moment of death for purposes of the law of inheritance, for example, just as it can declare that life begins before birth in order to allow people to inherit through a fetus. But it cannot change constitutional rights by its decisions about when life begins or death happens. It cannot escape its constitutional responsibilities to death-row prisoners by declaring them already dead, or improve its congressional representation by declaring deceased citizens still alive for that purpose. I cannot think of any significant constitutional rights that would be curtailed by treating someone as dead when his brain was dead, however. So none of Posner's examples suggest that he really accepts the position I reject."

9. *When, if ever,* may *a state override a woman's privacy rights by "adopting a theory of life"?* Consider Jed Rubenfeld, note 7 supra, at 628–30, 634–35:

"[T]he right at issue here is the freedom to decide whether and when to bear children. * * * Precisely because it would render abortion completely unavailable, a state determination that life begins at conception would not place an outer limit on this right; it would eviscerate the right at its core. [C]ontraception is no guarantee against pregnancy. Studies indicate that over half of the women who currently obtain abortions do use some form of contraception. Even in the strongest of cases—assuming women to be fully informed and vigilantly using one of the more effective contraceptive devices—the odds of pregnancy would by no means be negligible. [When] abortion is prohibited, no woman is guaranteed the right to decide whether or when to have children, and a large number of women will in fact have childbearing forced upon them against their will. * * *

"In light of the state's inability to demonstrate that a fetus is a person, the [*Roe* Court] did 'not agree that, by adopting one theory of life, [a state] may override the rights of pregnant women at stake.' Too strictly construed, this formulation would be incorrect. A state *may* override a woman's privacy rights (indeed may *only* override them) by 'adopting [a] theory of life'—that is, by determining a point at which to recognize the fetus as an independent human being. The Court's essential holding, however, was and remains valid: A state may not completely eviscerate the women's privacy rights by adopting a theory of life that bars abortion altogether. * * *

"[A]ssuming the Court preserves the right to privacy, it can announce as a new constitutional standard that states may deem the fetus a person at any point in pregnancy they choose, *so long as this point affords women a reasonable length of time in which to discover their pregnancy and obtain an abortion.* [This] standard would, however, have obvious disadvantages. It would lack definiteness, invite additional litigation, result in differing state rules, and so forth. On the other hand, the Court would be going no further than it had to go and would be allowing antiabortion states as much leeway in prohibiting abortion as the Constitution could tolerate." [d]

d. See also Dworkin, note 8 supra, at 428–32.

10. *Was the state's justification for interference with individual decision a "moral" one? A "religious" one?* Asks Professor Henkin, note 4 supra, at 1431–32: "Once, [the] promotion and protection of morals was clearly a proper concern of government; does the Right of Privacy imply that it is no longer? While the rights to use contraceptives, to have an abortion, to read obscene materials, were held not offset by hypothesized, particular public goods, were they not all essentially 'morals legislation'? And does it essentially all come down to the Court's saying [in effect] that these are not 'the law's business'? Does the Constitution, then, permit government to be only utilitarian not 'moral'? Or, if that inference is unwarranted, which morals may society promote, by what means? How much attention may it give in legislation to national history, to ancestral or contemporary religion, to the prevailing morality of the time?"

But compare Archibald Cox, *The Role of the Supreme Court* 113–14 (1976): "My criticism of *Roe* is that the Court failed to establish the legitimacy of the decision by not articulating a precept of sufficient abstractness to lift the ruling above the level of a political judgment based upon the evidence currently available from the medical, physical and social sciences. Nor can I articulate such a principle—unless it be that a State cannot interfere with the individual decisions relating to sex, procreation, and family with only a moral or philosophical State justification: a principle which I cannot accept or believe will be accepted by the American people."

"[A]ll normative judgments," observes Tribe *Treatise* 130, "are rooted in moral premises: surely the judgment that it is wrong to kill a two-week old infant is no less 'moral' in inspiration than the judgment, less frequently made but no less strongly felt by many of those who make it, that it is wrong to kill a two-day old fetus. Archibald Cox seems correct, therefore, when he concludes that *Roe* must be wrong if it rests on the premise that a state can never interfere with individual decisions relating to sex or procreation 'with only moral justification.' But it is clear that *Roe* rests on no such premise."

Is the judgment that it is wrong to kill a two-day old fetus a moral judgment or a *religious* one? How does one distinguish between "moral" and "religious" judgments? Aren't people who hold strong religious beliefs likely to *call them* moral convictions? And to believe sincerely that they *are* moral convictions? If the Court adopted, or allowed a state to adopt, the view that a fetus is in all stages of pregnancy a moral person on a par with an actual person, wouldn't that be the kind of endorsement of nonneutral values which the religion clauses forbid? See David Richards, *Constitutional Privacy, Religious Disestablishment, and the Abortion Decisions,* in *Abortion: Moral and Legal Perspectives* 148, 171–73 (Garfield & Hennessey eds. 1984). See also Thomas Emerson, *The Power of Congress to Change Constitutional Decisions of the Supreme Court: The Human Life Bill,* 77 Nw.U.L.Rev. 129, 131 (1982); Sylvia Law, *Rethinking Sex and the Constitution,* 132 U.Pa.L.Rev. 955, 1026 n. 249 (1984).

11. *What is the most difficult constitutional issue in the abortion controversy?* According to Professor Dworkin, note 8 supra, at 407, it is not some question about the moral personality or rights or interests of a fetus, but "whether states can legitimately claim a detached interest in protecting the intrinsic value, or sanctity, of human life. Does our Constitution allow states to decide [whether] human life is inherently valuable, why it is so, and how that inherent value can be respected?" Continues Dworkin, id. at 411:

"The real question decided in *Roe,* and the heart of the national debate, is the question of conformity [i.e., whether a state can require all its citizens to obey rules and practices that the majority believes best capture and respect the sanctity of life]. I said that government sometimes acts properly when it coerces people in order to protect values the majority endorses: when it collects taxes to support art, or when it requires businessmen to spend money to avoid endangering a species, for example. Why (I asked) can the state not forbid abortion on the same ground: that the majority of its citizens thinks that aborting a fetus, except when the mother's own life is at stake, is an intolerable insult to the inherent value of human life? [The] belief that the value of human life transcends its value for the creature whose life it is—that human life is objectively valuable from the point of view, as it were, of the universe—is plainly a religious belief, even when it is held by people who do not believe in a personal deity" and thus people's beliefs about the inherent value of human life, beliefs deployed in their opinions about abortion (and suicide and euthanasia as well) "should be deemed religious within the meaning of the First Amendment." Do you agree?

12. *The impact of Roe on a pluralistic society.* Consider Guido Calabresi, *Ideals, Beliefs, Attitudes, and the Law* 95–97 (1985): "[When] the Court proclaimed [that] anti-abortion beliefs as to commencement of life, *whether true or not,* are not part of our Constitution [it] said to highly defensive groups composed in significant part of recent immigrants that their highest beliefs [are] not part of *our* law as represented by its most fundamental statement, the Constitution. [This] was catastrophic because it reinforced doubts which the holders of anti-abortion beliefs already had about their full acceptance in American society.

"[*Roe*] opened wounds one wishes were closed. The decision made it impossible for the opposing views to live with each other, and created a situation in which one side seemed to need to *win* over the other. And, while that may be the side the Court supported, the losers will not quickly forget their exclusion (just as they have not forgotten their treatment as recent immigrants) to the detriment of our pluralistic society."

13. *A defense of Roe even assuming that the fetus is a person.* Agreeing with Professor Ely (see p. 431 infra) that "constitutional argument ought to be based on values that can be inferred from the text of the Constitution, the thinking of the Framers, or the structure of our national government," DONALD REGAN, note 2 supra, at 1618–42, maintains that such constitutional argument against laws prohibiting abortion may be made, based on three constitutional values: "non-subordination, freedom from physical invasion, and equal protection":[e]

"The non-subordination value that is implicit in the bad-samaritan principle of the common law[f] is at the core of the thirteenth amendment [which] speaks not merely of slavery, but of 'involuntary servitude.' * * * Unwilling pregnancy is not slavery in its fullest sense, [but] it certainly involves the disposition and coercion of the (intensely) personal service of one 'man' for another's benefit.

e. As Professor Regan acknowledges, his article builds on an argument made in Judith Thomson, *A Defense of Abortion,* 1 Phil. & Pub.Aff. 47 (1971).

f. At the outset of his article, id. at 1569, Professor Regan contends that "abortion should be viewed as presenting a problem in what we might call 'the law of samaritanism,' that is, the law concerning obligations imposed on certain individuals to give aid to others. It is a deeply rooted principle of American law that an individual is ordinarily not required to volunteer aid to another individual who is in

danger or in need of assistance. [I]f we require a pregnant woman to carry the fetus to term and deliver it—if we forbid abortion, in other words—we are compelling her to be a Good Samaritan. [I]f we consider the special nature of the burdens imposed on pregnant women by laws forbidding abortion, we must eventually conclude that the equal protection clause forbids imposition of these burdens on pregnant women." Regan refers to "the established principle that one does not have to volunteer aid" as the "bad-samaritan principle," id. at 1572.

The second value, freedom from physical invasion or imposed physical pain or hardship, is embodied in the eighth amendment and also plainly counts among those fundamental values of our society which are traditionally subsumed under fifth and fourteenth amendment due process. [There] is no other case, I believe, in which the law imposes comparable physical invasion and hardship as an obligation of samaritanism. * * *

"[E]ven if those parts of our tradition which forbid subordination or physical invasion have historically included an exception for abortion laws, the exception is impermissible. It creates an inequality that is inconsistent with an even more fundamental part of our tradition. [The] objection to an anti-abortion statute is that it picks out certain potential samaritans, namely women who want abortions, and treats them in a way that is at odds with the law's treatment of other potential samaritans. Women who want abortions are required to give aid in circumstances where closely analogous potential samaritans are not. And they are required to give aid of a *kind* and an *extent* that is required of no other potential samaritan.

"[I]t is important that the inequality of treatment between pregnant women and other potential samaritans touches on the constitutional values of non-subordination and freedom from physical invasion. A woman who is denied an abortion is compelled to serve the fetus and to suffer physical invasion, pain, and hardship. [That it can plausibly] be argued that the Constitution prohibits this imposition outright, [surely] means that any inequality of treatment we can point to becomes harder to justify. * * *

"Other reasons for the Court to give the abortion problem special attention are related to the suspect classification idea. Only women need abortions. [T]he one potential samaritan who is singled out for specially burdensome treatment is a potential samaritan who must, given human physiology, be female. Why is this important?

"First, any inequality that flows from an unchosen and unalterable characteristic is likely to be specially resented. [Since] no one has any choice about whether to be a woman, susceptibility to pregnancy (and to being in the position of wanting an abortion) is a nonchosen characteristic. (It is not an unalterable characteristic, since a woman might have herself sterilized, but this method of altering the characteristic itself involves a significant physical invasion.) [Moreover,] the only method of avoiding pregnancy with certainty requires, for many people, extraordinary self-denial [and] does not, to my mind, eliminate the force of the suggestion that pregnancy is often sufficiently 'unchosen' so that laws specially disadvantaging pregnant women limit women's control of their lives, are justifiably resented, and deserve more-than-minimal judicial attention.[g]

g. Consider Catharine MacKinnon, *Roe v. Wade: A Study in Male Ideology*, in *Abortion: Moral and Legal Perspectives* 45, 46–48 (Garfield & Hennessey eds. 1984): "Feminist investigations suggest [that women do not significantly control sex]. Feminism has found that women feel compelled to preserve the appearance—which, acted upon, becomes the reality—of male direction of sexual expression, as if it is male initiative itself that we want: it is that which turns us on. Men enforce this. It is much of what men want in a woman.

"[Under] these conditions, women often do not use birth control because [it] means acknowledging and planning and taking direction of intercourse, accepting one's sexual availability, and appearing nonspontaneous. [A] good user of contraception is a bad girl. She can be presumed sexually available and, among other consequences, raped with relative impunity. (If you think this isn't true, you should consider rape cases in which the fact that a woman had a diaphragm in is taken as an indication that what happened to her was intercourse, not rape. 'Why did you have your diaphragm in?') * * * I wonder if a woman can be presumed to control access to her sexuality if she feels unable to interrupt intercourse to insert a

"[M]ost legislatures would defend laws against abortion on the ground that they protect human life (or potential life). [But the] inequality between the treatment of pregnant women and the treatment of other potential samaritans who are not required to undertake burdens (often very much smaller burdens) in order to save life is too great. The inequality trenches on two distinct constitutionally protected interests—the interest in non-subordination and the interest in freedom from serious physical invasion. In addition, the inequality disadvantages a class that is defined by a non-chosen characteristic (whether sex or unwanted pregnancy) and that has suffered from a history of discrimination. This is more than any reasonable American legislature would tolerate. * * *

"Perhaps the greatest advantage of my argument is that it makes it possible to avoid the question of whether the fetus is, or may be treated by the state as, a person. Justice Blackmun claims at one point that the Court need not decide 'when life begins'. But his general argument [seems] plainly to assume that the fetus is *not* a person until the point of viability (at the earliest). Indeed, Blackmun elsewhere suggests that if the fetus were a person within the meaning of the fourteenth amendment, the woman's claim to an abortion would be foreclosed by the Constitution itself.

"On the last point, I think Blackmun is mistaken. [The] people who need the assistance of potential samaritans in ordinary samaritan cases are persons under the fourteenth amendment, and yet the general common law bad-samaritan principle is not unconstitutional. * * *

"[M]y argument justifies more clearly than the Court's argument [its] conclusion that abortion may not be forbidden even in the third trimester when the life or health of the mother is at stake. If the problem is ultimately one of balancing, as the Court's opinion suggests, it is not clear why the state's compelling interest (as the Court describes it) in protecting the potential life of a fetus already capable of 'meaningful life outside the mother's womb' (in the Court's phrase) is outweighed even by the woman's life, much less by her health. On my approach, however, the matter is clear. Even the reader who rejects my general conclusions must admit that there is no other case in which we would even consider requiring one individual to sacrifice his life or health to rescue another." [h]

14. *"Privacy"* or *"sex equality"*? "Nothing the Supreme Court has ever done," observes Sylvia Law, *Rethinking Sex and the Constitution*, 132 U.Pa.L.Rev. 955, 981 (1984), "has been more concretely important for women [than the decision in *Roe*]. Laws restricting abortion have a devastating sex-specific impact." Yet, as Professor Law notes, not only was the abortion decision not grounded on the principle of sex equality, the plaintiffs in *Roe* and *Doe* did not even challenge the abortion restrictions as sex discriminatory. But a growing number of commentators,[i] including Judge (now Justice) Ruth Bader Ginsburg,[j]

---

diaphragm; or worse, cannot even want to, aware that she risks a pregnancy she knows she does not want. * * *. [Yet] abortion policy has never been explicitly approached in the context of how women get pregnant; that is, as a consequence of intercourse under conditions of gender inequality; that is, as an issue of forced sex."

h. See also Laurence Tribe, *Abortion: The Clash of Absolutes* 129–35 (1990). But the "Good Samaritan" argument has not escaped criticism. See, e.g., Philip Bobbitt, *Constitutional Fate* 163 (1982); McConnell, note 5 supra, at 1185–86 & n. 8; Rubenfeld, note 7

supra, at 604 n. 35; David Strauss, *Abortion, Toleration, and Moral Uncertainty*, 1992 Sup. Ct.Rev. 1, 10–14.

i. See Calabresi, note 12 supra, at 99–102; Cass Sunstein, *The Partial Constitution* 272–85 (1993); Tribe, *Abortion* 105; Tribe *Treatise* 1353–55; Kenneth Karst, *Foreword: Equal Citizenship under the Fourteenth Amendment*, 91 Harv.L.Rev. 1, 57–59 (1977); Seth Kreimer, *Does Pro–Choice Mean Pro–Kevorkian? An Essay on Roe, Casey, and the Right to Die*, 44 Am.U.L.Rev. 803, 849 (1995); Law, supra at

---

See note j. on page 332.

are maintaining that the best argument for the right to abortion is based on principles of sexual equality, not "due process" or "privacy." CATHARINE MacKINNON, Note 6 supra, at 1319, puts it powerfully:

"Because the social organization of reproduction is a major bulwark of women's social inequality, any constitutional interpretation of a sex equality principle must prohibit laws, state policies, or official practices and acts that deprive women of reproductive control or punish women for their reproductive role or capacity. * * * Women's right to reproductive control is a sex equality right because it is inconsistent with an equality mandate for the state, by law, to collaborate with or mandate social inequality on the basis of sex, as [denials of abortion through criminalization or lack of public funding where needed] do. This is not so much an argument for an extension of the meaning of constitutional sex equality as a recognition that if it does not mean this, it does not mean anything at all.

"Under this sex equality analysis, criminal abortion statutes of the sort invalidated in *Roe* violate equal protection of the laws. They make women criminals for a medical procedure only women need, or make others criminals for performing a procedure on women that only women need, when much of the need for this procedure as well as barriers to access to it have been created by social conditions of sex inequality. Forced motherhood is sex inequality. Because pregnancy can be experienced only by women, and because of the unequal social predicates and consequences pregnancy has for women, any forced pregnancy will always deprive and hurt one sex only as a member of her gender."

But consider MICHAEL McCONNELL, note 5 supra, at 1187–88: "[A] law does not violate the Equal Protection Clause merely because it burdens one race or sex more heavily than another. Such a law is subject to heightened judicial scrutiny only if the legislature had an intent to discriminate. There exists no substantial evidence that abortion laws, as a matter of historical fact, were motivated by such an intent to discriminate against women. Indeed, the history of abortion laws shows that they were principally a response by the medical profession to improvements in the technology of abortion and to newly-discovered information about embryology. [More] interestingly, the nineteenth century anti-abortion movement was strongly supported by the women's movement. [In his book, *Abortion: The Clash of Values* 33 (1990), Professor Tribe] calls it '[i]ntriguing' that 'abortion rights [were] not really on the agenda of the early feminists.' It is even more intriguing that they were on the opposite side." Adds Professor McConnell, id. at 1189–90:

987–1002; Frances Olsen, *Unraveling Compromise,* 103 Harv.L.Rev. 105, 117–26 (1989); Reva Siegel, *Reasoning from the Body: A Historical Perspective on Abortion Regulation and Questions of Equal Protection,* 44 Stan.L.Rev. 261, 350–80 (1992); David Strauss, *Abortion, Toleration, and Moral Uncertainty,* 1992 Sup. Ct.Rev. 1, 18–22.

j. In a lecture delivered shortly before her nomination to the Supreme Court, Judge Ginsburg noted that in *Planned Parenthood v. Casey* (p. 363 infra), which reaffirmed "the essential holding" of *Roe,* the controlling Justices (O'Connor, Kennedy and Souter), speaking for the Court on this point, "added an important strand to the Court's opinions on abortion"— they "acknowledged the intimate connection between a woman's 'ability to control [her] reproductive li[fe]' and her 'ability [to] participate equally in the economic and social life of the Nation.'" Ginsburg, *Speaking in a Judicial Voice,* 67 N.Y.U.L.Rev. 1185, 1199 (1992) (quoting *Casey,* 112 S.Ct. at 2809). See also Ruth Bader Ginsburg, *Some Thoughts on Autonomy and Equality in Relation to Roe v. Wade,* 63 N.C.L.Rev. 375, 382, 386 (1985).

"On Tribe's assumption that 'the fetus [is] a person,'[k] the more natural implication of the Equal Protection Clause is that it stands *against* abortion rights. The Equal Protection Clause is designed to protect members of vulnerable and politically unrepresented minorities from the oppressive measures of the dominant majority. Abortion laws are designed to protect fetuses or unborn children, surely a vulnerable and unrepresented group, from private violence. It is an odd interpretation of the Equal Protection Clause to say that it *prevents* states from extending protection to the vulnerable and unrepresented."

15. *In Roe did the woman patient take a back seat to the male physician?* In *Roe,* maintains ANDREA ASARO, *The Judicial Portrayal of the Physician in Abortion and Sterilization Decisions,* 6 Harv. Women's L.J. 51, 53–55 (1983), "[for] Blackmun, the key issue was quite simply one of medical discretion, in other words: '[F]or the period of pregnancy prior to the "compelling" point, the attending physician, in consultation with his patient, is free to determine [that], in his medical judgment, the patient's pregnancy should be terminated.' Interestingly, the abortion decision is characterized here neither as primarily the woman's nor as fundamentally or initially a moral or personal one. Blackmun's perspective is clinical, and the woman patient has taken a back seat to the male physician-protagonist. [Concluding his *Roe* opinion, Justice Blackmun states]: '[The] decision vindicates the right of the physician to administer medical treatment according to his professional judgment up to the points where important state interests provide compelling justifications for intervention. Up to these points, *the abortion decision in all its aspects is inherently, and primarily, a medical decision, and basic responsibility for it must rest with the physician.'* [Emphasis added by Ms. Asaro.] Blackmun has neglected even to mention the pregnant woman as party to the abortion decision! The state, the physician, and the court have displaced Ms. Roe altogether."

16. *The "peculiar nature" of the Burger Court's activism.* Unlike the Warren Court, whose justices' doctrinal compromises "took place against a background in which the direction of constitutional development was both clear and, to many, inspiring," observes VINCENT BLASI, *The Rootless Activism of the Burger Court,* in *The Burger Court: The Counter-Revolution that Wasn't* 198, 212–13 (V. Blasi ed. 1983), the *Roe* justices "could not plausibly justify their decision as the working out of a theme implicit in several previous decisions, still less as the vindication of values deeply embedded in the nation's constitutional tradition. [T]he peculiar nature of the Burger Court's activism can be seen from the fact that even so fundamental an issue as abortion was treated by this Court as a conflict of particularized, material interests—a conflict that could be resolved by accommodating those interests in the spirit of compromise. Thus, third trimester abortions can be prohibited but earlier abortions cannot. The state cannot prohibit all abortions outright, but can refuse to fund them [see *Maher v. Roe* and *Harris v. McRae,* infra], even while funding the alternative of childbirth and thereby encouraging pregnant women to forgo the abortion option. The woman's husband cannot veto her choice to have an abortion [*Planned Parenthood v. Danforth,* infra] but a minor's parents can do so under certain limited circumstances. These doctrinal lines are not necessarily incoherent. But each has in fact taken on a highly arbitrary character because in grappling with the issues

---

k. At this point, Professor McConnell is referring to a passage in Professor Tribe's book on abortion (p. 135) where Tribe maintains that "even if the fetus * * * is regarded as a person," "a powerful case" can be made for the conclusion that laws prohibiting abortion "deny women the equal protection of the laws." As Tribe puts it, the Court might have said that "[e]ven if the fetus *is* a person, our Constitution forbids compelling a woman to carry it for nine months and become a mother."

that followed in *Roe*'s wake, the justices were unable to draw upon any sort of theory, or vision, or even framework for determining the contours of the right they had recognized. Each variation on the abortion issue was treated by the Court as an isolated, practical problem."

17. *The impact of Roe—some surprising aspects.* Although *Roe* increased women's access to safe abortions, "surprisingly," notes CASS SUNSTEIN, *The Partial Constitution* 147 (1993) "it did not dramatically increase the actual number and rate of abortions. [In] fact most states were moving in the direction of liberal abortion laws well before *Roe,* resulting in 600,000 lawful abortions per year. Astonishingly, the rate of increase in *legal* abortions was higher in the three years before that decision than in the three years after. It may well have been the case that states would generally have legalized abortion without *Roe.* Perhaps more fundamentally, the decision probably contributed to the creation of the 'moral majority'; helped defeat the Equal Rights Amendment; prevented the eventual achievement of consensual solutions to the abortion problem; and severely undermined the women's movement, by defining that movement in terms of the single issue of abortion, by spurring and organizing opposition, and by demobilizing potential adherents."

ROE v. WADE AND THE DEBATE IT STIRRED OVER "NONINTERPRETIVIST" OR "NONORIGINALIST" CONSTITUTIONAL DECISIONMAKING[a]

1. Consider Ira Lupu, *Constitutional Theory and the Search for the Workable Premise,* 8 Dayton L.Rev. 579, 583 (1983): "*Roe* clarified, as had no other case

a. Although the materials in this section inevitably overlap to some extent with the preceding set of Notes & Questions, it seems useful to focus separately on the general constitutional debate generated by the 1973 *Abortion Cases.*

"Interpretivism" indicates that "judges deciding constitutional issues should confine themselves to enforcing norms that are stated or clearly implicit in the written Constitution"; "noninterpretivism" indicates that "courts should go beyond that set of references and enforce norms that cannot be discovered within the four corners of the document." John Ely, *Democracy and Distrust* 1 (1980). "What distinguishes interpretivism from its opposite is its insistence that the work of the political branches is to be invalidated only in accord with an inference whose starting point, whose underlying premise, is fairly discoverable in the Constitution. That the complete inference will not be found there—because the situation is not likely to have been foreseen—is general common ground." Id. at 1–2.

As might be expected, there is disagreement over the appropriate terminology. In recent years, according to Peter Linzer, *The Carolene Products Footnote and the Preferred Position of Individual Rights,* 12 Const.Comm. 277, 286 (1995), "the term 'originalist' seems to have

replaced the awkward 'interpretivist.'" See also Robert Bennett, *Objectivity in Constitutional Law,* 132 U.Pa.L.Rev. 445, 446 & n. 3 (1984), preferring the term "originalists" to describe those who "argue that constitutional language, understood in light of the substantive intentions or values behind its enactment, is the sole proper source for constitutional interpretation," because this term "better captures the static pretense of the approach that seems to me to be its principal flaw." "On the other side of the debate are 'noninterpretivists' or 'nonoriginalists' who believe it is legitimate for judges to look beyond text and original intention in interpreting constitutional language," but they "are divided on what particular sources should replace or supplement originalist sources and on how to justify their use." Id. at 446.

Richard Fallon, *A Constructivist Coherence Theory of Constitutional Interpretation,* 100 Harv.L.Rev. 1189, 1211 (1987), divides "interpretivists" into two camps: "On one side stand 'originalists.' [They] take the rigid view that only the original understanding of the framers' specific intent ought to count. On the other side, 'moderate interpretivists' allow contemporary understandings and the framers' general or abstract intent to enter the constitutional calculus."

since World War II, the Supreme Court's willingness to reach results which no defensible interpretivist position could support. Although rhetorically tied to the meaning of 'liberty' in the fourteenth amendment due process clause, and loosely aligned with the penumbral analysis developed in *Griswold, Roe* cut fundamental rights adjudication loose from the constitutional text. [There followed] a vast array of doctrinal, methodological, and theoretical inquiries into the outcome in *Roe.* More or less detached from the case itself, these scholarly efforts offered a variety of justifications for noninterpretive review—natural law underpinnings of the 1787 Constitution, [the] search for enduring or traditional unwritten norms, [and] judicial manifestation of consensus morality."

2. *What happened on January 22, 1973?* "The subject of abortion," observes ROBERT BORK, *The Tempting of America* 111–16 (1990), "had been fiercely debated in state legislatures for many years. It raises profound moral issues upon which people of good will can and do disagree * * *. Whatever the proper resolution of the moral debate, [few] imagined that the Constitution resolved it. In 1973, a majority of the Supreme Court did imagine just that in *Roe.* [The] discovery this late in our history that the question was not one for democratic decision but one of constitutional law was so implausible that it certainly deserved a fifty-one page explanation. Unfortunately, in the entire opinion there is not one line of explanation, not one sentence that qualifies as legal argument. [Nor has the Court] ever provided the explanation lacking in 1973. It is unlikely that it ever will, because the right to abort, whatever one thinks of it, is not to be found in the Constitution. * * *

"Attempts to overturn *Roe* will continue as long as the Court adheres to it. And, just so long as the decision remains, the Court will be perceived, correctly, as political * * *. *Roe,* as the greatest example and symbol of the judicial usurpation of democratic prerogatives in this century, should be overturned. The Court's integrity requires that."

Professor Fallon has some unkind words for "originalism," id. at 1211, 1214: "[Its] purity proves its undoing, because originalism cannot satisfy the standards that it sets for itself. The problem is that arguments from text and the framers' intent cannot be kept independent of other kinds of factors that originalists, with their conception of what the rule requires, insist on excluding. [The] questions of when, how, and to what extent the rule-of-law ideals associated with a written constitution should accommodate needs for adaptation and change are notoriously difficult. [It] is a normative deficiency of originalism that its premises deny any scope whatever for accommodation."

Nor is Professor Fallon a fan of "moderate interpretivism," id. at 1215, 1217: "[It] also fails to provide a viable theory. [It] recognizes the legitimacy of arguments of original as well as contemporary meaning and of specific as well as general intent. But this recognition raises the problem of how to decide which meaning or which type of intent should govern in any particular situation. * * * Recognition that moderate interpretivism relies on factors besides text and history—and in particular that judges must make delicate moral and political judgments to determine the contemporary meaning of numerous constitutional con-

cepts and the level of abstraction at which the framers' intent ought to be stated—reveals the theory as failed in its own terms."

Thomas Grey, *Do We Have an Unwritten Constitution?*, 27 Stan.L.Rev. 703 (1975), probably originated the use of the "interpretivist-noninterpretivist" terminology, but he has since concluded that these labels "distort the debate": "If the current interest in interpretive theory [does] nothing else, at least it shows that the concept of interpretation is broad enough to encompass any plausible mode of constitutional adjudication. We are all interpretivists; the real arguments are not over whether judges should stick to interpreting, but over what they should interpret and what interpretive attitudes they should adopt. Repenting past errors, I will therefore use the less misleading labels 'textualists' and 'supplementers' for, respectively, those who consider the text the sole legitimate source of operative norms in constitutional adjudication, and those who accept supplementary sources of constitutional law [such as 'conventional morality']." Grey, *The Constitution as Scripture,* 37 Stan.L.Rev. 1 (1984).

But consider LAURENCE TRIBE, *Abortion* 99: "Judge Bork says that 'the right to abort, whatever one thinks of it, is not to be found in the Constitution.' In a sense this is obviously right. Indeed, not one of the words 'abortion,' 'pregnancy,' 'reproduction,' 'sex,' 'privacy,' 'bodily integrity,' and 'procreation' appears anywhere in [the] Constitution.[b] But neither do such phrases as 'freedom of thought,' 'rights of parenthood,' 'liberty of association,' 'family self-determination,' and 'freedom of marital choice.' Yet nearly everyone supposes that at least some of these dimensions of personal autonomy and independence are aspects of the 'liberty' which the Fourteenth Amendment says no state may deny to any person 'without due process of law.'

"The 'right to abortion' was first *announced*, it's true, in *Roe v. Wade*. [But the] 'right to privacy,' whatever its outer bounds, was suggested as early as 1923 in the case of *Meyer v. Nebraska*. *Roe* was simply the first case in which the general question of state regulation of abortion was squarely considered by the Supreme Court. To argue that for this reason, the Constitution does not protect the right to abortion, or that it did not do so until January 22, 1973, is no better than to argue that it does not protect the 'right to contribute money to a political campaign.' Although that right was not *announced* until the Supreme Court's 1976 decision in *Buckley v. Valeo* [p. 918 infra], it is beyond doubt that the right is, and has long been, a right protected by the free speech guarantee of the First Amendment."

3. Consider JOSEPH GRANO, *Judicial Review and a Written Constitution in a Democratic Society,* 28 Wayne L.Rev. 1, 25, 59 (1981): [An objection to criticisms of *Roe*] might be that the Court's poor choice of methodology is not a valid argument against noninterpretivism. The truth, however, is that the Court's methodology is basically all there is. Noninterpretivism is a methodology of *fundamental* rights, [for] no one maintains that the judiciary should require "compelling" reasons for all laws, including those that prohibit swindling or murder. Noninterpretivism's first requirement is that the judiciary separate that which is fundamental from that which is not, and it is this very task that requires the judiciary to take normative and moral positions that cannot be demonstrated.

"[*Roe*] is as wrong as the proposed constitutional amendment to protect the fetus, and for the same reason: it seeks to bind succeeding generations to our generation's thinking, or at least to the thinking of a segment of it. Through the Supreme Court, our generation has dictated to future generations that they can prohibit abortions only by mustering the requisite super-majority to amend the Constitution. [*Roe*] is just one example of judicial noninterpretivism, a methodology that permits the judiciary to decide the difficult moral issues of our time under the rubric of constitutional law. Whether the issue be abortion, the right of the family or unrelated individuals to share living quarters,[c] [or] the right to a greater share of the wealth, every noninterpretivist decision recognizing one of these claims adds, in effect, a new provision to the written constitution and thereby imposes an additional moral restraint on subsequent generations.[267]"

b. On the other hand, the *Lochner* Court did rely on words that appeared in the Constitution. As Professor Tribe notes elsewhere, see *Treatise* at 771, "the *Lochner* error" "was not in invoking a value the Constitution did not mark as special; the text evinces the most explicit concern with 'liberty,' 'contract,' and 'property.' The error lay in giving that value a perverse content."

c. See *Moore v. East Cleveland,* p. 407 infra.

[267]. Noninterpretivism is sometimes defended by positing horribles that only noninterpretivism can correct. Professor Karst, for example, invited us to imagine legislation prohibiting marriage: "All would agree—even Justice Rehnquist, I suppose—that an arbitrary denial by the state of the freedom to

4. *Are the Abortion Cases "bad constitutional law" or "not constitutional law"?* Consider JOHN ELY, *The Wages of Crying Wolf: A Comment on Roe v. Wade,* 82 Yale L.J. 920, 935–37, 939, 943, 947–49 (1973): "What is unusual about *Roe* is that the liberty involved is accorded [a] protection more stringent [than] that the present Court accords the freedom of the press explicitly guaranteed by the First Amendment. What is frightening about *Roe* is that this super-protected right is not inferable from the language of the Constitution, the framers' thinking respecting the specific problem in issue, any general value derivable from the provisions they included, or the nation's governmental structure. Nor is it explainable in terms of the unusual political impotence of the group judicially protected vis-á-vis the interest that legislatively prevailed over it.[d]

"[The] problem with *Roe* is not so much that it bungles the question it sets itself, but rather that it sets itself a question the Constitution has not made the Court's business. It *looks* different from *Lochner*—it has the shape if not the substance of a judgment that is very much the Court's business, one vindicating an interest the Constitution marks as special—and it is for that reason perhaps more dangerous. Of course in a sense it is more candid than *Lochner*. But the employment of a higher standard of judicial review, no matter how candid the recognition that it is indeed higher, loses some of its admirability when it is accompanied by neither a coherent account of why such a standard is appropriate nor any indication of why it has not been satisfied.

marry would violate the Fourteenth Amendment." Kenneth Karst, *The Freedom of Intimate Association,* 89 Yale L.J. 624, 667 (1980). Thus, extremely confident, Karst concluded, "*Of course* there is a right to marry." Id. [I] am quite certain I do not agree. I cannot conceive of a legislature prohibiting marriage, but the reason is that I cannot foresee the circumstances that would prompt such legislation. Presumably, however, such a decision would occur only after some event convinced a majority or supermajority of the population that marriage should be banned. Assuming such a society (again, one we cannot really conceive), it cannot be obvious that such a ban should be struck down as unconstitutional. "Ah!," you answer, "but suppose the legislature passes such a law without popular support?" Anyone who believes that noninterpretivism or anything else in constitutional law, or in any other law, can safeguard society from such a legislature is welcome to his views, for I have nothing further to say to such a person. Cf. John Ely, *Democracy and Distrust* 182 (1980) (discussing hypothetical law banning gall bladder operations) * * *.

d. Elsewhere in his article, id. at 933–35, Professor Ely argues that Justice Stone's suggestion in his famous *Carolene Products* footnote that the Court provide extraordinary constitutional protection for " 'discrete and insulate minorities' unable to form effective political alliances" does not apply to *Roe*: "Compared with men, very few women sit in our legislatures, [but] *no* fetuses sit [there]. Of course they have their champions, but so have women. The two interests have clashed re-

peatedly in the political arena, and had continued to do so up to the date of [*Roe*], generating quite a wide variety of accommodations. [Stone's suggestion] was clearly intended and should be reserved for those interests which, as compared with the interests to which they have been subordinated, constitute minorities usually incapable of protecting themselves. Compared with men, women may constitute such a 'minority'; compared with the unborn, they do not."

Professor Ely's challenge of the appropriateness of judicial intervention in *Roe* "is misguided, however," maintains Robert Bennett, *Abortion and Judicial Review,* 75 Nw.U.L.Rev. 978, 995–96 n. 71 (1981), "because it assumes that fetuses are political actors—indeed a political minority—whose 'powerlessness' is relevant to assessing the Court's appropriate role in the abortion controversy. Each political system must define, explicitly or implicitly, the universe of relevant political actors. [But] outside the abortion context there are no indications that fetuses are considered relevant political actors. [E]ven within the context of abortion-related issues, the suggestion that fetuses are a part of the larger political community appears, as in Ely's formulation, only incidentally and as part of the abortion discussion. It is, of course, possible for a legislature to take into account interests outside its own political community. [But] with fetuses, as with other interests outside the relevant universe of political actors, the legislative process can only take them into account insofar as relevant political actors subsume those interests into their own."

"[*Roe* is] a very bad decision. [It] is bad because it is bad constitutional law, or rather because it is *not* constitutional law and gives almost no sense of an obligation to try to be. [A] neutral and durable principle may be a thing of beauty and joy forever. But if it lacks connection with any value the Constitution marks as special, it is not a constitutional principle and the Court has no business imposing it."[e]

5. *Is it a question of "inventing" a new right, or of the state having to justify an invasion of liberty?* Consider the remarks of Professor Tribe in Choper, Kamisar & Tribe, *The Supreme Court: Trends and Developments 1982–83* (1984) at 215: "[The *Roe* Court] is said to have invented the right to abortion. [But once] one concedes that the word 'liberty' has substantive content in its application against the states through the Fourteenth Amendment—and it must, if any substantive provisions of the Bill of Rights are to be enforced against the states through the Fourteenth Amendment—it becomes not a question of inventing a new right, but of asking what the justification is for a state intrusion into what is indisputably an aspect of someone's personal liberty."[f]

6. *"Enumerated" and "unenumerated" rights.* Although many view the distinction between enumerated and unenumerated rights as presenting the important question whether and when courts have authority to enforce rights not actually enumerated in the Constitution (e.g., the right to travel and the right to privacy, from which the right to an abortion is said to derive), RONALD DWORKIN, *Unenumerated Rights,* 59 U.Chi.L.Rev. 381, 387–88 (1992), finds the question "unintelligible":

"The Bill of Rights * * * consists of broad and abstract principles of political morality, which together encompass, in exceptionally abstract form, all the dimensions of political morality that in our political culture can ground an individual constitutional right. The key issue in applying these abstract principles to particular political controversies is not one of reference but of *interpretation,* which is very different.

"Consider the following three constitutional arguments, each of which is very controversial. The first argues that the Equal Protection Clause creates a right of equal concern and respect, from which it follows that women have a right against gender-based discriminations unless such discriminations are required by important state interests. The second argues that the First Amendment grants a right of symbolic protest, from which it follows that individuals have a right to burn the American flag. The third argues that the Due Process Clause protects the basic freedoms central to the very concept of 'ordered liberty,' including the right of privacy, from which it follows that women have a constitutional right to abortion. By convention, the first two are arguments (good or bad) for enumerated rights: each claims that some right—the right against gender discrimination or the right to burn the flag—is an instance of some more general right set out, in suitably abstract form, in the text of the Constitution. The third argument, on the other hand, is thought to be different and more suspect, because it is thought to be an argument for an unenumerated right. The right it claims—the right to an abortion—is thought to bear a more tenuous or distant relationship to the

e. See also Ray Forrester, *Are We Ready for Truth in Judging?,* 63 A.B.A.J. 1212 (1977); Louis Lusky, *By What Right?* 14, 16–17, 20 (1975); Henry Monaghan, *The Constitution Goes to Harvard,* 13 Harv.Civ.Rts.—Civ. Lib.L.Rev. 116, 131 (1978); Richard Posner, *The Uncertain Protection of Privacy in the Supreme Court,* 1979 Sup.Ct.Rev. 173, 199–200.

f. Cf. Walter Dellinger & Gene Sperling, *Abortion and the Supreme Court: The Retreat from Roe v. Wade,* 138 U.Pa.L.Rev. 83, 90–91 (1989).

language of the Constitution. It is said to be at best implied by, rather than stated in, that language.

"But the distinction cannot be sustained. Each of the three arguments is interpretive in a way that excludes the kind of semantic constraints the distinction assumes. No one thinks that it follows just from the meaning of the words 'freedom of speech' either that people are free to burn flags, or that they are not. No one thinks it follows just from the meaning of the words 'equal protection' that laws excluding women from certain jobs are unconstitutional, or that they are not. [Nor] are the three arguments different in how they are interpretive. Each conclusion (if sound) follows, not from some historical hope or belief or intention of a 'framer,' but because the political principle that supports that conclusion best accounts for the general structure and history of constitutional law. Someone who thinks that this manner of constitutional argument is inappropriate—who thinks, for example, that framers' expectations should play a more decisive role than this view of constitutional argument allows—will have the reservation about all three arguments, not distinctly about the third. If he thinks that the third argument is wrong, because he abhors, for example, the idea of substantive due process, then he will reject it, but because it is wrong, not because the right it claims would be an unenumerated one." [g]

7. *Why noninterpretive review is a "necessary postulate" for constitutional adjudication.* Consider ROBERT SEDLER, *The Legitimacy Debate in Constitutional Adjudication,* 44 Ohio St.L.J. 110, 118–19, 122 (1983): "[The Court] has engaged in noninterpretive review throughout its history, convinced that its actions were legitimate and consistent with the Court's function under our constitutional system. [The] meaning of a constitutional provision develops incrementally, and that provision's line of growth strongly influences its application in particular cases.[167] The framework within which constitutional decision making has operated, then, is a significant constraint on the results that the Court will reach when it is engaged in that decision making.

"[The] argument that noninterpretive review is fully supportive of constitutional governance established by the Constitution proceeds as follows: (1) The overriding principle in the structure of constitutional governance established by the Constitution is the limitation on governmental power. (2) Many of the limitations on governmental power designed to protect individual rights that are contained in the Constitution are broadly phrased and open ended, and these majestic generalities directed toward the protection of individual rights are a part of our constitutional tradition.[h] (3) [These] limitations cannot be fully operable in

---

g. Cf. Thomas Grey, *Do We Have an Unwritten Constitution?,* 27 Stan.L.Rev. 703, 710–14 (1975).

167. [I]t would not have been inconsistent with the line of growth of constitutional protection for reproductive freedom for the Court to have held that the asserted governmental interest in protecting potential human life was constitutionally more important than the woman's interest in reproductive freedom. [But] because the Court had previously held that reproductive freedom is entitled to constitutional protection, the holding in *Roe,* extending that protection to the abortion decision, was fully consistent with the line of growth of constitutional protection for reproductive freedom.

h. "But," maintains Henry Monaghan, *Commentary* (panel discussion), 56 N.Y.U.L.Rev. 525, 526 (1981), "the Constitution doesn't contain generalities. The due process clause and the ninth amendment in my judgment are judge-made and commentator-made generalities. Take the phrase 'due process of law.' If there was ever a phrase that had a fixed, certain meaning when it was introduced in the Constitution and adopted in 1868, it was that phrase. It was the judges who transformed it into a general license to review the substance of legislation. [Let's] assume that the Constitution contains some generalities like freedom of speech and let's assume that you are going to need a Hercules to interpret such provisions. Even if that Hercules

contemporary society as a limitation on governmental power if their meaning is determined solely or even primarily by referring to values purportedly constitutionalized by the framers at an earlier time. (4) Therefore, given items (1) and (3) above, noninterpretive review is not only legitimate, but is also a necessary postulate for constitutional adjudication under our constitutional system."

ABORTION FUNDING

1. MAHER v. ROE, 432 U.S. 464, 97 S.Ct. 2376, 53 L.Ed.2d 484 (1977) (also discussed at p. 1408 infra), per POWELL, J., sustained Connecticut's use of Medicaid funds to reimburse women for the costs of childbirth and "medically necessary" first trimester abortions (defined to include "psychiatric necessity"), but not for the costs of elective or nontherapeutic first trimester abortions.[a]

On "the central question"—"whether the regulation 'impinges upon a fundamental right explicitly or implicitly protected by the Constitution' "—the Court held that *Roe* did not establish "an unqualified 'constitutional right to an abortion,' " but only a "right protect[ing] the woman from unduly burdensome interference with her freedom to decide whether to terminate her pregnancy. It implies no limitation on the authority of a State to make a value judgment favoring childbirth over abortion, and to implement that judgment by the allocation of public funds. [The] State may have made childbirth a more attractive alternative, thereby influencing the woman's decision, but it has imposed no restriction on access to abortions that was not already there. The indigency that may make it difficult—and in some cases, perhaps, impossible—for some women to have abortions is neither created nor in any way affected by the [regulation.]

"Our conclusion signals no retreat from *Roe* or the cases applying it. There is a basic difference between direct state interference with a protected activity and state encouragement of an alternative activity consonant with legislative policy. * * * We think it abundantly clear that a State is not required to show a compelling interest for its policy choice to favor normal childbirth any more than a State must so justify its election to fund public but not private education."

The Court then sustained the regulation "under the less demanding test of rationality that applies in the absence of a suspect classification or the impingement of a fundamental right." It had little difficulty finding the distinction drawn between childbirth and nontherapeutic abortion " 'rationally related' to a 'constitutionally permissible' purpose." "*Roe* itself explicitly acknowledged the State's strong interest in protecting the potential life of the fetus. [The] State unquestionably has a 'strong and legitimate interest in encouraging normal childbirth' " and subsidizing the substantial and significantly increasing costs

has to rely on some external political theory, which can't be fairly related or thought to underlie the constitutional text, at least the first amendment is a stopping point: it limits the subjects about which judges ought to be concerned. But take the question of abortion. There's nothing in the constitutional text or in its history to 'constitutionalize.' Nor is the theory that would authorize review containable."

a. In a companion case, *Beal v. Doe*, 432 U.S. 438, 97 S.Ct. 2366, 53 L.Ed.2d 464 (1977), per Powell, J., held that the Medicaid Act does

not require state funding of nontherapeutic first trimester abortions as a condition of participation in the joint federal-state program.

In another companion case, *Poelker v. Doe*, 432 U.S. 519, 97 S.Ct. 2391, 53 L.Ed.2d 528 (1977), per curiam, for the reasons set forth in *Maher*, found "no constitutional violation by the city of St. Louis in electing, as a policy choice, to provide publicly financed hospital services for childbirth without providing corresponding services for nontherapeutic abortions."

incident to childbirth is "a rational means of encouraging childbirth." [13]

BRENNAN, J., joined by Marshall and Blackmun, JJ., dissented, accusing the majority of "a distressing insensitivity to the plight of impoverished pregnant women." The "disparity in funding [clearly] operates to coerce indigent pregnant women to bear children they would not otherwise choose to have, and just as clearly, this coercion can only operate upon the poor, who are uniquely the victims of this form of financial pressure." *Roe* and its progeny held that "an area of privacy invulnerable to the State's intrusion surrounds the decision of a pregnant woman whether or not to carry her pregnancy to term. The Connecticut scheme clearly infringes upon that area of privacy."

As for *Poelker,* fn. a supra, "the fundamental right of a woman freely to choose to terminate her pregnancy has been infringed by the city of St. Louis through a deliberate policy based on opposition to elective abortions on moral grounds by city officials. [The] city policy is a significant, and in some cases insurmountable, obstacle to indigent pregnant women who cannot pay for abortions in [clinics or private hospitals].

In a second dissent, MARSHALL, J., thought it "all too obvious that the governmental actions in these cases, ostensibly taken to 'encourage' women to carry pregnancies to term, are in reality intended to impose a moral viewpoint that no State may constitutionally enforce. [The] impact of the regulations here fall tragically upon those among us least able to help or defend themselves."

In a third dissent, BLACKMUN, J., joined by Brennan and Marshall, JJ., charged that "the Court concedes the existence of a constitutional right but denies the realization and enjoyment of that right on the ground that existence and realization are separate and distinct. [Implicit in today's holdings] is the condescension that [the indigent woman] may go elsewhere for her abortion. I find that disingenuous and alarming, almost reminiscent of: 'Let them eat cake.' "

2. *More on abortion funding; The Hyde Amendment.* Title XIX of the Social Security Act established the Medicaid program to provide federal financial assistance to states choosing to reimburse certain costs of medical treatment for needy persons. Since 1976, various versions of the so-called Hyde Amendment have limited federal funding of abortions under the Medicaid program to those necessary to save the life of the mother and certain other exceptional circumstances.[a] HARRIS v. McRAE, 448 U.S. 297, 100 S.Ct. 2671, 65 L.Ed.2d 784 (1980), per STEWART, J., found no constitutional violation:

"The present case does differ factually from *Maher* insofar as that case involved a failure to fund nontherapeutic abortions, whereas the Hyde Amendment withholds funding of certain medically necessary abortions. [But] regard-

---

13. Much of the rhetoric of the three dissenting opinions would be equally applicable if Connecticut had elected not to fund either abortions or childbirth. Yet none of the dissents goes so far as to argue that the Constitution *requires* such assistance for all indigent pregnant women.

[Compare Gary Simson, *Abortion, Poverty and the Equal Protection of the Laws,* 13 Ga. L.Rev. 505, 508 (1979): "[I]f Connecticut funded neither childbirth nor abortion, poverty would not lead indigent women to prefer childbirth to abortion. Rather, since a safe abortion in the early months of pregnancy is materially cheaper than a safe childbirth, financial considerations probably would militate strongly *in favor of* abortion."]

a. The version of the Hyde Amendment applicable for fiscal year 1980 prohibited federal funding of abortions "except where the life of the mother would be endangered if the fetus were carried to term" or except for cases of rape or incest "when such rape or incest has been reported promptly to a law enforcement agency or public health service." But the initial version of the Hyde Amendment, which triggered the instant case, did not include the "rape or incest" exception.

less of [how] the freedom of a woman to choose to terminate her pregnancy for health reasons [is characterized], it simply does not follow that [this freedom] carries with it a constitutional entitlement to the financial resources to avail herself of the full range of protected choices. The reason why was explained in *Maher:* although government may not place obstacles in the path of a woman's exercise of her freedom of choice, it need not remove those not of its own creation. [T]he Hyde Amendment leaves an indigent woman with at least the same range of choice in deciding whether to obtain a medically necessary abortion as she would have had if Congress had chosen to subsidize no health costs at all.

"[Acceptance of appellees' argument] would mark a drastic change in our understanding of the Constitution. It cannot be that because government may not prohibit the use of contraceptives, *Griswold,* or prevent parents from sending their child to a private school, *Pierce,* government, therefore, has an affirmative constitutional obligation to assure that all persons have the financial resources to obtain contraceptives or send their children to private [schools.]" [b]

Four justices dissented—Brennan, Marshall and Blackmun, JJ. (the three *Maher* dissenters), and Stevens, J. who had joined the opinion of the Court in *Maher.*

Stevens, J., maintained that the instant case presented "[a] fundamentally different question" than the one decided in *Maher:* "This case involves the pool of benefits that Congress created by enacting [Title XIX]. Individuals who satisfy two neutral criteria—financial need and medical need—are entitled to equal access to that pool. The question is whether certain persons who satisfy those criteria may be denied access to benefits solely because they must exercise the constitutional right to have an abortion in order to obtain the medical care they need. Our prior cases plainly dictate [the answer].

"Unlike these plaintiffs, [those] in *Maher* did not satisfy the neutral criterion of medical need; they sought a subsidy for nontherapeutic abortions—medical procedures which by definition they did not need. [This case] involves a special exclusion of women who, by definition, are confronted with a choice between two serious harms: serious health damage to themselves on the one hand and abortion on the other. The competing interests are the interest in maternal health and the interest in protecting potential human life. It is now part of our law that the pregnant woman's decision as to which of these conflicting interests shall prevail is entitled to constitutional protection.

"[If] a woman has a constitutional right to place a higher value on avoiding

b. The Court then rejected the contention that the Hyde Amendment violates the Establishment Clause because, as the argument ran, "it incorporates into law the doctrines of the Roman Catholic Church": A statute does not run afoul of the Establishment Clause "because it 'happens to coincide or harmonize with the tenets of some or all religions,' *McGowan v. Maryland* [discussed at p. 1046 infra]"; the Hyde Amendment "is as much a reflection of 'traditionalist' values toward abortion, as it is an embodiment of the views of any particular religion."

"Again draw[ing] guidance from" *Maher,* the Court also rejected the argument that the

Hyde Amendment "violates the equal protection component of the Fifth Amendment": The Hyde Amendment "is not predicated on a constitutionally suspect classification. [Here,] as in *Maher,* the principal impact of [the] Amendment falls on the indigent. But that fact alone does not itself render the funding restriction constitutionally invalid, for this Court has held repeatedly that poverty, standing alone, is not a suspect classification." See also pp. 1314–17 infra. The Hyde Amendment need only satisfy the rational-basis standard of review and it does—"by encouraging childbirth except in the most urgent circumstances, [it] is rationally related to the legitimate governmental objective of protecting potential life."

either serious harm to her own health or perhaps an abnormal childbirth [3] than on protecting potential life, the exercise of that right cannot provide the basis for the denial of a benefit to which she would otherwise be entitled. The Court's sterile equal protection analysis evades this critical though simple point. The Court focuses exclusively on the 'legitimate interest in protecting the potential life of the fetus.' [*Roe*] squarely held that the States may not protect that interest when a conflict with the interest in a pregnant woman's health exists. [The] Court totally fails to explain why this reasoning is not dispositive here.[4]

"[Nor] can it be argued that the exclusion of this type of medically necessary treatment of the indigent can be justified on fiscal grounds. [For] the cost of an abortion is only a small fraction of the costs associated with childbirth. Thus, the decision to tolerate harm to indigent persons who need an abortion in order to avoid 'serious and long lasting health damage' is one that is financed by draining money out of the pool that is used to fund all other necessary medical procedures. Unlike most invidious classifications, this discrimination harms not only its direct victims but also the remainder of the class of needy persons that the pool was designed to benefit. * * *

"Having decided to alleviate some of the hardships of poverty by providing necessary medical care, the Government must use neutral criteria in distributing benefits. [It] may not create exceptions for the sole purpose of furthering a governmental interest that is constitutionally subordinate to the individual interest that the entire program was designed to protect."

The other three dissenters wrote separately, each voicing agreement with Stevens, J.'s analysis. BRENNAN, J., joined by Marshall and Blackmun, JJ., expressed his "continuing disagreement with the Court's mischaracterization of the nature of the fundamental right recognized in *Roe* and its misconception of the manner in which that right is infringed [by] legislation withdrawing all funding for medically necessary abortions": "[W]hat the Court fails to appreciate is that it is not simply the woman's indigency that interferes with her freedom of choice, but the combination of her own poverty and the government's unequal subsidization of abortion and childbirth." [c]

Notes and Questions

(a) *The logic of the abortion funding cases.* "There is," notes Tribe, *Treatise* at 1346, "a certain logic [to the abortion funding cases]: if the abortion choice is

---

3. The Court relies heavily on the premise [that] the State's legitimate interest in preserving potential life provides a sufficient justification for funding medical services that are necessarily associated with normal childbirth without also funding abortions that are not medically necessary. The *Maher* opinion repeatedly referred to the policy of favoring "normal childbirth." But this case involves a refusal to fund abortions which are medically necessary to avoid abnormal childbirth.

4. [In] responding to my analysis of this case, Justice White [in a separate opinion] has described the constitutional right recognized in *Roe* as "the right to choose to undergo an abortion without coercive interference by the Government" or a right "only to be free from unreasonable official interference with private choice." No such language is found in the *Roe* opinion itself. Rather, that case squarely held

that State interference is unreasonable if it attaches a greater importance to the interest in potential life than to the interest in protecting the mother's health. One could with equal justification describe the right protected by the First Amendment as the right to make speeches without coercive interference by the Government and then sustain a Government subsidy for all medically needy persons except those who publicly advocate a change of administration.

c. The Court extended *Maher* and *McRae* in *Rust v. Sullivan* (1991) (p. 349 infra), upholding federal regulations prohibiting private physicians receiving federal funds for "family planning services" from providing abortion information to a woman client except when a pregnancy places her life in peril. (The free speech aspects of this case are discussed at p. 915 infra.)

constitutionally private, why should the state be prevented from declining to make it a matter for public funding?" "But," continues Tribe, "this logic is far from inexorable":

"The government obviously has the constitutional *authority* to make abortion, like childbirth, available at no charge to the woman, either in a public facility or by public subsidy. The government's *affirmative* choice *not* to do so can fairly be characterized as a decision to enforce alienation of the woman's right to end her pregnancy, whether that alienation—or 'waiver'—was brought about voluntarily (by the woman's failure to save money for an abortion), or involuntarily (by economic circumstances beyond her control). After all, the unavailability of abortion to such a woman follows from her lack of funds only by virtue of the government's quite conscious decision to treat that medical procedure in particular as a purely private commodity available only to those who can pay the market price. The constitutionality of that decision is rendered dubious by the government's simultaneous decision to take *childbirth* procedures for the same poor woman *off* the private market: the result, as Justice Stevens put it, [dissenting in *McRae,*] is a government program that self-consciously 'require[s] the expenditure of millions and millions of dollars in order to thwart the exercise of a constitutional right.' The state's position with respect to reproductive rights—rights it is bound to respect—is therefore neither as neutral nor as passive as a majority of the Court supposed in *Maher* and *McRae.*" [a]

(b) *Preventing constitutional caste.* Where "rights are too important to be reserved for selected privileged groups," observes Kathleen Sullivan, *Unconstitutional Conditions,* 102 Harv.L.Rev. 1413, 1498–99 (1989), "conditions on benefits that affect their exercise can pose a similar danger of hierarchy. * * * Government cannot universally criminalize abortion, nor universally burden it with heavy restrictions, at least in the first trimester. The only difference between such general bans and the selective subsidization of childbirth but not abortion for indigent women is the class affected. Dependency on government defines the class here. But what the government cannot restrict for all, it may not restrict for those over whom it has special leverage because of their dependency—especially where the displacement of private alternatives creates special responsibility. To hold otherwise would sanction a two-tier system of constitutional rights—a system of constitutional caste."

(c) *Abortion as a private privilege, not a public right.* Consider Catharine MacKinnon, *Privacy v. Equality: Beyond Roe v. Wade*, in *Feminism Unmodified* 93, 100–01 (1987): "[*Roe*] presumes that government nonintervention into the private sphere promotes a woman's freedom of choice. When the alternative is jail, there is much to be said for this argument. But the [*McRae*] result sustains the meaning of privacy in *Roe*: women are guaranteed by the public no more than what we can get in private—that is, what we can extract through our intimate associations with men. Women with privileges get rights. [The] women in [*McRae*], women whose sexual refusal has counted for particularly little, needed something to make their privacy effective. The logic of the Court's response resembles the logic by which women are supposed to consent to sex. Preclude the alternatives, then call the sole remaining option 'her choice'. The point is that the alternatives are precluded *prior* to the reach of the chosen legal doctrine.

---

a. See also Susan Estrich & Kathleen Sullivan, *Abortion Politics: Writing for an Audience of One,* 138 U.Pa.L.Rev. 119, 150 (1989).

They are precluded by conditions of sex, race, and class—the very conditions the privacy frame not only leaves tacit but exists to *guarantee*."

(d) *On looking at the government's purpose.* Michael Perry, *Why the Supreme Court Was Plainly Wrong in the Hyde Amendment Case,* 32 Stan.L.Rev. 1113, 1122 (1980), observes that, although *Roe* does not forbid all government actions that might have the effect of making a woman prefer childbirth to abortion (e.g., the government could decide to fund childbirth *solely* in order to increase the size of the labor force), "*Roe* does require that government take no action, including the selective withholding of Medicaid funds, predicated on the view that abortion is per se morally objectionable—just as government has an undisputed obligation (to borrow one of the Court's own examples) not to take action predicated on the view that sending one's children to a private school is morally objectionable. [This means] that the central question in *McRae* ought to have been whether the Hyde Amendment is predicated on the illicit view. [The *McRae* majority] never even addressed that crucial question." After pointing out, inter alia, that Congressman Hyde stated that the purpose of his Amendment was "not to fund abortion because it's the killing of an innocently inconvenient pre-born child," Professor Perry concludes, id. at 1126, that "[i]t strains credulity to the breaking point to suggest that those charged with defending the Hyde Amendment in court could possibly establish that the view that abortion is per se morally objectionable did not play a but-for role in passage of the Amendment." [b]

POST–*ROE* STATUTORY RESTRICTIONS ON ABORTION

1. *Spousal and parental consent.* PLANNED PARENTHOOD v. DANFORTH, 428 U.S. 52, 96 S.Ct. 2831, 49 L.Ed.2d 788 (1976), per BLACKMUN, J., struck down, inter alia, provisions of a post-*Roe* Missouri abortion statute requiring the spouse's consent to abortion and, in the case of an unmarried woman under 18, parental consent. (These consents were required when a woman sought an abortion during the first trimester unless a physician certified that the abortion was "necessary [to] preserve the life of the mother.")

As for "spousal consent," "the State cannot 'delegate to a spouse a veto power which the state itself is absolutely and totally prohibited from exercising during the first trimester of pregnancy.' * * * Since it is the woman who physically bears the child and who is the more directly and immediately affected by the pregnancy, as between the two, the balance weighs in her favor." As for "parental consent," here, too, "the State does not have the constitutional authority to give a third party an absolute, and possibly arbitrary veto over the decision of the physician and his patient to terminate the patient's pregnancy regardless of the reason for withholding consent." The Court emphasized, however, that its holding "does not suggest that every minor, regardless of age or maturity, may give effective consent for termination of her pregnancy."

WHITE, J., joined by Burger, C.J., and Rehnquist J., dissented, baffled how the Court could find anything in the Constitution or the 1973 *Abortion Cases* *requiring* a state to "assign a greater value to a mother's decision to cut off a potential human life by abortion than to a father's decision to let it mature into a live child." As for parental consent, a state may "protect a minor unmarried

---

b. But consider the remarks of Professor Tribe in Choper, Kamisar & Tribe, *The Supreme Court: Trends and Developments* 1979–80 (1981) at 286–87 (ascertaining government purpose is a "treacherous" and "manipulable" inquiry and outside the limited area of suspect classes, "where purpose is critical because we're talking about symbolism and stigma, a strong case can be made for junking the whole issue of purpose."

woman from making the decision [whether or not to obtain an abortion] in a way which is not in her own best interests, and it seeks to achieve this goal by requiring consultation and consent." Stevens, J., joined the Court's invalidation of other provisions, but dissented on parental consent.

2. *Parental consent or notification requirements and the judicial bypass option.* Taken together, *Bellotti v. Baird* (*Bellotti II*), 443 U.S. 622, 99 S.Ct. 3035, 61 L.Ed.2d 797 (1979) (striking down a Massachusetts parental consent requirement) and *Planned Parenthood v. Ashcroft,* 462 U.S. 476, 103 S.Ct. 2517, 76 L.Ed.2d 733 (1983) (upholding a Missouri law requiring that minors secure parental consent or authorization from the juvenile court for abortion) established that "a state could restrict the ability of a minor female to obtain an abortion by requiring notification to, or the consent of, a parent if, but only if, the state established a procedure whereby the female could bypass the consent or notification requirement." John Nowak & Ronald Rotunda, *Constitutional Law* 838 (5th ed. 1995). See also Daniel Farber & John Nowak, *Beyond the Roe Debate: Judicial Experience with the 1980's "Reasonableness" Test,* 76 Va.L.Rev. 519, 524 (1990).

In order for a parental consent or notification requirement to pass constitutional muster, "[t]he judicial bypass procedure must allow the minor to have an abortion if the court found either that the minor is mature enough to make the abortion decision for herself, or, if she is not mature, that the abortion is in her best interest. The bypass procedure must not be such that the minor's identity would be divulged to her parents, or others, in a way that would deter the use of the procedure and, thereby, effectively give a veto power to parents." Nowak & Rotunda 838.

Although Justice Powell only wrote for himself and Chief Justice Burger in *Ashcroft* and his opinion in *Bellotti II* was only joined by three other justices (Burger, C.J., and Stewart and Rehnquist, JJ.), for many years the criteria Powell set forth in his plurality opinion in *Bellotti II* constituted the de facto constitutional standard for parental consent and notification laws.

Did Powell's plurality opinion in *Bellotti II* reflect an unwarranted confidence in the ability of judges to make wise decisions on behalf of pregnant minors and sound policy for society as a whole. Consider Robert H. Mnookin, *In the Interest of Children* 262–63 (1985):

"Powell's opinion seemed a high water mark of judicial arrogance. Neither legislatures nor families are to be trusted; nor are pregnant minors and their doctors. Only the modern-day secular priest, a judge, is to be trusted with the abortion decision for young women. My recent examination of the actual operation of the [post-*Bellotti II* Massachusetts statute] revealed that the new judicial process does not involve a careful individualized assessment, but is instead a rubber-stamp, administrative operation. [Between April 1981, when the statute first went into effect, and February 1983], [n]one of the 1,300 young women who have gone to court have been successfully refused an abortion.[a] [This finding] is perhaps not so surprising. After all, the proceedings before the judges are not contested, and the judge has no independent source of information. More fundamentally, even if the judge decides that the young woman before him is not

a. Although the requirement of judicial authorization did not lead to the denial of abortion *for those who went to court,* "the business of Massachusetts abortion clinics has significantly declined. It would appear that many girls who formerly would have secured abortions in Massachusetts are now going to other states, particularly New Hampshire." *Id.* at 242.

mature [about 10 percent of the cases], on what basis (other than moral revulsion to abortion) could he possibly decide that it is not in the best interests of an immature minor to have a first-trimester abortion?"

3(a). *Requirement that attending physician provide specified information to woman to insure that consent to abortion is "truly informed"; mandatory 24–hour waiting periods; second-trimester hospitalization requirement.* In AKRON v. AKRON CENTER FOR REPRODUCTIVE HEALTH (*Akron I*), 462 U.S. 416, 103 S.Ct. 2481, 76 L.Ed.2d 687 (1983), a 6–3 majority, per POWELL, J., struck down various sections of an ordinance regulating abortions. In order to insure that a woman's consent to an abortion was "truly informed," an informed consent provision required the attending physician to inform her patient, inter alia, of the physical and emotional complications that may result from an abortion, the particular risks associated with the abortion technique to be utilized, and that "the unborn child is a human life from the moment of conception." Much of the information required, observed the Court, "is designed not to inform the woman's consent but rather to persuade her to withhold it altogether. [A]n additional, and equally decisive, objection to [this provision] is its intrusion upon the discretion of the pregnant woman's physician. * * * [By] insisting upon recitation of a lengthy and inflexible list of information, Akron unreasonably has placed 'obstacles in the path of the doctor upon whom [the woman] is entitled to rely for advice in connection with her decision.' " [b]

As for a mandatory 24–hour waiting period after the pregnant woman signs a consent form, a provision that increases the cost of obtaining an abortion by requiring the woman to make two separate trips to the abortion facility, "Akron has failed to demonstrate that any legitimate state interest is furthered by an arbitrary and inflexible waiting period. [I]f a woman, after appropriate counseling, is prepared to give her written informed consent and proceed with the abortion, a State may not demand that she delay the effectuation of that decision."

As for a provision requiring that after the first trimester all abortions be performed in a hospital, thus preventing abortions in outpatient clinics, Akron's defense of it as a reasonable health regulation had "strong support at the time of *Roe.*" Since then, however, "the safety of second-trimester abortions has increased dramatically. The principal reason is that the [dilation and evacuation] D & E procedure is now widely and successfully used for the second-trimester abortions. [Thus], 'present medical knowledge' convincingly undercuts Akron's justification for requiring that *all* second-trimester abortions be performed in a hospital." By imposing "a heavy, and unnecessary, burden on women's access to a relatively inexpensive [and] safe abortion procedure," the hospitalization requirement "unreasonably infringes upon a woman's constitutional right to obtain an abortion."

3(b). *First suggestion of the "undue burden" standard.* Akron I marked the first time the "undue burden" standard, a test that was to attract much attention later, was suggested. Justice O'Connor (joined by White and Rehnquist, JJ.), who would have upheld all the regulations at issue, maintained that this standard

---

b. In *Thornburgh v. American College of Obstetricians and Gynecologists,* 476 U.S. 747, 106 S.Ct. 2169, 90 L.Ed.2d 779 (1986), a 5–4 majority, per Blackmun, J., struck down Pennsylvania's "informed consent" and "printed information" provisions for essentially the same reasons the Court invalidated similar provi-sions in *Akron.* That Pennsylvania "does not, and surely would not, compel similar disclosures of every possible peril of necessary surgery or of simple vaccination," observed the *Thornburgh* Court, "reveals the anti-abortion character of the statute and its real purpose."

"should be applied to the challenged regulations throughout the entire pregnancy without reference to the particular 'stage' of pregnancy involved" and that if the particular regulation "does not 'unduly burden' the fundamental right, then our evaluation of that regulation is limited to our determination that the regulation rationally relates to a legitimate state purpose." She continued:

"[The] 'undue burden' required in the abortion cases represents the required threshold inquiry that must be conducted before this Court can require a State to justify its legislative actions under the exacting 'compelling state interest' standard. [In] determining whether the State imposes an 'undue burden,' we must keep in mind that when we are concerned with extremely sensitive issues, such as the one involved here, 'the appropriate forum for their resolution in a democracy is the legislature.'"

4. *Requirement that physician report identities of performing and referring physicians and detailed information about woman seeking abortion; provision requiring presence of second physician and other standards of care for post-viability abortions.* THORNBURGH v. AMERICAN COLLEGE OF OBSTETRICIANS AND GYNECOLOGISTS, 476 U.S. 747, 106 S.Ct. 2169, 90 L.Ed.2d 779 (1986) (also discussed at p. 350 infra), invalidated, inter alia, the "reporting requirements" of a Pennsylvania statute and various restrictions of post-viability abortions.

As for what the Court called the statute's "extreme reporting requirements" (requiring information as to the identities of the performing and referring physicians and the woman seeking an abortion), these requirements went well beyond the state's interest in maternal health, and public disclosure of the information obtained might lead to harassment of women who had abortions or physicians who performed them. Thus these requirements posed "an unacceptable danger of deterring the exercise of an [intensely private] right."

As for the requirement that a physician performing a post-viability abortion use the medical technique providing the best opportunity for the unborn child to be aborted alive, unless it would present a "significantly greater medical risk" to the woman's life or health, the statutory language "is not susceptible to a construction that does not require the mother to bear an increased medical risk in order to save her viable fetus." Thus the statute required a "trade-off" between the woman's health and fetal survival rather than require that "maternal health be the physician's paramount consideration." As for the requirement that a second physician be present during an abortion performed when viability is possible, such physician to take all reasonable steps necessary to preserve the child's life and health, the provision was constitutionally defective because it cannot be construed to contain an exception for those emergency situations where the health of the mother would be endangered by delay in the arrival of the second physician.

5. *Prohibiting the use of public facilities or employees to perform abortions not necessary to save the woman's life; prohibiting the use of public funds, employees or facilities to counsel a woman to have an abortion not necessary to save her life; requiring a physician, after 20 weeks pregnancy, to perform certain examinations and tests to determine whether a fetus is viable.* WEBSTER v. REPRODUCTIVE HEALTH SERVICES, fn. b. supra (also discussed at p. 355 infra), upheld various provisions of a Missouri statute. As for the ban on the use of public facilities or employees to perform abortions, REHNQUIST, C.J., observed for a 5–4 majority:

"As we said earlier this Term in *DeShaney v. Winnebago County* [p. 1370 infra], 'our cases have recognized that the Due Process Clauses generally confer no affirmative right to governmental aid, even where such aid may be necessary to secure life, liberty, or property interests of which the government itself may not deprive the individual.' * * *

"Just as Congress' refusal to fund abortions in *McRae* left 'an indigent woman with at least the same range of choice in deciding whether to obtain a medically necessary abortion as she would have had if Congress had chosen to subsidize no health care costs at all,' Missouri's refusal to allow public employees to perform abortions in public hospitals leaves a pregnant woman with the same choices as if the State had chosen not to operate any public hospitals at all. * * * Having held that the State's refusal to fund abortions does not violate *Roe,* it strains logic to reach a contrary result for the use of public facilities and employees." [c]

The Court of Appeals had struck down state provisions prohibiting the use of public employees, public facilities and public funds to encourage or counsel a woman to have a nontherapeutic abortion—holding all three provisions unconstitutionally vague and violative of a woman's right to choose an abortion. But the state appealed only the invalidation of the public fund prohibition. In light of the state's contention, which the Court accepted for purposes of decision, that the ban on the use of public funds "is not directed at the primary conduct of physicians or health providers," but simply an instruction to the state's fiscal officers not to allocate public funds for abortion counseling, appellees (state-employed health professionals) maintained that they were not "adversely" affected by the provision and therefore that there was no longer a case or controversy before the Court on this question. The Court agreed.

c. See also *Rust v. Sullivan* (1991) (the free speech aspects of which are discussed at p. 822 infra), upholding federal regulations that implement Title X of the Public Health Services Act by (1) prohibiting a Title X project from providing counseling concerning the use of abortion (or providing referral for abortion) as a method of family planing; (2) prohibiting a Title X project from engaging in activities that "encourage, promote or advocate abortion as a matter of family planning"; and (3) requiring that Title X projects be organized so that they are "physically and financially separate" from prohibited abortion activities. Relying heavily on *Webster* and the "abortion funding" cases, *Maher* and *McRae,* the Court, per Rehnquist, C.J., rejected, inter alia, the arguments (as the majority described them) that the regulations violate a woman's "Fifth Amendment right to medical self-determination and to make informed medical decisions free of government-imposed harm":

"The Government has no constitutional duty to subsidize an activity merely because the activity is constitutionally protected and may validly choose to fund childbirth over abortion and 'implement that judgment by the allocation of public funds' for medical services relating to childbirth but not to those relating to abortion. *Webster.*

"[That] the regulations do not impermissibly burden a woman's Fifth Amendment rights is evident from the line of cases beginning with *Maher* and *McRae* and culminating in our most recent decision in *Webster.* [The] difficulty that a woman encounters when a Title X project does not provide abortion counseling or referral leaves her in no different position than she would have been if the government had not enacted Title X.

"In *Webster* we stated that '[h]aving held that the State's refusal [in *Maher*] to fund abortions does not violate *Roe,* it strains logic to reach a contrary result for the use of public facilities and employees.' It similarly would strain logic, in light of the more extreme restrictions in those cases, to find that the mere decision to exclude abortion-related services from a federally funded *pre-conceptual* family planning program, is unconstitutional."

On this issue, Blackmun, J., joined by Marshall and Stevens, JJ., dissented: "Even if one accepts as valid the Court's theorizing in [*McRae* and *Webster*], the majority's reasoning in the present cases is flawed. Until today, the Court has allowed to stand only those restrictions upon reproductive freedom that, while limiting the availability of abortion, have left intact a woman's ability to decide without coercion whether she will continue her pregnancy to term. * * * Today's decision abandons that principle and with disastrous results."

Also at issue in *Webster* was a viability-testing provision, a requirement that prior to performing an abortion on any woman a physician has "reason to believe is carrying an unborn child of 20 or more weeks gestational age," the physician shall determine if the "unborn child" is viable and "in making this determination" "shall perform" such examinations and tests "as are necessary."[d] The Court upheld the provision, but there was no majority opinion on this issue. Rehnquist, C.J., joined by White and Kennedy, JJ., read the provision as not requiring a physician to perform the tests in all circumstances, but only requiring her to exercise "reasonable professional judgment" in determining whether such tests are necessary or appropriate.

The Rehnquist plurality recognized that a provision for tests that will often show that the fetus is *not* viable was in conflict with *Roe* and cases following it. For *Roe* limited state involvement in second-trimester abortions "to protecting maternal health" and "allowed states to regulate or proscribe abortions to protect the unborn child only after viability." But the plurality considered this not so much a flaw in the challenged provision as a reflection of the fact that the "rigid trimester analysis" of *Roe* has proved "unsound in principle and unworkable in practice." (For a more comprehensive discussion of this issue, see pp. 355–58 infra.)

Unlike the Rehnquist plurality, concurring Justice O'Connor "[did] not understand these viability testing requirements to conflict with any of the Court's past decisions concerning state regulation of abortion." (She thus saw no need to reexamine the constitutionality of *Roe*.) She thought it "clear" that "requiring the performance of examinations and tests useful to determining whether a fetus is viable, when viability is possible, and when it would not be medically imprudent to do so, does not impose an undue burden on a woman's abortion decision."

O'Connor, J., distinguished the second-trimester requirement invalidation in *Akron I*. The requirement at issue in that case greatly increased the cost of an abortion whereas the viability-testing requirement did so "only marginally, if at all." (For a fuller discussion of O'Connor's views on this issue, see pp. 358–59 infra.)

Concurring Justice Scalia voted to uphold the viability-testing provision, but agreed with dissenting Justice Blackmun (joined by Brennan and Marshall, JJ.) that the portion of the plurality opinion sustaining this provision "effectively would overrule *Roe*." Scalia thought "that should be done, but would do it more explicitly."

CONTINUING CONTROVERSY OVER *ROE*: *THORNBURGH, WEBSTER* AND *HODGSON*

I. Dissenting in THORNBURGH (p. 348 supra), which invalidated various restrictions on abortion, WHITE, J., joined by Rehnquist, J., launched a strong attack on the premises of the majority's decision—and the premises of *Roe*:

"In my view, the time has come to recognize that [*Roe*] 'departs from a proper understanding' of the Constitution and to overrule it. I do not claim that the arguments in support of this proposition are new ones or that they were not

---

d. The plurality opinion noted that "the District Court found that 'the medical evidence is uncontradicted that a 20–week fetus is *not* viable' and that '23½ to 24 weeks gestation is the earliest point in pregnancy where a reason- able possibility of viability exists.' " But, add- ed the plurality, the district court "also found that there may be a 4–week error in estimating gestational age, which supports testing at 20 weeks."

considered by the Court in *Roe* or in the cases that succeeded it. But if an argument that a constitutional decision is erroneous must be novel in order to justify overruling that precedent, the Court's decisions in *Lochner* and *Plessy* would remain the law, for the doctrines announced in those decisions were nowhere more eloquently or incisively criticized than in the dissenting opinions of Justices Holmes (in *Lochner*) and Harlan (in both cases).

"[I] can certainly agree with the proposition—which I deem indisputable— that a woman's ability to choose an abortion is a species of 'liberty' that is subject to the general protections of the Due Process Clause. I cannot agree, however, that this liberty is so 'fundamental' that restrictions upon it call into play anything more than the most minimal judicial scrutiny.

"Fundamental liberties and interests are most clearly present when the Constitution provides specific textual recognition of their existence and importance. Thus, the Court is on relatively firm ground when it deems certain of the liberties set forth in the Bill of Rights to be fundamental and therefore finds them incorporated in the Fourteenth Amendment's guarantee that no State may deprive any person of liberty without due process of law. When the Court ventures further and defines as 'fundamental' liberties that are nowhere mentioned in the Constitution (or that are present only in the so-called 'penumbras' of specifically enumerated rights), it must, of necessity, act with more caution, lest it open itself to the accusation that, in the name of identifying constitutional principles to which the people have consented in framing their Constitution, the Court has done nothing more than impose its own controversial choices of value upon the people.[a]

"[The] Court has justified the recognition of a woman's fundamental right to terminate her pregnancy by invoking decisions upholding claims of personal autonomy in connection with the conduct of family life, the rearing of children, marital privacy, the use of contraceptives, and the preservation of the individual's capacity to procreate [citing *Griswold, Eisenstadt, Carey* and other cases]. Even if each of these cases was correctly decided and could be properly grounded in rights that are 'implicit in the concept of ordered liberty' or 'deeply rooted in this Nation's history and tradition,' the issues in the cases cited differ from those at stake where abortion is concerned. As the Court appropriately recognized in *Roe*, '[t]he pregnant woman cannot be isolated in her privacy'; the termination of a pregnancy typically involves the destruction of another entity: the fetus. However, one answers the metaphysical or theological question whether the fetus is a 'human being' or the legal question whether it is a 'person' as that term is used in the Constitution, one must at least recognize, first, that the fetus is an entity that bears in its cells all the genetic information that characterizes a member of the species homo sapiens and distinguishes an individualized member of that species from all others, and second, that there is no nonarbitrary line separating a fetus from a child or, indeed, an adult human being. Given that the continued existence and development—that is to say, the *life*—of such an entity are so directly at stake in the woman's decision whether or not to terminate her pregnancy, that decision must be recognized as sui generis, different in kind from the others that the Court has protected under the rubric of personal or family privacy and autonomy.[2]

---

a. Compare the language Justice White used later the same term in his opinion of the Court in *Bowers v. Hardwick* (p. 422 infra), upholding a prohibition against consensual sodomy as applied to homosexuals.

2. That the abortion decision, like the decisions in *Griswold, Eisenstadt,* and *Carey,* concerns childbearing (or, more generally, family life) in no sense necessitates a holding that the

"[If] the woman's liberty to choose an abortion is fundamental, then, it is not because any of our precedents (aside from *Roe* itself) commands or justifies that result; it can only be because protection for this unique choice is itself 'implicit in the concept of ordered liberty' or, perhaps, 'deeply rooted in this Nation's history and tradition.' It seems clear to me that it is neither. The Court's opinion in *Roe* itself convincingly refutes the notion that the abortion liberty is deeply rooted in the history or tradition of our people, as does the continuing and deep division of the people themselves over the question of abortion. As for the notion that choice in the matter of abortion is implicit in the concept of ordered liberty, it seems apparent to me that a free, egalitarian, and democratic society does not presuppose any particular rule or set of rules with respect to abortion. And again, the fact that many men and women of good will and high commitment to constitutional government place themselves on both sides of the abortion controversy strengthens my own conviction that the values animating the Constitution do not compel recognition of the abortion liberty as fundamental. In so denominating that liberty, the Court engages not in constitutional interpretation, but in the unrestrained imposition of its own, extraconstitutional value preferences.

"A second, equally basic error infects the Court's decision in *Roe*. The detailed set of rules governing state restrictions on abortion that the Court first articulated in *Roe* and has since refined and elaborated presupposes not only that the woman's liberty to choose an abortion is fundamental, but also that the state's countervailing interest in protecting fetal life (or, as the Court would have it, 'potential human life') becomes 'compelling' only at the point at which the fetus is viable. As Justice O'Connor pointed out three years ago in her dissent in *Akron,* the Court's choice of viability as the point at which the State's interest becomes compelling is entirely arbitrary.

"[The] governmental interest at issue is in protecting those who will be citizens if their lives are not ended in the womb. The substantiality of this interest is in no way dependent on the probability that the fetus may be capable of surviving outside the womb at any given point in its development, as the possibility of fetal survival is contingent on the state of medical practice and technology, factors that are in essence morally and constitutionally irrelevant. The State's interest is in the fetus as an entity in itself, and the character of this entity does not change at the point of viability under conventional medical wisdom. Accordingly, the State's interest, if compelling after viability, is equally compelling before viability.

" * * * Abortion is a hotly contested moral and political issue. Such issues, in our society, are to be resolved by the will of the people, either as expressed through legislation or through the general principles they have already incorporated into the Constitution they have adopted. *Roe* implies that the people have already resolved the debate by weaving into the Constitution the values and principles that answer the issue. As I have argued, I believe it is clear that the people have never—not in 1787, 1791, 1868, or at any time since—done any such thing. I would return the issue to the people by overruling *Roe*."

Concurring Justice STEVENS responded:

"[If] Justice White were correct in regarding the postconception decision of the question whether to bear a child as a relatively unimportant, second-class sort of interest, I might agree with his view that the individual should be required to

liberty to choose abortion is "fundamental." That the decision involves the destruction of the fetus renders it different in kind from the   decision not to conceive in the first place. * * *

conform her decision to the will of the majority. But if that decision commands the respect that is traditionally associated with the 'sensitive areas of liberty' protected by the Constitution, as Justice White characterized reproductive decisions in *Griswold,* no individual should be compelled to surrender the freedom to make that decision for herself simply because her 'value preferences' are not shared by the majority. In a sense, the basic question is whether the 'abortion decision' should be made by the individual or by the majority 'in the unrestrained imposition of its own, extraconstitutional value preferences.' But surely Justice White is quite wrong in suggesting that the Court is imposing value preferences on anyone else.[6]

"Justice White is also surely wrong in suggesting that the governmental interest in protecting fetal life is equally compelling during the entire period from the moment of conception until the moment of birth. Again, I recognize that a powerful theological argument can be made for that position, but I believe our jurisdiction is limited to the evaluation of secular state interests.[7] I should think it obvious that the State's interest in the protection of an embryo—even if that interest is defined as 'protecting those who will be citizens'—increases progressively and dramatically as the organism's capacity to feel pain, to experience pleasure, to survive, and to react to its surroundings increases day by day. The development of a fetus—and pregnancy itself—are not static conditions, and the assertion that the government's interest is static simply ignores this reality.

"Nor is it an answer to argue that life itself is not a static condition, and that 'there is no nonarbitrary line separating a fetus from a child, or indeed, an adult human being.' For, unless the religious view that a fetus is a 'person' is adopted—a view Justice White refuses to embrace—there is a fundamental and well-recognized difference between a fetus and a human being; indeed, if there is not such a difference, the permissibility of terminating the life of a fetus could scarcely be left to the will of the state legislatures.[8] And if distinctions may be drawn between a fetus and a human being in terms of the state interest in their protection—even though the fetus represents one of 'those who will be citizens'— it seems to me quite odd to argue that distinctions may not also be drawn between the state interest in protecting the freshly fertilized egg and the state interest in protecting the 9–month–gestated, fully sentient fetus on the eve of birth. Recognition of this distinction is supported not only by logic, but also by history and by our shared experiences.

"Turning to Justice White's comments on stare decisis, he is of course correct in pointing out that the Court 'has not hesitated to overrule decisions, or even whole lines of cases, where experience, scholarship, and reflection demonstrated that their fundamental premises were not to be found in the Constitution.' But Justice White has not disavowed the 'fundamental premises' on which the decision

---

6. Justice White's characterization of the governmental interest as "protecting those who will be citizens if their lives are not ended in the womb" reveals that his opinion may be influenced as much by his own value preferences as by his view about the proper allocation of decisionmaking responsibilities between the individual and the State. For if federal judges must allow the State to make the abortion decision, presumably the State is free to decide that a woman may *never* abort, may *sometimes* abort, or, as in the People's Republic of China, must *always* abort if her family is already too large. In contrast, our cases represent a consistent view that the individual is primarily responsible for reproductive decisions, whether the State seeks to prohibit reproduction, *Skinner,* or to require it, *Roe.*

7. The responsibility for nurturing the soul of the newly born, as well as the unborn, rests with individual parents, not with the State. No matter how important a sacrament such as baptism may be, a State surely could not punish a mother for refusing to baptize her child.

8. No member of this Court has ever suggested that a fetus is a "person" within the meaning of the Fourteenth Amendment.

in *Roe* rests. He has not disavowed the Court's prior approach to the interpretation of the word 'liberty' or, more narrowly, the line of cases that culminated in the unequivocal holding, applied to unmarried persons and married persons alike, 'that the Constitution protects individual decisions in matters of childbearing from unjustified intrusion by the State.' *Carey* (White, J., concurring in pertinent part).

"[In] the final analysis, the holding in *Roe* presumes that it is far better to permit some individuals to make incorrect decisions than to deny all individuals the right to make decisions that have a profound effect upon their destiny. Arguably a very primitive society would have been protected from evil by a rule against eating apples; a majority familiar with Adam's experience might favor such a rule. But the lawmakers who placed a special premium on the protection of individual liberty have recognized that certain values are more important than the will of a transient majority."

In a series of footnotes, WHITE, J., (joined by Rehnquist, J.), responded to Justice Stevens' criticism of his views as follows:

"[That the abortion decision involves the destruction of the fetus] does not go merely to the weight of the state interest in regulating abortion; it affects as well the characterization of the liberty interest itself. For if the liberty to make certain decisions with respect to contraception without governmental constraint is 'fundamental,' it is not only because those decisions are 'serious' and 'important' to the individual, but also because some value of privacy or individual autonomy that is somehow implicit in the scheme of ordered liberties established by the Constitution supports a judgment that such decisions are none of government's business. The same cannot be said where, as here, the individual is not 'isolated in her privacy.' * * *

"Justice Stevens asserts that I am 'quite wrong in suggesting that the Court is imposing value preferences on anyone else' when it denominates the liberty to choose abortion as 'fundamental' (in contradistinction to such other, nonfundamental liberties as the liberty to use dangerous drugs or to operate a business without governmental interference) and thereby disempowers state electoral majorities from legislating in this area. I can only respond that I cannot conceive of a definition of the phrase 'imposing value preferences' that does not encompass the Court's action.

"Justice Stevens also suggests that it is the legislative majority that has engaged in 'the unrestrained imposition of its own, extraconstitutional value choices,' when a state legislature restricts the availability of abortion. But a legislature, unlike a court, has the inherent power to do so unless its choices are constitutionally *forbidden*, which, in my view, is not the case here. * * *

"[It] is self-evident that neither the legislative decision to assert a state interest in fetal life before viability nor the judicial decision to recognize that interest as compelling constitutes an impermissible 'religious' decision merely because it coincides with the belief of one or more religions. Certainly the fact that the prohibition of murder coincides with one of the Ten Commandments does not render a State's interest in its murder statutes less than compelling, nor are legislative and judicial decisions concerning the use of the death penalty tainted by their correspondence to varying religious views on that subject. The simple, and perhaps unfortunate, fact of the matter is that in determining whether to assert an interest in fetal life, a State cannot avoid taking a position that will correspond to some religious beliefs and contradict others. The same is true to some extent with respect to the choice this Court faces in characterizing an asserted state interest in fetal life, for denying that such an interest is a 'compelling' one necessarily entails a negative resolution of the 'religious' issue of the humanity of the fetus, whereas accepting the State's interest as compelling reflects at least tolerance for a state decision that is congruent with the equally 'religious' position that human life begins at conception. Faced with such a decision, the most appropriate course of action for the Court is to defer to a legislative resolution of the issue: in other words, if a state legislature asserts an interest in protecting fetal life, I can see no satisfactory basis for *denying* that it is compelling."

II. WEBSTER (p. 348 supra) upheld, inter alia, a Missouri viability-testing requirement providing that certain examinations and tests should be performed when a physician has "reason to believe" that a woman is "carrying an unborn child of 20 or more weeks gestational age." There was no majority opinion on this issue. REHNQUIST, C.J., joined by White and Kennedy, JJ., observed:

"We think the doubt cast upon the [viability-testing provision by our earlier cases] is a reflection of the fact that the rigid trimester analysis of the course of a pregnancy enunciated in *Roe* has [made] constitutional law in this area a virtual procrustean bed. * * *

"Stare decisis is a cornerstone of our legal system, but it has less power in constitutional cases, where, save for constitutional amendments, this Court is the only body able to make needed changes. We have not refrained from reconsideration of a prior construction of the Constitution that has proved 'unsound in principle and unworkable in practice.' We think the *Roe* trimester framework falls into that category.

"In the first place, the rigid *Roe* framework is hardly consistent with the notion of a Constitution cast in general terms, as ours is, and usually speaking in general principles, as ours does. The key elements of the *Roe* framework— trimesters and viability—are not found in the text of the Constitution or in any place else one would expect to find a constitutional principle. Since the bounds of the inquiry are essentially indeterminate, the result has been a web of legal rules that have become increasingly intricate, resembling a code of regulations rather than a body of constitutional doctrine.

"In the second place, we do not see why the State's interest in protecting human life should come into existence only at the point of viability, and that there should therefore be a rigid line allowing state regulation after viability, but prohibiting it before viability. [The plurality then quoted from the dissents of White, J., and O'Connor, J., in *Thornburgh*.]

"It is true that the tests in question increase the expense of abortion, and regulate the discretion of the physician in determining the viability of the fetus. Since the tests will undoubtedly show in many cases that the fetus is not viable, the tests will have been performed for what were in fact second-trimester abortions. But we are satisfied that the requirement of these tests permissibly furthers the State's interest in protecting potential human life and we therefore believe [the provision] to be constitutional. * * *

"Both appellants and the United States as Amicus Curiae have urged that we overrule [*Roe*]. The facts of the present case, however, differ from those at issue in *Roe*. Here, Missouri has determined that viability is the point at which its interest in potential human life must be safeguarded. In *Roe,* on the other hand, the Texas statute criminalized the performance of *all* abortions, except when the mother's life was at stake. This case therefore affords us no occasion to revisit the holding of *Roe*, [and] we leave it undisturbed. To the extent indicated in our opinion, we would modify and narrow *Roe* and succeeding cases."

Dissenting Justice BLACKMUN, joined by Brennan and Marshall, JJ., directed his fire at the Rehnquist plurality's consideration of the statute's viability-testing requirement. Contrary to the plurality, he agreed with the Court of Appeals that the "plain language" of the viability-testing provision required that after 20 weeks the specified tests *must* be performed. "By mandating tests to determine fetal weight and lung maturity for every fetus thought to be more than 20 weeks gestational age, the statute requires physicians to undertake procedures [that] have no medical justification, impose significant additional health risks on both the pregnant woman and the fetus, and bear no rational relation to the State's interest in protecting fetal life. [Thus,] were it not for the plurality's tortured effort to avoid the plain import of [the provision], it could have struck [it down] as patently irrational irrespective of the *Roe* framework. The plurality eschews this straightforward resolution, in the hope of precipitating a constitutional crisis." Continued Blackmun:

"In the plurality's view, the viability-testing provision imposes a burden on second-trimester abortions as a way of furthering the State's interest in protecting the potential life of the fetus. Since under the *Roe* framework, the State may not fully regulate abortion in the interest of potential life (as opposed to maternal health) until the third trimester, the plurality finds it necessary, in order to save the Missouri testing provision, to throw out *Roe's* trimester framework. In flat contradiction to *Roe*, the plurality concludes that the State's interest in potential life is compelling before viability, and upholds the testing provision because it 'permissibly furthers' that state interest.

"[The] plurality does not even mention, much less join, the true jurisprudential debate underlying this case: whether the Constitution includes an 'unenumerated' general right to privacy as recognized in many of our decisions, most notably *Griswold* and *Roe*, and, more specifically, whether and to what extent such a right to privacy extends to matters of childbearing and family life, including abortion. [On] these grounds, abandoned by the plurality, the Court should decide this case.

"But rather than arguing that the text of the Constitution makes no mention of the right to privacy, the plurality complains that the critical elements of the *Roe* framework—trimesters and viability—do not appear in the Constitution and are, therefore, somehow inconsistent with a Constitution cast in general terms. Were this a true concern, we would have to abandon most of our constitutional jurisprudence. [The] Constitution makes no mention, for example, of the First Amendment's 'actual malice' standard for proving certain libels or of the standard for determining when speech is obscene. * * *

"With respect to the *Roe* framework, [the] trimester framework simply defines and limits that right to privacy in the abortion context to accommodate, not destroy, a State's legitimate interest in protecting the health of pregnant women and in preserving potential human life. Fashioning such accommodations between individual rights and the legitimate interests of government, establishing benchmarks and standards with which to evaluate the competing claims of individuals and government, lies at the very heart of constitutional adjudication. To the extent that the trimester framework is useful in this enterprise, it is not only consistent with constitutional interpretation, but necessary to the wise and just exercise of this Court's paramount authority to define the scope of constitutional rights.

"[In] answering the plurality's claim that the State's interest in the fetus is uniform and compelling throughout pregnancy, I cannot improve upon what Justice Stevens has written [quoting at length from Justice Stevens' concurring opinion in *Thornburgh*.]

"For my own part, I remain convinced [that] the *Roe* framework, and the viability standard in particular, fairly, sensibly, and effectively functions to safeguard the constitutional liberties of pregnant women while recognizing and accommodating the State's interest in potential human life. The viability line reflects the biological facts and truths of fetal development; it marks that threshold moment prior to which a fetus cannot survive separate from the woman and cannot reasonably and objectively be regarded as a subject of rights or interests distinct from, or paramount to, those of the pregnant woman. At the same time, the viability standard takes account of the undeniable fact that as the fetus evolves into its postnatal form, and as it loses its dependence on the uterine environment, the State's interest in the fetus' potential human life, and in fostering a regard for human life in general, becomes compelling. As a practical matter, because viability follows "quickening"—the point at which a woman feels movement in her womb—and because viability occurs no earlier than 23 weeks gestational age, it establishes an easily applicable standard for regulating abortion while providing a pregnant woman ample time to exercise her fundamental right with her responsible physician to terminate her pregnancy.[9] [The] plurality today advances not one reasonable argument as to why our judgment in [*Roe*] was wrong and should be abandoned.

"Having contrived an opportunity to reconsider the *Roe* framework, and then having discarded that framework, the plurality finds the testing provision unobjectionable because it 'permissibly furthers the State's interest in protecting potential human life.' [The] plurality's novel test appears to be nothing more than a dressed-up version of rational-basis review, this Court's most lenient level of scrutiny. One thing is clear, however: were the plurality's 'permissibly furthers' standard adopted by the Court, for all practical purposes, *Roe* would be overruled.

"The 'permissibly furthers' standard completely disregards the irreducible minimum of *Roe:* the Court's recognition that a woman has a limited fundamental constitutional right to decide whether to terminate a pregnancy. That right receives no meaningful recognition in the plurality's written opinion. Since, in the plurality's view, the State's interest in potential life is compelling as of the moment of conception, and is therefore served only if abortion is abolished, every hindrance to a woman's ability to obtain an abortion must be 'permissible.'

"[The] plurality pretends that *Roe* survives, explaining that the facts of this case differ from those in *Roe:* here, Missouri has chosen to assert its interest in potential life only at the point of viability, whereas, in *Roe*, Texas had asserted

---

9. Notably, neither the plurality nor Justice O'Connor advance the now-familiar catchphrase criticism of the *Roe* framework that because the point of viability will recede with advances in medical technology, *Roe* "is clearly on a collision course with itself." This critique has no medical foundation. As the medical literature and the amicus briefs filed in this case conclusively demonstrate, "there is an 'anatomic threshold' for fetal viability of about 23–24 weeks gestation." Prior to that time, the crucial organs are not sufficiently mature to provide the mutually sustaining functions that are prerequisite to extrauterine survival, or viability. Moreover, "no technology exists to bridge the development gap between the three-day embryo culture and the 24th week of gestation." Nor does the medical community believe that the development of any such technology is possible in the foreseeable future. In other words, the threshold of fetal viability is, and will remain, no different from what it was at the time *Roe* was decided. Predictions to the contrary are pure science fiction. See Brief for A Group of American Law Professors as Amici Curiae 23–25.

that interest from the point of conception, criminalizing all abortions, except where the life of the mother was at stake. This, of course, is a distinction without a difference. [If] the Constitution permits a State to enact any statute that reasonably furthers its interest in potential life, and if that interest arises as of conception, why would the Texas statute fail to pass muster? One suspects that the plurality agrees. It is impossible to read the plurality opinion * * * without recognizing its implicit invitation to every State to enact more and more restrictive abortion laws, and to assert their interest in potential life as of the moment of conception.

"[For] today, at least, the law of abortion stands undisturbed. For today, the women of this Nation still retain the liberty to control their destinies. But the signs are evident and very ominous, and a chill wind blows." [b]

Concurring Justice O'CONNOR agreed with the Rehnquist plurality that the viability-testing provision did not require a physician to perform examinations and tests when it would be careless and imprudent to do so, but only when useful to make subsidiary findings as to viability. Unlike the plurality, however, Justice O'Connor did not understand the viability testing provision (as so construed) to conflict with any of the Court's past decisions concerning state regulation of abortion. (Thus, there was no need to reexamine the constitutionality of *Roe.*) She thought it "clear" that "requiring the performance of examinations and tests useful to determining whether a fetus is viable, when viability is possible, and when it would not be medically imprudent to do so, does not impose an undue burden on a woman's abortion decision."

She distinguished the second-trimester requirement invalidated in *Akron I,* which more than doubled the cost of a woman's access to a relatively inexpensive and safe abortion procedure. "By contrast, the cost of examinations and tests that could usefully and prudently be performed when a woman is 20–24 weeks pregnant to determine whether the fetus is viable would only marginally, if at all, increase the cost of an abortion." Moreover, the tests required by the Missouri provision are to be performed "when viability is possible." This feature distinguishes the provision from the second-trimester hospitalization requirement invalidated in *Akron.*

Concurring Justice SCALIA voted to uphold the viability testing requirement, but agreed with dissenting Justice Blackmun (joined by Brennan and Marshall, JJ.) that the portion of the plurality opinion sustaining this provision "effectively would overrule *Roe.*" He thought "that should be done," but he would "do it more explicitly."

b. In a separate dissent, Stevens, J., agreed with the lower courts that the viability-testing provision was designed to "protect the potential human life of nonviable fetuses by making the abortion decision more costly" and, therefore, for the reasons stated by Justice Blackmun, "is manifestly unconstitutional * * * 'irrespective of the *Roe* framework.'" Stevens maintained that "the plain language [of the provision] is supported by the structure of the statute as a whole, particularly the preamble, which 'finds' that life 'begins at conception' and further commands that state laws shall be construed to maximize protection to 'the unborn child at every stage of development.'" Because he was unaware of "any secular basis for differentiating between contraceptive procedures that are effective immediately before and those that are effective immediately after fertilization," Stevens thought the preamble invalid under *Griswold* and its progeny. Moreover, "the absence of any secular purpose for the declarations that life begins at conception and that conception occurs at fertilization" made the relevant portion of the preamble invalid under the Establishment Clause of the First Amendment.

However, the *Webster* majority saw no need to pass on the constitutionality of the preamble because it "does not by its terms regulate abortion" and can be read simply as expressing a permissible "value judgment" favoring childbirth over abortion.

Noting that Justice O'Connor would uphold the provision because "it does not impose an undue burden on a woman's abortion decision," Scalia, J., expressed his unhappiness with that test: "The fact that the challenged regulation is less costly than [the second-trimester hospitalization requirement] we struck down in *Akron* tells us only that we cannot decide the present case on the basis of that earlier decision. It does not tell us whether the present requirement is an 'undue burden,' and I know of no basis for determining that this particular burden (or any other for that matter) is 'due.' One could with equal justification conclude that it is not.[c] To avoid the question of *Roe*'s validity, with the attendant costs that this will have for the Court and for the principles of self-governance, on the basis of a standard that offers 'no guide but the Court's own discretion' [quoting from a Holmes dissent] merely adds to the irrationality of what we do today."

Notes and Questions

1. *The significance of Webster.* Consider Susan Estrich & Kathleen Sullivan, *Abortion Politics: Writing for an Audience of One,* 138 U.Pa.L.Rev. 119–20 (1989): "The majority was able to avoid any ruling at all on Missouri's declaration that life begins at conception by concluding that the passage merely expressed a value judgment.[d] Restrictions on using public facilities for abortion, particularly as narrowly although perhaps inaccurately framed by the state's Attorney General, fit within the Court's precedents upholding the exclusion of public support for abortion. Finally, the state's seeming viability testing requirement at twenty weeks or more became, with a little interpretive twisting, no more than a recommendation that doctors perform such tests where medically appropriate.[e]

"Of course, if little was decided in *Webster,* a good deal was nonetheless said. The Chief Justice, writing for three members of the Court, made plain that he was ready to jettison [the] trimester approach of *Roe,* presumably finding the state's interest in potential life as compelling in the first month as the last, and leaving it to the state to balance its own interest against the woman's, subject only to some rationality review. The genius of the approach, if you can call it that, is that it effectively overrules *Roe* without ever even suggesting that a woman lacks a privacy or autonomy interest in her own body."

2. *The state's interest in protecting potential human life before viability.* "There is," observe Professors Estrich and Sullivan, id. at 146–47, "only one way

---

c. Cf. Laurence Tribe, *Abortion: The Clash of Absolutes* 24 (1990): "*Webster* was and remains an open invitation to state legislators to see just how strictly they can regulate abortion without Justice O'Connor finding the burden on the abortion right 'undue.' " At the time Professor Tribe made this remark, Justice O'Connor had never found a restriction on the abortion right "unduly burdensome" and thus constitutionally defective. But shortly thereafter, she did—in *Hodgson,* p. 455 infra.

d. See the discussion in fn. b supra.

e. But see Laurence Tribe, *The Curvature of Constitutional Space: What Lawyers Can Learn From Modern Physics,* 103 Harv.L.Rev. 1, 16 (1989): "In *Webster,* the Supreme Court went further than it had in the abortion funding cases: *Webster* upheld a ban on *privately* financed abortions in a public facility, under a statute that defined the concept of 'public facil-

ity' broadly enough to include essentially the only hospital in a large part of the state of Missouri—a hospital that was privately owned but happened to be located in a space rented from the government."

See also Frances Olsen, *Unraveling Compromise,* 103 Harv.L.Rev. 105, 116 (1989): "In a sense, *Webster* turns [*McRae*] upside down. [*McRae*] began from the idea that the right to abortion was a private right and concluded that deprivation of public funding was constitutional; the *Webster* plurality and Justice O'Connor began from the premise that deprivation of funding is constitutional to conclude that less burdensome restrictions on abortion—even burdens not related to funding, such as viability testing—are constitutional as well."

to protect potential life before a fetus has the potential to survive outside the womb: forbid or discourage abortion. After viability, there are surely other ways abortion regulations can preserve an interest in potential life. For example, the state may require two doctors' presence or forbid saline procedures in late abortions to enhance survival if an attempted abortion turns into a live birth. Imposing any 'undue burdens,' or indeed any burdens at all, on a woman's right *prior* to viability in the name of preserving life, though, is to say that a woman has a right and then to take it away. By definition, her right is to control her bodily autonomy *even at the expense of potential human life.*"

3. *More on the significance of fetal viability.* "Any time limit is inherently arbitrary to some degree," observes Laurence Tribe, *Abortion: The Clash of Absolutes* 208 (1990), "but at least *Roe*'s focus on fetal viability—when the fetus, given current technology, can survive independently—reflects the special concern that a woman not be forced to use her body to bring a new life to the point where *it* can lead a separate existence but *she* no longer can." Responds Michael McConnell, *How Not to Promote Serious Deliberation about Abortion* (essay review of Tribe's book), 58 U.Chi.L.Rev. 1181, 1198–99 (1991):

"Tribe half-heartedly defends the *Roe* Court's focus on fetal viability. But this is one of the least plausible alternatives. The theory is that at viability the fetus can survive on its own (with the help of extraordinary medical intervention). In fact, most fetuses do *not* survive abortion even after viability. But paradoxically, if it were true that fetuses *did* routinely survive abortion after viability, that would not, logically, be a reason to forbid abortions, because it would mean the abortion (that is, the termination of pregnancy) could be accomplished without the taking of human life. If viability really meant survivability, it would suggest exactly the opposite from Tribe's conclusion: women should be free to terminate their pregnancies at will after viability, so long as their doctors take proper steps to protect the life of the premature infant. Only prior to viability is there a strong justification for prohibiting the termination of pregnancy, because before that point it is not possible to terminate the pregnancy without killing the child. On the other hand, if (as is actually the case), viability does not really mean survivability, it carries no moral weight. * * * Viability depends entirely on the technology at a given time and place and not on any characteristic of the fetus; the moral-legal status of a being should not depend on such contingent factors."

Compare Jed Rubenfeld, *On the Legal Status of the Proposition that "Life Begins at Conception,"* 43 Stan.L.Rev. 599, 622–23, 635 (1991): "The stage in human development currently marked by 'viability' (in its traditional sense) has always carried an implicit significance quite apart from the fetus's chances of survival. Precisely due to the undeveloped state of our medical technology, 'viability' denotes a fairly advanced state in fetal development. Viability occurs not only at the time when the fetus's pulmonary capability begins, but also when its brain begins to take on the cortical structure capable of higher mental functioning. These two important developments provide indicia both of *independent* beingness and of distinctly *human* beingness. * * * The reason for *Roe*'s success (such as it was) is that, despite its vocabulary of potential life, the Court in all essential respects made a determination about when the states could deem the fetus a person. Viability never made sense as the point at which the state interest in potential human life becomes compelling. Its appeal lies in its demarcation of a stage at which the fetus, having become 'capable of meaningful life outside the mother's womb,' may be regarded as a distinct life-in-being with interests of its own—as, in short, a person. Viability, in this sense, is by no means a unique or flawless solution to the problem of locating such a stage in the fetus's development. It is only a *good* solution. Under the circumstances, however, that is an excellent recommendation."

3. In HODGSON v. MINNESOTA, 497 U.S. 417, 110 S.Ct. 2926, 111 L.Ed.2d 344 (1990), a 5–4 majority (Stevens, J., joined in principal part by Brennan, Marshall, Blackmun, and O'Connor, JJ.) struck down a state law requiring *both* parents of an unemancipated minor to be notified at least 48 hours before she underwent an abortion.[f] But a different 5–4 majority—Justice O'Connor and the four justices who would have sustained the two-parent notification requirement *without* a judicial bypass alternative (Kennedy, J., joined by Rehnquist, C.J., and White and Scalia, JJ.) (the Kennedy group)—upheld the two-parent notification requirement *combined with* a judicial bypass.[g] Thus *Hodgson* produced two distinct majorities and in each instance Justice O'Connor provided the crucial vote. In addition, six justices—Stevens and O'Connor, JJ., and the Kennedy group—upheld a provision that, before proceeding with an abortion, a minor must wait 48 hours after notifying a *single* parent of her intention to obtain an abortion.[h]

In striking down the two-parent notification requirement unaccompanied by a judicial bypass procedure, STEVENS, J., pointed to its many adverse effects, especially on both the minor and the custodial parent when, as is often the case, the parents are divorced or separated. He thought it "clear that the requirement that *both* parents be notified, whether or not both wish to be notified or have assumed responsibility for the upbringing of the child, does not reasonably further any legitimate state interest. [Not] only does two-parent notification fail to serve any state interest with respect to functioning families, [the] record reveals that in the thousands of dysfunctional families affected by this statute, the two-parent notice requirement proved positively harmful to the minor and her family, [resulting] in major trauma to the child, and often to a parent as well.

"[The] second parent may well have an interest in the minor's abortion decision, making full communication among all members of a family desirable in some cases, but such communication may not be decreed by the State. The State has no more interest in requiring all family members to talk with one another than it has in requiring certain of them to live together [citing *Moore v. East Cleveland,* p. 407 infra]."

Applying her "undue burden" test, concurring Justice O'CONNOR concluded that the obstacles imposed by Minnesota's two-parent notice requirement "are not reasonably related to legitimate state interests" and that the requirement "is all the more unreasonable when one considers that only half of the minors [in the state] reside with both biological parents [and a] third live with only one parent."

---

f. There were two exceptions: if an immediate abortion was necessary to prevent the minor's death or if she declared she was a victim of parental abuse or neglect (in which event the appropriate authorities had to be notified).

g. The first part of the challenged statute, which required the two-parent notification, provided no alternative means for a pregnant minor to obtain authorization for an abortion. However, the second part of the statute provided that if the first part were ever judicially enjoined the same two-parent notice requirement would be enforced with the addition of a judicial bypass procedure. Under this provision the minor can avoid notifying either parent if she can persuade a judge that she is a "mature" minor or, if immature, that an abortion without notice to her parents would be in her "best interests."

h. In *Ohio v. Akron Center for Reproductive Health,* 497 U.S. 502, 110 S.Ct. 2972, 111 L.Ed.2d 405 (1990), a companion case to *Hodgson,* the same six justices rejected a facial challenge to a state law prohibiting a physician or other person from performing an abortion on an unemancipated minor absent notice to one of the minor's parents or a court order authorizing the minor to consent.

KENNEDY, J., joined by Rehnquist, C.J., and White and Scalia, JJ., dissented on this issue, reminding his colleagues that the Court "must defer to a reasonable judgment by the state legislature when it determines what is sound public policy." "All must acknowledge," he continued, "that it was reasonable for the legislature to conclude that in most cases notice to both parents will work to the minor's benefit" (not only where the minor lives in the "ideal family setting," but also where she no longer lives with both parents).

Because Justice O'Connor agreed with the "Kennedy group" that the constitutional objection to the two-parent notification requirement is removed by the judicial bypass—"the interference with the internal operation of the family [simply] does not exist where the minor can avoid notifying one or both parents by use of the bypass procedure"—KENNEDY, J., joined by the Chief Justice, and White and Scalia, JJ., wrote the principal opinion upholding that provision: "In providing for the bypass, Minnesota has done nothing other than attempt to fit its legislation into the framework that we have supplied in our previous cases. The simple fact is that [Bellotti II] stands for the proposition that a two-parent consent law is constitutional if it provides for a sufficient judicial bypass alternative, and it requires us to sustain the statute before us here. [Although] eight members of the [Bellotti] Court concluded that the statute was unconstitutional, five indicated that they would uphold a two-parent consent statute with an adequate judicial bypass."

MARSHALL, J., joined by Brennan and Blackmun, JJ., dissented from the judgment of the Court that the judicial bypass renders the parental notice and 48–hour delay requirements constitutional: "Even if I did not believe that a judicial bypass procedure was facially unconstitutional, the experience of Minnesota's procedure in operation demonstrates that the bypass provision before us cannot save the parental notification and delay requirements. This Court has addressed judicial bypass procedures only in the context of facial challenges. The Court has never considered the actual burdens a particular bypass provision imposes on a woman's right to choose an abortion. Such consideration establishes that, even if judges authorized every abortion sought by petitioning minors,[i] Minnesota's judicial bypass is far too burdensome to remedy an otherwise unconstitutional statute. [It] forces a young woman in an already dire situation to choose between two fundamentally unacceptable alternatives: notifying a possibly dictatorial or even abusive parent and justifying her profoundly personal decision in an intimidating judicial proceeding to a blackrobed stranger. For such a woman, this dilemma is more likely to result in trauma and pain than in an informed and voluntary decision."

In a separate opinion, STEVENS, J., also maintained that the two-parent notice requirement was not saved by the judicial bypass option. He distinguished Bellotti II, inter alia, on the ground that "neither the arguments of the parties, nor any of the opinions in the case, considered the significant difference between a statute requiring the involvement of *both* parents in the abortion decision and a statute that merely requires the involvement of one. [A] rule requiring consent or notification of both parents is not reasonably related to the state interest in giving the pregnant minor the benefit of parental advice. [T]he fact that one-parent consent is the virtually uniform rule for any other activity which affects the minor's health, safety or welfare emphasizes the aberrant quality of the two-

---

i. Of 3,573 judicial bypass petitions filed in Minnesota courts during a period of four and a half years, all but 15 were granted. Recall Professor Mnookin's characterization of the utilization of the post-*Bellotti II* Massachusetts statute (see p. 346 supra)—"a rubber-stamp, administrative operation."

parent notice requirement. [T]he requirement that the bypass procedure must be invoked when the minor and one parent agree that the other parent should not be notified represents [an] unjustified governmental intrusion into the family's decisional process."

In a separate opinion, SCALIA, J., who dissented from the Court's invalidation of the two-parent notification requirement without a bypass but concurred in the Court's other rulings, commented: "One will search in vain the document we are supposed to be construing for text that provides the basis for the argument over these distinctions; and will find in our society's tradition regarding abortion no hint that the distinctions are constitutionally relevant, much less any indication how a constitutional argument about them ought to be resolved. The random and unpredictable results of our consequently unchanneled individual views make it increasingly evident, Term after Term, that the tools for this job are not to be found in the lawyer's—and hence not in the judge's—workbox. I continue to dissent from this enterprise of devising an Abortion Code, and from the illusion that we have authority to do so."

Notes and Questions

1. In *Hodgson,* did six justices "demote abortion from its fundamental status"? Did they ignore the traditional strict scrutiny applied to fundamental rights and analyze the state restrictions on abortion "under what amounted to a rational basis standard"? See 104 Harv.L.Rev. 253–54 (1990).

2. *Are "the tools for this job" not to be found in the judge's workbox?* Is Justice Scalia right? Consider Jed Rubenfeld, *On the Legal Status of the Proposition that "Life Begins at Conception,"* 43 Stan.L.Rev. 599, 615 (1991): "The 'tools' for this job are not in anyone's workbox. But a judge is not a handyman, and he cannot call in state legislators as professionals whenever he feels out of his depth. Has anyone ever imagined that the tools to determine what counts as 'religion' are ready to the jurist's hand? Yet, when this determination becomes dispositive of first amendment rights, the great difficulty of the question permits the judiciary neither to evade it nor to allow the states to answer it. In determining that life begins at a certain gestational point, a state establishes a compelling interest and thereby delineates the outer limit of a constitutional right. Courts cannot simply defer to state law on this point. They can no more defer here than in the case of a state's enactment of a certain definition of 'clear and present danger' allowing the legislature to prohibit constitutionally protected speech."

THE COURT REAFFIRMS "THE ESSENTIAL HOLDING OF *ROE* "

PLANNED PARENTHOOD OF SOUTHEASTERN PENNSYLVANIA v. CASEY

505 U.S. 833, 112 S.Ct. 2791, 120 L.Ed.2d 674 (1992).

JUSTICE O'CONNOR, JUSTICE KENNEDY, and JUSTICE SOUTER announced the judgment of the Court and delivered the opinion of the Court with respect to Parts I, II, III, V–A, V–C, and VI, an opinion with respect to Part V–E, in which JUSTICE STEVENS joins, and an opinion with respect to Parts IV, V–B, and V–D.

I. Liberty finds no refuge in a jurisprudence of doubt. Yet 19 years after our holding that the Constitution protects a woman's right to terminate her pregnancy in its early stages, *Roe v. Wade,* that definition of liberty is still questioned. Joining the respondents as amicus curiae, the United States, as it has done in five other cases in the last decade, again asks us to overrule *Roe*.

At issue in these cases are five provisions of the Pennsylvania Abortion Control Act of 1982 as amended in 1988 and 1989. [The] Act requires that a woman seeking an abortion give her informed consent prior to the abortion procedure, and specifies that she be provided with certain information at least 24 hours before the abortion is performed. § 3205. For a minor to obtain an abortion, the Act requires the informed consent of one of her parents, but provides for a judicial bypass option if the minor does not wish to or cannot obtain a parent's consent. § 3206. Another provision of the Act requires that, unless certain exceptions apply, a married woman seeking an abortion must sign a statement indicating that she has notified her husband of her intended abortion. § 3209. The Act exempts compliance with these three requirements in the event of a "medical emergency," which is defined in § 3203 of the Act. In addition to the above provisions regulating the performance of abortions, the Act imposes certain reporting requirements on facilities that provide abortion services. §§ 3207(b), 3214(a), 3214(f).

Before any of these provisions took effect, the petitioners, who are five abortion clinics and one physician representing himself as well as a class of physicians who provide abortion services, brought this suit seeking declaratory and injunctive relief. [The District Court held all the provisions at issue unconstitutional, but the Court of Appeals sustained all of them except for the husband notification requirement.]

[At] oral argument in this Court, the attorney for the parties challenging the statute took the position that none of the enactments can be upheld without overruling *Roe*. We disagree with that analysis; but we acknowledge that our decisions after *Roe* cast doubt upon the meaning and reach of its holding. Further, the Chief Justice admits that he would overrule the central holding of *Roe* and adopt the rational relationship test as the sole criterion of constitutionality. State and federal courts as well as legislatures throughout the Union must have guidance as they seek to address this subject in conformance with the Constitution. Given these premises, we find it imperative to review once more the principles that define the rights of the woman and the legitimate authority of the State respecting the termination of pregnancies by abortion procedures.

After considering the fundamental constitutional questions resolved by *Roe*, principles of institutional integrity, and the rule of *stare decisis*, we are led to conclude this: the essential holding of *Roe* should be retained and once again reaffirmed.

It must be stated at the outset and with clarity that *Roe*'s essential holding, the holding we reaffirm, has three parts. First is a recognition of the right of the woman to choose to have an abortion before viability and to obtain it without undue interference from the State. Before viability, the State's interests are not strong enough to support a prohibition of abortion or the imposition of a substantial obstacle to the woman's effective right to elect the procedure. Second is a confirmation of the State's power to restrict abortions after fetal viability, if the law contains exceptions for pregnancies which endanger a woman's life or health. And third is the principle that the State has legitimate interests from the outset of the pregnancy in protecting the health of the woman and the life of the fetus that may become a child. These principles do not contradict one another; and we adhere to each.

II. Constitutional protection of the woman's decision to terminate her pregnancy derives from the Due Process Clause of the Fourteenth Amendment. [The] controlling word in the case before us is "liberty." Although a literal reading of the Clause might suggest that it governs only the procedures by which a State may deprive persons of liberty, for at least 105 years [the] Clause has been understood to contain a substantive component as well, one "barring certain government actions regardless of the fairness of the procedures used to implement them."

[It] is tempting, as a means of curbing the discretion of federal judges, to suppose that liberty encompasses no more than those rights already guaranteed to the individual against federal interference by the express provisions of the first eight amendments to the Constitution. But of course this Court has never accepted that view.

It is also tempting, for the same reason, to suppose that the Due Process Clause protects only those practices, defined at the most specific level, that were protected against government interference by other rules of law when the Fourteenth Amendment was ratified. See *Michael H. v. Gerald D.*, n. 6 [p. 417 infra] (opinion of Scalia, J.). But such a view would be inconsistent with our law. It is a promise of the Constitution that there is a realm of personal liberty which the government may not enter. We have vindicated this principle before. Marriage is mentioned nowhere in the Bill of Rights and interracial marriage was illegal in most States in the 19th century, but the Court was no doubt correct in finding it to be an aspect of liberty protected against state interference by the substantive component of the Due Process Clause in *Loving v. Virginia* [p. 1086 infra].

Neither the Bill of Rights nor the specific practices of States at the time of the adoption of the Fourteenth Amendment marks the outer limits of the substantive sphere of liberty which the Fourteenth Amendment protects. See U.S. Const., Amend. 9. As the second Justice Harlan recognized:

> "[T]he full scope of the liberty guaranteed by the Due Process Clause cannot be found in or limited by the precise terms of the specific guarantees elsewhere provided in the Constitution. This 'liberty' is not a series of isolated points pricked out in terms of the taking of property; the freedom of speech, press, and religion; the right to keep and bear arms; the freedom from unreasonable searches and seizures; and so on. It is a rational continuum which, broadly speaking, includes a freedom from all substantial arbitrary impositions and purposeless restraints [and] which also recognizes, what a reasonable and sensitive judgment must, that certain interests require particularly careful scrutiny of the state needs asserted to justify their abridgment." *Poe v. Ullman* [p. 303 supra] (Harlan, J., dissenting from dismissal on jurisdictional grounds).

Justice Harlan wrote these words in addressing an issue the full Court did not reach in *Poe*, but the Court adopted his position four Terms later in *Griswold*. [It] is settled now, as it was when the Court heard arguments in *Roe*, that the Constitution places limits on a State's right to interfere with a person's most basic decisions about family and parenthood, as well as bodily integrity.

The inescapable fact is that adjudication of substantive due process claims may call upon the Court in interpreting the Constitution to exercise that same capacity which by tradition courts always have exercised: reasoned judgment. Its boundaries are not susceptible of expression as a simple rule. That does not mean we are free to invalidate state policy choices with which we disagree; yet neither does it permit us to shrink from the duties of our office. As Justice Harlan observed:

> "Due process has not been reduced to any formula; its content cannot be determined by reference to any code. The best that can be said is that through the course of this Court's decisions it has represented the balance which our Nation, built upon postulates of respect for the liberty of the individual, has struck between that liberty and the demands of organized society. If the supplying of content to this Constitutional concept has of necessity been a rational process, it certainly has not been one where judges have felt free to roam where unguided speculation might take them. The balance of which I speak is the balance struck by this country, having regard to what history teaches are the traditions from which it developed as well as the traditions from which it broke. That tradition is a living thing. A decision of this Court which radically departs from it could not long survive, while a decision which builds on what has survived is likely to be sound. No formula could serve as a substitute, in this area, for judgment and restraint." *Poe* (Harlan, J., dissenting). * * *

Men and women of good conscience can disagree, and we suppose some always shall disagree, about the profound moral and spiritual implications of terminating a pregnancy, even in its earliest stage. Some of us as individuals find abortion offensive to our most basic principles of morality, but that cannot control our decision. Our obligation is to define the liberty of all, not to mandate our own moral code. The underlying constitutional issue is whether the State can resolve these philosophic questions in such a definitive way that a woman lacks all choice in the matter, except perhaps [where] the pregnancy is itself a danger to her own life or health, or is the result of rape or incest. * * *

Our law affords constitutional protection to personal decisions relating to marriage, procreation, contraception, family relationships, child rearing, and education. [These] matters, involving the most intimate and personal choices a person may make in a lifetime, choices central to personal dignity and autonomy, are central to the liberty protected by the Fourteenth Amendment. At the heart of liberty is the right to define one's own concept of existence, of meaning, of the universe, and of the mystery of human life. Beliefs about these matters could not define the attributes of personhood were they formed under compulsion of the State.

These considerations begin our analysis of the woman's interest in terminating her pregnancy but cannot end it, for this reason: though the abortion decision may originate within the zone of conscience and belief, it is more than a philosophic exercise. Abortion is a unique act. It is an act fraught with consequences for others: for the woman who must live with the implications of her decision; for the persons who perform and assist in the procedure; for the spouse, family, and society which must confront the knowledge that these procedures exist, procedures some deem nothing short of an act of violence against innocent human life; and, depending on one's beliefs, for the life or potential life that is aborted. Though abortion is conduct, it does not follow that the State is entitled to proscribe it in all instances. That is because the liberty of the woman is at stake in a sense unique to the human condition and so unique to the law. The mother who carries a child to full term is subject to anxieties, to physical constraints, to pain that only she must bear. That these sacrifices have from the beginning of the human race been endured by woman with a pride that ennobles her in the eyes of others and gives to the infant a bond of love cannot alone be grounds for the State to insist she make the sacrifice. Her suffering is too intimate and personal for the State to insist, without more, upon its own vision of the woman's role, however dominant that vision has been in the course of our history and our culture. The destiny of the woman must be shaped to a large extent on her own conception of her spiritual imperatives and her place in society.

It should be recognized, moreover, that in some critical respects the abortion decision is of the same character as the decision to use contraception, to which [our cases] afford constitutional protection. We have no doubt as to the correctness of those decisions. They support the reasoning in *Roe* relating to the woman's liberty because they involve personal decisions concerning not only the meaning of procreation but also human responsibility and respect for it. As with abortion, reasonable people will have differences of opinion about these matters. One view is based on such reverence for the wonder of creation that any pregnancy ought to be welcomed and carried to full term no matter how difficult it will be to provide for the child and ensure its well-being. Another is that the inability to provide for the nurture and care of the infant is a cruelty to the child and an anguish to the parent. These are intimate views with infinite variations, and their deep, personal character underlay our decisions in *Griswold, Eisenstadt,* and *Carey.* The same concerns are present when the woman confronts the reality that, perhaps despite her attempts to avoid it, she has become pregnant.

[While] we appreciate the weight of the arguments made on behalf of the State in the case before us, arguments [which] conclude that *Roe* should be overruled, the reservations any of us may have in reaffirming the central holding of *Roe* are outweighed by the explication of individual liberty we have given combined with the force of stare decisis. We turn now to that doctrine.

III. The obligation to follow precedent begins with necessity, and a contrary necessity marks its outer limit. With Cardozo, we recognize that no judicial system could do society's work if it eyed each issue afresh in every case that raised it. See Benjamin Cardozo, *The Nature of the Judicial Process* 149 (1921). Indeed, the very concept of the rule of law underlying our own Constitution requires such continuity over time that a respect for precedent is, by definition, indispensable. At the other extreme, a different necessity would make itself felt if a prior judicial ruling should come to be seen so clearly as error that its enforcement was for that very reason doomed.

Even when the decision to overrule a prior case is not, as in the rare, latter instance, virtually foreordained, it is common wisdom that the rule of stare decisis is not an "inexorable command," and certainly it is not such in every constitutional case. Rather, when this Court reexamines a prior holding, its judgment is customarily informed by a series of prudential and pragmatic considerations designed to test the consistency of overruling a prior decision with the ideal of the rule of law, and to gauge the respective costs of reaffirming and overruling a prior case. Thus, for example, we may ask whether the rule has proved to be intolerable simply in defying practical workability; whether the rule is subject to a kind of reliance that would lend a special hardship to the consequences of overruling and add inequity to the cost of repudiation; whether related principles of law have so far developed as to have left the old rule no more than a remnant of abandoned doctrine; or whether facts have so changed or come to be seen so differently, as to have robbed the old rule of significant application or justification.

So in this case we may inquire whether *Roe*'s central rule has been found unworkable; whether the rule's limitation on state power could be removed without serious inequity to those who have relied upon it or significant damage to the stability of the society governed by the rule in question; whether the law's growth in the intervening years has left *Roe*'s central rule a doctrinal anachronism discounted by society; and whether *Roe*'s premises of fact have so far changed in the ensuing two decades as to render its central holding somehow irrelevant or unjustifiable in dealing with the issue it addressed.

Although *Roe* has engendered opposition, it has in no sense proven "unworkable," representing as it does a simple limitation beyond which a state law is unenforceable.

[While] neither respondents nor their amici in so many words deny that the abortion right invites some reliance prior to its actual exercise, one can readily imagine an argument stressing the dissimilarity of this case to one involving property or contract. Abortion is customarily chosen as an unplanned response to the consequence of unplanned activity or to the failure of conventional birth control, and except on the assumption that no intercourse would have occurred but for *Roe*'s holding, such behavior may appear to justify no reliance claim. Even if reliance could be claimed on that unrealistic assumption, the argument might run, any reliance interest would be de minimis. This argument would be premised on the hypothesis that reproductive planning could take virtually immediate account of any sudden restoration of state authority to ban abortions.

To eliminate the issue of reliance that easily, however, one would need to limit cognizable reliance to specific instances of sexual activity. But to do this would be simply to refuse to face the fact that for two decades of economic and social developments, people have organized intimate relationships and made choices that define their views of themselves and their places in society, in reliance on the availability of abortion in the event that contraception should fail. The ability of women to participate equally in the economic and social life of the Nation has been facilitated by their ability to control their reproductive lives. The Constitution serves human values, and while the effect of reliance on *Roe* cannot be exactly measured, neither can the certain cost of overruling *Roe* for people who have ordered their thinking and living around that case be dismissed.

No evolution of legal principle has left *Roe*'s doctrinal footings weaker than they were in 1973. No development of constitutional law since the case was decided has implicitly or explicitly left *Roe* behind as a mere survivor of obsolete constitutional thinking.

It will be recognized, of course, that *Roe* stands at an intersection of two lines of decisions, but in whichever doctrinal category one reads the case, the result for present purposes will be the same. The *Roe* Court itself placed its holding in the succession of cases most prominently exemplified by *Griswold*. When it is so seen, *Roe* is clearly in no jeopardy, since subsequent constitutional developments have neither disturbed, nor do they threaten to diminish, the scope of recognized protection accorded to the liberty relating to intimate relationships, the family, and decisions about whether or not to beget or bear a child.

Roe, however, may be seen not only as an exemplar of *Griswold* liberty but as a rule (whether or not mistaken) of personal autonomy and bodily integrity, with doctrinal affinity to cases recognizing limits on governmental power to mandate medical treatment or to bar its rejection. If so, our cases since *Roe* accord with *Roe*'s view that a State's interest in the protection of life falls short of justifying any plenary override of individual liberty claims. *Cruzan v. Director, Missouri Dept. of Health* [p. 436 infra].

Finally, one could classify *Roe* as *sui generis*. If the case is so viewed, then there clearly has been no erosion of its central determination. [In] *Webster,* although two of the present authors questioned the trimester framework in a way consistent with our judgment today, a majority of the Court either decided to reaffirm or declined to address the constitutional validity of the central holding of *Roe.*

Nor will courts building upon *Roe* be likely to hand down erroneous decisions as a consequence. Even on the assumption that the central holding of *Roe* was in error, that error would go only to the strength of the state interest in fetal protection, not to the recognition afforded by the Constitution to the woman's liberty. The latter aspect of the decision fits comfortably within the framework of the Court's prior decisions including *Skinner, Griswold, Loving,* and *Eisenstadt,* the holdings of which are "not a series of isolated points," but mark a "rational continuum." *Poe v. Ullman* (Harlan, J., dissenting). * * *

The soundness of this prong of the *Roe* analysis is apparent from a consideration of the alternative. If indeed the woman's interest in deciding whether to bear and beget a child had not been recognized as in *Roe,* the State might as readily restrict a woman's right to choose to carry a pregnancy to term as to terminate it, to further asserted state interests in population control, or eugenics, for example. Yet *Roe* has been sensibly relied upon to counter any such suggestions. [In] any event, because *Roe*'s scope is confined by the fact of its concern with postconception potential life, a concern otherwise likely to be implicated only by some forms of contraception protected independently under *Griswold* and later cases, any error in *Roe* is unlikely to have serious ramifications in future cases.

We have seen how time has overtaken some of *Roe*'s factual assumptions: advances in maternal health care allow for abortions safe to the mother later in pregnancy than was true in 1973, and advances in neonatal care have advanced viability to a point somewhat earlier. But these facts go only to the scheme of time limits on the realization of competing interests, and the divergences from the factual premises of 1973 have no bearing on the validity of *Roe*'s central holding, that viability marks the earliest point at which the State's interest in fetal life is constitutionally adequate to justify a legislative ban on nontherapeutic abortions. The soundness or unsoundness of that constitutional judgment in no sense turns on whether viability occurs at approximately 28 weeks, as was usual at the time of *Roe,* at 23 to 24 weeks, as it sometimes does today, or at some moment even slightly earlier in pregnancy, as it may if fetal respiratory capacity can somehow be enhanced in the future. Whenever it may occur, the attainment of viability may continue to serve as the critical fact, just as it has done since *Roe* was decided; which is to say that no change in *Roe*'s factual underpinning has left its central holding obsolete, and none supports an argument for overruling it.

The sum of the precedential inquiry to this point shows *Roe*'s underpinnings unweakened in any way affecting its central holding. While it has engendered disapproval, it has not been unworkable. An entire generation has come of age free to assume *Roe*'s concept of liberty in defining the capacity of women to act in society, and to make reproductive decisions; no erosion of principle going to liberty or personal autonomy has left *Roe*'s central holding a doctrinal remnant; *Roe* portends no developments at odds with other precedent for the analysis of personal liberty; and no changes of fact have rendered viability more or less appropriate as the point at which the balance of interests tips. Within the bounds of normal stare decisis analysis, then, and subject to the considerations on which it customarily turns, the stronger argument is for affirming *Roe*'s central holding, with whatever degree of personal reluctance any of us may have, not for overruling it.

In a less significant case, *stare decisis* analysis could, and would, stop at the point we have reached. But the sustained and widespread debate *Roe* has provoked calls for some comparison between that case and others of comparable dimension that have responded to national controversies and taken on the impress of the controversies addressed. Only two such decisional lines from the past century present themselves for examination, and in each instance the result reached by the Court accorded with the principles we apply today.

The first example is that line of cases identified with *Lochner v. New York* (1905), which imposed substantive limitations on legislation limiting economic autonomy in favor of health and welfare regulation, adopting, in Justice Holmes' view, the theory of *laissez-faire*. The *Lochner* decisions were exemplified by *Adkins v. Children's Hospital* (1923), in which this Court held it to be an infringement of constitutionally protected liberty of contract to require the employers of adult women to satisfy minimum wage standards. Fourteen years later, *West Coast Hotel Co. v. Parrish* (1937) signalled the demise of *Lochner* by overruling *Adkins*. In the meantime, the Depression had come and, with it, the lesson that seemed unmistakable to most people by 1937, that the interpretation of contractual freedom protected in *Adkins* rested on fundamentally false factual assumptions about the capacity of a relatively unregulated market to satisfy minimal levels of human welfare. [The] facts upon which the earlier case had premised a constitutional resolution of social controversy had proved to be untrue, and history's demonstration of their untruth not only justified but required the new choice of constitutional principle that *West Coast Hotel* announced. Of course, it was true that the Court lost something by its misperception, or its lack of prescience, and the Court-packing crisis only magnified the loss; but the clear demonstration that the facts of economic life were different from those previously assumed warranted the repudiation of the old law.

The second comparison that 20th century history invites is with the cases employing the separate-but-equal rule for applying the Fourteenth Amendment's equal protection guarantee. They began with *Plessy v. Ferguson* [p. 1075 infra], holding that legislatively mandated racial segregation in public transportation works no denial of equal protection, rejecting the argument that racial separation enforced by the legal machinery of American society treats the black race as inferior. The *Plessy* Court considered "the underlying fallacy of the plaintiff's argument to consist in the assumption that the enforced separation of the two races stamps the colored race with a badge of inferiority. If this be so, it is not by reason of anything found in the act, but solely because the colored race chooses to put that construction upon it." Whether, as a matter of historical fact, the Justices in the *Plessy* majority believed this or not, this understanding of the implication of segregation was the stated justification for the Court's opinion. But this understanding of the facts and the rule it was stated to justify were repudiated in *Brown v. Board of Education* [p. 1078 infra]. As one commentator observed, the question before the Court in *Brown* was "whether discrimination inheres in that segregation which is imposed by law in the twentieth century in certain specific states in the American Union. And that question has meaning and can find an answer only on the ground of history and of common knowledge about the facts of life in the times and places aforesaid." Charles Black, *The Lawfulness of the Segregation Decisions*, 69 Yale L.J. 421, 427 (1960).

The Court in *Brown* addressed these facts of life by observing that whatever may have been the understanding in *Plessy*'s time of the power of segregation to stigmatize those who were segregated with a "badge of inferiority," it was clear by 1954 that legally sanctioned segregation had just such an effect, to the point that racially separate public educational facilities were deemed inherently unequal. Society's understanding of the facts upon which a constitutional ruling was sought in 1954 was thus fundamentally different from the basis claimed for the decision in 1896. While we think *Plessy* was wrong the day it was decided, we must also recognize that the *Plessy* Court's explanation for its decision was so clearly at odds with the facts apparent to the Court in 1954 that the decision to reexamine *Plessy* was on this ground alone not only justified but required.

West Coast Hotel and *Brown* each rested on facts, or an understanding of facts, changed from those which furnished the claimed justifications for the earlier constitutional resolutions. [As] the decisions were thus comprehensible they were also defensible, not merely as the victories of one doctrinal school over another by dint of numbers (victories though they were), but as applications of constitutional principle to facts as they had not been seen by the Court before. In constitutional adjudication as elsewhere in life, changed circumstances may impose new obligations, and the thoughtful part of the Nation could accept each decision to overrule a prior case as a response to the Court's constitutional duty.

Because [neither] the factual underpinnings of *Roe*'s central holding nor our understanding of it has changed (and because no other indication of weakened precedent has been shown) the Court could not pretend to be reexamining the prior law with any justification beyond a present doctrinal disposition to come out differently from the Court of 1973. To overrule prior law for no other reason than that would run counter to the view repeated in our cases, that a decision to overrule should rest on some special reason over and above the belief that a prior case was wrongly decided. * * *

The examination of the conditions justifying the repudiation of *Adkins* by *West Coast Hotel* and *Plessy* by *Brown* is enough to suggest the terrible price that would have been paid if the Court had not overruled as it did. In the present case, however, as our analysis to this point makes clear, the terrible price would be paid for overruling. Our analysis would not be complete, however, without explaining why overruling *Roe*'s central holding would not only reach an unjustifiable result under principles of stare decisis, but would seriously weaken the Court's capacity to exercise the judicial power and to function as the Supreme Court of a Nation dedicated to the rule of law. [As] Americans of each succeeding generation are rightly told, the Court cannot buy support for its decisions by spending money and, except to a minor degree, it cannot independently coerce obedience to its decrees. The Court's power lies, rather, in its legitimacy, a product of substance and perception that shows itself in the people's acceptance of the Judiciary as fit to determine what the Nation's law means and to declare what it demands.

The underlying substance of this legitimacy is of course the warrant for the Court's decisions in the Constitution and the lesser sources of legal principle on which the Court draws. That substance is expressed in the Court's opinions, and our contemporary understanding is such that a decision without principled justification would be no judicial act at all. But even when justification is furnished by apposite legal principle, something more is required. Because not every conscientious claim of principled justification will be accepted as such, the justification claimed must be beyond dispute. The Court must take care to speak and act in ways that allow people to accept its decisions on the terms the Court claims for them, as grounded truly in principle, not as compromises with social and political pressures having, as such, no bearing on the principled choices that the Court is obliged to make.   Thus, the Court's legitimacy depends on making legally principled decisions under circumstances in which their principled character is sufficiently plausible to be accepted by the Nation.

* * * However upsetting it may be to those most directly affected when one judicially derived rule replaces another, the country can accept some correction of error without necessarily questioning the legitimacy of the Court.

In two circumstances, however, the Court would almost certainly fail to receive the benefit of the doubt in overruling prior cases.   There is, first, [a] limit to the amount of error that can plausibly be imputed to prior courts.   If that limit should be exceeded, disturbance of prior rulings would be taken as evidence that justifiable reexamination of principle had given way to drives for particular results in the short term.   The legitimacy of the Court would fade with the frequency of its vacillation.

That first circumstance can be described as hypothetical; the second is to the point here and now.   Where, in the performance of its judicial duties, the Court decides a case in such a way as to resolve the sort of intensely divisive controversy reflected in *Roe* and those rare, comparable cases, its decision has a dimension that the resolution of the normal case does not carry.   It is the dimension present whenever the Court's interpretation of the Constitution calls the contending sides of a national controversy to end their national division by accepting a common mandate rooted in the Constitution.

The Court is not asked to do this very often, having thus addressed the Nation only twice in our lifetime, in the decisions of *Brown* and *Roe*.   But when the Court does act in this way, its decision requires an equally rare precedential force to counter the inevitable efforts to overturn it and to thwart its implementation.   Some of those efforts may be mere unprincipled emotional reactions; others may proceed from principles worthy of profound respect.   But whatever the premises of opposition may be, only the most convincing justification under accepted standards of precedent could suffice to demonstrate that a later decision overruling the first was anything but a surrender to political pressure, and an unjustified repudiation of the principle on which the Court staked its authority in the first instance.   So to overrule under fire in the absence of the most compelling reason to reexamine a watershed decision would subvert the Court's legitimacy beyond any serious question.

[The] country's loss of confidence in the judiciary would be underscored by an equally certain and equally reasonable condemnation for another failing in overruling unnecessarily and under pressure.   Some cost will be paid by anyone who approves or implements a constitutional decision where it is unpopular, or who refuses to work to undermine the decision or to force its reversal.   The price may be criticism or ostracism, or it may be violence.   An extra price will be paid by those who themselves disapprove of the decision's results when viewed outside of constitutional terms, but who nevertheless struggle to accept it, because they respect the rule of law.   To all those who will be so tested by following, the Court implicitly undertakes to remain steadfast, lest in the end a price be paid for nothing.   [N]o Court that broke its faith with the people could sensibly expect credit for principle in the decision by which it did that.

It is true that diminished legitimacy may be restored, but only slowly.   Unlike the political branches, a Court thus weakened could not seek to regain its position with a new mandate from the voters, and even if the Court could somehow go to the polls, the loss of its principled character could not be retrieved by the casting of so many votes. Like the character of an individual, the legitimacy of the Court must be earned over time. So, indeed, must be the character of a Nation of people who aspire to live according to the rule of law. Their belief in themselves as such a people is not readily separable from their understanding of the Court invested with the authority to decide their constitutional cases and speak before all others for their constitutional ideals. If the Court's legitimacy should be undermined, then, so would the country be in its very ability to see itself through its constitutional ideals. The Court's concern with legitimacy is not for the sake of the Court but for the sake of the Nation to which it is responsible.

The Court's duty in the present case is clear. In 1973, it confronted the already-divisive issue of governmental power to limit personal choice to undergo abortion, for which it provided a new resolution based on the due process guaranteed by the Fourteenth Amendment. Whether or not a new social consensus is developing on that issue, its divisiveness is no less today than in 1973, and pressure to overrule the decision, like pressure to retain it, has grown only more intense. A decision to overrule *Roe*'s essential holding under the existing circumstances would address error, if error there was, at the cost of both profound and unnecessary damage to the Court's legitimacy, and to the Nation's commitment to the rule of law. It is therefore imperative to adhere to the essence of *Roe*'s original decision, and we do so today.

IV. From what we have said so far it follows that it is a constitutional liberty of the woman to have some freedom to terminate her pregnancy. We conclude that the basic decision in *Roe* was based on a constitutional analysis which we cannot now repudiate. The woman's liberty is not so unlimited, however, that from the outset the State cannot show its concern for the life of the unborn, and at a later point in fetal development the State's interest in life has sufficient force so that the right of the woman to terminate the pregnancy can be restricted.

That brings us, of course, to the point where much criticism has been directed at *Roe,* a criticism that always inheres when the Court draws a specific rule from what in the Constitution is but a general standard. We conclude, however, that the urgent claims of the woman to retain the ultimate control over her destiny and her body, claims implicit in the meaning of liberty, require us to perform that function. Liberty must not be extinguished for want of a line that is clear. And it falls to us to give some real substance to the woman's liberty to determine whether to carry her pregnancy to full term.

We conclude the line should be drawn at viability, so that before that time the woman has a right to choose to terminate her pregnancy. We adhere to this principle for two reasons. First [is] the doctrine of stare decisis. [We] have twice reaffirmed [*Roe*] in the face of great opposition. See *Thornburgh; Akron I.* Although we must overrule those parts of *Thornburgh* and *Akron I* [which] are inconsistent with *Roe*'s statement that the State has a legitimate interest in promoting the life or potential life of the unborn, the central premise of those cases represents an unbroken commitment by this Court to the essential holding of *Roe.* It is that premise which we reaffirm today.

The second reason is that the concept of viability, as we noted in *Roe,* is the time at which there is a realistic possibility of maintaining and nourishing a life outside the womb, so that the independent existence of the second life can in reason and all fairness be the object of state protection that now overrides the rights of the woman. Consistent with other constitutional norms, legislatures may draw lines which appear arbitrary without the necessity of offering a justification. But courts may not. We must justify the lines we draw. And there is no line other than viability which is more workable.

[The] woman's right to terminate her pregnancy before viability is the most central principle of *Roe v. Wade*. It is a rule of law and a component of liberty we cannot renounce.

On the other side of the equation is the interest of the State in the protection of potential life. The *Roe* Court recognized the State's "important and legitimate interest in protecting the potentiality of human life." The weight to be given this state interest, not the strength of the woman's interest, was the difficult question faced in *Roe*. We do not need to say whether each of us, had we been Members of the Court when the valuation of the State interest came before it as an original matter, would have concluded, as the *Roe* Court did, that its weight is insufficient to justify a ban on abortions prior to viability even when it is subject to certain exceptions. The matter is not before us in the first instance, and coming as it does after nearly 20 years of litigation in *Roe*'s wake we are satisfied that the immediate question is not the soundness of *Roe*'s resolution of the issue, but the precedential force that must be accorded to its holding. And we have concluded that the essential holding of *Roe* should be reaffirmed.

Yet it must be remembered that *Roe* speaks with clarity in establishing not only the woman's liberty but also the State's "important and legitimate interest in potential life." That portion [of] *Roe* has been given too little acknowledgement and implementation by the Court in its subsequent cases. Those cases decided that any regulation touching upon the abortion decision must survive strict scrutiny, to be sustained only if drawn in narrow terms to further a compelling state interest. Not all of the cases decided under that formulation can be reconciled with the holding in *Roe* itself that the State has legitimate interests in the health of the woman and in protecting the potential life within her. In resolving this tension, we choose to rely upon *Roe,* as against the later cases.

Roe established a trimester framework to govern abortion regulations. Under this elaborate but rigid construct, almost no regulation at all is permitted during the first trimester of pregnancy; regulations designed to protect the woman's health, but not to further the State's interest in potential life, are permitted during the second trimester; and during the third trimester, when the fetus is viable, prohibitions are permitted provided the life or health of the mother is not at stake.

[The] trimester framework no doubt was erected to ensure that the woman's right to choose not become so subordinate to the State's interest in promoting fetal life that her choice exists in theory but not in fact. We do not agree, however, that the trimester approach is necessary to accomplish this objective.

[Though] the woman has a right to choose to terminate or continue her pregnancy before viability, it does not at all follow that the State is prohibited from taking steps to ensure that this choice is thoughtful and informed. Even in the earliest stages of pregnancy, the State may enact rules and regulations designed to encourage her to know that there are philosophic and social arguments of great weight that can be brought to bear in favor of continuing the pregnancy to full term and that there are procedures and institutions to allow adoption of unwanted children as well as a certain degree of state assistance if the mother chooses to raise the child herself. [It] follows that States are free to enact laws to provide a reasonable framework for a woman to make a decision that has such profound and lasting meaning. This, too, we find consistent with *Roe*'s central premises, and indeed the inevitable consequence of our holding that the State has an interest in protecting the life of the unborn.

We reject the trimester framework, which we do not consider to be part of the essential holding of *Roe*. Measures aimed at ensuring that a woman's choice contemplates the consequences for the fetus do not necessarily interfere with the right recognized in *Roe*, although those measures have been found to be inconsistent with the rigid trimester framework announced in that case. A logical reading of the central holding in *Roe* itself, and a necessary reconciliation of the liberty of the woman and the interest of the State in promoting prenatal life, require [that] we abandon the trimester framework as a rigid prohibition on all previability regulation aimed at the protection of fetal life. The trimester framework suffers from these basic flaws: in its formulation it misconceives the nature of the pregnant woman's interest; and in practice it undervalues the State's interest in potential life, as recognized in *Roe*.

As our jurisprudence relating to all liberties save perhaps abortion has recognized, not every law which makes a right more difficult to exercise is, ipso facto, an infringement of that right. An example clarifies the point. We have held that not every ballot access limitation amounts to an infringement of the right to vote. Rather, the States are granted substantial flexibility in establishing the framework within which voters choose the candidates for whom they wish to vote.

The abortion right is similar. Numerous forms of state regulation might have the incidental effect of increasing the cost or decreasing the availability of medical care, whether for abortion or any other medical procedure. The fact that a law which serves a valid purpose, one not designed to strike at the right itself, has the incidental effect of making it more difficult or more expensive to procure an abortion cannot be enough to invalidate it. Only where state regulation imposes an undue burden on a woman's ability to make this decision does the power of the State reach into the heart of the liberty protected by the Due Process Clause.

[These] considerations of the nature of the abortion right illustrate that it is an overstatement to describe it as a right to decide whether to have an abortion "without interference from the State," *Danforth*. All abortion regulations interfere to some degree with a woman's ability to decide whether to terminate her pregnancy. [The] right recognized by *Roe* is a right "to be free from unwarranted governmental intrusion into matters so fundamentally affecting a person as the decision whether to bear or beget a child." *Eisenstadt*. Not all governmental intrusion is of necessity unwarranted; and that brings us to the other basic flaw in the trimester framework: even in *Roe*'s terms, in practice it undervalues the State's interest in the potential life within the woman.

* * * *Roe* began the contradiction by using the trimester framework to forbid any regulation of abortion designed to advance that interest before viability. [This is] incompatible with the recognition that there is a substantial state interest in potential life throughout pregnancy. [The] undue burden standard is the appropriate means of reconciling the State's interest with the woman's constitutionally protected liberty.

[A] finding of an undue burden is a shorthand for the conclusion that a state regulation has the purpose or effect of placing a substantial obstacle in the path of a woman seeking an abortion of a nonviable fetus. A statute with this purpose is invalid because the means chosen by the State to further the interest in potential life must be calculated to inform the woman's free choice, not hinder it. And a statute which, while furthering the interest in potential life or some other valid state interest, has the effect of placing a substantial obstacle in the path of a woman's choice cannot be considered a permissible means of serving its legitimate ends. To the extent that the opinions of the Court or of individual Justices use the undue burden standard in a manner that is inconsistent with this analysis, we set out what in our view should be the controlling standard. [In] our considered judgment, an undue burden is an unconstitutional burden. Understood another way, we answer the question, left open in previous opinions discussing the undue burden formulation, whether a law designed to further the State's interest in fetal life which imposes an undue burden on the woman's decision before fetal viability could be constitutional. The answer is no.

Some guiding principles should emerge. What is at stake is the woman's right to make the ultimate decision, not a right to be insulated from all others in doing so. Regulations which do no more than create a structural mechanism by which the State, or the parent or guardian of a minor, may express profound respect for the life of the unborn are permitted, if they are not a substantial obstacle to the woman's exercise of the right to choose. [Unless] it has that effect on her right of choice, a state measure designed to persuade her to choose childbirth over abortion will be upheld if reasonably related to that goal. Regulations designed to foster the health of a woman seeking an abortion are valid if they do not constitute an undue burden.

Even when jurists reason from shared premises, some disagreement is inevitable. [That] is to be expected in the application of any legal standard which must accommodate life's complexity. We do not expect it to be otherwise with respect to the undue burden standard. We give this summary:

(a) To protect the central right recognized by *Roe* while at the same time accommodating the State's profound interest in potential life, we will employ the undue burden analysis as explained in this opinion. An undue burden exists, and therefore a provision of law is invalid, if its purpose or effect is to place a substantial obstacle in the path of a woman seeking an abortion before the fetus attains viability.

(b) We reject the rigid trimester framework of *Roe.* To promote the State's profound interest in potential life, throughout pregnancy the State may take measures to ensure that the woman's choice is informed, and measures designed to advance this interest will not be invalidated as long as their purpose is to persuade the woman to choose childbirth over abortion. These measures must not be an undue burden on the right.

(c) As with any medical procedure, the State may enact regulations to further the health or safety of a woman seeking an abortion. Unnecessary health regulations that have the purpose or effect of presenting a substantial obstacle to a woman seeking an abortion impose an undue burden on the right.

(d) Our adoption of the undue burden analysis does not disturb the central holding of *Roe,* and we reaffirm that holding. [A] State may not prohibit any woman from making the ultimate decision to terminate her pregnancy before viability.

(e) We also reaffirm *Roe* 's holding that "subsequent to viability, the State in promoting its interest in the potentiality of human life may, if it chooses, regulate, and even proscribe, abortion except where it is necessary, in appropriate medical judgment, for the preservation of the life or health of the mother."

These principles control our assessment of the Pennsylvania statute, and we now turn to the issue of the validity of its challenged provisions.

V. The Court of Appeals applied what it believed to be the undue burden standard and upheld each of the provisions except for the husband notification requirement. We agree generally with this conclusion, but refine the undue burden analysis in accordance with the principles articulated above. We now consider the separate statutory sections at issue.

A. Because it is central to the operation of various other requirements, we begin with the statute's definition of medical emergency. Under the statute, a medical emergency is

"[t]hat condition which, on the basis of the physician's good faith clinical judgment, so complicates the medical condition of a pregnant woman as to necessitate the immediate abortion of her pregnancy to avert her death or for which a delay will create serious risk of substantial and irreversible impairment of a major bodily function."

Petitioners argue that the definition is too narrow, contending that it forecloses the possibility of an immediate abortion despite some significant health risks.

[But the Court of Appeals read the definition as] "intended to assure that compliance with [the] abortion regulations would not in any way pose a significant threat to the life or health of a woman." [We conclude that as so construed] the medical emergency definition imposes no undue burden on a woman's abortion right.

B. [Except] in a medical emergency, the statute requires that at least 24 hours before performing an abortion a physician inform the woman of the nature of the procedure, the health risks of the abortion and of childbirth, and the "probable gestational age of the unborn child." The physician or a qualified nonphysician must inform the woman of the availability of printed materials published by the State describing the fetus and providing information about medical assistance for childbirth, information about child support from the father, and a list of agencies which provide adoption and other services as alternatives to abortion. An abortion may not be performed unless the woman certifies in writing that she has been informed of the availability of these printed materials and has been provided them if she chooses to view them.

[To] the extent *Akron I* and *Thornburgh* find a constitutional violation when the government requires, as it does here, the giving of truthful, nonmisleading information about the nature of the procedure, the attendant health risks and those of childbirth, and the "probable gestational age" of the fetus, those cases go too far, are inconsistent with *Roe*'s acknowledgment of an important interest in potential life, and are overruled. [Further,] requiring that the woman be informed of the availability of information relating to fetal development and the assistance available should she decide to carry the pregnancy to full term is a reasonable measure to insure an informed choice, one which might cause the woman to choose childbirth over abortion. This requirement cannot be considered a substantial obstacle to obtaining an abortion, and, it follows, there is no undue burden.

[The] Pennsylvania statute also requires us to reconsider the holding in *Akron I* that the State may not require that a physician, as opposed to a qualified assistant, provide information relevant to a woman's informed consent. Since there is no evidence on this record that requiring a doctor to give the information as provided by the statute would amount in practical terms to a substantial obstacle to a woman seeking an abortion, we conclude that it is not an undue burden. * * *

Our analysis of Pennsylvania's 24–hour waiting period between the provision of the information deemed necessary to informed consent and the performance of an abortion under the undue burden standard requires us to reconsider the premise behind the decision in *Akron I* invalidating a parallel requirement. In *Akron I* we said: "Nor are we convinced that the State's legitimate concern that the woman's decision be informed is reasonably served by requiring a 24–hour delay as a matter of course."

We consider that conclusion to be wrong. The idea that important decisions will be more informed and deliberate if they follow some period of reflection does not strike us as unreasonable, particularly where the statute directs that important information become part of the background of the decision.

[Whether] the mandatory 24–hour waiting period is nonetheless invalid because in practice it is a substantial obstacle to a woman's choice to terminate her pregnancy is a closer question. The findings of fact [indicate] that because of the distances many women must travel to reach an abortion provider, the practical effect will often be a delay of much more than a day because the waiting period requires that a woman seeking an abortion make at least two visits to the doctor. The District Court also found that in many instances this will increase the exposure of women seeking abortions to "the harassment and hostility of anti-abortion protestors demonstrating outside a clinic." As a result, [for] those women who have the fewest financial resources, those who must travel long distances, and those who have difficulty explaining their whereabouts to husbands, employers, or others, the 24–hour waiting period will be "particularly burdensome."

These findings are troubling in some respects, but they do not demonstrate that the waiting period constitutes an undue burden. We do not doubt that, as the District Court held, the waiting period has the effect of "increasing the cost and risk of delay of abortions," but the District Court did not conclude that the increased costs and potential delays amount to substantial obstacles. Rather, [it] concluded that the waiting period does not further the state "interest in maternal health" and "infringes the physician's discretion to exercise sound medical judgment." Yet, [under] the undue burden standard a State is permitted to enact persuasive measures which favor childbirth over abortion, even if those measures do not further a health interest. And while the waiting period does limit a physician's discretion, that is not, standing alone, a reason to invalidate it. In light of the construction given the statute's definition of medical emergency by the Court of Appeals, and the District Court's findings, we cannot say that the waiting period imposes a real health risk.

We also disagree with the District Court's conclusion that the "particularly burdensome" effects of the waiting period on some women require its invalidation. A particular burden is not of necessity a substantial obstacle. Whether a burden falls on a particular group is a distinct inquiry from whether it is a substantial obstacle even as to the women in that group. * * *

We are left with the argument that the various aspects of the informed consent requirement are unconstitutional because they place barriers in the way of abortion on demand. Even the broadest reading of *Roe,* however, has not suggested that there is a constitutional right to abortion on demand. Rather, the right protected by *Roe* is a right to decide to terminate a pregnancy free of undue interference by the State. Because the informed consent requirement facilitates the wise exercise of that right it cannot be classified as an interference with the right *Roe* protects. The informed consent requirement is not an undue burden on that right.

C. Section 3209 of Pennsylvania's abortion law provides, except in cases of medical emergency, that no physician shall perform an abortion on a married woman without receiving a signed statement from the woman that she has notified her spouse that she is about to undergo an abortion. The woman has the option of providing an alternative signed statement certifying that her husband is not the man who impregnated her; that her husband could not be located; that the pregnancy is the result of spousal sexual assault which she has reported; or that the woman believes that notifying her husband will cause him or someone else to inflict bodily injury upon her. A physician who performs an abortion on a married woman without receiving the appropriate signed statement will have his or her license revoked, and is liable to the husband for damages.

The District Court heard the testimony of numerous expert witnesses, and made detailed findings of fact regarding the effect of this statute. These included:

"273. The vast majority of women consult their husbands prior to deciding to terminate their pregnancy * * *.

"279. The 'bodily injury' exception could not be invoked by a married woman whose husband, if notified, would, in her reasonable belief, threaten to (a) publicize her intent to have an abortion to family, friends or acquaintances; (b) retaliate against her in future child custody or divorce proceedings; (c) inflict psychological intimidation or emotional harm upon her, her children or other persons; (d) inflict bodily harm on other persons such as children, family members or other loved ones; or (e) use his control over finances to deprive of necessary monies for herself or her children * * *.

"281. Studies reveal that family violence occurs in two million families in the United States. This figure, however, is a conservative one that substantially understates (because battering is usually not reported until it reaches life-threatening proportions) the actual number of families affected by domestic violence. In fact, researchers estimate that one of every two women will be battered at some time in their life * * *.

"286. Married women, victims of battering, have been killed in Pennsylvania and throughout the United States * * *.

"287. Battering can often involve a substantial amount of sexual abuse, including marital rape and sexual mutilation * * *.

"288. In a domestic abuse situation, it is common for the battering husband to also abuse the children in an attempt to coerce the wife * * *.

"289. Mere notification of pregnancy is frequently a flashpoint for battering and violence within the family. [The] battering husband may deny parentage and use the pregnancy as an excuse for abuse * * *.

"290. Secrecy typically shrouds abusive families. Family members are instructed not to tell anyone, especially police or doctors, about the abuse and violence. Battering husbands often threaten their wives or her children with further abuse if she tells an outsider of the violence and tells her that nobody will believe her. A battered woman, therefore, is highly unlikely to disclose the violence against her for fear of retaliation by the abuser * * *.

"294. A woman in a shelter or a safe house unknown to her husband is not 'reasonably likely' to have bodily harm inflicted upon her by her batterer, however her attempt to notify her husband pursuant to section 3209 could accidentally disclose her whereabouts to her husband. Her fear of future ramifications would be realistic under the circumstances.

"295. Marital rape is rarely discussed with others or reported to law enforcement authorities, and of those reported only few are prosecuted * * *.

"296. It is common for battered women to have sexual intercourse with their husbands to avoid being battered. While this type of coercive sexual activity would be spousal sexual assault as defined by the Act, many women may not consider it to be so and others would fear disbelief * * *.

"297. The marital rape exception to section 3209 cannot be claimed by women who are victims of coercive sexual behavior other than penetration. The 90–day reporting requirement of the spousal sexual assault statute further narrows the class of sexually abused wives who can claim the exception, since many of these women may be psychologically unable to discuss or report the rape for several years after the incident * * *.

"298. Because of the nature of the battering relationship, battered women are unlikely to avail themselves of the exceptions to section 3209 of the Act, regardless of whether the section applies to them."

These findings are supported by studies of domestic violence. [According] to the American Medical Association [AMA], "[r]esearchers on family violence agree that the true incidence of partner violence is probably *double* the above estimates; or four million severely assaulted women per year. Studies suggest that from one-fifth to one-third of all women will be physically assaulted by a partner or ex-partner during their lifetime." Thus on an average day in the United States, nearly 11,000 women are severely assaulted by their male partners. Many of these incidents involve sexual assault. * * *

Other studies fill in the rest of this troubling picture. Physical violence is only the most visible form of abuse. Psychological abuse, particularly forced social and economic isolation of women, is also common. Many victims of domestic violence remain with their abusers, perhaps because they perceive no superior alternative. Many abused women who find temporary refuge in shelters return to their husbands, in large part because they have no other source of income. Returning to one's abuser can be dangerous. * * * Thirty percent of female homicide victims are killed by their male partners.

[This] information and the District Court's findings reinforce what common sense would suggest. In well-functioning marriages, spouses discuss important intimate decisions such as whether to bear a child. But there are millions of women in this country who are the victims of regular physical and psychological abuse at the hands of their husbands. Should these women become pregnant, they may have very good reasons for not wishing to inform their husbands of their decision to obtain an abortion. Many may have justifiable fears of physical abuse, but may be no less fearful of the consequences of reporting prior abuse to the Commonwealth of Pennsylvania. Many may have a reasonable fear that notifying their husbands will provoke further instances of child abuse; these women are not exempt from § 3209's notification requirement. Many may fear devastating forms of psychological abuse from their husbands, including verbal harassment, threats of future violence, the destruction of possessions, physical confinement to the home, the withdrawal of financial support, or the disclosure of the abortion to family and friends. [If] anything in this field is certain, it is that victims of spousal sexual assault are extremely reluctant to report the abuse to the government; hence, a great many spousal rape victims will not be exempt from the notification requirement imposed by § 3209.

The spousal notification requirement is thus likely to prevent a significant number of women from obtaining an abortion. It does not merely make abortions a little more difficult or expensive to obtain; for many women, it will impose a substantial obstacle. We must not blind ourselves to the fact that the significant number of women who fear for their safety and the safety of their children are likely to be deterred from procuring an abortion as surely as if the Commonwealth had outlawed abortion in all cases.

Respondents [maintain that the spousal notification provision] imposes almost no burden at all for the vast majority of women seeking abortions. They begin by noting that only about 20 percent of the women who obtain abortions are married. They then note that of these women about 95 percent notify their husbands of their own volition. Thus, respondents argue, the effects of § 3209 are felt by only one percent of the women who obtain abortions. [Since] some of these women will be able to notify their husbands without adverse consequences or will qualify for one of the exceptions, the statute affects fewer than one percent of women seeking abortions. [But the] analysis does not end with the one percent of women upon whom the statute operates; it begins there. Legislation is measured for consistency with the Constitution by its impact on those whose conduct it affects. For example, we would not say that a law which requires a newspaper to print a candidate's reply to an unfavorable editorial is valid on its face because most newspapers would adopt the policy even absent the law. The proper focus of constitutional inquiry is the group for whom the law is a restriction, not the group for whom the law is irrelevant.

[Section] 3209's real target is narrower even than the class of women seeking abortions identified by the State: it is married women seeking abortions who do not wish to notify their husbands of their intentions and who do not qualify for one of the statutory exceptions to the notice requirement. The unfortunate yet persisting conditions we document above will mean that in a large fraction of the cases in which § 3209 is relevant, it will operate as a substantial obstacle to a woman's choice to undergo an abortion. It is an undue burden, and therefore invalid.

This conclusion is in no way inconsistent with our decisions upholding parental notification or consent requirements. Those enactments, and our judgment that they are constitutional, are based on the quite reasonable assumption that minors will benefit from consultation with their parents and that children will often not realize that their parents have their best interests at heart. We cannot adopt a parallel assumption about adult women.

[If] this case concerned a State's ability to require the mother to notify the father before taking some action with respect to a living child raised by both, [it] would be reasonable to conclude as a general matter that the father's interest in the welfare of the child and the mother's interest are equal.

Before birth, however, the issue takes on a very different cast. It is an inescapable biological fact that state regulation with respect to the child a woman is carrying will have a far greater impact on the mother's liberty than on the father's. The effect of state regulation on a woman's protected liberty is doubly deserving of scrutiny in such a case, as the State has touched not only upon the private sphere of the family but upon the very bodily integrity of the pregnant woman. Cf. *Cruzan*. [The] Constitution protects individuals, men and women alike, from unjustified state interference, even when that interference is enacted into law for the benefit of their spouses.

There was a time, not so long ago, when a different understanding of the family and of the Constitution prevailed. In *Bradwell v. Illinois*, 16 Wall. 130 (1873), three Members of this Court reaffirmed the common-law principle that "a woman had no legal existence separate from her husband, who was regarded as her head and representative in the social state; and, notwithstanding some recent modifications of this civil status, many of the special rules of law flowing from and dependent upon this cardinal principle still exist in full force in most states." Only one generation has passed since this Court observed that "woman is still regarded as the center of home and family life," with attendant "special responsibilities" that precluded full and independent legal status under the Constitution. *Hoyt v. Florida* (1961) [p. 1178 infra]. These views, of course, are no longer consistent with our understanding of the family, the individual, or the Constitution.

In keeping with our rejection of the common-law understanding of a woman's role within the family, the Court held in *Danforth* that the Constitution does not permit a State to require a married woman to obtain her husband's consent before undergoing an abortion. The principles that guided the Court in *Danforth* should be our guides today. For the great many women who are victims of abuse inflicted by their husbands, or whose children are the victims of such abuse, a spousal notice requirement enables the husband to wield an effective veto over his wife's decision.

[The] husband's interest in the life of the child his wife is carrying does not permit the State to empower him with this troubling degree of authority over his wife. The contrary view leads to consequences reminiscent of the common law. A husband has no enforceable right to require a wife to advise him before she exercises her personal choices. If a husband's interest in the potential life of the child outweighs a wife's liberty, the State could require a married woman to notify her husband before she uses a postfertilization contraceptive. Perhaps next in line would be a statute requiring pregnant married women to notify their husbands before engaging in conduct causing risks to the fetus. After all, if the husband's interest in the fetus' safety is a sufficient predicate for state regulation, the State could reasonably conclude that pregnant wives should notify their husbands before drinking alcohol or smoking. Perhaps married women should notify their husbands before using contraceptives or before undergoing any type of surgery that may have complications affecting the husband's interest in his wife's reproductive organs. And if a husband's interest justifies notice in any of these cases, one might reasonably argue that it justifies exactly what the *Danforth* Court held it did not justify—a requirement of the husband's consent as well. A State may not give to a man the kind of dominion over his wife that parents exercise over their children.

Section 3209 embodies a view of marriage consonant with the common-law status of married women but repugnant to our present understanding of marriage and of the nature of the rights secured by the Constitution. Women do not lose their constitutionally protected liberty when they marry. The Constitution protects all individuals, male or female, married or unmarried, from the abuse of governmental power, even where that power is employed for the supposed benefit of a member of the individual's family. These considerations confirm our conclusion that § 3209 is invalid.

D. [Except] in a medical emergency, an unemancipated young woman under 18 may not obtain an abortion unless she and one of her parents (or guardian) provides informed consent as defined above. If neither a parent nor a guardian provides consent, a court may authorize the performance of an abortion upon a determination that the young woman is mature and capable of giving informed consent and has in fact given her informed consent, or that an abortion would be in her best interests.

We have been over most of this ground before. Our cases establish, and we reaffirm today, that a State may require a minor seeking an abortion to obtain the consent of a parent or guardian, provided that there is an adequate judicial bypass procedure. * * *

E. [E]very facility which performs abortions is required to file a report stating its name and address as well as the name and address of any related entity, such as a controlling or subsidiary organization. In the case of state-funded institutions, the information becomes public.

For each abortion performed, a report must be filed identifying: the physician (and the second physician where required); the facility; the referring physician or agency; the woman's age; the number of prior pregnancies and prior abortions she has had; gestational age; the type of abortion procedure; the date of the abortion; whether there were any pre-existing medical conditions which would complicate pregnancy; medical complications with the abortion; where applicable, the basis for the determination that the abortion was medically necessary; the weight of the aborted fetus; and whether the woman was married, and if so, whether notice was provided or the basis for the failure to give notice. Every abortion facility must also file quarterly reports showing the number of abortions performed broken down by trimester. In all events, the identity of each woman who has had an abortion remains confidential.

In *Danforth,* we held that recordkeeping and reporting provisions "that are reasonably directed to the preservation of maternal health and that properly respect a patient's confidentiality and privacy are permissible." We think that under this standard, all the provisions at issue here except that relating to spousal notice are constitutional. Although they do not relate to the State's interest in informing the woman's choice, they do relate to health. The collection of information with respect to actual patients is a vital element of medical research, and so it cannot be said that the requirements serve no purpose other than to make abortions more difficult. Nor do we find that the requirements impose a substantial obstacle to a woman's choice. At most they might increase the cost of some abortions by a slight amount. * * *

VI. Our Constitution is a covenant running from the first generation of Americans to us and then to future generations. It is a coherent succession. Each generation must learn anew that the Constitution's written terms embody ideas and aspirations that must survive more ages than one. We accept our responsibility not to retreat from interpreting the full meaning of the covenant in light of all of our precedents. We invoke it once again to define the freedom guaranteed by the Constitution's own promise, the promise of liberty. * * *

JUSTICE STEVENS, concurring in part and dissenting in part.

The portions of the Court's opinion that I have joined are more important than those with which I disagree. I shall therefore first comment on significant areas of agreement, and then explain the limited character of my disagreement.

The Court is unquestionably correct in concluding that the doctrine of stare decisis has controlling significance in a case of this kind, notwithstanding an individual justice's concerns about the merits.[1] The central holding of *Roe* has been a "part of our law" for almost two decades. It was a natural sequel to the protection of individual liberty established in *Griswold*. The societal costs of overruling *Roe* at this late date would be enormous. *Roe* is an integral part of a correct understanding of both the concept of liberty and the basic equality of men and women.

Stare decisis also provides a sufficient basis for my agreement with the joint opinion's reaffirmation of *Roe* 's post-viability analysis. Specifically, I accept the proposition that "[i]f the State is interested in protecting fetal life after viability, it may go so far as to proscribe abortion during that period, except when it is necessary to preserve the life or health of the mother."

I also accept what is implicit in the Court's analysis, namely, a reaffirmation of *Roe* 's explanation of *why* the State's obligation to protect the life or health of the mother must take precedence over any duty to the unborn. The Court in *Roe* carefully considered, and rejected, the State's argument "that the fetus is a 'person' within the language and meaning of the Fourteenth Amendment." * * * Accordingly, an abortion is not "the termination of life entitled to Fourteenth Amendment protection." From this holding, there was no dissent; indeed, no member of the Court has ever questioned this fundamental proposition. Thus, as a matter of federal constitutional law, a developing organism that is not yet a "person" does not have what is sometimes described as a "right to life." [2] This has been and, by the Court's holding today, remains a fundamental premise of our constitutional law governing reproductive autonomy.

My disagreement with the joint opinion begins with its understanding of the trimester framework established in *Roe*. Contrary to the suggestion of the joint opinion, it is not a "contradiction" to recognize that the State may have a legitimate interest in potential human life and, at the same time, to conclude that that interest does not justify the regulation of abortion before viability (although other interests, such as maternal health, may). The fact that the State's interest is legitimate does not tell us when, if ever, that interest outweighs the pregnant woman's interest in personal liberty. It is appropriate, therefore, to consider more carefully the nature of the interests at stake.

First, it is clear that, in order to be legitimate, the State's interest must be secular; consistent with the First Amendment the State may not promote a

---

1. It is sometimes useful to view the issue of stare decisis from a historical perspective. In the last nineteen years, fifteen Justices have confronted the basic issue presented in *Roe*. Of those, eleven have voted as the majority does today: Chief Justice Burger, Justices Douglas, Brennan, Stewart, Marshall, and Powell, and Justices Blackmun, O'Connor, Kennedy, Souter, and myself. Only four—all of whom happen to be on the Court today—have reached the opposite conclusion.

2. Professor Dworkin has made this comment on the issue:

"The suggestion that states are free to declare a fetus a person * * * assumes that a state can curtail some persons' constitutional rights by adding new persons to the constitutional population. * * *

"If a state could declare trees to be persons with a constitutional right to life, it could prohibit publishing newspapers or books in spite of the First Amendment's guarantee of free speech, which could not be understood as a license to kill * * *. Once we understand that the suggestion we are considering has that implication, we must reject it. If a fetus is not part of the constitutional population, under the national constitutional arrangement, then states have no power to overrule that national arrangement by themselves declaring that fetuses have rights competitive with the constitutional rights of pregnant women." Ronald Dworkin, *Unenumerated Rights: Whether and How Roe Should be Overruled*, 59 U.Chi.L.Rev. 381, 400–401 (1992).

theological or sectarian interest. Moreover, [the] state interest in potential human life is not an interest in loco parentis, for the fetus is not a person.

Identifying the State's interests—which the States rarely articulate with any precision—makes clear that the interest in protecting potential life is not grounded in the Constitution. It is, instead, an indirect interest supported by both humanitarian and pragmatic concerns. Many of our citizens believe that any abortion reflects an unacceptable disrespect for potential human life and that the performance of more than a million abortions each year is intolerable; many find third-trimester abortions performed when the fetus is approaching personhood particularly offensive. The State has a legitimate interest in minimizing such offense. The State may also have a broader interest in expanding the population, believing society would benefit from the services of additional productive citizens—or that the potential human lives might include the occasional Mozart or Curie. These are the kinds of concerns that comprise the State's interest in potential human life.

In counterpoise is the woman's constitutional interest in liberty. One aspect of this liberty is a right to bodily integrity, a right to control one's person. This right is neutral on the question of abortion: The Constitution would be equally offended by an absolute requirement that all women undergo abortions as by an absolute prohibition on abortions. * * *

The woman's constitutional liberty interest also involves her freedom to decide matters of the highest privacy and the most personal nature. [As] the joint opinion so eloquently demonstrates, a woman's decision to terminate her pregnancy is nothing less than a matter of conscience.

Weighing the State's interest in potential life and the woman's liberty interest, I agree with the joint opinion that the State may " 'expres[s] a preference for normal childbirth,' " that the State may take steps to ensure that a woman's choice "is thoughtful and informed," and that "States are free to enact laws to provide a reasonable framework for a woman to make a decision that has such profound and lasting meaning." Serious questions arise, however, when a State attempts to "persuade the woman to choose childbirth over abortion." Decisional autonomy must limit the State's power to inject into a woman's most personal deliberations its own views of what is best. The State may promote its preferences by funding childbirth, by creating and maintaining alternatives to abortion, and by espousing the virtues of family; but it must respect the individual's freedom to make such judgments.

[Under the principles established in the Court's previous cases, Justice Stevens deemed unconstitutional those sections requiring a woman to be provided with a wide range of materials "clearly designed to persuade her to choose not to undergo the abortion. While the State may produce and disseminate such material, it "may not inject such information into the woman's deliberations just as she is weighing such an important choice." But he did not find constitutionally objectionable those sections requiring the physician to inform a woman of the nature and risks of the abortion procedure and the medical risks of carrying to term for these "are neutral requirements comparable to those imposed in other medical procedures. These sections indicate no effort by the State to influence the woman's choice in any way."]

The 24–hour waiting period [raises] even more serious concerns. Such a requirement arguably furthers the State's interests in two ways, neither of which is constitutionally permissible.

First, it may be argued that the 24–hour delay is justified by the mere fact that it is likely to reduce the number of abortions, thus furthering the State's interest in potential life. But such an argument would justify any form of coercion that placed an obstacle in the woman's path. The State cannot further its interests by simply wearing down the ability of the pregnant woman to exercise her constitutional right.

Second, it can more reasonably be argued that the 24–hour delay furthers the State's interest in ensuring that the woman's decision is informed and thoughtful. But there is no evidence that the mandated delay benefits women or that it is necessary to enable the physician to convey any relevant information to the patient. The mandatory delay thus appears to rest on outmoded and unacceptable assumptions about the decisionmaking capacity of women. While there are well-established and consistently maintained reasons for the State to view with skepticism the ability of minors to make decisions, none of those reasons applies to an adult woman's decisionmaking ability. Just as we have left behind the belief that a woman must consult her husband before undertaking serious matters, so we must reject the notion that a woman is less capable of deciding matters of gravity.

In the alternative, the delay requirement may be premised on the belief that the decision to terminate a pregnancy is presumptively wrong. This premise is illegitimate. [A] woman who has, in the privacy of her thoughts and conscience, weighed the options and made her decision cannot be forced to reconsider all, simply because the State believes she has come to the wrong conclusion.[5]

[In] my opinion, a correct application of the "undue burden" standard leads to the same conclusion concerning the constitutionality of these requirements. A state-imposed burden on the exercise of a constitutional right is measured both by its effects and by its character: A burden may be "undue" either because the burden is too severe or because it lacks a legitimate, rational justification.[6]

The 24–hour delay requirement fails both parts of this test. The findings of the District Court establish the severity of the burden that the 24–hour delay imposes on many pregnant women. Yet even in those cases in which the delay is not especially onerous, it is, in my opinion, "undue" because there is no evidence that such a delay serves a useful and legitimate purpose.

[The] counseling provisions are similarly infirm. Whenever government commands private citizens to speak or to listen, careful review of the justification for that command is particularly appropriate. [The] statute requires that [information concerning alternatives to abortion, the availability of medical assistance benefits, and the possibility of child-support payments] be given to *all* women seeking abortions, including those for whom such information is clearly useless, such as those who are married, those who have undergone the procedure in the past and are fully aware of the options, and those who are fully convinced that

5. The joint opinion's reliance on the indirect effects of the regulation of constitutionally protected activity is misplaced; [as I explained in *Hodgson*] what matters is not only the effect of a regulation but also the reason for the regulation.

6. The meaning of any legal standard can only be understood by reviewing the actual cases in which it is applied. For that reason, I discount both Justice Scalia's comments on past descriptions of the standard and the attempt to give it crystal clarity in the joint opinion. The several opinions supporting the judgment in *Griswold* are less illuminating than the central holding of the case, which appears to have passed the test of time. The future may also demonstrate that a standard that analyzes both the severity of a regulatory burden and the legitimacy of its justification will provide a fully adequate framework for the review of abortion legislation even if the contours of the standard are not authoritatively articulated in any single opinion.

abortion is their only reasonable option.   * * * I conclude that [these] requirements do not serve a useful purpose and thus constitute an unnecessary—and
therefore undue—burden on the woman's constitutional liberty to decide to
terminate her pregnancy.

Accordingly, while I disagree with Parts IV, V–B, and V–D of the joint
opinion,[8] I join the remainder of the Court's opinion.

JUSTICE BLACKMUN, concurring in part, concurring in the judgment in part, and
dissenting in part.

I join parts I, II, III, V–A, V–C, and VI of the joint opinion * * *.

Three years ago, in *Webster,* four Members of this Court appeared poised to
"cas[t] into darkness the hopes and visions of every woman in this country" who
had come to believe that the Constitution guaranteed her the right to reproductive
choice. (Blackmun, J., dissenting). All that remained between the promise of
Roe and the darkness of the plurality was a single, flickering flame. Decisions
since *Webster* gave little reason to hope that this flame would cast much light.
But now, just when so many expected the darkness to fall, the flame has grown
bright.

I do not underestimate the significance of today's joint opinion. Yet I remain
steadfast in my belief that the right to reproductive choice is entitled to the full
protection afforded by this Court before *Webster.* And I fear for the darkness as
four Justices anxiously await the single vote necessary to extinguish the light.

Make no mistake, the joint opinion of Justices O'Connor, Kennedy, and
Souter is an act of personal courage and constitutional principle. In contrast to
previous decisions in which Justices O'Connor and Kennedy postponed reconsideration of *Roe,* the authors of the joint opinion today join Justice Stevens and me in
concluding that "the essential holding of *Roe* should be retained and once again
reaffirmed."   In brief, five Members of this Court today recognize that "the
Constitution protects a woman's right to terminate her pregnancy in its early
stages." * * *

Today, no less than yesterday, the Constitution and decisions of this Court
require that a State's abortion restrictions be subjected to the strictest of judicial
scrutiny. Our precedents and the joint opinion's principles require us to subject
all non-de-minimis abortion regulations to strict scrutiny. Under this standard,
the Pennsylvania statute's provisions requiring content-based counseling, a 24–
hour delay, informed parental consent, and reporting of abortion-related information must be invalidated. [R]estrictive abortion laws force women to endure
physical invasions far more substantial than those this Court has held to violate
the constitutional principle of bodily integrity in other contexts.[3]

Further, when the State restricts a woman's right to terminate her pregnancy, it deprives a woman of the right to make her own decision about reproduction
and family planning—critical life choices that this Court long has deemed central
to the right to privacy. The decision to terminate or continue a pregnancy has no

---

8. Although I agree that a parental-consent
requirement (with the appropriate bypass) is
constitutional, I do not join Part V–D of the
joint opinion because its approval of Pennsylvania's informed parental-consent requirement
is based on the reasons given in Part V–B, with
which I disagree.

3. As the joint opinion acknowledges, this
Court has recognized the vital liberty interest
of persons in refusing unwanted medical treatment. *Cruzan.* Just as the Due Process
Clause protects the deeply personal decision of
the individual to *refuse* medical treatment, it
also must protect the deeply personal decision
to *obtain* medical treatment, including a woman's decision to terminate a pregnancy.

less an impact on a woman's life than decisions about contraception or marriage. Because motherhood has a dramatic impact on a woman's educational prospects, employment opportunities, and self-determination, restrictive abortion laws deprive her of basic control over her life.

[A] State's restrictions on a woman's right to terminate her pregnancy also implicate constitutional guarantees of gender equality. [By] restricting the right to terminate pregnancies, the State conscripts women's bodies into its service, forcing women to continue their pregnancies, suffer the pains of childbirth, and in most instances, provide years of maternal care. The State does not compensate women for their services; instead, it assumes that they owe this duty as a matter of course. This assumption—that women can simply be forced to accept the "natural" status and incidents of motherhood—appears to rest upon a conception of women's role that has triggered the protection of the Equal Protection Clause.[4] The joint opinion recognizes that these assumptions about women's place in society "are no longer consistent with our understanding of the family, the individual, or the Constitution."

The Court has held that limitations on the right of privacy are permissible only if they survive "strict" constitutional scrutiny—that is, only if the governmental entity imposing the restriction can demonstrate that the limitation is both necessary and narrowly tailored to serve a compelling governmental interest. *Griswold.* We have applied this principle specifically in the context of abortion regulations. *Roe.*[5]

[In] my view, application of [the] analytical framework [set forth in *Roe*] is no less warranted than when it was approved by seven Members of this Court in *Roe.* Strict scrutiny of state limitations on reproductive choice still offers the most secure protection of the woman's right to make her own reproductive decisions, free from state coercion. No majority of this Court has ever agreed upon an alternative approach. The factual premises of the trimester framework have not been undermined and the *Roe* framework is far more administrable, and far less manipulable, than the "undue burden" standard adopted by the joint opinion. * * *

Roe 's trimester framework does not ignore the State's interest in prenatal life. Like Justice Stevens, I agree that the State may take steps to ensure that a woman's choice "is thoughtful and informed" and that "States are free to enact laws to provide a reasonable framework for a woman to make a decision that has such profound and lasting meaning." But "[s]erious questions arise when a State attempts to 'persuade the woman to choose childbirth over abortion.' Decisional autonomy must limit the State's power to inject into a woman's most personal deliberations its own views of what is best. * * *" (Opinion of Stevens, J.). As the joint opinion recognizes, "the means chosen by the State to further the interest in potential life must be calculated to inform the woman's free choice, not hinder it."

In sum, *Roe* 's requirement of strict scrutiny as implemented through a trimester framework should not be disturbed. No other approach has gained a

---

4. A growing number of commentators are recognizing this point. * * *

5. To say that restrictions on a right are subject to strict scrutiny is not to say that the right is absolute. Regulations can be upheld if they have no significant impact on the woman's exercise of her right and are justified by important state health objectives. See, *e.g.,*

Danforth (upholding requirements of a woman's written consent and record keeping). But the Court today reaffirms the essential principle of *Roe* that a woman has the right "to choose to have an abortion before viability and to obtain it without undue interference from the State." Under *Roe,* any more than *de minimis* interference is undue.

majority, and no other is more protective of the woman's fundamental right. Lastly, no other approach properly accommodates the woman's constitutional right with the State's legitimate interests.

Application of the strict scrutiny standard results in the invalidation of all the challenged provisions. Indeed, as this Court has invalidated virtually identical provisions in prior cases, stare decisis requires that we again strike them down.

This Court has upheld informed and written consent requirements only where the State has demonstrated that they genuinely further important health-related state concerns. * * *

Measured against these principles, some aspects of the Pennsylvania informed-consent scheme are unconstitutional. While it is unobjectionable for the Commonwealth to require that the patient be informed of the nature of the procedure, the health risks of the abortion and of childbirth, and the probable gestational age of the unborn child, I remain unconvinced that there is a vital state need for insisting that the information be provided by a physician rather than a counselor. [Moreover,] *Thornburgh* invalidated biased patient-counseling requirements virtually identical to the one at issue here. What we said of those requirements fully applies in this case * * *.

The 24–hour waiting period [is] also clearly unconstitutional. The District Court found that the mandatory 24–hour delay could lead to delays in excess of 24 hours, thus increasing health risks, and that it would require two visits to the abortion provider, thereby increasing travel time, exposure to further harassment, and financial cost. Finally, the District Court found that the requirement would pose especially significant burdens on women living in rural areas and those women that have difficulty explaining their whereabouts. In *Akron* this Court invalidated a similarly arbitrary or inflexible waiting period because, as here, it furthered no legitimate state interest.[8]

As Justice Stevens insightfully concludes, the mandatory delay rests either on outmoded or unacceptable assumptions about the decisionmaking capacity of women or the belief that the decision to terminate the pregnancy is presumptively wrong. The requirement that women consider this obvious and slanted information for an additional 24 hours contained in these provisions will only influence the woman's decision in improper ways. The vast majority of women will know this information—of the few that do not, it is less likely that their minds will be changed by this information than it will be either by the realization that the State opposes their choice or the need once again to endure abuse and harassment on return to the clinic. * * *

Finally, [the] statute requires every facility performing abortions to report its activities to the Commonwealth. Pennsylvania [attempts] to justify its required reports on the ground that the public has a right to know how its tax dollars are spent. A regulation designed to inform the public about public expenditures does not further the Commonwealth's interest in protecting maternal health. Accordingly, such a regulation cannot justify a legally significant burden on a woman's right to obtain an abortion. * * *

At long last, The Chief Justice admits it. Gone are the contentions that the issue need not be (or has not been) considered. There, on the first page, for all to

---

8. The Court's decision in *Hodgson v. Minnesota,* validating a 48–hour waiting period for minors seeking an abortion to permit parental involvement does not alter this conclusion. Here the 24–hour delay is imposed on an *adult* woman. Moreover, the statute in *Hodgson* did not require any delay once the minor obtained the affirmative consent of either a parent or the court.

see, is what was expected: "We believe that *Roe* was wrongly decided, and that it can and should be overruled consistently with our traditional approach to *stare decisis* in constitutional cases." If there is much reason to applaud the advances made by the joint opinion today, there is far more to fear from The Chief Justice's opinion.

The Chief Justice's criticism of *Roe* follows from his stunted conception of individual liberty. While recognizing that the Due Process Clause protects more than simply physical liberty, he then goes on to construe this Court's personal-liberty cases as establishing only a laundry list of particular rights, rather than a principled account of how these particular rights are grounded in a more general right of privacy. This constricted view is reinforced by The Chief Justice's exclusive reliance on tradition as a source of fundamental rights. [P]eople using contraceptives seem the next likely candidate for his list of outcasts.

Even more shocking than The Chief Justice's cramped notion of individual liberty is his complete omission of any discussion of the effects that compelled childbirth and motherhood have on women's lives. The only expression of concern with women's health is purely instrumental—for The Chief Justice, only women's *psychological* health is a concern, and only to the extent that he assumes that every woman who decides to have an abortion does so without serious consideration of the moral implications of their decision. In short, The Chief Justice's view of the State's compelling interest in maternal health has less to do with health than it does with compelling women to be maternal.

Nor does The Chief Justice give any serious consideration to the doctrine of stare decisis. For The Chief Justice, the facts that gave rise to *Roe* are surprisingly simple: "women become pregnant, there is a point somewhere, depending on medical technology, where a fetus becomes viable, and women give birth to children." This characterization of the issue thus allows The Chief Justice quickly to discard the joint opinion's reliance argument by asserting that "reproductive planning could take ... virtually immediate account of a decision overruling *Roe.*"

The Chief Justice's narrow conception of individual liberty and stare decisis leads him to propose the same standard of review proposed by the plurality in *Webster.*

[Under] his standard, States can ban abortion if that ban is rationally related to a legitimate state interest—a standard which the United States calls "deferential, but not toothless." Yet when pressed at oral argument to describe the teeth, the best protection that the Solicitor General could offer to women was that a prohibition, enforced by criminal penalties, *with no exception for the life of the mother,* "could raise very serious questions." Perhaps, the Solicitor General offered, the failure to include an exemption for the life of the mother would be "arbitrary and capricious." If, as The Chief Justice contends, the undue burden test is made out of whole cloth, the so-called "arbitrary and capricious" limit is the Solicitor General's "new clothes."

Even if it is somehow "irrational" for a State to require a woman to risk her life for her child, what protection is offered for women who become pregnant through rape or incest? Is there anything arbitrary or capricious about a State's prohibiting the sins of the father from being visited upon his offspring? [12]

---

12. Justice Scalia urges the Court to "get out of this area" and leave questions regarding abortion entirely to the States. Putting aside the fact that what he advocates is nothing short of an abdication by the Court of its constitutional responsibilities, Justice Scalia is

But, we are reassured, there is always the protection of the democratic process. While there is much to be praised about our democracy, our country since its founding has recognized that there are certain fundamental liberties that are not to be left to the whims of an election. A woman's right to reproductive choice is one of those fundamental liberties. Accordingly, that liberty need not seek refuge at the ballot box.

In one sense, the Court's approach is worlds apart from that of The Chief Justice and Justice Scalia. And yet, in another sense, the distance between the two approaches is short—the distance is but a single vote.

I am 83 years old. I cannot remain on this Court forever, and when I do step down, the confirmation process for my successor well may focus on the issue before us today. That, I regret, may be exactly where the choice between the two worlds will be made.

CHIEF JUSTICE REHNQUIST, with whom JUSTICE WHITE, JUSTICE SCALIA, and JUSTICE THOMAS join, concurring in the judgment in part and dissenting in part.

The joint opinion, following its newly-minted variation on stare decisis, retains the outer shell of *Roe* but beats a wholesale retreat from the substance of that case. We believe that *Roe* was wrongly decided, and that it can and should be overruled consistently with our traditional approach to stare decisis in constitutional cases. We would adopt the approach of the plurality in *Webster* and uphold the challenged provisions of the Pennsylvania statute in their entirety. * * *

In *Roe* the Court recognized a "guarantee of personal privacy" which "is broad enough to encompass a woman's decision whether or not to terminate her pregnancy." We are now of the view that, in terming this right fundamental, the Court in *Roe* read the earlier opinions upon which it based its decision much too broadly. Unlike marriage, procreation and contraception, abortion "involves the purposeful termination of potential life." The abortion decision must therefore "be recognized as sui generis, different in kind from the others that the Court has protected under the rubric of personal or family privacy and autonomy." *Thornburgh* (White, J., dissenting). One cannot ignore the fact that a woman is not isolated in her pregnancy, and that the decision to abort necessarily involves the destruction of a fetus.

[Nor] do the historical traditions of the American people support the view that the right to terminate one's pregnancy is "fundamental." The common law which we inherited from England made abortion after "quickening" an offense. At the time of the adoption of the Fourteenth Amendment, statutory prohibitions or restrictions on abortion were commonplace; in 1868, at least 28 of the then–37 States and 8 Territories had statutes banning or limiting abortion. By the turn of the century virtually every State had a law prohibiting or restricting abortion on its books. By the middle of the present century, a liberalization trend had set in. But 21 of the restrictive abortion laws in effect in 1868 were still in effect in 1973

uncharacteristically naive if he thinks that overruling *Roe* and holding that restrictions on a woman's right to an abortion are subject only to rational-basis review will enable the Court henceforth to avoid reviewing abortion-related issues. State efforts to regulate and prohibit abortion in a post-*Roe* world undoubtedly would raise a host of distinct and important constitutional questions meriting review by this Court. For example, does the Eighth Amendment impose any limits on the degree or kind of punishment a State can inflict upon physicians who perform, or women who undergo, abortions? What effect would differences among States in their approaches to abortion have on a woman's right to engage in interstate travel? Does the First Amendment permit States that choose not to criminalize abortion to ban all advertising providing information about where and how to obtain abortions?

when *Roe* was decided, and an overwhelming majority of the States prohibited abortion unless necessary to preserve the life or health of the mother. On this record, it can scarcely be said that any deeply rooted tradition of relatively unrestricted abortion in our history supported the classification of the right to abortion as "fundamental" under the Due Process Clause of the Fourteenth Amendment.

[The joint opinion] cannot bring itself to say that *Roe* was correct as an original matter, but [instead] contains an elaborate discussion of stare decisis. [This discussion] appears to be almost entirely dicta, because the joint opinion does not apply that principle in dealing with *Roe*. *Roe* decided that a woman had a fundamental right to an abortion. The joint opinion rejects that view. *Roe* decided that abortion regulations were to be subjected to "strict scrutiny" and could be justified only in the light of "compelling state interests." The joint opinion rejects that view. *Roe* analyzed abortion regulation under a rigid trimester framework, a framework which has guided this Court's decisionmaking for 19 years. The joint opinion rejects that framework.

Stare decisis is defined in Black's Law Dictionary as meaning "to abide by, or adhere to, decided cases." Whatever the "central holding" of *Roe* that is left after the joint opinion finishes dissecting it is surely not the result of that principle. While purporting to adhere to precedent, the joint opinion instead revises it. *Roe* continues to exist, but only in the way a storefront on a western movie set exists: a mere facade to give the illusion of reality. Decisions following *Roe,* such as *Akron* and *Thornburgh,* are frankly overruled in part under the "undue burden" standard expounded in the joint opinion.

In our view, authentic principles of stare decisis do not require that any portion of the reasoning in *Roe* be kept intact. "Stare decisis is not [a] universal, inexorable command," especially in cases involving the interpretation of the Federal Constitution. Erroneous decisions in such constitutional cases are uniquely durable, because correction through legislative action, save for constitutional amendment, is impossible. * * * Our constitutional watch does not cease merely because we have spoken before on an issue; when it becomes clear that a prior constitutional interpretation is unsound we are obliged to reexamine the question.

The joint opinion discusses several stare decisis factors which, it asserts, point toward retaining a portion of *Roe.* Two of these factors are that the main "factual underpinning" of *Roe* has remained the same, and that its doctrinal foundation is no weaker now than it was in 1973. Of course, what might be called the basic facts which gave rise to *Roe* have remained the same—women become pregnant, there is a point somewhere, depending on medical technology, where a fetus becomes viable, and women give birth to children. But this is only to say that the same facts which gave rise to *Roe* will continue to give rise to similar cases. It is not a reason, in and of itself, why those cases must be decided in the same incorrect manner as was the first case to deal with the question.

[The] joint opinion also points to the reliance interests involved in this context in its effort to explain why precedent must be followed for precedent's sake. [But,] as the joint opinion apparently agrees, any traditional notion of reliance is not applicable here. The Court today cuts back on the protection afforded by *Roe,* and no one claims that this action defeats any reliance interest in the disavowed trimester framework. Similarly, reliance interests would not be diminished were the Court to go further and acknowledge the full error of *Roe,* as "reproductive planning could take virtually immediate account of" this action.

[In] the end, having failed to put forth any evidence to prove any true reliance, the joint opinion's argument is based solely on generalized assertions about the national psyche, on a belief that the people of this country have grown accustomed to the *Roe* decision over the last 19 years and have "ordered their thinking and living around" it. As an initial matter, one might inquire how the joint opinion can view the "central holding" of *Roe* as so deeply rooted in our constitutional culture, when it so casually uproots and disposes of that same decision's trimester framework. Furthermore, at various points in the past, the same could have been said about this Court's erroneous decisions that the Constitution allowed "separate but equal" treatment of minorities or that "liberty" under the Due Process Clause protected "freedom of contract." The "separate but equal" doctrine lasted 58 years after *Plessy,* and *Lochner* 's protection of contractual freedom lasted 32 years. However, the simple fact that a generation or more had grown used to these major decisions did not prevent the Court from correcting its errors in those cases, nor should it prevent us from correctly interpreting the Constitution here.

[The joint opinion states] that when the Court "resolve[s] the sort of intensely divisive controversy reflected in *Roe* and those rare, comparable cases," its decision is exempt from reconsideration under established principles of stare decisis in constitutional cases. [This] is truly novel principle, one which is contrary to both the Court's historical practice and to the Court's traditional willingness to tolerate criticism of its opinions. Under this principle, when the Court has ruled on a divisive issue, it is apparently prevented from overruling that decision for the sole reason that it was incorrect, *unless opposition to the original decision has died away.*

The first difficulty with this principle [is that the] question of whether a particular issue is "intensely divisive" enough to qualify for special protection is entirely subjective and dependent on the individual assumptions of the Members of this Court. In addition, because the Court's duty is to ignore public opinion and criticism on issues that come before it, its members are in perhaps the worst position to judge whether a decision divides the Nation deeply enough to justify such uncommon protection.

[The] joint opinion picks out and discusses two prior Court rulings that it believes are of the "intensely divisive" variety, and concludes that they are of comparable dimension to *Roe* [referring to *Lochner* and *Plessy*]. It appears to us very odd indeed that the joint opinion chooses as benchmarks two cases in which the Court chose *not* to adhere to erroneous constitutional precedent, but instead enhanced its stature by acknowledging and correcting its error, apparently in violation of the joint opinion's "legitimacy" principle.

[The] joint opinion agrees that the Court's stature would have been seriously damaged if in *Brown* and *West Coast Hotel* it had dug in its heels and refused to apply normal principles of stare decisis to the earlier decisions. But the opinion contends that the Court was entitled to overrule *Plessy* and *Lochner* in those cases, despite the existence of opposition to the original decisions, only because both the Nation and the Court had learned new lessons in the interim. This is at best a feebly supported, post hoc rationalization for those decisions.

For example, the opinion asserts that the Court could justifiably overrule its decision in *Lochner* only because the Depression had convinced "most people" that constitutional protection of contractual freedom contributed to an economy that failed to protect the welfare of all. Surely the joint opinion does not mean to suggest that people saw this Court's failure to uphold minimum wage statutes as the cause of the Great Depression! In any event, the *Lochner* Court did not base its rule upon the policy judgment that an unregulated market was fundamental to a stable economy; it simply believed, erroneously, that "liberty" under the Due Process Clause protected the "right to make a contract." Nor is it the case that the people of this Nation only discovered the dangers of extreme laissez faire economics because of the Depression. State laws regulating maximum hours and minimum wages were in existence well before that time.

[When] the Court finally recognized its error in *West Coast Hotel,* it did not engage in the *post hoc* rationalization that the joint opinion attributes to it today; it did not state that *Lochner* had been based on an economic view that had fallen into disfavor, and that it therefore should be overruled. Chief Justice Hughes in his opinion for the Court simply recognized what Justice Holmes had previously recognized in his *Lochner* dissent, that "[t]he Constitution does not speak of freedom of contract."

[The] joint opinion also agrees that the Court acted properly in rejecting the doctrine of "separate but equal" in *Brown.* In fact, the opinion lauds *Brown* in comparing it to *Roe.* This is strange, in that under the opinion's "legitimacy" principle the Court would seemingly have been forced to adhere to its erroneous decision in *Plessy* because of its "intensely divisive" character. To us, adherence to *Roe* today under the guise of "legitimacy" would seem to resemble more closely adherence to *Plessy* on the same ground. Fortunately, the Court did not choose that option in *Brown,* and instead frankly repudiated *Plessy.* The joint opinion concludes that such repudiation was justified only because of newly discovered evidence that segregation had the effect of treating one race as inferior to another. But [it] is clear that the same arguments made before the Court in *Brown* were made in *Plessy* as well. The Court in *Brown* simply recognized, as Justice Harlan had recognized beforehand, that the Fourteenth Amendment does not permit racial segregation. The rule of *Brown* is not tied to popular opinion about the evils of segregation; it is a judgment that the Equal Protection Clause does not permit racial segregation, no matter whether the public might come to believe that it is beneficial. On that ground it stands, and on that ground alone the Court was justified in properly concluding that the *Plessy* Court had erred.

There is also a suggestion in the joint opinion that the propriety of overruling a "divisive" decision depends in part on whether "most people" would now agree that it should be overruled. [How] such agreement would be ascertained, short of a public opinion poll, the joint opinion does not say. But surely even the suggestion is totally at war with the idea of "legitimacy" in whose name it is invoked. The Judicial Branch derives its legitimacy, not from following public opinion, but from deciding by its best lights whether legislative enactments of the popular branches of Government comport with the Constitution. The doctrine of *stare decisis* is an adjunct of this duty, and should be no more subject to the vagaries of public opinion than is the basic judicial task. * * *

Roe is not this Court's only decision to generate conflict. Our decisions in some recent capital cases, and in *Bowers v. Hardwick* (1986), have also engendered demonstrations in opposition. The joint opinion's message to such protesters appears to be that they must cease their activities in order to serve their cause, because their protests will only cement in place a decision which by normal standards of stare decisis should be reconsidered. * * * Strong and often misguided criticism of a decision should not render the decision immune from reconsideration, lest a fetish for legitimacy penalize freedom of expression.

The end result of the joint opinion's paeans of praise for legitimacy is the enunciation of a brand new standard for evaluating state regulation of a woman's right to abortion—the "undue burden" standard. As indicated above, *Roe* adopted a "fundamental right" standard under which state regulations could survive only if they met the requirement of "strict scrutiny." While we disagree with that standard, it at least had a recognized basis in constitutional law at the time *Roe* was decided. The same cannot be said for the "undue burden" standard, which is created largely out of whole cloth by the authors of the joint opinion. It is a standard which even today does not command the support of a majority of this Court. And it will not, we believe, result in the sort of "simple limitation," easily applied, which the joint opinion anticipates. In sum, it is a standard which is not built to last.

* * * Because the undue burden standard is plucked from nowhere, the question of what is a "substantial obstacle" to abortion will undoubtedly engender a variety of conflicting views. For example, in the very matter before us now, the authors of the joint opinion would uphold Pennsylvania's 24–hour waiting period, concluding that a "particular burden" on some women is not a substantial obstacle. But the authors would at the same time strike down Pennsylvania's spousal notice provision, after finding that in a "large fraction" of cases the provision will be a substantial obstacle. And, while the authors conclude that the informed consent provisions do not constitute an "undue burden," Justice Stevens would hold that they do.

Furthermore, while striking down the spousal *notice* regulation, the joint opinion would uphold a parental *consent* restriction that certainly places very substantial obstacles in the path of a minor's abortion choice. The joint opinion is forthright in admitting that it draws this distinction based on a policy judgment that parents will have the best interests of their children at heart, while the same is not necessarily true of husbands as to their wives. This may or may not be a correct judgment, but it is quintessentially a legislative one. The "undue burden" inquiry does not in any way supply the distinction between parental consent and spousal consent which the joint opinion adopts. Despite the efforts of the joint opinion, the undue burden standard presents nothing more workable than the trimester framework which it discards today. Under the guise of the Constitution, this Court will still impart its own preferences on the States in the form of a complex abortion code.

The sum of the joint opinion's labors in the name of *stare decisis* and "legitimacy" is this: *Roe* stands as a sort of judicial Potemkin Village, which may be pointed out to passers by as a monument to the importance of adhering to precedent. But behind the facade, an entirely new method of analysis, without any roots in constitutional law, is imported to decide the constitutionality of state laws regulating abortion. Neither *stare decisis* nor "legitimacy" are truly served by such an effort.

We have stated above our belief that the Constitution does not subject state abortion regulations to heightened scrutiny. Accordingly, we think that the correct analysis is that set forth by the plurality opinion in *Webster*. A woman's interest in having an abortion is a form of liberty protected by the Due Process Clause, but States may regulate abortion procedures in ways rationally related to a legitimate state interest.

[The Chief Justice then discussed each of the challenged provisions and concluded that each should be upheld. His comments on the spousal notification provision follow.]

We first emphasize that Pennsylvania has not imposed a spousal *consent* requirement of the type the Court struck down in *Danforth.* [T]his case involves a much less intrusive requirement of spousal *notification,* not consent. * * * *Danforth* thus does not control our analysis.

[The] question before us is [whether] the spousal notification requirement rationally furthers any legitimate state interests. We conclude that it does. First, a husband's interests in procreation within marriage and in the potential life of his unborn child are certainly substantial ones. [The] State itself has legitimate interests both in protecting these interests of the father and in protecting the potential life of the fetus, and the spousal notification requirement is reasonably related to advancing those state interests. [Second,] the spousal notice requirement is a rational attempt by the State to improve truthful communication between spouses and encourage collaborative decisionmaking, and thereby fosters marital integrity. [The] Pennsylvania Legislature was in a position to weigh the likely benefits of the provision against its likely adverse effects, and presumably concluded, on balance, that the provision would be beneficial. Whether this was a wise decision or not, we cannot say that it was irrational. * * *

JUSTICE SCALIA, with whom THE CHIEF JUSTICE, JUSTICE WHITE, and JUSTICE THOMAS join, concurring in the judgment in part and dissenting in part.

[The] States may, if they wish, permit abortion-on-demand, but the Constitution does not *require* them to do so. The permissibility of abortion, and the limitations upon it, are to be resolved like most important questions in our democracy: by citizens trying to persuade one another and then voting. [A] State's choice between two positions on which reasonable people can disagree is constitutional even when (as is often the case) it intrudes upon a "liberty" in the absolute sense. Laws against bigamy, for example—which entire societies of reasonable people disagree with—intrude upon men and women's liberty to marry and live with one another. But bigamy happens not to be a liberty specially "protected" by the Constitution.

That is, quite simply, the issue in this case: not whether the power of a woman to abort her unborn child is a "liberty" in the absolute sense; or even whether it is a liberty of great importance to many women. Of course it is both. The issue is whether it is a liberty protected by the Constitution of the United States. I am sure it is not. I reach that conclusion not because of anything so exalted as my views concerning the "concept of existence, of meaning, of the universe, and of the mystery of human life." Rather, I reach it for the same reason I reach the conclusion that bigamy is not constitutionally protected—because of two simple facts: (1) the Constitution says absolutely nothing about it, and (2) the longstanding traditions of American society have permitted it to be legally proscribed.[1]

1. The Court's suggestion that adherence to tradition would require us to uphold laws against interracial marriage is entirely wrong. Any tradition in that case was contradicted *by a text*—an Equal Protection Clause that explicitly establishes racial equality as a constitutional value. [The] enterprise launched in *Roe,* by contrast, sought to *establish*—in the teeth of a clear, contrary tradition—a value found nowhere in the constitutional text.

There is, of course, no comparable tradition barring recognition of a "liberty interest" in carrying one's child to term free from state efforts to kill it. For that reason, it does not follow that the Constitution does not protect childbirth simply because it does not protect abortion. The Court's contention that the only way to protect childbirth is to protect abortion shows the utter bankruptcy of constitutional analysis deprived of tradition as a validating factor. It drives one to say that the only way to protect the right to eat is to acknowledge the constitutional right to starve oneself to death.

The Court destroys the proposition, evidently meant to represent my position, that "liberty" includes "only those practices, defined at the most specific level, that were protected against government interference by other rules of law when the Fourteenth Amendment was ratified" (citing *Michael H. v. Gerald D.*) (opinion of Scalia, J.). That is not, however, what *Michael H.* says; it merely observes that, in defining "liberty," we may not disregard a specific, "relevant tradition protecting, or denying protection to, the asserted right." But the Court does not wish to be fettered by any such limitation on its preferences. The Court's statement that it is "tempting" to acknowledge the authoritativeness of tradition in order to "cur[b] the discretion of federal judges" is of course rhetoric rather than reality; no government official is "tempted" to place restraints upon his own freedom of action, which is why Lord Acton did not say "Power tends to purify." The Court's temptation is in the quite opposite and more natural direction—towards systematically eliminating checks upon its own power; and it succumbs.

Beyond that brief summary of the essence of my position, I [must] respond to a few of the more outrageous arguments in today's opinion, which it is beyond human nature to leave unanswered. I shall discuss each of them under a quotation from the Court's opinion to which they pertain.

"The inescapable fact is that adjudication of substantive due process claims may call upon the Court in interpreting the Constitution to exercise that same capacity which by tradition courts always have exercised: reasoned judgment."

* * * "[R]easoned judgment" does not begin by begging the question, as *Roe* and subsequent cases unquestionably did by assuming that what the State is protecting is the mere "potentiality of human life." The whole argument of abortion opponents is that what the Court calls the fetus and what others call the unborn child *is a human life*. Thus, whatever answer *Roe* came up with after conducting its "balancing" is bound to be wrong, unless it is correct that the human fetus is in some critical sense merely potentially human. There is of course no way to determine that as a legal matter; it is in fact a value judgment. Some societies have considered newborn children not yet human, or the incompetent elderly no longer so.

The authors of the joint opinion, of course, do not squarely contend that *Roe* was a *correct* application of "reasoned judgment"; merely that it must be followed, because of stare decisis. But in their exhaustive discussion of all the factors that go into the determination of when stare decisis should be observed and when disregarded, they never mention "how wrong was the decision on its face?"

[The] emptiness of the "reasoned judgment" that produced *Roe* is displayed in plain view by the fact that, after more than 19 years of effort by some of the brightest (and most determined) legal minds in the country, after more than 10 cases upholding abortion rights in this Court, and after dozens upon dozens of amicus briefs submitted in this and other cases, the best the Court can do to explain how it is that the word "liberty" *must* be thought to include the right to destroy human fetuses is to rattle off a collection of adjectives that simply decorate a value judgment and conceal a political choice. The right to abort, we are told, inheres in "liberty" because it is among "a person's most basic decisions," it involves a "most intimate and personal choic[e]," it is "central to personal dignity and autonomy," it "originate[s] within the zone of conscience and belief," it is "too intimate and personal" for state interference, it reflects "intimate views" of a "deep, personal character," it involves "intimate relationships," and notions of "personal autonomy and bodily integrity," and it concerns a particularly " 'important decisio[n].' " But it is obvious to anyone applying "reasoned judgment" that the same adjectives can be applied to many forms of conduct that this Court (including one of the Justices in today's majority, see *Bowers v. Hardwick*) has held are *not* entitled to constitutional protection— because, like abortion, they are forms of conduct that have long been criminalized in American society. Those adjectives might be applied, for example, to homosexual sodomy, polygamy, adult incest, and suicide * * *.

"Liberty finds no refuge in a jurisprudence of doubt."

One might have feared to encounter this august and sonorous phrase in an opinion defending the real *Roe v. Wade,* rather than the revised version fabricated today by the authors of the joint opinion. The shortcomings of *Roe* did not include lack of clarity: Virtually all regulation of abortion before the third trimester was invalid. But to come across this phrase in the joint opinion—which calls upon federal district judges to apply an "undue burden" standard as doubtful in application as it is unprincipled in origin—is really more than one should have to bear.

[The] joint opinion explains that a state regulation imposes an "undue burden" if it "has the purpose or effect of placing a substantial obstacle in the path of a woman seeking an abortion of a nonviable fetus." An obstacle is "substantial," we are told, if it is "calculated[,] [not] to inform the woman's free choice, [but to] hinder it." [4] This latter statement cannot possibly mean what it says. *Any* regulation of abortion that is intended to advance what the joint opinion concedes is the State's "substantial" interest in protecting unborn life will be "calculated [to] hinder" a decision to have an abortion. It thus seems more accurate to say that the joint opinion would uphold abortion regulations only if they do not *unduly* hinder the woman's decision. That, of course, brings us right back to square one: Defining an "undue burden" as an "undue hindrance" (or a "substantial obstacle") hardly "clarifies" the test. Consciously or not, the joint opinion's verbal shell game will conceal raw judicial policy choices concerning what is "appropriate" abortion legislation.

The ultimately standardless nature of the "undue burden" inquiry is a reflection of the underlying fact that the concept has no principled or coherent legal basis. [W]hat is remarkable about the joint opinion's fact-intensive analysis is that it does not result in any measurable clarification of the "undue burden" standard. Rather, the approach of the joint opinion is, for the most part, simply to highlight certain facts in the record that apparently strike the three Justices as particularly significant in establishing (or refuting) the existence of an undue burden; after describing these facts, the opinion then simply announces that the provision either does or does not impose a "substantial obstacle" or an "undue burden." We do not know whether the same conclusions could have been reached on a different record, or in what respects the record would have had to differ before an opposite conclusion would have been appropriate. The inherently standardless nature of this inquiry invites the district judge to give effect to his personal preferences about abortion. By finding and relying upon the right facts, he can invalidate, it would seem, almost any abortion restriction that strikes him

4. The joint opinion further asserts that a law imposing an undue burden on abortion decisions is not a "permissible" means of serving "legitimate" state interests. This description of the undue burden standard in terms more commonly associated with the rational-basis test will come as a surprise even to those who have followed closely our wanderings in this forsaken wilderness. * * *

as "undue"—subject, of course, to the possibility of being reversed by a Circuit Court or Supreme Court that is as unconstrained in reviewing his decision as he was in making it.

To the extent I can discern *any* meaningful content in the "undue burden" standard as applied in the joint opinion, it appears to be that a State may not regulate abortion in such a way as to reduce significantly its incidence. The joint opinion repeatedly emphasizes that an important factor in the "undue burden" analysis is whether the regulation "prevent[s] a significant number of women from obtaining an abortion," whether a "significant number of women [are] likely to be deterred from procuring an abortion," and whether the regulation often "deters" women from seeking abortions. We are not told, however, what forms of "deterrence" are impermissible or what degree of success in deterrence is too much to be tolerated. [As] Justice Blackmun recognizes (with evident hope), the "undue burden" standard may ultimately require the invalidation of each provision upheld today if it can be shown, on a better record, that the State is too effectively "express[ing] a preference for childbirth over abortion." Reason finds no refuge in this jurisprudence of confusion.

"While we appreciate the weight of the arguments * * * that *Roe* should be overruled, the reservations any of us may have in reaffirming the central holding of *Roe* are outweighed by the explication of individual liberty we have given combined with the force of stare decisis."

The Court's reliance upon stare decisis can best be described as contrived. It insists upon the necessity of adhering not to all of *Roe,* but only to what it calls the "central holding." It seems to me that stare decisis ought to be applied even to the doctrine of stare decisis, and I confess never to have heard of this new, keep-what-you-want-and-throw-away-the-rest version. I wonder whether, as applied to *Marbury v. Madison,* for example, the new version of stare decisis would be satisfied if we allowed courts to review the constitutionality of only those statutes that (like the one in *Marbury*) pertain to the jurisdiction of the courts.

I am certainly not in a good position to dispute that the Court *has saved* the "central holding" of *Roe,* since to do that effectively I would have to know what the Court has saved, which in turn would require me to understand (as I do not) what the "undue burden" test means. I must confess, however, that I have always thought, and I think a lot of other people have always thought, that the arbitrary trimester framework, which the Court today discards, was quite as central to *Roe* as the arbitrary viability test, which the Court today retains. It seems particularly ungrateful to carve the trimester framework out of the core of *Roe,* since its very rigidity (in sharp contrast to the utter indeterminability of the "undue burden" test) is probably the only reason the Court is able to say, in urging *stare decisis,* that *Roe* "has in no sense proven 'unworkable.' " I suppose the Court is entitled to call a "central holding" whatever it wants to call a "central holding"—which is, come to think of it, perhaps one of the difficulties with this modified version of *stare decisis.* I thought I might note, however, that the following portions of *Roe* have not been saved:

• Under *Roe,* requiring that a woman seeking an abortion be provided truthful information about abortion before giving informed written consent is unconstitutional, if the information is designed to influence her choice, *Thornburgh.* Under the joint opinion's "undue burden" regime (as applied today, at least) such a requirement is constitutional.

• Under *Roe,* requiring that information be provided by a doctor, rather than by nonphysician counselors, is unconstitutional, *Akron I.* Under the "undue burden" regime (as applied today, at least) it is not.

• Under *Roe,* requiring a 24–hour waiting period between the time the woman gives her informed consent and the time of the abortion is unconstitutional, *Akron I.* Under the "undue burden" regime (as applied today, at least) it is not.

• Under *Roe,* requiring detailed reports that include demographic data about each woman who seeks an abortion and various information about each abortion is unconstitutional, *Thornburgh.* Under the "undue burden" regime (as applied today, at least) it generally is not.

"Where, in the performance of its judicial duties, the Court decides a case in such a way as to resolve the sort of intensely divisive controversy reflected in *Roe* * * *, its decision has a dimension that the resolution of the normal case does not carry. It is the dimension present whenever the Court's interpretation of the Constitution calls the contending sides of a national controversy to end their national division by accepting a common mandate rooted in the Constitution."

[Not] only did *Roe* not, as the Court suggests, *resolve* the deeply divisive issue of abortion; it did more than anything else to nourish it, by elevating it to the national level where it is infinitely more difficult to resolve. National politics were not plagued by abortion protests, national abortion lobbying, or abortion marches on Congress, before *Roe* was decided. Profound disagreement existed among our citizens over the issue—as it does over other issues, such as the death penalty—but that disagreement was being worked out at the state level. As with many other issues, the division of sentiment within each State was not as closely balanced as it was among the population of the Nation as a whole, meaning not only that more people would be satisfied with the results of state-by-state resolution, but also that those results would be more stable. Pre–*Roe,* moreover, political compromise was possible.

Roe's mandate for abortion-on-demand destroyed the compromises of the past, rendered compromise impossible for the future, and required the entire issue to be resolved uniformly, at the national level. At the same time, *Roe* created a vast new class of abortion consumers and abortion proponents by eliminating the moral opprobrium that had attached to the act. ("If the Constitution *guarantees* abortion, how can it be bad?"—not an accurate line of thought, but a natural one.) Many favor all of those developments, and it is not for me to say that they are wrong. But to portray *Roe* as the statesmanlike "settlement" of a divisive issue, a jurisprudential Peace of Westphalia that is worth preserving, is nothing less than Orwellian. *Roe* fanned into life an issue that has inflamed our national politics in general, and has obscured with its smoke the selection of Justices to this Court in particular, ever since. And by keeping us in the abortion-umpiring business, it is the perpetuation of that disruption, rather than of any pax Roeana, that the Court's new majority decrees.

"[T]o overrule under fire [would] subvert the Court's legitimacy * * *.

"To all those who will be * * * tested by following, the Court implicitly undertakes to remain steadfast * * *. The promise of constancy, once given, binds its maker for as long as the power to stand by the decision survives [and] the commitment [is not] obsolete * * *.

"[The American people's] belief in themselves as * * * a people [who aspire to live according to the rule of law] is not readily separable from their understanding of the Court invested with the authority to decide their constitutional cases and speak before all others for their constitutional ideals. If the Court's legitimacy should be undermined, then, so would the country be in its very ability to see itself through its constitutional ideals."

The Imperial Judiciary lives. It is instructive to compare this Nietzschean vision of us unelected, life-tenured judges—leading a Volk who will be "tested by following," and whose very "belief in themselves" is mystically bound up in their "understanding" of a Court that "speak[s] before all others for their constitutional ideals"—with the somewhat more modest role envisioned for these lawyers by the Founders.

[It] is particularly difficult, in the circumstances of the present decision, to sit still for the Court's lengthy lecture upon the virtues of "constancy," of "remain[ing] steadfast," of adhering to "principle." Among the five Justices who purportedly adhere to *Roe*, at most three agree upon the *principle* that constitutes adherence (the joint opinion's "undue burden" standard)—and that principle is inconsistent with *Roe*.[7] To make matters worse, two of the three, in order thus to remain steadfast, had to abandon previously stated positions. [The] only principle the Court "adheres" to, it seems to me, is the principle that the Court must be seen as standing by *Roe*. That is not a principle of law (which is what I thought the Court was talking about), but a principle of *Realpolitik*—and a wrong one at that.

I cannot agree with, indeed I am appalled by, the Court's suggestion that the decision whether to stand by an erroneous constitutional decision must be strongly influenced—*against* overruling, no less—by the substantial and continuing public opposition the decision has generated. [In] my history-book, the Court was covered with dishonor and deprived of legitimacy by *Dred Scott*, an erroneous (and widely opposed) opinion that it did not abandon, rather than by *West Coast Hotel*, which produced the famous "switch in time" from the Court's erroneous (and widely opposed) constitutional opposition to the social measures of the New Deal. (Both *Dred Scott* and one line of the cases resisting the New Deal rested upon the concept of "substantive due process" that the Court praises and employs today. Indeed, *Dred Scott* was "very possibly the first application of substantive due process in the Supreme Court, the original precedent for *Lochner* and *Roe*." David Currie, *The Constitution in the Supreme Court* 271 (1985).)

But whether it would "subvert the Court's legitimacy" or not, the notion that we would decide a case differently from the way we otherwise would have in order to show that we can stand firm against public disapproval is frightening. [As] The Chief Justice points out, we have been subjected to what the Court calls "political pressure" by *both* sides of this issue. Maybe today's decision *not* to overrule *Roe* will be seen as buckling to pressure from *that* direction. Instead of engaging in the hopeless task of predicting public perception—a job not for lawyers but for political campaign managers—the Justices should do what is *legally* right by asking two questions: (1) Was *Roe* correctly decided? (2) Has *Roe*

---

7. Justice Blackmun's effort to preserve as much of *Roe* as possible leads him to read the joint opinion as more "constan[t]" and "steadfast" than can be believed. He contends that the joint opinion's "undue burden" standard requires the application of strict scrutiny to "all non-de-minimis" abortion regulations, but that could only be true if a "substantial obstacle" (joint opinion), were the same thing as a non-de-minimis obstacle—which it plainly is not.

succeeded in producing a settled body of law? If the answer to both questions is no, *Roe* should undoubtedly be overruled.

* * * All manner of "liberties," the Court tells us, inhere in the Constitution and are enforceable by this Court—not just those mentioned in the text or established in the traditions of our society. Why even the Ninth Amendment— which says only that "[t]he enumeration in the Constitution of certain rights shall not be construed to deny or disparage others retained by the people"—is, despite our contrary understanding for almost 200 years, a literally boundless source of additional, unnamed, unhinted-at "rights," definable and enforceable by us, through "reasoned judgment."

What makes all this relevant to the bothersome application of "political pressure" against the Court are the twin facts that the American people love democracy and the American people are not fools. As long as this Court thought (and the people thought) that we Justices were doing essentially lawyers' work up here—reading text and discerning our society's traditional understanding of that text—the public pretty much left us alone. Texts and traditions are facts to study, not convictions to demonstrate about. But if in reality our process of constitutional adjudication consists primarily of making *value judgments;* if we can ignore a long and clear tradition clarifying an ambiguous text, as we did, for example, five days ago in declaring unconstitutional invocations and benedictions at public-high-school graduation ceremonies, *Lee v. Weisman* [p. 1098 infra]; if, as I say, our pronouncement of constitutional law rests primarily on value judgments, then a free and intelligent people's attitude towards us can be expected to be (*ought* to be) quite different. The people know that their value judgments are quite as good as those taught in any law school—maybe better. If, indeed, the "liberties" protected by the Constitution are, as the Court says, undefined and unbounded, then the people *should* demonstrate, to protest that we do not implement *their* values instead of *ours*. Not only that, but confirmation hearings for new Justices *should* deteriorate into question-and-answer sessions in which Senators go through a list of their constituents' most favored and most disfavored alleged constitutional rights, and seek the nominee's commitment to support or oppose them. Value judgments, after all, should be voted on, not dictated; and if our Constitution has somehow accidentally committed them to the Supreme Court, at least we can have a sort of plebiscite each time a new nominee to that body is put forward. Justice Blackmun not only regards this prospect with equanimity, he solicits it. * * *

There is a poignant aspect to today's opinion. Its length, and what might be called its epic tone, suggest that its authors believe they are bringing to an end a troublesome era in the history of our Nation and of our Court. "It is the dimension" of authority, they say, to "cal[l] the contending sides of national controversy to end their national division by accepting a common mandate rooted in the Constitution."

There comes vividly to mind a portrait [that] hangs in the Harvard Law School: Roger Brooke Taney, painted in 1859, the 82d year of his life, the 24th of his Chief Justiceship, the second after his opinion in *Dred Scott*. [He] sits facing the viewer, and staring straight out. There seems to be on his face, and in his deep-set eyes, an expression of profound sadness and disillusionment. [Those] of us who know how the lustre of his great Chief Justiceship came to be eclipsed by *Dred Scott* cannot help believing that he had that case—its already apparent consequences for the Court, and its soon-to-be-played-out consequences for the Nation—burning on his mind. I expect that two years earlier he, too, had thought himself "call[ing] the contending sides of national controversy to end their national division by accepting a common mandate rooted in the Constitution."

It is no more realistic for us in this case, than it was for him in that, to think that an issue of the sort they both involved—an issue involving life and death, freedom and subjugation—can be "speedily and finally settled" by the Supreme Court, as President James Buchanan in his inaugural address said the issue of slavery in the territories would be. Quite to the contrary, by foreclosing all democratic outlet for the deep passions this issue arouses, by banishing the issue from the political forum that gives all participants, even the losers, the satisfaction of a fair hearing and an honest fight, by continuing the imposition of a rigid national rule instead of allowing for regional differences, the Court merely prolongs and intensifies the anguish.

We should get out of this area, where we have no right to be, and where we do neither ourselves nor the country any good by remaining.

Notes and Questions

1. *Was continuity and stability given undue prominence?* The authors of the joint opinion in *Casey* "were moved by the need for continuity and stability in constitutional law," observes Charles Fried, *Constitutional Doctrine,* 107 Harv. L.Rev. 1140, 1143 (1994), "yet paradoxically they seemed to give this factor undue prominence relative to their conviction of the rightness of the actual decision— almost as if the decision could not stand on its own and needed an apology." Do you agree?

2. *Roe, Lochner and Brown,* "How," asks Cass Sunstein, *The Partial Constitution* 259–60 (1993), "can one approve of *Roe,* recognizing the abortion right, while disapproving of *Lochner?* The question seems hard to answer if *Lochner* is understood as a case [interpreting] the due process clause to protect a 'fundamental right.' *Roe* used the due process clause in this very way. The case might therefore be thought to stand or fall together." But, continues Sunstein, "This is a crude and ahistorical approach to the *Lochner* period. To a nonlawyer who simply reads the text of the Constitution, it would seem odd indeed to suggest that if we think that maximum-hours laws are constitutionally valid, we must also accept laws restricting abortion. The two problems appear to have little to do with each other. Maximum hours plausibly promote human liberty. [At] the very least, abortion restrictions raise a set of wholly different questions. "[If] we shift our field of vision a little bit, we might as reasonably ask: If you approve of *Brown* 's invalidation of segregation, how can you disapprove of *Roe?* On this view, *Brown* represented a judicial invalidation of a law contributing to second-class citizenship for a group of Americans defined in terms of a morally irrelevant characteristic (race)—and *Roe* represented exactly the same thing (with respect to gender). Of course *Roe* can be distinguished from *Brown*[, but] it is probably more fruitful to think of *Roe,* not as a rerun of *Lochner,* but as raising many of the same sorts of questions at issue in *Brown.* "

3. *Why should the abortion issue be decided on the level of the individual rather than on the level of the state?* Answers David Strauss, *Abortion, Toleration, and Moral Uncertainty,* 1992 Sup.Ct.Rev. 1, 18–20:

"This is the point at which the status of women, properly emphasized by *Casey,* becomes important. Allowing the abortion decision to be made at the political level, instead of the individual level, would create an impermissible risk of subordinating women. [Although] the Court has never made it entirely clear why discrimination against women is unconstitutional, it seems plausible to suppose that at least three aspects of the status of women in society, all relevant to the abortion issue, underlie this principle.

"First, the political process has a persistent tendency generally to undervalue the interests of women. [Second,] women's bodily integrity, in particular, is systematically undervalued. The Court's opinion in *Casey* alluded to this aspect of women's status. [Third,] women are treated as people whose principal responsibility is childbearing and child rearing. They are not seen as full participants in the labor market. [*Casey* did not] make clear the exact connection between the status of women and the abortion issue. The connection, I believe, is this: the tendency to subordinate women in these three ways disqualifies the political process from resolving the moral uncertainty that is central to the abortion debate. There is too great a danger that if the political process decides the abortion issue, that decision will be an act of subordinating women in one or more of these ways."

4. *The worst of all possible worlds?* Consider Sylvia Law, *Abortion Compromise—Inevitable and Impossible,* 1992 U.Ill.L.Rev. 921, 931: "From a pro-choice point of view, one plausible assessment of the *Casey* decision is that is represents the worst of all possible worlds. The joint opinion affirmed a woman's 'fundamental constitutional right' to abortion, but simultaneously allowed the state to adopt measures that effectively curtail *many* women's exercise of the abortion right. This curtailment hits hardest those women who are most vulnerable, i.e., the poor, the unsophisticated, the young, and women who live in rural areas. The abstract recognition of a right to abortion could dampen political enthusiasm in support of reproductive choice.[a] The initial reaction to the *Casey* decision, however, suggests that this is not the case. The margin of Supreme Court support for even the abstract affirmation of reproductive freedom is only one vote. Further it seems that most Americans are not so naive as to believe that their rights to control their bodies and lives have been secured by this decision. Only time will tell."

5. *Spousal notification vs. parental consent.* Consider 106 Harv.L.Rev. 163, 206–08 (1992): "Surface distinctions between pregnant adolescents and pregnant adults notwithstanding, the Court provided no principled basis for striking down the spousal notification clause because of the recognized potential for domestic violence while nonetheless upholding the parental consent requirement. * * * Tragically, in its application of the undue burden test, the Court failed to accord pregnant adolescent victims of family violence the same protection it granted similarly victimized pregnant women. [When] inflicted on adolescents, however, domestic violence has even more devastating consequences. * * * Given that '[m]illions of children in the United States are victims of physical, sexual and emotional abuse,' [*Casey*'s] assumption that 'minors will benefit from consultation with their parents and that children will often not realize that their parents have their best interests at heart' must seem a cruel irony to pregnant adolescents trapped in violent homes."[b]

a. "It is much harder to mobilize pro-choice lobbying, voting and fund-raising efforts, "observes Kathleen Sullivan, *Foreword: The Justices of Rules and Standards,* 106 Harv.L.Rev. 24, 110 (1992), "if *Roe* is nickel-and-dimed away rather than frankly overruled. * * * Why didn't pro-choice activists celebrate when five Justices reaffirmed 'the essential holding of *Roe*'? Because the Court stole their thunder by adopting a moderate, difference-splitting standard."

b. The Note goes on to say, id. at 208–09, that the obstacles posed by parental consent are not relieved by a judicial bypass option: "In order to exercise the judicial bypass option, a pregnant minor must navigate the judicial

6. *The spousal notification requirement vs. the 24–hour waiting period.*
According to Martha Field, *Abortion Law Today*, 14 J.Legal Med. 3, 13 (1993),
"the most serious issue *Casey* leaves open" is the scope of the cutback on *Roe*.
She continues, id. at 13–14:

"One reason the scope of the cutback is unknowable is that *Casey* itself seems
utterly inconsistent. The spousal notification requirement is analyzed as posing
an undue burden—a substantial obstacle to abortion—while the waiting period is
not. [It] was irrelevant that only a small fraction of women seeking abortion
would be burdened by the [spousal notification requirement], because '[t]he
proper focus of constitutional inquiry is the group for whom the law is a
restriction, not the group for whom the law is irrelevant.' But the same
conditions obtain with respect to the requirement that a woman wait 24 hours
after the 'informed consent' lecture before she can have an abortion. For most or
many [the] waiting period may not pose a serious problem, but for rural women
who must travel to an urban area to obtain an abortion, the cost of the additional
day may be prohibitive. Similarly those who must travel for abortion services and
who must be secretive about obtaining an abortion may have much more difficulty
explaining their absence if they must be away an extra 24 hours. With a waiting
period, these women are as impeded from obtaining an abortion as those who fear
husband notification."

But consider James Boyd White, *Acts of Hope* 181 (1994): "The part of the
[joint] opinion approving [the waiting period] requirement seems written by an
altogether different hand from the portion striking down the requirement that the
husband be notified, where the Court seems to recognize with some fullness both
the plight of the woman and what it would mean for the law to tell her what to do
in this case. On these grounds in particular, [some] have been infuriated with the
opinion. But this argument does not address the central moral fact of *Casey*,
which is that the writers of the Joint Opinion would presumably not have
supported *Roe* when it was first decided—a position to which they are surely
entitled—yet are compelled by a combination of its merits, as they now see and
define them, with their sense of obligation to the past, to uphold it."

7. *The alternative to an undue burden approach.* "[T]he adoption of an
expansively applied undue burden standard is hardly a panacea for the protection
of fundamental rights," recognizes Alan Brownstein, *How Rights Are Infringed:
The Role of Undue Burden Analysis in Constitutional Doctrine*, 45 Hast.L.J. 867,
958 (1994), for the balancing of burdens against the state's interests "is far more
conducive to judicial deference to the legislature than are categorical rules of
review." [c] The alternative, however, warns Professor Brownstein, "may be even
more limited and restrictive":

"If the only choice is between protecting the exercise of a right against all
burdens under strict scrutiny review or interpreting the interest at stake as
something other than a right and providing it no constitutional protection at all,

system. The assumption that this process
does not present substantial obstacles ignores
some basic realities. Teenagers are intimidated by the courts and find them inaccessible. A
confused pregnant teen who feels isolated and
frightened will be greatly deterred in her abortion choice by the prospect of bypassing her
parents and discussing intimate details about
her sexual activity with a judge."

  c. See also Sullivan, fn. a supra, at 111,
noting (shortly after the case was decided) that

"*Casey*'s undue burden test will be applied
principally by the lower federal courts, and
Presidents Reagan and Bush, who ran on anti-
abortion platforms, have appointed nearly 70%
of the sitting judges. No wonder lawyers for
the pro-choice side predict that the undue burden test will be applied in practice to uphold
more antiabortion measures than the test will
strike down."

the latter option may be selected in far too many circumstances. It may be implicit in the framework offered by the critics of the 'undue burden' standard that rights are rarely recognized, although they receive aggressive protection in those few circumstances when they are found to exist."

FAMILY LIVING ARRANGEMENTS, PARENTAL RIGHTS, AND THE "RIGHT TO MARRY"

As illustrated by WHALEN v. ROE, 429 U.S. 589, 97 S.Ct. 869, 51 L.Ed.2d 64 (1977) (sustaining a New York law that doctors disclose the names of persons obtaining certain drugs for storage in a central computer file), those attacking legislation can often cast their challenge in terms of an invasion of a constitutionally protected "zone of privacy." But the Court upheld the legislation as "a reasonable exercise of New York's broad police powers," holding that the program did not require extraordinary justification because it "does not, on its face, pose a sufficiently grievous threat" to either the "privacy" interest "in avoiding disclosure of personal matters" [a] or the "privacy" interest "in independence in making certain kinds of important decisions [e.g., abortion, marriage]." The cases discussed below deal with the latter "privacy" interest.

1. *Zoning; choice of household companions; "extended family" relationships.* Relying on earlier decisions sustaining local zoning regulations, BELLE TERRE v. BORAAS, 416 U.S. 1, 94 S.Ct. 1536, 39 L.Ed.2d 797 (1974), per DOUGLAS, J., upheld a village ordinance restricting land use to one-family dwellings (defining "family" to mean not more than two unrelated persons living together as a single housekeeping unit, and expressly excluding from the term lodging, boarding, fraternity or multiple-dwelling houses). Appellees, who had leased their houses to six unrelated college students, challenged the ordinance, inter alia, on the ground that it "trenches on the newcomers' rights of privacy." The Court disagreed: "We deal with economic and social legislation where legislatures have historically drawn lines which we respect [if the law] bears 'a rational relationship to a [permissible] state objective.' " "[B]oarding houses, fraternity houses, and the like present urban problems. [The] police power is not confined to elimination of filth, stench, and unhealthy places."

MARSHALL, J., dissented: The ordinance burdened "fundamental rights of association and privacy," and thus required extraordinary justification, not a mere

---

a. The Court, however, specifically did *not* decide "any question which might be presented by the unwarranted disclosure of accumulated private data—whether intentional or unintentional—or by a system that did not contain [adequate] security provisions."

See also *Paul v. Davis,* per Rehnquist, J., Sec. 5, I infra, holding that police disclosure of a person's shoplifting arrest did not violate his right of privacy: "His claim is based not upon any challenge to the State's ability to restrict his freedom of action in a sphere contended to be 'private,' but instead on a claim that the State may not publicize a record of an official

act such as an arrest. None of our substantive privacy decisions hold this or anything like this and we decline to enlarge them in this manner." Brennan, J., joined by Marshall, J., observed that "a host of state and federal courts, relying on both privacy notions and the presumption of innocence, have begun to develop a line of cases holding that there are substantive limits on the power of the Government to disseminate unresolved arrest records outside the law enforcement [system]. I fear that after today's decision, these nascent doctrines will never have the opportunity for full growth and analysis."

showing that the ordinance "bears a rational relationship to the accomplishment of legitimate governmental objectives." He viewed "the right to 'establish a home'" as an "essential part" of fourteenth amendment liberty and maintained that "the choice of household companions"—which "involves deeply personal considerations as to the kind and quality of intimate relationships within the home"—"surely falls within the right to privacy protected by the Constitution." The state's purposes "could be as effectively achieved by means of an ordinance that did not discriminate on the basis of constitutionally protected choices of life style." [b]

Distinguishing *Belle Terre* as involving an ordinance "affect[ing] only *unrelated* individuals," MOORE v. EAST CLEVELAND, 431 U.S. 494, 97 S.Ct. 1932, 52 L.Ed.2d 531 (1977), invalidated a housing ordinance that limited occupancy to single families, but defined "family" so as to forbid appellant from having her two grandsons live with her. (It did not permit living arrangements if, as in this case, the grandchildren were cousins rather than brothers.) [a] POWELL, J., announcing the Court's judgment and joined by Brennan, Marshall, and Blackmun, JJ., struck down the ordinance on substantive due process grounds:

"[O]n its face [the ordinance] selects certain categories of relatives who may live together and declares that others may not. [When] a city undertakes such intrusive regulation of the family [the] usual judicial deference to the legislature is inappropriate. 'This Court has long recognized that freedom of personal choice in matters of marriage and family life is one of the liberties protected by [due process].' Of course the family is not beyond regulation. But when the government intrudes on choices concerning family living arrangements, this Court must examine carefully the importance of the governmental interests advanced and the extent to which they are served by the challenged regulation [referring to Harlan, J.'s dissent in *Poe v. Ullman*]." "[T]hus examined, this ordinance cannot survive." [3] Although the city's goals—preventing overcrowding, minimizing congestion and avoiding financial strain on its school system—were "legitimate," the ordinance served them "marginally at best."

"[T]he history of the *Lochner* [era] counsels caution and restraint [but] it does [not] require what the city urges here: cutting off any family rights at the first convenient, if arbitrary boundary—the boundary of the nuclear family. * * * Appropriate limits on substantive due process come not from drawing arbitrary lines but rather from careful 'respect for the teachings of history [and] solid recognition of the basic values that underlie our society.' *Griswold* (Harlan, J., concurring). Our decisions teach that the Constitution protects the sanctity of the family precisely because the institution of the family is deeply rooted in this Nation's history and tradition. [Ours] is by no means a tradition limited to respect for [the] nuclear family. The tradition of uncles, aunts, cousins, and especially grandparents sharing a household along with parents and children [especially in times of adversity] has roots equally venerable and equally deserving of constitutional recognition. [In *Pierce*, the Constitution prevented a state from] 'standardiz[ing] its children by forcing them to accept instruction from public

---

b. Compare Marshall, J.'s views in *Belle Terre* with the Court's discussion of "freedom of intimate association" in *Roberts v. United States Jaycees,* p. 894 infra. See also the Court's discussion of "the freedom to enter into and carry on certain intimate of private relationships" in *Board of Directors of Rotary International v. Rotary Club of Duarte*, p. 899 infra.

a. The second grandson came to live with his grandmother after the death of his mother.

3. Appellant also claims that the ordinance contravenes the Equal Protection Clause, but it is not necessary for us to reach that contention.

teachers only.' By the same token the Constitution prevents East Cleveland from standardizing its children—and its adults—by forcing all to live in certain narrowly defined family patterns."[b]

STEWART, J., joined by Rehnquist, J., dissented, rejecting the argument that "the importance of the 'extended family' in American society" renders appellant's "decision to share her residence with her grandsons," like the decisions involved in bearing and raising children, "an aspect of 'family life' " entitled to substantive constitutional protection. To equate appellant's interest in sharing her residence with some of her relatives "with the fundamental decisions to marry and to bear children," he maintained, "is to extend the limited substantive contours of the Due Process Clause beyond recognition." He thought the challenged "family" definition "rationally designed to carry out the legitimate governmental purposes identified in *Belle Terre*." A different line "could hardly be drawn that would not sooner or later become the target of a challenge like the appellant's," such as "the hard case of an orphaned niece or nephew."

Nor could he understand why "the traditional importance of the extended family in America" need imply "that the residents of East Cleveland are constitutionally prevented from following what Justice Brennan calls the 'pattern' of 'white suburbia,' even though that choice may reflect 'cultural myopia.' In point of fact, East Cleveland is a predominantly Negro community, with a Negro City Manager and City Commission."[c]

WHITE, J., dissenting, voiced disbelief "that the interest in residing with more than one set of grandchildren is one that calls for any kind of heightened protection under the Due Process Clause. [The] present claim is hardly one of which it could be said that 'neither liberty nor justice would exist if [it] were sacrificed.' *Palko*."

He maintained that Powell, J.'s approach—construing the Due Process Clause to protect from all but "quite important" state interests any right "that in his estimate is deeply rooted in the country's traditions"—"suggests a far too expansive charter for this Court. [What] the deeply rooted traditions of the country are

---

b. Brennan, J., joined by Marshall, J., concurred, characterizing the ordinance as "senseless," "arbitrary" and "eccentric" and as reflecting "cultural myopia" and "a distressing insensitivity toward the economic and emotional needs of a very large part of our society." He called the "extended family" "virtually a means of survival" for many poor and black families. [The] 'nuclear family' is the pattern so often found in much of white suburbia," but "the Constitution cannot * * * tolerate the imposition by government upon the rest of us of white suburbia's preference in patterns of family living." But see dissenting Justice Stewart's response, infra.

Stevens, J., concurring, thought this "unprecedented ordinance" unconstitutional even under the "limited standard of review of zoning decisions": "The city has failed totally to explain the need for a rule which would allow a homeowner to have two grandchildren live with her if they are brothers, but not if they are cousins. Since the ordinance has not been shown to have any 'substantial relation to

[East Cleveland's] public health, safety, morals or general welfare' [and] since it cuts so deeply into a fundamental right normally associated with the ownership of residential property— that of an owner to decide who may reside on his or her property—it must fall [as] a taking of property without due process and without just compensation."

c. "[I]n assessing [appellant's] claim that the ordinance is 'arbitrary' and 'irrational,' " Stewart, J., considered a provision permitting her to request a variance "particularly persuasive evidence to the contrary. [The] variance procedure, a traditional part of American land-use law, bends the straight lines of East Cleveland's ordinance, shaping their contours to respond more flexibly to the hard cases that are the inevitable byproduct of legislative line-drawing."

Burger, C.J., dissented on the ground that appellant should have pursued the "plainly adequate administrative remedy" of seeking a variance, thus finding it "unnecessary to reach the difficult constitutional issue."

is arguable; which of them deserve [due process protection] is even more debatable. The suggested view would broaden enormously the horizons of the Clause." [d]

Notes and Questions

(a) *The elusiveness of the search for sources of fundamental rights. Moore v. East Cleveland,* maintains Joseph Grano, *Judicial Review and a Written Constitution in a Democratic Society,* 28 Wayne L.Rev. 1, 25–27 (1981), "demonstrates both how elusive the search for sources of fundamental rights can be and how unsatisfying the Court's attempts at demonstration necessarily are. Justice Powell's plurality opinion concluded that 'the Constitution protects the sanctity of the family precisely because the institution of the family is deeply rooted in the Nation's history and tradition.' Societies do change, however, and cognizant of this, the Court could not have intended to become constitutionally committed to every practice rooted in our history and tradition. In particular, progress toward racial and sexual equality depends upon success in freeing ourselves from the yoke of history and tradition. Moreover, by implication, Justice Powell's opinion suggested that the result would have been different had an unrelated neighbor taken charge of Mrs. Moore's grandson, [but did not explain] why history and tradition would not protect a neighbor's decision to do what Mrs. Moore did. Nor did he explain why, if it would not, history and tradition should be determinative. [Justice White's dissent], while accepting noninterpretivism with caution, rejected Justice Powell's history and tradition test for defining fundamental rights. [T]he issue that prompted [the Powell-White] exchange is intractable: freed from the need to use the written Constitution as a source of judgment, noninterpretivist judges may select any source that is personally appealing." [a]

(b) *Should Moore have been decided on "naked substantive due process grounds"?* *Moore*'s choice of rationale, comments Ira Lupu, *Untangling the Strands of the Fourteenth Amendment,* 77 Mich.L.Rev. 981, 1017 (1979), "reversed a pattern that had endured for four decades: it was the first decision since the 1937 revolution to invalidate a statute on naked substantive due process grounds when equal protection grounds seemed readily available. [*Griswold* and *Roe*] had not presented such alternatives; in both cases, the complained-of prohibition swept broadly across the state's entire population, and thus offered no classification readily subject to equal protection attack. In *Moore,* by contrast, the 'family' definition in the ordinance seemed perfect for invalidation as an arbitrary [classification]. The plurality opinion stood at least thirty years of conventional wisdom on its head by adopting a substantive due process theory and proclaiming in a one-sentence footnote that the due process holding rendered it unnecessary for the Court to reach the equal protection claims."

If *Moore* had invalidated the ordinance on equal protection grounds, observes Lupu, at 1019, it might have suggested "the permissibility of other, less arbitrary definitions of 'family.' Instead, *Moore* holds that families, defined by blood and marriage relations, cannot be carved up unless such limitations are critically necessary to achieve substantial zoning objectives." [b]

---

d. "[A]n approach grounded in history," replied Justice Powell [fn. 12], "imposes limits on the judiciary that are more meaningful than any based on [White, J.'s] abstract formula taken from *Palko.*"

a. But see Robert Sedler, *The Legitimacy Debate in Constitutional Adjudication,* 44 Ohio St.L.J. 93, 111–13 (1983) (neither White, J.,

who alluded to the legitimacy question in *Moore,* nor any other justice on the Court "has ever disputed that it was legitimate for the Court to have imputed a substantive meaning to the due process clause").

b. But see Thomas Gerety, *Doing Without Privacy,* 42 Ohio St.L.J. 143, 156–59 (1981) (*Moore* demonstrates need for "privacy" ratio-

(c) *Was the purpose of the ordinance quite straightforward?* How significant is it that "East Cleveland is a predominantly Negro community, with a Negro City Manager and City Commissioner"? Consider Robert Burt, *The Constitution of the Family,* 1979 Sup.Ct.Rev. 329, 389: "The plurality viewed the ordinance as directed against [over-crowding, minimizing traffic and the like, but] did not consider that the purpose of the ordinance was quite straightforward: to exclude from a middle-class, predominantly black community, that saw itself as socially and economically upwardly mobile, other black families most characteristic of lower-class ghetto life. Perhaps the Court did not see this purpose or, if it did, considered this an 'illegitimate goal,' though in other cases the Court had been exceedingly solicitous of white middle-class communities' attempts to preserve a common social identity—'zones,' as the Court had put the matter three years earlier [in *Belle Terre*]—'where family values, youth values, and the blessings of the quiet seclusion and clean air make the area a sanctuary for people.' [Although Brennan, J., had dissented in *Belle Terre*], I find in his characterization of the East Cleveland ordinance as 'senseless' and 'eccentric,' precisely what he alleges in it: 'a depressing insensitivity toward the economic and emotional needs' of the current majority of residents in East Cleveland."

(d) *Was Moore a dispute about the meaning of "family"?* Which way does it cut that the East Cleveland ordinance was "unusual" or even "eccentric"? Was victory for Mrs. Moore "total defeat" for the other city residents, but victory for them "not total defeat for her, except insofar as she wished to remain in their community while transferring its membership to her taste"? Consider Burt, supra, at 391: "[T]he very oddity of the East Cleveland ordinance suggests that Mrs. Moore is not alone in her opposition to it, that the city residents are more the vulnerable, isolated dissenters than she in the broader society, that they more than she deserve special judicial solicitude as a 'discrete and insular minority.' The Court in *Moore* myopically saw the case as a dispute between 'a family' and 'the state' rather than as a dispute among citizens about the meaning of 'family.' "

(e) *The blood relationship of the parties.* The *Moore* plurality emphasized the blood relationship of the parties. Should this factor be regarded as decisive? Consider Tribe, *Treatise* at 1420: "If a city or town may require that every home be occupied by a single 'family' consisting entirely of persons related by blood or marriage, it would be difficult to respond to the argument that the same city or town may also decide what a 'family' is: If longtime friends can be excluded by ordinance, why not second cousins? And if second cousins, why not certain grandchildren?" Should governmental interference with *any* "enduring relationships" be invalidated unless compellingly justified? See id. Could a town prohibit unmarried people or homosexuals from living together? Compare Kenneth Karst, *The Freedom of Intimate Association,* 89 Yale L.J. 624, 686–89 (1980) with Bruce Hafen, *The Constitutional Status of Marriage, Kinship, and Sexual Privacy,* 81 Mich.L.Rev. 463, 487, 559 (1983).

2. *Adoption and rights of the natural father.* QUILLOIN v. WALCOTT, 434 U.S. 246, 98 S.Ct. 549, 54 L.Ed.2d 511 (1978): Under Georgia law, if the natural father has not "legitimated" his offspring (appellant had not sought to do so during the 11 years between the child's birth and the adoption petition), only the mother's consent is required for the adoption of the illegitimate child. When the child was 11, the mother consented to his adoption by her husband with whom she and her son were living. Appellant attempted to block the adoption, but did

nale and inadequacy of "pure equal protection   theory of individual rights").

not seek custody or object to the child's continuing to live with his mother and stepfather. On the basis of various findings (e.g., appellant had provided support only on an irregular basis, the child himself expressed a desire to be adopted by his stepfather who was found to be fit to adopt the child), the trial court concluded that the adoption would be in the "best interests of the child."

A unanimous Court, per MARSHALL, J., affirmed: "We have recognized on numerous occasions that the relationship between parent and child is constitutionally protected, e.g. *Wisconsin v. Yoder* [discussed at pp. 1107, 1108 infra]; *Stanley v. Illinois,* 405 U.S. 645, 92 S.Ct. 1208, 31 L.Ed.2d 551 (1972) [and] [w]e have little doubt that the Due Process Clause would be offended '[i]f a State were to attempt to force the breakup of a natural family, over the objection of the parents and their children, without some showing of unfitness and for the sole reason that to do so was thought to be in the children's best interests.' *Smith v. Organization of Foster Families,* 431 U.S. 816, 862, 97 S.Ct. 2094, 2118, 53 L.Ed.2d 14 (1977) (Stewart, J., concurring). But this is not a case [where] the unwed father had, or sought [custody, or where] the proposed adoption would place the child with a new set of parents with whom the child had never before lived. Rather, the result of the adoption in this case is to give full recognition to a family unit already in existence, a result desired by all concerned, except appellant. [Under these circumstances it suffices that the state found] that the adoption, and denial of legitimation, was in the 'best interests of the child.' "

3. *Right to marry.* ZABLOCKI v. REDHAIL, 434 U.S. 374, 98 S.Ct. 673, 54 L.Ed.2d 618 (1978): A Wisconsin law forbade marriage by any resident with minor children not in his custody whom he is under court order to support, unless he proves compliance with the support obligation and that the children "are not then and are not likely thereafter to become public charges." Appellee and the woman he desired to marry were expecting a child, but he was denied a marriage license because he had not satisfied his support obligations to his illegitimate child who had been a public charge since birth. In striking down the marriage prohibition under the "fundamental rights" branch of equal protection doctrine (see Ch. 11, Sec. 4) the Court, per MARSHALL, J., observed:

"Since our past decisions make clear that the right to marry is of fundamental importance, and since the classification at issue here significantly interferes with the exercise of that right, we believe that 'critical examination' of the state's interests advanced in support of the classification is required. [Cases] subsequent to *Griswold* and *Loving v. Virginia* (1967) [p. 1086 infra, invalidating state miscegenation laws] have routinely categorized the decision to marry as among the personal decisions protected by the right of privacy. [It] is not surprising that the decision to marry has been placed on the same level of importance as decisions relating to procreation, childbirth, child rearing, and family relationships [for] it would make little sense to recognize a right of privacy with respect to other matters of family life and not with respect to the decision to enter the relationship that is the foundation of the family in our society. The woman whom appellee desired to marry had a fundamental right to seek an abortion of their expected child or to bring the child into life to suffer [the] disabilities that the status of illegitimacy brings. Surely, a decision to marry and raise the child in a traditional family setting must receive equivalent protection. And, if appellee's right to procreate means anything at all, it must imply some right to enter the only relationship in which [the state] allows sexual relations legally to take place.

"By reaffirming the fundamental character of the right to marry, we do not mean to suggest that every state regulation which relates in any way to the incidents of or prerequisites for marriage must be subjected to rigorous scrutiny. [R]easonable regulations that do not significantly interfere with decisions to enter into the marital relationships may legitimately be imposed. See *Califano v. Jobst,* 434 U.S. 47, 98 S.Ct. 95, 54 L.Ed.2d 228 (1977), n. 12 infra." However, because the statute prevents any Wisconsin resident in the affected class from marrying anywhere without a court order, some in the affected class, like appellee, "are absolutely prevented from ever getting married," for "they either lack the financial means to meet their support obligations or cannot prove that their children will not become public charges"; and because "many others [will] be sufficiently burdened by having to [satisfy the statute's requirements] that they will in effect be coerced into foregoing their right to marry," this statute "clearly does interfere directly and substantially with the right to marry.[12]

"When a statutory classification significantly interferes with the exercise of a fundamental right, it cannot be upheld unless it is supported by sufficiently important state interests and is closely tailored to effectuate only those interests. [Assuming that the state interests said to be served by the statute—furnishing an opportunity to counsel the applicant as to the need to fulfill his prior support obligations, and protecting the welfare of the out-of-custody children—] are legitimate and substantial interests, [since] the means selected by the State for achieving these interests unnecessarily impinge on the right to marry, the statute cannot be sustained.

"[The counseling interest] obviously cannot support the withholding of court permission to marry once counseling is completed. [As for the argument that the statute provides incentive for the applicant to make support payments to his children], with respect to [those] unable to meet the statutory requirements, the statute merely prevents the applicant from getting married, without delivering any money at all into the hands of the [children]. More importantly, [the] State already has numerous other means for exacting compliance with support obligations, means that are at least as effective as the instant statute's and yet do not impinge upon the right to marry [such as wage assignments, civil contempt proceedings and criminal penalties]."

As for the suggestion that the statute protects the ability of marriage applicants to meet prior support obligations by preventing the applicants from incurring new ones, the statute is "grossly underinclusive" since it in no way limits other new financial commitments and "substantially overinclusive as well," for the new spouse may actually improve the applicant's financial situation. "[P]reventing the marriage may only result in [new] children being born out of wedlock, as in fact occurred in appellee's case. Since the support obligation is the same whether the child is born in or out of wedlock, the net result of preventing the marriage is simply more illegitimate children." [a]

12. The directness and substantiality of the interference with the freedom to marry distinguish the instant case from *Jobst.* In *Jobst* [applying the "rationality" standard of review] we upheld sections of the Social Security Act providing, inter alia, for termination of a dependent child's benefits upon marriage to an individual not entitled to benefits under the Act. As the opinion for the Court expressly noted, the rule terminating benefits upon marriage was not "an attempt to interfere with the individual's freedom to make a decision as important as marriage." The Social Security provisions placed no direct legal obstacle in the path of persons desiring to get married, [and] there was no evidence that the laws significantly discouraged, let alone made "practically impossible," any marriages. Indeed, the provisions had not deterred the individual who challenged the statute from getting married, even though he and his wife were both disabled.
* * *

a. Burger, C.J., joined the Court's opinion and briefly concurred.

STEWART, J., concurred: "I do not agree [that] there is a 'right to marry' in the constitutional sense. [A] State may not only 'significantly interfere with decisions to enter into the marriage relationship,' but may in many circumstances absolutely prohibit it. Surely, for example, a State may legitimately say that no one can marry his or her sibling, that no one can marry who is not at least 14 years old, that no one can marry without first passing an examination for venereal disease, or that no one can marry who has a living husband or wife. But, just as surely, in regulating the intimate human relationship of marriage, there is a limit beyond which a State may not constitutionally go.

"[S]ome people simply cannot afford to meet the statute's financial requirements. To deny these people permission to marry penalizes them for failing to do that which they cannot do. Insofar as it applies to indigents, the state law is an irrational means of achieving these objectives of the State. As directed against either the indigent or the delinquent parent, the law is substantially more rational if viewed as a means of assuring the financial viability of future marriages. [But] the State's legitimate concern with the financial soundness of prospective marriages must stop short of telling people they may not marry because they are too poor or because they might persist in their financial irresponsibility. The invasion of constitutionally protected liberty and the chance of erroneous prediction are simply too great. A legislative judgment so alien to our traditions and so offensive to our shared notions of fairness offends the Due Process Clause of the Fourteenth Amendment.

"[E]qual protection doctrine has become the Court's chief instrument for invalidating state laws. Yet, in a case like this one, the doctrine is no more than substantive due process by another name. [T]he effect of the Court's decision in this case is not to require Wisconsin to draw its legislative classifications with greater precision or to afford similar treatment to similarly situated persons. Rather, the message of the Court's opinion is that Wisconsin may not use its control over marriage to achieve the objectives of the state statute. Such restrictions on basic governmental power are at the heart of substantive due process. The Court is understandably reluctant to rely on substantive due process. But to embrace the essence of that doctrine under the guise of equal protection serves no purpose but obfuscation."

POWELL, J., concurred in the judgment, but wrote separately "because the majority's rationale sweeps too broadly in an area which traditionally has been subject to state regulation": "The Court apparently would subject all state regulation which 'directly and substantially' interferes with the decision to marry in a traditional family setting to 'critical examination' or 'compelling state interest' analysis. Presumably, 'reasonable regulations that do not significantly interfere with decisions to enter into the marital relationship may legitimately be imposed.' The Court does not present, however, any principled means for distinguishing between the two types of regulations. Since state regulation in this area typically takes the form of a prerequisite or barrier to marriage or divorce, the degree of 'direct' interference with the decision to marry or to divorce is unlikely to provide either guidance for state legislatures or a basis for judicial oversight.

"[State] regulation has included bans on incest, bigamy, and homosexuality, as well as various preconditions to marriage, such as blood tests. Likewise, a showing of fault on the part of one of the partners traditionally has been a prerequisite to the dissolution of an unsuccessful union. A 'compelling state purpose' inquiry would cast doubt on the network of restrictions that the States have fashioned to govern marriage and divorce.

"State power over domestic relations is not without constitutional limits. The Due Process Clause requires a showing of justification 'when the government intrudes on choices concerning family living arrangements' in a manner which is contrary to deeply rooted traditions, *Moore v. East Cleveland,* [and it also limits] the extent to which the State may monopolize the process of ordering certain human relationships while excluding the truly indigent from that process. *Boddie v. Connecticut* [p. 1294 infra]. Furthermore, under the Equal Protection Clause, the means chosen by the State in this case must bear 'a fair and substantial relation' to the object of the legislation [citing *Reed v. Reed* and his concurring opinion in *Craig v. Boren,* both in Ch. 11, Sec. 3, I.].

"The Wisconsin measure in this case does not pass muster under either due process or equal protection standards. [As for the state's 'collection device' justification, the] vice inheres [in] the failure to make provision for those without the means to comply with child-support obligations. [As for the state interest in preserving 'the ability of marriage applicants to support their prior issue by preventing them from incurring new obligations,' the law is] so grossly underinclusive with respect to this objective, given the many ways that additional financial obligations may be incurred by the applicant quite apart from a contemplated marriage, that the classification 'does not bear a fair and substantial relation to the object of the legislation.' *Craig* (Powell, J., concurring)."

STEVENS, J., concurred: "Under this statute, a person's economic status may determine his eligibility to enter into a lawful marriage. A noncustodial parent whose children are 'public charges' may not marry even if he has met his court-ordered obligations. Thus, within the class of parents who have fulfilled their court-ordered obligations, the rich may marry and the poor may not. This type of statutory discrimination is, I believe, totally unprecedented, as well as inconsistent with our tradition of administering justice equally to the rich and to the [poor.]" [b]

Notes and Questions

(a) Consider Lupu, supra, at 1072: "[If *Zablocki*] had assessed the Wisconsin statute by analogy to the libertarian principles governing free expression, it would have discovered a significant threat to preferred liberty: the delegation to judges of power to authorize the marriage under the highly discretionary standard 'that such children [are] not likely thereafter to become public charges.' Once the liberty to marry is recognized as fundamental, doctrines requiring clear and imminent danger to legitimate state interests and confining the discretion to make that determination should play as critical a role as they traditionally do in speech cases."

(b) In response to the district court's invalidation of the statute at issue in *Zablocki,* Wisconsin enacted a replacement statute limited to *previously married persons* who had incurred support obligations and who now intended to marry, establishing a *rebuttable presumption* that the remarriage of a person with support obligations for children not in custody would substantially affect the children's welfare and, finally, providing that the applicant who submits proof that "for

---

b. Rehnquist, J., dissented, "view[ing] this legislative judgment in the light of the traditional presumption of validity [, just as] the traditional standard of review was applied in *Jobst,* despite the claim that the statute there in question burdened [the] right to marry." He concluded that the challenged statute, "despite its imperfections, is sufficiently rational to satisfy the demands of the Fourteenth Amendment."

reasonable cause" he was unable to meet support obligations may remarry. Under *Zablocki,* would this replacement statute (subsequently repealed) pass constitutional muster? See Note, 1979 Wis.L.Rev. 682.

(c) *"Significant interference."* Is the key to a clear application of *Zablocki* "the identification of what constitutes a significant interference with the right to marry"? Does the Court's reconciliation of *Zablocki* and *Jobst* provide much guidance on this point? See Note, *The Constitution and the Family,* 93 Harv. L.Rev. 1156, 1251–55 (1980): "[*Zablocki*] explicitly identifies directness as important to the determination of significance. [A] direct interference makes the state an actual participant in the decision to marry, [i.e.], represents a determination by the state that an individual should not be permitted to marry unless he meets some condition prior to marriage. An indirect interference, on the other hand, weighs the choice by imposing certain consequences upon marriage but leaves the ultimate choice with the individual. It is consistent with the concept of a free society to let the individual determine whether he can meet the burdens of marriage rather than, as in [*Zablocki*], to have the state decide whether the burdens of marriage will make it too difficult to manage problems like meeting child support payments."

4. *Civil commitment of children by their parents.* In rejecting the argument that only a formal hearing prior to parents' commitment of their minor children to a mental institution could adequately protect a child's rights, *Parham v. J.R.* (1979), per Burger, C.J. (a case treated more fully in the "procedural due process" section, infra), applied "the traditional presumption that the parents act in the best interests of the child." That some parents may act against the interests of the child some times "is hardly a reason to discard wholesale those pages of human experience that teach that parents generally do act in the child's best interests."

Is *Parham,* like *Planned Parenthood v. Danforth,* p. 345 supra, a situation in which the parents cannot be relied on to speak for the child's interests? Consider Note, 93 Harv.L.Rev. 89, 94 (1979): "[The *Danforth* Court] ruled that parents cannot prevent their daughters from having abortions [, reasoning] that the existence of the pregnancy itself fractured the family unit too severely to suggest that parental authority should be upheld to preserve the family structure. This reasoning is clearly applicable to a situation in which parents seek to remove a child from the family." Cf. Burt, supra, at 336; John Garvey, *Children and the Idea of Liberty,* 68 Ky.L.J. 809, 832–33 (1979–80).

MICHAEL H. v. GERALD D.

491 U.S. 110, 109 S.Ct. 2333, 105 L.Ed.2d 91 (1989).

JUSTICE SCALIA announced the judgment of the Court and delivered an opinion in which the CHIEF JUSTICE joins, and in all but footnote 6 of which JUSTICE O'CONNOR and JUSTICE KENNEDY join.

[Claiming to be the father of Victoria, the child of Carole D. and Gerald D., a married couple, Michael H. brought an action in California to establish his paternity and visitation rights. Although Gerald was listed as the father on the birth certificate and has always claimed the child as her father, blood tests showed a 98.07% probability that Michael, with whom the mother had had an adulterous affair, was the father. During the first three years of the child's life, she and her mother resided at times with Michael, who held the child out as his own. During this time, mother and child also resided at times with another man and with

Gerald. [Under California law, a child born to a married woman living with her husband, who is neither impotent nor sterile, is presumed to be a child of the marriage, a presumption that may be rebutted only in very limited circumstances. Relying on this presumption, the California courts rejected Michael's claims. The U.S. Supreme Court affirmed.]

Michael contends as a matter of substantive due process that because he has established a parental relationship with Victoria, protection of Gerald's and Carole's marital union is an insufficient state interest to support termination of that relationship. This argument is, of course, predicated on the assertion that Michael has a constitutionally protected liberty interest in his relationship with Victoria. [In] an attempt to limit and guide interpretation of the [Due Process] Clause, we have insisted not merely that the interest denominated as a "liberty" be "fundamental" (a concept that, in isolation, is hard to objectify), but also that it be an interest traditionally protected by our society.[2] As we have put it, the Due Process Clause affords only those protections "so rooted in the traditions and conscience of our people as to be ranked as fundamental." * * *

This insistence that the asserted liberty interest be rooted in history and tradition is evident, as elsewhere, in our cases according constitutional protection to certain parental rights. Michael [reads] *Stanley v. Illinois* [p. 505 supra, infra, invalidating an irrebuttable statutory presumption that unwed fathers are unfit parents, and such subsequent cases as *Quilloin*], as establishing that a liberty interest is created by biological fatherhood plus an established parental relationship—factors that exist in the present case as well. [As] we view [these cases], they rest not upon such isolated factors but upon the historic respect—indeed, sanctity would not be too strong a term—traditionally accorded to the relationships that develop within the unitary family.

[Thus,] the legal issue in the present case reduces to whether the relationship between persons in the situation of Michael and Victoria has been treated as a protected family unit under the historic practices of our society, or whether on any other basis it has been accorded special protection. We think it impossible to find that it has. In fact, quite to the contrary, our traditions have protected the marital family (Gerald, Carole, and the child they acknowledge to be theirs) against the sort of claim Michael asserts.[4]

We have found nothing in the older sources, nor in the older cases, addressing specifically the power of the natural father to assert parental rights over a child born into a woman's existing marriage with another man. Since it is Michael's

2. We do not understand what Justice Brennan has in mind by an interest "that society traditionally has thought important * * * without protecting it." The protection need not take the form of an explicit constitutional provision or statutory guarantee, but it must at least exclude (all that is necessary to decide the present case) a societal tradition of enacting laws *denying* the interest. Nor do we understand why our practice of limiting the Due Process Clause to traditionally protected interests turns the clause "into a redundancy." Its purpose is to prevent future generations from lightly casting aside important traditional values—not to enable this Court to invent new ones.

4. Justice Brennan insists that in determining whether a liberty interest exists we must look at Michael's relationship with Victoria in isolation, without reference to the circumstance that Victoria's mother was married to someone else when the child was conceived, and that that woman and her husband wish to raise the child as their own. We cannot imagine what compels this strange procedure of looking at the act which is assertedly the subject of a liberty interest in isolation from its effect upon other people—rather like inquiring whether there is a liberty interest in firing a gun where the case at hand happens to involve its discharge into another person's body. The logic of Justice Brennan's position leads to the conclusion that if Michael had begotten Victoria by rape, that fact would in no way affect his possession of a liberty interest in his relationship with her.

burden to establish that such a power (at least where the natural father has established a relationship with the child) is so deeply embedded within our traditions as to be a fundamental right, the lack of evidence alone might defeat his case. But the evidence shows that even in modern times [the] ability of a person in Michael's position to claim paternity has not been generally acknowledged.

[What] Michael asserts here is a right to have himself declared the natural father *and thereby to obtain parental prerogatives.* What he must establish, therefore, is not that our society has traditionally allowed a natural father in his circumstances to establish paternity, but that it has traditionally accorded such a father parental rights, or at least has not traditionally denied them. [What] counts is whether the States in fact award substantive parental rights to the natural father of a child conceived within and born into an extant marital union that wishes to embrace the child. We are not aware of a single case, old or new, that has done so. This is not the stuff of which fundamental rights qualifying as liberty interests are made.[6] * * *

Justice O'Connor, with whom Justice Kennedy joins, concurring in part.

I concur in all but footnote 6 of Justice Scalia's opinion. This footnote sketches a mode of historical analysis to be used when identifying liberty interests protected by the Due Process Clause of the Fourteenth Amendment that may be somewhat inconsistent with our past decisions in this area. See *Griswold; Eisenstadt.* On occasion the Court has characterized relevant traditions protecting asserted rights at levels of generality that might not be "the most specific level" available [quoting from fn. 6 of Justice Scalia's opinion]. See *Loving v. Virginia* [p. 1086 infra, invalidating state antimiscegenation laws]; *Turner v. Safley,* 482 U.S. 78, 107 S.Ct. 2254, 96 L.Ed.2d 64 (1987) [where, relying on

---

6. Justice Brennan criticizes our methodology in using historical traditions specifically relating to the rights of an adulterous natural father, rather than inquiring more generally "whether parenthood is an interest that historically has received our attention and protection." There seems to us no basis for the contention that this methodology is "nove[l]." For example, in *Bowers v. Hardwick* [p. 422 infra], we noted that at the time the Fourteenth Amendment was ratified all but 5 of the 37 States had criminal sodomy laws, that all 50 of the States had such laws prior to 1961, and that 24 States and the District of Columbia continued to have them; and we concluded from that record, regarding that very specific aspect of sexual conduct, that "to claim that a right to engage in such conduct is 'deeply rooted in this Nation's history and tradition' or 'implicit in the concept of ordered liberty' is, at best, facetious." In *Roe* we spent about a fifth of our opinion negating the proposition that there was a longstanding tradition of laws proscribing abortion.

We do not understand why, having rejected our focus upon the societal tradition regarding the natural father's rights vis-à-vis a child whose mother is married to another man, Justice Brennan would choose to focus instead upon "parenthood." Why should the relevant category not be even more general—perhaps "family relationships"; or "personal relationships"; or even "emotional attachments in

general"? Though the dissent has no basis for the level of generality it would select, we do: We refer to the most specific level at which a relevant tradition protecting, or denying protection to, the asserted right can be identified. If, for example, there were no societal tradition, either way, regarding the rights of the natural father of a child adulterously conceived, we would have to consult, and (if possible) reason from, the traditions regarding natural fathers in general. But there is such a more specific tradition, and it unqualifiedly denies protection to such a parent.

[Because] general traditions provide such imprecise guidance, they permit judges to dictate rather than discern the society's views. The need, if arbitrary decision-making is to be avoided, to adopt the most specific tradition as the point of reference—or at least to announce, as Justice Brennan declines to do, some other criterion for selecting among the innumerable relevant traditions that could be consulted—is well enough exemplified by the fact that in the present case Justice Brennan's opinion and Justice O'Connor's opinion, which disapproves this footnote, *both* appeal to tradition, but on the basis of the tradition they select reach opposite results. Although assuredly having the virtue (if it be that) of leaving judges free to decide as they think best when the unanticipated occurs, a rule of law that binds neither by text nor by any particular, identifiable tradition, is no rule of law at all. * * *

Zablocki, a unanimous Court struck down a prison regulation permitting inmates to marry only when there were "compelling reasons" to do so]. I would not foreclose the unanticipated by the prior imposition of a single mode of historical analysis. *Poe* (Harlan, J., dissenting).[a]

JUSTICE BRENNAN, with whom JUSTICE MARSHALL and JUSTICE BLACKMUN join, dissenting. * * *

Once we recognized that the "liberty" protected by the Due Process Clause of the Fourteenth Amendment encompasses more than freedom from bodily restraint, today's plurality opinion emphasizes, the concept was cut loose from one natural limitation on its meaning. This innovation paved the way, so the plurality hints, for judges to substitute their own preferences for those of elected officials. Dissatisfied with this supposedly unbridled and uncertain state of affairs, the plurality casts about for another limitation on the concept of liberty.

It finds this limitation in "tradition." Apparently oblivious to the fact that this concept can be as malleable and as elusive as "liberty" itself, the plurality pretends that tradition places a discernible border around the Constitution. The pretense is seductive; it would be comforting to believe that a search for "tradition" involves nothing more idiosyncratic or complicated than poring through dusty volumes on American history. Yet, as Justice White observed in his dissent in *Moore v. East Cleveland:* "What the deeply rooted traditions of the country are is arguable." [Because] reasonable people can disagree about the content of particular traditions, and because they can disagree even about which traditions are relevant to the definition of "liberty," the plurality has not found the objective boundary that it seeks.

Even if we could agree, moreover, on the content and significance of particular traditions, we still would be forced to identify the point at which a tradition becomes firm enough to be relevant to our definition of liberty and the moment at which it becomes too obsolete to be relevant any longer. The plurality supplies no objective means by which we might make these determinations.

[The plurality] does not ask whether parenthood is an interest that historically has received our attention and protection; the answer to that question is too clear for dispute. Instead, the plurality asks whether the specific variety of parenthood under consideration—a natural father's relationship with a child whose mother is married to another man—has enjoyed such protection.

If we had looked to tradition with such specificity in past cases, many a decision would have reached a different result. Surely the use of contraceptives by unmarried couples, *Eisenstadt;* or even by married couples, *Griswold;* [and] even the right to raise one's natural but illegitimate children, *Stanley v. Illinois,* were not "interest[s] traditionally protected by our society" at the time of their consideration by this Court.

[The] plurality's interpretive method is more than novel; it is misguided. It ignores the good reasons for limiting the role of "tradition" in interpreting the Constitution's deliberately capacious language. In the plurality's constitutional universe, we may not take notice of the fact that the original reasons for the conclusive presumption of paternity are out of place in a world in which blood tests can prove virtually beyond a shadow of a doubt who sired a particular child

a. Stevens, J., who concurred in the judgment, was "willing to assume for the purpose of deciding this case that Michael's relationship with Victoria is strong enough to give him a constitutional right to try to convince a trial judge that Victoria's best interest would be served by granting him visitation rights. I am satisfied, however, that the California statute, as applied in this case, gave him that opportunity."

and in which the fact of illegitimacy no longer plays the burdensome and stigmatizing role it once did. [By] describing the decisive question as whether Michael and Victoria's interest is one that has been "traditionally *protected by* our society" (emphasis added), rather than one that society traditionally has thought important (with or without protecting it), and by suggesting that our sole function is to "*discern* the society's views," n. 6 (emphasis added), the plurality acts as if the only purpose of the Due Process Clause is to confirm the importance of interests already protected by a majority of the States. Transforming the protection afforded by the Due Process Clause into a redundancy mocks those who, with care and purpose, wrote the Fourteenth Amendment.

In construing the Fourteenth Amendment to offer shelter only to those interests specifically protected by historical practice, moreover, the plurality ignores the kind of society in which our Constitution exists. We are not an assimilative, homogeneous society, but a facilitative, pluralistic one, in which we must be willing to abide someone else's unfamiliar or even repellant practice because the same tolerant impulse protects our own idiosyncracies. Even if we can agree, therefore, that "family" and "parenthood" are part of the good life, it is absurd to assume that we can agree on the content of those terms and destructive to pretend that we do. In a community such as ours, "liberty" must include the freedom not to conform. The plurality today squashes this freedom by requiring specific approval from history before protecting anything in the name of liberty.

The document that the plurality construes today is unfamiliar to me. It is not the living charter that I have taken to be our Constitution; it is instead a stagnant, archaic, hidebound document steeped in the prejudices and superstitions of a time long past. * * * [b]

DETERMINING THE APPROPRIATE LEVEL OF GENERALITY IN DEFINING RIGHTS; USING TRADITION AS A SUBSTITUTE FOR VALUE CHOICES: CRITICISM OF JUSTICE SCALIA'S APPROACH

1. *Looking to "tradition."* Are legally cognizable "traditions" likely to "mirror majoritarian, middle-class conventions"? Are historical traditions susceptible to as much manipulation—or even greater manipulation—than are legal precedents? What if it could be demonstrated unequivocally that public flogging and handbranding were widely accepted forms of punishment in 1791? How does one know when to *reject* an historical pattern or understanding? See Laurence Tribe & Michael Dorf, *Levels of Generality in the Definition of Rights*, 57 U.Chi.L.Rev. 1057, 1087, 1090 (1990).

2. *What is "tradition"? Does tradition ever speak with one voice?* Consider JACK BALKIN, *Tradition, Betrayal, and the Politics of Deconstruction*, 11 Cardozo L.Rev. 1613, 1617 (1990):

"If there is a tradition of protecting marital privacy, but not a more specific tradition protecting marital purchase of contraceptives, how do we know whether the latter situation is nevertheless subsumed under the former for purposes of constitutionally protected liberty? Might one not conclude instead that the *real* historical tradition was protection of marital privacy in the home, so that the purchase of contraceptives in the open marketplace could be regulated or even

b. White, J., also dissented.

proscribed consistent with the tradition? Would this not be more consistent with the experiences of Margaret Sanger and her followers, who publicly advocated birth control in the early twentieth century, and were met with incredible resistance? Again, if sexual harassment directed toward women in the workplace and respect for marital privacy are both traditions, but only one is worth protecting, how do we tell the difference? If back alley abortions are a tradition in response to the 'traditional' prohibition on abortion in America, does this make abortion (in or out of a back alley) a tradition worth protecting and sustaining? In short, what normative status should be assigned to a set of values given the fact that many people have held these values at one point or another in our nation's history?

"[W]hat is most troubling about Justice Scalia's call for respecting the most specific tradition available is that our most specific historical traditions may often be opposed to our more general commitments to liberty or equality. Curiously, then, different parts of the American tradition may conflict with each other. And indeed, this is one of the untidy facts of historical experience. The fourteenth amendment's abstract commitment to racial equality was accompanied by simultaneous acceptance of segregated public schools in the District of Columbia and acquiescence in antimiscegenation laws. The establishment clause and the principle of separation of church and state have coexisted with presidential proclamations of national days of prayer, official congressional chaplains, and national Christmas trees. Traditions do not exist as integrated wholes. They are a motley collection of principles and counterprinciples, standing for one thing when viewed narrowly and standing for another when viewed more generally. Tradition never speaks with one voice, although, to be sure, persons of particular predelictions may hear only one."

3. *In formulating the rights at stake, what information does one "abstract away"?* Consider LAURENCE TRIBE & MICHAEL DORF, note 1 supra, at 1092–93:

"* * * Justice Scalia's formulation of the rights at stake [in *Michael H.*] as the rights of "the natural father of a child adulterously conceived" [is] already a considerable abstraction. He has abstracted away lots of information that virtually everybody would agree is irrelevant. But he has also abstracted away some information that many people would see as quite relevant. The natural father in *Michael H.* had a longstanding, albeit adulterous and sporadic, relationship with the mother of his child. He also had fairly extensive, if sporadic, contact with his child. Surely this information is more significant than the plaintiff's race or age. A more specific formulation of the issue than Justice Scalia gives us would be: *what are the rights of the natural father of a child conceived in an adulterous but longstanding relationship, where the father has played a major, if sporadic, role in the child's early development?*

"It is unlikely that any tradition addresses this very question at this precise level of specificity. Thus, we are left with the problem of specifying the *next* most specific tradition. [Do] we abstract away the father's relationship with his child and her mother, as Justice Scalia does? Or do we instead abstract away the fact that the relationship with the mother was an adulterous one, as Justice Brennan does? If we do the latter, then we will find ourselves consulting traditions regarding natural fathers who play major roles in their children's development. This sounds an awful lot like 'traditions regarding natural fathers in general,' which Justice Scalia regarded as less specific than his formulation of the problem. By starting from an even *more* specific description of the case than did Justice

Scalia, we have seen that he had no greater justification for abstracting away the father-child relationship than Justice Brennan had for abstracting away the adultery."

4. *The role of "tradition" in due process analysis.* "Cases such as *Michael H.*" notes FRANK EASTERBROOK, *Abstraction and Authority,* 59 U.Chi.L.Rev. 349, 352 (1992), "show the importance of picking a level of generality. [By] choosing narrowly the Court may find no problem in the law. By choosing broadly the Court may find a problem with any law it pleases—invoking 'tradition' to demonstrate that adultery and other things that society has long deprecated are actually *protected* by some traditional freedom,[a] that practices traditionally scorned and punished are no different from practices traditionally praised, such as providing a home for one's grandchild. By reserving the right to choose a level of generality to fit the circumstances, as Justices O'Connor and Kennedy did, the Court makes a virtue of 'the understandable temptation to vary the relevant tradition's level of abstraction to make it come out right' [quoting John Ely]. Justices O'Connor and Kennedy worried that a rule for selecting a level of generality would change the outcome of some cases. Exactly so, but it is less than clear why that should be troubling.

"Although *Michael H.* vividly demonstrates the importance of the level of abstraction, the Justices' dispute was driven by the need to identify a 'tradition,' which would be used to define a fundamental right. If you assume that the purpose of that enterprise is to increase the number of protected interests, then 'it is crucial to define the liberty at a high enough level to permit unconventional variants to claim protection' [quoting Laurence Tribe]. If you believe that tradition serves to restrict the powers of judges to pursue their vision of a good society, then you will choose a lower level of generality. In either case the selection depends on conclusions about the role of 'tradition' in due process analysis rather than about the function of abstraction in understanding the Constitution itself."

6. *Justice Scalia's footnote 4 approach: incorporating the state's interest into an asserted liberty.* Although footnote 6 to Justice Scalia's plurality opinion in *Michael H.* has generated much comment, worthy of attention, too, is footnote 4— criticizing the Court's practice of first deciding whether a liberty is fundamental and then asking whether a government practice restricting that liberty can be justified. Consider Tribe & Dorf, supra, at 1096–97:

"When we automatically incorporate the factors that provide the state's possible justification for its regulation into the initial definition of a liberty, the fundamental nature of that liberty nearly vanishes. Unless the state's interest is facially absurd, when it is suitably incorporated into an asserted liberty it will render that liberty so specific as to seem insupportable, or at least radically disconnected from precedent. At a minimum, the privacy right protected in *Roe* becomes the implausible 'right' to destroy a living fetus. If one takes footnote 4 to its logical limit in the interpretation of *enumerated* rights, then the free speech right protected in *New York Times Co. v. Sullivan* [p. 571 infra] becomes the dubious 'right' to libel a public official and the right to an exclusionary remedy

---

a. Earlier in his article, id. at 351–52, Judge Easterbrook maintains that Brennan, J., dissenting in *Michael H.*, had "proceeded to define the [relevant] tradition as the right of biological parents to raise their children, coupled with 'freedom not to conform'—presumably a fundamental right to commit adultery."

"With 'freedom not to conform' as a 'fundamental right,'" adds Easterbrook, "the Court holds the whip hand, for *all* law abridges this freedom, and a judge may deem insufficient the justification asserted by the state for any rule at all."

protected in *Mapp v. Ohio* [p. 386 supra] becomes the counter-intuitive 'right' of a criminal to suppress the truth. To state these cases this way is to decide them in the government's favor. Anyone is free to argue that each of these cases was wrongly decided. But arguments to this effect must explain why the state interest overcomes the liberty interest. Under Justice Scalia's footnote 4 approach, by contrast, the state interest obliterates, without explanation and at the outset, any trace of the individual liberty at stake."

WHAT SHALL WE CALL THIS SEGMENT—THE RIGHT TO ENGAGE IN HOMOSEXUAL SODOMY? ADULT, CONSENSUAL SEXUAL CONDUCT IN THE HOME? THE AUTONOMY OF PRIVATE SEXUAL CHOICES? SEXUAL EXPRESSION AND CONTROL OF ONE'S BODY? UNCONVENTIONAL SEXUAL LIFESTYLES? THE RIGHT TO CONTROL ONE'S INTIMATE ASSOCIATIONS? THE RIGHT TO BE LET ALONE?

BOWERS v. HARDWICK

478 U.S. 186, 106 S.Ct. 2841, 92 L.Ed.2d 140 (1986).

JUSTICE WHITE delivered the opinion of the Court.

In August 1982, respondent was charged with violating the Georgia statute criminalizing sodomy[1] by committing that act with another adult male in the bedroom of respondent's home. After a preliminary hearing, the District Attorney decided not to present the matter to the grand jury unless further evidence developed.

Respondent then brought suit in the Federal District Court, challenging the constitutionality of the statute insofar as it criminalized consensual sodomy.[2] He asserted that he was a practicing homosexual, that the Georgia statute, as administered by the defendants, placed him in imminent danger of arrest, and that the statute [violated the Constitution]. The District Court granted the defendant's motion to dismiss for failure to state a claim. [The U.S. Court of Appeals for the Eleventh Circuit reversed, holding] that the Georgia statute violated respondent's fundamental rights because his homosexual activity is a private and intimate association that is beyond the reach of state regulation by reason of the Ninth Amendment and the Due Process Clause. [We reverse.]

---

1. Ga.Code Ann. § 16–6–2 (1984) provides, in pertinent part, as follows:

"(a) A person commits the offense of sodomy when he performs or submits to any sexual act involving the sex organs of one person and the mouth or anus of [another].

"(b) A person convicted of the offense of sodomy shall be punished by imprisonment for not less than one nor more than 20 [years]."

2. John and Mary Doe were also plaintiffs in the action. They alleged that they wished to engage in sexual activity proscribed by § 16–6–2 in the privacy of their home, and that they had been "chilled and deterred" from engaging in such activity by both the existence

of the statute and Hardwick's arrest. The District Court held, however, that because they had neither sustained, nor were in immediate danger of sustaining, any direct injury from the enforcement of the statute, they did not have proper standing to maintain the action. The Court of Appeals affirmed [and] the Does do not challenge that holding in this Court.

The only claim properly before the Court, therefore, is Hardwick's challenge to the Georgia statute as applied to consensual homosexual sodomy. We express no opinion on the constitutionality of the Georgia statute as applied to other acts of sodomy.

This case does not require a judgment on whether laws against sodomy between consenting adults in general, or between homosexuals in particular, are wise or desirable. [T]he issue presented is whether the Federal Constitution confers a fundamental right upon homosexuals to engage in sodomy and hence invalidates the laws of the many States that still make such conduct illegal and have done so for a very long time. The case also calls for some judgment about the limits of the Court's role in carrying out its constitutional mandate.

We first register our disagreement with the Court of Appeals [that] the Court's prior cases have construed the Constitution to confer a right of privacy that extends to homosexual sodomy and for all intents and purposes have decided this case. [We] think it evident that none of the rights announced in [such cases as *Skinner, Griswold* and *Roe*] bears any resemblance to the claimed constitutional right of homosexuals to engage in acts of sodomy that is asserted in this case. No connection between family, marriage, or procreation on the one hand and homosexual activity on the other has been [demonstrated]. Moreover, any claim that these cases nevertheless stand for the proposition that any kind of private sexual conduct between consenting adults is constitutionally insulated from state proscription is unsupportable. * * *

Precedent aside, however, respondent would have us announce [a] fundamental right to engage in homosexual sodomy. This we are quite unwilling to do. * * *

Striving to assure itself and the public that announcing rights not readily identifiable in the Constitution's text involves much more than the imposition of the Justices' own choice of values on the States and the Federal Government, the Court has sought to identify the nature of the rights qualifying for heightened judicial protection. In *Palko* it was said that this category includes those fundamental liberties that are "implicit in the concept of ordered liberty," such that "neither liberty nor justice would exist if [they] were sacrificed." A different description of fundamental liberties appeared in *Moore v. East Cleveland* (opinion of Powell, J.), where they are characterized as those liberties that are "deeply rooted in this Nation's history and tradition."

It is obvious to us that neither of these formulations would extend a fundamental right to homosexuals to engage in acts of consensual sodomy. Proscriptions against that conduct have ancient roots. Sodomy was a criminal offense at common law and was forbidden by the laws of the original thirteen States when they ratified the Bill of Rights. In 1868, when the Fourteenth Amendment was ratified, all but 5 of the 37 States in the Union had criminal sodomy laws. In fact, until 1961, all 50 States outlawed sodomy, and today, 24 States and the District of Columbia continue to provide criminal penalties for sodomy performed in private and between consenting adults. Against this background, to claim that a right to engage in such conduct is "deeply rooted in this Nation's history and tradition" or "implicit in the concept of ordered liberty" is, at best, facetious.

Nor are we inclined to take a more expansive view of our authority to discover new fundamental rights imbedded in the Due Process Clause. The Court is most vulnerable and comes nearest to illegitimacy when it deals with judge-made constitutional law having little or no cognizable roots in the language or design of the Constitution. That this is so was painfully demonstrated by the face-off between the Executive and the Court in the 1930's, which resulted in the repudiation of much of the substantive gloss that the Court had placed on the Due Process Clause of the Fifth and Fourteenth Amendments. There should be, therefore, great resistance to expand the substantive reach of those Clauses, particularly if it requires redefining the category of rights deemed to be fundamental. Otherwise, the Judiciary necessarily takes to itself further authority to govern the country without express constitutional authority. The claimed right pressed on us today falls far short of overcoming this resistance.

Respondent, however, asserts that the result should be different where the homosexual conduct occurs in the privacy of the home. He relies on *Stanley v. Georgia,* where the Court held that the First Amendment prevents conviction for possessing and reading obscene material in the privacy of [one's home].

Stanley did protect conduct that would not have been protected outside the home, and it partially prevented the enforcement of state obscenity laws; but the decision was firmly grounded in the First Amendment. The right pressed upon us here has no similar support in the text of the Constitution, and it does not qualify for recognition under the prevailing principles for construing the Fourteenth Amendment. Its limits are also difficult to discern. Plainly enough, otherwise illegal conduct is not always immunized whenever it occurs in the home. Victimless crimes, such as the possession and use of illegal drugs do not escape the law where they are committed at home. *Stanley* itself recognized that its holding offered no protection for the possession in the home of drugs, firearms, or stolen goods. And if respondent's submission is limited to the voluntary sexual conduct between consenting adults, it would be difficult, except by fiat, to limit the claimed right to homosexual conduct while leaving exposed to prosecution adultery, incest, and other sexual crimes even though they are committed in the home. We are unwilling to start down that road.

Even if the conduct at issue here is not a fundamental right, respondent asserts that there must be a rational basis for the law and that there is none in this case other than the presumed belief of a majority of the electorate in Georgia that homosexual sodomy is immoral and unacceptable. [The] law, however, is constantly based on notions of morality, and if all laws representing essentially moral choices are to be invalidated under the Due Process Clause, the courts will be very busy indeed. Even respondent makes no such claim, but insists that majority sentiments about the morality of homosexuality should be declared inadequate. We do not agree, and are unpersuaded that the sodomy laws of some 25 States should be invalidated on this basis.[8] [Reversed.]

CHIEF JUSTICE BURGER, concurring.

I join the Court's opinion, but I write separately to underscore my view that in constitutional terms there is no such thing as a fundamental right to commit homosexual sodomy. [To] hold that the act of homosexual sodomy is somehow protected as a fundamental right would be to cast aside millennia of moral teaching. * * *

JUSTICE POWELL, concurring.

I join the opinion of the Court. [But the] The Georgia statute at issue in this case authorizes a court to imprison a person for up to 20 years for a single private, consensual act of sodomy. In my view, a prison sentence for such conduct— certainly a sentence of long duration—would create a serious Eighth Amendment issue. Under the Georgia statute a single act of sodomy, even in the private setting of a home, is a felony comparable in terms of the possible sentence

8. Respondent does not defend the judgment below based on the Ninth Amendment, the Equal Protection Clause or the Eighth Amendment.

imposed to serious felonies such as aggravated battery, first degree arson, and robbery.

In this case, however, respondent has not been tried, much less convicted and sentenced.[2] Moreover, respondent has not raised the Eighth Amendment issue below. For these reasons this constitutional argument is not before us.

JUSTICE BLACKMUN, with whom JUSTICE BRENNAN, JUSTICE MARSHALL, and JUSTICE STEVENS join, dissenting.

This case is no more about "a fundamental right to engage in homosexual sodomy," as the Court purports to declare, than *Stanley* was about a fundamental right to watch obscene movies, or *Katz v. United States,* 389 U.S. 347, 88 S.Ct. 507, 19 L.Ed.2d 576 (1967), was about a fundamental right to place interstate bets from a telephone booth.[a] Rather, this case is about "the most comprehensive of rights and the right most valued by civilized men," namely, "the right to be let alone." *Olmstead v. United States,* 277 U.S. 438, 478, 48 S.Ct. 564, 572, 72 L.Ed. 944 (1928) (Brandeis, J., dissenting).

[T]he fact that the moral judgments expressed by statutes like § 16–6–2 may be "natural and familiar [should not] conclude our judgment upon the question whether statutes embodying them conflict with the Constitution of the United States." *Roe,* quoting *Lochner* (Holmes, J., dissenting). [We] must analyze respondent's claim in the light of the values that underlie the constitutional right to privacy. If that right means anything, it means that, before Georgia can prosecute its citizens for making choices about the most intimate aspects of their lives, it must do more than assert that the choice they have made is an " 'abominable crime not fit to be named among Christians.' " * * *

[T]he Court's almost obsessive focus on homosexual activity is particularly hard to justify in light of the broad language Georgia has used. Unlike the Court, the Georgia Legislature has not proceeded on the assumption that homosexuals are so different from other citizens that their lives may be controlled in a way that would not be tolerated if it limited the choices of those other citizens. Rather, Georgia has provided that "[a] person commits the offense of sodomy when he performs or submits to any sexual act involving the sex organs of one person and the mouth or anus of another." The sex or status of the persons who engage in the act is irrelevant as a matter of state law. In fact, to the extent I can discern a legislative purpose for Georgia's 1968 enactment, that purpose seems to have been to broaden the coverage of the law to reach heterosexual as well as homosexual activity. I therefore see no basis for the Court's decision to treat this case as an "as applied" challenge to § 16–6–2, see n. 2, or for Georgia's attempt, both in its brief and at oral argument, to defend § 16–6–2 solely on the grounds that it prohibits homosexual activity. * * *

---

2. It was conceded at oral argument that, prior to the complaint against respondent Hardwick, there had been no reported decision involving prosecution for private homosexual sodomy under this Statute for several decades. Moreover, the State has declined to present the criminal charge against Hardwick to a grand jury, and this is a suit for declaratory judgment brought by respondents challenging the validity of the statute. The history of nonenforcement suggests the moribund character today of laws criminalizing this type of private, consensual conduct. Some 26 states have repealed similar statutes. But the constitutional validity of the Georgia statute was put in issue by respondents, and for the reasons stated by the Court, I cannot say that conduct condemned for hundreds of years has now become a fundamental right.

a. *Katz* held that electronic surveillance of defendant violated the privacy upon which he justifiably relied when using a telephone booth and thus constituted a "search and seizure" within the meaning of the Fourth Amendment, even though the challenged surveillance technique involved no physical penetration of the phone booth from which defendant placed his calls.

"Our cases long have recognized that the Constitution embodies a promise that a certain private sphere of individual liberty will be kept largely beyond the reach of government." *Thornburgh*. In construing the right to privacy, the Court has proceeded along two somewhat distinct, albeit complementary, lines. First, it has recognized a privacy interest with reference to certain *decisions* that are properly for the individual to make. E.g., *Roe, Pierce*. Second, it has recognized a privacy interest with reference to certain *places* without regard for the particular activities in which the individuals who occupy them are engaged. The case before us implicates both the decisional and the spatial aspects of the right to privacy. * * *

Only the most willful blindness could obscure the fact that sexual intimacy is "a sensitive, key relationship of human existence, central to family life, community welfare, and the development of human personality." The fact that individuals define themselves in a significant way through their intimate sexual relationships with others suggests, in a Nation as diverse as ours, that there may be many "right" ways of conducting those relationships, and that much of the richness of a relationship will come from the freedom an individual has to *choose* the form and nature of these intensely personal bonds. See Kenneth Karst, *The Freedom of Intimate Association*, 89 Yale L.J. 624, 637 (1980).

In a variety of circumstances we have recognized that a necessary corollary of giving individuals freedom to choose how to conduct their lives is acceptance of the fact that different individuals will make different choices. [The] Court claims that its decision today merely refuses to recognize a fundamental right to engage in homosexual sodomy; what the Court really has refused to recognize is the fundamental interest all individuals have in controlling the nature of their intimate associations with others.

The behavior for which Hardwick faces prosecution occurred in his own home, a place to which the Fourth Amendment attaches special significance. The Court's treatment of this aspect of the case is symptomatic of its overall refusal to consider the broad principles that have informed our treatment of privacy in specific cases. Just as the right to privacy is more than the mere aggregation of a number of entitlements to engage in specific behavior, so too, protecting the physical integrity of the home is more than merely a means of protecting specific activities that often take place there. * * *

The Court's interpretation of the pivotal case of *Stanley v. Georgia* is entirely unconvincing. *Stanley* held that Georgia's undoubted power to punish the public distribution of constitutionally unprotected, obscene material did not permit the State to punish the private possession of such material. According to the majority here, *Stanley* relied entirely on the First Amendment, and thus, it is claimed, sheds no light on cases not involving printed materials. But that is not what *Stanley* said. Rather, the *Stanley* Court anchored its holding in the Fourth Amendment's special protection for the individual in his home.

[The] central place that *Stanley* gives Justice Brandeis' dissent in *Olmstead*, a case raising *no* First Amendment claim, shows that *Stanley* rested as much on the Court's understanding of the Fourth Amendment as it did on the First. * * * "The right of the people to be secure in [their] houses," expressly guaranteed by the Fourth Amendment, is perhaps the most "textual" of the various constitutional provisions that inform our understanding of the right to privacy, and thus I cannot agree with the Court's statement that "[t]he right pressed upon us here has [no] support in the text of the Constitution." Indeed, the right of an individual to conduct intimate relationships in the intimacy of his or her own home seems to me to be the heart of the Constitution's protection of privacy.

The Court's failure to comprehend the magnitude of the liberty interests at stake in this case leads it to slight the question whether [petitioner] has justified Georgia's infringement on these interests. I believe that neither of the two general justifications for § 16–6–2 that petitioner has advanced warrants dismissing respondent's challenge for failure to state a claim.

First, petitioner asserts that the acts made criminal by the statute may have serious adverse consequences for "the general public health and welfare," such as spreading communicable diseases or fostering other criminal activity. [Nothing in the record] provides any justification for finding the activity forbidden [to] be physically dangerous, either to the persons engaged in it or to others.[4]

The core of petitioner's defense of § 16–6–2, however, is that respondent and others who engage in the conduct prohibited by § 16–6–2 interfere with Georgia's exercise of the " 'right of the Nation and of the States to maintain a decent society,' " *Paris Adult Theatre*. Essentially, petitioner argues, and the Court agrees, that the fact that the acts described in § 16–6–2 "for hundreds of years, if not thousands, have been uniformly condemned as immoral" is a sufficient reason to permit a State to ban them today.

I cannot agree that either the length of time a majority has held its convictions or the passions with which it defends them can withdraw legislation from this Court's scrutiny. See, e.g., *Roe; Loving; Brown v. Board of Education.*[5] [It] is precisely because the issue raised by this case touches the heart of what makes individuals what they are that we should be especially sensitive to the rights of those whose choices upset the majority.

The assertion that "traditional Judeo–Christian values proscribe" the conduct involved cannot provide an adequate justification for § 16–6–2. That certain, but by no means all, religious groups condemn the behavior at issue gives the State no license to impose their judgments on the entire citizenry. The legitimacy of secular legislation depends instead on whether the State can advance some

4. Although I do not think it necessary to decide today issues that are not even remotely before us, it does seem to me that a court could find simple, analytically sound distinctions between certain private, consensual sexual conduct, on the one hand, and adultery and incest (the only two vaguely specific "sexual crimes" to which the majority points), on the other. For example, marriage, in addition to its spiritual aspects, is a civil contract that entitles the contracting parties to a variety of governmentally provided benefits. A State might define the contractual commitment necessary to become eligible for these benefits to include a commitment of fidelity and then punish individuals for breaching that contract. Moreover, a State might conclude that adultery is likely to injure third persons, in particular, spouses and children of persons who engage in extramarital affairs. With respect to incest, a court might well agree with respondent that the nature of familial relationships renders true consent to incestuous activity sufficiently problematical that a blanket prohibition of such activity is warranted. Notably, the Court makes no effort to explain why it has chosen to group private, consensual homosexual activity with adultery and incest rather than with private, consensual heterosexual activity by unmarried persons or, indeed, with oral or anal sex within marriage.

5. The parallel between *Loving* [which invalidated a Virginia antimiscegenation law] and this case is almost uncanny. There, too, the State relied on a religious justification for its law. [There], too, defenders of the challenged statute relied heavily on the fact that when the Fourteenth Amendment was ratified, most of the States had similar prohibitions. There, too, at the time the case came before the Court, many of the States still had criminal statutes concerning the conduct at issue. [Yet] the Court held, not only that the invidious racism of Virginia's law violated the Equal Protection Clause, but also that the law deprived the Lovings of due process by denying them the "freedom of choice to marry" that had "long been recognized as one of the vital personal rights essential to the orderly pursuit of happiness by free men."

justification for its law beyond its conformity to religious doctrine. A State can no more punish private behavior because of religious intolerance than it can punish such behavior because of racial animus. * * *

Nor can § 16–6–2 be justified as a "morally neutral" exercise of Georgia's power to "protect the public environment," *Paris Adult Theatre.* * * * Petitioner and the Court fail to see the difference between laws that protect public sensibilities and those that enforce private morality. Statutes banning public sexual activity are entirely consistent with protecting the individual's liberty interest in decisions concerning sexual relations: the same recognition that those decisions are intensely private which justifies protecting them from governmental interference can justify protecting individuals from unwilling exposure to the sexual activities of others. But the mere fact that intimate behavior may be punished when it takes place in public cannot dictate how States can regulate intimate behavior that occurs in intimate places.[7]

This case involves no real interference with the rights of others, for the mere knowledge that other individuals do not adhere to one's value system cannot be a legally cognizable interest, let alone an interest that can justify invading the houses, hearts, and minds of citizens who choose to live their lives differently. * * *

JUSTICE STEVENS, with whom JUSTICE BRENNAN and JUSTICE MARSHALL join, dissenting.

Like the statute that is challenged in this case, the rationale of the Court's opinion applies equally to the prohibited conduct regardless of whether the parties who engage in it are married or unmarried, or are of the same or different sexes. Sodomy was condemned as an odious and sinful type of behavior during the formative period of the common law. That condemnation was equally damning for heterosexual and homosexual sodomy. Moreover, it provided no special exemption for married couples. The license to cohabit and to produce legitimate offspring simply did not include any permission to engage in sexual conduct that was considered a "crime against nature."

The history of the Georgia statute before us clearly reveals this traditional prohibition of heterosexual, as well as homosexual, sodomy. Indeed, at one point in the 20th century, Georgia's law was construed to permit certain sexual conduct between homosexual women even though such conduct was prohibited between heterosexuals. The history of the statutes cited by the majority as proof for the proposition that sodomy is not constitutionally protected similarly reveals a prohibition on heterosexual, as well as homosexual, sodomy.

Because the Georgia statute expresses the traditional view that sodomy is an immoral kind of conduct regardless of the identity of the persons who engage in it, I believe that a proper analysis of its constitutionality requires consideration of two questions: First, may a State totally prohibit the described conduct by means of a neutral law applying without exception to all persons subject to its jurisdic-

---

7. At oral argument a suggestion appeared that, while the Fourth Amendment's special protection of the home might prevent the State from enforcing § 16–6–2 against individuals who engage in consensual sexual activity there, that protection would not make the statute invalid. The suggestion misses the point entirely. If the law is not invalid, then the police *can* invade the home to enforce it, provided, of course, that they obtain a determination of probable cause from a neutral magistrate. One of the reasons for the Court's holding in *Griswold* was precisely the possibility, and repugnancy, of permitting searches to obtain evidence regarding the use of contraceptives. Permitting the kinds of searches that might be necessary to obtain evidence of the sexual activity banned by § 16–6–2 seems no less intrusive, or repugnant.

tion? If not, may the State save the statute by announcing that it will only enforce the law against homosexuals? The two questions merit separate discussion.

Our prior cases make two propositions abundantly clear. First, the fact that the governing majority in a State has traditionally viewed a particular practice as immoral is not a sufficient reason for upholding a law prohibiting the practice; neither history nor tradition could save a law prohibiting miscegenation from constitutional attack.[9] Second, individual decisions by married persons, concerning the intimacies of their physical relationship, even when not intended to produce offspring, are a form of "liberty" protected by the Due Process Clause of the Fourteenth Amendment. *Griswold.* Moreover, this protection extends to intimate choices by unmarried as well as married persons. *Carey; Eisenstadt.* * * *

Society has every right to encourage its individual members to follow particular traditions in expressing affection for one another and in gratifying their personal desires. It, of course, may prohibit an individual from imposing his will on another to satisfy his own selfish interests. It also may prevent an individual from interfering with, or violating, a legally sanctioned and protected relationship, such as marriage. And it may explain the relative advantages and disadvantages of different forms of intimate expression. But when individual married couples are isolated from observation by others, the way in which they voluntarily choose to conduct their intimate relations is a matter for them—not the State—to decide.[10] The essential "liberty" that animated the development of the law in cases like *Griswold, Eisenstadt,* and *Carey* surely embraces the right to engage in nonreproductive, sexual conduct that others may consider offensive or immoral.

Paradoxical as it may seem, our prior cases thus establish that a State may not prohibit sodomy within "the sacred precincts of marital bedrooms," *Griswold,* or, indeed, between unmarried heterosexual adults. *Eisenstadt.* [If] the Georgia statute cannot be enforced as it is written—if the conduct it seeks to prohibit is a protected form of liberty for the vast majority of Georgia's citizens—the State must assume the burden of justifying a selective application of its law. Either the persons to whom Georgia seeks to apply its statute do not have the same interest in "liberty" that others have, or there must be a reason why the State may be permitted to apply a generally applicable law to certain persons that it does not apply to others.

The first possibility is plainly unacceptable. Although the meaning of the principle that "all men are created equal" is not always clear, it surely must mean that every free citizen has the same interest in "liberty" that the members of the majority share. From the standpoint of the individual, the homosexual and the heterosexual have the same interest in deciding how he will live his own life, and, more narrowly, how he will conduct himself in his personal and voluntary associations with his companions. State intrusion into the private conduct of either is equally burdensome.

The second possibility is similarly unacceptable. A policy of selective application must be supported by a neutral and legitimate interest—something more substantial than a habitual dislike for, or ignorance about, the disfavored group.

---

9. See *Loving.* Interestingly, miscegenation was once treated as a crime similar to sodomy.

10. Indeed, the Georgia Attorney General concedes that Georgia's statute would be un-

constitutional if applied to a married couple. * * * Significantly, Georgia passed the current statute three years after the Court's decision in *Griswold.*

Neither the State nor the Court has identified any such interest in this case. The Court has posited as a justification for the Georgia statute "the presumed belief of a majority of the electorate in Georgia that homosexual sodomy is immoral and unacceptable." But the Georgia electorate has expressed no such belief—instead, its representatives enacted a law that presumably reflects the belief that *all* *sodomy* is immoral and unacceptable. Unless the Court is prepared to conclude that such a law is constitutional, it may not rely on the work product of the Georgia Legislature to support its holding. For the Georgia statute does not single out homosexuals as a separate class meriting special disfavored treatment. [Moreover, the] record of nonenforcement, in this case and in the last several decades, belies the Attorney General's representations about the importance of the State's selective application of its generally applicable law.

Both the Georgia statute and the Georgia prosecutor thus completely fail to provide the Court with any support for the conclusion that homosexual sodomy, *simpliciter,* is considered unacceptable conduct in that State, and that the burden of justifying a selective application of the generally applicable law has been met.

The Court orders the dismissal of respondent's complaint even though the State's statute prohibits all sodomy; even though that prohibition is concededly unconstitutional with respect to heterosexuals; and even though the State's post hoc explanations for selective application are belied by the State's own actions. At the very least, I think it clear at this early stage of the litigation that respondent has alleged a constitutional claim sufficient to withstand a motion to dismiss. * * *

CRITICISM OF *BOWERS v. HARDWICK*

1. *"Sever[ing] the roots of the privacy doctrine."* Consider Jed Rubenfeld, *The Right of Privacy,* 102 Harv.L.Rev. 737, 748 (1989): "Justice White stated that the Court's prior cases have recognized three categories of activity protected by the right to privacy: marriage, procreation, and family relationships[, but he] neither sought nor found any unifying principle underlying his three categories. It was as if the Court had said, 'We in the majority barely understand why even these three areas are constitutionally protected; we simply acknowledge them and note that they are not involved here.' The device of compartmentalizing precedent is an old jurisprudential strategy for limiting unruly doctrines. The effect here is that, after *Hardwick,* we know that the right to privacy protects some aspects of marriage, procreation, and child-rearing, but we do not know why. By identifying three disparate applications ungrounded by any unifying principle, the majority effectively severed the roots of the privacy doctrine, leaving only the branches * * *."

2. *Are Roe and Hardwick irreconcilable?* Consider Frank Easterbrook, *Abstraction and Authority,* 59 U.Chi.L.Rev. 349, 365–66 (1992): "These are irreconcilable decisions—Tribe and Dorf [cited in fn. d infra] think so, I think so, the Justices themselves think so. At least seven of the Justices who voted in *Hardwick* would have treated the abortion and sodomy questions identically: Justices Brennan, Marshall, Blackmun, and Stevens, by protecting both; Justices Burger, White, and Rehnquist (perhaps Justice O'Connor, too), by protecting neither. Only Justice Powell saw a difference—adhering to *Roe* while joining the majority in *Hardwick*—and he is reputed to have changed his mind about *Hardwick* after he left the Court."

Suppose *Hardwick* had been decided in 1973 and the abortion question had come to the Court for the first time in 1986. Would the Court be compelled to decide against the right to abortion in '86? See Easterbrook, supra at 367.

3. *Why didn't the Court dismiss the* Hardwick *case as moot?* Consider Richard Posner, *Sex and Reason* 341–42 (1992): "It is unclear whether anyone had been prosecuted in Georgia for a violation of the sodomy law not involving aggravated circumstances for forty years or more. [In] any event, the district attorney's policy was not to prosecute adult consensual violators of the law. [Hardwick] did not try to show that there was a significant probability of his being arrested for sodomy in the future. It was a fluke that the police had seen him commit the crime in the privacy of his own home.

"One might in these circumstances have expected the Court, under its precedents,[a] to dismiss the case as moot, especially given the controversiality of the issue. [The] Court may not have done this because it wanted to cut back on the concept of sexual privacy in a case that some of the justices may have thought an ideal vehicle for doing so—a veritable reductio ad absurdum of the concept. [Had Justice White] noted that besides being about family, marriage and procreation, cases such as *Griswold, Eisenstadt* [and] *Roe* had been about sex, he could not have polished them off so easily. Nor if he had remarked the fact that, on its face anyway, the Georgia statute made sodomy illegal even when heterosexual—even, indeed, when practiced by married persons." [b]

4. *Under the circumstances of the* Hardwick *case, was sexuality "an anatomical irrelevance"?* Criticizing what he calls "Justice White's stunningly harsh and dismissive opinion [in] *Hardwick*," former Solicitor General Charles Fried, *Order and Law* 82–84 (1991), observes: "Unless one takes the implausible line that people generally choose their sexual orientation, then to criminalize any enjoyment of the sexual powers by a whole category of persons is either an imposition of very great cruelty or an exercise in hypocrisy inviting arbitrary and abusive applications of the criminal law. *Poe* [v. Ullman] and *Griswold* did emphasize the sanctity of marital intimacy, so that a step beyond these cases would have had to be taken to reach the conclusion Justice Blackmun urged in a particularly moving dissent. But it is a short step, and one authorized by reason and tradition: Hardwick was threatened with prosecution for having consensual sex with another man behind a closed bedroom door in his own home. The police found out about it by an uninvited accident. Here the conduct was truly private. It concerned no one else except in the question-begging sense that some may be offended by the very knowledge that such conduct goes unpunished. What is left is an act of private association and communication. The fact that sexuality is implicated seems an anatomical irrelevance."

5. *What was the specific act for which Hardwick has been arrested? Does it matter?* "Overlooked by both opinions," points out Posner, note 3 supra, at 343, "is the fact that at common law sodomy did not include fellatio, the specific act for which Hardwick had been arrested; sodomy at common law was limited to anal intercourse. The extension of the proscription to oral sex came late in the nineteenth century, after the Bill of Rights and the Fourteenth Amendment. White is correct nevertheless that the right to engage in homosexual acts is not deeply rooted in America's history and tradition. [But the] same thing could have

---

a. See, e.g., *DeFunis v. Odegaard*, 416 U.S. 312, 94 S.Ct. 1704, 40 L.Ed.2d 164 (1974).

b. "Evidently," observes Judge Posner, id. at 345, "the Georgia legislature that passed the sodomy law was concerned not about homosexuality as such but about 'unnatural' sexual acts by or on whomever committed. Whatever the arguments that might be marshaled in

favor of attempts to suppress homosexuality, they are not available as arguments for suppressing 'unnatural' sex acts between men and women—except for the theological arguments, by 1986 made only by orthodox Roman Catholics, and not by many of them, and those are a thin reed to support criminal punishment."

been said of the rights recognized in the earlier sexual privacy cases (had, indeed, been said by White himself, in his dissent in *Roe*) * * *."

6. *More on the level of generality in defining rights.* Did *Hardwick* define the claim of liberty at the wrong level of generality? Yes, maintains Laurence Tribe (who, as he notes, argued the case for Hardwick in the Supreme Court), *Treatise* at 1427–28: "Obviously, the history of homosexuality has been largely a history of opprobrium; indeed, it would not be implausible to find on this basis that homosexuals constitute a discrete and insular minority entitled to heightened protection under the equal protection clause.[c] Yet when the Court uses the history of violent disapproval of the behavior that forms part of the very definition of homosexuality as the basis for denying homosexuals' claim to protection, it effectively inverts the equal protection axiom of heightened judicial solicitude for despised groups and their characteristic activities and uses that inverted principle to bootstrap antipathy toward homosexuality into a tautological rationale for continuing to criminalize homosexuality. Therefore, in asking whether an alleged right forms part of a traditional liberty, it is crucial to define the liberty at a high enough level of generality to permit unconventional variants to claim protection along with mainstream versions of protected conduct. The proper question, as the dissent in *Hardwick* recognized, is not whether oral sex as such has long enjoyed a special place in the pantheon of constitutional rights, but whether private, consensual, adult sexual acts partake of traditionally revered liberties of intimate association and individual autonomy."

But consider Robert Bork, *The Tempting of America*, 203–04 (1990): "Tribe [thinks that a] constitutional right to homosexual conduct within the home [is] part of a broader right to sexual intimacies between consenting adults. [The] Court [, he tells us,] must choose the level of generality at which it states 'traditional liberty' at any level that results in a constitutional right for unconventional behavior. This bypasses the question of whether the Constitution contains protection for any sexual conduct or whether that is left to the moral sense of the people. It also fails to come to grips with the central question[:] How can any individual, professor, judge, or moral philosopher tell us convincingly that, regardless of law or our own moral sense, certain forms of unconventional behavior must be allowed? There is no apparent reason why the Court should manipulate the level of generality to protect unconventional sexual behavior any more than liberty should be taken at a high enough level of abstraction to protect kleptomania. Tribe has more sympathy for one than for the other, but that hardly rises to the level of a constitutional principle." [d]

7. *Drawing guidance from the text itself; Hardwick, Roe, and the "right" to use a sperm bank.* "The basic choice," maintain Tribe and Dorf, fn. a supra, at 1107 "—and neither the Constitution's text nor its structure nor its history can make it for us—is between emphasizing the 'conservative' functions of both the liberty and equality clauses (as well as others), and emphasizing their potential as generators of critique and change." They continue, id. at 1107–08:

"We must justify the choice extratextually, but we may and should then implement it in ways that draw as much guidance as possible from the text itself.

---

c. Cf. Frank Michelman, *Law's Republic,* 97 Yale L.J. 1493, 1532–33 (1988). Consider, too, Posner, note 3 supra, at 346–48; Sylvia Law, *Homosexuality and the Social Meaning of Gender,* 1988 Wisc. L.Rev. 1; David Richards, *Constitutional Legitimacy and Constitutional* *Privacy,* 61 NYU.L.Rev. 800 (1986). See also pp. 1321–23 infra.

d. For a partial response to Judge Bork, see Tribe & Dorf, *Levels of Generality in the Definitions of Rights,* 57 U.Chi.L.Rev. 1057, 1099–1100 (1990).

Justice Harlan exemplified such a program in his [*Poe v. Ullman*] dissent, in which he opted for a moderately conservative orientation toward generalization (one considerably less tradition-conserving than Justice Scalia's, however) and sought unifying structures for specified rights in an intermediate level of generality, drawing heavily upon textual points of reference.

"In the *Hardwick* context, if one is willing to generalize much at all, the Constitution's text—in the First Amendment's protection of peaceful assembly and in the Fourth Amendment's protection of the home—points toward generalizing in the direction of intimate personal association in the privacy of the home rather than generalizing in the direction of, let us say, freedom of choice in matters of procreation. It is for this reason that *Hardwick* seems to us so egregiously wrong; that *Roe* seems a closer and more difficult case; that a supposed 'fundamental right' to use a sperm bank would represent a particularly bold leap; and that a 'right' to enforce a surrogacy contract against a woman who has changed her mind and wishes to keep her gestational child entails a leap across a constitutionally unbridgeable void."

MORE ON PRIVACY AND AUTONOMY

1. *Personal appearance and lifestyles.* KELLEY v. JOHNSON, 425 U.S. 238, 96 S.Ct. 1440, 47 L.Ed.2d 708 (1976), per Rehnquist, J., held that regulations directed at the style and length of male police officers' hair, sideburns and mustaches, and prohibiting beards and goatees except for medical reasons, violated no " 'liberty' interest protected by the Fourteenth Amendment": "The 'liberty' interest claimed [here] is distinguishable from [those] protected in *Roe, Eisenstadt* [and] *Griswold,* [which] involved a substantial claim of infringement on the individual's freedom of choice with respect to certain basic matters of procreation, marriage, and family life."

Assuming that "the citizenry at large has some sort of 'liberty' interest within the Fourteenth Amendment in matters of personal appearance," this assumption is insufficient to topple the regulation, for respondent has sought constitutional protection "as an employee of the county and, more particularly, as a policeman. [T]he county has chosen a mode of organization which it undoubtedly deems the most efficient in enabling its police to carry out the duties assigned to them under state and local law. Such a choice necessarily gives weight to the overall need for discipline, esprit de corps, and uniformity.

"The promotion of safety of persons and property is unquestionably at the core of the State's police [power]. Choice of organization, dress and equipment for law enforcement personnel is a decision entitled to the same sort of presumption of legislative validity as are state choices designed to promote other aims within the cognizance of the State's police power. [Thus] the question is not [whether] the State can 'establish' a 'genuine public need' for the specific regulation [but] whether respondent can demonstrate that there is no rational connection between the regulation, based as it is on petitioner's method of organizing its police force, and the promotion of safety of persons and property.

"[The courts are not] in a position to weigh the policy arguments in favor of and against a rule regulating hairstyles as a part of regulations governing a uniformed civilian service. The constitutional issue [is whether the] determination that such regulations should be enacted is so irrational that it may be branded 'arbitrary,' and therefore a deprivation of respondent's 'liberty' interest in freedom to choose his own hairstyle. *Williamson v. Lee Optical Co.*

The overwhelming majority of state and local police of the present day are uniformed. This fact itself testifies to the recognition by those who direct those operations, and by the people of the States and localities who directly or indirectly choose such persons, that similarity in appearance of police officers is desirable. This choice may be based on a desire to make police officers readily recognizable to the members of the public, or a desire for the esprit de corps which such similarity is felt to inculcate within the police force itself. Either one is a sufficiently rational justification for" the regulations.[a]

Marshall, J., joined by Brennan, J., dissented: "An individual's personal appearance may reflect, sustain, and nourish his personality and may well be used as a means of expressing his attitude and lifestyle.[2] In taking control over a citizen's personal appearance, the Government forces him to sacrifice substantial elements of his integrity and identity as well. To say that the liberty guarantee of the Fourteenth Amendment does not encompass matters of personal appearance would be fundamentally inconsistent with the values of privacy, self-identity, autonomy, and personal integrity that I have always assumed the Constitution was designed to protect [referring, e.g., to *Roe* and *Griswold*].[b]

"[While] fully accepting the aims of 'identifiability' and maintenance of esprit de corps, I find no rational relationship between the challenged regulation and these goals. As for the first justification offered by the Court, I simply do not see how requiring policemen to maintain hair of under a certain length could rationally be argued to contribute to making them identifiable to the public as policemen. [As] for the Court's second justification, the fact that it is the President of the Patrolmen's Benevolent Association, in his official capacity, who has challenged the regulation here would seem to indicate that the regulation would if anything, decrease rather than increase the police force's esprit de corps.[6] And even if one accepted the argument that substantial similarity in appearance would increase a force's esprit de corps, I simply do not understand how implementation of this regulation could be expected to create any increment in similarity of appearance among members of a uniformed police force. While the regulation prohibits hair below the ears or the collar and limits the length of sideburns, it allows the maintenance of any type of hair style, other than a pony tail. Thus, as long as their hair does not go below their collars, two police officers, with an 'Afro' hair style and the other with a crew cut could both be in full compliance with the regulation.[7] * * * [8]"

a. Powell, J., joined the Court's opinion, but underscored that, unlike the dissenters, he found "no negative implications in the opinion with respect to a liberty interest within the Fourteenth Amendment as to matters of personal appearance."

2. While the parties did not address any First Amendment issues in any detail in this Court, governmental regulation of a citizen's personal appearance may in some circumstances not only deprive him of liberty under the Fourteenth Amendment but violate his First Amendment rights as well. *Tinker v. Des Moines School District* [p. 829 infra].

b. See also J. Harvie Wilkinson & G. Edward White, [*Constitutional Protection for Personal Lifestyles*, 62 Corn.L.Rev. 562, 605 (1977): "Appearance, like speech, is a chief medium of self-expression that involves important choices about how we wish to project ourselves and be perceived by others. To link

appearance with privacy and speech values is not, of course, to require similar constitutional treatment. It does imply, however, that we deal with a substantive constitutional liberty."

6. Nor, to say the least, is the esprit de corps argument bolstered by the fact that the International Brotherhood of Police Officers, a 25,000 member union representing uniformed police officers, has filed a brief as amicus curiae arguing that the challenged regulation is unconstitutional.

7. The regulation itself eschews what would appear to be a less intrusive means of achieving similarity in the hair length of on-duty officers. According to the regulation, a policeman cannot comply with the hair length requirements by wearing a wig with hair of the proper length while on duty. The regulation prohibits the wearing of wigs or hair pieces

8. See note 8. on page 435.

2. *The substantive due process rights of involuntarily-committed mentally retarded persons.* YOUNGBERG v. ROMEO, 457 U.S. 307, 102 S.Ct. 2452, 73 L.Ed.2d 28 (1982), considered for the first time the substantive due process rights of involuntarily-committed mentally retarded persons. On his mother's petition, Romeo, a profoundly retarded 33-year-old was involuntarily committed to a Pennsylvania state institution (Pennhurst). Subsequently, concerned about injuries Romeo had suffered at Pennhurst, his mother sued institution officials claiming that her son had constitutional rights to (1) safe conditions of confinement, (2) freedom from bodily restraint, and (3) "a constitutional right to minimally adequate habilitation," i.e., minimal training and development of needed skills. (In light of his severe retardation, however, respondent conceded that no amount of training would make his release possible.) The Court, per POWELL, J., pointed out that respondent's first two claims "involve liberty interests recognized by prior decisions of this Court, interests that involuntary commitment proceedings do not extinguish," but found respondent's remaining claim "more troubling":

"[If,] as seems the case, respondent seeks only training related to safety and freedom from restraints, this case does not present the difficult question whether a mentally retarded person, involuntarily committed to a state institution, has some general constitutional right to training per se, even when no type or amount of training would lead to freedom. [On the basis of the record], we conclude that respondent's liberty interests require the State to provide minimally adequate or reasonable training to ensure safety and freedom from undue restraint. [W]e need go no further in this case.

"[But the question] is not simply whether a liberty interest has been infringed but whether the extent or nature of the restraint or lack of absolute safety is such as to violate due process. In determining whether a substantive right protected by the Due Process Clause has been violated, it is necessary to balance 'the liberty of the individual' and 'the demands of an organized society.'"

The Court then considered "the proper standard for determining whether a State adequately has protected the rights of the involuntarily-committed mentally retarded." It agreed with the concurring judge below "that 'the Constitution only requires that the courts make certain that professional judgment was in fact exercised. It is not appropriate for the courts to specify which of several professionally acceptable choices should have been made.' Persons who have been involuntarily committed are entitled to more considerate treatment [than] criminals whose conditions of confinement are designed to punish. At the same time, the standard is lower than [a] 'compelling' or 'substantial' necessity [test for justifying restraints] that would place an undue burden on the administration of [state institutions] and also would restrict unnecessarily the exercise of professional judgment as to the needs of residents.

"on duty in uniform except for cosmetic reasons to cover natural baldness or physical disfiguration." Thus, while the regulation in terms applies to grooming standards of policemen while on duty, the hair length provision effectively controls both on-duty and off-duty appearance.

[Why did the *Kelley* majority see no need to respond to the dissent's point that simply requiring a police officer to wear an appropriate wig while on duty would serve all of the county's articulated interests? See Tribe *Treatise* at 1387 n. 26.]

8. Because, to my mind, the challenged regulation fails to pass even a minimal degree of scrutiny, there is no need to determine whether, given the nature of the interests involved and the degree to which they are affected, the application of a more heightened scrutiny would be appropriate.

"[In] determining what is 'reasonable'—in this and in any case presenting a claim for training by a state—we emphasize that courts must show deference to the judgment exercised by a qualified professional. [The] decision, if made by a professional, is presumptively valid; liability may be imposed only when the decision by the professional is such a substantial departure from accepted professional judgment, practice or standards as to demonstrate that the person responsible actually did not base the decision on such a judgment.[a] In an action for damages against a professional in his individual capacity, however, the professional will not be liable if he was unable to satisfy his normal professional standards because of budgetary constraints; in such a situation, good-faith immunity would bar liability."

BLACKMUN, J., joined by Brennan and O'Connor, JJ., joined the Court's opinion, but concurred separately to clarify why, because of the uncertainty in the record, "that opinion properly leaves open two difficult and important questions." He believed that whether Pennsylvania could accept respondent for "care and treatment" and then constitutionally refuse to provide him any "treatment," as that term is defined by state law, would, if properly before the Court, present "a serious issue." As for the second difficult question left open—whether respondent had an "independent constitutional claim [to] that 'habilitation' or training necessary to *preserve* those basic self-care skills he possessed when he first entered Pennhurst"—he believed that "it would be consistent with the Court's reasoning today to include within the 'minimally adequate training required by the Constitution' such training as is reasonably necessary to prevent a person's pre-existing self-care skills from *deteriorating* because of his commitment" and he viewed such deterioration "because of the State's unreasonable refusal to provide him training [a] loss of liberty quite distinct from—and as serious as—the loss of safety and freedom from unreasonable restraints."

BURGER, C.J., concurring, agreed with much of the Court's opinion, but "would hold flatly that respondent has no constitutional right to training, or 'habilitation,' per se." He agreed that "some amount of self-care instruction may be necessary to avoid unreasonable infringement of a mentally-retarded person's interests in safety and freedom from restraint"; but he thought it "clear" that "the Constitution does not otherwise place an affirmative duty on the State to provide any particular kind of training or habilitation—even such as might be encompassed under the essentially standardless rubric 'minimally adequate training,' to which the Court refers." Since respondent had asserted "a right to 'minimally adequate' habilitation '[q]uite apart from its relationship to decent care,'" unlike the Court he saw "no way to avoid the issue." [b]

THE "RIGHT TO DIE"

CRUZAN v. DIRECTOR, MISSOURI DEP'T. OF HEALTH

497 U.S. 261, 110 S.Ct. 2841, 111 L.Ed.2d 224 (1990).

CHIEF JUSTICE REHNQUIST delivered the opinion of the Court.

[The case arose as follows: Since 1983, when, at the age of 25, she suffered severe injuries during an automobile accident, Nancy Beth Cruzan has been in a

a. Does this place "a seemingly insurmountable burden" on plaintiff mental patients? See Note, 96 Harv.L.Rev. 77, 85 (1982).

b. Consider, too, *DeShaney v. Winnebago County*, p. 1370 infra.

persistent vegetative state, a condition in which a person exhibits motor reflexes, but evinces no indications of significant cognitive function. (Some 10,000 persons are being maintained in a persistent vegetative state (PVS) in the United States and the number is expected to increase significantly in the near future.) Although the trial court found that Nancy is "oblivious to her environment except for reflective responses to sound and perhaps painful stimuli," medical experts testified that if her life support were not removed she could be kept alive another 30 years.

[Nancy is able to breathe on her own, but for a number of years she has received all her nutrition and fluids through a gastrostomy tube (a feeding and hydration tube inserted into her stomach). About a month after the accident, when Nancy was unconscious, surgeons implanted the feeding tube with the consent of Nancy's then husband. This step was taken in order to ease feeding and improve chances of possible recovery. When it became apparent that Nancy had virtually no chance of regaining her cognitive faculties, co-petitioners Lester and Joyce Cruzan, Nancy's parents and co-guardians, sought to discontinue the tubal feeding. They were rebuffed by officials of the state hospital, where Nancy is a patient. Nancy's parents then sought a court order directing the removal of the feeding tube. The trial court so ordered, maintaining that a person in Nancy's condition had a fundamental right to refuse or to direct removal of her life support and that no state interest outweighed Nancy's "right to liberty."

[Before lapsing into her present condition, Nancy had neither executed a living will nor designated anyone to make health-care decisions for her in the event she became incompetent. But when still a vibrant person Nancy had once remarked that she did not want to live "as a vegetable." In another conversation, she had stated that if she couldn't do things for herself "even halfway, let alone not at all," she "wouldn't want to live that way." The trial court concluded that such evidence "suggests that given her present condition [Nancy] would not wish to continue on with her nutrition and hydration." The Missouri Supreme Court reversed (4–3). The majority considered Nancy's remarks so remote, general and casual as to be "unreliable for the purposes of establishing her intent." For a guardian to exercise whatever right an incompetent patient may have to be free of life support, ruled the court, the patient must have complied with "the formalities required under Missouri's living will statutes" or there must be "clear and convincing, inherently reliable evidence" of her wishes. Such evidence, concluded the court, was lacking in this case. The U.S. Supreme Court affirmed.]

As [various state] cases demonstrate, the common-law doctrine of informed consent is viewed as generally encompassing the right of a competent individual to refuse medical treatment. [State] courts have available to them for decision a number of sources—state constitutions, statutes, and common law—which are not available to us. In this Court, the question is simply and starkly whether the United States Constitution prohibits Missouri from choosing the rule of decision which it did.

[The] principle that a competent person has a constitutionally protected liberty interest in refusing unwanted medical treatment may be inferred from our prior decisions. [But] determining that a person has a "liberty interest" under the Due Process Clause does not end the inquiry;[7] "whether respondent's

---

7. Although many state courts have held that a right to refuse treatment is encompassed by a generalized constitutional right of privacy, we have never so held. We believe this issue is more properly analyzed in terms of a Fourteenth Amendment liberty interest. See *Bowers v. Hardwick*.

constitutional rights have been violated must be determined by balancing his liberty interests against the relevant state interests." *Youngberg v. Romeo.*

Petitioners insist that under the general holdings of our cases, the forced administration of life-sustaining medical treatment, and even of artificially-delivered food and water essential to life, would implicate a competent persons' liberty interest. Although we think the logic of the cases discussed above would embrace such a liberty interest, the dramatic consequences involved in refusal of such treatment would inform the inquiry as to whether the deprivation of that interest is constitutionally permissible. But for purposes of this case, we assume that the United States Constitution would grant a competent person a constitutionally protected right to refuse lifesaving hydration and nutrition.

Petitioners assert that an incompetent person should possess the same right in this respect as is possessed by a competent person. [The] difficulty with petitioners' claim is that in a sense it begs the question: an incompetent person is not able to make an informed and voluntary choice to exercise a hypothetical right to refuse treatment or any other right. Such a "right" must be exercised for her, if at all, by some sort of surrogate. Here, Missouri has in effect recognized that under certain circumstances a surrogate may act for the patient in electing to have hydration and nutrition withdrawn in such a way as to cause death, but it has established a procedural safeguard to assure that the action of the surrogate conforms as best it may to the wishes expressed by the patient while competent. Missouri requires that evidence of the incompetent's wishes as to the withdrawal of treatment be proved by clear and convincing evidence. The question, then, is whether the United States Constitution forbids the establishment of this procedural requirement by the State. We hold that it does not.

Whether or not Missouri's clear and convincing evidence requirement comports with [the] Constitution depends in part on what interests the State may properly seek to protect in this situation. Missouri relies on its interest in the protection and preservation of human life, and there can be no gainsaying this interest. As a general matter, the States—indeed, all civilized nations—demonstrate their commitment to life by treating homicide as serious crime. Moreover, the majority of States in this country have laws imposing criminal penalties on one who assists another to commit suicide. We do not think a State is required to remain neutral in the face of an informed and voluntary decision by a physically-able adult to starve to death.

But in the context presented here, a State has more particular interests at stake. The choice between life and death is a deeply personal decision of obvious and overwhelming finality. We believe Missouri may legitimately seek to safeguard the personal element of this choice through the imposition of heightened evidentiary requirements. It cannot be disputed that the Due Process Clause protects an interest in life as well as an interest in refusing life-sustaining medical treatment. Not all incompetent patients will have loved ones available to serve as surrogate decisionmakers. And even where family members are present, "[t]here will, of course, be some unfortunate situations in which family members will not act to protect a patient." A State is entitled to guard against potential abuses in such situations. Similarly, a State is entitled to consider that a judicial proceeding to make a determination regarding an incompetent's wishes may very well not be an adversarial one, with the added guarantee of accurate factfinding that the adversary process brings with it. Finally, we think a State may properly decline to make judgments about the "quality" of life that a particular individual may enjoy, and simply assert an unqualified interest in the preservation of human life to be weighed against the constitutionally protected interests of the individual.

In our view, Missouri has permissibly sought to advance these interests through the adoption of a "clear and convincing" standard of proof to govern such proceedings. [The] more stringent the burden of proof a party must bear, the more that party bears the risk of an erroneous decision. We believe that Missouri may permissibly place an increased risk of an erroneous decision on those seeking to terminate an incompetent individual's life-sustaining treatment. An erroneous decision not to terminate results in a maintenance of the status quo; the possibility of subsequent developments such as advancements in medical science, the discovery of new evidence regarding the patient's intent, changes in the law, or simply the unexpected death of the patient despite the administration of life-sustaining treatment, at least create the potential that a wrong decision will eventually be corrected or its impact mitigated. An erroneous decision to withdraw life-sustaining treatment, however, is not susceptible of correction.

[The] Supreme Court of Missouri held that in this case the testimony adduced at trial did not amount to clear and convincing proof of the patient's desire to have hydration and nutrition withdrawn. [The] testimony adduced at trial consisted primarily of Nancy Cruzan's statements made to a housemate about a year before her accident that she would not want to live should she face life as a "vegetable," and other observations to the same effect. The observations did not deal in terms with withdrawal of medical treatment or of hydration and nutrition. We cannot say that the Supreme Court of Missouri committed constitutional error in reaching the conclusion that it did.

Petitioners alternatively contend that Missouri must accept the "substituted judgment" of close family members even in the absence of substantial proof that their views reflect the views of the patient. [But] we do not think the Due Process Clause requires the State to repose judgment on these matters with anyone but the patient herself. Close family members may have a strong feeling—a feeling not at all ignoble or unworthy, but not entirely disinterested, either—that they do not wish to witness the continuation of the life of a loved one which they regard as hopeless, meaningless, and even degrading. But there is no automatic assurance that the view of close family members will necessarily be the same as the patient's would have been had she been confronted with the prospect of her situation while competent. * * *

JUSTICE O'CONNOR, concurring.

I agree that a protected liberty interest in refusing unwanted medical treatment may be inferred from our prior decisions and that the refusal of artificially delivered food and water is encompassed within that liberty interest. I write separately to clarify why I believe this to be so.

[Because] our notions of liberty are inextricably entwined with our idea of physical freedom and self-determination, the Court has often deemed state incursions into the body repugnant to the interests protected by the Due Process Clause. [The] State's imposition of medical treatment on an unwilling competent adult necessarily involves some form of restraint and intrusion. A seriously ill or dying patient whose wishes are not honored may feel a captive of the machinery required for life-sustaining measures or other medical interventions. Such forced treatment may burden that individual's liberty interests as much as any state coercion.

[The] State's artificial provision of nutrition and hydration implicates identical concerns. Artificial feeding cannot readily be distinguished from other forms of medical treatment. [Requiring] a competent adult to endure such procedures against her will burdens the patient's liberty, dignity, and freedom to determine the course of her own treatment. Accordingly, the liberty guaranteed by the Due Process Clause must protect, if it protects anything, an individual's deeply personal decision to reject medical treatment, including the artificial delivery of food and water.

I also write separately to emphasize that the Court does not today decide the issue whether a State must also give effect to the decisions of a surrogate decisionmaker. In my view, such a duty may well be constitutionally required to protect the patient's liberty interest in refusing medical treatment. Few individuals provide explicit oral or written instructions regarding their intent to refuse medical treatment should they become incompetent. * * * Delegating the authority to make medical decisions to a family member or friend is becoming a common method of planning for the future. * * *

[Today's decision] does not preclude a future determination that the Constitution requires the States to implement the decisions of a patient's duly appointed surrogate. Nor does it prevent States from developing other approaches for protecting an incompetent individual's liberty interest in refusing medical treatment. [N]o national consensus has yet emerged on the best solution for this difficult and sensitive problem. Today we decide only that one State's practice does not violate the Constitution * * *.

JUSTICE SCALIA, concurring.

The various opinions in this case portray quite clearly the difficult, indeed agonizing, questions that are presented by the constantly increasing power of science to keep the human body alive for longer than any reasonable person would want to inhabit it. The States have begun to grapple with these problems through legislation. I am concerned, from the tenor of today's opinions, that we are poised to confuse that enterprise as successfully as we have confused the enterprise of legislating concerning abortion—requiring it to be conducted against a background of federal constitutional imperatives that are unknown because they are being newly crafted from Term to Term. That would be a great misfortune.

While I agree with the Court's analysis today, and therefore join in its opinion, I would have preferred that we announce, clearly and promptly, that the federal courts have no business in this field; that American law has always accorded the State the power to prevent, by force if necessary, suicide—including suicide by refusing to take appropriate measures necessary to preserve one's life; that the point at which life becomes "worthless," and the point at which the means necessary to preserve it become "extraordinary" or "inappropriate," are neither set forth in the Constitution nor known to the nine Justices of this Court any better than they are known to nine people picked at random from the Kansas City telephone directory; and hence, that even when it *is* demonstrated by clear and convincing evidence that a patient no longer wishes certain measures to be taken to preserve her life, it is up to the citizens of Missouri to decide, through their elected representatives, whether that wish will be honored. It is quite impossible (because the Constitution says nothing about the matter) that those citizens will decide upon a line less lawful than the one we would choose; and it is unlikely (because we know no more about "life-and-death" than they do) that they will decide upon a line less reasonable.

The text of the Due Process Clause does not protect individuals against deprivations of liberty simpliciter. It protects them against deprivations of liberty "without due process of law." [It] is at least true that no "substantive due process" claim can be maintained unless the claimant demonstrates that the State has deprived him of a right historically and traditionally protected against State interference. *Michael H.* (plurality opinion); *Hardwick.* [That] cannot possibly be established here.

At common law in England, a suicide [was] criminally liable. [And] most States that did not explicitly prohibit assisted suicide in 1868 recognized, when the issue arose in the 50 years following the Fourteenth Amendment's ratification, that assisted and (in some cases) attempted suicide were unlawful. Thus, "there is no significant support for the claim that a right to suicide is so rooted in our tradition that it may be deemed 'fundamental' or 'implicit in the concept of ordered liberty.'"

Petitioners rely on three distinctions to separate Nancy Cruzan's case from ordinary suicide: (1) that she is permanently incapacitated and in pain; (2) that she would bring on her death not by any affirmative act but by merely declining treatment that provides nourishment; and (3) that preventing her from effectuating her presumed wish to die requires violation of her bodily integrity. None of these suffices. Suicide was not excused even when committed "to avoid those ills which [persons] had not the fortitude to endure."

[The] second asserted distinction [relies] on the dichotomy between action and inaction. Suicide, it is said, consists of an affirmative act to end one's life; refusing treatment is not an affirmative act "causing" death, but merely a passive acceptance of the natural process of dying. I readily acknowledge that the distinction between action and inaction has some bearing upon the legislative judgment of what ought to be prevented as suicide—though even there it would seem to me unreasonable to draw the line precisely between action and inaction, rather than between various forms of inaction.

[But] to return to the principal point for present purposes: the irrelevance of the action-inaction distinction. Starving oneself to death is no different from putting a gun to one's temple as far as the common-law definition of suicide is concerned; the cause of death in both cases is the suicide's conscious decision to "pu[t] an end to his own existence." Of course the common law rejected the action-inaction distinction in other contexts involving the taking of human life as well. In the prosecution of a parent for the starvation death of her infant, it was no defense that the infant's death was "caused" by no action of the parent but by the natural process of starvation, or by the infant's natural inability to provide for itself. A physician, moreover, could be criminally liable for failure to provide care that could have extended the patient's life, even if death was immediately caused by the underlying disease that the physician failed to treat.

[The] third asserted basis of distinction—that frustrating Nancy Cruzan's wish to die in the present case requires interference with her bodily integrity—is likewise inadequate, because such interference is impermissible only if one begs the question whether her refusal to undergo the treatment on her own is suicide. It has always been lawful not only for the State, but even for private citizens, to interfere with bodily integrity to prevent a felony. That general rule has of course been applied to suicide.

[The] dissents of Justices Brennan and Stevens make a plausible case for our intervention here only by embracing—the latter explicitly and the former by implication—a political principle that the States are free to adopt, but that is demonstrably not imposed by the Constitution. [I]nsofar as balancing the relative interests of the State and the individual is concerned, there is nothing distinctive about accepting death through the refusal of "medical treatment," as opposed to accepting it through the refusal of food, or through the failure to shut off the engine and get out of the car after parking in one's garage after work. [Justice] Brennan's position ultimately rests upon the proposition that it is none of the State's business if a person wants to commit suicide. Justice Stevens is explicit on the point. [This] is a view that some societies have held, and that our States are free to adopt if they wish. But it is not a view imposed by our constitutional traditions, in which the power of the State to prohibit suicide is unquestionable.

What I have said above is not meant to suggest that I would think it desirable, if we were sure that Nancy Cruzan wanted to die, to keep her alive by the means at issue here. I assert only that the Constitution has nothing to say about the subject. To raise up a constitutional right here we would have to create out of nothing (for it exists neither in text nor tradition) some constitutional principle whereby, although the State may insist that an individual come in out of the cold and eat food, it may not insist that he take medicine; and although it may pump his stomach empty of poison he has ingested, it may not fill his stomach with food he has failed to ingest. Are there, then, no reasonable and humane limits that ought not to be exceeded in requiring an individual to preserve his own life? There obviously are, but they are not set forth in the Due Process Clause. What assures us that those limits will not be exceeded is the same constitutional guarantee that is the source of most of our protection—what protects us, for example, from being assessed a tax of 100% of our income above the subsistence level, from being forbidden to drive cars, or from being required to send our children to school for 10 hours a day, none of which horribles is categorically prohibited by the Constitution. Our salvation is the Equal Protection Clause, which requires the democratic majority to accept for themselves and their loved ones what they impose on you and me. This Court need not, and has no authority to, inject itself into every field of human activity where irrationality and oppression may theoretically occur, and if it tries to do so it will destroy itself.

Justice Brennan, with whom Justice Marshall and Justice Blackmun join, dissenting.

[Because] I believe that Nancy Cruzan has a fundamental right to be free of unwanted artificial nutrition and hydration, which right is not outweighed by any interests of the State, and because I find that the improperly biased procedural obstacles imposed by the Missouri Supreme Court impermissibly burden that right, I respectfully dissent. Nancy Cruzan is entitled to choose to die with dignity.

[If] a competent person has a liberty interest to be free of unwanted medical treatment, as both the majority and Justice O'Connor concede, it must be fundamental. [The] right to be free from medical attention without consent, to determine what shall be done with one's own body, *is* deeply rooted in this Nation's traditions, as the majority acknowledges. [Thus,] freedom from unwanted medical attention is unquestionably among those principles "so rooted in the traditions and conscience of our people as to be ranked as fundamental."

[Although] the right to be free of unwanted medical intervention, like other constitutionally protected interests, may not be absolute, [w]hatever a State's possible interests in mandating life-support treatment under other circumstances, there is no good to be obtained here by Missouri's insistence that Nancy Cruzan remain on life-support systems if it is indeed her wish not to do so. Missouri does not claim, nor could it, that society as a whole will be benefited by Nancy's receiving medical treatment. No third party's situation will be improved and no harm to others will be averted.

The only state interest asserted here is a general interest in the preservation of life. But the State has no legitimate general interest in someone's life, completely abstracted from the interest of the person living that life, that could outweigh the person's choice to avoid medical treatment. [Thus,] the State's general interest in life must accede to Nancy Cruzan's particularized and intense interest in self-determination in her choice of medical treatment. There is simply nothing legitimately within the State's purview to be gained by superseding her decision.

[This] is not to say that the State has no legitimate interests to assert here. As the majority recognizes, Missouri has a parens patriae interest in providing Nancy Cruzan, now incompetent, with as accurate as possible a determination of how she would exercise her rights under these circumstances. [In doing so, however,] Missouri may constitutionally impose only those procedural requirements that serve to enhance the accuracy of a determination of Nancy Cruzan's wishes or are at least consistent with an accurate determination. The Missouri "safeguard" that the Court upholds today does not meet that standard [and] imposes a markedly asymmetrical evidentiary burden. Only evidence of specific statements of treatment choice made by the patient when competent is admissible to support a finding that the patient, now in a persistent vegetative state, would wish to avoid further medical treatment. Moreover, this evidence must be clear and convincing. No proof is required to support a finding that the incompetent person would wish to continue treatment.

[An] erroneous decision to terminate life-support is irrevocable, says the majority, while an erroneous decision not to terminate "results in a maintenance of the status quo." [17] But, from the point of view of the patient, an erroneous decision in either direction is irrevocable. [An] erroneous decision not to terminate [life-support] robs a patient of the very qualities protected by the right to avoid unwanted medical treatment. His own degraded existence is perpetuated; his family's suffering is protracted; the memory he leaves behind becomes more and more distorted. * * *

Too few people execute living wills or equivalently formal directives [for] an evidentiary rule [such as Missouri's] to ensure adequately that the wishes of incompetent persons will be honored. [Even] someone with a resolute determination to avoid life-support under circumstances such as Nancy's would still need to know that such things as living wills exist and how to execute one. Often legal help would be necessary, especially given the majority's apparent willingness to permit States to insist that a person's wishes are not truly known unless the particular medical treatment is specified.

[The] testimony of close friends and family members, on the other hand, may often be the best evidence available of what the patient's choice would be. [The] Missouri court's decision to ignore this whole category of testimony is also at odds with the practices of other States.

---

17. The majority's definition of the "status quo," of course, begs the question. Artificial delivery of nutrition and hydration represents the "status quo" only if the State has chosen to permit doctors and hospitals to keep a patient on life-support systems over the protests of his family or guardian. The "status quo" absent that state interference would be the natural result of his accident or illness (and the family's decision). * * *

[A] State may ensure that the person who makes the decision on the patient's behalf is the one whom the patient himself would have selected to make that choice for him. And a State may exclude from consideration anyone having improper motives. But a State generally must either repose the choice with the person whom the patient himself would most likely have chosen as proxy or leave the decision to the patient's family.

* * * Missouri and this Court [have] discarded evidence of [Nancy's] will, ignored her values, and deprived her of the right to a decision as closely approximating her own choice as humanly possible. They have done so disingenuously in her name, and openly in Missouri's own. * * *

JUSTICE STEVENS, dissenting.

[The Court] permits the State's abstract, undifferentiated interest in the preservation of life to overwhelm the best interests of Nancy Beth Cruzan, interests which would, according to an undisputed finding, be served by allowing her guardian to exercise her constitutional right to discontinue medical treatment.

* * * Choices about death touch the core of liberty. Our duty, and the concomitant freedom, to come to terms with the conditions of our own mortality are undoubtedly "so rooted in the traditions and conscience of our people as to be ranked as fundamental," and indeed are essential incidents of the unalienable rights to life and liberty endowed us by our Creator. The more precise constitutional significance of death is difficult to describe; not much may be said with confidence about death unless it is said from faith, and that alone is reason enough to protect the freedom to conform choices about death to individual conscience. We may also, however, justly assume that death is not life's simple opposite, or its necessary terminus, but rather its completion.

[These] considerations cast into stark relief the injustice, and unconstitutionality, of Missouri's treatment of Nancy Beth Cruzan. [Her] interest in life, no less than that of any other person, includes an interest in how she will be thought of after her death by those whose opinions mattered to her. There can be no doubt that her life made her dear to her family, and to others. How she dies will affect how that life is remembered. The trial court's order authorizing Nancy's parents to cease their daughter's treatment would have permitted the family that cares for Nancy to bring to a close her tragedy and her death. Missouri's objection to that order subordinates Nancy's body, her family, and the lasting significance of her life to the State's own interests. The decision we review thereby interferes with constitutional interests of the highest order.

[It] seems to me that the Court errs insofar as it characterizes this case as involving "judgments about the 'quality' of life that a particular individual may enjoy." Nancy Cruzan is obviously "*alive*" in a physiological sense. But for patients like Nancy Cruzan, who have no consciousness and no chance of recovery, there is a serious question as to whether the mere persistence of their bodies is "*life*" as that word is commonly understood, or as it is used in both the Constitution and the Declaration of Independence. The State's unflagging determination to perpetuate Nancy Cruzan's physical existence is comprehensible only as an effort to define life's meaning, not as an attempt to preserve its sanctity.

[My] disagreement with the Court [is] unrelated to its endorsement of the clear and convincing standard of proof for cases of this kind. Indeed, I agree that the controlling facts must be established with unmistakable clarity. The critical question, however, is not how to prove the controlling facts but rather what proven facts should be controlling. In my view, the constitutional answer is clear:

the best interests of the individual, especially when buttressed by the interests of all related third parties, must prevail over any general state policy that simply ignores those interests. Indeed, the only apparent secular basis for the State's interest in life is the policy's persuasive impact upon people other than Nancy and her family. * * *

Only because Missouri has arrogated to itself the power to define life, and only because the Court permits this usurpation, are Nancy Cruzan's life and liberty put into disquieting conflict. If Nancy Cruzan's life were defined by reference to her own interests, so that her life expired when her biological existence ceased serving *any* of her own interests, then her constitutionally protected interest in freedom from unwanted treatment would not come into conflict with her constitutionally protected interest in life. Conversely, if there were *any* evidence that Nancy Cruzan herself defined life to encompass every form of biological persistence by a human being, so that the continuation of treatment would serve Nancy's own liberty, then once again there would be no conflict between life and liberty. The opposition of life and liberty in this case are thus not the result of Nancy Cruzan's tragic accident, but are instead the artificial consequence of Missouri's effort, and this Court's willingness, to abstract Nancy Cruzan's life from Nancy Cruzan's person.

[The] Cruzan family's continuing concern provides a concrete reminder that Nancy Cruzan's interests did not disappear with her vitality or her consciousness. However commendable may be the State's interest in human life, it cannot pursue that interest by appropriating Nancy Cruzan's life as a symbol for its own purposes. Lives do not exist in abstraction from persons, and to pretend otherwise is not to honor but to desecrate the State's responsibility for protecting life. * * *

REFLECTIONS ON *CRUZAN* AND THE *"RIGHT TO DIE"*

1. *The death of Nancy Cruzan.* Two months after the Supreme Court's decision, Nancy's parents asked the state probate court for a second hearing. At this new hearing, three of Nancy's former co-workers recalled conversations in which she said she never would want to live "like a vegetable" on medical machines. See N.Y. Times, Nov. 2, 1990, p. A12. Since the State of Missouri withdrew from the case and Nancy's court-appointed guardian sought to disconnect the feeding tube, see N.Y. Times, Dec. 7, 1990, p. A12, all remaining parties agreed that artificial nutrition and hydration should cease. A week later, the probate judge ruled that there was "clear evidence" that the "intent" of Nancy, "if mentally able, would be to terminate her nutrition and hydration" and that there was "no evidence of substance" to the contrary. He then authorized the cessation of nutrition and hydration. See N.Y. Times, Dec. 15, 1990, p. 1. Twelve days later, and nearly eight years after she had lost consciousness and a feeding tube had first been implanted in her stomach, Nancy Cruzan died. Did the probate court take the "substituted judgment" seriously or did it really apply an objective test? Cf. Baron, note 2 infra.

2. *What upsets critics of the Cruzan case? What really drives death decisions in PVS cases?* CHARLES BARON, *On Taking Substituted Judgment Seriously*, Hastings Center Rep., Sept.-Oct., 1990, at 7–8: "By requiring clear and convincing evidence of substituted judgment, Missouri prevents death decisions for some persons who are in PVS. But so do those states [that] do not allow death decisions where there is *no* evidence for substituted judgment, or where the patient's family has not reached a death decision for the patient. What reason is

there for thinking that Missouri's procedural safeguards that cause many PVS patients to be continued on life support are unconstitutionally burdensome but those of other states are not? What upsets critics of *Cruzan,* is that Missouri has taken the substituted judgment test seriously. What actually drives death decisions in PVS cases is an objective test based on the convergence of 'best interests' and economic criteria. [But] the extreme discomfort of making death decisions for other people and our fear of the slippery slope * * * leads us to pretend that we are merely complying (however reluctantly) with the wishes of the patient. The result in most states is mere lip service to substituted judgment: Almost any evidence is deemed sufficient to establish a preference for death over PVS. Or families are empowered to express patient preferences for death—with few questions asked." Adds Baron: "What everyone *ought* to be upset about is that virtually all our states (including Missouri) have not adopted rules that openly and honestly apply the objective criteria really driving death decisions in PVS cases."

3. *Abortion, the "right to die," and the intrinsic value of life.* Did Chief Justice Rehnquist and Justice Scalia draw a distinction between the intrinsic value of life and its personal value for the patient? Did these justices maintain that it is *"intrinsically* a bad thing" to bring about a person's death even if it is not in the person's own interest to continue living? If so, is this similar to the notion that it is wrong to destroy a fetus *whether or not* a fetus has any interests to protect? See Ronald Dworkin, *Life's Dominion* 12, 198 (1993).[a]

4. *Analogy to suicide.* Consider Note, 104 Harv.L.Rev. 257, 262 (1990): "[T]he common law right to refuse medical treatment has long existed alongside anti-suicide laws. Acting outside the purview of the legal system, doctors have traditionally withheld certain treatments that would delay death on the grounds that the treatment was unnecessarily painful, that it would not improve the patient's condition, or that it was against the patient's wishes. Further, courts have explicitly rejected the notion that terminating treatment constitutes homicide and have held that the right to refuse treatment exists even if the consequence of refusal is death. Thus, even under Justice Scalia's narrow historical test [referring to fn. 6 of the plurality opinion in *Michael H.*], a competent person has a liberty interest in refusing life-sustaining medical treatment. Justice Scalia's zeal for avoiding the entire 'right to die' area led him to evaluate the interest with a history not specifically applicable to the facts of *Cruzan.*"

5. *More on the level of generality in defining rights or liberty interests. How might Chief Justice Rehnquist have been expected to frame the issue in Cruzan?* Rehnquist, C.J., joined Justice Scalia's plurality opinion in *Michael H.,* including fn. 6. In light of this, would one have expected, or at least not have been surprised, if the Chief Justice had defined the right or liberty interest at issue in *Cruzan* something as follows: "Is the liberty (or right) of an incompetent patient *who is neither dying nor terminally ill,* as those terms are commonly defined, to refuse *lifesaving artificial hydration and nutrition* deeply rooted in the Nation's history and tradition?" Did the Chief Justice assign any particular significance to the fact that the lifesaving measure involved in the *Cruzan* case was artificial feeding? Did he give any weight to the fact that Nancy Cruzan was neither "dying" nor "terminally ill," as those terms are defined by Missouri and many other states?[b] At any point, did he expressly discuss the level of generality at

a. Cf. Tribe, *Abortion* 231. But see Seth Kreimer, *Does Pro–Choice Mean Pro–Kevorkian? An Essay on Roe, Casey, and the Right to Die* (1995) (quoted at length at p. 453 infra);

Thomas Mayo, *Constitutionalizing the "Right to Die,"* 49 Md.L.Rev. 103 (1990).

b. Consider Yale Kamisar, *The "Right to Die": Green Lights and Yellow Lights,* Law

which the liberty interest in *Cruzan* should be defined (and why)? [c]

6. *Inconsistent views of families: can Cruzan and Akron Center be harmonized?* In *Cruzan*, Chief Justice Rehnquist noted that close family members might not act to protect a patient, but he joined Justice Kennedy's lead opinion in *Ohio v. Akron Center*, p. 361 supra, where the majority deemed it fair for a state to assume that "in most instances, the family will strive to give a lonely or even terrified minor advice that is both compassionate and mature." Consider Martha Minow, *The Role of Families in Medical Decisions*, 1991 Utah L.Rev. 1, 8–11:

"[The] dissenting views in *Cruzan* and *Akron Center* reconfirm the inconsistency [noted] in the majority opinions; indeed, we seem to have something like a musical round. The majority in *Cruzan* emphasizes the danger that some families may not act in concert with the incompetent patient's wishes or even in violation of that person's interests; the *Akron Center* dissent does the same, and stresses the danger that some parents may actually threaten abuse of a minor upon discovering her pregnancy. [The] majority in *Akron Center* focuses instead on 'good' families—assumed to be most families—who will provide warmth and helpful assistance to the pregnant minor who has sought help from a doctor. And the dissent in *Cruzan* speculates that family members may know more about the patient and care more about her than anyone else. The inconsistency is complete: the majorities and the dissents have simply swapped places in the two cases when it comes to expressing attitudes and assumptions about the families' participation in the medical decisions at issue." [d]

IS THERE A CONSTITUTIONAL RIGHT TO PHYSICIAN–ASSISTED SUICIDE?

In COMPASSION IN DYING v. WASHINGTON, 79 F.3d 790, 1996 WL 94848 (9th Cir.1996) (en banc), the Ninth Circuit became the first American appellate court to rule that there is a constitutional right to physician-assisted suicide under certain circumstances. An 8–3 majority, per REINHARDT, J., held (a) that "there is a constitutionally-protected liberty interest in determining the time and manner of one's death, an interest that must be weighed against the state's legitimate and countervailing interests"; and, after balancing the competing interests, (b) that insofar as a Washington statute totally banning assisted suicide [a] "prohibits physicians from prescribing life-ending medication for use by terminally ill, competent adults who wish to hasten their own death, it violates

Quadrangle Notes, Fall, 1990, pp. 3, 5: "I venture to say that in some future case the Court will make plain what I think is implicit in *Cruzan*: A patient's 'right to die' cannot be denied solely on the ground that she is neither 'dying' nor 'terminally ill'—no more than it can be denied solely for the reason that the life support involved is a feeding tube rather than a respirator."

c. The Chief Justice might have said, for example, that even under the narrow approach Scalia, J., took in *Michael H.*, "the liberty interest at issue is properly defined at the level of generality of medical treatment, not medical sustenance [because] that is 'the most specific level at which a relevant tradition protecting, or denying protection to, the asserted right can be identified.' Because the technology by

which food and water may be routinely provided by means other than oral intake is of relatively recent origin, no societal tradition exists either permitting or prohibiting individuals to deny themselves medically provided nutrition and hydration." *Developments in the Law—Medical Technology and the Law*, 103 Harv. L.Rev. 1520, 1662 n. 142 (1990). But see Note 6(a) supra.

d. Professor Minow goes on to say, id. at 23–24, that the Court was wrong in both cases.

a. The Washington statute provides that one who "knowingly causes or aids another person to attempt suicide" is guilty of "promoting a suicide," a felony punishable by as much as five years imprisonment.

the Due Process Clause." [b] In the course of its long opinion, the court observed:

"In examining whether a liberty interest exists in determining the time and manner of one's death, we begin with the compelling similarities between right-to-die cases and abortion cases. In the former as in the latter, the relative strength of the competing interests changes as physical, medical, or related circumstances vary. In right-to-die cases the outcome of the balancing test may differ at different points along the life cycle as a person's physical or medical condition deteriorates, just as in abortion cases the permissibility of restrictive state legislation may vary with the progression of the pregnancy. Equally important, both types of cases raise issues of life and death, and both arouse similar religious and moral concerns. Both also present basic questions about an individual's right of choice.

"[In] deciding right-to-die cases, we are guided by the Court's approach to the abortion cases. *Casey* in particular provides a powerful precedent. [Although] *Casey* was influenced by the doctrine of stare decisis, the fundamental message of that case lies in its statements regarding the type of issue that confronts us here: 'These matters, involving the most intimate and personal choices a person may make in a lifetime, choices central to personal dignity and autonomy, are central to the liberty protected by the Fourteenth Amendment.' [c]

" * * * We do not ask simply whether there is a liberty interest in receiving 'aid in killing oneself' because such a narrow interest could not exist in the absence of a broader and more important underlying interest—the right to die. In short, it is the end and not the means that defines the liberty interest. * * * We use the broader and more accurate terms 'the right to die,' 'determining the time and manner of one's death' and 'hastening one's death' for an important reason. The liberty interest we examine encompasses a whole range of acts that are generally not considered to constitute 'suicide.' Included within the liberty interest we examine, is for example, the act of refusing or terminating unwanted medical treatment. [A] competent adult has a liberty interest in refusing to be connected to a respirator or in being disconnected from one, even if he is terminally ill and cannot live without mechanical assistance. The law does not classify the death of a patient that results from the granting of his wish to decline or discontinue treatment as 'suicide.' Nor does the law label the acts of those who help the patient carry out that wish [as] assistance in suicide. Accordingly,

b. The court did not reach the question whether the Washington prohibition, in conjunction with other state laws permitting the termination of life-sustaining medical treatment, also violates the Equal Protection Clause. But consider *Quill v. Vacco*, p. 452 infra, answering this question in the affirmative.

c. At a subsequent point in its opinion, the Ninth Circuit called the decision how and when to die "one of the most, if not the most, 'intimate and personal choices a person may make in a lifetime,' a choice that 'is central to personal dignity and autonomy,' *Casey*." Some proponents of physician-assisted suicide have also relied on other language in the same paragraph of the *Casey* opinion quoted above, such as "[a]t the heart of liberty is the right to define one's own concept of existence." The paragraph from *Casey* reads in full:

"Our law affords constitutional protection to personal decisions relating to marriage, procreation, contraception, family relationships, child rearing, and education. Our cases recognize 'the right of the *individual*, married or single, to be free from unwarranted governmental intrusion into matters so fundamentally affecting a person as the decision whether to bear or beget a child.' Our precedents 'have respected the private realm of family life which the state cannot enter.' These matters, involving the most intimate and personal choices a person may make in a lifetime, choices central to personal dignity and autonomy, are central to the liberty protected by the Fourteenth Amendment. At the heart of liberty is the right to define one's own concept of existence, of meaning, of the universe, and of the mystery of human life. Beliefs about these matters could not define the attributes of personhood were they formed under compulsion of the State."

we believe that the broader terms * * * more accurately describe the liberty interest at issue here.

" * * * We believe that a careful examination of [the substantive due process] decisions demonstrates that there is a strong liberty interest in determining how and when one's life shall end, and that an explicit recognition of that interest follows naturally, indeed inevitably, from their reasoning. [A] common thread running through [such cases as *Pierce, Griswold, Loving* and *Roe*] is that they involve decisions that are highly personal and intimate, as well as of great importance to the individual.[65] Certainly few decisions are more personal, intimate or important than the decision to end one's life, especially when the reason for doing so is to avoid excessive and protracted pain. Accordingly, we believe the cases from *Pierce* through *Roe* provide strong general support for our conclusion that a liberty interest in controlling the time and manner of one's death is protected by [due process].

"*Casey* and *Cruzan* provide persuasive evidence that the Constitution encompasses a due process liberty interest in controlling the time and manner of one's death—that there is, in short, a constitutionally recognized 'right to die.' Our conclusion is strongly influenced by, but not limited to, the plight of mentally competent, terminally ill adults. We are influenced as well by the plight of others, such as those whose existence is reduced to a vegetative state or a permanent and irreversible state of unconsciousness.

"Our conclusion that there is a liberty interest in determining the time and manner of one's death does not mean that there is a concomitant right to exercise that interest in all circumstances or to do so free from state regulation. To the contrary, we explicitly recognize that some prohibitory and regulatory state action is fully consistent with constitutional principles.

"In short, finding a liberty interest constitutes a critical first step toward answering the question before us. The determination that must now be made is whether the state's attempt to curtail the exercise of that interest is constitutionally justified.

[The court then considered six related state interests and found them insufficient to outweigh the terminally ill individual's interest in deciding whether to end his or her suffering by hastening death with medication prescribed by his or her physician. The six state interests identified by the court were: "1) the state's general interest in preserving life; 2) the state's more specific interest in preventing suicide; 3) the state's interest in avoiding the involvement of third parties and in precluding the use of arbitrary, unfair, or undue influence; 4) the state's interest in protecting family members and loved ones; 5) the state's interest in protecting the integrity of the medical profession; and, 6) the state's interest in avoiding adverse consequences that might ensue if the statutory provision at issue is declared unconstitutional."

[As for the primary justification offered for the challenged statute, the state's interest in preventing suicide, the court concluded that the distinctions suggested by the state failed to distinguish physician-assisted suicide from other currently acceptable medical practices: "[W]e see little, if any, difference for constitutional

---

65. In this respect, *Bowers v. Hardwick* would appear to be aberrant and to turn on the specific sexual act at issue. * * * We do not believe that the *Bowers* holding controls the outcome here or is in any way inconsistent with our conclusion that there is a liberty interest in dying peacefully and with dignity. We also note, without surprise, that in the decade since *Bowers* was handed down the Court has never cited its central holding approvingly.

or ethical purposes between providing medication with a double effect [i.e., reducing the patient's pain, but at the same time hastening or increasing the risk of death] and providing medication with a single effect [causing death], as long as one of the known effects in each case is to hasten the end of the patient's life. Similarly, we see no ethical or constitutionally cognizable difference between a doctor's pulling the plug on a respirator and his prescribing drugs which will permit a terminally ill patient to end his own life. [To] us, what matters most is that the death of the patient is the intended result as surely in one case as in the other. In sum, we find the state's interests in preventing suicide do not make its interests substantially stronger here than in cases involving other forms of death-hastening medical intervention."]

"The liberty interest at issue here is an important one and, in the case of the terminally ill, is at its peak. Conversely, the state interests, while equally important in the abstract, are for the most part at a low point here. We recognize that in the case of life and death decisions the state has a particularly strong interest in avoiding undue influence and other forms of abuse. Here, that concern is ameliorated in large measure because of the mandatory involvement in the decision-making process of physicians, who have a strong bias in favor of preserving life, and because the process itself can be carefully regulated and rigorous safeguards adopted. Under these circumstances, we believe that the possibility of abuse, even when considered along with the other state interests, does not outweigh the liberty interest at issue.

"The state has chosen to pursue its interests by means of what for terminally ill patients is effectively a total prohibition, even though its most important interests could be adequately served by a far less burdensome measure. The consequences of rejecting the as-applied challenge would be disastrous for the terminally ill, while the adverse consequences for the state would be of a far lesser order. This, too, weighs in favor of upholding the liberty interest.

"[There] is one final point we must emphasize. Some argue strongly that decisions regarding matters affecting life or death should not be made by the courts. Essentially, we agree with that proposition. In this case, by permitting the *individual* to exercise the right to *choose* we are following the constitutional mandate to take such decisions out of the hands of the government, both state and federal, and to put them where they rightly belong, in the hands of the people. We are allowing individuals to make the decisions that so profoundly affect their very existence—and precluding the state from intruding excessively into that critical realm. The Constitution and the courts stand as a bulwark between individual freedom and arbitrary and intrusive governmental power. Under our constitutional system, neither the state nor the majority of the people in a state can impose its will upon the individual in a matter so highly 'central to personal dignity and autonomy,' *Casey.* Those who believe strongly that death must come without physician assistance are free to follow that creed, be they doctors or patients. They are not free, however, to force their views, their religious convictions, or their philosophies on all the other members of a democratic society, and to compel those whose values differ with theirs to die painful, protracted, and agonizing deaths."

There were three separate dissenting opinions. BEEZER, J., who wrote the principal dissent, observed:

"Plaintiffs ask us to blur the line between withdrawal of life-sustaining treatment and physician-assisted suicide. At the same time, some proponents of physician-assisted suicide would maintain a conceptual distinction between physician-assisted suicide and euthanasia. Associating physician-assisted suicide with a relatively accepted procedure and dissociating it from an unpalatable one are rhetorically powerful devices, but run counter to U.S. Supreme Court precedent,[1] Washington State statutory law, medical ethics guidelines of the American Medical Association and the American College of Physicians, and legal reasoning.

"The proper place to draw the line is between withdrawing life-sustaining treatment (which is based on the right to be free from unwanted intrusion) and physician-assisted suicide and euthanasia (which implicate the assistance of others in controlling the timing and manner of death). The former is constitutionally protected (under *Cruzan*); the latter are not.

" * * * The Supreme Court has repeatedly indicated an unwillingness to expand the list of rights deemed fundamental. Physician-assisted suicide is not currently on that list. To be fundamental, a liberty interest must be central to personal autonomy or deeply rooted in history. The district court relies on language in *Casey's* plurality opinion to hold that substantive due process protects a wide range of autonomy-based liberty interests, including physician-assisted suicide. Such a reading of *Casey* is permissible, provided it is clearly understood that the liberty interests so protected are not fundamental. *Casey's* reaffirmation of the abortion right is best understood as a decision that relies heavily on stare decisis; the abortion right, uniquely protected under the undue burden standard, is sui generis. The second test for determining the existence of fundamental rights, whether the interest is rooted in the nation's history, similarly militates against a fundamental right to physician-assisted suicide.

" * * * Given the tremendous advances in twentieth-century medical technology and public health, it is now possible to live much longer than at any time in recorded history. We have controlled most of the swift and merciful diseases that caused most deaths in the past. In their place are a host of diseases that cause a slow deterioration of the human condition: cancer, Alzheimer's disease, and AIDS are but a few. This change has forced us to step back and reexamine the historic presumption that all human lives are equally and intrinsically valuable. Viewed most charitably, this reexamination may be interpreted as our struggle with the question whether we as a society are willing to excuse the terminally ill for deciding that their lives are no longer worth living. Viewed less charitably, the reexamination may be interpreted as a mere rationalization for housecleaning, cost-cutting and burden-shifting—a way to get rid of those whose lives we deem worthless. Whether the charitable or uncharitable characterization ultimately prevails is a question that must be resolved by the people through deliberative decisionmaking in the voting booth, as in Washington in 1991, California in 1992 and Oregon in 1994, or in the legislatures, as recently undertaken in Michigan and New York. This issue we, the courts, need not—and should not—decide."[d]

1. *Cruzan* (assuming the existence of a constitutional right to be free from unwanted life-sustaining medical treatment, but implying the constitutionality of prohibitions of assisted suicide).

d. In a separate dissent, Kleinfeld, J., who joined Judge Beezer's opinion with two qualifications, remarked: "That a question is important does not imply that it is constitutional. The Founding Fathers did not establish the United States as a democratic republic so that elected officials would decide trivia, while all great questions would be decided by the judiciary. The majority treats [some language in *Casey*] as a basis for constitutionalizing any really important personal decision. That an issue is important does not mean that the people, through their democratically elected representatives, do not have the power to decide it. One might suppose that the general rule in a democratic republic would be the opposite, with a few exceptions. Judge Beezer's view, that the statement is made in the *sui generis* context of abortion law, is sounder than the majority's. There is a difficulty with expanding the quoted language from *Casey* beyond abortion, in the face of *Bowers v. Hardwick*, and we lack authority to overrule that decision of a higher court."

A month later, in QUILL v. VACCO, 80 F.3d 716, 1996 WL 148605 (2d Cir.1996), the U.S. Court of Appeals for the Second Circuit, per MINER, J., struck down two New York state statutes criminalizing assisted suicide insofar as they prevent physicians from helping terminally ill, mentally competent patients commit suicide. But the Second Circuit did so on equal protection, rather than due process grounds. As for the substantive due process argument:

"As in *Bowers v. Hardwick*, the right contended for here cannot be considered so implicit in our understanding of ordered liberty that neither justice nor liberty would exist if it were sacrificed. Nor can it be said that the right to assisted suicide claimed by plaintiffs is deeply rooted in the nation's traditions and history. Indeed, the very opposite is true. * * * Clearly, no 'right' to assisted suicide ever has been recognized in any state of the United States."

As for the argument that the state violates the Equal Protection Clause because it does not treat "similarly circumstanced" persons alike:

"While rational basis scrutiny governs judicial review of the constitutionality of legislation in the areas of social welfare and economics, strict scrutiny is the standard of review where a classification 'impermissibly interferes with the exercise of a fundamental right or operates to the peculiar disadvantage of a suspect class,' *Massachusetts Bd. of Retirement v. Murgia* [p. 1226 infra]. [For] the reasons [given earlier, the challenged laws] do not impinge on any fundamental rights nor can it be said they involve suspect classifications. * * * Applying the foregoing principles to the [instant case], it seems clear that: (1) the statutes in question fall within the category of social welfare legislation and therefore are subject to rational basis scrutiny upon judicial review; (2) New York law does not treat equally all competent persons who are in the final stages of fatal illness and wish to hasten their deaths; (3) the distinctions made by New York law with regard to such persons do not further any legitimate purpose; and (4) accordingly, to the extent that the statutes in question prohibit persons in the final stages of terminal illness from having assistance in ending their lives by the use of self-administered, prescribed drugs, [they] lack any rational basis and are violative of the Equal Protection Clause.

" * * * [It] seems clear that New York does not treat similarly circumstanced persons alike: those in the final stages of terminal illness who are on life-support systems are allowed to hasten their deaths by directing the removal of such systems; but those who are similarly situated, except for the previous attachment of life-sustaining equipment, are not allowed to [do so]. The district judge has identified 'a difference between allowing nature to take its course [and] intentionally using an artificial death-producing device.' But Justice Scalia, for one, has remarked upon 'the irrelevance of the action-inaction distinction,' noting that 'the cause of death in both cases is the suicide's conscious decision to pu[t] an end to his own existence.' *Cruzan* (concurring opinion).

"Indeed, there is nothing 'natural' about causing death by means other than the original illness or its complications. The withdrawal of nutrition brings on death by starvation, the withdrawal of hydration brings on death by dehydration, and the withdrawal of ventilation brings about respiratory failure. [Withdrawal of life support] is nothing more nor less than assisted suicide. It simply cannot be said that those mentally competent, terminally-ill persons who seek to hasten death but whose treatment does not include life support are treated equally.

"A finding of unequal treatment does not, of course, end the inquiry, unless it is determined that the inequality is not rationally related to some legitimate state interest. [But] what interest can the state possibly have in requiring the prolongation of a life that is all but ended? [And] what business is it of the state to require the continuation of agony when the result is imminent and inevitable? What concern prompts the state to interfere with a mentally competent patient's 'right to define [his] own concept of existence, of meaning, of the universe, and of the mystery of human life,' *Casey*, when the patient seeks to have drugs prescribed to end life during the final stages of a terminal illness? The greatly reduced interest of the state in preserving life compels the answer to these questions: 'None.' "

CALABRESI, J., who wrote a concurring opinion, maintained that "it cannot be denied that the laws here involved, whether tested by Due Process or by Equal Protection, are highly suspect. It is also the case, however, that neither *Cruzan*, nor *Casey*, nor the language of our Constitution, nor our constitutional tradition clearly makes these laws invalid. What, then, should be done?" He continued:

"[W]hen a law is neither plainly unconstitutional [nor] plainly constitutional, the courts ought not to decide the ultimate validity of the law without current and clearly expressed statements, by the people or by their elected officials, of the state interests involved. [Absent] such statements, the courts have frequently struck down such laws, while leaving open the possibility of reconsideration if appropriate statements were subsequently made.

"[The] rationale for the New York assisted-suicide prohibition has eroded with the passage of time. In the nineteenth century, both suicide and attempted suicide were crimes and assisting in those crimes was, derivatively, a crime as well. But suicide and attempted suicide are no longer crimes. Nevertheless, the prohibitions on assisted suicide might serve other valid ends.

"[Some parties] contend that the difference between what they call 'active' assisted suicide (making lethal drugs available to those terminally ill who would self-administer them) and what they call 'passive' behavior (actively removing life supports or feeding tubes, on demand, so that the patient may die) is fundamental. Even if I were to accept the distinction in the face of the powerful arguments made against it both by the majority today and by Justice Scalia in his *Cruzan* concurrence, there is no reason to believe that New York has consciously made such a judgment. Certainly New York has never enacted a law based on a reasoned defense of the difference. [Whether] under Equal Protection or Due Process, [the] absence of a recent, affirmative, lucid and unmistakable statement of why the state wishes to interfere with what has been held by the Supreme Court to be a significant individual right, dooms these statutes."

Notes and Questions

1. *Building on the abortion cases.* As pointed out by Professor Seth Kreimer, quoted infra, every judge who has found constitutional support for a right to assisted suicide has relied on the abortion cases. If a woman has a right to control her own body that allows her to avoid pregnancy and the trauma of childbirth, does it follow that one suffering intolerable pain or great loss of dignity should have a similar right to bring an end to his or her condition—and to do so by means of physician-assisted suicide? SETH KREIMER, *Does Pro–Choice Mean Pro–Kevorkian? An Essay on Roe, Casey, and the Right to Die*, 44 Am.U.L.Rev. 803, 809–10 (1995), thinks not:

"The value of self-determination in situations of intimate and personal moral conflict is engaged by claims for assisted suicide in ways that differ significantly from the abortion cases. Assisted suicide and voluntary active euthanasia, unlike abortion, involve the extinction of what all involved agree is a human life. The societal values attached to avoiding the killing of those who do not desire to die, whether because of medical error, the effects of a blurring of norms, or the pervasive connection between treatable clinical depression and suicide are absent in the case of abortion.

"Legalization of euthanasia and assisted suicide, unlike abortion, raises the specter of an increasingly cost-conscious medical system advertently or unconsciously tracking vulnerable populations away from expensive and personally demanding medical treatment or palliative care toward less expensive and easier medical suicide. Desperately ill citizens may feel themselves forced to justify their decision to remain alive. And unlike legalized abortion, the prospect of medical suicide threatens to taint pervasively the relations between doctor and patient.

"The principles of bodily autonomy that undergird *Casey* guard against the 'plenary override' of a citizen's considered choices regarding her own body. Yet both the moral force of the prohibitions against killing conceded human beings and the practical dangers of legalizing assisted suicide provide justifications for interference, which are absent in the case of abortion.

"Finally, the concerns of women's equality that are implicated by abortion are absent from the arguments for assisted suicide or euthanasia. Indeed, while prohibition of assistance denies to some handicapped individuals the practical option of suicide available to the nonhandicapped, it also arguably shields other handicapped individuals against lethal abuses to which they are disproportionately vulnerable." [a]

2. *Suppose a woman is likely to die if she has an abortion.* Suppose, because of a pregnant woman's special disability or particular illness, physicians agree there is a strong probability that even an abortion *before* fetal viability will cause her death. Suppose, further, that, despite this, the woman still wants an abortion. Could the state override the woman's wishes? If the state could, does it follow that consistently with the abortion cases, a state could prohibit physician-assisted suicide—a "medical procedure" *intended* to and *designed* to end a person's life? See Marc Spindelman, *Roe vs. Wade Recognizes No "Right to Die,"* The Detroit News, Oct. 16, 1994, at 3B.

3. *Does the policy against assisted suicide or euthanasia rest on the absolute sanctity of human life? Is this essentially a religious concept?* Consider RONALD DWORKIN, *Life's Dominion* 214, 217 (1993):

"[The] instinct that deliberate death is a savage insult to the intrinsic value of life, even when it is in the patient's interest, is the deepest, most important part of the conservative revulsion against euthanasia. Justices Rehnquist and Scalia [both] relied on that instinct [in] the *Cruzan* case. The instinct is central to many religious traditions. In its most straightforward formulation, [the] appeal to the sanctity of life uses the image of property: a person's life belongs not to him but to God. But some religious leaders and scholars have put the point more formally: by distinguishing, as I have, between the question of when

---

a. See also New York State Task Force on Life and the Law, *When Death is Sought: Assisted Suicide and Euthanasia in the Medical Context* (1994) (180–page report unanimously rejecting proposals to legalize assisted suicide and voluntary active euthanasia); Yale Kamisar, *Against Assisted Suicide—Even a Very Limited Form,* 72 U.Det.Mercy L.Rev. 735 (1995); Thomas Mayo, *Constitutionalizing the "Right to Die,"* 49 Md.L.Rev. 103 (1990).

keeping someone alive is good for him and when it is good because it respects a value he embodies.

"[It] is widely supposed that active euthanasia—doctors killing patients who beg to die—is always offensive to [the sanctity of life], and should be prohibited for that reason. But the question posed by euthanasia is not whether the sanctity of life should yield to some other value, like humanity or compassion, but how life's sanctity should be understood and respected. The great moral issues of abortion and euthanasia, which bracket life in earnest, have a similar structure. Each involves decisions [about] the intrinsic, cosmic importance of human life itself. In each case, opinions divide [because] the values in question are at the center of everyone's lives, and no one can treat them as trivial enough to accept other people's orders about what they mean." [b]

Compare Kreimer, supra at 812–13, 826, 853–54: "Professor Dworkin is wrong in asserting that [a state law prohibiting euthanasia or assisted suicide] 'fails to recognize that forcing people to live who genuinely want to die causes serious damage to them.' A legislature may acknowledge the tragic sacrifice it imposes on some of its citizens, yet still decide that the sacrifice is warranted by the interests of others. Dworkin is right when he asserts that '[t]here are dangers both in legalizing and refusing to legalize; the rival dangers must be balanced, and neither should be ignored.' But whether one balance or another is chosen seems in the first instance to be a matter of empirical investigation rather than abstract constitutional inference. * * *

"The State need not rely on a contested argument about the absolute sanctity of human life to adopt the proposition that public policy should minimize the pressures that impel citizens to seek death, and maximize the forces that support them in choosing life. Arguments for the prohibition of euthanasia and assisted suicide are rooted in part in the fear that legalization will unleash the opposite incentives. * * *

"To prohibit assistance enshrines the State's responsibility to protect the vulnerable and to affirm their connection to society. [When] a patient asks 'May I die?,' she may be seeking assurance that her doctors and family still value her. When the State says 'legally, you may not,' it tells the sufferer that she is still a valued member of the community. [The] Constitution does not prevent the State from embracing the ideals of autonomy and compassion. [But] the choice embedded in today's legal structure is also constitutionally legitimate. The very real costs to the liberty of some citizens do not constitutionally require the State to abandon its policy of protecting the vulnerable in choosing to live." [c]

---

b. See also Tom Stacy, *Euthanasia and the Supreme Court's Competing Conceptions of Religious Liberty,* 10 Issues in Law & Med. 55 (1994) (assisted suicide-active voluntary euthanasia debate encompasses issues that are inherently and intensely "religious"). But see David Smolin, *The Free Exercise Clause, the Religious Freedom Restoration Act, and the Right to Active and Passive Euthanasia,* 10 Issues in Law & Med. 3 (1994).

c. See also New York State Task Force Report, fn. a supra; Daniel Callahan & Margot White, *The Legalization of Physician-assisted*

Suicide: Creating a Regulatory Potemkin Village, 30 U.Rich.L.Rev. 1 (1995); Yale Kamisar, *Are Laws Against Assisted Suicide Unconstitutional?,* Hastings Center Rep., May–June 1993, p. 32; Edward Larson, *Prescription for Death: A Second Opinion,* 44 DePaul L.Rev. 461 (1995); Thomas Marzen, *"Out, Out Brief Candle": Constitutionally Prescribed Suicide for the Terminally Ill,* 21 Hast. Con. L.Q. 799 (1994). But see Robert Sedler, *Constitutional Challenges to Bans on "Assisted Suicide": The View from Without and Within,* 21 Hast. Con. L.Q. 777 (1994).

Chapter 6
THE RIGHT TO TRAVEL

INTRODUCTION

"The 'right to travel' from state to state has been a favorite of both the Warren and Burger Courts. The Constitution makes no mention of any such right. By now we know that cannot be determinative, but we are entitled to some sort of explanation of why the right is appropriately attributable. In recent years the Court has been almost smug in its refusal to provide one." [a]

—John Hart Ely, *Democracy and Distrust* 177 (1980).

Dissenting in *Shapiro v. Thompson* (1969) (discussed at p. 1276 infra), Harlan, J., observed: "Opinions of the Court and of individual Justices have suggested four provisions of the Constitution as possible sources of a right to travel enforceable against the federal or state governments: the Commerce Clause; the Privileges and Immunities Clause of Art. IV, § 2; the Privileges and Immunities Clause of the Fourteenth Amendment; and the Due Process Clause of the Fifth Amendment." (He concluded that "the right to travel interstate is a 'fundamental' right which, for present purposes, should be regarded as having its source in [the fifth amendment due process clause].") Other possible sources for the constitutional right to travel are the equal protection clause, the "penumbra" of the first amendment, the ninth amendment and "the nature of the federal union." [b] One recent constitutional law text discusses the right to travel in its "equal protection" chapter,[c] another treats the subject primarily in a chapter on "rights of privacy and personhood." [d]

APTHEKER v. SECRETARY OF STATE, 378 U.S. 500, 84 S.Ct. 1659, 12 L.Ed.2d 992 (1964), concerned an attack by top-ranking leaders of the Communist Party on § 6 of the Subversive Activities Control Act of 1950, which denied passports to members of an organization "with knowledge or notice" that it was

a. At this point Professor Ely refers to language in *Shapiro v. Thompson* and *United States v. Guest,* both quoted infra. See also Note, 40 U.M.K.C.L.Rev. 66, 77 (1971).

b. See generally Ira Lupu, *Untangling the Strands of the Fourteenth Amendment,* 77 Mich.L.Rev. 981, 993, 1031, 1060–64 (1979);

Notes, 22 U.C.L.A.L.Rev. 1129, 1140–45 (1975); 55 Neb.L.Rev. 117–22, 132 (1975) and authorities collected therein.

c. John Nowak & Ronald Rotunda, *Constitutional Law* § 14.38 (5th ed.1995).

d. Tribe *Treatise* § 15–14.

required to register as "a Communist organization." The Court, per GOLDBERG, J., struck down § 6 as "unconstitutional on its face" because it "too broadly and indiscriminately restricts the right to travel and thereby abridges the liberty guaranteed by the Fifth Amendment." It pointed to the dictum in *Kent v. Dulles,* 357 U.S. 116, 78 S.Ct. 1113, 2 L.Ed.2d 1204 (1958), that "The right to travel is a part of the 'liberty' of which the citizen cannot be deprived without [fifth amendment due process]. Freedom of movement across frontiers in either direction, and inside frontiers as well, was a part of our heritage. Travel abroad, like travel within the country [is] basic in our scheme of values." "Since freedom of association is itself guaranteed in the First Amendment, restrictions imposed upon the right to travel cannot be dismissed by asserting that the right to travel could be fully exercised if the individual would first yield up his membership in a given association." [a]

As for the government's argument that § 6 should be held constitutional as applied to "the top-ranking Party leaders involved here," such a "construction" would require "substantial rewriting" of the statute and would "inject an element of vagueness into the statute's scope," a course neither proper nor desirable "in dealing with a section which so severely curtails personal liberty." Since "freedom of travel is a constitutional liberty closely related to rights of free speech and association, [appellants] should not be required to assume the burden of demonstrating that Congress could not have written a statute constitutionally prohibiting their travel."

DOUGLAS, J., joined the Court's opinion, adding that "the right to move freely from State to State is a privilege and immunity of national citizenship." "Absent war, I see no way to keep a citizen from traveling within or without the country [unless] he has been convicted of a crime [or] there is probable cause for issuing a warrant [to arrest him]. Freedom of movement [is] the very essence of our free society, setting us apart. Like the right of assembly and the right of association, it often makes all other rights meaningful—knowing, studying, arguing, exploring, conversing, observing and even thinking." [b]

ZEMEL v. RUSK, 381 U.S. 1, 85 S.Ct. 1271, 14 L.Ed.2d 179 (1965), concerned refusal to issue passports to United States citizens for travel to Cuba "unless specifically endorsed [by] the Secretary of State." Appellant sought a passport "to satisfy my curiosity about the state of affairs in Cuba and to make me a better informed citizen." The Court, per WARREN, C.J., affirmed denial of the request: "The requirements of due process are a function not only of the extent of the governmental restriction imposed, but also of the extent of the necessity for the restriction. [The] United States and other members of the Organization of American States have determined that travel between Cuba and the other countries of the Western Hemisphere is an important element in the spreading of subversion. [In light of this factor and others], the Secretary has justifiably concluded that travel to Cuba by American citizens might involve the Nation in

---

a. *Kent* invalidated State Department regulations denying passports to Communists on the ground they exceeded the congressional grant of authority, thus avoiding the constitutional question.

b. Clark, J., joined by Harlan and White, JJ., dissented, maintaining that the Due Process Clause does not prohibit "reasonable regulation" of the right to travel abroad and that Congress had "a rational basis" for denying passports to members of the Communist Party.

dangerous international incidents, and that the Constitution does not require him to validate passports for such travel.

"The right to travel *within* the United States is of course also constitutionally protected. But that freedom does not mean that areas ravaged by flood, fire or pestilence cannot be quarantined when it can be demonstrated that unlimited travel to the area would directly and materially interfere with the safety and welfare of the area or the Nation as a whole. So it is with international travel. [That the challenged restriction] is supported by the weightiest considerations of national security is perhaps best pointed up by recalling that the Cuban Missile crisis of October 1962 preceded the filing of appellant's complaint by less than two months."

DOUGLAS, J., joined by Goldberg, J., dissented: "[T]here are areas [such as those stricken by pestilence or war] to which Congress can [prohibit] travel. [But] the only so-called danger present here is the Communist regime in Cuba. The world, however, is filled with Communist thought [and] if we are to know them and understand them, we must mingle with [them]. Restrictions on the right to travel in times of peace should be so particularized that a First Amendment right is not precluded unless some clear countervailing national interest stands in the way of its assertion." [a]

————

HAIG v. AGEE, 453 U.S. 280, 101 S.Ct. 2766, 69 L.Ed.2d 640 (1981) (other aspects of which are discussed at p. 782 infra), arose as follows: Agee, a former CIA employee then residing in West Germany, announced and engaged in a campaign to expose undercover CIA agents stationed abroad and "to drive them out of the countries where they are operating." In carrying out his campaign he travelled in various countries. On several occasions, his public identifications of alleged CIA agents in foreign countries were "followed by episodes of violence against the persons and organizations." Because of Agee's activities, his passport was revoked on the basis of a 1966 regulation authorizing passport revocation when the Secretary of State determines that an American citizen's activities abroad "are causing or likely to cause serious damage to the national security or the foreign policy of the United States." [a] After holding that the Passport Act of

---

a. Compare *Zemel* with *Regan v. Wald*, 468 U.S. 222, 104 S.Ct. 3026, 82 L.Ed.2d 171 (1984). In 1982, in order to "reduce Cuba's hard currency earnings from travel by U.S. persons to and from Cuba," a treasury regulation was amended to restrict travel-related economic transactions. Respondents, American citizens who wanted to travel to Cuba, challenged the amendment on both statutory and constitutional grounds. After devoting most of its opinion to a discussion of why the regulation was authorized by Congress, a 5–4 majority, per Rehnquist, J., rejected the constitutional challenge:

"We see no reason to differentiate between the travel restrictions imposed by the President in the present case and the passport restrictions imposed by the Secretary of State in *Zemel*. [Respondents] apparently feel that only a Cuban missile crisis in the offing will make area restrictions on international travel

constitutional. [The] holding in *Zemel*, however, was not tied to the Court's independent foreign policy analysis, [but] merely an example of [our] classical deference to the political branches in matters of foreign policy."

Blackmun, J., joined by Brennan, Marshall and Powell, JJ., dissented, maintaining that the restrictions on travel-related expenditures in Cuba were not authorized by Congress.

a. As a condition for his employment by the CIA, Agee contracted not to make any public statements about Agency matters, either during or after the term of his employment by the Agency, "without specific approval by the Agency." In a separate action brought by the government to enforce Agee's agreement, a federal district court held that "Agee has shown a flagrant disregard for the requirements of the Secrecy Agreement."

1926 authorized the revocation of Agee's passport pursuant to the policy announced by the challenged regulation, such policy being " 'sufficiently substantial and consistent' to compel the conclusion that Congress has approved it," [b] a 7–2 majority, per BURGER, C.J., rejected Agee's contention that the revocation violated, inter alia, his "right to travel," stressing the distinction between interstate and international travel:

"Revocation of a passport undeniably curtails travel, but the freedom to travel abroad with a 'letter of introduction' in the form of a passport issued by the sovereign is subordinate to national security and foreign policy considerations; as such, it is subject to reasonable governmental regulation. The Court has made it plain that the *freedom* to travel outside the United States must be distinguished from the *right* to travel within the United States. This was underscored in *Califano v. Aznavorian.* 439 U.S. 170, 99 S.Ct. 471, 58 L.Ed.2d 435 (1978).[c]

"It is 'obvious and unarguable' that no governmental interest is more compelling than the security of the Nation. [Not] only has Agee jeopardized the security of the United States, but he has endangered the interests of countries other than the United States—thereby creating serious problems for American foreign relations and foreign policy. Restricting Agee's foreign travel, although perhaps not certain to prevent all of Agee's harmful activities, is the only avenue open to the Government to limit these activities.[60]"

BRENNAN, J., joined by Marshall, J., dissenting, devoted most of his opinion to the argument that the regulation under which Agee's passport had been revoked was "invalid as an unlawful exercise of authority by the Secretary [of State] under

b. Relying on *Kent v. Dulles,* Agee argued that "the only way the Executive can establish implicit congressional approval is by proof of longstanding and consistent *enforcement* of the claimed power: that is by showing that many passports were revoked on national security and foreign policy grounds." The Court disagreed, pointing out that there were few occasions to call the Secretary's authority into play: "The exercise of a power emerges only in relation to a factual situation, and the continued validity of the power is not diluted simply because there is no need to use it. [Although] a pattern of actual enforcement is one indicator of Executive policy, it suffices that the Executive has 'openly asserted' the power at issue. *Kent* is not to the contrary. [In that case, the] Court had serious doubts as to whether there was in reality any definite policy in which Congress could have acquiesced."

Relying on language in *Kent* that "illegal conduct" and problems of allegiance were "the only [grounds] which it could fairly be argued were adopted by Congress in light of prior administrative practice," Agee also contended that "this enumeration was exclusive and is controlling here." Again the Court disagreed: "The *Kent* Court had no occasion to consider whether the Executive had the power to revoke the passport of an individual whose *conduct* is damaging the national security and foreign policy of the United States. *Kent* involved denials of passports solely on the basis of political beliefs entitled to First Amendment protection.

[As *Aptheker* illustrates, the] protections accorded beliefs standing alone is very different from the protection accorded conduct. [But] [b]eliefs and speech are only part of Agee's 'campaign to fight the United States CIA.' In that sense, this case contrasts markedly with the facts in *Kent* and *Aptheker.* No presumptions, rebuttable or otherwise, are involved, for Agee's conduct in foreign countries presents a serious danger to the national security.

c. In upholding a provision of the Social Security Act denying certain benefits for any month during all of which the recipient is outside the United States, the *Aznavorian* Court, per Stewart, J., rejected the view that international travel, no less than interstate travel, is "a basic constitutional right." In light of the "crucial distinction between the *freedom* to travel internationally and the *right* of interstate travel" (emphasis added), a statute "said to infringe the freedom to travel abroad is not to be judged by the same standard applied to laws that penalize the right of interstate travel, such as durational residency requirements imposed by the States [referring to the cases discussed at pp. 1421–32 infra]." See generally Note, 19 Va.J.Int'l L. 707 (1979).

60. Agee argues that the Government should be limited to an injunction ordering him to comply with his secrecy agreement [see fn. a]. This argument ignores the governmental interests at stake. As Agee concedes, such an injunction would not be enforceable outside of the United States.

the Passport Act of 1926." [d]   He then cited *Agee* as "a prime example of the adage that 'bad facts make bad law.'"

Notes and Questions

1. *The shift from Kent to Agee.* Consider Daniel Farber, *National Security, The Right to Travel, and the Court,* 1981 Sup.Ct.Rev. 263, 285–87: "[*Agee*] represents a major shift from previous travel cases such as *Kent* [which] laid heavy stress on the importance of the right to travel and took a correspondingly grudging approach to discretionary travel controls. *Agee,* on the other hand, distinguishes the *right* to travel within the United States from the mere *freedom* to travel outside the United States. It takes a correspondingly generous view of executive discretion. For three reasons, the *Kent* approach is preferable, even ignoring the matter of stare decisis.

"First is the importance of the right to travel itself. [One] important aspect of international travel is its relation to freedom of speech. Without the right to travel, criticism of foreign policy is greatly impeded. [Second,] *Kent*'s grudging attitude toward executive discretion is amply supported by history. [The] *Agee* Court seems to have assumed that the discretion to control travel had only been exercised on a principled basis. Too many counterexamples exist to allow reliance on this assumption. The third reason for preferring *Kent* to *Agee* is that *Kent* aligns more closely with congressional intent. Since *Kent,* Congress has strongly supported the principle of freedom of travel. Despite urgent pleas from [President Eisenhower], Congress refused to supply the statutory power held lacking in *Kent.* * * * Twenty years later, Congress abolished the other major elements of the Cold War program of travel control [area restrictions and a penalty for travel without a passport]. In sum, not only the holding but also the underlying policies of *Kent* have received congressional endorsement. This is of critical importance, because both *Kent* and *Agee* proceed from the premise that the President's power flows from Congress. Indeed, even if the President did have some inherent power in the area, that power would be greatly diminished by Congressional disapproval."

2. *The right to travel intrastate.* Is *intrastate* travel entitled to as much protection as travel across state lines? See *King v. New Rochelle Municipal Housing Auth.,* 442 F.2d 646 (2d Cir.1971) (it "would be meaningless to describe the right to travel between states as a fundamental precept of personal liberty and not to acknowledge a correlative constitutional right to travel within a state"). See also Tribe *Treatise* at 1380; Note, 22 U.C.L.A.L.Rev. 1129, 1145–46 (1975). But see Comment, 55 Neb.L.Rev. 117, 128–29 (1975) ("intrastate travel is not a fundamental right" and statutes limiting such travel will be upheld on "reasonable basis" test).

3. *Zoning ordinances.* The "one-family dwellings" zoning ordinance upheld in *Belle Terre,* Sec. 2 supra, was challenged, inter alia, on the ground that "it interferes with the right to migrate to and settle within a State." The Court, per Douglas, J., made short shrift of this contention, noting that the ordinance "is not aimed at transients." Professor Tribe, supra, at 1381, agrees that "qualitative as opposed to quantitative restraints on how a jurisdiction's land may be developed or used should [be] immune to challenge on right-to-travel grounds so long as they do not discriminate against new residents." At some point, however, "local laws making towns and municipalities homogeneous enclaves might cumulatively lead to a society in which migration from one jurisdiction to another, as a practical

---

d. See fn. b. supra.

matter, becomes extremely difficult. If a showing is made that persons must in effect choose between changing their way of life and staying put, a right-to-travel challenge should succeed. Cf. *Aptheker.*" Id. at n. 19. See generally Notes, 39 U.Chi.L.Rev. 612 (1972); 12 Harv.J.Leg. 244 (1975); 84 Yale L.J. 1564 (1975).

4. *A rationale for the right to travel.* Consider John Hart Ely, *Democracy and Distrust* 178–79 (1980): "The right at issue in the modern cases [is] not simply a right to travel to or through a state but rather a right to move there—the right, if you will, to relocate. [To] a large extent America was founded by persons escaping from environments they found oppressive. Mobility was quite free during the colonial period, and '[a]s a result, most colonials who dissented from their own community's conception of right and justice could move without great difficulty to a more congenial community.' And of course the symbolism, and indeed the reality, of 'the frontier' took much of its sustenance from the notion that a person should have the option of pulling up stakes and starting over elsewhere. [I think this tradition] points us in the right direction, one that associates the right to relocate not with the idea that it is some kind of handmaiden of majoritarian democracy but, quite to the contrary, with the notion that one should have an option of escaping an incompatible majority. [A dissenting member of a community] should have the option of exiting and relocating in a community whose values he or she finds more compatible. [S]ome differences remain [among the states]—relating perhaps most pertinently to the extent to which deviance of various sorts is tolerated or represented by law or enforcement policy, and indeed to the scope of such government services as education and welfare. [I]t's an old idea, dating back at least as far as Rousseau's 'droit d'emigration': it's just that the Court hasn't fixed on it. That is unfortunate, since it provides something the Court hasn't, a rationale for the right to travel it in fact has established."

See also Tribe at 1383–84: "[C]lose surveillance and control of travel in both its senses [as an aspect of expression or education and as a means of changing one's residence and starting life anew] has always been a central technique of the totalitarian state, but centuries of experience should suffice to mark as especially suspect any governmental measure designed to prevent the emigration of those dissatisfied with the existing order, or the immigration of those who might alter the status quo. Just as government should be forbidden to expel the citizen who has become a source of unrest, so it cannot be permitted to imprison the citizen who seeks freedom in another land."

Chapter 7
THE DEATH PENALTY AND
RELATED PROBLEMS: CRUEL AND
UNUSUAL PUNISHMENT

INTRODUCTION

"The question of capital punishment has been the subject of endless discussion and will probably never be settled so long as men believe in punishment. [The] reasons why it cannot be settled are plain. There is first of all no agreement as to the objects of punishment. Next there is no way to determine the results of punishment. [Moreover,] questions of this sort, or perhaps of any sort, are not settled by reason; they are settled by prejudices and sentiments or by emotion. When they are settled they do not stay settled, for the emotions change as new stimuli are applied to the machine."

—Clarence Darrow, *Crime, Its Cause and Treatment* 166 (1922).

At the time he made it, Darrow's prediction that the question of capital punishment "will probably never be settled" appeared well-founded. That the issue might ever be settled as a matter of constitutional law seemed almost inconceivable. The Court had already specifically sanctioned death by firing squad and by electrocution. Indeed, 25 years after Darrow's remarks, *Louisiana ex rel. Francis v. Resweber,* 329 U.S. 459, 67 S.Ct. 374, 91 L.Ed. 422 (1947), sustained what the dissenters called the horror of "death by installments." (After a first attempt to electrocute petitioner had failed because of mechanical difficulties, the state strapped him in the electric chair a second time and threw the switch again.) And in the 1950s the Court twice upheld the execution of men whose sanity was in doubt, leaving the question to the judgment of a governor and a warden. See Yale Kamisar, *The Reincarnation of the Death Penalty: Is it Possible?* Student Lawyer, May 1973, pp. 22–23.

In *Trop v. Dulles,* 356 U.S. 86, 78 S.Ct. 590, 2 L.Ed.2d 630 (1958), speaking for four justices, (Brennan, J., had found the "expatriation" provision invalid on other grounds), Warren, C.J., deemed deprivation of a native-born American's citizenship because of wartime desertion from the army—leaving him "stateless"—a "fate forbidden by the principle of civilized treatment guaranteed by the Eighth Amendment," but was quick to add: "[W]hatever the arguments may be against the [death penalty, it] has been employed throughout our history, and, in a day when it is still widely accepted, it cannot be said to violate the constitutional concept of cruelty." As late as 1968, a close student of the problem, observed: "[N]ot a single death penalty statute, not a single statutorily imposed mode of execution, not a single attempted execution has ever been held by any court to be 'cruel and unusual punishment' under any state or federal constitution. Nothing less than a mighty counterthrust would appear to be required to alter the direction of these decisions." Hugo Bedau, *The Courts, the Constitution, and Capital Punishment,* 1968 Utah L.Rev. 201.

In the 1960s the NAACP Legal Defense and Educational Fund, Inc. (LDF), led by Professor Anthony Amsterdam, did launch a major constitutional assault on the death penalty. Convinced that "each year the United States went without executions, the more hollow would ring claims that the American people could not do without them" and that "the longer death-row inmates waited, the greater their numbers, the more difficult it would be for the courts to permit the first execution," the LDF developed a "moratorium strategy," creating "a death-row logjam." Michael Meltsner, *Cruel and Unusual: The Supreme Court and Capital Punishment* 107 (1973).

Largely as a result of LDF efforts in blocking all executions on every conceivable legal ground, when the Court handed down *Furman,* infra, in 1972, there had not been a single execution in five years.

Actually, the number of executions had started to decline as early as the 1940s and had dropped dramatically in the 1960s, several years before the LDF had successfully developed its moratorium strategy. After peaking in the 1930s (152 per year during this decade, and reaching an all-time high of 199 executions in 1935), the annual rate of executions averaged 128 in the 1940s and 72 in the 1950s. There were only 21 executions in 1963, 15 in 1964 and a mere seven in 1965. (In the 1930–50 period, executions had averaged more than ten *a month*). See D. Baldus, G. Woodworth & C. Pulaski, *Equal Justice and the Death Penalty* 9 (1990); Jack Greenberg, *Capital Punishment as a System,* 91 Yale L.J. 908, 924–25 (1982).

SECTION 1. IS THE DEATH PENALTY ALWAYS—OR EVER—"CRUEL AND UNUSUAL"?

FURMAN v. GEORGIA, 408 U.S. 238, 92 S.Ct. 2726, 33 L.Ed.2d 346 (1972), considered the death sentence in three cases (all involving black defendants), two dealing with a murderer and rapist in Georgia, the third a rapist in Texas.[a] (Each had been sentenced to death after trial by jury. Under the applicable state statutes, the judge or jury had discretion to impose the death penalty.) Also at stake, however, were the lives of almost 600 condemned persons who had "piled up" in "death rows" throughout the land in recent years. Striking down the laws of 39 states[b] and various federal statutory provisions, a 5–4 majority, per curiam, held that "the imposition and carrying out" of the death penalty under the current arbitrarily and randomly administered system constitutes "cruel and unusual" punishment in violation of the eighth and fourteenth amendments.

a. Since 1930, murder and rape had accounted for nearly 99% of total executions and murder alone for about 87%. But various jurisdictions also permitted capital punishment for other crimes, e.g., kidnapping, treason, espionage, aircraft piracy.

b. Forty states authorized capital punishment for a variety of crimes, but since Rhode Island's only capital statute, murder by a life term prisoner, carried a mandatory death sentence, it was not invalidated by the instant case.

Each of the justices wrote a separate concurring or dissenting opinion explaining his reasons for invalidating or upholding the death penalty. (The nine opinions totalled 230 pages in the official reports.) *Furman* has been called "not so much a case as a badly orchestrated opera, with nine characters taking turns to offer their own arias." Robert Weisberg, *Deregulating Death,* 1983 Sup.Ct.Rev. 305, 315.

The pivotal opinions of Stewart and White, JJ., left open the question whether *any* system of capital punishment, as opposed to the presently capriciously administered one, would be unconstitutional. A third member of the majority, Douglas, J., also reserved for another day whether a nondiscriminatorily operated mandatory death penalty would be constitutional.

STEWART, J.: "If we were reviewing death sentences imposed under [laws making death the mandatory punishment for every person convicted of engaging in certain designated criminal conduct] we would be faced with the need to decide whether capital punishment is unconstitutional for all crimes and under all circumstances. We would need to decide whether a legislature—state or federal—could constitutionally determine that certain criminal conduct is so atrocious that society's interest in deterrence and retribution wholly outweighs any considerations of reform or rehabilitation of the perpetrator, and that, despite the inconclusive empirical evidence, only the automatic penalty of death will provide maximum deterrence.

"On that score I would say only that I cannot agree that retribution is a constitutionally impermissible ingredient in the imposition of punishment. The instinct for retribution is part of the nature of man, and channeling that instinct in the administration of criminal justice serves an important purpose in promoting the stability of a society governed by law. When people begin to believe that organized society is unwilling or unable to impose upon criminal offenders the punishment they 'deserve,' then there are sown the seeds of anarchy—of self-help, vigilante justice, and lynch law.

"The constitutionality of capital punishment in the abstract is not, however, before us in these cases. For the Georgia and Texas legislatures have not provided that the death penalty shall be imposed upon all those who are found guilty of forcible rape [or] murder. In a word, neither State has made a legislative determination that forcible rape and murder can be deterred only by imposing the penalty of death upon all who perpetrate those offenses. As [concurring] Justice White so tellingly puts it, the 'legislative will is not frustrated if the penalty is never imposed.'

"Instead, the death sentences now before us are the product of a legal system that brings them, I believe, within the very core of the Eighth Amendment's guarantee against cruel and unusual punishments, a guarantee applicable against the States through the Fourteenth Amendment. In the first place, it is clear that these sentences are 'cruel' in the sense that they excessively go beyond, not in degree but in kind, the punishments that the state legislatures have determined to be necessary. In the second place, it is equally clear that these sentences are 'unusual' in the sense that the penalty of death is infrequently imposed for murder, and that its imposition for rape is extraordinarily rare. But I do not rest my conclusion upon these two propositions alone.

"These death sentences are cruel and unusual in the same way that being struck by lightning is cruel and unusual. For, of all the people convicted of rapes and murders in 1967 and 1968, many just as reprehensible as these, the petitioners are among a capriciously selected random handful upon whom the sentence of death has in fact been imposed. My concurring Brothers have demonstrated that, if any basis can be discerned for the selection of these few to be sentenced to die, it is the constitutionally impermissible basis of race. But racial discrimination has not been proved, and I put it to one side. I simply conclude that the Eighth and Fourteenth Amendments cannot tolerate the inflicting of a sentence of death under legal systems that permit this unique penalty to be so wantonly and so freakishly imposed."

WHITE, J.: "The imposition and execution of the death penalty are obviously cruel in the dictionary sense. But the penalty has not been considered cruel and unusual punishment in the constitutional sense because it was thought justified by the social ends it was deemed to serve. At the moment that it ceases realistically to further these purposes, however, the emerging question is whether its imposition in such circumstances would violate the Eighth Amendment. It is my view that it would, for its imposition would then be the pointless and needless extinction of life with only marginal contributions to any discernible social or public purposes. A penalty with such negligible returns to the State would be patently excessive and cruel and unusual punishment violative of the Eighth Amendment.

"It is also my judgment that this point has been reached with respect to capital punishment as it is presently administered under the statutes involved in these cases. [A]s the statutes before us are now administered, the penalty is so infrequently imposed that the threat of execution is too attenuated to be of substantial service to criminal justice.

" * * * I must arrive at judgment; and I can do no more than state a conclusion based on 10 years of almost daily exposure to the facts and circumstances of hundreds and hundreds of federal and state criminal cases involving crimes for which death is the authorized penalty. [T]he death penalty is exacted with great infrequency even for the most atrocious crimes [and] there is no meaningful basis for distinguishing the few cases in which it is imposed from the many cases in which it is not.[c] The short of it is that the policy of vesting sentencing authority primarily in juries—a decision largely motivated by the desire to mitigate the harshness of the law and to bring community judgment to bear on the sentence as well as guilt or innocence—has so effectively achieved its aims that capital punishment within the confines of the statutes now before us has for all practical purposes run its course.

"[P]ast and present legislative judgment with respect to the death penalty loses much of its force when viewed in light of the recurring practice of delegating sentencing authority to the jury and the fact that a jury, in its own discretion and without violating its trust or any statutory policy, may refuse to impose the death penalty no matter what the circumstances of the crime. Legislative 'policy' is thus necessarily defined not by what is legislatively authorized but by what juries and judges do in exercising the discretion so regularly conferred upon them. In my judgment what was done in these cases violated the Eighth Amendment."

c. But consider Carol Vance, *The Death Penalty after Furman*, 48 Notre Dame Law. 850, 858 (1973): "Actually there is a fairly universal consensus on which cases should receive the harshest penalties. [It] is only in the bizarre murder, the killing for hire or during another serious crime, and a few other isolated instances that the people of this country want to see the death penalty applied. [Any prosecutor] (as well as any judge or defense attorney) can listen to a set of facts and tell you whether it is a death penalty case. [T]here *should* be very few death penalty sentences. Only a very few cases warrant this extreme measure. It takes two essential [ingredients]: (1) overwhelming proof [of] guilt and (2) an extremely aggravated fact situation. What is so surprising is Justice White's and Justice Stewart's conclusion that there is something highly improper in so few people receiving the death penalty."

DOUGLAS, J.: "The words 'cruel and unusual' certainly include penalties that are barbaric. But the words, at least when read in light of the English proscription against selective and irregular use of penalties, suggest that it is 'cruel and unusual' to apply the death penalty—or any other penalty—selectively to minorities whose numbers are few, who are outcasts of society, and who are unpopular, but whom society is willing to see suffer though it would not countenance general application of the same penalty across the board. * * *

"[T]hese discretionary statutes are unconstitutional in their operation. They are pregnant with discrimination and discrimination is an ingredient not compatible with the idea of equal protection of the laws that is implicit in the ban on 'cruel and unusual' punishments."

As BRENNAN, J., perceived the question, there are four principles "recognized in our cases and inherent in" the eighth amendment prohibition "sufficient to permit a judicial determination whether a challenged punishment" "does not comport with human dignity" and therefore is "cruel and unusual": (1) "a punishment must not be so severe as to be degrading to the dignity of human beings"; (2) the government "must not arbitrarily inflict a severe punishment"; (3) "a severe punishment must not be unacceptable to contemporary society"; and (4) "a severe punishment must not be excessive," i.e., "unnecessary." Applying the first and "primary" principle, Brennan, J., concluded that capital punishment "involves by its very nature a denial of the executed person's humanity" and, in comparison to all other punishments today, "is uniquely degrading to human dignity." He "would not hesitate to hold, on that ground alone, that death is today a 'cruel and unusual punishment,' *were it not that death is a punishment of longstanding usage and acceptance in this country.*" [Emphasis added.] He then turned to a discussion of the other three principles and, relying heavily upon the fact that today the death sentence is inflicted very rarely and most arbitrarily, concluded that the death penalty is inconsistent with these other principles as well. * * * "The function of these principles is to enable a court to determine whether a punishment comports with human dignity. Death, quite simply, does not."

MARSHALL, J.'s "historical foray" led to the question "whether American society has reached a point where abolition is not dependent on a successful grass roots movement in particular jurisdictions, but is demanded by the Eighth Amendment." He concluded that the death penalty constitutes "cruel and unusual" punishment on two independent grounds: (1) "it is excessive and serves no valid legislative purpose," i.e., it is not a more effective deterrent than life imprisonment; (2) "it is abhorrent to currently existing moral values."

As for the first ground: "Punishment for the sake of retribution" is "not permissible under the Eighth Amendment. [At] times a cry is heard that morality requires vengeance to evidence society's abhorrence of the act. But the Eighth Amendment is our insulation from our baser selves. The cruel and unusual language limits the avenues through which vengeance can be channeled.[d] Were

d. But consider Daniel Polsby, *The Death of Capital Punishment*, 1972 Sup.Ct.Rev. 1, 37, 39–40: "The confusion between the proposition that the death penalty deters and the proposition that it is appropriate is a fairly stable feature of retentionist argument. [I submit] that the declaration that the death penalty is a superior deterrent to serious crime, in spite of evidence to the contrary, amounts to nothing more than the expression of a value preference that, whether the penalty is a superior deterrent or not, it ought to be used. A priori, I can find nothing wrong with this value preference. It may be flinty and stern, but it does not seem to me necessarily barbaric, that someone might believe that certain criminals ought to be put to death, the inhuman brutality of their crimes being so

this not so, the language would be empty and a return to the rack and other tortures would be possible in a given case." Nor, "in light of the massive amount of evidence before us, [showing no correlation between the rate of murder or other capital crimes and the presence or absence of the death penalty, can capital punishment] be justified on the basis of its deterrent effect."

As for the second independent ground: Although recent opinion polls indicate that Americans are about equally divided on the question of capital punishment, "whether or not a punishment is cruel or unusual depends, not on whether its mere mention 'shocks the conscience and sense of justice of the people,' but on whether people who were fully informed as to the purposes of the penalty and its liabilities would find the penalty shocking, unjust and unacceptable." Marshall, J., then concluded that *if* the average citizen possessed "knowledge of all the facts presently available" (for example, that death is no more effective a deterrent than life imprisonment; "convicted murderers are rarely executed"; "no attempt is made in the sentencing process to ferret out likely recidivists for execution"; the punishment "is imposed discriminatorily against certain identifiable classes of people"; "innocent people have been executed";) "the average citizen *would,* in my opinion, find [capital punishment] shocking to his conscience and sense of justice. [Emphasis added.]ᵉ For this reason alone capital punishment cannot stand."

There were four separate dissenting opinions. Burger, C.J., warned that "it is essential to our role as a court that we not seize upon the enigmatic character of the [eighth amendment] guarantee as an invitation to enact our personal predilictions into law." As for the argument that the death penalty was "excessive" or "unnecessary," he found "no authority suggesting that the Eighth Amendment was intended to purge the law of its retributive elements" nor any basis for prohibiting "all punishments the States are unable to prove necessary to deter crime."

"Real change," maintained the Chief Justice, "could clearly be brought about [by legislatures responding to today's ruling if they] provided mandatory death sentences in such a way as to deny juries the opportunity to bring in a verdict on a lesser charge; under such a system, the death sentence could only be avoided by a verdict of acquittal. If this is the only alternative that the legislatures can safely pursue under today's ruling, I would have preferred that the Court opt for total abolition. * * *

"Quite apart from the limitations of the Eighth Amendment itself, the preference for legislative action is justified by the inability of the courts to participate in the debate at the level where the controversy is focused. The case against capital punishment is not the product of legal dialectic but rests primarily on factual claims, the truth of which cannot be tested by conventional judicial processes."

great as to outrun all possibility of forgiveness or amends. But if the argument is to rest upon straight moralistic dogma [why] should it dress itself up in the guise of a utilitarian argument instead? [One] answer may be that retentionists would be ashamed to admit to having such values. If so, surely it is relevant to a judgment whether death is a cruel and unusual punishment." Cf. Charles Black, *Capital Punishment: The Inevitability of Caprice and Mistake* 23–28 (1974).

e. Is this a valid means of ascertaining whether "popular sentiment" or "the average citizen" abhors capital punishment? Or does Marshall, J.'s approach represent excessive speculation or inappropriate "elitism" about moral judgment? Compare Kamisar, supra, at 48, and Polsby, supra, at 23–24 with Margaret Radin, *The Jurisprudence of Death,* 126 U.Pa. L.Rev. 989, 1040–42 (1978).

BLACKMUN, J., filed a separate dissent, "personally rejoicing" at the Court's result, but unable to accept it "as a matter of history, of law, or of constitutional pronouncement."

In a third dissent, POWELL, J., called the Court's ruling "the very sort of judgment that the legislative branch is competent to make and for which the judiciary is ill-equipped." He maintained that "the sweeping judicial action undertaken today reflects a basic lack of faith and confidence in the democratic process."

In a fourth dissent, REHNQUIST, J., concluded that the majority's ruling "significantly lack[ed]" the "humility" and "deference to legislative judgment" with which the task of judging constitutional cases must be approached; indeed, "it is not an act of judgment, but rather an act of will."

Notes and Questions

1. Of *"life"* and *"limb."* Consider Leonard Levy, *Against the Law* 396 (1974): "To argue as a matter of public morality or policy that the state should not take a life as a penalty for crime is an appropriate task for legislation. The responsible [Supreme Court justice] has a different task. In this case the text of the Constitution itself seemed confining, indeed, seemed to erect an insuperable barricade against acceptance of the abolitionist position. The [Eighth Amendment prohibition] appears in the same Bill of Rights that clearly sanctions the death penalty. The Fifth Amendment begins with a guarantee [that] '[n]o person shall be held to answer for a *capital,* or otherwise infamous crime, unless * * *.' The same amendment [also provides]: 'nor shall any person be subject for the same offense to be twice put in jeopardy of *life* or limb' [nor] 'be deprived of *life,* liberty, or property without due process * * *.' In 1868 the Fourteenth Amendment made an identical due-process clause applicable to the [states]. Thus, the Constitution itself in four places recognizes and permits capital punishment, a penalty that was common when the Fifth, Eighth and Fourteenth Amendments were adopted." See also Raoul Berger, *Death Penalties: The Supreme Court's Obstacle Course* 43–50 (1982). But cf. Levy, supra, at 402: "[Brennan, J.,] relegated to one of his footnotes a stunning retort to the dissenters who so heavily stressed the fact that the language of the Fifth Amendment authorized the death penalty. One of its clauses prohibited placing any person in double jeopardy of life 'or limb,' [but] Brennan asserted correctly that no one now contends that the reference to jeopardy of limb 'provides a perpetual constitutional sanction for such corporal punishments as branding and earcropping, which were common punishments when the Bill of Rights was adopted' [n. 28]. Not one of the four dissenters took note of the point; it was irrefutable."

2. *The "analytic" and "normative" approaches of the Furman majority.* Daniel Polsby has called "the Douglas-Stewart-White approach to the Eighth Amendment 'analytic' to distinguish it from the 'normative' approach of Brennan and Marshall." He observes, Polsby, fn. d supra at 24–25: "[The analytic approach's chief virtue is at the same time its chief vice: it avoids the core normative question whether the 'evolving standards of decency that mark the progress of a maturing society' have now risen high enough to wash the death penalty away. [W]hatever the analytic approach gains in avoiding subjective and impressionistic sallies into the shadow world of language, it also fails to meet Mr. Justice Brennan's implicit objection that the Eighth Amendment—whatever it means—must mean something, and, indeed, must mean something different from the other provisions of the Constitution. The arguments of Justices Douglas, Stewart, and White seem rather intent on avoiding, if possible, that core question.

Rather, they prefer to emphasize the use of the Eighth Amendment as a tool for testing whether the penalty of death is evenhandedly applied. Why they should have done this is obscure in view of the fact that existing doctrines of equal protection (which was the emphasis of the Douglas opinion) or due process of law should have furnished more than adequate ground for striking down the death penalty, once the factual premises which these three Justices proffer (relating to the arbitrariness or irrationality of the penalty's use, or in Douglas's case, to its use on despised or dispossessed minorities) are accepted.[f] To view the Eighth Amendment in those terms deprives it of a dimension which is latent in almost all of the previous [decisions]—as an independently potent moral force which is at the disposal of the least dangerous branch of government and which may be used to make the most dangerous branch a little less so.''

GREGG v. GEORGIA, 428 U.S. 153, 96 S.Ct. 2909, 49 L.Ed.2d 859 (1976), upheld the constitutionality of Georgia's post-*Furman* capital-sentencing procedures, rejecting the basic contention that "the punishment of death always, regardless of the enormity of the offense or the procedure followed in imposing the sentence, is cruel and unusual punishment in violation of the Constitution." STEWART, POWELL and STEVENS, JJ., who announced the judgment of the Court and filed an opinion delivered by Stewart, J., concluded that "the concerns expressed in *Furman* that the penalty of death not be imposed in an arbitrary or capricious manner can be met by a carefully drafted statute that ensures that the sentencing authority is given adequate information and guidance. As a general proposition these concerns are best met by a system [such as Georgia's] that provides for a bifurcated proceeding at which the sentencing authority is apprised of the information relevant to the imposition of sentence and provided with standards to guide its use of the information."

Unlike the procedures before the Court in *Furman*, the new Georgia sentencing procedures "focus the jury's attention on the particularized nature of the crime and the particularized characteristics of the individual defendant. While the jury is permitted to consider any aggravating or mitigating circumstances,[a] it must find and identify at least one [of 10 statutory aggravating circumstances [b] beyond a reasonable doubt] before it may impose a penalty of death. In this way the jury's discretion is channelled. No longer can a jury wantonly and freakishly impose the death sentence; it is always circumscribed by the legislative guidelines. In addition, the review function of the Supreme Court of Georgia [which is

---

f. But in *Furman* and companion cases certiorari was granted limited to the following question: "Does the imposition and carrying out of the death penalty in [these cases] constitute cruel and unusual punishment in violation of the Eighth and Fourteenth Amendments?"

a. The plurality pointed out that the jury is not *required* to find any mitigating circumstance in order to make a recommendation of mercy that is binding on the court, "but it must find a *statutory* aggravating circumstance before recommending a sentence of death."

b. Georgia authorized the death penalty for six categories of crime: murder, kidnapping under certain circumstances, rape, treason and aircraft hijacking. The statutory aggravating circumstances for murder include "a prior record of conviction for a capital offense" or "a substantial history of serious assaultive criminal convictions"; commission of the crime against a police officer or fireman while performing his official duties; commission of the crime while engaged in certain other felonies; or commission of an "outrageously or wantonly vile, horrible or inhuman" murder (§ (b)(7)). *Godfrey v. Georgia*, 446 U.S. 420, 100 S.Ct. 1759, 64 L.Ed.2d 398 (1980), held that the Georgia courts had "adopted such a broad and vague construction" of the § (b)(7) aggravating circumstance as to violate the eighth and fourteenth amendments. But cf. *Walton v. Arizona*, 497 U.S. 639, 110 S.Ct. 3047, 111 L.Ed.2d 511 (1990).

required to review every death sentence to determine, inter alia, whether it was imposed under the influence of passion or prejudice and whether it is 'excessive or disproportionate to the penalty imposed in similar cases, considering both the crime and the defendant'] affords additional assurance that the concerns that prompted our decision in *Furman* are not present to any significant degree in the Georgia procedure applied here.''

At the guilt stage (or guilt trial) of Georgia's bifurcated procedure, the jury found petitioner guilty of two counts of armed robbery and two counts of murder. At the sentencing stage, which took place before the same jury, the judge instructed the jury that it would not be authorized to consider the death penalty unless it first found beyond a reasonable doubt one of these statutorily defined "aggravating circumstances": (1) that murder was committed while the offender was engaged in the commission of "another capital felony," to-wit armed robbery; (2) the offender committed murder "for the purpose of receiving money"; (3) the murder was "outrageously or wantonly vile [in] that it [involved] depravity of the mind." Finding the first two "aggravating circumstances," the jury returned verdicts of death on each count. The Georgia Supreme Court affirmed the convictions. After reviewing the record and comparing the evidence and sentences in similar cases, the court upheld the death sentences for the murders, but vacated the armed robbery sentences on the ground, inter alia, that the death penalty had rarely been imposed in Georgia for that crime. In rejecting petitioner's claim that his death sentence under the Georgia statute constituted "cruel and unusual" punishment, the plurality observed:

"[A]n assessment of contemporary values concerning the infliction of a challenged sanction is relevant to the application of the Eighth Amendment, [but] our cases also make clear that public perceptions of standards of decency with respect to criminal sanctions are not conclusive. A penalty also must accord with 'the dignity of man,' which is the 'basic concept underlying the Eighth Amendment.' *Trop* (plurality opinion). This means, at least, that the punishment not be 'excessive.' When a form of punishment in the abstract [is challenged], the inquiry into 'excessiveness' has two aspects. First, the punishment must not involve the unnecessary and wanton infliction of pain. Second, the punishment must not be grossly out of proportion to the severity of the crime.

"[I]n assessing a punishment selected by a democratically elected legislature against the constitutional measure, we presume its validity. We may not require the legislature to select the least severe penalty possible so long as the penalty selected is not cruelly inhumane or disproportionate to the crime involved. And a heavy burden rests on those who would attack the judgment of the representatives of the people.

"[Petitioners renew the argument made in *Furman* that 'standards of decency' have evolved to the point where capital punishment no longer can be tolerated, a view accepted only by Justices Brennan and Marshall four years ago], but developments [since] *Furman* have undercut substantially the assumptions upon which [this] argument rested. [It] is now evident that a large proportion of American society continues to regard [capital punishment] as an appropriate and necessary criminal sanction.

"The most marked indication of society's endorsement of the death penalty for murder is the legislative response to *Furman*. The legislatures of at least 35 States have enacted new statutes that provide for the death penalty for at least some crimes that result in the death of another person.[c]   And the Congress of the United States, in 1974, enacted a statute providing the death penalty for aircraft piracy that results in death.

"[The] jury also is a significant and reliable objective index of contemporary values because it is so directly involved.   [It] may be true that evolving standards have influenced juries in recent decades to be more discriminating in imposing the sentence of death.   But the relative infrequency of jury verdicts imposing the death sentence does not indicate rejection of capital punishment per se.   Rather, [it] may well reflect the humane feeling that this most irrevocable of sanctions should be reserved for a small number of extreme cases.

"[H]owever, the Eighth Amendment demands more than that a challenged punishment be acceptable to contemporary society.   The Court also must ask whether is comports with the basic concept of human dignity at the core of the Amendment.   *Trop* (plurality opinion).

"[The] death penalty is said to serve two principal social purposes: retribution and deterrence of capital crimes by prospective offenders.   In part, capital punishment is an expression of society's moral outrage at particularly offensive conduct.   This function [is] essential in an ordered society that asks its citizens to rely on legal processes rather than self-help to vindicate their wrongs.   'The instinct for retribution is part of the nature of man, and channeling that instinct in the administration of criminal justice serves an important purpose in promoting the stability of a society governed by law.   * * *'

"[The] value of capital punishment as a deterrent of crime is a complex factual issue the resolution of which properly rests with the legislatures, which can evaluate the results of statistical studies in terms of their own local conditions and with a flexibility of approach that is not available to the courts.   Indeed, many of the post-*Furman* statutes reflect just such a responsible effort to define those crimes and those criminals for which capital punishment is most probably an effective deterrent.

"In sum, we cannot say that the judgment of the Georgia legislature that capital punishment may be necessary in some cases is clearly wrong.   Considerations of federalism, as well as respect for the ability of a legislature to evaluate, in terms of its particular state the moral consensus concerning the death penalty and its social utility as a sanction, require us to conclude, in the absence of more convincing evidence, that the infliction of death as a punishment for murder is not without justification and thus is not unconstitutionally severe.

"[Petitioner contends] that the changes in the Georgia sentencing procedures are only cosmetic, [focusing] on the opportunities for discretionary action that are inherent in the processing of any murder case under Georgia law.   He notes that the state prosecutor has unfettered authority to select those persons whom he wishes to prosecute for a capital offense and to plea bargain with them.   Further, at the trial the jury may choose to convict a defendant of a lesser included offense

---

c.   But consider Franklin Zimring & Gordon Hawkins, *Capital Punishment and the Eighth Amendment: Furman and Gregg in Retrospect*, 18 U.C.Davis L.Rev., 927, 950 (1985): The "legislative extravaganza" of post-*Furman* death penalty statutes "is reminiscent of the 'pouring panic of capital statutes' which was a feature of the history of the criminal law in eighteenth-century England.   Whatever the social psychology of that development may have been, the post-*Furman* reaction in America would probably be best characterized as a typical frustration-aggression response.   Like parallel incidents in school prayer and pornography, legislative backlash was entirely to be expected by anyone familiar with the history of judicial invalidation in this country."

For a useful summary of the post-*Furman* statutes, see Stephen Gillers, *Deciding Who Dies*, 129 U.Pa.L.Rev. 1, 13, 101–10 (1980).

rather than find him guilty of a crime punishable by death, even if the evidence would support a capital verdict. And finally, a defendant who is convicted and sentenced to die may have his sentence commuted by the Governor of the State and the Georgia Board of Pardons and Paroles.[d]

"The existence of these discretionary stages is not determinative of the issues before us. [*Furman*] dealt with the decision to impose the death sentence on a specific individual who had been convicted of a capital offense. Nothing in any of our cases suggests that the decision to afford an individual defendant mercy violates the Constitution. *Furman* held only that, in order to minimize the risk that the death penalty would be imposed on a capriciously selected group of offenders, the decision to impose it had to be guided by standards so that the sentencing authority would focus on the particularized circumstances of the crime and the defendant.[50]"

WHITE, J., joined by Burger, C.J., and Rehnquist, J., concurred in the judgment: "Petitioner's argument that there is an unconstitutional amount of discretion in the system which separates those suspects who receive the death penalty from those who receive life imprisonment, a lesser penalty, or are acquitted or never charged, seems to be in final analysis an indictment of our entire system of justice. Petitioner has argued, in effect, that no matter how effective the death penalty may be as a punishment, government, created and run as it must be by humans, is inevitably incompetent to administer it. This cannot be accepted as a proposition of constitutional law. [I] decline to interfere with the manner in which Georgia has chosen to enforce [the death penalty] on what is simply an assertion of lack of faith in the ability of the system of justice to operate in a fundamentally fair manner."[e]

BRENNAN, J., dissented: "In *Furman*, I read 'evolving standards of decency' as requiring focus upon the essence of the death penalty itself and not primarily or solely upon the procedures under which the determination to inflict the penalty upon a particular person was made. [That] continues to be my view."

MARSHALL, J., also dissented: "The two purposes that sustain the death penalty as nonexcessive in the Court's view are general deterrence and retribution. [The] evidence I reviewed in *Furman* remains convincing, in my view, that 'capital punishment is not necessary as a deterrent to crime in our society.' The justification for the death penalty must be found elsewhere.

---

d. For a forceful statement of the view that the post-*Furman* statutes do not effectively restrict jury discretion by any real standards and that capital sentencing statutes "never will"—"no society is going to kill everybody who meets certain present verbal requirements"—see Charles Black, *Capital Punishment: The Inevitability of Caprice and Mistake* 67–68 (1974).

50. The petitioner's argument is nothing more than a veiled contention that *Furman* indirectly outlawed capital punishment by placing totally unrealistic conditions on its use. In order to repair the alleged defects pointed to by the petitioner, it would be necessary to require that prosecuting authorities charge a capital offense whenever arguably there had been a capital murder and that they refuse to plea bargain with the defendant. If a jury

refused to convict even though the evidence supported the charge, its verdict would have to be reversed and a verdict of guilty entered or a new trial ordered, since the discretionary act of jury nullification would not be permitted. Finally, acts of executive clemency would have to be prohibited. Such a system, of course, would be totally alien to our notions of criminal justice.

Moreover, it would be unconstitutional. Such a system in many respects would have the vices of the mandatory death penalty statutes we hold unconstitutional today in *Woodson* and *Stanislaus Roberts* [infra].

e. Blackmun, J., concurred in the judgment, referring solely to his dissenting opinion in *Furman*.

"[The plurality's view of the important purpose served by 'channeling' 'the instinct for retribution' in the administration of criminal justice] is wholly inadequate to justify the death penalty. [It] simply defies belief to suggest that the death penalty is necessary to prevent the American people from taking the law into their own hands.

"[The contention] that the expression of moral outrage through the imposition of the death penalty serves to reinforce basic moral values [also] provides no support for the death penalty. It is inconceivable that any individual concerned about conforming his conduct to what society says is 'right' would fail to realize that murder is 'wrong' if the penalty were simply life imprisonment.

"[There] remains for consideration, however, what might be termed the purely retributive justification for the death penalty—that the death penalty is appropriate, not because of its beneficial effect on society, but because the taking of the murderer's life is itself morally good. Some of the language of the plurality's opinion appears positively to embrace this notion of retribution for its own sake as a justification for capital punishment.

"[T]hat society's judgment that the murderer 'deserves' death must be respected not simply because the preservation of order requires it, but because it is appropriate that society make the judgment and carry it out [is a notion] fundamentally at odds with the Eighth Amendment. The mere fact that the community demands the murderer's life in return for the evil he has done cannot sustain the death penalty, for as the plurality reminds us, 'the Eighth Amendment demands more than that a challenged punishment be acceptable to contemporary society.' [Under appropriate Eighth Amendment] standards, the taking of life 'because the wrong-doer deserves it' surely must fall, for such a punishment has as its very basis the total denial of the wrong-doer's dignity and worth."

Notes and Questions

1. *The Texas statute upheld in Jurek.* In companion cases to *Gregg,* dividing the same way, the Court upheld the constitutionality of two other state capital-sentencing procedures which, it concluded, essentially resembled the Georgia system. *Proffitt v. Florida,* 428 U.S. 242, 96 S.Ct. 2960, 49 L.Ed.2d 913 (1976); *Jurek v. Texas,* 428 U.S. 262, 96 S.Ct. 2950, 49 L.Ed.2d 929 (1976). For forceful criticism of *Jurek* and for the view that the Texas statute is "much worse than either the Georgia or the Florida statutes, bad as they are," see Charles Black, *Due Process for Death,* 26 Cath.U.L.Rev. 1, 2 (1976).

2. *Gregg, Jurek* and *Proffitt* reached the question reserved in *Furman* —"the constitutionality of capital punishment in the abstract"—and upheld it. But consider Charles Black, *Reflections on Opposing the Penalty of Death,* 10 St. Mary's L.J. 1, 7 (1978): "[T]he *only* question that actually confronts us [is] whether it is right to kill such people as are chosen by our system as it stands. [I]t doesn't really make any difference at all what I think about the abstract rightness of capital punishment. There exists no abstract capital punishment." See also Anthony Amsterdam, *Capital Punishment,* in Bedau, *The Death Penalty in America* 346, 349–51 (3rd ed. 1982).

3. *Public endorsement of the death penalty.* "The critical holding in *Gregg,*" observe Samuel Gross & Robert Mauro, *Death & Discrimination: Racial Disparities in Capital Sentencing* 216 (1990), "was not the endorsement of 'guided discretion' but the decision that the use of the death penalty is consistent with 'contemporary values' and 'public attitude[s]' toward crime, and therefore that it is not constitutionally 'cruel and unusual.' By 1976 the evidence of public

endorsement of the death penalty was undeniable." In 1972, when *Furman* was decided, 57 percent of a national sample favored the death penalty for murder. In 1976, when Gregg was decided, support for the death penalty had increased to 65 percent. A decade later, the level of support was between 70–75 percent. See id. at 255 n. 14. See also Hugo Bedau, "The Half Empty Glass" (1988), in *A Punishment in Search of a Crime* 255, 229 (Gray & Stanley ed. 1989), noting the high level of support for the death penalty "all across the board, academics, non-academics, men, women, white, non-white, college-educated, not college-educated. [The] incoming college freshmen support the death penalty by about three to one, which is extraordinary. Historically, [it] was the young who, by and large, were opposed to capital punishment. Not now."

4. *The continuing reluctance to impose the death penalty in all death-eligible cases.* "[O]ne obstacle to eliminating excessive or discriminatory death sentences under the post-*Furman* statutes," note David Baldus, George Woodworth & Charles Pulaski, *Equal Justice and the Death Penalty* 413–14 (1990), "is the continuing reluctance of prosecutors and juries to favor imposition of death sentences in all death-eligible cases. Not only is this reluctance contrary to the Supreme Court's expectations when it decided *Gregg*, but there is no practical remedy for this inaction. No one involved in the criminal-justice process is going to argue that the Eighth Amendment requires the more frequent imposition of death sentences. The fact remains, however, that when only a few of the many defendants convicted of capital murder actually receive death sentences the ability of the selection process to operate rationally and consistently in each case undergoes substantial strain."

5. *Assuming that evidence whether the death penalty is a better deterrent than life imprisonment is "inconclusive," what follows?* Consider Amsterdam, note 2 supra, at 355: *"Because* the [Supreme Court deemed the evidence] inconclusive, [it] held that the Constitution did not forbid judgment either way. But if the evidence is inconclusive, is it *your* judgment that we should conclusively kill people on a factual theory that the evidence does not conclusively sustain?" But see Ernest van den Haag in van den Haag & Conrad, *The Death Penalty: A Debate* 69 (1983).

6. *Whatever the answer when the issue is one of legislative policy, once a state enacts a death penalty statute, is it plain who has the "burden of proof"?* The *Gregg* plurality thought so. It "presumed" the "validity" of the challenged statute, put "a heavy burden [on] those who would attack the judgment of the representatives of the people" and framed the issue in terms of whether the Georgia legislature's judgment was "clearly wrong." But see Margaret Radin, *The Jurisprudence of Death,* 126 U.Pa.L.Rev. 989, 1029–30, 1064 & n. 280 (1978): "The conjunction of the factors of irrevocability, enormity and fundamental right peculiar to the death penalty demands a searching analysis with no initial presumptions in favor of the past. The death penalty should be subject to strict scrutiny for cruelty. [If] we as a society are seriously divided on whether a fundamental interest may be invaded by the government under certain circumstances, it is morally wrong to behave as if there existed a moral consensus that justified invading that interest. [*Roe v. Wade*] recognized that in a conflict between fundamental rights of individuals and the interests of the state, questions of the validity of a moral theory concerning which there exists no consensus should be resolved against the state."

7. *"Mercy."* Consider Black, note 1 supra, at 12: "[T]he question posed is not whether [as the *Gregg* plurality put it] 'the decision to afford an individual

defendant mercy violates the Constitution,' [but] whether a 'legal system' which regularly, and in great numbers, runs the death question through a gauntlet of decisions in no way even formally standard-bound, so that, at the end of the process, no one can say why some were selected and others were not selected for death, rises to due process. That is not a trivial question and it cannot [be] answered by calling it, [as Justice White does, concurring in *Gregg*], 'in final analysis an indictment of our entire system of justice.' If it is that, it is an indictment pleading to which would present some difficulty, for it is hard to find informed persons today who think very well of our 'entire system' of criminal justice. But death is unique, and the procedures we must use, having no better, in our entire system of justice—and that is really the kindest thing one can say of that system—may still not be good enough for the death choice. The Court has not really focused on and answered that question—in reason, I mean, and not by fiat." See also Radin, note 6 supra, at 1024.

But consider Ernest van den Haag, *Refuting Reiman and Nathanson,* 14 Philosophy & Public Affairs 165, 173–74 (1985): "Guilt is personal. No murderer becomes less guilty, or less deserving of punishment, because another murderer was punished leniently, or escaped punishment altogether. We should try our best to bring every murderer to justice. But if one got away with murder wherein is that a reason to let anyone else get away? A group of murderers does not become less deserving of punishment because another equally guilty group is not punished, or punished less. We can punish only a very small proportion of all criminals. Unavoidably they are selected accidentally. We should reduce this accidentality as much as possible but we cannot eliminate it."

SECTION 2. MANDATORY DEATH SENTENCES; REQUIRING CONSTRAINTS ON THE SENTENCER'S DISCRETION TO IMPOSE THE DEATH PENALTY vs. FORBIDDING RESTRICTIONS ON THE SENTENCER'S DISCRETION TO BE MERCIFUL

1. Unlike Georgia, Florida and Texas, whose post-*Furman* capital-sentencing procedures were designed to guide and to channel sentencing authority, 10 states responded to *Furman* by replacing discretionary jury sentencing in capital cases with *mandatory death penalties.* These mandatory death statutes were invalidated in WOODSON v. NORTH CAROLINA, 428 U.S. 280, 96 S.Ct. 2978, 49 L.Ed.2d 944 (1976) and ROBERTS (STANISLAUS) v. LOUISIANA, 428 U.S. 325, 96 S.Ct. 3001, 49 L.Ed.2d 974 (1976), both decided the same day as *Gregg.* As occurred in *Gregg,* in both *Woodson* and *Roberts,* STEWART, POWELL and STEVENS, JJ., announced the judgment of the Court. (In each case, for the reasons stated in their *Gregg* dissents, Brennan and Marshall, JJ., concurred in the result.) The history of mandatory death penalty laws in this country, observed the *Woodson* plurality, reveals that the practice "has been rejected as unduly harsh and unworkably rigid." Post–*Furman* enactments were dismissed as merely "attempts [to] retain the death penalty in a form consistent with the Constitution, rather than a renewed social acceptance of mandatory death sentencing."

"A separate deficiency" of the North Carolina statute was its failure to respond adequately to "*Furman's* rejection of unbridled jury discretion in the imposition of capital sentences." In light of the widespread and persistent jury resistance to mandatory death penalties—and the high probability that many juries, despite their oaths, would exercise discretion in deciding which murderers "shall live and which shall die" under these "mandatory" statutes—North Carolina had not remedied "the problem of unguided and unchecked jury discretion" that was "central to the limited holding in *Furman*," but "simply papered over" it. Not only does North Carolina's mandatory death penalty statute provide "no standards to guide the jury in its inevitable exercise" of discretion, but "there is no way under [state law] for the judiciary to check arbitrary and capricious exercise of that power through a review of death sentences. Instead of rationalizing the sentencing process, a mandatory scheme may well exacerbate the problem identified in *Furman* by resting the penalty determination on the particular jury's willingness to act lawlessly."

Another constitutional shortcoming of the statute was "its failure to allow the particularized consideration of relevant aspects of the character and record of each convicted defendant before the imposition upon him of a sentence of death. [D]eath is a punishment different from all other sanctions in kind rather than degree. A process that accords no significance to relevant facets of the character and record of the individual offender or the circumstances of the particular offense excludes from consideration in fixing the ultimate punishment of death the possibility of compassionate or mitigating factors stemming from the diverse frailties of humankind. It treats all persons convicted of a designated offense not as uniquely individual human beings, but as members of a faceless, undifferentiated mass to be subjected to the blind infliction of the penalty of death." [a]

Dissenting, Rehnquist, J., rejected the view that the 10 post-*Furman* mandatory death statutes merely represented "a wrong-headed reading [of] *Furman*. While those States may be presumed to have preferred their prior systems reposing sentencing discretion in juries or judges, they indisputably preferred mandatory capital punishment to no capital punishment at all. Their willingness to enact statutes providing that penalty is utterly inconsistent with the notion that they regarded mandatory capital sentencing as beyond 'evolving standards of decency.'" [b]

Dissenting in *Roberts* (which invalidated a Louisiana mandatory death sentence statute the *Woodson* plurality deemed fatally similar to North Carolina's), White, J., joined by Burger, C.J., and Blackmun and Rehnquist, JJ., maintained: "As the plurality now interprets the Eighth Amendment, the Louisiana and North Carolina statutes are infirm because the jury is deprived of all discretion once it finds the defendant guilty. Yet in the next breath it invalidates these statutes because they are said to invite or allow too much discretion: despite their instructions, when they feel that defendants do not deserve to die, juries will so often and systematically disobey their instructions and find the defendant not guilty or guilty of a noncapital offense that the statute fails to satisfy the standards of *Furman*. If it is truly the case that Louisiana juries will exercise *too*

---

a. The *Woodson* Court reserved judgment on the constitutionality of a mandatory death penalty statute "limited to an extremely narrow category of homicide, such as murder by a prisoner serving a life sentence." A decade later, in *Sumner v. Shuman*, 483 U.S. 66, 107 S.Ct. 2716, 97 L.Ed.2d 56 (1987), a 6–3 majority, per Blackmun, J., held that "a departure from the individualized capital-sentencing doctrine is not justified" even in such a case.

b. White, J., joined by Burger, C.J., and Rehnquist, J., also dissented, rejecting the Court's analysis for the reasons stated in his dissent in *Roberts*, infra. Blackmun, J., also dissented in *Woodson* for the reasons stated in his *Furman* dissent. All four *Woodson* dissenters also dissented in *Roberts*.

much discretion—and I do not agree that it is—then it seems strange indeed that the statute is also invalidated because it purports to give the jury *too little* discretion by making the death penalty mandatory. Furthermore, if there is danger of freakish and too infrequent imposition of capital punishment under a mandatory system such as Louisiana's, there is very little ground for believing that juries will be any more faithful to their instructions under the Georgia and Florida systems where the opportunity is much, much greater for juries to practice their own brand of unbridled discretion."

2. *Gregg and the "mandatory death" cases.* Are *Gregg* and *Woodson* and *Roberts,* handed down the same day, reconcilable? The *Woodson* plurality points out that "instead of rationalizing the sentencing process, a mandatory scheme may well exacerbate the problem identified in *Furman* by resting the penalty determination on the particular jury's willingness to act lawlessly." But are not "these lawless juries, whose lawlessness will taint and bend a mandatory system," the very same juries who are supposed "to follow with patient care the intricacies of the Georgia and Florida statutes [upheld the same day in *Gregg* and *Proffitt*], and the unfathomed mysteries of the Texas statute [upheld the same day in *Jurek*], and base these answers on nothing but sound discretion guided by law"? See Charles Black, *Due Process for Death,* 26 Cath.U.L.Rev. 1, 10 (1976); Charles Black, *The Death Penalty Now,* 51 Tul.L.Rev. 429, 441 (1977). See also Hugo Bedau, *Are Mandatory Capital Statutes Unconstitutional?,* in *The Courts, the Constitution, and Capital Punishment* 106 (1977).

3. LOCKETT v. OHIO, 438 U.S. 586, 98 S.Ct. 2954, 57 L.Ed.2d 973 (1978), struck down a post–*Furman* statute that required the trial judge, once a verdict of aggravated murder with specifications had been returned, to impose the death sentence unless he found one of three narrowly defined mitigating circumstances present. A four-justice plurality, BURGER, C.J., joined by Stewart, Powell and Stevens, JJ., concluded that "the sentencer, in all but the rarest kind of capital case, [must] not be precluded from considering *as a mitigating factor,* any aspect of a defendant's character or record and any of the circumstances of the offense that the defendant proffers as a basis for a sentence less than death. [The] nonavailability of corrective or modifying mechanisms with respect to an executed capital sentence underscores the need for individualized consideration as a constitutional requirement in imposing the death sentence." Dissenting Justice REHNQUIST protested: "By encouraging defendants in capital cases, and presumably sentencing judges and juries, to take into consideration anything under the sun as a 'mitigating circumstance,' it will not guide sentencing discretion but will totally unleash it."

4. EDDINGS v. OKLAHOMA, 455 U.S. 104, 102 S.Ct. 869, 71 L.Ed.2d 1 (1982), underscored the Court's commitment to the principle that *all* mitigating evidence must be considered by the sentencer. The defense offered in mitigation the fact that the defendant, who was 16 at the term of the murder, had a history of beatings by a brutal father and a serious emotional disturbance. Although the state statute permitted consideration of *any* mitigating circumstances, the trial judge refused to consider, as a matter of law, either defendant's emotional disturbance or the circumstances of his unhappy upbringing. The state appellate court found the excluded evidence irrelevant because it did not tend to provide a legal excuse from criminal responsibility. A 5–4 majority, per POWELL, J., vacated the death sentence: "[T]he rule in *Lockett* [reflects] the law's effort to develop a system of capital punishment at once consistent and principled but also humane and sensible to the uniqueness of the individual. [By] holding that the sentencer in capital cases must be permitted to consider any relevant mitigating factor, the

rule in *Lockett* recognizes that a consistency produced by ignoring individual differences is a false consistency. [Just] as the State may not by statute preclude the sentencer from considering any mitigating factor, neither may the sentencer refuse to consider, *as a matter of law,* any relevant mitigating evidence. [The] sentencer, and [the state appellate court] on review, may determine the weight to be given relevant mitigating evidence. But they may not give it no weight by excluding such evidence from their consideration."

5. *Exacerbating the disparity in capital defendant's representation.* The sentencer need only consider and, of course, *can* only consider the mitigating evidence that is *introduced.* And the quantity and quality of the mitigating evidence presented turns largely on the skill, dedication, resourcefulness and funding of the capital defendant's attorney. See *Special Project: The Constitutionality of the Death Penalty in New Jersey,* 15 Rutgers L.J. 261, 293–94 (1984). Thus, although the penalty trial affords an able defense lawyer the opportunity to present an enormous amount of material "personalizing" and "humanizing" the capital defendant, "it also exacerbates the disparity in capital defendants' representation at trial, which, in turn, may be expected to exacerbate the death penalty's uneven application." Welsh White, *The Death Penalty in the Eighties* 69 (1987).

IS THE COURT FACED WITH TWO INCOMPATIBLE SETS OF COMMANDS?

Several months before stepping down from the Supreme Court, dissenting from the denial of certiorari in a death penalty case, CALLINS v. COLLINS, ___ U.S. ___, 114 S.Ct. 1127, 127 L.Ed.2d 435 (1994), Blackmun, J., maintained that "the death penalty experiment has failed": "Experience has taught us that the constitutional goal of eliminating arbitrariness and discrimination from the administration of death can never be achieved without compromising an equally essential component of fundamental fairness—individualized sentencing. See *Lockett.* It is tempting, when faced with conflicting constitutional commands, to sacrifice one for the other or to assume that an acceptable balance between them already has been struck. In the context of the death penalty, however, such jurisprudential maneuvers are wholly inappropriate. The death penalty must be imposed 'fairly, and with reasonable consistency, or not at all.' *Eddings.*

"[From] this day forward, I no longer shall tinker with the machinery of death. For more than 20 years I have endeavored—indeed, I have struggled—along with a majority of this Court, to develop procedural and substantive rules that would lend more than the mere appearance of fairness to the death penalty endeavor. Rather than continue to coddle the Court's delusion that the desired level of fairness has been achieved and the need for regulation eviscerated, I feel morally and intellectually obligated simply to concede that the death penalty experiment has failed. It is virtually self-evident to me now that no combination of procedural rules or substantive regulations ever can save the death penalty from its inherent constitutional deficiencies. The basic question—does the system accurately and consistently determine which defendants 'deserve' to die?—cannot be answered in the affirmative. [The] problem is that the inevitability of factual, legal, and moral error gives us a system that we know must wrongly kill some defendants, a system that fails to deliver the fair, consistent, and reliable sentences of death required by the Constitution.

"In the years following *Furman,* serious efforts were made to comply with its mandate. State legislatures and appellate courts struggled to provide judges and juries with sensible and objective guidelines for determining who should live and who should die. * * *

"Unfortunately, all this experimentation and ingenuity yielded little of what *Furman* demanded. It soon became apparent that discretion could not be eliminated from capital sentencing without threatening the fundamental fairness due a defendant when life is at stake. Just as contemporary society was no longer tolerant of the random or discriminatory infliction of the penalty of death, evolving standards of decency required due consideration of the uniqueness of each individual defendant when imposing society's ultimate penalty.

"This development in the American conscience would have presented no constitutional dilemma if fairness to the individual could be achieved without sacrificing the consistency and rationality promised in *Furman*. But over the past two decades, efforts to balance these competing constitutional commands have been to no avail. Experience has shown that the consistency and rationality promised in *Furman* are inversely related to the fairness owed the individual when considering a sentence of death. A step toward consistency is a step away from fairness. * * *

"I believe the *Woodson–Lockett* line of cases to be fundamentally sound and rooted in American standards of decency that have evolved over time. [Yet,] as several Members of the Court have recognized, there is real 'tension' between the need for fairness to the individual and the consistency promised in *Furman*. [The] power to consider mitigating evidence that would warrant a sentence less than death is meaningless unless the sentencer has the discretion and authority to dispense mercy based on that evidence. Thus, the Constitution, by requiring a heightened degree of fairness to the individual, and also a greater degree of equality and rationality in the administration of death, demands sentencer discretion that is at once generously expanded and severely restricted.

"[The] arbitrariness inherent in the sentencer's discretion to afford mercy is exacerbated by the problem of race. Even under the most sophisticated death penalty statutes, race continues to play a major role in determining who shall live and who shall die. Perhaps it should not be surprising that the biases and prejudices that infect society generally would influence the determination of who is sentenced to death, even within the narrower pool of death-eligible defendants selected according to objective standards. No matter how narrowly the pool of death-eligible defendants is drawn according to objective standards, *Furman's* promise still will go unfulfilled so long as the sentencer is free to exercise unbridled discretion within the smaller group and thereby to discriminate. ' "The power to be lenient [also] is the power to discriminate." ' *McCleskey v. Kemp* [p. 481 infra], quoting Kenneth C. Davis, *Discretionary Justice* 170 (1973).

"[In] the years since *McCleskey,* I have come to wonder whether there was truth in the majority's suggestion that discrimination and arbitrariness could not be purged from the administration of capital punishment without sacrificing the equally essential component of fairness—individualized sentencing. Viewed in this way, the consistency promised in *Furman* and the fairness to the individual demanded in *Lockett* are not only inversely related, but irreconcilable in the context of capital punishment. Any statute or procedure that could effectively eliminate arbitrariness from the administration of death would also restrict the sentencer's discretion to such an extent that the sentencer would be unable to give full consideration to the unique characteristics of each defendant and the circumstances of the offense. By the same token, any statute or procedure that would provide the sentencer with sufficient discretion to consider fully and act upon the unique circumstances of each defendant would 'thro[w] open the back door to arbitrary and irrational sentencing.' All efforts to strike an appropriate balance between these conflicting constitutional commands are futile because there is a heightened need for both in the administration of death.

"But even if the constitutional requirements of consistency and fairness are theoretically reconcilable in the context of capital punishment, it is clear that this Court is not prepared to meet the challenge. In apparent frustration over its inability to strike an appropriate balance between the *Furman* promise of consistency and the *Lockett* requirement of individualized sentencing, the Court has retreated from the field, allowing relevant mitigating evidence to be discarded, vague aggravating circumstances to be employed, and providing no indication that the problem of race in the administration of death will ever be addressed. [In] my view, the proper course when faced with irreconcilable constitutional commands is not to ignore one or the other, nor to pretend that the dilemma does not exist, but to admit the futility of the effort to harmonize them. This means accepting the fact that the death penalty cannot be administered in accord with our Constitution."

Justice Blackmun's dissenting opinion produced a sharp response by concurring Justice SCALIA: "Justice Blackmun [explains] why the death penalty 'as currently administered,' is contrary to the Constitution. [That] explanation often refers to 'intellectual, moral and personal' perceptions, but never to the text and tradition of the Constitution. It is the latter rather than the former that ought to control.

"[As] Justice Blackmun describes, however, over the years since 1972 this Court has attached to the imposition of the death penalty two quite incompatible sets of commands. [These] commands were invented without benefit of any textual or historical support; they are the products of just such 'intellectual, moral, and personal' perceptions as Justice Blackmun expresses today, some of which (viz., those that have been 'perceived' simultaneously by five members of the Court) have been made part of what is called 'the Court's Eighth Amendment jurisprudence.'

"Though Justice Blackmun joins those of us who have acknowledged the incompatibility of the Court's *Furman* and *Lockett–Eddings* lines of jurisprudence, he unfortunately draws the wrong conclusion from the acknowledgment [quoting Blackmun's statement about 'accepting the fact that the death penalty cannot be administered in accord with our Constitution']. "Surely a different conclusion commends itself—to wit, that at least one of these judicially announced irreconcilable commands which cause the Constitution to prohibit what its text explicitly permits must be wrong.[a]

a. Concurring in *Walton v. Arizona,* 497 U.S. 639, 110 S.Ct. 3047, 111 L.Ed.2d 511 (1990), Justice Scalia left no doubt as to which irreconcilable command must be rejected:

"Our decision in *Furman* was arguably supported by [the text of the Eighth Amendment]. I am therefore willing to adhere to the precedent established by our *Furman* line of cases.

"[The] *Woodson–Lockett* line of cases is another matter. [T]hat bears no relation whatever to the text of the Eighth Amendment. The mandatory imposition of death—without sentencing discretion—for a crime which

States have traditionally punished with death cannot possibly violate the Eighth Amendment, because it will not be 'cruel' (neither absolutely nor for the particular crime) and it will not be 'unusual' (neither in the sense of being a type of penalty that is not traditional nor in the sense of being rarely or 'freakishly' imposed). "[My problem] is not that *Woodson* and *Lockett* are wrong, but that [they] are rationally irreconcilable with *Furman.* [Since] I cannot possibly be guided by what seem to me incompatible principles, I must reject the one that is plainly in error."

"Convictions in opposition to the death penalty are often passionate and deeply held. That would be no excuse for reading them into a Constitution that does not contain them, even if they represented the convictions of a majority of Americans. Much less is there any excuse for using that course to thrust a minority's views upon the people. [Justice] Blackmun did not select as the vehicle for his announcement that the death penalty is always unconstitutional [one of the other cases currently before us], for example, the case of the 11-year-old girl raped by four men and then killed by stuffing her panties down her throat. How enviable [the] quiet death [of a convicted murderer] by lethal injection compared with that! If the people conclude that such more brutal deaths may be deterred by capital punishment; indeed, if they merely conclude that justice requires such brutal deaths to be avenged by capital punishment; the creation of false, untextual and unhistorical contradictions within 'the Court's Eighth Amendment jurisprudence' should not prevent them."

SECTION 3. ADMINISTERING THE DEATH PENALTY IN A RACIALLY DISCRIMINATORY MANNER

McCLESKEY v. KEMP

481 U.S. 279, 107 S.Ct. 1756, 95 L.Ed.2d 262 (1987).

JUSTICE POWELL delivered the opinion of the Court.

[Petitioner, a black man, was convicted in a Georgia trial court of armed robbery and the murder of a white police officer in the course of the robbery and sentenced to death. He sought federal habeas corpus relief, contending that the Georgia capital sentencing process was administered in a racially discriminatory manner in violation of the Eighth Amendment and the Equal Protection Clause of the Fourteenth Amendment.[a] In support of his claim, petitioner proffered a statistical study by David Baldus, Charles Pulaski and George Woodworth (the Baldus study).

[This study examined over 2,000 murder cases that occurred in Georgia during the 1970s and concluded that, even after taking account of many nonracial variables, defendants charged with killing white victims were 4.3 times as likely to receive a death sentence as those charged with killing blacks. Moreover, according to this study, black defendants were 1.1 times as likely to receive a death sentence as other defendants. Thus, the study indicates that black defendants, such as petitioner, who kill whites have the greatest likelihood of being sentenced to death.

[The federal district court ruled that the Baldus study "failed to contribute anything of value" to petitioner's claim and denied relief. The U.S. Court of Appeals for the Eleventh Circuit assumed that the Baldus study "showed that systematic and substantial disparities existed in the penalties imposed upon homicide victims in Georgia based on race of the homicide victim, that the disparities existed at a less substantial rate in death sentencing based on race of defendants and that [these factors] were at work in [the county in which petitioner was tried]." Even assuming the validity of the study, however, the Court of Appeals found the statistics "insufficient to demonstrate discriminatory

---

a. For discussion of the portion of Justice Powell's opinion for the Court rejecting petitioner's equal protection claim, see p. 1092 infra.

intent or unconstitutional discrimination in the Fourteenth Amendment context [and] insufficient to show irrationality, arbitrariness and capriciousness under any kind of Eighth Amendment analysis." Thus, it affirmed the district court's denial of habeas corpus relief.]

[McCleskey argues, inter alia,] that the Baldus study demonstrates that the Georgia capital sentencing system violates the Eighth Amendment.[b] * * *

[O]ur decisions since *Furman* have identified a constitutionally permissible range of discretion in imposing the death penalty. First, there is a required threshold below which the death penalty cannot be imposed. In this context, the State must establish rational criteria that narrow the decisionmaker's judgment as to whether the circumstances of a particular defendant's case meet the threshold. Moreover, a societal consensus that the death penalty is disproportionate to a particular offense prevents a State from imposing the death penalty for that offense. Second, States cannot limit the sentencer's consideration of any relevant circumstance that could cause it to decline to impose the penalty. In this respect, the State cannot channel the sentencer's discretion, but must allow it to consider any relevant information offered by the defendant.

In light of our precedents under the Eighth Amendment, McCleskey cannot argue successfully that his sentence is "disproportionate to the crime in the traditional sense." He does not deny that he committed a murder in the course of a planned robbery, a crime for which this Court has determined that the death penalty constitutionally may be imposed. [He argues, rather,] that the sentence in his case is disproportionate to the sentences in other murder cases.

On the one hand, he cannot base a constitutional claim on an argument that his case differs from other cases in which defendants *did* receive the death penalty. On automatic appeal, the Georgia Supreme Court found that McCleskey's death sentence was not disproportionate to other death sentences imposed in the State. [Moreover,] where the statutory procedures adequately channel the sentencer's discretion, such proportionality review is not constitutionally required.

On the other hand, absent a showing that the Georgia capital punishment system operates in an arbitrary and capricious manner, McCleskey cannot prove a constitutional violation by demonstrating that other defendants who may be similarly situated did *not* receive the death penalty. In *Gregg*, the Court confronted the argument that "the opportunities for discretionary action that are inherent in the processing of any murder case under Georgia law," specifically the opportunities for discretionary leniency, rendered the capital sentences imposed arbitrary and capricious. We rejected this contention. * * *

Because McCleskey's sentence was imposed under Georgia sentencing procedures that focus discretion "on the particularized nature of the crime and the particularized characteristics of the individual defendant," we lawfully may presume that McCleskey's death sentence was not "wantonly and freakishly" imposed and thus that the sentence is not disproportionate within any recognized meaning under the Eighth Amendment.

b. The Court noted [fn. 7]: "As did the Court of Appeals, we assume the [Baldus] study is valid statistically without reviewing the factual findings of the District Court. Our assumption that the Baldus study is statistically valid does not include the assumption that the study shows that racial considerations actually enter into any sentencing decisions in Georgia. Even a sophisticated multiple regression analysis such as the Baldus study can only demonstrate a *risk* that the factor of race entered into some capital sentencing decisions and a necessarily lesser risk that race entered into any particular sentencing decision."

Although our decision in *Gregg* as to the facial validity of the Georgia capital punishment statute appears to foreclose McCleskey's disproportionality argument, he further contends that the Georgia capital punishment system is arbitrary and capricious in *application,* and therefore his sentence is excessive, because racial considerations may influence capital sentencing decisions in Georgia. We now address this claim.

To evaluate McCleskey's challenge, we must examine exactly what the Baldus study may show. Even Professor Baldus does not contend that his statistics *prove* that race enters into any capital sentencing decisions or that race was a factor in McCleskey's particular case. Statistics at most may show only a likelihood that a particular factor entered into some decisions. There is, of course, some risk of racial prejudice influencing a jury's decision in a criminal case. There are similar risks that other kinds of prejudice will influence other criminal trials. The question "is at what point that risk becomes constitutionally unacceptable." McCleskey asks us to accept the likelihood allegedly shown by the Baldus study as the constitutional measure of an unacceptable risk of racial prejudice influencing capital sentencing decisions. This we decline to do.

[At] most, the Baldus study indicates a discrepancy that appears to correlate with race. Apparent disparities in sentencing are an inevitable part of our criminal justice system. The discrepancy indicated by the Baldus study is "a far cry from the major systemic defects identified in *Furman.*" [O]ur consistent rule has been that constitutional guarantees are met when "the mode [for determining guilt or punishment] itself has been surrounded with safeguards to make it as fair as possible." Where the discretion that is fundamental to our criminal process is involved, we decline to assume that what is unexplained is invidious. In light of the safeguards designed to minimize racial bias in the process, the fundamental value of jury trial in our criminal justice system, and the benefits that discretion provides to criminal defendants, we hold that the Baldus study does not demonstrate a constitutionally significant risk of racial bias affecting the Georgia capital-sentencing process.[37]

---

37. * * * We have held that discretion in a capital punishment system is necessary to satisfy the Constitution. *Woodson.* Yet, the dissent now claims that the "discretion afforded prosecutors and jurors in the Georgia capital sentencing system" violates the Constitution by creating "opportunities for racial considerations to influence criminal proceedings." The dissent contends that in Georgia "[n]o guidelines govern prosecutorial decisions [and] that Georgia provides juries with no list of aggravating and mitigating factors, nor any standard for balancing them against one another." Prosecutorial decisions necessarily involve both judgmental and factual decisions that vary from case to case. Thus, it is difficult to imagine guidelines that would produce the predictability sought by the dissent without sacrificing the discretion essential to a humane and fair system of criminal justice. Indeed, the dissent suggests no such guidelines for prosecutorial discretion.

[The] dissent repeatedly emphasizes the need for "a uniquely high degree of rationality in imposing the death penalty." Again, no suggestion is made as to how greater "rational-ity" could be achieved under any type of statute that authorizes capital punishment. The *Gregg*-type statute imposes unprecedented safeguards in the special context of capital punishment. These include: (i) a bifurcated sentencing proceeding; (ii) the threshold requirement of one or more aggravating circumstances; and (iii) mandatory state Supreme Court review. All of these are administered pursuant to this Court's decisions interpreting the limits of the Eighth Amendment on the imposition of the death penalty, and all are subject to ultimate review by this Court. These ensure a degree of care in the imposition of the sentence of death that can be described only as unique. Given these safeguards already inherent in the imposition and review of capital sentences, the dissent's call for greater rationality is no less than a claim that a capital-punishment system cannot be administered in accord with the Constitution. As we reiterate, the requirement of heightened rationality in the imposition of capital punishment does not "plac[e] totally unrealistic conditions on its use." *Gregg.*

Two additional concerns inform our decision in this case. First, McCleskey's claim, taken to its logical conclusion, throws into serious question the principles that underlie our entire criminal justice system. The Eighth Amendment is not limited in application to capital punishment, but applies to all penalties. Thus, if we accepted McCleskey's claim that racial bias has impermissibly tainted the capital sentencing decision, we could soon be faced with similar claims as to other types of penalty. Moreover, the claim that his sentence rests on the irrelevant factor of race easily could be extended to apply to claims based on unexplained discrepancies that correlate to membership in other minority groups, and even to gender. Similarly, since McCleskey's claim relates to the race of his victim, other claims could apply with equally logical force to statistical disparities that correlate with the race or sex of other actors in the criminal justice system, such as defense attorneys, or judges. Also, there is no logical reason that such a claim need be limited to racial or sexual bias. If arbitrary and capricious punishment is the touchstone under the Eighth Amendment, such a claim could—at least in theory— be based upon any arbitrary variable, such as the defendant's facial characteristics, or the physical attractiveness of the defendant or the victim, that some statistical study indicates may be influential in jury decisionmaking. As these examples illustrate, there is no limiting principle to the type of challenge brought by McCleskey.[45] The Constitution does not require that a State eliminate any demonstrable disparity that correlates with a potentially irrelevant factor in order to operate a criminal justice system that includes capital punishment. * * *

Second, McCleskey's arguments are best presented to the legislative bodies. It is not the responsibility—or indeed even the right—of this Court to determine the appropriate punishment for particular crimes. * * * Despite McCleskey's wide ranging arguments that basically challenge the validity of capital punishment in our multi-racial society, the only question before us is whether in his case, the law of Georgia was properly applied. We agree with the [courts below] that this was carefully and correctly done in this case. * * *

JUSTICE BRENNAN, with whom JUSTICE MARSHALL joins, and with whom JUSTICE BLACKMUN and JUSTICE STEVENS join in all but Part I, dissenting. * * *

II. At some point in this case, Warren McCleskey doubtless asked his lawyer whether a jury was likely to sentence him to die. A candid reply to this question would have been disturbing. First, counsel would have to tell McCleskey that few of the details of the crime or of McCleskey's past criminal conduct were more important than the fact that his victim was white. Furthermore, counsel would feel bound to tell McCleskey that defendants charged with killing white victims in

---

45. Justice Stevens, who would not over-rule *Gregg,* suggests in his dissent that the infirmities alleged by McCleskey could be remedied by narrowing the class of death-eligible defendants to categories identified by the Baldus study where "prosecutors consistently seek, and juries consistently impose, the death penalty without regard to the race of the victim or the race of the offender." This proposed solution is unconvincing. First, "consistently" is a relative term, and narrowing the category of death-eligible defendants would simply shift the borderline between those defendants who received the death penalty and those who did not. A borderline area would continue to exist and vary in its boundaries. Moreover, because the discrepancy between

borderline cases would be difficult to explain, the system would likely remain open to challenge on the basis that the lack of explanation rendered the sentencing decisions unconstitutionally arbitrary.

Second, even assuming that a category with theoretically consistent results could be identified, it is difficult to imagine how Justice Stevens' proposal would or could operate on a case-by-case basis. Whenever a victim is white and the defendant is a member of a different race, what steps would a prosecutor be required to take—in addition to weighing the customary prosecutorial considerations—before concluding in the particular case that he lawfully could prosecute? * * *

Georgia are 4.3 times as likely to be sentenced to death as defendants charged with killing blacks. [The] story could be told in a variety of ways, but McCleskey could not fail to grasp its essential narrative line: there was a significant chance that race would play a prominent role in determining if he lived or died.

[The Court] finds no fault in a system in which lawyers must tell their clients that race casts a large shadow on the capital sentencing process. [It] arrives at this conclusion by stating that the Baldus study cannot "prove that race enters into any capital sentencing decisions or that race was a factor in McCleskey's particular case." [The likelihood that race influenced some decisions], holds the Court, is insufficient to establish a constitutional violation. The Court reaches this conclusion by placing four factors on the scales opposite McCleskey's evidence: the desire to encourage sentencing discretion, the existence of "statutory safeguards" in the Georgia scheme, the fear of encouraging widespread challenges to other sentencing decisions, and the limits of the judicial role. The Court's evaluation of the significance of petitioner's evidence is fundamentally at odds with our consistent concern for rationality in capital sentencing, and the considerations that the majority invokes to discount that evidence cannot justify ignoring its force.

III. It is important to emphasize at the outset that the Court's observation that McCleskey cannot prove the influence of race on any particular sentencing decision is irrelevant in evaluating his Eighth Amendment claim. Since *Furman,* the Court has been concerned with the *risk* of the imposition of an arbitrary sentence, rather than the proven fact of one. * * * This emphasis on risk acknowledges the difficulty of divining the jury's motivation in an individual case. In addition, it reflects the fact that concern for arbitrariness focuses on the rationality of the system as a whole, and that a system that features a significant probability that sentencing decisions are influenced by impermissible considerations cannot be regarded as rational.[1]

[The] Court assumes the statistical validity of the Baldus study, and acknowledges that McCleskey has demonstrated a risk that racial prejudice plays a role in capital sentencing in Georgia. Nonetheless, it finds the probability of prejudice insufficient to create constitutional concern. Close analysis of the Baldus study, however, in light of both statistical principles and human experience, reveals that the risk that race influenced McCleskey's sentence is intolerable by any imaginable standard. * * *

McCleskey's statistics have particular force because most of them are the product of sophisticated multiple-regression analysis. Such analysis is designed precisely to identify patterns in the aggregate, even though we may not be able to reconstitute with certainty any individual decision that goes to make up that pattern.

---

1. Once we can identify a pattern of arbitrary sentencing outcomes, we can say that a defendant runs a risk of being sentenced arbitrarily. It is thus immaterial whether the operation of an impermissible influence such as race is intentional. While the Equal Protection Clause forbids racial discrimination, and intent may be critical in a successful claim under that provision, the Eighth Amendment has its own distinct focus: whether punishment comports with social standards of rationality and decency. It may be, as in this case, that on occasion an influence that makes punishment arbitrary is also proscribed under another constitutional provision. That does not mean, however, that the standard for determining an Eighth Amendment violation is superseded by the standard for determining a violation under this other provision. Thus, the fact that McCleskey presents a viable Equal Protection claim does not require that he demonstrate intentional racial discrimination to establish his Eighth Amendment claim.

[The] statistical evidence in this case thus relentlessly documents the risk that McCleskey's sentence was influenced by racial considerations. This evidence shows that there is a better than even chance in Georgia that race will influence the decision to impose the death penalty: a majority of defendants in white-victim crimes would not have been sentenced to die if their victims had been black. [In] determining the guilt of a defendant, a state must prove its case beyond a reasonable doubt. That is, we refuse to convict if the chance of error is simply less likely than not. Surely, we should not be willing to take a person's life if the chance that his death sentence was irrationally imposed is *more* likely than not. In light of the gravity of the interest at stake, petitioner's statistics on their face are a powerful demonstration of the type of risk that our Eighth Amendment jurisprudence has consistently condemned.

Evaluation of McCleskey's evidence cannot rest solely on the numbers themselves. We must also ask whether the conclusion suggested by those numbers is consonant with our understanding of history and human experience. Georgia's legacy of a race-conscious criminal justice system, as well as this Court's own recognition of the persistent danger that racial attitudes may affect criminal proceedings, indicate that McCleskey's claim is not a fanciful product of mere statistical artifice. * * *

History and its continuing legacy * * * buttress the probative force of McCleskey's statistics. Formal dual criminal laws may no longer be in effect, and intentional discrimination may no longer be prominent. Nonetheless, as we acknowledged in *Turner v. Murray,* 476 U.S. 28, 106 S.Ct. 1683, 90 L.Ed.2d 27 (1986), "subtle, less consciously held racial attitudes" continue to be of concern, and the Georgia system gives such attitudes considerable room to operate. The conclusions drawn from McCleskey's statistical evidence are therefore consistent with the lessons of social experience. * * *

IV. The Court cites four reasons for shrinking from the implications of McCleskey's evidence: the desirability of discretion for actors in the criminal-justice system, the existence of statutory safeguards against abuse of that discretion, the potential consequences for broader challenges to criminal sentencing, and an understanding of the contours of the judicial role. While these concerns underscore the need for sober deliberation, they do not justify rejecting evidence as convincing as McCleskey has presented.

[The Court] also declines to find McCleskey's evidence sufficient in view of "the safeguards designed to minimize racial bias in the [capital sentencing] process." [It] is clear that *Gregg* bestowed no permanent approval on the Georgia system. It simply held that the State's statutory safeguards were assumed sufficient to channel discretion without evidence otherwise.

[The] challenge to the Georgia system is not speculative or theoretical; it is empirical. As a result, the Court cannot rely on the statutory safeguards in discounting McCleskey's evidence, for it is the very effectiveness of those safeguards that such evidence calls into question.

[In] fairness, the Court's fear that McCleskey's claim is an invitation to descend a slippery slope also rests on the realization that any humanly imposed system of penalties will exhibit some imperfection. Yet to reject McCleskey's powerful evidence on this basis is to ignore both the qualitatively different character of the death penalty and the particular repugnance of racial discrimination, considerations which may properly be taken into account in determining whether various punishments are "cruel and unusual." Furthermore, it fails to take account of the unprecedented refinement and strength of the Baldus study.

[The] Court also maintains that accepting McCleskey's claim would pose a threat to all sentencing because of the prospect that a correlation might be demonstrated between sentencing outcomes and other personal characteristics. Again, such a view is indifferent to the considerations that enter into a determination of whether punishment is "cruel and unusual." Race is a consideration whose influence is expressly consistently proscribed. We have expressed a moral commitment, as embodied in our fundamental law, that this specific characteristic should not be the basis for allotting burdens and benefits. * * *

Certainly, a factor that we would regard as morally irrelevant, such as hair color, at least theoretically could be associated with sentencing results to such an extent that we would regard as arbitrary a system in which that factor played a significant role. [However,] the evaluation of evidence suggesting such a correlation must be informed not merely by statistics, but by history and experience. One could hardly contend that this nation has on the basis of hair color inflicted upon persons deprivation comparable to that imposed on the basis of race. Recognition of this fact would necessarily influence the evaluation of data suggesting the influence of hair color on sentencing, and would require evidence of statistical correlation even more powerful than that presented by the Baldus study.

[Finally,] the Court justifies its rejection of McCleskey's claim by cautioning against usurpation of the legislatures' role in devising and monitoring criminal punishment. [The] judiciary's role in this society counts for little if the use of governmental power to extinguish life does not elicit close scrutiny. [The Court] fulfills, rather than disrupts, the scheme of separation of powers by closely scrutinizing the imposition of the death penalty, for no decision of a society is more deserving of the "sober second thought." * * * c

Notes and Questions

1. *The end of doubts?* Consider Robert Burt, *Disorder in the Court: The Death Penalty and the Constitution,* 85 Mich.L.Rev. 1741 (1987): "For twenty years, the Court has struggled to determine the constitutional status of capital punishment. Broadly speaking, there have been three distinct phases in this effort: the first, beginning in 1968, when the Court announced substantial doubts about the constitutional validity of the death penalty; the second, beginning in 1976, when the Court attempted to appease those doubts by rationalizing and routinizing the administration of the penalty; and the third, beginning in 1983

c. In a separate dissent, Justice Blackmun, with whom Marshall and Stevens, JJ., joined and with whom Brennan, J., joined in all but Part IV–B (maintaining that acceptance of petitioner's claim would not eliminate capital punishment in Georgia because "in extremely aggravated murders the risk of discriminatory enforcement of the death penalty is minimized"), concluded that if one assumes that the data presented by petitioner is valid, "as we must in light of the Court of Appeals' assumption, there exists in the Georgia capital-sentencing scheme a risk of racially based discrimination that is so acute that it violates the Eighth Amendment." But the great bulk of Justice Blackmun's opinion was devoted to a discussion of why he believed the Georgia capital punishment system violates the Equal Protection Clause. See p. 1092 infra.

In a third dissenting opinion, Justice Stevens, joined by Blackmun, J., called the majority's evident fear "that the acceptance of McCleskey's claim would sound the death knell for capital punishment in Georgia unfounded": "One of the lessons of the Baldus study is that there exist certain categories of extremely serious crimes for which prosecutors consistently seek, and juries consistently impose, the death penalty without regard to the race of the victim or the race of the offender. If Georgia were to narrow the class of death-eligible defendants to those categories, the danger of arbitrary and discriminatory imposition of the death penalty would be significantly decreased, if not eradicated."

and culminating [in] *McCleskey,* when the Court proclaimed the end of its doubts and correspondingly signalled its intention to turn away from any continuing scrutiny of the enterprise."

2. *The reluctance to "find" racial discrimination.* According to Randall Kennedy, *McCleskey v. Kemp: Race, Capital Punishment and the Supreme Court,* 101 Harv.L.Rev. 1388, 1418 (1988), the *McCleskey* majority manifested a "lack of concern for the feelings of blacks," an attitude that may be related to the Court's "very keen concern for the sensitivities of those—mainly whites—subject to being labeled 'racist.' " Continues Professor Kennedy:

"One of the great achievements of social reform in American history has involved the stigmatization of overt racial prejudice. But this triumph in principle has produced an unforeseen consequence in application: it is precisely the sense that racial discrimination is a terrible evil that inhibits the Justices from 'finding' it in all but the clearest circumstances. Perhaps they assume that conduct so horrible must be plainly observable. Or perhaps their sense of the shamefulness of racism is so intense that they find it difficult to burden an official or agency with the moral opprobrium that the 'racist' label connotes without absolutely positive proof of culpability."

3. *Discretion, arbitrariness and discrimination.* Although the information on discrimination and on arbitrariness was much sketchier in 1972 than in 1988, "to the extent that [comparisons] can be made, they certainly show no marked improvement. The courts' determined assertions that the pre-*Furman* problems have been solved must be seen as statements of faith rather than fact, or perhaps as wishful thinking, since the evidence, if it shows anything, shows remarkable constancy rather than change." Samuel Gross & Robert Mauro, *Death & Discrimination: Racial Disparities in Capital Sentencing* 200 (1989). "Whatever else might be said for the use of death as a punishment," warn Gross and Mauro, "one lesson is clear from experience: this is a power that we cannot exercise fairly and without discrimination."

Chapter 8
PROCEDURAL DUE PROCESS IN
NON–CRIMINAL CASES [a]

SECTION 1. DEPRIVATION OF "LIBERTY" AND "PROPERTY" INTERESTS [b]

"When a litigant is adversely affected entirely as a predictable consequence of procedural grossness and not as a consequence of ulterior design by government (or by its agents) to utilize constitutionally impermissible substantive standards, he is in serious difficulty. The essence of his complaint is to the felt unfairness of procedural grossness itself—that it builds in such a large margin of probable mistake as itself to be intolerable in a humane society. [But] *unlike* his freedom [of expression and religion] (sheltered by the first amendment), and *unlike* his entitlement to privacy (sheltered by the fourth and fifth amendments), [the litigant] cannot anchor a claim to freedom from procedural grossness per se in any clause of the Constitution.

"He cannot rely upon the equal protection clause, for we are here dealing with situations in which all similarly situated persons are uniformly subject to the same degree of procedural grossness * * *. Nor can one say (as doubtless is one's first impulse) that the individual's entitlement to 'due' process is obviously anchored in the very clauses sheltering due process. The difficulty is that such reasoning (ironically akin to the reasoning that created the right-privilege distinction) must imagine a clause *which in fact is not there.* It imagines that the fourteenth amendment (or the same phrase in the fifth amendment) provides something like this: 'No State [shall] deprive any person of life, liberty, property, or of due process of law, without due process of law * * *.' Alternatively, it imagines that the next clause of the fourteenth amendment provides something like this '[Nor shall any State] deny to any person [either] due process of law or the equal protection of the laws.'

"[But as the amendments] read in fact, due process is not itself a protected entitlement. [It] stands in relation to ['life, liberty, [and] property'] not as an equivalent constitutionally established entitlement, but only as a condition to be observed insofar as the state may move to imperil one of the named [interests]. [P]rocedural due process appears never to be anything more than a kind of 'constitutional condition.' It is evidently not a free standing human interest."

a. The creditors' remedies cases are briefly considered in *Flagg Bros. v. Brooks,* p. 1361 infra.

b. See also *DeShaney v. Winnebago County Dep't of Social Servs.*, p. 1370 infra.

—William Van Alstyne, *Cracks in "The New Property": Adjudicative Due Process in the Administrative State,* 62 Corn.L.Rev. 445, 450–52 (1977).[c]

———

1. According to most commentators, the "procedural due process revolution" began with GOLDBERG v. KELLY, 397 U.S. 254, 90 S.Ct. 1011, 25 L.Ed.2d 287 (1970), holding that due process requires that welfare recipients be afforded an evidentiary hearing *prior* to the termination of benefits. As pointed out in Simon, fn. c supra, at 150, *Goldberg* "did not in fact present the issue of whether welfare benefits were within the 'life, liberty or property' protected by the due process clauses, because [the Social Services Commissioner] conceded that 'the protections of the due process clause apply.' [a] Nevertheless, [the Court] addressed this issue [suggesting] that whether the right to continue receiving a government benefit was within the protection of the due process clause turned upon the importance of the benefit to the individual." Thus, the Court, per Brennan, J., observed:

"[Welfare] benefits are a matter of statutory entitlement for persons qualified to receive them.[b] Their termination involves state action that adjudicates impor-

c. But Professor Van Alstyne goes on to say, id. at 487, that "it is plausible [to] treat *freedom from arbitrary adjudicative procedures* as a substantive element of one's liberty"—"a freedom whose abridgement government must sustain the burden of justifying, even as it must do when it seeks to subordinate other freedoms, such as those of speech and privacy"—"that the protected essences of personal freedom include a freedom from fundamentally unfair modes of governmental action, an immunity (if you will) from procedural arbitrariness." But see Peter Simon, *Liberty and Property in the Supreme Court: A Defense of Roth and Perry,* 71 Calif.L.Rev. 146, 186 (1983). See also Rodney Smolla, *The Reemergency of the Right-Privilege Distinction in Constitutional Law,* 35 Stan.L.Rev. 69, 85–86 (1982); Stephen Williams, *Liberty and Property: The Problem of Government Benefit,* 12 J.Legal Stud. 3, 17–19 (1983).

Compare Van Alstyne, supra, with Ely, *Democracy and Distrust* 19 (1980), maintaining that the phrase "life, liberty or property" used to be, and ought to be, "read as a unit and given an open-ended, functional interpretation," meaning that the government cannot "*seriously hurt* you without due process of law" (emphasis added). But consider Timothy Terrell, *"Property," "Due Process," and the Distinction Between Definition and Theory in Legal Analysis,* 70 Geo.L.J. 861, 899–900 (1982): "[I]f the phrase seriously hurt [has] discoverable substance, then its content necessarily would develop [judicially] in the same manner that the substance of 'life, liberty, or property' has developed. [The] analysis would raise the same sort of questions previously raised about property: what is the definition of 'seriously hurt'? [And] why do we use this phrase rather than one which is more restrictive, such as 'extremely seriously hurt,' or less

restrictive, such as 'slightly hurt'? That is, what is the justificatory theory for Ely's substitute phrase?

"This analysis indicates that Ely's objection to the Court's treatment of 'life, liberty, or property' is based on an apparent belief that the Court should not engage in a definitional exercise at all. In effect, he argues that the purpose of the due process clause is to protect citizens from government arbitrariness, and, therefore, that these terms should relate solely to that justification. [Ely] recognizes by his use of the phrase seriously hurt the need for a trigger mechanism that must precede any due process inquiry. Yet if arbitrariness is the evil to avoid, why have any preliminary obstacle to judicial scrutiny, much less the one he has rather casually identified?"

a. "[W]hile there were three dissents in *Goldberg* respecting the *fullness* of the procedure that government would be required to observe before terminating an allegedly ineligible welfare recipient, no one (not even the government itself, as Justice Brennan observed) dissented from the proposition that the due process clause was applicable to the case." Van Alstyne 456.

b. At this point, the Court noted [fn. 8] that "[i]t may be more realistic today to regard welfare entitlements as more like 'property' than a 'gratuity,'" citing Charles Reich, *The New Property,* 73 Yale L.J. 733 (1964), and quoting extensively from Charles Reich, *Individual Rights and Social Welfare: The Emerging Social Issues,* 74 Yale L.J. 1245 (1965). In these articles Professor Reich maintained that public employment, welfare assistance, franchises, licenses and other forms of governmental largess should be given the kind of protection afforded traditional property rights.

tant rights. The constitutional challenge cannot be answered by an argument that public assistance benefits are 'a "privilege" and not a "right." ' Relevant constitutional restraints apply as much to the withdrawal of public assistance benefits as to disqualification for unemployment compensation or to denial of a tax exemption or to discharge from public employment. The extent to which procedural due process must be afforded the recipient is influenced by the extent to which he may be 'condemned to suffer grievous loss,' and depends upon whether the recipient's interest in avoiding the loss outweighs the governmental interest in summary adjudication."

2. As observed in Henry Monaghan, *Of "Liberty" and "Property,"* 62 Corn. L.Rev. 401, 407 (1977), BELL v. BURSON, 402 U.S. 535, 91 S.Ct. 1586, 29 L.Ed.2d 90 (1971), "represented the high-water mark of [the] approach [that] whether an interest deserved due process clause process protection involved a simple pragmatic assessment of its 'importance' to the individual." The Court, per BRENNAN, J., invalidated a Georgia statute providing that the vehicle registration and driver's license of an uninsured motorist involved in an accident shall be suspended unless he posts security to cover the damages claimed by agreed parties in accident reports: "[Although a state could bar] the issuance of licenses to all motorists who did not carry liability insurance [or] post security, [o]nce licenses are issued, as in petitioner's case [a clergyman whose ministry requires him to cover three rural communities by car], their continued possession may become *essential* in the pursuit of a livelihood. Suspension of issued licenses thus involves state action that adjudicates *important interests* of the licensees. In such cases the licenses are not to be taken away without that procedural due process required by the Fourteenth Amendment." (Emphasis added.)

Bell "could have said that the license was sufficient to qualify as 'property,' or that a suspension of an individual's freedom to drive was a restriction on his 'liberty.' The Court said neither; the importance of the interest alone sufficed, and 'importance' was determined as a matter of federal, not state, law." Monaghan 407–08.

3. But "*Bell*'s latitudinarian approach to 'liberty' and 'property,' " Monaghan 408, did not prevail. Stressing that before deciding what form of hearing is required by procedural due process the Court must "determine whether due process requirements apply in the first place," i.e., whether one has been deprived of "liberty" or "property"—and in doing so "we must look not to the 'weight' but to the nature of the interest at stake"—BOARD OF REGENTS v. ROTH, 408 U.S. 564, 92 S.Ct. 2701, 33 L.Ed.2d 548 (1972), per STEWART, J., for the first time, rejected a procedural due process claim because it implicated neither "liberty" nor "property." Hired by Wisconsin State University for a fixed term of one year, and given no tenure rights to continued employment, Roth had been informed that he would not be rehired for the next academic year. The Court rejected his contention that the University's failure to give him any reason for its decision or any opportunity to challenge it at any sort of hearing violated procedural due process: "The requirements of procedural due process apply only to the deprivation of interests encompassed within the Fourteenth Amendment's protection of liberty and property. [T]he range of interests protected by procedural due process is not infinite.

"[The] State, in declining to rehire [Roth], did not make any charge against him that might seriously damage his standing and associations in his community [e.g., accuse him of dishonesty or immorality,] [a] [nor] impose on him a stigma or

---

a. "Had it done so," noted the Court, "this would be a different case. For '[w]here a person's good name, reputation, honor, or integrity is at stake because of what the govern-

other disability that foreclosed his freedom to take advantage of other employment opportunities. [It did not, for example, bar him] from all other public employment in State universities.[b] [O]n the record before us,[c] all that clearly appears is that [Roth] was not rehired for one year at one University. It stretches the concept too far to suggest that [one] is deprived of 'liberty' when he simply is not rehired in one job but remains as free as before to seek another.

"[As for 'property' interests protected by procedural due process, to] have a property interest in a benefit, [one] must have more than a unilateral expectation of it. He must, instead, have a legitimate claim of entitlement to [it]. Property interests, of course, are not created by the Constitution, [but by, and] defined by existing rules or understandings that stem from an independent source such as state law—rules or understandings that secure certain benefits and that support claims of entitlement to those benefits. [But the terms of Roth's employment] specifically provided that [his] employment was to terminate on June 30. They did not provide for contract renewal absent 'sufficient cause.' Indeed, they made no provision for renewal whatsoever.[d] [Thus, although Roth] surely had an abstract concern in being rehired, [he lacked] a *property* interest sufficient to require the University [to] give him a hearing when [declining] to renew his contract of employment." [e]

4. *"The bitter with the sweet."* ARNETT v. KENNEDY, 416 U.S. 134, 94 S.Ct. 1633, 40 L.Ed.2d 15 (1974): Kennedy, a nonprobationary federal civil service

ment is doing to him, notice and an opportunity to be heard are essential.' *Wisconsin v. Constantineau,* 400 U.S. 433, 91 S.Ct. 507, 27 L.Ed.2d 515 (1971)." *Constantineau* (Burger, C.J., and Black and Blackmun, JJ., dissenting on procedural grounds), invalidated on due process grounds a state law providing that when, by "excessive drinking," one produces certain conditions or exhibits certain traits (e.g., exposing himself or family "to want" or becoming "dangerous to the peace"), designated officials may—without notice or hearing to the person involved—post a notice in all retail liquor stores that sales or gifts of liquor to him are forbidden for one year. But cf. *Paul v. Davis* (1976), infra.

b. "Had it done so," noted the Court, "this, again, would be a different case."

c. Roth had also alleged that non-renewal of his contract was based on his exercise of his right to freedom of speech, but this allegation was not before the Court. *Perry v. Sindermann,* 408 U.S. 593, 92 S.Ct. 2694, 33 L.Ed.2d 570 (1972), a companion case, made clear that the lack of a public employee's "right" to reemployment "is immaterial to his free speech claim." For "even though a person has no 'right' to a valuable governmental benefit and even though the government may deny him the benefit for any number of reasons, there are some reasons upon which the government may not act. It may not deny a benefit to a person on a basis that infringes his constitutionally protected interests—especially, his interest in freedom of speech."

d. But *Sindermann,* fn. c supra, involving another state college teacher serving on a year-to-year basis whose appointment had not been renewed and who had not received a hearing, per Stewart, J., held that a "lack of a contractual or tenure right to re-employment, taken alone," does not defeat one's claim that nonrenewal of his contract violated procedural due process. Sindermann had ten years service and had alleged, but not been permitted to prove, that the college had a de facto tenure program and that he had tenure under that program. He must, ruled the Court, be given an opportunity to prove the legitimacy of his claim of entitlement to continued employment absent "sufficient cause" "in light of 'the policies and practices of the institution.'" (Roth, on the other hand, had failed to establish "anything approaching a 'common law' of re-employment.")

e. Dissenting, Marshall, J., maintained that "every citizen who applies for a government job is entitled to it unless the government can establish some reason for denying the employment. This is the 'property' right [that] is protected by the Fourteenth Amendment and that cannot be denied 'without due process of law.' And it is also liberty—liberty to work—which is the 'very essence of the personal freedom and opportunity' secured by the Fourteenth Amendment."

Dissenting, Brennan, J., joined by Douglas, J., agreed with Marshall, J., that Roth had been denied due process when his contract had not been renewed without being informed of the reasons or given a chance to respond. Powell, J., did not participate.

employee in a regional OEO office, was removed by the Regional Director for allegedly publicly accusing the Director of bribery "in reckless disregard" of the facts. The relevant statutes provided, inter alia, that, prior to removal the employee had a right to reply to the charges orally and in writing and to submit affidavits to the official authorized to remove him (the Regional Director).[a] Instead of responding to the charges against him in a proceeding to be conducted and decided by the very person he had allegedly slandered, and who had filed the complaint against him, Kennedy instituted a federal suit, asserting that the discharge procedures denied him procedural due process because they failed to provide for a trial-type hearing before an impartial agency official prior to removal. The Court, with no majority opinion, held that the procedures satisfied due process.

The plurality opinion was by REHNQUIST, J., joined by Burger, C.J., and Stewart, J., but (as pointed out by White, J. joined by three other justices, dissenting in *Bishop v. Wood*, infra) the two justices who concurred in *Arnett*, as well as the four who dissented on this issue, rejected the plurality's analysis. As described by Van Alstyne, supra, at 582, according to Rehnquist, J., it was unnecessary to reach step two and "decide whether submitting Mr. Kennedy's fate to the judgment of his accuser was incompatible with [due process] because a close examination of Mr. Kennedy's property interest made it clear that *nothing* was in fact being taken from him to which he had *any* legally recognizable entitlement. In short, he failed at step one." Observed Rehnquist, J.:

"[A]ppellee did have a statutory expectancy that he not be removed other than for 'such cause as will promote the efficiency of the service.' But the very section of the statute [granting him that right] expressly provided also for the procedure by which 'cause' was to be determined, and expressly omitted the procedural guarantees [appellee claims]. [W]here the grant of a substantive right is inextricably intertwined with the limitations on the procedures which are to be employed in determining that right, a litigant in the position of appellee must take the bitter with the sweet."

As for appellee's contention that the charges on which his dismissal was based "in effect accused [him] of dishonesty, and that therefore a hearing was required before he could be deprived of this element of his 'liberty'": "Since the purpose of [such a hearing] is to provide the person 'an opportunity to clear his name,' a hearing afforded by administrative appeal procedures after the actual dismissal is a sufficient compliance with [due process requirements]."

POWELL, J., joined by Blackmun, J., concurred in the result, but criticized the plurality's approach: "[The Rehnquist analysis] would lead directly to the conclusion that whatever the nature of [one's] statutorily created property interest, deprivation of that interest could be accomplished without notice or a hearing at any time. This view misconceives the origin of the right to procedural due process. That right is conferred not by legislative grace, but by constitutional guarantee. While the legislature may elect not to confer a property interest in federal employment, it may not constitutionally authorize the deprivation of such an interest, once conferred, without appropriate procedural safeguards." [b]

---

a. The employee may also appeal an adverse decision to a reviewing authority within the agency. Only on appeal is he entitled to an evidentiary trial-type hearing, but if reinstated on appeal he receives full back pay.

b. This passage was quoted with approval by the Court in *Vitek v. Jones* (1980), *Logan v. Zimmerman Brush Co.* (1982), and *Cleveland Board of Education v. Loudermill* (1985), all discussed infra.

But after "weighing" the government's interest against the affected employee's,[c] Powell concluded that "a prior evidentiary hearing" was not required before removal. "The Government's interest in being able to act expeditiously to remove an unsatisfactory employee is substantial" and, since he would be reinstated and awarded back pay if he prevailed on the merits, Kennedy's "actual injury" would consist only of "a temporary interruption of his income during the interim." Thus, the challenged statutes and regulations "comport with due process by providing a reasonable accommodation of the competing interests." [d]

Notes and Questions

(a) *Circumventing Goldberg.* "The only difference" between *Arnett* and *Goldberg,* comments David Shapiro, *Mr. Justice Rehnquist: A Preliminary View,* 90 Harv.L.Rev. 293, 324 (1976), "is that [in *Goldberg*] the statutes and regulations governing eligibility were not 'inextricably intertwined' with [those] providing for post-termination but not pre-termination hearings. Thus, under Justice Rehnquist's approach all the legislature would have to do to circumvent [*Goldberg*] would be to place the procedural limitations (which presumably could deny *any* opportunity to be heard at any time) in the same statutory section with the substantive provisions on eligibility. Surely, as six members of the Court seemed to agree, the effect would be to turn what looked like a landmark constitutional decision into the flimsiest of trivia."

(b) *Did Powell miss Rehnquist's point?* Consider Van Alstyne at 464–65: In *Arnett,* Powell, J., "fully recognized the devastating effect of the Rehnquist treatment of the new property, [but] seemed to miss Rehnquist's point in his own reply." Recall that Powell, J., stated that the legislature "may not constitutionally authorize the deprivation of [a property interest in employment], *once conferred,* without appropriate safeguards" (emphasis added). Comments Van Alstyne: "But to speak of '[a property] interest, *once conferred,*' plainly begs the question Justice Rehnquist had raised: What 'interest' *was* 'conferred'? Show us a title or a jot of 'interest' actually 'conferred' by the legislature apart from the interest Kennedy held—the interest exactly bounded, as Rehnquist said, by the procedural provisions of the only source giving it any substance at all."

(c) *Must a government employee always "take the bitter with the sweet"?* "It is clear," comments Van Alstyne at 462, that he "need *not* [if] the bitter is a substantive restriction forbidden to government by the Constitution (which applies, of course, even when the government is operating as an employer), whether the bitter requires one to abstain from insisting upon one's first amendment rights or to relinquish one's rights to due process."

5. BISHOP v. WOOD, 426 U.S. 341, 96 S.Ct. 2074, 48 L.Ed.2d 684 (1976), per STEVENS, J., held—over the protest of the dissenters that the majority was

---

c. For a more extensive articulation of Powell, J.'s "balancing process," see his opinion for the Court in *Mathews v. Eldridge,* Sec. 2 infra.

d. White, J., concurring in part and dissenting in part, rejected the Rehnquist plurality's analysis and largely agreed with Powell, J.'s constitutional analysis. (Consider his opinion for the Court in *Vitek v. Jones,* infra). Although he found the pretermination procedures involved in *Arnett* generally adequate, White, J., would affirm the lower court's judgment, ordering reinstatement and backpay,

"due to the failure to provide an impartial hearing officer at the pretermination hearing"—a right he maintained that the challenged statute, although silent on the matter, should be construed as requiring in this case.

Dissenting, Marshall, J., joined by Douglas and Brennan, JJ., rejected the plurality's analysis on grounds similar to Powell's, but as Marshall "balanced" the interests involved (stressing the long delay in the processing of adverse personnel actions), Kennedy was entitled to "an evidentiary hearing before an impartial decision-maker prior to dismissal."

adopting an analysis rejected by six members of the Court in *Arnett*—that the dismissal of a city policeman implicated neither the "property" or "liberty" interests protected by due process. The City Manager of Marion, North Carolina, terminated petitioner's employment as a policeman without affording him a hearing to determine the sufficiency of the cause for his dismissal. Petitioner brought suit, contending that since he was classified as a "permanent employee" he had a constitutional right to a pretermination hearing.[a] During pretrial discovery he was informed that he had been discharged for insubordination, "causing low morale," and "conduct unsuited to an officer."

"[T]he sufficiency of the claim of entitlement," observed the Court, "must be decided by reference to state law. The [state supreme court] has held that an enforceable expectation of continued [state employment] can exist only if the employer, by statute or contract, has actually granted some form of guarantee. [Based] on his understanding of state law, [the federal district court] concluded that petitioner 'held his position at the will and pleasure of the city.' [As the ordinance was thus construed], the City Manager's determination of the adequacy of the grounds for discharge is not subject to judicial review; the employee is merely given certain procedural rights which the District Court found not to have been violated in this case. The District Court's reading of the ordinance is tenable; [and] it was accepted by [the] Fourth Circuit. These reasons are sufficient to foreclose our independent examination of the state law issue. Under [this view], petitioner's discharge did not deprive him of a property interest protected by the Fourteenth Amendment.[b]

"Petitioner's claim that he has been deprived of liberty has two components. He contends that the reasons given for his discharge are so serious as to constitute a stigma that may severely damage his reputation in the community [and] that those reasons were false.[c]

"[In] *Roth,* we recognized that the nonretention of an untenured college teacher might make him somewhat less attractive to other employers, but nevertheless concluded that it would stretch the concept too far 'to suggest that a person is deprived of "liberty" when he simply is not retained in one position but remains as free as before to seek another.' This same conclusion applies to the discharge of a public employee whose position is terminable at the will of the employer when [prior to his instituting a law suit] there is no public disclosure of the reasons for the discharge.

"[Even if the reasons given for petitioner's discharge were false], the reasons stated to him in private had no different impact on his reputation than if they had been true. And the answers to his interrogatories, whether true or false, did not

a. The relevant provision of the city ordinance provided:

"*Dismissal.* A permanent employee whose work is not satisfactory over a period of time shall be notified in what way his work is deficient and what he must do if his work is to be satisfactory. If a permanent employee fails to perform work up to the standard of the classification held, or continues to be negligent, inefficient, or unfit to perform his duties, he may be dismissed by the City Manager. Any discharged employee shall be given written notice of his discharge setting forth the effective date and reasons for his discharge if he shall request such a notice."

b. In *Arnett*, noted Stevens, J., "the Court concluded that because the employee could only be discharged for cause, he had a property interest which was entitled to constitutional protection. In this case, a holding that as a matter of state law the employee 'held his position at the will and pleasure of the city' necessarily establishes that he had *no* property interest."

c. Since the District Court granted summary judgment against petitioner, noted the Court, "we [must] assume that his discharge was a mistake and based on incorrect information."

cause the discharge. The truth or falsity of the City Manager's statement determines whether or not his decision to discharge the petitioner was correct or prudent, but neither enhances nor diminishes petitioner's claim that his constitutionally protected interest in liberty has been impaired.[13] A contrary evaluation of his contention would enable every discharged employee to assert a constitutional claim merely by alleging that his former supervisor made a mistake.

"The federal court is not the appropriate forum in which to review the multitude of personnel decisions that are made daily by public agencies.[14] [In] the absence of any claim that the public employer was motivated by a desire to curtail or to penalize the exercise of an employee's constitutionally protected rights, we must presume that official action was regular and, if erroneous, can best be corrected in other ways. [Due Process] is not a guarantee against incorrect or ill-advised personnel decisions." [d]

BRENNAN, J., joined by Marshall, J., dissented: "Petitioner was discharged as a policeman on the grounds of insubordination, 'causing low morale,' and 'conduct unsuited to an officer.' It is difficult to imagine a greater 'badge of infamy' that could be imposed on one following petitioner's calling. [Yet the Court holds] that a State may tell an employee that he is being fired for some nonderogatory reason, and then turn around and inform prospective employers that [he] was in fact discharged for a stigmatizing reason that will effectively preclude future employment.

"The Court purports to limit its holding to situations in which there is 'no public disclosure of the reasons for the discharge,' but in this case the stigmatizing reasons have been disclosed, and there is no reason to believe that respondents will not convey these actual reasons to petitioner's prospective employers. [The stigma was not imposed until after petitioner brought suit, but] the 'claim' does not arise until the State has officially branded petitioner in some way, and the purpose of the due process hearing is to accord him an opportunity to clear his [name].

"[T]he strained reading of the local ordinance, which the Court deems to be 'tenable,' cannot be dispositive of the existence vel non of petitioner's 'property' interest. There is certainly a federal dimension to the definition of 'property' in the Federal Constitution [and] at least before a state law is definitively construed as not securing a 'property' interest, the relevant inquiry is whether it was

13. Indeed, the impact on petitioner's constitutionally protected interest in liberty is no greater even if we assume that the City Manager deliberately lied. Such fact might conceivably provide the basis for a state law claim, the validity of which would be entirely unaffected by our analysis of the federal constitutional question.

14. [U]nless we were to adopt Justice Brennan's remarkably innovative suggestion that we develop a federal common law of property rights, or his equally far reaching view that almost every discharge implicates a constitutionally protected liberty interest, the ultimate control of state personnel relationships is, and will remain, with the States; they may grant or withhold tenure at their unfettered discretion. In this case, whether we accept or reject the construction of the ordinance adopted by the two lower courts, the power to change or

clarify that ordinance will remain in the hands of the City Council of the city of Marion.

[But see Robert Rabin, *Job Security and Due Process: Monitoring Discretion Through a Reasons Requirement*, 44 U.Chi.L.Rev. 60, 72 (1976) "[*Bishop's* reference to] 'Justice Brennan's remarkably innovative suggestion that we develop a federal common law of property' [goes] to the heart of the matter. For if the cases beginning with *Goldberg* were not developing 'a federal common law of property rights' it is impossible to comprehend the decisions. One would have thought that the dialogue sparked by Justice Rehnquist in *Arnett* made that clear."]

d. Smolla, first fn. c supra, 88–89, points to this "profoundly honest passage" as providing "the best insights into the motivations that underlie the Court's adoption of the entitlement doctrine."

objectively reasonable for the employee to believe he could rely on continued employment.[4] [At] a minimum, this would require in this case an analysis of the common practices utilized and the expectations generated by respondents, and the manner in which the local ordinance would reasonably be read by respondents' employees."

WHITE, J., joined by Brennan, Marshall and Blackmun, JJ., also dissented: "The majority's holding that petitioner had no property interest in his job in spite of the unequivocal language in the city ordinance that he may be dismissed only for certain kinds of cause rests [on] the fact that state law provides no *procedures* for assuring that the City Manager dismiss him only for cause.

"[This] is precisely the reasoning which was embraced by only three and expressly rejected by six Members of this Court in [*Kennedy*]. [The] ordinance plainly grants petitioner a right to his job unless there is cause to fire him. Having granted him such a right it is the Federal Constitution,[3] not state law, which determines the process to be applied in connection with any state decision to deprive him of it." [e]

Notes and Questions

(a) Consider Van Alstyne at 468–69: "[According to the Court], Bishop, as a 'permanent employee,' had even less fourteenth amendment property than had Roth, probationary employee at Oshkosh, Wisconsin. Roth had the enforceable assurance of at least the one year of assistant professor status (which he had completed) before encountering the hazard of nonrenewal. Although unknown to him, Bishop as a 'permanent employee' literally had no job *even from day to day,* but was dependent upon the non-happening of an event (receipt of notice of dismissal from the City Manager) as a condition precedent to vest affirmatively in him each day's entitlement to his status."

(b) Does *Roth* leave the courts a role that would allow them to decide for themselves whether interests defined by the state are fourteenth amendment "property"? Compare Monaghan 440 with Simon, first fn. c supra, at 182–83.

[4]. By holding that States have "unfettered discretion" in defining "property" for purposes of the Due Process Clause, [the] Court is, as my Brother White argues, effectively adopting the analysis rejected by a majority of the Court in *Arnett.* More basically, the Court's approach is a resurrection of the discredited rights/privileges distinction, for a State may now avoid all due process safeguards attendant upon the loss of even the necessities of life, cf. *Goldberg,* merely by labeling them as not constituting "property."

3. The majority intimates in [fn. b] that the views of the three plurality Justices in *Arnett* were rejected because the other six Justices disagreed on the question of how the federal *statute* involved in that case should be construed. This is incorrect. All Justices agreed on the meaning of the statute. [I]t was the constitutional significance of the statute on which the six disagreed with the plurality.

Similarly, here, I do not disagree with the majority or the courts below on the meaning of the state law. If I did, I might be inclined to defer to the judgments of the two lower courts. The state law says that petitioner may be dismissed by the City Manager only for certain kinds of cause and then provides that he will receive notice and an explanation, but no hearing and no review. I agree that as a matter of state law petitioner has no remedy no matter how arbitrarily or erroneously the City Manager has acted. This is what the lower courts say the statute means. I differ with those courts and the majority only with respect to the constitutional significance of an unambiguous state law. A majority of the Justices in *Arnett* stood on the proposition that the Constitution requires procedures *not* required by state law when the state conditions dismissal on "cause."

e. In a third dissent, Blackmun, J., joined by Brennan, J., maintained that the Marion ordinance "contains a 'for cause' standard for dismissal and [thus] creates a proper expectation of privacy of continued employment so long as [the employee] performs his work satisfactorily. At this point, the Federal Constitution steps in and requires that appropriate procedures be followed before the employee may be deprived of his property interest."

(c) *Is there a degree of circularity to the Bishop dissent?* "If the Court were to focus on real expectations and the role a government job actually plays in someone's life," observes Tribe, *Treatise* 698–99, "then it would have to move well beyond the positivist framework it first adopted in *Bishop*. Yet the [*Bishop* dissenters do] not offer a practical alternative. [They] attempt to find a statutory entitlement to a job as a policeman. But there is a degree of circularity to their argument that there may have been 'reasonable expectations' in *Bishop* that justified a finding of a property interest: it is questionable whether a person can truly be said to 'justifiably rely' on continued employment where the person's contract or statute expressly indicates either that the employment can be terminated without cause, or that cause is theoretically required but no hearing is to be allowed. This circle can be broken only by an assertion of substantive values or norms in the name of the Constitution—norms as to what an employee, for example, is *entitled* to expect *whatever* the contract or statute may say. Indeed, breaking the circle would require an acceptance of the proposition that due process is not merely a means to the end of implementing the state's own substantive rules and allocations but either a means to some very different and larger purpose, or—as in the intrinsic approach to procedural safeguards—an end in itself."

(d) Since the civil service bureaucracy has great potential for adversely affecting constitutional rights and civil service tenure would help free lower level bureaucrats from political control, should civil service employment be recognized as constitutionally protected? Compare Mark Tushnet, *The Newer Property: Suggestions for the Revival of Substantive Due Process,* 1975 Sup.Ct.Rev. 261, 284 with Van Alstyne at 482–87.

(e) *Public employment, welfare benefits, and the "government as monopolist" theory.* Consider Terrell, first fn. c supra, at 864–65, 902–04, 907–08, "propos[ing] a threshold inquiry for determining whether a particular government entitlement should be considered a protected property interest under the due process clause[,] [the] 'government as monopolist' theory. [W]hen government acts as a 'monopolist' [then] the due process constraint is properly applied to balance the power of government over the individual's life. When the individual is not forced to deal with government, however, but chooses to do so freely and voluntarily, the constitutional protection of due process is misplaced.

"[Based] on this factor of individual choice, cases involving government employment—such as *Roth, Bishop,* and *Arnett*—and potentially other contractual relations would seem to fall generally into the permissible arbitrariness, not the due process, set. Government is rarely a monopolist in these contractual situations, as either the only available employer or the only supplier or purchaser of a particular item. [O]nce an individual voluntarily accepts a job that has less than full due process protections for termination, then the individual has indeed taken 'the bitter with the sweet' and should not be able to base a cause of action on the inadequacy of these protections. [Welfare] benefits cases, like professional licenses cases, should fall in the due process set, just as the Court concluded in *Goldberg*. [The position of welfare recipients] is probably best seen as one of forced association automatically attended by some degree of procedural protection."

6. *Reading "liberty" narrowly.* PAUL v. DAVIS, 424 U.S. 693, 96 S.Ct. 1155, 47 L.Ed.2d 405 (1976), arose as follows: After respondent Davis had been arrested on a shoplifting charge, petitioner police officials circulated a "flyer" to 800 merchants in the Louisville, Ky. area designating him an "active shoplifter."

When the shoplifting charge was dismissed, Davis brought a § 1983 action alleging that the police officials' action under color of law had deprived him of his constitutional rights, by inhibiting him from entering business establishments and by impairing his employment opportunities. A 5–3 majority, per REHNQUIST, J., was unimpressed:

"[R]espondent's complaint would appear to state a classical claim for defamation actionable in the courts of virtually every State, [but he] brought his action [not] in the state courts of Kentucky, but in a [federal court]. [He contends that since petitioners are government officials] his action is thereby transmuted into one for deprivation by the State of rights secured under the Fourteenth Amendment. [It] is hard to perceive any logical stopping place to [respondent's] line of reasoning. [His] construction would seem almost necessarily to result in every legally cognizable injury which may have been inflicted by a state official acting under 'color of law' establishing a violation of the Fourteenth Amendment. [But our cases do] not establish the proposition that reputation alone, apart from some more tangible interests such as employment, is either 'liberty' or 'property' by itself sufficient to invoke the procedural protection of the Due Process Clause." Thus, no inquiry had to be made as to whether the police officials had followed adequate procedures before issuing the flyers."

The Court distinguished *Constantineau*, fn. a in *Bell v. Burson*, supra, as dependent on the fact that posting the person's name in liquor stores as a chronic drinker "deprived [him] of a right previously held under state law—the right [to] obtain liquor in common with the rest of the citizenry"—and thus "significantly altered his status as a matter of state law. [I]t was that alteration of legal status which, combined with the injury resulting from the defamation, justified the invocation of procedural safeguards." Interests "comprehended within the meaning of either 'liberty' or 'property' as meant in the Due Process Clause attain this constitutional status by virtue of the fact that they have been initially recognized and protected by state law, and we have repeatedly ruled that the procedural guarantees of the Fourteenth Amendment apply whenever the State seeks to remove or significantly alter that protected status. [But] the interest in reputation alone which respondent seeks to vindicate [is] quite different from the 'liberty' or 'property' recognized in [such decisions as *Bell v. Burson*]. [Although the interest in reputation is protected by the state by virtue of its tort law], any harm or injury to that interest, even where as here inflicted by an officer of the State, does not result in a deprivation of any 'liberty' or 'property' recognized by state or federal law, nor has it worked any change of respondent's status as theretofore recognized under the State's laws."

BRENNAN, J., joined by White and Marshall, JJ., dissented: "The Court today holds that public officials, acting in their official capacities as law enforcers, may on their own initiative and without trial constitutionally condemn innocent individuals as criminals and thereby brand them with one of the most stigmatizing and debilitating labels in our society. "[There] is no attempt by the Court to analyze the question as one of reconciliation of constitutionally protected personal rights and the exigencies of law enforcement. [Rather,] the Court by mere fiat and with no analysis wholly excludes personal interest in reputation from the ambit of 'life, liberty, or property' under the Fifth and Fourteenth Amendments, thus rendering due process concerns *never* applicable to the official stigmatization, however arbitrary, of an individual. The logical and disturbing corollary of this holding is that no due process infirmities would inhere in a statute constituting a commission to conduct *ex parte* trials of individuals, so long as the only official judgment pronounced was limited to the public condemnation and branding of a person as a Communist, a traitor, an 'active murderer,' a homosexual, or any other mark that 'merely' carries social opprobrium. The potential of today's decision is frightening for a free people."

Despite the majority's efforts to distinguish them, cases such as *Roth, Constantineau* [a] and *Goss v. Lopez,* [b] maintained Brennan, J., "are cogent authority that a person's interest in his good name and reputation falls within the broad term 'liberty' and clearly require that the government afford procedural protections before infringing that name and reputation by branding a person as a criminal. [It] is inexplicable how the Court can say that a person's status is 'altered' when the State suspends him from school, revokes his driver's license, fires him from a job, or denies him the right to purchase a drink of alcohol, but is in no way 'altered' when it officially pins upon him the brand of a criminal." [c]

Notes and Questions

(a) *"An unsettling conception of liberty."* Consider Monaghan at 424–27: "[I]t is an unsettling conception of 'liberty' that protects an individual against state interference with his access to liquor but not with his reputation in the community. * * * Defamation is a serious assault upon an individual's sense of 'self-identity,' and has from ancient times been viewed as 'psychic mayhem.' Accordingly, the Court's conclusion that such an assault implicates no constitutionally protected interest stands wholly at odds with our ethical, political, and constitutional assumption about the worth of each individual."

(b) *A defense of the result in, but not the reasoning of, Paul v. Davis.* Consider RODNEY SMOLLA, fn. a supra, at 841–47: "The critics of *Paul* have never explained satisfactorily how a section 1983 action is in any substantive law sense an improvement on the law of libel. [A § 1983] action shifts the substantive focus of the lawsuit away from the two issues that have always been at the core of libel actions: the truth or falsity of the defamatory language, and the conduct of the defendant in publishing it. [The] critics of *Paul* have also failed to build a convincing case for construing the fourteenth amendment as mandating an alternate federal forum for what are essentially defamation actions. [Rehnquist, J.,] might have argued, as he would eventually come to argue, that there is no need to treat deprivations of interests in liberty or property as matters of federal concern as long as the state has an adequate system in place to compensate

a. For the view that "the heart of the complaint" in *Constantineau* was "defamation, not restriction of access to liquor," see Monaghan at 431. See also id. at 423–24; Jerry Mashaw, *Due Process in the Administrative State* 95 (1985); David Shapiro, *Mr. Justice Rehnquist: A Preliminary View,* 90 Harv.L.Rev. 293, 326 (1976); Rodney Smolla, *The Displacement of Federal Due Process Claims by State Tort Remedies,* 1982 U.Ill.L.F. 831, 839–40, 845.

b. *Goss v. Lopez,* 419 U.S. 565, 95 S.Ct. 729, 42 L.Ed.2d 725 (1975) (also discussed in Sec. 2 infra), held that students suspended from public high schools for up to ten days were entitled to procedural protections against unfair suspensions. The *Goss* Court, per White, J., pointed out that state law had established a "property interest" in educational benefits, but also recognized "the liberty interest in reputation" implicated by suspensions: "The Due Process Clause also forbids arbitrary

deprivations of liberty. 'Where a person's good name, reputation, honor, or integrity is at stake because of what the government is doing to him,' the minimal requirements of the Clause must be satisfied. *Constantineau.* [If] sustained and recorded, [the charges of misconduct] could seriously damage the students' standing with their fellow pupils and their teachers as well as interfere with later opportunities for higher education and employment. [Neither] the property interest in educational benefits temporarily denied nor the liberty interest in reputation, which is also implicated, is so insubstantial that suspensions may constitutionally be imposed by any procedure the school chooses, no matter how arbitrary."

c. Stevens, J., did not participate, but a year later, dissenting in *Ingraham v. Wright,* discussed in fn. e infra, he suggested that *Paul* "may have been correctly decided on an incorrect rationale."

victims of those deprivations.[d]   This reasoning would not have denied that reputation was a sufficiently substantial interest to deserve characterization as property or liberty; such a position would merely have held that the interest in reputation was not deprived 'without due process of law' as long as the state courts remain ready, willing and able to provide 'due process' in the form of post-deprivation compensation.

"[In *Constantineau*] the Wisconsin posting statute may very well have pre-empted the normal remedies of the common law by authorizing the very posting procedure used by the police chief against Mrs. Constantineau, in all likelihood

d. Consider Justice Rehnquist's opinion for the Court in *Parratt v. Taylor*, 451 U.S. 527, 101 S.Ct. 1908, 68 L.Ed.2d 420 (1981). Although the state had a torts claim procedure which provided a remedy for tortious losses at the hands of the state, a state inmate brought a § 1983 action against prison officials, alleging that they had negligently lost certain hobby materials he had ordered by mail, thus depriving him of property without due process of law. The Court thought it plain that the prison officials had acted under color of state law; the lost materials constituted "property"; and that the alleged loss, although negligently caused, amounted to a "deprivation." But standing alone, "these three elements do not establish a violation of the Fourteenth Amendment. Nothing in that Amendment protects against all deprivations of life, liberty, or property by the State. [The Amendment] protects only against deprivations 'without due process of law.'" The Court then addressed the question whether "the tort remedies which Nebraska provides as a means of redress for property deprivations satisfy the requirements of procedural due process" and concluded that they did.

Does *Parratt's* analysis rest on a confusion of *substantive* and *procedural* due process? Consider Richard Fallon, *Some Confusions About Due Process, Judicial Review, and Constitutional Remedies*, 93 Colum.L.Rev. 309, 310–11, (1993): "According to [*Parratt*], the prisoner presented a procedural due process claim, [but] in fact, the inmate's strongest claim sounded in substantive due process: questions of procedure aside, state officials had deprived him of property without adequate justification. Once the substantive element of the inmate's claim is acknowledged, *Parratt* cannot be rationalized as a constitutional case holding that post-deprivation remedies in state court sometimes supply all the procedural due process to which an aggrieved party is entitled. *Parratt* makes most sense if viewed as an abstention decision, which calls upon federal courts to withhold substantive due process rulings in cases in which state tort law adequately protects constitutional values."

According to Fallon, id. at 341–42, *Hudson v. Palmer*, infra, which extended *Parratt* to intentional torts, "reflects a similar confusion of substantive and procedural due process. [In *Hudson*, the] gravamen of the claim, clearly, was that the guard had engaged in substantively arbitrary conduct and thereby deprived the claimant of constitutionally protected property."

In *Hudson v. Palmer*, 468 U.S. 517, 104 S.Ct. 3194, 82 L.Ed.2d 393 (1984), a state inmate brought a § 1983 action against a prison guard, alleging that the latter had engaged in an unreasonable "shakedown" search of the inmate's locker and cell and that, during the search, had intentionally destroyed some of his noncontraband personal property. The Court, per Burger, C.J., deemed the reasoning of *Parratt* applicable to intentional deprivation of property:

"The State can no more anticipate and control in advance the random and unauthorized intentional conduct of its employees than it can anticipate similar negligent conduct. [If] negligent deprivations of property do not violate [due process] because predeprivation process is impracticable, it follows that intentional deprivations do not [either] [provided that] adequate state postdeprivation remedies are available." Because Virginia did furnish such an adequate remedy, "even if [the guard] intentionally destroyed [the inmate's] personal property during the challenged shakedown search, the destruction did not violate the Fourteenth Amendment."

But see Tribe, supra, at 727–29: "[T]he magnitude of the [*Hudson*] opinion's apparent leap beyond *Parratt* seems unwarranted. It is one thing to say that no deprivation of life, liberty, or property without due process of law has occurred simply because a state agent negligently injures someone in the course of carrying out his official duties—as the Court was later to hold in *Daniels v. Williams* [474 U.S. 327, 106 S.Ct. 662, 88 L.Ed.2d 662 (1986)] and *Davidson v. Cannon* [474 U.S. 344, 106 S.Ct. 668, 88 L.Ed.2d 677 (1986)]. It is quite another thing to suggest that even an intentional abuse of state authority cannot inflict any constitutional injury unless and until the state has failed to provide redress. * * * Dirty Harry violated the Constitution even if the state made it possible for his victims to sue him. Any contrary intimation in the needlessly broad language of *Hudson* ought to be regard-

immunizing the police chief from the 'common law process' to which the police chiefs in Kentucky were still subject. [The] constitutional fault in Wisconsin's posting statute was thus systemic. It is precisely in cases in which the state enacts a regime that allows the state to visit substantial harm on its citizens without traditional recourse to the courts for compensation that federal constitutional law *should* be activated to override that system and 'superimpose a font of tort law' on the deficient state.

"[Rehnquist, J.,] could have finished off Davis' claim by simply pointing out that Davis continued to enjoy precisely the right and status that he always had under Kentucky law: the right to sue the police chiefs in a common law action for damages. [If] Kentucky had taken away from Davis his common law tort cause of action, *then* it would have extinguished 'a right or status previously recognized by state law.' But Kentucky did not.

"[As] much as Paul's language and logic were muddled and misleading, [its] result was sound. The result, however, was not justified by the reason Justice Rehnquist gave—that Kentucky law did not extend its protection to Mr. Davis' reputation—but by precisely the opposite fact: because Kentucky law *did* protect Davis, Kentucky did nothing to violate the due process clause." [e]

7. (a) *In some situations, at least, a litigant need not "take the bitter with the sweet."* A Nebraska law, § 83–180(1), provides that if a designated physician finds that a prisoner "suffers from a mental disease or defect" that cannot be properly treated in prison the Director of Correctional Services may transfer a prisoner to a mental hospital. Jones maintained that a prisoner is entitled to certain procedural protections, including notice, an adversary hearing and provision of counsel, before he is transferred to a state mental hospital for treatment. The Court agreed, VITEK v. JONES, 445 U.S. 480, 100 S.Ct. 1254, 63 L.Ed.2d 552 (1980), per WHITE, J. The involuntary transfer of a state prisoner to a mental hospital implicates a constitutionally protected "liberty interest" and once a state grants prisoners such an interest "due process protections are necessary 'to insure that the state-created right is not arbitrarily abrogated' "—these protections "being a matter of federal law, they are not diminished by the fact that the State may have specified its own procedures that it may deem adequate for determining the preconditions to adverse official action":

"We have repeatedly held that state statutes may create liberty interests that are entitled to the procedural protections of the Due Process Clause of the

ed as dictum, and should be reconsidered when a suitable case presents itself."

e. Professor Smolla then turns to *Ingraham v. Wright*, 430 U.S. 651, 97 S.Ct. 1401, 51 L.Ed.2d 711 (1977) (also discussed in Part II infra), a case finding that the "paddling" of students as a means of maintaining discipline in the public schools "implicates a constitutionally protected liberty interest," but concluding that the Due Process Clause does not require notice and hearing prior to imposition of corporal punishment as that practice is authorized and limited by the common law— the state's traditional common-law constraints and remedies "are fully adequate to afford due process." Comments Smolla at 847–48:

"As was true in *Paul,* in *Ingraham* state law had in place a remedial scheme that provided redress for the harm that was alleged to form the basis of the due process violation. The Court in *Ingraham* avoided the confusion of *Paul,* however, by steering clear of the notion that the existence of state tort law remedies somehow automatically displaced the due process clause. Instead [*Ingraham*] conceded the logical point that *Paul* had irrationally and stubbornly seemed to deny, recognizing that at a threshold level, common law protection and constitutional protection could be duplicative. [U]nlike the reputational interest at issue in *Paul,* an interest without independent federal content, the liberty interest in *Ingraham* was undeniably 'constitutional'—the right to be free of physical restraint and punishment, *Ingraham* thus made it clear that state common law remedies could serve as an adequate surrogate for due process safeguards even

Fourteenth Amendment. There is no 'constitutional or inherent right' to parole, *Greenholtz v. Nebraska Penal Inmates,* 442 U.S. 1, 7, 99 S.Ct. 2100, 2103, 60 L.Ed.2d 668 (1979),[a] but once a State grants a prisoner the conditional liberty properly dependent on the observance of special parole restrictions, due process protections attach to the decision to revoke parole. *Morrissey v. Brewer,* 408 U.S. 471, 92 S.Ct. 2593, 33 L.Ed.2d 484 (1972). The same is true of the revocation of probation. *Gagnon v. Scarpelli,* 411 U.S. 778, 93 S.Ct. 1756, 36 L.Ed.2d 656 (1973). In *Wolff v. McDonnell,* 418 U.S. 539, 94 S.Ct. 2963, 41 L.Ed.2d 935 (1974), we held that a state-created right to good-time credits, which could be forfeited only for serious misbehavior, constituted a liberty interest protected by the Due Process Clause.

"[In] *Meachum v. Fano,* 427 U.S. 215, 96 S.Ct. 2532, 49 L.Ed.2d 451 (1976), and *Montanye v. Haymes,* 427 U.S. 236, 96 S.Ct. 2543, 49 L.Ed.2d 466 (1976), we held that the transfer of a prisoner from one prison to another does not infringe a protected liberty interest. But in those cases transfers were discretionary with the prison authorities, and in neither case did the prisoner possess any right or justifiable expectation that he would not be transferred except for misbehavior or upon the occurrence of other specified events.[b]

"[The] 'objective expectation, firmly fixed in state law and official penal complex practice,' that a prisoner would not be transferred unless he suffered from a mental disease or defect that could not be adequately treated in the prison, gave Jones a liberty interest that entitled him to the benefits of appropriate procedures in connection with determining the conditions that warranted his transfer to a mental hospital. [If] the State grants a prisoner a right or expectation that adverse action will not be taken against him except upon the occurrence of specified behavior, 'the determination of whether such behavior has occurred becomes critical, and the minimum requirements of procedural due process appropriate for the circumstances must be observed.' *Wolff.* These minimum requirements being a matter of federal law, they are not diminished by

when 'hard core' constitutional interests in property or liberty were at stake."

a. The *Greenholtz* Court observed, per Burger, C.J., that, absent a statutory entitlement, "there is no constitutional right of a convicted person to be conditionally released before the expiration of a valid sentence. [We] can accept respondents' view that the expectancy of release provided by this statute is entitled to some measure of constitutional protection. However, we emphasize that this statute has unique structure and language and thus whether any other state statute provides a protectible entitlement must be decided on a case-by-case basis." Consider also Professor Nowak's criticism of *Greenholtz,* p. 519 infra.

Cf. *Connecticut Bd. of Pardons v. Dumschat,* 452 U.S. 458, 101 S.Ct. 2460, 69 L.Ed.2d 158 (1981), per Burger, C.J., rejecting the argument that "the fact that the Connecticut Board of Pardons has granted approximately three-fourths of the applications for commutation of life sentences creates a constitutional 'liberty interest' or 'entitlement' in life-term inmates so as to require that Board to explain its reasons for denial of an application for commutation."

b. The *Meachum* Court, per Rehnquist, J., rejected the contention that "*any* change in the conditions of confinement having a substantial adverse impact on the prisoner involved" invokes due process protections, maintaining instead that the original valid conviction and imprisonment decision "sufficiently extinguished the defendant's liberty interest to empower the State to confine him in *any* of its prisons." The *Meachum,* Court, observes Tribe at 694, "was wary of subjecting to 'judicial review a wide spectrum of discretionary actions that traditionally have been the business of prison administrations rather than of federal courts.' "

See also *Olim v. Wakinekona,* 461 U.S. 238, 103 S.Ct. 1741, 75 L.Ed.2d 813 (1983), per Blackmun, J., ruling that the transfer of a state prisoner from Hawaii to a maximum security facility in California "does not deprive an inmate of any liberty interest protected by the Due Process Clause in and of itself". Cf. *Hewitt v. Helms,* 459 U.S. 460, 103 S.Ct. 864, 74 L.Ed.2d 675 (1983) (transfer of inmate from general prison population to administrative segregation implicates no liberty interest "independently protected by the Due Process Clause").

the fact that the State may have specified its own procedures that it may deem adequate for determining the preconditions to adverse official action. [The state's] reliance on the opinion of a designated physician [for] determining whether the conditions warranting a transfer exist neither removes the prisoner's interest from due process protection nor answers the question of what process is due under the Constitution."

(b) *Recognizing a protected 'liberty interest' independently of state law.* The *Vitek* Court went on to hold that "independently of § 83–180(1), the transfer of a prisoner from a prison to a mental hospital must be accompanied by appropriate procedural protections":

"[F]or the ordinary citizen, [an involuntary] commitment to a mental hospital produces 'a massive curtailment of liberty' [and thus] 'requires due process protection.' [A] convicted felon [as well as an ordinary citizen] is entitled to the benefit of procedures appropriate in the circumstances before he is found to have a mental disease and transferred to a mental hospital. [A] criminal conviction and sentence of imprisonment extinguish an individual's right to freedom from confinement for the term of his sentence, but they do not authorize the State to classify him as mentally ill and to subject him to involuntary psychiatric treatment without affording him additional due process protections." [c]

See also *Foucha v. Louisiana,* 504 U.S. 71, 112 S.Ct. 1780, 118 L.Ed.2d 437 (1992) (also discussed at p. 516 infra), where a 5–4 majority, per White, J., struck down a state statute permitting a person acquitted of a crime by reason of insanity who no longer suffers from a mental illness to be committed indefinitely to a mental institution until he is able to demonstrate that he is not dangerous to himself or to others. Under the Due Process Clause, a state depriving someone of liberty in this way must establish the conditions justifying commitment by "clear and convincing evidence." The Court rejected the state's contention that an insanity acquittee could be confined on the basis of his antisocial personality, a condition that is not a mental disease and that is untreatable:

"First, even if his continued confinement were constitutionally permissible, keeping Foucha against his will in a mental institution is improper absent a determination in civil commitment proceedings of current mental illness and dangerousness. [Due process] requires that the nature of commitment bear some reasonable relation to the purpose for which the individual is committed. [Second,] if Foucha can no longer be held as an insanity acquittee in a mental hospital, he is entitled to constitutionally adequate procedures to establish the grounds for his confinement. [Third,] 'the Due Process Clause contains a substantive component that bars certain arbitrary wrongful government actions "regardless of the fairness of the procedures used to implement them." '

"[A State may] confine a mentally ill person if it shows 'by clear and convincing evidence that the individual is mentally ill and dangerous.' [Here,] the State has not carried that burden; indeed, the State does not claim that Foucha is now mentally ill."

c. Cf. *Washington v. Harper,* 494 U.S. 210, 110 S.Ct. 1028, 108 L.Ed.2d 178 (1990) (also discussed in Part II infra). The Court recognized that a state prisoner had a "significant liberty interest," protected by the Due Process Clause, in avoiding the forced administration of antipsychotic drugs. Thus, such treatment could be refused unless certain preconditions were met and procedural safeguards were established to ensure that the prisoners' interests were taken into account. But the Court went on to hold that the state's administrative hearing procedures (an unconsenting prisoner was entitled to a hearing before a committee of medical professionals) satisfied procedural due process; a judicial hearing is not a prerequisite for the involuntary treatment of prison inmates.

8.   (a) *A state is not free to employ such procedures as it pleases for adjudicating a claim it need not have created.*   In LOGAN v. ZIMMERMAN BRUSH CO., 455 U.S. 422, 102 S.Ct. 1148, 71 L.Ed.2d 265 (1982), appellant filed a charge with the Illinois Employment Practices Commission, alleging that his employment had been lawfully terminated because of his physical handicap.   This triggered the Commission's statutory obligation to convene a fact-finding conference within 120 days, but, apparently through inadvertence, the conference was scheduled five days *after* expiration of the statutory period.   The state court held that the failure to convene a conference within 120 days deprived the Commission of jurisdiction to consider appellant's claim under the Illinois Fair Employment Practices Act (FEPA).   The Court, per BLACKMUN, J., reversed, deeming appellant's FEPA claim "a species of property" protected by fourteenth amendment due process and holding that the state scheme had deprived appellant of his property right.

The Court pointed out that its recent cases had emphasized that "[t]he hallmark of property [is] an individual entitlement grounded in state law, which cannot be removed except 'for cause.'   [And] an FEPA claim, which presumably can be surrendered for value, is at least as substantial as the right to an education labeled as property in *Goss v. Lopez.*   Certainly, it would require a remarkable reading of a 'broad and majestic term' to conclude that a horse trainer's license is a protected property interest under the Fourteenth Amendment, while a state-created right to redress discrimination is not."

"Because the entitlement arises from statute, the [state supreme court] reasoned, it was the legislature's prerogative to establish the 'procedures to be followed upon a charge.'   [This analysis] misunderstands the nature of the Constitution's due process guarantee.   [B]ecause 'minimum [procedural] requirements [are] a matter of federal law, they are not diminished by the fact that the State may have specified its own procedures that it may deem adequate for determining the preconditions to adverse official action.'   *Vitek.*   Indeed, any other conclusion would allow the State to destroy at will virtually any state-created property interest.   The Court has considered and rejected such an approach [quoting from that portion of the *Vitek* opinion quoting with approval from Powell, J.'s concurring opinion in *Arnett*].

"Of course, the State remains free to create substantive defenses or immunities for use in adjudication—or to eliminate its statutorily created causes of action altogether—just as it can amend or terminate its welfare or employment programs [or adjust benefit levels].   [But the 120-day limitation] is a procedural limitation on the claimant's ability to assert his rights, not a substantive element of the FEPA claim."

(b) *Why can't a state "enfeeble" any entitlement it creates?*   Consider FRANK EASTERBROOK, *Substance and Due Process*, 1982 Sup.Ct.Rev. 85–86, 109–110, 120: "The process a legislature describes for vindicating the entitlements that it creates is a way of indicating how effective its plan should be.   The more process it affords, the more the legislature values the entitlements and thus is willing to sacrifice to avoid mistakes.   A court that protects the legislative power to define substantive entitlements ought to give it control of process as well.

"[The] Court's justification for specifying process once the statute has specified substance is that 'any other conclusion would allow the State to destroy at will virtually any state-created property interest.'   This would be a good argument if the Court could explain why a state may not destroy the interest it creates, at least prospectively.   But the Court has never so argued.   Under the Court's decisions legislatures are free to enact precatory statutes, statutes that contain no rules of decision, retroactive statutes, statutes that lack any methods of enforcement, statutes creating absolute immunities, and otherwise to have vacuous 'entitlements.' To use some invented numbers, if states may elect ten percent reliability in enforcement (the amount of adherence to a precatory statute), why can they not elect ninety percent (the amount obtained from rudimentary procedures)? Why, in other words, is the expedient of enfeebling a statutory entitlement by providing 'deficient' procedures out of bounds? The Court's cases contain no answers to this question because they are not consistent. There is no single view that could be respected in the name of stare decisis.

"[Illinois] need not have created any right to be free of discrimination because of handicap or given the right of any particular dimensions. That being so, [Illinois] also should have been allowed to employ such procedure as it pleased for adjudicating (or not adjudicating) Logan's claim.[105] "

(c) *Why wasn't Logan's right to sue the Commission in tort for its negligence in losing his claim sufficient to satisfy due process?* The Zimmerman Brush Company had another argument in support of the Illinois Supreme Court's decision. As described in Smolla, p. 500 fn. a supra, at 860, the Company argued that even if Logan possessed an "entitlement" under Illinois law "no federal due process violation existed, because Logan could sue the Commission for damages under the Illinois Court of Claims Act for having negligently destroyed his 'property'—his [FEPA cause of action]. Logan in effect had an action for 'malpractice' against the Commission, just as he would have had an action against his own attorney if the attorney had negligently caused Logan's claim to lapse. Under the reasoning in *Parratt v. Taylor* [p. 501 fn. d supra], the Company argued, the state had not deprived Logan of property without due process since the state's own tort remedies were adequate to make Logan whole." This argument, responded the Court, "misses *Parratt's* point":

"In *Parratt,* the Court emphasized that it was dealing with 'a tortious loss [of] property as a result of a random and unauthorized act by a state employee [rather than] some established procedure.' Here, in contrast, it is the state system itself that destroys a complainant's property interest, by operation of law, whenever the Commission fails to convene a timely conference—whether the Commission's action is taken through negligence, maliciousness, or otherwise. *Parratt* was not designed to reach such a situation. Unlike the complainant in *Parratt,* Logan is challenging not the Commission's error, but the 'established state procedure' that destroys his entitlement without according him proper procedural safeguards.

"In any event, the Court's decisions suggest that, absent 'the necessity of quick action by the State or the impracticality of providing any predeprivation process,' a post-deprivation hearing here would be constitutionally inadequate. *Parratt.* [That] is particularly true where, as here, the State's only post-termination process comes in the form of an independent tort action.[10] Seeking redress

---

105. [As] the Supreme Court of Illinois saw things, the statute (effectively) allowed Logan's claim to be distinguished for no reason at all. Thus the statute gave Logan no property right. *Bishop.* The Court never told us why it was disregarding the state court's construction of the state's statute.

10. In *Ingraham v. Wright* [p. 502 fn. e supra] the Court concluded that state tort remedies provided adequate process for students subjected to corporal punishment in school, [but it] emphasized that the state scheme "preserved what 'has always been the law of the land,'" [and] that adding additional safeguards would be unduly burdensome. Here neither of those rationales is available. Terminating potentially meritorious claims in a random manner is hardly a practice in line with our common-law traditions. And the State's abandonment of the challenged practice [after the inception of the present litigation] makes it difficult to argue that requiring a determination on the merits will impose undue burdens on the state administrative process.

through a tort suit is apt to be a lengthy and speculative process, which in a situation such as this one will never make the complainant entirely whole: the Illinois Court of Claims Act does not provide for reinstatement [and] even a successful suit will not vindicate entirely Logan's right to be free from discriminatory treatment."

(d) *The post-deprivation due process doctrine: reconciling Zimmerman Brush and Parratt.* The relationship between *Zimmerman Brush* and *Parratt,* observes Smolla at 861–62, "parallels the relationship that arguably existed between *Constantineau* and *Paul.* Random and unauthorized harm caused by the state, for which the state itself provides a remedy, does not implicate the Constitution. But when the state consciously enacts a system that places its imprimatur on arbitrary conduct, whether it be through a bizarre posting statute or a capricious administrative structure for handling handicap discrimination, federal court intervention under the due process clause is warranted."

9. *"[I]t is settled that the 'bitter with the sweet' approach misconceives the [due process] guarantee."* CLEVELAND BOARD OF EDUCATION v. LOUDERMILL, 470 U.S. 532, 105 S.Ct. 1487, 84 L.Ed.2d 494 (1985): Under Ohio law, respondents Loudermill and Donnelly were "classified civil servants" who could be discharged only for cause. Loudermill, a security guard, was dismissed because of dishonesty in filling out his employment application. He was not afforded an opportunity to respond to the dishonesty charge or to challenge the dismissal.[a] Donnelly was fired as a bus mechanic because he had failed an eye examination. He appealed to the Civil Service Commission, which ordered him reinstated without pay. "The statute plainly supports the conclusion [that] respondents possessed property rights in continued employment," but petitioners [stress] that in addition to specifying the grounds for termination, the statute sets out procedures by which termination may take place [and that these procedures were followed]. [Therefore,] '[t]o require additional procedures would in effect expand the scope of the property interest itself.' " The Court, per WHITE, J., disagreed:

"[Petitioners' argument] has its genesis in the plurality opinion in *Arnett.* [This approach] garnered three votes in *Arnett,* but was specifically rejected by the other six Justices. [I]n light of [*Vitek* and *Zimmerman Brush*], it is settled that the 'bitter with the sweet' approach misconceives the [due process] guarantee. If a clearer holding is needed, we provide it today. The point is straight-forward: the Due Process Clause provides that certain substantive rights—life, liberty, and property—cannot be deprived except pursuant to constitutionally adequate procedures. The categories of substance and procedure are distinct. Were the rule otherwise, the Clause would be reduced to a mere tautology. 'Property' cannot be defined by the procedures provided for its deprivation any more than can life or liberty. The right to due process 'is conferred, not by legislative grace, but by constitutional guarantee. While the legislature may elect not to confer a property interest in [public] employment, it may not constitutionally authorize the deprivation of such an interest, once conferred, without appropriate procedural safeguards.' *Arnett* (Powell, J., [concurring opinion]); see id. (White, J., [concurring in part]). [O]nce it is determined that the Due Process Clause applies, 'the question remains what process is due.' The answer is not to be found in the Ohio

a. On his 1979 job application, Loudermill stated that he had never been convicted of a felony. Eleven months later it was discovered that he had been convicted of grand larceny in 1968. Loudermill maintained that he had thought his larceny conviction was for a misdemeanor rather than a felony.

statute."[b]

REHNQUIST, J., the sole Justice to dissent on this issue, maintained that the Fourteenth Amendment "does not support the conclusion that Ohio's effort to confer a limited form of tenure upon respondents resulted in the creation of a 'property right' in their employment":

"Here, as in *Arnett*, '[t]he employee's statutorily defined right is not a guarantee against removal without cause in the abstract, but such a guarantee as enforced by the procedures which [the Ohio legislature] has designated for the determination of cause' (opinion of Rehnquist, J.). [We] ought to recognize the totality of the State's definition of the property right in question, and not merely seize upon one of several paragraphs in a unitary statute to proclaim that in that paragraph the State has inexorably conferred upon a civil service employee something which it is powerless to qualify in the next paragraph of the statute. [While] it does not impose a federal definition of property, the Court departs from the full breadth of the holding in *Roth* by its selective choice from among the sentences the Ohio legislature chooses to use in establishing and qualifying a right."

10. *A hard look at Loudermill's substance-procedure distinction.* Did the *Loudermill* majority provide a convincing basis for its rejection of Justice Rehnquist's position? Can procedural problems, as the majority seemed to think, be neatly separated from substantive choices? See Tribe at 709–12. If the state is free to define and limit underlying substantive entitlements, why shouldn't it be equally free to define the procedure that goes with each entitlement? If substantive restrictions on entitlements can be adopted which have the effect of limiting procedural rights, why can't the government take the "intermediate course of limiting public benefits and opportunities in an explicitly procedural way"? See id. at 711. "Ultimately," concludes Professor Tribe, id. at 713, "the clarity of the demarcation the Court declared in *Loudermill* between the rights-conferring function and the process-prescribing function is illusory; the Court must eventually move toward more deference on matters of procedure or less deference on matters of substance. Since the former course would leave the due process clause with little content in the modern state, where so much has come to depend on relationships with government, the latter seems preferable, certainly in relationships created to meet the needs of the individuals involved, and probably also in relationships created to meet the needs of others."

SECTION 2. WHAT KIND OF HEARING—AND WHEN?

GOLDBERG v. KELLY, 397 U.S. 254, 90 S.Ct. 1011, 25 L.Ed.2d 287 (1970), per BRENNAN, J. (Burger, C.J., and Black and Stewart, JJ., dissenting) held that due process requires an evidentiary hearing prior to termination of welfare benefits, stressing the "crucial factor [that] termination of aid pending resolution of a controversy over eligibility may deprive an *eligible* recipient of the very means by which to live while he waits. Since he lacks independent resources, his situation becomes immediately desperate. His need to concentrate upon [surviv-

b. The Court then held that respondents were not entitled to a "full adversarial hearing prior to adverse governmental action. [A]ll the process that is due is provided by a preter- mination opportunity to respond, coupled with [a full post-termination hearing] as provided by the Ohio statute." This aspect of *Loudermill* is treated in Sec. 2 infra.

al], in turn, adversely affects his ability to seek redress from the welfare bureaucracy." The hearing "need not take the form of a judicial or quasi-judicial trial," but a recipient must have "timely and adequate notice detailing the reasons for a proposed termination, and an effective opportunity to defend by confronting any adverse witnesses and by presenting his own arguments and evidence orally." The Court declined to "say that counsel must be provided" but the recipient must be allowed to retain counsel.

Consider JERRY MASHAW, *Due Process in the Administrative State* 35–36 (1985): "[T]he underprotectionist critic may claim that the due process revolution has stopped short of its essential goals: building legal security and democratic control into the administrative state. Legal security for the welfare claimant, for example, would at a minimum require that the hearing right be oriented to the issues that produce erroneous deprivations and that the recipient class has the necessary resources to make use of hearings to protect its interests. Yet neither condition seems to obtain. A careful study of errors suggests that they occur at least as often through misinterpretation of policy as through mistakes on questions of fact. The *Goldberg* decision limits due process hearings to facts. Moreover, welfare recipients generally lack the human or material resources to make use of the hearings *Goldberg* provided. Except for an occasional flurry of political activism expressed through appeals requests, hearings have been utilized about as infrequently after *Goldberg* as before.

"This sort of criticism may be pressed further to suggest that the hearing technique—the demand for individualized and detailed attention through quasi-judicial process—simply misses the point of the welfare state. The problem has become one of mass, not individual, justice. Legal security for the class of welfare claimants lies, not in hearings, but in good management. Unless due process, therefore, comes to terms with administration, becomes systems—rather than case-oriented, it will be irrelevant.

"The underprotectionist case goes further. *Goldberg*'s hearing rights extend only to the protection of what can be termed 'positive entitlements,' substantive interests already enjoying common law or statutory legal significance. Due process hearings are thus only an addition to the legal security of existing rights. They provide no access to the administrative forums in which rights are being created and no opportunity to avoid the application of general rules on the basis of individual circumstances. *Goldberg*'s hearing rights thus leave untouched the contemporary concern with (1) the remoteness of administrative policy making from immediate participation by affected interests and (2) the unfairness and irrationality that seem to attend bureaucratic implementation of general rules." [a]

---

a. At this point, Professor Mashaw turns to *O'Bannon v. Town Court Nursing Center*, 447 U.S. 773, 100 S.Ct. 2467, 65 L.Ed.2d 506 (1980), per Stevens, J., holding that, because nursing home residents had no government-established entitlement to continued residence at a particular home, they had no right to a hearing before the government decertified the home as provider of services at government expenses under Medicare and Medicaid agreements. Decertification would force the patients to seek care elsewhere and would probably mean that they would be separated from each and might mean that they would have to relocate away from their friends and families. But, responded the Court, Medicaid provisions only give recipients "the right to choose among a range of *qualified* providers, without government interference, [not the right] to enter an unqualified home and demand a hearing to certify it, nor [the right] to continue to receive benefits for care in a home that has been decertified. [A]lthough the regulations do protect patients by limiting the circumstances under which a *home* may transfer or discharge a Medicaid recipient, they do not purport to limit the Government's right to make a transfer

MATHEWS v. ELDRIDGE, 424 U.S. 319, 96 S.Ct. 893, 47 L.Ed.2d 18 (1976), per POWELL, J., held that although Social Security disability benefits constitute "a statutorily created 'property' interest protected by the Fifth Amendment," due process does not require a *Goldberg*-type hearing prior to their termination on the ground that "the worker is no longer disabled": "In recent years this Court increasingly has had occasion to consider the extent to which due process requires an evidentiary hearing prior to the deprivation of some type of property interest even if such a hearing is provided thereafter. In only one case, *Goldberg*, has the Court held that a hearing closely approximating a judicial trial is necessary. [For example,] *Bell v. Burson* [held] that due process required only that the prerevocation hearing involve a probable-cause determination as to the fault of the licensee, noting that the hearing 'need not take the form of a full adjudication of the question of liability.' [O]ur prior decisions indicate that identification of the specific dictates of due process generally requires consideration of three distinct factors: First, the private interest that will be affected by the official action; second, the risk of an erroneous deprivation of such interest through the procedures used, and the probable value, if any, of additional or substitute procedural safeguards; and finally, the government's interest, including the function involved and the fiscal and administrative burdens that the additional or substitute procedural requirement would entail." [a]

First, in contrast to *Goldberg*, "eligibility for disability benefits [is] not based upon financial need." Rather, such benefits are "wholly unrelated to the worker's income or support from many other sources, such as earnings of other family members, workmen's compensation awards, tort claims awards, savings, [insurance, pensions and public assistance.]" Thus, "there is less reason here than in *Goldberg* to depart from the ordinary principle, established by our decisions, that

necessary by decertifying a facility. [Whatever rights the patients may have against the nursing home] for failing to maintain its status[,] enforcement by [state and federal agencies] of their valid regulations did not directly affect their legal rights or deprive them of any constitutionally protected interest in life, liberty or property."

Blackmun, J., concurred, but found the Court's analysis "simplistic and unsatisfactory." For extensive criticism of *O'Bannon*, see Mashaw, supra, at 36–41; Tribe, supra, at 766–67; Terrell, supra, at 927–35.

a. The Court subsequently utilized the factors set forth in *Eldridge* in analyzing *Ingraham v. Wright* (corporal punishment in public schools) and *Parham v. J.R.* (parents' commitment of minor children), both discussed in the notes following this case. The *Eldridge* "balancing approach" was also utilized in, e.g., *Dixon v. Love*, 431 U.S. 105, 97 S.Ct. 1723, 52 L.Ed.2d 172 (1977) (Blackmun, J.) (no prior evidentiary hearing required for driver license revocation pursuant to regulation mandating such revocation if license had been suspended three times within 10 years for conviction of traffic violations); *Memphis Light, Gas & Water Division v. Craft*, 436 U.S. 1, 98 S.Ct. 1554, 56 L.Ed.2d 30 (1978) (Powell, J.) (municipal utility must provide its customers with some administrative procedure for entertaining com-

plaints before cutting off services); *Mackey v. Montrym*, 443 U.S. 1, 99 S.Ct. 2612, 61 L.Ed.2d 321 (1979) (Burger, C.J.) (license of driver lawfully arrested for drunk driving may be suspended for 90 days without prior hearing for refusing to take breath-analysis test so long as immediate post-suspension hearing is available; *Little v. Streater*, 452 U.S. 1, 101 S.Ct. 2202, 68 L.Ed.2d 627 (1981) (Burger, C.J.) (state's refusal to pay cost of blood grouping test for indigent defendant in paternity action, a proceeding with " 'quasi-criminal' overtones," denies him "meaningful opportunity to be heard" and thus violates procedural due process); *Walters v. National Association of Radiation Survivors*, 473 U.S. 305, 105 S.Ct. 3180, 87 L.Ed.2d 220 (1985) (Rehnquist, J.) (federal statute limiting to $10 the fee that may be paid an attorney or agent representing one seeking benefits from Veterans Administration (VA) for service-connected death or disability does not violate procedural due process; since benefits are not granted on basis of need, they are more like social security benefits involved in *Eldridge* than welfare benefits involved in *Goldberg*; elimination of fee limitation "would bid fair to complicate a proceeding which Congress wished to keep as simple as possible").

something less than an evidentiary hearing is sufficient prior to adverse administrative action."

Second, "the potential value of an evidentiary hearing, or even oral presentation to the decisionmaker, is substantially less in this context than in *Goldberg*." Here, "a medical assessment of the worker's physical or mental condition is required. This is a more sharply focused and easily documented decision than the typical determination of welfare entitlement [where] a wide variety of information may be deemed relevant, and issues of witness credibility and veracity often are critical to the decision-making process." Further, "the information critical [in the disability case] usually is derived from medical sources, [which are likely] to communicate more effectively through written documents than are welfare recipients or the lay witnesses supporting their cause."

Third, as to the "additional cost in terms of money and administrative burden" if pretermination hearings were required, "at some point the benefit of an additional safeguard to the individual affected by the administrative action and to society in terms of increased assurance that the action is just, may be outweighed by the cost. Significantly, the cost of protecting those whom the preliminary administrative process has identified as likely to be found undeserving may in the end come out of the pockets of the deserving since resources available for any particular program of social welfare are not unlimited."

Finally, "in assessing what process is due in this case, substantial weight must be given to the good-faith judgments of the individuals charged by Congress with the administration of the social welfare system that the procedures they have provided assure fair consideration of the entitlement claims of individuals."[b]

The *Eldridge* approach, observes Jerry Mashaw, *The Supreme Court's Due Process Calculus for Administrative Adjudication in Mathews v. Eldridge*, 44 U.Chi.L.Rev. 28, 39 (1976), "is subjective and impressionistic. [The Court] assumes that disability recipients are less dependent on income support than welfare recipients. This assumption is buttressed only by the notion that welfare is for the needy and disability insurance is for prior taxpayers. [But], any number of circumstances might make a terminated welfare recipient's plight less desperate than that of his disabled SSA counterpart,[42] or vice versa." Mashaw finds several of the *Eldridge* conclusions questionable, especially that it was dealing with an essentially medical determination. Id. at 40. "The *Goldberg* decision's approach to prescribing due process—specification of the attributes of adjudicatory hearings by analogy to judicial trial—makes the Court resemble an administrative engineer with an outdated professional education. It is at once intrusive and ineffectual. Retreating from this stance, [*Eldridge*] relies on the administrator's good faith— an equally troublesome posture in a political system that depends heavily on judicial review for the protection of countermajoritarian values." Id. at 58.

---

b. Brennan, J., joined by Marshall, J., dissented: "[I]n the present case, it is indicated that because disability benefits were terminated there was a foreclosure upon the Eldridge home and the family's furniture was repossessed, forcing Eldridge, his wife and children to sleep in one bed. [It] is also no argument that a worker, who has been placed in the untenable position of having been denied disability benefits, may still seek other forms of public assistance." Stevens, J., did not participate.

42. The terminated [welfare] recipient may have access to home or general relief depending upon his residence, whereas the disability claimant in a different state or locality may not. The disability claimant may be totally dependent for his livelihood on the disability payments, whereas the welfare recipient who is terminated may have been receiving a small AFDC payment to supplement inadequate family earnings.

Consider, too, Tribe at 718: "[The *Eldridge*] Court's unwillingness to consider values beyond accuracy of result in the context of a utilitarian balancing test when deciding what process is due, and the Court's grant of a strong presumption of constitutionality to statutory procedural provisions, amount to a serious abdication of traditional notions of judicial responsibility under the due process clauses. Like many other provisions of the Constitution, the due process requirement represented a decision on the part of the Framers to safeguard certain rights and values, those considered fundamental in a free society and yet unusually vulnerable to the risk of denial by the majority. Adequate protection of such 'core' concerns cannot be afforded by 'balancing' the general interests of the majority against those of the individual. [Moreover, there] is no reason to believe that the judiciary would be better suited to that task of utilitarian comparison than the legislature even if it were called for."

"Although the Supreme Court has treated *Mathews v. Eldridge* as furnishing a test for all seasons," the test, points out Richard Fallon, *Some Confusions about Due Process, Judicial Review, and Constitutional Remedies,* 93 Colum.L.Rev. 309, 331 (1993), "was designed for resolving claims of entitlement to particular types of *administrative,* rather than judicial, procedures. Claims of a right to judicial review raise issues lying beyond the [*Eldridge*] framework."

––––––––

1. *"Educational due process" cases.* (a) GOSS v. LOPEZ, 419 U.S. 565, 95 S.Ct. 729, 42 L.Ed.2d 725 (1975) (also discussed at p. 500 fn. b supra), per WHITE, J., held that "as a general rule," before a student is given a temporary suspension (ten days or less) from public school, due process requires "that the student be given oral or written notice of the charges against him and, if he denies them, an explanation of the evidence the authorities have and an opportunity to present his side of the story": "[T]otal exclusion from the educational process for more than a trivial period, and certainly if the suspension is for 10 days, is a serious event in the life of the suspended child. [T]he State is constrained to recognize a student's legitimate entitlement to a public education as a property interest which is protected by the Due Process Clause and which may not be taken away for misconduct without adherence to the minimum procedures required by that clause. [Due process] also forbids arbitrary deprivations of liberty. [Many] charges could seriously damage the students' standing with their fellow pupils and their teachers as well as interfere with later opportunities for higher education and employment."

POWELL, J., joined by Burger, C.J., and Blackmun and Rehnquist, JJ., dissented: "Whether *any* procedural protections are due" turns on the extent to which one will be "condemned to suffer *grievous* loss," [but] the record in this case reflects no educational injury to appellees. Each completed the semester in which the suspension occurred and performed at least as well as he or she had in previous years. [Few] rulings would interfere more extensively in the daily functioning of schools than subjecting routine discipline to the formalities and judicial oversight of due process." [a]

a. Compare *Goss* with *Bethel School Dist. v. Fraser* (1986) (also discussed at p. 834 infra). Fraser, a high school senior, was suspended for two days for making a sexually suggestive speech at a school-sponsored assembly. The Court, per Burger, C.J., rejected Fraser's con- tention that his suspension violated due process because he had no way of knowing that his speech would subject him to disciplinary sanctions: "Given the school's need to be able to impose disciplinary sanctions for a wide range of unanticipated conduct disruptive of

(b) But cf. INGRAHAM v. WRIGHT, 430 U.S. 651, 97 S.Ct. 1401, 51 L.Ed.2d 711 (1977) (also discussed at p. 502 fn. e supra), per Powell, J., holding that disciplinary corporal punishment in public school "implicates a constitutionally protected liberty interest," but that procedural due process does not require notice and an opportunity to be heard prior to imposition of that punishment as it is authorized and limited by Florida common law: "Were it not for the common-law privilege permitting teachers to inflict reasonable corporal punishment [and] the availability of the traditional remedies for abuse, the case for requiring advance procedural safeguards would be strong indeed. [But the disciplinarian] must exercise prudence and restraint. [And if] the punishment inflicted is later found to have been excessive [the] school authorities inflicting it may be held liable in damages to the child and, if malice is shown, they may be subject to criminal penalties.

"[Moreover,] because paddlings are usually inflicted in response to conduct directly observed by teachers in their presence, the risk that a child will be paddled without cause is typically insignificant. In the ordinary case, a disciplinary paddling neither threatens seriously to violate any substantive rights nor condemns the child 'to suffer grievous loss of any kind.'

"[T]he low incidence of abuse, and the availability of established judicial remedies in the event of abuse, distinguish this case from *Goss*. [The] subsequent [proceedings] available in this case may be viewed as affording substantially greater protection to the child than the informal conference mandated by *Goss*. [E]ven if the need for advance procedural safeguards were clear, the question would remain whether the incremental benefit could justify the [cost.] 'At some point the benefit of an additional safeguard [may] be outweighed by the cost.' *Eldridge*. We think that point has been reached in this case."

WHITE, J., joined by Brennan, Marshall and Stevens, JJ., dissented: "[The common law] tort action is utterly inadequate to protect against erroneous infliction of punishment for two reasons. First, under Florida law [the] student has no remedy at all for punishment imposed on the basis of mistaken facts, at least as long as the punishment was reasonable from the point of view of the disciplinarian, uninformed by any prior hearing. [Second], [the] lawsuit occurs after the punishment has been finally imposed. The infliction of physical pain is final and irreparable; it cannot be undone in a subsequent proceeding." [b]

(c) *Criticism of Ingraham.* "Government's interests in punishing guilty students first and asking questions about guilt later," maintain Lawrence Alexander & Paul Horton, *Ingraham v. Wright: A Primer for Cruel and Unusual Jurisprudence*, 52 S.Cal.L.Rev. 1305, 1384–85 (1979), "surely pale in significance when compared to the interests of innocent students in avoiding punishment.[282] Usually no emergency is averted by instantaneous corporal punishment.[283] The

---

the educational process, the school disciplinary rules need not be as detailed as a criminal code which imposes criminal sanctions. Cf. *Arnett*. Two days' suspension from school does not rise to the level of a penal sanction calling for the full panoply of procedural due process protections applicable to a criminal prosecution. Cf. *Goss*. The school disciplinary rule proscribing 'obscene' language and the prespeech admonition of teachers gave adequate warning to Fraser that his lewd speech could subject him to sanctions."

b. Compare *Ingraham* and *Parratt* (p. 501 fn. d supra) with *Zimmerman Brush* (p. 505 supra).

282. [*Ingraham*] is an easy case in this respect, considering that a more reparable student interest (freedom from 10-day suspension) outweighed similar government interests in *Goss*."

283. In that respect, corporal punishment differs from temporary suspensions, without pre-deprivation hearings, which may avert dangers to persons and property.

costs—monetary and otherwise—of providing pre-punishment hearings for the guilty are more than justified by the savings to the innocent. Finally, the burden imposed on the innocent in bringing post-deprivation actions is undoubtedly heavier than the burden imposed on government by a requirement of pre-punishment hearings. [In] none of the cases [upholding] a post-deprivation hearing was there both the strong likelihood of irreparable injury and the absence of a compelling justification for prompt action precluding a prior hearing."

"In other cases in which a post-deprivation hearing has been held adequate," emphasizes Irene Rosenberg, *Ingraham v. Wright: The Supreme Court's Whipping Boy,* 78 Colum.L.Rev. 75, 91 (1978), "the interest involved was 'property' rather than 'liberty.' [Where] a liberty interest is invoked, the injured person is considerably less likely to be made whole by a belated award of damages. Particularly is this true in the case of corporal punishment, where the liberty interest is freedom from 'infliction of appreciable physical pain.' " Professor Rosenberg continues, id. at 93–94:

"To [the] very real barriers impairing vindication of the child's rights [by bringing a tort action] [c] must be added not only the defense of sovereign immunity available to school boards, and the possible defense of good faith mistake available to teachers, but also the inadequacy of money damages as a means of repairing physical and psychological injury deliberately inflicted on a child.

"[The *Ingraham* Court] refused to attempt to distinguish between trivial and severe corporal punishment, while at the same time invoking [the] existence of common law and statutory restraints against *unreasonable* corporal punishment. In effect, the majority was asking the nation's school teachers to make the sorts of decisions about reasonableness that, if erroneous, could lead to tort liability, while at the same time acknowledging its own inability (or unwillingness) to make such judgments."

(d) *In defense of Ingraham.* "Tort law," observes Rodney Smolla, *The Displacement of Federal Due Process Claims by State Tort Remedies,* 1982 U.Ill. L.Rev. 831, 850–51, "has always awarded money for the taking of interests without any objectively discernable value—millions of dollars are awarded for lost reputation, for emotional distress, and for pain and suffering. [A] substantial damage award against a school teacher for excessive corporal punishment is easily conceivable, particularly in communities in which a consensus against such conduct prevails. It is not at all obvious that the threat of such awards is any less a deterrent to misconduct than internal administrative hearings, in which teachers who know the administrative ropes may often be able to prevail in proceedings stacked against students.

"[Professor Rosenberg's point] that the Supreme Court preferred to allow school teachers to make decisions about the reasonableness of discipline that the Court felt unable or unwilling to make is correct, but the Court's reticence is grounds for criticism only if one first assumes that federal court judges are or should be better qualified than school teachers to make such judgments.

"[*Ingraham*] did not totally eliminate federal concern with paddling—a due process violation could still exist if a state were to disable its own courts in their

c. Rosenberg notes, e.g., that it may prove difficult to secure an attorney willing to accept a case of this sort; completion of state court actions may take years, during which time "the child's memory of the controverted events may dim"; the formality of a jury trial is "considerably less conducive to articulate testimony by the public than an informal pre-punishment hearing would be"; and that a teacher is more likely to be believed than his or her ex-pupil. See id. at 92–93.

policing of local practices—but it placed federal law in a back-up role. *Ingraham* is in this sense consistent with the Court's general movement in procedural due process cases, toward initial deference to local prerogative in setting procedural norms when the substantive interests at stake are heavily imbued with localized values."

(e) BOARD OF CURATORS v. HOROWITZ, 435 U.S. 78, 98 S.Ct. 948, 55 L.Ed.2d 124 (1978), per REHNQUIST, J., "decline[d] to ignore the historic judgment of educators [and] formalize the academic dismissal process by requiring a hearing." Because of dissatisfaction with her clinical performance and personal hygiene, and after notice from and discussion with the dean of the medical school, a state medical school student was put on probation. After continued dissatisfaction with her work, and pursuant to a faculty-student council recommendation (supported by the dean and the provost), she was dismissed from school in her final year. Assuming but not deciding that there was "a liberty interest" in pursuing a medical career, "respondent has been awarded at least as much due process as the Fourteenth Amendment requires." The Court underscored the distinction between "academic evaluations of a student" and "disciplinary determinations," contrasting the instant case with *Goss*, where "[t]he requirement of a hearing [could] 'provide a meaningful hedge against erroneous action.' The decision to dismiss respondent, by comparison, rested on the academic judgment of school officials," a judgment "by its nature more subjective and evaluative than the typical factual questions presented in the average disciplinary decision."

2. *"Family due process."* (a) Balancing the three factors set forth in *Eldridge*, PARHAM v. J.R., 442 U.S. 584, 99 S.Ct. 2493, 61 L.Ed.2d 101 (1979) (also discussed at p. 510 fn. a and p. 415 supra), per BURGER, C.J., held that a preadmission adversary hearing is not required when parents (or a state agency acting in loco parentis) seek to commit their minor children to a mental institution—so long as the commitment is approved by an "independent medical judgment." The Court "assume[d] that a child has a protectible interest not only in being free of unnecessary bodily restraints but also in not being labelled erroneously" as "mentally ill," but concluded that "our precedents permit the parents to retain a substantial, if not the dominant, role in the decision, absent a finding of neglect or abuse, and that the traditional presumption that the parents act in the best interests of the child should apply. [But the] child's rights and the nature of the commitment decision are such that parents cannot always have absolute and unreviewable discretion [to institutionalize their child]. [They] retain plenary authority [to do so], subject to a physician's independent examination and medical judgment." In the course of a wide-ranging opinion the Court observed:

"That some parents 'may at times be acting against the interests of their children' [is reason] for caution, [but] hardly a reason to discard wholesale those pages of human experience that teach that parents generally do act in the child's best interests. The statist notion that governmental power should supersede parental authority in *all* cases because *some* parents abuse and neglect children is repugnant to American tradition.

"[Appellees] place particular reliance on *Planned Parenthood v. Danforth* [p. 345 supra], arguing that its holding indicates how little deference to parents is appropriate when the child is exercising a constitutional right. [But that case] involved an absolute parental veto over the child's ability to obtain an abortion. Parents in Georgia in no sense have an absolute right to commit their children to state mental hospitals; the statute requires [each regional hospital superintendent] to exercise independent judgment as to the child's need for confinement.

"[W]hat process is constitutionally due cannot be divorced from the nature of the ultimate decision that is being made. [Here,] the questions are essentially medical in character. [W]e recently stated in *Addington v. Texas,* 439 U.S. 908, 99 S.Ct. 276, 58 L.Ed.2d 254 (1978),[a] that the determination of 'whether a person is mentally ill turns on the *meaning* of the facts which must be interpreted by expert psychiatrists and psychologists.' [We reject] the notion that the shortcomings of specialists can always be avoided by shifting the decision [to] an untrained judge or administrative hearing officer after a judicial-type hearing. Even after a hearing, the nonspecialist decisionmaker must make a medical-psychiatric decision. Common human experience and scholarly opinions suggest that the supposed protections of an adversary proceeding to determine the appropriateness of medical decisions for the commitment and treatment of mental and emotional illness may well be more illusory than real. * * *

" '[P]rocedural due process rules are shaped by the risk of error inherent in the truthfinding process as applied to the generality of cases, not the rare exceptions.' *Eldridge.* In general, we are satisfied that an independent medical decision-making process, [followed] by additional periodic review of a child's condition, will protect children who should not be admitted; we do not believe the risks of error in that process would be significantly reduced by a more formal, judicial-type hearing."

Concurring and dissenting in part, BRENNAN, J., joined by Marshall and Stevens, JJ., agreed that the parent-child relationship "militate[s] in favor of postponement of formal commitment proceedings and against mandatory adversary preconfinement commitment hearings." But "[w]hile the question of the frequency of postadmission review hearings may properly be deferred, the right to at least one post-admission hearing can and should be affirmed now." "This case is governed by the rule of *Danforth.* The right to be free from wrongful incarceration, physical intrusion, and stigmatization has significance for the individual surely as great as the right to an abortion. [Indeed,] *Danforth* involved only a potential dispute between parent and child, whereas here a break in family autonomy has actually resulted in the parents' decision to surrender custody of their child to a state mental institution. [A] child who has been ousted from his family has even greater need for an independent advocate."[b]

(b) *Parental prerogatives and governmental intrusions: Parham and Ingraham compared.* Consider Robert Burt, *The Constitution of the Family,* 1979 Sup.Ct.Rev. 329, 332–33: "The Court spoke in *Parham* as if it were upholding parental prerogatives against governmental intrusions. [But the parents in that case] were not seeking to resist governmental power over their children; they were invoking that power by attempting to confine their children in state psychiatric institutions.

"This paean to parental prerogatives would have had greater relevance if state officials had sought to impose behavioral controls on children against their

---

a. *Addington* held that one's interest in the outcome of a civil commitment proceeding is so important that due process requires the state to justify confinement by "clear and convincing" evidence, rather than the normal "preponderance of the evidence" standard. See also *Foucha v. Louisiana,* p. 504 supra. Consider Note, 93 Harv.L.Rev. 89, 98 (1979): "It is difficult to reconcile *Parham* with *Addington.* [In] insisting on a strict standard of proof [*Addington*] assumed that an individual could

not be confined without an adversary hearing. In *Parham,* by contrast, the Court allowed minors to be institutionalized with fewer procedural standards than is required for the termination of welfare benefits. The presumption that parents or state agencies will act in a child's best interests is too tenuous a rationale to justify the denial of an adversary hearing."

b. See also Note, 93 Harv.L.Rev. 89, 94 (1979).

parent's wishes. The Court did consider a case two years earlier that directly implicated that question. School officials had administered corporal punishment to children. [In *Ingraham,* the] Court majority, composed of the same conservative nucleus as in *Parham* [but here joined by Stewart, J., with White, J., dissenting], ruled that school officials were free to disregard parental objections to this form of behavior control of their children. Justice Powell [said this] for the Court: 'Although the early cases viewed the authority of the teacher as deriving from the parents, [this concept] has been replaced by the view [that] the State itself may impose such corporal punishment as is reasonably necessary for the proper education of the child and for the maintenance of group discipline.' So much for the American tradition—paraded in *Parham* as well as 'the early cases'—that 'governmental power should [not] supersede parental authority.' "

(c) *"The subtleties and nuances of psychiatric diagnoses": Parham and Vitek compared.* The *Parham* Court, observes Jerry Mashaw, *Due Process in the Administrative State* 111 (1985), did not believe that a minor need be given a hearing prior to commitment to a mental institution, "apparently in substantial part because a hearing could provide little additional protection from error. [Yet,] somehow, when in *Vitek* [p. 502 supra] the question was whether a prisoner should have a hearing prior to being transferred to a mental hospital, the suggestion that psychiatric judgment was involved elicited the following judicial response: 'The medical nature of the [inquiry] does not justify dispensing with due process requirements. *It is precisely the subtleties and nuances of psychiatric diagnoses that justify the requirement of adversary hearings.'* " [Emphasis added by Mashaw.] See also John Garvey, *Children and the Idea of Liberty*, 68 Ky.L.J. 809, 826–30 (1979–80).

(d) *Parental status termination proceedings.* LASSITER v. DEPARTMENT OF SOCIAL SERVICES, 452 U.S. 18, 101 S.Ct. 2153, 68 L.Ed.2d 640 (1981), per STEWART, J., rejected the view that due process requires the appointment of counsel in every parental status termination proceeding involving indigent parents and left the appointment of counsel in such proceedings to be determined by the state courts on a case-by-case basis: "The pre-eminent generalization that emerges from this Court's precedents on an indigent's right to appointed counsel is that such a right has been recognized to exist only where the litigant may lose his physical liberty if he loses the litigation. * * * Significantly, as a litigant's interest in personal liberty diminishes, so does his right to appointed counsel. [Thus, *Gagnon v. Scarpelli*, 411 U.S. 778, 93 S.Ct. 1756, 36 L.Ed.2d 656 (1973),] declined to hold that indigent probationers have, per se, a right to counsel at revocation hearings, and instead left the decision whether counsel should be appointed to be made on a case-by-case basis."

The Court then held that in the circumstances of this case the trial judge did not deny Ms. Lassiter due process when he failed to appoint counsel for her: "[The] case presented no specially troublesome points of law, either procedural or substantive. While hearsay evidence was no doubt admitted, and while Ms. Lassiter no doubt left incomplete her defense that the Department had not adequately assisted her in rekindling her interest in her son, the weight of the evidence that she had few sparks of such an interest was sufficiently great that the presence of counsel for [her] could not have made a determinative difference.' " [c]

c. Burger, C.J., who joined the Court's opinion, also added, in a brief concurrence responding to the dissenters, that the purpose of the parental status termination proceeding "was not 'punitive' " but "*protective* of the child's best interests."

BLACKMUN, J., joined by Brennan and Marshall, JJ., dissented: "In this case, the State's aim is not simply to influence the parent-child relationship but to *extinguish* it. A termination of parental rights is both total and irrevocable. [It] is hardly surprising that this forced dissolution of the parent-child relationship has been recognized as a punitive sanction by courts, Congress, and commentators.

"[Faced] with a formal accusatory adjudication, with an adversary—the State—that commands great investigative and prosecutorial resources, with standards that involve ill-defined notions of fault and adequate parenting, and with the inevitable tendency of a court to apply subjective values or to defer to the State's 'expertise,' the defendant parent plainly is outstripped if he or she is without the assistance of 'the guiding hand of counsel.' When the parent is indigent, lacking in education, and easily intimidated by figures of authority, the imbalance may well become insuperable. [W]here as here, the threatened loss of liberty is severe and absolute, the State's role is so clearly adversarial and punitive, and the cost involved is relatively slight, there is no sound basis for refusing to recognize the right to counsel as a requisite of due process in a proceeding initiated by the State to terminate parental rights." [d]

STEVENS, J., also dissented: "[The] reasons supporting the conclusion that [due process] entitle the defendant in a criminal case to representation by counsel apply with equal force to a case of this kind. The issue is one of fundamental fairness, not of weighing the pecuniary costs against the societal benefits. Accordingly, even if the costs to the State were not relatively insignificant but rather were just as great as the costs of providing prosecutors, judges, and defense counsel to ensure the fairness of criminal proceedings, I would reach the same result in this category of cases. For the value of protecting our liberty from deprivation by the State without due process of law is priceless." [e]

Compare *Lassiter* with SANTOSKY v. KRAMER, 455 U.S. 745, 102 S.Ct. 1388, 71 L.Ed.2d 599 (1982). Under New York law, the state may terminate, over parental objection, the rights of parents in their natural child upon a finding that the child is "permanently neglected," a finding that need be supported only by a "fair preponderance of the evidence." Because "the private interest affected is commanding; the risk of error from using a preponderance standard is substantial; and the countervailing government interest favoring that standard is comparatively slight," a 5–4 majority, per BLACKMUN, J., held that a "fair preponderance of the evidence" standard in such proceedings violates due process. Thus, before a state may terminate permanently the rights of parents in their natural child, it must support its allegations by at least "clear and convincing evidence. [Unlike] a constitutional requirement of hearings or court-appointed counsel, a stricter standard of proof [than 'preponderance'] would reduce factual error without imposing substantial fiscal burdens upon the State."

Given the flexibility of the due process principle, dissenting JUSTICE REHNQUIST, joined by Burger, C.J., and White and O'Connor, JJ., thought it "obvious that a proper due process inquiry cannot be made by focusing upon one narrow provision

---

d. The dissent then examined the termination hearing in considerable detail and, "[i]n light of the unpursued avenues of defense, and of the experience petitioner underwent at this hearing," found "virtually incredible" the Court's conclusion that the termination proceeding was fundamentally fair.

e. For the view that the *Lassiter* Court forgot the teaching of *Gideon*—a reviewing court *cannot* conclude that "the case presented no specially troublesome points of law" on the basis of a record made *without* the assistance of counsel—see Yale Kamisar, *Gideon v. Wainwright A Quarter-Century Later*, 10 Pace L.Rev. 343, 354–55 (1990).

of the challenged statutory scheme. [Courts] must examine *all* procedural protections offered by the State, and must assess the *cumulative* effect of such safeguards." The dissent then pointed to the "host of procedural protections" the state had "placed around parental rights and interests." In addition to the basic fairness of the statutory scheme, "the standard of proof chosen by New York clearly reflects a constitutionally permissible balance of the interests at stake in this case. [When] the interests of the child and the State in a stable, nurturing homelife are balanced against the interests of the parents in the rearing of their child, it cannot be said that either set of interests is so clearly paramount as to require that the risk of error be allocated to one side or the other."

3. *"Open analysis of the values at stake."* Consider John Nowak, *Foreword—Due Process Methodology in the Postincorporation World*, 70 J.Crim.L. & C. 397, 403 (1979): "Although one may disagree with the results in [cases such as *Parham*, which employed the *Eldridge* 'balancing test,'] the Court's open analysis of the values at stake [and] its attempt to accommodate the competing values of liberty and efficient administrative procedures certainly is preferable to the masking of such decisions through vaguely worded opinions or formalistic interpretations of constitutional provisions. [By contrast], in *Greenholtz v. Nebraska Prison Inmates* (1979) [p. 503 fn. a supra], [holding] that inmates of penal institutions were not entitled to due process protection in decisionmaking processes related to their possible release on parole, a majority of the Justices totally failed to analyze the basic due process question. [*Greenholtz*, per Burger, C.J., found] no liberty interest meriting protection by the due process clause at issue in these proceedings. The four Justices [Brennan, Marshall, Powell and Stevens] who dissented, at least in part, found that the individual prisoners had a liberty interest at stake [and thus] struggled openly with the problem of determining what, if any, procedural safeguards should be given to [them]. Even if one agreed with the majority's conclusion[,] [it is] easier to accept the separate opinion of Justice Powell, [recognizing] that inmates had an interest worthy of protection by the due process clause [but finding] that the need of efficiently processing inmate files outweighed the interest in freedom preceding the expiration of a properly imposed sentence. [Powell, J.'s] balancing approach is more satisfying than the majority's simple assertion that the possibility of parole is no more than a hope— 'a hope which is not protected by due process.' By failing to adopt the Powell approach it was possible to avoid questions of fairness and value identification even in due process decisions."

4. *Separating the "property" or "liberty" issue from that of "what process is due."* While recent cases "fall short of providing the full inventory of procedural safeguards required by *Goldberg*," observes ROBERT RABIN, *Job Security and Due Process: Monitoring Administrative Discretion Through A Reasons Requirement*, 44 U.Chi.L.Rev. 60, 74–79 (1976), they proceed from the same basic assumption about the relationship between property interests and procedural due process: at a minimum, procedural due process contemplates some kind of a hearing—an opportunity to join issue, through the presentation of evidence to a decision maker who is then obliged to reach a reasoned determination on the basis of the submissions. Underlying this conception is the vital interest in promoting an accurate decision, in assuring that facts have been correctly established and properly characterized in conformity with the applicable legal [standard.]

"By equating procedural due process with a value that seems to require a right to some kind of a hearing, the Court has correspondingly been driven to set too high a threshold when arriving at an initial determination of whether a property interest exists. In theory, of course, the inquiry into whether a form of government largess creates a property interest can, as the Court and commentators [and, in a way, the editors of this casebook] suggest, be neatly separated from the question of 'what process is due.' In practice, however, whether an entitlement is established or not is determined with an eye to the minimum procedural requirements that would follow as a consequence of a decision in favor of the recipient's claim. A threshold perception of security of interest focuses both on the existence of a 'property' interest and the procedural safeguards attendant upon its recognition. [The] result, as *Roth* and *Bishop* illustrate, is that when the state equivocates about job security, a court cognizant of the high costs of a hearing requirement in terms of administrative efficiency is likely to be reluctant to recognize a property interest. The court then ends up affording no procedural protection at all, even though the employee in such a case may be on a tenure track or even in a 'permanent' position. * * *

"Fundamental to the concept of procedural due process is the right to a reasoned explanation of government conduct that is contrary to the expectations the government has created by conferring a special status upon an individual. [It] is crucial that this value be seen as distinct from the concern about administrative accuracy—the interest in correcting wrong decisions. Obviously, the two are related[, but] I would insist that the respect for individual autonomy that is at the foundation of procedural due process imposes a distinct obligation upon the government to explain fully its adverse status decision. * * *

"Procedural due process can be viewed as a layered approach aimed at accomplishing a fundamental objective—protection against arbitrary conduct by the state. One could view the [various rights] [a] as various layers intended to provide increasingly effective insulation from arbitrariness: each layer adds something to the defensive capacity to ward off an arbitrary effort to destroy a status relationship. In some cases—a job security case involving a first amendment claim, for example—the balance struck between the individual values to be protected and the costs of administration weighs so heavily in favor of the individual claimant that a many-layered approach, some form of 'evidentiary hearing,' seems clearly required. But as we respond to less exigent claims by peeling away the layers of protection—indeed as we strip away any semblance of a 'hearing'—it is essential that we retain the core safeguard against arbitrariness, the right to receive a meaningful explanation of what is being done to the individual."

a. For factors—"roughly in order of priority"—that have been considered to be elements of a fair hearing, see Henry Friendly, *"Some Kind of Hearing,"* 123 U.Pa.L.Rev. 1267, 1279–95 (1975): (1) "an unbiased tribunal" (but recall *Arnett v. Kennedy*); (2) "notice of the proposed action and the grounds asserted for it"; (3) "an opportunity to present reasons why the proposed action should not be taken"; (4), (5) and (6) "the right to call witnesses, to know the evidence against one, and to have decision based only on the evidence presented"; (7) "counsel"; (8) and (9), "the making of a record and a statement of reasons"; (10) "public attendance"; and (11) "judicial review."

Chapter 9
FREEDOM OF EXPRESSION
AND ASSOCIATION

SECTION 1. WHAT SPEECH IS NOT PROTECTED?

The first amendment provides that "Congress shall make no law * * * abridging the freedom of speech, or of the press." Some have stressed that no law means NO LAW. For example, Black, J., dissenting in *Konigsberg v. State Bar*, 366 U.S. 36, 81 S.Ct. 997, 6 L.Ed.2d 105 (1961) argued that the "First Amendment's unequivocal command * * * shows that the men who drafted our Bill of Rights did all the 'balancing' that was to be done in this field."

Laws forbidding speech, however, are commonplace. Laws against perjury, blackmail, and fraud prohibit speech.[a] So does much of the law of contracts. Black, J., himself conceded that speech pursued as an integral part of criminal conduct was beyond first amendment protection. Indeed no one contends that citizens are free to say anything, anywhere, at any time. As Holmes, J., observed, citizens are not free to yell "fire" falsely in a crowded theater.

The spectre of a man crying fire falsely in the theater, however, has plagued first amendment theory. The task is to formulate principles that separate the protected from the unprotected. But speech interacts with too many other values in too many complicated ways to expect that a single formula will prove productive.

Are advocates of illegal action, pornographers selling magazines, or publishers of defamation like that person in the theater or are they engaged in freedom of speech? Do citizens have a right to speak on government property? Which property? Is there a right of access to the print or broadcast media? Can government force private owners to grant access for speakers? Does the first amendment offer protection for the wealthy, powerful corporations, and media conglomerates against government attempts to assure greater equality in the intellectual marketplace? Can government demand information about private political associations or reporters' confidential sources without first amendment limits? Does the first amendment require government to produce information it might otherwise withhold?

The Court has approached questions such as these without much attention to

---

a. Nonetheless, for a sophisticated defence of Black, J.'s position, see Charles Black, *Mr.* *Justice Black, the Supreme Court, and the Bill of Rights,* 222 Harper's Mag. 63 (1961).

the language [b] or history [c] of the first amendment and without a commitment to any general theory.[d] Rather it has sought to develop principles on a case-by-case basis and has produced a complex and conflicting body of constitutional precedent. Many of the basic principles were developed in a line of cases involving the advocacy of illegal action.[e]

I. ADVOCACY OF ILLEGAL ACTION

A. EMERGING PRINCIPLES

SCHENCK v. UNITED STATES, 249 U.S. 47, 39 S.Ct. 247, 63 L.Ed. 470 (1919): Defendants were convicted of a conspiracy to violate the 1917 Espionage Act by conspiring to cause and attempting to cause insubordination in the armed forces of the United States, and obstruction of the recruiting and enlistment service of the United States, when at war with Germany, by printing and circulating to men accepted for military service approximately fifteen thousand copies of the document described in the opinion. In affirming, HOLMES, J., said for a unanimous Court: "The document in question upon its first printed side recited the first section of the Thirteenth Amendment, said that the idea embodied in it was violated by the conscription act and that a conscript is little better than a convict. In impassioned language it intimated that conscription was despotism in its worst form and a monstrous wrong against humanity in the interest of Wall Street's chosen few. It said, 'Do not submit to intimidation,' but in form at least confined itself to peaceful measures such as a petition for the repeal of the act. The other and later printed side of the sheet was headed 'Assert Your Rights.' It stated reasons for alleging that any one violated the Constitution when he refused to recognize 'your right to assert your opposition to the draft,' and went on, 'If you do not assert and support your rights, you are helping to deny or disparage

b. But compare for fn. b. in *Roth v. United States,* p. 604 infra.

c. But see, *McIntyre v. Ohio Elections Comm'n,* p. 877 infra (Thomas, J., concurring) (Scalia, J., dissenting). See, e.g., Michael Perry, *The Constitution, The Courts, and Human Rights,* 63–64 (1982). For a variety of views about the history surrounding the adoption of the first amendment, compare Leonard Levy, *Legacy of Suppression* (1960) with Leonard Levy, *Emergence of a Free Press* (1985); Leonard Levy, *The Legacy Reexamined,* 37 Stan. L.Rev. 767 (1985); Leonard Levy, *On the Origins of the Free Press Clause,* 32 U.C.L.A.L.Rev. 177 (1984) and George Anastaplo, *Book Review,* 39 N.Y.U.L.Rev. 735 (1964); David Anderson, *The Origins of the Press Clause,* 30 U.C.L.A.L.Rev. 455 (1983); Phillip Hamburger, *The Development of the Law of Seditious Libel and the Control of the Press,* 37 Stan.L.Rev. 661 (1985); William Mayton, *Seditious Libel and the Lost Guarantee of a Freedom of Expression,* 84 Colum.L.Rev. 91 (1984); William Mayton, *From a Legacy of Suppression to the 'Metaphor of the Fourth Estate,'* 39 Stan. L.Rev. 139 (1986); Lucas Powe, *The Fourth Estate and the Constitution* 22–50 (1991). David Rabban, *The Ahistorical Historian: Leonard Levy on Freedom of Expression in Early American History,* 37 Stan.L.Rev. 795 (1985).

For an ambitious attempt to marry history, philosophy, and the first amendment, see David Richards, *A Theory of Free Speech,* 34 UCLA L.Rev. 1837 (1987).

d. On the difficulties involved in developing general theory, see Larry Alexander & Paul Horton, *The Impossibility of a Free Speech Principle,* 78 Nw.U.L.Rev. 1319 (1983); Daniel Farber & Phillip Frickey, *Practical Reason and the First Amendment,* 34 UCLA L.Rev. 1615 (1987); Steven Shiffrin, *The First Amendment and Economic Regulation: Away From a General Theory of the First Amendment,* 78 Nw. U.L.Rev. 1212 (1983); Laurence Tribe, *Toward A Metatheory of Free Speech,* 10 Sw.U.L.Rev. 237 (1978).

e. For discussion of the case law preceding *Schenck v. United States,* infra, see Michael Gibson, *The Supreme Court and Freedom of Expression from 1791 to 1917,* 55 Fordham L.Rev. 263 (1986); David Rabban, *The First Amendment in Its Forgotten Years,* 90 Yale L.J. 514 (1981). A general history of free speech and suppression is much needed. For useful commentary see Zechariah Chafee, *Free Speech in the United States* (1941); Leon Whipple, *The Story of Civil Liberty in the United States* (1927); David Kairys, *Freedom of Speech* in The Politics of Law 160 (Kairys ed. 1982).

rights which it is the solemn duty of all citizens and residents of the United States to retain.' It described the arguments on the other side as coming from cunning politicians and a mercenary capitalist press, and even silent consent to the conscription law as helping to support an infamous conspiracy. It denied the power to send our citizens away to foreign shores to shoot up the people of other lands, and added that words could not express the condemnation such coldblooded ruthlessness deserves, &c., &c., winding up, 'You must do your share to maintain, support and uphold the rights of the people of this country.' Of course the document would not have been sent unless it had been intended to have some effect, and we do not see what effect it could be expected to have upon persons subject to the draft except to influence them to obstruct the carrying of it out. The defendants do not deny that the jury might find against them on this point.

"But it is said, suppose that that was the tendency of this circular, it is protected by the First Amendment to the Constitution. [We] admit that in many places and in ordinary times the defendants in saying all that was said in the circular would have been within their constitutional rights. But the character of every act depends upon the circumstances in which it is done. The most stringent protection of free speech would not protect a man in falsely shouting fire in a theatre and causing a panic. [The] question in every case is whether the words used are used in such circumstances and are of such a nature as to create a clear and present danger that they will bring about the substantive evils that Congress has a right to prevent. It is a question of proximity and degree.[a] When a nation is at war many things that might be said in time of peace are such a hindrance to its effort that their utterance will not be endured so long as men fight and that no Court could regard them as protected by any constitutional right. It seems to be admitted that if an actual obstruction of the recruiting service were proved, liability for words that produced that effect might be enforced. The statute of 1917 punishes conspiracies to obstruct as well as actual obstruction. If the act, (speaking, or circulating a paper), its tendency and the intent with which it is done are the same, we perceive no ground for saying that success alone warrants making the act a crime."[b]

---

a. Although Schenck was convicted for violating a conspiracy statute, Holmes appears to have used the occasion to import the law of criminal attempts into the freedom of expression area. "In *Schenck*, 'clear and present danger,' 'a question of proximity and degree' bridged the gap between the defendant's acts of publication and the [prohibited interferences with the war.] This connection was strikingly similar to the Holmesian analysis of the requirement of 'dangerous proximity to success' [quoting from an earlier Holmes opinion] that, in the law of attempts, bridges the gap between the defendant's acts and the completed crime. In either context, innocuous efforts are to be ignored." Yogal Rogat, *Mr. Justice Holmes: Some Modern Views—The Judge as Spectator,* 31 U.Chi.L.Rev. 213, 215 (1964). See also Chafee, *Free Speech in the United States* 81–82 (1941); Shapiro, *Freedom of Speech* 55–58 (1966). But see Holmes, J., dissenting in *Abrams* infra, and fn. b below.

b. See also *Frohwerk v. United States,* 249 U.S. 204, 39 S.Ct. 249, 63 L.Ed. 561 (1919), where a unanimous Court, per Holmes, J., sustained a conviction for conspiracy to obstruct recruiting in violation of the Espionage Act, by means of a dozen newspaper articles praising the spirit and strength of the German nation, criticizing the decision to send American troops to France, maintaining that the government was giving false and hypocritical reasons for its course of action and implying that "the guilt of those who voted the unnatural sacrifice" is greater than the wrong of those who seek to escape by resistance: "[*Schenck* decided] that a person may be convicted of a conspiracy to obstruct recruiting by words of persuasion. [S]o far as the language of the articles goes there is not much to choose between expressions to be found in them and those before us in *Schenck*." Consider Powe, supra, at 71: "The case against Frohwerk was [weaker] than that against Schenck on both contested points; the recipients of the writing

DEBS v. UNITED STATES, 249 U.S. 211, 39 S.Ct. 252, 63 L.Ed. 566 (1919): Defendant was convicted of violating the Espionage Act for obstructing and attempting to obstruct the recruiting service and for causing and attempting to cause insubordination and disloyalty in the armed services. He was given a ten-year prison sentence on each count, to run concurrently. His criminal conduct consisted of giving the anti-war speech described in the opinion at the state convention of the Socialist Party of Ohio, held at a park in Canton, Ohio, on a June 16, 1918 Sunday afternoon before a general audience of 1,200 persons. At the time of the speech, defendant was a national political figure.[a] In affirming, HOLMES, J., observed for a unanimous Court:

"The main theme of the speech was socialism, its growth, and a prophecy of its ultimate success. With that we have nothing to do, but if a part or the manifest intent of the more general utterances was to encourage those present to obstruct the recruiting service and if in passages such encouragement was directly given, the immunity of the general theme may not be enough to protect the speech. [Defendant had come to the park directly from a nearby jail, where he had visited three socialists imprisoned for obstructing the recruiting service. He expressed sympathy and admiration for these persons and others convicted of similar offenses, and then] said that the master class has always declared the war and the subject class has always fought the battles—that the subject class has had nothing to gain and all to lose, including their lives; [and that] 'You have your lives to lose; you certainly ought to have the right to declare war if you consider a war necessary.' [He next said of a woman serving a ten-year sentence for obstructing the recruiting service] that she had said no more than the speaker had said that afternoon; that if she was guilty so was [he].

"There followed personal experiences and illustrations of the growth of socialism, a glorification of minorities, and a prophecy of the success of [socialism], with the interjection that 'you need to know that you are fit for something better than slavery and cannon fodder.' [Defendant's] final exhortation [was] 'Don't worry about the charge of treason to your masters; but be concerned about the treason that involves yourselves.' The defendant addressed the jury himself, and while contending that his speech did not warrant the charges said 'I have been accused of obstructing the war. I admit it. Gentlemen, I abhor war. I would oppose the war if I stood alone.' The statement was not necessary to warrant the jury in finding that one purpose of the speech, whether incidental or not does not matter, was to oppose not only war in general but this war, and that the opposition was so expressed that its natural and intended effect would be to obstruct recruiting. If that was intended and if, in all the circumstances, that would be its probable effect, it would not be protected by reason of its being part of a general program and expressions of a general and conscientious belief.

"[Defendant's constitutional objections] based upon the First Amendment [were] disposed of in *Schenck*.

"[T]he admission in evidence of the record of the conviction [of various persons he mentioned in his speech was proper] to show what he was talking

and the intensity of the writing. [Even] the government attorney who prevailed in *Frohwerk* [concluded that he was] 'one of the clearest examples of the political prisoner.' "

a. Debs had run for the Presidency on the Socialist ticket for the fourth time in 1912. At the 1920 election, while in prison, Debs ran again and received over 900,000 votes as the Socialist candidate, a significant portion of all votes cast in that election. Consider Harry Kalven, *Ernst Freund and the First Amendment Tradition*, 40 U.Chi.L.Rev. 235, 237 (1973): "To put the case in modern context, it is somewhat as though George McGovern had been sent to prison for his criticism of the [Vietnam] war."

about, to explain the true import of his expression of sympathy and to throw light on the intent of the address. [Properly admitted, too, was an 'Anti-war Proclamation and Program' adopted the previous year, coupled with testimony that shortly before his speech defendant had stated that he approved it]. Its first recommendation was, 'continuous, active, and public opposition to the war, through demonstrations, mass petitions, and all other means within our power.' Evidence that the defendant accepted this view and this declaration of his duties at the time that he made his speech is evidence that if in that speech he used words tending to obstruct the recruiting service he meant that they should have that effect. [T]he jury were most carefully instructed that they could not find the defendant guilty for advocacy of any of his opinions unless the words used had as their natural tendency and reasonably probable effect to obstruct the recruiting service [and] unless the defendant had the specific intent to do so in his mind."

Notes and Questions

1. *The Man in the Theater.* Consider Harry Kalven, *A Worthy Tradition* 133–34 (1988): "*Schenck*—and perhaps even Holmes himself—are best remembered for the example of the man 'falsely shouting fire' in a crowded theater. Judge Hand said in *Masses* that 'words are not only the keys of persuasion, but the triggers of action.' Justice Holmes makes the same point by means of the 'fire' example, an image which was to catch the fancy of the culture. But the example has long seemed to me trivial and misleading. It is as if the only conceivable controversy over speech policy were with an adversary who asserts that *all* use of words is absolutely immunized under the First Amendment. The 'fire' example then triumphantly impeaches this massive major premise. Beyond that, it adds nothing to our understanding. If the point were that *only* speech which is a comparable 'trigger of action' could be regulated, the example might prove a stirring way of drawing the line at incitement, but it is abundantly clear that Justice Holmes is not comparing Schenck's leaflet to the shouting of 'fire.' Moreover, because the example is so wholly apolitical, it lacks the requisite complexity for dealing with any serious speech problem likely to confront the legal system. The man shouting 'fire' does not offer premises resembling those underlying radical political rhetoric—premises that constitute criticism of government."

2. *Schenck and Debs.* Consider Harry Kalven, *Ernst Freund and the First Amendment Tradition,* 40 U.Chi.L.Rev. 235, 236–38 (1973): "It has been customary to lavish care and attention on the *Schenck* case, [but *Debs,* argued well before *Schenck* was handed down and decided just one week later,] represented the first effort by Justice Holmes to apply what he had worked out about freedom of speech in *Schenck.* The start of the law of the first amendment is not *Schenck;* it is *Schenck* and *Debs* read together. [Deb's speech] fell into the genre of bitter criticism of government and government policy, sometimes called seditious libel; freedom of such criticism from government marks, we have come to understand, 'the central meaning of the First Amendment' [*New York Times v. Sullivan,* p. 674 infra]. During the Vietnam War thousands of utterances strictly comparable in bitterness and sharpness of criticism, if not in literacy, were made; it was pretty much taken for granted they were beyond the reach of government.[b] [*Debs*] raises serious questions as to what the first amendment, and more especially, what the clear and present danger formula can possibly have meant at the time. [Holmes] does not comment on the fact difference between [*Schenck* and *Debs*]: the defendant in *Schenck* had sent his leaflets directly to men who

b. Compare *Debs* with *Bond v. Floyd,* p. 562 infra.

awaited draft call whereas [Debs] was addressing a general audience at a public meeting. Holmes offers no discussion of the sense in which Debs's speech presented a clear and present danger. [In fact, *Debs*] did not move [Holmes] to discuss free speech at all; his brief opinion is occupied with two points about admissibility of [evidence]. It was for Holmes a routine criminal appeal."

3. *"Breathing space" for free speech under the Espionage Act.* Consider Zechariah Chafee, *Free Speech in the United States* 50–51 (1941): "[With a few exceptions, notably Judge Learned Hand's opinion in *Masses,* infra, the lower federal courts] allowed conviction [under the Espionage Act] for any words which had an indirect effect to discourage recruiting and the war spirit [so long as] the intention to discourage existed. [Moreover, the] requirement of intention became a mere form since it could be inferred from the existence of the indirect injurious effect. [T]he words of the Espionage Act of 1917 bear slight resemblance to the Sedition Law of 1798, but the judicial construction is much the same, except that under the Sedition Law truth was a defense."

Consider Ernst Freund's criticism of *Debs, The Debs Case and Freedom of Speech,* The New Republic, May 3, 1919, p. 13 reprinted in 40 U.Chi.L.Rev. 239, 240–41 (1973): "To know what you may do and what you may not do, and how far you may go in criticism, is the first condition of political liberty; to be permitted to agitate at your own peril, subject to a jury's guessing at motive, tendency and possible effect, makes the right of free speech a precarious gift. [For] arbitrary executive, [the Espionage Act] practically substitutes arbitrary, judicial power; since a jury's findings, within the limits of a conceivable psychological nexus between words and deeds, are beyond scrutiny and control; and while the jury may have been a protection against governmental power when the government was a thing apart from the people, its checking function fails where government policies are supported by majority opinion."

Holmes, J.'s response, in private correspondence, see Douglas Ginsburg, *Afterword,* 40 U.Chi.L.Rev. 243, 245 (1973), to Professor Freund's objection, in his article on *Debs,* to a jury "guessing at motive, tendency and possible effect" was that this could be said about "pretty much the whole body of the law, which for thirty years I have made my brethren smile by insisting to be everywhere a matter of degree." Holmes recalled the comment he made in a case involving a criminal prosecution under the Sherman Act that "the law is full of instances where a man's fate depends on his estimating rightly, that is, as the jury subsequently estimates it, some matter of degree. If his judgment is wrong, not only may he incur a fine or [prison term, but] the penalty of death."

4. MASSES PUBLISHING CO. v. PATTEN, 244 Fed. 535 (S.D.N.Y.1917): The Postmaster of New York advised plaintiff that an issue of his monthly revolutionary journal, *The Masses,* would be denied the mails under the Espionage Act since it tended to encourage the enemies of the United States and to hamper the government in its conduct of the war. The Postmaster subsequently specified as objectionable several cartoons entitled, e.g., "Conscription," "Making the World Safe for Capitalism"; several articles admiring the "sacrifice" of conscientious objectors and a poem praising two persons imprisoned for conspiracy to resist the draft. Plaintiff sought a preliminary injunction against the postmaster from excluding its magazine from the mails. LEARNED HAND, D.J., granted relief:

"[The postmaster maintains] that to arouse discontent and disaffection among the people with the prosecution of the war and with the draft tends to promote a mutinous and insubordinate temper among the troops. This [is] true; men who become satisfied that they are engaged in an enterprise dictated by the unconscionable selfishness of the rich, and effectuated by a tyrannous disregard for the will of those who must suffer and die, will be more prone to insubordination than those who have faith in the cause and acquiesce in the means. Yet to interpret the word 'cause' [in the statutory language forbidding one to 'willfully cause' insubordination in the armed forces] so broadly would [necessarily involve] the suppression of all hostile criticism, and of all opinion except what encouraged and supported the existing policies, or which fell within the range of temperate argument. It would contradict the normal assumption of democratic government that the suppression of hostile criticism does not turn upon the justice of its substance or the decency and propriety of its temper. Assuming that the power to repress such opinion may rest in Congress in the throes of a struggle for the very existence of the state, its exercise is so contrary to the use and wont of our people that only the clearest expression of such a power justifies the conclusion that it was intended.

"The defendant's position, therefore, in so far as it involves the suppression of the free utterance of abuse and criticism of the existing law, or of the policies of the war, is not, in my judgment, supported by the language of the statute. Yet there has always been a recognized limit to such expressions, incident indeed to the existence of any compulsive power of the state itself. One may not counsel or advise others to violate the law as it stands. Words are not only the keys of persuasion, but the triggers of action, and those which have no purport but to counsel the violation of law cannot by any latitude of interpretation be a part of that public opinion which is the final source of government in a democratic state. [To] counsel or advise a man to an act is to urge upon him either that it is his interest or his duty to do it. While, of course, this may be accomplished as well by indirection as expressly, since words carry the meaning that they impart, the definition is exhaustive, I think, and I shall use it. Political agitation, by the passions it arouses or the convictions it engenders, may in fact stimulate men to the violation of law. Detestation of existing policies is easily transformed into forcible resistance of the authority which puts them in execution, and it would be folly to disregard the causal relation between the two. Yet to assimilate agitation, legitimate as such, with direct incitement to violent resistance, is to disregard the tolerance of all methods of political agitation which in normal times is a safeguard of free government. The distinction is not a scholastic subterfuge, but a hard-bought acquisition in the fight for freedom, and the purpose to disregard it must be evident when the power exists. If one stops short of urging upon others that it is their duty or their interest to resist the law, it seems to me one should not be held to have attempted to cause its violation. If that be not the test, I can see no escape from the conclusion that under this section every political agitation which can be shown to be apt to create a seditious temper is illegal. I am confident that by such language Congress had no such revolutionary purpose in view.

"It seems to me, however, quite plain that none of the language and none of the cartoons in this paper can be thought directly to counsel or advise insubordination or mutiny, without a violation of their meaning quite beyond any tolerable understanding. I come, therefore to the [provision of the Act forbidding] any one from willfully obstructing [recruiting or enlistment]. I am not prepared to assent to the plaintiff's position that this only refers to acts other than words, nor that the act thus defined must be shown to have been successful. One may obstruct without preventing, and the mere obstruction is an injury to the service; for it throws impediments in its way. Here again, however, since the question is of the expression of opinion, I construe the sentence, so far as it restrains public utterance, [as] limited to the direct advocacy of resistance to the recruiting and enlistment service. If so, the inquiry is narrowed to the question whether any of the challenged matter may be said to advocate resistance to the draft, taking the meaning of the words with the utmost latitude which they can bear.

"As to the cartoons it seems to me quite clear that they do not fall within such a test. [T]he most that can be said [is that they] may breed such animosity to the draft as will promote resistance and strengthen the determination of those disposed to be recalcitrant. There is no intimation that, however, hateful the draft may be, one is in duty bound to resist it, certainly none that such resistance is to one's interest. I cannot, therefore, even with the limitations which surround the power of the court, assent to the assertion that any of the cartoons violate the act.

"[As for the text], it is plain enough that the [magazine] has the fullest sympathy for [those who resist the draft or obstruct recruiting], that it admires their courage, and that it presumptively approves their conduct. [Moreover,] these passages, it must be remembered, occur in a magazine which attacks with the utmost violence the draft and the war. That such comments have a tendency to arouse emulation in others is clear enough, but that they counsel others to follow these examples is not so plain. Literally at least they do not, and while, as I have said, the words are to be taken, not literally, but according to their full import, the literal meaning is the starting point for interpretation. One may admire and approve the course of a hero without feeling any duty to follow him. There is not the least implied intimation in these words that others are under a duty to follow. The most that can be said is that, if others do follow, they will get the same admiration and the same approval. Now, there is surely an appreciable distance between esteem and emulation; and unless there is here some advocacy of such emulation, I cannot see how the passages can be said to fall within the [law.] Surely, if the draft had not excepted Quakers, it would be too strong a doctrine to say that any who openly admire their fortitude or even approved their conduct was willfully obstructing the draft.

"When the question is of a statute constituting a crime, it seems to me that there should be more definite evidence of the act. The question before me is quite the same as what would arise upon a motion to dismiss an indictment at the close of the proof: Could any reasonable man say, not that the indirect result of the language might be to arouse a seditious disposition, for that would not be enough, but that the language directly advocated resistance to the draft? I cannot think that upon such language any verdict would stand." [c]

What result if the Court had applied the *Masses* test in *Schenck* or *Debs*? In *Abrams* or *Gitlow,* infra?

JUSTICE HOLMES—DISSENTING IN
ABRAMS v. UNITED STATES

250 U.S. 616, 624, 40 S.Ct. 17, 20, 63 L.Ed. 1173, 1178 (1919).

[In the summer of 1918, the United States sent a small body of marines to Siberia. Although the defendants maintained a strong socialist opposition to

---

c. In reversing, 246 Fed. 24 (1917), the Second Circuit observed: "If the natural and probable effect of what is said is to encourage resistance to a law, and the words are used in an endeavor to persuade to resistance, it is immaterial that the duty to resist is not mentioned, or the interest of the person addressed in resistance is not suggested. That one may willfully obstruct the enlistment service, without advising in direct language against enlistments, and without stating that to refrain from

enlistment is a duty or in one's interest, seems to us too plain for controversy."

For diverse views concerning Judge Hand's opinion and its importance, see Gerald Gunther, *Learned Hand* 151–70, 603 (1994); Bernard Schwartz, *Holmes v. Hand,* 1994 S.Ct. Rev. 209; Vincent Blasi, *Learned Hand and the Self–Government Theory of the First Amendment,* 61 U.Col.L.Rev. 1 (1990).

"German militarism," they opposed the "capitalist" invasion of Russia, and characterized it as an attempt to crush the Russian Revolution. Shortly thereafter, they printed two leaflets and distributed several thousand copies in New York City. Many of the copies were thrown from a window where one defendant was employed; others were passed around at radical meetings. Both leaflets supported Russia against the United States; one called upon workers to unite in a general strike. There was no evidence that workers responded to the call.

[The Court upheld the defendants' convictions for conspiring to violate two provisions of the 1918 amendments to the Espionage Act. One count prohibited language intended to "incite, provoke and encourage resistance to the United States"; the other punished those who urged curtailment of war production. As the Court interpreted the statute, an intent to interfere with efforts against a *declared* war was a necessary element of both offenses. Since the United States had not declared war upon Russia, "the main task of the government was to establish an [*intention*] *to interfere with the war with Germany.*" Chafee, supra, at 115. The Court found intent on the principle that "Men must be held to have intended, and to be accountable for, the effects which their acts were likely to produce. Even if their primary purpose and intent was to aid the cause of the Russian Revolution, the plan of action which they adopted necessarily involved, before it could be realized, defeat of the war program of the United States * * *."

[HOLMES, J., dissented in an opinion with which Brandeis, J., concurred:]

[I] am aware of course that the word "intent" as vaguely used in ordinary legal discussion means no more than knowledge at the time of the act that the consequences said to be intended will ensue. [But,] when words are used exactly, a deed is not done with intent to produce a consequence unless that consequence is the aim of the deed. It may be obvious, and obvious to the actor, that the consequence will follow, and he may be liable for it even if he regrets it, but he does not do the act with intent to produce it unless the aim to produce it is the proximate motive of the specific act although there may be some deeper motive behind.

It seems to me that this statute must be taken to use its words in a strict and accurate sense. They would be absurd in any other. A patriot might think that we were wasting money on aeroplanes, or making more cannon of a certain kind than we needed, and might advocate curtailment with success, yet even if it turned out that the curtailment hindered and was thought by other minds to have been obviously likely to hinder the United States in the prosecution of the war, no one would hold such conduct a crime. * * *

I never have seen any reason to doubt that the questions of law that alone were before this Court in the cases of *Schenck, Frohwerk* and *Debs* were rightly decided. I do not doubt for a moment that by the same reasoning that would justify punishing persuasion to murder, the United States constitutionally may punish speech that produces or is intended to produce a clear and imminent danger that it will bring about forthwith certain substantive evils that the United States constitutionally may seek to prevent. The power undoubtedly is greater in time of war than in time of peace because war opens dangers that do not exist at other times.

But as against dangers peculiar to war, as against others, the principle of the right to free speech is always the same. It is only the present danger of immediate evil or an intent to bring it about that warrants Congress in setting a limit to the expression of opinion where private rights are not concerned. Congress certainly cannot forbid all effort to change the mind of the country. Now nobody can suppose that the surreptitious publishing of a silly leaflet by an unknown man, without more, would present any immediate danger that its opinions would hinder the success of the government arms or have any appreciable tendency to do so.[a] Publishing those opinions for the very purpose of obstructing, however, might indicate a greater danger and at any rate would have the quality of an attempt.[b] * * *

I do not see how anyone can find the intent required by the statute in any of the defendants' words. The leaflet advocating a general strike is the only one that affords even a foundation for the charge, and [its only object] is to help Russia and stop American intervention there against the popular government— not to impede the United States in the war that it was carrying on. * * *

In this case sentences of twenty years imprisonment have been imposed for the publishing of two leaflets that I believe the defendants had as much right to publish as the Government has to publish the Constitution of the United States now vainly invoked by them. [E]ven if what I think the necessary intent were shown; the most nominal punishment seems to me all that possibly could be inflicted, unless the defendants are to be made to suffer not for what the indictment alleges but for the creed that they avow—[which,] although made the

a. See also Zechariah Chafee, supra, at 140: "The maximum sentence available against a formidable pro-German plot [20 years] was meted out [for] the silly, futile circulars of five obscure and isolated young aliens, misguided by their loyalty to their endangered country and ideals, who hatched their wild scheme in a garret, and carried it out in a cellar." But cf. John Wigmore, *Abrams v. U.S.: Freedom of Speech and Freedom of Thuggery in War-Time and Peace-Time,* 14 Ill.L.Rev. 539, 549–50 (1920): "[The *Abrams* dissent] is dallying with the facts and the law. None know better than judges that what is lawful for one is lawful for a thousand others. If these five men could, without the law's restraint, urge munition workers to a general strike and armed violences then others could lawfully do so; and a thousand disaffected undesirables, aliens and natives alike, were ready and waiting to do so. Though this circular was 'surreptitious,' the next ones need not be so. If such urgings were lawful, every munitions factory in the country could be stopped by them. The relative amount of harm that one criminal act can effect is no measure of its criminality, and no measure of the danger of its criminality. To put forward such a palliation is merely to reveal more clearly the indifference to the whole crisis. [At a time] when the fate of the civilized world hung in the balance, how could the Minority Opinion interpret law and conduct in such a way as to let loose men who were doing their hardest to paralyze the supreme war efforts of our country?"

b. Would it, if, under the circumstances, the defendant had no reasonable prospect of success? If his efforts were utterly ineffectual? Is bad intention or purpose, without more, an attempt? Or even everything done in furtherance of that bad intention? Or is unlawful "intention" or "purpose" merely one factor in determining whether defendant's conduct comes dangerously near success or stamps the actor as sufficiently dangerous? Cf. Oliver Wendall Holmes, *The Common Law* 65–66, 68–69 (1881): "Intent to commit a crime is not itself criminal. [Moreover], the law does not punish every act which is done with the intent to bring about a crime. [We] have seen what amounts to an attempt to burn a haystack [lighting a match with intent to start fire to a haystack]; but it was said in the same case, that, if the defendant had gone no further than to buy a box of matches for the purpose, he would not have been liable. [Relevant considerations are] the nearness of the danger, the greatness of the harm and the degree of apprehension felt." See also Holmes, C.J., in *Commonwealth v. Peaslee,* 177 Mass. 267, 59 N.E. 55 (1901) ("if the preparation comes very near to the accomplishment of the act, the intent to complete it renders the crime so probable" that the conduct will constitute an attempt); Holmes, J., dissenting in *Hyde v. United States,* 225 U.S. 347, 387, 32 S.Ct. 793, 56 L.Ed. 1114 (1912) (preliminary acts become an attempt when "so near to the result [completed crime] that if coupled with an intent to produce that result, the danger is very great"). See generally Chafee, supra, at 46–47; Hans Linde, *"Clear and Present Danger" Reexamined,* 22 Stan. L.Rev. 1163, 1168–69, 1183–86 (1970); Martin Shapiro, *Freedom of Speech* 55–58 (1966).

subject of examination at the trial, no one has a right even to consider in dealing with the charges before the Court.

Persecution for the expression of opinions seems to me perfectly logical. If you have no doubt of your premises or your power and want a certain result with all your heart you naturally express your wishes in law and sweep away all opposition. To allow opposition by speech seems to indicate that you think the speech impotent, as when a man says that he has squared the circle, or that you do not care whole-heartedly for the result, or that you doubt either your power or your premises. But when men have realized that time has upset many fighting faiths, they may come to believe even more than they believe the very foundations of their own conduct that the ultimate good desired is better reached by free trade in ideas—that the best test of truth is the power of the thought to get itself accepted in the competition of the market, and that truth is the only ground upon which their wishes safely can be carried out.[c] That at any rate is the theory of our Constitution. It is an experiment, as all life is an experiment. Every year if not every day we have to wager our salvation upon some prophecy based upon imperfect knowledge. While that experiment is part of our system I think that we should be eternally vigilant against attempts to check the expression of opinions that we loathe and believe to be fraught with death, unless they so imminently threaten immediate interference with the lawful and pressing purposes of the law that an immediate check is required to save the country. [Only] the emergency that makes it immediately dangerous to leave the correction of evil counsels to time warrants making any exception to the sweeping command, "Congress shall make no law * * * abridging the freedom of speech." Of course I am speaking only of expressions of opinion and exhortations, which were all that were uttered [here].[d]

Notes and Questions

1. *"Marketplace of ideas."* (a) Consider G. Edward White, *Justice Holmes and the Modernization of Free Speech Jurisprudence: The Human Dimension*, 80 Calif.L.Rev. 439 (1992): "For Chafee and those who emphasized the social interest in free speech, the search for truth was part of a process in which public opinion could become more informed and enlightened. For Holmes, 'truth' was the equivalent of majoritarian prejudice at any point in time. He defined it to Laski as 'the prevailing can't help of the majority,' and to Learned Hand as 'the majority vote of that nation that can lick all others.' The optimistic, democratic vision of Chafee and his progressive contemporaries had resonated with Holmes'

---

c. But see Wigmore, fn. a supra, at 550–51: "This apotheosis of Truth, however, shows a blindness to the deadly fact that meantime the 'power of the thought' of these circulars might 'get itself accepted in the competition of the market,' by munitions workers, so as to lose the war; in which case, the academic victory which Truth, 'the ultimate good,' might later secure in the market, would be too 'ultimate' to have any practical value for a defeated America. [To] weigh in juxtaposition the dastardly sentiments of these circulars and the great theme of world-justice for which [we were fighting], and then to assume the sacred cause of Truth as equally involved in both, is to misuse high ideals. This [dissenting opinion, if it had commanded a majority], would have ended by our letting soldiers die helpless in France, through our anxiety to protect the distribution of a leaflet whose sole purpose was to cut off the soldiers' munitions and supplies. How would this have advanced the cause of Truth?"

d. Consider Sheldon Novick, *Honorable Justice, The Life of Oliver Wendell Holmes* 331 (1989): "The majority did very highly disapprove of Holmes's dissent, and White tried to persuade him to be silent. When Holmes clung to what he thought his duty, three of the justices came to call on him in his library, and [his wife] Fanny joined them in trying to dissuade him from publishing his dissent." For illuminating discussion of *Abrams* and the period of which it is a part, see Richard Polenberg, *Fighting Faiths* (1987).

skeptical resignation about the primacy of majoritarian sentiment. The 'search for truth' metaphor, embodying both of those perspectives, had arrived in American free speech jurisprudence." Compare Isaac Kramnick and Barry Sheerman, *Harold Laski: A Life on the Left* 127 (1993): "Holmes's magisterial defence of free speech in his dissent was almost verbatim Laski's own amalgam of J.S. Mill and Charles Darwin. Political ideas are adequate for the moment they were formulated, but since men are various and move in varied directions, no one single scheme of interpreting life ever lasts. 'Political good refuses the swaddling clothes of finality. It is a shifting conception,' Laski writes. It is 'in the clash of ideas that we shall find the means of truth. There is no other safeguard of progress.'"

(b) Contrast Holmes' statement of the "marketplace of ideas" argument with John Milton's statement in *Areopagitica:* "And though all the winds of doctrine were let loose to play upon the earth, so Truth be in the field, we do injuriously by licensing and prohibiting to misdoubt her strength. Let her and Falsehood grapple; who ever knew Truth put to the worse, in a free and open encounter?" [e] Holmes claims that the competition of the market is the best test of truth; Milton maintains that truth will emerge in a free and open encounter. How would one verify either hypothesis?

Is the "marketplace of ideas" a "free and open encounter"? Consider Charles Lindblom, *Politics and Markets* 207 (1977): "Early, persuasive, unconscious conditioning—[to] believe in the fundamental politico-economic institutions of one's society is ubiquitous in every society. These institutions come to be taken for granted. Many people grow up to regard them not as institutions to be tested but as standards against which the correctness of new policies and institutions can be tested. When that happens, as is common, processes of critical judgment are short-circuited." Consider also Laurence Tribe, *American Constitutional Law* 786 (2d Ed.1988): "Especially when the wealthy have more access to the most potent media of communication than the poor, how sure can we be that 'free trade in ideas' is likely to generate truth?"

For a specific example, see Steven Shiffrin, *The First Amendment and Economic Regulation: Away From A General Theory of the First Amendment,* 78 Nw.U.L.Rev. 1212, 1281 (1983): "Living in a society in which children and adults are daily confronted with multiple communications that ask them to purchase products inevitably places emphasis on materialistic values. The authors of the individual messages may not intend that general emphasis, but the whole is greater than the sum of the parts. [Advertisers] spend some sixty billion dollars per year. [Those] who would oppose the materialist message must combat forces that have a massive economic advantage. Any confidence that we will know what is truth by seeing what emerges from such combat is ill placed."

Do the different market failure considerations offered by Lindblom, Tribe, and Shiffrin add up to a rebuttal of the marketplace argument? Consider Melvin Nimmer, *Nimmer on Freedom of Speech* 1–12 (1984): "If acceptance of an idea in the competition of the market is not the 'best test' [what] is the alternative? It can only be acceptance of an idea by some individual or group narrower than that of the public at large. Thus, the alternative to competition in the market must be some form of elitism. It seems hardly necessary to enlarge on the dangers of that

e. For commentary explaining Milton's argument, suggesting that Milton's most important contributions to free speech lie elsewhere, see Vincent Blasi, *Milton's Areopagitica and the Modern First Amendment* (1995).

path." Is elitism the only alternative to the marketplace perspective? Is elitism always wrong?

(c) Evaluate the following hypothetical commentary: "Liberals have favored government intervention in the economic marketplace but pressed for laissez-faire in the intellectual marketplace. Conservatives have done the reverse. Liberals and conservatives have one thing in common: inconsistent positions."

(d) Does the marketplace argument overvalue truth? Consider Frederick Schauer, *Free Speech: A Philosophical Enquiry* 23 (1982). Government may seek to suppress opinions "because their expression is thought to impair the authority of a lawful and effective government, interfere with the administration of justice (such as publication of a defendant's criminal record in advance of a jury trial), cause offence, invade someone's privacy, or cause a decrease in public order. When these are the motives for suppression, the possibility of losing some truth is relevant but hardly dispositive. [In such circumstances] the argument from truth [is] not wholly to the point." Is Holmes persuasive when he maintains that before we can suppress opinion we must wait until "an immediate check is required to save the country"?

(e) Does the marketplace argument threaten first amendment values? Consider Stanley Ingber, *The Marketplace of Ideas: A Legitimizing Myth*, 1984 Duke L.J. 1, 4–5 "[C]ourts that invoke the marketplace model of the first amendment justify free expression because of the aggregate benefits to society, and not because an individual speaker receives a particular benefit. Courts that focus their concern on the audience rather than the speaker relegate free expression to an instrumental value, a means toward some other goal, rather than a value unto itself. Once free expression is viewed solely as an instrumental value, however, it is easier to allow government regulation of speech if society as a whole 'benefits' from a regulated system of expression."

(f) Does the marketplace argument slight other important free speech values? Consider Robert Wolff, *The Poverty of Liberalism* 18 (1968) "[I]t is not to assist the advance of knowledge that free debate is needed. Rather, it is in order to guarantee that every legitimate interest shall make itself known and felt in the political [process]. Justice, not truth, is the ideal served by liberty of speech." Compare Paul Chevigny, *Philosophy of Language and Free Expression*, 55 N.Y.U.L.Rev. 157 (1980); Mark Leitner, *Liberalism, Separation and Speech*, 1985 Wis.L.Rev. 79, 89–90 & 103–04. The standard starting place for discussion of free speech values continues to be Thomas Emerson, *The System of Freedom of Expression* 6–9 (1970).

(g) Would an emphasis on dissent be preferable to an emphasis on the marketplace metaphor? Consider Steven Shiffrin, *The First Amendment, Democracy, and Romance* (1990): "[A] commitment to sponsoring dissent does not require a belief that what emerges in the 'market' is usually right or that the 'market' is the best test of truth. Quite the contrary, the commitment to sponsor dissent assumes that societal pressures to conform are strong and that incentives to keep quiet are often great. If the marketplace metaphor encourages the view that an invisible hand or voluntaristic arrangements have guided us patiently, but slowly, to Burkean harmony, the commitment to sponsoring dissent encourages us to believe that the cozy arrangements of the status quo have settled on something less than the true or the just. If the marketplace metaphor encourages the view that conventions, habits, and traditions have emerged as our best sense of the truth from the rigorous testing ground of the marketplace of ideas, the commitment to sponsoring dissent encourages the view that conventions, habits, and traditions are compromises open to challenge. If the marketplace metaphor counsels us that the market's version of truth is more worthy of trust than any that the government might dictate, a commitment to sponsoring dissent counsels us to be suspicious of both. If the marketplace metaphor encourages a sloppy form of relativism (whatever has emerged in the marketplace is right for now), the commitment to sponsoring dissent emphasizes that truth is not decided in public opinion polls."

(h) For a powerful critique of marketplace models, see C. Edwin Baker, *Human Liberty and Freedom of Speech* 6–24, 37–46 (1989). For qualified defenses, see Kent Greenawalt, *Free Speech Justifications*, 89 Colum.L.Rev. 119, 130–41, 153–54 (1989); Frederick Schauer, *Language, Truth, and the First Amendment*, 64 Va.L.Rev. 263 (1978). For commentary on metaphors in general and the marketplace metaphor in particular, see Steven Winter, *Transcendental Nonsense, Metaphoric Reasoning, and the Cognitive Stakes for Law*, 137 U.Pa.L.Rev. 1105 (1989).

2. Why did *Abrams,* but not *Debs,* stir Holmes to speak seriously and eloquently about freedom of speech? One suggestion is that "Holmes was biding his time until the Court should have before it a conviction so clearly wrong as to let him speak out his deepest thoughts about the First Amendment" and that "the opportunity [came] eight months after Debs went to prison, in *Abrams,*" Chafee, supra, at 86. See generally David Bogen, *The Free Speech Metamorphosis of Mr. Justice Holmes*, 11 Hof.L.Rev. 97 (1982). For the view that the criticism of *Debs* in both the Ernst Freund article and in Learned Hand's correspondence with Holmes may have contributed to a marked change in Holmes' thinking about the first amendment between *Debs* and *Abrams,* see Douglas Ginsburg, *Afterword,* 40 U.Chi.L.Rev. 243 (1973). The literature on Holmes' first amendment views and their connection to his larger world view is substantial. See, e.g., G. Edward White, *Justice Oliver Wendell Holmes* 412–54 (1993); Yogal Rogat & James O'Fallon, *Mr. Justice Holmes: A Dissenting Opinion—The Speech Cases,* 36 Stan.L.Rev. 1349 (1984); David Rabban, *The Emergence of Modern First Amendment Doctrine,* 50 U.Chi.L.Rev. 1205 (1983). For further analysis of the Holmes-Hand correspondence, see Gerald Gunther, *Learned Hand and the Origins of Modern First Amendment Doctrine: Some Fragments of History,* 27 Stan.L.Rev. 719 (1975).

B. STATE SEDITION LAWS

The second main group of cases in the initial development of first amendment doctrine involved state "sedition laws" of two basic types: criminal anarchy laws, typified by the New York statute in *Gitlow,* infra, and criminal syndicalism laws similar to the California statute in *Whitney,* infra. Most states enacted anarchy and syndicalism statutes between 1917 and 1921, in response to World War I and the fear of Bolshevism that developed in its wake, but the first modern sedition law was passed by New York in 1902, soon after the assassination of President McKinley. The law, which prohibited not only actual or attempted assassinations or conspiracies to assassinate, but advocacy of anarchy as well, lay idle for nearly twenty years, until the *Gitlow* prosecution.

GITLOW v. NEW YORK, 268 U.S. 652, 45 S.Ct. 625, 69 L.Ed. 1138 (1925): Defendant was a member of the Left Wing Section of the Socialist Party and a member of its National Council, which adopted a "Left Wing Manifesto," condemning the dominant "moderate Socialism" for its recognition of the necessity of the democratic parliamentary state; advocating the necessity of accomplishing the "Communist Revolution" by a militant and "revolutionary Socialism" based on "the class struggle"; and urging the development of mass political strikes for the destruction of the parliamentary state. Defendant arranged for printing and distributing, through the mails and otherwise, 16,000 copies of the Manifesto in the Left Wing's official organ, The Revolutionary Age. There was no evidence of any effect from the publication and circulation of the Manifesto.

In sustaining a conviction under the New York "criminal anarchy" statutes, prohibiting the "advocacy, advising or teaching the duty, necessity or propriety of overthrowing or overturning organized government by force or violence" and the publication or distribution of such matter, the majority, per SANFORD, J., stated that for present purposes we may and do assume [a] that first amendment freedoms of expression "are among the fundamental personal rights and 'liberties' protected by the due process clause of the Fourteenth Amendment from impairment by the States," but ruled:

"By enacting the present statute the State has determined, through its legislative body, that utterances advocating the overthrow of organized government by force, violence and unlawful means, are so inimical to the general welfare and involve such danger of substantive evil that they may be penalized in the exercise of its police power. That determination must be given great weight. Every presumption is to be indulged in favor of the validity of the statute. And the case is to be considered 'in the light of the principle that the State is primarily the judge of regulations required in the interest of public safety and welfare'; and that its police 'statutes may only be declared unconstitutional where they are arbitrary or unreasonable attempts to exercise authority vested in the State in the public interest.' That utterances inciting to the overthrow of organized government by unlawful means, present a sufficient danger of substantive evil to bring their punishment within the range of legislative discretion, is clear. Such utterances, by their very nature, involve danger to the public peace and to the security of the State. They threaten breaches of the peace and ultimate revolution. And the immediate danger is none the less real and substantial, because the effect of a given utterance cannot be accurately foreseen. The State cannot reasonably be required to measure the danger from every such utterance in the nice balance of a jeweler's scale. A single revolutionary spark may kindle a fire that, smoldering for a time, may burst into a sweeping and destructive conflagration. It cannot be said that the State is acting arbitrarily or unreasonably when in the exercise of its judgment as to the measures necessary to protect the public peace and safety, it seeks to extinguish the spark without waiting until it has enkindled the flame or blazed into the conflagration. It cannot reasonably be required to defer the adoption of measures for its own peace and safety until the revolutionary utterances lead to actual disturbances of the public peace or imminent and immediate danger of its own destruction; but it may, in the exercise of its judgment, suppress the threatened danger in its incipiency.

"[It] is clear that the question in [this case] is entirely different from that involved in those cases where the statute merely prohibits certain acts involving the danger of substantive evil, without any reference to language itself, and it is

---

a. Although *Gitlow* is often cited for the proposition that first amendment freedoms apply to restrict state conduct, its language is dictum. Some would say the first case so holding is *Fiske v. Kansas*, 274 U.S. 380, 47 S.Ct. 655, 71 L.Ed. 1108 (1927) (no evidence to support criminal syndicalism conviction) even though no reference to the first amendment appears in the opinion. See Zechariah Chafee at 352. Perhaps the honor belongs to *Near v. Minnesota* (1931), p. 759 infra.

sought to apply its provisions to language used by the defendant for the purpose of bringing about the prohibited results. There, if it be contended that the statute cannot be applied to the language used by the defendant because of its protection by the freedom of speech or press, it must necessarily be found, as an original question, without any previous determination by the legislative body, whether the specific language used involved such likelihood of bringing about the substantive evil as to deprive it of the constitutional protection. In such cases it has been held that the general provisions of the statute may be constitutionally applied to the specific utterance of the defendant if its natural tendency and probable effect was to bring about the substantive evil which the legislative body might prevent. *Schenck; Debs.* And the general statement in the *Schenck* case that the 'question in every case is whether the words are used in such circumstances and are of such a nature as to create a clear and present danger that they will bring about the substantive evils,' [was] manifestly intended, as shown by the context, to apply only in cases of this class, and has no application to those like the present, where the legislative body itself has previously determined the danger of substantive evil arising from utterances of a specified character.''

HOLMES, J., joined by Brandeis, J., dissented: ''The general principle of free speech, it seems to me, must be taken to be included in the Fourteenth Amendment, in view of the scope that has been given to the word 'liberty' as there used, although perhaps it may be accepted with a somewhat larger latitude of interpretation than is allowed to Congress by the sweeping language that governs or ought to govern the laws of the United States. If I am right then I think that the criterion sanctioned by the full Court in *Schenck* applies. [It] is true that in my opinion this criterion was departed from in *Abrams,* but the convictions that I expressed in that case are too deep for it to be possible for me as yet to believe that it [has] settled the law. If what I think the correct test is applied it is manifest that there was no present danger of an attempt to overthrow the government by force on the part of the admittedly small minority who shared the defendant's views. It is said that this manifesto was more than a theory, that it was an incitement. Every idea is an incitement. It offers itself for belief and if believed it is acted on unless some other belief outweighs it or some failure of energy stifles the movement at its birth. The only difference between the expression of an opinion and an incitement in the narrower sense is the speaker's enthusiasm for the result. Eloquence may set fire to reason. But whatever may be thought of the redundant discourse before us it had no chance of starting a present conflagration.[b] If in the long run the beliefs expressed in proletarian

b. Consider Harry Kalven, *A Worthy Tradition* 156 (1988): ''This famous passage points up the ironies in tradition building. The basic problem of finding an accommodation between speech too close to action and censorship too close to criticism might, we have argued, have been tolerably solved by settling on 'incitement' as the key term. It is a term which came easily to the mind of Learned Hand. But for Holmes it does not resonate as it did for Hand. It strikes his ear as a loose, expansible term. At an inopportune moment in the history of free speech the great master of the common law turns poet: 'Every idea is an incitement.' There is of course a sense in which this is true and in which it is a 'scholastic subterfuge' to pretend that speech can be arrayed in firm categories. But the defendants' proposed instruction had offered a sense in which it was not true, in which incitement required advocacy of some definite and immediate acts of force. The weakness of the prosecution's case was not that the defendants' radicalism was not dangerous; it was that their manifesto was not concrete enough to be an incitement.

''Justice Holmes's dissent in *Gitlow,* like his *Abrams* peroration, is extraordinary prose to find in a judicial opinion, and I suspect it has contributed beyond measure to the charisma of the First Amendment. But it also carries the disturbing suggestion that the defendants' speech is to be protected precisely because it is harmless and unimportant. It smacks, as will the later protections of Jehovah's Witnesses, of a luxury civil liberty.''

dictatorship are destined to be accepted by the dominant forces of the community, the only meaning of free speech is that they should be given their chance and have their way.[c]

"If the publication of this document had been laid as an attempt to induce an uprising against government at once and not at some indefinite time in the future it would have presented a different question. The object would have been one with which the law might deal, subject to the doubt whether there was any danger that the publication could produce any result, or in other words, whether it was not futile and too remote from possible consequences. But the indictment alleges the publication and nothing more."

Notes and Questions

1. The statute in *Schenck* was not aimed directly at expression, but at conduct, i.e., certain actual or attempted interferences with the war effort. Thus, an analysis in terms of proximity between the words and the conduct prohibited (by a concededly valid law) seemed useful. But in *Gitlow* (and in *Dennis,* p. 651 infra) the statute was directed expressly against *advocacy* of a certain doctrine. Once the legislature *designates the point at which words became unlawful,* how helpful is the clear and present danger test? Is the question still how close words come to achieving certain consequences? In *Gitlow,* did Holmes "evade" the difficulty of applying an unmodified *Schenck* test to a different kind of problem? See Yogal Rogat, *Mr. Justice Holmes: Some Modern Views—The Judge as Spectator,* 31 U.Chi.L.Rev. 213, 217 (1964). See also Walter Berns, *Freedom, Virtue and the First Amendment* 63 (Gateway ed. 1965); Hans Linde, *"Clear and Present Danger" Reexamined,* 22 Stan.L.Rev. 1163, 1169–79 (1970).

2. Consider Linde, supra, at 1171: "Since New York's law itself defined the prohibited speech, the [*Gitlow*] Court could choose among three positions. It could (1) accept this legislative judgment of the harmful potential of the proscribed words, subject to conventional judicial review; (2) independently scrutinize the facts to see whether a 'danger,' as stated in *Schenck,* justified suppression of the particular expression; or (3) hold that by legislating directly against the words rather than the effects, the lawmaker had gone beyond the leeway left to trial and proof by the holding in *Schenck* and had made a law forbidden by the first amendment." Which course did the *Gitlow* majority choose? The dissenters? Which position should the Court have chosen?

––––––

Cases such as *Whitney,* infra, raise questions not only about freedom of speech, but also about the right of assembly. In turn, *Whitney* raises the issue of the existence and scope of a right not mentioned in the first amendment: freedom of association. Freedom of association is explored in Sec. 9 infra. Several of the cases which follow are primarily characterized as speech cases because the assemblies or associations at issue were designed for the purpose of organizing future speech activity.

c. But see Richard Posner, *Free Speech in an Economic Perspective,* 20 Suff.L.Rev. 1, 7 (1986): "If those beliefs are destined to prevail, free speech is irrelevant. Holmes is not describing a competitive market in ideas but a natural monopoly."

WHITNEY v. CALIFORNIA

274 U.S. 357, 47 S.Ct. 641, 71 L.Ed. 1095 (1927).

JUSTICE SANFORD delivered the opinion of the Court.

[Charlotte Anita Whitney was convicted of violating the 1919 Criminal Syndicalism Act of California whose pertinent provisions were]:

"Section 1. The term 'criminal syndicalism' as used in this act is hereby defined as any doctrine or precept advocating, teaching or aiding and abetting the commission of crime, sabotage (which word is hereby defined as meaning willful and malicious physical damage or injury to physical property), or unlawful acts of force and violence or unlawful methods of terrorism as a means of accomplishing a change in industrial ownership or control, or effecting any political change.

"Sec. 2. Any person who: * * * 4. Organizes or assists in organizing, or is or knowingly becomes a member of, any organization, society, group or assemblage of persons organized or assembled to advocate, teach or aid and abet criminal syndicalism; * * *

"Is guilty of a felony and punishable by imprisonment."

The first count of the information, on which the conviction was had, charged that on or about November 28, 1919, in Alameda County, the defendant, in violation of the Criminal Syndicalism Act, "did then and there unlawfully, willfully, wrongfully, deliberately and feloniously organize and assist in organizing, and was, is, and knowingly became a member of [a group] organized and assembled to advocate, teach, aid and abet criminal syndicalism." * * *

1. While it is not denied that the evidence warranted the jury in finding that the defendant became a member of and assisted in organizing the Communist Labor Party of California, and that this was organized to advocate, teach, aid or abet criminal syndicalism as defined by the Act, it is urged that the Act, as here construed and applied, deprived the defendant of her liberty without due process of law. [Defendant's] argument is, in effect, that the character of the state organization could not be forecast when she attended the convention; that she had no purpose of helping to create an instrument of terrorism and violence; that she "took part in formulating and presenting to the convention a resolution which, if adopted, would have committed the new organization to a legitimate policy of political reform by the use of the ballot"; that it was not until after the majority of the convention turned out to be "contrary minded, and other less temperate policies prevailed" that the convention could have taken on the character of criminal syndicalism; and that as this was done over her protest, her mere presence in the convention, however violent the opinions expressed therein, could not thereby become a crime. This contention [is in effect] an effort to review the weight of the evidence for the purpose of showing that the defendant did not join and assist in organizing the Communist Labor Party of California with a knowledge of its unlawful character and purpose. This question, which is foreclosed by the verdict of the jury, [is] one of fact merely which is not open to review in this Court, involving as it does no constitutional question whatever. * * *

[That a state] may punish those who abuse [freedom of speech] by utterances inimical to the public welfare, tending to incite to crime, disturb the public peace, or endanger the foundations of organized government and threaten its overthrow by unlawful means, is not open to question. [*Gitlow*].

The essence of the offense denounced by the Act is the combining with others in an association for the accomplishment of the desired ends through the advocacy and use of criminal and unlawful methods. It partakes of the nature of a criminal conspiracy. That such united and joint action involves even greater danger to the public peace and security than the isolated utterances and acts of individuals is clear. We cannot hold that, as here applied, the Act is an unreasonable or arbitrary exercise of the police power of the State, unwarrantably infringing any right of free speech, assembly or association, or that those persons are protected from punishment by the due process clause who abuse such rights by joining and furthering an organization thus menacing the peace and welfare of the State. * * *

Affirmed.

JUSTICE BRANDEIS (concurring.) * * *

The felony which the statute created is a crime very unlike the old felony of conspiracy or the old misdemeanor of unlawful assembly. The mere act of assisting in forming a society for teaching syndicalism, of becoming a member of it, or assembling with others for that purpose is given the dynamic quality of crime. There is guilt although the society may not contemplate immediate promulgation of the doctrine. Thus the accused is to be punished, not for attempt, incitement or conspiracy, but for a step in preparation, which, if it threatens the public order at all, does so only remotely. The novelty in the prohibition introduced is that the statute aims, not at the practice of criminal syndicalism, nor even directly at the preaching of it, but at association with those who propose to preach it.

Despite arguments to the contrary which had seemed to me persuasive, it is settled that the due process clause of the Fourteenth Amendment applies to matters of substantive law as well as to matters of procedure. Thus all fundamental rights comprised within the term liberty are protected by the federal Constitution from invasion by the states. The right of free speech, the right to teach and the right of assembly are, of course, fundamental rights. These may not be denied or abridged. But, although the rights of free speech and assembly are fundamental, they are not in their nature absolute. Their exercise is subject to restriction, if the particular restriction proposed is required in order to protect the state from destruction or from serious injury, political, economic or moral. That the necessity which is essential to a valid restriction does not exist unless speech would produce, or is intended to produce,[a] a clear and imminent danger of some substantive evil which the state constitutionally may seek to prevent has been settled. See *Schenck*.

[The] Legislature must obviously decide, in the first instance, whether a danger exists which calls for a particular protective measure. But where a statute is valid only in case certain conditions exist, the enactment of the statute cannot alone establish the facts which are essential to its validity. Prohibitory legislation has repeatedly been held invalid, because unnecessary, where the denial of liberty involved was that of engaging in a particular business. The powers of the courts to strike down an offending law are no less when the interests involved are not property rights, but the fundamental personal rights of free speech and assembly.

This Court has not yet fixed the standard by which to determine when a danger shall be deemed clear; how remote the danger may be and yet be deemed present; and what degree of evil shall be deemed sufficiently substantial to justify

a. Unless speech would produce, *or* is intended to produce? Unless speech *would produce* a clear and imminent danger, although the harm produced was neither advocated nor intended by the speaker? Unless the speaker *intended* to produce a clear and imminent danger, even under extrinsic conditions of actual harmlessness? Compare *Brandenburg v. Ohio*, p. 656 infra. See generally Linde, supra, at 1168–69, 1181, 1185.

resort to abridgment of free speech and assembly as the means of protection. To reach sound conclusions on these matters, we must bear in mind why a state is, ordinarily, denied the power to prohibit dissemination of social, economic and political doctrine which a vast majority of its citizens believes to be false and fraught with evil consequence.

Those who won our independence believed that the final end of the state was to make men free to develop their faculties, and that in its government the deliberative forces should prevail over the arbitrary. They valued liberty both as an end and as a means. They believed liberty to be the secret of happiness and courage to be the secret of liberty. They believed that freedom to think as you will and to speak as you think are means indispensable to the discovery and spread of political truth; [b] that without free speech and assembly discussion would be futile; that with them, discussion affords ordinarily adequate protection against the dissemination of noxious doctrine; [c] that the greatest menace to freedom is an inert people; that public discussion is a political duty; and that this should be a fundamental principle of the American government. They recognized the risks to which all human institutions are subject. But they knew that order cannot be secured merely through fear of punishment for its infraction; that it is hazardous to discourage thought, hope and imagination; that fear breeds repression; that repression breeds hate; that hate menaces stable government; that the path of safety lies in the opportunity to discuss freely supposed grievances and proposed remedies; and that the fitting remedy for evil counsels is good ones. Believing in the power of reason as applied through public discussion, they eschewed silence coerced by law—the argument of force in its worst form. Recognizing the occasional tyrannies of governing majorities, they amended the Constitution so that free speech and assembly should be guaranteed.

Fear of serious injury cannot alone justify suppression of free speech and assembly. Men feared witches and burnt women. It is the function of speech to free men from the bondage of irrational fears. To justify suppression of free speech there must be reasonable ground to fear that serious evil will result if free speech is practiced. There must be reasonable ground to believe that the danger apprehended is imminent. There must be reasonable ground to believe that the evil to be prevented is a serious one.[d] Every denunciation of existing law tends in some measure to increase the probability that there will be violation of it. Condonation of a breach enhances the probability. Expressions of approval add to the probability. Propagation of the criminal state of mind by teaching syndical-

b. Consider Vincent Blasi, *The First Amendment and the Ideal of Civic Courage,* 29 Wm. & Mary L.Rev. 653, 673–74 (1988): "This is as close as Brandeis gets to the claim that unregulated discussion yields truth. Notice that, in contrast to Holmes, Brandeis never tells us what is 'the best test of truth.' He never employs the metaphor of the market-place. He speaks only of 'political truth,' and he uses the phrase 'means indispensable' to link activities described in highly personal terms—'think as you will,' 'speak as you think'—with the collective social goal of 'political truth.' I think his emphasis in this passage is on the attitudes and atmosphere that must prevail if the ideals of self-government and happiness through courage are to be realized. Brandeis is sketching a good society here, but not, I think, an all-conquering dialectic."

c. Consider Blasi, supra, at 674–75: "It is noteworthy that Brandeis never speaks of noxious doctrine being refuted or eliminated or defeated. He talks of societal self-protection and the fitting remedy. He warns us not to underestimate the value of discussion, education, good counsels. To me, his point is that noxious doctrine is most likely to flourish when its opponents lack the personal qualities of wisdom, creativity, and confidence. And those qualities, he suggests, are best developed by discussion and education, not by lazy and impatient reliance on the coercive authority of the state."

d. Does this suffice, regardless of the intent of the speaker? Regardless of the nature of the words he uses?

ism increases it. Advocacy of lawbreaking heightens it still further. But even advocacy of violation, however reprehensible morally, is not a justification for denying free speech where the advocacy falls short of incitement and there is nothing to indicate that the advocacy would be immediately acted on. The wide difference between advocacy and incitement, between preparation and attempt, between assembling and conspiracy, must be borne in mind. In order to support a finding of clear and present danger it must be shown either that immediate serious violence was to be expected or was advocated,[e] or that the past conduct furnished reason to believe that such advocacy was then contemplated.

Those who won our independence by revolution were not cowards. They did not fear political change. They did not exalt order at the cost of liberty. To courageous, self-reliant men, with confidence in the power of free and fearless reasoning applied through the processes of popular government, no danger flowing from speech can be deemed clear and present, unless the incidence of the evil apprehended is so imminent that it may befall before there is opportunity for full discussion. If there be time to expose through discussion the falsehood and fallacies, to avert the evil by the processes of education, the remedy to be applied is more speech, not enforced silence.[f] Only an emergency can justify repression. Such must be the rule if authority is to be reconciled with freedom. Such, in my opinion, is the command of the Constitution. It is therefore always open to Americans to challenge a law abridging free speech and assembly by showing that there was no emergency justifying it.

Moreover, even imminent danger cannot justify resort to prohibition of these functions essential to effective democracy, unless the evil apprehended is relatively serious. Prohibition of free speech and assembly is a measure so stringent that it would be inappropriate as the means for averting a relatively trivial harm to society. A police measure may be unconstitutional merely because the remedy, although effective as means of protection, is unduly harsh or oppressive. Thus, a state might, in the exercise of its police power, make any trespass upon the land of another a crime, regardless of the results or of the intent or purpose of the trespasser. It might, also, punish an attempt, a conspiracy, or an incitement to commit the trespass. But it is hardly conceivable that this court would hold constitutional a statute which punished as a felony the mere voluntary assembly with a society formed to teach that pedestrians had the moral right to cross uninclosed, unposted, waste lands and to advocate their doing so, even if there was imminent danger that advocacy would lead to a trespass. The fact that speech is likely to result in some violence or in destruction of property is not enough to justify its suppression. There must be the probability of serious injury to the State.[g] Among free men, the deterrents ordinarily to be applied to prevent crime are education and punishment for violations of the law, not abridgement of the rights of free speech and assembly.

e. What if violence is advocated, but the advocacy is utterly ineffectual? What if the speaker neither desires nor advocates violence, but, under the circumstances the speech nevertheless is "expected" to produce violence?

f. But see Richard Delgado & Jean Stefanic, *Images of the Outsider in American Law and Culture: Can Free Expression Remedy Systematic Social Ills?*, 77 Corn.L.Rev. 1258 (1992); Lawrence Lessig, *The Regulation of Social Meaning*, 62 U.Chi.L.Rev. 943, 1036–39 (1995).

g. But see Robert Bork, *Neutral Principles and Some First Amendment Problems*, 47 Ind. L.J. 1, 34 (1971): "It is difficult to see how a constitutional court could properly draw the distinction proposed. Brandeis offered no analysis to show that advocacy of law violation merited protection by the Court. Worse, the criterion he advanced is the importance, in the judge's eye, of the law whose violation is urged."

* * * Whenever the fundamental rights of free speech and assembly are alleged to have been invaded, it must remain open to a defendant to present the issue whether there actually did exist at the time a clear danger, whether the danger, if any, was imminent, and whether the evil apprehended was one so substantial as to justify the stringent restriction interposed by the Legislature. The legislative declaration, like the fact that the statute was passed and was sustained by the highest court of the State, creates merely a rebuttable presumption that these conditions have been satisfied.

Whether in 1919, when Miss Whitney did the things complained of, there was in California such clear and present danger of serious evil, might have been made the important issue in the case. She might have required that the issue be determined either by the court or the jury. She claimed below that the statute as applied to her violated the federal Constitution; but she did not claim that it was void because there was no clear and present danger of serious evil, nor did she request that the existence of these conditions of a valid measure thus restricting the rights of free speech and assembly be passed upon by the court or a jury. On the other hand, there was evidence on which the court or jury might have found that such danger existed. I am unable to assent to the suggestion in the opinion of the court that assembling with a political party, formed to advocate the desirability of a proletarian revolution by mass action at some date necessarily far in the future, is not a right within the protection of the Fourteenth Amendment. In the present case, however, there was other testimony which tended to establish the existence of a conspiracy, on the part of members of the International Workers of the World, to commit present serious crimes, and likewise to show that such a conspiracy would be furthered by the activity of the society of which Miss Whitney was a member. Under these circumstances the judgment of the State court cannot be disturbed. * * *

JUSTICE HOLMES joins in this opinion.

Notes and Questions

1. *"They valued liberty both as an end and as a means."* Should recognition of the value of liberty [h] as an end augment the marketplace perspective or replace it? Compare C. Edwin Baker, *Scope of the First Amendment Freedom of Speech,*

---

h. For literature contending that the related value of autonomy should play a central role in most (or all) aspects of first amendment law, see C. Edwin Baker, *Human Liberty and Freedom of Speech* 47–51 (1989); David Richards, *Toleration and the Constitution* 165–77 (1986); Robert Post, *Constitutional Domains* 268–331 (1995); Charles Fried, *The New First Amendment Jurisprudence: A Threat to Liberty,* 59 U.Chi.L.Rev. 225, 233–37 (1992); Robert Post, *Managing Deliberation: The Quandary of Democratic Dialogue,* 103 Ethics 654, 664–66 (1993); Robert Post, *Racist Speech, Democracy, and the First Amendment,* 32 Wm. & Mary L.Rev. 267, 279–85 (1991); Thomas Scanlon, *A Theory of Freedom of Expression,* 1 Phil. & Pub.Aff. 204, 215–22 (1972); David Strauss, *Persuasion, Autonomy, and Freedom of Expression,* 91 Colum.L.Rev. 334, 353–71 (1991).

For discussion of the value of autonomy and its connection to the problem of advocacy of illegal action, compare Scanlon, supra, with Thomas Scanlon, *Freedom of Expression and*

Categories of Expression, 40 U.Pitt.L.Rev. 519 (1979). For commentary on the differences between speaker and listener autonomy, see Cass Sunstein, *Democracy and the Problem of Free Speech* 139–44 (1993); C. Edwin Baker, *Turner Broadcasting: Content–Based Regulation of Persons and Presses,* 1994 Sup.Ct.Rev. 57, 72–80. For the contention that the literature confuses philosophical assumptions of autonomy and empirical claims of autonomy and for doubts about the resolving power of either conception, see Richard Fallon, *Two Senses of Autonomy,* 46 Stan.L.Rev. 875 (1994). For the suggestion that the value of autonomy depends upon open and rich public discussion, see Sunstein, supra. For the contention that the value of autonomy should be subservient to open and rich discussion, see Owen Fiss, *State Activism and State Censorship,* 100 Yale L.J. 2087 (1991). Owen Fiss, *Why the State,* 100 Harv. L.Rev. 781 (1987); Owen Fiss, *Free Speech and Social Structure,* 71 Iowa L.Rev. 1405 (1986).

25 U.C.L.A.L.Rev. 964 (1978) (liberty theory should replace marketplace theory) with Martin Redish, *The Value of Free Speech,* 130 U.Pa.L.Rev. 591 (1982) (self-realization should be regarded as the first amendment's exclusive value) and Rodney Smolla, *Free Speech in an Open Society* 5 (1992) ("There is no logical reason, however, why the preferred position of freedom of speech might not be buttressed by multiple rationales. Acceptance of one rationale need not bump another from the list, as if this were First Amendment musical chairs"); Steven Shiffrin, *The First Amendment and Economic Regulation: Away From a General Theory of the First Amendment,* 78 Nw.U.L.Rev. 1212 (1983) (many values including liberty and self-realization underpin the first amendment; single valued orientations are reductionist). But see Frederick Schauer, *Must Speech Be Special,* 78 Nw.U.L.Rev. 1284 (1983) (neither liberty nor self-realization should play *any* role in first amendment theory). For original discussions of free speech values, see Joshua Cohen, *Freedom of Expression,* 19 Phil. & Pub.Aff. 207 (1993); Joseph Raz, *Free Expression and Personal Identification,* 11 Oxford J.Legal St. 311 (1991).

2. *Brandeis and Republicanism.* Consider Pnina Lahav, *Holmes and Brandeis: Libertarian and Republican Justifications for Free Speech,* 4 J.L. & Pol. 451, 460–461 (1987): "[I]n his *Whitney* concurrence, Brandeis tells us, that in the American polity, 'the deliberative forces should prevail over the arbitrary,' that 'public discussion is a political duty,' and that 'the occasional tyranny of governing majorities' should be thwarted. This is radically different from the notion that individuals are free to remain aloof from politics if they so choose (a notion espoused by Holmes), and from the principle of the separation of the state from society. Implied here is the notion of civic virtue—the duty to participate in politics, the importance of deliberation, and the notion that the end of the state is not neutrality but active assistance in providing conditions of freedom which in turn are the 'secret of happiness.' One may even speculate that Brandeis, the progressive leader, believed that the final end of the state was the happiness of mankind.

"These ingredients of the Brandeis position in *Whitney* resonate with republican theory. The theory rests on two central themes: the idea of civic virtue and the idea that the end of politics (or the state) is the common good, which in turn is more than the sum of individual wills. Thus, the state is not separated from society, but rather is committed to the public good, and to a substantive notion of public morality. The members of society are not individuals encased in their autonomous zones, but rather social beings who recognize that they are an integral part of the society. This organic sense of belonging implicitly rejects the notion of combat zones. The republic and its citizens care for the welfare of all. Correctly understood, Brandeis' concurrence in *Whitney* is more than a justification from self-fulfillment or from self-rule. It is a justification from civic virtue." [i]

3. *Scope of the opinions.* Did Brandeis, J., simply reaffirm the clear and present danger test? Significantly clarify it? Significantly change it? Did Sanford, J., modify the position he had taken in *Gitlow?* Did he at least make it plain in *Whitney* that some state sedition convictions may be set aside under the first and fourteenth amendments? See Chafee, supra, at 351.

4. Ten years after *Whitney, DeJonge v. Oregon,* 299 U.S. 353, 57 S.Ct. 255, 81 L.Ed. 278 (1937) held that mere participation in a meeting called by the

i. For further background comparing the views of Brandeis and Holmes, JJ., see Blasi, fn. b supra; Robert Cover, *The Left, The Right* *and the First Amendment: 1919–28,* 40 Md. L.Rev. 349 (1981).

Communist party could not be made a crime. The right of peaceable assembly was declared to be "cognate to those of free speech and free press and is equally fundamental."

C. COMMUNISM AND ILLEGAL ADVOCACY

Kent Greenawalt has well described the pattern of decisions for much of the period between *Whitney* and *Dennis* infra: "[T]he clear and present danger formula emerged as the applicable standard not only for the kinds of issues with respect to which it originated but also for a wide variety of other First Amendment problems. If the Court was not always very clear about the relevance of that formula to those different problems, its use of the test, and its employment of ancillary doctrines, did evince a growing disposition to protect expression." *Speech and Crime,* 1980 Am.B.Found.Res.J. 645, 706. By 1951, however, anti-communist sentiment was a powerful theme in American politics. The Soviet Union had detonated a nuclear weapon; communists had firm control of the Chinese mainland; the Korean War had reached a stalemate; Alger Hiss had been convicted of perjury in congressional testimony concerning alleged spying activities for the Soviet Union while he was a State Department official; and Senator Joseph McCarthy of Wisconsin had created a national sensation by accusations that many "card carrying Communists" held important State Department jobs. In this context, the top leaders of the American Communist Party asked the Court to reverse their criminal conspiracy convictions.

DENNIS v. UNITED STATES

341 U.S. 494, 71 S.Ct. 857, 95 L.Ed. 1137 (1951).

CHIEF JUSTICE VINSON announced the judgment of the Court and an opinion in which JUSTICE REED, JUSTICE BURTON and JUSTICE MINTON join.

Petitioners were indicted in July, 1948, for violation of the conspiracy provisions of the Smith Act during the period of April, 1945, to July, 1948. * * * A verdict of guilty as to all the petitioners was [affirmed by the Second Circuit]. We granted certiorari, limited to the following two questions: (1) Whether either § 2 or § 3 of the Smith Act, inherently or as construed and applied in the instant case, violates the First Amendment and other provisions of the Bill of Rights; (2) whether either § 2 or § 3 of the Act, inherently or as construed and applied in the instant case, violates the First and Fifth Amendments, because of indefiniteness.

Sections 2 and 3 of the Smith Act provide as follows:

"Sec. 2.

"(a) It shall be unlawful for any person—

"(1) to knowingly or willfully advocate, abet, advise, or teach the duty, necessity, desirability, or propriety of overthrowing or destroying any government in the United States by force or violence, or by the assassination of any officer of any such government; * * *

"Sec. 3. It shall be unlawful for any person to attempt to commit, or to conspire to commit, any of the acts prohibited by the provisions [of] this title."

The indictment charged the petitioners with wilfully and knowingly conspiring (1) to organize as the Communist Party of the United States of America a society, group and assembly of persons who teach and advocate the overthrow and destruction of the Government of the United States by force and violence, and (2) knowingly and wilfully to advocate and teach the duty and necessity of overthrowing and destroying the Government of the United States by force and violence. The indictment further alleged that § 2 of the Smith Act proscribes these acts and that any conspiracy to take such action is a violation of § 3 of the Act.

The trial of the case extended over nine months, six of which were devoted to the taking of evidence, resulting in a record of 16,000 pages. Our limited grant of the writ of certiorari has removed from our consideration any question as to the sufficiency of the evidence to support the jury's determination that petitioners are guilty of the offense charged. Whether on this record petitioners did in fact advocate the overthrow of the Government by force and violence is not before us, and we must base any discussion of this point upon the conclusions stated in the opinion of the Court of Appeals, which treated the issue in great detail [and] held that the record supports the following broad conclusions: [that] the Communist Party is a highly disciplined organization, adept at infiltration into strategic positions, use of aliases, and double-meaning language; that the Party is rigidly controlled; that Communists, unlike other political parties, tolerate no dissension from the policy laid down by the guiding [forces]; that the literature of the Party and the statements and activities of its leaders, petitioners here, advocate, and the general goal of the Party was, during the period in question, to achieve a successful overthrow of the existing order by force and violence. * * *

The obvious purpose of the statute is to protect existing Government, not from change by peaceable, lawful and constitutional means, but from change by violence, revolution and terrorism. That it is within the *power* of the Congress to protect the Government of the United States from armed rebellion is a proposition which requires little discussion. Whatever theoretical merit there may be to the argument that there is a "right" to rebellion against dictatorial governments is without force where the existing structure of the government provides for peaceful and orderly change. We reject any principle of governmental helplessness in the face of preparation for revolution, which principle, carried to its logical conclusion, must lead to anarchy. No one could conceive that it is not within the power of Congress to prohibit acts intended to overthrow the Government by force and violence. The question with which we are concerned here is not whether Congress has such *power,* but whether the *means* which it has employed conflict with the First and Fifth Amendments to the Constitution.

One of the bases for the contention that the means which Congress has employed are invalid takes the form of an attack on the face of the statute on the grounds that by its terms it prohibits academic discussion of the merits of Marxism-Leninism, that it stifles ideas and is contrary to all concepts of a free speech and a free press. [This] is a federal statute which we must interpret as well as judge. Herein lies the fallacy of reliance upon the manner in which this Court has treated judgments of state courts. Where the statute as construed by the state court transgressed the First Amendment, we could not but invalidate the judgments of conviction.

The very language of the Smith Act negates the interpretation which petitioners would have us impose on that Act. It is directed at advocacy, not discussion. Thus, the trial judge properly charged the jury that they could not convict if they found that petitioners did "no more than pursue peaceful studies and discussions or teaching and advocacy in the realm of ideas." * * * Congress did not intend to eradicate the free discussion of political theories, to destroy the traditional rights of Americans to discuss and evaluate ideas without fear of governmental sanction. * * *

But although the statute is not directed at the hypothetical cases which petitioners have conjured, its application in this case has resulted in convictions for the teaching and advocacy of the overthrow of the Government by force and violence, which, even though coupled with the intent to accomplish that overthrow, contains an element of speech. For this reason, we must pay special heed to the demands of the First Amendment marking out the boundaries of speech.

[T]he basis of the First Amendment is the hypothesis that speech can rebut speech, propaganda will answer propaganda, free debate of ideas will result in the wisest governmental policies. [An] analysis of the leading cases in this Court which have involved direct limitations on speech, however, will demonstrate that both the majority of the Court and the dissenters in particular cases have recognized that this is not an unlimited, unqualified right, but that the societal value of speech must, on occasion, be subordinated to other values and considerations. * * *

Although no case subsequent to *Whitney* and *Gitlow* has expressly overruled the majority opinions in those cases, there is little doubt that subsequent opinions have inclined toward the Holmes-Brandeis rationale. * * *

In this case we are squarely presented with the application of the "clear and present danger" test, and must decide what that phrase imports.[a] We first note that many of the cases in which this Court has reversed convictions by use of this or similar tests have been based on the fact that the interest which the State was attempting to protect was itself too insubstantial to warrant restriction of speech. * * * Overthrow of the Government by force and violence is certainly a substantial enough interest for the Government to limit speech. Indeed, this is the ultimate value of any society, for if a society cannot protect its very structure from armed internal attack, it must follow that no subordinate value can be protected. If, then, this interest may be protected, the literal problem which is presented is what has been meant by the use of the phrase "clear and present danger" of the utterances bringing about the evil within the power of Congress to punish.

Obviously, the words cannot mean that before the Government may act, it must wait until the putsch is about to be executed, the plans have been laid and the signal is awaited. If Government is aware that a group aiming at its overthrow is attempting to indoctrinate its members and to commit them to a course whereby they will strike when the leaders feel the circumstances permit, action by the Government is required. The argument that there is no need for Government to concern itself, for Government is strong, it possesses ample powers to put down a rebellion, it may defeat the revolution with ease needs no answer. For that is not the question. Certainly an attempt to overthrow the Government by force, even though doomed from the outset because of inadequate numbers or power of the revolutionists, is a sufficient evil for Congress to prevent. The damage which such attempts create both physically and politically to a nation makes it impossible to measure the validity in terms of the probability of success, or the immediacy of a successful attempt. In the instant case the trial judge charged the jury that they could not convict unless they found that petitioners intended to overthrow the Government "as speedily as circumstances would permit." This does not mean, and could not properly mean, that they would not strike until there was certainty of success. What was meant was that the

a. Consider Harry Kalven, *A Worthy Tradition* 190–91 (1988): "The [Vinson opinion] acknowledges clear and present danger as the constitutional measure of free speech, but in the process, to meet the political exigencies of the case, it officially adjusts the test, giving it the kiss of death."

revolutionists would strike when they thought the time was ripe. We must therefore reject the contention that success or probability of success is the criterion.

The situation with which Justices Holmes and Brandeis were concerned in *Gitlow* was a comparatively isolated event, bearing little relation in their minds to any substantial threat to the safety of the community. [They] were not confronted with any situation comparable to the instant one—the development of an apparatus designed and dedicated to the overthrow of the Government, in the context of world crisis after crisis.

Chief Judge Learned Hand, writing for the majority below, interpreted the phrase as follows: "In each case [courts] must ask whether the gravity of the 'evil,' discounted by its improbability, justifies such invasion of free speech as is necessary to avoid the danger." We adopt this statement of the rule. As articulated by Chief Judge Hand, it is as succinct and inclusive as any other we might devise at this time. * * *

Likewise, we are in accord with the court below, which affirmed the trial court's finding that the requisite danger existed. The mere fact that from the period 1945 to 1948 petitioners' activities did not result in an attempt to overthrow the Government by force and violence is of course no answer to the fact that there was a group that was ready to make the attempt. The formation by petitioners of such a highly organized conspiracy, with rigidly disciplined members subject to call when the leaders, these petitioners, felt that the time had come for action, coupled with the inflammable nature of world conditions, similar uprisings in other countries, and the touch-and-go nature of our relations with countries with whom petitioners were in the very least ideologically attuned, convince us that their convictions were justified on this score. And this analysis disposes of the contention that a conspiracy to advocate, as distinguished from the advocacy itself, cannot be constitutionally restrained, because it comprises only the preparation. It is the existence of the conspiracy which creates the danger. * * *

Although we have concluded that the finding that there was a sufficient danger to warrant the application of the statute was justified on the merits, there remains the problem of whether the trial judge's treatment of the issue was correct. He charged the jury, in relevant part, as follows:

"In further construction and interpretation of the statute I charge you that it is not the abstract doctrine of overthrowing or destroying organized government by unlawful means which is denounced by this law, but the teaching and advocacy of action for the accomplishment of that purpose, by language reasonably and ordinarily calculated to incite persons to such action. Accordingly, you cannot find the defendants or any of them guilty of the crime charged unless you are satisfied beyond a reasonable doubt that they conspired to organize a society, group and assembly of persons who teach and advocate the overthrow or destruction of the Government of the United States by force and violence and to advocate and teach the duty and necessity of overthrowing or destroying the Government of the United States by force and violence, with the intent that such teaching and advocacy be of a rule or principle of action and by language reasonably and ordinarily calculated to incite persons to such action, all with the intent to cause the overthrow or destruction of the Government of the United States by force and violence as speedily as circumstances would permit. * * *

"If you are satisfied that the evidence establishes beyond a reasonable doubt that the defendants, or any of them, are guilty of a violation of the statute, as I have interpreted it to you, I find as matter of law that there is sufficient danger of a substantive evil that the Congress has a right to prevent to justify the application of the statute under the First Amendment of the Constitution. This is matter of law about which you have no concern. * * * "

It is thus clear that he reserved the question of the existence of the danger for his own determination, and the question becomes whether the issue is of such a nature that it should have been submitted to the jury.

[When] facts are found that establish the violation of a statute, the protection against conviction afforded by the First Amendment is a matter of law. The doctrine that there must be a clear and present danger of a substantive evil that Congress has a right to prevent is a judicial rule to be applied as a matter of law by the courts. The guilt is established by proof of facts. Whether the First Amendment protects the activity which constitutes the violation of the statute must depend upon a judicial determination of the scope of the First Amendment applied to the circumstances of the case.

[In] *Schenck* this Court itself examined the record to find whether the requisite danger appeared, and the issue was not submitted to a jury. And in every later case in which the Court has measured the validity of a statute by the "clear and present danger" test, that determination has been by the court, the question of the danger not being submitted to the jury. * * * Petitioners intended to overthrow the Government of the United States as speedily as the circumstances would permit. Their conspiracy to organize the Communist Party and to teach and advocate the overthrow of the Government of the United States by force and violence created a "clear and present danger" of an attempt to overthrow the Government by force and violence. They were properly and constitutionally convicted * * *.

Affirmed.

JUSTICE CLARK took no part in the consideration or decision of this case.

JUSTICE FRANKFURTER, concurring in affirmance of the judgment.

[The] demands of free speech in a democratic society as well as the interest in national security are better served by candid and informed weighing of the competing interests, within the confines of the judicial process, than by announcing dogmas too inflexible for the non-Euclidian problems to be solved.

But how are competing interests to be assessed? Since they are not subject to quantitative ascertainment, the issue necessarily resolves itself into asking, who is to make the adjustment?—who is to balance the relevant factors and ascertain which interest is in the circumstances to prevail? Full responsibility for the choice cannot be given to the courts. Courts are not representative bodies. They are not designed to be a good reflex of a democratic society. Their judgment is best informed, and therefore most dependable, within narrow limits. Their essential quality is detachment, founded on independence. History teaches that the independence of the judiciary is jeopardized when courts become embroiled in the passions of the day and assume primary responsibility in choosing between competing political, economic and social pressures.

Primary responsibility for adjusting the interests which compete in the situation before us of necessity belongs to the Congress. [We] are to set aside the judgment of those whose duty it is to legislate only if there is no reasonable basis for [it]. Free-speech cases are not an exception to the principle that we are not legislators, that direct policy-making is not our province. How best to reconcile competing interests is the business of legislatures, and the balance they strike is a judgment not to be displaced by ours, but to be respected unless outside the pale of fair judgment. [A] survey of the relevant decisions indicates that the results which we have reached are on the whole those that would ensue from careful weighing of conflicting interests. The complex issues presented by regulation of speech in public places by picketing, and by legislation prohibiting advocacy of crime have been resolved by scrutiny of many factors besides the imminence and gravity of the evil threatened. The matter has been well summarized by a reflective student of the Court's work. "The truth is that the clear-and-present-danger test is an oversimplified judgment unless it takes account also of a number of other factors: the relative seriousness of the danger in comparison with the value of the occasion for speech or political activity; the availability of more moderate controls than those which the state has imposed; and perhaps the specific intent with which the speech or activity is launched. No matter how rapidly we utter the phrase 'clear and present danger,' or how closely we hyphenate the words, they are not a substitute for the weighing of values. They tend to convey a delusion of certitude when what is most certain is the complexity of the strands in the web of freedoms which the judge must disentangle." Paul Freund, *On Understanding the Supreme Court* 27–28 [1949]. * * *

To make validity of legislation depend on judicial reading of events still in the womb of time—a forecast, that is, of the outcome of forces at best appreciated only with knowledge of the topmost secrets of nations—is to charge the judiciary with duties beyond its equipment. * * *

Even when moving strictly within the limits of constitutional adjudication, judges are concerned with issues that may be said to involve vital finalities. The too easy transition from disapproval of what is undesirable to condemnation as unconstitutional, has led some of the wisest judges to question the wisdom of our scheme in lodging such authority in courts. But it is relevant to remind that in sustaining the power of Congress in a case like this nothing irrevocable is done. The democratic process at all events is not impaired or restricted. Power and responsibility remain with the people and immediately with their representation. All the Court says is that Congress was not forbidden by the Constitution to pass this enactment and that a prosecution under it may be brought against a conspiracy such as the one before us. * * *

JUSTICE JACKSON, concurring.

[E]ither by accident or design, the Communist stratagem outwits the antianarchist pattern of statute aimed against "overthrow by force and violence" if qualified by the doctrine that only "clear and present danger" of accomplishing that result will sustain the prosecution.

The "clear and present danger" test was an innovation by Mr. Justice Holmes in the *Schenck* case, reiterated and refined by him and Mr. Justice Brandeis in later cases, all arising before the era of World War II revealed the subtlety and efficacy of modernized revolutionary techniques used by totalitarian parties. In those cases, they were faced with convictions under so-called criminal syndicalism statutes aimed at anarchists but which, loosely construed, had been applied to punish socialism, pacifism, and left-wing ideologies, the charges often resting on farfetched inferences which, if true, would establish only technical or trivial violations. They proposed "clear and present danger" as a test for the sufficiency of evidence in particular cases.

I would save it, unmodified, for application as a "rule of reason" in the kind of case for which it was devised. When the issue is criminality of a hotheaded speech on a street corner, or circulation of a few incendiary pamphlets, or parading by some zealots behind a red flag, or refusal of a handful of school children to salute our flag, it is not beyond the capacity of the judicial process to gather, comprehend, and weigh the necessary materials for decision whether it is a clear and present danger of substantive evil or a harmless letting off of steam. It is not a prophecy, for the danger in such cases has matured by the time of trial or it was never present. The test applies and has meaning where a conviction is sought to be based on a speech or writing which does not directly or explicitly advocate a crime but to which such tendency is sought to be attributed by construction or by implication from external circumstances. The formula in such cases favors freedoms that are vital to our society, and, even if sometimes applied too generously, the consequences cannot be grave. But its recent expansion has extended, in particular to Communists, unprecedented immunities. Unless we are to hold our Government captive in a judge-made verbal trap, we must approach the problem of a well-organized, nation-wide conspiracy, such as I have described, as realistically as our predecessors faced the trivialities that were being prosecuted until they were checked with a rule of reason.

I think reason is lacking for applying that test to this case.

If we must decide that this Act and its application are constitutional only if we are convinced that petitioner's conduct creates a "clear and present danger" of violent overthrow, we must appraise imponderables, including international and national phenomena which baffle the best informed foreign offices and our most experienced politicians. We would have to foresee and predict the effectiveness of Communist propaganda, opportunities for infiltration, whether, and when, a time will come that they consider propitious for action, and whether and how fast our existing government will deteriorate. And we would have to speculate as to whether an approaching Communist coup would not be anticipated by a nationalistic fascist movement. No doctrine can be sound whose application requires us to make a prophecy of that sort in the guise of a legal decision. The judicial process simply is not adequate to a trial of such far-flung issues. The answers given would reflect our own political predilections and nothing more.

The authors of the clear and present danger test never applied it to a case like this, nor would I. If applied as it is proposed here, it means that the Communist plotting is protected during its period of incubation; its preliminary stages of organization and preparation are immune from the law; the Government can move only after imminent action is manifest, when it would, of course, be too late.

The highest degree of constitutional protection is due to the individual acting without conspiracy. But even an individual cannot claim that the Constitution protects him in advocating or teaching overthrow of government by force or violence. I should suppose no one would doubt that Congress has power to make such attempted overthrow a crime. But the contention is that one has the constitutional right to work up a public desire and will to do what it is a crime to attempt. I think direct incitement by speech or writing can be made a crime, and I think there can be a conviction without also proving that the odds favored its success by 99 to 1, or some other extremely high ratio. * * *

What really is under review here is a conviction of conspiracy, after a trial for conspiracy, on an indictment charging conspiracy, brought under a statute outlawing conspiracy. With due respect to my colleagues, they seem to me to discuss anything under the sun except the law of conspiracy. * * *

The Constitution does not make conspiracy a civil right. [Although] I consider criminal conspiracy a dragnet device capable of perversion into an instrument of injustice in the hands of a partisan or complacent judiciary, it has an established place in our system of law, and no reason appears for applying it only to concerted action claimed to disturb interstate commerce and withholding it from those claimed to undermine our whole Government. * * *

I do not suggest that Congress could punish conspiracy to advocate something, the doing of which it may not punish. Advocacy or exposition of the doctrine of communal property ownership, or any political philosophy unassociated with advocacy of its imposition by force or seizure of government by unlawful means could not be reached through conspiracy prosecution. But it is not forbidden to put down force or violence, it is not forbidden to punish its teaching or advocacy, and the end being punishable, there is no doubt of the power to punish conspiracy for the purpose. * * *

JUSTICE BLACK, dissenting. * * *

So long as this Court exercises the power of judicial review of legislation, I cannot agree that the First Amendment permits us to sustain laws suppressing freedom of speech and press on the basis of Congress' or our own notions of mere "reasonableness." Such a doctrine waters down the First Amendment so that it amounts to little more than an admonition to Congress. The Amendment as so construed is not likely to protect any but those "safe" or orthodox views which rarely need its protection. I must also express my objection to the holding because, as Mr. Justice Douglas' dissent shows, it sanctions the determination of a crucial issue of fact by the judge rather than by the jury. * * *

Public opinion being what it now is, few will protest the conviction of these Communist petitioners. There is hope, however, that in calmer times, when present pressures, passions and fears subside, this or some later Court will restore the First Amendment liberties to the high preferred place where they belong in a free society.

JUSTICE DOUGLAS, dissenting.

If this were a case where those who claimed protection under the First Amendment were teaching the techniques of sabotage, the assassination of the President, the filching of documents from public files, the planting of bombs, the art of street warfare, and the like, I would have no doubts. The freedom to speak is not absolute; the teaching of methods of terror and other seditious conduct should be beyond the pale along with obscenity and immorality. This case was argued as if those were the facts. The argument imported much seditious conduct into the record. That is easy and it has popular appeal, for the activities of Communists in plotting and scheming against the free world are common knowledge. But the fact is that no such evidence was introduced at the trial. There is a statute which makes a seditious conspiracy unlawful. Petitioners, however, were not charged with a "conspiracy to overthrow" the Government. They were charged with a conspiracy to form a party and groups and assemblies of people who teach and advocate the overthrow of our Government by force or violence and with a conspiracy to advocate and teach its overthrow by force and violence. It may well be that indoctrination in the techniques of terror to destroy the Government would be indictable under either statute. But the teaching which is condemned here is of a different character.

So far as the present record is concerned, what petitioners did was to organize people to teach and themselves teach the Marxist-Leninist doctrine contained chiefly in four books: *Foundations of Leninism* by Stalin (1924); *The Communist Manifesto* by Marx and Engels (1848); *State and Revolution* by Lenin (1917); *History of the Communist Party of the Soviet Union* (B.) (1939).

Those books are to Soviet Communism what *Mein Kampf* was to Nazism. If they are understood, the ugliness of Communism is revealed, its deceit and cunning are exposed, the nature of its activities becomes apparent, and the chances of its success less likely. That is not, of course, the reason why petitioners chose these books for their classrooms. They are fervent Communists to whom these volumes are gospel. They preached the creed with the hope that some day it would be acted upon.

The opinion of the Court does not outlaw these texts nor condemn them to the fire, as the Communists do literature offensive to their creed. But if the books themselves are not outlawed, if they can lawfully remain on library shelves, by what reasoning does their use in a classroom become a crime? It would not be a crime under the Act to introduce these books to a class, though that would be teaching what the creed of violent overthrow of the Government is. The Act, as construed, requires the element of intent—that those who teach the creed believe in it. The crime then depends not on what is taught but on who the teacher is. That is to make freedom of speech turn not on *what is said,* but on the *intent* with which it is said. Once we start down that road we enter territory dangerous to the liberties of every citizen. * * *

The vice of treating speech as the equivalent of overt acts of a treasonable or seditious character is emphasized by a concurring opinion, which by invoking the law of conspiracy makes speech do service for deeds which are dangerous to society. [N]ever until today has anyone seriously thought that the ancient law of conspiracy could constitutionally be used to turn speech into seditious conduct. Yet that is precisely what is suggested. I repeat that we deal here with speech alone, not with speech *plus* acts of sabotage or unlawful conduct. Not a single seditious act is charged in the indictment. To make a lawful speech unlawful because two men conceive it is to raise the law of conspiracy to appalling proportions. * * *

There comes a time when even speech loses its constitutional immunity. Speech innocuous one year may at another time fan such destructive flames that it must be halted in the interests of the safety of the Republic. That is the meaning of the clear and present danger test. When conditions are so critical that there will be no time to avoid the evil that the speech threatens, it is time to call a halt. Otherwise, free speech which is the strength of the Nation will be the cause of its destruction.

Yet free speech is the rule, not the exception. The restraint to be constitutional must be based on more than fear, on more than passionate opposition against the speech, on more than a revolted dislike for its contents. There must be some immediate injury to society that is likely if speech is allowed. * * *

I had assumed that the question of the clear and present danger, being so critical an issue in the case, would be a matter for submission to the jury. [The] Court, I think, errs when it treats the question as one of law.

Yet, whether the question is one for the Court or the jury, there should be evidence of record on the issue. This record, however, contains no evidence whatsoever showing that the acts charged viz., the teaching of the Soviet theory of revolution with the hope that it will be realized, have created any clear and present danger to the Nation. The Court, however, rules to the contrary. [The majority] might as well say that the speech of petitioners is outlawed because Soviet Russia and her Red Army are a threat to world peace.

The nature of Communism as a force on the world scene would, of course, be relevant to the issue of clear and present danger of petitioners' advocacy within the United States. But the primary consideration is the strength and tactical position of petitioners and their converts in this country. On that there is no evidence in the record. If we are to take judicial notice of the threat of Communists within the nation, it should not be difficult to conclude that *as a political party* they are of little consequence. Communists in this country have never made a respectable or serious showing in any election. I would doubt that there is a village, let alone a city or county or state, which the Communists could carry. Communism in the world scene is no bogeyman; but Communism as a political faction or party in this country plainly is. Communism has been so thoroughly exposed in this country that it has been crippled as a political force. Free speech has destroyed it as an effective political party. It is inconceivable that those who went up and down this country preaching the doctrine of revolution which petitioners espouse would have any success. In days of trouble and confusion, when bread lines were long, when the unemployed walked the streets, when people were starving, the advocates of a short-cut by revolution might have a chance to gain adherents. But today there are no such conditions. The country is not in despair; the people know Soviet Communism; the doctrine of Soviet revolution is exposed in all of its ugliness and the American people want none of it.

[Unless] and until extreme and necessitous circumstances are shown our aim should be to keep speech unfettered and to allow the processes of law to be invoked only when the provocateurs among us move from speech to action. * * * b

Notes and Questions

1. What was the "substantive evil" in the *Dennis* case, the danger of which was sufficiently "clear and present" to warrant the application of the rule as originally formulated by Holmes and Brandeis? A *successful* revolution? An *attempted* revolution, however futile such an attempt might be? A *conspiracy* to plan the overthrow of the government by force and violence? A "conspiracy *to advocate*" such overthrow? See John Gorfinkel & John Mack, *Dennis v. United States and the Clear and Present Danger Rule,* 39 Calif.L.Rev. 475, 496–501 (1951); Nathaniel Nathanson, *The Communist Trial and the Clear-and-Present-Danger Test,* 63 Harv.L.Rev. 1167, 1168, 1173–75 (1950). Suppose it were established in *Dennis* that the odds were 99–1 against the Communists attempting an overthrow of the Government until 1961? 1971? Same result?

2. *Suppression of "totalitarian movements".* Consider Carl Auerbach, *The Communist Control Act of 1954,* 23 U.Chi.L.Rev. 173, 188–89 (1956): "[I]n suppressing totalitarian movements a democratic society is not acting to protect the status quo, but the very same interests which freedom of speech itself seeks to secure—the possibility of peaceful progress under freedom. That suppression may

b. Eighteen years later, concurring in *Brandenburg,* p. 563 infra, Douglas, J., declared: "I see no place in the regime of the First Amendment for any 'clear and present danger' test whether strict and tight as some would make it or free-wheeling as the Court in *Dennis* rephrased it. When one reads the opinions closely and sees when and how the 'clear and present danger' test has been applied, great misgivings are aroused. First, the threats were often loud but always puny and made serious only by judges so wedded to the status quo that critical analysis made them nervous. Second, the test was so twisted and perverted in *Dennis* as to make the trial of those teachers of Marxism an all-out political trial which was part and parcel of the cold war that has eroded substantial parts of the First Amendment."

sometimes have to be the means of securing and enlarging freedom is a paradox which is not unknown in other areas of the law of modern democratic states. The basic 'postulate,' therefore, which should 'limit and control' the First Amendment is that it is part of the framework for a constitutional democracy and should, therefore, not be used to curb the power of Congress to exclude from the political struggle those groups which, if victorious, would crush democracy and impose totalitarianism. See also Robert Bork, *Neutral Principles and Some First Amendment Problems,* 47 Ind.L.J. 1, 30–33 (1971).[c]

3. Does the second amendment guarantee individuals (or groups) the right to bear arms for protection including protection against government tyranny?[d] If the second amendment is so construed, does the second amendment shed light on the first?

4. *Deference to legislative judgment.* Consider Hans Linde, *"Clear and Present Danger" Reexamined,* 22 Stan.L.Rev. 1163, 1176–78 (1970): "The Smith Act in 1940 wrote into federal law almost the exact terms of the New York Criminal Anarchy Act sustained in *Gitlow.* New York had enacted that law in 1902, soon after the assassination of [President McKinley]. Between the occupation of Czechoslovakia and the Ribbentrap-Molotov pact of 1939, the House of Representatives was working on a bill [H.R. 5138] whose provenance was the fear of anarchist agitation in 1900 and the hatred of alien radicalism in 1919. It became law in 1940. * * *

"What was the legislative judgment that would deserve deference for its assessment of the danger from revolutionary speech? [A] member of the 76th Congress presumably might stand up in 1940 and demand to know whether H.R. 5138 [violated the first amendment]. Constitutional law, in its original function antecedent to judicial review, owes him an answer. The Congressman's decision must be constitutionally right or wrong, in that place and at that time—not only a prosecutor's, a jury's, or a judge's decisions at the time of a later trial.

"The answer the Congressman would get in 1940, of course, would be that in 1925 the Supreme Court had held that the New York legislature could reasonably have believed in 1902 that advocacy of violent overthrow of government was too dangerous to be permitted. [That theory] simply accepts a lawmaker's judgment of danger intrinsic in the content of such advocacy, quite independent of any extrinsic conditions. This answer would not pretend to anticipate in 1940 the external dangers in an atomic age that were invoked to sustain the act in 1951, nor would it need to. [I]s the answer Holmes and Brandeis would give the member of the 76th Congress more satisfactory—that it all depended on the circumstances; that the constitutionality of H.R. 5138 could be determined only in the context of future eventualities of clear and present danger which he might

c. For different perspectives, see John Rawls, *A Theory of Justice* 216–21 (1971); Steven Shiffrin, *Racist Speech Outsider Jurisprudence, and the Meaning of America,* 80 Cornell L.Rev. 43, 88 n. 220, 90 n. 232 (1994); Stephen Smith, *Radically Subversive Speech and the Authority of Law,* 94 Mich.L.Rev. 348 (1995).

d. Is the second amendment an embarrassment to liberals? See Sanford Levinson, *The Embarrassing Second Amendment,* 99 Yale L.J. 637 (1989). For a variety of perspectives on the second amendment, see Symposium, *A Second Amendment Symposium Issue,* 62 Tenn. L.Rev. 443 (1995); Lawrence Cress, *An Armed Community,* 71 J.Am.Hist. 22 (1984); Robert Cottrol & Raymond Diamond, *The Second Amendment: Toward an Afro–Americanist Reconsideration,* 90 Geo.L.Rev. 309 (1991); Andrew Hertz, *Gun Crazy,* 75 B.U.L.Rev. 57 (1995); Donald Kates, *Handgun Prohibition and the Original Meaning of the Second Amendment,* 82 Mich.L.Rev. 204 (1983); William Van Alstyne, *The Second Amendment and the Personal Right to Bear Arms,* 43 Duke L.J. 1236 (1994); David Williams, *Civic Republicanism and the Citizen Militia,* 101 Yale L.J. 551 (1991).

now be unable to foresee; that the danger which would justify his law to suppress revolutionary speech and organization might shift from indigenous rampages to foreign military menaces and back again so that the bill presently before him for enactment might well be unconstitutional now but might be constitutional in the light of diverse events in 1945, in 1948, in 1951, in 1957, and in 1961, perhaps not in 1966, but again in 1968?''

————

In 1954, Senator McCarthy was censured by the United States Senate for acting contrary to its ethics and impairing its dignity. In 1957, when the convictions of the "second string" communist leaders reached the Supreme Court in *Yates,* McCarthy had died, and so had McCarthyism. Although strong anti-communist sentiment persisted, the political atmosphere in *Yates'* 1957 was profoundly different from that of *Dennis'* 1951.

YATES v. UNITED STATES, 354 U.S. 298, 77 S.Ct. 1064, 1 L.Ed.2d 1356 (1957), reversed the convictions of 14 "second-string" Communist Party officials for conspiring, in violation of §§ 2(a)(1) and (3) of the Smith Act, (1) to advocate and teach the duty and necessity of overthrowing the federal government by force and violence, and (2) to organize, as the Communist Party of the United States, a group who so advocate and teach, all with the intent of causing the overthrow of the government by force and violence as speedily as circumstances would permit.

The trial judge, as the Court described it, "regarded as immaterial, and intended to withdraw from the jury's consideration, any issue as to the character of the advocacy in terms of its capacity to stir listeners to forcible action," by instructing the jury: "The kind of advocacy and teaching which is charged and upon which your verdict must be reached is not merely a desirability but a necessity that the Government of the United States be overthrown and destroyed by force and violence and not merely a propriety but a duty to overthrow [by] force and violence." Both the petitioners and the Government had submitted proposed instructions "which would have required the jury to find that the proscribed advocacy was not of a mere abstract doctrine of forcible overthrow, but of action to that end, by the use of language reasonably and ordinarily calculated to incite persons to such action," but the trial court had rejected these instructions on the basis of *Dennis.*

The Court was "thus faced with the question whether the Smith Act prohibits advocacy and teaching of forcible overthrow, as an abstract principle, divorced from any effort to instigate action to that end, so long as such advocacy or teaching is engaged in with evil intent." In holding that it did not, the Court, per HARLAN, J., avoided resolution of the issue "in terms of constitutional compulsion" [a] and construed the Smith Act—in light of the legislative history showing "beyond all question that Congress was aware of the distinction between the advocacy or teaching of abstract doctrine and the advocacy or teaching of action, and that it did not intend to disregard it"—as "aimed at the advocacy and teaching of concrete action for the forcible overthrow of the Government, and not of principles divorced from action":

"The Government's reliance on this Court's decision in *Dennis* is misplaced. The jury instructions which were refused here were given there, and were referred to by this Court as requiring 'the jury to find the facts *essential* to establish the substantive crime.' (Emphasis added). It is true that at one point in the late

a. But see *Brandenburg*, Part D infra.

Chief Justice's opinion it is stated that the Smith Act 'is directed at advocacy, not discussion,' but it is clear that the reference was to advocacy of action, not ideas, for in the very next sentence the opinion emphasizes that the jury was properly instructed that there could be no conviction for 'advocacy in the realm of ideas.'
* * *

"In failing to distinguish between advocacy of forcible overthrow as an abstract doctrine and advocacy of action to that end, the District Court appears to have been led astray by the holding in *Dennis* that advocacy of violent action to be taken at some future time was enough. [T]he District Court apparently thought that *Dennis* obliterated the traditional dividing line between advocacy of abstract doctrine and advocacy of action.

"This misconceives the situation confronting the Court in *Dennis* and what was held there. Although the jury's verdict, interpreted in light of the trial court's instructions, did not justify the conclusion that the defendants' advocacy was directed at, or created any danger of, immediate overthrow, it did establish that the advocacy was aimed at building up a seditious group and maintaining it in readiness for action at a propitious time. [The] essence of the *Dennis* holding was that indoctrination of a group in preparation for future violent action, as well as exhortation to immediate action, by advocacy found to be directed to 'action for the accomplishment' of forcible overthrow, to violence as 'a rule or principle of action,' and employing 'language of incitement,' is not constitutionally protected when the group is of sufficient size and cohesiveness, is sufficiently oriented towards action, and other circumstances are such as reasonably to justify apprehension that action will occur. This is quite a different thing from the view of the District Court here that mere doctrinal justification of forcible overthrow, if engaged in with the intent to accomplish overthrow, is punishable per se under the Smith Act. That sort of advocacy, even though uttered with the hope that it may ultimately lead to violent revolution, is too remote from concrete action to be regarded as the kind of indoctrination preparatory to action which was condemned in *Dennis*.

"[*Dennis* was] not concerned with a conspiracy to engage at some future time in seditious advocacy, but rather with a conspiracy to advocate presently the taking of forcible action in the future. It was action, not advocacy, that was to be postponed until 'circumstances' would 'permit.' * * *

"In light of the foregoing we are unable to regard the District Court's charge upon this aspect of the case as adequate. [T]he trial court's statement that the proscribed advocacy must include the 'urging,' 'necessity,' and 'duty' of forcible overthrow, and not merely its 'desirability' and 'propriety,' may not be regarded as a sufficient substitute for charging that the Smith Act reaches only advocacy of action for the overthrow of government by force and violence. The essential distinction is that those to whom the advocacy is addressed must be urged to *do* something, now or in the future, rather than merely to *believe* in something.
* * *

"We recognize that distinctions between advocacy or teaching of abstract doctrines, with evil intent, and that which is directed to stirring people to action, are often subtle and difficult to grasp, for in a broad sense, as Mr. Justice Holmes said in his dissenting opinion in *Gitlow*: 'Every idea is an incitement.' But the very subtlety of these distinctions required the most clear and explicit instructions with reference to them, for they concerned an issue which went to the very heart of the charges against these petitioners. The need for precise and understandable instructions on this issue is further emphasized by the equivocal character of the evidence in this [record]. Instances of speech that could be considered to amount to 'advocacy of action' are so few and far between as to be almost completely overshadowed by the hundreds of instances in the record in which overthrow, if mentioned at all, occurs in the course of doctrinal disputation so remote from action as to be almost wholly lacking in probative value. Vague references to 'revolutionary' or 'militant' action of an unspecified character, which are found in the evidence, might in addition be given too great weight by the jury in the absence of more precise instructions. Particularly in light of this record, we must regard the trial court's charge in this respect as furnishing wholly inadequate guidance to the jury on this central point in the case."

On the basis of its interpretation of the Smith Act, the Court ordered an acquittal of five of the 14 petitioners,[b] finding "no adequate evidence in the record" to sustain their convictions on retrial.[c]

BLACK, J., joined by Douglas, J., dissented in part, maintaining, as they had in *Dennis*, that the Smith Act provisions on which the prosecutions were based violated the first amendment and that therefore acquittal should have been directed for all 14 petitioners.

CLARK, J., dissented: "*Dennis* merely held that a charge was sufficient where it requires a finding that 'the Party advocates the theory that there is a duty and necessity to overthrow the Government by force and violence [as] a program for winning adherents and as a policy to be translated into action' as soon as the circumstances permit [concurring opinion of Frankfurter, J.]." Thus, "the trial judge charged in essence all that was required under the *Dennis* opinion." He also maintained that instead of freeing five of the petitioners "solely on the *facts*"—which he regarded an unprecedented usurpation of the jury's function—the Court should have afforded the Government an opportunity, on remand, to present its evidence against petitioners "under the new theories announced by the Court for Smith Act prosecutions." [d]

Notes and Questions

1. *Dennis and Yates compared.* (a) On what did *Yates* focus: whether a *conspiracy* itself presents a "clear and present" danger or whether the *speech* of the conspirators does? On what did *Dennis* focus? Did *Yates* attach the same significance as did *Dennis* to membership in the Communist Party, as either an indication of intent or proof of membership in a conspiracy? To what extent does the fact that the *Yates* petitioners were not first-string leaders of the Party account for the result?

(b) Is it understandable that the *Yates* trial judge was "misled" by language in Vinson, C.J.'s *Dennis* opinion into thinking that punishment of the advocacy of abstract doctrine was permissible under the first amendment? Consider Gerald Gunther, *Learned Hand* 603 (1994): "Harlan claimed to be reinterpreting *Dennis;* in fact, Harlan's opinion represented a doctrinal evolution in a new direction, a

b. None of the remaining nine petitioners were ever tried again. Upon remand, the government requested dismissal of the indictments, explaining that a "comprehensive review [establishes] that we cannot satisfy the evidentiary requirements laid down by" the Court in *Yates*. See Robert Mollan, *Smith Act Prosecutions: The Effect of the Dennis and Yates Decisions*, 26 U.Pitt.L.Rev. 705, 732 (1965).

c. The type of evidence which led the Court to order the acquittal of the five petitioners and the kind of evidence which caused it to deny directed acquittals as to the nine others are summarized in *Scales* infra.

d. Brennan and Whittaker, JJ., took no part. Burton, J.'s concurrence is omitted.

direction back to the *Masses* 'incitement' standard." Consider Kent Greenawalt, *Speech and Crime*, 1980 Am.B.Found.Res.J. 645, 720 n. 279: "In defense of the trial court's instruction, it might be said that if someone is told he has a duty to participate in the forcible overthrow of the government, that signifies that he should perform illegal actions when the time arises. If all the Supreme Court opinion demanded is an explicit urging that listeners perform illegal actions at some future time, it is hard to distinguish that from what is clearly implied in advocacy of the ' "duty" of forcible overthrow.' But Justice Harlan may have meant that the advocacy must be more closely linked with action, either in the sense of recommending specific action or in the sense of being more positively directed to producing action among listeners."

2. *Advocating "doctrine" and advocating "action."* Consider Walter Gellhorn, *American Rights* 80–81 (1960): "[O]ne can recognize a qualitative distinction between a speaker who expresses the opinion before a student audience that all law professors are scoundrels whose students should band together to beat them within an inch of their lives, and a second speaker who, taking up that theme, urges the audience to obtain baseball bats, meet behind the law faculty building at three o'clock next Thursday afternoon, and join him in attacking any professor who can then be found. The first speaker, in [the *Yates*] view, should not be prosecuted; the second has stepped over the line between advocating a belief and advocating an illegal action." Cf. Hand, *The Bill of Rights* 59–60 (1958).

In an effort to avoid the demanding evidentiary requirements of *Yates*, the government began prosecuting communists under the "membership clause" of the Smith Act, 18 U.S.C.A. § 2385. After *Scales* and *Noto*, infra, the government abandoned Smith Act prosecutions altogether.

SCALES v. UNITED STATES, 367 U.S. 203, 81 S.Ct. 1469, 6 L.Ed.2d 782 (1961) affirmed the conviction of the Chairman of the North and South Carolina Districts of the Communist Party under the "membership clause" of the Smith Act, 18 U.S.C.A. § 2385, described by the Court, per HARLAN, J., as making a felony "the acquisition or holding of knowing membership in any organization which advocates the overthrow of the [federal] Government by force or violence."[1] The trial judge had instructed the jury that, as the Supreme Court described it, "in order to convict it must find [that] (1) the Communist Party advocated the violent overthrow of the Government, in the sense of 'present advocacy of action' to accomplish that end as soon as circumstances were propitious; and (2) petitioner was an 'active' member of the Party, and not merely 'a nominal, passive * * *' member, with knowledge of the Party's illegal advocacy and a specific intent to bring about violent overthrow 'as speedily as circumstances would permit.'"

The Court held that "the membership clause permissibly bears the construction put upon it below" and as thus construed neither "imputes guilt to an

---

1. Section 2385 (whose membership clause we place in italics) reads: "Whoever organizes or helps or attempts to organize any society, group, or assembly of persons who teach, advocate, or encourage the overthrow or destruction of any such government by force or violence; *or becomes or is a member of*, or affiliates with, *any such society, group, or as-* *sembly of persons, knowing the purposes there-of—*

"Shall be fined not more than $20,000 or imprisoned not more than twenty years, or both, and shall be ineligible for employment by the United States or any department or agency thereof, for the five years next following his conviction. * * * "

individual merely on the basis of his associations and sympathies" in violation of due process nor infringes First Amendment freedoms:

"It was settled in *Dennis* that the advocacy with which we are here concerned is not constitutionally protected speech, and it was further established that a combination to promote such advocacy, albeit under the aegis of what purports to be a political party, is not such association as is protected by the First Amendment. We can discern no reason why membership, when it constitutes a purposeful form of complicity in a group engaging in this same forbidden advocacy, should receive any greater degree of protection from the guarantees of that Amendment.

"The [membership] clause does not make criminal all association with an organization, which has been shown to engage in illegal advocacy. There must be clear proof that a defendant 'specifically intend[s] to accomplish [the aims of the organization] by resort to violence.' *Noto* [this Part infra]. Thus the member for whom the organization is a vehicle for the advancement of legitimate aims and policies does not fall within the ban of the statute: he lacks the requisite specific intent 'to bring about the overthrow of the government as speedily as circumstances would permit.' Such a person may be foolish, deluded, or perhaps merely optimistic, but he is not by this statute made a criminal."

The Court also rejected the contention "that the evidence was insufficient to establish that the Communist Party was engaged in present advocacy of violent overthrow of the Government in the sense required by the Smith Act": "[T]he evidentiary question here is controlled in large part by *Yates* [which] rested on the view (not articulated in the opinion, though perhaps it should have been) that the Smith Act offenses, involving as they do subtler elements than are present in most other crimes, call for strict standards in assessing the adequacy of the proof needed to make out a case of illegal advocacy. This premise is as applicable to prosecutions under the membership clause of the Smith Act as it is to conspiracy prosecutions under that statute as we had in *Yates*. [*Yates*] indicates what type of evidence is needed to permit a jury to find that (a) there was 'advocacy of action' and (b) the Party was responsible for such advocacy.

"First, *Yates* makes clear what type of evidence is not *in itself* sufficient to show illegal advocacy. This category includes evidence of the following: the teaching of Marxism-Leninism and the connected use of Marxist 'classics' as textbooks; the official general resolutions and pronouncements of the Party at past conventions; dissemination of the Party's general literature, including the standard outlines on Marxism; the Party's history and organizational structure; the secrecy of meetings and the clandestine nature of the Party generally; statements by officials evidencing sympathy for and alliance with the U.S.S.R. It was the predominance of evidence of this type which led the Court to order the acquittal of several *Yates* [defendants].

"Second, *Yates* also indicates what kind of evidence is sufficient. There the Court pointed to two series of events which justified the denial of directed acquittals as to nine of the *Yates* defendants. The Court noted that with respect to seven of the defendants, meetings in San Francisco might be considered to be 'the systematic teaching and advocacy of illegal action which is condemned by the statute.' In those meetings, a small group of members were not only taught that violent revolution was inevitable, but they were also taught techniques for achieving that end. [T]he Court [also] referred to certain activities in the Los Angeles area 'which might be considered to amount to "advocacy of action"' and with which two *Yates* defendants were linked. Here again, the participants did not stop with teaching of the inevitability of eventual revolution, but went on to explain techniques, both legal and illegal, to be employed in preparation for or in connection with the revolution. [Viewed] together, these events described in *Yates* indicate at least two patterns of evidence sufficient to show illegal advocacy: (a) the teaching of forceful overthrow, accompanied by directions as to the type of illegal action which must be taken when the time for the revolution is reached; and (b) the teaching of forceful overthrow, accompanied by a contemporary, though legal, course of conduct clearly undertaken for the specific purpose of rendering effective the later illegal activity which is advocated."

After examining the *Scales* record, the Court concluded "this evidence sufficed to make a case for the jury on the issue of illegal Party advocacy. *Dennis* and *Yates* have definitely laid at rest any doubt that present advocacy of *future* action for violent overthrow satisfies statutory and constitutional requirements equally with advocacy of *immediate* action to that end. Hence this record cannot be considered deficient because it contains no evidence of advocacy for immediate overthrow. [T]he evidence amply showed that Party leaders were continuously preaching during the indictment period the inevitability of eventual forcible overthrow [and] the jury, under instructions which fully satisfied the requirements of *Yates*,[27] was entitled to infer from this systematic preaching [that] the doctrine of violent revolution [was] put forward as a guide to future action * * *; in short that 'advocacy of action' was engaged in." And "such advocacy was sufficiently broadly based to permit its attribution to the Party."

DOUGLAS, J., dissented: "When we allow petitioner to be sentenced to prison for six years for being a 'member' of the Communist Party, we make a sharp break with traditional concepts of First Amendment [rights]. Even the Alien and Sedition Laws—shameful reminders of an early chapter in intolerance—never went so far as we go today. They were aimed at conspiracy and advocacy of insurrection and at the publication of 'false, scandalous and malicious' writing against the Government. [There] is here no charge of conspiracy, no charge of any overt act to overthrow the Government by force and violence, no charge of any other criminal act. The charge is being a 'member' of the Communist Party, 'well-knowing' that it advocated the overthrow of the Government by force and violence, 'said defendant intending to bring about such overthrow by force and

---

27. The trial court charged: "Moreover, the teaching in the abstract or teaching objectively, that is, teaching, discussing, explaining, or expounding what is meant by the aim or purpose of any author, group, or society of overthrowing the Government by force and violence is not criminal. * * *

"However, if the Party went further, and with the intention of overthrowing the Government by force and violence, it taught, or advocated a rule or principle of action which both, one, called on its members to take forcible and concrete action at some advantageous time thereafter to overthrow the Government by force and violence, and, two, expressed that call in such written or oral words as would reasonably and ordinarily be calculated to incite its members to take concrete and forcible action for such overthrow; then, if the Communist Party did that, the Party became such a society or group, as was outlawed by the Smith Act.

"To be criminal the teaching or advocacy, or the call to action just described need not be for

immediate action, that is, for action today, tomorrow, next month, or next year. It is criminal, nonetheless, if the action is to be at an unnamed time in the future, to be fixed by the circumstances or on signal from the Party.

"It is criminal if it is a call upon the members to be ready, or to stand in readiness for action, or for a summons to action at a favorable, or opportune time in the future, or as speedily as circumstances will permit, provided always that the urging of such readiness be by words which would reasonably and ordinarily be calculated to spur a person to ready himself for, and to take action towards, the overthrow of the Government. But those to whom the advocacy or urging is addressed must be urged to do something now or in the future, rather than merely to believe in something. In other words, the advocacy must be of concrete action, and not merely a belief in abstract doctrine. However, the immediate concrete action urged should be intended to lead towards the forcible overthrow, and be so understood by those to whom the advocacy is addressed."

violence as speedily as circumstances would permit.' That falls far short of a charge of conspiracy. Conspiracy rests not in intention alone but in an agreement with one or more others to promote an unlawful project. * * *

"The case is not saved by showing that petitioner was an active member. None of the activity constitutes a crime. [Scales] recruited new members into the Party, and promoted the advanced education of selected young Party members in the theory of communism to be undertaken at secret schools. He was a director of one such school [at which] students were told (by someone else) that one of the Party's weaknesses was in failing to place people in key industrial positions. One witness told of a meeting arranged by Scales at which the staff of the school urged him to remain in his position in an industrial plant rather than return to college. In Scales' presence, students at the school were once shown how to kill a person with a pencil, a device which, it was said, might come in handy on a picket line. Other evidence showed Scales [at different times to have said or distributed literature which said] that the Party line was that the Negroes in the South and the working classes should be used to foment a violent revolution; that a Communist government could not be voted into power in this country because the Government controlled communication media, newspapers, the military, and the educational system, and that force was the only way to achieve the revolution; [that] the revolution would come within a generation; that it would be easier in the United States than in Russia to effectuate the revolution because of assistance and advice from Russian Communists. * * *

"Not one single illegal act is charged to petitioner. That is why the essence of the crime covered by the indictment is merely belief—belief in the proletarian revolution, belief in Communist creed."

BLACK, J., dissented primarily for the reasons of Douglas and Brennan, JJ. He also maintained that although the Court had suggested in other cases in which it had applied the "balancing test," that it was justified "because no direct abridgment of First Amendment freedoms was involved," in the instant case "petitioner is being sent to jail for the express reason that he has associated with people who have entertained unlawful ideas and said unlawful things, and that of course is a *direct* abridgment of his freedoms of speech and assembly * * *. Nevertheless, [the] Court relies upon its prior decisions to the effect that the Government has power to abridge speech and assembly if its interest in doing so is sufficient to outweigh the interest in protecting these First Amendment freedoms. This, I think, demonstrates the unlimited breadth and danger of the 'balancing test' as it is currently being employed by a majority of this Court." [a]

In another Smith Act "membership clause" case, the same day as *Scales*, NOTO v. UNITED STATES, 367 U.S. 290, 81 S.Ct. 1517, 6 L.Ed.2d 836 (1961), per HARLAN, J., reversed the conviction of a communist worker in upstate New York, finding that the record "bears much of the infirmity that we found in the *Yates* record, and requires us to conclude that the evidence of illegal Party advocacy was insufficient to support this conviction." There was much evidence of "the Party's teaching of abstract doctrine that revolution is an inevitable product of the 'proletarian' effort to achieve communism in a capitalistic society," but testimony of evidence which supported an inference of " 'advocacy of action'

a. Brennan, J., joined by Warren, C.J., and Douglas, J., dissented on the ground that sub-sequent legislation had superseded the membership provision of the Smith Act.

to accomplish that end" was "sparse indeed" and "lacked the compelling quality which in *Scales* was supplied by the petitioner's utterances and systematic course of conduct as a high Party official."

Notes and Questions

1. See Martin Shapiro, *Freedom of Speech* 119 (1966) for the view that when Congress had prohibited "membership" in organizations advocating the forcible overthrow of the government, it plainly had *not* meant "active" membership with "specific intent" and "the acrobatic display of statutory interpretation necessary to have made it mean all that simply demonstrated again the paradox of modest Justices who cannot bring themselves to challenge Congress, but yet cannot completely escape the feeling that they owe some independent duty to the Constitution."

2. Could Scales have been convicted under the advocacy or conspiracy to advocate clauses of the Smith Act? Could any really "active" Party member probably be? Without sufficient proof to satisfy *Yates*, can the government prove "membership" of the sort required for conviction in *Scales* and *Noto*? As a practical matter, did the Court eliminate the membership clause of the Smith Act as a separate means of prosecuting Communist Party members? See Shapiro, supra, at 120; 75 Harv.L.Rev. 116–17 (1961).

3. *Spock.* Dr. Spock, Rev. Coffin and others were convicted of conspiring to counsel and abet Selective Service registrants to refuse to have their draft cards in their possession and to disobey other duties imposed by the Selective Service Act of 1967. Spock signed a document entitled "A Call to Resist Illegitimate Authority," which "had 'a double aspect: in part it was a denunciation of governmental policy [in Vietnam] and, in part, it involved a public call to resist the duties imposed by the [Selective Service] Act.'" Several weeks later, Spock attended a demonstration in Washington, D.C., where an unsuccessful attempt was made to present collected draft cards to the Attorney General. *United States v. Spock,* 416 F.2d 165 (1st Cir.1969), per Aldrich, J., ruled that Spock should have been acquitted: "[Spock] was one of the drafters of the Call, but this does not evidence the necessary intent to adhere to its illegal aspects. [H]is speech was limited to condemnation of the war and the draft, and lacked any words or content of counselling. The jury could not find proscribed advocacy from the mere fact [that] he hoped the frequent stating of his views might give young men 'courage to take active steps in draft resistance.' This is a natural consequence of vigorous speech. Similarly, Spock's actions lacked the clear character necessary to imply specific intent under the First Amendment standard. [H]e was at the Washington demonstration, [but took] no part in its planning. [His statements at this demonstration did not extend] beyond the general anti-war, anti-draft remarks he had made before. His attendance is as consistent with a desire to repeat this speech as it is to aid a violation of the law. The dissent would fault us for drawing such distinctions, but it forgets the teaching of [*Bond v. Floyd* [b]] that expressing one's views in broad areas is not foreclosed by knowledge of the consequences, and the important lesson of *Noto, Scales* and *Yates* that one may belong to a group, knowing of its illegal aspects, and still not be found to adhere thereto."

b. *Bond v. Floyd,* 385 U.S. 116, 87 S.Ct. 339, 17 L.Ed.2d 235 (1966) found ambiguity in expressions of support for those unwilling to respond to the draft that earlier opinions would have characterized as clear advocacy of illegal action. As Thomas Emerson puts it "the distance traversed [from *Schenck* and *Debs* to *Bond*] is quite apparent." *Freedom of Expression in Wartime,* 116 U.Pa.L.Rev. 975, 988 (1968).

D. A MODERN "RESTATEMENT"

BRANDENBURG v. OHIO

395 U.S. 444, 89 S.Ct. 1827, 23 L.Ed.2d 430 (1969).

PER CURIAM.[a]

The appellant, a leader of a Ku Klux Klan group, was convicted under [a 1919] Ohio Criminal Syndicalism statute of "advocat[ing] the duty, necessity, or propriety of crime, sabotage, violence, or unlawful methods of terrorism as a means of accomplishing industrial or political reform" and of "voluntarily assembl[ing] with any society, group or assemblage of persons formed to teach or advocate the doctrines of criminal syndicalism." He was fined $1,000 and sentenced to one to 10 years' imprisonment. * * *

The record shows that a man, identified at trial as the appellant, telephoned an announcer-reporter on the staff of a Cincinnati television station and invited him to come to a Ku Klux Klan "rally" to be held at a farm in Hamilton County. With the cooperation of the organizers, the reporter and a cameraman attended the meeting and filmed the events. Portions of the films were later broadcast on the local station and on a national network.

The prosecution's case rested on the films and on testimony identifying the appellant as the person who communicated with the reporter and who spoke at the rally. The State also introduced into evidence several articles appearing in the film, including a pistol, a rifle, a shotgun, ammunition, a Bible, and a red hood worn by the speaker in the films.

One film showed 12 hooded figures, some of whom carried firearms. They were gathered around a large wooden cross, which they burned. No one was present other than the participants and the newsmen who made the film. Most of the words uttered during the scene were incomprehensible when the film was projected, but scattered phrases could be understood that were derogatory of Negroes and, in one instance, of Jews. Another scene on the same film showed the appellant, in Klan regalia, making a speech. The speech, in full, was as follows:

"This is an organizers' meeting. We have had quite a few members here today which are—we have hundreds, hundreds of members throughout the State of Ohio. I can quote from a newspaper clipping from the Columbus Ohio Dispatch, five weeks ago Sunday morning. The Klan has more members in the State of Ohio than does any other organization. We're not a revengent organization, but if our President, our Congress, our Supreme Court, continues to suppress the white, Caucasian race, it's possible that there might have to be some revengence taken.

a. See Bernard Schwartz, *Holmes Versus Hand: Clear and Present Danger or Advocacy of Unlawful Action?* 1995 S.Ct.Rev. 237: "*Brandenburg* was assigned to Justice Fortas. The draft opinion that he circulated stated a modified version of the Clear and Present test. [As] it turned out, *Brandenburg* did not come down as a Fortas opinion. Though the Justice had circulated his draft opinion in April 1969 and quickly secured the necessary votes, he followed Justice Harlan's suggestion to delay its announcement. Before then, the events occurred that led to Justice Fortas's forced resignation from the Court. The *Brandenburg* opinion was then redrafted by Justice Brennan, who eliminated all references to the Clear and Present Danger test and substituted the present *Brandenburg* language: 'where such advocacy is directed to inciting or producing imminent lawless action and is likely to incite or produce such action.' The Brennan redraft was issued as a per curiam opinion."

"We are marching on Congress July the Fourth, four hundred thousand strong. From there we are dividing into two groups, one group to march on St. Augustine, Florida, the other group to march into Mississippi. Thank you."

The second film showed six hooded figures one of whom, later identified as the appellant, repeated a speech very similar to that recorded on the first film. The reference to the possibility of "revengence" was omitted, and one sentence was added: "Personally, I believe the nigger should be returned to Africa, the Jew returned to Israel." Though some of the figures in the films carried weapons, the speaker did not.

[*Whitney*] sustained the constitutionality of California's Criminal Syndicalism Act, the text of which is quite similar to that of the laws of Ohio. The Court upheld the statute on the ground that, without more, "advocating" violent means to effect political and economic change involves such danger to the security of the State that the State may outlaw it. But *Whitney* has been thoroughly discredited by later decisions [such as *Dennis* which] have fashioned the principle that the constitutional guarantees of free speech and free press do not permit a State to forbid or proscribe advocacy of the use of force or of law violation except where such advocacy is directed to inciting or producing imminent lawless action and is likely to incite or produce such action.[2] As we said in *Noto*, "the mere abstract teaching [of] the moral propriety or even moral necessity for a resort to force and violence, is not the same as preparing a group for violent action and steeling it to such action." See also *Bond v. Floyd*. A statute which fails to draw this distinction impermissibly intrudes upon the freedoms guaranteed by the First and Fourteenth Amendments. It sweeps within its condemnation speech which our Constitution has immunized from governmental control. Cf. *Yates* * * *.

Measured by this test, Ohio's Criminal Syndicalism Act cannot be sustained. The Act punishes persons who "advocate or teach the duty, necessity, or propriety" of violence "as a means of accomplishing industrial or political reform"; or who publish or circulate or display any book or paper containing such advocacy; or who "justify" the commission of violent acts "with intent to exemplify, spread or advocate the propriety of the doctrines of criminal syndicalism"; or [who] "voluntarily assemble" with a group formed "to teach or advocate the doctrines of criminal syndicalism." Neither the indictment nor the trial judge's instructions to the jury in any way refined the statute's bald definition of the crime in terms of mere advocacy not distinguished from incitement to imminent lawless action.[3]

Accordingly, we are here confronted with a statute which, by its own words and as applied, purports to punish mere advocacy and to forbid, on pain of criminal punishment, assembly with others merely to advocate the described type of action.[4] Such a statute falls within the condemnation of the First and

---

2. It was on the theory that the Smith Act embodied such a principle and that it had been applied only in conformity with it that this Court sustained the Act's constitutionality. That this was the basis for *Dennis* was emphasized in *Yates*, in which the Court overturned convictions for advocacy of the forcible overthrow of the Government under the Smith Act, because the trial judge's instructions had allowed conviction for mere advocacy, unrelated to its tendency to produce forcible action.

3. The first count of the indictment charged that appellant "did unlawfully by word of mouth advocate the necessity, or pro-

priety of crime, violence, or unlawful methods of terrorism as a means of accomplishing political reform * * *." The second count charged that appellant "did unlawfully voluntarily assemble with a group or assemblage of persons formed to advocate the doctrines of criminal syndicalism * * *." The trial judge's charge merely followed the language of the indictment. * * *

4. Statutes affecting the right of assembly, like those touching on freedom of speech, must observe the established distinctions between mere advocacy and incitement to lawless action * * *.

Fourteenth Amendments. The contrary teaching of *Whitney* cannot be supported, and that decision is therefore overruled.

Reversed.

Justice Black, concurring.

I agree with the views expressed by Mr. Justice Douglas in his concurring opinion in this case that the "clear and present danger" doctrine should have no place in the interpretation of the First Amendment. I join the Court's opinion, which, as I understand it, simply cites *Dennis*, but does not indicate any agreement on the Court's part with the "clear and present danger" doctrine on which *Dennis* purported to rely.

Justice Douglas, concurring.

While I join the opinion of the Court, I desire to enter a caveat.

[Whether] the war power—the greatest leveler of them all—is adequate to sustain [the "clear and present danger"] doctrine is debatable. The dissents in *Abrams* [and other cases] show how easily "clear and present danger" is manipulated to crush what Brandeis called "the fundamental right of free men to strive for better conditions through new legislation and new institutions" by argument and discourse even in time of war. Though I doubt if the "clear and present danger" test is congenial to the First Amendment in time of a declared war, I am certain it is not reconcilable with the First Amendment in days of peace. * * *

Mr. Justice Holmes, though never formally abandoning the "clear and present danger" test, moved closer to the First Amendment ideal when he said in dissent in *Gitlow* [quoting the passage beginning, "Every idea is an incitement."] We have never been faithful to the philosophy of that dissent.

"[In *Dennis*, we distorted] the "clear and present danger" test beyond recognition. [I] see no place in the regime of the First Amendment for any "clear and present danger" test whether strict and tight as some would make it or free-wheeling as the Court in *Dennis* rephrased it.

Notes and Questions

1. What pre-*Brandenburg* decisions, if any, "have fashioned the principle" that advocacy may not be prohibited "except [where] directed to inciting or producing *imminent* lawless action *and * * * likely* to incite or produce such action"? (Emphasis added.) Did *Dennis*, *Yates* and *Scales* take pains to *deny* that the unlawful action advocated need be "imminent" or that the advocacy must be "likely" to produce the forbidden action? See Hans Linde, *"Clear and Present Danger" Reexamined*, 22 Stan.L.Rev. 1163, 1166–67, 1183–86 (1970).

2. Does *Brandenburg* adopt the *Masses* incitement test as a major part of the required showing? Consider Gerald Gunther, *Learned Hand and the Origins of Modern First Amendment Doctrine: Some Fragments of History*," 27 Stan. L.Rev. 719, 754–55 (1975): "An incitement-nonincitement distinction had only fragmentary and ambiguous antecedents in the pre-*Brandenburg* era; it was *Brandenburg* that really 'established' it; and, it was essentially an establishment of the legacy of Learned Hand. [Under] *Brandenburg*, probability of harm is no longer the central criterion for speech limitations. The inciting language of the speaker—the Hand focus on 'objective' words—is the major consideration. And punishment of the harmless inciter is prevented by the *Schenck*–derived requirement of a likelihood of dangerous consequences." (citing *Brandenburg*'s note 4.) But see Steven Shiffrin, *Defamatory Non-Media Speech and First Amendment*

Methodology, 25 U.C.L.A.L.Rev. 915, 947 n. 206 (1978): "Several leading commentators assume that *Brandenburg* adopts an incitement requirement. [The] conclusion is apparently based on this line from *Brandenburg:* 'Neither the indictment nor the trial judge's instructions to the jury in any way refined the statute's bald definition of the crime in terms of mere advocacy, not distinguished from incitement to imminent lawless action' [also citing note 4]. The difficulty with attaching significance to this ambiguous statement is that the term 'incitement' is used in the alternative in the Court's statement of its test. Thus, advocacy of imminent lawless action is protected unless it is directed to inciting *or* producing imminent lawless action and is likely to incite *or* produce imminent lawless action. Thus, even assuming that the use of the word incitement refers to express use of language, as opposed to the nature of results (an interpretation which is strained in light of the Court's wording of the test), incitement is not necessary to divorce the speech from first amendment protection. It is enough that the speech is directed to producing imminent lawless action and is likely to produce such action."

If one wants to argue that *Brandenburg* adopted *Masses,* is there anything to be made of the phrase "directed to" in the *Brandenburg* test? Alternatively, did *Yates* adopt the *Masses* test? If so, does its favorable citation in *Brandenburg* constitute an adoption of the *Masses* test?

3. The *Brandenburg* "inciting or producing imminent lawless action" standard was the basis for reversal of a disorderly conduct conviction in HESS v. INDIANA, 414 U.S. 105, 94 S.Ct. 326, 38 L.Ed.2d 303 (1973) (per curiam). After antiwar demonstrators on the Indiana University campus had blocked a public street, police moved them to the curbs on either side. As an officer passed him, appellant stated loudly, "We'll take the fucking street later (or again)," which led to his disorderly conduct conviction. His statement, observed the Court, "was not addressed to any person or group in particular" and "his tone, although loud, was no louder than that of the other people in the area. [At] best, [the] statement could be taken as counsel for present moderation; at worst, it amounted to nothing more than advocacy of illegal action at some indefinite future time." This was insufficient, under *Brandenburg,* to punish appellant's words, as the State had, on the ground that they had a "tendency to produce violence." It could not be said that appellant "was advocating, in the normal sense, any action" and there was "no evidence" that "his words were intended to produce, and likely to produce, *imminent* disorder."

REHNQUIST, J., joined by Burger, C.J., and Blackmun, J., dissented: "The simple explanation for the result in this case is that the majority has interpreted the evidence differently from the courts below." The dissenters quarrelled with the Court's conclusion that appellant's advocacy "was not directed towards inciting imminent action. [T]here are surely possible constructions of the statement which would encompass more or less immediate and continuing action against the police. They should not be rejected out of hand because of an unexplained preference for other acceptable alternatives." [b]

b. See also *NAACP v. Claiborne Hardware Co.,* 458 U.S. 886, 102 S.Ct. 3409, 73 L.Ed.2d 1215 (1982). The Court stated that the remarks of Charles Evers "might have been understood" as inviting violence, but stated that when "such appeals do not incite lawless action, they must be regarded as protected speech." If violent action had followed his remarks, a "substantial question" of liability would have been raised. The Court also observed, however, that the defendant might be held criminally liable for the acts of others if the speeches could be taken as evidence that the defendant gave "other specific instructions to carry out violent acts or threats." Compare *Watts v. United States,* 394 U.S. 705, 89 S.Ct.

4. Does *Yates* survive *Brandenburg*'s emphasis on *imminent* lawless action? Consider Harry Kalven, *A Worthy Tradition* 234 (1988): "It is [possible] that [*Brandenburg*] has preserved the group/individual distinction. Under such an approach the *Yates* incitement-to-future-action standard would apply to group speech and the *Brandenburg* incitement-to-immediate-action standard would apply to the individual speaker." Is light shed on the question by *Communist Party of Indiana v. Whitcomb,* 414 U.S. 441, 94 S.Ct. 656, 38 L.Ed.2d 635 (1974), invalidating an Indiana statute denying a political party or its candidates access to the ballot unless the party files an affidavit that it "does not advocate the overthrow of local, state or national government by force or violence"? The Court, per Brennan J., maintained that the required oath (which had been interpreted to include advocacy of abstract doctrine) violated the principle of *Brandenburg* and stated that the principle applied not only to attempted denials of public employment, bar licensing, and tax exemption, but also to ballot access denials. The flaw with the state's position was that it furnished access to the ballot "not because the Party urges others 'to *do* something now *or in the future* [but] merely to believe in something,' [*Yates*]" (Second emphasis added).

What happened to the "imminent lawless action" requirement? Does the *Whitcomb* language clarify *Brandenburg*? Modify it?

5. Does *Brandenburg* apply to the advocacy of trivial crimes? Suppose the advocacy of trespass across a lawn? What result under *Brandenburg*? What result under *Dennis*? Is *Dennis* potentially more speech protective than *Brandenburg*?

6. Does *Brandenburg* apply to solicitation of crime in private or non-ideological contexts? Consider Shiffrin, note 2 supra, at 950: "How different it might be if the factual context were to involve advocacy of murder in a non-socio-political context. One suspects that little rhetoric about the marketplace of ideas or other first amendment values would be employed and that the serious and explicit advocacy of murder in a concrete way would suffice to divorce the speech from first amendment protection even in the absence of a specific showing of likelihood." Would it matter if it were not explicit or not concrete? For trenchant analysis of the issues raised by the shift in context from public to private or in subject matter from ideological to non-ideological, see Kent Greenawalt, *Speech and Crime,* 1980 Am.B.Found.Res.J. 645.

7. Should the line of cases from *Schenck* to *Brandenburg* fuel cynicism about the binding force of legal doctrine and about the willingness or capacity of the judiciary to protect dissent? [c] To what extent does the focus on Supreme Court cases exaggerate the frailty of legal doctrine? [d]

1399, 22 L.Ed.2d 664 (1969) (statute prohibiting knowing and wilful threat of bodily harm upon the President is constitutional on its face) (dictum); *Rankin v. McPherson*, p. 981 infra (clerical employee's private expression of desire that Presidential assassination attempt be successful is insufficient justification for dismissal even in a law enforcement agency). For commentary on threats and the first amendment, compare Justice Linde's opinion in *State v. Robertson*, 293 Or. 402, 649 P.2d 569 (1982) with Kent Greenawalt, *Criminal Coercion and Freedom of Speech,* 78 Nw.U.L.Rev. 1081 (1984).

c. In fashioning first amendment doctrine, should the overriding objective be at "all times [to] equip the first amendment to do maximum service in those historical periods when intolerance of unorthodox ideas is most prevalent and when governments are most able and most likely to stifle dissent systematically"? Should the first amendment "be targeted for the worst of times"? What impact would such a perspective have on the general development of first amendment doctrine? See Vincent Blasi, *The Pathological Perspective and the First Amendment,* 85 Colum.L.Rev. 449 (1985).

d. For a comprehensive review and critical analysis of the problems and policies raised by

II. REPUTATION AND PRIVACY

In an important article, Harry Kalven coined the phrase "two level theory." Kalven, *The Metaphysics of the Law of Obscenity,* 1960 Sup.Ct.Rev. 1, 11. As he described it, *Beauharnais,* infra, and other cases employed a first amendment methodology that classified speech at two levels. Some speech—libel, obscenity, "fighting words"—was thought to be so bereft of social utility as to be beneath first amendment protection. At the second level, speech of constitutional value was thought to be protected unless it presented a clear and present danger of a substantive evil.

In considering libel and privacy, we will witness the collapse of "two level theory." The purpose is not a detailed examination of libel and privacy law. Our interests include the initial exclusion of defamation from first amendment protection, the themes and methods contributing to the erosion of that exclusion, and the articulation of basic first amendment values having implications and applications beyond defamation and the right to privacy.

A. GROUP LIBEL

BEAUHARNAIS v. ILLINOIS, 343 U.S. 250, 72 S.Ct. 725, 96 L.Ed. 919 (1952), per FRANKFURTER, J., sustained a statute prohibiting exhibition in any public place of any publication portraying "depravity, criminality, unchastity, or lack of virtue of a class of citizens, of any race, color, creed or religion [which exposes such citizens] to contempt, derision or obloquy or which is productive of breach of the peace or riots." The Court affirmed a conviction for organizing the distribution of a leaflet which petitioned the Mayor and City Council of Chicago "to halt the further encroachment, harassment and invasion of white people, their property, neighborhoods and persons by the Negro"; called for "one million self respecting white people in Chicago to unite"; and warned that if "the need to prevent the white race from becoming mongrelized by the Negro will not unite us, then the [aggressions], rapes, robberies, knives, guns, and marijuana of the Negro, surely will.":

"Today every American jurisdiction [punishes] libels directed at individuals. '[There] are certain well-defined and narrowly limited classes of speech, the prevention and punishment of which have never been thought to raise any constitutional problem. These include the lewd and obscene, the profane, the libelous, and the insulting or "fighting" words—those which by their very utterance inflict injury or tend to incite to an immediate breach of the peace. It has been well observed that such utterances are no essential part of any exposition of ideas, and are of such slight social value as a step to truth that any benefit that may be derived from them is clearly outweighed by the social interest in order and morality. "Resort to epithets or personal abuse is not in any proper sense communication of information or opinion safeguarded by the Constitution, and its punishment as a criminal act would raise no question under that instrument." *Cantwell v. Connecticut,* [p. 1013 infra].' Such were the views of a unanimous Court in *Chaplinsky v. New Hampshire,* p. 630 infra.[6]

advocacy of illegal action, see Greenawalt, note 7 supra. See generally Kent Greenawalt, *Speech, Crime, and the Uses of Language* (1989); Harry Kalven, *A Worthy Tradition* (1987).

6. In all but five States, the constitutional guarantee of free speech to every person is explicitly qualified by holding him "responsible for the abuse of that right." * * *

"No one will gainsay that it is libelous falsely to charge another with being a rapist, robber, carrier of knives and guns, and user of marijuana. The [question is whether the fourteenth amendment] prevents a State from punishing such libels—as criminal libel has been defined, limited and constitutionally recognized time out of mind—directed at designated collectivities and flagrantly disseminated. [I]f an utterance directed at an individual may be the object of criminal sanctions, we cannot deny to a State power to punish the same utterance directed at a defined group, unless we can say that this is a wilful and purposeless restriction unrelated to the peace and well-being of the State.

"Illinois did not have to look beyond her own borders to await the tragic experience of the last three decades to conclude that wilful purveyors of falsehood concerning racial and religious groups promote strife and tend powerfully to obstruct the manifold adjustments required for free, orderly life in a metropolitan, polyglot community. From the murder of the abolitionist Lovejoy in 1837 to the Cicero riots of 1951, Illinois has been the scene of exacerbated tension between races, often flaring into violence and destruction. In many of these outbreaks, utterances of the character here in question, so the Illinois legislature could conclude, played a significant [part.]

"In the face of this history and its frequent obligato of extreme racial and religious propaganda, we would deny experience to say that the Illinois legislature was without reason in seeking ways to curb false or malicious defamation of racial and religious groups, made in public places and by means calculated to have a powerful emotional impact on those to whom it was presented.

"[It would] be arrant dogmatism, quite outside the scope of our authority [for] us to deny that the Illinois Legislature may warrantably believe that a man's job and his educational opportunities and the dignity accorded him may depend as much on the reputation of the racial and religious group to which he willynilly belongs, as on his own merits. This being so, we are precluded from saying that speech concededly punishable when immediately directed at individuals cannot be outlawed if directed at groups with whose position and esteem in society the affiliated individual may be inextricably involved. * * *[18]

"As to the defense of truth, Illinois in common with many States requires a showing not only that the utterance state the facts, but also that the publication be made 'with good motives and for justifiable ends'. Both elements are necessary if the defense is to prevail. [The] teaching of a century and a half of criminal libel prosecutions in this country would go by the board if we were to hold that Illinois was not within her rights in making this combined requirement. Assuming that defendant's offer of proof directed to a part of the defense was adequate, it did not satisfy the entire requirement which Illinois could exact."

The Court ruled that the trial court properly declined to require the jury to find a "clear and present danger": "Libelous utterances not being within the area of constitutionally protected speech, it is unnecessary, either for us or for the State courts, to consider the issues behind the phrase 'clear and present danger.' Certainly no one would contend that obscene speech, for example, may be punished only upon a showing of such circumstances. Libel, as we have seen, is in the same class."

18. [If] a statute sought to outlaw libels of political parties, quite different problems not now before us would be raised. For one thing, the whole doctrine of fair comment as indispensable to the democratic political process would come into play. Political parties, like public men, are, as it were, public property.

BLACK, J., joined by Douglas, J., dissented: "[The Court] acts on the bland assumption that the First Amendment is wholly irrelevant. [Today's] case degrades First Amendment freedoms to the 'rational basis' level. [We] are cautioned that state legislatures must be left free to 'experiment' and to make legislative judgments. [State] experimentation in curbing freedom of expression is startling and frightening doctrine in a country dedicated to self-government by its people.

"[As] 'constitutionally recognized,' [criminal libel] has provided for punishment of false, malicious, scurrilous charges against individuals, not against huge groups. This limited scope of the law of criminal libel is of no small importance. It has confined state punishment of speech and expression to the narrowest of areas involving nothing more than private feuds. Every expansion of the law of criminal libel so as to punish discussion of matters of public concern means a corresponding invasion of the area dedicated to free expression by the First Amendment.

"[If] there be minority groups who hail this holding as their victory, they might consider the possible relevancy of this ancient remark: 'Another such victory and I am undone.' "

REED, J., joined by Douglas, J., dissenting, argued that the statute was unconstitutionally vague: "These words—'virtue,' 'derision,' and 'obloquy'—have neither general nor special meanings well enough known to apprise those within their reach as to limitations on speech. Philosophers and poets, thinkers of high and low degree from every age and race have sought to expound the meaning of virtue. * * * Are the tests of the Puritan or the Cavalier to be applied, those of the city or the farm, the Christian or non-Christian, the old or the young?"

DOUGLAS, J., dissented: "Hitler and his Nazis showed how evil a conspiracy could be which was aimed at destroying a race by exposing it to contempt, derision, and obloquy. I would be willing to concede that such conduct directed at a race or group in this country could be made an indictable offense. For such a project would be more than the exercise of free speech. [It] would be free speech plus.

"I would also be willing to concede that even without the element of conspiracy there might be times and occasions when the legislative or executive branch might call a halt to inflammatory talk, such as the shouting of 'fire' in a school or a theatre.

"My view is that if in any case other public interests are to override the plain command of the First Amendment, the peril of speech must be clear and present, leaving no room for argument, raising no doubts as to the necessity of curbing speech in order to prevent disaster."

JACKSON, J., dissenting, argued that the fourteenth amendment does not incorporate the first, as such, but permits the states more latitude than the Congress. He concluded, however, that due process required the trier of fact to evaluate the evidence as to the truth and good faith of the speaker and the clarity and presence of the danger. He was unwilling to assume danger from the tendency of the words and felt that the trial court had precluded the defendant's efforts to show truth and good motives.

Notes and Questions

1. *The right to petition.* Should it make a difference that the leaflet was in the form of a petition to the mayor and city council? Does the right of the people

"to petition the Government for a redress of grievances" add anything of substance to Beauharnais' other first amendment arguments? Consider Harry Kalven, *The Negro and the First Amendment* 40 (1965): "If it would make a difference whether the petition was genuine and not just a trick of form, can the Court penetrate the form and appraise the true motivation or must it, as it does with congressional committees accept the official motivation?" [a]

2. *Equality and freedom of speech.* Consider the following hypothetical commentary: "Group libel statutes pose uniquely difficult issues for they involve a clash between two constitutional commitments: the principle of equality and the principle of free speech. They force us to decide what we want to express as a nation: Do we want a powerful symbol of our belief in uninhibited debate or do we want to be the kind of nation that will not tolerate the public calumny of religious, ethnic, and racial groups?" Compare Loren Beth, *Group Libel and Free Speech,* 39 Minn.L.Rev. 167, 180–81 (1955).

3. *Tolerance and freedom of speech.* Should the first amendment be a means of institutionalizing a national commitment to the value of tolerance? By tolerating the intolerable, would we carve out one area of social interaction for extraordinary self-restraint and thereby develop [b] and demonstrate a vital social capacity? See generally Lee Bollinger, *The Tolerant Society: Freedom of Speech and Extremist Speech in America* (1986); Lee Bollinger, *Free Speech and Intellectual Values,* 92 Yale L.J. 438 (1983); Lee Bollinger, *Book Review,* 80 Mich.L.Rev. 617 (1982).

4. *Libel, group libel, and seditious libel.* Consider Kalven, supra, at 15, 16 and 50–51: Seditious libel "is the doctrine that criticism of government officials and policy may be viewed as defamation of government and may be punished as a serious crime. [On] my view, the absence of seditious libel as a crime is the true pragmatic test of freedom of speech. This I would argue is what freedom of speech is about. [The] most revealing aspect of the opinions, and particularly that of Justice Frankfurter, is the absence of any sense of the proximity of the case before them to seditious libel. The case presents almost a perfect instance of that competition among analogies which Edward Levi has emphasized as the essential circumstance of legal reasoning. In the middle we have group libel and Justice Frankfurter's urging its many resemblances to individual libel. [If] the Court's speech theory had been more grounded, as it seems to me it should be, on the relevance of the concept of seditious libel and less on the analogy to the law of attempts found in the slogan 'clear and present danger,' it is difficult to believe that either the debate or the result in *Beauharnais* would have been the same."

B. PUBLIC OFFICIALS AND SEDITIOUS LIBEL

NEW YORK TIMES CO. v. SULLIVAN

376 U.S. 254, 84 S.Ct. 710, 11 L.Ed.2d 686 (1964).

JUSTICE BRENNAN delivered the opinion of the Court.

[Sullivan, the Montgomery, Ala. police commissioner, sued the New York Times and four black Alabama clergymen for alleged libelous statements in a paid, full-page fund-raising advertisement signed by a "Committee to defend Martin

a. See *McDonald v. Smith,* 472 U.S. 479, 105 S.Ct. 2787, 86 L.Ed.2d 384 (1985) (denying any special first amendment status for the Petition Clause).

b. For skepticism about the capacity of courts to achieve any substantial impact in promoting tolerance, see Robert Nagel, *Constitutional Cultures* 27–59 (1989).

Luther King and the struggle for freedom in the South." The advertisement stated that "truckloads of police armed with shotguns and tear-gas ringed Alabama State College Campus" in Montgomery, and that "the Southern violators [have] bombed [Dr. King's] home, assaulted his person [and] arrested him seven times." In several respects the statements were untrue. Several witnesses testified that they understood the statements to refer to Sullivan because he supervised Montgomery police. Sullivan proved he did not participate in the events described. He offered no proof of pecuniary loss.[3] Pursuant to Alabama law, the trial court submitted the libel issue to the jury, giving general and punitive damages instructions. It returned a $500,000 verdict for Sullivan against all of the defendants.] We hold that the rule of law applied by the Alabama courts is constitutionally deficient for failure to provide the safeguards for freedom of speech and of the press that are required by the First and Fourteenth Amendments in a libel action brought by a public official against critics of his official conduct.[4] We further hold that under the proper safeguards the evidence presented in this case is constitutionally insufficient to support the judgment for respondent.

I. [The] publication here [communicated] information, expressed opinion, recited grievances, protested claimed abuses, and sought financial support on behalf of a movement whose existence and objectives are matters of the highest public interest and concern. That the Times was paid for publishing the advertisement is as immaterial in this connection as is the fact that newspapers and books are sold. *Smith v. California.* Any other conclusion would discourage newspapers from carrying "editorial advertisements" of this type, and so might shut off an important outlet for the promulgation of information and ideas by persons who do not themselves have access to publishing facilities.

II. Under Alabama law [once] "libel per se" has been established, the defendant has no defense as to stated facts unless he can persuade the jury that they were true in all their particulars. [His] privilege of "fair comment" for expressions of opinion depends on the truth of the facts upon which the comment is based. [Unless] he can discharge the burden of proving truth, general damages are presumed, and may be awarded without proof of pecuniary injury.

[Respondent] relies heavily, as did the Alabama courts, on statements of this Court to the effect that the Constitution does not protect libelous publications. Those statements do not foreclose our inquiry here. None of the cases sustained the use of libel laws to impose sanctions upon expression critical of the official conduct of public officials. [L]ibel can claim no talismanic immunity from constitutional limitations. It must be measured by standards that satisfy the First Amendment.

3. Approximately 394 copies of the edition of the Times containing the advertisement were circulated in Alabama. Of these, about 35 copies were distributed in Montgomery County. The total circulation of the Times for that day was approximately 650,000 copies.

4. [The] Times contends that the assumption of jurisdiction over its corporate person by the Alabama courts overreaches the territorial limits of the Due Process Clause. The latter claim is foreclosed from our review by the ruling of the Alabama courts that the Times entered a general appearance in the action and thus waived its jurisdictional objection. * * *

[Since *New York Times* the Court has upheld expansive personal jurisdiction against media defendants. *Calder v. Jones*, 465 U.S. 783, 104 S.Ct. 1482, 79 L.Ed.2d 804 (1984); *Keeton v. Hustler*, 465 U.S. 770, 104 S.Ct. 1473, 79 L.Ed.2d 790 (1984). *Calder* rejected the suggestion that first amendment concerns enter into jurisdictional analysis. It feared complicating the inquiry and argued that because first amendment concerns are taken into account in limiting the substantive law of defamation, "to reintroduce those concerns at the jurisdictional stage would be a form of double counting."]

The First Amendment, said Judge Learned Hand, "presupposes that right conclusions are more likely to be gathered out of a multitude of tongues, than through any kind of authoritative selection. To many this is, and always will be, folly; but we have staked upon it our all." [Thus] we consider this case against the background of a profound national commitment to the principle that debate on public issues should be uninhibited, robust, and wide-open, and that it may well include vehement, caustic, and sometimes unpleasantly sharp attacks on government and public officials. The present advertisement, as an expression of grievance and protest on one of the major public issues of our time, would seem clearly to qualify for the constitutional protection. The question is whether it forfeits that protection by the falsity of some of its factual statements and by its alleged defamation of respondent.

Authoritative interpretations of the First Amendment guarantees have consistently refused to recognize an exception for any test of truth—whether administered by judges, juries, or administrative officials—and especially not one that puts the burden of proving truth on the speaker. [E]rroneous statement is inevitable in free debate, and [it] must be protected if the freedoms of expression are to have the "breathing space" that they "need [to] survive."

[Injury] to official reputation affords no more warrant for repressing speech that would otherwise be free than does factual error. Where judicial officers are involved, this Court has held that concern for the dignity and reputation of the courts does not justify the punishment as criminal contempt of criticism of the judge or his decision. This is true even though the utterance contains "half-truths" and "misinformation." Such repression can be justified, if at all, only by a clear and present danger of the obstruction of justice. If judges are to be treated as "men of fortitude, able to thrive in a hardy climate," surely the same must be true of other government officials, such as elected city commissioners. Criticism of their official conduct does not lose its constitutional protection merely because it is effective criticism and hence diminishes their official reputations.

If neither factual error nor defamatory content suffices to remove the constitutional shield from criticism of official conduct, the combination of the two elements is no less inadequate. This is the lesson to be drawn from the great controversy over the Sedition Act of 1798, 1 Stat. 596, which first crystallized a national awareness of the central meaning of the First Amendment. [Although] the Sedition Act was never tested in this Court, the attack upon its validity has carried the day in the court of history. Fines levied in its prosecution were repaid by Act of Congress on the ground that it was unconstitutional. * * * Jefferson, as President, pardoned those who had been convicted and sentenced under the Act and remitted their fines. [Its] invalidity [has] also been assumed by Justices of this Court. [These] views reflect a broad consensus that the Act, because of the restraint it imposed upon criticism of government and public officials, was inconsistent with the First Amendment. * * *

What a State may not constitutionally bring about by means of a criminal statute is likewise beyond the reach of its civil law of libel. The fear of damage awards under a rule such as that invoked by the Alabama courts here may be markedly more inhibiting than the fear of prosecution under a criminal statute. [The] judgment awarded in this case—without the need for any proof of actual pecuniary loss—was one thousand times greater than the maximum fine provided by the Alabama criminal [libel law], and one hundred times greater than that provided by the Sedition Act. And since there is no double-jeopardy limitation applicable to civil lawsuits, this is not the only judgment that may be awarded against petitioners for the same publication.[18] Whether or not a newspaper can survive a succession of such judgments, the pall of fear and timidity imposed upon those who would give voice to public criticism is an atmosphere in which the First Amendment freedoms cannot [survive].

The state rule of law is not saved by its allowance of the defense of truth. A defense for erroneous statements honestly made is no less essential here than was the requirement of proof of guilty knowledge which, in *Smith v. California,* we held indispensable to a valid conviction of a bookseller for possessing obscene writings for [sale].

A rule compelling the critic of official conduct to guarantee the truth of all his factual assertions—and to do so on pain of libel judgments virtually unlimited in amount—leads to a comparable "self-censorship." Allowance of the defense of truth, with the burden of proving it on the defendant, does not mean that only false speech will be deterred.[19] [Under] such a rule, would-be critics of official conduct may be deterred from voicing their criticism, even though it is believed to be true and even though it is in fact true, because of doubt whether it can be proved in court or fear of the expense of having to do so. They tend to make only statements which "steer far wider of the unlawful zone." The rule thus dampens the vigor and limits the variety of public [debate].

The constitutional guarantees require, we think, a federal rule that prohibits a public official from recovering damages for a defamatory falsehood relating to his official conduct unless he proves that the statement was made with "actual malice"—that is, with knowledge that it was false or with reckless disregard of whether it was false or [not].[a]

Such a privilege for criticism of official conduct is appropriately analogous to the protection accorded a public official when *he* is sued for libel by a private citizen. In *Barr v. Matteo,* 360 U.S. 564, 575, 79 S.Ct. 1335, 1341, 3 L.Ed.2d 1434 (1959), this Court held the utterance of a federal official to be absolutely privileged if made "within the outer perimeter" of his duties. The States accord the same immunity to statements of their highest officers, although some differentiate their lesser officials and qualify the privilege they enjoy. But all hold that all officials are protected unless actual malice can be proved. The reason for the official privilege is said to be that the threat of damage suits would otherwise "inhibit the fearless, vigorous, and effective administration of policies of government" and "dampen the ardor of all but the most resolute, or the most irresponsible, in the

---

18. The Times states that four other libel suits based on the advertisement have been filed against it by [others]; that another $500,-000 verdict has been awarded in [one]; and that the damages sought in the other three total $2,000,000.

19. Even a false statement may be deemed to make a valuable contribution to the public debate, since it brings about "the clearer perception and livelier impression of truth, produced by its collision with error." Mill, *On Liberty* 15 (1955).

a. Compare *St. Amant v. Thompson,* 390 U.S. 727, 88 S.Ct. 1323, 20 L.Ed.2d 262 (1968) (publishing while "in fact entertain[ing] serious doubts about the truth of the publication" satisfies standard) with *Garrison v. Louisiana,* 379 U.S. 64, 85 S.Ct. 209, 13 L.Ed.2d 125 (1964) (standard requires "high degree of

awareness of probable falsity"). See also *Masson v. New Yorker Magazine, Inc.,* 501 U.S. 496, 111 S.Ct. 2419, 115 L.Ed.2d 447 (1991) ("a deliberate alteration of the words uttered by a plaintiff does not equate with knowledge of falsity [unless] the alteration results in a material change of meaning conveyed by the statement"). For discussion of malice and docudrama, see Rodney Smolla, *Harlot's Ghost and JFK: A Fictional Conversation with Norman Mailer, Oliver Stone, Earl Warren and Hugo Black,* 26 Suffolk U.L.Rev. 587 (1992).

For discussion of the malice doctrine's operation in practice, see Murchison, John Soloski, Randall Bezanson, Gilbert Cranberg, & Roselle Wissler, *Sullivan's Paradox: The Emergence of Judicial Standards of Journalism,* 73 N.C.L.Rev. 7 (1994).

unflinching discharge of their duties." *Barr.* Analogous considerations support the privilege for the citizen-critic of government. It is as much his duty to criticize as it is the official's duty to administer. [It] would give public servants an unjustified preference over the public they serve, if critics of official conduct did not have a fair equivalent of the immunity granted to the officials themselves. We conclude that such a privilege is required by the First and Fourteenth Amendments.[23]

III. [W]e consider that the proof presented to show actual malice lacks the convincing clarity [b] which the constitutional standard demands, and hence that it would not constitutionally sustain the judgment for respondent under the proper rule of law. [T]here is evidence that the Times published the advertisement without checking its accuracy against the news stories in the Times' own files. The mere presence of the stories in the files does [not] establish that the Times "knew" the advertisement was false, since the state of mind required for actual malice would have to be brought home to the persons in the Times' organization having responsibility for the publication of the advertisement. With respect to the failure of those persons to make the check, the record shows that they relied upon their knowledge of the good reputation of many [whose] names were listed as sponsors of the advertisement, and upon the letter from A. Philip Randolph, known to them as a responsible individual, certifying that the use of the names was authorized. There was testimony that the persons handling the advertisement saw nothing in it that would render it unacceptable under the Times' policy of rejecting advertisements containing "attacks of a personal character"; their failure to reject it on this ground was not unreasonable. We think the evidence against the Times supports at most a finding of negligence in failing to discover the misstatements, and is constitutionally insufficient to show the recklessness that is required for a finding of actual malice.

[T]he evidence was constitutionally defective in another respect: [c] it was incapable of supporting the jury's finding that the allegedly libelous statements were made "of and concerning" respondent. [On this point, the Supreme Court of Alabama] based its ruling on the proposition that: "[The] average person knows that municipal agents, such as police and firemen, and others, are under the control and direction of the city governing body, and more particularly under the direction and control of a single commissioner. In measuring the performance or deficiencies of such groups, praise or criticism is usually attached to the official in complete control of the body."

This proposition has disquieting implications for criticism of governmental conduct. [It would transmute] criticism of government, however impersonal it may seem on its face, into personal criticism, and hence potential libel, of the

---

23. We have no occasion here to determine how far down into the lower ranks of government employees the "public official" designation would extend for purposes of this rule, or otherwise to specify categories of persons who would or would not be included. [Nor] need we here determine the boundaries of the "official conduct" concept. * * *

b. Compare *Bose Corp. v. Consumers Union*, 466 U.S. 485, 104 S.Ct. 1949, 80 L.Ed.2d 502 (1984) (appellate courts "must exercise independent judgment and determine whether the record establishes actual malice with convincing clarity."). Accord *Harte–Hanks Communications, Inc. v. Connaughton*, 491 U.S.

657, 109 S.Ct. 2678, 105 L.Ed.2d 562 (1989). See also *Anderson v. Liberty Lobby, Inc.*, 477 U.S. 242, 106 S.Ct. 2505, 91 L.Ed.2d 202 (1986) (same standard at summary judgment). Should independent appellate judgment be required in all first amendment cases? All constitutional cases? For broad-ranging commentary, see Henry Monaghan, *Constitutional Fact Review*, 85 Colum.L.Rev. 229 (1985).

c. Implicitly, the Court left open the possibility of a new trial with new evidence. For discussion of the Court's internal debate on the question, see Bernard Schwartz, *Super Chief* 531–41 (1983).

officials of whom the government is composed. [Raising] as it does the possibility that a good-faith critic of government will be penalized for his criticism, the proposition relied on by the Alabama courts strikes at the very center of the constitutionally protected area of free expression. We hold that such a proposition may not constitutionally be utilized to establish that an otherwise impersonal attack on governmental operations was a libel of an official responsible for those operations. Since it was relied on exclusively here, and there was no other evidence to connect the statements with respondent, the evidence was constitutionally insufficient to support a finding that the statements referred to respondent. * * * [d]

JUSTICE BLACK, with whom JUSTICE DOUGLAS joins (concurring).

* * * "Malice," even as defined by the Court, is an elusive, abstract concept, hard to prove and hard to disprove. The requirement that malice be proved provides at best an evanescent protection for the right critically to discuss public affairs and certainly does not measure up to the sturdy safeguard embodied in the First Amendment. Unlike the Court, therefore, I vote to reverse exclusively on the ground that the Times and the individual defendants had an absolute, unconditional constitutional right to publish in the Times advertisement their criticisms of the Montgomery agencies and [officials].

The half-million-dollar verdict [gives] dramatic proof [that] state libel laws threaten the very existence of an American press virile enough to publish unpopular views on public affairs and bold enough to criticize the conduct of public officials. [B]riefs before us show that in Alabama there are now pending eleven libel suits by local and state officials against the Times seeking $5,600,000, and five such suits against the Columbia Broadcasting System seeking $1,700,000. Moreover, this technique for harassing and punishing a free press—now that it has been shown to be possible—is by no means limited to cases with racial overtones; it can be used in other fields where public feelings may make local as well as out-of-state newspapers easy prey for libel verdict seekers.

In my opinion the Federal Constitution has dealt with this deadly danger to the press in the only way possible without leaving the press open to destruction— by granting the press an absolute immunity for criticism of the way public officials do their public duty.

[This] Nation, I suspect, can live in peace without libel suits based on public discussions of public affairs and public officials. But I doubt that a country can live in freedom where its people can be made to suffer physically or financially for criticizing their government, its actions, or its officials. * * * [e]

---

d. For a similar ruling that impersonal criticism of a government operation cannot be the basis for defamation "of and concerning" the supervisor of the operation, see *Rosenblatt v. Baer*, 383 U.S. 75, 86 S.Ct. 669, 15 L.Ed.2d 597 (1966): "[T]antamount to a demand for recovery based on libel of government."

e. Goldberg, J., joined by Douglas, J., concurring, also asserted for "the citizen and [the] press an absolute unconditional privilege to criticize official conduct," but maintained that the imposition of liability for "[p]urely private defamation" did not abridge the first amendment because it had "little to do with the political ends of a self-governing society." For background on the *New York Times* case, see Anthony Lewis, *Make No Law* (1991); Rodney Smolla, *Suing The Press* 26–52 (1986). For the Canadian approach, see *Hill v. Church of Scientology of Ontario* [1995], 126 D.L.R. 4th 129.

Professor Kalven observed that the Court in *New York Times* was moving toward "the theory of free speech that Alexander Meiklejohn has been offering us for some fifteen years now." Harry Kalven, *The New York Times Case: A Note On "The Central Meaning of the First Amendment,"* 1964 Sup.Ct.Rev. 191, 221. Indeed Kalven reported Alexander Meiklejohn's view that the case was " 'an occasion for dancing in the streets.' " Id. at 221 n. 125. Consider the following excerpts from Meiklejohn's most significant work and Zechariah Chafee's pointed response.

ALEXANDER MEIKLEJOHN—FREE SPEECH AND ITS RELATION TO SELF–GOVERNMENT

3, 26–27, 93–94, 89–91 (1948), reprinted in Meiklejohn, *Political Freedom* 9,
27–28, 79–80, 75–77 (1960).
Reprinted with permission of the publisher; copyright © 1948, 1960
by Harper Collins Publishers.

We Americans think of ourselves as politically free. We believe in self-government. If men are to be governed, we say, then that governing must be done, not by others, but by themselves. So far, therefore, as our own affairs are concerned, we refuse to submit to alien control. That refusal, if need be, we will carry to the point of rebellion, of revolution. And if other men, within the jurisdiction of our laws, are denied their right to political freedom, we will, in the same spirit, rise to their defense. Governments, we insist, derive their just powers from the consent of the governed. If that consent be lacking, governments have no just powers.

[The] principle of the freedom of speech springs from the necessities of the program of self-government. It is not a Law of Nature or of Reason in the abstract. It is a deduction from the basic American agreement that public issues shall be decided by universal suffrage.[a]

If, then, on any occasion in the United States it is allowable to say that the Constitution is a good document it is equally allowable, in that situation, to say that the Constitution is a bad document. If a public building may be used in which to say, in time of war, that the war is justified, then the same building may be used in which to say that it is not justified. If it be publicly argued that conscription for armed service is moral and necessary, it may likewise be publicly argued that it is immoral and unnecessary. If it may be said that American political institutions are superior to those of England or Russia or Germany, it may, with equal freedom, be said that those of England or Russia or Germany are superior to ours. These conflicting views may be expressed, must be expressed, not because they are valid, but because they are relevant. If they are responsibly entertained by anyone, we, the voters, need to hear them. When a question of policy is "before the house," free men choose to meet it not with their eyes shut, but with their eyes open. To be afraid of ideas, any idea, is to be unfit for self-government. Any such suppression of ideas about the common good, the First

---

a. Consider David Cole, *Beyond Unconstitutional Conditions: Charting Spheres of Neutrality in Government–Funded Speech,* 67 N.Y.U.L.Rev. 675, 710 (1992): "If Holmes's 'free trade' metaphor represents the paradigmatic liberal vision of free speech, Meiklejohn's town meeting captures the republican vision of an inclusive public exchange in which ordinary people actively participate as citizens, engaged in an ongoing dialogue about public values and norms. Where the liberal view sees an 'invisible hand' reaching truth through the self-interested behavior of atomistic individuals, the republican vision emphasizes the constitutive role of public dialogue in shaping our collective identity as a community, and the importance of maintaining public institutions for speech to that end."

Amendment condemns with its absolute disapproval. The freedom of ideas shall not be abridged. * * *

If, however, as our argument has tried to show, the principle of the freedom of speech is derived, not from some supposed "Natural Right," but from the necessities of self-government by universal suffrage, there follows at once a very large limitation of the scope of the principle. The guarantee given by the First Amendment is not, then, assured to all speaking. It is assured only to speech which bears, directly or indirectly, upon issues with which voters have to deal— only, therefore, to the consideration of matters of public interest. Private speech, or private interest in speech, on the other hand, has no claim whatever to the protection of the First Amendment. If men are engaged, as we so commonly are, in argument, or inquiry, or advocacy, or incitement which is directed toward our private interests, private privileges, private possessions, we are, of course, entitled to "due process" protection of those activities. But the First Amendment has no concern over such protection. * * *

Here, then, are the charges which I would bring against the "clear and present danger" theory. They are all, it is clear, differing forms of the basic accusation that the compact of self-government has been ignored or repudiated.

First, the theory denies or obscures the fact that free citizens have two distinct sets of civil liberties. As the makers of the laws, they have duties and responsibilities which require an absolute freedom. As the subjects of the laws, they have possessions and rights, to which belongs a relative freedom.

Second, the theory fails to keep clear the distinction between the constitutional status of discussions of public policy and the corresponding status of discussions of private policy.

Third, the theory fails to recognize that, under the Constitution, the freedom of advocacy or incitement to action *by the government* may never be abridged. It is only advocacy or incitement to action by individuals or nonpolitical groups which is open to regulation.

Fourth, the theory regards the freedom of speech as a mere device which is to be abandoned when dangers threaten the public welfare. On the contrary, it is the very presence of those dangers which makes it imperative that, in the midst of our fears, we remember and observe a principle upon whose integrity rests the entire structure of government by consent of the governed.

Fifth, the Supreme Court, by adopting a theory which annuls the First Amendment, has struck a disastrous blow at our national education. It has denied the belief that men can, by processes of free public discussion, govern themselves. * * *

The unabridged freedom of public discussion is the rock on which our government stands. With that foundation beneath us, we shall not flinch in the face of any clear and present—or, even, terrific—danger.

ZECHARIAH CHAFEE, JR.—BOOK REVIEW

62 Harv.L.Rev. 891, 894–901 (1949).
Reprinted with permission of the publisher; copyright © 1949, by the
Harvard Law Review Association.

[M]y main objection to Mr. Meiklejohn's book [is that he] places virtually all his argument against current proposals for suppression on a constitutional position which is extremely dubious. Whereas the supporters of these measures are genuinely worried by the dangers of Communism, he refuses to argue that these dangers are actually small.   Instead, his constitutional position obliges him to argue that these dangers are irrelevant.   No matter how terrible and immediate the dangers may be, he keeps saying, the First Amendment will not let Congress or anybody else in the Government try to deal with Communists who have not yet committed unlawful [acts.]

Mr. Meiklejohn's basic proposition is that there are two distinct kinds of freedom of speech, protected by quite different clauses of the Constitution. Freedom of speech on matters affecting self-government is protected by the First Amendment and is not open to restrictions by the Government.   [By] contrast, private discussion is open to restrictions because it is protected by [fifth amendment due process].

The truth is, I think, that the framers had no very clear idea as to what they meant by "the freedom of speech or of the press," but we can say three things with reasonable assurance.   First, these politicians, lawyers, scholars, churchgoers and philosophers, scientists, agriculturalists, and wide readers used the phrase to embrace the whole realm of thought.   Second, they intended the First Amendment to give all the protection they desired, and had no idea of supplementing it by the Fifth Amendment.   Finally, the freedom which Congress was forbidden to abridge was not, for them, some absolute concept which had never existed on earth.   It was the freedom which they believed they already had—what they had wanted before the Revolution and had acquired through independence.   In thinking about it, they took for granted the limitations which had been customarily applied in the day-to-day work of colonial courts.   Now, they were setting up a new federal government of great potential strength, and (as in the rest of Bill of Rights) they were determined to make sure that it would not take away the freedoms which they then enjoyed in their thirteen sovereign states.

Still, the First Amendment has the power of growing to meet new needs.   As Marshall said, it is a *Constitution* which we are interpreting.   Although in 1791 the Amendment did not mean what Mr. Meiklejohn says, perhaps it ought to mean that now.   But the Supreme Court is unlikely to think so in any foreseeable future.   The author condemns the clear and present danger test as "a peculiarly inept and unsuccessful attempt to formulate an exception" to the constitutional protection of public discussion, but he does not realize how unworkable his own views would prove when applied in litigation.

In the first place, although it may be possible to draw a fairly bright line between speech which is completely immune and action which may be punished, some speech on public questions is so hateful that the Court would be very reluctant to protect it from statutory penalties.   We are not dealing with a philosopher who can write what he pleases, but with at least five men who are asked to block legislators and prosecutors.   The history of the Court Plan in 1937 shows how sure judges have to be of their ground to do that.   Take a few examples.   A newspaper charges the mayor with taking bribes.   Ezra Pound broadcasts from an Italian radio station that our participation in the war is an abominable mistake.   A speaker during a very bad food shortage tells a hungry mass of voters that the rationing board is so incompetent and corrupt that the best way to avoid starvation is to demand the immediate death of its members, unless they are ready to resign.   Plainly few judges can grant constitutional protection to such speeches.

Even the author begins to hedge.   Although his main insistence is on immunity for all speech connected with self-government, as my examples surely are, occasionally he concedes that "repressive action by the government is imperative for the sake of the general welfare," e.g., against libelous assertions, slander, words inciting men to crime, sedition, and treason by words. Here he is diving into very deep water. Once you push punishment beyond action into the realm of language, then you have to say pretty plainly how far back the law should go. You must enable future judges and jurymen to know where to stop. That is just what Holmes did when he drew his line at clear and present danger and the author gives us no substitute test for distinguishing between good public speech and bad public speech. He never faces the problem of Mark Anthony's Oration— discussion which is calculated to produce unlawful acts without ever mentioning them.

At times he hints that the line depends on the falsity of the assertions or the bad motives of the speakers. In the mayor's case, it is no answer to say that false charges are outside the Constitution; the issue is whether a jury shall be permitted to find them false even if they are in fact true. Moreover, in such charges a good deal of truth which might be useful to the voters is frequently mixed with some falsehood, so that the possibility of a damage action often keeps genuine information away from voters. And the low character of speakers and writers does not necessarily prevent them from uttering wholesome truths about politics. Witness the Essays of Francis Bacon. Mr. Meiklejohn has a special dislike for paid "lobbyists for special interests." But if discussing public questions with money in sight is outside the First Amendment, how about speeches by aspirants to a $75,000 job in Washington or editorials in newspapers or books on Free Speech? Dr. Johnson declared that any man who writes except for money is a fool. In short, the trouble with the bad-motive test is that courts and juries would apply it only to the exponents of unpopular views. If what is said happens to be our way, the speaker is as welcome as an ex-revolutionist to the Un-American Committee.

The most serious weakness in Mr. Meiklejohn's argument is that it rests on his supposed boundary between public speech and private speech. That line is extremely blurred. Take the novel *Strange Fruit*, which was lately suppressed in Massachusetts. It did not discuss any question then before the voters, but it dealt thoughtfully with many problems of the relations between whites and Negroes, a matter of great national concern. Was this under the First Amendment or the Fifth? [The] truth is that there are public aspects to practically every subject. [The] author recognizes this when he says that the First Amendment is directed against "mutilation of the thinking process of the community." [This] attitude, however, offers such a wide area for the First Amendment that very little is left for his private speech under the Fifth Amendment. For example, if books and plays are public speech, how can they be penalized for gross obscenity or libels?

On the other hand, if private speech does include scholarship (as the author suggests) and also art and literature, it is shocking to deprive these vital matters of the protection of the inspiring words of the First Amendment. The individual interest in freedom of speech, which Socrates voiced when he said that he would rather die than stop talking, is too precious to be left altogether to the vague words of the due process clause. Valuable as self-government is, it is in itself only a small part of our lives. That a philosopher should subordinate all other activities to it is indeed surprising.

[Even] if Holmes had agreed with Mr. Meiklejohn's view of the First Amendment, his insistence on such absolutism would not have persuaded a single colleague, and scores of men would have gone to prison who have been speaking freely for three decades. After all, a judge who is trying to establish a doctrine which the Supreme Court will promulgate as law cannot write like a solitary philosopher. He has to convince at least four men in a specific group and convince them very soon. The true alternative to Holmes' view of the First Amendment was not at all the perfect immunity for public discussion which Mr. Meiklejohn desires. It was no immunity at all in the face of legislation. Any danger, any tendency in speech to produce bad acts, no matter how remote, would suffice to validate a repressive statute, and the only hope for speakers and writers would lie in being tried by liberal jurymen. * * * Holmes worked out a formula which would invalidate a great deal of suppression, and won for it the solid authority of a unanimous Court. Afterwards, again and again, when his test was misapplied by the majority, Holmes restated his position in ringing words which, with the help of Brandeis and Hughes, eventually inspired the whole Court.

Notes and Questions

1. To what extent does *New York Times* incorporate Meiklejohn's perspective?[b] What is the "central meaning" of the first amendment?

Consider Lee Bollinger, *Images of a Free Press* 6–7 (1994): "On one hand, [*New York Times*] portrayed the citizen as reluctant to enter public debate, timid before the prospect of a lawsuit, fearful of the costs. One naturally imagines a citizenry composed of people with other things to do, who see participation in public affairs as a duty, not a joy, as something to be avoided when an excuse is at hand. Yet [*New York Times*] also provides the image of a citizen who is naturally disposed to enter public debate—in fact, too disposed. Believing deeply and finding opposing beliefs threatening, this person is inclined to resort to 'exaggeration, to vilification * * * [and] even to false statement.' Public discussion is not a pretty thing because belief pushes people to adversarial extremes and citizens cannot control themselves."

3. *New York Times, definitional balancing, and the two-level theory of the first amendment.* By holding that some libel was within the protection of the first amendment, did the Court dismantle its two-level theory? See Kalven, supra, at 217–218. Or did the Court merely rearrange its conception of what was protected and what was not?

Does *Garrison v. Louisiana,* 379 U.S. 64, 85 S.Ct. 209, 13 L.Ed.2d 125 (1964) shed light on the question? The Court stated: "Calculated falsehood falls into

b. For elaboration and modification of Meiklejohn's views, see Alexander Meiklejohn, *The First Amendment Is an Absolute,* 1961 Sup.Ct.Rev. 245. For commentary, see Lee Bollinger, *Free Speech and Intellectual Values,* 92 Yale L.J. 438 (1983); Kalven, p. 669 supra. For work proceeding from a politically based interpretation of the first amendment, see George Anastaplo, *The Constitutionalist* (1971); Cass Sunstein, *Democracy and the Problem of Free Speech* (1993); Lillian BeVier, *The First Amendment and Political Speech: An Inquiry Into the Substance and Limits of Principle,* 30 Stan.L.Rev. 299 (1978); Edward Bloustein, *The First Amendment and Privacy: The Supreme Court Justice and the Philosopher,* 28 Rutg.L.Rev. 41 (1974); Robert Bork, *Neutral Principles and Some First Amendment Problems,* 47 Ind.L.J. 1 (1971); Owen Fiss, *State Activism and State Censorship,* 100 Yale

L.J. 2087 (1991). Owen Fiss, *Why the State,* 100 Harv.L.Rev. 781 (1987); Owen Fiss, *Free Speech and Social Structure,* 71 Iowa L.Rev. 1405 (1986). See also William Brennan, *The Supreme Court and the Meiklejohn Interpretation of the First Amendment,* 79 Harv.L.Rev. 1 (1965); Daniel Farber, *Free Speech Without Romance,* 105 Harv.L.Rev. 554 (1991) (arriving at a politically centered perspective after applying economic analysis).

For criticism of Sunstein's position, see J.M. Balkin, *Populism and Progressivism as Constitutional Categories,* 104 Yale L.J. (1995); Robert Lipkin, *The Quest for the Common Good: Neutrality and Deliberative Democracy in Sunstein's Conception of American Constitutionalism,* 26 Conn.L.Rev. 1039 (1994); William Marshall, *Free Speech and the "Problem" of Democracy,* 89 Nw.U.L.Rev. 191 (1994).

that class of utterances '[of] such slight social value as a step to truth that any benefit that may be derived from them is clearly outweighed by the social interest in order and morality.' *Chaplinsky.*"

Could the judicial process here fairly be called *definitional* classification—defining which categories of libel are to be viewed as "speech" within the first amendment, and which are not? Consider Melville Nimmer, *The Right to Speak from Times to Time: First Amendment Theory Applied to Libel and Misapplied to Privacy,* 56 Calif.L.Rev. 935, 942–43 (1968): "[*New York Times*] points the way to the employment of the balancing process on the definitional rather than the litigation or ad hoc level, [that is,] balancing not for the purpose of determining which litigant deserves to prevail in the particular case, but only for the purpose of defining which forms of speech are to be regarded as 'speech' within the meaning of the first amendment. [By] in effect holding that knowingly and recklessly false speech was not 'speech' within the meaning of the first amendment, the Court must have implicitly (since no explicit explanation was offered) referred to certain competing policy considerations. This is surely a kind of balancing, but it is just as surely not ad hoc balancing." [c]

4. *The scope of New York Times.* Professor Kalven argued that given the Court's conception of freedom of speech, its holding could not be confined: "the invitation to follow a dialectic progression from public official to government policy to public policy to matters in the public domain, like art, seems * * * overwhelming." Kalven, supra, at 221.

(a) *Public officials. New York Times,* fn. 23 left open "how far down into the lower ranks of governmental employees" the rule would extend, and *Rosenblatt v. Baer,* 383 U.S. 75, 86 S.Ct. 669, 15 L.Ed.2d 597 (1966) suggested the rule might apply to the supervisor of a publicly owned ski resort, saying it applies to those who "appear to the public to [have] substantial responsibility for or control over the conduct of government affairs." Should criticism of the official conduct of *very* high ranking government officials (e.g., the President, the Secretary of State, a general commanding troops in war) be given greater protection than that afforded in *New York Times*?

(b) *Private conduct of public officials and candidates. Garrison,* extended *New York Times* to "anything which might touch on an official's fitness for

c. The literature about balancing is voluminous. Compare, e.g., Laurent Frantz, *The First Amendment in the Balance,* 71 Yale L.J. 1424 (1962); Laurent Frantz, *Is the First Amendment Law? —A Reply to Professor Mendelson,* 51 Calif.L.Rev. 729 (1963) with Wallace Mendelson, *On the Meaning of the First Amendment: Absolutes in the Balance,* 50 Calif.L.Rev. 821 (1962); Wallace Mendelson, *The First Amendment and the Judicial Process: A Reply to Mr. Frantz,* 17 Vand.L.Rev. 479 (1984). For recent criticism of balancing, see T. Alexander Aleinikoff, *Constitutional Law in the Age of Balancing,* 96 Yale L.J. 943 (1987); Robert Nagel, *Constitutional Cultures* (1989); Robert Nagel, *Rationalism in Constitutional Law,* 4 Const.Comm. 9 (1987); Robert Nagel, *The Formulaic Constitution,* 84 Mich.L.Rev. 165 (1985). For a philosophical attack on cost benefit analysis, see Laurence Tribe, *Policy Science: Analysis or Ideology?,* 2 Phil. & Pub. Aff. 66 (1972); Laurence Tribe, *Technology Assessment and the Fourth Discontinuity: The*

Limits of Instrumental Rationality, 46 So.Cal. L.Rev. 617 (1973). For philosophical defenses of balancing, see Pierre Schlag, *An Attack on Categorical Approaches to Freedom of Speech,* 30 U.C.L.A.L.Rev. 671 (1983); Steven Shiffrin, *Liberalism, Radicalism, and Legal Scholarship,* 30 U.C.L.A.L.Rev. 1103 (1983) (both resisting any necessary connection between balancing and instrumentalism or cost-benefit analysis). For more doctrinally focused analysis, compare, e.g., Thomas Emerson, *First Amendment Doctrine and the Burger Court,* 68 Calif.L.Rev. 422 (1980); Laurence Tribe, *Constitutional Calculus: Equal Justice or Economic Efficiency?,* 98 Harv.L.Rev. 592 (1985) with Frederick Schauer, *Categories and the First Amendment: A Play in Three Acts,* 34 Vand. L.Rev. 265 (1981); Steven Shiffrin, *The First Amendment and Economic Regulation: Away From a General Theory of the First Amendment,* 78 Nw.U.L.Rev. 1212 (1983); William Van Alstyne, *A Graphic Review of the Free Speech Clause,* 70 Calif.L.Rev. 107 (1982).

office," even if the defamation did not concern official conduct in office. Invoking that standard, *Monitor Patriot Co. v. Roy*, 401 U.S. 265, 91 S.Ct. 621, 28 L.Ed.2d 35 (1971) applied *New York Times* to a news column describing a candidate for public office as a "former small-time bootlegger."

(c) *Public figures.* In CURTIS PUB. CO. v. BUTTS and ASSOCIATED PRESS v. WALKER, 388 U.S. 130, 87 S.Ct. 1975, 18 L.Ed.2d 1094 (1967), HARLAN, J., contended that because public figures were not subject to the restraints of the political process, any criticism of them was not akin to seditious libel and was, therefore, a step removed from the central meaning of the first amendment. Nonetheless, he argued that public figure actions should not be left entirely to the vagaries of state defamation law and would have required that public figures show "highly unreasonable conduct constituting an extreme departure from the standards of investigation and reporting ordinarily adhered to by responsible publishers" as a prerequisite to recovery. In response, WARREN, C.J., argued that the inapplicability of the restraints of the political process to public figures underscored the importance for uninhibited debate about their activities since "public opinion may be the only instrument by which society can attempt to influence their conduct." He observed that increasingly "the distinctions between governmental and private sectors are blurred," that public figures, like public officials, "often play an influential role in ordering society," and as a class have a ready access to the mass media "both to influence policy and to counter criticism of their views and activities." He accordingly concluded that the *New York Times* rule should be extended to public figures. Four other justices in *Butts* and *Walker* were willing to go at least as far as Warren, C.J., and subsequent cases have settled on the position that public figures must meet the *New York Times* requirements in order to recover in a defamation action. The critical issues are how to define the concept of public figure and how to apply it in practice. See *Gertz*, infra.

(d) *Private plaintiffs and public issues.* Without deciding whether any first amendment protection should extend to matters not of general or public interest, a plurality led by BRENNAN, J., joined by Burger, C.J., and Blackmun, J., argued in ROSENBLOOM v. METROMEDIA, INC., 403 U.S. 29, 91 S.Ct. 1811, 29 L.Ed.2d 296 (1971), that the *New York Times* rule should be extended to defamatory statements involving matters of public or general interest "without regard to whether the persons involved are famous or anonymous." Black, J., would have gone further, opining that the first amendment "does not permit the recovery of libel judgments against the news media even when statements are broadcast with knowledge they are false," and Douglas, J., shared Black, J.'s approach (at least with respect to matters of public interest, although he did not participate in *Rosenbloom*.) WHITE, J., felt that the *New York Times* rule should apply to reporting on the official actions of public servants and to reporting on those involved in or affected by their official action. That principle was broad enough to cover Rosenbloom, a distributor of nudist magazines who had been arrested by the Philadelphia police for distributing obscene materials. The defamatory broadcast wrongly assumed his guilt. Dissenting, Harlan, Stewart and Marshall, JJ., counselled an approach similar to that taken in *Gertz*, infra.

After *Rosenbloom* the lower courts rather uniformly followed the approach taken by the plurality. By 1974, however, the composition of the Court had changed and so had the minds of some of the justices.

C. PRIVATE INDIVIDUALS AND PUBLIC FIGURES
GERTZ v. ROBERT WELCH, INC.
418 U.S. 323, 94 S.Ct. 2997, 41 L.Ed.2d 789 (1974).

JUSTICE POWELL delivered the opinion of the Court.

[Respondent published *American Opinion,* a monthly outlet for the John Birch Society. It published an article falsely stating that Gertz, a lawyer, was the "architect" in a "communist frameup" of a policeman convicted of murdering a youth whose family Gertz represented in resultant civil proceedings, and that Gertz had a "criminal record" and had been an officer in a named "Communist-fronter" organization that advocated violent seizure of our government. In Gertz' libel action there was evidence that *Opinion* 's managing editor did not know the statements were false and had relied on the reputation of the article's author and prior experience with the accuracy of his articles. After a $50,000 verdict for Gertz, the trial court entered judgment n.o.v., concluding that the *New York Times* rule applied to any discussion of a "public issue." The court of appeals affirmed, ruling that the publisher did not have the requisite "awareness of probable falsity." The Court held that *New York Times* did not apply to defamation of private individuals, but remanded for a new trial "because the jury was allowed to impose liability without fault [and] to presume damages without proof of injury."]

II. The principal issue in this case is whether a newspaper or broadcaster that publishes defamatory falsehoods about an individual who is neither a public official nor a public figure may claim a constitutional privilege against liability for the injury inflicted by those statements. * * *

In his opinion for the plurality in *Rosenbloom,* Mr. Justice Brennan took the *Times* privilege one step further [than *Butts* and *Walker*]. He concluded that its protection should extend to defamatory falsehoods relating to private persons if the statements concerned matters of general or public interest. He abjured the suggested distinction between public officials and public figures on the one hand and private individuals on the other. He focused instead on society's interest in learning about certain issues: "If a matter is a subject of public or general interest, it cannot suddenly become less so merely because a private individual is involved or because in some sense the individual did not choose to become involved." Thus, under the plurality opinion, a private citizen involuntarily associated with a matter of general interest has no recourse for injury to his reputation unless he can satisfy the demanding requirements of the *Times* [test].

III. [Under] the First Amendment there is no such thing as a false idea. However pernicious an opinion may seem, we depend for its correction not on the conscience of the judges and juries but on the competition of other ideas.[a] But there is no constitutional value in false statements of fact. Neither the intentional lie nor the careless error materially advances society's interest in "uninhibited, robust, and wide-open" debate on public issues. * * *

---

a. For many years the lower courts took this language seriously and deemed opinion to be absolutely protected (see, e.g., *Ollman v. Evans,* 750 F.2d 970 (D.C.Cir.1984)), but *Milkovich v. Lorain Journal Co.,* 497 U.S. 1, 110 S.Ct. 2695, 111 L.Ed.2d 1 (1990), per Rehnquist, C.J., ultimately denied that there is any "wholesale defamation exception for anything that might be labelled 'opinion.' " For the impact of *Milkovich,* see Kathryn Dix Sowle, *A Matter of Opinion,* 3 Wm. & Mary L.Rev. 467 (1994).

Although the erroneous statement of fact is not worthy of constitutional protection, it is nevertheless inevitable in free debate. [P]unishment of error runs the risk of inducing a cautious and restrictive exercise of the constitutionally guaranteed freedoms of speech and press. [The] First Amendment requires that we protect some falsehood in order to protect speech that matters.

The need to avoid self-censorship by the news media is, however, not the only societal value at issue. [The] legitimate state interest underlying the law of libel is the compensation of individuals for the harm inflicted on them by defamatory falsehoods. We would not lightly require the State to abandon this purpose, for, as Mr. Justice Stewart has reminded us, the individual's right to the protection of his own good name "reflects no more than our basic concept of the essential dignity and worth of every human being—a concept at the root of any decent system of ordered liberty. * * * " *Rosenblatt*.[b]

Some tension necessarily exists between the need for a vigorous and uninhibited press and the legitimate interest in redressing wrongful injury. [In] our continuing effort to define the proper accommodation between these competing concerns, we have been especially anxious to assure to the freedoms of speech and press that "breathing space" essential to their fruitful exercise. To that end this Court has extended a measure of strategic protection to defamatory falsehood.

The *New York Times* standard defines the level of constitutional protection appropriate to the context of defamation of [public figures and those who hold governmental office]. Plainly many deserving plaintiffs, including some intentionally subjected to injury, will be unable to surmount the barrier of the *New York Times* test. [For] the reasons stated below, we conclude that the state interest in compensating injury to the reputation of private individuals requires that a different rule should obtain with respect to them.

[W]e have no difficulty in distinguishing among defamation plaintiffs. The first remedy of any victim of defamation is self-help—using available opportunities to contradict the lie or correct the error and thereby to minimize its adverse impact on reputation. Public officials and public figures usually enjoy significantly greater access to the channels of effective communication and hence have a more realistic opportunity to counteract false statements than private individuals normally enjoy.[9] Private individuals are therefore more vulnerable to injury, and the state interest in protecting them is correspondingly greater.

---

b. Stewart J., continued: "The protection of private personality, like the protection of life itself, is left primarily to the individual States under the Ninth and Tenth Amendments. But this does not mean that the right is entitled to any less recognition by this Court as a basic of our constitutional system." Consider Robert Post, *The Social Foundations of Defamation Law*, 74 Calif.L.Rev. 691, 708 (1986): "[I]t is not immediately clear how reputation, which is social and public, and which resides in the 'common or general estimate of person,' can possibly affect the 'essential dignity' of a person's 'private personality.' The gulf that appears to separate reputation from dignity can be spanned only if defamation law contains an implicit theory of the relationship between the private and public aspects of the self."

9. Of course, an opportunity for rebuttal seldom suffices to undo harm of defamatory falsehood. Indeed, the law of defamation is rooted in our experience that the truth rarely catches up with a lie. But the fact that the self-help remedy of rebuttal, standing alone, is inadequate to its task does not mean that it is irrelevant to our inquiry. [Consider Steven Shiffrin, *Defamatory Non-Media Speech and First Amendment Methodology*, 25 U.C.L.A.L.Rev. 915, 952–53 (1978): "[F]ootnote nine, has seemingly left the first amendment in a peculiar spot. *Gertz* holds that the first amendment offers some protection for defamatory utterances presumably so that our Constitution can continue 'to preserve an uninhibited marketplace of ideas in which truth will ultimately prevail. * * * ' And yet the Court recognizes that 'an opportunity for rebuttal seldom suffices to undo [the] harm of defamatory falsehood,' i.e., truth does not emerge in the marketplace of ideas. Is the Court trapped in an obvious contradiction?"]

More important than the likelihood that private individuals will lack effective opportunities for rebuttal, there is a compelling normative consideration underlying the distinction between public and private defamation plaintiffs. An individual who decides to seek governmental office must accept certain necessary consequences of that involvement in public affairs. He runs the risk of closer public scrutiny than might otherwise be the case. [Those] classed as public figures stand in a similar [position.] [c]

Even if the foregoing generalities do not obtain in every instance, the communications media are entitled to act on the assumption that public officials and public figures have voluntarily exposed themselves to increased risk of injury from defamatory falsehoods concerning them. No such assumption is justified with respect to a private individual. He has not accepted public office nor assumed an "influential role in ordering society." *Butts.* He has relinquished no part of his interest in the protection of his own good name, and consequently he has a more compelling call on the courts for redress of injury inflicted by defamatory falsehood. Thus, private individuals are not only more vulnerable to injury than public officials and public figures; they are also more deserving of recovery.

For these reasons we conclude that the States should retain substantial latitude in their efforts to enforce a legal remedy for defamatory falsehood injurious to the reputation of a private individual. The extension of the *Times* test proposed by the *Rosenbloom* plurality would abridge this legitimate state interest to a degree that we find unacceptable. And it would occasion the additional difficulty of forcing state and federal judges to decide on an ad hoc basis which publications address issues of "general or public interest" and which do not—to determine, in the words of Mr. Justice Marshall, "what information is relevant to self-government." *Rosenbloom.* We doubt the wisdom of committing this task to the conscience of judges. [The] "public or general interest" test for determining the applicability of the *Times* standard to private defamation actions inadequately serves both of the competing values at stake. On the one hand, a private individual whose reputation is injured by defamatory falsehood that does concern an issue of public or general interest has no recourse unless he can meet the rigorous requirements of *Times.* This is true despite the factors that distinguish the state interest in compensating private individuals from the analogous interest involved in the context of public persons. On the other hand, a publisher or broadcaster of a defamatory error which a court deems unrelated to an issue of public or general interest may be held liable in damages even if it took every reasonable precaution to ensure the accuracy of its assertions. And liability may far exceed compensation for any actual injury to the plaintiff, for the jury may be permitted to presume damages without proof of loss and even to award punitive damages.

We hold that, so long as they do not impose liability without fault, the States may define for themselves the appropriate standard of liability for a publisher or broadcaster of defamatory falsehood injurious to a private individual. This

---

c. Consider Lee Bollinger, *Images of a Free Press* 25–26 (1994): "Essentially, the Court has said that, since these individuals have freely chosen a public life, what happens to them is their own doing, just as it is for a man who breaks his leg while hiking in the wilderness. Putting aside for the moment the fact that we also have an interest in encouraging people to enter public affairs, it simply is wrong to suppose that the pain inflicted by defamatory statements about public officials and figures is not our responsibility or concern. It should always be open to people to object to the way the world works under the rules we create, and not be dismissed by the claim that they have chosen to continue living in that world and, therefore, can be taken as having assented to it."

approach provides a more equitable boundary between the competing concerns involved here. It recognizes the strength of the legitimate state interest in compensating private individuals for wrongful injury to reputation, yet shields the press and broadcast media from the rigors of strict liability for defamation. At least this conclusion obtains where, as here, the substance of the defamatory statement "makes substantial danger to reputation apparent." *Butts*. This phrase places in perspective the conclusion we announce today. Our inquiry would involve considerations somewhat different from those discussed above if a State purported to condition civil liability on a factual misstatement whose content did not warn a reasonably prudent editor or broadcaster of its defamatory potential. Cf. *Time, Inc. v. Hill* [Part D infra]. Such a case is not now before us, and we intimate no view as to its proper resolution.

IV. [T]he strong and legitimate state interest in compensating private individuals for injury to reputation [extends] no further than compensation for actual injury. For the reasons stated below, we hold that the States may not permit recovery of presumed or punitive damages, at least when liability is not based on a showing of knowledge of falsity or reckless disregard for the truth.

The common law of defamation is an oddity of tort [law]. Juries may award substantial sums as compensation for supposed damage to reputation without any proof that such harm actually occurred. [This] unnecessarily compounds the potential of any system of liability for defamatory falsehood to inhibit the vigorous exercise of First Amendment freedoms [and] invites juries to punish unpopular opinion rather than to compensate individuals for injury sustained by the publication of a false fact. More to the point, the States have no substantial interest in securing for plaintiffs such as this petitioner gratuitous awards of money damages far in excess of any actual injury.

We would not, of course, invalidate state law simply because we doubt its wisdom, but here we are attempting to reconcile state law with a competing interest grounded in the constitutional command of the First Amendment. It is therefore appropriate to require that state remedies for defamatory falsehood reach no farther than is necessary to protect the legitimate interest involved. It is necessary to restrict defamation plaintiffs who do not prove knowledge of falsity or reckless disregard for the truth to compensation for actual injury. We need not define "actual injury," as trial courts have wide experience in framing appropriate jury instructions in tort action. Suffice it to say that actual injury is not limited to out-of-pocket loss. Indeed, the more customary types of actual harm inflicted by defamatory falsehood include impairment of reputation and standing in the community, personal humiliation, and mental anguish and suffering. Of course, juries must be limited by appropriate instructions, and all awards must be supported by competent evidence concerning the injury, although there need be no evidence which assigns an actual dollar value to the injury.

We also find no justification for allowing awards of punitive damages against publishers and broadcasters held liable under state-defined standards of liability for defamation. In most jurisdictions jury discretion over the amounts awarded is limited only by the gentle rule that they not be excessive. Consequently, juries assess punitive damages in wholly unpredictable amounts bearing no necessary relation to the actual harm caused. And they remain free to use their discretion selectively to punish expressions of unpopular views. [J]ury discretion to award punitive damages unnecessarily exacerbates the danger of media self-censorship; [punitive] damages are wholly irrelevant to the state interest that justifies a negligence standard for private defamation actions. They are not compensation for injury. Instead, they are private fines levied by civil juries to punish reprehensible conduct and to deter its future occurrence. In short, the private defamation plaintiff who establishes liability under a less demanding standard than that stated by *Times* may recover only such damages as are sufficient to compensate him for actual injury.[d]

V. Notwithstanding our refusal to extend the *New York Times* privilege to defamation of private individuals, respondent contends that we should affirm the judgment below on the ground that petitioner is [a] public figure. [That] designation may rest on either of two alternative bases. In some instances an individual may achieve such pervasive fame or notoriety that he becomes a public figure for all purposes and in all contexts. More commonly, an individual voluntarily injects himself or is drawn into a particular public controversy and thereby becomes a public figure for a limited range of issues. In either case such persons assume special prominence in the resolution of public questions.

Petitioner has long been active in community and professional affairs. He has served as an officer of local civic groups and of various professional organizations, and he has published several books and articles on legal subjects. Although petitioner was consequently well known in some circles, he had achieved no general fame or notoriety in the community. None of the prospective jurors called at the trial had ever heard of petitioner prior to this litigation, and respondent offered no proof that this response was atypical of the local population. We would not lightly assume that a citizen's participation in community and professional affairs rendered him a public figure for all purposes. Absent clear evidence of general fame or notoriety in the community, and pervasive involvement in the affairs of society, an individual should not be deemed a public personality for all aspects of his life. It is preferable to reduce the public-figure question to a more meaningful context by looking to the nature and extent of an individual's participation in the particular controversy giving rise to the defamation.

In this context it is plain that petitioner was not a public figure. He played a minimal role at the coroner's inquest, and his participation related solely to his representation of a private client. He took no part in the criminal prosecution of Officer Nuccio. Moreover, he never discussed either the criminal or civil litigation with the press and was never quoted as having done so. He plainly did not thrust himself into the vortex of this public issue, nor did he engage the public's attention in an attempt to influence its outcome. We are persuaded that the trial court did not err in refusing to characterize petitioner as a public figure for the purpose of this litigation.

We therefore conclude that the *New York Times* standard is inapplicable to this case and that the trial court erred in entering judgment for respondent. Because the jury was allowed to impose liability without fault and was permitted to presume damages without proof of injury, a new trial is necessary.[e]

---

d. On remand, Gertz was awarded $100,-000 in compensatory damages and $300,000 in punitive damages. In the prior trial, he had been awarded only $50,000 in damages.

e. Blackmun, J., concurred: "[Although I joined Brennan, J.'s plurality opinion in *Rosenbloom,* from which the Court's opinion in the present case departs, I join] the Court's opinion and its judgment for two reasons:

"1. By removing the spectres of presumed and punitive damages in the absence of *Times* malice, the Court eliminates significant and

powerful motives for self-censorship that otherwise are present in the traditional libel action. By so doing, the Court leaves what should prove to be sufficient and adequate breathing space for a vigorous press. What the Court has done, I believe, will have little, if any, practical effect on the functioning of responsible journalism.

"2. The Court was sadly fractionated in *Rosenbloom.* A result of that kind inevitably leads to uncertainty. I feel that it is of profound importance for the Court to come to rest

JUSTICE BRENNAN, dissenting.

[While the Court's] arguments are forcefully and eloquently presented, I cannot accept them for the reasons I stated in *Rosenbloom:* "The *New York Times* standard was applied to libel of a public official or public figure to give effect to the Amendment's function to encourage ventilation of public issues, not because the public official has any less interest in protecting his reputation than an individual in private life. [In] the vast majority of libels involving public officials or public figures, the ability to respond through the media will depend on the same complex factor on which the ability of a private individual depends: the unpredictable event of the media's continuing interest in the story. Thus the unproved, and highly improbable, generalization that an as yet [not fully defined] class of 'public figures' involved in matters of public concern will be better able to respond through the media than private individuals also involved in such matters seems too insubstantial a reed on which to rest a constitutional distinction."

[Adoption], by many States, of a reasonable care standard in cases where private individuals are involved in matters of public interest—the probable result of today's decision—[will] lead to self-censorship since publishers will be required carefully to weigh a myriad of uncertain factors before publication. The reasonable care standard is "elusive," *Time, Inc. v. Hill;* it saddles the press with "the intolerable burden of guessing how a jury might assess the reasonableness of steps taken by it to verify the accuracy of every reference to a name, picture or portrait." Ibid. Under a reasonable care regime, publishers and broadcasters will have to make pre-publication judgments about juror assessment of such diverse considerations as the size, operating procedures, and financial condition of the newsgathering system, as well as the relative costs and benefits of instituting less frequent and more costly reporting at a higher level of accuracy. [And] most hazardous, the flexibility which inheres in the reasonable care standard will create the danger that a jury will convert it into "an instrument for the suppression of those 'vehement, caustic, and sometimes unpleasantly sharp attacks,' [which] must be protected if the guarantees of the First and Fourteenth Amendments are to prevail." *Monitor Patriot Co.*

[A] jury's latitude to impose liability for want of due care poses a far greater threat of suppressing unpopular views than does a possible recovery of presumed or punitive damages. Moreover, the Court's broad-ranging examples of "actual injury" [allow] a jury bent on punishing expression of unpopular views a formidable weapon for doing so. [E]ven a limitation of recovery to "actual injury"—however much it reduces the size or frequency of recoveries—will not provide the necessary elbow room for First Amendment expression. "[The] very possibility of having to engage in litigation, an expensive and protracted process, is threat enough to cause discussion and debate to 'steer far wider of the unlawful zone' thereby keeping protected discussion from public cognizance. * * * " *Rosenbloom.*

[I] reject the argument that my *Rosenbloom* view improperly commits to judges the task of determining what is and what is not an issue of "general or public interest." [3] I noted in *Rosenbloom* that performance of this task would not

in the defamation area and to have a clearly defined majority position that eliminates the unsureness engendered by *Rosenbloom's* diversity. If my vote were not needed to create a majority, I would adhere to my prior view. A definitive ruling, however, is paramount."

3. The Court, taking a novel step, would not limit application of First Amendment protection to private libels involving issues of general or public interest, but would forbid the States from imposing liability without fault in any case where the substance of the defamato-

always be easy. But surely the courts, the ultimate arbiters of all disputes concerning clashes of constitutional values, would only be performing one of their traditional functions in undertaking this duty. [The] public interest is necessarily broad; any residual self-censorship that may result from the uncertain contours of the "general or public interest" concept should be of far less concern to publishers and broadcasters than that occasioned by state laws imposing liability for negligent falsehood. * * * f

JUSTICE WHITE, dissenting.

[T]he Court, in a few printed pages, has federalized major aspects of libel law by declaring unconstitutional in important respects the prevailing defamation law in all or most of the 50 States. * * *

I. [These] radical changes in the law and severe invasions of the prerogatives of the States [should] at least be shown to be required by the First Amendment or necessitated by our present circumstances. Neither has been [demonstrated.]

The central meaning of *New York Times,* and for me the First Amendment as it relates to libel laws, is that seditious libel—criticism of government and public officials—falls beyond the police power of the State. In a democratic society such as ours, the citizen has the privilege of criticizing his government and its officials. But neither *New York Times* nor its progeny suggest that the First Amendment intended in all circumstances to deprive the private citizen of his historic recourse to redress published falsehoods damaging to reputation or that, contrary to history and precedent, the amendment should now be so interpreted. Simply put, the First Amendment did not confer a "license to defame the citizen." Douglas, *The Right of the People* 38 (1958).

[T]he law has heretofore put the risk of falsehood on the publisher where the victim is a private citizen and no grounds of special privilege are invoked. The Court would now shift this risk to the victim, even though he has done nothing to invite the calumny, is wholly innocent of fault, and is helpless to avoid his injury. I doubt that jurisprudential resistance to liability without fault is sufficient ground for employing the First Amendment to revolutionize the law of libel, and in my view, that body of legal rules poses no realistic threat to the press and its

ry statement made substantial danger to reputation apparent. As in *Rosenbloom,* I would leave open the question of what constitutional standard, if any, applies when defamatory falsehoods are published or broadcast concerning either a private or public person's activities not within the scope of the general or public interest.

Parenthetically, my Brother White argues that the Court's view and mine will prevent a plaintiff—unable to demonstrate some degree of fault—from vindicating his reputation by securing a judgment that the publication was false. This argument overlooks the possible enactment of statutes, not requiring proof of fault, which provide for an action for retraction or for publication of a court's determination of falsity if the plaintiff is able to demonstrate that false statements have been published concerning his activities. Although it may be that questions could be raised concerning the constitutionality of such statutes, certainly nothing I have said today (and, as I read the Court's opinion, nothing said there) should be read to imply that a private plaintiff, unable to prove fault, must inevitably be denied the opportunity to secure a judgment upon the truth or falsity of statements published about him.

f. Douglas, J., dissented, objecting to "continued recognition of the possibility of state libel suits for public discussion of public issues" as diluting first amendment protection. He added: "Since this case involves a discussion of public affairs, I need not decide at this point whether the First Amendment prohibits all libel actions. 'An unconditional right to say what one pleases about public affairs is what I consider to be *the minimum guarantee* of the First Amendment.' *New York Times* (Black, J., concurring) (emphasis added). But 'public affairs' includes a great deal more than merely political affairs. Matters of science, economics, business, art, literature, etc., are all matters of interest to the general public. Indeed, any matter of sufficient general interest to prompt media coverage may be said to be a public affair. Certainly police killings, 'Communist conspiracies,' and the like qualify."

service to the public. The press today is vigorous and robust. To me, it is quite incredible to suggest that threats of libel suits from private citizens are causing the press to refrain from publishing the truth. I know of no hard facts to support that proposition, and the Court furnishes none.

[I]f the Court's principal concern is to protect the communications industry from large libel judgments, it would appear that its new requirements with respect to general and punitive damages would be ample protection. Why it also feels compelled to escalate the threshold standard of liability I cannot fathom, particularly when this will eliminate in many instances the plaintiff's possibility of securing a judicial determination that the damaging publication was indeed false, whether or not he is entitled to recover money damages. [I] find it unacceptable to distribute the risk in this manner and force the wholly innocent victim to bear the injury; for, as between the two, the defamer is the only culpable party. It is he who circulated a falsehood that he was not required to publish. * * * [g]

V. [I] fail to see how the quality or quantity of public debate will be promoted by further emasculation of state libel laws for the benefit of the news media.[41] If anything, this trend may provoke a new and radical imbalance in the communications process. Cf. Jerome Barron, *Access to the Press—A New First Amendment Right,* 80 Harv.L.Rev. 1641, 1657 (1967). It is not at all inconceivable that virtually unrestrained defamatory remarks about private citizens will discourage them from speaking out and concerning themselves with social problems. This would turn the First Amendment on its head. * * * [h]

Notes and Questions

1. *Gertz and Meiklejohn.* By affording some constitutional protection to all media defamatory speech whether or not it relates to public issues, does the Court squarely reject the Meiklejohn theory of the first amendment? Consider Steven Shiffrin, *Defamatory Non-Media Speech and First Amendment Methodology,* 25 U.C.L.A.L.Rev. 915, 929 (1978): "It may be that the Court has refused to adopt the Meiklejohn 'public issues' test not because it believes that private speech (i.e., speech unrelated to public issues) is as important as public speech but rather because it doubts its ability to distinguish unerringly between the two. [B]y placing all defamatory media speech within the scope of the first amendment, the Court may believe it has protected relatively little non-public speech. On the other hand, [putting aside comments about public officials and public figures], the Court may fear that if *Gertz* were extended to non-media speech, the result would be to protect much speech having nothing to do with public issues, while

g. White, J., also argued strongly against the Court's rulings on actual and punitive damages.

41. Cf. Willard Pedrick, *Freedom of the Press and the Law of Libel: The Modern Revised Translation,* 49 Cornell L.Q. 581, 601–02 (1964): "A great many forces in our society operate to determine the extent to which men are free in fact to express their ideas. Whether there is a privilege for good faith defamatory misstatements on matters of public concern or whether there is strict liability for such statements may not greatly affect the course of public discussion. How different has life been in those states which heretofore followed the majority rule imposing strict liability for misstatements of fact defaming public figures from life in the minority states where the good faith privilege held sway?"

h. Burger, C.J., also dissented: "I am frank to say I do not know the parameters of a 'negligence' doctrine as applied to the news media. [I] would prefer to allow this area of law to continue to evolve as it has up to now with respect to private citizens rather then embark on a new doctrinal theory which has no jurisprudential ancestry. [I would remand] for reinstatement of the verdict of the jury and the entry of an appropriate judgment on that verdict."

safeguarding relatively little that does."[i] For consideration of the distinction between public and private speech and of the media non-media distinction, see *Greenmoss*, p. 739 infra. See also *Philadelphia Newspapers, Inc. v. Hepps*, 475 U.S. 767, 106 S.Ct. 1558, 89 L.Ed.2d 783 (1986) (private figure plaintiff has burden of showing falsity at least when issue is of "public concern" and leaving open the question of what standards apply to non-media defendants).

2. *Public figures.* TIME, INC. v. FIRESTONE, 424 U.S. 448, 96 S.Ct. 958, 47 L.Ed.2d 154 (1976), per REHNQUIST, J., declared that persons who have not assumed a role of especial prominence in the affairs of society are not public figures unless they have " 'thrust themselves to the forefront of particular public controversies in order to influence the resolution of the issues involved.' " It held that a divorce proceeding involving one of America's wealthiest industrial families and containing testimony concerning the extramarital sexual activities of the parties did not involve a "public controversy," "even though the marital difficulties of extremely wealthy individuals may be of interest to some portion of the reading public." Nor was the filing of a divorce suit, or the holding of press conferences ("to satisfy inquiring reporters") thought to be freely publicizing the issues in order to influence their outcome. Recall *Gertz* doubted the wisdom of forcing judges to determine on an ad hoc basis what is and is not of "general or public interest." Is there a basis for distinguishing a public figure test requiring judges to determine on an ad hoc basis what is or is not a "public controversy"?

What does it mean to assume a role of especial prominence in the affairs of society? If Elmer Gertz, a prominent Illinois attorney, does not qualify, does Johnny Carson? Julia Child? Mr. Rogers? If so, is the slide from public officials to television chefs and personalities too precipitous because the latter "have little, if any effect, on questions of politics, public policy, or the organization and determination of societal affairs"? See Frederick Schauer, *Public Figures*, 25 Wm. & Mary L.Rev. 905 (1984). For replies, see Gerald Ashdown, *Of Public Figures and Public Interest—The Libel Law Conundrum*, id. at 937; Diana Daniels, *Public Figures Revisited*, id. at 957. Does a narrow definition of public figures discriminate in favor of orthodox media and discourage attempts "to illuminate previously unexposed aspects of society." Does the negligence concept itself threaten to discriminate "against media or outlets whose philosophies and methods deviate from those of the mainstream"? See generally David Anderson, *Libel and Press Self-Censorship*, 53 Tex.L.Rev. 422, 453, 455 (1975).

3. *Taking reputation too seriously?* Consider Rodney Smolla, *Suing the Press* 257 (1986): "[I]f we take the libel suit too seriously, we are in danger of raising our collective cultural sensitivity to reputation to unhealthy levels. We are in danger of surrendering a wonderful part of our national identity—our strapping, scrambling, free-wheeling individualism, in danger of becoming less American, less robust, wild-eyed, pluralistic and free, and more decorous, image-conscious, and narcissistic. The media is itself partly to blame for this direction,

i. For the claim that speech on private matters deserves as much protection as speech on public matters, see id. at 938–42. For discussion of the different meanings of public and private speech, see Frederick Schauer, *"Private" Speech and the "Private" Forum: Givhan v. Western Line School District*, 1979 Sup.Ct.Rev. 217. For additional commentary on the question of whether *Gertz* should extend to non-media defendants see, e.g., Albert Hill, *Defamation and Privacy Under the First Amendment*, 76 Colum.L.Rev. 1205 (1976); David Lange, *The Speech and Press Clauses*, 23 U.C.L.A.L.Rev. 77 (1975); Melville Nimmer, *Is Freedom of the Press a Redundancy: What Does It Add to Freedom of Speech?*, 26 Hast. L.J. 639 (1975); William Van Alstyne, Comment: *The Hazards to the Press of Claiming a "Preferred Position,"* 28 Hast.L.J. 761 (1977); Note, *Mediaocracy and Mistrust: Extending New York Times Defamation Protection to Non-media Defendants*, 95 Harv.L.Rev. 1876 (1982).

and it would be dangerous to release it totally from the important check and balance that the libel laws provide. But in the United States, the balance that must be struck between reputation and expression should never be tilted too far against expression, for the right to defiantly, robustly, and irreverently speak one's mind just because it is one's mind is quintessentially what it means to be an American."[j]

D. FALSE LIGHT PRIVACY

TIME, INC. v. HILL, 385 U.S. 374, 87 S.Ct. 534, 17 L.Ed.2d 456 (1967), applied the *New York Times* knowing and reckless falsity standard to a right of privacy action for publishing an erroneous but not defamatory report about private individuals involved in an incident of public interest. In 1952 the Hill family was the subject of national news coverage when held hostage in its home for 19 hours by three escaped convicts who treated the family courteously with no violence. This incident formed part of the basis for a novel, later made into a play, which involved violence against the hostage family. In 1955 *Life* published a picture story that showed the play's cast reenacting scenes from the play in the former Hill home. According to *Life*, the play "inspired by the [Hill] family's experience" "is a heartstopping account of how a family arose to heroism in a crisis." Hill secured a $30,000 judgment for compensatory damages against the publisher under the New York Right to Privacy statute, which, as interpreted, made truth a complete defense to actions based on "newsworthy people or events" but gave a right of action to one whose name or picture was the subject of an article containing "material and substantial falsification." The Court, per BRENNAN, J., reversed, holding that "the constitutional protections for speech and press preclude the application of the New York statute to redress false reports of matters of public interest in the absence of proof that the defendant published the report with knowledge of its falsity or in reckless disregard of the truth," and that the instructions did not adequately advise the jury that a verdict for Hill required a finding of knowing or reckless falsity:

j. For historical perspective on the social messages communicated by defamation law, see Norman Rosenberg, *Protecting the Best Men* (1986). For valuable material on how the *Gertz* rules work in practice, see Randall Bezanson, Gilbert Cranberg & John Soloski, *Libel Law and the Press: Myth and Reality* (1987); Henry Kaufman, *Libel 1980–85: Promises and Realities,* 90 Dick.L.Rev. 545 (1985); Marc Franklin, *Suing Media for Libel: A Litigation Study,* 1981 Am.B.Found.Res.J. 795; Marc Franklin, *Winners and Losers and Why: A Study of Defamation Litigation,* 1980 Am. B.Found.Res.J. 455. For commentary suggesting reforms, see Annenberg Washington Program, *Libel Law* (1988). See also Robert Ackerman, *Bringing Coherence to Defamation Law Through Uniform Legislation: The Search for an Elegant Solution,* 72 N.C.L.Rev. 291 (1994); David Anderson, *Is Libel Law Worth Reforming?,* 140 U.Pa.L.Rev. 487 (1991); Randall Bezanson, *The Libel Tort Today,* 45 Wash. & Lee L.Rev. 535 (1988); C. Thomas Dienes, *Libel Reform: An Appraisal,* 23 U.Mich.J.L.Ref. (1989); Richard Epstein, *Was New York Times v. Sullivan Wrong?,* 53 U.Chi.L.Rev. 782 (1986); Bruce Fein, *New York Times v. Sulli-* *van: An Obstacle to Enlightened Public Discourse and Government Responsiveness to the People* (1984); Marc Franklin, *Public Officials and Libel: In Defense of New York Times Co. v. Sullivan,* 5 Cardozo Arts & Ent.L.J. 51 (1986); Marc Franklin, *Constitutional Libel Law: The Role of Content,* 34 UCLA L.Rev. 1657 (1987); Marc Franklin, *A Declaratory Judgment Alternative to Current Libel Law,* 74 Calif.L.Rev. 809 (1986); Stanley Ingber, *Defamation: A Conflict Between Reason and Decency,* 65 Va.L.Rev. 785 (1979); Pierre Leval, *The No–Money, No–Fault Libel Suit: Keeping Sullivan in Its Proper Place,* 101 Harv.L.Rev. 1287 (1988); Lee Levine, *Book Review,* 56 G.W.U.L.Rev. 246 (1987); Anthony Lewis, *New York Times v. Sullivan Reconsidered: Time to Return to "The Central Meaning of the First Amendment,"* 83 Colum.L.Rev. 603 (1983); John Martin, *The Role of Retraction in Defamation Suits,* 1993 U.Chi. Legal F. 293; Frederick Schauer, *Uncoupling Free Speech,* 92 Colum.L.Rev. 1321 (1992); Rodney Smolla, *Let the Author Beware: The Rejuvenation of the American Law of Libel,* 132 U.Pa.L.Rev. 1 (1983).

"The guarantees for speech and press are not the preserve of political expression or comment upon public affairs, essential as those are to healthy government. One need only pick up any newspaper or magazine to comprehend the vast range of published matter which exposes persons to public view, both private citizens and public officials. Exposure of the self to others in varying degrees is a concomitant of life in a civilized community. The risk of this exposure is an essential incident of life in a society which places a primary value on freedom of speech and press. [We] have no doubt that the subject of the *Life* article, the opening of a new play linked to an actual incident, is a matter of public interest. 'The line between the informing and the entertaining is too elusive for the protection of [freedom of the press.]' Erroneous statement is no less inevitable in such case than in the case of comment upon public affairs, and in both, if innocent or merely negligent, '[it] must be protected if the freedoms of expression are to have the "breathing space" that they "need [to] survive".' [*New York Times.*] We create a grave risk of serious impairment of the indispensable service of a free press in a free society if we saddle the press with the impossible burden of verifying to a certainty the facts associated in news articles with a person's name, picture or portrait, particularly as related to non-defamatory matter. Even negligence would be a most elusive standard, especially when the content of the speech itself affords no warning of prospective harm to another through falsity. A negligence test would place on the press the intolerable burden of guessing how a jury might assess the reasonableness of steps taken by it to verify the accuracy of every reference to a name, picture or [portrait].

"We find applicable here the standard of knowing or reckless falsehood not through blind application of *New York Times,* relating solely to libel actions by public officials, but only upon consideration of the factors which arise in the particular context of the application of the New York statute in cases involving private individuals."

BLACK, J., joined by Douglas, J., concurred in reversal on the grounds stated in the Brennan opinion "in order for the Court to be able at this time to agree on an opinion in this important case based on the prevailing constitutional doctrine expressed in *New York Times,*" but reaffirmed their belief that the "malicious," "reckless disregard of the truth" and "knowing and reckless falsity" exceptions were impermissible "abridgments" of freedom of expression. Douglas, J., also filed a separate concurrence, deeming it "irrelevant to talk of any right of privacy in this context. Here a private person is catapulted into the news by events over which he had no control. He and his activities are then in the public domain as fully as the matters at issue in *New York Times.* Such privacy as a person normally has ceases when his life has ceased to be private."

HARLAN, J., concurring in part and dissenting in part, would have made the test of liability negligence, rather than the *New York Times* "reckless falsity": "It would be unreasonable to assume that Mr. Hill could find a forum for making a successful refutation of the *Life* material or that the public's interest in it would be sufficient for the truth to win out by comparison as it might in that area of discussion central to a free society. Thus the state interest in encouraging careful checking and preparation of published material is far stronger than in *Times.* The dangers of unchallengeable untruth are far too well documented to be summarily dismissed.

"Second, there is a vast difference in the state interest in protecting individuals like Mr. Hill from irresponsibly prepared publicity and the state interest in similar protection for a public official. In *Times* we acknowledged public officials to be a breed from whom hardiness to exposure to charges, innuendos, and criticisms might be demanded and who voluntarily assumed the risk of such things by entry into the public arena. But Mr. Hill came to public attention through an unfortunate circumstance not of his making rather than his voluntary actions and he can in no sense be considered to have 'waived' any protection the State might justifiably afford him from irresponsible publicity. Not being inured to the vicissitudes of journalistic scrutiny such an individual is more easily injured and his means of self-defense are more limited. The public is less likely to view with normal skepticism what is written about him because it is not accustomed to seeing his name in the press and expects only a disinterested report.

"The coincidence of these factors in this situation leads me to the view that a State should be free to hold the press to a duty of making a reasonable investigation of the underlying facts and limiting itself to 'fair comment' on the materials so gathered. Theoretically, of course, such a rule might slightly limit press discussion of matters touching individuals like Mr. Hill. But, from a pragmatic standpoint, until now the press, at least in New York, labored under the more exacting handicap of the existing New York privacy law and has certainly remained robust. Other professional activity of great social value is carried on under a duty of reasonable care and there is no reason to suspect the press would be less hardy than medical practitioners or attorneys." [a]

Notes and Questions

1. Compare ZACCHINI v. SCRIPPS–HOWARD BROADCASTING CO., 433 U.S. 562, 97 S.Ct. 2849, 53 L.Ed.2d 965 (1977): Zacchini performed as a "human cannonball," being shot from a cannon into a net some 200 feet away. Without Zacchini's permission to film or broadcast his act, Scripps-Howard obtained and broadcast the tape of his "shot" on the news. The Ohio Supreme Court held the telecast was protected under *Time, Inc. v. Hill* as a newsworthy event. The Court, per WHITE, J., reversed. *Hill* was distinguishable because Zacchini's claim was based not on privacy or reputation but "in protecting the proprietary interest," an interest "closely analogous to the goals of patent and copyright law." Unlike *Hill*, the issue was not whether Zacchini's act would be available to the public: "[T]he only question is who gets to do the publishing." [b]

2. Does *Hill* survive *Gertz*? Consider the following statement: "In *Hill* and *Gertz* the same class of plaintiffs have to meet different constitutional standards in order to recover. Only the name of the tort has changed. This makes no sense." Is the state interest significantly different in *Gertz* than in *Hill*? Should it matter whether the statement at issue would appear innocuous to a reasonable editor? Offensive? See Diane Zimmerman, *False Light Invasion of Privacy: The Light that Failed*, 64 N.Y.U.L.Rev. 364 (1989).

3. *False news.* Should injury to any particular person be a prerequisite to state regulation of false publications? Consider *Keeton v. Hustler Magazine, Inc.*, 465 U.S. 770, 104 S.Ct. 1473, 79 L.Ed.2d 790 (1984): "False statements of fact harm both the subject of the falsehood *and* the readers of the statement. New

---

a. Fortas, J., joined by Warren, C.J., and Clark, J., dissented, because "the jury instructions, although [not] a textbook model, satisfied [the *New York Times*] standard." For cogent commentary concerning false light privacy, see Gary Schwartz, *Explaining and Justifying a Limited Tort of False Light Invasion of Privacy*, 41 Case West.L.Rev. 886 (1991).

b. Powell, J., joined by Brennan and Marshall, JJ., dissented, observing that there was no showing that the broadcast was a "subterfuge or cover for private or commercial exploitation." Stevens, J., dissented on procedural grounds.

Hampshire may rightly employ its libel laws to discourage the deception of its citizens." Could New Hampshire make it a criminal offense to publish false statements with knowledge of their falsity without any requirement of injury to any particular person? See Zimmerman, supra.

E.   EMOTIONAL DISTRESS

HUSTLER MAGAZINE v. FALWELL, 485 U.S. 46, 108 S.Ct. 876, 99 L.Ed.2d 41 (1988), per Rehnquist, C.J., held that public figures and public officials offended by a mass media parody could not recover for the tort of intentional infliction of emotional distress without a showing of *New York Times* malice. Parodying a series of liquor advertisements in which celebrities speak about their "first time," the editors of *Hustler* chose plaintiff Jerry Falwell (a nationally famous minister, host of a nationally syndicated television show, and founder of the Moral Majority political organization) "as the featured celebrity and drafted an alleged 'interview' with him in which he states that his 'first time' was during a drunken incestuous rendezvous with his mother in an outhouse. The *Hustler* parody portrays [Falwell] and his mother [a] 'as drunk and immoral,' and suggests that [Falwell] is a hypocrite who preaches only when he is drunk. In small print at the bottom of the page, the ad contains the disclaimer, 'ad parody—not to be taken seriously.' The magazine's table of contents also lists the ad as 'Fiction; Ad and Personality Parody.' * * *

"We must decide whether a public figure may recover damages for emotional harm caused by the publication of an ad parody offensive to him, and doubtless gross and repugnant in the eyes of most.[3] [Falwell] would have us find that a State's interest in protecting public figures from emotional distress is sufficient to deny First Amendment protection to speech that is patently offensive and is intended to inflict emotional injury, even when that speech could not reasonably have been interpreted as stating actual facts about the public figure involved. * * *

"Generally speaking the law does not regard the intent to inflict emotional distress as one which should receive much solicitude, and it is quite understandable that most if not all jurisdictions have chosen to make it civilly culpable where the conduct in question is sufficiently 'outrageous.' But in the world of debate about public affairs, many things done with motives that are less than admirable are protected by the First Amendment. '[Debate] on public issues will not be uninhibited if the speaker must run the risk that it will be proved in court that he spoke out of hatred; even if he did speak out of hatred, utterances honestly believed contribute to the free interchange of ideas and the ascertainment of truth.' *Garrison.* Thus while such a bad motive may be deemed controlling for purposes of tort liability in other areas of the law, we think the First Amendment prohibits such a result in the area of public debate about public figures.

"Were we to hold otherwise, there can be little doubt that political cartoonists and satirists would be subjected to damage awards without any showing that their work falsely defamed its subject. * * *

---

a. Falwell's mother was not a plaintiff. What result if she were?

3. Under Virginia law, in an action for intentional infliction of emotional distress a plaintiff must show that the defendant's con-duct (1) is intentional or reckless; (2) offends generally accepted standards of decency or morality; (3) is causally connected with the plaintiff's emotional distress; and (4) caused emotional distress that was severe.

"There is no doubt that the caricature of [Falwell] and his mother published in Hustler is at best a distant cousin of [traditional] political cartoons * * * and a rather poor relation at that. If it were possible by laying down a principled standard to separate the one from the other, public discourse would probably suffer little or no harm. But we doubt that there is any such standard, and we are quite sure that the pejorative description 'outrageous' does not supply one. 'Outrageousness' in the area of political and social discourse has an inherent subjectiveness about it which would allow a jury to impose liability on the basis of the jurors' tastes or views, or perhaps on the basis of their dislike of a particular expression.

"We conclude that public figures and public officials may not recover for the tort of intentional infliction of emotional distress by reason of publications such as the one here at issue without showing in addition that the publication contains a false statement of fact which was made with 'actual malice,' i.e., with knowledge that the statement was false or with reckless disregard as to whether or not it was true." [b]

Notes and Questions

1. Does the rationale sweep beyond the holding? If debate on public issues should be uninhibited and if speakers filled with hatred have a place in that debate, why is the holding confined to suits brought by public officials and public figures? Is the holding likely to follow a "dialectic progression" from public official and public figure to all matters in the public domain? Should it? Is that far enough? Should the holding encompass all media speech? All non-media speech? Consider Rodney Smolla, *Emotional Distress and the First Amendment*, 20 Ariz.St.L.J. 423, 427 (1988): "The intellectual challenge posed by Falwell's suit is not how to construct a convincing rationale for rejecting his claim, but rather how to articulate limits on that rationale that will permit suits for emotional distress inflicted through speech in other contexts to survive." See generally Rodney Smolla, *Jerry Falwell v. Larry Flynt: The First Amendment on Trial* (1988). To what extent should the tort of intentional infliction of emotional distress raise constitutional problems? Compare Franklyn Haiman, *Speech and Law in a Free Society* 148–56 (1981) with Donald Downs, *Skokie Revisited: Hate Group Speech and the First Amendment*, 60 Not.D.Law. 629, 673–85 (1985). See generally Kent Greenawalt, *Speech, Crime, and the Uses of Language* 143–48 (1989) (discussing personal insults).

2. Is the problem with the outrageousness standard less its subjectivity than its enabling "a single community to use the authority of the state to confine speech within its own notions of propriety." Does *Falwell* exhibit a need to respect a "marketplace of communities?" Can we respect that marketplace without "blunt[ing the] rules of civility that define the essence of reason and dignity within community life?" Compare Robert Post, *The Constitutional Concept of Public Discourse*, 103 Harv.L.Rev. 601, 632, 643 (1990) with Joshua Cohen, 21 Phil. & Pub. Aff. 207, 227 n. 62 (1963).

3. Is there any distinction to be made between persons and trademarks? The Second Circuit permitted an injunction to issue against exhibition of the film *Debbie Does Dallas* on the ground that it infringed on the trademarked uniform of the Dallas Cowboys Cheerleaders. *Dallas Cowboys Cheerleaders, Inc. v. Pussycat Cinema, Ltd.* 604 F.2d 200 (2d Cir.1979). The movie involves women performing

b. White, J., concurred, but stated that *New York Times* was irrelevant because of the jury's finding that the parody contained no assertion of fact. Kennedy, J., took no part.

sexual services for a fee so they can go to Dallas to become "Texas Cowgirls." Consistent with *Falwell?* Consider Robert Kravitz, *Trademarks, Speech, and the Gay Olympics Case,* 69 B.U.L.Rev. 131 (1989): "If Rev. Jerry Falwell cannot succeed on a cause of action against an advertising parody suggesting he had a sexual encounter with his mother while drunk in an outhouse, why should an inanimate trademark enjoy greater protection against similar slurs? If Falwell cannot recover, surely Campari, whose trademark was also parodied in the fake ad, should not. [Broadly] interpreted, the holding in *Dallas Cowboys Cheerleaders* suggests that Ford Motor Company might enjoin the distribution of a book or a film that portrayed teenagers having sex in the back of a Ford car." See also Robert Denicola, *Trademarks as Speech,* 1982 Wis.L.Rev. 158.

F. DISCLOSURE OF PRIVATE FACTS

FLORIDA STAR v. B.J.F.

491 U.S. 524, 109 S.Ct. 2603, 105 L.Ed.2d 443 (1989).

JUSTICE MARSHALL delivered the opinion of the Court.

Florida Stat. § 794.03 (1987) makes it unlawful to "print, publish, or broadcast [in] any instrument of mass communication" the name of the victim of a sexual offense. Pursuant to this statute, appellant The Florida Star was found civilly liable for publishing the name of a rape victim which it had obtained from a publicly released police report. [B.J.F.] testified that she had suffered emotional distress from the publication of her name. She stated that she had heard about the article from fellow workers and acquaintances; that her mother had received several threatening phone calls from a man who stated that he would rape B.J.F. again; and that these events had forced B.J.F. to change her phone number and residence, to seek police protection, and to obtain mental health counseling. [The jury] awarded B.J.F. $75,000 in compensatory damages and $25,000 in punitive damages. * * *

[We do not] accept appellant's invitation to hold broadly that truthful publication may never be punished consistent with the First Amendment. Our cases have carefully eschewed reaching this ultimate question, mindful that the future may bring scenarios which prudence counsels our not resolving anticipatorily. See, e.g., *Near v. Minnesota,* [Section 4, I, B] (hypothesizing "publication of the sailing dates of transports or the number and location of troops"); see also *Garrison v. Louisiana* (endorsing absolute defense of truth "where discussion of public affairs is concerned," but leaving unsettled the constitutional implications of truthfulness "in the discrete area of purely private libels"). Indeed, in [*Cox Broadcasting v. Cohn,* 420 U.S. 469, 95 S.Ct. 1029, 43 L.Ed.2d 328 (1975)], we pointedly refused to answer even the less sweeping question "whether truthful publications may ever be subjected to civil or criminal liability" for invading "an area of privacy" defined by the State. [We] continue to believe that the sensitivity and significance of the interests presented in clashes between First Amendment and privacy rights counsel relying on limited principles that sweep no more broadly than the appropriate context of the instant case.

In our view, this case is appropriately analyzed with reference to such a limited First Amendment principle. It is the one, in fact, which we articulated in *Smith v. Daily Mail Pub. Co.,* [Section 5, I] in our synthesis of prior cases involving attempts to punish truthful publication: "[I]f a newspaper lawfully obtains truthful information about a matter of public significance then state officials may not constitutionally punish publication of the information, absent a need to further a state interest of the highest order." [a]   * * *

Applied to the instant case, the *Daily Mail* principle clearly commands reversal. The first inquiry is whether the newspaper "lawfully obtain[ed] truthful information about a matter of public significance." It is undisputed that the news article describing the assault on B.J.F. was accurate. In addition, appellant lawfully obtained B.J.F.'s name. Appellee's argument to the contrary is based on the fact that under Florida law, police reports which reveal the identity of the victim of a sexual offense are not among the matters of "public record" which the public, by law, is entitled to inspect. But the fact that state officials are not required to disclose such reports does not make it unlawful for a newspaper to receive them when furnished by the government. Nor does the fact that the Department apparently failed to fulfill its obligation under § 794.03 not to "cause or allow to [be] published" the name of a sexual offense victim make the newspaper's ensuing receipt of this information unlawful. Even assuming the Constitution permitted a State to proscribe *receipt* of information, Florida has not taken this step. It is, clear, furthermore, that the news article concerned "a matter of public significance[.]" That is, the article generally, as opposed to the specific identity contained within it, involved a matter of paramount public import: the commission, and investigation, of a violent crime which had been reported to authorities.

The second inquiry is whether imposing liability on appellant pursuant to § 794.03 serves "a need to further a state interest of the highest order." Appellee argues that a rule punishing publication furthers three closely related interests: the privacy of victims of sexual offenses; the physical safety of such victims, who may be targeted for retaliation if their names become known to their assailants; and the goal of encouraging victims of such crimes to report these offenses without fear of exposure.

At a time in which we are daily reminded of the tragic reality of rape, it is undeniable that these are highly significant interests. [We] accordingly do not rule out the possibility that, in a proper case, imposing civil sanctions for publication of the name of a rape victim might be so overwhelmingly necessary to advance these interests as to satisfy the *Daily Mail* standard. For three independent reasons, however, imposing liability for publication under the circumstances of this case is too precipitous a means of advancing these interests to convince us that there is a "need" within the meaning of the *Daily Mail* formulation for Florida to take this extreme step.

First is the manner in which appellant obtained the identifying information in question. [B.J.F.'s] identity would never have come to light were it not for the erroneous, if inadvertent, inclusion by the Department of her full name in an incident report made available in a press room open to the public. [Where] as here, the government has failed to police itself in disseminating information, it is clear [that] the imposition of damages against the press for its subsequent publication can hardly be said to be a narrowly tailored means of safeguarding anonymity.

a. Suppose a newspaper publishes the name of a confidential source who it believes has misled it for political reasons and suppose the source sues the newspaper for breach of contract? Should the *Daily Mail* principle apply? See *Cohen v. Cowles Media Co.,* 501 U.S. 663, 111 S.Ct. 2513, 115 L.Ed.2d 586 (1991). Should the *Daily Mail* principle apply in copyright cases?

That appellant gained access to the information in question through a government news release makes it especially likely that, if liability were to be imposed, self-censorship would result. Reliance on a news release is a paradigmatically "routine newspaper reporting techniqu[e]." The government's issuance of such a release, without qualification, can only convey to recipients that the government considered dissemination lawful, and indeed expected the recipients to disseminate the information further. Had appellant merely reproduced the news release prepared and released by the Department, imposing civil damages would surely violate the First Amendment. The fact that appellant converted the police report into a news story by adding the linguistic connecting tissue necessary to transform the report's facts into full sentences cannot change this result.

A second problem with Florida's imposition of liability for publication is the broad sweep of the negligence per se standard applied under the civil cause of action implied from § 794.03. Unlike claims based on the common law tort of invasion of privacy, civil actions based on § 794.03 require no case-by-case findings that the disclosure of a fact about a person's private life was one that a reasonable person would find highly offensive. On the contrary, under the per se theory of negligence adopted by the courts below, liability follows automatically from publication. This is so regardless of whether the identity of the victim is already known throughout the community; whether the victim has voluntarily called public attention to the offense; or whether the identity of the victim has otherwise become a reasonable subject of public concern—because, perhaps, questions have arisen whether the victim fabricated an assault by a particular person. Nor is there a scienter requirement of any kind under § 794.03, engendering the perverse result that truthful publications challenged pursuant to this cause of action are less protected by the First Amendment than even the least protected defamatory falsehoods: those involving purely private figures, where liability is evaluated under a standard, usually applied by a jury, of ordinary negligence. See *Gertz.* * * *

Third, and finally, the facial underinclusiveness of § 794.03 raises serious doubts about whether Florida is, in fact, serving, with this statute, the significant interests which appellee invokes in support of affirmance. Section 794.03 prohibits the publication of identifying information only if this information appears in an "instrument of mass communication," a term the statute does not define. Section 794.03 does not prohibit the spread by other means of the identities of victims of sexual offenses. An individual who maliciously spreads word of the identity of a rape victim is thus not covered, despite the fact that the communication of such information to persons who live near, or work with, the victim may have consequences equally devastating as the exposure of her name to large numbers of strangers.

When a State attempts the extraordinary measure of punishing truthful publication in the name of privacy, it must demonstrate its commitment to advancing this interest by applying its prohibition evenhandedly, to the small-time disseminator as well as the media giant. Where important First Amendment interests are at stake, the mass scope of disclosure is not an acceptable surrogate for injury. Without more careful and inclusive precautions against alternative forms of dissemination, we cannot conclude that Florida's selective ban on publication by the mass media satisfactorily accomplishes its stated purpose.

Our holding today is limited. We do not hold that truthful publication is automatically constitutionally protected, or that there is no zone of personal privacy within which the State may protect the individual from intrusion by the press, or even that a State may never punish publication of the name of a victim of a sexual offense. We hold only that where a newspaper publishes truthful information which it has lawfully obtained, punishment may lawfully be imposed, if at all, only when narrowly tailored to a state interest of the highest order, and that no such interest is satisfactorily served by imposing liability under § 794.03 to appellant under the facts of this case. * * *

JUSTICE SCALIA, concurring in part and concurring in the judgment.

I think it sufficient to decide this case to rely upon the third ground set forth in the Court's opinion: that a law cannot be regarded as protecting an interest "of the highest order" and thus as justifying a restriction upon truthful speech, when it leaves appreciable damage to that supposedly vital interest unprohibited. In the present case, I would anticipate that the rape victim's discomfort at the dissemination of news of her misfortune among friends and acquaintances would be at least as great as her discomfort at its publication by the media to people to whom she is only a name. Yet the law in question does not prohibit the former in either oral or written form. Nor is it at all clear, as I think it must be to validate this statute, that Florida's general privacy law would prohibit such gossip. Nor, finally, is it credible that the interest meant to be served by the statute is the protection of the victim against a rapist still at large—an interest that arguably would extend only to mass publication. There would be little reason to limit a statute with that objective to rape alone; or to extend it to all rapes, whether or not the felon has been apprehended and confined. In any case, the instructions here did not require the jury to find that the rapist was at large.

This law has every appearance of a prohibition that society is prepared to impose upon the press but not upon itself. Such a prohibition does not protect an interest "of the highest order." For that reason, I agree that the judgment of the court below must be reversed.

JUSTICE WHITE, with whom THE CHIEF JUSTICE and JUSTICE O'CONNOR join, dissenting.

"Short of homicide, [rape] is the 'ultimate violation of self.'" *Coker v. Georgia*, [433 U.S. 584, 97 S.Ct. 2861, 53 L.Ed.2d 982 (1977)] (opinion of White, J.). For B.J.F., however, the violation she suffered at a rapist's knife-point marked only the beginning of her ordeal. [Yet] today, the Court holds that a jury award of $75,000 to compensate B.J.F. for the harm she suffered due to the Star's negligence is at odds with the First Amendment. I do not accept this result.

[T]he three "independent reasons" the Court cites for reversing the judgment for B.J.F. [do not] support its result.

The first of these reasons [is] the fact "appellant gained access to [B.J.F.'s name] through a government news release." [But the] "release" of information provided by the government was not, as the Court says, "without qualification." As the Star's own reporter conceded at trial, the crime incident report that inadvertently included B.J.F.'s name was posted in a room that contained signs making it clear that the names of rape victims were not matters of public record, and were not to be published. The Star's reporter indicated that she understood that she "[was not] allowed to take down that information" (i.e., B.J.F.'s name) and that she "[was] not supposed to take the information from the police department." Thus, by her own admission the posting of the incident report did not convey to the Star's reporter the idea that "the government considered dissemination lawful"; the Court's suggestion to the contrary is inapt. * * *

Unfortunately, as this case illustrates, mistakes happen: even when States take measures to "avoid" disclosure, sometimes rape victim's names are found out. As I see it, it is not too much to ask the press, in instances such as this, to respect simple standards of decency and refrain from publishing a victim's name, address, and/or phone number.

Second, the Court complains [that] a newspaper might be found liable under the Florida courts' negligence per se theory without regard to a newspaper's scienter or degree of fault. The short answer to this complaint is that whatever merit the Court's argument might have, it is wholly inapposite here, where the jury found that appellant acted with "reckless indifference towards the rights of others," a standard far higher than the *Gertz* standard the Court urges as a constitutional minimum today.

But even taking the Court's concerns in the abstract, they miss the mark. [The] Court says that negligence per se permits a plaintiff to hold a defendant liable without a showing that the disclosure was "of a fact about a person's private life [that] a reasonable person would find highly offensive." But the point here is that the legislature—reflecting popular sentiment—has determined that disclosure of the fact that a person was raped is categorically a revelation that reasonable people find offensive. And as for the Court's suggestion that the Florida courts' theory permits liability without regard for whether the victim's identity is already known, or whether she herself has made it known—these are facts that would surely enter into the calculation of damages in such a case. In any event, none of these mitigating factors was present [here].

Third, the Court faults the Florida criminal statute for being underinclusive. [But] our cases which have struck down laws that limit or burden the press due to their underinclusiveness have involved situations where a legislature has singled out one segment of the news media or press for adverse treatment. Here, the Florida law evenhandedly covers all "instrument[s] of mass communication" no matter their form, media, content, nature or purpose. It excludes neighborhood gossips because presumably the Florida Legislature has determined that neighborhood gossips do not pose the danger and intrusion to rape victims that "instrument[s] of mass communication" do. Simply put: Florida wanted to prevent the widespread distribution of rape victim's names, and therefore enacted a statute tailored almost as precisely as possible to achieving that end. * * *

At issue in this case is whether there is any information about people, which—though true—may not be published in the press. [The] Court accepts appellant's invitation to obliterate one of the most note-worthy legal inventions of the 20th–Century: the tort of the publication of private facts. William Prosser, John Wade, & Victor Schwartz, *Torts* 951–952 (8th ed. 1988). Even if the Court's opinion does not say as much today, such obliteration will follow inevitably from the Court's conclusion here. [The] Court's ruling has been foreshadowed. In *Time, Inc. v. Hill,* we observed that—after a brief period early in this century where Brandeis' view was ascendant—the trend in "modern" jurisprudence has been to eclipse an individual's right to maintain private any truthful information that the press wished to publish. More recently, in *Cox Broadcasting,* we acknowledged the possibility that the First Amendment may prevent a State from ever subjecting the publication of truthful but private information to civil liability. Today, we hit the bottom of the slippery slope.

I would find a place to draw the line higher on the hillside: a spot high enough to protect B.J.F.'s desire for privacy and peace-of-mind in the wake of a horrible personal tragedy. There is no public interest in publishing the names, addresses, and phone numbers of persons who are the victims of crime—and no public interest in immunizing the press from liability in the rare cases where a State's efforts to protect a victim's privacy have failed. Consequently, I respectfully dissent.[5]

Notes and Questions

1. *Journalistic practice.* Consider Paul Marcus & Tara McMahon, *Limiting Disclosure of Rape Victims' Identities,* 64 S.Cal.L.Rev. 1019, 1046–47 (1991): "The journalists' code of ethics and the policies of most members of the media currently prohibit publication of a rape victim's name. [T]he New York Times calls the policy 'one of modern journalism's few conspiracies of silence.' And even though a few members of the media, such as [former] NBC News president Michael Gartner, disagree with the policy because, as Gartner says, 'it's not the job of the media to keep secrets,' the majority supports exercising such restraint. Furthermore, it is doubtful many would argue that as a result of working within this established policy of not disclosing rape victims' names, members of the media have become more timid in their endeavor to investigate and report the [news]. Codifying in a rule of law what is already the prevailing practice would not have a chilling effect on the media."

2. *Outing.* Should the first amendment preclude a privacy cause of action against those who publicly disclose that a private person is gay? What if the person is a public official, e.g., a member of a board of education? For diverse perspectives, see Rodney Smolla, *Free Speech in an Open Society,* 137–39 (1992); Susan Becker, *The Immorality of Publicly Outing Private People,* 73 Ore.L.Rev. 159 (1994); Barbara Moretti, *Outing: Justifiable or Unwarranted Invasion of Privacy? The Private Facts Tort As a Remedy for Disclosures of Sexual Orientation,* 11 Cardozo Arts & Ent.L.J. 857 (1993); Comment, *Forced Out of the Closet,* 46 U.Miami L.Rev. 413 (1992); Note, *Outing, Privacy, and the First Amendment,* 102 Yale L.J. 747 (1992); Note, *"Outing" and Freedom of the Press: Sexual Orientation's Challenge to the Supreme Court's Categorical Jurisprudence,* 77 Corn.L.Rev. 103 (1992).

III. OBSCENITY

A. THE SEARCH FOR A RATIONALE

Roth v. United States, infra, contains the Court's first extended discussion of the constitutionality of obscenity laws. The Court's opinion was framed by briefs that proceeded from sharply different visions of first amendment law. Roth argued that no speech including obscenity could be prohibited without meeting the clear and present danger test, that a danger of lustful thoughts was not the type of evil with which a legislature could be legitimately concerned, and that no danger of anti-social conduct had been shown. On the other hand, the government urged the Court to adopt a balancing test that prominently featured a consideration of the value of the speech involved. The government tendered an illustrative hierarchy of nineteen speech categories with political, religious, economic, and scientific speech at the top; entertainment, music, and humor in the middle; and libel, obscenity, profanity, and commercial pornography at the bottom.

5. The Court does not address the distinct constitutional questions raised by the award of punitive damages in this case. Consequently, I do not do so either. That award is more troublesome than the compensatory award discussed above. Cf. Note, *Punitive Damages and Libel Law,* 98 Harv.L.Rev. 847 (1985).

ROTH v. UNITED STATES
ALBERTS v. CALIFORNIA

354 U.S. 476, 77 S.Ct. 1304, 1 L.Ed.2d 1498 (1957).

JUSTICE BRENNAN delivered the opinion of the Court. [Roth and Alberts were convicted of violating the federal and California obscenity laws respectively. The issues raised were whether the statutes, *"on their faces and in a vacuum,* violated the freedom of expression and definiteness requirements of the Constitution." [a]]

The dispositive question is whether obscenity is utterance within the area of protected speech and press.[8] Although this is the first time the question has been squarely presented to this Court [expressions] found in numerous opinions indicate that this Court has always assumed that obscenity is not protected by the freedoms of speech and press.

The guaranties of freedom of expression in effect in 10 of the 14 States which by 1792 had ratified the Constitution, gave no absolute protection for every utterance. Thirteen of the 14 States provided for the prosecution of libel, and all of those States made either blasphemy or profanity, or both, statutory crimes. As early as 1712, Massachusetts made it criminal to publish "any filthy, obscene, or profane song, pamphlet, libel or mock sermon" in imitation or mimicking of religious services. * * *

In light of this history, it is apparent that the unconditional phrasing of the First Amendment was not intended to protect every utterance. This phrasing did not prevent this Court from concluding that libelous utterances are not within the area of constitutionally protected speech. *Beauharnais.* At the time of the adoption of the First Amendment, obscenity law was not as fully developed as libel law, but there is sufficiently contemporaneous evidence to show that obscenity, too, was outside the protection intended for speech and press.[b]

The protection given speech and press was fashioned to assure unfettered interchange of ideas for the bringing about of political and social changes desired by the people. [All] ideas having even the slightest redeeming social importance—unorthodox ideas, controversial ideas, even ideas hateful to the prevailing climate of opinion—have the full protection of the guaranties, unless excludable because they encroach upon the limited area of more important interests. But implicit in the history of the First Amendment is the rejection of obscenity as utterly without

---

a. See William Lockhart & Robert McClure, *Censorship of Obscenity: The Developing Constitutional Standards,* 45 Minn. L.Rev. 5, 13 (1960).

8. No issue is presented in either case concerning the obscenity of the material involved.

b. The Court here cited three state court decisions (1808 to 1821) recognizing as a common law offense the distribution or display of obscene or indecent materials, and four state statutes aimed at similar conduct (1800 to 1842). For the contention that obscenity is not "speech" within the meaning of the first amendment (let alone, not *protected* speech), see Frederick Schauer, *Free Speech: A Philosophical Enquiry* 181–84 (1982) (a sex aid, not speech). See generally Frederick Schauer, *Speech and "Speech"—Obscenity and "Obscen-*

ity": An Exercise in the Interpretation of Constitutional Language, 67 Geo.L.J. 899 (1979). But see Larry Alexander & Paul Horton, *The Impossibility of a Free Speech Principle,* 78 Nw.U.L.Rev. 1319, 1331–34 (1984). Compare Kent Greenawalt, *Criminal Coercion and Freedom of Speech,* 78 Nw.U.L.Rev. 1081 (1984) (discussing the question of whether all ordinary language should be included within the scope of the first amendment, even if much is ultimately unprotected, and contending that some ordinary language should be wholly outside the scope of the first amendment); Kent Greenawalt, *Speech, Crime and the Uses of Language.* But see Franklyn Haiman, *Comments on Kent Greenawalt's Criminal Coercion and Freedom of Speech,* 78 Nw.U.L.Rev. 1125 (1983).

redeeming social importance. This rejection for that reason is mirrored in the universal judgment that obscenity should be restrained, reflected in the international agreement of over 50 nations, in the obscenity laws of all of the 48 States, and in the 20 obscenity laws enacted by the Congress from 1842 to 1956. This is the same judgment expressed by this Court in *Chaplinsky* [p. 630 infra]: "There are certain well-defined and narrowly limited classes of speech, the prevention and punishment of which have never been thought to raise any Constitutional problem. *These include the lewd and obscene. [It] has been well observed that such utterances are no essential part of any exposition of ideas, and are of such slight social value as a step to truth that any benefit that may be derived from them is clearly outweighed by the social interest in order and morality.*" (Emphasis added [by Court].)

We hold that obscenity is not within the area of constitutionally protected speech or press.

It is strenuously urged that these obscenity statutes offend the constitutional guaranties because they punish incitation to impure sexual *thoughts,* not shown to be related to any overt antisocial conduct which is or may be incited in the persons stimulated to such *thoughts.* [It] is insisted that the constitutional guaranties are violated because convictions may be had without proof either that obscene material will perceptibly create a clear and present danger of antisocial conduct, or will probably induce its recipients to such conduct. But, in light of our holding that obscenity is not protected speech, the complete answer to this argument is in the holding of this Court in *Beauharnais:* "Libelous utterances not being within the area of constitutionally protected speech, it is unnecessary, either for us or for the State courts, to consider the issues behind the phrase 'clear and present danger.' Certainly no one would contend that obscene speech, for example, may be punished only upon a showing of such circumstances. * * *"

However, sex and obscenity are not synonymous. Obscene material is material which deals with sex in a manner appealing to prurient interest.[20] The portrayal of sex, e.g., in art, literature and scientific works, is not itself sufficient reason to deny material the constitutional protection of freedom of speech and press. Sex, a great and mysterious motive force in human life, has indisputably been a subject of absorbing interest to mankind through the ages; it is one of the vital problems of human interest and public [concern].

The fundamental freedoms of speech and press have contributed greatly to the development and well-being of our free society and are indispensable to its continued growth. [It] is therefore vital that the standards for judging obscenity safeguard the protection of freedom of speech and press for material which does not treat sex in a manner appealing to prurient interest.

The early leading standard of obscenity allowed material to be judged merely by the effect of an isolated excerpt upon particularly susceptible persons. *Regina v. Hicklin,* [1868] L.R. 3 Q.B. 360. Some American courts adopted this standard

---

20. I.e., material having a tendency to excite lustful thoughts. *Webster's New International Dictionary* (Unabridged, 2d ed., 1949) defines *prurient,* in pertinent part, as follows:

"Itching; longing; uneasy with desire or longing; of persons, having itching, morbid, or lascivious longings; of desire, curiosity, or propensity, lewd * * *."

We perceive no significant difference between the meaning of obscenity developed in the case law and the definition of the A.L.I., *Model Penal Code,* § 207.10(2) (Tent. Draft No. 6, 1957), viz.: "[A] thing is obscene if, considered as a whole, its predominant appeal is to prurient interest, i.e. a shameful or morbid interest in nudity, sex, or excretion, and if it goes substantially beyond customary limits of candor in description or representation of such [matters]." See Comment, id. at 10, and the discussion at page 29 et seq.

but later decisions have rejected it and substituted this test: whether to the average person, applying contemporary community standards, the dominant theme of the material taken as a whole appeals to prurient interest. The *Hicklin* test, judging obscenity by the effect of isolated passages upon the most susceptible persons, might well encompass material legitimately treating with sex, and so it must be rejected as unconstitutionally restrictive of the freedoms of speech and press. On the other hand, the substituted standard provides safeguards adequate to withstand the charge of constitutional infirmity. Both trial courts below sufficiently followed the proper standard. Both courts used the proper definition of obscenity.[c]

[It] is argued that the statutes do not provide reasonably ascertainable standards of guilt and therefore violate the constitutional requirements of due process. *Winters v. New York,* 333 U.S. 507, 68 S.Ct. 665, 92 L.Ed. 840 (1948). The federal obscenity statute makes punishable the mailing of material that is "obscene, lewd, lascivious, or filthy [or] other publication of an indecent character." The California statute makes punishable, inter alia, the keeping for sale or advertising material that is "obscene or indecent." The thrust of the argument is that these words are not sufficiently precise because they do not mean the same thing to all people, all the time, everywhere. Many decisions have recognized that these terms of obscenity statutes are not precise. This Court, however, has consistently held that lack of precision is not itself offensive to the requirements of due process. "[T]he Constitution does not require impossible standards"; all that is required is that the language "conveys sufficiently definite warning as to the proscribed conduct when measured by common understanding and [practices.]" * * *

In summary, then, we hold that these statutes, applied according to the proper standard for judging obscenity, do not offend constitutional safeguards against convictions based upon protected material, or fail to give men in acting adequate notice of what is prohibited. * * *[d]

Affirmed.

CHIEF JUSTICE WARREN, concurring in the result.

[It] is not the book that is on trial; it is a person. The conduct of the defendant is the central issue, not the obscenity of a book or picture. The nature of the materials is, of course, relevant as an attribute of the defendant's conduct. [The] defendants in both these cases were engaged in the business of purveying textual or graphic matter openly advertised to appeal to the erotic interest of their customers. They were plainly engaged in the commercial exploitation of the morbid and shameful craving for materials with prurient effect. * * *

JUSTICE DOUGLAS, with whom JUSTICE BLACK concurs, dissenting.

c. The opinion quoted with apparent approval from the trial court's instruction in *Roth:* "[The] test is not whether it would arouse sexual desires or sexual impure thoughts in those comprising a particular segment of the community, the young, the immature or the highly prudish or would leave another segment, the scientific or highly educated or the so-called worldly-wise and sophisticated indifferent and unmoved. [The] test in each case is the effect of the book, picture or publication considered as a whole, not upon any particular class, but upon all those whom it is likely to reach. In other words, you determine its impact upon the average person in the community. The books, pictures and circulars must be judged as a whole, in their entire context, and you are not to consider detached or separate portions in reaching a conclusion. You judge the circulars, pictures and publications which have been put in evidence by present-day standards of the community. You may ask yourselves does it offend the common conscience of the community by present-day standards."

d. Harlan, J., dissented in *Roth* and concurred in *Alberts.*

When we sustain these convictions, we make the legality of a publication turn on the purity of thought which a book or tract instills in the mind of the reader. I do not think we can approve that standard and be faithful to the command of the First Amendment * * *.

I would give the broad sweep of the First Amendment full support. I have the same confidence in the ability of our people to reject noxious literature as I have in their capacity to sort out the true from the false in theology, economics, politics, or any other field.

Notes and Questions

1. *Non-obscene advocacy of "sexual immorality."* Two years after *Roth*, KINGSLEY INT'L. PICTURES CORP. v. REGENTS, 360 U.S. 684, 79 S.Ct. 1362, 3 L.Ed.2d 1512 (1959), per STEWART, J., underlined the distinction between obscenity and non-obscene "portrayal of sex" in art and literature. *Kingsley* held invalid New York's denial of a license to exhibit the film *Lady Chatterley's Lover* pursuant to a statute requiring such denial when a film "portrays acts of sexual immorality [as] desirable, acceptable or proper patterns of behavior":

"The Court of Appeals unanimously and explicitly rejected any notion that the film is obscene [but] found that the picture as a whole 'alluringly portrays adultery as proper behavior.' [What] New York has done, [is] to prevent the exhibition of a motion picture because that picture advocates an idea—that adultery under certain circumstances may be proper behavior. Yet the First Amendment's basic guarantee is of freedom to advocate ideas. The State, quite simply, has thus struck at the very heart of constitutionally protected liberty.

"[T]he guarantee is not confined to the expression of ideas that are conventional or shared by a majority. It protects advocacy of the opinion that adultery may sometimes be proper, no less than advocacy of socialism or the single tax. And in the realm of ideas it protects expression which is eloquent no less than that which is unconvincing. Advocacy of conduct proscribed by law is not, as Mr. Justice Brandeis long ago pointed out, 'a justification for denying free speech where the advocacy falls short of incitement and there is nothing to indicate that the advocacy would be immediately acted on.' *Whitney*." [e]

2. *Ideas and the first amendment.* Consider Harry Kalven, *The Metaphysics of the Law of Obscenity*, 1960 Sup.Ct.Rev. 1, 15–16: "The classic defense of John Stuart Mill and the modern defense of Alexander Meiklejohn do not help much when the question is why the novel, the poem, the painting, the drama, or the piece of sculpture falls within the protection of the First Amendment. Nor do the famous opinions of Hand, Holmes, and Brandeis. [The] people do not need novels or dramas or paintings or poems because they will be called upon to vote. Art and belles-lettres do not deal in such ideas—at least not good art or belles-lettres—and it makes little sense here to talk [of] whether there is still time for counter-speech.

"[B]eauty has constitutional status too, [and] the life of the imagination is as important to the human adult as the life of the intellect. I do not think that the Court would find it difficult to protect Shakespeare, even though it is hard to

e. While joining the opinion, Black and Douglas, JJ., also stated that prior censorship of motion pictures violates the first amendment. See discussion of this issue in Sec. 4, II infra. Harlan, J., joined by Frankfurter and Whittaker, JJ., concurred in the result. While "granting that abstract public discussion [of] adultery, unaccompanied by obscene portrayal or actual incitement [may] not constitutionally be proscribed," they concluded that the New York Court of Appeals had found the film obscene, but on viewing the film they concluded it was not obscene. Clark, J., concurred in the result because the statutory standard was too vague.

enumerate the important ideas in the plays and poems. I am only suggesting that Mr. Justice Brennan might not have found it so easy to dismiss obscenity because it lacked socially useful ideas if he had recognized that as to this point, at least, obscenity is in the same position as all art and literature." See generally Sheldon Nahmod, *Artistic Expression and Aesthetic Theory: The Beautiful, The Sublime and The First Amendment,* 1987 Wisc.L.Rev. 221.

3. *The moral rationale for prohibition.* Consider Harry Clor, *Obscenity and Public Morality* 41–43 (1969): *Roth* "rejected the government's formula for the decision of obscenity cases, a formula which would have involved it in judgments concerning the importance of public morality and the role of government, as well as judgments concerning the effects of obscenity and the relative value of different forms of speech. The Court preferred to decide the case on the narrow and negative grounds that obscenity is without redeeming social importance. [W]hile the idea of redeeming social importance can be valuable as a definition of what should be protected, it cannot serve as a defense of regulation. Justices Harlan and Douglas can be answered only by a course of reasoning which provides some grounds for government activity in the area of morality, showing that the ends are legitimate and important, which provides some justification for the claims of community conscience, and which explores, more thoroughly than does the Court, the character of the 'thoughts' with which the law is here concerned."

The Court does assert that any value of obscenity as a step to truth is "outweighed by the social interest in order and morality.'" But consider David Richards, *Free Speech and Obscenity Law: Toward A Moral Theory of the First Amendment,* 123 U.Pa.L.Rev. 45, 81 (1974): "[P]ornography can be seen as the unique medium of a vision of sexuality [a] view of sensual delight in the erotic celebration of the body, a concept of easy freedom without consequences, a fantasy of timelessly repetitive indulgence. In opposition to the Victorian view that narrowly defines proper sexual function in a rigid way that is analogous to ideas of excremental regularity and moderation, pornography builds a model of plastic variety and joyful excess in sexuality. In opposition to the sorrowing Catholic dismissal of sexuality as an unfortunate and spiritually superficial concomitant of propagation, pornography affords the alternative idea of the independent status of sexuality as a profound and shattering ecstasy." [f]

Even if these characterizations were somewhat overwrought with respect to Roth's publications (e.g., *Wild Passion* and *Wanton By Night*) what of the view that individuals should be able to decide what they want to read and make moral decisions for themselves? Consider John Stuart Mill's statement of the harm principle in *On Liberty:* "[T]he only purpose for which power can be rightfully exercised over any member of a civilized community, against his will is to prevent harm to others."

Does the liberal view overestimate human rational capacity and underestimate the importance of the state in promoting a virtuous citizenry? See generally

---

f. For the view that pornography can best be defended as a form of anti-social dissent, consider Steven Gey, *The Apologetics of Suppression,* 86 Mich.L.Rev. 1564, 1630 (1988): "Porn exposes a rot in the framework of society, and the great popularity of porn makes the burghers uneasily suspicious that the surface rot may evidence a more deeply rooted degeneration of their moral and political primacy. Thus, the imperative to suppress pornography reveals a much deeper and more insidious inse-curity than the moralists will ever acknowledge." Cf. Robin West, *The Feminist–Conservative Anti–Pornography Alliance and the 1986 Attorney General's Commission on Pornography Report,* 1987 Am.B.Found.Res.J. 681, 686–99 (discussing victimizing and liberating aspects of pornography from the perspectives of women while contending that women's experience of pornography, albeit diverse, is different from that of men).

Clor, supra. Do liberals fail to appreciate the morally corrosive effects of obscenity? Consider the following observation: "Obscenity emphasizes the base animality of our nature, reduces the spirituality of humanity to mere bodily functions, and debases civilization by transforming the private into the public." Consider Irving Kristol, *Reflections of a Neoconservative* 45, 47 (1983): "Bearbaiting and cockfighting are prohibited only in part out of compassion for the suffering animals; the main reason they were abolished was because it was felt that they debased and brutalized the citizenry who flocked to witness such spectacles. And the question we face with regard to pornography and obscenity is whether [they] can or will brutalize and debase our citizenry. We are, after all, not dealing with one passing incident—one book, or one play, or one movie. We are dealing with a general tendency that is suffusing our entire culture. [W]hen men and women make love, as we say, they prefer to be alone—because it is only when you are alone that you can make love, as distinct from merely copulating in an animal and casual way. And that, too, is why those who are voyeurs, if they are not irredeemably sick, also feel ashamed at what they are witnessing. When sex is a public spectacle, a human relationship has been debased into a mere animal connection." See also Harry Clor, supra; Walter Berns, *Pornography vs. Democracy: The Case for Censorship,* 22 Pub.Int. 13 (1971). For the relationship between pornography, commerce, and culture, see Ronald Collins & David Skover, *The Pornographic State,* 107 Harv.L.Rev. 1374 (1994).

4. *Obscenity and deliberation.* Consider Cass Sunstein, *Words, Conduct, Caste,* 60 U.Chi.L.Rev. 795, 807–08 (1993): "Such materials fall in the same category as misleading commercial speech, libel of private persons, conspiracies, unlicensed medical or legal advice, bribes, perjury, threats, and so forth. These forms of speech do not appeal to deliberative capacities about public matters, or about matters at all—even if this category is construed quite broadly, as it should be, and even if we insist, as we should, that emotive and cognitive capacities are frequently intertwined in deliberative processes and that any sharp split between 'emotion' and 'cognition' would be untrue to political discussion. Many forms of pornography are not an appeal to the exchange of ideas, political or otherwise; they operate as masturbatory aids and do not qualify for top-tier First Amendment protection under the prevailing theories." But see David Cole, *Playing by Pornography's Rules: The Regulation of Sexual Expression,* 143 U.Pa.L.Rev. 111, 126–27 (1994): "Sexual expression, like human sexuality itself, cannot be 'purely physical.' Rather, it is deeply and inextricably interwoven with our identities, our emotions, our upbringing, our relationships to other human beings, and the ever-changing narratives and images that our community finds stimulating. [Thus], the argument that sexual expression can be usefully distinguished from political speech because it lacks 'cognitive' appeal is insupportable. Both political and sexual expression work in rational and irrational ways and contribute to our culture, our ideology, and our individual and collective identities through their rational and irrational communicative content."

Compare Sunstein, supra, at 808 & 808 n. 45: "Those who write or read sexually explicit material can often claim important expressive and deliberative interests. Sexually explicit works can be highly relevant to the development of human capacities. [But] no one has set out an approach to free speech based on expression and deliberative value. [To] be sure, pornography is political in the sense that it has political consequences. But this does not mean that it is political in the First Amendment sense of that word. Much speech that does not belong in the top tier—misleading commercial speech, attempted bribery of public officials—has political consequences. If speech qualified for the top tier whenever it has such consequences, almost all speech would so qualify, and First Amendment doctrine would be made senseless. Instead, the test is whether it is intended and received as a contribution to democratic deliberation—and much pornography fails that test. It is true that the recent attack on pornography has drawn attention to its political character, but this fact does not undermine the First Amendment argument, since the First Amendment conception of 'the political' is properly and importantly different from the conception of 'the political' in popular discussion."

5. *Feminism and pornography.* Does the Court's cryptic recitation of the interests in order and morality obscure the implications of pornography for women in a male-dominated culture? Consider Susan Brownmiller, *Against Our Will: Men, Women & Rape* 442–43, 444 (1976): Pornography is a "systematized commercially successful propaganda machine" encouraging males to get a "sense of power from viewing females as anonymous, panting playthings, adult toys, dehumanized objects to be used, abused, broken and discarded." See also Catharine MacKinnon, *Not a Moral Issue,* 2 Yale L. & Pol.Rev. 321, 327 (1984): "[T]he liberal defense of pornography as human sexual liberation, as de-repression— whether by feminists, lawyers, or neo-Freudians—is a defense not only of force and sexual terrorism, but of the subordination of women. Sexual liberation in the liberal sense frees male sexual aggression in the feminist sense. What in the liberal view looks like love and romance looks a lot like hatred and torture to the feminist. Pleasure and eroticism become violation. Desire appears as lust for dominance and submission."

STANLEY v. GEORGIA, 394 U.S. 557, 89 S.Ct. 1243, 22 L.Ed.2d 542 (1969), per MARSHALL, J., reversed a conviction for knowing "possession of obscene matter," based on three reels of obscene films found in Stanley's home when police entered under a search warrant for other purposes: "[*Roth*] and the cases following it discerned [an] 'important interest' in the regulation of commercial distribution of obscene material. That holding cannot foreclose an examination of the constitutional implications of a statute forbidding mere private possession of such material. [The constitutional] right to receive information and ideas, regardless of their social worth [*Winters*] is fundamental to our free society. Moreover, in the context of this case—a prosecution for mere possession of printed or filmed matter in the privacy of a person's own home—that right takes on an added dimension. For also fundamental is the right to be free, except in very limited circumstances, from unwanted governmental intrusions into one's privacy.

" 'The makers of our Constitution undertook to secure conditions favorable to the pursuit of happiness. They recognized the significance of man's spiritual nature, of his feelings and of his intellect. [They] sought to protect Americans in their beliefs, their thoughts, their emotions and their sensations. They conferred, as against the government, the right to be let alone—the most comprehensive of rights and the right most valued by civilized man.' *Olmstead v. United States,* 277 U.S. 438, 48 S.Ct. 564, 72 L.Ed. 944 (1928) (Brandeis, J., dissenting). * * *

"These are the rights that appellant is asserting in the case before us. He is asserting the right to read or observe what he pleases—the right to satisfy his intellectual and emotional needs in the privacy of his own home. He is asserting the right to be free from state inquiry into the contents of his library. Georgia contends that appellant does not have these rights, that there are certain types of materials that the individual may not read or even possess. [W]e think that mere categorization of these films as 'obscene' is insufficient justification for such a drastic invasion of personal liberties guaranteed by the First and Fourteenth Amendments. Whatever may be the justifications for other statutes regulating obscenity, we do not think they reach into the privacy of one's own home. If the First Amendment means anything, it means that a State has no business telling a man, sitting alone in his own house, what books he may read or what films he may watch. Our whole constitutional heritage rebels at the thought of giving government the power to control men's minds.

"[I]n the face of these traditional notions of individual liberty, Georgia asserts the right to protect the individual's mind from the effects of obscenity. We are not certain that this argument amounts to anything more than the assertion that the State has the right to control the moral content of a person's thoughts.[8] To some, this may be a noble purpose, but it is wholly inconsistent with the philosophy of the First Amendment. [*Kingsley Pictures.*] Nor is it relevant that obscenity in general, or the particular films before the Court, are arguably devoid of any ideological content. The line between the transmission of ideas and mere entertainment is much too elusive for this Court to draw, if indeed such a line can be drawn at all. [*Winters*]. Whatever the power of the state to control public dissemination of ideas inimical to the public morality, it cannot constitutionally premise legislation on the desirability of controlling a person's private thoughts.

"[Georgia] asserts that exposure to obscenity may lead to deviant sexual behavior or crimes of sexual violence. There appears to be little empirical basis for that assertion. But more importantly, if the State is only concerned about literature inducing antisocial conduct, we believe that in the context of private consumption of ideas and information we should adhere to the view that '[a]mong free men, the deterrents ordinarily to be applied to prevent crime are education and punishment for violations of the [law].' *Whitney* (Brandeis, J., concurring). See Emerson, *Toward a General Theory of the First Amendment*, 72 Yale L.J. 877, 938 (1963). Given the present state of knowledge, the State may no more prohibit mere possession of obscenity on the ground that it may lead to antisocial conduct than it may prohibit possession of chemistry books on the ground that they may lead to the manufacture of homemade spirits.

"It is true that in *Roth* this Court rejected the necessity of proving that exposure to obscene material would create a clear and present danger of antisocial conduct or would probably induce its recipients to such conduct. But that case dealt with public distribution of obscene materials and such distribution is subject to different objections. For example, there is always the danger that obscene material might fall into the hands of children, see *Ginsberg,* [fn. d, p. 619 infra], or that it might intrude upon the sensibilities or privacy of the general public. No such dangers are present in this [case.]

"We hold that the First and Fourteenth Amendments prohibit making mere private possession of obscene material a crime. *Roth* and the cases following that decision are not impaired by today's holding. As we have said, the States retain

---

8. "Communities believe, and act on the belief, that obscenity is immoral, is wrong for the individual, and has no place in a decent society. They believe, too, that adults as well as children are corruptible in morals and character, and that obscenity is a source of corruption that should be eliminated. Obscenity is not suppressed primarily for the protection of others. Much of it is suppressed for the purity of the community and for the salvation and welfare of the 'consumer.' Obscenity, at bottom, is not crime. Obscenity is sin." Louis Henkin, *Morals and the Constitution: The Sin of Obscenity,* 63 Col.L.Rev. 391, 395 (1963).

broad power to regulate obscenity; that power simply does not extend to mere possession by the individual in the privacy of his own home." [a]

Notes and Questions

1. *Obscenity and the first amendment.* Is *Stanley* consistent with the constitutional theory of *Roth?* Can the first amendment rationally be viewed as applicable to *private use* but not to *public distribution* of obscenity? Cf. Al Katz, *Privacy and Pornography,* 1969 Sup.Ct.Rev. 203, 210–11. Might the definitional two-level approach reconcile *Stanley* with *Roth?*

2. *Implications of Stanley.* Could *Stanley's* recognition of a first amendment right to "receive" and use obscene matter in the home fairly be viewed as implying a right to purchase it from commercial suppliers, or to import it for personal use, or to view it in a theater limited to consenting adults?

PARIS ADULT THEATRE I v. SLATON

413 U.S. 49, 93 S.Ct. 2628, 37 L.Ed.2d 446 (1973).

[The entrance to Paris Adult Theatres I & II was conventional and inoffensive without any pictures. Signs read: "Adult Theatre—You must be 21 and able to prove it. If viewing the nude body offends you, Please Do Not Enter." The District Attorney, nonetheless, had brought an action to enjoin the showing of two films that the Georgia Supreme Court described as "hard core pornography" leaving "little to the imagination." The Georgia Supreme Court assumed that the adult theaters in question barred minors and gave a full warning to the general public of the nature of the films involved, but held that the showing of the films was not constitutionally protected.]

CHIEF JUSTICE BURGER delivered the opinion of the Court.

[We] categorically disapprove the theory [that] obscene, pornographic films acquire constitutional immunity from state regulation simply because they are exhibited for consenting adults only. [Although we have] recognized the high importance of the state interest in regulating the exposure of obscene materials to juveniles and unconsenting adults, this Court has never declared these to be the only legitimate state interests permitting regulation of obscene material.

[W]e hold that there are legitimate state interests at stake in stemming the tide of commercialized obscenity, even assuming it is feasible to enforce effective safeguards against exposure to juveniles and to the passerby.[7] [These] include the interest of the public in the quality of life and the total community environment, the tone of commerce in the great city centers, and, possibly, the public safety itself. The Hill-Link Minority Report of the Commission on Obscenity and Pornography indicates that there is at least an arguable correlation between

---

a. Black, J., concurred separately. Stewart, J., joined by Brennan and White, JJ., concurred in the result on search and seizure grounds.

7. It is conceivable that an "adult" theatre can—if it really insists—prevent the exposure of its obscene wares to juveniles. An "adult" bookstore, dealing in obscene books, magazines, and pictures, cannot realistically make this claim. The Hill-Link Minority Report of the Commission on Obscenity and Pornography emphasizes evidence (the Abelson National Survey of Youth and Adults) that, although

most pornography may be bought by elders, "the heavy users and most highly exposed people to pornography are adolescent females (among women) and adolescent and young males (among men)." *The Report of the Commission on Obscenity* 401 (1970). The legitimate interest in preventing exposure of juveniles to obscene materials cannot be fully served by simply barring juveniles from the immediate physical premises of "adult" bookstores, when there is a flourishing "outside business" in these materials.

obscene material and crime. Quite apart from sex crimes, however, there remains one problem of large proportions aptly described by Professor Bickel: "It concerns the tone of the society, the mode, or to use terms that have perhaps greater currency, the style and quality of life, now and in the future. A man may be entitled to read an obscene book in his room, or expose himself indecently there. [We] should protect his privacy. But if he demands a right to obtain the books and pictures he wants in the market, and to foregather in public places—discreet, if you will, but accessible to all—with others who share his tastes, *then to grant him his right is to affect the world about the rest of us, and to impinge on other privacies.* Even supposing that each of us can, if he wishes, effectively avert the eye and stop the ear (which, in truth, we cannot), what is commonly read and seen and heard and done intrudes upon us all, want it or not." 22 *The Public Interest* 25, 25–26 (Winter, 1971). (Emphasis supplied.) [T]here is a "right of the Nation and of the States to maintain a decent [society]," *Jacobellis* (Warren, C.J., dissenting).

But, it is argued, there is no scientific data which conclusively demonstrates that exposure to obscene materials adversely affects men and women or their society. It is urged [that], absent such a demonstration, any kind of state regulation is "impermissible." We reject this argument. It is not for us to resolve empirical uncertainties underlying state legislation, save in the exceptional case where that legislation plainly impinges upon rights protected by the Constitution itself. [Although] there is no conclusive proof of a connection between antisocial behavior and obscene material, the legislature of Georgia could quite reasonably determine that such a connection does or might exist. In deciding *Roth*, this Court implicitly accepted that a legislature could legitimately act on such a conclusion to protect *"the social interest in order and morality."*

From the beginning of civilized societies, legislators and judges have acted on various unprovable assumptions. Such assumptions underlie much lawful state regulation of commercial and business affairs. The same is true of the federal securities, antitrust laws and a host of other federal regulations. [Likewise], when legislatures and administrators act to protect the physical environment from pollution and to preserve our resources of forests, streams and parks, they must act on such imponderables as the impact of a new highway near or through an existing park or wilderness area. [The] fact that a congressional directive reflects unprovable assumptions about what is good for the people, including imponderable aesthetic assumptions, is not a sufficient reason to find that statute unconstitutional.

If we accept the unprovable assumption that a complete education requires certain books, and the well nigh universal belief that good books, plays, and art lift the spirit, improve the mind, enrich the human personality and develop character, can we then say that a state legislature may not act on the corollary assumption that commerce in obscene books,[a] or public exhibitions focused on

---

a. The only case after *Roth* in which the Court upheld a conviction based upon books was in *Mishkin* [p. 619 infra] and most, if not all, of those books were illustrated. *Kaplan v. California*, 413 U.S. 115, 93 S.Ct. 2680, 37 L.Ed.2d 492 (1973) held that books without pictures can be legally obscene "in the sense of being unprotected by the First Amendment." It observed that books are "passed hand to hand, and we can take note of the tendency of widely circulated books of this category to reach the impressionable young and have a continuing impact. A State could reasonably regard the 'hard core' conduct described by *Suite 69* as capable of encouraging or causing antisocial behavior, especially in its impact on young people." Is *Kaplan*'s explanation in tension with *Butler v. Michigan* [p. 619 infra]? Why should the obscenity standard focus on the average adult if the underlying worry is that books will fall in the hands of children?

obscene conduct, have a tendency to exert a corrupting and debasing impact leading to antisocial behavior? [The] sum of experience, including that of the past two decades, affords an ample basis for legislatures to conclude that a sensitive, key relationship of human existence, central to family life, community welfare, and the development of human personality, can be debased and distorted by crass commercial exploitation of sex. Nothing in the Constitution prohibits a State from reaching such a conclusion and acting on it legislatively simply because there is no conclusive evidence or empirical data.

[Nothing] in this Court's decisions intimates that there is any "fundamental" privacy right "implicit in the concept of ordered liberty" to watch obscene movies in places of public accommodation. [W]e have declined to equate the privacy of the home relied on in *Stanley* with a "zone" of "privacy" that follows a distributor or a consumer of obscene materials wherever he goes.[b]

[W]e reject the claim that Georgia is here attempting to control the minds or thoughts of those who patronize theatres. Preventing unlimited display or distribution of obscene material, which by definition lacks any serious literary, artistic, political, or scientific value as communication, is distinct from a control of reason and the intellect. Cf. John Finnis, *"Reason and Passion": The Constitutional Dialectic of Free Speech and Obscenity,* 116 U.Pa.L.Rev. 222, 229–230, 241–243 (1967).

[Finally], petitioners argue that conduct which directly involves "consenting adults" only has, for that sole reason, a special claim to constitutional protection. Our Constitution establishes a broad range of conditions on the exercise of power by the States, but for us to say that our Constitution incorporates the proposition that conduct involving consenting adults only is always beyond state regulation,[14] is a step we are unable to take.[15] [The] issue in this context goes beyond whether someone, or even the majority, considers the conduct depicted as "wrong" or "sinful." The States have the power to make a morally neutral judgment that public exhibition of obscene material, or commerce in such material, has a tendency to injure the community as a whole, to endanger the public safety, or to jeopardize, in Mr. Chief Justice Warren's words, the States' "right [to] maintain a decent society." *Jacobellis* (dissenting). * * *

---

b. In a series of cases, the Court limited *Stanley* to its facts. It held that *Stanley* did not protect the mailing of obscene material to consenting adults, *United States v. Reidel,* 402 U.S. 351, 91 S.Ct. 1410, 28 L.Ed.2d 813 (1971) or the transporting or importing of obscene materials for private use, *United States v. Orito,* 413 U.S. 139, 93 S.Ct. 2674, 37 L.Ed.2d 513 (1973) (transporting); *United States v. 12 200–Ft. Reels,* 413 U.S. 123, 93 S.Ct. 2665, 37 L.Ed.2d 500 (1973) (importing). Dissenting in *Reels,* Douglas, J., argued that *Stanley* rights could legally be realized "only if one wrote or designed a tract in his attic and printed or processed it in his basement, so as to be able to read it in his study." Do these decisions take the first amendment out of *Stanley*? Are they justified by the rationale in *Paris Adult Theatre*? For example, does importation for personal use intrude "upon us all"? Affect the total community environment?

For the declaration that *Stanley's* "privacy of the home" principle is "firmly grounded" in the first amendment while resisting the principle's expansion to protect consensual adult homosexual sodomy in the home, see *Bowers v. Hardwick,* p. 422 supra. But see Blackmun, J., joined by Brennan, Marshall, and Stevens, JJ., dissenting in *Bowers* ("*Stanley* rested as much on the Court's understanding of the Fourth Amendment as it did on the First").

14. Cf. John Stuart Mill, *On Liberty* 13 (1955).

15. The state statute books are replete with constitutionally unchallenged laws against prostitution, suicide, voluntary self-mutilation, brutalizing "bare fist" prize fights, and duels, although these crimes may only directly involve "consenting adults." Statutes making bigamy a crime surely cut into an individual's freedom to associate, but few today seriously claim such statutes violate the First Amendment or any other constitutional provision.

JUSTICE BRENNAN, with whom JUSTICE STEWART and JUSTICE MARSHALL join, dissenting.

[I] am convinced that the approach initiated 15 years ago in *Roth* and culminating in the Court's decision today, cannot bring stability to this area of the law without jeopardizing fundamental First Amendment values, and I have concluded that the time has come to make a significant departure from that [approach.]

[The] decision of the Georgia Supreme Court rested squarely on its conclusion that the State could constitutionally suppress these films even if they were displayed only to persons over the age of 21 who were aware of the nature of their contents and who had consented to viewing them. [I] am convinced of the invalidity of that conclusion [and] would therefore vacate the [judgment]. I have no occasion to consider the extent of State power to regulate the distribution of sexually oriented materials to juveniles or to unconsenting [adults.] [*Stanley*] reflected our emerging view that the state interests in protecting children and in protecting unconsenting adults may stand on a different footing from the other asserted state interests. It may well be, as one commentator has argued, that "exposure to [erotic material] is for some persons an intense emotional experience. A communication of this nature, imposed upon a person contrary to his wishes, has all the characteristics of a physical assault * * *. [And it] constitutes an invasion of his [privacy]." [24] [But] whatever the strength of the state interests in protecting juveniles and unconsenting adults from exposure to sexually oriented materials, those interests cannot be asserted in defense of the holding of the Georgia Supreme Court, [which] assumed for the purposes of its decision that the films in issue were exhibited only to persons over the age of 21 who viewed them willingly and with prior knowledge of the nature of their contents. [The] justification for the suppression must be found, therefore, in some independent interest in regulating the reading and viewing habits of consenting [adults].

In *Stanley* we pointed out that "[t]here appears to be little empirical basis for" the assertion that "exposure to obscene materials may lead to deviant sexual behavior or crimes of sexual violence." In any event, we added that "if the State is only concerned about printed or filmed materials inducing antisocial conduct, we believe that in the context of private consumption of ideas and information we should adhere to the view that '[a]mong free men, the deterrents ordinarily to be applied to prevent crime are education and punishment for violations of the [law].' "

Moreover, in *Stanley* we rejected as "wholly inconsistent with the philosophy of the First Amendment," the notion that there is a legitimate state concern in the "control [of] the moral content of a person's thoughts." [The] traditional description of state police power does embrace the regulation of morals as well as the health, safety, and general welfare of the citizenry. [But] the State's interest in regulating morality by suppressing obscenity, while often asserted, remains essentially unfocused and ill-defined. And, since the attempt to curtail unprotected speech necessarily spills over into the area of protected speech, the effort to serve this speculative interest through the suppression of obscene material must tread heavily on rights protected by the First Amendment. * * * [27]

In short, while I cannot say that the interests of the State—apart from the question of juveniles and unconsenting adults—are trivial or nonexistent, I am

---

24. Thomas Emerson, *The System of Freedom of Expression* 496 (1970).

27. See Louis Henkin, *Morals and the Constitution: The Sin of Obscenity,* 63 Col.L.Rev. 391, 395 (1963).

compelled to conclude that these interests cannot justify the substantial damage to constitutional rights and to this Nation's judicial machinery that inevitably results from state efforts to bar the distribution even of unprotected material to consenting adults.[c]

MR. JUSTICE DOUGLAS, dissenting. * * *

"Obscenity" at most is the expression of offensive ideas. There are regimes in the world where ideas "offensive" to the majority (or at least to those who control the majority) are suppressed. There life proceeds at a monotonous pace. Most of us would find that world offensive. One of the most offensive experiences in my life was a visit to a nation where bookstalls were filled only with books on mathematics and books on religion.

I am sure I would find offensive most of the books and movies charged with being obscene. But in a life that has not been short, I have yet to be trapped into seeing or reading something that would offend me. I never read or see the materials coming to the Court under charges of "obscenity," because I have thought the First Amendment made it unconstitutional for me to act as a censor. * * *

B. A REVISED STANDARD

MILLER v. CALIFORNIA

413 U.S. 15, 93 S.Ct. 2607, 37 L.Ed.2d 419 (1973).

CHIEF JUSTICE BURGER delivered the opinion of the Court. [The Court remanded, "for proceedings not inconsistent" with the opinion's obscenity standard, Miller's conviction under California's obscenity law for mass mailing of unsolicited pictorial advertising brochures depicting men and women in a variety of group sexual activities.]

This is one of a group of "obscenity-pornography" cases being reviewed by the Court in a re-examination of standards enunciated in earlier cases involving what Mr. Justice Harlan called "the intractable obscenity problem." [I]n this context [a] [we] are called on to define the standards which must be used to identify obscene material that a State may [regulate].

[Nine years after *Roth*], in *Memoirs v. Massachusetts*, 383 U.S. 413, 86 S.Ct. 975, 16 L.Ed.2d 1 (1966), the Court veered sharply away from the Roth concept and, with only three Justices in the plurality opinion, articulated a new test of obscenity. The plurality held that under the Roth definition "as elaborated in subsequent cases, three elements must coalesce: it must be established that (a) the dominant theme of the material taken as a whole appeals to a prurient interest in sex; (b) the material is patently offensive because it affronts contemporary community standards relating to the description or representation of sexual matters; and (c) the material is utterly without redeeming social value." * * *

While *Roth* presumed "obscenity" to be "utterly without redeeming social importance," *Memoirs* required that to prove obscenity it must be affirmatively established that the material is "*utterly* without redeeming social value."

c. For the portion of Brennan, J.'s dissent addressing the difficulties of formulating an acceptable constitutional standard, see *Miller v. California*, infra.

a. The "context" was that in *Miller* "sexually explicit materials have been thrust by aggressive sales action upon unwilling recipients." But nothing in *Miller* limited the revised standard to that context, and the companion case, *Paris Adult Theatre*, applied the same standard to dissemination limited to consenting adults.

Thus, even as they repeated the words of *Roth,* the *Memoirs* plurality produced a drastically altered test that called on the prosecution to prove a negative, i.e., that the material was *"utterly* without redeeming social value"—a burden virtually impossible to discharge under our criminal standards of proof. [Apart] from the initial formulation in *Roth,* no majority of the Court has at any given time been able to agree on a standard to determine what constitutes obscene, pornographic material subject to regulation under the States' police power. See, e.g., *Redrup v. New York,* 386 U.S. 767, 87 S.Ct. 1414, 18 L.Ed.2d 515 (1967).[3] This is not remarkable, for in the area of freedom of speech and press the courts must always remain sensitive to any infringement on genuinely serious literary, artistic, political, or scientific expression. * * *

II. This much has been categorically settled by the Court, that obscene material is unprotected by the First Amendment. [We] acknowledge, however, the inherent dangers of undertaking to regulate any form of expression. State statutes designed to regulate obscene materials must be carefully limited. As a result, we now confine the permissible scope of such regulation to works which depict or describe sexual conduct. That conduct must be specifically defined by the applicable state law, as written or authoritatively construed.[6] A state offense must also be limited to works which, taken as a whole, appeal to the prurient interest in sex, which portray sexual conduct in a patently offensive way, and which, taken as a whole, do not have serious literary, artistic, political, or scientific value.

The basic guidelines for the trier of fact must be: (a) whether "the average person, applying contemporary community standards" would find that the work, taken as a whole, appeals to the prurient interest, (b) whether the work depicts or describes, in a patently offensive way, sexual conduct specifically defined by the applicable state law, and (c) whether the work, taken as a whole, lacks serious literary, artistic, political, or scientific value. We do not adopt as a constitutional standard the *"utterly* without redeeming social value" test of *Memoirs;* that concept has never commanded the adherence of more than three Justices at one time.[7] If a state law that regulates obscene material is thus limited, as written or construed, the First Amendment values applicable to the States [are] adequately protected by the ultimate power of appellate courts to conduct an independent review of constitutional claims when necessary.

3. In the absence of a majority view, this Court was compelled to embark on the practice of summarily reversing convictions for the dissemination of materials that at least five members of the Court, applying their separate tests, found to be protected by the First Amendment. *Redrup.* [Beyond] the necessity of circumstances, however, no justification has ever been offered in support of the *Redrup* "policy." The *Redrup* procedure has cast us in the role of an unreviewable board of censorship for the 50 States, subjectively judging each piece of material brought before us.

6. See, e.g., Oregon Laws 1971, c. 743, Art. 29, §§ 255–262, and Hawaii Penal Code, Tit. 37, §§ 1210–1216, 1972 Hawaii Session Laws, pp. 126–129, Act 9, Pt. II, as examples of state laws directed at depiction of defined physical conduct, as opposed to expression. [We] do not hold, as Mr. Justice Brennan intimates, that all States other than Oregon must now enact new obscenity statutes. Other existing state statutes, as construed heretofore or hereafter, may well be adequate.

7. "[We] also reject, as a constitutional standard, the ambiguous concept of 'social importance'." [*Hamling v. United States,* 418 U.S. 87, 94 S.Ct. 2887, 41 L.Ed.2d 590 (1974) upheld a conviction in which the jury had been instructed to find that the material was "utterly without redeeming social value." Defendant argued that the latter phrase was unconstitutionally vague and cited *Miller.* The Court rejected the vagueness challenge: "[O]ur opinion in *Miller* plainly indicates that we rejected the '[social] value' formulation, not because it was so vague as to deprive criminal defendants of adequate notice, but instead because it represented a departure from [*Roth*], and because in calling on the prosecution to 'prove a negative,' it imposed a '[prosecutorial] burden virtually impossible to discharge' and which was not constitutionally required."]

We emphasize that it is not our function to propose regulatory schemes for the States. [It] is possible, however, to give a few plain examples of what a state statute could define for regulation under the second part (b) of the standard announced in this opinion, supra:

(a) Patently offensive representations or descriptions of ultimate sexual acts, normal or perverted, actual or simulated.

(b) Patently offensive representations or descriptions of masturbation, excretory functions, and lewd exhibition of the genitals.[b]

Sex and nudity may not be exploited without limit by films or pictures exhibited or sold in places of public accommodation any more than live sex and nudity can be exhibited or sold without limit in such public places.[8] At a minimum, prurient,[c] patently offensive depiction or description of sexual conduct must have serious literary, artistic, political, or scientific value to merit First Amendment protection. For example, medical books for the education of physicians and related personnel necessarily use graphic illustrations and descriptions of human anatomy. In resolving the inevitably sensitive questions of fact and law, we must continue to rely on the jury system, accompanied by the safeguards that judges, rules of evidence, presumption of innocence and other protective features [provide].

Mr. Justice Brennan [has] abandoned his former positions and now maintains that no formulation of this Court, the Congress, or the States can adequately distinguish obscene material unprotected by the First Amendment from protected expression, *Paris Adult Theatre I v. Slaton* (Brennan, J., dissenting). Paradoxically, Mr. Justice Brennan indicates that suppression of unprotected obscene material is permissible to avoid exposure to unconsenting adults, as in this case, and to juveniles, although he gives no indication of how the division between protected and nonprotected materials may be drawn with greater precision for these purposes than for regulation of commercial exposure to consenting adults only. Nor does he indicate where in the Constitution he finds the authority to distin-

---

b. *Jenkins v. Georgia,* 418 U.S. 153, 94 S.Ct. 2750, 41 L.Ed.2d 642 (1974) held the film *Carnal Knowledge* not obscene because it did not " 'depict or describe patently offensive "hard core" sexual conduct' " as required by *Miller:* "[While there] are scenes in which sexual conduct including 'ultimate sexual acts' is to be understood to be taking place, the camera does not focus on the bodies of the actors at such times. There is no exhibition whatever of the actors' genitals, lewd or otherwise, during these scenes. There are occasional scenes of nudity, but nudity alone is not enough to make material legally obscene under the *Miller* standards." *Ward v. Illinois,* 431 U.S. 767, 97 S.Ct. 2085, 52 L.Ed.2d 738 (1977) held that it was not necessary for the legislature or the courts to provide an "exhaustive list of the sexual conduct [the] description of which may be held obscene." It is enough that a state adopt *Miller*'s explanatory examples. Stevens, J., joined by Brennan, Stewart and Marshall, JJ., dissented: "[I]f the statute need only describe the 'kinds' of proscribed sexual conduct, it adds no protection to what the Constitution itself creates. [The] specificity requirement as described in *Miller* held out the promise of a principled effort to respond to [the vagueness] argument. By abandoning that effort today, the Court withdraws the cornerstone of the *Miller* [structure]."

8. Although we are not presented here with the problem of regulating lewd public conduct itself, the States have greater power to regulate nonverbal, physical conduct than to suppress depictions or descriptions of the same behavior. * * *

c. *Brockett v. Spokane Arcades, Inc.,* 472 U.S. 491, 105 S.Ct. 2794, 86 L.Ed.2d 394 (1985) held that appeals to prurient interest could not be taken to include appeals to "normal" interests in sex. Only appeals to a "shameful or morbid interest in sex" are prurient. Although the Court was resolute in its position that appeals to "good, old fashioned, healthy" interests in sex were constitutionally protected, it did not further specify how "normal" sex was to be distinguished from the "shameful" or "morbid."

guish between a willing "adult" one month past the state law age of majority and a willing "juvenile" one month younger.[d]

Under the holdings announced today, no one will be subject to prosecution for the sale or exposure of obscene materials unless these materials depict or describe patently offensive "hard core" sexual conduct specifically defined by the regulating state law, as written or construed. We are satisfied that these specific prerequisites will provide fair notice to a dealer in such materials that his public and commercial activities may bring prosecution. If the inability to define regulated materials with ultimate, god-like precision altogether removes the power of the States or the Congress to regulate, then "hard core" pornography may be exposed without limit to the juvenile, the passerby, and the consenting adult alike, as indeed, Mr. Justice Douglas contends.

[N]o amount of "fatigue" should lead us to adopt a convenient "institutional" rationale—an absolutist, "anything goes" view of the First Amendment—because it will lighten our burdens. [Nor] should we remedy "tension between state and federal courts" by arbitrarily depriving the States of a power reserved to them under the Constitution, a power which they have enjoyed and exercised continuously from before the adoption of the First Amendment to this day. See *Roth.* "Our duty admits of no 'substitute for facing up to the tough individual problems of constitutional judgment involved in every obscenity case.'" *Jacobellis* (opinion of Brennan, J.).

III. Under a national Constitution, fundamental First Amendment limitations on the powers of the States do not vary from community to community, but this does not mean that there are, or should or can be, fixed, uniform national standards of precisely what appeals to the "prurient interest" or is "patently offensive." These are essentially questions of fact, and our nation is simply too big and too diverse for this Court to reasonably expect that such standards could be articulated for all 50 States in a single formulation, even assuming the prerequisite consensus exists. When triers of fact are asked to decide whether "the average person, applying contemporary community standards" would consider certain materials "prurient," it would be unrealistic to require that the answer be based on some abstract formulation. The adversary system, with lay jurors as the usual ultimate factfinders in criminal prosecutions, has historically permitted triers-of-fact to draw on the standards of their community, guided always by limiting instructions on the law. To require a State to structure obscenity

---

d. The suggestion that the same book may be obscene in some contexts but not in others has been endorsed in several different contexts. *Butler v. Michigan,* 352 U.S. 380, 77 S.Ct. 524, 1 L.Ed.2d 412 (1957) held that the state could not ban sales to the general public of material unsuitable for children: "The State insists that [by] quarantining the general reading public against books not too rugged for grown men and women in order to shield juvenile innocence, it is exercising its power to promote the general welfare. Surely, this is to burn the house to roast the pig. [The] incidence of this enactment is to reduce the adult population of Michigan to reading only what is fit for children." *Ginsberg v. New York,* 390 U.S. 629, 88 S.Ct. 1274, 20 L.Ed.2d 195 (1968), however, held that the state could bar the distribution to children of books that were suitable for adults, the Court recognizing it

was adopting a "variable" concept of obscenity. See also *Ginzburg v. United States,* 383 U.S. 463, 86 S.Ct. 942, 16 L.Ed.2d 31 (1966) ("pandering" method of marketing supports obscenity conviction even though the materials might not otherwise have been considered obscene); *Mishkin v. New York,* 383 U.S. 502, 86 S.Ct. 958, 16 L.Ed.2d 56 (1966) (material designed for and primarily disseminated to deviant sexual group can meet prurient appeal requirement even if the material lacks appeal to an average member of the general public; appeal is to be tested with reference to the sexual interests of the intended and probable recipient group).

The variable obscenity approach had previously been advocated and elaborated by William Lockhart & Robert McClure, *Censorship of Obscenity: The Developing Constitutional Standards,* 45 Minn.L.Rev. 5, 77 (1960).

proceedings around evidence of a *national* "community standard" would be an exercise in [futility].

We conclude that neither the State's alleged failure to offer evidence of "national standards," nor the trial court's charge that the jury consider state community standards, were constitutional errors. Nothing in the First Amendment requires that a jury must consider hypothetical and unascertainable "national standards" when attempting to determine whether certain materials are obscene as a matter of [fact].

It is neither realistic nor constitutionally sound to read the First Amendment as requiring that the people of Maine or Mississippi accept public depiction of conduct found tolerable in Las Vegas, or New York City. People in different States vary in their tastes and attitudes, and this diversity is not to be strangled by the absolutism of imposed uniformity. As the Court made clear in *Mishkin,* the primary concern with requiring a jury to apply the standard of "the average person, applying contemporary community standards" is to be certain that, so far as material is not aimed at a deviant group, it will be judged by its impact on an average person, rather than a particularly susceptible or sensitive person—or indeed a totally insensitive one.[e] [We] hold the requirement that the jury evaluate the materials with reference to "contemporary standards of the State of California" serves this protective purpose and is constitutionally adequate.[f] * * *

In sum we (a) reaffirm the *Roth* holding that obscene material is not protected by the First Amendment, (b) hold that such material can be regulated by the States, subject to the specific safeguards enunciated above, without a showing that the material is "*utterly* without redeeming social value," and (c) hold that obscenity is to be determined by applying "contemporary community standards," not "national standards." * * *

JUSTICE DOUGLAS, dissenting. * * *

My contention is that until a civil proceeding has placed a tract beyond the pale, no criminal prosecution should be sustained. For no more vivid illustration of vague and uncertain laws could be designed than those we have fashioned. [If] a specific book [or] motion picture has in a civil proceeding been condemned as obscene and review of that finding has been completed, and thereafter a person publishes [or] displays that particular book or film, then a vague law has been

---

e. *Pinkus v. United States,* 436 U.S. 293, 98 S.Ct. 1808, 56 L.Ed.2d 293 (1978) upheld a jury instruction stating "you are to judge these materials by the standard of the hypothetical average person in the community, but in determining this average standard you must include the *sensitive and the insensitive,* in other words, [everyone] in the community." On the other hand, in the absence of evidence that "children were the intended recipients" or that defendant "had reason to know children were likely to receive the materials," it was considered erroneous to instruct the jury that children were part of the relevant community. *Butler.* When the evidence would support such a charge, the Court stated that prurient appeal to deviant sexual groups could be substituted for appeal to the average person; moreover, the jury was entitled to take pandering into account. *Ginzburg.*

f. *Jenkins,* fn. b supra, stated that a judge may instruct a jury to apply "contemporary

community standards" without any further specification. Alternatively, the state may choose "to define the standards in more precise geographic terms, as was done by California in *Miller.*" *Hamling v. United States,* fn. 7 supra, interpreted a federal obscenity statute to make the relevant community the one from which the jury was drawn. The judge's instruction to consider the "community standards of the 'nation as a whole' delineated a wider geographical area than would be warranted by [*Miller*]" or the Court's construction of the statute, but the error was regarded as harmless under the circumstances. See also *Sable Communications v. FCC,* p. 870, infra ("dial-a-porn" company bears burden of complying with congressional obscenity ban despite diverse local community standards). After these decisions, what advice should lawyers give to publishers who distribute in national markets?

made specific.   There would remain the underlying question whether the First Amendment allows an implied exception in the case of obscenity.   I do not think it does and my views on the issue have been stated over and again.   But at least a criminal prosecution brought at that juncture would not violate the time-honored void-for-vagueness test.[8]

No such protective procedure has been designed by California in this case. Obscenity—which even we cannot define with precision—is a hodge-podge.   To send men to jail for violating standards they cannot understand, construe, and apply is a monstrous thing to do in a Nation dedicated to fair trials and due process.   * * *

JUSTICE BRENNAN, with whom JUSTICE STEWART and JUSTICE MARSHALL join, dissenting.

In my dissent in *Paris Adult Theatre,* decided this date, I noted that I had no occasion to consider the extent of state power to regulate the distribution of sexually oriented material to juveniles or the offensive exposure of such material to unconsenting adults.   [I] need not now decide whether a statute might be drawn to impose, within the requirements of the First Amendment, criminal penalties for the precise conduct at issue here.   For it is clear that under my dissent in *Paris Adult Theatre,* the statute under which the prosecution was brought is unconstitutionally overbroad, and therefore invalid on its face.   * * *

[In his *Paris Adult Theatre* dissent, Brennan, J., joined by Stewart and Marshall, JJ., argued that the state interests in regulating obscenity were not strong enough to justify the degree of vagueness.   He criticized not only the Court's standard in *Miller,* but also a range of alternatives:]

II.   [The] essence of our problem [is] that we have been unable to provide "sensitive tools" to separate obscenity from other sexually oriented but constitutionally protected speech, so that efforts to suppress the former do not spill over into the suppression of the latter.   [The dissent traced the Court's experience with *Roth* and its progeny.]

III.   Our experience with the *Roth* approach has certainly taught us that the outright suppression of obscenity cannot be reconciled with the fundamental principles of the First and Fourteenth Amendments.   For we have failed to formulate a standard that sharply distinguishes protected from unprotected speech, and out of necessity, we have resorted to the *Redrup* approach, which resolves cases as between the parties, but offers only the most obscure guidance to legislation, adjudication by other courts, and primary conduct.   [T]he vagueness problem would be largely of our own creation if it stemmed primarily from our failure to reach a consensus on any one standard.   But after 15 years of experimentation and debate I am reluctantly forced to the conclusion that none of the available formulas, including the one announced today, can reduce the vagueness to a tolerable level while at the same time striking an acceptable balance between the protections of the First and Fourteenth Amendments, on the one hand, and on the other the asserted state interest in regulating the dissemination of certain sexually oriented materials.   Any effort to draw a constitutionally acceptable boundary on state power must resort to such indefinite concepts as "prurient interest," "patent offensiveness," "serious literary value," and the like. The meaning of these concepts necessarily varies with the experience, outlook, and even idiosyncracies of the person defining them.   Although we have assumed

8.   The Commission on Obscenity and Pornography has advocated such a procedure.   [See] *Report of the Commission on Obscenity and Pornography* 70–71 (1970).

that obscenity does exist and that we "know it when [we] see it," *Jacobellis* (Stewart, J., concurring), we are manifestly unable to describe it in advance except by reference to concepts so elusive that they fail to distinguish clearly between protected and unprotected speech.

[Added to the inherent vagueness of standards] is the further complication that the obscenity of any particular item may depend upon nuances of presentation and the context of its dissemination. See *Ginzburg*. [N]o one definition, no matter how precisely or narrowly drawn, can possibly suffice for all situations, or carve out fully suppressible expression from all media without also creating a substantial risk of encroachment upon the guarantees of the Due Process Clause and the First Amendment.

[The] resulting level of uncertainty is utterly intolerable, not alone because it makes "[b]ookselling [a] hazardous profession," *Ginsberg* (Fortas, J., dissenting), but as well because it invites arbitrary and erratic enforcement of the law. [We] have indicated that "stricter standards of permissible statutory vagueness may be applied to a statute having a potentially inhibiting effect on speech; a man may the less be required to act at his peril here, because the free dissemination of ideas may be the loser." * * *

The problems of fair notice and chilling protected speech are very grave standing alone. But [a] vague statute in this area creates a third [set] of problems. These [concern] the institutional stress that inevitably results where the line separating protected from unprotected speech is excessively vague. [Almost] every obscenity case presents a constitutional question of exceptional difficulty. [As] a result of our failure to define standards with predictable application to any given piece of material, there is no probability of regularity in obscenity decisions by state and lower federal courts. [O]ne cannot say with certainty that material is obscene until at least five members of this Court, applying inevitably obscure standards, have pronounced it [so].

We have managed the burden of deciding scores of obscenity cases by relying on per curiam reversals or denials of certiorari—a practice which conceals the rationale of decision and gives at least the appearance of arbitrary action by this Court. More important, [the] practice effectively censors protected expression by leaving lower court determinations of obscenity intact even though the status of the allegedly obscene material is entirely unsettled until final review here. In addition, the uncertainty of the standards creates a continuing source of tension between state and federal [courts].

The severe problems arising from the lack of fair notice, from the chill on protected expression, and from the stress imposed on the state and federal judicial machinery persuade me that a significant change in direction is urgently required. I turn, therefore, to the alternatives that are now open.

IV. 1. The approach requiring the smallest deviation from our present course would be to draw a new line between protected and unprotected speech, still permitting the States to suppress all material on the unprotected side of the line. In my view, clarity cannot be obtained pursuant to this approach except by drawing a line that resolves all doubts in favor of state power and against the guarantees of the First Amendment. We could hold, for example, that any depiction or description of human sexual organs, irrespective of the manner or purpose of the portrayal, is outside the protection of the First Amendment and therefore open to suppression by the States. That formula would, no doubt, offer much fairer notice [and] give rise to a substantial probability of regularity in most judicial determinations under the standard. But such a standard would be appallingly overbroad, permitting the suppression of a vast range of literary, scientific, and artistic masterpieces. Neither the First Amendment nor any free community could possibly tolerate such a standard.

2. [T]he Court today recognizes that a prohibition against any depiction or description of human sexual organs could not be reconciled with the guarantees of the First Amendment. But the Court [adopts] a restatement of the *Roth-Memoirs* definition of obscenity [that] permits suppression if the government can prove that the materials lack "*serious* literary, artistic, political or scientific value." [In] *Roth* we held that certain expression is obscene, and thus outside the protection of the First Amendment, precisely *because* it lacks even the slightest redeeming social value. [The] Court's approach necessarily assumes that some works will be deemed obscene—even though they clearly have *some* social value— because the State was able to prove that the value, measured by some unspecified standard, was not sufficiently "serious" to warrant constitutional protection. That result [is] nothing less than a rejection of the fundamental First Amendment premises and rationale of the *Roth* opinion and an invitation to widespread suppression of sexually oriented speech. Before today, the protections of the First Amendment have never been thought limited to expressions of *serious* literary or political value. *Gooding v. Wilson; Cohen v. California; Terminiello v. Chicago* [Part V infra].

[T]he Court's approach [can] have no ameliorative impact on the cluster of problems that grow out of the vagueness of our current standards. Indeed, even the Court makes no argument that the reformulation will provide fairer notice to booksellers, theatre owners, and the reading and viewing public. Nor does the Court contend that the approach will provide clearer guidance to law enforcement officials or reduce the chill on protected expression [or] mitigate [the] institutional [problems].

Of course, the Court's restated *Roth* test does limit the definition of obscenity to depictions of physical conduct and explicit sexual acts. And that limitation may seem, at first glance, a welcome and clarifying addition to the *Roth-Memoirs* formula. But just as the agreement in *Roth* on an abstract definition of obscenity gave little hint of the extreme difficulty that was to follow in attempting to apply that definition to specific material, the mere formulation of a "physical conduct" test is no assurance that it can be applied with any greater facility. [The] Court surely demonstrates little sensitivity to our own institutional problems, much less the other vagueness-related difficulties, in establishing a system that requires us to consider whether a description of human genitals is sufficiently "lewd" to deprive it of constitutional protection; whether a sexual act is "ultimate"; whether the conduct depicted in materials before us fits within one of the categories of conduct whose depiction the state or federal governments have attempted to suppress; and a host of equally pointless inquiries. * * *

If the application of the "physical conduct" test to pictorial material is fraught with difficulty, its application to textual material carries the potential for extraordinary abuse. Surely we have passed the point where the mere written description of sexual conduct is deprived of First Amendment protection. Yet the test offers no guidance to us, or anyone else, in determining which written descriptions of sexual conduct are protected, and which are not.

Ultimately, the reformulation must fail because it still leaves in this Court the responsibility of determining in each case whether the materials are protected by the First Amendment. * * *

3. I have also considered the possibility of reducing our own role, and the role of appellate courts generally, in determining whether particular matter is obscene. Thus, [we] might adopt the position that where a lower federal or state court has conscientiously applied the constitutional standard, its finding of obscenity will be no more vulnerable to reversal by this Court than any finding of fact. [E]ven if the Constitution would permit us to refrain from judging for ourselves the alleged obscenity of particular materials, that approach would solve at best only a small part of our problem. For while it would mitigate the institutional stress, [it] would neither offer nor produce any cure for the other vices of vagueness. Far from providing a clearer guide to permissible primary conduct, the approach would inevitably lead to even greater uncertainty and the consequent due process problems of fair notice. And the approach would expose much protected, sexually oriented expression to the vagaries of jury determinations. Plainly, the institutional gain would be more than offset by the unprecedented infringement of First Amendment rights.

4. Finally, I have considered the view, urged so forcefully since 1957 by our Brothers Black and Douglas, that the First Amendment bars the suppression of any sexually oriented expression. That position would effect a sharp reduction, although perhaps not a total elimination, of the uncertainty that surrounds our current approach. Nevertheless, I am convinced that it would achieve that desirable goal only by stripping the States of power to an extent that cannot be justified by the commands of the Constitution, at least so long as there is available an alternative approach that strikes a better balance between the guarantee of free expression and the States' legitimate interests.

[I] would hold, therefore, that at least in the absence of distribution to juveniles or obtrusive exposure to unconsenting adults, the First and Fourteenth Amendments prohibit the state and federal governments from attempting wholly to suppress sexually oriented materials on the basis of their allegedly "obscene" contents.[g] Nothing in this approach precludes those governments from taking action to serve what may be strong and legitimate interests through regulation of the manner of distribution of sexually oriented material.

VI. [I] do not pretend to have found a complete and infallible [answer]. Difficult questions must still be faced, notably in the areas of distribution to juveniles and offensive exposure to unconsenting adults. Whatever the extent of state power to regulate in those areas,[29] it should be clear that the view I espouse today would introduce a large measure of clarity to this troubled area, would reduce the institutional pressure on this Court and the rest of the State and Federal judiciary, and would guarantee fuller freedom of expression while leaving room for the protection of legitimate governmental interests. * * *

Notes and Questions

1. *Serious value.* Consider Harry Clor, *Obscenity and the First Amendment: Round Three,* 7 Loy.L.A.L.Rev. 207, 210, 218 (1974): "The *Miller* decision abandons the requirement that a censorable work must be '*utterly* without redeeming social value' and substitutes the rule of 'serious value'—literary, artistic, political, or scientific. This is the most important innovation in the law

---

g. For the portion of Brennan, J.'s dissent addressing the strength and legitimacy of the state interests, see *Paris Adult Theatre,* supra.

29. The Court erroneously states, *Miller,* that the author of this opinion "indicates that suppression of unprotected obscene material is permissible to avoid exposure to unconsenting adults [and] to juveniles * * *." I defer expression of my views as to the scope of state power in these areas until cases squarely presenting these questions are before the Court.

of obscenity introduced by these decisions. [Serious] literature is to be protected regardless of majority opinions about prurience and offensiveness. *This* is the national principle which is not subject to variation from community to community. If it is to perform this function, the rule will have to be elaborated and the meaning of 'serious value' articulated in some measure. This is the most important item on the legal agenda."

(a) *An independent factor?* Under *Miller* would material found to have "serious artistic value" be entitled to first amendment protection regardless of how offensive or prurient? Must each factor in the *Miller* guidelines be independently satisfied, as in *Memoirs? Should* that be so? Would or should that preclude the degree of offensiveness or prurient appeal from affecting the conclusion on the value factor?

(b) *"Serious."* Do you find any guidance for determining when a first amendment value in material depicting sexual conduct is sufficiently "serious" to preclude finding it obscene? Does *Pope v. Illinois,* 481 U.S. 497, 107 S.Ct. 1918, 95 L.Ed.2d 439 (1987) assist?: "The proper inquiry is not whether an ordinary member of any given community would find serious literary, artistic, political, or scientific value[,] but whether a reasonable person would find such value in the material taken as a whole."

(c) *Scope of protected values.* Could the Court consistent with the first amendment exclude serious educational value from those that preclude a finding of obscenity? Serious entertainment value? Could the guidelines be interpreted to include such values? What might explain their omission?

2. *Vagueness and scienter.* Is the *Miller* test intolerably vague? Are there any alternatives that could mitigate the problem? Consider William Lockhart, *Escape from the Chill of Uncertainty: Explicit Sex and the First Amendment,* 9 Ga.L.Rev. 533, 563 (1975): "[E]ither legislative action, or constitutional adjudication, could establish as a defense to a criminal obscenity prosecution that the defendant *reasonably believed* that the material involved was not obscene, that is, was constitutionally protected. [Material] that would support such a court or jury finding is not the kind that requires or justifies quick action by the police and prosecutor. The public interest in preventing distribution of borderline material that can reasonably be believed not obscene is not so pressing as to require immediate criminal sanctions and can adequately be protected by a declaratory judgment or injunction action to establish the obscenity of the material."

Smith v. California, 361 U.S. 147, 80 S.Ct. 215, 4 L.Ed.2d 205 (1959) invalidated an ordinance that dispensed with any requirement that a seller of an obscene book have knowledge of its contents, but did not decide what sort of mental element was needed to prosecute. *Hamling v. United States,* supra, stated that it was constitutionally sufficient to show that a distributor of an advertising collage of pictures of sexual acts "had knowledge of the contents of the materials [and] that he knew the character and nature of the materials." Would it be consistent with *Hamling* to afford constitutional protection to a distributor who reasonably believed the material disseminated was not obscene? See Lockhart, supra, at 568.

3. *The practical impact of Miller.* Consider David Cole, *Playing by Pornography's Rules: The Regulation of Sexual Expression,* 143 U.Pa.L.Rev. 111, 170, 173 (1994): "Because this prohibition is so narrow, it serves in practice not so much to purge the community of explicit sexually arousing speech as to validate everything that remains as nonoffensive, 'normal,' or socially valuable. In this way, obscenity doctrine collectively assures the community that the pornography

it consumes at such a high rate is acceptable. [There] are the few who are actually prosecuted; given the remarkable amount and variety of sexual expression that goes without prosecution, to be prosecuted for obscenity these days is akin to being struck by lightning."

C. VAGUENESS AND OVERBREADTH: AN OVERVIEW

In *Paris Adult Theatre,* Brennan, J., dissents on the ground that the obscenity statute is unconstitutionally vague. He envisions the possibility that an obscenity statute might overcome his vagueness objection if it were tailored to combat distribution to unconsenting adults or to children. In *Miller,* the materials were in fact distributed to unconsenting adults. There Brennan, J., does not reach the vagueness question but objects on the ground that the statute is overbroad,—i.e., it is not confined to the protection of unconsenting adults and children, but also prohibits distribution of obscene materials to consenting adults. In Brennan, J.'s view, even if the particular conduct at issue in *Miller* might be constitutionally prohibited by a narrower statute, it cannot be reached under a statute that sweeps so much protected speech within its terms.

The doctrines of "vagueness" and "overbreadth" referred to in Brennan, J.'s dissents are deeply embedded in first amendment jurisprudence. At first glance, the doctrines appear discrete. A statute that prohibits the use of the words "kill" and "President" in the same sentence may not be vague, but it is certainly overbroad even though some sentences using those words may be unprotected. Conversely, a vague statute may not be overbroad; it may not pertain to first amendment freedoms at all, or it may clearly be intended to exclude all protected speech from its prohibition but use vague language to accomplish that purpose.

Ordinarily, however, the problems of "vagueness" and "overbreadth" are closely related; indeed the two concepts often merge. Consider, for example, an actual and a hypothetical "red flag" ban. A statute prohibiting anyone from "publicly display[ing] a red flag [or] device of any color or form whatever [as] a sign, symbol or emblem of opposition to organized government" was held fatally vague in *Stromberg v. California,* 283 U.S. 359, 51 S.Ct. 532, 75 L.Ed. 1117 (1931). The statute purported to be less than a total ban, but how much less was ambiguous and uncertain. The "opposition to organized government" language was vague because it might (or might not) be read as banning constitutionally protected red flag displays, e.g., those flown as an expression of peaceful and orderly opposition to the political party currently in power by members of another political party. But a hypothetical "absolute ban" on red flag displays, for any reason or under any circumstances, although *superficially* clear, would presumably also be struck down—for "overbreadth." The same may be said for a hypothetical statute "absolutely banning" picketing or parades—or the sale of literature containing any description of human sexual organs, regardless of the manner or purpose of the portrayal, the dominant theme of the material, the primary audience to which it is sold, or the social, literary, scientific or artistic value of the work.

The *language* of these hypothetical bans may not be vague, but if the language literally covers a variety of constitutionally protected activities, it *cannot be read literally.* Thus, the clarity of the language "is delusive, since it will have to be recast in order to separate the constitutional from the unconstitutional applications. If it is read as applicable only where constitutionally so, the reading uncovers the vagueness that is latent in its terms" and the problem of an "overbroad" law can emerge as "a special case of the problem of vagueness." See

Paul Freund, *The Supreme Court of the United States* 67–68 (1961). In other words, one may regard the aforementioned "overbroad" hypothetical statutes as no less vague and indefinite than laws whose very language forbids the public display of a red flag "except where one is constitutionally entitled to display it" or bans picketing "unless, under the circumstances, such conduct is constitutionally protected" or bars literature containing descriptions of human sexual organs "except where such descriptions do not constitute sufficient cause to deny the material the constitutional protection of freedom of speech and press."

Of course, statutes may be interpreted in ways that will avoid vagueness or overbreadth difficulties. See, e.g., *Scales v. United States,* p. 661 supra. It is established doctrine, for example, that an attack based either upon vagueness or overbreadth will be unsuccessful in federal court if the statute in question is "readily subject to a narrowing construction by the state courts." *Young v. American Mini-Theatres, Inc.; Erznoznik v. Jacksonville,* p. 703 infra. Moreover, "[f]or the purpose of determining whether a state statute is too vague and indefinite to constitute valid legislation [the Court takes] 'the statute as though it read precisely as the highest court of the State has interpreted it.'" *Wainwright v. Stone,* 414 U.S. 21, 94 S.Ct. 190, 38 L.Ed.2d 179 (1973). Under this policy, a litigant can be prosecuted successfully for violating a statute that by its terms appears vague or overbroad but is interpreted by the state court in the same prosecution to mean something clearer or narrower than its literal language would dictate. *Cox v. New Hampshire,* p. 801 infra. The harshness of this doctrine is mitigated somewhat by the fact that "unexpected" or "unforeseeable" judicial constructions in such contexts violate due process. See *Marks v. United States,* 430 U.S. 188, 97 S.Ct. 990, 51 L.Ed.2d 260 (1977).[a]

Somewhat more complicated is the issue of when general attacks on a statute are permitted. Plainly litigants may argue that statutes are vague as to their own conduct or that their own speech is protected. In other words, litigants are always free to argue that a statute is invalid "as applied" to their own conduct. The dispute concerns when litigants can attack a statute without reference to their own conduct, an attack sometimes called "on its face."

A separate question is: when should such attacks result in partial or total invalidation of a statute? The terminology here has become as confused as the issues. In the past, the Court has frequently referred to facial attacks on statutes in a way that embraces attempts at either partial or total invalidation. In some recent opinions, however, including those quoted below, it uses the term "facial attack" or "on its face" to refer only to arguments seeking total invalidation of a statute.

Terminology aside, one of the recurrent questions has been the extent to which litigants may argue that a statute is unconstitutionally overbroad even though their own conduct would not otherwise be constitutionally protected. This is often characterized as a standing issue. Ordinarily litigants do not have standing to raise the rights of others. See Ch. 13, Sec. 1, II, B. But, it has been argued that "[u]nder 'conventional' standing principles, a litigant has always had the right to be judged in accordance with a constitutionally valid rule of law." Henry Monaghan, *Overbreadth,* 1981 S.Ct.Rev. 1, 3. On this view, if a statute is unconstitutionally overbroad, it is not a valid rule of law, and any defendant

a. For commentary on overbreadth with special focus on the implications of the doctrine mentioned in this paragraph, see Richard Fallon, *Making Sense of Overbreadth,* 100 Yale L.J. 853 (1991).

prosecuted under the statute has standing to raise the overbreadth issue.[b] However the issue may be characterized, White, J., has contended for many years that a litigant whose own conduct is unprotected should not prevail on an overbreadth challenge without a showing that the statute's overbreadth is "real and substantial." After much litigation, White, J., has finally prevailed. The "substantial" overbreadth doctrine now burdens all litigants who argue that a statute should be declared overbroad when their own conduct is unprotected.[c] *Brockett v. Spokane Arcades, Inc.; New York v. Ferber*, p. 641 infra.

Less clear are the circumstances in which a litigant whose conduct *is* protected can go beyond a claim that the statute is unconstitutional "as applied." Again, litigants are always free to argue that their own conduct is protected. Moreover, the Court has stated that "[t]here is no reason to limit challenges to case-by-case 'as applied' challenges when the statute [in] all its applications falls short of constitutional demands." [d] *Maryland v. Joseph H. Munson Co.*, 467 U.S. 947, 104 S.Ct. 2839, 81 L.Ed.2d 786 (1984). How far beyond this the Court will go is unclear. In *Brockett v. Spokane Arcades, Inc.*, p. 618 supra, it referred to the "normal rule that partial, rather than facial invalidation" of statutes is to be preferred and observed that: "[A]n individual whose own speech or expressive conduct may validly be prohibited or sanctioned is permitted to challenge a statute on its face because it also threatens others not before the court—those who desire to engage in legally protected expression but who may refrain from doing so rather than risk prosecution or undertake to have the law declared partially invalid. If the overbreadth is 'substantial,' the law may not be enforced against anyone, including the party before the court, until it is narrowed to reach only unprotected activity, whether by legislative action or by judicial construction or partial invalidation.

"It is otherwise where the parties challenging the statute are those who desire to engage in protected speech that the overbroad statute purports to punish, or who seek to publish both protected and unprotected material. There is then no want of a proper party to challenge the statute, no concern that an attack on the statute will be unduly delayed or protected speech discouraged. The statute may forthwith be declared invalid to the extent that it reaches too far, but otherwise left intact." [e]

Brockett takes the view that it must give standing to the otherwise unprotected to raise an overbreadth challenge, in order to secure the rights of those whose

b. For more recent elaboration, see Henry Monaghan, *Third Party Standing*, 84 Colum.L.Rev. 277 (1984). See also Robert Sedler, *The Assertion of Constitutional Jus Tertii: A Substantive Approach*, 70 Calif.L.Rev. 1308, 1327 (1982) ("It may be the potential chilling effect upon others' expression that makes the statute invalid, but the litigant has his own right not to be subject to the operation of an invalid statute.").

c. For commentary on the concept of "substantial" overbreadth, see Fallon, supra; Martin Redish, *The Warren Court, The Burger Court and the First Amendment Overbreadth Doctrine*, 78 Nw.U.L.Rev. 1031, 1056–69 (1983).

d. There is a terminological dispute here. Compare *Los Angeles City Council v. Taxpayers For Vincent*, p. 906 infra (such challenges are not overbreadth challenges) with *Munson*, supra (such challenges are properly called overbreadth challenges).

e. After the Court has declared that the statute is invalid to the extent it reaches too far, the remaining portion of the statute will be examined to determine whether that portion is severable. That is, it could well be the intent of the legislature that the statute stands or falls as a single package. To invalidate a part, then, could be to invalidate the whole. Alternatively, the legislature may have intended to salvage whatever it might. The question of severability is regarded as one of legislative intent, but, at least with respect to federal legislation, courts will presume that severability was intended. See, e.g., *Regan v. Time, Inc.*, 468 U.S. 641, 104 S.Ct. 3262, 82 L.Ed.2d 487 (1984). The question of whether a provision of a state statute is severable is one of state law.

speech should be protected. But it sees no purpose in giving standing to the protected in order to secure rights for those whose speech should not be protected. This position is not without its ironies. In some circumstances, a litigant whose speech is unprotected will be in a better position than one whose speech is protected, at least if the litigant's goal is completely to stop enforcement of a statute.

Finally, what of the cases when it is uncertain whether the litigant's speech is protected? Should courts consider as applied attacks before proceeding to overbreadth attacks? *Board of Trustees v. Fox,* p. 732 infra, declared it "not the usual judicial practice" and "generally undesirable" to proceed to an overbreadth challenge without first determining whether the statute would be valid as applied.[f] Yet the Court has frequently (see, e.g., pp. 639–40 infra (fighting words cases)); declared statutes overbroad without an as applied determination. The Court has yet systematically to detail the considerations relevant to separating the "usual" judicial practice from the unusual.

The issues with respect to vagueness challenges are similar. It remains possible, however, that the Court will resolve them in ways different from the approaches it has fashioned in the law of overbreadth. White, J., clearly would pursue a different course. He has suggested that vagueness challenges should be confined to "as applied" attacks unless a statute is vague in all of its applications. Accordingly, if a statute clearly proscribes the conduct of a particular defendant, to allow that defendant to challenge a statute for vagueness is in his view "to confound vagueness and overbreadth." *Kolender v. Lawson,* 461 U.S. 352, 103 S.Ct. 1855, 75 L.Ed.2d 903 (1983) (White, J., dissenting). In response, the Court has stated that a facial attack upon a statute need not depend upon a showing of vagueness in all of a statute's applications: "[W]e permit a facial challenge if a law reaches 'a substantial amount of constitutionally protected conduct,' " *Kolender,* supra. Moreover, the Court has previously allowed litigants to raise the vagueness issue "even though there is no uncertainty about the impact of the ordinances on their own rights." *Young.* But see, e.g., *Broadrick v. Oklahoma,* p. 644 infra, in which White, J., writing for the Court suggests that standing to raise the vagueness argument should not be permitted in this situation.

Much less clear are the circumstances in which litigants whose conduct is *not* clearly covered by a statute can go beyond an "as applied" attack.[g] One approach would be to apply the same rule to all litigants, e.g., allowing total invalidation of statutes upon a showing of a "substantial" vagueness. In *Kolender,* the Court made no determination whether the statute involved was vague as to the defendant's own conduct; arguably, the opinion implied that it made no difference. Another approach would analogize to the approach suggested in *Brockett* for overbreadth challenges. Thus, a court might refrain from total invalidation of a statute and confine itself to striking the vague part insofar as the vague part seems to cover protected speech, leaving the balance of the statute intact. *Kolender* itself recites that the Court has "traditionally regarded vagueness and overbreadth as logically related and similar doctrines," but the Court's attitudes toward vagueness remain unclear. The questions of what standards should govern challenges to statutes that go beyond the facts before the Court, who

---

f. The case arose in the federal courts, and the Court might be less likely to remand to a state court for an as applied determination, but the Court did not address that distinction.

g. Conceivably, it could make a difference whether the litigants in this class of those "not clearly covered" have engaged in protected or unprotected conduct.

should be able to raise the challenges, and under what circumstances continue to divide the Court.[h]

IV. "FIGHTING WORDS," OFFENSIVE WORDS AND HOSTILE AUDIENCES

A. FIGHTING WORDS

CHAPLINSKY v. NEW HAMPSHIRE, 315 U.S. 568, 62 S.Ct. 766, 86 L.Ed. 1031 (1942): In the course of proselytizing on the streets, appellant, a Jehovah's Witness, denounced organized religion. Despite the city marshal's warning to "go slow" because his listeners were upset with his attacks on religion, appellant continued and a disturbance occurred. At this point, a police officer led appellant toward the police station, without arresting him. While enroute, appellant again encountered the city marshal who had previously admonished him. Appellant then said to the marshal (he claimed, but the marshal denied, in response to the marshal's cursing him): "You are a God damned racketeer" and "a damned Fascist and the whole government of Rochester are Fascists or agents of Fascists." He was convicted of violating a state statute forbidding anyone to address "any offensive, derisive or annoying word to any other person who is lawfully in any [public place] [or] call[ing] him by any offensive or derisive name." The Court, per MURPHY, J., upheld the conviction:

"There are certain well-defined and narrowly limited classes of speech, the prevention and punishment of which have never been thought to raise any Constitutional problem.[a] These include the lewd and obscene, the profane, the libelous, and the insulting or 'fighting' words—those which by their very utterance inflict injury or tend to incite an immediate breach of the peace. [S]uch utterances are no essential part of any exposition of ideas, and are of such slight social value as a step to truth that any benefit that may be derived from them is clearly outweighed by the social interest in order and morality. * * *

"On the authority of its earlier decisions, the state court declared that the statute's purpose was to preserve the public peace, no words being 'forbidden

h. For commentary on vagueness and overbreadth, see, e.g., Melville Nimmer, *Nimmer on Freedom of Speech*, 4–147—4–162 (1984); Larry Alexander, *Is There an Overbreadth Doctrine?*, 22 San Diego L.Rev. 541 (1985); Anthony Amsterdam, *The Void-For-Vagueness Doctrine in the Supreme Court*, 109 U.Pa.L.Rev. 67 (1960); David Bogen, *First Amendment Ancillary Doctrines*, 37 Md.L.Rev. 679, 705–26 (1978); Monaghan, supra; Redish, supra; Note, *The First Amendment Overbreadth Doctrine*, 83 Harv.L.Rev. 844 (1970). On the relationship between the overbreadth doctrine and the less drastic means test, see fn. b in *Central Hudson Gas & Elec. Corp. v. Public Serv. Comm'n*, p. 822 infra.

a. See Franklyn Haiman, *How Much of Our Speech is Free?*, The Civ.Lib.Rev., Winter, 1975, pp. 111, 123: "[T]his discrimination between two classes of speech made its first U.S. Supreme Court appearance in *Cantwell v. Connecticut* (1940) [p. 1105 infra]." Jehovah's Witnesses had been convicted of religious solicitation without a permit and of breach of the peace. The Court set aside both convictions.

It invalidated the permit system for "religious" solicitation, because it permitted the licensing official to determine what causes were "religious," thus allowing a "censorship of religion." In setting aside the breach of peace conviction, because the offense covered much protected conduct and left "too wide a discretion in its application," the Court, per Roberts, J., noted: "One may, however, be guilty of [breach of the peace] if he commits acts or makes statements likely to provoke violence and disturbance of good order. [I]n practically all [such decisions to this effect], the provocative language [held to constitute] a breach of the peace consisted of profane, indecent or abusive remarks directed to the person of the hearer. *Resort to epithets or personal abuse is not in any proper sense communication of information or opinion safeguarded by the Constitution,* and its punishment as a criminal act [under a narrowly drawn statute] would raise no question under that instrument." (Emphasis added). For commentary, see Robert Post, *Cultural Heterogeneity and Law*, 76 Calif.L.Rev. 297 (1988).

except such as have a direct tendency to cause acts of violence by the person to whom, individually, the remark is addressed'. It was further said: 'The word "offensive" is not to be defined in terms of what a particular addressee thinks. [The] test is what men of common intelligence would understand would be words likely to cause an average addressee to fight. [The] English language has a number of words and expressions which by general consent are "fighting words" when said without a disarming smile. [Such] words, as ordinary men know, are likely to cause a fight. So are threatening, profane or obscene revilings. Derisive and annoying words can be taken as coming within the purview of the statute as heretofore interpreted only when they have this characteristic of plainly tending to excite the addressee to a breach of the peace. [The] statute, as construed, does no more than prohibit the face-to-face words plainly likely to cause a breach of the peace by the addressee, words whose speaking constitute a breach of the peace by the speaker—including "classical fighting words", words in current use less "classical" but equally likely to cause violence, and other disorderly words, including profanity, obscenity and threats.'

"[A] statute punishing verbal acts, carefully drawn so as not unduly to impair liberty of expression, is not too vague for a criminal law. * * * [8]

"Nor can we say that the application of the statute to the facts disclosed by the record substantially or unreasonably impinges upon the privilege of free speech. Argument is unnecessary to demonstrate that the appellations 'damn racketeer' and 'damn Fascist' are epithets likely to provoke the average person to retaliation, and thereby cause a breach of the peace.

"The refusal of the state court to admit evidence of provocation and evidence bearing on the truth or falsity of the utterances is open to no Constitutional objection. Whether the facts sought to be proved by such evidence constitute a defense to the charge or may be shown in mitigation are questions for the state court to determine. Our function is fulfilled by a determination that the challenged statute, on its face and as applied, does not contravene the Fourteenth Amendment."

Notes and Questions

1. *Fighting words and free speech values.* (a) *Self realization.* Does speech have to step toward truth to be of first amendment value? Consider Martin Redish, *The Value of Free Speech,* 130 U.Pa.L.Rev. 591, 626 (1982): "Why not view Chaplinsky's comments as a personal catharsis, as a means to vent his frustration at a system he deemed—whether rightly or wrongly—to be oppressive? Is it not a mark of individuality to be able to cry out at a society viewed as crushing the individual? Under this analysis, so-called 'fighting words' represent a significant means of self-realization, whether or not they can be considered a means of attaining some elusive 'truth.' "

(b) *Fighting words and truth.* Are fighting words always false? Should truth be a defense? Always?

(c) *Fighting words and self-government.* Was Chaplinsky's statement *something other than* the expression of an idea? Did he wish to inform the marshal of his opinion of him and did he do so "in a way which was not only unquestionably

---

8. [Even] if the interpretative gloss placed on the statute by the court below be disregarded, the statute had been previously construed as intended to preserve the public peace by punishing conduct, the direct tendency of which was to provoke the person against whom it was directed to acts of violence.

Appellant need not therefore have been a prophet to understand what the statute condemned.

clear, [but] all too clear"? Arnold Loewy, *Punishing Flag Desecrators,* 49 N.C.L.Rev. 48, 82 (1970). How significant is it that Chaplinsky's remarks were not made in the context of a public debate or discussion of political or social issues? Taking into account the events preceding Chaplinsky's remarks, and that the addressee was "an important representative of the Rochester city government," may Chaplinsky's epithets be viewed as "a sharply-expressed form of political protest against indifferent or biased police services in the enforcement of his right to free speech"? Mark Rutzick, *Offensive Language and the Evolution of First Amendment Protection,* 9 Harv.Civ.Rts.—Civ.Lib.L.Rev. 1 (1974). If the speech is directed at a police officer or other official in his representative capacity, is "the real target the government"? See id.

2. *The social interest in order and morality.* What was the social interest in this case? (a) *The likelihood and immediacy of violent retaliation?* Should the Court have considered whether a *law enforcement officer* so reviled would have been provoked to retaliate? Whatever is assumed about the reaction of an average citizen to offensive words, may it be assumed that police are "trained to remain calm in the face of citizen anger such as that expressed by Chaplinsky"? Rutzick, supra, at 10. See also Powell, J., concurring in *Lewis v. New Orleans,* p. 733 infra; Note, 53 B.U.L.Rev. 834, 847 (1973).

(b) *The highly personal nature of the insult, delivered face to face?* Was the marshal "verbally slapped in the face"? May the *Chaplinsky* statute be viewed as "a special type of assault statute"? See Loewy, supra, at 83–84. See also Thomas Emerson, *The System of Freedom of Expression* 337–38 (1970).

B. HOSTILE AUDIENCES

TERMINIELLO v. CHICAGO, 337 U.S. 1, 69 S.Ct. 894, 93 L.Ed. 1131 (1949): Petitioner "vigorously, if not viciously" criticized various political and racial groups and condemned "a surging, howling mob" gathered in protest outside the auditorium in which he spoke. He called his adversaries "slimy scum," "snakes," "bedbugs," and the like. Those inside the hall could hear those on the outside yell, "Fascists, Hitlers!" The crowd outside tried to tear the clothes off those who entered. About 28 windows were broken; stink bombs were thrown. But in charging the jury, the trial court defined "breach of the peace" to include speech which "stirs the public to anger, *invites dispute,* [or] brings about a condition of unrest (emphasis added)." A 5–4 majority, per DOUGLAS, J., struck down the breach of peace ordinance as thus construed: "[A] function of free speech under our system of government is to invite dispute. It may indeed best serve its high purpose when it induces a condition of unrest, creates dissatisfaction with conditions as they are, or even stirs people to anger. [That] is why freedom of speech, though not absolute, *Chaplinsky,* is nevertheless protected against censorship or punishment, unless shown likely to produce a clear and present danger of a serious substantive evil that rises far above public inconvenience, annoyance, or unrest."

———

FEINER v. NEW YORK, 340 U.S. 315, 71 S.Ct. 303, 95 L.Ed. 295 (1951): Petitioner made a speech on a street corner in a predominantly black residential section of Syracuse, N.Y. A crowd of 75 to 80 persons, black and white, gathered around him, and several pedestrians had to go into the highway in order to pass by. A few minutes after he started, two police officers arrived and observed the rest of the meeting. In the course of his speech, publicizing a meeting of the Young Progressives of America to be held that evening in a local hotel and protesting the revocation of a permit to hold the meeting in a public school auditorium, petitioner referred to the President as a "bum," to the American Legion as "a Nazi Gestapo," and to the Mayor of Syracuse as a "champagne-sipping bum" who "does not speak for the Negro people." He also indicated in an excited manner: "The Negroes don't have equal rights; they should rise up in arms and fight for them."

These statements "stirred up a little excitement." One man indicated that if the police did not get that "S ... O ... B ..." off the stand, he would do so himself. There was not yet a disturbance, but according to police testimony "angry muttering and pushing." In the words of the arresting officer whose testimony was accepted by the trial judge, he "stepped in to prevent it from resulting in a fight." After disregarding two requests to stop speaking, petitioner was arrested and convicted for disorderly conduct. The Court, per VINSON, C.J., affirmed: "The language of *Cantwell* is appropriate here. '[Nobody would] suggest that the principle of freedom of speech sanctions incitement to riot or that religious liberty connotes the privilege to exhort others to physical attack upon those belonging to another sect. When clear and present danger of riot, disorder, interference with traffic upon the public street or other immediate threat to public safety, peace, or order, appears, the power of the State to prevent or punish is obvious.'

"[It] is one thing to say that the police cannot be used as an instrument for the suppression of unpopular views, and another to say that, when as here the speaker passes the bounds of argument or persuasion and undertakes incitement to riot, they are powerless to prevent a breach of the peace. Nor in this case can we condemn the considered judgment of three New York courts approving the means which the police, faced with a crisis, used in the exercise of their power and duty to preserve peace and order."

BLACK, J., dissented: "The Court's opinion apparently rests on this reasoning: The policeman, under the circumstances detailed, could reasonably conclude that serious fighting or even riot was imminent; therefore he could stop petitioner's speech to prevent a breach of peace; accordingly, it was 'disorderly conduct' for petitioner to continue speaking in disobedience of the officer's request. As to the existence of a dangerous situation on the street corner, it seems far-fetched to suggest that the 'facts' show any imminent threat of riot or uncontrollable disorder. It is neither unusual nor unexpected that some people at public street meetings mutter, mill about, push, shove, or disagree, even violently, with the speaker. Indeed, it is rare where controversial topics are discussed that an outdoor crowd does not do some or all of these things. Nor does one isolated threat to assault the speaker forebode disorder. Especially should the danger be discounted where, as here, the person threatening was a man whose wife and two small children accompanied him and who, so far as the record shows, was never close enough to petitioner to carry out the threat.

"Moreover, assuming that the 'facts' did indicate a critical situation, I reject the implication of the Court's opinion that the police had no obligation to protect petitioner's constitutional right to talk. The police of course have power to prevent breaches of the peace. But if, in the name of preserving order, they ever can interfere with a lawful public speaker, they first must make all reasonable efforts to protect him. Here the policemen did not even pretend to try to protect petitioner. According to the officers' testimony, the crowd was restless but there is no showing of any attempt to quiet it; pedestrians were forced to walk into the street, but there was no effort to clear a path on the sidewalk; one person threatened to assault petitioner but the officers did nothing to discourage this when even a word might have sufficed. Their duty was to protect petitioner's right to talk, even to the extent of arresting the man who threatened to interfere. Instead, they shirked that duty and acted only to suppress the right to speak.

"Finally, I cannot agree with the Court's statement that petitioner's disregard of the policeman's unexplained request amounted to such 'deliberate defiance' as would justify an arrest or conviction for disorderly conduct. On the contrary, I think that the policeman's action was a 'deliberate defiance' of ordinary official duty as well as of the constitutional right of free speech. For at least where time allows, courtesy and explanation of commands are basic elements of good official conduct in a democratic society. Here petitioner was 'asked' then 'told' then 'commanded' to stop speaking, but a man making a lawful address is certainly not required to be silent merely because an officer directs it.[a] Petitioner was entitled to know why he should cease doing a lawful act. Not once was he told."

Douglas, J., joined by Minton, J., dissented: "A speaker may not, of course, incite a riot any more than he may incite a breach of the peace by the use of 'fighting words'. But this record shows no such extremes. It shows an unsympathetic audience and the threat of one man to haul the speaker from the stage. It is against that kind of threat that speakers need police protection. If they do not receive it and instead the police throw their weight on the side of those who would break up the meetings, the police become the new censors of speech. Police censorship has all the vices of the censorship from city halls which we have repeatedly struck down."

Notes and Questions

1. What was the subject of disagreement in *Feiner*? (1) The standard for police interruption of a speech when danger of violence exists and the speaker intends to create disorder rather than to communicate ideas? (2) The standard when such danger exists, but the speaker only desires to communicate ideas? (3) Whether the danger of disorder and violence *was* plain and imminent? (4) Whether the speaker *did* intend to create disorder and violence?

May *Feiner* be limited to the proposition that when a speaker "incites to riot"—but only then—police may stop him without bothering to keep his audience in check? Cf. *Sellers v. Johnson,* 163 F.2d 877 (8th Cir.1947), cert. denied, 332 U.S. 851, 68 S.Ct. 356, 92 L.Ed. 421 (1948). See Richard Stewart, *Public Speech and Public Order in Britain and the United States,* 13 Vand.L.Rev. 625, 632–33 (1960).

Should the speech *always* be prohibitable when the speaker intends to create disorder, rather than communicate ideas? Should the speech be prohibitable *only* under these circumstances? Should a speech *ever* be prohibitable because listeners arrive or will arrive, as they would have in *Sellers,* with a preconceived intent to create disturbance? Is the only really difficult problem in this area posed when *neither* the speaker *nor* the audience which gathers intends to create disorder, but the audience becomes *genuinely* aroused, honestly—whether or not justifiably—enraged? Here, should the police protect the speechmaking to the fullest extent possible? If they are firmly told they must before they can arrest the speaker,

a. Compare *Houston v. Hill,* p. 733 infra (ordinance forbidding speech that in any man-   ner interrupts a police officer in the performance of duties is overbroad).

what is the likelihood that adequate preventive steps will be taken? See Walter Gellhorn, *American Rights* 55–62 (1960); Note, 49 Colum.L.Rev. 1118, 1123–24 (1949).

2. *Edwards v. South Carolina,* 372 U.S. 229, 83 S.Ct. 680, 9 L.Ed.2d 697 (1963) reversed a breach of the peace conviction of civil rights demonstrators who refused to disperse within 15 minutes of a police command. The Court maintained that the 200 to 300 onlookers did not threaten violence and that the police protection was ample. It described the situation as a "far cry from [*Feiner*]." Clark, J., dissenting, pointed to the racially charged atmosphere ("200 youthful Negro demonstrators were being aroused to a 'fever pitch' before a crowd of some 300 people who undoubtedly were hostile.") and concluded that city officials in good faith believed that disorder and violence were imminent. Did *Edwards* miss a golden opportunity to clarify *Feiner*? What if the crowd had been pushing, shoving and pressing more closely around the demonstrators in *Edwards*? Would the case still be a "far cry" from *Feiner* because the demonstrators had not "passed the bounds of argument or persuasion and undertaken incitement to riot"?

3. In the advocacy of illegal action context, the fear of violence arises from audience cooperation with the speaker. In the hostile audience context, the fear of violence arises from audience conflict with the speaker. How do the elements set out in *Brandenburg* relate to those implied in *Feiner*? How should they relate? Should the standard for "fighting words" cases be different from the "hostile audience" cases?

4. Should police be able to prosecute or silence disruptive audiences? Heckling audiences? In what contexts? See generally *In re Kay,* 1 Cal.3d 930, 83 Cal.Rptr. 686, 464 P.2d 142 (1970).

C. OFFENSIVE WORDS

COHEN v. CALIFORNIA

403 U.S. 15, 91 S.Ct. 1780, 29 L.Ed.2d 284 (1971).

JUSTICE HARLAN delivered the opinion of the Court.

[Defendant was convicted of violating that part of a general California disturbing-the-peace statute which prohibits "maliciously and willfully disturb[ing] the peace or quiet of any neighborhood or person" by "offensive conduct." He had worn a jacket bearing the plainly visible words "Fuck the Draft" in a Los Angeles courthouse corridor, where women and children were present. He testified that he did so as a means of informing the public of the depth of his feelings against the Vietnam War and the draft. He did not engage in, nor threaten, any violence, nor was anyone who saw him violently aroused. Nor was there any evidence that he uttered any sound prior to his arrest. In affirming, the California Court of Appeal construed "offensive conduct" to mean "behavior which has a tendency to provoke *others* to acts of violence or to in turn disturb the peace" and held that the state had proved this element because it was "reasonably foreseeable" that defendant's conduct "might cause others to rise up to commit a violent act against [him] or attempt to forceably remove his jacket."]

In order to lay hands on the precise issue which this case involves, it is useful first to canvass various matters which this record does *not* present.

The conviction quite clearly rests upon the asserted offensiveness of the *words* Cohen used to convey his message to the public. The only "conduct" which the State sought to punish is the fact of communication. Thus, we deal here with a conviction resting solely upon "speech," not upon any separately identifiable conduct which allegedly was intended by Cohen to be perceived by others as expressive of particular views but which, on its face, does not necessarily convey any message and hence arguably could be regulated without effectively repressing Cohen's ability to express himself. Cf. *United States v. O'Brien* [p. 669 infra]. Further, the State certainly lacks power to punish Cohen for the underlying content of the message the inscription conveyed. At least so long as there is no showing of an intent to incite disobedience to or disruption of the draft, Cohen could not, consistently with the First and Fourteenth Amendments, be punished for asserting the evident position on the inutility or immorality of the draft his jacket reflected. *Yates*.

Appellant's conviction, then, rests squarely upon his exercise [of] "freedom of speech" [and] can be justified, if at all, only as a valid regulation of the manner in which he exercised that freedom, not as a permissible prohibition on the substantive message it conveys. This does not end the inquiry, of course, for the First and Fourteenth Amendments have never been thought to give absolute protection to every individual to speak whenever or wherever he pleases, or to use any form of address in any circumstances that he chooses. In this vein, too, however, we think it important to note that several issues typically associated with such problems are not presented here.

In the first place, Cohen was tried under a statute applicable throughout the entire State. Any attempt to support this conviction on the ground that the statute seeks to preserve an appropriately decorous atmosphere in the courthouse where Cohen was arrested must fail in the absence of any language in the statute that would have put appellant on notice that certain kinds of otherwise permissible speech or conduct would nevertheless, under California law, not be tolerated in certain places. No fair reading of the phrase "offensive conduct" can be said sufficiently to inform the ordinary person that distinctions between certain locations are thereby created.[3]

In the second place, as it comes to us, this case cannot be said to fall within those relatively few categories of instances where prior decisions have established the power of government to deal more comprehensively with certain forms of individual expression simply upon a showing that such a form was employed. This is not, for example, an obscenity case. Whatever else may be necessary to give rise to the States' broader power to prohibit obscene expression, such expression must be, in some significant way, erotic. *Roth*. It cannot plausibly be maintained that this vulgar allusion to the Selective Service System would conjure up such psychic stimulation in anyone likely to be confronted with Cohen's crudely defaced jacket.

This Court has also held that the States are free to ban the simple use, without a demonstration of additional justifying circumstances, of so-called "fighting words," those personally abusive epithets which, when addressed to the ordinary citizen, are, as a matter of common knowledge, inherently likely to provoke violent reaction. *Chaplinsky*. While the four-letter word displayed by Cohen in relation to the draft is not uncommonly employed in a personally provocative fashion, in this instance it was clearly not "directed to the person of

---

3. It is illuminating to note what transpired when Cohen entered a courtroom in the building. He removed his jacket and stood with it folded over his arm. Meanwhile, a policeman sent the presiding judge a note suggesting that Cohen be held in contempt of court. The judge declined to do so and Cohen was arrested by the officer only after he emerged from the courtroom.

the hearer." No individual actually or likely to be present could reasonably have regarded the words on appellant's jacket as a direct personal insult. Nor do we have here an instance of the exercise of the State's police power to prevent a speaker from intentionally provoking a given group to hostile reaction. Cf. *Feiner; Terminiello.* There is, as noted above, no showing that anyone who saw Cohen was in fact violently aroused or that appellant intended such a result.

[T]he mere presumed presence of unwitting listeners or viewers does not serve automatically to justify curtailing all speech capable of giving offense. While this Court has recognized that government may properly act in many situations to prohibit intrusion into the privacy of the home of unwelcome views and ideas which cannot be totally banned from the public dialogue, we have at the same time consistently stressed that "we are often 'captives' outside the sanctuary of the home and subject to objectionable speech." The ability of government, consonant with the Constitution, to shut off discourse solely to protect others from hearing it is, in other words, dependent upon a showing that substantial privacy interests are being invaded in an essentially intolerable manner. Any broader view of this authority would effectively empower a majority to silence dissidents simply as a matter of personal predilections.

[Given] the subtlety and complexity of the factors involved if Cohen's "speech" was otherwise entitled to constitutional protection, we do not think the fact that some unwilling "listeners" in a public building may have been briefly exposed to it can serve to justify this breach of the peace conviction where, as here, there was no evidence that persons powerless to avoid appellant's conduct did in fact object to it, and where [unlike another portion of the same statute barring the use of "vulgar, profane or indecent language within [the] hearing of women or children, in a loud and boisterous manner"], the [challenged statutory provision] evinces no concern [with] the special plight of the captive auditor, but, instead, indiscriminately sweeps within its prohibitions all "offensive conduct" that disturbs "any neighborhood or person."

Against this background, the issue flushed by this case stands out in bold relief. It is whether California can excise, as "offensive conduct," one particular scurrilous epithet from the public discourse, either upon the theory of the court below that its use is inherently likely to cause violent reaction or upon a more general assertion that the States, acting as guardians of public morality, may properly remove this offensive word from the public vocabulary.

The rationale of the California court is plainly untenable. At most it reflects an "undifferentiated fear or apprehension of disturbance [which] is not enough to overcome the right to freedom of expression." *Tinker* [p. 829 infra]. We have been shown no evidence that substantial numbers of citizens are standing ready to strike out physically at whoever may assault their sensibilities with execrations like that uttered by Cohen. There may be some persons about with such lawless and violent proclivities, but that is an insufficient base upon which to erect, consistently with constitutional values, a governmental power to force persons who wish to ventilate their dissident views into avoiding particular forms of expression. The argument amounts to little more than the self-defeating proposition that to avoid physical censorship of one who has not sought to provoke such a response by a hypothetical coterie of the violent and lawless, the States may more appropriately effectuate that censorship themselves.

Admittedly, it is not so obvious that the First and Fourteenth Amendments must be taken to disable the States from punishing public utterance of this unseemly expletive in order to maintain what they regard as a suitable level of discourse within the body politic. We think, however, that examination and reflection will reveal the shortcomings of a contrary viewpoint.

[The] constitutional right of free expression is powerful medicine in a society as diverse and populous as ours. It is designed and intended to remove governmental restraints from the arena of public discussion, putting the decision as to what views shall be voiced largely into the hands of each of us, in the hope that use of such freedom will ultimately produce a more capable citizenry and more perfect polity and in the belief that no other approach would comport with the premise of individual dignity and choice upon which our political system rests.

To many, the immediate consequence of this freedom may often appear to be only verbal tumult, discord, and even offensive utterance. These are, however, within established limits, in truth necessary side effects of the broader enduring values which the process of open debate permits us to achieve. That the air may at times seem filled with verbal cacophony is, in this sense not a sign of weakness but of strength. We cannot lose sight of the fact that, in what otherwise might seem a trifling and annoying instance of individual distasteful abuse of a privilege, these fundamental societal values are truly implicated. * * *

Against this perception of the constitutional policies involved, we discern certain more particularized considerations that peculiarly call for reversal of this conviction. First, the principle contended for by the State seems inherently boundless. How is one to distinguish this from any other offensive word? Surely the State has no right to cleanse public debate to the point where it is grammatically palatable to the most squeamish among us. Yet no readily ascertainable general principle exists for stopping short of that result were we to affirm the judgment below. For, while the particular four-letter word being litigated here is perhaps more distasteful than most others of its genre, it is nevertheless often true that one man's vulgarity is another's lyric. Indeed, we think it is largely because governmental officials cannot make principled distinctions in this area that the Constitution leaves matters of taste and style so largely to the individual.

Additionally, we cannot overlook the fact, because it is well illustrated by the episode involved here, that much linguistic expression serves a dual communicative function: it conveys not only ideas capable of relatively precise, detached explication, but otherwise inexpressible emotions as well. In fact, words are often chosen as much for their emotive as their cognitive force. We cannot sanction the view that the Constitution, while solicitous of the cognitive content of individual speech, has little or no regard for that emotive function which, practically speaking, may often be the more important element of the overall message sought to be communicated. * * *

Finally, and in the same vein, we cannot indulge the facile assumption that one can forbid particular words without also running a substantial risk of suppressing ideas in the process. Indeed, governments might soon seize upon the censorship of particular words as a convenient guise for banning the expression of unpopular views. We have been able [to] discern little social benefit that might result from running the risk of opening the door to such grave results.

It is, in sum, our judgment that, absent a more particularized and compelling reason for its actions, the State may not, consistently with the First and Fourteenth Amendments, make the simple public display here involved of this single four-letter expletive a criminal offense. * * *

[BLACKMUN, J., joined by Burger, C.J., and Black, J., dissented for two reasons: (1) "Cohen's absurd and immature antic [was] mainly conduct and little speech" and the case falls "well within the sphere of *Chaplinsky*"; (2) although it declined to review the state court of appeals' decision in *Cohen*, the California Supreme Court subsequently narrowly construed the breach-of-the-peace statute in another case and *Cohen* should be remanded to the California Court of Appeal in the light of this subsequent construction. White, J., concurred with the dissent on the latter ground.]

Notes and Questions

1. For criticism of *Cohen*, see Alexander Bickel, *The Morality of Consent* 72 (1975) (Cohen's speech "constitutes an assault" and this sort of speech "may create [an] environment [in which] actions that were not possible before become possible"); Archibald Cox, *The Role of the Supreme Court in American Government* 47–48 (1976) (state has interest in "level at which public discourse is conducted"; state should not have to "allow exhibitionists and [others] trading upon our lower prurient interests to inflict themselves upon the public consciousness and dull its sensibilities"). For a defense (but what not a few would consider a narrow reading) of *Cohen*, see Daniel Farber, *Civilizing Public Discourse: An Essay on Professor Bickel, Justice Harlan, and the Enduring Significance of Cohen v. California*, 1980 Duke L.J. 283. See also John Hart Ely, *Democracy and Distrust* 114 (1980); Laurence Tribe, *American Constitutional Law* 787–88, 851–52, 916–17, 953–54 (2d Ed.1988). For an overview of Harlan, J.'s approach to the first amendment, see Daniel Farber & John Nowak, *Justice Harlan and the First Amendment,* 2 Const.Comm. 425 (1985).

2. To what extent, if at all, and in what ways, if any, does *Cohen* restrict the "fighting words" doctrine? Consider Hadley Arkes, *Civility and the Restriction of Speech: Rediscovering the Defamation of Groups,* 1974 Sup.Ct.Rev. 281, 316: *Cohen* turned "the presumptions in *Chaplinsky* around: instead of presuming that profane or defamatory speech was beneath constitutional protection, he presumed that the speech was protected and that the burden of proof lay with those who would restrict it." If "one man's vulgarity is another's lyric," how are discriminations to be made in the "fighting words" area? See Rutzick, p. 725 supra, at 20.

3. Does the "use of elaborate explanations and high sounding principles to resolve" cases like *Cohen* erect "obstacles to an enhanced public appreciation of free speech?" Does systematic judicial protection of "seemingly silly, unsavory, or dangerous activities" ultimately undermine public support for the idea of free speech? See Robert Nagel, *Constitutional Cultures* 47 (1989).

4. What does *Cohen* decide? Consider William Cohen, *A Look Back at Cohen v. California,* 34 UCLA L.Rev. 1595, 1602–03 (1987): "Unless it is overruled or dishonestly distinguished, *[Cohen]* has settled the proposition that a criminal statute is unconstitutional if it punishes all public use of profanity without reference to details such as the nature of the location and the audience. The opinion, however, left much to be decided about government controls on the use of profanity based on considerations of time, place, and manner. To what extent can profanity be punished because of the nature of the audience, the nature of the occasion on which it is uttered or displayed, or the manner of its utterance or display."

5. A series of cases in the early 1970s reversed convictions involving abusive language. *Gooding v. Wilson,* 405 U.S. 518, 92 S.Ct. 1103, 31 L.Ed.2d 408 (1972), invalidated a Georgia ordinance primarily because it had been previously applied to "utterances where there was no likelihood that the person addressed would

make an immediate violent utterance." *Lewis v. New Orleans,* 415 U.S. 130, 94 S.Ct. 970, 39 L.Ed.2d 214 (1974), ruled that vulgar or offensive speech was protected under the first amendment. Because the statute punished "opprobrious language," it was deemed by the Court to embrace words that do not " 'by their very utterance inflict injury or tend to invite an immediate breach of the peace.' "

Although *Gooding* seemed to require a danger of immediate violence, *Lewis* recited that infliction of injury was sufficient. Dissenting in both cases, Burger, C.J., and Blackmun and Rehnquist, JJ., complained that the majority invoked vagueness and overbreadth analysis "indiscriminately without regard to the nature of the speech in question, the possible effect the statute or ordinance has upon such speech, the importance of the speech in relation to the exposition of ideas, or the purported or asserted community interest in preventing that speech." The dissenters focused upon the facts of the cases (e.g., Gooding to a police officer: "White son of a bitch, I'll kill you," "You son of a bitch, I'll choke you to death," and "You son of a bitch, if you ever put your hands on me again, I'll cut you to pieces."). They complained that the majority had relegated the facts to "footnote status, conveniently distant and in less disturbing focus." In *Gooding, Lewis,* and the other cases, Powell, J., insisted upon the importance of context in decisionmaking. Dissenting in *Rosenfeld v. New Jersey,* 408 U.S. 901, 92 S.Ct. 2479, 33 L.Ed.2d 321 (1972), he suggested that *Chaplinsky* be extended to the "wilful use of scurrilous language calculated to offend the sensibilities of an unwilling audience"; concurring in *Lewis,* he maintained that allowing prosecutions for offensive language directed at police officers invited law enforcement abuse. Finally, he suggested in *Rosenfeld* that whatever the scope of the "fighting words" doctrine, overbreadth analysis was inappropriate in such cases. He doubted that such statutes deter others from exercising first amendment rights.[a]

Without questioning the power of states or municipalities to proscribe fighting words, or the failure to disperse in response to a valid police order, or the physical obstruction of an officer's investigation, or disorderly conduct, HOUSTON v. HILL, 482 U.S. 451, 107 S.Ct. 2502, 96 L.Ed.2d 398 (1987), per BRENNAN, J., invalidated as overbroad a Houston ordinance forbidding speech that in any manner interrupts a police officer in the performance of his or her duties: "The ordinance's plain language is admittedly violated scores of times daily, [yet] only some individuals—those chosen by the police in their unguided discretion—are arrested." [b]

POWELL, J., concurring in part and dissenting in part, argued that if the state were to construe the ordinance to require proof of intent to interfere with an officer's duties, overbreadth and vagueness difficulties might be overcome. In order to narrow the focus of the constitutional question, he would have certified that state law question to the appropriate Texas court.[c] Bowing to the court's determination to consider the ordinance without such a narrowing construction, he concluded that the ordinance was unconstitutionally vague.[d]

a. For commentary on Powell, J.'s approach, see Gerald Gunther, *In Search of Judicial Quality on a Changing Court: The Case of Justice Powell,* 24 Stan.L.Rev. 1001, 1029–35 (1972).

b. Blackmun, J., concurring, joined the Court's opinion, but reaffirmed his view that *Gooding* and *Lewis* were wrongly decided.

c. O'Connor, J., and Rehnquist, C.J., joined this portion of Powell, J.'s opinion.

d. Scalia, J., joined with Powell, J., on the vagueness issue and on some procedural issues, but thought the ordinance was properly before the Court. Rehnquist, C.J., dissenting, stated that he did not agree that the ordinance "in the absence of an authoritative construction by the Texas courts, is unconstitutional."

V. SHOULD NEW CATEGORIES BE CREATED?

Suppose a legislature were to outlaw speech whose dominant theme appeals to a morbid interest in violence, that is patently offensive to contemporary community standards, and that lacks serious literary, artistic, political or scientific value. Constitutional? One approach would be to contend that speech is protected unless it falls into already established categorical exceptions to first amendment protection. Another would be to argue by analogy, e.g., if obscenity is beneath first amendment protection, this speech should (or should not) be beneath such protection. Similarly, one could argue that exceptions to first amendment protection has been fashioned by resort to a balancing methodology and that balancing the relevant interests is the right approach. Alternatively, one could proceed from a particular substantive vision of the first amendment, such as the Meiklejohn view. Which approach has been applied by the Court? [a]

New York v. Ferber, infra, is interesting because it involves the question of whether to create a new category.

A. HARM TO CHILDREN AND THE OVERBREADTH DOCTRINE

NEW YORK v. FERBER, 458 U.S. 747, 102 S.Ct. 3348, 73 L.Ed.2d 1113 (1982), per WHITE, J., upheld conviction of a seller of films depicting young boys masturbating, under N.Y.Penal Law § 263.15, for "promoting [a] a sexual performance," defined as "any performance [which] includes sexual conduct [b] by a child" under 16. The Court addressed the "single question": " 'To prevent the abuse of children who are made to engage in sexual conduct for commercial purposes, could the New York State Legislature, consistent with the First Amendment, prohibit the dissemination of material which shows children engaged in sexual conduct, regardless of whether such material is obscene?' [c] * * *

"The *Miller* standard, like its predecessors, was an accommodation between the state's interests in protecting the 'sensibilities of unwilling recipients' from

a. For commentary on the Court's methodology, see Martin Redish, *Freedom of Expression: A Critical Analysis* (1984); Steven Shiffrin, *The First Amendment, Democracy, and Romance* (1990); William Van Alstyne, *Interpretations of the First Amendment* (1984); William Van Alstyne, *A Graphic Review of the Free Speech Clause,* 70 Calif.L.Rev. 107 (1982); T. Alexander Aleinikoff, *Constitutional Law in the Age of Balancing,* 96 Yale L.J. 943 (1987); Richard Fallon, *A Constructivist Coherence Theory of Constitutional Interpretation,* 100 Harv.L.Rev. 1189, 1228 n.191 (1987); Daniel Farber, *Content Regulation and the First Amendment: A Revisionist View,* 68 Geo.L.J. 727 (1980); Frederick Schauer, *Mrs. Palsgraf and the First Amendment,* 47 Wash.& Lee L.Rev. 161 (1990); Frederick Schauer, *The Second-Best First Amendment,* 31 Wm.& M.L.Rev. 1 (1989); Frederick Schauer, *Categories and the First Amendment: A Play in Three Acts,* 34 Vand.L.Rev. 265 (1981); Pierre Schlag, *Rules and Standards,* 33 U.C.L.A.L.Rev. 379 (1985); Geoffrey Stone, *Content Regulation and the First Amendment,* 25 Wm.& Mary L.Rev. 189 (1983); Geoffrey Stone, *Content–Neutral Restrictions,* 54 U.Chi. L.Rev. 46 (1987).

a. "Promote" was defined to include all aspects of production, distribution, exhibition and sale.

b. Sec. 263.3 defined "sexual conduct" as "actual or simulated sexual intercourse, deviate sexual intercourse, sexual bestiality, masturbation, sado-masochistic abuse, or lewd exhibition of the genitals."

c. The opinion gave the background for such legislation: "In recent years, the exploitive use of children in the production of pornography has become a serious national problem. The federal government and forty-seven States have sought to combat the problem with statutes specifically directed at the production of child pornography. At least half of such statutes do not require that the materials produced be legally obscene. Thirty-five States and the United States Congress have also passed legislation prohibiting the distribution of such materials; twenty States prohibit the distribution of material depicting children engaged in sexual conduct without requiring that the material be legally obscene. New York is one of the twenty."

exposure to pornographic material and the dangers of censorship inherent in unabashedly content-based laws. Like obscenity statutes, laws directed at the dissemination of child pornography run the risk of suppressing protected expression by allowing the hand of the censor to become unduly heavy. For the following reasons, however, we are persuaded that the States are entitled to greater leeway in the regulation of pornographic depictions of children.

"First. [The] prevention of sexual exploitation and abuse of children constitutes a government objective of surpassing importance. The legislative findings accompanying passage of the New York laws reflect this concern. * * *

"We shall not second-guess this legislative judgment. Respondent has not intimated that we do so. Suffice it to say that virtually all of the States and the United States have passed legislation proscribing the production of or otherwise combatting 'child pornography.' The legislative judgment, as well as the judgment found in the relevant literature, is that the use of children as subjects of pornographic materials is harmful to the physiological, emotional, and mental health of the child. That judgment, we think, easily passes muster under the First Amendment.

"Second. The distribution of photographs and films depicting sexual activity by juveniles is intrinsically related to the sexual abuse of children in at least two ways. First, the materials produced are a permanent record of the children's participation and the harm to the child is exacerbated by their circulation. Second, the distribution network for child pornography must be closed if the production of material which requires the sexual exploitation of children is to be effectively controlled. Indeed, there is no serious contention that the legislature was unjustified in believing that it is difficult, if not impossible, to halt the exploitation of children by pursuing only those who produce the photographs and movies. While the production of pornographic materials is a low-profile, clandestine industry, the need to market the resulting products requires a visible apparatus of distribution. The most expeditious if not the only practical method of law enforcement may be to dry up the market for this material by imposing severe criminal penalties on persons selling, advertising, or otherwise promoting the product. Thirty-five States and Congress have concluded that restraints on the distribution of pornographic materials are required in order to effectively combat the problem, and there is a body of literature and testimony to support these legislative conclusions.

"[The] *Miller* standard, like all general definitions of what may be banned as obscene, does not reflect the State's particular and more compelling interest in prosecuting those who promote the sexual exploitation of children. Thus, the question under the *Miller* test of whether a work, taken as a whole, appeals to the prurient interest of the average person bears no connection to the issue of whether a child has been physically or psychologically harmed in the production of the work. Similarly, a sexual explicit depiction need not be 'patently offensive' in order to have required the sexual exploitation of a child for its production. In addition, a work which, taken on the whole, contains serious literary, artistic, political, or scientific value may nevertheless embody the hardest core of child pornography. 'It is irrelevant to the child [who has been abused] whether or not the material [has] a literary, artistic, political, or social value.' We therefore cannot conclude that the *Miller* standard is a satisfactory solution to the child pornography problem.

"Third.   The advertising and selling of child pornography provides an economic motive for and is thus an integral part of the production of such materials, an activity illegal throughout the nation. 'It rarely has been suggested that the constitutional freedom for speech and press extends its immunity to speech or writing used as an integral part of conduct in violation of a valid criminal statute.' * * *

"Fourth.   The value of permitting live performances and photographic reproductions of children engaged in lewd sexual conduct is exceedingly modest, if not de minimis.   We consider it unlikely that visual depictions of children performing sexual acts or lewdly exhibiting their genitals would often constitute an important and necessary part of a literary performance or scientific or educational work.   As the trial court in this case observed, if it were necessary for literary or artistic value, a person over the statutory age who perhaps looked younger could be utilized.   * * *

"Fifth.   Recognizing and classifying child pornography as a category of material outside the protection of the First Amendment is not incompatible with our earlier decisions.   'The question whether speech is, or is not protected by the First Amendment often depends on the content of the speech.' *Young v. American Mini Theatres, Inc.* [p. 789 infra]. '[I]t is the content of an utterance that determines whether it is a protected epithet or [an] unprotected "fighting comment"'.   Leaving aside the special considerations when public officials are the target, *New York Times Co. v. Sullivan,* a libelous publication is not protected by the Constitution. *Beauharnais.* [It] is not rare that a content-based classification of speech has been accepted because it may be appropriately generalized that within the confines of the given classification, the evil to be restricted so overwhelmingly outweighs the expressive interests, if any, at stake, that no process of case-by-case adjudication is required.   When a definable class of material, such as that covered by § 263.15, bears so heavily and pervasively on the welfare of children engaged in its production, we think the balance of competing interests is clearly struck and that it is permissible to consider these materials as without the protection of the First Amendment.

"There are, of course, limits on the category of child pornography which, like obscenity, is unprotected by the First Amendment.   As with all legislation in this sensitive area, the conduct to be prohibited must be adequately defined by the applicable state law, as written or authoritatively construed.   Here the nature of the harm to be combatted requires that the state offense be limited to works that *visually* depict sexual conduct by children below a specified age.   The category of 'sexual conduct' proscribed must also be suitably limited and described.

"The test for child pornography is separate from the obscenity standard enunciated in *Miller,* but may be compared to it for purpose of clarity.   The *Miller* formulation is adjusted in the following respects: A trier of fact need not find that the material appeals to the prurient interest of the average person;   it is not required that sexual conduct portrayed be done so in a patently offensive manner; and the material at issue need not be considered as a whole.   We note that the distribution of descriptions or other depictions of sexual conduct, not otherwise obscene, which do not involve live performance or photographic or other visual reproduction of live performances, retains First Amendment protection.   As with obscenity laws, criminal responsibility may not be imposed without some element of scienter on the part of the defendant.   * * *

"It remains to address the claim that the New York statute is unconstitutionally overbroad because it would forbid the distribution of material with serious literary, scientific, or educational value or material which does not threaten the harms sought to be combated by the State. * * *

"The traditional rule is that a person to whom a statute may constitutionally be applied may not challenge that statute on the ground that it may conceivably be applied unconstitutionally to others in situations not before the Court. *Broadrick v. Oklahoma,* 413 U.S. 601, 93 S.Ct. 2908, 37 L.Ed.2d 830 (1973). In *Broadrick,* we recognized that this rule reflects two cardinal principles of our constitutional order: the personal nature of constitutional rights and prudential limitations on constitutional adjudication.[20] [By] focusing on the factual situation before us, and similar cases necessary for development of a constitutional rule,[21] we face 'flesh-and-blood' legal problems with data 'relevant and adequate to an informed judgment.' This practice also fulfills a valuable institutional purpose: it allows state courts the opportunity to construe a law to avoid constitutional infirmities.

"What has come to be known as the First Amendment overbreadth doctrine is one of the few exceptions to this principle and must be justified by weighty countervailing policies. The doctrine is predicated on the sensitive nature of protected expression: persons whose expression is constitutionally protected may well refrain from exercising their rights for fear of criminal sanctions by a statute susceptible of application to protected expression. * * *

"In *Broadrick,* we explained [that]: '[T]he plain import of our cases is, at the very least, that facial overbreadth adjudication is an exception to our traditional rules of practice and that its function, a limited one at the outset, attenuates as the otherwise unprotected behavior that it forbids the State to sanction moves from "pure speech" toward conduct and that conduct—even if expressive—falls within the scope of otherwise valid criminal laws that reflect legitimate state interests in maintaining comprehensive controls over harmful, constitutionally unprotected conduct. * * *'

"[*Broadrick*] examined a regulation involving restrictions on political campaign activity, an area not considered 'pure speech,' and thus it was unnecessary to consider the proper overbreadth test when a law arguably reaches traditional forms of expression such as books and films. As we intimated in *Broadrick,* the requirement of substantial overbreadth extended 'at the very least' to cases involving conduct plus speech. This case, which poses the question squarely, convinces us that the rationale of *Broadrick* is sound and should be applied in the present context involving the harmful employment of children to make sexually explicit materials for distribution.

"The premise that a law should not be invalidated for overbreadth unless it reaches a substantial number of impermissible applications is hardly novel. On most occasions involving facial invalidation, the Court has stressed the embracing sweep of the statute over protected expression.[26] Indeed, Justice Brennan observed in his dissenting opinion in *Broadrick*: 'We have never held that a statute

20. In addition to prudential restraints, the traditional rule is grounded in Art. III limits on the jurisdiction of federal courts to actual cases and controversies. * * *

21. Overbreadth challenges are only one type of facial attack. A person whose activity may be constitutionally regulated nevertheless may argue that the statute under which he is convicted or regulated is invalid on its face. See, e.g., *Terminiello.* See generally Henry

Monaghan, *Overbreadth,* 1981 S.Ct.Rev. 1, 10–14.

26. In *Gooding v. Wilson,* the Court's invalidation of a Georgia statute making it a misdemeanor to use " 'opprobrious words or abusive language, tending to cause a breach of the peace' " followed from state judicial decisions indicating that "merely to speak words offensive to some who hear them" could constitute a "breach of the peace." * * *

should be held invalid on its face merely because it is possible to conceive of a single impermissible application, and in that sense a requirement of substantial overbreadth is already implicit in the doctrine.'

"The requirement of substantial overbreadth is directly derived from the purpose and nature of the doctrine. While a sweeping statute, or one incapable of limitation, has the potential to repeatedly chill the exercise of expressive activity by many individuals, the extent of deterrence of protected speech can be expected to decrease with the declining reach of the regulation. This observation appears equally applicable to the publication of books and films as it is to activities, such as picketing or participation in election campaigns, which have previously been categorized as involving conduct plus speech. We see no appreciable difference between the position of a publisher or bookseller in doubt as to the reach of New York's child pornography law and the situation faced by the Oklahoma state employees with respect to the State's restriction on partisan political activity.[d]
* * *

"Applying these principles, we hold that § 263.15 is not substantially overbroad. We consider this the paradigmatic case of a state statute whose legitimate reach dwarfs its arguably impermissible applications. [While] the reach of the statute is directed at the hard core of child pornography, the Court of Appeals was understandably concerned that some protected expression, ranging from medical textbooks to pictorials in the National Geographic would fall prey to the statute. How often, if ever, it may be necessary to employ children to engage in conduct clearly within the reach of § 263.15 in order to produce educational, medical, or artistic works cannot be known with certainty. Yet we seriously doubt, and it has not been suggested, that these arguably impermissible applications of the statute amount to more than a tiny fraction of the materials within the statute's reach."[e]

d. *Brockett v. Spokane Arcades, Inc.*, p. 618 supra, stated: "The Court of Appeals erred in holding that the *Broadrick* substantial overbreadth requirement is inapplicable where pure speech rather than conduct is at issue. *Ferber* specifically held to the contrary." For commentary on the overbreadth discussion in *Broadrick* and *Ferber*, see Martin Redish, *The Warren Court, The Burger Court and the First Amendment Overbreadth Doctrine*, 78 Nw. U.L.Rev. 1031, 1056–69 (1983).

e. Brennan, J., joined by Marshall, J., agreed "with much of what is said in the Court's opinion. [This] special and compelling interest (in protecting the well-being of the State's youth), and the particular vulnerability of children, afford the State the leeway to regulate pornographic material, the promotion of which is harmful to children, even though the State does not have such leeway when it seeks only to protect consenting adults from exposure to such materials. * * * I also agree with the Court that the 'tiny fraction' of material of serious artistic, scientific or educational value that could conceivably fall within the reach of the statute is insufficient to justify striking the statute on grounds of overbreadth." But the concurrence stated that application of the statute to such materials as "do have serious artistic, scientific or medical value would violate the First Amendment."

On that issue O'Connor, J., wrote a short concurrence: "Although I join the Court's opinion, I write separately to stress that the Court does not hold that New York must except 'material with serious literary, scientific or educational value' from its statute. The Court merely holds that, even if the First Amendment shelters such material, New York's current statute is not sufficiently overbroad to support respondent's facial attack. The compelling interests identified in today's opinion suggest that the Constitution might in fact permit New York to ban knowing distribution of works depicting minors engaged in explicit sexual conduct, regardless of the social value of the depictions. For example, a 12-year-old child photographed while masturbating surely suffers the same psychological harm whether the community labels the photograph 'edifying' or 'tasteless.' The audience's appreciation of the depiction is simply irrelevant to New York's asserted interest in protecting children from psychological, emotional, and mental harm."

Stevens, J., also concurred in the judgment in a short opinion that noted his conclusion that the films in the case were not entitled to first amendment protection, and his view that overbreadth analysis should be avoided by waiting until the hypothetical case actually arises.

Notes and Questions

1. Consider Frederick Schauer, *Codifying the First Amendment: New York v. Ferber,* 1982 Sup.Ct.Rev. 285, 295: The new category created in *Ferber* "bears little resemblance to the category of obscenity delineated by *Miller.* The Court in *Ferber* explicitly held that child pornography need not appeal to the prurient interest, need not be patently offensive, and need not be based on a consideration of the material as a whole. This last aspect is most important, because it means that the presence of some serious literary, artistic, political, or scientific matter will not constitutionally redeem material containing depictions of sexual conduct by children. The Court referred to the foregoing factors in terms of having 'adjusted' the *Miller* test, but that is like saying a butterfly is an adjusted camel." What precisely is the new category created in *Ferber* ?

2. What test or standard of review did the Court use to determine whether the speech should be protected? For general discussion, see Schauer, supra. Did it apply a different test or a standard of review when it formulated its rules in *Gertz* ? Are tests or standards of review needed in these contexts? Desirable? Consider Steven Shiffrin, *The First Amendment and Economic Regulation: Away From a General Theory of the First Amendment,* 78 Nw.U.L.Rev. 1212, 1268 (1983): "The complex set of rules produced in *Gertz,* right or wrong, resulted from an appreciation that the protection of truth was important but that the protection of reputation also was important. The Court wisely avoided discussion of levels of scrutiny because any resort to such abstractions would have constitutionalized reductionism." Is "constitutionalized reductionism" desirable because it protects speech and provides guidance to the lower courts?

3. *The absence of children.* SIMON AND SCHUSTER, INC. v. MEMBERS OF NEW YORK STATE CRIME VICTIMS BD., 502 U.S. 105, 112 S.Ct. 501, 116 L.Ed.2d 476 (1991), per O'CONNOR, J., struck down a law requiring that income derived from works in which individuals admit to crime involving victims be used to compensate the victims: "[T]he State has a compelling interest in compensating victims from the fruits of the crime, but little if any interest in limiting such compensation to the proceeds of the wrongdoer's speech about the crime." [f]

4. *Overbreadth without a chilling effect?* Massachusetts prohibited adults from posing or exhibiting nude children for purposes of photographs, publications, or pictures, moving or otherwise. Bona fide scientific or medical purposes were excepted as were educational or cultural purposes for a bona fide school, museum, or library. Douglas Oakes was prosecuted for taking 10 color photographs of his 14–year–old stepdaughter in a state of nudity covered by the statute. The Massachusetts Supreme Judicial Court declared the statute overbroad. After certiorari was granted in MASSACHUSETTS v. OAKES, 491 U.S. 576, 109 S.Ct. 2633, 105 L.Ed.2d 493 (1989), Massachusetts added a "lascivious intent" requirement to the statute and eliminated the exemptions. O'CONNOR, J., joined by Rehnquist, C.J., and White and Kennedy, JJ., accordingly refused to entertain the overbreadth challenge and voted to remand the case for determination of the statute's constitutionality as applied: "Because it has been repealed, the former version of [the Massachusetts law] cannot chill protected speech."

Blackmun, J., concurred in the result without opinion.

f. Kennedy, J., concurring, would have stricken the statute without reference to the compelling state interest test which he condemned as ad hoc balancing. Blackmun, J., also concurred. Thomas, J., did not participate.

SCALIA, J., joined by Blackmun, Brennan, Marshall, and Stevens, JJ., disagreed:[g] "It seems to me strange judicial theory that a conviction initially invalid can be resuscitated by postconviction alteration of the statute under which it was obtained. [Even as a policy matter, the] overbreadth doctrine serves to protect constitutionally legitimate speech not merely *ex post,* that is, after the offending statute is enacted, but also *ex ante,* that is, when the legislature is contemplating what sort of statute to enact. If the promulgation of overbroad laws affecting speech was cost free[,] if *no* conviction of constitutionally proscribable conduct would be lost, so long as the offending statute was narrowed before the final appeal—then legislatures would have significantly reduced incentive to stay within constitutional bounds in the first place. [More] fundamentally, however, [it] seems to me that we are only free to pursue policy objectives through the modes of action traditionally followed by the courts and by the law. [I] have heard of a voidable contract, but never of a voidable law. The notion is bizarre."

5. *How substantial is substantial overbreadth?* Five justices addressed the overbreadth question in *Oakes,* but the substantive issue was not resolved. BRENNAN, J., joined by Marshall and Stevens, JJ., objected that the statute would make it criminal for parents "to photograph their infant children or toddlers in the bath or romping naked on the beach." More generally, he argued that the first amendment "blocks the prohibition of nude posing by minors in connection with the production of works of art not depicting lewd behavior. * * * Many of the world's great artists—Degas, Renoir, Donatello, to name but a few—have worked from models under 18 years of age, and many acclaimed photographs have included nude or partially clad minors."

SCALIA, J., joined by Blackmun, J., disagreed: "[G]iven the known extent of the kiddie-porn industry[,] I would estimate that the legitimate scope [of the statute] vastly exceeds the illegitimate. [Even] assuming that proscribing artistic depictions of preadolescent genitals and postadolescent breasts is impermissible,[2] the body of material that would be covered is, as far as I am aware, insignificant compared with the lawful scope of the statute. That leaves the family photos. [Assuming] that it is unconstitutional (as opposed to merely foolish) to prohibit such photography, I do not think it so common as to make the statute *substantially* overbroad. [My] perception differs, for example, from Justice Brennan's belief that there is an 'abundance of baby and child photographs taken every day' depicting genitals."[b]

---

g. Although these five justices agreed that the overbreadth challenge should be entertained, they divided on the merits of the challenge. Scalia, J., joined by Blackmun, J., found no merit in the overbreadth claim (see note 5 infra) and voted to reverse and to remand for determination of the statute's constitutionality as applied. The three remaining justices (see note 5 infra) agreed with the overbreadth challenge and voted to affirm the judgment below. O'Connor, J.'s opinion, therefore, became the plurality opinion, and the Court's judgment was to vacate the judgment below and to remand. In the end, six justices voted against the overbreadth challenge: four because it was moot; two because it did not meet the requirement of substantial overbreadth.

2. [Most] adults, I expect, would not hire themselves out as nude models, whatever the intention of the photographer or artist, and however unerotic the pose. There is no cause to think children are less sensitive. It is not unreasonable, therefore, for a State to regard parents' using (or permitting the use) of their children as nude models, or other adults' use of consenting minors, as a form of child exploitation.

b. For the argument that the Court should balance a number of factors including the "state's substantive interest in being able to impose sanctions for a particular kind of conduct under a particular legal standard, as opposed to being forced to rely on other, less restrictive substitutes" instead of trying to determine the number of constitutional and un-

Ohio prohibited possession of material showing a minor in a state of nudity, subject to exceptions.[a] Clyde Osborne was convicted for possessing photographs of a nude male adolescent in a variety of sexually explicit poses.[b] The photographs were secured in his home pursuant to a valid search warrant. The Ohio Supreme Court narrowed the statute to apply only to depictions of nudity involving a lewd exhibition or a graphic focus on the genitals.

OSBORNE v. OHIO, 495 U.S. 103, 110 S.Ct. 1691, 109 L.Ed.2d 98 (1990), per WHITE, J., upheld the statute as construed: "In *Stanley,* we struck down a Georgia law outlawing the private possession of obscene material. We recognized that the statute impinged upon Stanley's right to receive information in the privacy of his home, and we found Georgia's justifications for its law inadequate.[3]

"*Stanley* should not be read too broadly. We have previously noted that *Stanley* was a narrow holding and, since the decision in that case, the value of permitting child pornography has been characterized as 'exceedingly modest, if not *de minimis.*' *Ferber.* But assuming, for the sake of argument, that Osborne has a First Amendment interest in viewing and possessing child pornography, we nonetheless find this case distinct from *Stanley* because the interests underlying child pornography prohibitions far exceed the interests justifying the Georgia law at issue in *Stanley.* * * *

"In *Stanley,* Georgia primarily sought to proscribe the private possession of obscenity because it was concerned that obscenity would poison the minds of its viewers. [The] difference here is obvious: the State does not rely on a paternalistic interest in regulating Osborne's mind. Rather, Ohio has [acted] in order to protect the victims of child pornography; it hopes to destroy a market for the exploitative use of children. [*Stanley*] itself emphasized that we did not 'mean to express any opinion on statutes making criminal possession of other types of printed, filmed, or recorded materials. * * * [In] such cases, compelling reasons may exist for overriding the right of the individual to possess those materials.'[5]

"Given the importance of the State's interest in protecting the victims of child pornography, we cannot fault Ohio for attempting to stamp out this vice at all levels in the distribution chain. * * *

"Osborne contends that it was impermissible for the Ohio Supreme Court to apply its [narrowed] construction of the statute when evaluating his overbreadth claim.[c] Our cases, however, have long held that a statute as construed 'may be applied to conduct occurring prior to the construction, provided such application

constitutional applications, see Richard Fallon, *Making Sense of Overbreadth,* 100 Yale L.J. 853, 894 (1991).

a. Ohio excepted material possessed for "bona fide" purposes (e.g., artistic or scientific) or that showed the possessor's child or ward or where the possessor knew that the parents or guardians had consented in writing to the photography and to the manner in which it had been transferred.

b. Two of the photographs focused on the anus of the boy, one with a plastic object apparently inserted; another on his erect penis with an electric object in his hand.

3. We have since indicated that our decision in *Stanley* was "firmly grounded in the

First Amendment." *Bowers v. Hardwick,* p. 516 supra.

5. [T]he *Stanley* Court cited illicit possession of defense information as an example of the type of offense for which compelling state interests might justify a ban on possession. *Stanley,* however, did not suggest that this crime exhausted the entire category of proscribable offenses.

c. Given the statutory limitations and exceptions (see fn. a supra), the Court expressed doubt that the statute was substantially overbroad even without the Ohio Supreme Court's limiting construction although it conceded that the statute by its terms seemed to criminalize some constitutionally protected conduct.

affords fair warning to the defendan[t].'[12]　[That] Osborne's photographs of adolescent boys in sexually explicit situations constitute child pornography hardly needs elaboration.　Therefore, although [Ohio's statute] as written may have been imprecise at its fringes, someone in Osborne's position would not be surprised to learn that his possession of the four photographs at issue in this case constituted a crime.　* * *

"Finally, despite Osborne's contention to the contrary, we do not believe that *Massachusetts v. Oakes,* supports his theory of this case.

"[F]ive of the *Oakes* Justices feared that if we allowed a legislature to correct its mistakes without paying for them (beyond the inconvenience of passing a new law), we would decrease the legislature's incentive to draft a narrowly tailored law in the first place.　[But] a similar effect will not be likely if a judicial construction of a statute to eliminate overbreadth is allowed to be applied in the case before the Court.　This is so primarily because the legislatures cannot be sure that the statute, when examined by a court, will be saved by a narrowing construction rather than invalidated for overbreadth.　In the latter event, there could be no convictions under that law even of those whose own conduct is unprotected by the First Amendment.　Even if construed to obviate overbreadth, applying the statute to pending cases might be barred by the Due Process Clause.　Thus, careless drafting cannot be considered to be cost free based on the power of the courts to eliminate overbreadth by statutory construction.　* * *

"To conclude, although we find Osborne's First Amendment arguments unpersuasive, we reverse his conviction and remand for a new trial in order to ensure that Osborne's conviction stemmed from a finding that the State had proved each of the elements of the Ohio statute."[d]

Brennan, J., joined by Marshall, J., and Stevens, J., dissented: "As written, the Ohio statute is plainly overbroad.[2]　* * *

12.　This principle, of course, accords with the rationale underlying overbreadth challenges.　We normally do not allow a defendant to challenge a law as it is applied to others.　In the First Amendment context, however, we have said that "[b]ecause of the sensitive nature of constitutionally protected expression, we have not required that all those subject to overbroad regulations risk prosecution to test their rights.　For free expression—of transcendent value to all society, and not merely to those exercising their rights—might be the loser."　But once a statute is authoritatively construed, there is no longer any danger that protected speech will be deterred and therefore no longer any reason to entertain the defendant's challenge to the statute on its face.

d.　Defendant's attorney did not ask for a scienter instruction (even though Ohio law generally provides for a scienter requirement in criminal cases) and the Court stated that Osborne could be precluded from raising the question on remand.　But Osborne did raise the overbreadth issue and was, therefore, entitled to dispute the application of the statute, as construed, to the photographs in his possession even though Osborne's attorney had not specifically objected to the jury instructions.

Blackmun, J., concurring, agreed with the dissent's position that due process entitled the defendant to instructions on "lewd exhibition" and "graphic focus" without regard to whether an objection had been lodged at trial.

2.　The Court hints that § 2907.323's exemptions and "proper purposes" provisions might save it from being overbroad.　I disagree.　The enumerated "proper purposes" (e.g., a "bona fide artistic, medical, scientific, educational * * * or other proper purpose") are simultaneously too vague and too narrow. What is an acceptable "artistic" purpose? Would erotic art along the lines of Robert Mapplethorpe's qualify?　What is a valid "scientific" or "educational" purpose?　What about sex manuals?　What is a permissible "other proper purpose"?　What about photos taken for one purpose and recirculated for other, more prurient purposes?　The "proper purposes" standard appears to create problems analogous to those this Court has encountered in describing the "redeeming social importance" of obscenity.

At the same time, however, Ohio's list of "proper purposes" is too limited; it excludes such obviously permissible uses as the commercial distribution of fashion photographs or the simple exchange of pictures among family and friends.　Thus, a neighbor or grandparent who receives a photograph of an unclothed toddler might be subject to criminal sanctions.

"Wary of the statute's use of the 'nudity' standard, the Ohio Supreme Court construed § 2907.323(A)(3) to apply only 'where such nudity constitutes a lewd exhibition or involves a graphic focus on the genitals.' The 'lewd exhibition' and 'graphic focus' tests not only fail to cure the overbreadth of the statute, but they also create a new problem of vagueness. * * *

"The Ohio law is distinguishable [from *Ferber*] for several reasons. First, the New York statute did not criminalize materials with a '*graphic focus* ' on the genitals, and, as discussed further below, Ohio's 'graphic focus' test is impermissibly capacious. Even setting aside the 'graphic focus' element, the Ohio Supreme Court's narrowing construction is still overbroad because it focuses on 'lewd exhibitions of *nudity* ' rather than 'lewd exhibitions of *the genitals* ' in the context of *sexual conduct,* as in the New York statute at issue in *Ferber.*[e] Ohio law defines 'nudity' to include depictions of pubic areas, buttocks, the female breast, and covered male genitals 'in a discernibly turgid state,' *as well as* depictions of the genitals. On its face, then, the Ohio law is much broader than New York's. * * *

"Indeed, the broad definition of nudity in the Ohio statutory scheme means that 'child pornography' could include any photograph depicting a 'lewd exhibition' of even a small portion of a minor's buttocks or any part of the female breast below the nipple. Pictures of topless bathers at a Mediterranean beach, of teenagers in revealing dresses, and even of toddlers romping unclothed, all might be prohibited.[5]

"It might be objected that many of these depictions of nudity do not amount to 'lewd exhibitions.' But in the absence of *any* authoritative definition of that phrase by the Ohio Supreme Court, we cannot predict which ones. * * *

"The Ohio Supreme Court, moreover, did not specify the perspective from which 'lewdness' is to be determined. A 'reasonable' person's view of 'lewdness'? A reasonable pedophile's? An 'average' person applying contemporary local community standards? Statewide standards? Nationwide standards? In sum, the addition of a 'lewd exhibition' standard does not narrow adequately the statute's reach. If anything, it creates a new problem of vagueness, affording the public little notice of the statute's ambit and providing an avenue for 'policemen, prosecutors, and juries to pursue their personal predilections.'[12] Given the important First Amendment interests at issue, the vague, broad sweep of the 'lewd exhibition' language means that it cannot cure [the overbreadth problem].

"The Ohio Supreme Court also added a 'graphic focus' element to the nudity definition. This phrase, a stranger to obscenity regulation, suffers from the same vagueness difficulty as 'lewd exhibition.' Although the Ohio Supreme Court failed to elaborate what a 'graphic focus' might be, the test appears to involve nothing more than a subjective estimation of the centrality or prominence of the genitals in a picture or other representation. Not only is this factor dependent on the perspective and idiosyncrasies of the observer, it also is unconnected to whether

---

e. The Court read the Ohio Court's opinion to refer to the lewd exhibition of the genitals rather than the lewd exhibition of nudity, but maintained that the distinction was not important anyway.

5. [A] well-known commercial advertisement for a suntan lotion shows a dog pulling down the bottom half of a young girl's bikini, revealing a stark contrast between her suntanned back and pale buttocks. That this advertisement might be illegal in Ohio is an absurd yet altogether too conceivable conclusion under the language of the [statute.]

12. The danger of discriminatory enforcement assumes particular importance of the context of the instant case, which involves child pornography with male homosexual overtones. Sadly, evidence indicates that the overwhelming majority of arrests for violations of "lewdness" laws involve male homosexuals.

the material at issue merits constitutional protection. Simple nudity, no matter how prominent or 'graphic,' is within the bounds of the First Amendment. Michelangelo's 'David' might be said to have a 'graphic focus' on the genitals, for it plainly portrays them in a manner unavoidable to even a casual observer. Similarly, a painting of a partially clad girl could be said to involve a 'graphic focus,' depending on the picture's lighting and emphasis, as could the depictions of nude children on the friezes that adorn our Courtroom. Even a photograph of a child running naked on the beach or playing in the bathtub might run afoul of the law, depending on the focus and camera angle. * * *

"Even if the statute was not overbroad, our decision in *Stanley* forbids the criminalization of appellant's private possession in his home of the materials at issue. [Appellant] testified that he had been given the pictures in his home by a friend. There was no evidence that the photographs had been produced commercially or distributed. All were kept in an album that appellant had assembled for his personal use and had possessed privately for several years.

"In these circumstances, the Court's focus on *Ferber* rather than *Stanley* is misplaced. [*Ferber*] did nothing more than place child pornography on the same level of First Amendment protection as *obscene* adult pornography, meaning that its production and distribution could be proscribed. The distinction established in *Stanley* between *what* materials may be regulated and *how* they may be regulated still stands. * * *

"At bottom, the Court today is so disquieted by the possible exploitation of children in the *production* of the pornography that it is willing to tolerate the imposition of criminal penalties for simple *possession*. While I share the majority's concerns, I do not believe that it has struck the proper balance between the First Amendment and the State's interests, especially in light of the other means available to Ohio to protect children from exploitation and the State's failure to demonstrate a causal link between a ban on possession of child pornography and a decrease in its production. * * *

"When speech is eloquent and the ideas expressed lofty, it is easy to find restrictions on them invalid. But were the First Amendment limited to such discourse, our freedom would be sterile indeed. Mr. Osborne's pictures may be distasteful, but the Constitution guarantees both his right to possess them privately and his right to avoid punishment under an overbroad law."

B. HARM TO WOMEN: FEMINISM AND PORNOGRAPHY

Catharine MacKinnon and Andrea Dworkin have drafted an anti-pornography ordinance that has been considered in a number of jurisdictions.[a]

PROPOSED LOS ANGELES COUNTY ANTI–PORNOGRAPHY CIVIL RIGHTS LAW

Section 1. Statement of Policy

Pornography is sex discrimination. It exists in the County of Los Angeles, posing a substantial threat to the health, safety, welfare and equality of citizens in

a. The ordinance was first considered in Minneapolis. For political, rhetorical, and sociological discussion, see Paul Brest & Ann Vandenberg, *Politics, Feminism, and the Constitution: The Anti–Pornography Movement in Minneapolis,* 39 Stan.L.Rev. 607 (1987). Different versions of the ordinance were passed in Indianapolis, Indiana (see *Hudnut,* p. 658 infra) and Bellingham, Washington (see Margaret Baldwin, *Pornography and the Traffic in Women,* 1 Yale J.L. & Fem. 111 (1989)). Both versions were declared unconstitutional.

the community. Existing state and federal laws are inadequate to solve these problems in the County of Los Angeles.

Section 2. Findings

Pornography is a systematic practice of exploitation and subordination based on sex which differentially harms women. The harm of pornography includes dehumanization, sexual exploitation, forced sex, forced prostitution, physical injury, and social and sexual terrorism and inferiority presented as entertainment. The bigotry and contempt pornography promotes, with the acts of aggression it fosters, diminish opportunities for equality of rights in employment, education, property, public accommodations and public services; create public and private harassment, persecution and denigration; promote injury and degradation such as rape, battery, child sexual abuse, and prostitution and inhibit just enforcement of laws against these acts; contribute significantly to restricting women in particular from full exercise of citizenship and participation in public life, including in neighborhoods; damage relations between the sexes; and undermine women's equal exercise of rights to speech and action guaranteed to all citizens under the Constitutions and laws of the United States, the State of California and the County of Los Angeles.

Section 3. Definitions

1. *Pornography* is the graphic sexually explicit subordination of women through pictures and/or words that also includes one or more of the following: (i) women are presented dehumanized as sexual objects, things or commodities; or (ii) women are presented as sexual objects who enjoy pain or humiliation; or (iii) women are presented as sexual objects who experience sexual pleasure in being raped; or (iv) women are presented as sexual objects tied up or cut up or mutilated or bruised or physically hurt; or (v) women are presented in postures of sexual submission, servility, or display; or (vi) women's body parts—including but not limited to vaginas, breasts, or buttocks—are exhibited such that women are reduced to those parts; or (vii) women are presented as whores by nature; or (viii) women are presented as being penetrated by objects or animals; or (ix) women are presented in scenarios of degradation, injury, torture, shown as filthy or inferior, bleeding, bruised or hurt in a context that makes these conditions sexual.

2. The use of men, children, or transsexuals in the place of women in (1) above is also pornography for purposes of this law.

Section 4. Unlawful Practices

1. *Coercion into pornography*: It shall be sex discrimination to coerce, intimidate, or fraudulently induce (hereafter, "coerce") any person, including transsexual, into performing for pornography, which injury may date from any appearance or sale of any product(s) of such performance(s). The maker(s), seller(s), exhibitor(s) and/or distributor(s) of said pornography may be sued, including for an injunction to eliminate the product(s) of the performance(s) from the public view.

Proof of one or more of the following facts or conditions shall not, without more, negate a finding of coercion:

    (i) that the person is a woman; or

    (ii) that the person is or has been a prostitute; or

(iii) that the person has attained the age of majority; or

(iv) that the person is connected by blood or marriage to anyone involved in or related to the making of the pornography; or

(v) that the person has previously had, or been thought to have had, sexual relations with anyone, including anyone involved in or related to the making of the pornography; or

(vi) that the person has previously posed for sexually explicit pictures with or for anyone, including anyone involved in or related to the making of the pornography at issue; or

(vii) that anyone else, including a spouse or other relative, has given permission on the person's behalf; or

(viii) that the person actually consented to a use of the performance that is changed into pornography; or

(ix) that the person knew that the purpose of the acts or events in question was to make pornography; or

(x) that the person showed no resistance or appeared to cooperate actively in the photographic sessions or in the events that produced the pornography; or

(xi) that the person signed a contract, or made statements affirming a willingness to cooperate in the production of pornography; or

(xii) that no physical force, threats, or weapons were used in the making of the pornography; or

(xiii) that the person was paid or otherwise compensated.

2. *Trafficking in pornography:* It shall be sex discrimination to produce, sell, exhibit, or distribute pornography, including through private clubs.

(i) City, state, and federally funded public libraries or private and public university and college libraries in which pornography is available for study, including on open shelves but excluding special display presentations, shall not be construed to be trafficking in pornography.

(ii) Isolated passages or isolated parts shall not be actionable under this section.

(iii) Any woman has a claim hereunder as a woman acting against the subordination of women. Any man, child, or transsexual who alleges injury by pornography in the way women are injured by it also has a claim.

3. *Forcing pornography on a person:* It shall be sex discrimination to force pornography on a person, including child or transsexual, in any place of employment, education, home, or public place. Only the perpetrator of the force and/or institution responsible for the force may be sued.

4. *Assault or physical attack due to pornography:* It shall be sex discrimination to assault, physically attack or injure any person, including child or transsexual, in a way that is directly caused by specific pornography. The perpetrator of the assault or attack may be sued. The maker(s), distributor(s), seller(s), and/or exhibitor(s) may also be sued, including for an injunction against the specific pornography's further exhibition, distribution or sale.

Section 5. Defenses

1. It shall not be a defense that the defendant in an action under this law did not know or intend that the materials were pornography or sex discrimination.

2. No damages or compensation for losses shall be recoverable under Sec. 4(2) or other than against the perpetrator of the assault or attack in Sec. 4(4) unless the defendant knew or had reason to know that the materials were pornography.

3. In actions under Sec. 4(2) or other than against the perpetrator of the assault or attack in Sec. 4(4), no damages or compensation for losses shall be recoverable against maker(s) for pornography made, against distributor(s) for pornography distributed, against seller(s) for pornography sold, or against exhibitor(s) for pornography exhibited, prior to the effective date of this law.

Section 6. Enforcement

a. Civil Action: Any person, or their estate, aggrieved by violations of this law may enforce its provisions by means of a civil action. No criminal penalties shall attach for any violation of the provisions of this law. Relief for violations of this law, except as expressly restricted or precluded herein, may include compensatory and punitive damages and reasonable attorney's fees, costs and disbursements.

b. Injunction: Any person who violates this law may be enjoined except that:

(i) In actions under Sec. 4(2), and other than against the perpetrator of the assault or attack under Sec. 4(4), no temporary or permanent injunction shall issue prior to a final judicial determination that the challenged activities constitute a violation of this law.

(ii) No temporary or permanent injunction shall extend beyond such material(s) that, having been described with reasonable specificity by the injunction, have been determined to be validly proscribed under this law.

Section 7. Severability

Should any part(s) of this law be found legally invalid, the remaining part(s) remain valid. A judicial declaration that any part(s) of this law cannot be applied validly in a particular manner or to a particular case or category of cases shall not affect the validity of that part(s) as otherwise applied, unless such other application would clearly frustrate the intent of the Board of Supervisors in adopting this law.

Section 8. Limitation of Action

Actions under this law must be filed within one year of the alleged discriminatory acts.

Notes and Questions

1. *Relationship between obscenity and pornography.* Consider Andrea Dworkin, *Against the Male Flood: Censorship, Pornography, and Equality,* 8 Harv. Women's L.J. 1, 8–9 (1985): "What is at stake in obscenity law is always erection: under what conditions, in what circumstances, how, by whom, by what materials men want it produced in themselves. Men have made this public policy. Why they want to regulate their own erections through law is a question of endless interest and importance to feminists. * * *

"The insult pornography offers, invariably, to sex is accomplished in the active subordination of women: the creation of a sexual dynamic in which the putting-down of women, the suppression of women, and ultimately the brutalization of women, *is* what sex is taken to be. Obscenity in law, and in what it does socially, is erection. Law recognizes the act in this. Pornography, however, is a broader, more comprehensive act, because it crushes a whole class of people through violence and subjugation: and sex is the vehicle that does the crushing. The penis is not the test, as it is in obscenity. Instead, the status of women is the issue. Erection is implicated in the subordinating, but who it reaches and how are the pressing legal and social questions. Pornography, unlike obscenity, is a discrete, identifiable system of sexual exploitation that hurts women as a class by creating inequality and abuse."

Consider Catharine MacKinnon, *Pornography, Civil Rights, and Speech*, 20 Harv.Civ.Rts.—Civ.Lib.L.Rev. 1, 50–52 & 16–17 (1985): "Under the obscenity rubric, much legal and psychological scholarship has centered on a search for the elusive link between pornography defined as obscenity and harm. They have looked high and low—in the mind of the male consumer, in society or in its 'moral fabric,' in correlations between variations in levels of anti-social acts and liberalization of obscenity laws. The only harm they have found has been one they have attributed to 'the social interests in order and morality.' Until recently, no one looked very persistently for harm to women, particularly harm to women through men. The rather obvious fact that the sexes *relate* has been overlooked in the inquiry into the male consumer and his mind. The pornography doesn't just drop out of the sky, go into his head and stop there. Specifically, men rape, batter, prostitute, molest, and sexually harass women. Under conditions of inequality, they also hire, fire, promote, and grade women, decide how much or whether or not we are worth paying and for what, define and approve and disapprove of women in ways that count, that determine our lives.

"In pornography, there it is, in one place, all of the abuses that women had to struggle so long even to begin to articulate, all the *unspeakable* abuse: the rape, the battery, the sexual harassment, the prostitution, and the sexual abuse of children. Only in the pornography it is called something else: sex, sex, sex, sex, and sex, respectively. Pornography sexualizes rape, battery, sexual harassment, prostitution, and child sexual abuse; it thereby celebrates, promotes, authorizes, and legitimizes them. More generally, it eroticizes the dominance and submission that is the dynamic common to them all. It makes hierarchy sexy and calls that 'the truth about sex' or just a mirror of reality." See generally Andrea Dworkin, *Pornography: Men Possessing Women* (1981). Catharine MacKinnon, *Only Words* (1993); Catharine MacKinnon, *Toward a Feminist Theory of the State* 195–214 (1989); Catharine MacKinnon, *Feminism Unmodified* 127–228 (1987).

2. *The trafficking section.* Is the trafficking section constitutional under *Miller?* Consider the following hypothetical commentary: "The Dworkin-MacKinnon proposal focuses on a narrower class of material than *Miller* because it excludes erotic materials that do not involve subordination. That class of material upon which it does focus appeals to prurient interest because it is graphic and sexually explicit. Moreover, the eroticization of dominance in the ways specified in the ordinance is so patently offensive to community standards that it can be said as a matter of law that this class of materials lacks *serious* literary, artistic, political, or scientific value as a matter of law." Do you agree?

Is there a good analogy to *Beauharnais?* To *Ferber?* Did more or less harm exist in *Gertz? Miller? Ferber?* Was there more or less of a threat to first amendment values in *Gertz? Miller? Ferber?* Should this be accepted as a new category? Consider Wendy Kaminer, *Pornography and the First Amendment: Prior Restraints and Private Action,* 239, 245 in *Take Back the Night: Women on Pornography* (Laura Lederer ed. 1980): "The Women's Movement is a civil rights movement, and we should appreciate the importance of individual freedom of choice and the danger of turning popular sentiment into law in areas affecting individual privacy.

"Legislative or judicial control of pornography is simply not possible without breaking down the legal principles and procedures that are essential to our own right to speak and, ultimately, our freedom to control our own lives. We must continue to organize against pornography and the degradation and abuse of women, but we must not ask the government to take up our struggle for us. The power it will assume to do so will be far more dangerous to us all than the 'power' of pornography." [b]

3. *Pornography and Dissent.* See Rae Langton, *Speech Acts and Unspeakable Acts,* 22 Phil. & Pub.Aff. 293, 311–312 (1993): "What is important here is not whether the speech of pornographers is universally held in high esteem: it is not—hence the common assumption among liberals that in defending pornographers they are defending the underdog. What is important is whether it is authoritative in the domain that counts—the domain of speech about sex—and whether it is authoritative for the hearers that count: people, men, boys, who in addition to wanting 'entertainment,' want to discover the right way to do things, want to know which moves in the sexual game are legitimate. What is important is whether it is authoritative for those hearers who—one way or another—do seem to learn that violence is sexy and coercion legitimate: the fifty percent of boys who 'think it is okay for a man to rape a woman if he is sexually aroused by her,' the

b. Compare Nan Hunter & Sylvia Law, *Brief Amici Curiae of Feminist Anti-Censorship Taskforce* (on appeal in *Hudnut,* below), 21 U.Mich.J.L.Ref. 69, 109 & 129–30 (1987–88). The ordinance conceivably "would require the judiciary to impose its views of correct sexuality on a diverse community. The inevitable result would be to disapprove those images that are least conventional and privilege those that are closest to majoritarian beliefs about proper sexuality. [Moreover] [b]y defining sexually explicit images of women as subordinating and degrading to them, the ordinance reinforces the stereotypical view that 'good' women do not seek and enjoy sex. [Finally], the ordinance perpetuates a stereotype of women as helpless victims, incapable of consent, and in need of protection."

For collections of feminist perspectives, see *Take Back the Night,* supra; Varda Burstyn, ed., *Women Against Censorship* (1985); Ann Snitow, Christine Stansell & Sharon Thompson, etc., *Powers of Desire* 419–67 (1983). For a variety of views (including feminist views), see Joshua Cohen, *Freedom of Expression,* 21 Phil.&Pub.Aff. 207 (1993). Deborah Rhode, *Justice and Gender,* 263–73 (1989); Mark Tushnet, *Red, White, and Blue* 293–312 (1988); Donald Downs, *The Attorney General's Commission and the New Politics of Pornography,* 1987 Am.B.Found.Res.J. 641; Steven Gey, *The Apologetics of Suppression,* 86 Mich.L.Rev.

1564 (1988); Eric Hoffman, *Feminism, Pornography, and the Law,* 133 U.Pa.L.Rev. 497 (1985); Robert Post, *Cultural Heterogeneity and the Law,* 76 Calif.L.Rev. 297 (1988); David Richards, *Pornography Commissions and the First Amendment,* 39 Me.L.Rev. 275 (1987); Frederick Schauer, *Causation Theory and the Causes of Sexual Violence,* 1987 Am.B.Found. Res.J. 737; Suzanna Sherry, *An Essay Concerning Toleration,* 71 Minn.L.Rev. 963 (1987); Geoffrey Stone, *Anti–Pornography Legislation as Viewpoint–Discrimination,* 9 Harv.J.Pub. Pol'y 461 (1986); Nadine Strossen, *The Convergence of Feminist and Civil Liberties Principles in the Pornography Debate,* 62 N.Y.U.L.Rev. 201 (1987); Cass Sunstein, *Pornography and the First Amendment,* 1986 Duke L.J. 589; Robin West, *The Feminist–Conservative Anti–Pornography Alliance and the 1986 Attorney General's Commission on Pornography Report,* 1987 Am.B.Found.Res.J. 681; Note, *Violent Pornography and the Obscenity Doctrine,* 75 Geo.L.J. 1475 (1987); Note, *Anti-Pornography Laws and First Amendment Values,* 98 Harv.L.Rev. 460 (1984). See also *American Booksellers Ass'n v. Hudnut,* 771 F.2d 323 (7th Cir.1985) (declaring Indianapolis ordinance unconstitutional). For the Canadian approach, see *Regina v. Butler,* [1992] 1 S.C.R. 452. For comparative commentary, see Kent Greenawalt, *Fighting Words* 99–123 (1995).

fifteen percent of male college undergraduates who say they have raped a woman on a date, the eighty-six percent who say that they enjoy the conquest part of sex, the thirty percent who rank faces of women displaying pain and fear to be more sexually attractive than faces showing pleasure."

4. *Subordination.* Is the absence of subordination an appropriate ideal? Consider Carlin Meyer, *Sex, Sin, and Women's Liberation: Against Porn–Suppression,* 72 Tex.L.Rev. 1097, 1133 n. 156, 1154–55 (1994): "I am not suggesting that sex accompanied by intimacy, respect, and caring is not an appropriate ideal. Rather, I mean to argue that the sort of equality in which no one is ever the aggressor in fantasy or in reality is, at best, a 'utopian vision of sexual relations: sex without power, sex without persuasion, sex without pursuit.' [S]exual discourse needs to be free-wheeling and uncontrolled because of the hotly contested nature of issues concerning sexuality. Such issues as what constitutes pleasure for women and its connection to danger, to power, to men, and to aggression and inequality; of what sex is 'good' and 'bad'; and of whether women can escape inequality and coercion within Western sexual culture are debated and dissected with little agreement across boundaries of class, race, and nationality. Allies on other issues disagree about whether all violence is bad, over what constitutes violence or pleasure, and over the meaning of such terms as 'objectified,' 'degraded,' or 'demeaned.' " See also Susan Keller, *Viewing and Doing: Complicating Pornography's Meaning,* 81 Geo.L.J. 2195, 2231 (1993): "[R]obin West critiques MacKinnon and Dworkin for their failure to acknowledge the 'meaning and the value, to women, of the pleasure we take in our fantasies of eroticized submission.' Some like Jessica Benjamin and Kate Ellis have attempted to explain psychologically why pleasure can be found by women, as well as men, in submission and power. Of the various meanings pornography could have for a variety of audience members, one meaning for women could be pleasure in depictions of power."

5. *The pornography definition.* Is the proposed definition too vague? Is it more or less vague than the terminology employed in *Miller?* Is there a core of clear meaning? How would you clarify its meaning? Is the definition overbroad? What revisions, if any, would you suggest to narrow its scope?

Consider Thomas Emerson, *Pornography and the First Amendment: A Reply to Professor MacKinnon,* 3 Yale L. & Pol. Rev. 130, 131–32 (1985): "The sweep of the Indianapolis Ordinance is breathtaking. It would subject to governmental ban virtually all depictions of rape, verbal or pictorial, and a substantial proportion of other presentations of sexual encounters. More specifically, it would outlaw such works of literature as the *Arabian Nights,* John Cleland's *Fanny Hill,* Henry Miller's *Tropic of Cancer,* William Faulkner's *Sanctuary,* and Norman Mailer's *Ancient Evenings,* to name but a few. The ban would extend from Greek mythology and Shakespeare to the millions of copies of 'romance novels' now being sold in the supermarkets. It would embrace much of the world's art, from ancient carvings to Picasso, well-known films too numerous to mention, and a large amount of commercial advertising.

"The scope of the Indianapolis Ordinance is not accidental. Nor could it be limited by more precise drafting without defeating the purpose of its authors. As Professor MacKinnon emphasizes, male domination has deep, pervasive and ancient roots in our society, so it is not surprising that our literature, art, entertainment and commercial practices are permeated by attitudes and behavior that create and reflect the inferior status of women. If the answer to the problem, as Professor MacKinnon describes it, is government suppression of sexual expression that contributes to female subordination, then the net of restraint has to be cast on a nearly limitless scale. Even narrowing the proscribed area to depictions of sexual activities involving violence would outlaw a large segment of the world's literature and art."

Is the proposed ordinance susceptible to a narrower construction than that offered by Professor Emerson?

6. *The Ferber analogy.* Consider Cass Sunstein, *Neutrality in Constitutional Law (With Special Reference to Pornography, Abortion, and Surrogacy)*, 92 Colum.L.Rev. 1, 24 (1992): "A successful action for rape and sexual assault is difficult enough. The difficulty becomes all the greater when the victims are young women coerced into, and abused during, the production of pornography. Often those victims will be reluctant to put themselves through the experience and possible humiliation and expense of initiating a proceeding. Often prosecutors will be reluctant to act on their behalf. Often they will have extremely little credibility even if they are willing to come forward. In this light, the only realistically effective way to eliminate the practice is to eliminate or reduce the financial benefits."

7. *The assault provision.* Should the maker of a pornographic work be responsible for assaults prompted by the work? Should the maker of non-pornographic works be responsible for imitative assaults. In *Olivia N. v. NBC*, 126 Cal.App.3d 488, 178 Cal.Rptr. 888 (1981), the victim of a sexual assault allegedly imitating a sexual assault in NBC's "Born Innocent" sued the network. Olivia N. claimed that NBC negligently exposed her to serious risk because it knew or should have known that someone would imitate the act portrayed in the movie. Suppose Olivia N. could show that NBC had been advised that such an assault was likely if the movie were shown? Should a court analogize to cases like *Gertz?* The California court ruled that Olivia N. could not prevail unless she met the *Brandenburg* standard.[c]

———

The Indianapolis version of the anti-pornography civil rights ordinance was struck down in AMERICAN BOOKSELLERS ASS'N v. HUDNUT, 771 F.2d 323 (7th Cir.1985), affirmed, 475 U.S. 1001, 106 S.Ct. 1172, 89 L.Ed.2d 291 (1986). The Seventh Circuit, per Easterbrook, J., ruled that the definition of pornography infected the entire ordinance (including provisions against trafficking, coercion into pornography, forcing pornography on a person, and assault or physical attack due to pornography) because it impermissibly discriminated on the basis of point of view: "Indianapolis enacted an ordinance defining 'pornography' as a practice that discriminates against women. * * *

"The Indianapolis ordinance does not refer to the prurient interest, to offensiveness, or to the standards of the community. It demands attention to particular depictions, not to the work judged as a whole. It is irrelevant under the ordinance whether the work has literary, artistic, political, or scientific value. The City and many amici point to these omissions as virtues. They maintain that pornography influences attitudes, and the statute is a way to alter the socialization of men and women rather than to vindicate community standards of offensiveness. And as one of the principal drafters of the ordinance has asserted, 'if a

c. For relevant commentary, see J.M. Balkin, *The Rhetoric of Responsibility*, 76 Va. L.Rev. 197 (1990); Frederick Schauer, *Uncoupling Free Speech*, 92 Colum.L.Rev. 1321 (1992); Frederick Schauer, *Mrs. Palsgraf and the First Amendment*, 47 Wash. & Lee L.Rev. 161 (1990).

woman is subjected, why should it matter that the work has other value?'
Catharine MacKinnon, *Pornography, Civil Rights, and Speech,* 20 Harv.Civ.Rts.—
Civ.Lib.L.Rev. 1, 21 (1985).

"Civil rights groups and feminists have entered this case as amici on both
sides. Those supporting the ordinance say that it will play an important role in
reducing the tendency of men to view women as sexual objects, a tendency that
leads to both unacceptable attitudes and discrimination in the workplace and
violence away from it. Those opposing the ordinance point out that much radical
feminist literature is explicit and depicts women in ways forbidden by the
ordinance and that the ordinance would reopen old battles. It is unclear how
Indianapolis would treat works from James Joyce's *Ulysses* to Homer's *Iliad;*
both depict women as submissive objects for conquest and domination.

"We do not try to balance the arguments for and against an ordinance such as
this. The ordinance discriminates on the ground of the content of the speech.
Speech treating women in the approved way—in sexual encounters 'premised on
equality' (MacKinnon, supra, at 22)—is lawful no matter how sexually explicit.
Speech treating women in the disapproved way—as submissive in matters sexual
or as enjoying humiliation—is unlawful no matter how significant the literary,
artistic, or political qualities of the work taken as a whole. The state may not
ordain preferred viewpoints in this way. The Constitution forbids the state to
declare one perspective right and silence opponents.[a] [Under] the First Amendment the government must leave to the people the evaluation of ideas. Bald or
subtle, an idea is as powerful as the audience allows it to be. A belief may be
pernicious—the beliefs of Nazis led to the death of millions, those of the Klan to
the repression of millions. A pernicious belief may prevail. Totalitarian governments today rule much of the planet, practicing suppression of billions and
spreading dogma that may enslave others. One of the things that separates our
society from theirs is our absolute right to propagate opinions that the government finds wrong or even hateful. * * *

"Under the ordinance graphic sexually explicit speech is 'pornography' or not
depending on the perspective the author adopts. Speech that 'subordinates'
women and also, for example, presents women as enjoying pain, humiliation, or
rape, or even simply presents women in 'positions of servility or submission or
display' is forbidden, no matter how great the literary or political value of the
work taken as a whole. Speech that portrays women in positions of equality is
lawful, no matter how graphic the sexual content. This is thought control. It
establishes an 'approved' view of women, of how they may react to sexual
encounters, of how the sexes may relate to each other. Those who espouse the
approved view may use sexual images; those who do not, may not.

"Indianapolis justifies the ordinance on the ground that pornography affects
thoughts. Men who see women depicted as subordinate are more likely to treat
them so. Pornography is an aspect of dominance.[1] It does not persuade people so

---

a. But consider Alon Harel, *Bigotry, Pornography, and The First Amendment: A Theory of Unprotected Speech,* 65 S.Cal.L.Rev. 1887,
1889 (1992): "Some ideas and values cannot
aid in the process of shaping our political obligations. This is not because these 'values' do
not, as a matter of fact, influence the output of
the political process but because any influence
they do exert does not generate legitimate political obligations. Racist and sexist values
cannot participate in the shaping of political

obligations because the legal obligations they
generate do not have morally binding force."

1. "Pornography constructs what a woman
is in terms of its view of what men want
sexually. * * * Pornography's world of equality is a harmonious and balanced place. Men
and women are perfectly complementary and
perfectly bipolar. [All] the ways men love to
take and violate women, women love to be
taken and violated. [What] pornography *does*

much as change them. It works by socializing, by establishing the expected and the permissible. In this view pornography is not an idea; pornography is the injury.

"There is much to this perspective. Beliefs are also facts. People often act in accordance with the images and patterns they find around them. People raised in a religion tend to accept the tenets of that religion, often without independent examination. People taught from birth that black people are fit only for slavery rarely rebelled against that creed; beliefs coupled with the self-interest of the masters established a social structure that inflicted great harm while enduring for centuries. Words and images act at the level of the subconscious before they persuade at the level of the conscious. Even the truth has little chance unless a statement fits within the framework of beliefs that may never have been subjected to rational study.

"Therefore we accept the premises of this legislation. Depictions of subordination tend to perpetuate subordination. The subordinate status of women in turn leads to affront and lower pay at work, insult and injury at home, battery and rape on the streets.[2] * * *

"Yet this simply demonstrates the power of pornography as speech. All of these unhappy effects depend on mental intermediation. Pornography affects how people see the world, their fellows, and social relations. If pornography is what pornography does, so is other speech. Hitler's orations affected how some Germans saw Jews. Communism is a world view, not simply a *Manifesto* by Marx and Engels or a set of speeches. Efforts to suppress communist speech in the United States were based on the belief that the public acceptability of such ideas would increase the likelihood of totalitarian government. [Many] people believe that the existence of television, apart from the content of specific programs, leads to intellectual laziness, to a penchant for violence, to many other ills. The Alien and Sedition Acts passed during the administration of John Adams rested on a sincerely held belief that disrespect for the government leads to social collapse and

goes beyond its content: It eroticizes hierarchy, it sexualizes inequality. It makes dominance and submission sex. Inequality is its central dynamic; the illusion of freedom coming together with the reality of force is central to its working. [P]ornography is neither harmless fantasy nor a corrupt and confused misrepresentation of an otherwise neutral and healthy sexual situation. It institutionalizes the sexuality of male supremacy, fusing the erotization of dominance and submission with the social construction of male and female. * * * Men treat women as who they see women as being. Pornography constructs who that is. Men's power over women means that the way men see women defines who women can be. Pornography [is] a sexual reality." MacKinnon, supra, at 17–18 (note omitted, emphasis in original). See also Andrea Dworkin, *Pornography: Men Possessing Women* (1981). A national commission in Canada recently adopted a similar rationale for controlling pornography. Special Commission on Pornography and Prostitution, 1 *Pornography and Prostitution in Canada* 49–59 (1985).

2. MacKinnon's article collects empirical work that supports this proposition. The social science studies are very difficult to interpret, however, and they conflict. Because much of the effect of speech comes through a process of socialization, it is difficult to measure incremental benefits and injuries caused by particular speech. Several psychologists have found, for example, that those who see violent, sexually explicit films tend to have more violent thoughts. But how often does this lead to actual violence? National commissions on obscenity here, in the United Kingdom, and in Canada have found that it is not possible to demonstrate a direct link between obscenity and rape or exhibitionism. The several opinions in *Miller* discuss the U.S. commission. See also *Report of the Committee on Obscenity and Film Censorship* 61–95 (Home Office, Her Majesty's Stationery Office, 1979); 1 *Pornography and Prostitution in Canada* 71–73, 95–103. In saying that we accept the finding that pornography as the ordinance defines it leads to unhappy consequences, we mean only that there is evidence to this effect, that this evidence is consistent with much human experience, and that as judges we must accept the legislative resolution of such disputed empirical questions.

revolution—a belief with support in the history of many nations. Most governments of the world act on this empirical regularity, suppressing critical speech. In the United States, however, the strength of the support for this belief is irrelevant. Seditious libel is protected speech unless the danger is not only grave but also imminent. See *New York Times*; cf. *Brandenburg*.

"Racial bigotry, anti-semitism, violence on television, reporters' biases—these and many more influence the culture and shape our socialization. None is directly answerable by more speech, unless that speech too finds its place in the popular culture. Yet all is protected as speech, however insidious. Any other answer leaves the government in control of all of the institutions of culture, the great censor and director of which thoughts are good for us.

"Sexual responses often are unthinking responses, and the association of sexual arousal with the subordination of women therefore may have a substantial effect. But almost all cultural stimuli provoke unconscious responses. Religious ceremonies condition their participants. Teachers convey messages by selecting what not to cover; the implicit message about what is off limits or unthinkable may be more powerful than the messages for which they present rational argument. Television scripts contain unarticulated assumptions. People may be conditioned in subtle ways. If the fact that speech plays a role in a process of conditioning were enough to permit governmental regulation, that would be the end of freedom of speech. * * *

"Much of Indianapolis's argument rests on the belief that when speech is 'unanswerable,' and the metaphor that there is a 'marketplace of ideas' does not apply, the First Amendment does not apply either. The metaphor is honored; Milton's *Aeropagitica* and John Stewart Mill's *On Liberty* defend freedom of speech on the ground that the truth will prevail, and many of the most important cases under the First Amendment recite this position. The Framers undoubtedly believed it. As a general matter it is true. But the Constitution does not make the dominance of truth a necessary condition of freedom of speech. To say that it does would be to confuse an outcome of free speech with a necessary condition for the application of the amendment.

"A power to limit speech on the ground that truth has not yet prevailed and is not likely to prevail implies the power to declare truth. At some point the government must be able to say (as Indianapolis has said): 'We know what the truth is, yet a free exchange of speech has not driven out falsity, so that we must now prohibit falsity.' If the government may declare the truth, why wait for the failure of speech? Under the First Amendment, however, there is no such thing as a false idea, *Gertz*, so the government may not restrict speech on the ground that in a free exchange truth is not yet dominant. * * *

"We come, finally, to the argument that pornography is 'low value' speech, that it is enough like obscenity that Indianapolis may prohibit it. Some cases hold that speech far removed from politics and other subjects at the core of the Framers' concerns may be subjected to special regulation. E.g., *FCC v. Pacifica Foundation* [p. 954 infra]; *Young v. American Mini Theatres*; *Chaplinsky*. These cases do not sustain statutes that select among viewpoints, however. In *Pacifica* the FCC sought to keep vile language off the air during certain times. The Court held that it may; but the Court would not have sustained a regulation prohibiting scatological descriptions of Republicans but not scatological descriptions of Democrats, or any other form of selection among viewpoints.

"At all events, pornography is not low value speech within the meaning of these cases. Indianapolis seeks to prohibit certain speech because it believes this speech influences social relations and politics on a grand scale, that it controls attitudes at home and in the legislature. This precludes a characterization of the speech as low value. True, pornography and obscenity have sex in common. But Indianapolis left out of its definition any reference to literary, artistic, political, or scientific value. The ordinance applies to graphic sexually explicit subordination in works great and small.[3] The Court sometimes balances the value of speech against the costs of its restriction, but it does this by category of speech and not by the content of particular works. See John Hart Ely, *Flag Desecration: A Case Study in the Roles of Categorization and Balancing in First Amendment Analysis*, 88 Harv.L.Rev. 1482 (1975); Geoffrey Stone, *Restrictions of Speech Because of its Content: The Strange Case of Subject–Matter Restrictions*, 46 U.Chi.L.Rev. 81 (1978). Indianapolis has created an approved point of view and so loses the support of these cases.

"Any rationale we could imagine in support of this ordinance could not be limited to sex discrimination. Free speech has been on balance an ally of those seeking change. Governments that want stasis start by restricting speech. Culture is a powerful force of continuity; Indianapolis paints pornography as a part of the culture of power. Change in any complex system ultimately depends on the ability of outsiders to challenge accepted views and the reigning institutions. Without a strong guarantee of freedom of speech, there is no effective right to challenge what is." [a]

Notes and Questions

1. In response to the last paragraph, supra, Professor Frank Michelman observes: "[I]t is a fair and obvious question why preservation of 'effective right[s] to challenge what is' does not require protection of a 'freedom of speech' more broadly conceived to protect social critics—'outsiders,' in Judge Easterbrook's phrase—against suppression by nongovernmental as well as by governmental power. It is a fair and obvious question why the assertion that '[g]overnments that want stasis start by restricting speech' does not apply equally to the nongovernmental agencies of power in society. It is a fair and obvious question why our society's openness to challenge does not need protection against repressive private as well as public action." *Conceptions of Democracy in American Constitutional Argument: The Case of Pornography Regulation*, 56 Tenn.L.Rev. 291 (1989), citing MacKinnon, *Feminism Unmodified* 155–58 (1987).

2. *Free speech and silence.* Consider Catharine MacKinnon, *Toward a Feminist Theory of the State* 206 (1989): "That pornography chills women's

---

3. Indianapolis briefly argues that *Beauharnais*, which allowed a state to penalize "group libel," supports the ordinance. In *Collin v. Smith*, [p. 757 infra], we concluded that cases such as *New York Times v. Sullivan* had so washed away the foundations of *Beauharnais* that it could not be considered authoritative. If we are wrong in this, however, the case still does not support the ordinance. It is not clear that depicting women as subordinate in sexually explicit ways, even combined with a depiction of pleasure in rape, would fit within the definition of a group libel. The well received film *Swept Away* used explicit sex, plus taking pleasure in rape, to make a political statement, not to defame. Work must be an insult or slur for its own sake to come within the ambit of *Beauharnais,* and a work need not

be scurrilous at all to be pornography under the ordinance.

a. The balance of the opinion suggested ways that parts of the ordinance might be salvaged, if redrafted. It suggested, for example, that the city might forbid coerced participation in any film or in "any film containing explicit sex." If the latter were adopted, would it make a difference if the section applied to persons coerced into participation in such films without regard to whether they were forced into explicit sex scenes? Swygert, J., concurring, joined part of Easterbrook, J.'s opinion for the court, but objected both to the "questionable and broad assertions regarding how human behavior can be conditioned" and to the "advisory" opinion on how parts of the ordinance might be redrafted.

expression is difficult to demonstrate empirically because silence is not eloquent. Yet on no more of the same kind of evidence, the argument that suppressing pornography might chill legitimate speech has supported its protection. [T]he law of the First Amendment comprehends that freedom of expression, in the abstract, is a system but fails to comprehend that sexism (and racism), in the concrete, are also systems."

3. *"We do not try to balance * * *."* Does the existence of point of view discrimination preclude balancing under existing law? Consider MacKinnon, supra at 213: In *Hudnut,* "[o]bscenity law, which is based on nothing but value judgments about morality, was presented as the standard for constitutional point-of-viewlessness. The Court saw legal intervention against acts (most of which are already crimes) as 'point of view' discrimination without doubting the constitutionality of state intervention against obscenity, which has no connection with acts and is expressly defined on the basis of point of view about sex. [When] is a point of view not a point of view? When it is yours * * *. In the epistemologically hermetic doublethink of the male point of view, prohibiting advances toward sex equality under law is state neutrality."

4. Does pornography as defined by Indianapolis (or some part of that category) implicate such little first amendment value as to foreclose constitutional protection? How should such value be assessed? Consider Cass Sunstein, *Pornography and the First Amendment,* 1986 Duke Law Journal 603–04: "First, the speech must be far afield from the central concern of the first amendment, which, broadly speaking, is effective popular control of public affairs. Speech that concerns governmental processes is entitled to the highest level of protection; speech that has little or nothing to do with public affairs may be accorded less protection. Second, a distinction is drawn between cognitive and noncognitive aspects of speech. Speech that has purely noncognitive appeal will be entitled to less constitutional protection.[b] Third, the purpose of the speaker is relevant: if the speaker is seeking to communicate a message, he will be treated more favorably than if he is not. Fourth, the various classes of low-value speech reflect judgments that in certain areas, government is unlikely to be acting for constitutionally impermissible reasons or producing constitutionally troublesome harms."

How do Sunstein's factors apply to the Indianapolis ordinance?

To what extent is it desirable to consider the value of speech in forging a balance? Compare, e.g., Martin Redish, *The Value of Free Speech,* 130 U.Pa. L.Rev. 591, 596–611 (1982) and Larry Alexander, *Low Value Speech,* 83 Nw. U.L.Rev. 547 (1989) with Cass Sunstein, *Low Value Speech Revisited,* 83 Nw. U.L.Rev. 555 (1989). Reconsider the question after completing Section 3.

C. RACIST SPEECH REVISITED: THE NAZIS

"What do you want to sell in the marketplace? What idea? The idea of murder?"

Erna Gans, a concentration camp survivor and active leader in the Skokie B'nai B'rith.[a]

---

b. For debate about this factor compare Paul Chevigny, *Pornography and Cognition,* 1989 Duke L.J. 420 with Cass Sunstein, *The First Amendment and Cognition,* 1989 Duke L.J. 433. See also Kenneth Karst, *Boundaries and Reasons: Freedom of Expression and the Subordination of Groups,* 1990 U.Ill.L.Rev. 95.

a. Quoted in Fred Friendly & Martha Elliot, *The Constitution: That Delicate Balance* 83 (1984).

COLLIN v. SMITH, 578 F.2d 1197 (7th Cir.), cert. denied, 439 U.S. 916, 99 S.Ct. 291, 58 L.Ed.2d 264 (1978), per PELL, J., struck down a Village of Skokie *"Racial Slur" Ordinance,* making it a misdemeanor to disseminate any material (defined to include "public display of markings and clothing of symbolic significance") promoting and inciting racial or religious hatred. The Village would apparently apply this ordinance to the display of swastikas and military uniforms by the NSPA, a "Nazi organization" which planned to peacefully demonstrate for some 20–30 minutes in front of the Skokie Village Hall.

Although there was some evidence that some individuals "might have difficulty restraining their reactions to the Nazi demonstration," the Village "does not rely on a fear of responsive violence to justify the ordinance, and does not even suggest that there will be any physical violence if the march is held. This confession takes the case out of the scope of *Brandenburg* and *Feiner*. [It] also eliminates any argument based on the fighting words doctrine of *Chaplinsky*, [which] applied only to words with a direct tendency to cause violence by the persons to whom, individually, the words were addressed."

The court rejected, inter alia, the argument that the Nazi march, with its display of swastikas and uniforms, "will create a substantive evil that it has a right to prohibit: the infliction of psychic trauma on resident holocaust survivors [some 5,000] and other Jewish residents. [The] problem with engrafting an exception on the First Amendment for such situations is that they are indistinguishable in principle from speech that 'invite[s] dispute [or] induces a condition of unrest [or] even stirs people to anger,' *Terminiello*. Yet these are among the 'high purposes' of the First Amendment. [Where,] as here, a crime is made of a silent march, attended only by symbols and not by extrinsic conduct offensive in itself, we think the words of *Street v. New York* [p. 677 infra] are very much on point: '[A]ny shock effect [must] be attributed to the content of the ideas expressed. [P]ublic expression of ideas may not be prohibited merely because the ideas are themselves offensive to some of their hearers.' "

Nor was the court impressed with the argument that the proposed march was "not speech, [but] rather an invasion, intensely menacing no matter how peacefully conducted" (most of Skokie's residents are Jewish): "There *need be* no captive audience, as Village residents may, if they wish, simply avoid the Village Hall for thirty minutes on a Sunday afternoon, which no doubt would be their normal course of conduct on a day when the Village Hall was not open in the regular course of business. Absent such intrusion or captivity, there is no justifiable substantial privacy interest to save [the ordinance], when it attempts, by fiat, to declare the entire Village, at all times, a privacy zone that may be sanitized from the offensiveness of Nazi ideology and symbols." [b]

Notes and Questions

1. Is *Beauharnais,* p. 568 supra, still "good law"?

b. See also *Skokie v. National Socialist Party,* 69 Ill.2d 605, 14 Ill.Dec. 890, 373 N.E.2d 21 (1978). For commentary relating the Skokie issue to regulation of pornography, and of commercial speech, for the purpose of asking whether there are general principles of freedom of expression and whether freedom of expression should be category-dependent, see Thomas Scanlon, *Freedom of Expression and Categories of Expression,* 40 U.Pitt.L.Rev. 519 (1979). For assessment of the complicated connection between Skokie and equality values especially in light of the rest of first amendment law, see Laurence Tribe, *Constitutional Choices* 219–20 (1985). Compare Donald Downs, *Skokie Revisited: Hate Group Speech and the First Amendment,* 60 Not.D.Law. 629 (1985). More generally, see David Kretzmer, *Freedom of Speech and Racism,* 8 Cardozo L.Rev. 445 (1987).

2. *Abstraction and the first amendment.* Consider Frederick Schauer, *Harry Kalven and the Perils of Particularism,* 56 U.Chi.L.Rev. 397, 408 (1989): "[O]ne sees in the *Skokie* litigation an available distinction between Nazis and others, an equally available distinction between speech designed to persuade and speech designed to assault, and a decision made by the people rather than a decision designed to interfere with the people's wishes. If doctrinal development under the free speech clause were merely an instance of common law decision making, one might expect to see some or all of these factors treated as relevant, and new distinctions developed in order to make relevant those factors, such as the ones just enumerated, that had been suppressed by previous formulations. Yet we know that this is not what happened. The particular events were abstracted in numerous ways. Nazis became political speakers, a suburban community populated by Holocaust survivors became a public forum, and popularly inspired restrictions became governmental censorship. The resolution of the controversy, therefore, stands not as a monument to the ever-more-sensitive development of common law doctrine, but instead as an embodiment of the way in which the First Amendment operates precisely by the entrenchment of categories whose breadth prevents the consideration of some number of relevant factors, and prevents the free speech decision maker from 'thinking small.' "

3. *Toleration and the Nazis.* Consider Lee Bollinger, *Book Review,* 80 Mich.L.Rev. 617, 631 (1982) (reviewing Aryeh Neier, *Defending My Enemy: American Nazis, The Skokie Case, and the Risks of Freedom* (1979)): "One can understand [a] choice to protect the free speech activities of Nazis, but not because people should value their message in the slightest or believe it should be seriously entertained, not because a commitment to self-government or rationality logically demands that such ideas be presented for consideration, not because of a simple hope *qua* conviction that anti-Nazi sentiment will win in the end, not because the anti-Nazi belief will be stimulated by open confrontation and argument with the Nazi belief, not because a line could not be drawn that would exclude this ideology without inevitably encroaching on ideas that one likes—not for any of these reasons nor others related to them that are a part of the traditional baggage of the free speech argumentation; but rather because the danger of intolerance toward ideas is so pervasive an issue in our social lives, the process of mastering a capacity for tolerance so difficult, that it makes sense somewhere in the system to attempt to confront that problem and exercise more self-restraint than may be otherwise required. We should be, in short, more concerned with addressing through the act of tolerance the potential problems of intolerance than with valuing the act of speech itself.

"On this basis, then, tolerance becomes not merely a futile attempt at shoring up the legal barricades, a response devoid of intrinsic value and meaning, but instead a symbolic act indicating an awareness of the risks and dangers of intolerance and a commitment to developing a certain attitude toward the ideas and beliefs of others. At least a part of this attitude is a willingness to recognize the existence of ideas within society that we might otherwise prefer to ignore, and to see the risks involved in succumbing to the wish to refuse to acknowledge their existence. Self-knowledge may be the best defense available against the ideas that we hate." For rich elaboration of this perspective, see Lee Bollinger, *The Tolerant Society: Freedom of Speech and Extremist Speech in America* (1986).

4. Should the first amendment bar an action for intentional infliction of emotional distress for face-to-face racial insults? [c] Is it enough that the words in

---

c. On the relationship between discriminatory speech and the tort of intentional inflic- tion of emotional distress, see Jean Love, *Discriminatory Speech and the Tort of Intentional*

question inflict injury or must the victim show that the words were likely to promote a fight? Suppose a crowd of whites gathers to taunt a young black child on the way to a previously all white school? Suppose short of using violence, they do everything they can to harm the child? Is it the case that "no government that would call itself a decent government would fail to intervene [and] disperse the crowd" and that "the rights of the crowd [cannot] really stand on the same plane" as the child on the way to school? See Hadley Arkes, *Civility and the Restriction of Speech: Rediscovering the Defamation of Groups,* 1974 Sup.Ct.Rev. 281, 310–11. Should the first amendment bar state criminal or civil actions precisely tailored to punish racial insults? Insults directed against the handicapped? For the case in favor of a tort action against racial insults, see Richard Delgado, *Words That Wound: A Tort Action for Racial Insults, Epithets, and Name–Calling,* 17 Harv.Civ.Rts.—Civ.Lib.L.Rev. 133 (1982). For a spirited exchange, see Marjorie Heins, *Banning Words: A Comment on "Words that Wound,"* 18 Harv.Civ.Rts.—Civ.Lib.L.Rev. 585 (1983) and *Professor Richard Delgado Replies,* Id. at 593.

5. Consider Donald Downs, *Nazis in Skokie* 147 (1985): "[N]either Cohen nor Beauharnais intentionally directed his speech to definite targets, so their speech acts were less assaultive than the speech acts of Collin[.] Had Beauharnais passed his leaflets out in front of black homes or given them directly to blacks in similar settings, the very nature of his speech act would have been transformed from a racialist plea into an act of intimidation."

6. Is one person's "racialist's plea" another person's act of intimidation? Are these responses patterned? Consider Mari Matsuda, *Public Response to Racist Speech: Considering the Victim's Story,* 87 Mich.L.Rev. 2320, 2326–27 (1989): "[I] am forced to ask why the world looks so different to me from how it looks to many of the civil libertarians whom I consider my allies. [In] advocating legal restriction of hate speech, I have found my most sympathetic audience in people who identify with target groups, while I have encountered incredulity, skepticism, and even hostility from others.

"This split in reaction is also evident in case studies of hate speech. The typical reaction of target-group members to an incident of racist propaganda is alarm and immediate calls for redress. The typical reaction of non-target-group members is to consider the incidents isolated pranks,[d] the product of sick-but-harmless minds. This is in part a defensive reaction: a refusal to believe that real people, people just like us, are racists. This disassociation leads logically to the claim that there is no institutional or state responsibility to respond to the incident.[e] It is not the kind of real and pervasive threat that requires the state's power to quell."

See also Charles Lawrence, *If He Hollers Let Him Go: Regulating Racist Speech on Campus,* 1990 Duke L.J. 431, 474–75: "If one asks why we always begin by asking whether we can afford to fight racism rather than asking whether

Infliction of Emotional Distress, 47 Wash. & Lee L.Rev. 123 (1990).

d. For discussion of the extent and character of the harm, see Matsuda, supra; Lawrence, infra; Richard Delgado, *Campus Anti-racism Rules Constitutional Narratives in Collision,* 85 Nw.U.L.Rev. 343, 384 (1991) ("The ubiquity and incessancy of harmful racial depiction are [the] source of its virulence. Like water dripping on sandstone, it is a per-

vasive harm which only the most hardy can resist. Yet the prevailing first amendment paradigm predisposes us to treat racist speech as individual harm, as though we only had to evaluate the effect of a single drop of water.").

e. For the argument that the best interpretation of *Brown v. Board of Education requires* government to respond, see Lawrence, infra. For response, see Strossen, infra.

we can afford not to, or if one asks why my colleagues who oppose all regulation of racist speech do not feel the burden is theirs (to justify a reading of the first amendment that requires sacrificing rights guaranteed under the equal protection clause), then one sees an example of how unconscious racism operates in the marketplace of ideas. [O]ur unconscious racism causes us (even those of us who are the direct victims of racism) to view the first amendment as the 'regular' amendment—an amendment that works for all people—and the equal protection clause and racial equality as a special interest-amendment important to groups that are less valued."

7.   Consider Steven Shiffrin, *Racist Speech, Outsider Jurisprudence, and the Meaning of America,* 80 Corn.L.Rev. 43, 96–97, 103 (1994): "From the perspective of many millions of Americans, to enact racist speech regulations would be to pass yet another law exhibiting special favoritism for people of color. What makes this kind of law so potentially counterproductive is that its transformation of public racists into public martyrs would tap into widespread political traditions and understanding in our culture. In short, the case of the martyr would be appealingly wrapped in the banner of the American flag. Millions of white Americans already resent people of color to some degree. To fuse that resentment with Americans' love for the first amendment is risky business. [America] would still have a FIRST AMENDMENT and a strong first amendment tradition even if it enacted general racist speech regulations. The problem is not the first amendment; the problem is that racism is now and always has been a central part of the meaning of America."

8.   Consider Kenneth Karst, *Boundaries and Reasons: Freedom of Expression and the Subordination of Groups,* 1990 U.Ill.L.Rev. 95, 140–41: "Group libel and pornography each respond to a sense of inadequacy, but the two types of hate literature are circulated differently. Where the defamation of racial or religious groups is driven by the felt inadequacies of its distributors, today's pornography is largely driven by the inadequacies of its consumers, with most distributors simply profiting from that demand and seeking to increase it. In neither case will elimination of the literature cause the underlying sense of inadequacy to disappear. Anxious hatemongers, thwarted in purveying their racist leaflets, can find plenty of other ways to express their fear and hate, as the Ku Klux Klan and the Nazis have made clear. And anxious men, thwarted in the consumption of pornography, can find substitute symbols of sexual objectification not just in magazine ads or on television but in every woman they see."

9.   Consider Stanford University's definition of harassment by personal vilification: "Speech or other expression constitutes harassment by personal vilification if it a) is intended to insult or stigmatize an individual or a small number of individuals on the basis of their sex, race, color, handicap, religion, sexual orientation, or national and ethnic origin; and b) is addressed directly to the individual or individuals whom it insults or stigmatizes; and c) makes use of insulting or 'fighting words' or non-verbal symbols." Is this appropriate? See Thomas Grey, *Civil Rights v. Civil Liberties,* Soc. Phil. & Pol'y 81 (Spring 1991). Does this go too far? See Nadine Strossen, *Regulating Racist Speech on Campus: A Modest Proposal?* 1990 Duke L.J. 484. Does it not go far enough? See Lawrence, supra at 450 n. 82: "I supported a proposal which would have been broader in scope by prohibiting speech of this nature in all common areas, excepting organized rallies and speeches. It would have been narrower in its protection in that it would not have protected persons who were vilified on the basis of their membership in dominant majority groups." Compare Matsuda, supra at 2357, arguing that speech with a message of racial inferiority, that is

directed against a historically oppressed group, and that is persecutorial, hateful, and degrading should be outlawed.[f]

SECTION 2. DISTINGUISHING BETWEEN CONTENT REGULATION AND MANNER REGULATION: UNCONVENTIONAL FORMS OF COMMUNICATION

Special first amendment questions are often said to arise by regulation of the time, place, and manner of speech as opposed to regulation of its content. But the two types of regulation are not mutually exclusive. It is possible to regulate time, place, manner, and content in the same regulation. For example, in *Linmark*, p. 821 infra, the township outlawed signs (but not leaflets) advertising a house for sale (but not other advertisements or other messages) on front lawns (but not other places).

Further, the terms, manner and content are strongly contested concepts. Indeed, an issue recurring in this section is whether the regulations in question are of manner or content. To the extent this section is about manner regulation, it is not exhaustive—much comes later. Most of the cases in this section involve unconventional forms of expression. Speakers claim protection for burning draft cards, wearing armbands, mutilating flags, nude dancing, wearing long hair. Fact patterns such as these fix renewed attention on the question of how "speech" should be defined. It may be a nice question as to whether obscenity is not speech within the first amendment lexicon, whether it is such speech but has been balanced into an unprotected state, or whether it is not *freedom* of speech or *the* freedom of speech.[a] But assassinating a public figure, even to send a message, raises no first amendment problem. Robbing a bank does not raise a free speech issue. What does? How do we decide?

The fact patterns in this section also invite scrutiny of other issues that appear in succeeding sections. Should it make a difference if the state's interest in regulating speech is unrelated to what is being said? Suppose the state's concern arises from the non-communicative impact of the speech act—from its manner. Should that distinction make a constitutional difference, and, if so, how much? These questions become more complicated because in context it is often difficult to determine what the state interest is and sometimes difficult to determine whether there is a meaningful distinction between what is said and how it is said.

---

f. For other relevant literature, see, e.g., p. 695 supra; Kent Greenawalt, *Fighting Words* (1995); Mari Matsuda, Charles Lawrence, Richard Delgado, & Kimberle Crenshaw, eds., *Words that Wound* (1993); Laura Lederer & Richard Delgado, eds., *The Price We Pay: The Case Against Racist Speech, Hate Propaganda and Pornography* (1995); Samuel Walker, *Hate Speech: The History of an American Controversy* (1994); Symposium, *Campus Hate Speech and the Constitution in the Aftermath of Doe v. University of Michigan*, 37 Wayne L.Rev. 1309 (1991); Symposium, *Free Speech & Religious, Racial & Sexual Harassment*, 32 Wm.&Mary L.Rev. 207 (1991); Symposium, *Frontiers of Legal Thought: The New First Amendment*, 1990 Duke L.J. 375; Symposium, *Hate Speech and the First Amendment: On A Collision Course?*, 37 Vill.L.Rev. 723 (1992); Symposium, *Hate Speech After R.A.V.: More Conflict Between Free Speech and Equality*, 18 Wm. Mitchell L.Rev. 889 (1992); See also sources cited in connection with *R.A.V. v. City of St. Paul*, p. 837 infra and sources cited in Steven Shiffrin, *Racist Speech, Outsider Jurisprudence, and the Meaning of America*, 80 Corn. L.Rev. 43, 44 n. 6 (1994). For the Canadian perspective, see *Regina v. Keegstra*, [1990] 3 S.C.R. 697. For commentary, see Greenawalt, supra; Lorraine Weinrib, *Hate Promotion in a Democratic Society*, 36 McGill L.Rev. 1416 (1991).

a. See fn. b in *Roth*, p. 604 supra.

Even when the distinction between the manner of the speech and the content of the speech is clear, further doctrinal complications abound. Sometimes the regulation considered by the Court is described as one regulating the "time, place, or manner" of speech, and the Court employs the "time, place, or manner test" which is itself differently phrased in different cases. On other occasions the regulation is described as having an "incidental" impact on freedom of speech, and the Court turns to a different test. These different tests are sometimes described by the Court as functional equivalents. Should there be different tests? In what circumstances? [b]

Finally, in this and succeeding sections the question arises of the extent to which freedom of speech should require special sensitivity to the methods and communications needs of the less powerful.

UNITED STATES v. O'BRIEN

391 U.S. 367, 88 S.Ct. 1673, 20 L.Ed.2d 672 (1968).

CHIEF JUSTICE WARREN delivered the opinion of the Court.

On the morning of March 31, 1966, David Paul O'Brien and three companions burned their Selective Service registration certificates on the steps of the South Boston Courthouse. A sizable crowd, including several [FBI agents] witnessed the event. Immediately after the burning, members of the crowd began attacking O'Brien [and he was ushered to safety by an FBI agent.] O'Brien stated to FBI agents that he had burned his registration certificate because of his beliefs, knowing that he was violating federal law.

[For this act, O'Brien was convicted in federal court.] He [told] the jury that he burned the certificate publicly to influence others to adopt his antiwar beliefs, as he put it, "so that other people would reevaluate their positions with Selective Service, with the armed forces, and reevaluate their place in the culture of today, to hopefully consider my position."

The indictment upon which he was tried charged that he "wilfully and knowingly did mutilate, destroy, and change by burning [his] Registration Certificate; in violation of [§ 462(b)(3) of the Universal Military Training and Service Act of 1948], amended by Congress in 1965 (adding the words italicized below), so that at the time O'Brien burned his certificate an offense was committed by any person, "who forges, alters, *knowingly destroys, knowingly mutilates,* or in any manner changes any such certificate * * *." (Italics supplied.)

[On appeal, the] First Circuit held the 1965 Amendment unconstitutional as a law abridging freedom of speech. At the time the Amendment was enacted, a regulation of the Selective Service System required registrants to keep their registration certificates in their "personal possession at all times." Wilful violations of regulations promulgated pursuant to the Universal Military Training and Service Act were made criminal by statute. The Court of Appeals, therefore, was of the opinion that conduct punishable under the 1965 Amendment was already punishable under the nonpossession regulation, and consequently that the Amendment served no valid purpose; further, that in light of the prior regulation, the Amendment must have been "directed at public as distinguished from private destruction." On this basis, the Court concluded that the 1965 Amendment ran

b. See generally Susan Williams, *Content Discrimination and the First Amendment,* 139 U.Pa.L.Rev. 201 (1991).

afoul of the First Amendment by singling out persons engaged in protests for special treatment. * * *

When a male reaches the age of 18, he is required by the Universal Military Training and Service Act to register with a local draft board. He is assigned a Selective Service number, and within five days he is issued a registration certificate. Subsequently, and based on a questionnaire completed by the registrant, he is assigned a classification denoting his eligibility for induction, and "[a]s soon as practicable" thereafter he is issued a Notice of Classification. * * *

Both the registration and classification certificates bear notices that the registrant must notify his local board in writing of every change in address, physical condition, and occupational, marital, family, dependency, and military status, and of any other fact which might change his classification. Both also contain a notice that the registrant's Selective Service number should appear on all communications to his local board.

[The 1965] Amendment does not distinguish between public and private destruction, and it does not punish only destruction engaged in for the purpose of expressing views.[a] A law prohibiting destruction of Selective Service certificates no more abridges free speech on its face than a motor vehicle law prohibiting the destruction of drivers' licenses, or a tax law prohibiting the destruction of books and records.

O'Brien nonetheless argues [first] that the 1965 Amendment is unconstitutional [as] applied to him because his act of burning his registration certificate was protected "symbolic speech" within the First Amendment. [He claims that] the First Amendment guarantees include all modes of "communication of ideas by conduct," and that his conduct is within this definition because he did it in "demonstration against the war and against the draft."

We cannot accept the view that an apparently limitless variety of conduct can be labelled "speech" whenever the person engaging in the conduct intends thereby to express an idea. However, even on the assumption that the alleged communicative element in O'Brien's conduct is sufficient to bring into play the First Amendment, it does not necessarily follow that the destruction of a registration certificate is constitutionally protected activity. This Court has held that when "speech" and "nonspeech" elements are combined in the same course of conduct, a sufficiently important governmental interest in regulating the nonspeech element can justify incidental limitations on First Amendment freedoms. To characterize the quality of the governmental interest which must appear, the Court has employed a variety of descriptive terms: compelling; substantial; subordinating; paramount; cogent; strong. [W]e think it clear that a government regulation is sufficiently justified if it is within the constitutional power of the government; if it furthers an important or substantial governmental interest; if the governmental interest is unrelated to the suppression of free expression;[b] and if the incidental restriction on alleged First Amendment freedom is no greater

---

a. But compare Chief Judge Aldrich below, 376 F.2d at 541: "We would be closing our eyes in the light of the prior law if we did not see on the face of the amendment that it was precisely directed at public as distinguished from private destruction. [In] singling out persons engaging in protest for special treatment the amendment strikes at the very core of what the First Amendment protects."

b. For the contention that the many tests formulated by the Court are best regarded as

prophylactic rules designed to assure that the forbidden purpose of suppressing ideas does not underlie government acts, see David Bogen, *Balancing Freedom of Speech,* 38 Md. L.Rev. 387 (1979); David Bogen, *The Supreme Court's Interpretation of the Guarantee of Freedom of Speech,* 35 Md.L.Rev. 555 (1976). See generally David Bogen, *Bulwark of Liberty: The Court and the First Amendment* (1984).

than is essential to the furtherance of that interest. We find that the 1965 Amendment meets all of these requirements, and consequently that O'Brien can be constitutionally convicted for violating it. [Pursuant to its power to classify and conscript manpower for military service], Congress may establish a system of registration for individuals liable for training and service, and may require such individuals within reason to cooperate in the registration system. The issuance of certificates indicating the registration and eligibility classification of individuals is a legitimate and substantial administrative aid in the functioning of this system. And legislation to insure the continuing availability of issued certificates serves a legitimate and substantial purpose in the system's administration.

[O'Brien] essentially adopts the position that [Selective Service] certificates are so many pieces of paper designed to notify registrants of their registration or classification, to be retained or tossed in the wastebasket according to the convenience or taste of the registrant. Once the registrant has received notification, according to this view, there is no reason for him to retain the certificates. [However, the registration and classification certificates serve] purposes in addition to initial notification. Many of these purposes would be defeated by the certificates' destruction or mutilation. Among these are [simplifying verification of the registration and classification of suspected delinquents, evidence of availability for induction in the event of emergency, ease of communication between registrants and local boards, continually reminding registrants of the need to notify local boards of changes in status].

The many functions performed by Selective Service certificates establish beyond doubt that Congress has a legitimate and substantial interest in preventing their wanton and unrestrained destruction and assuring their continuing availability by punishing people who knowingly and wilfully destroy or mutilate them. And we are unpersuaded that the pre-existence of the nonpossession regulations in any way negates this interest.

In the absence of a question as to multiple punishment, it has never been suggested that there is anything improper in Congress providing alternative statutory avenues of prosecution to assure the effective protection of one and the same interest. Here, the pre-existing avenue of prosecution was not even statutory. Regulations may be modified or revoked from time to time by administrative discretion. Certainly, the Congress may change or supplement a regulation.

[The] gravamen of the offense defined by the statute is the deliberate rendering of certificates unavailable for the various purposes which they may serve. Whether registrants keep their certificates in their personal possession at all times, as required by the regulations, is of no particular concern under the 1965 Amendment, as long as they do not mutilate or destroy the certificates so as to render them unavailable. [The 1965 amendment] is concerned with abuses involving *any* issued Selective Service certificates, not only with the registrant's own certificates. The knowing destruction or mutilation of someone else's certificates would therefore violate the statute but not the nonpossession regulations.

We think it apparent that the continuing availability to each registrant of his Selective Service certificates substantially furthers the smooth and proper functioning of the system that Congress has established to raise armies. * * *

It is equally clear that the 1965 Amendment specifically protects this substantial governmental interest. We perceive no alternative means that would more precisely and narrowly assure the continuing availability of issued Selective Service certificates than a law which prohibits their wilful mutilation or destruction. The 1965 Amendment prohibits such conduct and does nothing more.

[The] governmental interest and the scope of the 1965 Amendment are limited to preventing a harm to the smooth and efficient functioning of the Selective Service System. When O'Brien deliberately rendered unavailable his registration certificate, he wilfully frustrated this governmental interest. For this noncommunicative impact of his conduct, and for nothing else, he was convicted.

The case at bar is therefore unlike one where the alleged governmental interest in regulating conduct arises in some measure because the communication allegedly integral to the conduct is itself thought to be harmful [distinguishing *Stromberg,* p. 626 supra].

[B]ecause of the Government's substantial interest in assuring the continuing availability of issued Selective Service certificates, because amended § 462(b) is an appropriately narrow means of protecting this interest and condemns only the independent noncommunicative impact of conduct within its reach, and because the noncommunicative impact of O'Brien's act of burning his registration certificate frustrated the Government's interest, a sufficient governmental interest has been shown to justify O'Brien's conviction.

O'Brien finally argues that the 1965 Amendment is unconstitutional as enacted because what he calls the "purpose" of Congress was "to suppress freedom of speech." We reject this argument because under settled principles the purpose of Congress, as O'Brien uses that term, is not a basis for declaring this legislation unconstitutional.

It is a familiar principle of constitutional law that this Court will not strike down an otherwise constitutional statute on the basis of an alleged illicit legislative motive.[c]

[I]f we were to examine legislative purpose in the instant case, we would be obliged to consider not only [the statements of the three members of Congress who addressed themselves to the amendment, all viewing draft-card burning as a brazen display of unpatriotism] but also the more authoritative reports of the Senate and House Armed Services Committees. [B]oth reports make clear a concern with the "defiant" destruction of so-called "draft cards" and with "open" encouragement to others to destroy their cards, [but they] also indicate that this concern stemmed from an apprehension that unrestrained destruction of cards would disrupt the smooth functioning of the Selective Service System. * * *

Reversed.[d]

JUSTICE HARLAN concurring. * * *

I wish to make explicit my understanding that [the Court's analysis] does not foreclose consideration of First Amendment claims in those rare instances when an "incidental" restriction upon expression, imposed by a regulation which furthers an "important or substantial" governmental interest and satisfies the Court's other criteria, in practice has the effect of entirely preventing a "speaker" from reaching a significant audience with whom he could not otherwise lawfully communicate. This is not such a case, since O'Brien manifestly could have conveyed his message in many ways other than by burning his draft card.

JUSTICE DOUGLAS, dissenting.

[Douglas, J., thought that "the underlying and basic problem in this case" was the constitutionality of a draft "in the absence of a declaration of war" and that the case should be put down for reargument on this question. The following

c. See generally Ch. 11, Sec. 2, III.   d. Marshall, J., took no part.

Term, concurring in *Brandenburg,* p. 563 supra, he criticized *O'Brien* on the merits. After recalling that the Court had rejected O'Brien's first amendment argument on the ground that "legislation to insure the continuing availability of issued certificates serves a legitimate and substantial purpose in the [selective service] system's administration," he commented: "But O'Brien was not prosecuted for not having his draft card available when asked for by a federal agent. He was indicted, tried, and convicted for burning the card. And this Court's affirmance [was not] consistent with the First Amendment." He observed, more generally in *Brandenburg:*

["Action is often a method of expression and within the protection of the First Amendment. Suppose one tears up his own copy of the Constitution in eloquent protest to a decision of this Court. May he be indicted? Suppose one rips his own Bible to shreds to celebrate his departure from one 'faith' and his embrace of atheism. May he be indicted? * * *

["The act of praying often involves body posture and movement as well as utterances. It is nonetheless protected by the Free Exercise Clause. Picketing [is] 'free speech plus.' [Therefore], it can be regulated when it comes to the 'plus' or 'action' side of the protest. It can be regulated as to the number of pickets and the place and hours, because traffic and other community problems would otherwise suffer. But none of these considerations are implicated in the symbolic protest of the Vietnam war in the burning of a draft card."]

Notes and Questions

1. *Expression vs. action.* What of the Court's rejection of the idea that conduct is speech "whenever the person engaging in the conduct intends thereby to express an idea." Was it right to question whether O'Brien's conduct was speech? What was it about O'Brien's conduct that made the Court doubt that it was speech? What if O'Brien had burned a copy of the Constitution? Consider Thomas Emerson, *The System of Freedom of Expression* 80 & 84 (1970): "To some extent expression and action are always mingled; most conduct includes elements of both. Even the clearest manifestations of expression involve some action, as in the case of holding a meeting, publishing a newspaper, or merely talking. At the other extreme, a political assassination includes a substantial mixture of expression. The guiding principle must be to determine which element is predominant in the conduct under consideration. Is expression the major element and the action only secondary? Or is the action the essence and the expression incidental? The answer, to a great extent, must be based on a common-sense reaction, made in light of the functions and operations of a system of freedom of expression. * * *

"The burning of a draft card is, of course, conduct that involves both communication and physical acts. Yet it seems quite clear that the predominant element in such conduct is expression (opposition to the draft) rather than action (destruction of a piece of cardboard). The registrant is not concerned with secret or inadvertent burning of his draft card, involving no communication with other persons. The main feature, for him, is the public nature of the burning, through which he expresses to the community his ideas and feelings about the war and the draft."

Compare John Hart Ely, *Flag Desecration: A Case Study in the Roles of Categorization and Balancing in First Amendment Analysis,* 88 Harv.L.Rev. 1482, 1495 (1975): "[B]urning a draft card to express opposition to the draft is an undifferentiated whole, 100% action and 100% expression. It involves no conduct that is not at the same time communication, and no communication that does not result from conduct. Attempts to determine which element 'predominates' will therefore inevitably degenerate into question-begging judgments about whether the activity should be protected. The *O'Brien* Court thus quite wisely dropped the 'speech-conduct' distinction as quickly as it had picked it up." [e]

Consider, too, C. Edwin Baker, *Scope of the First Amendment Freedom of Speech,* 25 U.C.L.A.L.Rev. 964, 1010–12 (1978): "[S]ince both verbal and nonverbal conduct advances first amendment values, the purpose of the [expression-action] distinction is unclear. Moreover, only an extremely crabbed reading of other clauses of the first amendment will be consistent with implementing an expression-action dichotomy. If religion plays a significant role in one's life, its *free exercise* normally will require doing or abstaining from certain conduct. And people typically assemble and associate to multiply their power in order to do something. Nevertheless, even if his 'expression-action' dichotomy is not very helpful, Emerson consistently makes very perceptive analyses of concrete situations; and these analyses frequently appear to make a different distinction: whether or not the conduct is, or is intended to be, coercive or physically injurious to another. All Emerson's examples of unprotected conduct, 'action,' involve coercion or injury to or physical interference with another or damage to physical property. * * *

"Expressive political protests sometimes involve acts of physical obstruction like lying down in front of troop trains, blocking traffic in a city, or pouring blood over files. Emerson argues that these must be considered 'action,' [but] [n]either the physical activity nor the motives of the actor distinguish these 'action' cases from draft card burning, which Emerson characterizes as expression. Rather, Emerson classifies the first examples of civil disobedience 'action' because the '[c]ivil disobedience attempts to achieve results through a kind of *coercion or pressure* * * *.' However, [draft-card burning], unlike failing to carry a draft card [which presumably 'interferes' or 'obstructs' the working of the selective service system], does not involve coercing or directly injuring or physically obstructing any person or government activity. This fact apparently explains why Emerson concludes that the expression element clearly predominates in draft card burning." [f] See generally C. Edwin Baker, *Human Liberty and Freedom of Speech* 70–91 (1989).

2. *Nature of the state interest and first amendment methodology.* Melville Nimmer, *The Meaning of Symbolic Speech under the First Amendment,* 21 U.C.L.A.L.Rev. 29 (1973), followed by John Hart Ely, note 1 supra, and Laurence Tribe, infra, has proposed that the crucial starting point for first amendment methodology is and should be the nature of the state interest.[g] As Ely puts it, at 1497: "The critical question would therefore seem to be whether the harm that the state is seeking to avert is one that grows out of the fact that the defendant is communicating, and more particularly out of the way people can be expected to

---

e. But, as Professor Ely recognizes, the Court picked it up again in *Cohen,* p. 728 supra: "[W]e deal here with a conviction resting solely upon 'speech', cf. *Stromberg,* not upon any separately identifiable conduct which allegedly was intended by Cohen to be perceived by others as expressive of particular views but which, on its face, does not necessarily convey any message and hence arguably could be regulated without effectively repress-

ing Cohen's ability to express himself. Cf. *O'Brien.*"

f. For discussion of Professor Baker's approach and refinement of the expression-action dichotomy, see Thomas Emerson, *First Amendment Doctrine and the Burger Court,* 68 Calif.L.Rev. 422, 474–80 (1980).

g. The distinction is a major organizing principle in Rodney Smolla, *Smolla and Nimmer on Freedom of Speech* (1984).

react to his message, or rather would arise even if the defendant's conduct had no communicative significance whatever."

For one view of the difference that the distinction makes, see Laurence Tribe, *American Constitutional Law* 791–92 (2d ed. 1988): "The Supreme Court has evolved two distinct approaches to the resolution of first amendment claims; the two correspond to the two ways in which government may 'abridge' speech. If a government regulation is aimed at the communicative impact of an act, analysis should proceed along what we will call *track one*. On that track, a regulation is unconstitutional unless government shows that the message being suppressed poses a 'clear and present danger,' constitutes a defamatory falsehood, or otherwise falls on the unprotected side of one of the lines the Court has drawn to distinguish those expressive acts privileged by the first amendment from those open to government regulation with only minimal due process scrutiny. If a government regulation is aimed at the noncommunicative impact of an act, its analysis proceeds on what we will call *track two*. On that track, a regulation is constitutional, even as applied to expressive conduct, so long as it does not unduly constrict the flow of information and ideas. On track two, the 'balance' between the values of freedom of expression and the government's regulatory interests is struck on a case-by-case basis, guided by whatever unifying principles may be articulated."

Professor Nimmer, in distinguishing between anti-speech interests (track one) and non-speech interests (track two), would apply definitional balancing (with a presumption in favor of speech) to the former and the *O'Brien* test to the latter. Dean Ely would prevent all regulations on track one except for speech that falls "within a few clearly and narrowly defined categories." John Hart Ely, *Democracy and Distrust* 110 (1980) (emphasis deleted). On track two, Ely insists that balancing is desirable and unavoidable. Ely, note 1 supra, at 1496–1502.

(a) *Normative value of the distinction.* Is balancing unavoidable on either track? How does one decide what the categories should be without balancing? Does the metaphor of balancing wrongly imply that all values are reduced to a single measure and imply non-existent quantitative capacities? Is the distinction between the tracks important enough to require rules on track one, even if ad hoc procedures are allowable on track two?

Is the distinction between the two tracks at least strong enough to justify a rebuttable presumption that regulation on track one is invalid, but regulation on track two is not? Consider a regulation governing express warranties in commercial advertising. Is much of contract law on track one?[h] Consider "a nationwide ban on *all* posters (intended to conserve paper)." Isn't that on track two? Do these examples suggest that too much emphasis is being placed on a single factor? See Daniel Farber, *Content Regulation and the First Amendment: A Revisionist View*, 68 Geo.U.L.Rev. 727, 746–47 (1980).[i]

(b) *Application to O'Brien.* Consider Ely, note 1 supra, at 1498–99: "The interests upon which the government relied were interests, having mainly to do with the preservation of selective service records, that would have been equally threatened had O'Brien's destruction of his draft card totally lacked communica-

h. For the suggestion that virtually all laws have information effects and that track two embraces virtually all laws not covered by track one, see Larry Alexander, *Trouble on Track Two: Incidental Regulations of Speech and Free Speech*, 44 Hastings L.J. 921 (1993) (arguing that track two countenances an un-

constitutional evaluation of the value of speech).

i. See generally Martin Redish, *The Content Distinction in First Amendment Analysis*, 34 Stan.L.Rev. 113 (1981). See notes after *Chicago Police Dept. v. Mosley,* p. 895 infra.

tive significance—had he, for example, used it to start a campfire for a solitary cookout or dropped it in his garbage disposal for a lark. (The law prohibited all knowing destructions, public or private)."

Compare Melville Nimmer, note 2 supra, at 41—contending that the *O'Brien* statute was "overnarrow": "[An overnarrow statute] may be said to create a conclusive presumption that in fact the state interest which the statute serves is an anti-rather than a non-speech interest. If the state interest asserted in *O'Brien* were truly the non-speech interest of assuring availability of draft cards, why did Congress choose not to prohibit any knowing conduct which leads to unavailability, rather than limiting the scope of the statute to those instances in which the proscribed conduct carries with it a speech component hostile to governmental policy? The obvious inference to be drawn is that in fact the Congress was completely indifferent to the 'availability' objective, and was concerned only with an interest which the *O'Brien* opinion states is impermissible— an interest in the suppression of free expression." [j]

(c) *Descriptive value of the distinction.* Does the distinction between the two tracks fully explain the Court's approach in *O'Brien*? Suppose again that an assassin truthfully claims that his or her killing was intended to and did communicate an idea? The assassin's first amendment claim would not prevail, but would it fail because the *O'Brien* test was not met or because no first amendment problem was implicated at all? Is a speech/conduct distinction a necessary prerequisite to the application of the *O'Brien* test? [k]

How different is the *O'Brien* test from the methods used to make decisions on track one? Is the *O'Brien* test as phrased potentially more speech protective than its application in the principal case would suggest? More speech protective than tests sometimes used on track one? Does the application in *O'Brien* offer "little more than the minimal rational-basis test applied in economic due process cases"? See Keith Werhan, *The O'Briening of First Amendment Methodology*, 19 Ariz.St. L.J. 635, 641 (1987): "There is no speech side to the Court's balance. [T]he absence of true balancing within the *O'Brien* methodology can be traced to the origins of the *O'Brien* test. [Having] avoided deciding whether O'Brien's act was protected expression, the Court hardly was in a position to take the next step of incorporating expressive interests into its balance." Id. at 641–42.

3. Does *O'Brien* shortchange the value of dissent? Consider Steven Shiffrin, *The First Amendment, Democracy, and Romance* 5–6, 81 (1990): "If an organizing symbol makes sense in first amendment jurisprudence, it is not the image of a content-neutral government; it is not a town hall meeting or even a robust marketplace of ideas; still less is it liberty, equality, self-realization, respect, dignity, autonomy, or even tolerance. If the first amendment is to have an organizing symbol, let it be an Emersonian [l] symbol, let it be the image of the dissenter. A major purpose of the first amendment [is] to protect the romantics— those who would break out of classical forms: the dissenters, the unorthodox, the outcasts. [That] Emersonian ideal of freedom of speech has deep roots in the nation's culture, but it has been subtly denigrated in recent first amendment theory and seriously abused in practice.

j. On the inadequacy of the *O'Brien* methodology to serve as a proxy for problematic motivation, see Lee Bollinger, *The Tolerant Society* 206–12 (1986). On its inadequacy as an organizing principle for first amendment doctrine, see Shiffrin, note 3 infra, ch. 1.

k. For commentary on the difficulties in defining speech, see Larry Alexander & Paul Horton, *The Impossibility of a Free Speech Principle,* 78 Nw.U.L.Rev. 1319 (1984).

l. See generally Joel Porte ed., *Ralph Waldo Emerson: Essays and Lectures* (1983).

"[N]either the town hall metaphor nor the marketplace of ideas metaphor[, for example,] is quite apt as a symbol for why *O'Brien* is a first amendment horror story. Town hall meetings can function without the burning of draft cards. And it is hard to claim that truth was kept from the marketplace of ideas. *O'Brien* is one of those not infrequent cases where government prosecutions assist the dissemination of the dissenter's message. Yet, *O'Brien* is perhaps the ultimate first amendment insult. O'Brien is jailed because the authorities find his manner of expression unpatriotic, threatening, and offensive. When he complains that his freedom of speech has been abridged, the authorities deny that he has spoken."

4. *Scope of O'Brien.* Should the *O'Brien* test be confined to unconventional forms of communication? Would a distinction of this type be defensible? See Ely, note 1 supra, at 1489: "The distinction is its own objection." See also Dean Alfange, *Free Speech and Symbolic Conduct: The Draft-Card Burning Case,* 1968 Sup.Ct.Rev. 1, 23–24; Lawrence Velvel, *Freedom of Speech and the Draft Card Burning Cases,* 16 U.Kan.L.Rev. 149, 153 (1968); Louis Henkin, *On Drawing Lines,* 82 Harv.L.Rev. 63, 79 (1968).

TEXAS v. JOHNSON

491 U.S. 397, 109 S.Ct. 2533, 105 L.Ed.2d 342 (1989).

JUSTICE BRENNAN delivered the opinion of the Court.

[Gregory] Lee Johnson was convicted of desecrating a flag in violation of Texas law.[1]

I. While the Republican National Convention was taking place in Dallas in 1984, respondent Johnson participated in a political demonstration dubbed the "Republican War Chest Tour." [The] demonstration ended in front of Dallas City Hall, where Johnson unfurled the American flag, doused it with kerosene, and set it on fire. While the flag burned, the protestors chanted, "America, the red, white, and blue, we spit on you." [No] one was physically injured or threatened with injury, though several witnesses testified that they had been seriously offended by the flag-burning. * * *

II. Johnson was convicted of flag desecration for burning the flag rather than for uttering insulting words.[2] [We] must first determine whether Johnson's burning of the flag constituted expressive conduct, permitting him to invoke the First Amendment in challenging his conviction. If his conduct was expressive, we

---

1. Tex.Penal Code Ann. § 42.09 (1989) provides in full: "§ 42.09. Desecration of Venerated Object

"(a) A person commits an offense if he intentionally or knowingly desecrates:

"(1) a public monument;

"(2) a place of worship or burial; or

"(3) a state or national flag.

"(b) For purposes of this section, 'desecrate' means deface, damage, or otherwise physically mistreat in a way that the actor knows will seriously offend one or more persons likely to observe or discover his action.

"(c) An offense under this section is a Class A misdemeanor."

2. Because the prosecutor's closing argument observed that Johnson had led the protestors in chants denouncing the flag while it burned, Johnson suggests that he may have been convicted for uttering critical words rather than for burning the flag. He relies on *Street v. New York,* 394 U.S. 576, 89 S.Ct. 1354, 22 L.Ed.2d 572 (1969), in which we reversed a conviction obtained under a New York statute that prohibited publicly defying or casting contempt on the flag "either by words or act" because we were persuaded that the defendant may have been convicted for his words alone. Unlike the law we faced in *Street,* however, the Texas flag-desecration statute does not on its face permit conviction for remarks critical of the flag, as Johnson himself admits. Nor was the jury in this case told that it could convict Johnson of flag desecration if it found only that he had uttered words critical of the flag and its referents. * * *

next decide whether the State's regulation is related to the suppression of free expression. *O'Brien.* If the State's regulation is not related to expression, then the less stringent standard we announced in *O'Brien* for regulations of noncommunicative conduct controls. If it is, then we are outside of *O'Brien*'s test, and we must ask whether this interest justifies Johnson's conviction under a more demanding standard.[3] A third possibility is that the State's asserted interest is simply not implicated on these facts, and in that event the interest drops out of the picture. * * *

In deciding whether particular conduct possesses sufficient communicative elements to bring the First Amendment into play, we have asked whether "[a]n intent to convey a particularized message was present, and [whether] the likelihood was great that the message would be understood by those who viewed it."[a] [In] *Spence v. Washington,* 418 U.S. 405, 94 S.Ct. 2727, 41 L.Ed.2d 842 (1974), for example, we emphasized that Spence's taping of a peace sign to his flag was "roughly simultaneous with and concededly triggered by the Cambodian incursion and the Kent State tragedy." The State of Washington had conceded, in fact, that Spence's conduct was a form of communication, and we stated that "the State's concession is inevitable on this record."

The State of Texas conceded for purposes of its oral argument in this case that Johnson's conduct was expressive conduct and this concession seems to us as prudent as was Washington's in *Spence.* * * *

III. In order to decide whether *O'Brien*'s test [applies] we must decide whether Texas has asserted an interest in support of Johnson's conviction that is unrelated to the suppression of expression.

A. Texas claims that its interest in preventing breaches of the peace justifies Johnson's conviction for flag desecration.[4] However, no disturbance of the peace actually occurred or threatened to occur because of Johnson's burning of the flag. [The] only evidence offered by the State at trial to show the reaction to Johnson's actions was the testimony of several persons who had been seriously offended by the flag-burning.

The State's position, therefore, amounts to a claim that an audience that takes serious offense at particular expression is necessarily likely to disturb the

---

3. [Johnson] has raised a facial challenge to Texas' flag-desecration [statute]. Section 42.09 regulates only physical conduct with respect to the flag, not the written or spoken word, and although one violates the statute only if one "knows" that one's physical treatment of the flag "will seriously offend one or more persons likely to observe or discover his action," this fact does not necessarily mean that the statute applies only to *expressive* conduct protected by the First Amendment. A tired person might, for example, drag a flag through the mud, knowing that this conduct is likely to offend others, and yet have no thought of expressing any idea; neither the language nor the Texas courts' interpretations of the statute precludes the possibility that such a person would be prosecuted for flag desecration. Because the prosecution of a person who had not engaged in expressive conduct would pose a different case, and because we are capable of disposing of this case on narrower grounds, we address only Johnson's claim that

§ 42.09 as applied to political expression like his violates the First Amendment.

a. For criticism of this standard, see Robert Post, *Recuperating First Amendment Doctrine,* 47 Stan.L.Rev. 1249 (1995).

4. Relying on our decision in *Boos v. Barry,* [p. 772 infra,] Johnson argues [that] the violent reaction to flag-burning feared by Texas would be the result of the message conveyed by them, and that this fact connects the State's interest to the suppression of expression. This view has found some favor in the lower courts. Johnson's theory may overread *Boos* insofar as it suggests that a desire to prevent a violent audience reaction is "related to expression" in the same way that a desire to prevent an audience from being offended is "related to expression." Because we find that the State's interest in preventing breaches of the peace is not implicated on these facts, however, we need not venture further into this area.

peace and that the expression may be prohibited on this basis. [W]e have not permitted the Government to assume that every expression of a provocative idea will incite a riot, but have instead required careful consideration of the actual circumstances surrounding such expression, asking whether the expression "is directed to inciting or producing imminent lawless action and is likely to incite or produce such action." *Brandenburg.* To accept Texas' arguments that it need only demonstrate "the potential for a breach of the peace," and that every flag-burning necessarily possesses that potential, would be to eviscerate our holding in *Brandenburg.* This we decline to do.

Nor does Johnson's expressive conduct fall within that small class of "fighting words" that are "likely to provoke the average person to retaliation, and thereby cause a breach of the peace." *Chaplinsky.* No reasonable onlooker would have regarded Johnson's generalized expression of dissatisfaction with the policies of the Federal Government as a direct personal insult or an invitation to exchange fisticuffs.

We thus conclude that the State's interest in maintaining order is not implicated on these facts. * * *

B. The State also asserts an interest in preserving the flag as a symbol of nationhood and national unity. [The] State, apparently, is concerned that such conduct will lead people to believe either that the flag does not stand for nationhood and national unity, but instead reflects other, less positive concepts, or that the concepts reflected in the flag do not in fact exist, that is, we do not enjoy unity as a Nation. These concerns blossom only when a person's treatment of the flag communicates some message, and thus are related "to the suppression of free expression" within the meaning of *O'Brien.* We are thus outside of *O'Brien*'s test altogether.

IV. It remains to consider whether the State's interest in preserving the flag as a symbol of nationhood and national unity justifies Johnson's conviction. [If Johnson] had burned the flag as a means of disposing of it because it was dirty or torn, he would not have been convicted of flag desecration under this Texas law: federal law designates burning as the preferred means of disposing of a flag "when it is in such condition that it is no longer a fitting emblem for display," 36 U.S.C. § 176(k), and Texas has no quarrel with this means of disposal. The Texas law is thus not aimed at protecting the physical integrity of the flag in all circumstances, but is designed instead to protect it only against impairments that would cause serious offense to others.[6]

Whether Johnson's treatment of the flag violated Texas law thus depended on the likely communicative impact of his expressive conduct. Our decision in *Boos v. Barry,* 485 U.S. 312, 108 S.Ct. 1157, 99 L.Ed.2d 333 (1988), tells us that this restriction on Johnson's expression is content-based. In *Boos,* we considered the constitutionality of a law prohibiting "the display of any sign within 50 feet of a foreign embassy if that sign tends to bring that foreign government into 'public odium' or 'public disrepute.' " Rejecting the argument that the law was content-neutral because it was justified by "our international law obligation to shield diplomats from speech that offends their dignity," we held that "[t]he emotive

---

6. *Cf. Smith v. Goguen,* 415 U.S. 566, 94 S.Ct. 1242, 39 L.Ed.2d 605 (1974) (Blackmun, J., dissenting) (emphasizing that lower court appeared to have construed state statute so as to protect physical integrity of the flag in all circumstances); id. (Rehnquist, J., dissenting) (same). [In *Goguen,* Blackmun, J., argued that "Goguen's punishment was constitutionally permissible for harming the physical integrity of the flag by wearing it affixed to the seat of his pants" and emphasized that such punishment would not be for "speech—a communicative element."].

impact of speech on its audience is not a 'secondary effect' '' unrelated to the content of the expression itself.

According to the principles announced in *Boos,* Johnson's political expression was restricted because of the content of the message he conveyed. We must therefore subject the State's asserted interest in preserving the special symbolic character of the flag to "the most exacting scrutiny." *Boos*.[8] * * *

If there is a bedrock principle underlying the First Amendment, it is that the Government may not prohibit the expression of an idea simply because society finds the idea itself offensive or disagreeable. [We] have not recognized an exception to this principle even where our flag has been involved. [We] never before have held that the Government may ensure that a symbol be used to express only one view of that symbol or its referents. Indeed, in *Schacht v. United States*, 398 U.S. 58, 90 S.Ct. 1555, 26 L.Ed.2d 44 (1970), we invalidated a federal statute permitting an actor portraying a member of one of our armed forces to " 'wear the uniform of that armed force if the portrayal does not tend to discredit that armed force.' " This proviso, we held, "which leaves Americans free to praise the war in Vietnam but can send persons like Schacht to prison for opposing it, cannot survive in a country which has the First Amendment."

We perceive no basis on which to hold that the principle underlying our decision in *Schacht* does not apply to this case. To conclude that the Government may permit designated symbols to be used to communicate only a limited set of messages would be to enter territory having no discernible or defensible boundaries. Could the Government, on this theory, prohibit the burning of state flags? Of copies of the Presidential seal? Of the Constitution? In evaluating these choices under the First Amendment, how would we decide which symbols were sufficiently special to warrant this unique status? To do so, we would be forced to consult our own political preferences, and impose them on the citizenry, in the very way that the First Amendment forbids us to do.

There is, moreover, no indication—either in the text of the Constitution or in our cases interpreting it—that a separate judicial category exists for the American flag alone. Indeed, we would not be surprised to learn that the persons who framed our Constitution and wrote the Amendment that we now construe were not known for their reverence for the Union Jack. The First Amendment does not guarantee that other concepts virtually sacred to our Nation as a whole—such as the principle that discrimination on the basis of race is odious and destructive—will go unquestioned in the marketplace of ideas. See *Brandenburg*. We decline, therefore, to create for the flag an exception to the joust of principles protected by the First Amendment.

It is not the State's ends, but its means, to which we object. It cannot be gainsaid that there is a special place reserved for the flag in this Nation, and thus we do not doubt that the Government has a legitimate interest in making efforts to "preserv[e] the national flag as an unalloyed symbol of our country." We reject the suggestion, urged at oral argument by counsel for Johnson, that the Government lacks "any state interest whatsoever" in regulating the manner in which the flag may be displayed. Congress has, for example, enacted precatory

---

8. Our inquiry is, of course, bounded by the particular facts of this case and by the statute under which Johnson was convicted. There was no evidence that Johnson himself stole the flag he burned, nor did the prosecution or the arguments urged in support of it depend on the theory that the flag was stolen. [Thus] nothing in our opinion should be taken to suggest that one is free to steal a flag so long as one later uses it to communicate an idea. We also emphasize that Johnson was prosecuted *only* for flag desecration—not for trespass, disorderly conduct, or arson.

regulations describing the proper treatment of the flag, see 36 U.S.C. §§ 173–177, and we cast no doubt on the legitimacy of its interest in making such recommendations. To say that the Government has an interest in encouraging proper treatment of the flag, however, is not to say that it may criminally punish a person for burning a flag as a means of political protest. "National unity as an end which officials may foster by persuasion and example is not in question. The problem is whether under our Constitution compulsion as here employed is a permissible means for its achievement."

[W]e submit that nobody can suppose that this one gesture of an unknown man will change our Nation's attitude towards its flag. See *Abrams* (Holmes, J., dissenting). Indeed, Texas' argument that the burning of an American flag " 'is an act having a high likelihood to cause a breach of the peace,' " and its statute's implicit assumption that physical mistreatment of the flag will lead to "serious offense," tend to confirm that the flag's special role is not in danger; if it were, no one would riot or take offense because a flag had been burned.

We are tempted to say, in fact, that the flag's deservedly cherished place in our community will be strengthened, not weakened, by our holding today. Our decision is a reaffirmation of the principles of freedom and inclusiveness that the flag best reflects, and of the conviction that our toleration of criticism such as Johnson's is a sign and source of our strength. Indeed, one of the proudest images of our flag, the one immortalized in our own national anthem, is of the bombardment it survived at Fort McHenry. It is the Nation's resilience, not its rigidity, that Texas sees reflected in the flag—and it is that resilience that we reassert today.

The way to preserve the flag's special role is not to punish those who feel differently about these matters. It is to persuade them that they are wrong. [We] can imagine no more appropriate response to burning a flag than waving one's own, no better way to counter a flag-burner's message than by saluting the flag that burns, no surer means of preserving the dignity even of the flag that burned than by—as one witness here did—according its remains a respectful burial. * * *

Justice Kennedy, concurring. * * *

Our colleagues in dissent advance powerful arguments why respondent may be convicted for his expression, reminding us that among those who will be dismayed by our holding will be some who have had the singular honor of carrying the flag in battle. And I agree that the flag holds a lonely place of honor in an age when absolutes are distrusted and simple truths are burdened by unneeded apologetics.

With all respect to those views, I do not believe the Constitution gives us the right to rule as the dissenting members of the Court urge, however painful this judgment is to announce. Though symbols often are what we ourselves make of them, the flag is constant in expressing beliefs Americans share, beliefs in law and peace and that freedom which sustains the human spirit. The case here today forces recognition of the costs to which those beliefs commit us. It is poignant but fundamental that the flag protects those who hold it in contempt.

For all the record shows, this respondent was not a philosopher and perhaps did not even possess the ability to comprehend how repellent his statements must be to the Republic itself. But whether or not he could appreciate the enormity of the offense he gave, the fact remains that his acts were speech, in both the technical and the fundamental meaning of the Constitution. So I agree with the Court that he must go free.

CHIEF JUSTICE REHNQUIST, with whom JUSTICE WHITE and JUSTICE O'CONNOR join, dissenting.

In holding this Texas statute unconstitutional, the Court ignores Justice Holmes' familiar aphorism that "a page of history is worth a volume of logic." *New York Trust Co. v. Eisner,* 256 U.S. 345, 41 S.Ct. 506, 65 L.Ed. 963 (1921). * * *

The American flag [throughout] more than 200 years of our history, has come to be the visible symbol embodying our Nation.[b] It does not represent the views of any particular political party, and it does not represent any particular political philosophy. The flag is not simply another "idea" or "point of view" competing for recognition in the marketplace of ideas. Millions and millions of Americans regard it with an almost mystical reverence regardless of what sort of social, political, or philosophical beliefs they may have. I cannot agree that the First Amendment invalidates the Act of Congress, and the laws of 48 of the 50 States, which make criminal the public burning of the flag.

More than 80 years ago in *Halter v. Nebraska* [205 U.S. 34, 27 S.Ct. 419, 51 L.Ed. 696 (1907)], this Court upheld the constitutionality of a Nebraska statute that forbade the use of representations of the American flag for advertising purposes upon articles of merchandise. The Court there said: "For that flag every true American has not simply an appreciation but a deep affection. * * * Hence, it has often occurred that insults to a flag have been the cause of war, and indignities put upon it, in the presence of those who revere it, have often been resented and sometimes punished on the spot."

Only two Terms ago, in *San Francisco Arts & Athletics, Inc. v. United States Olympic Committee,* [483 U.S. 522, 107 S.Ct. 2971, 97 L.Ed.2d 427 (1987)], the Court held that Congress could grant exclusive use of the word "Olympic" to the United States Olympic Committee. The Court thought that this "restrictio[n] on expressive speech properly [was] characterized as incidental to the primary congressional purpose of encouraging and rewarding the USOC's activities." As the Court stated, "when a word [or symbol] acquires value 'as the result of organization and the expenditure of labor, skill, and money' by an entity, that entity constitutionally may obtain a limited property right in the word [or symbol]." Surely Congress or the States may recognize a similar interest in the flag.[c]

[T]he public burning of the American flag by Johnson was no essential part of any exposition of ideas, and at the same time it had a tendency to incite a breach of the peace. Johnson was free to make any verbal denunciation of the flag that

---

b. Rehnquist, C.J., invoked a legacy of prose, poetry, and law in honor of flags in general and the American flag in particular both in peace and in war, quoting from, among others, Ralph Waldo Emerson and John Greenleaf Whittier. Emerson's poem referred to the Union Jack, but he did not always speak warmly of the American flag. After passage of the Fugitive Slave Law Emerson wrote, "We sneak about with the infamy of crime in the streets, & cowardice in ourselves and frankly once for all the Union is sunk, the flag is hateful, and shall be hissed." *Emerson in His Journals* 421 (J. Porte ed. 1982).

c. In response, Brennan, J., observed that *Halter* was decided "nearly twenty years" before the first amendment was applied to the states and "[m]ore important" that *Halter* involved "purely commercial rather than political speech." Similarly, he stated that the authorization "to prohibit certain commercial and promotional uses of the word 'Olympic' [does not] even begin to tell us whether the Government may criminally punish physical conduct towards the flag engaged in as a means of political protest."

he wished; indeed, he was free to burn the flag in private. He could publicly burn other symbols of the Government or effigies of political leaders. He did lead a march through the streets of Dallas, and conducted a rally in front of the Dallas City Hall. He engaged in a "die-in" to protest nuclear weapons. He shouted out various slogans during the march, including: "Reagan, Mondale which will it be? Either one means World War III"; "Ronald Reagan, killer of the hour, Perfect example of U.S. power"; and "red, white and blue, we spit on you, you stand for plunder, you will go under." For none of these acts was he arrested or prosecuted. [As] with "fighting words," so with flag burning, for purposes of the First Amendment: It is "no essential part of any exposition of ideas, and [is] of such slight social value as a step to truth that any benefit that may be derived from [it] is clearly outweighed" by the public interest in avoiding a probable breach of the peace. * * *

The result of the Texas statute is obviously to deny one in Johnson's frame of mind one of many means of "symbolic speech." Far from being a case of "one picture being worth a thousand words," flag burning is the equivalent of an inarticulate grunt or roar that, it seems fair to say, is most likely to be indulged in not to express any particular idea, but to antagonize others. [The] Texas statute [left Johnson] with a full panoply of other symbols and every conceivable form of verbal expression to express his deep disapproval of national policy. Thus, in no way can it be said that Texas is punishing him because his hearers—or any other group of people—were profoundly opposed to the message that he sought to convey. Such opposition is no proper basis for restricting speech or expression under the First Amendment. It was Johnson's use of this particular symbol, and not the idea that he sought to convey by it or by his many other expressions, for which he was punished. * * *

The Court concludes its opinion with a regrettably patronizing civics lecture, presumably addressed to the Members of both Houses of Congress, the members of the 48 state legislatures that enacted prohibitions against flag burning, and the troops fighting under that flag in Vietnam who objected to its being burned: "The way to preserve the flag's special role is not to punish those who feel differently about these matters. It is to persuade them that they are wrong." The Court's role as the final expositor of the Constitution is well established, but its role as a platonic guardian admonishing those responsible to public opinion as if they were truant school children has no similar place in our system of government. * * *

Uncritical extension of constitutional protection to the burning of the flag risks the frustration of the very purpose for which organized governments are instituted. The Court decides that the American flag is just another symbol, about which not only must opinions pro and con be tolerated, but for which the most minimal public respect may not be enjoined. The government may conscript men into the Armed Forces where they must fight and perhaps die for the flag, but the government may not prohibit the public burning of the banner under which they fight. I would uphold the Texas statute as applied in this case.[2]

JUSTICE STEVENS, dissenting. * * *

---

2. In holding that the Texas statute as applied to Johnson violates the First Amendment, the Court does not consider Johnson's claims that the statute is unconstitutionally vague or overbroad. I think those claims are without merit. [By] defining "desecrate" as "deface," "damage" or otherwise "physically mistreat" in a manner that the actor knows will "seriously offend" others, § 42.09 only prohibits flagrant acts of physical abuse and destruction of the flag of the sort at issue here—soaking a flag with lighter fluid and igniting it in public—and not any of the examples of improper flag etiquette cited in Respondent's brief.

Even if flag burning could be considered just another species of symbolic speech under the logical application of the rules that the Court has developed in its interpretation of the First Amendment in other contexts, this case has an intangible dimension that makes those rules inapplicable.

A country's flag is a symbol of more than "nationhood and national unity." [T]he American flag * * * is more than a proud symbol of the courage, the determination, and the gifts of nature that transformed 13 fledgling Colonies into a world power. It is a symbol of freedom, of equal opportunity, of religious tolerance, and of goodwill for other peoples who share our aspirations. The symbol carries its message to dissidents both at home and abroad who may have no interest at all in our national unity or survival.

The value of the flag as a symbol cannot be measured. Even so, I have no doubt that the interest in preserving that value for the future is both significant and legitimate. Conceivably that value will be enhanced by the Court's conclusion that our national commitment to free expression is so strong that even the United States as ultimate guarantor of that freedom is without power to prohibit the desecration of its unique symbol. But I am unpersuaded. The creation of a federal right to post bulletin boards and graffiti on the Washington Monument might enlarge the market for free expression, but at a cost I would not pay. Similarly, in my considered judgment, sanctioning the public desecration of the flag will tarnish its value—both for those who cherish the ideas for which it waves and for those who desire to don the robes of martyrdom by burning it. That tarnish is not justified by the trivial burden on free expression occasioned by requiring that an available, alternative mode of expression—including uttering words critical of the flag be employed.

It is appropriate to emphasize certain propositions that are not implicated by this case. [The] statute does not compel any conduct or any profession of respect for any idea or any symbol. [Nor] does the statute violate "the government's paramount obligation of neutrality in its regulation of protected communication." The content of respondent's message has no relevance whatsoever to the case. The concept of "desecration" does not turn on the substance of the message the actor intends to convey, but rather on whether those who view the act will take serious offense. Accordingly, one intending to convey a message of respect for the flag by burning it in a public square might nonetheless be guilty of desecration if he knows that others—perhaps simply because they misperceive the intended message—will be seriously offended. Indeed, even if the actor knows that all possible witnesses will understand that he intends to send a message of respect, he might still be guilty of desecration if he also knows that this understanding does not lessen the offense taken by some of those witnesses. The case has nothing to do with "disagreeable ideas." It involves disagreeable conduct that, in my opinion, diminishes the value of an important national asset.

[Had respondent] chosen to spray paint—or perhaps convey with a motion picture projector—his message of dissatisfaction on the facade of the Lincoln Memorial, there would be no question about the power of the Government to prohibit his means of expression. The prohibition would be supported by the legitimate interest in preserving the quality of an important national asset. Though the asset at stake in this case is intangible, given its unique value, the same interest supports a prohibition on the desecration of the American flag.*

---

* The Court suggested that a prohibition against flag desecration is not content-neutral because this form of symbolic speech is only used by persons who are critical of the flag or the ideas it represents. In making this suggestion the Court does not pause to consider the

The ideas of liberty and equality have been an irresistible force in motivating leaders like Patrick Henry, Susan B. Anthony, and Abraham Lincoln, schoolteachers like Nathan Hale and Booker T. Washington, the Philippine Scouts who fought at Bataan, and the soldiers who scaled the bluff at Omaha Beach. If those ideas are worth fighting for—and our history demonstrates that they are—it cannot be true that the flag that uniquely symbolizes their power is not itself worthy of protection from unnecessary desecration.

Notes and Questions

1. *Patriotism.* Consider George Fletcher, *Loyalty* 141 (1993): "The [question] is whether the Congress has a sufficiently clear interest in promoting national loyalty to interpret the crime of flag burning as a sanction aimed not at the message of protest, but at the act, regardless of its political slant. Whether Congress and the country possess this interest depends, of course, on what one thinks of loyalty and devotion to country as a value. A high regard for patriotism, for sharing a common purpose in cherishing our people and seeking to solve our problems, leads one easily to perceive the expression of our unity as a value important in itself. The flag is at least as important—to go from the sublime to the ridiculous—as protecting draft cards so that the Selective Service System can function efficiently."

2. *Dissent.* Consider Steven Shiffrin, *The First Amendment and the Meaning of America,* in *Identities, Politics, and Rights* 318 (Austin Sarat & Thomas Kearnes eds. 1996): "The flag-burning prohibition is uniquely troubling not because it interferes with the metaphorical marketplace of ideas, not because it topples our image of a content neutral government (*that* has fallen many times), and not merely because it suppresses political speech. The flag-burning prohibition is a naked attempt to smother dissent. If we must have a 'central meaning' of the first amendment, we should recognize that the dissenters—those who attack existing customs, habits, traditions and authorities—stand at the center of the first amendment and not at its periphery. Gregory Johnson was attacking a symbol which the vast majority of Americans regard with reverence. But that is *exactly* why he deserved first amendment protection. The first amendment has a special regard for those who swim against the current, for those who would shake us to our foundations, for those who reject prevailing authority. In burning the flag, Gregory Johnson rejected, opposed, even blasphemed the Nation's most important political, social, and cultural icon. Clearly Gregory Johnson's alleged act of burning the flag was a quintessential act of dissent. A dissent centered conception of the first amendment would make it clear that *Johnson* was an easy case—rightly decided."

3. *The meaning of the flag.* Consider Kenneth Karst, *Law's Promise, Law's Expression: Visions of Power in the Politics of Race, Gender, and Religion* 165 (1993): "According to those opinions the flag stands for our nationhood or

far-reaching consequences of its introduction of disparate impact analysis into our First Amendment jurisprudence. It seems obvious that a prohibition against the desecration of a gravesite is content-neutral even if it denies some protesters the right to make a symbolic statement by extinguishing the flame in Arlington Cemetery where John F. Kennedy is buried while permitting others to salute the flame by bowing their heads. Few would doubt that a protester who extinguishes the flame has desecrated the gravesite, regardless of whether he prefaces that act with a speech explaining that his purpose is to express deep admiration or unmitigated scorn for the late President. Likewise, few would claim that the protester who bows his head has desecrated the gravesite, even if he makes clear that his purpose is to show disrespect. In such a case, as in a flag burning case, the prohibition against desecration has absolutely nothing to do with the content of the message that the symbolic speech is intended to convey.

national unity (Brennan, paraphrasing the state's lawyers); for principles of freedom or inclusiveness (Brennan); for the nation's resiliency (Brennan); for the nation itself (Rehnquist); for something men will die for in war (Rehnquist); for 'America's imagined past and present' (Rehnquist, in Sheldon Nahmod's apt paraphrase); for courage, freedom, equal opportunity, religious tolerance, and 'goodwill for other peoples who share our aspirations' (Stevens); and for shared beliefs in law and peace and 'the freedom that sustains the human spirit' (Kennedy). So, even within the Supreme Court, the flag stands at once for freedom and for obedience to law, for war and for peace, for unity and for tolerance of difference."

4. *The flag's "physical integrity."* Brennan, J., observes that the Texas law is "not aimed at protecting the physical integrity of the flag in all circumstances. * * *" What if it were?[d]

In response to *Johnson*, Congress passed the Flag Protection Act of 1989 which attached criminal penalties to the knowing mutilation, defacement, burning, maintaining on the floor or ground, or trampling upon any flag of the United States. UNITED STATES v. EICHMAN, 496 U.S. 310, 110 S.Ct. 2404, 110 L.Ed.2d 287 (1990), per BRENNAN, J., invalidated the statute: "Although the Flag Protection Act contains no explicit content-based limitation on the scope of prohibited conduct, it is nevertheless clear that the Government's asserted *interest* is 'related "to the suppression of free expression"' and concerned with the content of such expression. The Government's interest in protecting the 'physical integrity' of a privately owned flag rests upon a perceived need to preserve the flag's status as a symbol of our Nation and certain national ideals. But the mere destruction or disfigurement of a particular physical manifestation of the symbol, without more, does not diminish or otherwise affect the symbol itself in any way. For example, the secret destruction of a flag in one's own basement would not threaten the flag's recognized meaning. Rather, the Government's desire to preserve the flag as a symbol for certain national ideals is implicated 'only when a person's treatment of the flag communicates [a] message' to others that is inconsistent with those ideals."

STEVENS, J., joined by Rehnquist, C.J., White and O'Connor, JJ., dissenting, argued that the government's "legitimate interest in protecting the symbolic value of the American flag" outweighed the free speech interest. In describing the flag's symbolic value he stated that the flag "inspires and motivates the average citizen to make personal sacrifices in order to achieve societal goals of overriding importance; at all times, it serves as a reminder of the paramount importance of pursuing the ideals that characterize our society. * * * [T]he communicative value of a well-placed bomb in the Capital does not entitle it to the protection of the First Amendment. Burning a flag is not, of course, equivalent to burning a public building. Assuming that the protester is burning his own flag, it causes no physical harm to other persons or to their property. The impact is purely symbolic, and it is apparent that some thoughtful persons believe that impact far from depreciating the value of the symbol, will actually decrease its meaning. I most respectfully disagree."[e]

d. For commentary concerning the extent to which a focus on physical integrity can be separated from a concern with content, see Kent Greenawalt, *O'er the Land of the Free: Flag Burning as Speech*, 37 UCLA L.Rev. 925 (1990); Frank Michelman, *Saving Old Glory: On Constitutional Iconography*, 42 Stan.L.Rev.

1337 (1990); Geoffrey Stone, *Flag Burning and the Constitution*, 75 Ia.L.Rev. 111 (1989); Mark Tushnet, *The Flag–Burning Episode: An Essay on the Constitution*, 61 U.Col.L.Rev. 39 (1990).

e. But see Arnold Loewy, *The Flag–Burning Case: Freedom of Speech When We Need It*

5. Prior to adopting the Flag Protection Act, the Senate by a vote of 97–3 had passed a resolution expressing "profound disappointment with the [*Johnson*] decision." The House had approved a similar resolution by a vote of 411–5, and President Bush had proposed a constitutional amendment to overrule *Johnson*. Opponents of the amendment argued that a carefully drawn statute might (or would) be upheld by the Court. Suppose you were a member of the House or Senate at that time. Suppose you supported *Johnson* but believed that the statute might be held constitutional, even though you did not think it should be. Suppose you also believed that if a statute were not passed an amendment would.[f]

Consider this exchange during hearings of the House Subcommittee on Civil and Constitutional Rights on *Statutory and Constitutional Responses to the Supreme Court Decision in Texas v. Johnson* (1989): Former Solicitor General Charles Fried: "My good friends and colleagues, Rex Lee and Laurence Tribe, have testified that a statute might be drawn that would pass constitutional muster. [I] hope and urge and pray that we will not act—that no statute be passed and of course that the Constitution not be amended. In short, I believe that *Johnson* is right [in] principle." * * *

Representative Schroeder: "I thought your testimony was eloquent. I think in a purist world, that is where we should go. But [we] are not talking about a purist world. We are talking about a very political world." * * *

Mr. Fried: "There are times when you earn your rather inadequate salary by just doing the right thing, and where you seem to agree with me is that the right thing to do is to do neither one of these. * * * It is called leadership."

Representative Schroeder: "It is called leadership. * * * But I guess what I am saying is if we can't stop a stampede on an amendment without something, isn't it better to try to save the Bill of Rights and the Constitution?"

Community for Creative Non–Violence (CCNV) sought to conduct a wintertime demonstration near the White House in Lafayette Park and the Mall to dramatize the plight of the homeless. The National Park Service authorized the erection of two symbolic tent cities for purposes of the demonstration, but denied CCNV's request that demonstrators be permitted to sleep in the tents. National Park Service regulations permit camping (the "use of park land for living accommodation purposes such as sleeping activities") in National Parks only in campgrounds designated for that purpose.

CLARK v. COMMUNITY FOR CREATIVE NON–VIOLENCE, 468 U.S. 288, 104 S.Ct. 3065, 82 L.Ed.2d 221 (1984), per WHITE, J., rejected CCNV's claim that the regulations could not be constitutionally applied against its demonstration: "We need not differ with the view of the Court of Appeals that overnight sleeping in connection with the demonstration is expressive conduct protected to some extent by the First Amendment.[5] We assume for present purposes, but do not

Most, 68 N.C.L.Rev. 165, 174 (1989): "Perhaps the ultimate irony is that *Johnson* has done more to preserve the flag as a symbol of liberty than any prior decision, while the decision's detractors would allow real desecration of the flag by making it a symbol of political oppression." Compare Robin West, *Foreword: Taking Freedom Seriously,* 104 Harv.L.Rev. 43,

97–98 (1990) (the militaristic patriotism associated with the flag menaces dissent); see also Greenawalt, fn. c supra.

f. For commentary, see Michelman, fn. d supra.

5. We reject the suggestion of the plurality below, however, that the burden on the demonstrators is limited to "the advancement of a

decide, that such is the case, cf. *O'Brien,* but this assumption only begins the inquiry. Expression, whether oral or written or symbolized by conduct, is subject to reasonable time, place, or manner restrictions. We have often noted that restrictions of this kind are valid provided that they are justified without reference to the content of the regulated speech, that they are narrowly tailored to serve a significant governmental interest, and that they leave open ample alternative channels for communication of the information.

"It is also true that a message may be delivered by conduct that is intended to be communicative and that, in context, would reasonably be understood by the viewer to be communicative. Symbolic expression of this kind may be forbidden or regulated if the conduct itself may constitutionally be regulated, if the regulation is narrowly drawn to further a substantial governmental interest, and if the interest is unrelated to the suppression of free speech. *O'Brien.*

"[That] sleeping, like the symbolic tents themselves, may be expressive and part of the message delivered by the demonstration does not make the ban any less a limitation on the manner of demonstrating, for reasonable time, place, or manner regulations normally have the purpose and direct effect of limiting expression but are nevertheless valid. Neither does the fact that sleeping, arguendo, may be expressive conduct, rather than oral or written expression, render the sleeping prohibition any less a time, place, or manner regulation. To the contrary, the Park Service neither attempts to ban sleeping generally nor to ban it everywhere in the parks. It has established areas for camping and forbids it elsewhere, including Lafayette Park and the Mall. Considered as such, we have very little trouble concluding that the Park Service may prohibit overnight sleeping in the parks involved here.

"The requirement that the regulation be content-neutral is clearly satisfied. The courts below accepted that view, and it is not disputed here that the prohibition on camping, and on sleeping specifically, is content-neutral and is not being applied because of disagreement with the message presented.[a] Neither was the regulation faulted, nor could it be, on the ground that without overnight sleeping the plight of the homeless could not be communicated in other ways. The regulation otherwise left the demonstration intact, with its symbolic city, signs, and the presence of those who were willing to take their turns in a day-and-night vigil. Respondents do not suggest that there was, or is, any barrier to delivering to the media, or to the public by other means, the intended message concerning the plight of the homeless.

"It is also apparent to us that the regulation narrowly focuses on the Government's substantial interest in maintaining the parks in the heart of our Capital in an attractive and intact condition, readily available to the millions of people who wish to see and enjoy them by their presence. To permit camping—using these areas as living accommodations—would be totally inimical to these purposes, as would be readily understood by those who have frequented the

plausible contention" that their conduct is expressive. Although it is common to place the burden upon the Government to justify impingements on First Amendment interests, it is the obligation of the person desiring to engage in assertedly expressive conduct to demonstrate that the First Amendment even applies. To hold otherwise would be to create a rule that all conduct is presumptively expressive.

a. Marshall, J., dissenting, observed that CCNV had held a demonstration the previous winter in which it set up nine tents and slept in Lafayette Park. The D.C. Circuit held that the regulations did not preclude such a demonstration. According to Marshall, J., "The regulations at issue in this case were passed in direct response" to that holding.

National Parks across the country and observed the unfortunate consequences of the activities of those who refuse to confine their camping to designated areas.

"It is urged by [CCNV] that if the symbolic city of tents was to be permitted and if the demonstrators did not intend to cook, dig, or engage in aspects of camping other than sleeping, the incremental benefit to the parks could not justify the ban on sleeping, which was here an expressive activity said to enhance the message concerning the plight of the poor and homeless. We cannot agree. In the first place, we seriously doubt that the First Amendment requires the Park Service to permit a demonstration in Lafayette Park and the Mall involving a 24–hour vigil and the erection of tents to accommodate 150 people. Furthermore, although we have assumed for present purposes that the sleeping banned in this case would have an expressive element, it is evident that its major value to this demonstration would be facilitative. Without a permit to sleep, it would be difficult to get the poor and homeless to participate or to be present at all.[b]

"Beyond this, however, it is evident from our cases that the validity of this regulation need not be judged solely by reference to the demonstration at hand.[c] Absent the prohibition on sleeping, there would be other groups who would demand permission to deliver an asserted message by camping in Lafayette Park. Some of them would surely have as credible a claim in this regard as does CCNV, and the denial of permits to still others would present difficult problems for the Park Service. With the prohibition, however, as is evident in the case before us, at least some around-the-clock demonstrations lasting for days on end will not materialize, others will be limited in size and duration, and the purposes of the regulation will thus be materially served. Perhaps these purposes would be more effectively and not so clumsily achieved by preventing tents and 24–hour vigils entirely in the core areas. But the Park Service's decision to permit nonsleeping demonstrations does not, in our view, impugn the camping prohibition as a valuable, but perhaps imperfect, protection to the parks. If the Government has a legitimate interest in ensuring that the National Parks are adequately protected, which we think it has, and if the parks would be more exposed to harm without the sleeping prohibition than with it, the ban is safe from invalidation under the First Amendment as a reasonable regulation of the manner in which a demonstration may be carried out. * * *

"[The] foregoing analysis demonstrates that the Park Service regulation is sustainable under the four-factor standard of *O'Brien,* for validating a regulation of expressive conduct, which, in the last analysis is little, if any, different from the standard applied to time, place, or manner restrictions.[8] No one contends that

b. What if it were the exclusive value? For discussion, see Gary Francione, *Experimentation and the Marketplace Theory of the First Amendment,* 136 U.Pa.L.Rev. 417 (1987).

c. For debate about this point and its implications, compare Frank Easterbrook, *Foreword: The Court and the Economic System,* 98 Harv.L.Rev. 4, 19–21 (1984) with Laurence Tribe, *Constitutional Calculus: Equal Justice or Economic Efficiency?* 98 Harv.L.Rev. 592, 599–603 (1985) and Frank Easterbrook, *Method, Result, and Authority: A Reply,* 98 Harv. L.Rev. 622, 626 (1985).

8. Reasonable time, place, or manner restrictions are valid even though they directly limit oral or written expression. It would be odd to insist on a higher standard for limita-

tions aimed at regulable conduct and having only an incidental impact on speech. Thus, if the time, place, or manner restriction on expressive sleeping, if that is what is involved in this case, sufficiently and narrowly serves a substantial enough governmental interest to escape First Amendment condemnation, it is untenable to invalidate it under *O'Brien* on the ground that the governmental interest is insufficient to warrant the intrusion on First Amendment concerns or that there is an inadequate nexus between the regulation and the interest sought to be served. We note that only recently, in a case dealing with the regulation of signs, the Court framed the issue under *O'Brien* and then based a crucial part of its analysis on the time, place, or manner cases.

aside from its impact on speech a rule against camping or overnight sleeping in public parks is beyond the constitutional power of the Government to enforce. And for the reasons we have discussed above, there is a substantial Government interest in conserving park property, an interest that is plainly served by, and requires for its implementation, measures such as the proscription of sleeping that are designed to limit the wear and tear on park properties. That interest is unrelated to suppression of expression.

"We are unmoved by the Court of Appeals' view that the challenged regulation is unnecessary, and hence invalid, because there are less speech-restrictive alternatives that could have satisfied the Government interest in preserving park lands. [The] Court of Appeals' suggestions that the Park Service minimize the possible injury by reducing the size, duration, or frequency of demonstrations would still curtail the total allowable expression in which demonstrators could engage, whether by sleeping or otherwise, and these suggestions represent no more than a disagreement with the Park Service over how much protection the core parks require or how an acceptable level of preservation is to be attained. We do not believe, however, that either *United States v. O'Brien* or the time, place, or manner decisions assign to the judiciary the authority to replace the Park Service as the manager of the Nation's parks or endow the judiciary with the competence to judge how much protection of park lands is wise and how that level of conservation is to be [attained.]"

BURGER, C.J., joined in the Court's opinion, adding: "[CCNV's] attempt at camping in the park is a form of 'picketing'; it is conduct, not speech. [It] trivializes the First Amendment to seek to use it as a shield in the manner asserted here."

MARSHALL, J., joined by Brennan, J., dissented: "The majority assumes, without deciding, that the respondents' conduct is entitled to constitutional protection. The problem with this assumption is that the Court thereby avoids examining closely the reality of respondents' planned expression. The majority's approach denatures respondents' asserted right and thus makes all too easy identification of a Government interest sufficient to warrant its abridgment.

"[Missing] from the majority's description is any inkling that Lafayette Park and the Mall have served as the sites for some of the most rousing political demonstrations in the Nation's history.[2] [The] primary purpose for making *sleep* an integral part of the demonstration was 'to re-enact the central reality of homelessness' and to impress upon public consciousness, in as dramatic a way as possible, that homelessness is a widespread problem, often ignored, that confronts its victims with life-threatening deprivations. As one of the homeless men seeking to demonstrate explained: 'Sleeping in Lafayette Park or on the Mall, for me, is to show people that conditions are so poor for the homeless and poor in this city that we would actually sleep *outside* in the winter to get the point across.' * * * Here respondents clearly intended to protest the reality of homelessness by sleeping outdoors in the winter in the near vicinity of the magisterial residence of the President of the United States. In addition to accentuating the political character of their protest by their choice of location and mode of communication, respondents also intended to underline the meaning of their protest by giving their demonstration satirical names. Respondents planned to name the demon-

---

2. At oral argument, the Government informed the Court "that on any given day there will be an average of three or so demonstrations going on" in the Mall–Lafayette Park area. Respondents accurately describe Lafayette Park "as the American analogue to 'Speaker's Corner' in Hyde Park."

stration on the Mall 'Congressional Village,' and the demonstration in Lafayette Park, 'Reaganville II.' * * *

"Although sleep in the context of this case is symbolic speech protected by the First Amendment, it is nonetheless subject to reasonable time, place, and manner restrictions. I agree with the standard enunciated by the majority.[6] I conclude, however, that the regulations at issue in this case, as applied to respondents, fail to satisfy this [standard].

"[T]here are no substantial Government interests advanced by the Government's regulations as applied to respondents. All that the Court's decision advances are the prerogatives of a bureaucracy that over the years has shown an implacable hostility toward citizens' exercise of First Amendment [rights].

"The disposition of this case impels me to make two additional observations. First, in this case, as in some others involving time, place, and manner restrictions, the Court has dramatically lowered its scrutiny of governmental regulations once it has determined that such regulations are content-neutral.[d] The result has been the creation of a two-tiered approach to First Amendment cases: while regulations that turn on the content of the expression are subjected to a strict form of judicial review, regulations that are aimed at matters other than expression receive only a minimal level of scrutiny. [The] Court has seemingly overlooked the fact that content-neutral restrictions are also capable of unnecessarily restricting protected expressive activity.[13] [The] Court [has] transformed the ban against content distinctions from a floor that offers all persons at least equal liberty under the First Amendment into a ceiling that restricts persons to the protection of First Amendment equality—but nothing more.[14] The consistent imposition of silence upon all may fulfill the dictates of an evenhanded content-neutrality. But it offends our 'profound national commitment to the principle that debate on public issues should be uninhibited, robust, and wide-open'. *New York Times Co. v. Sullivan.*

"Second, the disposition of this case reveals a mistaken assumption regarding the motives and behavior of Government officials who create and administer content-neutral regulations. The Court's salutary skepticism of governmental decisionmaking in First Amendment matters suddenly dissipates once it determines that a restriction is not content-based. The Court evidently assumes that the balance struck by officials is deserving of deference so long as it does not appear to be tainted by content discrimination. What the Court fails to recognize is that public officials have strong incentives to overregulate even in the absence of an intent to censor particular views. This incentive stems from the fact that of the two groups whose interests officials must accommodate—on the one hand, the

6. I also agree with the majority that no substantial difference distinguishes the test applicable to time, place, and manner restrictions and the test articulated in *O'Brien.*

d. In support of Marshall, J.'s contention, see generally William Lee, *Lonely Pamphleteers, Little People, and the Supreme Court,* 54 G.W.U.L.Rev. 757 (1986).

13. See Martin Redish, *The Content Distinction in First Amendment Analysis,* 34 Stan. L.Rev. 113 (1981).

14. Furthermore, [a] content-neutral regulation that restricts an inexpensive mode of communication will fall most heavily upon relatively poor speakers and to points of view that

such speakers typically espouse. [See Lee, fn. d supra.] This sort of latent inequality is very much in evidence in this case, for respondents lack the financial means necessary to buy access to more conventional modes of persuasion.

A disquieting feature about the disposition of this case is that it lends credence to the charge that judicial administration of the First Amendment, in conjunction with a social order marked by large disparities of wealth and other sources of power, tends systematically to discriminate against efforts by the relatively disadvantaged to convey their political ideas. * * *

interests of the general public and, on the other, the interests of those who seek to use a particular forum for First Amendment activity—the political power of the former is likely to be far greater than that of the latter.[16] "

Notes and Questions

1. Consider Mark Tushnet, *Character as Argument,* 14 Law and Social Inquiry 539, 549 (1989) (reviewing Harry Kalven, *A Worthy Tradition*): "To capture the attention of a public accustomed to dignified protest, and able to screen it from consciousness, dissidents may have to adopt novel forms of protest, such as sleeping in a national park overnight to draw attention to the disgrace of a national policy that deprives many people of decent shelter. Yet, precisely because their protests take a novel form, they may not be covered by the worthy tradition that Kalven honors. In this sense the dynamics of protest may make the protection of free speech what Kalven tellingly calls a 'luxury civil liberty,' a civil liberty to be enjoyed when nothing of consequence turns on protecting speech and to be abandoned when it really matters."

2. Should the Court have decided whether sleeping in the park in these circumstances was a form of expression entitled to some degree of first amendment protection? Should all forms of expression receive some level of first amendment protection?

(a) *Terrorism.* Would a political assassination be unprotected expression because it is not within the scope of the first amendment or because the government interests outweigh the expressive values. Does it matter?

(b) *The absence of "ideas."* Is the presence of an "idea" a necessary condition for expression to come within the first amendment's scope? Should nude dancing be excluded from the first amendment's scope because it is not intended to communicate ideas? Should protection for paintings depend upon whether "ideas" are expressed? See *Schad v. Mount Ephraim,* p. 702 infra: "[N]ude dancing is not without its First Amendment protections from official regulation." Should hair styles be afforded first amendment protection? Are hair styles distinguishable from nude dancing on the ground that the latter is a form of expressive entertainment? If so, should video games be afforded first amendment protection? See Note, *The First Amendment Side Effects of Curing Pac–Man Fever,* 84 Colum.L.Rev. 744 (1984). But see Frederick Schauer, *Free Speech and the Demise of the Soapbox* Book Review, 84 Colum.L.Rev. 558, 565 (1984) ("[T]he first amendment importance of the messages from an automatic teller to the bank's central computer completely escapes me, as does the first amendment importance of the mutual exchange of electronic and visual symbols between me and the Pac–Man machine.").[e]

3. The "time, place, or manner" test set out in *Clark* is differently stated in different cases. For example, *U.S. Postal Service v. Council of Greenburgh,* 453 U.S. 114, 101 S.Ct. 2676, 69 L.Ed.2d 517 (1981), speaks of "adequate" as opposed to "ample" alternative channels of communication, and *City of Renton v. Playtime Theatres, Inc.,* p. 702 infra, transcends the difference by requiring that the

16. See David Goldberger, *Judicial Scrutiny in Public Forum Cases: Misplaced Trust in the Judgment of Public Officials,* 32 Buffalo L.Rev. 175, 208 (1983).

e. See Robert Post, *Recuperating First Amendment Doctrine,* 47 Stan.L.Rev. 1249 (1995) (speech in its ordinary language sense has no inherent constitutional value and

should be defined to include only those social practices which implicate free speech values). Cf. Stanley Fish, *There's No Such Thing as Free Speech,* 102 (1994) (" 'Free speech' is just the name we give to verbal behavior that serves the substantive agendas we wish to advance").

restriction not "unreasonably limit" alternative channels of communication. Beyond these differences, a number of cases state that the regulation must serve a significant government interest without stating that it must be "narrowly tailored" to serve a significant government interest. See e.g., *Heffron v. International Soc. For Krishna Consciousness,* p. 801 infra. But see *Ward v. Rock Against Racism,* p. 801 infra (reaffirming and defining narrowly tailored requirement). Assuming sleeping in the *Clark* context implicates first amendment values, what test should apply?

New York Public Health law authorizes the forced closure of a building for one year if it has been used for the purpose of "lewdness, assignation or prostitution." A civil complaint alleged that prostitution solicitation and sexual activities by patrons were occurring at an adult bookstore within observation of the proprietor. Accordingly, the complaint called for the closure of the building for one year. There was no claim that any books in the store were obscene. The New York Court of Appeals held that the closure remedy violated the first amendment because it was broader than necessary to achieve the restriction against illicit sexual activities. It reasoned that an injunction against the alleged sexual conduct could further the state interest without infringing on first amendment values.

ARCARA v. CLOUD BOOKS, Inc., 478 U.S. 697, 106 S.Ct. 3172, 92 L.Ed.2d 568 (1986), per BURGER, C.J., reversed, holding that the closure remedy did not require any first amendment scrutiny: "This Court has applied First Amendment scrutiny to a statute regulating conduct which has the incidental effect of burdening the expression of a particular political opinion. *United States v. O'Brien.* * * *

"We have also applied First Amendment scrutiny to some statutes which, although directed at activity with no expressive component, impose a disproportionate burden upon those engaged in protected First Amendment activities. In *Minneapolis Star & Tribune v. Minnesota Commissioner of Revenue,* 460 U.S. 575, 103 S.Ct. 1365, 75 L.Ed.2d 295 (1983), we struck down a tax imposed on the sale of large quantities of newsprint and ink because the tax had the effect of singling out newspapers to shoulder its burden. [Even] while striking down the tax in *Minneapolis Star,* we emphasized: 'Clearly, the First Amendment does not prohibit all regulation of the press. It is beyond dispute that the States and the Federal Government can subject newspapers to generally applicable economic regulations without creating constitutional problems.'

"The New York Court of Appeals held that the *O'Brien* test for permissible governmental regulation was applicable to this case because the closure order sought by petitioner would also impose an incidental burden upon respondents' bookselling activities. [But] unlike the symbolic draft card burning in *O'Brien,* the sexual activity carried on in this case manifests absolutely no element of protected expression.[a] In *Paris Adult Theatre,* we underscored the fallacy of seeking to use the First Amendment as a cloak for obviously unlawful public sexual conduct by the diaphanous device of attributing protected expressive

---

a. In an earlier section of the opinion, Burger, C.J., stated that, "petitioners in *O'Brien* had, as respondents here do not, at least the semblance of expressive activity in their claim that the otherwise unlawful burning of a draft card was to 'carry a message' of the actor's opposition to the draft."

attributes to that conduct. First Amendment values may not be invoked by merely linking the words 'sex' and 'books.'

"Nor does the distinction drawn by the New York Public Health Law inevitably single out bookstores or others engaged in First Amendment protected activities for the imposition of its burden, as did the tax struck down in *Minneapolis Star*. [If] the city imposed closure penalties for demonstrated Fire Code violations or health hazards from inadequate sewage treatment, the First Amendment would not aid the owner of premises who had knowingly allowed such violations to persist.   * * *

"It is true that the closure order in this case would require respondents to move their bookselling business to another location. Yet we have not traditionally subjected every criminal and civil sanction imposed through legal process to 'least restrictive means' scrutiny simply because each particular remedy will have some effect on the First Amendment activities of those subject to sanction.[4]" **b**

O'CONNOR, J., joined by Stevens, J., concurred: "I agree that the Court of Appeals erred in applying a First Amendment standard of review where, as here, the government is regulating neither speech nor an incidental, non-expressive effect of speech. Any other conclusion would lead to the absurd result that any government action that had some conceivable speech-inhibiting consequences, such as the arrest of a newscaster for a traffic violation, would require analysis under the First Amendment."

BLACKMUN, J., joined by Brennan and Marshall, JJ., dissented: "Until today, this Court has never suggested that a State may suppress speech as much as it likes, without justification, so long as it does so through generally applicable regulations that have 'nothing to do with any expressive conduct.'   * * *

"At some point, of course, the impact of state regulation on First Amendment rights become so attenuated that it is easily outweighed by the state interest. But when a State directly and substantially impairs First Amendment activities, such as by shutting down a bookstore, I believe that the State must show, at a minimum, that it has chosen the least restrictive means of pursuing its legitimate objectives. The closure of a bookstore can no more be compared to a traffic arrest of a reporter than the closure of a church could be compared to the traffic arrest of its clergyman.

"A State has a legitimate interest in forbidding sexual acts committed in public, including a bookstore. An obvious method of eliminating such acts is to arrest the patron committing them. But the statute in issue does not provide for that. Instead, it imposes absolute liability on the bookstore simply because the activity occurs on the premises. And the penalty—a mandatory 1–year closure—imposes an unnecessary burden on speech. Of course 'linking the words "sex" and "books"' is not enough to extend First Amendment protection to illegal sexual activity, but neither should it suffice to remove First Amendment protec-

---

4. [T]here is no suggestion on the record before us that the closure of respondents' bookstore was sought under the public health nuisance statute as a pretext for the suppression of First Amendment protected material. Were respondents able to establish the existence of such a speech suppressive motivation or policy on the part of the District Attorney, they might have a claim of selective prosecution. Respondents in this case made no such assertion before the trial court.

b. On remand, the New York Court of Appeals held that, in the absence of a showing that the state had chosen a course no broader than necessary to accomplish its purpose, any forced closure of the bookstore would unduly impair the bookseller's rights of free expression under the New York State constitution. From New York's perspective, the question is not "who is aimed at but who is hit." *People ex rel. Arcara v. Cloud Books, Inc.*, 68 N.Y.2d 553, 510 N.Y.S.2d 844, 503 N.E.2d 492 (1986).

tion from books situated near the site of such activity. The State's purpose in stopping public lewdness cannot justify such a substantial infringement of First Amendment rights. * * *

"Petitioner has not demonstrated that a less restrictive remedy would be inadequate to abate the nuisance. The Court improperly attempts to shift to the bookseller the responsibility for finding an alternative site. But surely the Court would not uphold a city ordinance banning all public debate on the theory that the residents could move somewhere else.

Notes and Questions

1. Should the state's closing of a bookstore *always* trigger heightened judicial scrutiny? Is the first amendment really "not implicated" in *Arcara?* Should fire code regulations trigger first amendment scrutiny? Consider Comment, *Padlock Orders and Nuisance Laws,* 51 Albany L.Rev. 1007, 1026–27 (1987): "Closure penalties for fire code violations or health hazards from inadequate sewage treatment were offered as examples of generally applicable regulations which could constitutionally be applied to bookstores where the owner 'had knowingly allowed such violations to persist.' Few would argue with this conclusion. These generally applicable regulations would be within the state's constitutional power, would further a substantial governmental interest unrelated to the suppression of free expression, and the incidental restriction on first amendment freedoms, where the owner knowingly allowed the violations to persist, would be no greater than is essential to further the state's interest. Concluding that the *O'Brien* test is satisfied, however, does not support the conclusion that the test does not apply."

2. *Negative theory.* Should the scope of the first amendment be confined to instances in which government may have acted in a biased way? Consider Ronald Cass, *Commercial Speech, Constitutionalism, Collective Choice,* 56 U.Cin.L.Rev. 1317, 1352 (1988): "There is widespread agreement that limitation of official bias is the principal aim of the first amendment, historically and as amplified over the past half-century by the courts." See generally Ronald Cass, *The Perils of Positive Thinking: Constitutional Interpretation and Negative First Amendment Theory,* 34 U.C.L.A. L.Rev. 1405 (1987) (emphasizing official self interest and, to a lesser extent, intolerance as the principal motives of concern).

Professor Schauer has also attempted a justification for freedom of speech not based on any positive aspects of speech, but based on the premise that governments are "less capable of regulating speech than they are of regulating other forms of conduct." He suggests that bias, self-interest, and a general urge to suppress that with which one disagrees are significant reasons for this incapability. Frederick Schauer, *Free Speech: A Philosophical Enquiry* 80–86 (1982). See also Frederick Schauer, *Must Speech Be Special?,* 78 Nw.U.L.Rev. 1284 (1983). As he interprets the first amendment, therefore, its "focus * * * is on the motivations of the government." Frederick Schauer, *Cuban Cigars, Cuban Books, and the Problem of Incidental Restrictions on Communications,* 26 Wm. & Mary L.Rev. 779, 780 (1985).[c]

Is negative theory consistent with what the Court has *said* about free speech? With the doctrine it has produced? Consider, e.g., *Arcara. O'Brien.* The defama-

---

c. See also Frederick Schauer, *The Phenomenology of Speech and Harm,* 103 Ethics 635 (1993) (disputing the hypothesis that the harmful consequences of speech are less than those associated with other forms of conduct); Frederick Schauer, *The Sociology of the Hate Speech Debate,* 37 Vill.L.Rev. 805 (1992).

tion line of cases. Compare Frederick Schauer, *Cuban Cigars,* supra with Steven Shiffrin, *The First Amendment, Democracy, and Romance* (1990). Is the content-based/content-neutral distinction founded exclusively on a concern with government motive? See generally Geoffrey Stone, *Content Regulation and the First Amendment,* 25 Wm. & Mary L.Rev. 189 (1983) (arguing that the basis for the distinction is more complicated). Does an emphasis on motive or content unreasonably downplay the notion that the *effect* of government conduct on the quantity or quality of speech is of independent first amendment value? See generally Martin Redish, *The Content Distinction in First Amendment Analysis,* 34 Stan. L.Rev. 113 (1981); Susan Williams, *Content Discrimination and the First Amendment,* 139 U.Pa.L.Rev. 201 (1991).

3. Could *Arcara's* failure to find the first amendment implicated be justified without resort to negative theory or motive theory? Consider Laurence Tribe, *American Constitutional Law* 978–79 n. 2 (2d ed. 1988): "[W]hen *neither* the law, *nor* the act triggering its enforcement has any significant first amendment dimension, the fact that the law *incidentally* operates to restrict first amendment activity, and that some alternative state measure might offer a less restrictive means of pursuing the state's legitimate objectives, should not serve to condemn what the state has done as unconstitutional." Why not?

SECTION 3. IS SOME PROTECTED SPEECH LESS EQUAL THAN OTHER PROTECTED SPEECH?

I. NEAR OBSCENE SPEECH

YOUNG v. AMERICAN MINI THEATRES, INC.

427 U.S. 50, 96 S.Ct. 2440, 49 L.Ed.2d 310 (1976).

JUSTICE STEVENS delivered the opinion of the Court.*

[Detroit "Anti-Skid Row" ordinances prohibited "adult motion picture theaters" and "adult book stores" within 1,000 feet of any two other "regulated uses," which included such theaters and book stores, liquor stores, pool halls, pawnshops, and the like. The ordinances defined "adult motion picture theater" as one "presenting material distinguished or characterized by an emphasis on matter depicting, describing or relating to 'Specified Sexual Activities' [a] or 'Specified Anatomical Areas' " [b] and "adult book store" in substantially the same terms. The Court upheld the ordinances, reversing a decision in a federal declaratory judgment action by two theater owners wishing regularly to exhibit "adult" motion pictures.]

I. [R]espondents claim that the ordinances are too vague [because] they cannot determine how much of the ["specified"] activity may be permissible

---

* Part III of this opinion is joined only by The Chief Justice, Mr. Justice White, and Mr. Justice Rehnquist.

a. "Specified Sexual Activities" were defined thus:

"1. Human genitals in a state of sexual stimulation or arousal;

"2. Acts of human masturbation, sexual intercourse or sodomy;

"3. Fondling or other erotic touching of human genitals, pubic region, buttock or female breast."

b. "Specified Anatomical Areas" were defined thus:

"1. Less than completely and opaquely covered: (a) human genitals, pubic region, (b) buttock, and (c) female breast below a point immediately above the top of the areola, and

"2. Human male genitals in a discernibly turgid state, even if completely and opaquely covered."

before the exhibition is "characterized by an emphasis" on such matter. [We] find it unnecessary to consider the validity of [this argument. Both] theaters propose to offer adult fare on a regular basis. [Therefore], the element of vagueness in these ordinances has not affected these respondents. * * *

Because the ordinances affect communication protected by the First Amendment, respondents argue that they may raise the vagueness issue even though there is no uncertainty about the impact of the ordinances on their own rights. On several occasions we have determined that a defendant whose own speech was unprotected had standing to challenge the constitutionality of a statute which purported to prohibit protected speech, or even speech arguably protected. *Broadrick*. The exception is justified by the overriding importance of maintaining a free and open market for the interchange of ideas. Nevertheless, if the statute's deterrent effect of legitimate expression is not "both real and substantial" and if the statute is "readily subject to a narrowing construction by the state courts" the litigant is not permitted to assert the rights of third parties.

We are not persuaded that the Detroit Zoning Ordinances will have a significant deterrent effect on the exhibition of films protected by the First Amendment. [T]he only vagueness in the ordinances relates to the amount of sexually explicit activity that may be portrayed before the material can be said to be "characterized by an emphasis" on such matter. For most films the question will be readily answerable; to the extent that an area of doubt exists, we see no reason why the statute is not "readily subject to a narrowing construction by the state courts." Since there is surely a less vital interest in the uninhibited exhibition of material that is on the borderline between pornography and artistic expression than in the free dissemination of ideas of social and political significance,[c] and since the limited amount of uncertainty in the statute is easily susceptible of a narrowing construction, we think this is an inappropriate case in which to adjudicate the hypothetical claims of persons not before the Court. * * *

III. [T]he use of streets and parks for the free expression of views on national affairs may not be conditioned upon the sovereign's agreement with what a speaker may intend to say. [If] picketing in the vicinity of a school is to be allowed to express the point of view of labor, that means of expression in that place must be allowed for other points of view as well. As we said in [*Chicago Police Dep't v. Mosley,* p. 802 infra], "The central problem with Chicago's ordinance is that it describes permissible picketing in terms of its subject matter. [A]bove all else, the First Amendment means that government has no power to restrict expression because of its message, its ideas, its subject matter, or its content. [Any] restriction on expressive activity because of its content would completely undercut the 'profound national commitment to the principle that debate on public issues should be uninhibited, robust, and wide-open.' [*New York Times*]. Selective exclusions from a public forum may not be based on content alone, and may not be justified by reference to content alone."

---

c. But see Hunter & Law, p. 656 supra, at 119–20: "[S]exual speech is political. One core insight of modern feminism is that the person is political. The question of who does the dishes and rocks the cradle affects both the nature of the home and the composition of the legislature. The dynamics of intimate relations are likewise political, both to the individuals involved and by their multiplied effects to the wider society. To argue [that] sexually explicit speech is less important than other categories of discourse reinforces the conceptual structures that have identified women's concerns with relationships and intimacy as less significant and valuable precisely because those concerns are falsely regarded as having no bearing on the structure of social and political life."

This statement, and others to the same effect, read literally and without regard for the facts of the case in which it was made, would absolutely preclude any regulation of expressive activity predicated in whole or in part on the content of the communication. But we learned long ago that broad statements of principle, no matter how correct in the context in which they are made, are sometimes qualified by contrary decisions before the absolute limit of the stated principle is reached. When we review this Court's actual adjudications in the First Amendment area, we find this to have been the case with the stated principle that there may be no restriction whatever on expressive activity because of its content. * * *

The question whether speech is, or is not, protected by the First Amendment often depends on the content of the speech. Thus, the line between permissible advocacy and impermissible incitation to crime or violence depends, not merely on the setting in which the speech occurs, but also on exactly what the speaker had to say. Similarly, it is the content of the utterance that determines whether it is a protected epithet or an unprotected "fighting comment." * * *

Even within the area of protected speech, a difference in content may require a different governmental response. [*New York Times*] held that a public official may not recover damages from a critic of his official conduct without proof of "malice" as specially defined in that opinion. Implicit in the opinion is the assumption that if the content of the newspaper article had been different—that is, if its subject matter had not been a public official—a lesser standard of proof would have been adequate. [We] have recently held that the First Amendment affords some protection to commercial speech. [The] measure of [protection] to commercial speech will surely be governed largely by the content of the communication.[32] * * *

More directly in point are opinions dealing with the question whether the First Amendment prohibits the state and federal governments from wholly suppressing sexually oriented materials on the basis of their "obscene character." In *Ginsberg,* the Court upheld a conviction for selling to a minor magazines which were concededly not "obscene" if shown to adults. Indeed, the Members of the Court who would accord the greatest protection to such materials have repeatedly indicated that the State could prohibit the distribution or exhibition of such materials to juveniles and unconsenting adults. Surely the First Amendment does not foreclose such a prohibition; yet it is equally clear that any such prohibition must rest squarely on an appraisal of the content of material otherwise within a constitutionally protected area.

Such a line may be drawn on the basis of content without violating the Government's paramount obligation of neutrality in its regulation of protected communication. For the regulation of the places where sexually explicit films may be exhibited is unaffected by whatever social, political, or philosophical message the film may be intended to communicate; whether the motion picture ridicules or characterizes one point of view or another, the effect of the ordinances is exactly the same.

Moreover, even though we recognize that the First Amendment will not tolerate the total suppression of erotic materials that have some arguably artistic value, it is manifest that society's interest in protecting this type of expression is

---

32. As Mr. Justice Stewart pointed out in *Virginia Pharmacy* [p. 716 infra], the "differences between commercial price and product advertising [and] ideological communication" permits regulation of the former that the First Amendment would not tolerate with respect to the latter (concurring opinion).

of a wholly different, and lesser, magnitude than the interest in untrammeled political debate that inspired Voltaire's immortal comment.[d] Whether political oratory or philosophical discussion moves us to applaud or to despise what is said, every school-child can understand why our duty to defend the right to speak remains the same. But few of us would march our sons and daughters off to war to preserve the citizen's right to see "Specified Sexual Activities" exhibited in the theaters of our choice. Even though the First Amendment protects communication in this area from total suppression, we hold that the State may legitimately use the content of these materials as the basis for placing them in a different classification from other motion pictures.

The remaining question is whether the line drawn by these ordinances is justified by the city's interest in preserving the character of its neighborhoods. [The] record discloses a factual basis for the Common Council's conclusion that this kind of restriction will have the desired effect.[34] It is not our function to appraise the wisdom of its decision to require adult theaters to be separated rather than concentrated in the same areas. In either event, the city's interest in attempting to preserve the quality of urban life is one that must be accorded high respect. Moreover, the city must be allowed a reasonable opportunity to experiment with solutions to admittedly serious problems.

Since what is ultimately at stake is nothing more than a limitation on the place where adult films may be exhibited,[35] even though the determination of whether a particular film fits that characterization turns on the nature of its content, we conclude that the city's interest in the present and future character of its neighborhoods adequately supports its classification of motion pictures. * * *

JUSTICE POWELL, concurring in the judgment and portions of the opinion.

Although I agree with much of what is said in the plurality opinion, [my] approach to the resolution of this case is sufficiently different to prompt me to write separately.[1] I view the case as presenting an example of innovative land-use regulation, implicating First Amendment concerns only incidentally and to a limited extent. * * *

In this case, there is no indication that the application of the Anti–Skid Row Ordinance to adult theaters has the effect of suppressing production of or, to any significant degree, restricting access to adult movies. Nortown concededly will not be able to exhibit adult movies at its present location, and the ordinance limits the potential location of the proposed Pussy Cat. The constraints of the ordinance with respect to location may indeed create economic loss for some who are

---

d. The opinion had earlier quoted Voltaire: "I disapprove of what you say, but I will defend to the death your right to say it."

34. The City Council's determination was that a concentration of "adult" movie theaters causes the area to deteriorate and become a focus of crime, effects which are not attributable to theaters showing other types of films. It is this secondary effect which this zoning ordinance attempts to avoid, not the dissemination of "offensive" speech. In contrast, in *Erznoznik*, the justifications offered by the city rested primarily on the city's interest in protecting its citizens from exposure to unwanted "offensive" speech. * * *

35. The situation would be quite different if the ordinance had the effect of suppressing, or greatly restricting access to, lawful speech.

Here, however, the District Court specifically found that "[t]he Ordinances do not affect the operation of existing establishments but only the location of new ones. There are myriad locations in the City of Detroit which must be over 1000 feet from existing regulated establishments. This burden on First Amendment rights is slight." * * *

1. I do not think we need reach, nor am I inclined to agree with, the holding in Part III (and supporting discussion) that nonobscene, erotic materials may be treated differently under First Amendment principles from other forms of protected expression. I do not consider the conclusions in Part I of the opinion to depend on distinctions between protected speech.

engaged in this business. But in this respect they are affected no differently than any other commercial enterprise that suffers economic detriment as a result of land-use regulation. The cases are legion that sustained zoning against claims of serious economic damage.

The inquiry for First Amendment purposes is not concerned with economic impact; rather, it looks only to the effect of this ordinance upon freedom of expression. This prompts essentially two inquiries: (i) does the ordinance impose any content limitation on the creators of adult movies or their ability to make them available to whom they desire, and (ii) does it restrict in any significant way the viewing of these movies by those who desire to see them? On the record in this case, these inquiries must be answered in the negative. At most the impact of the ordinance on these interests is incidental and minimal.[2] Detroit has silenced no message, has invoked no censorship, and has imposed no limitation upon those who wish to view them. The ordinance is addressed only to the places at which this type of expression may be presented, a restriction that does not interfere with content. Nor is there any significant overall curtailment of adult movie presentations, or the opportunity for a message to reach an audience. On the basis of the District Court's finding, it appears that if a sufficient market exists to support them the number of adult movie theaters in Detroit will remain approximately the same, free to purvey the same message. To be sure some prospective patrons may be inconvenienced by this dispersal. But other patrons, depending upon where they live or work, may find it more convenient to view an adult movie when adult theaters are not concentrated in a particular section of the city.

In these circumstances, it is appropriate to analyze the permissibility of Detroit's action under the four-part test of *United States v. O'Brien* [p. 669 supra]. Under that test, a governmental regulation is sufficiently justified, despite its incidental impact upon First Amendment interests, "if it is within the constitutional power of the Government; if it furthers an important government interest; if the government interest is unrelated to the suppression of free expression; and if the incidental restriction [on] First Amendment freedoms is no greater than is essential to the furtherance of that interest." [Powell, J., concluded that the Detroit ordinance satisfied the *O'Brien* test.]

JUSTICE STEWART, with whom JUSTICE BRENNAN, JUSTICE MARSHALL and JUSTICE BLACKMUN join, dissenting.

[This case involves] the constitutional permissibility of selective interference with protected speech whose content is thought to produce distasteful effects. It is elementary that a prime function of the First Amendment is to guard against just such interference. By refusing to invalidate Detroit's ordinance the Court rides roughshod over cardinal principles of First Amendment law, which require that time, place and manner regulations that affect protected expression be content-neutral except in the limited context of a captive or juvenile audience. In place of these principles the Court invokes a concept wholly alien to the First Amendment. Since "few of us would march our sons and daughters off to war to preserve the citizen's right to see 'Specified Sexual Activities' exhibited in the theaters of our choice," the Court implies that these films are not entitled to the full protection of the Constitution. This stands "Voltaire's immortal comment," on its head. For if the guarantees of the First Amendment were reserved for expression that more than a "few of us" would take up arms to defend, then the

---

2. The communication involved here is not a kind in which the content or effectiveness of the message depends in some measure upon where or how it is conveyed. * * *

right of free expression would be defined and circumscribed by current popular opinion. The guarantees of the Bill of Rights were designed to protect against precisely such majoritarian limitations on individual liberty.

The fact that the "offensive" speech here may not address "important" topics—"ideas of social and political significance," in the Court's terminology— does not mean that it is less worthy of constitutional protection. "Wholly neutral futilities [come] under the protection of free speech as fully as do Keats' poems or Donne's sermons." *Winters* (Frankfurter, J., dissenting), accord, *Cohen v. California*. Moreover, in the absence of a judicial determination of obscenity, it is by no means clear that the speech is not "important" even on the Court's terms [*Roth; Kingsley Pictures*].

I can only interpret today's decision as an aberration. The Court is undoubtedly sympathetic, as am I, to the well-intentioned efforts of Detroit to "clean up" its streets and prevent the proliferation of "skid rows." But it is in those instances where protected speech grates most unpleasantly against the sensibilities that judicial vigilance must be at its [height].

The factual parallels between [*Erznoznik* and this case] are striking. There, as here, the ordinance did not forbid altogether the "distasteful" expression but merely required an alteration in the physical setting of the forum. There, as here, the city's principal asserted interest was in minimizing the "undesirable" effects of speech having a particular content. [And] the particular content of the restricted speech at issue in *Erznoznik* precisely parallels the content restricted in [Detroit's] definition of "Specified Anatomical Areas." * * *

The Court must never forget that the consequences of rigorously enforcing the guarantees of the First Amendment are frequently unpleasant. Much speech that seems to be of little or no value will enter the marketplace of ideas, threatening the quality of our social discourse and, more generally, the serenity of our lives. But that is the price to be paid for constitutional freedom. * * * *e*

Notes and Questions

1. *A hierarchy of protected speech.* Stevens, J., contends that as a matter of law some "protected" speech is less worthy than other protected speech. The dissenters and Powell, J., reject that view. Which approach is more likely to preserve First Amendment values? Would treating all protected speech equally invite a dilution of the force of the First Amendment with respect to the speech that "really" matters? Is the process of allowing judges to pick and choose between types of protected speech too dangerous? Would it be dangerous to protect political speech more than sexually explicit speech? Is sexually explicit speech non-political? If the plaintiff's approach were accepted, would the Court ultimately "rank speech in all its myriad forms, in order of its perceived importance," with new rankings being "created and old ones rejected depending on the Court's view of the worthiness of the speech at issue"? Roger Goldman, *A Doctrine of Worthier Speech: Young v. American Mini Theatres, Inc.,* 21 St. Louis U.L.J. 281, 300–01 (1977).

e. Blackmun, J., joined by the other three dissenters, also filed a dissent that protested the rejection of the vagueness argument, concluding on this issue: "As to the third reason, that 'adult' material is simply entitled to less protection, it certainly explains the lapse in applying settled vagueness principles, as indeed it explains this whole case. In joining Mr. Justice Stewart I have joined his forthright rejection of the notion that First Amendment protection is diminished for 'erotic materials' that only a 'few of us' see the need to protect."

2. *The exhibitor's free expression.* Did Powell, J., assume that the "first amendment rights [involved] in *Young* were primarily vested in creator and audience"? Note, 42 Mo.L.Rev. 461, 468 (1977); Note, 28 Case W.Res.L.Rev. 456, 482 (1978). Does the plurality opinion and its fn. 35 reflect similar lack of concern for exhibitor's interests? How would a record be built to distinguish *Young* from a similar ordinance in another city?

3. *Exclusionary zoning. Schad v. Mt. Ephraim,* 452 U.S. 61, 101 S.Ct. 2176, 68 L.Ed.2d 671 (1981) invalidated a Borough ordinance that permitted adult theaters and bookstores, but excluded live entertainment from its commercial zone. Even as applied to nude dancing, the Court found that the ordinance was not narrowly drawn to serve a sufficiently substantial state interest.[f] The Court observed that there was no evidence to show that the entertainment at issue was available in reasonably nearby areas. What if it were? Suppose the Borough banned adult theaters and bookstores, but could show they were available nearby?

RENTON v. PLAYTIME THEATRES, INC., 475 U.S. 41, 106 S.Ct. 925, 89 L.Ed.2d 29 (1986), per REHNQUIST, J., upheld a zoning ordinance that prohibited adult motion picture theaters from locating within 1,000 feet of any residential zone, church, park, or school. The effect was to exclude such theaters from approximately 94% of the land in the city. Of the remaining 520 acres, a substantial part was occupied by a sewage disposal and treatment plant, a horse racing track and environs, a warehouse and manufacturing facilities, a Mobil Oil tank farm, and a fully-developed shopping center: "[T]he resolution of this case is largely dictated by our decision in *Young v. American Mini Theatres, Inc.* There, although five Members of the Court did not agree on a single rationale for the decision, we held that the city of Detroit's zoning ordinance, which prohibited locating an adult theater within 1,000 feet of any two other 'regulated uses' or within 500 feet of any residential zone, did not violate the First and Fourteenth Amendments. The Renton ordinance, like the one in *Young,* does not ban adult theaters altogether, but merely provides that such theaters may not be located within 1,000 feet of any residential zone, single- or multiple-family dwelling, church, park, or school. The ordinance is therefore properly analyzed as a form of time, place, and manner regulation.

This Court has long held that regulations enacted for the purpose of restraining speech on the basis of its content presumptively violate the First Amendment. See *Chicago Police Dept. v. Mosley,* [p. 802 infra].[a] On the other hand, so-called 'content-neutral' time, place, and manner regulations are acceptable so long as they are designed to serve a substantial governmental interest and do not unreasonably limit alternative avenues of communication.[b]

"At first glance, the Renton ordinance, like the ordinance in *Young,* does not appear to fit neatly into either the 'content-based' or the 'content-neutral' category. To be sure, the ordinance treats theaters that specialize in adult films

---

f. But cf. *Newport v. Iacobucci,* 479 U.S. 92, 107 S.Ct. 383, 93 L.Ed.2d 334 (1986) (upholding ordinance prohibiting nude or nearly nude dancing in establishments serving liquor).

a. *Mosley* involved an ordinance that banned picketing near a school building except the "peaceful picketing of any school involved in a labor dispute." The Court stated: "The

regulation '[slips] from the neutrality of time, place, and circumstance into a concern about content.' This is never permitted."

b. Compare the statement of the time, place, and manner test in *Clark,* p. 687 supra. For commentary, see David Day, *The Hybridization of the Content–Neutral Standards for the Free Speech Clause,* 19 Ariz.St.L.J. 195 (1987).

differently from other kinds of theaters. Nevertheless, [the] City Council's 'predominate concerns' were with the secondary effects of adult theaters, and not with the content of adult films themselves. * * *

"[This] finding as to 'predominate' intent is more than adequate to establish that the city's pursuit of its zoning interests here was unrelated to the suppression of free expression.[c] The ordinance by its terms is designed to prevent crime, protect the city's retail trade, maintain property values,[d] and generally 'protec[t] and preserv[e] the quality of [the city's] neighborhoods, commercial districts, and the quality of urban life,' not to suppress the expression of unpopular views. As Justice Powell observed in *Young,* '[i]f [the city] had been concerned with restricting the message purveyed by adult theaters, it would have tried to close them or restrict their number rather than circumscribe their choice as to location.'

"In short, the [ordinance] does not contravene the fundamental principle that underlies our concern about 'content-based' speech regulations: that 'government may not grant the use of a forum to people whose views it finds acceptable, but deny use to those wishing to express less favored or more controversial views.' *Mosley.*

"It was with this understanding in mind that, in *Young,* a majority of this Court decided that at least with respect to businesses that purvey sexually explicit materials,[e] zoning ordinances designed to combat the undesirable secondary effects of such businesses are to be reviewed under the standards applicable to 'content-neutral' time, place, and manner regulations.[2]

"The appropriate inquiry in this case, then, is whether the Renton ordinance is designed to serve a substantial governmental interest and allows for reasonable alternative avenues of communication."

After concluding that the ordinance was designed to serve substantial government interests, the Court ruled that the Renton ordinance allowed "for reasonable alternative avenues of communication": "[W]e note that the ordinance leaves some 520 acres, or more than five percent of the entire land area of Renton, open to use as adult theater sites. [Respondents] argue, however, that some of the land in question is already occupied by existing businesses, that 'practically none' of the undeveloped land is currently for sale or lease, and that in general there are no 'commercially viable' adult theater sites within the 520 acres left open by the Renton ordinance. The Court of Appeals accepted these arguments. * * *

---

c. The Court interpreted the court of appeals opinion to require the invalidation of the ordinance if a "motivating factor" to restrict the exercise of first amendment rights was present "apparently no matter how small a part this motivating factor may have played in the City Council's decision." This view of the law, the Court continued, "was rejected in *O'Brien:* 'It is a familiar principle of constitutional law that this Court will not strike down an otherwise constitutional statute on the basis of an alleged illicit legislative motive. [What] motivates one legislator to make a speech about a statute is not necessarily what motivates scores of others to enact it, and the stakes are sufficiently high for us to eschew guesswork.' "

d. For support, see Charles Clarke, *Freedom of Speech and the Problem of the Lawful*

Harmful Public Reaction, 20 Akron L.Rev. 187 (1986).

e. The secondary effects justification was deemed to distinguish *Erznoznik v. City of Jacksonville,* 422 U.S. 205, 95 S.Ct. 2268, 45 L.Ed.2d 125 (1975) (invalidating ordinance prohibiting drive-in theaters from showing films containing nudity) and *Schad v. Mount Ephraim,* p. 795 supra (invalidating ordinance prohibiting live entertainment, as applied to nude dancing, in commercial zone).

2. See *Young* (plurality opinion) ("[I]t is manifest that society's interest in protecting this type of expression is of a wholly different, and lesser, magnitude than the interest in untrammeled political debate * * *.").

"We disagree. [That] respondents must fend for themselves in the real estate market, on an equal footing with other prospective purchasers and lessees, does not give rise to a First Amendment violation. And although we have cautioned against the enactment of zoning regulations that have 'the effect of suppressing, or greatly restricting access to, lawful speech,' *Young* (plurality opinion), we have never suggested that the First Amendment compels the Government to ensure that adult theaters, or any other kinds of speech-related businesses for that matter, will be able to obtain sites at bargain prices. [T]he First Amendment requires only that Renton refrain from effectively denying respondents a reasonable opportunity to open and operate an adult theater within the city, and the ordinance before us easily meets this requirement. * * * [4]" [f]

BRENNAN, J., joined by Marshall, J., dissented: "The fact that adult movie theaters may cause harmful 'secondary' land use effects may arguably give Renton a compelling reason to regulate such establishments; it does not mean, however, that such regulations are content-neutral. * * *

"The ordinance discriminates on its face against certain forms of speech based on content. Movie theaters specializing in 'adult motion pictures' may not be located within 1,000 feet of any residential zone, single- or multiple-family dwelling, church, park, or school. Other motion picture theaters, and other forms of 'adult entertainment,' such as bars, massage parlors, and adult bookstores, are not subject to the same restrictions. This selective treatment strongly suggests that Renton was interested not in controlling the 'secondary effects' associated with adult businesses, but in discriminating against adult theaters based on the content of the films they exhibit. [Moreover,] [a]s the Court of Appeals observed, '[b]oth the magistrate and the district court recognized that many of the stated reasons for the ordinance were no more than expressions of dislike for the subject matter.' [3] That some residents may be offended by the *content* of the films shown at adult movie theaters cannot form the basis for state regulation of speech. See *Terminiello*.

"Some of the 'findings' [do] relate to supposed 'secondary effects' associated with adult movie theaters [4] [but they were added by the City Council only after this law suit was filed and the Court should not] accept these post-hoc statements at face value. [As] the Court of Appeals concluded, '[t]he record presented by

---

4. [We] reject respondents' "vagueness" argument for the same reasons that led us to reject a similar challenge in *Young*. There, the Detroit ordinance applied to theaters "used to present material distinguished or characterized by an emphasis on [sexually explicit matter]." We held that "even if there may be some uncertainty about the effect of the ordinances on other litigants, they are unquestionably applicable to these respondents." We also held that the Detroit ordinance created no "significant deterrent effect" that might justify invocation of the First Amendment "overbreadth" doctrine.

f. Blackmun, J., concurred in the result without opinion.

3. For example, "finding" number 2 states that "[l]ocation of adult entertainment land uses on the main commercial thoroughfares of the City gives an impression of legitimacy to, and causes a loss of sensitivity to the ad-

verse effect of pornography upon children, established family relations, respect for marital relationship and for the sanctity of marriage relations of others, and the concept of nonaggressive, consensual sexual relations."

"Finding" number 6 states that "[l]ocation of adult land uses in close proximity to residential uses, churches, parks, and other public facilities, and schools, will cause a degradation of the community standard of morality. Pornographic material has a degrading effect upon the relationship between spouses."

4. For example, "finding" number 12 states that "[l]ocation of adult entertainment land uses in proximity to residential uses, churches, parks and other public facilities, and schools, may lead to increased levels of criminal activities, including prostitution, rape, incest and ass. lts in the vicinity of such adult entertainment land uses."

Renton to support its asserted interest in enacting the zoning ordinance is very thin.' [5] * * * 7

"Even assuming that the ordinance should be treated like a content-neutral time, place, and manner restriction, I would still find it unconstitutional. [T]he ordinance is invalid because it does not provide for reasonable alternative avenues of communication.ᵍ [The] facts serve to distinguish this case from *Young,* where there was no indication that the Detroit zoning ordinance seriously limited the locations available for adult businesses. See *Young,* (plurality opinion) ('The situation would be quite different if the ordinance had the effect of * * * greatly restricting access to, lawful speech').

"[R]espondents are not on equal footing with other prospective purchasers and lessees, but must conduct business under severe restrictions not imposed upon other establishments. [R]espondents do not ask Renton to guarantee low-price sites for their businesses, but seek, only a reasonable opportunity to operate adult theaters in the city. By denying them this opportunity, Renton can effectively ban a form of protected speech from its borders. The ordinance 'greatly restrict[s] access to, lawful speech,' *Young* (plurality opinion), and is plainly unconstitutional."

Notes and Questions

1. Does *Renton*—see fn. 2—endorse a hierarchy of categories among types of protected speech? Consider Laurence Tribe, *American Constitutional Law* 939 n. 66 (2d ed. 1988): "[I]t is doubtful that *Renton* can fairly be read as endorsing the concept of a hierarchy of intermediate categories, because the case turned on the majority's characterization of the restriction as content-neutral, and the issue of the relative importance of the speech involved, was, strictly speaking, irrelevant." But cf. Philip Prygoski, *Low Value Speech: From Young to Fraser,* 32 St. Louis Univ.L.J. 317, 345 (1987) (despite the content-neutral language, "antipathy toward the kind of expression involved" swayed the case).

2. Was the ordinance fairly characterized as content-neutral? Is the focus on "secondary effects" convincing? Consider Geoffrey Stone, *Content–Neutral Restrictions,* 54 U.Chi.L.Rev. 46, 115–117 (1987): "[T]he Court had never before *Renton* suggested that the absence of a constitutionally disfavored justification is in itself a justification for treating an expressly content-based restriction as if it

---

5. As part of the amendment passed after this lawsuit commenced, the City Council added a statement that it had intended to rely on the Washington Supreme Court's opinion in *Northend Cinema, Inc. v. Seattle,* 90 Wash.2d 709, 585 P.2d 1153 (1978), cert. denied, 441 U.S. 946, 99 S.Ct. 2166, 60 L.Ed.2d 1048 (1979), which upheld Seattle's zoning regulations against constitutional attack. Again, despite the suspicious coincidental timing of the amendment, the Court holds that "Renton was entitled to rely [on] the 'detailed findings' summarized in [the] *Northend Cinema* opinion." In *Northend Cinema,* the court noted that "[t]he record is replete with testimony regarding the effects of adult movie theater locations on residential neighborhoods." The opinion however, does not explain the evidence it purports to summarize, and provided no basis for determining whether Seattle's experience is relevant to Renton's.

7. As one commentator has noted: "[A]nyone with any knowledge of human nature should naturally assume that the decision to adopt almost any content-based restriction might have been affected by an antipathy on the part of at least some legislators to the ideas or information being suppressed. The logical assumption, in other words, is not that there is not improper motivation but, rather, because legislators are only human, that there is a substantial risk that an impermissible consideration has in fact colored the deliberative process." Geoffrey Stone, *Restrictions on Speech Because of its Content: The Peculiar Case of Subject–Matter Restrictions,* 46 U.Chi. L.Rev. 81, 106 (1978).

g. Brennan, J., argued that the ordinance also failed as an acceptable time, place, and manner restriction because it was not narrowly tailored to serve a significant governmental interest.

were content-neutral. To the contrary, with the single exception of *Renton,* the Court in such circumstances has always invoked the stringent standards of content-based review. [For example, in] *Ferber* the Court treated as content-based a law prohibiting 'child pornography,' even though the government defended the law not in terms of communicative impact, but on the ground that the law was necessary to protect children who participate in 'sexual performances.' [I]f taken seriously, and extended to other contexts, the Court's transmogrification in *Renton* of an expressly content-based restriction into one that is content-neutral threatens to undermine the very foundation of the content-based/content-neutral distinction. This would in turn erode the coherence and predictability of first amendment doctrine. One can only hope that this aspect of *Renton* is soon forgotten."

But cf. Daniel Farber & Philip Frickey, *The Jurisprudence of Public Choice,* 65 Tex.L.Rev. 873 (1987): "*[Renton]* appears to adopt the view that the government generally may take into account the content of speech when channeling speech, but may only rarely consider content when the purpose is censorship. We believe that in doing so *Renton* merely states explicitly what was implicit in a long line of prior cases."

Are subject matter restrictions as a class less problematic than other forms of content discrimination in that they often do not discriminate on the basis of point of view? Should *Renton's* secondary effects emphasis be limited to subject-matter-based restrictions? See Note, *The Content Distinction in Free Speech Analysis After Renton,* 102 Harv.L.Rev. 1904 (1989). Even if some subject matter restrictions are less problematic, is the Renton ordinance neutral as to point of view? Consider Geoffrey Stone, *Restrictions of Speech Because of its Content: The Peculiar Case of Subject–Matter Restrictions,* 46 U.Chi.L.Rev. 81, 111–12 (1978): "[T]he speech suppressed by restrictions such as those involved in [cases like *Erznoznik* and *Young*] will almost invariably carry an implicit, if not explicit, message in favor of more relaxed sexual mores. Such restrictions, in other words, have a potent viewpoint-differential impact. [I]n our society, the very presence of sexual explicitness in speech seems ideologically significant, without regard to whatever other messages might be intended. To treat such restrictions as viewpoint-neutral seems simply to ignore reality. Finally, [a] large percentage of citizens apparently feel threatened by nonobscene, sexually-explicit speech and believe it to be morally reprehensible. If it were not for the Court's relatively narrow construction of the obscenity concept, much of this speech would undoubtedly be banned outright. Thus, any restriction along these lines will carry an extraordinarily high risk that its enactment was tainted by this fundamentally illegitimate consideration. Such restrictions, although superficially viewpoint-neutral, pose a uniquely compelling case for content-based scrutiny." Are feminist or neo-conservative objections to near obscene speech both "fundamentally illegitimate." Should all content-based scrutiny be the same? Does *Renton* reconstruct the Court's "narrow construction of the obscenity concept?"

Is the concept of viewpoint neutrality itself problematic? Consider Cass Sunstein, *Pornography and the First Amendment,* 1986 Duke L.J. 589, 615: "One does not 'see' a viewpoint-based restriction when the harms invoked in defense of a regulation are obvious and so widely supported by social consensus that they allay any concern about impermissible government motivation. Whether a classification is viewpoint-based thus ultimately turns on the viewpoint of the decision-maker." See generally Catharine MacKinnon, *Feminism, Marxism, Method, and the State,* 7 Signs 515, 535–36 (1981).

3. *Renton's* "secondary effects" notion was revisited by several justices in *BOOS v. BARRY,* p. 679 supra. A District of Columbia ordinance banned the display of any sign within 500 feet of a foreign embassy that would tend to bring the embassy into "public odium" or "public disrepute." O'CONNOR, J., joined by Stevens and Scalia, JJ., distinguished *Renton:* "Respondents and the United States do not point to the 'secondary effects' of picket signs in front of embassies. They do not point to congestion, to interference with ingress or egress, to visual clutter, or to the need to protect the security of embassies. Rather, they rely on the need to protect the dignity of foreign diplomatic personnel by shielding them from speech that is critical of their governments. This justification focuses *only* on the content of the speech and the direct impact that speech has on its listeners. The emotive impact of speech on its audience is not a 'secondary effect.' Because the display clause regulates speech due to its potential primary impact, we conclude it must be considered content-based." [h]

BRENNAN, J., joined by Marshall, J., agreed with the conclusion that the ordinance was content-based, but objected to O'Connor, J.'s "assumption that the *Renton* analysis applies not only outside the context of businesses purveying sexually explicit materials but even to political speech." [i]

BARNES v. GLEN THEATRE, INC., 501 U.S. 560, 111 S.Ct. 2456, 115 L.Ed.2d 504 (1991) held that an Indiana statute prohibiting the knowing or intentional appearing in a public place in a state of nudity could constitutionally be applied to require that female dancers at a minimum wear "pasties" and a "G-string" when they dance. REHNQUIST, C.J., delivered the judgment of the Court in an opinion joined by O'Connor, J., and Kennedy, J.: "In *Doran v. Salem Inn, Inc.,* 422 U.S. 922, 95 S.Ct. 2561, 45 L.Ed.2d 648 (1975), we said: '[A]lthough the customary "barroom" type of nude dancing may involve only the barest minimum of protected expression, we recognized in *California v. LaRue,* 409 U.S. 109, 93 S.Ct. 390, 34 L.Ed.2d 342 (1972), that this form of entertainment might be entitled to First and Fourteenth Amendment protection under some circumstances.' In *Schad v. Mount Ephraim,* we said that [nude] dancing is not without its First Amendment protections from official regulation. These statements support the conclusion [that] nude dancing of the kind sought to be performed

---

h. In an earlier passage O'Connor, J., responded to the argument that the ordinance was not content-based on the theory that the government was not selecting between viewpoints. The argument was instead that "the permissible message on a picket sign is determined solely by the policies of a foreign government. We reject this contention, although we agree the provision is not viewpoint-based. The display clause determines which viewpoint is acceptable in a neutral fashion by looking to the policies of foreign governments. While this prevents the display clause from being directly viewpoint-based, a label with potential First Amendment ramifications of its own, it does not render the statute content-neutral. Rather, we have held that a regulation that 'does not favor either side of a political controversy' is nonetheless impermissible because the 'First Amendment's hostility to content-based regulation extends [to] prohibition of public discussion of an entire topic.' Here the government has determined that an entire category of speech—signs or displays critical of foreign governments—is not to be permitted."

i. Rehnquist, J., joined by White and Blackmun, JJ., voted to uphold the ordinance on the basis of Bork, J's opinion below in *Finzer v. Barry,* 798 F.2d 1450 (D.C.Cir.1986). Bork, J., stated that the need to adhere to principles of international law might constitute a secondary effect under *Renton* but was not "entirely sure" whether *Renton* alone could dictate that result and did not resolve the issue. Id. at 1469–70 n. 15. For a review of secondary effects doctrine see Philip Prygoski, The Supreme Court's "Secondary Effects" Analysis in Free Speech Cases, 6 Cooley L.Rev. 1 (1989).

here is expressive conduct within the outer perimeters of the First Amendment, though we view it as only marginally so.

"Indiana, of course, has not banned nude dancing as such, but has proscribed public nudity across the board. The Supreme Court of Indiana has construed the Indiana statute to preclude nudity in what are essentially places of public accommodation such as the Glen Theatre and the Kitty Kat Lounge. In such places, respondents point out, minors are excluded and there are no non-consenting viewers. Respondents contend that while the state may license establishments such as the ones involved here, and limit the geographical area in which they do business, it may not in any way limit the performance of the dances within them without violating the First Amendment. The petitioner contends, on the other hand, that Indiana's restriction on nude dancing is a valid 'time, place or manner' restriction under cases such as *Clark*.

"The 'time, place, or manner' test was developed for evaluating restrictions on expression taking place on public property which had been dedicated as a 'public forum,' although we have on at least one occasion applied it to conduct occurring on private property. See *Renton*. In *Clark* we observed that this test has been interpreted to embody much the same standards as those set forth in *O'Brien*. We turn, therefore, to the rule enunciated in *O'Brien*. * * *

"Applying the [*O'Brien*] test, we find that Indiana's public indecency statute is justified despite its incidental limitations on some expressive activity. The public indecency statute is clearly within the constitutional power of the State and furthers substantial governmental interests. It is impossible to discern, other than from the text of the statute, exactly what governmental interest the Indiana legislators had in mind when they enacted this statute, for Indiana does not record legislative history, and the state's highest court has not shed additional light on the statute's purpose. Nonetheless, the statute's purpose of protecting societal order and morality is clear from its text and history. Public indecency statutes of this sort are of ancient origin, and presently exist in at least 47 States. [They] reflect moral disapproval of people appearing in the nude among strangers in public places. [The] history of Indiana's public indecency statute shows that it predates barroom nude dancing and was enacted as a general prohibition. * * *

"[The] traditional police power of the States is defined as the authority to provide for the public health, safety, and morals, and we have upheld such a basis for legislation. In *Paris Adult Theatre,* we said: 'In deciding [*Roth*], this Court implicitly accepted that a legislature could legitimately act on such a conclusion to protect "the social interest in order and morality."' And in *Bowers v. Hardwick,* we said: 'The law, however, is constantly based on notions of morality, and if all laws representing essentially moral choices are to be invalidated under the Due Process Clause, the courts will be very busy indeed.'

"Thus, the public indecency statute furthers a substantial government interest in protecting order and morality.

"Some may view restricting nudity on moral grounds as necessarily related to expression. We disagree. It can be argued, of course, that almost limitless types of conduct—including appearing in the nude in public—are 'expressive,' and in one sense of the word this is true. People who go about in the nude in public may be expressing something about themselves by so doing. But the court rejected this expansive notion of 'expressive conduct' in *O'Brien,* saying: 'We cannot accept the view that an apparently limitless variety of conduct can be labelled "speech" whenever the person engaging in the conduct intends thereby to express an idea.'

"And in *Dallas v. Stanglin* we further observed: 'It is possible to find some kernel of expression in almost every activity a person undertakes—for example, walking down the street or meeting one's friends at a shopping mall—but such a kernel is not sufficient to bring the activity within the protection of the First Amendment. * * *'

"Respondents contend that even though prohibiting nudity in public generally may not be related to suppressing expression, prohibiting the performance of nude dancing is related to expression because the state seeks to prevent its erotic message. Therefore, they reason that the [statute] fails the third part of the *O'Brien* test, viz: the governmental interest must be unrelated to the suppression of free expression.

"But we do not think that when Indiana applies its statute to the nude dancing in these nightclubs it is proscribing nudity because of the erotic message conveyed by the dancers. Presumably numerous other erotic performances are presented at these establishments and similar clubs without any interference from the state, so long as the performers wear a scant amount of clothing. Likewise, the requirement that the dancers don pasties and a G-string does not deprive the dance of whatever erotic message it conveys; it simply makes the message slightly less graphic. The perceived evil that Indiana seeks to address is not erotic dancing, but public nudity. The appearance of people of all shapes, sizes and ages in the nude at a beach, for example, would convey little if any erotic message, yet the state still seeks to prevent it. Public nudity is the evil the state seeks to prevent, whether or not it is combined with expressive activity. * * *

"The fourth part of the *O'Brien* test requires that the incidental restriction on First Amendment freedom be no greater than is essential to the furtherance of the governmental interest. As indicated in the discussion above, the governmental interest served by the text of the prohibition is societal disapproval of nudity in public places and among strangers. The statutory prohibition is not a means to some greater end, but an end in itself. It is without cavil that the public indecency statute is 'narrowly tailored;' Indiana's requirement that the dancers wear at least pasties and a G-string is modest, and the bare minimum necessary to achieve the state's purpose."

SCALIA, J., concurred in the judgment: "[T]he challenged regulation must be upheld, not because it survives some lower level of First–Amendment scrutiny, but because, as a general law regulating conduct and not specifically directed at expression, it is not subject to First–Amendment scrutiny at all.[3]

"Were it the case that Indiana *in practice* targeted only expressive nudity, while turning a blind eye to nude beaches and unclothed purveyors of hot dogs and machine tools, it might be said that what posed as a regulation of conduct in general was in reality a regulation of only communicative conduct. Respondents have adduced no evidence of that. Indiana officials have brought many public indecency prosecutions for activities having no communicative element. * * *

3. The dissent [misunderstands] what is meant by the term "general law." I do not mean that the law restricts the targeted conduct in all places at all times. A law is "general" for the present purposes if it regulates conduct without regard to whether that conduct is expressive. Concededly, Indiana bans nudity in public places, but not within the privacy of the home. (That is not surprising, since the common law offense, and the traditional moral prohibition, runs against *public* nudity, not against all nudity.) But that confirms, rather than refutes, the general nature of the law: one may not go nude in public, whether or not one intends thereby to convey a message, and similarly one *may* go nude in private, again whether or not that nudity is expressive.

"The dissent confidently asserts that the purpose of restricting nudity in public places in general is to protect nonconsenting parties from offense; and argues that since only consenting, admission-paying patrons see respondents dance, that purpose cannot apply and the only remaining purpose must relate to the communicative elements of the performance. Perhaps the dissenters believe that 'offense to others' *ought* to be the only reason for restricting nudity in public places generally, but there is no basis for thinking that our society has ever shared that Thoreauvian 'you-may-do-what-you-like-so-long-as-it-does-not-injure-some-one-else' beau ideal—much less for thinking that it was written into the Constitution. The purpose of Indiana's nudity law would be violated, I think, if 60,000 fully consenting adults crowded into the Hoosierdome to display their genitals to one another, even if there were not an offended innocent in the crowd. Our society prohibits, and all human societies have prohibited, certain activities not because they harm others but because they are considered, in the traditional phrase, 'contra bonos mores,' *i.e.,* immoral. In American society, such prohibitions have included, for example, sadomasochism, cockfighting, bestiality, suicide, drug use, prostitution, and sodomy. While there may be great diversity of view on whether various of these prohibitions should exist (though I have found few ready to abandon, in principle, all of them) there is no doubt that, absent specific constitutional protection for the conduct involved, the Constitution does not prohibit them simply because they regulate 'morality.' See *Bowers v. Hardwick* (upholding prohibition of private homosexual sodomy enacted solely on 'the presumed belief of a majority of the electorate in [the jurisdiction] that homosexual sodomy is immoral and unacceptable'). * * *

"The First Amendment explicitly protects 'the freedom of speech [and] of the press'—oral and written speech—not 'expressive conduct.' When any law restricts speech, even for a purpose that has nothing to do with the suppression of communication (for instance, to reduce noise, see *Saia v. New York,* 334 U.S. 558, 68 S.Ct. 1148, 92 L.Ed. 1574 (1948), to regulate election campaigns, see *Buckley,* or to prevent littering, see *Schneider*), we insist that it meet the high, First-Amendment standard of justification. But virtually *every* law restricts conduct, and virtually *any* prohibited conduct can be performed for an expressive purpose— if only expressive of the fact that the actor disagrees with the prohibition. It cannot reasonably be demanded, therefore, that every restriction of expression incidentally produced by a general law regulating conduct pass normal First-Amendment scrutiny, or even—as some of our cases have suggested, see e.g., *O'Brien*—that it be justified by an 'important or substantial' government interest. Nor do our holdings require such justification: we have never invalidated the application of a general law simply because the conduct that it reached was being engaged in for expressive purposes and the government could not demonstrate a sufficiently important state interest.

"This is not to say that the First Amendment affords no protection to expressive conduct. Where the government prohibits conduct *precisely because of its communicative attributes,* we hold the regulation unconstitutional. See, e.g., *United States v. Eichman* (burning flag); *Texas v. Johnson* (same); *Tinker v. Des Moines* (wearing black arm bands).[4] In each of the foregoing cases, we explicitly

---

4. It is easy to conclude that conduct has been forbidden because of its communicative attributes when the conduct in question is what the Court has called 'inherently expressive,' and what I would prefer to call 'conventionally expressive'—such as flying a red flag.

I mean by that phrase (as I assume the Court means by 'inherently expressive') conduct that is normally engaged in for the purpose of communicating an idea, or perhaps an emotion, to someone else. I am not sure whether dancing fits that description, see *Dallas v. Stanglin*

found that suppressing communication was the object of the regulation of conduct. Where that has not been the case, however—where suppression of communicative use of the conduct was merely the incidental effect of forbidding the conduct for other reasons—we have allowed the regulation to stand.

"All our holdings (though admittedly not some of our discussion) support the conclusion that 'the only First Amendment analysis applicable to laws that do not directly or indirectly impede speech is the threshold inquiry of whether the purpose of the law is to suppress communication. If not, that is the end of the matter so far as First Amendment guarantees are concerned; if so, the court then proceeds to determine whether there is substantial justification for the proscription.' *Community for Creative Non–Violence v. Watt,* 703 F.2d 586 (D.C.Cir.1983) (en banc) (Scalia, J., dissenting), (emphasis omitted), rev'd *Clark v. Community for Creative Non–Violence.* Such a regime ensures that the government does not act to suppress communication, without requiring that all conduct-restricting regulation (which means in effect all regulation) survive an enhanced level of scrutiny." [a]

SOUTER, J., concurred in the judgment: This Court has previously categorized ballroom dancing as beyond the Amendment's protection, *City of Dallas v. Stanglin,* and dancing as aerobic exercise would likewise be outside the First Amendment's concern. But dancing as a performance directed to an actual or hypothetical audience gives expression at least to generalized emotion or feeling, and where the dancer is nude or nearly so the feeling expressed, in the absence of some contrary clue, is eroticism, carrying an endorsement of erotic experience. Such is the expressive content of the dances described in the record.

"Although such performance dancing is inherently expressive, nudity per se is not. It is a condition, not an activity, and the voluntary assumption of that condition, without more, apparently expresses nothing beyond the view that the condition is somehow appropriate to the circumstances. But every voluntary act implies some such idea, and the implication is thus so common and minimal that calling all voluntary activity expressive would reduce the concept of expression to the point of the meaningless. A search for some expression beyond the minimal in the choice to go nude will often yield nothing: a person may choose nudity, for example, for maximum sunbathing. But when nudity is combined with expressive activity, its stimulative and attractive value certainly can enhance the force of expression, and a dancer's acts in going from clothed to nude, as in a strip-tease, are integrated into the dance and its expressive function. Thus I agree with the plurality and the dissent that an interest in freely engaging in the nude dancing at issue here is subject to a degree of First Amendment protection.

"I also agree with the plurality that the appropriate analysis to determine the actual protection required by the First Amendment is the four-part enquiry described in *United States v. O'Brien* for judging the limits of appropriate state action burdening expressive acts as distinct from pure speech or representation. I

(social dance group 'do[es] not involve the sort of expressive association that the First Amendment has been held to protect'). But even if it does, this law is directed against nudity, not dancing. Nudity is *not* normally engaged in for the purpose of communicating an idea or an emotion.

a. Scalia, J., observed that his analysis was consistent with that in the peyote case, [p. 1020 infra] which he described as holding that

"general laws not specifically targeted at religious practices did not require heightened First Amendment scrutiny even though they diminished some people's ability to practice their religion." Scalia, J., also argued that the plurality had overread the precedents involving state interests in morality. As he read the cases, they only stood for the proposition that such interests were rational, not important or substantial.

nonetheless write separately to rest my concurrence in the judgment, not on the possible sufficiency of society's moral views to justify the limitations at issue, but on the State's substantial interest in combating the secondary effects of adult entertainment establishments of the sort typified by respondents' establishments.

"It is, of course, true that this justification has not been articulated by Indiana's legislature or by its courts. [I] think [we may] legitimately consider petitioners' assertion that the statute is applied to nude dancing because such dancing 'encourag[es] prostitution, increas[es] sexual assaults, and attract[s] other criminal activity.'

"This asserted justification for the statute may not be ignored merely because it is unclear to what extent this purpose motivated the Indiana Legislature in enacting the statute. Our appropriate focus is not an empirical enquiry into the actual intent of the enacting legislature, but rather the existence or not of a current governmental interest in the service of which the challenged application of the statute may be constitutional. In my view, the interest asserted by petitioners in preventing prostitution, sexual assault, and other criminal activity, although presumably not a justification for all applications of the statute, is sufficient under *O'Brien* to justify the State's enforcement of the statute against the type of adult entertainment at issue here. * * *

"In light of *Renton*'s recognition that legislation seeking to combat the secondary effects of adult entertainment need not await localized proof of those effects, the State of Indiana could reasonably conclude that forbidding nude entertainment of the type offered at the Kitty Kat Lounge [furthers] its interest in preventing prostitution, sexual assault, and associated crimes. Given our recognition that 'society's interest in protecting this type of expression is of a wholly different, and lesser, magnitude than the interest in untrammeled political debate,' *Young*, I do not believe that a State is required affirmatively to undertake to litigate this issue repeatedly in every case. The statute as applied to nudity of the sort at issue here therefore satisfies the second prong of *O'Brien*.[2] * * *

"The dissent contends, however, that Indiana seeks to regulate nude dancing as its means of combating such secondary effects 'because ... creating or emphasizing [the] thoughts and ideas [expressed by nude dancing] in the minds of the spectators may lead to increased prostitution' and that regulation of expressive conduct because of the fear that the expression will prove persuasive is inherently related to the suppression of free expression.

"[But] to say that pernicious secondary effects are associated with nude dancing establishments is not necessarily to say that such effects result from the persuasive effect of the expression inherent in nude dancing. It is to say, rather, only that the effects are correlated with the existence of establishments offering such dancing, without deciding what the precise causes of the correlation actually are. It is possible, for example, that the higher incidence of prostitution and sexual assault in the vicinity of adult entertainment locations results from the

---

2. Because there is no overbreadth challenge before us, we are not called upon to decide whether the application of the statute would be valid in other contexts. It is enough, then, to say that the secondary effects rationale on which I rely here would be open to question if the State were to seek to enforce the statute by barring expressive nudity in classes of productions that could not readily be analogized to the adult films at issue in *Ren-* *ton*. It is difficult to see, for example, how the enforcement of Indiana's statute against nudity in a production of 'Hair' or 'Equus' somewhere other than an 'adult' theater would further the State's interest in avoiding harmful secondary effects, in the absence of evidence that expressive nudity outside the context of *Renton*-type adult entertainment was correlated with such secondary effects.

concentration of crowds of men predisposed to such activities, or from the simple viewing of nude bodies regardless of whether those bodies are engaged in expression or not.   In neither case would the chain of causation run through the persuasive effect of the expressive component of nude dancing.

"Because the State's interest in banning nude dancing results from a simple correlation of such dancing with other evils, rather than from a relationship between the other evils and the expressive component of the dancing, the interest is unrelated to the suppression of free expression.[3]

"The fourth *O'Brien* condition, that the restriction be no greater than essential to further the governmental interest, requires little discussion. Pasties and a G-string moderate the expression to some degree, to be sure, but only to a degree. Dropping the final stitch is prohibited, but the limitation is minor when measured against the dancer's remaining capacity and opportunity to express the erotic message. Nor, so far as we are told, is the dancer or her employer limited by anything short of obscenity laws from expressing an erotic message by articulate speech or representational means; a pornographic movie featuring one of respondents, for example, was playing nearby without any interference from the authorities at the time these cases arose.

"Accordingly, I find *O'Brien* satisfied and concur in the judgment."

WHITE, J., joined by Marshall, Blackmun, and Stevens, JJ., dissented: "Both the Court and Justice Scalia in his concurring opinion overlook a fundamental and critical aspect of our cases upholding the States' exercise of their police powers. None of the cases they rely upon, including *O'Brien* and *Bowers v. Hardwick* involved anything less than truly *general* proscriptions on individual conduct. In *O'Brien,* for example, individuals were prohibited from destroying their draft cards at any time and in any place, even in completely private places such as the home. Likewise, in *Bowers,* the State prohibited sodomy, regardless of where the conduct might occur, including the home as was true in that case. By contrast, in this case Indiana does not suggest that its statute applies to, or could be applied to, nudity wherever it occurs, including the home. We do not understand the Court or Justice Scalia to be suggesting that Indiana could constitutionally enact such an intrusive prohibition, nor do we think such a suggestion would be tenable in light of our decision in *Stanley v. Georgia,* in which we held that States could not punish the mere possession of obscenity in the privacy of one's own home.

"We are told by the Attorney General of Indiana that, in *State v. Baysinger,* 272 Ind. 236, 397 N.E.2d 580 (1979), the Indiana Supreme Court held that the statute at issue here cannot and does not prohibit nudity as a part of some larger form of expression meriting protection when the communication of ideas is involved. Petitioners also state that the evils sought to be avoided by applying the statute in this case would not obtain in the case of theatrical productions, such as *Salome* or *Hair.* Neither is there any evidence that the State has attempted to apply the statute to nudity in performances such as plays, ballets or operas. 'No arrests have ever been made for nudity as part of a play or ballet.'

"Thus, the Indiana statute is not a *general* prohibition of the type we have upheld in prior cases. As a result, the Court's and Justice Scalia's simple references to the State's general interest in promoting societal order and morality is not sufficient justification for a statute which concededly reaches a significant

---

3. I reach this conclusion again mindful, as was the Court in *Renton,* that the protection of sexually explicit expression may be of lesser societal importance than the protection of other forms of expression.

amount of protected expressive activity. Instead, [when] the State enacts a law which draws a line between expressive conduct which is regulated and nonexpressive conduct of the same type which is not regulated, *O'Brien* places the burden on the State to justify the distinctions it has made. Closer inquiry as to the purpose of the statute is surely appropriate.

"Legislators do not just randomly select certain conduct for proscription; they have reasons for doing so and those reasons illuminate the purpose of the law that is passed. Indeed, a law may have multiple purposes. The purpose of forbidding people from appearing nude in parks, beaches, hot dog stands, and like public places is to protect others from offense. But that could not possibly be the purpose of preventing nude dancing in theaters and barrooms since the viewers are exclusively consenting adults who pay money to see these dances. The purpose of the proscription in these contexts is to protect the viewers from what the State believes is the harmful message that nude dancing communicates. [As] the State now tells us, and as Justice Souter agrees, the State's goal in applying what it describes as its 'content neutral' statute to the nude dancing in this case is 'deterrence of prostitution, sexual assaults, criminal activity, degradation of women, and other activities which break down family structure.' The attainment of these goals, however, depends on preventing an expressive activity.

[Since] the State permits the dancers to perform if they wear pasties and G-strings but forbids nude dancing, it is precisely because of the distinctive, expressive content of the nude dancing performances at issue in this case that the State seeks to apply the statutory prohibition. It is only because nude dancing performances may generate emotions and feelings of eroticism and sensuality among the spectators that the State seeks to regulate such expressive activity, apparently on the assumption that creating or emphasizing such thoughts and ideas in the minds of the spectators may lead to increased prostitution and the degradation of women. But generating thoughts, ideas, and emotions is the essence of communication. The nudity element of nude dancing performances cannot be neatly pigeonholed as mere 'conduct' independent of any expressive component of the dance.[2] * * *

"That the performances in the Kitty Kat Lounge may not be high art, to say the least, and may not appeal to the Court, is hardly an excuse for distorting and ignoring settled doctrine. The Court's assessment of the artistic merits of nude dancing performances should not be the determining factor in deciding this case. * * *

"The Court and Justice Souter do not go beyond saying that the state interests asserted here are important and substantial. But even if there were compelling interests, the Indiana statute is not narrowly drawn. If the State is genuinely concerned with prostitution and associated evils, as Justice Souter seems to think, [it] can adopt restrictions that do not interfere with the expressiveness of nonobscene nude dancing performances. For instance, the State could perhaps require that, while performing, nude performers remain at all times a certain minimum distance from spectators, that nude entertainment be limited to certain hours, or even that establishments providing such entertainment be

---

2. [If] Justice Souter is correct that there is no causal connection between the message conveyed by the nude dancing at issue here and the negative secondary effects that the State desires to regulate, the State does not have even a rational basis for its absolute prohibition on nude dancing that is admittedly expressive. Furthermore, if the real problem is the 'concentration of crowds of men predisposed to the' designated evils, then the First Amendment requires that the State address that problem in a fashion that does not include banning an entire category of expressive activity. See *Renton.*

dispersed throughout the city. Cf. *Renton*. Likewise, the State clearly has the authority to criminalize prostitution and obscene behavior. Banning an entire category of expressive activity, however, generally does not satisfy the narrow tailoring requirement of strict First Amendment scrutiny. Furthermore, if nude dancing in barrooms, as compared with other establishments, is the most worrisome problem, the State could invoke its Twenty-first Amendment powers and impose appropriate regulation.

"As I see it, our cases require us to affirm absent a compelling state interest supporting the statute. Neither the Court nor the State suggest that the statute could withstand scrutiny under that standard.

"[T]he premise for [Scalia, J.'s] position—that the statute is a *general* law of the type our cases contemplate—is nonexistent in this case. Reference to Justice Scalia's own hypothetical makes this clear. We agree with Justice Scalia that the Indiana statute would not permit 60,000 consenting Hoosiers to expose themselves to each other in the Hoosierdome. No one can doubt, however, that those same 60,000 Hoosiers would be perfectly free to drive to their respective homes all across Indiana and, once there, to parade around, cavort, and revel in the nude for hours in front of relatives and friends. It is difficult to see why the State's interest in morality is any less in that situation, especially if, as Justice Scalia seems to suggest, nudity is inherently evil, but clearly the statute does not reach such activity. As we pointed out earlier, the State's failure to enact a truly general proscription requires closer scrutiny of the reasons for the distinctions the State has drawn."

Notes and Questions

1. Is Scalia, J., correct in arguing that no first amendment test should apply in *Barnes*? Suppose a bookstore is closed for one year because the premises were knowingly used for purposes of prostitution. Is Arcara v. Cloud Books, Inc., 478 U.S. 697, 106 S.Ct. 3172, 92 L.Ed.2d 568 (1986) (no first amendment scrutiny; statute directed at prostitution and premises used regardless of other uses) consistent with *Barnes*?

2. *Is nude dancing speech?* Consider Robert Post, *Recuperating First Amendment Doctrine,* 47 Stan.L.Rev. 1249, 1259 (1995): "[T]he outcome in *Barnes* would have been different if Indiana were to have applied its statute to accepted media for the communication of ideas, as for example by attempting to prohibit nudity in movies or in the theater. Any such prohibition would serve interests deemed highly problematic by fully elaborated principles of First Amendment jurisprudence. Crucial to the result in *Barnes,* then, is the distinction between what the Court is prepared to accept as a medium for the communication of ideas, and its implicit understanding of nude dancing in nightclubs, which at least three of the majority Justices explicitly characterized as merely 'expressive conduct.' "

3. *Law and morals.* Consider Vincent Blasi, *Six Conservatives in Search of the First Amendment: The Revealing Case of Nude Dancing,* 33 Wm. and Mary L.Rev. 611, 621–22 (1992): "Can a principled conservative approve the enforcement of morals in the context of group vilification? Can a principled liberal argue that topless dancing is protected by the First Amendment but not the shouting of racial epithets? Important differences between the two categories of speech regulation may exist—hate speech ordinarily is not confined to settings in which every member of the audience has made a choice to receive the message, but hate speech also seems more political in character—but the response of many conserva-

tives to the hate speech issue at least suggests that they do not invariably prefer a narrow interpretation of the First Amendment and do not always take a broad view of the state's power to enforce morality."

II. COMMERCIAL SPEECH

VIRGINIA STATE BOARD OF PHARMACY v. VIRGINIA CITIZENS CONSUMER COUNCIL

425 U.S. 748, 96 S.Ct. 1817, 48 L.Ed.2d 346 (1976).

Justice Blackmun delivered the opinion of the Court.

[The Court held invalid a Virginia statute that made advertising the prices of prescription drugs "unprofessional conduct," subjecting pharmacists to license suspension or revocation. Prescription drug prices strikingly varied within the same locality, in Virginia and nationally, sometimes by several hundred percent. Such drugs were dispensed exclusively by licensed pharmacists but 95% were prepared by manufacturers, not compounded by the pharmacists.]

[Appellants] contend that the advertisement of prescription drug prices is outside the protection of the First Amendment because it is "commercial speech." There can be no question that in past decisions the Court has given some indication that commercial speech is unprotected.[a]

Last Term, in *Bigelow v. Virginia,* 421 U.S. 809, 95 S.Ct. 2222, 44 L.Ed.2d 600 (1975), the notion of unprotected "commercial speech" all but passed from the scene. We reversed a conviction for violation of a Virginia statute that made the circulation of any publication to encourage or promote the processing of an abortion in Virginia a misdemeanor. The defendant had published in his newspaper the availability of abortions in New York. The advertisement in question, in addition to announcing that abortions were legal in New York, offered the services of a referral agency in that State. [We] concluded that "the Virginia courts erred in their assumptions that advertising, as such, was entitled to no First Amendment protection," and we observed that the "relationship of speech to the marketplace of products or of services does not make it valueless in the marketplace of ideas."

Some fragment of hope for the continuing validity of a "commercial speech" exception arguably might have persisted because of the subject matter of the advertisement in *Bigelow.* We noted that in announcing the availability of legal abortions in New York, the advertisement "did more than simply propose a commercial transaction. It contained factual material of clear 'public interest.'" And, of course, the advertisement related to activity with which, at least in some respects, the State could not interfere. See *Roe v. Wade* [p. 314 infra]. Indeed, we observed: "We need not decide in this case the precise extent to which the First Amendment permits regulation of advertising that is related to activities the State may legitimately regulate or even prohibit."

a. Starting with *Valentine v. Chrestensen,* 316 U.S. 52, 62 S.Ct. 920, 86 L.Ed. 1262 (1942), the opinion summarized the decisions and dicta that gave such "indication." Long after *Chrestensen,* strong arguments against a first amendment exception for commercial speech had appeared. See Martin Redish, *The First Amendment in the Market Place,* 39 Geo. Wash.L.Rev. 420 (1971); Note, 50 Ore.L.Rev. 177 (1971); cf. Note, 78 Harv.L.Rev. 1191 (1965).

Here, [the] question whether there is a First Amendment exception for "commercial speech" is squarely before us. Our pharmacist does not wish to editorialize on any subject, cultural, philosophical, or political. He does not wish to report any particularly newsworthy fact, or to make generalized observations even about commercial matters. The "idea" he wishes to communicate is simply this: "I will sell you the X prescription drug at the Y price." Our question, then, is whether this communication is wholly outside the protection of the First Amendment.

V. [Speech] does not lose its First Amendment protection because money is spent to project it, as in a paid advertisement of one form or another. *New York Times Co. v. Sullivan.* Speech likewise is protected even though it is carried in a form that is "sold" for profit. *Smith v. California.* [Our] question is whether speech which does "no more than propose a commercial transaction," is so removed from any "exposition of ideas," and from "truth, science, morality, and arts in general, in its diffusion of liberal sentiments on the administration of Government", *Roth*, that it lacks all protection. Our answer is that it is not.

Focusing first on the individual parties to the transaction that is proposed in the commercial advertisement, we may assume that the advertiser's interest is a purely economic one. That hardly disqualifies him for protection under the First Amendment. The interests of the contestants in a labor dispute are primarily economic, but it has long been settled that both the employee and the employer are protected by the First Amendment when they express themselves on the merits of the dispute in order to influence its outcome.   * * * [17]

As to the particular consumer's interest in the free flow of commercial information, that interest may be as keen, if not keener by far, than his interest in the day's most urgent political debate.[b] Appellees' case in this respect is a convincing one. Those whom the suppression of prescription drug price information hits the hardest are the poor, the sick, and particularly the aged. A disproportionate amount of their income tends to be spent on prescription drugs; yet they are the least able to learn, by shopping from pharmacist to pharmacist, where their scarce dollars are best spent. When drug prices vary as strikingly as they do, information as to who is charging what becomes more than a convenience. It could mean the alleviation of physical pain or the enjoyment of basic necessities.

Generalizing, society also may have a strong interest in the free flow of commercial information. Even an individual advertisement, though entirely "commercial," may be of general public interest. The facts of decided cases furnish illustrations: advertisements stating that referral services for legal abortions are available, *Bigelow;* that a manufacturer of artificial furs promotes his

---

17. The speech of labor disputants, of course, is subject to a number of restrictions. The Court stated in *NLRB v. Gissel Packing Co.*, 395 U.S., at 618, 89 S.Ct., at 1942, 23 L.Ed.2d, at 581 (1969), for example, that an employer's threats of retaliation for the labor actions of his employees are "without the protection of the First Amendment." The constitutionality of restrictions upon speech in the special context of labor disputes is not before us here. We express no views on that complex subject, and advert to cases in the labor field only to note that in some circumstances speech of an entirely private and economic character enjoys the protection of the First Amendment.

[For the contention that labor speech receives less protection than commercial speech, see James Pope, *The Three-Systems Ladder of First Amendment Values: Two Rungs and a Black Hole,* 11 Hast.Con.L.Q. 189 (1984)].

b. Consider Mark Tushnet, *Red, White, and Blue* 290 (1988): "The listener's interest in receiving information, a private interest, thus prevails over a more republican vision of politics, in which political discussion is, at least on the level of public norms, 'keener by far' than private interest."

product as an alternative to the extinction by his competitors of fur-bearing mammals, see *Fur Information & Fashion Council, Inc. v. E.F. Timme & Son,* 364 F.Supp. 16 (S.D.N.Y.1973); and that a domestic producer advertises his product as an alternative to imports that tend to deprive American residents of their jobs, cf. *Chicago Joint Board v. Chicago Tribune Co.,* 435 F.2d 470 (C.A.7 1970), cert. denied, 402 U.S. 973 (1971). Obviously, not all commercial messages contain the same or even a very great public interest element. There are few to which such an element, however, could not be added. Our pharmacist, for example, could cast himself as a commentator on store-to-store disparities in drug prices, giving his own and those of a competitor as proof. We see little point in requiring him to do so, and little difference if he does not.

Moreover, there is another consideration that suggests that no line between publicly "interesting" or "important" commercial advertising and the opposite kind could ever be drawn. Advertising, however tasteless and excessive it sometimes may seem, is nonetheless dissemination of information as to who is producing and selling what product, for what reason, and at what price. So long as we preserve a predominantly free enterprise economy, the allocation of our resources in large measure will be made through numerous private economic decisions. It is a matter of public interest that those decisions, in the aggregate, be intelligent and well informed. To this end, the free flow of commercial information is indispensable. And if it is indispensable to the proper allocation of resources in a free enterprise system, it is also indispensable to the formation of intelligent opinions as to how that system ought to be regulated or altered. Therefore, even if the First Amendment were thought to be primarily an instrument to enlighten public decisionmaking in a democracy, we could not say that the free flow of information does not serve that goal.

Arrayed against these substantial individual and societal interests are a number of justifications for the advertising ban. These have to do principally with maintaining a high degree of professionalism on the part of licensed pharmacists. [Price] advertising, it is argued, will place in jeopardy the pharmacist's expertise and, with it, the customer's health. It is claimed that the aggressive price competition that will result from unlimited advertising will make it impossible for the pharmacist to supply professional services in the compounding, handling, and dispensing of prescription drugs. Such services are time-consuming and expensive; if competitors who economize by eliminating them are permitted to advertise their resulting lower prices, the more painstaking and conscientious pharmacist will be forced either to follow suit or to go out of business. [It] is further claimed that advertising will lead people to shop for their prescription drugs among the various pharmacists who offer the lowest prices, and the loss of stable pharmacist-customer relationships will make individual [attention] impossible. Finally, it is argued that damage will be done to the professional image of the pharmacist. This image, that of a skilled and specialized craftsman, attracts talent to the profession and reinforces the better habits of those who are in [it].

The strength of these proffered justifications is greatly undermined by the fact that high professional standards, to a substantial extent, are guaranteed by the close regulation to which pharmacists in Virginia are subject. [At] the same time, we cannot discount the Board's justifications entirely. The Court regarded justifications of this type sufficient to sustain the advertising bans challenged on due process and equal protection [grounds].[c]

---

c. The Court referred here to cases upholding bans on advertising prices for eyeglass frames and optometrist and dental services.

The challenge now made, however, is based on the First Amendment. This casts the Board's justifications in a different light, for on close inspection it is seen that the State's protectiveness of its citizens rests in large measure on the advantages of their being kept in ignorance. The advertising ban does not directly affect professional standards one way or the other. It affects them only through the reactions it is assumed people will have to the free flow of drug price information. There is no claim that the advertising ban in any way prevents the cutting of corners by the pharmacist who is so inclined. That pharmacist is likely to cut corners in any event. The only effect the advertising ban has on him is to insulate him from price competition and to open the way for him to make a substantial, and perhaps even excessive, profit in addition to providing an inferior service. The more painstaking pharmacist is also protected but, again, it is a protection based in large part on public ignorance.

It appears to be feared that if the pharmacist who wishes to provide low cost, and assertedly low quality, services is permitted to advertise, he will be taken up on his offer by too many unwitting customers. They will choose the low-cost, low-quality service and drive the "professional" pharmacist out of business. [They] will go from one pharmacist to another, following the discount, and destroy the pharmacist-customer relationship. They will lose respect for the profession because it advertises. All this is not in their best interests, and all this can be avoided if they are not permitted to know who is charging what.

[A]n alternative to this highly paternalistic [d] approach [is] to assume that this information is not in itself harmful, that people will perceive their own best interests if only they are well enough informed, and that the best means to that end is to open the channels of communication rather than to close them. If they are truly open, nothing prevents the "professional" pharmacist from marketing his own assertedly superior product, and contrasting it with that of the low-cost, high-volume prescription drug retailer. But the choice among these alternative approaches is not ours to make or the Virginia General Assembly's. It is precisely this kind of choice, between the dangers of suppressing information, and the dangers of its misuse if it is freely available, that the First Amendment makes for [us].

VI. In concluding that commercial speech, like other varieties, is protected, we of course do not hold that it can never be regulated in any way. Some forms of commercial speech regulation are surely permissible. We mention a few. [There] is no claim, for example, that the prohibition on prescription drug price advertising is a mere time, place, and manner restriction. We have often approved restrictions of that kind provided that they are justified without reference to the content of the regulated speech, that they serve a significant governmental interest, and that in so doing they leave open ample alternative channels for communication of the information. Whatever may be the proper bounds of time, place, and manner restrictions on commercial speech, they are plainly exceeded by this Virginia statute, which singles out speech of a particular content and seeks to prevent its dissemination completely.

d. Consider Frederick Schauer, *The Role of the People in First Amendment Theory,* 74 Calif.L.Rev. 761, 788 (1986): "We ought to recognize that popular control over nonpolitical speech may in some circumstances be a bad idea and address directly just why this is so. Perhaps it is time to face up to the paternalism of the first amendment, and maybe much of the rest of the Constitution as well." Is the Court's anti-paternalism paternalistic? For the contention that the Virginia price advertising ban was not paternalistic, see Daniel Lowenstein, *"Too Much Puff": Persuasion, Paternalism, and Commercial Speech,* 56 U.Cin.L.Rev. 1205, 1238 (1988).

Nor is there any claim that prescription drug price advertisements are forbidden because they are false or misleading in any way. Untruthful speech, commercial or otherwise, has never been protected for its own sake. *Gertz*. Obviously much commercial speech is not provably false, or even wholly false, but only deceptive or misleading. We foresee no obstacle to a State's dealing effectively with this problem.[24] The First Amendment, as we construe it today, does not prohibit the State from insuring that the stream of commercial information flows cleanly as well as freely.

Also, there is no claim that the transactions proposed in the forbidden advertisements are themselves illegal in any way. Finally, the special problems of the electronic broadcast media are likewise not in this case.

What is at issue is whether a State may completely suppress the dissemination of concededly truthful information about entirely lawful activity, fearful of that information's effect upon its disseminators and its recipients. Reserving other questions,[25] we conclude that the answer to this one is in the [negative].

JUSTICE STEWART, concurring.[e]

[I] write separately to explain why I think today's decision does not preclude [governmental regulation of false or deceptive advertising]. The Court has on several occasions addressed the problems posed by false statements of fact in libel cases. [Factual] errors are inevitable in free debate, and the imposition of liability for [such errors] can "dampe[n] the vigor and limi[t] the variety of public debate" by inducing "self-censorship." [In] contrast to the press, which must often attempt to assemble the true facts from sketchy and sometimes conflicting sources under the pressure of publication deadlines, the commercial advertiser generally knows the product or service he seeks to sell and is in a position to verify the accuracy of his factual representations before he disseminates them. The advertiser's access to the truth about his product and its price substantially eliminates any danger that governmental regulation of false or misleading price or product advertising will chill accurate and nondeceptive commercial [expression].

24. [C]ommon sense differences between speech that does "no more than propose a commercial transaction," *Pittsburgh Press* [p. 862 infra,] and other varieties [suggest] that a different degree of protection is necessary to insure that the flow of truthful and legitimate commercial information is unimpaired. The truth of commercial speech, for example, may be more easily verifiable by its disseminator than, let us say, news reporting or political commentary, in that ordinarily the advertiser seeks to disseminate information about a specific product or service that he himself provides and presumably knows more about than anyone else. Also, commercial speech may be more durable than other kinds. Since advertising is the sine qua non of commercial profits, there is little likelihood of its being chilled by proper regulation and foregone entirely.

Attributes such as these, the greater objectivity and hardiness of commercial speech, may make it less necessary to tolerate inaccurate statements for fear of silencing the speaker. They may also make it appropriate to require that a commercial message appear in such a form, or include such additional information,

warnings and disclaimers, as are necessary to prevent its being deceptive. They may also make inapplicable the prohibition on prior restraints. Compare *New York Times v. United States* [p. 867 infra] with *Donaldson v. Read Magazine*, 333 U.S. 178, 68 S.Ct. 591, 92 L.Ed. 628 (1948).

25. We stress that we have considered in this case the regulation of commercial advertising by pharmacists. Although we express no opinion as to other professions, the distinctions, historical and functional, between professions, may require consideration of quite different factors. Physicians and lawyers, for example, do not dispense standardized products; they render professional *services* of almost infinite variety and nature, with the consequent enhanced possibility for confusion and deception if they were to undertake certain kinds of advertising.

e. Burger, C.J., separately concurring, stressed the reservation in fn. 25 of the opinion with respect to advertising by attorneys and physicians. Stevens, J., took no part.

Since the factual claims contained in commercial price or product advertisements relate to tangible goods or services, they may be tested empirically and corrected to reflect the truth without in any manner jeopardizing the free dissemination of thought. Indeed, the elimination of false and deceptive claims serves to promote the one facet of commercial price and product advertising that warrants First Amendment protection—its contribution to the flow of accurate and reliable information relevant to public and private decisionmaking.

JUSTICE REHNQUIST, dissenting.

[Under] the Court's opinion the way will be open not only for dissemination of price information but for active promotion of prescription drugs, liquor, cigarettes and other products the use of which it has previously been thought desirable to discourage. Now, however, such promotion is protected by the First Amendment so long as it is not misleading or does not promote an illegal product or [enterprise].

The Court speaks of the consumer's interest in the free flow of commercial information. [This] should presumptively be the concern of the Virginia Legislature, which sits to balance [this] and other claims in the process of making laws such as the one here under attack. The Court speaks of the importance in a "predominantly free enterprise economy" of intelligent and well-informed decisions as to allocation of resources. While there is again much to be said for the Court's observation as a matter of desirable public policy, there is certainly nothing in the United States Constitution which requires the Virginia Legislature to hew to the teachings of Adam Smith in its legislative decisions regulating the pharmacy profession. E.g., *Nebbia v. New York; Olsen v. Nebraska* [Ch. 6, Sec. 3].

[There] are undoubted difficulties with an effort to draw a bright line between "commercial speech" on the one hand and "protected speech" on the other, and the Court does better to face up to these difficulties than to attempt to hide them under labels. In this case, however, the Court has unfortunately substituted for the wavering line previously thought to exist between commercial speech and protected speech a no more satisfactory line of its own—that between "truthful" commercial speech, on the one hand, and that which is "false and misleading" on the other. The difficulty with this line is not that it wavers, but on the contrary that it is simply too Procrustean to take into account the congeries of factors which I believe could, quite consistently with the First and Fourteenth Amendments, properly influence a legislative decision with respect to commercial advertising.

[S]uch a line simply makes no allowance whatever for what appears to have been a considered legislative judgment in most States that while prescription drugs are a necessary and vital part of medical care and treatment, there are sufficient dangers attending their widespread use that they simply may not be promoted in the same manner as hair creams, deodorants, and toothpaste. The very real dangers that general advertising for such drugs might create in terms of encouraging, even though not sanctioning, illicit use of them by individuals for whom they have not been prescribed, or by generating patient pressure upon physicians to prescribe them are simply not dealt with in the Court's [opinion].

Notes and Questions

1. As compared to political decisionmaking, is commercial advertising "neither more nor less significant than a host of other market activities that legislatures concededly may regulate"? Is there an "absence of any principled distinc-

tion between commercial soliciting and other aspects of economic activity"? Has economic due process been "resurrected, clothed in the ill-fitting garb of the first amendment"? See Thomas Jackson & John Jeffries, *Commercial Speech: Economic Due Process and the First Amendment,* 65 Va.L.Rev. 1, 18 and 30 (1979). Why may government "be paternalistic regarding the purchase of goods but may not be paternalistic regarding information about those goods"? Larry Alexander, *Speech in the Local Marketplace: Implications of Virginia State Board of Pharmacy v. Virginia Citizens Consumer Council, Inc. for Local Regulatory Power,* 14 San Diego L.Rev. 357, 376 (1977).

2.   Does the rationale of *Virginia Pharmacy* extend to image or non-informational advertising? Should such advertising be protected? For doubts, see Daniel Lowenstein, *"Too Much Puff": Persuasion, Paternalism, and Commercial Speech,* 56 U.Cin.L.Rev. 1205 (1988). For the cultural implications of image advertising, see Ronald Collins & David Skover, *Commerce and Communication,* 71 Tex.L.Rev. 697 (1993).[f] But see Sylvia Law, *Addiction, Autonomy, and Advertising,* 77 Iowa L.Rev. 909, 932 (1992): "A broad-sweeping principle denying constitutional protection to noninformational commercial speech reinforces a narrow vision of First Amendment values focusing on political participation and rationality. * * * Film, music, and novels are protected, not because they necessarily provide 'information' or facilitate participation in formal political processes, but because the First Amendment protects 'not only ideas capable of relatively precise, detached explication, but otherwise inexpressible emotions as well.' "

3.   Footnote 24 suggests that *deceptive* commercial speech may be regulated in ways that would be barred if the speech were political. Sound distinction?

(a) *"Commonsense" differences between commercial speech and other speech.* (1) *Verifiability.* Consider Daniel Farber, *Commercial Speech and First Amendment Theory,* 74 Nw.U.L.Rev. 372, 385–86 (1979): "[C]ommercial speech is not necessarily more verifiable than other speech. There may well be uncertainty about some quality of a product, such as the health effect of eggs. On the other hand, political speech is often quite verifiable by the speaker. A political candidate knows the truth about his own past and his present intentions, yet misrepresentations on these subjects are immune from state regulation." (2) *Durability.* Consider Martin Redish, *The Value of Free Speech,* 130 U.Pa.L.Rev. 591, 633 (1982): "[I]t is also incorrect to distinguish commercial from political expression on the ground that the former is somehow hardier because of the inherent profit motive. It could just as easily be said that we need not fear that commercial magazines and newspapers will cease publication for fear of governmental regulation, because they are in business for profit. Of course, the proper response to this contention is that our concern is not *whether* they will publish, but *what* they will publish: fear of regulation might deter them from dealing with controversial subjects." But see Ronald Cass, *Commercial Speech, Constitutionalism, Collective Choice,* 56 U.Cin.L.Rev. 1317, 1368–73 (1988).

(b) *Commercial speech and self-expression.* Is commercial speech distinguishable from political speech because it is unrelated to self-expression? Consider C. Edwin Baker, *Commercial Speech: A Problem in the Theory of Freedom,* 62 Iowa L.Rev. 1, 17 (1976): In commercial speech, the dissemination of the profit motive "breaks the connection between speech and any vision, or attitude, or value of the

---

f.   For the negative implications of advertising (informational or non-informational) for democratic politics and culture, see C. Edwin Baker, *Advertising and a Democratic Press* (1994). See also Ronald Collins, *Dictating Content: How Advertising Pressure Can Corrupt A Free Press* (1992).

individual or group engaged in advocacy. Thus the content and form of commercial speech cannot be attributed to individual value allegiances." See generally C. Edwin Baker, *Human Liberty and Freedom of Speech* chs. 3, 9, 10 (1989). For criticism, see, e.g., Pierre Schlag, *An Attack on Categorical Approaches to Freedom of Speech,* 30 U.C.L.A.L.Rev. 671, 710–21 (1983); Steven Shiffrin, *The First Amendment and Economic Regulation: Away From A General Theory of the First Amendment,* 78 Nw.U.L.Rev. 1212 (1983). Even if commercial speech is divorced from self expression (or dignity), should it merit substantial protection, nonetheless. See Aleita Estreicher, *Securities Regulation and the First Amendment,* 24 Ga.L.Rev. 223 (1990); Burt Neuborne, *The First Amendment and Government Regulation of Capital Markets,* 55 Brooklyn L.Rev. 5 (1989).

(c) *Contract approach to commercial speech.* Is commercial advertising distinguishable from other forms of speech because of the state interest in regulating contracts? Consider Farber, supra, at 389: "The unique aspect of commercial speech is that it is a prelude to, and therefore becomes integrated into, a contract, the essence of which is the presence of a promise. Because a promise is an undertaking to ensure that a certain state of affairs takes place, promises obviously have a closer connection with conduct than with self-expression. Second, [in] a fundamentally market economy, the government understandably is given particular deference in its enforcement of contractual expectations. Indeed, the Constitution itself gives special protection to contractual expectations in the contract clause. Finally, [the] technicalities of contract law, with its doctrines of privity, consideration, and the like, should not be blindly translated into first amendment jurisprudence. The basic doctrines of contract law, however, provide a helpful guide in considering commercial speech problems." For discussion, see Larry Alexander & Daniel Farber, *Commercial Speech and First Amendment Theory: A Critical Exchange,* 75 Nw.U.L.Rev. 307 (1980).

(d) *Error costs.* Is commercial speech distinguishable because the risks of error are less? Consider Cass, supra at 1360: "[T]he inquiry can be framed as asking four questions: (1) will officials err less systematically or less often in regulation of commercial speech than in regulation of other speech?; (2) will officials err less systematically or less often in regulation of commerce than in regulation of speech?; (3) will the consequences of errors in regulation of one sort of activity generally be less significant than the consequences of errors in the other?; and (4) will the process costs associated with error correction be lower in respect of one activity than the other?" On the risks of error, see generally Cass, supra; Fred McChesney, *A Positive Regulatory Theory of the First Amendment,* 20 Conn.L.Rev. 335 (1988). See also Ronald Coase, *Advertising and Free Speech,* 6 J.Legal Stud. 1 (1977); Richard Posner, *Free Speech in an Economic Perspective,* 20 Suffolk U.L.Rev. 1 (1986); Thomas Scanlon, *Freedom of Expression and Categories of Expression,* 40 U.Pitt.L.Rev. 519 (1979).

4. *Limits on regulation of deceptive advertising.* Bates v. State Bar, 433 U.S. 350, 51 Ohio Misc. 1, 97 S.Ct. 2691, 53 L.Ed.2d 810 (1977), struck down an Arizona Supreme Court rule against a lawyer "publicizing himself" through advertising. It rejected the claim that attorney price advertising was inherently misleading, but left open the "peculiar problems" associated with advertising claims regarding the quality of legal services.[f] Could a lawyer truthfully advertise

---

f. *Zauderer v. Office of Disciplinary Counsel,* p. 876 infra, held that a state may not discipline attorneys who solicit legal business through newspaper advertisements containing "truthful and nondeceptive information and advice regarding the legal rights of potential clients" or for the advertising use of "accurate and nondeceptive" illustrations. Zauderer had

that he or she has (1) tried twice as many personal injury cases as any other lawyer in the country? (2) averaged $10,000 more in recoveries per case than any other lawyer in the county? (3) graduated from Harvard Law School in the upper 10% of the class? (4) received "the best legal education this country offers"? Should an advertisement be protected if it is "sufficiently factual to be subject to verification" even if "implications of quality might be drawn from it"? See William Canby and Ernest Gellhorn, *Physician Advertising: The First Amendment and the Sherman Act,* 1978 Duke L.J. 543, 560–62. Should the Court have deferred to the judgment of the State Bar of Arizona? If not, should it defer to the SEC when it regulates the advertising of securities? The FTC when it regulates automobile advertising? The Virginia Board of Pharmacy when it regulates quality advertising by pharmacists? For deferential treatment of a state ban on the use of tradenames by optometrists, see *Friedman v. Rogers,* 440 U.S. 1, 99 S.Ct. 887, 59 L.Ed.2d 100 (1979).

5. *Truth and commercial advertising.* Should Mercedes Benz be able to truthfully advertise that Frank Sinatra drives its car without getting Sinatra's permission? See Wesley Liebeler, *A Property Rights Approach to Judicial Decision Making,* 4 Cato J. 783, 802–03 (1985); Shiffrin, supra note 3, at 1257–58 n. 275; Peter Felcher & Edward Rubin, *Privacy, Publicity, and the Portrayal of Real People by the Media,* 88 Yale L.J. 1577 (1979); James Treece, *Commercial Exploitation of Names, Likenesses, and Personal Histories,* 51 Tex.L.Rev. 637 (1973). Should the state be able to prevent homeowners from posting "for sale" signs in order to prevent panic selling in order to maintain an integrated neighborhood? See *Linmark Associates v. Willingboro,* 431 U.S. 85, 97 S.Ct. 1614, 52 L.Ed.2d 155 (1977). May a state regulate the content of contraceptive advertising in order to minimize its offensive character? Cf. *Carey v. Population Services Int'l.,* p. 406 supra (total ban on contraceptive advertising unconstitutional).

———

OHRALIK v. OHIO STATE BAR ASS'N, 436 U.S. 447, 98 S.Ct. 1912, 56 L.Ed.2d 444 (1978) upheld the indefinite suspension of an attorney for violating the anti-solicitation provisions of the Ohio Code of Professional Responsibility. Those provisions generally do not allow lawyers to recommend themselves to anyone who has not sought "their advice regarding employment of a lawyer." Albert Ohralik had approached two young accident victims to solicit employment—Carol McClintock in a hospital room where she lay in traction and Wanda Lou Holbert on the day she came home from the hospital. He employed a concealed tape recorder with Holbert, apparently to insure he would have evidence of her assent to his representation. The next day, when Holbert's mother informed Ohralik that she and her daughter did not want to have appellant represent them, he insisted that the daughter had entered into a binding agreement. McClintock also discharged Ohralik, and Ohralik sued her for breach of

placed illustrated ads in 36 Ohio newspapers publicizing his availability to represent women who had suffered injuries from use of a contraceptive device known as the Dalkon Shield Intrauterine Device. In the ad Zauderer stated that he had represented other women in Dalkon Shield litigation. The Court observed that accurate statements of fact cannot be proscribed "merely because it is possible that some readers will infer that he has some expertise in those areas." But it continued to "leave open the possibility that States may prevent attorneys from making non-verifiable claims regarding the quality of their services. *Bates.*"

contract. The Court ruled, per POWELL, J., that a state may forbid in-person solicitation of clients by lawyers for pecuniary gain:

"Expression concerning purely commercial transactions has come within the ambit of the Amendment's protection only recently. In rejecting the notion that such speech is wholly outside the protection of the First Amendment, *Virginia Pharmacy,* we were careful not to hold that it is wholly undifferentiable from other forms of speech.

"We have not discarded the common sense distinction between speech proposing a commercial transaction, which occurs in an area traditionally subject to government regulation, and other varieties of speech. To require a parity of constitutional protection for commercial and noncommercial speech alike could invite dilution, simply by a leveling process, of the force of the Amendment's guarantee with respect to the latter kind of speech. Rather than subject the First Amendment to such a devitalization, we instead have afforded commercial speech a limited measure of protection, commensurate with its subordinate position in the scale of First Amendment values, while allowing modes of regulation that might be impermissible in the realm of noncommercial expression.

"Moreover, 'it has never been deemed an abridgment of freedom of speech or press to make a course of conduct illegal merely because the conduct was in part initiated, evidenced, or carried out by means of language, either spoken, written, or printed.' *Giboney v. Empire Storage & Ice Co.,* 336 U.S. 490, 502, 69 S.Ct. 684, 691, 93 L.Ed. 834 (1949). Numerous examples could be cited of communications that are regulated without offending the First Amendment, such as the exchange of information about securities, *SEC v. Texas Gulf Sulphur Co.,* 401 F.2d 833 (C.A.2 1968), cert. denied, 394 U.S. 976, 89 S.Ct. 1454, 22 L.Ed.2d 756 (1969), corporate proxy statements, *Mills v. Electric Auto-Lite Co.,* 396 U.S. 375, 90 S.Ct. 616, 24 L.Ed.2d 593 (1970), the exchange of price and production information among competitors, *American Column & Lumber Co. v. United States,* 257 U.S. 377, 42 S.Ct. 114, 66 L.Ed. 284 (1921), and employers' threats of retaliation for the labor activities of employees, *NLRB v. Gissel Packing Co.,* 395 U.S. 575, 618, 89 S.Ct. 1918, 1942, 23 L.Ed.2d 547 (1969). Each of these examples illustrates that the State does not lose its power to regulate commercial activity deemed harmful to the public whenever speech is a component of that activity. Neither *Virginia Pharmacy* nor *Bates* purported to cast doubt on the permissibility of these kinds of commercial regulation.

"In-person solicitation by a lawyer of remunerative employment is a business transaction in which speech is an essential but subordinate component. While this does not remove the speech from the protection of the First Amendment, as was held in *Bates* and *Virginia Pharmacy,* it lowers the level of appropriate judicial scrutiny. [A] lawyer's procurement of remunerative employment is a subject only marginally affected with First Amendment concerns. It falls within the State's proper sphere of economic and professional regulation. While entitled to some constitutional protection, appellant's conduct is subject to regulation in furtherance of important state [interests].

" 'The interest of the States in regulating lawyers is especially great since lawyers are essential to the primary function of administering justice and have historically been officers of the courts' [and] act 'as trusted agents of their clients and as assistants to the court in search of a just solution to disputes.'

"[The] substantive evils of solicitation have been stated over the years in sweeping terms: stirring up litigation, assertion of fraudulent claims, debasing the legal profession, and potential harm to the solicited client in the form of overreaching, overcharging, underrepresentation, and misrepresentation." In providing information about the availability and terms of proposed legal services "in-person solicitation serves much the same function as the advertisement at issue in *Bates.* But there are significant differences as well. Unlike a public advertisement, which simply provides information and leaves the recipient free to act upon it or not, in-person solicitation may exert pressure and often demands an immediate response, without providing an opportunity for comparison or reflection. The aim and effect of in-person solicitation may be to provide a one-sided presentation and to encourage speedy and perhaps uninformed decisionmaking; there is no opportunity for intervention or counter-education by agencies of the Bar, supervisory authorities, or persons close to the solicited individual. The admonition that 'the fitting remedy for evil counsels is good ones' is of little value when the circumstances provide no opportunity for any remedy at all. In-person solicitation is as likely as not to discourage persons needing counsel from engaging in a critical comparison of the 'availability, nature, and prices' of legal services; it actually may disserve the individual and societal interest, identified in *Bates,* in facilitating 'informed and reliable decisionmaking.'

"[Appellant's argument that none of the evils of solicitation was found in his case] misconceives the nature of the State's interest. The rules prohibiting solicitation are prophylactic measures whose objective is the prevention of harm before it occurs.[a] The rules were applied in this case to discipline a lawyer for soliciting employment for pecuniary gain under circumstances likely to result in the adverse consequences the State seeks to avert. In such a situation, which is inherently conducive to overreaching and other forms of misconduct, the State has a strong interest in adopting and enforcing rules of conduct designed to protect the public from harmful solicitation by lawyers whom it has [licensed].

"The efficacy of the State's effort to prevent such harm to prospective clients would be substantially diminished if, having proved a solicitation in circumstances like those of this case, the State were required in addition to prove actual injury. Unlike the advertising in *Bates,* in-person solicitation is not visible or otherwise open to public scrutiny. Often there is no witness other than the lawyer and the lay person whom he has solicited, rendering it difficult or impossible to obtain reliable proof of what actually took place. This would be especially true if the lay person were so distressed at the time of the solicitation that he or she could not recall specific details at a later date. If appellant's view were sustained, in-person solicitation would be virtually immune to effective oversight and regulation by the State or by the legal profession, in contravention of the State's strong interest in regulating members of the Bar in an effective, objective, and self-enforcing manner. It therefore is not unreasonable, or violative of the Constitution, for a State to respond with what in effect is a prophylactic rule." [b]

Notes and Questions

1. *Companion case.* IN RE PRIMUS, 436 U.S. 412, 98 S.Ct. 1893, 56 L.Ed.2d 417 (1978), per POWELL, J., held that a state could not constitutionally discipline an ACLU "cooperating lawyer" who, after advising a gathering of allegedly illegally sterilized women of their rights, initiated further contact with one of the women by writing her a letter informing her of the ACLU's willingness to provide free legal representation for women in her situation and of the

a. But see Fred McChesney, *Commercial Speech in the Professions,* 134 U.Pa.L.Rev. 45 (1985) (anti-solicitation provisions may be motivated by anti-competitive considerations).

b. Marshall and Rehnquist, JJ., each separately concurred in the judgment. Brennan, J., did not participate.

organization's desire to file a lawsuit on her behalf. "South Carolina's action in punishing appellant for soliciting a prospective litigant by mail, on behalf of ACLU, must withstand the 'exacting scrutiny applicable to limitations on core First Amendment rights.' [Where] political expression or association is at issue, this Court has not tolerated the degree of imprecision that often characterizes government regulation of the conduct of commercial affairs. The approach we adopt today in *Ohralik* that the State may proscribe in-person solicitation for pecuniary gain under circumstances likely to result in adverse consequences, cannot be applied to appellant's activity on behalf of the ACLU. Although a showing of potential danger may suffice in the former context, appellant may not be disciplined unless her activity in fact involved the type of misconduct at which South Carolina's broad prohibition is said to be directed. The record does not support appellee's contention that undue influence, overreaching, misrepresentation, or invasion of privacy actually occurred in this case."

2. *Related cases. Edenfield v. Fane*, 507 U.S. 761, 113 S.Ct. 1792, 123 L.Ed.2d 543 (1993) held that direct personal solicitation of prospective business clients by Certified Public Accountants is protected under the first amendment,[1] but *Florida Bar v. Went For It, Inc.*, ___ U.S. ___, 115 S.Ct. 2371, 132 L.Ed.2d 541 (1995) held that targeted direct-mail solicitations by personal injury attorneys to victims and their relatives for thirty days following an accident were not protected under the first amendment.

3. *A hierarchy of protected speech.* Consider Steven Shiffrin, supra, at 1218–21 (1983). In *Virginia Pharmacy,* "the Court never admitted that commercial speech was less valuable than political speech. The 'commonsense differences' had nothing to do with value. [Although] Justice Blackmun labored to defend the asserted equal relationship between commercial speech and political speech for the *Virginia Pharmacy* majority, Justice Powell in *Ohralik* was content to lead the Court to an opposite position without explanation. In so doing, Justice Powell steered the Court to accept a hierarchy of protected speech for the first time, despite his own stated opposition [in *Young*] to creating any such hierarchy." Does the concern that the protection of non-commercial speech would be subject to dilution if it were placed on a par with commercial speech presuppose an unexplained difference between the two types of speech? See id. at 1221 n. 59. For discussion of the dilution argument, see William Marshall, *The Dilution of the First Amendment and the Equality of Ideas*, 38 Case W.Res.L.Rev. 566 (1988).

4. *Muddying the hierarchy.* Cincinnati permitted 1,500–2,000 newsracks throughout the city for publications not classified as commercial speech, but refused to allow an additional 62 newsracks that contained two publications classified as commercial speech. CINCINNATI v. DISCOVERY NETWORK, 507 U.S. 410, 113 S.Ct. 1505, 123 L.Ed.2d 99 (1993), per STEVENS, J., held that this discrimination violated the first amendment: "The major premise supporting the city's argument is the proposition that commercial speech has only a low value. Based on that premise, the city contends that the fact that assertedly more valuable publications are allowed to use newsracks does not undermine its judgment that its esthetic and safety interests are stronger than the interest in

---

1. Blackmun, J., concurred; O'Connor, J., dissented. Compare Ibanez v. Florida Dep't of Business and Professional Regulation, ___ U.S. ___, 114 S.Ct. 2084, 129 L.Ed.2d 118 (1994) (attorney's references in advertising, business cards and stationery to her credentials as a CPA and a Certified Financial Planner are not deceptive or misleading and are protected commercial speech); Accord, Peel v. Attorney Registration and Disciplinary Comm'n, 496 U.S. 91, 110 S.Ct. 2281, 110 L.Ed.2d 83 (1990) (reference on letterhead to prestigious certification is protected speech).

allowing commercial speakers to have similar access to the reading public. [In] our view, the city's argument attaches more importance to the distinction between commercial and non-commercial speech than our cases warrant and seriously underestimates the value of commercial speech." [20] c

5. *The reach of discovery network.*

(a) In *MARTIN v. STRUTHERS*, 319 U.S. 141, 63 S.Ct. 862, 87 L.Ed. 1313 (1943), a city forbade knocking on the door or ringing the doorbell of a resident in order to deliver handbills (in an industrial community where many worked night shifts and slept during the day). In striking down the ordinance, the Court, per BLACK, J., pointed out that the city's objectives could be achieved by means of a law making it an offense for any person to ring the doorbell of a householder who has "appropriately indicated that he is unwilling to be disturbed. This or any similar regulation leaves the decision as to whether distributors of literature may lawfully call at a home where it belongs—with the homeowner himself." By contrast, *Breard v. Alexandria*, 341 U.S. 622, 71 S.Ct. 920, 95 L.Ed. 1233 (1951) upheld an ordinance forbidding the practice of going door to door to solicit orders for the sale of goods. The commercial element was said to distinguish *Martin*. Does *Breard* survive *Virginia Pharmacy?* Does (should) *Discovery Network* settle the issue? What if, as in *Breard*, the solicitor is selling subscriptions for magazines?

(b) Compare *Schneider*, p. 799 infra (prohibition against leaflet distribution on streets unconstitutional) with *Valentine*, p. 716 supra (prohibition against distribution of commercial leaflets upheld). Does (should) the *holding* of *Valentine* survive *Virginia Pharmacy?* Does *Discovery Network* settle the issue? d

(c) The Court has held it unconstitutional for a locality to prohibit "For Sale" signs on residential property. *Linmark*. Similarly, the Court has held it unconstitutional to prohibit property owners from displaying political signs at their residences. *Ladue v. Gilleo*, ___ U.S. ___, 114 S.Ct. 2038, 129 L.Ed.2d 36 (1994). After *Linmark*, *Ladue*, and *Discovery Network*, would it be unconstitutional to

---

20. Metromedia, Inc. v. San Diego, 453 U.S. 490, 101 S.Ct. 2882, 69 L.Ed.2d 800 (1981), upon which the city heavily relies, is not to the contrary. In that case, a plurality of the Court found as a permissible restriction on commercial speech a city ordinance that, for the most part, banned outdoor "offsite" advertising billboards, but permitted "onsite" advertising signs identifying the owner of the premises and the goods sold or manufactured on the site. Unlike this case, which involves discrimination between commercial and noncommercial speech, the "offsite-onsite" distinction involved disparate treatment of two types of commercial speech. Only the onsite signs served both the commercial and public interest in guiding potential visitors to their intended destinations; moreover, the plurality concluded that a "city may believe that offsite advertising, with its periodically changing content, presents a more acute problem than does onsite advertising." Neither of these bases has any application to the disparate treatment of newsracks in this case.

The Chief Justice is correct that seven Justices in the Metromedia case were of the view that San Diego could completely ban offsite commercial billboards for reasons unrelated to the content of those billboards. Those seven Justices did not say, however, that San Diego could distinguish between commercial and noncommercial offsite billboards that cause the same esthetic and safety concerns. That question was not presented in Metromedia, for the regulation at issue in that case did not draw a distinction between commercial and noncommercial offsite billboards; with a few exceptions, it essentially banned all offsite billboards.

c. Rehnquist, J., joined by White & Thomas, JJ., dissented.

d. For relevant commentary on the normative issues, see C. Edwin Baker, *Commercial Speech: A Problem in the Theory of Freedom*, 62 Iowa L.Rev. 1 (1976); Martin Redish, *The First Amendment in the Marketplace: Commercial Speech and the Values of Free Expression*, 39 Geo.Wash.L.Rev. 429 (1971); Martin Redish, *The Value of Free Speech*, 130 U.Pa.L.Rev. 591 (1982); Steven Shiffrin, *The First Amendment and Economic Regulation: Away From a General Theory of the First Amendment*, 78 Nw.U.L.Rev. 1212, 1220, 1276–82 (1983).

prohibit signs on residential property that advertise goods and services sold elsewhere?

CENTRAL HUDSON GAS & ELEC. CORP. v. PUBLIC SERVICE COM'N, 447 U.S. 557, 100 S.Ct. 2343, 65 L.Ed.2d 341 (1980), per POWELL, J., invalidated a Commission regulation that, in an effort to conserve power, prohibited promotional advertising by an electric utility except for encouraging shifts of consumption from peak demand times: "The Commission's order restricts only commercial speech, that is, expression related solely to the economic interests of the speaker and its audience. [In] commercial speech cases, [a] four-part analysis has developed. At the outset, we must determine whether the expression is protected by the First Amendment. For commercial speech to come within that provision, it at least must concern lawful activity [a] and not be misleading. Next, we ask whether the asserted governmental interest is substantial. If both inquiries yield positive answers, we must determine whether the regulation directly advances the governmental interest asserted, and whether it is not more extensive than is necessary to serve that interest.[b]

"[T]he State's interest in energy conservation is directly advanced by the Commission order at issue here. There is an immediate connection between advertising and the demand for electricity. [Thus], we find a direct link between the state interest in conservation and the Commission's order.

"[T]he critical inquiry [is] whether the Commission's complete suppression of speech ordinarily protected by the First Amendment is no more extensive than necessary to further the State's interest in energy conservation. The Commission's order reaches all promotional advertising, regardless of the impact of the touted service on overall energy use. But the energy conservation rationale, as important as it is, cannot justify suppressing information about electric devices or services that would cause no net increase in total energy use. In addition, no showing has been made that a more limited restriction on the content of promotional advertising would not serve adequately the State's interests.

"Appellant insists that but for the ban, it would advertise products and services that use energy efficiently. These include the 'heat pump,' which both parties acknowledge to be a major improvement in electric heating, and the use of electric heat as a 'back-up' to solar and other heat sources. Although the Commission has questioned the efficiency of electric heating before this Court, neither the Commission's Policy Statement nor its order denying rehearing made findings on this issue. In the absence of authoritative findings to the contrary, we

a. *Pittsburgh Press Co. v. Human Relations Comm'n,* p. 720 infra, upheld an order forbidding publication of sex-designated help-wanted columns as a forbidden "aid" to prohibited sex discrimination in employment: "Discrimination in employment is *illegal* commercial activity under the ordinance. We have no doubt that a newspaper constitutionally could be forbidden to publish a want-ad proposing a sale of narcotics or soliciting prostitutes."

b. In an earlier footnote, the Court emphasized that this requirement was "not an application of the 'overbreadth' doctrine. The

latter theory permits the invalidation of regulations on First Amendment grounds even when the litigant challenging the regulation has engaged in no constitutionally protected activity. [In] this case, the Commission's prohibition acts directly against the promotional activities of Central Hudson, and to the extent the limitations are unnecessary to serve the state's interest, they are invalid." For a different perspective on the overbreadth doctrine, see Martin Redish, *The Warren Court, The Burger Court and the First Amendment Overbreadth Doctrine,* 78 Nw.U.L.Rev. 1031 (1983).

must credit as within the realm of possibility the claim that electric heat can be an efficient alternative in some circumstances.

"The Commission's order prevents appellant from promoting electric services that would reduce energy use by diverting demand from less efficient sources, or that would consume roughly the same amount of energy as do alternative sources. In neither situation would the utility's advertising endanger conservation or mislead the public. To the extent that the Commission's order suppresses speech that in no way impairs the State's interest in energy conservation, the Commission's order violates the First and Fourteenth Amendments and must be invalidated.

"The Commission also has not demonstrated that its interest in conservation cannot be protected adequately by more limited regulation of appellant's commercial expression. To further its policy of conservation, the Commission could attempt to restrict the format and content of Central Hudson's advertising. It might, for example, require that the advertisements include information about the relative efficiency and expense of the offered service, both under current conditions and for the foreseeable future.[13] In the absence of a showing that more limited speech regulation would be ineffective, we cannot approve the complete suppression of Central Hudson's advertising."

BLACKMUN, J., joined by Brennan, J., concurring in the judgment, saw in the Court's "four-part analysis" approval of "an intermediate level of scrutiny" whenever a restraint on commercial speech " 'directly advance[s]' a 'substantial' governmental interest and is 'not more extensive than is necessary to serve that interest.' I agree with the Court that this level of intermediate scrutiny is appropriate for a restraint on commercial speech designed to protect consumers from misleading or coercive speech, or a regulation related to the time, place, or manner of commercial speech. I do not agree, however, that the Court's four-part test is the proper one to be applied when a State seeks to suppress information about a product in order to manipulate a private economic decision that the State cannot or has not regulated or outlawed directly.   * * *

"I seriously doubt whether suppression of information concerning the availability and price of a legally offered product is ever a permissible way for the State to 'dampen' demand for or use of the product. Even though 'commercial' speech is involved, such a regulatory measure strikes at the heart of the First Amendment. This is because it is a covert attempt by the State to manipulate the choices of its citizens, not by persuasion or direct regulation, but by depriving the public of the information needed to make a free choice. As the Court recognizes, the State's policy choices are insulated from the visibility and scrutiny that direct regulation would entail and the conduct of citizens is molded by the information that government chooses to give [them].

"It appears that the Court would permit the State to ban all direct advertising of air conditioning, assuming that a more limited restriction on such advertising would not effectively deter the public from cooling its homes. In my view, our cases do not support this type of suppression. If a governmental unit believes that use or over-use of air conditioning is a serious problem, it must attack that problem directly, by prohibiting air conditioning or regulating thermostat levels."

---

13. The Commission also might consider a system of previewing advertising campaigns to insure that they will not defeat conservation policy. It has instituted such a program for approving "informational" advertising under the Policy Statement challenged in this case. We have observed that commercial speech is such a sturdy brand of expression that traditional prior restraint doctrine may not apply to it. *Virginia Pharmacy.* * * *

STEVENS, J., joined by Brennan, J., also concurred: "Because 'commercial speech' is afforded less constitutional protection than other forms of speech, it is important that the commercial speech concept not be defined too broadly lest speech deserving of greater constitutional protection be inadvertently suppressed. The issue in this case is whether New York's prohibition on the promotion of the use of electricity through advertising is a ban on nothing but commercial [speech].

"This case involves a governmental regulation that completely bans promotional advertising by an electric utility. This ban encompasses a great deal more than mere proposals to engage in certain kinds of commercial transactions. It prohibits all advocacy of the immediate or future use of electricity. It curtails expression by an informed and interested group of persons of their point of view on questions relating to the production and consumption of electrical energy—questions frequently discussed and debated by our political leaders. For example, an electric company's advocacy of the use of electric heat for environmental reasons, as opposed to wood-burning stoves, would seem to fall squarely within New York's promotional advertising ban and also within the bounds of maximum First Amendment protection. The breadth of the ban thus exceeds the boundaries of the commercial speech concept, however that concept may be defined.

"The justification for the regulation is nothing more than the expressed fear that the audience may find the utility's message persuasive. Without the aid of any coercion, deception, or misinformation, truthful communication may persuade some citizens to consume more electricity than they otherwise would. I assume that such a consequence would be undesirable and that government may therefore prohibit and punish the unnecessary or excessive use of electricity. But if the perceived harm associated with greater electrical usage is not sufficiently serious to justify direct regulation, surely it does not constitute the kind of clear and present danger that can justify the suppression of [speech].

"In sum, I concur in the result because I do not consider this to be a 'commercial speech' case. Accordingly, I see no need to decide whether the Court's four-part analysis adequately protects commercial speech—as properly defined—in the face of a blanket ban of the sort involved in this case."

REHNQUIST, J., dissented in a long opinion, summarized in his introduction: "The Court's analysis in my view is wrong in several respects. Initially, I disagree with the Court's conclusion that the speech of a state-created monopoly, which is the subject of a comprehensive regulatory scheme, is entitled to protection under the First Amendment. I also think that the Court errs here in failing to recognize that the state law is most accurately viewed as an economic regulation and that the speech involved (if it falls within the scope of the First Amendment at all) occupies a significantly more subordinate position in the hierarchy of First Amendment values than the Court gives it today. Finally, the Court in reaching its decision improperly substitutes its own judgment for that of the State in deciding how a proper ban on promotional advertising should be drafted. With regard to this latter point, the Court adopts as its final part of a four-part test a 'no more extensive than necessary' analysis that will unduly impair a state legislature's ability to adopt legislation reasonably designed to promote interests that have always been rightly thought to be of great importance to the State."

In commenting on the Court's four part test, Rehnquist, J., stated: "The [test] elevates the protection accorded commercial speech that falls within the scope of the First Amendment to a level that is virtually indistinguishable from that of noncommercial speech. I think the Court in so doing has effectively accomplished the 'devitalization' of the First Amendment that it counseled against in *Ohralik*. I think it has also by labeling economic regulation of business conduct as a restraint on 'free speech' gone far to resurrect the discredited doctrine of cases such as *Lochner*. New York's order here is in my view more akin to an economic regulation to which virtually complete deference should be accorded by this Court.

"I doubt there would be any question as to the constitutionality of New York's conservation effort if the Public Service Commission had chosen to raise the price of electricity, to condition its sale on specified terms, or to restrict its production. In terms of constitutional values, I think that such controls are virtually indistinguishable from the State's ban on promotional advertising."

Notes and Questions

1. *The four part test.* Is Rehnquist, J., correct in stating that the Court's test "elevates the protection of commercial speech to a level that is virtually indistinguishable from that of noncommercial speech"? Is it possible to state "the" test that has been applied to noncommercial speech?

2. *Paternalism and Central Hudson.* Consider Vincent Blasi, *The Pathological Perspective and the First Amendment*, 85 Colum.L.Rev. 449, 487 (1985): "[T]he claim of the regulators in the drug and lawyer advertising cases was that consumers would be influenced by the advertising to act against their own self-interest; in the promotional advertising case, the fear was that consumers would act against the public interest in pursuit of their own short range self-interest. The rationale in the first type of case is more paternalistic because it necessarily assumes that listeners cannot evaluate the message even when they have every incentive to try to do so. The rationale in the promotional advertising case is consistent with respect for the message-screening capacities of listeners; what the rationale doubts is the capacity of listeners to behave as public-spirited citizens when prompted to act selfishly by sophisticated advertising techniques."

3. In what sense was the speech in *Central Hudson* solely in the economic interests of speaker and audience?[c] Should the Court decide on an ad hoc basis which advertisements have political impact and which do not? In addressing this question, *Central Hudson,* noted that any product could be tied to public concerns and that since companies are otherwise free to speak about public issues,[d] "there is no reason for providing similar protection when such statements are made only in the context of commercial transactions." Compare *Bolger v. Youngs Drug Products Corp.,* 463 U.S. 60, 103 S.Ct. 2875, 77 L.Ed.2d 469 (1983) ("advertisers should not be permitted to immunize false or misleading product information from government regulation simply by including references to public issues"); *Board of Trustees v. Fox,* 492 U.S. 469, 109 S.Ct. 3028, 106 L.Ed.2d 388 (1989) (housewares sales presentations are commercial speech even though they provide information on matters of financial responsibility and how to run an efficient home).[e]

---

c. Is this category intended to be larger than the category of proposing a commercial transaction? Consider the question in connection with *Greenmoss,* p. 739 infra.

d. See Sec. 11 infra.

e. On the definitional difficulties, see Alex Kozinski & Stuart Banner, *Who's Afraid of Commercial Speech?*, 76 Va.L.Rev. 627 (1990).

Puerto Rico makes advertising of casino gambling, subject to a complicated body of regulations enforced by the Tourism Company of Puerto Rico (a public company with regulatory powers). These regulations allow casino advertising designed to attract tourists; they prohibit casino advertising aimed at Puerto Rican residents. For example, casino advertising is permitted when distributed in airports or on docks where cruise ships arrive and is permitted in media that primarily reach tourists, e.g., The New York Times, trade magazines, even advertisements on network television (that reaches Puerto Rico via cable). Advertising of the hotels containing the casinos is permitted in the local Puerto Rican media "when the trade name of the hotel is used even though it may contain a reference to the casino provided that the word casino is never used alone nor specified." But advertisements designed to attract residents of Puerto Rico to the casinos are expressly prohibited.

POSADAS DE PUERTO RICO ASSOCIATES v. TOURISM CO., 478 U.S. 328, 106 S.Ct. 2968, 92 L.Ed.2d 266 (1986), per REHNQUIST, J., upheld the advertising restrictions: "[A]dvertising of casino gambling aimed at the residents of Puerto Rico, concerns a lawful activity and is not misleading or fraudulent, at least in the abstract. We must therefore proceed to the three remaining steps of the *Central Hudson* analysis. [The government] interest at stake in this case, as determined by the Superior Court, is the reduction of demand for casino gambling by the residents of Puerto Rico. [The] Tourism Company's brief before this Court explains the legislature's belief that '[e]xcessive casino gambling among local residents—[would] produce serious harmful effects on the health, safety and welfare of the Puerto Rican citizens, such as the disruption of moral and cultural patterns, the increase in local crime, the fostering of prostitution, the development of corruption, and the infiltration of organized crime.' These are some of the very same concerns, of course, that have motivated the vast majority of the 50 States to prohibit casino gambling. We have no difficulty in concluding that the Puerto Rico Legislature's interest in the health, safety, and welfare of its citizens constitutes a 'substantial' governmental interest. Cf. *Renton*.

"The last two steps of the *Central Hudson* analysis basically involve a consideration of the 'fit' between the legislature's ends and the means chosen to accomplish those ends. [The] Puerto Rico Legislature obviously believed, when it enacted the advertising restrictions at issue here, that advertising of casino gambling aimed at the residents of Puerto Rico would serve to increase the demand for the product advertised. We think the legislature's belief is a reasonable one, and the fact that appellant has chosen to litigate this case all the way to this Court indicates that appellant shares the legislature's view.

"Appellant argues, however, that the challenged advertising restrictions are underinclusive because other kinds of gambling such as horse racing, cockfighting, and the lottery may be advertised to the residents of Puerto Rico. Appellant's argument is misplaced for two reasons. First, whether other kinds of gambling are advertised in Puerto Rico or not, the restrictions on advertising of casino gambling 'directly advance' the legislature's interest in reducing demand for games of chance. Second, the legislature's interest, as previously identified, is not necessarily to reduce demand for all games of chance, but to reduce demand for casino gambling. According to the Superior Court, horse racing, cockfighting, 'picas,' or small games of chance at fiestas, and the lottery 'have been traditionally part of the Puerto Rican's roots,' so that 'the legislator could have been more flexible than in authorizing more sophisticated games which are not so widely sponsored by the people.' In other words, the legislature felt that for Puerto Ricans the risks associated with casino gambling were significantly greater than those associated with the more traditional kinds of gambling in Puerto Rico. In our view, the legislature's separate classification of casino gambling, for purposes of the advertising ban, satisfies the third step of the *Central Hudson* analysis.

"We also think it clear beyond peradventure that the challenged statute and regulations satisfy the fourth and last step of the *Central Hudson* analysis. [The] narrowing constructions of the advertising restrictions announced by the Superior Court ensure that the restrictions will not affect advertising of casino gambling aimed at tourists, but will apply only to such advertising when aimed at the residents of Puerto Rico. Appellant contends, however, that the First Amendment requires the Puerto Rico Legislature to reduce demand for casino gambling among the residents of Puerto Rico not by suppressing commercial speech that might *encourage* such gambling, but by promulgating additional speech designed to *discourage* it. We reject this contention. We think it is up to the legislature to decide whether or not such a 'counterspeech' policy would be as effective in reducing the demand for casino gambling as a restriction on advertising. * * * [9]

"Appellant argues, [in addition], that the challenged advertising restrictions are constitutionally defective under our decisions in *Carey* [p. 312 supra,] and *Bigelow*. In *Carey,* this Court struck down a ban on any 'advertisement or display' of contraceptives, and in *Bigelow,* we reversed a criminal conviction based on the advertisement of an abortion clinic. [In] *Carey* and *Bigelow,* the underlying conduct that was the subject of the advertising restrictions was constitutionally protected and could not have been prohibited by the State. Here, on the other hand, the Puerto Rico Legislature surely could have prohibited casino gambling by the residents of Puerto Rico altogether. In our view, the greater power to completely ban casino gambling necessarily includes the lesser power to ban advertising of casino gambling, and *Carey* and *Bigelow* are hence inapposite.

"Appellant also makes the related argument that, having chosen to legalize casino gambling for residents of Puerto Rico, the First Amendment prohibits the legislature from using restrictions on advertising to accomplish its goal of reducing demand for such gambling. We disagree. In our view, appellant has the argument backwards. As we noted in the preceding paragraph, it is precisely *because* the government could have enacted a wholesale prohibition of the underlying conduct that it is permissible for the government to take the less intrusive step of allowing the conduct, but reducing the demand through restrictions on advertising. It would surely be a Pyrrhic victory for casino owners such as appellant to gain recognition of a First Amendment right to advertise their casinos to the residents of Puerto Rico, only to thereby force the legislature into banning

9. It should be apparent from our discussion of the First Amendment issue, and particularly the third and fourth prongs of the *Central Hudson* test, that appellant can fare no better under the equal protection guarantee of the Constitution. Cf. *Renton.* If there is a sufficient "fit" between the legislature's means and ends to satisfy the concerns of the First Amendment, the same "fit" is surely adequate under the applicable "rational basis" equal protection analysis.

Justice Stevens, in dissent, asserts the additional equal protection claim, not raised by appellant either below or in this Court, that the Puerto Rico statute and regulations impermissibly discriminate between different kinds of publications. [But according] to the Superi-

or Court, "[i]f the object of [an] advertisement is the tourist, it passes legal scrutiny." It is clear from the court's opinion that this basic test applies *regardless of whether the advertisement appears in a local or non-local publication.* Of course, the likelihood that a casino advertisement appearing in The New York Times will be primarily addressed to tourists, and not Puerto Rico residents, is far greater than would be the case for a similar advertisement appearing in the San Juan Star. But it is simply the demographics of the two newspapers' readerships, and not any form of "discrimination" on the part of the Puerto Rico Legislature or the Superior Court, which produces this result.

casino gambling by residents altogether. It would just as surely be a strange constitutional doctrine which would concede to the legislature the authority to totally ban a product or activity, but deny to the legislature the authority to forbid the stimulation of demand for the product or activity through advertising on behalf of those who would profit from such increased demand. Legislative regulation of products or activities deemed harmful, such as cigarettes, alcoholic beverages, and prostitution, has varied from outright prohibition on the one hand, to legalization of the product or activity with restrictions on stimulation of its demand on the other hand, see e.g., Nev.Rev.Stat. (authorizing licensing of houses of prostitution except in counties with more than 250,000 population), (prohibiting advertising of houses of prostitution '[i]n any public theater, on the public streets of any city or town, or on any public highway,' or 'in [a] place of business'). To rule out the latter, intermediate kind of response would require more than we find in the First Amendment.[11]"

BRENNAN, J., joined by Marshall and Blackmun, JJ., dissented: "[N]o differences between commercial and other kinds of speech justify protecting commercial speech less extensively where, as here, the government seeks to manipulate private behavior by depriving citizens of truthful information concerning lawful activities. [Accordingly,] where the government seeks to suppress the dissemination of nonmisleading commercial speech relating to legal activities, for fear that recipients will act on the information provided, such regulation should be subject to strict judicial scrutiny.

"The Court, rather than applying strict scrutiny, evaluates Puerto Rico's advertising ban under the relaxed standards normally used to test government regulation of commercial speech. Even under these standards, however, I do not believe that Puerto Rico constitutionally may suppress all casino advertising directed to its residents. [Neither] the statute on its face nor the legislative history indicates that the Puerto Rico Legislature thought that serious harm would result if residents were allowed to engage in casino gambling;[2] indeed, the available evidence suggests exactly the opposite. Puerto Rico has legalized gambling casinos, and permits its residents to patronize them. Thus, the Puerto Rico legislature has determined that permitting residents to engage in casino gambling will not produce the 'serious harmful effects' that have led a majority of States to ban such activity. Residents of Puerto Rico are also permitted to engage in a variety of other gambling activities [all] of which are allowed to advertise freely to residents.[3] Indeed, it is surely not far-fetched to suppose that the

11. Justice Stevens claims that the Superior Court's narrowing construction creates an impermissible "prior restraint" on protected speech, because that court required the submission of certain casino advertising to appellee for its prior approval. This argument was not raised [and] we therefore express no view on the constitutionality of the particular portion of the Superior Court's narrowing construction cited by Justice Stevens.

2. The Act's Statement of Motives says only that: "The purpose of this Act is to contribute to the development of tourism by means of the authorization of certain games of chance—[and] by the establishment of regulations for and the strict surveillance of said games by the government, in order to ensure for tourists the best possible safeguards, while at the same time opening for the Treasurer of

Puerto Rico an additional source of income." There is no suggestion that discouraging residents from patronizing gambling casinos would further Puerto Rico's interests in developing tourism, ensuring safeguards for tourists, or producing additional revenue.

3. [Appellee] has failed to show that casino gambling presents risks different from those associated with other gambling activities, such that Puerto Rico might, consistently with the First Amendment, choose to suppress only casino advertising directed to its residents. For this reason, I believe that Puerto Rico's selective advertising ban also violates appellant's rights under the Equal Protection Clause. In rejecting appellant's equal protection claim, the Court erroneously uses a "rational basis" analysis, thereby ignoring the important First Amendment interests implicated by this case.

legislature chose to restrict casino advertising not because of the 'evils' of casino gambling, but because it preferred that Puerto Ricans spend their gambling dollars on the Puerto Rico lottery. In any event, in light of the legislature's determination that serious harm will *not* result if residents are permitted and *encouraged* to gamble, I do not see how Puerto Rico's interest in discouraging its residents from engaging in casino gambling can be characterized as 'substantial,' even if the legislature had actually asserted such an interest which, of course, it has not.

"The Court nevertheless sustains Puerto Rico's advertising ban because the legislature *could* have determined that casino gambling would seriously harm the health, safety, and welfare of the Puerto Rican citizens.[4] This reasoning is contrary to this Court's long established First Amendment jurisprudence. When the government seeks to place restrictions upon commercial speech, a court may not, as the Court implies today, simply speculate about valid reasons that the government might have for enacting such restrictions.

"[E]ven assuming that an advertising ban would effectively reduce residents' patronage of gambling casinos,[5] it is not clear how it would directly [affect] local crime, prostitution, the development of corruption, or the infiltration of organized crime. Because Puerto Rico actively promotes its casinos to tourists, these problems are likely to persist whether or not residents are also encouraged to gamble. * * *

"Finally, [r]ather than suppressing constitutionally protected expression, Puerto Rico could seek directly to address the specific harms thought to be associated with casino gambling. Thus, Puerto Rico could continue carefully to monitor casino operations to guard against 'the development of corruption, and the infiltration of organized crime.' It could vigorously enforce its criminal statutes to combat 'the increase in local crime [and] the fostering of prostitution.' It could establish limits on the level of permissible betting, or promulgate additional speech designed to discourage casino gambling among residents, in order to avoid the 'disruption of moral and cultural patterns,' that might result if residents were to engage in excessive casino gambling. [I]t is incumbent upon the government to *prove* that more limited means are not sufficient to protect its interests, and for a *court* to decide whether or not the government has sustained this burden. See *Central Hudson*. In this case, nothing suggests that the Puerto Rico Legislature ever considered the efficacy of measures other than suppressing protected expression. * * * [6]"

---

4. The Court reasons that because Puerto Rico could legitimately decide to prohibit casino gambling entirely, it may also take the "less intrusive step" of legalizing casino gambling but restricting speech. [However,] having decided to legalize casino gambling, Puerto Rico's decision to ban truthful speech concerning entirely lawful activity raises serious First Amendment problems. Thus, the "constitutional doctrine" which bans Puerto Rico from banning advertisements concerning lawful casino gambling is not so strange a restraint—it is called the First Amendment.

5. Unlike the Court, I do not read the fact that appellant has chosen to litigate the case here necessarily to indicate the appellant itself believes that Puerto Rico residents would respond to casino advertising. In light of appel-

lee's arbitrary and capricious application of § 8, appellant could justifiably have believed that, notwithstanding the Superior Court's "narrowing" construction, its First Amendment rights could be safeguarded effectively only if the Act was invalidated on its face.

6. The Court seeks to buttress its holding by noting that some States have regulated other "harmful" products, such as cigarettes, alcoholic beverages, and legalized prostitution, by restricting advertising. While I believe that Puerto Rico may not prohibit all casino advertising directed to its residents, I reserve judgment as to the constitutionality of the variety of advertising restrictions adopted by other jurisdictions.

STEVENS, J., joined by Marshall and Blackmun, JJ., also dissented: "Whether a State may ban all advertising of an activity that it permits but could prohibit—such as gambling, prostitution, or the consumption of marijuana or liquor—is an elegant question of constitutional law.[2] It is not, however, appropriate to address that question in this case because Puerto Rico's rather bizarre restraints on speech are so plainly forbidden by the First Amendment. * * *

"With respect to the publisher, in stark, unabashed language, the Superior Court's construction favors certain identifiable publications and disfavors others. If the publication (or medium) is from outside Puerto Rico, it is very favored indeed. [If] the publication is native to Puerto Rico, however—the San Juan Star, for instance—it is subject to a far more rigid system of restraints and controls regarding the manner in which a certain form of speech (casino ads) may be carried in its pages. Unless the Court is prepared to uphold an Illinois regulation of speech that subjects The New York Times to one standard and The Chicago Tribune to another, I do not understand why it is willing to uphold a Puerto Rico regulation that applies one standard to The New York Times and another to the San Juan Star.

"With respect to the audience, [the] Regulations [pose] what might be viewed as a Reverse Privileges and Immunities problem: Puerto Rico's residents are singled out for disfavored treatment in comparison to all other Americans. [I] cannot imagine that this Court would uphold an Illinois regulation that forbade advertising 'addressed' to Illinois residents while allowing the same advertiser to communicate his message to visitors and commuters * * *

"With respect to the message, the regulations now take one word of the English language—'casino'—and give it a special opprobrium. Use of that suspicious six letter word is permitted only 'where the trade name of the hotel is used even though it may contain a reference to the casino.' * * * Singling out the use of a particular word for official sanctions raises grave First Amendment concerns, and Puerto Rico has utterly failed to justify the disfavor in which that particular six-letter word is held. [S]anctions for speech [should not] be as unpredictable and haphazardous as the role of dice in a casino."

Notes and Questions

1. *The greater includes the lesser.* Consider, Floyd Abrams, *Commercial Free Speech in the Marketplace of Ideas,* 41 Rutgers L.Rev. 737, 739 (1989): Rehnquist, J.'s opinion said that "because casino gambling could be banned, it therefore followed that the advertising of it could be banned. That is, simply and totally, an inversion of first amendment theory. Usually we say [that] we control speech last, not first; that we control conduct first, not last. [Usually] we say to legislatures: bite the bullet. If you really care enough, [do] something about the *thing* that you are concerned about. That thing is not speech, it is people engaging in casino gambling." Consider Ronald Rotunda, *The Constitutional Future of the Bill of Rights,* 65 N.C.L.Rev. 917 (1987): "What about [*Central Hudson*]? No one has a constitutional right to waste electricity. New York, in *Central Hudson,* could have simply banned the use of all electric hair dryers, or all energy inefficient heat pumps, or all electric toothbrushes. Yet *Central Hudson* teaches us that New York could not [prohibit] advertising that promotes the

2. Moreover, the Court has relied on an inappropriate major premise. The fact that Puerto Rico might prohibit all casino gambling does not necessarily mean that it could prohibit residents from patronizing casinos that are open to tourists. Even under the Court's reasoning, discriminatory censorship cannot be justified as a less restrictive form of economic regulation unless discriminatory regulation is itself permissible.

wasteful (but lawful) use of electricity." Is the *Posadas* dictum consistent with *Virginia Pharmacy?* [a]

2. Does *Posadas* adopt a "vice" or "morals" exception to *Central Hudson?* See Richard Epstein, *Foreword: Unconstitutional Conditions, State Power, and the Limits of Consent,* 102 Harv.L.Rev. 5, 67 (1988). But cf. Philip Kurland, *Posadas de Puerto Rico v. Tourism Company,* 1986 Sup.Ct.Rev. 1, 15: "Perhaps *Posadas* was intended to further a new moral code, which tolerates government restraint not only on speech that is conducive to illegal behavior but also on speech that may lead to immoral though legal conduct. The difficulty here is that we know or can find out, more or less, what has been made illegal. We cannot know what the courts will determine to be immoral until they tell us. Is gambling immoral? Only casino gambling? Is wine drinking immoral? When do purchases of luxuries become immoral? Doing any business with South Africa, Libya, Syria? If immorality is to be the guide to legitimating censorship, we have entered on a long and rocky road indeed."

RUBIN v. COORS BREWING CO., ___ U.S. ___, 115 S.Ct. 1585, 131 L.Ed.2d 532 (1995), per THOMAS, J., held that a federal provision prohibiting the display of alcoholic content on beer labels violated the first amendment. The Court argued among other things that the overall federal scheme was irrational in that it permitted alcoholic beverage advertising to mention alcoholic content in many circumstances and required disclosures of alcoholic content in the labelling of wines in some circumstances.

It also rejected the argument that the *Central Hudson* test was too stringent or inapplicable to the regulation of vices: [b] "*Edge Broadcasting* specifically avoided reaching the argument the Government makes here because the Court found that the regulation in question passed muster under *Central Hudson*. To be sure, *Posadas* did state that the Puerto Rican government could ban promotional advertising of casino gambling because it could have prohibited gambling altogether. But the Court reached this argument only after it already had found that the state regulation survived the *Central Hudson* test. The Court raised the Government's point in response to an alternative claim that Puerto Rico's regulation was inconsistent with *Carey v. Population Services Int'l* and *Bigelow*." [c]

a. For criticism of the "greater includes the lesser" argument, see John Garvey, *The Power and the Duties of Government,* 26 San Diego L.Rev. 209, 215–19 (1989); Seth Kreimer, *Allocational Sanctions: The Problem of Negative Rights in a Positive State,* 132 U.Pa.L.Rev. 1293, 1304–14 (1984).

b. *United States v. Edge Broadcasting Co.,* 509 U.S. 418, 113 S.Ct. 2696, 125 L.Ed.2d 345 (1993), upheld federal legislation prohibiting the broadcast of lottery advertising if the broadcaster is licensed in a state that does not permit lotteries (even in circumstances where 92% of the broadcaster's audience resided in a state that permitted lotteries).

For a sampling of views concerning a ban on tobacco advertising, see, e.g., Rebecca Arbogast, *A Proposal to Regulate the Manner of Tobacco Advertising,* 11 J.Health Pol., Pol'y & L. 393 (1986); Vincent Blasi & Henry Monaghan, *The First Amendment and Cigarette Advertising,* 256 J.A.M.A. 502 (1986); Vincent Blasi & Henry Monaghan, *Posadas and the*

Prohibition of Cigarette Advertising, 2 Tobacco Prod.Lit.Rep. 4.38 (1987); Kurland, supra; Lowenstein, supra; Jef Richards, *Clearing the Air About Cigarettes: Will Advertisers' Rights Go Up in Smoke,* 19 Pac.L.J. 1 (1987); Steven Shiffrin, *Alcohol and Cigarette Advertising: A Legal Primer,* 4 Adolescent Medicine 623 (1993); Comment, *First Amendment Values and the Constitutional Protection of Tobacco Advertising,* 82 N.W.U.L.Rev. 145 (1987). For the Canadian perspective on cigarette advertising, see *RJR–MacDonald, Inc. v. Canada,* [1995] 100 C.C.C.3d 1 (1995).

c. Stevens, J., concurred, arguing that the commercial speech doctrine is unsuited to those cases where the problems of misleading speech or incomplete information are not present. In the absence of such problems, he would give full first amendment protection rather than employing the *Central Hudson* test.

4. *Less restrictive alternatives?* *Central Hudson* insisted that the Commission "demonstrat[e] that its interest in conservation cannot be protected adequately by more limited regulation of appellant's commercial expression." Moreover, it listed a number of alternatives the Commission might consider. *Posadas* settled for the conclusion that the legislature "could" conclude as it "apparently did" that a suggested alternative would be ineffective. Should the legislature have been forced to demonstrate that the suggested alternative would be ineffective?

BOARD OF TRUSTEES v. FOX (1989), p. 732 supra, per SCALIA, J., held that the *Central Hudson* test does not require government to foreclose the possibility of all less restrictive alternatives. It is enough if the fit between means and ends is "reasonable." It need not be "perfect." Like time, place, and manner regulations, however, the relationship between means and end must be "narrowly tailored to achieve the desired objective." Under that standard, as interpreted (see p. 894 infra), government may not " 'burden substantially more speech than is necessary to further the government's legitimate interest,' "[d] but need not foreclose "all conceivable alternatives." The Court argued that to have a more demanding test in commercial speech than that used for time, place, and manner regulations would be inappropriate because time, place, and manner regulations can apply to political speech.[e]

III. PRIVATE SPEECH

Before studying *Dun & Bradstreet,* below, review *Gertz,* p. 584 supra.

Dun & Bradstreet, Inc., a credit reporting agency, falsely and negligently reported to five of its subscribers that Greenmoss Builders, Inc. had filed a petition for bankruptcy and also negligently misrepresented Greenmoss' assets and liabilities. In the ensuing defamation action, Greenmoss recovered $50,000 in compensatory damages and $300,000 in punitive damages. Dun & Bradstreet argued that, under *Gertz,* its first amendment rights had been violated because presumed and punitive damages had been imposed without instructions requiring a showing of *New York Times* malice. Greenmoss argued that the *Gertz* protections did not extend to non-media defendants and, in any event, did not extend to commercial speech. DUN & BRADSTREET, INC. v. GREENMOSS BUILDERS, INC., 472 U.S. 749, 105 S.Ct. 2939, 86 L.Ed.2d 593 (1985), rejected Dun & Bradstreet's contention, but there was no opinion of the Court. The common theme of the five Justices siding with Greenmoss was that the First Amendment places less value on "private" speech than upon "public" speech. POWELL, J. joined by Rehnquist and O'Connor, JJ., did not reach the media-non-media issue, relying instead on a public-private distinction: "We have never considered whether the *Gertz* balance obtains when the defamatory statements involve no issue of public concern. To make this determination, we must employ the approach approved in *Gertz* and balance the State's interest in compensating private individuals for injury to their reputation against the First Amendment interest in protecting this type of expression. This state interest is identical to the one weighed in *Gertz.* * * *

"The First Amendment interest, on the other hand, is less important than the one weighed in *Gertz.* We have long recognized that not all speech is of equal

---

d. Quoting *Ward v. Rock Against Racism,* p. 801 infra.

e. Blackmun, J., joined by Brennan and Marshall, JJ., dissenting, did not reach this issue.

First Amendment importance.[5] It is speech on 'matters of public concern' that is 'at the heart of the First Amendment's protection.' [In] contrast, speech on matters of purely private concern is of less First Amendment concern. As a number of state courts, including the court below, have recognized, the role of the Constitution in regulating state libel law is far more limited when the concerns that activated *New York Times* and *Gertz* are absent.[6] In such a case, '[t]here is no threat to the free and robust debate of public issues; there is no potential interference with a meaningful dialogue of ideas concerning self-government; and there is no threat of liability causing a reaction of self-censorship by the press. * * * *Harley-Davidson Motorsports, Inc. v. Markley*, 279 Or. 361, 366, 568 P.2d 1359, 1363 (1977). [In] light of the reduced constitutional value of speech involving no matters of public concern, we hold that the state interest adequately supports awards of presumed and punitive damages—even absent a showing of 'actual malice.' [7]

"[In] a related context, we have held that '[w]hether [speech] addresses a matter of public concern must be determined by [the expression's] content, form, and context [as] revealed by the whole record.' *Connick v. Myers* [p. 884 infra]. These factors indicate that petitioner's credit report concerns no public issue.[8] It was speech solely in the individual interest of the speaker and its specific business audience. Cf. *Central Hudson*. This particular interest warrants no special protection when—as in this case—the speech is wholly false and clearly damaging to the victim's business reputation. Moreover, since the credit report was made available to only five subscribers, who, under the terms of the subscription agreement, could not disseminate it further, it cannot be said that the report involves any 'strong interest in the free flow of commercial information.' *Virginia*

---

5. * * * Obscene speech and "fighting words" long have been accorded no protection. *Roth; Chaplinsky.* In the area of protected speech, the most prominent example of reduced protection for certain kinds of speech concerns commercial speech. Such speech, we have noted, occupies a "subordinate position in the scale of First Amendment values." Other areas of the law provide further examples. In *Ohralik* we noted that there are "[n]umerous examples [of] communications that are regulated without offending the First Amendment, such as the exchange of information about securities, * * * corporate proxy statements, [the] exchange of price and production information among competitors, [and] employers' threats of retaliation for the labor activities of employees." Yet similar regulation of political speech is subject to the most rigorous scrutiny. Likewise, while the power of the State to license lawyers, psychiatrists, and public school teachers—all of whom speak for a living—is unquestioned, this Court has held that a law requiring licensing of union organizers is unconstitutional under the First Amendment. *Thomas v. Collins*, [p. 759 infra].

6. As one commentator has remarked with respect to "the case of a commercial supplier of credit information that defames a person applying for credit"—the case before us today— "If the first amendment requirements outlined in *Gertz* apply, there is something clearly wrong with the first amendment or with

Gertz." Steven Shiffrin, *The First Amendment and Economic Regulation: Away From a General Theory of the First Amendment*, 78 Nw. L.Rev. 1212, 1268 (1983).

7. The dissent, purporting to apply the same balancing test that we do today, concludes that even speech on purely private matters is entitled to the protections of *Gertz*. [If] the dissent were the law, a woman of impeccable character who was branded a "whore" by a jealous neighbor would have no effective recourse unless she could prove "actual malice" by clear and convincing evidence. This is not malice in the ordinary sense, but in the more demanding sense of *New York Times*. The dissent would, in effect, constitutionalize the entire common law of libel.

8. The dissent suggests that our holding today leaves all credit reporting subject to reduced First Amendment protection. This is incorrect. The protection to be accorded a particular credit report depends on whether the report's "content, form, and context" indicate that it concerns a public matter. We also do not hold, as the dissent suggests we do, that the report is subject to reduced constitutional protection because it constitutes economic or commercial speech. We discuss such speech, along with advertising, only to show how many of the same concerns that argue in favor of reduced constitutional protection in those areas apply here as well.

Pharmacy. There is simply no credible argument that this type of credit reporting requires special protection to ensure that 'debate on public issues [will] be uninhibited, robust, and wide-open.' *New York Times*.

"In addition, the speech here, like advertising, is hardy and unlikely to be deterred by incidental state regulation. See *Virginia Pharmacy*. It is solely motivated by the desire for profit, which, we have noted, is a force less likely to be deterred than others. Arguably, the reporting here was also more objectively verifiable than speech deserving of greater protection. In any case, the market provides a powerful incentive to a credit reporting agency to be accurate, since false credit reporting is of no use to creditors. Thus, any incremental 'chilling' effect of libel suits would be of decreased significance."

Although expressing the view that *Gertz* should be overruled and that the *New York Times* malice definition should be reconsidered, BURGER, C.J., concurred: I agree that *Gertz* is limited to circumstances in which the alleged defamatory expression concerns a matter of general public importance, and that the expression in question here relates to a matter of essentially private concern."

WHITE, J., who had dissented in *Gertz,* was prepared to overrule that case or to limit it, but disagreed that the plurality's resolution of the case was faithful to *Gertz*: "I had thought that the decision in *Gertz* was intended to reach cases that involve any false statements of fact injurious to reputation, whether the statement is made privately or publicly and whether or not it implicates a matter of public importance. [Wisely,] Justice Powell does not rest his application of a different rule here on a distinction drawn between media and non-media defendants. On that issue, I agree with Justice Brennan that the First Amendment gives no more protection to the press in defamation suits than it does to others exercising their freedom of speech. None of our cases affords such a distinction; to the contrary, the Court has rejected it at every turn. It should be rejected again, particularly in this context, since it makes no sense to give the most protection to those publishers who reach the most readers and therefore pollute the channels of communication with the most misinformation and do the most damage to private reputation. [Although] Justice Powell speaks only of the inapplicability of the *Gertz* rule with respect to presumed and punitive damages, it must be that the *Gertz* requirement of some kind of fault on the part of the defendant is also inapplicable in cases such as this."

BRENNAN, J., joined by Marshall, Blackmun and Stevens, JJ., dissented: "[Respondent urged that *Gertz* be restricted] to cases in which the defendant is a 'media' entity. Such a distinction is irreconcilable with the fundamental First Amendment principle that '[t]he inherent worth [of] speech in terms of its capacity for informing the public does not depend upon the identity of its source, whether corporation, association, union, or individual.' *First National Bank v. Bellotti* [p. 930 infra]. First Amendment difficulties lurk in the definitional questions such an approach would generate. And the distinction would likely be born an anachronism.[7] Perhaps most importantly, [w]e protect the press to ensure the vitality of First Amendment guarantees. This solicitude implies no endorsement of the principle that speakers other than the press deserve lesser First Amendment protection. [Accordingly,] at least six Members of this Court (the four who join this opinion and Justice White and The Chief Justice) agree today that, in the context of defamation law, the rights of the institutional media

---

7. Owing to transformations in the technological and economic structure of the communications industry, there has been an increasing convergence of what might be labeled "media" and "nonmedia."

are no greater and no less than those enjoyed by other individuals or organizations engaged in the same activities.[10]   * * *

"The five Members of the Court voting to affirm the damage award in this case have provided almost no guidance as to what constitutes a protected 'matter of public concern.' [11] Justice White offers nothing at all, but his opinion does indicate that the distinction turns on solely the subject matter of the expression and not on the extent or conditions of dissemination of that expression. Justice Powell adumbrates a rationale that would appear to focus primarily on subject matter.[12] The opinion relies on the fact that the speech at issue was 'solely in the individual interest of the speaker and its *business* audience.' Analogizing explicitly to advertising, the opinion also states that credit reporting is 'hardy' and 'solely motivated by the desire for profit.' These two strains of analysis suggest that Justice Powell is excluding the subject matter of credit reports from 'matters of public concern' because the speech is predominantly in the realm of matters of economic concern."

Brennan, J., pointed to precedents (particularly labor cases) protecting speech on economic matters and argued that, "the breadth of this protection evinces recognition that freedom of expression is not only essential to check tyranny and foster self-government but also intrinsic to individual liberty and dignity and instrumental in society's search for truth." * * *

"The credit reporting of Dun & Bradstreet falls within any reasonable definition of 'public concern' consistent with our precedents. [W]e have made clear that speech loses none of its constitutional protection 'even though it is carried in a form that is "sold" for profit.' *Virginia Pharmacy.* More importantly, an announcement of the bankruptcy of a local company is information of potentially great concern to residents of the community where the company is [located]. And knowledge about solvency and the effect and prevalence of bankruptcy certainly would inform citizen opinions about questions of economic regulation. It is difficult to suggest that a bankruptcy is not a subject matter of public concern when federal law requires invocation of judicial mechanisms to effectuate it and makes the fact of the bankruptcy a matter of public record. * * *

"Even if the subject matter of credit reporting were properly considered—in the terms of Justice White and Justice Powell—as purely a matter of private

10. Justice Powell's opinion does not expressly reject the media/nonmedia distinction, but does expressly decline to apply that distinction to resolve this case.

11. One searches *Gertz* in vain for a single word to support the proposition that limits on presumed and punitive damages obtained only when speech involved matters of public concern. *Gertz* could not have been grounded in such a premise. Distrust of placing in the courts the power to decide what speech was of public concern was precisely the rationale *Gertz* offered for rejecting the *Rosenbloom* plurality approach. * * *

12. Justice Powell also appears to rely in part on the fact that communication was limited and confidential. Given that his analysis also relies on the subject matter of the credit report, it is difficult to decipher exactly what role the nature and extent of dissemination plays in Justice Powell's analysis. But because

the subject matter of the expression at issue is properly understood as a matter of public concern, it may well be that this element of confidentiality is crucial to the outcome as far as Justice Powell's opinion is concerned. In other words, it may be that Justice Powell thinks this particular expression could not contribute to public welfare because the public generally does not receive it. This factor does not suffice to save the analysis. See n. 18 infra.

[In fn. 18, Brennan, J., indicated that, "Dun & Bradstreet doubtless provides thousands of credit reports to thousands of subscribers who receive the information pursuant to the same strictures imposed on the recipients in this case. As a systemic matter, therefore, today's decision diminishes the free flow of information because Dun & Bradstreet will generally be made more reticent in providing information to all its subscribers."]

discourse, this speech would fall well within the range of valuable expression for which the First Amendment demands protection. Much expression that does not directly involve public issues receives significant protection. Our cases do permit some diminution in the degree of protection afforded one category of speech about economic or commercial matters. 'Commercial speech'—defined as advertisements that 'do no more than propose a commercial transaction'—may be more closely regulated than other types of speech. [Credit] reporting is not 'commercial speech' as this Court has defined the term. [W]e have been extremely chary about extending the 'commercial speech' doctrine beyond this narrowly circumscribed category of advertising because often vitally important speech will be uttered to advance economic interests and because the profit motive making such speech hardy dissipates rapidly when the speech is not advertising." [a]

Finally, Brennan, J., argued that even if credit reports were characterized as commercial speech, "unrestrained" presumed and punitive damages would violate the commercial speech requirement that "the regulatory means chosen be narrowly tailored so as to avoid any unnecessary chilling of protected expression. [Accordingly,] Greenmoss Builders should be permitted to recover for any actual damage it can show resulted from Dun & Bradstreet's negligently false credit report, but should be required to show actual malice to receive presumed or punitive damages."

Notes and Questions

1. *"Public" vs. "private" speech.* Which of the following are "private" according to the opinions of Powell, J., Burger, C.J., and White, J.? (a) a report in the Wall Street Journal that Greenmoss has gone bankrupt; (b) a confidential report by Dun & Bradstreet to a bank that a famous politician has poor credit. Would the answer be different if the subject of the report were an actor? (c) a statement in the campus newspaper, or by one student to another, that a law professor is an alcoholic. Would it make a difference if the law professor was being considered for a Supreme Court appointment?

Consider the relationship between the public/private focus of the *Greenmoss* decision and the "public controversy" aspect of the public figure definition. If the speech does not relate to a "public" controversy, can it be "public" within the terms of *Greenmoss*? See Rodney Smolla, *Law of Defamation* 3–15 (1986). Reconsider *Time, Inc. v. Firestone*, p. 592 supra.[b]

Finally, does it matter why the D & B subscribers received the information about Greenmoss? Suppose, for investment or insurance purposes, the subscrib-

---

a. Brennan, J., cited *Consolidated Edison,* which invalidated a regulation that prohibited a utility company from inserting its views on "controversial issues of public policy" into its monthly electrical bill mailings. The mailing that prompted the regulation advocated nuclear power.

b. For discussion of the different meanings of public and private speech, see Frederick Schauer, *"Private" Speech and the "Private" Forum: Givhan v. Western Line School District,* 1979 Sup.Ct.Rev. 217. Compare Michael Perry, *Freedom of Expression: An Essay on Theory and Doctrine,* 78 Nw.U.L.Rev. 1137 (1983) (denying any meaningful distinction between personal and political decisions). See generally Symposium, *The Public/Private Dis-*

tinction, 130 U.Pa.L.Rev. 1289 (1982); Robert Drechsel, *Defining "Public Concern" in Defamation Cases Since Dun & Bradstreet v. Greenmoss Builders,* 43 Fed.Com.L.J. 1 (1990); Risa Lieberwitz, *Freedom of Speech in Public Sector Employment: The Deconstitutionalization of the Public Sector Workplace,* 19 U.C.Davis L.Rev. 597 (1986); Toni Massaro, *Significant Silences: Freedom of Speech in the Public Sector Workplace,* 61 S.Cal.L.Rev. 1, 68–76 (1987). Comment, *A Conflict in the Public Interest,* 31 Santa Clara L.Rev. 997 (1991). For commentary on the question of whether Gertz should extend to non-media defendants see e.g. sources cited in note 1 after *Gertz,* p. 715 supra.

ers had asked for reports on all aspects of the construction industry in Vermont? Compare *Lowe v. SEC,* p. 770 infra.

2. *Focus of the decision.* Would an expansion of the commercial speech definition have been preferable to the promotion of ad hoc decisionmaking about the nature of "private" speech? Consider Steven Shiffrin, *The First Amendment and Economic Regulation: Away From A General Theory of the First Amendment,* 78 Nw.U.L.Rev. 1212, 1269 n. 327 (1983): "[D]rawing lines based on underlying first amendment values is a far cry from sending out the judiciary on a general ad hoc expedition to separate matters of general public interest from matters that are not. A commitment to segregate certain commercial speech from *Gertz* protection is not a commitment to general ad hoc determinations."

3. According to Powell, J., in fn. 5, are the *Ohralik* examples, i.e., exchange of information about securities, corporate proxy statements and the like, examples of protected speech subject to regulation? In what sense, are those examples of communication protected? What is the significance of Powell, J.'s suggestion that they are something other than commercial speech?[c] Where do those examples fit into Brennan, J.'s view of the first amendment? For general discussion, see Shiffrin, note 2 supra; Nicholas Wolfson, *The First Amendment and the SEC,* 20 Conn.L.Rev. 265 (1988). See also Comment, *A Political Speech Exception to the Regulation of Proxy Solicitations,* 86 Colum.L.Rev. 1453 (1986).

SECTION 4.   CONCEIVING AND RECONCEIVING THE STRUCTURE OF FIRST AMENDMENT DOCTRINE: HATE SPEECH REVISITED—AGAIN

R.A.V. v. ST. PAUL

505 U.S. 377, 112 S.Ct. 2538, 120 L.Ed.2d 305 (1992).

JUSTICE SCALIA delivered the opinion of the Court.

In the predawn hours of June 21, 1990, petitioner and several other teenagers allegedly assembled a crudely-made cross by taping together broken chair legs. They then allegedly burned the cross inside the fenced yard of a black family that lived across the street from the house where petitioner was staying. Although this conduct could have been punished under any of a number of laws, one of the two provisions under which respondent city of St. Paul chose to charge petitioner (then a juvenile) was the St. Paul Bias–Motivated Crime Ordinance, which provides: "Whoever places on public or private property a symbol, object, appellation, characterization or graffiti, including, but not limited to, a burning cross or Nazi swastika, which one knows or has reasonable grounds to know arouses anger, alarm or resentment in others on the basis of race, color, creed, religion or gender commits disorderly conduct and shall be guilty of a misdemeanor." * * *

I. [W]e accept the Minnesota Supreme Court's authoritative statement that the ordinance reaches only those expressions that constitute "fighting words" within the meaning of Chaplinsky. [W]e nonetheless conclude that the ordinance is facially unconstitutional in that it prohibits otherwise permitted speech solely on the basis of the subjects the speech addresses.

---

c. Consider *Board of Trustees v. Fox,* (dictum stating that attorneys or tutors dispensing advice for a fee do not engage in commercial speech and strongly suggesting that regulations prohibiting such speech in college dormitories may be unconstitutional).

[From] 1791 to the present, our society, like other free but civilized societies, has permitted restrictions upon the content of speech in a few limited areas, which are "of such slight social value as a step to truth that any benefit that may be derived from them is clearly outweighed by the social interest in order and morality." *Chaplinsky.* * * *

We have sometimes said that these categories of expression are "not within the area of constitutionally protected speech," *Roth; Beauharnais; Chaplinsky;* or that the "protection of the First Amendment does not extend" to them, *Bose Corp. v. Consumers Union of United States, Inc.* [p. 668 supra]; *Sable Communications of Cal., Inc. v. FCC* [p. 963 supra]. Such statements must be taken in context, however, and are no more literally true than is the occasionally repeated shorthand characterizing obscenity "as not being speech at all," Sunstein, *Pornography and the First Amendment,* 1986 Duke L.J. 589, 615, n. 146. What they mean is that these areas of speech can, consistently with the First Amendment, be regulated *because of their constitutionally proscribable content* (obscenity, defamation, etc.)—not that they are categories of speech entirely invisible to the Constitution, so that they may be made the vehicles for content discrimination unrelated to their distinctively proscribable content. Thus, the government may proscribe libel; but it may not make the further content discrimination of proscribing *only* libel critical of the government. * * *

Our cases surely do not establish the proposition that the First Amendment imposes no obstacle whatsoever to regulation of particular instances of such proscribable expression, so that the government "may regulate [them] freely," (White, J., concurring in judgment). That would mean that a city council could enact an ordinance prohibiting only those legally obscene works that contain criticism of the city government or, indeed, that do not include endorsement of the city government. Such a simplistic, all-or-nothing-at-all approach to First Amendment protection is at odds with common sense and with our jurisprudence as well.[4] It is not true that "fighting words" have at most a "de minimis" expressive content or that their content is *in all respects* "worthless and undeserving of constitutional protection"; sometimes they are quite expressive indeed. We have not said that they constitute "*no* part of the expression of ideas," but only that they constitute "no *essential* part of any exposition of ideas." *Chaplinsky.*

The proposition that a particular instance of speech can be proscribable on the basis of one feature (e.g., obscenity) but not on the basis of another (e.g., opposition to the city government) is commonplace, and has found application in many contexts. We have long held, for example, that nonverbal expressive activity can be banned because of the action it entails, but not because of the ideas it expresses—so that burning a flag in violation of an ordinance against outdoor fires could be punishable, whereas burning a flag in violation of an ordinance against dishonoring the flag is not. See *Johnson.* See also *Barnes* (Scalia, J., concurring in judgment) (Souter, J., concurring in judgment); *O'Brien.* Similarly, we have upheld reasonable "time, place, or manner" restrictions, but only if they

---

4. Justice White concedes that a city council cannot prohibit only those legally obscene works that contain criticism of the city government, but asserts that to be the consequence, not of the First Amendment, but of the Equal Protection Clause. Such content-based discrimination would not, he asserts, "be rationally related to a legitimate government interest." But of course the only *reason* that government interest is not a "legitimate" one is that it violates the First Amendment. This Court itself has occasionally fused the First Amendment into the Equal Protection Clause in this fashion, but at least with the acknowledgment (which Justice White cannot afford to make) that the First Amendment underlies its analysis. * * *

are "justified without reference to the content of the regulated speech." *Ward;* see also *Clark* (noting that the *O'Brien* test differs little from the standard applied to time, place, or manner restrictions). And just as the power to proscribe particular speech on the basis of a noncontent element (e.g., noise) does not entail the power to proscribe the same speech on the basis of a content element; so also, the power to proscribe it on the basis of *one* content element (e.g., obscenity) does not entail the power to proscribe it on the basis of *other* content elements.

In other words, the exclusion of "fighting words" from the scope of the First Amendment simply means that, for purposes of that Amendment, the unprotected features of the words are, despite their verbal character, essentially a "non-speech" element of communication. Fighting words are thus analogous to a noisy sound truck: Each [is,] a "mode of speech,"; both can be used to convey an idea; but neither has, in and of itself, a claim upon the First Amendment. As with the sound truck, however, so also with fighting words: The government may not regulate use based on hostility—or favoritism—towards the underlying message expressed.

The concurrences describe us as setting forth a new First Amendment principle that prohibition of constitutionally proscribable speech cannot be "underinclusiv[e]" (White, J., concurring in judgment)—a First Amendment "absolutism" whereby "within a particular 'proscribable' category of expression, [a] government must either proscribe *all* speech or no speech at all" (Stevens, J., concurring in judgment). That easy target is of the concurrences' own invention. In our view, the First Amendment imposes not an "underinclusiveness" limitation but a "content discrimination" limitation upon a State's prohibition of proscribable speech. There is no problem whatever, for example, with a State's prohibiting obscenity (and other forms of proscribable expression) only in certain media or markets, for although that prohibition would be "underinclusive," it would not discriminate on the basis of content. See, e.g., *Sable Communications* (upholding 47 U.S.C. § 223(b)(1) (1988), which prohibits obscene *telephone* communications).

Even the prohibition against content discrimination that we assert the First Amendment requires is not absolute. It applies differently in the context of proscribable speech than in the area of fully protected speech. The rationale of the general prohibition, after all, is that content discrimination "rais[es] the specter that the Government may effectively drive certain ideas or viewpoints from the marketplace," *Simon & Schuster,* [p. 646 infra].[a] But content discrimi-

a. Consider Steven Shiffrin, *Racist Speech, Outsider Jurisprudence, and the Meaning of America,* 80 Corn.L.Rev. 43, 59, 57 (1994): "If the argument is that a particular subject matter implicates the very risks the category was designed to cover, but in a more severe way, what difference does it make that the category of speech involved is not the most offensive *mode* of speech? The question is whether it causes the most serious form of injury. Since when is the mere possibility of idea discrimination in regulating less than fully protected speech of such enormous constitutional import? [Scalia, J.'s] description of the case law breathes new life into the expression about ostriches hiding their heads in the sand. When the government outlaws threats against the President, advertisements for casino gambling or alcoholic beverages, or the burning of draft cards, or when it engages in a campaign of zoning adult theaters out of neighborhoods, no one but a person wearing a black robe with a strong will to believe or befuddle could possibly suppose that 'there is no realistic possibility that official suppression of ideas is afoot.' Point-of-view discrimination permeates these categories. If point-of-view discrimination were as major an evil as the Court often supposes, one would think that a demanding test would have been applied in some of these cases. But many of the justices presumably share the governmental view that advertisements for casino gambling or alcoholic beverages, the burning of draft cards, and the kind of films shown in adult theaters are not worth much. They either do not look for point-of-view discrimination or devise tests that command them not to look. Perhaps they cannot see the ways in which they themselves discriminate."

nation among various instances of a class of proscribable speech often does not pose this threat.

When the basis for the content discrimination consists entirely of the very reason the entire class of speech at issue is proscribable, no significant danger of idea or viewpoint discrimination exists. Such a reason, having been adjudged neutral enough to support exclusion of the entire class of speech from First Amendment protection, is also neutral enough to form the basis of distinction within the class. To illustrate: A State might choose to prohibit only that obscenity which is the most patently offensive *in its prurience*—i.e., that which involves the most lascivious displays of sexual activity. But it may not prohibit, for example, only that obscenity which includes offensive *political* messages. And the Federal Government can criminalize only those threats of violence that are directed against the President, see 18 U.S.C. § 871—since the reasons why threats of violence are outside the First Amendment (protecting individuals from the fear of violence, from the disruption that fear engenders, and from the possibility that the threatened violence will occur) have special force when applied to the person of the President. See *Watts* [p. 659 supra] (upholding the facial validity of § 871 because of the "overwhelmin[g] interest in protecting the safety of [the] Chief Executive and in allowing him to perform his duties without interference from threats of physical violence"). But the Federal Government may not criminalize only those threats against the President that mention his policy on aid to inner cities. And to take a final example (one mentioned by Justice Stevens), a State may choose to regulate price advertising in one industry but not in others, because the risk of fraud (one of the characteristics of commercial speech that justifies depriving it of full First Amendment protection) is in its view greater there. Cf. *Morales v. Trans World Airlines, Inc.,* 504 U.S. 374, 112 S.Ct. 2031, 119 L.Ed.2d 157 (1992) (state regulation of airline advertising); *Ohralik* (state regulation of lawyer advertising). But a State may not prohibit only that commercial advertising that depicts men in a demeaning fashion.

Another valid basis for according differential treatment to even a content-defined subclass of proscribable speech is that the subclass happens to be associated with particular "secondary effects" of the speech, so that the regulation is "*justified* without reference to the content of [the] speech," *Renton*. A State could, for example, permit all obscene live performances except those involving minors. Moreover, since words can in some circumstances violate laws directed not against speech but against conduct (a law against treason, for example, is violated by telling the enemy the nation's defense secrets), a particular content-based subcategory of a proscribable class of speech can be swept up incidentally within the reach of a statute directed at conduct rather than speech. Thus, for example, sexually derogatory "fighting words," among other words, may produce a violation of Title VII's general prohibition against sexual discrimination in employment practices. Where the government does not target conduct on the basis of its expressive content, acts are not shielded from regulation merely because they express a discriminatory idea or philosophy.

These bases for distinction refute the proposition that the selectivity of the restriction is "even arguably 'conditioned upon the sovereign's agreement with what a speaker may intend to say.'" There may be other such bases as well. Indeed, to validate such selectivity (where totally proscribable speech is at issue) it may not even be necessary to identify any particular "neutral" basis, so long as the nature of the content discrimination is such that there is no realistic possibility that official suppression of ideas is afoot. (We cannot think of any First Amendment interest that would stand in the way of a State's prohibiting only those obscene motion pictures with blue-eyed actresses.)   Save for that limitation, the regulation of "fighting words," like the regulation of noisy speech, may address some offensive instances and leave other, equally offensive, instances alone.   See *Posadas*.[6]

II.   [Although] the phrase in the ordinance, "arouses anger, alarm or resentment in others," has been limited by the Minnesota Supreme Court's construction to reach only those symbols or displays that amount to "fighting words," the remaining, unmodified terms make clear that the ordinance applies only to "fighting words" that insult, or provoke violence, "on the basis of race, color, creed, religion or gender."   Displays containing abusive invective, no matter how vicious or severe, are permissible unless they are addressed to one of the specified disfavored topics.   Those who wish to use "fighting words" in connection with other ideas—to express hostility, for example, on the basis of political affiliation, union membership, or homosexuality—are not covered.   The First Amendment does not permit St. Paul to impose special prohibitions on those speakers who express views on disfavored subjects.

In its practical operation, moreover, the ordinance goes even beyond mere content discrimination, to actual viewpoint discrimination.   Displays containing some words—odious racial epithets, for example—would be prohibited to proponents of all views.   But "fighting words" that do not themselves invoke race, color, creed, religion, or gender—aspersions upon a person's mother, for example—would seemingly be usable ad libitum in the placards of those arguing *in favor* of racial, color, etc. tolerance and equality, but could not be used by that speaker's opponents.   One could hold up a sign saying, for example, that all "anti-Catholic bigots" are misbegotten; but not that all "papists" are, for that would insult and provoke violence "on the basis of religion."   St. Paul has no such authority to license one side of a debate to fight freestyle, while requiring the other to follow Marquis of Queensbury Rules.

What we have here, it must be emphasized, is not a prohibition of fighting words that are directed at certain persons or groups (which would be *facially* valid if it met the requirements of the Equal Protection Clause); but rather, a prohibition of fighting words that contain (as the Minnesota Supreme Court repeatedly emphasized) messages of "bias-motivated" hatred and in particular, as applied to this case, messages "based on virulent notions of racial supremacy." One must wholeheartedly agree with the Minnesota Supreme Court that "[i]t is the responsibility, even the obligation, of diverse communities to confront such notions in whatever form they appear," but the manner of that confrontation cannot consist of selective limitations upon speech.   St. Paul's brief asserts that a general "fighting words" law would not meet the city's needs because only a content-specific measure can communicate to minority groups that the "group hatred" aspect of such speech "is not condoned by the majority."   The point of the First Amendment is that majority preferences must be expressed in some fashion other than silencing speech on the basis of its content.   * * *

[T]he reason why fighting words are categorically excluded from the protection of the First Amendment is not that their content communicates any particular idea, but that their content embodies a particularly intolerable (and socially

---

6. Justice Stevens cites a string of opinions as supporting his assertion that "selective regulation of speech based on content" is not presumptively invalid.   [A]ll that their contents establish is what we readily concede: that presumptive invalidity does not mean invariable invalidity, leaving room for such exceptions as reasonable and viewpoint-neutral content-based discrimination in nonpublic forums, or with respect to certain speech by government employees.

unnecessary) *mode* of expressing *whatever* idea the speaker wishes to convey. St. Paul has not singled out an especially offensive mode of expression—it has not, for example, selected for prohibition only those fighting words that communicate ideas in a threatening (as opposed to a merely obnoxious) manner. Rather, it has proscribed fighting words of whatever manner that communicate messages of racial, gender, or religious intolerance. Selectivity of this sort creates the possibility that the city is seeking to handicap the expression of particular ideas.

* * * St. Paul argues that the ordinance [is] aimed only at the "secondary effects" of the speech, see *Renton*. According to St. Paul, the ordinance is intended, "not to impact on *[sic]* the right of free expression of the accused," but rather to "protect against the victimization of a person or persons who are particularly vulnerable because of their membership in a group that historically has been discriminated against." Even assuming that an ordinance that completely proscribes, rather than merely regulates, a specified category of speech can ever be considered to be directed only to the secondary effects of such speech, it is clear that the St. Paul ordinance is not directed to secondary effects within the meaning of *Renton*. As we said in *Boos* "[l]isteners' reactions to speech are not the type of 'secondary effects' we referred to in *Renton*." * * * [7]

Finally, St. Paul [asserts] that the ordinance helps to ensure the basic human rights of members of groups that have historically been subjected to discrimination, including the right of such group members to live in peace where they wish. We do not doubt that these interests are compelling, and that the ordinance can be said to promote them. But the "danger of censorship" presented by a facially content-based statute requires that that weapon be employed only where it is "*necessary* to serve the asserted [compelling] interest". The existence of adequate content-neutral alternatives thus "undercut[s] significantly" any defense of such a statute, casting considerable doubt on the government's protestations that "the asserted justification is in fact an accurate description of the purpose and effect of the law." [An] ordinance not limited to the favored topics, for example, would have precisely the same beneficial effect. In fact the only interest distinctively served by the content limitation is that of displaying the city council's special hostility towards the particular biases thus singled out. That is precisely what the First Amendment forbids. The politicians of St. Paul are entitled to express that hostility—but not through the means of imposing unique limitations upon speakers who (however benightedly) disagree. * * *

Let there be no mistake about our belief that burning a cross in someone's front yard is reprehensible. But St. Paul has sufficient means at its disposal to prevent such behavior without adding the First Amendment to the fire. * * *

JUSTICE WHITE, with whom JUSTICE BLACKMUN and JUSTICE O'CONNOR join, and with whom JUSTICE STEVENS joins except as to Part I(A), concurring in the judgment. * * *

I.A. [T]he majority holds that the First Amendment protects those narrow categories of expression long held to be undeserving of First Amendment protec-

---

7. St. Paul has not argued in this case that the ordinance merely regulates that subclass of fighting words which is most likely to provoke a violent response. But even if one assumes (as appears unlikely) that the categories selected may be so described, that would not justify selective regulation under a "secondary effects" theory. The only reason why such expressive conduct would be especially correlated with violence is that it conveys a particularly odious message; because the "chain of causation" thus *necessarily* "run[s] through the persuasive effect of the expressive component" of the conduct, it is clear that the St. Paul ordinance regulates on the basis of the "primary" effect of the speech—i.e., its persuasive (or repellent) force.

tion—at least to the extent that lawmakers may not regulate some fighting words more strictly than others because of their content. [Should] the government want to criminalize certain fighting words, the Court now requires it to criminalize all fighting words.

To borrow a phrase, "Such a simplistic, all-or-nothing-at-all approach to First Amendment protection is at odds with common sense and with our jurisprudence as well." It is inconsistent to hold that the government may proscribe an entire category of speech because the content of that speech is evil, but that the government may not treat a subset of that category differently without violating the First Amendment; the content of the subset is by definition worthless and undeserving of constitutional protection.

The majority's observation that fighting words are "quite expressive indeed," is no answer. Fighting words are not a means of exchanging views, rallying supporters, or registering a protest; they are directed against individuals to provoke violence or to inflict injury. Therefore, a ban on all fighting words or on a subset of the fighting words category would restrict only the social evil of hate speech, without creating the danger of driving viewpoints from the marketplace.

Therefore, the Court's insistence on inventing its brand of First Amendment underinclusiveness puzzles me.[3] [T]he Court's new "underbreadth" creation [invites] the continuation of expressive conduct that in this case is evil and worthless in First Amendment terms until the city of St. Paul cures the under-breadth by adding to its ordinance a catch-all phrase such as "and all other fighting words that may constitutionally be subject to this ordinance."

Any contribution of this holding to First Amendment jurisprudence is surely a negative one, since it necessarily signals that expressions of violence, such as the message of intimidation and racial hatred conveyed by burning a cross on someone's lawn, are of sufficient value to outweigh the social interest in order and morality that has traditionally placed such fighting words outside the First Amendment.[4] Indeed, by characterizing fighting words as a form of "debate" the majority legitimates hate speech as a form of public discussion. * * *

B. [Although] the First Amendment does not apply to categories of unprotected speech, such as fighting words, the Equal Protection Clause requires that the regulation of unprotected speech be rationally related to a legitimate government interest. A defamation statute that drew distinctions on the basis of political affiliation or "an ordinance prohibiting only those legally obscene works that contain criticism of the city government" would unquestionably fail rational basis review.[9]

---

3. The assortment of exceptions the Court attaches to its rule belies the majority's claim that its new theory is truly concerned with content discrimination. See Part I(C), infra (discussing the exceptions).

4. This does not suggest, of course, that cross burning is always unprotected. Burning a cross at a political rally would almost certainly be protected expression. Cf. *Brandenburg.* But in such a context, the cross burning could not be characterized as a "direct personal insult or an invitation to exchange fisticuffs," *Texas v. Johnson,* to which the fighting words doctrine, see Part II, infra, applies.

9. The majority is mistaken in stating that a ban on obscene works critical of government would fail equal protection review only because the ban would violate the First Amendment. While decisions such as *Mosley* recognize that First Amendment principles may be relevant to an equal protection claim challenging distinctions that impact on protected expression, there is no basis for linking First and Fourteenth Amendment analysis in a case involving unprotected expression. Certainly, one need not resort to First Amendment principles to conclude that the sort of improbable legislation the majority hypothesizes is based on senseless distinctions.

Turning to the St. Paul ordinance and assuming arguendo, as the majority does, that the ordinance is not constitutionally overbroad (but see Part II, infra), there is no question that it would pass equal protection review. The ordinance [reflects] the City's judgment that harms based on race, color, creed, religion, or gender are more pressing public concerns than the harms caused by other fighting words. In light of our Nation's long and painful experience with discrimination, this determination is plainly reasonable. Indeed, as the majority concedes, the interest is compelling.

C. The Court has patched up its argument with an apparently nonexhaustive list of ad hoc exceptions, in what can be viewed either as an attempt to confine the effects of its decision to the facts of this case, or as an effort to anticipate some of the questions that will arise from its radical revision of First Amendment law. * * *

To save the statute [making it illegal to threaten the life of the President], the majority has engrafted the following exception onto its newly announced First Amendment rule: Content-based distinctions may be drawn within an unprotected category of speech if the basis for the distinctions is "the very reason the entire class of speech at issue is proscribable." * * *

The exception swallows the majority's rule. Certainly, it should apply to the St. Paul ordinance, since "the reasons why [fighting words] are outside the First Amendment [have] special force when applied to [groups that have historically been subjected to discrimination]."

To avoid the result of its own analysis, the Court suggests that fighting words are simply a mode of communication, rather than a content-based category, and that the St. Paul ordinance has not singled out a particularly objectionable mode of communication. Again, the majority confuses the issue. A prohibition on fighting words is not a time, place, or manner restriction; it is a ban on a class of speech that conveys an overriding message of personal injury and imminent violence, a message that is at its ugliest when directed against groups that have long been the targets of discrimination. Accordingly, the ordinance falls within the first exception to the majority's theory.

As its second exception, the Court posits that certain content-based regulations will survive under the new regime if the regulated subclass "happens to be associated with particular 'secondary effects' of the speech" which the majority treats as encompassing instances in which "words [can] violate laws directed not against speech but against conduct."[11] Again, there is a simple explanation for the Court's eagerness to craft an exception to its new First Amendment rule: Under the general rule the Court applies in this case, Title VII hostile work environment claims would suddenly be unconstitutional.

Title VII * * * regulations covering hostile workplace claims forbid "sexual harassment," which includes "[u]nwelcome sexual advances, requests for sexual favors, and other verbal or physical conduct of a sexual nature" which creates "an intimidating, hostile, or offensive working environment." The regulation does not prohibit workplace harassment generally; it focuses on what the majority would characterize as the "disfavored topi[c]" of sexual harassment. In this way, Title VII is similar to the St. Paul ordinance that the majority condemns because

---

11. The consequences of the majority's conflation of the rarely-used secondary effects standard and the *O'Brien* test for conduct incorporating "speech" and "nonspeech" elements, see generally *O'Brien*, present another question that I fear will haunt us and the lower courts in the aftermath of the majority's opinion.

it "impose[s] special prohibitions on those speakers who express views on disfavored subjects." * * *

Hence, the majority's second exception, which the Court indicates would insulate a Title VII hostile work environment claim from an underinclusiveness challenge because "sexually derogatory 'fighting words' [may] produce a violation of Title VII's general prohibition against sexual discrimination in employment practices." But application of this exception to a hostile work environment claim does not hold up under close examination.

First, the hostile work environment regulation is not keyed to the presence or absence of an economic quid pro quo, but to the impact of the speech on the victimized worker. Consequently, the regulation would no more fall within a secondary effects exception than does the St. Paul ordinance. Second, the majority's focus on the statute's general prohibition on discrimination glosses over the language of the specific regulation governing hostile working environment, which reaches beyond any "incidental" effect on speech. If the relationship between the broader statute and specific regulation is sufficient to bring the Title VII regulation within *O'Brien*, then all St. Paul need do to bring its ordinance within this exception is to add some prefatory language concerning discrimination generally.

As the third exception to the Court's theory for deciding this case, the majority concocts a catchall exclusion to protect against unforeseen problems. [It] would apply in cases in which "there is no realistic possibility that official suppression of ideas is afoot." As I have demonstrated, this case does not concern the official suppression of ideas. The majority discards this notion out-of-hand. * * *

II. * * * I would decide the case on overbreadth grounds. * * *

In construing the St. Paul ordinance, [I understand the Minnesota Supreme Court] to have ruled that St. Paul may constitutionally prohibit expression that "by its very utterance" causes "anger, alarm or resentment."

Our fighting words cases have made clear, however, that [t]he mere fact that expressive activity causes hurt feelings, offense, or resentment does not render the expression unprotected. See *Eichman; Texas v. Johnson; Falwell.* * * * [13] The ordinance is therefore fatally overbroad and invalid on its face.

JUSTICE BLACKMUN, concurring in the judgment.

[B]y deciding that a State cannot regulate speech that causes great harm unless it also regulates speech that does not (setting law and logic on their heads), the Court seems to abandon the categorical approach, and inevitably to relax the level of scrutiny applicable to content-based laws. [The] simple reality is that the Court will never provide child pornography or cigarette advertising the level of protection customarily granted political speech. If we are forbidden from categorizing, as the Court has done here, we shall reduce protection across the board. * * *

[There] is the possibility that this case will not significantly alter First Amendment jurisprudence, but, instead, will be regarded as an aberration—a case

---

13. Although the First Amendment protects offensive speech, it does not require us to be subjected to such expression at all times, in all settings. We have held that such expression may be proscribed when it intrudes upon a "captive audience." And expression may be limited when it merges into conduct. *O'Brien.* However, because of the manner in which the Minnesota Supreme Court construed the St. Paul ordinance, those issues are not before us in this case.

where the Court manipulated doctrine to strike down an ordinance whose premise it opposed, namely, that racial threats and verbal assaults are of greater harm than other fighting words. I fear that the Court has been distracted from its proper mission by the temptation to decide the issue over "politically correct speech" and "cultural diversity," neither of which is presented here. If this is the meaning of today's opinion, it is perhaps even more regrettable.

I see no First Amendment values that are compromised by a law that prohibits hoodlums from driving minorities out of their homes by burning crosses on their lawns, but I see great harm in preventing the people of Saint Paul from specifically punishing the race-based fighting words that so prejudice their community. * * *

JUSTICE STEVENS, with whom JUSTICE WHITE and JUSTICE BLACKMUN join as to Part I, concurring in the judgment.

Conduct that creates special risks or causes special harms may be prohibited by special rules. Lighting a fire near an ammunition dump or a gasoline storage tank is especially dangerous; such behavior may be punished more severely than burning trash in a vacant lot. Threatening someone because of her race or religious beliefs may cause particularly severe trauma or touch off a riot, and threatening a high public official may cause substantial social disruption; such threats may be punished more severely than threats against someone based on, say, his support of a particular athletic team. There are legitimate, reasonable, and neutral justifications for such special rules.

This case involves the constitutionality of one such ordinance. * * *

I. [Our] First Amendment decisions have created a rough hierarchy in the constitutional protection of speech. Core political speech occupies the highest, most protected position; commercial speech and nonobscene, sexually explicit speech are regarded as a sort of second-class expression; obscenity and fighting words receive the least protection of all. Assuming that the Court is correct that this last class of speech is not wholly "unprotected," it certainly does not follow that fighting words and obscenity receive the *same* sort of protection afforded core political speech. Yet in ruling that proscribable speech cannot be regulated based on subject matter, the Court does just that. Perversely, this gives fighting words *greater* protection than is afforded commercial speech. If Congress can prohibit false advertising directed at airline passengers without also prohibiting false advertising directed at bus passengers and if a city can prohibit political advertisements in its buses while allowing other advertisements, it is ironic to hold that a city cannot regulate fighting words based on "race, color, creed, religion or gender" while leaving unregulated fighting words based on "union membership or homosexuality." * * * Perhaps because the Court recognizes these perversities, it quickly offers some ad hoc limitations on its newly extended prohibition on content-based regulations.[b]

b. In an earlier passage and footnote of his opinion, Stevens, J., argued: "[W]hile the Court rejects the 'all-or-nothing-at-all' nature of the categorical approach, it promptly embraces an absolutism of its own: within a particular 'proscribable' category of expression, the Court holds, a government must either proscribe all speech or no speech at all. The Court disputes this characterization because it has crafted two exceptions, one for 'certain media or markets' and the other for content discrimination based upon 'the very reason that the entire class of speech at issue is proscribable.' These exceptions are, at best, ill-defined. The Court does not tell us whether, with respect to the former, fighting words such as cross-burning could be proscribed only in certain neighborhoods where the threat of violence is particularly severe, or whether, with respect to the second category, fighting words that create a particular risk of harm (such as a race riot) would be proscribable. The hypothetical and illusory category of these two ex-

[T]he Court recognizes that a State may regulate advertising in one industry but not another because "the risk of fraud (one of the characteristics that justifies depriving [commercial speech] of full First Amendment protection)" in the regulated industry is "greater" than in other industries. "[O]ne of the characteristics that justifies" the constitutional status of fighting words is that such words "by their very utterance inflict injury or tend to incite an immediate breach of the peace." *Chaplinsky.* Certainly a legislature that may determine that the risk of fraud is greater in the legal trade than in the medical trade may determine that the risk of injury or breach of peace created by race-based threats is greater than that created by other threats.

Similarly, it is impossible to reconcile the Court's analysis of the St. Paul ordinance with its recognition that "a prohibition of fighting words that are directed at certain persons or groups [would] be facially valid." A selective proscription of unprotected expression designed to protect "certain persons or groups" (for example, a law proscribing threats directed at the elderly) would be constitutional if it were based on a legitimate determination that the harm created by the regulated expression differs from that created by the unregulated expression (that is, if the elderly are more severely injured by threats than are the nonelderly). Such selective protection is no different from a law prohibiting minors (and only minors) from obtaining obscene publications. St. Paul has determined—reasonably in my judgment—that fighting-word injuries "based on race, color, creed, religion or gender" are qualitatively different and more severe than fighting-word injuries based on other characteristics. Whether the selective proscription of proscribable speech is defined by the protected target ("certain persons or groups") or the basis of the harm (injuries "based on race, color, creed, religion or gender") makes no constitutional difference: what matters is whether the legislature's selection is based on a legitimate, neutral, and reasonable distinction. * * *

III. [Unlike] the Court, I do not believe that all content-based regulations are equally infirm and presumptively invalid; unlike Justice White, I do not believe that fighting words are wholly unprotected by the First Amendment. To the contrary, I believe our decisions establish a more complex and subtle analysis, one that considers the content and context of the regulated speech, and the nature and scope of the restriction on speech. * * * Whatever the allure of absolute doctrines, it is just too simple to declare expression "protected" or "unprotected" or to proclaim a regulation "content-based" or "content-neutral."

In applying this analysis to the St. Paul ordinance, I assume arguendo—as the Court does—that the ordinance regulates *only* fighting words and therefore is *not* overbroad. Looking to the content and character of the regulated activity, two things are clear. First, by hypothesis the ordinance bars only low-value speech, namely, fighting words. * * * Second, the ordinance regulates "expressive conduct [rather] than [the] written or spoken word."

Looking to the context of the regulated activity, it is again significant that the statute (by hypothesis) regulates *only* fighting words. Whether words are fighting words is determined in part by their context. Fighting words are not words that merely cause offense; fighting words must be directed at individuals so as to "by their very utterance inflict injury." By hypothesis, then, the St. Paul ordinance restricts speech in confrontational and potentially violent situations. The case at hand is illustrative. The cross-burning in this case—directed as it was to a single

ceptions persuades me that either my description of the Court's analysis is accurate or that the Court does not in fact mean much of what it says in its opinion."

African–American family trapped in their home—was nothing more than a crude form of physical intimidation. That this cross-burning sends a message of racial hostility does not automatically endow it with complete constitutional protection.

Significantly, the St. Paul ordinance regulates speech not on the basis of its subject matter or the viewpoint expressed, but rather on the basis of the *harm* the speech causes. * * * Contrary to the Court's suggestion, the ordinance regulates only a subcategory of expression that causes *injuries based on* "race, color, creed, religion or gender," not a subcategory that involves *discussions* that concern those characteristics.[9] * * *

Finally, it is noteworthy that the St. Paul ordinance is, as construed by the Court today, quite narrow. The St. Paul ordinance does not ban all "hate speech," nor does it ban, say, all cross-burnings or all swastika displays. Rather it only bans a subcategory of the already narrow category of fighting words. Such a limited ordinance leaves open and protected a vast range of expression on the subjects of racial, religious, and gender equality. As construed by the Court today, the ordinance certainly does not " 'raise the specter that the Government may effectively drive certain ideas or viewpoints from the marketplace.' " Petitioner is free to burn a cross to announce a rally or to express his views about racial supremacy, he may do so on private property or public land, at day or at night, so long as the burning is not so threatening and so directed at an individual as to "by its very [execution] inflict injury." Such a limited proscription scarcely offends the First Amendment. * * *[c]

Notes and Questions

1. At the capital sentencing phase of a murder case, the prosecution sought to introduce evidence that the defendant was a member of the Aryan Brotherhood which was stipulated to be a "white racist gang." DAWSON v. DELAWARE, 503 U.S. 159, 112 S.Ct. 1093, 117 L.Ed.2d 309 (1992), per Rehnquist, C.J., held that its admission violated the first amendment: "Even if the Delaware group to which Dawson allegedly belongs is racist, those beliefs, so far as we can determine, had no relevance to the sentencing proceeding in this case. For example, the Aryan Brotherhood evidence was not tied in any way to the murder of Dawson's [white] victim. [Moreover], we conclude that Dawson's First Amendment rights were violated by the admission of the Aryan Brotherhood evidence in this case, because

---

9. The Court contends that this distinction is "wordplay," reasoning that "[w]hat makes [the harms caused by race-based threats] distinct from [the harms] produced by other fighting words [is] the fact that, [the former are] caused by a *distinctive idea.*" In this way, the Court concludes that regulating speech based on the injury it causes is no different from regulating speech based on its subject matter. This analysis fundamentally miscomprehends the role of "race, color, creed, religion [and] gender" in contemporary American society. One need look no further than the recent social unrest in the Nation's cities to see that race-based threats may cause more harm to society and to individuals than other threats. Just as the statute prohibiting threats against the President is justifiable because of the place of the President in our social and political order, so a statute prohibiting race-based threats is justifiable because of the place of race in our social and political order. * * * [S]uch a place and is so incendiary an issue, until the Nation matures beyond that condition, laws such as St. Paul's ordinance will remain reasonable and justifiable.

c. For background on *R.A.V.*, see Edward Cleary, *Beyond the Burning Cross* (1994). For additional commentary, see Symposium, *Hate Speech After R.A.V.: More Conflict Between Free Speech and Equality,* 18 Wm. Mitchell L.Rev. 889 (1992); Akhil Amar, *The Case of the Missing Amendments,* 106 Harv.L.Rev. 124 (1992); Joshua Cohen, *Freedom of Expression,* 19 Phil.&Pub.Aff. 207 (1993); Elena Kagan, *The Changing Faces of First Amendment Neutrality,* 1992 Sup.Ct.Rev. 29; Elena Kagan, *Regulation of Hate Speech and Pornography After R.A.V.,* 60 U.Chi.L.Rev. 873 (1993); Charles Lawrence, *Crossburning and the Sound of Silence,* 37 Vill.L.Rev. 787 (1992); Shiffrin, supra.

the evidence proved nothing more than Dawson's abstract beliefs. [Delaware] might have avoided this problem if it had presented evidence showing more than mere abstract beliefs on Dawson's part, but on the present record one is left with the feeling that the Aryan Brotherhood evidence was employed simply because the jury would find these beliefs morally reprehensible."

THOMAS, J., dissented: "Dawson introduced mitigating character evidence that he had acted kindly toward his family. The stipulation tended to undercut this showing by suggesting that Dawson's kindness did not extend to members of other racial groups. Although we do not sit in judgment of the morality of particular creeds, we cannot bend traditional concepts of relevance to exempt the antisocial."

WISCONSIN v. MITCHELL, 508 U.S. 476, 113 S.Ct. 2194, 124 L.Ed.2d 436 (1993), per REHNQUIST, C.J., found no first amendment violation when Wisconsin permitted a sentence for aggravated battery to be enhanced on the ground that the white victim had been selected because of his race. The Court observed that, unlike *R.A.V.*, the Wisconsin statute was aimed at conduct, not speech, that a chilling effect on speech was unlikely, that the focus on motive was no different than that employed in anti-discrimination statutes, and that bias-inspired conduct is more likely "to provoke retaliatory crimes, inflict distinct emotional harms on their victims, and incite community unrest." Consistent with *R.A.V.?* [d]

2. Consider Shiffrin, fn. a supra, at 65: "Justice Scalia [maintains] that the rationale of the prohibition against content discrimination is the 'specter that the government may effectively drive certain ideas or viewpoints from the market-place.' That concern, however, is difficult to take seriously in the context of *R.A.V.* St. Paul prohibited only a small class of 'fighting words,' words which make a slight contribution to truth—just a particular socially unacceptable *mode* of presentation in Justice Scalia's view. It is hard to see how that raises the 'specter that the Government may effectively drive certain ideas or viewpoints from the marketplace.' Even more telling is Justice Scalia's 'content-neutral' alternative to the St. Paul ordinance: a 'pure' fighting words statute, which, he maintains, could serve the valid government interests in protecting basic human rights of members of groups historically subject to discrimination. But this content-neutral alternative would drive the very same ideas and viewpoints (along with others) from the marketplace." Is there a better rationale?

3. In distinguishing Title VII law, Scalia, J., states that if government does not target discriminatory conduct on the basis of its expressive content, government may regulate, apparently without first amendment scrutiny, even if the conduct expresses a discriminatory idea or philosophy. Is this consistent with *O'Brien*? The opinions in *Barnes* other than Scalia, J.'s? Suppose St. Paul outlawed all conduct that tended to create a racially or sexually hostile environment. Consider Richard Fallon, *Sexual Harassment, Content Neutrality, and the First Amendment Dog That Didn't Bark*, 1994 Sup.Ct.Rev. 1, 16: "A statute of this kind, which would restrict the press, political orators, and private citizens engaged in conversation in their homes, would surely offend the First Amendment. Certainly Justice Scalia [does] not believe otherwise." Could St. Paul outlaw racial harassment under Scalia, J.'s rationale and apply it to the facts of *R.A.V.* without first amendment scrutiny?

d. See Susan Gellman, *Sticks and Stones Can Put You in Jail, But Can Words Increase Your Sentence?*, 39 U.C.L.A.L.Rev. 333 (1991); Frederick Lawrence, *Resolving the Hate/Crimes Hate Speech Paradox*, 68 Notre Dame L.Rev. 673 (1993); See generally Laurence Tribe, *The Mystery of Motive, Private and Public: Some Notes Inspired by the Problems of Hate Crime and Animal Sacrifice*, 1993 Sup.Ct. Rev. 1.

Are many applications of sexual harassment law problematic under the first amendment? For a variety of views, see Kingsley Browne, *Title VII as Censorship: Hostile–Environment Harassment and the First Amendment*, 52 Ohio St.L.J. 481 (1991); Fallon, supra; Marcy Strauss, *Sexist Speech in the Workplace*, 25 Harv.C.R.–C.LL.Rev. 1 (1990); Nadine Strossen, *Regulating Workplace Sexual Harassment and Upholding the First Amendment—Avoiding a Collision*, 37 VillL.Rev. 757 (1992); Eugene Volokh, *Freedom of Speech and Workplace Harassment*, 39 U.C.L.A.L.Rev. 1791 (1992); Note, *Political Speech, Sexual Harassment, and a Captive Workforce*, 83 Calif.L.Rev. 637 (1995).

SECTION 5. PRIOR RESTRAINTS

Prior restraint is a technical term in first amendment law. A criminal statute prohibiting all advocacy of violent action would *restrain* speech and would have been enacted *prior* to any restrained communication. The statute would be overbroad, but it would not be a prior restraint. A prior restraint refers only to closely related, distinctive methods of regulating expression that are said to have in common their own peculiar set of evils and problems, in addition to those that accompany most any governmental interference with free expression. "The issue is not whether the government may impose a particular restriction of substance in an area of public expression, such as forbidding obscenity in newspapers, but whether it may do so by a particular method, such as advance screening of newspaper copy. In other words, restrictions which could be validly imposed when enforced by subsequent punishment are, nevertheless, forbidden if attempted by prior restraint." Thomas Emerson, *The Doctrine of Prior Restraint*, 20 Law and Contemp.Prob. 648 (1955).

The classic prior restraints were the English licensing laws which required a license in advance to print any material or to import or to sell any book.[a] One of the questions raised in this chapter concerns the types of government conduct beyond the classic licensing laws that should be characterized as prior restraints. Another concerns the question of when government licensing of speech, press, or assembly should be countenanced. Perhaps, most important, the Section explores the circumstances in which otherwise protected speech may be restrained on an ad hoc basis.

I. FOUNDATION CASES

A. LICENSING

LOVELL v. GRIFFIN, 303 U.S. 444, 58 S.Ct. 666, 82 L.Ed. 949 (1938), per Hughes, C.J., invalidated an ordinance prohibiting the distribution of handbooks, advertising or literature within the city of Griffin, Georgia without obtaining written permission of the City Manager: "[T]he ordinance is invalid on its face. Whatever the motive which induced its adoption, its character is such that it strikes at the very foundation of the freedom of the press by subjecting it to license and censorship. The struggle for the freedom of the press was primarily directed against the power of the licensor. It was against that power that John Milton directed his assault by his 'Appeal for the Liberty of Unlicensed Printing.' And the liberty of the press became initially a right to publish '*without* a license what formerly could be published only *with* one.' While this freedom from

---

a. For a persuasive chronicling of the abuses in a modern licensing system, see generally Lucas Powe, *American Broadcasting and the First Amendment* (1987).

previous restraint upon publication cannot be regarded as exhausting the guaranty of liberty, the prevention of that restraint was a leading purpose in the adoption of the constitutional provision. Legislation of the type of the ordinance in question would restore the system of license and censorship in its baldest form.

"The liberty of the press is not confined to newspapers and periodicals. It necessarily embraces pamphlets and leaflets. These indeed have been historic weapons in the defense of liberty, as the pamphlets of Thomas Paine and others in our own history abundantly attest. The press in its historic connotation comprehends every sort of publication which affords a vehicle of information and opinion. * * *

"The ordinance cannot be saved because it relates to distribution and not to publication. 'Liberty of circulating is as essential to that freedom as liberty of publishing; indeed, without the circulation, the publication would be of little value.' *Ex parte Jackson,* 96 U.S. (6 Otto) 727, 733, 24 L.Ed. 877 (1877).

"[As] the ordinance is void on its face, it was not necessary for appellant to seek a permit under it. She was entitled to contest its validity in answer to the charge against her." [a]

Notes and Questions

1. *First amendment procedure.* Notice that Lovell would get the benefit of the prior restraint doctrine even if the material she distributed was obscene or otherwise unprotected. In that respect, the prior restraint doctrine is similar to the doctrines of overbreadth and vagueness. For particular concerns that underlie the prior restraint doctrine, consider Thomas Emerson, *The System of Freedom of Expression* 506 (1970): "A system of prior restraint is in many ways more inhibiting than a system of subsequent punishment: It is likely to bring under government scrutiny a far wider range of expression; it shuts off communication before it takes place; suppression by a stroke of the pen is more likely to be applied than suppression through a criminal process; the procedures do not require attention to the safeguards of the criminal process; the system allows less opportunity for public appraisal and criticism; the dynamics of the system drive toward excesses, as the history of all censorship shows." [b]

2. *Scope and character of the doctrine.* What is the vice of the licensing scheme in *Lovell*? Is the concern that like vague statutes it affords undue discretion and potential for abuse? Is the real concern the uncontrolled power of the licensor to deny licenses? Suppose licenses were automatically issued to anyone who applied?

To what extent should the prior restraint doctrine apply to non-press activities? To a licensing ordinance that otherwise forbids soliciting membership in organizations that exact fees of their members? See *Staub v. Baxley,* 355 U.S. 313, 78 S.Ct. 277, 2 L.Ed.2d 302 (1958) (yes). To a licensing ordinance that otherwise prohibits attempts to secure contributions for charitable or religious causes? See *Cantwell v. Connecticut,* 310 U.S. 296, 60 S.Ct. 900, 84 L.Ed. 1213 (1940) (yes).

a. Cardozo, J., took no part.

b. But see Richard Posner, *Free Speech in an Economic Perspective,* 20 Suff.L.Rev. 1, 13 (1986): "The conventional arguments for why censorship is worse than criminal punishment are little better than plausible (though I think there is at least one good argument)" [observing that speech ordinarily does not produce sufficient damage to justify sifting through massive materials].

Should the prior restraint doctrine apply to all aspects of newspaper circulation? See *Lakewood v. Plain Dealer Publishing Co.,* 486 U.S. 750, 108 S.Ct. 2138, 100 L.Ed.2d 771 (1988) (invalidating ordinance granting Mayor power to grant or deny annual permits to place newsracks on public property).[c]

Suppose, in the above cases, that the authority of the licensor were confined by narrow, objective, and definite standards or that licenses were automatically issued to anyone who applied. *Hynes v. Mayor,* 425 U.S. 610, 96 S.Ct. 1755, 48 L.Ed.2d 243 (1976), per Burger, C.J., stated in dictum that a municipality could regulate house to house soliciting by requiring advance notice to the police department in order to protect its citizens from crime and undue annoyance: "A narrowly drawn ordinance, that does not vest in municipal officials the undefined power to determine what messages residents will hear, may serve these important interests without running afoul of the First Amendment." But cf. *Thomas v. Collins,* 323 U.S. 516, 65 S.Ct. 315, 89 L.Ed. 430 (1945) (registration requirement for paid union organizers invalid prior restraint); *Talley v. California,* 362 U.S. 60, 80 S.Ct. 536, 4 L.Ed.2d 559 (1960) (ban on anonymous handbills "void on its face," noting that the "obnoxious press licensing law of England, which was also enforced on the Colonies was due in part to the knowledge that exposure of the names of printers, writers and distributors would lessen the circulation of literature critical of the government").

B. INJUNCTIONS

NEAR v. MINNESOTA

283 U.S. 697, 51 S.Ct. 625, 75 L.Ed. 1357 (1931).

CHIEF JUSTICE HUGHES delivered the opinion of the Court.

[The *Saturday Press* published articles charging that through graft and incompetence named public officials failed to expose and punish gangsters responsible for gambling, bootlegging, and racketeering in Minneapolis. It demanded a special grand jury and special prosecutor to deal with the situation and to investigate an alleged attempt to assassinate one of its publishers. Under a statute that authorized abatement of a "malicious, scandalous and defamatory newspaper" the state secured, and its supreme court affirmed, a court order that "abated" the Press and perpetually enjoined the defendants from publishing or circulating "any publication whatsoever which is a malicious, scandalous or defamatory newspaper." The order did not restrain the defendants from operating a newspaper "in harmony with the general welfare."]

The object of the statute is not punishment, in the ordinary sense, but suppression of the offending newspaper. [In] the case of public officers, it is the reiteration of charges of official misconduct, and the fact that the newspaper [is] principally devoted to that purpose, that exposes it to suppression. [T]he operation and effect of the statute [is] that public authorities may bring the owner or publisher of a newspaper or periodical before a judge upon a charge of conducting a business of publishing scandalous and defamatory matter—in particular that the matter consists of charges against public officers of official dereliction—and, unless the owner or publisher is able and disposed to bring competent evidence to satisfy the judge that the charges are true and are published with good motives

---

c. White, J., joined by Stevens and O'Connor, JJ., dissenting, contended that *Lovell* should apply only if the newspaper had a constitutional right to place newsracks on public sidewalks. Otherwise, the newspaper should be required to show that a denial was based on improper reasons.

and for justifiable ends, his newspaper or periodical is suppressed and further publication is made punishable as a contempt. This is of the essence of censorship.

The question is whether a statute authorizing such proceedings [is] consistent with the conception of the liberty of the press as historically conceived and guaranteed. [I]t has been generally, if not universally, considered that it is the chief purpose of the guaranty to prevent previous restraints upon publication. The struggle in England, directed against the legislative power of the licenser, resulted in renunciation of the censorship of the press. The liberty deemed to be established was thus described by Blackstone: "The liberty of the press is indeed essential to the nature of a free state; but this consists in laying no *previous* restraints upon publications, and not in freedom from censure for criminal matter when published. Every freeman has an undoubted right to lay what sentiments he pleases before the public; to forbid this, is to destroy the freedom of the press; but if he publishes what is improper, mischievous or illegal, he must take the consequence of his own temerity." [The] criticism upon Blackstone's statement has not been because immunity from previous restraint upon publication has not been regarded as deserving of special emphasis, but chiefly because that immunity cannot be deemed to exhaust the conception of the liberty guaranteed by State and Federal Constitutions.

[T]he protection even as to previous restraint is not absolutely unlimited. But the limitation has been recognized only in exceptional cases. [N]o one would question but that a government might prevent actual obstruction to its recruiting service or the publication of the sailing dates of transports or the number and location of troops. On similar grounds, the primary requirements of decency may be enforced against obscene publications. The security of the community life may be protected against incitements to acts of violence and the overthrow by force of orderly [government].[a] * * *

The fact that for approximately one hundred and fifty years there has been almost an entire absence of attempts to impose previous restraints upon publications relating to the malfeasance of public officers is significant of the deep-seated conviction that such restraints would violate constitutional right. Public officers, whose character and conduct remain open to debate and free discussion in the press, find their remedies for false accusations in actions under libel laws providing for redress and punishment, and not in proceedings to restrain the publication of newspapers and periodicals. [The] fact that the liberty of the press may be abused by miscreant purveyors of scandal does not make any the less necessary the immunity of the press from previous restraint in dealing with official misconduct. Subsequent punishment for such abuses as may exist is the appropriate remedy, consistent with constitutional [privilege].

The statute in question cannot be justified by reason of the fact that the publisher is permitted to show, before injunction issues, that the matter published is true and is published with good motives and for justifiable ends. If such a statute, authorizing suppression and injunction on such a basis, is constitutionally valid, it would be equally permissible for the Legislature to provide that at any time the publisher of any newspaper could be brought before a court, or even an administrative officer (as the constitutional protection may not be regarded as resting on mere procedural details), and required to produce proof of the truth of

---

a. For critical commentary on the concessions in *Near,* see Hans Linde, *Courts and Censorship,* 66 Minn.L.Rev. 171 (1981); Jeffery Smith, *Prior Restraint: Original Intentions and Modern Interpretations,* 28 Wm. & M.Rev. 439, 462 (1987).

his publication, or of what he intended to publish and of his motives, or stand enjoined. If this can be done, the Legislature may provide machinery for determining in the complete exercise of its discretion what are justifiable ends and restrain publication accordingly. And it would be but a step to a complete system of censorship.

[For] these reasons we hold the statute, so far as it authorized the proceedings in this action, [to] be an infringement of the liberty of the press guaranteed by the Fourteenth Amendment. * * *

JUSTICE BUTLER (dissenting).

[T]he *previous restraints* referred to by [Blackstone] subjected the press to the arbitrary will of an administrative officer. [The] Minnesota statute does not operate as a *previous* restraint on publication within the proper meaning of that phrase. It does not authorize administrative control in advance such as was formerly exercised by the licensers and censors, but prescribes a remedy to be enforced by a suit in equity. In this case [t]he business and publications unquestionably constitute an abuse of the right of free press. [A]s stated by the state Supreme Court [they] threaten morals, peace, and good order. [The] restraint authorized is only in respect of continuing to do what has been duly adjudged to constitute a nuisance. [It] is fanciful to suggest similarity between the granting or enforcement of the decree authorized by this statute to prevent *further* publication of malicious, scandalous, and defamatory articles and the *previous restraint* upon the press by licensers as referred to by Blackstone and described in the history of the times to which he alludes. * * *

It is well known, as found by the state supreme court, that existing libel laws are inadequate effectively to suppress evils resulting from the kind of business and publications that are shown in this case. The doctrine [of this decision] exposes the peace and good order of every community and the business and private affairs of every individual to the constant and protracted false and malicious assaults of any insolvent publisher who may have purpose and sufficient capacity to contrive and put into effect a scheme or program for oppression, blackmail or extortion. * * *

JUSTICE VAN DEVANTER, JUSTICE McREYNOLDS, and JUSTICE SUTHERLAND concur in this opinion.[b]

Notes and Questions

1. *Near and seditious libel: a misuse of prior restraint? Near* was decided three decades before *New York Times v. Sullivan,* p. 674 supra. Should the Court have looked to the substance of the regulation rather than its form? Consider John Jeffries, *Rethinking Prior Restraint,* 92 Yale L.J. 409, 416–17 (1983): "In truth, *Near* involved nothing more or less than a repackaged version of the law of seditious libel, and this the majority rightly refused to countenance. Hence, there was pressure, so typical of this doctrine, to cram the law into the disfavored category of prior restraint, even though it in fact functioned very differently from a scheme of official licensing. Here there was no license and no censor, no ex parte determination of what was prohibited, and no suppression of publication based on speculation about what somebody might say. Here the decision to suppress was made by a judge (not a bureaucrat), after adversarial (not ex parte) proceedings, to determine the legal character of what had been (and not what

b. For background on the *Near* case, see Fred Friendly, *Minnesota Rag* (1981); Paul Murphy, *Near v. Minnesota in the Context of* *Historical Developments,* 66 Minn.L.Rev. 95, 133–60 (1981).

might be) published. The only aspect of prior restraint was the incidental fact that the defendants were commanded not to repeat that which they were proved to have done.

"[I]f *Near* reached the right result, does it really matter that it gave the wrong reason? The answer [is that] *Near* has become a prominent feature of the First Amendment landscape—a landmark, as the case is so often called, from which we chart our course to future decisions. [T]he Court has yet to explain (at least in terms that I understand) what it is about an injunction that justifies this independent rule of constitutional disfavor."

Should a court be able to enjoin the continued distribution of material it has finally adjudicated to be unprotected defamation under existing law? Suppose it enjoins the publication of any material that does not comply with the mandates of *New York Times* and *Gertz*?

2. *The collateral bar rule.* Does the collateral bar rule shed light on the relationship between prior restraints and injunctions? That rule insists "that a court order must be obeyed until it is set aside, and that persons subject to the order who disobey it may not defend against the ensuing charge of criminal contempt on the ground that the order was erroneous or even unconstitutional." Stephen Barnett, *The Puzzle of Prior Restraint,* 29 Stan.L.Rev. 539, 552 (1977). WALKER v. BIRMINGHAM, 388 U.S. 307, 87 S.Ct. 1824, 18 L.Ed.2d 1210 (1967) upheld the rule against a first amendment challenge in affirming the contempt conviction of defendants for violating an ex parte injunction issued by an Alabama court enjoining them from engaging in street parades without a municipal permit issued pursuant to the city's parade ordinance. The Court, per STEWART, J., (Warren, C.J., Brennan, Douglas, and Fortas, JJ., dissenting) held that because the petitioners neither moved to dissolve the injunction nor sought to comply with the city's parade ordinance, their claim that the injunction and ordinance were unconstitutional [c] did not need to be considered: "This Court cannot hold that the petitioners were constitutionally free to ignore all the procedures of the law and carry their battle to the streets. [R]espect for judicial process is a small price to pay for the civilizing hand of law, which alone can give abiding meaning to constitutional freedom." Although *Walker* suggested that its holding might be different if the court issuing the injunction lacked jurisdiction or if the injunction were "transparently invalid or had only a frivolous pretense to validity," it held that Alabama's invocation of the collateral bar rule was not itself unconstitutional.

Cf. *Poulos v. New Hampshire,* 345 U.S. 395, 73 S.Ct. 760, 97 L.Ed. 1105 (1953) (claim of arbitrary refusal to issue license for open air meeting need not be entertained when a licensing statute is considered to be valid on its face in circumstance where speaker fails to seek direct judicial relief and proceeds without a license).[d] Does *Poulos* pose considerable danger to first amendment interests because the low visibility of the administrative decision permits easy abridgement of free expression? See Henry Monaghan, *First Amendment "Due Process,"* 83 Harv.L.Rev. 518, 543 (1970). Do *Lovell, Walker,* and *Poulos* fit easily together? Consider Vincent Blasi, *Prior Restraints on Demonstrations,* 68 Mich. L.Rev. 1482, 1555 (1970): "A refuses to apply for a permit; he undertakes a

---

c. Indeed, the ordinance in question was declared unconstitutional two years later. *Shuttlesworth v. Birmingham,* 394 U.S. 147, 89 S.Ct. 935, 22 L.Ed.2d 162 (1969) (ordinance conferring unbridled discretion to prohibit any parade or demonstration is unconstitutional prior restraint).

d. For consideration of when licensing statutes for assemblies are valid, see *Cox v. New Hampshire,* p. 801 infra.

march that could have been prohibited in the first place; he is prosecuted for parading without a permit under a statute that is defective for overbreadth. B applies for a permit; he is rudely rebuffed by a city official in clear violation of the state permit statute (which is not invalid on its face); he marches anyway in a manner that would be protected by the first amendment, he is prosecuted for parading without a permit. C applies for a permit; he is rudely rebuffed; he notifies city officials that he will march anyway; the officials obtain an injunction against the march; the injunction is overbroad and is also based on a state statute that is overbroad; C marches in a manner ordinarily within his constitutional rights; he is prosecuted for contempt. Under the law as it now stands, A wins, but B and C lose!"

3. *Time, place, and manner regulations.* Should injunctions that impose time, place, or manner regulations in response to proven wrongdoing be subjected to more stringent examination than that ordinarily applied to general regulations imposed by legislative or executive action? See *Madsen v. Women's Health Center,* ___ U.S. ___, 114 S.Ct. 2516, 129 L.Ed.2d 593 (1994).

4. *The commentators, injunctions, and prior restraint.* Should the link between prior restraint doctrine and injunctions depend upon the collateral bar rule? Does the analogy between licensing systems and injunctions hold only in that event? See Owen Fiss, *The Civil Rights Injunction* 30, 69–74 (1978); Barnett, note 2 supra, at 553–54. Should the prior restraint doctrine be wholly inapplicable to injunctions so long as "expedited appellate review allows an immediate opportunity to test the validity of an injunction against speech and only so long as that opportunity is genuinely effective to allow timely publication should the injunction ultimately be adjudged invalid"? Jeffries, note 1 supra, at 433.[e] Indeed should the whole concept of prior restraint be abandoned? Consider id. at 433–34: "In the context of administrative preclearance, talking of prior restraint is unhelpful, though not inapt. A more informative frame of reference would be overbreadth, the doctrine that explicitly identifies why preclearance is specially objectionable. In the context of injunctions, however, the traditional doctrine of prior restraint is not merely unhelpful, but positively misleading. It focuses on a constitutionally inconsequential consideration of form and diverts attention away from the critical substantive issues of First Amendment coverage. The result is a two-pronged danger. On the one hand, vindication of First Amendment freedoms in the name of prior restraint may exaggerate the legitimate reach of official competence to suppress by subsequent punishment. On the other hand, insistence on special disfavor for prior restraints outside the realm of substantive protection under the First Amendment may deny to the government an appropriate choice of means to vindicate legitimate interests. In my view, neither risk is justified by any compelling reason to continue prior restraint as a doctrinally independent category of contemporary First Amendment analysis."[f]

For a nuanced argument that the prior restraint doctrine should apply to injunctions even in those jurisdictions that reject the applicability of the collateral

e. For the argument that regulation by injunction is generally more speech protective than regulation via subsequent punishment, see William Mayton, *Toward A Theory of First Amendment Process: Injunctions of Speech, Subsequent Punishment, and the Costs of the Prior Restraint Doctrine,* 67 Corn.L.Rev. 245 (1982). For the contention that this should count in favor of subsequent punishment in many contexts, see Martin Redish, *The Proper Role of the Prior Restraint Doctrine in First Amendment Theory,* 70 Va.L.Rev. 53, 92–93 (1984).

f. See also Marin Scordato, *Distinction Without a Difference,* 68 N.C.L.Rev. 1 (1989) (generally agreeing with Jeffries but arguing that a small part of prior restraint doctrine should be salvaged).

bar rule to first amendment arguments, see Vincent Blasi, *Toward a Theory of Prior Restraint: The Central Linkage,* 66 Minn.L.Rev. 11 (1981). Except in particular contexts, Professor Blasi does not claim that the chilling effect of injunctions on speech is more severe than those associated with criminal laws and civil liability rules. He does argue that unlike criminal laws and civil liability rules, regulation of speech by licensing and injunctions requires abstract and unduly speculative adjudication, stimulates overuse by regulatory agents, can to some extent distort the way in which audiences perceive the message at issue, and unreasonably implies that the activity of disseminating controversial communications is "a threat to, rather than an integral feature of, the social order." Id. at 85. He argues that many of these factors are aggravated if the collateral bar rule applies and that other undesirable features are added. For example, speakers are forced to reveal planned details about their communication. He concludes that the "concept of prior restraint is coherent at the core." Id. at 93.[g]

II. PRIOR RESTRAINTS, OBSCENITY, AND COMMERCIAL SPEECH

KINGSLEY BOOKS, INC. v. BROWN, 354 U.S. 436, 77 S.Ct. 1325, 1 L.Ed.2d 1469 (1957), per FRANKFURTER, J., upheld a state court decree, issued pursuant to a New York statute, enjoining the publisher from further distribution of 14 booklets the state court found obscene. On appeal to the Supreme Court the publisher challenged only the prior restraint, not the obscenity finding: "The phrase 'prior restraint' is not a self-wielding sword. Nor can it serve as a talismatic test. The duty of closer analysis and critical judgment in applying the thought behind the phrase has thus been authoritatively put by one who brings weighty learning to his support of constitutionally protected liberties: 'What is needed,' writes Professor Paul A. Freund, 'is a pragmatic assessment of its operation in the particular circumstances. The generalization that prior restraint is particularly obnoxious in civil liberties cases must yield to more particularistic analysis.' *The Supreme Court and Civil Liberties,* 4 Vand.L.Rev. 533, 539.

"Wherein does § 22–a differ in its effective operation from the type of statute upheld in *Alberts,* [p. 604 supra]. One would be bold to assert that the in terrorem effect of [criminal] statutes less restrains booksellers in the period before the law strikes than does § 22–a. Instead of requiring the bookseller to dread that the offer for sale of a book may, without prior warning, subject him to a criminal prosecution with the hazard of imprisonment, the civil procedure assures him that such consequences cannot follow unless he ignores a court order specifically directed to him for a prompt and carefully circumscribed determination of the issue of obscenity. Until then, he may keep the book for sale and sell it on his own judgment rather than steer 'nervously among the treacherous shoals.'[a]

"Criminal enforcement and the proceeding under § 22–a interfere with a book's solicitation of the public precisely at the same stage. In each situation the law moves after publication; the book need not in either case have yet passed into the hands of the public. [H]ere as a matter of fact copies of the booklets whose distribution was enjoined had been on sale for several weeks when process was

---

g. For detailed criticism of Blasi's position, all in defense of a different core, see Redish, fn. e supra, at 59–75.

a. In fact, § 22–a did not require a civil adjudication before criminal prosecution, as in-

timated by the opinion. The feasibility of such a requirement is considered in William Lockhart, *Escape from the Chill of Uncertainty,* 9 Ga.L.Rev. 533, 569–86 (1975).

served. In each case the bookseller is put on notice by the complaint that sale of the publication charged with obscenity in the period before trial may subject him to penal consequences. In the one case he may suffer fine and imprisonment for violation of the criminal statute, in the other, for disobedience of the temporary injunction. The bookseller may of course stand his ground and confidently believe that in any judicial proceeding the book could not be condemned as obscene, but both modes of procedure provide an effective deterrent against distribution prior to adjudication of the book's content—the threat of subsequent penalization.[2]"

The Court pointed out that in both criminal misdemeanor prosecutions and injunction proceedings a jury could be called as a matter of discretion, but that defendant did not request a jury trial and did not attack the statute for its failure to require a jury.

"Nor are the consequences of a judicial condemnation for obscenity under § 22–a more restrictive of freedom of expression than the result of conviction for a misdemeanor. In *Alberts,* the defendant was fined $500, sentenced to sixty days in prison, and put on probation for two years on condition that he not violate the obscenity statute. Not only was he completely separated from society for two months but he was also seriously restrained from trafficking in all obscene publications for a considerable time. Appellants, on the other hand, were enjoined from displaying for sale or distributing only the particular booklets theretofore published and adjudged to be obscene. Thus, the restraint upon appellants as merchants in obscenity was narrower than that imposed on *Alberts.*

"Section 22–a's provision for the seizure and destruction of the instruments of ascertained wrongdoing expresses resort to a legal remedy sanctioned by the long history of Anglo-American law. See Oliver Holmes, *The Common Law,* 24–26.

"[It] only remains to say that the difference between *Near* and this case is glaring in fact. The two cases are no less glaringly different when judged by the appropriate criteria of constitutional law. Minnesota empowered its courts to enjoin the dissemination of future issues of a publication because its past issues had been found offensive. In the language of Mr. Chief Justice Hughes, 'This is of the essence of censorship.' As such, it was enough to condemn the statute wholly apart from the fact that the proceeding in *Near* involved not obscenity but matters deemed to be derogatory to a public officer. Unlike *Near,* § 22–a is concerned solely with obscenity and, as authoritatively construed, it studiously withholds restraint upon matters not already published and not yet found to be offensive." [b]

TIMES FILM CORP. v. CHICAGO

365 U.S. 43, 81 S.Ct. 391, 5 L.Ed.2d 403 (1961).

JUSTICE CLARK delivered the opinion of the Court.

2. This comparison of remedies takes note of the fact that we do not have before us a case where, although the issue of obscenity is ultimately decided in favor of the bookseller, the State nevertheless attempts to punish him for disobedience of the interim injunction. For all we know, New York may impliedly condition the temporary injunction so as not to subject the bookseller to a charge of contempt if he prevails on the issue of obscenity.

b. Warren, C.J., dissented, objecting that the New York law "places the book on trial" without any consideration of its "manner of use." Black and Douglas, JJ., dissented, objecting to a state-wide decree depriving the publisher of separate trials in different communities, and to substituting "punishment by contempt for punishment by jury trial." Brennan, J., dissenting, contended that a jury trial is required to apply properly the *Roth* standard for obscenity.

Petitioner challenges on constitutional grounds the validity on its face of that portion of § 155–4 [1] of the Municipal Code of the City of Chicago which requires submission of all motion pictures for examination prior to their public exhibition. Petitioner is a New York corporation owning the exclusive right to publicly exhibit in Chicago the film known as "Don Juan." It applied for a permit, as Chicago's ordinance required, and tendered the license fee but refused to submit the film for examination. The appropriate city official refused to issue the permit and his order was made final on appeal to the Mayor. The sole ground for denial was petitioner's refusal to submit the film for examination as required. Petitioner then brought this suit seeking injunctive relief ordering the issuance of the permit without submission of the [film] * * *. Its sole ground is that the provision of the ordinance requiring submission of the film constitutes, on its face, a prior restraint [2] * * * [Admittedly,] the challenged section of the ordinance imposes a previous restraint, and the broad justiciable issue is therefore present as to whether the ambit of constitutional protection includes complete and absolute freedom to exhibit, at least once, any and every kind of motion picture. It is that question alone which we decide.

[T]here is not a word in the record as to the nature and content of "Don Juan." We are left entirely in the dark in this regard, as were the city officials and the other reviewing courts. Petitioner claims that the nature of the film is irrelevant, and that even if this film contains the basest type of pornography, or incitement to riot, or forceful overthrow of orderly government, it may nonetheless be shown without prior submission for examination. The challenge here is to the censor's basic authority; it does not go to any statutory standards employed by the censor or procedural requirements as to the submission of the film. * * *

Petitioner would have us hold that the public exhibition of motion pictures must be allowed under any circumstances. The State's sole remedy, it says, is the invocation of criminal process under the Illinois pornography statute and then only after a transgression. But this position [is] founded upon the claim of absolute privilege against prior restraint under the First Amendment—a claim without sanction in our cases. To illustrate its fallacy, we need only point to one of the "exceptional cases" which Chief Justice Hughes enumerated in *Near*, namely, "the primary requirements of decency [that] may be enforced against obscene publications." Moreover, we later held specifically "that obscenity is not within the area of constitutionally protected speech or press." *Roth*. Chicago emphasizes here its duty to protect its people against the dangers of obscenity in the public exhibition of motion pictures. To this argument petitioner's only answer is that regardless of the capacity for, or extent of, such an evil, previous restraint cannot be justified. With this we cannot agree. We recognized in [*Joseph Burstyn, Inc. v. Wilson*, 343 U.S. 495, 72 S.Ct. 777, 96 L.Ed. 1098 (1952)]

1. The portion of the section here under attack is as follows: "Such permit shall be granted only after the motion picture film for which said permit is requested has been produced at the office of the commissioner of police for examination or [censorship]."

2. That portion of § 155–4 of the Code providing standards is as follows: "If a picture or series of pictures, for the showing or exhibition of which an application for a permit is made, is immoral or obscene, or portrays, depravity, criminality, or lack of virtue of a class of citizens of any race, color, creed, or religion and exposes them to contempt, derision, or obloquy, or tends to produce a breach of the peace or riots, or purports to represent any hanging, lynching, or burning of a human being, it shall be the duty of the commissioner of police to refuse such permit; otherwise it shall be his duty to grant such permit.

"In case the commissioner of police shall refuse to grant a permit as hereinbefore provided, the applicant for the same may appeal to the mayor. Such appeal shall be presented in the same manner as the original application to the commissioner of police. The action of the mayor on any application for a permit shall be final." * * *

that "capacity for evil [may] be relevant in determining the permissible scope of community control," and that motion pictures were not "necessarily subject to the precise rules governing any other particular method of expression.   Each method," we said, "tends to present its own peculiar problems."   [It] is not for this Court to limit the State in its selection of the remedy it deems most effective to cope with such a problem, absent, of course, a showing of unreasonable strictures on individual liberty resulting from its application in particular circumstances. * * *

As to what may be decided when a concrete case involving a specific standard provided by this ordinance is presented, we intimate no opinion.   [At] this time we say no more than this—that we are dealing only with motion pictures and, even as to them, only in the context of the broadside attack presented on this record.

Affirmed.

CHIEF JUSTICE WARREN, with whom JUSTICE BLACK, JUSTICE DOUGLAS and JUSTICE BRENNAN join, dissenting.

I cannot agree either with the conclusion reached by the Court or with the reasons advanced for its support.   To me, this case clearly presents the question of our approval of unlimited censorship of motion pictures before exhibition through a system of administrative licensing.   Moreover, the decision presents a real danger of eventual censorship for every form of communication, be it newspapers, journals, books, magazines, television, radio or public speeches.   The Court purports to leave these questions for another day, but I am aware of no constitutional principle which permits us to hold that the communication of ideas through one medium may be censored while other media are immune.   Of course each medium presents its own peculiar problems, but they are not of the kind which would authorize the censorship of one form of communication and not others.   * * *

I hesitate to disagree with the Court's formulation of the issue before us, but, with all deference, I must insist that the question presented in this case is *not* whether a motion picture exhibitor has a constitutionally protected, "complete and absolute freedom to exhibit, at least once, any and every kind of motion picture."   [The] question here presented is whether the City of Chicago—or, for that matter, any city, any State or the Federal Government—may require all motion picture exhibitors to submit all films to a police chief, mayor or other administrative official, for licensing and censorship prior to public exhibition within the jurisdiction.

[In *Near*,] the Court recognized that the First Amendment's rejection of prior censorship through licensing and previous restraint is an inherent and basic principle of freedom of speech and press.   Now, the Court strays from that principle; it strikes down that tenet without requiring any demonstration that this is an "exceptional case," whatever that might be, and without any indication that Chicago has sustained the "heavy burden" which was supposed to have been placed upon it.   Clearly, this is neither an exceptional case nor has Chicago sustained *any* burden.   * * *

The booklets enjoined from distribution in *Kingsley* were concededly obscene.   There is no indication that this is true of the moving picture here.   This was treated as a particularly crucial distinction.   Thus, the Court has suggested that, in times of national emergency, the Government might impose a prior restraint upon "the publication of the sailing dates of transports or the number and location of troops." *Near.* But, surely this is not to suggest that the Government might require that all newspapers be submitted to a censor in order to assist it in preventing such information from reaching print. Yet in this case the Court gives its blessing to the censorship of all motion pictures in order to prevent the exhibition of those it feels to be constitutionally unprotected.

[E]ven if the impact of the motion picture is greater than that of some other media, that fact constitutes no basis for the argument that motion pictures should be subject to greater suppression. This is the traditional argument made in the censor's behalf; this is the argument advanced against newspapers at the time of the invention of the printing press. The argument was ultimately rejected in England, and has consistently been held to be contrary to our Constitution.[a] No compelling reason has been predicated for accepting the contention now. * * *[b]

Notes and Questions

1. Should the producers of *Bambi* be forced to submit their film to show it in a particular city? Should they be forced to pay a license fee? Suppose hundreds of cities adopted the Chicago system? If films must be submitted before exhibition, can a city constitutionally require that books be submitted before distribution? What are the "peculiar problems" associated with films?

2. *Procedural safeguards.* FREEDMAN v. MARYLAND, 380 U.S. 51, 85 S.Ct. 734, 13 L.Ed.2d 649 (1965), per Brennan, J., set out procedural safeguards designed to reduce the dangers associated with prior restraints of films. It required that the procedure must "assure a prompt final judicial decision, to minimize the deterrent effect of an interim and possibly erroneous denial of a license," that the censor must promptly institute the proceedings, that the burden of proof to show that the speech in question is unprotected must rest on the censor, and that the proceedings be adversarial. The *Freedman* standards have been applied in other contexts. *Blount v. Rizzi,* 400 U.S. 410, 91 S.Ct. 423, 27 L.Ed.2d 498 (1971) (postal stop orders of obscene materials); *United States v. Thirty-Seven Photographs,* 402 U.S. 363, 91 S.Ct. 1400, 28 L.Ed.2d 822 (1971) (customs seizure of obscene materials); *Southeastern Promotions Ltd. v. Conrad,* 420 U.S. 546, 95 S.Ct. 1239, 43 L.Ed.2d 448 (1975) (denial of permit to use municipal theater for the musical, Hair); *Carroll v. President and Commissioners,* 393 U.S. 175, 89 S.Ct. 347, 21 L.Ed.2d 325 (1968) (10 day restraining order against particular rallies or meetings invalid because *ex parte*). But cf. *FW/PBS v. Dallas,* 493 U.S. 215, 110 S.Ct. 596, 107 L.Ed.2d 603 (1990) (suggesting that partial application of *Freedman* standards (dispensing with burden of going to court and burden of proof, but retaining assurance of timely decisionmaking by licensor and prompt judicial review) to ordinance licensing sexually oriented businesses ostensibly without regard to content of films or books would be appropriate). Should the collateral bar rule apply to *Carroll* ? Do the *Freedman* standards make the *Times Film* decision palatable?[c] For thorough discussion of the procedural issues, see Henry Monaghan, *First Amendment "Due Process,"* 83 Harv.L.Rev. 518 (1970).

a. For the contention that the argument has in fact received a warm reception in the twentieth century, see Donald Lively, *Fear and the Media: A First Amendment Horror Show,* 69 Minn.L.Rev. 1071 (1985).

b. Douglas, J., joined by Warren, C.J., and Black, J., dissenting, elaborated on the evils connected with systems of censorship.

c. For the contention that *Freedman* procedures fail to address the main concern of the prior restraint doctrine, see Martin Redish, *The Proper Role of the Prior Restraint Doctrine in First Amendment Theory,* 70 Va.L.Rev. 53, 75–89 (1984).

3. *Enjoining habitual use of premises to exhibit obscene films.* Could a state authorize state courts to "abate" the "nuisance" of "habitual use [of premises for] commercial exhibition of obscene" films by enjoining future exhibition of any obscene films at the theater, once a finding of such habitual use is made, based on two or more convictions under the obscenity laws? Cf. *Vance v. Universal Amusement Co.,* 445 U.S. 308, 100 S.Ct. 1156, 63 L.Ed.2d 413 (1980).

4. *Comparing obscenity and commercial speech.* To combat deception, could commercial advertising be constitutionally subjected to a *Times Film* regime? Would such a scheme be permissible for advertising via some media, but not others? Reconsider fn. 24 in *Virginia Pharmacy,* p. 809 supra. Should the prohibition on prior restraints be inapplicable to injunctions against commercial advertising? Should *Freedman* standards be required? Should injunctions be permitted against a newspaper that carries unprotected advertising in addition to the advertiser? PITTSBURGH PRESS CO. v. PITTSBURGH COMM'N ON HUMAN RELATIONS, 413 U.S. 376, 93 S.Ct. 2553, 37 L.Ed.2d 669 (1973), per Powell, J., upheld an order forbidding Pittsburgh Press to carry sex-designated "help wanted" ads, except for exempt jobs: "As described by Blackstone, the protection against prior restraint at common law barred only a system of administrative censorship. [While] the Court boldly stepped beyond this narrow doctrine in *Near* [it] has never held that all injunctions are impermissible. See *Lorain Journal Co. v. United States,* 342 U.S. 143, 72 S.Ct. 181, 96 L.Ed. 162 (1951).[d] The special vice of a prior restraint is that communication will be suppressed, either directly or by inducing excessive caution in the speaker, before an adequate determination that it is unprotected by the First Amendment.

"The present order does not endanger arguably protected speech. Because the order is based on a continuing course of repetitive conduct, this is not a case in which the Court is asked to speculate as to the effect of publication. Moreover, the order is clear and sweeps no more broadly than necessary. And because no interim relief was granted, the order will not have gone into effect until it was finally determined that the actions of Pittsburgh Press were unprotected."

Stewart, J., joined by Douglas, J., dissented: Putting to one side "the question of governmental power to prevent publication of information that would clearly imperil the military defense of our Nation," "no government agency can tell a newspaper in advance what it can print and what it cannot." [e]

5. *Informal prior restraints.* BANTAM BOOKS, INC. v. SULLIVAN, 372 U.S. 58, 83 S.Ct. 631, 9 L.Ed.2d 584 (1963), per Brennan, J., (Harlan, J. dissenting) held unconstitutional the activities of a government commission that would identify "objectionable" books (some admittedly not obscene), notify the distributor in writing, inform the distributor of the Commission's duty to recommend obscenity prosecutions to the Attorney General and that the Commission's list of objectionable books was distributed to local police departments. The Commission thanked distributors in advance for their "cooperation," and a police officer usually visited the distributor to learn what action had been taken. In characterizing these practices as a system of prior administrative restraints, rather than mere legal advice, the Court observed that it did not mean to foreclose private consultation between law enforcement officers and distributors so long as such

---

d. *Lorain* upheld a Sherman Act injunction restraining a newspaper from seeking to monopolize commerce by refusing to carry advertising from merchants who advertised through a competing radio station.

e. Blackmun, J., dissented "for substantially the reasons stated by" Stewart, J. Burger, C.J., dissenting, argued that the majority had mischaracterized the character and interim effect of the Commission's order.

consultations were "genuinely undertaken with the purpose of aiding the distributor to comply" with the laws and avoid prosecution. What if the Commission circulated its list to distributors, police and prosecutors without mentioning prosecution? What if the prosecutor circulates a list of sixty books he or she regards as obscene and subject to prosecution?

6. *Bookstore and theater closings for obscenity violations.* An owner of more than a dozen stores and theaters was convicted of seventeen obscenity violations and three Racketeer Influenced and Corrupt Organizations Act (RICO) counts based on the obscenity convictions. In addition to a prison term and a substantial fine, the owner forfeited his rights to property he was found to have acquired through his racketeering offenses, including 10 pieces of commercial real estate, 31 businesses, and almost $9 million. The overwhelming majority of the speech materials forfeited were not obscene. Is this a prior restraint, a subsequent sanction, or both? If it is not a traditional prior restraint, should the traditional categories be expanded to include such forfeiture proceedings? Should protected free speech materials be subject to confiscation and destruction as a penalty for the distribution of unprotected materials? See *Alexander v. United States,* 509 U.S. 544, 113 S.Ct. 2766, 125 L.Ed.2d 441 (1993) (no prior restraint; no first amendment violation for confiscation and destruction of protected materials; but case remanded to determine if the forfeiture proceeding produced an excessive fine in violation of the eighth amendment).[a]

III. LICENSING "PROFESSIONALS": A DICHOTOMY BETWEEN SPEECH AND PRESS?

LOWE v. SEC, 472 U.S. 181, 105 S.Ct. 2557, 86 L.Ed.2d 130 (1985): The Investment Advisors Act of 1940 provides for injunctions and criminal penalties against anyone using the mails in conjunction with the advisory business who is not registered with the SEC or otherwise exempt from registration. The SEC sought an injunction against Lowe and his affiliated businesses primarily alleging that Lowe's registration with the SEC had been properly revoked because of various fraudulent activities,[a] and that by publishing investment newsletters, Lowe was using the mails as an investment advisor. The SEC did not claim that any information in the newsletters had been false or materially misleading or that Lowe had yet profited from the advice tendered. The SEC did contend that Lowe's prior criminal conduct showed his "total lack of fitness" to remain in an occupation with "numerous opportunities for dishonesty and self-dealing." Lowe denied that his newsletters were covered by the act and argued that, in any event, they were protected against registration and restraint under the first amendment.

The Court, per STEVENS, J., denied that Lowe's publication of financial newsletters made him an investment advisor under the act. The Court's interpretation was strongly influenced by first amendment considerations. The doctrine against prior restraints and the notion that freedom of the press includes everything from distributing leaflets to mass circulation of magazines was said to support a "broad reading" of the exclusion "that encompasses any newspaper,

a. Rehnquist, C.J., authored the majority opinion. Kennedy, J., joined by Blackmun and Stevens, JJ., dissenting, argued that prior restraint doctrine should apply in this circumstance, and that, in any event, the confiscation and destruction of magazines and videotapes not adjudicated to be obscene was an impermissible remedy. Souter, J., concurring in part and dissenting in part, accepted the latter conclusion, but not the former.

a. For example, during the period that he was giving personal investment advice, Lowe had been convicted of misappropriating funds of a client, tampering with evidence to cover up fraud of a client, and stealing from a bank.

business publication, or financial publication provided that two conditions are met. The publication must be 'bona fide,' and it must be 'of regular and general circulation.' Neither of these conditions is defined, but the two qualifications precisely differentiate 'hit and run tipsters' and 'touts' from genuine publishers. Presumably a 'bona fide' publication would be genuine in the sense that it would contain disinterested commentary and analysis as opposed to promotional material disseminated by a 'tout.' Moreover, publications with a 'general and regular' circulation would not include 'people who send out bulletins from time to time on the advisability of buying and selling stocks' or 'hit and run tipsters.' Because the content of petitioners' newsletters was completely disinterested, and because they were offered [b] to the general public on a regular schedule, they are described by the plain language of the [exclusion].

"The dangers of fraud, deception, or overreaching that motivated the enactment of the statute are present in personalized communications but are not replicated in publications that are advertised and sold in an open market.[57] To the extent that the chart service contains factual information about past transactions and market trends, and the newsletters contain commentary on general market conditions, there can be no doubt about the protected character of the communications,[58] a matter that concerned Congress when the exclusion was drafted. The content of the publications and the audience to which they are directed in this case reveal the specific limits of the exclusion. As long as the communications between petitioners and their subscribers remain entirely impersonal and do not develop into the kind of fiduciary, person-to-person relationships that were discussed at length in the legislative history of the Act and that are characteristic of investment adviser-client relationships, we believe the publications are, at least presumptively, within the exclusion." [c]

WHITE, J., joined by Burger, C.J., and Rehnquist, J., concurring, argued that the Court's statutory interpretation was "improvident" and "based on a thinly disguised conviction" that the Act was unconstitutional as applied to prohibit publication by unregistered advisors. "[While] purporting not to decide the question, the Court bases its statutory holding in large measure on the assumption that Congress already knew the answer to it when the statute was enacted. The Court thus attributes to the 76th Congress a clairvoyance the Solicitor General and the Second Circuit apparently lack—that is, the ability to predict our constitutional holdings 45 years in advance of our declining to reach them." Finding it necessary to reach the constitutional question, White, J., argued that an injunction against Lowe's publications would violate the first amendment: "The power of government to regulate the professions is not lost whenever the practice of a profession entails speech. The underlying principle was expressed by the Court in *Giboney v. Empire Storage & Ice Co.*, 336 U.S. 490, 69 S.Ct. 684, 93 L.Ed. 834 (1949): 'it has never been deemed an abridgment of freedom of speech or

---

b. Lowe's newsletters in fact did not appear according to schedule. White, J., concurring, remarked: "As is evident from the Court's conclusion that petitioner's publications meet the regularity requirement, the Court's construction of the requirement adopts the view of our major law reviews on the issue of regular publication: good intentions are enough."

57. Cf. *Ohralik.* It is significant that the Commission has not established that petitioners have had authority over the funds of subscribers; that petitioners have been delegated

decisionmaking authority to handle subscribers' portfolios or accounts; or that there have been individualized, investment-related interactions between petitioners and subscribers.

58. Moreover, because we have squarely held that the expression of opinion about a commercial product such as a loudspeaker is protected by the First Amendment, *Bose Corp.*, p. 668 supra, it is difficult to see why the expression of an opinion about a marketable security should not also be protected.

c. Powell, J., took no part.

press to make a course of conduct illegal merely because the conduct was in part initiated, evidenced, or carried out by means of language, either spoken, written, or printed.'

"Perhaps the most obvious example of a 'speaking profession' that is subject to governmental licensing is the legal profession. Although a lawyer's work is almost entirely devoted to the sort of communicative acts that, viewed in isolation, fall within the First Amendment's protection, we have never doubted that '[a] State can require high standards of qualification, such as good moral character or proficiency in its law, before it admits an applicant to the [bar].' [To] protect investors, the Government insists, it may require that investment advisers, like lawyers, evince the qualities of truth-speaking, honor, discretion, and fiduciary responsibility.

"But the principle that the government may restrict entry into professions and vocations through licensing schemes has never been extended to encompass the licensing of speech per se or of the press. At some point, a measure is no longer a regulation of a profession but a regulation of speech or of the press; beyond that point, the statute must survive the level of scrutiny demanded by the First Amendment. "[It] is for us, then, to find some principle by which to answer the question whether the Investment Advisers Act as applied to petitioner operates as a regulation of speech or of professional conduct.

"This is a problem Justice Jackson wrestled with in his concurring opinion in *Thomas v. Collins* [p. 852 supra]. His words are instructive: '[A] rough distinction always exists, I think, which is more shortly illustrated than explained. A state may forbid one without its license to practice law as a vocation, but I think it could not stop an unlicensed person from making a speech about the rights of man or the rights of labor, or any other kind of right, including recommending that his hearers organize to support his views. Likewise, the state may prohibit the pursuit of medicine as an occupation without its license, but I do not think it could make it a crime publicly or privately to speak urging persons to follow or reject any school of medical thought. So the state to an extent not necessary now to determine may regulate one who makes a business or a livelihood of soliciting funds or memberships for unions. But I do not think it can prohibit one, even if he is a salaried labor leader, from making an address to a public meeting of workmen, telling them their rights as he sees them and urging them to unite in general or to join a specific union.'

"Justice Jackson concluded that the distinguishing factor was whether the speech in any particular case was 'associat[ed] [with] some other factor which the state may regulate so as to bring the whole within its official control.' If 'in a particular case the association or characterization is a proven and valid one,' he concluded, the regulation may stand.

"These ideas help to locate the point where regulation of a profession leaves off and prohibitions on speech begin. One who takes the affairs of a client personally in hand and purports to exercise judgment on behalf of the client in the light of the client's individual needs and circumstances is properly viewed as engaging in the practice of a profession. Just as offer and acceptance are communications incidental to the regulable transaction called a contract, the professional's speech is incidental to the conduct of the profession. [Where] the personal nexus between professional and client does not exist, and a speaker does not purport to be exercising judgment on behalf of any particular individual with whose circumstances he is directly acquainted, government regulation ceases to function as legitimate regulation of professional practice with only incidental impact on speech; it becomes regulation of speaking or publishing as such, subject to the First Amendment's [command].

"[E]ven where mere 'commercial speech' is concerned, the First Amendment permits restraints on speech only when they are narrowly tailored to advance a legitimate governmental interest. The interest here is certainly legitimate: the Government wants to prevent investors from falling into the hands of scoundrels and swindlers. The means chosen, however, is extreme. [Our] commercial speech cases have consistently rejected the proposition that such drastic prohibitions on speech may be justified by a mere possibility that the prohibited speech will be fraudulent. See *Zauderer; Bates.* * * *

"I emphasize the narrowness of the constitutional basis on which I would decide this case. [I] would by no means foreclose the application of, for example, the Act's antifraud or reporting provisions to investment advisers (registered or unregistered) who offer their advice through publications. Nor do I intend to suggest that it is unconstitutional to invoke the Act's provisions for injunctive relief and criminal penalties against unregistered persons who, for compensation, offer personal investment advice to individual clients. I would hold only that the Act may not constitutionally be applied to prevent persons who are unregistered (including persons whose registration has been denied or revoked) from offering impersonal investment advice through publications such as the newsletters published by petitioner."

Notes and Questions

1. Is White, J.'s speech/profession dichotomy persuasive? Should the existence of a "profession" justify prior restraints?

2. Does White, J., suggest an element of special privilege for the press? Consider Steven Shiffrin, *The First Amendment and Economic Regulation: Away From a General Theory of the First Amendment,* 78 Nw.U.L.Rev. 1212, 1276 (1983): "The doctrine of prior restraint may have been designed to put the press on an equal footing. People could speak or write without a license and that ought not to change merely because they used a printing press. Yet we now license a good deal of speech (for example, of lawyers), and those licenses are clearly prior restraints. So we have turned the law upside down. To speak you sometimes need a license; to use the press you almost never do. A doctrine designed to create equality for the press has evolved into one that gives it a special place."

3. If lawyers, psychiatrists, and investment advisors can be licensed, what about fortune tellers? Union organizers? Journalists?

4. Does *Lowe* threaten the "foundations of SEC financial disclosure regulation [and cast] a pall on the validity of government regulation of the professions." See generally Nicholas Wolfson, *The First Amendment and the SEC,* 20 Conn. L.Rev. 265 (1988) (arguing that much securities and professional regulation violates the first amendment). See also Aleta Estreicher, *Securities Regulation and the First Amendment,* 24 Ga.L.Rev. 223 (1990) (arguing against restrictions of securities' advertising). For general commentary, see Symposium, *The First Amendment and Federal Securities Regulation,* 20 Conn.L.Rev. 261 (1988).

RILEY v. NATIONAL FEDERATION OF THE BLIND, 487 U.S. 781, 108 S.Ct. 2667, 101 L.Ed.2d 669 (1988), per BRENNAN, J., invalidated a scheme for licensing professional fundraisers who were soliciting on behalf of charitable organizations: "[North Carolina's] provision requires professional fundraisers to await a determination regarding their license application before engaging in solicitation, while volunteer fundraisers, or those employed by the charity, may solicit immediately upon submitting an application. [It] is well settled that a speaker's rights are not lost merely because compensation is received; a speaker is no less a speaker because he or she is paid to speak. [Generally,] speakers need not obtain a license to speak. However, that rule is not absolute. For example, states may impose valid time, place, or manner restrictions. North Carolina seeks to come within the exception by alleging a heightened interest in regulating those who solicit money. Even assuming that the State's interest does justify requiring fundraisers to obtain a license before soliciting, such a regulation must provide that the licensor 'will, within a specified brief period, either issue a license or go to court.' *Freedman.* [The] statute on its face does not purport to require when a determination must be made, nor is there an administrative regulation or interpretation doing so."

REHNQUIST, C.J., joined by O'Connor, J., dissented: "It simply is not true that [fundraisers] are prevented from engaging in any protected speech on their own behalf by the State's licensing requirements; the requirements only restrict their ability to engage in the profession of 'solicitation' without a license. We do not view bar admission requirements as invalid because they restrict a prospective lawyer's 'right' to be hired as an advocate by a client. So in this case we should not subject to strict scrutiny the State's attempt to license a business—professional fundraising—some of whose members might reasonably be thought to pose a risk of fraudulent activity." [a]

IV. PRIOR RESTRAINTS AND NATIONAL SECURITY

NEW YORK TIMES CO. v. UNITED STATES
[THE PENTAGON PAPERS CASE]

403 U.S. 713, 91 S.Ct. 2140, 29 L.Ed.2d 822 (1971).

PER CURIAM.

We granted certiorari in these cases in which the United States seeks to enjoin the *New York Times* and the *Washington Post* from publishing the contents of a classified study entitled "History of U.S. Decision-Making Process on Viet Nam Policy." [a]

"Any system of prior restraints of expression comes to this Court bearing a heavy presumption against its constitutional validity." *Bantam Books;* see also *Near.* The Government "thus carries a heavy burden of showing justification for the enforcement of such a restraint." [The district court in the *Times* case and both lower federal courts] in the *Post* case held that the Government had not met that burden. We agree. [T]he stays entered [by this Court five days previously] are vacated. * * *

JUSTICE BLACK, with whom JUSTICE DOUGLAS joins, concurring.

a. Stevens, J., also dissented from the Court's treatment of the licensing issue. For other aspects of the case, see p. 969 infra.

a. On June 12–14, 1971 the *New York Times* and on June 18 the *Washington Post* published portions of this "top secret" Pentagon study. Government actions seeking temporary restraining orders and injunctions progressed through two district courts and two courts of appeals between June 15–23. After a June 26 argument, ten Supreme Court opinions were issued on June 30, 1971.

I adhere to the view that the Government's case against the *Post* should have been dismissed and that the injunction against the *Times* should have been vacated without oral argument when the cases were first presented to this Court. I believe that every moment's continuance of the injunctions against these newspapers amounts to a flagrant, indefensible, and continuing violation of the First Amendment.   Furthermore, after oral arguments, I agree [with] the reasons stated by my Brothers Douglas and Brennan.   In my view it is unfortunate that some of my Brethren are apparently willing to hold that the publication of news may sometimes be enjoined.   Such a holding would make a shambles of the First Amendment.

[F]or the first time in the 182 years since the founding of the Republic, the federal courts are asked to hold that the First Amendment does not mean what it says, but rather means that the Government can halt the publication of current news of vital importance to the people of this country.   * * *

The Government does not even attempt to rely on any act of Congress. Instead it makes the bold and dangerously far-reaching contention that the courts should take it upon themselves to "make" a law abridging freedom of the press in the name of equity, presidential power and national security, even when the representatives of the people in Congress have adhered to the command of the First Amendment and refused to make such a law.   To find that the President has "inherent power" to halt the publication of news by resort to the courts would wipe out the First Amendment and destroy the fundamental liberty and security of the very people the Government hopes to make "secure."   [The] word "security" is a broad, vague generality whose contours should not be invoked to abrogate the fundamental law embodied in the First Amendment.   * * *

JUSTICE DOUGLAS, with whom JUSTICE BLACK joins, concurring.

While I join the opinion of the Court I believe it necessary to express my views more fully.

[The First Amendment leaves] no room for governmental [b] restraint on the press.   There is, moreover, no statute barring the publication by the press of the material which the *Times* and *Post* seek to use.   [These] disclosures may have a serious impact.   But that is no basis for sanctioning a previous restraint on the press * * *.

The dominant purpose of the First Amendment was to prohibit the widespread practice of governmental suppression of embarrassing information.   [A] debate of large proportions goes on in the Nation over our posture in Vietnam. That debate antedated the disclosure of the contents of the present documents. The latter are highly relevant to the debate in progress.

Secrecy in government is fundamentally anti-democratic, perpetuating bureaucratic errors.   Open debate and discussion of public issues are vital to our national health.   [The] stays in these cases that have been in effect for more than a week constitute a flouting of the principles of the First Amendment as interpreted in *Near*.

JUSTICE BRENNAN, concurring.

I write separately [to] emphasize what should be apparent: that our judgment in the present cases may not be taken to indicate the propriety, in the future, of

b.   But see Mark Denbeaux, *The First Word*   (1986).
of the First Amendment, 80 Nw.U.L.Rev. 1156

issuing temporary stays and restraining orders to block the publication of material sought to be suppressed by the Government. So far as I can determine, never before has the United States sought to enjoin a newspaper from publishing information in its possession. * * *

The entire thrust of the Government's claim throughout these cases has been that publication of the material sought to be enjoined "could," or "might," or "may" prejudice the national interest in various ways. But the First Amendment tolerates absolutely no prior judicial restraints of the press predicated upon surmise or conjecture that untoward consequences may result.* Our cases, it is true, have indicated that there is a single, extremely narrow class of cases in which the First Amendment's ban on prior judicial restraint may be overridden. Our cases have thus far indicated that such cases may arise only when the Nation "is at war," [*Schenck*]. Even if the present world situation were assumed to be tantamount to a time of war, or if the power of presently available armaments would justify even in peacetime the suppression of information that would set in motion a nuclear holocaust, in neither of these actions has the Government presented or even alleged that publication of items from or based upon the material at issue would cause the happening of an event of that nature. [Thus,] only governmental allegation and proof that publication must inevitably, directly and immediately cause the occurrence of an event kindred to imperiling the safety of a transport already at sea can support even the issuance of an interim restraining order. In no event may mere conclusions be sufficient: for if the Executive Branch seeks judicial aid in preventing publication, it must inevitably submit the basis upon which that aid is sought to scrutiny by the judiciary. And therefore, every restraint issued in this case, whatever its form, has violated the First Amendment—and not less so because that restraint was justified as necessary to afford the courts an opportunity to examine the claim more thoroughly. Unless and until the Government has clearly made out its case, the First Amendment commands that no injunction may issue.

JUSTICE STEWART, with whom JUSTICE WHITE joins, concurring.

[I]n the cases before us we are asked neither to construe specific regulations nor to apply specific laws. [We] are asked, quite simply, to prevent the publication by two newspapers of material that the Executive Branch insists should not, in the national interest, be published. I am convinced that the Executive is correct with respect to some of the documents involved. But I cannot say that disclosure of any of them will surely result in direct, immediate, and irreparable damage to our Nation or its people. That being so, there can under the First Amendment be but one judicial resolution of the issues before us. I join the judgments of the Court.

JUSTICE WHITE, with whom JUSTICE STEWART joins, concurring.

I concur in today's judgments, but only because of the concededly extraordinary protection against prior restraints enjoyed by the press under our constitutional system. I do not say that in no circumstances would the First Amendment permit an injunction against publishing information about government plans or operations. Nor, after examining the materials the Government characterizes as the most sensitive and destructive, can I deny that revelation of these documents

---

* *Freedman* and similar cases regarding temporary restraints of allegedly obscene materials are not in point. For those cases rest upon the proposition that "obscenity is not protected by the freedoms of speech and press." *Roth.* Here there is no question but that the material sought to be suppressed is within the protection of the First Amendment; the only question is whether, notwithstanding that fact, its publication may be enjoined for a time because of the presence of an overwhelming national interest. * * *

will do substantial damage to public interests. Indeed, I am confident that their disclosure will have that result. But I nevertheless agree that the United States has not satisfied the very heavy burden which it must meet to warrant an injunction against publication in these cases, at least in the absence of express and appropriately limited congressional authorization for prior restraints in circumstances such as these.

The Government's position is simply stated: The responsibility of the Executive for the conduct of the foreign affairs and for the security of the Nation is so basic that the President is entitled to an injunction against publication of a newspaper story whenever he can convince a court that the information to be revealed threatens "grave and irreparable" injury to the public interest; and the injunction should issue whether or not the material to be published is classified, whether or not publication would be lawful under relevant criminal statutes enacted by Congress and regardless of the circumstances by which the newspaper came into possession of the information.

At least in the absence of legislation by Congress, based on its own investigations and findings, I am quite unable to agree that the inherent powers of the Executive and the courts reach so far as to authorize remedies having such sweeping potential for inhibiting publications by the press. [To] sustain the Government in these cases would start the courts down a long and hazardous road that I am not willing to travel at least without congressional guidance and direction.

* * * Prior restraints require an unusually heavy justification under the First Amendment; but failure by the Government to justify prior restraints does not measure its constitutional entitlement to a conviction for criminal publication. That the Government mistakenly chose to proceed by injunction does not mean that it could not successfully proceed in another way.

* * * Congress has addressed itself to the problems of protecting the security of the country and the national defense from unauthorized disclosure of potentially damaging information. It has not, however, authorized the injunctive remedy against threatened publication. It has apparently been satisfied to rely on criminal sanctions and their deterrent effect on the responsible as well as the irresponsible press. * * *

JUSTICE HARLAN, with whom THE CHIEF JUSTICE and JUSTICE BLACKMUN join, dissenting. * * *

With all respect, I consider that the Court has been almost irresponsibly feverish in dealing with these cases. Both [the] Second Circuit and [the] District of Columbia Circuit rendered judgment on June 23. [This] Court's order setting a hearing before us on June 26 at 11 a.m., a course which I joined only to avoid the possibility of even more peremptory action by the Court, was issued less than 24 hours before. The record in the *Post* case was filed with the Clerk shortly before 1 p.m. on June 25; the record in the *Times* case did not arrive until 7 or 8 o'clock that same night. The briefs of the parties were received less than two hours before argument on June 26.

This frenzied train of events took place in the name of the presumption against prior restraints created by the First Amendment. Due regard for the extraordinarily important and difficult questions involved in these litigations should have led the Court to shun such a precipitate timetable. In order to decide the merits of these cases properly, some or all of the following questions should have been faced: * * *

2. Whether the First Amendment permits the federal courts to enjoin publication of stories which would present a serious threat to national security. See *Near* (dictum). * * *

4. Whether the unauthorized disclosure of any of these particular documents would seriously impair the national security.

5. What weight should be given to the opinion of high officers in the Executive Branch of the Government with respect to [question 4]. * * *

7. Whether the threatened harm to the national security or the Government's possessory interest in the documents justifies the issuance of an injunction against publication in light of—

a. The strong First Amendment policy against prior restraints on publication; b. The doctrine against enjoining conduct in violation of criminal statutes; and c. The extent to which the materials at issue have apparently already been otherwise disseminated.

These are difficult questions of fact, of law, and of judgment; the potential consequences of erroneous decision are enormous. The time which has been available to us, to the lower courts, and to the parties has been wholly inadequate for giving these cases the kind of consideration they deserve. It is a reflection on the stability of the judicial process that these great issues—as important as any that have arisen during my time on the Court—should have been decided under the pressures engendered by the torrent of publicity that has attended these litigations from their inception.

Forced as I am to reach the merits of these cases, I dissent from the opinion and judgments of the Court. Within the severe limitations imposed by the time constraints under which I have been required to operate, I can only state my reasons in telescoped form, even though in different circumstances I would have felt constrained to deal with the cases in the fuller sweep indicated above.

[It] is plain to me that the scope of the judicial function in passing upon the activities of the Executive Branch of the Government in the field of foreign affairs is very narrowly restricted. This view is, I think, dictated by the concept of separation of powers upon which our constitutional system [rests.] I agree that, in performance of its duty to protect the values of the First Amendment against political pressures, the judiciary must review the initial Executive determination to the point of satisfying itself that the subject matter of the dispute does lie within the proper compass of the President's foreign relations power. Constitutional considerations forbid "a complete abandonment of judicial control." Moreover, the judiciary may properly insist that the determination that disclosure of the subject matter would irreparably impair the national security be made by the head of the Executive Department concerned—here the Secretary of State or the Secretary of Defense—after actual personal consideration by that officer.[c] This safeguard is required in the analogous area of executive claims of privilege for secrets of state.

c. Consider Stanley Godofsky & Howard Rogatnick, *Prior Restraints: The Pentagon Papers Case Revisited,* 18 Cum.L.Rev. 527, 536–37 (1988): "Ironically, Justice Harlan's view of the Constitution might, ultimately, have presented more problems for the Government than those of most of the other Justices. Realistically, how often can the Secretary of State or Secretary of Defense devote 'actual personal consideration' to the question of whether material about to be published should be suppressed? And of what does 'actual personal consideration' consist? Must the Secretary himself read the documents? Is it sufficient 'consideration' by a Cabinet officer to act on the advice of his subordinates? If so, is not the 'actual personal consideration' test substantially meaningless? Could a Cabinet officer be required to testify as to the basis for his decision in order to test his 'bona fides'?"

But in my judgment the judiciary may not properly go beyond these two inquiries and redetermine for itself the probable impact of disclosure on the national security. "[T]he very nature of executive decisions as to foreign policy is political, not judicial. Such decisions are wholly confided by our Constitution to the political departments of the government, Executive and Legislative. They are delicate, complex, and involve large elements of prophecy. They are and should be undertaken only by those directly responsible to the people whose welfare they advance or imperil. They are decisions of a kind for which the judiciary has neither aptitude, facilities nor responsibility and which has long been held to belong in the domain of political power not subject to judicial intrusion or inquiry." *Chicago & S. Air Lines v. Waterman S.S. Corp.* (Jackson, J.), 333 U.S. 103, 68 S.Ct. 431, 92 L.Ed. 568 (1948).

Even if there is some room for the judiciary to override the executive determination, it is plain that the scope of review must be exceedingly narrow. I can see no indication in the opinions of either the District Court or the Court of Appeals in the *Post* litigation that the conclusions of the Executive were given even the deference owing to an administrative agency, much less that owing to a co-equal branch of the Government operating within the field of its constitutional prerogative. * * *

Pending further hearings in each case conducted under the appropriate ground rules, I would continue the restraints on publication. I cannot believe that the doctrine prohibiting prior restraints reaches to the point of preventing courts from maintaining the status quo long enough to act responsibly in matters of such national importance as those involved here.

JUSTICE BLACKMUN, dissenting.

[The First Amendment] is only one part of an entire Constitution. Article II of the great document vests in the Executive Branch primary power over the conduct of foreign affairs and places in that branch the responsibility for the Nation's safety. Each provision of the Constitution is important, and I cannot subscribe to a doctrine of unlimited absolutism for the First Amendment at the cost of downgrading other provisions. First Amendment absolutism has never commanded a majority of this Court. What is needed here is a weighing, upon properly developed standards, of the broad right of the press to print and of the very narrow right of the Government to prevent. Such standards are not yet developed. The parties here are in disagreement as to what those standards should be. But even the newspapers concede that there are situations where restraint is in order and is constitutional. Mr. Justice Holmes gave us a suggestion when he said in *Schenck*, "It is a question of proximity and degree. When a nation is at war many things that might be said in time of peace are such a hindrance to its effort that their utterance will not be endured so long as men fight and that no Court could regard them as protected by any constitutional right."

I therefore would remand these cases to be developed expeditiously, of course, but on a schedule permitting the orderly presentation of evidence from both sides [and] with the preparation of briefs, oral argument and court opinions of a quality better than has been seen to this point. [T]hese cases and the issues involved and the courts, including this one, deserve better than has been produced thus far. * * * d

---

d. Marshall, J., concurring, did not deal with first amendment issues but only with separation of powers—the government's at-

Notes and Questions

1. *What did the case decide?* Do you agree that "the case [did] not make any law at all, good or bad"? That on the question "whether injunctions against the press are permissible, it is clear that [the case] can supply no precedent?" See Peter Junger, *Down Memory Lane: The Case of the Pentagon Papers,* 23 Case W.Res.L.Rev. 3, 4–5 (1971). Or do you find in several concurring opinions a discernible standard that must be satisfied before a majority of the Court would permit an injunction against the press on national security grounds? Cf. 85 Harv.L.Rev. 199, 205–06 (1971). Do you find guidance as to the outcome if Congress were to authorize an injunction in narrow terms to protect national security? Cf. id. at 204–05. Might it fairly be said that this is a separation of powers decision, like the *Steel Seizure* case, as well as a first amendment decision? See Junger, supra, at 19.

2. *"De facto" prior restraint.* One difficulty with viewing the prior restraint doctrine as "simply creat[ing] a 'presumption' against the validity of the restraint" (Emerson's characterization of the current approach) rather than as "a prohibition on all restraints subject to certain categorical exceptions," observes Thomas Emerson, *First Amendment Doctrine and the Burger Court,* 68 Calif.L.Rev. 422, 457–58 (1980), is that "the requirement of ad hoc scrutiny of prior restraints is itself likely to result in a 'de facto' prior restraint." Pointing to Brennan, J.'s comment in *Pentagon Papers* that "every restraint issued in this case [has] violated the First Amendment—and not less so because that restraint was justified as necessary to afford the courts an opportunity to examine the claim more thoroughly," Emerson notes that "[t]his is exactly what happened when the government sought to enjoin *The Progressive* magazine from publishing an article on the manufacture of the hydrogen bomb. The Supreme Court refused to order an expedited appeal from the [federal district court] injunction against publication [and, although the case was ultimately dismissed by the Seventh Circuit,] *The Progressive* remained under effective prior restraint for nearly seven months."

Compare *Near* and *Pentagon Papers* with UNITED STATES v. PROGRESSIVE, INC., 467 F.Supp. 990 (W.D.Wis.1979) (preliminary injunction issued Mar. 28, 1979), request for writ of mandamus den. sub nom. *Morland v. Sprecher,* 443 U.S. 709, 99 S.Ct. 3086, 61 L.Ed.2d 860 (1979), case dismissed, 610 F.2d 819 (7th Cir.1979).[e] *The Progressive* planned to publish an article entitled, "The H-Bomb Secret—How We Got It, Why We're Telling It," maintaining that the article would contribute to informed opinion about nuclear weapons and demonstrate the inadequacies of a system of secrecy and classification. Although the government conceded that at least some of the information contained in the article was "in the public domain" or had been "declassified," it argued that "national security" permitted it to censor information originating in the public domain "if when drawn together, synthesized and collated, such information acquires the character of presenting immediate, direct and irreparable harm to the interests of the United States." The Secretary of State stated that publication would increase thermonuclear proliferation and that this would "irreparably impair the national

---

tempt to secure through the Court injunctive relief that Congress had refused to authorize.

Burger, C.J., dissenting, complained that because of "unseemly haste," "we do not know the facts of this case. [W]e literally do not know what we are acting on." He expressed no views on the merits, apart from his joinder in Harlan, J.'s opinion, and a statement that

he would have continued the temporary restraints in effect while returning the cases to the lower courts for more thorough exploration of the facts and issues.

e. The government's action against *The Progressive* was abandoned after information similar to that it sought to enjoin was published elsewhere.

security of the United States." The Secretary of Defense maintained that dissemination of the Morland article would lead to a substantial increase in the risk of thermonuclear proliferation and to use or threats that would "adversely affect the national security of the United States."

Although recognizing that this constituted "the first instance of prior restraint against a publication in this fashion in the [nation's history]," the district court enjoined defendants, pending final resolution of the litigation, from publishing or otherwise disclosing any information designated by the government as "restricted data" within the meaning of The Atomic Energy Act of 1954: "What is involved here is information dealing with the most destructive weapon in the history of mankind, information of sufficient destructive potential to nullify the right to free speech and to endanger the right to life itself. [Faced] with a stark choice between upholding the right to continued life and the right to freedom of the press, most jurists would have no difficulty in opting for the chance to continue to breathe and function as they work to achieve perfect freedom of expression.

"[A] mistake in ruling against *The Progressive* will seriously infringe cherished First Amendment rights. [A] mistake in ruling against the United States could pave the way for thermonuclear annihilation for us all. In that event, our right to life is extinguished and the right to publish becomes moot.

"[W]ar by foot soldiers has been replaced in large part by machines and bombs. No longer need there be any advance warning or any preparation time before a nuclear war could be commenced. [In light of these factors] publication of the technical information on the hydrogen bomb contained in the article is analogous to publication of troop movements or locations in time of war and falls within the extremely narrow exception to the rule against prior restraint [recognized in *Near*].[f]

"The government has met its burden under § 2274 of The Atomic Energy Act [which authorizes injunctive relief against one who would communicate or disclose restricted data 'with reason to believe such data will be utilized to injure the United States or to secure an advantage to any foreign nation.'] [I]t has also met the test enunciated by two Justices in *Pentagon Papers,* namely grave, direct, immediate and irreparable harm to the United States."

The court distinguished *Pentagon Papers* as follows: "[T]he study involved [there] contained historical data relating to events some three to twenty years previously. Secondly, the Supreme Court agreed with the lower court that no cogent reasons were advanced by the government as to why the article affected national security except that publication might cause some embarrassment to the United States. A final and most vital difference between these two cases is the fact that a specific statute is involved here [§ 2274 of The Atomic Energy Act]."

3. *CIA secrecy agreement.* The Central Intelligence Agency requires employees to sign a "secrecy agreement" as a condition of employment, an agreement committing the employee not to reveal classified information nor to publish any information obtained during the course of employment without prior approval of the Agency. In SNEPP v. UNITED STATES, 444 U.S. 507, 100 S.Ct. 763, 62

---

f. One of the reasons the court gave for finding that the objected-to technical portions of the article fell within the *Near* exception was that it was "unconvinced that suppression of [these portions] would in any plausible fashion impede the defendants in their laudable crusade to stimulate public knowledge of nuclear armament and bring about enlightened debate on national policy questions." Should this have been a factor in the decision to issue the preliminary injunction?

L.Ed.2d 704 (1980), Snepp had published a book called *Decent Interval* about certain CIA activities in South Vietnam based on his experiences as an agency employee without seeking prepublication review. At least for purposes of the litigation, the government conceded that Snepp's book divulged no confidential information. The Court, per curiam (Stevens, J., joined by Brennan and Marshall, JJ., dissenting) held that Snepp's failure to submit the book was a breach of trust and the government was entitled to a constructive trust on the proceeds of the book: "[E]ven in the absence of an express agreement, the CIA could have acted to protect substantial government interests by imposing reasonable restrictions on employee activities that in other contexts might be protected by the First Amendment. The Government has a compelling interest in protecting both the secrecy of information important to our national security and the appearance of confidentiality so essential to the effective operation of our foreign intelligence service." [g] When employees or past employees do submit publications for clearance, should *Freedman* standards apply? Can former CIA employees be required to submit all public speeches relating to their former employment for clearance? Are extemporaneous remarks permitted? To what extent can secrecy agreements be required of public employees outside the national security area? [h]

SECTION 6. FAIR ADMINISTRATION OF JUSTICE AND THE FIRST AMENDMENT AS SWORD

This section poses two connected problems. The first implicates familiar themes, albeit in a different context. The government seeks to deter or punish speech it regards as threatening to the fair administration of justice, but the speech at issue falls into no recognized category of unprotected speech. Thus, the courts must consider whether absolute protection is called for, or, alternatively, whether new categories or ad hoc determinations are appropriate, and whether prior restraints are permissible.

A second problem is unique. Government seeks not to punish speech, but to administer justice in private. It refuses to let the public or press witness its handling of prisoners, or its conduct of trial or pre-trial proceedings. The question is whether the first amendment can serve as a sword allowing citizen-critics to gather information. Assuming it can, what are its limits within the justice system? Does a right of access reach beyond the justice system?

Finally, a recurring issue concerns the role of the press. If the press cannot be prevented from speaking about trials, can prosecutors, defense attorneys, litigants and potential witnesses be prevented from speaking to the press? Is this one problem or many problems? Does the first amendment require that the press

g. Compare *Haig v. Agee*, 453 U.S. 280, 101 S.Ct. 2766, 69 L.Ed.2d 640 (1981), stating that "repeated disclosures of intelligence operations and names of intelligence personnel" for the "purpose of obstructing intelligence operations and the recruiting of intelligence personnel" are "clearly not protected by the Constitution." What if the publisher of the information merely has "reason to believe that such activities would impair or impede the foreign intelligence activities of the United States"? See 50 U.S.C. § 421.

h. For discussion of *Snepp*, see Mary Cheh, *Judicial Supervision of Executive Secrecy,* 69 Corn.L.Rev. 690 (1984); Frank Easterbrook,

Insider Trading, Secret Agents, Evidentiary Privileges, and the Production of Information, 1981 Sup.Ct.Rev. 309, 339–53; Stanley Godofsky & Howard Rogatnick, *Prior Restraints: The Pentagon Papers Case Revisited,* fn. c supra, at 543–54 (1988); Judith Koffler & Bennett Gershman, *The New Seditious Libel,* 69 Corn.L.Rev. 816 (1984); Jonathan Medow, *The First Amendment and the Secrecy State: Snepp v. United States,* 130 U.Pa.L.Rev. 775 (1982). For a thorough exploration of the occasions in which secrecy has been preferred over public knowledge, see Benjamin DuVal, *The Occasions of Secrecy,* 47 U.Pitt.L.Rev. 579 (1986).

be granted access not afforded the public? Does the first amendment permit differential access? If so, what are the limits on how government defines the press?

I. JUSTICE AND THE FIRST AMENDMENT AS SHIELD

In a number of cases, defendants have asserted that their rights to a fair trial have been abridged by newspaper publicity. SHEPPARD v. MAXWELL, 384 U.S. 333, 6 Ohio Misc. 231, 86 S.Ct. 1507, 16 L.Ed.2d 600 (1966), is probably the most notorious "trial by newspaper" case. The Court, per CLARK, J., (Black, J. dissenting) agreed with the "finding" of the Ohio Supreme Court that the atmosphere of defendant's murder trial was that of a " 'Roman holiday' for the news media." The courtroom was jammed with reporters. And in the corridors outside the courtroom, "a host of photographers and television personnel" photographed witnesses, counsel and jurors as they entered and left the courtroom. Throughout the trial, there was a deluge of publicity, much of which contained information never presented at trial, yet the jurors were not sequestered until the trial was over and they had begun their deliberations.

The Court placed the primary blame on the trial judge. He could "easily" have prevented "the carnival atmosphere of the trial" since "the courtroom and courthouse premises" were subject to his control. For example, he should have provided privacy for the jury, insulated witnesses from the media, instead of allowing them to be interviewed at will, and "made some effort to control the release of leads, information, and gossip to the press by police officers, witnesses, and the counsel for both sides." No one "coming under the jurisdiction of the court should be permitted to frustrate its function."

The Court recognized that "there is nothing that proscribes the press from reporting events that transpire in the courtroom. But where there is a reasonable likelihood that prejudicial news prior to trial will prevent a fair trial, the judge should continue the case until the threat abates, or transfer it to another county not so permeated with publicity. In addition, sequestration of the jury was something the judge should have raised sua sponte with counsel. If publicity during the proceedings threatens the fairness of the trial, a new trial should be ordered. But we must remember that reversals are but palliatives; the cure lies in those remedial measures that will prevent the prejudice at its inception."

The Court, however, reiterated its extreme reluctance "to place any direct limitations on the freedom traditionally exercised by the news media for '[w]hat transpires in the courtroom is public property.' " The press "does not simply publish information about trials but guards against the miscarriage of justice by subjecting the police, prosecutors, and judicial processes to extensive public scrutiny and criticism."

In anticipation of the trial of Simants for a mass murder which had attracted widespread news coverage, the county court prohibited everyone in attendance from, inter alia, releasing or authorizing for publication "any testimony given or evidence adduced." Simants' preliminary hearing (open to the public) was held the same day, subject to the restrictive order. Simants was bound over for trial. Respondent Nebraska state trial judge then entered an order which, as modified by the state supreme court, restrained the press and broadcasting media from reporting any confessions or incriminating statements made by Simants to law enforcement officers or third parties, except members of the press, and from reporting other facts "strongly implicative" of the defendant. The order expired when the jury was impaneled. NEBRASKA PRESS ASS'N v. STUART, 427 U.S. 539, 96 S.Ct. 2791, 49 L.Ed.2d 683 (1976), per BURGER, C.J., struck down the state court order: "To the extent that the order prohibited the reporting of evidence adduced at the open preliminary hearing, it plainly violated settled principles: 'There is nothing that proscribes the press from reporting events that transpire in the courtroom.' *Sheppard.*" [a] To the extent that the order prohibited publication "based on information gained from other sources, [the] heavy burden imposed as a condition to securing a prior restraint was not met." The portion of the order regarding "implicative" information was also "too vague and too broad" to survive scrutiny of restraints on first amendment rights.

"[P]retrial publicity—even pervasive, adverse publicity—does not inevitably lead to an unfair trial. The capacity of the jury eventually impaneled to decide the case fairly is influenced by the tone and extent of the publicity, which is in part, and often in large part, shaped by what attorneys, police and other officials do to precipitate news coverage. [T]he measures a judge takes or fails to take to mitigate the effects of pretrial publicity—the measures described in *Sheppard*— may well determine whether the defendant receives a trial consistent [with] due process.

"[The] Court has interpreted [first amendment] guarantees to afford special protection against orders that prohibit the publication or broadcast of particular information or commentary—orders that impose [a] 'prior' restraint on speech. None of our decided cases on prior restraint involved restrictive orders entered to protect a defendant's right to a fair and impartial jury, but [they] have a common thread relevant to this case. * * *

"The thread running through [*Near* and *Pentagon Papers*], is that prior restraints on speech and publication are the most serious and the least tolerable infringement on First Amendment rights. A criminal penalty or a judgment in a defamation case is subject to the whole panoply of protections afforded by deferring the impact of the judgment until all avenues of appellate review have been exhausted. [But] a prior restraint [has] an immediate and irreversible sanction. If it can be said that a threat of criminal or civil sanctions after publication 'chills' speech, prior restraint 'freezes' it at least for the time.

"[I]f the authors of [the first and sixth amendments], fully aware of the potential conflicts between them, were unwilling or unable to resolve the issue by assigning to one priority over the other, it is not for us to rewrite the Constitution by undertaking what they declined. [Yet] it is nonetheless clear that the barriers to prior restraint remain high unless we are to abandon what the Court has said for nearly a quarter of our national existence and implied throughout all of [it.]

"We turn now to the record in this case to determine whether, as Learned Hand put it, 'the gravity of the "evil," discounted by its improbability, justifies such invasion of free speech as is necessary to avoid the danger,' *Dennis* [2d Cir.], aff'd. To do so, we must examine the evidence before the trial judge when the order was entered to determine (a) the nature and extent of pretrial news coverage; (b) whether other measures would be likely to mitigate the effects of unrestrained pretrial publicity; (c) how effectively a restraining order would operate to prevent the threatened danger. The precise terms of the restraining

a. The Court added, however, that the county court "could not know that closure of the preliminary hearing was an alternative open to it until the Nebraska Supreme Court so construed state law."

order are also important. We must then consider whether the record supports the entry of a prior restraint on publication, one of the most extraordinary remedies known to our jurisprudence.''

As to (a), although the trial judge was justified in concluding there would be extensive pretrial publicity concerning this case, he "found only 'a clear and present danger that pretrial publicity *could* impinge upon the defendant's right to a fair trial.' [Emphasis added by the Court]. His conclusion as to the impact of such publicity on prospective jurors was of necessity speculative, dealing as he was with factors unknown and unknowable.''

As to (b), "there is no finding that alternative means [e.g., change of venue, postponement of trial to allow public attention to subside, searching questions of prospective jurors] would not have protected Simants' rights, and the Nebraska Supreme Court did no more than imply that such measures might not be adequate. Moreover, the record is lacking in evidence to support such a finding.''

As to (c), in view of such practical problems as the limited territorial jurisdiction of the trial court issuing the order, the difficulties of predicting what information "will in fact undermine the impartiality of jurors,'' the problem of drafting an order that will "effectively keep prejudicial information from prospective jurors,'' and that the events "took place in a community of only 850 people''—throughout which, "it is reasonable to assume,'' rumors that "could well be more damaging than reasonably accurate news accounts'' would "travel swiftly by word of mouth''—"it is far from clear that prior restraint on publication would have protected Simants' rights.''

"[It] is significant that when this Court has reversed a state conviction because of prejudicial publicity, it has carefully noted that some course of action short of prior restraint would have made a critical difference. However difficult it may be, we need not rule out the possibility of showing the kind of threat to fair trial rights that would possess the requisite degree of certainty to justify restraint. [We] reaffirm that the guarantees of freedom of expression are not an absolute prohibition under all circumstances, but the barriers to prior restraint remain high and the presumption against its use continues intact. We hold that, with respect to the order entered in this case [the] heavy burden imposed as a condition to securing a prior restraint was not [met].''

BRENNAN, J., joined by Stewart and Marshall, JJ., concurring, would hold that "resort to prior restraints on the freedom of the press is a constitutionally impermissible method for enforcing [the right to a fair trial by a jury]; judges have at their disposal a broad spectrum of devices for ensuring that fundamental fairness is accorded the accused without necessitating so drastic an incursion on the equally fundamental and salutary constitutional mandate that discussion of public affairs in a free society cannot depend on the preliminary grace of judicial censors'': "* * * Settled case law concerning the impropriety and constitutional invalidity of prior restraints on the press compels the conclusion that there can be no prohibition on the publication by the press of any information pertaining to pending judicial proceedings or the operation of the criminal justice system, no matter how shabby the means by which the information is obtained.[15] This does not imply, however, any subordination of Sixth Amendment rights, for an ac-

---

15. Of course, even if the press cannot be enjoined from reporting certain information, that does not necessarily immunize it from civil liability for libel or invasion of privacy or from criminal liability for transgressions of general criminal laws during the course of obtaining that information.

cused's right to a fair trial may be adequately assured through methods that do not infringe First Amendment values.

"[The narrow national security exception mentioned in *Near* and *Pentagon Papers*] does not mean, as the Nebraska Supreme Court assumed, that prior restraints can be justified on an ad hoc balancing approach that concludes that the 'presumption' must be overcome in light of some perceived 'justification.' Rather, this language refers to the fact that, as a matter of procedural safeguards and burden of proof, prior restraints even within a recognized exception to the rule against prior restraints will be extremely difficult to justify; but as an initial matter, the purpose for which a prior restraint is sought to be imposed 'must fit within one of the narrowly defined exceptions to the prohibition against prior restraints.' Indeed, two Justices in [*Pentagon Papers*] apparently controverted the existence of even a limited 'military security' exception to the rule against prior restraints on the publication of otherwise protected material. (Black, J., concurring); (Douglas, J., concurring). And a majority of the other Justices who expressed their views on the merits made it clear that they would take cognizance only of a 'single, extremely narrow class of cases in which the First Amendment's ban on prior judicial restraint may be overridden.' (Brennan, J., concurring). * * *

"The only exception that has thus far been recognized even in dictum to the blanket prohibition against prior restraints against publication of material which would otherwise be constitutionally shielded was the 'military security' situation addressed in [*Pentagon Papers*]. But unlike the virtually certain, direct, and immediate harm required for such a restraint [the] harm to a fair trial that might otherwise eventuate from publications which are suppressed pursuant to orders such as that under review must inherently remain speculative."

Although they joined the Court's opinion, White and Powell, JJ., also filed brief concurrences. WHITE, J., expressed "grave doubts" that these types of restrictive orders "would ever be justifiable." POWELL, J., "emphasize[d] the unique burden" resting upon one who "undertakes to show the necessity for prior restraint on pretrial publicity." In his judgment, a prior restraint "requires a showing that (i) there is a clear threat to the fairness of trial, (ii) such a threat is posed by the actual publicity to be restrained, and (iii) no less restrictive alternatives are available. Notwithstanding such a showing, a restraint may not issue unless it also is shown that previous publicity or publicity from unrestrained sources will not render the restraint inefficacious. [A]ny restraint must comply with the standards of specificity always required in the First Amendment context."

STEVENS, J., concurred in the judgment. He agreed with Brennan, J., that the "judiciary is capable of protecting the defendant's right to a fair trial without enjoining the press from publishing information in the public domain, and that it may not do so." But he reserved judgment, until further argument, on "[w]hether the same absolute protection would apply no matter how shabby or illegal the means by which the information is obtained, no matter how serious an intrusion on privacy might be involved, no matter how demonstrably false the information might be, no matter how prejudicial it might be to the interests of innocent persons, and no matter how perverse the motivation for publishing it." He indicated that "if ever required to face the issue squarely" he "may well accept [Brennan, J.'s] ultimate conclusion." [b]

b. For background on *Nebraska Press*, see Fred Friendly & Martha Elliot, *The Constitu-*   *tion: That Delicate Balance* 148–58 (1984).

Notes and Questions

1. *Why the prior restraint reliance?* Does "the reasoning used by all of the justices premised solely on the traditional aversion to prior restraints, insufficiently" protect the press? Robert Sack, *Principle and Nebraska Press Association v. Stuart,* 29 Stan.L.Rev. 411, 411 (1977). Would the *Nebraska Press* order have been "equally objectionable" if "framed as a statutory sanction punishing publication after it had occurred"? Id. at 415. See also Stephen Barnett, *The Puzzle of Prior Restraint,* 29 Stan.L.Rev. 539, 542–44, 560 (1977).

2. *Why the Dennis citation?* Consider Benno Schmidt, *Nebraska Press Association: An Expansion of Freedom and Contraction of Theory,* 29 Stan.L.Rev. 431, 459–60 (1977): Burger, C.J.'s reliance on *Dennis* "is remarkable, almost unbelievable, because that test is both an exceedingly odd means of determining the validity of a prior restraint and a controversial and recently neglected technique of first amendment adjudication. [If] the [*Dennis*] test is the right one for prior restraints, what tests should govern a subsequent punishment case resting on legislation?" See also Barnett, note 1 supra, at 542–44. Burger, C.J.'s citation to *Dennis* should be read in conjunction with dictum in his majority opinion in *Landmark Communications, Inc. v. Virginia,* note 6 infra. There he questioned reliance upon the clear and present danger standard but observed: "Properly applied, the test requires a court to make its own inquiry into the imminence and magnitude of the danger said to flow from the particular utterance and then to balance the character of the evil, as well as its likelihood, against the need for free and unfettered expression. The possibility that other measures will serve the State's interests should also be weighed."

3. *Future press restraints.* Was *Nebraska Press* a strong case for restraint? Is it "difficult to believe that any other case will provide an exception to the rule against prior restraints in fair trial/free press cases"? James Goodale, *The Press Ungagged: The Practical Effect on Gag Order Litigation of Nebraska Press,* 29 Stan.L.Rev. 497, 504 (1977). If so, does the dispute between the justices over the right standard make a difference? Does the collateral bar rule shed light on that question? See id. at 511–12; Barnett, note 1 supra, at 553–58. Should the collateral bar rule apply in this situation?

4. *Application to non-press defendants.* Should *Nebraska Press* standards apply to court orders preventing prosecutors, witnesses, potential witnesses, jurors,[c] defendants, or defense attorneys from talking to the press about the case? Should different standards apply to each category—e.g., do defense attorneys deserve as much protection as the press? See *Gentile v. State Bar,* 501 U.S. 1030, 111 S.Ct. 2720, 115 L.Ed.2d 888 (1991) (less stringent standard ("substantial likelihood of material prejudice") applies to defense attorneys not clear and present danger). See also Monroe Freedman & Janet Starwood, *Prior Restraints on Freedom of Expression by Defendants and Defense Attorneys: Ratio Decidendi v. Obiter Dictum,* 29 Stan.L.Rev. 607 (1977); Comment, *First Amendment Protection of Criminal Defense Attorneys' Extrajudicial [Statements],* 8 Whittier L.Rev. 1021 (1987).

5. *Obstructing justice.* A series of cases have held that the first amendment greatly restricts contempt sanctions against persons whose comments on pending cases were alleged to have created a danger of obstruction of the judicial process.

c. Marcy Strauss, *Juror Journalism,* 12 Yale L. & Pol'y Rev. 389 (1994); Comment, *Checkbook Journalism, Free Speech, and Fair Trials,* 143 U.Pa.L.Rev. 1739 (1995).

"Such repression can be justified, if at all, only by a clear and present danger of the obstruction of justice." *New York Times,* p. 674 supra. In *Bridges v. California,* 314 U.S. 252, 62 S.Ct. 190, 86 L.Ed. 192 (1941), union leader Bridges had caused publication or acquiesced in publication of a telegram threatening a strike if an "outrageous" California state decision involving Bridges' dock workers were enforced. The Court reversed Bridges' contempt citation. Consider Laurence Tribe, *American Constitutional Law* 624 (1978): "If Bridges' threat to cripple the economy of the entire West Coast did not present danger enough, the lesson of the case must be that almost nothing said outside the courtroom is punishable as contempt." [d]

Would it make a difference if a petit jury were impaneled? Suppose Bridges published an open letter to petit jurors? What if copies were sent by Bridges to each juror? Cf. *Wood v. Georgia,* 370 U.S. 375, 82 S.Ct. 1364, 8 L.Ed.2d 569 (1962) (open letter to press and grand jury—contempt citation reversed). But cf. *Cox v. Louisiana,* p. 919 infra (statute forbidding parades near courthouse with intent to interfere with administration of justice upheld): ("[W]e deal not with the contempt power [but] a statute narrowly drawn to punish" not a pure form of speech but expression mixed with conduct "that infringes a substantial state interest in protecting the judicial process.").

6. *Confidentiality and privacy.* A series of cases has rebuffed state efforts to protect confidentiality or privacy by prohibiting publication. *Cox Broadcasting Corp. v. Cohn,* p. 691 supra (state could not impose liability for public dissemination of the name of rape victim derived from public court documents); *Oklahoma Pub. Co. v. District Court,* 430 U.S. 308, 97 S.Ct. 1045, 51 L.Ed.2d 355 (1977) (pretrial order enjoining press from publishing name or picture of 11-year-old boy accused of murder invalid when reporters had been lawfully present at a prior public hearing and had photographed him en route from the courthouse); *Landmark Communications, Inc. v. Virginia,* 435 U.S. 829, 98 S.Ct. 1535, 56 L.Ed.2d 1 (1978) (statute making it a crime to publish information about particular confidential proceedings invalid as applied to non-participant in the proceedings, at least when the information had been lawfully acquired); *Smith v. Daily Mail Pub. Co.,* 443 U.S. 97, 99 S.Ct. 2667, 61 L.Ed.2d 399 (1979) (statute making it a crime for newspapers (but not broadcasters) to publish the name of any youth charged as a juvenile offender invalid as applied to information lawfully acquired from private sources). But cf. *Seattle Times Co. v. Rhinehart,* 467 U.S. 20, 104 S.Ct. 2199, 81 L.Ed.2d 17 (1984) (order enjoining newspaper from disseminating information acquired as a litigant in pretrial discovery valid so long as order is entered on a showing of good cause and does not restrict the dissemination of the information if gained from other sources).

II. JUSTICE AND THE FIRST AMENDMENT AS SWORD

By 1978, no Supreme Court holding contradicted Burger, C.J.'s contention for the plurality in *Houchins v. KQED,* 438 U.S. 1, 98 S.Ct. 2588, 57 L.Ed.2d 553 (1978) that, "neither the First Amendment nor the Fourteenth Amendment mandates a right of access to government information or sources of information within the government's control." Or as Stewart, J., put it in an often-quoted statement, "The Constitution itself is neither a Freedom of Information Act nor

d. Compare Carol Rieger, *Lawyers' Criticism of Judges: Is Freedom of Speech A Figure* of Speech?, 2 Const.Comm. 69 (1985).

an Official Secrets Act." *"Or of the Press,"* 26 Hast.L.J. 631, 636 (1975). *Richmond Newspapers, infra,* constitutes the Court's first break with its past denials of first amendment rights to information within governmental control.

RICHMOND NEWSPAPERS, INC. v. VIRGINIA

448 U.S. 555, 100 S.Ct. 2814, 65 L.Ed.2d 973 (1980).

[At the commencement of his fourth trial on a murder charge (his first conviction having been reversed and two subsequent retrials having ended in mistrials), defendant moved, without objection by the prosecutor or two reporters present, that the trial be closed to the public—defense counsel stating that he did not "want any information being shuffled back and forth when we have a recess as [to] who testified to what." The trial judge granted the motion, stating that "the statute gives me that power specifically." He presumably referred to Virginia Code § 19.2–266, providing that in all criminal trials "the court may, in its discretion, exclude [any] persons whose presence would impair the conduct of a fair trial, provided that the [defendant's right] to a public trial shall not be violated." Later the same day the trial court granted appellants' request for a hearing on a motion to vacate the closure order. At the closed hearing, appellants observed that prior to the entry of its closure order the court had failed to make any evidentiary findings or to consider any other, less drastic measures to ensure a fair trial. Defendant stated that he "didn't want information to leak out," be published by the media, perhaps inaccurately, and then be seen by the jurors. Noting inter alia that "having people in the Courtroom is distracting to the jury" and that if "the rights of the defendant are infringed in any way [and if his closure motion] doesn't completely override all rights of everyone else, then I'm inclined to go along with" the defendant, the court denied the motion to vacate the closure order. Defendant was subsequently found not guilty.]

CHIEF JUSTICE BURGER announced the judgment of the Court and delivered an opinion in which JUSTICE WHITE and JUSTICE STEVENS joined.

[T]he precise issue presented here has not previously been before this Court for decision. [*Gannett Co. v. DePasquale,* 443 U.S. 368, 99 S.Ct. 2898, 61 L.Ed.2d 608 (1979)] was not required to decide whether a right of access to *trials,* as distinguished from hearings on *pretrial* motions, was constitutionally guaranteed. The Court held that the Sixth Amendment's guarantee to the accused of a public trial gave neither the public nor the press an enforceable right of access to a *pretrial* suppression hearing. One concurring opinion specifically emphasized that "a hearing on a motion before trial to suppress evidence is not a *trial.*" (Burger, C.J., concurring). Moreover, the Court did not decide whether the First and Fourteenth Amendments guarantee a right of the public to attend trials; nor did the dissenting opinion reach this issue. [H]ere for the first time the Court is asked to decide whether a criminal trial itself may be closed to the public upon the unopposed request of a defendant, without any demonstration that closure is required to protect the defendant's superior right to a fair trial, or that some other overriding consideration requires closure.

[T]he historical evidence demonstrates conclusively that at the time when our organic laws were adopted, criminal trials both here and in England had long been presumptively open [, thus giving] assurance that the proceedings were conducted fairly to all concerned, [and] discourag[ing] perjury, the misconduct of participants, and decisions based on secret bias or partiality. [Moreover, the] early history of open trials in part reflects the widespread acknowledgment [that] public trials had significant therapeutic value. [When] a shocking crime occurs, a community reaction of outrage and public protest often follows. Thereafter the open processes of justice serve an important prophylactic purpose, providing an outlet for community concern, hostility, and emotion.

[The] crucial prophylactic aspects of the administration of justice cannot function in the dark; no community catharsis can occur if justice is "done in a corner [or] in any covert manner." [To] work effectively, it is important that society's criminal process "satisfy the appearance of justice," and the appearance of justice can best be provided by allowing people to observe it.

[From] this unbroken, uncontradicted history, supported by reasons as valid today as in centuries past, we are bound to conclude that a presumption of openness inheres in the very nature of a criminal trial under our system of criminal justice. [Nevertheless,] the State presses its contention that neither the Constitution nor the Bill of Rights contains any provision which by its terms guarantees to the public the right to attend criminal trials. Standing alone, this is correct, but there remains the question whether, absent an explicit provision, the Constitution affords protection against exclusion of the public from criminal trials.

[The] expressly guaranteed [first amendment] freedoms share a common core purpose of assuring freedom of communication on matters relating to the functioning of government. Plainly it would be difficult to single out any aspect of government of higher concern and importance to the people than the manner in which criminal trials are conducted * * *.

The Bill of Rights was enacted against the backdrop of the long history of trials being presumptively open. [In] guaranteeing freedoms such as those of speech and press, the First Amendment can be read as protecting the right of everyone to attend trials so as to give meaning to those explicit guarantees. * * * Free speech carries with it some freedom to listen. "In a variety of contexts this Court has referred to a First Amendment right to 'receive information and ideas.'" *Kleindienst v. Mandel,* 408 U.S. 753, 762, 92 S.Ct. 2576, 2581, 33 L.Ed.2d 683 (1972).[a] What this means in the context of trials is that the First Amendment guarantees of speech and press, standing alone, prohibit government from summarily closing courtroom doors which had long been open to the public at the time that amendment was adopted.

[It] is not crucial whether we describe this right to attend criminal trials to hear, see, and communicate observations concerning them as a "right of access," cf. *Gannett* (Powell, J., concurring); *Saxbe v. Washington Post Co.,* 417 U.S. 843, 94 S.Ct. 2811, 41 L.Ed.2d 514 (1974); *Pell v. Procunier,* 417 U.S. 817, 94 S.Ct. 2800, 41 L.Ed.2d 495 (1974),[11] or a "right to gather information," for we have recognized that "without some protection for seeking out the news, freedom of the press could be eviscerated." *Branzburg v. Hayes,* [p. 998 infra]. The explicit, guaranteed rights to speak and to publish concerning what takes place at a trial

---

a. *Mandel* held that the Executive had plenary power to exclude a Belgium journalist from the country, at least so long as it operated on the basis of a facially legitimate and bona fide reason for exclusion. Although the Court decided ultimately not to balance the government's particular justification against the first amendment interest, it recognized that those who sought personal communication with the excluded alien did have a first amendment interest at stake. The Court apparently assumed that the excluded speaker had no rights at stake, and none were asserted on his behalf.

11. *Procunier* and *Saxbe* are distinguishable in the sense that they were concerned with penal institutions which, by definition, are not "open" or public places. * * * See

would lose much meaning if access to observe the trial could, as it was here, be foreclosed arbitrarily.

The right of access to places traditionally open to the public, as criminal trials have long been, may be seen as assured by the amalgam of the First Amendment guarantees of speech and press; and their affinity to the right of assembly is not without relevance. From the outset, the right of assembly was regarded not only as an independent right but also as a catalyst to augment the free exercise of the other First Amendment rights with which it was deliberately linked by the draftsmen. * * * Subject to the traditional time, place, and manner restrictions, streets, sidewalks, and parks are places traditionally open, where First Amendment rights may be exercised [see generally Sec. 6 infra]; a trial courtroom also is a public place where the people generally—and representatives of the media—have a right to be present, and where their presence historically has been thought to enhance the integrity and quality of what takes place.

* * * Notwithstanding the appropriate caution against reading into the Constitution rights not explicitly defined, the Court has acknowledged that certain unarticulated rights are implicit in enumerated guarantees [referring, inter alia, to the rights of association and of privacy and the right to travel. See generally Ch. 7, Secs. 2 & 3]. [T]hese important but unarticulated rights [have] been found to share constitutional protection in common with explicit guarantees. The concerns expressed by Madison and others have thus been [resolved].[b]

We hold that the right to attend criminal trials [17] is implicit in the guarantees of the First Amendment; without the freedom to attend such trials, which people have exercised for centuries, important aspects of freedom of speech and "of the press could be eviscerated." *Branzburg.*

[In the present case,] the trial court made no findings to support closure; no inquiry was made as to whether alternative solutions would have met the need to ensure fairness; there was no recognition of any right under the Constitution for the public or press to attend the trial. In contrast to the pretrial proceeding dealt with in *Gannett,* there exist in the context of the trial itself various tested alternatives to satisfy the constitutional demands of fairness. [For example, there was nothing] to indicate that sequestration of the jurors would not have guarded against their being subjected to any improper information.[c] * * * Absent an overriding interest articulated in findings, the trial of a criminal case must be open to the public. * * *

Reversed.[d]

Justice Brennan, with whom Justice Marshall joins, concurring in the judgment.

also *Greer v. Spock* (military bases) 424 U.S. 828, 96 S.Ct. 1211, 47 L.Ed.2d 505 (1976).

b. The Chief Justice noted "the perceived need" of the Constitution's draftsmen "for some sort of constitutional 'saving clause' [which] would serve to foreclose application to the Bill of Rights of the maxim that the affirmation of particular rights implies a negation of those not expressly defined. Madison's efforts, culminating in the Ninth Amendment, served to allay the fears of those who were concerned that expressing certain guarantees could be read as excluding others."

17. Whether the public has a right to attend [civil trials is] not raised by this case, but we note that historically both civil and criminal trials have been presumptively open.

c. Once the jurors are selected, when, if ever, will their sequestration *not* be a satisfactory alternative to closure?

d. Powell, J., took no part. In *Gannett,* he took the position that a first amendment right of access applied to courtroom proceedings, albeit subject to overriding when justice so demanded or when confidentiality was necessary.

[*Gannett*] held that the Sixth Amendment right to a public trial was personal to the accused, conferring no right of access to pretrial proceedings that is separately enforceable by the public or the press. [This case] raises the question whether the First Amendment, of its own force and as applied to the States through the Fourteenth Amendment, secures the public an independent right of access to trial proceedings. Because I believe that [it does secure] such a public right of access, I agree [that], without more, agreement of the trial judge and the parties cannot constitutionally close a trial to the public.[1]

While freedom of expression is made inviolate by the First Amendment, and with only rare and stringent exceptions, may not be suppressed, the First Amendment has not been viewed by the Court in all settings as providing an equally categorical assurance of the correlative freedom of access to information.[2] Yet the Court has not ruled out a public access component to the First Amendment in every circumstance. Read with care and in context, our decisions must therefore be understood as holding only that any privilege of access to governmental information is subject to a degree of restraint dictated by the nature of the information and countervailing interests in security or confidentiality. [Cases such as *Houchins, Saxbe* and *Pell*] neither comprehensively nor absolutely deny that public access to information may at times be implied by the First Amendment and the principles which animate it.

The Court's approach in right of access cases simply reflects the special nature of a claim of First Amendment right to gather information. Customarily, First Amendment guarantees are interposed to protect communication between speaker and listener. When so employed against prior restraints, free speech protections are almost insurmountable. See generally Brennan, *Address*, 32 Rutg.L.Rev. 173, 176 (1979). But the First Amendment embodies more than a commitment to free expression and communicative interchange for their own sakes; it has a *structural* role to play in securing and fostering our republican system of self-government. Implicit in this structural role is not only "the principle that debate on public issues should be uninhibited, robust, and wide-open," but the antecedent assumption that valuable public debate—as well as other civic behavior—must be informed. The structural model links the First Amendment to that process of communication necessary for a democracy to survive, and thus entails solicitude not only for communication itself, but for the indispensable conditions of meaningful communication.

[A]n assertion of the prerogative to gather information must [be] assayed by considering the information sought and the opposing interests invaded. This judicial task is as much a matter of sensitivity to practical necessities as it is of abstract reasoning. But at least two helpful principles may be sketched. First, the case for a right of access has special force when drawn from an enduring and

---

1. Of course, the Sixth Amendment remains the source of the *accused's* own right to insist upon public judicial proceedings. *Gannett.*

That the Sixth Amendment explicitly establishes a public trial right does not impliedly foreclose the derivation of such a right from other provisions of the Constitution. The Constitution was not framed as a work of carpentry, in which all joints must fit snugly without overlapping. * * *

2. A conceptually separate, yet related, question is whether the media should enjoy greater access rights than the general public. But no such contention is at stake here. Since the media's right of access is at least equal to that of the general public, this case is resolved by a decision that the state statute unconstitutionally restricts public access to trials. As a practical matter, however, the institutional press is the likely, and fitting, chief beneficiary of a right of access because it serves as the "agent" of interested citizens, and funnels information about trials to a large number of individuals.

vital tradition of public entree to particular proceedings or information. Such a tradition commands respect in part because the Constitution carries the gloss of history. More importantly, a tradition of accessibility implies the favorable judgment of experience. Second, the value of access must be measured in specifics. Analysis is not advanced by rhetorical statements that all information bears upon public issues; what is crucial in individual cases is whether access to a particular government process is important in terms of that very process.

[This Court has] persistently defended the public character of the trial process. *In re Oliver,* 333 U.S. 257, 68 S.Ct. 499, 92 L.Ed. 682 (1948), established that [fourteenth amendment due process] forbids closed criminal trials [and] acknowledged that open trials are indispensable to First Amendment political and religious freedoms.

By the same token, a special solicitude for the public character of judicial proceedings is evident in the Court's rulings upholding the right to report about the administration of justice. While these decisions are impelled by the classic protections afforded by the First Amendment to pure communication, they are also bottomed upon a keen appreciation of the structural interest served in opening the judicial system to public inspection. So, in upholding a privilege for reporting truthful information about judicial misconduct proceedings, *Landmark* emphasized that public scrutiny of the operation of a judicial disciplinary body implicates a major purpose of the First Amendment—"discussion of governmental affairs." Again, *Nebraska Press* noted that the traditional guarantee against prior restraint "should have particular force as applied to reporting of criminal proceedings." And *Cox Broadcasting* instructed that "[w]ith respect to judicial proceedings in particular, the function of the press serves to guarantee the fairness of trials and to bring to bear the beneficial effects of public scrutiny upon the administration of justice."

[Open] trials play a fundamental role in furthering the efforts of our judicial system to assure the criminal defendant a fair and accurate adjudication of guilt or innocence. But, as a feature of our governing system of justice, the trial process serves other, broadly political, interests, and public access advances these objectives as well. To that extent, trial access possesses specific structural significance.

[For] a civilization founded upon principles of ordered liberty to survive and flourish, its members must share the conviction that they are governed equitably. That necessity * * * mandates a system of justice that demonstrates the fairness of the law to our citizens. One major function of the trial is to make that demonstration.

Secrecy is profoundly inimical to this demonstrative [purpose]. Public access is essential, therefore, if trial adjudication is to achieve the objective of maintaining public confidence in the administration of justice. But the trial [also] plays a pivotal role in the entire judicial process, and, by extension, in our form of government. Under our system, judges are not mere umpires, but, in their own sphere, lawmakers—a coordinate branch of *government.* [Thus], so far as the trial is the mechanism for judicial factfinding, as well as the initial forum for legal decisionmaking, it is a genuine governmental proceeding.

[More] importantly, public access to trials acts as an important check, akin in purpose to the other checks and balances that infuse our system of government. "The knowledge that every criminal trial is subject to contemporaneous review in the forum of public opinion is an effective restraint on possible abuse of judicial power," *Oliver*—an abuse that, in many cases, would have ramifications beyond the impact upon the parties before the court. * * *

Popular attendance at trials, in sum, substantially furthers the particular public purposes of that critical judicial proceeding. In that sense, public access is an indispensable element of the trial process itself. Trial access, therefore, assumes structural importance in our "government of laws."

As previously noted, resolution of First Amendment public access claims in individual cases must be strongly influenced by the weight of historical practice and by an assessment of the specific structural value of public access in the circumstances. With regard to the case at hand, our ingrained tradition of public trials and the importance of public access to the broader purposes of the trial process, tip the balance strongly toward the rule that trials be open.[23] What countervailing interests might be sufficiently compelling to reverse this presumption of openness need not concern us now,[24] for the statute at stake here authorizes trial closures at the unfettered discretion of the judge and parties.[25] [Thus it] violates the First and Fourteenth Amendments * * *.

JUSTICE STEWART, concurring in the judgment.

Whatever the ultimate answer [may] be with respect to pretrial suppression hearings in criminal cases, the First and Fourteenth Amendments clearly give the press and the public a right of access to trials themselves, civil as well as criminal. * * *

In conspicuous contrast to a military base, *Greer*; a jail, *Adderley v. Florida*, 385 U.S. 39, 87 S.Ct. 242, 17 L.Ed.2d 149 (1966); or a prison, *Pell*, a trial courtroom is a public place. Even more than city streets, sidewalks, and parks as areas of traditional First Amendment activity, a trial courtroom is a place where representatives of the press and of the public are not only free to be, but where their presence serves to assure the integrity of what goes on.

But this does not mean that the First Amendment right of members of the public and representatives of the press to attend civil and criminal trials is absolute. Just as a legislature may impose reasonable time, place and manner restrictions upon the exercise of First Amendment freedoms, so may a trial judge impose reasonable limitations upon the unrestricted occupation of a courtroom by representatives of the press and members of the public. Moreover, [there] may be occasions when not all who wish to attend a trial may do so.[3] And while there exist many alternative ways to satisfy the constitutional demands of a fair trial, those demands may also sometimes justify limitations upon the unrestricted presence of spectators in the courtroom.[5]

---

23. The presumption of public trials is, of course, not at all incompatible with reasonable restrictions imposed upon courtroom behavior in the interests of decorum. Thus, when engaging in interchanges at the bench, the trial judge is not required to allow public or press intrusion upon the huddle. Nor does this opinion intimate that judges are restricted in their ability to conduct conferences in chambers, inasmuch as such conferences are distinct from trial proceedings.

24. For example, national security concerns about confidentiality may sometimes warrant closures during sensitive portions of trial proceedings, such as testimony about state secrets.

25. Significantly, closing a trial lacks even the justification for barring the door to pretrial hearings: the necessity of preventing dissemination of suppressible prejudicial evidence to the public before the jury pool has become, in a practical sense, finite and subject to sequestration.

3. In such situations, representatives of the press must be assured access, *Houchins* (concurring opinion).

5. This is not to say that only constitutional considerations can justify such restrictions. The preservation of trade secrets, for example, might justify the exclusion of the public from at least some segments of a civil trial. And the sensibilities of a youthful prosecution witness,

Since in the present case the trial judge appears to have given no recognition to the right [of] the press and [the] public to be present at [the] murder trial over which he was presiding, the judgment under review must be [reversed.]

JUSTICE WHITE, concurring.

This case would have been unnecessary had *Gannett* construed the Sixth Amendment to forbid excluding the public from criminal proceedings except in narrowly defined circumstances. But the Court there rejected the submission of four of us to this effect, thus requiring that the First Amendment issue involved here be addressed. On this issue, I concur in the opinion of the Chief Justice.

JUSTICE BLACKMUN, concurring in the judgment.

My opinion and vote in partial dissent [in] *Gannett* compels my vote to reverse the judgment. [It] is gratifying [to] see the Court now looking to and relying upon legal history in determining the fundamental public character of the criminal trial. * * *

The Court's ultimate ruling in *Gannett,* with such clarification as is provided by the opinions in this case today, apparently is now to the effect that there is no *Sixth* Amendment right on the part of the public—or the press—to an open hearing on a motion to suppress. I, of course, continue to believe that *Gannett* was in error, both in its interpretation of the Sixth Amendment generally, and in its application to the suppression hearing, for I remain convinced that the right to a public trial is to be found where the Constitution explicitly placed it—in the Sixth Amendment.

[But] with the Sixth Amendment set to one side in this case, I am driven to conclude, as a secondary position, that the First Amendment must provide some measure of protection for public access to the trial. The opinion in partial dissent in *Gannett* explained that the public has an intense need and a deserved right to know about the administration of justice in general; about the prosecution of local crimes in particular; about the conduct of the judge, the prosecutor, defense counsel, police officers, other public servants, and all the actors in the judicial arena; and about the trial itself. It is clear and obvious to me, on the approach the Court has chosen to take, that, by closing this criminal trial, the trial judge abridged these First Amendment interests of the public. * * *

JUSTICE STEVENS, concurring.

This is a watershed case. Until today the Court has accorded virtually absolute protection to the dissemination of information or ideas, but never before has it squarely held that the acquisition of newsworthy matter is entitled to any constitutional protection whatsoever. An additional word of emphasis is therefore appropriate.

Twice before, the Court has implied that any governmental restriction on access to information, no matter how severe and no matter how unjustified, would be constitutionally acceptable so long as it did not single out the press for special disabilities not applicable to the public at large. In a dissent joined by [Brennan and Marshall, JJ.] in *Saxbe,* Justice Powell unequivocally rejected [that conclusion.] And in *Houchins,* I explained at length why [Brennan, Powell, JJ.] and I were convinced that "[a]n official prison policy of concealing * * * knowledge from the public by arbitrarily cutting off the flow of information at its source abridges [first amendment freedoms]." Since [Marshall and Blackmun, JJ.] were

for example, might justify similar exclusion in a criminal trial for rape, so long as the defen- dant's Sixth Amendment right to a public trial were not impaired.

unable to participate in that case, a majority of the Court neither accepted nor rejected that conclusion or the contrary conclusion expressed in the prevailing opinions. Today, however, for the first time, the Court unequivocally holds that an arbitrary interference with access to important information is an abridgment of the freedoms of speech and of the press protected by the First Amendment.

It is somewhat ironic that the Court should find more reason to recognize a right of access today than it did in *Houchins*. For *Houchins* involved the plight of a segment of society least able to protect itself, an attack on a longstanding policy of concealment, and an absence of any legitimate justification for abridging public access to information about how government operates. In this case we are protecting the interests of the most powerful voices in the community, we are concerned with an almost unique exception to an established tradition of openness in the conduct of criminal trials, and it is likely that the closure order was motivated by the judge's desire to protect the individual defendant from the burden of a fourth criminal trial.[2]

In any event, for the reasons stated [in] my *Houchins* opinion, as well as those stated by the Chief Justice today, I agree that the First Amendment protects the public and the press from abridgment of their rights of access to information about the operation of their government, including the Judicial Branch; given the total absence of any record justification for the closure order entered in this case, that order violated the First Amendment * * *.

JUSTICE REHNQUIST, dissenting.

[I] do not believe that [anything in the Constitution] require[s] that a State's reasons for denying public access to a trial, where both [the prosecution and defense] have consented to [a court-approved closure order], are subject to any additional constitutional review at our hands.

[The] issue here is not whether the "right" to freedom of the press * * * overrides the defendant's "right" to a fair trial, [but] whether any provision in the Constitution may fairly be read to prohibit what the [trial court] did in this case. Being unable to find any such prohibition in the First, Sixth, Ninth, or any other Amendments [or] in the Constitution itself, I dissent.

Notes and Questions

1. *Beyond the justice system.* May (should) "public access to information about how government operates" (to use Stevens, J.'s phrase) be denied, as the Chief Justice suggests, simply on the ground that the place at issue has not been *traditionally* open to the public (recall how the Chief Justice distinguishes penal institutions from criminal trials) or should the government also have to advance, as Stevens, J., suggests, "legitimate justification" for "abridging" public access? Compare the controversy over whether "the right to a public forum" should turn on whether the place at issue has *historically* been dedicated to the exercise of first amendment rights or on whether the manner of expression is *basically incompatible* with the normal activity of the place at a particular time. See generally the materials on the Public Forum: New Forums, Sec. 6, II infra. See

---

2. Neither that likely motivation nor facts showing the risk that a fifth trial would have been necessary without closure of the fourth are disclosed in this record, however. The absence of any articulated reason for the closure order is a sufficient basis for distinguishing this case from *Gannett*. The decision today is in no way inconsistent with the perfectly unambiguous holding in *Gannett* that the rights guaranteed by the Sixth Amendment are rights that may be asserted by the accused rather than members of the general public. * * *

also Note, *The First Amendment Right to Gather State-Held Information,* 89 Yale L.J. 923, 933–39 (1979). Consider, too, Vincent Blasi, *The Checking Value in First Amendment Theory,* 1977 Am.B.Found.Res.J. 521, 609–10: "[U]nder the checking value, the interest of the press (and ultimately the public) in learning certain information relevant to the abuse of official power would sometimes take precedence over perfectly legitimate and substantial government interests such as efficiency and confidentiality. Thus, the First Amendment may require that journalists have access as a general matter to some records, such as certain financial documents, which anyone investigating common abuses of the public trust would routinely want to inspect, even though the granting of such access would undoubtedly entail some costs and risks. Also, the balance might be tilted even more in the direction of access if a journalist could demonstrate that there are reasonable grounds to believe that certain records contain evidence of misconduct by public officials."

But cf. Yale Kamisar, *Right of Access to Information Generated or Controlled by the Government: Richmond Newspapers Examined and Gannett Revisited* in Jesse Choper, Yale Kamisar & Lawrence Tribe, The Supreme Court: Trends and Developments, 1979–80 145, 166 (1981): "I am sure I am not alone when I say that these law review commentaries go quite far. But *someday* the views they advance may be the law of the land. In the meantime, however, many more battles will have to be fought. *Someday* we may look back on *Richmond Newspapers* as the '*Powell v. Alabama*' of the right of access to government-controlled information—but it was a long, hard road from *Powell* to *Gideon*." [e]

2. *Within the justice system.* How far does (should) *Richmond Newspapers* extend within the justice system? To criminal pre-trial proceedings? [f] How is a trial defined? Should it extend to conferences in chambers or at the bench? To grand jury hearings? To civil trials? To depositions? To records of any or all of the above? Should it apply outside judicial proceedings? Should wardens be permitted to completely preclude access by the public and press to prisons? To executions? What if the prisoner wants to close the execution? For wide-ranging discussion of these and related questions, see Jesse Choper, Yale Kamisar, and Laurence Tribe, note 1 supra, at 145–206 (Professor Tribe was winning counsel in *Richmond Newspapers*). See also G. Michael Fenner & James Koley, *Access to Judicial Proceedings: To Richmond Newspapers and Beyond,* 16 Harv.Civ.Rts—Civ.Lib.L.Rev. 415 (1981).

3. *Closing trials.* After *Richmond Newspapers,* what showing should suffice to justify closure of a criminal trial? See *Globe Newspaper Co. v. Superior Court,* 457 U.S. 596, 102 S.Ct. 2613, 73 L.Ed.2d 248 (1982) (routine exclusion of press and public during testimony of minor victim of sex offense unconstitutional); *Press-Enterprise Co. v. Superior Court,* 464 U.S. 501, 104 S.Ct. 819, 78 L.Ed.2d 629 (1984) (extending *Richmond Newspapers* to voir dire examination of jurors).

e. For endorsements of generous access, see Franklyn Haiman, *Speech and Law in a Free Society* 108–14, 368–97 (1981); Mark Yudof, *When Government Speaks* 246–55 (1983); Thomas Emerson, *Legal Foundations of the Right to Know,* 1976 Wash.U.L.Q. 1, 14–17; Anthony Lewis, *A Public Right to Know about Public Institutions: The First Amendment as Sword,* 1980 Sup.Ct.Rev. 1. But see Lillian Bevier, *An Informed Public, an Informing Press: The Search for a Constitutional Principle,* 68 Calif.L.Rev. 482 (1980).

f. See *Press–Enterprise Co. v. Superior Court,* 478 U.S. 1, 106 S.Ct. 2735, 92 L.Ed.2d 1 (1986) ("California preliminary hearings are sufficiently like a trial" to implicate *Richmond Newspapers'* "qualified First Amendment right of access"), in addition, see *El Vocero de Puerto Rico v. Puerto Rico,* 508 U.S. 147, 113 S.Ct. 2004, 124 L.Ed.2d 60 (1993) (reaching same conclusion as to Puerto Rican preliminary hearings).

To overcome either the first amendment or the sixth amendment right to a public trial, the Court has required that the party seeking to close the proceedings "must advance an overriding interest that is likely to be prejudiced, the closure must be no broader than necessary to protect that interest, the trial court must consider reasonable alternatives to closing the proceeding, and it must make findings adequate to support the closure." *Waller v. Georgia,* 467 U.S. 39, 104 S.Ct. 2210, 81 L.Ed.2d 31 (1984).

4. *Special access rights for the press.* Is a press section in public trials required when the seating capacity would be exhausted by the public? Is a press section permitted? What limits attach to government determinations of who shall get press passes? See, e.g., *Sherrill v. Knight,* 569 F.2d 124 (D.C.Cir.1977) (denial of White House press pass infringes upon first amendment guarantees in the absence of adequate process); *Borreca v. Fasi,* 369 F.Supp. 906 (D.Haw.1974) (preliminary injunction against denial of access of a reporter to Mayor's press conferences justified when basis for exclusion is allegedly "inaccurate" and "irresponsible" reporting); *Los Angeles Free Press, Inc. v. Los Angeles,* 9 Cal. App.3d 448, 88 Cal.Rptr. 605 (1970) (exclusion of weekly newspaper from scenes of disaster and police press conferences upheld when newspaper did not report police and fire events "with some regularity"). When access is required, may the press be prevented from taking notes? Is the right to bring tape recorders into public trials protected under *Richmond Newspapers?* What about "unobtrusive" television cameras? Consider Charles Ares, *Chandler v. Florida: Television, Criminal Trials, and Due Process,* 1981 Sup.Ct.Rev. 157, 174: "Television in the courtroom expands public access to public institutions both qualitatively, because of its immediacy, and quantitatively, because of its reach. It is reported that a majority of Americans acquire their news primarily from television rather than from newspapers. To exclude the most important source of information about the working of courts without some compelling reason cannot be squared with the First Amendment." Cf. *Chandler v. Florida,* 449 U.S. 560, 101 S.Ct. 802, 66 L.Ed.2d 740 (1981) (subject to certain safeguards a state may *permit* electronic media and still photography coverage of public criminal proceedings over the objection of the accused).

Does *Chandler's* holding demean the interest in fair trials? Consider Griswold, *The Standards of the Legal Profession: Canon 35 Should Not Be Surrendered,* 48 A.B.A.J. 615, 617 (1962): "The presence of cameras and television [has] an inhibiting effect on some people, and an exhilarating effect on others. In either event, there would be distortion, and an inevitable interference with the administration of justice. With all the improved techniques in the world, the introduction of radio and television to the courtroom will surely and naturally convert it into a stage for those who can act, and into a place of additional burden for those who cannot." Do these objections apply with the same force to appellate proceedings?[g] Consider Yale Kamisar, *Chandler v. Florida: What Can Be Said for a "Right of Access" to Televise Judicial Proceedings?* in Jesse Choper, Yale Kamisar, & Laurence Tribe, The Supreme Court: Trends and Developments 1980–81, at 149, 168 (1982): "At the present time, no federal court allows TV coverage. *The place to begin* may well be the place that is likely to be the last holdout—the United States Supreme Court."

g. See Ares, supra, at 189–90.

SECTION 7. GOVERNMENT PROPERTY AND THE PUBLIC FORUM [a]

The case law treating the question of when persons can speak on public property has come to be known as public forum doctrine. But "[t]he public forum saga began, and very nearly ended," Geoffrey Stone, *Fora Americana: Speech in Public Places,* 1974 Sup.Ct.Rev. 233, 236, with an effort by Holmes, J., then on the Supreme Judicial Court of Massachusetts, "to solve a difficult first amendment problem by simplistic resort to a common-law concept," Vincent Blasi, *Prior Restraints on Demonstrations,* 68 Mich.L.Rev. 1482, 1484 (1970). For holding religious meetings on the Boston Common, a preacher was convicted under an ordinance prohibiting "any public address" upon publicly-owned property without a permit from the mayor. In upholding the permit ordinance Holmes, J., observed: "For the legislature absolutely or conditionally to forbid public speaking in a highway or public park is no more an infringement of rights of a member of the public than for the owner of a private house to forbid it in the house." *Massachusetts v. Davis,* 162 Mass. 510, 511, 39 N.E. 113, 113 (1895). On appeal, a unanimous Supreme Court adopted the Holmes position, 167 U.S. 43, 17 S.Ct. 731, 42 L.Ed. 71 (1897): "[T]he right to absolutely exclude all right to use [public property], necessarily includes the authority to determine under what circumstances such use may be availed of, as the greater power contains the lesser."

This view survived until *Hague v. CIO,* 307 U.S. 496, 59 S.Ct. 954, 83 L.Ed. 1423 (1939), which rejected Jersey City's claim that its ordinance requiring a permit for an open air meeting was justified by the "plenary power" rationale of *Davis.* In rejecting the implications of the *Davis* dictum, Roberts, J., in a plurality opinion, uttered a famous "counter dictum," which has played a central role in the evolution of public forum theory: "Wherever the title of streets and parks may rest, they have immemorially been held in trust for the use of the public and, time out of mind, have been used for purposes of assembly, communicating thoughts between citizens, and discussing public questions. Such use of the streets and public places has, from ancient times, been a part of the privileges, immunities, rights, and liberties of citizens. [This privilege of a citizen] is not absolute, but relative, and must be exercised in subordination to the general comfort and convenience, and in consonance with peace and good order; but it must not, in the guise of regulation, be abridged or denied." Eight months later, the *Hague* dictum was given impressive content by Roberts, J., for the Court, in *Schneider* infra.

I. FOUNDATION CASES

A. MANDATORY ACCESS

SCHNEIDER v. IRVINGTON, 308 U.S. 147, 60 S.Ct. 146, 84 L.Ed. 155 (1939), per ROBERTS, J., invalidated several ordinances prohibiting leafleting on public streets or other public places: "Municipal authorities, as trustees for the public, have the duty to keep their communities' streets open and available for movement of people and property, the primary purpose to which the streets are dedicated. So long as legislation to this end does not abridge the constitutional liberty of one rightfully upon the street to impart information through speech or the distribution of literature, it may lawfully regulate the conduct of those using

---

a. For treatment of the related question whether, and if so under what circumstances, there is a first amendment right of access to privately-owned facilities, such as shopping centers, see *Marsh v. Alabama,* p. 1323 infra; *Hudgens v. NLRB,* p. 1324 infra; *PruneYard Shopping Center v. Robins,* p. 873 infra.

the streets. For example, a person could not exercise this liberty by taking his stand in the middle of a crowded street, contrary to traffic regulations, and maintain his position to the stoppage of all traffic; a group of distributors could not insist upon a constitutional right to form a cordon across the street and to allow no pedestrian to pass who did not accept a tendered leaflet; nor does the guarantee of freedom of speech or of the press deprive a municipality of power to enact regulations against throwing literature broadcast in the streets. Prohibition of such conduct would not abridge the constitutional liberty since such activity bears no necessary relationship to the freedom to speak, write, print or distribute information or opinion. * * *

"In *Lovell* [p. 757 supra] this court held void an ordinance which forbade the distribution by hand or otherwise of literature of any kind without written permission from the city manager. [Similarly] in *Hague v. C.I.O.*, an ordinance was held void on its face because it provided for previous administrative censorship of the exercise of the right of speech and assembly in appropriate public places. "The [ordinances] under review do not purport to license distribution but all of them absolutely prohibit it in the streets and, one of them, in other public places as well.

"The motive of the legislation under attack in Numbers 13, 18 and 29 is held by the courts below to be the prevention of littering of the streets and, although the alleged offenders were not charged with themselves scattering paper in the streets, their convictions were sustained upon the theory that distribution by them encouraged or resulted in such littering. We are of opinion that the purpose to keep the streets clean and of good appearance is insufficient to justify an ordinance which prohibits a person rightfully on a public street from handing literature to one willing to receive it. Any burden imposed upon the city authorities in cleaning and caring for the streets as an indirect consequence of such distribution results from the constitutional protection of the freedom of speech and press. This constitutional protection does not deprive a city of all power to prevent street littering. There are obvious methods of preventing littering. Amongst these is the punishment of those who actually throw papers on the streets.

"It is suggested that [the] ordinances are valid because their operation is limited to streets and alleys and leaves persons free to distribute printed matter in other public places. But, as we have said, the streets are natural and proper places for the dissemination of information and opinion; and one is not to have the exercise of his liberty of expression in appropriate places abridged on the plea that it may be exercised in some other place."

McREYNOLDS, J., "is of opinion that the judgment in each case should be affirmed."

Notes and Questions

1. *Leaflets and the streets as public forum.* Consider Harry Kalven, *The Concept of the Public Forum: Cox v. Louisiana*, 1965 S.Ct.Rev. 1, 18 & 21: "Leaflet distribution in public places in a city is a method of communication that carries as an inextricable and expected consequence substantial littering of the streets, which the city has an obligation to keep clean. It is also a method of communication of some annoyance to a majority of people so addressed; that its impact on its audience is very high is doubtful. Yet the constitutional balance in *Schneider* was struck emphatically in favor of keeping the public forum open for this mode of communication. "[The] operative theory of the Court, at least for

the leaflet situation, is that, although it is a method of communication that interferes with the public use of the streets, the right to the streets as a public forum is such that leaflet distribution cannot be prohibited and can be regulated only for weighty reasons."

2. *Litter prevention as a substantial interest.* Does the interest in distributing leaflets always outweigh the interest in preventing littering? Suppose helicopters regularly dropped tons of leaflets on the town of Irvington?

3. *Beyond leaflets.* COX v. NEW HAMPSHIRE, 312 U.S. 569, 61 S.Ct. 762, 85 L.Ed. 1049 (1941), per HUGHES, C.J., upheld convictions of sixty-eight Jehovah's Witnesses for parading without a permit. They had marched in four or five groups (with perhaps twenty others) along the sidewalk in single file carrying signs and handing out leaflets: "[T]he state court considered and defined the duty of the licensing authority and the rights of the appellants to a license for their parade, with regard only to consideration of time, place and manner so as to conserve the public convenience." The licensing procedure was said to "afford opportunity for proper policing" and " 'to prevent confusion by overlapping parades, [to] secure convenient use of the streets by other travelers, and to minimize the risk of disorder.' " A municipality "undoubtedly" has "authority to control the use of its public streets for parades or processions." But see C. Edwin Baker, *Unreasoned Reasonableness: Mandatory Parade Permits and Time, Place, and Manner Regulations,* 78 Nw.U.L.Rev. 937, 992 (1984): Approximately 26,000 people walked on the same sidewalks during the same hour the defendants in *Cox* "marched." "This single difference in what [the defendants] did—'marching in formation,' which they did for expressive purposes and which presumably is an 'assembly' that the first amendment protects—turned out to have crucial significance. This sole difference, engaging in first amendment protected conduct, made them guilty of a criminal offense. [Surely] something is wrong with this result."

4. *Charging for use of public forum. Cox* said there was nothing "contrary to the Constitution" in the exaction of a fee " 'incident to the administration of the [licensing] Act and to the maintenance of public order in the matter licensed.' " Could leafleters be charged for the costs of cleaning up litter? Controversial speakers for the expense of police protection? See generally David Goldberger, *A Reconsideration of Cox v. New Hampshire: Can Demonstrators Be Required to Pay the Costs of Using America's Public Forums?,* 62 Tex.L.Rev. 403 (1983); Blasi, *Demonstrations,* supra at 1527–32.

5. *Reasonable time, place, and manner regulations.* As *Cox* reveals, a right of access to a public forum does not guarantee immunity from reasonable time, place, and manner regulations. In HEFFRON v. INTERNATIONAL SOC. FOR KRISHNA CONSCIOUSNESS, 452 U.S. 640, 101 S.Ct. 2559, 69 L.Ed.2d 298 (1981), for example, the Court, per WHITE, J., upheld a state fair rule prohibiting the distribution of printed material or the solicitation of funds except from a duly licensed booth on the fairgrounds. The Court noted that consideration of a forum's special attributes is relevant to the determination of reasonableness, and the test of reasonableness is whether the restrictions "are justified without reference to the content of the regulated speech, that they serve a significant governmental interest, and that in doing so they leave open ample alternative channels for communication of the information" [a]

WARD v. ROCK AGAINST RACISM, 491 U.S. 781, 109 S.Ct. 2746, 105 L.Ed.2d 661 (1989), per KENNEDY, J., observes that "[E]ven in a public forum the

---

a. Brennan, J., joined by Marshall and Stevens, JJ., dissented in part as did Blackmun, J., in a separate opinion. Their dispute was not with the Court's test, but its application.

government may impose reasonable restrictions on the time, place, or manner of protected speech, provided the restrictions 'are justified without reference to the content of the regulated speech, that they are narrowly tailored to serve a significant governmental interest, and that they leave open ample alternative channels for communication of the information.' " The case reasserts that the *O'Brien* test is little different from the time, place, and manner test, and then states: "[A] regulation of the time, place, or manner of protected speech must be narrowly tailored to serve the government's legitimate content-neutral interests but [it] need not be the least-restrictive or least-intrusive means of doing so. Rather, the requirement of narrow tailoring is satisfied 'so long as [the] regulation promotes a substantial government interest that would be achieved less effectively absent the regulation.' To be sure, this standard does not mean that a time, place, or manner regulation may burden substantially more speech than is necessary to further the government's legitimate interests. Government may not regulate expression in such a manner that a substantial portion of the burden on speech does not serve to advance its goals.[7]" Marshall, J., dissenting, joined by Brennan and Stevens, JJ., complains of the Court's "serious distortion of the narrowly tailoring requirement" and states that the Court's rejection of the less restrictive alternative test relies on "language in a few opinions [taken] out of context." Should the time, place, and manner test be different from the *O'Brien* test? Is there any difference between those tests and the approach employed in *Schneider*?

B. EQUAL ACCESS

CHICAGO POLICE DEPT. v. MOSLEY, 408 U.S. 92, 92 S.Ct. 2286, 33 L.Ed.2d 212 (1972), invalidated an ordinance banning all picketing within 150 feet of a school building while the school is in session and one half-hour before and afterwards, except "the peaceful picketing of any school involved in a labor dispute." The suit was brought by a federal postal employee who, for seven months prior to enactment of the ordinance, had frequently picketed a high school in Chicago. "During school hours and usually by himself, Mosley would walk the public sidewalk adjoining the school, carrying a sign that read: 'Jones High School practices black discrimination. Jones High School has a black quota.' His lonely crusade was always peaceful, orderly, and [quiet]." The Court, per MARSHALL, J., viewed the ordinance as drawing "an impermissible distinction between labor picketing and other peaceful picketing": "The central problem with Chicago's ordinance is that it describes permissible picketing in terms of its subject matter. Peaceful picketing on the subject of a school's labor-management dispute is permitted, but all other peaceful picketing is prohibited. The operative distinction is the message on a picket sign. But, above all else, the First Amendment means that government has no power to restrict expression because of its message, its ideas, its subject matter, or its content.

"[U]nder the Equal Protection Clause, not to mention the First Amendment itself,[a] government may not grant the use of a forum to people whose views it

7. A ban on handbilling, of course, would suppress a great quantity of speech that does not cause the evils that it seeks to eliminate, whether they be fraud, crime, litter, traffic congestion, or noise. For that reason, a complete ban on handbilling would be substantially broader than necessary to achieve the interests justifying it.

a. *Consolidated Edison Co. v. Public Service Comm'n,* p. 931 infra, abandoned equal protection and cited *Mosley* as a first amendment case: "The First Amendment's hostility to content-based regulation extends not only to restrictions on particular viewpoints, but also to prohibition of public discussion of an entire

finds acceptable, but deny use to those wishing to express less favored or more controversial views. And it may not select which issues are worth discussing or debating in public facilities. There is an 'equality of status in the field of ideas,' and government must afford all points of view an equal opportunity to be heard. Once a forum is opened up to assembly or speaking by some groups, government may not prohibit others from assembling or speaking on the basis of what they intend to say. Selective exclusions from a public forum may not be based on content alone, and may not be justified by reference to content alone.

"[Not] all picketing must always be allowed. We have continually recognized that reasonable 'time, place and manner' regulations of picketing may be necessary to further significant governmental interests. Similarly, under an equal protection analysis, there may be sufficient regulatory interests justifying selective exclusions or distinctions among picketers. [But] [b]ecause picketing plainly involves expressive conduct within the protection of the First Amendment, discriminations among picketers must be tailored to serve a substantial governmental interest. In this case, the ordinance itself describes impermissible picketing not in terms of time, place and manner, but in terms of subject matter. The regulation 'thus slip[s] from the neutrality of time, place and circumstance into a concern about content.' This is never permitted. * * *

"Although preventing school disruption is a city's legitimate concern, Chicago itself has determined that peaceful labor picketing during school hours is not an undue interference with school. Therefore, under the Equal Protection clause, Chicago may not maintain that other picketing disrupts the school unless that picketing is clearly more disruptive than the picketing Chicago already permits. If peaceful labor picketing is permitted, there is no justification for prohibiting all nonlabor picketing, both peaceful and nonpeaceful. 'Peaceful' labor picketing, however the term 'peaceful' is defined, is obviously no less disruptive than 'peaceful' nonlabor picketing. But Chicago's ordinance permits the former and prohibits the latter.

"[We also] reject the city's argument that, although it permits peaceful labor picketing, it may prohibit all nonlabor picketing because, as a class, nonlabor picketing is more prone to produce violence than labor picketing. Predictions about imminent disruption from picketing involve judgments appropriately made on an individualized basis, not by means of broad classifications, especially those based on subject matter. Freedom of expression, and its intersection with the guarantee of equal protection, would rest on a soft foundation indeed if government could distinguish among picketers on such a wholesale and categorical basis. '[I]n our system, undifferentiated fear or apprehension of disturbance is not enough to overcome the right to freedom of expression.' *Tinker*. Some labor picketing is peaceful, some disorderly; the same is true for picketing on other themes. No labor picketing could be more peaceful or less prone to violence than Mosley's solitary vigil. In seeking to restrict nonlabor picketing which is clearly more disruptive than peaceful labor picketing, Chicago may not prohibit all nonlabor picketing at the school forum." [b]

Notes and Questions

1. Consider Kenneth Karst, *Equality as a Central Principle in the First Amendment*, 43 U.Chi.L.Rev. 20, 28 (1975): "*Mosley* is a landmark first amend-

topic." But see, e.g., *Minnesota State Board v. Knight*, 465 U.S. 271, 104 S.Ct. 1058, 79 L.Ed.2d 299 (1984) (stating that *Mosley* is an equal protection case).

[b] Burger, C.J., joined the Court's opinion, but also concurred. Blackmun and Rehnquist, JJ., concurred in the result.

ment decision. It makes two principal points: (1) the essence of the first amendment is its denial to government of the power to determine which messages shall be heard and which suppressed * * *. (2) Any 'time, place and manner' restriction that selectively excludes speakers from a public forum must survive careful judicial scrutiny to ensure that the exclusion is the minimum necessary to further a significant government interest. Taken together, these statements declare a principle of major importance. The Court has explicitly adopted the principle of equal liberty of expression. [The] principle requires courts to start from the assumption that all speakers and all points of view are entitled to a hearing, and permits deviation from this basic assumption only upon a showing of substantial necessity."

2. What if the *Mosley* ordinance had not excepted labor picketing, but had banned *all* picketing within 150 feet of a school during school hours? Consider Karst 37–38: "The burden of this restriction would fall most heavily on those who have something to communicate to the school [population]. Student picketers presenting a grievance against a principal, or striking custodians with a message growing out of a labor dispute, would be affected more seriously by this ostensibly content-neutral ordinance than would, say the proponents of a candidate for Governor [who could just as effectively carry their message elsewhere]. This differential impact amounts to de facto content discrimination, presumptively invalid under the first amendment equality principle. "[The city faces] an apparent dilemma. [If it] bars all picketing within a certain area, it will effectively discriminate against those groups that can communicate to their audience only by picketing within that area. But if the city adjusts its ordinance to this differential impact, as by providing a student-picketing or labor-picketing exemption, [it runs] afoul of *Mosley* itself. The city can avoid the dilemma by amending the ordinance to ban not all picketing but only noisy picketing." [c]

3. Does equality fully explain the special concern with content regulation? Consider Geoffrey Stone, *Content Regulation and the First Amendment*, 25 Wm. & Mary L.Rev. 189, 207 (1983): "The problem, quite simply, is that restrictions on expression are rife with 'inequalities,' many of which have nothing whatever to do with content. The ordinance at issue in *Mosley,* for example, restricted picketing near schools, but left unrestricted picketing near hospitals, libraries, courthouses, and private homes. The ordinance at issue in *Erznoznik* restricted drive-in theaters that are visible from a public street, but did not restrict billboards. [Whatever] the effect of these content-neutral inequalities on first amendment analysis, they are not scrutinized in the same way as content-based inequalities. Not all inequalities, in other words, are equal. And although the concern with equality may support the content-based/content-neutral distinction, it does not in itself have much explanatory power."

Is the concern with content discrimination explainable because of concerns about communicative impact, distortion of public debate, or government motivation? See generally Stone, supra. See also sources cited in notes 1 & 2 after *O'Brien*, Sec. 4 supra and Ronald Cass, *First Amendment Access to Government Facilities*, 65 Va.L.Rev. 1287, 1323–25 (1979); Paul Stephan, *The First Amendment and Content Discrimination*, 68 Va.L.Rev. 203 (1982); Geoffrey Stone, *Restrictions of Speech Because of its Content: The Peculiar Case of Subject-Matter Restrictions*, 46 U.Chi.L.Rev. 81 (1978).

c. As Professor Karst notes, such an ordinance was upheld in *Grayned v. Rockford,* 408 U.S. 104, 92 S.Ct. 2294, 33 L.Ed.2d 222 (1972), the companion case to *Mosley.*

4. An Illinois statute prohibited picketing residences or dwellings—except when the dwelling is "used as a place of business," or is "a place of employment involved in a labor dispute or the place of holding a meeting [on] premises commonly used to discuss subjects of general public interest," or when a "person is picketing his own [dwelling]. Can a conviction for picketing the Mayor of Chicago's home be upheld? Is *Mosley* distinguishable? See *Carey v. Brown*, 447 U.S. 455, 100 S.Ct. 2286, 65 L.Ed.2d 263 (1980).

II. NEW FORUMS

Are first amendment rights on government property confined to streets and parks? "[W]hat about other publicly owned property, ranging from the grounds surrounding a public building, to the inside of a welfare office, publicly run bus, or library, to a legislative gallery?" Stone, *Fora Americana*, supra, at 245.

INTERNATIONAL SOCIETY FOR KRISHNA CONSCIOUSNESS, INC. v. LEE

505 U.S. 672, 112 S.Ct. 2701, 120 L.Ed.2d 541 (1992).

CHIEF JUSTICE REHNQUIST delivered the opinion of the Court.

* * * Petitioner International Society for Krishna Consciousness, Inc. (ISK-CON) is a not-for-profit religious corporation whose members perform a ritual known as sankirtan. The ritual consists of " 'going into public places, disseminating religious literature and soliciting funds to support the religion.' " The primary purpose of this ritual is raising funds for the movement.

Respondent [was] the police superintendent of the Port Authority of New York and New Jersey and was charged with enforcing the regulation at issue. The Port Authority owns and operates three major airports in the greater New York City area [which] collectively form one of the world's busiest metropolitan airport complexes. By decade's end they are expected to serve at least 110 million passengers annually. * * *

The Port Authority has adopted a regulation forbidding within the terminals the repetitive solicitation of money or distribution of literature [but] permits solicitation and distribution on the sidewalks outside the terminal buildings. The regulation effectively prohibits petitioner from performing sankirtan in the terminals. * * *

It is uncontested that the solicitation at issue in this case is a form of speech protected under the First Amendment.[3] But it is also well settled that the government need not permit all forms of speech on property that it owns and controls.

United States Postal Service v. Council of Greenburgh Civic Assns., 453 U.S. 114, 129, 101 S.Ct. 2676, 2685, 69 L.Ed.2d 517 (1981); [a] *Greer v. Spock*, 424 U.S. 828, 96 S.Ct. 1211, 47 L.Ed.2d 505 (1976).[b] Where the government is acting as a

---

3. We deal here only with ISKCON's petition raising the permissibility of solicitation. Respondent's cross-petition concerning the leafletting ban is disposed of in the companion case, *Lee v. International Society for Krishna Consciousness, Inc.*, 91–339 [p. 906 *infra*].

a. *Greenburgh* held that the post office could prevent individuals from placing unstamped material in residential mail boxes.

b. *Greer* held that the military could bar a presidential candidate from speaking on a military base even though members of the public were free to visit the base, the President had spoken on the base, and other speakers (e.g.,

proprietor, managing its internal operations, rather than acting as lawmaker with the power to regulate or license, its action will not be subjected to the heightened review to which its actions as a lawmaker may be subject. Thus, we have upheld a ban on political advertisements in city-operated transit vehicles, *Lehman v. City of Shaker Heights,* 418 U.S. 298, 94 S.Ct. 2714, 41 L.Ed.2d 770 (1974), even though the city permitted other types of advertising on those vehicles. Similarly, we have permitted a school district to limit access to an internal mail system used to communicate with teachers employed by the district. *Perry Education Assn. v. Perry Local Educators' Ass'n,* 460 U.S. 37, 103 S.Ct. 948, 74 L.Ed.2d 794 (1983).[c]

These cases reflect, either implicitly or explicitly, a "forum-based" approach for assessing restrictions that the government seeks to place on the use of its property. *Cornelius v. NAACP Legal Defense and Educational Fund, Inc.,* 473 U.S. 788, 800, 105 S.Ct. 3439, 3448, 87 L.Ed.2d 567 (1985).[d] Under this approach, regulation of speech on government property that has traditionally been available for public expression is subject to the highest scrutiny. Such regulations survive only if they are narrowly drawn to achieve a compelling state interest. *Perry.* The second category of public property is the designated public forum, whether of a limited or unlimited character—property that the state has opened for expressive activity by part or all of the public. *Id.*[e] Regulation of such property is subject to the same limitations as that governing a traditional public forum. Finally, there is all remaining public property. Limitations on expressive activity conducted on this last category of property must survive only a much more limited review. The challenged regulation need only be reasonable, as long as the regulation is not an effort to suppress the speaker's activity due to disagreement with the speaker's view.

entertainers and anti-drug speakers) had spoken by invitation on the base.

c. *Perry* held it permissible to deny access to the mailboxes for a competing union despite permitting access for the duly elected union and access for various community groups such as the cub scouts, the YMCA, and other civic and church organizations. *Mosley* and *Carey* were distinguished: "[The] key to those decisions [was] the presence of a public forum." Compare *Lamb's Chapel v. Center Moriches Union Free School Dist.,* 508 U.S. 384, 113 S.Ct. 2141, 124 L.Ed.2d 352 (1993) (school could not exclude religious groups from access to school property for after school meetings so long as it held the property generally open for meetings by social, civic, and recreation groups).

d. *Cornelius* upheld an executive order that included organizations providing direct health and welfare services to individuals or their families in a charity drive in the federal workplace while excluding legal defense and political advocacy organizations.

A 4–3 majority, per O'Connor, J., determined that "government does not create a public forum by inaction or by permitting limited discourse, but only by intentionally opening a non-traditional forum for public discourse." Observing that the Court will look to the policy and practice of the government, the nature of

the property and its compatibility with expressive activity in discerning intent, O'Connor, J., insisted that "we will not find that a public forum has been created in the face of clear evidence of a contrary intent, nor will we infer that the Government intended to create a public forum when the nature of the property is inconsistent with expressive activity."

Blackmun, J., dissented: "If the Government does not create a limited public forum unless it intends to provide an 'open forum' for expressive activity, and if the exclusion of some speakers is evidence that the Government did not intend to create such a forum, no speaker challenging denial of access will ever be able to prove that the forum is a limited public forum. The very fact that the Government denied access to the speaker indicates that the Government did not intend to provide an open forum for expressive activity, and [that] fact alone would demonstrate that the forum is not a limited public forum."

e. In interpreting this approach, *Perry* also stated in footnote 7 that: "a public forum may be created for a limited purpose such as use by certain groups, e.g., *Widmar v. Vincent* [p. 966 infra] (student groups), or for the discussion of certain subjects, e.g., *City of Madison Joint School District v. Wisconsin Pub. Employ. Relat. Comm'n,* 429 U.S. 167, 97 S.Ct. 421, 50 L.Ed.2d 376 (1976) (school board business).

[Our] precedents foreclose the conclusion that airport terminals are public fora. Reflecting the general growth of the air travel industry, airport terminals have only recently achieved their contemporary size and character. [Moreover,] even within the rather short history of air transport, it is only "[i]n recent years [that] it has become a common practice for various religious and non-profit organizations to use commercial airports as a forum for the distribution of literature, the solicitation of funds, the proselytizing of new members, and other similar activities." 45 Fed.Reg. 35314 (1980). Thus, the tradition of airport activity does not demonstrate that airports have historically been made available for speech activity. Nor can we say that these particular terminals, or airport terminals generally, have been intentionally opened by their operators to such activity; the frequent and continuing litigation evidencing the operators' objections belies any such claim. * * *

Petitioner attempts to circumvent the history and practice governing airport activity by pointing our attention to the variety of speech activity that it claims historically occurred at various "transportation nodes" such as rail stations, bus stations, wharves, and Ellis Island. Even if we were inclined to accept petitioner's historical account[,] we think that such evidence is of little import for two reasons. First, much of the evidence is irrelevant to *public* fora analysis, because sites such as bus and rail terminals traditionally have had *private* ownership. The development of privately owned parks that ban speech activity would not change the public fora status of publicly held parks. But the reverse is also true. The practices of privately held transportation centers do not bear on the government's regulatory authority over a publicly owned airport.

Second, the relevant unit for our inquiry is an airport, not "transportation nodes" generally. When new methods of transportation develop, new methods for accommodating that transportation are also likely to be needed. And with each new step, it therefore will be a new inquiry whether the transportation necessities are compatible with various kinds of expressive activity. [The] "security magnet," for example, is an airport commonplace that lacks a counterpart in bus terminals and train stations. And public access to air terminals is also not infrequently restricted—just last year the Federal Aviation Administration required airports for a 4–month period to limit access to areas normally publicly accessible. To blithely equate airports with other transportation centers, therefore, would be a mistake. [T]he record demonstrates that Port Authority management considers the purpose of the terminals to be the facilitation of passenger air travel, not the promotion of expression. Even if we look beyond the intent of the Port Authority to the manner in which the terminals have been operated, the terminals have never been dedicated (except under the threat of court order) to expression in the form sought to be exercised [here]. Thus, we think that neither by tradition nor purpose can the terminals be described as satisfying the standards we have previously set out for identifying a public forum.

The restrictions here challenged, therefore, need only satisfy a requirement of reasonableness. * * *

We have on many prior occasions noted the disruptive effect that solicitation may have on business. "Solicitation requires action by those who would respond: The individual solicited must decide whether or not to contribute (which itself might involve reading the solicitor's literature or hearing his pitch), and then, having decided to do so, reach for a wallet, search it for money, write a check, or produce a credit card." *Kokinda.* Passengers who wish to avoid the solicitor may have to alter their path, slowing both themselves and those around them. The result is that the normal flow of traffic is impeded. This is especially so in an airport, where "air travelers, who are often weighted down by cumbersome baggage [may] be hurrying to catch a plane or to arrange ground transportation." Delays may be particularly costly in this setting, as a flight missed by only a few minutes can result in hours worth of subsequent inconvenience.

In addition, face to face solicitation presents risks of duress that are an appropriate target of regulation. The skillful, and unprincipled, solicitor can target the most vulnerable, including those accompanying children or those suffering physical impairment and who cannot easily avoid the solicitation. The unsavory solicitor can also commit fraud through concealment of his affiliation or through deliberate efforts to shortchange those who agree to purchase. Compounding this problem is the fact that, in an airport, the targets of such activity frequently are on tight schedules. This in turn makes such visitors unlikely to stop and formally complain to airport authorities. As a result, the airport faces considerable difficulty in achieving its legitimate interest in monitoring solicitation activity to assure that travelers are not interfered with unduly.

[T]he sidewalk areas outside the terminals [are] frequented by an overwhelming percentage of airport users. [W]e think it would be odd to conclude that the Port Authority's terminal regulation is unreasonable despite the Port Authority having otherwise assured access to an area universally traveled. * * *

Moreover, "[if] petitioner is given access, so too must other groups. "Obviously, there would be a much larger threat to the State's interest in crowd control if all other religious, nonreligious, and noncommercial organizations could likewise move freely." As a result, we conclude that the solicitation ban is reasonable. * * *

Justice O'Connor, concurring in 91–155 [on the solicitation issue] and concurring in the judgment in 91–339 [on the distribution of literature issue]. * * *

I concur in the Court's opinion in No. 91–155 and agree that publicly owned airports are not public fora.

[This], however, does not mean that the government can restrict speech in whatever way it likes. * * *

"The reasonableness of the Government's restriction [on speech in a nonpublic forum] must be assessed in light of the purpose of the forum and all the surrounding circumstances." *Cornelius.* " '[C]onsideration of a forum's special attributes is relevant to the constitutionality of a regulation since the significance of the governmental interest must be assessed in light of the characteristic nature and function of the particular forum involved.' " *Kokinda.* In this case, the "special attributes" and "surrounding circumstances" of the airports operated by the Port Authority are determinative. Not only has the Port Authority chosen *not* to limit access to the airports under its control, it has created a huge complex open to travelers and nontravelers alike. The airports house restaurants, cafeterias, snack bars, coffee shops, cocktail lounges, post offices, banks, telegraph offices, clothing shops, drug stores, food stores, nurseries, barber shops, currency exchanges, art exhibits, commercial advertising displays, bookstores, newsstands, dental offices and private clubs. The International Arrivals Building at JFK Airport even has two branches of Bloomingdale's.

We have said that a restriction on speech in a nonpublic forum is "reasonable" when it is "consistent with the [government's] legitimate interest in 'preserv[ing] the property [for] the use to which it is lawfully dedicated.' " *Perry.* [The] reasonableness inquiry, therefore, is not whether the restrictions on speech are "consistent [with] preserving the property" for air travel, but whether they are reasonably related to maintaining the multipurpose environment that the Port Authority has deliberately created.

Applying that standard, I agree with the Court in No. 91–155 that the ban on solicitation is reasonable.   * * *

In my view, however, the regulation banning leafletting [cannot] be upheld as reasonable on this record. I therefore concur in the judgment in No. 91–339 striking down that prohibition. [W]e have expressly noted that leafletting does not entail the same kinds of problems presented by face-to-face solicitation. Specifically, "[o]ne need not ponder the contents of a leaflet or pamphlet in order mechanically to take it out of someone's [hand]. 'The distribution of literature does not require that the recipient stop in order to receive the message the speaker wishes to convey; instead the recipient is free to read the message at a later time.' " With the possible exception of avoiding litter, it is difficult to point to any problems intrinsic to the act of leafletting that would make it naturally incompatible with a large, multipurpose forum such as those at issue here.   * * *

Moreover, the Port Authority has not offered any justifications or record evidence to support its ban on the distribution of pamphlets alone. Its argument is focused instead on the problems created when literature is distributed in conjunction with a solicitation plea. Although we do not "requir[e] [that] proof be present to justify the denial of access to a nonpublic forum on grounds that the proposed use may disrupt the property's intended function," *Perry*, we have required some explanation as to why certain speech is inconsistent with the intended use of the forum.   * * *

Of course, it is still open for the Port Authority to promulgate regulations of the time, place, and manner of leafletting which are "content-neutral, narrowly tailored to serve a significant government interest, and leave open ample alternative channels of communication." For example, during the many years that this litigation has been in progress, the Port Authority has not banned sankirtan completely from JFK International Airport, but has restricted it to a relatively uncongested part of the airport terminals, the same part that houses the airport chapel. In my view, that regulation meets the standards we have applied * * *.

JUSTICE KENNEDY, with whom JUSTICE BLACKMUN, JUSTICE STEVENS, and JUSTICE SOUTER join as to Part I, concurring in the judgment.

I. [The Court] leaves the government with almost unlimited authority to restrict speech on its property by doing nothing more than articulating a non-speech-related purpose for the area, and it leaves almost no scope for the development of new public forums absent the rare approval of the government. The Court's error [in] analysis is a classification of the property that turns on the government's own definition or decision, unconstrained by an independent duty to respect the speech its citizens can voice there. The Court acknowledges as much, by reintroducing today into our First Amendment law a strict doctrinal line between the proprietary and regulatory functions of government which I thought had been abandoned long ago. *Schneider; Grayned v. Rockford,* 408 U.S. 104, 92 S.Ct. 2294, 33 L.Ed.2d 222 (1972).[f]

f. *Grayned* stated that: "The crucial question is whether the manner of expression is basically incompatible with the normal activity of a particular place at a particular time." Applying that test, the Court held constitutional an ordinance forbidding the making of noise which disturbs or tends to disturb the peace or good order of a school session.

[Public] places are of necessity the locus for discussion of public issues, as well as protest against arbitrary government action. At the heart of our jurisprudence lies the principle that in a free nation citizens must have the right to gather and speak with other persons in public places. The recognition that certain government-owned property is a public forum provides open notice to citizens that their freedoms may be exercised there without fear of a censorial government, adding tangible reinforcement to the idea that we are a free people. * * *

The Court's analysis rests on an inaccurate view of history. The notion that traditional public forums are property which have public discourse as their principal purpose is a most doubtful fiction. The types of property that we have recognized as the quintessential public forums are streets, parks, and sidewalks. It would seem apparent that the principal purpose of streets and sidewalks, like airports, is to facilitate transportation, not public discourse. [Similarly,] the purpose for the creation of public parks may be as much for beauty and open space as for discourse. Thus under the Court's analysis, even the quintessential public forums would appear to lack the necessary elements of what the Court defines as a public forum. * * *

One of the places left in our mobile society that is suitable for discourse is a metropolitan airport [because] in these days an airport is one of the few government-owned spaces where many persons have extensive contact with other members of the public. Given that private spaces of similar character are not subject to the dictates of the First Amendment, it is critical that we preserve these areas for protected speech. [If] the objective, physical characteristics of the property at issue and the actual public access and uses which have been permitted by the government indicate that expressive activity would be appropriate and compatible with those uses, the property is a public forum. [The] possibility of some theoretical inconsistency between expressive activities and the property's uses should not bar a finding of a public forum, if those inconsistencies can be avoided through simple and permitted regulations.

The second category of the Court's jurisprudence, the so-called designated forum, provides little, if any, additional protection for speech. [I] do not quarrel with the fact that speech must often be restricted on property of this kind to retain the purpose for which it has been designated. And I recognize that when property has been designated for a particular expressive use, the government may choose to eliminate that designation. But this increases the need to protect speech in other places, where discourse may occur free of such restrictions. In some sense the government always retains authority to close a public forum, by selling the property, changing its physical character, or changing its principal use. Otherwise the State would be prohibited from closing a park, or eliminating a street or sidewalk, which no one has understood the public forum doctrine to require. The difference is that when property is a protected public forum the State may not by fiat assert broad control over speech or expressive activities; it must alter the objective physical character or uses of the property, and bear the attendant costs, to change the property's forum status.

Under this analysis, it is evident that the public spaces of the Port Authority's airports are public forums. First, the District Court made detailed findings [that] show that the public spaces in the airports are broad, public thoroughfares full of people and lined with stores and other commercial activities. An airport corridor is of course not a street, but that is not the proper inquiry. The question is one of physical similarities, sufficient to suggest that the airport corridor should be a public forum for the same reasons that streets and sidewalks have been treated as public forums by the people who use them.

Second, the airport areas involved here are open to the public without restriction. Plaintiffs do not seek access to the secured areas of the airports, nor do I suggest that these areas would be public forums. And while most people who come to the Port Authority's airports do so for a reason related to air travel, [this] does not distinguish an airport from streets or sidewalks, which most people use for travel. * * *

Third, and perhaps most important, it is apparent from the record, and from the recent history of airports, that when adequate time, place, and manner regulations are in place, expressive activity is quite compatible with the uses of major airports. The Port Authority [argues] that the problem of congestion in its airports' corridors makes expressive activity inconsistent with the airports' primary purpose, which is to facilitate air travel. The First Amendment is often inconvenient. But that is besides the point. Inconvenience does not absolve the government of its obligation to tolerate speech. * * *

[A] grant of plenary power allows the government to tilt the dialogue heard by the public, to exclude many, more marginal voices. [We] have long recognized that the right to distribute flyers and literature lies at the heart of the liberties guaranteed by the Speech and Press Clauses of the First Amendment. The Port Authority's rule, which prohibits almost all such activity, is among the most restrictive possible of those liberties. The regulation is in fact so broad and restrictive of speech, Justice O'Connor finds it void even under the standards applicable to government regulations in nonpublic forums. I have no difficulty deciding the regulation cannot survive the far more stringent rules applicable to regulations in public forums. The regulation is not drawn in narrow terms and it does not leave open ample alternative channels for communication. * * *

II. It is my view, however, that the Port Authority's ban on the "solicitation and receipt of funds" [may] be upheld as either a reasonable time, place, and manner restriction, or as a regulation directed at the nonspeech element of expressive conduct. The two standards have considerable overlap in a case like this one. * * *

I am in full agreement with the statement of the Court that solicitation is a form of protected speech. If the Port Authority's solicitation regulation prohibited all speech which requested the contribution of funds, I would conclude that it was a direct, content-based restriction of speech in clear violation of the First Amendment. The Authority's regulation does not prohibit all solicitation, however; it prohibits the "solicitation and receipt of funds." [It] reaches only personal solicitations for immediate payment of money. [The] regulation does not cover, for example, the distribution of preaddressed envelopes along with a plea to contribute money to the distributor or his organization. As I understand the restriction it is directed only at the physical exchange of money, which is an element of conduct interwoven with otherwise expressive solicitation.

[T]he government interest in regulating the sales of literature[, however,] is not as powerful as in the case of solicitation. The danger of a fraud arising from such sales is much more limited than from pure solicitation, because in the case of a sale the nature of the exchange tends to be clearer to both parties. Also, the Port Authority's sale regulation is not as narrowly drawn as the solicitation rule, since it does not specify the receipt of money as a critical element of a violation. And perhaps most important, the flat ban on sales of literature leaves open fewer alternative channels of communication than the Port Authority's more limited prohibition on the solicitation and receipt of funds. Given the practicalities and ad hoc nature of much expressive activity in the public forum, sales of literature must be completed in one transaction to be workable. Attempting to collect money at another time or place is a far less plausible option in the context of a sale than when soliciting donations, because the literature sought to be sold will under normal circumstances be distributed within the forum. * * *

Against all of this must be balanced the great need, recognized by our precedents, to give the sale of literature full First Amendment protection. We have long recognized that to prohibit distribution of literature for the mere reason that it is sold would leave organizations seeking to spread their message without funds to operate. "It should be remembered that the pamphlets of Thomas Paine were not distributed free of charge." *Murdock v. Pennsylvania,* 319 U.S. 105, 63 S.Ct. 870, 87 L.Ed. 1292 (1943). The effect of a rule of law distinguishing between sales and distribution would be to close the marketplace of ideas to less affluent organizations and speakers, leaving speech as the preserve of those who are able to fund themselves. One of the primary purposes of the public forum is to provide persons who lack access to more sophisticated media the opportunity to speak. [And] while the same arguments might be made regarding solicitation of funds, the answer is that the Port Authority has not prohibited all solicitation, but only a narrow class of conduct associated with a particular manner of solicitation. * * *

JUSTICE SOUTER, with whom JUSTICE BLACKMUN and JUSTICE STEVENS join, concurring in the judgment in No. 91–339 [on the distribution of literature issue] and dissenting in No. 91–155 [on the solicitation issue].

[R]espondent comes closest to justifying the [total ban on solicitation of money for immediate payment] as one furthering the government's interest in preventing coercion and fraud.[1] [While] a solicitor can be insistent, a pedestrian on the street or airport concourse can simply walk [away]. Since there is here no evidence of any type of coercive conduct, over and above the merely importunate character of the open and public solicitation, that might justify a ban, the regulation cannot be sustained to avoid coercion.

As for fraud, our cases do not provide government with plenary authority to ban solicitation just because it could be [fraudulent.] The evidence of fraudulent conduct here is virtually nonexistent. It consists of one affidavit describing eight complaints, none of them substantiated, "involving some form of fraud, deception, or larceny" over an entire 11–year period between 1975 and 1986, during which the regulation at issue here was, by agreement, not enforced. [B]y the Port Authority's own calculation, there has not been a single claim of fraud or misrepresentation since 1981. * * *

---

1. Respondent also attempts to justify its regulation on the alternative basis of "interference with air travelers," referring in particular to problems of "annoyance," and "congestion." The First Amendment inevitably requires people to put up with annoyance and uninvited persuasion. Indeed, in such cases we need to scrutinize restrictions on speech with special care. In their degree of congestion, most of the public spaces of these airports are probably more comparable to public streets than to the fairground as we described it in *Heffron.* Consequently, the congestion argument, which was held there to justify a regulation confining solicitation to a fixed location, should have less force here. Be that as it may, the conclusion of a majority of the Court today that the Constitution forbids the ban on the sale [Ed. Does the majority of the Court conclude that the Constitution forbids the ban on the *sale* of literature?] as well as the distribution, of leaflets puts to rest respondent's argument that congestion justifies a total ban on solicitation. While there may, of course, be congested locations where solicitation could severely compromise the efficient flow of pedestrians, the proper response would be to tailor the restrictions to those choke points.

Even assuming a governmental interest adequate to justify some regulation, the present ban would fall when subjected to the requirement of narrow tailoring. Thus, in *Schaumburg v. Citizens for a Better Environment,* 444 U.S. 620, 100 S.Ct. 826, 63 L.Ed.2d 73 (1980), we said: "The Village's legitimate interest in preventing fraud can be better served by measures less intrusive than a direct prohibition on solicitation. Fraudulent misrepresentations can be prohibited and the penal laws used to punish such conduct directly."

[Finally,] I do not think the Port Authority's solicitation ban leaves open the "ample" channels of communication required of a valid content-neutral time, place and manner restriction. A distribution of preaddressed envelopes is unlikely to be much of an alternative. The practical reality of the regulation, which this Court can never ignore, is that it shuts off a uniquely powerful avenue of communication for organizations like the International Society for Krishna Consciousness, and may, in effect, completely prohibit unpopular and poorly funded groups from receiving funds in response to protected solicitation. * * *

LEE v. INTERNATIONAL SOCIETY FOR KRISHNA CONSCIOUSNESS, INC.

505 U.S. 830, 112 S.Ct. 2709, 120 L.Ed.2d 669 (1992).

PER CURIAM.

For the reasons expressed in the opinions of Justice O'Connor, Justice Kennedy, and Justice Souter in *ISKCON v. Lee,* the judgment of the Court of Appeals holding that the ban on distribution of literature in the Port Authority airport terminals is invalid under the First Amendment is affirmed.

CHIEF JUSTICE REHNQUIST, with whom JUSTICE WHITE, JUSTICE SCALIA and JUSTICE THOMAS join, dissenting.

Leafletting [must] be evaluated against a backdrop of the substantial congestion problem facing the Port Authority and with an eye to the cumulative impact that will result if all groups are permitted terminal access. Viewed in this light, I conclude that the distribution ban, no less than the solicitation ban, is reasonable.

[The] weary, harried, or hurried traveler may have no less desire and need to avoid the delays generated by having literature foisted upon him than he does to avoid delays from a financial solicitation. And while a busy passenger perhaps may succeed in fending off a leafletter with minimal disruption to himself by agreeing simply to take the proffered material, this does not completely ameliorate the dangers of congestion flowing from such leafletting. Others may choose not simply to accept the material but also to stop and engage the leafletter in debate, obstructing those who follow. Moreover, those who accept material may often simply drop it on the floor once out of the leafletter's range, creating an eyesore, a safety hazard, and additional cleanup work for airport staff. See *Los Angeles City Council v. Taxpayers for Vincent,* 466 U.S. 789, 104 S.Ct. 2118, 80 L.Ed.2d 772 (1984) (aesthetic interests may provide basis for restricting speech).

[Under] the regime that is today sustained, the Port Authority is obliged to permit leafletting. But monitoring leafletting activity in order to ensure that it is *only* leafletting that occurs, and not also soliciting, may prove little less burdensome than the monitoring that would be required if solicitation were permitted. At a minimum, therefore, I think it remains open whether at some future date the Port Authority may be able to reimpose a complete ban, having developed evidence that enforcement of a differential ban is overly burdensome. * * *

Notes and Questions

1. In order to prevent voter intimidation and election fraud, Tennessee prohibits the soliciting of votes and the display or distribution of campaign materials within 100 feet of the entrance to a polling place. Is the campaign-free zone, a public forum? Is the permitting of charitable or religious speech (including solicitation) or commercial speech while banning election speech (but not exit polling) impermissible content discrimination?

BURSON v. FREEMAN, 504 U.S. 191, 112 S.Ct. 1846, 119 L.Ed.2d 5 (1992) upheld the statute. BLACKMUN, J., joined by Rehnquist, C.J., and White and Kennedy, JJ., argued that the 100 foot zone was a public forum, that the regulation was based on the content of the speech, that the state was required to show that its statute was necessary to achieve a compelling state interest and narrowly drawn to achieve that end, and determined that this was the "rare case" in which strict scrutiny against content regulation could be satisfied: "There is [ample evidence] that political candidates have used campaign workers to commit voter intimidation or electoral fraud. In contrast, there is simply no evidence that political candidates have used other forms of solicitation or exit polling to commit such electoral abuses. [The] First Amendment does not require States to regulate for problems that do not exist. * * *

"Here, the State, as recognized administrator of elections, has asserted that the exercise of free speech rights conflicts with another fundamental right, the right to cast a ballot in an election free from the taint of intimidation and fraud. A long history, a substantial consensus, and simple common sense shows that some restricted zone around polling places is necessary to protect that fundamental right. Given the conflict between those two rights, we hold that requiring solicitors to stand 100 feet[g] from the entrances to polling places does not constitute an unconstitutional compromise."[h]

SCALIA, J., agreed with Blackmun, J., that the regulation was justified, but maintained that the area around a polling place is not a public forum: "If the category of 'traditional public forum' is to be a tool of analysis rather than a conclusory label, it must remain faithful to its name and derive its content from *tradition*. Because restrictions on speech around polling places are as venerable a part of the American tradition as the secret ballot, [Tennessee's statute] does not restrict speech in a traditional public forum. [I] believe that the [statute] though content-based, is constitutional because it is a reasonable, viewpoint-neutral regulation of a non-public forum."

STEVENS, J., joined by O'Connor and Souter, JJ., did not address the question of whether the area around a polling place was a public forum, but agreed with Blackmun, J., that the regulation could not be upheld without showing that it was necessary to serve a compelling state interest by means narrowly tailored to that end. He contended that the existence of the secret ballot was a sufficient safeguard against intimidation[i] and that the fear of fraud from last minute

---

g. Blackmun, J., argued that the question of whether the state should be required to set a smaller zone, perhaps 25 feet, would put the state to an unreasonable burden of proof, and that the difference between such zones was not of constitutional moment.

h. Kennedy, J., concurring, reaffirmed the views he had put forward in *Simon and Schuster,* but noted that the first amendment must appropriately give way in some cases where other constitutional rights are at stake. Thomas, J., took no part.

i. Stevens, J., argued that the record showed no evidence of intimidation or abuse, nor did it offer a basis for denying election advocacy, while permitting other forms of political advocacy, e.g., environmental advocacy. He maintained that the plurality had shifted the strict scrutiny standard from the state to the candidate who wished to speak.

campaigning could not be reconciled with *Mills v. Alabama,* 384 U.S. 214, 86 S.Ct. 1434, 16 L.Ed.2d 484 (1966)(prohibition on election day editorials unconstitutional). In addition, Stevens, J., argued that the prohibition disproportionately affects candidates with "fewer resources, candidates from lesser visibility offices, and 'grassroots' candidates" who specially profit from "last-minute campaigning near the polling place. [The] hubbub of campaign workers outside a polling place may be a nuisance, but it is also the sound of a vibrant democracy."

2. *The first amendment and geography.* Consider Daniel Farber & John Nowak, *The Misleading Nature of Public Forum Analysis: Content and Context in First Amendment Adjudication,* 70 Va.L.Rev., 1219, 1234–35 (1984): "Classification of public places as various types of forums has only confused judicial opinions by diverting attention from the real first amendment issues involved in the cases. Like the fourth amendment, the first amendment protects people, not places. Constitutional protection should depend not on labeling the speaker's physical location but on the first amendment values and governmental interests involved in the case. Of course, governmental interests are often tied to the nature of the place. [To] this extent, the public forum doctrine is a useful heuristic [device]. But when the heuristic device becomes the exclusive method of analysis, only confusion and mistakes can result." Compare Robert Post, *Between Governance and Management: The History and Theory of the Public Forum,* 34 U.C.L.A.L.Rev. 1713, 1777 (1987): "*Grayned's* 'incompatibility' test takes into account only the specific harm incident to a plaintiff's proposed speech; it does not recognize the generic damage to managerial authority flowing from the very process of independent judicial review of institutional decisionmaking. [The Court's] present focus 'on the character of the property at issue' is a theoretical dead end, because there is no satisfactory theory connecting the classification of government property with the exercise of first amendment rights. But there is great potential for a rich and principled jurisprudence if the Court were to focus instead on the relationship between judicial review and the functioning of institutional authority."

3. *Judicial role.* Is it the Court's responsibility "to ensure that speech is not unduly curtailed and to devise rules that will maximize the opportunities for expression" or "only to determine whether the challenged practice reflects deliberate governmental discrimination against disfavored viewpoints?" Should the Court focus its "energy on the kinds of places where denials of access tend systematically to trigger well-founded concerns about deliberate governmental abuse and distortion"? See Lillian BeVier, *Rehabilitating Public Forum Doctrine: In Defense of Categories,* 1993 Sup.Ct.Rev. 79.

4. *The private residence.* Anti-abortion demonstrators picketed on a number of occasions outside a doctor's home. In response, the Town Board passed an ordinance that was interpreted to prohibit picketing taking place solely in front of a residence and directed at a residence. FRISBY v. SCHULTZ, 487 U.S. 474, 108 S.Ct. 2495, 101 L.Ed.2d 420 (1988), per O'CONNOR, J., upheld the ordinance: "The state's interest in protecting the well-being, tranquility, and privacy of the home is certainly of the highest order in a free and civilized society." [j]

j. Brennan, joined by Marshall, dissenting, would have permitted the town to regulate the number of residential picketers, the hours, and the noise level of the pickets. Stevens, J., dissenting, would have limited the ban to conduct that "unreasonably interferes with the privacy of the home and does not serve a reasonable communicate purpose." He worried that a sign such as "GET WELL CHARLIE—OUR TEAM NEEDS YOU," would fall within the sweep of the ordinance.

On the other hand, MADSEN v. WOMEN'S HEALTH CENTER, p. 763 supra per REHNQUIST, C.J., struck down an injunction creating a 300–foot buffer zone around the homes of those who worked in abortion clinics: "The 300–foot zone around the residence is much larger than the zone approved in *Frisby*. [The] 300–foot zone would ban '[g]eneral marching through residential neighborhoods, or even walking a route in front of an entire block of houses.' The record before us does not contain sufficient justification for this broad a ban on picketing; it appears that a limitation on the time, duration of picketing, and number of pickets outside a smaller zone could have accomplished the desired result." [k]

5. *Footnote 7 forums.* What is the relationship between the Court's second category of property in *Perry* and its fn. 7 (see fn. e. supra)? Is the discretion to create forums limited? Is it necessary to show that restrictions on such forums are necessary to achieve a compelling state interest? If a restriction (to certain speakers or subjects) is challenged, can the restrictions be used to show that that the property is not a public forum of the second category? Is this inadmissible circularity? See Lawrence Tribe, *Equality as a First Amendment Theme: The "Government-as-Private Actor" Exception* in Jesse Choper, Yale Kamisar & Lawrence Tribe, The Supreme Court: Trends and Developments 1982–1983, at 221, 226 (1984); Post, supra at 1752–56. In any event, does fn. 7 create a fourth category of property without setting guiding stands? Are the *Perry* mailboxes fn. 7 forums?

LEHMAN v. SHAKER HEIGHTS, 418 U.S. 298, 94 S.Ct. 2714, 41 L.Ed.2d 770 (1974), held that a public transit system could sell commercial advertising space for cards on its vehicles while refusing to sell space for "political" or "public issue" advertising. BLACKMUN, J., joined by Burger, C.J., White and Rehnquist, JJ., ruled the bus cards not be a public forum and found the city's decision reasonable because it minimized "chances of abuse, the appearance of favoritism, and the risk of imposing upon a captive audience."

DOUGLAS, J., concurring, maintained that political messages and commercial messages were both offensive and intrusive to captive audiences, noted that the commercial advertising policy was not before the Court, and voted to deny a right to spread a political message to a captive audience.

BRENNAN, J., joined by Stewart, Marshall, and Powell, JJ., dissenting, observed that the "city's solicitous regard for 'captive riders' [has] a hollow ring in the present case where [it] has opened its rapid transit system as a forum for communication."

Is *Lehman* a fn. 7 forum?

6. *The relationship between the public forum tests and other tests.* In *Vincent*, a political candidate had placed signs on publicly owned utility poles, and the Court assessed the constitutionality of an ordinance that prohibited the placing of signs on public property. What test applies? A public forum test? A time, place, and manner test? The *O'Brien* test?

7. For additional commentary on public forum issues, see Curtis Berger, *Pruneyard Revisited: Political Activity on Private Lands*, 66 N.Y.U.L.Rev. 650 (1991); G. Sidney Buchanan, *The Case of the Vanishing Public Forum*, 1991 U.Ill.L.Rev. 949 (1991); David Day, *The End of the Public Forum Doctrine*, 78

---

k. Stevens, J., concurring and dissenting in part, joined the opinion of the Court on this issue; Souter, J., concurring, joined the opinion of the Court on this issue; Scalia, J., joined by Kennedy and Thomas, JJ., concurring and dissenting in part, joined in the judgment of the Court on this issue.

Iowa L.Rev. 143 (1992); David Goldstone, *The Public Forum Doctrine in the Age of the Information Superhighway (Where Are the Public Forums on the Information Superhighway?)*, 46 Hastings L.J. 335 (1995); Ronald Krotoszynski, Jr., *Celebrating Selma: The Importance of Context in Public Forum Analysis*, 104 Yale L.J. 1411 (1995); Edward Naughton, *Is Cyberspace A Public Forum? Computer Bulletin Boards, Free Speech, and State Action*, 81 Geo.L.J. 409 (1992); Note, 46 Okla.L.Rev. 155 (1993). For commentary on speaker-based restrictions, see Geoffrey Stone, *Content Regulation and the First Amendment*, 25 Wm. & Mary L.Rev. 189, 244–51 (1983).

SECTION 8. GOVERNMENT SUPPORT OF SPEECH

Public forum doctrine recognizes that government is obligated to permit some of its property to be used for communicative purposes without content discrimination, but public forum doctrine also allows other government property to be restricted to some speakers or for talk about selected subjects. In short, in some circumstances government can provide resources for some speech while denying support for other speech. Indeed, government is a significant actor in the marketplace of ideas. Sometimes the government speaks as government; sometimes it subsidizes speech without purporting to claim that the resulting message is its own. It supports speech in many ways: official government messages; statements of public officials at publicly subsidized press conferences; artistic, scientific, or political subsidies, even the classroom communications of public school teachers.

If content distinctions are suspect when government acts as censor, they are the norm when government speaks or otherwise subsidizes speech. Government makes editorial judgments; it decides that some content is appropriate for the occasion and other content is not. The public museum curator makes content decisions in selecting exhibits; the librarian in selecting books; the public board in selecting recipients for research grants; the public official in composing press releases.

The line between support for speech and censorship of speech is not always bright, however. In any event, the Constitution limits the choices government may make in supporting speech. For example, government support of religious speech is limited under the establishment clause. See Ch. 9. This section explores the extent to which the speech clause or constitutional conceptions of equality should limit government discretion in supporting speech.

I. SUBSIDIES AND TAX EXPENDITURES

REGAN v. TAXATION WITH REPRESENTATION OF WASHINGTON

461 U.S. 540, 103 S.Ct. 1997, 76 L.Ed.2d 129 (1983).

JUSTICE REHNQUIST delivered the opinion of the Court.

[Section 501(c) of the Internal Revenue Code affords tax exempt status to various nonprofit organizations. Section 501(c)(19) affords exemption to veterans' organizations. Moreover, contributions to veterans' organizations are treated by the IRS as deductible (up to 20% of adjusted gross income) even if the veterans organizations engage in substantial lobbying activity at state or federal levels. Section 501(c)(3) grants exempt status to various groups commonly called "charitable" organizations that are "organized and operated exclusively for religious, charitable, scientific [or] educational purposes [,] no substantial part of the activities of which is carrying on propaganda, or otherwise attempting to influence legislation [and] which does not participate in, or intervene in (including the publishing or distributing of statements), any political campaign on behalf of any candidate for public office." Section 501(c)(4) grants exempt status to groups organized for the purposes identified in 501(c)(3) (and for some other purposes) regardless of the amount of lobbying or political activity. Contributions made to groups meeting 501(c)(3) standards are deductible (up to 50% of adjusted gross income); contributions to 501(c)(4) groups are not deductible.

[TWR, a group organized to represent the taxpayer's public interest in Washington, was denied 501(c)(3) status because of its lobbying activities. It argued that affording tax deductible contributions to the substantial lobbying activities of veterans while denying such benefits to charitable organizations involved in similar activities was unconstitutional discrimination. The District of Columbia Court of Appeals agreed with TWR: "If veterans' organizations and organizations such as Taxation lobby on different sides of the same questions, Congress has chosen to favor one lobbyist on a particular issue over another. If veterans' organizations and [charitable] organizations lobby on entirely distinct matters, Congress has ensured that greater attention will be devoted to some causes than others. [A] First Amendment concern must inform the equal protection analysis in this case. [This] does not mean, however, that its application in a legal dispute is always simple. The lines will seem clearer when Congress directly prohibits a particular group from speaking in a particular place, and more confused when Congress subsidizes First Amendment expression unevenly through the intricacies of the Internal Revenue Code. Nevertheless, the principle remains the same."

[The Supreme Court reversed:]   * * *

Both tax exemptions and tax-deductibility are a form of subsidy[b] that is administered through the tax system. A tax exemption has much the same effect as a cash grant to the organization of the amount of tax it would have to pay on its income. Deductible contributions are similar to cash grants of the amount of a portion of the individual's contributions.[5] The system Congress has enacted provides this kind of subsidy to non profit civic welfare organizations generally, and an additional subsidy to those charitable organizations that do not engage in substantial lobbying. In short, Congress chose not to subsidize lobbying as extensively as it chose to subsidize other activities that non profit organizations undertake to promote the public welfare.

It appears that TWR could still qualify for a tax exemption under § 501(c)(4). It also appears that TWR can obtain tax-deductible contributions for its nonlobbying activity by returning to the dual structure it used in the past, with a § 501(c)(3) organization for nonlobbying activities and a § 501(c)(4) organization

---

b. The IRS accepted "the analogy between tax exemptions and direct government subsidies" for purposes of the case, but the question of what should be characterized as a subsidy is much debated in tax circles. Compare e.g., Boris Bittker & Kenneth Kaufman, *Taxes and Civil Rights: "Constitutionalizing" the Internal Revenue Code*, 82 Yale L.J. 51, 63–68 (1972) with Stanley Surrey & Paul McDaniel, *The Tax Expenditure Concept and the Budget Reform Act of 1974*, 17 B.C. Indust. & Comm. L.Rev. 679 (1976).

5. In stating that exemptions and deductions, on one hand, are like cash subsidies, on the other, we of course do not mean to assert that they are in all respects identical. See, e.g., *Walz v. Tax Commission* [p. 1062 infra].

for lobbying. TWR would, of course, have to ensure that the § 501(c)(3) organization did not subsidize the § 501(c)(4) organization; otherwise, public funds might be spent on an activity Congress chose not to subsidize.

TWR [claims,] relying on *Speiser v. Randall,* 357 U.S. 513, 78 S.Ct. 1332, 2 L.Ed.2d 1460 (1958), that the prohibition against substantial lobbying by § 501(c)(3) organizations imposes an "unconstitutional condition" on the receipt of tax-deductible contributions. In *Speiser,* California established a rule requiring anyone who sought to take advantage of a property tax exemption to sign a declaration stating that he did not advocate the forcible overthrow of the Government of the United States. This Court stated that "[t]o deny an exemption to claimants who engage in certain forms of speech is in effect to penalize them for such speech."

TWR is certainly correct when it states that we have held that the government may not deny a benefit to a person because he exercises a constitutional right. See *Perry v. Sindermann,* p. 1005 infra. But TWR is just as certainly incorrect when it claims that this case fits the *Speiser–Perry* model. The Code does not deny TWR the right to receive deductible contributions to support its nonlobbying activity, nor does it deny TWR any independent benefit on account of its intention to lobby. Congress has merely refused to pay for the lobbying out of public moneys. This Court has never held that Congress must grant a benefit such as TWR claims here to a person who wishes to exercise a constitutional right.

[The] case would be different if Congress were to discriminate invidiously in its subsidies in such a way as to "aim[ ] at the suppression of dangerous ideas." But the veterans' organizations that qualify under § 501(c)(19) are entitled to receive tax-deductible contributions regardless of the content of any speech they may use, including lobbying. We find no indication that the statute was intended to suppress any ideas or any demonstration that it has had that effect. The sections of the Internal Revenue Code here at issue do not employ any suspect classification. The distinction between veterans' organizations and other charitable organizations is not at all like distinctions based on race or national origin.

The Court of Appeals nonetheless held that "strict scrutiny" is required because the statute "*affect[s]* First Amendment rights on a discriminatory basis." Its opinion suggests that strict scrutiny applies whenever Congress subsidizes some speech, but not all speech. This is not the law. Congress could, for example, grant funds to an organization dedicated to combatting teenage drug abuse, but condition the grant by providing that none of the money received from Congress should be used to lobby state legislatures. [S]uch a statute would be valid. Congress might also enact a statute providing public money for an organization dedicated to combatting teenage alcohol abuse, and impose no condition against using funds obtained from Congress for lobbying. The existence of the second statute would not make the first statute subject to strict scrutiny.
* * *

These are scarcely novel principles. We have held [that] a legislature's decision not to subsidize the exercise of a fundamental right does not infringe the right, and thus is not subject to strict scrutiny. *Buckley v. Valeo,* [p. 1011 infra] upheld a statute that provides federal funds for candidates for public office who enter primary campaigns, but does not provide funds for candidates who do not run in party primaries. We rejected First Amendment and equal protection challenges to this provision without applying strict scrutiny.[c]

c. In *Buckley,* Rehnquist, J., dissenting, complained that the scheme for public funding of Presidential candidates "enshrined the Republican and Democratic Parties in a perma-

The reasoning [is] simple: "although government may not place obstacles in the path of a [person's] exercise [of] freedom of [speech], it need not remove those not of its own creation." * * * Congress—not TWR or this Court—has the authority to determine whether the advantage the public would receive from additional lobbying by charities is worth the money the public would pay to subsidize that lobbying, and other disadvantages that might accompany that lobbying. It appears that Congress was concerned that exempt organizations might use tax-deductible contributions to lobby to promote the private interests of their members.[d] It is not irrational for Congress to decide that tax exempt charities such as TWR should not further benefit at the expense of taxpayers at large by obtaining a further subsidy for lobbying.

It is also not irrational for Congress to decide that, even though it will not subsidize substantial lobbying by charities generally, it will subsidize lobbying by veterans' organizations. Veterans have "been obliged to drop their own affairs and take up the burdens of the nation," "subjecting themselves to the mental and physical hazards as well as the economic and family detriments which are peculiar to military service and which do not exist in normal civil life." Our country has a long standing policy of compensating veterans for their past contributions by providing them with numerous advantages.[e] This policy has "always been deemed to be legitimate."[f] * * *

Notes and Questions

1. Consider Kathleen Sullivan, *Unconstitutional Conditions*, 102 Harv.L.Rev. 1413, 1436, 1441 (1989). "[T]he characterization of a condition as a 'penalty' or as a 'nonsubsidy' depends on the baseline from which one measures. [As] in the abortion funding cases, [none] of the *TWR* opinions explained why the Court assumed a baseline of no subsidy for lobbying activities (in which case there is tautologically no penalty), rather than subsidy for all nonprofit activities (in which case the exclusion of the lobbying strand of those activities resembles a penalty). Nor did the opinions seriously discuss the potential deterrent effect on the lobbying activities of nonprofit organizations.

"In contrast to [*TWR*,] the Court in *FCC v. League of Women Voters* [p. 962 infra] invalidated a condition denying federal public broadcasting funds to stations that engage in editorializing. Treating this condition as flatly coercive, the majority repeatedly referred to it as a 'ban' or 'restriction' rather than an offer to the stations to choose between entirely private funding and a federal subsidy. Justice Rehnquist, in a biting dissent, depicted it as just such an offer: 'Congress simply ha[d] decided not to subsidize stations which engage in [editorializing].' In

---

nently preferred position, and has established requirements for funding minor-party and independent candidates to which the two major parties are not subject. [B]ecause of the First Amendment overtones of the appellants' Fifth Amendment equal protection claim, something more than a merely rational basis for the difference in treatment must be shown, as the Court apparently recognizes." *Buckley* found the funding scheme to be "in furtherance of *sufficiently important* government interests and has not unfairly or unnecessarily burdened the political opportunity of any party or candidate." (Emphasis added).

d. Does this concern apply equally to veterans' organizations? See Note, *Charitable Lobbying Restraints and Tax Exempt Organizations: Old Problems, New Directions?*, 1984 Utah L.Rev. 337, 357–59 (1984).

e. Is it a sufficient response to note that veterans can be rewarded in many ways that do not tread on first amendment equality values?

f. Blackmun, J., joined by Brennan and Marshall, JJ., joined the opinion, but concurred to emphasize the importance of the tax code being administered in a manner that did not discourage lobbying by TWR or other groups.

light of such divisions, the Court's current penalty/nonsubsidy distinction seems no more helpful than its other attempts to use coercion as the ordering principle of unconstitutional conditions doctrine." [g]

2. The Court observes that veterans' organizations receive tax benefits "regardless of the content of any speech they may use." Is this disingenuous because the content of veterans' organizations' speech is predictable? Could the Congress give money to Republican party organizations "regardless of the content of any speech they may use." What if Congress said it was benefiting veterans' organizations in part because Congress thought such organizations were delivering a message that deserved to be heard? Does it matter that favorable tax treatment assists veterans' lobbying at local, state, and federal levels? Could Congress withdraw favorable tax treatment from some veterans' organizations on the ground that their lobbying was not "worth the money"? Could Congress benefit charitable organizations, but not the veterans? Some charitable organizations, but not others? Could Congress give favorable tax treatment to lobbying of the Moral Majority, but no other group? [h]

3. Was TWR the wrong plaintiff? Was its claim weak because it failed to show viewpoint discrimination? Should a group whose primary purpose conflicts with that of veterans' groups be granted relief? See Note, *The Tax Code's Differential Treatment of Lobbying Under Section 501(c)(3): A Proposed First Amendment Analysis*, 66 Va.L.Rev. 1513 (1980).

4. Suppose that nothing in the tax law bars veterans' organizations from using tax deductible contributions for participation in political campaigns on behalf of candidates for public office. Is this more troublesome than the lobbying benefits? Suppose instead of supporting the political speech of others, government itself enters the political fray. Should a city government be able to buy media time to speak on behalf of candidates? To influence the outcome of initiative campaigns? [i]

5. *Taxation and the press.* Discriminatory taxation against the press or segments of it has generally been invalidated. *Arkansas Writers' Project, Inc. v.*

g. On the penalty/subsidy distinction, see Laurence Tribe, *American Constitutional Law* 781–84 (2d ed. 1988); Seth Kreimer, *Allocational Sanctions: The Problem of Negative Rights in a Positive State*, 132 U.Pa.L.Rev. 1293, 1351–78 (1984); Michael McConnell, *Unconstitutional Conditions: Unrecognized Implications for the Establishment Clause*, 26 San Diego L.Rev. 255, 261–63 (1989); Kathleen Sullivan, *Unconstitutional Conditions and the Distribution of Liberty*, 26 San Diego L.Rev. 367 (1989). See also Louis Seidman, *Reflections on Context and the Constitution*, 73 Minn. L.Rev. 73 (1988).

h. For general criticism of the tax code's treatment of charitable organizations, see Elias Clark, *The Limitation on Political Activities: A Discordant Note in the Law of Charities*, 46 Va.L.Rev. 439 (1960); Theodore Garrett, *Federal Tax Limitations on Political Activities of Public Interest and Educational Organizations*, 59 Geo.L.J. 561 (1971); Thomas Troyer, *Charities, Law-Making, and the Constitution: The Validity of the Restrictions on Influencing Legislation*, 31 N.Y.U.Inst. on Fed. Tax'n 1415 (1973).

i. For relevant commentary, see Mark Yudof, *When Government Speaks: Politics, Law, and Government Expression in America* (1983); David Cole, *Beyond Unconstitutional Conditions: Charting Spheres of Neutrality in Government–Funded Speech*, 67 N.Y.U.L.Rev. 675 (1992). Richard Delgado, *The Language of the Arms Race*, 64 B.U.L.Rev. 961 (1984); Thomas Emerson, *The Affirmative Side of the First Amendment*, 15 Ga.L.Rev. 795 (1981); Robert Kamenshine, *The First Amendment's Implied Political Establishment Clause*, 67 Calif.L.Rev. 1104 (1979); Steven Shiffrin, *Government Speech*, 27 U.C.L.A.L.Rev. 565 (1980); Frederick Schauer, *Book Review*, 35 Stan.L.Rev. 373 (1983); Mark Yudof, *When Governments Speak: Toward A Theory of Government Expression and the First Amendment*, 57 Tex. L.Rev. 863 (1979); Edward Ziegler, *Government Speech and the Constitution: The Limits of Official Partisanship*, 21 B.C.L.Rev. 578 (1980); Note, *The Constitutionality of Municipal Advocacy in Statewide Referendum Campaigns*, 93 Harv.L.Rev. 535 (1980).

Ragland, 481 U.S. 221, 107 S.Ct. 1722, 95 L.Ed.2d 209 (1987) (sales tax on general interest magazines while exempting newspapers, religious, professional, trade, and sports journals); *Minneapolis Star & Tribune v. Minnesota Comm'r of Rev.,* 460 U.S. 575, 103 S.Ct. 1365, 75 L.Ed.2d 295 (1983) (some press treated more favorably and press treated differently from other enterprises); *Grosjean v. American Press Co.,* 297 U.S. 233, 56 S.Ct. 444, 80 L.Ed. 660 (1936) (same).[j] But see *Leathers v. Medlock,* 499 U.S. 439, 111 S.Ct. 1438, 113 L.Ed.2d 494 (1991) (upholding general sales tax extension to cable that was not applicable to the print media on the grounds that it did not suppress ideas and that the tax did not target a small group of speakers).

RUST v. SULLIVAN

500 U.S. 173, 111 S.Ct. 1759, 114 L.Ed.2d 233 (1991).

CHIEF JUSTICE REHNQUIST delivered the opinion of the Court. * * *

In 1970, Congress enacted Title X of the Public Health Service Act (Act), [which] authorizes the Secretary to "make grants to and enter into contracts with public or non-profit private entities to assist in the establishment and operation of voluntary family planning projects which shall offer a broad range of acceptable and effective family planning methods and services." [Section] 1008 of the Act, however, provides that "[n]one of the funds appropriated under this subchapter shall be used in programs where abortion is a method of family planning." * * *

In 1988, the Secretary promulgated new regulations [that] attach three principal conditions on the grant of federal funds for Title X projects. First, the regulations specify that a "Title X project may not provide counseling concerning the use of abortion as a method of family planning or provide referral for abortion as a method of family planning." Because Title X is limited to preconceptional services, the program does not furnish services related to childbirth. Only in the context of a referral out of the Title X program is a pregnant woman given transitional information. Title X projects must refer every pregnant client "for appropriate prenatal and/or social services by furnishing a list of available providers that promote the welfare of the mother and the unborn child." The list may not be used indirectly to encourage or promote abortion, "such as by weighing the list of referrals in favor of health care providers which perform abortions, by including on the list of referral providers health care providers whose principal business is the provision of abortions, by excluding available providers who do not provide abortions, or by 'steering' clients to providers who offer abortion as a method of family planning." The Title X project is expressly prohibited from referring a pregnant woman to an abortion provider, even upon specific request. One permissible response to such an inquiry is that "the project does not consider abortion an appropriate method of family planning and therefore does not counsel or refer for abortion."

Second, the regulations broadly prohibit a Title X project from engaging in activities that "encourage, promote or advocate abortion as a method of family planning." Forbidden activities include lobbying for legislation that would in-

j. Are these cases consistent with *TRW?* See Richard Epstein, *Foreward, Unconstitutional Conditions, State Power, and the Limits of Consent,* 102 Harv.L.Rev. 4, 76–79 (1988). For a variety of views bearing on the general problem of subsidies, see Laurence Tribe, *American Constitutional Law* 781–84 (2nd ed., 1988); Epstein, supra; Seth Kreimer, *Allocational Sanctions: The Problem of Negative Rights in a Positive State,* 132 U.Pa.L.Rev. 1293 (1984); Steven Shiffrin, *Government Speech,* 27 UCLA L.Rev. 565 (1980); Sullivan, supra.

crease the availability of abortion as a method of family planning, developing or disseminating materials advocating abortion as a method of family planning, providing speakers to promote abortion as a method of family planning, using legal action to make abortion available in any way as a method of family planning, and paying dues to any group that advocates abortion as a method of family planning as a substantial part of its activities.

Third, the regulations require that Title X projects be organized so that they are "physically and financially separate" from prohibited abortion activities.

[Petitioners,] Title X grantees and doctors who supervise Title X funds suing on behalf of themselves and their patients[,] contend that the regulations violate the First Amendment by impermissibly discriminating based on viewpoint because they prohibit "all discussion about abortion as a lawful option—including counseling, referral, and the provision of neutral and accurate information about ending a pregnancy—while compelling the clinic or counselor to provide information that promotes continuing a pregnancy to term." [They] also assert that while the Government may place certain conditions on the receipt of federal subsidies, it may not "discriminate invidiously in its subsidies in such a way as to 'ai[m] at the suppression of dangerous ideas.'" *Regan.*

There is no question but that the statutory prohibition contained in § 1008 is constitutional. [The] Government can, without violating the Constitution, selectively fund a program to encourage certain activities it believes to be in the public interest, without at the same time funding an alternate program which seeks to deal with the problem in another way.[a] In so doing, the Government has not discriminated on the basis of viewpoint; it has merely chosen to fund one activity to the exclusion of the other. "[A] legislature's decision not to subsidize the exercise of a fundamental right does not infringe the right." *Regan.* * * *

[The] Title X program is designed not for prenatal care, but to encourage family planning. A doctor who wished to offer prenatal care to a project patient who became pregnant could properly be prohibited from doing so because such service is outside the scope of the federally funded program. The regulations prohibiting abortion counseling and referral are of the same ilk; "no funds appropriated for the project may be used in programs where abortion is a method of family planning," and a doctor employed by the project may be prohibited in the course of his project duties from counseling abortion or referring for abortion. This is not a case of the Government "suppressing a dangerous idea," but of a prohibition on a project grantee or its employees from engaging in activities outside of its scope.

To hold that the Government unconstitutionally discriminates on the basis of viewpoint when it chooses to fund a program dedicated to advance certain permissible goals, because the program in advancing those goals necessarily discourages alternate goals, would render numerous government programs constitutionally suspect. When Congress established a National Endowment for Democracy to encourage other countries to adopt democratic principles, it was not constitutionally required to fund a program to encourage competing lines of political philosophy such as Communism and Fascism. Petitioners' assertions ultimately boil down to the position that if the government chooses to subsidize one protected right, it must subsidize analogous counterpart rights. But the Court has soundly rejected that proposition. Within far broader limits than

a. The Court cited *Maher v. Roe* [(constitutional for government to subsidize childbirth without subsidizing abortions)] and *Harris v. McRae.*

petitioners are willing to concede, when the government appropriates public funds to establish a program it is entitled to define the limits of that program.

We believe that petitioners' reliance upon our decision in *Arkansas Writers' Project* is misplaced. That case involved a state sales tax which discriminated between magazines on the basis of their content. Relying on this fact, and on the fact that the tax "targets a small group within the press," contrary to our decision in *Minneapolis Star,* the Court held the tax invalid. But we have here not the case of a general law singling out a disfavored group on the basis of speech content, but a case of the Government refusing to fund activities, including speech, which are specifically excluded from the scope of the project funded.

Petitioners rely heavily on their claim that the regulations would not, in the circumstance of a medical emergency, permit a Title X project to refer a woman whose pregnancy places her life in imminent peril to a provider of abortions or abortion-related services. This case, of course, involves only a facial challenge to the regulations, and we do not have before us any application by the Secretary to a specific fact situation. On their face, we do not read the regulations to bar abortion referral or counseling in such circumstances. * * *

Petitioners also contend that the [regulations] condition the receipt of a benefit, in this case Title X funding, on the relinquishment of a constitutional right, the right to engage in abortion advocacy and counseling. * * *

[H]ere the government is not denying a benefit to anyone, but is instead simply insisting that public funds be spent for the purposes for which they were authorized. The Secretary's regulations do not force the Title X grantee to give up abortion-related speech; they merely require that the grantee keep such activities separate and distinct from Title X activities. Title X expressly distinguishes between a Title X *grantee* and a Title X *project.* The grantee, which normally is a health care organization, may receive funds from a variety of sources for a variety of purposes. The grantee receives Title X funds, however, for the specific and limited purpose of establishing and operating a Title X project. The regulations govern the scope of the Title X *project's* activities, and leave the grantee unfettered in its other activities. The Title X *grantee* can continue to perform abortions, provide abortion-related services, and engage in abortion advocacy; it simply is required to conduct those activities through programs that are separate and independent from the project that receives Title X funds.

In contrast, our "unconstitutional conditions" cases involve situations in which the government has placed a condition on the *recipient* of the subsidy rather that on a particular program or service, thus effectively prohibiting the recipient from engaging in the protected conduct outside the scope of the federally funded program. [By] requiring that the Title X grantee engage in abortion-related activity separately from activity receiving federal funding, Congress has, consistent with our teachings in *League of Women Voters* and *Regan,* not denied it the right to engage in abortion-related activities. Congress has merely refused to fund such activities out of the public fisc, and the Secretary has simply required a certain degree of separation from the Title X project in order to ensure the integrity of the federally funded program.

The same principles apply to petitioners' claim that the regulations abridge the free speech rights of the grantee's staff. * * *

This is not to suggest that funding by the Government, even when coupled with the freedom of the fund recipients to speak outside the scope of the Government-funded project, is invariably sufficient to justify government control over the content of expression. For example, this Court has recognized that the existence of a Government "subsidy," in the form of Government-owned property, does not justify the restriction of speech in areas that have "been traditionally open to the public for expressive activity," or have been "expressly dedicated to speech activity." Similarly, we have recognized that the university is a traditional sphere of free expression so fundamental to the functioning of our society that the Government's ability to control speech within that sphere by means of conditions attached to the expenditure of Government funds is restricted by the vagueness and overbreadth doctrines of the First Amendment, *Keyishian v. Board of Regents* [p. 971 infra]. It could be argued by analogy that traditional relationships such as that between doctor and patient should enjoy protection under the First Amendment from government regulation, even when subsidized by the Government. We need not resolve that question here, however, because the Title X program regulations do not significantly impinge upon the doctor-patient relationship. Nothing in them requires a doctor to represent as his own any opinion that he does not in fact hold. Nor is the doctor-patient relationship established by the Title X program sufficiently all-encompassing so as to justify an expectation on the part of the patient of comprehensive medical advice. The program does not provide post-conception medical care, and therefore a doctor's silence with regard to abortion cannot reasonably be thought to mislead a client into thinking that the doctor does not consider abortion an appropriate option for her. The doctor is always free to make clear that advice regarding abortion is simply beyond the scope of the program. In these circumstances, the general rule that the Government may choose not to subsidize speech applies with full force. * * *

JUSTICE BLACKMUN, with whom JUSTICE MARSHALL joins, with whom JUSTICE STEVENS joins as to Parts II [b] and III,[c] and with whom JUSTICE O'CONNOR joins as to Part I,[d] dissenting. * * *

II

A

Until today, the Court never has upheld viewpoint-based suppression of speech simply because that suppression was a condition upon the acceptance of public funds. Whatever may be the Government's power to condition the receipt of its largess upon the relinquishment of constitutional rights, it surely does not extend to a condition that suppresses the recipient's cherished freedom of speech based solely upon the content or viewpoint of that speech. * * *

It cannot seriously be disputed that the counseling and referral provisions at issue in the present cases constitute content-based regulation of speech. Title X grantees may provide counseling and referral regarding any of a wide range of family planning and other topics, save abortion.

The Regulations are also clearly viewpoint-based. While suppressing speech favorable to abortion with one hand, the Secretary compels anti-abortion speech with the other. For example, the Department of Health and Human Services' own description of the Regulations makes plain that "Title X projects are *required* to facilitate access to prenatal care and social services, including adoption services, that might be needed by the pregnant client to promote her well-being and that of her child, while making it abundantly clear that the project is not permitted to

---

b. Part II discussed freedom of speech and portions of it are set out below.

c. Part III argued that the regulations violated the fifth amendment due process clause.

d. Part I contended that the regulations were not authorized by the statute. O'Connor, and Stevens, JJ., each filed separate dissents advancing the same contention.

promote abortion by facilitating access to abortion through the referral process."
* * *

The Regulations pertaining to "advocacy" are even more explicitly viewpoint-based. These provide: "A Title X project may not *encourage, promote or advocate* abortion as a method of family planning." [The] Regulations do not, however, proscribe or even regulate anti-abortion advocacy. These are clearly restrictions aimed at the suppression of "dangerous ideas."

[T]he majority's claim that the Regulations merely limit a Title X project's speech to preventive or preconceptional services rings hollow in light of the broad range of non-preventive services that the Regulations authorize Title X projects to provide.[2] By refusing to fund those family-planning projects that advocate abortion *because* they advocate abortion, the Government plainly has targeted a particular viewpoint. [Clearly,] there are some bases upon which government may not rest its decision to fund or not to fund. For example, the Members of the majority surely would agree that government may not base its decision to support an activity upon considerations of race. As demonstrated above, our cases make clear that ideological viewpoint is a similarly repugnant ground upon which to base funding decisions.

[*Regan*] stands for the proposition that government has no obligation to subsidize a private party's efforts to petition the legislature regarding its views. Thus, if the challenged Regulations were confined to non-ideological limitations upon the use of Title X funds for lobbying activities, there would exist no violation of the First Amendment. The advocacy Regulations at issue here, [however,] intrude upon a wide range of communicative conduct, including the very words spoken to a woman by her physician. By manipulating the content of the doctor/patient dialogue, the Regulations upheld today force each of the petitioners "to be an instrument for fostering public adherence to an ideological point of view [he or she] finds unacceptable." *Wooley v. Maynard* [p. 871 infra].[3]

B. The Court concludes that the challenged Regulations do not violate the First Amendment rights of Title X staff members [by] emphasizing that Title X physicians and counselors "remain free [to] pursue abortion-related activities when they are not acting under the auspices of the Title X project." "The regulations," the majority explains, "do not in any way restrict the activities of those persons acting as private individuals." Under the majority's reasoning, the First Amendment could be read to tolerate *any* governmental restriction upon an employee's speech so long as that restriction is limited to the funded workplace. This is a dangerous proposition, and one the Court has rightly rejected in the past.

2. In addition to requiring referral for prenatal care and adoption services, the Regulations permit general health services such as physical examinations, screening for breast cancer, treatment of gynecological problems, and treatment for sexually transmitted diseases. None of the latter are strictly preventive, preconceptional services.

3. [That] the doctor-patient relationship is substantially burdened by a rule prohibiting the dissemination by the physician of pertinent medical information is beyond serious dispute. This burden is undiminished by the fact that the relationship at issue here is not an "all-encompassing" one. A woman seeking the services of a Title X clinic has every reason to expect, as do we all, that her physician will not withhold relevant information regarding the very purpose of her visit. To suggest otherwise is to engage in uninformed fantasy. Further, to hold that the doctor-patient relationship is somehow incomplete where a patient lacks the resources to seek comprehensive healthcare from a single provider is to ignore the situation of a vast number of Americans. As Justice Marshall has noted in a different context: "It is perfectly proper for judges to disagree about what the Constitution requires. But it is disgraceful for an interpretation of the Constitution to be premised upon unfounded assumptions about how people live."

In *Abood,* it was no answer to the petitioners' claim of compelled speech as a condition upon public employment that their speech outside the workplace remained unregulated by the State.[e] Nor was the public employee's First Amendment claim in *Rankin* derogated because the communication that her employer sought to punish occurred during business hours.[f] At the least, such conditions require courts to balance the speaker's interest in the message against those of government in preventing its dissemination.

In the cases at bar, the speaker's interest in the communication is both clear and vital. In addressing the family-planning needs of their clients, the physicians and counselors who staff Title X projects seek to provide them with the full range of information and options regarding their health and reproductive freedom. Indeed, the legitimate expectations of the patient and the ethical responsibilities of the medical profession demand no less. * * *

The Government's articulated interest in distorting the doctor/patient dialogue—ensuring that federal funds are not spent for a purpose outside the scope of the program—falls far short of that necessary to justify the suppression of truthful information and professional medical opinion regarding constitutionally protected conduct.[4] Moreover, the offending Regulation is not narrowly tailored to serve this interest. For example, the governmental interest at stake could be served by imposing rigorous bookkeeping standards to ensure financial separation or adopting content-neutral rules for the balanced dissemination of family-planning and health information. * * *

C. Finally, it is of no small significance that the speech the Secretary would suppress is truthful information regarding constitutionally protected conduct of vital importance to the listener. One can imagine no legitimate governmental interest that might be served by suppressing such information. * * *

Notes and Questions

1. *Deception.* Consider Dorothy E. Roberts, *Rust v. Sullivan and the Control of Knowledge* 61 Geo.Wash.L.Rev. 587, 594–95 (1993): "[P]regnancy may accelerate the progression of certain serious medical conditions, such as heart disease, hypertension, diabetes, sickle cell anemia, cancer and AIDS. For example, a woman with diabetic retinopathy who becomes pregnant may go blind. The regulations prohibited doctors from advising women suffering from these conditions that abortion may reduce the long-term risks to their health. Moreover, the recommendation of prenatal care may give the false impression that pregnancy does not jeopardize these women's health."

2. *Domination.* Note, *Unconstitutional Conditions as "Nonsubsidies": When is Deference Inappropriate?* 80 Geo.L.J. 131, 135 (1991): "*Rust* was wrongly decided because the government's domination of the entire family planning dialogue for many of those who seek such information has made private alternatives unavailable. Poor women have a right to this information because the Constitution respects the interests of those who want to receive a particular message, not just the interests of those who speak. In the limited context of the exchange between the family planning counselor and the poor pregnant woman

---

e. *Abood v. Detroit Board of Education* (compelled funding of ideological activities of union violates freedom of speech).

f. *Rankin v. McPherson* (expressed hope that assassination attempt of president be successful is protected speech when uttered in private to fellow employee during working hours).

4. It is to be noted that the Secretary has made no claim that the Regulations at issue reflect any concern for the health or welfare of Title X clients.

who wants information concerning a range of options, government has gone far toward creating a monopoly. By contrast, a broad portion of government's speech-related subsidies, such as those for the Kennedy Center, do not involve 'crowding out' of private alternatives and thus do not raise analogous First Amendment concerns."

3. *Quantity and quality of speech.* When does funding for the arts raise free speech concerns? Is it enough that "professional" standards are followed? Consider Owen Fiss, *State Activism and State Censorship*, 100 Yale L.J. 2087, 2101 (1991): "The constitutional wrong of an obscenity prosecution arises from the effect such an exercise of state power has upon public discourse, and although there is an analytic difference in the subsidy situation, arising from the scarcity factor, the focus should remain on the effect of the government action. The difference between the two situations requires not an abandonment of the concern with effect, but a more refined conception of effect and the introduction of a more qualitative perspective in the allocative context: A court [must] ascertain whether the allocative decision would contribute to a debate on national issues that is 'uninhibited, robust, and wide-open,' or whether its effect would be just the opposite. [When] a criterion such as 'artistic excellence' is used in such a way as to have the consequence of keeping from public view art that presents ideas and positions otherwise absent from public discourse, and thus to constrain public debate, it will have to be qualified in order to fulfill the purposes of the First Amendment." For criticism, see Amy Sabrin, *Thinking About Content: Can It Play An Appropriate Role in Government Funding of the Arts?* 102 Yale L.J. 1209 (1993).

4. *Rust distinguished.* The University of Virginia subsidized the printing costs of a wide variety of student organizations, but refused to fund religious publications (those that "primarily promote or manifest a particular belief in or about a deity or an ultimate reality"). ROSENBERGER v. UNIVERSITY OF VIRGINIA, (1995), per KENNEDY, J., held that the refusal to fund religious speech violated the free speech clause: "[In *Rust* p. 822 infra], the government did not create a program to encourage private speech but instead used private speakers to transmit specific information pertaining to its own program. We recognized that when the government appropriates public funds to promote a particular policy of its own it is entitled to say what it wishes. It does not follow, however, [that] viewpoint-based restrictions are proper when the University does not itself speak or subsidize transmittal of a message it favors but instead expends funds to encourage a diversity of views from private speakers." [g]

SOUTER, J., joined by Stevens, Ginsburg and Breyer, JJ., dissented: "If the Guidelines were written or applied so as to limit only such Christian advocacy and no other evangelical efforts that might compete with it, the discrimination would be based on viewpoint. But that is not what the regulation authorizes; it applies to Muslim and Jewish and Buddhist advocacy as well as to Christian and to agnostics and atheists as well as it does to deists and theists. The Guidelines [thus] do not skew debate by funding one position but not its competitors. [They] deny] funding for the entire subject matter of religious apologetics."

---

g. O'Connor, and Thomas, J., filed concurring opinions.

II. GOVERNMENT AS EDUCATOR AND EDITOR

TINKER v. DES MOINES SCHOOL DISTRICT

393 U.S. 503, 89 S.Ct. 733, 21 L.Ed.2d 731 (1969).

JUSTICE FORTAS delivered the opinion of the Court.

[Petitioners, two high school students and one junior high student, wore black armbands to school to publicize their objections to the Vietnam conflict and their advocacy of a truce. They refused to remove the armbands when asked to do so. In accordance with a ban on armbands which the city's school principals had adopted two days before in anticipation of such a protest, petitioners were sent home and suspended from school until they would return without the armbands. They sought a federal injunction restraining school officials from disciplining them, but the lower federal courts upheld the constitutionality of the school authorities' action on the ground that it was reasonable in order to prevent a disturbance which might result from the wearing of the armbands.]

[T]he wearing of armbands in the circumstances of this case was entirely divorced from actually or potentially disruptive conduct by those participating in it. It was closely akin to "pure speech" which, we have repeatedly held, is entitled to comprehensive protection under the First Amendment. * * *

First Amendment rights, applied in light of the special characteristics of the school environment, are available to teachers and students. It can hardly be argued that either students or teachers shed their constitutional rights to freedom of speech or expression at the schoolhouse gate. This has been the unmistakable holding of this Court for almost 50 years. In *Meyer v. Nebraska* [1923] [discussed in *Griswold v. Connecticut,* p. 299 supra], this Court [held that fourteenth amendment due process] prevents States from forbidding the teaching of a foreign language to young students. Statutes to this effect, the Court held, unconstitutionally interfere with the liberty of teacher, student, and parent. * * *

The problem presented by the present case does not relate to regulation of the length of skirts or the type of clothing, to hair style or deportment. [It] does not concern aggressive, disruptive action or even group demonstrations. Our problem involves direct, primary First Amendment rights akin to "pure speech."

The school officials banned and sought to punish petitioners for a silent, passive, expression of opinion, unaccompanied by any disorder or disturbance on the part of petitioners. There is here no evidence whatever of petitioners' interference, actual or nascent, with the school's work or of collision with the rights of other students to be secure and to be let alone. Accordingly, this case does not concern speech or action that intrudes upon the work of the school or the rights of other students.

Only a few of the 18,000 students in the school system wore the black armbands. Only five students were suspended for wearing them. There is no indication that the work of the school or any class was disrupted. Outside the classrooms, a few students made hostile remarks to the children wearing armbands, but there were no threats or acts of violence on school premises.

[I]n our system, undifferentiated fear or apprehension of disturbance [the District Court's basis for sustaining the school authorities' action] is not enough to overcome the right to freedom of expression. Any departure from absolute regimentation may cause trouble. Any variation from the majority's opinion may inspire fear. Any words spoken, in class, in the lunchroom or on the campus, that deviates from the views of another person, may start an argument or cause a disturbance. But our Constitution says we must take this risk [and] our history says that it is this sort of hazardous freedom—this kind of openness—that is the basis of our national strength and of the independence and vigor of Americans who grow up and live in this relatively permissive, often disputatious society.

In order for the State in the person of school officials to justify prohibition of a particular expression of opinion, it must be able to show that its action was caused by something more than a mere desire to avoid the discomfort and unpleasantness that always accompany an unpopular viewpoint. Certainly where there is no finding and no showing that the exercise of the forbidden right would "materially and substantially interfere with the requirements of appropriate discipline in the operation of the school," the prohibition cannot be sustained.

In the present case, the District Court made no such finding, and our independent examination of the record fails to yield evidence that the school authorities had reason to anticipate that the wearing of the armbands would substantially interfere with the work of the school or impinge upon the rights of other students. Even an official memorandum prepared after the suspension that listed the reasons for the ban on wearing the armbands made no reference to the anticipation of such disruption.[3]

On the contrary, the action of the school authorities appears to have been based upon an urgent wish to avoid the controversy which might result from the expression, even by the silent symbol of armbands, of opposition to this Nation's part in the conflagration in Vietnam. * * *

It is also relevant that the school authorities did not purport to prohibit the wearing of all symbols of political or controversial significance. The record shows that students in some of the schools wore buttons relating to national political campaigns, and some even wore the Iron Cross, traditionally a symbol of nazism. The order prohibiting the wearing of armbands did not extend to these. Instead, a particular symbol—black armbands worn to exhibit opposition to this Nation's involvement in Vietnam—was singled out for prohibition. Clearly, the prohibition of expression of one particular opinion, at least without evidence that it is necessary to avoid material and substantial interference with school work or discipline, is not constitutionally permissible.[a]

---

3. The only suggestions of fear of disorder in the report are these: "A former student of one of our high schools was killed in Viet Nam. Some of his friends are still in school and it was felt that if any kind of a demonstration existed, it might evolve into something which would be difficult to control.

"Students at one of the high schools were heard to say they would wear arm bands of other colors if the black bands prevailed."

Moreover, the testimony of school authorities at trial indicates that it was not fear of disruption that motivated the regulation prohibiting the armbands; the regulation was directed against "the principle of the demonstration" itself. School authorities simply felt that "the schools are no place for demonstrations," and if the students "didn't like the way our elected officials were handling things, it should be handled with the ballot box and not in the halls of our public schools."

a. Cf. *Guzick v. Drebus*, 305 F.Supp. 472 (N.D.Ohio 1969), upholding "a long-standing and consistently-applied rule prohibiting the

wearing of buttons and other insignia on school grounds during school hours unless these are related to a school-sponsored activity" as "reasonably related to the prevention of the distractions and disruptive and violent conduct" at a racially tense high school; although the button in the instant case did not convey an inflammatory message, the blanket prohibition avoids a situation "in which inflammatory and often insulting buttons would be worn"; a policy permitting certain buttons and excluding others would be "unworkable" in the context of the particular school and "would very likely lead to disruption itself"; a selective policy could not "practically be enforced, for it would require the school authorities to patrol the halls and classes in search of offending buttons"; moreover, such a policy would "necessarily involve the school administration in the controversies" at the school, destroy its "image of complete neutrality," "undermine the structure of discipline" and "materially and substantially affect the educational process"; and any attempt to enforce such a selec-

In our system, state-operated schools may not be enclaves of totalitarianism. School officials do not possess absolute authority over their students. Students in school as well as out of school are "persons" under our Constitution. They are possessed of fundamental rights which the State must respect, just as they themselves must respect their obligations to the State. In our system, students may not be regarded as closed-circuit recipients of only that which the State chooses to communicate. They may not be confined to the expression of those sentiments that are officially approved. In the absence of a specific showing of constitutionally valid reasons to regulate their speech, students are entitled to freedom of expression of their views.

[The principle of prior cases underscoring the importance of diversity and exchange of ideas in the schools,] is not confined to the supervised and ordained discussion which takes place in the classroom. The principal use to which the schools are dedicated is to accommodate students during prescribed hours for the purpose of certain types of activities. Among those activities is personal intercommunication among the students.[6] This is not only an inevitable part of the process of attending school. It is also an important part of the educational process.

A student's rights therefore, do not embrace merely the classroom hours. When he is in the cafeteria, or on the playing field, or on the campus during the authorized hours, he may express his opinions, even on controversial subjects like the conflict in Vietnam, if he does so "[without] materially and substantially interfering [with] appropriate discipline in the operation of the school" and without colliding with the rights of others. *Burnside.* But conduct by the student, in class or out of it, which for any reason—whether it stems from time, place, or type of behavior—materially disrupts classwork or involves substantial disorder or invasion of the rights of others is, of course, not immunized by the [first amendment].

We properly read [the first amendment] to permit reasonable regulation of speech-connected activities in carefully restricted circumstances. But we do not confine the permissible exercise of First Amendment rights to a telephone booth or the four corners of a pamphlet, or to supervised and ordained discussion in a school classroom.[b] * * *

Reversed and remanded.

JUSTICE STEWART, concurring.[c]

Although I agree with much of what is said in the Court's opinion, and with its judgment in this case, I cannot share the Court's uncritical assumption that, school discipline aside, the First Amendment rights of children are co-extensive with those of adults. Indeed, I had thought the Court decided otherwise just last Term in *Ginsberg v. New York* [p. 619 supra.] I continue to hold the view I expressed in that case: "[A] State may permissibly determine that, at least in some precisely delineated areas, a child—like someone in a captive audience—is

tive policy "would likely entangle the school authorities in the First Amendment prohibition against prior restraints on free speech."

6. In *Hammond v. South Carolina State College,* 272 F.Supp. 947 (D.C.S.C.1967). District Judge Hemphill had before him a case involving a meeting on campus of 300 students to express their views on school practices. He pointed out that a school is not like a hospital or a jail enclosure. It is a public place and its dedication to specific uses does not imply that the constitutional rights of persons entitled to be there are to be gauged as if the premises were purely private property.

b. See also Mark Yudof, *When Governments Speak: Toward a Theory of Government Expression and the First Amendment,* 57 Tex. L.Rev. 863, 884–85 (1979).

c. White, J., also briefly concurred.

not possessed of that full capacity for individual choice which is the presupposition of First Amendment guarantees." (concurring opinion). * * *

JUSTICE BLACK, dissenting. * * *

Assuming that the Court is correct in holding that the conduct of wearing armbands for the purpose of conveying political ideas is protected by the First Amendment [the] crucial remaining questions are whether students and teachers may use the schools at their whim as a platform for the exercise of free speech—"symbolic" or "pure"—and whether the Courts will allocate to themselves the function of deciding how the pupils' school day will be spent. * * *

While the record does not show that any of these armband students shouted, used profane language, or were violent in any manner, detailed testimony by some of them shows their armbands caused comments, warnings by other students, the poking of fun at them, and a warning by an older football player that other, nonprotesting students had better let them alone. There is also evidence that the professor of mathematics had his lesson period practically "wrecked" chiefly by disputes with Beth Tinker, who wore her armband for her "demonstration." Even a casual reading of the record shows that this armband did divert students' minds from their regular lessons, and that talk, comments, etc., made John Tinker "self-conscious" in attending school with his armband. While the absence of obscene or boisterous and loud disorder perhaps justifies the Court's statement that the few armband students did not actually "disrupt" the classwork, I think the record overwhelmingly shows that the armbands did exactly what the elected school officials and principals foresaw it would, that is, took the students' minds off their classwork and diverted them to thoughts about the highly emotional subject of the Vietnam war.

[E]ven if the record were silent as to protests against the Vietnam war distracting students from their assigned class work, members of this Court, like all other citizens, know, without being told, that the disputes over the wisdom of the Vietnam war have disrupted and divided this country as few other issues ever have. Of course students, like other people, cannot concentrate on lesser issues when black armbands are being ostentatiously displayed in their presence to call attention to the wounded and dead of the war, some of the wounded and the dead being their friends and neighbors. It was, of course, to distract the attention of other students that some students insisted up to the very point of their own suspension from school that they were determined to sit in school with their symbolic armbands. * * *

JUSTICE HARLAN, dissenting.

I certainly agree that state public school authorities in the discharge of their responsibilities are not wholly exempt from the requirements of the Fourteenth Amendment respecting the freedoms of expression and association. At the same time I am reluctant to believe that there is any disagreement between the majority and myself on the proposition that school officials should be accorded the widest authority in maintaining discipline and good order in their institutions. To translate that proposition into a workable constitutional rule, I would, in cases like this, cast upon those complaining the burden of showing that a particular school measure was motivated by other than legitimate school concerns—for example, a desire to prohibit the expression of an unpopular point of view, while permitting expression of the dominant opinion.

Finding nothing in this record which impugns the good faith of respondents in promulgating the arm band regulation, I would affirm the judgment below.

Notes and Questions

1. Should the government's interest in education trump the school child's interest in speaking in the classroom? Are the two interests compatible in this case? May students be prohibited from voicing their opinions of the Vietnam War in the middle of a math class? If so, why can't they be prevented from expressing their views on the same issue in the same class by means of "symbolic speech"? Cf. Sheldon Nahmod, *Beyond Tinker: The High School as an Educational Public Forum,* 5 Harv.Civ.Rts. & Civ.Lib.L.Rev. 278 (1970).

2. Could school authorities adopt a regulation forbidding *teachers* to wear black armbands in the classroom? Or prohibiting teachers from wearing *all* symbols of political or controversial significance in the classroom or anywhere on school property? Are students a "captive" group? Do the views of a teacher occupying a position of authority carry much more influence with a student than would those of students inter sese? Consider *James v. Board of Educ.,* 461 F.2d 566 (2d Cir.1972), holding that school officials violated a high school teacher's constitutional rights by discharging him because he had worn a black armband in class in symbolic protest of the Vietnam War. But the court stressed that "the armband did not disrupt classroom activities [nor] have any influence on any students and did not engender protest from any student, teacher or parent." What if it had? By implication, did the court confirm the potency of the "heckler's veto"? See Note, 39 Brook.L.Rev. 918 (1973). Same result if appellant had been a 3rd grade teacher rather than an 11th grade teacher? See Steven Shiffrin, *Government Speech,* 27 U.C.L.A.L.Rev. 565, 647–53 (1980).

HAZELWOOD SCHOOL DISTRICT v. KUHLMEIER

484 U.S. 260, 108 S.Ct. 562, 98 L.Ed.2d 592 (1988).

JUSTICE WHITE delivered the opinion of the Court. * * *

Petitioners are the Hazelwood School District in St. Louis County, Missouri; various school officials; Robert Eugene Reynolds, the principal of Hazelwood East High School, and Howard Emerson, a teacher in the school district. Respondents are three former Hazelwood East students who were staff members of Spectrum, the school newspaper. * * *

The practice at Hazelwood East during the spring 1983 semester was for the journalism teacher to submit page proofs of each Spectrum issue to Principal Reynolds for his review prior to publication. On May 10, Emerson delivered the proofs of the May 13 edition to Reynolds, who objected to two of the articles scheduled to appear in that edition. One of the stories described three Hazelwood East students' experiences with pregnancy; the other discussed the impact of divorce on students at the school.

Reynolds was concerned that, although the pregnancy story used false names "to keep the identity of these girls a secret," the pregnant students still might be identifiable from the text. He also believed that the article's references to sexual activity and birth control were inappropriate for some of the younger students at the school. In addition, Reynolds was concerned that a student identified by name in the divorce story had complained [about] her father * * *. Reynolds believed that the student's parents should have been given an opportunity to respond to these remarks or to consent to their publication. He was unaware that Emerson had deleted the student's name from the final version of the article.

Reynolds believed that there was no time to make the necessary changes in the stories before the scheduled press run and that the newspaper would not appear before the end of the school year if printing were delayed to any significant extent. He concluded that his only options under the circumstances were to publish a four-page newspaper instead of the planned six-page newspaper, eliminating the two pages on which the offending stories appeared, or to publish no newspaper at all. Accordingly, he directed Emerson to withhold from publication the two pages containing the stories on pregnancy and divorce.[1] He informed his superiors of the decision, and they concurred. * * *

[T]he First Amendment rights of students in the public schools "are not automatically coextensive with the rights of adults in other settings," *Bethel School District No. 403 v. Fraser,* 478 U.S. 675, 106 S.Ct. 3159, 92 L.Ed.2d 549 (1986), and must be "applied in light of the special characteristics of the school environment." *Tinker.* A school need not tolerate student speech that is inconsistent with its "basic educational mission," *Fraser,* even though the government could not censor similar speech outside the school. Accordingly, we held in *Fraser* that a student could be disciplined for having delivered a speech that was "sexually explicit" but not legally obscene at an official school [assembly]. We thus recognized that "[t]he determination of what manner of speech in the classroom or in school assembly is inappropriate properly rests with the school board," rather than with the federal courts. * * *

A

We deal first with the question whether Spectrum may appropriately be characterized as a forum for public expression. [T]he evidence relied upon by the Court of Appeals fails to demonstrate the "clear intent to create a public forum," *Cornelius,* that existed in cases in which we found public forums to have been created. School [officials] "reserve[d] the forum for its intended purpos[e]," *Perry,* as a supervised learning experience for journalism students. Accordingly, school officials were entitled to regulate the contents of Spectrum in any reasonable manner. * * *

The question whether the First Amendment requires a school to tolerate particular student speech—the question that we addressed in *Tinker*—is different from the question whether the First Amendment requires a school affirmatively to promote particular student speech. The former question addresses educators' ability to silence a student's personal expression that happens to occur on the school premises. The latter question concerns educators' authority over school-sponsored publications, theatrical productions, and other expressive activities that students, parents, and members of the public might reasonably perceive to bear the imprimatur of the school. These activities may fairly be characterized as part of the school curriculum, whether or not they occur in a traditional classroom setting, so long as they are supervised by faculty members and designed to impart particular knowledge or skills to student participants and audiences.

[A] school may in its capacity as publisher of a school newspaper or producer of a school play "disassociate itself," *Fraser,* not only from speech that would "substantially interfere with [its] work [or] impinge upon the rights of other students," *Tinker,* but also from speech that is, for example, ungrammatical, poorly written, inadequately researched, biased or prejudiced, vulgar or profane,

---

1. The two pages deleted from the newspaper also contained articles on teenage marriage, runaways, and juvenile delinquents, as well as a general article on teenage pregnancy. Reynolds testified that he had no objection to these articles and that they were deleted only because they appeared on the same pages as the two objectionable articles.

or unsuitable for immature audiences.[4] A school must be able to set high standards for the student speech that is disseminated under its auspices— standards that may be higher than those demanded by some newspaper publishers or theatrical producers in the "real" world—and may refuse to disseminate student speech that does not meet those standards. [Otherwise,] the schools would be unduly constrained from fulfilling their role as "a principal instrument in awakening the child to cultural values, in preparing him for later professional training, and in helping him to adjust normally to his environment." *Brown v. Board of Education.*

Accordingly, we conclude that the standard articulated in *Tinker* for determining when a school may punish student expression need not also be the standard for determining when a school may refuse to lend its name and resources to the dissemination of student expression. Instead, we hold that educators do not offend the First Amendment by exercising editorial control over the style and content of student speech in school-sponsored expressive activities so long as their actions are reasonably related to legitimate pedagogical concerns.[7] * * * a

JUSTICE BRENNAN, with whom JUSTICE MARSHALL and JUSTICE BLACKMUN join, dissenting.

[Under] *Tinker,* school officials may censor only such student speech as would "materially disrup[t]" a legitimate curricular function. Manifestly, student speech is more likely to disrupt a curricular function when it arises in the context of a curricular activity—one that "is designed to teach" something—than when it arises in the context of a noncurricular activity. Thus, under *Tinker,* the school may constitutionally punish the budding political orator if he disrupts calculus class but not if he holds his tongue for the cafeteria. That is not because some more stringent standard applies in the curricular context. (After all, this Court applied the same standard whether the Tinkers wore their armbands to the "classroom" or the "cafeteria.") It is because student speech in the noncurricular context is less likely to disrupt materially any legitimate pedagogical purpose.

I fully agree with the Court that the First Amendment should afford an educator the prerogative not to sponsor the publication of a newspaper article that is "ungrammatical, poorly written, inadequately researched, biased or prejudiced," or that falls short of the "high standards [for] student speech that is disseminated under [the school's] auspices." But we need not abandon *Tinker* to reach that conclusion; we need only apply it. The enumerated criteria reflect the

---

4. [The] decision in *Fraser* rested on the "vulgar," "lewd," and "plainly offensive" character of a speech delivered at an official school assembly rather than on any propensity of the speech to "materially disrupt[ ] classwork or involve[ ] substantial disorder or invasion of the rights of others." Indeed, the *Fraser* Court cited as "especially relevant" a portion of Justice Black's dissenting opinion in *Tinker* "disclaim[ing] any purpose [to] hold that the Federal Constitution compels the teachers, parents and elected school officials to surrender control of the American public school system to public school students." Of course, Justice Black's observations are equally relevant to the instant case.

7. A number of lower federal courts have similarly recognized that educators' decisions with regard to the content of school sponsored newspapers, dramatic productions, and other expressive activities are entitled to substantial deference. We need not now decide whether the same degree of deference is appropriate with respect to school-sponsored expressive activities at the college and university level.

a. White, J., concluded that Principal Reynolds acted reasonably in requiring deletion of the pages from the newspaper. In addition to concerns about privacy and failure to contact persons discussed in the stories, it was "not unreasonable for the principal to have concluded that [frank talk about sexual histories, albeit not graphic, with comments about use or nonuse of birth control] was inappropriate in a school-sponsored publication distributed to 14–year–old freshmen and presumably taken home to be read by students' even younger brothers and sisters."

skills that the curricular newspaper "is designed to teach." The educator may, under *Tinker,* constitutionally "censor" poor grammar, writing, or research because to reward such expression would "materially disrup[t]" the newspaper's curricular purpose. * * *

The Court relies on bits of testimony to portray the principal's conduct as a pedagogical lesson to Journalism II students who "had not sufficiently mastered those portions of [the] curriculum that pertained to the treatment of controversial issues and personal attacks, the need to protect the privacy of individuals [and] 'the legal, moral, and ethical restrictions imposed upon journalists * * *.'"

But the principal never consulted the students before censoring their work. [T]hey learned of the deletions when the paper was released. [Further,] he explained the deletions only in the broadest of generalities. In one meeting called at the behest of seven protesting Spectrum staff members (presumably a fraction of the full class), he characterized the articles as " 'too sensitive' for 'our immature audience of readers,'" and in a later meeting he deemed them simply "inappropriate, personal, sensitive and unsuitable for the newspaper." The Court's supposition that the principal intended (or the protesters understood) those generalities as a lesson on the nuances of journalistic responsibility is utterly incredible. If he did, a fact that neither the District Court nor the Court of Appeals found, the lesson was lost on all but the psychic Spectrum staffer.

The Court's second excuse for deviating from precedent is the school's interest in shielding an impressionable high school audience from material whose substance is "unsuitable for immature audiences." [*Tinker*] teaches us that the state educator's undeniable, and undeniably vital, mandate to inculcate moral and political values is not a general warrant to act as "thought police" stifling discussion of all but state-approved topics and advocacy of all but the official position. [The] mere fact of school sponsorship does not, as the Court suggests, license such thought control in the high school, whether through school suppression of disfavored viewpoints or through official assessment of topic sensitivity. [Moreover, the] State's prerogative to dissolve the student newspaper entirely (or to limit its subject matter) no more entitles it to dictate which viewpoints students may express on its pages, than the State's prerogative to close down the schoolhouse entitles it to prohibit the nondisruptive expression of antiwar sentiment within its gates.

Official censorship of student speech on the ground that it addresses "potentially sensitive topics" is, for related reasons, equally impermissible. I would not begrudge an educator the authority to limit the substantive scope of a school-sponsored publication to a certain, objectively definable topic, such as literary criticism, school sports, or an overview of the school year. Unlike those determinate limitations, "potential topic sensitivity" is a vaporous nonstandard [that] invites manipulation to achieve ends that cannot permissibly be achieved through blatant viewpoint discrimination and chills student speech to which school officials might not object. * * * [b]

Notes and Questions

1. Consider Bruce Hafen, *Hazelwood School District and the Role of First Amendment Institutions,* 1988 Duke L.J. 685, 701, 704–05: "[T]he question whether authoritarian or anti-authoritarian approaches will best develop the minds and expressive powers of children is more a matter of educational philoso-

---

b. Brennan, J. further argued that the material deleted was not conceivably tortious and that less restrictive alternatives, such as more precise deletions, were readily available.

phy and practice than of constitutional law. For that reason alone, first amendment theories applied by courts largely on the basis of anti-authoritarian assumptions are at best a clumsy and limited means of ensuring optimal educational development, whether the goal is an understanding of democratic values or a mastery of basic intellectual skills. Thus, one of *Hazelwood's* major contributions is its reaffirmation of schools' institutional role—and their accountability to the public for fulfilling it responsibly—in nurturing the underlying values of the first amendment. "The first amendment must [protect] not only individual writers, but newspapers; not only religious persons, but churches; not only individual students and teachers, but schools. These 'intellectual and moral associations' form a crucial part of the constitutional structure, for they help teach the peculiar and sometimes paradoxical blend of liberty and duty that sustains both individual freedom and the entire culture from one generation to the next."

2. *School sponsorship. Fraser* involved a speech on behalf of a candidate in a student election at an official school assembly. Was that speech "school-sponsored?" Or is the Court suggesting in fn. 4 that *Tinker's* standard is inadequate even for non-school-sponsored speech?

3. *A narrow holding?* Consider J. Marc Abrams & S. Mark Goodman, *End of an Era? The Decline of Student Press [Rights]*, 1988 Duke L.J. 706, 728: "*Hazelwood* is limited by its own terms to secondary-school-sponsored publications that are not public forums for student expression. [Publications] at institutions of higher education and independent (or forum) publications in secondary schools retain, for the time being, extensive first amendment protections." See also William Buss, *School Newspapers, Public Forum, and the First Amendment*, 74 Iowa L.Rev. 505 (1989).

4. Consider Martha Minow & Elizabeth Spellman, *Passion For Justice,* 10 Cardozo L.Rev. 37, 68–69 (1988): "The majority does not acknowledge the power it is exercising in the act of deferring to the 'reasonable' judgments of the [principal:] the power to signal to school officials all around the country, that it is all right to err on the side of eliminating student speech, it is all right to indulge your paternalistic attitudes toward the students; you do not need to guard against your own discomfort with what students want to discuss, for the 'rights' really lie within your own judgment about what they need. [The] dissent is acutely sensitive to the impact of censorship on students, but less attentive to the impact of judicial review on the school officials. Although equal attention to competing sides may make a decision more difficult, refraining from seeing the power of competing arguments itself may lead to tragic blindness."

BOARD OF EDUC. v. PICO, 457 U.S. 853, 102 S.Ct. 2799, 73 L.Ed.2d 435 (1982): On ascertaining that its school libraries contained eleven books that they described as "objectionable" and "improper fare for school students," [a] the Board

a. As the plurality opinion noted: "The nine [listed] books in the High School library were: *Slaughter House Five*, by Kurt Vonnegut, Jr.; *The Naked Ape*, by Desmond Morris; *Down These Mean Streets*, by Piri Thomas; *Best Short Stories of Negro Writers*, edited by Langston Hughes; *Go Ask Alice*, of anonymous authorship; *Laughing Boy*, by Oliver LaFarge; *Black Boy*, by Richard Wright; *A Hero Ain't Nothin' But A Sandwich*, by Alice Childress;

and *Soul On Ice*, by Eldridge Cleaver. The [listed] book in the Junior High School library was *A Reader for Writers*, edited by Jerome Archer. Still another listed book, *The Fixer*, by Bernard Malamud, was found to be included in the curriculum of a twelfth grade literature course."

The Board subsequently decided that only *Laughing Boy* should be returned to the li-

informally directed, over the objection of the school superintendent, that the books be delivered to the Board's offices so that Board members could read them. The Board characterized the listed books as "anti-American, anti-Christian, anti-Semitic, and just plain filthy" and concluded that it had a "duty" and a "moral obligation" "to protect the children in our school from this moral danger." Although an appointed parent-teacher "Book Review Committee" recommended that only two books be removed and a third be available to students only with parental approval, the Board decided that nine books should be removed and that another should be made available subject to parental approval. Respondent students contended that the Board's actions violated their first amendment rights. The district court granted summary judgment for the Board, stating that the Board had "restricted access only to certain books which [it] believed to be, in essence, vulgar." A 2–1 majority of the Second Circuit reversed. One member of the majority concluded that at least at the summary judgment stage, the Board had not offered sufficient justification for its action. A second member of the majority "viewed the case as turning on the contested factual issue of whether [the Board's] removal decision was motivated by a justifiable desire to remove books containing vulgarities and sexual explicitness, or rather by an impermissible desire to suppress ideas." Affirming, BRENNAN, J., announced the judgment of the Court in an opinion joined by Marshall and Stevens, JJ., and in part by Blackmun, J.: "Respondents do not seek [to] impose limitations upon their school Board's discretion to prescribe the curricula of the Island Trees schools. On the contrary, the only books at issue in this case are *library* books, books that by their nature are optional rather than required reading. [Furthermore,] even as to library books, the action before us does not involve the *acquisition* of books. [Rather,] the only action challenged in this case is the *removal* from school libraries of books originally placed there by the school authorities, or without objection from them.

[W]e do not deny that local school boards have a substantial legitimate role to play in the determination of school library content. [But] that discretion may not be exercised in a narrowly partisan or political manner. If a Democratic school board, motivated by party affiliation, ordered the removal of all books written by or in favor of Republicans, few would doubt that the order violated the constitutional rights of the students denied access to those books. The same conclusion would surely apply if an all-white school board, motivated by racial animus, decided to remove all books authored by blacks or advocating racial equality and integration. Our Constitution does not permit the official suppression of *ideas*. [If] petitioners *intended* by their removal decision to deny respondents access to ideas with which petitioners disagreed, and if this intent was the decisive factor in petitioners' decision,[22] then petitioners have exercised their discretion in violation of the Constitution. [On] the other hand, respondents implicitly concede that an unconstitutional motivation would *not* be demonstrated if it were shown that petitioners had decided to remove the books at issue because those books were pervasively vulgar. And again, respondents concede that if it were demonstrated that the removal decision was based solely upon the 'educational suitability' of the books in question, then their removal would be 'perfectly permissible.' "[This] would be a very different case if the record demonstrated that petitioners had employed established, regular, and facially unbiased procedures for the review of controversial materials. But [respondents'] allegations and some of the evidentia-

brary without restriction, and that *Black Boy* should be made available subject to parental approval.

22. By "decisive factor" we mean a "substantial factor" in the absence of which the opposite decision would have been reached.

ry materials presented below do not rule out the possibility that petitioners' removal procedures were highly irregular and ad hoc—the antithesis of those procedures that might tend to allay suspicions regarding petitioners' motivations.

"Construing these claims, affidavit statements, and other evidentiary materials in a manner favorable to respondents, we cannot conclude that petitioners were 'entitled to a judgment as a matter of law.' The evidence plainly does not foreclose the possibility that petitioners' decision to remove the books rested decisively upon disagreement with constitutionally protected ideas in those books, or upon a desire on petitioners' part to impose upon the students of the Island Trees High School and Junior High School a political orthodoxy to which petitioners and their constituents adhered." [b]

BLACKMUN, J., concurred, "I do not believe, as the plurality suggests, that the right at issue here is somehow associated with the peculiar nature of the school library; if schools may be used to inculcate ideas, surely libraries may play a role in that process. [S]chool officials may seek to instill certain values 'by persuasion and example,' or by choice of emphasis. That sort of positive educational action, however, is the converse of an intentional attempt to shield students from certain ideas that officials find politically distasteful.

WHITE, J., who concurred in the judgment, noted that "[t]he unresolved factual issue [is] the reason or reasons underlying the school board's removal of the books" and he was "not inclined to disagree with the Court of Appeals on such a fact-bound issue. [The] Court seems compelled to go further and issue a dissertation on the extent to which the First Amendment limits the discretion of the school board to remove books from the school library. I see no necessity for doing so at this point."

BURGER, C.J., joined by Powell, Rehnquist, and O'Connor, JJ., dissented: "[The] plurality concludes that under the Constitution school boards cannot choose to retain or dispense with books if their discretion is exercised in a 'narrowly partisan or political manner.' The plurality concedes that permissible factors are whether the books are 'pervasively vulgar' or educationally unsuitable. 'Educational suitability,' however, is a standardless phrase. * * * Ultimately the federal courts will be the judge of whether the motivation for book removal was 'valid' or 'reasonable.' Undoubtedly the validity of many book removals will ultimately turn on a judge's evaluation of the books. Discretion must be used, and the appropriate body to exercise that discretion is the local elected school board, not judges."

POWELL, J., also dissented: "In different contexts and in different times, the destruction of written materials has been the symbol of despotism and intolerance. But the removal of nine vulgar or racist books from a high school library by a concerned local school board does not raise this specter." [c]

REHNQUIST, J., joined by Burger, C.J., and Powell, J., dissented: "The nine books removed undoubtedly did contain 'ideas,' but in the light of the excerpts from them found in the dissenting opinion [in the court below], it is apparent that eight of them contained demonstrable amounts of vulgarity and profanity and the ninth contained nothing that could be considered partisan or political. [R]espondents admitted as much. Petitioners did not, for the reasons stated hereafter, run afoul of the First and Fourteenth Amendments by removing these particular

---

b. For criticism of Brennan, J.'s opinion, see William Lee, *The Supreme Court and the Right to Receive Expression,* 1987 Sup.Ct.Rev. 303, 323–27.

c. Powell, J., appended a summary of excerpts from the books at issue collected in the opinion of Judge Mansfield dissenting below.

books from the library in the manner in which they did. I would save for another day—feeling quite confident that that day will not arrive—the extreme examples posed in Justice Brennan's opinion.

[Had] petitioners been the members of a town council, I suppose all would agree that, absent a good deal more than is present in this record, they could not have prohibited the sale of these books by private booksellers within the munici-pality. But we have also recognized that the government may act in other capacities than as sovereign, and when it does the First Amendment may speak with a different voice. [By] the same token, expressive conduct which may not be prohibited by the State as sovereign may be proscribed by the State as property owner [quoting from *Adderley*, p. 867 supra].

When it acts as an educator, at least at the elementary and secondary school level, the government is engaged in inculcating social values and knowledge in relatively impressionable young people. Obviously there are innumerable deci-sions to be made as to what courses should be taught, what books should be purchased, or what teachers should be employed. In every one of these areas the members of a school board will act on the basis of their own personal or moral values, will attempt to mirror those of the community, or will abdicate the making of such decisions to so-called 'experts.' [In] the very course of administering the many-faceted operations of a school district, the mere decision to purchase some books will necessarily preclude the possibility of purchasing others. The decision to teach a particular subject may preclude the possibility of teaching another subject. A decision to replace a teacher because of ineffectiveness may by implication be seen as a disparagement of the subject matter taught. In each of these instances, however, the book or the exposure to the subject matter may be acquired elsewhere. The managers of the school district are not proscribing it as to the citizenry in general, but are simply determining that it will not be included in the curriculum or school library. In short, actions by the government as educator do not raise the same First Amendment concerns as actions by the government as sovereign. * * *

"Education consists of the selective presentation and explanation of ideas. The effective acquisition of knowledge depends upon an orderly exposure to relevant information. Nowhere is this more true than in elementary and second-ary schools, where, unlike the broad-ranging inquiry available to university students, the courses taught are those thought most relevant to the young students' individual development. [Determining] what information *not* to present to the students is often as important as identifying relevant material. This winnowing process necessarily leaves much information to be discovered by students at another time or in another place, and is fundamentally inconsistent with any constitutionally required eclecticism in public education.

"[Unlike] university or public libraries, elementary and secondary school libraries are not designed for free-wheeling inquiry; they are tailored, as the public school curriculum is tailored, to the teaching of basic skills and [ideas.]"

In a brief separate dissent, O'CONNOR, J., observed: "If the school board can set the curriculum, select teachers, and determine initially what books to purchase for the school library, it surely can decide which books to discontinue or remove from the school library so long as it does not also interfere with the right of students to read the material and to discuss it. As Justice Rehnquist persuasively argues, the plurality's analysis overlooks the fact that in this case the government is acting in its special role as educator."

Notes & Question

1. Consider Mark Yudof, *Library Book Selection and Public Schools: The Quest for the Archimedean Point,* 59 Ind.L.J. 527, 530 (1984): The critical questions in *Pico* are "who will control socialization of the young, what are the values to which they will be socialized, and how will cultural grounding and critical reflection be accommodated." On the latter point, see Mendelson, *The Habermas-Gadamer Debate,* New German Critique 18 (1979). See also Roberto Unger, *Knowledge and Politics* (1975); Drucilla Cornell, *Toward a Modern/Postmodern Reconstruction of Ethics,* 133 U.Pa.L.Rev. 291 (1985).[d]

2. Should librarians have a first amendment right to select and retain books against the objections of a school board? Against a city council in a non-school context? See Robert O'Neil, *Libraries, Librarians and First Amendment Freedoms,* 4 Hum.Rts. 295 (1975); Robert O'Neil, *Libraries, Liberties and the First Amendment,* 42 U.Cin.L.Rev. 209 (1973). Should elementary school teachers have a first amendment right to resist interference with their teaching by "politically" motivated administrators or school boards? At secondary levels? See William Canby, *The First Amendment and the State as Editor: Implications for Public Broadcasting,* 52 Tex.L.Rev. 1123 (1974). What of an approach that allows (requires?) administrators to set policies and procedures but prohibits ad hoc intervention?

3. Every justice recognizes that some content discrimination is permitted in selecting books and making curricular decisions. The line between a public forum and a facility subject to the government's editorial discretion, however, may be hard to draw. In SOUTHEASTERN PROMOTIONS, LTD. v. CONRAD, 420 U.S. 546, 95 S.Ct. 1239, 43 L.Ed.2d 448 (1975), reacting to reports that the musical *Hair* included nudity and was obscene, a publicly-appointed board denied *Hair's* producers a permit to use a theater dedicated for "cultural advancement and for clean, healthful, entertainment which will make for the upbuilding of a better citizenship." The Court, per BLACKMUN, J., held that the theater was a public forum "designed for and dedicated to expressive activities" and that the board's procedures amounted to a prior restraint in violation of *Freedman* requirements, p. 861 supra. One of the dissenters, REHNQUIST, J., asked: "May a municipal theater devote an entire season to Shakespeare, or is it required to book any

d. For a range of views on the scope and propriety of government promotion of particular values, see sources collected in fn. i after *Regan* supra. See also Ronald Dworkin, *A Matter of Principle* 181–204, 221–33 (1985); David Moshman, *Children, Education, and the First Amendment* (1989); Joseph Tussman, *Government and the Mind* (1977); Susan Bitensky, *A Contemporary Proposal for Reconciling the Free Speech Clause With Curricular Values Inculcation in the Public Schools,* 70 Notre Dame L.Rev. 769 (1995); David Diamond, *The First Amendment and Public Schools: The Case Against Judicial Intervention,* 59 Tex.L.Rev. 477 (1981); John Garvey, *Children and the First Amendment,* 57 Tex. L.Rev. 321 (1979); Stephen Goldstein, *The Asserted Constitutional Right of Public School Teachers to Determine What They Teach,* 124 U.Pa.L.Rev. 1293 (1976); Stephen Gottlieb, *In The Name of Patriotism: The Constitutionality of "Bending" History in Public Secondary Schools,* 62 N.Y.U.L.Rev. 497 (1987); Stanley Ingber, *Socialization, Indoctrination, or the "Pall of Orthodoxy": Value Training in the Public Schools,* 1987 U.Ill.L.Rev. 15; Joel Moskowitz, *The Making of the Moral Child: Legal Implications of Values Education,* 6 Pepp. L.Rev. 105 (1978); Sheldon Nahmod, *Controversy in the Classroom: The High School Teacher and Freedom of Expression,* 39 Geo. Wash.L.Rev. 1032 (1971); Suzanna Sherry, *Responsible Republicanism: Educating for Citizenship,* 62 U.Chi.L.Rev. 131 (1995); Tyll van Geel, *The Search for Constitutional Limits on Governmental Authority to Inculcate Youth,* 62 Tex.L.Rev. 197 (1983); Note, *Education and the Court: The Supreme Court's Educational Ideology,* 40 Vand.L.Rev. 939 (1987); Note, *The Promise of Pico: A New Definition of Orthodoxy,* 97 Yale L.J. 1805 (1988); Note, *State Indoctrination and the Protection of Non-State Voices in the Schools: Justifying a Prohibition of School Library Censorship,* 35 Stan. L.Rev. 497 (1983).

potential producer on a first come, first served basis? [T]he Court's opinion [seems] to give no constitutionally permissible role in the way of selection to the municipal authorities." For commentary, see Kenneth Karst, *Public Enterprise and the Public Forum: A Comment on Southeastern Promotions, Ltd. v. Conrad,* 37 Ohio St.L.J. 247 (1976); Steven Shiffrin, fn. i after *Regan,* supra, at 581–88; Comment, *Access to State-Owned Communications Media—The Public Forum Doctrine,* 26 U.C.L.A.L.Rev. 1410, 1440–44 (1979).

4. Blackmun, J., states in fn. 2 that the crucial point is the state's decision to "single out an idea for disapproval and then deny access to it." Suppose the government does not deny access to speech but officially denounces it. Constitutional? [e]

LAMONT v. POSTMASTER GENERAL, 381 U.S. 301, 85 S.Ct. 1493, 14 L.Ed.2d 398 (1965), per DOUGLAS, J., invalidated a federal statute permitting delivery of "communist political propaganda" only if the addressee specifically requested in writing that it be delivered: "We rest on the narrow ground that the addressee in order to receive his mail must request in writing that it be delivered. [The] addressee carries an affirmative obligation which we do not think the Government may impose on him. This requirement is almost certain to have a deterrent effect, especially as respects those who have sensitive positions. [Public] officials, like school teachers who have no tenure, might think they would invite disaster if they read what the Federal Government says contains the seeds of treason. Apart from them, any addressee is likely to feel some inhibition in sending for literature which federal officials have condemned as 'communist political propaganda.' "

MEESE v. KEENE, 481 U.S. 465, 107 S.Ct. 1862, 95 L.Ed.2d 415 (1987), per STEVENS, J., held that the government could label a film as "political propaganda" without violating the first amendment: "The Foreign Agents Registration Act [uses] the term 'political propaganda,' [f] [to] identify those expressive materials that must comply with the Act's registration, filing, and disclosure requirements." The government had identified three Canadian films as "political propaganda." Keene maintained that he should be free to exhibit the three films without being considered an exhibitor of governmentally designated "propaganda." Without otherwise reaching the Act's requirements, the Court rejected Keene's claim:

e. Consider Professor Lawrence's suggestion that segregation's *"only* purpose is to label or define blacks as inferior." Charles Lawrence, " *'One More River to Cross'—Recognizing the Real Injury in Brown," in* Shades of Brown 49, 50 (Bell ed. 1980). See also Charles Lawrence, *If He Hollers Let Him Go: Regulating Racist Speech on Campus,* 1990 Duke L.J. 431. When should governmental denunciation of persons or groups be considered a violation of the first amendment?

f. The Act defines political propaganda to include: "any oral, visual, graphic, written, pictorial, or other communication or expression by any person (1) which is reasonably adapted to, or which the person disseminating the same believes will, or which he intends to, prevail upon, indoctrinate, convert, induce, or in any other way influence a recipient or any section of the public within the United States with reference to the political or public interests, policies, or relations of a government or a foreign country or a foreign political party or

with reference to the foreign policies of the United States or promote in the United States racial, religious, or social dissensions, or (2) which advocates, advises, instigates, or promotes any racial, social, political, or religious disorder, civil riot, or other conflict involving the use of force or violence in any other American republic or the overthrow of any government or political subdivision of any other American republic by any means involving the use of force or violence."

Stevens, J., commented, "As defined in the Act, the term political propaganda includes misleading advocacy. [But] it also includes advocacy materials that are completely accurate and merit the closest attention and the highest respect. Standard reference works include both broad, neutral definitions of the word 'propaganda' that are consistent with the way the word is defined in this statute, and also the narrower, pejorative definition."

"The statute itself neither prohibits nor censors the dissemination of advocacy materials by agents of foreign principals.[g] [To] the contrary, Congress simply required the disseminators of such material to make additional disclosures that would better enable the public to evaluate the import of the propaganda. The statute does not prohibit appellee from advising his audience that the films have not been officially censured in any way. Disseminators of propaganda may go beyond the disclosures required by statute and add any further information they think germane to the public's viewing of the materials. By compelling some disclosure of information and permitting more, the Act's approach recognizes that the best remedy for misleading or inaccurate speech contained within materials subject to the Act is fair, truthful, and accurate speech. * * * Ironically, it is the injunction entered by the District Court that withholds information from the public. The suppressed information is the fact that the films fall within the category of materials that Congress has judged to be 'political propaganda'. A similar paternalistic strategy of protecting the public from information was followed by the Virginia Assembly, which enacted a ban on the advertising of prescription drug prices by pharmacists. See *Virginia Pharmacy*." [h]

BLACKMUN, J., joined by Brennan and Marshall, JJ., dissented: "[T]here is a significant difference between the 'paternalistic strategy of protecting the public from information,' by way of a *ban* on information and a prohibition of the government disparagement at issue in this case. [Under] the District Court's ruling, opponents of the viewpoint expressed by the [film] remained completely free to point out [its] foreign [source]. The difference was that dialogue on the value of the films and the viewpoints they express could occur in an atmosphere free of the constraint imposed by government condemnation. It is the Government's classification of those films as 'political propaganda' that is paternalistic. For that government action does more than simply provide additional information. It places the power of the Federal Government, with its authority, presumed neutrality, and assumed access to all the facts, behind an appellation *designed* to reduce the effectiveness of the speech in the eyes of the public."

g. The Court distinguished *Lamont* stating that the physical detention of mail, not its mere designation as "communist political propaganda" was the offending element of the statutory scheme. By contrast, the Court argued that the Foreign Agents Registration Act posed no obstacle to Keene's access to the materials. In response, Blackmun, J., dissenting, observed that the "communist political propaganda [detained in *Lamont*] and delivered only upon the addressee's request was defined by reference to the same 'neutral' definition of 'political propaganda' in the Act that is at issue here. Yet the Court examined the effects of the statutory requirements and had no trouble concluding that the need to request delivery of mail classified as 'communist political propaganda' was almost certain to have a deterrent effect upon debate."

h. Scalia, J., took no part. In *Block v. Meese*, 793 F.2d 1303 (D.C.Cir.1986), however, then Circuit Judge Scalia ruled on the issue. "[E]ven if classification as 'propaganda' constituted an expression of official government disapproval of the ideas in question, neither precedent nor reason would justify us in finding such an expression *in itself* unlawful. [W]e know of no case in which the first amendment has been held to be implicated by governmental action consisting of no more than governmental criticism of the speech's content. [A] rule excluding official praise or criticism of ideas would lead to the strange conclusion that it is permissible for the government to prohibit racial discrimination, but not to criticize racial bias; to criminalize polygamy, but not to praise the monogamous family; to make war on Hitler's Germany, but not to denounce Nazism. [The] line of permissibility [falls] not between criticism of ideas in general and criticism of the ideas contained in specific books or expressed by specific persons; but between the disparagement of ideas general or specific and the suppression of ideas through the exercise or threat of state power. If the latter is rigorously prescribed, see *Bantam Books,* the former can hold no terror."

SECTION 9. BROADCAST REGULATION AND ACCESS TO THE MASS MEDIA

The mass media are not invariably the most effective means of communication. For example, the right to place messages on utility poles concerning a lost dog may be more important than access to a radio or a television station. In some circumstances, picketing outside a school or placing leaflets in teachers' mailboxes may be the most effective communications medium. Nonetheless, the law regulating access to the mass media is of vital societal importance. This section considers first, cases in which government seeks to force newspapers and broadcasters to grant access; second, in *CBS v. DNC*, infra, a claim that the first amendment requires government to afford access for excluded groups to the broadcast media; third, a case in which government seeks to encourage diverse programming by promoting diversity among broadcast licensees; finally, cases in which government commands broadcasters not to carry particular programming at particular times or not to editorialize. A persistent theme is that broadcasting is "special," but whether it is, why it is, and what difference it should make are matters of considerable debate. Beyond this, attitudes about the most effective channel of communication raise questions about our commitment to and understanding of first amendment principles. If the assumption that broadcasting is special is a masquerade, why the masquerade?

I. ACCESS TO THE MASS MEDIA

MIAMI HERALD PUB. CO. v. TORNILLO, 418 U.S. 241, 94 S.Ct. 2831, 41 L.Ed.2d 730 (1974), per BURGER, C.J., unanimously struck down a Florida "right of reply" statute, which required any newspaper that "assails" the personal character or official record of a candidate in any election to print, on demand, free of cost, any reply the candidate may make to the charges, in as conspicuous a place and the same kind of type, provided the reply takes up no more space than the charges. The opinion carefully explained the aim of the statute to "ensure that a wide variety of views reach the public" even though "chains of newspapers, national newspapers, national wire and news services, and one-newspaper towns, are the dominant features of a press that has become noncompetitive and enormously powerful and influential in its capacity to manipulate popular opinion and change the course of events," placing "in a few hands the power to inform the American people and shape public opinion." [a] Nonetheless, the Court concluded that to require the printing of a reply violated the first amendment: "Compelling editors or publishers to publish that which ' "reason" tells them should not be published' is what is at issue in this case. The Florida statute operates as a command in the same sense as a statute or regulation forbidding appellant from publishing specified matter. [The] Florida statute exacts a penalty on the basis of the content of a newspaper. The first phase of the penalty resulting from the compelled printing of a reply is exacted in terms of the cost in printing and composing time and materials and in taking up space that could be devoted to other material the newspaper may have preferred to print. It is correct, as appellee contends, that a newspaper is not subject to the finite technological limitations of time that confront a broadcaster but it is not correct to say that, as an economic reality, a newspaper can proceed to infinite expansion of its column

a. The opinion developed these views at greater length, citing "generally" Jerome Barron, *Access to the Press—A New First Amendment Right*, 80 Harv.L.Rev. 1641 (1967); David Lange, *The Role of the Access Doctrine* in the Regulation of the Mass Media: A Critical Review and Assessment, 52 N.C.L.Rev. 1, 8–9 (1973). For historical background and a spirited criticism of the statute, see Lucas Powe, *Tornillo*, 1987 Sup.Ct.Rev. 345.

space to accommodate the replies that a government agency determines or a statute commands the readers should have available.

"Faced with the penalties that would accrue to any newspaper that published news or commentary arguably within the reach of the right of access statute, editors might well conclude that the safe course is to avoid controversy and that, under the operation of the Florida statute, political and electoral coverage would be blunted or reduced. Government enforced right of access inescapably 'dampens the vigor and limits the variety of public debate,' *New York Times*.

"Even if a newspaper would face no additional costs to comply with a compulsory access law and would not be forced to forego publication of news or opinion by the inclusion of a reply, the Florida statute fails to clear the barriers of the First Amendment because of its intrusion into the function of editors. A newspaper is more than a passive receptacle or conduit for news, comment, and advertising. The choice of material to go into a newspaper, and the decisions made as to limitations on the size of the paper, and content, and treatment of public issues and public officials—whether fair or unfair—constitutes the exercise of editorial control and judgment. It has yet to be demonstrated how governmental regulation of this crucial process can be exercised consistent with First Amendment guarantees of a free press as they have evolved to this time." [b]

The Federal Communications Commission for many years imposed on radio and television broadcasters the "fairness doctrine"—requiring that stations (1) devote a reasonable percentage of broadcast time to discussion of public issues and (2) assure fair coverage for each side.[c] At issue in RED LION BROADCASTING CO. v. FCC, 395 U.S. 367, 89 S.Ct. 1794, 23 L.Ed.2d 371 (1969), were the application of the fairness doctrine to a particular broadcast[d] and two specific access regulations promulgated under the doctrine: (1) the "political editorial" rule, requiring that when a broadcaster, in an editorial, "endorses or opposes" a political candidate, it must notify the candidate opposed, or the rivals of the

b. Brennan, J., joined by Rehnquist, J., joined the Court's opinion in a short statement to express the understanding that it "implies no view upon the constitutionality of 'retraction' statutes affording plaintiffs able to prove defamatory falsehoods a statutory action to require publication of a retraction."

White, J., concurred. After agreeing that "prior compulsion by government in matters going to the very nerve center of a newspaper—the decision as to what copy will or will not be included in any given edition—collides with the First Amendment," he returned to his attack on *Gertz*, decided the same day: "Reaffirming the rule that the press cannot be forced to print an answer to a personal attack made by it [throws] into stark relief the consequences of the new balance forged by the Court in the companion case also announced today. *Gertz* goes far toward eviscerating the effectiveness of the ordinary libel action, which has long been the only potent response available to the private citizen libeled by the press. [To] me it is a near absurdity to so deprecate individual dignity, as the Court does in *Gertz*, and to leave the people at the complete mercy

of the press, at least in this stage of our history when the press, as the majority in this case so well documents, is steadily becoming more powerful and much less likely to be deterred by threats of libel suits."

c. For helpful background on the origins, justification and administration of the fairness doctrine, see Roscoe Barrow, *The Fairness Doctrine: A Double Standard for Electronic and Print Media*, 26 Hast.L.J. 659 (1975); Benno Schmidt, *Freedom of the Press vs. Public Access* 157–98 (1976).

d. *Red Lion* grew out of a series of radio broadcasts by fundamentalist preacher Billy James Hargis, who had attacked Fred J. Cook, author of an article attacking Hargis and "hate clubs of the air." When Cook heard about the broadcast, he demanded that the station give him an opportunity to reply. Cook refused to pay for his "reply time" and the FCC ordered the station to give Cook the opportunity to reply whether or not he would pay for it. The Supreme Court upheld the order of free reply time. See Schmidt, fn. c supra, at 161–63.

candidate supported, and afford them a "reasonable opportunity" to respond; (2) the "personal attack" rule, requiring that "when, during the presentation of views on a controversial issue of public importance, an attack is made on the honesty, character [or] integrity [of] an identified person or group," the person or group attacked must be given notice, a transcript of the attack, and an opportunity to respond.[e] "[I]n view of [the] scarcity of broadcast frequencies, the Government's role in allocating those frequencies, and the legitimate claims of those unable without government assistance to gain access to those frequencies for expression of their views," a 7–0 majority, per WHITE, J., upheld both access regulations: [f]

"[The broadcasters] contention is that the First Amendment protects their desire to use their allotted frequencies continuously to broadcast whatever they choose, and to exclude whomever they choose from ever using that frequency. No man may be prevented from saying or publishing what he thinks, or from refusing in his speech or other utterances to give equal weight to the views of his opponents. This right, they say, applies equally to broadcasters.

"Although broadcasting is clearly a medium affected by a First Amendment interest, differences in the characteristics of new media justify differences in the First Amendment standards applied to [them]. Just as the Government may limit the use of sound-amplifying equipment potentially so noisy that it drowns out civilized private speech, so may the Government limit the use of broadcast equipment. The right of free speech of a broadcaster, the user of a sound truck, or any other individual does not embrace a right to snuff out the free speech of [others].

"Where there are substantially more individuals who want to broadcast than there are frequencies to allocate, it is idle to posit an unabridgeable First Amendment right to broadcast comparable to the right of every individual to speak, write, or publish. [It] would be strange if the First Amendment, aimed at protecting and furthering communications, prevented the Government from making radio communication possible by requiring licenses to broadcast and by limiting the number of licenses so as not to overcrowd the spectrum. * * *

"By the same token, as far as the First Amendment is concerned those who are licensed stand no better than those to whom licenses are refused. A license permits broadcasting, but the licensee has no constitutional right [to] monopolize a radio frequency to the exclusion of his fellow citizens. There is nothing in the First Amendment which prevents the Government from requiring a licensee to share his frequency with others and to conduct himself as a proxy or fiduciary with obligations to present those views and voices which are representative of his community and which would otherwise, by necessity, be barred from the airwaves.

"[The] people as a whole retain their interest in free speech by radio and their collective right to have the medium function consistently with the ends and purposes of the First Amendment. It is the right of the viewers and listeners, not the right of the broadcasters, which is paramount. [It] is the purpose of the First Amendment to preserve an uninhibited marketplace of ideas in which truth will ultimately prevail, rather than to countenance monopolization of that market, whether it be by the Government itself or a private licensee. [It] is the right of

---

e. Excepted were "personal attacks [by] legally qualified candidates [on] other such candidates" and "bona fide newscasts, bona fide news interviews, and on-the-spot coverage of a bona fide news event."

f. Surprisingly, none of the justices joining White, J.'s opinion felt the need to make additional remarks, but Douglas, J., who did not participate in *Red Lion,* expressed his disagreement with it in the *CBS* case, infra.

the public to receive suitable access to social, political, esthetic, moral, and other ideas and experiences which is crucial [here.]

"In terms of constitutional principle, and as enforced sharing of a scarce resource, the personal attack and political editorial rules are indistinguishable from the equal-time provision of § 315 [of the Communications Act], a specific enactment of Congress requiring [that stations allot equal time to qualified candidates for public office] and to which the fairness doctrine and these constituent regulations are important complements. [Nor] can we say that it is inconsistent with the First Amendment goal of producing an informed public capable of conducting its own affairs to require a broadcaster to permit answers to personal attacks occurring in the course of discussing controversial issues, or to require that the political opponents of those endorsed by the station be given a chance to communicate with the public. Otherwise, station owners and a few networks would have unfettered power to make time available only to the highest bidders, to communicate only their own views on public issues, people and candidates, and to permit on the air only those with whom they agreed. There is no sanctuary in the First Amendment for unlimited private censorship operating in a medium not open to all.

"[It is contended] that if political editorials or personal attacks will trigger an obligation in broadcasters to afford the opportunity for expression to speakers who need not pay for time and whose views are unpalatable to the licensees, then broadcasters will be irresistibly forced to self-censorship and their coverage of controversial public issues will be eliminated or at least rendered wholly ineffective. Such a result would indeed be a serious matter, [but] that possibility is at best speculative. [If these doctrines turn out to have this effect], there will be time enough to reconsider the constitutional implications. The fairness doctrine in the past has had no such overall effect. That this will occur now seems unlikely, however, since if present licensees should suddenly prove timorous, the Commission is not powerless to insist that they give adequate and fair attention to public issues. It does not violate the First Amendment to treat licensees given the privilege of using scarce radio frequencies as proxies for the entire community, obligated to give suitable time and attention to matters of great public concern. To condition the granting or renewal of licenses on a willingness to present representative community views on controversial issues is consistent with the ends and purposes of those constitutional provisions forbidding the abridgment of freedom of speech and freedom of the press." [g]

Notes and Questions

1. *Tension between Miami Herald and Red Lion.* Consider Lee Bollinger, *Freedom of the Press and Public Access: Toward a Theory of Partial Regulation of the Mass Media,* 75 Mich.L.Rev. 1, 4–6, 10–12 (1976): "What seems so remarkable

---

g. The Court noted that it "need not deal with the argument that even if there is no longer a technological scarcity of frequencies limiting the number of broadcasters, there nevertheless is an economic scarcity in the sense that the Commission could or does limit entry to the broadcasting market on economic grounds and license no more stations than the market will support. Hence, it is said, the fairness doctrine or its equivalent is essential to satisfy the claims of those excluded and of the public generally. A related argument, which we also put side, is that quite apart from scarcity of frequencies, technological or economic, Congress does not abridge freedom of speech or press by legislation directly or indirectly multiplying the voices and views presented to the public through time sharing, fairness doctrines, or other devices which limit or dissipate the power of those who sit astride the channels of communication with the general public." For background and discussion of *Red Lion,* see Fred Friendly, *The Good Guys, The Bad Guys and the First Amendment* (1975).

about the unanimous *Miami Herald* opinion is the complete absence of any reference to the Court's unanimous decision five years earlier in *Red Lion* [, upholding] the so-called personal attack rule, [which] is almost identical in substance to the Florida statute declared unconstitutional in *Miami Herald*. That omission, however, is no more surprising than the absence of any discussion in *Red Lion* of the cases in which the Court expressed great concern about the risks attending government regulation of the print media.

"[The] scarcity rationale [articulated in *Red Lion* does not] explain why what appears to be a similar phenomenon of natural monopolization within the newspaper industry does not constitute an equally appropriate occasion for access regulation. A difference in the cause of concentration—the exhaustion of a physical element necessary for communication in broadcasting as contrasted with the economic constraints on the number of possible competitors in the print media—would seem far less relevant from a first amendment standpoint than the fact of concentration itself. [Instead] of exploring the relevance for the print media of the new principle developed in broadcasting, the Court merely reiterated the opposing, more traditional, principle that the government cannot tell editors what to publish. It thus created a paradox, leaving the new principle unscathed while preserving tradition."

2. *The absence of balancing in Miami Herald.* Did *Miami Herald* present a confrontation between the rights of speech and press? "Nowhere does [*Miami Herald*] explicitly acknowledge [such a confrontation], but implicit recognition of the speech interest," observes Melville Nimmer, *Is Freedom of the Press a Redundancy? What Does it Add to Freedom of Speech?*, 26 Hast.L.J. 639, 645, 657 (1975), "may be found in the Court's reference to the access advocates' argument that, given the present semimonopolistic posture of the press, speech can be effective and therefore free only if enhanced by devices such as a right of reply statute. The Court in accepting the press clause argument in effect necessarily found it to be superior to any competing speech clause claims. [But] the issue cannot be resolved merely by noting, as did [*Miami Herald*], that a right of reply statute 'constitutes the [state] exercise of editorial control and judgment.' This is but one half of the equation. [*Miami Herald*] ignored the strong conflicting claims of 'speech.' Perhaps on balance the press should still prevail, but those who doubt the efficacy of such a result are hardly persuaded by an approach that apparently fails to recognize that any balancing of speech and press rights is required." [h]

3. *Scope of Miami Herald.* Consider Schmidt, supra, note c, at 233–35: "From the perspective of First Amendment law generally, *Miami Herald* would be a stark and unexplained deviation if one were to read the decision as creating absolute prohibitions on access obligations.[i] [The] fact the Court offers no discussion as to why First Amendment rules respecting access should be absolute, while all other rules emanating from that Amendment are relative, suggests that the principle of *Miami Herald* probably is destined for uncharted qualifications

h. Does *Miami Herald* demonstrate, as Professor Nimmer believes, at 644–46, that free speech and press can be distinct, even conflicting interests? Anthony Lewis, *A Preferred Position for Journalism?*, 7 Hof.L.Rev. 595, 603 (1979), thinks not: "[T]he vice of the [Florida right of reply] law lay in the compulsion to publish; and I think the result would be no different if the case involved a compulsion to speak. If a state statute required any

candidate who spoke falsely about another to make a corrective speech, would it survive challenge under the first amendment?"

i. "Even in the area of 'the central freedom of the First Amendment,' which is criticism of the governmental acts of public officials," recalls Professor Schmidt, fn. c supra, at 232, "there is no absolute protection for expression."

and exceptions." But see Lucas Powe, *Tornillo,* 1987 Sup.Ct.Rev. 345, 391, 390: "Quite frankly I do not believe that a twenty page Supreme Court opinion meeting all the standards of craft (all considerations are ventilated fully and the opinion be of publishable quality for a good legal journal) can as effectively protect the right of press autonomy as the blunt rejection in *Miami Herald.* Chief Justice Burger's failure to engage, so annoying to Schmidt and other commentators, is in fact a great strength of the opinion."

Would a statute requiring nondiscriminatory access to the classified ads section of a newspaper pass muster under *Miami Herald?* A requirement that legal notices be published?

4. *Absolute editorial autonomy—some of the time.* Is it ironic that *Gertz,* p. 677 supra was decided the same day as *Miami Herald?* Which poses a greater threat to editorial autonomy—a negligence standard in defamation cases or the guaranteed access contemplated by the Florida statute? Whose autonomy is important—the editors or the owners? May government protect editors from ad hoc intervention by corporate owners? See generally C. Edwin Baker, *Human Liberty and Freedom of Speech* 225–71 (1989).

5. *The threat to editorial autonomy in Red Lion.* Consider Schmidt, fn. c supra, at 166: *Red Lion* "left broadcaster autonomy almost entirely at the mercy of the FCC." See also William Van Alstyne, *The Möbius Strip of the First Amendment: Perspectives on Red Lion,* 29 S.C.L.Rev. 539, 571 (1978): "Indeed, if one continues to be troubled by *Red Lion,* I think it is not because one takes lightly the difficulty of forum allocation in a society of scarce resources. Rather, it is because one believes that the technique of the fairness doctrine in particular may represent a very trivial egalitarian gain and a major first amendment loss; that a twist has been given to the equal protection idea by a device the principal effect of which is merely to level down the most vivid and versatile forum we have, to flatten it out and to render it a mere commercial mirror of each community. What may have been lost is a willingness to risk the partisanship of licensees as catalysts and as active advocates with a freedom to exhort, a freedom that dares to exclaim 'Fuck the draft,' and not be made to yield by government at once to add, 'but on the other hand there is also the view, held by many.' "

6. *The best of both worlds.* "[T]he critical difference between what the Court was asked to do in *Red Lion* and what it was asked to do in *Miami Herald,*" maintains Professor Bollinger note 1 supra, at 27, "involved choosing between a partial regulatory system and a universal one. Viewed from that perspective, the Court reached the correct result in both cases." Continues Bollinger at 27, 32–33, 36–37: "[T]here are good first amendment reasons for being both receptive to and wary of access regulation. This dual nature of access legislation suggests the need to limit carefully the intrusiveness of the regulation in order safely to enjoy its remedial benefits. Thus, a proper judicial response is one that will permit the legislature to provide the public with access *somewhere* within the mass media, but not throughout the press. The Court should not, and need not, be forced into an all-or-nothing position on this matter; there is nothing in the first amendment that forbids having the best of both worlds."

For a powerful critique of the regulated world, see Lucas Powe, *American Broadcasting and the First Amendment* (1987). For a powerful critique of the unregulated world, see Stanley Ingber, *The First Amendment in Modern Garb,* 56 G.W.U.L.Rev. 187 (1987).

"Like many equal protection issues," observes Karst, p. 896 supra, at 45, "the media-access problem should be approached from two separate constitutional directions. First, what does the Constitution *compel* government to do in the way of equalizing? Second, what does the Constitution *permit* government to do in equalizing by statute?" *Red Lion* and *Miami Herald* presented the second question; the first is raised by COLUMBIA BROADCASTING SYSTEM, INC. v. DEMOCRATIC NAT'L. COMMITTEE, 412 U.S. 94, 93 S.Ct. 2080, 36 L.Ed.2d 772 (1973) (*CBS*): The FCC rejected the claims of Business Executives' Move for Vietnam Peace (BEM) and the Democratic National Committee (DNC) that "responsible" individuals and groups are entitled to purchase advertising time to comment on public issues, even though the broadcaster has complied with the fairness doctrine. The District of Columbia Circuit held that "a flat ban on paid public issue announcements" violates the first amendment "at least when other sorts of paid announcements are accepted," and remanded to the FCC to develop "reasonable procedures and regulations determining which and how many 'editorial advertisements' will be put on the air." The Supreme Court, per BURGER, C.J., reversed, holding that neither the "public interest" standard of the Communications Act (which draws heavily from the first amendment) nor the first amendment itself—assuming that refusal to accept such advertising constituted "governmental action" for first amendment purposes[a]—requires broadcasters to accept paid editorial announcements. As pointed out in Vincent Blasi, *The Checking Value in First Amendment Theory*, 1977 Am.B.Found.Res.J. 521, 613–14 although the Chief Justice "built to some extent" on *Red Lion,* his opinion "evinced a most important change of emphasis. For whereas Justice White based his argument in *Red Lion* on the premise that broadcasters are mere 'proxies' or 'fiduciaries' for the general public, the Chief Justice's opinion [in *CBS*] invoked a concept of 'journalistic independence' or 'journalistic discretion,' the essence of which is that broadcasters do indeed have special First Amendment interests which have to be considered in the constitutional calculus."

Observed the Chief Justice: "[From various provisions of the Communications Act of 1934] it seems clear that Congress intended to permit private broadcasting to develop with the widest journalistic freedom consistent with its public obligations. Only when the interests of the public are found to outweigh the private journalistic interests of the broadcasters will government power be asserted within the framework of the Act. License renewal proceedings, in which the listening public can be heard, are a principal means of such regulation.

"[W]ith the advent of radio a half century ago, Congress was faced with a fundamental choice between total Government ownership and control of the new medium—the choice of most other countries—or some other alternative. Long before the impact and potential of the medium was realized, Congress opted for a system of private broadcasters licensed and regulated by Government. The legislative history suggests that this choice was influenced not only by traditional attitudes toward private enterprise, but by a desire to maintain for licensees, so far as consistent with necessary regulation, a traditional journalistic [role.]

a. Burger, C.J., joined by Stewart and Rehnquist, JJ., concluded that a broadcast licensee's refusal to accept an advertisement was not "governmental action" for first amendment purposes. Although White, Blackmun and Powell, JJ., concurred in other parts of the Chief Justice's opinion, they did not decide this question for, *assuming* governmental action, they found that the challenged ban did not violate the first amendment. Douglas, J., who concurred in the result, assumed *no* governmental action. Dissenting, Brennan, J., joined by Marshall, J., found that the challenged ban did constitute "governmental action."

"The regulatory scheme evolved slowly, but very early the licensee's role developed in terms of a 'public trustee' charged with the duty of fairly and impartially informing the public audience. In this structure the Commission acts in essence as an 'overseer,' but the initial and primary responsibility for fairness, balance, and objectivity rests with the licensee. This role of the Government as an overseer and ultimate arbiter and guardian of the public interest and the role of the licensee as a journalistic 'free agent' call for a delicate balancing of competing interests. The maintenance of this balance for more than 40 years has called on both the regulators and the licensees to walk a 'tightrope' to preserve the First Amendment values written into the Radio Act and its successor, the Communications Act.

"The tensions inherent in such a regulatory structure emerge more clearly when we compare a private newspaper with a broadcast licensee. The power of a privately owned newspaper to advance its own political, social, and economic views is bounded by only two factors: first, the acceptance of a sufficient number of readers—and hence advertisers—to assure financial success; and, second, the journalistic integrity of its editors and publishers. A broadcast licensee has a large measure of journalistic freedom but not as large as that exercised by a newspaper. A licensee must balance what it might prefer to do as a private entrepreneur with what it is required to do as a 'public trustee.' To perform its statutory duties, the Commission must oversee without censoring. This suggests something of the difficulty and delicacy of administering the Communications Act—a function calling for flexibility and the capacity to adjust and readjust the regulatory mechanism to meet changing problems and needs.

"The licensee policy challenged in this case is intimately related to the journalistic role of a licensee for which it has been given initial and primary responsibility by Congress. The licensee's policy against accepting editorial advertising cannot be examined as an abstract proposition, but must be viewed in the context of its journalistic role. It does not help to press on us the idea that editorial ads are 'like' commercial ads, for the licensee's policy against editorial spot ads is expressly based on a journalistic judgment that 10- to 60-second spot announcements are ill-suited to intelligible and intelligent treatment of public issues; the broadcaster has chosen to provide a balanced treatment of controversial questions in a more comprehensive form. Obviously, the licensee's evaluation is based on its own journalistic judgment of priorities and newsworthiness.

"Moreover, the Commission has not fostered the licensee policy challenged here; it has simply declined to command particular action because it fell within the area of journalistic discretion. [The] Commission's reasoning, consistent with nearly 40 years of precedent, is that so long as a licensee meets its 'public trustee' obligation to provide balanced coverage of issues and events, it has broad discretion to decide how that obligation will be met. We do not reach the question whether the First Amendment or the Act can be read to preclude the Commission from determining that in some situations the public interest requires licensees to re-examine their policies with respect to editorial advertisements.[b] The Commis-

---

b. *Columbia Broadcasting System, Inc. v. FCC,* 453 U.S. 367, 101 S.Ct. 2813, 69 L.Ed.2d 706 (1981) upheld FCC administration of a statutory provision guaranteeing "reasonable" access to the airwaves for federal election candidates. The Court, per Burger, C.J., observed that "the Court has never approved a *general* right of access to the media. *Miami Herald;* *CBS v. DNC.* Nor do we do so today." But it found that the limited right of access "properly balances the First Amendment rights of federal candidates, the public, and broadcasters." White, J., joined by Rehnquist and Stevens, JJ., dissented on statutory grounds. For criticism, see Daniel Polsby, *Candidate Access to*

sion has not yet made such a determination; it has, for the present at least, found the policy to be within the sphere of journalistic discretion which Congress has left with the licensee.

"[I]t must constantly be kept in mind that the interest of the public is our foremost concern. With broadcasting, where the available means of communication are limited in both space and time, [Meiklejohn's admonition] that '[w]hat is essential is not that everyone shall speak, but that everything worth saying shall be said' is peculiarly appropriate.

"[Congress] has time and again rejected various legislative attempts that would have mandated a variety of forms of individual access. [It] has chosen to leave such questions with the Commission, to which it has given the flexibility to experiment with new ideas as changing conditions require. In this case, the Commission has decided that on balance the undesirable effects of the right of access urged by respondents would outweigh the asserted [benefits.]

"The Commission was justified in concluding that the public interest in providing access to the marketplace of 'ideas and experiences' would scarcely be served by a system so heavily weighted in favor of the financially affluent, or those with access to wealth. Even under a first-come-first-served system [the] views of the affluent could well prevail over those of others, since they would have it within their power to purchase time more frequently. Moreover, there is the substantial danger [that] the time allotted for editorial advertising could be monopolized by those of one political persuasion.

"These problems would not necessarily be solved by applying the Fairness Doctrine, including the *Cullman* doctrine [requiring broadcasters to provide free time for the presentation of opposing views if a paid sponsor is unavailable], to editorial advertising. If broadcasters were required to provide time, free when necessary, for the discussion of the various shades of opinion on the issue discussed in the advertisement, the affluent could still determine in large part the issues to be discussed. Thus, the very premise of the Court of Appeals' holding— that a right of access is necessary to allow individuals and groups the opportunity for self-initiated speech—would have little meaning to those who could not afford to purchase time in the first instance.

"If the Fairness Doctrine were applied to editorial advertising, there is also the substantial danger that the effective operation of that doctrine would be jeopardized. To minimize financial hardship and to comply fully with its public responsibilities a broadcaster might well be forced to make regular programming time available to those holding a view different from that expressed in an editorial advertisement. [The] result would be a further erosion of the journalistic discretion of broadcasters in the coverage of public issues, and a transfer of control over the treatment of public issues from the licensees who are accountable for broadcast performance to private individuals who are not. The public interest would no longer be 'paramount' but rather subordinate to private whim especially since, under the Court of Appeals' decision, a broadcaster would be largely precluded from rejecting editorial advertisements that dealt with matters trivial or insignificant or already fairly covered by the broadcaster. If the Fairness Doctrine and the *Cullman* doctrine were suspended to alleviate these problems, as respondents suggest might be appropriate, the question arises whether we would have abandoned more than we have gained. Under such a regime the congressional objective of balanced coverage of public issues would be seriously threatened.

the Air: The Uncertain Future of Broadcaster Discretion, 1981 Sup.Ct.Rev. 223.

"Nor can we accept the Court of Appeals' view that every potential speaker is 'the best judge' of what the listening public ought to hear or indeed the best judge of the merits of his or her views. All journalistic tradition and experience is to the contrary. For better or worse, editing is what editors are for; and editing is selection and choice of material. That editors—newspaper or broadcast—can and do abuse this power is beyond doubt, but that is not reason to deny the discretion Congress provided. Calculated risks of abuse are taken in order to preserve higher values. The presence of these risks is nothing new; the authors of the Bill of Rights accepted the reality that these risks were evils for which there was no acceptable remedy other than a spirit of moderation and a sense of responsibility—and civility—on the part of those who exercise the guaranteed freedoms of expression.

"It was reasonable for Congress to conclude that the public interest in being informed requires periodic accountability on the part of those who are entrusted with the use of broadcast frequencies, scarce as they are. In the delicate balancing historically followed in the regulation of broadcasting Congress and the Commission could appropriately conclude that the allocation of journalistic priorities should be concentrated in the licensee rather than diffused among many. This policy gives the public some assurance that the broadcaster will be answerable if he fails to meet their legitimate needs. No such accountability attaches to the private individual, whose only qualifications for using the broadcast facility may be abundant funds and a point of view. To agree that debate on public issues should be 'robust, and wide-open' does not mean that we should exchange 'public trustee' broadcasting, with all its limitations, for a system of self-appointed editorial commentators.

"[T]he risk of an enlargement of Government control over the content of broadcast discussion of public issues [is] inherent in the Court of Appeals' remand requiring regulations and procedures to sort out requests to be heard—a process involving the very editing that licensees now perform as to regular programming. [Under] a constitutionally commanded and government supervised right-of-access system urged by respondents and mandated by the Court of Appeals, the Commission would be required to oversee far more of the day-to-day operations of broadcasters' conduct, deciding such questions as whether a particular individual or group has had sufficient opportunity to present its viewpoint and whether a particular viewpoint has already been sufficiently aired. Regimenting broadcasters is too radical a therapy for the ailment respondents complain of. * * *

"The Commission is also entitled to take into account the reality that in a very real sense listeners and viewers constitute a 'captive audience.' [It] is no answer to say that because we tolerate pervasive commercial advertisement [we] can also live with its political counterparts.

"The rationale for the Court of Appeals' decision imposing a constitutional right of access on the broadcast media was that the licensee impermissibly discriminates by accepting commercial advertisements while refusing editorial advertisements. The court relied on [lower court cases] holding that state-supported school newspapers and public transit companies were forbidden by the First Amendment from excluding controversial editorial advertisements in favor of commercial advertisements.[c] The court also attempted to analogize this case to some of our decisions holding that States may not constitutionally ban certain protected speech while at the same time permitting other speech in public areas [citing e.g., *Grayned* and *Mosley*, Sec. 6 supra].

c. But see *Lehman v. Shaker Heights*, p. 816 supra.

"These decisions provide little guidance, however, in resolving the question whether the First Amendment required the Commission to mandate a private right of access to the broadcast media. In none of those cases did the forum sought for expression have an affirmative and independent statutory obligation to provide full and fair coverage of public issues, such as Congress has imposed on all broadcast licensees. In short, there is no 'discrimination' against controversial speech present in this case. The question here is not whether there is to be discussion of controversial issues of public importance on the broadcast media, but rather who shall determine what issues are to be discussed by whom, and when.''

DOUGLAS, J., concurred in the result, but "for quite different reasons." Because the Court did not decide whether a broadcast licensee is "a federal agency within the context of this case," he assumed that it was not. He "fail[ed] to see," then "how constitutionally we can treat TV and the radio differently than we treat newspapers": "I did not participate in [*Red Lion* and] would not support it. The Fairness Doctrine has no place in our First Amendment regime. It puts the head of the camel inside the tent and enables administration after administration to toy with TV or radio in order to serve its sordid or its benevolent ends. [The uniqueness of radio and TV] is due to engineering and technical problems. But the press in a realistic sense is likewise not available to all. [T]he daily newspapers now established are unique in the sense that it would be virtually impossible for a competitor to enter the field due to the financial exigencies of this era. The result is that in practical terms the newspapers and magazines, like the TV and radio, are available only to a select few. [That] may argue for a redefinition of the responsibilities of the press in First Amendment terms. But I do not think it gives us carte blanche to design systems of supervision and control nor empower [the government to] make 'some' laws 'abridging' freedom of the press. * * *

"Licenses are, of course, restricted in time and while, in my view, Congress has the power to make each license limited to a fixed term and nonreviewable, there is no power to deny renewals for editorial or ideological reasons [for] the First Amendment gives no preference to one school of thought over the others.

"The Court in today's decision by endorsing the Fairness Doctrine sanctions a federal saddle on broadcast licensees that is agreeable to the traditions of nations that never have known freedom of press and that is tolerable in countries that do not have a written constitution containing prohibitions as absolute as those in the First Amendment.'' [d]

BRENNAN, J., joined by Marshall, J., dissented, viewing "the *absolute* ban on the sale of air time for the discussion of controversial issues" as "governmental action'' [e] violating the first amendment: "As a practical matter, the Court's reliance on the Fairness Doctrine as an 'adequate' alternative to editorial advertising seriously overestimates the ability—or willingness—of broadcasters to expose the public to the 'widest possible dissemination of information from diverse and antagonistic sources.' [Indeed,] in light of the strong interest of broadcasters in maximizing their audience, and therefore their profits, it seems almost naive to expect the majority of broadcasters to produce the variety and controversiality of material necessary to reflect a full spectrum of viewpoints. Stated simply, angry customers are not good customers and, in the commercial world of mass communications, it is simply 'bad business' to espouse—or even to allow others to

d. Noting that his views "closely approach those expressed by Mr. Justice Douglas," Stewart, J., also concurred.

e. See fn. a supra.

espouse—the heterodox or the controversial. As a result, even under the Fairness Doctrine, broadcasters generally tend to permit only established—or at least moderated—views to enter the broadcast world's 'marketplace of ideas.' [24]

"Moreover, the Court's reliance on the Fairness Doctrine as the *sole* means of informing the public seriously misconceives and underestimates the public's interest in receiving ideas and information directly from the advocates of those ideas without the interposition of journalistic middlemen. Under the Fairness Doctrine, broadcasters decide what issues are 'important,' how 'fully' to cover them, and what format, time and style of coverage are 'appropriate.' The retention of such *absolute* control in the hands of a few government licensees is inimical to the First Amendment, for vigorous, free debate can be attained only when members of the public have at least *some* opportunity to take the initiative and editorial control into their own hands.

"[S]tanding alone, [the Fairness Doctrine] simply cannot eliminate the need for a further, complementary airing of controversial views through the limited availability of editorial advertising. Indeed, the availability of at least *some* opportunity for editorial advertising is imperative if we are ever to attain the 'free and general discussion of public matters [that] seems absolutely essential to prepare the people for an intelligent exercise of their rights as citizens.'

"Moreover, a proper balancing of the competing First Amendment interests at stake in this controversy must consider, not only the interests of broadcasters and of the listening and viewing public, but also the independent First Amendment interest of groups and individuals in effective self-expression. [I]n a time of apparently growing anonymity of the individual in our society, it is imperative that we take special care to preserve the vital First Amendment interest in assuring 'self-fulfillment [of expression] for each individual.' For our citizens may now find greater than ever the need to express their own views directly to the public, rather than through a governmentally appointed surrogate, if they are to feel that they can achieve at least some measure of control over their own destinies.

"[F]reedom of speech does not exist in the abstract. [It] can flourish only if it is allowed to operate in an effective forum—whether it be a public park, a schoolroom, a town meeting hall, a soapbox, or a radio and television frequency. For in the absence of an effective means of communication, the right to speak would ring hollow indeed. And, in recognition of these principles, we have consistently held that the First Amendment embodies not only the abstract right to be free from censorship, but also the right of an individual to utilize an appropriate and effective medium for the expression of his views.

"[W]ith the assistance of the Federal Government, the broadcast industry has become what is potentially the most efficient and effective 'marketplace of ideas' ever devised. [Thus], although 'full and free discussion' of ideas may have been a reality in the heyday of political pamphleteering, modern technological developments in the field of communications have made the soapbox orator and the leafleteer virtually obsolete. And, in light of the current dominance of the electronic media as the most effective means of reaching the public, any policy that *absolutely* denies citizens access to the airwaves necessarily renders even the concept of 'full and free discussion' practically meaningless.

"[T]he challenged ban can be upheld only if it is determined that such editorial advertising would unjustifiably impair the broadcaster's assertedly over-

24. [Citing many secondary sources to support this statement.]

riding interest in exercising *absolute* control over 'his' frequency. Such an analysis, however, hardly reflects the delicate balancing of interests that this sensitive question demands. Indeed, this 'absolutist' approach wholly disregards the competing First Amendment rights of all 'nonbroadcaster' citizens, ignores the teachings of our recent decision in *Red Lion,* and is not supported by the historical purposes underlying broadcast regulation in this Nation. [T]here is simply no overriding First Amendment interest of broadcasters that can justify the *absolute* exclusion of virtually all of our citizens from the most effective 'marketplace of ideas' ever devised.

"[T]his case deals *only* with the allocation of *advertising* time—airtime that broadcasters regularly relinquish to others without the retention of significant editorial control. Thus, we are concerned here not with the speech of broadcasters themselves but, rather, with their 'right' to decide which *other* individuals will be given an opportunity to speak in a forum that has already been opened to the public.

"Viewed in this context, the *absolute* ban on editorial advertising seems particularly offensive because, although broadcasters refuse to sell any airtime whatever to groups or individuals wishing to speak out on controversial issues of public importance, they make such airtime readily available to those 'commercial' advertisers who seek to peddle their goods and services to the public. [Yet an] individual seeking to discuss war, peace, pollution, or the suffering of the poor is denied this right to speak. Instead, he is compelled to rely on the beneficence of a corporate 'trustee' appointed by the Government to argue his case for him.

"It has been long recognized, however, that although access to public forums may be subjected to reasonable 'time, place, and manner' regulations, '[s]elective exclusions from a public forum, may not be based on *content* alone.' *Mosley* (emphasis added). Here, of course, the differential treatment accorded 'commercial' and 'controversial' speech clearly violates that principle. Moreover, and not without some irony, the favored treatment given 'commercial' speech under the existing scheme clearly reverses traditional First Amendment priorities. For it has generally been understood that 'commercial' speech enjoys *less* First Amendment protection than speech directed at the discussion of controversial issues of public importance."

Notes and Questions

1. *Confronting scarcity.* Consider Laurence Tribe, *American Constitutional Law* 1005 (2d ed.1988): "*CBS* took a step away from *Red Lion* by its treatment of broadcasters as part of the 'press' with an important editorial function to perform rather than as analogous to the postal or telephone systems, but *CBS* was firmly in the *Red Lion* tradition when it refused to consider the possibility that either the technologically scarce radio and television channels, or the finite time available on such channels, might be allocated much as economically scarce newspaper opportunities are allocated: by a combination of market mechanisms and chance rather than by government design coupled with broadcaster autonomy."

Suppose the government sold the airwaves to the highest bidder and allowed subsequent exchange according to property and contract law. Consider Note, *Reconciling Red Lion and Tornillo: A Consistent Theory of Media Regulation,* 28 Stan.L.Rev. 563, 583 (1976): "This regulatory strategy would remove the government from direct determination of the particular individuals who are allowed to broadcast, leaving this decision to market forces, and would avoid the need for specific behavioral commands and sanctions now necessary to secure compliance by broadcasters with the various obligations imposed by the public interest standard. [Under] strict scrutiny, then, the existence of this clearly identifiable less restrictive alternative indicates that the Communications Act is unconstitutional."

But see Van Alstyne, p. 849 supra, at 563: "Congress may indeed be free to 'sell off' the airwaves, and it may be wholly feasible to allocate most currently established broadcast signals by competitive bidding that, when done, may well produce private licensees operating truly without subsidy. But only a singularly insensitive observer would believe that this choice is not implicitly also a highly speech-restrictive choice by Congress. It is fully as speech-restrictive as though, in the case of land, government were to withdraw from *all* ownership and all subsidized maintenance of all land, including parks, auditoriums, and streets and to remain in the field exclusively as a policeman to enforce the proprietary decisions of all private landowners." [f]

Should it be constitutional for the government to exercise "ownership" over the entire broadcast spectrum? See Matthew Spitzer, *The Constitutionality of Licensing Broadcasters,* 64 N.Y.U.L.Rev. 990 (1989); Steven Shiffrin, *Government Speech,* 27 UCLA L.Rev. 565, 587 n. 122, 644–45 (1980).

2. *The "fairness" doctrine criticized.* The Court's assumption that the fairness doctrine works tolerably well has been roasted by the commentators. See, e.g., Ford Rowan, *Broadcast Fairness: Doctrine, Practice, Prospects* (1984); Steven Simmons, *The Fairness Doctrine and the Media* (1978); Johnson & Dystel, *A Day in the Life: The Federal Communications Commission,* 82 Yale L.J. 1575 (1973). Consider Thomas Krattenmaker & Lucas Powe, *The Fairness Doctrine Today: A Constitutional Curiosity and an Impossible Dream,* 1985 Duke L.J. 151, 175: "If the doctrine is to be taken seriously then suspected violations lurk everywhere and the FCC should undertake continuous oversight of the industry. If the FCC will not—or cannot—do that, then the doctrine must be toothless except for the randomly-selected few who are surprised to feel its bite after the fact." For a vigorous defense of the fairness doctrine, see Charles Ferris & James Kirkland, *Fairness—The Broadcaster's Hippocratic Oath,* 34 Cath.U.L.Rev. 605 (1985).

3. *The fairness doctrine repealed.* The FCC concluded a 15 month administrative proceeding with an official denunciation of the fairness doctrine, pointing in particular to the marked increase in the information services marketplace since *Red Lion* and the effects of the doctrine in application. FCC, [*General*] *Fairness Doctrine Obligations of Broadcast Licensees,* 102 F.C.C.2d 143 (1985). *Syracuse Peace Council,* 2 FCC Rcd 5043 (1987) held that "under the constitutional standard established by *Red Lion* and its progeny, the fairness doctrine contravenes the First Amendment and its enforcement is no longer in the public interest." [g]

4. *The worst of both worlds.* Evaluate the following hypothetical commentary: "*CBS v. DNC* allows government to grant virtually exclusive control over American's most valuable communication medium to corporations who regard it as their mission to 'deliver' audiences to advertisers. The system gives us the

---

f. For detailed criticism of the scarcity argument, see Matthew Spitzer, *Controlling the Content of Print and Broadcast,* 58 S.Cal. L.Rev. 1349 (1985).

g. *Syracuse Peace Council v. FCC,* 867 F.2d 654 (D.C.Cir.1989) affirmed the FCC's determination that the fairness doctrine no longer

serves the public interest without reaching constitutional issues. On June 20, 1987 President Reagan had vetoed congressional legislation designed to preserve the fairness doctrine on the ground that the legislation was unconstitutional.

worst of both worlds: the world of profit-seeking—without a free market; the world of regulation—without planning." For discussion of alternatives, see Ronald Cass, *Revolution in the Wasteland* (1981); Bruce Owen, *Economics and Freedom of Expression: Media Structure and the First Amendment* (1975); Charles Firestone & Phillip Jacklin, *Deregulation and the Pursuit of Fairness* in Telecommunications Policy and the Citizen 107 (Timothy Haight ed. 1979); Ralph Nader & Claire Riley, *Oh Say Can You See: A Broadcast Network for the Audience*, 5 J.L. & Pol. 1 (1988). Bruce Owen, *Structural Approaches to the Problem of Television Network Economic Dominance*, 1979 Duke L.J. 191.

5. Do access proposals miss the central problem? Is television at the heart of an "amusement-centered culture" that substitutes images and sound bites for serious public discourse while encouraging a privatized nonengaged citizenry? Consider Ronald Collins and David Skover, *The First Amendment in an Age of Paratroopers,* 68 Tex.L.Rev. 1087, 1088–89 (1990): "With entertainment as the paradigm for most public discourse, traditional first amendment values—which stress civic restraint and serious dialogue—are overshadowed. Given these core values and the anticensorial direction of first amendment theory, is there anything that could (or should) be done to thwart, rather than to feed, an amusement-centered culture?

"In attempting to answer this question, we confront a paradox: by saving itself, the first amendment destroys itself. On the one hand, to preserve its anticensorial ideals, the first amendment must protect both the old and new media cultures. Accordingly, it must constrain most governmental controls over expression, including those over the commercial use of electronic media. On the other hand, if the first amendment's protections do not differentiate between the old and new media cultures, the modern obsession with self-amusement will trivialize public discourse and undermine the traditional aim of the first amendment." [h]

6. Consider Henry Geller, *The Transformation of Television News: Articles and Comments: Fairness and the Public Trustee Concept: Time to Move On,* 47 Fed.Com.L.J. 79, 83–84 (1994): "It makes no sense to try to impose effective, behavioral regulation [when] conventional television faces such fierce and increasing competition, and viewership is declining rather than growing. It would be much sounder to truly deregulate broadcasting by eliminating the public trustee requirement and in its place substituting a reasonable spectrum fee imposed on existing stations (and an auction for all new frequency assignments), with the sums so obtained dedicated to public telecommunications. [For] the first time, we would have a structure that works to accomplish explicit policy goals. The commercial system would continue to do what it already does—deliver a great variety of entertainment and news-type programs. The noncommercial system would have the funds to accomplish its goals—to supply needed public service such as educational programming for children, cultural fare, minority presentations, and in-depth informational programs."

7. *Cable television.* Can government require cable operators to grant an access channel for the public, for the government, and for educational institutions? Which is the better analogy: *Red Lion* or *Miami Herald?* Need government lease space or otherwise afford access to utility poles under its control (and

h. For discussion of the Collins–Skover paradox by Max Lerner, David M. O'Brien, Martin Redish, Edward Rubin, Herbert Schiller, and Mark Tushnet, see Colloquy: *The First Amendment and the Paratroopers Paradox,* 68 Texas L.Rev. 1087 (1990).

grant rights of way) to all competing cable companies? Is the appropriate analogy to *Schneider? Perry? Vincent? Red Lion? Miami Herald?*

LOS ANGELES v. PREFERRED COMMUNICATIONS, INC., 476 U.S. 488, 106 S.Ct. 2034, 90 L.Ed.2d 480 (1986), per Rehnquist, J., upheld the refusal to dismiss a complaint brought by a cable company demanding access to a city's utility poles and asserting a right to be free of government-mandated channels: "Cable television partakes of some of the aspects of speech and the communication of ideas as do the traditional enterprises of newspapers and [book publishers]. Respondent's proposed activities would seem to implicate First Amendment interests as do the activities of wireless broadcasters, which were found to fall within the ambit of the First Amendment in [*Red Lion*]. Of course, ['Even'] protected speech is not equally permissible in all places and at all times.' *Cornelius.* Moreover, where speech and conduct are joined in a single course of action, the First Amendment values must be balanced against competing societal interests. See, e.g., *Vincent; O'Brien.*" The Court postponed fuller discussion of any cable rights until a factual record had been developed.[a]

The Cable Television and Consumer Protection and Competition Act of 1992 required cable television systems to devote a portion of their channels to local broadcasters including commercial stations and public broadcast stations.[a] Congress was concerned about the monopolistic character of cable operations in most localities and the economic incentives for cable operators to favor their own programming. It also pointed to the importance of maintaining local broadcasting. TURNER BROADCASTING SYSTEM, INC. v. FCC, ___ U.S. ___, 114 S.Ct. 2445, 129 L.Ed.2d 497 (1994), per Kennedy, J., joined by Rehnquist, C.J., and Blackmun and Souter, JJ., upheld the requirement so long as the Government could demonstrate on remand that in the absence of legislation, a large number of broadcast stations would not be carried or would be adversely repositioned, that such stations would be at serious risk of financial difficulty, that the cable operators' programming selections (as opposed to using unused channel capacity) would not be excessively affected, and that no less restrictive alternative means existed. The plurality, joined by Stevens, J., argued that the antitrust interests of government were content neutral, but concluded that "some measure of heightened First Amendment scrutiny" was appropriate because the act was not a generally applicable law but directed at cable operators: "The scope and operation of the challenged provisions make clear [that] Congress designed the must-carry provisions not to promote speech of a particular content, but to prevent cable operators from exploiting their economic power to the detriment of broadcasters,

a. For cogent discussion, see Daniel Brenner, *Cable Television and the Freedom of Expression,* 1988 Duke L.J. 329. See also Powe, supra, at 216–47; David Saylor, *Municipal Ripoff: The Unconstitutionality of Cable Television Franchise Fees and Access Support Payments,* 35 Cath.U.L.Rev. 671 (1986); Ithiel de Sola Pool, *Technologies of Freedom* 151–88 (1983); Monroe Price, *Taming Red Lion: The First Amendment and Structural Approaches to Media Regulation,* 31 Fed.Comm.L.J. 215 (1979); Comment, *Access to Cable Television:*

A Critique of the Affirmative Duty Theory of the First Amendment, 70 Calif.L.Rev. 1393 (1982). For discussion of other technologies, see Special Issue, *Videotex,* 36 Fed.Comm.L.J. 119 (1984). Monroe Price, *Free Expression and Digital Dreams: The Open and Closed Terrain of Speech,* 22 Critical Inquiry 64 (1995).

a. It also required that they be placed in the same numerical position as when broadcast over the air.

and thereby to ensure that all Americans, especially those unable to subscribe to cable, have access to free television programming—whatever its content." [b]

O'CONNOR, J., joined by Scalia, Ginsburg, and Thomas, JJ., concurring and dissenting in part, would have held the requirements unconstitutional without a remand. They argued that strict scrutiny was appropriate because the preference for broadcasters over cable programmers on many channels was based on content (referring to findings about local public affairs programming and public television). [c] Although the interest in public affairs programming was said to be weighty, O'Connor, J., observed that public affairs cable-programming could be displaced: "In the rare circumstances where the government may draw content-based distinctions to serve its goals, the restrictions must serve the goals a good deal more precisely than this." O'Connor, J., also argued that the requirements should fail content neutral scrutiny as well because the act disadvantaged cable operators with no anti-competitive motives and favored broadcasters who could financially survive even if dropped from a cable system. [d]

Notes and Questions

Has the United States "consistently and properly engaged in content-motivated structuring of the communications realm" in ways that have usually "benefited the nation." See C. Edwin Baker, *Turner Broadcasting: Content–Based Regulation of Persons and Presses,* 1994 Sup.Ct.Rev. 57, 94. Does the dissent's emphasis on content discrimination shortchange the government's interest in assuring a robust communications system? Would such an emphasis lead to the conclusion that commercial broadcasters deserved no preference but public broadcasters did? Consider Donald Hawthorne & Monroe Price, *Rewiring the First Amendment: Meaning, Content and Public Broadcasting,* 12 Cardozo Arts & Ent.L.J. 499, 504 (1994): "If the absence of a meaningful content basis for preferring commercial broadcasters should impair their entitlement to 'must-carry' treatment, precisely the converse is true for noncommercial broadcasters. These entities have been mandated to carry on government's historic responsibility to educate the citizenry and more recent undertaking to subsidize the arts." [e]

METRO BROADCASTING v. FCC, 497 U.S. 547, 110 S.Ct. 2997, 111 L.Ed.2d 445 (1990), per BRENNAN, J., reaffirmed the government's power to regulate the airwaves in the context of upholding minority ownership policies designed to effectuate more diverse programming: "The Government's role in distributing the limited number of broadcast licenses is not merely that of a 'traffic officer;' rather, it is axiomatic that broadcasting may be regulated in light of the rights of the viewing and listening audience and that 'the widest possible dissemination of

b. Blackmun, J., concurring, emphasized the importance of deferring to Congress during the new proceedings. Stevens, J., concurring, reluctantly joined the order to remand; he would have preferred to affirm the must-carry legislation without further proceedings. Ginsburg, J., concurred in parts of the Court's opinion (including the section arguing for intermediate first amendment scrutiny regarding the antitrust interest), filed a separate concurring opinion, and joined O'Connor, J's opinion.

c. Kennedy, J., argued that such findings showed "nothing more than the recognition

that the services provided by broadcast television have some intrinsic value and, thus, are worth preserving against the threats posed by cable."

d. Thomas, J., did not join this section of the opinion.

e. See also Monroe Price & Donald Hawthorne, *Saving Public Television,* Hast.Comm./ Ent.L.J. 65 (1994); Cass Sunstein, *The First Amendment in Cyberspace,* 104 Yale L.J. 1757 (1995).

information from diverse and antagonistic sources is essential to the welfare of the public.' Safeguarding the public's right to receive a diversity of views and information over the airwaves is [consistent] with 'the ends and purposes of the First Amendment' * * *.

"The benefits of such diversity are not limited to the members of minority groups who gain access to the broadcasting industry by virtue of the ownership policies; rather, the benefits redound to all members of the viewing and listening audience. [W]e conclude that the interest in enhancing broadcast diversity is, at the very least, an important governmental objective and is therefore a sufficient basis for the Commission's minority ownership policies. Just as a 'diverse student body' contributing to a 'robust exchange of ideas' is a 'constitutionally permissible goal' on which a race-conscious university admissions program may be predicated, *Bakke* (opinion of Powell, J.), the diversity of views and information on the airwaves serves important First Amendment values."

O'CONNOR, J., joined by Rehnquist, C.J., Scalia and Kennedy, JJ., dissenting, also recognized and reaffirmed governmental power to regulate broadcasting: "The Court has recognized an interest in obtaining diverse broadcasting viewpoints as a legitimate basis for the FCC, acting pursuant to its 'public interest' statutory mandate, to adopt limited measures to increase the number of competing licensees and to encourage licensees to present varied views on issues of public concern. See, e.g., *Red Lion*. [But] the conclusion that measures adopted to further the interest in diversity of broadcasting viewpoints are neither beyond the FCC's statutory authority nor contrary to the First Amendment hardly establishes the interest as important for equal protection purposes.

"The FCC's extension of the asserted interest in diversity of views in this case presents, at the very least, an unsettled First Amendment issue. The FCC has concluded that the American broadcasting public receives the incorrect mix of ideas and claims to have adopted the challenged policies to supplement programming content with a particular set of views. Although we have approved limited measures designed to increase information and views generally, the Court has never upheld a broadcasting measure designed to amplify a distinct set of views or the views of a particular class of speakers. [Even] if an interest is determined to be legitimate in one context, it does not suddenly become important enough to justify distinctions based on race."

II. BROADCASTING AND CONTENT REGULATION: INDECENT SPEECH

FCC v. PACIFICA FOUNDATION

438 U.S. 726, 98 S.Ct. 3026, 57 L.Ed.2d 1073 (1978).

JUSTICE STEVENS delivered the opinion of the Court (Parts I, II, III, and IV–C) and an opinion in which CHIEF JUSTICE BURGER and JUSTICE REHNQUIST joined (Parts IV–A and IV–B).

[In an early afternoon weekday broadcast which was devoted that day to contemporary attitudes toward the use of language, respondent's New York radio station aired a 12-minute selection called "Filthy Words," from a comedy album by a satiric humorist, George Carlin. The monologue, which had evoked frequent laughter from a live theater audience, began by referring to Carlin's thought about the seven words you can't say on the public airwaves, "the ones you definitely wouldn't say ever." He then listed the words ("shit," "piss," "fuck," "motherfucker," "cocksucker," "cunt," and "tits"), "the ones that will curve your spine, grow hair on your hands and (laughter) maybe, even bring us, God help us, peace without honor (laughter) um, and a bourbon (laughter)," and repeated them over and over in a variety of colloquialisms. Immediately prior to the monologue, listeners were advised that it included sensitive language which some might regard as offensive. Those who might be offended were advised to change the station and return in fifteen minutes.

[The FCC received a complaint from a man stating that while driving in his car with his young son he had heard the broadcast of the Carlin monologue. The FCC issued an order to be "associated with the station's license file, and in the event that subsequent complaints are received, the Commission will then decide whether it should utilize any of the available sanctions it has been granted by Congress."] [a]

The Commission characterized the language used in the Carlin monologue as "patently offensive," though not necessarily obscene, and expressed the opinion that it should be regulated by principles analogous to those found in the law of nuisance where the "law generally speaks to *channeling* behavior more than actually prohibiting [it]." [5]

Applying these considerations to the language used in the monologue as broadcast by respondent, the Commission concluded that certain words depicted sexual and excretory activities in a patently offensive manner, noted that they "were broadcast at a time when children were undoubtedly in the audience (i.e., in the early afternoon)," and that the prerecorded language, with these offensive words "repeated over and over," was "deliberately broadcast." In summary, the Commission stated: "We therefore hold that the language as broadcast was indecent [under 18 U.S.C. 1464]."

IV. Pacifica [argues] that the Commission's construction of the statutory language broadly encompasses so much constitutionally protected speech that reversal is required even if Pacifica's broadcast of the "Filthy Words" monologue is not itself protected by the First Amendment. * * *

A. The first argument fails because our review is limited to the question whether the Commission has the authority to proscribe this particular broadcast. As the Commission itself emphasized, its order was "issued in a specific factual context." That approach is appropriate for courts as well as the Commission when regulation of indecency is at stake, for indecency is largely a function of context—it cannot be adequately judged in the abstract. * * *

It is true that the Commission's order may lead some broadcasters to censor themselves. At most, however, the Commission's definition of indecency will deter only the broadcasting of patently offensive references to excretory and sexual organs and activities.[18] While some of these references may be protected, they surely lie at the periphery of First Amendment concern. * * * Invalidating any rule on the basis of its hypothetical application to situations not before the Court is "strong medicine" to be applied "sparingly and only as a last resort."

a. The FCC's action is placed in the context of other similar actions in Lucas Powe, *American Broadcasting and the First Amendment* 162–90 (1987).

5. Thus, the Commission suggested, if an offensive broadcast had literary, artistic, political or scientific value, and were preceded by warnings, it might not be indecent in the late evening, but would be so during the day, when children are in the audience.

18. A requirement that indecent language be avoided will have its primary effect on the form, rather than the content, of serious communication. There are few, if any, thoughts that cannot be expressed by the use of less offensive language.

Broadrick [p. 737 supra]. We decline to administer that medicine to preserve the vigor of patently offensive sexual and excretory speech.

B. [The] words of the Carlin monologue are unquestionably "speech" within the meaning of the First Amendment. [The] question in this case is whether a broadcast of patently offensive words dealing with sex and excretion may be regulated because of its content.[20] Obscene materials have been denied the protection of the First Amendment because their content is so offensive to contemporary moral standards. *Roth*. But the fact that society may find speech offensive is not a sufficient reason for suppressing it. Indeed, if it is the speaker's opinion that gives offense, that consequence is a reason for according it constitutional protection. For it is a central tenet of the First Amendment that the government must remain neutral in the marketplace of ideas. If there were any reason to believe that the Commission's characterization of the Carlin monologue as offensive could be traced to its political content—or even to the fact that it satirized contemporary attitudes about four letter words [22]—First Amendment protection might be required. But that is simply not this case. These words offend for the same reasons that obscenity offends. Their place in the hierarchy of First Amendment values was aptly sketched by Mr. Justice Murphy when he said, "such utterances are no essential part of any exposition of ideas, and are of such slight social value as a step to truth that any benefit that may be derived from them is clearly outweighed by the social interest in order and morality." *Chaplinsky*.

Although these words ordinarily lack literary, political, or scientific value, they are not entirely outside the protection of the First Amendment. Some uses of even the most offensive words are unquestionably protected. Indeed, we may assume, arguendo, that this monologue would be protected in other contexts. [It] is a characteristic of speech such as this that both its capacity to offend and its "social value," to use Mr. Justice Murphy's term, vary with the circumstances. Words that are commonplace in one setting are shocking in another. To paraphrase Mr. Justice Harlan, one occasion's lyric is another's vulgarity. Cf. *Cohen v. California*.[25]

In this case it is undisputed that the content of Pacifica's broadcast was "vulgar," "offensive," and "shocking." Because content of that character is not entitled to absolute constitutional protection under all circumstances, we must

20. Although neither Justice Powell nor Justice Brennan directly confronts this question, both have answered it affirmatively, the latter explicitly, at fn. 3, infra, and the former implicitly by concurring in a judgment that could not otherwise stand.

22. The monologue does present a point of view; it attempts to show that the words it uses are "harmless" and that our attitudes toward them are "essentially silly." The Commission objects, not to this point of view, but to the way in which it is expressed. The belief that these words are harmless does not necessarily confer a First Amendment privilege to use them while proselytizing just as the conviction that obscenity is harmless does not license one to communicate that conviction by the indiscriminate distribution of an obscene leaflet.

25. The importance of context is illustrated by the *Cohen* case. [So] far as the evidence showed no one in the courthouse was offended by [Cohen's jacket.]

In holding that criminal sanctions could not be imposed on Cohen for his political statement in a public place, the Court rejected the argument that his speech would offend unwilling viewers; it noted that "there was no evidence that persons powerless to avoid [his] conduct did in fact object to it." In contrast, in this case the Commission was responding to a listener's strenuous complaint, and Pacifica does not question its determination that this afternoon broadcast was likely to offend listeners. It should be noted that the Commission imposed a far more moderate penalty on Pacifica than the state court imposed on Cohen. Even the strongest civil penalty at the Commission's command does not include criminal prosecution.

consider its context in order to determine whether the Commission's action was constitutionally permissible.

C. We have long recognized that each medium of expression presents special First Amendment problems. And of all forms of communication, it is broadcasting that has received the most limited First Amendment [protection.]

The reasons for these distinctions are complex, but two have relevance to the present case. First, the broadcast media have established a uniquely pervasive presence in the lives of all Americans. Patently offensive, indecent material presented over the airwaves confronts the citizen, not only in public, but also in the privacy of the home, where the individual's right to be let alone plainly outweighs the First Amendment rights of an intruder. *Rowan v. Post Office Dept.,* 397 U.S. 728, 90 S.Ct. 1484, 25 L.Ed.2d 736. Because the broadcast audience is constantly tuning in and out, prior warnings cannot completely protect the listener or viewer from unexpected program content. To say that one may avoid further offense by turning off the radio when he hears indecent language is like saying that the remedy for an assault is to run away after the first blow.[27]
* * *

Second, broadcasting is uniquely accessible to children, even those too young to read. Although Cohen's written message might have been incomprehensible to a first grader, Pacifica's broadcast could have enlarged a child's vocabulary in an instant. Other forms of offensive expression may be withheld from the young without restricting the expression at its source. Bookstores and motion picture theaters, for example, may be prohibited from making indecent material available to children. We held in *Ginsberg* [p. 712 supra] that the government's interest in the "well being of its youth" and in supporting "parents' claim to authority in their own household" justified the regulation of otherwise protected expression.[28]
* * *

It is appropriate, in conclusion, to emphasize the narrowness of our holding. This case does not involve a two-way radio conversation between a cab driver and a dispatcher, or a telecast of an Elizabethan comedy. We have not decided that an occasional expletive in either setting would justify any sanction or, indeed, that this broadcast would justify a criminal prosecution. The Commission's decision rested entirely on a nuisance rationale under which context is all-important.

[R]eversed.

JUSTICE POWELL, with whom JUSTICE BLACKMUN joins, concurring.

[T]he language employed is, to most people, vulgar and offensive. It was chosen specifically for this quality, and it was repeated over and over as a sort of verbal shock treatment. [In] essence, the Commission sought to "channel" the monologue to hours when the fewest unsupervised children would be exposed to it. In my view, this consideration provides strong support for the Commission's holding.

27. Outside the home, the balance between the offensive speaker and the unwilling audience may sometimes tip in favor of the speaker, requiring the offended listener to turn away. See *Erznoznik.* * * *

28. The Commission's action does not by any means reduce adults to hearing only what is fit for children. Cf. *Butler v. Michigan* [p. 712 supra]. Adults who feel the need may purchase tapes and records or go to theatres and nightclubs to hear these words. In fact, the Commission has not unequivocally closed even broadcasting to speech of this sort; whether broadcast audiences in the late evening contain so few children that playing this monologue would be permissible is an issue neither the Commission nor this Court has decided.

[The] Commission properly held that the speech from which society may attempt to shield its children is not limited to that which appeals to the youthful prurient interest. The language involved in this case is as potentially degrading and harmful to children as representations of many erotic acts.

In most instances, the dissemination of this kind of speech to children may be limited without also limiting willing adults' access to it. Sellers of printed and recorded matter and exhibitors of motion pictures and live performances may be required to shut their doors to children, but such a requirement has no effect on adults' access. See *Ginsberg*. The difficulty is that [d]uring most of the broadcast hours, both adults and unsupervised children are likely to be in the broadcast audience, and the broadcaster cannot reach willing adults without also reaching children. This, as the Court emphasizes, is one of the distinctions between the broadcast and other media to which we often have adverted as justifying a different treatment of the broadcast media for First Amendment purposes. In my view, the Commission was entitled to give substantial weight to this difference in reaching its decision in this case.

[Another difference] is that broadcasting—unlike most other forms of communication—comes directly into the home, the one place where people ordinarily have the right not to be assaulted by uninvited and offensive sights and sounds. *Erznoznik; Cohen; Rowan.* * * * "That we are often 'captives' outside the sanctuary of the home and subject to objectionable speech and other sound does not mean we must be captives everywhere." *Rowan.* The Commission also was entitled to give this factor appropriate weight in the circumstances of the instant case. This is not to say, however, that the Commission has an unrestricted license to decide what speech, protected in other media, may be banned from the airwaves in order to protect unwilling adults from momentary exposure to it in their homes.[2] * * *

[M]y views are generally in accord with what is said in Part IV(C) of opinion. I therefore join that portion of his opinion. I do not join Part IV(B), however, because I do not subscribe to the theory that the Justices of this Court are free generally to decide on the basis of its content which speech protected by the First Amendment is most "valuable" and hence deserving of the most protection, and which is less "valuable" and hence deserving of less protection.[3] In my view, the result in this case does not turn on whether Carlin's monologue, viewed as a whole, or the words that comprise it, have more or less "value" than a candidate's campaign speech. This is a judgment for each person to make, not one for the judges to impose upon him.[4]

2. It is true that the radio listener quickly may tune out speech that is offensive to him. In addition, broadcasters may preface potentially offensive programs with warnings. But such warnings do not help the unsuspecting listener who tunes in at the middle of a program. In this respect, too, broadcasting appears to differ from books and records, which may carry warnings on their faces, and from motion pictures and live performances, which may carry warnings on their marquees.

3. The Court has, however, created a limited exception to this rule in order to bring commercial speech within the protection of the First Amendment. See *Ohralik* [p. 724 supra].

4. For much the same reason, I also do not join Part IV(A). I had not thought that the application vel non of overbreadth analysis should depend on the Court's judgment as to the value of the protected speech that might be deterred. Except in the context of commercial speech, see *Bates* [p. 723 supra], it has not in the past. See, e.g., *Lewis v. New Orleans; Gooding.*

As Justice Stevens points out, however, the Commission's order was limited to the facts of this case; "it did not purport to engage in formal rulemaking or in the promulgation of any regulations." In addition, since the Commission may be expected to proceed cautiously, as it has in the past, I do not foresee an undue "chilling" effect on broadcasters' exercise of their rights. I agree, therefore, that respondent's overbreadth challenge is meritless.

The result turns instead on the unique characteristics of the broadcast media, combined with society's right to protect its children from speech generally agreed to be inappropriate for their years, and with the interest of unwilling adults in not being assaulted by such offensive speech in their homes. Moreover, I doubt whether today's decision will prevent any adult who wishes to receive Carlin's message in Carlin's own words from doing so, and from making for himself a value judgment as to the merit of the message and words. These are the grounds upon which I join the judgment of the Court as to Part IV.

JUSTICE BRENNAN, with whom JUSTICE MARSHALL joins, dissenting.

[T]he Court refuses to embrace the notion, completely antithetical to basic First Amendment values, that the degree of protection the First Amendment affords protected speech varies with the social value ascribed to that speech by five Members of this Court. See opinion of Justice Powell. Moreover, [all] Members of the Court agree that [the monologue] does not fall within one of the categories of speech, such as "fighting words," or obscenity, that is totally without First Amendment protection. [Yet] a majority of the Court [1] nevertheless finds that, on the facts of this case, the FCC is not constitutionally barred from imposing sanctions on Pacifica for its airing of the Carlin monologue. * * *

[A]n individual's actions in switching on and listening to communications transmitted over the public airways and directed to the public at-large do not implicate fundamental privacy interests, even when engaged in within the home. Instead, because the radio is undeniably a public medium, these actions are more properly viewed as a decision to take part, if only as a listener, in an ongoing public discourse. Although an individual's decision to allow public radio communications into his home undoubtedly does not abrogate all of his privacy interests, the residual privacy interests he retains vis-à-vis the communication he voluntarily admits into his home are surely no greater than those of the people present in the corridor of the Los Angeles courthouse in *[Cohen]*.

Even if an individual who voluntarily opens his home to radio communications retains privacy interests of sufficient moment to justify a ban on protected speech if those interests are "invaded in an essentially intolerable manner," *Cohen*, the very fact that those interests are threatened only by a radio broadcast precludes any intolerable invasion of privacy; for unlike other intrusive modes of communication, such as sound trucks, "[t]he radio can be turned off"—and with a minimum of effort. [Whatever] the minimal discomfort suffered by a listener who inadvertently tunes into a program he finds offensive during the brief interval before he can simply extend his arm and switch stations or flick the "off" button, it is surely worth the candle to preserve the broadcaster's right to send, and the right of those interested to receive, a message entitled to full First Amendment protection. * * *

The Court's balance, of necessity, fails to accord proper weight to the interests of listeners who wish to hear broadcasts the FCC deems offensive. It permits majoritarian tastes completely to preclude a protected message from entering the homes of a receptive, unoffended minority. No decision of this Court supports such a result. Where the individuals comprising the offended majority may freely choose to reject the material being offered, we have never found their privacy interests of such moment to warrant the suppression of speech on privacy grounds. [In] *Rowan*, the Court upheld a statute, permitting householders to

1. Where I refer without differentiation to the actions of "the Court," my reference is to this majority, which consists of my Brothers Powell and Stevens and those Members of the Court joining their separate opinions.

require that mail advertisers stop sending them lewd or offensive materials and remove their names from mailing lists. Unlike the situation here, householders who wished to receive the sender's communications were not prevented from doing so. Equally important, the determination of offensiveness vel non under the statute involved in *Rowan* was completely within the hands of the individual householder; no governmental evaluation of the worth of the mail's content stood between the mailer and the householder. In contrast, the visage of the censor is all too discernable here. * * *

Because the Carlin monologue is obviously not an erotic appeal to the prurient interests of children, the Court, for the first time, allows the government to prevent minors from gaining access to materials that are not obscene, and are therefore protected, as to them.[2] It thus ignores our recent admonition that "[s]peech that is neither obscene as to youths nor subject to some other legitimate proscription cannot be suppressed solely to protect the young from ideas or images that a legislative body thinks unsuitable for them." *Erznoznik*.[3] The Court's refusal to follow its own pronouncements is especially lamentable since it has the anomalous subsidiary effect, at least in the radio context at issue here, of making completely unavailable to adults material which may not constitutionally be kept even from children. * * * *Yoder* and *Pierce*, [Ch. 9, Sec. 2, I], hold that parents, *not* the government, have the right to make certain decisions regarding the upbringing of their children. As surprising as it may be to individual Members of this Court, some parents may actually find Mr. Carlin's unabashed attitude towards the seven "dirty words" healthy, and deem it desirable to expose their children to the manner in which Mr. Carlin defuses the taboo surrounding the words. Such parents may constitute a minority of the American public, but the absence of great numbers willing to exercise the right to raise their children in this fashion does not alter the right's nature or its existence. Only the Court's regrettable decision does that.

As demonstrated above, neither of the factors relied on by both [Powell and Stevens, JJ.]—the intrusive nature of radio and the presence of children in the listening audience—can, when taken on its own terms, support the FCC's disapproval of the Carlin monologue. [A] neither of the opinions comprising the Court serve to clarify the extent to which the FCC may assert the privacy and children-in-the-audience rationales as justification for expunging from the airways protected communications the Commission finds offensive. Taken to their logical extreme, these rationales would support the cleansing of public radio of any "four-letter words" whatsoever, regardless of their context. The rationales could justify the banning from radio of a myriad of literary works, novels, poems, and plays by the likes of Shakespeare, Joyce, Hemingway, Ben Jonson, Henry Fielding, Robert Burns, and Chaucer; they could support the suppression of a good deal of political

---

2. Even if the monologue appealed to the prurient interest of minors, it would not be obscene as to them unless, as to them, "the work, taken as a whole, lacks serious literary, artistic, political, or scientific value." *Miller*.

3. It may be that a narrowly drawn regulation prohibiting the use of offensive language on broadcasts directed specifically at younger children constitutes one of the "other legitimate proscription[s]" alluded to in *Erznoznik*. This is so both because of the difficulties inherent in adapting the *Miller* formulation to communications received by young children, and because such children are "not possessed of

that full capacity for individual choice which is the presupposition of the First Amendment guarantees." *Ginsberg*. (Stewart, J., concurring). I doubt, as my Brother Stevens suggests, that such a limited regulation amounts to a regulation of speech based on its content, since, by hypothesis, the only persons at whom the regulated communication is directed are incapable of evaluating its content. To the extent that such a regulation is viewed as a regulation based on content, it marks the outermost limits to which content regulation is permissible.

speech, such as the Nixon tapes; and they could even provide the basis for imposing sanctions for the broadcast of certain portions of the Bible.

In order to dispel the spectre of the possibility of so unpalatable a degree of censorship, and to defuse Pacifica's overbreadth challenge, the FCC insists that it desires only the authority to reprimand a broadcaster on facts analogous to those present in this case. [Powell and Stevens, JJ.] take the FCC at its word, and consequently do no more than permit the Commission to censor the afternoon broadcast of the "sort of verbal shock treatment" involved [here]. I would place the responsibility and the right to weed worthless and offensive communications from the public airways where it belongs and where, until today, it resided: in a public free to choose those communications worthy of its attention from a marketplace unsullied by the censor's hand.　* * *

My Brother Stevens [finds] solace in his conviction that "[t]here are few, if any, thoughts that cannot be expressed by the use of less offensive language." The idea that the content of a message and its potential impact on any who might receive it can be divorced from the words that are the vehicle for its expression is transparently fallacious. A given word may have a unique capacity to capsule an idea, evoke an emotion, or conjure up an image. Indeed, for those of us who place an appropriately high value on our cherished First Amendment rights, the word "censor" is such a word. Mr. Justice Harlan, speaking for the Court, recognized the truism that a speaker's choice of words cannot surgically be separated from the ideas he desires to express when he warned that "we cannot indulge the facile assumption that one can forbid particular words without also running a substantial risk of suppressing ideas in the process."

[Stevens, J.] also finds relevant to his First Amendment analysis the fact that "[a]dults who feel the need may purchase tapes and records or go to theatres and nightclubs to hear [the tabooed] words." [Powell, J.,] agrees. [The] opinions of my Brethren display both a sad insensitivity to the fact that these alternatives involve the expenditure of money, time, and effort that many of those wishing to hear Mr. Carlin's message may not be able to afford, and a naive innocence of the reality that in many cases, the medium may well be the message.

The Court apparently believes that the FCC's actions here can be analogized to the zoning ordinances upheld in *American Mini Theatres*. For two reasons, it is wrong. First, the zoning ordinances found to pass constitutional muster [had] valid goals other than the channeling of protected speech. No such goals are present here. Second, [the] ordinances did not restrict the access of distributors or exhibitors to the market or impair the viewing public's access to the regulated material. Again, this is not the situation here.

[T]here runs throughout the opinions of my Brothers Powell and Stevens [a] depressing inability to appreciate that in our land of cultural pluralism, there are many who think, act, and talk differently from the Members of this Court, and who do not share their fragile sensibilities. It is only an acute ethnocentric myopia that enables the Court [to blink at] persons who do not share the Court's view as to which words or expressions are acceptable and who, for a variety of reasons, including a conscious desire to flout majoritarian conventions, express themselves using words that may be regarded as offensive by those from different socio-economic backgrounds.[8] In this context, the Court's decision may be seen

---

8. Under the approach taken by my Brother Powell, the availability of broadcasts *about* groups whose members comprise such audiences might also be affected. Both news broadcasts about activities involving these groups and public affairs broadcasts about

for what, in the broader perspective, it really is: another of the dominant culture's inevitable efforts to force those groups who do not share its mores to conform to its way of thinking, acting, and speaking. * * *b

Notes and Questions

1. *Implications for broadcasting.* Consider Thomas Krattenmaker & Lucas Powe, *Televised Violence: First Amendment Principles and Social Science Theory,* 64 Va.L.Rev. 1123, 1228 (1978): *Pacifica* "marks the first time any theory other than scarcity has received the official imprimatur of the Court. [S]carcity could not have authorized the result in *Pacifica* because regardless of whether one thinks the incredible abundance of radio stations in the United States (and especially in New York City) is insufficient, scarcity supports adding voices not banning them." What is the significance of the Court's comment that "the broadcast media have established a uniquely pervasive presence in the lives of all Americans"? Consider Daniel Brenner, *Censoring the Airwaves: The Supreme Court's Pacifica Decision* in Free But Regulated: Conflicting Traditions in Media Law 175, 177 & 79 (1982): "[N]ewspapers, drive-in movies, direct mail advertisements and imprinted T-shirts are media that have also 'established a uniquely pervasive presence' in our lives, in and out of [home]. Offhand comments about broadcasting enjoying 'the most limited' First Amendment protection—What of comic books? Playing cards? Chinese cookie fortunes?—are not simply harmless baffle; they constitute Delphic pronouncements made at a watershed period in the development of electronic media." See also Powe, supra fn. a, at 210–11.

Is the Court suggesting that the broadcast media are uniquely powerful? If so, should that factor cut for or against government regulation? See Powe, supra, at 211–15; Lucas Powe, *"Or of the [Broadcast] Press,"* 55 Tex.L.Rev. 39, 58–62 (1976). Does *Pacifica* support regulation of sex and violence on television, of "offensive" commercials, of advertising directed toward children? See generally Matthew Spitzer, *Seven Dirty Words and Six Other Stories* (1986) (criticizing *Pacifica's* distinctions between print and broadcast).

FCC v. LEAGUE OF WOMEN VOTERS, 468 U.S. 364, 104 S.Ct. 3106, 82 L.Ed.2d 278 (1984), per BRENNAN, J., invalidated a federal law prohibiting editorializing on public broadcast stations: "As our cases attest, [broadcast restrictions] have been upheld only when we were satisfied that the restriction is narrowly tailored to further a substantial governmental interest, such as ensuring adequate and balanced coverage of public issues.[13] "

their concerns are apt to contain interviews, statements, or remarks by group leaders and members which may contain offensive language to an extent my Brother Powell finds unacceptable.

b. Stewart, J., joined by Brennan, White, and Marshall, JJ., dissenting maintained that the Commission lacked statutory authority to issue its order and did not reach the constitutional question.

13. [*Pacifica*] is consistent with the approach taken in our other broadcast cases. There, the Court focused on certain physical characteristics of broadcasting—specifically, that the medium's uniquely pervasive presence renders impossible any prior warning for those listeners who may be offended by indecent language, and, second, that the case with which children may gain access to the medium,

especially during daytime hours, creates a substantial risk that they may be exposed to such offensive expression without parental supervision. The governmental interest in reduction of those risks through Commission regulation of the timing and character of such "indecent broadcasting" was thought sufficiently substantial to outweigh the broadcaster's First Amendment interest in controlling the presentation of its programming. In this case, by contrast, we are faced not with indecent expression, but rather with expression that is at the core of First Amendment protections, and no claim is made by the Government that the expression of editorial opinion by noncommercial stations will create a substantial "nuisance" of the kind addressed in *Pacifica.*

2. *Public/Private.* David Cole, *Playing by Pornography's Rules: The Regulation of Sexual Expression,* 143 U.Pa.L.Rev. 111, 140 (1994); "The Court's sexual expression decisions can be organized along a similar public/private axis. The Court's zoning decisions allow communities to demand that when sexually explicit speech appears in public, it must be relegated to dark and distant parts of town. The Court's affirmance of the FCC's 'indecency' regulation permits the zoning of sexual speech to less 'public' times of day. And while private possession of obscenity cannot be regulated, the state is free to regulate obscenity in a public place even if it is enjoyed only by consenting adults, and even where it is only being transported through public channels for private home use. What is immune from regulation in private becomes suppressible in public, even if the very same speakers, listeners, and speech are involved."

3. *Telephonic "indecency" compared.* SABLE COMMUNICATIONS v. FCC, 492 U.S. 115, 109 S.Ct. 2829, 106 L.Ed.2d 93 (1989), per White, J., invalidated a congressional ban on "indecent" interstate commercial telephone messages, i.e., "dial-a-porn." [c] The Court thought *Pacifica* was "readily distinguishable from this case, most obviously because it did not involve a total ban on broadcasting indecent material. [Second,] there is no 'captive audience' problem here; callers will generally not be unwilling listeners. [Third,] the congressional record contains no legislative findings that would justify us in concluding that there is no constitutionally acceptable less restrictive means, short of a total ban, to achieve the Government's interest in protecting minors."

SECTION 10. THE RIGHT NOT TO SPEAK, THE RIGHT TO ASSOCIATE, AND THE RIGHT NOT TO ASSOCIATE

NAACP v. Alabama ex rel. Patterson, 357 U.S. 449, 78 S.Ct. 1163, 2 L.Ed.2d 1488 (1958), per Harlan, J., held that the first amendment barred Alabama from compelling production of NAACP membership lists. The opinion used the phrase freedom of association repeatedly, "elevat[ing] freedom of association to an independent right, possessing an equal status with the other rights specifically enumerated in the first amendment." Thomas Emerson, *Freedom of Association and Freedom of Expression,* 74 Yale L.J. 1, 2 (1964).

From the materials on advocacy of illegal action (Sec. 1, I supra) onward, it has been evident that individuals have rights to join with others for expressive purposes. This section explores other aspects of the freedom to associate and its corollary, the freedom not to associate. First, we explore cases which the Court bases on a right not to speak, but might better be understood as establishing a right not to be associated with particular ideas. Second, we explore aspects of free association in the employment context—in particular the claims of employees not to be associated with a political party, or a union or its policies. Those claims are to some extent derived from the cases establishing a right not to be associated with particular ideas. Third, instead of persons resisting forced membership in a group, we confront a group resisting members.

Finally, freedom of association is used to resist government mandated disclosure. There is no general right not to speak. Every day witnesses are sub-

---

c. The Court upheld a ban on "obscene" interstate commercial telephonic messages. See p. 620 supra. Scalia, J., concurring, noted: "[W]hile we hold the Constitution prevents Congress from banning indecent speech in this fashion, we do not hold that the Constitution requires public utilities to carry it." Brennan, J., joined by Marshall and Stevens, JJ., concurred on the indecency issue and dissented on the obscenity issue.

poenaed to testify against their will.   But the first amendment affords a particularized right not to speak when forced disclosure would jeopardize important associational rights.   One of the questions of the final part is whether press relationships with confidential sources are uniquely protected associations.   That issue carries beyond the subject of the section and back to the question of whether the Constitution contemplates a special role for the institutional press.

I.   THE RIGHT NOT TO BE ASSOCIATED WITH PARTICULAR IDEAS

"If there is any fixed star in our constitutional constellation, it is that no official, high or petty, can prescribe what shall be orthodox in politics, nationalism, religion, or other matter of opinion or force citizens to confess by word or act their faith therein."

West Virginia State Bd. of Educ. v. Barnette, p. 1013 infra (Jackson, J.) (upholding right of public school students to refuse to salute flag).

————

New Hampshire required that noncommercial vehicles bear license plates embossed with the state motto, "Live Free or Die."   "Refus[ing] to be coerced by the State into advertising a slogan which I find morally, ethically, religiously and politically abhorrent," appellee, a Jehovah's Witness, covered up the motto on his license plate, a misdemeanor under state law.   After being convicted several times of violating the misdemeanor statute, appellee sought federal injunctive and declaratory relief.   WOOLEY v. MAYNARD, 430 U.S. 705, 97 S.Ct. 1428, 51 L.Ed.2d 752 (1977), per Burger, C.J., held that requiring appellee to display the motto on his license plates violated his first amendment right to "refrain from speaking": "[T]he freedom of thought protected by the First Amendment [includes] both the right to speak freely and the right to refrain from speaking at all. See *Barnette.*   The right to speak and the right to refrain from speaking are complementary components of the broader concept of 'individual freedom of mind.'   This is illustrated [by] *Miami Herald Publishing Co. v. Tornillo* [p. 844 infra], where we held unconstitutional a Florida statute placing an affirmative duty upon newspapers to publish the replies of political candidates whom they had criticized.

"* * * Compelling the affirmative act of a flag salute [the situation in *Barnette*] involved a more serious infringement upon personal liberties than the passive act of carrying the state motto on a license plate, but the difference is essentially one of degree.   Here, as in *Barnette,* we are faced with a state measure which forces an individual as part of his daily life—indeed constantly while his automobile is in public view—to be an instrument for fostering public adherence to an ideological point of view he finds unacceptable.   In doing so, the State 'invades the sphere of intellect and spirit which it is the purpose of the First Amendment [to] reserve from all official control.'   *Barnette.*

"New Hampshire's statute in effect requires that appellees use their private property as a 'mobile billboard' for the State's ideological message—or suffer a penalty, as Maynard already has.   [The] fact that most individuals agree with the thrust of [the] motto is not the test; most Americans also find the flag salute acceptable.   The First Amendment protects the right of individuals to hold a point of view different from the majority and to refuse to foster, in the way New Hampshire commands, an idea they find morally objectionable."

The Court next considered whether "the State's countervailing interest" was "sufficiently compelling" to justify appellees to display the motto on their license plates. The two interests claimed by the state were (1) facilitating the identification of state license plates from those of similar colors of other states and (2) promoting "appreciation of history, state pride, [and] individualism." As to (1), the record revealed that these state license plates were readily distinguishable from others without reference to the state motto and, in any event, the state's purpose could be achieved by "less drastic means," i.e., by alternative methods less restrictive of first amendment freedoms. As to (2), where the State's interest is to communicate an "official view" as to history and state pride or to disseminate any other "ideology," "such interest cannot outweigh an individual's First Amendment right to avoid becoming the courier for such message."

REHNQUIST, J., joined by Blackmun, J., dissented, not only agreeing with what he called "the Court's implicit recognition that there is no protected 'symbolic speech' in this case," but maintaining that "that conclusion goes far to undermine the Court's ultimate holding that there is an element of protected expression here. The State has not forced appellees to 'say' anything; and it has not forced them to communicate ideas with nonverbal actions reasonably likened to 'speech,' such as wearing a lapel button promoting a political candidate or waving a flag as a symbolic gesture.[a] The State has simply required that *all* noncommercial automobiles bear license tags with the state motto. [Appellees] have not been forced to affirm or reject that motto; they are simply required by the State [to] carry a state auto license tag for identification and registration purposes. [The] issue, unconfronted by the Court, is whether appellees, in displaying, as they are required to do, state license tags, the format of which is known to all as having been prescribed by the State, would be considered to be advocating political or ideological views.

"[H]aving recognized the rather obvious differences between [*Barnette* and this case], the Court does not explain why the same result should obtain. The Court suggests that the test is whether the individual is forced 'to be an instrument for fostering public adherence to an ideological point of view he finds unacceptable,' [but] these are merely conclusory words. [For] example, were New Hampshire to erect a multitude of billboards, each proclaiming 'Live Free or Die,' and tax all citizens for the cost of erection and maintenance, clearly the message would be 'fostered' by the individual citizen-taxpayers and just as clearly those individuals would be 'instruments' in that communication. Certainly, however, that case would not fall within the ambit of *Barnette*. In that case, as in this case, there is no *affirmation* of belief. For First Amendment principles to be implicated, the State must place the citizen in the position of either appearing to, or actually, 'asserting as true' the message. This was the focus of *Barnette,* and clearly distinguishes this case from that one."[b]

Notes and Questions

1. Consider Laurence Tribe, *The Curvature of Constitutional Space: What Lawyers Can Learn From Modern Physics*, 103 Harv.L.Rev. 1, 22 (1989): "[T]he

a. Should compelled speech cases be characterized as personhood or autonomy cases rather than free speech cases? See Abner Greene, *The Pledge of Allegiance Problem,* 44 Fordham L.Rev. 451 (1995). Does *compelled* expression have to be understood by others to

be "speech" or does it suffice that the Maynards *subjectively believed* that they were being forced to make an expression? See note 1 following this case.

b. White, J., joined by Blackmun and Rehnquist, JJ., dissented on procedural grounds.

very existence of the challenged New Hampshire Law in a sense *protected* free speech rights. For it was well known that people had no choice about whether the state motto was to appear on their license plates. [Ironically], by requiring the state to give people the option whether or not to have its motto displayed on their license plates, the *Wooley* Court forced people into a symbolic expression. [An] adequate constitutional analysis cannot ignore the impact on social meaning of the Court's own action."

2. *Use of private property as a forum for the speech of others.* (a) Appellees sought to enjoin a shopping center from denying them access to the center's central courtyard in order to solicit signatures from passersby for petitions opposing a U.N. resolution. The California Supreme Court held they were entitled to conduct their activity at the center, construing the state constitution to protect "speech and petitioning, reasonably exercised, in shopping centers, even [when] privately owned." PRUNEYARD SHOPPING CENTER v. ROBINS, 447 U.S. 74, 100 S.Ct. 2035, 64 L.Ed.2d 741 (1980) per REHNQUIST, J., affirmed: "[In *Wooley,*] the government itself prescribed the message, required it to be displayed openly on appellee's personal property that was used 'as part of his daily life,' and refused to permit him [to] cover up the motto even though the Court found that the display of the motto served no important state interest. Here, by contrast, [the center] is not limited to the personal use of appellants, [but is] a business establishment that is open to the public to come and go as they please. The views expressed by members of the public in passing out pamphlets or seeking signatures for a petition thus will not likely be identified with those of the owner. Second, no specific message is dictated by the State to be displayed on appellants' property. There consequently is no danger of government discrimination for or against a particular message. Finally, [it appears] appellants can expressly disavow any connection with the message by simply posting signs in the area where the speakers or handbillers stand."

Unlike *Barnette,* appellants "are not [being] compelled to affirm their belief in any governmentally prescribed position or view, and they are free to publicly dissociate themselves from the views of the speakers or handbillers. [*Miami Herald*] rests on the principle that the State cannot tell a newspaper what it must print. [There was also a danger that the statute requiring a newspaper to publish a political candidate's reply to previously published criticism would deter] editors from publishing controversial political [statements]. Thus, the statute was found to be an 'intrusion into the function of editors.' These concerns obviously are not present here."

POWELL, J., joined by White, J., concurring in the judgment, maintained that "state action that transforms privately owned property into a forum for the expression of the public's views could raise serious First Amendment questions": "I do not believe that the result in *Wooley* would have changed had [the state] directed its citizens to place the slogan 'Live Free or Die' in their shop windows rather than on their automobiles. [*Wooley*] protects a person who refuses to allow use of his property as a market place for the ideas of others. [One] who has merely invited the public onto his property for commercial purposes cannot fairly be said to have relinquished his right 'to decline to be an instrument for fostering public adherence to an ideological point of view he finds unacceptable.' *Wooley.*

"[E]ven when [as here] no particular message is mandated by the State, First Amendment interests are affected by state action that forces a property owner to admit third-party speakers. [A] right of access [may be] no less intrusive than speech compelled by the State itself. [A] law requiring that a newspaper permit others to use its columns imposes an unacceptable burden upon the newspaper's First Amendment right to select material for publication. *Miami Herald.*

"[If] a state law mandated public access to the bulletin board of a freestanding store [or] small shopping center [or allowed soliciting or pamphleteering in the entrance area of a store,] customers might well conclude that the messages reflect the view of the proprietor. [He] either could permit his customers to receive a mistaken impression [or] disavow the messages. Should he take the first course, he effectively has been compelled to affirm someone else's belief. Should he choose the second, he has been forced to speak when he would prefer to remain silent. In short, he has lost control over his freedom to speak or not to speak on certain issues. The mere fact that he is free to dissociate himself from the views expressed on his property cannot restore his 'right to refrain from speaking at all.' *Wooley.*

"A property owner may also be faced with speakers who wish to use his premises as a platform for views that he finds morally repugnant [, for example, a] minority-owned business confronted with leafleteers from the American Nazi Party or the Ku Klux Klan, [or] a church-operated enterprise asked to host demonstrations in favor of abortion. [The] pressure to respond is particularly apparent [in the above cases, but] an owner who strongly objects to some of the causes to which the state-imposed right of access would extend may oppose ideological activities 'of *any* sort' that are not related to the purposes for which he has invited the public onto his property. See *Abood.* To require the owner to specify the particular ideas he finds objectionable enough to compel a response would force him to relinquish his 'freedom to maintain his own beliefs without public disclosure.' *Abood.* * * *

"[On this record] I cannot say that customers of this vast center [occupying several city blocks and containing more than 65 shops] would be likely to assume that appellees' limited speech activity expressed the views of [the center]. [Moreover, appellants] have not alleged that they object to [appellees' views, nor asserted] that some groups who reasonably might be expected to speak at [the center] will express views that are so objectionable as to require a response even when listeners will not mistake their source. [Thus,] I join the judgment of the Court, [but] I do not interpret our decision today as a blanket approval for state efforts to transform privately owned commercial property into public forums." [c]

PACIFIC GAS & ELECTRIC CO. v. PUBLIC UTILITIES COMM'N, 475 U.S. 1, 106 S.Ct. 903, 89 L.Ed.2d 1 (1986), per POWELL, J., joined by Burger, C.J., and Brennan and O'Connor, JJ., (together with MARSHALL, J., concurring), struck down a commission requirement that a private utility company include in its billing envelope materials supplied by a public interest group that were critical of some of the company's positions.[d] Was the result required by *Miami Herald*? Consistent with *PruneYard*?

3. *Paraders' rights.* The City of Boston authorized the South Boston Allied War Veterans Council to conduct the St. Patricks Day–Evacuation parade (commemorating the evacuation of British troops from the city in 1776). The Veterans Council refused to let the Irish–American Gay, Lesbian and Bisexual

---

c. For commentary, see Curtis Berger, *Pruneyard Revisited: Political Activity on Private Lands,* 66 N.Y.U.L.Rev. 633 (1991); Sanford Levinson, *Freedom of Speech and the Right of Access to Private Property Under State Constitutional Law* in Developments in State Constitutional Law 51 (McGraw ed. 1985).

d. Burger, C.J., filed a concurring opinion; Rehnquist, J., joined by White and Stevens, JJ., dissented; Stevens, J., filed a separate dissent; Blackmun, J., took no part.

Group of Boston march in the parade, but the Massachusetts courts ruled that the Council's refusal violated a public accommodations law in that the parade was an "open recreational event." HURLEY v. IRISH–AMERICAN GAY, LESBIAN AND BISEXUAL GROUP OF BOSTON, ___ U.S. ___, 115 S.Ct. 2338, 132 L.Ed.2d 487, 1995 WL 360192 (1995), per SOUTER, J., held that "[t]his use of the State's power violates the fundamental rule of protection under the First Amendment, that a speaker has the autonomy to choose the content of his own message. * * *

"[The Council's] claim to the benefit of this principle of autonomy to control one's own speech is as sound as the South Boston parade is expressive. Rather like a composer, the Council selects the expressive units of the parade from potential participants, and though the score may not produce a particularized message, each contingent's expression in the Council's eyes comports with what merits celebration on that day. Even if this view gives the Council credit for a more considered judgment than it actively made, the Council clearly decided to exclude a message it did not like from the communication it chose to make, and that is enough to invoke its right as a private speaker to shape its expression by speaking on one subject while remaining silent on another. * * *

"Unlike the programming offered on various channels by a cable network, the parade does not consist of individual, unrelated segments that happen to be transmitted together for individual selection by members of the audience. Although each parade unit generally identifies itself, each is understood to contribute something to a common theme, and accordingly there is no customary practice whereby private sponsors disavow any 'identity of viewpoint' between themselves and the selected participants. Practice follows practicability here, for such disclaimers would be quite curious in a moving parade. [*PruneYard* found] that the proprietors were running 'a business establishment that is open to the public to come and go as they please,' that the solicitations would 'not likely be identified with those of the owner,' and that the proprietors could 'expressly disavow any connection with the message by simply posting signs in the area where the speakers or handbillers stand.' " [e]

4. *Economic pressure to engage in political activity.* NAACP v. CLAIBORNE HARDWARE CO., 458 U.S. 886, 102 S.Ct. 3409, 73 L.Ed.2d 1215 (1982): The NAACP had organized a consumer boycott whose principal objective was, according to the lower court, "to force the white merchants [to] bring pressure upon [the government] to grant defendants' demands or, in the alternative, to suffer economic ruin." Mississippi characterized the boycott as a tortious and malicious interference with the plaintiffs' businesses. The Court, per STEVENS, J., held for the NAACP: Although labor boycotts organized for economic ends had long been subject to prohibition, "speech to protest racial discrimination" was "essential political speech lying at the core of the First Amendment" and was therefore distinguishable. Is the boycott protected association? Are there association rights on the other side? Does the state have a legitimate interest in protecting merchants from being forced to support political change they would otherwise oppose? Cf. *NLRB v. Retail Store Employees Union,* 447 U.S. 607, 100 S.Ct. 2372, 65 L.Ed.2d 377 (1980) (ban on labor picketing encouraging consumer boycott of neutral employer upheld). Are the white merchants neutral? [f] For commentary, compare Michael Harper, *The Consumer's Emerging Right to Boycott: NAACP v. Claiborne Hardware and Its Implications for American Labor*

e. For incisive pre-*Hurley* commentary, see Larry W. Yackle, *Parading Ourselves: Freedom of Speech at the Feast of St. Patrick,* 73 B.U.L.Rev. 791 (1993).

f. Stevens, J., also argued in *Claiborne* that the boycott was protected as a right to petition the government. Are the white merchants the government?

Law, 93 Yale L.J. 409 (1984) with Maimon Schwarzschild & Larry Alexander, *Consumer Boycotts and Freedom of Association: Comment on a Recently Proposed Theory,* 22 San Diego L.Rev. 555 (1985).

5. *Orthodoxy and commercial advertising.* ZAUDERER v. OFFICE OF DISCIPLINARY COUNSEL, 471 U.S. 626, 105 S.Ct. 2265, 85 L.Ed.2d 652 (1985), per WHITE, J., upheld an Ohio requirement that an attorney advertising availability on a contingency basis must disclose in the ad whether the clients would have to pay costs if their lawsuits should prove unsuccessful: "[T]he interests at stake in this case are not of the same order as those discussed in *Wooley, Miami Herald,* and *Barnette.* Ohio has not attempted to 'prescribe what shall be orthodox in politics, nationalism, religion, or other matters of opinion or force citizens to confess by word or act their faith therein.' The State has attempted only to prescribe what shall be orthodox in commercial advertising [regarding] purely factual and uncontroversial [g] information about the terms under which his services will be available. Because the extension of First Amendment protection to commercial speech is justified principally by the value to consumers of the information such speech provides, *Virginia Pharmacy,* appellant's constitutionally protected interest in *not* providing any particular factual information in his advertising is minimal. [We] recognize that unjustified or unduly burdensome disclosure requirements might offend the First Amendment by chilling protected commercial speech. But we hold that an advertiser's rights are adequately protected as long as disclosure requirements are reasonably related to the State's interest in preventing deception of consumers."

The Court stated that the first amendment interests "implicated by disclosure requirements are substantially weaker than those at stake when speech is f]actually suppressed." Accordingly it rejected any requirement that the advertisement in question be shown to be deceptive absent the disclosure or that the state meet a "least restrictive means" analysis.

BRENNAN, J., joined by Marshall, J., dissenting on this issue, conceded that the distinction between disclosure and suppression "supports some differences in analysis," but thought the Court had exaggerated the importance of the distinction: "[A]n affirmative publication requirement 'operates as a command in the same sense as a statute or regulation forbidding [someone] to publish specified matter,' and that [a] compulsion to publish that which 'reason tells [one] should not be published' therefore raises substantial first amendment concerns. *Miami Herald.*" Accordingly, he would have required a demonstration that the advertising was inherently likely to deceive or record evidence that the advertising was in fact deceptive, or a showing that another substantial interest was directly [advanced]. Applying this standard, Brennan, J., agreed with the Court that a state may require an advertising attorney to include a costs disclaimer, but concluded

g. What if the requested disclosures are controverted? Do cigarette companies have first amendment grounds to resist forced disclosures?

Do doctors have a first amendment right to resist state mandated disclosures to patients regarding abortion? Consider joint opinion of O'Connor, Kennedy, and Souter, JJ., in *Planned Parenthood v. Casey,* 505 U.S. 833, 112 S.Ct. 2791, 120 L.Ed.2d 674 (1992): "[This] is, for constitutional purposes, no different from a requirement that a doctor give certain specific information about any medical procedure. [To] be sure, the physician's First Amendment rights not to speak are implicated, see *Wooley,* but only as part of the practice of medicine, subject to reasonable licensing and regulation by the State."

Can professional fundraisers be required to disclose their professional status before soliciting funds? The percent of charitable contributions that have been turned over to charity in the past 12 months? See *Riley v. National Federation of the Blind,* p. 773 supra (the former can be required, not the latter).

that the state had provided Zauderer with inadequate notice of what he was required to include in the advertisement.

6. *Anonymous political speech.* McINTYRE v. OHIO ELECTIONS COMM'N, ___ U.S. ___, 115 S.Ct. 1511, 131 L.Ed.2d 426 (1995), per STEVENS, J., held that Ohio's prohibition against the distribution of anonymous campaign literature was unconstitutional: "Under our Constitution, anonymous, pamphleteering is not a pernicious, fraudulent practice, but an honorable tradition of advocacy and of dissent. [The] State may and does punish fraud directly. But it cannot seek to punish fraud indirectly by indiscriminately outlawing a category of speech, based on its content, with no necessary relationship to the danger sought to be prevented." [h]

THOMAS, J., concurred, but argued that instead of asking whether " 'an honorable tradition' of free speech has existed throughout American history, [we] should seek the original understanding when we interpret the Speech and Press clauses, just as we do when we read the Religion Clauses of the First Amendment." According to Thomas, J., this approach also protected anonymous speech.

SCALIA, J., joined by Rehnquist, C.J., dissenting, asserted that it was the "Court's (and society's) traditional view that the Constitution bears its original meaning and is unchanging." Applying that approach, he concluded that anonymous political speech is not protected under the first amendment.

II. FREEDOM OF ASSOCIATION AND EMPLOYMENT

ELROD v. BURNS, 427 U.S. 347, 96 S.Ct. 2673, 49 L.Ed.2d 547 (1976), (Stevens, J., not participating) declared unconstitutional the dismissal of nonpolicymaking and nonconfidential state and local government employees solely on the ground that they were not affiliated with or sponsored by a particular political party. (The newly elected Democratic Sheriff of Cook County, Illinois, had sought to replace noncivil-service employees in his office, all Republicans, with members of his own party. The employees who brought suit were process servers and a juvenile court bailiff). BRENNAN, J., announced the judgment and an opinion joined by White and Marshall, JJ.: "The cost of the practice of patronage is the restraint it places on freedoms of belief and association. [The] free functioning of the electoral process also suffers. Conditioning political employment on partisan support prevents support of competing public interests. [As] government employment, state or federal, becomes more pervasive, the greater the dependence on it becomes, and therefore the greater becomes the power to starve political [opposition]. Patronage thus tips the electoral process in favor of the incumbent party.

"[P]olitical belief and association constitute the core of those activities protected by the First Amendment. "[The] Court recognized in *United Public Workers v. Mitchell*, 330 U.S. 75, 100, 67 S.Ct. 556, 569, 91 L.Ed. 754 (1947), that 'Congress may not "enact a regulation providing that no Republican, Jew or Negro shall be appointed to federal office." ' This principle was reaffirmed in *Wieman v. Updegraff*, 344 U.S. 183, 73 S.Ct. 215, 97 L.Ed. 216 (1952), which held that a State could not require its employees to establish their loyalty by extracting an oath denying past affiliation with Communists. And in *Cafeteria & Restaurant Workers v. McElroy*, 367 U.S. 886, 898, 81 S.Ct. 1743, 1750, 6 L.Ed.2d 1230

h. Ginsburg, J., concurred. For broad-ranging commentary on the relationship between privacy and disclosure, see Seth Kreimer, *Sunlight, Secrets, and Scarlet Letters: The* *Tension Between Privacy and Disclosure in Constitutional Law,* 140 U.Pa.L.Rev. 1, 70 (1991).

(1961), the Court recognized again that the government could not deny employment because of previous membership in a particular party.[11]

"Particularly pertinent to the constitutionality of the practice of patronage dismissals are *Keyishian v. Board of Regents,* 385 U.S. 589, 87 S.Ct. 675, 17 L.Ed.2d 629 (1967), and *Perry v. Sindermann,* 408 U.S. 593, 92 S.Ct. 2694, 33 L.Ed.2d 570 (1972). In *Keyishian,* the Court invalidated New York statutes barring employment merely on the basis of membership in 'subversive' organizations. *Keyishian* squarely held that political association alone could not, consistently with the First Amendment, constitute an adequate ground for denying public employment.[12] In *Perry,* the Court broadly rejected the validity of limitations on First Amendment rights as a condition to the receipt of a governmental benefit, stating that the government 'may not deny a benefit to a person on a basis that infringes his constitutionally protected interests—especially, his interest in freedom of speech. For if the government could deny a benefit to a person because of his constitutionally protected speech or associations, his exercise of those freedoms would in effect be penalized and inhibited. This would allow the government to "produce a result which [it] could not command directly." *Speiser.* Such interference with constitutional rights is impermissible.' * * * [13]"

If the practice is to survive constitutional challenge, "it must further some vital government end by a means that is least restrictive of freedom of belief and association in achieving that end, and the benefit gained must outweigh the loss of constitutionally protected rights." The plurality then considered and rejected three interests offered in justification of patronage—(1) "the need to insure effective government"; (2) "the need for political loyalty of employees" to assure implementation of the new administration's policies; and (3) "the preservation of the democratic process" and the continued vitality of "party politics":

As to (1), the argument fails, inter alia, "because it is doubtful that the mere difference of political persuasion motivates poor performance; nor do we think it legitimately may be used for imputing such behavior. [At] all events, less drastic

11. Protection of First Amendment interests has not been limited to invalidation of conditions on government employment requiring allegiance to a particular political party. This Court's decisions have prohibited conditions on public benefits, in the form of jobs or otherwise, which dampen the exercise generally of First Amendment rights, however slight the inducement to the individual to forsake those rights.

[T]he First Amendment prohibits limiting the grant of a tax exemption to only those who affirm their loyalty to the State granting the exemption. *Speiser v. Randall,* 357 U.S. 513, 78 S.Ct. 1332, 2 L.Ed.2d 1460 (1958).

12. Thereafter, *United States v. Robel,* 389 U.S. 258, 88 S.Ct. 419, 19 L.Ed.2d 508 (1967), similarly held that mere membership in the Communist Party could not bar a person from employment in private defense establishments important to national security.

13. The increasingly pervasive nature of public employment provides officials with substantial power through conditioning jobs on partisan support, particularly in this time of high unemployment. Since the government

however, may not seek to achieve an unlawful end either directly or indirectly, the inducement afforded by placing conditions on a benefit need not be particularly great in order to find that rights have been violated. Rights are infringed both where the government fines a person a penny for being a Republican and where it withholds the grant of a penny for the same reason.

Petitioners contend that even though the government may not provide that public employees may retain their jobs only if they become affiliated with or provide support for the in-party, respondents here have waived any objection to such requirements. The difficulty with this argument is that it completely swallows the rule. Since the qualification may not be constitutionally imposed absent an appropriate justification, to accept the waiver argument is to say that the government may do what it may not do. A finding of waiver in this case, therefore, would be contrary to our view that a partisan job qualification abridges the First Amendment.

means for insuring [this interest] are available"—discharge for good cause, "such as insubordination or poor job performance, when those bases exist."

"[Moreover] the lack of any justification for patronage dismissals as a means of furthering government effectiveness and efficiency distinguishes this case from *U.S. Civil Service Comm'n v. Letter Carriers,* 413 U.S. 548, 93 S.Ct. 2880, 37 L.Ed.2d 796 (1973), and *Mitchell.* In both of those cases, legislative restraints on political management and campaigning by public employees were upheld despite their encroachment on First Amendment rights because, inter alia, they did serve in a necessary manner to foster and protect efficient and effective government. Interestingly, the activities that were restrained by the legislation involved in those cases are characteristic of patronage practices. As the Court observed in *Mitchell,* 'The conviction that an actively partisan governmental personnel threatens good administration has deepened since [1882]. Congress recognizes danger to the service in that political rather than official effort may earn advancement and to the public in that governmental favor may be channeled through political connections.' "

As for the second interest, the need for political loyalty and implementation of new policies "may be adequately met" by limiting patronage dismissals to "policy-making positions." As for the third interest—one "premised on the centrality of partisan politics in the democratic process"—"we are not persuaded [that] the interdiction of patronage dismissals [will cause] the demise of party politics." Political parties existed prior to active patronage and "they have survived substantial reduction in their patronage power through the establishment of the merit system.

"Patronage dismissals thus are not the least restrictive alternative to achieving the contributions they may make to the democratic process. The process functions as well without the practice, perhaps even better, for patronage dismissals clearly also retard that practice. [U]nlike the gain to representative government provided by the Hatch Act in *Letter Carriers* and *Mitchell,* the gain to representative government provided by [the practice], if any, would be insufficient to justify its sacrifice of First Amendment rights.

"To be sure, *Letter Carriers* and *Mitchell* upheld Hatch Act restraints sacrificing political campaigning and management, activities themselves protected by the First Amendment. But in those cases it was the Court's judgment that congressional subordination of those activities was permissible to safeguard the core interests of individual belief and association. Subordination of some First Amendment activity was permissible to protect other such activity. Today, we hold that subordination of other First Amendment activity, that is, patronage dismissals, not only is permissible, but also is mandated by the First Amendment. And since patronage dismissals fall within the category of political campaigning and management, this conclusion irresistibly flows from *Mitchell* and *Letter Carriers.* For if the First Amendment did not place individual belief and association above political campaigning and management, at least in the setting of public employment, the restraints on those latter activities could not have been judged permissible in *Mitchell* and *Letter Carriers.*"

STEWART, J., joined by Blackmun, J., concurred: "This case does not require us to consider the broad contours of the so-called patronage system, with all its variations and permutations. In particular, it does not require us to consider the constitutional validity of a system that confines the hiring of some governmental employees to those of a particular political party, and I would intimate no views whatever on that question.

"The single substantive question involved in this case is whether a nonpolicy-making, nonconfidential government employee can be discharged or threatened with discharge from a job that he is satisfactorily performing upon the sole ground of his political beliefs. I agree with the plurality that he cannot. See *Perry v. Sindermann*."

POWELL, J., joined by Burger, C.J., and Rehnquist, J., dissented: "[Here, we have] complaining employees who apparently accepted patronage jobs knowingly and willingly, while fully familiar with the 'tenure' practices long prevailing in the Sheriff's Office. Such employees have *benefited* from their political beliefs and activities; they have not been penalized for them. In these circumstances, I am inclined to [the view that they] may not be heard to challenge [the patronage system] when it comes their turn to be replaced."

Beyond waiver, he complained that the Court "unnecessarily constitutional-izes another element of American life—an element not without its faults but one which generations have accepted on balance as having merit." Powell, J., stressed the importance of political parties and their dependency upon patronage. "History and long prevailing practice across the country support the view that patronage hiring practices make a sufficiently substantial contribution to the practical functioning of our democratic system to support their relatively modest intrusion on First Amendment interests. * * *

"It is difficult to disagree with the view, as an abstract proposition, that government employment ordinarily should not be conditioned upon one's political beliefs or activities. But we deal here with a highly practical and rather fundamental element of our political system, not the theoretical abstraction of a political science seminar. [T]he plurality seriously underestimates the strength of the government interest—especially at the local level—in allowing some patronage hiring practices, and it exaggerates the perceived burden on First Amendment rights. * * *

"It is naive to think that [local political activity supporting parties is] motivated [by] some academic interest in 'democracy' or other public service impulse. For the most part, the hope of some reward generates a major portion of [such activity]. It is difficult to overestimate the contributions to our system by the major political parties, fortunately limited in number compared to the frac-tionalization that has made the continued existence of democratic government doubtful in some other countries. * * *

"It is against decades of experience to the contrary, then, that the plurality opinion concludes that patronage hiring practices interfere with the 'free function-ing of the electoral process.' This *ad hoc* judicial judgment runs counter to the judgments of the representatives of the people in state and local governments, representatives who have chosen, in most instances, to retain some patronage practices in combination with a merit-oriented civil service. One would think that elected representatives of the people are better equipped than we to weigh the need for some continuation of patronage practices in light of the interests above identified,[9] and particularly in view of local conditions. *Letter Carriers; Mitch-*

---

9. The plurality might be taken to concede some promotion of the democratic process by patronage hiring practices but to conclude that in net effect such practices will reduce political debate impermissibly by affecting some employees or potential employees and thereby depriving society of the 'unfettered judgment of each citizen on matters of political concern.' In the past the Court has upheld congressional actions designed to increase the overall level of political discourse but affecting adversely the First Amendment interests of some individuals. In *Letter Carriers* we indicated specifically that the First Amendment freedoms of federal

ell." [a]

Notes and Questions

1.   BRANTI v. FINKEL, 445 U.S. 507, 100 S.Ct. 1287, 63 L.Ed.2d 574 (1980), per STEVENS, J., applied *Elrod* to "protect an assistant public defender who is satisfactorily performing his job from discharge solely because of his political beliefs." [b] The Court rejected the argument that even if party sponsorship is an unconstitutional condition for retaining low-level public employees it is a permissible requirement for an assistant public defender: "[P]arty affiliation is not necessarily relevant to every policymaking or confidential position. The coach of a state university's football team formulates policy, but no one could seriously claim that Republicans make better coaches than Democrats, or vice versa, no matter which party is in control of the state government. On the other hand, it is equally clear that the governor of a state may appropriately believe that the official duties of various assistants who help him write speeches, explain his views to the press, or communicate with the legislature cannot be performed effectively unless those persons share his political beliefs and party commitments. In sum, the ultimate inquiry is not whether the label 'policymaker' or 'confidential' fits a particular position; rather, the question is whether the hiring authority can demonstrate that party affiliation is an appropriate requirement for the effective performance of the public office involved." The Court concluded that neither the policymaking of an assistant public defender nor the access of client's confidential information had any bearing on partisan political considerations.

2.   RUTAN v. REPUBLICAN PARTY OF ILLINOIS, 497 U.S. 62, 110 S.Ct. 2729, 111 L.Ed.2d 52 (1990), per BRENNAN, J., extended *Elrod* and *Branti* not only to promotion, transfer, and recall decisions, but also to hiring decisions: "It is unnecessary here to consider whether not being hired is less burdensome than being discharged because the government is not pressed to do *either* on the basis of political affiliation." [c]

STEVENS, J., concurred: "[T]he entire rationale for patronage hiring [rests] on the assumption that the patronage employee filling the government position must be paid a premium to reward him for his partisan services. [This assumes] that governmental power and public resources—in this case employment opportunities—may appropriately be used to subsidize partisan activities [4] even when the

employees could be limited in an effort to further the functioning of the democratic process. I do not believe that local legislative judgments as to what will further the democratic process in light of local conditions should receive less weight than these congressional judgments. Surely that should be the case until we have a record, if one could be created, showing the fears of the plurality to be justified.

a.   Burger, C.J., dissented, contending that the decision "represents a significant intrusion into the area of legislative and policy concerns."

b.   The Court noted that in *Elrod*, as in the instant case, "the only practice at issue was the *dismissal* of public employees for partisan reasons" and thus there was "no occasion to address petitioner's argument that there is a compelling governmental interest in maintaining a political sponsorship system for *filling*

vacancies in the public defender's office." (Emphasis added.)

c.   The opinion excepted employment decisions where party affiliation or support was an "appropriate requirement for the position involved." Illinois, according to the complaint, however, was operating a wholesale patronage system out of the governor's office that functioned broadly to limit state hiring to those supported by the Republican Party.

4.   [Scalia, J.'s opinion is devoid of reference to meaningful evidence that patronage practices have played a significant role in the preservation of the two-party system. In each of the examples that he cites—"the Boss Tweeds, the Tammany Halls, the Pendergast Machines, the Byrd Machines and the Daley Machines," patronage practices were used solely to protect the power of an entrenched majority. See Douglas Laycock, *Notes on the Role of Judicial Review, the Expansion of Federal Power, and*

political affiliation of the employee or the job applicant is entirely unrelated to his or her public service. The premise on which this position rests would justify the use of public funds to compensate party members for their campaign work, or conversely, a legislative enactment denying public employment to nonmembers of the majority party."

SCALIA, J., joined by Rehnquist, C.J., and Kennedy, J., and in part by O'Connor, J.,[d] dissenting, argued that *Elrod* and *Branti* were wrongly decided and opposed their extension: "As the merit principle [for government employment] has been extended and its effects increasingly felt; as the Boss Tweeds, the Tammany Halls, the Pendergast Machines, the Byrd Machines and the Daley Machines have faded into history; we find that political leaders at all levels increasingly complain of the helplessness of elected government, unprotected by 'party discipline,' before the demands of small and cohesive interest-groups.

"The choice between patronage and the merit principle—or, to be more realistic about it, the choice between the desirable mix of merit and patronage principles in widely varying federal, state, and local political contexts—is not so clear that I would be prepared, as an original matter, to chisel a single, inflexible prescription into the Constitution. * * *

"The provisions of the Bill of Rights were designed to restrain transient majorities from impairing long-recognized personal liberties. They did not create by implication novel individual rights overturning accepted political norms. Thus, when a practice not expressly prohibited by the text of the Bill of Rights bears the endorsement of a long tradition of open, wide-spread, and unchallenged use that dates back to the beginning of the Republic, we have no proper basis for striking it down.[1] Such a venerable and accepted tradition is not to be laid on the examining table and scrutinized for its conformity to some abstract principle of First–Amendment adjudication devised by this Court. To the contrary, such traditions are themselves the stuff out of which the Court's principles are to be formed. They are, in these uncertain areas, the very points of reference by which the

---

the Structure of Constitutional Rights, 99 Yale L.J. 1711, 1722 (1990) (describing the "hopelessness of contesting elections" in Chicago's "one-party system" when "half a dozen employees of the city and of city contractors were paid with public funds to work [a precinct] for the other side"); Richard Johnson, *Successful Reform Litigation: The Shakman Patronage Case,* 64 Chi.–Kent L.Rev. 479, 481 (1988) (the "massive Democratic patronage employment system" maintained a "noncompetitive political system" in Cook County in the 1960's).

Without repeating the Court's studied rejection of the policy arguments for patronage practices in *Elrod,* I note only that many commentators agree more with Justice Scalia's admissions of the systemic costs of patronage practices—the "financial corruption, such as salary kickbacks and partisan political activity on government-paid time," the reduced efficiency of government, and the undeniable constraint upon the expression of views by employees than with his belief that patronage is necessary to political stability and integration of powerless groups. * * *

d. O'Connor, J., did not join the sections of Scalia, J's opinion quoted infra, but did join

sections arguing that *Elrod* and *Branti* were wrongly decided.

1. The customary invocation of *Brown v. Board of Education* as demonstrating the dangerous consequences of this principle, (Stevens, J., concurring), is unsupportable. I argue for the role of tradition in giving content only to *ambiguous* constitutional text; no tradition can supersede the Constitution. In my view the Fourteenth Amendment's requirement of "equal protection of the laws," combined with the Thirteenth Amendment's abolition of the institution of black slavery, leaves no room for doubt that laws treating people differently because of their race are invalid. Moreover, even if one does not regard the Fourteenth Amendment as crystal clear on this point, a tradition of *unchallenged* validity did not exist with respect to the practice in *Brown.* To the contrary, in the 19th century the principle of "separate-but-equal" had been vigorously opposed on constitutional grounds, litigated up to this Court, and upheld only over the dissent of one of our historically most respected Justices. See *Plessy v. Ferguson* (Harlan, J., dissenting).

legitimacy or illegitimacy of *other* practices are to be figured out. When it appears that the latest 'rule,' or 'three-part test,' or 'balancing test' devised by the Court has placed us on a collision course with such a landmark practice, it is the former that must be recalculated by us, and not the latter that must be abandoned by our citizens. I know of no other way to formulate a constitutional jurisprudence that reflects, as it should, the principles adhered to, over time, by the American people, rather than those favored by the personal (and necessarily shifting) philosophical dispositions of a majority of this Court.

"I will not describe at length the claim of patronage to landmark status as one of our accepted political traditions. Justice Powell discussed it in his dissenting opinions in *Elrod* and *Branti*. Suffice it to say that patronage was, without any thought that it could be unconstitutional, a basis for government employment from the earliest days of the Republic until *Elrod*—and has continued unabated since *Elrod,* to the extent still permitted by that unfortunate decision. * * * [2] " [e]

3. Might Communists be treated differently from Republican or Democrats for some confidential employment? Consider White, J., dissenting in *Robel* (cited in Brennan, J.'s *Elrod* opinion fn. 12): "[D]enying the opportunity to be employed in some defense plants is a much smaller deterrent to the exercise of associational rights than [a] criminal penalty attached solely to membership, and the Government's interest in keeping potential spies and saboteurs from defense plants is much greater than its interest [in] committing all Party members to prison." Compare Gerald Israel, *Elfbrandt v. Russell: The Demise of the Oath?,* 1966 Sup.Ct.Rev. 193, 201–07 and Robert O'Neil, *Unconstitutional Conditions,* 54 Calif.L.Rev. 443 (1966) with William Van Alstyne, *The Constitutional Rights of Employees,* 16 U.C.L.A.L.Rev. 751 (1969).

COLE v. RICHARDSON, 405 U.S. 676, 92 S.Ct. 1332, 31 L.Ed.2d 593 (1972), per BURGER, C.J. (over the dissents of Douglas, J., and Marshall, J., joined by Brennan, J.), upheld the dismissal of Richardson's employment at a state hospital

2. Justice Stevens seeks to counteract this tradition by relying upon the supposed "unequivocal repudiation" of the right-privilege distinction. That will not do. If the right-privilege distinction was once used to explain the practice, and if that distinction is to be repudiated, then one must simply devise some other theory to explain it. The order of precedence is that a constitutional theory must be wrong if its application contradicts a clear constitutional tradition; not that a clear constitutional tradition must be wrong if it does not conform to the current constitutional theory. On Justice Stevens' view of the matter, this Court examines a historical practice, endows it with an intellectual foundation, and later, by simply undermining that foundation, relegates the constitutional tradition to the dustbin of history. That is not how constitutional adjudication works. I am not sure, in any event, that the right-privilege distinction has been as unequivocally rejected as Justice Stevens supposes. It has certainly been recognized that the fact that the government need not confer a certain benefit does not mean that it can attach any conditions whatever to the conferral of that benefit. But it remains true that cer-

tain conditions can be attached to benefits that cannot be imposed as prescriptions upon the public at large. If Justice Stevens chooses to call this something other than a right-privilege distinction, that is fine and good—but it is in any case what explains the nonpatronage restrictions upon federal employees that the Court continues to approve, and there is no reason why it cannot support patronage restrictions as well.

e. In addition to the arguments referred to in footnotes 1 and 2 of Scalia, J.'s opinion, Stevens, J., maintained in response: "The tradition that is relevant in this case is the American commitment to examine and reexamine past and present practices against the basic principles embodied in the Constitution. the inspirational command by our President in 1961 is entirely consistent with that tradition: 'Ask not what your country can do for you— ask what you can do for your country.' This case involves a contrary command: 'Ask not what job applicants can do for the State—ask what they can do for our party.' Whatever traditional support may remain for a command of that ilk, it is plainly an illegitimate excuse for the practices rejected by the Court today."

for refusing to sign a loyalty oath calling in part for an affirmation that "I will oppose the overthrow of the government [by] force, violence, or by any illegal or unconstitutional method": "Since there is no constitutionally protected right to overthrow a government by force, violence, or illegal or unconstitutional means, no constitutional right is infringed by an oath to abide by the constitutional system in the future."[f] Should the first amendment permit requiring public employees to oppose that which they have a right to advocate? Is *Cole* consistent with the cases cited in the plurality opinion? With *Robel*? With *Wooley*?

4. The plurality argues that its conclusion flows irresistibly from *Mitchell* and *Letter Carriers*? Were these cases rightly decided? Is a ban on active participation in political campaigns by government employees necessary (as the Court thought in *Letter Carriers*) to avoid the impression that the government practices "political justice" or to prevent the government work force from becoming a "peaceful, invincible, and perhaps corrupt political machine"? Would prohibitions against coercion (such as those commanded by *Elrod*) be sufficient? If not, is the concern about coercion relevant only to participation on behalf of incumbents? See Vincent Blasi, *The Checking Value in First Amendment Theory*, 1977 Am.B.Found.Res.J. 521, 634–35. Is it of major import that the restrictions are "not aimed at particular parties, groups or points of [view]"? *Letter Carriers*. Does an emphasis on this factor, denigrate the liberty and associational interests of government employees? See Martin Redish, *The Content Distinction in First Amendment Analysis*, 34 Stan.L.Rev. 113 (1981). See also Note, *"Un–Hatching" Federal Employee Political Endorsements*, 134 U.Pa.L.Rev. 1497 (1986) (criticizing Hatch Act policies).

5. *Beyond loyalty and partisanship.* A provision of the Ethics in Government Act prohibited receipt of honoraria for speeches or writings by federal employees. UNITED STATES v. NATIONAL TREASURY EMPLOYEES UNION, ___ U.S. ___, 115 S.Ct. 1003, 130 L.Ed.2d 964 (1995), per STEVENS, J., invalidated that provision as applied to lower level executive branch employees, the only parties before the Court.

O'CONNOR, J., concurring and dissenting, would have upheld the provision as applied to *work related* speeches and writings, by lower level executive branch employees (the majority thought this would rewrite the statute).[g]

———

When District Attorney Connick proposed to transfer Assistant D.A. Myers to a different section, she strongly opposed it. Myers prepared and distributed to the other assistants a questionnaire concerning office transfer policy, office morale, the need for a grievance committee and two questions Connick particularly objected to—the level of confidence in various supervisors and whether employees felt pressured to work in political campaigns. Connick terminated Myers for refusal to accept the transfer and for distributing the questionnaire. CONNICK v. MYERS, 461 U.S. 138, 103 S.Ct. 1684, 75 L.Ed.2d 708 (1983), per WHITE, J., held that her discharge "did not offend the first amendment:"

"For most of this century, the unchallenged dogma was that a public employee had no right to object to conditions placed upon the terms of employment—including those which restricted the exercise of constitutional rights. The classic formulation of this position was Justice Holmes', who, when sitting on the

---

f. Powell and Rehnquist, JJ., took no part.

g. Rehnquist, C.J., joined by Scalia and Thomas, JJ., dissented.

Supreme Judicial Court of Massachusetts, observed: 'A policeman may have a constitutional right to talk politics, but he has no constitutional right to be a policeman.' *McAuliffe v. Mayor,* 155 Mass. 216, 220, 29 N.E. 517, 517 (1892). For many years, Holmes' epigram expressed this Court's law. *Adler v. Bd. of Educ.,* 342 U.S. 485, 72 S.Ct. 380, 96 L.Ed. 517 (1952); *Garner v. Bd. of Pub. Works,* 341 U.S. 716, 71 S.Ct. 909, 95 L.Ed. 1317 (1951)."

The Court proceeded, however, to recount a series of cases[a] repudiating Holmes' epigram. Those cases stood for the idea that it was wholly impermissible to deny freedom of expression "by the denial of or placing of conditions upon a benefit or a privilege." As the Court characterized the public employee cases, they were all rooted in the rights of public employees to participate in public affairs.[b] In particular, the Court focused upon *Pickering v. Bd. of Educ.,* 391 U.S. 563, 88 S.Ct. 1731, 20 L.Ed.2d 811 (1968): "The repeated emphasis in *Pickering* on the right of a public employee 'as a citizen, in commenting upon matters of public concern,' [reflects] both the historical evolvement of the rights of public employees, and the common sense realization that government offices could not function if every employment decision became a constitutional matter.[5] * * *

"*Pickering* [held] impermissible under the First Amendment the dismissal of a high school teacher for openly criticizing the Board of Education on its allocation of school funds between athletics and education and its methods of informing taxpayers about the need for additional revenue. Pickering's subject was a matter of legitimate public concern upon which free and open debate is vital to informed decision-making by the electorate. [I]n *Givhan v. Western Line Cons. School Dist.,* 439 U.S. 410, 99 S.Ct. 693, 58 L.Ed.2d 619 (1979), we held that First Amendment protection applies when a public employee arranges to communicate privately with his employer rather than to express his views publicly. Although the subject-matter of Mrs. Givhan's statements were not the issue before the Court, it is clear that her statements concerning the school district's allegedly racially discriminatory policies involved a matter of public concern.

"*Pickering,* its antecedents and progeny, lead us to conclude that [w]hen employee expression cannot be fairly considered as relating to any matter of political, social, or other concern to the community, government officials should enjoy wide latitude in managing their offices, without intrusive oversight by the judiciary in the name of the First Amendment.[c] [We] do not suggest, however, [that] speech on private matters falls into one of the narrow and well-defined classes of expression which carries so little social value, such as obscenity, that the state can prohibit and punish such expression by all persons in its jurisdiction. See *Chaplinsky; Roth; Ferber.* For example, an employee's false criticism of his employer on grounds not of public concern may be cause for his discharge but would be entitled to the same protection in a libel action accorded an identical statement made by a man on the street. We hold only that when a public

---

a. Most of the cases involved the right of public employees to associate.

b. But see *Letter Carriers,* p. 879 supra.

5. The question of whether expression is of a kind that is of legitimate concern to the public is also the standard in determining whether a common-law action for invasion of privacy is present. See *Restatement (Second) of Torts,* § 652D. See also *Cox Broadcasting Co. v. Cohn* (action for invasion of privacy cannot be maintained when the subject-matter

of the publicity is matter of public record); *Time, Inc. v. Hill.*

c. If there is dispute about what an employee said, does the first amendment require the trier of fact to determine that the statement was made or is it enough that the employer reasonably thought the statement was made? See *Waters v. Churchill,* ___ U.S. ___, 114 S.Ct. 1878, 128 L.Ed.2d 686 (1994) (enough that employer reasonably thought statement was made).

employee speaks not as a citizen upon matters of public concern, but instead as an employee upon matters only of personal interest, absent the most unusual circumstances, a federal court is not the appropriate forum in which to review the wisdom of a personnel decision taken by a public agency allegedly in reaction to the employee's behavior. Our responsibility is to ensure that citizens are not deprived of fundamental rights by virtue of working for the government; this does not require a grant of immunity for employee grievances not afforded by the First Amendment to those who do not work for the state.

"Whether an employee's speech addresses a matter of public concern must be determined by the content, form, and context of a given statement, as revealed by the whole record. [We] view the questions pertaining to the confidence and trust that Myers' coworkers possess in various supervisors, the level of office morale, and the need for a grievance committee as mere extensions of Myers' dispute over her transfer to another section of the criminal court. [T]he questionnaire, if released to the public, would convey no information at all other than the fact that a single employee is upset with the status quo. [T]he focus of Myers' questions is not to evaluate the performance of the office but rather [to] reflect one employee's dissatisfaction with a transfer and an attempt to turn that displeasure into a cause celèbre.[8] * * *

"One question in Myers' questionnaire, however, [whether] assistant district attorneys 'ever feel pressured to work in political campaigns on behalf of office supported candidates,' [is] a matter of interest to the community upon which it is essential that public employees be able to speak out freely without fear of retaliatory dismissal.

"Because one of the questions in Myers' survey touched upon a matter of public concern, and contributed to her discharge we must determine whether Connick was justified in discharging Myers. [The] District Court viewed the issue of whether Myers' speech was upon a matter of 'public concern' as a threshold inquiry, after which it became the government's burden to 'clearly demonstrate' that the speech involved 'substantially interfered' with official responsibilities. Yet *Pickering* unmistakably states [that] the state's burden in justifying a particular discharge varies depending upon the nature of the employee's expression. Although such particularized balancing is difficult, the courts must reach the most appropriate possible balance of the competing interests. * * *

"We agree with the District Court that there is no demonstration here that the questionnaire impeded Myers' ability to perform her responsibilities. The District Court was also correct to recognize that 'it is important to the efficient and successful operation of the District Attorney's office for Assistants to maintain close working relationships with their superiors.' Connick's judgment, and apparently also that of his first assistant [who] characterized Myers' actions as causing a 'mini-insurrection', was that Myers' questionnaire was an act of insubordination which interfered with working relationships. When close working relationships are essential to fulfilling public responsibilities, a wide degree of

---

8. This is not a case like *Givhan,* where an employee speaks out as a citizen on a matter of general concern, not tied to a personal employment dispute, but arranges to do so privately. Mrs. Givhan's right to protest racial discrimination—a matter inherently of public concern—is not forfeited by her choice of a private forum. Here, however, a questionnaire not otherwise of public concern does not attain that status because its subject matter could, in different circumstances, have been the topic of a communication to the public that might be of general interest. The dissent's analysis of whether discussions of office morale and discipline could be matters of public concern is beside the point—it does not answer whether *this* questionnaire is such speech.

deference to the employer's judgment is appropriate. Furthermore, we do not see the necessity for an employer to allow events to unfold to the extent that the disruption of the office and the destruction of working relationships is manifest before taking action. We caution that a stronger showing may be necessary if the employee's speech more substantially involved matters of public [concern].

"Myers' questionnaire touched upon matters of public concern in only a most limited sense; her survey, in our view, is most accurately characterized as an employee grievance concerning internal office policy. The limited First Amendment interest involved here does not require that Connick tolerate action which he reasonably believed would disrupt the office, undermine his authority, and destroy close working relationships."

BRENNAN, J., joined by Marshall, Blackmun and Stevens, JJ., dissented: "[S]peech about 'the manner in which government is operated or should be operated' is an essential part of the communications necessary for self-governance the protection of which was a central purpose of the First Amendment. Because the questionnaire addressed such matters and its distribution did not adversely affect the operations of the District Attorney's Office or interfere with Myers' working relationship with her fellow employees, I dissent. * * *

"The balancing test articulated in *Pickering* comes into play only when a public employee's speech implicates the government's interests as an employer. When public employees engage in expression unrelated to their employment while away from the work place, their First Amendment rights are, of course, no different from those of the general public. Thus, whether a public employee's speech addresses a matter of public concern is relevant to the constitutional inquiry only when the statements at issue—by virtue of their content or the context in which they were made—may have an adverse impact on the government's ability to perform its duties efficiently.

"The Court's decision today is flawed in three respects. First, the Court distorts the balancing analysis required under *Pickering* by suggesting that one factor, the context in which a statement is made, is to be weighed *twice*—first in determining whether an employee's speech addresses a matter of public concern and then in deciding whether the statement adversely affected the government's interest as an employer. Second, in concluding that the effect of respondent's personnel policies on employee morale and the work performance of the District Attorney's Office is not a matter of public concern, the Court impermissibly narrows the class of subjects on which public employees may speak out without fear of retaliatory dismissal. Third, the Court misapplies the *Pickering* balancing test in holding that Myers could constitutionally be dismissed for circulating a questionnaire addressed to at least one subject that *was* 'a matter of interest to the community,' in the absence of evidence that her conduct disrupted the efficient functioning of the District Attorney's Office.

"[The] proper means to ensure that the courts are not swamped with routine employee grievances mischaracterized as First Amendment cases is not to restrict artificially the concept of 'public concern,' but to require that adequate weight be given to the public's important interests in the efficient performance of governmental functions and in preserving employee discipline and harmony sufficient to achieve that end.

"[The Court's] extreme deference to the employer's judgment is not appropriate when public employees voice critical views concerning the operations of the agency for which they work. Although an employer's determination that an employee's statements have undermined essential working relationships must be carefully weighed in the *Pickering* balance, we must bear in mind that 'the threat of dismissal from public employment is [a] potent means of inhibiting speech.' [As] a result, the public will be deprived of valuable information with which to evaluate the performance of elected officials.''

Notes and Questions

1. *Holmes' epigram.* Does the Court reject Holmes' epigram with one hand and embrace it with the other? Does it to some extent hold that because there is no right to hold a job, its retention is a revocable privilege? Consider Laurence Tribe, *Constitutional Choices* 208 (1985): "*Connick* resurrects the right-privilege doctrine for 'private' speech by government employees. By hinging protection on the distinction between public and private speech, the Court has embarked on a difficult definitional course. The stated test, which includes the 'content, form, and context' of the expression, provides little guidance. As Justice Brennan pointed out in dissent, the Court significantly narrowed the concept of a public issue in holding that criticism of governmental officials is not necessarily of public concern, but provided no clear alternative formulation. The mere fact that expression constitutes an employee grievance surely cannot be decisive, since the Court found that pressure upon employees to work on political campaigns was of public concern. Nor can the absence of partisan political concerns be determinative, since an employee grievance criticizing hiring and personnel management policies is of public concern if based upon a claim of racial discrimination. What is clear is that, at least until the precise reach of *Connick* is determined, public employees, who often possess unique information, will be discouraged from adding their voices to the debate on government performance." [d]

2. Consider the tension between *Letter Carriers* and *Pickering* or *Connick*. Consider also the relationship between *Pickering, Connick,* and *Elrod*. Suppose a deputy sheriff is discharged for meeting with a political opponent of the incumbent sheriff. Does *Elrod* apply or *Pickering–Connick?* [e] What is the difference? For discussion, see Note, *Politics and the Non–Civil Service Public Employee: A Categorical Approach to First Amendment Protection,* 85 Colum.L.Rev. 558 (1985).

3. Does *Connick* provide less protection for the public employee than is afforded to the school child in *Tinker,* p. 829 supra? Does the public/private distinction distinguish *Tinker?* If *Tinker's* black arm band symbolized criticism of the school principal, would the outcome have been different?

4. After hearing of an assassination attempt on the life of the President, a clerical employee in a county constable's office remarked to a friend in the office, "If they go after him again, I hope they get him." Free speech? See *Rankin v. McPherson,* 483 U.S. 378, 107 S.Ct. 2891, 97 L.Ed.2d 315 (1987). For discussion, see Steven Shiffrin, *The First Amendment, Democracy, and Romance* (1990); Toni

d. Much of the literature relevant to the "right-privilege" distinction is cited in Ch. 7, Sec. 5.

e. Should the standards for public teachers, professors, professionals, and non-professional employees each be controlled by *Connick?* Should academic freedom apply to "intramural" speech in ways that permit freer speech

than that available to other public employees? For discussion, see Matthew Finkin, *Intramural Speech, Academic Freedom, and the First Amendment,* 66 Texas L.Rev. 1323 (1988); Mark Yudof, *Intramural Musings on Academic Freedom,* 66 Texas L.Rev. 1351 (1988); Paul Brest, *Protecting Academic Freedom Through*

Massaro, *Significant Silences: Freedom of Speech in the Public Sector Workplace,* 61 S.Cal.L.Rev. 1, 68–76 (1987).[f]

––––––

A 1981 amendment to the Food Stamp Act provides that no family shall become eligible to participate in the program during the time that any member of the household is on strike nor shall receive any increase in food stamp allotments by virtue of decreased income of the striking member. LYNG v. UAW, 485 U.S. 360, 108 S.Ct. 1184, 99 L.Ed.2d 380 (1988), per WHITE, J., stated that associational rights included the "combination of workers together in order better to assert their lawful rights" but found no interference with such association: "[The statute] does not 'order' appellees not to associate together for the purpose of conducting a strike, or for any other purpose, and it does not 'prevent' them from associating together or burden their ability to do so in any significant manner. [I]t seems 'exceedingly unlikely' that this statute will prevent individuals from continuing to associate together in unions to promote their lawful objectives.[a] [A] 'legislature's decision not to subsidize the exercise of a fundamental right does not infringe the right.' *Regan*."[b]

MARSHALL, J., joined by Brennan and Blackmun, JJ., dissenting, saw no need to reach the first amendment issue (although he was "unconvinced" by the Court's treatment of the issue) because, he argued, the statute failed to meet even the most deferential scrutiny. In light of a variety of statutory benefits easing management's burden in labor disputes, he concluded: "Altering the backdrop of governmental support in this one-sided and devastating way amounts to a penalty on strikers, not neutrality."[c]

––––––

In ABOOD v. DETROIT BD. OF EDUC., 431 U.S. 209, 97 S.Ct. 1782, 52 L.Ed.2d 261 (1977), a Michigan statute permitted an "agency shop" arrangement, whereby all local governmental employees represented by a union, even though not themselves union members, must, as a condition of employment, pay to the union "service charges" equal in amount to union dues. Alleging that they were unwilling to pay union dues, that (1) they opposed public sector collective bargaining and that (2) the union was engaged in non-collective bargaining political-ideological activities which they disapproved, public school teachers challenged the validity of the agency-shop clause in a collective bargaining agreement between the Board of Education and the union. The Court, per STEWART, J., rejected plaintiffs' first contention, but sustained the second—the union's expendi-

––––––

the First Amendment, 66 Texas L.Rev. 1359 (1988).

f. For discussion of *Connick,* see eg., Shiffrin, supra, Massaro, supra, Risa Lieberwitz, *Freedom of Speech in Public Sector Employment: The Deconstitutionalization of the Public Sector Workplace,* 19 U.C.Davis L.Rev. 597 (1986); Robert Post, *Between Governance and Management,* 34 UCLA L.Rev. 1713, 1813–16 (1987); Comment, *The Public Employee's Right of Free Speech,* 55 U.Cin.L.Rev. 449 (1986). For relevant pre-*Connick* commentary, see Frederick Schauer, *"Private" Speech and the "Private" Forum: Givhan v. Western Line School District,* 1979 Sup.Ct.Rev. 217.

a. Should a penalty for the exercise of a right be unconstitutional even if it does not inhibit the exercise of that right?

b. How does one distinguish the mere failure to subsidize from a penalty? Is participation in a strike protected association? For commentary discussing and ranging beyond *Lyng,* see Kathleen Sullivan, *Unconstitutional Conditions,* 102 Harv.L.Rev. 1413, 1428–56, 1474 (1989).

c. The government had argued that the statute was justified by the interest of governmental neutrality in private labor disputes.

ture of a part of such "service charges" "to contribute to political candidates and to express political views unrelated to its duties as exclusive bargaining representative" violates the first amendment rights of non-union employees who oppose such causes.

"To compel employees financially to support their collective-bargaining representative has an impact upon their First Amendment interests. An employee may very well have ideological objections to a wide variety of activities undertaken by the union in its role as exclusive representative. His moral or religious views about the desirability of abortion may not square with the union's policy in negotiating a medical benefits plan. One individual might disagree with a union policy of negotiating limits on the right to strike, believing that to be the road to serfdom for the working class, while another might have economic or political objections to unionism itself. An employee might object to the union's wage policy because it violates guidelines designed to limit inflation, or might object to the union's seeking a clause in the collective-bargaining agreement proscribing racial discrimination. The examples could be multiplied. To be required to help finance the union as a collective-bargaining agent might well be thought, therefore, to interfere in some way with an employee's freedom to associate for the advancement of ideas, or to refrain from doing so, as he sees fit. But the judgment clearly made in [*Railway Employees' Dep't v. Hanson,* 351 U.S. 225, 76 S.Ct. 714, 100 L.Ed. 1112 (1956), upholding against first amendment challenge a union-shop clause, authorized by the Railway Labor Act (RLA), requiring financial support of the union by every member of the bargaining unit, and *International Ass'n of Machinists v. Street,* 367 U.S. 740, 81 S.Ct. 1784, 6 L.Ed.2d 1141 (1961), avoiding serious constitutional issues by construing RLA to prohibit the use of compulsory union dues for political purposes] is that such interference as exists is constitutionally justified by the legislative assessment of the important contribution of the union shop to the system of labor relations established by the Congress. '[As long as the union leadership acts] to promote the cause which justified bringing the group together, the individual cannot withdraw his financial support merely because he disagrees with the group's strategy.' *Street* (Douglas, J., concurring).

"[The] desirability of labor peace is no less important in the public sector, nor is the risk of 'free riders' any smaller. [Thus], insofar as the service charge is used to finance expenditures by the union for the purposes of collective bargaining, contract administration, and grievance adjustment, [*Hanson* and *Street*] appear to require validation of the agency-shop agreement before us."

In agreeing with plaintiffs' contention that they fall within the protection of *Elrod* and other cases guaranteeing the freedom to associate for the purpose of advancing ideas and forbidding the government to require one to relinquish first amendment rights as a condition of public employment "because they have been prohibited not from actively associating, but rather from refusing to associate," and in ruling that plaintiffs could constitutionally prevent the union's spending a part of their required service fees for political and ideological purposes unrelated to collective bargaining, the Court pointed out: "The fact that [plaintiffs] are compelled to make, rather than prohibited from making, contributions for political purposes works no less an infringement of their constitutional rights. For at the heart of the First Amendment is the notion that an individual should be free to believe as he will, and that in a free society one's beliefs should be shaped by his mind and his conscience rather than coerced by the State. See [*Elrod.*]

"These principles prohibit a State from compelling an individual [to] associate with a political party, *Elrod,* as a condition of employment. They are no less applicable to the case at bar, and they thus prohibit the [union] from requiring any [plaintiff] to contribute to the support of an ideological cause he may oppose as a condition of holding a job as a public school teacher.

"We do not hold that a union cannot constitutionally spend funds for the expression of political views, on behalf of political candidates, or towards the advancement of other ideological causes not germane to its duties as collective bargaining representative. Rather, the Constitution requires only that expenditures be financed from [charges] paid by employees who do not object to advancing those ideas and who are not coerced into doing so against their will by the threat of loss of government employment."

The Court remanded to devise an appropriate "way of preventing subsidization of ideological activity by employees who object thereto without restricting the union's ability to require every employee to contribute to the cost of collective-bargaining activities." [a]

POWELL, J., joined by Burger, C.J., and Blackmun, J., agreed that a state cannot constitutionally compel public employees to contribute to union political activities which they oppose and thus joined the Court's judgment remanding the case for further proceedings, but balked at the Court's apparent ruling "that public employees can be compelled by the State to pay full union dues to a union with which they disagree, subject only to a possible rebate or deduction if they are willing to step forward, declare their opposition to the union, and initiate a proceeding to establish that some portion of their dues has been spent on 'ideological activities unrelated to collective bargaining.' Such a sweeping limitation of First Amendment rights by the Court is not only unnecessary on this record; it [is] unsupported by either precedent or reason. * * *

"The Court's extensive reliance on *Hanson* and *Street* requires it to rule that there is no constitutional distinction between what the Government can require of its own employees and what it can permit private employees to do. To me the distinction is fundamental. Under the First Amendment the Government may authorize private parties to enter into voluntary agreements whose terms it could not adopt as its own.

"[The] collective-bargaining agreement to which a public agency is a party is not merely analogous to legislation; it has all of the attributes of legislation for the subjects [e.g., residency requirements for state employees] with which it deals. [The] State in this case has not merely authorized union-shop agreements between willing parties; it has negotiated and adopted such an agreement itself. [It] has undertaken to compel employees to pay full dues [to] a union as a condition of employment. Accordingly, the [Board of Education's] collective-bargaining agreement, like any other enactment of state law, is fully subject to the constraints that the Constitution imposes on coercive governmental regulation.

"[I] would make it more explicit [than has the majority] that compelling a government employee to give financial support to a union in the public sector—regardless of the use to which the union puts the contribution—impinges seriously upon interests in free speech and association protected by the First Amendment.

"[*Buckley* held that] limitations on political contributions 'impinge on protected associational freedoms.' [That] *Buckley* dealt with a contribution limitation

---

a. For procedural aspects of the implementation, see *Chicago Teachers Union v. Hudson,*   475 U.S. 292, 106 S.Ct. 1066, 89 L.Ed.2d 232 (1986).

requirement does not alter its importance for this case. An individual can no more be required to affiliate with a candidate by making a contribution than he can be prohibited from such affiliation. The only question after *Buckley* is whether a union in the public sector is sufficiently distinguishable from a political candidate or committee to remove the withholding of financial contributions from First Amendment protection. In my view no principled distinction exists.

"The ultimate objective of a union in the public sector, like that of a political party, is to influence public decisionmaking in accordance with the views and perceived interests of the membership. [In this sense], the public sector union is indistinguishable from the traditional political party in this country.

"[It] is possible that paramount governmental interests may be found—at least with respect to certain narrowly defined subjects of bargaining—that would support this restriction on First Amendment rights. But 'the burden is on the government to show the existence of such an interest.' *Elrod.* Because this appeal reaches this Court on a motion to dismiss, the record is barren of any demonstration by the State that excluding minority views from the processes by which governmental policy is made is necessary to serve overriding governmental objectives. * * *

"Before today it had been well established that when state law intrudes upon protected speech, the State itself must shoulder the burden of proving that its action is justified by overriding state interests. See *Elrod; Speiser v. Randall.* The Court, for the first time in a First Amendment case, simply reverses this principle. Under today's decision, a nonunion employee who would vindicate his First Amendment rights apparently must initiate a proceeding to prove that the union has allocated some portion of its budget to 'ideological activities unrelated to collective bargaining.' I would adhere to established First Amendment principles and require the State to come forward and demonstrate, as to each union expenditure for which it would exact support from minority employees, that the compelled contribution is necessary to serve overriding governmental objectives." [b]

REHNQUIST, J., concurring, noted that had he joined the *Elrod* plurality, he "would find it virtually impossible to join the Court's opinion in this case." He did not "read the Court's opinion as leaving intact the 'unfettered judgment of each citizen on matters of political concern' [*Elrod*] when it holds that Michigan [may] require an objecting member of a public employees' union to contribute to the funds necessary for the union to carry out its bargaining activities. Nor does the Court's opinion leave such a member free 'to believe as he will and to act and associate according to his beliefs' [*Elrod*]." He was "unable to see a constitutional distinction between a governmentally imposed requirement that a public employee be a Democrat or Republican or else lose his job, and a similar requirement that a public employee contribute to the collective-bargaining expenses of a labor union." [c]

b. Reading *Elrod* and *Abood* together, Powell, J., maintains that public employees may be forced to support a political party, but not the union which represents them in collective bargaining. For revealing commentary, see Paul Kahn, *The Court, the Community and the Judicial Balance: The Jurisprudence of Justice Powell,* 97 Yale L.J. 1, 45–47 (1987).

c. Stevens, J., also filed a brief concurrence: "The Court's opinion does not foreclose the argument that the Union should not be permitted to exact a service fee from nonmembers without first establishing a procedure which will avoid the risk that their funds will be used, even temporarily, to finance ideological activities unrelated to collective bargaining."

Notes and Questions

1. How should the *Abood* rules apply to forced employee payments for union conventions, union newsletters, union social activities or union organizing? See *Lehnert v. Ferris Faculty Ass'n*, 500 U.S. 507, 111 S.Ct. 1950, 114 L.Ed.2d 572 (1991); *Ellis v. Brotherhood of Railway, Airline & Steamship Clerks*, 466 U.S. 435, 104 S.Ct. 1883, 80 L.Ed.2d 428 (1984). See also *Communications Workers v. Beck*, 487 U.S. 735, 108 S.Ct. 2641, 101 L.Ed.2d 634 (1988) (forced expenditures for purposes other than collective bargaining including non-germane-non-ideological activities violates National Labor Relations Act). For exploration of the issues raised by *Abood*, see Norman Cantor, *Forced Payments to Service Institutions and Constitutional Interests in Ideological Non-Association*, 36 Rut.L.Rev. 3 (1984).

2. Does *Abood* exaggerate the first amendment interests? See generally, Gaebler, *First Amendment Protection Against Government Compelled Expression and Association*, 23 B.C.L.R. 995 (1982). If Michigan subsidized unions directly, would dissenting taxpayers have a first amendment claim? Suppose Michigan taxed those most likely to benefit from union activity, i.e., the employees? Are compelled contributions different from government taxation? See Steven Shiffrin, *Government Speech*, 27 U.C.L.A.L.Rev. 565, 594 (1980). Suppose the union contract provided for a direct payment from the employer and that union dues were not required of employees? Would this arrangement affect the rules set out in *Abood*?

3. Although *Abood* limits the sources of funding for union speech, it does not question union rights of free speech and association. Such rights include not only the endorsement of political candidates [b] and causes, but also associational rights to pursue legal claims. Even as against state bar regulations, for example, unions are free to recommend attorneys to their members and to hire or engage in contracts with attorneys to represent individual union members. See *United Transportation Union v. State Bar*, 401 U.S. 576, 91 S.Ct. 1076, 28 L.Ed.2d 339 (1971): "[C]ollective activity undertaken to obtain meaningful access to the courts is a fundamental right within the protection of the First Amendment. [T]hat right would be a hollow promise if courts could deny associations of workers or others the means of enabling their members to meet the costs of legal representation."

4. California requires all attorneys to join and pay dues to the State Bar, a regulated state agency authorized not only to examine prospective attorneys and to recommend bar admission or discipline, but also to use compulsory dues for a broad range of lobbying and amicus curiae activities. KELLER v. STATE BAR OF CALIFORNIA, 496 U.S. 1, 110 S.Ct. 2228, 110 L.Ed.2d 1 (1990), per REHN-QUIST, C.J., unanimously held that compulsory bar dues could only be used if "reasonably incurred for the purpose of regulating the legal profession or improving the quality of the legal service available to the people of the State." Recognizing that difficult line-drawing questions could arise, the Court observed that the case presented clear ends of a spectrum: "Compulsory dues may not be expended to endorse or advance a gun control or nuclear weapons freeze initiative; at the other end of the spectrum petitioners have no valid constitutional objection to their compulsory dues being spent for activities connected with disciplining members of the bar or proposing ethical codes for the profession.

b. See also *Eu v. San Francisco County Democratic Central Committee*, 489 U.S. 214, 109 S.Ct. 1013, 103 L.Ed.2d 271 (1989) (statute forbidding official governing bodies of political parties from endorsing or opposing candidates for partisan office in primary elections violates protected speech and association rights). For commentary, see Daniel Lowenstein, *Associational Rights of Major Political Parties: A Skeptical Inquiry*, 71 Tex.L.Rev. 1741 (1993).

"[The] State Bar of California is a good deal different from most other entities that would be regarded in common parlance as 'governmental agencies.' Its principal funding comes not from appropriations made to it by the legislature, but from dues levied on its members by the Board of Governors. [It] undoubtedly performs important and valuable services for the State by way of governance of the profession, but those services are essentially advisory in nature. The State Bar does not admit anyone to the practice of law, it does not finally disbar or suspend anyone, nor does it ultimately establish ethical codes of conduct. All of those functions are reserved by California law to the State Supreme Court. * * *

"The State Bar of California was created, not to participate in the general government of the State, but to provide specialized professional advice to those with the ultimate responsibility of governing the legal profession. Its members and officers are such not because they are citizens or voters, but because they are lawyers. We think that these differences between the State Bar, on the one hand, and traditional government agencies and officials, on the other hand, render unavailing respondent's argument that it is not subject to the same constitutional rule with respect to the use of compulsory dues as are labor unions representing public and private employees."

III. INTIMATE ASSOCIATION AND EXPRESSIVE ASSOCIATION

ROBERTS v. UNITED STATES JAYCEES, 468 U.S. 609, 104 S.Ct. 3244, 82 L.Ed.2d 462 (1984): Appellee U.S. Jaycees, a nonprofit national membership corporation whose objective is to pursue educational and charitable purposes that promote the growth and development of young men's civic organizations, limits regular membership to young men between the ages of 18 and 35. Associate membership is available to women and older men. An associate member may not vote or hold local or national office. Two local chapters in Minnesota violated appellee's bylaws by admitting women as regular members. When they learned that revocation of their charters was to be considered, members of both chapters filed discrimination charges with the Minnesota Department of Human Rights, alleging that the exclusion of women from full membership violated the Minnesota Human Rights Act (Act), which makes it an "unfair discriminatory practice" to deny anyone "the full and equal enjoyment of goods, services, facilities, privileges, advantages, and accommodations of a place of accommodation" because, inter alia, of sex.

Before a hearing on the state charge took place, appellee brought federal suit, alleging that requiring it to accept women as regular members would violate the male members' constitutional "freedom of association." A state hearing officer decided against appellee and the federal district court certified to the Minnesota Supreme Court the question whether appellee is "a place of public accommodation" within the meaning of the Act. With the record of the administrative hearing before it, the state Supreme Court answered that question in the affirmative. The U.S. Court of Appeals held that application of the Act to appellee's membership policies would violate its freedom of association.[a]

a. When the state supreme court held that appellee was "a place of public accommodation" within the meaning of the Act, it suggested that, unlike appellee, the Kiwanis Club might be sufficiently "private" to be outside the scope of the Act. Appellee then amended its complaint to allege that the state court's interpretation of the Act rendered it unconstitutionally vague. The Eighth Circuit so held, but the Supreme Court reversed.

In rejecting appellee's claims,[b] the Court, per BRENNAN, J., pointed out that the Constitution protects " 'freedom of association' in two distinct senses," what might be called "freedom of intimate association" and "freedom of expressive association": "In one line of decisions, the Court has concluded that choices to enter into and maintain certain intimate human relationships must be secured against undue intrusion by the State because of the role of such relationships in safeguarding the individual freedom that is central to our constitutional scheme. In this respect, freedom of association receives protection as a fundamental element of personal liberty. In another set of decisions, the Court has recognized a right to associate for the purpose of engaging in those activities protected by the First Amendment—speech, assembly, petition for the redress of grievances, [and] religion. The Constitution guarantees freedom of association of this kind as an indispensable means of preserving other individual liberties."

The freedom of intimate association was deemed important because, "certain kinds of personal bonds have played a critical role in the culture and traditions of the Nation by cultivating and transmitting shared ideals and beliefs; they thereby foster diversity and act as critical buffers between the individual and the power of the State.[c] Moreover, the constitutional shelter afforded such relationships reflects the realization that individuals draw much of their emotional enrichment from close ties with others. Protecting these relationships from unwarranted state interference therefore safeguards the ability independently to define one's identity that is central to any concept of liberty.

"The personal affiliations that exemplify these considerations [are] distinguished by such attributes as relative smallness, a high degree of selectivity in decisions to begin and maintain the affiliation, and seclusion from others in critical aspects of the relationship. [A]n association lacking these qualities—such as a large business enterprise—seems remote from the concerns giving rise to this constitutional protection. * * *

"Between these poles, of course, lies a broad range of human relationships that may make greater or lesser claims to constitutional protection from particular incursions by the State. [We] need not mark the potentially significant points on this terrain with any precision. We note only that factors that may be relevant include size, purpose, policies, selectivity, congeniality, and other characteristics that in a particular case may be pertinent. In this case, however, several features of the Jaycees clearly place the organization outside of the category of relationships worthy of this kind of constitutional protection.

"[T]he local chapters of the Jaycees are large and basically unselective groups. [Apart] from age and sex, neither the national organization nor the local chapters employs any criteria for judging applicants for membership, and new members are routinely recruited and admitted with no inquiry into their backgrounds. In fact, a local officer testified that he could recall no instance in which an applicant had been denied membership on any basis other than age or sex. [Furthermore], numerous non-members of both genders regularly participate in a substantial

---

b. There was no dissent. Rehnquist, J., concurred in the judgment. O'Connor, J., joined part of the Court's opinion and concurred in the judgment. See infra. Burger, C.J., and Blackmun, J., took no part.

c. For commentary on this aspect of association from a variety of perspectives, see Alisdair McIntyre, *After Virtue* (1981); Robert Nisbet, *The Quest For Community* (1969); Nancy

Rosenblum, *Another Liberalism* (1987); Roberto Unger, *Knowledge and Politics* (1975); Gerald Frug, *The City as a Legal Concept*, 93 Harv.L.Rev. 1057 (1980); Kenneth Karst, *Equality and Community: Lessons From the Civil Rights Era*, 56 Not.D.Law. 183 (1980); Kathleen Sullivan, *Rainbow Republicanism*, 97 Yale L.J. 1713 (1988).

portion of activities central to the decision of many members to associate with one another, including many of the organization's various community programs, awards ceremonies, and recruitment meetings.

"[We] turn therefore to consider the extent to which application of the Minnesota statute to compel the Jaycees to accept women infringes the group's freedom of expressive association. * * *

"Government actions that may unconstitutionally infringe upon [freedom of expressive association] can take a number of forms. Among other things, government may seek to impose penalties or withhold benefits from individuals because of their membership in a disfavored group; it may attempt to require disclosure of the fact of membership in a group seeking anonymity; and it may try to interfere with the internal organization or affairs of the group. [There] can be no clearer example of an intrusion into the internal structure or affairs of an association than a regulation that forces the group to accept members it does not desire. Such a regulation may impair the ability of the original members to express only those views that brought them together. Freedom of association therefore plainly presupposes a freedom not to associate. See *Abood*.

"The right to associate for expressive purposes is not, however, absolute. Infringements on that right may be justified by regulations adopted to serve compelling state interests, unrelated to the suppression of ideas, that cannot be achieved through means significantly less restrictive of associational freedoms.

"[I]n upholding Title II of the Civil Rights Act of 1964, which forbids race discrimination in public accommodations, we emphasized that its 'fundamental object [was] to vindicate "the deprivation of personal dignity that surely accompanies denials of equal access to public establishments."' *Heart of Atlanta Motel*. That stigmatizing injury, and the denial of equal opportunities that accompanies it, is surely felt as strongly by persons suffering discrimination on the basis of their sex as by those treated differently because of their race.

"Nor is the state interest in assuring equal access limited to the provision of purely tangible goods and services. A State enjoys broad authority to create rights of public access on behalf of its citizens. *PruneYard*. Like many States and municipalities, Minnesota has adopted a functional definition of public accommodations that reaches various forms of public, quasi-commercial conduct. This expansive definition reflects a recognition of the changing nature of the American economy and of the importance, both to the individual and to society, of removing the barriers to economic advancement and political and social integration that have historically plagued certain disadvantaged groups, including women. * * *

"In applying the Act to the Jaycees, the State has advanced those interests through the least restrictive means of achieving its ends. Indeed, the Jaycees have failed to demonstrate that the Act imposes any serious burdens on the male members' freedom of expressive association. See *Hishon v. King & Spalding*, 467 U.S. 69, 104 S.Ct. 2229, 81 L.Ed.2d 59 (1984) (law firm 'has not shown how its ability to fulfill [protected] function[s] would be inhibited by a requirement that it consider [a woman lawyer] for partnership on her merits'). To be sure, a 'not insubstantial part' of the Jaycees' activities constitutes protected expression on political, economic, cultural, and social affairs. [There] is, however, no basis in the record for concluding that admission of women as full voting members will impede the organization's ability to engage in these protected activities or to disseminate its preferred views. The Act requires no change in the Jaycees' creed of promoting the interests of young men, and it imposes no restrictions on the organization's ability to exclude individuals with ideologies or philosophies different from those of its existing members. Moreover, the Jaycees already invite women to share the group's views and philosophy and to participate in much of [its] activities. Accordingly, any claim that admission of women as full voting members will impair a symbolic message conveyed by the very fact that women are not permitted to vote is attenuated at best.

"[In] claiming that women might have a different attitude about such issues as the federal budget, school prayer, voting rights, and foreign relations, or that the organization's public positions would have a different effect if the group were not 'a purely young men's association,' the Jaycees rely solely on unsupported generalizations about the relative interests and perspectives of men and women. Although such generalizations may or may not have a statistical basis in fact with respect to particular positions adopted by the Jaycees, we have repeatedly condemned legal decisionmaking that relies uncritically on such assumptions. In the absence of a showing far more substantial than that attempted by the Jaycees, we decline to indulge in the sexual stereotyping [of appellees].

"In any event, even if enforcement of the Act causes some incidental abridgement of the Jaycees' protected speech, that effect is no greater than is necessary to accomplish the State's legitimate purposes. [A]cts of invidious discrimination in the distribution of publicly available goods, services, and other advantages cause unique evils that government has a compelling interest to prevent—wholly apart from the point of view such conduct may transmit. Accordingly, like violence or other types of potentially expressive activities that produce special harms distinct from their communicative impact, such practices are entitled to no constitutional protection."

O'CONNOR, J., concurring, joined the Court's opinion except for its analysis of freedom of expressive association: "[T]hat the Court has adopted a test that unadvisedly casts doubt on the power of States to pursue the profoundly important goal of ensuring nondiscriminatory access to commercial opportunities" yet "accords insufficient protection to expressive associations and places inappropriate burdens on groups claiming the protection of the First Amendment":

"[The] Court declares that the Jaycees' right of association depends on the organization's making a 'substantial' showing that the admission of unwelcome members 'will change the message communicated by the group's speech. [S]uch a requirement, especially in the context of the balancing-of-interests test articulated by the Court, raises the possibility that certain commercial associations, by engaging occasionally in certain kinds of expressive activities, might improperly gain protection for discrimination. The Court's focus raises other problems as well. [W]ould the Court's analysis of this case be different if, for example, the Jaycees membership had a steady history of opposing public issues thought (by the Court) to be favored by women? It might seem easy to conclude, in the latter case, that the admission of women to the Jaycees' ranks would affect the content of the organization's message, but I do not believe that should change the outcome of this case. Whether an association is or is not constitutionally protected in the selection of its membership should not depend on what the association says or why its members say it.

"The Court's readiness to inquire into the connection between membership and message reveals a more fundamental flaw in its analysis. The Court pursues this inquiry as part of its mechanical application of a 'compelling interest' test, [and] entirely neglects to establish at the threshold that the Jaycees is an association whose activities or purposes should engage the strong protections that the First Amendment extends to expressive associations.

"On the one hand, an association engaged exclusively in protected expression enjoys First Amendment protection of both the content of its message and the choice of its members. * * * Protection of the association's right to define its membership derives from the recognition that the formation of an expressive association is the creation of a voice, and the selection of members is the definition of that voice. [A] ban on specific group voices on public affairs violates the most basic guarantee of the First Amendment—that citizens, not the government, control the content of public discussion.

"On the other hand, there is only minimal constitutional protection of the freedom of *commercial* association. There are, of course, some constitutional protections of commercial speech—speech intended and used to promote a commercial transaction with the speaker. But the State is free to impose any rational regulation on the commercial transaction itself. The Constitution does not guarantee a right to choose employees, customers, suppliers, or those with whom one engages in simple commercial transactions, without restraint from the State.

"[A]n association should be characterized as commercial, and therefore subject to rationally related state regulation of its membership and other associational activities, when, and only when, the association's activities are not predominantly of the type protected by the First Amendment. It is only when the association is predominantly engaged in protected expression that state regulation of its membership will necessarily affect, change, dilute, or silence one collective voice that would otherwise be heard. An association must choose its market. Once it enters the marketplace of commerce in any substantial degree it loses the complete control over its membership that it would otherwise enjoy if it confined its affairs to the marketplace of ideas.

"[N]otwithstanding its protected expressive activities, [appellee] is, first and foremost, an organization that, at both the national and local levels, promotes and practices the art of solicitation and management. The organization claims that the training it offers its members gives them an advantage in business, and business firms do indeed sometimes pay the dues of individual memberships for their employees. Jaycees members hone their solicitation and management skills, under the direction and supervision of the organization, primarily through their active recruitment of new members. * * * [The] 'not insubstantial' volume of protected Jaycees activity found by the Court of Appeals is simply not enough to preclude state regulation of the Jaycees' commercial activities. The State of Minnesota has a legitimate interest in ensuring nondiscriminatory access to the commercial opportunity presented by membership in the Jaycees."

Notes and Questions

Freedom of intimate association. The reference to the freedom of intimate association is the first in the Court's history, but the notion that the concept should serve as an organizing principle is found in Kenneth Karst, *Freedom of Intimate Association,* 89 Yale L.J. 624 (1980). To what extent should freedom of intimate association itself be regarded as a first amendment right? Compare Karst with C. Edwin Baker, *Scope of the First Amendment Freedom of Speech,* 25 U.C.L.A.L.Rev. 964 (1978) and Reena Raggi, *An Independent Right to Freedom of Association,* 12 Harv.Civ.Rts.-Civ.Lib.L.Rev. 1 (1977).

Although the freedom of intimate association has limited relevance for the 295,000 member Jaycees, the concept "has important implications for other private associations with discriminatory membership policies." Douglas Linder, *Freedom of Association After Roberts v. United States Jaycees,* 82 Mich.L.Rev.

1878, 1885 (1984). What are (should be) the implications for golf and country clubs, fraternal societies, athletic clubs and downtown or city clubs? Consider Comment, *Discrimination in Private Social Clubs: Freedom of Association and Right to Privacy,* 1970 Duke L.J. 1181, 1222: "Whether this society is capable of free evolution to social equality seems irrelevant in light of the influence of the social club in perpetuating general racial and religious economic and social inferiority and in light of the urgent need for reversal of racial polarization. Many private social clubs have become so affected with the public interest that some regulation of their membership practices is not only a proper but also a necessary exercise of legislative power." [d] See generally Michael Burns, *The Exclusion of Women From Influential Men's Clubs: The Inner Sanctum and the Myth of Full Equality,* 18 Harv.Civ.Rts.-Civ.Lib.L.Rev. 321 (1983). How do O'Connor and Brennan, JJ., differ on such questions? For appreciation of O'Connor, J.'s perspective, see Linder, supra. For defense of Brennan, J.'s perspective, see Note, 98 Harv.L.Rev. 195 (1984).

IV. GOVERNMENT MANDATED DISCLOSURES AND FREEDOM OF ASSOCIATION

A. POLITICAL ASSOCIATION AND GOVERNMENT MANDATED DISCLOSURES

BARENBLATT v. UNITED STATES

360 U.S. 109, 79 S.Ct. 1081, 3 L.Ed.2d 1115 (1959).

Justice Harlan delivered the opinion of the Court. * * *

[In] the present case congressional efforts to learn the extent of a nationwide, indeed world-wide, problem have brought one of its investigating committees into the field of education. Of course, broadly viewed, inquiries cannot be made into the teaching that is pursued in any of our educational institutions. When academic teaching-freedom and its corollary learning-freedom, so essential to the well-being of the Nation, are claimed, this Court will always be on the alert against intrusion by Congress into this constitutionally protected domain. But this does not mean that the Congress is precluded from interrogating a witness merely because he is a teacher. An educational institution is not a constitutional sanctuary from inquiry into matters that may otherwise be within the constitutional legislative domain merely for the reason that inquiry is made of someone within its walls. * * *

We here review petitioner's conviction under 2 U.S.C. § 192 for contempt of Congress, arising from his refusal to answer certain questions put to him by a Subcommittee of the House Committee on Un-American Activities during the course of an inquiry concerning alleged Communist infiltration into the field of education. * * *

Pursuant to a subpoena, and accompanied by counsel, petitioner on June 28, 1954, appeared as a witness before this congressional Subcommittee. After

---

d. For cases following or extending *Roberts,* see *Board of Directors of Rotary International v. Rotary Club of Duarte,* 481 U.S. 537, 107 S.Ct. 1940, 95 L.Ed.2d 474 (1987); *New York State Club Ass'n v. New York,* 487 U.S. 1, 108 S.Ct. 2225, 101 L.Ed.2d 1 (1988) (upholding city ordinance against facial challenge that prohibits discrimination based on race, creed, or sex by institutions (except benevolent orders or religious corporations) with more than 400 members that provide regular meal service and receive payment from nonmembers for the furtherance of trade or business); *Dallas v. Stanglin,* 490 U.S. 19, 109 S.Ct. 1591, 104 L.Ed.2d 18 (1989) (upholding ordinance restricting admission to certain dance halls to persons between the ages of 14 and 18).

answering a few preliminary questions and testifying that he had been a graduate student and teaching fellow at the University of Michigan from 1947 to 1950 and an instructor in psychology at Vassar College from 1950 to shortly before his appearance before the Subcommittee, petitioner objected generally to the right of the Subcommittee to inquire into his "political" and "religious" beliefs or any "other personal and private affairs" or "associational activities," upon grounds set forth in a previously prepared memorandum which he was allowed to file with the Subcommittee.[2] Thereafter petitioner specifically declined to answer [the following questions]:

"Are you now a member of the Communist Party? (Count One.)

"Have you ever been a member of the Communist Party? (Count Two.)
* * *

"Were you ever a member of the Haldane Club of the Communist Party while at the University of Michigan? (Count Four.) * * *"

In each instance the grounds of refusal were those set forth in the prepared statement. Petitioner expressly disclaimed reliance upon "the Fifth Amendment." [Upon conviction under all counts in a federal court, petitioner was sentenced to 6 months imprisonment.]

Undeniably, the First Amendment in some circumstances protects an individual from being compelled to disclose his associational relationships. However, the protections of the First Amendment, unlike a proper claim of the privilege against self-incrimination under the Fifth Amendment, do not afford a witness the right to resist inquiry in all circumstances. Where First Amendment rights are asserted to bar governmental interrogation resolution of the issue always involves a balancing by the courts of the competing private and public interests at stake in the particular circumstances shown. * * *

The first question is whether this investigation was related to a valid legislative purpose, for Congress may not constitutionally require an individual to disclose his political relationships or other private affairs except in relation to such a purpose.

That Congress has wide power to legislate in the field of Communist activity in this Country, and to conduct appropriate investigations in aid thereof, is hardly debatable. The existence of such power has never been questioned by this Court, and it is sufficient to say, without particularization, that Congress has enacted or considered in this field a wide range of legislative measures, not a few of which have stemmed from recommendations of the very Committee whose actions have been drawn in question here. In the last analysis this power rests on the right of self-preservation, "the ultimate value of any society," *Dennis.* Justification for its exercise in turn rests on the long and widely accepted view that the tenets of the Communist Party include the ultimate overthrow of the Government of the United States by force and violence, a view which has been given formal expression by the Congress.

We think that investigatory power in this domain is not to be denied Congress solely because the field of education is involved. [Indeed] we do not understand petitioner here to suggest that Congress in no circumstances may inquire into

---

2. In the words of the panel of the Court of Appeals which first heard the case this memorandum "can best be described as a lengthy legal brief attacking the jurisdiction of the committee to ask appellant any questions or to conduct any inquiry at all, based on the First, Ninth and Tenth Amendments, the prohibition against bills of attainder, and the doctrine of separation of powers."

Communist activity in the field of education. Rather, his position is in effect that this particular investigation was aimed not at the revolutionary aspects but at the theoretical classroom discussion of communism.

In our opinion this position rests on a too constricted view of the nature of the investigatory process, and is not supported by a fair assessment of the record before us. An investigation of advocacy of or preparation for overthrow certainly embraces the right to identify a witness as a member of the Communist Party and to inquire into the various manifestations of the Party's tenets. The strict requirements of a prosecution under the Smith Act are not the measure of the permissible scope of a congressional investigation into "overthrow," for of necessity the investigatory process must proceed step by step. Nor can it fairly be concluded that this investigation was directed at controlling what is being taught at our universities rather than at overthrow. The statement of the Subcommittee Chairman at the opening of the investigation evinces no such intention,[31] and so far as this record reveals nothing thereafter transpired which would justify our holding that the thrust of the investigation later changed. [C]ertainly the conclusion would not be justified that the questioning of petitioner would have exceeded permissible bounds had he not shut off the Subcommittee at the threshold.

Nor can we accept the further contention that this investigation should not be deemed to have been in furtherance of a legislative purpose because the true objective of the Committee and of the Congress was purely "exposure." So long as Congress acts in pursuance of its constitutional power, the judiciary lacks authority to intervene on the basis of the motives which spurred the exercise of that power. [Having] scrutinized this record we cannot say that the unanimous panel of the Court of Appeals which first considered this case was wrong in concluding that "the primary purposes of the inquiry were in aid of legislative processes." * * *

Finally, the record is barren of other factors which in themselves might sometimes lead to the conclusion that the individual interests at stake were not subordinate to those of the state. There is no indication in this record that the Subcommittee was attempting to pillory witnesses. Nor did petitioner's appearance as a witness follow from indiscriminate dragnet procedures, lacking in probable cause for belief that he possessed information which might be helpful to the Subcommittee. And the relevancy of the questions put to him by the Subcommittee is not open to doubt.

We conclude that the balance between the individual and the governmental interests here at stake must be struck in favor of the latter, and that therefore the provisions of the First Amendment have not been offended. * * *

---

31. The following are excerpts from that statement: "[In] opening this hearing, it is well to make clear to you and others just what the nature of this investigation is.

"From time to time, the committee has investigated Communists and Communist activities within the entertainment, newspaper, and labor fields, and also within the professions and the Government. In no instance has the work of the committee taken on the character of an investigation of entertainment organizations, newspapers, labor unions, the professions, or the Government, as such, and it is not now the purpose of this committee to investigate education or educational institutions, as [such.]

"The Committee is equally concerned with the opportunities that the Communist Party has to wield its influence upon members of the teaching profession and students through Communists who are members of the teaching profession. Therefore, the objective of this investigation is to ascertain the character, extent and objects of Communist Party activities when such activities are carried on by members of the teaching profession who are subject to the directives and discipline of the Communist Party." * * *

Affirmed.

Justice Black, with whom The Chief Justice, and Justice Douglas concur, dissenting. * * *

I do not agree that laws directly abridging First Amendment freedoms can be justified by a congressional or judicial balancing process. There are, of course, cases [such as those involving the right of a city to control its streets] suggesting that a law which primarily regulates conduct but which might also indirectly affect speech can be upheld if the effect on speech is minor in relation to the need for control of the conduct. With these cases I agree. [But they do not] even remotely suggest that a law directly aimed at curtailing speech and political persuasion could be saved through a balancing process. * * *

But even assuming what I cannot assume, that some balancing is proper in this case, I feel that the Court after stating the test ignores it completely. At most it balances the right of the Government to preserve itself, against Barenblatt's right to refrain from revealing Communist affiliations. Such a balance, however, mistakes the factors to be weighed. In the first place, it completely leaves out the real interest in Barenblatt's silence, the interest of the people as a whole in being able to join organizations, advocate causes and make political "mistakes" without later being subjected to governmental penalties for having dared to think for themselves. It is this right, the right to err politically, which keeps us strong as a Nation. [It] is these interests of society, rather than Barenblatt's own right to silence, which I think the Court should put on the balance against the demands of the Government, if any balancing process is to be tolerated. Instead they are not mentioned, while on the other side the demands of the Government are vastly overstated and called "self preservation." [Such an approach] reduces "balancing" to a mere play on words and is completely inconsistent with the rules this Court has previously given for applying a "balancing test," where it is proper. * * *

Finally, I think Barenblatt's conviction violates the Constitution because the chief aim, purpose and practice of the House Un-American Activities Committee, as disclosed by its many reports, is to try witnesses and punish them because they are or have been Communists or because they refuse to admit or deny Communist affiliations. The punishment imposed is generally punishment by humiliation and public shame. [T]he proof that the Un-American Activities Committee is here undertaking a purely judicial function is [overwhelming].

It is the protection from arbitrary punishments through the right to a judicial trial with all these safeguards which over the years has distinguished America from lands where drum-head courts and other similar "tribunals" deprive the weak and the unorthodox of life, liberty and property without due process of law. It is this same right which is denied to Barenblatt, because the Court today fails to see what is here for all to see—that exposure and punishment is the aim of this Committee and the reason for its existence. To deny this aim is to ignore the Committee's own claims and the reports it has issued ever since it was established. * * *

Ultimately all the questions in this case really boil down to one—whether we as a people will try fearfully and futilely to preserve democracy by adopting totalitarian methods, or whether in accordance with our traditions and our Constitution we will have the confidence and courage to be free.

[Brennan, J., dissenting, expressed "complete agreement with my Brother Black that no purpose for the investigation [is] revealed by the record except exposure purely for the sake of exposure. This is not a purpose to which Barenblatt's rights under the First Amendment can validly be subordinated."]

Notes and Questions

1. *Compelling testimony vs. investigating.* Is the power of Congress to *compel testimony* in aid of legislation as broad as its power to *investigate* for this purpose. *Ought* it be? When Congress calls a hostile witness, is it concerned with this person's appraisal of the general problem or his advice? What does it contribute to legislative insight, how does it aid the consideration of general legislation, to call a witness who wishes to *conceal* some thing about his individual case or that of his friends? To "inventory the Communists in the United States one at a time"? Harry Kalven, *Mr. Alexander Meiklejohn and the Barenblatt Opinion,* 27 U.Chi.L.Rev. 315, 327 (1960). Consider also Seth Kreimer, *Sunlight, Secrets, and Scarlet Letters: The Tension Between Privacy and Disclosure in Constitutional Law,* 140 U.Pa.L.Rev. 1, 70 (1991): "The offensiveness of the inquiries by HUAC and the loyalty boards lay not only in their potential impact on the future political activities of the witnesses. The inquiries were experienced, and intended, as violations of witnesses' personal autonomy. So, too, the ritualistic requirement that former Communists 'name the names' of their leftist friends and colleagues as a condition of avoiding blacklists was objectionable even when the names had been published previously. The public betrayal of intimate relations assaulted both the witnesses and those they identified by denying their autonomy as citizens."

2. *"Balancing".* (a) In "balancing the interests," did *Barenblatt* adequately consider and weigh the *alternative methods* for achieving the investigative purpose? Did it consider the necessity of gathering the information sought by the Subcommittee in the particular way it attempted to obtain it from Barenblatt: by forcing him to disclose or deny Communist affiliation at a *public* hearing? See Paul Kauper, *Civil Liberties and the Constitution* 121 (1962).

(b) What *are* the "interests" on either side that the Court must "balance"? Whatever they are, on what basis can a judge compare them qualitatively without some independent standard to which they can be referred? Does the "balancing process" make it more—or less—difficult for judges to rest on their predispositions? See Laurent Frantz, *The First Amendment in the Balance,* 71 Yale L.J. 1424 (1962).

3. *Fifth vs. first amendments. Barenblatt* points out that "the protections of the First Amendment, unlike a proper claim of the privilege against self-incrimination [do] not afford a witness the right to resist inquiry in all circumstances. Where First Amendment rights are asserted [the] issue *always* involves a balancing by the courts of the competing private and public interests at stake." (Emphasis added.) Why, when confronted by the same national danger must the fifth amendment always prevail over the care for national security, but the first amendment give way to it? Should the interest of a citizen, and of the nation, in freedom of speech and association be entitled to less weight than the interest of a private individual in his safety from self-incrimination? See Alexander Meiklejohn, *The Balancing of Self-Preservation Against Political Freedom,* 49 Calif.L.Rev. 4, 6–7 (1961).

4. *The "Equality Principle."* Although disclosure cases do not follow a uniform course, the Court has manifested more concern about the impact of disclosure on private associations than is exhibited in *Barenblatt.* It has been especially protective of the NAACP. Consider Kenneth Karst, *Equality as a*

Central Principle in the First Amendment, 43 U.Chi.L.Rev. 20, 42–43 (1975): "In the late 1950s, when the civil rights movement was gathering momentum in the South, public disclosure of one's membership in the NAACP typically was followed by annoyances [and] often by more tangible reprisals like being fired. In a series of cases, the Court held that [government] could not constitutionally insist on such disclosure, either by the NAACP itself[a] or by individual members.[b]

"The governments' demands for information in these cases usually were presented for ostensibly neutral purposes. [The] Court, solemnly going along with the gag, took these asserted justifications at face value but concluded nonetheless that the required disclosures unconstitutionally invaded first amendment rights of political association.

"[The] Court's concern in these cases grows out of the first amendment's equality principle. If all the school teachers in Arkansas were to disclose their respective memberships in organizations, it is a safe bet that most Rotarians and Job's Daughters would not be greeted with heavy breathing when they answered the phone at night. The private harassment that concerned the Court was reserved for those associated with an unpopular challenge to the local orthodoxy."

5. *Election disclosure requirements.* BROWN v. SOCIALIST WORKERS, 459 U.S. 87, 103 S.Ct. 416, 74 L.Ed.2d 250 (1982), per MARSHALL, J., held that an Ohio statute requiring every political party to report the names and addresses of campaign contributors and recipients of campaign disbursements could not be applied to the Socialist Workers Party. Citing *Buckley v. Valeo,* p. 1011 infra, the Court held that the " 'evidence offered [by a minor party] need show only a reasonable probability that the compelled disclosure [of] names will subject them to threats, harassment, or reprisals from either Government officials or private parties.' " Consider Geoffrey Stone & William Marshall, *Brown v. Socialist Workers: Inequality As A Command of the First Amendment,* 1983 Sup.Ct.Rev. 583, 592: "[*Brown*] expressly exempted particular political parties from an otherwise content-neutral regulation for reasons directly related to the content of their expression. [The] constitutionally compelled exemption substitutes a content-based law for one that is content neutral. It stands the presumption in favor of 'content neutrality' on its head." Is the decision, nonetheless, consistent with first amendment values? See Stone & Marshall, supra.

a. *Gibson v. Florida Leg. Investig. Comm.,* 372 U.S. 539, 83 S.Ct. 889, 9 L.Ed.2d 929 (1963), per Goldberg, J., reversed a Florida Supreme Court holding that the custodian of NAACP records could be compelled to bring membership lists to legislative hearings so that he could be forced to refer to them in determining whether individuals suspected as being communists were NAACP members. This could not be required said the Court without a substantial relation between the NAACP and "conduct in which the State may have a compelling regulatory concern." Because no substantial relation was shown, compelling the NAACP to disclose its membership presented "a question wholly different from compelling the Communist Party to disclose its own membership." Harlan, J., joined by Clark, Stewart, and White, JJ., dissenting, complained that the

Court had required "an investigating agency to prove in advance the very things it is trying to find out."

b. *Shelton v. Tucker,* 364 U.S. 479, 81 S.Ct. 247, 5 L.Ed.2d 231 (1960) held that teachers could not be required as a condition of employment to list all of the organizations they had belonged to or contributed to during the preceding five years. Professor Karst suggests that Barenblatt should have received the same hospitality. But what standard should govern? Should the Court endorse a general right not to speak? A right not to speak about political associations? Suppose, after a wave of racially motivated bombings, the leader of a white racist organization is called before a grand jury and asked to reveal the group's membership. What standard should govern?

B.   REPORTER'S PRIVILEGE
BRANZBURG v. HAYES
408 U.S. 665, 92 S.Ct. 2646, 33 L.Ed.2d 626 (1972).

JUSTICE WHITE delivered the opinion of the Court.

[Branzburg, a Kentucky reporter, wrote articles describing his observations of local hashish-making and other drug violations. He refused to testify before a grand jury regarding his information. The state courts rejected his claim of a first amendment privilege.

[Pappas, a Massachusetts TV newsman-photographer, was allowed to enter and remain inside a Black Panther headquarters on condition he disclose nothing. When an anticipated police raid did not occur, he wrote no story. Summoned before a local grand jury, he refused to answer any questions about what had occurred inside the Panther headquarters or to identify those he had observed. The state courts denied his claim of a first amendment privilege.

[Caldwell, a N.Y. Times reporter covering the Black Panthers, was summoned to appear before a federal grand jury investigating Panther activities. A federal court issued a protective order providing that although he had to divulge information given him "for publication," he could withhold "confidential" information "developed or maintained by him as a professional journalist." Maintaining that absent a specific need for his testimony he should be excused from attending the grand jury altogether, Caldwell disregarded the order and was held in contempt. The Ninth Circuit reversed, holding that absent "compelling reasons" Caldwell could refuse even to attend the grand jury, because of the potential impact of such an appearance on the flow of news to the public.]

[Petitioners' first amendment claims] may be simply put: that to gather news it is often necessary to agree either not to identify [sources] or to publish only part of the facts revealed, or both; that if the reporter is nevertheless forced to reveal these confidences to a grand jury, the source so identified and other confidential sources of other reporters will be measurably deterred from furnishing publishable information, all to the detriment of the free flow of information protected by the First Amendment. Although petitioners do not claim an absolute privilege [they] assert that the reporter should not be forced either to appear or to testify before a grand jury or at trial until and unless sufficient grounds are shown for believing that the reporter possesses information relevant to a crime the grand jury is investigating, that the information the reporter has is unavailable from other sources, and that the need for the information is sufficiently compelling to override the claimed invasion of First Amendment interests occasioned by the disclosure. [The] heart of the claim is that the burden on news gathering resulting from compelling reporters to disclose confidential information outweighs any public interest in obtaining the information.

[We agree] that news gathering [qualifies] for First Amendment protection; without some protection for seeking out the news, freedom of the press could be eviscerated. But this case involves no intrusions upon speech [and no] command that the press publish what it prefers to withhold. [N]o penalty, civil or criminal, related to the content of published material is at issue here. The use of confidential sources by the press is not forbidden or restricted; reporters remain free to seek news from any source by means within the law. No attempt is made to require the press to publish its sources of information or indiscriminately to disclose them on request.

The sole issue before us is the obligation of reporters to respond to grand jury subpoenas as other citizens do and to answer questions relevant to an investigation into the commission of crime. The claim is, [that] reporters are exempt from [the average citizen's] obligations because if forced to respond to subpoenas and identify their sources or disclose other confidences, their informants will refuse or be reluctant to furnish newsworthy information in the future.

[T]he First Amendment does not guarantee the press a constitutional right of special access to information not available to the public generally. [Although] news gathering may be hampered, the press is regularly excluded from grand jury proceedings, our own conferences, the meetings of other official bodies gathered in executive session, and the meetings of private organizations. Newsmen have no constitutional right of access to the scenes of crime or disaster when the general public is excluded, and they may be prohibited from attending or publishing information about trials if such restrictions are necessary to assure a defendant a fair trial before an impartial tribunal. [It] is thus not surprising that the great weight of authority is that newsmen are not exempt from the normal duty of appearing before a grand jury and answering questions relevant to a criminal investigation.

[Because] its task is to inquire into the existence of possible criminal conduct and to return only well-founded indictments, [the grand jury's] investigative powers are necessarily broad. [T]he long standing principle that "the public has a right to every man's evidence," except for those persons protected by a constitutional, common law, or statutory privilege, is particularly applicable to grand jury proceedings.

A [minority] of States have provided newsmen a statutory privilege of varying breadth, [but] none has been provided by federal statute. [We decline to create one] by interpreting the First Amendment to grant newsmen a testimonial privilege that other citizens do not enjoy. [On] the records now before us, we perceive no basis for holding that the public interest in law enforcement and in ensuring effective grand jury proceedings is insufficient to override the consequential, but uncertain, burden on news gathering which is said to result from insisting that reporters, like other citizens, respond to relevant questions put to them in the course of a valid grand jury investigation or criminal trial.

This conclusion [does not] threaten the vast bulk of confidential relationships between reporters and their sources. Grand juries address themselves to the issues of whether crimes have been committed and who committed them. Only where news sources themselves are implicated in crime or possess information relevant to the grand jury's task need they or the reporter be concerned about grand jury subpoenas. Nothing before us indicates that a large number or percentage of *all* confidential news sources fall into either category and would in any way be deterred by [our holding].

It would be frivolous to assert—and no one does in these cases—that the First Amendment, in the interest of securing news or otherwise, confers a license on either the reporter or his news sources to violate otherwise valid criminal laws. [W]e cannot seriously entertain the notion that the First Amendment protects a newsman's agreement to conceal the criminal conduct of his source, or evidence thereof, on the theory that it is better to write about crime than to do something about [it.]

There remain those situations where a source is not engaged in criminal conduct but has information suggesting illegal conduct by others. [But] we remain unclear how often and to what extent informers are actually deterred from furnishing information when newsmen are forced to testify before a grand jury. The available data indicates that some newsmen rely a great deal on confidential sources and that some informants are particularly sensitive to the threat of exposure and may be silenced if it is held by this Court that, ordinarily, newsmen must testify pursuant to subpoenas, but the evidence fails to demonstrate that [our holding would cause] a significant constriction of the flow of news to the public * * *. Estimates of the inhibiting effect of such subpoenas on the willingness of informants to make disclosures to newsmen are widely divergent and to a great extent speculative. It would be difficult to canvass the views of the informants themselves; surveys of reporters on this topic are chiefly opinions of predicted informant behavior and must be viewed in the light of the professional self-interest of the interviewees.[33] Reliance by the press on confidential informants does not mean that all such sources will in fact dry up because of the later possible appearance of the newsman before a grand jury. The reporter may never be called and if he objects to testifying, the prosecution may not insist. Also, the relationship of many informants to the press is a symbiotic one which is unlikely to be greatly inhibited by the threat of subpoena: quite often, such informants are members of a minority political or cultural group which relies heavily on the media to propagate its views, publicize its aims, and magnify its exposure to the public. * * *

Accepting the fact, however, that an undetermined number of informants not themselves implicated in crime will nevertheless, for whatever reason, refuse to talk to newsmen if they fear identification by a reporter in an official investigation, we cannot accept the argument that the public interest in possible future news about crime from undisclosed, unverified sources must take precedence over the public interest in pursuing and prosecuting those crimes reported to the press by informants and in thus deterring the commission of such crimes in the future.

[C]oncealment of crime and agreements to do so are not looked upon with favor. Such conduct deserves no encomium, and we decline now to afford it First Amendment [protection].

[T]he common law recognized no [reporter's] privilege, and the constitutional argument was not even asserted until 1958. From the beginning of our country the press has operated without constitutional protection for press informants, and the press has [flourished.]

The argument for [a] constitutional privilege rests heavily on those cases holding that the infringement of protected First Amendment rights must be no broader than necessary to achieve a permissible governmental purpose. We do not deal, however, with a governmental institution that has abused its proper function, as a legislative committee does when it "expose[s] for the sake of exposure." [Nor is there any] attempt here by the grand juries to invade protected First Amendment rights by forcing wholesale disclosure of names and organizational affiliations for a purpose which is not germane to the determination of whether crime has been committed, and the characteristic secrecy of grand jury proceedings is a further protection against the undue invasion of such rights. * * *

33. In his *Press Subpoenas: An Empirical and Legal Analysis* 6–12 (1971), Prof. Blasi discusses these methodological problems. [His] survey found that slightly more than half of the 975 reporters questioned said that they relied on regular confidential sources for at least 10% of their stories. Of this group of reporters, only 8% were able to say with some certainty that their professional functioning had been adversely affected by the threat of subpoena; another 11% were not certain whether or not they had been adversely affected. [See also Vincent Blasi, *The Newsman's Privilege: An Empirical Study,* 70 Mich.L.Rev. 229 (1971).]

[The] requirements of those cases which hold that a State's interest must be "compelling" or "paramount" to justify even an indirect burden on First Amendment rights, are also met here. [If] the test is that the Government "convincingly show a substantial relation between the information sought and a subject of overriding and compelling state interest," *Gibson,* it is quite apparent (1) that the State has the necessary interest in extirpating the traffic in illegal drugs, in forestalling assassination attempts on the President, and in preventing the community from being disrupted by violent disorders endangering both persons and property; and (2) that, based on the stories Branzburg and Caldwell wrote and Pappas' admitted conduct, the grand jury called these reporters as they would others—because it was likely that they could supply information to help the Government determine whether illegal conduct had occurred and, if it had, whether there was sufficient evidence to return an indictment.

Similar considerations dispose of the reporters' claims that preliminary to requiring their grand jury appearance, the State must show that a crime has been committed and that they possess relevant information not available from other sources, for only the grand jury itself can make this determination. [A] grand jury investigation "is not fully carried out until every available clue has been run down and all witnesses examined in every proper way to find if a crime has been committed." * * *

[The] privilege claimed here is conditional, not absolute; given the suggested preliminary showings and compelling need, the reporter would be required to testify. [If] newsmen's confidential sources are as sensitive as they are claimed to be, the prospect of being unmasked whenever a judge determines the situation justifies it is hardly a satisfactory solution to the problem. For them, it would appear that only an absolute privilege would suffice.

We are unwilling to embark the judiciary on a long and difficult journey to such an uncertain destination. The administration of a constitutional newsman's privilege would present practical and conceptual difficulties of a high order. Sooner or later, it would be necessary to define those categories of newsmen who qualified for the privilege, a questionable procedure in light of the traditional doctrine that liberty of the press is the right of the lonely pamphleteer who uses carbon paper or a mimeograph just as much as of the large metropolitan publisher who utilizes the latest photocomposition methods. [The] informative function asserted by representatives of the organized press in the present cases is also performed by lecturers, political pollsters, novelists, academic researchers, and dramatists. Almost any author may quite accurately assert that he is contributing to the flow of information to the public, that he relies on confidential sources of information, and that these sources will be silenced if he is forced to make disclosures before a grand jury.

In each instance where a reporter is subpoenaed to testify, the courts would also be embroiled in preliminary factual and legal determinations with respect to whether the proper predicate had been laid for the reporters' appearance. [I]n the end, by considering whether enforcement of a particular law served a "compelling" governmental interest, the courts would be inextricably involved in distinguishing between the value of enforcing different criminal laws. By requiring testimony from a reporter in investigations involving some crimes but not in others, they would be making a value judgment which a legislature had declined to [make.]

At the federal level, Congress has freedom to determine whether a statutory newsman's privilege is necessary and desirable and to fashion standards and rules as narrow or broad as deemed necessary [and], equally important, to re-fashion those rules as experience from time to time may dictate. There is also merit in leaving state legislatures free, within First Amendment limits, to fashion their own standards in light of the conditions and problems with respect to the relations between law enforcement officials and press in their own [areas].

In addition, there is much force in the pragmatic view that the press has at its disposal powerful mechanisms of communication and is far from helpless to protect itself from harassment or substantial harm. Furthermore, if what the newsmen urged in these cases is true—that law enforcement cannot hope to gain and may suffer from subpoenaing newsmen before grand juries—prosecutors will be loath to risk so much for so little. Thus, at the federal level the Attorney General has already fashioned a set of rules for federal officials in connection with subpoenaing members of the press to testify before grand juries or at criminal trials.[a] These rules are a major step in the direction petitioners desire to move. They may prove wholly sufficient to resolve the bulk of disagreements and controversies between press and federal officials.

[G]rand jury investigations if instituted or conducted other than in good faith, would pose wholly different issues for resolution under the First Amendment. Official harassment of the press undertaken not for purposes of law enforcement but to disrupt a reporter's relationship with his news sources would have no justification. Grand juries are subject to judicial control and subpoenas to motions to quash. We do not expect courts will forget that grand juries must operate within the limits of the First Amendment as well as the Fifth.

We turn, therefore, to the disposition of the cases before us. [*Caldwell*] must be reversed. If there is no First Amendment privilege to refuse to answer the relevant and material questions asked during a good-faith grand jury investigation, then it is a fortiori true that there is no privilege to refuse to appear before such a grand jury until the Government demonstrates some "compelling need" for a newsman's testimony. [*Branzburg*] must be affirmed. [P]etitioner refused to answer questions that directly related to criminal conduct which he had observed and written about. [If] what petitioner wrote was true, he had direct information to provide the grand jury concerning the commission of serious crimes. [In *Pappas,* we] affirm [and] hold that petitioner must appear before the grand jury to answer the questions put to him, subject, of course, to the supervision of the presiding judge as to "the propriety, purposes, and scope of the grand jury inquiry and the pertinence of the probable testimony."

JUSTICE POWELL, concurring in the opinion of the Court.

I add this brief statement to emphasize what seems to me to be the limited nature of the Court's holding. The Court does not hold that newsmen, subpoenaed to testify before a grand jury, are without constitutional rights with respect to the gathering of news or in safeguarding their sources. [As] indicated in the concluding portion of the opinion, the Court states that no harassment of newsmen will be tolerated. If a newsman believes that the grand jury investigation is not being conducted in good faith he is not without remedy. Indeed, if the newsman is called upon to give information bearing only a remote and tenuous relationship to the subject of the investigation, or if he has some other reason to believe that his testimony implicates confidential source relationships without a

---

a. The "Guidelines for Subpoenas to the News Media," noted the Court, recognize that "compulsory process in some circumstances may have a limiting effect on the exercise of First Amendment rights" and provide, inter alia, that that factor "must [be] weight[ed]" in every case against the public interest to be served in administering justice.

legitimate need of law enforcement, he will have access to the Court on a motion to quash and an appropriate protective order may be entered. The asserted claim to privilege should be judged on its facts by the striking of a proper balance between freedom of the press and the obligation of all citizens to give relevant testimony with respect to criminal conduct. The balance of these vital constitutional and societal interests on a case-by-case basis accords with the tried and traditional way of adjudicating such questions.*

In short, the courts will be available to newsmen under circumstances where legitimate First Amendment interests require protection.

JUSTICE DOUGLAS, dissenting.

[T]here is no "compelling need" that can be shown [by the Government] which qualifies the reporter's immunity from appearing or testifying before a grand jury, unless the reporter himself is implicated in a crime. His immunity in my view is therefore quite complete, for absent his involvement in a crime, the First Amendment protects him against an appearance before a grand jury and if he is involved in a crime, the Fifth Amendment stands as a barrier. Since in my view there is no area of inquiry not protected by a privilege, the reporter need not appear for the futile purpose of invoking one to each [question.]

Two principles which follow from [Alexander Meiklejohn's] understanding of the First Amendment are at stake here. One is that the people, the ultimate governors, must have absolute freedom of and therefore privacy of their individual opinions and beliefs regardless of how suspect or strange they may appear to others. Ancillary to that principle is the conclusion that an individual must also have absolute privacy over whatever information he may generate in the course of testing his opinions and beliefs. In this regard, Caldwell's status as a reporter is less relevant than is his status as a student who affirmatively pursued empirical research to enlarge his own intellectual viewpoint. The second principle is that effective self-government cannot succeed unless the people are immersed in a steady, robust, unimpeded, and uncensored flow of opinion and reporting which are continuously subjected to critique, rebuttal, and re-examination. In this respect, Caldwell's status as a newsgatherer and an integral part of that process becomes critical.   * * *

Sooner or later any test which provides less than blanket protection to beliefs and associations will be twisted and relaxed so as to provide virtually no protection at [all]. Perceptions of the worth of state objectives will change with the composition of the Court and with the intensity of the politics of the [times.]

JUSTICE STEWART, with whom JUSTICE BRENNAN and JUSTICE MARSHALL join, dissenting.

---

* It is to be remembered that Caldwell asserts a constitutional privilege not even to appear before the grand jury unless a court decides that the government has made a showing that meets the three preconditions specified in [Stewart, J.'s dissent]. To be sure, this would require a "balancing" of interests by the Court, but under circumstances and constraints significantly different from the balancing that will be appropriate under the Court's decision. The newsman witness, like all other witnesses, will have to appear; he will not be in a position to litigate at the threshold the State's very authority to subpoena him. Moreover, absent the constitutional preconditions that [the dissent] would impose as heavy burdens of proof to be carried by the State, the court—when called upon to protect a newsman from improper or prejudicial questioning—would be free to balance the competing interests on their merits in the particular case. The new constitutional rule endorsed by [the dissent] would, as a practical matter, defeat such a fair balancing and the essential societal interest in the detection and prosecution of crime would be heavily subordinated.

The Court's crabbed view of the First Amendment reflects a disturbing insensitivity to the critical role of an independent press in our society. [While] Mr. Justice Powell's enigmatic concurring opinion gives some hope of a more flexible view in the future, the Court in these cases holds that a newsman has no First Amendment right to protect his sources when called before a grand jury. The Court thus invites state and federal authorities to undermine the historic independence of the press by attempting to annex the journalistic profession as an investigative arm of government. Not only will this decision impair performance of the press' constitutionally protected functions, but it will, I am convinced, in the long run, harm rather than help the administration of justice.

[As] private and public aggregations of power burgeon in size and the pressures for conformity necessarily mount, there is obviously a continuing need for an independent press to disseminate a robust variety of information and opinion through reportage, investigation and criticism, if we are to preserve our constitutional tradition of maximizing freedom of choice by encouraging diversity of expression. * * *

A corollary of the right to publish must be the right to gather news. [This right] implies, in turn, a right to a confidential relationship between a reporter and his source. This proposition follows as a matter of simple logic once three factual predicates are recognized: (1) newsmen require informants to gather news; (2) confidentiality—the promise or understanding that names or certain aspects of communications will be kept off-the-record—is essential to the creation and maintenance of a news-gathering relationship with informants; and (3) the existence of an unbridled subpoena power—the absence of a constitutional right protecting, in *any* way, a confidential relationship from compulsory process—will either deter sources from divulging information or deter reporters from gathering and publishing information. * * *

After today's decision, the potential informant can never be sure that his identity or off-the-record communications will not subsequently be revealed through the compelled testimony of a newsman. A public spirited person inside government, who is not implicated in any crime, will now be fearful of revealing corruption or other governmental wrong-doing, because he will now know he can subsequently be identified by use of compulsory process. The potential source must, therefore, choose between risking exposure by giving information or avoiding the risk by remaining silent.

The reporter must speculate about whether contact with a controversial source or publication of controversial material will lead to a subpoena. In the event of a subpoena, under today's decision, the newsman will know that he must choose between being punished for contempt if he refuses to testify, or violating his profession's ethics [10] and impairing his resourcefulness as a reporter if he discloses confidential information. * * *

The impairment of the flow of news cannot, of course, be proven with scientific precision, as the Court seems to demand. [But] we have never before demanded that First Amendment rights rest on elaborate empirical studies demonstrating beyond any conceivable doubt that deterrent effects exist; we have never before required proof of the exact number of people potentially affected by governmental action, who would actually be dissuaded from engaging in First Amendment activity.

---

10. The American Newspaper Guild has adopted the following rule as part of the newsman's code of ethics: "Newspaper men shall refuse to reveal confidences or disclose sources of confidential information in court or before other judicial or investigative bodies."

Rather, on the basis of common sense and available information, we have asked, often implicitly, (1) whether there was a rational connection between the cause (the governmental action) and the effect (the deterrence or impairment of First Amendment activity) and (2) whether the effect would occur with some regularity, i.e., would not be de minimus. And, in making this determination, we have shown a special solicitude towards the "indispensable liberties" protected by the First Amendment, *NAACP v. Alabama,* for "freedoms such as these are protected not only against heavy-handed frontal attack, but also from being stifled by more subtle government interference." Once this threshold inquiry has been satisfied, we have then examined the competing interests in determining whether there is an unconstitutional infringement of First Amendment freedoms.   * * *

We cannot await an unequivocal—and therefore unattainable—imprimatur from empirical studies. We can and must accept the evidence developed in the record, and elsewhere, that overwhelmingly supports the premise that deterrence will occur with regularity in important types of newsgathering relationships. Thus, we cannot escape the conclusion that when neither the reporter nor his source can rely on the shield of confidentiality against unrestrained use of the grand jury's subpoena power, valuable information will not be published and the public dialogue will inevitably be impoverished.

[W]hen an investigation impinges on First Amendment rights, the government must not only show that the inquiry is of "compelling and overriding importance" but it must also "convincingly" demonstrate that the investigation is "substantially related" to the information sought. Governmental officials must, therefore, demonstrate that the information sought is *clearly* relevant to a *precisely* defined subject of governmental inquiry. They must demonstrate that it is reasonable to think the witness in question has that information. And they must show that there is not any means of obtaining the information less destructive of First Amendment liberties.   * * *

I believe the safeguards developed in our decisions involving governmental investigations must apply to the grand jury inquiries in these cases. Surely the function of the grand jury to aid in the enforcement of the law is no more important than the function of the legislature, and its committees, to make the law. [T]he vices of vagueness and overbreadth which legislative investigations may manifest are also exhibited by grand jury inquiries, since grand jury investigations are not limited in scope to specific criminal acts.

[Thus,] when a reporter is asked to appear before a grand jury and reveal confidences, I would hold that the government must (1) show that there is probable cause to believe that the newsman has information which is clearly relevant to a specific probable violation of law; (2) demonstrate that the information sought cannot be obtained by alternative means less destructive of First Amendment rights; and (3) demonstrate a compelling and overriding interest in the information.   * * *

The crux of the Court's rejection of any newsman's privilege is its observation that only "where news sources themselves are implicated in crime or possess information *relevant* to the grand jury's task need they or the reporter be concerned about grand jury subpoenas." (emphasis supplied). But this is a most misleading construct. [G]iven the grand jury's extraordinarily broad investigative powers and the weak standards of relevance and materiality that apply during such inquiries, reporters, if they have no testimonial privilege, will be called to give information about informants who have neither committed crimes nor have information about crime. It is to avoid deterrence of such sources and thus to prevent needless injury to First Amendment values that I think the government must be required to show probable cause that the newsman has information which is clearly relevant to a specific probable violation of criminal law. * * *

Both the "probable cause" and "alternative means" requirements [would] serve the vital function of mediating between the public interest in the administration of justice and the constitutional protection of the full flow of information. These requirements would avoid a direct conflict between these competing concerns, and they would generally provide adequate protection for newsmen.[35] No doubt the courts would be required to make some delicate judgments in working out this accommodation. But that, after all, is the function of courts of law. Better such judgments, however difficult, than the simplistic and stultifying absolutism adopted by the Court in denying any force to the First Amendment in these cases.[36]

[I]n the name of advancing the administration of justice, the Court's decision, I think, will only impair the achievement of that goal. People entrusted with law enforcement responsibility, no less than private citizens, need general information relating to controversial social problems. [W]hen a grand jury may exercise an unbridled subpoena power, and sources involved in sensitive matters become fearful of disclosing information, the newsman will not only cease to be a useful grand jury witness; he will cease to investigate and publish information about issues of public import.

[In Stewart, J.'s view, the Ninth Circuit correctly ruled that in the circumstances of the case, Caldwell need not divulge confidential information and, moreover, that in this case Caldwell had established that "his very appearance [before] the grand jury would jeopardize his relationship with his sources, leading to a severance of the news gathering relationship and impairment of the flow of news to the public." But because "only in very rare circumstances would a confidential relationship between a reporter and his source be so sensitive [as to preclude] his mere appearance before the grand jury," Stewart, J., would confine "*this* aspect of the *Caldwell* judgment [to] its own facts." Thus, he would affirm in *Caldwell* and remand the other cases for further proceedings not inconsistent with his views.]

Notes and Questions

1. *The role of the press.* Consider Vincent Blasi, *The Checking Value in First Amendment Theory,* 1977 Am.B.Found.Res.J. 521, 593: The White, J., opinion "characterized the press as a private-interest group rather than an institution with a central function to perform in the constitutional system of checks and balances [and] labeled the source relationships that the reporters sought to maintain 'a private system of informers operated by the press to report on criminal conduct' [cautioning] that this system would be 'unaccountable to the public' were a reporter's privilege to be recognized." In contrast to White, J.'s perspective, consider the remarks of Stewart, J., in a much-discussed address, "*Or of the Press,*" 26 Hast.L.J. 631, 634 (1975): "In setting up the three branches of the Federal Government, the Founders deliberately created an internally competi-

---

35. We need not, therefore, reach the question of whether government's interest in these cases is "overriding and compelling." I do not, however, believe, as the Court does, that *all* grand jury investigations automatically would override the newsman's testimonial privilege.

36. The disclaimers in Mr. Justice Powell's concurring opinion leave room for the hope that in some future case the Court may take a less absolute position in this area.

tive [b] system. [The] primary purpose [c] of [the Free Press Clause] was a similar one: to create a fourth institution outside the Government as an additional check on the three official branches." [d] Proceeding from variations of this fourth estate view of the press, most commentators endorse a reporter's privilege. See, e.g., C. Edwin Baker, *Press Rights and Government Power to Structure the Press,* 34 U.Miami L.Rev. 819, 858 (1980) (absolute protection). But see Randall Bezanson, *The New Free Press Guarantee,* 63 Va.L.Rev. 731, 759–62 (1977) (press clause prevents special governmental assistance for press). Claims for an independent press-clause, however, need not interpret the press clause along fourth estate lines, see *Rodney Smolla, Smolla and Nimmer on Freedom of Speech* 2–104—2–129 (1984).[e]

2. Whatever role is assigned to the press, are press relationships with confidential sources not entitled to at least the same protections afforded to civil rights groups and minority parties? Does *Branzburg* exhibit insensitivity to free speech values? Consider Blasi, supra, at 593: Two of the journalists "were covering the Black Panther Party, [which] claimed to be the victim of an official nationwide policy of persecution and extermination. Yet the White opinion made no reference to the speech value of news about possible official misbehavior obtained from persons against whom abuses of power may have been directed. Instead, Justice White spoke only of the criminal activities of the sources themselves and their peers, and denigrated the speech value at stake as that in 'possible future news about crime from undisclosed, unverified sources.'"

3. *Evaluating Powell, J.'s concurrence.* Did five justices—or only four—hold that grand juries may pursue their goals by any means short of bad faith? May one conclude that the information sought bears "only a remote and tenuous relationship to the subject of investigation" on grounds falling short of demonstrating "bad faith"? Does Powell, J.'s suggested test—the privilege claim "should be judged on its facts by [balancing the] vital constitutional and societal interests on a case-by-case basis"—resemble Stewart, J.'s dissenting approach more than White, J.'s? Extrajudicially, Stewart, J., has referred to *Branzburg* as

---

b. For commentary on how the "cozy connections" between press and government demonstrate that the relationship is often more cooperative than adversarial, see Aviam Soifer, *Freedom of the Press in the United States* in Press Law in Modern Democracies 79, 108–110 (Pnina Lahav, ed., 1985).

c. For spirited debate about the historical evidence, compare David Anderson, *The Origins of the Press Clause,* 30 U.C.L.A.L.Rev. 455 (1983) with Leonard Levy, *On the Origins of the Free Press Clause,* 32 U.C.L.A.L.Rev. 177 (1984). See generally Leonard Levy, *Emergence of a Free Press* (1985).

d. For Brennan, J.'s views, see *Address,* 32 Rutg.L.Rev. 173 (1979).

e. For criticism of the notion of an independent press clause, see David Lange, *The Speech and Press Clauses,* 23 U.C.L.A.L.Rev. 77 (1975); Anthony Lewis, *A Preferred Position for Journalism?,* 7 Hof.L.Rev. 595 (1979); William Van Alstyne, *The First Amendment and the Free Press: A Comment on Some New Trends and Some Old Theories,* 9 Hof.L.Rev. 1 (1980); William Van Alstyne, *The Hazards to the Press of Claiming a "Preferred Position",* 28 Hast.L.J. 761 (1977). But see Floyd

Abrams, *The Press is Different: Reflections on Justice Stewart and the Autonomous Press,* 7 Hof.L.Rev. 563 (1979). For an effort to transcend the issues involved, see generally Robert Sack, *Reflections on the Wrong Question: Special Constitutional Privilege for the Institutional Press,* 7 Hof.L.Rev. 629 (1979). Finally, for commentary on the "tension between journalism as the political, sometimes partisan fourth estate and journalism as a profession" purporting to operate as a "neutral and objective medium," see Pnina Lahav, *An Outline for a General Theory of Press Law in Democracy* in Press Law in Modern Democracies 339, 352–54 (Lahav ed. 1985). See also Lee Bollinger, *The Press and the Public Interest: An Essay on the Relationship Between Social Behavior and the Language of First Amendment Theory,* 82 Mich.L.Rev. 1447, 1457 (1984) (commenting generally on the pitfalls connected with justifying a free press by arguing that it serves the public interest: "More than most groups (compare lawyers, for example) the press is in conflict over its relationship to the world on which it regularly reports.").

a case which rejected claims for a journalist's privilege "by a vote of 5–4, or, considering Mr. Justice Powell's concurring opinion, perhaps by a vote of 4½–4½." Potter Stewart, *"Or of the Press,"* 26 Hast.L.J. 631, 635 (1975). The majority of courts applying *Branzburg* have concluded that Powell, J.'s opinion read together with the dissents affords the basis for a qualified privilege. Among the issues litigated are whether the privilege should be confined to journalists (or extended e.g. to academics) and the related question of how to define journalists and whether the privilege belongs to the source, the reporter, or both. For an exhaustive survey, see James Goodale, Joseph Moodhe & Rodney Ott, *Reporter's Privilege Cases,* 421 PLI/PAT 63 (1995).

The Court's most recent expression on the subject unanimously refuses, at least in the absence of bad faith, to extend a qualified first amendment privilege to "confidential" tenure files and, in dictum, confines *Branzburg* to the recognition that the " 'bad faith' exercise of grand jury powers might raise First Amendment concerns." *University of Pennsylvania v. EEOC,* 493 U.S. 182, 110 S.Ct. 577, 107 L.Ed.2d 571 (1990) (gender discrimination claim). For relevant commentary, see Byrne, *Academic Freedom: A "Special Concern of the First Amendment,"* 99 Yale L.J. 251 (1989).

4. *Other contexts.* Does *Branzburg's* emphasis on the grand jury's special role in the American criminal justice system warrant different treatment of the journalist's privilege when a prosecutor seeks disclosure? See Donna Murasky, *The Journalist's Privilege: Branzburg and Its Aftermath,* 52 Tex.L.Rev. 829, 885 (1974). Are the interests of civil litigants in compelling disclosure of a journalist's confidences significantly weaker than those of criminal litigants? Should there be an absolute journalist's privilege in civil discovery proceedings? See id. at 898–903. What if the journalist is a party to the litigation?

5. *Reverse Branzburg.* Suppose a newspaper truthfully publishes the name of source it had promised anonymity. The newspaper contends that the information provided (which reflected badly upon a political candidate) was misleading and that the source's name is newsworthy because he was associated with the other side in the political campaign. The source sued for recovery on a theory of promissory estoppel. Would a recovery violate the principle that the press is free to publish the truth? See *Cohen v. Cowles Media Co.,* 501 U.S. 663, 111 S.Ct. 2513, 115 L.Ed.2d 586 (1991) (recovery not barred by first amendment).

6. *State "shield laws" and a criminal defendant's right to compulsory process.* As of 1984, 26 states had enacted "shield" laws. Some protect only journalists' sources; some (including New Jersey) protect undisclosed information obtained in the course of a journalist's professional activities as well as sources. See Goodale, Moodhe & Imes, note 3 supra.

In re Farber, 78 N.J. 259, 394 A.2d 330 (1978), cert. denied, 439 U.S. 997, 99 S.Ct. 598, 58 L.Ed.2d 670 (1978): *New York Times* investigative reporter Myron Farber wrote a series of articles claiming that an unidentified "Doctor X" had caused the death of several patients by poisoning. This led to the indictment and eventual prosecution of Dr. Jascalevich for murder. (He was ultimately acquitted.) In response to the defendant's request, the trial court demanded the disclosure of Farber's sources and the production of his interview notes and other information for his in camera inspection. Relying on the first amendment and the state shield law, Farber refused to comply with the subpoenas. After White, J., and then Marshall, J., had denied stays, each deeming it unlikely that four justices would grant certiorari at this stage of the case, Farber was jailed for civil contempt and the *Times* heavily fined.

The state supreme court (5–2) upheld civil and criminal convictions of the *Times* and Farber. Under the circumstances, it ruled, the first amendment did not protect Farber against disclosure. Nor did the New Jersey shield law, for Farber's statutory rights had to yield to Dr. Jascalevich's sixth amendment right "to have compulsory process for obtaining witnesses in his favor." [e]

ZURCHER v. STANFORD DAILY, 436 U.S. 547, 98 S.Ct. 1970, 56 L.Ed.2d 525 (1978), again declined to afford the press special protection—dividing very much as in *Branzburg*.[a] A student newspaper that had published articles and photographs of a clash between demonstrators and police brought this federal action, claiming that a search of its offices for film and pictures showing events at the scene of the police-demonstrators clash (the newspaper was not involved in the unlawful acts) had violated its first and fourth amendment rights. A 5–3 majority, per WHITE, J., held that the fourth amendment does not prevent the government from issuing a search warrant (based on reasonable cause to believe that the "things" to be searched for are located on the property) simply because the owner or possessor of the place to be searched is not reasonably suspected of criminal involvement. The Court also rejected the argument that "whatever may be true of third-party searches generally, where the third party is a newspaper, there are additional [first amendment factors justifying] a nearly per se rule forbidding the search warrant and permitting only the subpoena duces tecum. The general submission is that searches of newspaper offices for evidence of crime reasonably believed to be on the premises will seriously threaten the ability of the press to gather, analyze, and disseminate news.

"[Although] [a]ware of the long struggle between Crown and press and desiring to curb unjustified official intrusions, [the Framers] did not forbid warrants where the press was involved, did not require special showing that subpoenas would be impractical, and did not insist that the owner of the place to be searched, if connected with the press, must be shown to be implicated in the offense being investigated. Further, the prior cases do no more than insist that the courts apply the warrant requirements with particular exactitude when First Amendment interests would be endangered by the search. [N]o more than this is required where the warrant requested is for the seizure of criminal evidence reasonably believed to be on the premises occupied by a newspaper. Properly administered, the preconditions for a warrant—probable cause, specificity [as to] place [and] things to be seized and overall reasonableness—should afford [the press] sufficient protection * * *.

"[R]espondents and amici have pointed to only a very few instances [since] 1971 involving [newspaper office searches]. This reality hardly suggests abuse, and if abuse occurs, there will be time enough to deal with it. Furthermore, the press [is] not easily intimidated—nor should it be."

e. For an exhaustive analysis of the case, see Note, 32 Rutg.L.Rev. 545 (1979). The case is also discussed at length by *New York Times* columnist Anthony Lewis, *A Preferred Position for Journalism?*, 7 Hof.L.Rev. 595, 610–18 (1979).

a. In both cases, White, J., joined by Burger, C.J., Blackmun, Powell and Rehnquist, JJ., delivered the opinion of the Court and in both cases the "fifth vote"—Powell, J.,—also wrote a separate opinion which seemed to meet the concerns of the dissent part way. In both cases Stewart, J., dissented, maintaining that the Court's holding would seriously impair "newsgathering." Stevens, J., who had replaced Douglas, J., also dissented in *Zurcher*, as had Douglas in *Branzburg*. Brennan, J., who had joined Stewart, J.'s dissent in *Branzburg*, did not participate in *Zurcher*.

POWELL, J., concurring, rejected Stewart, J.'s dissenting view that the press is entitled to "a special procedure, not available to others," when the government requires evidence in its possession, but added: "This is not to say [that a warrant] sufficient to support the search of an apartment or an automobile would be reasonable in supporting the search of a newspaper office. [While] there is no justification for the establishment of a separate Fourth Amendment procedure for the press, a magistrate asked to issue a warrant for the search of press offices can and should take cognizance of the independent values protected by the First Amendment—such as those highlighted by [Stewart, J., dissenting]—when he weighs such factors." [b]

STEWART, joined by Marshall, J., dissented: "A search warrant allows police officers to ransack the files of a newspaper, reading each and every document until they have found the one named in the warrant, while a subpoena would permit the newspaper itself to produce only the specific documents requested. A search, unlike a subpoena, will therefore lead to the needless exposure of confidential information completely unrelated to the purpose of the investigation. The knowledge that police officers can make an unannounced raid on a newsroom is thus bound to have a deterrent effect on the availability of confidential news sources. [The result] will be a diminishing flow of potentially important information to the public.

"[Here, unlike *Branzburg,* the newspaper does] not claim that any of the evidence sought was privileged [, but] only that a subpoena would have served equally well to produce that evidence. Thus, we are not concerned with the principle, central to *Branzburg,* that ' "the public [has] a right to everyman's evidence," ' but only with whether any significant social interest would be impaired if the police were generally required to obtain evidence from the press by means of a subpoena rather than a search. * * *

"Perhaps as a matter of abstract policy a newspaper office should receive no more protection from unannounced police searches than, say, the office of a doctor or the office of a bank. But we are here to uphold a Constitution. And our Constitution does not explicitly protect the practice of medicine or the business of banking from all abridgement by government. It does explicitly protect the freedom of the press." [c]

Notes and Questions

1. The distinctions between search and subpoena are underscored in Laurence Tribe, *American Constitutional Law* 973 (2d ed. 1988): "When a subpoena is served on a newspaper, it has the opportunity to assert constitutional and statutory rights [such as 'shield laws,' enacted in many states, protecting reporters from divulging information given them in confidence] to keep certain materials confidential. Such protection is circumvented when officials can proceed *ex parte,* by search warrant. And the risk of abuse may be greatest exactly when the press plays its most vital and creative role in our political system, the role of watchdog on official corruption and abuse. Officials who find themselves the targets [of] media investigations may well be tempted to conduct searches to find out precisely

b. Powell, J., noted that his *Branzburg* concurrence may "properly be read as supporting the view expressed in the text above, and in the Court's [*Zurcher*] opinion," that under the warrant requirement "the magistrate should consider the values of a free press as well as the societal interest in enforcing the criminal laws."

c. Stevens, J., dissented on the general fourth amendment issue.

what various journalists have discovered, and to retaliate against reporters who have unearthed and reported official wrongdoing."

2. The difficulty in identifying suspects at the early stages of a criminal investigation, relied on by the *Zurcher* majority, does not, maintains Note, 92 Harv.L.Rev. 206–07 (1978), "require that the court refuse to adopt a special rule for those *classes* of witnesses who are so unlikely to destroy evidence as to deserve special protection from third party searches. [One reasonable approach] would be a narrow rule favoring the use of the subpoena only when the material is sought from neutral observers who possess evidence specifically because of the nature of their work, such as journalists, doctors, lawyers and accountants. Such parties are relatively easy to identify and are extremely unlikely to be either culpable or sympathetic to those who are culpable." [d]

SECTION 11. WEALTH AND THE POLITICAL PROCESS: CONCERNS FOR EQUALITY

The idea of equality has loomed large throughout this chapter. Some feel it should be a central concern of the first amendment. See Laurence Tribe, *Constitutional Choices* 188–220 (1985); Kenneth Karst, *Equality as a Central Principle in the First Amendment,* 43 U.Chi.L.Rev. 20 (1975). Equality has been championed by those who seek access to government property and to media facilities. It has been invoked in support of content regulation and against it. This section considers government efforts to prevent the domination of the political process by wealthy individuals and business corporations. In the end, it would be appropriate to reconsider the arguments for and against a marketplace conception of the first amendment, to ask whether the Court's interpretations overall (e.g., taking the public forum materials, the media materials, and the election materials together) have adequately considered the interest in equality, and to inquire generally about the relationship between liberty and equality in the constitutional scheme.

BUCKLEY v. VALEO
424 U.S. 1, 96 S.Ct. 612, 46 L.Ed.2d 659 (1976).

Per Curiam.

[In this portion of a lengthy opinion dealing with the validity of the Federal Election Campaign Act of 1971, as amended in 1974, the Court considers those parts of the Act limiting *contributions* to a candidate for federal office (all sustained), and those parts limiting *expenditures* in support of such candidacy (all held invalid).[a]]

A. *General Principles.* The Act's contribution and expenditure limitations operate in an area of the most fundamental First Amendment activities. Discussion of public issues and debate on the qualifications of candidates are integral to the operation of the system of government established by our Constitution.

[Appellees] contend that what the Act regulates is conduct, and that its effect on speech and association is incidental at most. Appellants respond that contri-

---

d. For discussion of executive and legislative response to *Zurcher,* see Goodale, Moodhe, and Ott, note 3 supra after *Branzburg.* In particular, see The Privacy Protection Act of 1980, 42 U.S.C. §§ 2000aa–2000aa–12 (limiting the impact of *Zurcher* on the media).

a. Other aspects of *Buckley* are briefly considered in Sec. 8, I supra (public funding); Sec. 10, IV supra (disclosure).

butions and expenditures are at the very core of political speech, and that the Act's limitations thus constitute restraints on First Amendment liberty that are both gross and [direct.]

We cannot share the view [that] the present Act's contribution and expenditure limitations are comparable to the restrictions on conduct upheld in *O'Brien* [p. 762 supra]. The expenditure of money simply cannot be equated with such conduct as destruction of a draft card. Some forms of communication made possible by the giving and spending of money involve speech alone, some involve conduct primarily, and some involve a combination of the two. Yet this Court has never suggested that the dependence of a communication on the expenditure of money operates itself to introduce a non-speech element or to reduce the exacting scrutiny required by the First Amendment. * * *

Even if the categorization of the expenditure of money as conduct were accepted, the limitations challenged here would not meet the *O'Brien* test because the governmental interests advanced in support of the Act involve "suppressing communication." The interests served by the Act include restricting the voices of people and interest groups who have money to spend and reducing the overall scope of federal election campaigns. [Unlike] *O'Brien*, where [the] interest in the preservation of draft cards was wholly unrelated to their use as a means of communication, it is beyond dispute that the interest in regulating the alleged "conduct" of giving or spending money "arises in some measure because the communication allegedly integral to the conduct is itself thought to be harmful."

Nor can the Act's contribution and expenditure limitations be sustained, as some of the parties suggest, by reference to the constitutional principles reflected in such decisions as *Cox v. Louisiana, Adderley,* and *Kovacs,* [Secs. 8, II and 9 supra]. [The] critical difference between this case and those time, place and manner cases is that the present Act's contribution and expenditure limitations impose direct quantity restrictions on political communication and association by persons, groups, candidates and political parties in addition to any reasonable time, place, and manner regulations otherwise imposed.

A restriction on the amount of money a person or group can spend on political communication during a campaign necessarily reduces the quantity of expression by restricting the number of issues discussed, the depth of their exploration, and the size of the audience reached. This is because virtually every means of communicating ideas in today's mass society requires the expenditure of [money].

The expenditure limitations contained in the Act represent substantial rather than merely theoretical restraints on the quantity and diversity of political speech. The $1,000 ceiling on spending "relative to a clearly identified candidate," 18 U.S.C. § 608(e)(1), would appear to exclude all citizens and groups except candidates, political parties and the institutional press from any significant use of the most effective modes of communication.[20] * * *

By contrast with a limitation upon expenditures for political expression, a limitation [on] the amount of money a person may give to a candidate or campaign organization [involves] little direct restraint on his political communication, for it permits the symbolic expression of support evidenced by a contribution but does not in any way infringe the contributor's freedom to discuss candidates and issues. While contributions may result in political expression if spent by a candidate or an

20. The record indicates that, as of January 1, 1975, one full-page advertisement in a daily edition of a certain metropolitan newspaper costs $6,971.04—almost seven times the annual limit on expenditures "relative to" a particular candidate imposed on the vast majority of individual citizens and associations by § 608(e)(1).

association to present views to the voters, the transformation of contributions into political debate involves speech by someone other than the contributor.

[There] is no indication [that] the contribution limitations imposed by the Act would have any dramatic adverse effect on the funding of campaigns and political associations.[23] The overall effect of the Act's contribution ceilings is merely to require candidates and political committees to raise funds from a greater number of persons and to compel people who would otherwise contribute amounts greater than the statutory limits to expend such funds on direct political expression, rather than to reduce the total amount of money potentially available to promote political expression. * * *

In sum, although the Act's contribution and expenditure limitations both implicate fundamental First Amendment interests, its expenditure ceilings impose significantly more severe restrictions on protected freedoms of political expression and association than do its limitations on financial contributions.

B. *Contribution Limitations.* [Section] 608(b) provides, with certain limited exceptions, that "no person shall make contributions to any candidate with respect to any election for Federal office which, in the aggregate, exceeds $1,000."[b] * * *

Appellants contend that the $1,000 contribution ceiling unjustifiably burdens First Amendment freedoms, employs overbroad dollar limits, and discriminates against candidates opposing incumbent officeholders and against minor-party candidates in violation of the Fifth Amendment.

[In] view of the fundamental nature of the right to associate, governmental "action which may have the effect of curtailing the freedom to associate is subject to the closest scrutiny." Yet, it is clear that "[n]either the right to associate nor the right to participate in political activities is absolute." *Letter Carriers* [p. 879 supra]. Even a " 'significant interference' with protected rights of political association" may be sustained if the State demonstrates a sufficiently important interest and employs means closely drawn to avoid unnecessary abridgment of associational freedoms. * * *

It is unnecessary to look beyond the Act's primary purpose—to limit the actuality and appearance of corruption resulting from large individual financial contributions—in order to find a constitutionally sufficient justification for the $1,000 contribution limitation. [The] increasing importance of the communications media and sophisticated mass mailing and polling operations to effective campaigning make the raising of large sums of money an ever more essential ingredient of an effective candidacy. To the extent that large contributions are given to secure political quid pro quos from current and potential office holders, the integrity of our system of representative democracy is undermined. Although the scope of such pernicious practices can never be reliably ascertained, the deeply

23. Statistical findings agreed to by the parties reveal that approximately 5.1% of the $73,483,613 raised by the 1161 candidates for Congress in 1974 was obtained in amounts in excess of $1,000. In 1974, two major-party senatorial candidates, Ramsey Clark and Senator Charles Mathias, Jr., operated large-scale campaigns on contributions raised under a voluntarily imposed $100 contribution limitation.

b. As defined, "person" includes "an individual, partnership, committee, association, corporation or any other organization or group." The limitation applies to: (1) anything of value, such as gifts, loans, advances, and promises to give, (2) contributions made direct to the candidate or to an intermediary, or a committee authorized by the candidate, (3) the aggregate amounts contributed to the candidate for each election, treating primaries, run-off elections and general elections separately and all Presidential primaries within a single calendar year as one election.

disturbing examples surfacing after the 1972 election demonstrate that the problem is not an illusory one.

Of almost equal concern as the danger of actual quid pro quo arrangements is the impact of the appearance of corruption stemming from public awareness of the opportunities for abuse inherent in a regime of large individual financial contributions. In *Letter Carriers,* the Court found that the danger to "fair and effective government" posed by partisan political conduct on the part of federal employees charged with administering the law was a sufficiently important concern to justify broad restrictions on the employees' right of partisan political association. Here, as there, Congress could legitimately conclude that the avoidance of the appearance of improper influence "is also critical [if] confidence in the system of representative Government is not to be eroded to a disastrous extent." [29]

Appellants contend that the contribution limitations must be invalidated because bribery laws and narrowly-drawn disclosure requirements constitute a less restrictive means of dealing with "proven and suspected quid pro quo arrangements." But laws [against] bribes deal with only the most blatant and specific attempts of those with money to influence governmental action. [And] Congress was surely entitled to conclude that disclosure was only a partial measure, and that contribution ceilings were a necessary legislative concomitant to deal with the reality or appearance of corruption inherent in a system permitting unlimited financial contributions, even when the identities of the contributors and the amounts of their contributions are fully disclosed.

The Act's $1,000 contribution limitation focuses precisely on the problem of large campaign contributions—the narrow aspect of political association where the actuality and potential for corruption have been identified—while leaving persons free to engage in independent political expression, to associate actively through volunteering their services. [The] Act's contribution limitations [do] not undermine to any material degree the potential for robust and effective discussion of candidates and campaign [issues].

We find that, under the rigorous standard of review established by our prior decisions, the weighty interests served by restricting the size of financial contributions to political candidates are sufficient to justify the limited effect upon First Amendment freedoms caused by the $1,000 contribution ceiling.[c]

---

29. Although the Court in *Letter Carriers* found that this interest was constitutionally sufficient to justify legislation prohibiting federal employees from engaging in certain partisan political activities, it was careful to emphasize that the limitations did not restrict an employee's right to express his views on political issues and candidates.

c. The Court rejected the challenges that the $1,000 limit was overbroad because (1) most large contributors do not seek improper influence over a candidate, and (2) much more than $1,000 would still not be enough to influence improperly a candidate or office holder. With respect to (1), "Congress was justified in concluding that the interest in safeguarding against the appearance of impropriety requires that the opportunity for abuse inherent in the process of raising large monetary contributions be eliminated." With respect to (2), "As the Court of Appeals observed, '[a] court has no

scalpel to probe, whether, say, a $2,000 ceiling might not serve as well as $1,000.' Such distinctions in degree become significant only when they can be said to amount to differences in kind."

The Court also rejected as without support in the record the claims that the contribution limitations worked invidious discrimination between incumbents and challengers to whom the same limitations applied.

The Court then upheld (1) exclusion from the $1,000 limit of the value of unpaid volunteer services and of certain expenses paid by the volunteer up to a maximum of $500; (2) the higher limit of $5,000 for contributions to a candidate by established, registered political committees with at least 50 contributing supporters and fielding at least five candidates for federal office; and (3) the $25,000 limit on total contributions to all candidates by one person in one calendar year.

C. *Expenditure Limitations.* [1.] Section 608(e)(1) provides that "[n]o person may make any expenditure [relative] to a clearly identified candidate during a calendar year which, when added to all other expenditures made by such person during the year advocating the election or defeat of such candidate, exceeds $1,000." [Its] plain effect [is] to prohibit all individuals, who are neither candidates nor owners of institutional press facilities, and all groups, except political parties and campaign organizations, from voicing their views "relative to a clearly identified candidate" through means that entail aggregate expenditures of more than $1,000 during a calendar year. The provision, for example, would make it a federal criminal offense for a person or association to place a single one-quarter page advertisement "relative to a clearly identified candidate" in a major metropolitan newspaper.

[Although] "expenditure," "clearly identified," and "candidate" are defined in the Act, there is no definition clarifying what expenditures are "relative to" a candidate. [But the "when" clause in § 608(e)(1)] clearly permits, if indeed it does not require, the phrase "relative to" a candidate to be read to mean "advocating the election or defeat of" a candidate.

But while such a construction of § 608(e)(1) refocuses the vagueness question, [it hardly] eliminates the problem of unconstitutional vagueness altogether. For the distinction between discussion of issues and candidates and advocacy of election or defeat of candidates may often dissolve in practical application. Candidates, especially incumbents, are intimately tied to public issues involving legislative proposals and governmental actions. Not only do candidates campaign on the basis of their positions on various public issues, but campaigns themselves generate issues of public interest.

[Constitutionally deficient uncertainty which "compels the speaker to hedge and trim"] can be avoided only by reading § 608(e)(1) as limited to communications that include explicit words of advocacy of election or defeat of a candidate, much as the definition of "clearly identified" in § 608(e)(2) requires that an explicit and unambiguous reference to the candidate appear as part of the communication. This is the reading of the provision suggested by the nongovernmental appellees in arguing that "[f]unds spent to propagate one's views on issues without expressly calling for a candidate's election or defeat are thus not covered." We agree that in order to preserve the provision against invalidation on vagueness grounds, § 608(e)(1) must be construed to apply only to expenditures for communications that in express terms advocate the election or defeat of a clearly identified candidate for federal office.

We turn then to the basic First Amendment question—whether § 608(e)(1), even as thus narrowly and explicitly construed, impermissibly burdens the constitutional right of free expression. * * *

We find that the governmental interest in preventing corruption and the appearance of corruption is inadequate to justify § 608(e)(1)'s ceiling on independent expenditures. First, assuming arguendo that large independent expenditures pose the same dangers of actual or apparent quid pro quo arrangements as do large contributions, § 608(e)(1) does not provide an answer that sufficiently relates to the elimination of those dangers. Unlike the contribution limitations' total ban on the giving of large amounts of money to candidates, § 608(e)(1) prevents only some large expenditures. So long as persons and groups eschew expenditures that in express terms advocate the election or defeat of a clearly identified candidate, they are free to spend as much as they want to promote the candidate and his views. The exacting interpretation of the statutory language necessary to avoid unconstitutional vagueness thus undermines the limitation's effectiveness as a loophole-closing provision by facilitating circumvention by those seeking to exert improper influence upon a candidate or office-holder. It would naively underestimate the ingenuity and resourcefulness of persons and groups desiring to buy influence to believe that they would have much difficulty devising expenditures that skirted the restriction on express advocacy of election or defeat but nevertheless benefited the candidate's campaign. * * *

Second, [the] independent advocacy restricted by the provision does not presently appear to pose dangers of real or apparent corruption comparable to those identified with large campaign contributions. The parties defending § 608(e)(1) contend that it is necessary to prevent would-be contributors from avoiding the contribution limitations by the simple expedient of paying directly for media advertisements or for other portions of the candidate's campaign activities. [Section] 608(b)'s contribution ceilings rather than § 608(e)(1)'s independent expenditure limitation prevent attempts to circumvent the Act through prearranged or coordinated expenditures amounting to disguised contributions.[53] By contrast, § 608(e)(1) limits expenditures for express advocacy of candidates made totally independently of the candidate and his campaign. [The] absence of prearrangement and coordination of an expenditure with the candidate or his agent not only undermines the value of the expenditure to the candidate, but also alleviates the danger that expenditures will be given as a quid pro quo for improper commitments from the candidate. Rather than preventing circumvention of the contribution limitations, § 608(e)(1) severely restricts all independent advocacy despite its substantially diminished potential for abuse.

While the independent expenditure ceiling thus fails to serve any substantial governmental interest in stemming the reality or appearance of corruption in the electoral process, it heavily burdens core First Amendment expression. [Advocacy] of the election or defeat of candidates for federal office is no less entitled to protection under the First Amendment than the discussion of political policy generally or advocacy of the passage or defeat of legislation.

It is argued, however, that the ancillary governmental interest in equalizing the relative ability of individuals and groups to influence the outcome of elections serves to justify the limitation on express advocacy of the election or defeat of candidates imposed by § 608(e)(1)'s expenditure ceiling. But the concept that government may restrict the speech of some elements of our society in order to enhance the relative voice of others [d] is wholly foreign to the First Amendment, which was designed "to secure 'the widest possible dissemination of information from diverse and antagonistic sources,'" and "'to assure unfettered interchange of ideas for the bringing about of political and social changes desired by the people.'" *New York Times Co. v. Sullivan.* The First Amendment's protection

---

53. Section 608(e)(1) does not apply to expenditures "on behalf of a candidate within the meaning of" § 608(2)(B). That section provides that expenditures "authorized or requested by the candidate, an authorized committee of the candidate, or an agent of the candidate" are to be treated as expenditures of the candidate and contributions by the person or group making the expenditure. [In] view of [the] legislative history and the purposes of the Act, we find that the "authorized or requested" standard of the Act operates to treat all expenditures placed in cooperation with or with the consent of a candidate, his agents, or an authorized committee of the candidate as contributions subject to the limitations set forth in § 608(b).

d. The lower court characterized the issue somewhat differently. Can "the wealthy few [claim] a constitutional guarantee to a stronger political voice than the unwealthy many because they are able to give and spend more money, and because the amounts they give and spend cannot be limited"? 519 F.2d 821, 841 (D.C.Cir.1975).

against governmental abridgement of free expression cannot properly be made to depend on a person's financial ability to engage in public discussion.[55]

[*Mills*] *v. Alabama,* 384 U.S. 214, 86 S.Ct. 1434, 16 L.Ed.2d 484 (1966), held that legislative restrictions on advocacy of the election or defeat of political candidates are wholly at odds with the guarantees of the First Amendment. [Yet] the prohibition on election day editorials invalidated in *Mills* is clearly a lesser intrusion on constitutional freedom than a $1,000 limitation on the amount of money any person or association can spend *during an entire election year* in advocating the election or defeat of a candidate for public office.

For the reasons stated, we conclude that § 608(e)(1)'s independent expenditure limitation is unconstitutional under the First Amendment.

2. [The] Act also sets limits on expenditures by a candidate "from his personal funds, or the personal funds of his immediate family, in connection with his campaigns during any calendar year." § 608(a)(1).[e]

The ceiling on personal expenditures by candidates on their own behalf [imposes] a substantial restraint on the ability of persons to engage in protected First Amendment expression. The candidate, no less than any other person, has a First Amendment right to engage in the discussion of public issues and vigorously and tirelessly to advocate his own election and the election of other candidates. Indeed, it is of particular importance that candidates have the unfettered opportunity to make their views known so that the electorate may intelligently evaluate the candidates' personal qualities and their positions on vital public issues before choosing among them on election day. [Section] 608(a)'s ceiling on personal expenditures by a candidate in furtherance of his own candidacy thus clearly and directly interferes with constitutionally protected freedoms.

The primary governmental interest served by the Act—the prevention of actual and apparent corruption of the political process—does not support the limitation on the candidate's expenditure of his own personal funds. [Indeed], the use of personal funds reduces the candidate's dependence on outside contributions and thereby counteracts the coercive pressures and attendant risks of abuse to which the Act's contribution limitations are directed.

The ancillary interest in equalizing the relative financial resources of candidates competing for elective office, therefore, provides the sole relevant rationale for Section 608(a)'s expenditure ceiling. That interest is clearly not sufficient to justify the provision's infringement of fundamental First Amendment rights. First, the limitation may fail to promote financial equality among candidates. [Indeed], a candidate's personal wealth may impede his [fundraising efforts]. Second, and more fundamentally, the First Amendment simply cannot tolerate § 608(a)'s restriction upon the freedom of a candidate to speak without legislative limit on behalf of his own candidacy. We therefore hold that § 608(a)'s restrictions on a candidate's personal expenditures is unconstitutional.

3. [Section] 608(c) of the Act places limitations on overall campaign expenditures by candidates [seeking] election to federal office. [For Presidential candi-

---

55. Neither the voting rights cases [Ch. 10, Sec. 4, I, A] nor the Court's decision upholding the FCC's fairness doctrine [p. 845 supra] lends support to appellees' position that the First Amendment permits Congress to abridge the rights of some persons to engage in politi-cal expression in order to enhance the relative voice of other segments of our [society].

e. $50,000 for Presidential or Vice Presidential candidates; $35,000 for Senate candidates; $25,000 for most candidates for the House of Representatives.

dates the ceiling is $10,000,000 in seeking nomination and $20,000,000 in the general election campaign; for House of Representatives candidates it is $70,000 for each campaign—primary and general; for candidates for Senator the ceiling depends on the size of the voting age population.]

No governmental interest that has been suggested is sufficient to justify [these restrictions] on the quantity of political expression. [The] interest in alleviating the corrupting influence of large contributions is served by the Act's contribution limitations and disclosure provisions rather than by § 608(c)'s campaign expenditure ceilings. [There] is no indication that the substantial criminal penalties for violating the contribution ceilings combined with the political repercussion of such violations will be insufficient to police the contribution provisions. Extensive reporting, auditing, and disclosure requirements applicable to both contributions and expenditures by political campaigns are designed to facilitate the detection of illegal contributions. * * *

The interest in equalizing the financial resources of candidates competing for federal office is no more convincing a justification for restricting the scope of federal election campaigns. Given the limitation on the size of outside contributions, the financial resources available to a candidate's campaign, like the number of volunteers recruited, will normally vary with the size and intensity of the candidate's support. There is nothing invidious, improper, or unhealthy in permitting such funds to be spent to carry the candidate's message to the electorate. Moreover, the equalization of permissible campaign expenditures might serve not to equalize the opportunities of all candidates but to handicap a candidate who lacked substantial name recognition or exposure of his views before the start of the campaign.

The campaign expenditure ceilings appear to be designed primarily to serve the governmental interests in reducing the allegedly skyrocketing costs of political campaigns. [But the] First Amendment denies government the power to determine that spending to promote one's political views is wasteful, excessive, or unwise. In the free society ordained by our Constitution it is not the government but the people individually as citizens and candidates and collectively as associations and political committees who must retain control over the quantity and range of debate on public issues in a political campaign.

For these reasons we hold that § 608(c) is constitutionally invalid. * * *

CHIEF JUSTICE BURGER, concurring in part and dissenting in part.

[I] agree fully with that part of the Court's opinion that holds unconstitutional the limitations the Act puts on campaign expenditures. [Yet] when it approves similarly stringent limitations on contributions, the Court ignores the reasons it finds so persuasive in the context of expenditures. For me contributions and expenditures are two sides of the same First Amendment coin.

[Limiting] contributions, as a practical matter, will limit expenditures and will put an effective ceiling on the amount of political activity and debate that the Government will permit to take place.[5]

5. The Court notes that 94.9% of the funds raised by congressional candidates in 1974 came in contributions of less than $1,000, n. 27, and suggests that the effect of the contribution limitations will be minimal. This logic ignores the disproportionate influence large contributions may have when they are made early in a campaign; "seed money" can be essential, and the inability to obtain it may effectively end some candidacies before they begin. Appellants have excerpted from the record data on nine campaigns to which large, initial contributions were critical. Campaigns such as these will be much harder, and perhaps impossible, to mount under the Act.

The Court attempts to separate the two communicative aspects of political contributions—the "moral" support that the gift itself conveys, which the Court suggests is the same whether the gift is of $10 or $10,000,[6] and the fact that money translates into communication. The Court dismisses the effect of the limitations on the second aspect of contributions: "[T]he transformation of contributions into political debate involves speech by someone other than the contributor." On this premise—that contribution limitations restrict only the speech of "someone other than the contributor"—rests the Court's justification for treating contributions differently from expenditures. The premise is demonstrably flawed; the contribution limitations will, in specific instances, limit exactly the same political activity that the expenditure ceilings limit, and at least one of the "expenditure" limitations the Court finds objectionable operates precisely like the "contribution" limitations.[8]

The Court's attempt to distinguish the communication inherent in political *contributions* from the speech aspects of political *expenditures* simply will not wash. We do little but engage in word games unless we recognize that people—candidates and contributors—spend money on political activity because they wish to communicate ideas, and their constitutional interest in doing so is precisely the same whether they or someone else utter the words.

[T]he restrictions are hardly incidental in their effect upon particular campaigns. Judges are ill-equipped to gauge the precise impact of legislation, but a law that impinges upon First Amendment rights requires us to make the attempt. It is not simply speculation to think that the limitations on contributions will foreclose some candidacies.[9] The limitations will also alter the nature of some electoral contests drastically.[10]

[In] striking down the limitations on campaign expenditures, the Court relies in part on its conclusion that other means—namely, disclosure and contribution ceilings—will adequately serve the statute's aim. It is not clear why the same analysis is not also appropriate in weighing the need for contribution ceilings in addition to disclosure requirements. Congress may well be entitled to conclude that disclosure was a "partial measure," but I had not thought until today that Congress could enact its conclusions in the First Amendment area into laws immune from the most searching review by this Court. * * *[f]

JUSTICE WHITE, concurring in part and dissenting in part. * * *

6. Whatever the effect of the limitation, it is clearly arbitrary—Congress has imposed the same ceiling on contributions to a New York or California senatorial campaign that it has put on House races in Alaska or Wyoming. Both the strength of support conveyed by the gift of $1,000 *and* the gift's potential for corruptly influencing the recipient will vary enormously from place to place. * * *

8. The Court treats the Act's provisions limiting a candidate's spending from his *personal resources* as *expenditure* limits, as indeed the Act characterizes them, and holds them unconstitutional. As Mr. Justice Marshall points out, infra, by the Court's logic these provisions could as easily be treated as limits on *contributions,* since they limit what the candidate can give to his own campaign.

9. Candidates who must raise large initial contributions in order to appeal for more funds to a broader audience will be handicapped.

See n. 5, supra. It is not enough to say that the contribution ceilings "merely require candidates [to] raise funds from a greater number of persons," where the limitations will effectively prevent candidates without substantial personal resources from doing just that.

10. Under the Court's holding, candidates with personal fortunes will be free to contribute to their own campaigns as much as they like, since the Court chooses to view the Act's provisions in this regard as unconstitutional "expenditure" limitations rather than "contribution" limitations. See n. 8, supra.

f. Blackmun, J., also dissented separately from that part of the Court's opinion upholding the Act's restrictions on campaign contributions, unpersuaded that "a principled constitutional distinction" could be made between the contribution and expenditure limitations involved.

I [agree] with the Court's judgment upholding the limitations on contributions. I dissent [from] the Court's view that the expenditure limitations [violate] the First Amendment. [This] case depends on whether the nonspeech interests of the Federal Government in regulating the use of money in political campaigns are sufficiently urgent to justify the incidental effects that the limitations visit upon the First Amendment interests of candidates and their supporters.

[The Court] accepts the congressional judgment that the evils of unlimited contributions are sufficiently threatening to warrant restriction regardless of the impact of the limits on the contributor's opportunity for effective speech and in turn on the total volume of the candidate's political communications by reason of his inability to accept large sums from those willing to give.

The congressional judgment, which I would also accept, was that other steps must be taken to counter the corrosive effects of money in federal election campaigns. One of these steps is § 608(e), which [limits] what a contributor may independently spend in support or denigration of one running for federal office. Congress was plainly of the view that these expenditures also have corruptive potential; but the Court strikes down the provision, strangely enough claiming more insight as to what may improperly influence candidates than is possessed by the majority of Congress that passed this Bill and the President who signed it. Those supporting the Bill undeniably included many seasoned professionals who have been deeply involved in elective processes and who have viewed them at close range over many years.

It would make little sense to me, and apparently made none to Congress, to limit the amounts an individual may give to a candidate or spend with his approval but fail to limit the amounts that could be spent on his behalf. Yet the Court permits the former while striking down the latter limitation. [I] would take the word of those who know—that limiting independent expenditures is essential to prevent transparent and widespread evasion of the contribution limits. * * *

The Court also rejects Congress' judgment manifested in § 608(c) that the federal interest in limiting total campaign expenditures by individual candidates justifies the incidental effect on their opportunity for effective political speech. I disagree both with the Court's assessment of the impact on speech and with its narrow view of the values the limitations will serve.

[M]oney is not always equivalent to or used for speech, even in the context of political campaigns. [There are] many expensive campaign activities that are not themselves communicative or remotely related to speech. Furthermore, campaigns differ among themselves. Some seem to spend much less money than others and yet communicate as much or more than those supported by enormous bureaucracies with unlimited financing. The record before us no more supports the conclusion that the communicative efforts of congressional and Presidential candidates will be crippled by the expenditure limitations than it supports the contrary. The judgment of Congress was that reasonably effective campaigns could be conducted within the limits established by the Act and that the communicative efforts of these campaigns would not seriously suffer. In this posture of the case, there is no sound basis for invalidating the expenditure limitations, so long as the purposes they serve are legitimate and sufficiently substantial, which in my view they are.

[E]xpenditure ceilings reinforce the contribution limits and help eradicate the hazard of corruption. [Without] limits on total expenditures, campaign costs will inevitably and endlessly escalate. Pressure to raise funds will constantly build and with it the temptation to resort in "emergencies" to those sources of large sums, who, history shows, are sufficiently confident of not being caught to risk flouting contribution [limits.]

The ceiling on candidate expenditures represents the considered judgment of Congress that elections are to be decided among candidates none of whom has overpowering advantage by reason of a huge campaign war chest. At least so long as the ceiling placed upon the candidates is not plainly too low, elections are not to turn on the difference in the amounts of money that candidates have to spend. This seems an acceptable purpose and the means chosen a common sense way to achieve [it.]

I also disagree with the Court's judgment that § 608(a), which limits the amount of money that a candidate or his family may spend on his campaign, violates the Constitution. Although it is true that this provision does not promote any interest in preventing the corruption of candidates, the provision does, nevertheless, serve salutary purposes related to the integrity of federal campaigns. By limiting the importance of personal wealth, § 608(a) helps to assure that only individuals with a modicum of support from others will be viable candidates. This in turn would tend to discourage any notion that the outcome of elections is primarily a function of money. Similarly, § 608(a) tends to equalize access to the political arena, encouraging the less wealthy, unable to bankroll their own campaigns, to run for political office.[g]

Notes and Questions

1. *Expenditure limitations.* Is it "foreign" to the first amendment to curb the spending of the wealthy in an effort to preserve the integrity of the elections process? Would it have been "foreign" to first amendment doctrine to engage in some type of balancing? Does the Court's expenditure ruling denigrate the interest in equality? See, e.g., Laurence Tribe, *Constitutional Choices* 193–94 (1985); Marlene Nicholson, *Buckley v. Valeo: The Constitutionality of the Federal Election Campaign Act Amendments of 1974,* 1977 Wis.L.Rev. 323, 336; J. Skelly Wright, *Money and the Pollution of Politics: Is the First Amendment an Obstacle to Political Equality?,* 82 Colum.L.Rev. 609 (1982). Even if the concept of political equity is a "legitimizing myth," is *Buckley* flawed because it underestimates the necessity of promoting political leadership that is autonomous and independent of pluralistic forces? Is government autonomy necessary for minimally adequate regulation of the economy? See Jeffrey Blum, *The Divisible First Amendment: A Critical Functionalist Approach to Freedom of Speech and Electoral Campaign Spending,* 58 N.Y.U.L.Rev. 1273, 1369–78 (1983). Alternatively, would it be better to solve the wealth problem by redistribution (and control of corporate power), while holding fast to a strong liberty principle? See C. Edwin Baker,

---

g. Marshall, J., dissented from that part of the Court's opinion invalidating the limitation on the amount a candidate or his family may spend on his campaign. He considered "the interest in promoting the reality and appearance of equal access to the political arena" sufficient to justify the limitation: "[T]he wealthy candidate's immediate access to a substantial personal fortune may give him an initial advantage that his less wealthy opponent can never overcome. [With the option of large contributions removed by § 608(b)], the less wealthy candidate is without the means to match the large initial expenditures of money

of which the wealthy candidate is capable. In short, the limitations on contributions put a premium on a candidate's personal wealth. "[Section 608(a) then] emerges not simply as a device to reduce the natural advantage of the wealthy candidate, but as a provision providing some symmetry to a regulatory scheme that otherwise enhances the natural advantage of the wealthy."

For background on the *Buckley* case, see Fred Friendly & Martha Elliot, *The Constitution: That Delicate Balance* 91–107 (1984).

Realizing Self-Realization: Corporate Political Expenditures and Redish's The Value of Free Speech, 130 U.Pa.L.Rev. 646, 652 (1982); C. Edwin Baker, *Scope of the First Amendment Freedom of Speech,* 25 U.C.L.A.L.Rev. 964, 983–90 (1978).

2. To what extent are campaign finance laws likely to advance equality values? [h] Aren't they most likely to benefit incumbents? See Richard Epstein, *Modern Republicanism—Or the Flight From Substance,* 97 Yale L.J. 1633, 1643–45 (1988); Jon Macey, *The Missing Element in the Republican Revival,* 97 Yale L.J. 1673, 1680–81 (1988). Consider this hypothetical response: "The system has always been stacked in favor of incumbents. Campaign finance legislation might free incumbents from the need to rely on interest group funding and could improve not only the quality of representation, but also the substantive fairness of legislation." Is increased legislative autonomy desirable? Compare Cass Sunstein, *Beyond the Republican Revival,* 97 Yale L.J. 1539 (1988) with Michael Fitts, *Look Before You Leap,* 97 Yale L.J. 1651 (1988); Michael Fitts, *The Vices of Virtue,* 136 U.Pa.L.Rev. 1567 (1988).

3. *Varying scrutiny.* (a) Did *Buckley* apply less exacting scrutiny to impairment of associational freedoms by contribution limits than to impairment of free expression by expenditure limits? Cf. 90 Harv.L.Rev. 178–79 (1976). "Granted that freedom of association is merely ancillary to speech, a means of amplifying and effectuating communication but logically secondary to speech," is this also "true of expenditures of money in aid of speech"? See Daniel Polsby, *Buckley v. Valeo: The Special Nature of Political Speech,* 1976 Sup.Ct.Rev. 1, 22. Can a lesser degree of scrutiny be justified for contributions? Or were the differing results based on the Court's perceiving a greater threat to first amendment interests in the expenditure limits and less risk of corruption and undue influence in unlimited independent expenditures? Cf. Nicholson, note 1 supra, at 340–45. Does the opinion indicate why greater deference was paid to congressional judgment on review of the contribution limits than on review of the expenditure limits? Cf. Note, 76 Colum.L.Rev. 852, 862 (1976). For a defense of strict scrutiny across the board, see Lillian BeVier, *Money and Politics: A Perspective on the First Amendment and Campaign Finance Reform,* 73 Calif.L.Rev. 1045 (1985).

(b) *The O'Brien analogy.* May the Court's rejection of the less-exacting *O'Brien* standard on the ground that the expenditure of money did not introduce a non-speech element fairly be criticized for asking the wrong question: whether *"pure speech* can be regulated where there is some incidental effect on *money,"* rather than whether "the use of *money* can be regulated, by analogy to such conduct as draft-card burning, where there is an undoubted incidental effect on *speech"*? See J. Skelly Wright, *Politics and the Constitution: Is Money Speech?,* 85 Yale L.J. 1001, 1007 (1976). But compare J.M. Balkin, *Some Realism About Pluralism: Legal Realist Approaches to the First Amendment,* 1990 Duke L.J. 375, 414: "I suspect that the slogan 'money is not speech' is attractive because it appeals to a certain humanistic vision—that there is something quite different between the situation of a lone individual expressing her views and the purchase of hired mouths using hired expressions created by hired minds to saturate the

---

h. Consider Paul Brest, *Further Beyond the Republican Revival,* 97 Yale L.J. 1623, 1627 (1988): " 'Those who are better off participate more, and by participating more they exercise more influence on government officials.' Unequal resources produce unequal influence in determining which issues get on the political [agenda]. Campaign finance regulations barely begin to remedy the systematic ways in which inequalities of wealth distort the political process." But see Edward B. Foley, *Equal-Dollars–Per Voter: A Constitutional Principle of Campaign Finance,* 94 Colum.L.Rev. 1204 (1994); Jamin Raskin & John Bonifaz, *Equal Protection and the Wealth Primary,* 11 Yale L. & Pol'y Rev. 273 (1993). For a variety of views, see *Symposium on Campaign Finance Reform,* 94 Colum.L.Rev. 1125 (1994).

airwaves with ideological drivel. Yet in one sense, this humanistic vision really turns upon a set of unstated egalitarian assumptions about economic and social power. Certainly we would have no objection to a person with a speech impediment hiring someone to do her talking for her; that is because we think that, under these circumstances, it is fair for such a person to boost her communicative powers. Modern political campaigns seem a far cry from this example because of the massive amounts of economic power expended to get the message across. I think we should isolate the egalitarian assumptions implicit in the 'money is not speech' position and put them to their best use—the justification of campaign finance reforms on the ground that gross inequalities of economic power destroy the integrity of the political process. [G]overnment is responsible for inequalities in access to the means of communication because it has created the system of property rights that makes such inequalities possible. Therefore, it is not only wrong but also incoherent for opponents of campaign finance reform to contend that the government should not regulate access to the political process. Government already regulates access to the political process—the first amendment simply demands that it do so fairly."

4. *Federal funding and expenditure limitations.* A separate section of the *Buckley* opinion seemed to approve expenditure limitations imposed upon candidates who accept federal funding: "[A]cceptance of federal funding entails voluntary acceptance of an expenditure ceiling." The existence of federal funding for a candidate has not, however, served to justify limitations on expenditures by groups who work on behalf of, but independently of, the candidate. FEC v. NATIONAL CONSERVATIVE POLITICAL ACTION COMM., 470 U.S. 480, 105 S.Ct. 1459, 84 L.Ed.2d 455 (1985), per REHNQUIST, J., invalidated a provision making it a political offense for such groups to expend more than $1000 to further the nomination or election of a candidate receiving federal financing. The Court argued that *Buckley* protected the freedom of association of "large numbers of individuals of modest means" to join together and amplify their voices.[i] The Court stressed that the case involved expenditures, not contributions within the meaning of *Buckley;* that the provision was not directed to the size of the contributions the organizations received, and was not confined to corporations.

In dissent, WHITE, J., noted his continuing objection to the distinction between contributions and expenditures, and Marshall, J., a new convert to that position, separately dissented on the same ground. Even assuming *Buckley* was correctly decided, White, J., argued that contributors to political committees were not engaging in speech to any greater extent than those who contribute directly to political campaigns: only the donee had changed. Moreover, he worried, as had Congress, that candidates would "go around hat in hand, begging for money from Washington-based special interest groups, political action committees whose sole purpose for existing is to seek a quid pro quo. [The] candidate may be forced to please the spenders rather than the voters, and the two groups are not identical." [j]

FIRST NAT'L. BANK v. BELLOTTI, 435 U.S. 765, 98 S.Ct. 1407, 55 L.Ed.2d 707 (1978), per POWELL, J., held invalid under the first and fourteenth amendments a Massachusetts criminal statute prohibiting banks or business corporations from

---

i. One defendant had received an average of $75 from 101,000 people during 1979–80; another, an average of $25 from approximately 100,000 people.

j. For discussion of the character evoked by the opinions of Rehnquist, J., and White, J., see Gerald Frug, *Argument as Character,* 40 Stan.L.Rev. 869, 896–921 (1988).

making contributions or expenditures to influence "the vote on any question submitted to the voters, other than one materially affecting any of the property, business or assets of the corporation," defined to exclude from the exception questions "concerning the taxation of the income, property or transactions of individuals": "The speech proposed by appellants is at the heart of the First Amendment's protection. [If] the speakers here were not corporations, no one would suggest that the state could silence their proposed speech. It is the type of speech indispensable to decisionmaking in a democracy, and this is no less true because the speech comes from a corporation rather than an individual. The inherent worth of the speech in terms of its capacity for informing the public does not depend upon the identity of its source, whether corporation, association, union or individual.

"The court below nevertheless held that corporate speech is protected by the First Amendment only when it pertains directly to the corporation's business interests. In deciding whether this novel and restrictive gloss on the First Amendment comports with the Constitution and the precedents of this Court, we need not survey the outer boundaries of the Amendment's protection of corporate speech, or address the abstract question whether corporations have the full measure of rights that individuals enjoy under the First Amendment.[13] The question in this case, simply put, is whether the corporate identity of the speaker deprives this proposed speech of what otherwise would be its clear entitlement to protection. We turn now to that question.

"[A]ppellee suggests that First Amendment rights generally have been afforded only to corporations engaged in the communications business or through which individuals express themselves. [But] the Court's decisions involving corporations in the business of communication or entertainment are based not only on the role of the First Amendment in fostering individual self-expression but also on its role in affording the public access to discussion, debate, and the dissemination of information and ideas. See *Red Lion*, [p. 845 supra]; *Stanley v. Georgia*, [p. 610 supra]; *Time, Inc. v. Hill*, [p. 593 supra].

"[We] find no support in the First or Fourteenth Amendments, or in the decisions of this Court, for the proposition that speech that otherwise would be within the protection of the First Amendment loses that protection simply because its source is a corporation that cannot prove [a] material effect on its business or property. The 'materially affecting' requirement is not an identification of the boundaries of corporate speech etched by the Constitution itself. Rather, it amounts to an impermissible legislative prohibition of speech based on the identity of the interests that spokesmen may represent in public debate over controversial issues and a requirement that the speaker have a sufficiently great interest in the subject to justify communication.

"[In] the realm of protected speech, the legislature is constitutionally disqualified from dictating the subjects about which persons may speak and the speakers who may address a public issue. *Chicago Police Dep't v. Mosley*, [p. 802 supra].

---

13. Nor is there any occasion to consider in this case whether, under different circumstances, a justification for a restriction on speech that would be inadequate as applied to individuals might suffice to sustain the same restriction as applied to corporations, unions, or like entities.

[*Consolidated Edison Co. v. Public Serv. Comm'n*, 447 U.S. 530, 100 S.Ct. 2326, 65 L.Ed.2d 319 (1980), held that neither Consolidated Edison's corporate status, nor its status as a government regulated monopoly precluded it from asserting a first amendment right to insert controversial messages in its billing envelopes. Citing *Bellotti*, the Court stressed that the worth of speech does not depend upon its source.]

If a legislature may direct business corporations to 'stick to business,' it also may limit other corporations—religious, charitable, or civic—to their respective 'business' when addressing the public. Such power in government to channel the expression of views is unacceptable under the First Amendment. Especially where, as here, the legislature's suppression of speech suggests an attempt to give one side of a debatable public question an advantage in expressing its views to the people, the First Amendment is plainly offended. * * *

"The constitutionality of § 8's prohibition of the 'exposition of ideas' by corporations turns on whether it can survive the exacting scrutiny necessitated by a state-imposed restriction of freedom of speech. Especially where, as here, a prohibition is directed at speech itself,[23] and the speech is intimately related to the process of governing, 'the State may prevail only upon showing a subordinating interest which is compelling.' *Bates v. Little Rock,* 361 U.S. 516, 80 S.Ct. 412, 4 L.Ed.2d 480 (1960).

"Preserving the integrity of the electoral process, preventing corruption, and 'sustain[ing] the active, alert responsibility of the individual citizen in a democracy for the wise conduct of government' are interests of the highest importance. *Buckley.* Preservation of the individual citizen's confidence in government is equally important.

"[Appellee's arguments] that these interests are endangered by corporate participation in discussion of a referendum [issue] hinge upon the assumption that such participation would exert an undue influence on the outcome of a referendum vote, and—in the end—destroy the confidence of the people in the democratic process and the integrity of government. According to appellee, corporations are wealthy and powerful and their views may drown out other points of view. If appellee's arguments were supported by record or legislative findings that corporate advocacy threatened imminently to undermine democratic processes, thereby denigrating rather than serving First Amendment interests,[a] these arguments would merit our consideration.[b] Cf. *Red Lion.* But there has been no showing that the relative voice of corporations has been overwhelming or even significant in influencing referenda in Massachusetts, or that there has been any threat to the confidence of the citizenry in government.

"[Referenda] are held on issues, not candidates for public office. The risk of corruption perceived in cases involving candidate elections simply is not present [c]

---

23. It is too late to suggest "that the dependence of a communication on the expenditure of money operates itself to introduce a nonspeech element or to reduce the exacting scrutiny required by the First Amendment." *Buckley.* Furthermore, § 8 is an "attempt directly to control speech [rather than] to protect, from an evil shown to be grave, some interest clearly within the sphere of governmental concern." *Speiser* [p. 819 supra]. Compare *O'Brien.*

a. Legislatures wishing to support such findings need not look far. See, e.g., Daniel Lowenstein, *Campaign Spending and Ballot Propositions: Recent Experience, Public Choice Theory and the First Amendment,* 29 U.C.L.A. L.Rev. 505 (1982); John Schockley, *Direct Democracy, Campaign Finance, and the Courts: Can Corruption, Undue Influence, and Declining Voter Confidence Be Found?,* 39 U.Miami

L.Rev. 377 (1985). For additional information and commentary, see Archibald Cox, *Constitutional Issues in the Regulation of the Financing of Election Campaigns,* 31 Clev.St.L.Rev. 395 (1982); Symposium, *Political Action Committees and Campaign Finance,* 22 Ariz.L.Rev. 351 (1981); Symposium, *Campaign Finance Reform,* 10 Hast.Con.L.Q. 463 (1983).

b. "[I]f *Tornillo* and *Buckley* slammed the door on excessive power arguments, [*Bellotti*] opened a window. [The] Court did not pause, however, to explain why factors found in *Buckley* and *Tornillo* to be foreign to the first amendment would have 'merited consideration' in *Bellotti.*" Steven Shiffrin, *Government Speech,* 27 U.C.L.A. L.Rev. 565, 598–99 (1980).

c. *Citizens Against Rent Control v. Berkeley,* 454 U.S. 290, 102 S.Ct. 434, 70 L.Ed.2d 492 (1981) (White, J., dissenting), struck down

in a popular vote on a public issue.[26]   To be sure, corporate advertising may influence the outcome of the vote; this would be its purpose.   But the fact that advocacy may persuade the electorate is hardly a reason to suppress [it.]   We noted [that] 'the concept that government may restrict the speech of some elements of our society in order to enhance the relative voice of others is wholly foreign to the First Amendment.'   *Buckley.*   Moreover, the people in our democracy are entrusted with the responsibility for judging and evaluating the relative merits of conflicting arguments.[31]   They may consider, in making their judgment, the source and credibility of the advocate.   But if there be any danger that the people cannot evaluate the information and arguments advanced by appellants, it is a danger contemplated by the Framers of the First Amendment."

The Court rejected the argument that § 8 was justified by the interest in preventing use of corporate resources to advance views with which some shareholders disagreed.   In this respect the statute was under-inclusive in not forbidding "the expenditure of corporate funds on any public issue until it becomes the subject of a referendum, though the displeasure of disapproving shareholders is unlikely to be any less.   The fact that a particular kind of ballot question has been singled out for special treatment undermines the likelihood of a genuine state interest in protecting shareholders.   It suggests instead that the legislature may have been concerned with silencing corporations on a particular subject.   Indeed, appellee has conceded that 'the legislative and judicial history of the statute indicates [that] the second crime was "tailor-made" to prohibit corporate campaign contributions to oppose a graduated income tax amendment.'

"[The] over-inclusiveness of the statute is demonstrated by the fact that § 8 would prohibit a corporation from supporting or opposing a referendum proposal even if its shareholders unanimously authorized the contribution or expenditure. Ultimately shareholders may decide, through the procedures of corporate democracy, whether their corporation should engage in debate on public issues.[34]"

a city ordinance placing a $250 limitation on contributions to committees formed to support or oppose ballot measures submitted to popular vote. The Court, per Burger, C.J., observed that the case did not involve an ordinance confined to contributions by corporations and that the case involved ballot measures, not candidate elections. Rehnquist, J., concurring noted the presence of a corporate petitioner, but emphasized that the ordinance was not aimed only at corporations. In separate concurrences Marshall, J., and Blackmun, J., joined by O'Connor, J., noted that the record did not contain the kind of evidence that would warrant consideration under *Bellotti.* For commentary, see Laurence Tribe, Constitutional Choices 195–97 (1985); Lowenstein, fn. a supra, at 584–602; Marlene Nicholson, *The Constitutionality of Contribution Limitations in Ballot Measure Elections,* 9 Ecol.L.Q. 683 (1981).

26. [Appellants] do not challenge the constitutionality of laws prohibiting or limiting corporate contributions to political candidates or committees, or other means of influencing candidate elections. About half of these laws, including the Federal Corrupt Practices Act, by their terms do not apply to referendum votes. [The] overriding concern behind the enactment

of statutes such as the Federal Corrupt Practices Act was the problem of corruption of elected representatives through the creation of political debts. [The] case before us presents no comparable problem, and our consideration of a corporation's right to speak on issues of general public interest implies no comparable right in the quite different context of participation in a political campaign for election to public office. Congress might well be able to demonstrate the existence of a danger of real or apparent corruption in independent expenditures by corporations to influence candidate elections. Cf. *Buckley.*

31. Government is forbidden to assume the task of ultimate judgment, lest the people lose their ability to govern themselves. The First Amendment rejects the "highly paternalistic" approach of statutes like § 8 which restrict what the people may hear. *Virginia Pharmacy* [p. 809 supra].

34. [White, J.'s] repeatedly expressed concern for corporate shareholders who may be "coerced" into supporting "causes with which they disagree" apparently is not shared by appellants' shareholders. Not a single shareholder has joined appellee in defending the Massachusetts statute, or so far as the record

BURGER, C.J., who joined the Court's opinion, concurred: "A disquieting aspect of Massachusetts' position is that it may carry the risk of impinging on the First Amendment rights of those who employ the corporate form—as most do—to carry on the business of mass communications, particularly the large media conglomerates. This is so because of the difficulty, and perhaps impossibility, of distinguishing, either as a matter of fact or constitutional law, media corporations from corporations such as appellants.

"Making traditional use of the corporate form, some media enterprises have amassed vast wealth and power and conduct many activities, some directly related—and some not—to their publishing and broadcasting activities. Today, a corporation might own the dominant newspaper in one or more large metropolitan centers, television and radio stations in those same centers and others, a newspaper chain, news magazines with nationwide circulation, national or worldwide wire news services, and substantial interests in book publishing and distribution enterprises. Corporate ownership may extend, vertically, to pulp mills and pulp timberlands to insure an adequate, continuing supply of newsprint and to trucking and steamship lines for the purpose of transporting the newsprint to the presses. Such activities would be logical economic auxiliaries to a publishing conglomerate. Ownership also may extend beyond to business activities unrelated to the task of publishing newspapers and magazines or broadcasting radio and television programs. Obviously, such far-reaching ownership would not be possible without the state-provided corporate form and its 'special rules relating to such matters as limited liability, perpetual life, and the accumulation, distribution, and taxation of assets'. (White, J., dissenting).

"In terms of 'unfair advantage in the political process' and 'corporate domination of the electoral process,' it could be argued that such media conglomerates as I describe pose a much more realistic threat to valid interests than do appellants and similar entities not regularly concerned with shaping popular opinion on public issues. See *Miami Herald*.

"In terms of Massachusetts' other concern, the interests of minority shareholders, I perceive no basis for saying that the managers and directors of the media conglomerates are more or less sensitive to the views and desires of minority shareholders than are corporate officers generally. Nor can it be said, even if relevant to First Amendment analysis—which it is not—that the former are more virtuous, wise, or restrained in the exercise of corporate power than are the latter. Thus, no factual distinction has been identified as yet that would

shows, has interposed any objection to the right asserted by the corporations to make the proscribed expenditures.

The dissent of Mr. Justice White relies heavily on *Abood* and *Street,* [Sec. 10, II supra]. These decisions involved the First Amendment rights of employees in closed or agency shops not to be compelled, as a condition of employment, to support with financial contributions the political activities of other union members with which the dissenters disagreed.

Street and *Abood* are irrelevant to the question presented in this case. In those cases employees were required, either by state law or by agreement between the employer and the union, to pay dues or a "service fee" to the exclusive bargaining representative. To the extent that these funds were used by the union in furtherance of political goals, unrelated to

collective bargaining, they were held to be unconstitutional because they compelled the dissenting union member "to furnish contributions of money for the propagation of opinions which he disbelieves."

The critical distinction here is that no shareholder has been "compelled" to contribute anything. Apart from the fact, noted by the dissent, that compulsion by the State is wholly absent, the [shareholder] invests in a corporation of his own volition and is [free to withdraw his investment at any time and for any reason.] A more relevant analogy, therefore, is to the situation where an employee voluntarily joins a union, or an individual voluntarily joins an association, and later finds himself in disagreement with its stance on a political issue.
* * *

justify government restraints on the right of appellants to express their views without, at the same time, opening the door to similar restraints on media conglomerates with their vastly greater influence."

WHITE, J., joined by Brennan and Marshall, JJ., dissented, stressing: (1) The statute was designed to protect first amendment rights by "preventing institutions which have been permitted to amass wealth as a result of special advantages extended by the State for certain economic purposes from using that wealth to acquire an unfair advantage in the political process, especially where, as here, the issue involved has no material connection with the business of the corporation. The State need not permit its own creation to consume it. Massachusetts could permissibly conclude that not to impose limits upon the political activities of corporations would have placed it in a position of departing from neutrality and indirectly assisting the propagation of corporate views because of the advantages its laws give to the corporate acquisition of funds to finance such activities. Such expenditures may be viewed as seriously threatening the role of the First Amendment as a guarantor of a free marketplace of ideas.

"[This] Nation has for many years recognized the need for measures designed to prevent corporate domination of the political process. The Corrupt Practices Act, first enacted in 1907, has consistently barred corporate contributions in connection with federal elections. This Court has repeatedly recognized that one of the principal purposes of this prohibition is 'to avoid the deleterious influences on federal elections resulting from the use of money by those who exercise control over large aggregations of capital.' *United States v. United Auto. Workers,* 352 U.S. 567, 585, 77 S.Ct. 529, 538, 1 L.Ed.2d 563 (1957). Although this Court has never adjudicated the constitutionality of the Act, there is no suggestion in its cases construing it that this purpose is in any sense illegitimate or deserving of other than the utmost respect; indeed, the thrust of its opinions, until today, has been to the contrary."

(2) The Massachusetts law advances the "overriding interest [of] assuring that shareholders are not compelled to support and financially further beliefs with which they disagree, where [the issue] does not materially affect the business, property, or other affairs of the corporation.[12] [The law] protects the very freedoms that this Court has held to be guaranteed by the First Amendment. [Last Term, in *Abood,* we] held that, a State may not, even indirectly, require an individual to contribute to the support of an ideological cause he may oppose as a condition of [employment].

"Presumably, unlike [*Street* and *Abood,*] the use of funds invested by shareholders with opposing views by Massachusetts corporations in connection with referenda or elections would not constitute state action and, consequently, not violate the First Amendment. Until now, however, the States have always been free to adopt measures designed to further rights protected by the Constitution even when not compelled to do so."

REHNQUIST, J., dissenting, argued that "the Fourteenth Amendment does not require a State to endow a business corporation with the power of political speech": "A State grants to a business corporation the blessings of potentially perpetual life and limited liability to enhance its efficiency as an economic entity. It might reasonably be concluded that those properties, so beneficial in the economic sphere, pose special dangers in the political sphere. [T]he States might

---

12. This, of course, is an interest that was not present in *Buckley,* and would not justify limitations upon the activities of associations, corporate or otherwise, formed for the express purpose of advancing a political or social cause.

reasonably fear that the corporation would use its economic power to obtain further benefits beyond those already bestowed. I would think that any particular form of organization upon which the State confers special privileges or immunities different from those of natural persons would be subject to like regulation, whether the organization is a labor union, a partnership, a trade association, or a corporation." [d]

Notes and Questions

1. *Protecting the privileged.* (a) Consider Mark Tushnet, *An Essay on Rights,* 62 Tex.L.Rev. 1363, 1387 (1984): "The first amendment has replaced the due process clause as the primary guarantor of the privileged. [Even] in its heyday the due process clause stood in the way only of specific legislation designed to reduce the benefits of privilege. Today, in contrast, the first amendment stands as a general obstruction to all progressive legislative efforts. To protect their positions of privilege, the wealthy can make prudent investments either in political action or, more conventionally, in factories or stocks. But since the demise of substantive due process, their investments in factories and stocks can be regulated by legislatures. Under *Buckley* and *Bellotti,* however, their investments in politics—or politicians—cannot be regulated significantly. Needless to say, careful investment in politics may prevent effective regulation of traditional investments." See also Mark Tushnet, *Corporations and Free Speech* in The Politics of Law 253 (David Kairys ed. 1982).[e] Compare Sanford Levinson, *Book Review,* 83 Mich.L.Rev. 939, 945 (1985): "Overtly, justifying restriction of campaign spending by reference to the idea of fair access to the public forum may seem content neutral. However, it is worth considering to what extent we in fact support such restrictions because of tacit assumptions about the contents of the views held by the rich, who would obviously feel most of the burden of the restrictions. If both political views and the propensity to spend money on politics were distributed randomly among the entire populace, it is hard to see why anyone would be very excited about the whole issue of campaign finance."

Does Levinson's observation shortchange participatory values? Consider Cass Sunstein, *Beyond the Republican Revival,* 97 Yale L.J. 1539, 1577 (1988):

d. Rehnquist, J., suggested that when the state creates a corporation such as a newspaper, "it necessarily assumes that the corporation is entitled to the liberty of the press essential to the conduct of its business." But a newspaper has "no greater right than any other corporation" to contribute money to political campaigns although its right to endorse a candidate in its editorial columns would be fully protected.

e. For suggestions that the first amendment may be generally harmful from a progressive perspective, see J.M. Balkin, *Some Realism About Pluralism: Legal Realist Approaches to the First Amendment,* 1990 Duke L.J. 375; Mary E. Becker, *The Politics of Women's Wrongs and the Bill of "Rights": A Bicentennial Perspective,* 59 U.Chi.L.Rev. 453, 486–94 (1992); Mary E. Becker, *Conservative Free Speech and the Uneasy Case for Judicial Review,* 64 U.Colo.L.Rev. 975 (1993); Richard Delgado, *Comments About Mary Becker,* 64 U.Colo.L.Rev. 1051 (1993); Morton Horwitz, *Rights,* 23 Harv. CR–CL L.Rev. 393, 397–98,

402–03 (1988); Frederick Schauer, *The Political Incidence of the Free Speech Principle,* 64 U.Colo.L.Rev. 935 (1993); Mark Tushnet, *An Essay on Rights,* 62 Tex.L.Rev. 1363, 1386–92 (1984). For contrary considerations, see Burt Neuborne, *Blues for the Left Hand,* 62 U.Chi. L.Rev. 423 (1995); Steven Shiffrin, *The Politics of the Mass Media and the Free Speech Principle,* 69 Ind.L.J. 689 (1994); Kathleen Sullivan, *Discrimination, Distribution and Free Speech,* 37 Ariz.L.Rev. 439 (1995); Kathleen Sullivan, *Free Speech and Unfree Markets,* 42 U.C.L.A.L.Rev. 949 (1995); Kathleen Sullivan, *Resurrecting Free Speech,* 63 Ford. L.Rev. 971 (1995); Kathleen Sullivan, *Free Speech Wars,* 48 S.M.U.L.Rev. 203 (1994). See also Mark Graber, *Old Wine in New Bottles,* 48 Vand.L.Rev. 349 (1995). For discussion on a broad range of issues concerning the relationship between speech values and property values in Burger Court decisions, see Norman Dorsen & Gara, *Free Speech, Property, and the Burger Court: Old Values, New Balances,* 1982 Sup.Ct.Rev. 195.

"[R]epublican understandings would point toward large reforms of the electoral process in an effort to improve political deliberation and to promote political equality and citizenship."

(b) Colorado made it a felony to pay persons to circulate initiative or referendum petitions. The purposes of the provision were to assure that a ballot measure had a sufficiently broad base of popular support to warrant its placement on the ballot and to eliminate an incentive to produce fraudulent signatures. Constitutional? See *Meyer v. Grant,* 486 U.S. 414, 108 S.Ct. 1886, 100 L.Ed.2d 425 (1988) (invalidating statute). For criticism, see Daniel Lowenstein & Robert Stern, *The First Amendment and Paid Initiative Petition Circulators: A Dissenting View and a Proposal,* 17 Hastings Con.L.Q. 175 (1989).

2. *Distinguishing media corporations.* Consider Marlene Nicholson, *The Constitutionality of the Federal Restrictions on Corporate and Union Campaign Contributions and Expenditures,* 65 Corn.L.Rev. 945, 959 (1980): "A solution may be to focus on the distinction between media activities and other activities. A diversified corporation, partially involved in the media, would be entitled to full first amendment protection for its media-related operations. Under this approach, a newspaper would not lose its first amendment rights because it purchased a pulp mill, but it could not extend these rights to its pulp mill operations. An oil company that purchased a newspaper would not gain first amendment rights for its oil operations, but it would be able to assert these first amendment rights in the operation of its newspaper. The problem is not, to paraphrase Chief Justice Burger, the impracticability of making a distinction, but rather the difficulty of finding a theory that will justify a distinction."

Can self-expression serve as a distinguishing factor? See id. at 959–60. Is there more freedom "to choose and create the content of the delivered speech in the communications industry than in other industries"? Does the communication industry "display less allegiance to the profit motive than other industries"? Does it matter that the communications industry's product is speech? Can a fourth estate theory distinguish the press? On that premise, is there no reason to expand the definition of the press to include business corporations? See generally C. Edwin Baker, *Human Liberty and Freedom of Speech,* Chs. 10, 11 (1989); C. Edwin Baker, *Commercial Speech: A Problem in the Theory of Freedom,* 62 Iowa L.Rev. 1, 25–40 (1976); C. Edwin Baker, *Press Rights and Government Power to Structure the Press,* 34 U.Miami L.Rev. 819, 822–36 (1980).

3. *Protecting shareholders.* After *Bellotti,* could government "authorize management to make some kinds of corporate speech, such as commercial speech, but not others, such as political or noncommercial speech, without the approval or express consent of stockholders"? See generally Victor Brudney, *Business Corporations and Stockholders' Rights Under the First Amendment,* 91 Yale L.J. 235 (1981).

4. *Protecting associational rights.* Should the Court have considered the possibly "stronger argument: corporate political expression should be protected as the speech and associational activity of the individual owners"? Cf. Note, 92 Harv.L.Rev. 163, 165–66 (1978). Does this argument slight the extent to which the state has altered political influence by creating corporations and conferring advantages upon them? See William Patton & Randall Bartlett, *Corporate "Persons" and Freedom of Speech: The Political Impact of Legal Mythology,* 1981 Wis.L.Rev. 494. Does the association argument also assume too much about the connection between the owners' views and the corporation's speech? See Baker, *Commercial Speech,* note 2 supra and Brudney note 3 supra.

5. *Protecting listeners.* Is *Bellotti* justifiable because of listeners' rights? See Martin Redish, *Self-Realization, Democracy, and Freedom of Expression: A Reply to Professor Baker,* 130 U.Pa.L.Rev. 678–79 (1982). But see Note, *Statutory Limitations on Corporate Spending in Ballot Measure Campaigns: The Case for Constitutionality,* 36 Hast.L.J. 433 (1985) (legal and market limitations on corporate speech inherently negate its value for listeners). Reconsider the arguments for and against the marketplace of ideas argument, Sec. 1, I supra.

6. *Aftermath of fn. 26.* 2 U.S.C.A. § 441(b) prohibits corporations or unions from making contributions or expenditures in connection with federal elections, but allows corporations and unions to establish and pay the expenses of segregated funds to be used for political purposes during federal elections. It prohibits corporations from soliciting contributions from persons other than its "stockholders and their families and its executive or administrative personnel and their families." In lieu of shareholders, corporations without capital stock are permitted to solicit contributions for such a fund from their "members." FEC v. NATIONAL RIGHT TO WORK COMM., 459 U.S. 197, 103 S.Ct. 552, 74 L.Ed.2d 364 (1982), per REHNQUIST, J., characterized these provisions as sufficiently tailored to prevent corruption or its appearance and to protect corporate contributors as to negate any judgment that restriction on associational interests was "undue." The National Right to Work Committee is an advocacy group organized as a nonprofit corporation without capital stock. It conceded that it was required to set up a segregated fund under § 441(b) but argued that it was entitled to solicit contributions from anyone that had previously responded to any of its prior mass mailings. The Court unanimously held that this conception of membership would render the statutory corporation "meaningless." Without requiring any evidentiary showing, the Court stated that the interest in avoiding corruption or its appearance justified "treating unions, corporations, and similar organizations differently from individuals."

FEC v. National Conservative Political Action Comm., p. 930 supra, per REHNQUIST, J., characterized *National Right to Work Comm.* as proceeding from the premise that "in return for the special advantages that the State confers on the corporate form, individuals acting jointly through corporations forgo some of the rights they have as individuals." But, citing *Bellotti's* fn. 26, he suggested that the question of whether a corporation could constitutionally be restricted in making independent expenditures to influence elections for public office was still open. Should advocacy groups organized in corporate form be treated like business corporations?

———

Michigan law prohibits corporations, profit or nonprofit, from making contributions to candidates or independent expenditures on behalf of or opposed to candidates. The law entitles such corporations, however, to solicit contributions for allowable expenditures from a segregated fund. The Michigan State Chamber of Commerce, a nonprofit corporation with more than 8,000 members (three quarters of whom are profit corporations), sought to place a newspaper advertisement in support of a Congressional candidate and argued that Michigan's prohibition of such corporate ads was unconstitutional. AUSTIN v. MICHIGAN STATE CHAMBER OF COMMERCE, 494 U.S. 652, 110 S.Ct. 1391, 108 L.Ed.2d 652 (1990), per MARSHALL, J., upheld the scheme as applied to these facts: "[T]he political advantage of corporations is unfair because '[t]he resources in the treasury of a business corporation [are] not an indication of popular support for the corporation's political ideas. They reflect instead the economically motivated decisions of investors and customers. The availability of these resources may make a corporation a formidable political presence, even though the power of the corporation may be no reflection of the power of its ideas.' *FEC v. Massachusetts Citizens for Life, Inc.,* 479 U.S. 238, 107 S.Ct. 616, 93 L.Ed.2d 539 (1986) [MCFL]. * * *

"The Chamber argues that this concern about corporate domination of the political process is insufficient to justify restrictions on independent expenditures. Although this Court has distinguished these expenditures from direct contributions in the context of federal laws regulating individual donors, it has also recognized that a legislature might demonstrate a danger of real or apparent corruption posed by such expenditures when made by corporations to influence candidate elections, *Bellotti,* n. 26. Regardless of whether this danger of 'financial quid pro quo' corruption may be sufficient to justify a restriction on independent expenditures, Michigan's regulation aims at a different type of corruption in the political arena: the corrosive and distorting effects of immense aggregations of wealth that are accumulated with the help of the corporate form and that have little or no correlation to the public's support for the corporation's political ideas. The Act does not attempt 'to equalize the relative influence of speakers on elections'; rather, it ensures that expenditures reflect actual public support for the political ideas espoused by corporations. We emphasize that the mere fact that corporations may accumulate large amounts of wealth is not the justification for [the statute]; rather, the unique state-conferred corporate structure that facilitates the amassing of large treasuries warrants the limit on independent expenditures. [We] therefore hold that the State has articulated a sufficiently compelling rationale to support its restriction on independent expenditures by corporations.

"We next turn to the question whether the Act is sufficiently narrowly tailored to achieve its goal. We find that the Act is precisely targeted to eliminate the distortion caused by corporate spending while also allowing corporations to express their political views. [T]he Act does not impose an *absolute* ban on all forms of corporate political spending but permits corporations to make independent political expenditures through separate segregated funds. Because persons contributing to such funds understand that their money will be used solely for political purposes, the speech generated accurately reflects contributors' support for the corporation's political views.

[Although] some closely held corporations, just as some publicly held ones, may not have accumulated significant amounts of wealth, they receive from the State the special benefits conferred by the corporate structure and present the potential for distorting the political process. This potential for distortion justifies § 54(1)'s general applicability to all corporations. The section therefore is not substantially overbroad.

"The Chamber contends that [the Act] cannot be applied to a nonprofit ideological corporation like a chamber of commerce. [The Chamber relied on *MCFL,* per Brennan, J., which held that 2 U.S.C. § 441b, prohibiting corporations from using their treasury funds for the purpose of influencing any election for public office, was unconstitutional as applied to the expenditures of a nonprofit, nonstock corporation. Specifically, MCFL an anti-abortion organization had printed and distributed some 100,000 "newsletters" advocating the election of a number of candidates. Rehnquist, C.J., joined by White, Blackmun, and Stevens, JJ., dissenting, argued that organizations opting for a corporate form could be barred from using treasury funds for election purposes.] [a] In *MCFL*, we held that the nonprofit organization there had 'features more akin to voluntary political associations than business firms, and therefore should not have to bear burdens on independent spending solely because of [its] incorporated status.' In reaching that conclusion, we enumerated three characteristics of the corporation that were 'essential' to our holding. * * *

"The first characteristic of MCFL that distinguished it from ordinary business corporations was that the organization 'was formed for the express purpose of promoting political ideas, and cannot engage in business activities.' [MCFL's] narrow political focus thus 'ensure[d] that [its] political resources reflect[ed] political support.'

"In contrast, the Chamber's bylaws set forth more varied purposes, several of which are not inherently political. For instance, the Chamber compiles and disseminates information relating to social, civic, and economic conditions, trains and educates its members, and promotes ethical business practices. Unlike MCFL's, the Chamber's educational activities are not expressly tied to political goals; many of its seminars, conventions, and publications are politically neutral and focus on business and economic issues. The Chamber's President and Chief Executive Officer stated that one of the corporation's main purposes is to provide 'service to [its] membership that includes everything from group insurance to educational seminars, [and] litigation activities on behalf of the business community.' * * *

"We described the second feature of MCFL as the absence of 'shareholders or other persons affiliated so as to have a claim on its assets or earnings. This ensures that persons connected with the organization will have no economic disincentive for disassociating with it if they disagree with its political activity.' Although the Chamber also lacks shareholders, many of its members may be similarly reluctant to withdraw as members even if they disagree with the Chamber's political expression, because they wish to benefit from the Chamber's nonpolitical [programs].[2]

"The final characteristic upon which we relied in *MCFL* was [that] the organization [was] not established by, and had a policy of not accepting contributions from, business corporations. Thus it could not 'serv[e] as [a] condui[t] for the type of direct spending that creates a threat to the political marketplace.' In striking contrast, more than three-quarters of the Chamber's members are business corporations, whose political contributions and expenditures can constitutionally be regulated by the [State].[3] Because the Chamber accepts money from for-profit corporations, it could, absent application of § 54(1), serve as a conduit for corporate political spending. * * *

"The Chamber also attacks § 54(1) as underinclusive because it does not regulate the independent expenditures of unincorporated labor unions.[4] Whereas

a. For commentary on *MCFL*, see Louis Seidman, *Reflections on Context and the Constitution*, 73 Minn.L.Rev. 73, 80–84 (1988).

2. A requirement that the Chamber disclose the nature and extent of its political activities would not eliminate the possible distortion of the political process inherent in independent expenditures from general corporate funds. Given the significant incentive for members to continue their financial support for the Chamber in spite of their disagreement with its political agenda, disclosure will not ensure that the funds in the Chamber's treasury correspond to members' support for its ideas.

3. A nonprofit corporation's segregated fund, on the other hand, apparently cannot receive contributions from corporations. * * *

4. The Federal Election Campaign Act restricts the independent expenditures of labor organizations as well as those of corporations. 2 U.S.C. § 441b(a).

unincorporated unions, and indeed individuals, may be able to amass large treasuries, they do so without the significant state-conferred advantages of the corporate structure; corporations are 'by far the most prominent example of entities that enjoy legal advantages enhancing their ability to accumulate wealth.' The desire to counterbalance those advantages unique to the corporate form is the State's compelling interest in this case * * *.

"[We now] address the Chamber's contention that the provision infringes its rights under the Fourteenth Amendment. The Chamber argues [that] the State should also restrict the independent expenditures of [corporations] engaged in the media business.[5] [But] media corporations differ significantly from other corporations in that their resources are devoted to the collection of information and its dissemination to the public. We have consistently recognized the unique role that the press plays in 'informing and educating the public, offering criticism, and providing a forum for discussion and debate.' *Bellotti*. See also *Mills v. Alabama* ('[T]he press serves and was designed to serve as a powerful antidote to any abuses of power by governmental officials and as a constitutionally chosen means for keeping officials elected by the people responsible to all the people whom they were selected to serve'). [The] media exception ensures that the Act does not hinder or prevent the institutional press from reporting on and publishing editorials about newsworthy events. Cf. 15 U.S.C. §§ 1801–1804 (enacting a limited exemption from the antitrust laws for newspapers in part because of the recognition of the special role of the press). [Although] the press' unique societal role may not entitle the press to greater protection under the Constitution, it does provide a compelling reason for the State to exempt media corporations from the scope of political expenditure limitations. We therefore hold that the Act does not violate the Equal Protection Clause."

BRENNAN, J., joined the Court's opinion, but referring to himself as "one of the 'Orwellian' 'censors' derided by the dissents and as the author of [*MCFL*]," also concurred to express his views: "The requirement that corporate independent expenditures be financed through a segregated fund or political action committee [may] be unconstitutional as applied to some corporations because they do not present the dangers at which expenditure limitations are aimed. Indeed, we determined that [*MCFL*] fell into this category.[3] [4]

"The Michigan law is concededly 'underinclusive' insofar as it does not ban other types of political expenditures to which a dissenting Chamber member or corporate shareholder might object. [A] corporation remains free, for example, to use general treasury funds to support an initiative proposal in a state referendum. See *Bellotti*.

5. The Federal Election Campaign Act contains a similar exemption that excludes from the definition of expenditure "any news story, commentary, or editorial distributed through the facilities of any broadcasting station, newspaper, magazine, or other periodical publication, unless such facilities are owned or controlled by any political party, political committee, or candidate." 2 U.S.C. § 431(9)(B)(i).

3. [Whether] an organization presents the threat at which the campaign finance laws are aimed has to do with the particular characteristics of the organization at issue and not with the content of its speech. Of course, if a correlation between the two factors could be shown to exist, a group would be free to mount a First Amendment challenge on that basis. * * *

4. According to Justice Kennedy's dissent, the majority holds that "it is now a felony in Michigan for the Sierra Club, or the American Civil Liberties Union" to make independent expenditures. This characterization [overlooks] the central lesson of *MCFL* that the First Amendment may require exemptions, on an as-applied basis, from expenditure restrictions. * * *

"I do not find this underinclusiveness fatal, for several reasons.[8] First, as the dissents recognize, discussions on candidate elections lie 'at the heart of political debate.' But just as speech interests are at their zenith in this area, so too are the interests of unwilling Chamber members and corporate shareholders forced to subsidize that speech. The State's decision to focus on this especially sensitive context is a justifiable one. Second, in light of our decisions in *Bellotti, Consolidated Edison Co. v. Public Service Comm'n,* and related cases, a State cannot prohibit corporations from making many other types of political expenditures. [T]o the extent that the Michigan statute is 'underinclusive' only because it does not regulate corporate expenditures in referenda or other corporate expression (besides merely commercial speech), this reflects the requirements of our decisions rather than the lack of an important state interest on the part of Michigan in regulating expenditures in *candidate* elections. In this sense, the Michigan law is not 'underinclusive' at all. Finally, the provision in Michigan corporate law authorizing shareholder actions against corporate waste might serve as a remedy for other types of political expenditures that have no legitimate connection to the corporation's business."

STEVENS, J., joined the Court's opinion and concurred: "[T]he distinction between individual expenditures and individual contributions that the Court identified in *Buckley,* should have little, if any, weight in reviewing corporate participation in candidate elections. In that context, I believe the danger of either the fact, or the appearance, of quid pro quo relationships provides an adequate justification for state regulation of both expenditures and contributions. Moreover, as we recognized in *Bellotti,* there is a vast difference between lobbying and debating public issues on the one hand, and political campaigns for election to public office on the other."

SCALIA, J., dissented: " 'Attention all citizens. To assure the fairness of elections by preventing disproportionate expression of the views of any single powerful group, your Government has decided that the following associations of persons shall be prohibited from speaking or writing in support of any candidate: _____'. In permitting Michigan to make private corporations the first object of this Orwellian announcement, the Court today endorses the principle that too much speech is an evil that the democratic majority can proscribe. I dissent because that principle is contrary to our case law and incompatible with the absolutely central truth of the First Amendment: that government cannot be trusted to assure, through censorship, the 'fairness' of political debate.

"The Court's opinion says that political speech of corporations can be regulated because '[s]tate law grants [them] special advantages' and because this 'unique state-conferred corporate structure * * * facilitates the amassing of large treasur-

---

8. [In] the context of labor unions, [r]ather than assuming that an employee accepts as "the deal," that the union will use his dues for any purpose that will advance the interests of the bargaining unit, including political contributions and expenditures, we have determined that "the authority to impose dues and fees [is] restricted at least to the 'extent of denying the unions the right, over the employee's objection, to use his money to support political causes which he opposes,' even though Congress was well aware that *unions had historically expended funds in the support of political candidates*

and issues." Ellis v. Railway Clerks [p. 893 supra].

Given the extensive state regulation of corporations, shareholder expectations are always a function of *state law.* It is circular to say, as does Justice Scalia, that *if* a State did not protect shareholders, they would have no expectation of being protected, and therefore that the State has no legitimate interest in protecting them. [I] believe it entirely proper for a State to decide to promote the ability of investors to purchase stock in corporations without fear that their money will be used to support candidates with whom they do not agree.

ies.' This analysis seeks to create one good argument by combining two bad ones. Those individuals who form that type of voluntary association known as a corporation are, to be sure, given special advantages—notably, the immunization of their personal fortunes from liability for the actions of the association—that the State is under no obligation to confer. But so are other associations and private individuals given all sorts of special advantages that the State need not confer, ranging from tax breaks to contract awards to public employment to outright cash subsidies. It is rudimentary that the State cannot exact as the price of those special advantages the forfeiture of First Amendment rights. The categorical suspension of the right of any person, or of any association of persons, to speak out on political matters must be justified by a compelling state need. Which is why the Court puts forward its second bad argument, the fact [t]hat corporations 'amas[s] large treasuries [is] also not sufficient justification for the suppression of political speech, unless one thinks it would be lawful to prohibit men and women whose net worth is above a certain figure from endorsing political candidates. Neither of these two flawed arguments is improved by combining them.

"In *FCC v. League of Women Voters of California*, [p. 869 supra], striking down a congressionally imposed ban upon editorializing by noncommercial broadcasting stations that receive federal funds, the *only* respect in which we considered the receipt of that 'special advantage' relevant was in determining whether the speech limitation could be justified under Congress' spending power, as a means of assuring that the subsidy was devoted only to the purposes Congress intended, which did not include political editorializing. We held it could not be justified on that basis, since 'a noncommercial educational station that receives only 1% of its overall income from [federal] grants is barred absolutely from all editorializing. [The] station has no way of limiting the use of its federal funds to all noneditorializing activities, and, more importantly, it is barred from using even wholly private funds to finance its editorial activity.' Of course the same is true here, even assuming that tax exemptions and other benefits accorded to incorporated associations constitute an exercise of the spending power. It is not just that portion of the corporation's assets attributable to the gratuitously conferred 'special advantages' that is prohibited from being used for political endorsements, but *all* of the corporation's [assets.] Commercial corporations may not have a public persona as sympathetic as that of public broadcasters, but they are no less entitled to this Court's concern.[a]

"As for the second part of the Court's argumentation, [c]ertain uses of 'massive wealth' in the electoral process—whether or not the wealth is the result of 'special advantages' conferred by the State—pose a substantial risk of corruption which constitutes a compelling need for the regulation of speech. Such a risk plainly exists when the wealth is given directly to the political candidate, to be used under his direction and control. [But the] "contention that prohibiting overt advocacy for or against a political candidate satisfies a 'compelling need' to avoid 'corruption' is easily dismissed. As we said in *Buckley*, '[i]t would naively underestimate the ingenuity and resourcefulness of persons and groups desiring to buy influence to believe that they would have much difficulty devising expenditures that skirted the restriction on express advocacy of election or defeat but nevertheless benefited the candidate's campaign.' Independent advocacy, moreover, unlike contributions, 'may well provide little assistance to the candidate's

a. Scalia, J., also argued that *Buckley* had decided the question of independent corporate political expenditures. He observed that *Buckley* had included corporate plaintiffs. Those plaintiffs apparently were the New York Civil Liberties Union, Inc. and Human Events, Inc. Can *Buckley* be distinguished?

campaign and indeed may prove counterproductive,' thus reducing the danger that it will be exchanged 'as a quid pro quo for improper commitments from the candidate.' The latter point seems even more plainly true with respect to corporate advocates than it is with respect to individuals. I expect I could count on the fingers of one hand the candidates who would generally welcome, much less negotiate for, a formal endorsement by AT & T or General Motors. The advocacy of such entities that have 'amassed great wealth' will be effective only to the extent that it brings to the people's attention *ideas* which—despite the invariably self-interested and probably uncongenial source—strike them as true.

"The Court does not try to defend the proposition that independent advocacy poses a substantial risk of political 'corruption,' as English-speakers understand that term. Rather, [its] opinion ultimately rests upon that proposition whose violation constitutes the New Corruption: expenditures must 'reflect actual public support for the political ideas espoused.' This illiberal free-speech principle of 'one man, one minute' was proposed and soundly rejected in *Buckley*. [And the Court's limitation of this principle to corporations] is of course entirely irrational. Why is it perfectly all right if advocacy by an individual billionaire is out of proportion with 'actual public support' for his positions? * * *

"Justice Brennan's concurrence would have us believe that the prohibition [is] a paternalistic measure to protect the corporate shareholder of America. [But] the Michigan [statute] permits corporations to take as many ideological and political positions as they please, so long as they are not 'in assistance of, or in opposition to, the nomination or election of a candidate.' That is indeed the Court's sole basis for distinguishing *Bellotti*, which invalidated restriction of a corporation's general political speech. The Michigan law appears to be designed, in other words, neither to protect shareholders, nor even (impermissibly) to 'balance' general political debate, but to protect political candidates. * * *

"But even if the object of the prohibition could plausibly be portrayed as the protection of shareholders (which the Court's opinion, at least, does not even assert), that would not suffice as a 'compelling need' to support this blatant restriction upon core political speech. A person becomes a member of that form of association known as a for-profit corporation in order to pursue economic objectives. [In] joining such an association, the shareholder knows that management may take any action that is ultimately in accord with what the majority (or a specified supermajority) of the shareholders wishes, so long as that action is designed to make a profit. That is the deal. The corporate actions to which the shareholder exposes himself, therefore, include many things that he may find politically or ideologically uncongenial: investment in South Africa, operation of an abortion clinic, publication of a pornographic magazine, or even publication of a newspaper that adopts absurd political views and makes catastrophic political endorsements. His only protections against such assaults upon his ideological commitments are (1) his ability to persuade a majority (or the requisite minority) of his fellow shareholders that the action should not be taken, and ultimately (2) his ability to sell his stock. (The latter course, by the way, does not ordinarily involve the severe psychic trauma or economic disaster that Justice Brennan's opinion suggests.) It seems to me entirely fanciful, in other words, to suggest that the Michigan statute makes any significant contribution towards insulating the exclusively profit-motivated shareholder from the rude world of politics and ideology.

"But even if that were not fanciful, it would be fanciful to think, as Justice Brennan's opinion assumes, that there is any difference between for-profit and not-for-profit corporations insofar as the need for protection of the individual member's ideological psyche is concerned. Would it be any more upsetting to a shareholder of General Motors that it endorsed the election of Henry Wallace (to stay comfortably in the past) than it would be to a member of the American Civil Liberties Union that it endorsed the election of George Wallace?

"Finally, a few words are in order concerning the Court's approval of the Michigan law's exception for 'media corporations.' [I]f one believes in the Court's rationale of 'compelling state need' to prevent amassed corporate wealth from skewing the political debate, surely that 'unique role' of the press does not give Michigan justification for *excluding* media corporations from coverage, but provides especially strong reason to *include* them. Amassed corporate wealth that regularly sits astride the ordinary channels of information is much more likely to produce the New Corruption (too much of one point of view) than amassed corporate wealth that is generally busy making money elsewhere. Such media corporations not only have vastly greater power to perpetrate the evil of overinforming, they also have vastly greater opportunity. General Motors, after all, will risk a stockholder suit if it makes a political endorsement that is not plausibly tied to its ability to make money for its shareholders. But media corporations make money *by* making political commentary, including endorsements. * * *

"Members of the institutional press, despite the Court's approval of their illogical exemption from the Michigan law, will find little reason for comfort in today's decision. The theory of New Corruption it espouses is a dagger at their throat. The Court today holds merely that media corporations *may* be excluded from the Michigan law, not that they *must* be." [b]

b. Kennedy, J., joined by O'Connor and Scalia, JJ., also dissented. For valuable commentary relevant to the issues raised in *Austin,* see C. Edwin Baker, *Turner Broadcasting: Content–Based Regulation of Persons and Presses,* 1994 Sup.Ct.Rev. 57; Victor Brudney, *Association, Advocacy, and the First Amendment,* 4 Wm. & Mary Bill of Rts.J. 3 (1995); Julian Eule, *Promoting Speaker Diversity: Austin and Metro Broadcasting,* 1990 Sup.Ct.

Rev. 105; Jill Fisch, *Frankenstein's Monster Hits the Campaign Trail: An Approach to Regulation of Corporate Political Expenditures,* 32 Wm. & Mary L.Rev. 587 (1991); Daniel Lowenstein, *A Patternless Mosaic,* 21 Capital U.L.Rev. 381 (1992); Andrew Stark, *Strange Bedfellows: Two Paradoxes in Constitutional Discourse Over Corporate and Individual Political Activity,* 14 Cardozo L.Rev. 1347 (1993).

Chapter 10
FREEDOM OF RELIGION

This chapter concerns the "religion clauses" of the first amendment, commonly known as the "establishment clause" (forbidding laws "respecting an establishment of religion") and the "free exercise clause" (forbidding laws "prohibiting the free exercise thereof"). It is difficult to explore either clause in isolation from the other. The extent to which the clauses interact may be illustrated by the matter of public financial aid to parochial schools, the subject of several cases that follow: On the one hand, does such aid violate the establishment clause? On the other hand, does a state's failure to provide such aid violate the free exercise clause? Another example of the potential conflict between the clauses—also considered in the materials below—is whether, on the one hand, a state's exemption of church buildings from property taxes contravenes the establishment clause or whether, on the other hand, a state's taxing these buildings contravenes the free exercise clause.

Despite this interrelationship of the two clauses, Sec. 1 deals almost exclusively with the establishment clause. Sec. 2, I then considers conventional problems under the free exercise clause. Sec. 2, II examines the complex issues of defining "religion" for purposes of the first amendment and determining the bona fides of an asserted "religious" belief—both matters usually presumed in the cases decided by the Supreme Court and the former never specifically addressed by a majority of the justices. Issues under each clause having been explored in some detail, Sec. 3 presents the subject of preference among religions that has both establishment and free exercise ramifications, and, finally, Sec. 4 discusses problems presented by government action that attempts to accommodate the seemingly opposing demands of the two religion clauses.

SECTION 1. ESTABLISHMENT CLAUSE

Prior to 1947, only two decisions concerning the establishment clause produced any significant consideration by the Court. *Bradfield v. Roberts*, 175 U.S. 291, 20 S.Ct. 121, 44 L.Ed. 168 (1899) upheld federal appropriations to a hospital in the District of Columbia, operated by the Catholic Church, for ward construction and care of indigent patients. *Quick Bear v. Leupp*, 210 U.S. 50, 28 S.Ct. 690, 52 L.Ed. 954 (1908) upheld federal disbursement of funds, held in trust for the Sioux Indians, to Catholic schools designated by the Sioux for payment of tuition costs. Since 1947, however, a substantial number of cases have dealt with the meaning of the establishment clause. The major areas of controversy have concerned public financial assistance to church-related institutions (mainly parochial schools) and religious practices in the public schools. Since the mid 1980s, several decisions have involved government action that publicly acknowledges religion.[a]

———

EVERSON v. BOARD OF EDUC., 330 U.S. 1, 67 S.Ct. 504, 91 L.Ed. 711 (1947): A New Jersey township reimbursed parents for the cost of sending their children "on regular buses operated by the public transportation system," to and from schools, including nonprofit private and parochial schools. The Court, per BLACK, J., rejected a municipal taxpayer's contention that payment for Catholic parochial school students violated the establishment clause, observing that the religion clauses of the first amendment, "as made applicable to the states by the Fourteenth," [b] "reflected in the minds of early Americans a vivid mental picture

a. For discussion of the various "articulated justifications for the special constitutional place of religion" by the Justices, see Michael E. Smith, *The Special Place of Religion in the Constitution,* 1983 Sup.Ct.Rev. 83.

b. *Application of the establishment clause to the states.* Is nonestablishment as "implicit in the concept of ordered liberty" as the freedoms of speech, press, religious exercise, and assembly? See *Palko v. Connecticut,* p. 370 supra. Is it "fundamental to the American scheme"? See *Duncan v. Louisiana,* p. 374 supra.

Brennan, J., has stated: "It has been suggested, with some support in history, that absorption of the First Amendment's ban against congressional legislation 'respecting an establishment of religion' is conceptually impossible because the Framers meant the Establishment Clause also to foreclose any attempt by Congress to disestablish the existing official state churches. [But] the last of the formal state establishments was dissolved more than three decades before the Fourteenth Amendment was ratified, and thus the problem of protecting official state churches from federal encroachments could hardly have been any concern of those who framed the post-Civil War Amendments. [T]he Fourteenth Amendment created a panoply of new federal rights for the protection of citizens of the various States. And among those rights was freedom from such state governmental involvement in the affairs of religion as the Establishment Clause had originally foreclosed on the part of Congress.

"It has also been suggested that the 'liberty' guaranteed by the Fourteenth Amendment logically cannot absorb the Establishment Clause because that clause is not one of the provisions of the Bill of Rights which in terms protects a 'freedom' of the individual. The fallacy in this contention, I think, is that it underestimates the role of the Establishment Clause as a co-guarantor, with the Free Exercise Clause, of religious liberty. * * *

"Finally, it has been contended that absorption of the Establishment Clause is precluded by the absence of any intention on the part of the Framers of the Fourteenth Amendment to circumscribe the residual powers of the States to aid religious activities and institutions in ways which fell short of formal establishments. That argument relies in part upon the express terms of the abortive Blaine Amendment—proposed several years after the adoption of the Fourteenth Amendment—which would have added to the First Amendment a provision that '[n]o state shall make any law respecting an establishment of religion.' Such a restriction would have been superfluous, it is said, if the Fourteenth Amendment had already made the Establishment Clause binding upon the States.

"The argument proves too much, for the Fourteenth Amendment's protection of the free exercise of religion can hardly be questioned; yet the Blaine Amendment would also have added an explicit protection against state laws abridging that liberty." *School Dist. v. Schempp,* Part I infra (concurring opinion).

Consider Mark D. Howe, *The Constitutional Question,* in Religion and the Free Society 49, 55 (1958): "The Court did not seem to be aware of the fact that some legislative enactments respecting an establishment of religion affect most remotely, if at all, the personal rights of religious liberty. [If the Court] reexamined its own interpretations of history [it might allow] the states to take such action in aid of religion as does not appreciably affect the religious or other constitutional rights of individuals * * *."

Compare Jesse H. Choper, *The Establishment Clause and Aid to Parochial Schools,* 56 Calif.L.Rev. 260, 274–75 (1968): "[Howe] assumes that while the fourteenth amendment prevents infringements of liberty which 'significantly affect' the individual, the first amendment forbids abridgements which do not do so. [A] central design of the establishment clause was that it [prevent] government generally from coercing religious belief and specifically from compulsorily taxing individuals for strictly religious purposes. If nonsecular federal action involves either of these consequences,

of conditions and practices which they fervently wished to stamp out in order to preserve liberty for themselves and for their posterity."

The Court detailed the history of religious persecution in Europe "before and contemporaneous with the colonization of America" and the "repetition of many of the old world practices" in the colonies—emphasizing the compulsion "to pay tithes and taxes to support government-sponsored churches whose ministers preached inflammatory sermons designed to strengthen and consolidate the established faith by generating a burning hatred against dissenters." The abhorrence of these practices "reached its dramatic climax in Virginia in 1785–86" when "Madison wrote his great Memorial and Remonstrance" against renewal of "Virginia's tax levy for support of the established church" and the Virginia Assembly "enacted the famous 'Virginia Bill for Religious Liberty' originally written by Thomas Jefferson. [T]he provisions of the First Amendment, in the drafting and adoption of which Madison and Jefferson played such leading roles, had the same objective and were intended to provide the same protection against governmental intrusion on religious liberty as the Virginia statute. [The] interrelationship of these complementary clauses was well summarized [in] *Watson v. Jones,* 13 Wall. 679, 730, 20 L.Ed. 666: 'The structure of our government has, for the preservation of civil liberty, rescued the temporal institutions from religious interference. On the other hand, it has secured religious liberty from the invasions of the civil authority.'

"The 'establishment of religion' clause of the First Amendment means at least this: Neither a state nor the Federal Government can set up a church. Neither can pass laws which aid one religion, aid all religions, or prefer one religion over another. Neither can force nor influence a person to go to or to remain away from church against his will or force him to profess a belief or disbelief in any religion. No person can be punished for entertaining or professing religious beliefs or disbeliefs, for church attendance or non-attendance. No tax in any amount, large or small can be levied to support any religious activities or institutions, whatever they may be called, or whatever form they may adopt to teach or practice religion. Neither a state nor the Federal Government can, openly or secretly, participate in the affairs of any religious organizations or groups and vice versa. In the words of Jefferson, the clause against establishment of religion by law was intended to erect 'a wall of separation between Church and State.' **c**

"We must [not invalidate the New Jersey statute] if it is within the state's constitutional power even though it approaches the verge of that power. New Jersey cannot consistently with the 'establishment of religion' clause of the First Amendment contribute tax-raised funds to the support of an institution which teaches the tenets and faith of any church. On the other hand, other language of the amendment commands that New Jersey cannot hamper its citizens in the free exercise of their own religion. Consequently, it cannot exclude individual Catho-

---

[it] has 'significantly' affected individual freedom. Thus, if such state action involves either, it has seemingly violated the fourteenth amendment by 'significantly' affecting personal liberty. However, if federal action involves neither consequence, then [the] establishment clause itself—as a matter of constitutional construction—has probably not been breached." See also Note, *Toward a Uniform Valuation of the Religion Guarantees,* 80 Yale L.J. 77 (1970).

c. For the view that "the religion clauses amounted to a decision by the national government not to address substantive questions concerning the proper relationship between religion and government," but rather "did no more and no less than confirm the constitutional allocation of jurisdiction over religion to the states," see Steven D. Smith, *Foreordained Failure: The Quest for a Constitutional Principle of Religious Freedom* (1995).

lics, Lutherans, Mohammedans, Baptists, Jews, Methodists, Non-believers, Presbyterians, or the members of any other faith, *because of their faith, or lack of it,* from receiving the benefits of public welfare legislation. While we do not mean to intimate that a state could not provide transportation only to children attending public schools, we must be careful, in protecting the citizens of New Jersey against state-established churches, to be sure that we do not inadvertently prohibit New Jersey from extending its general State law benefits to all its citizens without regard to their religious belief."

Noting that "the New Jersey legislature has decided that a public purpose will be served" by having children "ride in public buses to and from schools rather than run the risk of traffic and other hazards incident to walking or 'hitchhiking,' " the Court conceded "that children are helped to get to church schools. There is even a possibility that some of the children might not be sent to the church schools if the parents were compelled to pay their children's bus fares out of their own pockets when transportation to a public school would have been paid for by the State. [But] state-paid policemen, detailed to protect children going to and from church schools from the very real hazards of traffic, would serve much the same [purpose]. Similarly, parents might be reluctant to permit their children to attend schools which the state had cut off from such general government services as ordinary police and fire protection, connections for sewage disposal, public highways and sidewalks. Of course, cutting off church schools from these services, so separate and so indisputably marked off from the religious function, would make it far more difficult for the schools to operate. But such is obviously not the purpose of the First Amendment. That Amendment requires the state to be a neutral in its relations with groups of religious believers and nonbelievers; it does not require the state to be their adversary. State power is no more to be used so as to handicap religions, than it is to favor them.

"This Court had said that parents may, in the discharge of their duty under state compulsory education laws, send their children to a religious rather than a public school if the school meets the secular educational requirements which the state has power to impose. See *Pierce v. Society of Sisters*, [p. 299 supra]. It appears that these parochial schools meet New Jersey's requirements. The State contributes no money to the schools. It does not support them. Its legislation, as applied, does no more than provide a general program to help parents get their children, regardless of their religion, safely and expeditiously to and from accredited schools.

"The First Amendment has erected a wall between church and state. That wall must be kept high and impregnable. We could not approve the slightest breach. New Jersey has not breached it here."

Rutledge, J., joined by Frankfurter, Jackson and Burton, JJ., filed the principal dissent, arguing that the statute aided children "in a substantial way to get the very thing which they are sent to the particular school to secure, namely, religious training and teaching. * * * Commingling the religious with the secular teaching does not divest the whole of its religious permeation and emphasis or make them of minor part, if proportion were material. Indeed, on any other view, the constitutional prohibition always could be brought to naught by adding a modicum of the secular. [Transportation] cost is as much a part of the total expense, except at times in amount, as the cost of textbooks, of school lunches, of athletic equipment, of writing and other [materials]. Payment of transportation is [no] less essential to education, whether religious or secular, than payment for tuitions, for teachers' salaries, for buildings, equipment and necessary materials. [No] rational line can be drawn between payment for such larger, but not more necessary, items and payment for transportation. [Now], as in Madison's time, not the amount but the principle of assessment is wrong.

" * * * Public money devoted to payment of religious costs, educational or other, brings the quest for more. It brings too the struggle of sect against sect for the larger share or for any. Here one by numbers alone will benefit most, there another. That is precisely the history of societies which have had an established religion and dissident groups. It is the very thing Jefferson and Madison experienced and sought to guard against, whether in its blunt or in its more screened forms. The end of such strife cannot be other than to destroy the cherished liberty. The dominating group will achieve the dominant benefit; or all will embroil the state in their dissensions. * * *

"Nor is the case comparable to one of furnishing fire or police protection, or access to public highways. These things are matters of common right, part of the general need for safety. Certainly the fire department must not stand idly by while the church burns."

The Court did not again confront the subject of aid to parochial schools until 1968. These decisions are considered in Part II infra. During the intervening two decades, however, the Court was presented with other problems—the most prominent concerning religious influence in the public schools—that enabled it to further develop the establishment clause rationale begun in *Everson*.

I. RELIGION AND PUBLIC SCHOOLS

WALLACE v. JAFFREE

472 U.S. 38, 105 S.Ct. 2479, 86 L.Ed.2d 29 (1985).

JUSTICE STEVENS delivered the opinion of the Court.

[In 1978, Alabama enacted § 16–1–20 authorizing a one-minute period of silence in all public schools "for meditation"; in 1981, it enacted § 16–1–20.1 authorizing a period of silence "for meditation or voluntary prayer." Appellees] have not questioned the holding that § 16–1–20 is valid. Thus, the narrow question for decision [concerns § 16–1–20.1].

[T]he Court has unambiguously concluded that the individual freedom of conscience protected by the First Amendment embraces the right to select any religious faith or none at all.[37] This conclusion derives support not only from the interest in respecting the individual's freedom of conscience, but also from the conviction that religious beliefs worthy of respect are the product of free and voluntary choice by the faithful, and from recognition of the fact that the political interest in forestalling intolerance extends beyond intolerance among Christian sects—or even intolerance among "religions"—to encompass intolerance of the disbeliever and the uncertain. * * *

37. [See] *Torcaso v. Watkins*, [Sec. 2, II infra] ("We repeat and again reaffirm that neither a State nor the Federal Government can constitutionally force a person 'to profess a belief or disbelief in any religion.' Neither can constitutionally pass laws or impose require- ments which aid all religions as against non- believers, and neither can aid those religions based on a belief in the existence of God as against those religions founded on different beliefs").

When the Court has been called upon to construe the breadth of the Establishment Clause, it has examined the criteria developed over a period of many years. Thus, in *Lemon v. Kurtzman,* 403 U.S. 602, 612–613, 91 S.Ct. 2105, 2111, 29 L.Ed.2d 745 (1971), we wrote: " * * * Three such tests may be gleaned from our cases. First, the statute must have a secular legislative purpose; second, its principal or primary effect must be one that neither advances nor inhibits religion,[a] finally, the statute must not foster 'an excessive government entanglement with religion.' " It is the first of these three criteria that is most plainly implicated by this case. As the District Court correctly recognized, no consideration of the second or third criteria is necessary if a statute does not have a clearly secular purpose. For even though a statute that is motivated in part by a religious purpose may satisfy the first criterion, the First Amendment requires that a statute must be invalidated if it is entirely motivated by a purpose to advance religion.

In applying the purpose test, it is appropriate to ask "whether government's actual purpose is to endorse or disapprove of religion."[42] In this case, the answer to that question is dispositive. * * *

The sponsor of the bill that became § 16–1–20.1, Senator Donald Holmes, inserted into the legislative record—apparently without dissent—a statement indicating that the legislation was an "effort to return voluntary prayer" to the public schools. Later Senator Holmes confirmed this purpose before the District Court. In response to the question whether he had any purpose for the legislation other than returning voluntary prayer to public schools, he stated: "No, I did not have no other purpose in mind."[44] The State did not present evidence of *any* secular purpose.[45] * * *

a. Compare Douglas Laycock, *Towards a General Theory of the Religion Clauses: The Case of Church Labor Relations and the Right to Church Autonomy,* 81 Colum.L.Rev. 1373, 1381, 1384 (1981): "The 'inhibits' language is at odds with the constitutional text and with the Court's own statements of the origins and purposes of the [establishment] clause. Government support for religion is an element of every establishment claim, just as a burden or restriction on religion is an element of every free exercise claim. Regulation that burdens religion, enacted because of the government's general interest in regulation, is simply not establishment."

42. *Lynch v. Donnelly,* [Part III infra] (O'Connor, J., concurring) ("The purpose prong of the *Lemon* test asks whether government's actual purpose is to endorse or disapprove of religion. The effect prong asks whether, irrespective of government's actual purpose, the practice under review in fact conveys a message of endorsement or disapproval. An affirmative answer to either question should render the challenged practice invalid").

44. The District Court and the Court of Appeals agreed that the purpose of § 16–1–20.1 was "an effort on the part of the State of Alabama to encourage a religious activity." The evidence presented to the District Court elaborated on the express admission of the

Governor of Alabama (then Fob James) that the enactment of § 16–1–20.1 was intended to "clarify [the State's] intent to have prayer as part of the daily classroom activity," and that the "expressed legislative purpose in enacting Section 16–1–20.1 (1981) was to 'return voluntary prayer to public schools.' "

45. Appellant Governor George C. Wallace now argues that § 16–1–20.1 "is best understood as a permissible accommodation of religion" and that viewed even in terms of the *Lemon* test, the "statute conforms to acceptable constitutional criteria." These arguments seem to be based on the theory that the free exercise of religion of some of the State's citizens was burdened before the statute was enacted. The United States, appearing as amicus curiae in support of the appellants, candidly acknowledges that "it is unlikely that in most contexts a strong Free Exercise claim could be made that time for personal prayer must be set aside during the school day." There is no basis for the suggestion that § 16–1–20.1 "is a means for accommodating the religious and meditative needs of students without in any way diminishing the school's own neutrality or secular atmosphere." In this case, it is undisputed that at the time of the enactment of § 16–1–20.1 there was no governmental practice impeding students from silently praying for one minute at the beginning of each schoolday; thus, there was no need to "accommo-

The legislative intent to return prayer to the public schools is, of course, quite different from merely protecting every student's right to engage in voluntary prayer during an appropriate moment of silence during the schoolday. The 1978 statute already protected that right, containing nothing that prevented any student from engaging in voluntary prayer during a silent minute of meditation. [The] legislature enacted § 16–1–20.1, despite the existence of § 16–1–20 for the sole purpose of expressing the State's endorsement of prayer activities for one minute at the beginning of each schoolday. The addition of "or voluntary prayer" indicates that the State intended to characterize prayer as a favored practice. Such an endorsement is not consistent with the established principle that the government must pursue a course of complete neutrality toward religion.

The importance of that principle does not permit us to treat this as an inconsequential case involving nothing more than a few words of symbolic speech on behalf of the political majority.[51] For whenever the State itself speaks on a religious subject, one of the questions that we must ask is "whether the government intends to convey a message of endorsement or disapproval of religion." * * *

The judgment of the Court of Appeals is affirmed.

JUSTICE O'CONNOR concurring in the judgment.

* * * Although a distinct jurisprudence has enveloped each of [the Religion] Clauses, their common purpose is to secure religious liberty. On these principles the Court has been and remains unanimous. * * * I do believe, however, that the standards announced in *Lemon* should be reexamined and refined in order to make them more useful in achieving the underlying purpose of the First Amendment. [O]ur goal should be "to frame a principle for constitutional adjudication that is not only grounded in the history and language of the first amendment, but one that is also capable of consistent application to the relevant problems." Jesse H. Choper, *Religion in the Public Schools: A Proposed Constitutional Standard,* 47 Minn.L.Rev. 329, 332–333 (1963). Last Term, I proposed a refinement of the *Lemon* test with this goal in mind. *Lynch v. Donnelly* (concurring opinion).

The *Lynch* concurrence suggested that the religious liberty protected by the Establishment Clause is infringed when the government makes adherence to religion relevant to a person's standing in the political community. Direct government action endorsing religion or a particular religious practice is invalid under this approach because it "sends a message to nonadherents that they are outsiders, not full members of the political community, and an accompanying message to adherents that they are insiders, favored members of the political community." * * *

date" or to exempt individuals from any general governmental requirement because of the dictates of our cases interpreting the Free Exercise Clause. * * *

51. As this Court stated in *Engel v. Vitale,* [infra]: "The Establishment Clause, unlike the Free Exercise Clause, does not depend upon any showing of direct governmental compulsion and is violated by the enactment of laws which establish an official religion whether those laws operate directly to coerce nonobserving individuals or not." Moreover, this Court has noted that "[w]hen the power, prestige and financial support of government is placed behind a particular religious belief, the indirect coercive pressure upon religious minorities to conform to the prevailing officially approved religion is plain." Id. This comment has special force in the public-school context where attendance is mandatory. Justice Frankfurter acknowledged this reality in *McCollum v. Board of Education,* [note 1(a) infra] (concurring opinion): "That a child is offered an alternative may reduce the constraint; it does not eliminate the operation of influence by the school in matters sacred to conscience and outside the school's domain. The law of imitation operates, and non-conformity is not an outstanding characteristic of children." * * *

The endorsement test is useful because of the analytic content it gives to the *Lemon*-mandated inquiry into legislative purpose and effect. In this country, church and state must necessarily operate within the same community. Because of this coexistence, it is inevitable that the secular interests of government and the religious interests of various sects and their adherents will frequently intersect, conflict, and combine. A statute that ostensibly promotes a secular interest often has an incidental or even a primary effect of helping or hindering a sectarian belief. Chaos would ensue if every such statute were invalid under the Establishment Clause. For example, the State could not criminalize murder for fear that it would thereby promote the Biblical command against killing.[b] The task for the Court is to sort out those statutes and government practices whose purpose and effect go against the grain of religious liberty protected by the First Amendment.

The endorsement test does not preclude government from acknowledging religion or from taking religion into account in making law and policy. It does preclude government from conveying or attempting to convey a message that religion or a particular religious belief is favored or preferred. Such an endorsement infringes the religious liberty of the nonadherent, for "[w]hen the power, prestige and financial support of government is placed behind a particular religious belief, the indirect coercive pressure upon religious minorities to conform to the prevailing officially approved religion is plain." *Engel.* * * *

Twenty-five states permit or require public school teachers to have students observe a moment of silence in their classrooms. A few statutes provide that the moment of silence is for the purpose of meditation alone. The typical statute, however, calls for a moment of silence at the beginning of the schoolday during which students may meditate, pray, or reflect on the activities of the day. * * * Relying on this Court's decisions disapproving vocal prayer and Bible reading in the public schools, see *School Dist. v. Schempp,* 374 U.S. 203, 83 S.Ct. 1560, 10 L.Ed.2d 844 (1963); *Engel v. Vitale,* 370 U.S. 421, 82 S.Ct. 1261, 8 L.Ed.2d 601 (1962), the courts that have struck down the moment of silence statutes generally conclude that their purpose and effect are to encourage prayer in public schools.

The *Engel* and *Schempp* decisions are not dispositive on the constitutionality of moment of silence laws. In those cases, public school teachers and students led their classes in devotional exercises. In *Engel,* a New York statute required teachers to lead their classes in a vocal prayer.[c] The Court concluded that "it is no part of the business of government to compose official prayers for any group of the American people to recite as part of a religious program carried on by the

---

b. On this analysis, *McGowan v. Maryland,* 366 U.S. 420, 81 S.Ct. 1101, 6 L.Ed.2d 393 (1961), per Warren, C.J., held that the "present purpose and effect" of Maryland's Sunday Closing Laws were not religious and did not violate the establishment clause. Although "the original laws which dealt with Sunday labor were motivated by religious forces," the Court showed that secular emphases in language and interpretation have come about, that recent "legislation was supported by labor groups and trade associations," and that "secular justifications have been advanced for making Sunday a day of rest, a day when people may recover from the labors of the week just passed and may physically and mentally prepare for the week's work to come. [It] would

seem unrealistic for enforcement purposes and perhaps detrimental to the general welfare to require a State to choose a common day of rest other than that which most persons would select of their own accord."

Douglas, J., dissented: "No matter how much is written, no matter what is said," Sunday is a Christian holiday. "There is an 'establishment' of religion in the constitutional sense if any practice of any religious group has the sanction of law behind it."

c. The prayer, composed by the N.Y. Board of Regents, provided: "Almighty God, we acknowledge our dependence upon Thee, and we beg Thy blessings upon us, our parents, our teachers and our country."

government." [d]   In *Schempp,* the Court addressed Pennsylvania and Maryland statutes that authorized morning Bible readings in public schools.[e]   The Court reviewed the purpose and effect of the statutes, concluded that they required religious exercises, and therefore found them to violate the Establishment Clause. Under all of these statutes, a student who did not share the religious beliefs expressed in the course of the exercise was left with the choice of participating, thereby compromising the nonadherent's beliefs, or withdrawing, thereby calling attention to his or her nonconformity.   The decisions acknowledged the coercion implicit under the statutory schemes, see *Engel,*[f] but they expressly turned only on the fact that the government was sponsoring a manifestly religious exercise.[g]

A state-sponsored moment of silence in the public schools is different from state-sponsored vocal prayer or Bible reading.   First, a moment of silence is not inherently religious.   Silence, unlike prayer or Bible reading, need not be associated with a religious exercise.   Second, a pupil who participates in a moment of silence need not compromise his or her beliefs.   During a moment of silence, a student who objects to prayer is left to his or her own thoughts, and is not compelled to listen to the prayers or thoughts of others.   [It] is difficult to discern a serious threat to religious liberty from a room of silent, thoughtful schoolchildren.

By mandating a moment of silence, a State does not necessarily endorse any activity that might occur during the period.   Even if a statute specifies that a student may choose to pray silently during a quiet moment, the State has not thereby encouraged prayer over other specified alternatives.   Nonetheless, it is also possible that a moment of silence statute, either as drafted or as actually implemented, could effectively favor the child who prays over the child who does not.   For example, the message of endorsement would seem inescapable if the teacher exhorts children to use the designated time to pray.   Similarly, the fact of the statute or its legislative history may clearly establish that it seeks to encourage or promote voluntary prayer over other alternatives, rather than merely provide a quiet moment that may be dedicated to prayer by those so inclined. The crucial question is whether the State has conveyed or attempted to convey the message that children should use the moment of silence for prayer.[2]   This

---

d.   Stewart, J., dissented.   Frankfurter and White, JJ., did not participate.

e.   The reading of the Bible, without comment, was followed by recitation of the Lord's Prayer.   In Pennsylvania, various students read passages they selected from any version of the Bible.   Plaintiff father testified that "specific religious doctrines purveyed by a literal reading of the Bible" were contrary to the family's Unitarian religious beliefs; one expert testified that "portions of the New Testament were offensive to Jewish tradition" and, if "read without explanation, they could [be] psychologically harmful to the child and had caused a divisive force within the social media of the school"; a defense expert testified "that the Bible [was] non-sectarian within the Christian faiths."

Stewart, J., dissented.

f.   See fn. 51 in the Court's opinion, supra.

g.   *Engel* distinguished "the fact that school children and others are officially encouraged to express love for our country by reciting histori-

cal documents such as the Declaration of Independence which contain references to the Deity or by singing officially espoused anthems which include the composer's professions of faith in a Supreme Being, or with the fact that there are many manifestations in our public life of belief in God.   Such patriotic or ceremonial occasions bear no true resemblance to the unquestioned religious exercise that the State of New York has sponsored in this instance."

2.   Appellants argue that *Zorach v. Clauson,* [note 1(b) infra,] suggests there is no constitutional infirmity in a State's encouraging a child to pray during a moment of silence.   [There] the Court stated that "[w]hen the state encourages religious instruction—*[by] adjusting the schedule of public events to sectarian needs,* it follows the best of our traditions."   When the State provides a moment of silence during which prayer may occur at the election of the student, it can be said to be adjusting the schedule of public events to sectarian needs. But when the State also encourages the student to pray during a moment of silence, it

question cannot be answered in the abstract, but instead requires courts to examine the history, language, and administration of a particular statute to determine whether it operates as an endorsement of religion.

Before reviewing Alabama's moment of silence law to determine whether it endorses prayer, some general observations on the proper scope of the inquiry are in order. First, the inquiry into the purpose of the legislature in enacting a moment of silence law should be deferential and limited. In determining whether the government intends a moment of silence statute to convey a message of endorsement or disapproval of religion, a court has no license to psychoanalyze the legislators. If a legislature expresses a plausible secular purpose for a moment of silence statute in either the text or the legislative history, or if the statute disclaims an intent to encourage prayer over alternatives during a moment of silence, then courts should generally defer to that stated intent. It is particularly troublesome to denigrate an expressed secular purpose due to postenactment testimony by particular legislators or by interested persons who witnessed the drafting of the statute.[h] Even if the text and official history of a statute express no secular purpose, the statute should be held to have an improper purpose only if it is beyond purview that endorsement of religion or a religious belief "was and is the law's reason for existence." *Epperson v. Arkansas,* [note 3(b) infra]. Since there is arguably a secular pedagogical value to a moment of silence in public schools, courts should find an improper purpose behind such a statute only if the statute on its face, in its official legislative history, or in its interpretation by a responsible administrative agency suggests it has the primary purpose of endorsing prayer.

[It] is not a trivial matter [to] require that the legislature manifest a secular purpose and omit all sectarian endorsements from its laws. That requirement is precisely tailored to the Establishment Clause's purpose of assuring that government not intentionally endorse religion or a religious practice. It is of course possible that a legislature will enunciate a sham secular purpose for a statute. I have little doubt that our courts are capable of distinguishing a sham secular purpose from a sincere one, or that the *Lemon* inquiry into the effect of an enactment would help decide those close cases where the validity of an expressed secular purpose is in doubt. * * *

Second, the *Lynch* concurrence suggested that the effect of a moment of silence law is not entirely a question of [fact]. The relevant issue is whether an objective observer, acquainted with the text, legislative history, and implementation of the statute, would perceive it as a state endorsement of prayer in public schools. A moment of silence law that is clearly drafted and implemented so as to permit prayer, meditation, and reflection within the prescribed period, without endorsing one alternative over the others, should pass this test.

The analysis above suggests that moment of silence laws in many States should pass Establishment Clause scrutiny because they do not favor the child who chooses to pray during a moment of silence over the child who chooses to meditate or reflect. § 16–1–20.1 does not stand on the same footing. However deferentially one examines its text and legislative history, however objectively one views the message attempted to be conveyed to the public, the conclusion is

---

converts an otherwise inoffensive moment of silence into an effort by the majority to use the machinery of the State to encourage the minority to participate in a religious exercise.

h. For further discussion of this point, see Burger, C.J.'s opinion infra.

unavoidable that the purpose of the statute is to endorse prayer in public [schools.] [5] * * * i

CHIEF JUSTICE BURGER dissenting.

* * * Today's decision recalls the observations of Justice Goldberg: "[U]ntutored devotion to the concept of neutrality can lead to invocation or approval of results which partake not simply of that noninterference and noninvolvement with the religious which the Constitution commands, but of a brooding and pervasive dedication to the secular and a passive, or even active, hostility to the religious. Such results are not only not compelled by the Constitution, but, it seems to me, are prohibited by it." *Schempp* (concurring opinion). * * *

Curiously, the opinions do not mention that *all* of the sponsor's statements relied upon—including the statement "inserted" into the Senate Journal—were made *after* the legislature had passed the statute; [there] is not a shred of evidence that the legislature as a whole shared the sponsor's motive or that a majority in either house was even aware of the sponsor's view of the bill when it was passed. The sole relevance of the sponsor's statements, therefore, is that they reflect the personal, subjective motives of a single legislator. No case in the 195–year history of this Court supports the disconcerting idea that post-enactment statements by individual legislators are relevant in determining the constitutionality of legislation.

Even if an individual legislator's after-the-fact statements could rationally be considered relevant, all of the opinions fail to mention that the sponsor also testified that one of his purposes in drafting and sponsoring the moment-of-silence bill was to clear up a widespread misunderstanding that a schoolchild is legally *prohibited* from engaging in silent, individual prayer once he steps inside a public school building. That testimony is at least as important as the statements the Court relies upon, and surely that testimony manifests a permissible purpose. * * *

The several preceding opinions conclude that the principal difference between § 16–1–20.1 and its predecessor statute proves that the sole purpose behind the inclusion of the phrase "or voluntary prayer" in § 16–1–20.1 was to endorse and promote prayer. This reasoning is simply a subtle way of focusing exclusively on the religious component of the statute rather than examining the statute as a whole. Such logic—if it can be called that—would lead the Court to hold, for example, that a state may enact a statute that provides reimbursement for bus transportation to the parents of all schoolchildren, but may not *add* parents of parochial school students to an existing program providing reimbursement for parents of public school students. Congress amended the statutory Pledge of Allegiance 31 years ago to add the words "under God." Do the several opinions in support of the judgment today render the Pledge unconstitutional? [3]

---

5. The Chief Justice suggests that one consequence of the Court's emphasis on the difference between § 16–1–20.1 and its predecessor statute might be to render the Pledge of Allegiance unconstitutional because Congress amended it in 1954 to add the words "under God". I disagree. In my view, the words "under God" in the Pledge serve as an acknowledgement of religion with "the legitimate secular purposes of solemnizing public occasions, [and] expressing confidence in the future." *Lynch* (concurring opinion).

i. Powell, J., who was the fifth justice to join the Court's opinion, also separately concurred, agreeing "fully with Justice O'Connor's assertion that some moment-of-silence statutes may be constitutional, a suggestion set forth in the Court's opinion as well."

3. The House Report on the legislation amending the Pledge states that the purpose of the amendment was to affirm the principle that "our people and our Government [are dependent] upon the moral directions of the Creator." If this is simply "acknowledge-

* * * Without pressuring those who do not wish to pray, the statute simply creates an opportunity to think, to plan, or to pray if one wishes—as Congress does by providing chaplains and chapels. [The] statute "endorses" only the view that the religious observances of others should be tolerated and where possible, accommodated. If the government may not accommodate religious needs when it does so in a wholly neutral and noncoercive manner, the "benevolent neutrality" that we have long considered the correct constitutional standard will quickly translate into the "callous indifference" that the Court has consistently held the Establishment Clause does not require. * * *

JUSTICE REHNQUIST, dissenting.

[The historical evidence shows] that the Establishment Clause [forbade] establishment of a national religion, and forbade preference among religious sects or denominations. [It] did not require government neutrality between religion and irreligion nor did it prohibit the Federal Government from providing nondiscriminatory aid to religion. There is simply no historical foundation for the proposition that the Framers intended to build the "wall of separation" that was constitutionalized in *Everson*.

[I]n the 38 years since *Everson* our Establishment Clause cases have been neither principled nor unified. [The "purpose and effect" tests] have the same historical deficiencies as the wall concept itself: they are in no way based on either the language or intent of the drafters.

The secular purpose prong has proven mercurial in application because it has never been fully defined, and we have never fully stated how the test is to operate. If the purpose prong is intended to void those aids to sectarian institutions accompanied by a stated legislative purpose to aid religion, the prong will condemn nothing so long as the legislature utters a secular purpose and says nothing about aiding religion. Thus the constitutionality of a statute may depend upon what the legislators put into the legislative history and, more importantly, what they leave out. * * *

However, if the purpose prong is aimed to void all statutes enacted with the intent to aid sectarian institutions, whether stated or not, then most statutes providing any aid, such as textbooks or bus rides for sectarian school children, will fail because one of the purposes behind every statute, whether stated or not, is to aid the target of its largesse. * * *

If a constitutional theory has no basis in the history of the amendment it seeks to interpret, is difficult to apply and yields unprincipled results, I see little use in it. [It] would come as much of a shock to those who drafted the Bill of Rights as it will to a large number of thoughtful Americans today to learn that the Constitution, as construed by the majority, prohibits the Alabama Legislature from "endorsing" prayer. George Washington himself, at the request of the very Congress which passed the Bill of Rights, proclaimed a day of "public thanksgiving and prayer, to be observed by acknowledging with grateful hearts the many and signal favors of Almighty God." History must judge whether it was the

---

ment," not "endorsement," of religion, (O'Connor, J., concurring in the judgment), the distinction is far too infinitesimal for me to grasp.

[Compare Jefferson B. Fordham, *The Implications of the Supreme Court Decisions Dealing with Religious Practices in the Public Schools*, 6 J. of Chur. & St. 44, 56 (1964): "In view of the patriotic element here, one may suggest that the likelihood of indirect compulsion is much greater than in the simple prayer case. Here the individual dissenter is made to stand out as one unwilling to engage in a patriotic act and recital. Does this not overbalance the countervailing consideration that the prime purpose is promotion of patriotism and the religious element is secondary?"]

Father of his Country in 1789, or a majority of the Court today, which has strayed from the meaning of the Establishment Clause. * * * j

Notes and Questions

1. *Released time.* (a) McCOLLUM v. BOARD OF EDUC., 333 U.S. 203, 68 S.Ct. 461, 92 L.Ed. 649 (1948), per BLACK, J., held that a Champaign, Illinois public school released time program violated the establishment clause. Privately employed religious teachers held weekly classes, on public school premises, in their respective religions, for students whose parents signed request cards, while non-attending students pursued secular studies in other parts of the building. "Here not only are the state's tax-supported public school buildings used for the dissemination of religious doctrines. The State also affords sectarian groups an invaluable aid in that it helps to provide pupils for their religious classes through use of the state's compulsory public school machinery." [a]

(b) ZORACH v. CLAUSON, 343 U.S. 306, 72 S.Ct. 679, 96 L.Ed. 954 (1952), per DOUGLAS, J., upheld a New York City released time program in which the religious classes were held in church buildings: "[This] program involves neither religious instruction in public school classrooms nor the expenditure of public funds. All costs, including the application blanks, are paid by the religious organizations. The case is therefore unlike *McCollum.*

"[The] nullification of this law would have wide and profound effects. A Catholic student applies to his teacher for permission to leave the school during hours on a Holy Day of Obligation to attend a mass. A Jewish student asks his teacher for permission to be excused for Yom Kippur. A Protestant wants the afternoon off for a family baptismal ceremony. In each case the teacher requires parental consent in writing. In each case the teacher, in order to make sure the student is not a truant, goes further and requires a report from the priest, the rabbi, or the minister. The teacher in other words cooperates in a religious program to the extent of making it possible for her students to participate in it. Whether she does it occasionally for a few students, regularly for one, or pursuant to a systematized program designed to further the religious needs of all the students does not alter the character of the act.

"We are a religious people whose institutions presuppose a Supreme Being. We guarantee the freedom to worship as one chooses. [When] the state encourages religious instruction or cooperates with religious authorities by adjusting the schedule of public events to sectarian needs, [it] respects the religious nature of our people and accommodates the public service to their spiritual needs. To hold that it may not would be to find in the Constitution a requirement that the government show a callous indifference to religious groups. That would be preferring those who believe in no religion over those who do believe. [The] problem, like many problems in constitutional law, is one of degree."

JACKSON, J., dissented: "If public education were taking so much of the pupils' time as to injure the public or the students' welfare by encroaching upon their religious opportunity, simply shortening everyone's school day would facilitate

---

j. White, J., also dissented, "for the most part agreeing with the opinion of [Burger, C.J.]," and, noting that in light of Rehnquist, J.'s "explication of the history of the religion clauses, [it] would be quite understandable if we undertook to reassess our cases dealing with these clauses, particularly [the] Establishment Clause."

In *Rosenberger v. University of Virginia,* Sec. 1, II infra, Thomas, J., noted that he found "much to commend [the] view that the Framers saw the Establishment Clause simply as a prohibition on governmental preferences for some religious faiths over others."

a. Frankfurter and Jackson, JJ., each filed concurrences. Reed, J., dissented.

voluntary and optional attendance at Church classes. But that suggestion is rejected upon the ground that if they are made free many students will not go to the Church. [Here] schooling is more or less suspended during the 'released time' so the nonreligious attendants will not forge ahead of the churchgoing absentees. But it serves as a temporary jail for a pupil who will not go to Church. It takes more subtlety of mind than I possess to deny that this is governmental constraint in support of religion." [b]

(c) *Cost.* Can *Zorach* be reconciled with *McCollum* on the ground that the *McCollum* plan involved a significantly greater cost to the public? Brennan, J., has distinguished the cases "not [because] of the difference in public expenditures involved. True, the *McCollum* program involved the regular use of school facilities, classrooms, heat and light and time from the regular school day—even though the actual incremental cost may have been negligible. [But the] deeper difference was that the *McCollum* program placed the religious instructor in the public school classroom in precisely the position of authority held by the regular teachers of secular subjects, while the *Zorach* program did not. The *McCollum* program, in lending to the support of sectarian instruction all the authority of the governmentally operated public school system, brought government and religion into that proximity which the Establishment Clause forbids." *Schempp* (concurring opinion).

(d) *Coercion.* *Zorach* found "no evidence [that] the system involves the use of coercion to get public school students into religious classrooms. [If] it were established that any one or more teachers were using their office to persuade or force students to take the religious instruction, a wholly different case would be presented."' Would the *Zorach* plan be inherently coercive, and therefore unconstitutional, if it were shown that most children found religious instruction more appealing than remaining in the public schools? Even if the alternative for those remaining was secular instruction with academic credit? If so, would it be permissible to excuse children from classes to enable them to attend special religious services of their faith? Would the first amendment forbid attendance at parochial schools, as an alternative to public schools, on the ground that this was simply one hundred per cent released time?

Under this analysis, would a program of "dismissed time" as described by Jackson, J., in *Zorach* (all children released early permitting those who so wish to attend religious schools) be unconstitutional? Would "dismissed time" be nonetheless invalid if it could be shown that the *purpose* for the early school closing was to facilitate religious education? Or is this merely an accommodation "adjusting the schedule of public events to sectarian needs"?

What of the argument that the *Zorach* program is inherently coercive, and therefore unconstitutional, because, as Frankfurter, J., contended in *McCollum*, "the law of imitation operates" placing "an obvious pressure upon children to attend" religious classes? Under this analysis, what result in the case of excusing students to attend a religious service? In the case of parochial schools? In the case of "dismissed time"? Do you agree with Jackson, J.'s assertion in *McCollum*

---

b. Black and Frankfurter, JJ., also filed separate dissents.

For a description of the interaction of the justices in fashioning the *Everson, McCollum* and *Zorach* opinions, see Note, *The "Released Time" Cases Revisited: A Study of Group Decisionmaking by the Supreme Court,* 83 Yale L.J. 1202 (1974).

7. [The] only allegation in the complaint that bears on the issue is that the operation of the program "has resulted and inevitably results in the exercise of pressure and coercion upon parents and children to secure attendance by the children for religious instruction." But this charge does not even implicate the school authorities. * * *

that "it may be doubted whether the Constitution [protects] one from the embarrassment that always attends nonconformity, whether in religion, politics, behavior or dress"?

(e) *Use of public property.* Is the use of public school classrooms for religious purposes during nonschool hours distinguishable from *McCollum?* Consider Tribe *Treatise* 1175: "Religious instructors will no longer stand in 'the position of authority held by the regular teachers,' because the activities lie outside the mandatory school day. Although coercion is conceivable, it is not inherent, as it probably is with official school prayer; students who do not want to take part in the religious activities may take part in other activities or leave the campus. No symbolic mingling of church and state functions takes place, so long as access to the campus is entirely independent of the religious or other content of the meetings. Thus, the state neither lends power to religion, nor borrows legitimacy from religion. Permitting a religious group to use school facilities during nonschool hours, accordingly, conveys no message of endorsement."

2. *School prayer and the relevance of coercion.* (a) Should *Engel* and *Schempp* (and *McCollum*) have been explicitly based on "the coercion implicit under the statutory schemes"? Consider Stewart, J., dissenting in *Schempp:* "[T]he duty laid upon government in connection with religious exercises in the public schools is that of refraining from so structuring the school environment as to put any kind of pressure on a child to participate in those exercises; it is not that of providing an atmosphere in which children are kept scrupulously insulated from any awareness that some of their fellows may want to open the school day with prayer, or of the fact that there exist in our pluralistic society differences of religious belief.[c] [A] law which provided for religious exercises during the school day and which contained no excusal provision would obviously be unconstitutionally coercive upon those who did not wish to participate. And even under a law containing an excusal provision, if the exercises were held during the school day, and no equally desirable alternative were provided by the school authorities, the likelihood that children might be under at least some psychological compulsion to participate would be great. [Here,] the record shows no more than a subjective prophecy by a parent of what he thought would happen if a request were made to be excused from participation in the exercises under the amended statute. [It] is conceivable that these school boards, or even all school boards, might eventually find it impossible to administer a system of religious exercises during school hours in such a way as to meet this constitutional standard—in such a way as completely to free from any kind of official coercion those who do not affirmatively

---

c. Consider Erwin N. Griswold, *Absolute is in the Dark—A Discussion of the Approach of the Supreme Court to Constitutional Questions,* 8 Utah L.Rev. 167, 177, (1963): "When the prayer is recited, if [a] child or his parents feel that he cannot participate, he may stand or sit, in respectful attention, while the other children take part in the ceremony. Or he may leave the room. It is said that this is bad, because it sets him apart from other children. It is even said that there is an element of compulsion in this. [But] is this the way it should be looked at? The child of a nonconforming or minority group is, to be sure, different in his beliefs. That is what it means to be a member of a minority. Is it not desirable, and educational, for him to learn and observe this, in the atmosphere of the school—not so

much that he is different, as that other children are different from him? And is it not desirable that, at the same time, he experiences and learns the fact that his difference is tolerated and accepted? No compulsion is put upon him. He need not participate. But he, too, has the opportunity to be tolerant. He allows the majority of the group to follow their own tradition, perhaps coming to understand and to respect what they feel is significant to them." See also Arthur E. Sutherland, *Establishment According to Engel,* 76 Harv.L.Rev. 25 (1962); Philip B. Kurland, *The Regents' Prayer Case: "Full of Sound and Fury, Signifying * * *,"* 1962 Sup.Ct.Rev. 1; Ernest J. Brown, *Ouis Custodiet Ipsos Custodes?—The School Prayer Cases,* 1963 Sup.Ct.Rev. 1.

want to participate.[8] But I think we must not assume that school boards so lack the qualities of inventiveness and good will as to make impossible the achievement of that goal."

What evidence of coercion does Stewart, J. require? That the objectors first ask to be excused from participation and then show that social pressures were brought to bear on them? Would this force an objector to surrender his rights in order to vindicate them? Or would Stewart, J., accept the testimony of social scientists that the program was coercive? Could this be judicially noticed? Or would he require a showing that these particular objectors were coerced? Were likely to be coerced? If so, is this a desirable test?

(b) *Establishment vs. free exercise.* If the decisions *should* turn on the element of coercion, would it have been preferable to base them on "the narrower ground of freedom of religion or of conscience, explaining why the considerations advanced in support of the prayer were outweighed by the rights of the objectors, and why under the circumstances the feature of voluntary participation did not sufficiently protect the interests of objectors"? Paul Kauper, *Prayer, Public Schools and the Supreme Court,* 61 Mich.L.Rev. 1031, 1065–66 (1963). Would this analysis permit prayer in an elementary school where every child was willing to participate? In *any* high school? Consider Louis Pollak, *Public Prayers in Public Schools,* 77 Harv.L.Rev. 62, 70 (1963): "[T]o have pitched the decision [on the free exercise clause] would presumably have meant that the prayer programs were constitutionally unobjectionable unless and until challenged, and, therefore, that school boards would have been under no discernible legal obligation, as assuredly they now are, to suspend ongoing prayer programs on their own initiative. [Indeed,] the hypothetical schoolchild plaintiff, whose free exercise rights would thus be enforced, would have to be a child with the gumption not only to disassociate himself from the prayer program but to prefer litigation to the relatively expeditious exit procedure contemplated by the excusal proviso."

3. *Secular purpose.* Several decisions, in addition to *Jaffree,* have invalidated public school practices because their "purpose" has been found to be "religious":

(a) STONE v. GRAHAM, 449 U.S. 39, 101 S.Ct. 192, 66 L.Ed.2d 199 (1980), per curiam held that a Kentucky statute—requiring "the posting of a copy of the Ten Commandments, purchased with private contributions, on the wall of each public classroom in the State," with the notation at the bottom that "The secular application of the Ten Commandments is clearly seen in its adoption as the fundamental legal code of Western Civilization and the Common Law of the United States"—had "no secular legislative purpose": "The Ten Commandments is undeniably a sacred text in the Jewish and Christian faiths, and no legislative recitation of a supposed secular purpose can blind us to that [fact]. Posting of religious texts on the wall serves [no] educational function. If the posted copies of the Ten Commandments are to have any effect at all, it will be to induce the school children to read, meditate upon, perhaps to venerate and obey, the Commandments. However desirable this might be as a matter of private devotion, it is not a permissible state objective under the Establishment Clause."

8. For example, if the [record] contained proof (rather than mere prophecy) that the timing of morning announcements by the school was such as to handicap children who did not want to listen to the Bible reading, or that the excusal provision was so administered as to carry any overtones of social inferiority, then impermissible coercion would clearly exist.

REHNQUIST, J., dissented: "The Court's summary rejection of a secular purpose articulated by the legislature and confirmed by the state court is without precedent in Establishment Clause jurisprudence. [This] Court has recognized that 'religion has been closely identified with our history and government,' *Schempp*, and that 'the history of man is inseparable from the history of religion,' *Engel*. Kentucky has decided to make students aware of this fact by demonstrating the secular impact of the Ten Commandments." [a]

(b) EPPERSON v. ARKANSAS, 393 U.S. 97, 89 S.Ct. 266, 21 L.Ed.2d 228 (1968), per FORTAS, J., held that an "anti-evolution" statute, forbidding teachers in public schools "to teach the theory or doctrine that mankind ascended or descended from a lower order of animals," violated "the First Amendment's prohibition of laws respecting an establishment of religion or prohibiting the free exercise thereof": "Arkansas' law selects from the body of knowledge a particular segment which it proscribes for the sole reason that it is deemed to conflict with a particular religious doctrine." Citing newspaper advertisements and letters supporting adoption of the statute in 1928, the Court found it "clear that fundamentalist sectarian conviction was and is the law's reason for existence. Its antecedent, Tennessee's 'monkey law,' candidly stated" a religious purpose. "Perhaps the sensational publicity attendant upon the *Scopes* trial induced Arkansas to adopt less explicit language [but] there is no doubt that the motivation for the law was the same * * *. Arkansas' law cannot be defended as an act of religious neutrality. Arkansas did not seek to excise from the curricula of its schools and universities all discussion of the origin of man."

BLACK, J., concurring on the ground of "vagueness," found the first amendment questions "troublesome": "Since there is no indication that the literal Biblical doctrine of the origin of man is included in the curriculum of Arkansas schools, does not the removal of the subject of evolution leave the State in a neutral position toward these supposedly competing religious and anti-religious doctrines? [It] is plain that a state law prohibiting all teaching of human development or biology is constitutionally quite different from a law that compels a teacher to teach as true only one theory of a given doctrine. It would be difficult to make a First Amendment case out of a state law eliminating the subject of higher mathematics, or astronomy, or biology from its curriculum. [T]here is no reason I can imagine why a State is without power to withdraw from its curriculum any subject deemed too emotional and controversial for its public schools." [b]

(c) EDWARDS v. AGUILLARD, 482 U.S. 578, 107 S.Ct. 2573, 96 L.Ed.2d 510 (1987), per BRENNAN, J., held that a Louisiana statute, which forebade "the teaching of the theory of evolution in public schools unless accompanied by instruction in 'creation science,'" had "no clear secular purpose": "True, the Act's stated purpose is to protect academic freedom. [While] the Court is normally deferential to a State's articulation of a secular purpose, it is required that the statement of such purpose be sincere and not a sham. See *Jaffree; Stone v. Graham; Schempp*. [It] is clear from the legislative history [that] requiring schools to teach creation science with evolution does not advance academic freedom. The Act does not grant teachers a flexibility that they did not already possess to supplement the present science curriculum with the presentation of theories, besides evolution, about the origin of life. [While] requiring that

---

a. Stewart, J., also dissented. Burger, C.J., and Blackmun, J., dissented from not giving the case plenary consideration.

b. Harlan, J., concurred in the Court's "establishment of religion" rationale. Stewart, J., concurred on the ground of vagueness.

curriculum guides be developed for creation science, the Act says nothing of comparable guides for evolution. [The] Act forbids school boards to discriminate against anyone who 'chooses to be a creation-scientist' or to teach 'creationism,' but fails to protect those who choose to teach evolution or any other non-creation science theory, or who refuse to teach creation science.

"If the Louisiana legislature's purpose was solely to maximize the comprehensiveness and effectiveness of science instruction, it would have encouraged the teaching of all scientific theories about the origins of humankind. But [the] legislative history documents that the Act's primary purpose was to change the science curriculum of public schools in order to provide persuasive advantage to a particular religious doctrine that rejects the factual basis of evolution in its entirety [and that] embodies the religious belief that a supernatural creator was responsible for the creation of humankind. * * *

"We do not imply that a legislature could never require that scientific critiques of prevailing scientific theories be taught. [T]eaching a variety of scientific theories about the origins of humankind to school children might be validly done with the clear secular intent of enhancing the effectiveness of science instruction. But because the primary purpose of the Creationism Act is to endorse a particular religious doctrine, the Act furthers religion in violation of the Establishment Clause." [a]

SCALIA, J., joined by Rehnquist, C.J., dissented: "Even if I agreed with the questionable premise that legislation can be invalidated under the Establishment Clause on the basis of its motivation alone, without regard to its effects, I would still find no justification for today's decision. [The] Louisiana Legislature explicitly set forth its secular purpose ('protecting academic freedom') [which] meant: *students'* freedom from *indoctrination*. The legislature wanted to ensure that students would be free to decide for themselves how life began, based upon a fair and balanced presentation of the scientific evidence. [The] legislature did not care *whether* the topic of origins was taught; it simply wished to ensure that *when* the topic was taught, [it] be 'taught as a theory, rather than as proven scientific fact' and that scientific evidence inconsistent with the theory of evolution (viz., 'creation science') be taught as well. Living up to its title of '*Balanced Treatment for Creation–Science and Evolution–Science Act*,' it treats the teaching of creation the same way. It does *not* mandate instruction in creation science; *forbids* teachers to present creation science 'as proven scientific fact'; and *bans* the teaching of creation science unless the theory [is] 'discredit[ed] at every turn' with the teaching of evolution. It surpasses understanding how the Court can see in this a purpose 'to restructure the science curriculum to conform with a particular religious viewpoint,' 'to provide a persuasive advantage to a particular religious doctrine,' 'to promote the theory of creation science which embodies a particular religious tenet,' and 'to endorse a particular religious doctrine.'

"[The] Louisiana legislators had been told repeatedly that creation scientists were scorned by most educators and scientists, who themselves had an almost religious faith in evolution. It is hardly surprising, then, that in seeking to achieve a balanced, 'nonindoctrinating' curriculum, the legislators protected from discrimination only those teachers whom they thought were *suffering* from discrimination. [The] two provisions respecting the development of curriculum

a. Powell, J., joined by O'Connor, J., joined the Court's opinion but wrote separately "to emphasize that nothing in the Court's opinion diminishes the traditionally broad discretion accorded state and local school officials in the selection of the public school curriculum." White, J., concurred only in the judgment, with which he agreed "unless [we] are to reconsider the Court's decisions interpreting the Establishment Clause."

guides are also consistent with 'academic freedom' as the Louisiana Legislature understood the term. [In] light of the unavailability of works on creation science suitable for classroom use (a fact appellees concede) and the existence of ample materials on evolution, it was entirely reasonable for the Legislature to conclude that science teachers attempting to implement the Act would need a curriculum guide on creation science, but not on evolution. [Thus,] the provisions of the Act of so much concern to the Court *support* the conclusion that the Legislature acted to advance 'academic freedom.' * * *

"It is undoubtedly true that what prompted the Legislature to direct its attention to the misrepresentation of evolution in the schools (rather than the inaccurate presentation of other topics) was its awareness of the tension between evolution and the religious beliefs of many children. But even appellees concede that a valid secular purpose is not rendered impermissible simply because its pursuit is prompted by concern for religious sensitivities. [I] am astonished by the Court's unprecedented readiness to [disbelieve] the secular purpose set forth in the Act [and to conclude] that it is a sham enacted to conceal the legislators' violation of their oaths of office. [I] can only attribute [this] to an intellectual predisposition [and] an instinctive reaction that any governmentally imposed requirements bearing upon the teaching of evolution must be a manifestation of Christian fundamentalist repression. In this case, however, it seems to me the Court's position is the repressive one. The people of Louisiana, including those who are Christian fundamentalists, are quite entitled, as a secular matter, to have whatever scientific evidence there may be against evolution presented in their schools, just as Mr. Scopes was entitled to present whatever scientific evidence there was for it. Perhaps what the Louisiana Legislature has done is unconstitutional because there *is* no such evidence, and the scheme they have established will amount to no more than a presentation of the Book of Genesis. But we cannot say that on the evidence before us in this summary judgment context, which includes ample uncontradicted testimony that 'creation science' is a body of scientific knowledge rather than revealed belief.[b] *Infinitely less* can we say (or should we say) that the scientific evidence for evolution is so conclusive that no one could be gullible enough to believe that there is any real scientific evidence to the contrary, so that the legislation's stated purpose must be a lie. Yet that illiberal judgment, that *Scopes*-in-reverse, is ultimately the basis on which the Court's facile rejection of the Louisiana Legislature's purpose must rest. * * *

"I have to this point assumed the validity of the *Lemon* 'purpose' test. In fact, however, I think [it] is 'a constitutional theory [that] has no basis in the history of the amendment it seeks to interpret, is difficult to apply and yields unprincipled results.' *Jaffree* (Rehnquist, J., dissenting).

"[D]iscerning the subjective motivation of those enacting the statute is, to be honest, almost always an impossible task. The number of possible motivations, to begin with, is not binary, or indeed even finite. In the present case, for example, a particular legislator need not have voted for the Act either because he wanted to foster religion or because he wanted to improve education. He may have thought the bill would provide jobs for his district, or may have wanted to make amends with a faction of his party he had alienated on another vote, or he may have been a close friend of the bill's sponsor, or he may have been repaying a favor he owed

---

b. "The only evidence in the record [defining] 'creation science' is found in five affidavits filed by appellants. In those affidavits, two scientists, a philosopher, a theologian, and an educator, all of whom claim extensive knowl- edge of creation science, swear that it is essentially a collection of scientific data supporting the theory that the physical universe and life within it appeared suddenly and have not changed substantially since appearing.''

the Majority Leader, or he may have hoped the Governor would appreciate his vote and make a fundraising appearance for him, or he may have been pressured to vote for a bill he disliked by a wealthy contributor or by a flood of constituent mail, or he may have been seeking favorable publicity, or he may have been reluctant to hurt the feelings of a loyal staff member who worked on the bill, or he may have been settling an old score with a legislator who opposed the bill, or he may have been mad at his wife who opposed the bill, or he may have been intoxicated and utterly *un*motivated when the vote was called, or he may have accidentally voted 'yes' instead of 'no,' or, of course, he may have had (and very likely did have) a combination of some of the above and many other motivations. To look for *the sole purpose* of even a single legislator is probably to look for something that does not exist."

(d) Is it meaningful to distinguish between *secular* vs. *religious* purposes? Consider Phillip E. Johnson, *Concepts and Compromise in First Amendment Religious Doctrine,* 72 Calif.L.Rev. 817, 827 (1984): "Governments usually act out of secular motives, even when they are directly aiding a particular religious sect. An atheistic ruler might well create an established church because he thinks it a useful way of raising money, or of ensuring that the clergy do not preach seditious doctrines. In democratic societies, elected officials have an excellent secular reason to accommodate (or at least to avoid offending) groups and individuals who are religious, as well as groups and individuals who are not. They wish to be re-elected, and they do not want important groups to feel that the community does not honor their values."

(e) If the "purpose" of government action is found to be "religious," *should* that alone be enough to invalidate it under the establishment clause? If so, what result in *Zorach?* For a public school "dismissed time" program implemented to facilitate religious education?[c] Consider Tribe *Treatise* 1211: "The secular purpose requirement, partly because of its sketchy parameters, could raise two particularly important conceptual problems in application. First, it might be used to strike down laws whose effects are utterly secular. A legislature might, for example, vote to increase welfare benefits because individual legislators feel religiously compelled to do so. So too, when a legislature passes a neutral moment-of-silence statute, many legislators may hope that students will use the time for prayer. However improper these purposes may be, it is hard to see a meaningful establishment clause problem so long as the statute's effects are completely secular. A visible religious purpose may independently convey a message of endorsement or exclusion, but such a message, standing alone, should rarely if ever suffice to transform a secular action into an establishment clause violation. A religious message may be conveyed by the legislative debates concerning a bill, but the same result is possible from debates that lead to no legislation; it can hardly be said that the debates themselves establish a religion."

Compare Norman Redlich, *Separation of Church and State: The Burger Court's Tortuous Journey,* 60 Not.D.L.Rev. 1094, 1136 (1985): "When the state encourages silent prayer, it endorses a practice that is unacceptable to those whose faith requires that they pray only in a place of worship, or before some religious symbol. Some faiths may forbid praying with members of another faith, or with the opposite sex; some require believers to stand, or face a certain direction, or sit down, or wear certain apparel, or be led by ordained spiritual leaders—the variables reflect the infinite capacity of the human spirit to worship

---

c. For use of this test to invalidate the "religiously motivated" Utah firing squad, see Martin R. Gardner, *Illicit Legislative Motiva-* *tion as a Sufficient Condition for Unconstitutionality Under the Establishment Clause,* 1979 Wash.U.L.Q. 435.

God in different ways. Any state expression of preference for prayer, whether vocal or silent, destroys the neutral position of the [state]. All prescribed moments of silence are highly suspect."

Contrast Jesse H. Choper, *The Religion Clauses of the First Amendment: Reconciling the Conflict,* 41 U.Pitt.L.Rev. 673, 686–87 (1980): "[I]t is only when religious purpose is coupled with threatened impairment of religious freedom that government action should be held to violate the Establishment Clause. [Conceding] that the [*Epperson*] statute had a solely religious purpose, [there] was no evidence that religious beliefs were either coerced, compromised or influenced. That is, it was not shown, nor do I believe that it could be persuasively argued, that the anti-evolution law either (1) induced children of fundamentalist religions to accept the biblical theory of creation, or (2) conditioned other children for conversion to fundamentalism. [Thus,] the accommodation for religion in [*Epperson*] should have survived the Establishment Clause challenge."

Similarly, "I would find that the creation science law had a religious purpose [to] placate those religious fundamentalists whose beliefs rejected the Darwinian theory of evolution. But, under my approach, so long as the theory of creation science is taught in an objective rather than a proselytizing fashion, it does not seem to me to pose a danger to religious liberty [and] should not be held to violate the Establishment Clause." Jesse H. Choper, *Church, State and the Supreme Court: Current Controversy,* 29 Ariz.L.Rev. 551, 557 (1987).

4. *Purpose, primary effect, and equal access.* BOARD OF EDUC. v. MERGENS, 496 U.S. 226, 110 S.Ct. 2356, 110 L.Ed.2d 191 (1990), interpreted the Equal Access Act, passed by Congress in 1984, to apply to public secondary schools that (a) receive federal financial assistance, and (b) give official recognition to noncurriculum related student groups (e.g., chess club and scuba diving club in contrast to Latin club and math club) in such ways as allowing them to meet on school premises during noninstructional time. The Act prohibited these schools from denying equal access to, or otherwise discriminating against, student groups "on the basis of the religious, political, philosophical, or other content of the speech at [their] meetings." O'CONNOR, J., joined by Rehnquist, C.J., and White and Blackmun, JJ., held that the establishment clause did not forbid Westside High School from including within its thirty recognized student groups a Christian club "to read and discuss the Bible, to have fellowship and to pray together": "In *Widmar v. Vincent,* 454 U.S. 263, 102 S.Ct. 269, 70 L.Ed.2d 440 (1981), we applied the three-part *Lemon* test to hold that an 'equal access' policy, at the university level, does not violate the Establishment Clause. We concluded that 'an open-forum policy, including nondiscrimination against religious speech, would have a secular purpose,' and would in fact *avoid* entanglement with religion. See id. ("[T]he University would risk greater 'entanglement' by attempting to enforce its exclusion of 'religious worship' and 'religious speech' "). We also found that although incidental benefits accrued to religious groups who used university facilities, this result did not amount to an establishment of religion. First, we stated that a university's forum does not 'confer any imprimatur of state approval on religious sects or practices.' Indeed, the message is one of neutrality rather than endorsement; if a State refused to let religious groups use facilities open to others, then it would demonstrate not neutrality but hostility toward religion. Second, we noted that '[t]he [University's] provision of benefits to [a] broad spectrum of groups'—both nonreligious and religious speakers—was 'an important index of secular effect.'

"We think the logic of *Widmar* applies with equal force to the Equal Access [Act.] Congress' avowed purpose—to prevent discrimination against religious and other types of speech—is undeniably secular. Even if some legislators were motivated by a conviction that religious speech in particular was valuable and worthy of protection, that alone would not invalidate the Act, because what is relevant is the legislative *purpose* of the statute, not the possibly religious *motives* of the legislators who enacted the law. Because the Act on its face grants equal access to both secular and religious speech, we think it clear that the Act's purpose was not to 'endorse or disapprove of religion,' *Jaffree* (O'Connor, J., concurring).

"Petitioners' principal contention is that the Act has the primary effect of advancing religion. Specifically, petitioners urge that, because the student religious meetings are held under school aegis, and because the state's compulsory attendance laws bring the students together (and thereby provide a ready-made audience for student evangelists), an objective observer in the position of a secondary school student will perceive official school support for such religious meetings.

"We disagree. First, [there] is a crucial difference between *government* speech endorsing religion, which the Establishment Clause forbids, and *private* speech endorsing religion, which the Free Speech and Free Exercise Clauses protect. We think that secondary school students are mature enough and are likely to understand that a school does not endorse or support student speech that it merely permits on a nondiscriminatory basis. * * *

"Second, we note that the Act expressly limits participation by school officials at meetings of student religious groups, and that any such meetings must be held during 'noninstructional time.' The Act therefore avoids the problems of 'the students' emulation of teachers as role models' and 'mandatory attendance requirements,' *Aguillard;* see also *McCollum.* To be sure, the possibility of *student* peer pressure remains, but there is little if any risk of official state endorsement or coercion where no formal classroom activities are involved and no school officials actively participate. * * *

"Third, the broad spectrum of officially recognized student clubs at Westside, and the fact that Westside students are free to initiate and organize additional student clubs counteract any possible message of official endorsement of or preference for religion or a particular religious belief." [a]

KENNEDY, J., joined by Scalia, J., concurred, emphasizing his disagreement with the plurality's "endorsement test" developed more fully in *Allegheny County v. ACLU,* Part III infra: "I should think it inevitable that a public high school 'endorses' a religious club, in a common-sense use of the term, if the club happens to be one of many activities that the school permits students to choose in order to further the development of their intellect and character in an extracurricular setting. But no constitutional violation occurs if the school's action is based upon a recognition of the fact that membership in a religious club is one of many permissible ways for a student to further his or her own personal enrichment. The inquiry with respect to coercion must be whether the government imposes pressure upon a student to participate in a religious activity. This inquiry, of

---

a. See also *Lamb's Chapel v. Center Moriches Union Free School Dist.,* 508 U.S. 384, 113 S.Ct. 2141, 124 L.Ed.2d 352 (1993), relying on *Widmar* to unanimously hold that a school district did not violate the establishment clause in permitting a church's after-hours use of school facilities to show a religiously oriented film series on family values when the school district also permitted presentation of views on the subject by nonreligious groups.

course, must be undertaken with sensitivity to the special circumstances that exist in a secondary school where the line between voluntary and coerced participation may be difficult to draw. No such coercion, however, has been shown to exist as a necessary result of this statute, either on its face or as respondents seek to invoke it on the facts of this case."

MARSHALL, J., joined by Brennan, J., concurred "to emphasize the steps Westside must take to avoid appearing to endorse the Christian Club's goals."

STEVENS, J., dissented: "Under the Court's interpretation of the Act, Congress has imposed a difficult choice on public high schools receiving federal financial assistance. If such a school continues to allow students to participate in such familiar and innocuous activities as a school chess or scuba diving club, it must also allow religious groups to make use of school facilities. [The] Act, as construed by the majority, comes perilously close to an outright command to allow organized prayer, and perhaps the kind of religious ceremonies involved in *Widmar,* on school premises." [b]

5. *Military chaplains.* In rejecting the argument that Bible reading and prayer exercises in public schools furthered "the majority's right to free exercise of religion," *Schempp* did "not pass upon a situation such as military service, where the Government regulates the temporal and geographic environment of individuals to a point that, unless it permits voluntary religious services to be conducted with the use of government facilities, military personnel would be unable to engage in the practice of their faiths." Might it be that, while free exercise considerations may justify government provision for opportunity to worship, the establishment clause nonetheless bars a government subsidized ministry? "Could the governmental interest be satisfied merely by allowing free time for the serviceman to seek non-military worship or by merely giving the religious orders the right to come into the military environment, at their own expense, to provide the opportunity for worship?" M. Albert Figinski, *Military Chaplains—A Constitutionally Permissible Accommodation Between Church and State,* 24 Md. L.Rev. 377, 409 (1964). Or might it be "that the Government need not necessarily provide chapels and chaplains to those of its armed personnel who are *not* cut off from civilian church facilities"? Klaus J. Herrmann, *Some Considerations on the Constitutionality of the United States Military Chaplaincy,* 14 Am.U.L.Rev. 24, 34 (1964).

6. *Public school secularism.* *Schempp* emphasized that "it might well be said that one's education is not complete without a study of comparative religion or the history of religion and its relationship to the advancement of civilization. It certainly may be said that the Bible is worthy of study for its literary and historic qualities. Nothing we have said here indicates that such study of the Bible or of religion, when presented objectively as part of a secular program of education, may not be [effected]." Consider Leonard F. Manning, *The Douglas Concept of God in Government,* 39 Wash.L.Rev. 47, 63 (1964): "[I]f we forbid the teaching of recognized religions in our public schools and forbid a prayer which simply acknowledges the existence of God and at the same time permit—as, indeed, we must—the teaching of some code of ethical conduct, some system of value norms, does not the system which the school then sponsors become the

b. May elementary or secondary schools permit their facilities to be used for instruction by religious groups if they also permit instruction by outside teachers of art, music, crafts, dance, etc. (cf. *McCollum*)? May they post the Ten Commandments if they also post the symbols of other civic or charitable groups (cf. *Stone*)? See Douglas Laycock, *Equal Access and Moments of Silence: The Equal Status of Religious Speech by Private Speakers,* 81 Nw. U.L.Rev. 1, 33–35 (1986).

system of Secular Humanism or simply secular humanism? Do we not then prefer, in public education, one religion, Secular Humanism, over other religions which are founded upon a belief in the existence of God?" May it be argued in response that, simply because the religion of Secular Humanism "adopts" as its own a moral or ideological tenet that is also a publicly accepted behavioral standard, this does not make it a "religious" tenet under the establishment clause for the purpose of its being taught in the public schools? See note 4, Sec. 2, II infra. If government requires that public employees be of "good moral character," is this a "religious test" for public office? Contrast Stewart, J., dissenting in *Schempp:* "It might also be argued that parents who want their children exposed to religious influences can adequately fulfill that wish off school property and outside school time. [But] a compulsory state educational system so structures a child's life that if religious exercises are held to be an impermissible activity in schools, [this] is seen, not as the realization of state neutrality, but rather as the establishment of a religion of secularism, or at the least, as government support of the beliefs of those who think that religious exercises should be conducted only in private."

II. FINANCIAL AID TO RELIGION

WALZ v. TAX COM'N, 397 U.S. 664, 90 S.Ct. 1409, 25 L.Ed.2d 697 (1970), per BURGER, C.J., upheld state tax exemption for "real or personal property used exclusively for religious, educational or charitable purposes": "The legislative purpose of a property tax exemption is neither the advancement nor the inhibition of religion; it is neither sponsorship nor hostility. New York, in common with the other States, has determined that certain entities that exist in a harmonious relationship to the community at large, and that foster its 'moral or mental improvement,' should not be inhibited in their activities by property taxation or the hazard of loss of those properties for nonpayment of taxes. It [has] granted exemption to all houses of religious worship within a broad class of property owned by nonprofit, quasi-public corporations which include hospitals, libraries, playgrounds, scientific, professional, historical and patriotic groups. * * *

"We find it unnecessary to justify the tax exemption on the social welfare services or 'good works' that some churches perform for parishioners and others— family counselling, aid to the elderly and the infirm, and to children. [To] give emphasis to so variable an aspect of the work of religious bodies would introduce an element of governmental evaluation and standards as to the worth of particular social welfare programs, thus producing a kind of continuing day-to-day relationship which the policy of neutrality seeks to minimize. * * *

" * * * We must also be sure that the end result—the effect—is not an excessive government entanglement with religion. The test is inescapably one of degree. * * * Elimination of exemption would tend to expand the involvement of government by giving rise to tax valuation of church property, tax liens, tax foreclosures, and the direct confrontations and conflicts that follow in the train of those legal processes.

"Granting tax exemptions to churches necessarily operates to afford an indirect economic benefit and also gives rise to some, but yet a lesser, involvement than taxing [them]. Obviously a direct money subsidy would be a relationship pregnant with involvement and, as with most governmental grant programs, could encompass sustained and detailed administrative relationships for enforcement of statutory or administrative standards, but that is not this case. * * *

"It is obviously correct that no one acquires a vested or protected right in violation of the Constitution by long [use]. Yet an unbroken practice of according the exemption to churches [is] not something to be lightly cast aside."

BRENNAN, J., concurred: "Tax exemptions and general subsidies [both] provide economic assistance, [but a] subsidy involves the direct transfer of public monies to the subsidized enterprise and uses resources exacted from taxpayers as a whole. An exemption, on the other hand, involves no such transfer.[a] It assists the exempted enterprise only passively." [b]

DOUGLAS, J., dissented: "If history be our guide, then tax exemption of church property in this country is indeed highly suspect, as it arose in the early days when the church was an agency of the state. [The] financial support rendered here is to the church, the place of worship. A tax exemption is a subsidy."

Notes and Questions

1. *Direct subsidies vs. tax exemption.* Consider William W. Van Alstyne, *Constitutional Separation of Church and State: The Quest for a Coherent Position,* 57 Am.Pol.Sci.Rev. 865, 881 (1963): "To finance expanding government services, [taxes] may gradually divert an increasing fraction of total personal income, necessarily leaving proportionately less money in the private sector to each person to spend according to his individual choice, in support of religion or other undertakings. To the extent that the tax revenues thus collected may not be spent by government to support religious enterprises, but must be used exclusively for secular purposes, the net effect, arguably, is to reduce the relative supply of funds available to religion." Does this warrant tax exemption for "religion"? Does it "warrant the judicial junking of the establishment clause"? Id. Is it "equally arguable that government fiscal activity, far from reducing disposable personal income, actually increases it"? Id. See also Alan Schwarz, *The Nonestablishment Principle: A Reply to Professor Giannella,* 81 Harv.L.Rev. 1465, 1469–70 (1968).

2. *"Neutrality."* (a) TEXAS MONTHLY, INC. v. BULLOCK, 489 U.S. 1, 109 S.Ct. 890, 103 L.Ed.2d 1 (1989), held violative of the establishment clause a Texas sales tax exemption for books and "periodicals that are published or distributed by a religious faith and that consist wholly of writings promulgating the teaching of the faith." BRENNAN, J., joined by Marshall and Stevens, JJ., reasoned that *Walz* and *Widmar,* Part I supra, "emphasized that the benefits derived by religious organizations flowed to a large number of nonreligious groups as well": "However, when government directs a subsidy exclusively to religious organizations that is not required by the Free Exercise Clause and that either burdens nonbeneficiaries markedly or cannot reasonably be seen as removing a significant state-imposed deterrent to the free exercise of religion, as Texas has done, it 'provide[s] unjustifiable awards of assistance to religious organizations' and cannot but 'conve[y] a message of endorsement' to slighted members of the community. This is particularly true where, as here, the subsidy is targeted at writings that *promulgate* the teachings of religious faiths. It is difficult to view Texas' narrow exemption as anything but state sponsorship of religious belief [which] lacks a secular objective."

BLACKMUN, J., joined by O'Connor, J., concurred: "[A] tax exemption *limited* to the sale of religious literature * * * offends our most basic understanding of what the establishment clause is all about." White, J., concurred on freedom of

---

a. What of the fact that exemption for churches augments the tax bills of others?

b. Harlan, J., also concurred.

press grounds. Scalia, J., joined by Rehnquist, C.J., and Kennedy, J., dissented from Brennan, J.'s distinction of *Walz*.

(b) In BOARD OF EDUC. OF KIRYAS JOEL v. GRUMET, __ U.S. __, 114 S.Ct. 2481, 129 L.Ed.2d 546 (1994), a New York statute constituted the Village of Kiryas Joel—"a religious enclave of Satmar Hasidim, practitioners of a strict form of Judaism"—as a separate school district. Most of the children attend pervasively religious private schools. The newly created district "currently runs only a special education program for handicapped [Satmar] children" who reside both inside and outside the village. The statute was passed "to enable the village's handicapped children to receive a secular, public-school education" because when they previously attended public schools in the larger school district outside the village, they suffered "panic, fear and trauma [in] leaving their own community and being with people whose ways were so different." The Court, per SOUTER, J., invoked "a principle at the heart of the Establishment Clause, that government should not prefer one religion to another, or religion to irreligion. Because the religious community of Kiryas Joel did not receive its new governmental authority simply as one of many communities eligible for equal treatment under a general law, we have no assurance that the next similarly situated group seeking a school district of its own will receive one; [and] a legislature's failure to enact a special law is itself unreviewable.[a] [Here] the benefit flows only to a single sect, [and] whatever the limits of permissible legislative accommodations may be, compare *Texas Monthly*, it is clear that neutrality as among religions must be honored.[b] [The statute] therefore crosses the line from permissible accommodation to impermissible establishment."[c]

KENNEDY, J., concurred in the judgment: "[G]overnment may not use religion as a criterion to draw political or electoral lines. Whether or not the purpose is

a. Kennedy, J., disagreed, arguing that if another religious community were denied special legislative help, it "could sue the State of New York, contending that New York's discriminatory treatment of the two religious communities violated the Establishment Clause. To resolve this claim, the court would have only to determine whether the community does indeed bear the same burden on its religious practice as did the Satmars in Kiryas Joel. See *Olsen v. Drug Enforcement Admin.*, 878 F.2d 1458, 1463–1465 (D.C.Cir.1989) (R.B. Ginsburg, J.) (rejecting claim that the members of the Ethiopian Zion Coptic Church were entitled to an exemption from the marijuana laws on the same terms as the peyote exemption for the Native American Church). While a finding of discrimination would then raise a difficult question of relief, compare *Olsen* ('Faced with the choice between invalidation and extension of any controlled-substances religious exemption, which would the political branches choose? It would take a court bolder than this one to predict [that] extension, not invalidation, would be the probable choice'), with *Califano v. Westcott*, 443 U.S. 76, 89–93, 99 S.Ct. 2655, 2663–65, 61 L.Ed.2d 382 (1979) (curing gender discrimination in the AFDC program by extending benefits to children of unemployed mothers instead of denying benefits to children of unemployed fathers), the discrimination itself would not be beyond judicial remedy."

b. Compare Thomas C. Berg, *Slouching Towards Secularism*, 44 Emory L.J. 433, 468–69 (1995): "[T]he reason the legislature specifically accommodated the Satmars was simply that their plight was unique: no other group of children was being denied effective special education because they were traumatized by the atmosphere of the mainstream public schools. [Even] if the children of other groups had been harmed by the public school ethos, few if any such groups live together communally so as to permit the solution of a geographically based school district such as that drawn for the Satmars." But see Ira C. Lupu, *The Lingering Death of Separatism*, 62 Geo.Wash.L.Rev. 230, 269 (1994): "Is it imaginable that New York State would create a new public school district at the behest of an insular group of Branch Davidians or members of the Unification Church, whose children—like the Hasidim—may suffer panic, fear, and trauma at encountering those outside their own community?"

c. Within ten days of *Kiryas Joel*, the New York legislature passed a new law allowing "any municipality situated wholly within a single school district" to form its own district if it meets designated criteria regarding population, enrollment and property wealth. Constitutional when used by the Village of Kiryas Joel?

accommodation and whether or not the government provides similar gerrymanders to people of all religious faiths, the Establishment Clause forbids the government to use religion as a line-drawing criterion."

SCALIA, J., joined by Rehnquist, C.J., and Thomas, J., dissented: "[A]ll the residents of the Kiryas Joel Village School District are Satmars. But all its residents also wear unusual dress, have unusual civic customs, and have not much to do with people who are culturally different from them. [I]t was not theology but dress, language, and cultural alienation that posed the educational problem for the children [and caused the Legislature to] provide a public education for these students, in the same way it addressed, by a similar law, the unique needs of children institutionalized in a hospital.

"[T]he creation of a special, one-culture school district for the benefit of [children whose] parents were nonreligious commune dwellers, or American Indians, or gypsies [would] pose no problem. The neutrality demanded by the Religion Clauses requires the same indulgence towards cultural characteristics that are accompanied by religious belief." [d]

3. *Delegation of government power:* In *Kiryas Joel,* SOUTER, J., joined by Blackmun, Stevens and Ginsburg, JJ., found an additional ground for invalidating the statute: "delegating the State's discretionary authority over public schools to a group defined by its character as a religious community, in a legal and historical context that gives no assurance that governmental power has been or will be exercised neutrally." They relied on LARKIN v. GRENDEL'S DEN, INC., 459 U.S. 116, 103 S.Ct. 505, 74 L.Ed.2d 297 (1982), per BURGER, C.J., which held that a Massachusetts law (§ 16C), giving churches and schools the power "to veto applications for liquor licenses within a five hundred foot radius of the church or school, violates the Establishment Clause": § 16C is not simply a legislative exercise of zoning power [because it] delegates * * * discretionary governmental powers [to] religious bodies.

"[The] valid secular objectives [of protecting] spiritual, cultural, and educational centers from the 'hurly-burly' associated with liquor outlets [can] be readily accomplished by other means—either through an absolute legislative ban on liquor outlets within reasonable prescribed distances from churches, schools, hospitals and like institutions, or by ensuring a hearing for the views of affected institutions at licensing proceedings. [But the] churches' power under the statute is standardless [and] may therefore be used by churches [for] explicitly religious goals, for example, favoring liquor licenses for members of that congregation or adherents of that faith. [In] addition, the mere appearance of a joint exercise of legislative authority by Church and State provides a significant symbolic benefit to religion in the minds of some by reason of the power conferred. It does not strain our prior holdings to say that the statute can be seen as having a 'primary' and 'principal' effect of advancing religion. [Finally, § 16C] enmeshes churches in the processes of government and creates the danger of 'political fragmentation and divisiveness along religious lines.' "

REHNQUIST, J., dissented in *Grendel's Den:* A "flat ban [on] the grant of an alcoholic beverages license to any establishment located within 500 feet of a church or a [school], which the majority concedes is valid, is more protective of churches and more restrictive of liquor sales than the present § 16C. * * * Nothing in the Court's opinion persuades me why the more rigid prohibition would be constitutional, but the more flexible not. [It] does not sponsor or

d. Is this persuasive when there is total congruence between a religion and distinctive cultural needs *and* the cultural distinctiveness is defined by the religion?

subsidize any religious group or activity. It does not encourage, much less compel, anyone to participate in religious activities or to support religious institutions. To say that it 'advances' religion is to strain at the meaning of the word. [If] a church were to seek to advance the interests of its members [by favoring them for licenses], there would be an occasion to determine whether it had violated any right of an unsuccessful applicant for a liquor license. But our ability to discern a risk of such abuse does not render § 16C violative of the Establishment Clause."

Scalia, J., joined by Rehnquist, C.J., and Thomas, J., dissenting in *Kiryas Joel,* argued that *Grendel's Den* had ruled that "a state may not delegate its civil authority *to a church,*" and did not involve delegation to "groups of people sharing a common religious and cultural heritage": "If the conferral of governmental power upon a religious institution *as such* (rather than upon American citizens who belong to the religious institution) is not the test of *Grendel's Den* invalidity, there is no reason why giving power to a body that is overwhelmingly dominated by the members of one sect would not suffice to invoke the Establishment Clause. That might have made the entire States of Utah and New Mexico unconstitutional at the time of their admission to the Union."

Query: Does the "delegation" to church-related schools of the authority to satisfy state requirements for elementary and secondary education violate the establishment clause?

4. *"Excessive government entanglement" in ecclesiastical disputes.* (a) In JONES v. WOLF, 443 U.S. 595, 99 S.Ct. 3020, 61 L.Ed.2d 775 (1979), a majority of the Vineville Presbyterian Church of Macon, Ga. voted to separate from the Presbyterian Church in the United States (PCUS). A commission of PCUS, acting pursuant to the PCUS constitution (called the Book of Church Order), declared the Vineville minority to be "the true congregation." The minority sued to establish its right to the local church property. The Supreme Court of Georgia applied "the 'neutral principles of law' method for resolving church property disputes. The court examined the deeds to the properties, the state statutes dealing with implied trusts, and the Book of Church Order, to determine whether there was any basis for a trust in favor of the general church. Finding nothing that would give rise to a trust in any of these documents, the court awarded the property on the basis of legal title, which was in the local church, or in the names of trustees for the local church. [Without] further analysis or elaboration, [it] further decreed that the local congregation was represented by the majority faction, respondents herein."

The Court, per BLACKMUN, J., stated the established principle that "the First Amendment prohibits civil courts from resolving church property disputes on the basis of religious doctrine and practice. *Presbyterian Church v. Mary Elizabeth Blue Hull Memorial Presbyterian Church,* 393 U.S. 440, 89 S.Ct. 601, 21 L.Ed.2d 658 (1969). As a corollary to this commandment, the Amendment requires that civil courts defer to the resolution of issues of religious doctrine or polity by the highest court of a hierarchical church organization. *Serbian Orthodox Diocese v. Milivojevich,* 426 U.S. 696, 96 S.Ct. 2372, 49 L.Ed.2d 151 (1976)[a] Subject to

a. *Serbian,* per Brennan, J., reversed a state court decision that the Mother Church's removal of respondent as bishop of the American–Canadian diocese was "procedurally and substantively defective under the internal regulations of the Mother Church and were therefore arbitrary and invalid": "[W]hether or not there is room for 'marginal civil court review' under the narrow rubrics of 'fraud' or 'collusion' when church tribunals act in bad faith for secular purposes, no 'arbitrariness' exception— in the sense of an inquiry whether the deci-

these limitations, however, * * * 'a State may adopt *any* of various approaches for settling church property disputes so long as it involves no consideration of doctrinal matters, whether the ritual and liturgy of worship or the tenets of faith.' *Maryland & Va. Eldership v. Sharpsburg Church*, 396 U.S. 367, 90 S.Ct. 499, 24 L.Ed.2d 582 (1970) (Brennan, J., concurring) (emphasis in original).

"[W]e think the 'neutral principles of law' approach is consistent with the foregoing constitutional principles. [It] relies extensively on objective, well-established concepts of trust and property law familiar to lawyers and judges. It thereby promises to free civil courts completely from entanglement in questions of religious doctrine, polity, and practice. Furthermore, the neutral principles analysis [affords] flexibility in ordering private rights and obligations to reflect the intentions of the parties. Through appropriate reversionary clauses and trust provisions, religious societies can specify what is to happen to church property in the event of a particular contingency, or what religious body will determine the ownership in the event of a schism or doctrinal controversy. In this manner, a religious organization can ensure that a dispute over the ownership of church property will be resolved in accord with the desires of the members.

"[The] neutral principles method [does require] a civil court to examine certain religious documents, such as a church constitution, for language of trust in favor of the general church. In undertaking such an examination, a civil court must take special care to scrutinize the document in purely secular terms, and not to rely on religious precepts in determining whether the document indicates that the parties have intended to create a trust. In addition, there may be cases where the deed, the corporate charter, or the constitution of the general church incorporates religious concepts in the provisions relating to the ownership of property. If in such a case the interpretation of the instruments of ownership would require the civil court to resolve a religious controversy, then the court must defer to the resolution of the doctrinal issue by the authoritative ecclesiastical body. *Serbian.*"

The Court vacated the judgment, however, since "the grounds for the decision that respondents represent the Vineville church remain unarticulated": "If in fact Georgia has adopted a presumptive rule of majority representation, defeasible upon a showing that the identity of the local church is to be determined by some other means, we think this would be consistent with [the] First Amendment. Majority rule is generally employed in the governance of religious societies. Furthermore, the majority faction generally can be identified without resolving any question of religious doctrine or polity. [Most] importantly, any rule of majority representation can always be overcome, under the neutral principles approach, either by providing, in the corporate charter or the constitution of the general church, that the identity of the local church is to be established in some other way, or by providing that the church property is held in trust for the general church and those who remain loyal to it. Indeed, the State may adopt any method of overcoming the majoritarian presumption, so long as the use of that method does not impair free exercise rights or entangle the civil courts in matters of religious controversy.

sions of the highest ecclesiastical tribunal of a hierarchical church complied with church laws and regulations—is consistent with the constitutional mandate that civil courts are bound to accept the decisions of the highest judicatories of a religious organization of hierarchical polity on matters of discipline, faith, internal organization, or ecclesiastical rule, custom or law. [I]t is the essence of religious faith that ecclesiastical decisions are reached and are to be accepted as matters of faith whether or not rational or measurable by objective criteria."

Rehnquist and Stevens, JJ., dissented. See 1977 Utah L.Rev. 138.

"[But] there are at least some indications that under Georgia law the process of identifying the faction that represents the Vineville church [must] be determined according to terms of the Book of Church Order * * *. Such a determination, however, would appear to require a civil court to pass on questions of religious doctrine, and to usurp the function of the commission appointed by the Presbytery * * *. Therefore, if Georgia law provides that the identity of the Vineville church is to be determined according to the 'laws and regulations' of the PCUS, then the First Amendment requires that the Georgia courts give deference to the presbyterial commission's determination of that church's identity."

POWELL, J., joined by Burger, C.J., and Stewart and White, JJ., dissented, finding that the neutral principles "approach inevitably will increase the involvement of civil courts in church controversies": "Until today, [the] first question presented in a case involving an intrachurch dispute over church property was where within the religious association the rules of polity, accepted by its members before the schism, had placed ultimate authority over the use of the church property. The courts, in answering this question have recognized two broad categories of church government. One is congregational, in which authority over questions of church doctrine, practice, and administration rests entirely in the local congregation or some body within it. In disputes over the control and use of the property of such a church, the civil courts enforce the authoritative resolution of the controversy within the local church itself. *Watson v. Jones,* 80 U.S. (13 Wall) 679, 20 L.Ed. 666 (1871). The second is hierarchical, in which the local church is but an integral and subordinate part of a larger church and is under the authority of the general church. Since the decisions of the local congregation are subject to review by the tribunals of the church hierarchy, this Court has held that the civil courts must give effect to the duly made decisions of the highest body within the hierarchy that has considered the dispute. [By] doing so, the [civil] court avoids two equally unacceptable departures from the genuine neutrality mandated by the First Amendment. First, it refrains from direct review and revision of decisions of the church on matters of religious doctrine and practice that underlie the church's determination of intrachurch controversies, including those that relate to control of church property.[b] Equally important, by recognizing the authoritative resolution reached within the religious association, the civil court avoids interfering indirectly with the religious governance of those who have formed the association and submitted themselves to its authority."[c]

(b) *Scope of the decision.* After *Jones v. Wolf,* what results in the following situations: (i) A donor who made a bequest "to the First Methodist Church" seeks return of the money because subsequently a majority of the church's

---

b. In response, the Court pointed out that, under the dissent's approach, "civil courts would always be required to examine the polity and administration of a church to determine which unit of government has ultimate control over church property. In some cases, this task would not prove to be difficult. But in others, the locus of control would be ambiguous, and 'a careful examination of the constitutions of the general and local church, as well as other relevant documents, [would] be necessary to ascertain the form of governance adopted by the members of the religious association.' In such cases, the suggested rule would appear to require 'a searching and therefore impermissible inquiry into church polity.' *Serbian.* The neutral principles approach, in contrast, obviates entirely the need for an analysis or examination of ecclesiastical polity or doctrine in settling church property disputes."

c. In response, the Court contended that "the neutral principles approach cannot be said to 'inhibit' the free exercise of religion, any more than do other neutral provisions of state law governing the manner in which churches own property, hire employees, or purchase goods. Under the neutral principles approach, the outcome of a church property dispute is not foreordained. At any time before the dispute erupts, the parties can ensure, if they so desire, that the faction loyal to the hierarchical church will retain the church property" by using reversionary clauses, trust provisions, etc.

members decided to affiliate with another denomination. Suppose the bequest had been "to the First Methodist Church so long as it does not substantially deviate from existing doctrine"? (ii) A state statute makes it a crime for sellers to falsely represent food to be "kosher." See Note, 71 Mich.L.Rev. 1641 (1973).

(c) *Proposed approach.* "The solution most of the time is to honor internal church agreements, just as a court would honor the internal agreements of a secular organization. Only when doctrinal decisions [d] or the imposition of external policies are involved [e] need a court refrain from deciding a dispute. This approach serves both organizational autonomy and the other interests of the church and its members, while preserving the religious neutrality demanded by the first amendment." Ira M. Ellman, *Driven from the Tribunal: Judicial Resolution of Internal Church Disputes,* 69 Calif.L.Rev. 1378, 1444 (1981).[f]

MUELLER v. ALLEN

463 U.S. 388, 103 S.Ct. 3062, 77 L.Ed.2d 721 (1983).

JUSTICE REHNQUIST delivered the opinion of the Court.

Minnesota allows taxpayers, in computing their state income tax, to deduct certain expenses incurred in providing for the education of their children.[1] [A]bout 820,000 students attended [Minnesota's public] school system in the most recent school year. During the same year, approximately 91,000 elementary and secondary students attended some 500 privately supported schools located in Minnesota, and about 95% of these students attended schools considering themselves to be sectarian. * * *

Today's case is no exception to our oft-repeated statement that the Establishment Clause presents especially difficult questions of interpretation and application. [It] is not at all easy [to] apply this Court's various decisions construing the Clause to governmental programs of financial assistance to sectarian schools and the parents of children attending those schools. Indeed, in many of these decisions "we have expressly or implicitly acknowledged that we can only dimly perceive the lines of demarcation in this extraordinarily sensitive area of constitu-

---

d. "Few [cases] present the problem of governmental determination of religious doctrine. [More] common are a second group of cases in which the court is asked to determine which religious doctrine the embattled parties agreed to follow. This kind of question is very different and need not present the first amendment difficulties inherent in the first group of cases." Id. at 1414.

e. "[T]he application of judge-made rules of procedural fairness in associational governance, and the use of charitable trust rules of charitable assets [are issues that] present the potential for courts to impose government-created policies on religious organizations [rather than rules seeking to fulfill the parties' intentions]." Id. at 1421.

f. For the view that "freedom of church groups" should be preferred to "freedom of individual members," and therefore the rule of "deference" to church decisions should prevail over the "neutral principles" approach, see John H. Garvey, *Churches and the Free Exercise of Religion,* 4 Notre D.J.L.Eth & Pub.Pol. 567 (1990).

1. Minn.Stat. § 290.09(22) (1982) permits a taxpayer to deduct from his or her computation of gross income the following: "[The] amount he has paid to others, not to exceed $500 for each dependent in grades K to 6 and $700 for each dependent in grades 7 to 12, for tuition, textbooks and transportation of each dependent in attending an elementary or secondary school [wherein] a resident of this state may legally fulfill the state's compulsory attendance laws, which is not operated for profit, and which adheres to the provisions of the Civil Rights Act of 1964 * * *. As used in this subdivision, 'textbooks' shall mean and include books and other instructional materials and equipment used in elementary and secondary schools in teaching only those subjects legally and commonly taught in public elementary and secondary schools in this state and shall not include instructional books and materials used in the teaching of religious tenets, doctrines or worship * * *."

tional law." *Lemon.*[a]

One fixed principle in this field is our consistent rejection of the argument that "any program which in some manner aids an institution with a religious affiliation" violates the Establishment Clause. For example, it is now well established that a State may reimburse parents for expenses incurred in transporting their children to school, *Everson,* and that it may loan secular textbooks to all schoolchildren within the State, *Board of Educ. v. Allen,* 392 U.S. 236, 88 S.Ct. 1923, 20 L.Ed.2d 1060 (1968). [But] our decisions also have struck down arrangements resembling, in many respects, these forms of assistance. See, e.g., *Lemon; Levitt v. Committee for Pub. Educ.,* 413 U.S. 472, 93 S.Ct. 2814, 37 L.Ed.2d 736 (1973); *Meek v. Pittenger,* 421 U.S. 349, 95 S.Ct. 1753, 44 L.Ed.2d 217 (1975); *Wolman v. Walter,* 433 U.S. 229, 237–238, 97 S.Ct. 2593, 2599–2600, 53 L.Ed.2d 714 (1977).[3] Petitioners place particular reliance on our decision in *Committee for Pub. Educ. v. Nyquist,* 413 U.S. 756, 93 S.Ct. 2955, 37 L.Ed.2d 948 (1973), where we held invalid a New York [statute] granting thinly disguised "tax benefits," actually amounting to tuition grants, to the parents of children attending private schools. As explained below, we conclude that § 290.09(22) bears less resemblance to the arrangement struck down in *Nyquist* than it does to assistance programs upheld in our prior [decisions].

Little time need be spent on the question of whether the Minnesota tax deduction has a secular purpose. Under our prior decisions, governmental assistance programs have consistently survived this inquiry even when they have run afoul of other aspects of the *Lemon* framework. This reflects, at least in part, our reluctance to attribute unconstitutional motives to the states, particularly when a plausible secular purpose for the state's program may be discerned from the face of the statute.

A state's decision to defray the cost of educational expenses incurred by parents—regardless of the type of schools their children attend—evidences a purpose that is both secular and understandable. An educated populace is essential to the political and economic health of any community, and a state's efforts to assist parents in meeting the rising cost of educational expenses plainly serves this secular purpose of ensuring that the state's citizenry is well-educated. Similarly, Minnesota, like other states, could conclude that there is a strong public interest in assuring the continued financial health of private schools, both sectarian and non-sectarian. By educating a substantial number of students such schools relieve public schools of a correspondingly great burden—to the benefit of all taxpayers. In addition, private schools may serve as a benchmark for public schools * * *.

We turn therefore to the more difficult but related question whether the Minnesota statute has "the primary effect of advancing the sectarian aims of the

---

a. *Committee for Pub. Educ. v. Regan,* 444 U.S. 646, 100 S.Ct. 840, 63 L.Ed.2d 94 (1980), per White, J.,—holding that states may reimburse parochial schools for the cost of routine recordkeeping and administering state-prepared tests—observed that the "decisions have tended to avoid categorical imperatives and absolutist approaches at either end of the range of possible outcomes. This course sacrifices clarity and predictability for flexibility * * *."

3. In *Lemon,* the Court concluded that the State's reimbursement of nonpublic schools for the cost of teachers' salaries, textbooks, and instructional materials, and its payment of a salary supplement to teachers in nonpublic schools, resulted in excessive entanglement of church and state. In *Levitt,* we struck down on Establishment Clause grounds a state program reimbursing nonpublic schools for the cost of teacher-prepared examinations. Finally, in *Meek* and *Wolman,* we held unconstitutional a direct loan of instructional materials to nonpublic schools, while upholding the loan of textbooks to individual students.

non-public schools." In concluding that it does not, we find several features of the Minnesota tax deduction particularly significant. First, an essential feature of Minnesota's arrangement is the fact that § 290.09(22) is only one among many deductions—such as those for medical expenses and charitable contributions [b]— available under the Minnesota tax laws.[5] Our decisions consistently have recognized that [the] legislature's judgment that a deduction for educational expenses fairly equalizes the tax burden of its citizens and encourages desirable expenditures for educational purposes is entitled to substantial deference.[6]

Other characteristics of § 290.09(22) argue equally strongly for the provision's constitutionality. Most importantly, the deduction is available for educational expenses incurred by *all* parents, including those whose children attend public schools and those whose children attend non-sectarian private schools or sectarian private schools. Just as in *Widmar,* [so] here: "the provision of benefits to so broad a spectrum of groups is an important index of secular effect."

In this respect, as well as others, this case is vitally different from the scheme struck down in *Nyquist.* There, public assistance amounting to tuition grants, was provided only to parents of children in *nonpublic* schools. This fact had considerable bearing on our decision striking down the New York statute at issue; we explicitly distinguished both *Allen* and *Everson* on the grounds that "In both cases the class of beneficiaries included *all* schoolchildren, those in public as well as those in private schools." Moreover, we intimated that "public assistance (e.g., scholarships) made available generally without regard to the sectarian-nonsectarian or public-nonpublic nature of the institution benefited," might not offend the Establishment Clause. We think the tax deduction adopted by Minnesota is more

b. Compare Jesse H. Choper, *The Establishment Clause and Aid to Parochial Schools—An Update,* 75 Calif.L.Rev. 5, 8 (1987): "This [is] no different than saying that an appropriation to build a new Lutheran church in St. Paul would be only one of many appropriations by the Minnesota legislature. It follows from Justice Rehnquist's reasoning that since Minnesota appropriates money for the University of Minnesota and for all kinds of other things, an appropriation to build a Lutheran church should be treated just like one of many appropriations. But the establishment clause is plainly meant to prohibit some things, even though they are much like other things, if they involve religion."

5. Deductions for charitable contributions, allowed by Minnesota law, include contributions to religious institutions, and exemptions from property tax for property used for charitable purposes under Minnesota law include property used for wholly religious purposes. In each case, it may be that religious institutions benefit very substantially from the allowance of such deductions. The Court's holding in *Walz* indicates, however, that this does not require the conclusion that such provisions of a state's tax law violate the Establishment Clause.

6. Our decision in *Nyquist* is not to the contrary on this point. We expressed considerable doubt there that the "tax benefits" provided by New York law properly could be re-

garded as parts of a genuine system of tax laws. Plainly, the outright grants to low-income parents ["of $50 to $100 per child (but no more than 50% of tuition actually paid)"] did not take the form of ordinary tax benefits. As to the benefits provided to middle-income parents, the Court said: "The amount of the deduction is unrelated to the amount of money actually expended by any parent on tuition, but is calculated on the basis of a formula contained in the statute. The formula is apparently the product of a legislative attempt to assure that each family would receive a carefully estimated net benefit, and that the tax benefit would be comparable to, and compatible with, the tuition grant for lower income families." Indeed, the question whether a program having the elements of a "genuine tax deduction" would be constitutionally acceptable was expressly reserved in *Nyquist.* While the economic consequences of the program in *Nyquist* and that in this case may be difficult to distinguish, we have recognized on other occasions that "the form of the [state's assistance to parochial schools must be examined] for the light that it casts on the substance." The fact that the Minnesota plan embodies a "genuine tax deduction" is thus of some relevance, especially given the traditional rule of deference accorded legislative classifications in tax statutes.

similar to this latter type of program than it is to the arrangement struck down in *Nyquist.* * * *

We also agree with the Court of Appeals that, by channeling whatever assistance it may provide to parochial schools through individual parents, Minnesota has reduced the Establishment Clause objections to which its action is subject. It is true, of course, that financial assistance provided to parents ultimately has an economic effect comparable to that of aid given directly to the schools attended by their children. It is also true, however, that under Minnesota's arrangement public funds become available only as a result of numerous, private choices of individual parents of school-age children. [It] is noteworthy that all but one of our recent cases invalidating state aid to parochial schools have involved the direct transmission of assistance from the state to the schools themselves. The exception, of course, was *Nyquist,* which, as discussed previously is distinguishable from this case on other grounds. Where, as here, aid to parochial schools is available only as a result of decisions of individual parents no "imprimatur of State approval," *Widmar,* can be deemed to have been conferred on any particular religion, or on religion generally. * * *

Petitioners argue that, notwithstanding the facial neutrality of § 290.09(22), [most] parents of public school children incur no tuition expenses, and that other expenses deductible under § 290.09(22) are negligible in value; moreover, they claim that 96% of the children in private schools in 1978–1979 attended religiously-affiliated institutions. Because of all this, they reason, the bulk of deductions taken under § 290.09(22) will be claimed by parents of children in sectarian schools. Respondents reply that petitioners have failed to consider the impact of deductions for items such as transportation, summer school tuition, tuition paid by parents whose children attended schools outside the school districts in which they resided, rental or purchase costs for a variety of equipment, and tuition for certain types of instruction not ordinarily provided in public schools.

We need not consider these contentions in detail. We would be loath to adopt a rule grounding the constitutionality of a facially neutral law on annual reports reciting the extent to which various classes of private citizens claimed benefits under the law. Such an approach would scarcely provide the certainty that this field stands in need of, nor can we perceive principled standards by which such statistical evidence might be evaluated. Moreover, the fact that private persons fail in a particular year to claim the tax relief to which they are entitled—under a facially neutral statute—should be of little importance in determining the constitutionality of the statute permitting such relief.

Finally, [if] parents of children in private schools choose to take especial advantage of the relief provided by § 290.09(22), it is no doubt due to the fact that they bear a particularly great financial burden in educating their children. More fundamentally, whatever unequal effect may be attributed to the statutory classification can fairly be regarded as a rough return for the benefits, discussed above, provided to the state and all taxpayers by parents sending their children to parochial schools. In the light of all this, we believe it wiser to decline to engage in the type of empirical inquiry into those persons benefited by state law which petitioners urge. * * *

Turning to the third part of the *Lemon* inquiry, we have no difficulty in concluding that the Minnesota statute does not "excessively entangle" the state in religion.[c] [T]hat state officials must determine whether particular textbooks

---

c. In *Lemon,* "comprehensive, discriminating, and continuing state surveillance will inevitably be required [under statutory restrictions] to ensure [that] subsidized teachers do

qualify for a deduction [does] not differ substantially from making the types of decisions approved in [*Allen*].[11]

Affirmed.

JUSTICE MARSHALL, with whom JUSTICE BRENNAN, JUSTICE BLACKMUN and JUSTICE STEVENS join, dissenting. * * *

As we recognized in *Nyquist,* direct government subsidization of parochial school tuition is impermissible because "the effect of the aid is unmistakably to provide desired financial support for nonpublic, sectarian institutions." "[A]id to the educational function of [parochial schools] necessarily results in aid to the sectarian enterprise as a whole" because "[t]he very purpose of those schools is to provide an integrated secular and religious education." For this reason, aid to

---

not inculcate religion. [Unlike] a book, a teacher cannot be inspected once so as to determine the extent and intent of his or her personal beliefs and subjective acceptance of the limitations imposed by the First Amendment. These prophylactic contacts will involve excessive and enduring entanglement between state and church."

White, J., dissenting in *Lemon,* accused the Court of "creat[ing] an insoluble paradox for the State and the parochial schools. The State cannot finance secular instruction if it permits religion to be taught in the same classroom; but if it exacts a promise that religion not be so taught—a promise the school and its teachers are quite willing and on this record able to give—and enforces it, it is then entangled in the 'no entanglement' aspect of the Court's Establishment Clause jurisprudence."

11. No party to this litigation has urged that the Minnesota plan is invalid because it runs afoul of the rather elusive inquiry, subsumed under the third part of the *Lemon* test, whether the Minnesota statute partakes of the "divisive political potential" condemned in *Lemon.* * * *

The Court's language in *Lemon* respecting political divisiveness was made in the context of Pennsylvania and Rhode Island statutes which provided for either direct payments of, or reimbursement of, a proportion of teachers' salaries in parochial schools. We think, in the light of the treatment of the point in later cases discussed above, the language must be regarded as confined to cases where direct financial subsidies are paid to parochial schools or to teachers in parochial schools.

[*Lemon* reasoned: "In a community where such a large number of pupils are served by church-related schools, it can be assumed that state assistance will entail considerable political activity [by partisans and opponents]. Candidates will be forced to declare and voters to choose. It would be unrealistic to ignore the fact that many people confronted with issues of this kind will find their votes aligned with their faith.

["Ordinarily political debate and division, however vigorous or even partisan, are normal and healthy manifestations of our democratic system of government, but political division along religious lines was one of the principal evils against which the First Amendment was intended to protect. Paul A. Freund, *Public Aid to Parochial Schools,* 82 Harv.L.Rev. 1680, 1692 (1969)."]

[Compare Alan Schwarz, *No Imposition of Religion: The Establishment Clause Value,* 77 Yale L.J. 692, 711 (1968): "If avoidance of strife were an independent [establishment clause] value, no legislation could be adopted on any subject which aroused strong and divided [religious] feelings." See Jesse H. Choper, *The Establishment Clause and Aid to Parochial Schools,* 56 Calif.L.Rev. 260, 273 (1968): "Nor would a denial of aid to parochial schools largely diminish the extent of religious political activity. In fact, it 'might lead to greater political ruptures caused by the alienation of segments of the religious community.' Those who send their children to parochial schools might intensify opposition to increased governmental aid to public education." Contrast William D. Valente & William A. Stanmeyer, *Public Aid to Parochial Schools—A Reply to Professor Freund,* 59 Geo.L.J. 59, 70 n. 46 (1970): "[O]ne's assessment of the accuracy of the views of Professors Freund, Schwartz, and Choper as to likely political repercussions is itself a political judgment and not judicial, and [the] weighing of political reactions is a function of legislatures and not of courts." See also Kenneth F. Ripple, *The Entanglement Test of the Religion Clauses—A Ten Year Assessment,* 27 U.C.L.A.L.Rev. 1195 (1980). For the view that the historical evidence shows "that it is misguided to interpret the first amendment as prohibiting legislative consideration of an issue affecting religion on the ground that the very act of consideration will spawn impermissible religious division," see Peter M. Schotten, *The Establishment Clause and Excessive Governmental–Religious Entanglement: The Constitutional Status of Aid to Nonpublic Elementary and Secondary Schools,* 15 Wake For. L.Rev. 207, 225 (1979).]

sectarian schools must be restricted to ensure that it may not be used to further the religious mission of those schools. While "services such as police and fire protection, sewage disposal, highways, and sidewalks," may be provided to parochial schools in common with other institutions, because this type of assistance is clearly "marked off from the religious function" of those schools, unrestricted financial assistance, such as grants for the maintenance and construction of parochial schools, may not be provided. * * *

Indirect assistance in the form of financial aid to parents for tuition payments is similarly impermissible because it is not "subject [to] restrictions" which "guarantee the separation between secular and religious educational functions [and] ensure that State financial aid supports only the former." *Lemon.* [As] was true of the law struck down in *Nyquist,* "it is precisely the function of [Minnesota's] law to provide assistance to private schools, the great majority of which are sectarian. By reimbursing parents for a portion of their tuition bill, the State seeks to relieve their financial burdens sufficiently to assure that they continue to have the option to send their children to religion-oriented schools. And while the other purposes for that aid—to perpetuate a pluralistic educational environment and to protect the fiscal integrity of overburdened public schools— are certainly unexceptional, the effect of the aid is unmistakably to provide desired financial support for nonpublic, sectarian institutions."

* * * Financial assistance for tuition payments has a consequence that "is quite unlike the sort of 'indirect' and 'incidental' benefits that flowed to sectarian schools from programs aiding *all* parents by supplying bus transportation and secular textbooks for their children. *Such benefits were carefully restricted to the purely secular side of church-affiliated institutions* and provided no special aid for those who had chosen to support religious schools. Yet such aid approached the 'verge' of the constitutionally impermissible." * * *

ZOBREST v. CATALINA FOOTHILLS SCHOOL DIST.

509 U.S. 1, 113 S.Ct. 2462, 125 L.Ed.2d 1 (1993).

Chief Justice REHNQUIST delivered the opinion of the Court.

Petitioner James Zobrest, who has been deaf since birth, asked respondent school district to provide a sign-language interpreter to accompany him to classes at [Salpointe] Roman Catholic high school in Tucson, Arizona, pursuant to the Individuals with Disabilities Education Act (IDEA) and its Arizona counterpart. The United States Court of Appeals for the Ninth Circuit decided, however, that provision of such a publicly employed interpreter would violate the Establishment Clause * * * applying the three-part test announced in *Lemon.* It first found that the IDEA has a clear secular purpose: "to assist States and Localities to provide for the education of all handicapped children." Turning to the second prong of the *Lemon* inquiry, though, the Court of Appeals determined that the IDEA, if applied as petitioners proposed, would have the primary effect of advancing religion and thus would run afoul of the Establishment Clause. "By placing its employee in the sectarian school," the Court of Appeals reasoned, "the government would create the appearance that it was a 'joint sponsor' of the school's activities." This, the court held, would create the "symbolic union of government and religion" found impermissible in *School Dist. of Grand Rapids v. Ball,* 473 U.S. 373, 392, 105 S.Ct. 3216, 3227, 87 L.Ed.2d 267 (1985).

[W]e have consistently held that government programs that neutrally provide benefits to a broad class of citizens defined without reference to religion are not readily subject to an Establishment Clause challenge just because sectarian institutions may also receive an attenuated financial benefit. Nowhere have we stated this principle more clearly than in *Mueller* and *Witters v. Washington Dept. of Services for Blind,* 474 U.S. 481, 106 S.Ct. 748, 88 L.Ed.2d 846 (1986) [in which] we upheld against an Establishment Clause challenge the State of Washington's extension of vocational assistance, as part of a general state program, to a blind person studying at a private Christian college to become a pastor, missionary, or youth director. Looking at the statute as a whole, we observed that "[a]ny aid provided under Washington's program that ultimately flows to religious institutions does so only as a result of the genuinely independent and private choices of aid recipients." The program, we said, "creates no financial incentive for students to undertake sectarian education." We also remarked that, much like the law in *Mueller,* "Washington's program is 'made available generally without regard to the sectarian-nonsectarian, or public-nonpublic nature of the institution benefitted.' " In light of these factors, we held that Washington's program—even as applied to a student who sought state assistance so that he could become a pastor—would not advance religion in a manner inconsistent with the Establishment Clause.[a]

That same reasoning applies with equal force here. The service at issue in this case is part of a general government program that distributes benefits neutrally to any child qualifying as "handicapped" under the IDEA, without regard to the "sectarian-nonsectarian, or public-nonpublic nature" of the school the child attends. By according parents freedom to select a school of their choice, the statute ensures that a government-paid interpreter will be present in a sectarian school only as a result of the private decision of individual parents. In other words, because the IDEA creates no financial incentive for parents to choose a sectarian school, an interpreter's presence there cannot be attributed to state decisionmaking. [When] the government offers a neutral service on the premises of a sectarian school as part of a general program that "is in no way skewed towards religion," *Witters,* it follows under our prior decisions that provision of that service does not offend the Establishment Clause. Indeed, this is an even easier case than *Mueller* and *Witters* in the sense that, under the IDEA, no funds traceable to the government ever find their way into sectarian schools' coffers. The only indirect economic benefit a sectarian school might receive by dint of the IDEA is the handicapped child's tuition—and that is, of course, assuming that the school makes a profit on each student; that, without an IDEA interpreter, the child would have gone to school elsewhere; and that the school, then, would have been unable to fill that child's spot.

[R]espondent argues that this case more closely resembles *Meek* and *Grand Rapids.* In *Meek,* we struck down a statute that, inter alia, provided "massive aid" to private schools—more than 75% of which were church related—through a direct loan of teaching material and equipment [such as] maps, charts, and tape recorders. According to respondent, if the government could not place a tape recorder in a sectarian school in *Meek,* then it surely cannot place an interpreter in Salpointe. The statute in *Meek* also authorized state-paid personnel to furnish "auxiliary services"—which included remedial and accelerated instruction and guidance counseling—on the premises of religious schools. We determined that this part of the statute offended the First Amendment as well. *Grand Rapids*

a. On remand, the state court held that the aid in this case would violate the Washington constitution's provision that "no public money [shall] be appropriated for [any] religious instruction." *Witters v. State Commission for the Blind,* 112 Wash.2d 363, 771 P.2d 1119, cert. denied, 493 U.S. 850 (1989).

similarly involved two public programs that provided services on private school premises; there, public employees taught classes to students in private school classrooms.[9] We found that those programs likewise violated the Constitution, relying largely on *Meek*.[b] * * *

Respondent's reliance on *Meek* and *Grand Rapids* is misplaced for two reasons. First, the programs in *Meek* and *Grand Rapids*—through direct grants of government aid—relieved sectarian schools of costs they otherwise would have borne in educating their students. See *Witters* ("[T]he State may not grant aid to a religious school, whether cash or in kind, where the effect of the aid is 'that of a direct subsidy to the religious school' from the State") (quoting *Grand Rapids*). * * * "Substantial aid to the educational function of such schools," we explained, "necessarily results in aid to the sectarian school enterprise as a whole," and therefore brings about "the direct and substantial advancement of religious activity." So, too, was the case in *Grand Rapids:* The programs challenged there, which provided teachers in addition to instructional equipment and material, "in effect subsidize[d] the religious functions of the parochial schools by taking over a substantial portion of their responsibility for teaching secular subjects." "This kind of direct aid," we determined, "is indistinguishable from the provision of a direct cash subsidy to the religious school." [But] Salpointe is not relieved of an expense that it otherwise would have assumed in educating its students. And, as we noted above, [h]andicapped children, not sectarian schools, are the primary beneficiaries of the IDEA; to the extent sectarian schools benefit at all from the IDEA, they are only incidental beneficiaries. * * *

Second, the task of a sign-language interpreter seems to us quite different from that of a teacher or guidance counselor. [T]he Establishment Clause lays down no absolute bar to the placing of a public employee in a sectarian school.[10] * * * Nothing in this record suggests that a sign-language interpreter would do more than accurately interpret whatever material is presented to the class as a whole. * * * James' parents have chosen of their own free will to place him in a pervasively sectarian environment. The sign-language interpreter they have

---

9. Forty of the forty-one private schools involved in *Grand Rapids* were pervasively sectarian.

b. *Grand Rapids,* per Brennan, J., reasoned that the "program, if not subjected to a comprehensive, discriminating, and continuing state surveillance, *Lemon,* would entail an unacceptable risk that the state-sponsored instructional personnel would 'advance the religious mission of the church-related schools in which they serve.' Even though the teachers were paid by the State, '[t]he potential for impermissible fostering of religion under these circumstances, although somewhat reduced, is nonetheless present.' "

O'Connor, J., concurred: "When full-time parochial school teachers receive public funds to teach secular courses to their parochial school students under parochial school supervision, I agree that the program has the perceived and actual effect of advancing the religious aims of the church-related schools." But she disagreed when the teachers were regular public school employees: "Common sense suggests [that such] instructors are professional educators who can and do follow instructions not to inculcate religion in their classes. They are unlikely to be influenced by the sectarian nature of the parochial schools where they teach, not only because they are carefully supervised by public officials, but also because the vast majority of them visit several different schools each week and are not of the same religion as their parochial students."

In separate opinions in *Kiryas Joel,* O'Connor and Kennedy, JJ., called for reconsideration of *Grand Rapids* and its companion case of *Aguilar v. Felton,* 473 U.S. 402, 105 S.Ct. 3232, 87 L.Ed.2d 290 (1985). Scalia, J., joined by Rehnquist, C.J., and Thomas, J., urged that the cases be overruled.

10. For instance, in *Wolman,* we made clear that "the provision of health services to all schoolchildren—public and nonpublic—does not have the primary effect of aiding religion," even when those services are provided within sectarian schools. We accordingly rejected a First Amendment challenge to the State's providing diagnostic speech and hearing services on sectarian school premises.

requested will neither add to nor subtract from that environment, and hence the provision of such assistance is not barred by the Establishment Clause. * * *

Reversed.

JUSTICE BLACKMUN, with whom JUSTICE SOUTER joins, * * * dissenting.

Despite my disagreement with the majority's decision to reach the constitutional question,[c] its arguments on the merits deserve a response. Until now, the Court never has authorized a public employee to participate directly in religious indoctrination. Yet that is the consequence of today's decision. * * *

At Salpointe, where the secular and the sectarian are "inextricably intertwined," governmental assistance to the educational function of the school necessarily entails governmental participation in the school's inculcation of religion. A state-employed sign-language interpreter would be required to communicate the material covered in religion class, the nominally secular subjects that are taught from a religious perspective, and the daily Masses at which Salpointe encourages attendance for Catholic students. * * *

"Although Establishment Clause jurisprudence is characterized by few absolutes," at a minimum "the Clause does absolutely prohibit government-financed or government-sponsored indoctrination into the beliefs of a particular religious faith." *Grand Rapids.* * * *

Thus, the Court has upheld the use of public school buses to transport children to and from school, *Everson,* while striking down the employment of publicly funded buses for field trips controlled by parochial school teachers, *Wolman.* Similarly, the Court has permitted the provision of secular textbooks whose content is immutable and can be ascertained in advance, *Allen,* while prohibiting the provision of any instructional materials or equipment that could be used to convey a religious message, such as slide projectors, tape recorders, record players, and the like, *Wolman.* State-paid speech and hearing therapists have been allowed to administer diagnostic testing on the premises of parochial schools, *Wolman,* whereas state-paid remedial teachers and counselors have not been authorized to offer their services because of the risk that they may inculcate religious beliefs, *Meek.*[d]

These distinctions perhaps are somewhat fine, but "lines must be drawn." *Grand Rapids.* [When] government dispenses public funds to individuals who employ them to finance private choices, it is difficult to argue that government is actually endorsing religion. But the graphic symbol of the concert of church and state that results when a public employee or instrumentality mouths a religious message is likely to "enlis[t]—at least in the eyes of impressionable youngsters— the powers of government to the support of the religious denomination operating the school." *Grand Rapids.* And the union of church and state in pursuit of a common enterprise is likely to place the imprimatur of governmental approval upon the favored religion, conveying a message of exclusion to all those who do not adhere to its tenets. * * *

---

c. Stevens and O'Connor, JJ., dissented on this ground alone.

d. *Wolman,* however, upheld a program for similar services at neutral sites off the premises of the parochial school—even a portable classroom parked next to the school.

ROSENBERGER v. UNIVERSITY OF VIRGINIA, __ U.S. __, 115 S.Ct. 2510, 132 L.Ed.2d 700 (1995), per KENNEDY, J., held that the University's refusal to pay from its SAF (Student Activities Fund, which was used to fund various communications by student groups), the printing costs of a student newspaper ("Wide Awake, which offers a Christian perspective on both personal and community issues, especially those relevant to college students at the University of Virginia") because it promoted a "religious activity" (defined as "a particular belief in or about a deity or an ultimate reality") was "viewpoint discrimination" in violation of free speech (see p. 828 supra) and not justified by the establishment clause: "A central lesson of our decisions is that a significant factor in upholding governmental programs in the face of Establishment Clause attack is their neutrality towards religion. * * *

"The governmental program here is neutral toward religion. There is no suggestion that the University created it to advance religion or adopted some ingenious device with the purpose of aiding a religious cause. [The] apprehensions of our predecessors involved the levying of taxes upon the public for the sole and exclusive purpose of establishing and supporting specific sects. The exaction here, by contrast, is a student activity fee designed to reflect the reality that student life in its many dimensions includes the necessity of wide-ranging speech and inquiry and that student expression is an integral part of the University's educational mission. [The] SAF cannot be used for unlimited purposes, much less the illegitimate purpose of supporting one religion. Much like the arrangement in *Widmar,* the money goes to a special fund from which any group of students with [recognized] status can draw for purposes consistent with the University's educational mission; and to the extent the student is interested in speech, withdrawal is permitted to cover the whole spectrum of speech, whether it manifests a religious view, an antireligious view, or neither. Our decision, then, cannot be read as addressing an expenditure from a general tax fund. [The] University has taken pains to disassociate itself from the private speech involved in this case [and] there is no real likelihood that the speech in question is being either endorsed or coerced by the State.

"[If] the expenditure of governmental funds is prohibited whenever those funds pay for a service that is, pursuant to a religion-neutral program, used by a group for sectarian purposes, then *Widmar, Mergens,* and *Lamb's Chapel* would have to be overruled. Given our holdings in these cases, it follows that a public university may maintain its own computer facility and give student groups access to that facility, including the use of the printers, on a religion neutral, say first-come-first-served, basis. [There] is no difference in logic or principle, and no difference of constitutional significance, between a school using its funds to operate a facility to which students have access, and a school paying a third-party contractor to operate the facility on its behalf.[a] The latter occurs here. The University provides printing services to a broad spectrum of student newspapers. [Any] benefit to religion is incidental to the government's provision of secular services for secular purposes on a religion-neutral basis. Printing is a routine, secular, and recurring attribute of student life.

"[It] is, of course, true that if the State pays a church's bills it is subsidizing it, and we must guard against this abuse. That is not a danger here, based on the considerations we have advanced and for the additional reason that the student

a. Since the University made payments for publication costs directly to the printing companies, "we do not confront a case where, even under a neutral program that includes nonsectarian recipients, the government is making direct money payments to an institution or group that is engaged in religious activity."

publication is not a religious institution, at least in the usual sense of that term as used in our case law, and it is not a religious organization as used in the University's own regulations. It is instead a publication involved in a pure forum for the expression of ideas, ideas that would be both incomplete and chilled were the Constitution to be interpreted to require that state officials and courts scan the publication to ferret out views that principally manifest a belief in a divine being."

O'CONNOR, J., joined the Court's opinion subject to several comments: "This case lies at the intersection of the principle of government neutrality and the prohibition on state funding of religious activities. [Not] to finance Wide Awake, according to petitioners, violates the principle of neutrality by sending a message of hostility toward religion. To finance Wide Awake, argues the University, violates the prohibition on direct state funding of religious activities.

"When two bedrock principles so conflict, understandably neither can provide the definitive answer. Reliance on categorical platitudes is unavailing. Resolution instead depends on the hard task of judging—sifting through the details and determining whether the challenged program offends the Establishment Clause. Such judgment requires courts to draw lines, sometimes quite fine, based on the particular facts of each case. [C]ertain considerations specific to the program at issue lead me to conclude that by providing the same assistance to Wide Awake that it does to other publications, the University would not be endorsing the magazine's religious perspective." [b]

SOUTER, J., joined by Stevens, Ginsburg and Breyer, JJ., dissented: "The Court today, for the first time, approves direct funding of core religious activities by an arm of the State. [If the Establishment] Clause was meant to accomplish nothing else, it was meant to bar this use of public money. * * *

"The Court, accordingly, [has] categorically condemned state programs directly aiding religious activity, *Grand Rapids; Wolman; Meek; Nyquist,* (striking aid to nonpublic schools for maintenance and repair of facilities because "[n]o attempt is made to restrict payments to those expenditures related to the upkeep of facilities used exclusively for secular purposes"); *Levitt* (striking aid to nonpublic schools for state-mandated tests because the state had failed to "assure that the state-supported activity is not being used for religious indoctrination"); *Tilton v. Richardson,* 403 U.S. 672, 683, 91 S.Ct. 2091, 2098, 29 L.Ed.2d 790 (1971) (plurality opinion) (striking as insufficient a 20–year limit on prohibition for religious use in federal construction program for university facilities because unrestricted use even after 20 years "is in effect a contribution of some value to a religious body").

"Even when the Court has upheld aid to an institution performing both secular and sectarian functions, it has always made a searching enquiry to ensure that the institution kept the secular activities separate from its sectarian ones, with any direct aid flowing only to the former and never the latter. *Bowen v.*

b. "Unlike monies dispensed from state or federal treasuries, the Student Activities Fund is collected from students who themselves administer the fund and select qualifying recipients only from among those who originally paid the fee." Thus, "although the question is not presented here, I note the possibility that the student fee is susceptible to a Free Speech Clause challenge by an objecting student that she should not be compelled to pay for speech with which she disagrees. See, e.g., *Keller; Abood* pp. 889, 893 supra. The existence of such an opt-out possibility not available to citizens generally, provides a potential basis for distinguishing proceeds of the student fees in this case from proceeds of the general assessments in support of religion that lie at the core of the prohibition against religious funding, and from government funds generally."

Kendrick, 487 U.S. 589, 614–615, 108 S.Ct. 2562, 2577, 101 L.Ed.2d 520 (1988) (upholding grant program for services related to premarital adolescent sexual relations on ground that funds cannot be "used by the grantees in such a way as to advance religion"); *Roemer v. Board of Pub. Works of Md.,* 426 U.S. 736, 746–748, 755, 759–761, 96 S.Ct. 2337, 2344–2346, 2349, 2351–2352, 49 L.Ed.2d 179 (1976) (plurality opinion) (upholding general aid program restricting uses of funds to secular activities only); *Hunt v. McNair,* 413 U.S. 734, 742–745, 93 S.Ct. 2868, 2873–2875, 37 L.Ed.2d 923 (1973) (upholding general revenue bond program excluding from participation facilities used for religious purposes); *Tilton* (upholding general aid program for construction of academic facilities as "[t]here is no evidence that religion seeps into the use of any of these facilities"); see *Allen* (upholding textbook loan program limited to secular books requested by individual students for secular educational purposes). * * *

"Why does the Court not apply this clear law to these clear facts and conclude, as I do, that the funding scheme here is a clear constitutional violation? The answer must be in part that the Court fails to confront the evidence [about Wide Awake.] [c] Throughout its opinion, the Court refers uninformatively to Wide Awake's 'Christian viewpoint,' or its 'religious perspective,' and in distinguishing funding of Wide Awake from the funding of a church, the Court maintains that '[Wide Awake] is not a religious institution, at least in the usual sense.' The Court does not quote the magazine's adoption of Saint Paul's exhortation to awaken to the nearness of salvation, or any of its articles enjoining readers to accept Jesus Christ, or the religious verses, or the religious textual analyses, or the suggested prayers. [A further] answer is that the Court focuses on a subsidiary body of law, which it correctly states but ultimately misapplies. That subsidiary body of law accounts for the Court's substantial attention to the fact that the University's funding scheme is 'neutral,' in the formal sense that it makes funds available on an evenhanded basis to secular and sectarian applicants alike. While this is indeed true and relevant under our cases, it does not alone satisfy the requirements of the Establishment Clause, as the Court recognizes when it says that evenhandedness is only a 'significant factor' in certain Establishment Clause analysis, not a dispositive one. This recognition reflects the Court's appreciation of two general rules: that whenever affirmative government aid ultimately benefits religion, the Establishment Clause requires some justification beyond evenhandedness on the government's part; and that direct public funding of core sectarian activities, even if accomplished pursuant to an evenhanded program, would be entirely inconsistent with the Establishment Clause and would strike at the very heart of the Clause's protection. [In] the doubtful cases (those not involving direct public funding), where there is initially room for argument about a law's effect, evenhandedness serves to weed out those laws that impermissibly advance religion by channelling aid to it exclusively. [d] Evenhandedness is therefore a prerequisite to further enquiry into the constitutionality of a

---

c. "The character of the magazine is candidly disclosed on the opening page of the first issue, where the editor-in-chief announces Wide Awake's mission in a letter to the readership signed, 'Love in Christ': it is 'to challenge Christians to live, in word and deed, according to the faith they proclaim and to encourage students to consider what a personal relationship with Jesus Christ means.'" The dissent then quotes essays in Wide Awake on racism and eating disorders, concluding that "this writing is no merely descriptive examination of religious doctrine or even of ideal Christian practice in confronting life's social and personal problems. Nor is it merely the expression of editorial opinion that incidentally coincides with Christian ethics and reflects a Christian view of human obligation. It is straightforward exhortation to enter into a relationship with God as revealed in Jesus Christ, and to satisfy a series of moral obligations derived from the teachings of Jesus Christ."

d. The dissent then discussed *Mueller, Witters, Zobrest* and *Walz.*

doubtful law,[5] but evenhandedness goes no further. It does not guarantee success under Establishment Clause scrutiny.

"[O]ur cases have unsurprisingly repudiated any such attempt to cut the Establishment Clause down to a mere prohibition against unequal direct aid. See, e.g., *Wolman* (striking funding of field trips for nonpublic school students, such as are 'provided to public school students in the district,' because of unacceptable danger that state funds would be used to foster religion). And nowhere has the Court's adherence to the preeminence of the no-direct-funding principle over the principle of evenhandedness been as clear as in *Bowen*. * * *

"*Bowen* involved consideration of the Adolescent Family Life Act (AFLA), a federal grant program providing funds to institutions for counseling and educational services related to adolescent sexuality and pregnancy. [T]he District Court [held] the AFLA program unconstitutional both on its face and also insofar as religious institutions were involved in receiving grants under the Act. When this Court reversed on the issue of facial constitutionality under the Establishment Clause, we said that there was 'no intimation in the statute that at some point, or for some grantees, religious uses are permitted.' On the contrary, after looking at the legislative history and applicable regulations, we found safeguards adequate to ensure that grants would not be 'used [by] grantees in such a way as to advance religion.'

"With respect to the claim that the program was unconstitutional as applied, we remanded the case [to] 'consider [whether] in particular cases AFLA aid has been used to fund "specifically religious activit[ies]" in an otherwise substantially secular setting."' In giving additional guidance to the District Court, we suggested that application of the Act would be unconstitutional if it turned out that aid recipients were using materials 'that have an explicitly religious content or are designed to inculcate the views of a particular religious faith.'[e] At no point in our opinion did we suggest that the breadth of potential recipients, or distribution on an evenhanded basis, could have justified the use of federal funds for religious activities, a position that would have made no sense after we had pegged the Act's facial constitutionality to our conclusion that advancement of religion was not inevitable. * * *

"*Witters, Mueller,* and *Zobrest* expressly preserve the standard thus exhibited so often. Each of these cases explicitly distinguished the indirect aid in issue from contrasting examples in the line of cases striking down direct aid, and each thereby expressly preserved the core constitutional principle that direct aid to religion is impermissible. * * *

"The Court's claim of support from [the] forum-access cases [*Widmar; Mergens; Lamb's Chapel*] is ruled out by the very scope of their holdings. While they do indeed allow a limited benefit to religious speakers, they rest on the recognition that all speakers are entitled to use the street corner (even though the State paves the roads and provides police protection to everyone on the street) and on the

---

5. In a narrow band of cases at the polar extreme from direct funding cases, those involving essential public benefits commonly associated with living in an organized society (like police and fire protection, for example), evenhandedness may become important to ensuring that religious interests are not inhibited.

e. Blackmun, J., joined by Brennan, Marshall and Stevens, JJ., dissented: "Notwith-

standing the fact that government funds are paying for religious organizations to teach and counsel impressionable adolescents on a highly sensitive subject of considerable religious significance, often on the premises of a church or parochial school and without any effort to remove religious symbols from the sites, the majority concludes that the AFLA is not facially invalid."

analogy between the public street corner and open classroom space. Thus, the Court found it significant that the classroom speakers would engage in traditional speech activities in these forums, too, even though the rooms (like street corners) require some incidental state spending to maintain them. The analogy breaks down entirely, however, if the cases are read more broadly than the Court wrote them, to cover more than forums for literal speaking. There is no traditional street corner printing provided by the government on equal terms to all comers, and the forum cases cannot be lifted to a higher plane of generalization without admitting that new economic benefits are being extended directly to religion in clear violation of the principle barring direct aid. The argument from economic equivalence thus breaks down on recognizing that the direct state aid it would support is not mitigated by the street corner analogy in the service of free speech. Absent that, the rule against direct aid stands as a bar to printing services as well as printers. * * *

"Although it was a taxation scheme that moved Madison to write in the first instance, the Court has never held that government resources obtained without taxation could be used for direct religious support, and our cases on direct government aid have frequently spoken in terms in no way limited to tax revenues."

Notes and Questions

1. *Higher education.* The *Roemer, Hunt* and *Tilton* cases, described briefly in Souter, J.'s dissent, all upheld aid to church-related colleges and universities. *Roemer* noted "what is crucial to a nonentangling aid program: the ability of the State to identify and subsidize separate secular functions carried out at the school, without on-the-site inspections being necessary to prevent diversion of the funds to sectarian purposes." *Tilton* added: "There are generally significant differences between the religious aspects of church-related institutions of higher learning and parochial elementary and secondary schools. The 'affirmative, if not dominant, policy' of the instruction in pre-college church-schools is 'to assure future adherents to a particular faith by having control of their total education at an early age.' There is substance to the contention that college students are less impressionable and less susceptible to religious indoctrination. [Further], by their very nature, college and postgraduate courses tend to limit the opportunities for sectarian influence by virtue of their own internal disciplines. Many church-related colleges and universities are characterized by a high degree of academic freedom and seek to evoke free and critical responses from their students."

Compare Donald Giannella, *Lemon and Tilton: The Bitter and the Sweet of Church–State Entanglement,* 1971 Sup.Ct.Rev. 147, 175: "The Court's point is probably well taken that religion is more central to the activities of parochial schools than to those of most church-related colleges. But it is highly questionable to conclude that the risk of sectarian instruction creeping into a parochial school's physical education course is greater than the risk of a similar entry into a college history course."

Brennan, J., concurred in *Lemon* but dissented in *Tilton*: "[A] sectarian university is the equivalent in the realm of higher education of the Catholic elementary schools in Rhode Island; it is an educational institution in which the propagation and advancement of a particular religion is a primary function of the institution. [It] is not that religion 'permeates' the secular education that is provided. Rather, it is that the secular education is provided within the environment of religion; the institution is dedicated to two goals, secular education *and* religious instruction. When aid flows directly to the institution, both functions benefit."

White, J., concurred in *Tilton* but dissented in *Lemon:* "The Court strikes down the Rhode Island statute on its face [accepting] the model for the Catholic elementary and secondary schools that it rejected for the Catholic universities or colleges in [*Tilton.* It] strikes down this Rhode Island statute based primarily on its own model and its own suppositions and unsupported views of what is likely to happen in Rhode Island parochial school [classrooms]."

Consider Tribe *Treatise* 1221: "Another reason that religious colleges are treated differently from parochial schools is the *public's* view of the aid programs. Aid for secular programs in all colleges, including those with church affiliation, is generally perceived as assistance to non-religious activities. But the moment aid is sent to a parochial school as such, it is widely seen as aid to religion. The number of dollars released for religious purposes may be identical; the symbolism is not."

2. *Primary effect.* In *Tilton,* Douglas, J., joined by Black and Marshall, JJ., dissenting, argued that "religion pervades" parochial schools, which "operate on one budget" and "money not spent for one purpose becomes available for other purposes." If so, does bus transportation or secular textbooks for parochial school students "have a primary effect that advances religion"? If so, would this forbid stationing traffic police near parochial schools? Having the fire department put out fires in them? Furnishing sidewalks in front of them? If the public did not provide parochial schools with sidewalks and police and fire protection, would the schools have to include these items in their budgets? If so, does the public's supplying them "release" funds? May a public library lend books to parochial school students in which readings have been assigned by their teacher? Suppose it were shown that these books were "in fact instrumental in the teaching of religion"?

3. *Broad class of beneficiary groups.* (a) *Vouchers.* After *Mueller, Witters, Zobrest* and *Rosenberger,* would an "education voucher" plan pass muster if the vouchers were given to *all* parents for use in *any* school?

(b) *Political divisiveness.* To what extent does a "broad class" of beneficiary groups affect this criterion? Consider Note, *The Constitutionality of Tax Relief for Parents of Children Attending Public and Nonpublic Schools,* 67 Minn.L.Rev. 793, 820–21 (1983): "Legislation that primarily aids sectarian education disrupts political equality and promotes rivalry among religious sects by favoring those groups that emphasize private primary and secondary education. [In] contrast, aid which broadly benefits secular as well as sectarian groups is less likely to generate interfaith rivalries or imbalances of power. Even if only some sects receive aid directly, members of other faiths will probably benefit as members of the broader legislative class. Because particular religious groups will not be perceived as the primary beneficiaries of state aid, competition among sects for government funds will also be reduced." Compare Laura Underkuffler–Freund, *The Separation of the Religious and the Secular,* 36 Wm. & M.L.Rev. 837, 975 (1995): "The concerns of reformers—that governmental financial support of religious institutions would promote their involvement in government, their meddling with laws, their grasping for money, and their attempts to protect governmentally-bestowed privileges and emoluments—are presented no less by the public funding of all religious institutions than by the funding of few. Rather, the answer becomes [one] of degree: while incidental public support for sectarian institutions (on a basis equal to public institutions and to each other) probably presents little danger of institutional alliance of church and state, extensive funding may pose significant danger."

4. *Burden of proof.* Of what significance is the question of who—state or recipient—has the burden of proof in respect to each of the establishment clause criteria articulated in the decisions? In fact, to whom was the burden of proof assigned? Is the constitutionality of the programs invalidated still open on a showing that religion no more "permeates the secular education" in primary and secondary parochial schools than it does in church-related colleges?

5. *"Shared time."* Would a state "dual enrollment" plan, allowing parochial school students to take selected courses in the public schools, pass muster? Consider 85 Harv.L.Rev. 178 (1971): "[The] plan would have no impermissible effect, for public school teachers in public school buildings are unlikely to advance religion. However, the legislative purpose behind such a plan would be suspect: the obvious motive for releasing students for part of the day is to preserve the ability of their parents to give them religion-tinged instruction. In addition, such a plan might produce considerable conflict between public and parochial school authorities. If parochial school pupils were educated together with full-time public school pupils, accommodation of the scheduling needs of both systems could be quite difficult. Moreover, parochial school authorities might try to influence the content of the public school [courses]. Finally, since parochial schools would be the only beneficiaries of such legislation any modification of it would precipitate political controversy along religious lines." But see Paul G. Haskell, *The Prospects for Public Aid to Parochial Schools*, 56 Minn.L.Rev. 159 (1971).

6. *Other approaches.* Commentators have proposed various "tests" to measure the validity of public aid to church-related schools. In evaluating those that follow, what results would they produce in the decided cases?

(a) Murray A. Gordon, *The Unconstitutionality of Public Aid to Parochial Schools,* in The Wall Between Church and State 73, 92 (Oaks ed. 1963): "The [test] is whether it is the church (or church institution) or the state that performs or controls the performance of the services paid for by the state. [It] is reasonable to assume that services performed or controlled by a religious institution could and would be used to further the religious objectives of that institution, whereas services performed or controlled by a public body would be secular in purpose and form." What result in *Everson* if the buses were rented by the parochial school? What about lunches preceded by prayers in the parochial school cafeteria?

(b) Jesse H. Choper, *The Establishment Clause and Aid to Parochial Schools,* 56 Calif.L.Rev. 260, 265–66 (1968): "[G]overnmental financial aid may be extended directly or indirectly to support parochial schools [so] long as such aid does not exceed the value of the secular educational service rendered by the school." [c] Would such aid have "a secular legislative purpose and a primary effect that neither advances nor inhibits religion"? Compare Harold D. Hammett, *The Homogenized Wall*, 53 A.B.A.J. 929, 932–33 (1967): "If the net effect of the financial aid is to increase proportionally the influence of both the church and the state, so that their influence relative to each other remains at the same original ratio, the 'primary' effect on religion has been neutral." [d] Contrast Stephen D.

c. For further analysis, see Michael W. McConnell & Richard Posner, *An Economic Approach to Issues of Religious Freedom*, 56 U.Chi.L.Rev. 1 (1989); Note, *The Supreme Court, Effect Inquiry, and Aid to Parochial Education*, 37 Stan.L.Rev. 219 (1984).

d. See also William D. Valente, *Aid to Church Related Education—New Directions Without Dogma*, 55 Va.L.Rev. 579 (1969); Legal Dep't, NCWC, *The Constitutionality of the Inclusion of Church–Related Schools in Federal Aid to Education*, 50 Geo.L.J. 397 (1961).

Sugarman, *New Perspectives on "Aid" to Private School Users,* in Nonpublic School Aid 64, 66 (West ed. 1976): "Even if the [effect] principle were limited to cases in which there was (or the legislature knew there would be) a *large* beneficial impact on religion, it would intolerably inhibit secular government action. For example, perhaps building roads and running public transportation on Sunday may be shown to have large beneficial impacts on religion. [For] me the concerns underlying the Establishment clause could be satisfied with an affirmative answer to this hypothetical question: Would the legislature have acted as it did were there no interdependency with religion involved? If so, then I think it would be fair to say that there is no subsidy of religion, that the religious benefits are constitutionally permitted side effects." [e]

III. OFFICIAL ACKNOWLEDGMENT OF RELIGION

ALLEGHENY COUNTY v. ACLU

492 U.S. 573, 109 S.Ct. 3086, 106 L.Ed.2d 472 (1989).

JUSTICE BLACKMUN announced the judgment of the Court and delivered the opinion of the Court with respect to Parts III–A, IV, and V, an opinion with respect to Parts I and II, in which JUSTICE O'CONNOR and JUSTICE STEVENS join, an opinion with respect to Part III–B, in which JUSTICE STEVENS joins, and an opinion with respect to Part VI.

This litigation concerns the constitutionality of two recurring holiday displays located on public property in downtown Pittsburgh. The first is a crèche placed on the Grand Staircase of the Allegheny County Courthouse. The second is a Chanukah menorah placed just outside the City–County Building, next to a Christmas tree and a sign saluting liberty. The Court of Appeals for the Third Circuit ruled that each display violates the Establishment Clause [because] each has the impermissible effect of endorsing religion. We agree that the crèche display has that unconstitutional effect but reverse the Court of Appeals' judgment regarding the menorah display.

I.A. [The] crèche [is] a visual representation of the scene in the manger in Bethlehem shortly after the birth of Jesus, as described in the Gospels of Luke and Matthew. The crèche includes figures of the infant Jesus, Mary, Joseph, farm animals, shepherds, and wise men, all placed in or before a wooden representation of a manger, which has at its crest an angel bearing a banner that proclaims "Gloria in Excelsis Deo!"

[III.A.] Although "the myriad, subtle ways in which Establishment Clause values can be eroded," are not susceptible to a single verbal formulation, this Court has attempted to encapsulate the essential precepts of the Establishment Clause. Thus, in *Everson,* the Court gave this often-repeated summary [stating the third ¶ on p. 1092]. In *Lemon,* the Court sought to refine these principles by focusing on three "tests" for determining whether a government practice violates the Establishment Clause. [Our] subsequent decisions further have refined the definition of governmental action that unconstitutionally advances religion. In recent years, we have paid particularly close attention to whether the challenged governmental practice either has the purpose or effect of "endorsing" religion, a concern that has long had a place in our Establishment Clause jurisprudence. See *Engel.* * * *

e. Problems under the free exercise clause raised by the exclusion of parochial schools from public aid programs are considered in note 2, p. 1016 infra.

Of course, the word "endorsement" is not self-defining. Rather, it derives its meaning from other words that this Court has found useful over the years in interpreting the Establishment Clause. [Whether] the key word is "endorsement," "favoritism," or "promotion," the essential principle remains the same. The Establishment Clause, at the very least, prohibits government from appearing to take a position on questions of religious belief or from "making adherence to a religion relevant in any way to a person's standing in the political community." *Lynch v. Donnelly,* 465 U.S. 668, 687, 104 S.Ct. 1355, 1386, 79 L.Ed.2d 604 (1984) (O'Connor, J., concurring).

B. [In *Lynch,*] we considered whether the city of Pawtucket, R.I., had violated the Establishment Clause by including a crèche in its annual Christmas display, located in a private park within the downtown shopping district.[a] By a 5–4 decision in that difficult case, the Court upheld inclusion of the crèche in the Pawtucket display, holding, inter alia, that the inclusion of the crèche did not have the impermissible effect of advancing or promoting religion.

The rationale [contains] two strands, neither of which provides guidance for decision in subsequent cases. First, the opinion states that the inclusion of the crèche in the display was "no more an advancement or endorsement of religion" than other "endorsements" this Court has approved in the past—but the opinion offers no discernible measure for distinguishing between permissible and impermissible endorsements. Second, the opinion observes that any benefit the government's display of the crèche gave to religion was no more than "indirect, remote, and incidental"—without saying how or why.

Although Justice O'Connor joined the majority opinion in *Lynch,* she wrote a concurrence [that] provides a sound analytical framework for evaluating governmental use of religious symbols.

First and foremost, the concurrence [recognizes] any endorsement of religion as "invalid," because it "sends a message to nonadherents that they are outsiders, not full members of the political community, and an accompanying message to adherents that they are insiders, favored members of the political community."

Second, the concurrence articulates a method for determining whether the government's use of an object with religious meaning has the effect of endorsing religion. The effect of the display depends upon the message that the government's practice communicates: the question is "what viewers may fairly understand to be the purpose of the display." That inquiry, of necessity, turns upon the context in which the contested object appears: "a typical museum setting, though not neutralizing the religious content of a religious painting, negates any message of endorsement of that content." * * *

The concurrence applied this mode of analysis to the Pawtucket crèche, seen in the context of that city's holiday celebration as a whole. In addition to the crèche the city's display contained: a Santa Claus House with a live Santa distributing candy, reindeer pulling Santa's sleigh; a live 40–foot Christmas tree strung with lights; statues of carolers in old-fashioned dress; candy-striped poles; a "talking" wishing well; a large banner proclaiming "SEASONS GREETINGS"; a miniature "village" with several houses and a church, and various "cut-out" figures, including those of a clown, a dancing elephant, a robot, and a teddy bear. The concurrence concluded that both because the crèche is "a traditional symbol"

---

a. "[Ten years ago], when [the] crèche was acquired, it cost the City $1365; it now is valued at $200. The erection and dismantling of the crèche costs the City about $20 per year; nominal expenses are incurred in lighting the crèche. No money has been expended on its maintenance for the past 10 years."

of Christmas, a holiday with strong secular elements, and because the crèche was "displayed along with purely secular symbols," the crèche's setting "changes what viewers may fairly understand to be the purpose of the display" and "negates any message of endorsement" of "the Christian beliefs represented by the crèche."

The four *Lynch* dissenters agreed with the concurrence that the controlling question was "whether Pawtucket ha[d] run afoul of the Establishment Clause by endorsing religion through its display of the crèche." The dissenters also agreed with the general proposition that the context in which the government uses a religious symbol is relevant for determining the answer to that question. They simply reached a different answer: the dissenters concluded that the other elements of the Pawtucket display did not negate the endorsement of Christian faith caused by the presence of the crèche. * * *

Thus, despite divergence at the bottom line, the five Justices in concurrence and dissent in *Lynch* agreed upon the relevant constitutional principles [which] are sound, and have been adopted by the Court in subsequent cases. [*Grand Rapids*.]

IV. We turn first to the county's crèche display. [U]nlike *Lynch*, nothing in the context of the display detracts from the crèche's religious message. [Furthermore,] the crèche sits on the Grand Staircase, the "main" and "most beautiful part" of the building that is the seat of county government. No viewer could reasonably think that it occupies this location without the support and approval of the government. * * *

In sum, *Lynch* teaches that government may celebrate Christmas in some manner and form, but not in a way that endorses Christian doctrine. Here, Allegheny County has transgressed this line. It has chosen to celebrate Christmas in a way that has the effect of endorsing a patently Christian message: Glory to God for the birth of Jesus Christ. * * *

V. Justice Kennedy and the three Justices who join him would find the display of the crèche consistent with the Establishment Clause. [The] reasons for deciding otherwise are so far-reaching in their implications that they require a response in some depth:

A. In *Marsh v. Chambers*, 463 U.S. 783, 103 S.Ct. 3330, 77 L.Ed.2d 1019 (1983) [upholding the practice of legislative prayer], the Court relied specifically on the fact that Congress authorized legislative prayer at the same time that it produced the Bill of Rights.[b] Justice Kennedy, however, argues that *Marsh* legitimates all "practices with no greater potential for an establishment of religion" than those "accepted traditions dating back to the Founding." Otherwise, the Justice asserts, such practices as our national motto ("In God We Trust") and our Pledge of Allegiance (with the phrase "under God," added in 1954) are in danger of invalidity.

b. *Marsh* also pointed, inter alia, to the practice in the colonies (including Virginia after adopting its Declaration of Rights which has been "considered the precursor of both the Free Exercise and Establishment Clauses"), to the opening invocations in federal courts (including the Supreme Court), and to the Continental Congress and First Congress: "[T]he practice of opening sessions with prayer has continued without interruption ever since that early session of Congress. It has also been followed consistently in most of the states." Brennan, Marshall and Stevens, JJ., dissented.

Of what relevance is it that, subsequently, "Madison acknowledged that he had been quite mistaken in approving—as a member of the House, in 1789—bills for the payment of congressional chaplains"? William W. Van Alstyne, *Trends in the Supreme Court: Mr. Jefferson's Crumbling Wall*, 1984 Duke L.J. 770, 776.

Our previous opinions have considered in dicta the motto and the pledge, characterizing them as consistent with the proposition that government may not communicate an endorsement of religious belief. We need not return to the subject of "ceremonial deism," [c] because there is an obvious distinction between crèche displays and references to God in the motto and the pledge. However history may affect the constitutionality of nonsectarian references to religion by the government,[52] history cannot legitimate practices that demonstrate the government's allegiance to a particular sect or creed. [The] history of this Nation, it is perhaps sad to say, contains numerous examples of official acts that endorsed Christianity specifically [but] this heritage of official discrimination against non-Christians has no place in the jurisprudence of the Establishment Clause. * * *

C. Although Justice Kennedy repeatedly accuses the Court of harboring a "latent hostility" or "callous indifference" toward religion, nothing could be further from the truth. [The] government does not discriminate against any citizen on the basis of the citizen's religious faith if the government is secular in its functions and operations. On the contrary, the Constitution mandates that the government remain secular, rather than affiliating itself with religious beliefs or institutions, precisely in order to avoid discriminating among citizens on the basis of their religious faiths.

A secular state, it must be remembered, is not the same as an atheistic or antireligious state. A secular state establishes neither atheism nor religion as its official creed. * * * [59]

VI. The display of the Chanukah menorah in front of the City–County Building may well present a closer [issue. The] relevant question for Establishment Clause purposes is whether the combined display of the tree, the sign, and the menorah has the effect of endorsing both Christian and Jewish faiths, or rather simply recognizes that both Christmas and Chanukah are part of the same winter-holiday season, which has attained a secular status in our society. Of the two interpretations of this particular display, the latter seems far more plausible and is also in line with *Lynch*.[64]

c. Brennan, J., joined by Marshall, Blackmun and Stevens, JJ., dissenting in *Lynch* "suggest[ed] that such practices as the designation of 'In God We Trust' as our national motto, or the references to God contained in the Pledge of Allegiance can best be understood [as] a form of 'ceremonial deism,' protected from Establishment Clause scrutiny chiefly because they have lost through rote repetition any significant religious content."

52. It is worth noting that just because *Marsh* sustained the validity of legislative prayer, it does not necessarily follow that practices like proclaiming a National Day of Prayer are constitutional. Legislative prayer does not urge citizens to engage in religious practices, and on that basis could well be distinguishable from an exhortation from government to the people that they engage in religious conduct. But, as this practice is not before us, we express no judgment about its constitutionality.

59. In his attempt to legitimate the display of the crèche on the Grand Staircase, Justice Kennedy repeatedly characterizes it as an "accommodation" of religion. But an accommo-dation of religion, in order to be permitted under the Establishment Clause, must lift "an identifiable burden *on the exercise of religion.*" *Corporation of Presiding Bishop v. Amos*, [Sec. 3 infra]. Prohibiting the display of a crèche at this location [does] not impose a burden on the practice of Christianity (except to the extent some Christian sect seeks to be an officially approved religion), and therefore permitting the display is not an "accommodation" of religion in the conventional sense.

["Accommodation" of religion and the relationship between the establishment and free exercise clauses is considered in detail in Sec. 3 infra.]

64. [The] conclusion that Pittsburgh's combined Christmas–Chanukah display cannot be interpreted as endorsing Judaism alone does not mean, however, that it is implausible, as a general matter, for a city like Pittsburgh to endorse a minority faith. The display of a menorah alone might well have that effect.

The Christmas tree, unlike the menorah, is not itself a religious symbol. [The] widely accepted view of the Christmas tree as the preeminent secular symbol of the Christmas holiday season serves to emphasize the secular component of the message communicated by other elements of an accompanying holiday display, including the Chanukah menorah.[66]

The tree, moreover, is clearly the predominant element in the city's display. The 45–foot tree occupies the central position [in] the City–County Building; the 18–foot menorah is positioned to one side. Given this configuration, it is much more sensible to interpret the meaning of the menorah in light of the tree, rather than vice versa. * * *

Although the city has used a symbol with religious meaning as its representation of Chanukah, this is not a case in which the city has reasonable alternatives that are less religious in nature. [Where] the government's secular message can be conveyed by two symbols, only one of which carries religious meaning, an observer reasonably might infer from the fact that the government has chosen to use the religious symbol that the government means to promote religious faith. See *Schempp* (Brennan, J., concurring) (Establishment Clause forbids use of religious means to serve secular ends when secular means suffice). But where, as here, no such choice has been made, this inference of endorsement is not present.[68]

The Mayor's sign further diminishes the possibility that the tree and the menorah will be interpreted as a dual endorsement of Christianity and Judaism. The sign states that during the holiday season the city salutes liberty. Moreover, the sign draws upon the theme of light, common to both Chanukah and Christmas as winter festivals, and links that theme with this Nation's legacy of freedom, which allows an American to celebrate the holiday season in whatever way he wishes, religiously or otherwise. [While] an adjudication of the display's effect must take into account the perspective of one who is neither Christian nor Jewish, as well as of those who adhere to either of these religions, the constitutionality of its effect must also be judged according to the standard of a "reasonable observer." See Laurence H. Tribe, *American Constitutional Law* 1296 (2d ed. 1988) (challenged government practices should be judged "from the perspective of a 'reasonable non-adherent'"). When measured against this standard, the menorah need not be excluded from this particular display.

The conclusion here that, in this particular context, the menorah's display does not have an effect of endorsing religious faith does not foreclose the possibility that the display of the menorah might violate either the "purpose" or "entanglement" prong of the *Lemon* analysis. These issues were not addressed by the Court of Appeals and may be considered by that court on remand. * * *

66. Although the Christmas tree represents the secular celebration of Christmas, its very association with Christmas (a holiday with religious dimensions) makes it conceivable that the tree might be seen as representing Christian religion when displayed next to an object associated with Jewish religion. For this reason, I agree with Justice Brennan and Justice Stevens that one must ask whether the tree and the menorah together endorse the *religious* beliefs of Christians and Jews. For the reasons stated in the text, however, I conclude the city's overall display does not have this impermissible effect.

68. In *Lynch*, in contrast, there was no need for Pawtucket to include a crèche in order to convey a secular message about Christmas. (Blackmun, J., dissenting). [In] displaying the menorah next to the tree, the city has demonstrated no preference for the *religious* celebration of the holiday season. This conclusion, however, would be untenable had the city substituted a crèche for its Christmas tree or if the city had failed to substitute for the menorah an alternative, more secular, representation of Chanukah.

JUSTICE KENNEDY, with whom THE CHIEF JUSTICE, JUSTICE WHITE, and JUSTICE SCALIA join, concurring in the judgment in part and dissenting in part. * * *

I.   In keeping with the usual fashion of recent years, the majority applies the *Lemon* test to judge the constitutionality of the holiday displays here in question. * * * Persuasive criticism of *Lemon* has emerged. See *Aguillard* (Scalia, J., dissenting); *Aguilar v. Felton* (O'Connor, J., dissenting); *Jaffree* (Rehnquist, J., dissenting); *Roemer* (White, J., concurring in judgment). Our cases often question its utility in providing concrete answers to Establishment Clause questions, calling it but a "helpful signpos[t]" or "guidelin[e]", to assist our deliberations rather than a comprehensive test. *Mueller;* See *Lynch* ("we have repeatedly emphasized our unwillingness to be confined to any single test or criterion in this sensitive area").[d] Substantial revision of our Establishment Clause doctrine may be in order[e]; but it is unnecessary to undertake that task today, for even the *Lemon* test, when applied with proper sensitivity to our traditions and our caselaw, supports the conclusion that both the crèche and the menorah are permissible displays in the context of the holiday season. * * *

Rather than requiring government to avoid any action that acknowledges or aids religion, the Establishment Clause permits government some latitude in recognizing and accommodating the central role religion plays in our society. *Lynch; Walz.* Any approach less sensitive to our heritage would border on latent hostility toward religion, as it would require government in all its multifaceted roles to acknowledge only the secular, to the exclusion and so to the detriment of the religious. A categorical approach would install federal courts as jealous guardians of an absolute "wall of separation," sending a clear message of disapproval. In this century, as the modern administrative state expands to touch the lives of its citizens in such diverse ways and redirects their financial choices through programs of its own, it is difficult to maintain the fiction that requiring government to avoid all assistance to religion can in fairness be viewed as serving the goal of neutrality. * * *

The ability of the organized community to recognize and accommodate religion in a society with a pervasive public sector requires diligent observance of the border between accommodation and establishment. Our cases disclose two limiting principles: government may not coerce anyone to support or participate

---

d. In *Marsh,* Brennan, J., joined by Marshall, J. dissenting, noting that "the Court makes no pretense of subjecting Nebraska's practice of legislative prayer to any of the formal 'tests' that have traditionally structured our inquiry under the Establishment Clause": "I have no doubt that, if any group of law students were asked to apply the principles of *Lemon* to the question of legislative prayer, they would nearly unanimously find the practice to be unconstitutional. [W]e are faced here with the regularized practice of conducting official prayers, on behalf of the entire legislature, as part of the order of business constituting the formal opening of every single session of the legislative term."

e. Four year later, concurring in *Lamb's Chapel,* Scalia, J., joined by Thomas, J., noted that six "of the currently sitting Justices" have disagreed with *Lemon*—Rehnquist, C.J., and White, O'Connor, and Kennedy, JJ., in addition to themselves:

"For my part, I agree with the long list of constitutional scholars who have criticized *Lemon* and bemoaned the strange Establishment Clause geometry of crooked lines and wavering shapes its intermittent use has produced. See, e.g., Jesse H. Choper, *The Establishment Clause and Aid to Parochial Schools—An Update,* 75 Cal.L.Rev. 5 (1987); William P. Marshall, *"We Know It When We See It": The Supreme Court and Establishment,* 59 S.Cal.L.Rev. 495 (1986); Michael W. McConnell, *Accommodation of Religion,* 1985 S.Ct.Rev. 1; Philip B. Kurland, *The Religion Clauses and the Burger Court,* 34 Cath. U.L.Rev. 1 (1984); Robert Cord, *Separation of Church and State* (1982); Jesse H. Choper, *The Religion Clauses of the First Amendment: Reconciling the Conflict,* 41 U.Pitt.L.Rev. 673 (1980). I will decline to apply *Lemon*—whether it validates or invalidates the government action in question—and therefore cannot join the opinion of the Court today."

in any religion or its exercise; and it may not, in the guise of avoiding hostility or callous indifference, give direct benefits to religion in such a degree that it in fact "establishes a [state] religion or religious faith, or tends to do so." *Lynch.* These two principles, while distinct, are not unrelated, for it would be difficult indeed to establish a religion without some measure of more or less subtle coercion, be it in the form of taxation to supply the substantial benefits that would sustain a state-established faith, direct compulsion to observance, or governmental exhortation to religiosity that amounts in fact to proselytizing.

[The] freedom to worship as one pleases without government interference or oppression is the great object of both the Establishment and the Free Exercise Clauses. Barring all attempts to aid religion through government coercion goes far toward attainment of this object. [S]ome of our recent cases reject the view that coercion is the sole touchstone of an Establishment Clause violation. See *Engel* (dictum) (rejecting, without citation of authority, proposition that coercion is required to demonstrate an Establishment Clause violation); *Schempp; Nyquist.* That may be true if by "coercion" is meant *direct* coercion in the classic sense of an establishment of religion that the Framers knew. But coercion need not be a direct tax in aid of religion or a test oath. Symbolic recognition or accommodation of religious faith may violate the Clause in an extreme case.[1] I doubt not, for example, that the Clause forbids a city to permit the permanent erection of a large Latin cross on the roof of city hall. This is not because government speech about religion is per se suspect, as the majority would have it, but because such an obtrusive year-round religious display would place the government's weight behind an obvious effort to proselytize on behalf of a particular religion. Speech may coerce in some circumstances, but this does not justify a ban on all government recognition of religion. As Chief Justice Burger wrote for the Court in *Walz:* "[W]e will not tolerate either governmentally established religion or governmental interference with religion. Short of those expressly proscribed governmental acts there is room for play in the joints productive of a benevolent neutrality which will permit religious exercise to exist without sponsorship and without interference." * * * Absent coercion, the risk of infringement of religious liberty by passive or symbolic accommodation is minimal. [In] determining whether there exists an establishment, or a tendency toward one, we refer to the other types of church-state contacts that have existed unchallenged throughout our history, or that have been found permissible in our caselaw [discussing *Lynch* and *Marsh*].

II. These principles are not difficult to apply to the facts of the case before us. In permitting the displays on government property of the menorah and the crèche, the city and county sought to do no more than "celebrate the season," and to acknowledge, along with many of their citizens, the historical background and the religious as well as secular nature of the Chanukah and Christmas holidays. * * *

If government is to participate in its citizens' celebration of a holiday that contains both a secular and a religious component, enforced recognition of only the secular aspect would signify the callous indifference toward religious faith that our cases and traditions do not require; for by commemorating the holiday only as

---

1. [O]ur cases have held only that *direct* coercion need not always be shown to establish an Establishment Clause violation. The prayer invalidated in *Engel* was unquestionably coercive in an indirect manner, as the *Engel* Court itself recognized * * *.

[*Marsh* noted that "here, the individual claiming injury by the practice is an adult, presumably not readily susceptible to 'religious indoctrination,' see *Tilton,* or peer pressure, compare *Schempp* (Brennan, J., concurring)."]

it is celebrated by nonadherents, the government would be refusing to acknowledge the plain fact, and the historical reality, that many of its citizens celebrate its religious aspects as well. [The] Religion Clauses do not require government to acknowledge these holidays or their religious component; but our strong tradition of government accommodation and acknowledgment permits government to do so.

There is no suggestion here that the government's power to coerce has been used to further the interests of Christianity or Judaism in any way. No one was compelled to observe or participate in any religious ceremony or activity. Neither the city nor the county contributed significant amounts of tax money to serve the cause of one religious faith. The crèche and the menorah are purely passive symbols of religious holidays. Passersby who disagree with the message conveyed by these displays are free to ignore them, or even to turn their backs, just as they are free to do when they disagree with any other form of government speech.

[Crucial] to the Court's conclusion [in *Lynch*] was not the number, prominence, or type of secular items contained in the holiday display but the simple fact that, when displayed by government during the Christmas season, a crèche presents no realistic danger of moving government down the forbidden road toward an establishment of religion. Whether the crèche be surrounded by poinsettias, talking wishing wells, or carolers, the conclusion remains the same, for the relevant context is not the items in the display itself but the season as a whole. * * *

[III.] Even if *Lynch* did not control, I would not commit this Court to the test applied by the majority today. The notion that cases arising under the Establishment Clause should be decided by an inquiry into whether a " 'reasonable observer' " may " 'fairly understand' " government action to " 'sen[d] a message to nonadherents that they are outsiders, not full members of the political community,' " is a recent, and in my view most unwelcome, addition to our tangled Establishment Clause jurisprudence. * * *

[A.] *Marsh* stands for the proposition, not that specific practices common in 1791 are an exception to the otherwise broad sweep of the Establishment Clause, but rather that the meaning of the Clause is to be determined by reference to historical practices and understandings.[7] Whatever test we choose to apply must permit not only legitimate practices two centuries old but also any other practices with no greater potential for an establishment of religion. [Few] of our traditional practices recognizing the part religion plays in our society can withstand scrutiny under a faithful application [the endorsement test].

Some examples suffice to make plain my concerns. Since the Founding of our Republic, American Presidents have issued Thanksgiving Proclamations establishing a national day of celebration and prayer. The first such proclamation was issued by President Washington at the request of the First Congress [and] the forthrightly religious nature of these proclamations has not waned with the years. President Franklin D. Roosevelt went so far as to "suggest a nationwide reading of the Holy Scriptures during the period from Thanksgiving Day to Christmas" so that "we may bear more earnest witness to our gratitude to Almighty God." It requires little imagination to conclude that these proclamations would cause

---

7. Contrary to the majority's discussion, the relevant historical practices are those conducted by governmental units which were subject to the constraints of the Establishment Clause. Acts of "official discrimination against non-Christians" perpetrated in the eighteenth and nineteenth centuries by States and municipalities are of course irrelevant to this inquiry, but the practices of past Congresses and Presidents are highly informative.

nonadherents to feel excluded, yet they have been a part of our national heritage from the beginning.[9]

The Executive has not been the only Branch of our Government to recognize the central role of religion in our society. The fact that this Court opens its sessions with the request that "God save the United States and this honorable Court" has been noted elsewhere. The Legislature has gone much further, not only employing legislative chaplains, but also setting aside a special prayer room in the Capitol for use by Members of the House and Senate. The room is decorated with a large stained glass panel that depicts President Washington kneeling in prayer; around him is etched the first verse of the 16th Psalm: "Preserve me, O God, for in Thee do I put my trust." * * * Congress has directed the President to "set aside and proclaim a suitable day each year [as] a National Day of Prayer, on which the people of the United States may turn to God in prayer and meditation at churches, in groups, and as individuals." [Also] by statute, the Pledge of Allegiance to the Flag describes the United States as "one Nation under God." To be sure, no one is obligated to recite this phrase, see *West Virginia State Bd. of Educ. v. Barnette,* [Sec. 2, I infra] but it borders on sophistry to suggest that the " 'reasonable' " atheist would not feel less than a " 'full membe[r] of the political community' " every time his fellow Americans recited, as part of their expression of patriotism and love for country, a phrase he believed to be false. Likewise, our national motto, "In God we trust," which is prominently engraved in the wall above the Speaker's dias in the Chamber of the House of Representatives and is reproduced on every coin minted and every dollar printed by the Federal Government, must have the same effect.

If the intent of the Establishment Clause is to protect individuals from mere feelings of exclusion, then legislative prayer cannot escape invalidation. It has been argued that "[these] government acknowledgments of religion serve, in the only ways reasonably possible in our culture, the legitimate secular purposes of solemnizing public occasions, expressing confidence in the future, and encouraging the recognition of what is worthy of appreciation in society." *Lynch* (O'Connor, J., concurring). I fail to see why prayer is the only way to convey these messages; appeals to patriotism, moments of silence, and any number of other approaches would be as effective, were the only purposes at issue the ones described by the *Lynch* concurrence. Nor is it clear to me why "encouraging the recognition of what is worthy of appreciation in society" can be characterized as a purely secular purpose, if it can be achieved only through religious prayer. No doubt prayer is "worthy of appreciation," but that is most assuredly not because it is secular. Even accepting the secular-solemnization explanation at face value, moreover, it seems incredible to suggest that the average observer of legislative prayer who either believes in no religion or whose faith rejects the concept of God would not receive the clear message that his faith is out of step with the political norm.[10]

---

9. Similarly, our presidential inaugurations have traditionally opened with a request for divine blessing. * * *

10. If the majority's test were to be applied logically, it would lead to the elimination of all nonsecular Christmas caroling in public buildings or, presumably, anywhere on public property. It is difficult to argue that lyrics like "Good Christian men, rejoice," "Joy to the world! the Savior reigns," "This, this is Christ the King," "Christ, by highest heav'n adored," and "Come and behold Him, Born the King of angels," have acquired such a secular nature that nonadherents would not feel "left out" by a government-sponsored or approved program that included these carols. We do not think for a moment that the Court will ban such carol programs, however. Like Thanksgiving Proclamations, the reference to God in the Pledge of Allegiance, and invocations to God in sessions of Congress and of this Court, they constitute practices that the Court will not proscribe, but that the Court's reasoning today does not explain.

[B.] If there be such a person as the "reasonable observer," I am quite certain that he or she will take away a salient message from our holding in this case: the Supreme Court of the United States has concluded that the First Amendment creates classes of religions based on the relative numbers of their adherents. Those religions enjoying the largest following must be consigned to the status of least-favored faiths so as to avoid any possible risk of offending members of minority religions. I would be the first to admit that many questions arising under the Establishment Clause do not admit of easy answers, but whatever the Clause requires, it is not the result reached by the Court today.

[IV.] The case before us is admittedly a troubling one. It must be conceded that, however neutral the purpose of the city and county, the eager proselytizer may seek to use these symbols for his own ends. The urge to use them to teach or to taunt is always present. It is also true that some devout adherents of Judaism or Christianity may be as offended by the holiday display as are nonbelievers, if not more so. To place these religious symbols in a common hallway or sidewalk, where they may be ignored or even insulted, must be distasteful to many who cherish their meaning.

For these reasons, I might have voted against installation of these particular displays were I a local legislative official. But [the] principles of the Establishment Clause and our Nation's historic traditions of diversity and pluralism allow communities to make reasonable judgments respecting the accommodation or acknowledgment of holidays with both cultural and religious aspects. No constitutional violation occurs when they do so by displaying a symbol of the holiday's religious origins. * * *

JUSTICE O'CONNOR with whom JUSTICE BRENNAN and JUSTICE STEVENS join as to Part II, concurring in part and concurring in the judgment. * * *

II. In his separate opinion, Justice Kennedy asserts that the endorsement test "is flawed in its fundamentals and unworkable in practice." * * *

An Establishment Clause standard that prohibits only "coercive" practices or overt efforts at government proselytization, but fails to take account of the numerous more subtle ways that government can show favoritism to particular beliefs or convey a message of disapproval to others, would not, in my view, adequately protect the religious liberty or respect the religious diversity of the members of our pluralistic political community. Thus, this Court has never relied on coercion alone as the touchstone of Establishment Clause analysis. To require a showing of coercion, even indirect coercion, as an essential element of an Establishment Clause violation would make the Free Exercise Clause a redundancy. [Moreover,] as even Justice Kennedy recognizes, any Establishment Clause test limited to "*direct* coercion" clearly would fail to account for forms of "[s]ymbolic recognition or accommodation of religious faith" that may violate the Establishment Clause.

[To] be sure, the endorsement test depends on a sensitivity to the unique circumstances and context of a particular challenged practice and, like any test that is sensitive to context, it may not always yield results with unanimous agreement at the margins. But that is true of many standards in constitutional law, and even the modified coercion test offered by Justice Kennedy involves judgment and hard choices at the margin. He admits as much by acknowledging that the permanent display of a Latin cross at city hall would violate the Establishment Clause, as would the display of symbols of Christian holidays alone. Would the display of a Latin cross for six months have such an unconstitutional effect, or the display of the symbols of most Christian holidays and one Jewish holiday? Would the Christmas-time display of a crèche inside a courtroom be "coercive" if subpoenaed witnesses had no opportunity to "turn their backs" and walk away? Would displaying a crèche in front of a public school violate the Establishment Clause under Justice Kennedy's test? * * *

Justice Kennedy submits that the endorsement test is inconsistent with our precedents and traditions because, in his words, if it were "applied without artificial exceptions for historical practice," it would invalidate many traditional practices recognizing the role of religion in our society. * * * Historical acceptance of a practice does not in itself validate that practice under the Establishment Clause if the practice violates the values protected by that Clause, just as historical acceptance of racial or gender based discrimination does not immunize such practices from scrutiny under the 14th Amendment.[f] [On] the contrary, the "history and ubiquity" of a practice is relevant because it provides part of the context in which a reasonable observer evaluates whether a challenged governmental practice conveys a message of endorsement of religion. [Thus,] the celebration of Thanksgiving as a public holiday, despite its religious origins, is now generally understood as a celebration of patriotic values rather than particular religious beliefs.[g] * * *

III. For reasons which differ somewhat from those set forth in Part VI of Justice Blackmun's opinion, I also conclude that the city of Pittsburgh's combined holiday display of a Chanukah menorah, a Christmas tree, and a sign saluting liberty does not have the effect of conveying an endorsement of religion. [My] conclusion does not depend on whether or not the city had "a more secular alternative symbol" of Chanukah, just as the Court's decision in *Lynch* clearly did not turn on whether the city of Pawtucket could have conveyed its tribute to the Christmas holiday season by using a "less religious" alternative to the crèche symbol in its display of traditional holiday symbols. In my view, Justice Blackmun's new rule that an inference of endorsement arises every time government uses a symbol with religious meaning if a "more secular alternative" is available, is too blunt an instrument for Establishment Clause analysis, which depends on sensitivity to the context and circumstances presented by each case. * * *

JUSTICE BRENNAN, with whom JUSTICE MARSHALL and JUSTICE STEVENS join, concurring in part and dissenting in part.

* * * I continue to believe that the display of an object that "retains a specifically Christian [or other] religious meaning," is incompatible with the separation of church and state demanded by our Constitution. I therefore agree with the Court that Allegheny County's display of a crèche at the county

---

f. In contending that "specific historical practice should [not] override [the] clear constitutional imperative," Brennan, J., joined by Marshall, J., dissenting in *Marsh,* noted that "the sort of historical argument made by the Court should be advanced with some hesitation in light of certain other skeletons in the congressional closet. See, e.g., An Act for the Punishment of certain Crimes against the United States (1790) (enacted by the First Congress and requiring that persons convicted of certain theft offenses 'be publicly whipped, not exceeding thirty-nine stripes'); Act of July 23, 1866 (reaffirming the racial segregation of the public schools in the District of Columbia; enacted exactly one week after Congress proposed Fourteenth Amendment to the States)."

Brennan, J., concurring in *Schempp,* further observed that "today the Nation is far more heterogeneous religiously, including as it does substantial minorities not only of Catholics and Jews but as well of those who worship according to no version of the Bible and those who worship no God at all. In the face of such profound changes, practices which may have been objectionable to no one in the time of Jefferson and Madison may today be highly offensive to many persons, the deeply devout and the non-believers alike. [Thus], our use of the history of their time must limit itself to broad purposes, not specific practices."

g. Brennan, J.'s dissent in *Lynch,* supra, expressed a similar view.

courthouse signals an endorsement of the Christian faith in violation of the Establishment Clause, and join Parts III–A, IV, and V of the Court's opinion. I cannot agree, however, [with] the decision as to the menorah [which] rests on three premises: the Christmas tree is a secular symbol; Chanukah is a holiday with secular dimensions, symbolized by the menorah; and the government may promote pluralism by sponsoring or condoning displays having strong religious associations on its property. None of these is sound.

[I.]   Even though the tree alone may be deemed predominantly secular, it can hardly be so characterized when placed next to such a forthrightly religious symbol. Consider a poster featuring a star of David, a statue of Buddha, a Christmas tree, a mosque, and a drawing of Krishna. There can be no doubt that, when found in such company, the tree serves as an unabashedly religious symbol.
* * *

[II.]   The menorah is indisputably a religious symbol, used ritually in a celebration that has deep religious significance. That, in my view, is all that need be said. Whatever secular practices the holiday of Chanukah has taken on in its contemporary observance are beside the point. * * * Pittsburgh's secularization of an inherently religious symbol, aided and abetted here by Justice Blackmun's opinion, recalls the effort in *Lynch* to render the crèche a secular symbol. As I said then: "To suggest, as the Court does, that such a symbol is merely 'traditional' and therefore no different from Santa's house or reindeer is not only offensive to those for whom the crèche has profound significance, but insulting to those who insist for religious or personal reasons that the story of Christ is in no sense a part of 'history' nor an unavoidable element of our national 'heritage.'"
* * *

III.   Justice Blackmun, in his acceptance of the city's message of "diversity," and, even more so, Justice O'Connor, in her approval of the "message of pluralism and freedom to choose one's own beliefs," appear to believe that, where seasonal displays are concerned, more is better. Whereas a display might be constitutionally problematic if it showcased the holiday of just one religion, those problems vaporize as soon as more than one religion is included. I know of no principle under the Establishment Clause, however, that permits us to conclude that governmental promotion of religion is acceptable so long as one religion is not favored. We have, on the contrary, interpreted that Clause to require neutrality, not just among religions, but between religion and nonreligion.

Nor do I discern the theory under which the government is permitted to appropriate particular holidays and religious objects to its own use in celebrating "pluralism." The message of the sign announcing a "Salute to Liberty" is not religious, but patriotic; the government's use of religion to promote its own cause is undoubtedly offensive to those whose religious beliefs are not bound up with their attitude toward the Nation.

The uncritical acceptance of a message of religious pluralism also ignores the extent to which even that message may offend. Many religious faiths are hostile to each other, and indeed, refuse even to participate in ecumenical services designed to demonstrate the very pluralism Justices Blackmun and O'Connor extol. * * *

JUSTICE STEVENS, with whom JUSTICE BRENNAN and JUSTICE MARSHALL join, concurring in part and dissenting in part. * * *

Treatment of a symbol of a particular tradition demonstrates one's attitude toward that tradition. Thus the prominent display of religious symbols on government property falls within the compass of the First Amendment, even though interference with personal choices about supporting a church, by means of governmental tithing, was the primary concern in 1791. Whether the vice in such a display is characterized as "coercion," or "endorsement," or merely as state action with the purpose and effect of providing support for specific faiths, it is common ground that this symbolic governmental speech "respecting an establishment of religion" may violate the Constitution.

In my opinion the Establishment Clause should be construed to create a strong presumption against the display of religious symbols on public property. There is always a risk that such symbols will offend nonmembers of the faith being advertised as well as adherents who consider the particular advertisement disrespectful. [Even] though "[p]assersby who disagree with the message conveyed by these displays are free to ignore them, or even turn their backs," displays of this kind inevitably have a greater tendency to emphasize sincere and deeply felt differences among individuals than to achieve an ecumenical goal. The Establishment Clause does not allow public bodies to foment such disagreement.

Application of a strong presumption against the public use of religious symbols scarcely will "require a relentless extirpation of all contact between government and religion," (Kennedy, J., concurring and dissenting), for it will prohibit a display only when its message, evaluated in the context in which it is presented, is nonsecular. For example, a carving of Moses holding the Ten Commandments, if that is the only adornment on a courtroom wall, conveys an equivocal message, perhaps of respect for Judaism, for religion in general, or for law. The addition of carvings depicting Confucius and Mohammed may honor religion, or particular religions, to an extent that the First Amendment does not tolerate any more than it does "the permanent erection of a large Latin cross on the roof of city hall." Placement of secular figures such as Caesar Augustus, William Blackstone, Napoleon Bonaparte, and John Marshall alongside these three religious leaders, however, signals respect not for great proselytizers but for great lawgivers. It would be absurd to exclude such a fitting message from a courtroom,[13] as it would to exclude religious paintings by Italian Renaissance masters from a public museum.[h] Far from "border[ing] on latent hostility toward religion," this careful consideration of context gives due regard to religious and nonreligious members of our society. * * *

Notes and Questions

1. *Secular purpose under the "Lemon" test. Lynch* found that "Pawtucket has *a* secular purpose for its display": "The City [has] principally taken note of a significant historical religious event long celebrated in the Western World. [Were] the test that the government must have 'exclusively secular' objectives, much of the conduct and legislation this Court has approved in the past would have been invalidated."

Brennan, J.'s dissent in *Lynch,* reasoned: "When government decides to recognize Christmas day as a public holiday, it does no more than accommodate the calendar of public activities to the plain fact that many Americans will expect on that day to spend time visiting with their families, attending religious services,

---

13. All these leaders, of course, appear in friezes on the walls of our courtroom.

h. As an example of government "reference to our religious heritage," *Lynch* noted that "the National Gallery in Washington, maintained with Government support, for example, has long exhibited masterpieces with religious messages, notably the Last Supper, and paintings depicting the Birth of Christ, the Crucifixion, and the Resurrection, among many others with explicit Christian themes and messages."

and perhaps enjoying some respite from preholiday activities. [If] public officials go further and participate in the *secular* celebration of Christmas—by, for example, decorating public places with such secular images as wreaths, garlands or Santa Claus figures—they move closer to the limits of their constitutional power but nevertheless remain within the boundaries set by the Establishment Clause. But when those officials participate in or appear to endorse the distinctively religious elements of this otherwise secular event, they encroach upon First Amendment freedoms. [The] Court seems to assume that forbidding Pawtucket from displaying a crèche would be tantamount to forbidding a state college from including the Bible or Milton's Paradise Lost in a course on English literature. But in those cases the religiously-inspired materials are being considered solely as literature. [In] this case, by contrast, the crèche plays no comparable secular role. [It] would be another matter if the crèche were displayed in a museum setting, in the company of other religiously-inspired artifacts, as an example, among many, of the symbolic representation of religious myths. In that setting, we would have objective guarantees that the crèche could not suggest that a particular faith had been singled out for public favor and recognition.''

Does the dissent's approach require that government have ''exclusively secular'' objectives? If so, is this inconsistent with the Court's subsequent opinion in *Jaffree* (joined by all the *Lynch* dissenters) that ''a statute that is motivated in part by a religious purpose may satisfy the first [*Lemon*] criterion.''

2. *Differing interpretations of the ''coercion'' test.* LEE v. WEISMAN, 505 U.S. 577, 112 S.Ct. 2649, 120 L.Ed.2d 467 (1992), per KENNEDY, J., held violative of the establishment clause the practice of public school officials inviting members of the clergy to offer invocation and benediction prayers at graduation ceremonies: ''We can decide the case without reconsidering the general constitutional framework [in *Lemon*.] The government involvement with religious activity in this case is pervasive, to the point of creating a state-sponsored and state-directed religious exercise in the public school [where] subtle coercive pressures exist and where the student had no real alternative which would have allowed her to avoid the fact or appearance of participation.

''[The] undeniable fact is that the school district's supervision and control of a high school graduation ceremony places public pressure, as well as peer pressure, on attending students to stand as a group or, at least, maintain respectful silence during the Invocation and Benediction. This pressure, though subtle and indirect, can be as real as any overt compulsion. * * *

''Finding no violation under these circumstances would place objectors in the dilemma of participating, with all that implies, or protesting. * * * Research in psychology supports the common assumption that adolescents are often susceptible to pressure from their peers towards conformity, and that the influence is strongest in matters of social convention. [That] the intrusion was in the course of promulgating religion that sought to be civic or nonsectarian rather than pertaining to one sect does not lessen the offense or isolation to the objectors. At best it narrows their number, at worst increases their sense of isolation and affront.

''[I]n our society and in our culture high school graduation is one of life's most significant occasions. A school rule which excuses attendance is beside the point. Attendance may not be required by official decree, yet it is apparent that a student is not free to absent herself from the graduation exercise in any real sense of the term 'voluntary,' for absence would require forfeiture of these intangible benefits which have motivated the student through youth and all her high school years.[a] [To] say that a student must remain apart from the ceremony at the opening invocation and closing benediction is to risk compelling conformity in an environment analogous to the classroom setting, where we have said the risk of compulsion is especially high. See *Engel* and *Schempp.* * * *

"Inherent differences between the public school system and a session of a State Legislature distinguish this case from *Marsh*. [The] atmosphere at the opening of a session of a state legislature where adults are free to enter and leave with little comment and for any number of reasons cannot compare with the constraining potential of the one school event most important for the student to attend. * * *

"We do not hold that every state action implicating religion is invalid if one or a few citizens find it offensive. People may take offense at all manner of religious as well as nonreligious messages, but offense alone does not in every case show a violation. We know too that sometimes to endure social isolation or even anger may be the price of conscience or nonconformity. But, by any reading of our cases, the conformity required of the student in this case was too high an exaction to withstand the test of the Establishment Clause." [b]

BLACKMUN, J., joined by Stevens and O'Connor, JJ., who joined the Court's opinion, concurred: "[I]t is not enough that the government restrain from compelling religious practices: it must not engage in them either. [To] that end, our cases have prohibited government endorsement of religion, its sponsorship, and active involvement in religion, whether or not citizens were coerced to conform."

SOUTER, J., (who also joined the Court's opinion), joined by Stevens and O'Connor, JJ., concurred: "The Framers adopted the Religion Clauses in response to a long tradition of coercive state support for religion, particularly in the form of tax assessments, but their special antipathy to religious coercion did not exhaust their hostility to the features and incidents of establishment. Indeed, Jefferson and Madison opposed any political appropriation of religion, [and] saw that even without the tax collector's participation, an official endorsement of religion can impair religious liberty. [O]ne can call any act of endorsement a form of coercion, but only if one is willing to dilute the meaning of 'coercion' until there is no meaning left. [This] principle against favoritism and endorsement has become the foundation of Establishment Clause jurisprudence, ensuring that religious belief is irrelevant to every citizen's standing in the political community * * *.

"Religious students cannot complain that omitting prayers from their graduation ceremony would, in any realistic sense, 'burden' their spiritual callings. To

---

a. Consider Steven G. Gey, *Religious Coercion and the Establishment Clause,* 1994 U.Ill. L.Rev. 463, 503: "But a citizen of Allegheny County may also be compelled to transact business in the county courthouse, which would inevitably require that person to pass by the prominent display of the birth of the Christian savior. If the Allegheny County citizen is not coerced by being required to respectfully pass by the religious display, why is the Providence student coerced by respectfully remaining silent during a one-minute prayer? Conversely, if 'the act of standing or remaining silent' during a graduation prayer is 'an expression of participation' in the prayer, why is walking by an overtly Christian display in respectful si-

lence not also 'an expression of participation' in the display?"

b. After *Lee,* what result if school officials delegate the graduation program to the graduating class which decides that student volunteers will give invocation and benediction prayers? See Thomas A. Schweitzer, *The Progeny of Lee v. Weisman: Can Student-Invited Prayer at Public School Graduations Still Be Constitutional?*, 9 B.Y.U.J.Pub.L. 291 (1995)(discussing cases). See generally Christina E. Martin, *Student–Initiated Religious Expression after Mergens and Weisman,* 61 U.Chi.L.Rev. 1565 (1994). What result if the class valedictorian begins her speech with a prayer?

be sure, many of them invest this rite of passage with spiritual significance, but they may express their religious feelings about it before and after the ceremony. They may even organize a privately sponsored baccalaureate if they desire the company of likeminded students. Because they accordingly have no need for the machinery of the State to affirm their beliefs, the government's sponsorship of prayer at the graduation ceremony is most reasonably understood as an official endorsement of religion and, in this instance, of theistic religion."

SCALIA, J., joined by Rehnquist, C.J., and White and Thomas, JJ., dissented: "Three terms ago, I joined an opinion recognizing that 'the meaning of the [Establishment] Clause is to be determined by reference to historical practices and understandings.' * * * *Allegheny County* (Kennedy, J., concurring in judgment in part and dissenting in part).

"These views of course prevent me from joining today's opinion, which is conspicuously bereft of any reference to history [and] lays waste a tradition that is as old as public-school graduation ceremonies themselves, and that is a component of an even more longstanding American tradition of nonsectarian prayer to God at public celebrations generally.

"[Since] the Court does not dispute that students exposed to prayer at graduation ceremonies retain (despite 'subtle coercive pressures,') the free will to sit, there is absolutely no basis for the Court's decision. It is fanciful enough to say that 'a reasonable dissenter,' standing head erect in a class of bowed heads, 'could believe that the group exercise signified her own participation or approval of it.' It is beyond the absurd to say that she could entertain such a belief while pointedly declining to rise.

"But let us assume the very worst, that the nonparticipating graduate is 'subtly coerced' * * * to stand! Even that half of the disjunctive does not remotely establish a 'participation' (or an 'appearance of participation') in a religious exercise. * * *

"The deeper flaw in the Court's opinion does not lie in its wrong answer to the question whether there was state-induced 'peer-pressure' coercion; it lies, rather, in the Court's making violation of the Establishment Clause hinge on such a precious question. The coercion that was a hallmark of historical establishments of religion was coercion of religious orthodoxy and of financial support by force of *law and threat of penalty*. [I] concede that our constitutional tradition [has,] ruled out of order government-sponsored endorsement of religion—even when no legal coercion is present, and indeed even when no ersatz, 'peer-pressure' psycho-coercion is present—where the endorsement is sectarian, in the sense of specifying details upon which men and women who believe in a benevolent, omnipotent Creator and Ruler of the world, are known to differ (for example, the divinity of Christ). But there is simply no support for the proposition that the officially sponsored nondenominational invocation and benediction read by Rabbi Gutterman—with no one legally coerced to recite them—violated the Constitution of the United States.[c] To the contrary, they are so characteristically American they could have come from the pen of George Washington or Abraham Lincoln himself.

c. Compare Gey, supra, at 507: "If dissenting audience members at a state-sponsored public event may walk away from the affair without subjecting themselves to legal penalties, it should not matter whether a prayer given at that function incorporates the tenets of a particular sect, or comments unfavorably on the tenets of another sect. It should not matter even if the government sponsors a prayer overtly hostile to one or more faiths, so long as the dissenters are allowed to ignore the government's advice and practice their own beliefs freely."

"The Court relies on our 'school prayer' cases, *Engel* and *Schempp*. But whatever the merit of those cases, they do not support, much less compel, the Court's psycho-journey. In the first place, *Engel* and *Schempp* do not constitute an exception to the rule, distilled from historical practice, that public ceremonies may include prayer; rather, they simply do not fall within the scope of the rule (for the obvious reason that school instruction is not a public ceremony). Second, we have made clear our understanding that school prayer occurs within a framework in which legal coercion to attend school (i.e., coercion under threat of penalty) provides the ultimate backdrop. * * * Voluntary prayer at graduation—a one-time ceremony at which parents, friends and relatives are present— can hardly be thought to raise the same concerns." [d]

3. *Differing interpretations of the "endorsement" test.* (a) CAPITOL SQUARE REVIEW & ADVISORY BOARD v. PINETTE, ___ U.S. ___, 115 S.Ct. 2440, 132 L.Ed.2d 650 (1995), per Scalia, J., relying on *Widmar* and *Lamb's Chapel*, held that petitioner's permitting the Ku Klux Klan to place a Latin cross in Capitol Square—"A 10–acre, state-owned plaza surrounding the Statehouse in Columbus, Ohio"—when it had also permitted such other unattended displays as "a State-sponsored lighted tree during the Christmas season, a privately-sponsored menorah during Chanukah, a display showing the progress of a United Way fundraising campaign, and booths and exhibits during an arts festival," did not violate the establishment clause: "The State did not sponsor respondents' expression, the expression was made on government property that had been opened to the public for speech, and permission was requested through the same application process and on the same terms required of other private groups."

The seven-justice majority divided, however, on the scope of the "endorsement" test. Scalia, J., joined by Rehnquist, C.J., and Kennedy and Thomas, JJ., rejected petitioners' "endorsement test" claim based on "the forum's proximity to the seat of government, which, they contend, may produce the perception that the cross bears the State's approval": "[W]e have consistently held that it is no violation for government to enact neutral policies that happen to benefit religion. Where we have tested for endorsement of religion, the subject of the test was either expression by the government itself, *Lynch,* or else government action alleged to discriminate in favor of private religious expression or activity, *Kiryas Joel; Allegheny County.* The test petitioners propose, which would attribute to a neutrally behaving government private religious expression, has no antecedent in our jurisprudence, and would better be called a 'transferred endorsement' test. [O]ne can conceive of a case in which a governmental entity manipulates its administration of a public forum close to the seat of government (or within a government building) in such a manner that only certain religious groups take advantage of it, creating an impression of endorsement that is in fact accurate. But those situations, which involve governmental favoritism, do not exist here. * * *

"The contrary view, most strongly espoused by Justice Stevens [infra], but endorsed by Justice Souter and Justice O'Connor [and Breyer, J.] as well, [infra], exiles private religious speech to a realm of less-protected expression. [It] is no answer to say that the Establishment Clause tempers religious speech. By its terms that Clause applies only to the words and acts of government. It was never

d. How would the *Lee* Court—with Souter, J. replacing Brennan, J. and Thomas, J. replacing Marshall, J.—have decided the crèche issue in *Allegheny County?* See Jesse H. Choper, *Separation of Church and State: "New" Di-* *rections by the "New" Supreme Court,* 34 J. Church & State 363 (1992); Suzanna Sherry, *Lee v. Weisman: Paradox Redux,* 1992 Sup.Ct. Rev. 123.

meant, and has never been read by this Court, to serve as an impediment to purely private religious speech connected to the State only through its occurrence in a public forum.

"Since petitioners' 'transferred endorsement' principle cannot possibly be restricted to squares in front of state capitols, the Establishment Clause regime that it would usher in is most unappealing. [Every] proposed act of private, religious expression in a public forum would force officials to weigh a host of imponderables. How close to government is too close? What kind of building, and in what context, symbolizes state authority? If the State guessed wrong in one direction, it would be guilty of an Establishment Clause violation; if in the other, it would be liable for suppressing free exercise or free speech (a risk not run when the State restrains only its own expression)." [a]

O'CONNOR, J., joined by Souter and Breyer, JJ., concurred in part: "Where the government's operation of a public forum has the effect of endorsing religion, even if the governmental actor neither intends nor actively encourages that result, the Establishment Clause is violated [because] the State's own actions (operating the forum in a particular manner and permitting the religious expression to take place therein), and their relationship to the private speech at issue, actually convey a message of endorsement." [b]

STEVENS, J., dissented: "[W]hile this unattended, freestanding wooden cross was unquestionably a religious symbol, observers may well have received completely different messages from that symbol. Some might have perceived it as a message of love, others as a message of hate, still others as a message of exclusion—a Statehouse sign calling powerfully to mind their outsider status. [It] is especially important to take account of the perspective of a reasonable observer who may not share the particular religious belief it expresses. A paramount purpose of the Establishment Clause is to protect such a person from being made to feel like an outsider in matters of faith, and a stranger in the political community. If a reasonable person could perceive a government endorsement of religion from a private display, then the State may not allow its property to be used as a forum for that display. No less stringent rule can adequately protect non-adherents from a well-grounded perception that their sovereign supports a faith to which they do not subscribe." [c,5]

---

a. Thomas, J., filed a brief concurrence, emphasizing that "a cross erected by the Ku Klux Klan [is] a political act, not a Christian one."

b. Souter, J., joined by O'Connor and Breyer, JJ., concurred "in large part because of the possibility of affixing a sign to the cross adequately disclaiming any government sponsorship or endorsement of it.

"[As] long as the governmental entity does not 'manipulat[e]' the forum in such a way as to exclude all other speech, the plurality's opinion would seem to [invite] government encouragement [of religion], even when the result will be the domination of the forum by religious displays and religious speakers. By allowing government to encourage what it can not do on its own, the proposed per se rule would tempt a public body to contract out its establishment of religion, by encouraging the private enterprise of the religious to exhibit what the government could not display itself.

"Something of the sort, in fact, may have happened here. Immediately after the District

Court issued the injunction ordering petitioners to grant the Klan's permit, a local church council [invited] all local churches to erect crosses, and the Board granted 'blanket permission' for 'all churches friendly to or affiliated with' the council to do so. The end result was that a part of the square was strewn with crosses, and while the effect in this case may have provided more embarrassment than suspicion of endorsement, the opportunity for the latter is clear."

c. O'Connor, J., responded: "Under such an approach, a religious display is necessarily precluded so long as some passersby would perceive a governmental endorsement thereof. In my view, however, [the] reasonable observer in the endorsement inquiry must be deemed aware of the history and context of the community and forum in which the religious display appears. [An] informed member of the com-

---

5. See note 5 on page 1010.

"[The] very fact that a sign is installed on public property implies official recognition and reinforcement of its message. That implication is especially strong when the sign stands in front of the seat of the government itself. The 'reasonable observer' of any symbol placed unattended in front of any capitol in the world will normally assume that the sovereign—which is not only the owner of that parcel of real estate but also the lawgiver for the surrounding territory—has sponsored and facilitated its message. [Even] if the disclaimer at the foot of the cross (which stated that the cross was placed there by a private organization) were legible, that inference would remain, because a property owner's decision to allow a third party to place a sign on her property conveys the same message of endorsement as if she had erected it herself. [This] clear image of endorsement was lacking in *Widmar* and *Lamb's Chapel,* in which the issue was access to government facilities. Moreover, there was no question in those cases of an unattended display; private speakers, who could be distinguished from the state, were present. * * *

"The battle over the Klan cross underscores the power of such symbolism. The menorah prompted the Klan to seek permission to erect an anti-semitic symbol, which in turn not only prompted vandalism but also motivated other sects to seek permission to place their own symbols in the Square. These facts illustrate the potential for insidious entanglement that flows from state-endorsed proselytizing."

GINSBURG, J., also dissented, reserving the question of whether an unequivocal disclaimer, "legible from a distance," "that Ohio did not endorse the display's message" would suffice: "Near the stationary cross were the government's flags and the government's statues. No human speaker was present to disassociate the religious symbol from the State. No other private display was in sight. No plainly visible sign informed the public that the cross belonged to the Klan and that Ohio's government did not endorse the display's message."

(b) *"Reasonable observer."* Consider William P. Marshall, *"We Know It When We See It," The Supreme Court and Establishment,* 59 So.Cal.L.Rev. 495, 537 (1986): "Is the objective observer (or average person) a religious person, an agnostic, a separationist, a person sharing the predominate religious sensibility of the community, or one holding a minority view? Is there any 'correct' perception?" Compare Note, *Religion and the State,* 100 Harv.L.Rev. 1606, 1648 (1987): "[If the test] is governed by the perspective of the majority, it will be inadequately sensitive to the impact of government actions on religious minorities, thereby in effect basing the protection of religious minorities on the judgment of the very majority that is accused of infringing the minority's religious autonomy. If the establishment clause is to prohibit government from sending the message to religious minorities or nonadherents that the state favors certain beliefs and that

munity will know how the public space in question has been used in the past—and it is that fact, not that the space may meet the legal definition of a public forum, which is relevant to the endorsement inquiry. [The] reasonable observer would recognize the distinction between speech the government supports and speech that it merely allows in a place that traditionally has been open to a range of private speakers accompanied, if necessary, by an appropriate disclaimer."

5. [O'Connor, J.'s] 'reasonable person' comes off as a well-schooled jurist, a being

finer than the tort-law model. With respect, I think this enhanced tort-law standard is singularly out of place in the Establishment Clause context. It strips of constitutional protection every reasonable person whose knowledge happens to fall below some 'ideal' standard. * * * Justice O'Connor's argument that 'there is always someone' who will feel excluded by any particular governmental action, ignores the requirement that such an apprehension be objectively reasonable. A person who views an exotic cow at the zoo as a symbol of the Government's approval of the Hindu religion cannot survive this test.

as nonadherents they are not fully members of the political community, its application must turn on the message received *by the minority or nonadherent.*"

(c) *Ambiguities.* (i) Consider Steven D. Smith, *Symbols, Perceptions, and Doctrinal Illusions: Establishment Neutrality and the "No Endorsement" Test,* 86 Mich.L.Rev. 266, 283, 301–03, 310–12 (1987): "[E]vidence of the test's indeterminate character appears in [Arnold H. Loewy, *Rethinking Government Neutrality Towards Religion Under the Establishment Clause: The Untapped Potential of Justice O'Connor's Insight,* 64 N.C.L.Rev. 1049 (1986).] Loewy likes the 'no endorsement' test. In applying that test to particular controversies, however, he concludes that Pawtucket's sponsorship of a nativity scene violated the establishment clause, that Alabama's 'moment of silence' law probably did *not* violate the clause, and that ceremonial invocations of deity, such as those occurring in the Pledge of Allegiance or the opening of a Supreme Court session, *do* violate the "no endorsement" test. In each instance, Justice O'Connor would disagree. [From] the Continental Congress[139] through the framing of the Bill of Rights[140] and on down to the present day, government and government officials—including Presidents [not] to mention the Supreme Court itself[141]—have frequently expressed approval of religion and religious ideas. Such history [at] least demonstrates that many Americans, including some of our early eminent statesmen, have *believed* such approval was proper. That fact alone is sufficient to show that the 'no endorsement' principle is controversial, not easily self-evident. * * * Religious diversity in this country is rich enough to ensure that *any* governmental policy in an area that potentially concerns religion will probably alienate some people. If public institutions employ religious symbols, persons who do not adhere to the predominant religion may feel like 'outsiders.' But if religious symbols are banned from such contexts, some religious people will feel that their most central values and concerns—and thus, in an important sense, they themselves—have been excluded from a public culture devoted purely to secular concerns. [We] might conclude, however, that any alienation felt by [the latter] groups, although perfectly sincere, should be disregarded because their dissatisfaction actually results not from particular governmental actions but rather from the very meaning of the establishment clause." Contrast Jesse H. Choper, *Securing Religious Liberty: Principles for Judicial interpretation of the Religion Clauses* 28–29 (1995): "[T]his would grant something that I find too close to a self-interested veto for the minority. [An] effective solution here would be to entrust this 'perspective-dependent' inquiry to an independent judiciary * * *. Although justices of the Supreme Court 'cannot become someone else,' they should, with their own solicitude for the values of religious liberty, either assume the view of a reasonable member of the political community who is faithful to the Constitution's protection of individual rights or ask whether a *reasonable minority observer,* who would be 'acquainted with the text, legislative history, and implementation of the [challenged state action],' *should feel* less than a full member of the political community.[112]"

---

139. [The] Continental Congress "sprinkled its proceedings liberally with the mention of God, Jesus Christ, the Christian religion, and many other religious references."

140. Shortly after approving the Bill of Rights, which of course included the establishment clause, the first Congress resolved to observe a day of thanksgiving and prayer in appreciation of "the many signal favors of Almighty God."

141. See, e.g., *Zorach* ("We are a religious people whose institutions presuppose a Supreme Being."); *Church of the Holy Trinity v. United States,* 143 U.S. 457, 471, 12 S.Ct. 511, 516, 36 L.Ed. 226 (1892) (asserting that "this is a Christian nation").

112. Although this process is basically normative rather than empirical, the Court's judgment should obviously be influenced by the perception (if fairly discernible) of 'average'

(ii) Do government accommodations for religion (such as exempting the sacramental use of wine during Prohibition) violate the endorsement test? Consider Mark Tushnet, "Of Church and State and the Supreme Court": Kurland Revisited, 1989 Sup.Ct.Rev. 373, 395 n. 73: "They use religion as a basis for government classification, and they do [so] precisely in order to confer a benefit on some religions that does not flow either to nonbelievers or to all religions. [W]hat is the signal intended to be sent by these accommodations? It is difficult to avoid the conclusion that permissible accommodations, with their necessarily disparate impact, indicate some degree of government approval of the practices." Compare Michael W. McConnell, *Religious Freedom at a Crossroads,* 59 U.Chi.L.Rev. 115, 150 (1992): "Any action the government takes on issues of this sort inevitably sends out messages, and it is not surprising that reasonable observers from different legal and religious perspectives respond to these messages in different ways. These examples raise some of the most important and most often litigated issues under the Establishment Clause, and the concept of endorsement does not help to resolve them."

(d) *None* of the opinions in *Capitol Square* invoked the *Lemon* test, which was barely mentioned. How would the *Capitol Square* Court have decided the crèche issue in *Allegheny?*

SECTION 2. FREE EXERCISE CLAUSE AND RELATED PROBLEMS

I. CONFLICT WITH STATE REGULATION

The most common problem respecting free exercise of religion has involved a generally applicable government regulation, whose purpose is nonreligious, that either makes illegal (or otherwise burdens) conduct that is dictated by some religious belief, or requires (or otherwise encourages) conduct that is forbidden by some religious belief. REYNOLDS v. UNITED STATES, 98 U.S. 145, 25 L.Ed. 244 (1879), the first major decision on the free exercise clause, upheld a federal law making polygamy illegal as applied to a Mormon whose religious duty was to practice polygamy: "Congress was deprived of all legislative power over mere opinion, but was left free to reach actions which were in violation of social duties or subversive of good order." CANTWELL v. CONNECTICUT, 310 U.S. 296, 60 S.Ct. 900, 84 L.Ed. 1213 (1940), reemphasized this distinction between religious opinion or belief, on the one hand, and action taken because of religion, on the other, although the Court this time spoke more solicitously about the latter: "The [Constitution] forestalls compulsion by law of the acceptance of any creed or the practice of any form of worship. Freedom of conscience and freedom to adhere to such religious organization or form of worship as the individual may choose cannot be restricted by law. [Free exercise] embraces two concepts,—freedom to believe and freedom to act. The first is absolute but, in the nature of things, the second cannot be. [The] freedom to act must have appropriate definition to preserve the enforcement of that protection [although] the power to regulate must be so exercised as not, in attaining a permissible end, unduly to infringe the protected freedom."

Beginning with *Cantwell*—which first held that the fourteenth amendment made the free exercise guarantee applicable to the states—a number of cases

members of minority religious faiths and should be more strongly affected if their re-   sponse is very widely shared.

invalidated application of state laws to conduct undertaken pursuant to religious beliefs. Like *Cantwell*, these decisions, a number of which are set forth in Ch. 8,[a] rested in whole or in part on the freedom of expression protections of the first and fourteenth amendments. Similarly, WEST VIRGINIA STATE BD. OF EDUC. v. BARNETTE, 319 U.S. 624, 63 S.Ct. 1178, 87 L.Ed. 1628 (1943),[b] held that compelling a flag salute by public school children whose religious scruples forbade it violated the first amendment: "[The] freedoms of speech and of press, of assembly, and of worship [are] susceptible of restriction only to prevent grave and immediate danger to interests which the state may lawfully protect. [The] freedom asserted by these appellees does not bring them into collision with rights asserted by any other individual. It is such conflicts which most frequently require intervention of the State to determine where the rights of one end and those of another begin. [T]he compulsory flag salute and pledge requires *affirmation of a belief* and an *attitude of mind*. [If] there is any fixed star in our constitutional constellation, it is that no official, high or petty, can prescribe what shall be orthodox in politics, nationalism or other matters of opinion or force citizens to confess by word or act their faith therein."

It was not until 1963, in *Sherbert v. Verner* (discussed below), that the Court held conduct protected by the free exercise clause alone.

HOBBIE v. UNEMPLOYMENT APPEALS COM'N

480 U.S. 136, 107 S.Ct. 1046, 94 L.Ed.2d 190 (1987).

JUSTICE BRENNAN delivered the opinion of the Court.

Appellant's employer discharged her when she refused to work certain scheduled hours because of sincerely-held religious convictions adopted after beginning employment. * * * Under our precedents, the [Florida] Appeals Commission's disqualification of appellant from receipt of [unemployment compensation] benefits violates the Free Exercise Clause of the First Amendment, applicable to the States through the Fourteenth Amendment. *Sherbert v. Verner*, 374 U.S. 398, 83 S.Ct. 1790, 10 L.Ed.2d 965 (1963); *Thomas v. Review Board*, 450 U.S. 707, 101 S.Ct. 1425, 67 L.Ed.2d 624 (1981). In *Sherbert* we considered South Carolina's denial of unemployment compensation benefits to a Sabbatarian who, like Hobbie, refused to work on Saturdays. The Court held that the State's disqualification of Sherbert "force[d] her to choose between following the precepts of her religion and forfeiting benefits, on the one hand, and abandoning one of the precepts of her religion in order to accept work, on the other hand. Governmental imposition of such a choice puts the same kind of burden upon the free exercise of religion as would a fine imposed against [her] for her Saturday worship." * * *

In *Thomas*, [a] Jehovah's Witness, held religious beliefs that forbade his participation in the production of armaments. He was forced to leave his job when the employer closed his department and transferred him to a division that fabricated turrets for tanks. Indiana then denied Thomas unemployment compensation benefits. * * *

We see no meaningful distinction among the situations of Sherbert, Thomas, and Hobbie. We again affirm, as stated in *Thomas:* "Where the state conditions receipt of an important benefit upon conduct proscribed by a religious faith, *or*

---

a. E.g., *Schneider v. Irvington*, p. 799 supra; *Lovell v. Griffin*, p. 757 supra (involving distribution of religious literature). See also *Marsh v. Alabama*, p. 1323 infra.

b. Overruling *Minersville School Dist. v. Gobitis*, 310 U.S. 586, 60 S.Ct. 1010, 84 L.Ed. 1375 (1940).

where it denies such a benefit because of conduct mandated by religious belief, thereby putting substantial pressure on an adherent to modify his behavior and to violate his beliefs, a burden upon religion exists. While the compulsion may be indirect, the infringement upon free exercise is nonetheless substantial." (emphasis added).

Both *Sherbert* and *Thomas* held that such infringements must be subjected to strict scrutiny and could be justified only by proof by the State of a compelling interest. The Appeals Commission does not seriously contend that its denial of benefits can withstand strict scrutiny;[a] rather it urges that we hold that its justification should be determined under the less rigorous standard articulated in Chief Justice Burger's opinion in *Bowen v. Roy:* "the Government meets its burden when it demonstrates that a challenged requirement for governmental benefits, neutral and uniform in its application, is a reasonable means of promoting a legitimate public interest."[b] 476 U.S. 693, 707–08, 106 S.Ct. 2147, 2156, 90 L.Ed.2d 735 (1986). Five Justices expressly rejected this argument in *Roy.* See (Blackmun, J., concurring in part); (O'Connor, J., concurring in part and dissenting in part, joined by Brennan and Marshall, JJ.); (White, J., dissenting). We reject the argument again today. As Justice O'Connor pointed out in *Roy,* "[s]uch a test has no basis in precedent and relegates a serious First Amendment value to the barest level of minimal scrutiny that the Equal Protection Clause already provides." See also *Wisconsin v. Yoder,* 406 U.S. 205, 215, 92 S.Ct. 1526, 1533, 32 L.Ed.2d 15 (1972) ("[O]nly those interests of the highest order and those not otherwise served can overbalance legitimate claims to the free exercise of religion").[7] * * *

The Appeals Commission also attempts to distinguish this case by arguing that [in] *Sherbert* and *Thomas,* the employees held their respective religious beliefs at the time of hire; subsequent changes in the conditions of employment made *by the employer* caused the conflict between work and belief. In this case, Hobbie's beliefs changed during the course of her employment, creating a conflict between job and faith that had not previously existed. * * *

In effect, the Appeals Commission asks us to single out the religious convert for different, less favorable treatment than that given an individual whose adherence to his or her faith precedes employment. We decline to do so. * * *

a. In *Sherbert,* the state "suggest[ed] no more than a possibility that the filing of fraudulent claims by unscrupulous claimants feigning religious objections to Saturday work [might] dilute the unemployment compensation fund [but] there is no proof whatever to warrant such fears of malingering or deceit [and] it is highly doubtful whether such evidence would be sufficient to warrant a substantial infringement of religious liberties. For [it] would plainly be incumbent upon the [state] to demonstrate that no alternative forms of regulation would combat such abuses without infringing First Amendment rights."

b. Burger, C.J., joined by Powell and Rehnquist, JJ., prefaced this statement in *Roy* as follows: "[G]overnment regulation that indirectly and incidentally calls for a choice between securing a governmental benefit and adherence to religious beliefs is wholly different from government [action] that criminalizes religiously inspired activity or inescapably compels conduct that some find objectionable for religious reasons. Although the denial of governmental benefits over religious objection can raise serious Free Exercise problems, these two very different forms of government action are not governed by the same constitutional standard. * * * Absent proof of an intent to discriminate against particular religious beliefs or against religion in general, the Government meets its burden [etc.]"

7. In *Roy* [the parents of a two year old girl (named Little Bird of the Snow), for whom a social security number had been assigned at birth, contended that federal requirements— that recipients of AFDC and Food Stamps must submit their social security numbers, which shall be used by the government to prevent welfare fraud—violated their Native American religious beliefs. Five justices— O'Connor, Brennan, Marshall, Blackmun and White, JJ.—found that *Sherbert* and *Thomas* sustained the parents' claim.]

[Another issue in *Roy* is discussed in *Lyng,* note 4(d) infra.]

Finally, we reject the Appeals Commission's argument that the awarding of benefits to Hobbie would violate the Establishment Clause. This Court has long recognized that the government may (and sometimes must) accommodate religious practices and that it may do so without violating the Establishment Clause.[10] See e.g., *Yoder* (judicial exemption of Amish children from compulsory attendance at high school); *Walz* (tax exemption for churches). * * *

Reversed.[c]

CHIEF JUSTICE REHNQUIST, dissenting.

I adhere to the views I stated in dissent in *Thomas* [where Rehnquist, J., stated:

["As to the proper interpretation of the Free Exercise Clause, I would accept the decision of *Braunfeld v. Brown*, 366 U.S. 599, 81 S.Ct. 1144, 6 L.Ed.2d 563 (1961), and the dissent in *Sherbert*. In *Braunfeld*, we held that Sunday closing laws do not violate the First Amendment rights of Sabbatarians. Chief Justice Warren explained that the statute did not make unlawful any religious practices of appellants; it simply made the practice of their religious beliefs more expensive. We concluded that '[t]o strike down, without the most critical scrutiny, legislation which imposes only an indirect burden on the exercise of religion, i.e. legislation which does not make unlawful the religious practice itself, would radically restrict the operating latitude of the legislature.'[d] Likewise in this case, it cannot be said that the State discriminated against Thomas on the basis of his religious beliefs or that he was denied benefits *because* he was a Jehovah's Witness.[1] Where, as here, a State has enacted a general statute, the purpose and effect of which is to advance the State's secular goals, the Free Exercise Clause does not in my view require the State to conform that statute to the dictates of religious conscience of any group. As Justice Harlan recognized in his dissent in *Sherbert*: 'Those situations in which the Constitution may require special treatment on account of religion [are] few and far between.' "]

Notes and Questions

1. *Scope of decisions.* After *Sherbert, Thomas* and *Hobbie,* may a state deny unemployment benefits (a) to member of a pacifist religion who agreed to produce tanks as a condition of employment and who was fired for subsequently refusing to do so because of religious beliefs, see *Oregon Dep't of Human Resources v. Smith,* 485 U.S. 660, 108 S.Ct. 1444, 99 L.Ed.2d 753 (1988); (b) to a Sabbatarian

---

10. In the unemployment benefits context, the majorities *and* those dissenting have concluded that, were a state voluntarily to provide benefits to individuals in Hobbie's situation, such an accommodation would not violate the Establishment Clause. See *Thomas* (Rehnquist, J., dissenting); *Sherbert,* (Harlan, J., dissenting).

[The conflict between the establishment and free exercise clauses is considered in Sec. 4 infra.]

c. The opinions of Powell and Stevens, JJ., concurring in the judgment, are omitted.

d. *Braunfeld* continued: "Statutes which tax income and limit the amount which may be deducted for religious contributions impose an indirect economic burden on the observance of the religion of the citizen whose religion requires him to donate a greater amount to his church; statutes which require the courts to be closed on Saturday and Sunday impose a similar indirect burden on the observance of the religion of the trial lawyer whose religion requires him to rest on a weekday. The list of legislation of this nature is nearly limitless."

Query: If a statute makes a religious practice unlawful but the maximum penalty is a fine, does this impose a "direct" or "indirect" burden?

1. [In] this case, the Indiana Supreme Court *has* construed the State's unemployment statute to make every personal subjective reason for leaving a job a basis for disqualification. [Because] Thomas left his job for a personal reason, the State of Indiana should not be prohibited from disqualifying him from receiving benefits.

who is dismissed from a job in the post office for refusal to work on Saturday because to grant an exemption would require paying overtime to another employee?[a] May (c) a state deny worker's compensation to the widow of an employee who, after being injured at work, died because of his refusal on religious grounds to accept a blood transfusion?

2. *Aid to parochial schools.* (a) Is the Court's implicit conclusion, that denial of financial benefits to parochial schools does not infringe the free exercise rights of attending children,[b] consistent with *Sherbert, Thomas* and *Hobbie*? After *Everson*, could a student bus transportation program exclude children who attend parochial schools? See *Luetkemeyer v. Kaufmann,* 419 U.S. 888, 95 S.Ct. 167, 42 L.Ed.2d 134 (1974). If some religions impose a duty on parents to send children to religious schools, may these parents argue that, since they must pay public school taxes, the state's failure to support parochial as well as public schools and thus defray their parochial school tuition costs imposes a serious financial burden on their exercise of religion? That "if the state gives financial assistance only to the school where education is deliberately divorced from religion [this is] preferential treatment of irreligion"? See Robert F. Drinan, *The Constitutionality of Public Aid to Parochial Schools,* in The Wall Between Church and State 55, 68 (Oaks ed. 1963). That, "conditioning the availability of benefits upon their willingness to violate a cardinal principle of their religious faith effectively penalizes the free exercise of their constitutional liberties" (*Sherbert*); that there is no "compelling state interest to justify the substantial infringement of their First Amendment rights"? May these parents further argue that their position is stronger than *Sherbert, Thomas* and *Hobbie* because the purpose of granting an exemption in that case was *solely* to aid religion whereas there is a wholly nonreligious purpose in giving aid to all nonpublic schools—improving the quality of the secular education?

Consider Paul G. Kauper, *Religion and the Constitution* 36–37 (1964): "If the public policy of the state is to limit the use of educational funds to schools under public control, this involves no discrimination except the distinction between schools under public and those under private control—a distinction well recognized in our law. But if public funds are made available for all educational institutions whether public or private except those that are under the control of a religious body, it is indeed hard to avoid the conclusion that the religious factor is being used as a ground for disqualification from public benefits." Compare 25 U.Pitt.L.Rev. 713 (1964): Suppose that the statute in *Everson* had dictated that all those attending nonpublic schools should not obtain free transportation, except that those students who attended religious schools because of the dictates of their religion also should qualify for fare reimbursement. It is submitted that under the rationale of *Sherbert* such a statute would be constitutional."

3. *Other forms of government largesse.* If a state fluoridates drinking water, must it supply nonfluoridated water to persons whose religion forbids such "medicinal aids"? If a state gives financial support to various voluntary and eleemosynary institutions, does *Sherbert* require it to give such support to churches? Consider Tribe *Treatise* 1274: "Presumably the government could

---

a. See also *TWA v. Hardison,* 432 U.S. 63, 97 S.Ct. 2264, 53 L.Ed.2d 113 (1977), interpreting the Civil Rights Act prohibition against religious discrimination in employment as permitting dismissal of a Sabbatarian if accommodating his work schedule would require "more than a de minimis cost" by the employer. Brennan and Marshall, JJ., dissented.

b. See the dictum in *Sloan v. Lemon,* 413 U.S. 825, 93 S.Ct. 2982, 37 L.Ed.2d 939 (1973): "[V]alid aid to nonpublic, nonsectarian schools would provide no lever for aid to their sectarian counterparts."

provide subsidized loans to beef producers without facing a colorable free exercise claim brought by people whose religion requires them to raise and eat only vegetables; or provide tax benefits to medical or military professionals without facing a claim brought by people whose religious tenets forbid such work. But the principles underlying [the distinctions between these policies and that in *Sherbert, Thomas* and *Hobbie*] resist ready definition."

4. *Rejections of free exercise claims.* (a) *Taxation.* (i) JIMMY SWAGGART MINISTRIES v. BOARD OF EQUAL., 493 U.S. 378, 110 S.Ct. 688, 107 L.Ed.2d 796 (1990), per O'CONNOR, J., unanimously held that the free exercise clause does not prohibit imposing a generally applicable sales and use tax on the sale of religious materials by a religious organization. The Court distinguished *Murdock v. Pennsylvania*, 319 U.S. 105, 63 S.Ct. 870, 87 L.Ed. 1292 (1943) and *Follett v. McCormick*, 321 U.S. 573, 64 S.Ct. 717, 88 L.Ed. 938 (1944), which had invalidated license taxes for sellers as applied to Jehovah's Witnesses who went from house to house selling religious pamphlets, because of the "particular nature of the challenged taxes—flat license taxes that operated as a prior restraint on the exercise of religious liberty": "As the Court made clear in *Hernandez v. Commissioner* [Sec. 3 infra], holding that the Government's disallowance of a tax deduction for religious 'auditing' and 'training' services did not violate [free exercise], to the extent that imposition of a generally applicable tax merely decreases the amount of money appellant has to spend on its religious activities, any such burden is not constitutionally significant. * * *

"Finally, because appellant's religious beliefs do not forbid payment of the sales and use tax, appellant's reliance on *Sherbert* and its progeny is misplaced. [Although] it is of course possible to imagine that a more onerous tax, even if generally applicable, might effectively choke off an adherent's religious practices, cf. *Murdock* (the burden of a flat tax could render itinerant evangelism 'crushed and closed out by the sheer weight of the toll or tribute which is exacted town by town'), we face no such situation in this case."

(ii) UNITED STATES v. LEE, 455 U.S. 252, 102 S.Ct. 1051, 71 L.Ed.2d 127 (1982), per BURGER, C.J., held that the free exercise clause does not require an exemption for members of the Old Order Amish from payment of social security taxes even though "both payment and receipt of social security benefits is forbidden by the Amish faith": "The state may justify a limitation on religious liberty by showing that it is essential to accomplish an overriding governmental interest [and] mandatory participation is indispensable to the fiscal vitality of the social security system. [To] maintain an organized society that guarantees religious freedom to a great variety of faiths requires that some religious practices yield to the common good. [The] tax system could not function if denominations were allowed to challenge the tax system because tax payments were spent in a manner that violates their religious belief."

STEVENS, J., concurred in the judgment: "As a matter of fiscal policy, an enlarged exemption probably would benefit the social security system because the nonpayment of these taxes by the Amish would be more than offset by the elimination of their right to collect benefits.[c] * * * Nonetheless, I agree with the

c. Stevens, J., found the distinction between this case and *Yoder* "unconvincing because precisely the same religious interest is implicated in both cases and Wisconsin's inter- est in requiring its children to attend school until they reach the age of 16 is surely not inferior to the federal interest in collecting these social security taxes."

Court's conclusion that the difficulties associated with processing other claims to tax exemption on religious grounds justify a rejection of this claim.[2]"

(b) *Conscription.* (i) GILLETTE v. UNITED STATES, 401 U.S. 437, 91 S.Ct. 828, 28 L.Ed.2d 168 (1971), per MARSHALL, J., held that the free exercise clause does not forbid Congress from "conscripting persons who oppose a particular war on grounds of conscience and religion. * * * [23]": "The conscription laws [are] not designed to interfere with any religious ritual or practice, and do not work a penalty against any theological position. The incidental burdens felt by persons in petitioners' position are strictly justified by substantial governmental interests that relate directly to the very impacts questioned. And more broadly, of course, there is the Government's interest in procuring the manpower necessary for military purposes * * *."

DOUGLAS, J., dissented: "[M]y choice is the dicta of Chief Justice Hughes who, dissenting in *Macintosh,* spoke for Holmes, Brandeis, and Stone: '[Among] the most eminent statesmen here and abroad have been those who condemned the action of their country in entering into wars they thought to be unjustified. [If] the mere holding of religious or conscientious scruples against all wars should not disqualify a citizen from holding office in this country, or an applicant otherwise qualified from being admitted to citizenship, there would seem to be no reason why a reservation of religious or conscientious objection to participation in wars believed to be unjust should constitute such a disqualification.' " [d]

(ii) In JOHNSON v. ROBISON, 415 U.S. 361, 94 S.Ct. 1160, 39 L.Ed.2d 389 (1974), a federal statute granted educational benefits for veterans who served on active duty but disqualified conscientious objectors who performed alternate civilian service. The Court, per BRENNAN, J., found a "rational basis" for the classification and thus no violation of equal protection, because the "disruption caused by military service is quantitatively greater" and "qualitatively different." Further, the statute "involves only an incidental burden upon appellee's free exercise of religion—if, indeed, any burden exists at all.[19] [T]he Government's

2. In my opinion, the principal reason for adopting a strong presumption against such claims is not a matter of administrative convenience. It is the overriding interest in keeping the government—whether it be the legislature or the courts—out of the business of evaluating the relative merits of differing religious claims. The risk that governmental approval of some and disapproval of others will be perceived as favoring one religion over another is an important risk the Establishment Clause was designed to preclude.

23. We are not faced with the question whether the Free Exercise Clause itself would require exemption of any class other than objectors to particular wars. * * * We note that the Court has previously suggested that relief for conscientious objectors is not mandated by the Constitution. See *Hamilton v. Regents; United States v. Macintosh,* 283 U.S. 605, 623–24, 51 S.Ct. 570, 574–75, 75 L.Ed. 1302 (1931).

d. Did *Gillette* discard the "alternative means" approach found in *Sherbert?* Consider Tribe *Treatise* 1266: "In light of the relative ease with which the conscientious-objector exemption has been administered throughout our history without placing a noticeable burden on

the country's military manpower needs, a court might well require a concrete showing of threat to such needs in order to justify abolition of the exemption. The use of conscientious objectors—even selective conscientious objectors—in paramedical or other non-military roles could meet both the personnel argument and the morale argument well enough to constitute a required alternative under *Sherbert.*"

See generally Hugh C. Macgill, *Selective Conscientious Objection: Divine Will and Legislative Grace,* 54 Va.L.Rev. 1355 (1968); Theodore Hochstadt, *The Right to Exemption from Military Service of a Conscientious Objector to a Particular War,* 3 Harv.Civ.Rts.—Civ. Lib.L.Rev. 1 (1967).

19. * * * Congress has bestowed relative benefits upon conscientious objectors by permitting them to perform their alternate service obligation as civilians. Thus, Congress' decision to grant educational benefits to military servicemen might arguably be viewed as an attempt to equalize the burdens of military service and civilian alternate service, rather than an effort [to] place a relative burden upon a conscientious objector's free exercise of religion.

substantial interest in raising and supporting armies is of 'a kind and weight' clearly sufficient to sustain the challenged legislation, for the burden upon appellee's free exercise [is] not nearly of the same order or magnitude as" in *Gillette*. Douglas, J., dissented.

(c) *Tax exemption*. BOB JONES UNIV. v. UNITED STATES, 461 U.S. 574, 103 S.Ct. 2017, 76 L.Ed.2d 157 (1983), per BURGER, C.J., held that IRS denial of tax exempt status to private schools that practice racial discrimination on the basis of sincerely held religious beliefs does not violate the free exercise clause: "[T]he Government has a fundamental, overriding interest in eradicating racial discrimination in education [which] substantially outweighs whatever burden denial of tax benefits places on petitioners' exercise of their religious beliefs. The interests asserted by petitioners cannot be accommodated with that compelling governmental interest, see *Lee;* and no 'less restrictive means' are available to achieve the governmental interest." [e] Rehnquist, J., agreeing with the Court's free exercise analysis, dissented on the ground that Congress had not authorized the IRS denial of tax exemption.[f]

(d) *Internal government affairs*. LYNG v. NORTHWEST INDIAN CEMETERY PROTECTIVE ASS'N, 485 U.S. 439, 108 S.Ct. 1319, 99 L.Ed.2d 534 (1988), per O'CONNOR, J., held the federal government's building a road and allowing timber harvesting in a national forest did not violate the free exercise rights of American Indian tribes even though this would "virtually destroy the Indians' ability to practice their religion" because it would irreparably damage "sacred areas which are an integral and necessary part of [their] belief systems": "In *Bowen v. Roy*, we considered a challenge to a federal statute that required the States to use Social Security numbers in administering certain welfare programs. Two applicants for benefits under these programs contended that their religious beliefs prevented them from acceding to the use of a Social Security number for their two-year-old daughter because the use of a numerical identifier would ' "rob the spirit" of [their] daughter and prevent her from attaining greater spiritual power.' [The] Court rejected this kind of challenge in *Roy:* 'The Free Exercise Clause simply cannot be understood to require the Government to conduct its own internal affairs in ways that comport with the religious beliefs of particular citizens. Just as the Government may not insist that [the Roys] engage in any set form of religious observance, so [they] may not demand that the Government join in their chosen religious practices by refraining from using a number to identify their daughter. [The] Free Exercise Clause affords an individual protection from certain forms of governmental compulsion; it does not afford an individual a right to dictate the conduct of the Government's internal procedures.'

"The building of a road or the harvesting of timber on publicly owned land cannot meaningfully be distinguished from the use of a Social Security number in *Roy*. In both cases, the challenged government action would interfere significantly with private persons' ability to pursue spiritual fulfillment according to their own religious beliefs. In neither case, however, would the affected individuals be

---

e. For a contrary view, see Douglas Laycock, *Tax Exemptions for Racially Discriminatory Religious Schools*, 60 Tex.L.Rev. 259 (1982); Mayer G. Freed & Daniel D. Polsby, *Race, Religion, and Public Policy: Bob Jones University v. United States*, 1983 Sup.Ct.Rev. 1, 20–30.

f. Four justices also rejected the claim that Nebraska's denial of a driver's license to a

person whose sincerely held religious beliefs— pursuant to the Second Commandment prohibition of "graven images"—forbade her to be photographed, violated the free exercise clause. *Quaring v. Peterson*, 728 F.2d 1121 (8th Cir. 1984) (free exercise violation), affirmed by an equally divided Court, 472 U.S. 478, 105 S.Ct. 3492, 86 L.Ed.2d 383 (1985).

coerced by the Government's action into violating their religious beliefs; nor would either governmental action penalize religious activity by denying any person an equal share of the rights, benefits, and privileges enjoyed by other citizens.

"[However] much we might wish that it were otherwise, government simply could not operate if it were required to satisfy every citizen's religious needs and desires. A broad range of government activities—from social welfare programs to foreign aid to conservation projects—will always be considered essential to the spiritual well-being of some citizens, often on the basis of sincerely held religious beliefs. Others will find the very same activities deeply offensive, and perhaps incompatible with their own search for spiritual fulfillment and with the tenets of their religion. The First Amendment must apply to all citizens alike, and it can give to none of them a veto over public programs that do not prohibit the free exercise of religion. * * *

"[The] dissent now offers to distinguish [*Roy*] by saying that the Government was acting there 'in a purely internal manner,' whereas land-use decisions 'are likely to have substantial external effects.' [But robbing] the spirit of a child, and preventing her from attaining greater spiritual power, is both a 'substantial external effect' and one that is remarkably similar to the injury claimed by respondents in the case before us today." [g]

BRENNAN, J., joined by Marshall and Blackmun, JJ., dissented: "[R]espondents have claimed—and proved—that the desecration of the high country will prevent religious leaders from attaining the religious power or medicine indispensable to the success of virtually all their rituals and ceremonies. [T]oday's ruling sacrifices a religion at least as old as the Nation itself, along with the spiritual well-being of its approximately 5,000 adherents, so that the Forest Service can build a six-mile segment of road that two lower courts found had only the most marginal and speculative utility, both to the Government itself and to the private lumber interests that might conceivably use it." Kennedy, J., did not participate.

EMPLOYMENT DIVISION v. SMITH

494 U.S. 872, 110 S.Ct. 1595, 108 L.Ed.2d 876 (1990).

JUSTICE SCALIA delivered the opinion of the Court. * * *

Respondents Alfred Smith and Galen Black were fired from their jobs with a private drug rehabilitation organization because they ingested peyote for sacramental purposes at a ceremony of the Native American Church, of which both are members. When respondents applied to petitioner Employment Division for unemployment compensation, they were determined to be ineligible for benefits because they had been discharged for work-related "misconduct". [We believe] that "if a State has prohibited through its criminal laws certain kinds of religiously motivated conduct without violating the First Amendment, it certainly follows that it may impose the lesser burden of denying unemployment compensation benefits to persons who engage in that conduct." * * *

[The] free exercise of religion means, first and foremost, the right to believe and profess whatever religious doctrine one desires. Thus, the First Amendment obviously excludes all "governmental regulation of religious *beliefs* as such." The

g. *Nature of remedy.* Is there a difference between the remedy needed to satisfy the free exercise claim in *Roy* and that in *Lyng?* If so, what about the required remedy in the other instances in which the Court has sustained the free exercise claim?

government may not compel affirmation of religious belief, see *Torcaso v. Watkins,* [Part II infra], punish the expression of religious doctrines it believes to be false, *United States v. Ballard,* [Part II infra], impose special disabilities on the basis of religious views or religious status, see *McDaniel v. Paty* [state rule disqualifying clergy from being legislators]; cf. *Larson v. Valente,* [Sec. 3 infra] or lend its power to one or the other side in controversies over religious authority or dogma, see *Presbyterian Church v. Hull Church,* [Sec. 1, II supra.]

But the "exercise of religion" often involves not only belief and profession but the performance of (or abstention from) physical acts: assembling with others for a worship service, participating in sacramental use of bread and wine, proselytizing, abstaining from certain foods or certain modes of transportation. It would be true, we think (though no case of ours has involved the point), that a state would be "prohibiting the free exercise [of religion]" if it sought to ban such acts or abstentions only when they are engaged in for religious reasons, or only because of the religious belief that they display. It would doubtless be unconstitutional, for example, to ban the casting of "statues that are to be used for worship purposes," or to prohibit bowing down before a golden calf.

Respondents in the present case, however, seek to carry the meaning of "prohibiting the free exercise [of religion]" one large step further. They contend that their religious motivation for using peyote places them beyond the reach of a criminal law that is not specifically directed at their religious practice, and that is concededly constitutional as applied to those who use the drug for other reasons. [As] a textual matter, we do not think the words must be given that meaning. It is no more necessary to regard the collection of a general tax, for example, as "prohibiting the free exercise [of religion]" by those citizens who believe support of organized government to be sinful, than it is to regard the same tax as "abridging the freedom [of] the press" of those publishing companies that must pay the tax as a condition of staying in business. It is a permissible reading of the text, in the one case as in the other, to say that if prohibiting the exercise of religion (or burdening the activity of printing) is not the object of the tax but merely the incidental effect of a generally applicable and otherwise valid provision, the First Amendment has not been offended. Compare *Citizen Publishing Co. v. United States,* 394 U.S. 131, 89 S.Ct. 927, 22 L.Ed.2d 148 (1969) (upholding application of antitrust laws to press), with *Grosjean v. American Press Co.,* [p. 822 supra] (striking down license tax applied only to newspapers with weekly circulation above a specified level); see generally *Minneapolis Star & Tribune Co. v. Minnesota Commissioner of Revenue* [p. 822 supra].

Our decisions reveal that the latter reading is the correct one. We have never held that an individual's religious beliefs excuse him from compliance with an otherwise valid law prohibiting conduct that the State is free to regulate. [In] *Prince v. Massachusetts,* 321 U.S. 158, 64 S.Ct. 438, 88 L.Ed. 645 (1944), we held that a mother could be prosecuted under the child labor laws for using her children to dispense literature in the streets, her religious motivation notwithstanding. [The opinion also discusses *Braunfeld, Gillette,* and *Lee.*]

The only decisions in which we have held that the First Amendment bars application of a neutral, generally applicable law to religiously motivated action have involved not the Free Exercise Clause alone, but the Free Exercise Clause in conjunction with other constitutional protections, such as freedom of speech and of the press, see *Cantwell* (invalidating a licensing system for religious and charitable solicitations under which the administrator had discretion to deny a license to any cause he deemed nonreligious); *Murdock* (invalidating a flat tax on solicitation as applied to the dissemination of religious ideas); *Follett* (same), or the right of parents, acknowledged in *Pierce v. Society of Sisters* [Sec. 1 supra] to direct the education of their children, see *Yoder,* (invalidating compulsory school-attendance laws as applied to Amish parents who refused on religious grounds to send their children to school).[1] Some of our cases prohibiting compelled expression, decided exclusively upon free speech grounds, have also involved freedom of religion, cf. *Wooley v. Maynard* [p. 871 supra] (invalidating compelled display of a license plate slogan that offended individual religious beliefs); *Barnette.* And it is easy to envision a case in which a challenge on freedom of association grounds would likewise be reinforced by Free Exercise Clause concerns. Cf. *Roberts v. United States Jaycees* [p. 894 supra] ("An individual's freedom to speak, to worship, and to petition the government for the redress of grievances could not be vigorously protected from interference by the State [if] a correlative freedom to engage in group effort toward those ends were not also guaranteed."). * * *

Respondents argue that even though exemption from generally applicable criminal laws need not automatically be extended to religiously motivated actors, at least the claim for a religious exemption must be evaluated under the balancing test set forth in *Sherbert.* Under the *Sherbert* test, governmental actions that substantially burden a religious practice must be justified by a compelling governmental interest. [We] have never invalidated any governmental action on the basis of the *Sherbert* test except the denial of unemployment compensation. Although we have sometimes purported to apply the *Sherbert* test in contexts other than that, we have always found the test satisfied, see *Lee, Gillette.* In recent years we have abstained from applying the *Sherbert* test (outside the unemployment compensation field) at all [discussing *Roy* and *Lyng*]. In *Goldman v. Weinberger,* 475 U.S. 503, 106 S.Ct. 1310, 89 L.Ed.2d 478 (1986), we rejected application of the *Sherbert* test to military dress regulations that forbade the wearing of yarmulkes. In *O'Lone v. Shabazz,* 482 U.S. 342, 107 S.Ct. 2400, 96 L.Ed.2d 282 (1987), we sustained, without mentioning the *Sherbert* test, a prison's refusal to excuse inmates from work requirements to attend worship services.[a]

Even if we were inclined to breathe into *Sherbert* some life beyond the unemployment compensation field, we would not apply it to require exemptions from a generally applicable criminal law. The *Sherbert* test, it must be recalled, was developed in a context that lent itself to individualized governmental assessment of the reasons for the relevant conduct. As a plurality of the Court noted in *Roy,* a distinctive feature of unemployment compensation programs is that their eligibility criteria invite consideration of the particular circumstances behind an

---

1. [*Yoder*] said that "the Court's holding in *Pierce* stands as a charter of the rights of parents to direct the religious upbringing of their children. And, when the interests of parenthood are combined with a free exercise claim of the nature revealed by this record, more than merely a 'reasonable relation to some purpose within the competency of the State' is required to sustain the validity of the State's requirement under the First Amendment."

[Compare Jesse H. Choper, *The Rise and Decline of the Constitutional Protection of Religious Liberty,* 70 Neb.L.Rev. 651, 675–76 (1991): "[A]ttributing the result in *Yoder* to its combination of free exercise rights with a substantive due process right of parents to direct their children's education is especially ironic for Justice Scalia, who rejects use of the due process clause 'to invent new [constitutionally protected substantive interests],' especially—as in the case of compulsory education law—when there is 'a societal tradition of enacting laws *denying* the interest.' [citing *Michael H. v. Gerald D.,* p. 415 supra]"]

a. For a careful review of the cases, both in the Supreme Court and in the U.S. courts of appeals for ten years preceding *Smith,* concluding that "despite the apparent protection afforded claimants by the language of the compelling interest test, courts overwhelmingly sided with the government when applying that test," see James E. Ryan, *Smith and the Religious Freedom Restoration Act: An Iconoclastic Assessment,* 78 Va.L.Rev. 1407 (1992).

applicant's unemployment. [As] the plurality pointed out in *Roy,* our decisions in the unemployment cases stand for the proposition that where the State has in place a system of individual exemptions, it may not refuse to extend that system to cases of "religious hardship" without compelling reason.[b]

Whether or not the decisions are that limited, they at least have nothing to do with an across-the-board criminal prohibition on a particular form of conduct. [We] conclude today that the sounder approach, and the approach in accord with the vast majority of our precedents, is to hold the test inapplicable to such challenges. [To] make an individual's obligation to obey such a law contingent upon the law's coincidence with his religious beliefs, except where the State's interest is "compelling"—permitting him, by virtue of his beliefs, "to become a law unto himself," *Reynolds*—contradicts both constitutional tradition and common sense.[2]

The "compelling government interest" requirement seems benign, because it is familiar from other fields. But using it as the standard that must be met before the government may accord different treatment on the basis of race, see [p. 1074 infra], or before the government may regulate the content of speech, is not remotely comparable to using it for the purpose asserted here. What it produces in those other fields—equality of treatment, and an unrestricted flow of contending speech—are constitutional norms; what it would produce here—a private right to ignore generally applicable laws—is a constitutional anomaly.[3]

Nor is it possible to limit the impact of respondents' proposal by requiring a "compelling state interest" only when the conduct prohibited is "central" to the individual's religion. It is no more appropriate for judges to determine the "centrality" of religious beliefs before applying a "compelling interest" test in the free exercise field, than it would be for them to determine the "importance" of ideas before applying the "compelling interest" test in the free speech field. What principle of law or logic can be brought to bear to contradict a believer's assertion that a particular act is "central" to his personal faith? [I]n many different contexts, we have warned that courts must not presume to determine the place of a particular belief in a religion or the plausibility of a religious claim. See, e.g., *Thomas* [Part II infra]; *Jones v. Wolf,* [Sec. 1, II supra]; *Ballard.*[4]

b. For the view that the system of discretionary hearings involved in the unemployment cases presents "a fertile ground for the undervaluation of minority religious interests" and is therefore "vulnerable to a distinct constitutional objection," see Christopher L. Eisgruber & Lawrence G. Sager, *The Vulnerability of Conscience: The Constitutional Basis for Protecting Religious Conduct,* 61 U.Chi.L.Rev. 1245 (1994).

2. Justice O'Connor seeks to distinguish *Lyng* and *Roy* on the ground that those cases involved the government's conduct of "its own internal affairs." [But] it is hard to see any reason in principle or practicality why the government should have to tailor its health and safety laws to conform to the diversity of religious belief, but should not have to tailor its management of public lands, *Lyng,* or its administration of welfare programs, *Roy.*

3. [Just] as we subject to the most exacting scrutiny laws that make classifications based on race or on the content of speech, so too we

strictly scrutinize governmental classifications based on religion, see *McDaniel;* see also *Torcaso.* But we have held that race-neutral laws that have the *effect* of disproportionately disadvantaging a particular racial group do not thereby become subject to compelling-interest analysis under the Equal Protection Clause, see *Washington v. Davis* [p. 1093 infra] (police employment examination); and we have held that generally applicable laws unconcerned with regulating speech that have the *effect* of interfering with speech do not thereby become subject to compelling-interest analysis under the First Amendment, see *Citizen Publishing Co. v. United States* (antitrust laws). Our conclusion that generally applicable, religion-neutral laws that have the effect of burdening a particular religious practice need not be justified by a compelling governmental interest is the only approach compatible with these precedents.

4. [In] any case, dispensing with a "centrality" inquiry is utterly unworkable. It would

If the "compelling interest" test is to be applied at all, then, it must be applied across the board, to all actions thought to be religiously commanded. Moreover, if "compelling interest" really means what it says (and watering it down here would subvert its rigor in the other fields where it is applied), many laws will not meet the test. Any society adopting such a system would be courting anarchy, but that danger increases in direct proportion to the society's diversity of religious beliefs, and its determination to coerce or suppress none of them. Precisely because "we are a cosmopolitan nation made up of people of almost every conceivable religious preference," and precisely because we value and protect that religious divergence, we cannot afford the luxury of deeming *presumptively invalid,* as applied to the religious objector, every regulation of conduct that does not protect an interest of the highest order. The rule respondents favor would open the prospect of constitutionally required religious exemptions from civic obligations of almost every conceivable kind—ranging from compulsory military service, see, e.g., *Gillette,* to the payment of taxes, see, e.g., *Lee,* to health and safety regulation such as manslaughter and child neglect laws, see, *e.g., Funkhouser v. State,* 763 P.2d 695 (Okla.Crim.App.1988), compulsory vaccination laws, see, *e.g., Cude v. State,* 237 Ark. 927, 377 S.W.2d 816 (1964), drug laws, see, *e.g., Olsen v. Drug Enforcement Administration,* 878 F.2d 1458 (D.C.Cir.1989), and traffic laws, see *Cox v. New Hampshire,* [p. 801 supra], to social welfare legislation such as minimum wage laws, see *Tony and Susan Alamo Foundation v. Secretary of Labor,* 471 U.S. 290, 105 S.Ct. 1953, 85 L.Ed.2d 278 (1985), child labor laws, see *Prince;* animal cruelty laws, see, e.g., *Church of the Lukumi Babalu Aye Inc. v. Hialeah,* 723 F.Supp. 1467 (S.D.Fla.1989); environmental protection laws, see *United States v. Little,* 638 F.Supp. 337 (D.Mont.1986), and laws providing for equality of opportunity for the races, see e.g., *Bob Jones University.* The First Amendment's protection of religious liberty does not require this.[5]

[A] number of States have made an exception to their drug laws for sacramental peyote use. But to say that a nondiscriminatory religious-practice exemption is permitted, or even that it is desirable, is not to say that it is constitutionally required, and that the appropriate occasions for its creation can be discerned by the courts. It may fairly be said that leaving accommodation to the political process will place at a relative disadvantage those religious practices that are not widely engaged in; but that unavoidable consequence of democratic government must be preferred to a system in which each conscience is a law unto itself or in which judges weigh the social importance of all laws against the centrality of all religious beliefs. * * *

require, for example, the same degree of "compelling state interest" to impede the practice of throwing rice at church weddings as to impede the practice of getting married in church. There is no way out of the difficulty that, if general laws are to be subjected to a "religious practice" exception, *both* the importance of the law at issue *and* the centrality of the practice at issue must reasonably be considered. * * *

5. Justice O'Connor contends that the "parade of horribles" in the text only "demonstrates [that] courts have been quite capable of strik[ing] sensible balances between religious liberty and competing state interests." But the cases we cite have struck "sensible balances" only because they have all applied the general laws, despite the claims for religious

exemption. In any event, Justice O'Connor mistakes the purpose of our parade: it is not to suggest that courts would necessarily permit harmful exemptions from these laws (though they might), but to suggest that courts would constantly be in the business of determining whether the "severe impact" of various laws on religious practice (to use Justice Blackmun's terminology) or the "constitutiona[l] significan[ce]" of the "burden on the particular plaintiffs" (to use Justice O'Connor's terminology) suffices to permit us to confer an exemption. It is a parade of horribles because it is horrible to contemplate that federal judges will regularly balance against the importance of general laws the significance of religious practice.

JUSTICE O'CONNOR, with whom JUSTICE BRENNAN, JUSTICE MARSHALL, and JUSTICE BLACKMUN join as to [Part II], concurring in the judgment. * * *

II.   [A] law that prohibits certain conduct—conduct that happens to be an act of worship for someone—manifestly does prohibit that person's free exercise of his religion * * * regardless of whether the law prohibits the conduct only when engaged in for religious reasons, only by members of that religion, or by all persons.

[If] the First Amendment is to have any vitality, it ought not be construed to cover only the extreme and hypothetical situation in which a State directly targets a religious practice. As we have noted in a slightly different context, " '[s]uch a test has no basis in precedent and relegates a serious First Amendment value to the barest level of minimum scrutiny that the Equal Protection Clause already provides.' " *Hobbie*.

[I]n *Yoder* we expressly rejected the interpretation the Court now adopts: "[T]o agree that religiously grounded conduct must often be subject to the broad police power of the State is not to deny that there are areas of conduct protected by the Free Exercise Clause of the First Amendment and thus beyond the power of the State to control, *even under regulations of general applicability*. [A] regulation neutral on its face may, in its application, nonetheless offend the constitutional requirement for government neutrality if it unduly burdens the free exercise of religion."

The Court endeavors to escape from our decisions in *Cantwell* and *Yoder* by labeling them "hybrid" decisions but there is no denying that both cases expressly relied on the Free Exercise Clause and that we have consistently regarded those cases as part of the mainstream of our free exercise jurisprudence. Moreover, in each of the other cases cited by the Court to support its categorical rule, we rejected the particular constitutional claims before us only after carefully weighing the competing interests. [That] we rejected the free exercise claims in those cases hardly calls into question the applicability of First Amendment doctrine * * *. [I]t is surely unusual to judge the vitality of a constitutional doctrine by looking to the win-loss record of the plaintiffs who happen to come before us.

[W]e have never distinguished between cases in which a State conditions receipt of a benefit on conduct prohibited by religious beliefs and cases in which a State affirmatively prohibits such conduct. The *Sherbert* compelling interest test applies in both kinds of cases. [A] neutral criminal law prohibiting conduct that a State may legitimately regulate is, if anything, *more* burdensome than a neutral civil statute placing legitimate conditions on the award of a state benefit.

[Even] if, as an empirical matter, a government's criminal laws might usually serve a compelling interest in health, safety, or public order, the First Amendment at least requires a case-by-case determination of the question, sensitive to the facts of each particular claim. Given the range of conduct that a State might legitimately make criminal, we cannot assume, merely because a law carries criminal sanctions and is generally applicable, that the First Amendment *never* requires the State to grant a limited exemption for religiously motivated conduct.

Moreover, we have not "rejected" or "declined to apply" the compelling interest test in our recent cases. See, e.g., *Hobbie*. The cases cited by the Court signal no retreat from our consistent adherence to the compelling interest test. In both *Roy* and *Lyng*, for example, we expressly distinguished *Sherbert* on the ground that the First Amendment does not "require the Government *itself* to behave in ways that the individual believes will further his or her spiritual development. [The] Free Exercise Clause simply cannot be understood to require the Government to conduct its own internal affairs in ways that comport with the religious beliefs of particular citizens." This distinction makes sense because "the Free Exercise Clause is written in terms of what the government cannot do to the individual, not in terms of what the individual can exact from the government." *Sherbert* (Douglas, J., concerning).[a] Because the case sub judice, like the other cases in which we have applied *Sherbert,* plainly falls into the former category, I would apply those established precedents to the facts of this case.

Similarly, the other cases cited by the Court for the proposition that we have rejected application of the *Sherbert* test outside the unemployment compensation field are distinguishable because they arose in the narrow, specialized contexts in which we have not traditionally required the government to justify a burden on religious conduct by articulating a compelling interest. See *Goldman v. Weinberger* ("Our review of military regulations challenged on First Amendment grounds is far more deferential than constitutional review of similar laws or regulations designed for civilian society"); *O'Lone v. Shabazz* ("[P]rison regulations alleged to infringe constitutional rights are judged under a 'reasonableness' test less restrictive than that ordinarily applied to alleged infringements of fundamental constitutional rights"). That we did not apply the compelling interest test in these cases says nothing about whether the test should continue to apply in paradigm free exercise cases such as the one presented here.[b]

[We have] recognized that the Free Exercise Clause protects values distinct from those protected by the Equal Protection Clause. See *Hobbie.* As the language of the Clause itself makes clear, an individual's free exercise of religion is a preferred constitutional activity. A law that makes criminal such an activity therefore triggers constitutional concern—and heightened judicial scrutiny—even if it does not target the particular religious conduct at issue. Our free speech cases similarly recognize that neutral regulations that affect free speech values are subject to a balancing, rather than categorical, approach. See, e.g., *United States v. O'Brien,* [p. 669 supra]; *Renton v. Playtime Theatres, Inc.,* [p. 702 supra]; cf. *Anderson v. Celebrezze,* 460 U.S. 780, 103 S.Ct. 1564, 75 L.Ed.2d 547 (1983) (generally applicable laws may impinge on free association concerns). * * *

Finally, the Court today suggests that the disfavoring of minority religions is an "unavoidable consequence" under our system of government and that accommodation of such religions must be left to the political process. In my view, however, the First Amendment was enacted precisely to protect the rights of those whose religious practices are not shared by the majority and may be viewed with hostility. The history of our free exercise doctrine amply demonstrates the harsh

a. For the view that the *Lyng* approach, which "seems to involve neither social science nor theology" is attractive to the Court because it functions to "reduce the number of claims that must be afforded the searching inquiry demanded by the free exercise clause" and to permit the Court to avoid resolving the difficult issues of "cognizability of the asserted burden, the sincerity of the claimant, and religiosity of the claim," see Ira C. Lupu, *Where Rights Begin: The Problem of Burdens on The Free Exercise of Religion,* 102 Harv.L.Rev. 933 (1989).

b. See also Michael W. McConnell, *Free Exercise Revisionism and the Smith Decision,* 57

U.Chi.L.Rev. 1109, 1127 (1990): "The Court also failed to point out that in [*Roy*], five Justices expressed the view that adherents to a traditional Abenaki religion under which computer-generated numbers are deemed to rob the individual's spirit of its power were entitled to an exemption from the requirement that welfare recipients provide a social security number on their application. This did not become a holding of the Court because one of the five Justices supporting the result concluded that this aspect of the case had become moot."

impact majoritarian rule has had on unpopular or emerging religious groups such as the Jehovah's Witnesses and the Amish.[c] [The] compelling interest test reflects the First Amendment's mandate of preserving religious liberty to the fullest extent possible in a pluralistic society. For the Court to deem this command a "luxury," is to denigrate "[t]he very purpose of a Bill of Rights."

III. The Court's holding today not only misreads settled First Amendment precedent; it appears to be unnecessary to this case. I would reach the same result applying our established free exercise jurisprudence.

There is no dispute that Oregon's criminal prohibition of peyote places a severe burden on the ability of respondents to freely exercise their religion. Peyote is a sacrament of the Native American Church and is regarded as vital to respondents' ability to practice their religion. * * *

There is also no dispute that Oregon has a significant interest in enforcing laws that control the possession and use of controlled substances by its citizens. [Indeed,] under federal law (incorporated by Oregon law in relevant part), peyote is specifically regulated as a Schedule I controlled substance, which means that Congress has found that it has a high potential for abuse, that there is no currently accepted medical use, and that there is a lack of accepted safety for use of the drug under medical supervision. In light of our recent decisions holding that the governmental interests in the collection of income tax, *Hernandez,* a comprehensive social security system, see *Lee,* and military conscription, see *Gillette,* are compelling, respondents do not seriously dispute that Oregon has a compelling interest in prohibiting the possession of peyote by its citizens.

Thus, the critical question in this case is whether exempting respondents from the State's general criminal prohibition "will unduly interfere with fulfillment of the governmental interest." *Lee.* Although the question is close, I would conclude that uniform application of Oregon's criminal prohibition is "essential to accomplish," *Lee,* its overriding interest in preventing the physical harm caused by the use of a Schedule I controlled substance. Oregon's criminal prohibition represents that State's judgment that the possession and use of controlled substances, even by only one person, is inherently harmful and dangerous. Because the health effects caused by the use of controlled substances exist regardless of the motivation of the user, the use of such substances, even for religious purposes, violates the very purpose of the laws that prohibit them. Moreover, in view of the societal interest in preventing trafficking in controlled substances, uniform application of the criminal prohibition at issue is essential to the effectiveness of Oregon's stated interest in preventing any possession of peyote. * * *

c. See also Douglas Laycock, *Formal, Substantive, and Disaggregated Neutrality Toward Religion,* 39 De Paul L.Rev. 993, 1016 (1990): "Of course, inadvertence can interact with hostility, or with an insensitivity that borders on hostility. Consider what might happen when Frances Quaring [see fn.f supra] writes her legislator. She may get a sympathetic response and a legislated exemption. But her legislator may find it so impossible to empathize with her belief that he never seriously considers whether an exemption would be workable. Even if he empathizes, the legislative calendar is crowded, and the original statute having been enacted, all the burdens of legislative inertia now work against an exemption."

Compare Eisengruber & Sager, supra, at 1304: "[After *Lyng,*] the political process responded to interests the judiciary had not protected, and the Bureau of Land Management relocated the road. [After *Lee,*] Congress accommodated churches that had religious objections to participating in the social security system. [After *Goldman,*] Congress granted relief. And [after *Smith,*] Oregon legislated an exemption to its law."

Respondents contend that any incompatibility is belied by the fact that the Federal Government and several States provide exemptions for the religious use of peyote. But other governments may surely choose to grant an exemption without Oregon, with its specific asserted interest in uniform application of its drug laws, being *required* to do so by the First Amendment. Respondents also note that the sacramental use of peyote is central to the tenets of the Native American Church, but I agree with the Court, that because "[i]t is not within the judicial ken to question the centrality of particular beliefs or practices to a faith," our determination of the constitutionality of Oregon's general criminal prohibition cannot, and should not, turn on the centrality of the particular religious practice at issue. This does not mean, of course, that courts may not make factual findings as to whether a claimant holds a sincerely held religious belief that conflicts with, and thus is burdened by, the challenged law. The distinction between questions of centrality and questions of sincerity and burden is admittedly fine, but it is one that is an established part of our free exercise doctrine * * *.

JUSTICE BLACKMUN, with whom JUSTICE BRENNAN and JUSTICE MARSHALL join, dissenting.

This Court over the years painstakingly has developed a consistent and exacting standard to test the constitutionality of a state statute that burdens the free exercise of religion. Such a statute may stand only if the law in general, and the State's refusal to allow a religious exemption in particular, are justified by a compelling interest that cannot be served by less restrictive means.

In weighing respondents' clear interest in the free exercise of their religion against Oregon's asserted interest in enforcing its drug laws, it is important to articulate in precise terms the state interest involved. It is not the State's broad interest in fighting the critical "war on drugs" that must be weighed against respondents' claim, but the State's narrow interest in refusing to make an exception for the religious, ceremonial use of peyote. [The] State cannot plausibly assert that unbending application of a criminal prohibition is essential to fulfill any compelling interest, if it does not, in fact, attempt to enforce that prohibition. * * * Oregon has never sought to prosecute respondents, and does not claim that it has made significant enforcement efforts against other religious users of peyote.[3] The State's asserted interest thus amounts only to the symbolic preservation of an unenforced prohibition. * * *

Similarly, this Court's prior decisions have not allowed a government to rely on mere speculation about potential harms, but have demanded evidentiary support for a refusal to allow a religious exception. [In] this case, the State's justification for refusing to recognize an exception to its criminal laws for religious peyote use is entirely speculative.

The State [offers] no evidence that the religious use of peyote has ever harmed anyone.[4] The factual findings of other courts cast doubt on the State's assumption that religious use of peyote is harmful. See *State v. Whittingham,* 19 Ariz.App. 27, 30, 504 P.2d 950, 953 (1973) ("the State failed to prove that the quantities of peyote used in the sacraments of the Native American Church are

3. The only reported case in which the State of Oregon has sought to prosecute a person for religious peyote use is *State v. Soto,* 21 Ore.App. 794, 537 P.2d 142 (1975).

4. This dearth of evidence is not surprising, since the State never asserted this health and safety interest before the Oregon courts; thus, there was no opportunity for factfinding concerning the alleged dangers of peyote use. What has now become the State's principal argument for its view that the criminal prohibition is enforceable against religious use of peyote rests on no evidentiary foundation at all.

sufficiently harmful to the health and welfare of the participants so as to permit a legitimate intrusion under the State's police power"); *People v. Woody,* 61 Cal.2d 716, 722–723, 40 Cal.Rptr. 69, 74, 394 P.2d 813, 818 (1964) ("as the Attorney General [admits,] the opinion of scientists and other experts is 'that peyote [works] no permanent deleterious injury to the Indian' ").

The fact that peyote is classified as a Schedule I controlled substance does not, by itself, show that any and all uses of peyote, in any circumstance, are inherently harmful and dangerous. The Federal Government, which created the classifications of unlawful drugs from which Oregon's drug laws are derived, apparently does not find peyote so dangerous as to preclude an exemption for religious use.[5] Moreover, other Schedule I drugs have lawful uses. See *Olsen v. Drug Enforcement Admin.* (medical and research uses of marijuana).

The carefully circumscribed ritual context in which respondents used peyote is far removed from the irresponsible and unrestricted recreational use of unlawful drugs.[6] * * *[7]

Moreover, just as in *Yoder,* the values and interests of those seeking a religious exemption in this case are congruent, to a great degree, with those the State seeks to promote through its drug laws. See *Yoder* (since the Amish accept formal schooling up to 8th grade, and then provide "ideal" vocational education, State's interest in enforcing its law against the Amish is "less substantial than [for] children generally"). Not only does the Church's doctrine forbid nonreligious use of peyote; it also generally advocates self-reliance, familial responsibility, and abstinence from alcohol. There is considerable evidence that the spiritual and social support provided by the Church has been effective in combatting the tragic effects of alcoholism on the Native American population. * * *

The State also seeks to support its refusal to make an exception for religious use of peyote by invoking its interest in abolishing drug trafficking. There is, however, practically no illegal traffic in peyote. Also, the availability of peyote for religious use, even if Oregon were to allow an exemption from its criminal laws, would still be strictly controlled by federal regulations, see 21 U.S.C. §§ 821–823 (registration requirements for distribution of controlled substances); and by the State of Texas, the only State in which peyote grows in significant quantities. Peyote simply is not a popular drug; its distribution for use in religious rituals has nothing to do with the vast and violent traffic in illegal narcotics that plagues this country.

Finally, the State argues that, [if] it grants an exemption for religious peyote use, a flood of other claims to religious exemptions will follow. It would then be placed in a dilemma, it says, between allowing a patchwork of exemptions that would hinder its law enforcement efforts, and risking a violation of the Establishment Clause by arbitrarily limiting its religious exemptions. [This] Court, however, consistently has rejected similar arguments in past free exercise cases, and it

---

5. [Moreover,] 23 States, including many that have significant Native American populations, have statutory or judicially crafted exemptions in their drug laws for religious use of peyote.

6. In this respect, respondents' use of peyote seems closely analogous to the sacramental use of wine by the Roman Catholic Church. During Prohibition, the Federal Government exempted such use of wine from its general ban on possession and use of alcohol. However

er compelling the Government's then general interest in prohibiting the use of alcohol may have been, it could not plausibly have asserted an interest sufficiently compelling to outweigh Catholics' right to take communion.

7. The use of peyote is, to some degree, self-limiting. The peyote plant is extremely bitter, and eating it is an unpleasant experience, which would tend to discourage casual or recreational use.

should do so here as well. [And almost] half the States, and the Federal Government, have maintained an exemption for religious peyote use for many years, and apparently have not found themselves overwhelmed by claims to other religious exemptions.[8] Allowing an exemption for religious peyote use would not necessarily oblige the State to grant a similar exemption to other religious groups. The unusual circumstances that make the religious use of peyote compatible with the State's interests in health and safety and in preventing drug trafficking would not apply to other religious claims. Some religions, for example, might not restrict drug use to a limited ceremonial context, as does the Native American Church. See, e.g., *Olsen* ("the Ethiopian Zion Coptic Church [teaches] that marijuana is properly smoked 'continually all day' "). Some religious claims involve drugs such as marijuana and heroin, in which there is significant illegal traffic, with its attendant greed and violence, so that it would be difficult to grant a religious exemption without seriously compromising law enforcement efforts.[9] That the State might grant an exemption for religious peyote use, but deny other religious claims arising in different circumstances, would not violate the Establishment Clause. Though the State must treat all religions equally, and not favor one over another, this obligation is fulfilled by the uniform application of the "compelling interest" *test* to all free exercise claims, not by reaching uniform *results* as to all claims. * * *

Finally, although I agree with Justice O'Connor that courts should refrain from delving into questions of whether, as a matter of religious doctrine, a particular practice is "central" to the religion, I do not think this means that the courts must turn a blind eye to the severe impact of a State's restrictions on the adherents of a minority religion.

Respondents believe, and their sincerity has *never* been at issue, that the peyote plant embodies their deity, and eating it is an act of worship and communion. Without peyote, they could not enact the essential ritual of their religion. [This] potentially devastating impact must be viewed in light of the federal policy—reached in reaction to many years of religious persecution and intolerance—of protecting the religious freedom of Native Americans. See American Indian Religious Freedom Act. * * *

Notes and Questions

1. *"Generally applicable" regulations, "neutrality," and the religion clauses.* Are the positions of the justices comprising both the majority and dissent in *Smith* consistent with their positions in other religion cases? Consider Douglas Laycock, *The Remnants of Free Exercise,* 1990 Sup.Ct.Rev. 1, 12–13: "Four Justices [O'Connor, J., joined by Brennan, Marshall and Blackmun, JJ.] found religion-blindness undeniably neutral in the context of taxation [in *Swaggart*], but oppressive in the context of regulation [in *Smith*]. *Swaggart's* claim that formally neutral taxation 'neither advances nor inhibits religion' invokes the language of the cases on government payments to church-sponsored schools, but it is inconsistent with the substance of those cases. When government pays money to church-sponsored schools, the Court says the benefit advances religion; it is irrelevant

---

8. Over the years, various sects have raised free exercise claims regarding drug use. In no reported case, except those involving claims of religious peyote use, has the claimant prevailed.

9. Thus, this case is distinguishable from *Lee,* in which the Court concluded that there was "no principled way" to distinguish other exemption claims, and the "tax system could not function if denominations were allowed to challenge the tax system because tax payments were spent in a manner that violates their religious belief."

that government spends comparable sums on secular schools. But when government takes money from churches, the 'burden is not constitutionally significant,' and it is dispositive that government takes comparable sums from secular taxpayers."

2. *Discrimination.* CHURCH OF THE LUKUMI BABALU AYE, INC. v. HIALEAH, 508 U.S. 520, 113 S.Ct. 2217, 124 L.Ed.2d 472 (1993), per KENNEDY, J., held that city ordinances barring ritual animal sacrifice violated the free exercise clause: "[I]f the object of a law is to infringe upon or restrict practices because of their religious motivation, the law is not neutral, see *Smith;* and it is invalid unless it is justified by a compelling interest and is narrowly tailored to advance that interest. [The] ordinances had as their object the suppression of [the Santeria] religion. The [record] discloses animosity to Santeria adherents and their religious practices; the ordinances by their own terms target this religious exercise; the texts of the ordinances were gerrymandered with care to proscribe religious killings of animals but to exclude almost all secular killings; and the ordinances suppress much more religious conduct than is necessary in order to achieve the legitimate ends asserted in their defense. [A] law that targets religious conduct for distinctive treatment or advances legitimate governmental interests only against conduct with a religious motivation will survive strict scrutiny only in rare cases. It follows from what we have already said that these ordinances cannot withstand this scrutiny."

SOUTER, J., concurred specially "for I have doubts whether the *Smith* rule merits adherence": Because "*Smith* refrained from overruling prior free-exercise cases that contain a free-exercise rule fundamentally at odds with the rule *Smith* declared, [in] a case presenting the issue, the Court should re-examine the rule *Smith* declared."

BLACKMUN, J., joined by O'Connor, J., concurred only in the judgment: "I continue to believe that *Smith* was wrongly decided, because it ignored the value of religious freedom as an affirmative individual liberty and treated the Free Exercise Clause as no more than an antidiscrimination principle." Moreover, "when a law discriminates against religion as such, as do the ordinances in this case, it automatically will fail strict scrutiny [because] a law that targets religious practice for disfavored treatment both burdens the free exercise of religion and, by definition, is not precisely tailored to a compelling governmental interest.

"[This] case does not present, and I therefore decline to reach, the question whether the Free Exercise Clause would require a religious exemption from a law that sincerely pursued the goal of protecting animals from cruel treatment. The number of organizations that have filed amicus briefs on behalf of this interest, however, demonstrates that it is not a concern to be treated lightly."

3. *Congressional response to Smith and subsequent developments.* In SWANNER v. ANCHORAGE EQUAL RIGHTS COMM'N, ___ U.S. ___, 115 S.Ct. 460, 130 L.Ed.2d 368 (1994), THOMAS, J., dissented from denial of certiorari to the Alaska Supreme Court's ruling that neither the free exercise clause nor the state constitution entitled petitioner to an exemption from ordinances prohibiting landlords from refusing to rent because of the prospective tenants' marital status. Petitioner had refused "to rent to any unmarried couple who intended to live together on his property, based on his sincere religious belief that such cohabitation is a sin and that he would be facilitating the sin by renting to cohabitants."

"The Alaska Supreme Court also ruled that petitioner had no defense to the state and local ordinances under the Religious Freedom Restoration Act of 1993 (RFRA), 107 Stat. 1488, 42 U.S.C. § 2000bb et seq. (1988 ed., Supp. V) [which] provides that a governmental entity 'shall not substantially burden a person's exercise of religion even if the burden results from a rule of general applicability,' unless the entity 'demonstrates that application of the burden to the person [is] in furtherance of a compelling governmental interest [and is the least restrictive means of furthering that compelling governmental interest].' [1] In a footnote, the opinion below dismissed petitioner's invocation of this Act of Congress: 'Assuming that the Act is constitutional and applies to this case, it does not affect the outcome, because we hold in the next section that compelling state interests support the prohibitions on marital status discrimination.' 874 P.2d, at 280, n. 9. * * *

"RFRA explicitly adopted 'the compelling interest test as set forth in *Sherbert* [and] *Yoder*.' 42 U.S.C. § 2000bb(b)(1) * * *.

"I am quite skeptical that Alaska's asserted interest in preventing discrimination on the basis of marital status is 'compelling' enough to satisfy these stringent standards. Our decision in *Bob Jones University* is instructive in the context of asserted governmental interests in preventing private 'discrimination.' In that case, we held that 'the Government has a fundamental, overriding interest in eradicating racial discrimination in education.' We found such an interest fundamental and overriding—in a word, 'compelling,'—only because we had found that '[o]ver the past quarter of a century, every pronouncement of this Court and myriad Acts of Congress and Executive Orders attest a firm national policy to prohibit racial segregation and discrimination in public education.'

"By contrast, there is surely no 'firm national policy' against marital status discrimination in housing decisions. Chief Justice Moore, dissenting in the case below, correctly observed that 'marital status classifications have never been accorded any heightened scrutiny under the Equal Protection Clause of either the federal or the Alaska Constitutions.' Moreover, the federal Fair Housing Act does not prohibit people from making housing decisions based on marital status. See 42 U.S.C. § 3604 (outlawing housing discrimination on the basis of race, color, religion, sex, handicap, familial status, or national origin).

"Nor does Alaska law, apart from the statutes at issue in this case, attest to any firm *state* policy against marital status discrimination. Indeed, as the dissent below pointed out: 'Alaska law explicitly sanctions such discrimination. See, e.g., AS 13.11.015 (intestate succession does not benefit unmarried partner of decedent); AS 23.30.215(a) (workers' compensation death benefits only for surviving spouse, child, parent, grandchild, or sibling); Alaska R.Evid. 505 (no marital communication privilege between unmarried couples); *Serradell v. Hartford Accident & Indemn. Co.*, 843 P.2d 639, 641 (Alaska 1992) (no insurance coverage for unmarried partner under family accident insurance policy).' The majority admitted that these were 'areas in which the state itself discriminates based on marital status.'

"If, despite affirmative discrimination by Alaska on the basis of marital status and a complete absence of any national policy against such discrimination, the State's asserted interest in this case is allowed to qualify as a 'compelling' interest—that is, a 'paramount' interest, an interest 'of the highest order'—then I am at a loss to know what asserted governmental interests are not compelling. The decision of the Alaska Supreme Court drains the word *compelling* of any

---

1. RFRA was Congress' response to our decision in [*Smith*]. Thus, as a substitute for constitutional protection, RFRA grants a statu- tory "claim or defense to persons whose religious exercise is substantially burdened by government."

meaning and seriously undermines the protection for exercise of religion that Congress so emphatically mandated in RFRA.

"Although RFRA itself is a relatively new statute, the state courts have already exhibited considerable confusion in applying the *Sherbert–Yoder* test to the specific issue presented by this case. Apart from this case, the highest courts of Massachusetts and Minnesota are each deeply split on the question whether preventing 'marital status' discrimination is a 'compelling' interest under our precedents, and the California Court of Appeal has twice applied the compelling interest test adopted by RFRA in reaching decisions that are directly contrary to the decision below. See *Attorney General v. Desilets,* 418 Mass. 316, 636 N.E.2d 233 (1994); *State ex rel. Cooper v. French,* 460 N.W.2d 2 (Minn.1990); *Smith v. Fair Employ. and Hous. Comm'n,* 25 Cal.App.4th 251, 30 Cal.Rptr.2d 395, review granted, 33 Cal.Rptr.2d 567, 880 P.2d 111 (1994); *Donahue v. Fair Employ. and Hous. Comm'n,* 2 Cal.Rptr.2d 32 (Cal.App.1991), review granted, 5 Cal.Rptr.2d 781, 825 P.2d 766 (1992), review dism'd, cause remanded, 23 Cal.Rptr.2d 591, 859 P.2d 671 (1993). By itself, this confusion on an important and recurring question of federal law provides sufficient reason to grant certiorari in this case." [a]

4. *Balancing process.* Of what significance is it that all the decisions sustaining free exercise claims against government regulations of conduct (*Sherbert—Thomas—Hobbie, Yoder* and *Roy*) involved religious refusal to engage in conduct required by government rather than religiously dictated action forbidden by the state? What should be the results in respect to the religiously mandated *inaction* in the following: (a) Citing for contempt person who refuses to serve on jury. See *In re Jenison,* 265 Minn. 96, 120 N.W.2d 515 (1963), vacated, 375 U.S. 14, 84 S.Ct. 63, 11 L.Ed.2d 39 (1963), reversed, 267 Minn. 136, 125 N.W.2d 588 (1963); (b) Statute requiring smallpox vaccination applied to person whose religion forbids medicinal aids. See *Jacobson v. Massachusetts,* 197 U.S. 11, 25 S.Ct. 358, 49 L.Ed. 643 (1905); (c) Court order of blood transfusion, to save life of pregnant mother and child, for woman of Jehovah's Witness faith which obligates adherents to "abstain from blood." Suppose the woman were not pregnant but had infant children? See *Application of Georgetown College, Inc.,* 331 F.2d 1000 (D.C.Cir.1964), cert. denied, 377 U.S. 978, 84 S.Ct. 1883, 12 L.Ed.2d 746 (1964). Suppose the woman were neither pregnant nor had any children? Suppose there were only a slight chance that the transfusion would save the life? That the woman is a brilliant scientist whose work is vital to national security? Suppose the transfusion is thought necessary not to preserve life but to bring back to good health?

5. *Willingness of others.* In the case of *action* due to religious beliefs, should a distinction be drawn between action that is requested by the people affected and action that is imposed on others? Should the conviction of a religious Spiritualist for fortune telling be sustained despite the fact that fortunes were told only upon request? If not, how do you distinguish the polygamy cases?[b]

---

a. For careful consideration of major statutory interpretation issues under RFRA, see Ira C. Lupu, *Of Time and the RFRA: A Lawyer's Guide to the Religious Freedom Restoration Act,* 56 Mont.L.Rev. 171 (1995); Douglas Laycock & Oliver S. Thomas, *Interpreting the Religious Freedom Restoration Act,* 73 Texas L.Rev. 209 (1994).

b. For earlier reviews of the cases and refined "balancing" approaches, see Joseph M.

Dodge, II, *The Free Exercise of Religion: A Sociological Approach,* 67 Mich.L.Rev. 679 (1969); Donald Giannella, *Religious Liberty, Nonestablishment, and Doctrinal Development—Part I. The Religious Liberty Guarantee,* 80 Harv.L.Rev. 1381–1423 (1967); Robert E. Rodes, Jr., *Sub Deo et Lege: A Study of Free Exercise,* 4 Relig. & Pub.Or. 3 (1968); J. Morris Clark, *Guidelines for the Free Exercise Clause,* 83 Harv.L.Rev. 327 (1969); Paul Marcus, *The Forum of Conscience: Applying Stan-*

II. UNUSUAL RELIGIOUS BELIEFS AND PRACTICES

1. *Validity and sincerity of beliefs.* In UNITED STATES v. BALLARD, 322 U.S. 78, 64 S.Ct. 882, 88 L.Ed. 1148 (1944), defendant was indicted for mail fraud. He had solicited funds for the "I Am" movement, asserting, inter alia, that he had been selected as a divine messenger, had the divine power of healing incurable diseases, and had talked with Jesus and would transmit these conversations to mankind. The Court, per DOUGLAS, J., held that the first amendment barred submitting to the jury the question of whether these religious beliefs were true: "Men may believe what they cannot prove. * * * Religious experiences which are as real as life to some may be incomprehensible to others. [The] miracles of the New Testament, the Divinity of Christ, life after death, the power of prayer are deep in the religious convictions of many. If one could be sent to jail because a jury in a hostile environment found those teachings false, little indeed would be left of religious freedom."

(a) *Ballard* permits the prosecution to prove that, irrespective of whether the incidents described by defendant happened, he did not honestly believe that they had? Sound? If so, may the prosecution introduce evidence that the incidents did not in fact happen and that therefore defendant could not honestly believe that they did? Should this line of proof be permitted in the prosecution of an official of the Catholic church for soliciting funds to construct a shrine commemorating the Miracle of Fatima in 1930?

(b) Is it relevant that in *Ballard* the alleged divine revelation was made to defendant himself? Would it be material if the experiences had allegedly occurred at a definite time and place? Many Biblical happenings are so identified. Could the prosecution introduce evidence that Ballard was not physically present at the alleged place at the alleged time? If Protestant, Catholic or Jewish clergy were prosecuted and there was overwhelming scientific evidence disputing the Biblical doctrine, what would the jury be likely to find as to the honesty of the beliefs? Should the first amendment permit people to obtain money in the name of religion by knowingly making false statements? See Tribe *Treatise* 1243–47.

(c) Should the prosecution be able to prove that defendant had stated on many occasions that he believed none of his representations but that by saying that he did he was amassing great wealth? Suppose it can be shown that a priest or rabbi is *somewhat* skeptical as to the truth of certain Biblical occurrences? See John T. Noonan, Jr., *How Sincere Do You Have to Be to Be Religious,* 1988 U.Ill.L.Rev. 713. Could Ballard be convicted on the ground that fraudulent procurement of money, just like polygamy, is conduct which may be constitutionally prohibited even if done in the name of religion?

2. *What is "religion"?* May the Court determine that asserted religious beliefs and practices do not constitute a valid religion? Consider Jonathan Weiss, *Privilege, Posture and Protection—"Religion" in the Law,* 73 Yale L.J. 593, 604 (1964): "[A]ny definition of religion would seem to violate religious freedom in that it would dictate to religions, present and future, what they must [be]. Furthermore, an attempt to define religion, even for purposes of increasing freedom for religions, would run afoul of the 'establishment' clause as excluding some religions, or even as establishing a notion respecting religion."

Is it relevant that the beliefs of a group do not include the existence of God? TORCASO v. WATKINS, per BLACK, J., 367 U.S. 488, 81 S.Ct. 1680, 6 L.Ed.2d 982

dards Under the Free Exercise Clause, 1973
Duke L.J. 1217.

(1961), invalidating a Maryland provision requiring a declaration of belief in the existence of God as a test for public office, stated: "Neither [a state nor the federal government can] impose requirements which aid all religions as against nonbelievers, and neither can aid those religions based on a belief in the existence of God as against those religions founded on different beliefs." The Court noted that "among religions in this country which do not teach what would generally be considered a belief in the existence of God are Buddhism, Taoism, Ethical Culture, Secular Humanism and others."

What if the Communist Party claimed religious status? Consider Paul G. Kauper, *Religion and the Constitution* 31 (1964): "What makes secular humanism a religion? Is it because it is an ideology or system of belief that attempts to furnish a rationale of life? But if any ideology, creed, or philosophy respecting man and society is a religion, then must not democracy, fascism, and communism also qualify as religions? It is not uncommon to refer to these as secular or quasi religions, for some find in these systems an adequate explanation of the meaning and purpose of life and the source of values that command faith and devotion. Certainly in the case of communism, with its discipline, its cultus, its sense of community, and its obligation to duties owing to the system, the resemblance to religion in the conventional sense is [clear]."

May a single person establish his or her own religion? Consider Milton Konvitz, *Religious Liberty and Conscience* 84 (1968): "[Many religions] had their origin in a 'private and personal' religious experience. Mohammed did not take over an on-going, established religion; the history of Islam records the names of his first three converts. John Wesley is given credit as the founder of Methodism. Mrs. Mary Baker Eddy was the founder of the Christian Science church. Menno Simons organized a division of Anabaptists that in due course became the sect known as the Mennonites. Jacob Ammon broke away from the Mennonites and founded the sect known as the Amish."

How important is it that the group has regular weekly services? Designated leaders who conduct these services? Ceremonies for naming, marrying and burying members? Does the first amendment extend only to those groups that conform to the "conventional" concept of religion? Consider Harvey Cox (Harvard Divinity School), N.Y. Times 25 (Feb. 16, 1977): "[C]ourts [often] turn to some vague 'man-in-the-street' idea of what 'religion' should be. [But] a man-in-the-street approach would surely have ruled out early Christianity, which seemed both subversive and atheistic to the religious Romans of the day. The truth is that one man's 'bizarre cult' is another's true path to salvation, and the Bill of Rights was designed to safeguard minorities from the man-on-the-street's uncertain capacity for tolerance. The new challenge to our pluralism often comes from Oriental religious movements, because their views of religion differ so fundamentally from ours." To what extent should a group's "brainwashing," mental coercion techniques affect its constitutional status as a "religion"? Compare Richard Delgado, *Religious Totalism: Gentle and Ungentle Persuasion Under the First Amendment,* 51 So.Cal.L.Rev. 1 (1977) with Note, *Conservatorship and Religious Cults: Divining A Theory of Free Exercise,* 53 N.Y.U.L.Rev. 1247 (1978).

Suppose that a group has certain characteristics of "traditional" religions, such as a holy book, ministers, houses of worship, prescribed prayers, a strict moral code, a belief in the hereafter and an appeal to faith, but also has announced social and economic tenets? (Methodism developed originally out of social concerns.) Consider Note, *Toward a Constitutional Definition of Religion,* 91 Harv.L.Rev. 1056, 1069 (1978): "[A] spokesman for the new 'liberation theology' within Catholicism argues that true religion is to be found in liberation 'as the creation of a new social consciousness and as a social appropriation not only of the means of production, but also of the political processes.' The church, he says, seeks 'the abolition of the exploitation of man by man.' The views of these and other significant Christian theologians coalesce around one important theme: the Christian church will find itself only by discarding what until now has been perceived to be religious and by immersing itself in the secular world." Does the first amendment encompass any political, philosophical, moral or social doctrine that some group honestly espouses as its religion?

UNITED STATES v. SEEGER, 380 U.S. 163, 85 S.Ct. 850, 13 L.Ed.2d 733 (1965), interpreted § 6(j) of the Universal Military Training and Service Act, which exempted from combat any person "who, by reason of religious training and belief, is conscientiously opposed to participation in war in any form. Religious training and belief in this connection means an individual's belief in a relation to a Supreme Being involving duties superior to those arising from any human relation, but does not include essentially political, sociological or philosophical views or a merely personal moral code."[a] The Court, per CLARK, J., avoided constitutional questions and upheld claims for exemption of three conscientious objectors. One declared "that he preferred to leave the question as to his belief in a Supreme Being open, [and] that his was a 'belief in and devotion to goodness and virtue for their own sakes, and a religious faith in a purely ethical creed.' " Another said "that he felt it a violation of his moral code to take human life and that he considered this belief superior to his obligation to the state. As to whether his conviction was religious, he quoted with approval Reverend John Haynes Holmes' definition of religion as 'the consciousness of some power manifest in nature which helps man in the ordering of his life in harmony with its demands * * *; it is man thinking his highest, feeling his deepest, and living his best.' The source of his conviction he attributed to reading and meditation 'in our democratic American culture, with its values derived from the western religious and philosophical tradition.' As to his belief in a Supreme Being, Peter stated that he supposed 'you could call that a belief in the Supreme Being or God. These just do not happen to be the words I use.' "

The Court "concluded that Congress, in using the expression 'Supreme Being' rather than the designation 'God,' was merely clarifying the meaning of religious training and belief so as to embrace all religions and to exclude essentially political, sociological, or philosophical views [and that] the test of belief 'in a relation to a Supreme Being' is whether a given belief that is sincere and meaningful occupies a place in the life of its possessor parallel to that filled by the orthodox belief in God of one who clearly qualifies for the exemption. [No] party claims to be an atheist * * *. We do not deal with or intimate any decision on that situation in these cases. [The] use by Congress of the words 'merely personal' seems to us to restrict the exception to a moral code which [is] in no way related to a Supreme Being. [Congress did] not distinguish between externally and internally derived beliefs. Such a determination [would] prove impossible as a practical matter."

In WELSH v. UNITED STATES, 398 U.S. 333, 90 S.Ct. 1792, 26 L.Ed.2d 308 (1970), petitioner, in his application for exemption, "struck the word 'religious' entirely and later characterized his beliefs as having been formed 'by reading in

---

a. The statute was subsequently amended to omit the "belief in a Supreme Being" element.

the fields of history and sociology.' " BLACK, J., joined by Douglas, Brennan and Marshall, JJ., held that, under *Seeger,* "if an individual deeply and sincerely holds beliefs which are purely ethical or moral in source and content but that nevertheless impose upon him a duty of conscience to refrain from participating in any war at any time, those beliefs certainly occupy in the life of that individual 'a place parallel to that filled [by] God' in traditionally religious persons." "Although [Welsh] originally characterized his beliefs as nonreligious, he later upon reflection wrote a long and thoughtful letter to his Appeal Board in which he declared that his beliefs were 'certainly religious in the ethical sense of that word.' * * * § 6(j)'s exclusion of those persons with 'essentially political, sociological, or philosophical views or a merely personal moral code' should [not] be read to exclude those who hold strong beliefs about our domestic and foreign affairs or even those whose conscientious objection to participation in all wars is founded to a substantial extent upon considerations of public policy. The two groups of registrants which obviously do fall within these exclusions from the exemption are those whose beliefs are not deeply held and those whose objection to war does not rest at all upon moral, ethical, or religious principle but instead rests solely upon considerations of policy, pragmatism, or expediency." [b]

3. *What is "religious belief"?* (a) Of what significance is it that the practice is an "age-old form" of religious conduct (see *Murdock*)? Is a "cardinal principle" of the asserted religious faith (see *Sherbert*)? Consider Laycock, fn. a, p. 951 supra, at 1390–91: "Many activities that obviously are exercises of religion are not required by conscience or doctrine. Singing in the church choir and saying the Roman Catholic rosary are two common examples. Any activity engaged in by a church as a body is an exercise of religion. [Indeed,] many would say that an emphasis on rules and obligations misconceives the essential nature of some religions." Compare Giannella, fn. b, p. 1033 supra, at 1427–28: "[Use of hallucinogenics] should be denied the status of religious claims [because] denial [does] not create problems for the individual's conscience similar to those created by traditionally religious claims to freedom of worship. Personal alienation from one's Maker, frustration of one's ultimate mission in life, and violation of the religious person's integrity are all at stake when the right to worship is threatened. Although the seeker of new psychological worlds may feel equally frustrated when deprived of his gropings for a higher reality, there is not the same sense of acute loss—the loss of the Be-all and End-all of life. [A] different problem presents itself when an individual who does not believe in a supernatural or personal God asserts conscientious objection to certain conduct because of its injurious effects on his fellow man. [T]his ethical belief may be held with such a degree of intensity that its violation occasions the same interior revulsion and anguish as does violation of the law of God to the pious." Under this approach, on what evidence should these factual questions be determined? Suppose a drug-use defendant claims "that its use was essential to attain a unique level of spiritual consciousness [and] compared the effect of depriving him of marihuana with that of forbidding a Catholic to celebrate the Mass"? Joel J. Finer, *Psychedelics and Religious Freedom,* 19 Hast.L.J. 667, 692 (1968).

b. In separate opinions, Harlan, J., and White, J., (joined by Burger, C.J., and Stewart, J.) dissented on the issue of statutory construction. For their views on the constitutional issue, see Sec. 4 infra.

See generally Note, *Defining Religion,* 32 U.Chi.L.Rev. 533 (1965); Note, *The Sacred* *and the Profane: A First Amendment Definition of Religion,* 61 Tex.L.Rev. 139 (1982). For criticism of "sincerity," see Comment, *The Legal Relationship of Conscience to Religion: Refusals to Bear Arms,* 38 U.Chi.L.Rev. 583 (1971).

For the view that "belief [in] 'extratemporal consequences'—whether the effects of actions taken pursuant or contrary to the dictates of a person's beliefs extend in some meaningful way beyond his lifetime—is a sensible and desirable criterion (albeit plainly far short of ideal) for determining when the free exercise clause should trigger judicial consideration of whether an exemption from general government regulations of conduct is constitutionally required," see Jesse H. Choper, *Defining "Religion" in the First Amendment,* 1982 U.Ill.L.Rev. 579, 599, 603–04: [c] "It may be persuasively argued that *all* beliefs that invoke a transcendent reality—and especially those that provide their adherents with glimpses of meaning and truth that make them so important and so uncompromisable—should be encompassed by the special constitutional protection granted 'religion' by the free exercise clause. [In] many ways, however, transcendental explanations of worldly realities are essentially no different [than] conventional exegeses for temporal outcomes that are based on such 'rational' disciplines as economics, political science, sociology, or psychology, or even such 'hard' sciences [as] physics. When justifying competing government policies on such varied matters as social welfare, the economy, and military and foreign affairs, there is at bedrock only a gossamer line between 'rational' and 'supernatural' causation—the former really being little more capable of 'scientific proof' than the latter. [Therefore, government's] plenary authority to regulate the worldly affairs of society [should] not be restricted because of the nature of the causes, which are all basically unverifiable, that different groups believe will produce consequences that the state seeks to achieve."

For the view that this approach "does not promise to yield sound results for many free exercise cases," see Kent Greenawalt, *Religion as a Concept in Constitutional Law,* 72 Calif.L.Rev. 753, 763, 815 (1984): "No specification of essential conditions will capture all and only the beliefs, practices, and organizations that are regarded as religious in modern culture and should be treated as such under the Constitution. [Rather, determining] whether questionable beliefs, practices, and organizations are religious by seeing how closely they resemble what is undeniably religious is a method that has been implicitly used by courts in difficult borderline cases [and] is consonant with Supreme Court decisions." [d] See also George C. Freeman, III, *The Misguided Search for the Constitutional Definition of "Religion,"* 71 Geo.L.J. 1519 (1983).

(b) *Judicial role.* In THOMAS v. REVIEW BD., Part I supra, petitioner testified that, although his religious convictions forbade him to manufacture weapons, "he could, in good conscience, engage indirectly in the production, [for] example, as an employee of a raw material supplier or of a roll foundry." The Indiana Supreme Court, viewing petitioner's positions as inconsistent, ruled that "Thomas had made a merely 'personal philosophical choice rather than a religious choice.'" The Court, per BURGER, C.J. reversed: "The determination of what is a 'religious' belief or practice is more often than not a difficult and delicate task, [but] resolution of that question is not to turn upon a judicial perception of the particular belief or practice in question; religious beliefs need not be acceptable,

c. For criticism of this view, see Stanley Ingber, *Religion or Ideology: A Needed Clarification of the Religion Clauses,* 41 Stan.L.Rev. 233, 274–77 (1989); Note, *Religion and Morality Legislation: A Reexamination of Establishment Clause Analysis,* 59 N.Y.U.L.Rev. 301, 346–52 (1984); Note, *Defining "Religion" in the First Amendment: A Functional Approach,* 74 Corn.L.Rev. 532 (1989).

d. For the view that religion should be defined as dealing only with "quintessentially religious questions," "addressing the profound questions of human existence," "such as God's existence or the proper definition of life and death," see Tom Stacy, *Death, Privacy, and the Free Exercise of Religion,* 77 Corn.L.Rev. 490 (1992).

logical, consistent, or comprehensible to others in order to merit First Amendment protection.

" * * * Thomas drew a line and it is not for us to say that the line he drew was an unreasonable one. Courts should not undertake to dissect religious beliefs because the believer admits that he is 'struggling' with his position or because his beliefs are not articulated with the clarity and precision that a more sophisticated person might employ.

"The Indiana court also appears to have given significant weight to the fact that another Jehovah's Witness had no scruples about working on tank turrets; for that other Witness, at least, such work was 'scripturally' acceptable. Intrafaith differences of that kind are not uncommon among followers of a particular creed, and the judicial process is singularly ill equipped to resolve such differences in relation to the Religion Clauses. [The] narrow function of a reviewing court in this context is to determine whether there was an appropriate finding that petitioner terminated his work because of an honest conviction that such work was forbidden by his religion."

4. *Variable definition.* May "religion" be defined differently for purposes of the establishment clause than the free exercise clause? Consider Marc S. Galanter, *Religious Freedom in the United States: A Turning Point?* 1966 Wis.L.Rev. 217, 266–67: "[For purposes of the establishment clause, the] effect and purpose of government action are not to be assessed by the religious sensibilities of the person who is complaining of the alleged establishment. It must be essentially religious in some widely shared public understanding. [But, for the free exercise clause, the] claimants' view of religion controls the characterization of their objection as a religious one." Does this analysis solve the dilemma of Manning, note 6, p. 968 supra, at 66: "If religion need not be predicated on a belief in God or even in a god and if it may not be tested by the common consensus of what reasonable men would reasonably call religion, if it is so private that—so long as it does not inflict injury on society—it is immured from governmental interference and from judicial inquiry, [might] not a group of gymnasts proclaiming on their trampolines that physical culture is their religion be engaged in a religious exercise? And if Congress, in a particular Olympic year, appropriated funds to subsidize their calisthenics would this not [be] an establishment of religion?" See generally Note, *Transcendental Meditation and the Meaning of Religion Under the Establishment Clause,* 62 Minn.L.Rev. 887 (1978).

SECTION 3. PREFERENCE AMONG RELIGIONS

LARSON v. VALENTE, 456 U.S. 228, 102 S.Ct. 1673, 72 L.Ed.2d 33 (1982), involved a challenge by the Unification Church ("Moonies") to "a Minnesota statute, imposing certain registration and reporting requirements upon only those religious organizations that solicit more than fifty per cent of their funds from nonmembers." The Court, per BRENNAN, J., noting that "the clearest command of the Establishment Clause is that one religious denomination cannot be officially preferred over another, [Everson]," and that the "constitutional prohibition of denominational preferences is inextricably connected with the continuing vitality of the Free Exercise Clause," held that the statute violated the establishment clause because it did not survive "strict scrutiny." [a] Assuming that the state's

a. The Court rejected the argument that the statute was merely "a law based upon secular criteria which may not identically af-

fect all religious organizations." This "is not simply a facially neutral statute, the provisions of which happen to have a 'disparate impact'

"valid secular purpose [in] protecting its citizens from abusive practices in the solicitation of funds for charity" is "compelling," the state "failed to demonstrate that the fifty per cent rule [is] 'closely fitted'" to furthering that interest. Moreover, the statute failed the third *Lemon* "test": "The fifty per cent [rule] effects the *selective* legislative imposition of burdens and advantages upon particular denominations. The 'risk of politicizing religion' that inheres in such legislation is obvious, and indeed is confirmed by the provision's legislative history [which] demonstrates that the provision was drafted with the explicit intention of including particular religious denominations and excluding others."

WHITE, J., joined by Rehnquist, J., dissented,[b] disagreeing with the Court's view "that the rule on its face represents an explicit and deliberate preference for some religious beliefs over others": "The rule [names] no churches or denominations that are entitled to or denied the exemption. [Some] religions will qualify and some will not, but this depends on the source of their contributions, not on their brand of religion. [The Court's assertion] that the limitation might burden the less well-organized denominations [is contrary to the state's claim] that both categories include not only well-established, but also not so well-established organizations."[c] Further, "I cannot join the Court's easy rejection of the state's submission that a valid secular purpose justifies basing the exemption on the percentage of external funding."

Notes and Questions

1. *The Gillette rationale.* (a) Should the existence of a "neutral, secular basis" justify government preference—de jure or de facto—among religions? Consider Kent Greenawalt, *All or Nothing at All: The Defeat of Selective Conscientious Objection,* 1971 Sup.Ct.Rev. 31, 71: "If a sociological survey indicated that Protestants generally work harder than Catholics, the government might simplify its hiring problems by interviewing only Protestants. If the doctors of Catholic hospitals were determined to be on the average more qualified than those at Lutheran hospitals, aid might be limited to the Catholic hospitals. It is, of course, inconceivable that such legislation would be passed and its unconstitutionality is [apparent]." How significant was the Court's observation that the *Gillette* law "attempts to accommodate free exercise values"?

(b) Was the Draft Act of 1917, which exempted only conscientious objectors affiliated with some "well-recognized religious sect" whose principles forbade participation in war, also valid under the *Gillette* rationale? Consider 48 Minn.

upon different religious organizations. On the contrary [it] makes explicit and deliberate distinctions between different religious organizations [and] effectively distinguishes between 'well-established churches' that have 'achieved strong but not total financial support from their members,' on the one hand, and 'churches which are new and lacking in a constituency, or, which, as a matter of policy, may favor public solicitation over general reliance on financial support from members,' on the other hand."

The Court found *Gillette v. United States,* Sec. 2, I supra, "readily distinguishable": "In that case, we rejected an Establishment Clause attack upon § 6(j) of the Military Selective Service Act of 1967, which afforded 'conscientious objector' status to any person who, 'by reason of religious training and belief,' was

'conscientiously opposed to participation in war in any form * * *.' Section 6(j) 'focused on individual conscientious belief, not on sectarian affiliation.' Under § 6(j), conscientious objector status was available on an equal basis to both the Quaker and the Roman Catholic, despite the distinction drawn by the latter's church between 'just' and 'unjust' wars. [In] contrast, the statute challenged in the case before us focuses precisely and solely upon religious organizations."

b. Rehnquist, J., joined by Burger, C.J. and White and O'Connor, JJ., also dissented on the ground that appellee Unification Church had no standing.

c. *Gillette* held that there was no religious "gerrymander" if there was "a neutral, secular basis for the lines government has drawn."

L.Rev. 776–77 (1964): "Since pacifism often arises from religious beliefs, a workable method for ascertaining sincerity may have to be couched in terms of those beliefs. Such a test should be permissible, even though it may theoretically 'prefer' some sincere conscientious objectors over others, if it reasonably advances the [statute's] purpose by aiding local draft boards in administering the act. For example, since membership in an organized pacifist sect may be better evidence of sincerity than the mere assertion of pacificist beliefs, a requirement to that effect should be permissible." See also Comment, 64 Colum.L.Rev. 938 (1964).

2. *The Larson rationale.* (a) Consider Jesse H. Choper, *The Free Exercise Clause: A Structural Overview and An Appraisal of Recent Developments,* 27 Wm. & M.L.Rev. 943, 958–61 (1986): "*Larson* should be seen as a free exercise clause decision parading in an establishment clause disguise. [The] major thrust of the Court's opinion [used] classic free exercise clause analysis, [holding] that discrimination among religions must survive strict scrutiny. [Even if] the Minnesota statute did not specifically give preference to some religions over others, it did expressly deal with the subject of religion, and it resulted in favoring some and disfavoring others. In my view, it should have been as vulnerable—that is, subject to the same level of scrutiny—as a general, neutral law that says nothing about religion but that happens to have an adverse impact on some faiths, like the Wisconsin compulsory education law at issue in *Yoder.* The problem is that when the [pre-*Smith*] Court has invoked the establishment clause, it has applied a much more lenient test to laws that expressly deal with religion and subject some faiths to discriminatory treatment than it has applied under the free exercise clause to general, neutral laws that come into conflict with religious beliefs. [In] reality, I believe that the Selective Service Act survived strict scrutiny in *Gillette* [because of the] powerful government interest in raising an army and the difficulties in administering a draft exemption based on "just war" beliefs. [In] sum, the doctrine in *Gillette,* that a valid secular basis for de facto religious discrimination is enough to sustain it under the establishment clause, plainly supports Justice White's dissent in *Larson.* The *Gillette* doctrine, however, effectively has been abandoned, and rightly so."

(b) HERNANDEZ v. COMMISSIONER, 490 U.S. 680, 109 S.Ct. 2136, 104 L.Ed.2d 766 (1989), per MARSHALL, J., found no violation of the establishment clause in not permitting federal taxpayers to deduct as "charitable contributions" payments to the Church of Scientology for "auditing" and "training" sessions. A central tenet of the Church requires "fixed donations" for these sessions to study the faith's tenets and to increase spiritual awareness. The proceeds are the Church's primary source of income:

Larson was distinguished on the ground that IRS disallowance for payments made "with some expectation of a quid pro quo in terms of goods or services [makes] no 'explicit and deliberate distinctions between different religious organizations,' applying instead to all religious entities. [It] may be that a consequence of the quid pro quo orientation of the 'contribution or gift' requirement is to impose a disparate burden on those charitable and religious groups that rely on sales of commodities or services as a means of fund-raising, relative to those groups that raise funds primarily by soliciting unilateral donations. But a statute primarily having a secular effect does not violate the Establishment Clause merely because it 'happens to coincide or harmonize with the tenets of some or all religions.' *McGowan.*"

Because of the absence of "a proper factual record," the Court did not consider the contention of O'CONNOR, J., joined by Scalia, J., dissenting, that "at least some of the fixed payments which the IRS has treated as charitable deductions [are as much a 'quid pro quo exchange'] as the payments [here]": "In exchange for their payment of pew rents, Christians receive particular seats during worship services. Similarly, in some synagogues attendance at the worship services for Jewish High Holy Days is often predicated upon the purchase of a general admission ticket or a reserved seat ticket. Religious honors such as publicly reading from Scripture are purchased or auctioned periodically in some synagogues of Jews from Morocco and Syria. Mormons must tithe ten percent of their income as a necessary but not sufficient condition to obtaining a 'temple recommend,' i.e., the right to be admitted into the temple. A Mass stipend—a fixed payment given to a Catholic priest, in consideration of which he is obliged to apply the fruits of the Mass for the intention of the donor—has similar overtones of exchange. [Thus, the case] involves the differential application of a standard based on constitutionally impermissible differences drawn by the Government among religions." Brennan and Kennedy, JJ., did not participate.

3. *Preference for "religious" objectors.* Is Congress' limitation of draft exemption to "religious" conscientious objectors valid? Consider John H. Mansfield, *Conscientious Objection—1964 Term*, 1965 Relig. & Pub.Or. 3, 76: "[T]here are really no convincing reasons why the religious objector should be exempt and not the non-religious conscientious objector. [T]he religious objector's opposition rests on somewhat more fundamental grounds [and] makes reference to realities that can more easily be described as spiritual. But the non-religious conscientious objector's opposition does rest on basic propositions about the nature of reality and the significance of human existence; this is what distinguishes it from objection that is not even conscientious." See David M. Cohen & Robert S. Greenspan, *Conscientious Objection, Democratic Theory, and the Constitution*, 29 U.Pitt.L.Rev. 389, 403 (1968): "Nothing is more repugnant to a sense of fairness than the rejection of the claim of a conscientious objector because he does not believe in a transcendent reality. If his belief were coupled with a belief that the sun controlled man's destiny, communicating it through sun-spots, his exemption would be immediately granted. This places a premium upon madness and is a celebration of cranks and utopians. The concerned citizen, whose belief is intelligible and commends itself more to our understanding is turned away because he did not indulge in fantastic flights of imagination." Does the "religious" exemption result in more or less government "entanglement" with religion than an exemption for *all* conscientious objectors?

SECTION 4.   CONFLICT BETWEEN THE CLAUSES

The decision in *Employment Division v. Smith* appeared to have relieved some of the tension that had existed between the doctrines that the Court had developed under the establishment and free exercise clauses. But substantial questions remained, e.g., do (a) the decisions in *Sherbert (Thomas, Hobbie), Yoder* and *Roy,* and (b) statutes such as the Religious Freedom Restoration Act and other laws granting religious exemptions from laws of general applicability violate the establishment clause because they impermissibly aid religion?

CORPORATION OF THE PRESIDING BISHOP
OF THE CHURCH OF JESUS CHRIST OF
LATTER–DAY SAINTS v. AMOS

483 U.S. 327, 107 S.Ct. 2862, 97 L.Ed.2d 273 (1987).

JUSTICE WHITE delivered the opinion of the Court.

Section 702 of the Civil Rights Act of 1964 exempts religious organizations from Title VII's prohibition against discrimination in employment on the basis of religion. * * *

The Deseret Gymnasium (Gymnasium) in Salt Lake City, Utah, is a nonprofit facility, open to the public, run by [an] unincorporated religious association sometimes called the Mormon or LDS Church.

Appellee Mayson worked at the Gymnasium for some 16 years as an assistant building engineer and then building engineer. He was discharged in 1981 because he failed to qualify for a temple recommend, that is, a certificate that he is a member of the Church and eligible to attend its temples.

Mayson [contended] that if construed to allow religious employers to discriminate on religious grounds in hiring for nonreligious jobs, § 702 violates the Establishment Clause. * * *

"This Court has long recognized that the government may (and sometimes must) accommodate religious practices and that it may do so without violating the Establishment Clause." It is well established, too, that "[t]he limits of permissible state accommodation to religion are by no means co-extensive with the noninterference mandated by the Free Exercise Clause." *Walz.*[a] [At] some point, accommodation may devolve into "an unlawful fostering of religion," but this is not such a case, in our view. * * *

Lemon requires first that the law at issue serve a "secular legislative purpose." This does not mean that the law's purpose must be unrelated to religion * * *. Rather, *Lemon*'s "purpose" requirement aims at preventing the relevant governmental decisionmaker—in this case, Congress—from abandoning neutrality and acting with the intent of promoting a particular point of view in religious matters.

Under the *Lemon* analysis, it is a permissible legislative purpose to alleviate significant governmental interference with the ability of religious organizations to define and carry out their religious missions.[b] Appellees argue that there is no

---

a. Consider Michael W. McConnell, *Accommodation of Religion*, 1985 Sup.Ct.Rev. 1, 34: "[S]ome government employees may view attendance at religious services on a holy day a sacred duty; they could make out a plausible free exercise case if the government refused them leave. Others may view attendance at services as no more than a spiritually wholesome activity; their free exercise claim would be much weaker. It is not unreasonable for the government to disregard these distinctions—to implement a general policy permitting leave for employees on the holy days of their faith. There seems little reason to confine the government to the exacting standards appropriate to courts when they exercise their

function of judicial review. Religious liberty is not enhanced by a rule confining government accommodations to the minimum compelled under the Constitution."

b. See also Wilbur Katz, *Note on the Constitutionality of Shared Time,* 1964 Relig. & Pub.Or. 85, 88: "It is no violation of neutrality for the government to express its concern for religious freedom by measures which merely neutralize what would otherwise be restrictive effects of government action. Provision for voluntary worship in the armed forces is constitutional, not because government policy may properly favor religion, but because the government is not required to exercise its military powers in a manner restrictive of religious

such purpose here because § 702 provided adequate protection for religious employers prior to the 1972 amendment, when it exempted only the religious activities of such employers from the statutory ban on religious discrimination. We may assume for the sake of argument that the pre–1972 exemption was adequate in the sense that the Free Exercise Clause required no more. Nonetheless, it is a significant burden on a religious organization to require it, on pain of substantial liability, to predict which of its activities a secular court will consider religious. The line is hardly a bright one, and an organization might understandably be concerned that a judge would not understand its religious tenets and sense of mission. Fear of potential liability might affect the way an organization carried out what it understood to be its religious mission. * * *

The second requirement under *Lemon* is that the law in question have "a principal or primary effect [that] neither advances nor inhibits religion." Undoubtedly, religious organizations are better able now to advance their purposes than they were prior to the 1972 amendment to § 702. But religious groups have been better able to advance their purposes on account of many laws that have passed constitutional muster: for example, the property tax exemption at issue in *Walz,* or the loans of school books to school children, including parochial school students, upheld in *Allen.* A law is not unconstitutional simply because it *allows* churches to advance religion, which is their very purpose. For a law to have forbidden "effects" under *Lemon,* it must be fair to say that the *government itself* has advanced religion through its own activities and influence. [Moreover,] we find no persuasive evidence in the record before us that the Church's ability to propagate its religious doctrine through the Gymnasium is any greater now than it was prior to the passage of the Civil Rights Act in 1964. In such circumstances, we do not see how any advancement of religion achieved by the Gymnasium can be fairly attributed to the Government, as opposed to the Church.[15]

We find unpersuasive the District Court's reliance on the fact that § 702 singles out religious entities for a benefit. [The Court] has never indicated that statutes that give special consideration to religious groups are per se invalid. That would run contrary to the teaching of our cases that there is ample room for accommodation of religion under the Establishment Clause. Where, as here, government acts with the proper purpose of lifting a regulation that burdens the exercise of religion, we see no reason to require that the exemption come packaged with benefits to secular entities. * * * *Larson* indicates that laws discriminating *among* religions are subject to strict scrutiny, and that laws "affording a uniform benefit to *all* religions" should be analyzed under *Lemon.* In a case such as this, where a statute is neutral on its face and motivated by a permissible purpose of limiting governmental interference with the exercise of religion, we see no justification for applying strict scrutiny to a statute that passes the *Lemon* test. [A]s applied to the nonprofit activities of religious employers, § 702 is rationally related to the legitimate purpose of alleviating significant governmental interference with the ability of religious organizations to define and carry out their religious missions. * * *

The judgment of the District Court is reversed * * *.

freedom. Affirmative government action to maintain religious freedom in these instances serves the secular purpose of promoting a constitutional right, the free exercise of religion."

15. Undoubtedly, Mayson's freedom of choice in religious matters was impinged upon, but it was the Church [and] not the Government, who put him to the choice of changing his religious practices or losing his [job.]

JUSTICE BRENNAN, with whom JUSTICE MARSHALL joins, concurring in the judgment.

[Any] exemption from Title VII's proscription on religious discrimination [says] that a person may be put to the choice of either conforming to certain religious tenets or losing a job opportunity, a promotion, or, as in this case, employment itself. The potential for coercion created by such a provision is in serious tension with our commitment to individual freedom of conscience in matters of religious belief.

At the same time, religious organizations have an interest in autonomy in ordering their internal affairs * * *. Determining that certain activities are in furtherance of an organization's religious mission, and that only those committed to that mission should conduct them, is thus a means by which a religious community defines itself. Solicitude for a church's ability to do so reflects the idea that furtherance of the autonomy of religious organizations often furthers individual religious freedom as well. * * *

This rationale suggests that, ideally, religious organizations should be able to discriminate on the basis of religion *only* with respect to religious activities [because] the infringement on religious liberty that results from conditioning performance of *secular* activity upon religious belief cannot be defended as necessary for the community's self-definition. Furthermore, the authorization of discrimination in such circumstances is not an accommodation that simply enables a church to gain members by the normal means of prescribing the terms of membership for those who seek to participate in furthering the mission of the community. Rather, it puts at the disposal of religion the added advantages of economic leverage in the secular realm. * * *

What makes the application of a religious-secular distinction difficult is that the character of an activity is not self-evident. As a result, determining whether an activity is religious or secular requires a searching case-by-case analysis. This results in considerable ongoing government entanglement in religious affairs. Furthermore, this prospect of government intrusion raises concern that a religious organization may be chilled in its Free Exercise activity. * * *

The risk of chilling religious organizations is most likely to arise with respect to *nonprofit* activities. The fact that an operation is not organized as a profit-making commercial enterprise makes colorable a claim that it is not purely secular in orientation. * * *

Sensitivity to individual religious freedom dictates that religious discrimination be permitted only with respect to employment in religious activities. Concern for the autonomy of religious organizations demands that we avoid the entanglement and the chill on religious expression that a case-by-case determination would produce. We cannot escape the fact that these aims are in tension. Because of the nature of nonprofit activities, I believe that a categorical exemption for such enterprises appropriately balances these competing concerns. * * *

JUSTICE BLACKMUN, concurring in the judgment.

Essentially for the reasons set forth in Justice O'Connor's opinion, * * * I too, concur in the judgment of the Court. * * *

JUSTICE O'CONNOR, concurring in the judgment. * * *

In *Wallace v. Jaffree,* I noted a tension in the Court's use of the *Lemon* test to evaluate an Establishment Clause challenge to government efforts to accommodate the free exercise of religion: "On the one hand, a rigid application of the

Lemon test would invalidate legislation exempting religious observers from generally applicable government obligations. By definition, such legislation has a religious purpose and effect in promoting the free exercise of religion.[c] On the other hand, judicial deference to all legislation that purports to facilitate the free exercise of religion would completely vitiate the Establishment Clause. Any statute pertaining to religion can be viewed as an 'accommodation' of free exercise rights." [d]

In my view, the opinion for the Court leans toward the second of the two unacceptable options described [above.] Almost any government benefit to religion could be recharacterized as simply "allowing" a religion to better advance itself, unless perhaps it involved actual proselytization by government agents. In nearly every case of a government benefit to religion, the religious mission would not be advanced if the religion did not take advantage of the benefit; even a direct financial subsidy to a religious organization would not advance religion if for some reason the organization failed to make any use of the [funds.]

The necessary first step in evaluating an Establishment Clause challenge to a government action lifting from religious organizations a generally applicable regulatory burden is to recognize that such government action *does* have the effect of advancing religion. The necessary second step is to separate those benefits to religion that constitutionally accommodate the free exercise of religion from those

c. In her *Jaffree* concurrence, O'Connor, J., added: "Indeed, the statute at issue in *Lemon* [can] be viewed as an accommodation of the religious beliefs of parents who choose to send their children to religious schools."

In this connection, consider Kurland, *Religion and the Law* 12 (1962): "The [free exercise and establishment] clauses should be read as stating a single precept: that government cannot utilize religion as a standard for action or inaction because these clauses, read together as they should be, prohibit classification in terms of religion either to confer a benefit or to impose a burden." For thoughtful comment, see Kauper, *Book Review*, 41 Texas L.Rev. 467 (1963); Pfeffer, *Religion–Blind Government*, 15 Stan.L.Rev. 389 (1963); Mansfield, *Book Review*, 52 Calif.L.Rev. 212 (1964).

Similarly, for the view that the free exercise clause should generally only guarantee "equality of treatment for those who act out of sincere religious belief" and should afford special protection only for acts of "worship," as defined, see Fernandez, *The Free Exercise of Religion*, 36 So.Calif.L.Rev. 546 (1963). For the view that free exercise claims should be treated "no differently than free expression claims," see Marshall, *Solving the Free Exercise Dilemma: Free Exercise as Expression*, 67 Minn.L.Rev. 545 (1983).

d. In *Jaffree*, O'Connor, J. added: "It [is] difficult to square any notion of 'complete neutrality' with the mandate of the Free Exercise Clause that government must sometimes exempt a religious observer from an otherwise generally applicable obligation. A government that confers a benefit on an explicitly religious basis is not neutral toward religion. The solu-

tion [lies] in identifying workable limits to the Government's license to promote the free exercise of religion. [O]ne can plausibly assert that government pursues free exercise clause values when it lifts a government-imposed burden on the free exercise of religion. If a statute falls within this category, then the standard Establishment Clause test should be modified accordingly. [T]he Court should simply acknowledge that the religious purpose of such a statute is legitimated by the Free Exercise Clause."

See also Abner S. Greene, *The Political Balance of the Religion Clauses*, 102 Yale L.J. 1611, 1644 (1993): "[I]f we construe the Establishment Clause to prohibit legislation enacted for the express purpose of advancing religious values, then the predicate for universal obedience to law has been removed. A religious conscientious objector may legitimately claim that because she was thwarted from offering her values for majority acceptance as law, she should have at lest a prima facie right of exemption from law that conflicts with her religion. The Free Exercise Clause works as a counterweight to the Establishment Clause; it gives back what the Establishment Clause takes away." Compare Sherry, fn. d, p. 1008 supra, at 145: "This formulation can also be reversed: protecting the values of the Establishment Clause should constitute a compelling government interest sufficient to justify the impact of neutral laws on religious exercise. Whichever clause serves as the compelling interest trumps the other. Which formulation one prefers depends solely on whether one places a higher priority on the values of the Establishment Clause or on those of the Free Exercise Clause."

that provide unjustifiable awards of assistance to religious organizations. As I have suggested in earlier opinions, the inquiry framed by the *Lemon* test should be "whether government's purpose is to endorse religion and whether the statute actually conveys a message of endorsement." To ascertain whether the statute conveys a message of endorsement, the relevant issue is how it would be perceived by an objective observer, acquainted with the text, legislative history, and implementation of the statute.[e] [This] case involves a government decision to lift from a nonprofit activity of a religious organization the burden of demonstrating that the particular nonprofit activity is religious as well as the burden of refraining from discriminating on the basis of religion. Because there is a probability that a nonprofit activity of a religious organization will itself be involved in the organization's religious mission, in my view the objective observer should perceive the government action as an accommodation of the exercise of religion rather than as a government endorsement of religion.

* * * While I express no opinion on the issue, I emphasize that under the holding of the Court, and under my view of the appropriate Establishment Clause analysis, the question of the constitutionality of the § 702 exemption as applied to for-profit activities of religious organizations remains open.

Notes and Questions

1. *Draft exemption.* Did the statute in *Gillette,* exempting only "religious" conscientious objectors, impermissibly prefer religion over nonreligion? In WELSH v. UNITED STATES, Sec. 2, II supra, four justices addressed the issue. WHITE, J., joined by Burger, C.J., and Stewart, J., found it valid: "First, § 6(j) may represent a purely practical judgment that religious objectors, however admirable, would be of no more use in combat than many others unqualified for military service. [On] this basis, the exemption has neither the primary purpose nor the effect of furthering religion. * * *

"Second, Congress may have [believed that] to deny the exemption would violate the Free Exercise Clause or at least raise grave problems in this respect. True, this Court has more than once stated its unwillingness to construe the First Amendment, standing alone, as requiring draft exemptions for religious believers. [But] just as in *Katzenbach v. Morgan,* [p. 1386 infra], where we accepted the judgment of Congress as to what legislation was appropriate to enforce the Equal Protection Clause of the Fourteenth Amendment, here we should respect congressional judgment accommodating the Free Exercise Clause and the power to raise armies. This involves no surrender of the Court's function as ultimate arbiter in disputes over interpretation of the Constitution. But it was enough in *Katzenbach* 'to perceive a basis upon which the Congress might resolve the conflict as it did' * * *.

---

e. In *Jaffree,* O'Connor, J., added: "[C]ourts should assume that the 'objective observer,' is acquainted with the Free Exercise Clause and the values it promotes. Thus individual perceptions, or resentment that a religious observer is exempted from a particular government requirement, would be entitled to little weight if the Free Exercise Clause strongly supported the exemption."

Compare William P. Marshall, *The Religious Freedom Restoration Act: Establishment, Equal Protection and Free Speech Concerns,* 56 Mont.L.Rev. 227, 236 (1995): "Prior to *Smith,* one could argue that the Constitution demanded some accommodation from general laws of neutral applicability for free exercise interests. Legislative exemptions from neutral laws, which provided this accommodation, could therefore be defended as in accord with this constitutional mandate. The denial of the free exercise right in *Smith,* however, suggests that exempting religion from neutral laws is no longer based upon a constitutional requirement. Accordingly, after *Smith,* the strength of the state interest supporting the legislative exemption is necessarily diminished."

"[If] it is 'favoritism' and not 'neutrality' to exempt religious believers from the draft, is it 'neutrality' and not 'inhibition' of religion to compel religious believers to fight * * *? It cannot be ignored that the First Amendment itself contains a religious classification [and the free exercise clause] protects conduct as well as religious belief and speech. [It] was not suggested [in *Braunfeld*] that the Sunday closing laws in 21 States exempting Sabbatarians and others violated the Establishment Clause because no provision was made for others who claimed nonreligious reasons for not working on some particular day of the week. Nor was it intimated in *Zorach* that the no-establishment holding might be infirm because only those pursuing religious studies for designated periods were released from the public school routine; neither was it hinted that a public school's refusal to institute a released time program would violate the Free Exercise Clause. The Court in *Sherbert* construed the Free Exercise Clause to require special treatment for Sabbatarians under the State's unemployment compensation law. But the State could deal specially with Sabbatarians whether the Free Exercise Clause required it or not * * *." a

HARLAN, J., disagreed, believing that "having chosen to exempt, [Congress] cannot draw the line between theistic or nontheistic religious beliefs on the one hand and secular beliefs on the other. [I]t must encompass the class of individuals it purports to exclude, those whose beliefs emanate from a purely moral, ethical, or philosophical source.[9] The common denominator must be the intensity of moral conviction with which a belief is [held]. *Everson*, *McGowan* and *Allen*, all sustained legislation on the premise that it was neutral in its application and thus did not constitute an establishment, notwithstanding the fact that it may have assisted religious groups by giving them the same benefits accorded to nonreligious groups.[12] To the extent that *Zorach* and *Sherbert* stand for the proposition that the Government may (*Zorach*), or must (*Sherbert*), shape its secular programs to accommodate the beliefs and tenets of religious groups, I think these cases unsound.[13]"

2. *Unemployment compensation.* (a) Did the Court's decisions in *Sherbert*, *Thomas* and *Hobbie* impermissibly prefer religion? In THOMAS v. REVIEW BD., Sec. 2 supra, REHNQUIST, J., dissented, finding the result "inconsistent with many of our prior Establishment Clause cases"[2]. "If Indiana were to legislate what the

---

a. See generally Peter J. Donnici, *Governmental Encouragement of Religious Ideology: A Study of the Current Conscientious Objector Exemption from Military Service,* 13 J.Pub.L. 16, 43 (1964).

9. * * * I suggested [in *Sherbert*] that a State could constitutionally create exceptions to its program to accommodate religious scruples. [But] any such exception in order to satisfy the Establishment Clause [would] have to be sufficiently broad so as to be religiously neutral. This would require creating an exception for anyone who, as a matter of conscience, could not comply with the statute. * * *

12. [I] fail to see how [§ 6(j)] has "any substantial legislative purpose" apart from honoring the conscience of individuals who oppose war on only religious grounds. * * *

13. [At] the very least the Constitution requires that the State not excuse students early for the purpose of receiving religious instruction when it does not offer to nonreligious

students the opportunity to use school hours for spiritual or ethical instruction of a nonreligious nature. Moreover, whether a released-time program cast in terms of improving "conscience" to the exclusion of artistic or cultural pursuits, would be "neutral" and consistent with the requirement of "voluntarism," is by no means an easy question. * * *

2. To the extent *Sherbert* was correctly decided, it might be argued that cases such as *McCollum, Engel, Schempp, Lemon,* and *Nyquist* were wrongly decided. The "aid" rendered to religion in these latter cases may not be significantly different, in kind or degree, than the "aid" afforded Mrs. Sherbert or Thomas. For example, if the State in *Sherbert* could not deny compensation to one refusing work for religious reasons, it might be argued that a State may not deny reimbursement to students who choose for religious reasons to attend parochial schools. The argument would be that although a State need not allocate any funds to education, once it has done so, it may

Court today requires—an unemployment compensation law which permitted benefits to be granted to those persons who quit their jobs for religious reasons—the statute would 'plainly' violate the Establishment Clause as interpreted in such cases as *Lemon* and *Nyquist.* First, [the] proviso would clearly serve only a religious purpose. It would grant financial benefits for the sole purpose of accommodating religious beliefs. Second, there can be little doubt that the primary effect of the proviso would be to 'advance' religion by facilitating the exercise of religious belief. Third, any statute including such a proviso would surely 'entangle' the State in religion far more than the mere grant of tax exemptions, as in *Walz,* or the award of tuition grants and tax credits, as in *Nyquist.* By granting financial benefits to persons solely on the basis of their religious beliefs, the State must necessarily inquire whether the claimant's belief is 'religious' and whether it is sincerely held. [Just] as I think that Justice Harlan in *Sherbert* correctly stated the proper approach to free exercise questions, I believe that Justice Stewart, dissenting in *Schempp,* accurately stated the reach of the Establishment Clause [as] limited to 'government support of proselytizing activities of religious sects by throwing the weight of secular authorities behind the dissemination of religious tenets.' See *McCollum* (Reed, J., dissenting) (impermissible aid is only 'purposeful assistance directly to the church itself or to some religious [group] performing ecclesiastical functions'). Conversely, governmental assistance which does not have the effect of 'inducing' religious belief, but instead merely 'accommodates' or implements an independent religious choice does not impermissibly involve the government in religious choices and therefore does not violate the Establishment [Clause]. I would think that in this case, as in *Sherbert,* had the state voluntarily chosen to pay unemployment compensation benefits to persons who left their jobs for religious reasons, such aid would be constitutionally permissible because it redounds directly to the benefit of the individual."

(b) *Accommodation vs. inducement vs. imposition vs. coercion.* Consider Alan Schwarz, *No Imposition of Religion: The Establishment Clause Value,* 77 Yale L.J. 692, 693, 723, 728 (1968): "[T]he dilemma [between the religion clauses] results from an unnecessarily broad reading of the establishment clause; that clause should be read to prohibit only aid which has as its motive or substantial effect the imposition of religious belief or practice * * *. Conversely, aid which does not have the effect of inducing religious belief, but merely accommodates or implements an individual religious choice, does not increase the danger of religion and [does] not violate the no-imposition standard. * * * Exemption of Mrs. Sherbert [represents] a judgment that the exercise of Seventh-day Adventism is more worthy than bowling on Saturdays, but the exemption has no significant effect and arguably no effect at all upon whether someone becomes a Seventh-day Adventist. Similarly, the Sabbatarian exemption from Sunday closing laws does not induce one to become a Jew; draft exemption to conscientious objectors does not normally induce one to become a Quaker; closing the public schools on all religious holidays or on every Wednesday at 2 P.M. does not induce the adoption of religion; and compulsory Sunday closing, while implementing an independent desire to attend church services, has no substantial effect upon the creation of

not require any person to sacrifice his religious beliefs in order to obtain an equal education. There can be little doubt that to the extent secular education provides answers to important moral questions without reference to religion or teaches that there are no answers, a person in one sense sacrifices his religious belief by attending secular schools. And even if such "aid" were not constitutionally compelled by the Free Exercise Clause, Justice Harlan may well be right in *Sherbert* when he finds sufficient flexibility in the Establishment Clause to permit the States to voluntarily choose to grant such benefits to individuals.

such desire. The availability of preferential aid to religious exercise may, to be sure, induce false claims of religious belief, but the establishment clause is not concerned with false claims of belief, only with induced belief." Does this distinguish *McCollum, Engel* and *Schempp* from *Sherbert?* Do you agree with all of the *factual* assumptions made? Under this analysis, what result in *Epperson?* What of a small governmental payment to all persons who would lose salary because they have to be absent from their jobs in order to attend religious services? Would the state's failure to provide Mrs. Sherbert with unemployment compensation be the same as its not having on-premises released time and school prayer in that all of these actions simply "make the practice of religious beliefs more expensive"?

Compare Jesse H. Choper, *The Religion Clauses of the First Amendment: Reconciling the Conflict,* 41 U.Pitt.L.Rev. 673, 691, 697–700 (1980): "My proposal for resolving the conflict between the two Religion Clauses seeks to implement their historically and contemporarily acknowledged common goal: to safeguard religious liberty. [I]t is only when an accommodation would jeopardize religious liberty—when it would coerce, compromise, or influence religious choice—that it would fail. [For example, in *Yoder,* unless] it could be shown that relieving the Amish [would] tend to coerce, compromise, or influence religious choice—and it is extremely doubtful that it could—the exemption was permissible under the Establishment Clause. In contrast, in *Sherbert,* [the] exemption results in impairment of religious liberty because compulsorily raised tax funds must be used to subsidize Mrs. Sherbert's exercise of religion.[b] [In the draft exemption cases], professing a personal 'religion' (as opposed to 'essentially political, sociological or philosophical considerations') was enough to gain the enormous advantage of avoiding combat duty. [D]raftees seeking exemption would have to formulate a statement of personal doctrine that would pass muster. This endeavor would involve deep and careful thought, and perhaps reading in philosophy and religion. Some undoubtedly would be persuaded by what they read. Moreover, the theory of 'cognitive dissonance'—which posits that to avoid madness we tend to become what we hold ourselves to be and what others believe us to be—also suggests that some initially fraudulent claims of belief in a personal religion would develop into true belief. Thus, a draft exemption for religious objectors threatens values of religious freedom by encouraging the adoption of religious beliefs by those who seek to qualify for the benefit."

(c) *Breadth of exemption.* In TEXAS MONTHLY, INC. v. BULLOCK, Sec. 1, II supra, SCALIA, J., joined by Rehnquist, C.J., and Kennedy, J., charged that according to Brennan, J.'s plurality opinion, "no law is constitutional whose 'benefits [are] confined to religious organizations,' except, of course, those laws that are unconstitutional *unless* they contain benefits confined to religious organizations. [But] 'the limits of permissible state accommodation to religion are by no means co-extensive with the noninterference mandated by the Free Exercise Clause.' Breadth of coverage is essential to constitutionality whenever a law's benefiting of religious activity is sought to be defended not specifically (or not exclusively) as an intentional and reasonable accommodation of religion, but as merely the incidental consequence of seeking to benefit *all* activity that achieves a

b. See also Jesse H. Choper, *The Free Exercise Clause,* 27 Wm. & M.L.Rev. 943, 951 n. 25 (1986): "Under Justice Rehnquist's [and Professor Schwarz's] rationale, if a municipally-owned bus company wanted to waive the fare to take people to churches, it could do so. According to Justice Rehnquist, the waiver would not 'induce' religion, but would simply 'accommodate' a religious choice that already had been made. That may be true, but the waiver also would result in what the religion clauses protect against—the use of tax funds for exclusively religious purposes."

particular secular goal. But that is a different rationale—more commonly invoked than accommodation of religion but, as our cases show, not preclusive of it. Where accommodation of religion is the justification, by definition religion is being singled out." Finally, "the proper lesson to be drawn from" the fact that the free exercise clause may not require the Texas sales tax exemption and "that *Murdock* and *Follett* are narrowly distinguishable" is that "if the exemption comes so close to being a constitutionally required accommodation, there is no doubt that it is at least a permissible one." [c]

BRENNAN, J., joined by Marshall and Stevens, JJ., responded: "Contrary to the dissent's claims, we in no way suggest that *all* benefits conferred exclusively upon religious groups or upon individuals on account of their religious beliefs are forbidden by the Establishment Clause unless they are mandated by the Free Exercise Clause. Our decisions in *Zorach* and *Amos* offer two examples. Similarly, if the Air Force provided a sufficiently broad exemption from its dress requirements for servicemen whose religious faiths commanded them to wear certain headgear or other attire, see *Goldman v. Weinberger*, that exemption presumably would not be invalid under the Establishment Clause even though this Court has not found it to be required by the Free Exercise Clause.

"All of these cases, however, involve legislative exemptions that did not or would not impose substantial burdens on nonbeneficiaries while allowing others to act according to their religious beliefs, or that were designed to alleviate government intrusions that might significantly deter adherents of a particular faith from conduct protected by the Free Exercise Clause. New York City's decision to release students from public schools so that they might obtain religious instruction elsewhere, which we upheld in *Zorach,* was found not to coerce students who wished to remain behind to alter their religious beliefs, nor did it impose monetary costs on their parents or other taxpayers who opposed or were indifferent to the religious instruction given to students who were released. The hypothetical Air Force uniform exemption also would not place a monetary burden on those required to conform to the dress code or subject them to any appreciable privation. And the application of Title VII's exemption for religious organizations that we approved in *Amos* though it had some adverse effect on those holding or seeking employment with those organizations (if not on taxpayers generally), prevented potentially serious encroachments on protected religious freedoms.

"Texas' tax exemption, by contrast, does not remove a demonstrated and possible grave imposition on religious activity sheltered by the Free Exercise Clause. Moreover, it burdens nonbeneficiaries by increasing their tax bills by whatever amount is needed to offset the benefit bestowed on subscribers to religious publications."

3. *Sabbath observance.* THORNTON v. CALDOR, INC., 472 U.S. 703, 105 S.Ct. 2914, 86 L.Ed.2d 557 (1985), per BURGER, C.J., held that a Connecticut law— which provided "that those who observe a Sabbath any day of the week as a matter of religious conviction must be relieved of the duty to work on that day, no matter what burden or inconvenience this imposes on the employer or fellow workers"—"has a primary effect that impermissibly advances a particular religious practice" and thus violates the establishment clause: "The statute arms Sabbath observers with an absolute and unqualified right not to work on whatever

---

c. Why didn't Texas' exemption violate the establishment clause test articulated by Kennedy, J. (joined by Rehnquist, C.J., and White and Scalia, JJ.) in *Allegheny County v. ACLU,* Sec. I, III supra, because it gave "direct benefits to religion" and involved "subtle coercion [in] the form of taxation"?

day they designate as their Sabbath [and thus] goes beyond having an incidental or remote effect of advancing religion."[d]

O'CONNOR, J., joined by Marshall, J., concurred, distinguishing "the religious accommodation provisions of Title VII of the Civil Rights Act [which] require private employers to reasonably accommodate the religious practices of employees unless to do so would cause undue hardship to the employer's business": "In my view, a statute outlawing employment discrimination based on race, color, religion, sex or national origin has the valid secular purpose of assuring employment opportunity to all groups in our pluralistic society. Since Title VII calls for reasonable rather than absolute accommodation and extends that requirement to all religious beliefs and practices rather than protecting only the Sabbath observance, I believe an objective observer would perceive it as an anti-discrimination law rather than an endorsement of religion or a particular religious practice."

Was the purpose or effect of the *Caldor* statute any different than that of the *Amos* statute or the Court's decisions in *Sherbert, Thomas, Hobbie, Roy* and *Yoder?* *Amos* distinguished *Caldor* on the ground that in *Amos*, "appellee was not legally obligated to take the steps necessary to qualify for a temple recommend, and his discharge was not required by statute."

Does the *Caldor* statute "promote" and "endorse" a particular "religion" or "religious belief" or "religious practice" any more so than the Court's decisions in *Sherbert, Thomas, Hobbie, Yoder* and *Roy,* or than the statutory exemptions from the draft or Sunday Closing Laws? *Hobbie* distinguished *Caldor* as follows: "Florida's provision of unemployment benefits to religious observers does not single out a particular class of such persons for favorable treatment and thereby have the effect of implicitly endorsing a particular religious belief. Rather, the provision of unemployment benefits generally available within the State to religious observers who must leave their employment due to an irreconcilable conflict between the demands of work and conscience neutrally accommodates religious beliefs and practices, without endorsement."

In *Kiryas Joel,* Sec. I, II supra, SCALIA, J., joined by Rehnquist, C.J., and Thomas, J., disagreed with the Court's conclusion that New York had impermissibly preferred one religion: "[M]ost efforts at accommodation seek to solve a problem that applies to members of only one or a few religions. Not every religion uses wine in its sacraments, but that does not make an exemption from Prohibition for sacramental wine-use impermissible, nor does it require the State granting such an exemption to explain in advance how it will treat every other claim for dispensation from its controlled-substances laws. Likewise, not every religion uses peyote in its services, but we have suggested that legislation which exempts the sacramental use of peyote from generally applicable drug laws is not only permissible, but desirable, see *Smith,* without any suggestion that some 'up front' legislative guarantee of equal treatment for sacramental substances used by other sects must be provided."

---

d. Rehnquist, J., dissented without opinion.

Consider Richard A. Epstein, *Religious Liberty in the Welfare State*, 31 Wm.& M.L.Rev. 375, 406 (1990): "[It would plainly be unconstitutional] if the state offered to pay a small sum out of public funds to the employer to defray the additional costs it had to bear to keep the religious worker on its payroll. [If] a public subsidy of religious workers is not acceptable under the establishment clause, then

a public mandate of a private subsidy is unacceptable as well."

For the view that since "securing individual constitutional rights often (or almost always) imposes impediments to the smooth functioning of our system, if accommodations for religion impose only imprecise social/economic costs, then these prices of religious tolerance are permitted to be paid," see Jesse H. Choper, *Securing Religious Liberty*, 123–126 (1995).

Kennedy, J., expressed a similar view: "It is normal for legislatures to respond to problems as they arise—no less so when the issue is religious accommodation. Most accommodations cover particular religious practices."

4. *School prayer.* In *Jaffree,* O'CONNOR, J., applied her "solution" to Alabama's moment of silence law: "No law prevents a student who is so inclined from praying silently in public schools. [Of] course, the State might argue that § 16–1–20.1 protects not silent prayer, but rather group silent prayer under State sponsorship. Phrased in these terms, the burden lifted by the statute is not one imposed by the State of Alabama, but by the Establishment Clause as interpreted in *Engel* and *Schempp.* In my view, it is beyond the authority of the State of Alabama to remove burdens imposed by the Constitution itself."

5. *Reconciling the conflict.* Assuming the validity of the distinction between *McCollum, Engel, Schempp* and *Jaffree* on the one hand, and the programs such as that in *Amos* and exemption from the draft etc. on the other, are the above approaches nonetheless undesirable because they result not merely in protection of free exercise (or neutrality or accommodation) but in relieving persons with certain religious beliefs of significant burdens from which many other persons strongly desire to be exempted? That, in this sense, there is "preference" for minority religions and "discrimination" against the other persons because of their religion or lack of it? Should free exercise exemptions "be allowed only if the petitioner agrees to the imposition of some alternative duty or burden"? Note, 91 Harv.L.Rev. at 1082. Consider Galanter, p. 1039 supra, at 290–91: "[In *Sherbert*] it was clear that the state was already solicitous of the scruples of Sunday worshippers, though not of Saturday ones. In such a case, it is easy to appreciate that the exception [required by the decision] is restorative or equalizing. It puts the minority in the same position that the majority enjoys. [But] can it be said that the kind of disparity found in *Sherbert* between the treatment of majority and minority is a unique or unusual thing? Whatever seriously interferes with majority religious beliefs and practices is unlikely to become a legal requirement— for example, work on Sunday or Christmas. And whatever the majority considers necessary for its religious practice is quite unlikely to be prohibited by law. And whatever the majority finds religiously objectionable is unlikely to become a legal requirement—for example, medical practices which substantial groups find abhorrent, like contraception, sterilization, euthanasia, or abortion. Exceptions then, give to minorities what majorities have by virtue of suffrage and representative government. The question is not whether the state may prefer these minorities, but whether it may counterbalance the natural advantages of majorities."

Chapter 11
EQUAL PROTECTION

Virtually no legislation applies universally and treats all persons equally; all laws classify (or "discriminate") by imposing special burdens (or granting exemptions from such burdens) or by conferring special benefits on some people and not others. Under what circumstances do such laws violate the fourteenth amendment's command that no state shall "deny to any person within its jurisdiction the equal protection of the laws"? [a]

Despite the fact that the language of the equal protection clause is not confined to racial discrimination, the *Slaughter-House Cases,* p. 52 supra (the first decision interpreting the Civil War amendments), "doubt[ed] very much whether any action of a state not directed by way of discrimination against the negroes as a class, or on account of their race, will ever be held to come within the purview of this provision." Sec. 2 will concern the "strict scrutiny" given to racial (and ethnic) classifications which the Court has deemed to be "suspect." Sec. 3 will consider the extension of a nondeferential standard of review to government action that disadvantages several other discrete groups. At least as early as 1897, however, the Court invoked the equal protection clause to invalidate a commonplace economic regulation that obligated railroad defendants (but not others) to pay the attorneys' fees of successful plaintiffs. The Court acknowledged that "as a general proposition, [it] is undeniably true [that] it is not within the scope of the Fourteenth Amendment to withhold from States the power of classification." But "it must appear" that a classification is "based upon some reasonable ground— some difference which bears a just and proper relation to the attempted classifica-

---

a. By its terms, the equal protection clause does not apply to the federal government. A series of decisions, however, has held that the fifth amendment's due process clause—although not containing the language of equal protection—forbids "unjustifiable" discrimination (*Bolling v. Sharpe,* Sec. 2, II infra) and that—except under special circumstances (see Sec. 3, I infra: "Alienage")—the "approach to Fifth Amendment equal protection claims has always been precisely the same as to equal protection claims under the Fourteenth Amendment" (*Weinberger v. Wiesenfeld,* Sec. 3, IV infra).

In 1976, *Hampton v. Wong,* Sec. 3, I infra, advanced a different approach. It stated that "when a federal rule is applicable to only a limited territory, such as the District of Columbia, or an insular possession, and when there is no special national interest involved, the Due Process Clause has been construed as having the same significance as the Equal Protection Clause," but suggested a different standard for "a federal rule having a nationwide impact." Subsequent decisions, however, have continued to treat equal protection claims against the federal government under the fifth amendment in the same way as equal protection claims against the states under the fourteenth amendment, even though the challenged federal rule had "nationwide impact." See generally Kenneth L. Karst, *The Fifth Amendment's Guarantee of Equal Protection,* 55 N.C.L.Rev. 541 (1977).

tion—and is not a mere arbitrary selection." *Gulf, C. & S. F. Ry. v. Ellis,* 165 U.S. 150, 17 S.Ct. 255, 41 L.Ed. 666 (1897).[b]

Sec. 1 deals with this "traditional approach" under the equal protection clause to general economic and social welfare regulations, as distinguished from either "suspect" or "quasi-suspect" classifications (Secs. 2–3) or laws that affect what have come to be known as "fundamental rights" (Sec. 4).

SECTION 1.   TRADITIONAL APPROACH

As observed in Ch. 6, Sec. 1, III, the due process clause was the usual provision used by the Court in the first third of this century to overturn a great many economic and social welfare regulations. But despite Holmes, J.'s reference during this period to the equal protection clause as "the usual last resort of constitutional arguments," [a] the Court held that approximately twenty such state and local laws violated equal protection.[b] In doing so, the Court employed the deferential standard of judicial review called for by the "traditional approach" which granted a state "a broad discretion in classification in the exercise of its power of regulation" and interposed the "constitutional guaranty of equal protection" only "against discriminations that are entirely arbitrary." [c]

The materials that follow concern the Court's use of the "traditional approach" under equal protection to economic and social welfare regulations since the late 1930s when it abandoned active substantive due process review of such legislation.

FCC v. BEACH COMMUNICATIONS, INC.

508 U.S. 307, 113 S.Ct. 2096, 124 L.Ed.2d 211 (1993).

JUSTICE THOMAS delivered the opinion of the Court.

In providing for the regulation of cable television facilities, Congress has drawn a distinction between facilities that serve separately owned and managed buildings and those that serve one or more buildings under common ownership or management. [Under Cable Act § 602(7)(B), cable] facilities in the latter category are exempt from regulation as long as they provide services without using public rights-of-way. * * *

This case arises out of an FCC proceeding clarifying the agency's interpretation of the term "cable system" as it is used in the Cable Act. In this proceeding, the Commission addressed the application of the exemption codified in § 602(7)(B) to satellite master antenna television (SMATV) facilities. Unlike a traditional cable television system, which delivers video programming to a large community of subscribers through coaxial cables laid under city streets or along utility lines, an SMATV system typically receives a signal from a satellite through a small satellite dish located on a rooftop and then retransmits the signal by wire to units within a building or complex of buildings. The Commission ruled that an SMATV system that serves multiple buildings via a network of interconnected physical

b. For an even earlier invocation of the equal protection clause to invalidate a classification of transportation rates, see *Reagan v. Farmers' Loan & Trust Co.,* 154 U.S. 362, 14 S.Ct. 1047, 38 L.Ed. 1014 (1894). For an informative review of the Court's earliest use of the equal protection clause, see 2 Norman Dorsen, Paul Bender, Burt Neuborne & Sylvia Law, *Political and Civil Rights in the United States* 57–58 (Law School ed., 4th ed. 1979).

a. *Buck v. Bell,* 274 U.S. 200, 47 S.Ct. 584, 71 L.Ed. 1000 (1927).

b. 2 Dorsen et al., supra, at 336.

c. *Smith v. Cahoon,* 283 U.S. 553, 51 S.Ct. 582, 75 L.Ed. 1264 (1931).

transmission lines is a cable system, unless it falls within the § 602(7)(B) exemption. Consistent with the plain terms of the statutory exemption, the Commission concluded that such an SMATV system is [not exempt] if its transmission lines interconnect separately owned and managed buildings or if its lines use or cross any public right-of-way. * * *

[The court of appeals held that "the Cable Act violates the equal protection component of the Fifth Amendment."]

Whether embodied in the Fourteenth Amendment or inferred from the Fifth, equal protection is not a license for courts to judge the wisdom, fairness, or logic of legislative choices. In areas of social and economic policy, a statutory classification that neither proceeds along suspect lines [e.g., race, national origin, religion, or alienage] nor infringes fundamental constitutional rights must be upheld against equal protection challenge if there is any reasonably conceivable state of facts that could provide a rational basis for the classification. Where there are "plausible reasons" for Congress' action, "our inquiry is at an end." *United States Railroad Retirement Bd. v. Fritz*, 449 U.S. 166, 179, 101 S.Ct. 453, 461, 66 L.Ed.2d 368 (1980). This standard of review is a paradigm of judicial restraint. "The Constitution presumes that, absent some reason to infer antipathy, even improvident decisions will eventually be rectified by the democratic process and that judicial intervention is generally unwarranted no matter how unwisely we may think a political branch has acted." *Vance v. Bradley*, 440 U.S. 93, 97, 99 S.Ct. 939, 942–943, 59 L.Ed.2d 171 (1979) [sustaining mandatory retirement at age 60 for federal Foreign Service personnel].

On rational-basis review, a classification in a statute such as the Cable Act comes to us bearing a strong presumption of validity, and those attacking the rationality of the legislative classification have the burden "to negative every conceivable basis which might support it." Moreover, because we never require a legislature to articulate its reasons for enacting a statute, it is entirely irrelevant for constitutional purposes whether the conceived reason for the challenged distinction actually motivated the legislature. *Fritz*.[a] Thus, the absence of "legislative facts" explaining the distinction "[o]n the record," [citing the court below] has no significance in rational-basis analysis. In other words, a legislative choice is not subject to courtroom fact-finding and may be based on rational speculation unsupported by evidence or empirical data. * * *

These restraints on judicial review have added force "where the legislature must necessarily engage in a process of line-drawing." *Fritz*. Defining the class of persons subject to a regulatory requirement—much like classifying governmental beneficiaries—"inevitably requires that some persons who have an almost equally strong claim to favored treatment be placed on different sides of the line,

---

a. Brennan, J. joined by Marshall, J., dissented in *Fritz*: "[T]his Court has frequently recognized that the actual purposes of Congress, rather than the post hoc justifications offered by Government attorneys, must be the primary basis for analysis under the rational basis test," citing *San Antonio Ind. School Dist. v. Rodriguez,* p. 1297 infra and *Massachusetts Board of Retirement v. Murgia,* p. 1226 infra. Three months after *Fritz, Schweiker v. Wilson,* 450 U.S. 221, 101 S.Ct. 1074, 67 L.Ed.2d 186 (1981), per Blackmun, J., relied on "Congress' deliberate, considered choice" in upholding Congress' denial of SSI "comfort allowances" to needy aged, blind and disabled persons confined in public institutions unless the institutions received federal Medicaid funds. Powell, J., joined by Brennan, Marshall and Stevens, JJ., dissented: "In my view, the Court should receive with some skepticism post hoc hypotheses about legislative purpose, unsupported by the legislative history. When no indication of legislative purpose appears other than the current position of the Secretary, the Court should require that the classification bear a 'fair and substantial relation' to the asserted purpose. See *F.S. Royster Guano Co. v. Virginia,* 253 U.S. 412, 415, 40 S.Ct. 560, 561, 64 L.Ed. 989 (1920) [discussed at p. 1067 infra]."

and the fact [that] the line might have been drawn differently at some points is a matter for legislative, rather than judicial, consideration." Ibid. The distinction at issue here represents such a line: By excluding from the definition of "cable system" those facilities that serve commonly owned or managed buildings without using public rights-of-way, § 602(7)(B) delineates the bounds of the regulatory field. Such scope-of-coverage provisions are unavoidable components of most economic or social legislation. [This] necessity renders the precise coordinates of the resulting legislative judgment virtually unreviewable, since the legislature must be allowed leeway to approach a perceived problem incrementally. See, e.g., *Williamson v. Lee Optical* [p. 67 supra]: "The problem of legislative classification is a perennial one, admitting of no doctrinaire definition. Evils in the same field may be of different dimensions and proportions, requiring different remedies. Or so the legislature may think. Or the reform may take one step at a time, addressing itself to the phase of the problem which seems most acute to the legislative mind. The legislature may select one phase of one field and apply a remedy there, neglecting the others. The prohibition of the Equal Protection Clause goes no further than the invidious discrimination." [b, 7]

Applying these principles, we conclude that the common-ownership distinction is constitutional. There are at least two possible bases for the distinction; either one suffices. First, Congress borrowed § 602(7)(B) from pre-Cable Act regulations, and although the existence of a prior administrative scheme is certainly not necessary to the rationality of the statute, it is plausible that Congress also adopted the FCC's earlier rationale. Under that rationale, common ownership was thought to be indicative of those systems for which the costs of regulation would outweigh the benefits to consumers. Because the number of subscribers was a similar indicator, the Commission also exempted cable facilities that served fewer than 50 subscribers. * * *

Respondents argue that Congress did not intend common ownership to be a surrogate for small size, since Congress simultaneously rejected the FCC's 50–subscriber exemption by omitting it from the Cable Act. Whether the posited reason for the challenged distinction actually motivated Congress is "constitutionally irrelevant," and, in any event, the FCC's explanation indicates that both common ownership and number of subscribers were considered indicia of "very small" cable systems. * * *

Furthermore, small size is only one plausible ownership-related factor contributing to consumer welfare. Subscriber influence is another. Where an SMATV system serves a complex of buildings under common ownership or management, individual subscribers could conceivably have greater bargaining power vis-a-vis the cable operator (even if the number of dwelling units were large), since all the subscribers could negotiate with one voice through the common owner or manager. * * *

b. *Lee Optical* upheld a statute generally prohibiting the fitting of eyeglasses without a prescription exempted businesses that sold ready-to-wear glasses. See also *Ferguson v. Skrupa*, p. 67 supra, upholding a statute that barred all but lawyers from the business of debt adjusting.

7. See also *Dandridge v. Williams*, 397 U.S. 471, 485, 90 S.Ct. 1153, 1161, 25 L.Ed.2d 491 (1970) (classification does not violate equal protection simply because it "is not made with mathematical nicety or because in practice it results in some inequality"); *Metropolis Theater Co. v. Chicago*, 228 U.S. 61, 69–70, 33 S.Ct. 441, 443, 57 L.Ed. 730 (1913) ("The problems of government are practical ones and may justify, if they do not require, rough accommodations—illogical, it may be, and unscientific"); *Heath & Milligan Mfg. Co. v. Worst*, 207 U.S. 338, 354, 28 S.Ct. 114, 119, 52 L.Ed. 236 (1907) ("logical appropriateness of the inclusion or exclusion of objects or persons" and "exact wisdom and nice adaptation of remedies are not required").

There is a second conceivable basis for the statutory distinction. Suppose competing SMATV operators wish to sell video programming to subscribers in a group of contiguous buildings, such as a single city block, which can be interconnected by wire without crossing a public right-of-way. If all the buildings belong to one owner or are commonly managed, that owner or manager could freely negotiate a deal for all subscribers on a competitive basis. But if the buildings are separately owned and managed, the first SMATV operator who gains a foothold by signing a contract and installing a satellite dish and associated transmission equipment on one of the buildings would enjoy a powerful cost advantage in competing for the remaining subscribers: he could connect additional buildings for the cost of a few feet of cable, whereas any competitor would have to recover the cost of his own satellite headend facility. Thus, the first operator could charge rates well above his cost and still undercut the competition. This potential for effective monopoly power might theoretically justify regulating the latter class of SMATV systems and not the former. * * *

The judgment of the Court of Appeals is reversed * * *.

Justice Stevens, concurring in the judgment. * * *

The master antenna serving multiple units in an apartment building is less unsightly than a forest of individual antennas, each serving a separate apartment. It was surely sensible to allow owners to make use of such an improvement without incurring the costs of franchising and economic regulation. Even though regulation might have been justified, [a] justification for nonregulation would nevertheless remain: Whenever possible, property owners should be free to use improvements to their property as they see fit. [But this] does not apply to the situation in which the improvement—here, the satellite antenna—is being used to distribute signals to subscribers on other people's property. In that situation, the property owner, or the SMATV operator, has reached out beyond the property line and is seeking to employ the satellite antenna in the broader market for television programming. While the crossing of that line need not trigger regulatory intervention, and the absence of such a crossing may not prevent such intervention, it certainly cannot be said that government is disabled, by the Constitution, from regulating in the case of the former and abstaining in the case of the latter. [In] my judgment, it is reasonable to presume[3] that Congress was motivated by an interest in allowing property owners to exercise freedom in the use of their own property. Legislation so motivated surely does not violate the sovereign's duty to govern impartially. * * *

---

3. The Court states that a legislative classification must be upheld "if there is any reasonably conceivable state of facts that could provide a rational basis for the classification," and that "[w]here there are 'plausible reasons' for Congress' action, 'our inquiry is at an end.'" In my view, this formulation sweeps too broadly, for it is difficult to imagine a legislative classification that could not be supported by a "reasonably conceivable state of facts." Judicial review under the "conceivable set of facts" test is tantamount to no review at all.

[In *Fritz*, Stevens, J., concurring in the judgment, observed that a legislature's "actual purpose is sometimes unknown. Moreover, undue

emphasis on actual motivation may result in identically worded statutes being held valid in one State and invalid in a neighboring State."] I continue to believe that when [the] actual rationale for the legislative classification is unclear, we should inquire whether the classification is rationally related to "a legitimate purpose that we may *reasonably presume* to have motivated an impartial legislature." [For the view that if "rationality is to be a meaningful standard of review, the court must conceive of its task as identifying the legislature's *probable* goals based on the available evidence," see Scott H. Bice, *Rationality Analysis in Constitutional Law*, 65 Minn.L.Rev. 1, 30 (1980).]

RAILWAY EXPRESS AGENCY v. NEW YORK

336 U.S. 106, 69 S.Ct. 463, 93 L.Ed. 533 (1949).

JUSTICE DOUGLAS delivered the opinion of the Court.

[T]he Traffic Regulations of the City of New York [provide]: "No person shall operate [on] any street an advertising vehicle; [except for] business notices upon business delivery vehicles, so long as such vehicles are engaged in the usual business [of] the owner and not used merely or mainly for advertising."

Appellant [operates] about 1,900 trucks in New York City and sells the space on the exterior sides of these trucks for advertising [for] the most part unconnected with its own business. It was convicted * * *.

The court [below] concluded that advertising on [vehicles] constitutes a distraction to vehicle drivers and to pedestrians alike and therefore affects the safety of the public in the use of the streets. We do not sit to weigh evidence on the due process issue in order to determine whether the regulation is sound or appropriate; nor is it our function to pass judgment on its wisdom. See *Olsen v. Nebraska* [p. 65 supra]. We would be trespassing on one of the most intensely local and specialized of all municipal problems if we held that this regulation had no relation to the traffic problem of New York City. It is the judgment of the local authorities that it does have such a relation. And nothing has been advanced which shows that to be palpably false.

The question of equal protection of the laws is pressed more strenuously on us. [It] is said, for example, that one of appellant's trucks carrying the advertisement of a commercial house would not cause any greater distraction of pedestrians and vehicle drivers than if the commercial house carried the same advertisement on its own truck. Yet the regulation allows the latter to do what the former is forbidden from doing. It is therefore contended that the classification which the regulation makes has no relation to the traffic problem since a violation turns not on what kind of advertisements are carried on trucks but on whose trucks they are carried.

That, however, is a superficial way of analyzing the [problem]. The local authorities may well have concluded that those who advertised their own wares on their trucks do not present the same traffic problem in view of the nature or extent of the advertising which they use. * * *

We cannot say that that judgment is not an allowable one. Yet if it is, the classification has relation to the purpose for which it is made and does not contain the kind of discrimination against which the Equal Protection Clause affords protection. It is by such practical considerations based on experience rather than by theoretical inconsistencies that the question of equal protection is to be answered. And the fact that New York City sees fit to eliminate from traffic this kind of distraction but does not touch what may be even greater ones in a different category, such as the vivid displays on Times Square, is immaterial. It is no requirement of equal protection that all evils of the same genus be eradicated or none at all. * * *

Affirmed.

JUSTICE RUTLEDGE acquiesces in the Court's opinion and judgment, dubitante on the question of equal protection of the laws.

JUSTICE JACKSON, concurring. * * *

The burden should rest heavily upon one who would persuade us to use the due process clause to strike down a substantive [law]. Even its provident use against municipal regulations frequently disables all government—state, munici-

pal and federal—from dealing with the conduct in question because the requirement of due process is also applicable to State and Federal Governments. * * *

Invocation of the equal protection clause, on the other hand, does not disable
any governmental body from dealing with the subject at hand. It merely means
that the prohibition or regulation must have a broader impact. I regard it as a
salutary doctrine that cities, states and the Federal Government must exercise
their powers so as not to discriminate between their inhabitants except upon some
reasonable differentiation fairly related to the object of regulation. [T]here is no
more effective practical guaranty against arbitrary and unreasonable government
than to require that the principles of law which officials would impose upon a
minority must be imposed generally. Conversely, nothing opens the door to
arbitrary action so effectively as to allow those officials to pick and choose only a
few to whom they will apply legislation and thus to escape the political retribution
that might be visited upon them if larger numbers were affected. Courts can take
no better measure to assure that laws will be just than to require that laws be
equal in operation. * * *

In this case, if the City of New York should assume that display of any
advertising on vehicles tends and intends to distract the attention of persons using
the highways and to increase the dangers of its traffic, I should think it fully
within its constitutional powers to forbid it all. [Instead], however, the City seeks
to reduce the hazard only by saying that while some may, others may not exhibit
such appeals. The same display, for example, advertising cigarettes, which this
appellant is forbidden to carry on its trucks, may be carried on the trucks of a
cigarette dealer. [The] courts of New York have declared that the sole nature and
purpose of the regulation before us is to reduce traffic hazards. There is not even
a pretense here that the traffic hazard created by the advertising which is
forbidden is in any manner or degree more hazardous than that which is
permitted. * * *

* * * I do not think differences of treatment under law should be approved
on classification because of differences unrelated to the legislative purpose. The
equal protection clause ceases to assure either equality or protection if it is
avoided by any conceivable difference that can be pointed out between those
bound and those left free. This Court has often announced the principle that the
differentiation must have an appropriate relation to the object of the [legislation].

The question in my mind comes to this. Where individuals contribute to an
evil or danger in the same way and to the same degree, may those who do so for
hire be prohibited, while those who do so for their own commercial ends but not
for hire be allowed to continue? I think the answer has to be that the hireling
may be put in a class by himself and may be dealt with differently than those who
act on their own. But this is not merely because such a discrimination will enable
the lawmaker to diminish the evil. That might be done by many classifications,
which I should think wholly unsustainable. It is rather because there is a real
difference between doing in self-interest and doing for hire, so that it is one thing
to tolerate action from those who act on their own and it is another thing to
permit the same action to be promoted for a price. [I]n view of the control I
would concede to cities to protect citizens in quiet and orderly use for their proper
purposes of the highways and public places, I think the judgment below must be
affirmed.

Notes and Questions

1. *Legislative purpose.* (a) Of what relevance in *Railway Express* was it that
the state courts "declared that the sole purpose" of the law "is to reduce traffic

hazards"? Would it be more accurate (and realistic) to describe the purpose as being "to promote public safety slightly by reducing the number of distractions on the sides of moving vehicles to the extent this is feasible without jeopardizing the economic well-being of those merchants who advertise on their own trucks," Note, *Legislative Purpose, Rationality and Equal Protection*, 82 Yale L.J. 123, 144 (1972)—a purpose to which the classification unquestionably was "rationally related"? Is it not true that many government programs "involve goals that reflect an accommodation of various purposes which are determined by subtle or blatant policy trade-offs"? Id. That often "the legislature is simply a 'market-like arena' in which individuals and special interest groups trade with each other through representatives to further their own private ends"? Scott H. Bice, *Rationality Analysis in Constitutional Law*, 65 Minn.L.Rev. 1, 19 (1980).[a]

Are such legislative purposes (or goals) "rational"? "Legitimate"? "Constitutionally permissible"? Consider Cass R. Sunstein, *Interest Groups in American Public Law*, 38 Stan.L.Rev. 29, 49–50 (1985): "Under this conception of the political process, review of statutes for 'rationality' is incoherent. It demands of statutory enactments something inconsistent with their very nature as the product of self-interested efforts by competing groups seeking scarce social resources. The rationality requirement may, however, be understood precisely as a requirement that regulatory measures be something other than a response to political pressure. [In] many cases, modern and not-so-modern, the Court has indicated that [pluralist] compromise is impermissible if it is the sole reason for the legislative enactment at issue." See also Joseph Tussman & Jacobus tenBroek, *The Equal Protection of the Laws*, 37 Calif.L.Rev. 341, 350 (1949): "[T]he requirement that laws be equal rests upon a theory of legislation quite distinct from that of pressure groups—a theory which puts forward some conception of a 'general good' as the 'legitimate public purpose' at which legislation must aim, and according to which the triumph of private or group pressure marks the corruption of the legislative process." Compare Richard Posner, *The DeFunis Case and the Constitutionality of Preferential Treatment of Racial Minorities*, 1974 Sup.Ct.Rev. 1, 27: "[A] vast part of the output of the governmental process would be seen to consist of discrimination, in the sense of an effort to redistribute wealth (in one form or another) from one group in the community to another, founded on the superior ability of one group to manipulate the political process rather than on any principle of justice or efficiency. Yet it would be odd, indeed, to condemn as unconstitutional the most characteristic product of a democratic (perhaps of any) political system." See also Robert F. Nagel, *Constitutional Cultures* 119 (1989): "Legislative 'irrationality' [provides] real advantages to a democratic system [in that] legislators can serve many interests at once. They are free to respond to the intensity of constituents' beliefs, so that groups whose values are difficult to formalize or explain, but nevertheless are strongly held, can be accommodated. Even if no one objective is fully achieved, many groups can be partially satisfied and can therefore be expected to retain some sense of loyalty to the governmental process. Because negotiation and trading 'across substantive fields' are encouraged, the hard sacrifices that different allocations of resources require are implic-

---

a. Consider Michael Klarman, *An Interpretive History of Modern Equal Protection*, 90 Mich.L.Rev. 213, 250 (1991): "[The] facially bizarre classification [in *Railway Express*] probably was attributable primarily to the powerful lobbying arm of the city's newspapers. Several Justices were troubled by a classification difficult to justify in terms other than raw interest group power. While *Railway Express* came down unanimous as to result, the Court initially was divided five to four, with Justice Reed arguing (correctly) in his draft dissent that to sustain a law based on such a 'whimsical' distinction was essentially to render the Equal Protection Clause 'useless in state regulation of business practices.' "

itly recognized. In the bartering process, people with widely divergent interests are compelled to deal with each other and to recognize the probable costs that their own preferences will inflict on others; thus new understandings and new values emerge as citizens experience firsthand the processes of self-government. Because compromise is necessary and abstract argument is of limited value, groups are encouraged to find the common ground in their positions, rather than to insist on apparently irreconcilable differences of principle."

(b) The legislative history of state and local legislation is often unrecorded and not readily available. Should the Court assess the "actual purposes" of legislation rather than hypothesizing any "conceivable basis which might support it"? Consider Nagel, supra, at 116: "There are many sound reasons for embarking on an activity before finally formulating an objective. Because the potential consequences of an important program are often unlimited, decision makers lack the resources to gather or evaluate all the relevant information. Accordingly, it may be desirable to begin a tentative program and to reformulate incrementally both the objectives and the means chosen for their achievement in light of actual experience. The reformulated objectives can differ dramatically from the original, tentative objective. Thus, constitutionalism that requires a decision maker to identify consequences (and relate them to an articulated value) before acting can result in the abandonment of potentially useful activity." Contrast Gerald Gunther, *In Search of Evolving Doctrine on a Changing Court: A Model for a Newer Equal Protection,* 86 Harv.L.Rev. 1, 44–46 (1972): "If the Court were to require an articulation of purpose from an authoritative state source"—"a state court's or attorney general's office description of purpose should be acceptable"—"rather than hypothesizing one on its own, there would at least be indirect pressure on the legislature to state its own reasons for selecting particular means and classifications [and thus] improve the quality of the political process [by] encouraging a fuller airing in the political arena of the grounds for legislative action." Is improving the political process a proper function of the judiciary? Compare Laurence H. Tribe, *Toward a Model of Roles in the Due Process of Life and Law,* 87 Harv.L.Rev. 1, 6 n. 28 (1973): "A mismatch between means and ends, when the only ends examined are those argued in a law's defense by an executive officer, may indicate no more than that the officer did not advance the right ends in the law's defense. That his oversight or deliberate choice should be allowed thereby to frustrate the past efforts of his jurisdiction's legislature seems strange." See also Kent Greenawalt, *The Unresolved Problems of Reverse Discrimination,* 67 Calif.L.Rev. 87, 107 (1979): "If it is enough that a lawyer defending the classification state a purpose, then, since lawyers can be almost as imaginative as judges and are likely to suggest many purposes in complex and controversial cases, the requirement of articulated purpose is unlikely often to be crucial." See generally John H. Ely, *Democracy and Distrust* 125–31 (1980).

(c) In *Fritz,* Congress sought to bolster the financial basis of the railroad retirement system by reducing benefits for some (but not all) former railroad workers who also qualified for social security benefits. BRENNAN, J., dissenting, contended that Congress did not intend the result produced by the statute because "Congress may have been misled": this was an instance where "complex legislation was drafted by outside parties [railroad management and labor representatives] and Congress relied on them to explain it, where the misstatements are frequent and unrebutted, and where no Member of Congress can be found to have stated the effect of the classification correctly."[b] The Court, per REHNQUIST, J.,

---

b. "At issue was a statute that had been drafted by private parties, who sought to pro-tect their own interests, or those of their allies, and of no one else. As a result, a group not

replied: "If this test were applied literally to every member of any legislature that ever voted on a law, there would be very few laws which would survive it. The language of the statute is clear, and we have historically assumed that Congress intended what it enacted." BRENNAN, J. responded that "by presuming purpose from result, the Court reduces analysis to tautology. It may always be said that Congress intended to do what it in fact did. If that were the extent of our analysis, we would find every statute, no matter how arbitrary or irrational, perfectly tailored to achieve its purpose."

2. *"One step at a time."* (a) Does the Court's permitting legislatures to "implement their program step by step" immunize "pressure group" lawmaking from equal protection attack? Should it? Consider Note, *Equal Protection,* 82 Harv.L.Rev. 1065, 1085 (1969): "To require that the state remedy all aspects of a particular mischief or none at all might preclude a state from undertaking any program of correction until its resources were adequate to deal with the entire problem. Second, in some instances, the state may not be convinced that a particular policy is a wise one, or it may prove impossible to marshal a legislative majority in favor of extending the policy's coverage any further. Thus, to demand application of the policy to all whom it might logically encompass, would severely restrict the state's opportunities to experiment." [a]

(b) Does the Court's "step by step" approach, combined with its "minimum rationality" requirement for legislative classifications as reflected in *Beach Communications* and *Railway Express* mean that a "classification that neither proceeds along suspect lines nor infringes fundamental constitutional rights" will never be held to violate equal protection? May a law that was rationally related to the purpose that caused its enactment subsequently become irrational because of a change of factual circumstances? If so, suppose a present purpose (not even conceivable by the enacting legislature) now rationally supports the law? See generally Hans A. Linde, *Due Process of Lawmaking,* 55 Neb.L.Rev. 197, 215–22 (1976); Bice, note 1 supra, at 33–45.

3. *Underinclusion.* (a) Does the "step by step" approach, which permits "underinclusive" legislation [b]—allowing "officials to pick and choose only a few to whom they will apply legislation and thus to escape the political retribution that might be visited upon them if larger numbers were affected"—promote "arbitrary and unreasonable government"? Is it inconsistent with the *Carolene Products* concern, Ch. 1, Sec. 1, for "prejudice against discrete and insular minorities"? When "politically disadvantaged minorities are affected," should "the legislative judgment [be] more critically regarded, for such disadvantaged groups wield less influence in legislative councils than their proportion in the population would seem to warrant" and thus "it might be argued that the legislative decisions do not represent a proper majoritarian choice"? Note, 82 Harv.L.Rev. at 1125.

Consider Jesse H. Choper, *Judicial Review and the National Political Process* 75–77 (1980): "Majoritarians should have scant difficulty [with] the Court's

represented in the private negotiations was significantly harmed. Most important, Congress was unaware of that harm and indeed had sought to prevent it." Sunstein, supra, at 71.

a. If the legislature's "step by step" justification is based on (i) "presently inadequate resources" or (ii) a "desire to experiment," should the Court uphold the classification

"only for the specific period that corresponds to the nature of the legislature's timebound objective"? Note, *Reforming the One Step at a Time Justification in Equal Protection Cases,* 90 Yale L.J. 1777, 1784 (1981).

b. For the classic discussion of various types of legislative classifications, see Tussman & tenBroek, note 1 supra.

assistance of persons who are not represented in the political process *at all*—best illustrated by aliens [or] minority racial groups who were illegally disenfranchised in certain parts of the nation. But the matter becomes painfully more complicated [when] the judicially favored minority is one that, although fully enfranchised in accordance with its numbers, is nonetheless characterized as being 'politically impotent,' 'not adequately represented,' 'discrete and insular,' or the like. The initial complexity arises because almost all, if not all, groups and interests in the American political process are 'minorities.' Thus, each time any group loses any political battle in which it has an interest—and some group always does—it may lay claim to the label of 'political weakness' or 'submerged and beaten minority.' [It] is true that some minorities, because of their sophistication and combined arithmetical and financial strength, are more influential than others on most political issues; and that some groups with modest numbers may win powerful surrogates who give them forceful representation. Similarly, there are some minorities who are less effective than others on most legislative matters because of their geographic isolation, the general inexcitability or unpopularity of their ideas, their relative inarticulateness, their lack of numbers and resources, or because they are viewed with such resentment, distaste, or hatred that they can neither join working coalitions nor prevent hostile action. But there are many disparate groups who may legitimately claim to meet some or all of these varied criteria for judicial solicitude. Thus, the Court may have to be as sympathetic to the pleas of apartment dwellers in Iowa, tobacco farmers in Massachusetts, debt adjustors in Kansas, oil well producers in New York, and cedar tree owners in Virginia as it is to the complaints of Jehovah's Witnesses in Rhode Island, communists in New Hampshire, progressives in Ohio, Asian-Americans in California, and blacks in Mississippi—all these illustrations assuming a given temporal span, presumably also to be determined by the Court." See also Rehnquist, J., dissenting in *Sugarman v. Dougall* and *In re Griffiths*, Sec. 3, I infra, which held state discriminations against aliens subject to "strict scrutiny": "Our society, consisting of over 200 million individuals of multitudinous origins, customs, tongues, beliefs, and cultures is, to say the least, diverse. It would hardly take extraordinary ingenuity for a lawyer to find 'insular and discrete' minorities at every turn of the road. Yet, unless the Court can precisely define and constitutionally justify both the terms and analysis it uses, [the] Court can choose a 'minority' it 'feels' deserves 'solicitude' and thereafter prohibit the States from classifying that 'minority' differently from the 'majority.' I cannot find [any] constitutional authority for such a 'ward of the Court' approach to equal protection." See also Sandalow, *The Distrust of Politics,* 56 N.Y.U.L.Rev. 446, 466–67 (1981): "Corporations also do not vote, but those who argue that aliens should be accorded [special protection] do not frequently complain that corporations should also receive that protection because they lack political influence. Any attempt to appraise the inner workings of the political process must, as the illustration of the corporation suggests, examine the entire process to ascertain the extent of a group's influence. [But] what measure have we, other than an evaluation of outcomes [—i.e., the desirability of the substantive policies enacted by the legislature]?"

(b) Were the groups disadvantaged by the laws in the cases discussed to this point—*Beach Communications, Railway Express, Lee Optical, Ferguson*—"politically disadvantaged minorities"? What role, if any, should this factor play? In NEW YORK CITY TRANSIT AUTH. v. BEAZER, 440 U.S. 568, 99 S.Ct. 1355, 59 L.Ed.2d 587 (1979), which used the "rationality" test to uphold the exclusion of methadone users from any Transit Authority (TA) employment, White, J., joined by Marshall, J., dissented: [c] "[TA] stipulated that '[o]ne of the reasons for [the] drug policy is [that TA feels] an adverse public reaction would result if it were generally known that [TA] employed persons with a prior history of drug abuse, including persons participating in methadone maintenance programs.' It is hard for me to reconcile that stipulation of animus against former addicts with our past holdings that 'a bare [desire] to harm a politically unpopular group cannot constitute a *legitimate* governmental interest.' *Moreno* [infra]." [d]

UNITED STATES DEPT. OF AGRICULTURE v. MORENO, 413 U.S. 528, 93 S.Ct. 2821, 37 L.Ed.2d 782 (1973), per BRENNAN, J., applying " 'traditional' equal protection analysis," held that a provision of the Food Stamp Act—excluding "any household containing an individual who is unrelated to any other member of the household"—was "wholly without any rational basis": It "is clearly irrelevant to the stated purposes of the Act [which are to] raise levels of nutrition among low-income households. [Thus], the challenged classification must rationally further some legitimate governmental interest other than those specifically stated in the congressional 'declaration of policy.'

"[The] little legislative history [that] does exist" indicates that the provision "was intended to [prevent] 'hippie communes' from participating in the food stamp program. [But equal protection] at the very least mean[s] that a bare congressional desire to harm a politically unpopular group cannot constitute a *legitimate* governmental interest." Nor does the classification "operate so as rationally to further the prevention of fraud" because, under the Act, "two *unrelated* persons living together" may "avoid the 'unrelated person' exclusion simply by altering their living arrangements so as [to] create two separate 'households,' both of which are eligible for assistance. [Thus], in practical operation, the [provision] excludes from participation [not] those persons who are 'likely to abuse the program' but, rather, only those persons who are so desperately in need of aid that they cannot even afford to alter their living arrangements so as to retain their eligibility."

DOUGLAS, J., concurred: "I could not say that [this] provision has no 'rational' relation to control of fraud. We deal here, however, with the right of association, protected by the First Amendment." Thus, the classification "can be sustained only on a showing of a 'compelling' governmental interest."

REHNQUIST, J., joined by Burger, C.J., dissented: "Congress attacked the problem with a rather blunt instrument, [b]ut I do not think it is unreasonable for Congress to conclude that the basic unit which it was willing to support [with] food stamps is some variation on the family as we know it—a household consisting of related individuals. This unit provides a guarantee which is not provided by households containing unrelated individuals that the household exists for some purpose other than to collect federal food stamps.

c. White, J., joined by Brennan, J., also dissented on statutory grounds.

d. White, J., added: "Some weight should also be given to the history of the rule. Petitioners admit that it was not the result of a reasoned policy decision and stipulated that they had never studied the ability of those on methadone maintenance to perform petitioners' jobs. Petitioners are not directly accountable to the public, are not the type of official body that normally makes legislative judg-

ments of fact such as those relied upon by the majority today, and are by nature more concerned with business efficiency than with other public policies for which they have no direct responsibility. Both the State and City of New York, which do exhibit those democratic characteristics, hire persons in methadone programs for similar jobs. These factors together strongly point to a conclusion of invidious discrimination."

"Admittedly, [the] limitation will make ineligible many households which have not been formed for the purpose of collecting federal food stamps, and will [not] wholly deny food stamps to those households which may have been formed in large part to take advantage of the program. But, as the Court concedes, 'traditional' equal protection analysis does not require that every classification be drawn with precise mathematical nicety." [e]

For cases in addition to *Moreno,* finding an equal protection violation under the "rationality" test because of an illegitimate (or impermissible) state purpose, see *Zobel v. Williams,* p. 1285 infra; *Metropolitan Life Ins. Co. v. Ward,* 470 U.S. 869, 105 S.Ct. 1676, 84 L.Ed.2d 751 (1985) (state tax that discriminated against out-of-state insurance companies for the purpose of "promoting local industry" "constitutes the very sort of parochial discrimination that the Equal Protection Clause was intended to prevent").

4. *Overinclusion.* Many laws, based on a plausible (often persuasive) judgment that many or most persons within the classification pose the problem sought to be remedied, subject the entire class to the regulation even though not every person within the class may pose the problem. For example, in *Ferguson,* the law was not only underinclusive in permitting only lawyers to be debt adjusters, but was also overinclusive in that there were surely *some* nonlawyers who would not engage in abusive debt adjusting. A common justification for overinclusive laws is avoidance of the administrative cost and chance of error in making individualized determinations for each person within the class.

Should the Court be more deferential to overinclusiveness because it "poses less danger than underinclusiveness, at least from the viewpoint of political accountability, for overinclusiveness does not ordinarily exempt potentially powerful opponents from a law's reach"? Tribe, *American Constitutional Law* 1049 (2d ed. 1988). Or is overinclusion "less tolerable than underinclusion, for while the latter fails to impose the burden on some who should logically bear it, the former actually does impose the burden on some who do not belong in the class"? Note, 82 Harv.L.Rev. at 1086.[f]

5. *"Means/end fit."* To what extent should the Court employ a "strengthened 'rational' scrutiny" by requiring "that legislative means must substantially further legislative ends"? Gunther, note 1 after *Dukes,* supra: "Examination of means in light of asserted state purposes would directly promote public consideration of the benefits assertedly sought by the proposed legislation; indirectly, it

---

e. Compare *Lyng v. Castillo,* 477 U.S. 635, 106 S.Ct. 2727, 91 L.Ed.2d 527 (1986), per Stevens, J., holding that a Food Stamp Act provision—which treated "parents, children, and siblings who live together" *less* favorably than "distant relatives, or groups of unrelated persons who live together"—had a "rational basis": "Congress could reasonably determine that close relatives sharing a home—almost by definition—tend to purchase and prepare meals together while distant relatives and unrelated individuals might not be so inclined. [And] Congress might have reasoned that it would be somewhat easier for close relatives—again, almost by definition—to accommodate their living habits to a federal policy favoring common meal preparation than it would be for more distant relatives or unrelated persons to

do so." Brennan, Marshall and White, JJ., dissented.

f. For the view that the Court should use a "legitimacy principle" in determining equal protection claims—which "requires simply that in enacting classifications legislators must: (1) avoid palpably inaccurate factual judgments; (2) not act discriminatorily, classifying persons, for example, in ways that offend the individualist ethic; and (3) be sensitive to the need for some proportion between the advantages of avoiding individualized determinations and the costs of abridging certain important interests"—see Michael J. Perry, *Constitutional "Fairness": Notes on Equal Protection and Due Process,* 63 Va.L.Rev. 383 (1977).

would stimulate fuller political examination, in relation to those benefits, of the costs that would be incurred if the proposed means were adopted."

Compare REHNQUIST, J., dissenting in *Trimble v. Gordon*, Sec. 3, III infra, which held that an Illinois statute, forbidding illegitimate children to inherit from their fathers by intestate succession, violated equal protection: "[Judicial review of means/end fit] requires a conscious second-guessing of legislative judgment in an area where this Court has no special expertise whatever. [In] most cases, [the] 'fit' will involve a greater or lesser degree of imperfection. Then the Court asks itself how much 'imperfection' between means and ends is permissible? In making this judgment it must throw into the judicial hopper the whole range of factors which were first thrown into the legislative hopper. What alternatives were reasonably available? What reasons are there for the legislature to accomplish this 'purpose' in the way it did? What obstacles stood in the way of other solutions?

"[Without] any antecedent constitutional mandate, we have created on the premises of the Equal Protection Clause a school for legislators, whereby opinions of this Court are written to instruct them in a better understanding of how to accomplish their ordinary legislative tasks. [Since] Illinois' distinction is not mindless and patently irrational, I would [affirm]."[g]

The post 1930s cases considered to this point almost all invoke the extremely deferential "minimum rationality" standard of review. This approach has been used regularly in recent years in rejecting equal protection challenges to economic and social welfare legislation.[a] Several such decisions, in which the challengers unsuccessfully sought to have the classifications characterized as being "suspect" or involving "fundamental rights" (and thus subject to "strict scrutiny"), are considered in Sec. 4 infra. In some situations, however, although employing the traditional "rational basis" standard, the Court has held laws violative of equal protection.[b]

Furthermore, the Court has periodically articulated the "traditional" standard in a way that suggests a more active judicial examination of the challenged classification. For example, JOHNSON v. ROBISON, p. 1018 supra, per BRENNAN, J., upheld a federal statute granting educational benefits to military veterans but not to conscientious objectors who performed alternate civilian service under the "rational basis" standard, but stated the formulation of the *Royster Guano* case (also invoked by Powell, J., fn. a, p. 1056 supra) that the classification "must be reasonable, not arbitrary, and must rest upon some ground of difference having a fair and substantial relation to the object of the legislation, so that all persons similarly circumstanced shall be treated alike," and then devoted several pages to

---

g. For the view that the "rationality" requirement does—and should—function as a balance of costs, benefits, and alternatives as well as the legitimacy of legislative purpose and the closeness of fit between means and ends, see Robert W. Bennett, *"Mere" Rationality in Constitutional Law: Judicial Review and Democratic Theory*, 67 Calif.L.Rev. 1049 (1979). But see Edward L. Barrett, *The Rational Basis Standard for Equal Protection Re-*

view of Ordinary Legislative Classifications, 68 Ky.L.J. 845 (1980).

a. For descriptions and citations, see John E. Nowak and Ronald D. Rotunda *Constitutional Law* 607–608 (5th ed. 1995).

b. See, e.g., *Eisenstadt v. Baird* (1972), p. 404 supra; *Baxstrom v. Herold*, 383 U.S. 107, 86 S.Ct. 760, 15 L.Ed.2d 620 (1966) (extensive procedural rights prior to civil commitment

considering the justification.[c]

---

1. *Recent holdings of "irrationality."* (a) In LOGAN v. ZIMMERMAN BRUSH CO. (1982), p. 505 supra, for the first time in 25 years, a majority of the justices, without questioning the legitimacy of the state's purpose, employed "the lowest level of permissible equal protection scrutiny" and found a violation of equal protection. Appellant filed an employment discrimination complaint before an Illinois Commission which inadvertently scheduled the hearing at a date after the statutory time period expired. The state court held that this deprived the Commission of jurisdiction and terminated appellant's claim. BLACKMUN, J., joined by Brennan, Marshall and O'Connor, JJ., found this discrimination against those who did not get a hearing to be "patently irrational in light of [the law's] stated purpose": "I cannot agree that terminating a claim that the State itself has misscheduled is a rational way of expediting the resolution of disputes. [The] state's rationale must be something more than the exercise of a strained imagination; while the connection between means and ends need not be precise, it, at the least, must have some objective basis. That is not so here." POWELL, J., joined by Rehnquist, J., concurred as to "this unusual classification": "As appellants possessed no power to convene hearings, it is unfair and irrational to punish them for the Commission's failure to do so." [a]

(b) ALLEGHENY PITTSBURGH COAL CO. v. COUNTY COM'N, 488 U.S. 336, 109 S.Ct. 633, 102 L.Ed.2d 688 (1989), per REHNQUIST, C.J., unanimously found an equal protection violation when a West Virginia county tax assessor "valued petitioners' real property on the basis of its recent purchase price, but made only minor modifications in the assessments of land which had not been recently sold," resulting in the fact that "petitioners' property has been assessed at roughly 8 to 35 times more than comparable neighboring property, and these discrepancies have continued for more than 10 years with little change." The Court held that the county assessor's practice was not "rationally related" to West Virginia's rule "that all property of the kind held by petitioners shall be taxed at a rate uniform throughout the state according to its estimated market value." [b]

---

except for persons who are ending a prison term).

c. See also *Reed v. Reed* (1971), Sec. 3, II infra, per Burger, C.J., using this formulation in holding a law that discriminated against women violative of equal protection.

a. See also *G.D. Searle & Co. v. Cohn,* 455 U.S. 404, 102 S.Ct. 1137, 71 L.Ed.2d 250 (1982), for a dissent by Stevens, J., finding no "rational basis" for a statutory classification; *Lyng v. Intern. Union,* 485 U.S. 360, 108 S.Ct. 1184, 99 L.Ed.2d 380 (1988), for a dissent by Marshall, J., joined by Brennan and Blackmun, JJ., finding that Congress' denial of food stamps to persons who meet the low income test because they are on strike "cannot survive even rational basis scrutiny"; *Bankers Life & Casualty Co. v. Crenshaw,* 486 U.S. 71, 108 S.Ct. 1645, 100 L.Ed.2d 62 (1988), for a dissent by Blackmun, J., finding that a statutory classification was not "reasonably related" to the asserted state interests and was thus "arbitrary and irrational"; *Heller v. Doe,* p. 1224 infra, for a dissent by Souter, J., joined by Blackmun, Stevens and O'Connor, JJ., finding that a state's provision of different procedures for civil commitment of the mentally retarded and mentally ill "is not supported by any rational justification."

See also *Bowen v. Owens,* 476 U.S. 340, 106 S.Ct. 1881, 90 L.Ed.2d 316 (1986), for a dissent by Blackmun, J., finding no "rational basis" for a Social Security Act classification. Marshall and Brennan, JJ., also dissented on the ground that Congress had no "actual purpose" "for drawing this line other than its desire to find a point of compromise between the two Houses."

b. For the view that *Allegheny* "revived a doctrine that had lain dormant for fifty years," see Robert J. Glennon, *Taxation and Equal Protection,* 58 Geo.Wash.L.Rev. 261, 290

Compare NORDLINGER v. HAHN, 505 U.S. 1, 112 S.Ct. 2326, 120 L.Ed.2d 1 (1992), per BLACKMUN, J., which held that California's "acquisition value" system for initially assessing property (Proposition 13) "rationally furthers the State's ["legitimate"] interests in neighborhood stability and the protection of property owners' reliance interests." As in *Allegheny,* Proposition 13 "resulted in dramatic disparities in taxation of properties of comparable value." But "the Equal Protection Clause is satisfied so long as there is a plausible policy reason for the classification, *Fritz,* [and] *Allegheny* was the rare case where the facts precluded any plausible inference that the reason for the unequal assessment practice was to achieve the benefits of an acquisition-value tax scheme. By contrast, Proposition 13 was enacted precisely to achieve the benefits."

THOMAS, J., concurred in upholding Proposition 13 but would have "confronted [*Allegheny*] directly": "Even if the assessor did violate West Virginia law, she would not have violated the Equal Protection Clause. A violation of state law does not by itself constitute a violation of the Federal Constitution." [c]

2. *Legislative role.* Is the "traditional"—"rational basis"—"minimum rationality" approach premised "on the propriety of unelected federal judges' displacing the judgments of elected state officials, or upon the competence of federal courts to prescribe workable standards of state conduct and devise measures to enforce them"? See Lawrence G. Sager, *Fair Measure: The Legal Status of Underenforced Constitutional Norms,* 91 Harv.L.Rev. 1212, 1217 (1978). If either, of what relevance is the "traditional" approach to state and local legislators? State judges? Congress? Consider id. at 1218–21: "Institutional rather than analytical reasons appear to have prompted the broad exclusion of state tax and regulatory measures from the reach of the equal protection construct fashioned by the federal judiciary. This is what creates the disparity between this construct and a true conception of equal protection, and thus substantiates the claim that equal protection is an underenforced constitutional norm. [C]onstitutional norms which are underenforced by the federal judiciary should be understood to be legally valid to their full conceptual limits, and federal judicial decisions which stop short of these limits should be understood as delineating only the boundaries of the federal courts' role in enforcing the norm: By 'legally valid,' I mean that the unenforced margins of underenforced norms should have the full status of positive law which we generally accord to the norms of our Constitution, save only that the federal judiciary will not enforce these margins. Thus, the legal powers or legal obligations of government officials which are subtended in the unenforced margins of underenforced constitutional norms are to be understood to remain in full force." For further consideration, see *Katzenbach v. Morgan,* p. 1479 infra, and notes thereafter.[c]

(1990): "The systematic and intentional undervaluation test [is] at war both with rational basis review and with the broad latitude given states in creating tax schemes. [In] every instance that [the] Court [has] found that a tax scheme violated rational basis equal protection, [the] opinion was either poorly reasoned or over the dissents of Justices of great stature." Accord, William Cohen, *State Law in Equality Clothing,* 38 U.C.L.A.L.Rev. 87 (1990).

c. Stevens, J., dissented: "[T]he selective provision of benefits based on the timing of one's membership in a class (whether that class be the class of residents or the class of property owners) is rarely a 'legitimate state

interest.' Similarly situated neighbors have an equal right to share in the benefits of local government. It would obviously be unconstitutional to provide one with more or better fire or police protection than the other; it is just as plainly unconstitutional to require one to pay five times as much in property taxes as the other for the same government services. In my opinion, the severe inequalities created by Proposition 13 are arbitrary and unreasonable and do not rationally further a legitimate state interest."

c. For the view that the Court should defer to a *state court's* "factual conclusions" that a state law's classification "was not rationally

SECTION 2. RACE AND ETHNIC ANCESTRY

I. DISCRIMINATION AGAINST RACIAL AND ETHNIC MINORITIES

The "evil to be remedied" by the equal protection clause, declared the *Slaughter-House Cases,* was "the existence of laws in the States where the newly emancipated negroes resided, which discriminated with gross injustice and hardship against them as a class." STRAUDER v. WEST VIRGINIA, 100 U.S. (10 Otto) 303, 25 L.Ed. 664 (1900)—the first post-Civil War racial discrimination case to reach the Court—per STRONG, J., invalidating the state murder conviction of an African–American on the ground that state law forbade blacks from serving on grand or petit juries,[a] observed that "the true spirit and meaning" of the Civil War amendments was "securing to a race recently emancipated [the] enjoyment of all the civil rights that under the law are enjoyed by [whites]. What is [equal protection but] that all persons, whether colored or white, shall stand equal before the laws of the States, and, in regard to the colored race, for whose protection the amendment was primarily designed, that no discrimination shall be made against them by law because of their color? The words of the amendment [contain] a positive immunity or right, most valuable to the colored race,—the right to exemption from unfriendly legislation against them distinctively as colored,—exemption from legal discriminations, implying inferiority in civil society, lessening the security of their enjoyment of the rights which others enjoy, and discriminations which are steps towards reducing them to the condition of a subject race.

"That the West Virginia statute respecting juries [is] such a discrimination ought not to be doubted. [And if] in those States where the colored people constitute a majority of the entire population a law should be enacted excluding all white men from jury service, [we] apprehend no one would be heard to claim that it would not be a denial to white men of the equal protection of the laws.[b] Nor if a law should be passed excluding all naturalized Celtic Irishmen, would there be any doubt of its inconsistency with the spirit of the amendment. * * *

"We do not say that within the limits from which it is not excluded by the amendment a State may not prescribe the qualifications of its jurors, and in so doing make discriminations. It may confine the selection to males, to freeholders, to citizens, to persons within certain ages, or to persons having educational qualifications. We do not believe the Fourteenth Amendment was ever intended to prohibit this. Looking at its history, it is clear it had no such purpose. Its aim was against discrimination because of race or color."

Thus, as stated in *Brown v. Board of Education,* Part II infra, "in the first cases in this Court construing the Fourteenth Amendment, decided shortly after

---

related to a legitimate state purpose," see Stevens, J., dissenting in *Minnesota v. Clover Leaf Creamery Co.*

a. The Court emphasized that the question was *not* whether a black defendant "has a right to a grand or a petit jury composed in whole or in part of persons of his own race or color, but [whether] all persons of his race or color may be excluded by law solely because of their race or color."

The Court has adhered to *Strauder's* requirement of systematic exclusion. See note 1 following *Yick Wo v. Hopkins,* Sec. III infra. But it has permitted criminal defendants who

are not themselves members of the excluded group to challenge the jury's composition on the ground that it violates the defendant's sixth amendment right to a jury "selected from a fair cross section of the community." See, e.g., *Peters v. Kiff,* 407 U.S. 493, 92 S.Ct. 2163, 33 L.Ed.2d 83 (1972) (white challenging exclusion of blacks); *Duren v. Missouri,* 439 U.S. 357, 99 S.Ct. 664, 58 L.Ed.2d 579 (1979) (man challenging exclusion of women).

b. The issue of discrimination against the majority race—that of "favorable," "reverse," or "benign" discrimination—is considered in Part V infra.

its adoption, the Court interpreted it as proscribing all state-imposed discriminations against the Negro race." Subsequent decisions extended this proscription to state discrimination against persons because of their national origin, such as those of Chinese or Mexican ancestry.[c]

KOREMATSU v. UNITED STATES

323 U.S. 214, 65 S.Ct. 193, 89 L.Ed. 194 (1944).

JUSTICE BLACK delivered the opinion of the Court.

The petitioner, an American citizen of Japanese descent, was convicted in a federal district court for remaining in San Leandro, California, a "Military Area," contrary to Civilian Exclusion Order No. 34 of the Commanding General of the Western Command, U.S. Army, which directed that after May 9, 1942, all persons of Japanese ancestry should be excluded from that area. No question was raised as to petitioner's loyalty to the United States. * * *

[A]ll legal restrictions which curtail the civil rights of a single racial group are immediately suspect. That is not to say that all such restrictions are unconstitutional. It is to say that courts must subject them to the most rigid scrutiny. Pressing public necessity may sometimes justify the existence of such restrictions; racial antagonism never can. * * *

Exclusion Order No. 34 [was] one of a number of military orders [and a] curfew order, [also] promulgated pursuant to Executive Order 9066, subjected all persons of Japanese ancestry in prescribed West Coast military areas to remain in their residences from 8 p.m. to 6 a.m. [In] *Hirabayashi v. United States,* 320 U.S. 81, 63 S.Ct. 1365, 87 L.Ed. 1774 (1943), we sustained a conviction [for] violation of the curfew order [as] an exercise of the power [to] take steps necessary to prevent espionage and sabotage in an area threatened by Japanese attack.

In the light of the principles we announced in the *Hirabayashi* case, we are unable to conclude that it was beyond the war power of Congress and the Executive to exclude those of Japanese ancestry from the West Coast war area at the time they [did]. Nothing short of apprehension by the proper military authorities of the gravest imminent danger to the public safety can constitutionally justify either. But exclusion from a threatened area, no less than curfew, has a definite and close relationship to the prevention of espionage and sabotage. * * *

Here, as in *Hirabayashi,* "we cannot reject as unfounded the judgment of the military authorities and of Congress that there were disloyal members of that population, whose number and strength could not be precisely and quickly ascertained. We cannot say that the war-making branches of the Government did not have ground for believing that in a critical hour such persons could not readily be isolated and separately dealt with, and constituted a menace to the national defense and safety, which demanded that prompt and adequate measures be taken to guard against it."

[This] answers the contention that the exclusion was in the nature of group punishment based on antagonism to those of Japanese origin. That there were members of the group who retained loyalties to Japan has been confirmed by investigations made subsequent to the exclusion. Approximately five thousand American citizens of Japanese ancestry refused to swear unqualified allegiance to

---

c. *Yick Wo v. Hopkins* (1886), Sec. III infra;
Hernandez v. Texas, 347 U.S. 475, 74 S.Ct. 667,
98 L.Ed. 866 (1954).

the United States [and] several thousand evacuees requested repatriation to Japan.

[H]ardships are part of war, and war is an aggregation of hardships. [E]xclusion of large groups of citizens from their homes, except under circumstances of direst emergency and peril, is inconsistent with our basic governmental institutions. But when under conditions of modern warfare our shores are threatened by hostile forces, the power to protect must be commensurate with the threatened danger. * * *

It is said that we are dealing here with the case of imprisonment of a citizen in a concentration camp solely because of his ancestry, without evidence or inquiry concerning his loyalty and good disposition towards the United States. [But] we are dealing specifically with nothing but an exclusion order. To cast this case into outlines of racial prejudice, without reference to the real military dangers which were presented, merely confuses the issue. Korematsu was not excluded from the Military Area because of hostility to him or his race. He was excluded because we are at war with the Japanese Empire, because the properly constituted military authorities feared an invasion of our West Coast and felt constrained to take proper security measures, because they decided that the military urgency of the situation demanded that all citizens of Japanese ancestry be segregated from the West Coast temporarily, and finally, because Congress, reposing its confidence in this time of war in our military leaders—as inevitably it must—determined that they should have the power to do just this. * * * We cannot—by availing ourselves of the calm perspective of hindsight—now say that at that time these actions were unjustified.[a]

Affirmed.

JUSTICE FRANKFURTER [who joined the Court's opinion], concurring.

[To] find that the Constitution does not forbid the military measures now complained of does not carry with it approval of that which Congress and the Executive did. That is their business, not ours.

JUSTICE MURPHY, dissenting.

[T]he exclusion, either temporarily or permanently, of all persons with Japanese blood in their veins [must] rely for its reasonableness upon the assumption that *all* persons of Japanese ancestry may have a dangerous tendency to commit sabotage and espionage and [it] is difficult to believe that reason, logic or experience could be marshalled in support of such an assumption. [The] reasons appear, instead, to be largely an accumulation of much of the misinformation, half-truths and insinuations that for years have been directed against Japanese Americans by people with racial and economic prejudices—the same people who have been among the foremost advocates of the evacuation. A military judgment based upon such racial and sociological considerations is not entitled to the great weight ordinarily given the judgments based upon strictly military considerations. Especially is this so when every charge relative to race, religion, culture, geograph-

---

a. For the view that "notwithstanding the grandiose rhetoric [of "most rigid scrutiny"], the Court actually applied its most deferential brand of rationality review," see Michael J. Klarman, *An Interpretive History of Modern Equal Protection,* 90 Mich.L.Rev. 213, 232–233 (1991). Consider Larry G. Simon, *Racially Prejudiced Governmental Actions: A Motivation Theory of the Constitutional Ban Against Racial Discrimination,* 15 San Diego L.Rev. 1041, 1074 (1978): "The Japanese exclusion cases [are] most troubling not because the Court found that the challenged rules would have been promulgated even apart from prejudice, but because it refused seriously to consider whether maintaining the exclusionary system and continuing its enforcement as of the time the cases reached the Court could be explained on grounds other than racial prejudice." See fn. d. infra.

ical location, and legal and economic status has been substantially discredited by independent studies made by experts in these matters. * * *

Moreover, there was no adequate proof that the FBI and the military and naval intelligence services did not have the espionage and sabotage situation well in hand during this long period. Nor is there any denial of the fact that not one person of Japanese ancestry was accused or convicted of espionage or sabotage after Pearl Harbor while they were still free, a fact which is some evidence of the loyalty of the vast majority of these individuals and of the effectiveness of the established methods of combatting these evils. It seems incredible that under these circumstances it would have been impossible to hold loyalty hearings for the mere 112,000 persons involved—or at least for the 70,000 American citizens—especially when a large part of this number represented children and elderly men and women. Any inconvenience that may have accompanied an attempt to conform to procedural due process cannot be said to justify violations of constitutional [rights].

JUSTICE JACKSON, dissenting.

Korematsu was born on our soil, of parents born in Japan. [Had] Korematsu been one of four—the others being, say, a German alien enemy, an Italian alien enemy, and a citizen of American-born ancestors, convicted of treason but out on parole—only Korematsu's presence would have violated the order. The difference between their innocence and his crime would result, not from anything he did, said, or thought, different than they, but only in that he was born of different racial stock.

Now, if any fundamental assumption underlies our system, it is that guilt is personal and not inheritable. [If] Congress in peace-time legislation should enact such a criminal law, I should suppose this Court would refuse to enforce it.

But [it] would be impracticable and dangerous idealism to expect or insist that each specific military command in an area of probable operations will conform to conventional tests of constitutionality. When an area is so beset that it must be put under military control at all, the paramount consideration is that its measures be successful, rather than legal. * * * I cannot say, from any evidence before me, that the orders of General DeWitt were not reasonably expedient military precautions, nor could I say that they were. But even if they were permissible military procedures, I deny that it follows that they are constitutional. If, as the Court holds, it does follow, then we may as well say that any military order will be constitutional and have done with it.

The limitation under which courts always will labor in examining the necessity for a military order are illustrated by this case. How does the Court know that these orders have a reasonable basis in necessity? No evidence whatever on that subject has been taken by this or any other court. There is sharp controversy as to the credibility of the DeWitt report. So the Court, having no real evidence before it, has no choice but to accept General DeWitt's own unsworn, self-serving statement, untested by any cross-examination, that what he did was reasonable. And thus it will always be when courts try to look into the reasonableness of a military order. * * *

[A] judicial construction of the due process clause that will sustain this order is a far more subtle blow to liberty than the promulgation of the order itself. A military order, however unconstitutional, is not apt to last longer than the military emergency. [But] once a judicial opinion rationalizes [the] Constitution to show that the Constitution sanctions such an order, the Court for all time has validated the principle of racial discrimination in criminal procedure and of transplanting American citizens. The principle then lies about like a loaded weapon ready for the hand of any authority that can bring forward a plausible claim of an urgent need. * * * [b]

My duties as a justice as I see them do not require me to make a military judgment as to whether General DeWitt's evacuation and detention program was a reasonable military necessity. I do not suggest that the courts should have attempted to interfere with the Army in carrying out its task. But I do not think they may be asked to execute a military expedient that has no place in law under the Constitution. I would reverse the judgment and discharge the prisoner.[c]

Notes and Questions

1. *Standard of review.* *Hirabayashi* and *Korematsu* have been the last instances in which the Court has failed to invalidate intentional (or "de jure") government discrimination against a racial or ethnic minority.[d] In 1967, the Court observed that laws imposing "invidious racial discriminations" bear a "very heavy burden of justification" and "if they are ever to be upheld, they must be shown to be necessary to the accomplishment of some permissible state objective"; they are unlike statutes "involving no racial discrimination" where "the Court has merely asked whether there is any rational foundation for the discriminations, and has deferred to the wisdom of the state legislatures." [e]

2. *"Rigid scrutiny" and "special traits."* (a) Should state discrimination against a racial minority ever be upheld? Consider Douglas, J., *We the Judges* 399 (1956): "Experience shows that liquor has a devastating effect on the North American Indian and Eskimo. It is, therefore, commonly provided [that] no liquor should be sold to those races. Other regulations based on race may likewise be justified by reason of the special traits of those races [and] what at first blush may seem to be an invidious discrimination may on analysis be found to have plausible grounds justifying it." [f]

---

b. Compare Warren, C.J., *The Bill of Rights and the Military,* 37 N.Y.U.L.Rev. 181, 192–93 (1962): "[*Hirabayashi* and *Korematsu*] demonstrate dramatically that there are some circumstances in which the Court will, in effect, conclude that it is simply not in a position to reject descriptions by the Executive of the degree of military necessity. Thus, in a case like *Hirabayashi,* only the Executive is qualified to determine whether, for example, an invasion is imminent. In such a situation, where time is of the essence, if the Court is to deny the asserted right of the military authorities, it must be on the theory that the claimed justification, though factually unassailable, is insufficient. [S]uch cases would be extraordinary indeed. [To] put it another way, the fact that the Court rules in a case like *Hirabayashi* that a given program is constitutional, does not necessarily answer the question whether, in a broader sense, it actually is."

For a description of then-California Attorney General and later-Governor Earl Warren's "leading role" in the Japanese exclusion as the "one blot on his record * * * otherwise so admirable," see David Halberstam, *The Fifties* 417–18 (1993): "He was playing to the growing fear of sabotage and the country's anger

against the Japanese, particularly in California."

c. The dissenting opinion of Roberts, J., is omitted. The Japanese evacuation and *Korematsu* have been the subject of extensive criticism. See, e.g., Audrie Girdner & Anne Loftis, *The Great Betrayal* (1969); Morton Grodzins, *Americans Betrayed* (1949); Eugene V. Rostow, *The Japanese American Cases—A Disaster,* in The Sovereign Prerogative 193 (1962).

d. On the same day as *Korematsu, Ex parte Endo,* 323 U.S. 283, 65 S.Ct. 208, 89 L.Ed. 243 (1944), per Douglas, J., held that Executive Order 9066 did not authorize the continued detention of concededly loyal persons of Japanese ancestry: "This Court [has] favored that interpretation of legislation which gives it the greater chance of surviving the test of constitutionality."

e. *Loving v. Virginia,* Part II infra. For discussion of "refinements" of the "test," see note 1 after *Loving.*

f. For discussion of federal laws that specially classify members of American Indian tribes, see Tribe *Treatise* 1467–74; *Morton v. Mancari,* 417 U.S. 535, 94 S.Ct. 2474, 41

May a state require that all African–Americans undergo a blood test for sickle cell anemia? Suppose that "studies have indicated that seven to nine percent of the American Black population carries the sickle cell trait, while 0.3 percent suffer from the disease" and that "the incidence of sickle cell anemia in the White population is negligible"? Note, *Constitutional and Practical Considerations in Mandatory Sickle Cell Anemia Testing,* 7 U.C.D.L.Rev. 509, 519 (1974). Should it make a difference if the state, rather than the individual, pays for the blood test? May "overinclusive" racial laws be distinguished on the basis of the severity of the burden imposed? Compare *Hirabayashi, Korematsu* and *Endo.*

(b) Is a law providing "that anyone whose skin is darker than a certain shade (either attached as an exhibit or defined in terms of albedo or reflecting power) is negligent for walking on a road at night without wearing some light-colored item of clothing" distinguishable from the other situations referred to above? See John Kaplan, *Equal Justice in an Unequal World: Equality for the Negro—The Problem of Special Treatment,* 61 Nw.U.L.Rev. 363, 383 (1966).

(c) May the federal government consider racial (religious) differences in assigning personnel to official American posts in foreign countries?

II. SEGREGATION AND OTHER CLASSIFICATIONS

Part I involved laws that imposed burdens on racial and ethnic minorities. This section concerns laws that segregate or otherwise classify on a racial basis but, at least in a literal sense, treat all races identically. The principal question is whether (and, if so, why) such laws should be subject to the same "rigid" or "strict" standard of review.

PLESSY v. FERGUSON

163 U.S. 537, 16 S.Ct. 1138, 41 L.Ed. 256 (1896).

JUSTICE BROWN delivered the opinion of the Court.

[An 1890 Louisiana law required that railway passenger cars have "equal but separate accommodations for the white, and colored races." Plessy, alleging that he "was seven-eights Caucasian and one-eighth African blood; that the mixture of colored blood was not discernible in him; and that he was entitled to every right [of] the white race," was arrested for refusing to vacate a seat in a coach for whites.]

That it does not conflict with the thirteenth amendment [is] too clear for argument. Slavery implies involuntary servitude,—a state of bondage * * *. This amendment [was] regarded by the statesmen of that day as insufficient to protect the colored race from certain laws [imposing] onerous disabilities and burdens, and curtailing their rights in the pursuit of life, liberty, and property to such an extent that their freedom was of little value; [and] the fourteenth amendment was devised to meet this exigency. * * *

The object of the amendment was undoubtedly to enforce the absolute equality of the two races before the law, but, in the nature of things, it could not have been intended to abolish distinctions based upon color, or to enforce social, as distinguished from political, equality, or a commingling of the two races upon terms unsatisfactory to either. [Laws] requiring their separation, in places where

L.Ed.2d 290 (1974), upholding a hiring prefer-ence for qualified Indians in the Bureau of Indian Affairs of the Department of the Interi-or.

they are liable to be brought into contact [have] been generally, if not universally, recognized as within the competency of the state legislatures in the exercise of their police power. The most common instance of this is connected with the establishment of separate schools for white and colored children, which have been [upheld] even by courts of states where the political rights of the colored race have been longest and most earnestly enforced [citing cases from Mass., Ohio, Mo., Cal., La., N.Y., Ind. and Ky.].

Laws forbidding the intermarriage of the two races may be said in a technical sense to interfere with the freedom of contract, and yet have been universally recognized as within the police power of the state. [S]tatutes for the separation of the two races upon public conveyances were held to be constitutional in [federal decisions and cases from Pa., Mich., Ill., Tenn. and N.Y. It is suggested] that the same argument that will justify the state legislature in requiring railways to provide separate accommodations for the two races will also authorize them to require separate cars to be provided for people whose hair is of a certain color, or who are aliens, or who belong to certain nationalities, or to enact laws requiring colored people to walk upon one side of the street, and white people upon the other, or requiring white men's houses to be painted white, and colored men's black, or their vehicles or business signs to be of different colors, upon the theory that one side of the street is as good as the other, or that a house or vehicle of one color is as good as one of another color. The reply to all this is that every exercise of the police power must be reasonable, and extend only to such laws as are enacted in good faith for the promotion of the public good, and not for the annoyance or oppression of a particular class. [In] determining the question of reasonableness, [the state] is at liberty to act with reference to the established usages, customs, and traditions of the people, and with a view to the promotion of their comfort, and the preservation of the public peace and good order. Gauged by this standard, we cannot say [this law] is unreasonable, or more obnoxious to the fourteenth amendment than the [acts] requiring separate schools for colored children in the District of Columbia, the constitutionality of which does not seem to have been questioned or the corresponding acts of state legislatures.[a]

We consider the underlying fallacy of the plaintiff's argument to consist in the assumption that the enforced separation of the two races stamps the colored race with a badge of inferiority. If this be so, it is not by reason of anything found in the act, but solely because the colored race chooses to put that construction upon it. [The] argument also assumes that social prejudices may be overcome by legislation, and that equal rights cannot be secured to the negro except by an enforced commingling of the two races. We cannot accept this proposition. If the two races are to meet upon terms of social equality, it must be the result [of] voluntary consent of individuals. * * * Legislation is powerless to eradicate racial instincts, or to abolish distinctions based upon physical differences,[b] and the

a. Compare Robert J. Harris, *The Constitution, Education, and Segregation,* 29 Temp. L.Q. 409, 413 (1956): "[T]he dictum [that] reasonableness is to be construed with reference to established usages, customs and traditions of the people [wholly] ignores the fact that it was to prevent these customs and traditions from being enacted into law that the fourteenth amendment was adopted."

For the view that "*Plessy,* the case first introducing separate-but-equal to the Supreme Court, apparently contemplated that unequal segregated facilities would be subject to justifi-

cation just like any other sort of inequality," see Klarman, supra, at 229–230: "[E]quality was required in *Plessy* [only] because the Court could conceive of no rational explanation for a state's refusal to provide equal railway facilities for blacks. Racial classifications, in other words, were subjected to the same general rationality test which had come to govern equal protection review of economic regulation."

b. Consider Michael W. McConnell, *Originalism and the Desegregation Decisions,* 81 Va.L.Rev. 947, 1131 (1995): "That is a debata-

attempt to do so can only result in accentuating the difficulties of the present situation. * * *

Affirmed.

JUSTICE BREWER did [not] participate in the decision of this case.

JUSTICE HARLAN dissenting.

[No] legislative body or judicial tribunal may have regard to the race of citizens when the civil rights of those citizens are involved. * * *

It was said in argument that the statute of Louisiana does not discriminate against either race, but prescribes a rule applicable alike to white and colored citizens. But [e]very one knows that [it] had its origin in the purpose, not so much to exclude white persons from railroad cars occupied by blacks, as to exclude colored people from coaches occupied by or assigned to white persons. [The] fundamental objection, therefore, to the statute, is that it interferes with the personal freedom of citizens.[c] * * *

The white race deems itself to be the dominant race in this country. And so it is, in prestige, in achievements, in education, in wealth, and in power. So, I doubt not, it will continue to be for all time, if it remains true to its great heritage, and holds fast to the principles of constitutional liberty. But in view of the constitution, in the eye of the law, there is in this country no superior, dominant, ruling class of citizens. There is no caste here. Our constitution is color-blind * * *.

In my opinion, the judgment this day rendered will, in time, prove to be quite as pernicious as the decision made by this tribunal in the *Dred Scott Case* [that] the descendants of Africans who were imported into this country, and sold as slaves, were not included nor intended to be included under the word "citizens" in the constitution; [that,] at the time of the adoption of the constitution, they were "considered as a subordinate and inferior class of beings, who had been subjugated by the dominant race, and, whether emancipated or not, yet remained subject to their authority, and had no rights or privileges but such as those who held the power and the government might choose to grant them." 19 How. 393, 404. The recent amendments of the constitution, it was supposed, had eradicated these principles from our institutions. [What] can more certainly arouse race hate, what more certainly create and perpetuate a feeling of distrust between these races, than state enactments which, in fact, proceed on the ground that colored citizens are so inferior and degraded that they cannot be allowed to sit in public coaches occupied by white citizens? [The] thin disguise of "equal" accommoda-

ble proposition, but it turns the issue on its head. No one in *Plessy* was seeking 'legislation' to abolish distinctions; Plessy was challenging legislation *enforcing* racial distinctions imposed upon the private market by the state. The Court was wrong in framing the issue as whether the Fourteenth Amendment would '*enforce* social equality.' The question was whether the Amendment would tolerate state legislation to enforce social *inequality*."

c. See John P. Frank & Robert F. Munro, *The Original Understanding of "Equal Protection of the Laws,"* 1972 Wash.U.L.Q. 421, 455: "We believe that the equal protection clause, in the eyes of its contemporaries, froze into constitutional law the existing common law obligation of transportation companies to take all comers and to eliminate any possibility of their segregation. Congress decided so often in this period that color classifications were not permissible for purposes of transportation that it is difficult to understand how equal protection could possibly be given another meaning." For a discussion of "civil" rights in the fourteenth amendment's history, see Alexander M. Bickel, *The Original Understanding and the Segregation Decision*, 69 Harv.L.Rev. 1 (1955). Compare Raoul Berger, *Government By Judiciary: The Transformation of the Fourteenth Amendment* (1977).

tions for passengers in railroad coaches will not mislead any one, nor atone for the wrong this day done. * * *

I do not deem it necessary to review the decisions of state courts to which reference was made in argument. Some [are] inapplicable, because rendered prior to the adoption of the last amendments of the [constitution]. Others were made at a time [when] race prejudice was, practically, the supreme law of the land. Those decisions cannot be guides in the era introduced by the recent amendments of the supreme law, which established universal civil freedom * * *.[d]

BROWN v. BOARD OF EDUCATION

347 U.S. 483, 74 S.Ct. 686, 98 L.Ed. 873 (1954).

CHIEF JUSTICE WARREN delivered the opinion of the Court.

These cases come to us from the States of Kansas, South Carolina, Virginia, and Delaware. * * *

In each of the cases, minors of the Negro race [seek] the aid of the courts in obtaining admission to the public schools of their community on a nonsegregated basis. [In] each of the cases other than the Delaware case, a three-judge federal district court denied relief to the plaintiffs on the so-called "separate but equal" doctrine announced by this Court in [Plessy]. In the Delaware case, the Supreme Court of Delaware adhered to that doctrine, but ordered that the plaintiffs be admitted to the white schools because of their superiority to the Negro schools.

* * * Argument was heard in the 1952 Term, and reargument was heard this Term on certain questions propounded by the Court.

Reargument was largely devoted to the circumstances surrounding the adoption of the Fourteenth Amendment in 1868. It covered exhaustively consideration of the Amendment in Congress, ratification by the states, then existing practices in racial segregation, and the views of proponents and opponents of the Amendment. This discussion and our own investigation convince us that, although these sources cast some light, it is not enough to resolve the problem with which we are faced. At best, they are inconclusive. The most avid proponents of the post-War Amendments undoubtedly intended them to remove all legal distinctions among "all persons born or naturalized in the United States." Their opponents, just as certainly, were antagonistic to both the letter and the spirit of the Amendments and wished them to have the most limited effect. What others in Congress and the state legislatures had in mind cannot be determined with any degree of certainty.

An additional reason for the inconclusive nature of the Amendment's history, with respect to segregated schools, is the status of public education at that time. In the South, the movement toward free common schools, supported by general taxation, had not yet taken hold. Education of white children was largely in the hands of private groups. Education of Negroes was almost nonexistent, and practically all of the race were illiterate. In fact, any education of Negroes was forbidden by law in some states. Today, in contrast, many Negroes have achieved outstanding success in the arts and sciences as well as in the business and professional world. It is true that public school education at the time of the

---

d. How do you account for the Court's dramatic shift in perspective in the sixteen years between *Strauder* and *Plessy*? See generally C. Vann Woodward, *The Strange Career of Jim Crow* (2d ed. 1966). For discussion of *Plessy* and its background, see Charles A. Lofgren, *The Plessy Case: A Legal Historical Interpretation* (1987); Paul Oberst, *The Strange Career of Plessy v. Ferguson*, 15 Ariz.L.Rev. 389 (1973).

Amendment had advanced further in the North, but the effect of the Amendment on Northern States was generally ignored in the congressional debates. Even in the North, the conditions of public education did not approximate those existing today. The curriculum was usually rudimentary; ungraded schools were common in rural areas; the school term was but three months a year in many states; and compulsory school attendance was virtually unknown. As a consequence, it is not surprising that there should be so little in the history of the Fourteenth Amendment relating to its intended effect on public education.

In the first cases in this Court construing the Fourteenth Amendment, decided shortly after its adoption, the Court interpreted it as proscribing all state-imposed discriminations against the Negro race.[5] The doctrine of "separate but equal" did not make its appearance in this Court until 1896 in *Plessy,* involving not education but transportation. [In] this Court, there have been six cases involving the "separate but equal" doctrine in the field of public education. In *Cumming v. Board of Education,* 175 U.S. 528, 20 S.Ct. 197, 44 L.Ed. 262, and *Gong Lum v. Rice,* 275 U.S. 78, 48 S.Ct. 91, 72 L.Ed. 172, the validity of the doctrine itself was not challenged.[8] In more recent cases, all on the graduate school level, inequality was found in that specific benefits enjoyed by white students were denied to Negro students of the same educational qualifications. *Missouri ex rel. Gaines v. Canada,* 305 U.S. 337, 59 S.Ct. 232, 83 L.Ed. 208 [a]; *Sipuel v. Oklahoma,* 332 U.S. 631, 68 S.Ct. 299, 92 L.Ed. 247; *Sweatt v. Painter,* 339 U.S. 629, 70 S.Ct. 848, 94 L.Ed. 1114 [b]; *McLaurin v. Oklahoma State Regents,* 339 U.S. 637, 70 S.Ct. 851, 94 L.Ed. 1149.[c] In none of these cases was it necessary to re-examine the doctrine to grant relief to the Negro plaintiff. And in *Sweatt,* the Court expressly reserved decision on the question whether *Plessy* should be held inapplicable to public education.

---

5. *Slaughter-House Cases; Strauder * * *.* See also *Virginia v. Rives,* 1879, 100 U.S. 313, 318, 25 L.Ed. 667; *Ex parte Virginia,* 1879, 100 U.S. 339, 344–345, 25 L.Ed. 676. [See generally Brief for the Committee of Law Teachers Against Segregation in Legal Education, *Segregation and the Equal Protection Clause,* 34 Minn.L.Rev. 289 (1950).]

8. In *Cumming,* Negro taxpayers sought an injunction requiring the defendant school board to discontinue the operation of a high school for white children until the board resumed operation of a high school for Negro children. Similarly, in *Gong Lum,* the plaintiff, a child of Chinese descent, contended only that state authorities had misapplied the doctrine by classifying him with Negro children and requiring him to attend a Negro school.

a. *Gaines,* in 1938, invalidated the refusal to admit blacks to the University of Missouri School of Law, despite the state's offer to pay petitioner's tuition at an out-of-state law school pending establishment of a state law school for African–Americans.

b. *Sweatt,* in 1950, required admission of African–Americans to the University of Texas Law School despite the recent establishment of a state law school for blacks: "In terms of number of the faculty, variety of courses and opportunity for specialization, size of the student body, scope of the library, availability of

law review and similar activities, the University of Texas Law School is superior. What is more important, the University of Texas Law School possesses to a far greater degree those qualities which are incapable of objective measurement but which make for greatness in a law school. Such qualities, to name but a few, include reputation of the faculty, experience of the administration, position and influence of the alumni, standing in the community, traditions and prestige. [Moreover, the law school] cannot be effective in isolation from the individuals and institutions with which the law interacts. Few students and no one who has practiced law would choose to study in an academic vacuum, removed from the interplay of ideas and the exchange of views with which the law is concerned. The law school to which Texas is willing to admit petitioner excludes from its student body members of the racial groups which number 85% of the population of the State and include most of the lawyers, witnesses, jurors, judges and other officials with whom petitioner will inevitably be dealing when he becomes a member of the Texas Bar."

c. *McLaurin,* in 1950, held violative of equal protection requirements that African–American graduate students at the University of Oklahoma sit at separate desks adjoining the classrooms and separate tables outside the library reading room, and eat at separate times in the school cafeteria.

In the instant cases, that question is directly presented. [T]here are findings below that the Negro and white schools involved have been equalized, or are being equalized, with respect to buildings, curricula, qualifications and salaries of teachers, and other "tangible" factors. Our decision, therefore, cannot turn on merely a comparison of these tangible factors in the Negro and white schools involved in each of the cases. We must look instead to the effect of segregation itself on public education.

In approaching this problem, we cannot turn the clock back to 1868 when the Amendment was adopted, or even to 1896 when *Plessy* was written. We must consider public education in the light of its full development and its present place in American life throughout the Nation. Only in this way can it be determined if segregation in public schools deprives these plaintiffs of the equal protection of the laws.

Today, education is perhaps the most important function of state and local governments. Compulsory school attendance laws and the great expenditures for education both demonstrate our recognition of the importance of education to our democratic society. It is required in the performance of our most basic public responsibilities, even service in the armed forces. It is the very foundation of good citizenship. Today it is a principal instrument in awakening the child to cultural values, in preparing him for later professional training, and in helping him to adjust normally to his environment. In these days, it is doubtful that any child may reasonably be expected to succeed in life if he is denied the opportunity of an education. Such an opportunity, where the state has undertaken to provide it, is a right which must be made available to all on equal terms.

We come then to the question presented: Does segregation of children in public schools solely on the basis of race, even though the physical facilities and other "tangible" factors may be equal, deprive the children of the minority group of equal educational opportunities? We believe that it does.

In *Sweatt,* in finding that a segregated law school for Negroes could not provide them equal educational opportunities, this Court relied in large part on "those qualities which are incapable of objective measurement but which make for greatness in a law school." In *McLaurin,* the Court, in requiring that a Negro admitted to a white graduate school be treated like all other students, again resorted to intangible considerations: "[his] ability to study, to engage in discussions and exchange views with other students, and in general, to learn his profession." Such considerations apply with added force to children in grade and high schools. To separate them from others of similar age and qualifications solely because of their race generates a feeling of inferiority as to their status in the community that may affect their hearts and minds in a way unlikely ever to be undone. The effect of this separation on their educational opportunities was well stated by a finding in the Kansas case by a court which nevertheless felt compelled to rule against the Negro plaintiffs: "Segregation of white and colored children in public schools has a detrimental effect upon the colored children. The impact is greater when it has the sanction of the law; for the policy of separating the races is usually interpreted as denoting the inferiority of the Negro group. A sense of inferiority affects the motivation of a child to learn. Segregation with the sanction of law, therefore, has a tendency to [retard] the educational and mental development of Negro children and to deprive them of some of the benefits they would receive in a racial[ly] integrated school system."[10] Whatever may have

---

10. A similar finding was made in the Delaware case: "I conclude from the testimony that in our Delaware society, State-imposed segregation in education itself results in the

been the extent of psychological knowledge at the time of *Plessy,* this finding is amply supported by modern authority.[11] Any language in *Plessy* contrary to this finding is rejected.

We conclude that in the field of public education the doctrine of "separate but equal" has no place. Separate educational facilities are inherently unequal. Therefore, we hold that the plaintiffs and others similarly situated for whom the actions have been brought are, by reason of the segregation complained of, deprived of [equal protection].

Because these are class actions, because of the wide applicability of this decision, and because of the great variety of local conditions, the formulation of decrees in these cases presents problems of considerable complexity. On reargument, the consideration of appropriate relief was necessarily subordinated to the primary question—the constitutionality of segregation in public education. We have now announced that such segregation is a denial of the equal protection of the laws. In order that we may have the full assistance of the parties in formulating decrees, the cases will be restored to the docket, and the parties are requested to present further argument on Questions 4 and 5 previously propounded by the Court for the reargument this Term.[13] * * *

Notes and Questions

1. *The Court's rationale.* What was the specific basis for the decision?

(a) *Social science materials.* At trial in several of the cases, psychiatrists and social scientists testified as to the harmful effects of state-imposed segregation on black children. On appeal, appellants filed a statement to this effect by 32 sociologists, anthropologists, psychologists, and psychiatrists who worked in the area of American race relations—reprinted in 37 Minn.L.Rev. 427 (1953).

Was the decision based on this information? Is this desirable? Should *Brown* be modified or overruled if new social science data reaches different

Negro children, as a class, receiving educational opportunities which are substantially inferior to those available to white children otherwise similarly situated."

11. Kenneth B. Clark, *Effect of Prejudice and Discrimination on Personality Development* (Midcentury White House Conference on Children and Youth, 1950); Helen L. Witmer and Ruth Kotinsky, *Personality in the Making* (1952), c. VI; Max Deutscher and Isidor Chein, *The Psychological Effects of Enforced Segregation: A Survey of Social Science Opinion,* 26 J.Psychol. 259 (1948); Chein, *What are the Psychological Effects of Segregation Under Conditions of Equal Facilities?,* 3 Int.J. Opinion and Attitude Res. 229 (1949); Theodore Brameld, *Educational Costs in Discrimination and National Welfare* (MacIver, ed., 1949), 44–48; *Frazier,* The Negro in the United States *(1949), 674–681. And, see generally Gunnar Myrdal,* An American Dilemma *(1962).*

13. "4. Assuming it is decided that segregation in public schools violates the Fourteenth Amendment

"(a) would a decree necessarily follow providing that, within the limits set by normal geographic school districting, Negro children

should forthwith be admitted to schools of their choice, or

"(b) may this Court, in the exercise of its equity powers, permit an effective gradual adjustment to be brought about from existing segregated systems to a system not based on color distinctions?

"5. On the assumption on which questions 4(a) and (b) are based, and assuming further that this Court will exercise its equity powers to the end described in question 4(b),

"(a) should this Court formulate detailed decrees in these cases;

"(b) if so, what specific issues should the decrees reach;

"(c) should this Court appoint a special master to hear evidence with a view to recommending specific terms for such decrees;

"(d) should this Court remand to the courts of first instance with directions to frame decrees in these cases, and if so what general directions should the decrees of this Court include and what procedures should the courts of first instance follow in arriving at the specific terms of more detailed decrees?"

conclusions? [d] Consider Edmund Cahn, *Jurisprudence*, 30 N.Y.U.L.Rev. 150, 157–58, 167 (1955): "It is one thing to use the current scientific findings, however ephemeral they may be, in order to ascertain whether the legislature has acted reasonably in adopting some scheme of social or economic regulation; deference here is shown not so much to the findings as to the legislature. It would be quite another thing to have our fundamental rights rise, fall, or change along with the latest fashions of psychological literature."

(b) Does *Brown* rest on a finding that "in terms of the most familiar and universally accepted standards of right and wrong [racial] segregation under government auspices inevitably inflicts humiliation, [and] official humiliation of innocent, law-abiding citizens is psychologically injurious and morally evil"? Cahn, supra, at 159. If so, where are such "universally accepted standards" found? See Ronald Dworkin, *Social Sciences and Constitutional Rights—The Consequences of Uncertainty*, 6 J.L. & Ed. 3 (1977).

(c) *Historical considerations.* (i) Would it have been better for the Court to rely upon the original purpose of the fourteenth amendment as stated in *Strauder*: to grant African–Americans "the right to exemption from unfriendly legislation against them as distinctively colored"? If so, how should *Plessy* have been treated? Was the *Brown* Court in 1954 a better judge of fourteenth amendment intent than the *Plessy* Court in 1896? Than the *Strauder* Court in 1879?

(ii) Apart from the specific intentions of the framers and ratifiers of the fourteenth amendment in respect to school segregation,[e] of what significance is the fact that "every one of the twenty-six states that had any substantial racial differences among its people either approved the operation of segregated schools already in existence or subsequently established such schools by action of the same law-making body which considered the Fourteenth Amendment"? *Declaration of Constitutional Principles Issued by 19 Senators and 77 Representatives of the Congress*, N.Y. Times, p. 19, col. 2, March 12, 1956. What justified the Court's consideration of "public education in the light of its full development and its present place in American life throughout the Nation"? Consider Alexander M. Bickel, *The Original Understanding and the Segregation Decision*, 69 Harv.L.Rev. 1, 59 (1955): "If the fourteenth amendment were a statute, a court might very well hold [that] it was foreclosed from applying it to segregation in public schools. [But] we are dealing with a constitutional amendment, not a statute. The tradition of a broadly worded organic law not frequently or lightly amended was

---

d. For extensive discussion and comprehensive listing of the substantial and controversial research and literature on the subject, see Symposia, *School Desegregation: Lessons of the First Twenty-Five Years*, 42 Law & Contemp.Prob., nos. 3–4 (1978). In particular, see Mark G. Yudof, *School Desegregation: Legal Realism, Reasoned Elaboration, and Social Science Research in the Supreme Court*, 42 Law & Contemp.Prob. 57, 61 nn. 26–27 (no. 4, 1978). See also Frank I. Goodman, *De Facto School Segregation: A Constitutional and Empirical Analysis*, 60 Calif.L.Rev. 275 (1972).

e. For the view that the framers did not intend to prohibit it, see Raoul Berger, *Government by Judiciary* 117–33 (1977); Michael J. Perry, *The Constitution, the Courts, and Human Rights* 66–69 (1982). Compare Paul R. Dimond, *Strict Construction and Judicial Review of Racial Discrimination Under the Equal Protection Clause*, 80 Mich.L.Rev. 462 (1982); Joseph D. Grano, *Judicial Review and a Written Constitution in a Democratic Society*, 28 Wayne L.Rev. 1, 67–72 (1981). See generally Michael W. McConnell, *Originalism and the Desegregation Decisions*, 81 Va.L.Rev. 947, 952, 1093 (1995): "[Although] there is something very close to a consensus that *Brown* was inconsistent with the original understanding, [it] is clear beyond peradventure that a very substantial portion of the Congress, including leading framers of the Amendment, subscribed to the view that school segregation violates the Fourteenth Amendment." For appraisal of the significance of McConnell's conclusion, see Michael J. Klarman, *Brown, Originalism and Constitutional Theory*, 81 Va.L.Rev. 1881 (1995).

well-established by 1866, and [it] cannot be assumed that [anyone] expected or wished the future role of the Constitution in the scheme of American government to differ from the past. Should not the search for congressional purpose therefore, properly be twofold? One inquiry should be directed at the congressional understanding of the immediate effect of the enactment on conditions then present. Another should aim to discover what if any thought was given to the long-range effect, under future circumstances, of provisions necessarily intended for permanence."

2. *"Neutral principles."* Consider Herbert Wechsler, *Toward Neutral Principles of Constitutional Law,* 73 Harv.L.Rev. 1, 34 (1959): "[A]ssuming equal facilities, the question posed by state-enforced segregation is not one of discrimination at all. Its human and its constitutional dimensions lie [in] the denial by the state of freedom to associate, a denial that impinges in the same way on any groups or races that may be involved. [But] if the freedom of association is denied by segregation, integration forces an association upon those for whom it is unpleasant or repugnant. [W]here the state must practically choose between denying the association to those individuals who wish it or imposing it on those who would avoid it, is there a basis in neutral principles for holding that the Constitution demands that the claims for association should prevail?"

In reply, consider the following from a "draft opinion" of *Brown* by Louis Pollak, *Racial Discrimination and Judicial Integrity: A Reply to Professor Wechsler,* 108 U.Pa.L.Rev. 1, 27, 29–30 (1959): "[W]e start from the base point that in the United States 'all legal restrictions which curtail the civil rights of a single racial group are immediately suspect.' *Korematsu.* [T]here is special need for 'a searching judicial inquiry into the legislative judgment in situations where prejudice against discrete and insular minorities may tend to curtail the operation of those political processes ordinarily to be relied on to protect minorities.' See *United States v. Carolene Products,* n. 4 [p. 17 supra]. We could not, therefore, sustain the reasonableness of these racial distinctions and the absence of harm said to flow from them, unless we were prepared to say that no factual case can be made the other way. [To] the extent that implementation of this decision forces racial mingling on school children against their will, [this] consequence follows because the community through its political processes has [chosen] compulsory education. [The resulting] coerced association [cannot] be said to emanate from this Court or from the Constitution. In any event, parents sufficiently disturbed at the prospect of having their children educated in democratic fashion in company with their peers are presumably entitled to fulfill their educational responsibilities in other ways."

See also Charles Black, *The Lawfulness of the Segregation Decisions,* 69 Yale L.J. 421, 429 (1960): "The fourteenth amendment [forbids] disadvantaging the Negro race by law. It was surely anticipated that the following of this directive would entail some disagreeableness for some white southerners. [When] the directive of equality cannot be followed without displeasing the white, then something that can be called a 'freedom' of the white must be impaired. If the fourteenth amendment commands equality, and if segregation violates equality, then the status of the reciprocal 'freedom' is automatically settled." [f]

f. For the view that "the decision in *Brown* to break with the Court's long-held position on [segregation] cannot be understood without some consideration of the decision's value to whites [in] policymaking positions able to see the economic and political advances at home and abroad that would follow abandonment of segregation," see Derrick A. Bell, Jr., *Brown v. Board of Education and the Interest-Convergence Dilemma,* 93 Harv.L.Rev. 518 (1980). For amplification, see Mary L. Dudziak, *Deseg-*

3. *Extent of the decision.* (a) Did *Brown* bar all forms of state-imposed racial segregation? Or did it apply only to public schools? For comment immediately after *Brown,* consider Paul G. Kauper, *Segregation in Public Education,* 52 Mich.L.Rev. 1137, 1154–55 (1954): "[*Brown*] placed emphasis upon the intangible factors that make the *Plessy* doctrine inapplicable to public schools. Education is an experience and not simply an enjoyment of physical facilities. But with respect to common carrier and public recreational facilities, the emphasis is upon the enjoyment of the physical facilities and services so that it is more nearly possible to speak of equality of enjoyment within the pattern of segregation." [g] Compare Robert McKay, *Segregation and Public Recreation,* 40 Va.L.Rev. 697, 724 (1954): "[T]here appears to be no reason to believe that the sense of inferiority engendered by segregation in recreation is any less than in education." See Pollak, supra, at 29: "[W]here facilities are voluntary the community's asserted need to ordain segregation seems even less weighty [for] those for whom racial mingling is obnoxious are under no obligation to attend."

(b) After *Brown,* the Court, by means of rather summary per curiam decisions, citing *Brown,* consistently held invalid state imposed racial segregation in other public facilities—e.g., golf courses, parks, playgrounds.[h]

4. *Segregation by the federal government.* BOLLING v. SHARPE, 347 U.S. 497, 74 S.Ct. 693, 98 L.Ed. 884 (1954), per WARREN, C.J., held—on the same day as *Brown*—that public school segregation in the District of Columbia "constitutes an arbitrary deprivation [of] liberty in violation of the Due Process Clause" of the fifth amendment: "The Fifth Amendment [does] not contain an equal protection clause as does the Fourteenth Amendment which applies only to the states. But the concepts of equal protection and due process, both stemming from our American ideal of fairness, are not mutually exclusive. The 'equal protection of the laws' is a more explicit safeguard of prohibited unfairness than 'due process of law,' and, therefore, we do not imply that the two are always interchangeable phrases. But, as this Court has recognized, discrimination may be so unjustifiable as to be violative of due process.

"Classifications based solely upon race must be scrutinized with particular care, since they are contrary to our traditions and hence constitutionally suspect. ["Liberty"] extends to the full range of conduct which the individual is free to pursue, and it cannot be restricted except for a proper governmental objective. Segregation in public education is not reasonably related to any proper governmental objective * * *.

"In view of our decision that the Constitution prohibits the states from maintaining racially segregated public schools, it would be unthinkable that the same Constitution would impose a lesser duty on the Federal Government."

regation as a Cold War Imperative, 41 Stan. L.Rev. 61 (1988).

g. For the view that "most of the Fourteenth Amendment's drafters [intended] racial discrimination [to be] impermissible with regard to certain fundamental rights, rather than across the board," and that "rather than stating a racial classification rule, *Brown* elevated education to the level of other fundamental rights with regards to which the Equal Protection Clause forbade racial discrimination," see Klarman, fn. a, p. 1167 supra, at 235, 247.

h. For a detailed listing of these and lower court decisions, see William B. Lockhart, Yale Kamisar & Jesse H. Choper, *Constitutional Law: Cases—Comments—Questions* 1206 (3d ed. 1970).

BROWN v. BOARD OF EDUCATION

349 U.S. 294, 75 S.Ct. 753, 99 L.Ed. 1083 (1955).

CHIEF JUSTICE WARREN delivered the opinion of the Court.

These cases were decided on May 17, 1954. [There] remains for consideration the manner in which relief is to be accorded. * * *

Full implementation of these constitutional principles may require solution of varied local school problems. School authorities have the primary responsibility for elucidating, assessing, and solving [them]; courts will have to consider whether the action of school authorities constitutes good faith implementation of the governing constitutional principles. Because of their proximity to local conditions and the possible need for further hearings, the courts which originally heard these cases can best perform this judicial appraisal. Accordingly, we believe it appropriate to remand the cases to those courts.

In fashioning and effectuating the decrees, the courts will be guided by equitable principles. Traditionally, equity has been characterized by a practical flexibility in shaping its remedies and by a facility for adjusting and reconciling public and private needs. [A]t stake is the personal interest of the plaintiffs in admission to public schools as soon as practicable on a nondiscriminatory basis. To effectuate this interest may call for elimination of a variety of obstacles in making the transition to school systems operated in accordance with the constitutional principles set forth in our May 17, 1954, decision. Courts of equity may properly take into account the public interest in the elimination of such obstacles in a systematic and effective manner. But it should go without saying that the vitality of these constitutional principles cannot be allowed to yield simply because of disagreement with them.

While giving weight to these public and private considerations, the courts will require that the defendants make a prompt and reasonable start toward full compliance with our May 17, 1954, ruling. Once such a start has been made, the courts may find that additional time is necessary to carry out the ruling in an effective manner. The burden rests upon the defendants to establish that such time is necessary in the public interest and is consistent with good faith compliance at the earliest practicable date. To that end, the courts may consider problems related to administration, arising from the physical condition of the school plant, the school transportation system, personnel, revision of school districts and attendance areas into compact units to achieve a system of determining admission to the public schools on a nonracial basis, and revision of local laws and regulations which may be necessary in solving the foregoing problems. They will also consider the adequacy of any plans the defendants may propose to meet these problems and to effectuate a transition to a racially nondiscriminatory school system. During this period of transition, the courts will retain jurisdiction of these cases.

The [cases are remanded] to take such proceedings and enter such orders and decrees consistent with this opinion as are necessary and proper to admit to public schools on a racially nondiscriminatory basis with all deliberate speed the parties to these cases. * * *

Notes and Questions

1. *"Individual" vs. "race" rights.* Was the decree consistent with *Brown I?* Since plaintiffs had only a limited number of years of school remaining, did postponement of relief partially or totally destroy the very rights the decree was intended to enforce? Does the "deliberate speed" formula assume that "Negroes (unlike whites) possess rights as a race rather than as individuals, so that a

particular Negro can rightly be delayed in the enjoyment of his established rights if progress is being made in improving the legal status of Negroes generally"? Louis Lusky, *The Stereotype: Hard Core of Racism,* 13 Buf.L.Rev. 450, 457 (1963). See also Robert Carter, *The Warren Court and Desegregation,* 67 Mich.L.Rev. 237, 243 (1968). To what extent may the "deliberate speed" decree "have served the interests of blacks even while it accommodated the opposition of whites"? Paul D. Gewirtz, *Remedies and Resistance,* 92 Yale L.J. 585, 609–28 (1983).

2. *"Deliberate speed" and the slow pace of desegregation.* What of Black, J.'s view that this formula "delayed the process of outlawing segregation" and that it would have been preferable to treat *Brown* "as an ordinary law suit and force that judgment on the counties it affected that minute"? Transcript, *Justice Black and the Bill of Rights,* CBS News Special, Dec. 3, 1968. Should the Court have relied on social science data that "prompt, decisive action on the part of recognized authorities usually results in less anxiety and less resistance in cases where the public is opposed to the action than does a more hesitant and gradual procedure"? Kenneth B. Clark, *Introduction to Argument: The Complete Oral Argument in Brown, 1952–55,* xxxiii (Friedman ed. 1969). Compare Lino A. Graglia, *The Brown Cases Revisited: Where Are They Now?,* 1 Benchmark 23, 27 (Mar.–Apr. 1984): "There can be little doubt that if the Court had ordered the end of segregation in 1954 or 1955 the result would have been the closing of public schools in much of the South, about which the Court could have done nothing. The principal impact would have been on poor blacks, and *Brown* could have come to be seen as a blunder and symbol of judicial impotence." [a]

3. *Responsibility of local officials.* Was it wise to give *local* school authorities and *local* federal judges "primary responsibility" for effectuating desegregation? To permit "practical flexibility"? Were local school officials "most prone to resent and resist the changes ordered by the Court, and to look upon the newly enunciated constitutional doctrine as a personal repudiation"? Carter, supra, at 245. Were the district courts the sector of the federal judiciary most exposed to community pressures and least willing and able to challenge local mores? See Louis Lusky, *Racial Discrimination and the Federal Law: A Problem in Nullification,* 63 Colum.L.Rev. 1163 (1963). Was it wise to have the lower federal courts judge compliance under such broad standards as "good faith" and "public interest"? See Robert Carter, *Equal Educational Opportunities for Negroes—Abstraction or Reality,* 1968 U.Ill.L.F. 160, 177–80.[b]

LOVING v. VIRGINIA
388 U.S. 1, 87 S.Ct. 1817, 18 L.Ed.2d 1010 (1967).

CHIEF JUSTICE WARREN delivered the opinion of the Court.

This case presents a constitutional question never addressed by this Court: whether a statutory scheme adopted by Virginia to prevent marriages between persons solely on the basis of racial classifications violates [the] Fourteenth Amendment. [Appellants, a black woman and white man, were married in the

---

a. See also Alexander M. Bickel, *The Decade of School Desegregation: Progress and Prospects,* 64 Colum.L.Rev. 193, 201–02 (1964); John Kaplan, *Comment on School Desegregation,* 64 Colum.L.Rev. 223, 224–26 (1964).

b. The developments in implementing *Brown* are considered in Part IV infra.

For fascinating descriptions and interpretations of the Court's internal decisionmaking process in the segregation cases, see Dennis Hutchinson, *Unanimity and Desegregation: Decisionmaking in the Supreme Court, 1948–1958,* 68 Geo.L.J. 1 (1979); Mark Tushnet, *What Really Happened in Brown v. Board of Education,* 91 Colum.L.Rev. 1867 (1991).

District of Columbia, returned to reside in Virginia, and were convicted under the state antimiscegenation statute.]

Virginia is now one of 16 States which prohibit and punish marriages on the basis of racial classifications.[5] [The] state court concluded that the State's legitimate purposes were "to preserve the racial integrity of its citizens," and to prevent "the corruption of blood," "a mongrel breed of citizens," and "the obliteration of racial pride," obviously an endorsement of the doctrine of White Supremacy. [T]he State [argues] that the meaning of the Equal Protection Clause, as illuminated by the statements of the Framers, is only that state penal laws containing an interracial element as part of the definition of the offense must apply equally to whites and Negroes in the sense that members of each race are punished to the same degree. * * *

Because we reject the notion that the mere "equal application" of a statute containing racial classifications is enough to remove the classifications from the Fourteenth Amendment's proscription of all invidious racial discriminations, we do not accept the State's contention that these statutes should be upheld if there is any possible basis for concluding that they serve a rational purpose. [Here], we deal with statutes containing racial classifications, and the fact of equal application does not immunize the statute from the very heavy burden of justification which the Fourteenth Amendment has traditionally required of state statutes drawn according to race.

The State argues that statements in the Thirty-ninth Congress about the time of the passage of the Fourteenth Amendment indicate that the Framers did not intend the Amendment to make unconstitutional state miscegenation laws. Many of the statements [have] some relevance to the intention of Congress in submitting the Fourteenth Amendment, [but] it must be understood that they pertained to the passage of specific statutes and not to the broader, organic purpose of a constitutional amendment. As for the various statements directly concerning the Fourteenth Amendment, we have said in connection with a related problem, that although these historical sources "cast some light" they are not sufficient to resolve the problem; "[a]t best, they are inconclusive." *Brown.* We have rejected the proposition that the debates in the Thirty-ninth Congress or in the state legislatures which ratified the Fourteenth Amendment supported the theory [that equal protection] is satisfied by penal laws defining offenses based on racial classifications so long as white and Negro participants in the offense were similarly punished. *McLaughlin v. Florida,* 379 U.S. 184, 85 S.Ct. 283, 13 L.Ed.2d 222 (1964).[a]

The State finds support for its "equal application" theory [in] *Pace v. Alabama,* 106 U.S. 583, 1 S.Ct. 637, 27 L.Ed. 207 (1883). In that case, the Court upheld a conviction under an Alabama statute forbidding adultery or fornication between a white person and a Negro which imposed a greater penalty than that of a statute proscribing similar conduct by members of the same race. The Court reasoned that the statute could not be said to discriminate against Negroes because the punishment for each participant in the offense was the same. However, as recently as the 1964 Term, in rejecting the reasoning of that case, we stated *"Pace* represents a limited view of the Equal Protection Clause which has not withstood analysis in the subsequent decisions of this Court." *McLaughlin.* [The] clear and central purpose of the Fourteenth Amendment was to eliminate

---

5. [Over] the past 15 years, 14 States have repealed laws outlawing interracial marriages * * *.

a. *McLaughlin* invalidated a statute making interracial cohabitation a crime.

all official state sources of invidious racial discrimination in the States. [At] the very least, the Equal Protection Clause demands that racial classifications, especially suspect in criminal statutes, be subjected to the "most rigid scrutiny," and, if they are ever to be upheld, they must be shown to be necessary to the accomplishment of some permissible state objective, independent of the racial discrimination which it was the object of the Fourteenth Amendment to eliminate.[b] Indeed, two [justices] have already stated that they "cannot conceive of a valid legislative purpose [which] makes the color of a person's skin the test of whether his conduct is a criminal offense." *McLaughlin* (Stewart, J., joined by Douglas, J., concurring).

There is patently no legitimate overriding purpose independent of invidious racial discrimination which justifies this classification. The fact that Virginia only prohibits interracial marriages involving white persons demonstrates that the racial classifications must stand on their own justification, as measures designed to maintain White Supremacy.[11] We have consistently denied the constitutionality of measures which restrict the rights of citizens on account of race. There can be no doubt that restricting the freedom to marry solely because of racial classifications violates the central meaning of the Equal Protection Clause.

These statutes also deprive the Lovings of liberty without [due process].

Marriage is one of the "basic civil rights of man," fundamental to our very existence and survival. *Skinner v. Oklahoma* [p. 391 supra]. To deny this fundamental freedom on so unsupportable a basis as the racial classifications embodied in these statutes [surely denies due process].

Reversed.

JUSTICE STEWART, concurring.

I have previously expressed the belief that "it is simply not possible for a state law to be valid under our Constitution which makes the criminality of an act depend upon the race of the actor." *McLaughlin* (concurring opinion). Because I adhere to that belief, I concur in the judgment of the Court.

Notes and Questions

1. *Standard of review.* Is the constitutional test for laws that *classify* by race or ethnicity different from that for laws that *discriminate* against racial or ethnic minorities? Does *Loving* require only that the state purpose be "permissible" or "legitimate" in contrast to *Korematsu's* requirement of "pressing public necessity"? Compare *In re Griffiths*, Sec. 3, I infra: "In order to justify the use of a suspect classification, a State must show that its purpose or interest is both

---

b. *McLaughlin* also stated that racial classifications were " 'in most circumstances irrelevant' to any constitutionally acceptable legislative purpose." Harlan, J., concurring, added that "necessity, not mere reasonable relationship, is the proper test"; this "test which developed to protect free speech against state infringement should be equally applicable in a case involving state racial discrimination—prohibition of which lies at the very heart of the Fourteenth Amendment."

11. [While] Virginia prohibits whites from marrying any nonwhite (subject to the excep-

tion for the descendants of Pocahontas), Negroes, Orientals and any other racial class may intermarry without statutory interference. Appellants contend that this distinction renders Virginia's miscegenation statutes arbitrary and unreasonable even assuming the constitutional validity of an official purpose to preserve "racial integrity." We need not reach this contention because we find the racial classifications in these statutes repugnant to the Fourteenth Amendment, even assuming an evenhanded state purpose to protect the "integrity" of all races.

constitutionally permissible [8] and substantial,[9] and that its use of the classification is 'necessary to the accomplishment' of its purpose or the safeguarding of its interest."

2. *Racial information.* ANDERSON v. MARTIN, 375 U.S. 399, 84 S.Ct. 454, 11 L.Ed.2d 430 (1964), held violative of equal protection a statute requiring that the race of candidates for elective office be on the ballot: "The vice lies [in] the placing of the power of the State behind a racial classification that induces racial prejudice at the polls." Should the result turn on whether a black candidate is likely to receive more or less votes because of race being designated? On whether the statute contributes to a more informed electorate? See Comments, 15 Stan.L.Rev. 339 (1963); 111 U.Pa.L.Rev. 827 (1963). May a state collect racial statistics within school districts to effectuate a policy of integration? May a national census include racial information? May a state, for statistical purposes, require designation of the parties' race on every divorce decree? See *Tancil v. Woolls,* 379 U.S. 19, 85 S.Ct. 157, 13 L.Ed.2d 91 (1964).

3. *Family issues.* PALMORE v. SIDOTI, 466 U.S. 429, 104 S.Ct. 1879, 80 L.Ed.2d 421 (1984), per BURGER, C.J., held that Florida's denial of child custody to a white mother because her new husband was black violated equal protection: "There is a risk that a child living with a step-parent of a different race may be subject to a variety of pressures and stresses not present if the child were living with parents of the same racial or ethnic origin. [But the] effects of racial prejudice, however real, cannot justify a racial classification removing an infant child from the custody of its natural mother found to be an appropriate person to have such custody."[c]

4. *Law enforcement issues.* May a police department assign all black officers to black residential areas and all white officers to white residential areas? May it *ever* consider race in determining assignment? May prison officials take racial tensions among prisoners into account in maintaining security, discipline, or good order? Cf. *Lee v. Washington,* 390 U.S. 333, 88 S.Ct. 994, 19 L.Ed.2d 1212 (1968).

III. DE JURE VS. DE FACTO DISCRIMINATION

Part I involved laws that explicitly discriminated against racial and ethnic minorities. But intentional (or "de jure") discrimination may exist even though the law in question is racially "neutral" on its face: the law may be deliberately administered in a discriminatory way; or a law, although neutral in its language and applied in accordance with its terms, may have been enacted with a purpose (or motive) to disadvantage a "suspect" class. This section concerns these additional types of "de jure" discrimination as well as government action that is racially neutral in its terms, administration, and purpose but which has a discriminatory effect or impact ("de facto" discrimination).

8. Discrimination or segregation for its own sake is not, of course, a constitutionally permissible purpose.

9. The state interest required has been characterized as "overriding," *Loving,* "compelling," *Graham v. Richardson* [Sec. 3, II infra], "important," *Dunn v. Blumstein* [Sec. 4, II infra], or "substantial," ibid. We attribute no particular significance to these variations in diction.

c. What result if the new husband seeks to adopt the child and the natural father objects solely because of racial prejudice? See Note, *Race as a Factor in Custody and Adoption Disputes,* 71 Corn.L.Rev. 209 (1985).

YICK WO v. HOPKINS

118 U.S. 356, 6 S.Ct. 1064, 30 L.Ed. 220 (1886).

JUSTICE MATTHEWS delivered the opinion of the Court.

[A San Francisco ordinance made it unlawful to operate a laundry without the consent of the board of supervisors except in a brick or stone building. Yick Wo, a Chinese alien who had operated a laundry for 22 years, had certificates from the health and fire authorities, but was refused consent by the board. It was admitted that "there were about 320 laundries in the city [and] about 240 were owned [by] subjects of China, and of the whole number, viz., 320, about 310 were constructed of wood"; that "petitioner, and more than 150 of his countrymen, have been arrested" for violating the ordinance "while those who are not subjects of China, and who are conducting 80 odd laundries under similar conditions, are left unmolested."]

[T]he facts shown establish an administration directed so exclusively against a particular class of persons as to warrant and require the conclusion that, whatever may have been the intent of the ordinances as adopted, they are applied [with] a mind so unequal and oppressive as to amount to a practical denial by the State of [equal protection]. Though the law itself be fair on its face and impartial in appearance, yet, if it is applied and administered by public authority with an evil eye and an unequal hand, so as practically to make unjust and illegal discriminations between persons in similar circumstances, material to their rights, the denial of equal justice is still within the prohibition of the Constitution. [The] fact of this discrimination is admitted. No reason for it is shown, and the conclusion cannot be resisted that no reason for it exists except hostility to [Yick Wo's] race and nationality * * *.

Notes and Questions

1. *Proving intentional discrimination.* (a) *Jury selection.* In CASTANEDA v. PARTIDA, 430 U.S. 482, 97 S.Ct. 1272, 51 L.Ed.2d 498 (1977), respondent challenged the grand jury that indicted him in 1972. He showed that, although 79% of the county's population had Spanish surnames, the average percentage of Spanish-surnamed grand jurors between 1962–72 was 39%. In 1972, 52.5% of persons on the grand jury list had Spanish surnames as did 50% of those on respondent's grand jury list. The Court, per BLACKMUN, J., held that respondent had established a prima facie case of discrimination against Mexican-Americans: "While the earlier cases involved absolute exclusion of an identifiable group, later cases established the principle that substantial underrepresentation of the group constitutes a constitutional violation as well, if it results from purposeful discrimination. [T]he degree of underrepresentation must be proved, by comparing the proportion of the group in the total population to the proportion called to serve as grand jurors, over a significant period of time.[13] [A] selection procedure that is susceptible of abuse or is not racially neutral supports the presumption of discrimination raised by the statistical showing.[a] Once the defendant has shown substantial underrepresentation of his group, he has made out a prima facie case

13. [If] a disparity is sufficiently large, then it is unlikely that it is due solely to chance or accident, and, in the absence of evidence to the contrary, one must conclude that racial or other class-related factors entered into the selection process.

a. The Court observed that, "as in *Alexander v. Louisiana,* 405 U.S. 625, 92 S.Ct. 1221, 31 L.Ed.2d 536 (1972), the selection procedure [here] is not racially neutral with respect to Mexican-Americans; Spanish surnames are just as easily identifiable as race was from the questionnaires in *Alexander* or the notations and card colors in *Whitus v. Georgia,* 385 U.S. 545, 87 S.Ct. 643, 17 L.Ed.2d 599 (1967)."

of discriminatory purpose, and the burden then shifts to the State to rebut that case." [b]

Should the state's proof that a majority of the jury commissioners were Mexican-American rebut the prima facie case? A majority of elected officials in the county? See *Castaneda*.[c]

(b) *Deference to factfinder:* The trial court's decision on the ultimate question of discriminatory intent represents a finding of fact of the sort accorded great deference on appeal, particularly on issues of credibility. *Hernandez v. New York,* 500 U.S. 352, 111 S.Ct. 1859, 114 L.Ed.2d 395 (1991).

(c) *Executive appointments.* In MAYOR OF PHILA. v. EDUCATIONAL EQUALITY LEAGUE, 415 U.S. 605, 94 S.Ct. 1323, 39 L.Ed.2d 630 (1974), respondents contended that in 1971 the mayor had racially discriminated in appointments to the city's Nominating Panel for school board members. Under the city charter, the Panel had thirteen persons—four appointed from the citizenry at large and the others being the highest-ranking officers of nine city-wide organizations (e.g., labor union council, commerce group, parent-teacher association, etc.). Approximately "34% of the population of Philadelphia and approximately 60% of the students attending the city's various schools were Negroes" but "the 1971 Panel had 11 whites and two Negroes." The Court, per POWELL, J., held the proof "too fragmentary and speculative" to establish "a prima facie case of racial discrimination." The statistics were "simplistic percentage comparisons [in] the context of this case"; because of the designated qualifications for Panel members, it could not "be assumed that all citizens are fungible for purposes of determining whether members of a particular class have been unlawfully excluded." [d]

2. *Criminal enforcement.* If an African–American prosecuted for violating a gambling ordinance shows that the law is enforced only against blacks, may the police justify their conduct on the ground that, since *most* gambling was believed to be taking place in black residential areas, *all* the "gambling squad" was assigned there? Is this different from a state justifying its exclusion of *all* African–Americans from jury service because *most* did not possess adequate educational qualifications? See generally Sheri L. Johnson, *Race and the Decision to Detain a Suspect,* 93 Yale L.J. 214 (1983). Is *Yick Wo* distinguishable from the gambling hypothetical because, in *Yick Wo,* "*no* reason for [the discrimination was] shown" and "*no* reason for it exists except hostility to the race"?

3. *Peremptory challenge.* BATSON v. KENTUCKY, 476 U.S. 79, 106 S.Ct. 1712, 90 L.Ed.2d 69 (1986), per POWELL, J.—declining to follow *Swain v. Alabama,* 380 U.S. 202, 85 S.Ct. 824, 13 L.Ed.2d 759 (1965)—held that, using the same "combination of factors" as in cases like *Castaneda,* "a defendant may establish a prima facie case of purposeful discrimination in selection of the petit jury solely on evidence concerning the prosecutor's exercise of peremptory challenges at the defendant's trial. [Then], the burden shifts to the State to come forward with a neutral explanation for challenging black jurors. [T]he prosecution's explanation need not rise to the level justifying exercise of a challenge for cause. [B]ut the prosecutor may not rebut the defendant's prima facie case of discrimination by

b. Burger, C.J., and Stewart, Powell and Rehnquist, JJ., dissented.

c. See generally Michael O. Finkelstein, *The Application of Statistical Decision Theory to the Jury Discrimination Cases,* 80 Harv. L.Rev. 338 (1966); Comment, *The Civil Peti-*

tioner's Right to Representative Grand Juries and a Statistical Method of Showing Discrimination in Jury Selection Cases Generally, 20 U.C.L.A.L.Rev. 581 (1973).

d. White, J., joined by Douglas, Brennan and Marshall, JJ., dissented.

stating merely that he challenged jurors of the defendant's race on the assumption—or his intuitive judgment—that they would be partial to the defendant because of their shared race, [because the] core guarantee of equal protection, ensuring citizens that their State will not discriminate on account of race, would be meaningless" if this were permitted.

REHNQUIST, J., joined by Burger, C.J., dissented: "[T]here is simply nothing 'unequal' about the State using its peremptory challenges to strike blacks from the jury in cases involving black defendants, so long as such challenges are also used to exclude whites in cases involving white defendants, Hispanics in cases involving Hispanic defendants, Asians in cases involving Asian defendants, and so on." [e]

4. *Capital sentencing.* McCLESKEY v. KEMP, whose facts are set forth in detail at p. 482 supra, per POWELL, J., rejected petitioner's claim "that the Baldus study compels an inference that his sentence rests on purposeful discrimination." Unlike the jury selection cases, where "the factors that may be considered are limited, usually by state [statute], each particular decision to impose the death penalty is made by a [jury] unique in its composition, and the Constitution requires that its decision rest on consideration of innumerable factors that vary according to the characteristics of the individual defendant and the facts of the particular capital offense." Further, unlike the jury selection context, "here, the State has no practical opportunity to rebut the Baldus study" because "policy considerations" (1) "dictate that jurors [not] be called [to] testify to the motives and influences that led to their verdict" and (2) "suggest the impropriety of our requiring prosecutors to defend their decisions to seek death penalties, often years after they were made." [17] Finally, implementation of laws against murder, which are "at the heart of the State's criminal justice system, [requires] discretionary judgments. [W]e would demand exceptionally clear proof before we would infer that the discretion has been abused."

BLACKMUN, J., joined by Brennan, Marshall and Stevens, JJ., dissented, reviewing parts of the Baldus study in detail: "I concentrate on the decisions within the prosecutor's office through which the State decided to seek the death penalty and, in particular, the point at which the State proceeded to the penalty phase after conviction. This is a step at which the evidence of the effect of the racial factors was especially strong" and not adequately rebutted by the state.

"I agree [as] to the difficulty of examining the jury's decisionmaking process [but not with the] Court's refusal to require that the prosecutor provide an explanation for his actions * * *. Prosecutors undoubtedly need adequate discretion to allocate the resources of their offices and to fulfill their responsibilities to

---

e. *Georgia v. McCollum,* 505 U.S. 42, 112 S.Ct. 2348, 120 L.Ed.2d 33 (1992), per Blackmun, J., extended *Batson* and *Edmonson v. Leesville Concrete Co.,* p. 1461, infra (holding *Batson* applicable to civil litigants) to peremptory challenges by a criminal defendant: "Just as public confidence in criminal justice is undermined by a conviction in a trial where racial discrimination has occurred in jury selection, so is public confidence undermined where a defendant, assisted by racially discriminatory peremptory strikes, obtains an acquittal."

O'Connor and Scalia, JJ., dissented on the ground that there was no "state action" (as discussed in her dissent in *Edmonson*). Rehnquist, C.J. and Thomas, J., agreed, but con-

curred in the judgment because "*Edmonson* governs this case." On the merits, Thomas, J., added: "In *Strauder,* we put the rights of defendants foremost. Today's decision, while protecting jurors, leaves defendants with less means of protecting themselves. [B]lack criminal defendants will rue the day that this court ventured down this road that inexorably will lead to the elimination of peremptory strikes."

17. Requiring a prosecutor to rebut a study that analyzes the past conduct of scores of prosecutors is quite different from requiring a prosecutor to rebut a contemporaneous challenge to his own acts. See *Batson.*

the public in deciding how best to enforce the law, but this does not place them beyond the constraints imposed on state action under the Fourteenth Amendment.

WASHINGTON v. DAVIS

426 U.S. 229, 96 S.Ct. 2040, 48 L.Ed.2d 597 (1976).

JUSTICE WHITE delivered the opinion of the Court.

This case involves the validity of a qualifying test administered to applicants for positions as police officers in the District of Columbia. [T]he police recruit was required to satisfy certain physical and character standards, to be a high school graduate or its equivalent and to receive a grade of at least 40 out of 80 on "Test 21," which is "an examination that is used generally throughout the federal service," which "was developed by the Civil Service Commission, not the Police Department," and which was "designed to test verbal ability, vocabulary, reading and comprehension."

[The] District Court rejected the assertion that Test 21 was culturally slanted to favor whites and was "satisfied that the undisputable facts prove the test to be reasonably and directly related to the requirements of the police recruit training program and that it is neither so designed nor operates to discriminate against otherwise qualified blacks." [The Court of Appeals held] that lack of discriminatory intent in designing and administering Test 21 was irrelevant; the critical fact was rather [that] four times as many [blacks] failed the test than did whites. This disproportionate impact [was] held sufficient to establish a constitutional violation, absent proof by petitioners that the test was an adequate measure of job performance in addition to being an indicator of probable success in the training program, a burden which the court ruled petitioners had failed to discharge. * * *

The central purpose of the Equal Protection Clause [is] the prevention of official conduct discriminating on the basis of race. [But] our cases have not embraced the proposition that a law or other official act, without regard to whether it reflects a racially discriminatory purpose, is unconstitutional *solely* because it has a racially disproportionate impact.

Almost 100 years ago, *Strauder* established that the exclusion of Negroes from grand and petit juries in criminal proceedings violated the Equal Protection Clause, but the fact that a particular jury or a series of juries does not statistically reflect the racial composition of the community does not in itself make out an invidious discrimination forbidden by the Clause. "A purpose to discriminate must be present which may be proven by systematic exclusion of eligible jurymen of the prescribed race or by an unequal application of the law to such an extent as to show intentional discrimination." * * *

The school desegregation cases have also adhered to the basic equal protection principle that the invidious quality of a law claimed to be racially discriminatory must ultimately be traced to a racially discriminatory purpose. That there are both predominantly black and predominantly white schools in a community is not alone violative of the Equal Protection Clause. The essential element ["differentiating] between de jure segregation and so-called de facto segregation [is] *purpose* or *intent* to segregate." *Keyes v. School Dist.*, [Part IV infra].

This is not to say that the necessary discriminatory racial purpose must be express or appear on the face of the statute, or that a law's disproportionate impact is irrelevant. [A] statute, otherwise neutral on its face, must not be applied so as invidiously to discriminate on the basis of race. *Yick Wo.* It is also clear from the cases dealing with racial discrimination in the selection of juries that [a] prima facie case of discriminatory purpose may be proved [by] the absence of Negroes on a particular jury combined with the failure of the jury commissioners to be informed of eligible Negro jurors in a community, or with racially non-neutral selection procedures. With a prima facie case made out, "the burden of proof shifts to the State to rebut the presumption of unconstitutional action by showing that permissible racially neutral selection criteria and procedures have produced the monochromatic result."

Necessarily, an invidious discriminatory purpose may often be inferred from the totality of the relevant facts, including [that] the law bears more heavily on one race than another. It is also not infrequently true that the discriminatory impact—in the jury cases for example, the total or seriously disproportionate exclusion of Negroes from jury venires—may for all practical purposes demonstrate unconstitutionality because in various circumstances the discrimination is very difficult to explain on nonracial grounds. Nevertheless, we have not held that a law, neutral on its face and serving ends otherwise within the power of government to pursue, is invalid under the Equal Protection Clause simply because it may affect a greater proportion of one race than of another. Disproportionate impact [s]tanding alone [does] not trigger the rule that racial classifications are to be subjected to the strictest scrutiny and are justifiable only by the weightiest of considerations.

There are some indications to the contrary in our cases. In *Palmer v. Thompson,* 403 U.S. 217, 91 S.Ct. 1940, 29 L.Ed.2d 438 (1971), the city of Jackson, Miss., following a court decree to this effect, desegregated all of its public facilities save five swimming pools which [were] closed by ordinance pursuant to a determination by the city council that closure was necessary to preserve peace and order and that integrated pools could not be economically operated. [T]his Court rejected the argument that [the] otherwise seemingly permissible ends served by the ordinance could be impeached by demonstrating that racially invidious motivations had prompted the city council's action. [W]hatever dicta the opinion may contain, the decision did not involve, much less invalidate, a statute or ordinance having neutral purposes but disproportionate racial consequences.[11]

[Test 21] seeks to ascertain whether those who take it have acquired a particular level of verbal skill; and it is untenable that the Constitution prevents the government from seeking modestly to upgrade the communicative abilities of its employees rather than to be satisfied with some lower level of competence, particularly where the job requires special ability to communicate orally and in writing. Respondents, as Negroes, could no more successfully claim that the test denied them equal protection than could white applicants who also failed. The conclusion would not be different in the face of proof that more Negroes than whites had been disqualified by Test 21. * * *

Nor on the facts of the case before us would the disproportionate impact of Test 21 warrant the conclusion that it is a purposeful device to discriminate against Negroes * * *. [T]he test is neutral on its face and rationally may be said to serve a purpose the government is constitutionally empowered to pursue. Even

---

11. To the extent that *Palmer* suggests a generally applicable proposition that legislative purpose is irrelevant in constitutional adjudication, our prior cases—as indicated in the text—are to the contrary; and very shortly after *Palmer,* all Members of the Court majority in that case [joined] *Lemon v. Kurtzman,* [p. 951 supra], [that] the validity of public aid to church-related schools includes close inquiry into the purpose of the challenged statute.

agreeing with the District Court that the differential racial effect of Test 21 called for further inquiry, we think the District Court correctly held that the affirmative efforts of the Metropolitan Police Department to recruit black officers, the changing racial composition of the recruit classes and of the force in general, and the relationship of the test to the training program negated any inference that the Department discriminated on the basis of race * * *.

Under Title VII [of the Civil Rights Act of 1964], Congress provided that when hiring and promotion practices disqualifying substantially disproportionate numbers of blacks are challenged, discriminatory purpose need not be proved, and that it is an insufficient response to demonstrate some rational basis for the challenged practices. It is necessary, in addition, that they be "validated" in terms of job performance * * *. However this process proceeds, it involves a more probing judicial review of, and less deference to, the seemingly reasonable acts of administrators and executives than is appropriate under the Constitution where special racial impact, without discriminatory purpose, is claimed. We are not disposed to adopt this more rigorous standard for the purposes of applying the Fifth and the Fourteenth Amendments in cases such as this.

A rule that a statute designed to serve neutral ends is nevertheless invalid, absent compelling justification, if in practice it benefits or burdens one race more than another would be far-reaching and would raise serious questions about, and perhaps invalidate, a whole range of tax, welfare, public service, regulatory, and licensing statutes that may be more burdensome to the poor and to the average black than to the more affluent white.[14]

Given that rule, such consequences would perhaps be likely to follow. However, in our view, extension of the rule beyond those areas where it is already applicable by reason of statute, such as in the field of public employment, should await legislative prescription. * * * a

JUSTICE STEVENS [who joined the Court's opinion] concurring. * * *

The requirement of purposeful discrimination is a common thread running through the cases summarized [by the Court. But] in each of these contexts, the burden of proving a prima facie case may well involve differing evidentiary considerations. The extent of deference that one pays to the trial court's

---

14. Frank I. Goodman, *De Facto School Segregation: A Constitutional and Empirical Analysis,* 60 Calif.L.Rev. 275, 300 (1972), suggests that disproportionate-impact analysis might invalidate "tests and qualifications for voting, draft deferment, public employment, jury service, and other government-conferred [benefits]; [s]ales taxes, bail schedules, utility rates, bridge tolls, license fees, and other state-imposed charges." It has also been argued that minimum wage and usury laws as well as professional licensing requirements would require major modifications in light of the un-equal-impact rule. William Silverman, *Equal Protection, Economic Legislation, and Racial Discrimination,* 25 Vand.L.Rev. 1183 (1972). * * *

a. The Court also found no violation of the relevant statutory provisions. Stewart, J., joined only the constitutional aspects of the Court's opinion. Brennan, J., joined by Marshall, J., did not address the constitutional questions but dissented on statutory grounds.

For detailed criticism of this decision, as well as many others, for enshrining the "perpetrator perspective" of racial discrimination and ignoring the "victim perspective," see Alan D. Freeman, *Legitimizing Racial Discrimination Through Antidiscrimination Law: A Critical Review of Supreme Court Doctrine,* 62 Minn. L.Rev. 1049 (1978). For the view that *Davis* resolved two "competing institutional concerns"—(1) making "meaningful inquiries into legislative motive in order to discern the presence of discriminatory intent" is "difficult and inappropriate," and (2) "applying strict scrutiny in all disparate impact cases would engage the courts too extensively in overseeing social policy"—"in a direction adverse to the interests of substantive racial justice," see Barbara J. Flagg, *Enduring Principles: On Race, Process, and Constitutional Law,* 82 Calif.L.Rev. 935 (1994).

determination of the factual issue, and indeed, the extent to which one characterizes the intent issue as a question of fact or a question of law, will vary in different contexts.

Frequently the most probative evidence of intent will be objective evidence of what actually happened rather than evidence describing the subjective state of mind of the actor. For normally the actor is presumed to have intended the natural consequences of his deeds. This is particularly true in the case of governmental action which is frequently the product of compromise, of collective decisionmaking, and of mixed motivation. It is unrealistic, on the one hand, to require the victim of alleged discrimination to uncover the actual subjective intent of the decisionmaker or conversely, to invalidate otherwise legitimate action simply because an improper motive affected the deliberation of a participant in the decisional process. A law conscripting clerics should not be invalidated because an atheist voted for it.[b]

My point [is] to suggest that the line between discriminatory purpose and discriminatory impact is not nearly as bright, and perhaps not quite as critical, as the reader of the Court's opinion might assume. I agree [that] a constitutional issue does not arise every time some disproportionate impact is shown. On the other hand, when the disproportion is as dramatic as in *Gomillion v. Lightfoot*, 364 U.S. 339, 81 S.Ct. 125, 5 L.Ed.2d 110 (1960)[c] or *Yick Wo*, it really does not matter whether the standard is phrased in terms of purpose or effect. * * *

There are two reasons why I am convinced that the challenge to Test 21 is insufficient. First, the test serves the neutral and legitimate purpose of requiring all applicants to meet a uniform minimum standard of literacy. Reading ability is manifestly relevant to the police function, there is no evidence that the required passing grade was set at an arbitrarily high level, and there is sufficient disparity among high schools and high school graduates to justify the use of a separate uniform test. Second, the same test is used throughout the federal service. The applicants for employment in the District of Columbia Police Department represent such a small fraction of the total number of persons who have taken the test

---

b. See also Todd Rakoff, *Washington v. Davis and the Objective Theory of Contracts*, 29 Harv.Civ.Rts.Civ.Lib.L.Rev. 63, 72–73, 81–82, 86 (1994): "[I]n most decisions of consequence, there are many officials involved. [L]egislation is passed by a body with a large number of members, and usually bears the signature of a chief executive as well. Moreover, [a]nyone who thinks that an executive regulation, for example, represents the determination of a chief executive, or even of the official titularly in charge of the issuing department, rather than the corporate judgement of a large number of staff members, does not understand the administrative reality. [But] even if the intent of each official were known, and even if we had a calculus of official motives, would we know all that we need to know? Many officials, if they were candid—and after all, on this view what we want to know is exactly what they really did think—would tell us that they acted as they did in large part because of political pressures originating outside of government: pressures from constituents, from contributors and supporters, from organized lobbies. Should a court trace these pressures? [What *should* matter],

in addition to the effects of official action, is not the intent of the few officials, but the social meaning of what transpired [as measured by] the well-worn doctrinal formulation of the objective test—how would the reasonable person view the matter in light of the evidence—as referring to actual cultural interpretations without being necessarily fictitious."

c. In *Gomillion*, an Alabama statute changed the Tuskegee city boundaries from a square to a 28 sided figure, allegedly removing "all save only four or five of its 400 Negro voters while not removing a single white voter or resident." The Court held that the complaint "amply alleges a claim of racial discrimination" in violation of the fifteenth amendment: "If these allegations upon a trial remained uncontradicted or unqualified, the conclusion would be irresistible, tantamount for all practical purposes to a mathematical demonstration, that the legislation is solely concerned with segregating white and colored voters by fencing Negro citizens out of town so as to deprive them of their pre-existing municipal vote."

that their experience is of minimal probative value [to] overcome the presumption that a test which is this widely used by the Federal Government is in fact neutral in its effect as well as its "purpose" as that term is used in constitutional adjudication. * * *

———

ARLINGTON HEIGHTS v. METROPOLITAN HOUSING DEV. CORP., 429 U.S. 252, 97 S.Ct. 555, 50 L.Ed.2d 450 (1977), per POWELL, J.—holding that petitioner Village's refusal to rezone land from single-family (R–3) to multiple-family (R–5), so as to permit respondent MHDC's construction of racially integrated housing, did not violate equal protection—amplified *Davis:*

"*Davis* does not require a plaintiff to prove that the challenged action rested solely on racially discriminatory purposes. Rarely can it be said that a legislature or administrative body operating under a broad mandate made a decision motivated solely by a single concern, or even that a particular purpose was the 'dominant' or 'primary' one. In fact, it is because legislators and administrators are properly concerned with balancing numerous competing considerations that courts refrain from reviewing the merits of their decisions, absent a showing of arbitrariness or irrationality. But racial discrimination is not just another competing consideration. When there is proof that a discriminatory purpose has been a motivating factor in the decision, this judicial deference is no longer justified.[12]

"Determining whether invidious discriminatory purpose was a motivating factor demands a sensitive inquiry into such circumstantial and direct evidence of intent as may be available. The impact of the official action [may] provide an important starting point. Sometimes a clear pattern, unexplainable on grounds other than race, emerges from the effect of the state action even when the governing legislation appears neutral on its face. *Yick Wo; Guinn v. United States,* 238 U.S. 347, 35 S.Ct. 926, 59 L.Ed. 1340 (1915); *Lane v. Wilson,* 307 U.S. 268, 59 S.Ct. 872, 83 L.Ed. 1281 (1939);[a] *Gomillion.* The evidentiary inquiry is then relatively easy.[13] But such cases are rare. Absent a pattern as stark as that in *Gomillion* or *Yick Wo,* impact alone is not determinative,[14] and the Court must look to other evidence.[15]

12. For a scholarly discussion of legislative motivation, see Paul Brest, *Palmer v. Thompson: An Approach to The Problem of Unconstitutional Motive,* 1971 Sup.Ct. 95, 116–118. [See also John H. Ely, *Legislative and Administrative Motivation in Constitutional Law,* 79 Yale L.J. 1205 (1970).]

a. *Guinn* held that Oklahoma's literacy test for voting violated the fifteenth amendment because its "grandfather clause" effectively exempted whites. Oklahoma then immediately enacted a new law providing that all persons who previously voted were qualified for life but that all others must register within a twelve day period or be permanently disenfranchised. *Lane held that this new law violated the fifteenth amendment.*

13. Several of our jury selection cases fall into this category. Because of the nature of the jury selection task, however, we have permitted a finding of constitutional violation even when the statistical pattern does not approach the extremes of *Yick Wo* or *Gomillion.*

[For the view that the Court has used the allocation of burden of proof in respect to discriminatory purpose or intent to obscure its own "balancing of competing individual and public interests" and its own "making many of the ultimate value choices implicit in equal protection," see Daniel R. Ortiz, *The Myth of Intent in Equal Protection,* 41 Stan.L.Rev. 1105 (1989).]

14. This is not to say that a consistent pattern of official racial discrimination is a necessary predicate to a violation of [equal protection]. A single invidiously discriminatory governmental act—in the exercise of the zoning power as elsewhere—would not necessarily be immunized by the absence of such discrimination in the making of other comparable decisions.

15. In many instances, to recognize the limited probative value of disproportionate impact is merely to acknowledge the "heterogeneity" of the nation's population.

"The historical background of the decision is one evidentiary source, particularly if it reveals a series of official actions taken for invidious purposes. See *Lane*. The specific sequence of events leading up to the challenged decision also may shed some light on the decision-maker's purposes. *Reitman v. Mulkey*, [p. 1344 infra]. For example, if the property involved here always had been zoned R–5 but suddenly was changed to R–3 when the town learned of MHDC's plans to erect integrated housing, we would have a far different case. Departures from the normal procedural sequence also might afford evidence that improper purposes are playing a role. Substantive departures too may be relevant, particularly if the factors usually considered important by the decisionmaker strongly favor a decision contrary to the one reached.

"The legislative or administrative history may be highly relevant, especially where there are contemporary statements by members of the decisionmaking body, minutes of its meetings, or reports. In some extraordinary instances the members might be called to the stand at trial to testify concerning the purpose of the official action, although even then such testimony frequently will be barred by privilege. See *Tenney v. Brandhove*, 341 U.S. 367, 71 S.Ct. 783, 95 L.Ed. 1019 (1951); *United States v. Nixon*, 418 U.S. 683, 94 S.Ct. 3090, 41 L.Ed.2d 1039 (1974).[18]

"[This] summary identifies, without purporting to be exhaustive, subjects of proper inquiry in determining whether racially discriminatory intent existed."

Both courts below found that the rezoning denial was not racially motivated.

"We also have reviewed the evidence. The impact of the Village's decision does arguably bear more heavily on racial minorities. [But] there is little about the sequence of events leading up to the decision that would spark suspicion. The area [has] been zoned R–3 since 1959, the year when Arlington Heights first adopted a zoning map. Single-family homes surround the 80-acre site, and the Village is undeniably committed to single-family homes as its dominant residential land use. The rezoning request progressed according to the usual procedures. * * *

"The statements by the Plan Commission and Village Board members, as reflected in the official minutes, focused almost exclusively on the zoning aspects of the MHDC petition, and the zoning factors on which they relied are not novel criteria in the Village's rezoning decisions. * * * MHDC called one member of the Village Board to the stand at trial. Nothing in her testimony supports an inference of invidious purpose.

"In sum, [r]espondents simply failed to carry their burden of proving that discriminatory purpose was a motivating factor in the Village's decision.[21] This conclusion ends the constitutional inquiry." [b]

---

18. This Court has recognized, ever since *Fletcher v. Peck* [p. 48 supra], that judicial inquiries into legislative or executive motivation represent a substantial intrusion into the workings of other branches of government. Placing a decisionmaker on the stand is therefore "usually to be avoided."

21. Proof that the decision by the Village was motivated in part by a racially discriminatory purpose would not necessarily have required invalidation of the challenged decision. Such proof would, however, have shifted to the Village the burden of establishing that the same decision would have resulted even had the impermissible purpose not been considered. If this were established, the complaining party in a case of this kind no longer fairly could attribute the injury complained of to improper consideration of a discriminatory purpose.

b. The Court remanded for further consideration of respondents' claims under the Fair Housing Act. Marshall, J., joined by Brennan, J., concurred in the Court's substantive discussion but, along with White, J., would have

PERSONNEL ADMINISTRATOR v. FEENEY, 442 U.S. 256, 99 S.Ct. 2282, 60 L.Ed.2d 870 (1979), per STEWART, J.,—relying on *Davis* and *Arlington Heights*—upheld Massachusetts' "absolute lifetime preference to veterans" for state civil service positions, even though "the preference operates overwhelmingly to the advantage of males" [a]: "When a statute gender-neutral on its face is challenged on the ground that its effects upon women are disproportionately adverse, a two-fold inquiry [is] appropriate. The first question is whether the statutory classification is indeed neutral * * *. If the classification itself, covert or overt, is not based upon gender, the second question is whether the adverse effect reflects invidious gender-based discrimination. In this second inquiry, impact provides an 'important starting point,' *Arlington Heights,* but purposeful discrimination is 'the condition that offends the Constitution.'"

As to the first question, "The District Court [found] first, that ch. 31 serves legitimate and worthy purposes; second, that the absolute preference was not established for the purpose of discriminating against women. [Thus,] the distinction between veterans and nonveterans drawn by ch. 31 is not a pretext for gender discrimination. * * *

"If the impact of this statute could not be plausibly explained on a neutral ground, impact itself would signal that the real classification made by the law was in fact not neutral. But there can be but one answer to the question whether this veteran preference excludes significant numbers of women from preferred state jobs because they are women or because they are nonveterans. [Although] few women benefit from the preference, * * * significant numbers of nonveterans are men, and [too] many men are affected by ch. 31 to permit the inference that the statute is but a pretext for preferring men over women. * * *

"The dispositive question, then, is whether the appellee has shown that a gender-based discriminatory purpose has, at least in some measure, shaped [ch. 31. Her] contention that this veterans' preference is 'inherently non-neutral' or 'gender-biased' presumes that the State, by favoring veterans, intentionally incorporated into its public employment policies the panoply of sex-based and assertedly discriminatory federal laws that have prevented all but a handful of women from becoming veterans. There are two serious difficulties with this argument. First, it is wholly at odds with the District Court's central finding that Massachusetts has not offered a preference to veterans for the purpose of discriminating against women. Second, [t]o the extent that the status of veteran is one that few women have been enabled to achieve, every hiring preference for veterans, however modest or extreme, is inherently gender-biased. If Massachusetts by offering such a preference can be said intentionally to have incorporated into its state employment policies the historical gender-based federal military personnel practices, the degree of the preference would or should make no constitutional difference. Invidious discrimination does not become less so because the discrimination accomplished is of a lesser magnitude.[23] Discriminatory intent is simply

---

remanded "this entire case [for] further proceedings consistent with *Davis.*" Stevens, J., did not participate.

On remand, the court of appeals held that proof of a discriminatory purpose was not required to find a violation of the Fair Housing Act. 558 F.2d 1283 (7th Cir.1977), cert. denied, 434 U.S. 1025, 98 S.Ct. 752, 54 L.Ed.2d 772 (1978).

a. Sex discrimination is considered in Sec. 3, II infra. Although not been held to be

"suspect," it has been held to be subject to special judicial scrutiny and the Court's approach to the "purpose" vs. "impact" issue has been similar to cases involving discrimination against racial or ethnic minorities.

23. This is not to say that the degree of impact is irrelevant to the question of intent. But it is to say that a more modest preference, while it might well lessen impact and, as the State argues, might lessen the effectiveness of the statute in helping veterans, would not be

not amenable to calibration. It either is a factor that has influenced the legislative choice or it is not. The District Court's conclusion that the absolute veterans' preference was not originally enacted or subsequently reaffirmed for the purpose of giving an advantage to males as such necessarily compels the conclusion that the State intended nothing more than to prefer 'veterans.' * * *

"To be sure, this case is unusual in that it involves a law that by design is not neutral. [As] opposed to the written test at issue in *Davis,* it does not purport to define a job related characteristic. To the contrary, it confers upon a specifically described group—perceived to be particularly deserving—a competitive head start. But the District Court found, and the appellee has not disputed, that this legislative choice was legitimate. [Thus, it] must be analyzed as is any other neutral law that casts a greater burden upon women as a group than upon men as a group. The enlistment policies of the armed services may well have discriminated on the basis of sex. But the history of discrimination against women in the military is not on trial in this case.

"The appellee's ultimate argument rests upon the presumption, common to the criminal and civil law, that a person intends the natural and foreseeable consequences of his voluntary actions. * * *

" 'Discriminatory purpose,' however, implies more than intent as volition or intent as awareness of consequences. It implies that the decisionmaker, in this case a state legislature, selected or reaffirmed a particular course of action at least in part 'because of,' not merely 'in spite of,' its adverse effects upon an identifiable group.[25] Yet nothing in the record demonstrates that this preference for veterans was originally devised or subsequently re-enacted because it would accomplish the collateral goal of keeping women in a stereotypic and predefined place in the Massachusetts Civil Service."

STEVENS, J., joined by White, J., concurred in the Court's opinion, adding: "[F]or me the answer is largely provided by the fact that the number of males disadvantaged by Massachusetts' Veterans Preference (1,867,000) is sufficiently large—and sufficiently close to the number of disadvantaged females (2,954,000)— to refute the claim that the rule was intended to benefit males as a class over females as a class."

MARSHALL, J., joined by Brennan, J., dissented: "In my judgment, [ch. 31] evinces purposeful gender-based discrimination. * * *

"That a legislature seeks to advantage one group does not, as a matter of logic or of common sense, exclude the possibility that it also intends to disadvantage another. Individuals in general and lawmakers in particular frequently act for a variety of reasons. [S]ince reliable evidence of subjective intentions is seldom obtainable, resort to inference based on objective factors is generally unavoidable. To discern the purposes underlying facially neutral policies, this Court has therefore considered the degree, inevitability, and foreseeability of any disproportionate impact as well as the alternatives reasonably available.

any more or less "neutral" in the constitutional sense.

25. This is not to say that the inevitability or foreseeability of consequences of a neutral rule has no bearing upon the existence of discriminatory intent. Certainly, when the adverse consequences of a law upon an identifiable group are as inevitable as the gender-based consequences of ch. 31, a strong inference that the adverse effects were desired can

reasonably be drawn. But in this inquiry— made as it is under the Constitution—an inference is a working tool, not a synonym for proof. When as here, the impact is essentially an unavoidable consequence of a legislative policy that has in itself always been deemed to be legitimate, and when, as here, the statutory history and all of the available evidence affirmatively demonstrate the opposite, the inference simply fails to ripen into proof.

"[T]he impact of the Massachusetts statute on women is undisputed. Any veteran with a passing grade on the civil service exam must be placed ahead of a nonveteran, regardless of their respective scores. [Because] less than 2% of the women in Massachusetts are veterans, the absolute preference formula has rendered desirable state civil service employment an almost exclusively male prerogative. [Where] the foreseeable impact of a facially neutral policy is so disproportionate, the burden should rest on the State to establish that sex-based considerations played no part in the choice of the particular legislative scheme.

"Clearly, that burden was not sustained here. The legislative history of the statute reflects the Commonwealth's patent appreciation of the impact the preference system would have on women, and an equally evident desire to mitigate that impact only with respect to certain traditionally female occupations. Until 1971, the statute [and] regulations exempted from operation of the preference any job requisitions 'especially calling for women.' In practice, this exemption, coupled with the absolute preference for veterans, has created a gender-based civil service hierarchy, with women occupying low grade clerical and secretarial jobs and men holding more responsible and remunerative positions. [Particularly] when viewed against the range of less discriminatory alternatives available to assist veterans,[2] Massachusetts's choice of a formula that so severely restricts public employment opportunities for women cannot reasonably be thought gender-neutral. The Court's conclusion to the contrary—that 'nothing in the record' evinces a 'collateral goal of keeping women in a stereotypic and predefined place in the Massachusetts Civil Service'—displays a singularly myopic view of the facts established below.[3]"

MOBILE v. BOLDEN, Sec. 4, I, A infra, involved the question of whether a fifteenth amendment violation requires "discriminatory purpose." STEWART, J., joined by Burger, C.J., and Powell and Rehnquist, JJ., relying on *Guinn, Lane* and *Gomillion,* found that it did. WHITE, J., appeared to avoid explicitly addressing the question, finding that the election scheme at issue had a discriminatory purpose. BLACKMUN, J., "assuming that proof of intent is a prerequisite," agreed with White, J.'s finding. STEVENS, J., did not directly address the question, but disagreed with Stewart, J.'s "reach[ing] out to decide [it]."

MARSHALL, J., dissented: "*Davis* required a showing of discriminatory purpose to support racial discrimination claims largely because it feared that a standard based solely on disproportionate impact would unduly interfere with the far-ranging governmental distribution of constitutional gratuities [citing *Davis'* text at fn. 14]. Underlying the Court's decision was a determination that, since the Constitution does not entitle any person to such governmental benefits, courts should accord discretion to those officials who decide how the government shall allocate its scarce resources. * * *

2. Only four States afford a preference comparable in [scope]. Other States and the Federal Government grant point or tie-breaking preferences that do not foreclose opportunities for women.

3. Although it is relevant that the preference statute also disadvantages a substantial group of men, it is equally pertinent that 47% of Massachusetts men over 18 are veterans, as compared to 0.8% of Massachusetts women. Given this disparity, and the indicia of intent noted supra, the absolute number of men denied preference cannot be dispositive, especially since they have not faced the barriers to achieving veteran status confronted by women.

"Such judicial deference to official decisionmaking has no place under the Fifteenth Amendment. Section 1 of that Amendment differs from the Fourteenth Amendment's prohibition on racial discrimination in two crucial respects: it explicitly recognizes the right to vote free of hindrances related to race, and it sweeps no further. [The] right to vote is of such fundamental importance in the constitutional scheme that the Fifteenth Amendment's command that it shall not be 'abridged' on account of race must be interpreted as providing that the votes of citizens of all races shall be of substantially equal weight. Furthermore, a disproportionate-impact test under the Fifteenth Amendment would not lead to constant judicial intrusion into the process of official decisionmaking. Rather, the standard would reach only those decisions having a discriminatory effect upon the minority's vote. The Fifteenth Amendment cannot tolerate that kind of decision, even if made in good faith, because the Amendment grants racial minorities the full enjoyment of the right to vote, not simply protection against the unfairness of intentional vote dilution along racial lines.[32]

"In addition, it is beyond dispute that a standard based solely upon the motives of official decisionmakers creates significant problems of proof [and] creates the risk that officials will be able to adopt policies that are the products of discriminatory intent so long as they sufficiently mask their motives through the use of subtlety and illusion. [That] risk becomes intolerable [when] the precious right to vote protected by the Fifteenth Amendment is concerned." [a]

———

In MEMPHIS v. GREENE, 451 U.S. 100, 101 S.Ct. 1584, 67 L.Ed.2d 769 (1981), the city—at the behest of citizens of Hein Park, a white residential community within Memphis—closed a street, West Drive, that traversed Hein Park and was used mainly by African–Americans who lived in an adjacent area. The Court, per STEVENS, J., agreeing that "the adverse impact on blacks was greater than on whites," found no violation of 42 U.S.C.A. § 1982 [p. 1375 infra] or the thirteenth amendment: "[T]he critical facts established by the record are these: The city's decision to close West Drive was motivated by its interest in protecting the safety and tranquility of a residential neighborhood. The procedures followed in making the decision were fair and were not affected by any racial or other impermissible factors. The city has conferred a benefit on certain white property owners but there is no reason to believe that it would refuse to confer a comparable benefit on black property owners. The closing has not affected the value of property owned by black citizens, but it has caused some slight inconvenience to black motorists.

"[T]he record discloses no racially discriminatory motive on the part of the City Council [and] a review of the justification for the official action challenged in this case demonstrates that its disparate impact on black citizens could not [be] fairly characterized as a badge or incident of slavery.

32. Even if a municipal policy is shown to dilute the right to vote, however, the policy will not be struck down if the city shows that it serves highly important local interests and is closely tailored to effectuate only those interests.

a. In a brief opinion, Brennan, J., agreed with Marshall, J.'s conclusion.

For an opinion of the Court per White, J.—joined by Burger, C.J., and Brennan, Marshall, Blackmun and O'Connor, JJ.—even more strongly suggesting that a fifteenth amendment violation requires a "discriminatory purpose," see *Rogers v. Lodge*, Sec. 4, I, A infra.

"[To] decide the narrow constitutional question presented by this record we need not speculate about the sort of impact on a racial group that might be prohibited by the Amendment itself. We merely hold that the impact of the closing of West Drive on nonresidents of Hein Park [does] not reflect a violation of the Thirteenth Amendment."

MARSHALL, J., joined by Brennan and Blackmun, JJ., dissented: "I [do] not mean to imply that all municipal decisions that affect Negroes adversely and benefit whites are prohibited by the Thirteenth Amendment. I would, however, insist that the government carry a heavy burden of justification before I would sustain against Thirteenth Amendment challenge conduct as egregious as erection of a barrier to prevent predominantly-Negro traffic from entering a historically all-white neighborhood. [I] do not believe that the city has discharged that burden in this case, and for that reason I would hold that the erection of the barrier at the end of West Drive amounts to a badge or incident of slavery forbidden by the Thirteenth Amendment."

Notes and Questions

1. *The "discriminatory purpose" requirement.* (a) Should "racially disproportionate impact" alone trigger special judicial scrutiny? Consider Tribe *Treatise* 1516–20: "The goal of the equal protection clause is not to stamp out impure thoughts, but to guarantee a full measure of human dignity for all. [Beyond] the purposeful, affirmative adoption or use of rules that disadvantage [them,] minorities can also be injured when the government is 'only' indifferent to their suffering or 'merely' blind to how prior official discrimination contributed to it and how current official acts will perpetuate it. [S]trict judicial scrutiny [should be used] for those government acts that, given their history, context, source, and effect, seem most likely not only to perpetuate subordination but also to reflect a tradition of hostility toward an historically subjugated group, or a pattern of blindness or indifference to the interests of that group." Compare Robert W. Bennett, *"Mere" Rationality in Constitutional Law: Judicial Review and Democratic Theory,* 67 Calif.L.Rev. 1049, 1076 (1979): "If members of racial minorities statistically obtain benefits and suffer detriments as one or another piece of legislation is passed without attention to its racial impact, they are obtaining, not being deprived of, equal protection of the laws. To forbid all legislation that disadvantages them would give them the gains from political bargaining without the losses. This would be so regardless of the degree of the racially disproportionate impact or the importance of the interest affected."

To what extent "must equal protection doctrine address the unconscious racism that underlies much of the racially disproportionate impact of governmental policy"? Charles R. Lawrence III, *The Id, the Ego, and Equal Protection: Reckoning with Unconscious Racism,* 39 Stan.L.Rev. 317, 355 (1987). Consider id. at 364–65: "What does it mean [in *Memphis*] to construct a barrier between all-white and all-black sections of Memphis? In a city where just twenty years ago such barriers were built down the middle of rest rooms and restaurants with signs on them that read 'white' and 'colored' won't there be a considerable consensus as to whether the barrier speaks in racial terms? [The] meaning says that the peace and quiet of a white neighborhood has been weighed against the stigmatization of blacks. The decision to build a barrier issues the statement that white tranquility is more important than black pride. * * *

"At the opposite end of the spectrum is a hypothetical increase in the municipal railway fare [or] an increase in the sales tax, the fee for obtaining a driver's license, or the cost of a building permit. These are all cases where the impact on blacks in a particular instance may be greater than it is on whites. They are also cases where some stigma may attach to those who are excluded by the governmental action. But we are likely to think of the in-group and out-group in economic rather than racial terms. These actions do not contribute directly to the system of beliefs that labels blacks as inferior. Where the culture as a whole does not think of an action in racial terms, it is also unlikely that unconscious attitudes about race influenced the governmental decisionmaker."

Is there a "discriminatory purpose" if it is determined that the challenged law would not have been passed "if its racial impact had been reversed, i.e., if the disparate impact had been on whites rather than on blacks"? Eric Schnapper, *Two Categories of Discriminatory Intent,* 17 Harv.Civ.Rts.Civ.Lib.L.Rev. 31, 51 (1982). Consider id. at 55–56: "The central issue [in *Feeney*] is whether Massachusetts would have adopted in 1896 a veterans' preference [that would have excluded 98% of all male applicants] or would have amended its statutes successively in 1919, 1943, 1949, and 1968 to assure such preferential treatment for new generations of predominantly female veterans. The all too familiar history of discrimination on the basis of sex in this country renders implausible the suggestion * * *." [a]

Contrast Michael J. Perry, *The Disproportionate Impact Theory of Racial Discrimination,* 125 U.Pa.L.Rev. 540, 559–60 (1977): "Laws employing a racial criterion of selection are inherently more dangerous than laws involving no racial criterion. The former, unlike the latter, directly encourage racism [and] are usually difficult if not impossible to justify on legitimate grounds. By contrast, laws having a disproportionate racial impact are quite easy to explain on legitimate grounds because such laws serve a legitimate function in addition to the function of racial selection. Accordingly, the standard of review [should be] more rigorous than that required by the rational relationship test but less rigorous than that required by the strict scrutiny test. [In] determining whether a disproportionate disadvantage is justified, a court would weigh several factors: (1) the degree of disproportion in the impact; (2) the private interest disadvantaged; (3) the efficiency of the challenged law in achieving its objective and the availability of alternative means having a less disproportionate impact; and (4) the government objective sought to be advanced." [b]

(b) *First amendment freedoms.* In cases holding "neutral" laws that had an adverse impact on speech or association to violate the first amendment—such as *In re Primus* (p. 849 supra)—in which the Court required a "compelling state interest" or "more than merely a 'reasonable relation to some purpose within the competency of the state,'" did the Court find that the challenged state programs had a "discriminatory purpose"? If not, how is the disproportionate racial impact situation distinguishable? Consider Perry, supra, at 556: "The first amendment protects values and interests believed indispensable to the democratic functioning of the political process. Government is charged with the duty, under the first amendment, of safeguarding those values and interests [by] acting solicitously toward them as well as by refraining from deliberately abridging them. The equal

a. For detailed development of this approach, see also David A. Strauss, *Discriminatory Intent and the Taming of Brown,* 56 U.Chi.L.Rev. 935 (1989).

b. For a similar "balancing approach," see Theodore Eisenberg, *Disproportionate Impact and Illicit Motive: Theories of Constitutional Adjudication,* 52 N.Y.U.L.Rev. 36 (1977).

For the view that "serious scrutiny is preferable to ad hoc balancing," see Gayle Binion, *Intent and Equal Protection: A Reconsideration,* 1983 Sup.Ct.Rev. 397—comprehensively criticizing the "discriminatory purpose" requirement as developed and applied in the cases.

protection clause serves principally as a brake on the lamentable tendency of the majority race wilfully to oppress or exploit racial minorities, and in this regard it prohibits, absent compelling justification, the use of race as a criterion of selection. Traditionally, however, it has not been thought wrong—unfortunate, perhaps, but not wrong—that an individual or group is incidentally burdened by a law serving the public good. [Thus], with respect to racial discrimination equal protection doctrine has focused almost exclusively on *wilful* oppression or exploitation of minorities by the majority. This focus is especially understandable in light of what historically has been this society's severest moral affliction, racial animus." [c]

(c) *Burden of proof.* Who does (should) have the burden of proving a "discriminatory purpose"? What does (should) a challenger have to prove to shift the burden to the state "to rebut the presumption of unconstitutional action"? Consider Simon, fn. a in *Korematsu*, at 1111: "[A] showing of significant disproportionate disadvantage to a racial minority group, *without more*, gives rise to an inference that the action may have been taken or at least maintained or continued with knowledge that such groups would be relatively disadvantaged. [I]t raises a possibility sufficient to oblige the government to come forward with a credible explanation showing that the action was (or would have been) taken quite apart from prejudice. Depending upon the type of governmental action at issue, discharging this burden will often be easy for the government, but sometimes it will be difficult or impossible. In all cases, however, the government should be required to show more than that the action has some racially innocent 'conceivable basis in fact' because, as anyone familiar with this standard is aware, it can result in the validation of actions on the basis of explanations that are virtually incredible." Compare Kenneth L. Karst, *The Costs of Motive-Centered Inquiry,* 15 San Diego L.Rev. 1163, 1165 (1978): "Because an individual's behavior results from the interaction of a multitude of motives, and because racial attitudes often operate at the margin of consciousness, in any given case there almost certainly will be an opportunity for a government official to argue that his action was prompted by racially neutral considerations. When that argument is made, should we not expect the judge to give the official the benefit of the moral doubt? When the governmental action is the product of a group decision, will not that tendency toward generosity be heightened? The first objection to a motive-centered doctrine of racial discrimination, then, is that it places a 'very heavy burden' of persuasion on the wrong side of the dispute, to the severe detriment of the constitutional protection of racial equality." See generally James F. Blumstein, *Defining and Proving Race Discrimination: Perspectives on the Purpose vs. Results Approach from the Voting Rights Act,* 69 Va.L.Rev. 633 (1983).

2. *Prior state discrimination.* (a) Should there be special judicial scrutiny if the disproportionate racial impact of a law, whose purpose is racially neutral, is produced (influenced) by prior intentional state discrimination? See *Lane,* fn. a in *Arlington Heights.* Suppose a state requires that all applicants furnish recommendations from alumni and that there are no black alumni because the university admitted no blacks in the past? Suppose a state hires teachers wholly on the basis of merit and racial segregation in schools has rendered the quality of education of black teachers inferior to that of whites? Would (should) there have been special judicial scrutiny in *Feeney* if the disproportionate impact had been produced (influenced) by prior intentional discrimination by Massachusetts rather

---

c. As to whether "discriminatory purpose" is required in respect to laws that allegedly violate equal protection because they affect "fundamental rights," see *Mobile v. Bolden,* Sec. 4, I, A infra.

than military personnel practices of the federal government? If so, why should Massachusetts' "incorporation" of intentional discrimination by another government agency make a "constitutional difference"?

(b) Does the "prior discrimination" factor provide a limiting principle that ameliorates *Davis'* concern about the "far-reaching" consequences of "disproportionate-impact analysis"? Consider Perry, supra, at 557–58: "When disadvantage is suffered not merely as a consequence of a law, but [also] *as a consequence of prior governmental action that was constitutionally (and ethically) offensive,* it cannot be maintained that the disadvantage is ethically inoffensive. The disadvantage, in such a circumstance, is the fruit of prior government misdeeds and, accordingly, should bear a heavier burden of justification than that required of a truly neutral disadvantage. [The] failure of American society to outlaw racial discrimination—at least those instances of discrimination (in schooling, housing, and employment) most destructive to the social position of blacks—was hardly better, as a moral matter, than the discrimination itself. In terms of moral responsibility this failure, which endured for too long, amounted to complicity. Laws having a disproportionate racial impact burden blacks *because* of their especially disadvantaged position in American society. A failure to require government to take account of that especially disadvantaged social position by selecting and fine-tuning laws to avoid the unnecessary or thoughtless aggravation of the situation would effectively ignore American society's responsibility for that social position [and] would compound the responsibility."

Compare Owen M. Fiss, *Groups and the Equal Protection Clause,* 5 Phil. & Pub.Afrs. 107, 145 (1976): "A true inquiry into past discrimination [requires] the courts to construct causal connections that span significant periods of time, periods greater than those permitted under any general statute of limitations (a common device used to prevent the judiciary from undertaking inquiries where the evidence is likely to be stale, fragmentary, and generally unreliable). The difficulties of these backward-looking inquiries are compounded because the court must invariably deal with aggregate behavior, not just a single transaction; it must determine the causal explanation for the residential patterns of an entire community, or the skill levels of all the black applicants." See also Eric Schnapper, *Perpetuation of Past Discrimination,* 96 Harv.L.Rev. 828 (1983); Paul Brest, *In Defense of the Antidiscrimination Principle,* 90 Harv.L.Rev. 1, 42 (1976).

3. *Consequences of "discriminatory purpose."* If it is found that a law "was motivated by a racially discriminatory purpose," should the state be permitted to prove "that the same decision would have resulted had the impermissible purpose not been considered"? *Arlington Heights,* fn. 21. May a state defend a statute that discriminates on its face by proving that the same effect would have resulted even if the legislature had never taken race into account? Or should the Court invalidate a racially motivated law and "remand to the legislature for a reconsideration [on] the basis of purely legitimate factors"? Robert G. Schwemm, *From Washington to Arlington Heights and Beyond: Discriminatory Purpose in Equal Protection Litigation,* 1977 U.Ill.L.F. 961, 1020. Would the latter course be futile "because the legislature could immediately pass an identical statute for valid reasons"? Eisenberg, supra, at 116. Consider id.: "[I]t is absurd to assume that all legislators would completely ignore a court holding that the legislature used constitutionally impermissible criteria in initially passing a statute. Some legislators, after being informed that they initially acted unconstitutionally, may refuse to vote for reenactment. Furthermore, if a statute is invalidated on judicial review, the legislature often will decline or fail to consider a new law. In many situations, therefore, judicial action on the basis of motive results in an effective,

not a futile, invalidation." If there is a remand and the law is reenacted, should there be a presumption "that the decisionmaker continues to entertain the motives that led to the original decision (and to its invalidation)"? Brest, fn. 12 in *Arlington Heights,* at 125–26.

IV. REMEDYING SEGREGATION

Although there was prompt compliance with *Brown* in the District of Columbia and some border states, the initial response in the deep south was "massive resistance"—exemplified by the Governor's use of the Arkansas national guard in 1957 to prevent desegregation in Little Rock and Virginia's 1956 legislation closing any racially mixed public schools. See generally McKay, *"With All Deliberate Speed": Legislative Reaction and Judicial Development 1956–1957,* 43 Va.L.Rev. 1205 (1957).

COOPER v. AARON, 358 U.S. 1, 78 S.Ct. 1401, 3 L.Ed.2d 5 (1958), the first decision to follow the remands in *Brown,* involved the Little Rock school board's request to stay an integration plan that had been in operation at Central High School during the 1957–58 school year, but only after federal troops had been sent by the President to protect black students from "extreme public hostility" engendered largely by the Governor's and Legislature's opposition. The opinion, unprecedented in that it was signed by all nine justices (including those appointed since *Brown*), "unanimously reaffirmed" *Brown.* The Court agreed that "the educational progress of all the students [will] continue to suffer if the conditions which prevailed last year are permitted to continue," but denied the request for delay: "The constitutional rights of [black children] are not to be sacrificed or yielded to the violence and disorder which have followed upon the actions of the Governor and Legislature." The difficulties, created by state action, "can also be brought under control by state action." *Brown* "can neither be nullified openly and directly by state legislators or state executive or judicial officers, nor nullified indirectly by them through evasive schemes." [a]

GRIFFIN v. COUNTY SCHOOL BD., 377 U.S. 218, 84 S.Ct. 1226, 12 L.Ed.2d 256 (1964): In 1959, Prince Edward County, Va. closed its public schools rather than comply with a desegregation order. Private schools, supported by state and local tuition grants and tax credits, were operated for whites. The Court, per BLACK, J., held the closing denied African–Americans equal protection: States have "wide discretion in deciding whether laws shall operate statewide or shall operate only in certain counties [but whatever] nonracial grounds might support a State's allowing a county to abandon public schools, the object must be a constitutional one, and grounds of race and opposition to desegregation do not qualify as

a. Who determines whether public hostility may "be brought under control by state action"? May it ever be found that the hostility is so great that it is uncontrollable? Of what relevance is the financial cost to the state? Suppose the state, although *able,* is *unwilling* to quiet the hostility? See generally Paul D.

constitutional." [b]

In the late 1950s, some states sought to comply with *Brown* by simply permitting students to apply for transfer to another school. Procedures were complex and time-consuming; standards were vague, making it difficult to show that denials were due to race. See Note, *The Federal Courts and Integration of Southern Schools: Troubled Status of the Pupil Placement Act,* 62 Colum.L.Rev. 1448 (1962). By the early 1960s, most federal courts refused to accept these "tokenism" plans. See Alexander M. Bickel, *The Decade of School Desegregation: Progress and Prospects,* 64 Colum.L.Rev. 193 (1964). Finally, *Alexander v. Holmes Cty. Bd. of Educ.,* 396 U.S. 19, 90 S.Ct. 29, 24 L.Ed.2d 19 (1969), ordered denial of "all motions for additional time" and made clear that "the obligation of every school district is to terminate dual school systems at once and to operate now and hereafter only unitary schools." [c]

GREEN v. COUNTY SCHOOL BD., 391 U.S. 430, 88 S.Ct. 1689, 20 L.Ed.2d 716 (1968): The population of New Kent County in rural Virginia was about half black. Although there was no residential segregation, its two combined elementary and high schools, previously segregated by law, remained wholly segregated in fact until 1964. In 1965, the board adopted a "freedom-of-choice" plan to remain eligible for federal financial aid.[d] After three years, no white child chose to go to

Gewirtz, *Remedies and Resistance,* 92 Yale L.J. 585 (1983).

b. The Court affirmed the district court's order enjoining public financial aid to the private schools and held (Clark and Harlan, JJ. disagreeing) that "the District Court [may] require the Supervisors to exercise the power that is theirs to levy taxes to raise funds adequate to reopen, operate, and maintain without racial discrimination a public school system [like] that operated in other counties in Virginia." See also *Missouri v. Jenkins,* 495 U.S. 33, 110 S.Ct. 1651, 109 L.Ed.2d 31 (1990) ("District Court [also may] set aside state laws preventing local governments from raising funds sufficient to satisfy their constitutional obligations").

Griffin was subsequently distinguished in *Palmer v. Thompson* (1971)—involving the closing of swimming pools—discussed in *Washington v. Davis,* Part III supra.

c. For the view that "desegregation is not a remedy [merely] for schools [but also] a surprisingly successful remedy for a mortally serious, infrastructure-threatening malfunction [of] our plurality-protecting democratic political system," see James S. Liebman, *Desegregating Politics: "All–Out" Desegregation Explained,* 90 Colum.L.Rev. 1463, 1635–45 (1990).

d. The Civil Rights Act of 1964 bars federal financial assistance for any program adminis-

tered in a racially discriminatory manner. Pursuant thereto, eligibility for federal aid to local school districts was conditioned either on compliance with existing court desegregation orders or, in the absence of such an order, on submission of a desegregation plan consistent with federal "guidelines." See generally James Dunn, *Title VI, The Guidelines and School Desegregation in the South,* 53 Va. L.Rev. 42 (1967): Note, *The Courts, HEW, and Southern School Desegregation,* 77 Yale L.J. 321 (1967).

In the 1964–65 school year, before implementation of the guidelines, only 2.14% of black students in the eleven "southern states" attended schools in which they were not the racial majority. In 1968, the figure was reported at 20.3%. By the 1972–73 school year, it was 46.3%. Statistical Abstract of the United States 124 (1974). The comparable figure for 1972–73 in the six "border states and the District of Columbia" was 31.8%; for the 32 "northern and western states" it was 28.3%. Id.

For a pessimistic view of *Brown's* impact, see Gerald N. Rosenberg, *The Hollow Hope: Can Courts Bring About Social Change?* (1991). Compare Jesse H. Choper, *Consequences of Supreme Court Decisions Upholding Individual Constitutional Rights,* 83 Mich.L.Rev. 1, 25–28 (1984) ("although a congeries of complex factors contributed to the civil rights upheaval in the 1960s, [*Brown*] was the catalyst"). For

the black school which 85% of the black children continued to attend. School buses traveled "overlapping routes throughout the county to transport pupils to and from the two schools."

A unanimous Court, per BRENNAN, J., held "it is against this background that 13 years after *Brown II* commanded the abolition of dual systems we must measure the effectiveness of [respondent's plan]. School boards [then] operating state-compelled dual systems [were] clearly charged with the affirmative duty to take whatever steps might be necessary to convert to a unitary system in which racial discrimination would be eliminated root and branch. [It] is incumbent upon the school board to establish that its proposed plan promises meaningful and immediate progress toward disestablishing state-imposed segregation. [Where] more promising courses of action are open to the board, that may indicate a lack of good faith; and at the least it places a heavy burden upon the board to explain its preference for an apparently less effective method. [The instant] plan has operated simply to burden children and their parents with a responsibility which *Brown II* placed squarely on the School Board. The Board must be required [to] fashion steps which promise realistically to convert promptly to a system without a 'white' school and a 'Negro' school, but just schools."

SWANN v. CHARLOTTE–MECKLENBURG BD. OF EDUC.

402 U.S. 1, 91 S.Ct. 1267, 28 L.Ed.2d 554 (1971).

CHIEF JUSTICE BURGER delivered the opinion of the Court.

[This case concerned desegregation of the Charlotte, N.C. metropolitan area school district, which had had a statutorily mandated dual system. A companion case involved Mobile, Ala. The history included the district court's rejection in 1969 of three plans submitted by respondent board of education; its acceptance of a plan prepared at its request by "an expert in education administration"; modification of the district court decree by the court of appeals; and the district court's subsequent rejection of a plan prepared by federal officials and its conclusion that either the education expert's plan or a new plan submitted by a minority of the school board was "reasonable and acceptable."]

If school authorities fail in their affirmative obligations ["to eliminate from the public schools all vestiges of state-imposed segregation"] judicial authority may be invoked. Once a right and a violation have been shown, the scope of a district court's equitable powers to remedy past wrongs is broad, for breadth and flexibility are inherent in equitable remedies. [The] task is to correct, by a balancing of the individual and collective interests, the condition that offends the Constitution. [But] it is important to remember that judicial powers may be exercised only on the basis of a constitutional violation. * * *

School authorities are traditionally charged with broad power to formulate and implement educational policy and might well conclude, for example, that in order to prepare students to live in a pluralistic society each school should have a

the view that "racial change in America was inevitable owing to a variety of deep-seated social, political, and economic forces," and that "*Brown's* contribution to the civil rights movement of the 1960s was in creating a "political climate conducive to the brutal suppression of civil rights demonstrations" in the south, which, in turn, aroused "indifferent northern whites from their apathy, leading to demands

for national civil rights legislation which the Kennedy and Johnson administrations no longer deemed it politically expedient resist," see Michael J. Klarman, *Brown, Racial Change, and the Civil Rights Movement*, 80 Va.L.Rev. 7, 10–11 (1994). For diverse commentaries on this general thesis by David J. Garrow, Gerald N. Rosenberg, and Mark Tushnet, see 80 Va. L.Rev. 151–199 (1994).

prescribed ratio of Negro to white students reflecting the proportion for the district as a whole. To do this as an educational policy is within the broad discretionary powers of school authorities; absent a finding of a constitutional violation, however, that would not be within the authority of a federal court. * * *

The school authorities argue that the equity powers of federal district courts have been limited by Title IV of the Civil Rights Act of 1964, 42 U.S.C.A. [§ 2000c–6, which states]: "nothing herein shall empower any official or court of the United States to issue any order seeking to achieve a racial balance in any school by requiring the transportation of pupils [or] otherwise enlarge the existing power of the court to insure compliance with constitutional standards."[a]

* * * § 2000c–6 is in terms designed to foreclose any interpretation of the Act as expanding the *existing* powers of federal courts to enforce the Equal Protection Clause. There is no suggestion of an intention to restrict those powers or withdraw from courts their historic equitable remedial powers. The legislative history of Title IV indicates that Congress was concerned that the Act might be read as creating a right of action under the Fourteenth Amendment in the situation of so-called "de facto segregation," where racial imbalance exists in the schools but with no showing that this was brought about by discriminatory action of state authorities. * * *

The central issue in this case is that of student assignment, and there are essentially four problem areas: * * *

(1) *Racial Balances or Racial Quotas.* [I]t is urged that the District Court has imposed a racial balance requirement of 71%–29% on individual schools, [reflecting] the pupil constituency of the system. If we were to read the holding of the District Court to require, as a matter of substantive constitutional right, any particular degree of racial balance or mixing, that approach would be disapproved [for the] constitutional command to desegregate schools does not mean that every school in every community must always reflect the racial composition of the school system as a whole.

[But] the use made of mathematical ratios was no more than [a] useful starting point in shaping a remedy to correct past constitutional violations. In sum, the very limited use made of mathematical ratios was within the equitable remedial discretion of the District Court.[b]

(2) *One-Race Schools.* The record in this case reveals the familiar phenomenon that in metropolitan areas minority groups are often found concentrated in one part of the city. [T]he existence of some small number of one-race, or virtually one-race schools within a district is not in and of itself the mark of a system which still practices segregation by law. [But] the burden upon the school authorities will be to satisfy the court that their racial composition is not the result of present or past discriminatory action on their part.

---

a. Congress enacted a series of similar provisions during the 1970s. For example, the Education Amendments Act of 1974 required that federal courts and agencies give priority to nonbusing remedies, but also provided "that the provisions of this title are not intended to modify or diminish the authority of the courts of the United States to enforce fully the fifth and fourteenth amendments."

For consideration of the constitutionality of such legislation, see note 7(e) p. 1395 infra (§ 5 of the fourteenth amendment).

b. Cf. Rehnquist, J., joined by Burger, C.J., and Powell, J., dissenting from denial of certiorari in *Cleveland Bd. of Educ. v. Reed,* 445 U.S. 935, 100 S.Ct. 1329, 63 L.Ed.2d 770 (1980), in which the district court's remedy required that "every grade in every school [have] a ratio of black and white students in approximate proportion to the systemwide ratio."

An optional majority-to-minority transfer provision [is] an indispensable remedy for those students willing to transfer to other schools in order to lessen the impact on them of the state-imposed stigma of segregation. [S]uch a transfer arrangement must grant the transferring student free transportation and space must be made available in the school to which he desires to move. * * *

(3) *Remedial Altering of Attendance Zones.* [O]ne of the principal tools employed by school planners and by courts to break up the dual school system has been a frank—and sometimes drastic—gerrymandering of school districts and attendance zones. An additional step was pairing, "clustering," or "grouping" of schools with attendance assignments made deliberately to accomplish the transfer of Negro students out of formerly segregated Negro schools and transfer of white students to formerly all-Negro schools. More often than not, these zones are neither compact nor contiguous; indeed they may be on opposite ends of the city. As an interim corrective measure, this cannot be said to be beyond the broad remedial powers of a court.

Absent a constitutional violation there would be no basis for judicially ordering assignment of students on a racial basis. All things being equal, with no history of discrimination, it might well be desirable to assign pupils to schools nearest their homes. But all things are not equal in a system that has been deliberately constructed and maintained to enforce racial segregation. The remedy for such segregation may be administratively awkward, inconvenient and even bizarre in some situations and may impose burdens on some; but [this] cannot be avoided in the interim period when remedial adjustments are being made to eliminate the dual school systems.

No fixed or even substantially fixed guidelines can be established as to how far a court can go, but it must be recognized that there are limits. The objective is to dismantle the dual school system. [When] school authorities present a district court with a "loaded game board," affirmative action in the form of remedial altering of attendance zones is proper to achieve truly non-discriminatory assignments. [W]e must of necessity rely to a large extent, as this Court has for more than 16 years, on the informed judgment of the district courts in the first instance and on courts of appeals. * * *

(4) *Transportation of Students.* [No] rigid guidelines as to student transportation can be given for application to the infinite variety of problems presented in thousands of situations. Bus transportation has been an integral part of the public education system for [years]. Eighteen million of the nation's public school children, approximately 39%, were transported to their schools by bus in 1969–1970 in all parts of the country.

The importance of bus transportation as a normal and accepted tool of educational policy is readily discernible in this and the companion case.[11] * * *

The decree provided that [trips] for elementary school pupils average about seven miles and the District Court found that they would take "not over 35 minutes at the most."[12] This system compares favorably with the transportation

11. During 1967–1968, for example, the Mobile board used 207 buses to transport 22,094 students daily for an average round trip of 31 miles. During 1966–1967, 7,116 students in the metropolitan area were bused daily. In Charlotte-Mecklenburg [m]ore elementary school children than high school children were to be bused, and four- and five-year-olds travel the longest routes in the system.

12. The District Court found that the school system would have to employ 138 more buses than it had previously operated. But 105 of those buses were already available and the others could easily be obtained. Additionally, it should be noted that North Carolina

plan previously operated in Charlotte under which each day 23,600 students on all grade levels were transported an average of 15 miles one way for an average trip requiring over an hour. In these circumstances, we find no basis for holding that the local school authorities may not be required to employ bus transportation as one tool of school desegregation. Desegregation plans cannot be limited to the walk-in school.

An objection to transportation of students may have validity when the time or distance of travel is so great as to risk either the health of the children or significantly impinge on the educational process. District courts must weigh the soundness of any transportation plan in light of what is said in subdivisions (1), (2), and (3) above. [L]imits on time of travel will vary with many factors, but probably with none more than the age of the students. The reconciliation of competing values in a desegregation case is, of course, a difficult task with many sensitive facets but fundamentally no more so than remedial measures courts of equity have traditionally employed. * * * c

Notes and Questions

1. *Scope of duty.* Do *Green* and *Swann* require school boards that had de jure segregated systems to take "*whatever* steps might be necessary" for "meaningful and immediate progress toward disestablishing state-imposed segregation" (*Green*)? Or need they only adopt plans that are "reasonable, *feasible* and workable" (*Swann*)? Who determines what is "feasible"? Consider Frank I. Goodman, *Racial Imbalance in the Oakland Public Schools: A Legal Analysis* 69 (1966): "Whether a particular course of action is 'feasible' depends largely upon which elements of the situation are assumed to be fixed and unalterable and which are regarded as freely variable. If, for example, one accepts as a 'given' the basic validity of the neighborhood school concept and the existing facilities and financial resources of the school district, the range of 'feasible' desegregation measures is apt to be rather limited. Drop these assumptions and the range of feasibilities becomes broader. Assume, finally, that money is no obstacle, and that proximity to schools can be dismissed as a mere matter of 'convenience,' and nearly *everything* becomes feasible. [Black] children could be bused to predominantly white schools without regard to space limitations, and those schools placed on double sessions pending the construction of new facilities." Compare John Kaplan, *Segregation Litigation and the Schools—Part II: The General Northern Problem,* 58 Nw.U.L.Rev. 157, 183 (1963): "How can the courts weigh the value of a 30 per cent increase in integration against a requirement that students cross a dangerous traffic artery or walk five extra blocks? How could the courts weigh the achievement of integration through busing children against the greater cost and a somewhat larger class size?" Do courts often make judgments of this nature in constitutional litigation? See Owen M. Fiss, *The Charlotte-Mecklenburg Case—Its Significance for Northern School Desegregation,* 38 U.Chi.L.Rev. 697, 702 (1971): "[Under *Swann*,] if there is a conflict between integration and other values, integration will generally prevail. [In the *Mobile* case, the] Court rejected a desegregation plan that allowed some all-black schools to remain [whose elimination] required assigning students across a major highway that divided the

---

requires provision of transportation for all students who are assigned to schools more than one and one-half miles from their homes.

c. In a companion case, *North Carolina State Bd. of Educ. v. Swann,* 402 U.S. 43, 91 S.Ct. 1284, 28 L.Ed.2d 586 (1971), the Court held that an Anti-Busing Law, enacted during the instant litigation—barring (1) pupil assignment on the basis of race or to create a racial balance or ratio in the schools, and (2) busing for such purposes—contravened the doctrine "that all reasonable methods be available to formulate an effective remedy."

metropolitan area. [The] Court remanded because 'inadequate consideration was given to the possible use of bus transportation and split zoning.' "

2. *Scope of remedy.* Is the remedy mandated by *Brown II, Green,* and *Swann* limited to desegregation of schools? Consider Liebman, for c, p. 1108 supra, at 1514: "[A]s of 1954, 1970 (when school desegregation actually began in earnest), and even 1990, the majority of as yet uncompensated victims of school segregation have been adults, not children. Yet, [no] school desegregation remedy has ever compensated graduates of segregated elementary and secondary public schools for the educational, economic, psychological, or political harms they have continued to suffer throughout their adult lives as a result of their segregated and inferior schooling [or] for what we usually think of as the most compensable of all harms—the lost earnings and wealth that demonstrably flow from the poor schooling, confinement to neighborhoods with substandard [housing] and lost job opportunities that in turn demonstrably flow from officially mandated school segregation."

———

KEYES v. SCHOOL DIST., 413 U.S. 189, 93 S.Ct. 2686, 37 L.Ed.2d 548 (1973), was the first case of segregation that had never been statutorily mandated. The district court found that the Denver school board—by school construction, gerrymandering attendance zones, and excessive use of mobile classroom units— "had engaged over almost a decade after 1960 in an unconstitutional policy of deliberate racial segregation with respect to the Park Hill schools," and ordered their desegregation. However, although the "core city schools" were also segregated in fact, the district court found that the school board had no segregative policy as to them and declined to order their desegregation.

The Court, per BRENNAN, J., reversed, first holding that since, in the southwest, Negroes and Hispanos "suffer identical discrimination in treatment when compared with the treatment afforded Anglo[s,] schools with a combined predominance of Negroes and Hispanos [should be] included in the category of 'segregated' schools." It then held that "where plaintiffs prove that the school authorities have carried out a systematic program of segregation affecting a substantial portion of the students, schools, teachers and facilities [it] is only common sense to conclude that there exists a predicate for a finding of the existence of a dual school system" because "racially inspired school board actions have an impact beyond the particular schools that are the subjects of those actions. This is not to say, of course, that there can never be a case in which the geographical structure of or the natural boundaries within a school district may have the effect of dividing the district into separate, identifiable and unrelated units. Such a determination is essentially a question of fact to be resolved by the trial court [but] such cases must be rare."

Finally, emphasizing "that the differentiating factor between de jure segregation and so-called de facto segregation [is] *purpose* or *intent* to segregate," it held "that a finding of intentionally segregative school board actions in a meaningful portion of a school system [creates] a prima facie case of unlawful segregative design on the part of school authorities, and shifts to those authorities the burden of proving that other segregated schools within the system are not also the result of intentionally segregative actions. This is true even if it is determined that different areas of the school district should be viewed independently of each [other].[a] In discharging that burden, it is not enough, of course, that the school authorities rely upon some allegedly logical, racially neutral explanation [such as a "neighborhood school policy"] for their actions. Their burden is to adduce proof sufficient to support a finding that segregative intent was not among the factors that motivated their actions." Further, "if the actions of school authorities were to any degree motivated by segregative intent and the segregation resulting from those actions continues to exist, the fact of remoteness in time certainly does not make those actions any less 'intentional.'

"This is not to say, however, that the prima facie case may not be met by evidence supporting a finding that a lesser degree of segregated schooling in the core city area would not have resulted even if the Board had not acted as it [did]. Intentional school segregation in the past may have been a factor in creating a natural environment for the growth of further segregation. Thus, if respondent School Board cannot disprove segregative intent, it can rebut the prima facie case only by showing that its past segregative acts did not create or contribute to the current segregated condition of the core city schools." [b]

POWELL, J., filed a lengthy separate opinion: "[T]he familiar root cause of segregated schools in *all* the biracial metropolitan areas of our country is essentially the same: one of segregated residential and migratory patterns the impact of which on the racial composition of the schools was often perpetuated and rarely ameliorated by action of public school authorities. This is a national, not a southern phenomenon. And it is largely unrelated to whether a particular State had or did not have segregative school laws. * * *[c]

"I would hold [that] where segregated public schools exist within a school district to a substantial degree, there is a prima facie case that the duly constituted public authorities [are] sufficiently responsible to impose upon them a nationally applicable burden to demonstrate they nevertheless are operating a genuinely

a. What constitutes a "substantial" or "meaningful portion" of a school system? Consider Comment, *Unlocking the Northern Schoolhouse Doors,* 9 Harv.Civ.Rts.Civ. Lib.L.Rev. 124, 150 (1974): "Park Hill is a neighborhood of eight schools educating less than thirty-eight percent of Denver's black students and less than ten percent of all pupils in the district. [Thus], a decree compelling extensive desegregation will almost invariably flow from a finding of localized de jure practices." Does "a finding of intentionally segregative school board actions" for all elementary schools "create a prima facie case of unlawful segregative design" for all secondary schools?

b. Burger, C.J., concurred in the result. Douglas, J., joined the Court's opinion but stated "that there [is] no difference between de facto and de jure segregation." White, J., did not participate.

c. Powell, J., quoted from Frank I. Goodman, *De Facto School Segregation: A Constitutional and Empirical Analysis,* 60 Calif.L.Rev. 275, 297 (1972): "Ohio discarded [legally mandated segregation] in 1887, Indiana in 1949, [New York in 1938, New Mexico and Wyoming in 1954 (85 Harv.L.Rev. 85 n. 72 (1971))]. [T]here is no reason to suppose that 1954 is a universally appropriate dividing line between de jure segregation that may safely be assumed

to have spent itself and that which may not. For many remedial purposes, adoption of an arbitrary but easily administrable cutoff point might not be objectionable. But in a situation such as school desegregation, where both the rights asserted and the remedial burdens imposed are of such magnitude, and where the resulting sectional discrimination is passionately resented, it is surely questionable whether such arbitrariness is either politically or morally acceptable."

Consider also Kenneth L. Karst, *Not One Law at Rome and Another at Athens: The Fourteenth Amendment in Nationwide Application,* 1972 Wash.U.L.Q. 383, 388–89: "If the decisions of a southern school board concerning school location and school sizes can be said to have contributed to racial segregation among residential areas, then with far greater force it can be argued that official state action in northern and western cities has produced residential segregation. Until 1948, racially restrictive covenants in deeds were regularly enforced by state courts; governmental action has often located public housing [as] to intensify residential segregation; and, in a variety of ways, the federal government's programs of subsidy and loan guarantees have explicitly encouraged racial segregation in private housing."

integrated school system. [This] does not mean—and indeed could not mean in view of the residential patterns of most of our major metropolitan areas—that *every school* must in fact be an integrated unit." [d]

REHNQUIST, J., dissented: "[I]t would be a quite unprecedented application of principles of equitable relief to determine that if the gerrymandering of one attendance zone were proven, particular racial mixtures could be required by a federal district court for every school in the district. [U]nless the Equal Protection Clause [be] held to embody a principle of 'taint,' [such] a result can only be described as the product of judicial fiat. * * *

"The drastic extension of *Brown* which *Green* represented was barely, if at all, explicated in the latter opinion. To require that a genuinely 'dual' system be disestablished, in the sense that the assignment to a child of a particular school is not made to depend on his race, is one thing. To require that school boards affirmatively undertake to achieve racial mixing in schools where such mixing is not achieved in sufficient degree by neutrally drawn boundary lines is quite obviously something else."

COLUMBUS BOARD OF EDUC. v. PENICK

443 U.S. 449, 99 S.Ct. 2941, 61 L.Ed.2d 666 (1979).

JUSTICE WHITE delivered the opinion of the Court.

The public schools of Columbus, Ohio, are highly segregated by race. In 1976, over 32% of the 96,000 students in the system were black. About 70% of all students attended schools that were at least 80% black or 80% white. Half of the 172 schools were 90% black or 90% white. * * *

We have discovered no reason [to] disturb the judgment of the Court of Appeals, based on the findings and conclusions of the District Court, that the Board's conduct at the time of trial [in 1975] and before not only was animated by an unconstitutional, segregative purpose, but also had current, segregative impact that was sufficiently systemwide to warrant the [systemwide] remedy ordered by the District Court. * * *

First, [t]he Board insists that, since segregated schooling was not commanded by state law ["at least since 1888,"] and since not all schools were wholly black or wholly white in 1954, the District Court was not warranted in finding a dual system. But the District Court found that the "Columbus Public Schools were *officially* segregated by race in 1954"; and in any event, there is no reason to question the finding that as the "direct result of cognitive acts or omissions" the Board maintained "an enclave of separate, black schools on the near east side of Columbus." Proof of purposeful and effective maintenance of a body of separate black schools in a substantial part of the system itself is prima facie proof of a dual school system and supports a finding to this effect absent sufficient contrary proof by the Board, which was not forthcoming in this case. *Keyes.*

Second, both courts below declared that since the decision in *Brown II*, the Columbus Board has been under a continuous constitutional obligation to disestablish its dual school system. [Each] failure or refusal to fulfill this affirmative duty continues the violation of the Fourteenth Amendment. *United States v.*

---

d. Powell, J., further argued that "transportation orders should be applied with special caution to any proposal as disruptive of family life and interests—and ultimately of education itself—as extensive transportation of elementary age children solely for desegregation purposes."

Scotland Neck Bd. of Educ., 407 U.S. 484, 92 S.Ct. 2214, 33 L.Ed.2d 75 (1972) (creation of a new school district in a city that had operated a dual school system but was not yet the subject of court-ordered desegregation).[a] * * * Whatever the Board's current purpose with respect to racially separate education might be, it knowingly continued its failure to eliminate the consequences of its past intentionally segregative policies. * * *[b]

Third, the District Court [also] found that in the intervening years there had been a series of Board actions and practices that could not "reasonably be explained without reference to racial concerns," and that "intentionally aggravated, rather than alleviated," racial separation in the schools. These matters included the general practice of assigning black teachers only to those schools with substantial black student populations, a practice that was terminated only in 1974[;] the intentionally segregative use of optional attendance zones,[8] discontiguous attendance areas,[9] and boundary changes;[10] and the selection of sites for new school construction that had the foreseeable and anticipated effect of maintaining the racial separation of the schools.[11] * * *

[It] is urged that the courts below failed to heed the requirements of *Keyes, Washington v. Davis,* and *Arlington Heights,* that a plaintiff seeking to make out an equal protection violation on the basis of racial discrimination must show purpose. [But] the District Court correctly noted that actions having foreseeable and anticipated disparate impact are relevant evidence to prove the ultimate fact, forbidden purpose.[c] * * *

It is also urged that the District Court and the Court of Appeals failed to observe the requirements [of] *Dayton Bd. of Educ. v. Brinkman (Dayton I),* 433 U.S. 406, 97 S.Ct. 2766, 53 L.Ed.2d 851 (1977), which reiterated the accepted rule that the remedy imposed by a court of equity should be commensurate with the

---

a. In *Scotland Neck,* the school officials defended their action as "necessary to avoid 'white flight' [but this cannot] be accepted as a reason for achieving anything less than complete uprooting" of the dual system. For critical analysis, see Note, *White Flight as a Factor in Desegregation Analysis: A Judicial Recognition of Reality,* 66 Va.L.Rev. 961 (1980). For the view that the Court's "rejection of the white flight argument should not be understood as an absolute principle," see Paul D. Gewirtz, *Remedies and Resistance,* 92 Yale L.J. 585, 628–65 (1983).

b. In *Dayton Board of Education v. Brinkman (Dayton II),* 443 U.S. 526, 99 S.Ct. 2971, 61 L.Ed.2d 720 (1979), a companion case to *Columbus,* the Court, per White, J., added: "[T]he measure of the post-*Brown* conduct of a school board under an unsatisfied duty to liquidate a dual system is the effectiveness, not the purpose, of the actions in decreasing or increasing the segregation caused by the dual system. [T]he Board has a 'heavy burden' of showing that actions that increased or continued the effects of the dual system serve important and legitimate ends."

8. Despite petitioners' avowedly strong preference for neighborhood schools, in times of residential racial transition the Board created optional attendance zones to allow white students to avoid predominantly black schools, which were often closer to the homes of the white pupils. * * *

9. This technique was applied when neighborhood schools would have tended to desegregate the involved schools. In the 1960s, a group of white students were bused past their neighborhood school to a "whiter" school. The District Court could "discern no other explanation than a racial one for the existence of the Moler discontiguous attendance area for the period 1963 through 1969." * * *

10. Gerrymandering of boundary lines also continued after 1954. * * *

11. The District Court found that, of the 103 schools built by the Board between 1950 and 1975, 87 opened with racially identifiable student bodies and 71 remained that way at the time of trial. This result was reasonably foreseeable under the circumstances in light of the sites selected, and the Board was often specifically warned that it was, without apparent justification, choosing sites that would maintain or further segregation. * * *

c. For criticism of the Court's "subjective intent" approach and a supporting rationale for an "institutional segregative intent" test, see Note, *Reading the Mind of the School Board: Segregative Intent and the De Facto/De Jure Distinction,* 86 Yale L.J. 317 (1976).

violation ascertained, and held that the remedy for the violations that had then been established in that case should be aimed at rectifying the "incremental segregative effect" of the discriminatory acts identified. In *Dayton I*, only a few apparently isolated discriminatory practices had been found; yet a systemwide remedy had been imposed without proof of a systemwide impact.[d] Here, however, the District Court [and the Court of Appeals] repeatedly emphasized that it had found purposefully segregative practices with current, systemwide impact. * * *

Affirmed.[e]

JUSTICE REHNQUIST, with whom JUSTICE POWELL joins, dissenting.

The school desegregation remedy imposed [is] as complete and dramatic a displacement of local authority by the federal judiciary as is possible in our federal system [—] 42,000 of the system's 96,000 students are reassigned to new schools. There are like reassignment of teachers, staff, and administrators, reorganization of the grade structure of virtually every elementary school in the system, the closing of 33 schools, and the additional transportation of 37,000 students. * * *

Today the Court affirms [in] opinions so Delphic that lower courts will be hard pressed to fathom their implications for school desegregation litigation. I can only offer two suggestions. The first is that the Court, possibly chastened by the complexity and emotion that accompanies school desegregation cases, wishes to relegate the determination of a violation of [equal protection] in any plan of pupil assignment, and the formulation of a remedy for its violation, to the judgment of a single District Judge. * * * "Discriminatory purpose" and "systemwide violation" are to be treated as talismanic phrases which once invoked, warrant only the most superficial scrutiny by appellate courts.[f]

Such an [approach] holds out the disturbing prospect of very different remedies being imposed on similar school systems because of the predilections of individual judges and their good faith but incongruent efforts to make sense of this Court's confused pronouncements today. * * *

[Alternatively, the] Court suggests a radical new approach to desegregation cases in systems without a history of statutorily mandated separation of the races: if a district court concludes—employing what in honesty must be characterized as an irrebuttable presumption—that there was a "dual" school system at the time of *Brown I*, it must find post-1954 constitutional violations in a school board's failure to take every affirmative step to integrate the system. Put differently,

d. *Dayton I*, per Rehnquist, J., also observed: "The finding [that many Dayton] schools are either predominantly white or predominantly black"—"standing by itself, is not a violation of the Fourteenth Amendment in the absence of a showing that this condition resulted from intentionally segregative actions on the part of the Board. *Davis.*"

e. The concurring opinions of Burger, C.J., and Stewart, J., and the dissenting opinion of Powell, J., are omitted.

f. For a detailed review of the *Keyes* litigation, criticizing the district judge's findings of deliberate segregation and concluding that "perhaps nothing emerges more clearly [than] the fact of the almost totally unrestrained freedom of choice district judges possess in 'desegregation' litigation," see Lino A. Graglia, *Disaster By Decree* 162–99 (1976): "If this one judge had found—as he should have and as the

federal judges in New Jersey did find in *Spencer v. Kugler*, 404 U.S. 1027, 92 S.Ct. 707, 30 L.Ed.2d 723 (1972)—that the racial imbalance in the schools was not the result of racial discrimination by school officials, the travail of Denver would have been at an end. Never in our history has the fate of so many people so importantly depended on the whim of a single, unelected, lifetime official."

But see *Dayton II*, fn. b supra, upholding the conclusion of the court of appeals that the district court's finding—that "plaintiffs had failed to prove that acts of intentional segregation over 20 years old had any current incremental segregative effects [and that] plaintiffs had failed to show either discriminatory purpose or segregative effect, or both, with respect to the challenged practices and policies of the [school board]"—was "clearly erroneous."

racial imbalance at the time the complaint is filed is sufficient to support a systemwide, racial balance school busing remedy if the district court can find *some* evidence of discriminatory purpose prior to 1954, without any inquiry into the causal relationship between those pre-1954 violations and current segregation in the school system.

[As] a matter of history, 1954 makes no more sense as a benchmark—indeed it makes *less* sense—than 1968, 1971 or 1973. Perhaps the [last] year has the most to commend it, if one insists on a benchmark, because in *Keyes* this Court first confronted the problem of school segregation in the context of systems without a history of statutorily mandated separation of the races. * * *

Causality plays a central role in *Keyes* [which] held that before the burden of production shifts to the school board, the plaintiffs must prove "that the school authorities have carried out a systematic program of segregation *affecting a substantial portion of the students, schools, teachers and facilities within the school system.*" The Court recognized that a trial court might find "that [at] some point in time the relationship between past segregative acts and present segregation may become so attenuated as to be incapable of supporting a finding of de jure segregation warranting judicial intervention." The relevance of past acts of the school board was to depend on whether "segregation resulting from those actions continues to exist." That inquiry is not central under the approach approved by the Court today. * * *

The Court's use of the term "affirmative duty" implies that integration be the pre-eminent—indeed, the controlling—educational consideration in school board decisionmaking. It takes precedence over other legitimate educational objectives subject to some vague feasibility limitation. * * *

[O]bjective evidence [of segregative intent] must be carefully analyzed for it may otherwise reduce the "discriminatory purpose" requirement to a "discriminatory impact" test by another name. [In] a school system with racially imbalanced schools, *every* school board action regarding construction, pupil assignment, transportation, annexation and temporary facilities will promote integration, aggravate segregation or maintain segregation. Foreseeability follows from the obviousness of that proposition. Such a tight noose on school board decisionmaking will invariably move government of a school system [to] the courthouse. * * *

Once a showing is made that the District Court believes satisfies the *Keyes* requirement of purposeful discrimination in a substantial part of the school system, the school board will almost invariably rely on its neighborhood school policy and residential segregation to show that it is not responsible for the existence of certain predominantly black and white schools in other parts of the school system. [Here] the District Court relied on a general proposition that "there is often a substantial reciprocal effect between the color of the school and the color of the neighborhood it serves" to block any inquiry into whether racially identifiable schools were the product of racially identifiable neighborhoods or whether past discriminatory acts bore a "but for" relationship to current segregative conditions. [But] as the District Court recognized, other factors play an important role in determining segregated residential patterns. [Yet] today the School Board is called to task for all the forces beyond their control that shaped residential segregation in Columbus. There is thus no room for *Keyes* or *Swann* rebuttal either with respect to the school system today or that of 30 years ago. * * *

Notes and Questions

1. *Scope of the decisions.* (a) Do *Keyes* and *Columbus* "sweep away the distinction between de facto and de jure segregation"? In a district that presently has substantial racial imbalance in its schools, but that had no statutorily mandated segregation in 1954, if plaintiffs fail to prove "intentionally segregative school board actions in a meaningful portion of the school system" (*Keyes*), does the school board have an "affirmative duty" to desegregate? Does *Columbus* "leave open the possibility that if a school board operated a dual system prior to 1954, but abandoned its segregative policies before *Brown I* was decided, it might not be subject to an affirmative duty to desegregate"? 93 Harv.L.Rev. 126 n. 58 (1979). In these circumstances, must the school board prove that the segregation that existed in 1954 (or that exists today) was not "caused" by its earlier intentionally segregative actions? If so, is the presumption of causality "irrebutt-able" (Rehnquist, J.)? Is the task of overcoming the presumption "virtually impossible"? "Extraordinarily difficult"? See Jesse H. Choper, Yale Kamisar & Laurence H. Tribe, *The Supreme Court: Trends and Developments, 1978–1979,* 253–54 (1979).

(b) In *Keyes,* if plaintiffs make out "a prima facie case of unlawful segregative design on the part of school authorities," is the scope of the burden imposed on the school board "of proving that other segregated schools within the system are not also the result of intentionally segregative actions" consistent with the approach of *Arlington Heights* fn. 21? See Choper, Kamisar & Tribe, supra, at 241. Is the subject of intentional school segregation distinguishable from other forms of intentional racial discrimination?

(c) If, apart from school location and assignment policies, many "other factors play an important role in determining segregated residential patterns" (Rehn-quist, J.), do *Keyes* and *Columbus* answer a question left open in *Swann:* if plaintiffs prove "that school segregation is a consequence of other types of state action [see Karst, fn. c. in *Keyes*], without any discriminatory action by the school authorities, is there a constitutional violation requiring remedial action"? See generally Comment, *School Desegregation After Swann: A Theory of Government Responsibility,* 39 U.Chi.L.Rev. 421 (1972).

2. *Resegregation.* (a) In PASADENA CITY BD. OF EDUC. v. SPANGLER, 427 U.S. 424, 96 S.Ct. 2697, 49 L.Ed.2d 599 (1976), a court ordered plan to remedy de jure segregation resulted in no racially imbalanced schools in 1970. But this lasted only one year; by 1974, five of the district's 32 schools were over half black. The Court, per REHNQUIST, J., reversed the district judge's order "to require annual readjustment of attendance zones so that there would not be a majority of any minority in any Pasadena public school": "[The] quite normal pattern of human migration resulted in some changes in the demographics of Pasadena's residential patterns, with resultant shifts in the racial makeup of some of the schools. [But] these shifts were not attributed to any segregative actions on the part of the defendants. [H]aving once implemented a racially neutral attendance pattern in order to remedy the perceived constitutional violations on the part of the defendants, the District Court had fully performed its function of providing the appropriate remedy for previous racially discriminatory attendance patterns." [a]

a. Marshall, J., joined by Brennan, J., dissented on the ground that a "unitary system" had not been established. Stevens, J., did not participate.

Consider Paul D. Gewirtz, *Choice in the Transition: School Desegregation and the Corrective Ideal,* 86 Colum.L.Rev. 728, 753 (1986): "[R]equiring integration for a period of time is

(b) OKLAHOMA CITY BD. OF EDUC. v. DOWELL, 498 U.S. 237, 111 S.Ct. 630, 112 L.Ed.2d 715 (1991): Eight years after a federal court finding that "unitariness had been achieved," the school board adopted a new neighborhood assignment plan (SRP). Its asserted purpose was to alleviate greater busing burdens on young African–American children caused by demographic changes and to increase parental involvement. This resulted in about half the schools becoming primarily uniracial. The Court, per REHNQUIST, C.J., held that a desegregation decree should be dissolved if the board has "complied in good faith [since] it was entered" and "the vestiges of past discrimination have been eliminated to the extent practicable. [The] District Court should then evaluate the Board's decision to implement the SRP under appropriate equal protection principles. See *Washington v. Davis, Arlington Heights.*" [b]

(c) In FREEMAN v. PITTS, 503 U.S. 467, 112 S.Ct. 1430, 118 L.Ed.2d 108 (1992), the district court had found that the De Kalb County (GA) School System had "achieved unitary status [with] regard to student assignments, transportation, physical facilities, and extracurricular activities," but not in respect to "teacher and principal assignments, resource allocation, and quality of education." The Court, per KENNEDY, J.,—emphasizing that "returning schools to the control of local authorities at the earliest practicable date is essential to restore their true accountability in our government system"—remanded the case for more specific findings and held that "while retaining jurisdiction over the case, the court [may] withdraw judicial supervision with respect to discrete categories in which the school district has achieved compliance with a court-ordered desegregation plan [and] need not retain active control over every aspect of school administration until a school district has demonstrated unitary status in all facets of its system.

"[Among] the factors which must inform the sound discretion of the court in ordering partial withdrawal are the following: whether there has been full and satisfactory compliance with the decree in those aspects of the system where supervision is to be withdrawn; whether retention of judicial control is necessary or practicable to achieve compliance with the decree in other facets of the school system; and whether the school district has demonstrated, [its] good faith commitment to the whole of the court's decree * * *.

"As the de jure violation becomes more remote in time and these demographic changes intervene, it becomes less likely that a current racial imbalance in a school district is a vestige of the prior de jure system. The causal link between current conditions and the prior violation is even more attenuated if the school district has demonstrated its good faith. [It] was appropriate for the District Court to examine the reasons for the racial imbalance before ordering an impractical, and no doubt massive, expenditure of funds to achieve racial balance after 17 years of efforts to implement the comprehensive plan in a district where there were fundamental changes in demographics, changes not attributable to the former de jure regime or any later actions by school officials. The District Court's

a plausible precondition to having an untainted post-violation choice plan. [To] be untainted, choices must be made from among schools that are not racially identified; the segregated arrangements must be actually disestablished and attendance patterns transformed. Indeed, in order for the racial identity of the schools to be transformed, integration will have to be maintained for a period of time sufficient to change public perceptions and understandings."

b. Marshall, J., joined by Blackmun and Stevens, JJ., dissented: "I believe a desegregation decree cannot be lifted so long as conditions likely to inflict the stigmatic injury condemned in *Brown I* persist and there remain feasible methods of eliminating such conditions." Souter, J., did not participate.

determination to order instead the expenditure of scarce resources in areas such as the quality of education, where full compliance had not yet been achieved, underscores the uses of discretion in framing equitable remedies. * * *

"There was no showing that racial balance [in student assignments] was an appropriate mechanism to cure other deficiencies in this case. It is true that the school district was not in compliance with respect to faculty assignments, but the record does not show that student reassignments would be a feasible or practicable way to remedy this defect."

SCALIA, J., concurred: "Racially imbalanced schools are [the] product of a blend of public and private actions, and any assessment that they would not be segregated, or would not be *as* segregated, in the absence of a particular one of those factors is guesswork. [Only] in rare cases such as this one and *Spangler,* where the racial imbalance had been temporarily corrected after the abandonment of de jure segregation, can it be asserted with any degree of confidence that the past discrimination is no longer playing a proximate role. Thus, allocation of the burden of proof foreordains the result in almost all of the 'vestige of past discrimination' cases. [Our] post-*Green* cases provide that, once state-enforced school segregation is shown to have existed in a jurisdiction in 1954, there arises a presumption, effectively irrebuttable (because the school district cannot prove the negative), that any current racial imbalance is the product of that violation, at least if the imbalance has continuously existed.

"In the context of elementary and secondary education, [the] extent and recency of the prior discrimination, and the improbability that young children (or their parents) would use 'freedom of choice' plans to disrupt existing patterns 'warrant[ed] a presumption [that] schools that are substantially disproportionate in their racial composition' were remnants of the de jure system. *Swann.*

"But granting the merits of this approach at the time of *Green,* it is now 25 years later. [Since] a multitude of private factors has shaped school systems in the years after abandonment of de jure segregation—normal migration, population growth (as in this case), 'white flight' from the inner cities, increases in the costs of new facilities—the percentage of the current makeup of school systems attributable to the prior, government-enforced discrimination has diminished with each passing year, to the point where it cannot realistically be assumed to be a significant factor.

"[While] we must continue to prohibit, without qualification, all racial discrimination in the operation of public schools, and to afford remedies that eliminate not only the discrimination but its identified consequences, we should consider laying aside the extraordinary, and increasingly counterfactual, presumption of *Green.* We must soon revert to the ordinary principles [that] plaintiffs alleging Equal Protection violations must prove intent and causation and not merely the existence of racial disparity, see *Washington v. Davis.*"

SOUTER, J., concurred, emphasizing that "racial imbalance in student assignments caused by demographic change is not insulated from federal judicial oversight where the demographic change is itself caused ['by past school segregation and the patterns of thinking that segregation creates'], and before deciding to relinquish supervision and control over student assignments, a district court should make findings on the presence or absence of this relationship."

BLACKMUN, J., joined by Stevens and O'Connor, JJ., concurred only in the judgment of remand, stressing that "the District Court's jurisdiction should continue until the school board demonstrates full compliance with the Constitution." Thomas, J., did not participate.[b]

3. *"De facto" school segregation.* (a) Contrary to *Dayton I*, in the absence of any "intentionally segregative actions" on the part of any state agency, *should* the fact that many schools in a district "are either predominantly white or predominantly black" "standing by itself" violate equal protection? For an early view, see Owen M. Fiss, *Racial Imbalance in the Public Schools: The Constitutional Concepts,* 78 Harv.L.Rev. 564 (1965).

(b) *Effect on students.* Consider Note, *Racial Imbalance in the Public Schools: Constitutional Dimensions and Judicial Response,* 18 Vand.L.Rev. 1290, 1295–96 (1965): "Fiss points out 'that students in such schools are also deprived of the intellectual stimulation that comes from the exchange of ideas and the development of personal relationships in a racially and socially heterogeneous context.' [Because *Brown*] found that 'to separate [blacks] from others of similar age and qualifications solely because of their race generates a feeling of inferiority,' proponents of racial balance in the schools argue analogously that racial imbalance also breeds inferiority. [A] more damaging aspect of racial imbalance relates to [a] corollary goal of education [which is] 'to induct the young person systematically into the culture and society to which he is an heir and in which he should be a partner.' The Supreme Court recognized [this] in *Brown*. [It] seems clear that regardless of the cause of the separation of the races the isolation of a minority race will prevent the achievement of this educational goal." [c] Compare Kaplan, note 1 after *Swann,* at 174: "[V]irtually every bit of the sociological evidence of harm presented [in *Brown*] involved compulsory segregation based overtly on race in the social setting of the South where school segregation was merely one facet of the general exclusion of the Negro from the dominant life of the community. It is by no means obvious that harm will automatically follow where the segregation is of the de facto variety, occurring in the Northern setting, and is not purposely based on race." Consider Mark G. Yudof, *Equal Educational Opportunity and the Courts,* 51 Tex.L.Rev. 411, 436 (1973): "One study of

b. For the view that by permitting school districts to "take actions that aggravate existing racial imbalances," i.e., to "enact policies that have de facto segregatory effects," *Freeman* "offers little protection against incremental resegregation," see Note, *Killing Brown Softly: The Subtle Undermining of Effective Desegregation,* 46 Stan.L.Rev. 147 (1993). Consider id. at 166–67: "Because racial disparities in any aspect of a school system may perpetuate racial identifiability, incremental resegregation may lead to school districts never eliminating the racial identifiability of their schools. Consider, for instance, a school district that has successfully desegregated its student assignments but remains unlawfully segregated with respect to faculty and staff assignments. If returned to local control, enrollment may resegregate before the school district successfully desegregates its faculty and staff. Thus, a significant facet of the school system may remain segregated—either de jure or de facto—at all points before, during, and after the desegregation process.

"This problem is aggravated where a school district achieves compliance in different *Green* areas at widely disparate times. Large time

lags will inevitably increase the likelihood that areas released from supervision will resegregate prior to compliance in other areas. Yet, once the school district achieves unitary status in those areas that remain under judicial supervision, the district court can dissolve its desegregation order regardless of the continued racial identifiability of the schools."

c. See also David A. Strauss, *Discriminatory Intent and the Taming of Brown,* 56 U.Chi. L.Rev. 935, 962 (1989): "[T]he argument that conscious or obvious discrimination is especially debilitating is an argument about the effects of government actions, not about the intent or process that produced them. If this argument is correct, what follows is that any action that has the same effects as obvious discrimination—the same insulting, stigmatizing, or subordinating effects—should also be unconstitutional. [T]here is no reason to believe that the class of actions with those effects is limited to overt and covert racial classifications. Depending on how the crucial psychological effect is defined, race-neutral measures that leave blacks in an inferior position may be equally harmful."

the psychological impact of segregation on black children has found that the black child's self-concept is inversely related to the proportion of white students in the school; the whiter his school the lower the black child rated himself. Other studies have reached the opposite conclusion. Studies of the relationship between personality development and segregation are similarly conflicting. [Moreover,] available studies are inconclusive as to whether integration in fact accelerates academic achievement. Further complicating the evidence are the many additional variables that may alter the effect of integration or segregation: the degree of interracial hostility, the percentage of black students in relation to the school population, the socio-economic makeup of the student body, the existence of ability grouping, and the attitudes of parents, teachers, and administrators." [d] See also Goodman, fn. c. in *Keyes,* at 400–435 for an intensive review of various studies, concluding that "the influence of biracial schooling upon the achievement of black students is highly *uncertain.*" Compare James S. Liebman, *Implementing Brown in the Nineties: Political Reconstruction, Liberal Recollection, and Litigatively Enforced Legislative Reform,* 76 Va.L.Rev. 349, 356–57 (1990), reviewing studies in the 1980s which conclude that "northern desegregation has a substantial positive effect on black students' achievement," and that "more certain is desegregation's positive impact on dropout, teenage pregnancy, and delinquency rates; on the likelihood that blacks will attend and succeed at college (particularly four-year colleges), secure employment in predominantly white job settings, and live in integrated neighborhoods as adults; and on the salary levels blacks attain in the labor market."

(c) *Constitutional "values" and judicial interpretation.* Consider Goodman, note 1(b) after *Swann,* at 21–23: "[T]here is a *moral* difference of the first importance between a law which discriminates against citizens solely on the ground of race and one which, though based on racially neutral criteria, operates to the detriment of a minority group. [e] [A] second important difference between legislation requiring, and legislation merely resulting in, racial segregation is the absence in the former case of any legitimate State interest which might countervail the harm inflicted on Negro children. [The] only rationale for segregation which has even a semblance of plausibility is that it helps to avoid needless friction between the races and thus preserves tranquility both in the classroom and in the larger society. In the long run, however, by creating barriers to normal intergroup relations and arousing the resentment and frustration of the minority group, segregation probably does more to defeat than to promote racial peace. And even were this not so, it still could not be said that segregation is a necessary means to that end, for there are many other ways of dealing with the problem of racial conflict. [This] is not the case with de facto segregation. Here the psychological injury suffered by Negro children results from the use of otherwise legitimate means (geographical districting criteria) to accomplish an

d. For discussion of the constitutionality of all-African-American programs (and schools) for "solving the problems of young African–American males," see Note, *Some Constitutional Problems with the Resegregation of Public Schools,* 80 Geo.L.J. 363 (1991). See also Richard Cummings, *All Male Black Schools: Equal Protection, the New Separatism and Brown v. Board of Education,* 20 Hast.Con. L.Q. 725 (1993).

e. Compare Goodman, note (b) supra, at 319: "Is there really a decisive moral difference between the state of mind that produces de facto segregation and that which produced de jure segregation? Those who advocate the neighborhood school may not want segregation, but they well know their policy begets it; either they see no harm or they deem the harm an acceptable cost. On the other hand, if de facto segregation is rarely inadvertent, de jure segregation is not always malevolent. Many an avowed segregationist genuinely believes his policy benefits all, black and white alike, offering them a classroom free from racial friction."

otherwise legitimate end (the neighborhood school) which could not be accomplished in any other way."

Even if de jure and de facto segregation are distinguishable, should the school board at least be required "to take reasonable steps—as opposed to all possible steps [as with de jure segregation]—to eliminate" de facto segregation? Fiss, note 1 after *Swann,* at 706. Consider Kaplan, note b supra, at 180: "It is hard [to] argue that the cause of mixing Negro and white children, taken as it must be from the vague words of the equal protection clause, deserves the same standing as the right of free expression which not only is founded in the explicit wording of the first amendment, but also is at the very basis of any free [society]. Integration may be an important value [but] it is hard to argue that it is more fundamental than the right of the state to provide for the health, safety, and education of its children."

Does *Washington v. Davis* plainly reject the view that "other values" should be disregarded in "the cause of racial integration"? Consider Goodman, note b supra, at 306: "[If] it is true that de facto, like de jure segregation, generates feelings of racial inferiority in black school children, the injury is one they incur distinctively as blacks, solely on account of their race. A white child similarly situated would not be similarly affected. In that sense, the neighborhood school policy can be said to inflict a 'racially specific' harm, a harm differing in kind from that inflicted by [the] examples of state action [in fn. 14 of *Davis*] that hurt more blacks than whites, but hurt the individual black no more than his white counterpart." At the least, contrary to fn. 9 in *Dayton II,* should "the foreseeability of segregative consequences" make out "a prima facie case of purposeful racial discrimination" on the part of the school board and shift the burden to it to prove nonsegregative intent? [f]

3. *Interdistrict remedies.* (a) *Schools.* In MILLIKEN v. BRADLEY, 418 U.S. 717, 94 S.Ct. 3112, 41 L.Ed.2d 1069 (1974), the district court found that various actions of the Detroit Board of Education, the State Board of Education and the Michigan legislature (e.g., barring use of state funds for busing), produced de jure segregation in Detroit; that, because of the city's racial composition, desegregation plans limited to Detroit "would accentuate the racial identifiability of the district as a Black school system, and would not accomplish desegregation." Thus, the district judge ordered a plan encompassing 53 neighboring suburban school districts (in Oakland and Macomb counties). The Court, per BURGER, C.J.,—emphasizing that, apart from one "isolated instance affecting two of the school districts," the record "contains evidence of de jure segregated conditions only in" Detroit—reversed, stating the issue as "whether a federal court may impose a multidistrict [remedy] absent any finding that the other included school districts have failed to operate unitary school systems within their districts, [that] the boundary lines of any affected school district were established with the purpose of fostering racial segregation [, or that] the included districts committed acts which effected segregation within the other districts, and absent a meaningful opportunity for the included neighboring school districts to [be] heard on the propriety of a multidistrict remedy or on the question of constitutional violations by those neighboring districts":

"The controlling principle [is] that the scope of the remedy is determined by the nature and extent of the constitutional violation. *Swann.* [Before] imposing a cross-district remedy, it must first be shown that there has been a constitutional

---

f. The constitutional issues presented when school boards *voluntarily* undertake to remedy   de facto segregation are considered in Part V infra.

violation within one district that produces a significant segregative effect in [another].[a] The constitutional right of the Negro respondents residing in Detroit is to attend a unitary school system in that district."[b]

WHITE, J., joined by Douglas, Brennan and Marshall, JJ., dissented: "The Court of Appeals [concluded] that an interdistrict remedy 'is supported by the status of school districts under Michigan law and by the historical control exercised over local school districts by the legislature of Michigan and by State agencies and officials.' Obviously, whatever difficulties there might be, they are surmountable; for the Court itself concedes that had there been sufficient evidence of an interdistrict violation, the District Court could have fashioned a single remedy for the districts implicated * * *.

"I am even more mystified how the Court can ignore the legal reality that the constitutional violations, even if occurring locally, were committed by governmental entities for which the State is responsible and that it is the State that must respond to the command of the Fourteenth Amendment."

MARSHALL, J., joined by Douglas, Brennan, and White, JJ., dissented: "Ironically purporting to base its result on the principle that the scope of the remedy [should] be determined by the nature and the extent of the constitutional violation, the Court's answer is to provide no remedy at all [thus] guaranteeing that Negro children in Detroit will receive the same separate and inherently unequal education in the future as they have been unconstitutionally afforded in the past. * * *

"The State's creation, through de jure acts of segregation, of a growing core of all-Negro schools inevitably acted as a magnet to attract Negroes to the areas served by such schools [and] helped drive whites to other areas of the city or to the suburbs. [Having] created a system where whites and Negroes were intentionally kept apart so that they could not become accustomed to learning together, the State is responsible for the fact that many whites will react to the dismantling of that segregated system by attempting to flee to the suburbs."[c]

(b) MISSOURI v. JENKINS, ___ U.S. ___, 115 S.Ct. 2038, 132 L.Ed.2d 63 (1995), involved the 18–year school desegregation litigation for the Kansas City, Missouri School District (KCMSD). The Court, per REHNQUIST, C.J., found that "the District Court has set out on a program to create a school district that was equal to or superior to the surrounding [suburban ones]. This remedy has included an elaborate program of capital improvements, course enrichment, and extracurricular enhancement not simply in the formerly identifiable black schools, but in schools throughout the district. [The] District Court's remedial order has

---

a. Is this allocation of the burden of proof consistent with *Keyes*? Are there reasons for a presumption of segregative intent or effect in a *Keyes*-type situation but not in a *Milliken*-type one?

For a listing of subsequent cases imposing interdistrict remedies, see Note, *Interdistrict Remedies for Segregated Schools*, 79 Colum.L.Rev. 1168 n. 5 (1979). See generally Robert A. Sedler, *The Profound Impact of Milliken v. Bradley*, 33 Wayne L.Rev. 1693 (1987); Robert A. Sedler, *Metropolitan Desegregation in the Wake of Milliken—On Losing Big Battles and Winning Small Wars: The View Largely from Within*, 1975 Wash.U.L.Q. 535.

b. For the view that this states an improperly narrow perception of the constitutional right at issue, see Norman C. Amaker, *Milliken v. Bradley: The Meaning of the Constitution in School Desegregation Cases*, 2 Hast.Con.L.Q. 349 (1975); Charles R. Lawrence, *Segregation "Misunderstood": The Milliken Decision Revisited*, 12 U.S.F.L.Rev. 15 (1977).

c. Douglas, J., also filed a brief dissent. For evidence that it is doubtful whether metropolitan school desegregation remedies will produce integration without a permanent "ongoing system of student-quota reassignment," see Eleanor P. Wolf, *Northern School Desegregation and Residential Choice*, 1977 Sup.Ct.Rev. 63.

all but made the KCMSD itself into a magnet district [designed] to attract nonminority students from outside the KCMSD schools. But this inter district goal is beyond the scope of the intra district violation identified by the District Court." Consequently, "the District Court's order [of] across-the-board salary increases for instructional and noninstructional employees [and its] order requiring the State to continue to fund the quality education programs because student achievement levels were still 'at or below national norms at many grade levels' cannot be sustained."

THOMAS, J., added a concurrence: "Two threads in our jurisprudence have produced this unfortunate situation, in which a District Court has taken it upon itself to experiment with the education of the KCMSD's black youth. First, the court has read our cases to support the theory that black students suffer an unspecified psychological harm from segregation that retards their mental and educational development. This approach not only relies upon questionable social science research rather than constitutional principle, but it also rests on an assumption of black inferiority.[d] Second, we have permitted the federal courts to exercise virtually unlimited equitable powers to remedy this alleged constitutional violation.[e] The exercise of this authority has trampled upon principles of federalism and the separation of powers and has freed courts to pursue other agendas unrelated to the narrow purpose of precisely remedying a constitutional harm.[f]" O'Connor, J., also concurred separately.

SOUTER, J., joined by Stevens, Ginsburg and Breyer, JJ., dissented on the merits, but more forcefully on the ground that the Court's "addressing an important and complex question without adequate notice to the parties [leads] it to render an opinion anchored in neither the findings and evidence contained in the record, nor in controlling precedent, which is squarely at odds with the Court's holding today." Ginsburg, J., added a brief dissent.

(c) *Housing.* In HILLS v. GAUTREAUX, 425 U.S. 284, 96 S.Ct. 1538, 47 L.Ed.2d 792 (1976), the district court found that the federal Dep't of Housing (HUD) and the Chicago Housing Authority (CHA) had racially segregated public housing projects in Chicago. The Court, per STEWART, J., held that "nothing in [*Milliken*] suggests a per se rule that federal courts lack authority to order parties found to have violated the Constitution to undertake remedial efforts beyond the municipal boundaries of the city where the violation occurred. [The] proposed remedy in *Milliken* was impermissible because of the limits on the federal judicial power to interfere with the operation of state political entities that were not implicated in unconstitutional conduct. Here, [a] judicial order directing relief beyond the boundary lines of Chicago will not necessarily entail coercion of

---

d. "This misconception has drawn the courts away from the important goal in desegregation. The point of the Equal Protection Clause is not to enforce strict race-mixing, but to ensure that blacks and whites are treated equally by the State without regard to their skin color. [Because] of their 'distinctive histories and traditions,' black schools can function as the center and symbol of black communities, and provide examples of independent black leadership, success, and achievement."

e. "When a district court holds the State liable for discrimination almost 30 years after the last official state action, it must do more than show that there are schools with high black populations or low test scores."

f. "We have given the federal courts the freedom to use any measure necessary to reverse problems—such as racial isolation or low educational achievement—that have proven stubbornly resistant to government policies. [Thus,] the District Court here ordered massive expenditures by local and state authorities, without congressional or executive authorization and without any indication that such measures would attract whites back to KCMSD or raise KCMSD test scores. The time has come for us to put the genie back in the bottle."

uninvolved governmental units, because [both] CHA and HUD have the authority to operate outside the Chicago city limits.[14]" [a]

(d) *Other remedies.* In MILLIKEN v. BRADLEY (MILLIKEN II), 433 U.S. 267, 97 S.Ct. 2749, 53 L.Ed.2d 745 (1977), the district court, on remand, fashioned a new decree which required (in addition to a pupil assignment plan for the Detroit school system) a number of "educational components"—including remedial reading and revised testing and counseling programs for pupils, and a training program for teachers. The state, which was ordered to pay for part of these programs, appealed. The Court, per BURGER, C.J., affirmed: "[T]he District Court found that [the] educational components [were] necessary to restore the victims of discriminatory conduct to the position they would have enjoyed in terms of education had these four components been provided in a nondiscriminatory manner in a school system free from pervasive de jure racial segregation. [D]iscriminatory student assignment policies can themselves manifest and breed other inequalities built into a dual system founded on racial discrimination." [b]

4. *Beyond elementary and secondary schools.* (a) BAZEMORE v. FRIDAY, 478 U.S. 385, 106 S.Ct. 3000, 92 L.Ed.2d 315 (1986), per WHITE, J., held that *Green's* "affirmative duty to desegregate" has "no application" to the 4–H and Homemaker Clubs (which had been deliberately segregated until 1965) operated by the North Carolina Agricultural Extension Service, despite the fact that a majority of the clubs remained uniracial in 1980: "While school children must go to school, there is no compulsion to join 4–H or Homemaker Clubs, and while School Boards customarily have the power to create school attendance areas and otherwise designate the school that particular students may attend, there is no statutory or regulatory authority to deny a young person the right to join any Club he or she wishes to join."

BRENNAN, J., joined by Marshall, Blackmun and Stevens, JJ., dissented: "Nothing in our earlier cases suggests that the State's obligation to desegregate is confined only to those activities in which members of the public are compelled to participate." [c]

(b) UNITED STATES v. FORDICE, 505 U.S. 717, 112 S.Ct. 2727, 120 L.Ed.2d 575 (1992), per WHITE, J., involved Mississippi's public university system which maintained five almost completely white and three almost exclusively black schools: "That college attendance is by choice and not by assignment does not

---

14. [Although] the state officials in *Milliken* had the authority to operate across school district lines, the exercise of that authority [would] have eliminated numerous independent school districts or at least have displaced important powers granted those uninvolved governmental entities under state law.

a. Marshall, J., joined by Brennan and White, JJ., joined the Court's opinion "except insofar as it appears to reaffirm [*Milliken*]."

Is *Gautreaux* faithful to the principle that "the scope of the remedy is determined by the nature and extent of the constitutional violation"? See Stephen B. Kanner, *From Denver to Dayton: The Development of a Theory of Equal Protection Remedies*, 72 Nw.U.L.Rev. 382 (1977).

b. For the view that "providing unequal and inadequate school resources and excluding black parents from meaningful participation in school policymaking are at least as damaging

to black children as enforced separation," see Derrick A. Bell, Jr., *Serving Two Masters: Integration Ideals and Client Interests in School Desegregation Litigation*, 85 Yale L.J. 470 (1976).

For decisions concerning the validity of state aid to private schools that racially discriminate, see *Norwood v. Harrison* and *Gilmore v. Montgomery*, pp. 1510, 1511 infra.

c. For the view that the core harm of de jure school segregation was "distorting the socializing process of public schools" by "inculcating a belief in the inferiority of African-Americans," and, therefore, that "racial imbalance has less importance in an institution" like 4–H clubs, see Kevin Brown, *Has the Supreme Court Allowed the Cure for De Jure Segregation to Replicate the Disease*, 78 Corn. L.Rev. 1 (1992).

mean that a race-neutral admissions policy cures the constitutional violation of a dual system. [If] the State perpetuates policies and practices traceable to its prior system that continue to have segregative effects—whether by influencing student enrollment decisions or by fostering segregation in other facets of the university system—and such policies are without sound educational justification and can be practically eliminated, the State has not satisfied its burden of proving that it has dismantled its prior system."

The Court remanded the case for review "in light of the proper standard," but did "address four policies of the present system: * * *

"The present admission standards are not only traceable to the de jure system and were originally adopted for a discriminatory purpose, but they also have present discriminatory effects. Every Mississippi resident under 21 seeking admission to the university system must take the ACT. Any applicant who scores at least 15 qualifies for automatic admission to [the] historically white institutions. [I]n 1985, 72 percent of Mississippi's white high school seniors achieved an ACT composite score of 15 or better, while less than 30 percent of black high school seniors earned that score. It is not surprising then that Mississippi's universities remain predominantly identifiable by race.

"[The] courts below made little if any effort to justify in educational terms those particular disparities in entrance requirements or to inquire whether it was practicable to eliminate them.

"[The] record also indicated that the disparity between black and white students' high school grade averages was much narrower than the gap between their average ACT scores, thereby suggesting that an admissions formula which included grades would increase the number of black students eligible for automatic admission to all of Mississippi's public universities. * * *

"A second aspect of the present system that necessitates further inquiry is the widespread duplication of programs [that] was part and parcel of the prior dual system of higher education—the whole notion of 'separate but equal' required duplicative programs in two sets of [schools]. The court's holding that petitioners could not establish the constitutional defect of unnecessary duplication, therefore, improperly shifted the burden away from the State. * * *

"We next address [the fact that in] 1981, the State assigned certain missions to Mississippi's public universities as they then existed. [We] do not suggest that absent discriminatory purpose the assignment of different missions to various institutions in a State's higher education system would raise an equal protection issue where one or more of the institutions become or remain predominantly black or white. But here the issue is whether the State has sufficiently dismantled its prior dual system; and when combined with the differential admission practices and unnecessary program duplication, it is likely that the mission designations interfere with student choice and tend to perpetuate the segregated system. On remand, the court should inquire whether it would be practicable and consistent with sound educational practices to eliminate any such discriminatory effects of the State's present policy of mission assignments.

"Fourth, the State attempted to bring itself into compliance with the Constitution by continuing to maintain and operate all eight higher educational institutions. [O]n remand this issue should be carefully explored by inquiring and determining whether retention of all eight institutions itself affects student choice and perpetuates the segregated higher education system, whether maintenance of each of the universities is educationally justifiable, and whether one or more of them can be practicably closed or merged with other existing institutions."

THOMAS, J., concurred, emphasizing that "we do not foreclose the possibility that there exists 'sound educational justification' for maintaining historically black colleges as such. * * * Obviously, a State cannot maintain such traditions by closing particular institutions, historically white or historically black, to particular racial groups. Nonetheless, it hardly follows that a State cannot operate a diverse assortment of institutions—including historically black institutions—open to all on a race-neutral basis, but with established traditions and programs that might disproportionately appeal to one race or another. No one, I imagine, would argue that such institutional diversity is without 'sound educational justification,' or that it is even remotely akin to program duplication, which is designed to separate the races for the sake of separating the races." [a]

SCALIA, J., concurred on the ground that "the District Court should have required Mississippi to prove that its continued use of ACT requirements does not have a racially exclusionary purpose and effect," but dissented from "the Court's [applying] to universities the amorphous standard adopted for primary and secondary schools in *Green*. * * *

"*Bazemore's* standard for dismantling a dual system ought to control here: discontinuation of discriminatory practices and adoption of a neutral admissions policy. To use *Green* nomenclature, modern racial imbalance remains a 'vestige' of past segregative practices in Mississippi's universities, in that the previously mandated racial identification continues to affect where students choose to enroll—just as it surely affected which clubs students chose to join in *Bazemore*. [Like] the club attendance in *Bazemore* (and unlike the school attendance in *Green*), attending college is voluntary, not a legal obligation, and which institution particular students attend is determined by their own choice." O'Connor, J., also filed a brief concurrence.

V. REPEALS OF REMEDIES AND RESTRUCTURINGS OF THE POLITICAL PROCESS THAT BURDEN MINORITIES

In HUNTER v. ERICKSON, 393 U.S. 385, 89 S.Ct. 557, 21 L.Ed.2d 616 (1969), after the Akron, Ohio city council enacted a fair housing ordinance, the voters amended the city charter to prevent "any ordinance dealing with racial, religious, or ancestral discrimination in housing without the approval of the majority of the voters of Akron." The Court, per WHITE, J., held this "explicitly racial classification" violative of equal protection. Although the law "on its face" treated all races "in an identical manner, the reality [was] that the law's impact

---

a. For the view that "the Court's concepts of which practices are traceable to the prior system and foster segregation are so expansive that it will be difficult for any state to satisfy its duty under *Fordice* without eliminating some or all of its predominantly black institutions, either by closing the black institutions directly or by increasing their white enrollment through the close of predominantly white schools or eliminating program duplication," see 106 Harv.L.Rev. 235 (1992). Consider Note, *Mississippi Learning: Curriculum for the Post–Brown Era of Higher Education De-*

segregation, 104 Yale L.J. 243, 259–60 (1994): "In choosing which schools to maintain, states like Mississippi will close weaker schools due to scarcity of resources. Because the dual system shortchanged historically black schools for years, the weaker schools undoubtedly will be the historically black ones. [Thus,] *Fordice* has made it more difficult to argue simultaneously for the preservation or quality schools and for the maintenance of colleges with almost exclusively African–American enrollments."

[fell] on the minority," since "[t]he majority [needed] no protection against discrimination." Placing "special burdens on racial minorities in the governmental process [is] no more permissible than denying them the vote." Black, J., dissented.

———

In WASHINGTON v. SEATTLE SCHOOL DIST., 458 U.S. 457, 102 S.Ct. 3187, 73 L.Ed.2d 896 (1982), shortly after appellee implemented a mandatory busing plan to reduce de facto school segregation, the Washington electorate adopted Initiative 350, providing—with a number of broad exceptions—that "no school board [shall] directly or indirectly require any student to attend a school other than the school which is geographically nearest or next nearest the student's place of residence." The Court, per BLACKMUN, J., relied on *Hunter v. Erickson* in holding that Initiative 350 violated equal protection: "[T]he political majority may generally restructure the political process to place obstacles in the path of everyone seeking to secure the benefits of governmental action. But a different analysis is required when the State allocates governmental power non-neutrally, by explicitly using the *racial* nature of a decision to determine the decisionmaking process.

"[D]espite its facial neutrality there is little doubt that the initiative was effectively drawn for racial purposes. [T]he District Court found that the text [was] carefully tailored to interfere only with desegregative busing.[a] [It] in fact allows school districts to bus their students 'for most, if not all,' of the nonintegrative purposes required by their educational policies.[6] [It] is true [that] the proponents of mandatory integration cannot be classified by race: Negroes and whites may be counted among both the supporters and the opponents of Initiative 350. [But] desegregation of the public schools, like the Akron open housing ordinance, at bottom inures primarily to the benefit of the minority, and is designed for that purpose. [Given] the racial focus of Initiative 350, this suffices to trigger application of the *Hunter* doctrine.

"We are also satisfied that the practical effect of Initiative 350 is to work a reallocation of power of the kind condemned in *Hunter*. The initiative removes the authority to address a racial problem—and only a racial problem—from the existing decisionmaking body, in such a way as to burden minority interests. Those favoring the elimination of de facto school segregation now must seek relief from the state legislature, or from the statewide electorate. Yet authority over all other student assignment decisions, as well as over most other areas of educational policy, remains vested in the local school board. [As] in *Hunter,* then, the community's political mechanisms are modified to place effective decisionmaking authority over a racial issue at a different level of government.[17]"

POWELL, J., joined by Burger, C.J., and Rehnquist and O'Connor, JJ., dissented: "This is certainly not a case where a State [has] established a racially discriminatory requirement. Initiative 350 [is] neutral on its face, and racially

---

a. "The initiative envisioned busing for racial purposes in only one circumstance: it did not purport to 'prevent any court of competent jurisdiction from adjudicating constitutional issues relating to the public schools.' "

6. At the beginning of the 1978–1979 academic year, approximately 300,000 of the 769,040 students enrolled in Washington's public schools were bused to school. Ninety-five per-

cent of these students were transported for reasons unrelated to race.

17. [While] Justice Powell [finds] it crucial that the proponents of integrated schools remain free to use Washington's initiative system to further their ends, that was true in *Hunter* as well * * *.

neutral as public policy.   Children of all races benefit from neighborhood [schools].

"Nothing in *Hunter* supports the Court's extraordinary invasion into the State's distribution of authority.   [Initiative 350] simply does not place unique political obstacles in the way of racial minorities.   In this case, unlike in *Hunter,* the political system has *not* been redrawn or altered.   The authority of the State over the public school system, acting through Initiative or the legislature, is plenary.   Thus, the State's political system is not altered when it adopts for the first time a policy, concededly within the area of its authority, for the regulation of local school districts.   And certainly racial minorities are not uniquely or comparatively burdened by the State's adoption of a policy that would be lawful if adopted by any School District in the State.[13] * * *[14]"

In CRAWFORD v. LOS ANGELES BD. OF EDUC., 458 U.S. 527, 102 S.Ct. 3211, 73 L.Ed.2d 948 (1982), after the state courts had ordered substantial busing to remedy de facto school segregation which the state courts had found violative of the state constitution, the California electorate amended the state constitution by adopting Proposition I, providing that "state courts shall not order mandatory pupil assignment or transportation unless a federal court would do so to remedy a violation of the Equal Protection Clause."   The Court, per POWELL, J., found no violation of equal protection, "rejecting the contention that once a State chooses to do 'more' than the Fourteenth Amendment requires, it may never recede. [E]ven after Proposition I, the California Constitution still imposes a greater duty of desegregation than does the Federal Constitution.   The state courts of California continue to have an obligation under state law to order segregated school districts to use voluntary desegregation techniques, whether or not there has been a finding of intentional segregation.   The school districts themselves retain a state law obligation to take reasonably feasible steps to desegregate, and they remain free to adopt reassignment and busing plans to effectuate desegregation.[12]

"[Proposition I] does not embody a racial classification.   It neither says nor implies that persons are to be treated differently on account of their race.   * * *

13. The Court repeatedly states that the effect of Initiative 350 is "to redraw decision-making authority over racial matters—*and only over racial matters*—in such a way as to place *comparative* burdens on minorities." But the decision by the State to exercise its authority over the schools and over racial matters in the schools does not place a comparative burden on racial minorities.   In [*Hunter*,] "fair housing legislation *alone* was subject to an automatic referendum requirement."   By contrast, Initiative 350 merely places mandatory busing among the much larger group of matters—covering race relations, administration of the schools, and a variety of other matters—addressed at the State level.   Racial minorities, if indeed they are burdened by Initiative 350, are not *comparatively* burdened. In this respect, they are in the same position as any other group of persons who are disadvantaged by regulations drawn at the State level.

14. The Court's decision intrudes deeply into normal State decisionmaking.   Under its

holding the people [apparently] are forever barred from developing a different policy on mandatory busing where a School District previously has adopted one of its own.   This principle would not seem limited to the question of mandatory busing.   Thus, if the admissions committee of a State law school developed an affirmative action plan that came under fire, the Court apparently would find it unconstitutional for any higher authority to intervene unless that authority traditionally dictated admissions policies.   As a constitutional matter, the Dean of the Law School, the faculty of the University as a whole, the University President, the Chancellor of the University System, and the Board of Regents might be powerless to intervene despite their greater authority under State law. * * *

12. In this respect this case differs from the situation presented in *Seattle*.

"Were we to hold that the mere repeal of race related legislation is unconstitutional, we would limit seriously the authority of States to deal with the problems of our heterogeneous population. * * *

"*Hunter* involved more than a 'mere repeal' of the fair housing ordinance: persons seeking anti-discrimination housing laws—presumptively racial minorities—were 'singled out for mandatory referendums while no other [group] face[d] that obstacle.' By contrast, [Proposition I] is less than a 'repeal' of the California Equal Protection Clause. As noted above, after Proposition I, the State Constitution still places upon school boards a greater duty to desegregate than does the Fourteenth Amendment.

"Nor can it be said that Proposition I distorts the political process for racial reasons or that it allocates governmental or judicial power on the basis of a discriminatory principle. [The] remedies available for violation of the antitrust laws, for example, are different than those available for violation of the Civil Rights Acts. Yet a 'dual court system'—one for the racial majority and one for the racial minority—is not established simply because civil rights remedies are different from those available in other areas."

BLACKMUN, J., joined by Brennan, J., although joining the Court's opinion, concurred "to address [the] critical distinctions between this case [and] *Seattle*": "State courts do not create the rights they enforce; those rights originate elsewhere—in the state legislature, in the State's political subdivisions, or in the state constitution itself. When one of those rights is repealed, and therefore is rendered unenforceable in the courts, that action hardly can be said to restructure the State's decisionmaking mechanism. While the California electorate may have made it more difficult to achieve desegregation when it enacted Proposition I, [it] did so not by working a structural change in the political *process* so much as by simply repealing the right to invoke a judicial busing remedy. Indeed, ruling for petitioners on a *Hunter* theory seemingly would mean that statutory affirmative action or antidiscrimination programs never could be repealed, for a repeal of the enactment would mean that enforcement authority previously lodged in the state courts was being removed by another political entity.

"In short, the people of California—the same 'entity' that put in place the state constitution, and created the enforceable obligation to desegregate—have made the desegregation obligation judicially unenforceable. The 'political process or the decisionmaking mechanism used to *address* racially conscious legislation' has not been 'singled out for peculiar and disadvantageous treatment,' *Seattle,* for those political mechanisms that create and repeal the rights ultimately enforced by the courts were left entirely unaffected by Proposition I."

MARSHALL, J., dissented: "I fail to see how a fundamental redefinition of the governmental decisionmaking structure with respect to the same racial issue can be unconstitutional when the state seeks to remove the authority from local school boards [as in *Seattle*], yet constitutional when the state attempts to achieve the same result by limiting the power of its [courts].

"Proposition I is not a 'mere repeal.' [B]y denying full access to the only branch of government that has been willing to address this issue meaningfully, [Proposition I] is far worse for those seeking to vindicate the plainly unpopular cause of racial integration in the public schools than a simple reallocation of an often unavailable and unresponsive legislative process."

Notes and Questions

1. *Facially neutral statutes, disparate impact, and the political process.* Is the result in *Seattle* consistent with *Washington v. Davis*, p. 1093 supra? Why does a facially neutral statute trigger heightened judicial scrutiny?

(a) Did the proponents of Initiative 350 restructure the political process, or merely use it to achieve the outcome that they desired? Would it count as a "restructuring" of the political process if the voters adopted an initiative that, without generally withdrawing the power of local school districts to implement busing plans, simply forbade school busing in the Seattle district?

(b) What does the Court mean when it says in *Seattle* that "there is little doubt that the initiative was effectively drawn for racial purposes"? Does it mean that there was a racially invidious intent, such as underlay the antimiscegenation statute in *Loving v. Virginia*, p. 1086 supra? If so, couldn't the initiative have been invalidated on that ground alone?

Consider Cass R. Sunstein, *Public Values, Private Interests, and the Equal Protection Clause,* 1982 Sup.Ct.Rev. 127, 149, 157–58: "A classification [that] singles out a racial problem for special and disadvantageous treatment [is] peculiarly likely to be supported by invidious justifications. Like the heightened scrutiny applied to facial racial classifications, heightened scrutiny in *Hunter* is justified by a suspicion that improper justifications are at work. [But] arguments against busing are less likely to be animated by racial bias than are arguments against legislation preventing discrimination in housing. *Seattle* might therefore have been treated differently from *Hunter* on the ground that invidious motives may well not have been at work."

2. *Crawford and the political process.* Is *Crawford* persuasively distinguishable from *Seattle*? Does the distinction depend on the proposition that a restructuring of the remedies available through the judicial process is not a restructuring of the political process? That the busing remedy was withdrawn by the same, statewide electorate that adopted the California constitutional provision under which it was granted in the first place?

VI. AFFIRMATIVE ACTION AND "BENIGN" DISCRIMINATION

REGENTS OF UNIV. OF CALIFORNIA v. BAKKE

438 U.S. 265, 98 S.Ct. 2733, 57 L.Ed.2d 750 (1978).

Justice Powell announced the judgment of the Court.

This case presents a challenge to the special admissions program of the petitioner, the Medical School of the University of California at Davis * * *.

For the reasons stated in the following opinion, I believe that so much of the judgment of the California court as holds petitioner's special admissions program unlawful and directs that respondent be admitted to the Medical School must be affirmed. For the reasons expressed in a separate opinion, my Brothers The Chief Justice, Mr. Justice Stewart, Mr. Justice Rehnquist, and Mr. Justice Stevens concur in this judgment.

I also conclude [that] the portion of the court's judgment enjoining petitioner from according any consideration to race in its admissions process must be reversed. For reasons expressed in separate opinions, my Brothers Mr. Justice

Brennan, Mr. Justice White, Mr. Justice Marshall, and Mr. Justice Blackmun concur in this judgment. * * *

I.† [The medical school reserved 16 out of 100 places in its entering class for members of minority groups, apparently defined as "Blacks," "Chicanos," "Asians," and "American Indians."] Allan Bakke is a white male who applied [and was rejected, even though] applicants were admitted under the special program with grade point averages [and] Medical College Admissions Test scores significantly lower than Bakke's. * * *

II. [Powell, J., found that Title VI of the Civil Rights Act of 1964—which provides that "No person in the United States shall, on the ground of race, color, or national origin, be excluded from participation in, be denied the benefits of, or be subjected to, discrimination under any program or activity receiving Federal financial assistance"—proscribes "only those racial classifications that would violate the Equal Protection Clause or the Fifth Amendment."]

III. A. [P]etitioner argues that the court below erred in applying strict scrutiny to the special admissions programs because white males, such as respondent, are not a "discrete and insular minority" requiring extraordinary protection from the majoritarian political process. *Carolene Products Co.,* n. 4 [p. 17 supra. These] characteristics may be relevant in deciding whether or not to add new types of classifications to the list of "suspect" categories or whether a particular classification survives close examination. Racial and ethnic classifications, however, are subject to stringent examination without regard to these additional characteristics. [*Hirabayashi; Korematsu.*]

B. This perception of racial and ethnic distinctions is rooted in our Nation's constitutional and demographic history. The Court's initial view of the Fourteenth Amendment was that its "one pervading purpose" was "the freedom of the slave race * * *." *Slaughter-House Cases.* [Later, however, as] the Nation filled with the stock of many lands, the reach of the Clause was gradually extended to all ethnic groups seeking protection from official discrimination. * * *

Petitioner urges us to adopt for the first time a more restrictive view [and] hold that discrimination against members of the white "majority" cannot be suspect if its purpose can be characterized as "benign."[34] [But it] is far too late to argue that the guarantee of equal protection to *all* persons permits the recognition of special wards entitled to a degree of protection greater than that accorded others. * * *

Once the artificial line of a "two-class theory" of the Fourteenth Amendment is put aside, the difficulties entailed in varying the level of judicial review

---

† Justice Brennan, Mr. Justice White, Mr. Justice Marshall, and Mr. Justice Blackmun join Parts I and V–C of this opinion. Mr. Justice White also joins Part III–A of this opinion.

34. In the view of Mr. Justice Brennan, Mr. Justice White, Mr. Justice Marshall, and Mr. Justice Blackmun, the pliable notion of "stigma" is the crucial element in analyzing racial classifications. The Equal Protection Clause is not framed in terms of "stigma." Certainly the word has no clearly defined constitutional meaning. It reflects a subjective judgment that is standardless. *All* state-imposed classifications that rearrange burdens and benefits on the basis of race are likely to be viewed with deep resentment by the individuals burdened. The denial to innocent persons of equal rights and opportunities may outrage those so deprived and therefore may be perceived as invidious. These individuals are likely to find little comfort in the notion that the deprivation they are asked to endure is merely the price of membership in the dominant majority and that its imposition is inspired by the supposedly benign purpose of aiding others. One should not lightly dismiss the inherent unfairness of, and the perception of mistreatment that accompanies, a system of allocating benefits and privileges on the basis of skin color and ethnic origin. * * *

according to a perceived "preferred" status of a particular racial or ethnic minority are intractable. [T]he white "majority" itself is composed of various minority groups, most of which can lay claim to a history of prior discrimination at the hands of the state and private individuals. Not all of these groups can receive preferential treatment and corresponding judicial tolerance of distinctions drawn in terms of race and nationality, for then the only "majority" left would be a new minority of White Anglo–Saxon Protestants. There is no principled basis for deciding which groups would merit "heightened judicial solicitude" and which would not.[36] * * *

Moreover, there are serious problems of justice connected with the idea of preference itself. First, it may not always be clear that a so-called preference is in fact benign. Courts may be asked to validate burdens imposed upon individual members of particular groups in order to advance the group's general interest. Nothing in the Constitution supports the notion that individuals may be asked to suffer otherwise impermissible burdens in order to enhance the societal standing of their ethnic groups. Second, preferential programs may only reinforce common stereotypes holding that certain groups are unable to achieve success without special protection based on a factor having no relationship to individual worth. Third, there is a measure of inequity in forcing innocent persons in respondent's position to bear the burdens of redressing grievances not of their making. * * *

If it is the individual who is entitled to judicial protection against classifications based upon his racial or ethnic background because such distinctions impinge upon personal rights, rather than the individual only because of his membership in a particular group, then constitutional standards may be applied consistently. Political judgments regarding the necessity for the particular classification may be weighed in the constitutional balance, *Korematsu,* but the standard of justification will remain constant. [When legal classifications] touch upon an individual's race or ethnic background, he is entitled to a judicial determination that the burden he is asked to bear on that basis is precisely tailored to serve a compelling governmental interest. * * *

C. Petitioner contends that on several occasions this Court has approved preferential classifications without applying the most exacting scrutiny. * * *

The school desegregation cases are inapposite. Each involved remedies for clearly determined constitutional violations. [Here,] there was no judicial determination of constitutional violation as a predicate for [a] remedial classification.

The employment discrimination cases also do not advance petitioner's cause. For example, in *Franks v. Bowman Transportation Co.,* 424 U.S. 747, 96 S.Ct.

---

36. [M]y Brothers Brennan, White, Marshall, and Blackmun [would] require as a justification for a program such as petitioner's, only two findings: (i) that there has been some form of discrimination against the preferred minority groups "by society at large" (it being conceded that petitioner had no history of discrimination), and (ii) that "there is reason to believe" that the disparate impact sought to be rectified by the program is the "product" of such discrimination * * *.

[The] first step is easily taken. No one denies the regrettable fact that there has been societal discrimination in this country against various racial and ethnic groups. The second step, however, involves a speculative leap: but for this discrimination by society at large,

Bakke "would have failed to qualify for admission" because Negro applicants—nothing is said about Asians—would have made better scores. Not one word in the record supports this conclusion, and the plurality offers no standard for courts to use in applying such a presumption of causation to other racial or ethnic classifications. This failure is a grave one, since if it may be concluded *on this record* that each of the minority groups preferred by the petitioner's special program is entitled to the benefit of the presumption, it would seem difficult to determine that any of the dozens of minority groups that have suffered "societal discrimination" cannot also claim it, in any area of social intercourse.

1251, 47 L.Ed.2d 444 (1976), we approved a retroactive award of seniority to a class of Negro truck drivers who had been the victims of discrimination—not just by society at large, but by the respondent in that case. While this relief imposed some burdens on other employees, it was held necessary " 'to make [the victims] whole for injuries suffered on account of unlawful employment discrimination.' " [But] we have never approved preferential classifications in the absence of proven constitutional or statutory violations.[41] * * *

In this case, [there] has been no determination by the legislature or a responsible administrative agency that the University engaged in a discriminatory practice requiring remedial efforts. * * *

IV. [The] special admissions program purports to serve the purposes of: (i) "reducing the historic deficit of traditionally disfavored minorities in medical schools and the medical profession," (ii) countering the effects of societal discrimination; (iii) increasing the number of physicians who will practice in communities currently undeserved; and (iv) obtaining the educational benefits that flow from an ethnically diverse student body. It is necessary to decide which, if any, of these purposes is substantial enough to support the use of a suspect classification.

A. If petitioner's purpose is to assure within its student body some specified percentage of a particular group merely because of its race or ethnic origin, such a preferential purpose must be rejected not as insubstantial but as facially invalid. Preferring members of any one group for no reason other than race or ethnic origin is discrimination for its own sake. This the Constitution forbids. E.g., *Loving.*

B. The State certainly has a legitimate and substantial interest in ameliorating, or eliminating where feasible, the disabling effects of identified discrimination. [That] goal [is] far more focused than the remedying of the effects of "societal discrimination," an amorphous concept of injury that may be ageless in its reach into the past.

We have never approved a classification that aids persons perceived as members of relatively victimized groups at the expense of other innocent individuals in the absence of judicial, legislative, or administrative findings of constitutional or statutory violations. [Without] such findings of constitutional or statutory violations,[44] it cannot be said that the government has any greater interest in

---

41. This case does not call into question congressionally authorized administrative actions, such as consent decrees under Title VII or approval of reapportionment plans under § 5 of the Voting Rights Act of 1965. In such cases, there has been detailed legislative consideration of the various indicia of previous constitutional or statutory violations, e.g., *South Carolina v. Katzenbach,* [p. 1378 infra], and particular administrative bodies have been charged with monitoring various activities in order to detect such violations and formulate appropriate remedies.

Furthermore, we are not here presented with an occasion to review legislation by Congress pursuant to its powers under § 2 of the Thirteenth Amendment and § 5 of the Fourteenth Amendment to remedy the effects of prior discrimination. *Katzenbach v. Morgan* [p. 1386 infra]; *Jones v. Alfred H. Mayer Co.,* [p. 1406 infra].

44. Mr. Justice Brennan, Mr. Justice White, Mr. Justice Marshall, and Mr. Justice Blackmun misconceive the scope of this Court's holdings under Title VII when they suggest that "disparate impact" alone is sufficient to establish a violation of that statute and, by analogy, other civil rights measures. [This] was made quite clear in the seminal decision in this area, *Griggs v. Duke Power Co.,* 401 U.S. 424, 91 S.Ct. 849, 28 L.Ed.2d 158 (1971): "*Discriminatory preference* for any group, minority or majority, is precisely and only what Congress has proscribed. What is required by Congress is the removal of *artificial, arbitrary, and unnecessary barriers* to employment when the barriers operate invidiously to discriminate on the basis of racial or other impermissible classification." Thus, disparate impact is a basis for relief under Title VII only if the practice in question is not founded on "business necessity," or lacks "a manifest rela-

helping one individual than in refraining from harming another. Thus, the government has no compelling justification for inflicting such harm.

Petitioner does not purport to have made, and is in no position to make, such findings. Its broad mission is education, not the formulation of any legislative policy or the adjudication of particular claims of illegality. For reasons similar to those stated in Part III of this opinion, isolated segments of our vast governmental structures are not competent to make those decisions, at least in the absence of legislative mandates and legislatively determined criteria. Cf. *Hampton v. Mow Sun Wong* [Sec. 4, I infra]. Compare n. 41, supra. * * *

Hence, the purpose of helping certain groups whom the faculty of the Davis Medical School perceived as victims of "societal discrimination" does not justify a classification that imposes disadvantages upon persons like respondent, who bear no responsibility for whatever harm the beneficiaries of the special admissions program are thought to have suffered. To hold otherwise would be to convert a remedy heretofore reserved for violations of legal rights into a privilege that all institutions throughout the Nation could grant at their pleasure to whatever groups are perceived as victims of societal discrimination. That is a step we have never approved.

C. Petitioner identifies, as another purpose of its program, improving the delivery of health care services to communities currently underserved. It may be assumed that in some situations a State's interest in facilitating the health care of its citizens is sufficiently compelling to support the use of a suspect classification. But there is virtually no evidence in the record indicating that petitioner's special admissions program is either needed or geared to promote that goal. The court below addressed this failure of proof: "The University concedes it cannot assure that minority doctors who entered under the program, all of whom express an 'interest' in participating in a disadvantaged community, will actually do so. It may be correct to assume that some of them will carry out this intention, and that it is more likely they will practice in minority communities than the average white doctor. Nevertheless, there are more precise and reliable [ways to achieve this end]."

D. The fourth goal asserted by petitioner is the attainment of a diverse student body. * * * Academic freedom, though not a specifically enumerated constitutional right, long has been viewed as a special concern of the First Amendment. [Thus,] in arguing that its universities must be accorded the right to select those students who will contribute the most to the "robust exchange of ideas," petitioner invokes a countervailing constitutional interest, [and] must be viewed as seeking to achieve a goal that is of paramount importance in the fulfillment of its mission. * * *

Ethnic diversity, however, is only one element in a range of factors a university properly may consider in attaining the goal of a heterogeneous student body. Although a university must have wide discretion in making the sensitive

tionship to the employment in question." Nothing *in this record*—as opposed to some of the general literature cited by Mr. Justice Brennan, Mr. Justice White, Mr. Justice Marshall, and Mr. Justice Blackmun—even remotely suggests that the disparate impact of the general admissions program at Davis Medical School [is] without educational justification.

Moreover, the presumption in *Griggs*—that disparate impact without any showing of busi-

ness justification established the existence of discrimination in violation of the statute—was based on legislative determinations, wholly absent here, that past discrimination had handicapped various minority groups to such an extent that disparate impact could be traced to identifiable instances of past discrimination * * *.

judgments as to who should be admitted, constitutional limitations protecting individual rights may not be disregarded. [As] the interest of diversity is compelling in the context of a university's admissions program, the question remains whether the program's racial classification is necessary to promote this interest.

V. A. [P]etitioner's argument that this is the only effective means of serving the interest of diversity is seriously flawed. [The] diversity that furthers a compelling state interest encompasses a far broader array of qualifications and characteristics of which racial or ethnic origin is but a single though important element. Petitioner's special admissions program, focused *solely* on ethnic diversity, would hinder rather than further attainment of genuine diversity. * * *

The experience of other university admissions programs, which take race into account in achieving the educational diversity valued by the First Amendment, demonstrates that the assignment of a fixed number of places to a minority group is not a necessary means toward that end. An illuminating example is found in the Harvard College program:

"In recent years Harvard College has expanded the concept of diversity to include students from disadvantaged economic, racial and ethnic groups. [When] the Committee on Admissions reviews the large middle group of applicants who are 'admissible' and deemed capable of doing good work in their courses, the race of an applicant may tip the balance in his favor just as geographic origin or a life spent on a farm may tip the balance in other candidates' cases. * * *

"In Harvard College admissions the Committee has not set target-quotas for the number of blacks, or of musicians, football players, physicists or Californians to be admitted in a given year[a] [but] in choosing among thousands of applicants who are not only 'admissible' academically but have other strong qualities, the Committee, with a number of criteria in mind, pays some attention to distribution among many types and categories of students."

In such an admissions program, race or ethnic background may be deemed a "plus" in a particular applicant's file, yet it does not insulate the individual from comparison with all [others]. The file of a particular black applicant may be examined for his potential contribution to diversity without the factor of race being decisive when compared, for example, with that of an applicant identified as an Italian–American if the latter is thought to exhibit qualities more likely to promote beneficial educational pluralism. Such qualities could include exceptional personal talents, unique work or service experience, leadership potential, maturity, demonstrated compassion, a history of overcoming disadvantage, ability to communicate with the poor, or other qualifications deemed important. * * *

This kind of program treats each applicant as an individual in the admissions process. The applicant who loses out [to] another candidate receiving a "plus" on

---

a. The portion of this paragraph of the Harvard program—omitted by Powell, J., in his opinion but reprinted in full in an appendix to the opinion—is as follows: "At the same time the Committee is aware that if Harvard College is to provide a truly heterogeneous environment that reflects the rich diversity of the United States, it cannot be provided without some attention to numbers. It would not make sense, for example, to have 10 or 20 students out of 1,100 whose homes are west of the Mississippi. Comparably 10 or 20 black students could not begin to bring to their classmates and to each other the variety of points of view, backgrounds and experiences of blacks in the United States. Their small numbers might also create a sense of isolation [and] thus make it more difficult for them to develop and achieve their potential. Consequently, when making its decisions, the Committee on Admissions is aware that there is some relationship between numbers and achieving the benefits to be derived from a diverse student body, and between numbers and providing a reasonable environment for those students admitted."

the basis of ethnic background will not have been foreclosed from all consideration [simply] because he was not the right color or had the wrong surname. It would mean only that his combined qualifications, which may have included similar nonobjective factors, did not outweigh those of the other applicant. His qualifications would have been weighed fairly and competitively and he would have no basis to complain of unequal treatment under the Fourteenth Amendment.

It has been suggested that an admissions program which considers race only as one factor is simply a subtle and more sophisticated—but no less effective—means of according racial preference than the Davis program. A facial intent to discriminate, however, is evident [in] this case. No such facial infirmity exists in an admissions program where race or ethnic background is simply one element—to be weighed fairly against other elements—in the selection process. [And] a Court would not assume that a university, professing to employ a facially nondiscriminatory admissions policy, would operate it as a cover for the functional equivalent of a quota system. * * * 53

B. [W]hen a State's distribution of benefits or imposition of burdens hinges on the color of a person's skin or ancestry, that individual is entitled to a demonstration that the challenged classification is necessary to promote a substantial state interest. Petitioner has failed to carry this burden. For this reason, that portion of the California court's judgment holding petitioner's special admissions program invalid under the Fourteenth Amendment must be affirmed.

C. In enjoining petitioner from ever considering the race of any applicant, however, the courts below failed to recognize that the State has a substantial interest that legitimately may be served by a properly devised admissions program involving the competitive consideration of race and ethnic origin. For this reason, so much of the California court's judgment as enjoins petitioner from any consideration of the race of any applicant must be reversed.

VI. With respect to respondent's entitlement to an injunction directing his admission to the Medical School, petitioner has conceded that it could not carry its burden of proving that, but for the existence of its unlawful special admissions program, respondent still would not have been admitted. Hence, respondent is entitled to the injunction, and that portion of the judgment must be affirmed.

Opinion of JUSTICE BRENNAN, JUSTICE WHITE, JUSTICE MARSHALL, and JUSTICE BLACKMUN, concurring in the judgment in part and dissenting. * * *

I. [C]laims that law must be "color-blind" or that the datum of race is no longer relevant to public policy must be seen as aspiration rather than as description of reality. This is not to denigrate aspiration; for reality rebukes us that race has too often been used by those who would stigmatize and oppress minorities. Yet we cannot [let] color blindness become myopia which masks the reality that many "created equal" have been treated within our lifetimes as inferior both by the law and by their fellow citizens. * * *

III. [A] government practice or statute which [contains] "suspect classifications" is to be subjected to "strict scrutiny" * * *. [But] whites as a class [do not] have any of the "traditional indicia of suspectness: the class is not saddled with such disabilities, or subjected to such a history of purposeful unequal

---

53. [There] also are strong policy reasons that correspond to the constitutional distinction between petitioner's preference program and one that assures a measure of competition among all applicants. Petitioner's program will be viewed as inherently unfair by the public generally as well as by [applicants]. Fairness in individual competition for opportunities, especially those provided by the State, is a widely cherished American ethic. * * *

treatment, or relegated to such a position of political powerlessness as to commend extraordinary protection from the majoritarian political process."

Moreover, [this] is not a case where racial classifications are "irrelevant and therefore prohibited." *Hirabayashi.* Nor has anyone suggested that the University's purposes contravene the cardinal principle that racial classifications that stigmatize—because they are drawn on the presumption that one race is inferior to another or because they put the weight of government behind racial hatred and separatism—are invalid without more. See *Yick Wo.* * * *

On the other hand, the fact that this case does not fit neatly into our prior analytic framework for race cases does not mean that it should be analyzed by applying the very loose rational-basis [standard]. Instead, a number of considerations—developed in gender discrimination cases but which carry even more force when applied to racial classifications—lead us to conclude that racial classifications designed to further remedial purposes "must serve important governmental objectives and must be substantially related to achievement of those objectives." *Craig v. Boren,* [Sec. 3, I infra].

First, race, like "gender-based classifications too often [has] been inexcusably utilized to stereotype and stigmatize politically powerless segments of society." While a carefully tailored statute designed to remedy past discrimination could avoid these vices, see *Califano v. Webster,* [Sec. 3, infra] we nonetheless have recognized that the line between honest and thoughtful appraisal of the effects of past discrimination and paternalistic stereotyping is not so clear and that a statute based on the latter is patently capable of stigmatizing all women with a badge of inferiority. State programs designed ostensibly to ameliorate the effects of past racial discrimination obviously create the same hazard of stigma, since they may promote racial separatism and reinforce the views of those who believe that members of racial minorities are inherently incapable of succeeding on their own.

Second, race, like gender and illegitimacy, is an immutable characteristic which its possessors are powerless to escape or set aside. While a classification is not per se invalid because [of this], it is nevertheless true that such divisions are contrary to our deep belief that "legal burdens should bear some relationship to individual responsibility or wrongdoing," and that advancement sanctioned, sponsored, or approved by the State should ideally be based on individual merit or achievement, or at the least on factors within the control of an individual.

Because this principle is so deeply rooted it might be supposed that it would be considered in the legislative process and weighed against the benefits of programs preferring individuals because of their race. But [t]he "natural consequence of our governing processes [may well be] that the most 'discrete and insular' of whites [will] be called upon to bear the immediate, direct costs of benign discrimination." [Thus] our review under the Fourteenth Amendment should be strict—not " 'strict' in theory and fatal in fact," because it is stigma that causes fatality—but strict and searching nonetheless.

IV. Davis' articulated purpose of remedying the effects of past societal discrimination is, under our cases, sufficiently important to justify the use of race-conscious admissions programs where there is a sound basis for concluding that minority underrepresentation is substantial and chronic, and that the handicap of past discrimination is impeding access of minorities to the medical school.

A. At least since *Green v. County School Bd.,* [a] public body which has itself been adjudged to have engaged in racial discrimination cannot bring itself into compliance with the Equal Protection Clause simply by ending its unlawful acts and adopting a neutral stance. Three years later, *Swann* [held] that courts could enter desegregation orders which assigned students and faculty by reference to race, and that local school boards could *voluntarily* adopt desegregation plans which made express reference to race if this was necessary to remedy the effects of past discrimination. Moreover, we stated that school boards, even in the absence of a judicial finding of past discrimination, could voluntarily adopt plans which assigned students with the end of creating racial pluralism by establishing fixed ratios of black and white students in each school. *Swann*. * * *

[O]ur cases under Title VII [have also] held that, in order to achieve minority participation in previously segregated areas of public life, Congress may require or authorize preferential treatment for those likely disadvantaged by societal racial discrimination. Such legislation has been sustained even without a requirement of findings of intentional racial discrimination by those required or authorized to accord preferential treatment, or a case-by-case determination that those to be benefitted suffered from racial discrimination. These decisions compel the conclusion that States also may adopt race-conscious programs designed to overcome substantial, chronic minority underrepresentation where there is reason to believe that the evil addressed is a product of past racial discrimination.[42] * * *

B. [Davis] had a sound basis for believing that the problem of underrepresentation of minorities was substantial and chronic and that the problem was attributable to handicaps imposed on minority applicants by past and present racial discrimination. Until at least 1973, the practice of medicine in this country [was] largely the prerogative of whites. * * *

Moreover, Davis had very good reason to believe that the national pattern of underrepresentation of minorities in medicine would be perpetuated if it retained a single admissions standard. For example, the entering classes in 1968 and 1969, [when] such a standard was used, included only one Chicano and two Negroes out of 100 admittees. Nor is there any relief from this pattern of underrepresentation in the statistics for the regular admissions program in later years.

Davis clearly could conclude that the serious and persistent underrepresentation [is] the result of handicaps under which minority applicants labor as a consequence of a background of deliberate, purposeful discrimination against minorities in education and in society generally, as well as in the medical profession. From the inception of our national life, Negroes have been subjected to unique legal [disabilities]. The generation of minority students applying to Davis Medical School since it opened in 1968—most of whom were born before or about the time *Brown I* was decided—clearly have been victims of this discrimination. [T]he conclusion is inescapable that applicants to medical school must be few indeed who endured the effects of de jure segregation, the resistance to *Brown I*, or the equally debilitating pervasive private discrimination fostered by our long history of official discrimination, cf. *Reitman v. Mulkey,* [p. 1344], and yet come to the starting line with an education equal to whites. * * *

---

42. [Justice Powell] would not allow [the university] to exercise such power in the absence of "judicial, legislative, or administrative findings of constitutional or statutory violations." [But] the manner in which a State chooses to delegate governmental functions is for it to decide. California, by constitutional provision, has chosen to place authority over the operation of the University of California in the Board of Regents [who] have been vested with full legislative (including policymaking), administrative, and adjudicative powers. [W]e, unlike our Brother Powell, find nothing in the Equal Protection Clause that requires us to depart from established principle by limiting the scope of power the Regents may exercise more narrowly than the powers that may constitutionally be wielded by the Assembly. * * *

C. The second prong of our test—whether the Davis program stigmatizes any discrete group or individual and whether race is reasonably used in light of the program's objectives—is clearly satisfied by the Davis program. * * *

Unlike discrimination against racial minorities, the use of racial preferences for remedial purposes does not inflict a pervasive injury upon individual whites in the sense that wherever they go or whatever they do there is a significant likelihood that they will be treated as second-class citizens because of their color. This distinction does not mean that the exclusion of a white resulting from the preferential use of race is not sufficiently serious to require justification; but it does mean that the injury inflicted by such a policy is not distinguishable from disadvantages caused by a wide range of government actions, none of which has ever been thought impermissible for that reason alone.

In addition, there is simply no evidence that the Davis program discriminates intentionally or unintentionally against any minority group which it purports to benefit. The program does not establish a quota in the invidious sense of a ceiling on the number of minority applicants to be admitted. Nor can the program reasonably be regarded as stigmatizing the program's beneficiaries or their race as inferior. The Davis program does not simply advance less qualified applicants; rather, it compensates applicants, whom it is uncontested are fully qualified to study medicine, for educational disadvantage which it was reasonable to conclude was a product of state-fostered discrimination. Once admitted, these students must satisfy the same degree [requirements]; they are taught by the same faculty in the same classes; and their performance is evaluated by the same standards by which regularly admitted students are judged. Under these circumstances, their performance and degrees must be regarded equally with the regularly admitted students with whom they compete for standing.

D. We disagree with the lower courts' conclusion that the Davis program's use of race was unreasonable in light of its objectives. [A]s petitioner argues, there are no practical means by which it could achieve its ends in the foreseeable future without the use of race-conscious measures. With respect to any factor (such as poverty or family educational background) that may be used as a substitute for race as an indicator of past discrimination, whites greatly outnumber racial minorities simply because whites make up a far larger percentage of the total population and therefore far outnumber minorities in absolute terms at every socio-economic level. * * *

E. Finally, Davis' special admissions program cannot be said to violate the Constitution simply because it has set aside a predetermined number of places for qualified minority applicants rather than using minority status as a positive factor to be considered in evaluating the applications of disadvantaged minority applicants. For purposes of constitutional adjudication, there is no difference between the two approaches. In any admissions program which accords special consideration to disadvantaged racial minorities, a determination of the degree of preference to be given is unavoidable, and any given preference that results in the exclusion of a white candidate is no more or less constitutionally acceptable than a program such as that at Davis. Furthermore, the extent of the preference inevitably depends on how many minority applicants the particular school is seeking to admit in any particular year so long as the number of qualified minority applicants exceeds that number. There is no sensible, and certainly no constitutional, distinction between, for example, adding a set number of points to the admissions rating of disadvantaged minority applicants as an expression of the preference with the expectation that this will result in the admission of an approximately determined number of qualified minority applicants and setting a fixed number of places for such applicants as was done here.

[That] the Harvard approach does not also make public the extent of the preference and the precise workings of the system while the Davis program employs a specific, openly stated number, does not condemn the [latter]. It may be that the Harvard plan is more acceptable to the public than is the Davis "quota." If it is, any State [is] free to adopt it in preference to a less acceptable alternative, just as it is generally free [to] abjure granting any racial preferences in its admissions program. But there is no basis for preferring a particular preference program simply because in achieving the same goals that [Davis] is pursuing, it proceeds in a manner that is not immediately apparent to the public.[b]
* * *

JUSTICE MARSHALL.

[I]t must be remembered that, during most of the past 200 years, the Constitution as interpreted by this Court did not prohibit the most ingenious and pervasive forms of discrimination against the Negro. Now, when a State acts to remedy the effects of that legacy of discrimination, I cannot believe that this same Constitution stands as a barrier. * * *

The position of the Negro today in America is the tragic but inevitable consequence of centuries of unequal treatment. Measured by any benchmark of comfort or achievement, meaningful equality remains a distant dream for the Negro [—comparing Negro and white statistics on life expectancy, infant mortality, median income, poverty, unemployment, and percentages in professions].

In light of the sorry history of discrimination and its devastating impact on the lives of Negroes, bringing the Negro into the mainstream of American life should be a state interest of the highest order. To fail to do so is to ensure that America will forever remain a divided society. * * *

Since the Congress that considered and rejected the objections to the 1866 Freedmen's Bureau Act concerning special relief to Negroes also proposed the Fourteenth Amendment, it is inconceivable that the Fourteenth Amendment was intended to prohibit all race-conscious relief measures. [T]o hold that it barred state action to remedy the effects [of] discrimination [would] pervert the intent of the framers by substituting abstract equality for the genuine equality the amendment was intended to achieve.

[H]ad the Court [held in *Plessy*] that the Equal Protection Clause forbids differences in treatment based on race, we would not be faced with this dilemma in 1978. We must remember, however, that the principle that the "Constitution is color-blind" appeared only in the opinion of the lone dissenter. [F]or the next 60 years, from *Plessy* to *Brown,* ours was a Nation where, *by law,* an individual could be given "special" treatment based on the color of his skin. * * *

I fear that we have come full circle. After the Civil War our government started several "affirmative action" programs. This Court in the *Civil Rights Cases,* [p. 1318 infra], and *Plessy* destroyed the movement toward complete equality. For almost a century no action was taken, and this nonaction was with the tacit approval of the courts. Then we had *Brown* and the Civil Rights Acts of Congress, followed by numerous affirmative action programs. *Now,* we have this

---

b. The separate opinion of White, J.—concluding that Title VI does not provide for a private cause of action—is omitted.

Court again stepping in, this time to stop affirmative action programs of the type used by the University of California.

JUSTICE BLACKMUN. * * *

I yield to no one in my earnest hope that the time will come when an "affirmative action" program is unnecessary and is, in truth, only a relic of the past. I would hope that we could reach this stage within a decade at the most. But the story of *Brown,* decided almost a quarter of a century ago, suggests that that hope is a slim one. At some time, however, beyond any period of what some would claim is only transitional inequality, the United States must and will reach a stage of maturity where action along this line is no longer necessary. Then persons will be regarded as persons, and discrimination of the type we address today will be an ugly feature of history that is instructive but that is behind us. * * *

It is somewhat ironic to have us so deeply disturbed over a program where race is an element of consciousness, and yet to be aware of the fact, as we are, that institutions of higher learning, albeit more on the undergraduate than the graduate level, have given conceded preferences up to a point to those possessed of athletic skills, to the children of alumni, to the affluent who may bestow their largess on the institutions, and to those having connections with celebrities, the famous, and the powerful. * * *

[That] the Fourteenth Amendment has expanded beyond its original 1868 conception [does] not mean for me, however, that the Fourteenth Amendment has broken away from its moorings and its original intended purposes. [In] order to get beyond racism, we must first take account of race. There is no other way. And in order to treat some persons equally, we must treat them differently. We cannot—we dare not—let the Equal Protection Clause perpetrate racial supremacy. * * *

JUSTICE STEVENS, with whom THE CHIEF JUSTICE, JUSTICE STEWART, and JUSTICE REHNQUIST join, concurring in the judgment in part and dissenting in part.[1]

[Bakke] challenged petitioner's special admissions program [and the] California Supreme Court upheld his challenge and ordered him admitted. If the state court was correct in its view that the University's special program was illegal, and that Bakke was therefore unlawfully excluded from the medical school because of his race, we should affirm its judgment, regardless of our views about the legality of admissions programs that are not now before the Court.

[Stevens, J., then construed the state court opinion as containing no "outstanding injunction forbidding any consideration of racial criteria in processing applications."] It is therefore perfectly clear that the question whether race can ever be used as a factor in an admissions decision is not an issue in this case, and that discussion of that issue is inappropriate.

[Stevens, J., then interpreted Title VI as prohibiting "the exclusion of *any* individual from a federally funded program 'on the ground of race.'"] It is therefore our duty to affirm the judgment ordering Bakke admitted * * *.

---

1. Four Members of the Court have undertaken to announce the legal and constitutional effect of this Court's judgment. See opinion of Justice Brennan, White, Marshall, and Blackmun. [But] only a majority can speak for the Court or determine what is the "central meaning" of any judgment of the Court.

Notes and Questions

1. *"Benign" and "invidious" discrimination.* Should race-based classificatory schemes that aim to advantage previously disadvantaged minorities be evaluated under the same constitutional standard as schemes that are invidiously motivated and designed to stigmatize?

   a. *History.* Consider Louis Pollak, *"Mr. Chief Justice: May It Please the Court:"*, in Constitutional Government in America 247, 252 (Collins ed. 1980): "[T]he Freedmen's Bureau [authorized] a large remedial apparatus for the education and economic advancement [of] the freedmen. What could more clearly show that the fourteenth amendment, far from precluding remedial programs particularly designed to assist those groups battered by American history, was expected to be implemented in just such ways? "[a] Compare Charles Fried, *Metro Broadcasting, Inc. v. FCC: Two Concepts of Equality*, 104 Harv.L.Rev. 107, 111 n.21 (1990): "[R]eference to the Reconstruction-era Freedmen's Bureaus is not quite apposite: they no more accorded benefits in terms of race than did the Emancipation Proclamation."[b]

   b. *Moral relevance and permissibility.* Is the relevant constitutional principle that government should not classify by race? Or is it that government should not use race as a basis to demean, suppress, or stigmatize?[c]

Is it acceptable for public officials to treat integration—which requires race-consciousness—as a positive good? To draw school district lines or to adopt voluntary busing plans with an aim of achieving a greater integration of the races? Compare *Swann's* dictum that "school authorities might well conclude that in order to prepare students to live in a pluralistic society each school should have a prescribed ratio of Negro to white students reflecting the proportion for the district as a whole."

Consider David A. Strauss, *The Myth of Colorblindness,* 1986 Sup.Ct.Rev. 99, 131: "[T]here is unquestionably an undertone in the affirmative action debate that affirmative action is different from nondiscrimination because affirmative action causes innocent people to suffer. The assertion that there is a difference [is] incorrect. Prohibiting discrimination also causes, and has caused, innocent people to suffer [pointing to *Brown* and *Palmore v. Sidoti*]. [N]o one has justified the suffering of these victims of nondiscrimination in a way that would not also justify the suffering of victims of affirmative action."

   c. *Political representation.* Consider John H. Ely, *The Constitutionality of Reverse Racial Discrimination*, 41 U.Chi.L.Rev. 723, 735–36 (1974): "When the group that controls the decision making process classifies so as to advantage a minority and disadvantage itself, the reasons for being unusually suspicious, and, consequently, employing a stringent brand of review, are lacking. A White majority is unlikely to disadvantage itself for reasons of racial prejudice; nor is it likely to be tempted either to underestimate the needs and deserts of Whites

---

   a. See also Eric Schnapper, *Affirmative Action and the Legislative History of the Fourteenth Amendment*, 71 Va.L.Rev. 753, 784–89 (1985).

   b. See also Lino Graglia, *Racially Discriminatory Admission to Public Institutions of Higher Education,* in Constitutional Government in America, supra, 255, 263: "[T]his argument proves too much. It is equally clear that the fourteenth amendment was not intended to prohibit school segregation either."

   c. Cf. Jerome M. Culp, Jr., *Colorblind Remedies and the Intersectionality of Oppression: Policy Arguments Masquerading as Moral Claims,* 69 N.Y.U.L.Rev. 162, 171 (1994): "The genuine moral goal associated with race is to end race-based oppression. Colorblindness may sometimes accomplish this moral goal, but it is not the goal itself. Therefore, the color-blind principle [must] be seen as a policy argument and not a moral precept."

relative to those of others, or to overestimate the costs of devising an alternative classification that would extend to certain Whites the advantages generally extended to Blacks. [Whether] or not it is more blessed to give than to receive, it is surely less suspicious." Compare Terrance Sandalow, *Racial Preferences in Higher Education: Political Responsibility and the Judicial Role,* 42 U.Chi.L.Rev. 653, 694–99 (1975): "[This] analysis [is] troublesome on several grounds. First, in American politics majorities [typically] are coalitions of minorities which have varying [interests]. Resolution of the dispute depends upon which of the minorities is more successful in forging an alliance with those groups which are less immediately affected. The issue whether state schools ought to adopt preferential admissions policies is no exception. The immediate beneficiaries of these policies are the minorities which receive preferential treatment. But there is no reason to suppose that the costs of such policies are borne equally by sub-groups within the white population. To the extent that they are not, the discrimination—though nominally against a majority—is in reality against those sub-groups."

See also Kent Greenawalt, *Judicial Scrutiny of "Benign" Racial Preference in Law School Admissions,* 75 Colum.L.R. 559, 573–74 (1975): "We may safely suppose that the faculty of most state law schools is almost entirely white, but we may not assume that most faculty members will identify more with marginal white applicants than with black applicants. As most law teachers have done very well academically [they] may have trouble identifying themselves with marginal applicants. [M]any intellectuals may actually find it easier to identify with the plight of the 'oppressed' than the problems of the 'Philistine' middle and lower middle classes, from whom many marginal white applicants may come."

2. *Justifications for affirmative action.* Numerous justifications have been offered for affirmative action programs—that is, for programs that take race or group status into account for the purpose of increasing the participation of previously disadvantaged or excluded groups. Some of the asserted justifications are predominantly based on past injustices, while others emphasize anticipated future benefits. A third class of justifications views affirmative action as a safeguard against current, sometimes subconscious, bias.

(a) *Backward-looking justifications.* (i) Affirmative action is often defended as a *remedy* for past discrimination, but a remedy of a somewhat unusual kind. It is undeniable that there is a long and shameful national history of discrimination based on race. In many cases, however, the particular institution implementing an affirmative action program either has not engaged in or refuses to acknowledge that it has engaged in past discrimination. Moreover, even if the implementing institution has engaged in past discrimination, the beneficiaries of its affirmative action program are unlikely to be those particular individuals against whom it has discriminated. (The beneficiaries of the program may of course have been the victims of discrimination by other institutions and individuals—of "societal discrimination.") Finally, the costs of the remedy may be felt not by the institution itself, but by "innocent" whites.

(ii) A slightly different argument is that society itself, through acts of governmental commission (discriminatory acts) and omission (failure to forbid or remedy private discrimination), is substantially responsible for currently skewed patterns of distribution in which whites (on average) are much more materially and educationally advantaged than blacks (on average) and that affirmative action is therefore justified as a form of class-based reparations for society's wrongs. Are the premises of this argument, which depend on collective or group-based notions such as "societal" discrimination against a "class" defined by race, consistent with the proposition that the Constitution protects the rights of "individuals"? See Fried, supra. Is the entire theory of the equal protection clause—in particular, its focus on the acceptability of legal *classifications*—inherently group-based? See Owen M. Fiss, *Groups and the Equal Protection Clause*, 5 Phil. & Pub.Aff. 107, 108 (1976).

(b) *Forward-looking justifications.* Forward-looking justifications look less to past discrimination than to the anticipated benefits to be reaped from affirmative action programs.

(i) One view is that a more nearly proportionate distribution of opportunities and benefits to members of traditionally disadvantaged groups is a general good—either to break any association of race or ethnicity with subordinated social class, or to demonstrate the society's equal openness to members of groups that are socially salient.[d]

(ii) Another, narrower view is that race, in some situations, may be a powerful indicator of a person's capacity to perform a socially valuable function. In *Bakke*, for example, Powell, J., recognized that people from minority backgrounds might introduce a distinctive perspective in academic institutions. It is sometimes also argued that black teachers provide needed role models to black students (and thus, because of their race, are more effective teachers in some contexts than otherwise similarly talented whites) and that black police officers, other factors being equal, may be able to function more effectively than white police officers in some situations.[e] On this view, affirmative action is not, in some contexts, an exception to principles requiring merit-based distribution; on the contrary, race can sometimes be a component or indicator of "merit"—conceived as the capacity to perform socially valued functions effectively. See Richard H. Fallon, Jr., *To Each According to His Ability, From None According to His Race: The Concept of Merit in the Law of Antidiscrimination*, 60 B.U.L.Rev. 815 (1980); Kenneth L. Karst & Harold W. Horowitz, *Affirmative Action and Equal Protection*, 60 Va.L.Rev. 955 (1974).

Is race likely to be an accurate indicator of the distinctive views and perspectives underlying the aim of "diversity"? Of the capacity to generate distinctive insights that are valuable in practical deliberations or the search for truth?[f]

Is it morally objectionable to allow race to be treated as a measure of a person's capacity or merit? Is it dangerous to associate race with merit in a society that has often viewed whiteness as a sign of worth and membership in other races as an indicator of likely inability, vice, or treachery? See Randall L. Kennedy, *Racial Critiques of Legal Academia*, 102 Harv.L.Rev. 1745, 1807 (1989).

d. Cf. Kathleen M. Sullivan, *Sins of Discrimination: Last Term's Affirmative Action Cases*, 100 Harv.L.Rev. 78, 96–97 (1986).

e. Compare Terrance Sandalow, *Minority Preferences in Law School Admissions*, in *Constitutional Government in America*, supra, at 277, 282: "The ability to 'speak the language' of the client, to understand his perception of his problem, and to deal with others in the community on his behalf are qualities essential to being a 'good lawyer.' These qualifications are more likely to be found among lawyers who share the client's racial or ethnic identity, at least to the extent that the client's life is bound up in a community defined in these terms."

f. For affirmative answers, see, e.g., Kimberle Crenshaw, *Race, Reform, and Retrenchment: Transformation and Legitimation in Antidiscrimination Law*, 101 Harv.L.Rev. 1331, 1336 (1988); Mari Matsuda, *Affirmative Action and Legal Knowledge: Planting Seeds in Plowed–Up Ground*, 11 Harv. Women's L.J. 1, 12–13 (1988). See also Duncan Kennedy, *A Cultural Pluralist Case for Affirmative Action in Legal Academia*, 1990 Duke L.J. 705, 713.

Consider Fallon, supra, at 874–75: "Factors peculiar to the sphere of education indicate that Justice Powell's approach [in the *Bakke* case, which allows race to be treated as a 'plus' in considering a student's capacity to contribute to desired diversity and thus as a component of an applicant's 'merit,' is appropriate.] Almost uniquely among the objects of social distribution, education functions almost equally as, on the one hand, a benefit to be awarded on a merit basis, and, on the other, an element of merit itself. Education increases capacity for future performance, and provides a common and accepted merit criterion in competitions for scarce jobs and social resources. To whom, it might then be asked, should merit be given? Who merits merit? The oddity of these questions [suggests] that the situation of education is unique—and because of its uniqueness any conception of merit allowed by the law to obtain within that sphere is unlikely to alter conceptual usage and associations elsewhere."

(c) *Present and prophylactic justifications.* A final set of justifications for affirmative action maintains that existing, "meritocratic" distributive schemes are often skewed in several ways: (i) familiar merit measures often test for and reward traits that tend to be disproportionately possessed by whites, even when those traits are not relevant to performance; (ii) the same measures overlook *other* traits that are equally relevant to excellence in practical performance; (iii) merit testing frequently has a subjective component, and whites administering such tests may be culturally sensitized to recognize the merit of white more readily than of black candidates. On this view, affirmative action is a prophylactic needed to correct for predictable corruptions in the implementation of meritocratic ideals—again, not a departure from merit standards, but a corrective needed to achieve a more genuinely meritocratic distribution.

Among its implications, this asserted justification rejects the stigmatizing assumption that "affirmative action means that unqualified, or lesser qualified, individuals will be selected over more qualified individuals."[g] Indeed, it assumes that "[r]acial discrimination"—which affirmative action aims to correct—"is powerful precisely because of its frequent invisibility, its felt neutrality"[h] as reflected in "meritocratic" standards.[i]

Would this rationale for affirmative action, if persuasive, support a "quota" system? If so, how should the size of the quotas be fixed?

3. *The Bakke "standard."* A principal issue dividing the parties in *Bakke*, and to some extent the Court, was the question of the appropriate legal standard by which to judge the constitutionality of voluntarily adopted affirmative action programs. Four justices opted explicitly for an "intermediate" standard (between strict scrutiny and rational basis review). Powell, J., whose position was dispositive, instead purported to apply "strict scrutiny," under which even "benign" race-based classifications are impermissible unless necessary to serve a compelling government interest.

Do you agree with the way that Powell, J., applied the "strict scrutiny" standard to the various state interests asserted in *Bakke*? Does a public university, exercising its academic freedom, have a "compelling" interest in an ethnically

g. Michael Selmi, *Testing for Equality: Merit, Efficiency, and the Affirmative Action Debate,* 42 UCLA L.Rev. 1251, 1251 (1995).

h. Patricia J. Williams, *Metro Broadcasting, Inc. v. FCC: Regrouping in Singular Times,* 104 Harv.L.Rev. 525, 544 (1990).

i. See Richard Delgado, *Rodrigo's Tenth Chronicle: Merit and Affirmative Action,* 83 Geo.L.J. 1711 (1995); Luke Charles Harris & Uma Narayan, *Affirmative Action and the Myth of Equal Treatment: A Transformative Critique of the Terms of the Affirmative Action Debate,* 11 Harv. Blackletter L.J. 1 (1994).

"diverse student body" that would contribute to a "robust exchange of ideas". Consider Wayne McCormack, *Race and Politics in the Supreme Court: Bakke to Basics,* 1979 Utah L.Rev. 491, 530: "Most educators would agree that some element of diversity in a student body is healthy," but this "is simply not the most honest statement of the objective of [most affirmative action] programs. [Further,] it is hard to believe that racial classifications disfavoring racial or ethnic minorities could be justified by a school's claim of academic freedom. This justification would be considered ludicrous if advanced as a basis for preferring members of the white majority. These considerations rob the principle of the very neutrality that Justice Powell was seeking elsewhere in the opinion and suggest the instability of the rationale."

4. *Affirmative action and stigma.* Do affirmative action programs unfairly stigmatize minorities in general, and their intended beneficiaries in particular, by creating the impression that minorities could not be expected to satisfy meritocratic norms without special preferences? Do they give rise to what Professor Carter calls "the best black syndrome"—the perception that highly able and successful minorities have risen to coveted positions only as a result of affirmative action. Consider Stephen L. Carter, *Reflections of an Affirmative Action Baby* 69 (1991): "Supporters of [racial] preferences cite a whole catalogue of explanations for the inability of people of color to get along without them: institutional racism, inferior education, overt prejudice, the lingering effects of slavery and oppression, cultural bias in the criteria for admission and unemployment. All of these arguments are most sincerely pressed, and some of them are true. [But] they all entail the assumption that people of color cannot at present compete on the same playing field with people who are white." See also Richard Delgado, *The Imperial Scholar: Reflections on a Review of Civil Rights Literature,* 132 U.Pa.L.Rev. 561, 570 n.46 (1984), arguing that an affirmative action program designed to promote diversity in an academic institution "may well be perceived as treating the minority admittee as an ornament, a curiosity, one who brings an element of the piquant to the lives of white professors and students."

Compare T. Alexander Aleinikoff, *A Case for Race–Consciousness,* 91 Colum.L.Rev. 1060, 1091 (1991): "Despite assertions by whites that race-conscious programs 'stigmatize' beneficiaries, blacks remain overwhelmingly in favor of affirmative action. Would we not expect blacks to be the first to recognize such harms and therefore to oppose affirmative action if it produced serious stigmatic injury?"

Is the real point that affirmative action programs help some minorities, but hurt others, who would have competed successfully without affirmative action, and whose achievements are tainted by the suspicion that they succeeded only because of racial preferences?[j] If so, how should the balance be struck? Does the Constitution provide an answer? Is it "surprising that the Court would hold [affirmative action] policies unconstitutional on the basis of predictions [concerning stigmatizing effects] which [social] scientists could not confidently make"?

---

j. Most schools do not publish the relevant admissions data, but in *Bakke,* the Medical School reported that, with no race-based affirmative action program, its entering classes in 1968 and 1969 included "only 1 Chicano and 2 Negroes out of the 50 admittees." According to a report on a lawsuit challenging the admissions program at the University of Texas Law School, "[i]f the law school had based its 1992 admissions on a strictly colorblind standard [establishing minimum test scores that a candidate must achieve to enter the pool from which the entering class is selected], the entering class of 500 students would have included, at most, nine black and eighteen Mexican–American students, all of whom were being courted by the most prestigious law schools in America." Jeffrey Rosen, *Is Affirmative Action Doomed?,* The New Republic 25, 28 (October 17, 1994).

See Mark Strasser, *The Invidiousness of Invidiousness: On the Supreme Court's Affirmative Action Jurisprudence*, 21 Hast.Con.L.Q. 323, 401 (1994).

5. *Individualized judgments and quotas.* Is there any practical distinction between (a) a separate, identified program for minority admissions and (b) a program in which racial background can be counted as a "plus," and those administering the program—in order to get the desired "diversity"—monitor the number of admittees who fall within relevant categories? See Paul J. Mishkin, *The Uses of Ambivalence: Reflections on the Supreme Court and the Constitutionality of Affirmative Action,* 131 U.Pa.L.Rev. 907, 928 (1983): "The description of race as simply 'another factor' among a lot of others considered in seeking diversity tends to minimize the sense that minority students are separate and different and the recipients of special dispensations. [These] perceptions [can] facilitate or hamper the development of relationships among individuals and groups; they can advance or retard the educational process for all—including, particularly, minority students whose self-image is most crucially involved."[k] Compare Vincent Blasi, *Bakke as Precedent: Does Mr. Justice Powell Have a Theory?* 67 Calif.L.Rev. 21, 60 (1979): "[I]t is almost always a bad thing for constitutional standards to be based on the purported perceptions of the populace regarding what is fair or rational rather than on well-considered and explicitly defended arguments respecting fairness and rationality. [I]f admissions programs are to be evaluated not on the basis of what they really entail but instead in terms of how they are generally perceived, educational institutions can only regard the constitutional standard as a legitimation of subterfuge and hypocrisy."

6. *Which groups and individuals?* (a) If affirmative action is constitutionally justifiable for some minority groups, is it equally justifiable for all?[l] For all minority groups that have suffered historical discrimination? For the poor? Should lines be drawn, lest government promote race-consciousness and exacerbate racial divisions? Consider Deborah Ramirez, *Multicultural Empowerment: It's Not Just Black and White Anymore*, 47 Stan.L.Rev. 957, 962–63 (1995): "In 1960, blacks constituted 96 percent of the minority population. Today, the phenomenal growth in the Asian and Latino communities has altered the mix [so] dramatically that blacks now make up only about 50 percent of the population of people of color [and people of color represent about 25 percent of the total population according to the 1990 census]. [As] a result, affirmative action remedies originally designed to address the legacy of suffering and discrimination experienced by African–Americans are increasingly benefiting *other* people of color. [If] blacks are indeed uniquely disadvantaged, does the 'lesser' history of discrimination against Latinos and Asians entitle them to a lesser remedy, or no remedy at all? "

(b) Consider Ian F. Haney Lopez, *The Social Construction of Race: Some Observations on Illusion, Fabrication, and Choice*, 29 Harv.C.R.C.L. L.Rev. 1, 10 (1994): "I write as a Latino. [My] older brother, Garth, and I are the only children of a fourth-generation Irish father [and] a Salvadoran immigrant mother. [We] both have light but not white skin. [Interestingly], Garth and I conceive of ourselves in different racial terms. For the most part, he considers his race transparent, [and] he relates most easily with the Anglo side of the family. I, on

---

k. See also Michael J. Perry, *Modern Equal Protection: A Conceptualization and Appraisal,* 79 Colum.L.Rev. 1023, 1048 (1979).

l. For diverse views, see, e.g., Paul Brest & Miranda Oshige, *Affirmative Action for Whom?*, 47 Stan.L.Rev. 855 (1995); Michael Gottesman, *Twelve Topics to Consider Before Opting for Racial Quotas*, 79 Geo.L.J. 1737 (1991); Richard H. Fallon, Jr. & Paul C. Weiler, *Firefighters v. Stotts: Conflicting Models of Racial Justice*, 1984 Sup.Ct.Rev. 1, 44–50.

the other hand, consider myself Latino and am in greatest contact with my maternal family." How, generally, should race be defined for purposes of administering race-based classifications?[m] Under the framework laid out in *Bakke*, "if one were to consider the brothers as law school applicants," would it be acceptable for the school to conclude that "Ian Haney Lopez's presence would serve most of the goals of affirmative action," whereas that of Garth would not? See Brest & Oshigee, supra 875.

(c) Is it constitutionally permissible under *Bakke* for a state university to grant an admissions "plus" to an African–American applicant whose views on political issues are deemed to reflect a characteristic "black" or "minority" perspective, but to deny a similar preference to an African–American candidate whose views are deemed too mainstream?[n]

(d) In order to maintain a diverse student body, may a public educational institution with competitive entrance requirements place a cap (40 percent) on the maximum number of students that may be admitted from any racially defined group? Could it give race-based, individualized preferences (as in *Bakke*) to promote the same end—even if the effect was to exclude Chinese–Americans with higher scores than whites? See Selena Dong, Note, *"Too Many Asians": The Challenge of Fighting Discrimination Against Asian–Americans and Preserving Affirmative Action*, 47 Stan.L.Rev. 1027 (1995).

7. *Bakke's authority.* According to Brest & Oshiga, supra, at 857, "The constitutional and statutory permissibility of using race as an admissions criterion [in state and local educational institutions] continues to be determined by *Bakke*—particularly Justice Powell's opinion." As you read the remainder of this section, consider whether *Bakke* remains consonant with doctrines governing the constitutional permissibility of "benign" racial preferences in other contexts.

———

WYGANT v. JACKSON BD. OF EDUC., 476 U.S. 267, 106 S.Ct. 1842, 90 L.Ed.2d 260 (1986), involved a minority preference in teacher lay-offs. When a budget crisis required cutting teaching positions, the school board, pursuant to a contract with the local teachers union, laid off more senior white teachers in order to retain less senior minority teachers. The court of appeals upheld the school board's action as justified by its interest in "providing role models for its minority students, as an attempt to alleviate the effects of societal discrimination." Although there was no majority opinion, five justices agreed that the school board had violated the Constitution.

m. See Christopher A. Ford, *Administering Identity: The Determination of "Race" in Race–Conscious Law*, 82 Cal.L.Rev. 1231 (1994).

n. And if views or perspective are ultimately crucial, is it permissible to rely on race at all, rather than simply selecting people on the basis of their views or perspectives? See Sheila Foster, *Difference and Equality: A Critical Assessment of the Concept of "Diversity"*, 1993 Wis.L.Rev. 105 (probing the relationship between viewpoint and background as elements of diversity and endorsing a substantive conception of diversity aimed at including and empowering members of historically disadvantaged groups). Related questions concerning the relevance of authors' race to perspectives in and the resulting quality of legal scholarship have recently engendered heated debate. Compare, e.g., Delgado, supra 566–73 (asserting that a distinctive perspective and insights strongly correlate with race) and Mari J. Matsuda, *Looking at the Bottom: Critical Legal Studies and Reparations*, 22 Harv.C.R.–C.L.L.Rev. 323, 324 (1987) (same) with R. Kennedy, supra 1749 (denying the racial distinctiveness thesis). See also Colloquy, *Responses to Randall Kennedy's Racial Critiques of Legal Academia*, 103 Harv.L.Rev. 1844, 1844–86 (1990) (including articles by Scott Brewer, Milner S. Ball, Robin D. Barnes, Richard Delgado, and Leslie G. Espinoza).

Writing for a plurality,[a] POWELL, J., found that race-based preferences must be subjected to strict scrutiny. The plurality concluded that the school board had no compelling interest in remedying "societal discrimination," and suggested that "prior [institutional] discrimination" supplied the only permissible justification for "race-based remedies." But even if the school board had discriminated in the past, "the burden that a preferential-layoffs scheme imposes on innocent parties" would be too great to be constitutionally acceptable. "While hiring goals impose a diffuse burden, often foreclosing only one of several opportunities, layoffs impose the entire burden of achieving racial equality on particular individuals, often resulting in serious disruption of their lives. That burden is too intrusive" and therefore fails the requirement that a race-based remedy be "narrowly tailored" to achieve its ends.

O'CONNOR, J., concurring, subscribed to the view that "racial classifications of any sort must be subjected to 'strict scrutiny.'" Under this standard, she "agree[d] with the plurality that a governmental agency's interest in remedying 'societal' discrimination * * * cannot be deemed sufficiently compelling to pass constitutional muster." Even if the school board had discriminated in the past, it had attempted to justify its layoff program by reference to discrimination with respect to student assignments, not faculty hiring, and the remedy was not closely tailored to the violation. With respect to other possible compelling government interests: "[A]lthough its precise contours are uncertain, a state interest in the promotion of racial diversity has been found sufficiently 'compelling,' at least in the context of higher education, to support the use of racial considerations in furthering that interest. And certainly nothing the Court has said today necessarily forecloses the possibility that the Court will find other governmental interests which have been relied upon in the lower courts but which have not been passed on here to be sufficiently 'important' or 'compelling' to sustain the use of affirmative action policies."

WHITE, J., wrote a brief opinion concurring in the judgment, but did not specifically endorse any standard of review.

Dissenting, MARSHALL, J., joined by Brennan and Blackmun, JJ., found the school board's actions adequately justified by its interest in "preserv[ing] the levels of faculty integration" achieved during the 1970s by an affirmative action program of unchallenged validity. It was a mistake to regard laid off whites as singled out to bear a unique and disproportionate burden. The aim of the contract between the school board and the union was to apportion the burden of layoffs that were not deserved by anyone, and there was no basis for thinking that "the tradition of basing layoff decisions on seniority is so fundamental that its modification can never be permitted."

In a separate dissent, STEVENS, J., argued that the equal protection clause permits "inclusionary" but not "exclusionary" use of racial classifications to promote legitimate government purposes. He would not have asked whether the race-based preference was justified "as a remedy for sins that were committed in the past," but whether by maintaining "an integrated faculty" it provided educational benefits that "could not be provided by an all-white" faculty.

Notes and Questions

1. *Race and merit.* If the government, in *Bakke,* had a compelling interest in achieving a diverse student body, why did the school board, in *Wygant,* not have

_____

a. Burger, C.J., and Rehnquist, J., joined in all, and O'Connor, J., in parts, of the opinion.

a compelling interest in retaining a diverse faculty?[b] If layoff decisions had been based on individualized assessments, rather than seniority, could a faculty member's contribution to faculty diversity have been treated as a "plus"?

2. *Weight of burden.* Should it matter under the equal protection clause what "burden," if any, an affirmative action program imposes on "innocent whites"? Consider Richard H. Fallon, Jr. & Paul C. Weiler, *Firefighters v. Stotts: Conflicting Models of Racial Justice*, 1984 Sup.Ct.Rev. 1, 28–31: "Issues of racial justice can be viewed as subsuming at least two questions. One involves [the] conditions that must be satisfied to justify even in principle a program of race-conscious redistribution. Another involves the fairness of cost allocation. [The] wrongs of racial discrimination often having been social and legal, [the costs of affirmative action would ideally] be spread broadly across relevant segments of the economy or the political community. [Where] cost spreading would be difficult to achieve consistently with the ordinary practices of American government, we assume that the costs of affirmative discrimination—as of any other social policy— may be assigned to identifiable classes of citizens. The mandatory draft in wartime provides a relevant if extreme example of socially imposed individual burdens. [But] the moral dubiousness of an assignment of costs will increase with the burden imposed on particular individuals."

Compare Laurence H. Tribe, *American Constitutional Law* 1536–37 (2d ed. 1988): "The fact that implementing preferences in layoffs may be viewed as causing harms more focused and intrusive than those caused by preferences in allocating limited economic opportunities in the first place should not be deemed to make otherwise acceptable affirmative action violative of equal protection. To be sure, burdening vested employment rights of white workers might well amount to a taking for a public purpose and thus require just compensation. But [d]istinguishing between otherwise justified affirmative action plans on the basis of the degree of sacrifice they extract from equally innocent white workers unnecessarily confounds takings and equal-protection analyses and subordinates the achievement of racial justice to whatever pattern of economic distribution our discriminatory past happens to have produced."[c]

RICHMOND v. J.A. CROSON CO.

488 U.S. 469, 109 S.Ct. 706, 102 L.Ed.2d 854 (1989).

JUSTICE O'CONNOR announced the judgment of the Court and delivered the opinion of the Court with respect to Parts I, III–B, and IV, an opinion with respect to Part II, in which THE CHIEF JUSTICE and JUSTICE WHITE join, and an opinion with respect to Parts III–A and V, in which THE CHIEF JUSTICE, JUSTICE WHITE and JUSTICE KENNEDY join. * * *

I. On April 11, 1983, the Richmond City Council adopted the Minority Business Utilization Plan (the Plan). The Plan required prime contractors to

b. Compare Robert A. Sedler, *Racial Preference and the Constitution: The Societal Interest in the Equal Participation Objective*, 26 Wayne L.Rev. 1227, 1236, 1248, 1250, 1254 (1980) (arguing that, under the logic of Powell, J.'s opinion in *Bakke*, "there is strong societal interest in [the] equal participation of blacks * * * whenever a 'black [can] bring something that a white person cannot offer,' "and that this extends to *all* "institutions of government, the 'power professions,' such as law and medicine, [and] the economic system").

c. See also David Chang, *Discriminatory Impact, Affirmative Action, and Innocent Victims: Judicial Conservatism or Conservative Justices*, 91 Colum.L.Rev. 790, 793 (1991) (arguing that for courts to invalidate classifications established to serve permissible purposes because of their incidental effect in imposing burdens is a form of judicial activism incompatible with equal protection doctrine and especially *Washington v. Davis*, [p. 1093 supra]).

whom the city awarded construction contracts to subcontract at least 30% of the dollar amount of the contract to one or more Minority Business Enterprises (MBEs) [defined] as "[a] business at least fifty-one (51) percent of which is owned and controlled [by] minority group members." "Minority group members" were defined as "[c]itizens of the United States who are Blacks, Spanish-speaking, Orientals, Indians, Eskimos, or Aleuts." [The] Plan declared that it was "remedial" in nature, and enacted "for the purpose of promoting wider participation by minority business enterprises in the construction of public projects." The Plan expired on June 30, 1988, and was in effect for approximately five years.

The Plan authorized the Director of the Department of General Services to promulgate rules which "shall allow waivers in those individual situations where a contractor can prove to the satisfaction of the director that the requirements herein cannot be achieved." * * *

The Plan was adopted by the Richmond City Council after a public hearing. Seven members of the public spoke to the merits of the ordinance: five were in opposition, two in favor. Proponents of the set-aside provision relied on a study which indicated that, while the general population of Richmond was 50% black, only .67% of the city's prime construction contracts had been awarded to minority businesses in the 5–year period from 1978 to 1983. It was also established that a variety of contractors' associations, whose representatives appeared in opposition to the ordinance, had virtually no minority businesses within their membership. * * *

There was no direct evidence of race discrimination on the part of the city in letting contracts or any evidence that the city's prime contractors had discriminated against minority-owned subcontractors. * * * Representatives of various contractors' associations questioned whether there were enough MBEs in the Richmond area to satisfy the 30% set-aside requirement. [One] noted that only 4.7% of all construction firms in the United States were minority owned and that 41% of these were located in California, New York, Illinois, Florida, and Hawaii. He predicted that the ordinance would thus lead to a windfall for the few minority firms in Richmond. Council person Gillespie indicated his concern that many local labor jobs, held by both blacks and whites, would be lost because the ordinance put no geographic limit on the MBEs eligible for the 30% set-aside. * * *

[The case was brought by a contractor whose low bid on a city project was not accepted because of failure to comply with the Plan's requirements. A] divided panel of the Court of Appeals struck down the Richmond set-aside program as violating both prongs of strict scrutiny under the Equal Protection Clause * * *.

II. [In *Fullilove v. Klutznick,* 448 U.S. 448, 100 S.Ct. 2758, 65 L.Ed.2d 902 (1980)], we upheld the minority set-aside contained in § 103(f)(2) of the Public Works Employment Act of 1977 (the Act) against a challenge based on the equal protection component of the Due Process Clause. The Act authorized a four billion dollar appropriation for federal grants to state and local governments for use in public works projects [and] contained the following requirement: "Except to the extent the Secretary determines otherwise, no grant shall be made under this Act [unless] the applicant gives satisfactory assurance to the Secretary that at least 10 per centum of the amount of each grant shall be expended for minority business enterprises." MBEs were defined as businesses effectively controlled by "citizens of the United States who are Negroes, Spanish-speaking, Orientals, Indians, Eskimos, and Aleuts."

The principal opinion in *Fullilove*, written by Chief Justice Burger, did not employ "strict scrutiny" or any other traditional standard of equal protection review. The Chief Justice noted at the outset that although racial classifications call for close examination, the Court was at the same time, "bound to approach [its] task with appropriate deference to the Congress" [and that] Congress could mandate state and local government compliance with the set-aside program under its § 5 power to enforce the Fourteenth Amendment (citing *Katzenbach v. Morgan,* [p. 1386 infra]).

The Chief Justice next turned to the constraints on Congress' power to employ race-conscious remedial relief. His opinion stressed two factors in upholding the MBE set-aside. First was the unique remedial powers of Congress under § 5 of the Fourteenth Amendment: "[It] is fundamental that *in no organ of government, state or federal, does there repose a more comprehensive remedial power than in the Congress,* expressly charged by the Constitution with competence and authority to enforce equal protection guarantees." (Emphasis added).

[In] reviewing the legislative history behind the Act, the principal opinion focused on the evidence before Congress that a nationwide history of past discrimination had reduced minority participation in federal construction grants [and] concluded that "Congress had abundant historical basis from which it could conclude that traditional procurement practices, when applied to minority businesses, could perpetuate the effects of prior discrimination."

The second factor emphasized by the principal opinion in *Fullilove* was the flexible nature of the 10% set-aside. [A] waiver could be sought where minority businesses were not available to fill the 10% requirement or, more importantly, where an MBE attempted "to exploit the remedial aspects of the program by charging an unreasonable price, i.e., a price not attributable to the present effects of prior discrimination." The Chief Justice indicated that without this fine tuning to remedial purpose, the statute would not have "pass[ed] muster."

In his concurring opinion, Justice Powell relied on the legislative history adduced by the principal opinion in finding that "Congress reasonably concluded that private and governmental discrimination had contributed to the negligible percentage of public contracts awarded minority contractors." Justice Powell also found that the means chosen by Congress, particularly in light of the flexible waiver provisions, were "reasonably necessary" to address the problem identified. Justice Powell made it clear that other governmental entities might have to show more than Congress before undertaking race-conscious [measures].[a]

Appellant and its supporting amici rely heavily on *Fullilove* for the proposition that a city council, like Congress, need not make specific findings of discrimination to engage in race-conscious relief. Thus, appellant argues "[i]t would be a perversion of federalism to hold that the federal government has a compelling interest in remedying the effects of racial discrimination in its own public works program, but a city government does not."

What appellant ignores is that Congress, unlike any State or political subdivision, has a specific constitutional mandate to enforce the dictates of the Four-

a. Burger, C.J.'s opinion was joined by White and Powell, JJ. Powell, J., also concurred separately. Marshall, J., joined by Brennan and Blackmun, JJ., concurred. Stevens, J., dissented for reasons discussed below. Stewart, J., joined by Rehnquist, J., dissented on the ground that, generally, "under our Constitution, the government may never act to the detriment of a person solely because of that person's race," and that "a judicial decree that imposes burdens on the basis of race can be upheld only where its sole purpose is to eradicate the actual effects of illegal race discrimination."

teenth Amendment.   The power to "enforce" may at times also include the power
to define situations which *Congress* determines threaten principles of equality and
to adopt prophylactic rules to deal with those situations.   See *Katzenbach v.
Morgan.*   See also *South Carolina v. Katzenbach* [p. 1378 infra] (similar interpretation of congressional power under § 2 of the Fifteenth Amendment).   The Civil
War Amendments themselves worked a dramatic change in the balance between
congressional and state power over matters of race.   Speaking of the Thirteenth
and Fourteenth Amendments in *Ex parte Virginia,* the Court stated: "They were
intended to be, what they really are, limitations of the powers of the States and
enlargements of the power of Congress."

[It seems clear,] however, that a state or local subdivision (if delegated the
authority from the State) has the authority to eradicate the effects of private
discrimination within its own legislative jurisdiction.   This authority must, of
course, be exercised within the constraints of § 1 of the Fourteenth Amendment.
[As] a matter of state law, the city of Richmond has legislative authority over its
procurement policies, and can use its spending powers to remedy private discrimination, if it identifies that discrimination with the particularity required by the
Fourteenth Amendment.   * * *

Thus, if the city could show that it had essentially become a "passive
participant" in a system of racial exclusion practiced by elements of the local
construction industry, we think it clear that the city could take affirmative steps
to dismantle such a system.   It is beyond dispute that any public entity, state or
federal, has a compelling interest in assuring that public dollars, drawn from the
tax contributions of all citizens, do not serve to finance the evil of private
prejudice.   Cf. *Norwood v. Harrison* [p. 1353 infra].

III.   A.   [The] Richmond Plan denies certain citizens the opportunity to
compete for a fixed percentage of public contracts based solely upon their race.
To whatever racial group these citizens belong, their "personal rights" to be
treated with equal dignity and respect are implicated by a rigid rule erecting race
as the sole criterion in an aspect of public decisionmaking.

Absent searching judicial inquiry into the justification for such race-based
measures, there is simply no way of determining what classifications are "benign"
or "remedial" and what classifications are in fact motivated by illegitimate
notions of racial inferiority or simple racial politics.   Indeed, the purpose of strict
scrutiny is to "smoke out" illegitimate uses of race by assuring that the legislative
body is pursuing a goal important enough to warrant use of a highly suspect tool.
The test also ensures that the means chosen "fit" this compelling goal so closely
that there is little or no possibility that the motive for the classification was
illegitimate racial prejudice or stereotype.

Classifications based on race carry a danger of stigmatic harm.   Unless they
are strictly reserved for remedial settings, they may in fact promote notions of
racial inferiority and lead to a politics of racial hostility.   We thus reaffirm the
view expressed by the plurality in *Wygant v. Jackson Bd. of Educ.* that the
standard of review under the Equal Protection Clause is not dependent on the
race of those burdened or benefitted by a particular classification.   * * *

Even were we to accept a reading of the guarantee of equal protection under
which the level of scrutiny varies according to the ability of different groups to
defend their interests in the representative process, heightened scrutiny would
still be appropriate in the circumstances of this case.   [B]lacks comprise approximately 50% of the population of the city of Richmond.   Five of the nine seats on
the City Council are held by blacks.   The concern that a political majority will

more easily act to the disadvantage of a minority based on unwarranted assumptions or incomplete facts would seem to militate for, not against, the application of heightened judicial scrutiny in this case. * * *

Justice Powell's opinion [in *Bakke*] applied heightened scrutiny under the Equal Protection Clause to the racial classification at issue. His opinion [contrasted] the "focused" goal of remedying "wrongs worked by specific instances of racial discrimination" with "the remedying of the effects of 'societal discrimination,' an amorphous concept of injury that may be ageless in its reach into the past." He indicated that for the governmental interest in remedying past discrimination to be triggered "judicial, legislative, or administrative findings of constitutional or statutory violations" must be made. Only then does the Government have a compelling interest in favoring one race over another.

In *Wygant*, * * * Justice Powell, writing for the plurality, again drew the distinction between "societal discrimination" which is an inadequate basis for race-conscious classifications, and the type of identified discrimination that can support and define the scope of race-based relief. * * *

B. [The] District Court found the city council's "findings sufficient to ensure that, in adopting the Plan, it was remedying the present effects of past discrimination in the *construction industry*." [A] generalized assertion that there has been past discrimination in an entire industry provides no guidance for a legislative body to determine the precise scope of the injury it seeks to remedy. It "has no logical stopping point." *Wygant*. "Relief" for such an ill-defined wrong could extend until the percentage of public contracts awarded to MBEs in Richmond mirrored the percentage of minorities in the population as a whole.

Appellant argues that it is attempting to remedy various forms of past discrimination that are alleged to be responsible for the small number of minority businesses in the local contracting industry. [While] there is no doubt that the sorry history of both private and public discrimination in this country has contributed to a lack of opportunities for black entrepreneurs, this observation, standing alone, cannot justify a rigid racial quota in the awarding of public contracts in Richmond, Virginia. * * *

It is sheer speculation how many minority firms there would be in Richmond absent past societal discrimination, just as it was sheer speculation how many minority medical students would have been admitted to the medical school at Davis absent past discrimination in educational opportunities.[b] Defining these sorts of injuries as "identified discrimination" would give local governments license to create a patchwork of racial preferences based on statistical generalizations about any particular field of endeavor.

These defects are apparent in this case. The 30% quota cannot in any realistic sense be tied to any injury suffered by anyone. [None of the] "findings" [relied on by the district court,] singly or together, provide the city of Richmond with a "strong basis in evidence for its conclusion that remedial action was necessary." *Wygant*. There is nothing approaching a prima facie case of a constitutional or statutory violation by *anyone* in the Richmond construction industry.

The District Court accorded great weight to the fact that the city council designated the Plan as "remedial." But the mere recitation of a "benign" or

---

b. For criticism of the "notion [that] discrimination must be the decisive explanation of intergroup differences," see Thomas Sowell, *Weber and Bakke, and the Presuppositions of "Affirmative Action,"* 26 Wayne L.Rev. 1309, 1335 (1980).

legitimate purpose for a racial classification, is entitled to little or no weight. Racial classifications are suspect, and that means that simple legislative assurances of good intention cannot suffice.   * * *

In the employment context, we have recognized that for certain entry level positions or positions requiring minimal training, statistical comparisons of the racial composition of an employer's workforce to the racial composition of the relevant population may be probative of a pattern of discrimination. See *Teamsters v. United States,* 431 U.S. 324, 337–338, 97 S.Ct. 1843, 1855–1856, 52 L.Ed.2d 396 (1977) (statistical comparison between minority truck drivers and relevant population probative of discriminatory exclusion). But where special qualifications are necessary, the relevant statistical pool for purposes of demonstrating discriminatory exclusion must be the number of minorities qualified to undertake the particular task. *Hazelwood School Dist. v. United States,* 433 U.S. 299, 308, 97 S.Ct. 2736, 2741, 53 L.Ed.2d 768 (1977), *Johnson v. Transportation Agency,* 480 U.S. 616, 651–652, 107 S.Ct. 1442, 1462, 94 L.Ed.2d 615 (1987) (O'Connor, J., concurring).

In this case, the city does not even know how many MBEs in the relevant market are qualified to undertake prime or subcontracting work in public construction projects. Nor does the city know what percentage of total city construction dollars minority firms now receive as subcontractors on prime contracts let by the city. * * *

Finally, the city and the District Court relied on Congress' finding in connection with the set-aside approved in *Fullilove* that there had been nationwide discrimination in the construction industry. The probative value of these findings for demonstrating the existence of discrimination in Richmond is extremely limited. By its inclusion of a waiver procedure in the national program addressed in *Fullilove,* Congress explicitly recognized that the scope of the problem would vary from market area to market area. * * *

In sum, none of the evidence presented by the city points to any identified discrimination in the Richmond construction industry. We, therefore, hold that the city has failed to demonstrate a compelling interest in apportioning public contracting opportunities on the basis of race. * * *

The foregoing analysis applies only to the inclusion of blacks within the Richmond set-aside program. There is *absolutely no evidence* of past discrimination against Spanish-speaking, Oriental, Indian, Eskimo, or Aleut persons in any aspect of the Richmond construction industry. * * *

IV. As noted by the court below, it is almost impossible to assess whether the Richmond Plan is narrowly tailored to remedy prior discrimination since it is not linked to identified discrimination in any way. We limit ourselves to two observations in this regard.

First, there does not appear to have been any consideration of the use of race-neutral means to increase minority business participation in city contracting. * * *

Second, the 30% quota cannot be said to be narrowly tailored to any goal, except perhaps outright racial balancing. It rests upon the "completely unrealistic" assumption that minorities will choose a particular trade in lockstep proportion to their representation in the local population.

Since the city must already consider bids and waivers on a case-by-case basis, it is difficult to see the need for a rigid numerical quota. [But unlike] the program upheld in *Fullilove,* the Richmond Plan's waiver system focuses solely on the availability of MBEs; there is no inquiry into whether or not the particular MBE seeking a racial preference has suffered from the effects of past discrimination by the city or prime contractors. * * *

V. Nothing we say today precludes a state or local entity from taking action to rectify the effects of identified discrimination within its jurisdiction. If the city of Richmond had evidence before it that nonminority contractors were systematically excluding minority businesses from subcontracting opportunities it could take action to end the discriminatory exclusion. Where there is a significant statistical disparity between the number of qualified minority contractors willing and able to perform a particular service and the number of such contractors actually engaged by the locality or the locality's prime contractors, an inference of discriminatory exclusion could arise. Under such circumstances, the city could act to dismantle the closed business system by taking appropriate measures against those who discriminate on the basis of race or other illegitimate criteria. In the extreme case, some form of narrowly tailored racial preference might be necessary to break down patterns of deliberate exclusion. * * *

Proper findings in this regard are necessary to define both the scope of the injury and the extent of the remedy necessary to cure its effects. Such findings also serve to assure all citizens that the deviation from the norm of equal treatment of all racial and ethnic groups is a temporary matter, a measure taken in the service of the goal of equality itself. Absent such findings, there is a danger that a racial classification is merely the product of unthinking stereo-types or a form of racial politics. * * *

Affirmed.

JUSTICE STEVENS, concurring in part and concurring in the judgment.

* * * I believe the Constitution requires us to evaluate our policy decisions— including those that govern the relationships among different racial and ethnic groups—primarily by studying their probable impact on the future. I therefore do not agree with the premise that seems to underlie today's decision, as well as the decision in *Wygant,* that a governmental decision that rests on a racial classification is never permissible except as a remedy for a past wrong.[1] I do, however, agree with the Court's explanation of why the Richmond ordinance cannot be justified as a remedy for past discrimination, and therefore join Parts I, III–B, and IV of its opinion.

[T]he city makes no claim that the public interest in the efficient performance of its construction contracts will be served by granting a preference to minority-business enterprises. This case is therefore completely unlike *Wygant,* in which I thought it quite obvious that the School Board had reasonably concluded that an

---

1. In my view the Court's approach to this case gives unwarranted deference to race-based legislative action that purports to serve a purely remedial goal, and overlooks the potential value of race-based determinations that may serve other valid purposes. With regard to the former point—as I explained at some length in *Fullilove*—I am not prepared to assume that even a more narrowly tailored set-aside program supported by stronger findings would be constitutionally justified. Unless the legislature can identify both the particular victims and the particular perpetrators of past discrimination, which is precisely what a court does when it makes findings of fact and conclusions of law, a *remedial* justification for race-based legislation will almost certainly sweep too broadly. With regard to the latter point: I think it unfortunate that the Court in neither *Wygant* nor this case seems prepared to acknowledge that some race-based policy decisions may serve a legitimate public purpose. I agree, of course, that race is so seldom relevant to legislative decisions on how best to foster the public good that legitimate justifications for race-based legislation will usually not be available. But unlike the Court, I would not totally discount the legitimacy of race-based decisions that may produce tangible and fully justified future benefits.

integrated faculty could provide educational benefits to the entire student body that could not be provided by an all-white, or nearly all-white faculty.

[T]his litigation [also] involves an attempt by a legislative body, rather than a court, to fashion a remedy for a past wrong. Legislatures are primarily policy-making bodies that promulgate rules to govern future conduct. [It] is the judicial system, rather than the legislative process, that is best equipped to identify past wrongdoers and to fashion remedies that will create the conditions that presumably would have existed had no wrong been committed. * * *

The class of persons benefitted by the ordinance is not * * * limited to victims of [identified] discrimination—it encompasses persons who have never been in business in Richmond as well as minority contractors who may have been guilty of discriminating against members of other minority [groups.]

The ordinance is equally vulnerable because of its failure to identify the characteristics of the disadvantaged class of white contractors that justify the disparate treatment. That [class] presumably includes some who have been guilty of unlawful discrimination, some who practiced discrimination before it was forbidden by law, and some who have never discriminated against anyone on the basis of race. Imposing a common burden on such a disparate class merely because each member of the class is of the same race stems from reliance on a stereotype rather than fact or reason.[9] * * *

JUSTICE KENNEDY, concurring in part and concurring in the judgment.

I join all but Part II of Justice O'Connor's opinion * * *.

[The] process by which a law that is an equal protection violation when enacted by a State becomes transformed to an equal protection guarantee when enacted by Congress poses a difficult proposition for me; but as it is not before us, any reconsideration of that issue must await some further case. * * *

The moral imperative of racial neutrality is the driving force of the Equal Protection Clause. Justice Scalia's opinion underscores that proposition, quite properly in my view. The rule suggested in his opinion, which would strike down all preferences which are not necessary remedies to victims of unlawful discrimination, would serve important structural goals, as it would eliminate the necessity for courts to pass upon each racial preference that is enacted.

Nevertheless, given that a rule of automatic invalidity for racial preferences in almost every case would be a significant break with our precedents that require a case-by-case test, I am not convinced we need adopt it at this point. [My] reasons [are] as follows. First, I am confident that, in application, the strict scrutiny standard will operate in a manner generally consistent with the imperative of race neutrality, because it forbids the use even of narrowly drawn racial classifications except as a last resort. Second, the rule against race-conscious remedies is already less than an absolute one, for that relief may be the only adequate remedy after a judicial determination that a State or its instrumentality has violated the Equal Protection Clause. I note, in this connection, that evidence which would support a judicial finding of intentional discrimination may suffice also to justify remedial legislative action, for it diminishes the constitutional responsibilities of

---

9. There is, of course, another possibility that should not be overlooked. The ordinance might be nothing more than a form of patronage. But racial patronage, like a racial gerrymander, is no more defensible than political patronage or a political gerrymander. But unlike the Court, I would not totally discount the legitimacy of race-based decisions that may produce tangible and fully justified future benefits.

the political branches to say they must wait to act until ordered to do so by a court. * * *

JUSTICE SCALIA, concurring in the judgment.

I agree with much of the Court's opinion, and, in particular, with its conclusion that strict scrutiny must be applied to all governmental classification by race, whether or not its asserted purpose is "remedial" or "benign." I do not agree, however, with the Court's dicta suggesting that, despite the Fourteenth Amendment, state and local governments may in some circumstances discriminate on the basis of race in order (in a broad sense) "to ameliorate the effects of past discrimination." The benign purpose of compensating for social disadvantages, whether they have been acquired by reason of prior discrimination or otherwise, can no more be pursued by the illegitimate means of racial discrimination than can other assertedly benign purposes we have repeatedly rejected. See, e.g., [*Wygant*]. At least where state or local action is at issue, only a social emergency rising to the level of imminent danger to life and limb—for example, a prison race riot, requiring temporary segregation of inmates, cf. *Lee v. Washington*—can justify an exception to the principle embodied in the Fourteenth Amendment that "[o]ur Constitution is color-blind, and neither knows nor tolerates classes among citizens," *Plessy* (Harlan, J., dissenting) * * *.

A sound distinction between federal and state (or local) action based on race rests not only upon the substance of the Civil War Amendments, but upon social reality and governmental theory. It is a simple fact that what Justice Stewart described in *Fullilove* as "the dispassionate objectivity [and] the flexibility that are needed to mold a race-conscious remedy around the single objective of eliminating the effects of past or present discrimination"—political qualities already to be doubted in a national legislature—are substantially less likely to exist at the state or local level. The struggle for racial justice has historically been a struggle by the national society against oppression in the individual States. [What] the record shows, in other words, is that racial discrimination against any group finds a more ready expression at the state and local than at the federal level. To the children of the Founding Fathers, this should come as no surprise. An acute awareness of the heightened danger of oppression from political factions in small, rather than large, political units dates to the very beginning of our national history.

In my view there is only one circumstance in which the States may act *by race* to "undo the effects of past discrimination": where that is necessary to eliminate their own maintenance of a system of unlawful racial classification. [This] distinction explains our school desegregation cases, in which we have made plain that States and localities sometimes have an obligation to adopt race-conscious remedies. While there is no doubt that those cases have taken into account the continuing "effects" of previously mandated racial school assignment, we have held those effects to justify a race-conscious remedy only because we have concluded, in that context, that they perpetuate a "dual school system." We have stressed each school district's constitutional *"duty to dismantle* its dual system," and have found that "[e]ach instance of a failure or refusal to fulfill this affirmative duty *continues the violation* of the Fourteenth Amendment." *Columbus.* * * *

I agree with the Court's dictum that a fundamental distinction must be drawn between the effects of "societal" discrimination and the effects of "identified" discrimination, and that the situation would be different if Richmond's plan were "tailored" to identify those particular bidders who "suffered from the effects of past discrimination by the city or prime contractors." In my view, however, the reason that would make a difference is not, as the Court states, that it would justify race-conscious action but rather that it would enable race-neutral remediation. Nothing prevents Richmond from according a contracting preference to identified victims of discrimination. While most of the beneficiaries might be black, neither the beneficiaries nor those disadvantaged by the preference would be identified *on the basis of their race*. In other words, far from justifying racial classification, identification of actual victims of discrimination makes it less supportable than ever, because more obviously unneeded. * * *

It is plainly true that in our society blacks have suffered discrimination immeasurably greater than any directed at other racial groups. But those who believe that racial preferences can help to "even the score" display, and reinforce, a manner of thinking by race that was the source of the injustice and that will, if it endures within our society, be the source of more injustice still. The relevant proposition is not that it was blacks, or Jews, or Irish who were discriminated against, but that it was individual men and women, "created equal," who were discriminated against. And the relevant resolve is that that should never happen again. Racial preferences appear to "even the score" (in some small degree) only if one embraces the proposition that our society is appropriately viewed as divided into races, making it right that an injustice rendered in the past to a black man should be compensated for by discriminating against a white. Nothing is worth that embrace. Since blacks have been disproportionately disadvantaged by racial discrimination, any race-neutral remedial program aimed at the disadvantaged *as such* will have a disproportionately beneficial impact on blacks. Only such a program, and not one that operates on the basis of race, is in accord with the letter and the spirit of our Constitution. * * *

JUSTICE MARSHALL, with whom JUSTICE BRENNAN and JUSTICE BLACKMUN join, dissenting. * * *[a]

My view has long been that race-conscious classifications designed to further remedial goals "must serve important governmental objectives and must be substantially related to achievement of those objectives" in order to withstand constitutional scrutiny. Analyzed in terms of this two-prong standard, Richmond's set-aside, like the federal program on which it was modeled, is "plainly constitutional." *Fullilove* (Marshall, J., concurring in judgment).

Turning first to the governmental interest inquiry, Richmond has two powerful interests in setting aside a portion of public contracting funds for minority-owned enterprises. The first is the city's interest in eradicating the effects of past racial discrimination. * * *

Richmond has a second compelling interest in setting aside, where possible, a portion of its contracting dollars. [When] government channels all its contracting funds to a white-dominated community of established contractors whose racial homogeneity is the product of private discrimination, it does more than place its imprimatur on the practices which forged and which continue to define that community. It also provides a measurable boost to those economic entities that have thrived within it, while denying important economic benefits to those entities which, but for prior discrimination, might well be better qualified to receive valuable government contracts. In my view, the interest in ensuring that the government does not reflect and reinforce prior private discrimination in dispensing public contracts is every bit as strong as the interest in eliminating private

---

a. A brief dissent by Blackmun, J., joined by Brennan, J., is omitted.

discrimination—an interest which this Court has repeatedly deemed compelling. See, e.g., *Roberts v. United States Jaycees*, [p. 894 supra.]

The remaining question with respect to the "governmental interest" prong of equal protection analysis is whether Richmond has proffered satisfactory proof of past racial discrimination to support its twin interests in remediation and in governmental nonperpetuation.   * * * Richmond acted against a backdrop of congressional and Executive Branch studies which demonstrated with such force the nationwide pervasiveness of prior discrimination that Congress presumed that " 'present economic inequities' "in construction contracting resulted from " 'past discriminatory systems.' " The city's local evidence confirmed that Richmond's construction industry did not deviate from this pernicious national pattern.

[M]ore fundamentally, where the issue is not present discrimination but rather whether *past* discrimination has resulted in the *continuing exclusion* of minorities from an historically tight-knit industry, a contrast between population and work force is entirely appropriate to help gauge the degree of the exclusion. * * *

Finally, I vehemently disagree with the majority's dismissal of the congressional and Executive Branch findings noted in *Fullilove* as having "extremely limited" probative value in this case. * * *

In my judgment, Richmond's set-aside plan also comports with the second prong of the equal protection inquiry, for it is substantially related to the interests it seeks to serve in remedying past discrimination and in ensuring that municipal contract procurement does not perpetuate that discrimination. The most striking aspect of the city's ordinance is the similarity it bears to the "appropriately limited" federal set-aside provision upheld in *Fullilove*. Like the federal provision, Richmond's is limited to five years in duration, and was not renewed when it came up for reconsideration in 1988. Like the federal provision, Richmond's contains a waiver provision freeing from its subcontracting requirements those nonminority firms that demonstrate that they cannot comply with its provisions. Like the federal provision, Richmond's has a minimal impact on innocent third parties. While the measure affects 30% of *public* contracting dollars, that translates to only 3% of overall Richmond area contracting.

Finally, like the federal provision, Richmond's does not interfere with any vested right of a contractor to a particular contract; instead it operates entirely prospectively. * * *

[The] majority takes issue, however, with two aspects of Richmond's tailoring: the city's refusal to explore the use of race-neutral measures to increase minority business participation in contracting, and the selection of a 30% set-aside figure. [But] the majority overlooks the fact that since 1975, Richmond has barred both discrimination by the city in awarding public contracts and discrimination by public contractors. The virtual absence of minority businesses from the city's contracting rolls, indicated by the fact that such businesses have received less than 1% of public contracting dollars, strongly suggests that this ban has not succeeded in redressing the impact of past discrimination or in preventing city contract procurement from reinforcing racial homogeneity. * * *

As for Richmond's 30% target, the majority states that this figure "cannot be said to be narrowly tailored to any goal, except perhaps outright racial balancing." The majority ignores two important facts. First, the set-aside measure affects only 3% of overall city contracting; thus, any imprecision in tailoring has far less impact than the majority suggests. But more important, the majority ignores the fact that Richmond's 30% figure was patterned directly on the *Fullilove* precedent. Congress' 10% figure fell "roughly halfway between the present percentage of minority contractors and the percentage of minority group members in the Nation." The Richmond City Council's 30% figure similarly falls roughly halfway between the present percentage of Richmond-based minority contractors (almost zero) and the percentage of minorities in Richmond (50%). * * *

I am also troubled by the majority's assertion that, even if it did not believe generally in strict scrutiny of race-based remedial measures, "the circumstances of this case" require this Court to look upon the Richmond City Council's measure with the strictest scrutiny. The sole such circumstance which the majority cites, however, is the fact [that] "blacks comprise approximately 50% of the population of the city of Richmond" and that "[f]ive of the nine seats on the City Council are held by blacks."

While I agree that the numerical and political supremacy of a given racial group is a factor bearing upon the level of scrutiny to be applied, this Court has never held that numerical inferiority, standing alone, makes a racial group "suspect" and thus entitled to strict scrutiny review. * * *

It cannot seriously be suggested that nonminorities in Richmond have any "history of purposeful unequal treatment." Nor is there any indication that they have any of the disabilities that have characteristically afflicted those groups this Court has deemed suspect. Indeed, the numerical and political dominance of nonminorities within the State of Virginia and the Nation as a whole provide an enormous political check against the "simple racial politics" at the municipal level which the majority fears. If the majority really believes that groups like Richmond's nonminorities, which comprise approximately half the population but which are outnumbered even marginally in political fora, are deserving of suspect class status for these reasons alone, this Court's decisions denying suspect status to women and to persons with below-average incomes stand on extremely shaky ground.

In my view, the "circumstances of this case," underscore the importance of *not* subjecting to a strict scrutiny straitjacket the increasing number of cities which have recently come under minority leadership and are eager to rectify, or at least prevent the perpetuation of, past racial discrimination. In many cases, these cities will be the ones with the most in the way of prior discrimination to rectify. * * *

Nothing in the Constitution or in the prior decisions of this Court supports limiting state authority to confront the effects of past discrimination to those situations in which a prima facie case of a constitutional or statutory violation can be made out. [The] meaning of "equal protection of the laws" thus turns on the happenstance of whether a State or local body has previously defined illegal discrimination. Indeed, given that racially discriminatory cities may be the ones least likely to have tough, antidiscrimination laws on their books, the majority's constitutional incorporation of state and local statutes has the perverse effect of inhibiting those States or localities with the worst records of official racism from taking remedial action.

Similar flaws would inhere in the majority's standard even if it incorporated only federal anti-discrimination statutes. If Congress tomorrow dramatically expanded Title VII of the Civil Rights Act of 1964—or alternatively, if it repealed that legislation altogether—the meaning of equal protection would change precipitously along with it. Whatever the Framers of the Fourteenth Amendment had in mind in 1868, it certainly was not that the content of their Amendment would turn on the amendments to or the evolving interpretations of a federal statute passed nearly a century later. * * *

Notes and Questions

1. *Standard.* A clear majority in *Croson* agrees that affirmative action programs should be upheld only if closely tailored to serve a compelling government interest. But does a majority also agree on what this standard means in practice?

2. *Compelling interests.* (a) State and local governments have a compelling interest in remedying their own past discrimination, but how close must they (and should they have to) come to identifying specific violations—with the attendant risk of liability—in order to act on this basis? Must they show a "strong basis in evidence" for conclusions that "approach[] a prima facie case of a constitutional or statutory violation"?

(b) Does *Croson* permit a state or local lawmaking body to implement affirmative action remedies in exercising its "authority to eradicate the effects of private discrimination within its own legislative jurisdiction"? Or would such remedies go to "the remedying of the effects of societal discrimination"?

3. *Close tailoring.* Suppose that the City of Richmond could have established past discrimination that it had a compelling interest in remedying.[a] (a) Could it immediately have implemented race-based preferences, or would it need to have attempted other, race-neutral measures—or at least demonstrated their futility—first? (b) Could it have established numerical targets for minority subcontractors? If so, how large could such targets be? (c) What waiver mechanisms would have been necessary?[b]

4. *"Individual" and "group" justice.* (a) Consider the position of Charles Fried, *Metro Broadcasting, Inc. v. FCC: Two Concepts of Equality*, 104 Harv. L.Rev. 107, 108–09, 111 (1990), that O'Connor, J., for the *Croson* plurality, reads the equal protection clause as embodying an "individualistic" conception of fairness, whereas the position of the dissenters rests on a conception of "group" justice. On the individualistic conception, Fried says, race-based remedies are permissible only to compensate for past wrongs by an individual wrongdoer; this is why remedies for "societal" discrimination are inappropriate. But how "individualistic" is a position that requires identified wrongdoing as a predicate for race-based remedies, but then allows the benefit of those remedies to flow to persons not proven to be the victims of the identified wrongdoing? In other words, the position identified (and defended) as individualistic requires individually identified wrongdoing, but then—once the wrongdoing is identified—allows group-based remedies in at least some circumstances. Does this asymmetry make sense?

(b) Consider Kent Greenawalt, *The Unresolved Problems of Reverse Discrimination*, 67 Calif.L.Rev. 87, 127 (1979): "[G]iven the lingering effects of discrimination against earlier generations, given people's inevitable advancement through stages of life, and given the tremendous geographic mobility in the United States,

a. Does *Croson*'s analysis of the proof of specific discrimination substitute "adjectival dismissiveness" and "rhetorical devices" for analysis of "richly textured facts?" See Patricia Williams, *The Obliging Shell: An Informal Essay on Formal Equal Opportunity*, 87 Mich. L.Rev. 2128 (1989).

b. For debate concerning the scope of *Croson*, compare Joint Statement, *Constitutional Scholars' Statement on Affirmative Action After City of Richmond v. J.A. Croson Co.*, 98 Yale L.J. 1711 (1989) with Charles Fried, *Affirmative Action After City of Richmond v. J.A. Croson Co.: A Response to the Scholars' Statement*, 99 Yale L.J. 155 (1989). See also *Scholars' Reply to Professor Fried*, 99 Yale L.J. 163 (1989).

people whose opportunities are unequal because of earlier discrimination will typically have not been affected by any discrimination by the organization from which they now seek a job or other benefit. It is not sensible to demand as a matter of constitutional law that that organization itself have discriminated before racial preferences are permissible."[c]

(c) Compare the more consistently individualistic position taken by Scalia, J., concurring. Does the logic of individualism—including such notions as individual responsibility, merit, and desert—establish the correctness of his view?

(d) Does the dissenting position of Marshall, J., necessarily reflect the "collectivist" assumption that racial groups "hav[e] a status independent of and even superior to that of individual group members"? Fried, supra at 109.

5. *Preferences for majorities.* Should it have mattered to the analysis in *Croson* that blacks held more than half the seats on the Richmond city council? That the set-aside program benefitted a range of groups with diverse histories and current economic statuses? Did the facts illustrate a serious risk of race-based division and resentment engendered by "a form of racial politics"?[d]

6. *Judicial remedies for judicially identified discrimination.* In cases involving extreme circumstances, the Court has upheld judicially mandated, race-based remedies. Perhaps the leading case is UNITED STATES v. PARADISE, 480 U.S. 149, 107 S.Ct. 1053, 94 L.Ed.2d 203 (1987):[e] In 1972, a federal district court found that the Alabama Department of Public Safety had intentionally excluded all blacks from employment as state troopers during its entire 37 year history. The court enjoined the Department, inter alia, from engaging in any promotional practices "for the purpose or with the effect of discriminating against any employee [on] the ground of race or color." During the next eleven years, the court issued a series of further orders dealing with "attempts by the Department

---

c. The Court has held that a voluntary affirmative action plan adopted by a private employer, not subject to constitutional constraints, need not be predicated on past discrimination by the employer itself to be permissible under Title VII of the Civil Rights Act of 1964–which, inter alia, makes it "unlawful [for] any employer, labor organization, or joint labor-management committee [to] discriminate against any individual because of his race, color, religion, sex, or national origin in admission [to] any program established to provide apprenticeship or other training."

United Steelworkers v. Weber, 443 U.S. 193, 99 S.Ct. 2721, 61 L.Ed.2d 480 (1979), per Brennan, J., held that "an affirmative action plan—collectively bargained by an employer and a union—that reserve[d] for black employees 50% of the openings in an in-plant craft-training program until the percentage of black craftworkers in the plant is commensurate with the percentage of blacks in the local labor force," was justified by the interest in alleviating a racial imbalance in the employer's workplace. The Court found, 5–2, that "It would be ironic indeed if a law triggered by a Nation's concern over centuries of racial injustice [constituted] the first legislative prohibition of all voluntary, private, race-conscious efforts to abolish traditional patterns of racial segregation and hierarchy."

d. Compare Michael Rosenfeld, *Decoding Richmond: Affirmative Action and the Elusive Meaning of Constitutional Equality,* 87 Mich. L.Rev. 1729, 1774 (1989): "[S]o long as all members of society have a voice, one half of the population cannot, consistent with the premises underlying the *Carolene* approach, use the majoritarian process to subjugate the other half. Furthermore, although there may be a majority of blacks on the City Council, the fact that there is no black majority in Richmond should serve as a powerful incentive for black Council members not to act with disregard for the interests of one half of their constituents. In any event, the Richmond City Council's decision to adopt the Plan was not made strictly along racial lines. One white councilmember voted with the majority and another abstained." See also T. Alexander Aleinikoff, *A Case for Race–Consciousness,* 91 Colum.L.Rev. 1060, 1105–06 (1991): "It is a spectacular irony that black electoral successes are used to deny black elected officials an equal opportunity to fashion what they believe to be effective programs for ending second-class citizenship based on race." Do you agree?

e. See also *Local 28 of Sheet Metal Workers' Intern. Ass'n v. EEOC,* 478 U.S. 421, 106 S.Ct. 3019, 92 L.Ed.2d 344 (1986).

to delay or frustrate compliance." In 1983, "confronted with the Department's failure to develop promotion procedures" and with only four black corporals out of 66 and no blacks at any higher ranks, "the District Court ordered the promotion of one black trooper for each white trooper elevated in rank, as long as qualified black candidates were available, until the Department implemented an acceptable promotion procedure."

BRENNAN, J., joined by Marshall, Blackmun and Powell, JJ., found "that the relief ordered survives even strict scrutiny analysis." In response to the contention "that the Department was found guilty only of discrimination in hiring, and not in its promotional practices," the plurality held that "the race-conscious relief at issue here is justified by a compelling interest in remedying the discrimination. [It] is also supported by the societal interest in compliance with the judgments of federal courts."

In addition, "the one-for-one promotion requirement was narrowly tailored to serve its several purposes," and "it was *necessary* [in order] to eliminate the effects of the Department's 'long term, open, and pervasive' discrimination" without further delay.

"[Because] the one-for-one requirement is so limited in scope and duration, it only postpones the promotions of qualified whites. Consequently, like a hiring goal, it 'impose[s] a diffuse burden, * * * foreclosing only one of several opportunities.' *Wygant.* * * * Finally, the basic limitation, that black troopers promoted must be qualified, remains."

STEVENS, J., concurred in the judgment: "A party who has been found guilty of repeated and persistent violations of the law bears the burden of demonstrating that the chancellor's efforts to fashion effective relief exceed the bounds of 'reasonableness.' The burden of proof in a case like this is precisely the opposite of that in cases such as *Wygant* and *Fullilove,* which did not involve any proven violations of law."

O'CONNOR, J., joined by Rehnquist, C.J., and Scalia, J., agreed that "the Federal Government has a compelling interest in remedying past and present discrimination by the Department," but dissented "because the Court adopts a standardless view of 'narrowly tailored' far less stringent than that required by strict scrutiny." "[What] is most disturbing [is] that the District Court imposed the promotion quota *without consideration of any of the available alternatives.* [If this] can survive strict scrutiny as narrowly tailored, the requirement that a racial classification be 'narrowly tailored' for a compelling governmental purpose has lost most of its meaning."

WHITE, J., "agreeing with much of" O'Connor, J.'s opinion, found "it evident that the District Court exceeded its equitable powers in devising a remedy in this case."

———

METRO BROADCASTING, INC. v. FCC, 497 U.S. 547, 110 S.Ct. 2997, 111 L.Ed.2d 445 (1990), per BRENNAN, J., upheld minority preference policies of the Federal Communications Commission. The policies provided that minority ownership would be considered a plus in the consideration of mutually exclusive applications for stations and allowed potential minority owners to acquire licenses by sale and transfer under conditions not available to nonminorities.

"It is of overriding significance in these cases that the FCC's minority ownership programs have been specifically approved—indeed, mandated—by Congress. In *Fullilove*, [we] explained that deference was appropriate in light of Congress' institutional competence as the national legislature (opinion of Burger, C.J.); (Powell, J., concurring), as well as Congress' powers under the Commerce Clause (opinion of Burger, C.J.); (Powell, J., concurring), the Spending Clause (opinion of Burger, C.J.), and the Civil War Amendments (opinion of Burger, C.J.); (Powell, J., concurring).[11] [We] hold that benign race-conscious measures mandated by Congress—even if those measures are not 'remedial' in the sense of being designed to compensate victims of past governmental or societal discrimination—are constitutionally permissible to the extent that they serve important governmental objectives within the power of Congress and are substantially related to achievement of those objectives.

"Our decision last Term [in] *Croson* reaffirmed the lesson of *Fullilove* that race-conscious classifications adopted by Congress to address racial and ethnic discrimination are subject to a different standard than such classifications prescribed by state and local governments.   * * *

"We hold that the FCC minority ownership policies pass muster under the test we announce today.   [The interest] in enhancing broadcast diversity is, at the very least, an important governmental objective and is therefore a sufficient basis for the Commission's minority ownership policies.   Just as a 'diverse student body' contributing to a 'robust exchange of ideas' is a 'constitutionally permissible goal' on which a race-conscious university admissions program may be predicated, Bakke, (opinion of Powell, J.), the diversity of views and information on the airwaves serves important First Amendment values."[a]

O'CONNOR, J., joined by Rehnquist, C.J., and Scalia and Kennedy, JJ., dissented: "The Constitution's guarantee of equal protection binds the Federal Government as it does the States, and no lower level of scrutiny applies to the Federal Government's use of race classifications.   [*Bolling v. Sharpe.*]

"Congress has considerable latitude, presenting special concerns for judicial review, when it exercises its 'unique remedial powers [under] § 5 of the Fourteenth Amendment,' see *Croson,* but this case does not implicate those powers. Section 5 empowers Congress to act respecting the States, and of course this case concerns only the administration of federal programs by federal officials.   * * *

"The Court asserts that *Fullilove* supports its novel application of intermediate scrutiny to 'benign' race conscious measures adopted by Congress.   Three reasons defeat this claim.   First, *Fullilove* concerned an exercise of Congress' powers under § 5 of the Fourteenth Amendment.   * * * *Croson* resolved any doubt that might remain regarding this [point.]   *Croson* indicated that the decision in *Fullilove* turned on 'the unique remedial powers of Congress under § 5,' and that the latitude afforded Congress in identifying and redressing past discrimination rested on § 5's 'specific constitutional mandate to enforce the dictates of the Fourteenth Amendment.'   * * *

11. Justice O'Connor's suggestion that the deference to Congress described in *Fullilove* rested entirely on Congress' powers under § 5 of the Fourteenth Amendment is simply incorrect.   The Chief Justice expressly noted that in enacting the provision at issue, "Congress employed an amalgam of its specifically delegated powers."

a. Brennan, J.'s opinion also concluded that the minority ownership policies were substantially related to the achievement of the government's interest, that they were not based on impermissible stereotyping, and that they did not impose impermissible burdens on nonminorities.   Stevens, J., joined the opinion and wrote a separate concurring opinion.

"Second, *Fullilove* applies at most only to congressional measures that seek to remedy identified past discrimination. The Court upheld the challenged measures in *Fullilove* only because Congress had identified discrimination that had particularly affected the construction industry and had carefully constructed corresponding remedial measures. See *Fullilove* (opinion of Burger, C.J.); (opinion of Powell, J.). [The] FCC and Congress are clearly not acting for any remedial purpose, and the Court today expressly extends its standard to racial classifications that are not remedial in any sense.

"Finally, even if *Fullilove* applied outside a remedial exercise of Congress' § 5 power, it would not support today's adoption of the intermediate standard of [review]. Although the Court correctly observes that a majority did not apply strict scrutiny, six Members of the Court rejected intermediate scrutiny in favor of some more stringent form of review."[b]

Notes and Questions

1. *Diversity.* How likely is it that minority ownership will correlate strongly with the "diversity" of programming that is the minority preference's ostensible aim?[c]

Does the Court accept the broader proposition that Congress may utilize non-invidious schemes of racial classification, not to remedy past discrimination, but in the service of forward-looking goals? Under *Metro Broadcasting*, could Congress, for example, treat race as a "plus" in selecting candidates to be military officers under a "role model" theory analogous to that advanced (and rejected) in *Wygant*?

2. *Special deference to Congress.* Although Brennan, J.'s opinion for the Court asserted the "overriding significance" of the fact that Congress had mandated the preference involved in *Metro Broadcasting*, he applied the same "intermediate" standard of scrutiny that he and Marshall and Blackmun, JJ., had consistently championed for *all* cases involving "benign" racial classifications. Stevens, J., also joined the majority opinion, but wrote a concurrence emphasizing the significance for him of the distinction between forward-looking justifications for affirmative action (which in principle he approves) and backward-looking, remedial justifications (which he generally disapproves, since the "remedy" will seldom be tailored to reach the individual victims of the precise wrongs ostensibly being remedied). The fifth member of the *Metro Broadcasting* majority was White, J., who in *Croson* had joined O'Connor, J.'s opinion applying "strict" scrutiny to an affirmative action plan implemented by a state governmental subdivision. The four dissenters thought that strict scrutiny should apply. Would it be fair to say that it was only for White, J., that the difference between congressionally mandated and state implemented affirmative action—on which the distinction between the results in *Croson* and *Metro Broadcasting* ostensibly rested—was a material one?

b. O'Connor, J.'s opinion also concluded that the FCC's policy could not withstand even an intermediate form of scrutiny. Kennedy, J., joined by Scalia, J., also filed a separate dissenting opinion.

c. For the view that the FCC's preference "is primarily a remedial measure clothed in the garb of diversity," see Neal Devins, *Metro Broadcasting, Inc. v. FCC: Requiem for a Heavyweight,* 69 Tex.L.Rev. 125, 130 (1990). For a more equivocal view and a modeling of circumstances under which minority preferences might in fact enhance diversity, see Matthew L. Spitzer, *Justifying Minority Preferences in Broadcasting,* 64 So.Cal.L.Rev. 293 (1991).

ADARAND CONSTRUCTORS, INC. v. PENA
___ U.S. ___, 115 S.Ct. 2097, 132 L.Ed.2d 158 (1995).

JUSTICE O'CONNOR announced the judgment of the Court and delivered an opinion with respect to Parts I, II, III–A, III–B, III–D, and IV, which is for the Court except insofar as it might be inconsistent with the views expressed in JUSTICE SCALIA'S concurrence, and an opinion with respect to Part III–C in which JUSTICE KENNEDY joins. * * *

I. In 1989, the Central Federal Lands Highway Division (CFLHD), which is part of the United States Department of Transportation (DOT), awarded the prime contract for a highway construction project in Colorado to Mountain Gravel & Construction Company. Mountain Gravel then solicited bids from subcontractors for the guardrail portion of the contract. Adarand, a Colorado-based highway construction company specializing in guardrail work, submitted the low bid. Gonzales Construction Company also submitted a bid.

The prime contract's terms provide that Mountain Gravel would receive additional compensation if it hired subcontractors certified as small businesses controlled by "socially and economically disadvantaged individuals." Gonzales is certified as such a business; Adarand is not. Mountain Gravel awarded the subcontract to Gonzales, despite Adarand's low bid, and Mountain Gravel's Chief Estimator has submitted an affidavit stating that Mountain Gravel would have accepted Adarand's bid, had it not been for the additional payment it received by hiring Gonzales instead. Federal law requires that a subcontracting clause similar to the one used here must appear in most federal agency contracts, and it also requires the clause to state that "[t]he contractor shall presume that socially and economically disadvantaged individuals include Black Americans, Hispanic Americans, Native Americans, Asian Pacific Americans, and other minorities, or any other individual found to be disadvantaged by the [Small Business] Administration pursuant to section 8(a) of the Small Business Act." Adarand claims that the presumption set forth in that statute discriminates on the basis of race in violation of the Federal Government's Fifth Amendment obligation not to deny anyone equal protection of the laws. * * *

[Adarand's] claim arises under the Fifth Amendment to the Constitution, which provides that "No person shall [be] deprived of life, liberty, or property, without due process of law." Although this Court has always understood that Clause to provide some measure of protection against *arbitrary* treatment by the Federal Government, it is not as explicit a guarantee of *equal* treatment as the Fourteenth Amendment * * *. Our cases have accorded varying degrees of significance to the difference in the language of those two Clauses. We think it necessary to revisit the issue here.

A. Through the 1940s, this Court had routinely taken the view in non-race-related cases that, "[u]nlike the Fourteenth Amendment, the Fifth contains no equal protection clause and it provides no guaranty against discriminatory legislation by Congress." *Detroit Bank v. United States*, 317 U.S. 329, 337, 63 S.Ct. 297, 301, 87 L.Ed. 304 (1943). [But the Court departed from this view in *Korematsu*, which] began by noting that "all legal restrictions which curtail the civil rights of a single racial group are immediately suspect [and] courts must subject them to the most rigid scrutiny." * * *

In *Bolling v. Sharpe*, the Court for the first time explicitly questioned the existence of any difference between the obligations of the Federal Government and the States to avoid racial classifications [and] concluded that, "[i]n view of [the] decision [in *Brown*] that the Constitution prohibits the states from maintaining racially segregated public schools, it would be unthinkable that the same

Constitution would impose a lesser duty on the Federal Government." [After intervening decisions,] in 1975, the Court stated explicitly that "[t]his Court's approach to Fifth Amendment equal protection claims has always been precisely the same as to equal protection claims under the Fourteenth Amendment." *Weinberger v. Wiesenfeld*, [p. 1199 infra].

B. [After some disagreement about the standard for assessing race-based governmental action designed to benefit historically disadvantaged groups, a majority, in *Croson,*] finally agreed that the Fourteenth Amendment requires strict scrutiny of all race-based action by state and local governments. But *Croson* of course had no occasion to declare what standard of review the Fifth Amendment requires for such action taken by the Federal Government. *Croson* observed simply that the Court's "treatment of an exercise of congressional power in *Fullilove* cannot be dispositive here," because *Croson*'s facts did not implicate Congress' broad power under § 5 of the Fourteenth Amendment. * * *

Despite lingering uncertainty in the details, however, the Court's cases through *Croson* had established three general propositions with respect to governmental racial classifications. First, skepticism: " '[a]ny preference based on racial or ethnic criteria must necessarily receive a most searching examination.' " [*Wygant.*] Second, consistency: "the standard of review under the Equal Protection Clause is not dependent on the race of those burdened or benefitted by a particular classification." [*Croson.*] And third, congruence: "[e]qual protection analysis in the Fifth Amendment area is the same as that under the Fourteenth Amendment." [*Buckley v. Valeo*, p. 918 supra.] Taken together, these three propositions lead to the conclusion that any person, of whatever race, has the right to demand that any governmental actor subject to the Constitution justify any racial classification subjecting that person to unequal treatment under the strictest judicial scrutiny. * * *

A year later, however, the Court took a surprising turn. In *Metro Broadcasting*, the Court [held] that "benign" federal racial classifications need only satisfy intermediate scrutiny, [but] did not explain how to tell whether a racial classification should be deemed "benign," other than to express "confiden[ce] that an 'examination of the legislative scheme and its history' will separate benign measures from other types of racial classifications." * * *

By adopting intermediate scrutiny as the standard of review for congressionally mandated "benign" racial classifications, *Metro Broadcasting* departed from prior cases in two significant respects. First, it turned its back on *Croson*'s explanation of why strict scrutiny of all governmental racial classifications is essential. "Absent searching judicial inquiry into the justification for such race-based measures, there is simply no way of determining what classifications are 'benign' or 'remedial' and what classifications are in fact motivated by illegitimate notions of racial inferiority or simple racial politics. * * *" We adhere to that view today. * * *

Second, *Metro Broadcasting* squarely rejected one of the three propositions established by the Court's earlier equal protection cases, namely, congruence between the standards applicable to federal and state racial classifications, and in so doing also undermined the other two—skepticism of all racial classifications, and consistency of treatment irrespective of the race of the burdened or benefitted group. * * *

The three propositions undermined by *Metro Broadcasting* all derive from the basic principle that the Fifth and Fourteenth Amendments to the Constitution protect *persons*, not *groups*. It follows from that principle that all governmental action based on race—a *group* classification long recognized as "in most circumstances irrelevant and therefore prohibited"—should be subjected to detailed judicial inquiry to ensure that the *personal* right to equal protection of the laws has not been infringed.   These ideas have long been central to this Court's understanding of equal protection, and holding "benign" state and federal racial classifications to different standards does not square with them.   "[A] free people whose institutions are founded upon the doctrine of equality" should tolerate no retreat from the principle that government may treat people differently because of their race only for the most compelling reasons.   Accordingly, we hold today that all racial classifications, imposed by whatever federal, state, or local governmental actor, must be analyzed by a reviewing court under strict scrutiny.   In other words, such classifications are constitutional only if they are narrowly tailored measures that further compelling governmental interests.   To the extent that *Metro Broadcasting* is inconsistent with that holding, it is overruled.

[In his dissenting opinion,] Justice Stevens * * * claims that we have ignored any difference between federal and state legislatures.   But requiring that Congress, like the States, enact racial classifications only when doing so is necessary to further a "compelling interest" does not contravene any principle of appropriate respect for a co-equal Branch of the Government.   It is true that various Members of this Court have taken different views of the authority § 5 of the Fourteenth Amendment confers upon Congress to deal with the problem of racial discrimination, and the extent to which courts should defer to Congress' exercise of that authority.   We need not, and do not, address these differences today. * * *

C.   "Although adherence to precedent is not rigidly required in constitutional cases, any departure from the doctrine of stare decisis demands special justification."   [But] "stare decisis is a principle of policy and not a mechanical formula of adherence to the latest decision, however recent and questionable, when such adherence involves collision with a prior doctrine more embracing in its scope, intrinsically sounder, and verified by experience."   Remaining true to an "intrinsically sounder" doctrine established in prior cases better serves the values of stare decisis than would following a more recently decided case inconsistent with the decisions that came before it; the latter course would simply compound the recent error and would likely make the unjustified break from previously established doctrine complete.   In such a situation, "special justification" exists to depart from the recently decided case.

D.   [Finally,] we wish to dispel the notion that strict scrutiny is "strict in theory, but fatal in fact."   The unhappy persistence of both the practice and the lingering effects of racial discrimination against minority groups in this country is an unfortunate reality, and government is not disqualified from acting in response to it.   As recently as 1987, for example, every Justice of this Court agreed that the Alabama Department of Public Safety's "pervasive, systematic, and obstinate discriminatory conduct" justified a narrowly tailored race-based remedy.   See *United States v. Paradise*, [p. 1166 supra].   When race-based action is necessary to further a compelling interest, such action is within constitutional constraints if it satisfies the "narrow tailoring" test this Court has set out in previous cases.

IV.   Because our decision today alters the playing field in some important respects, we think it best to remand the case to the lower courts for further consideration in light of the principles we have announced.   The Court of Appeals, following *Metro Broadcasting* and *Fullilove*, analyzed the case in terms of intermediate scrutiny.   [It] did not decide the question whether the interests served by the use of subcontractor compensation clauses are properly described as "compelling." It also did not address the question of narrow tailoring in terms of our strict scrutiny cases, by asking, for example, whether there was "any consideration of the use of race-neutral means to increase minority business participation" in government contracting, [*Croson*,] or whether the program was appropriately limited such that it "will not last longer than the discriminatory effects it is designed to eliminate," *Fullilove*, (Powell, J., concurring). * * *

JUSTICE SCALIA, concurring in part and concurring in the judgment.

I join the opinion of the Court, except Part III–C, and except insofar as it may be inconsistent with the following. In my view, government can never have a "compelling interest" in discriminating on the basis of race in order to "make up" for past racial discrimination in the opposite direction. Individuals who have been wronged by unlawful racial discrimination should be made whole; but under our Constitution there can be no such thing as either a creditor or a debtor race. That concept is alien to the Constitution's focus upon the individual. To pursue the concept of racial entitlement—even for the most admirable and benign of purposes—is to reinforce and preserve for future mischief the way of thinking that produced race slavery, race privilege and race hatred. In the eyes of government, we are just one race here. It is American.

It is unlikely, if not impossible, that the challenged program would survive under this understanding of strict scrutiny, but I am content to leave that to be decided on remand.

JUSTICE THOMAS, concurring in part and concurring in the judgment.

I agree with the majority's conclusion that strict scrutiny applies to *all* government classifications based on race. I write separately, however, to express my disagreement with the premise underlying Justice Stevens' and Justice Ginsburg's dissents: that there is a racial paternalism exception to the principle of equal protection. I believe that there is a "moral [and] constitutional equivalence," (Stevens, J., dissenting), between laws designed to subjugate a race and those that distribute benefits on the basis of race in order to foster some current notion of equality. Government cannot make us equal; it can only recognize, respect, and protect us as equal before the law.

That these programs may have been motivated, in part, by good intentions cannot provide refuge from the principle that under our Constitution, the government may not make distinctions on the basis of race. As far as the Constitution is concerned, it is irrelevant whether a government's racial classifications are drawn by those who wish to oppress a race or by those who have a sincere desire to help those thought to be disadvantaged. There can be no doubt that the paternalism that appears to lie at the heart of this program is at war with the principle of inherent equality that underlies and infuses our Constitution. See Declaration of Independence ("We hold these truths to be self-evident, that all men are created equal, that they are endowed by their Creator with certain inalienable Rights, that among these are Life, Liberty, and the pursuit of Happiness").

These programs not only raise grave constitutional questions, they also undermine the moral basis of the equal protection principle. Purchased at the price of immeasurable human suffering, the equal protection principle reflects our Nation's understanding that such classifications ultimately have a destructive impact on the individual and our society. Unquestionably, "[i]nvidious [racial] discrimination is an engine of oppression." It is also true that "[r]emedial" racial preferences may reflect "a desire to foster equality in society." But there can be no doubt that racial paternalism and its unintended consequences can be as poisonous and pernicious as any other form of discrimination. So-called "benign" discrimination teaches many that because of chronic and apparently immutable handicaps, minorities cannot compete with them without their patronizing indulgence. Inevitably, such programs engender attitudes of superiority or, alternatively, provoke resentment among those who believe that they have been wronged by the government's use of race. These programs stamp minorities with a badge of inferiority and may cause them to develop dependencies or to adopt an attitude that they are "entitled" to preferences. * * *

In my mind, government-sponsored racial discrimination based on benign prejudice is just as noxious as discrimination inspired by malicious prejudice. In each instance, it is racial discrimination, plain and simple.

JUSTICE STEVENS, with whom JUSTICE GINSBURG joins, dissenting.

[There] is no moral or constitutional equivalence between a policy that is designed to perpetuate a caste system and one that seeks to eradicate racial subordination. Invidious discrimination is an engine of oppression, subjugating a disfavored group to enhance or maintain the power of the majority. Remedial race-based preferences reflect the opposite impulse: a desire to foster equality in society. No sensible conception of the Government's constitutional obligation to "govern impartially" should ignore this distinction. * * *

The consistency that the Court espouses would disregard the difference between a "No Trespassing" sign and a welcome mat. It would treat a Dixiecrat Senator's decision to vote against Thurgood Marshall's confirmation in order to keep African Americans off the Supreme Court as on a par with President Johnson's evaluation of his nominee's race as a positive factor. It would equate a law that made black citizens ineligible for military service with a program aimed at recruiting black soldiers. An attempt by the majority to exclude members of a minority race from a regulated market is fundamentally different from a subsidy that enables a relatively small group of newcomers to enter that market. An interest in "consistency" does not justify treating differences as though they were similarities. * * *

III.   [The] majority in *Metro Broadcasting* [was] not alone in relying upon a critical distinction between federal and state programs. In his separate opinion in [*Croson*], Justice Scalia discussed the basis for this distinction. He observed that "it is one thing to permit racially based conduct by the Federal Government— whose legislative powers concerning matters of race were explicitly enhanced by the Fourteenth Amendment—and quite another to permit it by the precise entities against whose conduct in matters of race that Amendment was specifically directed." [In] her plurality opinion in *Croson,* Justice O'Connor also emphasized the importance of this distinction when she responded to the City's argument that *Fullilove* was controlling. * * *

Presumably, the majority is now satisfied that its theory of "congruence" between the substantive rights provided by the Fifth and Fourteenth Amendments disposes of the objection based upon divided constitutional powers. But it is one thing to say (as no one seems to dispute) that the Fifth Amendment encompasses a general guarantee of equal protection as broad as that contained within the Fourteenth Amendment. It is another thing entirely to say that Congress' institutional competence and constitutional authority entitles it to no greater deference when it enacts a program designed to foster equality than the deference due a State legislature. * * *

JUSTICE SOUTER, with whom JUSTICE GINSBURG and JUSTICE BREYER join, dissenting.

[I] agree with Justice Stevens' conclusion that stare decisis compels the application of *Fullilove*. Although *Fullilove* did not reflect doctrinal consistency, its several opinions produced a result on shared grounds that petitioner does not attack: that discrimination in the construction industry had been subject to government acquiescence, with effects that remain and that may be addressed by some preferential treatment falling within the congressional power under § 5 of the Fourteenth Amendment. Once *Fullilove* is applied, [the] statutes in question here (which are substantially better tailored to the harm being remedied than the statute endorsed in *Fullilove*) pass muster under Fifth Amendment due process and Fourteenth Amendment equal protection.

The Court today, however, does not reach the application of *Fullilove* to the facts of this case, and on remand it will be incumbent on the Government and petitioner to address anew the facts upon which statutes like these must be judged on the Government's remedial theory of justification: facts about the current effects of past discrimination, the necessity for a preferential remedy, and the suitability of this particular preferential scheme. * * *

In assessing the degree to which today's holding portends a departure from past practice, it is also worth noting that nothing in today's opinion implies any view of Congress's § 5 power and the deference due its exercise that differs from the views expressed in the *Fullilove* plurality. The Court simply notes the observation in *Croson* "that the Court's 'treatment of an exercise of congressional power in *Fullilove* cannot be dispositive here,' because *Croson's* facts did not implicate Congress' broad power under § 5 of the Fourteenth Amendment," and explains that there is disagreement among today's majority about the extent of the § 5 power. * * * Thus, today's decision should leave § 5 exactly where it is as the source of an interest of the national government sufficiently important to satisfy the corresponding requirement of the strict scrutiny test.

* * * The Court has long accepted the view that constitutional authority to remedy past discrimination is not limited to the power to forbid its continuation, but extends to eliminating those effects that would otherwise persist and skew the operation of public systems even in the absence of current intent to practice any discrimination. * * *

When the extirpation of lingering discriminatory effects is thought to require a catch-up mechanism, like the racially preferential inducement under the statutes considered here, the result may be that some members of the historically favored race are hurt by that remedial mechanism, however innocent they may be of any personal responsibility for any discriminatory conduct. When this price is considered reasonable, it is in part because it is a price to be paid only temporarily; if the justification for the preference is eliminating the effects of a past practice, the assumption is that the effects will themselves recede into the past, becoming attenuated and finally disappearing. Thus, Justice Powell wrote in his concurring opinion in *Fullilove* that the "temporary nature of this remedy ensures that a race-conscious program will not last longer than the discriminatory effects it is designed to eliminate."

Surely the transition from the *Fullilove* plurality view (in which Justice Powell joined) to today's strict scrutiny (which will presumably be applied as Justice Powell employed it) does not signal a change in the standard by which the burden of a remedial racial preference is to be judged as reasonable or not at any given time. If in the District Court Adarand had chosen to press a challenge to the reasonableness of the burden of these statutes, more than a decade after *Fullilove* had examined such a burden, I doubt that the claim would have fared any differently from the way it will now be treated on remand from this Court.

Justice Ginsburg, with whom Justice Breyer joins, dissenting.

[I] agree with Justice Stevens that, in this area, large deference in owed by the Judiciary to "Congress' institutional competence and constitutional authority to overcome historic racial subjugation." * * *

The statutes and regulations at issue, as the Court indicates, were adopted by the political branches in response to an "unfortunate reality": "[t]he unhappy persistence of both the practice and the lingering effects of racial discrimination against minority groups in this country." The United States suffers from those lingering effects because, for most of our Nation's history, the idea that "we are just one race," (Scalia, J., concurring), was not embraced. For generations, our lawmakers and judges were unprepared to say that there is in this land no superior race, no race inferior to any other. * * *

The divisions in this difficult case should not obscure the Court's recognition of the persistence of racial inequality and a majority's acknowledgment of Congress' authority to act affirmatively, not only to end discrimination, but also to counteract discrimination's lingering effects. Those effects, reflective of a system of racial caste only recently ended, are evident in our workplaces, markets, and neighborhoods. Job applicants with identical resumes, qualifications, and interview styles still experience different receptions, depending on their race. White and African–American consumers still encounter different deals. People of color looking for housing still face discriminatory treatment by landlords, real estate agents, and mortgage lenders. Minority entrepreneurs sometimes fail to gain contracts though they are the low bidders, and they are sometimes refused work even after winning contracts. Bias both conscious and unconscious, reflecting traditional and unexamined habits of thought, keeps up barriers that must come down if equal opportunity and nondiscrimination are ever genuinely to become this country's law and practice.

Given this history and its practical consequences, Congress surely can conclude that a carefully designed affirmative action program may help to realize, finally, the "equal protection of the laws" the Fourteenth Amendment has promised since 1868. * * *

For a classification made to hasten the day when "we are just one race," (Scalia, J., concurring), [the] lead opinion has dispelled the notion that "strict scrutiny" is " 'fatal in fact.' " Properly, a majority of the Court calls for review that is searching, in order to ferret out classifications in reality malign, but masquerading as benign. (lead opinion). The Court's once lax review of sex-based classifications demonstrates the need for such suspicion. * * *

Close review also is in order for this further reason. As Justice Souter points out, and as this very case shows, some members of the historically favored race can be hurt by catch-up mechanisms designed to cope with the lingering effects of entrenched racial subjugation. Court review can ensure that preferences are not so large as to trammel unduly upon the opportunities of others or interfere too harshly with legitimate expectations of persons in once-preferred groups. * * *

While I would not disturb the programs challenged in this case, and would leave their improvement to the political branches, I see today's decision as one that allows our precedent to evolve, still to be informed by and responsive to changing conditions.

Notes and Questions

1. *Congruence.* Should congressionally mandated affirmative action be subject to the same standard of review as affirmative action implemented by state and local governments? O'Connor, J.'s plurality opinion had defended a divergence of standards in *Croson*, as had the majority opinion in *Metro Broadcasting*. Why did O'Connor, J., change her mind—or did she?

2. *Original understanding.* Why did Scalia and Thomas, JJ., who frequently insist upon the central significance of the original understanding of the Constitution's language, pay no apparent heed to the original understanding in this case? Should the original understanding matter? If so, should it also be relevant that *Adarand* arose under the due process clause of the fifth amendment (which contains no explicit "equal protection" clause) rather than the fourteenth amendment?

3. *Compelling governmental interests.* Which congressional grounds for implementing race-based affirmative action programs would count as "compelling"?

(a) *Remedying discrimination.* Remedying "societal" discrimination is not a "compelling" interest for the states, under *Croson*, but does Congress have a compelling interest in remedying discrimination occurring anywhere within the nation? If so, how specifically must Congress identify the area, or sector of the economy, within which identified discrimination occurs? Suppose that Congress purports to identify discrimination within some sector of the economy. Would its fact-finding receive special deference under § 5 of the fourteenth amendment?

(b) *Diversity and other interests.* Are there other compelling national interests—possibly forward-looking interests analogous to the diversity interest deemed compelling in *Bakke*? Would the diversity interest advanced in *Metro Broadcasting* count as "compelling"?

4. *Close tailoring.* Because of Congress' power to prescribe remedies under § 5 of the fourteenth amendment, are congressional judgments about the necessity of race-based remedies entitled to greater judicial deference *under* the strict scrutiny standard than the comparable judgments of state and local governments? Powell, J.'s concurring opinion in *Fullilove*, applying a strict scrutiny standard, observed that "the breadth of discretion in the choice of remedies [for identified discrimination] may vary with the nature and authority of the governmental body" and emphasized Congress' "unique constitutional power" to prescribe remedies under the thirteenth and fourteenth amendments. Will the Court adopt this approach? Should it?

SECTION 3. DISCRIMINATIONS BASED ON GENDER

I. DEFINING THE LEVEL OF SCRUTINY

Prior to 1971, the Court used the deferential "traditional approach" (see Sec. 1 supra) for classifications based on gender. The earliest case, *Bradwell v. Illinois,* 83 U.S. (16 Wall.) 130, 21 L.Ed. 442 (1873), upheld a law denying women the right to practice law. Bradley, J., concurring with Swayne and Field, JJ., explained that "the natural and proper timidity and delicacy which belongs to the female sex evidently unfits it for many of the occupations of civil life. [The] paramount destiny and mission of woman are to fulfill the noble and benign offices of wife and mother. This is the law of the Creator." *Muller v. Oregon,*

208 U.S. 412, 28 S.Ct. 324, 52 L.Ed. 551 (1908), per Brewer, J., upheld a law barring factory work by women for more than ten hours a day, reasoning that "as healthy mothers are essential to vigorous offspring, the physical well-being of a woman becomes an object of public interest and care."[a] *Goesaert v. Cleary,* 335 U.S. 464, 69 S.Ct. 198, 93 L.Ed. 163 (1948), per Frankfurter, J., upheld a law denying bartender's licenses to most women, reasoning that "the fact that women may now have achieved the virtues that men have long claimed as their prerogatives and now indulge in vices that men have long practiced, does not preclude the States from drawing a sharp line between the sexes, certainly in such matters as the regulation of the liquor traffic." Finally, *Hoyt v. Florida,* 368 U.S. 57, 82 S.Ct. 159, 7 L.Ed.2d 118 (1961), per Harlan, J., sustained a law placing women on the jury list only if they made special request, stating that "woman is still regarded as the center of home and family life."[b]

The first decision holding sex discrimination violative of equal protection, REED v. REED, 404 U.S. 71, 92 S.Ct. 251, 30 L.Ed.2d 225 (1971), per BURGER, C.J., involved a law preferring males to females when two persons were otherwise equally entitled to be the administrator of an estate: "A classification 'must be reasonable, not arbitrary, and must rest upon some ground of difference having a fair and substantial relation to the object of the [law].' *Royster Guano,* [Sec. 1 supra]. The question" is whether the classification "bears a rational relationship to a state objective that is sought to be advanced by the [law]." It was contended that the law had the reasonable "objective of reducing the workload on probate courts by eliminating one class of contests" and that the legislature might reasonably have "concluded that in general men are better qualified to act as an administrator than are women." But "to give a mandatory preference to members of either sex over members of the other, merely to accomplish the elimination of hearings on the merits, is to make the very kind of arbitrary legislative choice forbidden by [equal protection]."

Did *Reed* really involve "rational basis" review, or did the Court in fact apply elevated scrutiny? Consider Catharine A. MacKinnon, *Sexual Harassment of Working Women* 108 (1979): "It would have been considerably more rational, factually based, not arbitrary, and substantially related to the statutory purpose to presume that men would be the better administrators if most women were illiterate and wholly excluded from business affairs. Yet this reasoning would reveal a society in severe need of prohibitions on sex discrimination."

Reed was followed by FRONTIERO v. RICHARDSON, 411 U.S. 677, 93 S.Ct. 1764, 36 L.Ed.2d 583 (1973), which invalidated a federal statute permitting males in the armed services an automatic dependency allowance for their wives but requiring servicewomen to prove that their husbands were dependent. BRENNAN,

a. But see *Adkins v. Children's Hospital,* 261 U.S. 525, 43 S.Ct. 394, 67 L.Ed. 785 (1923) (minimum wage for women violates due process), overruled, *West Coast Hotel Co. v. Parrish,* p. 65 supra.

b. *Hoyt* was effectively overruled in *Taylor v. Louisiana,* 419 U.S. 522, 95 S.Ct. 692, 42 L.Ed.2d 690 (1975), holding that a similar statute, operating largely to exclude women from jury service, deprived a criminal defendant of the sixth and fourteenth amendment right to an impartial jury drawn from a fair cross section of the community.

J., joined by Douglas, White, and Marshall, JJ., argued that "classifications based upon sex [are] inherently suspect and must therefore be subjected to close judicial scrutiny," finding "at least implicit support for such an approach in [*Reed's*] departure from 'traditional' rational basis analysis": "[O]ur Nation has had a long and unfortunate history of sex discrimination. Traditionally, such discrimination was rationalized by an attitude of 'romantic paternalism' which, in practical effect, put women not on a pedestal, but in a cage. * * *

"As a result of notions such as these, [statutes] became laden with gross, stereotypical distinctions between the sexes and, indeed, throughout much of the 19th century the position of women in our society was, in many respects, comparable to that of blacks under the pre-Civil War slave codes. Neither slaves nor women could hold office, serve on juries, or bring suit in their own names, and married women traditionally were denied the legal capacity to hold or convey property or to serve as legal guardians of their own children. And although blacks were guaranteed the right to vote in 1870, women were denied even [that] until adoption of the Nineteenth Amendment half a century later.

"It is true, of course, that the position of women in America has improved markedly in recent decades. [But] in part because of the high visibility of the sex characteristic, women still face pervasive, although at times more subtle, discrimination in our educational institutions, on the job market and, perhaps most conspicuously, in the political arena.[17]

"Moreover, since sex, like race and national origin, is an immutable characteristic [the] imposition of special disabilities [would] seem to violate 'the basic concept of our system that legal burdens should bear some relationship to individual responsibility.' And what differentiates sex from such non-suspect statuses as intelligence or physical disability [is] that the sex characteristic frequently bears no relation to ability to perform or contribute to society.

"[The] Government [maintains] that, as an empirical matter, wives in our society frequently are dependent upon their husbands, while husbands rarely are dependent upon their wives. Thus, the Government argues that Congress might reasonably have concluded that it would be both cheaper and easier simply conclusively to presume that wives of male members are financially dependent upon their husbands, while burdening female members with the task of establishing dependency in fact.

"The Government offers no concrete evidence, however, tending to support its view that such differential treatment in fact saves the Government any money. [And any] statutory scheme which draws a sharp line between the sexes, *solely* [for] administrative convenience [violates equal protection]."

Powell, J., joined by Burger, C.J., and Blackmun, J., concurring, would rely "on the authority of *Reed* and reserve for the future any expansion of its rationale" because of the "Equal Rights Amendment, which if adopted will resolve [the] question." Stewart, J., concurred, "agreeing that the [statutes] work an invidious discrimination." Rehnquist, J., dissented.[a]

---

17. It is true [that] when viewed in the abstract, women do not constitute a small and powerless minority. Nevertheless, in part because of past discrimination, women are vastly underrepresented in this Nation's decision-making councils. * * *

a. See also *Stanton v. Stanton*, 421 U.S. 7, 95 S.Ct. 1373, 43 L.Ed.2d 688 (1975), per Blackmun, J., relying on *Reed*, holding that a statute requiring child support for males to age 21 but for females only to age 18 violated equal protection.

Notes and Questions

1. *Basis for heightened scrutiny.* Should women be treated as a "suspect" classification? If so, on what basis?

(a) *Economic disadvantage.* Women, on average, earn lower incomes than men;[b] own less property; and are more likely to be below the poverty line.[c]

(b) *Historical discrimination and prejudice.* How persuasive is the analogy of historically practiced gender-based discrimination to discrimination based on race?

In her brief in *Reed*, Ruth Bader Ginsburg wrote that being a woman, like being of a minority race, is "an unalterable identifying trait which the dominant culture views as a badge of inferiority justifying disadvantaged treatment in social, legal, economic and political contexts." The brief also quoted Note, *Sex Discrimination and Equal Protection: Do We Need a Constitutional Amendment?*, 84 Harv.L.Rev. 1499, 1507 (1971): "The similarities between race and sex discrimination are indeed striking. Both classifications create large, natural classes, membership in which is beyond the individual's control; both are highly visible characteristics on which legislators have found it easy to draw gross, stereotypical distinctions. Historically, the legal position of black slaves was justified by analogy to the legal status of women. Both slaves and wives were once subject to the all-encompassing paternalistic power of the male head of the house. Arguments justifying different treatment for the sexes on the grounds of female inferiority, need for male protection, and happiness in their assigned roles bear a striking resemblance to the half-truths surrounding the myth of the 'happy slave.' The historical patterns of race and sex discrimination have, in many instances, produced similar present day results."[d]

Compare Richard A. Wasserstrom, *Racism, Sexism, and Preferential Treatment: An Approach to the Topics*, 24 U.C.L.A.L.Rev. 581, 589–90 (1977): "[T]o be female, as opposed to being black, is not to be conceived of as simply a creature of

---

b. "In 1993, the average weekly wage for a full-time woman worker in the United States was 77 percent of the wage paid to a full-time male worker." Marion Crain, *Between Feminism and Unionism: Working Class Women, Sex Equality, and Labor Speech*, 82 Geo.L.J. 1903, 1910 (1994). This figure reflected an increase from 60% in 1960 and 62% in 1970. Among other possible explanations, "statistical discrimination" against women may be economically rational if women are less likely than men to be willing to work long hours or to work uninterruptedly for the same firms for long periods of years. See Samuel Issacharoff & Elyse Rosenblum, *Women and the Workplace: Accommodating the Demands of Pregnancy*, 94 Colum.L.Rev. 2154, 2159–71 (1994). On the other hand, it may be economically rational for women to "invest" less in job training and expend less effort in their jobs if they are in professions that "discriminate against women and thus reward their investment less than that of men." Cass R. Sunstein, *Why Markets Don't Stop Discrimination*, in *Reassessing Civil Rights* 22, 29 (Ellen Frankel Paul et al. eds. 1991). See also Edward J. McCaffrey, *Slouching Towards Equality: Gender Discrimination, Market Efficiency, and Social Change*, 103 Yale L.J. 595 (1993)

(arguing for a corrective to achieve the enhanced "social efficiency" that would result if the labor market provided greater incentives for women).

c. In 1991, 20.6 million females, compared to 15.1 million males, were below the poverty line. Bureau of the Census, U.S. Dep't of Com., Ser. P–60, No. 181, *Poverty in the United States: 1991* at 10 (1992). See also Peter B. Edelman, *Toward a Comprehensive Antipoverty Strategy: Getting Beyond the Silver Bullet*, 81 Geo.L.J. 1697 (1993).

d. But cf. Ruth Bader Ginsburg, *Speaking in a Judicial Voice*, 67 N.Y.U.L.Rev. 1185, 1198–1209 (1992), noting "a reason that distances race discrimination from discrimination based on sex": "Most women are life partners of men; women bear and raise both sons and daughters. Once women's own consciousness was awakened to the unfairness of allocating opportunity and responsibility on the basis of sex, education of others—of fathers, husbands, sons as well as daughters—could begin, or be reinforced, at home. When blacks were confined by law to a separate sector, there was no similar prospect for educating the white majority."

less worth. That is one important thing that differentiates sexism from racism: The ideology of sex, as opposed to the ideology of race, is a good deal more complex and confusing. Women are both put on a pedestal and deemed not fully developed persons. They are idealized; their approval and admiration is sought; and they are at the same time regarded as less competent than men and less able to live fully developed, fully human lives—for that is what men do." See also Catharine A. MacKinnon, *Reflections on Sex Equality Under Law*, 100 Yale L.J. 1281, 1289, 1298 (1991): "The African American struggle for social equality has been the crucible for equality law in America. [The] inequality of women to men deserves a theory of its own."

(c) *Lack of political power.* As of 1991, women held only 6% of the seats in the national legislature and roughly 18% of the places in state legislatures.[e] Moreover, historical discrimination against women might be taken to suggest that, within the terms of the *Carolene Products* footnote, p. 17, supra, gender-based prejudice and stereotypes of women constitute "a special condition, which tends seriously to curtail the operation of those political processes ordinarily to be relied upon to protect minorities, and which may call for a correspondingly more searching judicial inquiry." On the other hand, women are a not a minority, but a majority, of the national population.

Consider Note, supra, 84 Harv.L.Rev. at 1505 n. 48: "Political power is a difficult concept [to] define. Furthermore, many [women] are not aware of or do not care about the inequalities based on sex in the legal structure. Others may have decided that, on balance, they are benefitted rather than burdened by current laws distinguishing the sexes, and thus they may oppose the principle that no such distinctions should be allowed. These considerations weaken the argument that women can protect their interests through their political power, however defined. Even if women could use their political power to protect their interests, but do not choose to do so, the minority who feel they are discriminated against still should have a right to constitutional protection."

Compare John H. Ely, *Democracy and Distrust* 166–69 (1980): "[I]n assessing suspiciousness it cannot be enough simply to note that a group does not function as a political bloc. [We must] see if there are systemic bars [to] access. On that score it seems important that today discussion about the appropriate 'place' of women is common among both women and men, and between the sexes as well. The very stereotypes that gave rise to laws 'protecting' women by barring them from various activities are under daily and publicized attack, and are the subject of equally spirited defense. [Given] such open discussion [the] claim that the numerical majority is being 'dominated' [is] one it has become impossible to maintain except at the most inflated rhetorical level. It also renders the broader argument self-contradictory, since to make such a claim in the context of the current debate one must at least implicitly grant the validity of the stereotype, that women are in effect mental infants who will believe anything men tell them to believe.

"[But] most laws classifying by sex [probably pre-date woman suffrage]: they should be invalidated. [To] put on the group affected the burden of using its recently unblocked access to get the offending laws repealed would be to place in their path an additional hurdle that the rest of us do not have to contend with in order to protect ourselves—hardly an appropriate response to the realization that they have been unfairly blocked in the past. In fact I may be wrong in supposing

e. Mary E. Becker, *The Politics of Women's Wrongs and the Bill of "Rights": A Bicenten-* *nial Perspective*, 59 U.Chi.L.Rev. 453, 455 (1992).

that because women now are in a position to protect themselves they will, that we are thus unlikely to see in the future the sort of official gender discrimination that has marked our past. But if women don't protect themselves from sex discrimination in the future, [it] will be because for one reason or another—substantive disagreement or more likely the assignment of a low priority to the issue—they don't choose to."

(d) *Moral irrelevance.* Does it matter that, for many people, gender would be relevant for many purposes even in an ideal world? That separate men's and women's restrooms convey no inherent message of superiority or inferiority? For a probing and subtle discussion, see Wasserstrom, supra.

2. *Original intent or understanding.* No one suggests that the fourteenth amendment was originally intended or understood to bar gender discrimination. Is this relevant? Dispositive? Was Powell, J., right in thinking that the Court should hesitate to move too quickly while it appeared that the proposed Equal Rights Amendment might resolve the question? What are the implications, if any, of the failure of the Equal Rights Amendment to win adoption by the requisite number of states?[f]

CRAIG v. BOREN

429 U.S. 190, 97 S.Ct. 451, 50 L.Ed.2d 397 (1976).

JUSTICE BRENNAN delivered the opinion of the Court.

The interaction of two sections of an Oklahoma statute prohibits the sale of "nonintoxicating" 3.2% beer to males under the age of 21 and to females under the age of 18. The question to be decided is whether such a gender-based differential constitutes a denial to males 18–20 years of age the equal protection of the laws in violation of the Fourteenth Amendment.

[To] withstand constitutional challenge, previous cases establish that classifications by gender must serve important governmental objectives and must be substantially related to achievement of those objectives. * * * Decisions following *Reed* [have] rejected administrative ease and convenience as sufficiently important objectives to justify gender-based classifications. * * *[6]

Reed has also provided the underpinning for decisions that have invalidated statutes employing gender as an inaccurate proxy for other, more germane bases of classification. Hence, "archaic and overbroad" generalizations concerning the financial position of servicewomen, *Frontiero,* and working women, *Wiesenfeld* [p. 1199 infra], could not justify use of a gender line in determining eligibility for certain governmental entitlements. Similarly increasingly outdated misconceptions concerning the role of females in the home rather than in the 'marketplace and world of ideas' were rejected as loose-fitting characterizations incapable of supporting state statutory schemes that were premised upon their accuracy.

---

f. This proposed amendment—that "equality of rights under the law shall not be denied or abridged by the United States or by an State on account of sex"—was approved by 35 states (three less than required for ratification) at its expiration in 1982. See generally Barbara A. Brown, Thomas I. Emerson, Gail Falk, & Ann E. Freedman, *The Equal Rights Amendment: A Constitutional Basis for Equal Rights for Women,* 80 Yale L.J. 871 (1971).

6. *Kahn v. Shevin,* [p. 1198 infra] and *Schlesinger v. Ballard,* [p. 1198 infra], upholding the use of gender-based classifications, rested upon the Court's perception of the laudatory purposes of those laws as remedying disadvantageous conditions suffered by women in economic and military life. Needless to say, Oklahoma does not suggest that the age-sex differential was enacted to ensure the availability of 3.2% beer for women as compensation for previous deprivations.

Stanton. In light of the weak congruence between gender and the characteristic or trait that gender purported to represent, it was necessary that the legislatures choose either to realign their substantive laws in a gender-neutral fashion, or to adopt procedures for identifying those instances where the sex-centered generalization actually comported to fact.

[We] turn then to the question whether, under *Reed*, the difference between males and females with respect to the purchase of 3.2% beer warrants the differential in age drawn by the Oklahoma statute. * * *

We accept for purposes of discussion the District Court's identification of the objective underlying [the challenged statute] as the enhancement of traffic safety. [The] appellees introduced a variety of statistical surveys [to support the statute, but the] most focused and relevant of the statistical surveys, arrests of 18–20–year-olds for alcohol-related driving offenses, exemplifies the ultimate unpersuasiveness of this evidentiary record. Viewed in terms of the correlation between sex and the actual activity that Oklahoma seeks to regulate—driving while under the influence of alcohol—the statistics broadly establish that .18% of females and 2% of males in that age group were arrested for that offense. While such a disparity is not trivial in a statistical sense, it hardly can form the basis for employment of a gender line as a classifying device. Certainly if maleness is to serve as a proxy for drinking and driving, a correlation of 2% must be considered an unduly tenuous "fit." [Indeed,] prior cases have consistently rejected the use of sex as a decisionmaking factor even though the statutes in question certainly rested on far more predictive empirical relationships than this.

Moreover, the statistics exhibit a variety of other shortcomings that seriously impugn their value to equal protection analysis. * * *[14] None [of the surveys] purports to measure the use and dangerousness of 3.2% beer as opposed to alcohol generally, a detail that is of particular importance since, in light of its low alcohol level, Oklahoma apparently considers the 3.2% beverage to be "nonintoxicating."

[W]hen it is further recognized that Oklahoma's statute prohibits only the selling of 3.2% beer to young males and not their drinking the beverage once acquired (even after purchase by their 18–20–year-old female companions), the relationship between gender and traffic safety becomes far too tenuous to satisfy *Reed's* requirement that the gender-based difference be substantially related to achievement of the statutory objective. * * *

JUSTICE POWELL concurring.

I join the opinion of the Court as I am in general agreement with it. I do have reservations as to some of the discussion concerning the appropriate standard for equal protection analysis and the relevance of the statistical evidence. * * *

With respect to the equal protection standard, I agree that *Reed* is the most relevant precedent. But I find it unnecessary, in deciding this case, to read that decision as broadly as some of the Court's language may imply. *Reed* and subsequent cases involving gender-based classifications make clear that the Court subjects such classifications to a more critical examination than is normally applied when "fundamental" constitutional rights and "suspect classes" are not present.

---

14. The very social stereotypes that find reflection in age-differential laws are likely substantially to distort the accuracy of these comparative statistics. Hence, "reckless" young men who drink and drive are transformed into arrest statistics, whereas their female counterparts are chivalrously escorted home. * * *

I view this as a relatively easy case. [T]his gender-based classification does not bear a fair and substantial relation to the object of the legislation. * * *

JUSTICE STEVENS concurring.

I am inclined to believe that what has become known as the two-tiered analysis of equal protection claims [is] a method the Court has employed to explain decisions that actually apply a single standard in a reasonably consistent fashion. * * *

In this case, the classification [is] objectionable because it is based on an accident of birth, because it is a mere remnant of the now almost universally rejected tradition of discriminating against males in this age bracket, and because, to the extent it reflects any physical difference between males and females, it is actually perverse.[4] * * *

The classification is not totally irrational. For the evidence does indicate that there are more males than females in this age bracket who drive and also more who drink. Nevertheless, [i]t is difficult to believe that the statute was actually intended to cope with the problem of traffic safety, since it has only a minimal effect on access to a not-very-intoxicating beverage and does not prohibit its consumption. [But] even assuming some such slight benefit, it does not seem to me that an insult to all of the young men of the State can be justified by visiting the sins of the 2% on the 98%.

JUSTICE REHNQUIST, [with whom CHIEF JUSTICE BURGER was "in general agreement"] dissenting.

The Court's disposition of this case is objectionable on two grounds. First is its conclusion that *men* challenging a gender-based statute which treats them less favorably than women may invoke a more stringent standard of judicial review than pertains to most other types of classifications. Second is the Court's enunciation of this standard, without citation to any source, as being that "classifications by gender must serve *important* governmental objectives and must be *substantially* related to achievement of those objectives." The only redeeming feature of the Court's opinion, to my mind, is that it apparently signals a retreat by those who joined the plurality opinion in *Frontiero* from their view that sex is a "suspect" classification for purposes of equal protection analysis. I think the Oklahoma statute challenged here need pass only the "rational basis" equal protection analysis expounded in [prior cases].

[T]here being no plausible argument that this is a discrimination against females,[2] the Court's reliance on our previous sex-discrimination cases is ill-founded. It treats gender classification as a talisman which-without regard to the rights involved or the persons affected-calls into effect a heavier burden of judicial review.

The Court's [standard of review] apparently comes out of thin air. The Equal Protection Clause contains no such language, and none of our previous cases adopt that standard. I would think we have had enough difficulty with the two

---

4. Because males are generally heavier than females, they have a greater capacity to consume alcohol without impairing their driving ability than do females.

2. I am not aware of the argument from time to time advanced, that all discriminations between the sexes ultimately redound to the detriment of females, because they tend to reinforce "old notions" restricting the roles and opportunities of women. As a general proposition applying equally to all sex categorizations, I believe that this argument was implicitly found to carry little weight in our decisions upholding gender-based differences. See *Ballard; Kahn.* Seeing no assertion that it has special applicability to the situation at hand, I believe it can be dismissed as an insubstantial consideration.

standards of review which our cases have recognized—the norm of "rational basis," and the "compelling state interest" required where a "suspect classification" is involved—so as to counsel weightily against the insertion of still another "standard" between those two. How is this Court to divine what objectives are important? How is it to determine whether a particular law is "substantially" related to the achievement of such objective, rather than related in some other way to its achievement?

[Under the] applicable rational-basis test [the] evidence suggests clear differences between the drinking and driving habits of young men and women. Those differences are grounds enough for the State reasonably to conclude that young males pose by far the greater drunk-driving hazard, both in terms of sheer numbers and in terms of hazard on a per-driver basis. The gender-based difference in treatment in this case is therefore not irrational.

Notes and Questions

1. *Level of scrutiny.* Is the intermediate level of equal protection scrutiny applied in *Craig* soundly justified? If so, on what basis?

2. *Protection of men.* Is there any reason why statutes discriminating against *men* should be subject to heightened equal protection scrutiny? Is it plausible to think that both men and women are semi-suspect classes? Consider Laurence H. Tribe, *American Constitutional Law* 1564–65 (2d ed. 1988): "It is no surprise that many of [the leading] sex discrimination cases were brought by male plaintiffs, since legislative assumptions about traditional sex roles often impinge on the rights of both men and women [by impliedly derogating the capacity of women to function effectively outside the home]. [In defending gender-based classifications,] the government's almost uniform argument [has] emphasized the [benefits achieved by reliance on] the accurate and therefore 'rational' assumption of traditional male and female inclinations and capacities. The Supreme Court's thoughtful response [has] recognized the argument's essence as self-fulfilling prophecy: The 'accuracy' of government's assumption is derived in some significant degree from the chill on sex-role experimentation and change generated by the classifications themselves."[a]

3. *Application in Craig.* Did *Craig* rest on the conclusion that the challenged law was unlikely to save any lives through a reduction in traffic accidents attributable to drinking by 18–21 year-old males? That it was unlikely to save enough lives to be constitutionally tolerable?

Or was the point that the state, in order to be able to restrict the sale of 3.2 beer to young men, must also prohibit sales to women of the same age? Should the state, in order to achieve important ends (such as saving lives by improving highway safety), be required to impose restrictions that it regards as unnecessary

---

a. See also Kenneth L. Karst, *Woman's Constitution*, 1984 Duke L.J. 447, 449: "The prevailing construct of woman is largely a male product, for it is men who have held the power to define roles and institutions in our society. And the male stereotype of woman is crucially influenced by men's need to define woman in order to define themselves as men." See generally Catharine MacKinnon, *Feminism, Marxism, Method, and the State: Toward Feminist Jurisprudence*, 8 Signs 635, at 635 (1983) ("male and female are created through the erotization of dominance and submission. The man/woman difference and the dominance/submission dynamic define each other"); Catharine MacKinnon, *Feminism, Marxism, Method, and the State: An Agenda for Theory*, 7 Signs 515 (1982). On gender roles, see also Simone de Beauvoir, *The Second Sex* (1971); Dale Spender, *Man Made Language* (2d ed. 1985); Christine A. Littleton, *Reconstructing Sexual Equality*, 75 Calif.L.Rev. 1279 (1987); Frances E. Olsen, *The Family and the Market: A Study of Ideology and Legal Reform*, 96 Harv.L.Rev. 1497 (1983).

(as well as those it thinks vital)? What theory (or theories) of the equal protection clause would support such a view?

II. DIFFERENCES—REAL AND IMAGINED

DOTHARD v. RAWLINSON, 433 U.S. 321, 97 S.Ct. 2720, 53 L.Ed.2d 786 (1977), per Stewart, J., upheld the exclusion of women prison guards from duty in "contact positions" in all-male prisons: "In this environment of violence and disorganization, it would be an oversimplification to characterize [the exclusion of women] as an exercise in 'romantic paternalism.' [A] woman's relative ability to maintain order in a male, maximum-security, unclassified penitentiary could [be] directly reduced by her womanhood. There is a basis in fact for expecting that sex offenders who have criminally assaulted women in the past would be moved to do so again if access to women were established within the prison. There would also be a real risk that other inmates, deprived of a normal heterosexual environment, would assault women guards because they were women."[b]

MICHAEL M. v. SUPERIOR COURT, 450 U.S. 464, 101 S.Ct. 1200, 67 L.Ed.2d 437 (1981), upheld a "statutory rape" law that punished the male, but not the female, party to intercourse when the female was under 18 and not the male's wife. Rehnquist, J., joined by Burger, C.J., and Stewart and Powell, JJ., observed "that the traditional minimum rationality test takes on a somewhat 'sharper focus' when gender-based classifications are challenged. See Craig (Powell, J., concurring). [But] this court has consistently upheld statutes where the gender classification is not invidious, but rather realistically reflects the fact that the sexes are not similarly situated in certain circumstances. * * *

"We are satisfied not only that the prevention of illegitimate [teenage] pregnancy is at least one of the 'purposes' of the statute, but that the State has a strong interest in preventing such pregnancy.[7]

"Because virtually all of the significant harmful and inescapably identifiable consequences of teenage pregnancy fall on the young female, a legislature acts well within its authority when it elects to punish only the participant who, by nature, suffers few of the consequences of his conduct. It is hardly unreasonable for a legislature acting to protect minor females to exclude them from punishment. Moreover, the risk of pregnancy itself constitutes a substantial deterrence to young females. [A] criminal sanction imposed solely on males thus serves to roughly 'equalize' the deterrents on the sexes.

"[The] State persuasively contends that a gender-neutral statute would frustrate its interest in effective enforcement. Its view is that a female is surely less likely to report violations of the statute if she herself would be subject to criminal prosecution. In an area already fraught with prosecutorial difficulties,

---

b. For criticism, see Christine A. Littleton, *Equality and Feminist Legal Theory,* 48 U.Pitt.L.Rev. 1043, 1049–50 (1987).

7. Although petitioner concedes that the State has a "compelling" interest in preventing teenage pregnancy, he contends that the "true" purpose [is] to protect the virtue and chastity of young women. As such, the statute

is unjustifiable because it rests on archaic stereotypes. [Even] if the preservation of female chastity were one of the motives of the statute, and even if that motive be impermissible, petitioner's argument must fail because "[this] court will not strike down an otherwise constitutional statute on the basis of an alleged illicit legislative motive." *United States v. O'Brien,* [p. 669 supra].

we decline to hold that the Equal Protection Clause requires a legislature to enact a statute so broad that it may well be incapable of enforcement."[a]

BLACKMUN, J., concurred: "I [cannot] vote to strike down the California statutory rape law, for I think it is a sufficiently reasoned and constitutional effort to control the problem at its inception. [I] am persuaded that, although a minor has substantial privacy rights in intimate affairs connected with procreation, California's [efforts] to prevent teenage pregnancy are to be viewed differently from efforts to inhibit a woman from dealing with pregnancy once it has become an inevitability. * * *

"I think [it] is only fair, with respect to this particular petitioner, to point out that his partner, Sharon, appears not to have been an unwilling participant in at least the initial stages of the intimacies that took place the night of June 3, 1978.[*] Petitioner's and Sharon's nonacquaintance with each other before the incident: their drinking; their withdrawal from the others of the group; their foreplay, in which she willingly participated and seems to have encouraged; and the closeness of their ages (a difference of only one year and 18 days) are factors that should make this case an unattractive one to prosecute at all, and especially to prosecute as a felony, rather than as a misdemeanor. But the State has chosen to prosecute in that manner, and the facts, I reluctantly conclude, may fit the crime."

BRENNAN, J., joined by White and Marshall, JJ., dissented: "None of the three opinions upholding the California statute fairly applies the equal protection analysis this Court has so carefully developed since *Craig*. [The] plurality assumes that a gender-neutral statute would be less effective [in] deterring sexual activity because a gender-neutral statute would create significant enforcement problems. [But] a State's bare assertion [is] not enough to meet its burden of proof under *Craig*. Rather, the State must produce evidence that will persuade the Court that its assertion is true [and the] State has [not].

"The second flaw in the State's assertion is that even assuming that a gender-neutral statute would be more difficult to enforce, the State has still not shown

---

a. Stewart, J., also concurred, noting "that the statutory discrimination, when viewed as part of the wider scheme of California law, is not as clearcut as might at first appear. Females are not freed from criminal liability in California for engaging in sexual activity that may be harmful. It is unlawful, for example, for any person, of either sex, [to] contribute to the delinquency of anyone under 18 years of age. All persons are prohibited [from] consensual intercourse with a child under 14. [Finally,] females may be brought within the proscription of § 261.5 itself, since a female may be charged with aiding and abetting its violation. [A]pproximately 14% of the juveniles arrested for participation in acts made unlawful by § 261.5 between 1975 and 1979 were females. Moreover, an underage female who is as culpable as her male partner, or more culpable, may be prosecuted as a juvenile delinquent."

* Sharon at the preliminary hearing testified as follows: * * *

"We were drinking at the railroad tracks and we walked over to this bush and he started kissing me and stuff, and I was kissing him back, too, at first. Then, I was telling him to stop * * *.

"[T]hen he asked me if I wanted to walk him over to the park; so we walked over to the park and we sat down on a bench and then he started kissing me again and we were laying on the bench. And he told me to take my pants off.

"I said, 'No,' and I was trying to get up and he hit me back down on the bench and then I just said to myself, 'Forget it,' and I let him do what he wanted to do. * * *

"Q. Did you have sexual intercourse with the defendant?

"A. Yeah. * * *

"Q. You said that he hit you?

"A. Yeah.

"Q. How did he hit you?

"A. He slugged me in the face.

"[The Court]: Did he hit you one time or did he hit you more than once?

"The Witness: He hit me about two or three times. * * *"

that those enforcement problems would make such a statute less effective than a gender-based statute in deterring minor females from engaging in sexual intercourse. Common sense, however, suggests that a gender-neutral statutory rape law is potentially a *greater* deterrent of sexual activity than a gender-based law, for the simple reason that a gender-neutral law subjects both men and women to criminal sanctions and thus arguably has a deterrent effect on twice as many potential violators. Even if fewer persons were prosecuted under the gender-neutral law, as the State suggests, it would still be true that twice as many persons would be *subject* to arrest."

Stevens, J., also dissented: "[T]hat a female confronts a greater risk of harm than a male is a reason for applying the prohibition to her—not a reason for granting her a license to use her own judgment on whether or not to assume the risk. Surely, if we examine the problem from the point of view of society's interest in preventing the risk-creating conduct from occurring at all, it is irrational to exempt 50% of the potential violators. * * *

"Finally, even if my logic is faulty and there actually is some speculative basis for treating equally guilty males and females differently, I still believe that any such speculative justification would be outweighed by the paramount interest in even-handed enforcement of the law. A rule that authorizes punishment of only one of two equally guilty wrongdoers violates the essence of the constitutional requirement that the sovereign must govern impartially."

Notes and Questions

1. *Other discriminations based on differences.* In "high-rape" areas, may female students be subjected to an earlier curfew than males? May women employees, because women live longer, be required to make larger contributions than men to a state pension fund? See *Los Angeles Dep't of Water & Power v. Manhart,* 435 U.S. 702, 98 S.Ct. 1370, 55 L.Ed.2d 657 (1978) (violation of Title VII). May only women be required to wear tops while swimming?

Consider Laurence H. Tribe, *Constitutional Choices* 241 (1985): "That 'the sexes are not similarly situated' in such cases as *Michael M* and *Dothard* would not, to anyone less mesmerized [than the Supreme Court] by the ideal of law as a mirror of nature, be thought to *justify* a gender discrimination as noninvidious; it would instead raise the question whether such discrimination formed part of the law's systemic support for male supremacy." Viewing the problem through this different "lens," Professor Tribe concludes that "The law must be prepared to act [by] affirmatively combating the inequities that result when we all too casually allow biological differences to justify the imposition of legal disabilities on women." Laurence H. Tribe, *American Constitutional Law* 1577 (2d ed. 1988). Do you agree? How might this approach be applied to *Dothard*? To *Michael M*? What would be the costs?

2. *Feminist criticisms of statutory rape laws.* Consider Frances Olsen, *Statutory Rape: A Feminist Critique of Rights Analysis,* 63 Tex.L.Rev. 387, 404–07 (1984): "Feminists charge that [statutory rape laws] are harmful to women on both a practical and an ideological level. First, as an effort to control the sexual activities of young women, statutory rape [laws] interfere[] with the sexual freedom of the underage female. [They] violate the female's right [to] be as free sexually as her male counterpart. [Second, g]ender-based statutory rape laws reinforce the sexual stereotype of men as aggressors and women as passive victims. The laws perpetuate the double standard of sexual morality [in which] sex is an accomplishment [for men but a debasing activity for women]. * * *

"Unfortunately, [however,] invalidating statutory rape laws altogether [might] undermine the right of young women to be free of unwanted sexual conduct. [Since the stereotypes that statutory rape laws reinforce may have a basis in current social reality, underage] females might discover that although the abolition of [such] laws would protect their rights against the state, it would remove some of their already-minimal protection against individual men. [Among other needed protections,] statutory rape laws may prohibit certain instances of sexual assault that should be considered illegal, but cannot be prosecuted as forcible rape.[94]"

3. *Discrimination and the dissenting opinions.* On what basis did the dissenting justices object to the statute in *Michael M*? Consider Olsen, supra, at 418–19: "[T]he statute discriminates in two different ways: it outlaws sexual intercourse by minor females, but not by minor males, and it protects minor females from exploitative intercourse with anyone, but does not protect minor males from exploitative intercourse with females who are above the age of consent. The dissenters ignored the first discrimination altogether and appeared confused about the second."

According to Professor Olsen, the dissenting justices would have regarded the law as "gender-neutral" as long as it punished underage women and their sexual partners equally for engaging in the same sexual acts—even if it allowed minor males (but not minor females) to engage in intercourse with partners above the age of consent. Id. at 419. Should the latter discrimination be regarded as constitutionally objectionable? Why did none of the dissenting Justices allude to it?

Professor Olsen also argues that the "revision" that the dissenting justices would have found acceptable "would be the worst alternative for women, because it would increase the coercive aspects of the California law and diminish any protective elements it now might have. A woman would find it more difficult to use statutory rape laws as a shield against male aggression [because] the woman would have to admit that she had violated the law in order to prosecute the male * * *." Id. at 419–20.

Do you agree? (Consider the testimony in the *Michael M.* case as reported in the footnote to Blackmun, J.'s opinion.) What are the implications, if any, for what the content of statutory rape laws should have to be to pass constitutional muster?

4. *The focus on "difference."* Should the constitutionality of gender-based classifications be based on an assessment of whether males and females are relevantly "different"?

(a) Consider Deborah Rhode, *Gender and Justice* 2–3 (1989): "The law's conventional approach to gender issues has focused on gender difference. [Within] this framework, sex-based discrimination remains justifiable if the sexes are different in some sense that is related to valid regulatory objectives. [But] this difference-oriented approach has proved inadequate in both theory and practice. As a theoretical matter, it tends toward tautology. It permits different treatment for those who differ with respect to legitimate purposes but provides no standards for determining what differences are relevant and what counts as legitimate. As a practical matter, this approach has both over- and undervalued gender differences. In some instances, biology has determined destiny, while in other contexts,

---

94. [The] testimony [in *Michael M.*] provides one example. The man hit the female in the face two or three [times]. Presumably this could not be prosecuted as forcible rape because before intercourse took place the female gave what is considered legal consent.

women's particular needs have gone unacknowledged or unaddressed. [Reliance] on 'real difference' [has] often done more to reflect sex-based inequalities than to challenge them."

(b) Consider the suggestion of Martha Minow, *Introduction: Finding Our Paradoxes, Affirming Our Beyond*, 24 Harv.C.R.C.L.L.Rev. 1, 2–4 (1989), that feminist scholarship addressing issues of "difference" has included at least three stages: "[T]he first stage articulated women's claims to be granted the same rights and privileges as men [including] rights to vote and to hold the same jobs as men. The second stage advocated respect and accommodation for women's historical and contemporary differences. For those writing in this second stage, the problem needing redress was the undervaluation or disregard for women's historic and persistent interests, traits, and needs. Examples of second-stage goals include obtaining pregnancy and maternity leaves from paid employment, pursuing comparable worth to revalue traditional women's work, and elaborating special rights for women to respond to rape, battery of women by men, and self-determination about whether to conceive or bear a child.

"The third stage rejects the preoccupation with similarities and differences between men and women. As third-stage representatives see it, this preoccupation has itself helped perpetuate the degradation and subordination of women. Focusing on the similarities and differences between men and women threatens to preserve men as the starting point for analysis. For example, an unstated male norm makes pregnancy and maternity leaves 'special treatment,' contrasted to the 'normal treatment' given to employees. But these programs are special only in comparison with background rules that treat as the norm the person—a man—who never gets pregnant."[a]

(c) Would it be better to declare that a "rule or practice is discriminatory [if] it participates in the systemic social deprivation of one sex because of sex"? Should the "only question for litigation [be] whether the policy or practice in question integrally contributes to the maintenance of an underclass * * * because of gender"? See Catharine A. MacKinnon, *Sexual Harassment of Working Women* 117 (1979).

ROSTKER v. GOLDBERG, 453 U.S. 57, 101 S.Ct. 2646, 69 L.Ed.2d 478 (1981), per REHNQUIST, J., upheld a Military Selective Service Act (MSSA) provision "authorizing the President to require the registration of males and not females": "The case arises in the context of Congress' authority over national defense and military affairs, and perhaps in no other area has the Court accorded Congress greater deference. [This is not] to say that Congress is free to disregard the Constitution when it acts in the area of military affairs. [But in] deciding the question before us we must be particularly careful not to substitute our judgment of what is desirable for that of Congress, or our own evaluation of evidence for a reasonable evaluation by [Congress].

a. See also Martha Minow, *Making All the Difference* 230–39 (1990); Elizabeth V. Spellman, *Inessential Woman* (1988); Patricia A. Cain, *Feminist Jurisprudence: Grounding the Theories*, 4 Berk. Women's L.J. 191 (1989–90); Kimberle Crenshaw, *Demarginalizing the Intersection of Race and Sex: A Black Feminist Critique of Antidiscrimination Doctrine*, Feminist Theory and Antiracist Politics, 1989 U.Chi. Legal F. 139; Angela P. Harris, *Race and Essentialism in Feminist Legal Theory*, 42 Stan.L.Rev. 581 (1990); Carrie Menkel-Meadow, *Mainstreaming Feminist Legal Theory*, 23 Pac.L.J. 1493 (1992); Patricia Williams, *The Obliging Shell: An Informal Essay on Formal Equal Opportunity*, 87 Mich.L.Rev. 2128 (1989).

"No one could deny that under the test of *Craig,* the Government's interest in raising and supporting armies is an 'important governmental interest.' [Nor did Congress, in excluding women from draft registration,] act 'unthinkingly' or 'reflexively and not for any considered reason.' The question of registering women for the draft not only received considerable national attention and was the subject of wide-ranging public debate, but also was extensively considered by Congress in hearings, floor debate, and in committee. * * *

"Congress determined that any future draft, which would be facilitated by the registration scheme, would be characterized by a need for combat troops. [Since] women are [statutorily] excluded from combat, Congress concluded that they would not be needed in the event of a draft, and therefore decided not to register them. [The] exemption of women from registration is not only sufficiently but closely related to Congress' purpose in authorizing registration. See *Michael M.; Craig; Reed.* [As] was the case in *Ballard,* [p. 1198, infra] 'the gender classification is not invidious, but rather realistically reflects the fact that the sexes are not similarly situated' in this case. *Michael M.* The Constitution requires that Congress treat similarly situated persons similarly, not that it engage in gestures of superficial equality.

"In holding the MSSA constitutionally invalid the District Court relied heavily on the President's decision to seek authority to register women and the testimony of members of the Executive Branch and the military in support of that decision. As stated by the Administration's witnesses before Congress, however, the President's 'decision to ask for authority to register women is based on equity.' * * * Congress was certainly entitled, in the exercise of its constitutional powers to raise and regulate armies and navies, to focus on the question of military need rather than 'equity.' * * *

"Although the military experts who testified in favor of registering women uniformly opposed the actual drafting of women, there was testimony that in the event of a draft of 650,000 the military could absorb some 80,000 female inductees [to] fill noncombat positions, freeing men to go to the front. In relying on this testimony, [the] District Court palpably exceeded its authority when it ignored Congress' considered response to this line of reasoning.

"In the first place, assuming that a small number of women could be drafted for noncombat roles, Congress simply did not consider it worth the added burdens of including women in draft and registration plans. * * * Congress also concluded that whatever the need for women for noncombat roles during mobilization, [it] could be met by volunteers.

"Most significantly, Congress determined that staffing noncombat positions with women during a mobilization would be positively detrimental to the important goal of military flexibility. [The] District Court was quite wrong in undertaking an independent evaluation of this evidence, rather than adopting an appropriately deferential examination of *Congress'* evaluation of that evidence."

Marshall, J., joined by Brennan, J., dissented:[a] "The Court today places its imprimatur on one of the most potent remaining public expressions of 'ancient canards about the proper role of women.' [W]e are not called upon to decide whether either men or women can be drafted at all, whether they must be drafted in equal numbers, in what order they should be drafted, or once inducted, how they are to be trained for their respective functions. In addition, this case does not involve a challenge to the statutes or policies that prohibit female members of

---

a. White, J., joined by Brennan, J., dissented separately.

the Armed Forces from serving in combat. It is with this understanding that I turn to the task at hand. [In] my judgment, there simply is no basis for concluding in this case that excluding women from registration is substantially related to the achievement of a concededly important governmental interest in maintaining an effective defense. * * *

"[The Court's analysis] focuses on the wrong question. The relevant inquiry under the *Craig* test is not whether a *gender-neutral* classification would substantially advance important governmental interests. Rather, the question is whether the gender-based classification is itself substantially related to the achievement of the asserted governmental interest. Thus, the Government's task in this case is to demonstrate that excluding women from registration substantially furthers the goal of preparing for a draft of combat troops. Or to put it another way, the Government must show that registering women would substantially impede its efforts to prepare for such a draft. Under our precedents, the Government cannot meet this burden without showing that a gender neutral statute would be a less effective means of attaining this end. [In] this case, the Government makes no claim that preparing for a draft of combat troops cannot be accomplished just as effectively by *registering* both men and women but *drafting* only men if only men turn out to be needed.[11] Nor can the Government argue that this alternative entails the additional cost and administrative inconvenience of registering women. This Court has repeatedly stated that [administrative convenience] is not an adequate constitutional justification under the *Craig* test.

"The fact that registering women in no way obstructs the governmental interest in preparing for a draft of combat troops points up a second flaw in the Court's analysis. The Court essentially reduces the question of the constitutionality of male-only *registration* to the validity of a hypothetical program for *conscripting* only men. [If] it could indeed be guaranteed in advance that conscription would be reimposed by Congress only in circumstances where, and in a form under which, all conscripts would have to be trained for and assigned to combat or combat rotation positions from which women are categorically excluded, then it could be argued that registration of women would be pointless.

"But of course, no such guarantee is possible. Certainly, nothing about the MSSA limits Congress to reinstituting the draft only in such circumstances. For example, Congress may decide that the All-Volunteer Armed Forces are inadequate to meet the Nation's defense needs even in times of peace and reinstitute peacetime conscription. In that event, the hypothetical draft the Court relied [on] would presumably be of little relevance. [The] fact that registration is a first step in the conscription process does not mean that a registration law expressly discriminating between men and women may be justified by a valid conscription program which would, in retrospect, make the current discrimination appear functionally related to the program that emerged.

"But even addressing the Court's reasoning on its own terms, its analysis is flawed because the entire argument rests on a premise that is demonstrably false. As noted, the majority simply assumes that registration prepares for a draft in which *every* draftee must be available for assignment to combat. But [this] finds no support in either the testimony before Congress, or more importantly, in the findings of the Senate Report, [which] concluded [that] drafting '*very large*

---

11. Alternatively, the Government could employ a classification that is related to the statutory objective but is not based on gender, for example, combat eligibility. Under the current scheme, large subgroups of the male population who are ineligible for combat because of physical handicaps or conscientious objector status are nonetheless required to register.

numbers of women' would hinder military flexibility. [But the] testimony on this issue at the congressional hearings was that drafting a limited number of women is quite compatible with the military's need for flexibility. In concluding that the Armed Services could usefully employ at least 80,000 women conscripts out of a total of 650,000 draftees that would be needed in the event of a major European war, the Defense Department took into account both the need for rotation of combat personnel and the possibility that some support personnel might have to be sent into combat. [The] combat restrictions that would prevent a female draftee from serving in a combat or combat rotation position also apply to the 150,000–250,000 women volunteers in the Armed Services. If the presence of increasing but controlled numbers of female volunteers has not unacceptably 'divide[d] the military into two groups,' it is difficult to see how the induction of a similarly limited additional number of women could accomplish this result.

"[T]he Senate Report establishes that induction of a large number of men but only a limited number of women [would] be substantially related to important governmental interests. But the discussion and findings in the Senate Report do not enable the Government to carry its burden of demonstrating that *completely* excluding women from the draft by excluding them from registration substantially furthers important governmental objectives."

Notes and Questions

1. *Agreement and disagreement.* All justices in *Rostker* appear to agree that it is constitutionally permissible for the armed services (i) to exclude women from combat positions and (ii) in the event of a draft, to conscript males only. Why?[a] Would it be fair to say that the majority and dissenting justices differ mostly if not exclusively about the implications of their shared assumptions?

2. *Male burdens and benefits.* Consider Leo Kanowitz, *"Benign" Sex Discrimination: Its Troubles and Their Cure,* 31 Hast.L.J. 1379, 1394 (1980): "[A] casual glance at the treatment males have received at the hands of the law solely because they are males suggests that they have paid an awesome price for other advantages they have presumably enjoyed over females in our society. Whether one talks of the male's unique obligation of compulsory military service, his primary duty for spousal and child support, his lack of the same kinds of protective labor legislation that have traditionally been enjoyed by women, or the statutory or judicial preference in child custody disputes that has long been accorded to mothers vis-à-vis fathers of minor children, sex discrimination against males in statutes and judicial decisions has been widespread and severe."[b]

3. *Feminist divisions.* Consider Wendy W. Williams, *The Equality Crisis: Some Reflections on Culture, Courts, and Feminism,* 7 Women's Rts.L.Rep. 175, 189–90 (1982): "As for *Rostker,* the conflicts among feminists were overtly expressed. Some of us felt it essential that we support the notion that a single-sex draft was unconstitutional; others felt that feminists should not take such a

---

a. "Outside the services, [does] the exclusion of women from combat serve[ ] functions that are chiefly expressive, symbolizing and reinforcing a traditional view of femininity that subordinates women"? See Kenneth L. Karst, *The Pursuit of Manhood and the Desegregation of the Armed Forces,* 38 U.C.L.A.L.Rev. 499, 525 (1991).

b. Compare Catharine A. MacKinnon, *Feminism Unmodified: Discourses on Life and Law* 38 (1987): "Excluding women is always an option if equality feels in tension with the pursuit [of a desired end]. They never seem to think of excluding men. Take combat. Somehow it takes the glory out of the foxhole, the buddiness out of the trenches, to imagine us out there. You get the feeling they might rather end the draft, they might even rather not fight wars at all than have to do it with us."

position. These latter groups explicitly contrasted the female ethic of nurturance and life-giving with a male ethic of aggression and militarism and asserted that if we argued to the Court that single-sex registration is unconstitutional we would be betraying ourselves and supporting what we find least acceptable about the male world.[c]

"To me, this latter argument quite overtly taps qualities that the culture has ascribed to woman-as-childrearer and converts them to a normative value statement, one with which it is easy for us to sympathize. This is one of the circumstances in which the feeling that 'I want what he's got but I don't want to be what he's had to be in order to get it' comes quickly to the surface. But I also believe that the reflexive response based on these deeper cultural senses leads us to untenable positions. [To] me, *Rostker* never posed the question of whether women should be forced as men now are to fight wars, but whether we, like them, must take the responsibility for deciding whether or not to fight, whether or not to bear the cost of risking our lives, on the one hand, or resisting in the name of peace, on the other. And do we not, by insisting upon our differences at these crucial junctures, promote and reinforce the us-them dichotomy that permits the Rehnquists and the Stewarts to resolve matters of great importance and complexity by the simplistic, reflexive assertion that men and women 'are simply not similarly situated?' "

4. *Sex-specific traits.* (a) GEDULDIG v. AIELLO, 417 U.S. 484, 94 S.Ct. 2485, 41 L.Ed.2d 256 (1974), per Stewart, J., held that exclusion of "disability that accompanies normal pregnancy and childbirth" from California's disability insurance system "does not exclude [anyone] because of gender * * *. While it is true that only women can become pregnant, it does not follow that every legislative classification concerning pregnancy is [sex-based]. Absent a showing that distinctions involving pregnancy are mere pretexts designed to effect an invidious discrimination against the members of one sex or the other, lawmakers are constitutionally free to include or exclude pregnancy from the coverage of legislation such as this on any reasonable basis, just as with respect to any other physical condition. [The] program divides potential recipients into two groups—pregnant women and nonpregnant persons. While the first group is exclusively female, the second includes members of both sexes. The fiscal and actuarial benefits of the program thus accrue to members of both sexes. [There] is no risk from which men are protected and women are not. Likewise, there is no risk from which women are protected and men are not.[21]"

Brennan, J. joined by Douglas and Marshall, JJ., dissented, finding "sex discrimination" in the state's "singling out for less favorable treatment a gender-linked disability peculiar to women [while] men receive full compensation for all disabilities suffered, including those that affect only or primarily their sex, such as prostatectomies, circumcision, hemophilia and gout."

c. Compare Carol Gilligan, *In a Different Voice* (1982), suggesting that women tend to have a different moral framework—more concerned with issues of relationships and of caring—from the characteristically rights-based outlook of men. Questions raised about Gilligan's theory include (i) whether the characteristic difference that she identifies in fact exists; (ii) whether, even if it does, it is the result of social conditioning rather than reflective of a "natural" difference between men and women; and (iii) whether governmental action predicated on the notion that women have a distinctive moral perspective helps to perpetuate a stereotype that works to women's overall disadvantage. For opinionated commentary on the use of and debates about Gilligan's theory in feminist thought, see Mary Joe Frug, *Progressive Feminist Legal Scholarship: Can We Claim "A Different Voice"?*, 15 Harv. Women's L.J. 37 (1992). For caustic criticism, see MacKinnon, *supra*, at 32–45.

21. Indeed, the [data indicated] that both the annual claim rate and the annual claim cost are greater for women than for [men.]

(b) What result under *Geduldig* if the disability program excluded only sickle-cell anemia? Should this case, like *Geduldig*, be resolved under the rule of *Washington v. Davis* and its focus on the question whether there was an intent to discriminate?

(c) Could a state constitutionally forbid "pregnant persons" from teaching in the public schools? For the invalidation of an employment disability for pregnant women on the ground that an "irrebuttable presumption" of inability violated due process, see *Cleveland State Bd. of Educ. v. LaFleur*, 414 U.S. 632, 94 S.Ct. 791, 39 L.Ed.2d 52 (1974).

(d) Should legislation regulating abortions be scrutinized as effecting a form of gender-based discrimination? See pp. 331–33 supra.

5. *Discrimination against unmarried fathers.* The leading cases involving discrimination against unmarried fathers, both decided by 5–4, are hard to reconcile. Compare *Caban v. Mohammed*, 441 U.S. 380, 99 S.Ct. 1760, 60 L.Ed.2d 297 (1979) (holding violative of equal protection a New York statute granting the mother—but not the father—of an illegitimate child the right to veto the child's adoption) with *Parham v. Hughes*, 441 U.S. 347, 99 S.Ct. 1742, 60 L.Ed.2d 269 (1979) (upholding a law denying the father—but not the mother—of an illegitimate child the right to sue for the child's wrongful death unless he had legitimated the child).[d] Since the statutes involved distinctions between unmarried mothers and unmarried fathers, do both cases present straightforward issues of gender discrimination? Cf. *Geduldig v. Aiello*, supra.

Under the test applicable to statutes that discriminate on the basis of gender, is the state warranted in presuming that unmarried mothers do, but unmarried fathers do not, enjoy a "relationship" with their children that justifies their exercise of distinctive powers and enjoyment of distinctive rights? Consider the argument of Sylvia A. Law, *Rethinking Sex and the Constitution*, 132 U.Pa.L.Rev. 955, 995–98 (1984), that (i) "[t]he stereotype of women accepting the 'unshakable responsibility for the care of the child' is overwhelmingly accurate"; (ii) "[t]he stereotype of male irresponsibility in relation to the children they father is also distressingly accurate"; but (iii) the difference may be more attributable to "social patterns and sex-based stereotypes" than to "biology"; and (iv) law granting preferences to women may reinforce those stereotypes. But compare Mary L. Shanley, *Unwed Fathers' Rights, Adoption, and Sex Equality: Gender–Neutrality and the Perpetuation of Patriarchy*, 95 Colum.L.Rev. 60 (1995), arguing that allowing unmarried fathers to veto a child's adoption may frustrate the efforts of caring, unwed mothers—who in fact have much closer physical and emotional bonds—to protect the child's best interests. If a presumption that unmarried mothers stand on a different footing from unmarried fathers is permitted, should processes be required in which the presumption can be overcome?

6. *Child custody proceedings.* Should it be constitutionally permissible for states to grant a preference to mothers over fathers in child custody proceedings? Consider Joan C. Williams, *Deconstructing Gender*, 87 Mich.L.Rev. 797, 838

---

d. Compare *Lehr v. Robertson*, 463 U.S. 248, 103 S.Ct. 2985, 77 L.Ed.2d 614 (1983), per Stevens, J., upholding (6–3) a New York provision that denies a father, who never had any significant relationship with his illegitimate child, notice and opportunity to be heard before the child may be adopted. But see *Michael H. v. Gerald D.*, p. 415 supra (alleged father with significant relationship to child denied any paternal rights because mother was married to another man at time of conception and birth).

For another decision dealing with paternal rights in respect to adoption and custody of illegitimate children, see *Quilloin v. Walcott*, p. 410 supra.

(1989): "[T]he abolition of the maternal presumption in child-custody decisions has had two deleterious impacts on women. First, in the 90 percent of the cases where mothers received custody, mothers often find themselves bargaining away financial claims in exchange for custody of the children. Even if the father does not want custody, his lawyer will often advise him to claim it in order to have a bargaining chip with which to bargain down his wife's financial claims. Second, the abolition of the maternal preference has created situations where a father who wants custody often wins even if he was not the primary caretaker prior to the divorce—on the grounds that he can offer the children a better life because he is richer than his former wife."

———

Alabama sued J.E.B. for paternity and child support on behalf of T.B., the mother of a minor child. The state used 9 of its 10 preemptory strikes to remove male jurors.[a] J.E.B. v. ALABAMA ex rel. T.B., 511 U.S. 127, 114 S.Ct. 1419, 128 L.Ed.2d 89 (1994), per BLACKMUN, J., held that the state's action violated equal protection: "[T]he only question is whether discrimination on the basis of gender in jury selection substantially furthers the State's legitimate interest in achieving a fair and impartial trial.[6] [R]espondent maintains that its decision to strike virtually all the males from the jury in this case 'may reasonably have been based upon the perception, supported by history, that men otherwise totally qualified to serve upon a jury might be more sympathetic and receptive to the arguments of a man alleged in a paternity action to be the father of an out-of-wedlock child, while women equally qualified to serve upon a jury might be more sympathetic and receptive to the arguments of the complaining witness who bore the child.

"We shall not accept as a defense to gender-based peremptory challenges 'the very stereotype the law condemns.' [Respondent] urges this Court to condone the same stereotypes that justified the wholesale exclusion of women from juries and the ballot box.[11] Respondent seems to assume that gross generalizations that would be deemed impermissible if made on the basis of race are somehow permissible when made on the basis of gender. * * *

"When state actors exercise peremptory challenges in reliance on gender stereotypes, they ratify and reinforce prejudicial views of the relative abilities of men and women. Because these stereotypes have wreaked injustice in so many other spheres of our country's public life, active discrimination by litigants on the basis of gender during jury selection 'invites cynicism respecting the jury's neutrality and its obligation to adhere to the law.' [Our] conclusion that litigants may not strike potential jurors solely on the basis of gender does not imply the elimination of all peremptory challenges.[14] Neither does it conflict with a State's

a. J.E.B. used all but one of his preemptory strikes to remove female jurors, but any issue thus raised was not before the Court.

6. Because we conclude that gender-based peremptory challenges are not substantially related to an important government objective, we once again need not decide whether classifications based on gender are inherently suspect. See *Mississippi University for Women*, [p. 1202 infra]; *Harris v. Forklift Systems*, 510 U.S. 17, ___ 114 S.Ct. 367, 373, 126 L.Ed.2d 295 (1993) (Ginsburg, J., concurring) ("[I]t remains an

open question whether 'classifications based upon gender are inherently suspect.' ").

11. [The] Equal Protection Clause, as interpreted by decisions of this court, acknowledges that a shred of truth may be contained in some stereotypes, but requires that state actors look beyond the surface before making judgments about people that are likely to stigmatize as well as to perpetuate historical patterns of discrimination.

14. The popular refrain is that *all* peremptory challenges are based on stereotypes of some kind, expressing various intuitive and

legitimate interest in using such challenges in its effort to secure a fair and impartial jury. Parties still may remove jurors whom they feel might be less acceptable than others on the panel; gender simply may not serve as a proxy for bias. Parties may also exercise their peremptory challenges to remove from the venire any group or class of individuals normally subject to 'rational basis' review. Even strikes based on characteristics that are disproportionately associated with one gender could be appropriate, absent a showing of pretext.[16]"

O'CONNOR, J., concurred: "[T]oday's important blow against gender discrimination is not costless. [A] plethora of studies make clear that in rape cases, for example, female jurors are somewhat more likely to vote to convict than male jurors. Moreover, though there have been no similarly definitive studies regarding, for example, sexual harassment, child custody, or spousal or child abuse, one need not be a sexist to share the intuition that in certain cases a person's gender and resulting life experience will be relevant to his or her view of the [case.] Individuals are not expected to ignore as jurors what they know as men—or women. [These] concerns reinforce my conviction that today's decision should be limited to a prohibition on the government's use of gender-based peremptory challenges."[b]

SCALIA, J., joined by Rehnquist, C.J., and Thomas, J., dissented: "Today's opinion is an inspiring demonstration of how thoroughly up-to-date and right-thinking we Justices are in matters pertaining to the sexes (or as the Court would have it, the genders),[1] and how sternly we disapprove the male chauvinist attitudes of our predecessors. [The] hasty reader will be surprised to learn, for example, that this lawsuit involves a complaint about the use of peremptory challenges to exclude *men* from a petit jury. * * *

"The Court [spends] time establishing that the use of sex as a proxy for particular views or sympathies is unwise and perhaps irrational. The opinion stresses the lack of statistical evidence to support the widely held belief that, at least in certain types of cases, a juror's sex has some statistically significant predictive value as to how the juror will behave. This assertion seems to place the Court in opposition to its earlier Sixth Amendment 'fair cross-section' cases. See, e.g., *Taylor v. Louisiana* ('Controlled studies [have] concluded that women bring to juries their own perspectives and values that influence both jury deliberation and result'). But times and trends do change, and unisex is unquestionably in fashion. Personally, I am less inclined to demand statistics, and more inclined to

---

frequently erroneous biases. But where peremptory challenges are made on the basis of group characteristics other than race or gender (like occupation, for example), they do not reinforce the same stereotypes about the group's competence or predispositions that have been used to prevent them from voting, participating on juries, pursuing their chosen professions, or otherwise contributing to civic life. See Barbara Allen Babcock, *A Place in the Palladium, Women's Rights and Jury Service*, 61 U.Cinn.L.Rev. 1139, 1173 (1993).

16. For example, challenging all persons who have had military experience would disproportionately affect men at this time, while challenging all persons employed as nurses would disproportionately affect women. Without a showing of pretext, however, these challenges may well not be unconstitutional, since

they are not gender- or race-based. See *Hernandez v. New York*.

b. Kennedy, J., concurred. Rehnquist, C.J., filed a dissenting opinion.

1. Throughout this opinion, I shall refer to the issue as sex discrimination rather than (as the Court does) gender discrimination. The word "gender" has acquired the new and useful connotation of cultural or attitudinal characteristics (as opposed to physical characteristics) distinctive to the sexes. That is to say, gender is to sex as feminine is to female and masculine to male. The present case does not involve peremptory strikes exercised on the basis of femininity or masculinity (as far as it appears, effeminate men did not survive the prosecution's peremptories). The case involves, therefore, sex discrimination plain and simple.

credit the perceptions of experienced litigators who have had money on the line. But it does not matter. The Court's fervent defense of the proposition *il n'y a pas de différence entre les hommes et les femmes* (it stereotypes the opposite view as hateful 'stereotyping') turns out to be, like its recounting of the history of sex discrimination against women, utterly irrelevant. Even if sex was a remarkably good predictor in certain cases, the Court would find its use in peremptories unconstitutional. * * *

"The core of the Court's reasoning is that peremptory challenges on the basis of any group characteristic subject to heightened scrutiny are inconsistent with the guarantee of the Equal Protection Clause. That conclusion can be reached only by focusing unrealistically upon individual exercises of the peremptory challenge, and ignoring the totality of the practice. Since all groups are subject to the peremptory challenge (and will be made the object of it, depending upon the nature of the particular case) it is hard to see how any group is denied equal protection. That explains why peremptory challenges coexisted with the Equal Protection Clause for 120 years. This case is a perfect example of how the system as a whole is even-handed. [F]or every man struck by the government petitioner's own lawyer struck a woman. To say that men were singled out for discriminatory treatment in this process is preposterous. [That] is why the Court's characterization of respondent's argument as 'reminiscent of the arguments advanced to justify the total exclusion of women from juries,' is patently false. Women were categorically excluded from juries because of doubt that they were competent; women are stricken from juries by peremptory challenge because of doubt that they are well disposed to the striking party's case. There is discrimination and dishonor in the former, and not in the [latter]."

III. "BENIGN"—"COMPENSATORY"— "REMEDIAL" DISCRIMINATION

KAHN v. SHEVIN, 416 U.S. 351, 94 S.Ct. 1734, 40 L.Ed.2d 189 (1974), per Douglas, J., upheld a property tax exemption for widows (but not widowers). Unlike *Reed*, the law is "reasonably designed to further the state policy of cushioning the financial impact of spousal loss upon the sex for whom that loss imposes a disproportionately heavy burden." Unlike *Frontiero*, the classification here is not "*solely* for administrative convenience," nor were the statutes there "in any sense designed to rectify the effects of past discrimination against women."[a]

———

SCHLESINGER v. BALLARD, 419 U.S. 498, 95 S.Ct. 572, 42 L.Ed.2d 610 (1975), per Stewart, J., upheld a federal statute providing for the discharge of naval "line" officers who had not been promoted for nine years (males) or thirteen years (females): In "*Reed* and *Frontiero* the challenged classifications [were] premised on overbroad generalizations" and were sought to be justified solely on "administrative convenience." Here, because of Navy restrictions on combat and

a. Brennan, J., joined by Marshall, J., dissented: "[I]n providing special benefits for a needy segment of society long the victim of purposeful discrimination and neglect, the statute serves the compelling state interest of achieving equality for such groups." But it "is plainly overinclusive [because] the State could readily narrow the class of beneficiaries to those widows for whom the effects of past economic discrimination against women have been a practical reality." White, J., also dissented.

sea duty for women, "Congress [may] quite rationally have believed that women line officers had less opportunity for promotion than did their male counterparts, and that a longer period of tenure for women officers would, therefore, be consistent with the goal to provide women officers with 'fair and equitable career advancement programs.' Cf. *Kahn*."[b]

WEINBERGER v. WIESENFELD, 420 U.S. 636, 95 S.Ct. 1225, 43 L.Ed.2d 514 (1975), per BRENNAN, J., held that Social Security Act § 402(g)'s payment of benefits to the wife—but not to the husband—of a deceased wage earner with minor children violated equal protection because it "unjustifiably discriminated against women wage-earners":[c] As in *Frontiero*, an " 'archaic and overbroad' generalization [underlies] the distinction drawn by § 402(g), namely, that male [but not female] workers' earnings are vital to the support of their families." Unlike *Kahn*, "it is apparent both from the statutory scheme itself and from the legislative history of § 402(g) that Congress' purpose [was] not to provide an income to women who were, because of economic discrimination, unable to provide for themselves. Rather, § 402(g), linked as it is directly to responsibility for minor children, was intended to permit women to elect not to work and to devote themselves to the care of children. Since this purpose in no way is premised upon any special disadvantages of women, [the] gender-based distinction of § 402(g) is entirely irrational."[d]

CALIFANO v. GOLDFARB, 430 U.S. 199, 97 S.Ct. 1021, 51 L.Ed.2d 270 (1977), held that Social Security Act § 402(f)'s payment of benefits to a widow of a covered employee, but not to a widower unless he proves dependency on his deceased wife-employee, violated equal protection. Brennan, J., joined by White, Marshall, and Powell, JJ., found *Wiesenfeld* "dispositive."

STEVENS, J., concurred, noting his agreement with the dissent's contentions that "the relevant discrimination in this case is against surviving male spouses, rather than against deceased female wage earners" and that "a classification which treats certain aged widows more favorably than their male counterparts is not 'invidious.' " Nonetheless, since "the history of the statute is entirely consistent with the view that Congress simply assumed that all widows should be regarded as 'dependents' in some general sense," he was "persuaded that this discrimination against a group of males is merely the accidental by-product of a

---

b. Brennan, J., joined by Douglas and Marshall, JJ.—and "for the most part" by White, J.—dissented: "I find quite troublesome the notion that a gender-based difference in treatment can be justified by another, broader, gender-based difference in treatment imposed directly and currently by the Navy itself." See also Leo Kanowitz, *"Benign" Sex Discrimination: Its Troubles and Their Cure*, 31 Hast.L.J. 1379, 1407 (1980): "Nor did the Court in *Ballard* take into account another detrimental impact of the policy upon women: the easing of pressure on their superiors to promote them

precisely because women officers could stay in the service two years longer than men without being promoted."

c. Against which sex did the provision discriminate? Was the discrimination in *Frontiero* against servicewomen or their male spouses? What about *Kahn*?

d. Powell, J., joined by Burger, C.J., "concur[red] generally in the opinion of the Court." Rehnquist, J., disclaiming reliance on *Frontiero*, concurred in the result. Douglas, J., did not participate.

traditional way of thinking about females."[e]

REHNQUIST, J., joined by Burger, C.J., and Stewart and Blackmun, JJ., dissented: "Favoring aged widows is scarcely an invidious discrimination. [It] in no way perpetuates the economic discrimination which has been the basis for heightened scrutiny of gender-based classifications, and is, in fact, explainable as a measure to ameliorate the characteristically depressed condition of aged widows. *Kahn*."[f]

CALIFANO v. WEBSTER

430 U.S. 313, 97 S.Ct. 1192, 51 L.Ed.2d 360 (1977).

PER CURIAM.

[Social Security Act § 215(b)(3)'s formula—which has since been amended—afforded the chance of higher old-age benefits to female wage earners than to similarly situated males.]

To withstand scrutiny under [equal protection], "classifications by gender must serve important governmental objectives and must be substantially related to achievement of those objectives." *Craig.* Reduction of the disparity in economic condition between men and women caused by the long history of discrimination against women has been recognized as such an important governmental objective. *Ballard; Kahn.* But "the mere recitation of a benign, compensatory purpose is not an automatic shield which protects against any inquiry into the actual purposes underlying a statutory scheme." *Wiesenfeld.* Accordingly, we have rejected attempts to justify gender classifications as compensation for past discrimination against women when the classifications in fact penalized women wage earners, *Goldfarb; Wiesenfeld,* or when the statutory structure and its legislative history revealed that the classification was not enacted as compensation for past discrimination. *Goldfarb; Wiesenfeld.*

[This statute] is more analogous to those upheld in *Kahn* and *Ballard* than to those struck down in *Wiesenfeld* and *Goldfarb.* The more favorable treatment of the female wage earner enacted here was not a result of "archaic and overbroad generalizations" about women, or of "the role-typing society has long imposed" upon women such as casual assumptions that women are "the weaker sex" or are more likely to be child-rearers or dependents. Rather, "the only discernible purpose of [§ 215's more favorable treatment is] the permissible one of redressing our society's longstanding disparate treatment of women." *Goldfarb.*

The challenged statute operated directly to compensate women for past economic discrimination. Retirement benefits [are] based on past earnings. But as we have recognized, "[w]hether from overt discrimination or from the socialization process of a male-dominated culture, the job market is inhospitable to the woman seeking any but the lowest paid jobs." *Kahn.* Thus, allowing women, who as such have been unfairly hindered from earning as much as men, to

---

e. Stevens, J., also strongly suggested that he disagreed with *Kahn*.

f. *Wengler v. Druggists Mut. Ins. Co.,* 446 U.S. 142, 100 S.Ct. 1540, 64 L.Ed.2d 107 (1980), per White, J., held that a virtually identical state workers' compensation law discriminated against women (relying on *Goldfarb, Wiesenfeld* and *Frontiero*)—and against men (relying on Stevens, J.'s concurrence in *Goldfarb*)—and thus violated equal protection. Stevens, J., concurred on the basis of his *Gold-*

farb concurrence. Only Rehnquist, J., dissented.

See also *Califano v. Westcott,* 443 U.S. 76, 99 S.Ct. 2655, 61 L.Ed.2d 382 (1979), relying on *Goldfarb* and *Wiesenfeld* to hold violative of equal protection a provision of the Social Security Act providing benefits to families whose dependent children have been deprived of parental support because of the unemployment of the father, but not the mother.

eliminate additional low-earning years from the calculation of their retirement benefits works directly to remedy some part of the effect of past discrimination.[5]

[T]he legislative history is clear that the differing treatment of men and women in former § 215(b)(3) was not "the accidental byproduct of a traditional way of thinking about females," *Goldfarb* (Stevens, J., concurring in the result), but rather was deliberately enacted to compensate for particular economic disabilities suffered by women.[a] * * *

Reversed.

CHIEF JUSTICE BURGER, with whom JUSTICE STEWART, JUSTICE BLACKMUN, and JUSTICE REHNQUIST join, concurring in the judgment.

* * * I find it somewhat difficult to distinguish [*Goldfarb*]. I question whether certainty in the law is promoted by hinging the validity of important statutory schemes on whether five Justices view them to be more akin to the "offensive" provisions struck down in *Wiesenfeld* and *Frontiero,* or more like the "benign" provisions upheld in *Ballard* and *Kahn.* I therefore concur in the judgment [for] reasons stated by Mr. Justice Rehnquist in his dissenting opinion in *Goldfarb,* in which Mr. Justice Stewart, Mr. Justice Blackmun, and I joined.

Notes and Questions

1. *Permissible purposes and overbroad generalizations.* Consider the suggestion of Michael Klarman, *An Interpretive History of Modern Equal Protection*, 90 Mich.L.Rev. 213, 303–08 (1991), that the Court's 1976 decision in *Washington v. Davis*, p. 1093 supra, marked a general shift in equal protection jurisprudence from a focus on legislative "outputs"—i.e., on whether statutes had a discriminatory impact on groups entitled to special judicial solicitude—to a preoccupation with legislative "inputs"—i.e., with the deliberative process that led to the legislature's decision. Thus, Professor Klarman maintains, the Court's 1973 and 1974 decisions in *Kahn* and *Ballard* exhibited little or no concern with overbroad generalizations and stereotypes, whereas the legislature's actual thinking and motivation were of "overriding importance" in the post-*Washington v. Davis* decisions in *Goldfarb* and *Webster.* Is this analysis persuasive? If such a shift did occur, does it reflect a change for the better?

2. *Other "compensatory" statutes.* ORR v. ORR, 440 U.S. 268, 99 S.Ct. 1102, 59 L.Ed.2d 306 (1979), considered "two legislative objectives" for an Alabama statute providing that only husbands may be required to pay alimony— (1) to "provide help for needy spouses, using sex as a proxy for need," and (2) to "compensat[e] women for past discrimination during marriage, which assertedly has left them unprepared to fend for themselves." The Court, per BRENNAN, J., held that the statute failed the *Craig* standard: "Under the statute, individualized hearings at which the parties' relative financial circumstances are considered *already* occur. There is no reason, therefore, to use sex as a proxy for need. Needy males could be helped along with needy females with little if any additional burden on the [state]. Similarly, since individualized hearings can determine which women were in fact discriminated against vis-à-vis their husbands, as well

---

5. Even with the advantage[,] women on the average received lower retirement benefits than men. "As of December 1972, the average monthly retirement insurance benefit for males was $179.60 and for females, $140.50."

a. See also *Heckler v. Mathews,* 465 U.S. 728, 104 S.Ct. 1387, 79 L.Ed.2d 646 (1984),

unanimously upholding a "temporary revival" of the classification invalidated in *Goldfarb* "in order to protect[] the expectations of persons, both men and women, who had planned their retirements based on" it.

as which family units defied the stereotype and left the husband dependent on the wife, Alabama's alleged compensatory purpose may be effectuated without placing burdens solely on husbands."[b]

3. *Affirmative action for women.* Does *Webster* establish that affirmative action for women—with respect, for example, to educational opportunities, employment, and government contracts—will generally be tested under *Craig*'s mid-level scrutiny? If so, is it appropriate for gender-based affirmative action to be subject to less stringent scrutiny than race-based affirmative action?[c]

What "substantial" interests, if any, might support gender-based affirmative action? Remedying past "societal" discrimination?[d] "Diversity" in education? In employment?[e] In government contracting?

MISSISSIPPI UNIV. FOR WOMEN v. HOGAN
458 U.S. 718, 102 S.Ct. 3331, 73 L.Ed.2d 1090 (1982).

JUSTICE O'CONNOR delivered the opinion of the Court.

[MUW, "the oldest state-supported all-female college in the United States," denied Hogan admission to its School of Nursing solely because of his sex.[a]]

* * * Our decisions [establish] that the party seeking to uphold a statute that classifies individuals on the basis of their gender must carry the burden of showing an "exceedingly persuasive justification" for the classification. The burden is met only by showing at least that the classification serves "important governmental objectives and that the discriminatory means employed" are "substantially related to the achievement of those objectives."[9]

Although the test [is] straightforward, it must be applied free of fixed notions concerning the roles and abilities of males and females. [Thus,] if the statutory objective is to exclude or "protect" members of one gender because they are presumed to suffer from an inherent handicap or to be innately inferior, the objective itself is illegitimate. See *Frontiero*.

b. Blackmun, J., concurred. Burger, C.J., and Powell and Rehnquist, JJ., dissented on procedural grounds to which Stevens, J.'s concurrence responded.

c. According to Comment, *Gender-Based Affirmative Action: Where Does It Fit in the Tiered Scheme of Equal Protection Scrutiny?*, 41 Kan.L.Rev. 591 (1993), the circuits are split on this issue in the wake of *Croson*.

d. Compare *Johnson v. Transportation Agency*, 480 U.S. 616, 107 S.Ct. 1442, 94 L.Ed.2d 615 (1987), which upheld—against a challenge based exclusively on Title VII of the 1964 Civil Rights Act—the agency's promotion, under an affirmative action plan, of a woman in preference to a man who had received a slightly higher numerical rating on a mix of objective and subjective evaluations. The Court, per Brennan, J., found that no constitutional issue was properly before the Court and held that Title VII permits affirmative action when there is a "manifest imbalance" in an employer's work force. O'Connor, J., who concurred separately, argued that the constitutional and statutory standards were identical. Scalia, J., joined by Rehnquist, C.J., and White,

J. (in part), dissented on the ground that the statute forbids affirmative action preferences.

e. Does the validity of this interest depend on the controversial claim, often associated with Carol Gilligan's *In a Different Voice* (1982), discussed on p. 1194 supra, that women's characteristic moral framework tends to differ from that of men? Cf. Suzanna Sherry, *Civic Virtue and the Feminine Voice in Constitutional Adjudication*, 72 Va.L.Rev. 543, 592–613 (1986) (suggesting that O'Connor, J.'s approach to constitutional interpretation is partly a valuable and distinctive reflection of her gender).

a. The Court declined "to address the question of whether MUW's admissions policy, as applied to males seeking admission to schools other than the School of Nursing, violates the Fourteenth Amendment."

9. [Because] we conclude that the challenged statutory classification is not substantially related to an important objective, we need not decide whether classifications based upon gender are inherently suspect.

If the State's objective is legitimate and important, we next determine whether the requisite direct, substantial relationship between objective and means is present. The purpose of requiring that close relationship is to assure that the validity of a classification is determined through reasoned analysis rather than through the mechanical application of traditional, often inaccurate, assumptions about the proper roles of men and women. The need for the requirement is amply revealed by reference to the broad range of statutes already invalidated by this Court, statutes that relied upon the simplistic, outdated assumption that gender could be used as a "proxy for other, more germane bases of classification," *Craig,* to establish a link between objective and classification. * * *

The State's primary justification for maintaining the single-sex admissions policy of MUW's School of Nursing is that it compensates for discrimination against women and, therefore, constitutes educational affirmative action. [A] state can evoke a compensatory purpose to justify an otherwise discriminatory classification only if members of the gender benefitted by the classification actually suffer a disadvantage related to the classification. We considered such a situation in *Webster* [and *Ballard*].

In sharp contrast, Mississippi has made no showing that women lacked opportunities to obtain training in the field of nursing or to attain positions of leadership in that field when the MUW School of Nursing opened its door or that women currently are deprived of such opportunities. In fact, in 1970, the year before the School of Nursing's first class enrolled, women earned 94 percent of the nursing baccalaureate degrees conferred in Mississippi and 98.6 percent of the degrees earned nationwide.[14]

Rather than compensate for discriminatory barriers faced by women, MUW's [policy] tends to perpetuate the stereotyped view of nursing as an exclusively woman's job.[15] By assuring that Mississippi allots more openings in its state-supported nursing schools to women than it does to men, MUW's admissions policy lends credibility to the old view that women, not men, should become nurses, and makes the assumption that nursing is a field for women a self-fulfilling prophecy. Thus, we conclude that, although the State recited a "benign, compensatory purpose," it failed to establish that the alleged objective is the actual purpose underlying the discriminatory classification.

The policy is invalid also because [the] State has made no showing that the gender-based classification is substantially and directly related to its proposed compensatory objective. To the contrary, MUW's policy of permitting men to attend classes as auditors fatally undermines its claim that women, at least those in the School of Nursing, are adversely affected by the presence of men.[17]

---

14. Relatively little change has taken place during the past 10 years. In 1980, women received more than 94 percent of the baccalaureate degrees conferred nationwide and constituted 96.5 percent of the registered nurses in the labor force.

15. Officials of the American Nurses Association have suggested that excluding men from the field has depressed nurses' wages. To the extent the exclusion of men has that effect, MUW's admissions policy actually penalizes the very class the State purports to benefit. Cf. *Wiesenfeld.*

17. Justice Powell's dissent suggests that a second objective is served by the gender-based classification in that Mississippi has elected to provide women a choice of educational environments. Since any gender-based classification provides one class a benefit or choice not available to the other class, however, that argument begs the question. The issue is not whether the benefitted class profits from the classification, but whether the State's decision to confer a benefit only upon one class by means of a discriminatory classification is substantially related to achieving a legitimate and substantial goal.

Affirmed.[b]

CHIEF JUSTICE BURGER, dissenting.

I agree generally with Justice Powell's dissenting opinion. I write separately, however, to emphasize that [s]ince the Court's opinion relies heavily on its finding that women have traditionally dominated the nursing profession, it suggests that a State might well be justified in maintaining, for example, the option of an all-women's business school or liberal arts program.

JUSTICE POWELL, with whom JUSTICE REHNQUIST joins, dissenting.[c]

[T]he Court errs seriously by assuming [that] the equal protection standard generally applicable to sex discrimination is appropriate here. That standard was designed to free women from "archaic and overbroad generalizations." *Ballard.* In no previous case have we applied it to invalidate state efforts to *expand* women's choices. * * *

By applying heightened equal protection analysis to this case, the Court frustrates the liberating spirit of the Equal Protection Clause. It forbids the States from providing women with an opportunity to choose the type of university they prefer. And yet it is these women whom the Court regards as the *victims* of an illegal, stereotyped perception of the role of women in our society. The Court reasons this way in a case in which no woman has complained, and the only complainant is a man who advances no claims on behalf of anyone else. His claim [is] not that he is being denied a substantive educational opportunity, or even the right to attend an all-male or a coeducational college. It is *only* that the colleges open to him are located at inconvenient distances.

* * * I would sustain Mississippi's right to continue MUW on a rational basis analysis. But I need not apply this "lowest tier" of scrutiny. [More] than 2,000 women presently evidence their preference for MUW by having enrolled [there.] Generations of our finest minds, both among educators and students, have believed that single-sex, college-level institutions afford distinctive benefits. There are many persons, of course, who have different views. But simply because there are these differences is no reason—certainly none of constitutional dimension—to conclude that no substantial state interest is served when such a choice is made available.[17]

Notes and Questions

1. *Single-gender schools.* In *Hogan,* the Court stated that it was "not faced with the question of whether States can provide 'separate but equal' undergraduate institutions for males and females." Under what circumstances, if any, should a state be able to do so? Cf. *Vorchheimer v. School Dist. of Philadelphia,* 532 F.2d 880 (3d Cir.1976), affirmed by an equally divided Court, 430 U.S. 703, 97 S.Ct. 1671, 51 L.Ed.2d 750 (1977) (upholding "separate but equal" public schools for boys and girls; Rehnquist, J., not participating); Note, *Inner-City Single–Sex Schools: Educational Reform or Invidious Discrimination?*, 105 Harv.L.Rev. 1741 (1992).

---

b. The state's contention that Congress had authorized the MUW policy is considered at p. 1394 infra.

c. Blackmun, J.'s brief dissenting opinion—agreeing essentially with Powell, J.—is omitted.

17. [It] is understandable that MUW might believe that it could allow men to audit courses without materially affecting its environment. MUW charges tuition but gives no academic credit for auditing. The University evidently is correct in believing that few men will choose to audit under such circumstances. This deviation from a perfect relationship between means and ends is insubstantial.

2. *Single-sex athletic programs.* May public schools have separate athletic programs for boys and girls? May boys be excluded from "girls' teams"? Girls from "boys' teams"? According to Note, *Boys Muscling in on Girls' Sports,* 53 Ohio St.L.J. 891, 892–93 (1992), most lower courts have held that " 'separate but equal' teams remain a constitutionally permissible alternative to gender-integrated teams. [The] important governmental objective in denying boys access to girls' athletic teams has been articulated as: 'maintaining, fostering, and promoting athletic opportunities for girls' and 'redressing past discrimination against women in athletics and promoting equality of athletic opportunity between the sexes'; in short, 'redressing the disparate opportunities available to males and females.' Most courts addressing the issue have found a substantial relationship between excluding boys from girls' teams and providing equal opportunities for females. Hence, exclusion is considered a permissible means of achieving this objective."

Do you agree with this analysis? Is it consistent with the Court's frequent admonition in cases involving race-based affirmative action that equal protection rights attach to individuals, not groups?

3. *Pregnancy and maternity leaves. General Electric Co. v. Gilbert,* 429 U.S. 125, 97 S.Ct. 401, 50 L.Ed.2d 343 (1976), held that Title VII's prohibition of sex discrimination did not prevent companies from excluding pregnancy from their disability plans. In response, Congress enacted the Pregnancy Discrimination Act, 42 U.S.C.A. § 2000e(k) (1978), which defined sex discrimination to include pregnancy discrimination. Some states have given maternity leave rights that go beyond that afforded to non-pregnant employees who are unable to work. Is this sex discrimination? See *California Federal Savings & Loan Ass'n v. Guerra,* 479 U.S. 272, 107 S.Ct. 683, 93 L.Ed.2d 613 (1987) (protection for physical disabilities associated with pregnancy with no similar protection for disabilities unrelated to pregnancy is neither inconsistent with nor preempted by federal antidiscrimination statutes).

In order to pass muster under the equal protection clause, should a state statute providing post-natal maternity leaves also have to make identical provision for paternity leaves? Is an approach based upon "special treatment" for women a "double-edged sword"? See Wendy W. Williams, *The Equality Crisis: Some Reflections on Culture, Courts, and Feminism,* 7 Women's Rts.L.Rptr. 175, 196 (1982) ("[i]f we can't have it both ways, we need to think carefully about which way we want to have it"). Does the phrase "special treatment" presuppose a male perspective?[e]

Consider Katharine T. Bartlett, *Feminist Legal Methods,* 103 Harv.L.Rev. 829, 842 (1990): "Although feminists have split over whether women have more to lose than to gain from singling out pregnancy for different, some would say 'favored,' treatment, they agree on the critical question: what are the consequences for women of specific rules or practices?" Should this also be the critical question under the equal protection clause? Does a doctrine that ignores the biological differences between men and women regarding abortion, reproduction, and creation of another human being mean that "women can claim equality only

e. For further commentary, see, e.g., Lucinda M. Finley, *Transcending Equality Theory: A Way Out of the Maternity and the Workplace Debate,* 86 Colum.L.Rev. 1118 (1986); Christine A. Littleton, *Reconstructing Sexual Equality,* 75 Calif.L.Rev. 1279, 1297–1300 (1987); Herma Hill Kay, *Models of Equality,* 1985 U.Ill.L.Rev. 39; Herma Hill Kay, *Equality and Difference: The Case of Pregnancy,* 1 Berkeley Women's L.J. 1 (1985); Wendy W. Williams, *Equality's Riddle: Pregnancy and the Equal Treatment/Special Treatment Debate,* 13 N.Y.U. Rev. L. & Soc. Change 325, 351–80 (1984–85).

insofar as they are like men'"? Sylvia A. Law, *Rethinking Sex and the Constitution,* 132 U.Pa.L.Rev. 955, 1007 (1984).

SECTION 4. SPECIAL SCRUTINY FOR OTHER CLASSIFICATIONS

Are there are other classifications that should be subject to special scrutiny? If so, by what criteria should those classifications be identified?

I. ALIENAGE

Up to the late 1940s, the Supreme Court found a "special public interest"[a] in rejecting almost all challenges to state discriminations against aliens respecting such activities as land ownership, *Terrace v. Thompson,* 263 U.S. 197, 44 S.Ct. 15, 68 L.Ed. 255 (1923); killing wild game, *Patsone v. Pennsylvania,* 232 U.S. 138, 34 S.Ct. 281, 58 L.Ed. 539 (1914); operating poolhalls, *State of Ohio ex rel. Clarke v. Deckebach,* 274 U.S. 392, 47 S.Ct. 630, 71 L.Ed. 1115 (1927); and working on public construction projects, *Crane v. New York,* 239 U.S. 195, 36 S.Ct. 85, 60 L.Ed. 218 (1915).[b] But *Takahashi v. Fish & Game Com'n,* 334 U.S. 410, 68 S.Ct. 1138, 92 L.Ed. 1478 (1948), relying on both Congress' "broad constitutional powers in determining what aliens shall be admitted to the United States" and the fourteenth amendment's "general policy" of "equality," invalidated California's denial of licenses for commercial fishing in coastal waters to aliens lawfully residing in the state. *Graham v. Richardson,* 403 U.S. 365, 91 S.Ct. 1848, 29 L.Ed.2d 534 (1971), took a much further step. Reasoning that "aliens as a class are a prime example of a 'discrete and insular minority,'" the Court ruled in *Graham* that "classifications based on alienage [are] inherently suspect and subject to close judicial scrutiny" and held that state laws denying welfare benefits to aliens violate equal protection.

SUGARMAN v. DOUGALL, 413 U.S. 634, 93 S.Ct. 2842, 37 L.Ed.2d 853 (1973), applied the close scrutiny prescribed by *Graham* to Section 53 of New York's Civil Service Law, which required citizenship as a condition of public employment in positions subject to competitive examination. The Court, per BLACKMUN, J., held that section 53 unconstitutionally discriminated against aliens: "It is established, of course, that an alien is entitled to the shelter of the Equal Protection Clause[,] that aliens as a class 'are a prime example of a "discrete and insular" minority (see *United States v. Carolene Products Co.* [fn. 4, p. 17 supra]),' and that classifications based on alienage are 'subject to close judicial scrutiny.'

"[We] recognize a State's interest in establishing its own form of government, and in limiting participation in that government to those who are within 'the basic conception of a political community.' We recognize, too, the State's broad power to define its political community. But in seeking to achieve this substantial purpose, with discrimination against aliens, the means the State employs must be precisely drawn in light of the acknowledged purpose.

"Section 53 is neither narrowly confined nor precise in its application. Its imposed ineligibility may apply to the 'sanitation man, class B,' to the typist, and to the office worker, as well as to the person who directly participates in the formulation and execution of important state policy. The citizenship restriction

---

a. *Truax v. Raich,* 239 U.S. 33, 36 S.Ct. 7, 60 L.Ed. 131 (1915).

b. *Truax,* however, invalidated Arizona's forbidding employers of five or more persons from hiring over 20% aliens.

sweeps indiscriminately. [At the same time, other provisions] of the Civil Service Law, relating generally to persons holding elective and high appointive offices, contain no citizenship restrictions. Indeed, even § 53 permits an alien to hold a classified civil service position under certain circumstances. In view of the breadth and imprecision of § 53 in the context of the State's interest, we conclude that the statute does not withstand close judicial scrutiny. * * *

"While we rule that § 53 is unconstitutional, we do not hold that, on the basis of an individualized determination, an alien may not be refused, or discharged from, public employment, even on the basis of noncitizenship, if the refusal to hire, or the discharge, rests on legitimate state interests that relate to qualifications for a particular position or to the characteristics of the employee. [Neither] do we hold that a State may not, in an appropriately defined class of positions, require citizenship as a qualification for office. [Such] power inheres in the State by virtue of its obligation, already noted above, 'to preserve the basic conception of a political community.' [O]fficers who participate directly in the formulation, execution, or review of broad public policy perform functions that go to the heart of representative government."[a]

REHNQUIST, J., dissenting in *Sugarman* and *Griffiths*, stated: "The Court, by holding in these cases and in *Graham,* that a citizen-alien classification is 'suspect' in the eyes of our Constitution, fails to mention, let alone rationalize, the fact that the Constitution itself recognizes a basic difference between citizens and aliens. That distinction is constitutionally important in no less than 11 instances in a political document noted for its brevity. [Indeed,] the very Amendment which the Court reads to prohibit classifications based on citizenship establishes the very distinction which the Court now condemns as 'suspect.' [The] language of that Amendment carefully distinguishes between 'persons' who, whether by birth or naturalization, had achieved a certain status, and 'persons' in general. That a 'citizen' was considered by Congress to be a rationally distinct subclass of all 'persons' is obvious from the language of the Amendment. * * *

"The mere recitation of the words 'insular and discrete minority' is hardly a *constitutional* reason for prohibiting state legislative classifications such as are involved here. Our society, consisting of over 200 million individuals of multitudinous origins, customs, tongues, beliefs, and cultures is, to say the least, diverse. It would hardly take extraordinary ingenuity for a lawyer to find 'insular and discrete' minorities at every turn in the road. Yet, unless the Court can precisely define and constitutionally justify both the terms and analysis it uses, these decisions today stand for the proposition that the Court can choose a 'minority' it 'feels' deserves 'solicitude' and thereafter prohibit the States from classifying that 'minority' differently from the 'majority.' I cannot find, and the Court does not cite, any constitutional authority for such a 'ward of the Court' approach to equal protection."

AMBACH v. NORWICK

441 U.S. 68, 99 S.Ct. 1589, 60 L.Ed.2d 49 (1979).

JUSTICE POWELL delivered the opinion of the Court.

This case presents the question whether a State, consistently with the Equal Protection Clause, may refuse to employ as elementary and secondary school

---

a. The same day as *Sugarman, In re Griffiths*, 413 U.S. 717, 93 S.Ct. 2851, 37 L.Ed.2d 910 (1973), per Powell, J., invalidated Connecticut's attempt to totally exclude resident aliens from practicing law: "[T]he status of holding a license to practice law [does not] place one so close to the core of the political process as to make him a formulator of government policy." Burger, C.J., and Rehnquist, J., dissented in *Griffiths*.

teachers aliens who are eligible for United States citizenship but who refuse to seek naturalization. * * *

[*Graham* for] the first time treated classifications based on alienage as "inherently suspect and subject to close judicial scrutiny." Applying *Graham,* this Court has held invalid statutes that prevented aliens from entering a State's classified civil service, *Sugarman,* practicing law, *Griffiths,* working as an engineer, *Examining Bd. v. Flores de Otero,* 426 U.S. 572, 96 S.Ct. 2264, 49 L.Ed.2d 65 (1976), and receiving state educational benefits, *Nyquist v. Mauclet,* 432 U.S. 1, 97 S.Ct. 2120, 53 L.Ed.2d 63 (1977). * * *

In *Sugarman,* we recognized that a State could, "in an appropriately defined class of positions, require citizenship as a qualification for office." [*Sugarman* thus contemplated that the] exclusion of aliens from [influential] governmental positions would not invite as demanding scrutiny from this Court.

Applying the rational basis standard, we held last Term that New York could exclude aliens from the ranks of its police force. *Foley v. Connelie,* 435 U.S. 291, 98 S.Ct. 1067, 55 L.Ed.2d 287 (1978). Because the police function fulfilled "a most fundamental obligation of government to its constituency" and by necessity cloaked policemen with substantial discretionary powers, we viewed the police force as being one of those appropriately defined classes of positions for which a citizenship requirement could be imposed.[a] * * *

The rule for governmental functions, which is an exception to the general standard applicable to classifications based on alienage, rests on important principles inherent in the Constitution. The distinction between citizens and aliens, though ordinarily irrelevant to private activity, [denotes] an association with the polity which, in a democratic republic, exercises the powers of governance. The form of this association is important; an oath of allegiance or similar ceremony cannot substitute for the unequivocal legal bond citizenship represents. It is because of this special significance of citizenship that governmental entities, when exercising the functions of government, have wider latitude in limiting the participation of noncitizens.

In determining whether, for purposes of equal protection analysis, teaching in public schools constitutes a governmental function, we look to the role of public education and to the degree of responsibility and discretion teachers possess in fulfilling that role. Each of these considerations supports the conclusion that public school teachers may be regarded as performing a task "that go[es] to the heart of representative government."

Public education, like the police function, "fulfills a most fundamental obligation of government to its constituency." *Foley.* The importance of public schools in the preparation of individuals for participation as citizens, and in the preservation of the values on which our society rests, long has been recognized by our decisions [*Brown I*]. [In] shaping the students' experience to achieve educational goals, teachers by necessity have wide discretion over the way the course material is communicated to students. [Further], a teacher serves as a role model for his students, exerting a subtle but important influence over their perceptions and values. Thus, [a] teacher has an opportunity to influence the attitudes of students toward government, the political process, and a citizen's social responsi-

---

a. *Cabell v. Chavez–Salido,* 454 U.S. 432, 102 S.Ct. 735, 70 L.Ed.2d 677 (1982), extended *Folie* to probation officers. Marshall, J., joined by Brennan, Marshall, and Stevens, JJ., dis- sented in *Folie.* Blackmun, J., joined by Brennan, Marshall, and Stevens, JJ., dissented in *Cabell.*

bilities. This influence is crucial to the continued good health of a democracy. * * *

As the legitimacy of the State's interest in furthering the educational goals outlined above is undoubted, it remains only to consider whether [the statute] bears a rational relationship to this interest. The restriction is carefully framed to serve its purpose, as it bars from teaching only those aliens who have demonstrated their unwillingness to obtain United States citizenship. Appellees [in] effect have chosen to classify themselves. They prefer to retain citizenship in a foreign country with the obligations it entails of primary duty and loyalty.[14] [New York has] made a judgment that citizenship should be a qualification for teaching the young of the State in the public schools, and [the statute] furthers that judgment.

Reversed.

JUSTICE BLACKMUN, with whom JUSTICE BRENNAN, JUSTICE MARSHALL, and JUSTICE STEVENS, join, dissenting.

[T]he New York classification is irrational. Is it better to employ a poor citizen-teacher than an excellent resident alien teacher? Is it preferable to have a citizen who has never seen Spain or a Latin American country teach Spanish to eighth graders and to deny that opportunity to a resident alien who may have lived for 20 years in the culture of Spain or Latin America? The State will know how to select its teachers responsibly, wholly apart from citizenship, and can do so selectively and intelligently. * * *

[Further], it is logically impossible to differentiate between this case [and *Griffiths*]. One may speak proudly of the role model of the teacher, of his ability to mold young minds, of his inculcating force as to national ideals, and of his profound influence in the impartation of our society's values. Are the attributes of an attorney any the less? [The attorney] is an influence in legislation, in the community, and in the role model figure that the professional person enjoys. * * *

Notes and Questions

1. *Aliens as a suspect class.* How persuasive is the argument that discriminations against aliens should be subject to strict scrutiny?[a]

(a) Is it sufficient to justify strict scrutiny that aliens are a "discrete and insular" minority? Should it be relevant that the Constitution, as Rehnquist, J., pointed out in *Sugarman*, assumes the relevance of citizenship for at least some purposes—including the distribution of rights to vote and to hold some federal political offices? Compare T. Alexander Aleinikoff, *Citizens, Aliens, Membership and the Constitution*, 7 Const. Commentary 9, 21 (1990): "[T]he textual references to citizenship can be read two ways. Either the framers thought that their Constitution was really about citizens and therefore constantly reminded us of

---

14. As our cases have emphasized, resident aliens pay taxes, serve in the armed forces, and have made significant contributions to our country in private and public endeavors. No doubt [many] would make excellent public school teachers. But the legislature, having in mind the importance of education to state and local governments, may determine eligibility for the key position in discharging that function on the assumption that *generally* persons [who] have not declined the opportunity to

seek United States citizenship, are better qualified than are those who have elected to remain aliens. * * *

a. Would the rationale for strict scrutiny apply in a case involving discrimination against a foreign or alien corporation? See Hartwin Bungert, *Equal Protection for Foreign and Alien Corporations: Towards Intermediate Scrutiny for a Quasi–Suspect Classification*, 59 Mo.L.Rev. 569 (1994).

that; or they thought their document was primarily about persons, and therefore mentioned citizens in particular situations as a special case. [M]uch can be said for the latter [approach]."

Consider Laurence H. Tribe, *American Constitutional Law* 1545 (2d ed. 1988): "Because aliens are ordinarily eligible to become citizens, alienage [is] not an unalterable trait. That aliens do not vote might be seen as demonstrating their lack of political power; but, at least if it is alien disenfranchisement that is being challenged, it would seem oddly circular to rely on the very practice challenged to establish the propriety of so strictly scrutinizing it as to make very probable its invalidation."[b]

(b) Does the history of prejudice against aliens justify strict scrutiny?

(c) Does the relevance of alien status to some legitimate government purposes suggest that alienage-based classifications, like gender-based classifications, should be subject to a form of intermediate scrutiny? See *Developments in the Law—Immigration Policy and the Rights of Aliens*, 96 Harv.L.Rev. 1286, 1432–33 (1983).

2. *"Political function" exception.* (a) Is the Court's governing principle— that it is permissible for states to exclude aliens from functions related to "the process of self-government" but not to discriminate against aliens generally—a sound one? Consider Note, *A Dual Standard for State Discrimination Against Aliens*, 92 Harv.L.Rev. 1516, 1531–33 (1979): "Some dual standard [appears] fundamentally consistent with general equal protection doctrine interpreted in light of distinctions the Constitution makes on the basis of citizenship. [But despite *Foley's*] attempt to draw an analogy to exclusion of aliens from voting and holding high office, the existence of those exclusions only underscores the need for close review of other measures disadvantaging aliens. [Since] aliens are politically powerless because of their disenfranchisement and disqualification from high office, [the] political decision to bar aliens from the police should be stringently scrutinized."

(b) Are the Court's applications of the "political function exception" persuasively reasoned? With *Ambach* compare BERNAL v. FAINTER, 467 U.S. 216, 104 S.Ct. 2312, 81 L.Ed.2d 175 (1984), per MARSHALL, J., which held that Texas could not constitutionally preclude an alien from becoming a notary public: "We emphasize, as we have in the past, that the political-function exception must be narrowly construed; otherwise the exception will swallow the rule and depreciate the significance that should attach to the designation of the group as a 'discrete and insular' minority for whom heightened judicial solicitude is appropriate."[c] Was the political function exception narrowly construed in *Ambach*? *Foley*? *Cabell*?

3. *The role of the supremacy clause.* In addition to holding that classifications discriminating against aliens are constitutionally suspect, *Graham* found that "an additional reason why the state statutes [challenged in] these cases do not withstand constitutional scrutiny emerges from the area of federal-state

---

b. Compare Gerald M. Rosberg, *Aliens and Equal Protection: Why Not the Right to Vote?* 75 Mich.L.Rev. 1092, 1106 (1977): "[E]xcluding [aliens] from the political process clearly requires the strictest review of all, for it is the very fact of exclusion that made the classification suspect and necessitated strict scrutiny in the first place." But cf. Jamin B. Raskin, *Legal Aliens, Local Citizens: The Historical,*

Constitutional and Theoretical Meanings of Alien Suffrage, 141 U.Pa.L.Rev. 1391, 1395 (1993) (arguing that "state enfranchisement of noncitizens is neither forbidden by the Constitution, as is commonly assumed, nor compelled by it" and should be subject to local decision).

c. Rehnquist, J., dissented.

relations. [State] laws that restrict the eligibility of aliens for [welfare] conflict [with] overriding national policies in an area constitutionally entrusted to the Federal Government. [In] *Takahashi* it was said that the States 'can neither add to nor take from the conditions lawfully imposed by Congress upon admission, naturalization and residence of aliens in the United States or the several states.' "

TOLL v. MORENO, 458 U.S. 1, 102 S.Ct. 2977, 73 L.Ed.2d 563 (1982), per BRENNAN, J., held that a University of Maryland rule—flatly denying "in-state" tuition to nonimmigrant aliens with G–4 visas (issued to employees of certain international organizations and their immediate families)—violated the supremacy clause. The Court observed that "commentators have noted [that] many of the Court's decisions concerning alienage classifications, such as *Takahashi*, are better explained in preemption than equal protection terms. See, e.g., Michael J. Perry, *Modern Equal Protection; A Conceptualization and Appraisal*, 79 Colum.L.Rev. 1023, 1060–65 (1979). [Read] together, *Takahashi* and *Graham* stand for the broad principle that 'state regulation not congressionally sanctioned that discriminates against aliens lawfully admitted to the country is impermissible if it imposes additional burdens not contemplated by Congress.' To be sure, when Congress has done nothing more than permit a class of aliens to enter the country temporarily, the proper application of the principle is likely to be a matter of some dispute. But [in] light of Congress' explicit decision not to bar G–4 aliens from acquiring domicile, [the Maryland rule] surely amounts to an ancillary 'burden not contemplated by Congress.' [Further, as] a result of an array of treaties, international agreements, and federal statutes, G–4 visa holders employed by [various international organizations] are relieved of federal, and in many instances, state and local taxes, on the salaries paid by the organizations. [The Maryland rule] frustrates these federal policies."[d]

REHNQUIST, J., joined by Burger, C.J., dissented: "[T]hat a state statute can be said to discriminate against aliens does not, standing alone, demonstrate that the statute is preempted. [A] state law is invalid only if there is 'such actual conflict between the two schemes of regulation that both cannot stand in the same area,' or if Congress has in some other way unambiguously declared its intention to foreclose the state law in question. [The] Court offers no evidence that Congress' intent in permitting respondents to establish 'domicile in the United States' has any bearing at all on the tuition available to them at state universities." As for tax relief, "First, the Federal Government has not barred the States from collecting taxes from many, if not most, G–4 visa holders. Second, as to those G–4 nonimmigrants who *are* immune from state income taxes by treaty, Maryland's tuition policy cannot fairly be said to conflict with those treaties in a manner requiring its preemption."[e]

---

d. Blackmun, J., who joined the Court's opinion, concurred, vehemently denying the suggestion in Rehnquist, J.'s dissent that "decisions holding resident aliens to be a 'suspect class' no longer are good law."

e. O'Connor, J., concurred in part and dissented in part: "I conclude that the Supremacy Clause does not prohibit the University from charging out-of-state tuition to those G–4 aliens who are exempted by federal law from federal taxes only." See Jesse H. Choper, *Discrimination Against Aliens*, in Jesse H. Choper, Yale Kamisar & Laurence H. Tribe, 4 *The Supreme Court: Trends and Developments 1981–82* 5, 14–21 (1983) for the view that (1)

Toll's use of the supremacy clause was a "salutory development," but that (2) "the Court's major difficulty resulted from its going beyond its premise and getting into the gory details of whether the University of Maryland regulation actually came into some direct conflict with congressional policy"; "Justice Rehnquist's argument was fairly strong once you accept *his* premise" of what is required for preemption. For further discussions of the relation between federal immigration policy and state obligations to aliens, see Stephen H. Legomsky, *Immigration, Federalism, and the Welfare State*, 42 U.C.L.A.L.Rev. 1453 (1995); Evangeline A. Abriel, *Rethinking Preemption for Pur-*

4. *Discrimination against "illegal aliens."* PLYLER v. DOE, 457 U.S. 202, 102 S.Ct. 2382, 72 L.Ed.2d 786 (1982), p. 1310, infra, "reject[ed] the claim that 'illegal aliens' are a 'suspect class.' [U]ndocumented status is not irrelevant to any proper legislative goal. Nor is [it] an absolutely immutable characteristic since it is the product of conscious, indeed unlawful, action." But the Court, per BRENNAN, J., invalidated a Texas statute denying free public education to illegal alien *children,* stressing both the special status of the children—who can " 'affect neither their parents' conduct nor their own status' "—and "the importance of education," both to the children themselves and to the nation more generally, since so many undocumented residents were almost certain to remain in the United States.[f]

Under *Plyler,* may states permissibly deny welfare to illegal alien adults? To illegal alien adults with children?[g] May states permissibly refuse to furnish illegal aliens with emergency medical care? See Gerald L. Neuman, *Aliens as Outlaws: Government Services, Proposition 187, and the Structure of Equal Protection Doctrine,* 42 U.C.L.A.L.Rev. 1425 (1995) (arguing for "a limited extension of *Plyler* that forbids the states to exclude 'illegal' alien adults from a minimal level of government services"). Might the denial of some services to illegal aliens be impermissible under "rational basis" scrutiny?

5. *Federal discrimination.* (a) It has long been held that the national government has power "to exclude aliens altogether from the United States, or to prescribe the terms and conditions upon which they may come to this country." *Lem Moon Sing v. United States,* 158 U.S. 538, 15 S.Ct. 967, 39 L.Ed. 1082 (1895). Relying on this traditionally recognized authority, MATHEWS v. DIAZ, 426 U.S. 67, 96 S.Ct. 1883, 48 L.Ed.2d 478 (1976), per STEVENS, J., upheld a federal statute denying Medicare benefits to aliens unless they have (1) been admitted for permanent residence and (2) resided for at least five years in the United States. Although "aliens and citizens alike, are protected by the Due Process Clause, [i]n the exercise of its broad power over naturalization and immigration, Congress regularly makes rules that would be unacceptable if applied to citizens.

"[T]he responsibility for regulating the relationship between the United States and [aliens] has been committed to the political branches of the Federal Government. Since decisions in these matters may implicate our relations with foreign powers, and since a wide variety of classifications must be defined in the light of changing political and economic circumstances, such decisions are frequently of a character more appropriate to either the Legislature or the Executive than to the Judiciary. [The] reasons that preclude judicial review of political questions also dictate a narrow standard of review of decisions made by the Congress or the President in the area of immigration and naturalization.

"Since it is obvious that Congress has no constitutional duty to provide *all aliens* with the welfare benefits provided to citizens, the party challenging the constitutionality of the particular line Congress has drawn"[—allowing benefits to some aliens but not to others—]"has the burden of advancing principled reasoning that will at once invalidate that line and yet tolerate a different line separating some aliens from others. [Since neither of the two requirements] is wholly irrational, this case essentially involves nothing more than a claim that it would have been more reasonable for Congress to select somewhat different require-

---

poses of Aliens and Public Benefits, 42 U.C.L.A.L.Rev. 1597 (1995).

f. Burger, C.J., joined by White, Rehnquist, and O'Connor, JJ., dissented.

g. Compare *New Jersey Welfare Rights Org. v. Cahill,* p. 1215 infra.

ments of the same kind. [But] it remains true that some line is essential, that any line must produce some harsh and apparently arbitrary consequences, and, of greatest importance, that those who qualify under the test Congress has chosen may reasonably be presumed to have a greater affinity with the United States than those who do not."

Why do the arguments for treating aliens as a suspect class, if valid with respect to state legislation, not apply equally to the federal government and federal legislation? Does the disparity of standards for scrutinizing state and federal legislation survive *Adarand Constructors, Inc. v. Pena*, p. 1170 supra?

Congress' power to exclude aliens or impose conditions on their admission to the United States does not imply a power to deny them all constitutional rights while they are here. E.g., *Almeida-Sanchez v. United States*, 413 U.S. 266, 273, 93 S.Ct. 2535, 2539–2540, 37 L.Ed.2d 596, 602–603 (1973) (fourth amendment); *Wong Wing v. United States*, 163 U.S. 228, 237, 16 S.Ct. 977, 980–981, 41 L.Ed. 140, 143 (1896) (fifth and sixth amendments). Does the Constitution thus require that a line be drawn between Congress' relatively plenary power over immigration and its much more limited power to impose special disabilities on aliens once they are lawfully resident in the United States?[h] Consider the views that (i) "courts have wrongly assumed that every federal regulation based on *alienage* is necessarily sustainable as an exercise of the *immigration* power"[i] and (ii) the provision involved in *Mathews* "was not in any obvious way concerned with immigration."[j] Should a "substantive limit to the exercise of a federal power of national self-definition derive[ ] from the idea that alienage is a stage of transition from outsider to full member?"[k]

(b) HAMPTON v. MOW SUN WONG, 426 U.S. 88, 96 S.Ct. 1895, 48 L.Ed.2d 495 (1976), per STEVENS, J., held that a federal Civil Service Commission regulation, generally barring resident aliens from civil service employment, denied "liberty without due process of law": "[T]he federal power over aliens is [not] so plenary that any agent of the National Government may arbitrarily subject all resident aliens to different substantive rules than those applied to citizens. * * *

"When the Federal Government asserts an overriding national interest as justification for a discriminatory rule which would violate the Equal Protection Clause if adopted by a State, due process requires that there be a legitimate basis for presuming that the rule was actually intended to serve that interest. [We] may assume [that] if the Congress or the President had expressly imposed the citizenship requirement, it would be justified by the national interest in providing an incentive for aliens to become naturalized, or possibly even as providing the President with an expendable token for treaty negotiating purposes; but we are not willing to presume that the Chairman of [CSC] was deliberately fostering an interest so far removed from his normal responsibilities."

The Court reviewed the history of the regulation dating to 1884, concluding that it "cannot fairly be construed to evidence either congressional [or presidential] approval or disapproval of the [rule]. [Thus,] our inquiry is whether the national interests which the Government identifies as justifications for the Com-

h. See, e.g., Linda S. Bosniak, *Membership, Equality, and the Difference that Alienage Makes*, 69 N.Y.U.L.Rev. 1047 (1994).

i. T. Alexander Aleinikoff, *Federal Regulation of Aliens and the Constitution*, 83 Am. J.Int'l L. 862, 869 (1989).

j. Gerald M. Rosberg, *The Protection of Aliens From Discriminatory Treatment by the National Government*, 1977 Sup.Ct.Rev. 275, 334.

k. Hiroshi Motomura, *Immigration and Alienage, Federalism and Proposition 187*, 35 Va.J.Int'l L. 201 (1994).

mission rule are interests on which that agency may properly rely in making a decision implicating the constitutional and social values at stake in this litigation. * * *

"The only concern of [the] Commission is the promotion of an efficient federal service. In general it is fair to assume that its goal would be best served by removing unnecessary restrictions on the eligibility of qualified applicants for employment. With only one exception, the interests [put] forth as supporting the Commission regulation at issue in this case are not matters which are properly the business of the Commission. That one exception is the administrative desirability of having one simple rule excluding all noncitizens when it is manifest that citizenship is an appropriate and legitimate requirement for some important and sensitive positions. Arguably, therefore, administrative convenience may provide a rational basis for the general rule.

"[But there] is nothing [to] indicate that the Commission actually made any considered evaluation of the relative desirability of a simple exclusionary rule on the one hand, or the value to the service of enlarging the pool of eligible employees on the other. [Of] greater significance, however, is the quality of the interest at stake. Any fair balancing of the public interest in avoiding the wholesale deprivation of employment opportunities caused by the Commission's indiscriminate policy, as opposed to what may be nothing more than a hypothetical justification, requires rejection of the argument of administrative convenience in this case."[l]

REHNQUIST, J., joined by Burger, C.J., and White and Blackmun, JJ., dissented: "The Court's opinion enunciates a novel conception of the procedural due process guaranteed by the Fifth Amendment, and from this concept proceeds to evolve a doctrine of delegation of legislative authority which seems to me to be quite contrary to the doctrine established by a long [line of] decisions. * * *

"[Once] it is determined that [CSC] was properly delegated the power by Congress to make decisions regarding citizenship of prospective civil servants, then the reasons for which that power was exercised are as foreclosed from judicial scrutiny as if Congress had made the decision itself. The fact that Congress has delegated a power does not provide a back door through which to attack a policy which would otherwise have been immune from attack."

Did *Hampton* express a constitutional conclusion about powers that Congress may not permissibly delegate to the Civil Service Commission? A statutory conclusion about the powers that Congress actually had delegated? A judgment that the federal rule discriminating against aliens could be justified only by the considerations that actually motivated the decisionmaker?

(c) Could Congress, exercising its plenary power over immigration, require the states to engage in discrimination against aliens that would otherwise be barred by the equal protection clause? Can Congress authorize (without requiring) otherwise forbidden state discrimination?[m]

---

l. Brennan, J., joined by Marshall, J., joined the Court's opinion "understanding that there are reserved the equal protection questions that would be raised by congressional or Presidential enactment of a bar on employment of aliens by the Federal Government."

President Ford subsequently issued such an executive order. Valid? See *Vergara v. Hampton,* 581 F.2d 1281 (7th Cir.1978), cert. denied, 441 U.S. 905, 99 S.Ct. 1993, 60 L.Ed.2d 373 (1979); *Jalil v. Campbell,* 590 F.2d 1120 (D.C.Cir.1978).

m. For negative answers, see *Graham v. Richardson,* supra; Gilbert Paul Carrasco, *Congressional Arrogation of Power: Alien Constellation in the Galaxy of Equally Protection,* 74 B.U.L.Rev. 591 (1994).

II. ILLEGITIMACY AND RELATED CLASSIFICATIONS

NEW JERSEY WELFARE RIGHTS ORG. v. CAHILL

411 U.S. 619, 93 S.Ct. 1700, 36 L.Ed.2d 543 (1973).

PER CURIAM.

This case presents the question of the constitutionality under the Equal Protection Clause of the Fourteenth Amendment of the New Jersey "Assistance to Families of the Working Poor" program that allegedly discriminates against illegitimate children in the provision of financial assistance and other services. Specifically, appellants challenge that aspect of the program that limits benefits to only those otherwise qualified families "which consist of a household composed of two adults of the opposite sex ceremonially married to each other who have at least one minor child [of] both, the natural child of one and adopted by the other, or a child adopted by [both]." N.J.Stat.Ann. § 44:13–3(a). Appellants do not challenge the statute's "household" requirement. Rather, they argue that although the challenged classification turns upon the marital status of the parents as well as upon the parent-child relationship, in practical effect it operates almost invariably to deny benefits to illegitimate children while granting benefits to those children who are legitimate. Although apparently conceding the correctness of this position, the [lower court] upheld the statutory scheme on the ground that it was designed "to preserve and strengthen family life."[a]

Confronted with similar arguments in the past, we have specifically declared that: "The status of illegitimacy has expressed through the ages society's condemnation of irresponsible liaisons beyond the bonds of marriage. But visiting this condemnation on the head of an infant is illogical and unjust. Moreover, imposing disabilities on the illegitimate child is contrary to the basic concept of our system that legal burdens should bear some relationship to individual responsibility or wrongdoing. Obviously, no child is responsible for his birth and penalizing the illegitimate child is an ineffectual—as well as an unjust—way of deterring the parent." *Weber v. Aetna Casualty & Surety Co.*, 406 U.S. 164, 92 S.Ct. 1400, 31 L.Ed.2d 768 (1972). Thus, in *Weber* we held that under the Equal Protection Clause a State may not exclude illegitimate children from sharing equally with other children in the recovery of workmen's compensation benefits for the death of their parent. Similarly, in *Levy v. Louisiana*, 391 U.S. 68, 88 S.Ct. 1509, 20 L.Ed.2d 436 (1968), we held that a State may not create a right of action in favor of children for the wrongful death of a parent and exclude illegitimate children from the benefit of such a right. And only this Term, in *Gomez v. Perez*, 409 U.S. 535, 93 S.Ct. 872, 35 L.Ed.2d 56 (1973), we held that once a State posits a judicially enforceable right on behalf of children to needed support from their natural father, there is no constitutionally sufficient justification for denying such an essential right to illegitimate children.[b]

a. The lower court argued that it was appropriate for the state to limit its subsidy to "legitimate families, ones where the likelihood is greater for the instillment of social norms. It is certainly a proper and a compelling state interest to refuse to subsidize a living unit which may lead to the state of anomie and which violates its laws against fornication and adultery."

b. *Clark v. Jeter,* further discussed infra, invalidated a six year statute of limitations as applied to paternity actions required as a prerequisite for support actions. The Court pointed to "increasingly sophisticated tests for genetic markers [that] permit the exclusion of over 99% of those who might be accused of paternity."

Those decisions compel the conclusion that appellants' claim of the denial of equal protection must be sustained, for there can be no doubt that the benefits extended under the challenged program are as indispensable to the health and well-being of illegitimate children as to those who are legitimate. * * *

THE CHIEF JUSTICE concurs in the result.

JUSTICE REHNQUIST, dissenting. * * *

The Court relies on *Weber,* where a Louisiana statute that denied workmen's compensation benefits to an illegitimate child was invalidated. But the very language that the Court quotes from *Weber* shows how different this case is from that. There a disability was visited solely on an illegitimate child. Here the statute distinguishes among types of families. While the classification adopted by the New Jersey Legislature undoubtedly results in denying benefits to "families" consisting of a mother and father not ceremonially married who are living with natural children, whatever denial of benefits the classification makes is imposed equally on the parents as well as the children.

Here the New Jersey Legislature has determined that special financial assistance should be given to family units that meet the statutory definition of "working poor." It does not seem to me irrational in establishing such a special program to condition the receipt of such grants on the sort of ceremonial marriage that could quite reasonably be found to be an essential ingredient of the family unit that the New Jersey Legislature is trying to protect from dissolution due to the economic vicissitudes of modern life. The Constitution does not require that special financial assistance designed by the legislature to help poor families be extended to "communes" as well. [Here] the classification is based on a particular type of family unit, one of, if not the, core units of our social system. * * *

Notes and Questions

1. *Origins of discrimination.* Consider Harry D. Krause, *Equal Protection for the Illegitimate,* 65 Mich.L.Rev. 477, 498–99 (1967): "There has been a long history of discrimination against the illegitimate. The medieval church, in both its concern for the family and its aversion to illicit sex, reinforced the basic self-interest of the father, which self-interest may ultimately have been most directly responsible for the situation of the illegitimate. It was natural that men, as legislators, would have limited their accidental offsprings' claims against them, both economically and in terms of a family relationship, especially since the social status of the illegitimate mother often did not equal their own. Moreover, their legitimate wives had an interest in denying the illegitimate's claim on their husbands, since any such claim could be allowed only at the expense of the legitimate family. Against these forces have stood only the illegitimate mother and the helpless child, and thus it is not surprising that our laws are inconsiderate of the child's interests."

2. *The level of scrutiny.* Although the Court's decisions reveal somewhat less than perfect consistency in stating the equal protection standard applicable to illegitimacy cases, *Clark v. Jeter,* 486 U.S. 456, 108 S.Ct. 1910, 100 L.Ed.2d 465 (1988), unanimously concluded that between the "extremes of rational basis review and strict scrutiny lies a level of intermediate scrutiny, which generally has been applied to discriminatory classifications based on sex or illegitimacy. To withstand intermediate scrutiny, a statutory classification must be substantially related to an important governmental objective."

Should the standard be stricter? According to one expert, the Court's roughly thirty cases involving illegitimacy "and uncounted state court decisions establish the principle that the nonmarital child is entitled to all but complete legal equality with the legitimate child in *most* substantive areas of the law."[a]

3. *Administrative convenience.* (a) A recurrent issue in illegitimacy cases—which affords a partial exception to the suggestion that classifications based on illegitimacy have generally been invalidated—has involved the weight of the state's interest in avoiding the cost and uncertainty surrounding efforts to prove paternity, especially after the purported father is dead. Compare *Lalli v. Lalli*, 439 U.S. 259, 99 S.Ct. 518, 58 L.Ed.2d 503 (1978) (upholding bars to intestate inheritance by children born out of wedlock)[b] with *Trimble v. Gordon*, 430 U.S. 762, 97 S.Ct. 1459, 52 L.Ed.2d 31 (1977) (invalidating an Illinois law that permitted marital children to recover from either intestate parent, but permitted nonmarital children to inherit only from intestate mothers, not from intestate fathers). Although there are factual distinctions, the cases seem hard to reconcile in principle. See Laurence H. Tribe, *American Constitutional Law* 1554–57 (2d ed. 1988).

(b) MATHEWS v. LUCAS, 427 U.S. 495, 96 S.Ct. 2755, 49 L.Ed.2d 651 (1976), per BLACKMUN, J., upheld a provision of the Social Security Act that disadvantaged illegitimate children by conditioning their collection of survivors benefits "upon a showing that the deceased wage earner was the claimant child's parent and, at the time of his death, was living with the child or contributing to his support." STEVENS, J., joined by Brennan and Marshall, JJ., dissented: "[I]n the name of 'administrative convenience' the Court allows these survivors' benefits to be allocated on grounds which have only the most tenuous connection to the supposedly controlling factor—the child's dependency on his father. [T]he classification [is] more probably the product of a tradition of thinking of illegitimates as less deserving persons than legitimates."

(c) Compare MILLS v. HABLUETZEL, 456 U.S. 91, 102 S.Ct. 1549, 71 L.Ed.2d 770 (1982), per REHNQUIST, J., holding that a Texas statute—which then provided that, in order to obtain support, a paternity suit must be brought before the child is one year old—violated equal protection: "[I]n support suits by illegitimate children, more than in support suits by legitimate children, the State has an interest in preventing the prosecution of stale or fraudulent claims, and may impose greater restrictions on the former than it imposes on the latter. Such restrictions will survive equal protection scrutiny to the extent they are substantially related to a legitimate state interest. [But, first], the period for obtaining support granted by Texas to illegitimate children must be sufficiently long in duration to present a reasonable opportunity for those with an interest in such children to assert claims on their behalf. Second, any time limitation placed on that opportunity must be substantially related to the State's interest in avoiding the litigation of stale or fraudulent claims."[c]

A unanimous Court reached the same result for Tennessee's two-year statute of limitations. *Pickett v. Brown*, 462 U.S. 1, 103 S.Ct. 2199, 76 L.Ed.2d 372 (1983).

---

a. Harry D. Krause, *Family Law* 154–55 (2d ed. 1986) (emphasis added).

b. See also *Labine v. Vincent*, 401 U.S. 532, 91 S.Ct. 1017, 28 L.Ed.2d 288 (1971) (upholding a bar to intestate inheritance by unlegitimated children born out of wedlock and, inter alia, speculating that the state may view this rule as reflective of the wishes of most persons dying without a will).

c. O'Connor, J., joined by Burger, C.J., and Brennan and Blackmun, JJ.,—and by Powell, J., in his own brief opinion—wrote "separately because I fear that the [Court's] opinion may be misinterpreted as approving the four-year statute of limitations now used in Texas."

4. *Discrimination against families with illegitimate children.* Does the Court in *Cahill* have any adequate response to Rehnquist, J.'s argument that the challenged statute "distinguishes among types of families," not between legitimate and illegitimate children? Is *Cahill*'s treatment of the challenged statute as involving a discrimination against illegitimate children consistent with the holding of *Washington v. Davis*, p. 1093 supra?

Cf. CALIFANO v. BOLES, 443 U.S. 282, 99 S.Ct. 2767, 61 L.Ed.2d 541 (1979), per REHNQUIST, J., upholding a provision of the Social Security Act granting "mother's benefits" to a deceased's widow or divorced wife but not to the mother of his illegitimate child. The Court, noting that the illegitimate child received child's benefits, reasoned that the "mother's benefits" program "was not designed [for] child-care subsidies. Instead Congress sought to limit the category of beneficiaries to those who actually suffer economic dislocation upon the death of a wage earner and are likely to be confronted at that juncture with the choice between employment or the assumption of full-time child-care responsibilities. In this [light,] Congress could reasonably conclude that a woman who has never been married to the wage earner is far less likely to be dependent upon the wage earner at the time of his death."

MARSHALL, J., joined by Brennan, White, and Blackmun, JJ., dissented, finding that the program, "both in purpose and effect, is a form of assistance to children," and that its discrimination against illegitimates violates equal protection.

5. *Discrimination against unmarried mothers.* GLONA v. AMERICAN GUAR. & LIAB. INS. CO., 391 U.S. 73, 88 S.Ct. 1515, 20 L.Ed.2d 441 (1968), invalidated a Louisiana statutory provision barring a mother's suit to recover for the alleged wrongful death of her illegitimate child. Although acknowledging the state's legitimate interest in "dealing with 'sin,'" the Court, per DOUGLAS, J., held that there was no "rational basis for assuming that if [a] mother is allowed recovery [in a wrongful death case that] the cause of illegitimacy will be served." It was "farfetched to assume that women have illegitimate children so they can be compensated in damages for their death."

Do the interests underlying heightened scrutiny for statutes that discriminate against illegitimate children support similarly elevated scrutiny for statutes that discriminate against the *mothers* of illegitimate children?[d]

For discussion of cases involving discrimination against unwed fathers but not unwed mothers, see p. 1195 supra.

III. MENTAL RETARDATION

CLEBURNE v. CLEBURNE LIVING CENTER, INC.

473 U.S. 432, 105 S.Ct. 3249, 87 L.Ed.2d 313 (1985).

JUSTICE WHITE delivered the opinion of the Court.

A Texas city denied a special permit for the operation of a group home for the mentally retarded. [Permits under the zoning ordinance must be renewed annually and applicants must "obtain the signatures of the property owners within 200 feet of the property to be used."] It was anticipated that the [Featherston] home would house 13 retarded men and women, who would be under the constant supervision of CLC staff members. * * *

---

d. See Note, *Equal Protection for Unmarried Parents*, 65 Ia.L.Rev. 679 (1980).

[The] general rule [under the Equal Protection Clause] is that legislation is presumed to be valid and will be sustained if the classification drawn by the statute is rationally related to a legitimate state interest. *Schweiker v. Wilson; United States R.R. Retirement Bd. v. Fritz; Vance v. Bradley,* [Sec. 1 supra]. [White, J., then surveyed recognized exceptions to the general rule, involving discriminations based on race, alienage, national origin, gender, and illegitimacy.]

We have declined, however, to extend heightened review to differential treatment based on [age]. The lesson of *Murgia,* [p. 1226 infra], is that where individuals in the group affected by a law have distinguishing characteristics relevant to interests the state has the authority to implement, the courts have been very reluctant, as they should be in our federal system and with our respect for the separation of powers, to closely scrutinize legislative choices as to whether, how and to what extent those interests should be pursued. In such cases, the Equal Protection Clause requires only a rational means to serve a legitimate end.

Against this background, we conclude [that] the Court of Appeals erred in holding mental retardation a quasi-suspect classification. [First, those] who are mentally retarded have a reduced ability to cope with and function in the everyday world. [T]hey range from those whose disability is not immediately evident to those who must be constantly cared for. They are thus different, immutably so, in relevant respects, and the states' interest in dealing with and providing for them is plainly a legitimate one. How this large and diversified group is to be treated under the law is a difficult and often a technical matter, very much a task for legislators guided by qualified professionals and not by the perhaps ill-informed opinions of the judiciary. Heightened scrutiny inevitably involves substantive judgments about legislative decisions, and we doubt that the predicate for such judicial oversight is present where the classification deals with mental retardation.

Second, [both national and state] lawmakers have been addressing the[] difficulties [of the retarded] in a manner that belies a continuing antipathy or prejudice and a corresponding need for more intrusive oversight by the judiciary. Thus, the federal government has not only outlawed discrimination against the mentally retarded in federally funded programs, but it has also provided the retarded with the right to receive "appropriate treatment, services, and habilita-tion" in a setting that is "least restrictive of [their] personal liberty." * * * Texas has similarly enacted legislation that acknowledges the special status of the mentally retarded by conferring certain rights upon them, such as "the right to live in the least restrictive setting appropriate to [their] individual needs and abilities" * * *. [It] may be, as CLC contends, that legislation designed to benefit, rather than disadvantage, the retarded would generally withstand exami-nation under a test of heightened scrutiny. The relevant inquiry, however, is whether heightened scrutiny is constitutionally mandated in the first instance. Even assuming that many of these laws could be shown to be substantially related to an important governmental purpose, merely requiring the legislature to justify its efforts in these terms may lead it to refrain from acting at all. Much recent legislation intended to benefit the retarded also assumes the need for measures that might be perceived to disadvantage them. The Education of the Handi-capped Act, for example, requires an "appropriate" education, not one that is equal in all respects to the education of non-retarded children; clearly, admission to a class that exceeded the abilities of a retarded child would not be appropriate. * * *

Third, the legislative response, which could hardly have occurred and survived without public support, negates any claim that the mentally retarded are politically powerless in the sense that they have no ability to attract the attention of the lawmakers. * * *

Fourth, if the large and amorphous class of the mentally retarded were deemed quasi-suspect, [it] would be difficult to find a principled way to distinguish a variety of other groups who have perhaps immutable disabilities setting them off from others, who cannot themselves mandate the desired legislative responses, and who can claim some degree of prejudice from at least part of the public at large. One need mention in this respect only the aging, the disabled, the mentally ill, and the infirm. We are reluctant to set out on that course, and we decline to do so.

Doubtless, there have been and there will continue to be instances of discrimination against the retarded that are in fact invidious, and that are properly subject to judicial correction under constitutional norms. But the appropriate method of reaching such instances is [to] look to the likelihood that governmental action premised on a particular classification is valid as a general matter, not merely to the specifics of the case before us. Because mental retardation is a characteristic that the government may legitimately take into account in a wide range of decisions, and because both state and federal governments have recently committed themselves to assisting the retarded, we will not presume that any given legislative action, even one that disadvantages retarded individuals, is rooted in considerations that the Constitution will not tolerate.

Our refusal to recognize the retarded as a quasi-suspect class does not leave them entirely unprotected from invidious discrimination. To withstand equal protection review, legislation that distinguishes between the mentally retarded and others must be rationally related to a legitimate governmental purpose. This standard, we believe, affords government the latitude necessary both to pursue policies designed to assist the retarded in realizing their full potential, and to freely and efficiently engage in activities that burden the retarded in what is essentially an incidental manner. The State may not rely on a classification whose relationship to an asserted goal is so attenuated as to render the distinction arbitrary or irrational. See *Zobel v. Williams,* [Sec. 1285 infra]; *U.S. Dep't of Agriculture v. Moreno,* [p. 1065]. Furthermore, some objectives—such as "a bare * * * desire to harm a politically unpopular group," *Moreno*—are not legitimate state interests. * * *

The constitutional issue is clearly posed. The City does not require a special use permit in an R–3 zone for apartment houses, multiple dwellings, boarding and lodging houses, fraternity or sorority houses, dormitories, apartment hotels, hospitals, sanitariums, nursing homes for convalescents or the aged (other than for the insane or feeble-minded or alcoholics or drug addicts), private clubs or fraternal orders, and other specified uses. [I]n our view the record does not reveal any rational basis for believing that the Featherston home would pose any special threat to the city's legitimate interests * * *.

The District Court found that the City Council's insistence on the permit rested on several factors. First, the Council was concerned with the negative attitude of the majority of property owners located within 200 feet of the Featherston facility, as well as with the fears of elderly residents of the neighborhood. But mere negative attitudes, or fear, unsubstantiated by factors which are properly cognizable in a zoning proceeding, are not permissible bases for treating a home for the mentally retarded differently from apartment houses, multiple dwellings, and the like.   * * *

Second, the Council [was] concerned that the facility was across the street from a junior high school, and it feared that the students might harass the occupants of the Featherston home. But the school itself is attended by about 30 mentally retarded students, and denying a permit based on such vague, undifferentiated fears is again permitting some portion of the community to validate what would otherwise be an equal protection violation. The other objection to the home's location was that it was located on "a five hundred year flood plain." This concern with the possibility of a flood, however, can hardly be based on a distinction between the Featherston home and, for example, nursing homes, homes for convalescents or the aged, or sanitariums or hospitals, any of which could be located on the Featherston site without obtaining a special use permit. The same may be said of another concern of the Council—doubts about the legal responsibility for actions which the mentally retarded might take. If there is no concern about legal responsibility with respect to other uses that would be permitted in the area, such as boarding and fraternity houses, it is difficult to believe that the groups of mildly or moderately mentally retarded individuals who would live at 201 Featherston would present any different or special hazard.

Fourth, the Council was concerned with the size of the home and the number of people that would occupy it. [But] there would be no restrictions on the number of people who could occupy this home as a boarding house, nursing home, family dwelling, fraternity house, or dormitory. [At] least this record does not clarify how, in this connection, the characteristics of the intended occupants of the Featherston home rationally justify denying to those occupants what would be permitted to groups occupying the same site for different purposes.   * * *

The short of it is that requiring the permit in this case appears to us to rest on an irrational prejudice against the mentally retarded. [Thus, the] judgment of the Court of Appeals is affirmed insofar as it invalidates the zoning ordinance as applied to the Featherston home.   * * *

Justice Stevens, with whom The Chief Justice joins, concurring.

[O]ur cases reflect a continuum of judgmental responses to differing classifications which have been explained in opinions by terms ranging from "strict scrutiny" at one extreme to "rational basis" at the other. I have never been persuaded that these so called "standards" adequately explain the decisional process. Cases involving classifications based on alienage, illegal residency, illegitimacy, gender, age, or—as in this case—mental retardation, do not fit well into sharply defined classifications.

[I] have always asked myself whether I could find a "rational basis" for the classification at issue. The term "rational," of course, includes a requirement that an impartial lawmaker could logically believe that the classification would serve a legitimate public purpose that transcends the harm to the members of the disadvantaged class. Thus, the word "rational" * * * includes elements of legitimacy and neutrality that must always characterize the performance of the sovereign's duty to govern impartially. The rational basis test, properly understood, adequately explains why a law that deprives a person of the right to vote because his skin has a different pigmentation than that of other voters violates [equal protection]. We do not need to apply a special standard, or to apply "strict scrutiny," or even "heightened scrutiny," to decide such cases.

In every equal protection case, we have to ask certain basic questions. What class is harmed by the legislation, and has it been subjected to a "tradition of disfavor" by our laws? What is the public purpose that is being served by the law? What is the characteristic of the disadvantaged class that justifies the disparate treatment? In most cases the answer to these questions will tell us whether the statute has a "rational basis." The answers will result in the virtually automatic invalidation of racial classifications and in the validation of most economic classifications, but they will provide differing results in cases involving classifications based on alienage, gender, or illegitimacy. But that is not because we apply an "intermediate standard of review" in these cases; rather it is because the characteristics of these groups are sometimes relevant and sometimes irrelevant to a valid public purpose, or, more specifically, to the purpose that the challenged laws purportedly intended to serve.

Every law that places the mentally retarded in a special class is not presumptively irrational. The differences between mentally retarded persons and those with greater mental capacity are obviously relevant to certain legislative decisions. * * *

[The record in this case] convinces me that this permit was required because of the irrational fears of neighboring property owners, rather than for the protection of the mentally retarded persons who would reside in respondent's home. * * * I cannot believe that a rational member of this disadvantaged class could ever approve of the discriminatory application of the city's ordinance in this case. * * *

JUSTICE MARSHALL, with whom JUSTICE BRENNAN and JUSTICE BLACKMUN join, concurring in the judgment in part and dissenting in part.

The Court holds [the] ordinance invalid on rational basis grounds and disclaims that anything special, in the form of heightened scrutiny, is taking place. Yet Cleburne's ordinance surely would be valid under the traditional rational basis test applicable to economic and commercial regulation. [The] Court, for example, concludes that legitimate concerns for fire hazards or the serenity of the neighborhood do not justify singling out respondents to bear the burdens of these concerns, for analogous permitted uses appear to pose similar threats. Yet under the traditional and most minimal version of the rational basis test, "reform may take one step at a time, addressing itself to the phase of the problem which seems most acute to the legislative mind." * * *

The refusal to acknowledge that something more than minimum rationality review is at work here is, in my view, unfortunate in at least two respects.[4] The suggestion that the traditional rational basis test allows this sort of searching inquiry creates precedent for this Court and lower courts to subject economic and commercial classifications to similar and searching "ordinary" rational basis review—a small and regrettable step back toward the days of *Lochner v. New York*. Moreover, by failing to articulate the factors that justify today's "second order" rational basis review, the Court provides no principled foundation for determining when more searching inquiry is to be invoked. Lower courts are thus left in the dark on this important question, and this Court remains unac-

---

4. The two cases the Court cites in its rational basis discussion, *Zobel* and *Moreno*, expose the special nature of the rational basis test employed today. As two of only a handful of modern equal protection cases striking down legislation under what purports to be a rational basis standard, these cases must be and generally have been viewed as intermediate review decisions masquerading in rational basis language. See, e.g., Laurence H. Tribe, *American Constitutional Law* 1090, n. 10 (1978) (discussing *Moreno*); see also *Moreno* (Douglas, J., concurring); *Zobel* (Brennan, J., concurring).

countable for its decisions employing, or refusing to employ, particularly searching scrutiny. * * *

I have long believed the level of scrutiny employed in an equal protection case should vary with "the constitutional and societal importance of the interest adversely affected and the recognized invidiousness of the basis upon which the particular classification is drawn." *San Antonio Ind. Sch. Dist. v. Rodriguez* [p. 1296 infra] (Marshall, J., dissenting). See also *Dandridge v. Williams* [p. 1287 infra] (Marshall, J., dissenting). When a zoning ordinance works to exclude the retarded from all residential districts in a community, these two considerations require that the ordinance be convincingly justified as substantially furthering legitimate and important purposes.

First, the interest [in] establishing group homes is substantial, [for] as deinstitutionalization has progressed, group homes have become the primary means by which retarded adults can enter life in the community. * * *

Second, the mentally retarded have been subject to a "lengthy and tragic history" of segregation and discrimination that can only be called grotesque. [E]ven when judicial action *has* catalyzed legislative change, that change certainly does not eviscerate the underlying constitutional principle. The Court, for example, has never suggested that race-based classifications became any less suspect once extensive legislation had been enacted on the subject.

For the retarded, just as for Negroes and women, much has changed in recent years, but much remains the same; outdated statutes are still on the books, and irrational fears or ignorance, traceable to the prolonged social and cultural isolation of the retarded, continue to stymie recognition of the dignity and individuality of retarded people. * * *

The Court's [assumption] that the standard of review must be fixed with reference to the number of classifications to which a characteristic would validly be relevant [is] flawed. [Our] heightened scrutiny precedents belie the claim that a characteristic must virtually always be irrelevant to warrant heightened scrutiny. * * * Heightened but not strict scrutiny is considered appropriate in areas such as gender, illegitimacy, or alienage because the Court views the trait as relevant under some circumstances but not others. [An] inquiry into constitutional principle, not mathematics, determines whether heightened scrutiny is appropriate. Whenever evolving principles of equality, rooted in the Equal Protection Clause, require that certain classifications be viewed as *potentially* discriminatory, and when history reveals systemic unequal treatment, more searching judicial inquiry than minimum rationality becomes relevant. * * *[24]

---

24. No single talisman can define those groups likely to be the target of classifications offensive to the Fourteenth Amendment and therefore warranting heightened or strict scrutiny; experience, not abstract logic, must be the primary guide. The "political powerlessness" of a group may be relevant, but that factor is neither necessary, as the gender cases demonstrate, nor sufficient, as the example of minors illustrates. [W]e see few statutes reflecting prejudice or indifference to minors, and I am not aware of any suggestion that legislation affecting them be viewed with the suspicion of heightened scrutiny. Similarly, immutability of the trait at issue may be relevant, but many immutable characteristics, such as height or blindness, are valid bases of

governmental action and classifications under a variety of circumstances.

The political powerlessness of a group and the immutability of its defining trait are relevant insofar as they point to a social and cultural isolation that gives the majority little reason to respect or be concerned with that group's interests and needs. Statutes discriminating against the young have not been common nor need be feared because those who do vote and legislate were once themselves young, typically have children of their own, and certainly interact regularly with minors. Their social integration means that minors, unlike discrete and insular minorities, tend to be treated in legislative arenas with full concern

In light of the scrutiny that should be applied here, Cleburne's ordinance sweeps too broadly to dispel the suspicion that it rests on a bare desire to treat the retarded as outsiders, pariahs who do not belong in the community. The Court, while disclaiming that special scrutiny is necessary or warranted, reaches the same conclusion. Rather than striking the ordinance down, however, the Court invalidates it merely as applied to respondents. I must dissent from the novel proposition that "the preferred course of adjudication" is to leave standing a legislative act resting on "irrational prejudice," thereby forcing individuals in the group discriminated against to continue to run the act's gauntlet. * * *

Notes and Questions

1. *Tiers of scrutiny.* Are the Court's justifications for refusing to apply heightened scrutiny persuasive?[a] Is the dissent persuasive that the Court *in fact* applies heightened scrutiny? That equal protection analysis both is and should be too complex to be captured in a short list of tiers or standards of review?

2. *"Rationality" and morality.* Do you agree with Stevens, J., that inquiry into the "rationality" of a law "includes elements of legitimacy and neutrality" and assessment of whether the sovereign has acted "impartially"? Is this approach consistent with the *Carolene Products* footnote, p. 17 supra, and the limitation of the judicial role in equal protection cases to the protection of discrete and insular minorities? Consider the suggestion of Bruce A. Ackerman, *Beyond Carolene Products*, 98 Harv.L.Rev. 713, 737, 741 (1985), that *"Carolene's* emphasis on 'prejudice' "* as a factor triggering heightened judicial scrutiny suggests that "there are certain substantive principles" that courts, in implementing the equal protection clause, must identify and enforce—for "[o]ne person's 'prejudice' is, notoriously, another's 'principle.' " According to Professor Ackerman, this responsibility for substantive oversight cannot be limited to cases involving discrete and insular minorities. Women are not a minority at all, and illegitimates, in Ackerman's terms, are neither discrete (readily identifiable) nor insular (geographically clustered).

Do you agree with Marshall, J., that equal protection analysis should depend on both the classification used by government and the nature of the burden or benefit being distributed?

3. *Retreat from Cleburne?* The Court appears to have applied a much less stringent form of "rational basis" review in its one post-*Cleburne* case involving the equal protection rights of the mentally retarded. HELLER v. DOE, 509 U.S. 312, 113 S.Ct. 2637, 125 L.Ed.2d 257 (1993), per KENNEDY, J., upheld a Kentucky

---

and respect, despite their formal and complete exclusion from the electoral process.

The discreteness and insularity warranting a "more searching judicial inquiry" must therefore be viewed from a social and cultural perspective as well as a political one. To this task judges are well suited, for the lessons of history and experience are surely the best guide as to when, and with respect to what interests, society is likely to stigmatize individuals as members of an inferior caste or view them as not belonging to the community. Because prejudice spawns prejudice, and stereotypes produce limitations that confirm the stereotype on which they are based, a history of unequal treatment requires sensitivity to the prospect that its vestiges endure. In separating those

groups that are discrete and insular from those that are not, as in many important legal distinctions, "a page of history is worth a volume of logic."

a. In the Americans with Disabilities Act, Congress, invoking its "power to enforce the fourteenth amendment," purports to "find[ ]" that "individuals with disabilities"—including the mentally retarded—"are a discrete and insular minority." 42 U.S.C. § 12101(a)(7) & (b)(4). Should this "finding" affect the determination whether "strict scrutiny" applies? See Note, *Normalization as a Goal: The Americans with Disabilities Act and Individuals with Mental Retardation*, 73 Tex.L.Rev. 409, 423–30 (1994).

scheme that allows the involuntary commitment of the mentally retarded under less stringent standards than those employed for the involuntary commitment of the mentally ill. Because of the case's procedural posture, the Court did not revisit the issue of whether standards disadvantaging the retarded should receive heightened scrutiny; the only question was whether differences in the standard of proof (clear and convincing evidence in cases involving the retarded, compared with proof beyond a reasonable doubt in mental illness cases) and concerning intervention rights (family members could intervene as parties in retardation, but not mental illness, cases) satisfied rational basis review.[b]

Treating as canonical the formulation that "a classification 'must be upheld against equal protection challenge if there is any reasonably conceivable state of facts that could provide a rational basis for the classification,'" the Court concluded that the lesser standard of proof was justified because it was "reasonably conceivable" that violent behavior by the mentally retarded was easier to predict than such behavior by the mentally ill, and because the treatment afforded to the mentally retarded is less invasive than that provided to the mentally ill. The participation of family members or guardians in the proceedings was also rationally supported. Retardation can have effects on a person's daily living about which parents and guardians may have special insights. By contrast, mental illness may have a later onset, about which parents could have no knowledge, and there might be a greater need for privacy.

Souter, J., joined by Blackmun and Stevens, JJ., dissented; "While the Court cites *Cleburne* once, and does not purport to overrule it, neither does the Court apply it, and at the end of the day *Cleburne*'s status is left uncertain. * * *

"While difficulty of proof, and of interpretation of evidence, could legitimately counsel against setting the standard so high that the State may be unable to satisfy it (thereby effectively thwarting efforts to satisfy legitimate interests in protection, care, and treatment), that would at most justify a lower standard in the allegedly more difficult cases of illness, not in the easier cases of retardation. We do not lower burdens of proof merely because it is easy to prove the proposition at issue, nor do we raise them merely because it is difficult."

Souter, J., argued that both the mentally retarded and the mentally ill are subjected to invasive techniques during confinement and that no differences plausibly justified different commitment procedures. He also objected to the participation of parents or guardians as parties: "Where the third party supports commitment, someone who is alleged to be retarded is faced not only with a second advocate for institutionalization, but with a second prosecutor with the capacity to call and cross-examine witnesses, to obtain expert testimony and to raise an appeal that might not otherwise be taken, whereas a person said to require commitment on the basis of mental illness is not. [The] Court simply points to no characteristic of mental retardation that could rationally justify imposing this burden of a second prosecutor on those alleged to be mentally retarded where the State has decided not to impose it upon those alleged to be mentally ill."

"Without plausible justification, Kentucky is being allowed to draw a distinction that is difficult to see as resting on anything other than the stereotypical assumption that the retarded are 'perpetual children,' an assumption that has

---

b. The plaintiffs also challenged the parent and guardian procedures as a violation of pro- cedural due process. See Chap. VIII, Sec. 2 supra.

historically been taken to justify the disrespect and 'grotesque mistreatment' to which the retarded have been subjected. See *Cleburne* (Stevens, J., concurring)."[c]

IV. OTHER, CHALLENGED BASES FOR DISCRIMINATION

1. *Age.* MASSACHUSETTS BD. OF RETIREMENT v. MURGIA, 427 U.S. 307, 96 S.Ct. 2562, 49 L.Ed.2d 520 (1976), per curiam, upheld—"under the rational basis standard"—a law requiring uniformed state police officers to retire at age 50. After first rejecting the contention "that a right of governmental employment per se is fundamental" so as to make the legislative classification subject to "strict scrutiny" (see Sec. 5 of this Chapter), the Court continued: "While the treatment of the aged in this Nation has not been wholly free of discrimination, such persons, unlike, say, those who have been discriminated against on the basis of race or national origin, have not experienced a 'history of purposeful unequal treatment' or been subjected to unique disabilities on the basis of stereotyped characteristics not truly indicative of their abilities. The [Massachusetts statute] cannot be said to discriminate only against the elderly. Rather, it draws the line at a certain age in middle life. But even old age does not define a 'discrete and insular' group, *Carolene Products Co.,* n. 4, in need of 'extraordinary protection from the majoritarian political process.' Instead, it marks a stage that each of us will reach if we live out our normal span. Even if the statute could be said to impose a penalty upon a class defined as the aged, it would not impose a distinction sufficiently akin to those classifications that we have found suspect to call for strict judicial scrutiny."

MARSHALL, J., dissented from "the rigid two-tier model [that] still holds sway as the Court's articulated description of the equal protection test," urging the "flexible equal protection standard" developed in his earlier opinions in *Dandridge v. Williams,* p. 1287 infra, and *San Antonio Ind. School Dist. v. Rodriguez,* p. 1296, infra—which would focus "upon the character of the classification in question, the relative importance to individuals in the class discriminated against of the governmental benefits that they do not receive, and the state interests asserted in the support of the classification": "[T]he Court is quite right in suggesting that distinctions exist between the elderly and traditional suspect classes such as [blacks]. The elderly are protected not only by certain antidiscrimination legislation, but by legislation that provides them with positive benefits not enjoyed by the public at large. Moreover, the elderly are not isolated in society, and discrimination against them is not pervasive but is centered primarily in employment. The advantage of a flexible equal protection standard, however, is that it can readily accommodate such variables. The elderly are undoubtedly discriminated against, and when legislation denies them an important benefit— employment—I conclude that to sustain the legislation the Commonwealth must show a reasonably substantial interest and a scheme reasonably closely tailored to achieving that interest."

See also *Vance v. Bradley,* 440 U.S. 93, 99 S.Ct. 939, 59 L.Ed.2d 171 (1979) (upholding mandatory retirement at age 60 for federal Foreign Service personnel); *Gregory v. Ashcroft,* 501 U.S. 452, 111 S.Ct. 2395, 115 L.Ed.2d 410 (1991) (upholding Missouri's mandatory retirement for judges at age 70). On discrimina-

c. Blackmun, J., dissenting, observed that he would subject laws discriminating against individuals with mental retardation to heightened review. O'Connor, J., concurring and dissenting in part, agreed with Souter, J.'s analysis of the differential burden of proof requirements, but concluded that there was a rational basis for the differential rules regarding the participation of parents and guardians as parties.

tions against children, see Laurence H. Tribe, *American Constitutional Law* 1588–93 (2d ed. 1988).

2. *Wealth.* Laws that explicitly distinguish on the basis of wealth or poverty, and work directly to the disadvantage of the poor, are rare.[a] Today, laws seldom if ever prescribe that the poor cannot vote, attend public universities, utilize legal processes, or receive medical care in public hospitals. The disadvantage experienced by the poor more typically arises from the discriminatory impact of statutes that condition opportunities on the payment of money, or that draw lines—such as those separating relatively poor from relatively wealthy school districts—that strongly correlate with wealth. A variety of equal protection issues involving discriminatory impact on the poor are discussed in Sec. 5 infra.

Rare though they may be, should explicit discriminations against poor people be held "suspect"? Although the Warren Court had *stated* on several occasions that "lines drawn on the basis of wealth or property" "render a classification highly suspect,"[b] the Burger Court observed in 1973 that the Court had "never held that wealth discrimination alone provides an adequate basis for invoking strict scrutiny,"[c] and, in 1980, *Harris v. McRae,* p. 341 supra, said that "this Court has held repeatedly that poverty, standing alone, is not a suspect classification. See, e.g. *James v. Valtierra* [infra]."

JAMES v. VALTIERRA, 402 U.S. 137, 91 S.Ct. 1331, 28 L.Ed.2d 678 (1971), per Black, J., upheld Art. 34 of the California constitution, which provided that no "low-rent housing project"—defined as any development "for persons of low income"—could be constructed unless approved by local referendum: "Provisions for referendums demonstrate devotion to democracy, not to bias, discrimination, or prejudice." A "law making procedure that 'disadvantages' a particular group does not always deny equal protection." Nor were "persons advocating low-income housing * * * singled out": mandatory referendums were "required for approval of state constitutional amendments, for the issuance of general obligation long-term bonds by local governments, and for certain municipal territorial annexations."[d]

Marshall, J., joined by Brennan and Blackmun, JJ., dissented. Under California law, "publicly assisted housing developments designed to accommodate the aged, veterans, state employees, persons of moderate income, or any class of citizens other than the poor, need not be approved by prior referenda. [Art. 34 is] an explicit classification on the basis of poverty—a suspect classification which demands exacting judicial scrutiny."[e]

Do you agree that *James* involved "an explicit classification on the basis of poverty"?

What result if the state were to make it a crime for a person without visible means of support to refuse employment? If it were to discriminate against the poor in offering admissions to prestigious state universities, because of the risk that those without minimum resources would drop out for financial reasons (and thus squander some of the state's investment in their education)?

a. But cf. *Edwards v. California,* 314 U.S. 160, 62 S.Ct. 164, 86 L.Ed. 119 (1941), invalidating, under the commerce clause, a California statute making it a misdemeanor knowingly to transport a non-resident indigent into the state.

b. *Harper v. Virginia Bd. of Elections* and *McDonald v. Board of Elec. Comm'rs,* p. 1231 infra, 394 U.S. 802, 89 S.Ct. 1404, 22 L.Ed.2d 739 (1969).

c. *San Antonio Ind. School Dist. v. Rodriguez,* p. 1296 infra.

d. Cf. *Hunter v. Erickson,* p. 429, supra.

e. Douglas, J., did not participate.

Consider Frank I. Michelman, *On Protecting the Poor Through the Fourteenth Amendment*, 83 Harv.L.Rev. 7, 21 (1969): "[I]f money is power, then a class deliberately defined so as to include everyone who has less wealth or income than any person outside it may certainly be deemed [to] be especially susceptible to abuse by majoritarian process; and classification of 'the poor' as such, may, like classification of racial minorities as such, be popularly understood as a badge of inferiority. Especially is this so in light of the extreme difficulty of imagining proper governmental objectives which require for their achievement the explicit carving out, for relatively disadvantageous treatment, of a class defined by relative paucity of wealth or income."[f] Compare Ralph K. Winter, Jr. *Poverty, Economic Equality, and the Equal Protection Clause,* 1972 Sup.Ct.Rev. 41, 97–98: "Race is [the] basis of a stereotype which served as a systematic vehicle of governmental discrimination. Moreover, it is not a stereotype with a pretense at being related to individual merit, even though it [is] unalterable by the individual. [But] poverty is not absolutely unalterable for all those afflicted by it. The history of this nation is a history of virtually all of its people bettering themselves [economically].[g] Beyond that, [t]here simply has not been any legislation invoking a poverty classification even remotely resembling the widespread, official, racial segregation of schools and other facilities. To the contrary, there is an enormous amount of legislation [to] help the poor. [Finally], to the extent low income is related to low productivity—and it is to a large extent—poverty is not entirely unrelated to individual merit. One need not adopt productivity as the sole criterion of merit to say that poverty resulting from low productivity is far different from legal exclusion from public facilities because of one's race." See also Robert H. Bork, *The Impossibility of Finding Welfare Rights in the Constitution*, 1979 Wash.U.L.Q. 695, 701: "In the past two decades we have witnessed an explosion of welfare legislation, massive income redistributions, and civil rights laws of all kinds. The poor and the minorities have had access to the political process and have done very well through it."

3. *Sexual orientation. Bowers v. Hardwick*, p. 422 supra, upheld a Georgia anti-sodomy statute against attack under the due process clause, but expressly declined to consider equal protection challenges to the statute and its application. Are governmental classifications that disfavor homosexuals vulnerable to challenge under the equal protection clause? The question has a variety of dimensions.[h]

(a) *Definition of the affected class.* Governmental classifications relating to "homosexuality," "homosexuals," and so forth may refer either to homosexual "status"—a disposition or orientation—or to homosexual "acts." *Bowers* at least casts doubt on the argument that a class defined by its commission of criminally proscribable acts is constitutionally "suspect"—though it can still be questioned whether it is "rational" for government to discriminate against those who commit this particular type of constitutionally proscribable act if it does not impose similar disabilities on those who engage in other prohibitable conduct. Moreover, it is a separate question whether it should be constitutionally suspect for govern-

---

f. See also Stephen Loffredo, *Poverty Democracy, and Constitutional Law*, 141 U.Pa. L.Rev. 1277 (1993).

g. See also Comment, 85 Harv.L.Rev. 129 (1971): "The poor seem to be a less cohesive and less readily identifiable group than are racial minorities. Because the class of 'poor' is constantly in flux, the reinforced sense of stigma which characterizes de jure racial classifica-

tions is probably mitigated even where explicit wealth classifications are concerned."

h. Two recent symposia provide useful introductions: *Symposium on Sexual Orientation and the Law*, 79 Va.L.Rev. 1419 (1993); and *Symposium: Stonewall at 25*, 29 Harv. C.R.C.L.L.Rev. 277 (1994).

ment to discriminate against a class of people defined solely by their homosexual disposition, proclivities, or state of mind, regardless of whether they have engaged in sexual acts of the kind held prohibitable in *Bowers*.

(b) *Equal protection categories.* (i) Are homosexuals—at least insofar as defined by status, not conduct—a paradigmatic discrete and insular minority who have been the victims of historic "prejudice"?[i] See John H. Ely, *Democracy and Distrust* 162–63 (1980). Would a determination to this effect require a moral judgment? If so, is such a moral judgment barred by *Bowers*, or can *Bowers* be distinguished on either or both of the grounds that (a) it involved conduct, not "status," and (b) whereas due process methodology looks backward at "tradition" and traditional morality, equal protection analysis is appropriately critical of traditional, stereotyped, and prejudicial thinking. See Cass R. Sunstein, *Sexual Orientation and the Constitution: A Note on the Relationship between Due Process and Equal Protection*, 55 U.Chi.L.Rev. 1161 (1988).

(ii) Is discrimination against homosexuals a form of sex discrimination appropriately subject to intermediate scrutiny? Consider Andrew Koppelman, *Why Discrimination Against Lesbians and Gay Men is Sex Discrimination*, 69 N.Y.U.L.Rev. 197, 208 (1994): "If a business fires Ricky, or if the state prosecutes him, because of his sexual activities with Fred, while these actions would not be taken against Lucy if she did exactly the same things with Fred, then Ricky is being discriminated against because of his sex."[j] See also Sylvia A. Law, *Homosexuality and the Social Meaning of Gender*, 1988 Wisc.L.Rev. 187; Cass R. Sunstein, *Homosexuality and the Constitution*, 70 Ind.L.J. 1 (1994) (arguing that discrimination against homosexuals reinforces traditional assumptions concerning the general superiority of heterosexual males and devalues the sexual "passivity" traditionally associated with women). Compare Craig M. Bradley, *The Right Not to Endorse Gay Rights: A Reply to Sunstein*, 70 Ind.L.J. 29 (1994).

(iii) Do some discriminatory classifications reflect no more than the "bare * * * desire to hurt a politically unpopular group" that the Court has found not to be a legitimate state interest at all. See *United States Dep't of Agriculture v. Moreno*, p. 1065 supra. If other classifications reflect no other basis than the desire of some not to have to associate with homosexuals, is this the sort of "irrational prejudice" dismissed by the Court in *Cleburne* as inadequate to justify legislation even under a rational basis standard?

(c) *Religion and self-expression.* Consider the arguments of David A.J. Richards, *Sexual Preference as a Suspect (Religious) Classification: An Alternative Perspective on the Unconstitutionality of Anti–Lesbian/Gay Initiatives*, 55 Ohio St.L.J. 491 (1994), that: (i) anti-homosexual legislation is suspect because reflective of sectarian religious beliefs; and (ii) homosexual sexual activity is inherently expressive, and classifications burdening this expression intrude impermissibly on freedom of conscience.[k]

---

i. Does it matter whether homosexuality is an "immutable" characteristic? For a negative answer, see Janet E. Halley, *Sexual Orientation and the Politics of Biology: A Critique of the Argument from Immutability*, 46 Stan. L.Rev. 503 (1994).

j. Would this argument also support a right to homosexual marriage? Cf. *Baehr v. Lewin*, 74 Haw. 530, 852 P.2d 44 (1993) (finding denial of marriage rights to same-sex couples presumptively unconstitutional under the Hawaiian constitution and remanding for inquiry concerning the state's interests). See also William N. Eskridge, Jr., *A History of Same Sex Marriage*, 79 Va.L.Rev. 1419 (1993) (arguing that same sex marriages have existed historically).

k. See also David Cole & William N. Eskridge, Jr., *From Hand–Holding to Sodomy: First Amendment Protection of Homosexual (Expressive) Conduct*, 29 Harv.Civ.Rts.Civ. Lib.L.Rev. 319 (1994).

(d) *"Don't ask, don't tell."* The United States military now observes a "don't ask, don't tell" policy, codified in 10 U.S.C.A. § 654(b), under which homosexuals remain subject to exclusion from the armed services,[l] but the military will not seek to discover evidence of homosexual acts or orientation when it is not openly disclosed. Is this the type of military judgment that deserves special deference from the judiciary? Is the policy rationally justified? Does it explicitly and impermissibly burden free speech rights?[m]

SECTION 5. "FUNDAMENTAL RIGHTS"

I. VOTING

A. DENIAL OR QUALIFICATION OF THE RIGHT

FORTSON v. MORRIS, 385 U.S. 231, 87 S.Ct. 446, 17 L.Ed.2d 330 (1966): In the 1966 Georgia gubernatorial election, no candidate received a majority of the popular vote. Georgia provided that in such case the Georgia legislature shall elect the governor from the two candidates receiving the highest popular vote. The Court, per BLACK, J., upheld the election: There is no federal constitutional provision "which either expressly or impliedly dictates the method a State must use to select its Governor. A method which would be valid if initially employed is equally valid when employed as an alternative."

DOUGLAS, J., joined by Warren, C.J., and Brennan and Fortas, JJ., dissented, viewing "the legislative choice" as "only a part of the popular election machinery. [A] candidate who received a minority of the popular vote might receive a clear majority of the votes cast in the legislature," thus "contrary to the principle of 'one person, one vote.'"

Notes and Questions

Scope of the decision. May a state provide that a popularly elected governor shall appoint the entire legislature? Appoint the legislator from any district in which no candidate received a majority (⅔) (¾) of the popular vote? That all local officials shall be appointed by the legislature or some part thereof? What provision(s) of the Constitution are most germane in considering these issues? See generally John Hart Ely, *Democracy and Distrust* 116–25 (1980); Sanford Levinson, *Judicial Review and the Problem of the Comprehensible Constitution*, 59 Tex.L.Rev. 395, 413–15 (1981).

Compare Janet E. Halley, *The Politics of the Closet: Towards Equal Protection for Gay, Lesbian, and Bisexual Identity*, 36 U.C.L.A.L.Rev. 915 (1989), arguing that sexual identity is mutable, created partly through social and political discourse, and that the political process loses legitimacy if it systematically silences those disposed to challenge heterosexual orthodoxy.

l. The prohibition extends (i) to those who have engaged in or solicited homosexual acts, unless "such conduct is a departure from a member's usual and customary behavior" and the member's continued service "is consistent [with] discipline, good order, and morale," and (ii) to anyone who "has stated that he or she is a homosexual or bisexual," unless there is evidence that the member does not engage in and does not have "a propensity to engage in" homosexual acts.

m. Recent cases raising many of the issues identified above include: *Steffan v. Perry*, 41 F.3d 677 (D.C.Cir.1994) (en banc) (upholding forced discharge from the Naval Academy under a rational basis standard); *Meinhold v. United States Dept. of Defense*, 34 F.3d 1469 (9th Cir.1994) (applying narrowing construction of military regulations to preserve their constitutionality); *Able v. United States*, 880 F.Supp. 968 (E.D.N.Y.1995) (finding "don't ask, don't tell" policy invalid under both first and fifth amendments); *Philips v. Perry*, 883 F.Supp. 539 (W.D.Wash.1995) (rejecting a free speech challenge to a military discharge).

CARRINGTON v. RASH, 380 U.S. 89, 85 S.Ct. 775, 13 L.Ed.2d 675 (1965), per STEWART, J., held a Texas provision, barring members of the military who moved to Texas from voting in state elections so long as they remained in the military, "an invidious discrimination": "We deal here with matters close to the core of our constitutional system." Only "where military personnel are involved has Texas been unwilling to develop more precise tests to determine the bona fides of an individual claiming to have actually made his home in the State long enough to vote." " 'Fencing out' from the franchise a sector of the population because of the way they may vote is constitutionally impermissible." [a]

———

HARPER v. VIRGINIA BD. OF ELEC., 383 U.S. 663, 86 S.Ct. 1079, 16 L.Ed.2d 169 (1966), per DOUGLAS, J., overruling *Breedlove v. Suttles,* 302 U.S. 277, 58 S.Ct. 205, 82 L.Ed. 252 (1937), held that Virginia's $1.50 poll tax as "a prerequisite of voting" was "an 'invidious' discrimination": "[T]he right to vote in state elections is nowhere expressly mentioned" in the Constitution, but "once the franchise is [granted] lines may not be drawn which [violate equal protection].[3]"

"Long ago in *Yick Wo,* [Sec. 2, III supra], the Court referred to 'the political franchise of voting' as a 'fundamental political right, because preservative of all rights.' * * * Wealth, like race, creed, or color, is not germane to one's ability to participate intelligently in the electoral process. Lines drawn on the basis of wealth or property, like those of race, are traditionally disfavored. See *Edwards v. California,* [p. 252 supra] (Jackson, J., concurring); *Griffin v. Illinois; Douglas v. California,* [Part III infra]. To introduce wealth or payment of a fee as a measure of a voter's qualifications is to introduce a capricious or irrelevant factor. * * *

"In determining what lines are unconstitutionally discriminatory, we have never been confined to historic notions of equality" and "notions of what constitutes equal treatment for purposes of the Equal Protection Clause *do* change [citing *Plessy* and *Brown,* Sec. 2, II supra]. Our conclusion, like that in *Reynolds,* is founded not on what we think governmental policy should be, but on what the Equal Protection Clause requires.

"We have long been mindful that where fundamental rights and liberties are asserted under the Equal Protection Clause, classifications which might invade or restrain them must be closely scrutinized and carefully confined. See, e.g., *Reynolds; Carrington.*"

BLACK, J., dissented: "[U]nder a proper interpretation of the Equal Protection Clause States are to have the broadest kind of leeway in areas where they have a general constitutional competence to act. [P]oll tax legislation can 'reasonably,' 'rationally' and without an 'invidious' or evil purpose to injure anyone be found to rest on a number of state policies including (1) the State's desire to collect its revenue, and (2) its belief that voters who pay a poll tax will be interested in furthering the State's welfare when they vote. [And] history is on the side of

a. Harlan, J., dissented: The classification was "rational" in treating such persons as "transients for voting purposes" because the "vast majority" will leave "when the military compulsion ends." Finally, Texas "could rationally decide to protect local politics against the influences of military voting strength." Warren, C.J., did not participate.

3. [While] the "Virginia poll tax was born of a desire to disenfranchise the Negro," we do not stop to determine whether [the] Virginia tax in its modern setting serves the same end.

'rationality' of the State's poll tax policy. Property qualifications existed in the Colonies and were continued by many States after the Constitution was adopted. [The Court] seems to be using the old 'natural-law-due-process formula' to justify striking down state laws as violations of [equal protection]."

HARLAN, J., joined by Stewart, J., dissented: "The [equal protection] test evolved by this Court [is whether] a classification can be deemed to be founded on some rational and otherwise constitutionally permissible state [policy].[3] *Reynolds* [also] marked a departure from these traditional and wise principles. [I]t was probably accepted as sound political theory by a large percentage of Americans through most of our history, that people with some property have a deeper stake in community affairs, and are consequently more responsible, more educated, more knowledgeable, more worthy of [confidence. It] is all wrong, in my view, for the Court to adopt the political doctrines popularly accepted at a particular moment of our history and to declare all others to be irrational and invidious * * *."

Notes and Questions

1.   Should (does?) the Constitution embrace a right to vote or simply a right of equality in voting?

2.   *Denial of voting to residents.* Should a state be able to deny the vote to those who can not pass a literacy test? *Lassiter v. Northampton County Board of Elections,* 360 U.S. 45, 79 S.Ct. 985, 3 L.Ed.2d 1072 (1959) (constitutional).[b]   To smart seventeen year olds?[c]   To felons? *Richardson v. Ramirez,* 418 U.S. 24, 94 S.Ct. 2655, 41 L.Ed.2d 551 (1974) (constitutional).

3.   *Denial of voting to non-residents.* Alabama extended a city's police and sanitary regulations and its business-licensing powers (at reduced fees) to residents of adjacent, unincorporated communities, but did not permit them to vote in city elections. Constitutional? See *Holt Civic Club v. Tuscaloosa,* 439 U.S. 60, 99 S.Ct. 383, 58 L.Ed.2d 292 (1978) (constitutional).

4.   Do voting exclusions necessarily make assumptions about the character and purpose of democratic politics? What assumptions?[d]   Should the community be permitted to confine the franchise to those likely to focus on its long range interests? Would this mean that students of voting age could be excluded?[e] Assuming an appropriate test could be devised, should the community be permitted to confine the vote to those with substantial knowledge of its customs, habits, and traditions? Should the community be permitted to confine the vote to those with a commitment to its shared values? If not, why are resident aliens forced to take an oath on becoming citizens?[f]   Should the oath be abandoned? Should all those with an interest in voting be permitted to do so? Should all those directly

---

3.   I think the somewhat different application of the Equal Protection Clause to racial discrimination cases finds justification in the fact that insofar as that clause may embody a particular value in addition to rationality, the historical origins of the Civil War Amendments might attribute to racial equality this special status. * * *

b.   Does *Lassiter* survive *Harper* ?

c.   Compare *Oregon v. Mitchell,* p. 1397 infra.

d.   See generally Frank Michelman, *Conceptions of Democracy in American Constitutional*

Argument: Voting Rights, 41 Fla.L.Rev. 443 (1989). See also C. Edwin Baker, *Republican Liberalism,* 41 Fla.L.Rev. 491 (1989).

e.   May a state single out certain groups (students) for a presumption of nonresidency (in the district in which they attend college)? See generally Note, *Student Voting and the Constitution,* 72 Colum.L.Rev. 162 (1972).

f.   See Sanford Levinson, *Suffrage and Community: Who Should Vote,* 41 Fla.L.Rev. 545 (1989).

regulated by the state be permitted to vote? If the latter, what is the best argument for the majority position in *Holt*?

KRAMER v. UNION FREE SCHOOL DISTRICT

395 U.S. 621, 89 S.Ct. 1886, 23 L.Ed.2d 583 (1969).

CHIEF JUSTICE WARREN delivered the opinion of the Court.

[§ 2012 of the New York Education Law] provides that in certain New York school districts residents [may] vote in the school district election only if they [or their spouse] (1) own (or lease) taxable real property within the district, or (2) are parents (or have custody of) children enrolled in the local public schools. Appellant, a bachelor who neither owns nor leases taxable real property, [claimed] § 2012 denied him equal protection * * *.

[I]t is important to note what is *not* at issue in this case. The requirements of § 2012 that school district voters must (1) be citizens of the United States, (2) be bona fide residents of the school district, and (3) be at least 21 years of age are not challenged. * * *

[S]tatutes distributing the franchise constitute the foundation of our representative society. Any unjustified discrimination in determining who may participate in political affairs or in the selection of public officials undermines the legitimacy of representative government. [Therefore,] if a [statute] grants the right to vote to some bona fide residents of requisite age and citizenship and denies the franchise to others, the Court must determine whether the exclusions are necessary to promote a compelling state interest. See *Carrington*.

[The] presumption of constitutionality and the approval given "rational" classifications in other types of enactments are based on an assumption that the institutions of state government are structured so as to represent fairly all the people. However, when the challenge to the statute is in effect a challenge of this basic assumption, the assumption can no longer serve as the basis for presuming constitutionality. And, the assumption is no less under attack because the legislature which decides who may participate at the various levels of political choice is fairly elected. * * * [10]

The need for exacting judicial scrutiny of statutes distributing the franchise is undiminished simply because, under a different statutory scheme, the offices subject to election might have been filled through appointment [11] [since] "once the franchise is granted to the electorate, lines may not be drawn which are inconsistent with [equal protection]." *Harper*.

Nor is the need for close judicial examination affected because the district [and] the school board do not have "general" legislative powers. Our exacting examination is necessitated not by the subject of the election [but] because some resident citizens are permitted to participate and some are not. * * *

Besides appellant and others who similarly live in their parents' homes, the statute also disenfranchises the following persons (unless they are parents or guardians of children enrolled in the district public school): senior citizens and others living with children or relatives; clergy, military personnel and others who live on tax-exempt property; boarders and lodgers; parents who neither own nor

10. [See] *Avery v. Midland County.*

11. Similarly, no less a showing of a compelling justification for disenfranchising resi-

dents is required merely because the questions scheduled for the election need not have been submitted to the voters.

lease qualifying property and whose children are too young to attend school [or] attend private schools.

[A]ppellees argue that the State has a legitimate interest in limiting the franchise in school district elections [to] those "primarily interested in such elections" [and] that the State may reasonably and permissibly conclude that "property taxpayers" (including lessees of taxable property who share the tax burden through rent payments) and parents of the children enrolled in the district's schools are those "primarily interested" in school affairs. * * *

[A]ssuming, arguendo, that New York legitimately might limit the franchise in these school district elections to those "primarily interested in school affairs," close scrutiny of the § 2012 classifications demonstrates that they do not accomplish this purpose with sufficient precision to justify denying appellant the franchise.

[T]he classifications must be tailored so that the exclusion of appellant and members of his class is necessary to achieve the articulated state goal.[14] Section 2012 does not meet the exacting standard of precision [because it permits] inclusion of many persons who have, at best, a remote and indirect interest in school affairs and on the other hand, exclude[s] others who have a distinct and direct interest in the school meeting decisions.[15] * * *[a]

JUSTICE STEWART, with whom JUSTICE BLACK and JUSTICE HARLAN join, dissenting. * * *

Clearly a State may reasonably assume that its residents have a greater stake in the outcome of elections held within its boundaries than do other persons [and] that residents, being generally better informed regarding state affairs than are nonresidents, will be more likely [to] vote responsibly. And the same may be said of legislative assumptions regarding the electoral competence of adults and literate persons on the one hand, and of minors and illiterates on the other. It is clear, of course, that lines thus drawn cannot infallibly perform their intended legislative function. Just as "[i]lliterate people may be intelligent voters," nonresidents or minors might also in some instances be interested, informed, and intelligent participants in the electoral process. Persons who commute across a state line to work may well have a great stake in the affairs of the State in which they are employed; some college students under 21 may be both better informed and more passionately interested in political affairs than many adults. But such discrepancies are the inevitable concomitant of the line-drawing that is essential to lawmaking.[b] So long as the classification is rationally related to a permissible legislative end, therefore—as are residence, literacy, and age requirements imposed with respect to voting—there is no denial of equal protection.

14. Of course, if the exclusions are necessary to promote the articulated state interest, we must then determine whether the interest promoted by limiting the franchise constitutes a compelling state interest. We do not reach that issue in this case.

15. For example, appellant resides with his parents in the school district, pays state and federal taxes and is interested in and affected by school board decisions [but] an uninterested unemployed young man who pays no state or federal taxes, but who rents an apartment in the district, can [vote].

a. See also *Cipriano v. Houma*, 395 U.S. 701, 89 S.Ct. 1897, 23 L.Ed.2d 647 (1969) (invalidating statute confining vote to property taxpayers in elections for issuance of municipal bonds by a municipal utility); *Phoenix v. Kolodziejski*, 399 U.S. 204, 90 S.Ct. 1990, 26 L.Ed.2d 523 (1970) (invalidating statute confining vote to real property taxpayers in elections for issuance of general obligation bonds for financing various municipal improvements).

b. See Rex Lee, *Mr. Herbert Spencer and the Bachelor Stockbroker*, 15 Ariz.L.Rev. 457 (1973).

Thus judged, the statutory classification involved here seems to me clearly to be valid [and] the Court does not really argue the contrary. Instead, it [asserts] that the traditional equal protection standard is [inapt]. But the asserted justification for applying [a stricter] standard cannot withstand analysis. [The] voting qualifications at issue have been promulgated not by Union Free School District, but by the New York State Legislature, and the appellant is of course fully able to participate in the election of representatives in that body. There is simply no claim whatever here that the state government is not "structured so as to represent fairly all the people," including the appellant.

[§ 2012] does not involve racial classifications [and] is not one that impinges upon a constitutionally protected right, and that consequently can be justified only by a "compelling" state interest. For "the Constitution of the United States does not confer the right of suffrage upon any one."

In any event, it seems to me that under *any* equal protection standard, short of a doctrinaire insistence that universal suffrage is somehow mandated by the Constitution, the appellant's claim must be rejected. * * *

B. "DILUTION" OF THE RIGHT: APPORTIONMENT

The Court's initial hesitancy to consider malapportioned legislatures—largely the product of districts drawn when the nation's rural/urban population ratio was vastly different than in mid 20th century—and its subsequent assertion of jurisdiction are presented in BAKER v. CARR, p. 34 supra.

The first full post-*Baker* opinion on the problem was GRAY v. SANDERS, 372 U.S. 368, 83 S.Ct. 801, 9 L.Ed.2d 821 (1963), invalidating the "county unit system" employed in Georgia primaries for statewide officers. The candidate receiving the highest number of votes in each county obtained "two votes for each representative to which the county is entitled in the lower House of the General Assembly," and the winner was determined on the basis of the county unit vote. Because counties were not represented in the state legislature in accordance with their population, "combination of the units from the counties having the smallest population gives counties having population of one-third of the total in the state a clear majority of county units." The Court, per DOUGLAS, J., emphasizing that the case did not involve legislative districting, held that equal protection requires that "once the geographical unit for which a representative is to be chosen is designated, all who participate in the election are to have an equal vote. [The] conception of political equality from the Declaration of Independence, to Lincoln's Gettysburg Address, to the Fifteenth, Seventeenth, and Nineteenth Amendments can mean only one thing—one person, one vote." [a]

WESBERRY v. SANDERS, 376 U.S. 1, 84 S.Ct. 526, 11 L.Ed.2d 481 (1964), per BLACK, J., struck down the Georgia congressional districting statute which

---

a. Harlan, J., dissented. Is there a distinction between the issue in *Gray* and legislative apportionment? See 77 Harv.L.Rev. 131 (1963).

Is a state primary for selecting delegates to the national political parties' presidential nominating conventions, which awards all of the state's delegates to the candidate with the highest number of votes, valid after *Gray*? See James Blumstein, *Party Reform, the Winner-Take-All Primary, and the California Delegate Challenge: The Gold Rush Revisited*, 25 Vand. L.Rev. 975 (1972).

accorded some districts more than twice the population of others: "[T]he command of Art. I, § 2, that Representatives be chosen 'by the People of the several States' means that as nearly as is practicable one man's vote in a congressional election is to be worth as much as another's." [b]

Notes and Questions

1. *Commitment to Congress.* Has Art. I—as argued by Harlan, J., in *Wesberry*—"conferred upon Congress exclusive authority to secure fair representation by the States" in the House of Representatives? Consider Anthony Lewis, *Legislative Apportionment and the Federal Courts,* 71 Harv.L.Rev. 1057, 1074 (1958): "[That Art. I] casts the right to equal representation in the House in terms of affirmative congressional power should not preclude judicial enforcement of the right in the absence of legislation. Such judicial action is commonplace in other areas, [e.g.,] the commerce clause, which is phrased in the most general language and entirely in terms of congressional power." Is *Wesberry* premised, sub silentio, on the commerce clause analogy? May Congress "overrule" *Wesberry* as it may a commerce clause decision?

2. *Equal representation.* What does *Wesberry* portend for the effective power of some congressional committees to "pigeon-hole" legislation? The Senate filibuster? Are these practices consistent with the principle that "one man's vote in a congressional election is to be worth as much as another's"?

REYNOLDS v. SIMS

377 U.S. 533, 84 S.Ct. 1362, 12 L.Ed.2d 506 (1964).

CHIEF JUSTICE WARREN delivered the opinion of the Court.

[Although the Alabama constitution required the legislature to reapportion decennially on the basis of population, none had taken place since 1901. The federal district court held the existing malapportionment violative of equal protection. Under] 1960 census figures, only 25.1% of the State's total population resided in districts represented by a majority of the members of the Senate, and only 25.7% lived in counties which could elect a majority of the members of the House of Representatives. Population-variance ratios of up to about 41-to-1 existed in the Senate, and up to about 16-to-1 in the House. * * *

Gray and *Wesberry* are of course not dispositive [of] these cases involving state legislative [apportionment]. But neither are they wholly inapposite. [*Gray*] established the basic principle of equality among voters within a State, [and] *Wesberry* clearly established that the fundamental principle of representative government in this country is one of equal representation for equal numbers of people, without regard to race, sex, economic status, or place of residence within a State. Our problem, then, is to ascertain [whether] there are any constitutionally cognizable principles which would justify departures from the basic standard of equality among voters in the apportionment of seats in state legislatures.

A predominant consideration in determining whether a State's legislative apportionment scheme constitutes an invidious discrimination [is] that the rights allegedly impaired are individual and personal in nature. [Since] the right of suffrage is a fundamental matter in a free and democratic society [and] is

---

b. Clark, J., would have remanded for consideration "against the requirements of the Equal Protection Clause." Harlan, J., would have adhered to *Colegrove* and, on the merits (joined by Stewart, J.,) dissented, finding the Court's theory "demonstrably unsound historically."

preservative of other basic civil and political rights, any alleged infringement [must] be carefully and meticulously scrutinized. * * *

Legislators represent people, not trees or acres. Legislators are elected by voters, not farms or cities or economic interests. As long as ours is a representative form of government, [the] right to elect legislators in a free and unimpaired fashion is a bedrock of our political system. [It] is inconceivable that a state law to the effect that, in counting votes for legislators, the votes of citizens in one part of the State would be multiplied by two, five, or 10, while the votes of persons in another area would be counted only at face value, could be [constitutional]. Of course, the effect of state legislative districting schemes which give the same number of representatives to unequal numbers of constituents is identical. * * *

Logically, in a society ostensibly grounded on representative government, it would seem reasonable that a majority of the people of a State could elect a majority of that State's legislators. [T]o sanction minority control of state legislative bodies would appear to deny majority rights in a way that far surpasses any possible denial of minority rights that might otherwise be thought to result.[a] [T]he concept of equal protection has been traditionally viewed as requiring the uniform treatment of persons standing in the same relation to the governmental action questioned or challenged. With respect to the allocation of legislative representation, all voters, as citizens of a State, stand in the same relation regardless of where they live. Any suggested criteria for the differentiation of citizens are insufficient to justify any discrimination, as to the weight of their votes, unless relevant to the permissible purposes of legislative apportionment. Since the achieving of fair and effective representation for all citizens is concededly the basic aim of legislative apportionment, we conclude that the Equal Protection Clause guarantees the opportunity for equal participation by all voters in the election of state legislators. Diluting the weight of votes because of place of residence impairs basic constitutional rights under the Fourteenth Amendment just as much as invidious discriminations based upon factors such as race, or economic status. Our constitutional system amply provides for the protection of minorities by means other than giving them majority control of state legislatures. * * *

We are told that the matter of apportioning representation in a state legislature is a complex and many-faceted one. We are advised that States can rationally consider factors other than [population]. We are admonished not to restrict the power of the States to impose differing views as to political philosophy on their citizens. We are cautioned about the dangers of entering into political thickets and mathematical quagmires. Our answer is this: a denial of constitutionally protected rights demands judicial protection; our oath and our office require no less of us. [To] the extent that a citizen's right to vote is debased, he is that much less a citizen. [A] nation once primarily rural in character becomes predominantly urban. Representation schemes once fair and equitable become archaic and outdated. But the basic principle of representative government [remains]—the weight of a citizen's vote cannot be made to depend on where he

---

a. But see Alexander Bickel, *The Supreme Court and Reapportionment,* in Reapportionment in the 1970's, 57, 58–59 (Nelson Polsby ed. 1971): "[A] rigorous majoritarianism is not what our institutions rest [on]. American government [includes] a Supreme Court which wields political power and [is] not elected at all. Our government includes a Senate [in] which each state, regardless of population, has an equal vote that not even a duly enacted and ratified constitutional amendment can, without its own consent, deprive it of. Our government includes a House of Representatives in which each state has at least one vote, even though the whole state may be (as some are) considerably smaller in population than the average congressional district."

lives. Population is, of necessity, [the] controlling criterion for judgment in legislative [apportionment]. This is the clear and strong command of our Constitution's Equal Protection Clause. This is an essential part of the concept of a government of laws and not men. This is at the heart of Lincoln's vision of "government of the people, by the people, [and] for the people." * * *

We hold that, as a basic constitutional standard, the Equal Protection Clause requires that the seats in both houses of a bicameral state legislature must be apportioned on a population basis. [We] find the federal analogy inapposite and irrelevant to state legislative districting schemes. [T]he Founding Fathers clearly had no intention of establishing a pattern or model for the apportionment of seats in state legislatures when the system of representation in the Federal Congress was adopted. Demonstrative of this is the fact that the Northwest Ordinance, adopted in the same year, 1787, as the Federal Constitution, provided for the apportionment of seats in territorial legislatures solely on the basis of population.

The system of representation in the two Houses of the Federal Congress [is] based on the consideration that in establishing our type of federalism a group of formerly independent States bound themselves together under one national government. [A] compromise between the larger and smaller States on this matter averted a deadlock in the constitutional convention * * *.

Political subdivisions of States [never] have been considered as sovereign entities. Rather, they have been traditionally regarded as subordinate governmental instrumentalities created by the State. * * *

[The] right of a citizen to equal representation and to have his vote weighted equally with those of all other citizens in the election of members of one house of a bicameral state legislature would amount to little if States could effectively submerge the equal-population principle in the apportionment of seats in the other house. * * * Deadlock between the two bodies might result in compromise and concession on some issues. But in all too many cases the more probable result would be frustration of the majority will through minority veto in the house not apportioned on a population [basis].

We do not believe that the concept of bicameralism is rendered anachronistic and meaningless when the predominant basis of representation in the two state legislative bodies is required to be the same—population. A prime reason for bicameralism, modernly considered, is to insure mature and deliberate consideration of, and to prevent precipitate action on, proposed legislative measures. Simply because the controlling criterion for apportioning representation is required to be the same in both houses does not mean that there will be no differences in the composition and complexion of the two bodies. [The] numerical size of the two bodies could be made to differ, even significantly, and the geographical size of districts from which legislators are elected could also be made to differ. [T]he Equal Protection Clause requires that a State make an honest and good faith effort to construct districts, in both houses of its legislature, as nearly of equal population as is practicable. We realize that it is a practical impossibility to arrange legislative districts so that each one has an identical number of residents, or citizens, or voters. Mathematical exactness or precision is hardly a workable constitutional requirement.

[So] long as the divergences from a strict population standard are based on legitimate considerations incident to the effectuation of a rational state policy, some deviations from the equal-population principle are constitutionally permissible, [b]ut neither history alone, nor economic or other sorts of group interests, are permissible factors in attempting to justify disparities from population-based representation. Citizens, not history or economic interests, cast votes. Considerations of area alone provide an insufficient justification for deviations from the equal-population principle. Again, people, not land or trees or pastures, vote. Modern developments and improvements in transportation and communications make rather hollow, in the mid-1960's, most claims [for] allowing such deviations in order to insure effective representation for sparsely settled areas and to prevent legislative districts from becoming so large that the availability of access of citizens to their representatives is impaired. * * *

A consideration that appears to be of more substance [is] according political subdivisions some independent representation in at least one body of the state legislature, as long as the basic standard of equality of population among districts is maintained. [In] many States much of the legislature's activity involves the enactment of so-called local legislation, directed only to the concerns of particular political subdivisions. And a State may legitimately desire to construct districts along political subdivision lines to deter the possibilities of gerrymandering. However, permitting deviations from population-based representation does not mean that each local governmental unit or political subdivision can be given separate representation, regardless of [population].[b]

* * * Decennial reapportionment appears to be a rational approach to readjustment of legislative representation in order to take into account population shifts and growth [and] if reapportionment were accomplished with less frequency, it would assuredly be constitutionally suspect. * * *

[T]he court below acted with proper judicial restraint, after the Alabama Legislature had failed to act effectively in remedying the constitutional deficiencies in the State's legislative apportionment scheme, in ordering its own temporary reapportionment plan into effect, at a time sufficiently early to permit the holding of elections pursuant to that plan without great difficulty, and in prescribing a plan admittedly provisional in purpose so as not to usurp the primary responsibility for reapportionment which rests with the legislature.[c]

b. Under *Reynolds,* could Colorado give [small] counties [representation] by permitting them each to have a representative in the legislature, but granting that legislator only a fractional vote determined on a population basis (or granting him a full vote but giving legislators from larger counties a more heavily weighted vote)? Consider Robert Dixon, *Reapportionment Perspectives: What is Fair Representation?*, 51 A.B.A.J. 319, 322 (1965): "[W]eighted voting may be nullified for several reasons. One of the most important reasons would be the consideration that one man casting nineteen votes is not as effective in terms of representation as nineteen separate voices (or lobbyists). Another would be that nineteen men separately elected would provide more opportunity for expression of divergent views. [B]oth of these arguments involve going beyond the simple mathematical tenor of the Supreme Court's 'one-man, one-vote' decisions. They involve putting reapportionment in the context of the actual complexities of representation—and the difficulties in determining what is fair and effective representation." Does this objection go similarly to fractional voting? If not, should fractional voting also extend to committee voting? Assignment to committee? Compensation? What else? See generally John Banzhaf, *One Man, ? Votes: Mathematical Analysis of Voting Power and Effective Representation,* 36 Geo.Wash.L.Rev. 808 (1968); Note, *Equal Representation and the Weighted Voting Alternatives,* 79 Yale L.J. 311 (1969).

c. *Travia v. Lomenzo,* 381 U.S. 431, 85 S.Ct. 1582, 14 L.Ed.2d 480 (1965), refused to stay a district court's order that New York hold a special legislative election—thus shortening the terms of legislators elected under an invalid apportionment—under a reapportionment plan enacted by the legislature but held invalid by the state court because it provided for more legislators than permitted under the state constitution.

May a court order that a convention be called to amend the state constitution apportionment provisions? Require that all plans be submitted to it for approval? Cf. *Burns v. Richardson,* 384 U.S. 73, 86 S.Ct. 1286, 16 L.Ed.2d 376 (1966). Require changing the size of the legislature? See *67th Minnesota State Senate v. Beens,* 406 U.S. 187, 92 S.Ct. 1477, 32 L.Ed.2d 1 (1972). Order that a malappor-

[Clark and Stewart, JJ., concurred in the result in *Reynolds,* but Justice Stewart, joined by Justice Clark, dissented in two of the companion cases in an opinion sharply at odds with the *Reynolds'* rationale:] [d]

First, says the Court, it is "established that the fundamental principle of representative government in this country is one of equal representation for equal numbers of [people]." [But] this "was not the colonial system, it was not the system chosen for the national government by the Constitution, it was not the system exclusively or even predominantly practiced by the States at the time of adoption of the Fourteenth Amendment, it is not predominantly practiced by the States today." Secondly, says the Court, unless legislative districts are equal in population, voters in the more populous districts will suffer a 'debasement' amounting to a constitutional injury. [I] find it impossible to understand how or why a voter in California, for instance, either feels or is less a citizen than a voter in Nevada, simply because, despite their population disparities, each of those States is represented by two United States Senators.

[My] own understanding of the various theories of representative government is that no one theory has ever commanded unanimous [assent]. But even if it were thought that the rule announced today by the Court is, as a matter of political theory, the most desirable, [I] could not join in the fabrication of a constitutional mandate which imports and forever freezes one theory of political thought into our Constitution, and forever denies to every State any opportunity for enlightened and progressive innovation * * *.

Representative government is a process of accommodating group interests through democratic institutional arrangements. * * * Appropriate legislative apportionment, therefore, should ideally be designed to insure effective representation in the State's legislature, in cooperation with other organs of political power, of the various groups and interests making up the electorate. In practice, of course, this ideal is approximated in the particular apportionment system of any State by a realistic accommodation of the diverse and often conflicting political forces operating within the State.

[The] fact of geographic districting, the constitutional validity of which the Court does not question, carries with it an acceptance of the idea of legislative representation of regional needs and interests. Yet if geographical residence is irrelevant, as the Court suggests, and the goal is solely that of equally "weighted" votes, I do not understand why the Court's constitutional rule does not require the abolition of districts and the holding of all elections at large.

The fact is, of course, that population factors must often to some degree be subordinated in devising a legislative apportionment plan which is to achieve the important goal of ensuring a fair, effective, and balanced representation of the regional, social, and economic interests within a State. And the further fact is that throughout our history the apportionments of State Legislatures have re-

---

tioned legislature meet only for limited purposes? See *Fortson v. Toombs,* 379 U.S. 621, 85 S.Ct. 598, 13 L.Ed.2d 527 (1965).

d. In addition to *Reynolds,* the Court invalidated apportionments in Colorado, *Lucas v. Forty-Fourth Gen. Assembly,* 377 U.S. 713, 84 S.Ct. 1459, 12 L.Ed.2d 632 (1964); Delaware, *Roman v. Sincock,* 377 U.S. 695, 84 S.Ct. 1449, 12 L.Ed.2d 620; Maryland, *Maryland Comm. for Fair Rep. v. Tawes,* 377 U.S. 656, 84 S.Ct. 1429, 12 L.Ed.2d 595; New York, *WMCA, Inc.*

v. Lomenzo, 377 U.S. 633, 84 S.Ct. 1418, 12 L.Ed.2d 568 (1964); Virginia, *Davis v. Mann,* 377 U.S. 678, 84 S.Ct. 1441, 12 L.Ed.2d 609.

Stewart, J., joined by Clark, dissented in *Lucas* and *Lomenzo* in the opinion partially set out in the text infra. Stewart, J., also dissented in *Davis.* In *Lucas,* Clark, J., stated: "[I]f one house is fairly apportioned by population [then] the people should have some latitude in providing on a rational basis, for representation in the other house."

flected the strongly felt American tradition that the public interest is composed of many diverse interests, and that in the long run it can better be expressed by a medley of component voices than by the majority's monolithic command. [I] think the cases should be decided by application of accepted principles of constitutional adjudication under the Equal Protection Clause [and that] demands but two basic attributes of any plan of state legislative apportionment. First, it demands that, in the light of the State's own characteristics and needs, the plan must be a rational one. Secondly, it demands that the plan must be such as not to permit the systematic frustration of the will of a majority of the electorate of the State. * * *

JUSTICE HARLAN, dissenting [in all the cases decided that day.]

The Court's constitutional discussion [is] remarkable [for] its failure to address itself at all to the Fourteenth Amendment as a whole or to the legislative history of the Amendment pertinent to the matter at hand. [I] am unable to understand the Court's utter disregard of [§ 2 of the fourteenth amendment], which expressly recognizes the States' power to deny "or in any way" abridge the right of their inhabitants to vote for "the members of the [State] Legislature," and its express provision of a remedy for such denial or abridgement. The comprehensive scope of the second section and its particular reference to the state legislatures precludes the suggestion that the first section was intended to have the result reached by the [Court].

The history of the adoption of the Fourteenth Amendment provides conclusive evidence that neither those who proposed nor those who ratified the Amendment believed that the Equal Protection Clause limited the power of the States to apportion their legislatures as they saw fit. Moreover, the history demonstrates that the intention to leave this power undisturbed was deliberate and was widely believed to be essential to the adoption of the Amendment.[e] [N]ote should [also] be taken of the Fifteenth and Nineteenth Amendments. [If] constitutional amendment was the only means by which all men and, later, women, could be guaranteed the right to vote at all, even for *federal* officers, how can it be that the far less obvious right to a particular kind of apportionment of *state* legislatures—a right to which is opposed a far more plausible conflicting interest of the State than the interest which opposes the general right to vote—can be conferred by judicial construction of the Fourteenth Amendment?

[The] consequence of today's decision is that in all but the handful of States which may already satisfy the new requirements the [courts] are given blanket authority and the constitutional duty to supervise apportionment of the State Legislatures. It is difficult to imagine a more intolerable and inappropriate interference by the judiciary with the independent legislatures of the States. [No]

---

e. For refutation of Harlan, J.'s lengthy historical argument, see William Van Alstyne, *The Fourteenth Amendment, The "Right" to Vote, and the Understanding of the Thirty-Ninth Congress,* 1965 Sup.Ct.Rev. 33; Edward Goldberg, *Mr. Justice Harlan, The Uses of History, and the Congressional Globe,* 15 J.Pub.L. 181 (1966).

Consider Carl Auerbach, *The Reapportionment Cases: One Person, One Vote—One Vote, One Value,* 1964 Sup.Ct.Rev. 1, 31–34, 77–78: "To accept Mr. Justice Harlan's view would lead to the astonishing result that—apart from the complicated and never-used remedy provid-

ed by the second section of the Fourteenth Amendment—neither the federal courts, nor Congress under the fifth section, could act to prevent a state from denying the right to vote in a state or local election to a class of citizens, otherwise qualified to vote by state law, for reasons which have nothing to do with race, color, or previous condition of servitude, but which nevertheless result in an arbitrary classification, e.g., because the citizens disfranchised are residents of a particular county or because they migrated into the state from outside the state."

set of standards can guide a court which has to decide how many legislative districts a State shall have, or what the shape of the districts shall be, [or] whether a State should have single-member districts or multi-member districts or some combination of both. No such standard can control the balance between keeping up with population shifts and having stable districts. In all these respects, the courts will be called upon to make particular decisions with respect to which a principle of equally populated districts will be of no assistance whatsoever. * * *

Although the Court—necessarily, as I believe—provides only generalities in elaboration of its main thesis, its opinion nevertheless fully demonstrates how far removed these problems are from fields of judicial competence. Recognizing that "indiscriminate districting" is an invitation to "partisan gerrymandering," the Court nevertheless excludes virtually every basis for the formation of electoral districts other than "indiscriminate districting." In one or another of today's opinions, the Court declares it unconstitutional for a State to give effective consideration to any of the following in establishing legislative districts: (1) history; (2) "economic or other sorts of group interests"; (3) area; (4) geographical considerations; (5) a desire "to insure effective representation for sparsely settled areas"; (6) "availability of access of citizens to their representatives"; (7) theories of bicameralism (except those approved by the Court); (8) occupation; (9) "an attempt to balance urban and rural power"; (10) the preference of a majority of voters in the State. So far as presently appears, the *only* factor which a State may consider, apart from numbers, is political subdivisions. But even "a clearly rational state policy" recognizing this factor is unconstitutional if "population is submerged as the controlling consideration * * *."

I know of no principle of logic or practical or theoretical politics, still less any constitutional principle, which establishes all or any of these exclusions. [L]egislators can represent their electors only by speaking for their interests—economic, social, political—many of which do reflect the place where the electors live. The Court does not establish, or indeed even attempt to make a case for the proposition that conflicting interests within a State can only be adjusted by disregarding them when voters are grouped for purposes of [representation].

[The] Constitution is not a panacea for every blot upon the public welfare, nor [does] this Court [serve] its high purpose when it exceeds its authority, even to satisfy justified impatience with the slow workings of the political [process.] [f]

Notes and Questions

1. *Results.* By mid-1968, "congressional district lines were redrawn in thirty-seven states"; "only nine states had any district with a population deviation in excess of ten per cent from the state average, while twenty-four states had no deviation as large as five per cent from the state norm"; every state legislature "had made some adjustment, and it seemed probable that more than thirty of the state legislatures satisfied any reasonable interpretation of the equal-population principle." Robert McKay, *Reapportionment: Success Story of the Warren Court,* 67 Mich.L.Rev. 223, 229 (1968). A number of studies—as to the impact of reapportionment on state policy and the extent to which reapportioned legislatures are more likely than malapportioned ones to expend funds, be responsive to urban needs and have a competitive political system—have arrived at conflicting

f. A week later, the Court invalidated apportionments in nine additional states. The opinions begin at 378 U.S. 553, 84 S.Ct. 1904, 12 L.Ed.2d 1033. For thoughtful pre-*Reynolds* commentaries on apportionment standards, see William Lockhart, Yale Kamisar & Jesse Choper, *Constitutional Law: Cases—Comments—Questions* 1318 (3d. ed. 1970).

conclusions. For a collection and appraisal, see Alexander Bickel, *The Effects of Malapportionment in the States—A Mistrial,* in Reapportionment in the 1970's 151 (Nelson Polsby ed. 1971); Jesse Choper, *Consequences of Supreme Court Decisions Upholding Individual Constitutional Rights,* 83 Mich.L.Rev. 1, 90–94 (1984). But consider Pamela Karlan, *The Rights To Vote: Some Pessimism about Formalism,* 71 Tex.L.Rev. 1705, 1705 (1993): "Chief Justice Warren called *Reynolds v. Sims* his most important opinion 'because it insured that henceforth elections would reflect the collective public interest—embodied in the "one-man, one-vote" standard—rather than the machinations of special interests.' Measured against that ambition, *Reynolds* has been a spectacular failure. Advances in the technology of districting have stripped the substantive principles of one-person, one-vote of any real constraining force."

2. *High vote requirements.* GORDON v. LANCE, 403 U.S. 1, 91 S.Ct. 1889, 29 L.Ed.2d 273 (1971), per BURGER, C.J., upheld a West Virginia rule that forbade political subdivisions from incurring bonded indebtedness or increasing tax rates beyond designated limits without 60% approval in a referendum: "The defect [in *Gray v. Sanders* and *Cipriano v. Houma,* Part B infra] lay in the denial or dilution of voting power because of group characteristics—geographic location and property ownership—that bore no valid relation to the interest of those groups in the subject matter of the [election]. In contrast we can discern no independently identifiable group or category that favors bonded indebtedness over other forms of financing. Consequently no sector of the population may be said to be 'fenced out' from the franchise because of the way they will vote. [T]here is nothing in the language of the Constitution, our history or our cases that requires that a majority always prevail on every issue. [The] Constitution itself provides that a simple majority vote is insufficient on some issues [and] the Bill of Rights removes entire areas of legislation from the concept of majoritarian supremacy. * * * [6] " [g] Do you agree that in *Lance* "no independently identifiable group" was "fenced out"? See J. Harvie Wilkinson, *The Supreme Court, the Equal Protection Clause, and the Three Faces of Constitutional Equality,* 61 Va.L.Rev. 945, 972–75 (1975). After *Lance,* may a state require a 60% *legislative* vote to establish any public transit system? To enact laws affecting designated counties? Does *Lance* logically (constitutionally) extend to the situations in its fn. 6? May a state require a 60% vote to unseat any incumbent?

3. *Permissible population deviation.* The Court has permitted considerably less deviation from the one person one vote requirement for congressional districts than for state and local [h] elections. KARCHER v. DAGGETT, 462 U.S. 725, 103

---

6. We intimate no view on the constitutionality of a provision requiring unanimity or giving a veto power to a very small group. Nor do we decide whether a State [may] require extraordinary majorities for the election of public officers.

g. Harlan, J., concurred in the result. Brennan and Marshall, JJ., dissented.

h. *Avery v. Midland County,* 390 U.S. 474, 88 S.Ct. 1114, 20 L.Ed.2d 45 (1968) held that *Reynolds* applied to a county body with "general responsibility and power for local affairs" but left open the status of special purpose units of government "affecting definable groups of constituents more than other[s]." See also *Hadley v. Junior College Dist.,* 397 U.S. 50, 90 S.Ct. 791, 25 L.Ed.2d 45 (1970)

(extending *Avery* to junior college district). But cf. *Sailors v. Board of Educ.,* 387 U.S. 105, 87 S.Ct. 1549, 18 L.Ed.2d 650 (1967) (constitutional to permit school boards of component districts to select school board even though component districts served unequal populations); *Dusch v. Davis,* 387 U.S. 112, 87 S.Ct. 1554, 18 L.Ed.2d 656 (1967) (constitutional for city to require in at large elections for its legislative body that some candidates come from districts varying widely in population); *Wells v. Edwards,* 409 U.S. 1095, 93 S.Ct. 904, 34 L.Ed.2d 679 (1973) (summarily affirmed provisions for election of state supreme court judges from districts established without regard to population).

In connection with *Wells,* consider Note, 47 Notre Dame Law. 316, 326–27 (1971): "Some

S.Ct. 2653, 77 L.Ed.2d 133 (1983), per BRENNAN, J., invalidated a percentage deviation in New Jersey's congressional districts of 0.7%. But justifiable deviations were not ruled out: "Any number of consistently applied legislative policies might justify some ['minor population deviations'], including, for instance, making districts compact, respecting municipal boundaries, preserving the cores of prior districts, [preserving voting strength of racial minorities], and avoiding contests between incumbent Representatives. [The] state must, however, show with some specificity that a particular objective required the specific deviations in its plan rather than simply relying on general assertions [as here]." [i] On the other hand, GAFFNEY v. CUMMINGS, 412 U.S. 735, 93 S.Ct. 2321, 37 L.Ed.2d 298 (1973), per WHITE, J., held that a Connecticut state legislative reapportionment with a maximum deviation of 7.83% was "insignificant" and "required no justification by the state." [j]

MAHAN v. HOWELL, 410 U.S. 315, 93 S.Ct. 979, 35 L.Ed.2d 320 (1973), per REHNQUIST, J., upheld Virginia's state legislative apportionment, which had a maximum percentage deviation from the ideal of "16.4%—[one] district being overrepresented by 6.8% and [another] being underrepresented by 9.6%. [T]he minimum population necessary to elect a majority of the House of Delegates was 49.29%": [k] "In *Kirkpatrick v. Preisler,* 394 U.S. 526, 89 S.Ct. 1225, 22 L.Ed.2d

would argue [that] the entire rationale [of] 'one man, one vote' is to achieve maximum institutional responsiveness and that by common agreement judges need not be responsive to the popular will or whim and therefore the rule has no applicability to them. [But this would] overlook the more basic concept of political equality which underlies [*Reynolds*], namely, that irrespective of the elective office involved, full and effective citizenship requires that each man's vote count the same. It should also be noted that a requirement of equal judicial districts in no way implies that the judges elected from those districts need be responsive."

i. White, J., joined by Burger, C.J., Powell and Rehnquist, JJ., dissented.

j. Brennan, J., joined by Douglas and Marshall, JJ., dissented.

White v. Regester, 412 U.S. 755, 93 S.Ct. 2332, 37 L.Ed.2d 314 (1973) (similarly divided), used the same analysis as *Gaffney* to uphold a Texas apportionment in which "the total variation between largest and smallest district" was 9.9%—although "very likely larger differences would not be tolerable without qualification."

More recently, *Brown v. Thomson,* 462 U.S. 835, 103 S.Ct. 2690, 77 L.Ed.2d 214 (1983), per Powell, J., upheld Wyoming's allocation of one seat in its House of Representatives to its least populous county, resulting in a maximum deviation of 89%. The Court emphasized that "appellants deliberately have limited their challenge to the alleged dilution of their voting power resulting from the one representative given to Niobrara County" rather than "the state apportionment plan as a whole."

O'Connor, J., joined by Stevens, J., expressed "the gravest doubts that a statewide legislative

plan with an 85% maximum deviation would survive constitutional scrutiny despite the presence of the State's strong interest in preserving county boundaries. I join the Court's opinion on the understanding that nothing in it suggests that this Court would uphold such a scheme."

Brennan, J., joined by White, Marshall and Blackmun, JJ.,—although "stressing how extraordinarily narrow [the decision] is, and how empty of likely precedential value"—dissented.

k. *Abate v. Mundt,* 403 U.S. 182, 91 S.Ct. 1904, 29 L.Ed.2d 399 (1971) upheld the apportionment of Rockland County, N.Y.'s governing board. Each of the five constituent towns comprised one district and each had at least one representative. The most "underrepresented" district was by 7.1% and the most "overrepresented" by 4.8%—"a total deviation from population equality of 11.9%": "[V]iable local governments may need considerable flexibility [to] meet changing societal needs [and] a desire to preserve the integrity of political subdivisions may justify an apportionment plan which departs from numerical equality. *Reynolds.* [T]hat local legislative bodies frequently have fewer representatives than do their state and national counterparts and that some local legislative districts may have a much smaller population than do congressional and state legislative districts, lend support to the argument that slightly greater percentage deviations may be tolerable for local government [apportionment]." Would (should) the deviation permitted in *Abate* be equally precedential for Los Angeles (Cal.) County with 7,000,000 residents as for Hamilton (N.Y.) County with 4,700 residents? See Note, *Reapportionment—Nine Years into the "Revolution" and Still Struggling,* 70 Mich.L.Rev. 586 (1972).

519 (1969) and *Wells v. Rockefeller,* 394 U.S. 542, 89 S.Ct. 1234, 22 L.Ed.2d 535 (1969), this Court invalidated state reapportionment statutes for federal congressional districts having maximum percentage deviations of 5.97% and 13.1% respectively. [I]t was concluded that [*Wesberry's*] command 'permits only the limited population variances which are unavoidable despite a good-faith effort to achieve absolute equality, or for which justification is shown.'

"[*Reynolds* suggested] more flexibility was constitutionally permissible with respect to state legislative reapportionment than in congressional redistricting. Consideration was given to the fact [that] there is a significantly larger number of seats in state legislative bodies to be distributed within a State than Congressional seats, and that therefore it may be feasible for a State to use political subdivision lines to a greater [extent].[1] * * *

"Neither courts nor legislatures are furnished any specialized calipers which enable them to extract from the general language of the Equal Protection Clause [the] mathematical formula which establishes what range of percentage deviations are permissible, and what are not. [While] this percentage may well approach tolerable limits, we do not believe it exceeds them."

4. *Acres vote, not people.* SALYER LAND CO. v. TULARE LAKE BASIN WATER STORAGE DIST., 410 U.S. 719, 93 S.Ct. 1224, 35 L.Ed.2d 659 (1973), per REHNQUIST, J., upheld California statutes permitting only landowners to vote in "water storage districts" elections and apportioning votes according to the assessed valuation of the land within the districts. These districts planned projects for water acquisition, conservation and distribution; they were empowered to fix charges for use of water in proportion to services rendered; project costs were assessed against land in accordance with benefits accruing to each tract. Appellee district had a population of 77 (including 18 children), most employed by one of four corporations that farmed 85% of the land; there were also about 200 other small landowners; one of the corporations (Boswell Co.) held a majority of the votes.

"[Appellee], although vested with some typical governmental powers,[7] has relatively limited authority." Apart from water,[8] "it [does] not exercise what might be thought of as 'normal governmental' authority, [and] its actions disproportionately affect landowners" because of the method of allocating project costs and service charges. "In short, there is no way that the economic burdens of district operations can fall on residents qua residents, and the operations of the districts primarily affect the land within their boundaries." Thus, relying on the language of *Avery* and *Hadley* [p. 1337 supra] that some elections might not come within the doctrine in *Reynolds* and *Kramer,* "we conclude that [appellee], by reason of its special limited purpose and of the disproportionate effect of its activities on landowners as a group, is the sort of exception to the [rule] contemplated."

---

1. See also Douglas Hobbs, *Book Review,* 16 U.C.L.A.L.Rev. 659, 682 (1969): "[C]ongressmen are assumed to represent the state as a whole as well as their district; state legislators, on the other hand, are expected to be more parochial. Therefore, there is arguably a better case on the state [level] for allowing deviation based on local communities of interest. In addition, on the state level population variations in one house can be compensated for in the other. This [is] impossible in congressional districting."

7. The board [can] condemn private property [and] cooperate (including contract) with other agencies, state and federal. Both general obligations bonds and interest-bearing warrants may be authorized.

8. Appellants strongly urge that districts [engage] in flood control activities [but these] are incident to the exercise of the district's primary functions of water storage and distribution.

Thus, the franchise restriction is valid unless " 'wholly irrelevant to achievement of the regulation's objectives.' No doubt residents within the district may be affected by its activities. But [California] could quite reasonably have concluded that the number of landowners and owners of sufficient amounts of acreage whose consent was necessary to organize the district would not have subjected their land to the lien of its possibly very substantial assessments unless they had a dominant voice in its control." [b] As to appellants' "reliance on the various decisions of this Court holding that wealth has no relation to resident-voter qualifications," because "the benefits and burdens to each landowner in the District are in proportion to the assessed value of the land," "we cannot say that the California legislative decision to permit voting in the same proportion is not rationally based." [c]

Douglas, J., joined by Brennan and Marshall, JJ., dissented: In the past, floods were averted by storing water in Buena Vista Lake. "But that was not done in the great 1969 flood" because the board—"dominated [by] Boswell Co.— voted 6–4 to table the motion" because it had an "agricultural lease in the Buena Vista Lake Basin and flooding it would have interfered" with its crops. As a result, the residence of one of the non-landowner appellants "was 15½ feet below the water level of the crest of the flood." "Measured by the *Hadley* test," the district "surely performs 'important governmental functions' which 'have sufficient impact throughout the district' to justify the application of the *Avery* principle. [The] result [here] is a corporate political kingdom undreamed of [by] our Constitution."

5. BURNS v. RICHARDSON, 384 U.S. 73, 86 S.Ct. 1286, 16 L.Ed.2d 376 (1966), per BRENNAN, J., upheld a Hawaii plan that used *registered voters* as the population base, which, "probably because of uneven distribution of military residents—largely unregistered," produced results significantly different than if total population figures had been used: States are not "required to include aliens, transients, short-term or temporary residents, or persons denied the vote for conviction of crime in the apportionment [base]. The decision to include or exclude any such group involves choices about the nature of representation with which we have been shown no constitutionally founded reason to interfere. [But use] of a registered voter or actual voter basis [is] susceptible to improper influences by which those in political power might be able to perpetuate underrepresentation of groups constitutionally entitled to participate in the electoral [process]. [W]e hold that the present apportionment satisfies the Equal Protection Clause only because on this record it was found to have produced a distribution of legislators not substantially different from that which would have

b. Compare Note, 72 Mich.L.Rev. 868, 893–94 (1974): "[W]hether a unit provides an unusual or specialized service should not be determinative. [The] critical question is, rather, whether the impact on the citizens is so uniform that each citizen should participate equally in political decision-making. [*Salyer*] posed the choice as between a unit with specialized powers and disproportionate effects and a unit with general powers and equalized effects and ignored the possibility of a unit with specialized powers but equalized effects."

c. Compare 87 Harv.L.Rev. 100–01 (1973): "[*Salyer*] merely found that landowners were

disproportionately affected 'as a group' and made no claim that some landowners were disproportionately affected relative to other landowners. It is unlikely that disproportionate effects on those within the landowner group could be found, since a large landowner, although assessed more on an absolute basis than a small landowner, receives proportionately larger benefits from district activities." Ball v. James, 451 U.S. 355, 101 S.Ct. 1811, 68 L.Ed.2d 150 (1981) extended *Salyer* to a water district that had become a major supplier of hydroelectric power in the state.

resulted from the use of [state citizen population, which is] a permissible population base."

MOBILE v. BOLDEN

446 U.S. 55, 100 S.Ct. 1490, 64 L.Ed.2d 47 (1980).

JUSTICE STEWART announced the judgment of the Court and delivered an opinion in which THE CHIEF JUSTICE, JUSTICE POWELL, and JUSTICE REHNQUIST join.

The City of Mobile, Ala., has since 1911 been governed by a City Commission consisting of three members elected by the voters of the city at-large. [This] is the same basic electoral system that is followed by literally thousands of municipalities and other local governmental units throughout the Nation.[a]

[The] constitutional objection to multimember districts is not and cannot be that, as such, they depart from apportionment on a population basis in violation of *Reynolds* and its progeny. Rather the focus in such cases has been on the lack of representation multimember districts afford various elements of the voting population in a system of representative legislative democracy. "Criticism [of multimember districts] is rooted in their winner-take-all aspects, their tendency to submerge minorities, [a] general preference for legislatures reflecting community interests as closely as possible and disenchantment with political parties and elections as devices to settle policy differences between contending interests." *Whitcomb v. Chavis*, 403 U.S. 124, 91 S.Ct. 1858, 29 L.Ed.2d 363 (1971).[b]

Despite repeated constitutional attacks upon multimember legislative districts, the Court has consistently held that they are not unconstitutional per se, e.g., *White v. Regester; Whitcomb; Burns v. Richardson; Fortson v. Dorsey*, 379 U.S. 433, 85 S.Ct. 498, 13 L.Ed.2d 401 (1965).[12] We have recognized, however, that such legislative apportionments could violate the Fourteenth Amendment if their purpose were invidiously to minimize or cancel out the voting potential of racial or ethnic minorities. To prove such a purpose it is not enough to show that the group allegedly discriminated against has not elected representatives in proportion to its numbers. A plaintiff must prove that the disputed plan was "conceived or operated as [a] purposeful device[] to further racial discrimination." *Whitcomb*.

---

a. Consider Samuel Issacharoff, *Polarized Voting and the Political Process: The Transformation of Voting Rights Jurisprudence,* 90 Mich.L.Rev. 1833, 1839–40: "The widespread use of multimember electoral systems dates from the turn of the century, when an unusual alliance of northern Progressives and southern Redeemers endeavored to curtail the ability of community-based political machines, depicted pejoratively as ward heelers, to deliver the spoils of power to their local political bases. By eliminating the local bases of voting power of, respectively, urban working-class ethnics and freed slaves, the turn-of-the-century reformers hoped to centralize political power through the use of at-large and multimember election devices. These election schemes allow for serial voting that, in the context of a major-

ity voting bloc, will reward a cohesive majority with superordinate representation."

b. On the issue generally, see John Banzhaf, *Multi-Member Electoral Districts—Do They Violate the "One Man, One Vote" Principle,* 75 Yale L.J. 1309 (1966); Walter Carpeneti, *Legislative Apportionment: Multi-member Districts and Fair Representation,* 120 U.Pa. L.Rev. 666 (1972); Laurence Tribe, *American Constitutional Law* 750 (1978).

12. We have made clear, however, that a court in formulating an apportionment [plan] should, as a general rule, not permit multimember legislative districts. * * * *Connor v. Finch.* [See *Wise v. Lipscomb,* 437 U.S. 535, 98 S.Ct. 2493, 57 L.Ed.2d 411 (1978), on whether a reapportionment plan was "court-devised" or "legislatively enacted."]

This burden of proof is simply one aspect of the basic principle that only if there is purposeful discrimination can there be a violation of [equal protection]. See *Washington v. Davis; Arlington Heights; Personnel Adm'r v. Feeney,* [Sec. 2, III supra]. Although dicta may be drawn from a few of the Court's earlier opinions suggesting that disproportionate effects alone may establish a claim of unconstitutional racial vote dilution, the fact is that such a view is not supported by any decision of this Court.[13] More importantly, such a view is not consistent with the meaning of the Equal Protection Clause as it has been understood in a variety of other contexts involving alleged racial discrimination. *Davis* (employment); *Arlington Heights* (zoning); *Keyes,* [Sec. 2, IV supra] (public schools); *Akins v. Texas,* 325 U.S. 398, 65 S.Ct. 1276, 89 L.Ed. 1692 (1945) (jury selection).

In only one case has the Court sustained a claim that multimember legislative districts unconstitutionally diluted the voting strength of a discrete group. [*Regester*] upheld a constitutional challenge by Negroes and Mexican-Americans to parts of a legislative reapportionment plan adopted by the State of Texas. [T]he Court held that the plaintiffs had been able to "produce evidence to support the finding that the political processes leading to nomination and election were not equally open to participation by the group[s] in question." In so holding, the Court relied upon evidence in the record that included a long history of official discrimination against minorities as well as indifference to their needs and interests on the part of white elected officials. * * *

Regester is thus consistent with "the basic equal protection principle that the invidious quality of a law claimed to be racially discriminatory must ultimately be traced to a racially discriminatory purpose." [But] where the character of a law is readily explainable on grounds apart from race, as would nearly always be true where, as here, an entire system of local governance is brought into question, disproportionate impact alone cannot be decisive, and courts must look to other evidence to support a finding of discriminatory purpose. [I]t is clear that the evidence in the present case fell far short of showing that the appellants "conceived or operated [a] purposeful device[ ] to further racial discrimination." *Whitcomb.*

[T]he District Court [affirmed by the Court of Appeals] based its conclusion of unconstitutionality primarily on the fact that no Negro had ever been elected to the City Commission, apparently because of the pervasiveness of racially polarized voting in Mobile. The trial court also found that city officials had not been as responsive to the interests of Negroes as to those of white persons. On the basis of these findings, the court concluded that the political processes in Mobile were not equally open to Negroes, despite its seemingly inconsistent findings that there were no inhibitions against Negroes becoming candidates, and that in fact Negroes had registered and voted without hindrance. * * *

First, [i]t may be that Negro candidates have been defeated, but that fact alone does not work a constitutional deprivation.

---

13. The dissenting opinion of Mr. Justice Marshall reads the Court's opinion in *Dorsey* to say that a claim of vote dilution under the Equal Protection Clause could rest on either discriminatory purpose or effect. [Although] the Court recognized that "designedly or otherwise," multimember districting schemes might, under the circumstances of a particular case, minimize the voting strength of a racial group, an issue as to the constitutionality of such an arrangement "[w]as not [presented]."

The phrase "designedly or otherwise" [was] repeated, also in dictum, in *Burns.* But the constitutional challenge to the multimember constituencies failed in that case because the plaintiffs demonstrated neither discriminatory purpose nor effect.

Second, [evidence] of discrimination by white officials in Mobile is relevant only as the most tenuous and circumstantial evidence of the constitutional invalidity of the electoral system under which they attained their offices.

Third, the District Court and the Court of Appeals supported their conclusion by drawing upon the substantial history of official racial discrimination in Alabama. But past discrimination cannot, in the manner of original sin, condemn governmental action that is not itself unlawful. The ultimate question remains whether a discriminatory intent has been proved in a given [case].

Finally, the District Court and the Court of Appeals pointed to the mechanics of the at-large electoral system itself as proof that the votes of Negroes were being invidiously canceled out. But those features of that electoral system, such as the majority vote requirement, tend naturally to disadvantage any voting minority [and] are far from proof that the at-large electoral scheme represents purposeful discrimination against Negro voters.

We turn finally [to] Justice Marshall's dissenting opinion. The theory [appears] to be that every "political group," or at least every such group that is in the minority, has a federal constitutional right to elect candidates in proportion to its numbers.[22] Moreover, a political group's "right" to have its candidates elected is said to be a "fundamental interest," the infringement of which may be established without proof that a State has acted with the purpose of impairing anybody's access to the political process. This dissenting opinion finds the "right" infringed [because] no Negro has been elected to the Mobile City Commission.

Whatever appeal the dissenting opinion's view may have as a matter of political theory, it is not the law.[c] The Equal Protection Clause [does] not require proportional representation as an imperative of political organization.   * * *

It is of course true that a law that impinges upon a fundamental right explicitly or implicitly secured by the Constitution is presumptively unconstitutional. See *Shapiro v. Thompson,* [Part II infra]. See also *San Antonio Ind. School Dist. v. Rodriguez,* [Part IV infra]. But plainly "[i]t is not the province of this Court to create substantive constitutional rights in the name of guaranteeing equal protection of the laws," id. [In] *Whitcomb,* the trial court had found that a multimember state legislative district had invidiously deprived Negroes and poor persons of rights guaranteed them by the Constitution, notwithstanding the absence of any evidence whatever of discrimination against them. Reversing the trial court, this Court said: "The District Court's holding, although on the facts of this case limited to guaranteeing one racial group representation, is not easily

22. The dissenting opinion seeks to disclaim this description of its theory by suggesting that a claim of vote dilution may require, in addition to proof of electoral defeat, some evidence of "historical and social factors" indicating that the group in question is without political influence. Putting to the side the evident fact that these gauzy sociological considerations have no constitutional basis, it remains far from certain that they could, in any principled manner, exclude the claims of any discrete political group that happens, for whatever reason, to elect fewer of its candidates than arithmetic indicates it might. Indeed, the putative limits are bound to prove illusory if the express purpose informing their application would be, as the dissent assumes, to re-

dress the "inequitable distribution of political influence."

c. Consider Aviam Soifer, *Complacency and Constitutional Law,* 42 Ohio St.L.J. 383, 389–90 (1981): "It is forgotten, but not insignificant, that the group that Justice Stone identified first in his *Carolene Products* footnote as in need of special judicial concern were those persons without sufficient access to 'those political processes which can ordinarily be expected to bring about *repeal* of undesirable legislation.' That legislation already on the books might be particularly difficult to repeal seemed obvious and important in 1938. The Court now appears confident that, as a constitutional matter, whatever law is in place ought to remain there."

contained. It is expressive of the more general proposition that any group with distinctive interests must be represented in legislative halls if it is numerous enough to command at least one seat and represents a majority living in an area sufficiently compact to constitute a single-member district. This approach would make it difficult to reject claims of Democrats, Republicans, or members of any political [organization]. There are also union oriented workers, the university community, religious or ethnic groups occupying identifiable areas of our hetero-geneous cities and urban areas. Indeed, it would be difficult for a great many, if not most, multi-member districts to survive analysis under the District Court's view unless combined with some voting arrangement such as proportional repre-sentation or cumulative voting aimed at providing representation for minority parties or interests. At the very least, affirmance [would] spawn endless litigation concerning the multi-member district systems now widely employed in this country." * * *

JUSTICE BLACKMUN, concurring in the result.

Assuming that proof of intent is a prerequisite to appellees' prevailing on their constitutional claim of vote dilution, I am inclined to agree with Mr. Justice White that, in this case, "the findings of the District Court amply support an inference of purposeful discrimination." I concur in the Court's judgment of reversal, however, because I believe that the relief afforded appellees by the District Court [ordering a new form of government "of a Mayor and a City Council with members elected from single-member districts"] was not commensu-rate with the sound exercise of judicial discretion. * * *

JUSTICE STEVENS, concurring in the judgment.

[While] I agree with Mr. Justice Stewart that no violation of respondents' constitutional rights has been demonstrated, my analysis of the issue proceeds along somewhat different lines.

[T]his case draws into question a political structure that treats all individuals as equals but adversely affects the political strength of a racially identifiable group. Although I am satisfied that such a structure may be challenged under the Fifteenth Amendment as well as under the Equal Protection Clause of the Fourteenth Amendment, I believe that under either provision it must be judged by a standard that allows the political process to function effectively. * * *

[No] case decided by this Court establishes a constitutional right to propor-tional representation for racial minorities. What *Gomillion* [Sec. 2, III supra] holds is that a sufficiently "uncouth" or irrational racial gerrymander violates the Fifteenth Amendment. [The] fact that the "gerrymander" condemned in *Gomil-lion* was equally vulnerable under both Amendments indicates that the essential holding of that case is applicable, not merely to gerrymanders directed against racial minorities, but to those aimed at religious, ethnic, economic and political groups as well.[7]

---

7. [See], e.g., *Whitcomb* (districts that are "conceived or operated as purposeful devices to further racial *or economic* discrimination" are prohibited by the Fourteenth Amendment) (emphasis supplied); *Dorsey* (an apportion-ment scheme would be invalid [if] it "oper-ate[d] to minimize or cancel out the voting strength of racial *or political* elements of the voting population") (emphasis supplied).

[For the view that the right to "effective political representation" should be limited to racial groups under the fifteenth amendment and thus "avoid an uncontrolled expansion of the effectiveness principle to countless interest groups," see Note, *United Jewish Organiza-tions v. Carey and the Need to Recognize Aggre-gate Voting Rights,* 87 Yale L.J. 571 (1978).]

My conclusion that the same standard should be applied to racial groups as is applied to other groups leads me also to conclude that the standard cannot condemn every adverse impact on one or more political groups without spawning more dilution litigation than the judiciary can manage. [N]othing comparable to the mathematical yardstick used in apportionment cases is available to identify the difference between permissible and impermissible adverse impacts on the voting strength of political groups. * * *

In my view, the proper standard is suggested by three characteristics of the gerrymander condemned in *Gomillion:* (1) the 28-sided configuration [was] manifestly not the product of a routine or a traditional political decision; (2) it had a significant adverse impact on a minority group; and (3) it was unsupported by any neutral justification and thus was either totally irrational or entirely motivated by a desire to curtail the political strength of the minority. These characteristics suggest that a proper test should focus on the objective effects of the political decision rather than the subjective motivation of the decisionmaker. In this case, if the commission form of government in Mobile were extraordinary, or if it were nothing more than a vestige of history, with no greater justification than the grotesque figure in *Gomillion*, it would surely violate the Constitution. That conclusion would follow simply from its adverse impact on black voters plus the absence of any legitimate justification for the system, without reference to the subjective intent of the political body that has refused to alter it.

Conversely, I am also persuaded that a political decision that affects group voting rights may be valid even if it can be proved that irrational or invidious factors have played some part in its enactment or retention. The standard for testing the acceptability of such a decision must take into account the fact that the responsibility for drawing political boundaries is generally committed to the legislative process and that the process inevitably involves a series of compromises among different group interests. If the process is to work, it must reflect an awareness of group interests and it must tolerate some attempts to advantage or to disadvantage particular segments of the voting populace. [Accordingly], a political decision that is supported by valid and articulable justifications cannot be invalid simply because some participants in the decisionmaking process were motivated by a purpose to disadvantage a minority group.

The decision to retain the commission form of government in Mobile, Ala., is such a decision. [The] fact that these at-large systems characteristically place one or more minority groups at a significant disadvantage in the struggle for political power cannot invalidate all such systems. See *Whitcomb.* Nor can it be the law that such systems are valid when there is no evidence that they were instituted or maintained for discriminatory reasons, but that they may be selectively condemned on the basis of the subjective motivation of some of their supporters. A contrary view "would spawn endless litigation concerning the multimember districts now widely employed in this Country," and would entangle the judiciary in a voracious political thicket.

JUSTICE BRENNAN, dissenting.

I dissent because I agree with Mr. Justice Marshall that proof of discriminatory impact is sufficient in these cases. I also dissent because, even accepting the plurality's premise that discriminatory purpose must be shown, I agree with [Marshall and White, JJ.,] that the appellees have clearly met that burden.

JUSTICE WHITE, dissenting.

[Both] the District Court and the Court of Appeals properly found that an invidious discriminatory purpose could be inferred from the totality of facts in this case. The Court's cryptic rejection of their conclusions ignores the principles that an invidious discriminatory purpose can be inferred from objective factors of the kind relied on in *Regester* and that the trial courts are in a special position to make such intensely local appraisals.

[T]he plurality today rejects the inference of purposeful discrimination apparently because each of the factors relied upon by the courts below is alone insufficient to support the inference. [By] viewing each of the factors relied upon below in isolation, and ignoring the fact that racial bloc voting at the polls makes it impossible to elect a black commissioner under the at-large system, the plurality rejects the "totality of the circumstances" approach we endorsed in *Regester, Davis,* and *Arlington Heights* * * *.

JUSTICE MARSHALL, dissenting. * * *

The Court does not dispute the proposition that multimember districting can have the effect of submerging electoral minorities. [Further], we decided a series of vote-dilution cases under the Fourteenth Amendment that were designed to protect electoral minorities from precisely the combination of electoral laws and historical and social factors found in the present cases.[4] [Although] we have held that multimember districts are not unconstitutional per se, there is simply no basis for the plurality's conclusion that under our prior cases proof of discriminatory intent is a necessary condition for the invalidation of multimember districting.

[Under] this line of cases, an electoral districting plan is invalid if it has the effect of affording an electoral minority "less opportunity [than] other residents in the district to participate in the political processes and to elect legislators of their choice," *Regester*. It is also apparent that the Court in *Regester* considered equal access to the political process as meaning more than merely allowing the minority the opportunity to vote. *Regester* stands for the proposition that an electoral system may not relegate an electoral minority to political impotence by diminishing the importance of its [vote].

The plurality fails to apply the discriminatory effect standard of *Regester* because that approach conflicts with what the plurality takes to be an elementary principle of law. "[O]nly if there is purposeful discrimination," announces the plurality, "can there be a violation of [equal protection]." That proposition [fails] to distinguish between two distinct lines of equal protection decisions: those involving suspect classifications, and those involving fundamental rights. * * *

Under the Equal Protection Clause, if a classification "impinges upon a fundamental right explicitly or implicitly protected by the [Constitution], strict judicial scrutiny" is required, *Rodriguez,* regardless of whether the infringement was intentional. As I will explain, our cases recognize a fundamental right to equal electoral participation that encompasses protection against vote dilution.

---

4. [T]hough municipalities must be accorded some discretion in arranging their affairs, see *Abate,* there is all the more reason to scrutinize assertions that municipal, rather than State, multi-member districting dilutes the vote of an electoral minority: "In statewide elections, it is possible that a large minority group in one multi-member district will be unable to elect any legislators, while in another multi-member district where the same group is a slight majority, they will elect the entire slate of legislators. [In] at-large elections, [t]here is no way to balance out the discrimination against a particular minority group because the entire city is one huge election district. The minority's loss is absolute." Barbara Berry & Thomas Dye, *The Discriminatory Effects of At-Large Elections,* 7 Fla.St.U.L.Rev. 85, 87 (1979). * * *

Proof of discriminatory purpose is, therefore, not required to support a claim of vote dilution.[10] The plurality's erroneous conclusion to the contrary is the result of a failure to recognize the central distinction between *Regester* and *Davis:* the former involved an infringement of a constitutionally protected right, while the latter dealt with a claim of racially discriminatory distribution of an interest to which no citizen has a constitutional entitlement.[11] * * *

Reynolds and its progeny focused solely on the discriminatory *effects* of malapportionment. [In] the present cases, the alleged vote dilution, though caused by the combined effects of the electoral structure and social and historical factors rather than by unequal population distribution, is analytically the same concept: the unjustified abridgement of a fundamental right. It follows, then, that a showing of discriminatory intent is just as unnecessary under the vote-dilution approach adopted in *Dorsey* and applied in *Regester,* as it is under our reapportionment cases. * * *

The plurality's response is that my approach amounts to nothing less than a constitutional requirement of proportional representation for groups. That assertion amounts to nothing more than a red herring.[c] [Appellees] proved that no Negro had ever been elected to the Mobile City Commission, despite the fact that Negroes constitute about one-third of the electorate, and that the persistence of severe racial bloc voting made it highly unlikely that any Negro could be elected at-large in the foreseeable future. Contrary to the plurality's contention, however, I do not find unconstitutional vote dilution in this case simply because of that showing. The plaintiffs convinced the District Court that Mobile Negroes were unable to use alternative avenues of political influence. They showed that Mobile Negroes still suffered pervasive present effects of massive historical official and private discrimination, and that the city commission had been quite unresponsive to the needs of the minority community. Mobile has been guilty of such pervasive racial discrimination in hiring employees that extensive intervention by the Federal District Court has been required. Negroes are grossly underrepresented on city boards and committees. The city's distribution of public services is racially discriminatory. City officials and police were largely unmoved by Negro complaints about police brutality and "mock lynchings." The District Court concluded that "[t]his sluggish and timid response is another manifestation of the low priority given to the needs of the black citizens and of the [commissioners'] political fear of a white backlash vote when black citizens' needs are at stake."

[T]he protection against vote dilution recognized by our prior cases serves as a minimally intrusive guarantee of political survival for a discrete political

---

10. [Although] the right to vote is distinguishable for present purposes from the other fundamental rights our cases have recognized, surely the plurality would not require proof of discriminatory purpose in those cases. The plurality fails to articulate why the right to vote should receive such singular treatment. Furthermore, the plurality refuses to recognize the disutility of requiring proof of discriminatory purpose in fundamental rights cases. For example, it would make no sense to require such a showing when the question is whether a state statute regulating abortion violates the right of personal choice recognized in *Roe v. Wade.* The only logical inquiry is whether, regardless of the legislature's motive, the statute has the effect of infringing that right. See,

e.g., *Planned Parenthood v. Danforth,* [p. 459 supra].

11. [See] also Comment, *Proof of Racially Discriminatory Purpose Under the Equal Protection Clause,* 12 Harv.C.R.–C.L.L.Rev. 725, 758, n. 175 (1977); Note, *Racial Vote Dilution in Multimember Districts: The Constitutional Standard After Washington v. Davis,* 76 Mich. L.Rev. 694, 722–26 (1978); Comment, *Constitutional Challenges to Gerrymanders,* 45 U.Chi. L.Rev. 845, 869–77 (1978). * * *

c. For the view that "PR is the only electoral system that can give equal representation to all groups," see Note, *The Constitutional Imperative of Proportional Representation,* 94 Yale L.J. 163 (1984).

minority that is effectively locked out of governmental decisionmaking processes. So understood, the doctrine hardly " 'create[s] substantive constitutional rights in the name of guaranteeing equal protection of the laws,' " [but] is a simple reflection of the basic principle that the Equal Protection Clause protects "[t]he right of a citizen to equal representation and to have his vote weighted equally with those of all other citizens." *Reynolds*.

[The] plurality's requirement of proof of *intentional discrimination* [may] represent an attempt to bury the legitimate concerns of the minority beneath the soil of a doctrine almost as impermeable as it is specious. If so, the superficial tranquility created by such measures can be but short-lived. If this Court refuses to honor our long-recognized principle that the Constitution "nullifies sophisticated as well as simple-minded modes of discrimination," it cannot expect the victims of discrimination to respect political channels of seeking redress. I dissent.

ROGERS v. LODGE, 458 U.S. 613, 102 S.Ct. 3272, 73 L.Ed.2d 1012 (1982), per WHITE, J., affirmed a decision that the at-large election system for a Georgia county Board of Commissioners violated equal protection: "The District Court [demonstrated] its understanding of the controlling standard by observing that a determination of discriminatory intent is 'a requisite to a finding of unconstitutional vote dilution' [and] concluded that the [system] 'although racially neutral when adopted, is being *maintained* for invidious purposes.' [For] the most part, the District Court dealt with the evidence in terms of the factors [that had been used by the district court in *Mobile*], but as the Court of Appeals stated: 'Judge Alaimo [did] not treat [those factors] as absolute, but rather considered them only to the extent that they were relevant to the question of discriminatory intent.' Although a tenable argument can be made to the contrary, we are not inclined to disagree with the Court of Appeals' conclusion that the District Court applied the proper legal standard. * * *

"The Court of Appeals [stated that the] District Court correctly anticipated *Mobile* and required appellees to prove that the at-large voting system was maintained [a] for a discriminatory purpose. The Court of Appeals also held that the District Court's findings not only were not clearly erroneous, but its conclusion that the at-large system was maintained for invidious purposes was 'virtually mandated by the overwhelming proof.' [This Court has] noted that issues of intent are commonly treated as factual matters [and] has frequently noted its reluctance to disturb findings of fact concurred in by two lower courts."

POWELL, J., joined by Rehnquist, J., dissented: "[T]he Court's opinion cannot be reconciled persuasively with [*Mobile*]. There are some variances in the largely sociological evidence presented in the two cases. But *Mobile* held that this *kind* of evidence was not enough. * * *

"The Court's decision today relies heavily on the capacity of the federal district courts—essentially free from any standards prepounded by this Court—to determine whether at-large voting systems are 'being maintained for the invidious purpose of diluting the voting strength of the black population.' Federal courts thus are invited to engage in deeply subjective inquiries into the motivations of local officials in structuring local governments. Inquiries of this kind not only can

---

a. For commentary on the Court's handling of the intent issue, see C. Edwin Baker, *Outcome Equality or Equality of Respect: The Substantive Content of Equal Protection*, 131 U.Pa. L.Rev. 933, 983–84 (1983).

be 'unseemly,' they intrude the federal courts—with only the vaguest constitutional direction—into an area of intensely local and political concern.

"Emphasizing these considerations, Justice Stevens argues forcefully [that] subjective intent is irrelevant to the establishment of a case of racial vote [dilution].[b] I agree with much of what he says [but] would not accept this view. 'The central purpose of the Equal Protection Clause [is] the prevention of official conduct discriminating on the basis of race.' *Davis.* Because I am unwilling to abandon this central principle in cases of this kind, I cannot join Justice Stevens's opinion. [But] in the absence of proof of discrimination by reliance on the kind of objective factors identified by Justice Stevens, I would hold that the factors cited by the Court of Appeals are too attenuated as a matter of law to support an inference of discriminatory intent." [c]

DAVIS v. BANDEMER

478 U.S. 109, 106 S.Ct. 2797, 92 L.Ed.2d 85 (1986).

[Democrats challenged Indiana's 1981 state apportionment—enacted by Republican majorities in both houses of the legislature and signed by a Republican governor—on the ground that it "constituted a political gerrymander intended to disadvantage Democrats on a statewide basis." A majority of the Court, per White, J.—relying on cases such as *Baker* and *Reynolds* (indicating "the justiciability of claims going to the adequacy of state representation in state legislatures"); *Mobile, Whitcomb, Regester* and *Rogers* ("racial gerrymandering presents a justiciable equal protection claim"); and, particularly, *Gaffney v. Cummings,* [p. 1337 supra],[a]—held that a "political gerrymandering claim [is] justiciable."]

JUSTICE WHITE announced the judgment of the Court and delivered [an] opinion in which JUSTICE BRENNAN, JUSTICE MARSHALL, and JUSTICE BLACKMUN joined * * *.

We [agree] with the District Court that in order to succeed the Bandemer plaintiffs were required to prove both intentional discrimination against an identifiable political group and an actual discriminatory effect on that group. [As] long as redistricting is done by a legislature, it should not be very difficult to prove that the likely political consequences of the reapportionment were intended.[11]

---

b. Stevens, J.'s long dissent expanded his views expressed in *Mobile.*

c. In 1982 Congress amended the Voting Rights Act of 1965, p. 1538 infra, in a manner that has been interpreted to obviate the need for proof of discriminatory purpose.

a. *Gaffney* ruled that the fact "that virtually every Senate and House district line [in Connecticut] was drawn with the conscious intent to create a districting plan that would achieve a rough approximation of the statewide political strengths of the Democratic and Republican Parties, the only two parties in the state large enough to elect legislators from discernible geographic areas" did not invalidate the plan.

11. That discriminatory intent may not be difficult to prove in this context does not, of course, mean that it need not be proved at all to succeed on such a claim. [Would (should) state constitutional speech and debate clause

claims be respected in litigating the issue? For reflection on how the issue might be litigated, see Comment, *Politics and Purpose: Hide and Seek in the Gerrymandering Thicket After Davis v. Bandemer,* 136 U.Pa.L.Rev. 183, 184–85 (1987). See also Dixon, fn. b in *Reynolds* supra, at 322; Richard Engstrom, *The Supreme Court and Equipopulous Gerrymandering: A Remaining Obstacle in the Quest for Fair and Effective Representation,* 1976 Ariz. St.L.J. 277. Cf. Voting Rights Act of 1965, fn. a, (burden of proof on state with respect to changes in districting); Stanley Halpin & Richard Engstrom, *Racial Gerrymandering and Southern State Legislative Districting: Attorney General Determinations Under the Voting Rights Act,* 22 J.Pub.L. 37 (1973). For general commentary on the issue of purpose, see C. Edwin Baker, *Outcome Equality or Equality of Respect: The Substantive Content of Equal Protection,* 131 U.Pa.L.Rev. 933, 972–84 (1983)].

We do not accept, however, the District Court's legal and factual bases for concluding that the 1981 Act visited a sufficiently adverse effect on the appellees' constitutionally protected rights to make out a violation of the Equal Protection Clause. The District Court held that because any apportionment scheme that purposely prevents proportional representation is unconstitutional, Democratic voters need only show that their proportionate voting influence has been adversely affected. Our cases, however, clearly foreclose any claim that the Constitution requires proportional representation or that legislatures in reapportioning must draw district lines to come as near as possible to allocating seats to the contending parties in proportion to what their anticipated statewide vote will be. *Whitcomb; Regester.*

The typical election for legislative seats in the United States is conducted in described geographical districts, with the candidate receiving the most votes in each district winning the seat allocated to that district. If all or most of the districts are competitive, [even] a narrow statewide preference for either party would produce an overwhelming majority for the winning party in the state legislature. This consequence, however, is inherent in winner-take-all, district-based elections, and we cannot hold that such a reapportionment law would violate the Equal Protection Clause because the voters in the losing party do not have representation in the legislature in proportion to the statewide vote received by their party candidates. * * *

In cases involving individual multi-member districts, we have required a substantially greater showing of adverse effects than a mere lack of proportional representation to support a finding of unconstitutional vote dilution. Only where there is evidence that excluded groups have "less opportunity to participate in the political processes and to elect candidates of their choice" have we refused to approve the use of multi-member districts. *Rogers.* See also *United Jewish Orgs. v. Carey; Regester; Whitcomb.* In these cases, we have also noted the lack of responsiveness by those elected to the concerns of the relevant groups. *Rogers; Regester.*[12]

These holdings rest on a conviction that the mere fact that a particular apportionment scheme makes it more difficult for a particular group in a particular district to elect the representatives of its choice does not render that scheme constitutionally infirm. This conviction, in turn, stems from a perception that the power to influence the political process is not limited to winning elections. An individual or a group of individuals who votes for a losing candidate is usually deemed to be adequately represented by the winning candidate and to have as much opportunity to influence that candidate as other voters in the district. We cannot presume in such a situation, without actual proof to the contrary, that the candidate elected will entirely ignore the interests of those voters. This is true even in a safe district where the losing group loses election after election. Thus, a group's electoral power is not unconstitutionally diminished by the simple fact of an appointment scheme that makes winning elections more difficult,[b] and a failure

---

12. Although these cases involved racial groups, we believe that the principles developed in these cases would apply equally to claims by political groups in individual districts. We note, however, that the elements necessary to a successful vote dilution claim may be more difficult to prove in relation to a claim by a political group. For example, historical patterns of exclusion from the political processes, evidence which would support a vote dilution claim, are in general more likely to be present for a racial group than for a political group.

b. Consider Dean Alfange, "*Gerrymandering and the Constitution: Into the Thorns of the Thicket at Last,*" 1986 Sup.Ct.Rev. 175, 245–46: [It undoubtedly] "came as something of a surprise to the Republican National Committee to be told that whether their candidates

of proportional representation alone does not constitute impermissible discrimination under the Equal Protection Clause.

As with individual districts, where unconstitutional vote dilution is alleged in the form of statewide political gerrymandering, the mere lack of proportional representation will not be sufficient to prove unconstitutional discrimination. Again, without specific supporting evidence, a court cannot presume in such a case that those who are elected will disregard the disproportionately under-represented group. Rather, unconstitutional discrimination occurs only when the electoral system is arranged in a manner that will consistently degrade a voter's or a group of voters' influence on the political process as a [whole].

In a challenge to an individual district, this inquiry focuses on the opportunity of members of the group to participate in party deliberations in the slating and nomination of candidates, their opportunity to register and vote, and hence their chance to directly influence the election returns and to secure the attention of the winning candidate. Statewide, however, the inquiry centers on the voters' direct or indirect influence on the elections of the state legislature as a whole. And, as in individual district cases, an equal protection violation may be found only where the electoral system substantially disadvantages certain voters in their opportunity to influence the political process effectively. In this context, such a finding of unconstitutionality must be supported by evidence of continued frustration of the will of a majority of the voters or effective denial to a minority of voters of a fair chance to influence the political process.

Based on these views, we would reject the District Court's apparent holding that *any* interference with an opportunity to elect a representative of one's choice would be sufficient to allege or make out an equal protection violation, unless justified by some acceptable state interest that the State would be required to demonstrate. [S]uch a low threshold for legal action would invite attack on all or almost all reapportionment statutes. District-based elections hardly ever produce a perfect fit between votes and representation. [Inviting] attack on minor departures from some supposed norm would too much embroil the judiciary in second-guessing what has consistently been referred to as a political task for the legislature * * *.

The view that a prima facie case of illegal discrimination in reapportionment requires a showing of more than a *de minimis* effect is not unprecedented. Reapportionment cases involving the one person, one vote principle [provide] support for such a requirement. In the present, considerably more complex context, it is also appropriate to require allegations and proof that the challenged legislative plan has had or will have effects that are sufficiently serious to require intervention by the federal courts in state reapportionment decisions.

---

are able to win elections is not essentially relevant to the question whether they have been victims of a gerrymander."

But consider Daniel Lowenstein, *Bandemer's Gap: Gerrymandering and Equal Protection,* in Toward Fair and Effective Representation 64 (Groffman ed. 1990): "As Professor Alfange acknowledges, it makes an enormous difference to a minority group whether their representatives regard them as 'enemies to be overcome or as constituents to be wooed in the next election.' Democrats represented by Republican legislators ordinarily fall within the latter category. Blacks, communists, and homosexuals are examples of groups that have sometimes fallen within the former category. If the plurality opinion is read as contemplating an action brought by a group suffering from that sort of discriminatory treatment, Justice White's statement about representation for supporters of losing candidates is not bewildering [at] all." For the contention that the plurality engages in a suspect classifications' analysis (not fundamental rights) and that the likely beneficiaries, if any, would not be major parties, see id.

The District Court's findings do not satisfy this threshold condition to stating and proving a cause of action. In reaching its conclusion, the District Court relied primarily on the results of the 1982 elections: Democratic candidates for the State House of Representatives had received 51.9% of the votes cast statewide and Republican candidates 48.1%; yet, out of the 100 seats to be filled, Republican candidates won 57 and Democrats 43. In the Senate, 53.1% of the votes were cast for Democratic candidates and 46.9% for Republicans; of the 25 Senate seats to be filled, Republicans won 12 and Democrats 13. The court also relied upon the use of multi-member districts in Marion and Allen counties, where Democrats or those inclined to vote Democratic in 1982 amounted to 46.6% of the population of those counties but Republicans won 86 percent—18 of 21—seats allocated to the districts in those counties. These disparities were enough to require a neutral justification by the State, which in the eyes of the District Court was not forthcoming.[15]

Relying on a single election to prove unconstitutional discrimination is unsatisfactory. The District Court observed, and the parties do not disagree, that Indiana is a swing State. Voters sometimes prefer Democratic candidates, and sometimes Republican. The District Court did not find that because of the 1981 Act the Democrats could not in one of the next few elections secure a sufficient vote to take control of the assembly. Indeed, the District Court declined to hold that the 1982 election results were the predictable consequences of the 1981 Act and expressly refused to hold that those results were a reliable prediction of future ones. The District Court did not ask by what percentage the statewide Democratic vote would have had to increase to control either the House or the Senate. The appellants argue here, without a persuasive response from appellees, that had the Democratic candidates received an additional few percentage points of the votes cast statewide, they would have obtained a majority of the seats in both houses. Nor was there any finding that the 1981 reapportionment would consign the Democrats to a minority status in the Assembly throughout the 1980's or that the Democrats would have no hope of doing any better in the reapportionment that would occur after the 1990 census. Without findings of this nature, the District Court erred in concluding that the 1981 Act violated the Equal Protection Clause.

The District Court's discussion of the multi-member districts created by the 1981 Act does not undermine this conclusion. For the purposes of the statewide political gerrymandering claim, these districts appear indistinguishable from safe Republican and safe Democratic single-member districts. Simply showing that there are multi-member districts in the State and that those districts are constructed so as to be safely Republican or Democratic in no way bolsters the contention that there has been *statewide* discrimination against Democratic voters. It could be, were the necessary threshold effect to be shown, that multi-member districts could be demonstrated to be suspect on the ground that they are

---

15. The District Court apparently thought that the political group suffering discrimination was all those voters who voted for Democratic Assembly candidates in 1982. Judge Pell, in dissent, argued that the allegedly disfavored group should be defined as those voters who could be counted on to vote Democratic from election to election, thus excluding those who vote the Republican ticket from time to time. He would have counted the true believers by averaging the Democratic vote cast in two different elections for those statewide of-fices for which party-line voting is thought to be the rule and personality and issue-oriented factors are relatively unimportant. Although accepting Judge Pell's definition of Democratic voters would have strongly suggested that the 1981 reapportionment had no discriminatory effect at all, there was no response to his position. The appellees take up the challenge in this Court, claiming that Judge Pell chose the wrong election years for the purpose of averaging the Democratic votes. The dispute need not now be resolved.

particularly useful in attaining impermissibly discriminatory ends; at this stage of the inquiry, however, the multi-member district evidence does not materially aid the appellees' case. * * *

In response to our approach, Justice Powell suggests an alternative method for evaluating equal protection claims of political gerrymandering. In his view, courts should look at a number of factors in considering these claims: the nature of the legislative procedures by which the challenged redistricting was accomplished and the intent behind the redistricting; the shapes of the districts and their conformity with political subdivision boundaries; and "evidence concerning population disparities and statistics tending to show vote dilution." [T]he crux of Justice Powell's analysis seems to be that—at least in some cases—the intentional drawing of district boundaries for partisan ends and for no other reason violates the Equal Protection Clause in and of itself. We disagree, however, with this conception of a constitutional violation. Specifically, even if a state legislature redistricts with the specific intention of disadvantaging one political party's election prospects, we do not believe that there has been an unconstitutional discrimination against members of that party unless the redistricting does in fact disadvantage it at the polls.

Moreover, as we discussed above, a mere lack of proportionate results in one election cannot suffice in this regard. [E]qual protection violations may be found only where a history (actual or projected) of disproportionate results appears in conjunction with ["strong indicia of lack of political power and the denial of fair representation."] The mere lack of control of the General Assembly after a single election does not rise to the requisite level. [But] Justice Powell's view would allow a constitutional violation to be found where the only proven effect on a political party's electoral power was disproportionate results in one (or possibly two) elections. * * *

In rejecting Justice Powell's approach, we do not mean to intimate that the factors he considers are entirely irrelevant. The election results obviously are relevant to a showing of the effects required to prove a political gerrymandering claim under our view. And the district configurations may be combined with vote projections to predict future election results, which are also relevant to the effects showing. The other factors, even if not relevant to the effects issue, might well be relevant to an equal protection claim. The equal protection argument would proceed along the following lines: If there were a discriminatory effect and a discriminatory intent, then the legislation would be examined for valid underpinnings. Thus, evidence of exclusive legislative process and deliberate drawing of district lines in accordance with accepted gerrymandering principles would be relevant to intent, and evidence of valid and invalid configuration would be relevant to whether the districting plan met legitimate state interests.

This course is consistent with our equal protection cases generally and is the course we follow here: We assumed that there was discriminatory intent, found that there was insufficient discriminatory effect to constitute an equal protection violation,[19] and therefore did not reach the question of the state interests (legitimate or otherwise) served by the particular districts as they were created by the legislature. Consequently, the valid or invalid configuration of the districts was an issue we did not need to consider.

19. In most equal protection cases, it is true, a discriminatory effect will be readily apparent, and no heightened effect will be re-quired, but that is the only real difference between this type of equal protection claim and others.

* * * We recognize that our own view may be difficult of application. Determining when an electoral system has been "arranged in a manner that will consistently degrade a voter's or a group of voters' influence on the political process as a whole" is of necessity a difficult inquiry. Nevertheless, we believe that it recognizes the delicacy of intruding on this most political of legislative functions and is at the same time consistent with our prior cases regarding individual multi-member districts, which have formulated a parallel standard. * * *

JUSTICE POWELL, with whom JUSTICE STEVENS joins, concurring [on the issue of justiciability], and dissenting.

[T]he plurality expresses the view, with which I agree, that a partisan political gerrymander violates the Equal Protection Clause only on proof of "both intentional discrimination against an identifiable political group and an actual discriminatory effect on that group." The plurality acknowledges that the record in this case supports a finding that the challenged redistricting plan was adopted for the purpose of discriminating against Democratic voters. The plurality argues, however, that appellees failed to establish that their voting strength was diluted statewide despite uncontradicted proof that certain key districts were grotesquely gerrymandered to enhance the election prospects of Republican candidates. * * *

The Equal Protection Clause guarantees citizens that their state will govern them impartially. In the context of redistricting, that guarantee is of critical importance because the franchise provides most citizens their only voice in the legislative process. Since the contours of a voting district powerfully may affect citizens' ability to exercise influence through their vote, district lines should be determined in accordance with neutral and legitimate criteria. When deciding where those lines will fall, the state should treat its voters as standing in the same position, regardless of their political beliefs or party affiliation. [*Reynolds*] contemplated that "one person, one vote" would be only one among several neutral factors that serve the constitutional mandate of fair and effective representation. * * *

The [most] basic flaw in the plurality's opinion is its failure to enunciate any standard that affords guidance to legislatures and courts.[10] [This] places the plurality in the curious position of inviting further litigation even as it appears to signal the "constitutional green light" to would-be gerrymanderers. * * *

A court should look first to the legislative process by which the challenged plan was adopted. Here, the District Court found that the procedures used in redistricting Indiana were carefully designed to exclude Democrats from participating in the legislative process [which] consisted of nothing more than the majority party's private application of computer technology to mapmaking. [T]he only data used in the computer program were precinct population, race of precinct citizens, precinct political complexion, and statewide party voting trends. * * *

Next, the District Court found [how] the mapmakers carved up counties, cities, and even townships in their effort to draw lines beneficial to the majority

---

10. * * * I cannot agree, as the plurality suggests, that a standard requiring proof of "heightened effect," where invidious intent has been established directly, has support in any of our cases, or that an equal protection violation can be established "only where a history (actual or projected) of disproportionate results appears." If a racial minority establishes that the legislature adopted a redistricting law for no purpose other than to disadvantage that group, the plurality's new and erroneous standard would require plaintiffs to wait for the results of several elections, creating a history of discriminatory effect, before they can challenge the law in court.

party. [The] redistricting dissects counties into strange shapes lacking in common interests, on one occasion even placing the seat of one county in a voting district composed of townships from other counties. Under these conditions, the District Court expressly found that "the potential for voter disillusion and nonparticipation is great," as voters are forced to focus their political activities in artificial electoral units. Intelligent voters, regardless of party affiliation, resent this sort of political manipulation of the electorate for no public purpose. * * *

[When] the plan was completed, Republican leaders announced that the House map was designed to yield 56 "safe" Republican seats and 30 Democratic seats, with the remainder being "tossups." Republicans expected that their Senate map would regularly produce 30 Republican seats and 8 to 10 Democratic seats so that Republicans would maintain their grip on the Senate even if Democrats won the remaining seats. In short, the record unequivocally demonstrates that in 1981 the Republican-dominated General Assembly deliberately sought to design a redistricting plan under which members of the Democratic party would be deprived of a fair opportunity to win control of the General Assembly at least until 1991, the date of the next redistricting. * * *

Appellees further demonstrated through a statistical showing that the House Plan debased the effectiveness of their votes [reciting the 1982 election statistics in White, J.'s opinion. Moreover, since] half of the Senate membership is up for election every two years, the only election results under the challenged plan available at trial [showed] that, of the seats up for election in 1982, Democrats were elected to 13 seats and Republicans to 12. [It] was appellees' contention that most of the Senate seats won by Democrats in 1982 were "safe" Democratic seats so that their party's success at the polls in that year was fully consistent with the statewide Republican gerrymander. This contention is borne out by the results of the 1984 Senate election. In that election, Democratic candidates received 42.3 percent of the vote, and Republicans 57.7 percent. Yet, of the 25 Senate positions up for election, only 7 were captured by Democrats.

The District Court found, and I agree, that appellants failed to justify the discriminatory impact of the plan by showing that the plan had a rational basis in permissible neutral criteria. [As] the plurality opinion makes clear, [a] colorable claim of discriminatory gerrymandering presents a justiciable controversy under the Equal Protection Clause. Federal courts in exercising their duty to adjudicate such claims should impose a heavy burden of proof on those who allege that a redistricting plan violates the Constitution. [T]his case presents a paradigm example of unconstitutional discrimination against the members of a political party that happened to be out of power. The well-grounded findings of the District Court to this effect have not been, and I believe cannot be, held clearly erroneous. * * * [25]

JUSTICE O'CONNOR, with whom THE CHIEF JUSTICE and JUSTICE REHNQUIST join, concurring in the judgment.

[T]he legislative business of apportionment is fundamentally a political affair, and challenges to the manner in which an apportionment has been carried out—by the very parties that are responsible for this process—present a political question in the truest sense of the term.

---

25. As is evident from the several opinions filed today, there is no "Court" for a standard that properly should be applied in determining whether a challenged redistricting plan is an unconstitutional partisan political gerrymander. The standard proposed by the plurality is explicitly rejected by two Justices, and three Justices also have expressed the view that the plurality's standard will "prove unmanageable and arbitrary." (O'Connor, J., joined by Burger, C.J., and Rehnquist, J., concurring in the judgment).

To turn these matters over to the federal judiciary is to inject the courts into the most heated partisan issues. It is predictable that the courts will respond by moving away from the nebulous standard a plurality of the Court fashions today and toward some form of rough proportional representation for all political groups. The consequences of this shift will be as immense as they are unfortunate. I do not believe, and the Court offers not a shred of evidence to suggest, that the Framers of the Constitution intended the judicial power to encompass the making of such fundamental choices about how this Nation is to be governed. Nor do I believe that the proportional representation towards which the Court's expansion of equal protection doctrine will lead is consistent with our history, our traditions, or our political institutions.[c] * * *

The step taken today is a momentous one, which if followed in the future can only lead to political instability and judicial malaise. [Federal] courts will have no alternative but to attempt to recreate the complex process of legislative apportionment in the context of adversary litigation in order to reconcile the competing claims of political, religious, ethnic, racial, occupational, and socioeconomic groups. Even if there were some way of limiting such claims to organized political parties, the fact remains that the losing party or the losing group of legislators in every reapportionment will now be invited to fight the battle anew in federal court. [The] Equal Protection Clause does not supply judicially manageable standards for resolving purely political gerrymandering claims, and no group right to an equal share of political power was ever intended by the Framers. [Unlike racial minorities], members of the Democratic and Republican parties cannot claim that they are a discrete and insular group vulnerable to exclusion from the political process by some dominant group: these political parties *are* the dominant groups, and the Court has offered no reason to believe that they are incapable of fending for themselves through the political process. Indeed, there is good reason to think that political gerrymandering is a self-limiting enterprise. See Cain, *The Reapportionment Puzzle* 151–159 (1984). In order to gerrymander, the legislative majority must weaken some of its safe seats, thus exposing its own incumbents to greater risks of defeat—risks they may refuse to accept past a certain point. Similarly, an overambitious gerrymander can lead to disaster for the legislative majority: because it has created more seats in which it hopes to win relatively narrow victories, the same swing in overall voting strength will tend to cost the legislative majority more and more seats as the gerrymander becomes more ambitious. More generally, each major party presumably has ample weapons at its disposal to conduct the partisan struggle that often leads to a partisan apportionment, but also often leads to a bipartisan one. * * *

Furthermore, the Court fails to explain why a bipartisan gerrymander—which is what was approved in *Gaffney*—affects individuals any differently than a partisan gerrymander. [As] the plurality acknowledges, the scheme upheld in *Gaffney* tended to "deny safe district minorities any realistic chance to elect their own representatives." If this bipartisan arrangement between two groups of self-interested legislators is constitutionally permissible, as I believe and as the Court held in *Gaffney,* then—in terms of the rights of individuals—it should be equally permissible for a legislative majority to employ the same means to pursue its own interests over the opposition of the other party.

c. Burger, C.J.'s separate opinion, relying   omitted.
on Frankfurter, J.'s dissent in *Baker v. Carr,* is

* * * [The] Court has in effect decided that it is constitutionally acceptable for both parties to "waste" the votes of individuals through a bipartisan gerrymander, so long as the *parties* themselves are not deprived of their group voting strength to an extent that will exceed the plurality's threshold requirement. This choice confers greater rights on powerful political groups than on individuals; that cannot be the meaning of the Equal Protection Clause. * * *

Vote dilution analysis is far less manageable when extended to major political parties than if confined to racial minority groups. First, [d]esigning an apportionment plan that does not impair or degrade the voting strength of several groups is more difficult than designing a plan that does not have such an effect on one group for the simple reason that, as the number of criteria the plan must meet increases, the number of solutions that will satisfy those criteria will decrease. * * *

Second, while membership in a racial group is an immutable characteristic, voters can—and often do—move from one party to the other or support candidates from both parties. Consequently, the difficulty of measuring voting strength is heightened in the case of a major political party. * * *

Moreover, any such intervention is likely to move in the direction of proportional representation for political parties. This is clear by analogy to the problem that arises in racial gerrymandering cases: "in order to decide whether an electoral system has made it harder for minority voters to elect the candidates they prefer, a court must have an idea in mind of how hard it 'should' be for minority voters to elect their preferred candidates under an acceptable system." Any such norm must make some reference, even if only a loose one, to the relation between the racial minority group's share of the electorate and its share of the elected representatives. In order to implement the plurality's standard, it will thus be necessary for courts to adopt an analogous norm, in order to assess whether the voting strength of a political party has been "degraded" by an apportionment, either on a state-wide basis or in particular districts. Absent any such norm, the inquiry the plurality proposes would be so standardless as to make the adjudication of political gerrymandering claims impossible.

* * * [Because] the most easily measured indicia of political power relate solely to winning and losing elections, there is a grave risk that the plurality's various attempts to qualify and condition the group right the Court has created will gradually pale in importance. What is likely to remain is a loose form of proportionality, under which *some* deviations from proportionality are permissible, but any significant, persistent deviations from proportionality are suspect. Courts will be forced to look for some form of "undue" disproportionality with respect to electoral success if political gerrymandering claims are justiciable, because otherwise they will find their decisions turning on imponderables such as whether the legislators of one party have fairly represented the voters of the other.

Of course, in one sense a requirement of proportional representation, whether loose or absolute, is judicially manageable. If this Court were to declare that the Equal Protection Clause required proportional representation within certain fixed tolerances, I have no doubt that district courts would be able to apply this edict. The flaw in such a pronouncement, however, would be the use of the Equal Protection Clause as the vehicle for making a fundamental policy choice that is contrary to the intent of its Framers and to the traditions of this republic. The political question doctrine as articulated in *Baker* rightly requires that we refrain from making such policy choices in order to evade what would otherwise be a lack of judicially manageable standards. * * *

* * * [To] allow district courts to strike down apportionment plans on the basis of their prognostications as to the outcome of future elections or future apportionments invites "findings" on matters as to which neither judges nor anyone else can have any confidence. Once it is conceded that "a group's electoral power is not unconstitutionally diminished by the simple fact of an apportionment scheme that makes winning elections more difficult," the virtual impossibility of reliably predicting how difficult it will be to win an election in 2, or 4, or 10 years should, in my view, weigh in favor of holding such challenges nonjusticiable. Racial gerrymandering should remain justiciable, for the harms it engenders run counter to the central thrust of the Fourteenth Amendment. But no such justification can be given for judicial intervention on behalf of mainstream political parties, and the risks such intervention poses to our political institutions are unacceptable. * * *

Notes and Questions

1. Consider Tribe, *Treatise* 1083 (2d ed.1988): "Justice White's opinion for the Court on the justiciability issue [equated] the Court's decision to intervene in the case with the Court's determination in *Baker v. Carr* to hear claims relating to the disparate size of election districts. Yet the two kinds of intervention are surely distinct. Although the *Baker* Court did not itself announce the one person, one vote rule, that rule was looming on the near horizon; the *Baker* Court had no reason to fear that no judicially manageable standard could be found. The Court in *Bandemer* had every reason to fear such an eventuality."

2. Consider Pamela Karlan, p. 1336 supra, 1715–16 (1993): "In cases involving claims of racial vote dilution, the Court focused on the racial aspect of the cause of action, which allowed it to borrow the discriminatory purpose requirement from general equal protection doctrine. [This] stringent purpose requirement was extraordinarily difficult to meet. By contrast, when the Court was faced with a claim of political gerrymandering, in *Bandemer*, it could hardly use the purpose requirement to pretermit the claim; given the overtly partisan nature of the redistricting process, nearly every districting theme was intended to maximize the election of members of the redistricting party at the expense of other parties' candidates. So, in the area of political gerrymandering, the Court developed a heightened effects [requirement.] The test, like the purpose test in racial dilution cases was virtually impossible to meet."

3. Is one person's gerrymander another person's good government? Consider Ronald Brown & Daniel Lowenstein, *A Democratic Perspective on Legislative Districting*, 6 J. of Law & Politics 673, 679 (1990): "The most common 'neutral' criterion Republicans try to impose [is] compactness. The usual way of levying a political attack on a districting plan is to show diagrams of selected oddly-shaped districts. This is supposed to prove that the plan is an outrageous gerrymander. [The] real reason the Republicans promote the compactness requirement is that it tends to work systematically to their [benefit]. Inner-city areas tend to contain Democratic voters concentrated in extraordinarily high percentages. Many surrounding affluent areas are predominantly but not nearly so overwhelmingly Republican. Accordingly, it may be relatively easy to draw compact districts separating these areas and thereby to accomplish the objective of a Republican gerrymander—a small number of overwhelmingly democratic districts surrounded by a large number of much closer but still safely Republican districts." [d]

d. See Comment, *Politics and Purpose*, fn. 11 supra: "While the plaintiffs in [*Bandemer*] were Indiana Democrats, Republicans nationally hailed the justiciability of gerrymandering:

But cf. Martin Shapiro, *Gerrymandering, Unfairness, and the Supreme Court,* 33 UCLA L.Rev. 227, 240 (1985): "If geography favors the Republicans in an ungerrymandered world, that is a purely fortuitous result, unforeseeable by either party when it chose its ideologies and clienteles. Such stacking ought to be considered extraneous to the goal of constraining the self-serving actions of the legislatures." [e] For a comprehensive attempt to show that the removal of politics from redistricting is an illusory goal with the conclusion that judges should keep out, see Daniel Lowenstein & Jonathan Steinberg, *The Quest for Legislative Districting in the Public Interest: Elusive or Illusory,* 33 UCLA L.Rev. 1 (1985). [f] But see Bernard Groffman, *Criteria for Districting: A Social Science Perspective,* 33 UCLA L.Rev. 77 (1985).

4. Consider Schuck, fn. f supra, at 1372, 1375–76: "It is puzzling that the concern for [party] representation so evident in all of the [*Bandemer*] opinions [has] crested at this particular moment in our political history. * * * The partisan identification of American voters is probably weaker today than at any time since the founding of mass-based political parties * * *." Is the Court wasting judicial resources in *Bandemer?* Alternatively, does the existence of gerrymandering undercut the wisdom of the expending of judicial resources in *Reynolds?*

SHAW v. RENO

509 U.S. 630, 113 S.Ct. 2816, 125 L.Ed.2d 511 (1993).

JUSTICE O'CONNOR delivered the opinion of the Court.

[As] a result of the 1990 census, North Carolina became entitled to a twelfth seat in the United States House of Representatives. The General Assembly enacted a reapportionment plan that included one majority-black congressional district. After the Attorney General of the United States objected to the plan pursuant to § 5 of the Voting Rights Act of 1965, the General Assembly passed new legislation creating a second majority-black district. Appellants allege that the revised plan, which contains district boundary lines of dramatically irregular shape, constitutes an unconstitutional racial gerrymander. * * *

The voting age population of North Carolina is approximately 78% white, 20% black, and 1% Native American; the remaining 1% is predominantly Asian. The black population is relatively dispersed; blacks constitute a majority of the general population in only 5 of the State's 100 counties. [The] largest concentrations of black citizens live in the Coastal Plain, primarily in the northern part. The General Assembly's first redistricting plan contained one majority-black district centered in that area of the State. [I]t moves southward until it tapers to a narrow band; then, with finger-like extensions, it reaches far into the southern-

---

they believed that Democrats, who control most state legislatures, have drawn state and congressional district lines to Democratic advantage. National Democrats, however, have minimized the impact of the decision, taking the view that the high equal protection threshold in [*Bandemer*] would prevent drastic restructuring." For some indication of the threshold's height, see *Badham v. Eu,* 694 F.Supp. 664 (N.D.Cal.1988), affirmed mem., 488 U.S. 1024, 109 S.Ct. 829, 102 L.Ed.2d 962 (1989) (California reapportionment plan not violated under *Bandemer* standards).

e. For Shapiro's opposition to judicial intervention, nonetheless, see id. at 252–56.

f. See also Peter Schuck, *The Thickest Thicket: Partisan Gerrymandering and Judicial Regulation of Politics,* 87 Colum.L.Rev. 1325, 1337 (1987) (arguments against a structure permitting gerrymandering "overlook important complexities and values in our political life, project incomplete visions of democratic representation, and invite innovative political remedies that should not be mandated by our federal courts").

most part of the State near the South Carolina border. District 1 has been compared to a "Rorschach ink-blot test," and a "bug splattered on a windshield."

The second majority-black district, District 12, is even more unusually shaped. It is approximately 160 miles long and, for much of its length, no wider than the I–85 corridor. It winds in snake-like fashion through tobacco country, financial centers, and manufacturing areas "until it gobbles in enough enclaves of black neighborhoods." Northbound and southbound drivers on I–85 sometimes find themselves in separate districts in one county, only to "trade" districts when they enter the next county. Of the 10 counties through which District 12 passes, five are cut into three different districts; even towns are divided. At one point the district remains contiguous only because it intersects at a single point with two other districts before crossing over them. One state legislator has remarked that "[i]f you drove down the interstate with both car doors open, you'd kill most of the people in the district." * * *

An understanding of the nature of appellants' claim is critical to our resolution of the case. In their complaint, appellants did not claim that the General Assembly's reapportionment plan unconstitutionally "diluted" white voting strength. They did not even claim to be white. Rather, appellants' complaint alleged that the deliberate segregation of voters into separate districts on the basis of race violated their constitutional right to participate in a "color-blind" electoral process. [This] Court never has held that race-conscious state decisionmaking is impermissible in all circumstances. What appellants object to is redistricting legislation that is so extremely irregular on its face that it rationally can be viewed only as an effort to segregate the races for purposes of voting, without regard for traditional districting principles and without sufficiently compelling justification. For the reasons that follow, we conclude that appellants have stated a claim upon which relief can be granted under the Equal Protection Clause.

[R]edistricting differs from other kinds of state decisionmaking in that the legislature always is aware of race when it draws district lines, just as it is aware of age, economic status, religious and political persuasion, and a variety of other demographic factors. That sort of race consciousness does not lead inevitably to impermissible race discrimination. [W]hen members of a racial group live together in one community, a reapportionment plan that concentrates members of the group in one district and excludes them from others may reflect wholly legitimate purposes. The district lines may be drawn, for example, to provide for compact districts of contiguous territory, or to maintain the integrity of political subdivisions.

The difficulty of proof, of course, does not mean that a racial gerrymander, once established, should receive less scrutiny under the Equal Protection Clause than other state legislation classifying citizens by race. Moreover, it seems clear to us that proof sometimes will not be difficult at all. In some exceptional cases, a reapportionment plan may be so highly irregular that, on its face, it rationally cannot be understood as anything other than an effort to "segregat[e] voters" on the basis of race. *Gomillion,* in which a tortured municipal boundary line was drawn to exclude black voters, was such a case. So, too, would be a case in which a State concentrated a dispersed minority population in a single district by disregarding traditional districting principles such as compactness, contiguity, and respect for political subdivisions. We emphasize that these criteria are important not because they are constitutionally required—they are not—but because they are objective factors that may serve to defeat a claim that a district has been gerrymandered on racial lines.

[A] reapportionment plan that includes in one district individuals who belong to the same race, but who are otherwise widely separated by geographical and political boundaries, and who may have little in common with one another but the color of their skin, bears an uncomfortable resemblance to political apartheid. It reinforces the perception that members of the same racial group—regardless of their age, education, economic status, or the community in which they live—think alike, share the same political interests, and will prefer the same candidates at the polls. We have rejected such perceptions elsewhere as impermissible racial stereotypes. By perpetuating such notions, a racial gerrymander may exacerbate the very patterns of racial bloc voting that majority-minority districting is sometimes said to counteract.

The message that such districting sends to elected representatives is equally pernicious. When a district obviously is created solely to effectuate the perceived common interests of one racial group, elected officials are more likely to believe that their primary obligation is to represent only the members of that group, rather than their constituency as a whole. This is altogether antithetical to our system of representative democracy. * * *

For these reasons, we conclude that a plaintiff challenging a reapportionment statute under the Equal Protection Clause may state a claim by alleging that the legislation, though race-neutral on its face, rationally cannot be understood as anything other than an effort to separate voters into different districts on the basis of race, and that the separation lacks sufficient justification. It is unnecessary for us to decide whether or how a reapportionment plan that, on its face, can be explained in nonracial terms successfully could be challenged. Thus, we express no view as to whether "the intentional creation of majority-minority districts, without more" always gives rise to an equal protection claim. * * *

Justice Souter apparently believes that racial gerrymandering is harmless unless it dilutes a racial group's voting strength. As we have explained, however, reapportionment legislation that cannot be understood as anything other than an effort to classify and separate voters by race injures voters in other ways. It reinforces racial stereotypes and threatens to undermine our system of representative democracy by signaling to elected officials that they represent a particular racial group rather than their constituency as a whole. * * *.

The dissenters [also] suggest that a racial gerrymander of the sort alleged here is functionally equivalent to gerrymanders for nonracial purposes, such as political gerrymanders. This Court has held political gerrymanders to be justiciable under the Equal Protection Clause. See *Bandemer.* But nothing in our case law compels the conclusion that racial and political gerrymanders are subject to precisely the same constitutional scrutiny. In fact, our country's long and persistent history of racial discrimination in voting—as well as our Fourteenth Amendment jurisprudence, which always has reserved the strictest scrutiny for discrimination on the basis of race, would seem to compel the opposite conclusion.

[Finally,] nothing in the Court's highly fractured decision in *UJO*—[which] the dissenters evidently believe controls—forecloses the claim we recognize today. [The] plaintiffs in *UJO*—members of a Hasidic community split between two districts under New York's revised redistricting plan—did not allege that the plan, on its face, was so highly irregular that it rationally could be understood only as an effort to segregate voters by race. Indeed, the facts of the case would not have supported such a claim. Three Justices approved the New York statute, in part, precisely because it adhered to traditional districting principles: "[W]e think [it] permissible for a State, employing sound districting principles such as compactness and population equality, to attempt to prevent racial minorities from being repeatedly outvoted by creating districts that will afford fair representation to the members of those racial groups who are sufficiently numerous and whose residential patterns afford the opportunity of creating districts in which they will be in the majority."

[*UJO*] set forth a standard under which white voters can establish unconstitutional vote dilution. [Nothing] in the decision precludes white voters (or voters of any other race) from bringing the analytically distinct claim that a reapportionment plan rationally cannot be understood as anything other than an effort to segregate citizens into separate voting districts on the basis of race without sufficient justification. Because appellants here stated such a claim, the District Court erred in dismissing their complaint.

Justice Souter contends that exacting scrutiny of racial gerrymanders under the Fourteenth Amendment is inappropriate because reapportionment "nearly always require[s] some consideration of race for legitimate reasons." "As long as members of racial groups have [a] commonality of interest" and "racial block voting takes place," he argues, "legislators will have to take race into account" in order to comply with the Voting Rights Act. Justice Souter's reasoning is flawed.

[That] racial bloc voting or minority political cohesion may be found to exist in some cases, of course, is no reason to treat all racial gerrymanders differently from other kinds of racial classification. Justice Souter apparently views racial gerrymandering of the type presented here as a special category of "benign" racial discrimination that should be subject to relaxed judicial review. As we have said, however, the very reason that the Equal Protection Clause demands strict scrutiny of all racial classifications is because without it, a court cannot determine whether or not the discrimination truly is "benign." [We] therefore consider what that level of scrutiny requires in the reapportionment context.

[O]n remand North Carolina might claim that it adopted the revised plan in order to comply with the § 5 "nonretrogression" principle. Under that principle, a proposed voting change cannot be precleared if it will lead to "a retrogression in the position of racial minorities with respect to their effective exercise of the electoral franchise." [But none of our cases] give covered jurisdictions carte blanche to engage in racial gerrymandering in the name of nonretrogression. A reapportionment plan would not be narrowly tailored to the goal of avoiding retrogression if the State went beyond what was reasonably necessary to avoid retrogression. [T]he state appellees contend that the General Assembly's revised plan was necessary not to prevent retrogression, but to avoid dilution of black voting strength in violation of § 2, as construed in *Thornburg v. Gingles,* 478 U.S. 30, 106 S.Ct. 2752, 92 L.Ed.2d 25 (1986), [which] held that members of a racial minority group claiming § 2 vote dilution [must] prove three threshold conditions: that the minority group "is sufficiently large and geographically compact to constitute a majority in a single-member district," that the minority group is "politically cohesive," and that "the white majority votes sufficiently as a block to enable [it] usually to defeat the minority's preferred candidate." * * *

Appellants maintain that the General Assembly's revised plan could not have been required by § 2. They contend that the State's black population is too dispersed to support two geographically compact majority-black districts, as the bizarre shape of District 12 demonstrates, and that there is no evidence of black political cohesion. They also contend that recent black electoral successes demonstrate the willingness of white voters in North Carolina to vote for black candidates. Appellants point out that blacks currently hold the positions of State

Auditor, Speaker of the North Carolina House of Representatives, and chair of the North Carolina State Board of Elections. They also point out that in 1990 a black candidate defeated a white opponent in the Democratic Party run-off for a United States Senate seat before being defeated narrowly by the Republican incumbent in the general election. Appellants further argue that if § 2 did require adoption of North Carolina's revised plan, § 2 is to that extent unconstitutional. These arguments were not developed below, and the issues remain open for consideration on remand.

The state appellees alternatively argue that the General Assembly's plan advanced a compelling interest entirely distinct from the Voting Rights Act. We previously have recognized a significant state interest in eradicating the effects of past racial discrimination. * * *

The state appellees submit that two pieces of evidence gave the General Assembly a strong basis for believing that remedial action was warranted here: the Attorney General's imposition of the § 5 preclearance requirement on 40 North Carolina counties, and the *Gingles* District Court's findings of a long history of official racial discrimination in North Carolina's political system and of pervasive racial bloc voting. The state appellees assert that the deliberate creation of majority-minority districts is the most precise way—indeed the only effective way—to overcome the effects of racially polarized voting. This question also need not be decided at this stage of the litigation. We note, however, that only three Justices in *UJO* were prepared to say that States have a significant interest in minimizing the consequences of racial bloc voting apart from the requirements of the Voting Rights Act. And those three Justices specifically concluded that race-based districting, as a response to racially polarized voting, is constitutionally permissible only when the State "employ[s] sound districting principles," and only when the affected racial group's "residential patterns afford the opportunity of creating districts in which they will be in the majority."

Racial classifications of any sort pose the risk of lasting harm to our society. They reinforce the belief, held by too many for too much of our history, that individuals should be judged by the color of their skin. Racial classifications with respect to voting carry particular dangers. Racial gerrymandering, even for remedial purposes, may balkanize us into competing racial factions; it threatens to carry us further from the goal of a political system in which race no longer matters—a goal that the Fourteenth and Fifteenth Amendments embody, and to which the Nation continues to aspire. It is for these reasons that race-based districting by our state legislatures demands close judicial scrutiny. * * *

Justice White, with whom Justice Blackmun and Justice Stevens join, dissenting.

The facts of this case mirror those presented in *UJO,* [where] five of the Justices reasoned that members of the white majority could not plausibly argue that their influence over the political process had been unfairly cancelled or that such had been the State's intent. Accordingly, they held that plaintiffs were not entitled to relief under the Constitution's Equal Protection Clause. On the same reasoning, I would affirm the district court's dismissal of appellants' claim in this instance.

The Court today chooses not to overrule, but rather to sidestep, *UJO.* It does so by glossing over the striking similarities, focusing on surface differences, most notably the (admittedly unusual) shape of the newly created district, and imagining an entirely new cause of action. Because the holding is limited to such anomalous circumstances, it perhaps will not substantially hamper a State's legitimate efforts to redistrict in favor of racial minorities. Nonetheless, the notion that North Carolina's plan, under which whites remain a voting majority in a disproportionate number of congressional districts, and pursuant to which the State has sent its first black representatives since Reconstruction to the United States Congress, might have violated appellants' constitutional rights is both a fiction and a departure from settled equal protection principles. * * *

I summed up my views on this matter in the plurality opinion in *Bandemer*. Because districting inevitably is the expression of interest group politics, and because "the power to influence the political process is not limited to winning elections," the question in gerrymandering cases is "whether a particular group has been unconstitutionally denied its chance to effectively influence the political process." [By] this, I meant that the group must exhibit "strong indicia of lack of political power and the denial of fair representation," so that it could be said that it has "essentially been shut out of the political process." In short, even assuming that racial (or political) factors were considered in the drawing of district boundaries, a showing of discriminatory effects is a "threshold requirement" in the absence of which there is no equal protection violation, and no need to "reach the question of the state interests [served] by the particular districts."

To distinguish a claim that alleges that the redistricting scheme has discriminatory intent and effect from one that does not has nothing to do with dividing racial classifications between the "benign" and the malicious—an enterprise which, as the majority notes, the Court has treated with skepticism. Rather, the issue is whether the classification based on race discriminates against anyone by denying equal access to the political process.

[I]t strains credulity to suggest that North Carolina's purpose in creating a second majority-minority district was to discriminate against members of the majority group by "impair[ing] or burden[ing their] opportunity [to] participate in the political process." The State has made no mystery of its intent, which was to respond to the Attorney General's objections by improving the minority group's prospects of electing a candidate of its choice. I doubt that this constitutes a discriminatory purpose as defined in the Court's equal protection cases—i.e., an intent to aggravate "the unequal distribution of electoral power." But even assuming that it does, there is no question that appellants have not alleged the requisite discriminatory effects. Whites constitute roughly 76 percent of the total population and 79 percent of the voting age population in North Carolina. Yet, under the State's plan, they still constitute a voting majority in 10 (or 83 percent) of the 12 congressional districts. * * *

Racial gerrymanders come in various shades: At-large voting schemes, see, e.g., *White v. Regester*, [p. 1244 supra], the fragmentation of a minority group among various districts "so that it is a majority in none," otherwise known as "cracking;" the "stacking" of "a large minority population concentration [with] a larger white population;" and, finally, the "concentration of [minority voters] into districts where they constitute an excessive majority," also called "packing." In each instance, race is consciously utilized by the legislature for electoral purposes; in each instance, we have put the plaintiff challenging the district lines to the burden of demonstrating that the plan was meant to, and did in fact, exclude an identifiable racial group from participation in the political process.

Not so, apparently, when the districting "segregates" by drawing odd-shaped lines. In that case, we are told, such proof no longer is needed. Instead, it is the State that must rebut the allegation that race was taken into account, a fact that, together with the legislators' consideration of ethnic, religious, and other group characteristics, I had thought we practically took for granted. Part of the explanation for the majority's approach has to do, perhaps, with the emotions stirred by words such as "segregation" and "political apartheid." But their loose and imprecise use by today's majority has, I fear, led it astray. The consideration of race in "segregation" cases is no different than in other race-conscious districting; from the standpoint of the affected groups, moreover, the line-drawings all act in similar fashion. A plan that "segregates" being functionally indistinguishable from any of the other varieties of gerrymandering, we should be consistent in what we require from a claimant: Proof of discriminatory purpose and effect.

The other part of the majority's explanation of its holding is related to its simultaneous discomfort and fascination with irregularly shaped districts. Lack of compactness or contiguity, like uncouth district lines, certainly is a helpful indicator that some form of gerrymandering (racial or other) might have taken place. [But] they do no more than that. In particular, they have no bearing on whether the plan ultimately is found to violate the Constitution. Given two districts drawn on similar, race-based grounds, the one does not become more injurious than the other simply by virtue of being snake-like, at least so far as the Constitution is concerned and absent any evidence of differential racial impact. [A] regularly shaped district can just as effectively effectuate racially discriminatory gerrymandering as an odd-shaped one. By focusing on looks rather than impact, the majority "immediately casts attention in the wrong direction—toward superficialities of shape and size, rather than toward the political realities of district composition."

Limited by its own terms to cases involving unusually-shaped districts, the Court's approach nonetheless will unnecessarily hinder to some extent a State's voluntary effort to ensure a modicum of minority representation. This will be true in areas where the minority population is geographically dispersed. It also will be true where the minority population is not scattered but, for reasons unrelated to race—for example incumbency protection—the State would rather not create the majority-minority district in its most "obvious" location. * * *

Although I disagree with the holding that appellants' claim is cognizable, the Court's discussion of the level of scrutiny it requires warrants a few comments. I have no doubt that a State's compliance with the Voting Rights Act clearly constitutes a compelling interest.

The Court, while seemingly agreeing with this position, warns that the State's redistricting effort must be "narrowly tailored" to further its interest in complying with the law. It is evident to me, however, that what North Carolina did was precisely tailored to meet the objection of the Attorney General to its prior plan. Hence, I see no need for a remand at all, even accepting the majority's basic approach to this case.

Furthermore, how it intends to manage this standard, I do not know. Is it more "narrowly tailored" to create an irregular majority-minority district as opposed to one that is compact but harms other State interests such as incumbency protection or the representation of rural interests? Of the following two options—creation of two minority influence districts or of a single majority-minority district—is one "narrowly tailored" and the other not? Once the Attorney General has found that a proposed redistricting change violates § 5's nonretrogression principle in that it will abridge a racial minority's right to vote, does "narrow tailoring" mean that the most the State can do is preserve the status quo? Or can it maintain that change, while attempting to enhance minority voting power in some other manner? This small sample only begins to scratch the surface of the problems raised by the majority's test. But it suffices to illustrate the unworkability of a standard that is divorced from any measure of constitutional harm. In that, State efforts to remedy minority vote dilution are wholly unlike what typically has been labeled "affirmative action." To the extent that no other racial group is injured, remedying a Voting Rights Act violation does not involve preferential treatment. It involves, instead, an attempt to equalize treatment, and to provide minority voters with an effective voice in the political process. The Equal Protection Clause of the Constitution, surely, does not stand in the way. * * *

JUSTICE STEVENS, dissenting.

[I] believe that the Equal Protection Clause is violated when the State creates the kind of uncouth district boundaries seen in *Gomillion* and this case, for the sole purpose of making it more difficult for members of a minority group to win an election. The duty to govern impartially is abused when a group with power over the electoral process defines electoral boundaries solely to enhance its own political strength at the expense of any weaker group. That duty, however, is not violated when the majority acts to facilitate the election of a member of a group that lacks such power because it remains underrepresented in the state legislature—whether that group is defined by political affiliation, by common economic interests, or by religious, ethnic, or racial characteristics. [If] it is permissible to draw boundaries to provide adequate representation for rural voters, for union members, for Hasidic Jews, for Polish Americans, or for Republicans, it necessarily follows that it is permissible to do the same thing for members of the very minority group whose history in the United States gave birth to the Equal Protection Clause. A contrary conclusion could only be described as perverse.

JUSTICE SOUTER, dissenting.

[Unlike] other contexts in which we have addressed the State's conscious use of race, see, e.g., *Croson; Wygant,* electoral districting calls for decisions that nearly always require some consideration of race for legitimate reasons where there is a racially mixed population. As long as members of racial groups have the commonality of interest implicit in our ability to talk about concepts like "minority voting strength," and "dilution of minority votes," and as long as racial bloc voting takes place, legislators will have to take race into account in order to avoid dilution of minority voting strength in the districting plans they adopt. [A] second distinction between districting and most other governmental decisions in which race has figured is that those other decisions using racial criteria characteristically occur in circumstances in which the use of race to the advantage of one person is necessarily at the obvious expense of a member of a different race. * * *

In districting, by contrast, the mere placement of an individual in one district instead of another denies no one a right or benefit provided to others. [Under] our cases there is in general a requirement that in order to obtain relief under the Fourteenth Amendment, the purpose and effect of the districting must be to devalue the effectiveness of a voter compared to what, as a group member, he would otherwise be able to enjoy. * * *

There is thus no theoretical inconsistency in having two distinct approaches to equal protection analysis, one for cases of electoral districting and one for most other types of state governmental decisions. Nor, because of the distinctions between the two categories, is there any risk that Fourteenth Amendment districting law as such will be taken to imply anything for purposes of general

Fourteenth Amendment scrutiny about "benign" racial discrimination, or about group entitlement as distinct from individual protection, or about the appropriateness of strict or other heightened scrutiny. * * * [a]

———

MILLER v. JOHNSON, ___ U.S. ___, 115 S.Ct. 2475, 132 L.Ed.2d 762 (1995), involved Georgia's creation of three majority-minority congressional districts (out of a total of eleven), responding to the Justice Department's earlier refusals to grant preclearance under the Voting Rights Act to plans that created only two such districts. (Georgia's population was about 27% black.) "The dense population centers of the approved Eleventh District were all majority-black, all at the periphery of the district, and in the case of Atlanta, Augusta and Savannah, all tied to a sparsely populated rural core by even less populated land bridges. Extending from Atlanta to the Atlantic, the Eleventh covered 6,784.2 square miles, splitting eight counties and five municipalities along the way." The Court, per KENNEDY, J., held this violated equal protection because "race was the predominant factor motivating the drawing of the Eleventh District":

"Our observation in *Shaw* of the consequences of racial stereotyping was not meant to suggest that a district must be bizarre on its face before there is a constitutional violation. * * * Shape is relevant not because bizarreness is a necessary element of the constitutional wrong or a threshold requirement of proof, but because it may be persuasive circumstantial evidence that race for its own sake, and not other districting principles, was the legislature's dominant and controlling rationale in drawing its district lines. The logical implication, as courts applying *Shaw* have recognized, is that parties may rely on evidence other than bizarreness to establish race-based districting.

"[The] courts, in assessing the sufficiency of a challenge to a districting plan, must be sensitive to the complex interplay of forces that enter a legislature's redistricting calculus. Redistricting legislatures will, for example, almost always be aware of racial demographics; but it does not follow that race predominates in the redistricting process. [The] plaintiff's burden is to show, either through circumstantial evidence of a district's shape and demographics or more direct evidence going to legislative purpose, that [the] legislature subordinated traditional race-neutral districting principles, including but not limited to compactness, contiguity, respect for political subdivisions or communities defined by actual shared interests, to racial considerations. * * *

"[Whether] or not in some cases compliance with the Voting Rights Act, standing alone, can provide a compelling interest independent of any interest in remedying past discrimination, it cannot do so here. [When] a state governmental entity seeks to justify race-based remedies to cure the effects of past discrimination, we do not accept the government's mere assertion that the remedial action is required. Rather, we insist on a strong basis in evidence of the harm being remedied. [The] State does not argue, however, that it created the Eleventh District to remedy past discrimination, and with good reason: there is little doubt that the State's true interest in designing the Eleventh District was creating a third majority-black district to satisfy the Justice Department's preclearance demands. [It] does not follow, however, that the plan was required by the substantive provisions of the Voting Rights Act. * * *

a. The brief dissenting opinion of Blackmun, J., is omitted.

"Georgia's drawing of the Eleventh District was not required under the Act because there was no reasonable basis to believe that Georgia's earlier enacted plans violated [§ 5]. Georgia's first and second proposed plans increased the number of majority-black districts from 1 out of 10 (10%) to 2 out of 11 (18.18%). These plans were 'ameliorative' and could not have violated § 5's non-retrogression principle. [The] State's policy of adhering to other districting principles instead of creating as many majority-minority districts as possible does not support an inference that the plan 'so discriminates on the basis of race or color as to violate the Constitution,' and thus cannot provide any basis under § 5 for the Justice Department's objection.

"[T]he Justice Department's implicit command that States engage in presumptively unconstitutional race-based districting brings the Voting Rights Act, once upheld as a proper exercise of Congress' authority under § 2 of the Fifteenth Amendment, into tension with the Fourteenth Amendment. [We] need not, however, resolve these troubling and difficult constitutional questions today. There is no indication Congress intended such a far-reaching application of § 5, so we reject the Justice Department's interpretation of the statute and avoid the constitutional problems that interpretation raises."

O'CONNOR, J., added: "Application of the Court's standard does not throw into doubt the vast majority of the Nation's 435 congressional districts, where presumably the States have drawn the boundaries in accordance with their customary districting principles. That is so even though race may well have been considered in the redistricting process. But application of the Court's standard helps achieve *Shaw*'s basic objective of making extreme instances of gerrymandering subject to meaningful judicial review. I therefore join the Court's opinion."

GINSBURG, J., joined by Stevens, Souter and Breyer, JJ., dissented: "Although the Georgia General Assembly prominently considered race in shaping the Eleventh District, race did not crowd out all other factors, as the Court found it did in North Carolina's delineation of the *Shaw* district. [The] District covers a core area in central and eastern Georgia, and its total land area of 6,780 square miles is about average for the State. The border of the Eleventh District runs 1,184 miles, in line with Georgia's Second District, which has a 1,243-mile border, and the State's Eighth District, with a border running 1,155 miles. Of the 22 counties in the District, 14 are intact and 8 are divided. That puts the Eleventh District at about the state average in divided counties. [And] notably, the Eleventh District's boundaries largely follow precinct lines. Evidence at trial similarly shows that [political considerations] went into determining the Eleventh District's boundaries. * * * Tellingly, the District that the Court's decision today unsettles is not among those on a statistically calculated list of the 28 most bizarre districts in the United States, a study prepared in the wake of our decision in *Shaw*. * * *

"To accommodate the reality of ethnic bonds, legislatures have long drawn voting districts along ethnic lines. Our Nation's cities are full of districts identified by their ethnic character—Chinese, Irish, Italian, Jewish, Polish, Russian, for example. The creation of ethnic districts reflecting felt identity is not ordinarily viewed as offensive or demeaning to those included in the delineation. [If] Chinese–Americans and Russian–Americans may seek and secure group recognition in the delineation of voting districts, then African–Americans should not be dissimilarly treated. Otherwise, in the name of equal protection, we would shut out 'the very minority group whose history in the United States gave birth to the Equal Protection Clause.' " [a]

Notes and Questions

1. Consider Charles Fried, *Foreword: Revolutions?*, 109 Harv.L.Rev. 13, 66 (1995): "However difficult it may be to attribute motive to a legislature in such cases, the purpose of the Justice Department was unambiguous and avowed, and the Court found that its taint was transferred to the Georgia legislature which had acted in compliance with the pressure. So the 'bottom line' of the *Miller* case may be the very serious practical effect of chastening the Justice Department's relentless pursuit [of] guaranteed proportional representation through the creation of the greatest possible number of majority-minority districts."

2. Consider Note, *Trouble in Paradise: Equal Protection and the Dilemma of Interminority Group Conflict,* 47 Stan.L.Rev. 1059, 1077–78 (1995): "All of [O'Connor, J.'s] concerns have something in common: They see danger in living in a society where racial minorities have distinct identities and exercise political power accordingly. Justice O'Connor's worry about elected officials' loyalty to racial groups rather than to some theoretical, nonracial 'constituency' reflects a kind of Madisonian fear, not that minority groups will lack representation, but that their effective, cohesive representation will operate as factions to the detriment of national interests. Justice O'Connor seemed unconcerned that so-called national interests often boil down to legislative majority (white) interests; she similarly ignored the possibility that white representatives might occasionally consider themselves racial representatives too. The irony of *Shaw* is that while the Court recognized the existence of a multiracial polity in order to justify its holding, it did so precisely in order to destroy the legitimacy of competition and minority political strength within that polity."

3. Consider T. Alexander Aleinikoff & Samuel Issacharoff, *Race and Redistricting: Drawing Constitutional Lines After Shaw v. Reno,* 92 Mich.L.Rev. 588, 612–613 (1993): "What is the evidence that race-conscious districting exacerbates racial bloc voting, or that it sends a message to an elected representative that she need only represent members of her group? There is only rudimentary evidence of the relative quality of representation and responsiveness in racially drawn districts, none of which is referred to by the Court, and none of which supports the categorical assertion that representation from such districts is fundamentally different from that afforded other constituent groups who form a majority in a congressional district. The Court's description of democratic legitimacy also seems rather thin. It is certainly arguable that democratic processes are enhanced rather than degraded when previously excluded groups are able to elect representatives of their choice, even if those representatives primarily seek to further the interests that constituency. Indeed, claiming that representatives should look primarily to interests beyond their district calls into question the entire edifice of geographically based districting."

4. *Beyond territorial districting.* Lani Guinier, *The Tyranny of the Majority* 149, 153 (1994): "[M]odified at-large systems used in corporate governance, such as cumulative voting, should be considered. Under a modified at-large system, each voter is given the same number of votes as open seats, and the voter may plump or cumulate her votes to reflect the intensity of her preferences. Depend-

---

a. Stevens, J., added a brief dissent, arguing that respondents "have not suffered any legally cognizable injury."

ing on the exclusion threshold, political cohesive minority group are assured representation if they vote strategically. Similarly, all voters have the potential to form voluntary constituencies based on their own assessment of their interests. As a consequence, semiproportional systems such as cumulative voting give more voters, not just racial minorities, the opportunity to vote for a winning candidate.
* * *

"In balancing the fears of balkanization against observations about existing alienation, I conclude that exclusiveness is a greater evil than controversy, that passivity does not equal contentment, and that differences need not be permanently enshrined in the electoral configuration. Modified at-large election systems encourage continuous redistricting by the voters themselves based on the way they cast their votes at each election. Whatever differences emerge, therefore, are those chosen by the voters rather than imposed externally on the voters based on assumptions about demographic characteristics or incumbent self-interest. These voter-generated differences may infuse the process with new ideas; diversity of viewpoint can be enlightening. Finally, the modified at-large system may simply reflect a necessary transition phase from power politics to principled politics. But, whether it succeeds in that respect, it at least has the benefit in infusing the process with more legitimacy from the perspective of previously disenfranchised groups."

II. TRAVEL

SHAPIRO v. THOMPSON

394 U.S. 618, 89 S.Ct. 1322, 22 L.Ed.2d 600 (1969).

JUSTICE BRENNAN delivered the opinion of the Court.

These three appeals [are from federal courts] holding unconstitutional [Conn., Pa. and D.C. statutes denying welfare] to residents [who] have not resided within their jurisdictions for at least one [year].

There is no dispute that the effect of the waiting-period requirement [is] to create two classes of needy resident families indistinguishable from each other except that one is composed of residents who have resided a year or more, and the second of residents who have resided less than a year, in the jurisdiction. [T]he second class is denied welfare aid upon which may depend the ability of the families to obtain the very means to subsist—food, shelter, and other necessities of life. [We] agree [that the statutes deny equal protection]. The interests which appellants assert are promoted by the classification either may not constitutionally be promoted by government or are not compelling governmental interests.

Primarily, appellants justify the waiting-period requirement as a protective device to preserve the fiscal integrity of state public assistance programs. It is asserted that people who require welfare assistance during their first year of residence in a State are likely to become continuing burdens on state welfare programs. Therefore, the argument runs, if such people can be deterred from entering the jurisdiction by denying them welfare benefits during the first year, state programs to assist long-time residents will not be impaired. [But] the purpose of inhibiting migration by needy persons into the State is constitutionally impermissible.

This Court long ago recognized that the nature of our Federal Union and our constitutional concepts of personal liberty unite to require that all citizens be free to travel throughout the length and breadth of our land uninhibited by statutes, rules, or regulations which unreasonably burden or restrict this movement. [See *United States v. Guest*, p. 1381 infra.

Alternatively, appellants argue that even if it is impermissible for a State to attempt to deter the entry of all indigents, the challenged classification may be justified as a permissible state attempt to discourage those indigents who would enter the State solely to obtain larger benefits. [But] a State may no more try to fence out those indigents who seek higher welfare benefits than it may try to fence out indigents generally. [W]e do not perceive why a mother who is seeking to make a new life for herself and her children should be regarded as less deserving because she considers, among other factors, the level of a State's public assistance. Surely such a mother is no less deserving than a mother who moves into a particular State in order to take advantage of its better educational facilities.

Appellants argue further that the challenged classification may be sustained as an attempt to distinguish between new and old residents on the basis of the contribution they have made to the community through the payment of taxes. [But this] would logically permit the State to bar new residents from schools, parks, and libraries or deprive them of police and fire protection. Indeed it would permit the State to apportion all benefits and services according to the past tax contributions of its citizens. The Equal Protection Clause prohibits such an apportionment of state services.[10]

We recognize that a State [may] legitimately attempt to limit its expenditures, whether for public assistance, public education, or any other program. But a State may not accomplish such a purpose by invidious distinctions between classes of its citizens. It could not, for example, reduce expenditures for education by barring indigent children from its schools. [Thus], appellants must do more than show that denying welfare benefits to new residents saves [money.]

Appellants next advance as justification [four] administrative and related governmental objectives allegedly served by the waiting-period requirement. * * *

At the outset, we reject appellants' argument that a mere showing of a rational relationship between the waiting period and these four admittedly permissible state objectives will suffice, [for] in moving from State to State or to the District of Columbia appellees were exercising a constitutional right, and any classification which serves to penalize the exercise of that right, unless shown to be necessary to promote a *compelling* governmental interest, is unconstitutional. Cf. *Skinner v. Oklahoma,*; *Korematsu; Sherbert v. Verner*].

The argument that the waiting-period requirement facilitates budget predictability is wholly unfounded. The records in all three cases are utterly devoid of evidence [of use of] the one-year requirement as a means to predict the number of people who will require assistance in the budget year. * * *

The argument that the waiting period serves as an administratively efficient rule of thumb for determining residency similarly will not withstand scrutiny. [Before] granting an application, the welfare authorities investigate the applicant [and] in the course of the inquiry necessarily learn the facts upon which to determine whether the applicant is a resident.

Similarly, there is no need for a State to use the one-year waiting period as a safeguard against fraudulent receipt of benefits; for less drastic means are available, and are employed * * *.

---

10. We are not dealing here with state insurance programs which may legitimately tie the amount of benefits to the individual's contributions.

Pennsylvania suggests that the one-year waiting period is justified as a means of encouraging new residents to join the labor force promptly. But this logic would also require a similar waiting period for long-term [residents.]

We conclude therefore that appellants [have] no need to use the one-year requirement for the governmental purposes suggested. Thus, even under traditional equal protection tests [the classification] would seem irrational and unconstitutional. But [s]ince the classification here touches on the fundamental right of interstate movement, its constitutionality must be judged by the stricter standard of whether it promotes a *compelling* state interest. Under this standard, the waiting period requirement clearly violates the Equal Protection Clause.[21]

[The Court rejected the contention that Social Security Act § 402(b) approved imposition of one-year residence requirements. But] even if it could be argued that the constitutionality of § 402(b) is [in issue,] Congress may not authorize the States to violate the Equal Protection Clause. * * *

Affirmed.[a]

CHIEF JUSTICE WARREN with whom JUSTICE BLACK joins, dissenting.

[§ 402(b)] intended to authorize state residence requirements of up to one [year.] Congress, pursuant to its commerce power, has enacted a variety of restrictions upon interstate travel. It has taxed air and rail fares and [gasoline]. Many of the federal safety regulations of common carriers which cross state lines burden the right to travel. And Congress has prohibited by criminal statute interstate travel for certain purposes. * * *

The Court's right-to-travel cases lend little support to the view that congressional action is invalid merely because it burdens the right to travel. Most of our cases fall into two categories: those in which *state* imposed restrictions were involved, see e.g., *Edwards v. California,* and those concerning congressional decisions to remove impediments to interstate movement, see, e.g., [*Guest*]. *Aptheker v. Secretary of State,* is the only case in which this Court invalidated on a constitutional basis a congressionally imposed restriction. *Aptheker* also involved [a] claim that the congressional restriction compelled a potential traveler to choose between his right to travel and his First Amendment right of freedom of association. [*Aptheker*] thus contains two characteristics distinguishing it from the [instant case]: a combined infringement of two constitutionally protected rights and a flat prohibition upon travel. [Here], travel itself is not prohibited. Any burden inheres solely in the fact that a potential welfare recipient might take into consideration the loss of welfare benefits for a limited period of time if he changes his residence. Not only is this burden of uncertain degree,[5] but appellees themselves assert there is evidence that few welfare recipients have in fact been deterred by residence requirements.

---

21. We imply no view of the validity of waiting period *or* residence requirements determining eligibility to vote, [for] tuition-free education, to obtain a license to practice a profession, to hunt or fish, [etc. These] may promote compelling state interests on the one hand, or, on the other, may not be penalties upon the exercise of the constitutional right of interstate travel.

a. Stewart, J., joined the Court's opinion, emphasizing that "the Court simply recognizes" that the statutes impinge upon "the constitutional right of interstate travel." For discussion of attempts to circumvent *Shapiro,* see Note, *The Resurgence of Durational Residence Requirements for the Receipt of Welfare Funds,* 27 Loy.U.L.A.L.Rev. 305 (1993).

5. [I]ndigents who are disqualified from categorical assistance by residence requirements are not left wholly without assistance. Each of the appellees in these cases found alternative sources of assistance * * *.

The insubstantiality of the restriction imposed by residence requirements must then be evaluated in light of the possible congressional reasons for such requirements. [Given] the apprehensions of many States that an increase in benefits without minimal residence requirements would result in an inability to provide an adequate welfare system, Congress deliberately adopted the intermediate course of a cooperative program. [Our] cases require only that Congress have a rational basis for finding that a chosen regulatory scheme is necessary to the furtherance of interstate commerce. See, e.g., *Katzenbach v. McClung.* I conclude that residence requirements can be imposed by Congress as an exercise of its power to control interstate commerce consistent with the constitutionally guaranteed right to travel. * * * [b]

JUSTICE HARLAN, dissenting. * * *

In upholding the equal protection argument, the Court has applied an equal protection doctrine of relatively recent vintage [—the] "compelling interest" doctrine [which constitutes] an increasingly significant exception to the long-established rule that a statute does not deny equal protection if it is rationally related to a legitimate governmental objective. The "compelling interest" doctrine has two branches. [The] "suspect" criteria [branch today] apparently has been further enlarged to include classifications based upon recent interstate movement, and perhaps those based upon the exercise of *any* constitutional [right].

I think that this branch of the "compelling interest" doctrine is sound when applied to racial classifications, for historically the Equal Protection Clause was largely a product of the desire to eradicate legal distinctions founded upon race. However, I believe that the more recent extensions have been unwise. [When] a classification is based upon the exercise of rights guaranteed against state infringement by the federal Constitution, then there is no need for any resort to the Equal Protection Clause; in such instances, this Court may properly and straightforwardly invalidate any undue burden upon those rights under the Fourteenth Amendment's Due Process Clause.

The second branch of the "compelling interest" principle is even more troublesome. For it has been held that a statutory classification is subject to the "compelling interest" test if the result of the classification may be to affect a "fundamental right," regardless of the basis of the classification. This rule was foreshadowed in *Skinner* [and] re-emerged in *Reynolds v. Sims,* [again] in *Carrington v. Rash* [and] was also an alternate ground in *Harper* and apparently was a basis of the holding in *Williams v. Rhodes.* It has reappeared today in the Court's cryptic suggestion that the "compelling interest" test is applicable merely because the result of the classification may be to deny the appellees "food, shelter, and other necessities of life," as well as in the Court's statement that "[s]ince the classification here touches on the fundamental right of interstate movement, its constitutionality must be judged by the stricter standard of whether it promotes a *compelling* state interest."

I think this branch [is] unfortunate because it creates an exception which threatens to swallow the standard equal protection rule. Virtually every state statute affects important rights. This Court has repeatedly held, for example, that the traditional equal protection standard is applicable to statutory classifications affecting such fundamental matters as the right to pursue a particular

---

b. As to whether the "federalistic dimension" of the right to travel should limit Congress' power to affect it, see Kenneth Karst, *The Fifth Amendment's Guarantee of Equal Protection,* 55 N.C.L.Rev. 541, 558–60 (1977).

occupation, the right to receive greater or smaller wages or to work more or less hours, and the right to inherit property. Rights such as these are in principle indistinguishable from those involved here, and to extend the "compelling interest" rule to all cases in which such rights are affected would go far toward making this Court a "super-legislature." This branch of the doctrine is also unnecessary. When the right affected is one assured by the federal Constitution, any infringement can be dealt with under the Due Process Clause. But when a statute affects only matters not mentioned in the federal Constitution and is not arbitrary or irrational, I must reiterate that I know of nothing which entitles this Court to pick out particular human activities, characterize them as "fundamental," and give them added protection under an unusually stringent equal protection test. * * *

For reasons hereafter set forth, a legislature might rationally find that the imposition of a welfare residence requirement would aid in the accomplishment of at least four valid governmental objectives. It might also find that residence requirements have advantages not shared by other methods of achieving the same goals. [Thus], it cannot be said that the requirements are "arbitrary" or "lacking in rational justification." Hence, I can find no objection to these residence requirements under [equal protection].

The next issue [is] whether a one-year welfare residence requirement amounts to an undue burden upon the right of interstate travel [which I conclude] is a "fundamental" right [that] should be regarded as having its source in the Due Process Clause of the Fifth Amendment.

[In] my view, a number of considerations militate in favor of constitutionality. First, as just shown, four separate, legitimate governmental interests are furthered by residence requirements. Second, the impact of the requirements upon the freedom of individuals to travel interstate is indirect and, according to evidence put forward by the appellees themselves, insubstantial. Third, these are [cases] in which the States have acted within the terms of a limited authorization by the national government, and in which Congress itself has laid down a like rule for the District of Columbia. Fourth, the legislatures which enacted these statutes have been fully exposed to the arguments of the appellees as to why these residence requirements are unwise, and have rejected them. This is not, therefore, an instance in which legislatures have acted without mature deliberation.

Fifth, [the] field of welfare assistance is one in which there is a widely recognized need for fresh solutions and consequently for experimentation. Invalidation of welfare residence requirements might have the unfortunate consequence of discouraging the Federal and State Governments from establishing unusually generous welfare programs in particular areas on an experimental basis, because of fears that the program would cause an influx of persons seeking higher welfare payments. Sixth, [the] statutes come to us clothed with the authority of Congress and attended by a correspondingly heavy presumption of constitutionality. * * *

Notes and Questions

1. *Equal protection vs. due process.* If a state simply eliminated welfare, or granted lower payments than other states, would this "touch on the fundamental right of interstate movement" just as harshly as the programs in *Shapiro?* "Fence out indigents" at least as much? Would it be invalid under *Shapiro* "unless shown to be necessary to promote a *compelling* governmental interest"? See generally Bernard Harvith, *The Constitutionality of Residence Tests for General and Categorical Assistance Programs,* 54 Calif.L.Rev. 567, 593–95 (1966).

Or does *Shapiro* deal only with "invidious distinctions between classes of citizens"? Does Harlan, J.'s contention—that "when the right affected is one assured by the Constitution, any infringement can be dealt with under the Due Process Clause"—render the *Shapiro* approach superfluous? [a] Or does *Shapiro's* equal protection analysis add another dimension to the problem by distinguishing between the state interest needed to justify (a) reducing expenditures generally, and (b) reducing expenditures by denying benefits to recent travellers? See *Chicago Police Dep't. v. Mosley,* p. 895 supra. See generally Robert Reinstein, *The Welfare Cases: Fundamental Rights, The Poor, and the Burden of Proof in Constitutional Litigation,* 44 Temp.L.Q. 1, 36–40 (1970); Jesse Choper, Yale Kamisar & Laurence Tribe, *The Supreme Court: Trends and Developments 1978–1979,* 263–64, 311–12 (1979).

2. *Residence requirements.* (a) After *Shapiro,* may a state deny welfare assistance to transients who have no intention of remaining permanently in the state? Did *Shapiro* not really involve "the interest in freedom of travel" but rather "only the narrower interest in freedom of interstate migration"—i.e., to "resettle, find a new job, and start a new life"? See Edward Barrett, *Judicial Supervision of Legislative Classifications—A More Modest Role for Equal Protection,* 1976 B.Y.U.L.Rev. 89, 117. See also *Memorial Hosp. v. Maricopa Cty.,* note 3(b) infra. Consider Note, *Durational Residence Requirements from Shapiro Through Sosna,* 50 N.Y.U.L.Rev. 622, 675 (1975): "A classification scheme based [on] residency does not penalize exercise of the right to travel because it results in no denial of benefits or privileges: transient nonresidents remain eligible for benefits in the state in which they are residents."

(b) DOE v. BOLTON, p. 321 supra, invalidated the residency requirement of the Georgia abortion law: "Just as the Privileges and Immunities Clause, Art. IV, § 2, protects persons who enter other States to ply their trade, so must it protect persons who enter Georgia seeking the medical services that are available there. A contrary holding would mean that a State could limit to its own residents the general medical care available within its borders." Is *Doe* consistent with the analysis in note (a) supra? Compare *Carrington v. Rash,* Part I, B supra. On Art. IV, § 2, see generally Ch. 4, Sec. 1, VI.

(c) What of a residency requirement that affects both freedom of travel and freedom of interstate migration? McCARTHY v. PHILADELPHIA CIVIL SERVICE COM'N, 424 U.S. 645, 96 S.Ct. 1154, 47 L.Ed.2d 366 (1976), per curiam—involving a Philadelphia fireman who was terminated when he moved to New Jersey—held that "a municipal regulation requiring employees of the city [to] be residents of the city" did not impair the "right to travel interstate as defined in *Shapiro,*" which questioned neither "the validity of a condition placed upon municipal employment that a person be a resident *at the time* of his application," [6] nor "the validity of appropriately defined and uniformly applied bona fide residence requirements." [b] Is *McCarthy* consistent with *Shapiro* and *Doe?*

(d) MARTINEZ v. BYNUM, 461 U.S. 321, 103 S.Ct. 1838, 75 L.Ed.2d 879 (1983), per POWELL, J., upheld Texas' denial of free public education to children

---

a. For support of this view, see Arnold Loewy, *A Different and More Viable Theory of Equal Protection,* 57 N.C.L.Rev. 1 (1978); Michael Perry, *Modern Equal Protection: A Conceptualization and Appraisal,* 79 Colum.L.Rev. 1023 (1979).

6. Nor did [it] involve a public agency's relationship with its own employees which, of course, may justify greater control than over the citizenry at large. Cf. *Pickering v. Board of Educ.* [p. 885 supra]; *Broadrick v. Oklahoma,* [p. 644 supra].

b. Burger, C.J., and Brennan and Blackmun, JJ., would set the case for argument.

who, apart from their parents or guardians, reside in the school district "for the sole purpose of attending" the public schools: "A bona fide residence requirement [with] respect to attendance in public free schools does not violate the Equal Protection Clause [7] [nor does it] burden or penalize the constitutional right of interstate travel, for any person is free to move to a State and to establish residence there. [A]t the very least, a school district generally would be justified in requiring school-age children or their parents to satisfy the traditional, basic residence criteria—i.e., to live in the district with a bona fide intention of remaining there—before it treated them as residents." Marshall, J., dissented, mainly on the ground that an "intention of remaining" is not a proper criterion for a bona fide residence requirement. Is *Martinez* consistent with *Shapiro* and *Doe?*

(e) After *Shapiro,* may a state adopt a "one-year-waiting-period" in which the newcomer receives no more welfare than in the state from which he came?

3. *Other waiting-period requirements.* (a) *Voting.* DUNN v. BLUMSTEIN, 405 U.S. 330, 92 S.Ct. 995, 31 L.Ed.2d 274 (1972), per MARSHALL, J., held that Tennessee's voting registration requirements—of residence in the state for one year and in the county for three months—violate equal protection. Although "States have the power to require that voters be bona fide residents of the relevant political subdivision," it is the "additional *durational* residence requirement which appellee challenges. [Here], whether we look to the benefit withheld by the classification (the opportunity to vote) or the basis for the classification (recent interstate travel)," the classification must be "*necessary* to promote a *compelling* governmental interest. [In] pursuing that important interest, the State cannot choose means which unnecessarily burden or restrict constitutionally protected activity."

First, as for the state's interest in "preventing fraud [by] keeping nonresidents from voting, [the] record is totally devoid of any evidence that durational residence requirements are in fact necessary to identify bona fide residents." Second, "the State cannot seriously maintain that it is 'necessary' to reside for a year in the State and three months in the county in order to be minimally knowledgeable about congressional, state or even purely local elections. [T]he conclusive presumptions of durational residence requirements are much too crude." [c]

BURGER, C.J., dissented: "It is no more a denial of Equal Protection for a State to require newcomers to be exposed to state and local problems for a reasonable period such as one year before voting, than it is to require children to wait 18 years before [voting.] Some lines must be drawn. To challenge such lines by the 'compelling state interest' standard is to condemn them all." [d]

---

7. A bona fide residence requirement implicates no "suspect" classification, and therefore is not subject to strict scrutiny. Indeed, there is nothing invidiously discriminatory about a bona fide residence requirement if it is uniformly applied. Thus the question is simply whether there is a rational basis for it.

This view assumes, of course, that the "service" that the State would deny to nonresidents is not a fundamental right protected by the Constitution. * * *

c. Blackmun, J., concurred in the result. Powell and Rehnquist, JJ., did not participate.

d. *Marston v. Lewis,* 410 U.S. 679, 93 S.Ct. 1211, 35 L.Ed.2d 627 (1973), per curiam, upheld Arizona's 50-day durational residency requirement for state and local elections as "necessary to permit preparation of accurate voter lists." *Burns v. Fortson,* 410 U.S. 686, 93 S.Ct. 1209, 35 L.Ed.2d 633 (1973), upheld a similar Georgia provision, noting that "the 50-day registration period approaches the outer constitutional limits in this area" (Blackmun, J., concurring only in the result because of objection to this statement).

Marshall, J., joined by Douglas and Brennan, JJ., dissented, observing that *Dunn* "held that

(b) *Medical care.* MEMORIAL HOSPITAL v. MARICOPA COUNTY, 415 U.S. 250, 94 S.Ct. 1076, 39 L.Ed.2d 306 (1974), per MARSHALL, J., held an Arizona statute—requiring one year's residence in the county for indigents to receive nonemergency hospitalization or medical care at county expense—violative of equal protection: "Although any durational residence requirement impinges to some extent on the right to travel," *Shapiro* "did not declare such requirements to be per se unconstitutional." It is only a state classification that "operates to *penalize* [indigents] for exercising their right to migrate to and settle in that state" which "must be justified by a compelling state interest. [*Dunn*] found that the denial of the franchise, 'a fundamental political right,' was a penalty [and *Shapiro*] found denial of the basic 'necessities of life' to be a penalty. Nonetheless, the Court has declined to strike down state statutes requiring one year of residence as a condition to lower tuition at state institutions of higher education.[12] Whatever the ultimate parameters of the *Shapiro* penalty analysis, it is at least clear that medical care is as much 'a basic necessity of life' to an indigent as welfare assistance." For reasons similar to those in *Shapiro*, the state has not met its "heavy burden of justification." [e]

REHNQUIST, J., dissented: "[F]ees for use of transportation facilities such as taxes on airport users,[12] have been upheld [against] attacks based upon the right to travel. [T]he line to be derived from our prior cases is that some financial impositions on interstate travelers have such indirect or inconsequential impact on travel that they simply do not constitute the type of direct purposeful barriers struck down" in *Shapiro*. "The solicitude which the Court has shown in cases involving the right to vote, and the virtual denial of entry inherent in denial of welfare benefits—'the very means by which to live'—ought not be so casually extended to the alleged deprivation here. Rather the Court should examine, as it has done in the past, whether the challenged requirement erects a real and purposeful barrier to movement, [or] whether the effects on travel, viewed realistically, are merely incidental and remote."

(c) *Divorce.* SOSNA v. IOWA, 419 U.S. 393, 95 S.Ct. 553, 42 L.Ed.2d 532 (1975), per REHNQUIST, J., upheld a one-year residency requirement to file for divorce: The laws in *Shapiro* and *Maricopa* "were justified on the basis of budgetary or record-keeping considerations which were held insufficient to outweigh the constitutional claims of the individuals. But Iowa's divorce residency requirement is of a different stripe. [A] decree of divorce [will] affect [both spouses'] marital status and very likely their property rights. Where a married couple has minor children, a decree of divorce would usually include provisions for their custody and support. With consequences of such moment riding on a

---

a 30-day residency requirement provided the State with '[ample time to] complete whatever administrative tasks are necessary to prevent fraud' in the process of voter registration."

Compare *Rosario v. Rockefeller*, Part I, B supra.

12. See *Vlandis v. Kline* [412 U.S. 441, 93 S.Ct. 2230, 37 L.Ed.2d 63 (1973) invalidating the statutory conclusive presumption that a student who applied from out of state was, therefore, a non-resident for tuition purposes for the entire period of attendance at a public university. *Starns v. Malkerson*, 401 U.S. 985, 91 S.Ct. 1231, 28 L.Ed.2d 527 (1971) summarily affirmed a Minnesota Regulation denying a student the opportunity to show residency for tuition purposes until the student had lived in

the state for one year. *Vlandis* was part of series of cases invalidating legislation for enacting irrebuttable presumptions in violation of due process. The doctrine was sharply confined in *Weinberger v. Salfi*, 422 U.S. 749, 95 S.Ct. 2457, 45 L.Ed.2d 522 (1975)].

e. Burger, C.J., and Blackmun, J., concurred in the result. Douglas, J., filed a separate opinion: "So far as interstate travel per se is considered, I share the doubts of my Brother Rehnquist. [Here,] invidious discrimination against the poor [is] the critical issue."

12. See *Evansville-Vanderburgh Airport Auth. Dist. v. Delta Airlines*, 405 U.S. 707, 92 S.Ct. 1349, 31 L.Ed.2d 620 (1972).

divorce decree issued by its courts, Iowa may insist that one seeking to initiate such a proceeding have the modicum of attachment to the State required here. Such a requirement additionally furthers the State's parallel interests in both avoiding officious intermeddling in matters in which another State has a paramount interest, and in minimizing the susceptibility of its own divorce decrees to collateral attack." [f]

MARSHALL, J., joined by Brennan, J., dissented, relying on *Boddie v. Connecticut,* Part III infra: The right to divorce "is of such fundamental importance" that the law "penalizes interstate travel within the meaning of *Shapiro, Dunn,* and *Maricopa.* [The] Court has not only declined to apply the 'compelling interest' test to this case, it has conjured up possible justifications for the State's restriction in a manner much more akin to the lenient standard" of equal protection review. A "simple requirement of domicile—physical presence plus intent to remain—[would] remove the rigid one-year barrier while permitting the State to restrict the availability of its divorce process to citizens who are genuinely its own." [g]

(d) *The decisions' rationale.* Do the cases explain how the Court determines whether a "waiting-period" requirement "operates to *penalize* " the right to travel? In both *Dunn* and *Maricopa* the Court conceded "that there is no evidence in the record before us that anyone was actually deterred from traveling by the challenged restriction [but] *Shapiro* did not rest upon a finding that denial of welfare actually deterred travel. Nor have other 'right to travel' [cases] always relied on the presence of actual deterrence." Consider 88 Harv.L.Rev. 117–18 (1974): "[T]he Court should consider the deterrent effect [rather] than attempt, as does Justice Marshall's 'penalty' analysis, to assess the importance of various state benefits to immigrants. Insofar as the validity of a given requirement depends upon the latter, what is being protected is not the right to travel, but the right to the withheld benefit."

Does the Court *presume* that withholding of certain benefits (but not others) deters travel? Would this explain the "basic necessity of life" emphasis in *Shapiro* and *Maricopa?* Does it account for the result in *Sosna?* In *Dunn?* Are *Shapiro* and *Maricopa* distinguishable from *Dunn* and *Sosna* because only the former tend to "fence out indigents" (*Shapiro;* cf. Douglas, J., in *Maricopa*)? [h] See Part III infra. Is *Dunn* explicable on other grounds? See Part I, B supra.

Should the decisions turn on whether residency requirements reflect a "reasonable concern for proof of domiciliary intent"? See William Cohen, *Equal Treatment for Newcomers,* 1 Const.Comm. 9, 19 (1984).

(e) *Other problems.* What of the validity of waiting-period requirements to be eligible for public housing? To be a candidate for elective office? See Note, *Durational Residency Requirements for Candidates,* 40 U.Chi.L.Rev. 357 (1973). To be admitted to the bar? To obtain public employment? See Note, 67 Calif.L.Rev. 386 (1979).

f. White, J., dissented on procedural grounds.

g. For the view that "durational residency requirements for state benefits and services are permissible only to the extent they respond to a reasonable concern for proof of domiciliary intent," see William Cohen, *Equal Treatment for Newcomers: The Core Meaning of National and State Citizenship,* 1 Const.Comment. 9 (1984).

h. For the view that *Sosna* may be distinguished from *Shapiro* and *Maricopa* because of the absence of impermissible state "motivation," see Loewy, fn. a after *Shapiro,* at 38–39; J. Morris Clark, *Legislative Motivation and Fundamental Rights in Constitutional Law,* 15 San Diego L.Rev. 953, 984–90 (1978).

4. *Length of residence requirements.* ZOBEL v. WILLIAMS, 457 U.S. 55, 102 S.Ct. 2309, 72 L.Ed.2d 672 (1982), per BURGER, C.J., held that Alaska's scheme of distributing its revenue from state-owned oil reserves to its citizens "in varying amounts, retroactively based on the length of each citizen's residence, violates the equal protection rights of newer state citizens." The Court held that two of Alaska's stated objectives—"creating a financial incentive for individuals to establish and maintain Alaska residence, and assuring prudent management of the [oil revenues] and the State's natural and mineral resources"—were "not rationally related to the distinctions Alaska seeks to draw." And, under *Shapiro,* the objective of rewarding "contributions of various kinds, both tangible and intangible, which residents have made during their years of residence," was "not a legitimate state purpose. [Such] reasoning could open the door to state apportionment of other rights, benefits and services according to length of residency. It would permit the states to divide citizens into expanding numbers of permanent classes. Such a result would be clearly impermissible."

BRENNAN, J., joined by Marshall, Blackmun and Powell, JJ., joined the Court's opinion, adding that "the Citizenship Clause of the Fourteenth Amendment [bars] degrees of citizenship based on length of residence. And the Equal Protection Clause would not tolerate such distinctions. In short, as much as the right to travel, equality of citizenship is of the essence in our republic. [Thus], discrimination on the basis of residence must be supported by a valid state interest independent of the discrimination itself. [L]ength of residence may, for example, be used to test the bona fides of citizenship—and allegiance and attachment may bear some rational relationship to a very limited number of legitimate state purposes. Cf. *Chimento v. Stark,* 353 F.Supp. 1211 (D.N.H.), affirmed, 414 U.S. 802, 94 S.Ct. 125, 38 L.Ed.2d 39 (1973) (seven year citizenship requirement to run for governor); U.S. Const., art. I, § 2, cl. 2, § 3, cl. 3; art. II, § 1, cl. 4. But those instances in which length of residence could provide a legitimate basis for distinguishing one citizen from another are rare."

O'CONNOR, J., concurred: "A desire to compensate citizens for their prior contributions is neither inherently invidious nor irrational. Under some circumstances, the objective may be wholly reasonable.[1] Even a generalized desire to reward citizens for past endurance, particularly in a State where years of hardship only recently have produced prosperity, is not innately improper. The difficulty is that plans enacted to further this objective necessarily treat new residents of a State less favorably than the longer-term residents who have past contributions to 'reward.' * * * Stripped to its essentials, the plan denies non-Alaskans settling in the State the same privileges afforded longer-term residents. The Privileges and Immunities Clause of Article IV [addresses] just this type of discrimination.

" * * * I believe [that] application of the Privileges and Immunities Clause to controversies involving the 'right to travel' would at least begin the task of reuniting this elusive right with the constitutional principles it embodies. [I]

---

1. A State, for example, might choose to divide its largesse among all persons who previously have contributed their time to volunteer community organizations. If the State graded its dividends according to the number of years devoted to prior community service, it could be said that the State intended "to reward citizens for past contributions." Alternatively, a State might enact a tax credit for citizens who contribute to the State's ecology by building alternative fuel sources or establishing recycling plants. If the State made this credit retroactive, to benefit those citizens who launched these improvements before they became fashionable, the State once again would be rewarding past contributions. The Court's opinion would dismiss these objectives as wholly illegitimate. I would recognize them as valid goals and inquire only whether their implementation infringed any constitutionally protected interest.

conclude that Alaska's disbursement scheme violates [the] Privileges and Immunities Clause" because there is nothing "to indicate that noncitizens constitute a peculiar source of the evil at which the statute is aimed" and no " 'substantial relationship' between the evil and the discrimination practiced against the noncitizens. *Hicklin v. Orbeck.*" [i]

REHNQUIST, J., dissented: "[T]he illegitimacy of a State's recognizing past contributions of its citizens has been established by the Court only in certain cases considering an infringement of the right to travel, and the majority itself rightly declines to apply the strict scrutiny analysis of those right-to-travel cases. The distribution scheme at issue in this case impedes no person's right to travel to and settle in Alaska; if anything, the prospect of receiving annual cash dividends would encourage immigration to Alaska." [j]

ATTORNEY GENERAL v. SOTO–LOPEZ, 476 U.S. 898, 106 S.Ct. 2317, 90 L.Ed.2d 899 (1986), held violative of equal protection a New York civil service employment preference for residents who served in the military during time of war and who were New York residents when they entered the service. BRENNAN, J., joined by Marshall, Blackmun and Powell, JJ., recognized that "the benefit sought here may not rise to the same level of importance as the necessities of life and the right to vote, [but such] a permanent deprivation of a significant benefit, based only on the fact of nonresidence at a past point in time, clearly operates to penalize appellees' for exercising their rights to migrate. [The] State has not met its heavy burden of proving that it has selected a means of pursuing a compelling state interest which does not impinge unnecessarily on constitutionally protected interests."

BURGER, C.J.—with whom White, J., agreed—concurred in the judgment because, under *Zobel* and *Hooper*—in which "we had no occasion to reach the issues whether the classifications would survive heightened scrutiny or whether the right to travel was violated"—"the statutory scheme cannot pass even the minimum rationality test."

O'CONNOR, J., joined by Rehnquist and Stevens, JJ., dissented, reasoning along the lines of her concurrence in *Zobel* and the dissents in *Zobel* and *Hooper*: "[F]inding that this scheme in theory or practical effect constitutes a 'penalty' on appellees' fundamental right to settle in New York or on their 'right to migrate' seems to me ephemeral, and completely unnecessary to safeguard the constitutional purpose of 'maintaining a Union rather than a mere "league of states." ' *Zobel* (O'Connor, J., concurring in judgment). Thus, heightened scrutiny, either under the 'right to migrate' or the Equal Protection Clause is inappropriate. Under

---

i. For views generally supportive of O'Connor, J.'s analysis, see David Bogen, *The Privileges and Immunities Clause of Article IV*, 37 Case W.L.Rev. 794 (1987); Note, *State Parochialism, the Right to Travel, and the Privileges and Immunities Clause of Article IV*, 41 Stan.L.Rev. 1557 (1989).

j. See also *Hooper v. Bernalillo County Assessor*, 472 U.S. 612, 105 S.Ct. 2862, 86 L.Ed.2d 487 (1985), per Burger, C.J., holding that a New Mexico property tax exemption for only those Vietnam veterans who were state residents before May 1976 "is not rationally related to the State's asserted legislative goal[s]," and thus "suffers the same constitutional flaw [as] *Zobel*": "[T]he Equal Protection Clause [forbids] the State to prefer established resident veterans over newcomers in [the] apportionment of an economic benefit."

Stevens, J., joined by Rehnquist and O'Connor, JJ., dissented: The classification "rationally furthers a legitimate state purpose. [The] need to budget for the future is itself a valid reason for [a limit] on the size of potential beneficiaries."

rational basis review, New York [is] attempting to say 'thank you' to those who personified New York's sacrifice and effort to 'do its part' in supporting this Nation's war efforts."

III. WELFARE

DANDRIDGE v. WILLIAMS, 397 U.S. 471, 90 S.Ct. 1153, 25 L.Ed.2d 491 (1970): Maryland's Aid to Families with Dependent Children program gave most eligible families their computed "standard of need," but imposed a "maximum limitation" on the total amount any family could receive. The Court, per STEWART, J., held this did not violate equal protection: "[H]ere we deal with state regulation in the social and economic field, not affecting freedoms guaranteed by the Bill of Rights, and claimed to violate the Fourteenth Amendment only because the regulation results in some disparity in grants of welfare payments to the largest AFDC families.[16] In [this area] a State does not violate [equal protection] merely because the classifications made by its laws are imperfect." "It is enough that the State's action be rationally based and free from invidious discrimination."

"To be sure, [many cases] enunciating this [standard] have in the main involved state regulation of business or industry. The administration of public welfare assistance, by contrast, involves the most basic economic needs of impoverished human beings, [but] we can find no basis for applying a different constitutional standard. [By] combining a limit on the recipient's grant with permission to retain money earned, without reduction in the amount of the grant, Maryland provides an incentive to seek gainful employment. And by keeping the maximum family AFDC grants to the minimum wage a steadily employed head of a household receives, the State maintains some semblance of an equitable balance between families on welfare and those supported by an employed breadwinner.

"It is true that in some AFDC families there may be no person who is employable. It is also true that with respect to AFDC families whose determined standard of need is below the regulatory maximum, [the] employment incentive is absent. But the Equal Protection Clause does not require that a State must choose between attacking every aspect of a problem or not attacking the problem at all. [T]he intractable economic, social, and even philosophical problems presented by public welfare assistance programs are not the business of this Court." [a]

MARSHALL, J., joined by Brennan, J., dissented: [b] "[T]he only distinction between those children with respect to whom assistance is granted and those [denied] is the size of the family into which the child permits himself to be born. [This] is grossly underinclusive in terms of the class which the AFDC program was designed to assist, namely *all* needy dependent children, [and requires] a persuasive justification * * *.

"The Court never undertakes to inquire for such a justification; rather it avoids the task by focusing upon the abstract dichotomy between two different approaches to equal protection problems which have been utilized by this Court.

"[The] cases relied on by the Court, in which a 'mere rationality' test was actually used, e.g., *Williamson v. Lee Optical Co.* [Sec. 1 supra], [involve] regulation of business interests. The extremes to which the Court has gone in dreaming

---

16. Cf. *Shapiro,* where, by contrast, the Court found state interference with the constitutionally protected freedom of interstate travel.

a. See also Lindsey v. Normet, 405 U.S. 56, 92 S.Ct. 862, 31 L.Ed.2d 36 (1972) (the assur-

ance of adequate housing is not a fundamental right).

b. Douglas, J., dissented on the ground (agreed to also by Marshall and Brennan, JJ.) that the Maryland law was inconsistent with the Social Security Act.

up rational bases for state regulation in that area may in many instances be ascribed to a healthy revulsion from the Court's earlier excesses in using the Constitution to protect interests which have more than enough power to protect themselves in the legislative halls.[c] This case, involving the literally vital interests of a powerless minority—poor families without breadwinners—is far removed from the area of business regulation, as the Court concedes. * * *

"In my view, equal protection analysis of this case is not appreciably advanced by the a priori definition of a 'right,' fundamental [and thus invoking the "compelling" test] or otherwise.[14] Rather, concentration must be placed upon the character of the classification in question, the relative importance to individuals in the class discriminated against of the governmental benefits which they do not receive, and the asserted state interests in support of the classification. * * *

"It is the individual interests here [that] most clearly distinguish this case from the 'business regulation' [cases]. AFDC support to needy dependent children provides the stuff which sustains those children's lives: food, clothing, shelter. And this Court has already recognized [that] when a benefit, even a 'gratuitous' benefit, is necessary to sustain life, stricter constitutional standards, both procedural [17] and substantive,[18] are applied to the deprivation of that benefit.

"Nor is the distinction upon which the deprivation is here based—the distinction between large and small families—one which readily commends [itself].

c. Compare J. Harvie Wilkinson, *The Supreme Court, the Equal Protection Clause, and the Three Faces of Constitutional Equality,* 61 Va.L.Rev. 945, 1008–09 (1975): "*Lochner* and cases like it arose precisely because business was not getting its way, because what were then thought traditional employer prerogatives were succumbing to a rising tide of social and regulatory legislation. Conversely, [the] legislative trend ever since the New Deal has been running more and more toward social welfare programs, [whose] stated purpose is to help the poor and less well off. Indiscriminate application of [Marshall, J.'s] position, therefore, would invite the thought that the major change since *Lochner* is that the Court has switched political sides."

Is neutrality between these political sides desirable? Consider J.M. Balkin, *The Footnote,* 83 Nw.U.L.Rev. 275, 311: "The lesson of [repudiating] *Lochner* was that courts should not hinder legislatures from pursuing human rights through alteration of property rights; and that the state was responsible for the reproduction of disparities in economic power achieved through maintenance of the status quo. [By] understanding [the move away from *Lochner*], as the strict separation of political and economic liberty[,] the pluralist faith of *Carolene Products* reintroduced, at a new level, the very evil that *West Coast Hotel* found in *Lochner*. If the *Lochner* court had seen differences in economic status as natural and not seriously affecting human rights, so now *Carolene Products* saw differences in political power stemming from differences in economic power as prepolitical and not seriously threatening the purity of the democratic process."

14. Appellees do argue that their "fundamental rights" are infringed [and cite] *Skinner* for the proposition that the "right of procreation" is fundamental. [B]ut the effect of the maximum grant regulation upon the right of procreation is marginal and indirect at best, totally unlike the compulsory sterilization law [in] *Skinner*.

[T]he Court's insistence that equal protection analysis turns on the basis of a closed category of "fundamental rights" involves a curious value judgment. It is certainly difficult to believe that a person whose very survival is at stake would be comforted by the knowledge that his "fundamental" rights are preserved intact. * * *

17. See *Goldberg v. Kelly*.

18. [See] *Kirk v. Board of Regents,* 273 Cal.App.2d 430, 440–441, 78 Cal.Rptr. 260, 266–267 (1969), appeal dismissed, 396 U.S. 554, 90 S.Ct. 754, 24 L.Ed.2d 747 (1970), upholding a one-year residency requirement for tuition-free graduate education at state university, and distinguishing *Shapiro* on the ground that it "involved the immediate and pressing need for preservation of life and health of persons unable to live without public assistance, and their dependent children."

These cases and those cited n. 17, supra, suggest that whether or not there is a constitutional "right" to subsistence (as to which see n. 14, supra), deprivations of benefits necessary for subsistence will receive closer constitutional scrutiny, under both the Due Process and Equal Protection Clauses, than will deprivation of less essential forms of governmental entitlements.

Indeed, governmental discrimination between children on the basis of a factor over which they have no control [bears] some resemblance to the classification between legitimate and illegitimate children which we condemned [in Sec. 3, III supra]."

On examination, the asserted state interests were either "arbitrary," impermissible, of "minimum rationality," "drastically overinclusive," or "grossly underinclusive." "The existence of [other] alternatives [to satisfy asserted state interests] does not, of course, conclusively establish the invalidity of the maximum grant regulation. It is certainly relevant, however, in appraising the overall interest of the State in the maintenance of the regulation [against] a fundamental constitutional challenge." [d]

Notes and Questions

1. Consider Richard Fallon, *Individual Rights and the Powers of Government*, 27 Ga.L.Rev. 343, 377 (1993): "Perhaps the most pervasive strategy in constitutional law is for courts to distinguish between negative and positive freedoms; to insist that constitutional rights stand as barriers against government coercion and discrimination, but not require the government affirmatively to come to anyone's aid." Is the judiciary an inappropriate institution to manage and enforce positive rights such as rights to welfare or housing. If not, should a legislator who has taken an oath to defend the Constitution feel an obligation to recognize welfare rights on any of the following theories?

(a) Rights should be determined on the basis of what is important to human beings. Welfare rights are undeniably important.

(b) The Constitution assumes that persons are entitled to equal concern and respect. To deny welfare rights is to deny the concern and respect owed to every person.

(c) The Constitution assumes that persons are citizens who will participate meaningfully in the democratic process including political dialogue about the future direction of the country. Citizens deprived of welfare rights are unlikely to participate effectively in the democratic process.

(d) The state is responsible for much American poverty. In an effort to avoid inflation, it has knowingly created unemployment for millions of workers. Similarly, it has created much unemployment by closing defense plants and the like. At the same time the government engages in socialism for the rich while it tolerates capitalism for the poor. It subsidizes middle and upper class housing through tax breaks; it spends billions on behalf of corporations. Given that the state is a major player in the economy, and that it creates much unemployment as it otherwise distributes wealth through the economy, equal protection demands minimum welfare entitlements at the very least.

2. Does *Dandridge* wrongfully punish innocent children? Does it impinge on reproductive rights? Or do those arguments assume the existence of welfare rights?

---

d. See also *Richardson v. Belcher,* 404 U.S. 78, 92 S.Ct. 254, 30 L.Ed.2d 231 (1971), per Stewart, J., upholding a provision of the Social Security Act reducing disability benefits for those who receive state worker's compensation—but not for those who receive compensation from private insurance or from tort claim awards—as "rationally based." Douglas, J., and Marshall, J., joined by Brennan, J., dissented.

See generally Samuel Krislov, *The OEO Lawyers Fail to Constitutionalize a Right to Welfare: A Study in the Uses and Limits of the Judicial Process,* 58 Minn.L.Rev. 211 (1973).

3. Evaluate the following hypothetical commentary: "Poverty is a relative concept. The American "poor" are many times wealthier than the poor in other countries. Recognition of welfare rights would do little to remove the stigma of inequality, would provide incentives not to work and undermine the work ethic, would reward the wrong people while creating a needless bureaucracy, would discourage private giving, and would impair the efficiency of the American economy."

4. For a range of views, see Susan Frelich Appleton, *Beyond The Limits of Reproductive Choice: The Contributions of the Abortion–Funding Cases to Fundamental–Rights Analysis and to the Welfare–Rights Thesis*, 81 Colum.L.Rev. 721 (1981); Susan Frelich Appleton, *Professor Michelman's Quest for a Constitutional Welfare Right*, 3 Washington University Law Quarterly 715 (1979); Robert Bork, *The Impossibility of Finding Welfare Rights in the Constitution*, 1979 Wash.U.L.Q. 695; Erwin Chemerinsky, *Making the Right Case for A Constitutional Right to Minimum Entitlements*, 44 Mercer L.Rev. 525 (1993); Peter Edelman, *The Next Century of Our Constitution: Rethinking Our Duty to the Poor*, 39 Hast.L.J. 1 (1987); Stephen Loffredo, *Poverty, Democracy and Constitutional Law*, 141 U.Pa. L.Rev. 1277 (1993); Frank Michelman, *Welfare Rights in a Constitutional Democracy*, 1979 Wash.U.L.Q.; Frank Michelman, *On Protecting the Poor Under the Fourteenth Amendment*, 83 Harv.L.Rev. 7 (1969); Ralph Winter, Jr. *Changing Concepts of Equality: From Equality Before the Law to the Welfare State*, 1979 Wash.U.L.Q. 741.

IV. ACCESS TO THE COURTS

Several Warren Court decisions (in addition to *Harper v. Virginia Bd. of Elec.*, Part I, A supra) held that state laws or practices that operated to the disadvantage of poor people—in contrast to "de jure" discrimination against the poor—violated equal protection (and/or due process). Most of these rulings, as well as those of the Burger Court following this path, concern the question of whether states must waive fees (or provide certain services without charge) to poor people who could not otherwise effectively participate in criminal or civil litigation. These decisions are included in this section. Other kinds of laws that have a disproportionate impact on the poor are considered in the section that follows.

GRIFFIN v. ILLINOIS, 351 U.S. 12, 76 S.Ct. 585, 100 L.Ed. 891 (1956), held that a state must furnish an indigent criminal defendant with a free trial transcript (or its equivalent) if it were necessary for "adequate and effective appellate review" of the conviction. BLACK, J., joined by Warren, C.J., and Douglas and Clark, JJ., found that "both equal protection and due process emphasize [that in] criminal trials a State can no more discriminate on account of poverty than on account of religion, race, or color. Plainly the ability to pay costs in advance bears no rational relationship to a defendant's guilt or innocence and could not be used as an excuse to deprive a defendant of a fair trial. [It] is true that a State is not required by the federal constitution to provide appellate [review]. See, e.g., *McKane v. Durston*, 153 U.S. 684, 687–88, 14 S.Ct. 913, 914–15, 38 L.Ed. 867 (1894). But that is not to say that a State that does grant appellate review can do so in a way that discriminates against some convicted defendants on account of their poverty. * * *

"All of the States now provide some method of appeal from criminal convictions, recognizing the importance of appellate review to a correct adjudication of guilt or innocence. [Thus] to deny adequate review to the poor means that many of them may lose their life, liberty or property because of unjust convictions which appellate courts would set aside. [There] can be no equal justice where the kind of trial a man gets depends on the amount of money he has." [a]

DOUGLAS v. CALIFORNIA, 372 U.S. 353, 83 S.Ct. 814, 9 L.Ed.2d 811 (1963), per DOUGLAS, J., relying on *Griffin,* held that a state must appoint counsel for an indigent for "the first appeal, granted as a matter of [statutory right] from a criminal conviction." It disapproved California's system of appointing counsel only when the appellate court made "an independent investigation of the record and determine[d] it would be of advantage to the defendant or helpful to [the] court": "[A] state can, consistently with the Fourteenth Amendment, provide for differences so long as the result does not amount to a denial of due process or an 'invidious discrimination.' Absolute equality is not [required]. But where the merits of the one and only appeal an indigent has as of right are decided without benefit of counsel, we think an unconstitutional line has been drawn between rich and poor.

"When an indigent is forced to run this gantlet of a preliminary showing of merit, the right to appeal does not comport with fair procedure. [There] is lacking that equality demanded by the Fourteenth Amendment where the rich man, who appeals as of right, enjoys the benefit of counsel's examination into the record, research of the law, and marshalling of arguments on his behalf, while the indigent, already burdened by a preliminary determination that his case is without merit, is forced to shift for himself. The indigent, where the record is unclear or the errors are hidden, has only the right to a meaningless ritual, while the rich man has a meaningful appeal."

HARLAN, J., joined by Stewart, J., dissented from the Court's reliance, as in *Griffin,* "on a blend of the Equal Protection and Due Process Clauses," believing that "this case should be judged solely under the Due Process Clause": "States, of course, are prohibited by the Equal Protection Clause from discriminating between 'rich' and 'poor' *as such* in the formulation and application of their laws. But it is a far different thing to suggest that this provision prevents the State from adopting a law of general applicability that may affect the poor more harshly than it does the rich, or, on the other hand, from making some effort to redress economic imbalances while not eliminating them entirely.

"Every financial exaction which the State imposes on a uniform basis is more easily satisfied by the well-to-do than by the indigent. Yet I take it that no one would dispute the constitutional power of the State to levy a uniform sales tax, to charge tuition at a state university, to fix rates for the purchase of water from a municipal corporation, to impose a standard fine for criminal violations, or to establish minimum bail for various categories of offenses. Nor could it be contended that the State may not classify as crimes acts which the poor are more likely to commit than are the rich. And surely, there would be no basis for

---

a. Frankfurter, J., concurred in the result. Burton, Minton, Reed and Harlan, JJ., dissented.

For subsequent application of *Griffin,* see e.g., *Burns v. Ohio,* 360 U.S. 252, 79 S.Ct. 1164, 3 L.Ed.2d 1209 (1959) (indigent criminal defendant cannot be required to pay filing fee for appeal); *Long v. District Court,* 385 U.S. 192, 87 S.Ct. 362, 17 L.Ed.2d 290 (1966) (indigent must be furnished free transcript of state habeas corpus hearing for use on appeal from denial of habeas, although transcript not a sine qua non to access to appellate court). Cf. *Britt v. North Carolina,* 404 U.S. 226, 92 S.Ct. 431, 30 L.Ed.2d 400 (1971) (adequate alternative to transcript existed). For analysis of *Griffin,* see Michael Klarman, *An Interpretive History of Modern Equal Protection,* 90 Mich.L.Rev. 213, 265–67 (1991).

attacking a state law which provided benefits for the needy simply because those benefits fell short of the goods or services that others could purchase for themselves.

"Laws such as these do not deny equal protection to the less fortunate for one essential reason: the Equal Protection Clause does not impose on the States 'an affirmative duty to lift the handicaps flowing from differences in economic circumstances.' To so construe it would be to read into the Constitution a philosophy of leveling that would be foreign to many of our basic concepts of the proper relations between government and society. [N]o matter how far the state rule might go in providing counsel for indigents, it could never be expected to satisfy an affirmative duty—if one existed—to place the poor on the same level as those who can afford the best legal talent available."

As for due process, "we have today held [that] there is an absolute right to the services of counsel at trial. *Gideon v. Wainwright*, 372 U.S. 335, 83 S.Ct. 792, 9 L.Ed.2d 799 (1963). But [a]ppellate review is in itself not required by the Fourteenth Amendment, [and] thus the question presented is the narrow one whether the State's rules with respect to the appointment of counsel are so arbitrary or unreasonable, *in the context of the particular appellate procedure that it has established,* as to require their invalidation." Clark, J., also dissented.[b]

ROSS v. MOFFITT, 417 U.S. 600, 94 S.Ct. 2437, 41 L.Ed.2d 341 (1974), per REHNQUIST, J., held that *Douglas* does not require counsel for discretionary state appeals or for applications for review in the Supreme Court: As for due process, "it is clear that the State need not provide any appeal at all. The fact that an appeal *has* been provided does not automatically mean that a State then acts unfairly by refusing to provide counsel to indigent defendants at every stage of the way. Unfairness results only if indigents are singled out by the State and denied meaningful access to that system because of their poverty. That question is more profitably considered under an equal protection analysis [which] 'does not require absolute equality or precisely equal advantages,' [but] does require that the state appellate system be 'free of unreasoned distinctions' and that indigents have an adequate opportunity to present their claims fairly within the adversarial system.

"[P]rior to his seeking discretionary review in the State Supreme Court, [respondent's] claims 'had once been presented by a lawyer and passed upon by an [intermediate] appellate court.' *Douglas.* We do not believe that it can be said, therefore, that [respondent] is denied meaningful access to the North Carolina Supreme Court simply because the State does not appoint counsel to aid him in seeking review in that court. At that stage he will have, at the very least, [a record] of trial proceedings, a brief on his behalf in the Court of Appeals setting forth his claims of error, and in many cases an opinion by the Court of Appeals disposing of his case. These materials, supplemented by whatever submission respondent may make pro se, would appear to provide the Supreme Court of North Carolina with an adequate basis on which to base its decision to grant or deny [review].

"This is not to say, of course, that a skilled lawyer [would] not prove helpful to any litigant able to employ him. An indigent defendant seeking review in the

b. For exploration of the implications of *Griffin* and *Douglas*, see Yale Kamisar & Jesse Choper, *The Right to Counsel in Minnesota:* *Some Field Findings and Legal-Policy Observations*, 48 Minn.L.Rev. 1, 7–14 (1963).

Supreme Court of North Carolina is therefore somewhat handicapped in comparison with a wealthy [defendant].   But both the opportunity to have counsel prepare an initial brief in the Court of Appeals and the nature of discretionary review in the Supreme Court of North Carolina make this relative handicap far less than the handicap borne by the indigent defendant denied counsel on his initial appeal as of right in *Douglas*.   [The] duty of the State under our cases is not to duplicate the legal arsenal that may be privately retained by a criminal defendant, [but] only to assure the indigent defendant an adequate opportunity to present his claims fairly in the context of the State's appellate [process]."

Douglas, J., joined by Brennan and Marshall, JJ., dissented: "The right to discretionary review is a substantial one, and one where a lawyer can be of significant assistance to an indigent defendant.   It was correctly perceived below that the 'same concepts of fairness and equality, which require counsel in a first appeal of right, require counsel in other and subsequent discretionary appeals.' " c

---

TATE v. SHORT, 401 U.S. 395, 91 S.Ct. 668, 28 L.Ed.2d 130 (1971): An indigent accumulated $425 in fines for traffic offenses.   Texas law provided only for fines but required that those unable to pay be incarcerated to satisfy their fines at the rate of $5 per day.   The Court, per Brennan, J., reversed: Equal protection " 'requires that the statutory ceiling placed on imprisonment for any substantive offense be the same for all defendants irrespective of their economic status.' *Williams v. Illinois*, 399 U.S. 235, 90 S.Ct. 2018, 26 L.Ed.2d 586 (1970). [Thus, Texas cannot] limit the punishment to payment of the fine if one is able to pay it, yet convert the fine into a prison term for an [indigent].   Imprisonment in such a case is not imposed to further any penal objective of the State.   * * *

"There are, however, other alternatives [such as procedures for paying fines in installments] to which the State may constitutionally resort to serve its concededly valid interest in enforcing payment of fines.   [O]ur decision [should not] be understood as precluding imprisonment as an enforcement method when alternative means are unsuccessful despite the defendant's reasonable efforts to satisfy the fines by those means;   the determination of the constitutionality of [that] must await the presentation of a concrete case."   Black, J., concurred in the result.a

---

c.   See also *United States v. MacCollom*, 426 U.S. 317, 96 S.Ct. 2086, 48 L.Ed.2d 666 (1976) (5–4), relying on *Ross* to uphold provision of a free trial transcript for use in a collateral attack on a federal conviction only if a federal judge certifies that the claim is "not frivolous" and that the transcript is "needed to decide the issue."

See also *Lassiter v. Department of Social Servs.*, p. 641 supra (due process does not *always* require appointment of counsel for indigent parents in state suit to terminate parental status).

a.   Harlan, J., concurred on the basis of his concurrence in *Williams* where he "dissociated" himself from the Court's "equal protection rationale" which, if "fully realized," "would require that the consequence of punishment be the same for all individuals."

Compare William Clune, *The Supreme Court's Treatment of Wealth Discriminations Under the Fourteenth Amendment*, 1975 Sup. Ct.Rev. 289, 306: "The Court could require a schedule of fines fairly and thoughtfully designed to produce equal disutility on the average.   One possibility would be a fine of an equal percentage of [earnings].   Such a system would go most of the way toward curing the wrong but would not represent a great interference with the states' systems of criminal justice."

BEARDEN v. GEORGIA, 461 U.S. 660, 103 S.Ct. 2064, 76 L.Ed.2d 221 (1983), per O'CONNOR, J.,—noting that "due process and equal protection principles converge in these cases"—held that "it is fundamentally unfair" to "revoke a defendant's probation for failure to pay the imposed fine and restitution, absent evidence and findings that the defendant was somehow responsible for the failure or that alternative forms of punishment were inadequate": Probation "reflects a determination by the sentencing court that the State's penological interests do not require imprisonment. A probationer's failure to make reasonable efforts to repay his debt to society may indicate that this original determination needs reevaluation, [but 'only if alternate measures' such as 'extend[ing] the time for making payments, or reduc[ing] the fine, or direct[ing] that the probationer perform some form of labor or public service in lieu of the fine'] are not adequate to meet the State's interests in punishment and deterrence may the court imprison a probationer who has made sufficient bona fide efforts to pay." [b]

BODDIE v. CONNECTICUT, 401 U.S. 371, 91 S.Ct. 780, 28 L.Ed.2d 113 (1971), per HARLAN, J., sustained indigents' challenge to the state's requiring court fees and costs (averaging $60) in order to sue for divorce: "[M]arriage involves interests of basic importance in our society. [Without] a prior judicial imprimatur, individuals may freely enter into and rescind commercial contracts, for example, but we are unaware of any jurisdiction where private citizens may covenant for or dissolve marriages without state approval. [Thus], although they assert here due process rights as would-be plaintiffs, we think appellants' plight [is] akin to that of defendants faced with exclusion from the only forum effectively empowered to settle their disputes. [D]ue process requires, at a minimum, that absent a countervailing state interest of overriding significance, persons forced to settle their claims of right and duty through the judicial process must be given a meaningful opportunity to be heard." [d]

UNITED STATES v. KRAS, 409 U.S. 434, 93 S.Ct. 631, 34 L.Ed.2d 626 (1973), per BLACKMUN, J., held that the Bankruptcy Act's conditioning the right to discharge on payment of $50 fees does not violate fifth amendment due process, including "equal protection": "[A] debtor, in theory, and often in actuality, may adjust his debts by negotiated agreement with his creditors. [Thus,] *Boddie's* emphasis on [judicial] exclusivity finds no counterpart in the bankrupt's situation." Moreover, unlike free speech or marriage, bankruptcy is not a "fundamental" right demanding "the lofty requirement of a compelling governmental interest before [it] may be significantly regulated." Bankruptcy legislation "is in the area of economics and social welfare. See *Dandridge v. Williams* [Part IV infra]." Thus, the standard is "rational justification"—and "the rational basis for the fee

b. White, J., joined by Burger, C.J., and Powell and Rehnquist, JJ., concurred on the ground that the sentencing judge had "automatically" imposed a "long prison term" rather than making "a good-faith effort to impose a jail sentence that in terms of the state's sentencing objectives will be roughly equivalent to the fine and restitution that the defendant failed to pay."

May an indigent accused be denied pretrial release if he is incapable of posting required bail? See *Bandy v. United States,* 81 S.Ct. 197, 5 L.Ed.2d 218 (1960) (Douglas, J., as Circuit Justice).

d. Douglas, J., and Brennan, J., concurred, but relied on the equal protection rationale of *Griffin.* Black, J., dissented.

requirement is readily apparent": Congress' desire "to make the system self-sustaining and paid for by those who use [it]."

STEWART, J., joined by Douglas, Brennan and Marshall, JJ., dissented: "The bankrupt is bankrupt precisely for the reason that the State stands ready to exact all of his debts through garnishment, attachment, and the panoply of other creditor remedies. [I]n the unique situation of the indigent bankrupt the government provides the only effective means of his ever being free of these government imposed obligations. [While] the creditors of a bankrupt with assets might well desire to reach a compromise settlement, that possibility is foreclosed to the truly indigent bankrupt. [The] Court today holds that Congress may say that some of the poor are too poor even to go bankrupt." [e]

———

LITTLE v. STREATER, 452 U.S. 1, 101 S.Ct. 2202, 68 L.Ed.2d 627 (1981), per BURGER, C.J., held violative of due process Connecticut's refusal to pay the cost of blood grouping tests for indigent defendants in paternity actions. The Court stressed "the unique quality of blood grouping tests as a source of exculpatory evidence, the State's prominent role in the litigation,"—since the child was receiving welfare state law required the mother to institute the paternity action—"the 'quasi-criminal' overtones" of paternity proceedings, and the fact that state law made the defendant's testimony alone "insufficient to overcome the plaintiff's prima facie case": "Because appellant has no choice of an alternative forum and his interests, as well as those of the child, are constitutionally significant, this case is comparable to *Boddie* rather than to *Kras* and *Orwein*."

Notes and Questions

1. *Access to courts in civil proceedings.* (a) *Defendants.* Do the decisions (especially *Boddie*) establish that persons made defendants in civil suits cannot be denied the opportunity to defend—whether as a matter of due process or equal protection—because of their inability to pay a state imposed fee? See Comment, *The Heirs of Boddie: Court Access for Indigents After Kras and Ortwein,* 8 Harv.Civ.Rts.—Civ.Lib.L.Rev. 571 (1973).

(b) *Plaintiffs.* To what extent do the decisions invalidate court access fees for indigent plaintiffs? Does *Boddie* forbid such fees in *all* situations where state law makes courts "the only forum effectively empowered to settle the dispute"? Consider 85 Harv.L.Rev. 107 (1971): "Judicial approval is required to formalize legal relationships in [matters other than divorce]: adoption and custody of children, naturalization, change of a name, settlement of a decedent's estate, adjudication of incompetency, and awards of title to property in rem." Or do *Kras* (and *Ortwein*) also require that the right sought to be vindicated be "fundamental"? "Constitutional"? How do the cases line up in respect to these categories? Is the right to seek recovery for injury to person or property "fundamental"? See Part III infra. For the view that access to courts generally may be a right derived from the first amendment, see Note, *A First Amendment Right to Access to the Courts for Indigents,* 82 Yale L.J. 1055 (1973); or a right

---

e. Douglas, J., joined by Brennan, J., as well as Marshall, J., also dissented.

See also *Ortwein v. Schwab,* 410 U.S. 656, 93 S.Ct. 1172, 35 L.Ed.2d 572 (1973), upholding a requirement that indigents appealing an ad-verse decision in a welfare hearing pay a $25 state appellate court filing fee. (For further discussion of indigents and appeals, see *Lindsey v. Normet,* Part IV infra.)

analogous to voting, see Frank Michelman, *The Supreme Court and Litigation Access Fees: The Right to Protect One's Rights—Part II*, 1974 Duke L.J. 527.

Is the "judicial exclusivity" factor—that for bankruptcy but not for divorce "effective alternatives for the adjustment of differences remain"—meaningful? Desirable as a constitutional principle? Consider 85 Harv.L.Rev. 108 (1971): "Much of the incentive for parties to agree to private resolution of a dispute is supplied by the threat that either may resort to the judicial process. Moreover, an agreement is of small value to a party unable to enforce its terms in court. Thus, although a tort claimant does have power to resolve his dispute with the tortfeasor while a divorce plaintiff does not, the likelihood of a settlement for a tort claimant too poor to get into court seems no greater than the possibility that the *Boddie* plaintiffs will obtain the funds necessary to obtain judicial relief." See also Gary Goodpaster, *The Integration of Equal Protection, Due Process Standards, and the Indigent's Right of Free Access to the Courts*, 56 Ia.L.Rev. 223 (1970); Michelman, *supra—Part I*, 1973 Duke L.J. 1153, 1178–85.

2. *Other "payment requirements."* (a) May a state require indigents to pay a marriage license fee (n.b. the constitutional right of privacy)? A driver's license fee or interstate highway tolls or gasoline taxes (n.b. the constitutional right to travel)? May a state revoke the driver's license of an uninsured indigent who cannot post a security deposit after an accident? See Note, *Financial Responsibility Laws in Constitutional Perspective*, 61 Calif.L.Rev. 1072 (1973). Require a "court access fee" of an indigent plaintiff who seeks to enjoin an ordinance allegedly in violation of his first amendment rights? Require license fees from indigents to engage in certain occupations?

(b) May a public hospital deny abortions to indigents who cannot pay the established service charge? Cf. *Maher v. Roe*, Part V infra. May a state charge a fee to all those who use public streets or parks for "free speech" purposes to defray costs of cleaning up, etc.? See *Cox v. New Hampshire*, p. 914 supra. Are these situations distinguishable from *Harper* because they do not simply condition the right on payment of a tax but reimburse the state for costs? Compare *Griffin, Douglas* and *Lubin v. Panish* (Part I, C supra).

(c) For further consideration, see note 2 after *Rodriguez*, Part V infra. See generally Barbara Brudno, *Poverty, Inequality, and the Law* (1976).

V. EDUCATION

SAN ANTONIO IND. SCHOOL DIST. v. RODRIGUEZ
411 U.S. 1, 93 S.Ct. 1278, 36 L.Ed.2d 16 (1973).

Justice Powell delivered the opinion of the Court.

This suit attacking the Texas system of financing public education was initiated by Mexican-American parents [as] a class action on behalf of school children throughout the State who are members of minority groups or who are poor and reside in school districts having a low property tax base. * * *

Recognizing the need for increased state funding to help offset disparities in local spending [because of sizable differences in the value of assessable property between local school districts,] the state legislature [established the] Minimum Foundation School Program [which] accounts for approximately half of the total educational expenditures in Texas. [It] calls for state and local contributions to a fund earmarked specifically for teacher salaries, operating expenses, and transportation costs. The State [finances] approximately [80%]. The districts' share, known as the Local Fund Assignment, is apportioned among the school districts under a formula designed to reflect each district's relative taxpaying ability. * * *

The school district in which appellees reside, [Edgewood,] has been compared throughout this litigation with the Alamo Heights [District. Edgewood] is situated in the core-city sector of San Antonio in a residential neighborhood that has little commercial or industrial property. [A]pproximately 90% of the student population is Mexican-American and over 6% is Negro. The average assessed property value per pupil is $5,960—the lowest in the metropolitan area—and the median family income ($4,686) is also the lowest. At an equalized tax rate of $1.05 per $100 of assessed property—the highest in the metropolitan area—the district contributed $26 to the education of each child for the 1967–1968 school year above its Local Fund Assignment for the Minimum Foundation Program. The Foundation Program contributed $222 per pupil for a state-local total of $248. Federal funds added another $108 for a total of $356 per pupil.

Alamo Heights is the most affluent school district in San Antonio. [Its] school population [has] only 18% Mexican-Americans and less than 1% Negroes. The assessed property value per pupil exceeds $49,000 and the median family income is $8,001. In 1967–1968 the local tax rate of $.85 per $100 of valuation yielded $333 per pupil over and above its contribution to the Foundation Program. Coupled with the $225 provided from that Program, the district was able to supply $558 per student. Supplemented by a $36 per pupil grant from federal sources, Alamo Heights spent $594 per pupil.

[M]ore recent partial statistics indicate that [the] trend of increasing state aid has been significant. For the 1970–1971 school year, the Foundation School Program allotment for Edgewood was $356 per [pupil and] Alamo Heights [received] $491 per [pupil].[35] These recent figures also reveal the extent to which these two districts' allotments were funded from their own required contributions to the Local Fund Assignment. Alamo Heights, because of its relative wealth, was required to contribute out of its local property tax collections approximately $100 per pupil, or about 20% of its Foundation grant. Edgewood, on the other hand, paid only $8.46 per pupil, which is about 2.4% of its grant. [Finding] that wealth is a "suspect" classification and that education is a "fundamental" interest, the District Court held that the Texas system could be sustained only if the State could show that it was premised upon some compelling state interest. * * *

II. [The] wealth discrimination discovered [is] quite unlike any of the forms of wealth discrimination heretofore reviewed by this Court. [The] individuals who constituted the class discriminated against in our prior cases shared two distinguishing characteristics: because of their impecunity they were completely

---

35. [I]t is apparent that Alamo Heights has enjoyed a larger gain [due] to the emphasis in the State's allocation formula on the guaranteed minimum salaries for teachers. Higher salaries are guaranteed to teachers having more years of experience and possessing more advanced degrees. Therefore, Alamo Heights, which has a greater percentage of experienced personnel with advanced degrees, receives more State support. * * * Because more dollars have been given to districts that already spend more per pupil, such Foundation formulas have been described as "anti-equalizing." The formula, however, is anti-equalizing only if viewed in absolute terms. The percentage disparity between the two Texas districts is diminished substantially by State aid. Alamo Heights derived in 1967–1968 almost 13 times as much money from local taxes as Edgewood did. The State aid grants to each district in 1970–1971 lowered the ratio to approximately two to [one].

unable to pay for some desired benefit, and as a consequence, they sustained an absolute deprivation of a meaningful opportunity to enjoy that benefit [discussing *Griffin v. Illinois* and *Bullock v. Carter* [a]]. *Douglas v. California* [provides] no relief for those on whom the burdens of paying for a criminal defense are, relatively speaking, great but not insurmountable. Nor does it deal with relative differences in the quality of counsel acquired by the less wealthy. [And] *Williams* and *Tate* [do] not touch on the question whether equal protection is denied to persons with relatively less money on whom designated fines impose heavier burdens. * * *

[Even] a cursory examination however, demonstrates that neither of the two distinguishing characteristics of wealth classifications can be found here. First, [there] is reason to believe that the poorest families are not necessarily clustered in the poorest property districts. A [recent] Connecticut study found, not surprisingly, that the poor were clustered around commercial and industrial areas—those same areas that provide the most attractive sources of property tax income for school districts. Whether a similar pattern would be discovered in Texas is not known, but there is no basis on the record [for] assuming [otherwise].

Second, [lack] of personal resources has not occasioned an absolute deprivation of the desired benefit. The argument here is not that the children [are] receiving no public education; rather, it is that they are receiving a poorer quality education [than] children in districts having more assessable wealth. [A] sufficient answer to appellees' argument is that at least where wealth is involved the Equal Protection Clause does not require absolute equality or precisely equal advantages. Nor indeed, in view of the infinite variables affecting the educational process, can any system assure equal quality of education except in the most relative sense. Texas asserts that the Minimum Foundation Program provides an "adequate" education for all children in the State. [No] proof was offered at trial persuasively discrediting or refuting the State's assertion. * * * [60]

[Appellees] sought to prove that a direct correlation exists between the wealth of families within each district and the expenditures therein for education. [But] appellees' proof [fails].

This brings us [to] the third way in which the classification scheme might be defined—*district* wealth discrimination. Since the only correlation indicated by the evidence is between district property wealth and expenditures, it may be argued that discrimination might be found without regard to the individual income characteristics of district residents. * * *

However described, it is clear that appellees' suit asks this Court to extend its most exacting scrutiny to review a system that allegedly discriminates against a large, diverse, and amorphous class, unified only by the common factor of residence in districts that happen to have less taxable wealth than other districts.

---

a. As applied to an indigent plaintiff, *Bullock* invalidated a Texas statute requiring candidates to pay $50 plus their pro rata share of the cost of the election in order to get on the primary ballot, resulting in fees as high as $8,900.

60. [If] elementary and secondary education were made available by the State only to those able to pay a tuition assessed against each pupil, there would be a clearly defined class of "poor" people—definable in terms of their inability to pay the prescribed sum—who would be absolutely precluded from receiving an education. That case would present a far more compelling set of circumstances for judicial assistance than [this one].

[Does this extend to higher education as well? See Leonard Strickman, *The Tuition-Poor, the Public University, and Equal Protection,* 29 U.Fla.L.Rev. 595 (1977). For the view that "*Dandridge* and its *progeny*" do not apply to situations involving "a total cut-off of welfare that approaches denial of subsistence," see Note, *Intermediate Equal Protection Scrutiny of Welfare Laws that Deny Subsistence,* 132 U.Pa.L.Rev. 1547 (1984).]

The system of alleged discrimination and the class it defines have none of the traditional indicia of suspectness: the class is not saddled with such disabilities, or subjected to such a history of purposeful unequal treatment, or relegated to such a position of political powerlessness as to command extraordinary protection from the majoritarian political process.

We thus conclude that the Texas system does not operate to the peculiar disadvantage of any suspect class. But [recognizing] that this Court has never heretofore held that wealth discrimination alone provides an adequate basis for invoking strict scrutiny, appellees [also] assert that the State's system impermissibly interferes with the exercise of a "fundamental" right [requiring] the strict standard of judicial review. * * *

Nothing this Court holds today in any way detracts from our historic dedication to public education. [But] the importance of a service performed by the State does not determine whether it must be regarded as fundamental for purposes of examination under the Equal Protection Clause. [In *Shapiro,* the] right to interstate travel had long been recognized as a right of constitutional significance, and the Court's decision therefore did not require an ad hoc determination as to the social or economic importance of that right. *Lindsey* [as well as *Dandridge*] firmly reiterates that social importance is not the critical determinant for subjecting state legislation to strict scrutiny. * * *

The lesson of these cases [is that it] is not the province of this Court to create substantive constitutional rights in the name of guaranteeing equal protection of the laws. Thus the key to discovering whether education is "fundamental" is not to be found in comparisons of the relative societal significance of education as opposed to subsistence or housing [or] by weighing whether education is as important as the right to travel. Rather, the answer lies in assessing whether there is a right to education explicitly or implicitly guaranteed by the Constitution. *Dunn;*[74] *Skinner.*[76]

Education, of course, is not among the rights afforded explicit protection under [the] Constitution. Nor do we find any basis for saying it is implicitly so protected.[a] [But] appellees [contend] that education is distinguishable from other services and benefits provided by the State because it bears a peculiarly close relationship to other rights and liberties accorded protection under the Constitution [in that] it is essential to the effective exercise of First Amendment freedoms and to intelligent utilization of the right to vote. In asserting a nexus between

---

74. *Dunn* fully canvasses this Court's voting rights cases and explains that "this Court has made clear that a citizen has a *constitutionally protected right* to participate in elections on an equal basis with other citizens in the jurisdiction." (emphasis supplied). The constitutional underpinnings of [this right] can no longer be doubted even though, as the Court noted in *Harper,* "the right to vote in state elections is nowhere expressly mentioned."

76. *Skinner* applied the standard of close scrutiny to a state law permitting forced sterilization of "habitual criminals." Implicit in the Court's opinion is the recognition that the right of procreation is among the rights of personal privacy protected under the Constitution. See *Roe v. Wade.*

a. For the view that education *is* "fundamental," see John Coons, William Clune & Stephen Sugarman, *Educational Opportunity: A Workable Constitutional Test for State Financial Structures,* 57 Calif.L.Rev. 305 (1969). As to housing, see Lawrence Sager, *Tight Little Islands: Exclusionary Zoning, Equal Protection, and the Indigent,* 21 Stan.L.Rev. 767 (1969). As to various municipal services, see Gershon Ratner, *Inter-Neighborhood Denials of Equal Protection in the Provision of Municipal Services,* 4 Harv.Civ.Rts.—Civ.Lib.L.Rev. 1 (1968); Ralph Abascal, *Municipal Services and Equal Protection: Variations on a Theme by Griffin v. Illinois,* 20 Hast.L.J. 1367 (1969).

Massachusetts Bd. of Retirement v. Murgia (1976), Sec. 3, IV supra, held that a "right of governmental employment" is *not* fundamental.

speech and education, appellees urge that the right to speak is meaningless unless the speaker is capable of articulating his thoughts intelligently and persuasively. [A] similar line of reasoning is pursued with respect to the right to [vote]: a voter cannot cast his ballot intelligently unless his reading skills and thought processes have been adequately developed.

We need not dispute any of these propositions. [Yet] we have never presumed to possess either the ability or the authority to guarantee to the citizenry the most *effective* speech or the most *informed* electoral choice. That these may be desirable goals [is] not to be doubted. [But] they are not values to be implemented by judicial intrusion into otherwise legitimate state activities.

Even if it were conceded that some identifiable quantum of education is a constitutionally protected prerequisite to the meaningful exercise of either right, we have no indication that the [present] system fails to provide each child with an opportunity to acquire the basic minimal skills [necessary]. Furthermore, the logical limitations on appellees' nexus theory are difficult * * *. Empirical examination might well buttress an assumption that the ill-fed, ill-clothed, and ill-housed are among the most ineffective participants in the political process and that they derive the least enjoyment from the benefits of the First Amendment. * * *

[The] present case, in another basic sense, is significantly different from any of the cases in which the Court has applied strict scrutiny [to] legislation touching upon constitutionally protected rights. [These] involved legislation which "deprived," "infringed," or "interfered" with the free exercise of some such fundamental personal right or liberty. [Every] step leading to the establishment of the system Texas utilizes today [was] implemented in an effort to *extend* public education and to improve its quality. Of course, every reform that benefits some more than others may be criticized for what it fails to accomplish. But we think it plain that, in substance, the thrust of the Texas system is affirmative and reformatory and, therefore, should be scrutinized under judicial principles sensitive to the nature of the State's efforts and to the rights reserved to the States under the Constitution.

[A] century of Supreme Court adjudication under the Equal Protection Clause affirmatively supports the application of the traditional standard of review, which requires only that the State's system be shown to bear some rational relationship to legitimate state purposes. This case represents [a] direct attack on the way in which Texas has chosen to raise and disburse state and local tax revenues. [This] Court has often admonished against such interferences with the State's fiscal policies under the Equal Protection Clause [and] we continue to acknowledge that the Justices of this Court lack both the expertise and the familiarity with local problems so necessary to the making of wise decisions with respect to the raising and disposition of public revenues. Yet we are urged to direct the States either to alter drastically the present system or to throw out the property tax altogether in favor of some other form of taxation. No scheme of taxation [has] yet been devised which is free of all discriminatory impact. In such a complex arena in which no perfect alternatives exist, the Court does well not to impose too rigorous a standard of scrutiny lest all local fiscal schemes become subjects of criticism under the Equal Protection Clause.

[T]his case also involves the most persistent and difficult questions of educational policy, another area in which this Court's lack of specialized knowledge and experience counsels against premature interference with the informed judgments made at the state and local levels. [On] even the most basic questions in this area the scholars and educational experts are divided. Indeed, one of the hottest sources of controversy concerns the extent to which there is a demonstrable correlation between educational expenditures and the quality of education—an assumed correlation underlying virtually every legal conclusion drawn by the District [Court].

It must be remembered also that every claim arising under the Equal Protection Clause has implications for the relationship between national and state power under our federal system. [I]t would be difficult to imagine a case having a greater potential impact on our federal system than the one now before us, in which we are urged to abrogate systems of financing public education presently in existence in virtually every State. * * *

III. [The] State's contribution, under the Minimum Foundation Program, was designed to provide an adequate minimum educational offering in every school in the State. [T]o fulfill its local Fund Assignment, every district must impose an ad valorem tax on property located within its borders. The Fund Assignment was designed to remain sufficiently low to assure that each district would have some ability to provide a more enriched educational program. [In] large measure, these additional local revenues are devoted to paying higher salaries to more teachers. Therefore, the primary distinguishing attributes of schools in property-affluent districts are lower pupil-teacher ratios and higher salary schedules.[101] [In] part, local control [means] freedom to devote more money to the education of one's children. Equally important, however, is the opportunity it offers for participation in the decision-making process that determines how those local tax dollars will be spent. [No] area of social concern stands to profit more from a multiplicity of viewpoints and from a diversity of approaches than does public education.

[While] it is no doubt true that reliance on local property taxation for school revenues provides less freedom of choice with respect to expenditures for some districts than for others,[107] the existence of "some inequality" in the manner in which the State's rationale is achieved is not alone a sufficient basis for striking down the entire system. [Nor] must the financing system fail because, as appellees suggest, other methods of satisfying the State's interest, which occasion "less drastic" disparities in expenditures, might be conceived. Only where state action impinges on the exercise of fundamental constitutional rights or liberties must it be found to have chosen the least restrictive alternative. It is also well to remember that even those districts that have reduced ability to make free decisions with respect to how much they spend on education still retain under the present system a large measure of authority as to how available funds will be allocated. They further enjoy the power to make numerous other decisions with

---

101. [As] previously noted, the extent to which the quality of education varies with expenditure per pupil is debated inconclusively by the most thoughtful students of public education. While all would agree that there is a correlation up to the point of providing the recognized essentials, [the] issues of greatest disagreement include the effect on the quality of education of pupil-teacher ratios and of higher teacher [salaries].

107. Mr. Justice White suggests in his dissent that the Texas system violates [equal protection] because the means it has selected to effectuate its interest in local autonomy fail to guarantee complete freedom of choice to every district. He places special emphasis on the statutory provision that establishes a maximum rate of $1.50 per $100 valuation at which a local school district may tax for school maintenance. The maintenance rate in Edgewood when this case was litigated [was] $.55 per $100, barely one-third of the allowable rate. (The tax rate of $1.05 per $100 is the equalized rate for maintenance and for the retirement of bonds.) Appellees do not claim that the ceiling presently bars desired tax increases in Edgewood or in any other Texas district. Therefore, the constitutionality of that statutory provision is not before [us].

respect to the operation of the schools.[108]   The people of Texas may be justified in believing [that] along with increased control of the purse strings at the state level will go increased control over local policies.

[A]ny scheme of local taxation—indeed the very existence of identifiable local governmental units—requires the establishment of jurisdictional boundaries that are inevitably arbitrary.   It is equally inevitable that some localities are going to be blessed with more taxable assets than others.   Nor is local wealth a static quantity.   Changes [may] result from any number of events, some of which local residents can and do influence.   For instance, commercial and industrial enterprises may be encouraged to locate within a district by various actions—public and private.

Moreover, if local taxation for local expenditure is an unconstitutional method of providing for education then it may be an equally impermissible means of providing other necessary services customarily financed largely from local property taxes, including local police and fire protection, public health and hospitals, and public utility facilities of various kinds.   [It has] never been within the constitutional prerogative of this Court to nullify statewide measures for financing public services merely because the burdens or benefits thereof fall unevenly depending upon the relative wealth of the political subdivisions in which citizens live.

[In] its essential characteristics the Texas plan for financing public education reflects what many educators for a half century have thought was an enlightened approach to a problem for which there is no perfect solution.   We are unwilling to assume for ourselves a level of wisdom superior to that of legislators, scholars, and educational authorities in 49 States, especially where the alternatives proposed are only recently conceived and nowhere yet tested.   * * *

IV.   [T]his Court's action today is not to be viewed as placing its judicial imprimatur on the status quo.   The need is apparent for reform in tax systems which may well have relied too long and too heavily on the local property tax. And certainly innovative new thinking as to public education, its methods and its funding, is necessary to assure both a higher level of quality and greater uniformity of opportunity.   These matters merit the continued attention of the scholars who already have contributed much by their challenges.   But the ultimate solutions must come from the lawmakers and from the democratic pressures of those who elect them.

Reversed.[b]

Justice Brennan, dissenting.

Although I agree with my Brother White that the Texas statutory scheme is devoid of any rational basis, [I] also record my disagreement with the Court's rather distressing assertion that a right may be deemed "fundamental" for the purposes of equal protection analysis only if it is "explicitly or implicitly guaranteed by the Constitution."   As my Brother Marshall convincingly demonstrates our prior cases stand for the proposition that "fundamentality" is, in large measure, a function of the right's importance in terms of the effectuation of those rights which are in fact constitutionally guaranteed.   * * *

---

108. Mr. Justice Marshall['s] assertion, that genuine local control does not exist in Texas, simply cannot be supported.   It is abundantly refuted by the elaborate statutory division of responsibilities set out in the Texas Education Code.   Although policy decisionmaking and supervision in certain areas are reserved to the State, the day-to-day authority over the "management and control" of all public elementary and secondary schools is squarely placed on the local school boards [listing a number of their specific powers].

b. The concurring opinion of Stewart, J., who joined the Court's opinion, is omitted.

JUSTICE WHITE, with whom JUSTICE DOUGLAS and JUSTICE BRENNAN join, dissenting.

[T]his case would be quite different if it were true that the Texas system, while insuring minimum educational expenditures in every district through state funding, extends a meaningful option to all local districts to increase their per-pupil [expenditures. But for] districts with a low per-pupil real estate tax base [the] Texas system utterly fails to extend a realistic choice to parents, because the property tax, which is the only revenue-raising mechanism extended to school districts, is practically and legally unavailable. * * *

In order to equal the highest yield in any other Bexar County district, Alamo Heights would be required to tax at the rate of 68¢ per $100 of assessed valuation. Edgewood would be required to tax at the prohibitive rate of $5.76 per $100. But state law places a $1.50 per $100 ceiling on the maintenance tax [rate]. Requiring the State to establish only that unequal treatment is in furtherance of a permissible goal, without also requiring the State to show that the means chosen to effectuate that goal are rationally related to its achievement, makes equal protection analysis no more than an empty gesture. * * *

JUSTICE MARSHALL, with whom JUSTICE DOUGLAS, concurs, dissenting.

[T]he majority's holding can only be seen as a retreat from our historic commitment to equality of educational opportunity. [The issue] is not whether Texas is doing its best to ameliorate the worst features of a discriminatory scheme, but rather whether the scheme itself is in fact unconstitutionally discriminatory.[35] Authorities concerned with educational quality no doubt disagree as to the significance of variations in per pupil spending. [But it] is an inescapable fact that if one district has more funds available per pupil than another district, the former will have greater choice in educational [planning].

At the very least, in view of the substantial interdistrict disparities in funding, [the] burden of proving that these disparities do not in fact affect the quality of children's education must fall upon the appellants. Yet [they] have argued no more than that the relationship is ambiguous. * * *

Nor can I accept the appellants' apparent suggestion [that equal protection] cannot be offended by substantially unequal state treatment of persons who are similarly situated so long as the State provides everyone with some unspecified amount of education which evidently is "enough." [The] Equal Protection Clause is not addressed to the minimal sufficiency but rather to the unjustifiable inequalities of state action. [Even] if the Equal Protection Clause encompassed some theory of constitutional adequacy, discrimination in the provision of educational opportunity would certainly seem to be a poor candidate for its application. Neither the majority nor appellants informs us how judicially manageable standards are to be derived for determining how much education is "enough" to excuse constitutional discrimination. [In] light of the data introduced before the District Court, the conclusion that the school children of property poor districts constitute a sufficient class for our purposes seems indisputable to me. [Whether]

35. * * * Texas' financing scheme is hardly remedial legislation of the type for which we have previously shown substantial tolerance. Such legislation may in fact extend the vote to "persons who otherwise would be denied it by state law," *Katzenbach v. Morgan,* or it may eliminate the evils of the private bail bondsman, *Schilb v. Kuebel* [Part I, B supra]. But those are instances in which a legislative body has sought to remedy problems for which it cannot be said to have been directly responsible. By contrast, [it] is the State's own scheme which has caused the funding problem, and, thus viewed, that scheme can hardly be deemed remedial.

this discrimination, against [them] is violative of the Equal Protection Clause is the question to which we must now turn.

[The] Court apparently seeks to establish [that] equal protection cases fall into one of two neat categories which dictate the appropriate standard of review—strict scrutiny or mere rationality. But [a] principled reading of what this Court has done reveals that it has applied a spectrum of standards [which] clearly comprehends variations in the degree of care with which the Court will scrutinize particular classifications, depending [on] the constitutional and societal importance of the interest adversely affected and the recognized invidiousness of the basis upon which the particular classification is drawn.[c] * * *

I therefore cannot accept the majority's labored efforts to demonstrate that fundamental interests, which call for strict scrutiny of the challenged classification, encompass only established rights which we are somehow bound to recognize from the text of the Constitution itself. * * *[59]

I would like to know where the Constitution guarantees the right to procreate, *Skinner*, or the right to vote in state elections, e.g., *Reynolds v. Sims*,[60] or the right to an appeal from a criminal conviction, e.g., *Griffin*.[61] These are instances in which, due to the importance of the interests at stake, the Court has displayed a strong concern with the existence of discriminatory state treatment. But the Court has [never] indicated that these are interests which independently enjoy full-blown constitutional protection. * * *

The majority is, of course, correct when it suggests that the process of determining which interests are fundamental is a difficult one. But I do not think the problem is insurmountable. [The task] should be to determine the extent to which constitutionally guaranteed rights are dependent on interests not mentioned in the Constitution. As the nexus between the specific constitutional guarantee and the nonconstitutional interest draws closer, the nonconstitutional interest becomes more fundamental and the degree of judicial scrutiny applied when the interest is infringed on a discriminatory basis must be adjusted accordingly. * * * Procreation is now understood to be important because of its interaction with the established constitutional right of privacy. The exercise of the state franchise is closely tied to basic civil and political rights inherent in the First Amendment. And access to criminal appellate processes enhances the integrity of the range of rights implicit in the Fourteenth Amendment guarantee

c. In *Vlandis v. Kline,* Sec. 2 supra,—decided after *Rodriquez*—White, J., stated that he, too, agreed that this has been the Court's approach in applying the equal protection clause. See also the dissent of Marshall, J., joined by Brennan and Blackmun, JJ., in *Cleburne v. Cleburne Living Center, Inc.,* Sec. 4, III supra.

59. Indeed, the Court's theory would render the established concept of fundamental interests in the context of equal protection analysis superfluous, for the substantive constitutional right itself requires that this Court strictly scrutinize any asserted state interest for restricting or denying access to any particular guaranteed right.

60. It is interesting that in its effort to reconcile the state voting rights cases with its theory of fundamentality the majority can muster nothing more than the contention that

"[t]he constitutional underpinnings of the *right to equal treatment in the voting process* can no longer be doubted." If, by this, the Court intends to recognize a substantive constitutional "right to equal treatment in the voting process" independent of the Equal Protection Clause, the source of such a right is certainly a mystery to me.

61. It is true that *Griffin* and *Douglas* also involved discrimination against [indigents]. But, as the majority points out, the Court has never deemed wealth discrimination alone to be sufficient to require strict judicial scrutiny; rather, such review of wealth classifications has been applied only where the discrimination affects an important individual interest, see, e.g., *Harper.* Thus, I believe *Griffin* and *Douglas* can only be understood as premised on a recognition of the fundamental importance of the criminal appellate process.

of due process of law. Only if we closely protect the related interests from state discrimination do we ultimately ensure the integrity of the constitutional guarantee itself. This is the real lesson that must be taken from our previous decisions involving interests deemed to be fundamental.

The effect of the interaction of individual interests with established constitutional guarantees upon the degree of care exercised by this Court in reviewing state discrimination affecting such interests is amply illustrated [by] *Eisenstadt v. Baird.* [The] Court purported to test the statute under its traditional standard [but] clearly did not adhere to these highly tolerant standards of traditional rational review. [Yet] I think the Court's action was entirely appropriate for access to and use of contraceptives bears a close relationship to the individual's constitutional right of privacy.

A similar process of analysis with respect to the invidiousness of the basis on which a particular classification is drawn has also influenced the Court as to the appropriate degree of scrutiny to be accorded any particular case. [It] may be that all of [the] considerations, which make for particular judicial solicitude in the face of discrimination on the basis of race, nationality, or alienage, do not coalesce—or at least not to the same degree—in other forms of discrimination. Nevertheless, these considerations have undoubtedly influenced the care with which the Court has scrutinized other forms of discrimination. [Thus], in *Reed v. Reed,* [Sec. 3, II, A supra], the Court [resorted] to a more stringent standard of equal protection review than that employed in cases involving commercial matters. [T]he particularly invidious character of the classification caused the Court to pause and scrutinize with more than traditional care the rationality of state discrimination. Discrimination on the basis [of] sex posed for the Court the spectre of forms of discrimination which it implicitly recognized to have deep social and legal roots without necessarily having any basis in actual differences. Still, the Court's sensitivity to the invidiousness of the basis for discrimination is perhaps most apparent in its decisions protecting the interests of children born out of wedlock from discriminatory state action.

[In] the context of economic interests, we find that discriminatory state action is almost always sustained for such interests are generally far removed from constitutional guarantees. [But] the situation differs markedly when discrimination against important individual interests with constitutional implications and against particularly disadvantaged or powerless classes is involved.[d] The majority suggests, however, that a variable standard of review would give this Court the appearance of a "superlegislature." I cannot agree. Such an approach seems to me a part of the guarantees of our Constitution and of the historic experiences with oppression of and discrimination against discrete, powerless minorities which underlie that Document. In truth, the Court itself will be open to the criticism raised by the majority so long as it continues on its present course of effectively selecting in private which cases will be afforded special consideration without acknowledging the true basis of its action. [Such] obfuscated action may be appropriate to a political body such as a legislature, but it is not appropriate to

---

d. In *Massachusetts Bd. of Retirement v. Murgia,* Marshall, J., further explained his approach: "[T]here remain rights, not now classified as 'fundamental,' that remain vital to the flourishing of a free society, and classes, not now classified as 'suspect,' that are unfairly burdened by invidious discrimination unrelated to the individual worth of their members. Whatever we call these rights and classes, we simply cannot forgo all judicial protection against discriminatory legislation bearing upon them, but for the rare instances when the legislative choice can be termed 'wholly irrelevant' to the legislative goal."

this Court. Open debate of the bases for the Court's action is essential to the rationality and consistency of our decisionmaking process. * * *

[It] is true that this Court has never deemed the provision of free public education to be required by the Constitution. [But] the fundamental importance of education is amply indicated by the prior decisions of this Court, by the unique status accorded public education by our society, and by the close relationship between education and some of our most basic constitutional [values].

Education directly affects the ability of a child to exercise his First Amendment interests both as a source and as a receiver of information and [ideas]. Indeed, it has frequently been suggested that education is the dominant factor affecting political consciousness and participation.[72] * * *[74] [T]he issue is neither provision of the most *effective* speech nor of the most *informed* vote. Appellees do not now seek the best education Texas might provide [but] an end to state [discrimination].[75]

[We] are told that in every prior case involving a wealth classification, the members of the disadvantaged class have "shared two distinguishing characteristics: because of their impecunity they were completely unable to pay for some desired benefit, and as a consequence, they sustained an absolute deprivation of a meaningful opportunity to enjoy that benefit." I cannot agree. * * *

In *Harper,* the Court struck down [a] poll tax in toto; it did not order merely that those too poor to pay the tax be exempted; complete impecunity clearly was not determinative. [In] *Griffin* and *Douglas* [t]he right of appeal itself was not absolutely denied to those too poor to pay; but because of the cost of a transcript and of counsel, the appeal was a substantially less meaningful right for the poor than for the rich. [This] clearly encompassed degrees of discrimination on the basis of wealth which do not amount to outright denial of the affected right or interest.[77]

This is not to say that the form of wealth classification in this case does not differ significantly from those recognized [in] previous [decisions. Here], the

72. [I]t should be obvious that the political process, like most other aspects of social intercourse, is to some degree competitive. It is thus of little benefit to an individual from a property poor district to have "enough" education if those around him have more than "enough."

74. [Whatever] the severity of the impact of insufficient food or inadequate housing on a person's life, they have never been considered to bear the same direct and immediate relationship to constitutional concerns for free speech and for our political processes as education has long been recognized to bear. Perhaps, the best evidence of this fact is the unique status which has been accorded public education as the single public service nearly unanimously guaranteed in the constitutions of our States. Education, in terms of constitutional values, is much more analogous in my judgment, to the right to vote in state elections than to public welfare or public housing. [Indeed,] we have long recognized education as an essential step in providing the disadvantaged with the tools necessary to achieve economic self-sufficiency.

75. The majority's reliance on this Court's traditional deference to legislative bodies in matters of taxation falls wide of the mark [for] in this case we are presented with a claim [that] the revenue producing mechanism directly discriminates against the interests of some of the intended beneficiaries; and in contrast to the taxpayer suits, the interest adversely affected is of substantial constitutional and societal importance. * * *

77. Even putting aside its misreading of *Griffin* and *Douglas,* the Court fails to offer any reasoned constitutional basis for restricting cases involving wealth discrimination to instances in which there is an absolute deprivation of the interest affected. [Equal protection] guarantees equality of treatment of those persons who are similarly situated; it does not merely bar some form of excessive discrimination between such persons. Outside the context of wealth discrimination, the Court's reapportionment decisions clearly indicate that relative discrimination is within the purview of the Equal Protection Clause. * * *

children of the disadvantaged Texas school districts are being discriminated against not necessarily because of [the] wealth of their families, but because of the taxable property wealth of the residents of the district in which they happen to live. The appropriate question, then, is whether the same degree of judicial solicitude and scrutiny that has previously been afforded wealth classifications is warranted here.

[That] wealth classifications alone have not necessarily been considered to bear the same high degree of suspectness as have classifications based on, for instance, race or alienage may be explainable on a number of grounds. The "poor" may not be seen as politically powerless as certain discrete and insular minority groups. Personal poverty may entail much the same social stigma as historically attached to certain racial or ethnic groups [but it] is not a permanent disability; its shackles may be escaped. Perhaps, most importantly, though, personal wealth may not necessarily share the general irrelevance as a basis for legislative action that race or nationality is recognized to have. While the "poor" have frequently been a legally disadvantaged group, it cannot be ignored that social legislation must frequently take cognizance of the economic status of our citizens. Thus, we have generally gauged the invidiousness of wealth classifications with an awareness of the importance of the interests being affected and the relevance of personal wealth to those interests.

When evaluated with these considerations in mind, it seems to me that discrimination on the basis of group wealth in this case likewise calls for careful judicial scrutiny. First, [it] bears no relationship whatsoever to the interest of Texas school children in the educational opportunity afforded them [by] Texas. Given the importance of that interest, we must be particularly sensitive to the invidious characteristics of any form of discrimination that is not clearly intended to serve it, as opposed to some other distinct state interest. Discrimination on the basis of group wealth may not, to be sure, reflect the social stigma frequently attached to personal poverty. Nevertheless, insofar as group wealth discrimination involves wealth over which the disadvantaged individual has no significant control,[83] it represents in fact a more serious basis of discrimination than does personal wealth. For such discrimination is no reflection of the individual's characteristics or his abilities. And thus—particularly in the context of a disadvantaged class composed of children—we have previously treated discrimination on a basis which the individual cannot control as constitutionally disfavored. Cf. *Weber; Levy,* [Sec. 3, III supra].

The disability of the disadvantaged class in this case extends as well into the political processes upon which we ordinarily rely as adequate for the protection and promotion of all interests. Here legislative reallocation of the State's property wealth must be sought in the face of inevitable opposition from significantly advantaged districts that have a strong vested interest in the preservation of the status [quo]. *Griffin, Douglas, Williams, Tate,* and our other prior cases have dealt with discrimination on the basis of indigency which was attributable to the operation of the private sector. But we have no such simple de facto wealth discrimination here. The means for financing public education in Texas are selected and specified by the State. [At] the same time, governmentally imposed land use controls have undoubtedly encouraged and rigidified natural trends in the allocation of particular areas for residential or commercial use, and thus

---

83. True, a family may move to escape a property poor school district, assuming it has the means to do so. But such a view would itself raise a serious constitutional question concerning an impermissible burdening of the right to travel, or, more precisely, the concomitant right to remain where one is.

determined each district's amount of taxable property wealth. In short, this case, in contrast to the Court's previous wealth discrimination decisions, can only be seen as "unusual in the extent to which governmental action *is* the cause of the wealth classifications."

[Here] both the nature of the interest and the classification dictate close judicial [scrutiny. I] do not question that local control of public education, as an abstract matter, constitutes a very substantial state interest. [But] on this record, it is apparent that the State's purported concern with local control is offered primarily as an excuse rather than as a justification for interdistrict inequality.

In Texas statewide laws regulate [the] most minute details of local public education. For example, the State prescribes required courses. All textbooks must be submitted for state [approval]. The State has established the qualifications necessary for teaching in Texas public schools and the procedures for obtaining certification. The State has even legislated on the length of the school [day.]

Moreover, even if we accept Texas' general dedication to local control in educational matters, [i]f Texas had a system truly dedicated to local fiscal control one would expect the quality of the educational opportunity provided in each district to vary with the decision of the voters in that district as to the level of sacrifice they wish to make for public education. [But local] districts cannot choose to have the best education [by] imposing the highest tax rate. Instead, the quality of the educational opportunity offered by any particular district is largely determined by the amount of taxable property located in the district—a factor over which local voters can exercise no control.

The study introduced in the District Court showed a direct inverse relationship between equalized taxable district property wealth and district tax effort with the result that the property poor districts making the highest tax effort obtained the lowest per pupil yield. * * *

In my judgment, any substantial degree of scrutiny of the operation of the Texas financing scheme reveals that the State has selected means wholly inappropriate to secure its purported interest in assuring its school districts local fiscal control.[96] At the same time, appellees have pointed out a variety of alternative financing schemes which may serve the State's purported interest in local control as well as, if not better than, the present scheme without the current impairment of the educational opportunity of vast numbers of Texas schoolchildren.[98] * * *

---

96. [Although] my Brother White purports to reach this result by application of that lenient standard of mere rationality, [it] seems to be that the care with which he scrutinizes the practical effectiveness of the present local property tax as a device for affording local fiscal control reflects the application of a more stringent standard of [review].

98. * * * Central financing would leave in local hands the entire gamut of local educational policy-making—teachers, curriculum, school sites, the whole process of allocating resources among alternative educational objectives.

A second possibility is the much discussed theory of district power equalization put forth by Professors Coons, Clune, and Sugarman in their seminal work, *Private Wealth and Public*

Education 201–242 (1970). Such a scheme would truly reflect a dedication to local fiscal control. Under their system, each school district would receive a fixed amount of revenue per pupil for any particular level of tax effort regardless of the level of local property tax base. * * *

District wealth reapportionment is yet another alternative * * *.

A fourth possibility would be to remove commercial, industrial, and mineral property from local tax rolls, to tax this property on a statewide basis, and to return the resulting revenues to the local districts in a fashion that would compensate for remaining variations in the local tax bases.

Notes and Questions

1. PAPASAN v. ALLAIN, 478 U.S. 265, 106 S.Ct. 2932, 92 L.Ed.2d 209 (1986), per WHITE, J., held that a complaint alleging an equal protection violation because of "a state decision to divide state resources unequally among school districts" should survive a motion to dismiss. *Rodriguez* was deemed to set the proper standard of review—rational basis—but was distinguished because it "did not purport to validate all funding variations that might result from a State's public school funding decision. It held merely that the variations that resulted from allowing local control over local property tax funding of the public schools were constitutionally permissible in that case."

POWELL, joined by Burger, C.J., and Rehnquist, J., dissented finding that the system was substantially similar to that upheld in *Rodriguez* and further maintaining that the variations in funding to local districts were *de minimis*.[g]

2. *Wealth classifications*. (a) Does *Rodriguez* hold that de facto discriminations against poor people are subject to "strict scrutiny" only if the classification involves a right "explicitly or implicitly guaranteed by the Constitution"? May *all* the prior "wealth discrimination" cases be explained on this basis? Or does the Court's fn. 60 suggest that a state payment requirement resulting in "an absolute deprivation" of an "important" (albeit not "fundamental") right requires "strict scrutiny"? If so, what are other "important" rights?

Is education unique because it is compulsory—i.e., is the state barred from requiring it and at the same time imposing a "user-fee" even on those who can't pay? May the public schools impose a charge for all textbooks, even against indigents? May any of the broad range of municipal services—fire and police, parks and recreation, etc.—be conditioned on a "user-fee"? How about water?

(b) *Affirmative obligation*. Suppose a state simply shut its public schools and left the task to private entrepreneurs? In what way is this different than the situation posited in fn. 60? Suppose a state simply shut off all relief and welfare assistance? Is this state action subject to "strict scrutiny" under equal protection? Or does this beg the "state action" issue?

May a state bar impoverished citizens from public housing? If not, may it charge rentals for all public housing that the impoverished can't afford? If not, may it simply not construct public housing, leaving the impoverished to fend for themselves? Or does government have the affirmative obligation to afford at least "minimum protection" (if not "equal protection") to all citizens in respect to those services that are "of such fundamental importance" that "severe deprivation" would otherwise result? See generally Frank Michelman, *On Protecting the Poor Through the Fourteenth Amendment*, 83 Harv.L.Rev. 7 (1969). For the view that it is improper for the judiciary to decide issues of economic allocation, see Wilkinson, fn. c in *Dandridge;* Winter, p. 1383 supra. Compare generally John

---

None of these particular alternatives are necessarily constitutionally compelled; rather, they indicate the breadth of choice which remains to the State if the present interdistrict disparities were eliminated.

[For a collection of further commentaries, emphasizing the varying complexities of school finance in constitutional adjudication, see William Lockhart, Yale Kamisar & Jesse Choper, *Constitutional Law: Cases—Comments—Questions* 1552–53 (4th ed. 1975).]

g. In response, White, J., stated: "We [decline] to append to the general requirements of

an equal protection cause of action an additional threshold effects requirement." Compare *Bandemer,* p. 1348 supra. For discussion of state constitutional approaches, see Jonathan Banks, *State Constitutional Analyses of Public School Finance Reform Cases: Myth or Methodology?*, 45 Vand.L.Rev. 129 (1992); William Thro, *To Render Them Safe: The Analysis of State Constitutional Provisions in Public School Finance Reform Litigation*, 75 Va. L.Rev. 1639 (1989).

Rawls, *A Theory of Justice* (1971) with Robert Nozick, *Anarchy, State and Utopia* (1974).

Consider Albert Bendich, *Privacy, Poverty, and the Constitution*, 54 Calif.L.Rev. 407, 420–21 (1966): "It would be perverse to say that one has a fundamental right to be assisted by a lawyer when charged with crime, but that he has no right to such food or medicine as might be required to keep him reasonably healthy and attentive during the process of his trial. [But] if a person charged with crime has a right to such assistance, on what principle is one innocent of such a charge to be denied equal access to assistance? [What] constitutional guarantees other than those which are bound up with the criminal law are denied to persons because of their poverty? Does the fourth amendment's guarantee of the right to be secure in one's person, papers, house, and effects presuppose housing for the people of America? If it does, then clearly the condition of being unable to pay rent can deprive one of this aspect of the right to privacy as effectively as the inability to pay counsel fees [deprives] one of the right to counsel." Are there *any* "constitutional guarantees" that can be effectively exercised without "minimally adequate" food, clothing and shelter? Without "minimally adequate" education and medical assistance? Is the state constitutionally obligated to provide its impoverished citizens "minimally adequate" political campaign expenses? "Minimally adequate" funds to travel throughout the country and abroad? How are the terms "minimally adequate" and "impoverished" to be defined? By whom? Of what relevance does the "cost-to-the-state" factor bear on the "compelling" justification inquiry?

May the state bar indigents from public parks? Golf courses? Opera houses? If not, may it charge a "user-fee"? May it decline to engage in such activities without subsidizing those persons who can't pay their own way? See generally Note, *Discrimination Against the Poor and the Fourteenth Amendment*, 81 Harv. L.Rev. 435 (1967).

(c) Whatever the scope of "strict scrutiny" for de facto discriminations against (or among) poor people, does *Rodriguez* restrict the analysis to state action that imposes "payment requirements"? See *Jefferson v. Hackney* (1972), fn. a in *Washington v. Davis*, Sec. 2, III supra.

3. *"Implicitly guaranteed" rights.* (a) Apart from any issue of wealth discrimination, does *Rodriguez* suggest that there may be a "constitutional right" to a *minimum* education? E.g., must a state provide *some* meaningful education to mentally retarded children? To non-English speaking children? See Note, *The Constitutional Right of Bilingual Children to an Equal Educational Opportunity*, 47 So.Cal.L.Rev. 943 (1974).

(b) PLYLER v. DOE, 457 U.S. 202, 102 S.Ct. 2382, 72 L.Ed.2d 786 (1982), per BRENNAN, J., held that a Texas statute (§ 21.031) denying free public education to illegal alien children violated equal protection: "Persuasive arguments support the view that a State may withhold its beneficience from those whose very presence within the United States is the product of their own unlawful conduct. [But the children] in these cases 'can affect neither their parents' conduct nor their own status.' *Trimble v. Gordon*, [Sec. 3, III supra]. Even if the State found it expedient to control the conduct of adults by acting against their children, legislation directing the onus of a parent's misconduct against his children does not comport with fundamental conceptions of justice. * * * *Weber v. Aetna Casualty & Surety Co.* [Sec. 3, III supra].

"We reject the claim that 'illegal aliens' are a 'suspect class.' [U]ndocumented status is not irrelevant to any proper legislative goal. Nor is [it] an absolutely immutable characteristic since it is the product of conscious, indeed unlawful, action. But § 21.031 [imposes] its discriminatory burden on the basis of a legal characteristic over which children can have little control. It is thus difficult to conceive of a rational justification for penalizing these children for their presence within the United States. * * *

"Public education is not a 'right' granted to individuals by the Constitution.[a] *Rodriguez.* But neither is it merely some governmental 'benefit' indistinguishable from other forms of social welfare legislation. Both the importance of education in maintaining our basic institutions, and the lasting impact of its deprivation on the life of the child, mark the distinction. [We] cannot ignore the significant social costs borne by our Nation when select groups are denied the means to absorb the values and skills upon which our social order rests.[20] [Thus], the discrimination contained in § 21.031 can hardly be considered rational unless it furthers some substantial goal of the State.

" * * * Faced with an equal protection challenge respecting the treatment of aliens, we agree that the courts must be attentive to congressional policy; the exercise of congressional power might well affect the State's prerogatives to afford differential treatment to a particular class of aliens. [But] there is no indication that the disability imposed by § 21.031 corresponds to any identifiable congressional policy. The State does not claim that the conservation of state educational resources was ever a congressional concern in restricting immigration. More importantly, the classification reflected in § 21.031 does not operate harmoniously within the federal program. [In] light of the discretionary federal power to grant relief from deportation, a State cannot realistically determine that any particular undocumented child will in fact be deported until after deportation proceedings have been completed. It would of course be most difficult for the State to justify a denial of education to a child enjoying an inchoate federal permission to remain.

"We are reluctant to impute to Congress the intention to withhold from these children, for so long as they are present in this country through no fault of their own, access to a basic education. In other contexts, undocumented status, coupled with some articulable federal policy, might enhance State authority with respect to the treatment of undocumented aliens. But in the area of special constitutional sensitivity presented by this case, and in the absence of any contrary indication fairly discernible in the present legislative record, we perceive no national policy that supports the State in denying these children an elementary education.[b] [We] therefore turn to the state objectives that are said to support § 21.031. * * *

"First, appellants appear to suggest that the State may seek to protect the State from an influx of illegal immigrants. While a State might have an interest in mitigating the potentially harsh economic effects of sudden shifts in population,

---

a. Consider Michael Klarman, *An Interpretive History of Modern Equal Protection,* 90 Mich.L.Rev. 213, 288 (1991): "Internal documents suggest that four of the five Justices in the *Plyler* majority were prepared forthrightly to hold education a fundamental interest for equal protection purposes. * * * Justice Powell, however, who supplied the fifth [vote], balked at the idea of 'creating another heretofore unidentified right.' "

20. * * * Whatever the current status of these children, the courts below concluded that

many will remain here permanently and that some indeterminate number will eventually become citizens. * * *

b. For the view that "the Court should have followed the lead of *Toll v. Moreno,* [Sec. 3, I supra], and used the Supremacy Clause" to hold the *Plyler* statute invalid because it was neither "sanctioned nor contemplated by Congress," see Choper, fn. e, supra, at 21–32. See also 96 Harv.L.Rev. 130 (1982). Compare Tom Gerety, *Children in the Labyrinth: The Complexities of Plyler v. Doe,* 44 U.Pitt.L.Rev. 379, 380–87 (1983).

[t]here is no evidence in the record suggesting that illegal entrants impose any significant burden on the State's economy. To the contrary, the available evidence suggests that illegal aliens underutilize public services, while contributing their labor to the local economy and tax money to the State fisc. The dominant incentive for illegal entry [into] Texas is the availability of employment; few if any illegal immigrants come to this country [to] avail themselves of a free education. * * *

"Second, [appellants] suggest that undocumented children are appropriately singled out for exclusion because of the special burdens they impose on the State's ability to provide high quality public education. But the record in no way supports the claim [and], even if improvement in the quality of education were a likely result of barring some *number* of children from the schools of the State, the State must support its selection of *this* group as the appropriate target for exclusion. In terms of educational cost and need, however, undocumented children are 'basically indistinguishable' from legally resident alien children.

"Finally, appellants suggest that undocumented children are appropriately singled out because their unlawful presence within the United States renders them less likely than other children to remain within the boundaries of the State, and to put their education to productive social or political use within the State. Even assuming that such an interest is legitimate, it is an interest that is most difficult to quantify. The State has no assurance that any child, citizen or not, will employ the education provided by the State within the confines of the State's borders. In any event, the record is clear that many of the undocumented children disabled by this classification will remain in this country indefinitely, and that some will become lawful residents or citizens of the United States. It is difficult to understand precisely what the State hopes to achieve by promoting the creation and perpetuation of a subclass of illiterates within our boundaries, surely adding to the problems and costs of unemployment, welfare, and crime. It is thus clear that whatever savings might be achieved [are] wholly insubstantial in light of the costs involved to these children, the State, and the Nation."[c]

BLACKMUN, J., who joined the Court's opinion, concurred: "I joined [the] Court in *Rodriguez,* and I continue to believe that it provides the appropriate model for resolving most equal protection disputes. [But] I believe the Court's experience has demonstrated that the *Rodriguez* formulation does not settle every issue of 'fundamental rights' arising under the Equal Protection Clause. Only a pedant would insist that there are *no* meaningful distinctions among the multitude of social and political interests regulated by the States * * *. Children denied an education are placed at a permanent and insurmountable competitive [disadvantage]. And when those children are members of an identifiable group, that group—through the State's action—will have been converted into a discrete underclass. Other benefits provided by the State, such as housing and public assistance, are of course important: to an individual in immediate need, they may be more desirable than the right to be educated. But classifications involving the complete denial of education are .in a sense unique, for they strike at the heart of equal protection values by involving the State in the creation of permanent class distinctions. Cf. *Rodriguez* (Marshall, J., dissenting). In a sense, then, denial of an education is the analogue of denial of the right to vote: the former relegates the individual to second-class social status; the latter places him at a permanent political disadvantage.

c. Marshall, J., joined the Court's opinion but emphasized "that the facts of these cases demonstrate the wisdom of rejecting a rigidi- fied approach to equal protection analysis, and of employing" his suggested approach in *Dandridge* and *Rodriguez.*

"This conclusion is fully consistent with *Rodriguez*. The Court there reserved judgment on the constitutionality of a state system that 'occasioned an absolute denial of educational opportunities to any of its children,' noting that 'no charge fairly could be made that the system [at issue in *Rodriguez*] fails to provide each child with an opportunity to acquire * * * basic minimal skills.' [In] such circumstances, the voting decisions suggest that the State must offer something more than a rational basis for its classification."

POWELL, J., who joined the Court's opinion, concurred "to emphasize the unique character of the case": "Although the analogy is not perfect, our holding today does find support in decisions of this Court with respect to the status of illegitimates. [Thus,] review in a case such as this is properly heightened. [These children] have been singled out for a lifelong penalty and stigma. A legislative classification that threatens the creation of an underclass of future citizens and residents cannot be reconciled with one of the fundamental purposes of the Fourteenth Amendment. In these unique circumstances, the Court properly may require that the State's interests be substantial and that the means bear a 'fair and substantial relation' to these interests.[3]"

BURGER, C.J., joined by White, Rehnquist and O'Connor, JJ., dissented: "[B]y patching together bits and pieces of what might be termed quasi-suspect-class and quasi-fundamental-rights analysis, the Court spins out a theory custom-tailored to the facts [and its] opinion rests on such a unique confluence of theories and rationales that it will likely stand for little beyond the results in these particular [cases].[d]

"[I]n some circumstances persons generally, and children in particular, may have little control over or responsibility for such things as their ill health, need for public assistance, or place of residence. Yet a state legislature is not barred from considering, for example, relevant differences between the mentally-healthy and the mentally-ill, or between the residents of different counties,[5] simply because these may be factors unrelated to individual choice or to any 'wrongdoing.' The Equal Protection Clause protects against arbitrary and irrational classifications, and against invidious discrimination stemming from prejudice and hostility; it is not an all-encompassing 'equalizer' designed to eradicate every distinction for which persons are not 'responsible.' * * *[e]

"The Court's analogy to cases involving discrimination against illegitimate children is grossly misleading. The State has not thrust any disabilities upon appellees due to their 'status of birth.' Cf. *Weber*. Rather, appellees' status is

3. [I]n *Rodriguez* no group of children was singled out by the State and then penalized because of their parents' status. [Nor] was any group of children totally deprived of all education as in this case. If the resident children of illegal aliens were denied welfare assistance, made available by government to all other children who qualify, this also—in my opinion—would be an impermissible penalizing of children because of their parents' status.

d. See generally Dennis Hutchinson, *More Substantive Equal Protection? A Note on Plyler v. Doe*, 1982 Sup.Ct.Rev. 167.

5. Appellees "lack control" over their illegal residence in this country in the same sense as lawfully resident children lack control over the school district in which their parents reside. Yet in *Rodriguez*, [t]here was no suggestion [that] a child's "lack of responsibility" for his residence in a particular school district had any relevance to the proper standard of review of his [claims.]

e. Compare Choper, supra, at 29: "Although it is true that the children in *Rodriguez* had no effective choice as to where they lived, the statute in *Plyler* [is] much more stigmatizing. It [says] to a class of children that they are no good; that even though what is wrong with them is something over which they have no control, the state is going to penalize them nonetheless. I think [this] provided an effective doctrinal hook on which the Court could have more explicitly hung its decision."

predicated upon the circumstances of their concededly illegal presence in this [country].

"The central question in these cases, as in every equal protection case not involving truly fundamental rights 'explicitly or implicitly guaranteed by the Constitution,' *Rodriguez,* is whether there is some legitimate basis for a legislative distinction between different classes of persons. The fact that the distinction is drawn in legislation affecting access to public education—as opposed to legislation allocating other important governmental benefits, such as public assistance, health care, or housing—cannot make a difference in the level of scrutiny applied.

"Once it is conceded—as the Court does—that illegal aliens are not a suspect class, and that education is not a fundamental right, our inquiry should focus on and be limited to whether the legislative classification at issue bears a rational relationship to a legitimate state purpose. [I]t simply is not 'irrational' for a State to conclude that it does not have the same responsibility to provide benefits for persons whose very presence in the State and this country is illegal as it does to provide for persons lawfully present. * * *

"It is significant that the federal government has seen fit to exclude illegal aliens from numerous social welfare [programs]. Although these exclusions do not conclusively demonstrate the constitutionality of the State's use of the same classification for comparable purposes, at the very least they tend to support the rationality of excluding illegal alien residents of a State from such programs so as to preserve the State's finite revenues for the benefit of lawful residents. * * *

"Denying a free education to illegal alien children is not a choice I would make were I a legislator. Apart from compassionate considerations, the long-range costs of excluding any children from the public schools may well outweigh the costs of educating them. But [the] fact that there are sound *policy* arguments against the Texas legislature's choice does not render that choice an unconstitutional one. [While] the 'specter of a permanent caste' of illegal Mexican residents of the United States is indeed a disturbing one, it is but one segment of a larger problem, which is for the political branches to solve."

4. *Standards of equal protection review.* Does Marshall, J.'s *Rodriguez* dissent demonstrate that the Court "has applied a spectrum of standards" as to "the degree of care with which it will scrutinize particular classifications"? In addition to *Papasan* and *Plyler* supra, see also United States Dept. of Agriculture v. Moreno, Sec. 1 supra and fns. e and f following *New Orleans v. Dukes,* Sec. 1 supra; *Cleburne,* Sec. 3, IV supra.[a]

VI. MEDICAL CARE: ABORTIONS

MAHER v. ROE, p. 340 supra, per POWELL, J., held that Connecticut's refusal to give medicaid for nontherapeutic abortions, even though it gives medicaid for

---

a. For analysis urging that the Court use three levels of equal protection review and "should validate a statute [that "limits the exercise of a fundamental right by a class of persons"] only if the means used bear a factually demonstrable relationship to a state interest capable of withstanding analysis," see John Nowak, *Realigning the Standard of Review Under the Equal Protection Guarantee—Prohibited, Neutral, and Permissive Classifications,* 62 Geo.L.J. 1071 (1974): "The Court will scrutinize the factual support for the legislation to determine whether its ends are capable of withstanding analysis and whether its means are rationally related to that end."

For analysis urging that the Court weigh the "*nature* of the affected interest" and the "*magnitude* of disadvantage" against the "*nature* of the state's interest" and the "relationship between *means and ends,*" see Gary Simson, *A Method for Analyzing Discriminatory Effects Under the Equal Protection Clause,* 29 Stan.L.Rev. 663 (1977).

childbirth, does not violate equal protection: "The Constitution imposes no obligation on the States to pay the pregnancy-related medical expenses of indigent women, or indeed to pay any of the medical expenses of indigents.[5]   But when a State decides to alleviate some of the hardships of poverty by providing medical care, the manner in which it dispenses benefits is subject to constitutional limitations. * * *

"This case involves no discrimination against a suspect class. An indigent woman desiring an abortion does not come within the limited category of disadvantaged classes so recognized by our cases. Nor does the fact that the impact of the regulation falls upon those who cannot pay lead to a different conclusion. In a sense, every denial of welfare to an indigent creates a wealth classification as compared to nonindigents who are able to pay for the desired goods or services. But this Court has never held that financial need alone identifies a suspect [class]. See *Rodriguez; Dandridge.*[6]   Accordingly, the central question in this case is whether the regulation 'impinges upon a fundamental right explicitly or implicitly protected by the Constitution.' "

In reasoning that "the Connecticut regulation places no obstacles—absolute or otherwise—in the pregnant woman's path to an abortion" the Court also found that "appellees' reliance on the penalty analysis of *Shapiro* and *Maricopa* is misplaced.[8]"

In rejecting the Court's distinction between a state's direct interference with a fundamental right and encouraging an alternative activity, BRENNAN, J., joined by Marshall and Blackmun, JJ., dissenting, added that "First Amendment decisions have consistently held [that] the compelling state interest test is applicable not only to outright denials but also to restraints that make exercise of those rights more difficult. See, e.g., *Sherbert*. [The] compelling state interest test has been applied in voting cases, even where only relatively small infringements upon voting power, such as dilution of voting strength caused by malapportionment, have been involved. [The] Connecticut scheme cannot be distinguished from other grants and withholdings of financial benefits that we have held unconstitutionally burdened a fundamental right. [The] governing principle is the same [as

---

5. [Because] Connecticut has made no attempt to monopolize the means for terminating pregnancies through abortion the present case is easily distinguished from *Boddie*. [Does this similarly distinguish *Harper* and *Lubin v. Panish*?]

6. [*Griffin* and *Douglas*] are grounded in the criminal justice system, a governmental monopoly in which participation is compelled. Cf. n. 5, supra. Our subsequent decisions have made it clear that the principles underlying *Griffin* and *Douglas* do not extend to legislative classifications generally.

[For incisive comparison of *Maher* with *Griffin* and *Douglas* —and with *Shapiro* (see fn. 8 infra)—see Barbara Brudno, *Wealth Discrimination in the Supreme Court: Equal Protection for the Poor from Griffin to Maher*, in Constitutional Government in America 229 (Ronald Collins ed. 1980).]

8. * * * Penalties are most familiar to the criminal law, where criminal sanctions are imposed as a consequence of proscribed conduct. *Shapiro* and *Maricopa* recognized that denial of welfare to one who had recently exercised

the right to travel across state lines was sufficiently analogous to a criminal fine to justify strict judicial scrutiny.

If Connecticut denied general welfare benefits to all women who had obtained abortions and who were otherwise entitled to the benefits, we would have a close analogy to the facts in *Shapiro*, and strict scrutiny might be [appropriate]. But the claim here is that the State "penalizes" the woman's decision to have an abortion by refusing to pay for it. *Shapiro* and *Maricopa* did not hold that States would penalize the right to travel interstate by refusing to pay the bus fares of the indigent travelers. We find no support in the right to travel cases for the view that Connecticut must show a compelling interest for its decision not to fund elective abortions.

Sherbert v. Verner similarly is inapplicable here. In addition, that case was decided in the significantly different context of a constitutionally imposed "governmental obligation of neutrality" originating in [the] Religion Clauses of the First Amendment.

in *Sherbert*], for Connecticut grants and withholds financial benefits in a manner that discourages significantly the exercise of a fundamental constitutional right. Indeed, the case for application of the principle actually is stronger than in *Sherbert* since appellees are all indigents and therefore even more vulnerable to the financial pressures imposed by the Connecticut regulations."

MARSHALL, J., dissented: "[*Rodriguez*] stated a test for analyzing discrimination on the basis of wealth that would, if fairly applied here, strike down the regulations. The Court there held that a wealth discrimination claim is made out by persons ['who] because of their impecunity [are] completely unable to pay for some desired benefit, and as a consequence [sustain] an absolute deprivation of a meaningful opportunity to enjoy that benefit.' Medicaid recipients are, almost by definition, 'completely unable to pay for' abortions, and are thereby completely denied 'a meaningful opportunity' to obtain them."[6]

Notes and Questions

1. Does the Connecticut regulation "discriminate against," rather than simply "burden," a fundamental right? Is there a constitutional difference? See note 1 after *Shapiro*, Part II supra. Consider 91 Harv.L.Rev. 144 (1977): "It can hardly be [that] the state could provide a free forum for indigents' speech only on the condition that no unpopular views be espoused, even though this policy would deny only the specific costs of exercising disfavored speech rights. Similarly, it is difficult to imagine that the Court would uphold a policy of providing free justices of the peace for intraracial but not racially mixed marriages, thereby declining to pay the specific costs of a disfavored but constitutionally protected union, notwithstanding that the state has merely made intraracial marriage a more attractive alternative without creating an obstacle to private marriage opportunities."

See also Brennan, J., dissenting in *Harris v. McRae* (1980), p. 341 supra (which relied on *Maher* to sustain denial of medicaid even for "medically necessary" abortions): "Whether the State withholds only the special costs of a disfavored option or penalizes the individual more broadly for the manner in which she exercises her choice, it cannot interfere with a constitutionally protected decision through the coercive use of governmental largess."

Did *Dandridge* uphold a policy of providing welfare to indigent parents only for sustaining four children and no more? If so, is the law in *Maher* distinguishable?

2. Consider Michael Klarman, *An Interpretive History of Modern Equal Protection*, 90 Mich.L.Rev. 213, 289–90 (1991): "Given its latitudinarian interpre-

---

6. Application of the flexible equal protection standard [urged in Marshall, J.'s *Rodriguez* dissent] would allow the Court to strike down the regulations in these cases without calling into question laws funding public education or English language teaching in public schools. [See the majority's discussion of this point at p. 464 supra.] By permitting a court to weigh all relevant factors, the flexible standard does not logically require acceptance of any equal protection claim that is "identical in principle" under the traditional approach to those advanced here.

[Is there any way other than use of a "flexible equal protection standard" to distinguish *Maher* from the problems raised by the majority in respect to *Meyer* and *Pierce* ? Consider

Michael Perry, *The Abortion Funding Cases: A Comment on the Supreme Court's Role in American Government,* 66 Geo.L.J. 1191, 1199–1200 (1978): "One need not disapprove of private schools to acknowledge the wisdom of providing free, public education. [But the state's decision in *Maher*] is recognizable solely as a disapproval of and an effort to discourage abortion." See also Michael Perry, *Why the Supreme Court Was Plainly Wrong in the Hyde Amendment Case: A Brief Comment on Harris v. McRae,* 32 Stan.L.Rev. 1113 (1980). Laurence Tribe, *American Constitutional Law* 933 n. 77 (1978). Compare Charles Fahy, *The Abortion Funding Cases: A Response to Professor Perry,* 67 Geo.L.J. 1205 (1979).]

tations of the Fourteenth Amendment's Due Process Clause and certain Bill of Rights provisions, the Burger Court's constriction of the fundamental rights strand of equal protection cannot plausibly have been motivated by strict constructionist concerns. Rather, I think, the explanation must be that the Justices were more comfortable forbidding state regulation of certain spheres than requiring government equalization (or at least "minimum protection") of fundamental interests such as education, food, shelter, and medical care. The unpalatable aspect of fundamental rights equal protection, in other words, was not its recognition of unenumerated rights, but its reconceptualization of equal protection as an entitlement to affirmative governmental assistance. The abortion funding decisions both corroborate the Burger Court's hostility to the fundamental rights strand and confirm my [explanation]."

Chapter 12
THE CONCEPT OF STATE ACTION

SECTION 1. INTRODUCTION

The "state action" doctrine has long established that, because of their language or history, most provisions of the Constitution that protect individual liberty—including those set forth in Art. 1, §§ 9 and 10, the Bill of Rights, and the fourteenth and fifteenth amendments—impose restrictions or obligations only on government.   The subject received its first extensive treatment in the CIVIL RIGHTS CASES, 109 U.S. 3, 3 S.Ct. 18, 27 L.Ed. 835 (1883), which held, per BRADLEY, J., that neither the thirteenth nor fourteenth amendments empowered Congress to pass the Civil Rights Act of 1875, making racial discrimination unlawful in public accommodations (inns, public conveyances, places of public amusement, etc.)—"and no other ground of authority for its passage being suggested, it must necessarily be declared void."   Although the issue presented did not simply concern the authority granted the *Court* under § 1 of the thirteenth and fourteenth amendments, but rather involved the scope of *Congress'* power under the final sections of these amendments to enforce their substantive provisions "by appropriate legislation" (a topic to be considered in detail in Ch. 12), the Court's discussion of "state action" remains the classic exposition of the doctrine.

The Court held that, under the fourteenth amendment, "it is state action of a particular character that is prohibited. Individual invasion of individual rights is not the subject-matter of the amendment. [It] nullifies and makes void all state legislation, and state action of every kind, which impairs the privileges and immunities of citizens of the United States, or which injures them in life, liberty, or property without due process of law, or which denies to any of them the equal protection of the laws. [T]he last section of the amendment [does] not authorize congress to create a code of municipal law for the regulation of private rights; but to provide modes of redress against the operation of state laws, and the action of state officers, executive or judicial, when these are subversive of the fundamental rights specified in the amendment. * * *

"An inspection of the [Civil Rights Act of 1875] shows that [it] proceeds ex directo to declare that certain acts committed by individuals shall be deemed offenses, and shall be prosecuted [by] the United States. It does not profess to be corrective of any constitutional wrong committed by the states; [it] applies equally to cases arising in states which have the justest laws respecting the personal rights of citizens, and whose authorities are ever ready to enforce such laws as to those which arise in states that may have violated the prohibition of the amendment. In other words, it steps into the domain of local jurisprudence, and lays down rules for the conduct of individuals in society towards each other * * *. [C]ivil rights, such as are guarantied by the constitution against state aggression, cannot be impaired by the wrongful acts of individuals, unsupported by state authority in the shape of laws, customs, or judicial or executive proceedings. The wrongful act of an individual, unsupported by any such authority, is simply a private wrong, or a crime of that individual * * *. An individual cannot deprive a man of his right to vote, to hold property, to buy and to sell, to sue in the courts, or to be a witness or a juror; he may, by force or fraud, interfere with the enjoyment of the right in a particular case; [but] unless protected in these wrongful acts by some shield of state law or state authority, he cannot destroy or injure the right; he will only render himself amenable to satisfaction or punishment; and amenable therefor to the laws of the state where the wrongful acts are committed. [The] abrogation and denial of rights, for which the states alone were or could be responsible, was the great seminal and fundamental wrong which was intended to be remedied."

The Court recognized that the thirteenth amendment "is not a mere prohibition of state laws establishing or upholding slavery, but an absolute declaration that slavery or involuntary servitude shall not exist in any part of the United States [and] that the power vested in congress to enforce the article by appropriate legislation, clothes congress with power to pass all laws necessary and proper for abolishing all badges and incidents of slavery, in the United States * * *. [T]he civil rights bill of 1866, passed in view of the thirteenth amendment, before the fourteenth was adopted, undertook to wipe out these burdens and disabilities, * * * namely, the same right to make and enforce contracts, to sue, be parties, give evidence, and to inherit, purchase, lease, sell, and convey property, as is enjoyed by white citizens. [At] that time (in 1866) congress did not assume, under the authority given by the thirteenth amendment, to adjust what may be called the social rights of men and races in the community; but only to declare and vindicate those fundamental rights which appertain to the essence of citizenship, and the enjoyment or deprivation of which constitutes the essential distinction between freedom and slavery.

"[It] would be running the slavery argument into the ground to make it apply to every act of discrimination which a person may see fit to make as to the guests he will entertain, or as to the people he will take into his coach or cab or car, or admit to his concert or theater, or deal with in other matters of intercourse or business. Innkeepers and public carriers, by the laws of all the states, so far as we are aware, are bound, to the extent of their facilities, to furnish proper accommodation to all unobjectionable persons who in good faith apply for them. If the laws themselves make any unjust discrimination, amenable to the prohibitions of the fourteenth amendment, congress has full power to afford a remedy under that amendment and in accordance with it." [a]

a. In *Bell v. Maryland,* 378 U.S. 226, 84 S.Ct. 1814, 12 L.Ed.2d 822 (1964), Goldberg, J., joined by Warren, C.J., and Douglas, J., examining the "historical evidence" in detail, concluded that the *Civil Rights Cases* were based on the assumption of the framers of the fourteenth amendment that "under state law, when the Negro's disability as a citizen was removed, he would be assured the same public civil rights that the law had guaranteed white persons," and that "the duties of the proprietors of places of public accommodation would remain as they had long been and that the States would now be affirmatively obligated to insure that these rights ran to Negro as well as white citizens." Black, J., joined by Harlan and White, JJ., disagreed. Cf. Tribe *Treatise* 1694 n. 14. See generally John P. Frank & Robert F. Munro, *The Original Understanding of "Equal Protection of the Laws,"* 1972 Wash. U.L.Q. 421, 468–72. For the view that the *Civil Rights Cases* interpreted the fourteenth amendment to reflect the intent of its framers that the "prohibited state action is the *failure to protect fundamental interests,*" see Alan R.

HARLAN, J., dissented: "Was it the purpose of the nation [by the thirteenth amendment] simply to destroy the institution [of slavery], and remit the race, theretofore held in bondage, to the several states for such protection, in their civil rights, necessarily growing out of freedom, as those states, in their discretion, choose to provide? [S]ince slavery [was] the moving or principal cause of the adoption of that amendment, and since that institution rested wholly upon the inferiority, as a race, of those held in bondage, their freedom necessarily involved immunity from, and protection against, all discrimination against them, because of their race, in respect of such civil rights as belong to freemen of other races. Congress, therefore, under its express power to enforce that amendment, by appropriate legislation, may enact laws of a direct and primary character, operating upon states, their officers and agents, and also upon, at least, such individuals and corporations as exercise public functions and wield power and authority under the state. * * *

"It remains now to inquire what are the legal rights of colored persons in respect of the accommodations * * *.

"1. As to public conveyances on land and water. [In] *Olcott v. Sup'rs,* 16 Wall. 694, it was ruled that railroads [are] none the less public highways because controlled and owned by private corporations; that it is a part of the function of government to make and maintain highways for the conveyance of the public; that no matter who is the agent, and what is the agency, the function performed is *that of the state* * * *.

"Such being the relations these corporations hold to the public, it would seem that the right of a colored person to use an improved public highway, upon the terms accorded to freemen of other races, is as fundamental in the state of freedom, established in this country, as are any of the rights which my brethren concede to be so far fundamental as to be deemed the essence of civil freedom.

"2. As to inns. [The] authorities are sufficient to show that a keeper of an inn is in the exercise of a quasi public employment. The law gives him special privileges, and he is charged with certain duties and responsibilities to the public. The public nature of his employment forbids him from discriminating against any person asking admission as a guest on account of the race or color of that person.

"3. As to places of public amusement. [W]ithin the meaning of the act of 1875, [they] are such as are established and maintained under direct license of the law. [The] local government granting the license represents [the colored race] as well as all other races within its jurisdiction. A license from the public to establish a place of public amusement, imports, in law, equality of right, at such places, among all the members of that public." [b]

Madry, *Private Accountability and the Fourteenth Amendment; State Action; Federalism and Congress,* 59 Mo.L.Rev. 499 (1994).

b. For general support of Harlan, J.'s thirteenth amendment view, see Arthur Kinoy, *The Constitutional Right of Negro Freedom,* 21 Rutg.L.Rev. 387 (1967). Although the Court has since ruled that the thirteenth amendment grants broad enforcement power to *Congress* (see p. 1406 infra), the Court has confined its use of the amendment, absent congressional legislation, to holding state peonage laws invalid. See *Memphis v. Greene,*

p. 1102 supra. For application of the thirteenth amendment to the areas of "employment discrimination and affirmative action, jury selection and peremptory challenges, and capital crimes and the death penalty," and for a review of recent scholarship that applies the thirteenth amendment to "racial hate speech legislation, reproductive rights, and federal prosecution of racially motivated violence" and to "abused children, battered women, and women coerced into prostitution," see Douglas L. Colbert, *Liberating the Thirteenth Amendment,* 30 Harv.Civ.Rts.Civ.Lib.L.Rev. (1995).

Turning to the fourteenth amendment, "the first clause of the first section—
'all persons born or naturalized in the United States, and subject to the jurisdiction thereof, are citizens of the United States, and of the state wherein they reside'—is of a distinctly affirmative character. In its application to the colored race, previously liberated, it created and granted, as well citizenship of the United States, as citizenship of the state in which they respectively resided. [Further], they were brought, by this supreme act of the nation, within the direct operation of that provision of the constitution which declares that 'the citizens of each state shall be entitled to all privileges and immunities of citizens in the several states.' Article IV, § 2.

"The citizenship thus acquired [may be protected] by congressional legislation of a primary direct character; this, because the power of congress is not restricted to the enforcement of prohibitions upon state laws or state action. It is, in terms distinct and positive, to enforce 'the *provisions of this article* ' of amendment * * * *all* of the provisions,—affirmative and prohibitive * * *.

"But what was secured to colored citizens of the United States—as between them and their respective states—by the grant to them of state citizenship? With what rights, privileges, or immunities did this grant from the nation invest them? There is one, if there be no others—exemption from race discrimination in respect of any civil right belonging to citizens of the white race in the same state [by] the state, or its officers, or by individuals, or corporations exercising public functions or authority * * *. It was perfectly well known that the great danger to the equal enjoyment by citizens of their rights, as citizens, was to be apprehended, not altogether from unfriendly state legislation, but from the hostile action of corporations and individuals in the states. * * *

"But if it were conceded that the power of congress could not be brought into activity until the rights specified in the act of 1875 had been abridged or denied by some state law or state action, I maintain that the decision of the court is erroneous. [In] every material sense applicable to the practical enforcement of the fourteenth amendment, railroad corporations, keepers of inns, and managers of places of public amusement are agents of the state, because amenable, in respect of their public duties and functions, to public regulation. * * * I agree that if one citizen chooses not to hold social intercourse with another, he is not and cannot be made amenable to the law for his conduct in that regard; for no legal right of a citizen is violated by the refusal of others to maintain merely social relations with him, even upon grounds of race. [The] rights which congress, by the act of 1875, endeavored to secure and protect are legal, not social, rights. The right, for instance, of a colored citizen to use the accommodations of a public highway upon the same terms as are permitted to white citizens is no more a social right than his right, under the law, to use the public streets of a city, or a town, or a turnpike road, or a public market, or a post-office, or his right to sit in a public building with others, of whatever race, for the purpose of hearing the political questions of the day discussed."

The basic doctrine of the *Civil Rights Cases* —that it is "state action" that is prohibited by the fourteenth amendment—has remained undisturbed. But the question of what constitutes "state action" has generated significant controversy. It is settled that the term comprehends statutes enacted by national, state and local legislative bodies and the official actions of all government officers.[c] The more difficult problems arise when the conduct of private individuals or groups is challenged as being unconstitutional. Although—as will be pointed out in the materials that follow (see, e.g., note 7 after *Shelley v. Kraemer*, Sec. 3 infra)—it has often been argued that the inquiries are misperceived, the questions that the Court has asked are whether the private actor (a) is performing a "government function," or (b) is sufficiently "involved with" or "encouraged by" the state so as to be held to the state's constitutional obligations. These subjects will be developed in the next two sections of this chapter.

Until the past few decades, most of the cases involved racial discrimination (or, occasionally, denial of free speech). But, as will be detailed in Ch. 12, the enactment and strengthening of federal (and state) civil rights statutes since the 1960s has largely mooted the problem of private racial discrimination. Further, with the growth under the equal protection clause of the number of "suspect" and "quasi-suspect" classifications (see Ch. 10, Sec. 3) and the expansion under the due process clause of the procedural rights that the state must afford persons before depriving them of liberty or property (see Ch. 7, Sec. 5), an increasing number of cases (as will be seen in the final section of this chapter) have involved attempts to require "private" adherence to these constitutional responsibilities.

SECTION 2. "GOVERNMENT FUNCTION"

SMITH v. ALLWRIGHT, 321 U.S. 649, 64 S.Ct. 757, 88 L.Ed. 987 (1944), held the fifteenth amendment forebade exclusion of African–Americans from primary elections conducted by the Democratic Party of Texas, pursuant to party resolution. The Court, per REED, J., relied heavily on a case from Louisiana, *United States v. Classic* (1941), p. 1378 infra, which held "that Section 4 of Article I of the Constitution authorized Congress to regulate primary as well as general elections, 'where the primary is by law made an integral part of the election machinery.'" *Classic* "makes clear that state delegation to a party of the power to fix the qualifications of primary elections is delegation of a state function that may make the party's action the action of the state." The Court added that the extensive statutory control of primary elections in Texas "makes the party which is required to follow these legislative directions an agency of the state in so far as it determines the participants in a primary election. [The] right to participate in the choice of elected officials without restriction by any state because of race [is] not to be nullified by a state through casting its electoral process in a form which permits a private organization to practice racial discrimination in the election." Frankfurter, J., concurred in the result. Roberts, J., dissented.

TERRY v. ADAMS, 345 U.S. 461, 73 S.Ct. 809, 97 L.Ed. 1152 (1953), involved the exclusion of African–Americans from the "pre-primary" elections of the Jaybird Democratic Association, an organization of all the white voters in a Texas county that was run like a regular political party and whose candidates since 1889

---

c. On the question of what constitutes a "government" agency, *Lebron v. National R.R. Passenger Corp.*, ___ U.S. ___, 115 S.Ct. 961, 130 L.Ed.2d 902 (1995), per Scalia, J., held that Amtrak—created by a special federal statute as a corporation "for the furtherance of governmental objectives," with the President having "permanent authority to appoint a majority of the directors"—"is part of the government for purposes of the First Amendment," even though the authorizing statute disclaims this fact. O'Connor, J., dissented.

had nearly always run unopposed and won in the regular Democratic primary and the general election. The record showed "complete absence of any compliance with the state law or practice, or cooperation by or with the State." Although there was no majority opinion, the Court held the election subject to the fifteenth amendment.

BLACK, J., joined by Douglas and Burton, JJ., found that "the admitted party purpose" was "to escape the Fifteenth Amendment's command." The "Amendment excludes social or business clubs" but "no election machinery could be sustained if its purpose or effect was to deny Negroes on account of their race an effective voice in the governmental affairs. [The] only election that has counted in this Texas county for more than fifty years has been that held by the Jaybirds. [For] a state to permit such a duplication of its election processes is to permit a flagrant abuse [of] the Fifteenth Amendment."

CLARK, J., joined by Vinson, C.J., and Reed and Jackson, JJ., described the Jaybirds as not merely a "private club" "organized to influence public candidacies or political action," but rather a "part and parcel of the Democratic Party, an organization existing under the auspices of Texas law. [W]hen a state structures its electoral apparatus in a form which devolves upon a political organization the uncontested choice of public officials, that organization itself, in whatever disguise, takes on those attributes of government which draw the Constitution's safeguards into play." [a]

MINTON, J., dissented: The Jaybird's activity "seems to differ very little from situations common in many other places [where] a candidate must obtain the approval of a religious group. [E]lections and other public business are influenced by all sorts of pressures from carefully organized groups. [Far] from the activities of these groups being properly labeled as state action, [they] are to be considered as attempts to influence or obtain state action." [b]

MARSH v. ALABAMA, 326 U.S. 501, 66 S.Ct. 276, 90 L.Ed. 265 (1946), held that "a State, consistently with the First and Fourteenth Amendments," cannot "impose criminal punishment on a person who undertakes to distribute religious literature on the premises of a company-owned town contrary to the wishes of the town's management." The town, owned by a shipbuilding company, had "all the characteristics of any other American town." Appellant, a Jehovah's Witness, was warned that she could not distribute the literature and when she refused to leave the sidewalk of the town's "business block," a deputy sheriff, who was paid by the company to serve as the town's policeman, arrested her and she was convicted of trespass.

The Court, per BLACK, J., reversed: Under *Lovell v. Griffin,* p. 757 supra, an ordinary municipality could not have barred appellant's activities, and the fact

---

a. Frankfurter, J., stated that the "vital requirement is State responsibility" and found it as follows: "As a matter of practical politics," "we may assume" "those charged by State law with the duty of assuring all eligible voters an opportunity to participate in the selection of candidates at the primary—the county election officials who are normally leaders in their communities—participate by voting in the Jaybird primary" "and condone" "a wholly successful effort to withdraw signifi-

cance from the State-prescribed primary, to subvert the operation of what is formally the law of the State for primaries in this county."

b. Are these examples distinguishable because "the only election that has counted in this Texas county for more than fifty years has been that held by the Jaybirds"? Because the fifteenth amendment outlawed discrimination *on the basis of race or color* with respect to the right to vote?

that "a single company had legal title to all the town" may not result in impairing "channels of communication" of its inhabitants or those persons passing through. "Ownership does not always mean absolute dominion. The more an owner, for his advantage, opens up his property for use by the public in general, the more do his rights become circumscribed by the statutory and constitutional rights of those who use it. Thus, the owners of privately held bridges, ferries, turnpikes and railroads may not operate them as freely as a farmer does his farm. Since these facilities are built and operated primarily to benefit the public and since their operation is essentially a public function, it is subject to state regulation." In balancing property rights against freedom of press and religion, "the latter occupy a preferred position" and the former do not "justify the State's permitting a corporation to govern a community of citizens so as to restrict their fundamental liberties and the enforcement of such restraint by the application of a State statute." Frankfurter, J., concurred and Jackson, J., did not participate.[c]

AMALGAMATED FOOD EMPLOYEES UNION v. LOGAN VALLEY PLAZA, 391 U.S. 308, 88 S.Ct. 1601, 20 L.Ed.2d 603 (1968), per MARSHALL, J.,—reasoning that a large privately owned shopping center was the "functional equivalent of the business district [in] *Marsh*"—held that it could not enjoin peaceful union picketing on its property against a store located in the shopping center. Black and White, JJ., dissented; Harlan, J., did not reach the merits.

Four years later, LLOYD CORP. v. TANNER, 407 U.S. 551, 92 S.Ct. 2219, 33 L.Ed.2d 131 (1972), per POWELL, J., held that a shopping center's refusal to permit antiwar handbilling on its premises was not state action violative of the first and fourteenth amendments. *Logan Valley* was distinguished because the picketing there had been specifically directed to a store in the shopping center and the pickets had no other reasonable opportunity to reach their audience. *Marsh* "involved the assumption by a private enterprise of semi-official municipal functions as a delegate of the State. In effect, the owner of the company town was performing the full spectrum of municipal powers and stood in the shoes of the State. In the instant case there is no comparable assumption or exercise of municipal functions or power." Marshall, J., joined by Douglas, Brennan and Stewart, JJ., dissented, finding "no valid distinction" from *Logan Valley*.

Finally, HUDGENS v. NLRB, 424 U.S. 507, 96 S.Ct. 1029, 47 L.Ed.2d 196 (1976), per STEWART, J.,—involving picketing of a store in a shopping center by a union with a grievance against the store's warehouse (located elsewhere)— overruled *Logan Valley* on the ground that *"Lloyd* amounted to [its] total rejection."[a] MARSHALL, J., joined by Brennan, J., dissented: *"Logan Valley* [recognized] that the owner of the modern shopping center complex, by dedicating his property to public use as a business district, to some extent displaces the 'State' from control of historical First Amendment forums, and may acquire a virtual monopoly of places suitable for effective communication. The roadways, parking

---

c. Reed, J., joined by Vinson, C.J., and Burton, J., dissented, noting that "there was [no] objection to appellant's use of the nearby public highway and under our decisions she could rightfully have continued her activities [thirty feet parallel] from the spot she insisted upon using."

a. White, J., concurred in the result, finding that *Logan Valley* "does not cover the facts of this case [which concern] a warehouse not located on the center's premises. The picketing was thus not 'directly related in its purpose to the use to which the shopping center property was being put.'" Stevens, J., did not participate.

lots, and walkways of the modern shopping center may be as essential for effective speech as the streets and sidewalks in the municipal or company-owned town." [b]

EVANS v. NEWTON, 382 U.S. 296, 86 S.Ct. 486, 15 L.Ed.2d 373 (1966): In 1911, Senator A.O. Bacon devised land to Macon, Ga., to be used as a park for whites only. After *Pennsylvania v. Board of Trusts,* 353 U.S. 230, 77 S.Ct. 806, 1 L.Ed.2d 792 (1957)—holding that there is "state action" when public officials act as trustees under a private will requiring racial discrimination—the city permitted African–Americans to use the park. When Bacon's heirs sued to remove the city as trustee, the Georgia courts accepted the city's resignation and appointed private individuals as trustees so that the trust's purpose would not fail.

The Court, per DOUGLAS, J., reversed. Although "when private individuals or groups are endowed by the State with powers or functions governmental in nature, they become agencies or instrumentalities of the State," nonetheless, "the range of government activities is broad and varied, and the fact that government has engaged in a particular activity does not necessarily mean that an individual entrepreneur or manager of the same kind of undertaking suffers the same constitutional inhibitions. While a State may not segregate public schools so as to exclude one or more religious groups, those sects may maintain their own parochial educational systems."

"If a testator wanted to leave a school or center for the use of one race only and in no way implicated the State in the supervision, control, or management of that facility, we assume arguendo that no constitutional difficulty would be encountered. This park, however, is in a different posture" because "for years it was an integral part" of the city's activities, assumedly "granted tax exemption" and "swept, manicured, watered, patrolled, and maintained by the city." "The momentum it acquired as a public facility is certainly not dissipated ipso facto by the appointment of 'private' trustees. So far as this record shows, there has been no change in municipal maintenance and concern over this facility. [If] the municipality remains entwined in the management or control of the park, it remains subject to the restraints of the Fourteenth Amendment."

"This conclusion is buttressed by the" fact that "the service rendered even by a private park of this character is municipal in nature," "more like a fire department or police department" than like "golf clubs, social centers, luncheon clubs, schools such as Tuskegee was at least in origin, and other like organizations in the private sector." "Mass recreation through the use of parks is plainly in the public domain and state courts that aid private parties to perform that public function on a segregated basis implicate the State in conduct proscribed by the Fourteenth Amendment. Like the streets of the company town in *Marsh,* the elective process of *Terry,* and the transit system of *Pollak,*[c] the predominant

---

b. For a decision that the free speech and petition provisions of the California constitution require that "shopping center owners permit expressive activity on their property," see *Robins v. Pruneyard Shopping Center,* 23 Cal.3d 899, 153 Cal.Rptr. 854, 592 P.2d 341 (1979). For consideration under the National Labor Relations Act of the right of unions to engage in communicative activity on the employer's premises, see *Eastex, Inc. v. NLRB,* 437 U.S. 556, 98 S.Ct. 2505, 57 L.Ed.2d 428 (1978); *Scott Hudgens,* 230 N.L.R.B. 414 (1977).

c. In *Public Utilities Com'n v. Pollak,* 343 U.S. 451, 72 S.Ct. 813, 96 L.Ed. 1068 (1952), a city transit company subject to public regulation was considered in "sufficiently close relation" with the government as to cause the Court to determine whether the company's playing of radio programs on buses violated due process.

character and purpose of this park are municipal." White, J., concurred on a separate ground.

HARLAN, J., joined by Stewart, J., dissented: The majority's "real holding" is not based on any state involvement in the park, but "because a privately operated park whose only criterion for exclusion is racial is within the 'public domain.'" Precedent does "not support this novel state action theory." In *Pollak*, "state action was explicitly premised on the close legal regulation of the company by the public utilities commission and the commission's approval of the particular action under attack. The conclusion might alternatively have rested on the near-exclusive legal monopoly enjoyed by the company, but in all events nothing was rested on any 'public function' theory." In *Terry*, "none of the three prevailing opinions garnered a majority, and some commentators have simply concluded that the state action requirement was read out of the Fifteenth Amendment on that occasion." [d] *Marsh* is the "only Fourteenth Amendment case finding state action in the 'public function' performed by a technically private institution."

The failing of the majority's theory "can be shown by comparing [the] 'public function' of privately established schools with that of privately owned parks. Like parks, the purpose schools serve is important to the public. Like parks, private control exists, but there is also a very strong tradition of public control in this field. Like parks, schools may be available to almost anyone of one race or religion but to no others. Like parks, there are normally alternatives for those shut out but there may also be inconveniences and disadvantages caused by the restriction. Like parks, the extent of school intimacy varies greatly depending on the size and character of the institution." [e]

"While this process of analogy might be spun out to reach privately owned orphanages, libraries, garbage collection companies, detective agencies, and a host of other functions commonly regarded as nongovernmental though paralleling fields of governmental activity, the example of schools is, I think, sufficient to indicate the pervasive potentialities of this 'public function' theory of state action. It substitutes for the comparatively clear and concrete tests of state action a catch-phrase approach as vague and amorphous as it is far-reaching. [f] [And] it carries the seeds of transferring to federal authority vast areas of concerns whose regulation has wisely been left by the Constitution to the States." [g]

Notes and Questions

1. *Scope of decisions.* (a) In *Marsh*, could the shipbuilding company discriminate against African–Americans in hiring production workers? In hiring peace officers or street cleaners for the town? In *Smith v. Allwright*, could the

---

d. Harlan, J., cited Thomas P. Lewis, *The Meaning of State Action*, 60 Colum.L.Rev. 1083, 1094 (1960), who argues that "voting is a purely governmental function. No private organization can decree that a majority vote shall entitle a candidate to public office, while most of the functions involved in [other] cases are those traditionally performed by private organizations or at least within their performance capabilities." See also Note, *The Strange Career of State Action Under the Fifteenth Amendment*, 74 Yale L.J. 1448, 1456–59 (1965).

e. For further consideration of "private schools," see note 3 after *Moose Lodge v. Irvis*, Sec. 3 infra.

f. Is there a "strong tradition" of private as well as public operation of parks in cities? Is it likely that, if Senator Bacon had not provided the park in *Evans*, the city would have provided its own? Is this approach too "vague and amorphous" to serve as a constitutional standard?

g. Black, J., believing that "the Georgia courts decided no federal constitutional question," agreed with the position also stated by Harlan, J.'s opinion that "the writ of certiorari should have been dismissed as improvidently granted."

For subsequent litigation in respect to this park, see *Evans v. Abney*, Sec. 3 infra.

Democratic Party refuse to hire Jewish secretaries? In *Terry,* could the Jaybirds refuse to hire black secretaries? May "private organizations" that perform "government functions" be subject to some constitutional limitations but not others?

(b) *Migrant labor camps.* A company that has a large commercial farm owns a "residential community" adjacent to it that is several miles from the nearest municipality. It has duplex homes and apartments for about half of the 300 farmworkers (and their families) who work on the farm either seasonally or year-round. It also has a store that sells food, a cafeteria, and a recreation center. Does *Marsh* or *Hudgens* govern the question of whether the "residential community" may exclude union organizers? See Note, *First Amendment and the Problem of Access to Migrant Labor Camps,* 67 Corn.L.Rev. 560 (1976).

(c) *Apartment Complexes.* A company owns a "residential community of 129 acres with 12,000 family units for 35,000 people, in 171 adjoining and 'interrelated' apartment houses." Does *Marsh* or *Hudgens* govern the question of whether the company may refuse to rent to African–Americans? May refuse to permit nonresidents to distribute political pamphlets in the apartment houses? On the privately owned "sidewalks" within the community? See *Watchtower Bible & Tract Society v. Metropolitan Life Ins. Co.,* 297 N.Y. 339, 79 N.E.2d 433 (1948), cert. denied, 335 U.S. 886, 69 S.Ct. 232, 93 L.Ed. 425 (1948).[a]

2. *Statutory bargaining agents.* Suppose a labor union, acting as exclusive bargaining agent for all employees by authority of federal statute, does not bargain as strenuously for black employees? See generally Robert L. Hale, *Force and the State: A Comparison of Political and Economic Compulsion,* 35 Colum.L.Rev. 149, 192–98 (1935). Consider Murphy, J. concurring in *Steele v. Louisville & N.R.R.,* 323 U.S. 192, 208, 65 S.Ct. 226, 234, 89 L.Ed. 173, 186 (1944): "While such a union is essentially a private organization, its power to represent and bind all members of a class or craft is derived solely from Congress. [I]t cannot be assumed that Congress meant to authorize the representative to act so to ignore the rights guaranteed by the Constitution. Otherwise the Act would bear the stigma of unconstitutionality under the Fifth Amendment." May the union, although bargaining fairly for black employees, bar them from union membership?

3. *"Private" function.* (a) If the activities of private groups may rise to the performance of a "government function," may certain official activities of government ever be considered the performance of a "private function"? Such as acting as trustee under a private will? Is the nature of the trust property relevant? In any case, does the state's official "entwinement" end the matter?

(b) If a privately owned amusement park contracts with a state deputy sheriff, who is regularly employed by the park, to enforce its racial segregation policy, may the state convict African–Americans whom the deputy arrests when they refuse to leave the premises, for trespass? See *Griffin v. Maryland,* 378 U.S. 130, 84 S.Ct. 1770, 12 L.Ed.2d 754 (1964).

(c) *State scholarship funds.* May a state university constitutionally award scholarships which the donor has designated for whites only? For persons of a particular religion only? If the donor personally selects the scholarship recipients each year and racially discriminates, may the university constitutionally admit those selected? Is there a "difference of substance" between these two situations? May a state university constitutionally solicit scholarships to be awarded on racial

---

a. The "government function" issue is considered further in Sec. 4 infra.

bases?   See generally Note, *Constitutionality of Restricted Scholarships*, 33
N.Y.U.L.Rev. 604 (1958).

JACKSON v. METROPOLITAN EDISON CO.

419 U.S. 345, 95 S.Ct. 449, 42 L.Ed.2d 477 (1974).

JUSTICE REHNQUIST delivered the opinion of the Court.

Respondent [holds] a certificate of public convenience issued by the Pennsylvania Public Utility Commission empowering it to deliver electricity [and] is subject to extensive regulation by the Commission.   Under a provision of its general tariff filed with the Commission, it has the right to discontinue service to any customer on reasonable notice of nonpayment of bills.

Petitioner [sued] Metropolitan [under] 42 U.S.C. § 1983, seeking damages for the termination and an injunction requiring Metropolitan to continue providing power to her residence until she had been afforded notice, a hearing, and an opportunity to pay any amounts found due.   She urged that under state law she had an entitlement to reasonably continuous electrical service to her home and that Metropolitan's termination [was] "state action" depriving her of property in violation of the Fourteenth Amendment's guarantee of due process of law.

The District Court [and] Court of Appeals [found] an absence of state action.

[The] mere fact that a business is subject to state regulation does not by itself convert its action into that of the State for purposes of the Fourteenth Amendment.   [It] may well be that acts of a heavily regulated utility with at least something of a governmentally protected monopoly will more readily be found to be "state" acts than will the acts of an entity lacking these characteristics.   But the inquiry must be whether there is a sufficiently close nexus between the State and the challenged action of the regulated entity so that the action of the latter may be fairly treated as that of the State itself.   * * *

Petitioner first argues that "state action" is present because of the monopoly status allegedly conferred upon Metropolitan by the State of Pennsylvania.   As a factual matter, it may well be doubted that the State ever granted or guaranteed Metropolitan a monopoly.[8]   But assuming that it had, this fact is not determinative * * *.   In *Pollak,* where the Court dealt with the activities of the District of Columbia Transit Co., a congressionally established monopoly, we expressly disclaimed reliance on the monopoly status of the transit authority.   * * *

Petitioner next urges that state action is present because respondent provides an essential public service [and] hence performs a "public function."   We have, of course, found state action present in the exercise by a private entity of powers traditionally exclusively reserved to the State.   See, e.g., *Terry* (election); *Marsh* (company town); *Evans* (municipal park).   If we were dealing with the exercise by Metropolitan of some power delegated to it by the State which is traditionally associated with sovereignty, such as eminent domain, our case would be quite a different one.   But while the Pennsylvania statute imposes an obligation to furnish service on regulated utilities, it imposes no such obligation on the State. * * *

---

8. [In] fact Metropolitan does face competition within portions of its service area from another private utility company and from municipal utility companies.   [As] petitioner admits, such public utility companies are natural monopolies created by the economic forces of high threshold capital requirements and virtually unlimited economy of scale.   Regulation was superimposed on such natural monopolies as a substitute for competition and not to eliminate [it].

Perhaps in recognition of the fact that the supplying of utility service is not traditionally the exclusive prerogative of the State, petitioner invites the expansion of the doctrine of this limited line of cases into a broad principle that all businesses "affected with the public interest" are state actors in all their actions.

We decline the invitation for reasons stated long ago in *Nebbia v. New York,* [p. 62 supra], in the course of rejecting a substantive due process attack on state legislation: "It is clear that there is no closed class or category of businesses affected with a public interest * * *. The phrase 'affected with a public interest' can, in the nature of things, mean no more than that an industry, for adequate reason is subject to control for the public good. * * *"

Doctors, optometrists, lawyers, Metropolitan, and Nebbia's upstate New York grocery selling a quart of milk are all in regulated businesses, providing arguably essential goods and services, "affected with a public interest." We do not believe that such a status converts their every action, absent more, into that of the State.

We also reject the notion that Metropolitan's termination is state action because the State "has specifically authorized and approved" the termination practice. In the instant case, Metropolitan filed with the Public Utility Commission a general tariff—a provision of which states Metropolitan's right to terminate service for nonpayment. This provision has appeared in Metropolitan's previously filed tariffs for many years and has never been the subject of a hearing or other scrutiny by the Commission.[11] Although the Commission did hold hearings on portions of Metropolitan's general tariff relating to a general rate increase, it never even considered the reinsertion of this provision in the newly filed general tariff. * * *

The case most heavily relied on by petitioner is *Pollak.* There the Court dealt with the contention that Capital Transit's installation of a piped music system on its buses violated the First Amendment rights of the bus riders. [The] District of Columbia Public Utilities Commission, on its own motion, commenced an investigation of the effects of the piped music, and after a full hearing concluded [that] the practice "in fact, through the creation of better will among passengers, [tends] to improve the conditions under which the public ride." Here, on the other hand, there was no such imprimatur placed on the practice of Metropolitan about which petitioner complains. The nature of governmental regulation of private utilities is such that a utility may frequently be required by the state regulatory scheme to obtain approval for practices a business regulated in less detail would be free to institute without any approval from a regulatory body. Approval by a state utility commission of such a request from a regulated utility, where the commission has not put its own weight on the side of the proposed practice by ordering it, does not transmute a practice initiated by the utility and approved by the commission into "state action." At most, the Commission's failure to overturn this practice amounted to no more than a determination that a Pennsylvania utility was authorized to employ such a practice if it so desired. * * *

Affirmed.

Justice Marshall, dissenting. * * *

Our state-action cases have repeatedly relied on several factors clearly presented by this case: a state-sanctioned monopoly; an extensive pattern of cooperation between the "private" entity and the State; and a service uniquely public in

---

11. Petitioner does not contest the fact that Metropolitan had this right at common law before the advent of regulation.

nature. Today the Court takes a major step in repudiating this line of authority. [Even] when the Court has not found state action based solely on the State's conferral of a monopoly, it has suggested that the monopoly factor weighs heavily in determining whether constitutional obligations can be imposed on formally private entities. See *Steele v. Louisville & Nashville R. Co.* * * *

The majority distinguishes this line of cases with a cryptic assertion that public utility companies are "natural monopolies." * * * Initially, it is far from obvious that an electric company would not be subject to competition if the market were unimpeded by governmental restrictions. Certainly the "start-up" costs of initiating electric service are substantial, but the rewards available in a relatively inelastic market might well be sufficient under the right circumstances to attract competitive investment. Instead, the State has chosen to forbid the high profit margins that might invite private competition or increase pressure for state ownership and operation of electric power facilities.

* * * Encompassed within this policy is the State's determination not to permit governmental competition with the selected private company, but to cooperate with and regulate the company in a multitude of ways to ensure that the company's service will be the functional equivalent of service provided by the State.

* * * I question the wisdom [of] focusing solely on the extent of state support for the particular activity under challenge. In cases where the State's only significant involvement is through financial support or limited regulation of the private entity, it may be well to inquire whether the State's involvement suggests state approval of the objectionable conduct. But where the State has so thoroughly insinuated itself into the operations of the enterprise, it should not be fatal if the State has not affirmatively sanctioned the particular practice in question.

[I]t seems to me in any event that the State *has* given its approval to Metropolitan Edison's termination procedures. [That] it was not seriously questioned before approval [suggests] that the Commission was satisfied to permit the company to proceed in the termination area as it had done in the past. * * *

I agree with the majority that it requires more than a finding that a particular business is "affected with the public interest" before constitutional burdens can be imposed on that business. But when the activity in question is of such public importance that the State invariably either provides the service itself or permits private companies to act as state surrogates in providing it, much more is involved than just a matter of public interest. In those cases, the State has determined that if private companies wish to enter the field, they will have to surrender many of the prerogatives normally associated with private enterprise and behave in many ways like a governmental body. And when the State's regulatory scheme has gone that far, it seems entirely consistent to impose on the public utility the constitutional burdens normally reserved for the State.

Private parties performing functions affecting the public interest can often make a persuasive claim to be free of the constitutional requirements applicable to governmental institutions because of the value of preserving a private sector in which the opportunity for individual choice is maximized. See *Evans.* Maintaining the private status of parochial [schools] advances just this value. In the due process area, a similar value of diversity may often be furthered by allowing various private institutions the flexibility to select procedures that fit their particular needs. But it is hard to imagine any such interests that are furthered by protecting privately owned public utility companies from meeting the constitutional standards that would apply if the companies were state owned. The values of pluralism and diversity are simply not relevant when the private company is the only electric company in town. * * *

What is perhaps most troubling about the Court's opinion is that it would appear to apply to a broad range of claimed constitutional violations by the company. The Court has not adopted the notion, accepted elsewhere, that different standards should apply to state action analysis when different constitutional claims are presented. Thus, the majority's analysis would seemingly apply as well to a company that refused to extend service to Negroes, welfare recipients, or any other group that the company preferred, for its own reasons, not to serve. I cannot believe that this Court would hold that the State's involvement with the utility company was not sufficient to impose upon the company an obligation to meet the constitutional mandate of nondiscrimination. Yet nothing in the analysis of the majority opinion suggests otherwise.[a]

Notes and Questions

1. *The "power" theory.* (a) Of what significance should it be that Metropolitan was "the only public utility furnishing electricity to the city"? Might it be argued that the "power" held by certain organizations today was conceived by the framers of the fourteenth amendment to be only within the possession of government? That, under a "living Constitution," such "power" creates such a threat to individual freedom that it should fall within the purview of state action? See Note, *State Action: Theories for Applying Constitutional Restrictions to Private Activity,* 74 Colum.L.Rev. 656 (1974).

Does (should) the "power theory" approach extend to holding the only ice skating rink in town to the state's constitutional responsibilities? Or is it limited to an activity that "is of such public importance that the State invariably either provides the service itself or permits private companies to act as state surrogates in providing it"? Does this invoke the "public function"—or "government function"—approach (to be considered further in note 2 after *Flagg Bros. v. Brooks,* infra)? In any event, does *Jackson* preclude this line of analysis?

(b) Does (should) the "power theory" depend on state participation in conferring the status?

(i) *Corporations.* Consider Adolf A. Berle, *Constitutional Limitations on Corporate Activity—Protection of Personal Rights From Invasion Through Economic Power,* 100 U.Pa.L.Rev. 933, 942–43 (1952): "[A corporation should be] as subject to constitutional limitations which limit action as is the state itself. [The] preconditions of application are two: the undeniable fact that the corporation was created by the state and the existence of sufficient economic power concentrated in this vehicle to invade the constitutional right of an individual to a material degree. [The] principle is logical because [the] modern state has set up, and come to rely on, the corporate system to carry out functions for which in modern life by community demand the government is held ultimately responsible." See also Theodore J. St. Antoine, *Color Blindness But Not Myopia: A New Look at State Action, Equal Protection, and "Private" Racial Discrimination,* 59 Mich.L.Rev. 993 (1961); Arthur S. Miller, *The Constitutional Law of the "Security State,"* 10 Stan.L.Rev. 620, 661–66 (1958). Does this rationale apply to *all* corporations? Should it be restricted to entities "created by the state"?

a. Brennan, J., dissented on procedural grounds. Douglas, J.'s dissent is omitted.

For a decision finding state action under the California constitution when a privately owned utility discriminates in hiring, see *Gay Law Students Ass'n v. Pacific Telephone & Telegraph Co.,* 24 Cal.3d 458, 156 Cal.Rptr. 14, 595 P.2d 592 (1979).

(ii) *Labor organizations.* Suppose a large powerful union, without statutory authority or assistance, becomes the exclusive bargaining agent in a particular industry. May it constitutionally discriminate against African–Americans? See generally Harry H. Wellington, *The Constitution, The Labor Union, and "Governmental Action,"* 70 Yale L.J. 345, 346–50 (1961). If not, must such a union afford a member "due process" before expelling him? May such a union refuse to hire black secretaries?

(c) Does the "power theory" aid in analyzing the last series of questions? Might it be argued, for example, that a particular labor union has sufficient "power" in respect to job opportunities in the industry as to be constitutionally forbidden from racially discriminating among its members but insufficient power over general job opportunities as to be constitutionally barred from using a religious test for its office employees? That the "state's duty to take preventive action [or the "state action" issue] varies with the magnitude of the discrimination and the consequent problem it creates"? Henry Friendly, *The Dartmouth College Case and the Public-Private Penumbra* 22 (1969). See generally Jesse H. Choper, *Thoughts on State Action: The "Government Function" and "Power Theory" Approaches,* 1979 Wash.U.L.Q. 757; compare Gary C. Leedes, *State Action Limitations on Courts and Congressional Power,* 60 N.C.L.Rev. 747, 757–61 (1981).[b]

2. *Constitutional rights of "power holders."* (a) In COLUMBIA BROADCASTING SYSTEM v. DEMOCRATIC NAT'L COMM., p. 850 supra—in which the FCC had ruled that a broadcaster is not required to accept editorial advertisements—some justices addressed the question of whether the action of the broadcast licensee was "governmental action" for purposes of the first amendment. BURGER, C.J., joined by Stewart and Rehnquist, JJ., concluded that it was not: "The historic aversion to censorship led Congress [to] explicitly [prohibit] the Commission from interfering with the exercise of free speech over the broadcast frequencies. [T]he Commission acts in essence as an 'overseer,' but the initial and primary responsibility for fairness, balance and objectivity rests with the licensee. * * * Moreover, the Commission has not fostered the licensee policy challenged here; it has simply declined to command particular action because it fell within the area of journalistic discretion. * * *

"Were we to read the First Amendment to spell out governmental action in the circumstances presented here, few licensee decisions on the content of broadcasts or the processes of editorial evaluation would escape constitutional scrutiny. In this sensitive area so sweeping a concept of governmental action would go far in practical effect to undermine nearly a half century of unmistakable congressional purpose to maintain—no matter how difficult the task—essentially private broadcast journalism held only broadly accountable to public interest standards."

BRENNAN, J., joined by Marshall, J., disagreed: "[T]he public nature of the airwaves, the governmentally created preferred status of broadcast licensees, the pervasive federal regulation of broadcast programming, and the Commission's specific approval of the challenged broadcaster policy combine in this case to bring

---

b. For the view that the state action doctrine may be justified by values of private pluralism, see Maimon Schwarzschild, *Value Pluralism and the Constitution: In Defense of the State Action Doctrine,* 1988 Sup.Ct.Rev. 129, 146–47: "[T]he essence of the doctrine is that it distinguishes between exercises of choice by the monopoly institutions of the state—which must conform to the Constitution—and exercises of choice by private persons acting, as private persons always do, with the protection of the state. This is an essential distinction for a society that wants to safeguard the diversity of its own values by limiting the reach of the constitutional norms that govern its public institutions."

the promulgation and enforcement of that policy within the orbit of constitutional imperatives. [Here], as in *Pollak,* the broadcast licensees operate 'under the regulatory supervision of [an] agency authorized by Congress.' And, again as in *Pollak,* that agency received 'protests' against the challenged policy and, after formal consideration, 'dismissed' the complaints on the ground that the 'public interest, convenience, and necessity' were not 'impaired' by that policy. Indeed, the argument for finding 'governmental action' here is even stronger than in *Pollak,* for this case concerns not an incidental activity of a bus company but, rather, the primary activity of the regulated entities—communication. * * * 12 "

(b) *Newspapers.* Is the conduct of the only newspaper in a metropolitan area "state action"? May it offer free "society news" space to whites only? May it refuse to hire black employees? After the *CBS* case, may a licensed broadcaster engage in such actions?

SECTION 3. STATE "INVOLVEMENT" OR "ENCOURAGEMENT"

SHELLEY v. KRAEMER

334 U.S. 1, 68 S.Ct. 836, 92 L.Ed. 1161 (1948).

CHIEF JUSTICE VINSON delivered the opinion of the Court.

[In two cases from Missouri and Michigan, petitioners were African–Americans who had purchased houses from whites despite the fact that the properties were subject to restrictive covenants, signed by most property owners in the block, providing that for a specified time (in one case fifty years from 1911) the property would be sold only to Caucasians. Respondents, owners of other property subject to the covenants, sued to enjoin the buyers from taking possession and to divest them of title. The state courts granted the relief.]

Equality in the enjoyment of property rights was regarded by the framers of [the Fourteenth] Amendment as an essential pre-condition to the realization of other basic civil rights and liberties which the Amendment was intended to guarantee.[7] Thus, [42 U.S.C. § 1982] derived from § 1 of the Civil Rights Act of 1866 which was enacted by Congress while the Fourteenth Amendment was also under consideration, provides: "All citizens of the United States shall have the same right, in every State and Territory, as is enjoyed by white citizens thereof to inherit, purchase, lease, sell, hold, and convey real and personal property." * * *

It is likewise clear that restrictions on the right of occupancy of the sort sought to be created by the private agreements in these cases could not be squared with the requirements of the Fourteenth Amendment if imposed by state statute or local ordinance. * * *

---

12. [W]here, as here, the Government has implicated itself in the actions of an otherwise private individual, that individual must exercise his own rights with due regard for the First Amendment rights of others. In other words, an accommodation of competing rights is required, and "balancing" [is] the result. * * *

I might also note that [a] finding of governmental involvement in this case does not in any sense command a similar conclusion with respect to newspapers. [The] decision as to who shall operate newspapers is made in the free market, not by Government fiat. The newspaper industry is not extensively regulated and, indeed, in light of the differences between the electronic and printed media, such regulation would violate the First Amendment with respect to newspapers. * * *

7. *Slaughter-House Cases* [p. 52 supra]. See Horace E. Flack, *The Adoption of the Fourteenth Amendment.*

But the present cases [do] not involve action by state legislatures or city councils. Here the particular patterns of discrimination and the areas in which the restrictions are to operate, are determined, in the first instance, by the terms of agreements among private individuals. Participation of the State consists in the enforcement of the restrictions so defined. * * *

Since the decision of this Court in the *Civil Rights Cases,* the principle has become firmly embedded in our constitutional law that the action inhibited by the first section of the Fourteenth Amendment is only such action as may fairly be said to be that of the States. That Amendment erects no shield against merely private conduct, however discriminatory or wrongful.

We conclude, therefore, that the restrictive agreements standing alone cannot be regarded as a violation of any rights guaranteed to petitioners by the Fourteenth Amendment. So long as the purposes of those agreements are effectuated by voluntary adherence to their terms, it would appear clear that there has been no action by the State and the provisions of the Amendment have not been violated.

But here there was more. These are cases in which the purposes of the agreements were secured only by judicial enforcement by state courts of the restrictive terms of the agreements. * * *

That the action of state courts and of judicial officers in their official capacities is to be regarded as action of the State within the meaning of the Fourteenth Amendment, is a proposition which has long been established. [In] the *Civil Rights Cases,* this Court pointed out that the Amendment makes void "state action of every kind" which is inconsistent with the guaranties therein contained, and extends to manifestations of "state authority in the shape of laws, customs, or judicial or executive proceedings." * * *

One of the earliest applications of the prohibitions contained in the Fourteenth Amendment to action of state judicial officials occurred in cases in which Negroes had been excluded from jury service * * *. These cases demonstrate, also, the early recognition by this Court that state action in violation of the Amendment's provisions is equally repugnant to the constitutional commands whether directed by state statute or taken by a judicial official in the absence of statute. * * *

The action of state courts in imposing penalties or depriving parties of other substantive rights without providing adequate notice and opportunity to defend, has, of course, long been regarded as a denial of the due process of law guaranteed by the Fourteenth Amendment.

In numerous cases, this Court has reversed criminal convictions in state courts for failure of those courts to provide the essential ingredients of a fair hearing. Thus it has been held that convictions obtained in state courts under the domination of a mob are void. Convictions obtained by coerced confessions, by the use of perjured testimony known by the prosecution to be such, or without the effective assistance of counsel, have also been held to be exertions of state authority in conflict with the fundamental rights protected by the Fourteenth Amendment.

But the examples of state judicial action which have been held by this Court to violate the Amendment's commands are not restricted to situations in which the judicial proceedings were found in some manner to be procedurally unfair. It has been recognized that the action of state courts in enforcing a substantive common-law rule formulated by those courts, may result in the denial of rights guaranteed by the Fourteenth Amendment. [Thus,] in *AFL v. Swing,* 1941, 312 U.S. 321, 61 S.Ct. 568, 85 L.Ed. 855, enforcement by state courts of the common-law policy of the State, which resulted in the restraining of peaceful picketing, was held to be state action of the sort prohibited by the Amendment's guaranties of freedom of discussion. In *Cantwell v. Connecticut,* 1940, 310 U.S. 296, 60 S.Ct. 900, 84 L.Ed. 1213, a conviction in a state court of the common-law crime of breach of the peace was, under the circumstances of the case, found to be a violation of the Amendment's commands relating to freedom of religion. In *Bridges v. California,* 1941, 314 U.S. 252, 62 S.Ct. 190, 86 L.Ed. 192, enforcement of the state's common-law rule relating to contempts by publication was held to be state action inconsistent with the prohibitions of the Fourteenth Amendment. * * *

We have no doubt that there has been state action in these cases in the full and complete sense of the phrase. The undisputed facts disclose that petitioners were willing purchasers of properties upon which they desired to establish homes. The owners of the properties were willing sellers; and contracts of sale were accordingly consummated. It is clear that but for the active intervention of the state courts, supported by the full panoply of state power, petitioners would have been free to occupy the properties in question without restraint.

These are not cases, as has been suggested, in which the States have merely abstained from action, leaving private individuals free to impose such discriminations as they see fit. Rather, these are cases in which the States have made available to such individuals the full coercive power of government to deny to petitioners, on the grounds of race or color, the enjoyment of property rights in premises which petitioners are willing and financially able to acquire and which the grantors are willing to sell. * * *

The enforcement of the restrictive agreements by the state courts in these cases was directed pursuant to the common-law policy of the States as formulated by those courts in earlier decisions. [The] judicial action in each case bears the clear and unmistakable imprimatur of the State. We have noted that previous decisions of this Court have established the proposition that judicial action is not immunized from the operation of the Fourteenth Amendment simply because it is taken pursuant to the state's common-law policy. Nor is the Amendment ineffective simply because the particular pattern of discrimination, which the State has enforced, was defined initially by the terms of a private agreement. * * * We have noted that freedom from discrimination by the States in the enjoyment of property rights was among the basic objectives sought to be effectuated by the framers of the Fourteenth Amendment. That such discrimination has occurred in these cases is clear. * * *

Respondents urge, however, that since the state courts stand ready to enforce restrictive covenants excluding white persons[,] enforcement of covenants excluding colored persons may not be deemed a denial of equal protection of the laws to the colored persons who are thereby affected. [But the] rights created by the first section of the Fourteenth Amendment are, by its terms, guaranteed to the individual. The rights established are personal rights. It is, therefore, no answer to these petitioners to say that the courts may also be induced to deny white persons rights of ownership and occupancy on grounds of race or color. Equal protection of the laws is not achieved through indiscriminate imposition of inequalities. * * *

Reversed.

JUSTICE REED, JUSTICE JACKSON, and JUSTICE RUTLEDGE took no part in the consideration or decision of these cases.[a]

Notes and Questions

1. *Authority of prior decisions.* Do the cases holding that "judicial action is state action" call for the result in *Shelley*? Consider Comment, *The Impact of Shelley v. Kraemer on the State Action Concept*, 44 Calif.L.Rev. 718, 724 (1956): "In the cases exemplifying 'orthodox' judicial violation the prohibited activity [e.g., barring black jurors] was practiced by the judge himself. [But in *Shelley*] the discrimination originated with private persons." May this be said about "convictions obtained under the domination of a mob"?

As to those cases (*Swing, Cantwell, Bridges*) involving "the action of state courts in enforcing a substantive common-law rule," consider Comment, 45 Mich.L.Rev. 733, 742–43 (1947): "The difficulty of attributing the discrimination effected by the covenants to the enforcing tribunal is not to be escaped by pretending that it forms an element of the common law from which the right to enforcement is derived. The common law is simply the policy of the state in certain of its aspects, [and] that policy as seen in respect to these facts looks no further than to the protection of property and contract rights." Did the state policy in *Cantwell* look any further than to the protection of public tranquility? Did it, in *Bridges,* look any further than to the protection of the integrity of the court? For careful analysis, see William W. Van Alstyne, *Mr. Justice Black, Constitutional Review, and the Talisman of State Action*, 1965 Duke L.J. 219.

Are the considerations in *Shelley* different from all of these cases because it involves equal protection rather than due process? Because these other cases involve the right of free speech? Should there be a distinction between civil suits and criminal prosecutions? Consider Comment, 45 Mich.L.Rev. 733, 746 (1947): "The theory of civil remedies is that the interest of the state in the protection of property and contract rights is ordinarily secondary to that of the individual citizen, that the extent to which the protection of the law is obtained for them is largely discretionary with him. [A] criminal statute is an expression of state policy of a much higher order. In theory, the state pursues purposes of its own in criminal legislation."

2. *Zoning ordinances(?).* Is *Shelley* supportable because "so long as it is unconstitutional for a state to require racial segregation by zoning statutes [it] is equally unconstitutional for the state to bring it about by any other form of state action"? Dudley O. McGovney, *Racial Residential Segregation by State Court Enforcement of Restrictive Agreements, Covenants or Conditions in Deeds is Unconstitutional*, 33 Calif.L.Rev. 5, 30 (1945). Is the source of the discrimination the same in both instances? Or is this a variation of the "government function" approach? Consider Issac N. Groner & David M. Helfeld, *Race Discrimination in Housing*, 57 Yale L.J. 426, 454 (1948): "Where covenants do not presently cover entire areas, experience shows that, if encouraged by court enforcement, covenants do in time cover all of the area available for desirable residences." See also William R. Ming, *Racial Restrictions and the Fourteenth Amendment: The Restrictive Covenant Cases*, 16 U.Chi.L.Rev. 203 (1949).

3. BARROWS v. JACKSON, 346 U.S. 249, 73 S.Ct. 1031, 97 L.Ed. 1586 (1953), held that an action by a co-covenantor to recover damages from a property owner who sold to an African–American was barred by equal protection. Would

a. For a history of the battle against restrictive covenants, see Clement E. Vose, *NAACP Strategy in the Covenant Cases*, 6 W.Res.L.Rev. 101 (1955).

this suit, like the one in *Shelley,* involve "the full coercive power of government to deny [on] grounds of race [the] enjoyment of property rights"? Would the suit in *Barrows* have the same effect as a suit to enjoin a white property owner from breaching the covenant? See *Hurd v. Hodge,* 334 U.S. 24, 68 S.Ct. 847, 92 L.Ed. 1187 (1948).

4. *Other devices.* After *Shelley* and *Barrows,* consider the validity of:

(a) A deed conveying property on condition that if sold to an African–American it automatically reverts to the original grantor.

(i) Suppose the grantor sues to evict the black purchaser? Suppose the grantor retakes possession and the black purchaser sues to evict? Might a court deny relief in the latter situation on the ground that it had "merely abstained from action, leaving private individuals free to impose such discrimination as they see fit"?

(ii) Suppose a suit for declaratory judgment as to the validity of the reverter? If the reverter were declared invalid, could it be said "that the restrictive agreements standing alone cannot be regarded as a violation of [the] Fourteenth Amendment"? If it were declared valid, could a court deny the original grantor's suit to enjoin the black purchaser's taking possession? See generally Arthur S. Miller, *Racial Discrimination and Private Schools,* 41 Minn.L.Rev. 245, 276–80 (1957).

(b) A will devising property on condition that if the beneficiary marry a person "not born in the Hebrew faith" the property be paid over to someone else. Suppose the beneficiary marries a Catholic and the remainderman sues for the property?

(c) A child custody decree directing the father to pay private school tuition. Suppose the father refuses to pay because the school racially discriminates and the mother sues to enforce the decree.

5. *The limits of Shelley.* (a) Consider Comment, 44 Calif.L.Rev. 718, 733 (1956): "If obtaining court aid to carry out 'private' activity 'converts' such private action into 'state' action, then there could never be any private action in any practical sense. So entwined are our lives with the law that the logical result would be that almost *all* action, to be effective, must result in state action. Thus all private activity would be required to 'conform' with the standards of conduct imposed on the states by the fourteenth amendment."

(b) Evaluate the following analyses of *Shelley:*

(i) "[S]ince one's property rights in land are only powers delegated by higher state agencies [and] are legally effective only by virtue of authority granted by the state, then looking only to the face of the Fourteenth Amendment, it applies to all property [rights] used in a prohibited manner." Trayton L. Lathrop, *The Racial Covenant Cases,* 1948 Wis.L.Rev. 508, 515.

(ii) "[T]he *law* of contracts is not a matter of private agreement. The *agreements* entered may be classified as *private* affairs. However, when resort is had to a state court seeking enforcement for breach of such an agreement, it is the *law* of contracts which then must be invoked." Alfred L. Scanlan, *Racial Restriction in Real Estate—Property Values Versus Human Values,* 24 Not.D.Law. 157, 172–73 (1949).

(iii) "Professor Louis Pollak [*Racial Discrimination and Judicial Integrity,* 108 U.Pa.L.Rev. 1, 13 (1959)] would apply *Shelley* to prevent the state from enforcing a discrimination by one who does not wish to discriminate; [b] but he would allow the state to give its support to willing discrimination. [H]is proposal requires important limitation of *Shelley,* and raises a number of possible objections. [The equal protection] clause seems to be designed to protect the victim against discrimination, not to protect an unwilling 'actor' against being compelled to discriminate. It would seem also an eccentric constitutional provision which protected the aggrieved against involuntary discrimination by private persons but not against voluntary private discrimination. Moreover, the distinction is offered as a definition of 'state action.' But whether the judgment of a court enforces a voluntary discrimination or compels a no-longer-voluntary discrimination, the discrimination is private in origin; in both cases it requires a court judgment to make the discrimination effective. [Finally,] in *Shelley* itself, is it acceptable to think of the case as one in which the state was compelling discrimination by a grantor of property who no longer wished to discriminate? In essence, the state was enforcing discrimination by the other parties to the covenant." Louis Henkin, *Shelley v. Kraemer: Notes for a Revised Opinion,* 110 U.Pa.L.Rev. 473, 477–78 & n. 10 (1962).

Compare Harold W. Horowitz, *The Misleading Search for "State Action" Under the Fourteenth Amendment,* 30 So.Cal.L.Rev. 208, 213 (1957): "There is involved here a question of the degree of effect of different forms of state action on a prospective Negro buyer's opportunity to purchase and use [land]. The state does not substantially deny the Negro that opportunity by *permitting* a private person to refuse to deal with him because of his race. This would be the situation where there was 'voluntary adherence' to the restrictive covenant by the landowner. But the state does to a far greater degree deny the Negro the opportunity to acquire land, because of his race, if it *compels* a landowner not to deal with the Negro. This is the situation where the state enforces the restrictive covenant after a landowner has decided not to adhere to it."

(iv) Since restraints on alienation of property are presumptively void, being valid generally only if the court finds the restraint a reasonable one and consistent with public policy, Restatement, *Property* § 406 (1944), was there state action in *Shelley* because the court placed its imprimatur on a racially discriminatory restraint? Might it be argued that, due to this, the source of discrimination was public rather than private? See Jesse H. Choper, *Thoughts on State Action,* 1979 Wash.U.L.Q. 757, 769–71.

(v) Consider Barbara R. Snyder, *Private Motivation, State Action and the Allocation of Responsibility for Fourteenth Amendment Violations,* 75 Corn.L.Rev. 1053, 1985 (1990): "In ordering the enforcement of the covenant, the state court determined that the plaintiffs were entitled to judgment only after taking notice of the race of the Shelleys. [Thus], the Missouri court's decision was racially discriminatory on its face."

(c) Consider Comment, 44 Calif.L.Rev. 718, 735 (1956): "It is submitted that the doctrine of judicial enforcement as interpreted by *Shelley* is applicable only when the court action abets private discrimination which in the absence of such judicial aid would be ineffective. [Where] the private activity, admitted in *Shelley* to be valid in itself, is already effective, it is not to be said that the court, recognizing or failing to abolish the activity, is itself an arm of the discrimination; the situation has remained the same, court action or no. It is only where the

---

b. See *Moose Lodge v. Irvis,* infra, for this application of *Shelley*—in the only opinion of the Court (apart from *Barrows v. Jackson*) that has relied on *Shelley* to find state action. Cf. also fn. 10 in *Flagg Bros. v. Brooks,* Sec. 4 infra, and note 1 thereafter.

proponents of discrimination, unable to further their ends privately, seek court aid is the state itself causing discrimination under *Shelley.*"

(i) Suppose plaintiff is denied relief in a breach of contract suit against a cemetery for refusing to bury an African–American because the burial lot purchase contract was restricted to Caucasians? What result under *Shelley*? Under the above theory? Would denial of plaintiff's cause of action make the discrimination "effective"? If the body had already been interred, could the cemetery obtain the court's aid in removing it?

(ii) Suppose a collective bargaining agreement authorizes discharge of employees for "just cause" and an employee is so discharged because he is black. What result in the employee's suit for reinstatement? See *Black v. Cutter Lab.,* 351 U.S. 292, 301–03, 76 S.Ct. 824, 828, 100 L.Ed. 1188, 1197 (1956) (dissenting opinion). What result in the employer's suit to restrain the employee from continuing to appear on the job?

(iii) Suppose a landlord seeks the court's aid to evict a tenant whose defense is that the eviction is solely on the grounds of race (or religion, or speech)? Suppose the tenant seeks to restrain the landlord from recovering possession of the leased premises? If the tenant refuses to give up possession and is forcibly evicted by the landlord, what result in the tenant's suit for assault? Would a desirable rule produce different results in the above situations?

(iv) What result in a suit by the state real estate board to revoke a broker's license for having sold property to an African–American contrary to the owner's instructions? In a suit by a citizen to force the state real estate board to revoke a broker's license for having refused to show property to African–Americans pursuant to the owner's instructions?

(v) At common law, no person who offered his property for sale could be enjoined from arbitrarily refusing to sell to another. Suppose an owner refuses to sell solely because of the buyer's race. Consider Richard G. Huber, *Revolution in Private Law?* 6 S.C.L.Q. 8, 26 (1953): "It would seem, under *Shelley,* that he could bring suit alleging denial of equal protection of the laws. Even if the court wished to dismiss the suit as not stating a cause of action [it] would seem that the court could not do so without supporting the discrimination."

6. *Reconsideration of prior problems in light of Shelley.* (a) *Evans v. Newton.* (i) When the state court accepted the city's resignation and appointed private trustees to carry out the testator's discriminatory intent, was this state action that abetted otherwise private discrimination? If the city had not resigned and the state court had granted the relief sought to remove the city as trustee, would this be enforcing discrimination by one who did not wish to discriminate in violation of the *Shelley* rule?

If Senator Bacon had designated a private trustee who was unwilling or unable to act, a new trustee would be appointed by the court. Would discrimination by such an appointee be state action? In most states, charitable trusts are enforced by the attorney general. If Bacon's will had designated a private trustee who refused to discriminate, would an action by the attorney general to force the trustee to comply with terms of the trust violate equal protection? If the private trustee, in compliance with the terms, discriminates from the outset, would the attorney general's failure to seek to end the discrimination violate equal protection? What would be the effect of a court approving the trustee's accounts?

(ii) On remand, after *Evans,* the Georgia courts interpreted Senator Bacon's will and held that "because the park's segregated, whites-only character was an essential and inseparable part of the testator's plan," the "cy pres doctrine to amend the terms of the will by striking the racial restrictions" was inapplicable; that, therefore, the trust failed and the trust property "by operation of law reverted to the heirs of Senator Bacon." EVANS v. ABNEY, 396 U.S. 435, 90 S.Ct. 628, 24 L.Ed.2d 634 (1970), per BLACK, J., affirmed, finding that "the Georgia court had no alternative under its relevant trust laws, which are long standing and neutral with regard to race, but to end the Baconsfield trust": "[T]he Constitution imposes no requirement upon the Georgia court to approach Bacon's will any differently than it would approach any will creating any charitable trust of any kind. [T]here is not the slightest indication that any of the Georgia judges involved were motivated by racial animus or discriminatory intent of any sort in construing and enforcing Senator Bacon's will. Nor is there any indication that Senator Bacon in drawing up his will was persuaded or induced to include racial restrictions by the fact that such restrictions were permitted by the Georgia trust statutes." *Shelley* was "easily distinguishable" because here "the termination of the park was a loss shared equally by the white and Negro citizens of Macon."

BRENNAN, J., dissented: "For almost half a century Baconsfield has been a public park." When "a public facility would remain open but for the constitutional command that it be operated on a nonsegregated basis, the closing of that facility conveys an unambiguous message of community involvement in racial discrimination. [But] the Court finds that in this case it is not the State or city but 'a private party which is injecting the racially discriminatory motivation.'" Nonetheless, "this discriminatory closing is permeated with state action": "First, there is state action whenever a State enters into an arrangement which creates a private right to compel or enforce the reversion of a public facility" and, here, "in accepting title to the park," city officials agreed to that "if the city should ever incur a constitutional obligation to desegregate the park. [The] decision whether or not a public facility shall be operated in compliance with the Constitution is an essential *governmental* decision." Second, "nothing in the record suggests that after our decision in *Evans v. Newton* the City of Macon retracted its previous willingness to manage Baconsfield on a nonsegregated basis, or that the white beneficiaries of Senator Bacon's generosity were unwilling to share it with Negroes, rather than have the park revert to his heirs." Thus, contrary to *Shelley,* "this is a case of a state court's enforcement of a racial restriction to prevent willing parties from dealing with one another." Douglas, J., dissented; Marshall, J., did not participate.

(iii) Was the Georgia courts' action "a judicial choice between two incompatible terms of his will"—"(1) to keep Negroes out of the park; and (2) to keep Baconsfield a park forever"—thus, state action placing its imprimatur on racial discrimination (see note 5(b)(iv) supra)? Comment, 14 Kan.L.Rev. 613, 625 (1966).

(b) *De facto school segregation.* Consider Comment, 31 Mo.L.Rev. 391, 397 (1966): "[*Shelley*] stands for the proposition that the state may not give discriminatory acts of private persons the force of law. Does not the local school board violate that proposition when [it] assures private persons that if they are able to keep their neighborhoods segregated their schools will be segregated also." Does the school board thus also encourage private housing discrimination?

7. *The balancing approach.* Is the ultimate solution in *Shelley,* and other cases, a balancing of *all* of the particular interests involved? Consider William W. Van Alstyne & Kenneth L. Karst, *State Action,* 14 Stan.L.Rev. 3, 44–45 (1961): "[There has been] an attempt to discover or invent the *kind* of state connection

which will satisfy the state action requirement. It is suggested, for example, that the state acts in the sense of the amendment when it coerces private discrimination, but not when it simply lends its aid to such racial discrimination as private individuals may choose to practice. [This analysis] perpetuates the untenable distinction between the state action requirement on the one hand and the balance of 'substantive' constitutional interests on the other. This way of looking at the problem [is] even more dangerous than the suggestion's other unfortunate aspect: its assumption that every private discrimination is invalid once the right formal state connection has been found." See also Jerre Williams, *Mulkey v. Reitman and State Action,* 14 U.C.L.A.L.Rev. 26 (1966).

Compare Henkin, note 5(b)(iii) supra at 496: "Generally, the equal protection clause precludes state enforcement of private discrimination. There is, however, a small area of liberty favored by the Constitution even over claims to equality. Rights of liberty and property, of privacy and voluntary association, must be balanced, in close cases, against the right not to have the state enforce discrimination against the victim. In the few instances in which the right to discriminate is protected or preferred by the Constitution, the state may enforce it." [c] Is it the contention that the inquiry is not whether state action is present but whether the state policy preference, expressed through its laws, between conflicting claims of individuals, denies equal protection?

Contrast Martin G. Gilbert, *Theories of State Action as Applied to the "Sit-In" Cases,* 17 Ark.L.Rev. 147, 161 (1963): "The primary weakness in Henkin's approach would seem to be that the responsibility of the state arises from its *power* to act in a given situation. It would seem much sounder to impute responsibility where there is a *duty* on the part of the state to act. Thus, where traditional state functions, such as running elections or operating a town, are involved, the state would seem to have a duty to see that these activities are conducted in a constitutional manner. Beyond [this], the state might have a duty to insure nondiscrimination by enterprises which occupy important positions of public interest. For example, if all the milk producers in an area refused to sell to Negroes, it would seem that the state would have a duty to insure that Negroes could purchase milk on equal terms with whites. In the case of the small corner diner, especially in an area which offers other sources of similar meals to the Negro, it would seem that the state has no duty to insure the Negro a meal there, even though the state would clearly have the power to do so. Here again, an ad hoc approach would be required."

See Harold W. Horowitz, *Fourteenth Amendment Aspects of Racial Discrimination in "Private" Housing,* 52 Calif.L.Rev. 1, 12–20 (1964): "The determination of the constitutionality under the fourteenth amendment of state law permitting a private person to discriminate, on racial grounds, against another private person in a specific fact situation requires consideration of various interdependent factors: the nature and degree of injury to the person discriminated against, the interest of the discriminator in being permitted to discriminate, and the interest of the discriminatee in having opportunity of access equal to that of other persons to the benefits of governmental assistance to the discriminator * * *. If there is extensive state participation and involvement related to the activities of the discriminator, it is more likely that those activities will be public in nature, with consequent public indignity and humiliation suffered by the person discriminated against, and more likely that denial of access to those activities will be of some

---

c. See also Charles L. Black, *"State Action," Equal Protection, and California's Proposition 14,* 81 Harv.L.Rev. 69, 83–109 (1967); Frank S. Sengstock & Mary C. Sengstock, *Discrimination: A Constitutional Dilemma,* 9 Wm. & M.L.Rev. 59 (1967).

significance to the discriminatee. [When] there is governmental assistance to the discriminator in carrying on his activities, and the assistance is being provided to further the purposes of a governmental program designed to provide benefits for the public or a permissible segment of the public, the effect of the discrimination is to deny to the discriminatee the opportunity to have equal opportunity of access to the benefits of the governmental program." [d]

Compare Jesse H. Choper, *Thoughts on State Action,* 1979 Wash.U.L.Q. 757, 762: "[The balancing approaches] contradict a central feature of the fourteenth amendment. Although its major purpose was to augment the authority of the national government to secure certain constitutional rights, its primary thrust was to accomplish this goal by outlawing deprivations of these rights by state governments and their legal structures rather than by the impact of private choice. By effectively obliterating the distinction between state action and private action, these theories eviscerate the fourteenth amendment's restriction on the authority of the national government vis-à-vis the states regarding the regulation of the myriad relationships that occur between one individual and another. [A]t the initiative of any litigant who is offended by another person's behavior, these theories would subject to the scrutiny of federal judges, under substantive constitutional standards customarily developed for measuring the actions of government, all sorts of private conduct that because of political constraints and collective good sense would probably never be mandated by law. Further, by permitting private actors to violate constitutional norms when they have a constitutionally protected liberty interest to do so, these theories would delegate to federal judges the power to implement the vague mandate of the due process clause in speaking the final word about the validity of virtually all transactions between individuals. In doing so, the national judiciary would be required to determine whether private conduct was constitutionally immune from government control even though, because of general political sensitivity to individual autonomy, such private conduct probably would never be regulated by the state." See also Thomas P. Lewis, *The Role of Law in Regulating Discrimination in Places of Public Accommodation,* 13 Buf.L.Rev. 402, 416–18 (1964).

8. *"Sit-in" cases.* [e] (a) In PETERSON v. GREENVILLE, 373 U.S. 244, 83 S.Ct. 1119, 10 L.Ed.2d 323 (1963), an ordinance forebade restaurants to seat whites and blacks together. The Court, per WARREN, C.J., reversed trespass convictions of black youths who, when denied service at a lunch counter, refused to leave: "[T]hese convictions cannot stand, even assuming [that] the manager would have acted as he did independently of the existence of the ordinance. [When] a state agency passes a law compelling persons to discriminate [such] a

---

d. For other discussions of a balancing approach, see Robert J. Glennon & John E. Nowak, *A Functional Analysis of the Fourteenth Amendment "State Action" Requirement,* 1976 Sup.Ct.Rev. 221; Thomas G. Quinn, *State Action: A Pathology and a Proposed Cure,* 64 Calif.L.Rev. 146 (1976); Anthony Thompson, *Piercing the Veil of State Action: The Revisionist Theory and a Mythical Application to Self-Help Repossession.* 1977 Wis.L.Rev. 1; Arval A. Morris & L.A. Scot Powe, Jr., *Constitutional & Statutory Rights to Open Housing,* 44 Wash. L.Rev. 1–56 (1968); David Haber, *Notes on the Limits of Shelley v. Kraemer,* 18 Rutgers L.Rev. 811 (1964).

For recent consideration of "balancing," see Erwin Chemerinsky, *Rethinking State Action,*

80 Nw.U.L.Rev. 503 (1985); William P. Marshall, *Diluting Constitutional Rights: Rethinking "Rethinking State Action,"* 80 Nw.U.L.Rev. 558 (1985); Erwin Chemerinsky, *More Is Not Less: A Rejoinder to Professor Marshall,* 80 Nw.U.L.Rev. 571 (1985).

e. In the early 1960s, the Court—employing a variety of doctrines, but never relying on *Shelley*—reversed a long series of trespass convictions of "sit-in" demonstrators who were protesting racial discrimination by restaurants and other businesses. The Civil Rights Act of 1964 (p. 105 supra) largely mooted the constitutional problem of equal rights in public accommodations.

palpable violation of the Fourteenth Amendment cannot be saved by attempting to separate the mental urges of the discriminators." [f]   Douglas, J., concurred. [g] HARLAN, J., noting "a clash of competing constitutional claims of a high order: liberty and equality," would have "the issue of state action" turn on the "question of fact" whether the restaurant "might have preferred for reasons entirely of its own not to serve meals to Negroes along with whites, [or] whether the ordinance played some part in [the] decision to segregate." [h]

(b) In BELL v. MARYLAND, 378 U.S. 226, 84 S.Ct. 1814, 12 L.Ed.2d 822 (1964), GOLDBERG, J., joined by Warren, C.J., and Douglas, J., relying on the historical view in Sec. 1, fn. a, cited *Marsh, Shelley, Terry* and *Barrows* for the view that "a State, obligated under the Fourteenth Amendment to maintain a system of law in which Negroes are not denied protection in their claim to be treated as equal members of the community, may not use its criminal trespass laws to frustrate the constitutionally granted right.   Nor [may] a State frustrate this right by legitimating a proprietor's attempt at self-help." [i]

BLACK, J., joined by Harlan and White, JJ., dissented: Reliance on *Shelley* was "misplaced" because it established only these propositions: "(1) When an owner of property is willing to sell and a would-be purchaser is willing to buy, then the Civil Rights Act of 1866, which gives all persons the same right to 'inherit, lease, sell, hold, and convey' property, prohibits a State, whether through its legislature, executive, or judiciary, from preventing the sale on the grounds of the race or color of one of the parties.   * * * (2) Once a person has become a property owner, then he [may] sell his property to whom he pleases and admit to that property whom he will; so long as *both* parties are willing parties, then the principles

---

f.   See also *Lombard v. Louisiana,* 373 U.S. 267, 83 S.Ct. 1122, 10 L.Ed.2d 338 (1963) (statements by city officials that sit-ins "would not be permitted" had "as much coercive effect as an ordinance"); *Robinson v. Florida,* 378 U.S. 153, 84 S.Ct. 1693, 12 L.Ed.2d 771 (1964) (state health regulations, requiring racially separate toilets in restaurants, impose "burdens bound to discourage the serving of the two races together").

If a statute requires private colleges to enact regulations for maintenance of order on campus, must such a college's procedures for dismissal of students comport with procedural due process?

g.   See also Douglas, J.'s view that "state policy may be as effectively expressed in *customs* as in formal legislative, executive, or judicial action," *Garner v. Louisiana,* 368 U.S. 157, 82 S.Ct. 248, 7 L.Ed.2d 207 (1961) (concurring opinion) (cf. Kenneth L. Karst & William W. Van Alstyne, *Sit-Ins and State Action—Mr. Justice Douglas Concurring,* 14 Stan.L.Rev. 762 (1962)); and Brennan, J.'s view that *Peterson, Lombard,* and *Robinson* "together hold that a state policy of discouraging privately chosen integration or encouraging privately chosen segregation, even though the policy is expressed in a form nondiscriminatory on its face, is unconstitutional and taints the privately chosen segregation it seeks to bring about," *Adickes v. S.H. Kress & Co.,* 398 U.S. 144, 90 S.Ct. 1598, 26 L.Ed.2d 142 (1970) (separate

opinion).   See further, note 2 after *Reitman v. Mulkey,* infra.

h.   Consider Thomas P. Lewis, *The Sit-In Cases: Great Expectations,* 1963 Sup.Ct.Rev. 101, 110: "The Court [was] concerned with persons unknown and unknowable who might be affected by the cumulative pressure of such laws on a variety of proprietors in a variety of environments.   [When] only the proprietor can know what his 'mental urges' are, and when even he might find difficulty in separating them, judicial review will be more effective for the mass of cases [if] the Court by the announcement of its rule makes it as certain as it can that proprietors and officials alike appreciate the precise status of segregation laws."

If federal law requires airlines to search passengers for weapons, should the issue of whether such a search by an airline employee is "state action" under the fourth and fourteenth amendments turn on whether the airlines would have conducted the searches regardless of the federal legislation?

i.   See also Souter, J., dissenting in *Bray v. Alexandria Women's Health Clinic,* 506 U.S. 263, 113 S.Ct. 753, 122 L.Ed.2d 34 (1993): "[G]overnment enforcement of private segregation by use of a state trespass law, rather than 'securing to all persons [the] equal protection of the laws,' itself amounted to an unconstitutional act in violation of the Equal Protection Clause of the Fourteenth Amendment. Cf. *Shelley.*"

stated in *Buchanan v. Warley,* 245 U.S. 60, 38 S.Ct. 16, 62 L.Ed. 149 (1917) and *Shelley* protect this right. But equally, when one party is unwilling, as when the property owner chooses *not* to sell to a particular person or *not* to admit that person, [then] he is entitled to rely on the guarantee of due process of law [to] protect his free use and enjoyment of property and to know that only by valid legislation, passed pursuant to some constitutional grant of power, can anyone disturb this free use."

REITMAN v. MULKEY

387 U.S. 369, 87 S.Ct. 1627, 18 L.Ed.2d 830 (1967).

JUSTICE WHITE delivered the opinion of the Court.

[Section 26 of the California constitution], an initiated measure submitted to the people [in] a statewide ballot in 1964, provides in part as follows: "Neither the State nor any subdivision or agency thereof shall deny, limit or abridge, directly or indirectly, the right of any person, who is willing or desires to sell, lease or rent any part or all of his real property, to decline to sell, lease or rent such property to such person or persons as he, in his absolute discretion, chooses." The real property covered by § 26 is limited to residential property and contains an exception for state-owned real estate.

[Respondents] sued under § 51 and § 52 of the California Civil Code [forbidding racial discrimination "in all business establishments"] alleging that petitioners had refused to rent them an apartment solely on account of their race. An injunction and damages were demanded. Petitioners moved for summary judgment on the ground that §§ 51 and 52 [had] been rendered null and void by the adoption of [§ 26] after the filing of the complaint. [The California Supreme Court held that § 26] was invalid as denying [equal protection].

We affirm the judgment [which] quite properly undertook to examine the constitutionality of § 26 in terms of its "immediate objective," its "ultimate impact" and its "historical context and the conditions existing prior to its enactment." Judgments such as these we have frequently undertaken ourselves. *Yick Wo v. Hopkins; Lombard v. Louisiana; Anderson v. Martin.* But here the California Supreme Court has addressed itself to these matters and we should give careful consideration to its views because they concern the purpose, scope, and operative effect of a provision of the California Constitution.

First, the court considered whether § 26 was concerned at all with private discriminations in residential housing. [§ 26's] immediate design and intent, the California court said, was "to overturn state laws that bore on the right of private sellers and lessors to discriminate," [and] "to forestall future state action that might circumscribe this right." * * *

Second, the court conceded that the State was permitted a neutral position with respect to private racial discriminations and that the State was not bound by the Federal Constitution to forbid them. But [the] court deemed it necessary to determine whether [§ 26] invalidly involved the State in racial discriminations in the housing market. Its conclusion was that it did.

To reach this result, the state court [reasoned] that a prohibited state involvement could be found "even where the state can be charged with only encouraging," rather than commanding discrimination. [To] the California court "[t]he instant case [was one]" wherein the State had taken affirmative action designed to make private discriminations legally possible. Section 26 was said to have changed the situation from one in which discriminatory practices were restricted "to one wherein it is encouraged, within the meaning of the cited decisions"; § 26 was legislative action "which authorized private discrimination" and made the State "at least a partner in the instant act of discrimination * * *." The court could "conceive of no other purpose for an application of section 26 aside from authorizing the perpetration of a purported private discrimination * * *." * * *

There is no sound reason for rejecting this judgment. [It] did not read either our cases or the Fourteenth Amendment as establishing an automatic constitutional barrier to the repeal of an existing law prohibiting racial discriminations in housing; nor did the court rule that a State may never put in statutory form an existing policy of neutrality with respect to private discriminations. [It] dealt with § 26 as though it expressly authorized and constitutionalized the private right to discriminate [and] the court assessed the ultimate impact of § 26 in the California environment and concluded that the section would encourage and significantly involve the State in private racial discrimination contrary to the Fourteenth Amendment.

The California court could very reasonably conclude that § 26 would and did have wider impact than a mere repeal of existing statutes. [The] right to discriminate, including the right to discriminate on racial grounds, was now embodied in the State's basic charter, immune from legislative, executive, or judicial regulation at any level of the state government. Those practicing racial discriminations need no longer rely solely on their personal choice. They could now invoke express constitutional authority, free from censure or interference of any kind from official sources. * * *

This Court has never attempted the "impossible task" of formulating an infallible test for determining whether the State "in any of its manifestations" has become significantly involved in private discriminations. [Here] the California court, armed as it was with the knowledge of the facts and circumstances concerning the passage and potential impact of § 26, and familiar with the milieu in which that provision would operate, has determined that the provision would involve the State in private racial discriminations to an unconstitutional degree. We accept this holding of the California court. * * *

Affirmed.[a]

JUSTICE HARLAN, whom JUSTICE BLACK, JUSTICE CLARK, and JUSTICE STEWART join, dissenting.

[A]ll that has happened is that California has effected a pro tanto repeal of its prior statutes forbidding private discrimination. This runs no more afoul of the Fourteenth Amendment than would have California's failure to pass any such antidiscrimination statutes in the first instance. The fact that such repeal was also accompanied by a constitutional prohibition against future enactment of such laws by the California Legislature cannot well be thought to affect, from a federal constitutional standpoint, the validity of what California has done. [§ 26] is neutral on its face, and it is only by in effect asserting that this requirement of passive official neutrality is camouflage that the Court is able to reach its conclusion. * * *

a. Douglas, J., joined the Court's opinion, adding that "we deal here with a problem in the realm of zoning, similar to the one we had in *Shelley*. [When] the state leaves [the zoning] function to private agencies or institutions [including real estate brokers who are state licensees], it suffers a governmental function to be performed under private auspices in a way the State itself may not act. The present case is therefore kin to *Terry*."

There is no disagreement whatever but that § 26 was meant to nullify California's fair-housing legislation and thus to remove from private residential property transactions the state-created impediment upon freedom of choice. [But there was no finding] that the defendants' actions were anything but the product of their own private choice. [There] were no findings as to the general effect of § 26. The Court declares that the California court "held the purpose and intent of § 26 was to authorize private racial discriminations in the housing market," but there is no supporting fact in the record for this characterization.

[The] denial of equal protection emerges only from the conclusion reached by the Court that the implementation of a new policy of governmental neutrality [has] the effect of lending encouragement to those who wish to discriminate. In the context of the actual facts of the case, this conclusion appears to me to state only a truism: people who want to discriminate but were previously forbidden to do so by state law are now left free because the State has chosen to have no law on the subject at all. Obviously whenever there is a change in the law it will have resulted from the concerted activity of those who desire the change, and its enactment will allow those supporting the legislation to pursue their private goals.

[Every] act of private discrimination is either forbidden by state law or permitted by it. There can be little doubt that such permissiveness—whether by express constitutional or statutory provision, or implicit in the common law—to some extent "encourages" those who wish to discriminate to do so. Under this theory "state action" in the form of laws that do nothing more than passively permit private discrimination could be said to tinge *all* private discrimination with the taint of unconstitutional state encouragement. * * *

Notes and Questions

1. *Court's rationale.* (a) What was the specific basis for § 26's invalidity? Was it that it "constitutionalized the private right to discriminate" in housing, making it "immune from legislative, executive, or judicial regulation at any level of state government"—thus making it much more difficult for minorities to get governmental antidiscrimination help? Would this call for the same result even if California had never enacted anti-discrimination Laws? Suppose a state provides that *all* legislation requires approval by ⅔ of the voters? All legislation having *anything* to do with the sale and purchase of real and personal property? Was § 26 a less "neutral provision"? Sufficiently "nonneutral"? Was *this* the thrust of the opinion? If so, does *Reitman* hold that racial discrimination in housing by private individuals in California is "state action"?

(b) Or did the Court rest on the finding (whose finding?) that § 26, given "the milieu in which that provision would operate," "would involve the State in private racial discriminations to an unconstitutional degree"? If so, could "mere repeal of existing statutes" so operate? Failure to enact a proposed antidiscrimination law? The mere absence of an antidiscrimination law? Consider Archibald Cox, *The Warren Court* 45 (1968): "The truth would seem to be that the absence of legal restraints gives encouragement of a sort to anyone minded to engage in discrimination, and any defeat of proposed restraints after strong public debate will give moral support to some persons who might not otherwise have been ready to discriminate. The degree of support that is given seems likely to depend upon a congeries of factors far more diffuse and subtle than the differences between repeal of a statute and amendment of a constitution." Compare 42 Wash.L.Rev. 285 (1966). See generally Charles L. Black, *"State Action," Equal Protection, and California's Proposition 14,* 81 Harv.L.Rev. 69 (1967); Philip B. Kurland, *Egalitarianism and the Warren Court,* 68 Mich. 629, 668–70 (1970); Kenneth L. Karst

& Harold W. Horowitz, *Reitman v. Mulkey: A Telophase of Substantive Equal Protection,* 1967 Sup.Ct.Rev. 39.

Suppose a school board rescinds a resolution of its predecessor that recognized the boards' responsibility for segregation and called for—but did not enact—any remedial action? See *Dayton Bd. of Educ. v. Brinkman,* 433 U.S. 406, 413–14, 97 S.Ct. 2766, 2772, 53 L.Ed.2d 851, 859 (1977).

2. *State "encouragement" or "authorization."* (a) To what extent does *Reitman* establish the principle that state law which *encourages* (or *authorizes*) private conduct results in "state action"? Is this the basis for Brennan, J.'s view in *Adickes*? What result if "a state passed a statute which provided that individuals shall have the legal right to engage in racial discrimination in their own homes"? Jerre Williams, *The Twilight of State Action,* 41 Texas L.Rev. 347, 384 (1963). Consider William M. Burke & David J. Reber, *State Action, Congressional Power and Creditors' Rights: An Essay on the Fourteenth Amendment,* 46 So.Cal.L.Rev. 1003, 1105–09 (1973): "[The] basic principle limiting the scope of the fourteenth amendment would be destroyed by equating state action with action authorized or encouraged by state law. [California] statutory law authorizes [the] use of force in self-defense; the disposition of real and personal property; [the] creation of a contractual relationship; [the] execution of a will; the formation of a corporation [etc.]. If state authority or encouragement is a valid state action test, then all of the above forms of private conduct would present fourteenth amendment equal protection and due process problems. [The] fallacy in the thesis [is] most readily apparent when one considers the impact of judicial law. It is almost impossible to consider any form of activity that is not somehow authorized by state decisional law. [As] long as the law is permissive in nature and leaves the initial decision to take the action entirely within the realm of private choice, neither the state nor the individual should be held constitutionally responsible under the fourteenth amendment. [Further], constitutional significance should not attach to such extraneous considerations as whether the law restates a long-standing law, clarifies an existing law, changes the law, creates entirely new law or repeals existing law. [First], the effect of a statute as a form of state law authorizing private conduct is precisely the same regardless of the statute's longevity * * *. Second, untoward consequences would follow from a holding that the statute is unconstitutional because of its newness or because it repeals an existing law considered more socially desirable by the Court. Such a holding would constitutionally freeze into state law every form of social legislation or decisional or administrative law deemed constitutionally proper by the Court and would thereby discourage states from experimenting in this regard. It would also produce anomalous and illogical results since the identical private conduct authorized and encouraged by the identical statutory or judicial law would be valid in some states under the fourteenth amendment but invalid in others solely because of the age of the state law in each jurisdiction."

Compare Note, *State Action: Theories for Applying Constitutional Restrictions to Private Activity,* 74 Colum.L.Rev. 656, 665–66 (1974): "Statutes enlarging common law rights clearly amount to an increase of private powers, while mere statutory codification of common law rights does not amount to authorization [and the] argument that such 'authorizing' statutes involve government by increasing private powers implies that an increase in powers through expansion of common law rights effected by the courts will constitute a government grant of power. Since any particular decision expanding the previously existing common law would thus constitute 'authorization,' the question arises as against when present common law rights are to be measured. The most reasonable starting point for 'state action' cases arising under the fourteenth amendment would seem to be the common law as of adoption of that amendment." See also Harold W. Horowitz & Kenneth L. Karst, *The California Supreme Court and State Action Under the Fourteenth Amendment: The Leader Beclouds the Issue,* 21 U.C.L.A.L.Rev. 1421 (1974).

(b) The "state 'encouragement' or 'authorization' " issue is considered further in *Flagg Bros. v. Brooks,* Sec. 4 infra.

3. *Repeal of discriminatory legislation.* Recall *Lombard, Peterson* and *Robinson.* Suppose all official pronouncements *requiring* discrimination are repealed or retracted? Is subsequent "private" discrimination in respect to matters previously covered by official pronouncements "state action"? Is the state "significantly involved" because its repeals have now made "private discriminations legally possible"? Have they "authorized" and "encouraged" discrimination? Or is this "mere repeal of existing statutes"? Is discrimination more "authorized and encouraged" by repeal of laws requiring discrimination or by repeal of laws forbidding it?

MOOSE LODGE v. IRVIS

407 U.S. 163, 92 S.Ct. 1965, 32 L.Ed.2d 627 (1972).

JUSTICE REHNQUIST delivered the opinion of the Court.

Appellee Irvis, a Negro, [who] was refused service [as the guest of a member] by appellant Moose Lodge, [claimed] that because the Pennsylvania liquor board had issued appellant Moose Lodge a private club license that authorized the sale of alcoholic beverages on its premises, the refusal of service to him was "state action" * * *.

A three-judge district court [entered] a decree declaring invalid the liquor license issued to Moose Lodge "as long as it follows a policy of racial discrimination in its membership or operating policies or practices." * * *

Moose Lodge is a private club in the ordinary meaning of that term. [It] conducts all of its activities in a building that is owned by it. It is not publicly funded. Only members and guests are permitted in any lodge of the order; one may become a guest only by invitation * * *.

While the principle is easily stated, the question of whether particular discriminatory conduct is private, on the one hand, or amounts to "state action," on the other hand, frequently admits of no easy answer. "Only by sifting facts and weighing circumstances can the non-obvious involvement of the State in private conduct be attributed its true significance." *Burton v. Wilmington Parking Authority,* 365 U.S. 715, 81 S.Ct. 856, 6 L.Ed.2d 45 (1961).

[*Burton* held] that a private restaurant owner who refused service because of a customer's race violated the Fourteenth Amendment, where the restaurant was located in a building owned by a state-created parking authority and leased from the authority. The Court, after a comprehensive review of the relationship between the lessee and the parking authority concluded that the latter had "so far insinuated itself into a position of interdependence with Eagle [the restaurant owner] that it must be recognized as a joint participant in the challenged activity, which, on that account, cannot be considered to have been so 'purely private' as to fall without the scope of the Fourteenth Amendment."

The Court has never held, of course, that discrimination by an otherwise private entity would be violative of the Equal Protection Clause if the private entity receives any sort of benefit or service at all from the State, or if it is subject to state regulation in any degree whatever. Since state-furnished services include such necessities of life as electricity, water, and police and fire protection, such a holding would utterly emasculate the distinction between private as distinguished from State conduct set forth in *The Civil Rights Cases* and adhered to in subsequent decisions. Our holdings indicate that where the impetus for the discrimination is private, the State must have "significantly involved itself with invidious discriminations," *Reitman,* in order for the discriminatory action to fall within the ambit of the constitutional prohibition. * * *

In *Burton,* the Court's full discussion of the facts in its opinion indicates the significant differences between that case and this: "The land and building were publicly owned.[a] As an entity, the building was dedicated to 'public uses' in performance of the Authority's 'essential governmental functions.'[b] The costs of land acquisition, construction, and maintenance are defrayed entirely from donations by the City of Wilmington, from loans and revenue bonds and from the proceeds of rentals and parking services out of which the loans and bonds were payable. Assuming that the distinction would be significant, the commercially leased areas were not surplus state property, but constituted a physically and financially integral and, indeed, indispensable part of the State's plan to operate its project as a self-sustaining unit.[c] Upkeep and maintenance of the building, including necessary repairs, were responsibilities of the Authority and were payable out of public funds. It cannot be doubted that the peculiar relationship of the restaurant to the parking facility in which it is located confers on each an incidental variety of mutual benefits. Guests of the restaurant are afforded a convenient place to park their automobiles, even if they cannot enter the restaurant directly from the parking area. Similarly, its convenience for diners may well provide additional demand for the Authority's parking facilities.[d] Should any improvements effected in the leasehold by Eagle become part of the realty, there is no possibility of increased taxes being passed on to it since the fee is held by a tax-exempt government agency. Neither can it be ignored, especially in view of Eagle's affirmative allegation that for it to serve Negroes would injure its business, that profits earned by discrimination not only contribute to, but also are indispensable elements in, the financial success of a governmental agency."[e]

a. If the space has been leased to a law firm, could it constitutionally discriminate among its clients?

b. If the Authority had municipal immunity from tort liability, is Eagle liable for a customer's food poisoning?

c. "Other portions of the structure were leased to other tenants, including a bookstore, a retail jeweler, and a food store. Upon completion of the building, the Authority located at appropriate places thereon official signs indicating the public character of the building, and flew from mastheads on the roof both the state and national flags." *Burton.* Query: If Wilmington, instead of including rental space in the parking building, had relied on rental income from other of its properties located throughout the city to help finance the parking facility, could lessees of these properties refuse to do business with African–Americans?

d. Suppose Eagle were located in a private building immediately adjacent to the public parking building?

e. *Burton* added: "It is irony amounting to grave injustice that in one part of a single building, erected and maintained with public funds by an agency of the State to serve a public purpose, all persons have equal rights, while in another portion, also serving the public, a Negro is a second-class citizen [but] at the same time fully enjoys equal access to nearby restaurants in wholly privately owned buildings. [I]n its lease with Eagle the Authority could have affirmatively required Eagle to discharge the responsibilities under the Fourteenth Amendment imposed upon the private enterprise as a consequence of state participation. But no State may effectively abdicate its responsibilities by either ignoring them or by merely failing to discharge them whatever the motive may be." Query: If the state sells surplus property without requiring its nondiscriminatory use because such a requirement would bring the city a lower price, may the purchaser constitutionally discriminate? If such a requirement were financially irrelevant

Here there is nothing approaching the symbiotic relationship between lessor and lessee that was present in [*Burton*]. Moose Lodge quite ostentatiously proclaims the fact that it is not open to the public at large. Nor is it located and operated in such surroundings that although private in name, it discharges a function or performs a service that would otherwise in all likelihood be performed by the State. In short, while Eagle was a public restaurant in a public building, Moose Lodge is a private social club in a private building.

With the exception hereafter noted, the Pennsylvania Liquor Control Board plays absolutely no part in establishing or enforcing the membership or guest policies of the club which it licenses to serve liquor.[3] [The] only effect that the state licensing of Moose Lodge to serve liquor can be said to have on the right of any other Pennsylvanian to buy or be served liquor on premises other than those of Moose Lodge is that for some purposes club licenses are counted in the maximum number of licenses which may be issued in a given municipality. Basically each municipality has a quota of one retail license for each 1,500 inhabitants. Licenses issued to hotels, municipal golf courses and airport restaurants are not counted in this quota, nor are club licenses until the maximum number of retail licenses is reached. Beyond that point, neither additional retail licenses nor additional club licenses may be issued so long as the number of issued and outstanding retail licenses remains above the statutory maximum.

The District Court was at pains to [note that] an applicant for a club license must make such physical alterations in its premises as the board may require, must file a list of the names and addresses of its members and employees, and must keep extensive financial records. The board is granted the right to inspect the licensed premises at any time * * *.

However detailed this type of regulation may be in some particulars, it cannot be said to in any way foster or encourage racial discrimination. Nor can it be said to make the State in any realistic sense a partner or even a joint venturer in the club's enterprise. The limited effect of the prohibition against obtaining additional club licenses when the maximum number of retail licenses allotted to a municipality has been issued, when considered together with the availability of liquor from hotel, restaurant, and retail licensees falls far short of conferring upon club licensees a monopoly in the dispensing of liquor * * *. We therefore hold that, with the exception hereafter noted, the operation of the regulatory scheme enforced by the Pennsylvania Liquor Control Board does not sufficiently implicate the State in the discriminatory guest policies of Moose Lodge * * *.

The District Court found that [Regulations § 113.09] of the Liquor Control Board adopted pursuant to statute affirmatively require that "every club licensee shall adhere to all the provisions of its constitution and by-laws." Appellant argues that the purpose of this provision "is purely and simply and plainly the prevention of subterfuge." [There] can be no doubt that the label "private club" can and has been used to evade both regulations of State and local liquor

---

but the state neglected to include it, may the buyer discriminate?

Harlan, J., joined by Whittaker, J., dissented: "The Court's opinion, by a process of first undiscriminatingly throwing together various factual bits and pieces and then undermining the resulting structure by an equally vague disclaimer, seems to me to leave completely at sea just what it is in this record that satisfies the requirement of 'state action.'" See generally Thomas P. Lewis, *Burton v. Wilmington Parking Authority—A Case Without Precedent*, 61 Colum.L.Rev. 1458 (1961).

3. Unlike the situation in *Pollak*, where the regulatory agency had affirmatively approved the practice of the regulated entity after full investigation * * *.

authorities, and statutes requiring places of public accommodation to serve all persons without regard to race, color, religion, or national origin. * * *

[The Moose constitution and by-laws limit membership and guest privileges to male Caucasians.]

Even though the Liquor Control Board regulation in question is neutral in its terms, the result of its application in a case where the constitution and by-laws of a club required racial discrimination would be to invoke the sanctions of the State to enforce a concededly discriminatory private rule. * * * *Shelley v. Kraemer* makes it clear that the application of state sanctions to enforce such a rule would violate the Fourteenth Amendment. * * *

Appellee was entitled to a decree enjoining the enforcement of § 113.09 [but] no more. The judgment of the District Court is reversed * * *.

JUSTICE DOUGLAS, with whom JUSTICE MARSHALL joins, dissenting.

My view of the First Amendment and the related guarantees of the Bill of Rights is that they create a zone of privacy which precludes government from interfering with private clubs or groups.[1] The associational rights which our system honors permits all white, all black, all brown, and all yellow clubs to be formed. [And] the fact that a private club gets some kind of permit from the State or municipality does not make it ipso facto a public enterprise or undertaking, any more than the grant to a householder of a permit to operate an incinerator puts the householder in the public domain. We must therefore examine whether there are special circumstances involved in the Pennsylvania scheme which differentiate the liquor license possessed by Moose Lodge from the incinerator permit.

[The opinion then agrees with the Court's disposition of Regulations § 113.09]. But there is another flaw in the scheme not so easily cured. Liquor licenses in Pennsylvania [are] not freely available to those who meet racially neutral qualifications. There is a complex quota system, which the majority accurately describes. What the majority neglects to say is that the Harrisburg quota, where Moose Lodge No. 107 is located, has been full for many years. No more club licenses may be issued in that city.

This state-enforced scarcity of licenses restricts the ability of blacks to obtain liquor, for liquor is commercially available *only* at private clubs for a significant portion of each week.[3] [A] group desiring to form a nondiscriminatory club which would serve blacks must purchase a license held by an existing club, which can exact a monopoly price for the transfer. The availability of such a license is speculative at best, however, for, as Moose Lodge itself concedes, without a liquor license a fraternal organization would be hard-pressed to survive.

Thus, the State of Pennsylvania is putting the weight of its liquor license, concededly a valued and important adjunct to a private club, behind racial discrimination. * * *

JUSTICE BRENNAN, with whom JUSTICE MARSHALL joins, dissenting.

1. [There] was no occasion [below] to consider the question whether perhaps because of a role as a center of community activity, Moose Lodge No. 107 was in fact "private" for equal protection purposes. The decision today, therefore, leaves this question open.

3. Hotels and restaurants may serve liquor between 7:00 a.m. and 2:00 a.m. the next day, Monday through Saturday. On Sunday, such licensees are restricted to sales between 12:00 a.m. and 2:00 a.m., and between 1:00 p.m. and 10:00 p.m. * * * Club licensees, however, are permitted to sell liquor to members and guests from 7:00 a.m. to 3:00 a.m. the next day, seven-days-a-week. * * *

When Moose Lodge obtained its liquor license, the State of Pennsylvania became an active participant in the operation of the Lodge bar. Liquor licensing laws [are] primarily pervasive regulatory schemes under which the State dictates and continually supervises virtually every detail of the operation of the licensee's business. Very few, if any, other licensed businesses experience such complete state involvement. [The] opinion of the [court below] most persuasively demonstrates the "state action" present in this case: * * *

"[After describing the regulations, mentioned in the majority opinion, the court below continued:] It is only on compliance with these and numerous other requirements and if the Board is satisfied that the applicant is 'a person of good repute' and that the license will not be 'detrimental to the welfare, health, peace and morals of the inhabitants of the neighborhood,' that the license may issue.

"Once a license has been issued the licensee must comply with many detailed requirements or risk its suspension or revocation. He must in any event have it renewed periodically. Liquor licenses have been employed in Pennsylvania to regulate a wide variety of moral conduct, such as the presence and activities of homosexuals, performance by a topless dancer, lewd dancing, swearing, being noisy or disorderly. So broad is the state's power that the courts of Pennsylvania have upheld its restriction of freedom of expression of a licensee on the ground that in doing so it merely exercises its plenary power to attach conditions to the privilege of dispensing liquor which a licensee holds at the sufferance of the state. * * *" * * * f

Notes and Questions

1. *Court's rationale.* Does *Moose Lodge* rest ultimately on a "balancing approach"? See Note, *State Action and the Burger Court,* 60 Va.L.Rev. 840 (1974). Consider Note, *Developing Legal Vistas for the Discouragement of Private Club Discrimination,* 58 Iowa L.Rev. 108, 139 (1972): "[There is evidence that] large, nationwide fraternal orders which are segregated pursuant to national constitutions, [serve] substantially economic interests. Furthermore, a glance at the membership requirement and size of these clubs indicates they are not closely knit clubs involving a high quotient of intimacy. They are certainly not primarily religious or political in nature. Hence, under the balancing approach, the associational rights asserted by these clubs would not seem strong."

2. *Burton vs. Moose Lodge.* Consider Christopher D. Stone, *Corporate Vices and Corporate Virtues: Do Public/Private Distinctions Matter?,* 130 U.Pa.L.Rev. 1441, 1449–1501 (1982): "[W]e should be readier to deem an actor 'public' when [it is 'symbolically public' and] when the preponderant costs of doing so will be imposed on the benefitting public at-large. [There] are several ways to interpret the contrasting results in *Burton* and *Moose Lodge.* One way is to contrast the symbolic elements of the situation: after all, the parking authority building flew, quite literally, the flags of government. [Second,] in *Burton,* the government stood to capture essentially all the economic benefits of the discrimination, assuming perfect competition among bidders for the lease. Hence, the Court's decision prohibiting the arrangement eliminated from public revenues essentially the full measure of the ill-gotten gains. [T]he preponderant costs of setting a morally correct example will be borne by the public, which is exactly where they ought to lie. Note that the same consequence, the apportionment of essentially

f. Irvis also complained to the Pennsylvania Human Rights Commission. *Commonwealth v. Loyal Order of Moose,* 448 Pa. 451, 294 A.2d 594, appeal dismissed, 409 U.S. 1052 (1972), upheld the Commission's ruling that the Harrisburg Moose Lodge was a "public accommodation" under state law and could not bar guests on the basis of race.

all 'fairness' costs on general revenues, would not result from a plaintiff's victory when the government is insuring mortgages, or guaranteeing loans, or is a regulatory licensor, as in *Moose Lodge.* [In] those situations, extending state action would concentrate costs on a distinct sub-group, a result that courts have been reluctant to decree."

3. *Private schools.* (a) NORWOOD v. HARRISON, 413 U.S. 455, 93 S.Ct. 2804, 37 L.Ed.2d 723 (1973), per BURGER, C.J., enjoined Mississippi's lending of textbooks to all students in public and private schools as applied to racially segregated private schools: "[T]hat the Constitution may compel toleration of private discrimination in some circumstances does not mean that it requires state support for such discrimination."

The textbook program, "enacted first in 1940, long before [there] was any occasion to have a policy or reason to foster the development of racially segregated private academies," may have been "motivated by [a] sincere interest in the educational welfare of all Mississippi children. But good intentions as to one valid objective do not serve to negate the State's involvement in violation of a constitutional duty. 'The existence of a permissible purpose cannot sustain an action that has an impermissible effect.' [citing school desegregation cases]." The lower court had found "that the textbook loans did not interfere with or impede the State's acknowledged duty to establish a unitary school system" since "the State's public schools are now fully unitary." The Court, although casting doubt on the finding, held it "irrelevant": "A State's constitutional obligation requires it to steer clear, not only of operating the old dual system of racially segregated schools, but also of giving significant aid to institutions that practice racial or other invidious discrimination."

Plaintiffs had failed to show that "any child enrolled in private school, if deprived of free textbooks, would withdraw from private school and subsequently enroll in the public schools." But "the Constitution does not permit the State to aid discrimination even when there is no precise causal relationship between state financial aid to a private school and the continued well-being of that school. A State may not grant the type of tangible financial aid here involved if that aid has a significant tendency to facilitate, reinforce, and support private discrimination. * * * Textbooks are a basic educational tool and, like tuition grants, they are provided only in connection with schools; they are to be distinguished from generalized services government might provide to schools in common with others. Moreover, the textbooks provided to private school students by the State in this case are a form of assistance readily available from sources entirely independent of the State—unlike, for example, 'such necessities of life as electricity, water, and police and fire protection.'" Douglas and Brennan, JJ., concurred in the result.

(b) In GILMORE v. MONTGOMERY, 417 U.S. 556, 94 S.Ct. 2416, 41 L.Ed.2d 304 (1974), a federal court enjoined the city's "permitting the use of public park recreational facilities by private segregated school groups and by other non-school groups that racially discriminate in their membership." The Court, per BLACK-MUN, J., modified the decree in part: It "was wholly proper for the city to be enjoined from permitting *exclusive* access to public recreational facilities by segregated private schools" (emphasis added), which had been "formed in reaction against" the federal court's school desegregation order. "[T]his assistance significantly tended to undermine the federal court order mandating [a] unitary school system in Montgomery."

But, "upon this record, we are unable to draw a conclusion as to whether the use of zoos, museums, parks, and other recreational facilities by private school groups *in common with others,* and by private nonschool organizations, involves government so directly in the actions of those users as to warrant" intervention (emphasis added). "It is possible that certain uses of city facilities will be judged to be in contravention of the parks [or school] desegregation order, [or] in some way to constitute impermissible 'state action' ascribing to the city the discriminatory actions of the groups."

The latter issue concerns "whether there is significant state involvement in the private discrimination alleged. * * * Traditional state monopolies, such as electricity, water, and police and fire protection—all generalized governmental services—do not by their mere provision constitute a showing of state involvement in invidious discrimination. *Norwood.* The same is true of a broad spectrum of municipal recreational facilities * * *.

"If, however, the city or other governmental entity rations otherwise freely accessible recreational facilities, the case for state action will naturally be stronger than if the facilities are simply available to all comers without condition or reservation. Here, for example, petitioners allege that the city engages in scheduling softball games for an all-white church league and provides balls, equipment, fields, and lighting. The city's role in that situation would be dangerously close to what was found to exist in *Burton* * * *." [a]

WHITE, J., joined by Douglas, J., concurred: "[T]he question is not whether there is state action, but whether the conceded action by the city, and hence by the State, is such that the State must be deemed to have denied the equal protection of the laws. In other words, by permitting a segregated school or group to use city-owned facilities, has the State furnished such aid to the group's segregated policies or become so involved in them that the State itself may fairly be said to have denied equal protection? Under *Burton,* it is perfectly clear that to violate the Equal Protection Clause the State itself need not make, advise, or authorize the private decision to discriminate that involves the State in the practice of segregation or would appear to do so in the minds of ordinary citizens." Marshall, J. generally agreed with White, J.

(c) *Significance of remedy.* In contrast to *Burton* (where plaintiff sought an injunction against Eagle Coffee Shoppe), since the only remedy sought in *Norwood* and *Gilmore* was against the state or city itself, did these cases really present any "state action" issue at all? Was the issue in *Moose Lodge* whether the club's refusal to serve Irvis constituted "state action"? Or was it whether Pennsylvania could grant a liquor license to a club that practiced racial discrimination? Are these constitutional issues the same? What result in *Marsh* if the leafletter sued the shipbuilding company for violation of her constitutional rights? Consider Robert C. Brown, *State Action Analysis of Tax Expenditures,* 11 Harv.Civ.Rts.-Civ.Lib.L. 97, 115–19 (1976): "[T]wo kinds of 'state action' cases should [be] distinguished: only in suits in which relief is sought against a private actor should the private actor's interests be taken into account. [Thus,] it is quite possible that a plaintiff proceeding under a state action theory might prevail in enjoining the government's action but fail in his efforts to enjoin the private activity." Compare Thomas R. McCoy, *Current State Action Theories, the Jackson Nexus Requirement, and Employee Discharges by Semi-Public and State-Aided Institutions,* 31 Vand.L.Rev. 785, 802 (1978): "Although this theoretical distinction has considerable superficial appeal, primarily because it is formulated in terms of

---

a. Brennan, J., concurred in part but would enjoin *any* "school-sponsored or directed uses of the city recreational facilities that enable private segregated schools to duplicate public school operations at public expense."

balancing competing constitutional interests, closer inspection reveals no significant difference between the cases. [E]ither kind of suit presents the private actor with precisely the same basic option—either modify the private action to conform to fourteenth amendment standards or do without the state aid. In other words, the two kinds of suits are indistinguishable in terms of the private interest interfered with, and therefore they should not present significantly different standards for the level of state aid required." Contrast Brown, supra, at 119 n. 102: "It is of course true that the removal of the government aid will have a coercive effect on the private actor. In some cases the pressure to conform private behavior to constitutional standards generated by the loss of assistance will be as coercive as an injunction. In such a case, however, the fact that withdrawing the aid had a strong influence on private behavior would imply a high level of significance of government involvement with the private actor. In that case it would be appropriate to impose relief on the private actor as well as on the government, so the remedy distinction would not apply."

In any event, since the practices in *Norwood* and *Gilmore* were not shown to be "motivated" to perpetuate racial discrimination, can these decisions be squared with *Washington v. Davis,* p. 1093 supra? Given the doctrines that (1) public financial aid to parochial schools violates the establishment clause if either the *purpose or effect* advances religion (Ch. 9, Sec. 1, II), whereas (2) a racially discriminatory *purpose* must exist for violation of the equal protection clause (Ch. 10, Sec. 2, III), can *Norwood* be squared with *Board of Educ. v. Allen* (p. 977 supra).? See Jesse H. Choper, *Thoughts on State Action,* 1979 Wash.U.L.Q. 757, 765–69.

(d) What results in *Norwood* and *Gilmore* if the remedy sought had been to compel the private schools to desegregate? Should some or all private schools be held to the requirements of the equal protection clause? [b]

(i) *Financial aid.* If private schools receive extensive financial aid from the state, does it result in state action only in respect to a specific activity being funded? Consider Comment, *Tax Incentives as State Action,* 122 U.Pa.L.Rev. 414, 436 (1973): "This [theory] incorrectly assumes that government involvement that bears directly upon a specific activity of an entity can be meaningfully distinguished from government involvement that serves more generally to perpetuate that entity as a whole. It is an inescapable fact that general government assistance which perpetuates an entity operates indirectly to perpetuate the specific activities of that entity." May a person whose sole source of income is public relief constitutionally refuse to sell his home to African–Americans?

(ii) *Public control.* Suppose the private schools' curriculum and admission policy are subject to state regulation? If a state statute regulates election procedures of all voluntary organizations, is a social club barred from racially discriminating? If the state provides private schools with extensive financial aid and strict regulation, are the schools "state functions"? If the state licenses all barber schools and requires that all barbers attend such schools, are the schools "state functions"?

(iii) *"Government function."* Even without state aid or regulation, does "the spirit of [the segregation decisions] support the argument that education is a matter of such vital public concern that any action taken in regard to it must be subject to the prohibitions of the fourteenth amendment"? 56 Colum.L.Rev. 285,

---

b. See *Runyon v. McCrary,* p. 1408 infra, holding that a federal statute prohibits private schools from refusing to accept black students.

287 (1956). Consider Glenn Abernathy, *Expansion of the State Action Concept Under the Fourteenth Amendment,* 43 Corn.L.Q. 375, 407 (1958): "[T]he only purely privately operated functions which properly should be considered as governmental are those which are indispensable to the maintenance of democratic government. [S]uch a definition does not go so far as to cover operations which are merely useful or desirable as aids to a more efficient or intelligently controlled government. If these are to be included, then we are no better off than if we equate governmental action with operations affected with a public interest. Education is desirable and useful in a democratic system but it is not indispensable [in] the sense that access to the ballot and the processes of selecting public officials is." If the state closed all of its public schools, would that make private schools "indispensable to the maintenance of democratic government"? If so, would some (all) private schools be barred from racially (sexually, religiously) discriminating? [c]

4. *Tax exempt organizations.* May government give tax exemptions (or permit tax deductions for donations) to private schools, fraternal groups and charitable foundations that fail to adhere to fourteenth amendment requirements? See generally Boris I. Bittker & Kenneth M. Kaufman, *Taxes and Civil Rights: "Constitutionalizing" the Internal Revenue Code,* 82 Yale L.J. 51 (1972). Consider Note, *State Action and the United States Junior Chamber of Commerce,* 43 Geo.Wash.L.Rev. 1407, 1423–24 (1975): "[T]he Internal Revenue Code's tax exemptions for charitable organizations are based upon the theory that the Government is compensated for the loss of revenue by being relieved of the financial burden that would otherwise have to be met by appropriations of government funds. [Where] the private entity is thus acting as a surrogate for the government, any discrimination connected with the performance of public services, even if not affirmatively approved by the government, subjects the victims to discrimination that would not have occurred had the government performed the services directly. The government cannot avoid these constitutional limitations by delegating its functions to private entities, even if the delegation is well-intentioned." See also Frank R. Parker, *Evans v. Newton and the Racially Restricted Charitable Trust,* 13 How.L.J. 223 (1967). Reconsider note 4(c) supra.

5. *Redevelopment housing.* Are major urban redevelopment housing projects, undertaken pursuant to statutory authority with benefit of public condemnation power and tax exemption, constitutionally barred from racially discriminating? If so, what about ordinary private housing projects that receive public "aid" in the form of water and sewage disposal, police and fire protection? See generally Comment, *Application of the Fourteenth Amendment to Builders of Private Housing,* 12 Kan.L.Rev. 426 (1964); Note, *Nondiscrimination Implications of Federal Involvement in Housing,* 19 Vand.L.Rev. 865 (1966); 17 J.Pub.L. 175 (1968). Is urban redevelopment distinguishable from a small private housing project because the former has the effect of racial zoning? Is this a restatement of the "government function" theory? Is the issue of "state action" affected if the claim is that the housing project evicted a tenant without affording procedural due process?

c. See generally Note, *The Wall of Racial Separation: The Role of Private and Parochial Schools in Racial Integration,* 43 N.Y.U.L.Rev. 514 (1968); Note, *Segregation Academies and State Action,* 82 Yale L.J. 1436 (1973); O'Neil, *Private Universities and Public Law,* 19 Buf. L.Rev. 155 (1970).

For further consideration of this issue, see note 2(b) after *Flagg Bros. v. Brooks,* Sec. 4 infra.

SECTION 4. RECENT DEVELOPMENT

RENDELL–BAKER v. KOHN

457 U.S. 830, 102 S.Ct. 2764, 73 L.Ed.2d 418 (1982).

CHIEF JUSTICE BURGER delivered the opinion of the Court.

[New Perspectives is a private school that] specializes in dealing with students who have experienced difficulty completing public high [schools]. In recent years, nearly all of the students at the school have been referred to it by the Brookline or Boston school committees, or by the Drug Rehabilitation Division of the Massachusetts Department of Mental Health.[1] The school issues high school diplomas certified by the Brookline School Committee. In recent years, public funds have accounted for at least 90%, and in one year 99%, of respondent's operating budget. There were approximately 50 students at the school in those years and none paid tuition.

To be eligible for tuition funding under Chapter 766, the school must comply with a variety [of] detailed regulations concerning matters ranging from record-keeping to student-teacher ratios. Concerning personnel policies, [the] regulations require the school to maintain written job descriptions [and] statements describing personnel standards and procedures, but they impose few specific requirements.

[By] its contract with the Boston School Committee, [the] school must agree to carry out the individualized plan developed for each student referred to the school by the Committee. [The] contract with the State Drug Rehabilitation Division [provides] for reimbursement for services provided for students referred to the school [and] includes requirements concerning the services to be provided. Except for general requirements, such as an equal employment opportunity requirement, the agreement does not cover personnel policies.

[Petitioners were discharged by the school for, inter alia, supporting student criticisms against various school policies and sued under 42 U.S.C. § 1983.]

While five of the six petitioners were teachers at the school, petitioner Rendell-Baker was a vocational counselor hired under a grant from the federal Law Enforcement Assistance Administration, whose funds are distributed in Massachusetts through the State Committee on Criminal Justice. As a condition of the grant, the Committee on Criminal Justice must approve the school's initial hiring decisions. The purpose of this requirement is to insure that the school hires vocational counselors who meet the qualifications described in the school's grant proposal to the Committee; the Committee does not interview applicants for counselor positions.

Rendell-Baker * * * demanded reinstatement or a hearing. The school agreed to apply a new policy, calling for appointment of a grievance committee, to consider her claims. Rendell-Baker also complained to the State Committee on Criminal Justice, which asked the school to provide a written explanation for her discharge. After the school complied, the Committee responded that it was satisfied with the explanation, but notified the school that it would not pay any back pay or other damage award Rendell-Baker might obtain from it as a result of her discharge. The Committee told Rendell-Baker that it had no authority to order a hearing, although it would refuse to approve the hiring of another

---

1. Chapter 766, Mass.G.L., requires school committees to identify students with special needs and to develop suitable educational programs for such students. Mass.G.L. c. 71B, § 4 provides that school committees may "en-ter into an agreement with any public or private school, agency, or institution to provide the necessary special education" for these students. * * *

counselor if the school disregarded its agreement to apply its new grievance procedure in her case. [The] core issue presented [is] not whether petitioners were discharged because of their speech or without adequate procedural protections, but whether the school's action in discharging them can fairly be seen as state action. * * *

In *Blum v. Yaretsky,* 457 U.S. 991, 102 S.Ct. 2777, 73 L.Ed.2d 534 (1982), [t]he Court considered whether certain nursing homes were state actors for the purpose of determining whether decisions regarding transfers of patients could be fairly attributed to the state, and hence be subjected to Fourteenth Amendment due process requirements. The challenged transfers primarily involved decisions, made by physicians and nursing home administrators, to move patients from "skilled nursing facilities" to less expensive "health related facilities." Like the New Perspectives School, the nursing homes were privately owned and operated. [T]he Court held that, "[A] State normally can be held responsible for a private decision only when it has exercised coercive power or has provided such significant encouragement, either overt or covert, that the choice must in law be deemed to be that of the State." In determining that the transfer decisions were not actions of the state, the Court considered each of the factors alleged by petitioners here to make the discharge decisions of the New Perspective School fairly attributable to the state.

First, the nursing homes, like the school, depended on the State for funds; the State subsidized the operating and capital costs of the nursing homes, and paid the medical expenses of more than 90% of the patients. * * *

The school, like the nursing homes, is not fundamentally different from many private corporations whose business depends primarily on contracts to build roads, bridges, dams, ships, or submarines for the government. Acts of such private contractors do not become acts of the government by reason of their significant or even total engagement in performing public contracts.

The school is also analogous to the public defender found not to be a state actor in *Polk County v. Dodson,* [p. 1474 infra]. There we concluded that, although the State paid the public defender, her relationship with her client was "identical to that existing between any other lawyer and client." Here the relationship between the school and its teachers and counselors is not changed because the State pays the tuition of the students.

A second factor considered in *Blum* was the extensive regulation of the nursing homes by the State. There the State was indirectly involved in the transfer decisions challenged in that case because a primary goal of the State in regulating nursing homes was to keep costs down by transferring patients from intensive treatment centers to less expensive facilities when possible.[a] Both state and federal regulations encouraged the nursing homes to transfer patients to less expensive facilities when appropriate. The nursing homes were extensively regulated in many other ways as well. The Court relied on *Jackson,* where we held that state regulation, even if "extensive and detailed," did not make a utility's actions state action.

Here the decisions to discharge the petitioners were not compelled or even influenced by any state regulation. Indeed, in contrast to the extensive regulation

---

a. Brennan, J., joined by Marshall, J., dissented in *Blum:* "[Not] only has the State established the system of treatment levels and utilization review in order to further its own fiscal goals, [but] the State prescribes with as much precision as is possible the standards by which individual determinations are to be made. [The] Court thus fails to perceive the decisive involvement of the State in the private conduct challenged by the respondents."

of the school generally, the various regulators showed relatively little interest in the school's personnel matters. The most intrusive personnel regulation promulgated by the various government agencies was the requirement that the Committee on Criminal Justice had the power to approve persons hired as vocational counselors.[6] Such a regulation is not sufficient to make a decision to discharge, made by private management, state action.

The third factor asserted to show that the school is a state actor is that it performs a "public function." However, our holdings have made clear that the relevant question [is] whether the function performed has been "traditionally the *exclusive* prerogative of the State." There can be no doubt that the education of maladjusted high school students is a public function, but that is only the beginning of the inquiry. Chapter 766 [demonstrates] that the State intends to provide services for such students at public expense. That legislative policy choice in no way makes these services the exclusive province of the State. Indeed, [until] recently the State had not undertaken to provide education for students who could not be served by traditional public schools. That a private entity performs a function which serves the public does not make its acts state action.[7]

Fourth, petitioners argue that there is a "symbiotic relationship" [as] in *Burton*. Such a claim was rejected in *Blum,* and we reject it here. In *Burton,* [i]n response to the argument that the restaurant's profits, and hence the State's financial position, would suffer if it did not discriminate, the Court concluded that this showed that the State profited from the restaurant's discriminatory conduct. [Here] the school's fiscal relationship with the State is not different from that of many contractors performing services for the government.[b] * * *

Affirmed.[c]

JUSTICE MARSHALL, with whom JUSTICE BRENNAN joins, dissenting.

[I]t is difficult to imagine a closer relationship between a government and a private enterprise. [The] school's very survival depends on the State. If the State chooses, it may exercise complete control over the school's operations simply by threatening to withdraw financial support if the school takes action that it considers objectionable. [Almost] every decision the school makes is substantially affected in some way by the State's regulations.[1]

The fact that the school is providing a substitute for public education is also an important indicium of state action. [Under Ch. 766], the State is *required* to provide a free education to all children, including those with special needs. Clearly, if the State had decided to provide the service itself, its conduct would be

---

6. [The] Committee had no power to hire or discharge a counselor who had the qualifications specified in the school's grant application. Moreover, the Committee did not take any part in discharging Rendell-Baker; on the contrary, it attempted to use leverage to aid her. [T]here is no evidence that the Committee had any authority to take even those steps.

7. There is no evidence that the State has attempted to avoid its constitutional duties by a sham arrangement which attempts to disguise provision of public services as acts of private parties. Cf. *Evans v. Newton.*

[Compare Brennan, J., joined by Marshall, J., dissenting in *Blum:* "For many, the totality of their social network is the nursing home community. Within that environment, the

nursing home operator is the immediate authority, the provider of food, clothing, shelter, and health care, and, in every significant respect, the functional equivalent of a State. Cf. *Marsh.*"]

b. Does this adopt the "moral exemplar model" in note 2 after *Moose Lodge?*

c. White, J., concurred in the judgment (and in *Blum*): "For me, the critical factor is the absence of any allegation that the employment decision was itself based upon some rule of conduct or policy put forth by the State."

1. [By] analyzing the various indicia of state action separately, without considering their cumulative impact, the majority commits a fundamental error.

measured against constitutional standards. The State should not be permitted to avoid constitutional requirements simply by delegating its statutory duty to a private entity. * * *

The majority repeatedly compares the school to a private contractor * * *. Although shipbuilders and dambuilders, like the school, may be dependent on government funds, they are not so closely supervised by the government. And unlike most private contractors, the school is performing a statutory duty of the State. * * *

In SAN FRANCISCO ARTS & ATHLETICS, INC. v. UNITED STATES OLYMPIC COMM., 483 U.S. 522, 107 S.Ct. 2971, 97 L.Ed.2d 427 (1987), respondent USOC, to which Congress granted the right to prohibit certain commercial and promotional uses of the word "Olympic," secured relief enjoining petitioner from calling its athletic competitions the "Gay Olympic Games." Petitioner claimed that USOC's enforcement discriminated in violation of equal protection. The Court, per POWELL, J.—relying mainly on *Rendell–Baker, Blum* and *Jackson*— held that USOC is not a "governmental actor."

BRENNAN, J., joined by Marshall, J.—and "largely" by O'Connor and Blackmun, JJ.—dissented on the basis of *Burton:* "The USOC and the Federal Government exist in a symbiotic relationship sufficient to provide a nexus between the USOC's challenged action and the Government. First, as in *Burton,* the relationship here confers a variety of mutual benefits. [T]he Act gave the USOC authority and responsibilities that no private organization in this country had ever held. The Act also conferred substantial financial resources on the USOC, authorizing it to seek up to $16 million annually in grants from the Secretary of Commerce, and affording it unprecedented power to control the use of the word 'Olympic' and related emblems to raise additional funds. As a result of the Act, the United States obtained, for the first time in its history, an exclusive and effective organization to coordinate and administer all amateur athletics related to international competition, and to represent that program abroad.

"Second, in the eye of the public, both national and international, the connection between the decisions of the United States Government and those of the United States Olympic Committee is profound. The President of the United States has served as the Honorary President of the USOC. The national flag flies both literally and figuratively over the central product of the USOC, the United States Olympic Team.[d] [While] in *Burton* the restaurant was able to pursue a policy of discrimination because the State had failed to impose upon it a policy of non-discrimination, the USOC could pursue its alleged policy of selective enforcement only because Congress *affirmatively* granted it power that it would not otherwise have to control the use of the word 'Olympic.' "[e]

d. The Court responded that "all sorts of private organizations send 'national representatives' to participate in world competitions. Although many are of interest only to a select group, others, like the Davis Cup Competition, the America's Cup, and the Miss Universe Pageant, are widely viewed as involving representation of our country. The organizations that sponsor United States participation in these events all perform 'national representational,' as well as 'administrative [and] adjudicative role[s],' in selecting and presenting the national representatives."

e. The Court responded that petitioner "has failed to demonstrate that the Federal Government can or does exert any influence over the exercise of the USOC's enforcement decisions. Absent proof of this type of 'close nexus between the [Government] and the challenged action of the [USOC],' the challenged

FLAGG BROS., INC. v. BROOKS

436 U.S. 149, 98 S.Ct. 1729, 56 L.Ed.2d 185 (1978).

JUSTICE REHNQUIST delivered the opinion of the Court.

The question presented [is] whether a warehouseman's proposed sale of goods entrusted to him for storage, as permitted by New York Uniform Commercial Code § 7–210, is an action properly attributable to the State * * *.

[R]espondent Shirley Brooks and her family were evicted from their apartment in Mount Vernon, N.Y., on June 13, 1973. The city marshal arranged for Brooks' possessions to be stored by petitioner Flagg Brothers, Inc., in its warehouse. Brooks was informed of the cost of moving and storage, and she instructed the workmen to proceed, although she found the price too high. On August 25, 1973, after a series of disputes over the validity of the charges being claimed by petitioner Flagg Brothers, Brooks received a letter demanding that her account be brought up to date within 10 days "or your furniture will be sold." A series of subsequent letters from respondent and her attorneys produced no satisfaction.

Brooks thereupon initiated this class action in the District Court under 42 U.S.C. § 1983, seeking damages, an injunction against the threatened sale of her belongings, and the declaration that such a sale pursuant to § 7–210 would violate [due process]. She was later joined in her action by [Jones,] whose goods had been stored by Flagg Brothers following her eviction. [T]he District Court * * * dismissed the complaint [and] the Court of Appeals reversed. * * *

It must be noted that respondents have named no public officials as defendants in this action. The city marshal, who supervised their evictions, was dismissed from the case by the consent of all the parties. This total absence of overt official involvement plainly distinguishes this case from earlier decisions imposing procedural restrictions on creditors' remedies such as *North Georgia Finishing, Inc., v. Di-Chem, Inc.,* 419 U.S. 601, 95 S.Ct. 719, 42 L.Ed.2d 751 (1975); *Fuentes v. Shevin,* 407 U.S. 67, 92 S.Ct. 1983, 32 L.Ed.2d 556 (1972); *Sniadach v. Family Finance Corp.,* 395 U.S. 337, 89 S.Ct. 1820, 23 L.Ed.2d 349 (1969).[a] [While] any person with sufficient physical power may deprive a person

action may not be 'fairly treated as that of the [Government] itself.' *Jackson.*"

a. *Sniadach* held that a statute—authorizing a creditor to get a summons from a court clerk and thereby obtain prejudgment garnishment of a debtor's wages—violated due process because the statute did not provide the debtor with prior notice and opportunity for a hearing.

Fuentes held that a statute—authorizing a seller of goods under a conditional sales contract to get a writ from a court clerk and thereby obtain prejudgment repossession with the sheriff's help—violated due process because the statute did not provide the buyer with prior notice and opportunity for a hearing.

North Georgia Finishing held violative of due process a statute authorizing a creditor to obtain prejudgment garnishment of a debtor's assets by filing an affidavit with a court clerk stating reasons to fear that the property would otherwise be lost. The Court distinguished

Mitchell v. W.T. Grant Co., 416 U.S. 600, 94 S.Ct. 1895, 40 L.Ed.2d 406 (1974), which had upheld a statute that, without requiring prior notice to a buyer-debtor, permitted a seller-creditor holding a vendor's lien to secure a writ of sequestration and, having filed a bond, to cause the sheriff to take possession of the property at issue. *North Georgia Finishing* emphasized that under the sequestration statute in *Mitchell,* unlike the garnishment statute at bar, the writ "was issuable only by a judge upon the filing of an affidavit going beyond mere conclusory allegations and clearly setting out the facts entitling the creditor to sequestration" and that the *Mitchell* statute "expressly entitled the debtor to an immediate hearing after seizure and to dissolution of the writ absent proof by the creditor of the grounds on which the writ was issued."

For general discussion of these cases, see Robert E. Scott, *Constitutional Regulation of Provisional Creditor Remedies: The Cost of*

of his property, only a State or a private person whose action "may be fairly treated as that of the State itself," *Jackson,* may deprive him of "an interest encompassed within the Fourteenth Amendment's protection," *Fuentes* * * *.

Respondents' primary contention is that New York has delegated to Flagg Brothers a power "traditionally exclusively reserved to the State." *Jackson.* They argue that the resolution of private disputes is a traditional function of civil government, and that the State in § 7–210 has delegated this function to Flagg Brothers. Respondents, however, have read too much into the language of our previous cases. While many functions have been traditionally performed by governments, very few have been "exclusively reserved to the State."

One such area has been elections. * * * *Terry v. Adams; Smith v. Allwright.* Although the rationale of these cases may be subject to some dispute, their scope is carefully defined. The doctrine does not reach to all forms of private political activity, but encompasses only state-regulated elections or elections conducted by organizations which in practice produce "the uncontested choice of public officials." *Terry* (Clark, J., concurring). * * *

A second line of cases under the public-function doctrine originated with *Marsh.* Just as the Texas Democratic Party in *Smith* and the Jaybird Democratic Association in *Terry* effectively performed the entire public function of selecting public officials, so too the Gulf Shipbuilding Corp. performed all the necessary municipal functions in the town of Chickasaw, Ala., which it owned. * * *

These two branches of the public-function doctrine have in common the feature of exclusivity.[8] Although the elections held by the Democratic Party and its affiliates were the only meaningful elections in Texas, and the streets owned by the Gulf Shipbuilding Corp. were the only streets in Chickasaw, the proposed sale by Flagg Brothers under § 7–210 is not the only means of resolving this purely private dispute. Respondent Brooks has never alleged that state law barred her from seeking a waiver of Flagg Brothers' right to sell her goods at the time she authorized their storage. Presumably, respondent Jones, who alleges that she never authorized the storage of her goods, could have sought to replevy her goods at any time under state law. The challenged statute itself provides a damages remedy against the warehouseman for violations of its provisions. This system of rights and remedies, recognizing the traditional place of private arrangements in

---

Procedural Due Process, 61 Va.L.Rev. 807 (1975); Linda J. Silberman, *Shaffer v. Heitner: The End of an Era,* 53 N.Y.U.L.Rev. 33, 53–62 (1978).

More recently, *Connecticut v. Doehr,* 501 U.S. 1, 111 S.Ct. 2105, 115 L.Ed.2d 1 (1991), held that a state statute authorizing prejudgment attachment of real estate upon plaintiff's ex parte showing that there is probable cause to sustain the validity of his or her claim—without a showing of extraordinary circumstances, and without a requirement that the person seeking the attachment post a bond—violated due process. Petitioner sought an attachment on respondent's home in conjunction with a civil action for assault and battery that he was seeking to institute against respondent in the same court. On the strength of statements in petitioner's affidavit, the court ordered the attachment. Only after the sheriff attached his property did respondent receive

notice, which informed him of his right to a postattachment hearing. Instead, respondent filed a federal action, successfully arguing that the state statute violated due process.

8. Respondents also contend that *Evans v. Newton* establishes that the operation of a park for recreational purposes is an exclusively public function. We doubt that *Newton* intended to establish any such broad doctrine in the teeth of the experience of several American entrepreneurs who amassed great fortunes by operating parks for recreational purposes. We think *Newton* rests on a finding of ordinary state action under extraordinary circumstances. The Court's opinion emphasizes that the record showed "no change in the municipal maintenance and concern over this facility" after the transfer of title to private trustees. * * *

ordering relationships in the commercial world,[9] can hardly be said to have delegated to Flagg Brothers an exclusive prerogative of the sovereign.[10]

Whatever the particular remedies available under New York law, we do not consider a more detailed description of them necessary to our conclusion that the settlement of disputes between debtors and creditors is not traditionally an exclusive public function.[11] Creditors and debtors have had available to them historically a far wider number of choices than has one who would be an elected public official, or a member of Jehovah's Witnesses who wished to distribute literature in Chickasaw, Ala. * * *[12] This is true whether these commercial rights and remedies are created by statute or decisional law. To rely upon the historical antecedents of a particular practice would result in the constitutional condemnation in one State of a remedy found perfectly permissible in another.

[W]e would be remiss if we did not note that there are a number of state and municipal functions not covered by our election cases or governed by the reason-

---

9. Unlike the parade of horribles suggested by our Brother Stevens in dissent, this case does not involve state authorization of private breach of the peace.

10. [It] would intolerably broaden, beyond the scope of any of our previous cases, the notion of state action [to] hold that the mere existence of a body of property law in a State, whether decisional or statutory, itself amounted to "state action" even though no state process or state officials were ever involved in enforcing that body of law.

This situation is clearly distinguishable from cases such as *North Georgia Finishing; Fuentes;* and *Sniadach.* In each of those cases a government official participated in the physical deprivation of what had concededly been the constitutional plaintiff's property under state law before the deprivation occurred. The constitutional protection attaches not because, as in *North Georgia Finishing,* a clerk issued a ministerial writ out of the court, but because as a result of that writ the property of the debtor was seized and impounded by the affirmative command of the law of Georgia. The creditor in *North Georgia Finishing* had not simply sought to pursue the collection of his debt by private means permissible under Georgia law; he had invoked the authority of the Georgia court, which in turn had ordered the garnishee not to pay over money which previously had been the property of the debtor. See *Shelley v. Kraemer.* * * *

11. It may well be, as my Brother Stevens' dissent contends, that "[t]he power to order legally binding surrenders of property and the constitutional restrictions on that power are necessary correlatives in our system." But here New York, unlike Florida in *Fuentes,* Georgia in *North Georgia Finishing,* and Wisconsin in *Sniadach,* has not ordered respondents to surrender any property whatever. It has merely enacted a statute which provides that a warehouseman conforming to the provisions of the statute may convert his traditional lien into good title. There is no reason what-

ever to believe that either Flagg Brothers or respondents could not, if they wished, seek resort to the New York courts in order to either compel or prevent the "surrenders of property" to which that dissent refers, and that the compliance of Flagg Brothers with applicable New York property law would be reviewed after customary notice and hearing in such a proceeding.

The fact that such a judicial review of a self-help remedy is seldom encountered bears witness to the important part that such remedies have played in our system of property rights. This is particularly true of the warehouseman's lien, which is the source of this provision in the Uniform Commercial Code which is the law in 49 States and the District of Columbia. The lien in this case, particularly because it is burdened by procedural constraints and provides for a compensatory remedy and judicial relief against abuse, is not atypical of creditors' liens historically, whether created by statute or legislatively enacted. The conduct of private actors in relying on the rights established under these liens to resort to self-help remedies does not permit their conduct to be ascribed to the State.

12. This is not to say that dispute resolution between creditors and debtors involves a category of human affairs that is never subject to constitutional constraints. We merely address the public-function doctrine as respondents would apply it to this case.

Self-help of the type involved in this case is not significantly different from creditor remedies generally, whether created by common law or enacted by legislatures. New York's statute has done nothing more than authorize (and indeed without limit)—without participation by any public official—what Flagg Brothers would tend to do, even in the absence of such authorization, i.e., dispose of respondents' property in order to free up its valuable storage space. The proposed sale pursuant to the lien in this case is not a significant departure from traditional private arrangements.

ing of *Marsh* which have been administered with a greater degree of exclusivity by States and municipalities than has the function of so-called "dispute resolution." Among these are such functions as education, fire and police protection, and tax collection. We express no view as to the extent, if any, to which a city or State might be free to delegate to private parties the performance of such functions and thereby avoid the strictures of the Fourteenth Amendment. * * *

Respondents further urge that Flagg Brothers' proposed action is properly attributable to the State because the State has authorized and encouraged it in enacting § 7–210. Our cases state "that a State is responsible for [the] act of a private party when the State, by its law, has compelled the act." This Court, however, has never held that a State's mere acquiescence in a private action converts that action into that of the State. The Court rejected a similar argument in *Jackson* * * *. The clearest demonstration of this distinction appears in *Moose Lodge,* which held that the Commonwealth of Pennsylvania, although not responsible for racial discrimination voluntarily practiced by a private club, could not by law require the club to comply with its own discriminatory rules. These cases clearly rejected the notion that our prior cases permitted the imposition of Fourteenth Amendment restraints on private action by the simple device of characterizing the State's inaction as "authorization" or "encouragement."

It is quite immaterial that the State has embodied its decision not to act in statutory form. If New York had no commercial statutes at all, its courts would still be faced with the decision whether to prohibit or to permit the sort of sale threatened here the first time an aggrieved bailor came before them for relief. A judicial decision to deny relief would be no less an "authorization" or "encouragement" of that sale than the legislature's decision embodied in this statute. [If] the mere denial of judicial relief is considered sufficient encouragement to make the State responsible for those private acts, all private deprivations of property would be converted into public acts whenever the State, for whatever reason, denies relief sought by the putative property owner. * * *

Here, the State of New York has not compelled the sale of a bailor's goods, but has merely announced the circumstances under which its courts will not interfere with a private sale. Indeed, the crux of respondents' complaint is not that the State *has* acted, but that it has *refused* to act. This statutory refusal to act is no different in principle from an ordinary statute of limitations whereby the State declines to provide a remedy for private deprivations of property after the passage of a given period of time. * * *

Reversed.

JUSTICE STEVENS, with whom JUSTICE WHITE and JUSTICE MARSHALL join, dissenting.

[Under the Court's] approach a State could enact laws authorizing private citizens to use self-help in countless situations without any possibility of federal challenge. A state statute could authorize the warehouseman to retain all proceeds of the lien sale, even if they far exceeded the amount of the alleged debt; it could authorize finance companies to enter private homes to repossess merchandise; or indeed, it could authorize "any person with sufficient physical power" to acquire and sell the property of his weaker neighbor. An attempt to challenge the validity of any such outrageous statute would be defeated by the reasoning the Court uses today: The Court's rationale would characterize action pursuant to such a statute as purely private action, which the State permits but does not compel, in an area not exclusively reserved to the State.

As these examples suggest, the distinctions between "permission" and "compulsion" on the one hand, and "exclusive" and "non-exclusive," on the other, cannot be determinative factors in state-action analysis. There is no great chasm between "permission" and "compulsion" requiring particular state action to fall within one or the other definitional camp. [In] this case, the State of New York, by enacting § 7–210 of the Uniform Commercial Code, has acted in the most effective and unambiguous way a State can act. This section specifically authorizes petitioner Flagg Brothers to sell respondents' possessions; it details the procedures that petitioner must follow; and it grants petitioner the power to convey good title to goods that are now owned by respondents to a third party.

[P]etitioners have attempted to argue that the nonconsensual transfer of property rights is not a traditional function of the sovereign. The overwhelming historical evidence is to the contrary, however,[7] and the Court wisely does not adopt this position. Instead, the Court reasons that state action cannot be found because the State has not delegated to the warehouseman an *exclusive* sovereign function.[8] This distinction, however, is not consistent with our prior decisions on state action; is not even adhered to by the Court in this case;[10] and, most importantly, is inconsistent with the line of cases beginning with *Sniadach*.

Since *Sniadach* this Court has scrutinized various state statutes regulating the debtor-creditor relationship for compliance with the Due Process Clause. In each of these cases a finding of state action was a prerequisite to the Court's decision. The Court today seeks to explain these findings on the ground that in each case there was some element of "overt official involvement." [But] until today, this Court had never held that purely ministerial acts of "minor governmental functionaries" were sufficient to establish state action. The suggestion that this was the basis for due process review in *Sniadach, Fuentes,* and *North Georgia Finishing* marks a major and, in my judgment, unwise expansion of the state-action doctrine. The number of private actions in which a governmental functionary plays some ministerial role is legion;[12] to base due process review on the fortuity of such governmental intervention would demean the majestic purposes of the Due Process Clause.

7. The New York State courts have recognized that the execution of a lien is a traditional function of the State. * * *

8. As I understand the Court's notion of "exclusivity," the sovereign function here is not exclusive because there may be other state remedies, under different statutes or common-law theories, available to respondents. Even if I were to accept the notion that sovereign functions must be "exclusive," the Court's description of exclusivity is incomprehensible. The question is whether a particular action is a uniquely sovereign function, not whether state law forecloses any possibility of recovering for damages for such activity. For instance, it is clear that the maintenance of a police force is a unique sovereign function, and the delegation of police power to a private party will entail state action. Under the Court's analysis, however, there would be no state action if the State provided a remedy, such as an action for wrongful imprisonment, for the individual injured by the "private" policeman. This analysis is not based on "exclusivity," but on some vague, and highly inappropriate, notion that respondents should not complain about this state statute if the State offers them a glimmer of hope of redeeming their possessions, or at least the value of the goods, through some other state action. Of course, the availability of other state remedies may be relevant in determining whether the statute provides sufficient procedural protections under the Due Process Clause, but it is not relevant to the state-action issue.

10. As the Court is forced to recognize, its notion of exclusivity simply cannot be squared with the wide range of functions that are typically considered sovereign functions, such as "education, fire and police protection, and tax collection."

12. For instance, state officials often perform ministerial acts in the transferring of ownership in motor vehicles or real estate. It is difficult to believe that the Court would hold that all car sales are invested with state action.

Instead, cases such as *North Georgia Finishing* must be viewed as reflecting this Court's recognition of the significance of the State's role in defining *and controlling* the debtor-creditor relationship. [In *Fuentes*, the] statutes placed the state power to repossess property in the hands of an interested private party, just as the state statute in this case places the state power to conduct judicially binding sales in satisfaction of a lien in the hands of the warehouseman. "Private parties, serving their own private advantage, may unilaterally invoke state power to replevy goods from another. No state official participates in the decision to seek a writ; no state official reviews the basis for the claim to repossession; and no state official evaluates the need for immediate seizure. There is not even a requirement that the plaintiff provide any information to the court on these matters." Ibid. [Yet] the very defect that made the statutes in *Fuentes* and *North Georgia Finishing* unconstitutional—lack of state control—is, under today's decision, the factor that precludes constitutional review of the state statute. The Due Process Clause cannot command such incongruous results. If it is unconstitutional for a State to allow a private party to exercise a traditional state power because the state supervision of that power is purely mechanical, the State surely cannot immunize its actions from constitutional *scrutiny* by removing even the mechanical supervision. * * *

It is important to emphasize that, contrary to the Court's apparent fears, this conclusion does not even remotely suggest that "all private deprivations of property [will] be converted into public acts whenever the State, for whatever reason, denies relief sought by the putative property owner." The focus is not on the private deprivation but on the state authorization. [The] State's conduct in this case takes the concrete form of a statutory enactment, and it is that statute that may be challenged. * * *

Finally, it is obviously true that the overwhelming majority of disputes in our society are resolved in the private sphere. But it is no longer possible, if it ever was, to believe that a sharp line can be drawn between private and public actions. The Court['s] description of what is state action does not even attempt to reflect the concerns of the Due Process Clause, for the state-action doctrine is, after all, merely one aspect of this broad constitutional protection.

In the broadest sense, we expect government "to provide a reasonable and fair framework of rules which facilitate commercial transactions." This "framework of rules" is premised on the assumption that the State will control nonconsensual deprivations of property and that the State's control will, in turn, be subject to the restrictions of the Due Process Clause. * * * [b]

Notes and Questions

1. *Authority of prior decisions.* (a) Does the Court's use of *Shelley v. Kraemer* (in fn. 10) refute the dissent's objection that the Court's handling of the prior debtor-creditor decisions establishes the principle that "purely ministerial acts of minor governmental functionaries" constitute state action? If so, then would the Court have found state action in *Flagg Bros.* if the state courts had to be used to enforce the warehouseman's lien? Would this read *Shelley* for all it is worth? Does fn. 10 so read *Shelley*? In any event, is the dissent correct in complaining that "the very defect that made the statutes in *Fuentes* and *North Georgia Finishing* unconstitutional—lack of state control—is, under *Flagg Bros.*, the factor that precludes constitutional review of the state statute"?

b. The separate dissent of Marshall, J., is omitted. Brennan, J., did not participate.

(b) LUGAR v. EDMONDSON OIL CO., 457 U.S. 922, 102 S.Ct. 2744, 73 L.Ed.2d 482 (1982), per White, J.,—involving a statute that authorized a creditor to file a petition with a court clerk and thus obtain a prejudgment attachment of a debtor's property which was executed by the sheriff—relied on all the debtor-creditor decisions as establishing the doctrine "that a private party's joint participation with state officials in the seizure of disputed property is sufficient to characterize that party as a 'state actor' for purposes of the Fourteenth Amendment." Powell, J., joined by Rehnquist and O'Connor, JJ., dissented: "It is unclear why a private party engages in state action when filing papers seeking an attachment of property, but not [when] summoning police to investigate a suspected crime." Burger, C.J., also dissented.

(c) NATIONAL COLLEGIATE ATHLETIC ASS'N v. TARKANIAN, 488 U.S. 179, 109 S.Ct. 454, 102 L.Ed.2d 469 (1988): The NCAA is an association of virtually all colleges with major athletic programs, and its rules governing these programs are binding on its members. After its investigation that found 38 recruitment violations by the staff of the University of Nevada, Las Vegas (including 10 by Tarkanian, who was UNLV's basketball coach), NCAA imposed sanctions on UNLV and requested it to show cause why additional penalties should not be imposed if it failed to suspend Tarkanian. The Court, per STEVENS, J., conceded that UNLV's suspension of Tarkanian, which was clearly state action, "was influenced by the rules and recommendations of the NCAA," but held that this did not turn the NCAA's conduct into "state action" and thus the NCAA did not violate Tarkanian's right to procedural due process: Although, as a member of the NCAA, UNLV played a role in formulating its rules, "UNLV delegated no power to the NCAA to take specific action against any University employee. The commitment by UNLV to adhere to NCAA enforcement procedures was enforceable only by sanctions that the NCAA might impose on UNLV," and which UNLV could choose to ignore by withdrawing from the NCAA. And even if "the power of the NCAA is so great that the UNLV had no practical alternative to compliance with its demands," "it does not follow that such a private party [is] acting under color of state law." Finally, "in the case before us the state and private parties' relevant interests do not coincide, as they did in *Burton;* rather, they have clashed throughout the investigation, the attempt to discipline Tarkanian, and this litigation. UNLV and the NCAA were antagonists, not joint participants, and the NCAA may not be deemed a state actor on this ground."

WHITE, J., joined by Brennan, Marshall and O'Connor, JJ.,—emphasizing that UNLV, a public university is a "state actor"—dissented: "[I]t was the NCAA's findings that Tarkanian had violated NCAA rules, made at NCAA-conducted hearings, all of which were agreed to by UNLV in its membership agreement with the NCAA, that resulted in Tarkanian's suspension by UNLV. On these facts, the NCAA was 'jointly engaged with [UNLV] officials in the challenged action,' and therefore was a state actor."

2. *"Governmental function."* (a) *Dispute resolution.* Do you agree that the authority exercised by the warehouseman under the New York statute was not a "governmental function"? Consider 92 Harv.L.Rev. 128 (1978): "The exclusivity of the function's exercise may shed some light on this inquiry, but it does not give a final answer to the basic question. Regardless of the fact that there are many ways to go about resolving a private dispute, the ability to conclude unresolved disputes by making authoritative determinations of rights in property is central to our conception of government's role in society. If a state chose to assign part of its judicial function to private tribunals, giving them all the authority of trial

courts, there would be little doubt that a vital attribute of sovereignty was involved.''

What result in *Flagg Bros.* if the warehouseman's lien had not been "burdened by procedural constraints" and had not provided "for a compensatory remedy and judicial relief against abuse''?

(b) *Jury selection.* EDMONSON v. LEESVILLE CONCRETE CO., 500 U.S. 614, 111 S.Ct. 2077, 114 L.Ed.2d 660 (1991), per KENNEDY, J., held that use by a private litigant in a civil trial of a peremptory challenge to exclude jurors on the basis of race violated "the excluded jurors' equal protection rights": "[I]n determining whether a particular action or course of conduct is governmental in character, it is relevant to examine the following: the extent to which the actor relies on governmental assistance and benefits, see *Burton;* whether the actor is performing a traditional governmental function, see *Terry; Marsh;* and whether the injury caused is aggravated in a unique way by the incidents of governmental authority, see *Shelley* * * *.

"Although private use of state-sanctioned private remedies or procedures does not rise, by itself, to the level of state action, our cases have found state action when private parties make extensive use of state procedures with 'the overt, significant assistance of state officials.' See *Lugar.* It cannot be disputed that, without the overt, significant participation of the government, the peremptory challenge system, as well as the jury trial system of which it is a part, simply could not exist. [The] government summons jurors, constrains their freedom of movement, and subjects them to public scrutiny and examination. The party who exercises a challenge invokes the formal authority of the court, which must discharge the prospective juror, thus effecting the 'final and practical denial' of the excluded individual's opportunity to serve on the petit jury. [By] enforcing a discriminatory peremptory challenge, the court 'has not only made itself a party to the [biased act], but has elected to place its power, property and prestige behind the [alleged] discrimination.' *Burton.* In so doing, the government has 'create[d] the legal framework governing the [challenged] conduct,' [*Tarkanian*], and in a significant way has involved itself with invidious discrimination.

"[Further, a] traditional function of government is evident here. The peremptory challenge is used in selecting an entity that is a quintessential governmental body, having no attributes of a private actor. The jury exercises the power of the court and of the government that confers the court's jurisdiction. [If] a government confers on a private body the power to choose the government's employees or officials, the private body will be bound by the constitutional mandate of race neutrality [*Terry*]. If peremptory challenges based on race were permitted, persons could be required by summons to be put at risk of open and public discrimination as a condition of their participation in the justice system. The injury to excluded jurors would be the direct result of governmental delegation and participation.

"Finally, we note that the injury caused by the discrimination is made more severe because the government permits it to occur within the courthouse itself. Few places are a more real expression of the constitutional authority of the government than a courtroom, where the law itself unfolds.''

O'CONNOR, J., joined by Rehnquist, C.J., and Scalia, J., dissented: "It is the nature of a peremptory that its exercise is left wholly within the discretion of the litigant. [The] peremptory is, by design, an enclave of private action in a government-managed proceeding.

"The Court amasses much ostensible evidence of the Federal Government's 'overt, significant participation' in the peremptory process. [The] bulk of the practices the Court describes—the establishment of qualifications for jury service, the location and summoning of prospective jurors, the jury wheel, the voter lists, the jury qualification forms, the per diem for jury service—[is] in furtherance of the Government's distinct obligation to provide a qualified jury; the Government would do these things even if there were no peremptory challenges. [That] these actions may be necessary to a peremptory challenge—in the sense that there could be no such challenge without a venire from which to select—no more makes the challenge state action than the building of roads and provision of public transportation makes state action of riding on a bus.

"[The] government 'normally can be held responsible for a private decision only when it has exercised coercive power or has provided such significant encouragement, either overt or covert, that the choice must in law be deemed to be that of the State.' *Blum.* [A] judge does not 'significantly encourage' discrimination by the mere act of excusing a juror in response to an unexplained request. * * *

"A peremptory challenge by a private litigant [is] not a traditional government function. [In] order to constitute state action under this doctrine, private conduct must not only comprise something that the government traditionally does, but something that *only* the government traditionally does. Even if one could fairly characterize the use of a peremptory strike as the performance of the traditional government function of jury selection, it has never been exclusively the function of the government to select juries; peremptory strikes are older than the Republic. * * *

"Constitutional 'liability attaches only to those wrongdoers who carry a badge of authority of [the government] and represent it in some capacity.' *Tarkanian.* A government attorney who uses a peremptory challenge on behalf of the client is, by definition, representing the government. The challenge thereby becomes state action. It is antithetical to the nature of our adversarial process, however, to say that a private attorney acting on behalf of a private client represents the government for constitutional purposes."

(c) *Education.* Would (should) the Court hold that private schools perform a "government function"? If so, under what circumstances? Consider Choper, *Thoughts on State Action*, 1979 Wash.U.L.Q. 757, 778: "[I]t is clear that the operation of elementary and secondary schools is not an enterprise that is 'traditionally *exclusively* reserved to the State.' But a comprehensive survey of school districts in the United States would surely show that virtually all maintained at least one public elementary and secondary school unless, because of some peculiar development, the educational needs of the community's children were historically always met by a privately funded school. Such a school—or at least one of such schools if there are several in the hypothetical community (and which one is *the* one may present a nice question)—is, in effect, serving as a substitute for the conventional public school that the school district would otherwise provide. In this sense, it is performing a function 'traditionally *exclusively* reserved to the State.' "

3. *The limits (or lack of limits) of the state action concept.* Do you agree that "an ordinary statute of limitations whereby the State declines to provide a remedy for private deprivations of property after the passage of a given period of time" is *not* state action? If it *is* state action, then is New York's rule—that "its courts will not interfere with a private sale" pursuant to a warehouseman's lien—also

state action? If so, is it not true that "all private deprivations of property would be converted into public acts whenever the State, for whatever reason, denies relief sought by the putative property owner"? Of what relevance is it that "the State's conduct in *Flagg Bros.* takes the concrete form of a statutory enactment"? May a "state procedure" providing a "framework of rules which facilitate commercial transactions" be promulgated by common law as well as by statute? See generally Paul Brest, *State Action and Liberal Theory: A Casenote on Flagg Brothers v. Brooks,* 130 U.Pa.L.Rev. 1296 (1982); Frank I. Goodman, *Professor Brest on State Action and Liberal Theory,* 130 U.Pa.L.Rev. 1331–45 (1982).

DeSHANEY v. WINNEBAGO DEP'T OF SOCIAL SERV.

489 U.S. 189, 109 S.Ct. 998, 103 L.Ed.2d 249 (1989).

CHIEF JUSTICE REHNQUIST delivered the opinion of the Court.

[I]n January 1982, when [Joshua DeShaney's] father's second wife complained to the police, at the time of their divorce, that he had previously "hit the boy causing marks and [was] a prime case for child abuse." The Winnebago County Department of Social Services (DSS) interviewed the father, but he denied the accusations, and DSS did not pursue them further. In January 1983, Joshua was admitted to a local hospital with multiple bruises and abrasions. The examining physician suspected child abuse and notified DSS. [T]he county convened an ad hoc "Child Protection Team" [which] decided that there was insufficient evidence of child abuse to retain Joshua in the custody of the court. The Team did, however, decide to recommend several measures to protect Joshua, including enrolling him in a preschool program, providing his father with certain counselling services, and encouraging his father's girlfriend to move out of the home. Randy DeShaney entered into a voluntary agreement with DSS in which he promised to cooperate with them in accomplishing these goals.

[A month after] the juvenile court dismissed the child protection case and returned Joshua to the custody of his father * * * emergency room personnel called the DSS caseworker handling Joshua's case to report that he had once again been treated for suspicious injuries. The caseworker concluded that there was no basis for action. For the next six months, the caseworker made monthly visits to the DeShaney home, during which she observed a number of suspicious injuries on Joshua's head; she also noticed that he had not been enrolled in school and that the girlfriend had not moved out. The caseworker dutifully recorded these incidents in her files, along with her continuing suspicions that someone in the DeShaney household was physically abusing Joshua, but she did nothing more. In November 1983, the emergency room notified DSS that Joshua had been treated once again for injuries that they believed to be caused by child abuse. On the caseworker's next two visits to the DeShaney home, she was told that Joshua was too ill to see her. Still DSS took no action.

In March 1984, Randy DeShaney beat 4-year-old Joshua so severely that he fell into a life-threatening coma [and] is expected to spend the rest of his life confined to an institution for the profoundly retarded. Randy DeShaney was subsequently tried and convicted of child abuse.

Joshua and his mother brought this action under 42 U.S.C. § 1983 [alleging] that the State had deprived Joshua of his liberty interest in "free[dom] from unjustified intrusions on personal security" by failing to provide him with adequate protection against his father's violence. The claim is one invoking the substantive rather than procedural component of the Due Process Clause; petitioners do not claim that the State denied Joshua protection without according him appropriate procedural safeguards, but that it was categorically obligated to protect him in these circumstances.

But nothing in the language of the Due Process Clause itself requires the State to protect the life, liberty, and property of its citizens against invasion by private actors. The Clause is phrased as a limitation on the State's power to act, not as a guarantee of certain minimal levels of safety and security. [Nor] does history support such an expansive reading of the constitutional text. [The Clause's] purpose was to protect the people from the State, not to ensure that the State protected them from each other. The Framers were content to leave the extent of governmental obligation in the latter area to the democratic political processes. * * *

Petitioners contend, however, that even if the Due Process Clause imposes no affirmative obligation on the State to provide the general public with adequate protective services, such a duty may arise out of certain "special relationships" created or assumed by the State with respect to particular individuals [and] that such a "special relationship" existed here because the State knew that Joshua faced a special danger of abuse at his father's hands, and specifically proclaimed, by word and by deed, its intention to protect him against that danger. * * *

We reject this argument. It is true that in certain limited circumstances the Constitution imposes upon the State affirmative duties of care and protection with respect to particular individuals [discussing *Youngberg v. Romeo*, p. 529 supra; *Estelle v. Gamble*, 429 U.S. 97, 97 S.Ct. 285, 50 L.Ed.2d 251 (1976); and other cases.]

But these [cases] stand only for the proposition that when the State takes a person into its custody and holds him there against his will, the Constitution imposes upon it a corresponding duty to assume some responsibility for his safety and general well-being. [In] the substantive due process analysis, it is the State's affirmative act of restraining the individual's freedom to act on his own behalf— through incarceration, institutionalization, or other similar restraint of personal liberty—which is the "deprivation of liberty" triggering the protections of the Due Process Clause, not its failure to act to protect his liberty interests against harms inflicted by other means.

The *Estelle-Youngberg* analysis simply has no applicability in the present case. Petitioners concede that the harms Joshua suffered did not occur while he was in the State's custody, but while he was in the custody of his natural father, who was in no sense a state actor.[9] While the State may have been aware of the dangers that Joshua faced in the free world, it played no part in their creation, nor did it do anything to render him any more vulnerable to them. That the State once took temporary custody of Joshua does not alter the analysis, for when it returned him to his father's custody, it placed him in no worse position than that in which he would have been had it not acted at all; the State does not become the permanent guarantor of an individual's safety by having once offered

---

9. [Had] the State by the affirmative exercise of its power removed Joshua from free society and placed him in a foster home operated by its agents, we might have a situation sufficiently analogous to incarceration or institutionalization to give rise to an affirmative duty to protect. Indeed, several Courts of Appeals have [so held], by analogy to *Estelle* and *Youngberg*. * * * We express no view on the validity of this analogy, however, as it is not before us in the present case. [See Note 2, following this case.]

THE CONCEPT OF STATE ACTION

him shelter. Under these circumstances, the State had no constitutional duty to protect Joshua. * * *[10]

[The] most that can be said of the state functionaries in this case is that they stood by and did nothing when suspicious circumstances dictated a more active role for them. In defense of them it must also be said that had they moved too soon to take custody of the son away from the father, they would likely have been met with charges of improperly intruding into the parent-child relationship, charges based on the same Due Process Clause that forms the basis for the present charge of failure to provide adequate protection.

The people of Wisconsin may well prefer a system of liability which would place upon the State and its officials the responsibility for failure to act in situations such as the present one. They may create such a system, if they do not have it already, by changing the tort law of the State in accordance with the regular law-making process. But they should not have it thrust upon them by this Court's expansion of the Due Process Clause of the Fourteenth Amendment.

JUSTICE BRENNAN, with whom JUSTICE MARSHALL and JUSTICE BLACKMUN join, dissenting.

[T]o the Court, the only fact that seems to count as an "affirmative act of restraining the individual's freedom to act on his own behalf" is direct physical control. I would not however, give *Youngberg* and *Estelle* such a stingy scope. I would recognize, as the Court apparently cannot, that "the State's knowledge of [an] individual's predicament [and] its expressions of intent to help him" can amount to a "limitation of his freedom to act on his own behalf" or to obtain help from others. Thus, I would read *Youngberg* and *Estelle* to stand for the much more generous proposition that, if a State cuts off private sources of aid and then refuses aid itself, it cannot wash its hands of the harm that results from its inaction. * * *

Wisconsin has established a child-welfare system specifically designed to help children like Joshua. [While] other governmental bodies and private persons are largely responsible for the reporting of possible cases of child abuse, Wisconsin law channels all such reports to the local departments of social services for evaluation and, if necessary, further action. [In] this way, Wisconsin law invites—indeed, directs—citizens and other governmental entities to depend on local departments of social services such as respondent to protect children from abuse.

The specific facts before us bear out this view of Wisconsin's system of protecting children. Each time someone voiced a suspicion that Joshua was being abused, that information was relayed to the Department for investigation and possible action. [A] private citizen, or even a person working in a government agency other than DSS, would doubtless feel that her job was done as soon as she had reported her suspicions of child abuse to DSS. [If] DSS ignores or dismisses these suspicions, no one will step in to fill the gap. * * *

It simply belies reality, therefore, to contend that the State "stood by and did nothing" with respect to Joshua. Through its child-protection program, the State actively intervened in Joshua's life and, by virtue of this intervention, acquired ever more certain knowledge that Joshua was in grave danger. * * * My disagreement with the Court arises from its failure to see that inaction can be

---

10. Because we conclude that the Due Process Clause did not require the State to protect Joshua from his father, we need not address respondents' alternative argument that the in-

dividual state actors lacked the requisite "state of mind" to make out a due process violation. * * *

every bit as abusive of power as action, that oppression can result when a State undertakes a vital duty and then ignores it. * * *

JUSTICE BLACKMUN, dissenting. * * *

Like the antebellum judges who denied relief to fugitive slaves, the Court today claims that its decision, however harsh, is compelled by existing legal doctrine. On the contrary, the question presented by this case is an open one, and our Fourteenth Amendment precedents may be read more broadly or narrowly depending upon how one chooses to read them. Faced with the choice, I would adopt a "sympathetic" reading, one which comports with dictates of fundamental justice and recognizes that compassion need not be exiled from the province of judging. * * *

Notes and Questions

1. *"State of mind" of government officials.* (a) Consider David A. Strauss, *Due Process, Government Inaction and Private Wrongs,* 1989 Sup.Ct.Rev. 53, 57–59: "Suppose that police officers learn that a murder is about to occur that they can prevent with minimal cost. [They] decide not to [intervene] because the targeted victim is someone whom they believe is guilty of another crime. The officers would rather see him killed by private persons than brought to trial where, they fear, he might escape with an acquittal or a light sentence.

"This must be a case of government inaction, assuming that there is such a thing. The police officers did not instigate or facilitate the murder in any way, except to refrain from intervening. They did not make the victim worse off than he would have been if the officers had never become aware of the predicament." Do you agree that "this hypothetical case is indistinguishable from *DeShaney*"? Id. In light of fn. 10 in *DeShaney*, would "child protective service employees [not] violate the Due Process Clause even if they deliberately refuse to intervened because they wanted to see a child harmed (because of a grudge against a family or out of a bizarre belief that child abuse constitutes proper discipline, for example)"? Id.

(b) Is there (should there be) a constitutional difference between government inaction that is careless or inadvertent rather than deliberate? Consider Richard S. Kay, *The State Action Doctrine, the Public–Private Distinction, and the Independence of Constitutional Law,* 10 Const.Comm. 329, 357 (1993): "The harms that follow on a state's failure to act are, in a sense, happenstance. In the usual case no official person will have planned for those results to follow. Affirmative acts, on the other hand, are more likely to have been deliberate and, therefore, they are more likely to have been undertaken with a dangerous state of mind. They pose the hazard not merely of the injuries that follow in the particular instance but of a course of conduct which portends even greater harm. This need not be so in every case, but it is a reasonable enough assumption to explain why the state may be thought more threatening when it acts than when it fails to act."

2. *The exception for "custodial" situations.* Consider Strauss, supra, at 63–66: "The government actively supports the family unit in countless ways. State law imposes support obligations on parents and gives them vast rights to control and direct their lives. State law bars strangers from intervening in the family except in extraordinary circumstances. Many state laws [are] designed to promote the establishment and maintenance of families. Through schools and many other media, the government promotes the family unit and reinforces the authority of the parents. [What] is wrongful under the Due Process Clause, according [to] *DeShaney*, is to establish [prisons, state hospitals and other institutions]

without taking care to protect those who are 'confined' within them. Since the state plays a role in establishing the family, it owes a duty of care to persons in Joshua DeShaney's position as well.''

3. *Legally created monopolies.* Consider Laurence H. Tribe, *The Curvature of Constitutional Space: What Lawyers Can Learn from Modern Physics,* 103 Harv. L.Rev. 1, 11 (1989): In *Boddie v. Connecticut,* p. 1387 supra, holding that due process prohibits a state from denying those seeking divorce access to its courts solely because of inability to pay filing fees and costs, ''there had been no previous state action directed at the particular individual. It was the legal structure itself—combined, to be sure, with the economic and social circumstances of the individual—that had isolated the person from the fulfillment of an important need. [If] the law creates a state monopoly over the fulfillment of certain needs (dissolution of a failed marriage, protection from a violent parent) and thereby renders some, but not all, individuals particularly vulnerable, can the very act of creating this legal *structure* constitute state action violative of due process? * * * *Boddie* answers 'yes,' at least where the state's interest in preserving that legal structure inviolate is sufficient to 'override the interest' of the plaintiff. [As] in *Boddie,* the governmental act in *DeShaney* that isolated Joshua—that is, the establishment of a legal structure that narrowly channeled all information and action in regard to child abuse—was not a force directed at Joshua personally; his isolation was a result of the simple juxtaposition of Wisconsin law and his personal situation. And, again as in *Boddie,* it was the monopoly created by the legal structure in *DeShaney* that made the plaintiff peculiarly vulnerable.''

Chapter 13
CONGRESSIONAL ENFORCEMENT
OF CIVIL RIGHTS

The exercise of congressional authority under the commerce power to protect civil rights was upheld in *Heart of Atlanta Motel, Inc. v. United States,* 379 U.S. 241, 85 S.Ct. 348, 13 L.Ed.2d 258 (1964). But the potentially most pervasive sources of federal legislative power to enforce personal liberty are found in the final sections of the thirteenth, fourteenth, and fifteenth amendments which grant Congress power to enforce the substantive provisions of these amendments "by appropriate legislation."[a]

SECTION 1. HISTORICAL FRAMEWORK

I. LEGISLATION

The Civil Rights Act of 1866, enacted pursuant to the thirteenth amendment, was the first Reconstruction Act seeking "to protect all persons in the United States in their civil rights." (See "Historical Background," p. 320 supra.) Its current provisions are:

42 U.S.C. § 1981. *"Equal rights under the law.* All persons within the jurisdiction of the United States shall have the same right in every State and Territory to make and enforce contracts, to sue, be parties, give evidence, and to the full and equal benefit of all laws and proceedings for the security of persons and property as is enjoyed by white citizens, and shall be subject to like punishment, pains, penalties, taxes, licenses, and exactions of every kind, and to no other."

42 U.S.C. § 1982. *"Property rights of citizens.* All citizens of the United States shall have the same right, in every State and Territory, as is enjoyed by white citizens thereof to inherit, purchase, lease, sell, hold, and convey real and personal property."

The 1866 Act then provided criminal penalties against any person denying such rights under color of law. With certain changes (the most important being addition of the word "willfully" in 1909, 35 Stat. 1092, and the substantial

---

a. For a listing of some recent, frequent attempts by Congress to legislate under this authority, see Note, *When the Supreme Court* *Restricts Constitutional Rights, Can Congress Save Us?,* 141 U.Pa.L.Rev. 1029, 1031 n. 23 (1993).

increase of penalties in 1968, 82 Stat. 75), this has survived as a significant federal criminal statute enforcing civil rights:

18 U.S.C. § 242. *"Deprivation of rights under color of law.* Whoever, under color of any law, statute, ordinance, regulation, or custom, willfully subjects any inhabitant of any State, Territory, or District to the deprivation of any rights, privileges, or immunities secured or protected by the Constitution or laws of the United States, or to different punishments, pains or penalties, on account of such inhabitant being an alien, or by reason of his color, or race, than are prescribed for the punishment of citizens, shall be fined not more than $1,000 or imprisoned not more than one year, or both; and if death results shall be subject to imprisonment for any term of years or for life."

————

Doubt as to the adequacy of the thirteenth amendment to support the 1866 Act was a significant force leading to adoption of the fourteenth amendment. After ratification of the fifteenth amendment, Congress passed the Act of May 31, 1870, 16 Stat. 140, principally to enforce the right to vote guaranteed by the amendment.[a] One section, barring private conspiracies, evolved as an important existing protection:

18 U.S.C. § 241. *"Conspiracy against rights of citizens.* If two or more persons conspire to injure, oppress, threaten, or intimidate any citizen in the free exercise or enjoyment of any right or privilege secured to him by the Constitution or laws of the United States, or because of his having exercised the same; or

"If two or more persons go on the highway, or on the premises of another, with intent to prevent or hinder his free exercise or enjoyment of any right or privilege so secured—

"They shall be fined not more than $10,000 or imprisoned not more than ten years, or both; and if death results, they shall be subject to imprisonment for any term of years or for life."

————

Next came the Ku Klux Klan Act of 1871, 17 Stat. 13, which made criminal private conspiracies against the operations of government officials or courts, or to deprive persons of equal protection of the laws.[b] The Act also established civil liabilities that have evolved to be important existing provisions. One is the civil counterpart of 18 U.S.C.A. § 242:

42 U.S.C. § 1983. *"Civil action for deprivation of rights.* Every person who, under color of any statute, ordinance, regulation, custom, or usage, of any State or Territory, subjects, or causes to be subjected, any citizen of the United States or other persons within the jurisdiction thereof to the deprivation of any

---

a. Few of the protections afforded the right to vote survived. *United States v. Reese,* 92 U.S. (2 Otto) 214, 23 L.Ed. 563 (1876), held two sections unconstitutional, as not supported by the fifteenth amendment, because the offenses they created for interfering with voting were not limited to denial on the basis of race. Other sections were repealed by the anti-Reconstruction Congress in 1894, 28 Stat. 36–37.

b. The latter proviso was held unconstitutional, as not supported by the fourteenth amendment, in *United States v. Harris,* 106 U.S. 629, 1 S.Ct. 601, 27 L.Ed. 290 (1882), because "directed exclusively against the action of private persons, without reference to the laws of the State or their administration by her officers." The entire part was repealed in 1909, 35 Stat. 1153–54.

rights, privileges or immunities secured by the Constitution and laws, shall be liable to the person injured in an action of law, suit in equity, or other proper proceedings for redress.''

Another is roughly the civil counterpart of 18 U.S.C.A. § 241:

42 U.S.C. § 1985. *"Conspiracy to interfere with civil rights. * * * (3)* If two or more persons in any State or Territory conspire or go in disguise on the highway or on the premises of another, for the purpose of depriving, either directly or indirectly, any person or class of persons of the equal protection of the laws, or of equal privileges and immunities under the laws; or for the purpose of preventing or hindering the constituted authorities of any State or Territory from giving or securing to all persons within such State or Territory the equal protection of the laws; [the] party so injured or deprived may have an action for the recovery of damages, occasioned by such injury or deprivation, against any one or more of the conspirators.''

––––––––

The final Reconstruction enactment in this area was the Civil Rights Act of 1875, dealing with racial discrimination in public accommodations, held invalid in the *Civil Rights Cases,* p. 1318 supra.[c] No significant congressional action to enforce civil rights took place between 1875 and the Civil Rights Act of 1957. The principal thrust of the 1957 Act and of the Civil Rights Act of 1960 was against racial discrimination in voting. The Civil Rights Act of 1964, although principally concerned with matters already considered, also dealt with voting. But the most comprehensive federal legislation in aid of the franchise is the Voting Rights Act of 1965, 42 U.S.C. § 1973, and its later Amendments. Finally, the Civil Rights Act of 1968 provides protection against interference with designated "federally protected activities," 18 U.S.C. § 245, and against discrimination in housing, 42 U.S.C. §§ 3601–31—both considered at several points infra.

II. JUDICIAL DECISIONS

Necessity of "state action" for violation of constitutional rights. (a) *In general.* Shortly after enactment of the Reconstruction civil rights laws, a series of decisions culminating in the *Civil Rights Cases* significantly limited their impact by interpreting the fourteenth (and fifteenth) amendments as barring only "state action," thus precluding congressional legislation against "private individuals" for violating rights of persons created by these amendments.[a]

(b) *Sec. 241 exceptions.* But the Court has long recognized that there is a limited category of constitutional rights, protected by § 241, that, as stated in UNITED STATES v. WILLIAMS, 341 U.S. 70, 71 S.Ct. 581, 95 L.Ed. 758 (1951), "Congress can beyond doubt constitutionally secure against interference by private individuals. [T]his category includes rights which arise from the relationship of the individual and the Federal Government. The right of citizens to vote in congressional elections, for instance, may obviously be protected by Congress from

c. For general discussion and evolution of the Reconstruction civil rights legislation, see Eugene Gressman, *The Unhappy History of Civil Rights Legislation,* 50 Mich.L.Rev. 1323 (1952); Will Maslow & Joseph B. Robison, *Civil Rights Legislation and the Fight for Equality, 1862–1952,* 20 U.Chi.L.Rev. 363

(1953); U.S. Comm'n on Civil Rights, *Enforcement* 103–40 (1965).

a. See *United States v. Cruikshank,* 92 U.S. (2 Otto) 542, 23 L.Ed. 588 (1876); *Virginia v. Rives,* 100 U.S. (10 Otto) 313, 25 L.Ed. 667 (1879). See also fn. b supra.

individual as well as from State interference. *Ex parte Yarbrough,* 110 U.S. 651, 4 S.Ct. 152, 28 L.Ed. 274." [b] The Court has also included, as "attributes of national citizenship," "the right of the people peaceably to assemble for the purpose of petitioning Congress for a redress of grievances" [c] and the "constitutional right to travel from one State to another." [d]

(c) *"Custom or usage" under § 1983.* ADICKES v. S.H. KRESS & CO., 398 U.S. 144, 90 S.Ct. 1598, 26 L.Ed.2d 142 (1970), involved a damages action against a restaurant for having deprived plaintiff of equal protection—alleging that defendant acted "under color [of] custom, or usage, of any State." The Court (Douglas and Brennan, JJ., dissenting; Marshall, J., not participating) held "that a 'custom or usage' for purposes of § 1983 requires state involvement and is not simply a practice which reflects long-standing social habits, generally observed by the people in a locality"; it "must have the force of law by virtue of the persistent practices of state officials."

SECTION 2. MODERN DEVELOPMENTS

SOUTH CAROLINA v. KATZENBACH, 383 U.S. 301, 86 S.Ct. 803, 15 L.Ed.2d 769 (1966): South Carolina challenged the Voting Rights Act of 1965 (enacted pursuant to § 2 of the fifteenth amendment)—"the heart of [which] is a complex scheme of stringent remedies aimed at areas where voting discrimination has been most flagrant." The Court, per WARREN, C.J., referred to "the voluminous legislative history" that showed, inter alia, "unremitting and ingenious defiance of the Constitution," the enactment of literacy tests in Alabama, Georgia, Louisiana, Mississippi, North Carolina, South Carolina, and Virginia, still in use, which, because of their various qualifications, "were specifically designed to prevent Negroes from voting." It pointed out that "discriminatory application of voting tests" "pursuant to a widespread 'pattern or practice'" "is now the principal method used to bar Negroes from the polls," and gave a number of illustrations; that "case-by-case litigation against voting discrimination" under federal statutes of 1957, 1960 and 1964 has "done little to cure the problem."

"As against the reserved powers of the States, Congress may use any rational means to effectuate the constitutional prohibition of racial discrimination in voting. [The] basic test to be applied in a case involving § 2 of the Fifteenth Amendment is the same as in all cases concerning the express powers of Congress with relation to the reserved powers of the [states.] 'Let the end be legitimate, let it be within the scope of the constitution, and all means which are appropriate, which are plainly adapted to that end, which are not prohibited, but consist with the letter and spirit of the constitution, are constitutional.' *McCulloch v. Maryland,* 17 U.S. (4 Wheat.) 316, 4 L.Ed. 579 (1819). "We therefore reject South Carolina's argument that Congress may appropriately do no more than to forbid violations of the Fifteenth Amendment in general terms—that the task of fashion-

---

b. *United States v. Classic,* 313 U.S. 299, 61 S.Ct. 1031, 85 L.Ed. 1368 (1941), included within this category the right to vote in the Louisiana congressional primary: "Interference with [this right is] an interference with the effective choice of the voters at the only stage of the election procedure when their choice is of significance, since it is at the only stage when such interference could have any practical effect on the ultimate [result]."

c. *Cruikshank,* fn. a supra (dictum). For potential expansion, see Howard M. Feuerstein, *Civil Rights Crimes and the Federal Power to Punish Private Individuals for Interference With Federally Secured Rights,* 19 Vand.L.Rev. 641, 654–59 (1966).

d. *United States v. Guest,* Sec. 2 infra.

ing specific remedies or of applying them to particular localities must necessarily be left entirely to the courts.

The "coverage formula" of the Act applied "to any State, or to any separate political subdivision [for] which two findings have been made: (1) the Attorney General has determined that on November 1, 1964, it maintained a 'test or device,' and (2) the Director of the Census has determined that less than 50% of its voting-age residents were registered on November 1, 1964, or voted in the presidential election of November 1964. These findings are not reviewable * * *. § 4(b). [T]he phrase 'test or device' means any requirement that a registrant or voter must '(1) demonstrate the ability to read, write, understand, or interpret any matter, (2) demonstrate any educational achievement or his knowledge of any particular subject, (3) possess good moral character, or (4) prove his qualifications by the voucher of registered voters or members of any other class.' § 4(c)." Statutory coverage was terminated by a so-called "bail out" provision—if the area obtained a judgment from a three-judge federal court in the District of Columbia "that tests and devices have not been used during the preceding five years to abridge the franchise on racial grounds." "In acceptable legislative fashion, Congress chose to limit its attention to the geographic areas where immediate action seemed necessary."

The areas covered, "for which there was evidence of actual voting discrimination,"—Alabama, Louisiana, Mississippi, Georgia, South Carolina and much of North Carolina—shared the "two characteristics incorporated by Congress into the coverage formula." "It was therefore permissible to impose the new remedies on the few remaining States and political subdivisions covered by the formula, at least in the absence of proof that they have been free of substantial voting discrimination in recent years." That there are excluded areas "for which there is evidence of voting discrimination by other means" is irrelevant: "Congress strengthened existing remedies for voting discrimination in other areas of the country. Legislation need not deal with all phases of a problem in the same way, so long as the distinctions drawn have some basis in political experience." "There are no States or political subdivisions exempted from coverage under § 4(b) in which the record reveals recent racial discrimination involving tests and devices. This fact confirms the rationality of the formula." The findings "which trigger application of the coverage formula" "consist of objective statistical determinations" and the termination procedure "serves as a partial substitute for direct judicial review."

In areas covered, § 4(a) suspended "literacy tests and similar voting qualifications for a period of five years from the last occurrence of substantial voting discrimination," and § 5 suspended "all new voting regulations pending review by [the Attorney General or a three-judge court in the District of Columbia] to determine whether their use would perpetuate voting discrimination." [a] Both were upheld as a "legitimate response to the problem," the Court recounting the evidence Congress had before it of prior discriminatory administration of old tests and use of new tests to evade court decrees. "Congress knew that continuance of the tests and devices in use at the present time, no matter how fairly administered in the future, would freeze the effect of past discrimination in favor of unqualified white registrants. Congress permissibly rejected the alternatives of requiring a

---

a. For examples of the Court's subsequent broad interpretation of "voting regulations" that are subject to the suspension provision of section 5, see *United Jewish Orgs. v. Carey*, p. 1256 supra (new or revised reapportionment plan); *Rome v. United States*, infra (election of officials "at large" rather than by district; annexation of adjacent area thus increasing number of eligible voters).

complete re-registration of all voters, believing that this would be too harsh on many whites who had enjoyed the franchise for their entire adult lives." [b]

Notes and Questions

Enforcement provisions. Section 11(b) (with criminal penalties) provides that "no person, whether acting under color of law or otherwise, shall intimidate, threaten, or coerce [any] person for voting or attempting to vote, [or] for urging or aiding any person to vote or attempt to vote, or intimidate, threaten, or coerce any [federal official] for exercising any powers or duties under" the Act. Section 12(c) punishes "whoever conspires" to interfere with rights secured by the Act and § 12(d) authorizes injunctions against "any person" who engages or is about to engage in practices prohibited by the Act.[c] Constitutional? See generally L. Thorne McCarty & Russell B. Stevenson, *The Voting Rights Act of 1965: An Evaluation,* 3 Harv.Civ.Rts.Civ.Lib.L.Rev. 357 (1968).

UNITED STATES v. PRICE, 383 U.S. 787, 86 S.Ct. 1152, 16 L.Ed.2d 267 (1966), involved "appeals from the dismissal in part of two indictments," for conspiracy and substantive violations under §§ 241 and 242, against three Mississippi police officials and fifteen "nonofficial persons," for having willfully killed three civil rights workers—the police officials first jailing the victims, then releasing them and intercepting them and, then, all 18 defendants "punishing" the victims by shooting them—thus depriving "the victims due process of law."

The Court, treating the case as raising issues "of construction, not of constitutional power," held that, as to the conspiracy count against the "private persons" under § 242, " '[I]t is immaterial to the conspiracy that these private individuals were not acting under color of law' because the count charges that they were conspiring with persons who were so acting. See *United States v. Rabinowich,* 238 U.S. 78, 87, 35 S.Ct. 682, 684, 59 L.Ed. 1211 (1915)." As to the substantive counts against the "private persons" under § 242, the Court, stating that the statutory language "under color of law" has "consistently been treated as the same thing as the 'state action' required by the Fourteenth Amendment," held that "private persons, jointly engaged with state officials in the prohibited action, are acting 'under color' of law for purposes of the statute. To act 'under color' of law does not require that the accused be an officer of the State. It is enough that he is a wilful participant in joint activity with the State or its agents," citing *Burton v. Wilmington Parking Auth.,* p. 1506 supra. "[A]ccording to the indictment, the brutal joint adventure was made possible by state detention and calculated release of the prisoners by an officer of the State." "Those who took advantage of participation by state officers in accomplishment of the foul purpose alleged must suffer the consequences of that participation." [d]

---

b. Black, J., agreed "with substantially all of the Court's opinion" but dissented in respect to § 5: "[I]f all the provisions of our Constitution which limit the power of the Federal Government and reserve other power to the States are to mean anything, they mean at least that the States have power to pass laws [without] first sending their officials hundreds of miles away to beg federal authorities to approve them."

c. The Civil Rights Act of 1968, 18 U.S.C.A. § 245(b)(1), penalizes all persons who interfere, etc. (see note 2(b) infra) with "voting or qualifying to vote, qualifying or campaigning as a candidate for elective office, or qualifying or acting as a poll watcher or any legally authorized election official, in any primary, special, or general election."

d. See also *Screws v. United States,* 325 U.S. 91, 65 S.Ct. 1031, 89 L.Ed. 1495 (1945) holding that it was no defense under § 242

Notes and Questions

1. *"Participation" of private persons with state officers.* In *Price,* the "official" and "nonofficial" defendants all appeared to be actively and equally participating in the venture. Could private persons be constitutionally convicted under § 242 if they were "passive" participants with state officers? Suppose the private person were the "active" participant while the state officers were merely "passive"? See Thomas J. Klitgaard, *The Civil Rights Act and Mr. Monroe,* 49 Calif.L.Rev. 145, 168–69 (1961). Could the private person be convicted if all the state officers are acquitted?

2. Consider the constitutionality of the following prosecutions under § 242:

(a) Defendant sheriff beats prisoner to death because prisoner cursed the sheriff. Suppose the sheriff encounters a personal enemy on the street and beats him to death? Suppose this personal enemy declined to resist because he feared the consequences of a victory over a police officer? Suppose the sheriff first tells the personal enemy that he is under arrest?

(b) Defendant private citizen secretly enters a jail and beats a prisoner to death. Suppose the citizen joined the sheriff in beating the prisoner to death in order to obtain a confession?

(c) Defendant sheriff stands by while a private citizen beats to death the sheriff's prisoner, who is the citizen's personal enemy.

(d) Defendant private citizen is part of a mob that so intimidates parents of school children as to cause them to keep the children away from the school with the result that the school is closed.

(e) Defendant bus driver racially segregates passengers because he is commanded by state statute to do so.

(f) Defendant private citizen makes a "citizen's arrest" without probable cause. Suppose the citizen masqueraded as a policeman and made an arrest without probable cause? Suppose this citizen, dressed as a policeman, killed a personal enemy? Suppose the citizen, making an arrest without probable cause, were a private detective who became a "special police officer" by local law? See *Williams v. United States,* 341 U.S. 97, 71 S.Ct. 576, 95 L.Ed. 774 (1951).

(g) Defendant court-appointed trustee embezzles the funds.

(h) Defendant attorney, an "officer of the court," makes false statements in a sanity proceeding which result in the commitment of another person. Suppose defendant is court-appointed? See *Polk County v. Dodson,* 454 U.S. 312, 102 S.Ct. 445, 70 L.Ed.2d 509 (1981) (public defender does not act under color of law when performing traditional adversarial functions as appointed counsel).

UNITED STATES v. GUEST

383 U.S. 745, 86 S.Ct. 1170, 16 L.Ed.2d 239 (1966).

JUSTICE STEWART delivered the opinion of the Court.

[Defendants were indicted] for criminal conspiracy in violation of § 241 [to] deprive Negro citizens of the free exercise and enjoyment of several specified

that defendant's actions were in violation of state law: "Misuse of power, possessed by virtue of state law and made possible only because the wrongdoer is clothed with the authority of state law, is action taken 'under color of' state law. [It] is clear that under 'color' of law means under 'pretense' of law. Thus acts of officers in the ambit of their personal pursuits are plainly excluded. Acts of officers who undertake to perform their official duties are included whether they hew to the line of their authority or overstep it."

rights secured by the Constitution and laws of the United States. The defendants [successfully] moved to dismiss the indictment on the ground that it did not charge an offense under the laws of the United States. [As] in *Price,* decided today, we deal here with issues of statutory construction, not with issues of constitutional power. * * *

II. The second numbered paragraph of the indictment alleged that the defendants conspired to injure, oppress, threaten, and intimidate Negro citizens of the United States in the free exercise of enjoyment of: "The right to the equal utilization, without discrimination upon the basis of race, of public facilities in the vicinity of Athens, Georgia, owned, operated, or managed by [the State]." * * *

Unlike the indictment in *Price,* [the] indictment in the present case names no person alleged to have acted in any way under the color of state law. * * *

It is a commonplace that rights under the Equal Protection Clause itself arise only where there has been involvement of the State or of one acting under the color of its authority. [Here, one] of the means of accomplishing the object of the conspiracy, according to the indictment, was "By causing the arrest of Negroes by means of false reports that such Negroes had committed criminal acts." [The] allegation of the extent of official involvement in the present case is not clear. [But it] is broad enough to cover a charge of active connivance by agents of the State in the making of the "false reports," or other conduct amounting to official discrimination clearly sufficient to constitute denial of rights protected by the Equal Protection Clause. * * *

III. The fourth numbered paragraph of the indictment alleged that the defendants conspired to injure, oppress, threaten, and intimidate Negro citizens of the United States in the free exercise and enjoyment of: "The right to travel freely to and from the State of Georgia." [The] constitutional right to travel from one State to another, and necessarily to use the highways and other instrumentalities of interstate commerce in doing so, occupies a position fundamental to the concept of our Federal Union. [See Ch. 6.]

This does not mean, of course, that every criminal conspiracy affecting an individual's right of free interstate passage is within the sanction of § 241. A specific intent to interfere with the federal right must be [proved]. Thus, for example, a conspiracy to rob an interstate traveler would not, of itself, violate § 241. But if the predominant purpose of the conspiracy is to impede or prevent the exercise of the right of interstate travel, or to oppress a person because of his exercise of that right, then, whether or not motivated by racial discrimination, the conspiracy becomes a proper object of the federal law under which the indictment in this case was brought. * * * a

Reversed and remanded.

JUSTICE CLARK, with whom JUSTICE BLACK and JUSTICE FORTAS join, concurring.

I join the opinion of the Court in this case but believe it worthwhile to comment on [Part II]. The Court's interpretation of the indictment clearly avoids the question whether Congress, by appropriate legislation, has the power to punish private conspiracies that interfere with Fourteenth Amendment rights, such as the right to utilize public facilities. My Brother Brennan, however, [suggests] that the Court indicates sub silentio that Congress does not have the

---

a. The Civil Rights Act of 1968, 18 U.S.C.A. § 245(b), penalizes all persons who interfere etc. (see note 2(b) infra) with "any person because of his race, color, religion or national origin and because he is or has [been] traveling in or using any facility of interstate commerce, or using any vehicle, terminal, or facility of any common carrier by motor, rail, water, or air."

power to outlaw such conspiracies. Although the Court specifically rejects any such connotation, it is, I believe, both appropriate and necessary under the circumstances here to say that there now can be no doubt that the specific language of § 5 empowers the Congress to enact laws punishing all conspiracies—with or without state action—that interfere with Fourteenth Amendment rights.

JUSTICE BRENNAN, with whom THE CHIEF JUSTICE and JUSTICE DOUGLAS join, concurring in part and dissenting in part.

* * * I do not agree [with the rationale] of Part II, which holds, as I read the opinion, that a conspiracy to interfere with the exercise of the right to equal utilization of state facilities is not within the meaning of § 241 [unless] discriminatory conduct by state officers is involved in the alleged conspiracy.

* * * I believe that § 241 reaches such a private conspiracy, not because the Fourteenth Amendment of its own force prohibits such a conspiracy, but because § 241, as an exercise of congressional power under § 5 of that Amendment, prohibits *all* conspiracies to interfere with the exercise of a "right * * * secured [by] the Constitution" and because [the] right to use state facilities without discrimination on the basis of race is, within the meaning of § 241, a right created by, arising under and dependent upon the Fourteenth Amendment and hence is a right "secured" by that Amendment. It finds its source in the Amendment. [The] Fourteenth Amendment commands the State to provide the members of all races with equal access to the public facilities it owns or manages, and the right of a citizen to use those facilities without discrimination on the basis of race is a basic corollary of this command. Whatever may be the status of the right to equal utilization of *privately owned facilities,* it must be emphasized that we are here concerned with the right to equal utilization of *public facilities owned or operated by or on behalf of the State.* * * *

A majority of the members of the Court[6] express the view today that § 5 empowers Congress to enact laws punishing *all* conspiracies to interfere with the exercise of Fourteenth Amendment rights, whether or not state officers or others acting under the color of state law are implicated in the conspiracy. [§ 5] authorizes Congress to make laws that it concludes are reasonably necessary to protect a right created by and arising under that Amendment; and Congress is thus fully empowered to determine that punishment of private conspiracies interfering with the exercise of such a right is necessary to its full protection. * * *

I acknowledge that some of the decisions of this Court, most notably an aspect of the *Civil Rights Cases,* have declared that Congress' power under § 5 is confined to the adoption of "appropriate legislation for correcting the effects [of] prohibited state law and state [acts]." I do not accept—and a majority of the Court today rejects—this interpretation of § 5. It reduces the legislative power to enforce the provisions of the Amendment to that of the judiciary;[7] and it attributes a far too limited objective to the Amendment's sponsors.[8] Moreover,

6. The majority consists of the Justices joining my Brother Clark's opinion and the Justices joining this opinion. * * *

7. Congress, not the judiciary, was viewed as the more likely agency to implement fully the guarantees of equality, and thus it could be presumed the primary purpose of the Amendments was to augment the power of Congress, not the judiciary. See Joseph B. James, *The Framing of the Fourteenth Amendment,* 184

(1956); Robert J. Harris, *The Quest for Equality,* 53–54 (1960); Laurent B. Frantz, *Congressional Power to Enforce the Fourteenth Amendment Against Private Acts,* 73 Yale L.J. 1353, 1356 (1964).

8. As the first Mr. Justice Harlan said in dissent in the *Civil Rights Cases:* "It was perfectly well known that the great danger to equal enjoyment by citizens of their rights, as

the language of § 5 of the Fourteenth Amendment and § 2 of the Fifteenth Amendment are virtually the same, and we recently held in *South Carolina v. Katzenbach* that "[t]he basic test to be applied in a case involving § 2 of the Fifteenth Amendment is the same as in all cases concerning the express powers of Congress with relation to the reserved powers of the States." The classic formulation of that test by Chief Justice Marshall in *McCulloch v. Maryland,* was there adopted * * *.

Viewed in its proper perspective, § 5 appears as a positive grant of legislative power, authorizing Congress to exercise its discretion in fashioning remedies to achieve civil and political equality for all citizens. No one would deny [that] Congress has the power to punish state officers who, in excess of their authority and in violation of state law, conspire to threaten, harass and murder Negroes for attempting to use [state] facilities. And I can find no principle of federalism nor word of the Constitution that denies Congress power to determine that in order adequately to protect the right to equal utilization of state facilities, it is also appropriate to punish other individuals—neither state officers nor acting in concert with state officers—who engage in the same brutal conduct for the same misguided purpose. * * *[b]

Notes and Questions

1. *Interference with fourteenth (and fifteenth) amendment rights.* Are private persons, who intimidate state officials in an attempt to thwart their racial integration of public schools, subject to prosecution under § 241? Private persons who intimidate black school children or their parents in an attempt to stop them from going to integrated schools? Who lynch a prisoner, thus preventing his fair trial by the state? Who intimidate African-Americans in an effort to prevent them from voting? Cf. note after *South Carolina v. Katzenbach.* Who detain a judge in an effort to prevent him from setting bail?

2. *Scope of congressional power under § 5.* (a) Do you agree with "a majority of the members of the Court" in *Guest* that "§ 5 empowers Congress to enact laws punishing *all* conspiracies to interfere with the exercise of Fourteenth Amendment rights, whether or not state officers or others acting under color of state law are implicated in the conspiracy"? Consider Feuerstein, fn. c, Sec. 1, II supra, at 674–75: "[They] start with the proposition that there is a right to use state facilities without discrimination based upon race, when actually they are saying that there is a right to use state facilities without racial discrimination from any quarter—state or private. The traditional view of the equal protection clause is that it creates a right to be free of discrimination by the state. So defined, the right can only be infringed by state action, and legislation under § 5 must be directed at that infringement. Unfortunately, neither the Brennan nor the Clark opinion directly confronts this traditional approach."[c] Is the majority's

citizens, was to be apprehended, not altogether from unfriendly state legislation, but from the hostile action of corporations and individuals in the states. And it is to be presumed that it was intended, by [§ 5], to clothe congress with power and authority to meet that danger."

[For the view that the fourteenth amendment's "Privileges or Immunities Clause (coupled with the § 5 Enforcement Clause)" was intended "as an authorization of Federal legislation to prohibit private racial discrimination if the states did not," see Louis Lusky, *By What Right?* 181–203 (1975). See also Frantz, fn. 7 supra.]

b. Harlan, J.'s partial concurrence and dissent is omitted.

c. Compare Stevens, J., concurring in *Great American Fed. S. & L. Ass'n v. Novotny,* 442 U.S. 366, 99 S.Ct. 2345, 60 L.Ed.2d 957 (1979): "[I]f private persons take conspiratorial action that prevents or hinders the constituted authorities of any State from giving or securing equal treatment, the private persons would cause those authorities to violate the Four-

rationale limited to "conspiracies" or is Congress empowered, beyond § 241, to penalize individual private acts? Does Brennan, J.'s rationale extend to "the right to equal utilization of *privately owned facilities*"?

(b) *Civil Rights Act of 1968*. 18 U.S.C.A. § 245(b): "Whoever, whether or not acting under color of law, by force or threat of force willfully injures, intimidates or interferes with, or attempts to injure, intimidate or interfere with— * * *

"(2) any person because of his race, color, religion or national origin and because he is or has been—

"(A) enrolling in or attending any public school or public college;

"(B) participating in or enjoying any benefit, service, privilege, program, facility or activity provided or administered by any State or subdivision thereof;

"(C) applying for or enjoying employment, or any perquisite thereof, by any private employer or any agency of any State or subdivision thereof, or joining or using the services or advantages of any labor organization, hiring hall, or employment agency;

"(D) serving, or attending upon any court of any State in connection with possible service, as a grand or petit juror; * * *

"(F) enjoying the goods, services, facilities, privileges, advantages, or accommodations of any inn, hotel, motel, or other establishment which provides lodging to transient guests, or of any restaurant, cafeteria, lunchroom, lunch counter, soda fountain, or other facility which serves the public and which is principally engaged in selling food or beverages for consumption on the premises, or of any gasoline station, or of any motion picture house, theater, concert hall, sports arena, stadium, or any other place of exhibition or entertainment which serves the public, or of any other establishment which serves the public and (i) which is located within the premises of any of the aforesaid establishments or within the premises of which is physically located any of the aforesaid establishments, and (ii) which holds itself out as serving patrons of such establishments; or * * *

"(5) any citizen because he is or has been, or in order to intimidate such citizen or any other citizen from lawfully aiding or encouraging other persons to participate, without discrimination on account of race, color, religion or national origin, in any of the benefits or activities described [or] participating lawfully in speech or peaceful assembly opposing any denial of the opportunity to so participate—

"shall be fined not more than $1,000, or imprisoned not more than one year, or both; and if bodily injury results shall be fined not more than $10,000, or imprisoned not more than ten years, or both; and if death results shall be subject to imprisonment for any term of years or for life. * * * Nothing in subparagraph (2)(F) * * * of this subsection shall apply to the proprietor of any establishment which provides lodging to transient guests, or to any employee acting on behalf of such proprietor, with respect to the enjoyment of [the] accommodations of such establishment if such establishment is located within a building which contains not more than five rooms for rent or hire and which is actually occupied by the proprietor as his residence."

teenth Amendment; [but if] private persons engage in purely private acts of discrimination, [they] do not violate the Equal Protection Clause of the Fourteenth Amendment. The rights secured by the Equal Protection and Due Process Clauses of the Fourteenth Amendment are rights to protection against unequal or unfair treatment by the State, not by private parties."

(c) Suppose a private individual murders a black person. It is clear that the *effect* (irrespective of the murderer's *intent*) is to prevent the victim's equal use of state facilities; that it prevents his right to vote, etc. These facts would be equally true if the victim were white. May the murderer be punished under § 241? Under a more narrowly drawn federal criminal statute? Consider Archibald Cox, *Constitutional Adjudication and the Promotion of Human Rights,* 80 Harv.L.Rev. 91, 116 (1966): "It seems unlikely that much constitutional significance will attach to distinctions in terms of intent. The differences between purpose, awareness that a consequence must follow, conscious indifference, and responsibility for the natural and probable consequences of an act are far too elusive to measure the scope of congressional power. Furthermore, if violence and intimidation are actually interfering with the right to vote or to enjoy state facilities, there is scant practical relevance in the wrongdoers' motivation. The suggestion was once made that the power of Congress to regulate local activities under the commerce clause depended upon the intent with which the activities were conducted, but the idea was shortly abandoned in favor of legislative or administrative determination of the practical effects on commerce."

Does congressional power fail in the above instance because "its authority is confined to instances in which there is a special relationship between the person injured and the state"? Because there is "an utter lack of proportion between the federal punishment [and] the federal interest in safeguarding enjoyment of the constitutional right"? Or is "the responsibility for the federal system" left to Congress: "possession of congressional power should not be confused with its exercise"? Id. at 116–17, 119.

KATZENBACH v. MORGAN

384 U.S. 641, 86 S.Ct. 1717, 16 L.Ed.2d 828 (1966).

JUSTICE BRENNAN delivered the opinion of the Court.

[Section] 4(e) of the Voting Rights Act of 1965 [provides] that no person who has successfully completed the sixth primary grade in a [school] accredited by the Commonwealth of Puerto Rico in which the language of instruction was other than English shall be denied the right to vote in any election because of his inability to read or write English. Appellees, registered voters in New York City, brought this suit to challenge the constitutionality of § 4(e) insofar as it pro tanto prohibits the enforcement of the election laws of New York requiring an ability to read and write English * * *.

Under the distribution of powers effected by the Constitution, [the] qualifications established by the States for voting for members of the most numerous branch of the state legislature also determine who may vote for United States Representatives and Senators, Art. I, § 2; Seventeenth Amendment. But, of course, the States have no power to grant or withhold the franchise on conditions that are forbidden by the Fourteenth Amendment * * *.

The Attorney General of New York argues that an exercise of congressional power under § 5 of the Fourteenth Amendment that prohibits the enforcement of a state [law] cannot be sustained as appropriate legislation to enforce the Equal Protection Clause unless the judiciary decides—even with the guidance of a congressional judgment—that the application of the English literacy requirement prohibited by § 4(e) is forbidden by the Equal Protection Clause itself. We disagree. Neither the language nor history of § 5 supports such a construction.[7] [A] construction of § 5 that would require a judicial determination that the enforcement of the state law precluded by Congress violated the Amendment, as a condition of sustaining the congressional enactment [would] confine the legislative power in this context to the insignificant role of abrogating only those state laws that the judicial branch was prepared to adjudge unconstitutional, or of merely informing the judgment of the judiciary by particularizing the "majestic generalities" of [§ 1]. Accordingly, our decision in *Lassiter v. Northampton Cty. Bd. of Elec.*, 360 U.S. 45, 79 S.Ct. 985, 3 L.Ed.2d 1072 (1959), sustaining the North Carolina English literacy requirement as not in all circumstances prohibited by the first sections of the Fourteenth and Fifteenth Amendments, [did] not present the question before us here: Without regard to whether the judiciary would find that the Equal Protection Clause itself nullifies New York's English literacy requirement as so applied, could Congress prohibit the enforcement of the state law by legislating under § 5? In answering this question, our task is limited to determining whether such legislation is, as required by § 5, appropriate legislation to enforce the Equal Protection Clause.

By including § 5 the draftsmen sought to grant to Congress [the] same broad powers expressed in the Necessary and Proper Clause.[9] The classic formulation of the reach of those powers was established by Chief Justice Marshall in *McCulloch v. Maryland* * * *. *Ex parte Virginia*, 100 U.S. 339, 25 L.Ed. 676 (1879), decided 12 years after the adoption of the Fourteenth Amendment, held that congressional power under § 5 had this same broad scope * * *. Section 2 of the Fifteenth Amendment grants Congress a similar power [and] we recently held in *South Carolina v. Katzenbach* that [the test was] the one formulated in *McCulloch*. * * * Correctly viewed, § 5 is a positive grant of legislative power authorizing Congress to exercise its discretion in determining whether and what legislation is needed to secure the guarantees of the Fourteenth Amendment. * * *[10]

There can be no doubt that § 4(e) may be regarded as an enactment to enforce the Equal Protection Clause. [S]pecifically, § 4(e) may be viewed as a measure to secure for the Puerto Rican community residing in New York nondiscriminatory treatment by government—both in the imposition of voting qualifications and the provision or administration of governmental services, such as public schools, public housing and law enforcement.

---

7. For the historical evidence suggesting that the sponsors and supporters of the Amendment were primarily interested in augmenting the power of Congress, rather than the judiciary, see generally Jacobus tenBroek, *The Antislavery Origins of the Fourteenth Amendment* 187–217 (1951). [But see Robert A. Burt, *Miranda and Title II: A Morganatic Marriage*, 1969 Sup.Ct.Rev. 81–100.]

9. In fact, earlier drafts of the proposed Amendment employed the "necessary and proper" terminology to describe the scope of congressional power under the Amendment. The substitution of the "appropriate legislation" formula was never thought to have the effect of diminishing the scope of this congressional power. See, e.g., Cong. Globe, 42d Cong., 1st Sess., App. 83 * * *. [But see Note, *Theories of Federalism and Civil Rights*, 75 Yale L.J. 1007, 1046 n. 200 (1966). Compare discussion in *Argument: The Oral Argument*

Before the Supreme Court in Brown v. Board of Education of Topeka, 1952–55, 93–94 (Friedman ed. 1969).]

10. Contrary to the suggestion of the dissent, § 5 does not grant Congress power to exercise discretion in the other direction and to enact "statutes so as in effect to dilute equal protection and due process decisions of this Court." We emphasize that Congress' power under § 5 is limited to adopting measures to enforce the guarantees of the Amendment; § 5 grants Congress no power to restrict, abrogate, or dilute these guarantees. Thus, for example, an enactment authorizing the States to establish racially segregated systems of education would not be—as required by § 5—a measure "to enforce" the Equal Protection Clause since that clause of its own force prohibits such state laws.

Section 4(e) may be readily seen as "plainly adapted" to furthering these aims of the Equal Protection Clause. The practical effect of § 4(e) is to prohibit New York from denying the right to vote to large segments of its Puerto Rican community [—the] right that is "preservative of all rights." This enhanced political power will be helpful in gaining nondiscriminatory treatment in public services for the entire Puerto Rican community.[11] Section 4(e) thereby enables the Puerto Rican minority better to obtain "perfect equality of civil rights and equal protection of the laws." [It] was for Congress, as the branch that made this judgment, to assess and weigh the various conflicting considerations—the risk or pervasiveness of the discrimination in governmental services, the effectiveness of eliminating the state restriction on the right to vote as a means of dealing with the evil, the adequacy or availability of alternative remedies, and the nature and significance of the state interests that would be affected by the nullification of the English literacy requirement * * *. It is not for us to review the congressional resolution of these factors. It is enough that we be able to perceive a basis upon which the Congress might resolve the conflict as it did. There plainly was such a [basis]. Any contrary conclusion would require us to be blind to the realities familiar to the legislators.

The result is no different if we confine our inquiry to the question whether § 4(e) was merely legislation aimed at the elimination of an invidious discrimination in establishing voter qualifications. We are told that New York's English literacy requirement originated in the desire to provide an incentive for non-English speaking immigrants to learn the English language and in order to assure the intelligent exercise of the franchise. Yet Congress might well have questioned, in light of the many exemptions provided,[13] and some evidence suggesting that prejudice played a prominent role in the enactment of the requirement,[14] whether these were actually the interests being served. Congress might have also questioned whether denial of a right deemed so precious and fundamental in our society was a necessary or appropriate means of encouraging persons to learn English, or of furthering the goal of an intelligent exercise of the franchise.[15] Finally, Congress might well have concluded that as a means of furthering the intelligent exercise of the franchise, an ability to read or understand Spanish is as

---

11. Cf. * * * *United States v. Darby*, that the power of Congress to regulate interstate commerce "extends to those activities intra-state which so affect interstate commerce or the exercise of the power of Congress over it as to make regulation of them appropriate means to the attainment of a legitimate end * * *."

13. The principal exemption complained of is that for persons who had been eligible to vote before January 1, 1922.

14. This evidence consists in part of statements made in the Constitutional Convention first considering the English literacy requirement * * *. Congress was aware of this evidence. See, e.g., *Literacy Tests and Voter Requirements in Federal and State Elections*, Senate Hearings 507–513; *Voting Rights*, House Hearings 508–513.

15. Other States have found ways of assuring an intelligent exercise of the franchise short of total disenfranchisement of persons not literate in English. For example, in Ha-

waii, where literacy in either English or Hawaiian suffices, candidates' names may be printed in both languages; New York itself already provides assistance for those exempt from the literacy requirement and are literate in no language; and, of course, the problem of assuring the intelligent exercise of the franchise has been met by those States, more than 30 in number, that have no literacy requirement at all. Section 4(e) does not preclude resort to these alternative methods of assuring the intelligent exercise of the franchise. True, the statute precludes, for a certain class, disenfranchisement and thus limits the States' choice of means of satisfying a purported state interest. But our cases have held that the States can be required to tailor carefully the means of satisfying a legitimate state interest when fundamental liberties and rights are threatened, see, e.g., *Carrington v. Rash; Harper v. Virginia Board of Elections* [p. 1231 supra]; *United States v. Carolene Products Co.* [Ch. 1, I supra]; and Congress is free to apply the same principle in the exercise of its powers.

effective as ability to read English for those to whom Spanish-language newspapers and Spanish-language radio and television programs are available to inform them of election issues and governmental affairs.[16] Since Congress undertook to legislate so as to preclude the enforcement of the state law, and did so in the context of a general appraisal of literacy requirements for voting, see *South Carolina v. Katzenbach,* to which it brought a specially informed legislative competence,[17] it was Congress' prerogative to weigh these competing considerations. Here again, it is enough that we perceive a basis upon which Congress might predicate a judgment that the application of New York's English literacy requirement * * * constituted an invidious discrimination in violation of the Equal Protection Clause.

[The Court rejected the contention that the "American-flag schools" limitation itself violates "the letter and spirit of the Constitution"].

Reversed.

Justice Harlan, whom Justice Stewart joins, dissenting.

[Harlan, J., first argued that the New York law was not forbidden by the equal protection clause itself.] I believe the Court has confused the issue of how much enforcement power Congress possesses under § 5 with the distinct issue of what questions are appropriate for congressional determination and what questions are essentially judicial in nature.

When recognized state violations of federal constitutional standards have occurred, Congress is of course empowered by § 5 to take appropriate remedial measures * * *. But it is a judicial question whether the condition with which Congress has thus sought to deal is in truth an infringement of the Constitution, something that is the necessary prerequisite to bringing the § 5 power into play at all. Thus, in *Ex parte Virginia,* involving a federal statute making it a federal crime to disqualify anyone from jury service because of race, the Court first held as a matter of constitutional law that "the Fourteenth Amendment secures [an] impartial jury trial, by jurors indifferently selected or chosen without discrimination against such jurors because of their color." Only then did the Court hold that to enforce this prohibition upon state discrimination, Congress could enact a criminal statute of the type under consideration. [In] *South Carolina v. Katzenbach,* [we] reviewed first the "voluminous legislative history" as well as judicial precedents supporting the basic congressional finding that the clear commands of the Fifteenth Amendment had been infringed by various state subterfuges. Given the existence of the evil, we held the remedial steps taken by the legislature under the Enforcement Clause of the Fifteenth Amendment to be a justifiable exercise of congressional initiative.

[The] question here is not whether the statute is appropriate remedial legislation to cure an established violation of a constitutional command, but whether there has in fact been an infringement of that constitutional command, that is, whether a particular state practice or, as here, a statute is so arbitrary or irrational as to offend the command of [equal protection]. That question is one

---

16. See, e.g., 111 Cong.Rec. 10675 (May 20, 1965), 15102 (July 6, 1965), 15666 (July 9, 1965). The record in this case includes affidavits describing the nature of New York's two major Spanish-language newspapers [and] its three full-time Spanish-language radio stations and affidavits from those who have campaigned in Spanish speaking areas.

17. See, e.g., 111 Cong.Rec. 10676 (Senator Long of Louisiana and Senator Young), 10678 (Senator Holland) (May 20, 1965), drawing on their experience with voters literate in a language other than English. * * *

for the judicial branch ultimately to determine. [In] view of [*Lassiter*], I do not think it is open to Congress to limit the effect of that decision as it has undertaken to do by § 4(e). In effect the Court reads § 5 of the Fourteenth Amendment as giving Congress the power to define the *substantive* scope of the Amendment. If that indeed be the true reach of § 5, then I do not see why Congress should not be able as well to exercise its § 5 "discretion" by enacting statutes so as in effect to dilute equal protection and due process decisions of this Court. In all such cases there is room for reasonable men to differ as to whether or not a denial of equal protection or due process has occurred, and the final decision is one of judgment. Until today this judgment has always been one for the judiciary to resolve.

I do not mean to suggest in what has been said that a legislative judgment of the type incorporated in § 4(e) is without any force whatsoever. Decisions on questions of equal protection and due process are based not on abstract logic, but on empirical foundations. To the extent "legislative facts" are relevant to a judicial determination, Congress is well equipped to investigate them, and such determinations are of course entitled to due respect.[a] In *South Carolina v. Katzenbach,* such legislative findings were made to show that racial discrimination in voting was actually occurring. Similarly, in *Heart of Atlanta Motel, Inc. v. United States,* the congressional determination that racial discrimination in a clearly defined group of public accommodations did effectively impede interstate commerce was based on "voluminous testimony" which had been put before the Congress and in the context of which it passed remedial legislation.

But no such factual data provide a legislative record supporting § 4(e)[9] by way of showing that Spanish-speaking citizens are fully as capable of making informed decisions in a New York election as are English-speaking citizens. Nor was there any showing whatever to support the Court's alternative argument that § 4(e) should be viewed as but a remedial measure designed to cure or assure against unconstitutional discrimination of other varieties, e.g., in "public schools, public housing and law enforcement" * * *.

Thus, we have [here] what can at most be called a legislative announcement that Congress believes a state law to entail an unconstitutional deprivation of equal protection. Although this kind of declaration is of course entitled to the most respectful consideration, coming as it does from a concurrent branch and one that is knowledgeable in matters of popular political participation, I do not believe it lessens our responsibility to decide the fundamental issue of whether in fact the state enactment violates federal constitutional rights.

In assessing the deference we should give to this kind of congressional expression of policy, it is relevant that the judiciary has always given to congressional enactments a presumption of validity. However, it is also a canon of judicial review that state statutes are given a similar presumption, [and] although it has been suggested that this Court should give somewhat more deference to

---

a. For the view that "Congress cannot alter the *normative component* of a judicial decision" but that "the *empirical component* [is] the province of Congress," see Irving Gordon, *The Nature and Uses of Congressional Power Under Section Five of the Fourteenth Amendment to Overcome Decisions of the Supreme Court,* 72 Nw.U.L.Rev. 656 (1977). See note 7(b) infra.

9. There were no committee hearings or reports referring to this section, which was introduced from the floor during debate on the full Voting Rights Act.

Congress than to a State Legislature,[10] such a simple weighing of presumptions is hardly a satisfying way of resolving a matter that touches the distribution of state and federal power in an area so sensitive as that of the regulation of the franchise. Rather it should be recognized that while the Fourteenth Amendment is a "brooding omnipresence" over all state legislation, the substantive matters which it touches are all within the primary legislative competence of the States. Federal authority, legislative no less than judicial, does not intrude unless there has been a denial by state action of Fourteenth Amendment [limitations]. At least in the area of primary state concern a state statute that passes constitutional muster under the judicial standard of rationality should not be permitted to be set at naught by a mere contrary congressional pronouncement unsupported by a legislative record justifying that conclusion. * * *

Notes and Questions

1. *Congress and equal protection.* After *Morgan,* may Congress enact legislation prohibiting *all* state discrimination on the basis of alienage, illegitimacy and gender? Cf. Ch. 10, Sec. 3. Forbidding state discrimination against master antenna cable TV systems, opticians, debt adjustors and methadone users? Cf. Ch. 10, Sec. 1. Requiring that, in all instances in which state action has a racially disproportionate impact, the courts should balance the strength of the government interest against the disadvantage imposed on the racial minority? Cf. Ch. 10, Sec. 2, IV. For the view that, since the Court "underenforces" the provisions of § 1 of the fourteenth amendment because of "institutional" reasons "based upon questions of propriety or capacity," Congress has "the authority to enact legislation which fills in that body's conception" of those provisions, see Lawrence G. Sager, *Fair Measure: The Legal Status of Underenforced Constitutional Norms,* 91 Harv.L.Rev. 1212 (1978). For the view that "Congress may expand the judiciary's role by identifying additional suspect classes and fundamental rights and by increasing the level of scrutiny in specified types of equal protection cases," see Stephen F. Ross, *Legislative Enforcement of Equal Protection,* 72 Minn.L.Rev. 311, 335 (1987).

After *Morgan,* may Congress outlaw *all* age and residence requirements for voting? Consider Alexander M. Bickel, *The Voting Rights Cases,* 1966 Sup.Ct. Rev. 79, 100: "[S]uppose Congress decided that aliens or eighteen-year-olds or residents of New Jersey are being discriminated against in New York. The decision would be as plausible as the one concerning Spanish-speaking Puerto Ricans. Could Congress give these groups the vote? If Congress may freely bestow the vote as a means of curing other discriminations, which it fears may be practiced against groups deprived of the vote, essentially because of this deprivation and on the basis of no other evidence, then there is nothing left of state autonomy in setting qualifications for voting."

2. *Analogy to commerce power.* On the scope of Congress' power under the commerce clause, is Congress' discretion limited to determining what are "appropriate means" for regulating intrastate commerce that affects commerce in more than one state, or does it extend to determining *whether* intrastate commerce affects commerce in more than one state? See Comment, 20 Rutg.L.Rev. 826 (1966). Is the *Morgan* standard of judicial review of Congress' power under § 5 the same as the standard for reviewing Congress' power under the commerce clause? Consider Cox, p. 1386 supra, at 104: "Conclusory but qualifying phrases

---

10. See James B. Thayer, *The Origin and Scope of the American Doctrine of Constitutional Law,* 7 Harv.L.Rev. 129, 154–155 (1893).

like 'reasonable relation' and 'rational' are notably absent from the opinion, in contrast to the public accommodations and voting rights cases where [the opinions] were limited by the need to use terms acceptable to a unanimous bench. It is sufficient that the law 'may be viewed' as a measure for securing equal protection and that the Court can 'perceive a basis' upon which Congress might predicate its judgment. The choice of words cannot have been casual. Evidently, the Court intends to validate any legislation under section 5—at least any legislation dealing with state action—without judging the substantiality of its relation to a permissible federal objective."

3. *Need for a "legislative record."* What of Harlan, J.'s suggestion that other broad exertions of congressional power have been sustained only on the basis of "factual data" or "voluminous testimony"? Consider Cox, supra, at 105: "[His view] is at odds with the presumption of constitutionality and with a long line of precedents holding that a statute must be judged constitutional if any set of facts which can reasonably be conceived would sustain it. No case has ever held that a record is constitutionally required. [The] principle is not merely one of deference to Congress or the states. It rests upon appreciation of the fact that the fundamental basis for legislative action is the knowledge, experience, and judgment of the people's representatives only a small part, or even none, of which may come from the hearings and reports of committees or debates upon the floor."

4. *Congress and procedural due process.* After *Morgan,* may Congress impose the federal rules of civil and criminal procedure on the states on the ground that the fourteenth amendment requires that due process be accorded all litigants and that in "its discretion" the federal rules are "needed to secure the guarantees of the Fourteenth Amendment"? Apart from "specific" constitutional prohibitions, under *Morgan,* what are the limits of congressional power? See Note, *Congressional Power to Enforce Due Process Rights,* 80 Colum.L.Rev. 1265 (1980).

5. *Congress and substantive due process.* May Congress enact the proposed Freedom of Choice Act (FOCA), H.R. 25, 102d Cong., 1st Sess. (1991); S. 25, 102d Cong.2d Sess. (1992), which would respond to *Planned Parenthood v. Casey,* p. 363 supra, by codifying the holding of *Roe v. Wade?* May Congress grant a federal right to "abortion on demand"? Is the Religious Freedom Restoration Act (RFRA), p. 1031 supra—which responded to *Employment Division v. Smith* by adopting "the compelling interest test as set forth in *Sherbert* and *Yoder"*—within Congress' power? See Daniel O. Conkle, *The Religious Freedom Restoration Act: The Constitutional Significance of an Unconstitutional Statute,* 56 Mont.L.Rev. 39, 41–70 (1995): Does RFRA simply respond to the Court's "institutional concerns" in *Smith*—"that the judiciary is unsuited to decide when religious claimants are entitled to exemptions from neutral laws," Joanne C. Brant, *Taking the Supreme Court at Its Word: The Implications for RFRA and Separation of Powers,* 56 Mont.L.Rev. (1995)—and therefore not involve congressional definition of the "substantive" scope of the first or fourteenth amendments? Is this also true of FOCA? For the view that under "the text and history of the First Amendment," Congress "cannot prescribe the substantive content of first amendment rights in the states," see Jay S. Bybee, *Taking Liberties With the First Amendment: Congress, Section 5, and the Religious Freedom Restoration Act,* 48 Vand.L.Rev. 1539 (1995).

6. *Congress and state action.* If *Morgan* gives Congress "the power to define the *substantive* scope" of equal protection (and due process), does it similarly permit Congress to determine the question of what constitutes "state action"?

For example, might Congress, in "exercise of its discretion," determine that any judicial enforcement of racial discrimination shall be prohibited? That racial discrimination in the sale and rental of housing exists because of the failure of the states to make such discrimination illegal, and that this state "inaction" is state action under the fourteenth amendment that should "appropriately" be "remedied" by federal fair housing legislation? See fn. 8 in Brennan, J.'s opinion in *Guest*.

(a) For another post-*Morgan* approach re federal housing legislation, consider Cox, supra, at 120: "So long as Negroes are confined to racial ghettos, there will be actual or dangerously potential state discrimination in the quantity or quality of public services. First, the isolation of unpopular minorities in poverty-stricken, socially and economically isolated neighborhoods, lacking political influence, invites a lower quality of state services just as withholding the vote from many citizens in Puerto Rican neighborhoods made it less likely that they would receive equal services. Second, the very existence of the ghetto renders it more difficult [for] a state to provide equal services. Children in black ghettos, with an inferior cultural and economic background, lack the environment and associations essential to truly equal educational opportunity. [*Morgan* held that] Congress might legislate to remove an obstacle to the state's performance of its constitutional duty not to discriminate in providing public services, even though the immediate subject matter of the legislation—there the requirement of English literacy—was not itself a violation of the fourteenth amendment. It follows that Congress may likewise legislate to eliminate racial ghettos as obstacles to the states' performance of that same constitutional duty, even though the immediate subject matter of this legislation—the practices that result in ghettos—do not themselves involve violations of the fourteenth amendment. The only important difference is that in *Morgan* the obstacle was itself a state law whereas discrimination in housing has a private origin. [But] that difference in the source of the threat to performance of the state's obligation is irrelevant." [b]

(b) *Civil Rights Act of 1968, Title VIII: Fair Housing.* After declaring "the policy of the United States to provide, within constitutional limitations, for fair housing throughout the United States" (42 U.S.C.A. § 3601), the Act makes unlawful various discriminations "because of race, color, religion, or national origin" (§ 3604) "in the sale or rental of housing" that is "owned or operated by the Federal Government," or financed or supported by various federal programs (§ 3603(a)). It is also applicable "to all other dwellings" *except* "any single family house" when its owner then "does not own" nor have "any interest in" "more than three such," *and* the private owner does not use a real estate broker, or advertising that states a discriminatory preference (§ 3603(b)(1)). § 3603(b)(2) further exempts "rooms or units in dwellings containing living quarters occupied or intended to be occupied by no more than four families living independently of each other, if the owner actually maintains and occupies one of such living quarters as his residence." § 3607 permits certain sales and rentals by "religious" groups to be limited "to persons of the same religion" "unless membership in such religion is restricted on account of race, color, or national origin" and permits "a private club" that "provides lodgings" to limit them "to its members." Constitutional?

7. *Congressional dilution of fourteenth amendment rights.* (a) After *Morgan*, does Congress have power "to dilute equal protection and due process

b. See also Notes, *Toward Limits on Congressional Enforcement Power Under the Civil War Amendments,* 34 Stan.L.Rev. 453 (1982); *Congressional Power Under Section Five of the Fourteenth Amendment,* 25 Stan.L.Rev. 885 (1973).

decisions" of the Court? Consider Cox, supra, at 106 n. 86: "According to the conventional theory [enunciated in fn. 10 of *Morgan*], the Court has invalidated state statutes under the due process and equal protection clauses only when no state of facts which can reasonably be conceived would sustain them. Where that is true, a congressional effort to withdraw the protection granted by the clause would lack the foundation of a reasonably conceivable set of facts and would therefore be just as invalid as the state legislation. But while that is true in the realm of economic regulation, the Court has often substituted its own evaluation of actual conditions in reviewing legislation dealing with 'preferred rights.' It is hard to see how the Court can consistently give weight to the congressional judgment in expanding the definition of equal protection in the area of human rights but refuse to give it weight in narrowing the definition where the definition depends upon appraisal of the facts." Does the "answer" lie in a theory that justifies judicial review principally on the need to afford protection to certain minority "rights" from the majority will? Consider William Cohen, *Congressional Power to Interpret Due Process and Equal Protection*, 27 Stan.L.Rev. 603, 614 (1975): "[A] theory that distinguishes between congressional competence to make 'liberty' and 'federalism' judgments resolves the dilemma. A congressional judgment rejecting a judicial interpretation of the due process or equal protection clauses—an interpretation that had given the individual procedural or substantive protection from state and federal government alike—is entitled to no more deference than the identical decision of a state legislature.[c] Congress is no more immune to momentary passions of the majority than are the state legislatures. But a congressional judgment resolving at the national level an issue that could— without constitutional objection—be decided in the same way at the state level, ought normally to be binding on the courts, since Congress presumably reflects a balance between both national and state interests and hence is better able to adjust such conflicts." See also Jesse H. Choper, *Judicial Review and the National Political Process* 198–200 (1980). For the view that this reasoning is supported by both constitutional structure and original intent, see Douglas Laycock, *RFRA, Congress, and the Ratchet*, 56 Mont.L.Rev. 145, 157–165 (1995).

In MISSISSIPPI UNIV. FOR WOMEN v. HOGAN, p. 1202 supra, "the State contended that Congress, in enacting [the] Education Amendments of 1972, expressly had authorized MUW to continue its single-sex admissions policy by exempting public undergraduate institutions that traditionally have used single-sex admissions policies from the gender discrimination prohibition of Title IX. Through that provision, the State argued, Congress limited the reach of the Fourteenth Amendment by exercising its power under § 5 of the Amendment." The Court, relying on fn. 10 of *Morgan,* responded: "Although we give deference to congressional decisions and classifications, neither Congress nor a State can validate a law that denies the rights guaranteed by the Fourteenth Amendment." The four dissenting justices did not address the issue.

(b) *Competence as to "facts."* Does *Miranda v. Arizona*, 384 U.S. 436, 10 Ohio Misc. 9, 86 S.Ct. 1602, 16 L.Ed.2d 694 (1966), rest on the *factual* assumption that there is "compulsion inherent in custodial surroundings" and thus "no statement obtained from the defendant can truly be the product of his free choice"? Does *Mapp v. Ohio*, p. 386 supra, rest on the *factual* assumption that the exclusionary rule is a "deterrent safeguard without insistence upon which the

---

c. For the view that equal protection challenges to congressional action should be judged by a more lenient (but not "toothless") standard of review than state action, see Robert A. Bohrer, *Bakke, Weber and Fullilove: Benign Discrimination and Congressional Power to Enforce the Fourteenth Amendment*, 56 Ind.L.J. 473 (1981).

Fourth Amendment would have been reduced to 'a form of words'"? Does *Gideon v. Wainwright,* 372 U.S. 335, 83 S.Ct. 792, 9 L.Ed.2d 799 (1963), rest on the *factual* assumption that a person "who is too poor to hire a lawyer, cannot be assured a fair trial unless counsel is provided for him"? Does *Brown v. Board of Education,* p. 1078 supra, rest on the *factual* assumption that racially "separate educational facilities are inherently unequal"? Does *Planned Parenthood v. Casey* rest on *factual* assumptions that "informed consent" requirements and 24–hour waiting periods do *not* "impose an undue burden on a woman's abortion right"? See generally Ira C. Lupu, *Statutes Revolving in Constitutional Law Orbits,* 79 Va.L.Rev. 1, 37–46 (1993). If so, may Congress, pursuant to § 5, find the *facts* to be otherwise and legislate a contrary rule? See S.Rep. No. 1097, 90th Cong., 2d Sess. 59–63 (1968).

(c) *Line-drawing.* What deference is owed congressional action, pursuant to § 5, that precisely defines (i) how long a delay constitutes denial of the "right to a speedy trial," see *Barker v. Wingo,* 407 U.S. 514, 92 S.Ct. 2182, 33 L.Ed.2d 101 (1972); (ii) how great a deviation from absolute population equality among legislative districts constitutes a violation of the "one person-one vote" requirement, see Ch. 10, Sec. 1, A?

(d) *Conflicting constitutional provisions.* May de facto racial segregation in the schools arguably violate equal protection; may use of racial criteria to alleviate de facto segregation arguably violate equal protection (see Ch. 10, Secs. 2, III and 2, V? If so, what deference is owed congressional action, pursuant to § 5, dealing with these matters? See opinion of White, J., in *Welsh v. United States,* p. 1047 supra.

(e) *Rights vs. remedies.* May Congress, pursuant to § 5, withdraw (or replace) the "exclusionary rule" of *Mapp v. Ohio* on the ground that this does not "dilute" any substantive constitutional right but merely modifies a remedy for its violation? On similar analysis, may Congress forbid busing (or substitute alternatives) to remedy school segregation? See fn. a, p. 1110 supra. Consider Note, *The Nixon Busing Bills and Constitutional Power,* 81 Yale L.J. 1542, 1570–71 (1972): "Because busing is one remedy among many, Robert Bork [*Constitutionality of the President's Busing Proposals* 21–22 (1972)] argues [that the anti-busing bill] leaves intact the duty *Brown* imposed upon formerly segregated school districts. Such an argument creates an artificial distinction between rights and remedies; the right which cannot be vindicated is not a right at all, and the most that can be said for the distinction is that it may be useful where a right can be vindicated in several ways. [If] busing is in some cases—as it was in *Swann*—the only remedy that would produce desegregation in any real sense, then Bork's argument falls. The real question about the constitutionality of the busing bills is the question that Bork hesitates to answer directly: to what extent does the Equal Protection Clause require that once segregated schools achieve a racial balance? *Swann,* of course, had a simple and direct answer: to the greatest extent possible." See also Ronald D. Rotunda, *Congressional Power to Restrict the Jurisdiction of the Lower Federal Courts and the Problem of School Busing,* 64 Geo.L.J. 839 (1976).

For the view that many judicial decisions implementing constitutional rights are not "true constitutional interpretations" but rather only "constitutional common law" rules that may be modified by Congress, see Henry P. Monaghan, *Constitutional Common Law,* 89 Harv.L.Rev. 1 (1975). Compare Thomas S. Schrock & Robert C. Welsh, *Reconsidering the Constitutional Common Law,* 91 Harv.L.Rev. 1117 (1978).

(f) *Definition of "dilution."* If Congress believed that more wrongdoers would be convicted and crime deterred by changing the *Miranda* rule, would such legislation "dilute" the due process rights of the accused, or "secure" the rights of the public generally not to be denied life or property without due process of law? Who should *ultimately* determine these issues? See generally J. Edmond Nathanson, *Congressional Power to Contradict the Supreme Court's Constitutional Decisions. Accommodation of Rights in Conflict,* 27 Wm. & M.L.Rev. 331 (1986).

(g) *"Human Life Bill."* What of the constitutionality of the following proposed statute, S. 158 and H.R. 900, 97th Cong., 1st Sess. (1981):

"Sec. 1. The Congress finds that present day scientific evidence indicates a significant likelihood that actual human life exists from conception.

"The Congress further finds that the fourteenth amendment to the Constitution of the United States was intended to protect all human beings.

"Upon the basis of these findings, and in the exercise of the powers of the Congress, including its power under section 5 of the fourteenth amendment to the Constitution of the United States, the Congress hereby declares that for the purpose of enforcing the obligation of the States under the fourteenth amendment not to deprive persons of life without due process of law, human life shall be deemed to exist from conception, without regard to race, sex, age, health, defect, or condition of dependency; and for this purpose 'person' shall include all human life as defined herein. * * * " [d]

(i) *Questions of "fact."* Do the issues of when "human life" begins and what is a "person" involve questions of fact? Consider Laurence H. Tribe, *Prepared Statement,* Hearings on S. 158 at 251: "Such questions [call] at bottom for normative judgments no less profound than those involved in defining 'liberty' or 'equality.' [They] entail 'question[s] to which science can provide no answer,' as the National Academy of Sciences itself acknowledged * * *. Congress cannot transform an issue of religion, morality, and law into one of fact by waving the magic wand of Section 5 [which] no more authorizes Congress to transmute a matter of values into a matter of scientific observation than it authorizes Congress to announce a mathematical formula for human freedom." See also Archibald Cox, *Prepared Statement,* id. at 340–41.

(ii) *"Dilution" vs. "expansion."* Does the Bill dilute the right to an abortion? Consider John T. Noonan, Jr., *Prepared Statement,* id. at 266–67: "In recognizing the unborn as persons, [the] Act treats no one unequally but gives equal protection to one class of humanity now unequally treated. * * * Necessarily, the expression of the rights of one class of human beings has an impact on the rights of others. The elimination of literacy tests in this way 'diluted' the voting rights of the literate. It is inescapable that congressional expression of the right to life will have an impact on the abortion right; but in the eyes of Congress, [there] will be a net gain for Fourteenth Amendment rights by the expansion and the attendant diminution."

---

d. For argument in favor of its validity, see Stephen H. Galebach, *A Human Life Statute,* 7 Human Life Rev. 3 (1981), reprinted in Hearings on S. 158, before the Subcomm. on Separation of Powers of the Senate Comm. on the Judiciary, 97th Cong., 1st Sess. 205 (1981); Thomas Nagel, *Prepared Statement,* id. 321. For exhaustive consideration, see Samuel Estr- eicher, *Congressional Power and Constitutional Rights: Reflections on Proposed "Human Life" Legislation,* 68 Va.L.Rev. 333 (1982). For an "institutional" perspective, see Stephen L. Carter, *The Morgan "Power" and the Forced Reconsideration of Constitutional Decisions,* 53 U.Chi.L.Rev. 819 (1986).

OREGON v. MITCHELL

400 U.S. 112, 91 S.Ct. 260, 27 L.Ed.2d 272 (1970).

[In original jurisdiction suits, brought by Oregon and Texas against the Attorney General and by the United States against Arizona and Idaho, the states challenged Congress' power to enact Titles II and III of the Voting Rights Act Amendments of 1970. (1) Section 302 forbade states to deny any citizen, otherwise qualified to vote, the right to vote in any federal, state or local election "on account of age if such citizen is eighteen years of age or older." Black, Douglas, Brennan, White and Marshall, JJ., voted to uphold this provision as to federal elections; Burger, C.J., and Black, Harlan, Stewart and Blackmun, JJ., voted to hold it unconstitutional as to state and local elections. (2) Section 201 extended the Voting Rights Act of 1965 for an additional five years (to 1975) and also extended nationwide § 4(a)'s prohibition of "any test or device" (including literacy tests) "as a prerequisite for voting or registration." This was upheld unanimously.[a] (3) Sec. 202 abolished any state "durational residency requirement as a precondition to voting for President and Vice President" and required uniform rules for the provision of "absentee ballots". Only Harlan, J., voted to hold this provision invalid.]

JUSTICE BLACK, announcing the judgments of the Court in an opinion expressing his own view of the cases.

[T]he responsibility of the States for setting the qualifications of voters in congressional elections [in Art. I, § 2] was made subject to the power of Congress to make or alter such regulations [in Art. I, § 4].[b] * * * Similarly, it is the prerogative of Congress to oversee the conduct of presidential and vice presidential elections and to set the qualifications for voters for electors for those offices. It cannot be seriously contended that Congress has less power over the conduct of presidential elections than it has over congressional elections.[7]

On the other hand, [n]o function is more essential to the separate and independent existence of the States [than] the power to determine within the limits of the Constitution the qualifications of their own voters for state, county, and municipal [offices]. Amendments Fourteen, Fifteen, Nineteen, and Twenty-Four, each of which has assumed that the States had general supervisory power over state elections, are examples of express limitations on the power of the States to govern themselves. * * *

In enacting the 18-year-old vote provisions of the Act now before the Court, Congress made no legislative findings that 21-year-old vote requirements were used by the States to disenfranchise voters on account of race. I seriously doubt

---

a. In 1975, the Act was amended to extend for an additional seven years, to make § 4(a)'s suspension of "any test or device" indefinite, and to greatly expand the geographic coverage (including, inter alia, areas with at least 5% language minorities) of the requirement that new voting regulations be reviewed by the Attorney General or a federal court. See generally David E. Hunter, *The 1975 Voting Rights Act and Language Minorities,* 25 Cath. U.L.Rev. 250 (1976). The seven year extension was upheld in *Rome v. United States,* note 4 infra. In 1982, the Act's preclearance mechanism was extended for 25 years.

b. Could the substance of the 24th amendment, barring payment of a poll tax as a condition to vote in federal elections, have been enacted simply by a federal statute?

7. [I]nherent in the very concept of a supreme national government with national officers is a residual power in Congress to insure that those officers represent their national constituency as responsively as possible. This power arises from the nature of our constitutional system of government and from the Necessary and Proper Clause.

that such a finding, if made, could be supported by substantial evidence. Since Congress has attempted to invade an area preserved to the States by the Constitution without a foundation for enforcing the Civil War Amendments' ban on racial discrimination, I would hold that Congress has exceeded its powers in attempting to lower the voting age in state and local elections. On the other hand, [i]n enacting the literacy test ban of Title II Congress had before it a long history of the discriminatory use of literacy tests to disfranchise voters on account of their race. [A]s to the Nation as a whole, Congress had before it statistics which demonstrate that voter registration and voter participation are consistently greater in States without literacy tests.

Congress also had before it this country's history of discriminatory educational opportunities in both the North and the South. [There] is substantial, if not overwhelming, evidence from which Congress could have concluded that it is a denial of equal protection to condition the political participation of children educated in a dual school system upon their educational achievement. [Finally in enacting the residency and absentee voting] regulations for national elections Congress was attempting to insure a fully effective voice to all citizens in national elections. What I said [about Congress' power to regulate federal elections] applies with equal force here. * * *

JUSTICE BRENNAN, JUSTICE WHITE, and JUSTICE MARSHALL dissent from the judgment insofar as it declares § 302 unconstitutional as applied to state and local elections * * *.

[Residency:] Whether or not the Constitution vests Congress with particular power to set qualifications for voting in strictly federal elections, we believe there is an adequate constitutional basis for § 202 in § 5 of the Fourteenth Amendment. [A] durational residence requirement operates to penalize those persons, and only those persons, who have exercised their constitutional right of interstate migration. [I]n such a case, governmental action may withstand constitutional scrutiny only upon a clear showing that the burden imposed is necessary to protect a compelling and substantial governmental interest. *Shapiro v. Thompson* [p. 1276 supra]. [W]e find ample justification for the congressional conclusion that § 202 is a reasonable means for eliminating an unnecessary burden on the right of interstate migration. *Guest.*

[Age:] We believe there is serious question whether a statute [denying] the franchise to citizens [between] the ages of 18 and 21 could, in any event, withstand present scrutiny under the Equal Protection Clause. Regardless of the answer to this question, however, it is clear to us that proper regard for the special function of Congress in making determinations of legislative fact compels this Court to respect those determinations unless they are contradicted by evidence far stronger than anything that has been adduced in these [cases.]

A. [W]hen exclusions from the franchise are challenged as violating [equal protection] "the Court must determine whether the exclusions are necessary to promote a compelling state interest."

In the present cases, the States justify exclusion of 18- to 21-year-olds from the voting rolls solely on the basis of the States' interests in promoting intelligent and responsible exercise of the franchise. [But each] of the 50 States has provided special mechanisms for dealing with persons who are deemed insufficiently mature and intelligent to understand, and to conform their behavior to, the criminal laws of the State. Forty-nine of the States have concluded that, in this regard, 18-year-olds are invariably to be dealt with according to precisely the same standards prescribed for their elders [in] the critically important matter of criminal responsibility. Similarly, every State permits 18-year-olds to marry, and 39 States do not require parental consent for such persons of one or both sexes. [No] State in the Union requires attendance at school beyond the age of 18. [T]hat 18-year-olds as a class may be less educated than some of their elders cannot justify restriction of the franchise for the States themselves have determined that this incremental education is irrelevant to voting qualifications. And finally, we have been cited to no material whatsoever that would support the proposition that intelligence, as opposed to educational attainment, increases between the ages of 18 and 21.

[No] State seeking to uphold its denial of the franchise to 18-year-olds has adduced anything beyond the mere difference in age. [But] perhaps more important is the uniform experience of those States—Georgia since 1943, and Kentucky since 1955—that have permitted 18-year-olds to vote. [E]very person who spoke to the issue in either the House or Senate was agreed that 18-year-olds in both States were at least as interested, able, and responsible in voting as were their elders. * * *

B. [When] a state legislative classification is subjected to judicial challenge as violating the Equal Protection Clause, it comes before the courts cloaked by the presumption that the legislature has, as it should, acted within constitutional limitations. [But] this limitation on judicial review of state legislative classifications is a limitation stemming not from the Fourteenth Amendment itself, but from the nature of [the] judicial process [which] makes it an inappropriate forum for the determination of complex factual questions of the kind so often involved in constitutional adjudication. [Should Congress, however, pursuant to § 5] undertake an investigation in order to determine whether the factual basis necessary to support a state legislative discrimination actually exists, it need not stop once it determines that some reasonable men could believe the factual basis exists. Section 5 empowers Congress to make its own determination on the matter. See *Morgan.* It should hardly be necessary to add that if the asserted factual basis necessary to support a given state discrimination does not exist, § 5 of the Fourteenth Amendment vests Congress with power to remove the discrimination by appropriate means.

["Where] we find that the legislators, in light of the facts and testimony before them, have a rational basis for finding a chosen regulatory scheme necessary [our] investigation is at an end." *Katzenbach v. McClung; Morgan.*[32] * * *

C. [T]he language of the Fourteenth Amendment [applies] on its face to all assertions of state power, however made. [I]t seems to us, the historical record will not bear the weight our Brother Harlan has placed upon it. [Our] reading of the historical background [results] in a somewhat imperfect picture of an era of constitutional confusion, confusion which the Amendment did little to resolve. [The opinion examines in some detail the historical setting, the "politics of the day," the changes in language of the proposed Amendment made in the Joint Congressional Committee on Reconstruction, and the "obscure" and sometimes "incongruous" statements made in congressional debates, campaign speeches and

---

32. As we emphasized in *Morgan,* "§ 5 does not grant Congress power [to] enact 'statutes so as in effect to dilute equal protection and due process decisions of this Court.'" As indicated above, a decision of this Court striking down a state statute expresses, among other things, our conclusion that the legislative findings upon which the statute is based are so far wrong as to be unreasonable. Unless Congress were to unearth new evidence in its investigation, its identical findings on the identical issue would be no more reasonable than those of the state legislature.

the press. It suggests] that the Amendment was framed by men who possessed differing views on the great question of the suffrage and [who] papered over their differences with the broad, elastic language of § 1 and left to future interpreters of their Amendment the task of resolving in accordance with future vision and future needs the issues which they left unresolved. [Those] who submitted the Fifteenth Amendment [could] well have desired that any prohibition against racial discrimination in voting stand upon a firmer foundation than mere legislative action capable of repeal or the vagaries of judicial decision. [At] least some of the supporters of the Nineteenth Amendment believed that sex discrimination in voting was itself proscribed by the Fourteenth Amendment [and] the Twenty-fourth Amendment was not proposed to the States until this Court had held [that] state laws requiring payment of a poll tax as a prerequisite to voting did not ipso facto violate [equal protection]. Accordingly, we see no reason that the mere enactment of these amendments can be thought to imply that their proponents believed the Fourteenth Amendment did not apply to state allocations of political power. * * *

Nor do we find persuasive our Brother Harlan's argument that § 2 of the Fourteenth Amendment was intended as an exclusive remedy for state restrictions on the franchise * * *. [I]t is at least equally plausible that congressional legislation pursuant to §§ 1 and 5 was thought by the framers of the Amendment to be another potential remedy. Section 2, in such a scheme, is hardly superfluous: it was of critical importance in assuring that, should the Southern States deny the franchise to Negroes, the Congress called upon to remedy that discrimination would not be controlled by the beneficiaries of discrimination themselves. * * *

In sum, Congress had ample evidence upon which it could have based the conclusion [under § 5] that exclusion of citizens 18 to 21 years of age from the franchise is wholly unnecessary to promote any legitimate interest the States may have in assuring intelligent and responsible voting. * * *

JUSTICE HARLAN, concurring in part and dissenting in part.

[Similar to his dissent in *Reynolds v. Sims,* [p. 1241 supra], Harlan, J., argued at length "that the history of the Fourteenth Amendment makes it clear beyond any reasonable doubt" that § 1 was never intended to "reach discriminatory voting qualifications," again emphasizing § 2—providing for reduced congressional representation for states denying 21-year old male citizens the right to vote.[c] [That] constitutional amendments were deemed necessary to bring about federal abolition of state restrictions on voting by reason of race (Amend. XV), sex (Amend. XIX), and, even with respect to federal elections, the failure to pay state poll taxes (Amend. XXIV), is itself forceful evidence of the common understanding in 1869, 1919, and 1962, respectively, that the Fourteenth Amendment did not empower Congress to legislate in these respects. * * *

[Although] Congress' expression of the view that it does have power to alter state suffrage qualifications is entitled to the most respectful consideration by the judiciary, [this] cannot displace the duty of this Court to make an independent determination whether Congress has exceeded its powers. * * *

c. "To be sure, one might argue that § 2 is simply a rhetorical flourish, and that the qualifications listed there are merely the ones which the Framers deemed to be consistent with the alleged prohibition of § 1. This argument is not only unreasonable on its face and untenable in light of the historical record; it is fatal to the validity of the reduction of the voting age [before] us.

"The only sensible explanation of § 2, therefore, is that the racial voter qualifications it was designed to penalize were understood to be permitted by § 1 * * *."

It is suggested that the proper basis for the doctrine enunciated in *Morgan* lies in the relative fact-finding competence of Court, Congress, and state legislatures. [But the] disagreement in these cases revolves around the evaluation [of] largely uncontested factual material. On the assumption that maturity and experience are relevant to intelligent and responsible exercise of the elective franchise, are the immaturity and inexperience of the average 18-, 19-, or 20-year-old sufficiently serious to justify denying such a person a direct voice in decisions affecting his or her life? Whether or not this judgment is characterized as "factual," it calls for striking a balance between incommensurate interests. Where the balance is to be struck depends ultimately on the values and the perspective of the decisionmaker. It is a matter as to which men of good will can and do reasonably differ.

I fully agree that judgments of the sort involved here are beyond the institutional competence and constitutional authority of the judiciary. [But judicial] deference is based, not on relative fact-finding competence, but on due regard for the decision of the body constitutionally appointed to decide. Establishment of voting qualifications is a matter for state legislatures. Assuming any authority at all, only when the Court can say with some confidence that the legislature has demonstrably erred in adjusting the competing interests is it justified in striking down the legislative judgment. * * *

The same considerations apply, and with almost equal force, to Congress' displacement of state decisions with its own ideas of wise policy. The sole distinction between Congress and the Court in this regard is that Congress, being an elective body, presumptively has popular authority for the value judgment it makes. But since the state legislature has a like authority, this distinction between Congress and the judiciary falls short of justifying a congressional veto on the state judgment. The perspectives and values of national legislators on the issue of voting qualifications are likely to differ from those of state legislators, but I see no reason a priori to prefer those of the national figures, whose collective decision, applying nationwide, is necessarily less able to take account of peculiar local conditions. Whether one agrees with this judgment or not, it is the one expressed by the Framers in leaving voter qualifications to the States. The Supremacy Clause does not, as my colleagues seem to argue, represent a judgment that federal decisions are superior to those of the States whenever the two may differ. * * *

JUSTICE STEWART, with whom THE CHIEF JUSTICE and JUSTICE BLACKMUN join, concurring in part and dissenting in part. * * *

[Literacy:] Because the justification for extending the ban on literacy tests to the entire Nation need not turn on whether literacy tests unfairly discriminate against Negroes in every State in the Union, Congress was not required to make state-by-state findings * * *. In the interests of uniformity, Congress may paint with a much broader brush than may this Court, which must confine itself to the judicial function of deciding individual cases and controversies upon individual records. * * * Experience gained under the 1965 Act has now led Congress to conclude that it should go the whole distance. This approach to the problem is a rational one; consequently it is within [the] power of Congress under § 2 of the Fifteenth Amendment. * * *

[Residency:] Contrary to the submission of my Brother Black, Article I, § 4 does not create in the federal legislature the power to alter the constitutionally established qualifications to vote in congressional elections. [The] "manner" of holding elections can hardly be read to mean the *qualifications* for voters, when it is remembered that § 2 of the same Article I explicitly speaks of the "qualifications" for voters in elections to choose Representatives. It is plain, in short, that when the Framers meant qualifications they said "qualifications." That word does not appear in Article I, § 4. Moreover, § 4 does not give Congress the power to do anything that a State might not have done [and] the States are not free to prescribe qualifications for voters in federal elections which differ from those prescribed for the most numerous branch of the state legislature.[d] * * *

* * * I am persuaded that the constitutional provisions discussed above are not sufficient to prevent Congress from protecting a person who exercises his constitutional right to enter and abide in any State in the Union from losing his opportunity to vote, when Congress may protect the right of interstate travel from other less fundamental disabilities. The power of the States with regard to the franchise is subject to the power of the Federal Government to vindicate the unconditional personal rights secured to the citizen by the Federal Constitution. The power which Congress has exercised in enacting § 202 is not a general power to prescribe qualifications for voters in either federal or state elections. It is confined to federal action against a particular problem clearly within the purview of congressional authority. Finally, [w]e should strive to avoid an interpretation of the Constitution that would withhold from Congress the power to legislate for the protection of those constitutional rights which the States are unable effectively to secure. * * *

[Age: Recent] decisions have established that state action regulating suffrage is not immune from the impact of the Equal Protection Clause. But we have been careful in those decisions to note the undoubted power of a State to establish a qualification for voting based on age. See, e.g., *Kramer* [p. 1233 supra]. Indeed, none of the opinions filed today suggest that the States have anything but a constitutionally unimpeachable interest in establishing some age qualification as such. Yet to test the power to establish an age qualification by the "compelling interest" standard is really to deny a State any choice at all, because no State could demonstrate a "compelling interest" in drawing the line with respect to age at one point rather than another. * * *[14]

Morgan does not hold that Congress has the power to determine what are and what are not "compelling state interests" for equal protection purposes. [*Morgan*] upheld the statute on two grounds: that Congress could conclude that enhancing the political power of the Puerto Rican community by conferring the right to vote was an appropriate means of remedying discriminatory treatment in public services; and that Congress could conclude that the New York statute was tainted by the impermissible purpose of denying the right to vote to Puerto Ricans, an undoubted invidious discrimination under the Equal Protection Clause. Both of these decisional grounds were far-reaching. The Court's opinion made clear that Congress could impose on the States a remedy for the denial of equal protection which elaborated upon the direct command of the Constitution, and that it could override state laws on the ground that they were in fact used as instruments of invidious discrimination even though a court in an individual lawsuit might not have reached that factual conclusion.

But it is necessary to go much further to sustain § 302. The state laws which it invalidates do not invidiously discriminate against any discrete and insular minority. Unlike the statute considered in *Morgan,* § 302 is valid only if

---

d. Harlan, J., expressed a similar view.

14. [S]o long as a State does not set the voting age higher than 21, the reasonableness of its choice is confirmed by the very Fourteenth Amendment upon which the Government relies [see § 2].

Congress has the power not only to provide the means of eradicating situations which amount to a violation of the Equal Protection Clause, but also to determine as a matter of substantive constitutional law what situations fall within the ambit of the clause, and what state interests are "compelling." * * * e

Notes and Questions

1. *Mitchell's "interpretation" of Morgan.* (a) To what extent do the opinions in *Mitchell* clarify (or cloud) the scope of Congress' power delineated in *Morgan*? Do either Brennan or Harlan, JJ., do more in *Mitchell* than restate their *Morgan* analyses? Do Black and Stewart, JJ., accurately "read" *Morgan*? Consider Archibald Cox, *The Role of Congress in Constitutional Determinations*, 40 U.Cin.L.Rev. 199, 237 (1971): "Justice Stewart's summary of *Morgan* [is] historically inaccurate: the New York literacy statute antedates by decades the arrival of numerous Puerto Ricans. Second, [the] *Morgan* opinion barely hints that Congress was concerned to ascribe a racist purpose to the New York lawmakers. [Finally], even by Justice Stewart's own account, the *Morgan* case sustained a congressional finding of substantive unconstitutionality and thus belies his later assertion that Congress lacks power to make a substantive determination of constitutional law." Do you agree? If Congress believed that "prejudice played a prominent role in the enactment" of the state literacy law in *Morgan*, is it important against which minority group the prejudice was directed? If this was the basis of Congress' "constitutional determination" in *Morgan*, is it the same kind of "substantive determination of constitutional law" by Congress that Brennan, J. sought to uphold in *Mitchell*?

(b) In any event, does Stewart, J.'s "reading" of *Morgan*—that Congress may "override state laws on the ground that they were in fact used as instruments of invidious discrimination"—mean that Congress may outlaw all "de facto" discriminations against "any discrete and insular minority"? Consider 85 Harv.L.Rev. 162 (1971): "Congress might be able to revamp a host of state benefit programs that impose particular disabilities on the poor on the rational basis that, in fact, a large fraction of the poor were blacks or members of ethnic minorities. [T]he literacy test analogy seems instructive: the class of citizens to whom the device was a serious obstacle was surely wider than merely blacks, yet Congress' conclusion that a large number of blacks were seriously disadvantaged [was] sufficient to uphold abolishing the practice under Congress' enforcement powers." Do you agree? Or does Stewart, J.'s "reading" of *Morgan* only comprehend congressional power over state laws it finds "tainted by [an] impermissible purpose"? See note 4 infra. See generally Jesse H. Choper, *Congressional Power to Expand Judicial Definitions of the Substantive Terms of the Civil War Amendments*, 67 Minn.L.Rev. 299, 328–34 (1982).

2. *Present status of Morgan.* In EEOC v. WYOMING, 460 U.S. 226, 103 S.Ct. 1054, 75 L.Ed.2d 18 (1983), BURGER, C.J., joined by Powell, Rehnquist and O'Connor, JJ., dissenting—after pointing out that the Court had rejected equal protection challenges to mandatory retirement schemes (p. 1226 supra)—denied that Congress had power under § 5 to apply the Age Discrimination in Employment Act to state hiring: "Allowing Congress [to] define rights wholly independently of our case law * * * fundamentally alters our scheme of government. Although the *South Carolina v. Katzenbach* line of cases may be read to allow Congress a degree of flexibility in deciding what the Fourteenth Amendment safeguards, I have always read *Mitchell* as finally imposing a limitation on the

e. The separate opinion of Douglas, J., is omitted.

extent to which Congress may substitute its own judgment for that of the states and assume this Court's 'role of final arbiter,' (Harlan, J., dissenting)." [f]

3. *Alternative rationale.* Consider David E. Engdahl, *Constitutionality of the Voting Age Statute,* 39 Geo.Wash.L.Rev. 1, 38–39 (1970): "A *state* classification which denies to a significant 'stake-holder' the right to vote in a *national* election cannot be justified unless the citizen's exclusion from the national election sufficiently promotes some sufficient *state* interest. Since no *state,* as such, has a legitimate interest in protecting the integrity of *national* elections, it is difficult to imagine any state interest sufficient to justify, under the equal protection clause, any *state* exclusion of a significant 'stake-holder' in *national* elections. The significant stake which 18, 19 and 20-year-olds hold in federal elections, with their impact upon war and peace, is shown by their peculiar susceptibility to conscription for military service. Under section five of the fourteenth amendment, Congress may act to eliminate any state impediments which prevent these young citizens from participating in the *national* elections in which they have such a substantial stake. * * *

"In view of the fact that [federal elections] ordinarily occur at the same time and even on the same ballot as elections not only for state legislators, but also for other state and local officials as well, the coexistence of different age qualifications for voting for these various officials would produce a good deal of confusion. In its discretion, Congress may therefore determine that to make removal of an unconstitutional impediment to voting in federal elections fully effective, it is necessary to adjust the minimum age for voting in *all* elections—federal, state and local."

Even if § 5 does *not* empower Congress to lower the voting age in federal *or* state elections, if Art. I, § 4 *does* empower Congress to lower the voting age in *federal* elections, does the latter part of this analysis justify Congress' also lowering the voting age in *state* elections? [g]

4. *De facto discrimination.* (a) ROME v. UNITED STATES, 446 U.S. 156, 100 S.Ct. 1548, 64 L.Ed.2d 119 (1980), involved the Attorney General's refusal to approve, under § 5 of the Voting Rights Act, various changes in the Rome, Ga.'s electoral system and a number of city annexations. A federal court found that the city had not employed any discriminatory barriers to black voting or black candidacy in the past 17 years and that the city had proved that the electoral changes and annexations were not discriminatorily motivated, but that they were prohibited by the Act because they had a discriminatory effect. The Court, per MARSHALL, J., affirmed: "[T]he Act's ban on electoral changes that are discriminatory in effect is an appropriate method of promoting the purposes of the Fifteenth Amendment, even if it is assumed that § 1 of the Amendment prohibits only intentional discrimination in voting. [See *Mobile v. Bolden,* p. 1247 supra.] Congress could rationally have concluded that, because electoral changes by jurisdictions with a demonstrable history of intentional racial discrimination in voting create the risk of purposeful discrimination, it was proper to prohibit changes that have a discriminatory impact. See *South Carolina v. Katzenbach.*"

---

f. For the view that "the scope of the definitional power" granted Congress in *Morgan,* "although by no means insignificant, may nonetheless be quite limited," see Choper, note 1(b) supra.

g. For an historical view that, pursuant to Art. I, §§ 2 and 4 and Art. IV, § 4 (the guaran-

tee clause), Congress has "ultimate supervisory authority over voter qualifications in both state and national elections," see Richard S. Greene, *Congressional Power Over the Elective Franchise: The Unconstitutional Phases of Oregon v. Mitchell,* 52 B.U.L.Rev. 505 (1972).

REHNQUIST, J., joined by Stewart, J., dissented: "The Court today identifies the constitutional wrong which was the object of this congressional exercise of power as purposeful discrimination by local governments in structuring their political processes in an effort to reduce black voting strength. [What] the Court explicitly ignores is that in this case the city has proven that these changes are not discriminatory in purpose. * * *

"Congress had before it evidence that various governments were enacting electoral changes and annexing territory to prevent the participation of blacks in local government by measures other than outright denial of the franchise. [G]iven the difficulties of proving that an electoral change or annexation has been undertaken for the purpose of discriminating against blacks, Congress could properly conclude that as a remedial matter it was necessary to place the burden of proving lack of discriminatory purpose on the localities. But all of this does not support the conclusion that Congress is acting remedially when it continues the presumption of purposeful discrimination even after the locality has disproved that presumption. Absent other circumstances, it would be a topsy-turvy judicial system which held that electoral changes which have been affirmatively proven to be permissible under the Constitution nonetheless violate the Constitution. [Thus,] the result of the Court's holding is that Congress effectively has the power to determine for itself that this conduct violates the Constitution. This result violates previously well-established distinctions between the Judicial Branch and the Legislative or Executive Branches of the Federal Government." Powell, J., dissented on narrower grounds.

(b) Do you agree that *Rome* empowers Congress "to determine for itself [what] conduct violates the Constitution"? Consider Choper, note 1(b) supra, at 331–32: "[*Rome's*] rationale permits Congress to create a 'conclusive presumption' of racial motivation with respect to specified state or local practices that Congress finds have been widely or consistently employed for the purpose of disadvantaging racial minorities—and thus effectively authorizes a congressional conclusion that such practices violate the substance of the fourteenth amendment. But this is a much narrower license than empowering Congress to declare that all state or local rules with a racially disproportionate impact violate equal protection for that reason alone. [A] variety of factors make it extremely difficult for plaintiffs to prove that a state legislative or administrative body has acted with discriminatory intent and make it much more appropriate for Congress than for the judiciary to combat the problem of illicit motivation. Thus, there are powerful reasons for Congress to choose not to rely upon district judges for the highly sensitive task of ascertaining racially discriminatory intent on a case by case basis in respect to state of local schemes whose real purpose Congress has grounds to suspect. [*Rome*] did no more than recognize this reality when is [used] what is principally a remedial or prophylactic rationale."

(c) Does *Rome* establish the validity of the Religious Freedom Restoration Act? Consider Douglas Laycock, *RFRA, Congress, and the Ratchet,* 56 Mont. L.Rev. 145, 166 (1995): "Many facially neutral, generally applicable laws are in fact based on hostility to a particular religion or to religion in general. * * * Congress found in the committee reports that neutral laws have been used to suppress religion, that litigating motive is not a reliable way to protect religious liberty, and that therefore we need RFRA."

JONES v. ALFRED H. MAYER CO.

392 U.S. 409, 88 S.Ct. 2186, 20 L.Ed.2d 1189 (1968).

JUSTICE STEWART delivered the opinion of the Court.

[P]etitioners filed a complaint [that] respondents had refused to sell them a home [for] the sole reason that petitioner [is] a Negro. Relying in part upon 42 U.S.C. § 1982 [Sec. 1, I supra], the petitioners sought injunctive and other relief.[1] The [courts below] sustained the respondents' motion to dismiss [concluding] that § 1982 applies only to state action * * *.

[I]t is important to make clear precisely what this case does *not* involve. Whatever else it may be, § 1982 is not a comprehensive open housing law. In sharp contrast to the Fair Housing Title (Title VIII) of the Civil Rights Act of 1968, the statute in this case deals only with racial discrimination and does not address itself to discrimination on grounds of religion or national origin. It does not deal specifically with discrimination in the provision of services or facilities in connection with the sale or rental of a dwelling. It does not prohibit advertising or other representations that indicate discriminatory preferences. It does not refer explicitly to discrimination in financing arrangements or in the provision of brokerage services.[10] It does not empower a federal administrative agency to assist aggrieved parties. It makes no provision for intervention by the Attorney General. And, although it can be enforced by injunction, it contains no provision expressly authorizing a federal court to order the payment of damages.

Thus, although § 1982 contains none of the exemptions that Congress included in the Civil Rights Act of 1968, it would be a serious mistake to suppose that § 1982 in any way diminishes the significance of the law recently enacted by Congress. * * *

[It] is true that a dictum in [*Hurd v. Hodge,* 334 U.S. 24, 68 S.Ct. 847, 92 L.Ed. 1187 (1948)] said that § 1982 was directed only toward "governmental action," but neither *Hurd* nor any other case before or since has presented that precise issue for adjudication in this Court.[25] * * *

On its [face] § 1982 appears to prohibit *all* discrimination against Negroes in the sale or rental of property—discrimination by private owners as well as discrimination by public authorities. * * * Stressing what they consider to be the revolutionary implications of so literal a reading of § 1982, the respondents argue that Congress cannot possibly have intended any such result. Our examination of the relevant history, however, persuades us that Congress meant exactly what it said.

In its original form, § 1982 was part [of] the Civil Rights Act of 1866. [The Court then extensively examined antecedent statutes and studies and debate in the Congress, contemporaneous with the proposal and ratification of the thirteenth amendment, in support of its conclusion respecting § 1982.]

1. To vindicate their rights under § 1982, the petitioners invoked the jurisdiction of the District Court to award "damages [or] equitable or other relief under any Act of Congress providing for the protection of civil rights * * *." 28 U.S.C. § 1343(4). * * *

10. In noting that § 1982 differs from the Civil Rights Act of 1968 [we] intimate no view upon the question whether ancillary services or facilities of this sort might in some situations constitute "property" as that term is employed in § 1982. * * *

25. Two of this Court's early opinions contain dicta to the general effect that § 1982 is limited to state action. *Virginia v. Rives,* 100 U.S. 313, 317–318, 25 L.Ed. 667; *Civil Rights Cases.* * * *

Nor was the scope of the 1866 Act altered when it was re-enacted in 1870, some two years after the ratification of the Fourteenth Amendment. It is quite true that some members of Congress supported the Fourteenth Amendment "in order to eliminate doubt as to the constitutional validity of the Civil Rights Act as applied to the States." *Hurd.* But it certainly does not follow that the adoption of the Fourteenth Amendment or the subsequent readoption of the Civil Rights Act were meant somehow to *limit* its application to state action. The legislative history furnishes not the slightest factual basis for any such speculation, and the conditions prevailing in 1870 make it highly implausible. * * *

The remaining question is whether Congress has power under the Constitution to do what § 1982 purports to [do]. Our starting point is the Thirteenth Amendment, for it was pursuant to that constitutional provision that Congress originally enacted what is now § 1982. [It] has never been [doubted] "that the power vested in Congress to enforce the article by appropriate legislation," [*Civil Rights Cases,*] includes the power to enact laws "direct and primary, operating upon the acts of individuals, whether sanctioned by State legislation or not." *Id.* * * *

"By its own unaided force and effect," the Thirteenth Amendment "abolished slavery, and established universal freedom." *Civil Rights Cases.* Whether or not the Amendment *itself* did any more than that—a question not involved in this case—it is at least clear that the Enabling Clause of that Amendment empowered Congress to do much more.[a] For that clause clothed "Congress with power to pass *all laws necessary and proper for abolishing all badges and incidents of slavery in the United States.*" Ibid. (Emphasis added.)

Those who opposed passage of the Civil Rights Act of 1866 argued in effect that the Thirteenth Amendment merely authorized Congress to dissolve the legal bond by which the Negro slave was held to his master. Yet [the] majority leaders in Congress—who were, after all, the authors of the Thirteenth Amendment—had no doubt that its Enabling Clause contemplated the sort of positive legislation that was embodied in the 1866 Civil Rights Act. Their chief spokesman, Senator Trumbull of Illinois, the Chairman of the Judiciary Committee, [argued] that, if the narrower construction of the Enabling Clause were correct, then "the trumpet of freedom that we have been blowing throughout the land has given an 'uncertain sound,' and the promised freedom is a delusion. [I] have no doubt that under this provision [we] may destroy all these discriminations in civil rights against [black people]. Who is to decide what that appropriate legislation is to be? The Congress * * *."

Surely Senator Trumbull was right. Surely Congress has the power under the Thirteenth Amendment rationally to determine what are the badges and the incidents of slavery, and the authority to translate that determination into effective legislation. Nor can we say that the determination Congress has made is an irrational one. For this Court recognized long ago that, whatever else they may have encompassed, the badges and incidents of slavery—its "burdens and disabilities"—included restraints upon "those fundamental rights which are the essence of civil freedom, namely the same right [to] inherit, purchase, lease, sell and convey property, as is enjoyed by white citizens." *Civil Rights Cases.* Just as the Black Codes, enacted after the Civil War to restrict the free exercise of those rights, were substitutes for the slave system, so the exclusion of Negroes

---

a. For discussion of the use of judicial power under § 1 of the amendment, see fn. b, p. 1320 supra.

from white communities became a substitute for the Black Codes. And when racial discrimination herds men into ghettos and makes their ability to buy property turn on the color of their skin, then it too is a relic of slavery.

[At] the very least, the freedom that Congress is empowered to secure under the Thirteenth Amendment includes the freedom to buy whatever a white man can buy, the right to live wherever a white man can live. If Congress cannot say that being a free man means at least this much, then the Thirteenth Amendment made a promise the Nation cannot keep. * * *

Reversed.

JUSTICE HARLAN, whom JUSTICE WHITE joins, dissenting.

[The] issue of the constitutionality of § 1982, as construed by the Court, and of liability under the Fourteenth Amendment alone, [present] formidable difficulties. [In a lengthy opinion, Harlan, J., relied on statements in prior Supreme Court opinions, the use of the word "right" in § 1982, the legislative history and debates of the Civil Rights Act of 1866 and of companion legislation, and on the ethics of the times to demonstrate that the Court's construction of § 1982 was "open to the most serious doubt" if not "wholly untenable."] [b]

———

RUNYON v. McCRARY, 427 U.S. 160, 96 S.Ct. 2586, 49 L.Ed.2d 415 (1976), per Stewart, J., relying on *Mayer's* interpretation of § 1982, held that § 1981 Sec. 1, I supra, prohibits private schools—that were operated commercially and open to the public in that they engaged in general advertising to attract students—from refusing to accept black students. POWELL, J., joined the opinion, but added that "choices, including those involved in entering into a contract, that are 'private' in the sense that they are not part of a commercial relationship offered generally or widely, and that reflect the selectivity exercised by an individual entering into a personal relationship, certainly were never intended to be restricted by" § 1981. Stevens, J., joined the Court's opinion, feeling bound by, but disagreeing with, the statutory interpretation in *Mayer*. White, J., joined by Rehnquist, J., dissented on grounds of statutory interpretation.

Notes and Questions

1. *Scope of §§ 1982 and 1981.* (a) What other discriminations against blacks are presently prohibited by these provisions? Consider Louis Henkin, *On Drawing Lines,* 82 Harv.L.Rev. 63, 85–86 (1968): "Will no bequest stand up which includes a racial discrimination since that would deprive Negroes of 'the same right [to] inherit'? Has there been an easier answer to [Senator Bacon's] will all this time while the Court struggled with theories of state action to find escape from his discrimination [see *Newton* and *Abney,* pp. 1418, 1433 supra.]? Indeed, [Title II of the Civil Rights Act of 1964] provides that certain places of public accommodations may not discriminate on the basis of race in selling goods and services; the Court's construction of § 1982, when applied to personal property, renders the title (and its limitations) superfluous. Moreover, by the

b. The concurring opinion of Douglas, J., is omitted. For conflicting views as to § 1982's legislative history, compare Charles Fairman, *Reconstruction and Reunion: 1864–1888, Part One* (1971) with Sanford Levinson, *Book Review,* 26 Stan.L.Rev. 461 (1974); Robert L.

Kohl, *The Civil Rights Act of 1866, Its Hour Come Round at Last,* 55 Va.L.Rev. 272 (1969) with Gerhard Casper, *Jones v. Mayer: Clio, Bemused and Confused Muse,* 1968 Sup.Ct. Rev. 89.

Court's technique of construction, the right 'to make and enforce contracts' guaranteed by [§ 1981] should prevent a restaurant or hotel management from refusing on grounds of race to 'make a contract' for service with a Negro. Indeed, that construction should prevent any employer from refusing 'to make a contract' of employment with a Negro; and the fair employment provisions of the 1964 Act likewise become superfluous, as does the entire struggle, since the days of the New Deal, to enact adequate fair employment legislation." ᶜ

(b) *Constitutionality.* Are the above racial discriminations "badges and incidents of slavery"? What of the practice by sellers of certain goods or services of charging African–Americans higher prices? See Note, *Discriminatory Housing Markets, Racial Unconscionability, and Section 1988,* 80 Yale L.J. 516 (1971). Is the initial question inaccurately stated? Do these instances "run the slavery argument into the ground" (*Civil Rights Cases*)?

Does the thirteenth amendment empower Congress to prohibit action that has a racially disproportionate impact, regardless of its purpose? Do §§ 1981–82 do so? See Note, *Section 1981: Discriminatory Purpose or Disproportionate Impact?* 80 Colum.L.Rev. 137 (1980); *Memphis v. Greene,* p. 1102 supra.

2. *Scope of § 1985.* GRIFFIN v. BRECKENRIDGE, 403 U.S. 88, 91 S.Ct. 1790, 29 L.Ed.2d 338 (1971), was a damage action under § 1985. Allegedly, respondents had wilfully conspired to assault and terrorize petitioners—who "were travelling upon the federal, state and local highways"—in order to prevent petitioners "and other Negro-Americans [from] seeking the equal protection of the laws and from enjoying the equal rights, privileges and immunities of citizens under the laws"—including rights to free speech, association, petition for redress of grievances, "their rights not to be enslaved nor deprived of life, liberty or property other than by due process of law, and their rights to travel the public highways without restraint in the same terms as white citizens." The Court, per STEWART, J., held "that all indicators—text, companion provisions, and legislative history—point unwaveringly to § 1985's coverage of private conspiracies." And the "constitutional shoals that would lie in the path of interpreting § 1985 as a general federal tort law can be avoided" because the "language requiring intent to deprive of *equal* protection, or *equal* privileges and immunities, means that there must be some racial, or perhaps otherwise class-based, invidiously discriminatory animus behind the conspirators' action.⁹"

The Court then found *at least* two sources of "congressional power to reach the private conspiracy alleged." First, under § 2 of the thirteenth amendment, "the varieties of private conduct which [Congress] may make criminally punishable or civilly remediable extend far beyond the actual imposition of slavery [*Mayer*]." Thus, Congress was "wholly within its powers [in] creating a statutory cause of action for Negro citizens who have been the victims of conspiratorial, racially discriminatory private action aimed at depriving them of the basic rights that the law secures to all free men." Second, "the right of interstate travel is

---

c. Does § 1981 make *Moose Lodge v. Irvis,* p. 1348 supra, incorrect? Or do other constitutional provisions (values) justify the decision?

9. We need not decide, given the facts of this case, whether conspiracy motivated by invidiously discriminatory intent other than racial bias would be actionable under the portion of § 1985(3) before us. [See *Carpenters, Local 610 v. Scott,* infra, holding that § 1985 does not "reach conspiracies motivated by economic or commercial animus."]

[See also *Bray v. Alexandria Women's Health Clinic,* p. 1343 supra, leaving open the question of whether "an invidiously discriminatory animus" against women comes within § 1985, but holding that opposition to abortion does not reflect such animus because it does not involve "a purpose that focuses upon women *by reason of their sex.*" Blackmun, Stevens and O'Connor, JJ., disagreed.]

constitutionally protected [against] private as well as governmental interference." Since "it is open to the petitioners to prove at trial that they had been engaging in interstate travel or intended to do so, that [the] conspirators intended to drive out-of-state civil rights workers from the State, or that they meant to deter the petitioners from associating with such persons," this "could make it clear that the petitioners had suffered from conduct which Congress may reach under its power to protect the right of interstate travel." [d]

3. *Beyond racial discrimination.* (a) CARPENTERS, LOCAL 610 v. SCOTT, 463 U.S. 825, 103 S.Ct. 3352, 77 L.Ed.2d 1049 (1983), per WHITE, J., held "that an alleged conspiracy to infringe First Amendment rights is not a violation of § 1985 unless it is proved that the state is involved in the conspiracy or that the aim of the conspiracy is to influence the activity of the state": "*Griffin* did not hold that even when the alleged conspiracy is aimed at a right [such as in the first amendment] that is by definition a right only against state interference the plaintiff in a § 1985 suit nevertheless need not prove that the conspiracy contemplated state involvement of some sort. The complaint in *Griffin* alleged, among other things, a deprivation of First Amendment rights but we did not sustain the action on the basis of that allegation and paid it scant attention. Instead, we upheld the application of § 1985 to private conspiracies aimed at interfering with rights [such as the freedom from slavery and the right to travel] constitutionally protected against private, as well as official, encroachment." Blackmun, J., joined by Brennan, Marshall and O'Connor, JJ., dissented. Does § 1985 provide a cause of action to whites who suffer injury because of their espousal of the rights of African–Americans?

In BRAY v. ALEXANDRIA WOMEN'S HEALTH CLINIC, p. 1343 supra, an injunction was sought against anti-abortion demonstrators' trespassing on, and obstructing access to, the premises of abortion clinics. The Court per SCALIA, J., held that § 1985 does not apply to private conspiracies aimed against abortion because that involves "a right only against state interference." STEVENS, J., joined by Blackmun, J., dissented on the ground that § 1985 covers "a large-scale conspiracy that violates the victims' constitutional rights by overwhelming the local authorities." O'Connor and Souter, JJ., agreed with Stevens, J., in separate opinions.

(b) To what extent does *Mayer* empower Congress to define the terms of the Civil War amendments? For example, pursuant to § 2 of the thirteenth amendment, may Congress "rationally determine" that discriminations against groups other than African–Americans are "badges and incidents of slavery"? See *McDonald v. Santa Fe Trail Trans. Co.*, 427 U.S. 273, 96 S.Ct. 2574, 49 L.Ed.2d 493 (1976) ("Congress is authorized under [§ 2] to legislate in regard to 'every race and individual' "). Consider Note, *Jones v. Mayer: The Thirteenth Amendment and the Federal Anti-Discrimination Laws,* 69 Colum.L.Rev. 1019, 1025–26 (1969): "[T]he Court's conclusion that housing discrimination *today* is a badge or incident of slavery is itself a recognition that the 'slavery' referred to in the thirteenth amendment now encompasses the second class citizenship imposed on members of disparate minority groups. By doing so, the Court has implicitly interpreted 'slavery' as the word has come to mean. [A] victim's people need not have been enslaved in order to invoke its protection. He need only be suffering today under conditions that could reasonably be called symptoms of a slave society, inability to

---

d. Harlan, J., joined the Court's opinion but found it unnecessary to rely on the "right of interstate travel."

raise a family with dignity caused by unemployment, poor schools and housing, and lack of a place in the body politic. By removing the time element from badges and incidents of slavery, an aggrieved party need not show a continuous link between his plight and actual slavery in order to benefit from the guarantees of the thirteenth amendment." [e] Compare Note, *The "New" Thirteenth Amendment: A Preliminary Analysis,* 82 Harv.L.Rev. 1294 (1969). Consider Choper, note 1(b) p. 1403 supra, at 313–14: "*Mayer* need not be interpreted as conferring any *definitional* authority on Congress. Rather, it can be persuasively argued on either of two theories that the Court upheld the Civil Rights Act of 1866 as only a *remedial* exercise of Congress's enforcement power under the thirteenth amendment. First, 'slavery' may be regarded as a status to be defined by the Court, [and] the 'badges and incidents of slavery' may be regarded, not as elements of that definition, but as stigmas and disabilities related to slavery. [Thus] to say that Congress may rationally determine the badges and incidents of slavery is nothing more than to say that Congress may prohibit certain practices, although those practices themselves do not constitute slavery, when Congress rationally finds that their prohibition will help to *prevent* slavery.[83] Alternatively, since Congress's power under *Morgan*'s remedial branch encompasses eradicating the *effects* of constitutional violations as well as preventing future ones, the congressional prohibition in *Mayer* may be readily sustained as an effort to eliminate the persistent legacies of the past condition of slavery."

4. *Self-executing force of thirteenth amendment.* Apart from federal legislation pursuant to § 2, are any (all) of the discriminations referred to above made unconstitutional by § 1 of "the Amendment *itself* "? If so, by what means should (can) the Court enforce § 1?

---

e. For the view that *McDonald* strongly supports this approach, see Emily Calhoun, *The Thirteenth and Fourteenth Amendments: Constitutional Authority for Federal Legislation Against Private Sex Discrimination,* 61 Minn.L.Rev. 313 (1977). For criticism of *McDonald,* see Note, *The Thirteenth Amendment and Private Affirmative Action,* 89 Yale L.J. 399 (1979).

The Court has interpreted § 1981 "to protect from discrimination identifiable classes of persons who are subjected to intentional discrimination solely because of their ancestry or ethnic characteristics." *Saint Francis College v. Al-Khazraji,* 481 U.S. 604, 107 S.Ct. 2022, 95 L.Ed.2d 582 (1987) (Arabs); *Shaare Tefila Congregation v. Cobb,* 481 U.S. 615, 107 S.Ct. 2019, 95 L.Ed.2d 594 (1987) (Jews).

83. David E. Engdahl, *Constitutional Power: Federal and State in a Nutshell* 247–48 (1974) (emphasis added).

Chapter 14
LIMITATIONS ON JUDICIAL POWER AND REVIEW: STANDING TO SUE

The judicial power under article III is limited to the resolution of "cases" or "controversies." These terms are hardly self-defining, and the Supreme Court, in giving meaning to them, has developed a complex set of what are often called "justiciability" doctrines. These doctrines are typically studied intensively in courses on Federal Courts, and reasons of space preclude a detailed examination here. But one justiciability doctrine is of sufficient importance, and raises sufficiently representative themes and issues, to merit consideration in a course on Constitutional Law. This is the doctrine of "standing," which addresses the frequently crucial question of who, if anyone, is entitled to invoke the jurisdiction of a federal court—including the Supreme Court—to procure a ruling on a constitutional claim.

SECTION 1. THE STRUCTURE OF STANDING DOCTRINE

ALLEN v. WRIGHT
468 U.S. 737, 104 S.Ct. 3315, 82 L.Ed.2d 556 (1984).

JUSTICE O'CONNOR delivered the opinion of the Court.

Parents of black public school children allege in this nation-wide class action that the Internal Revenue Service (IRS) has not adopted sufficient standards and procedures to fulfill its obligation to deny tax-exempt status to racially discriminatory private schools. They assert that the IRS thereby harms them directly and interferes with the ability of their children to receive an education in desegregated public schools. The issue before us is whether plaintiffs have standing to bring this suit. We hold that they do not.

[Respondents] allege in their complaint that many racially segregated private schools were created or expanded in their communities at the time the public schools were undergoing desegregation. According to the complaint, many such private schools, including 17 schools or school systems identified by name in the complaint (perhaps some 30 schools in all), receive tax exemptions either directly or through the tax-exempt status of "umbrella" organizations that operate or support the [schools.][11] Respondents allege that the IRS grant of tax exemptions

11. * * * Contrary to Justice Brennan's statement, the complaint does not allege that each desegregating district in which they reside contains one or more racially discriminatory private schools unlawfully receiving a tax exemption.

1412

to such racially discriminatory schools is unlawful [under federal statutes and the Constitution, and they seek declaratory and injunctive relief].

[R]espondents do not allege that their children have been the victims of discriminatory exclusion from the schools whose tax exemptions they challenge as unlawful. [Rather,] respondents claim a direct injury from the mere fact of the challenged Government conduct and, as indicated by the restriction of the plaintiff class to parents of children in desegregating school districts, injury to their children's opportunity to receive a desegregated education. * * *

II.   Article III of the Constitution confines the federal courts to adjudicating actual "cases" and "controversies." As the Court explained in *Valley Forge Christian College v. Americans United for Separation of Church and State, Inc.,* [infra] the "case or controversy" requirement defines with respect to the Judicial Branch the idea of separation of powers on which the Federal Government is founded. The several doctrines that have grown up to elaborate that requirement are "founded in concern about the proper—and properly limited—role of the courts in a democratic society." *Warth v. Seldin,* [infra]. * * *

The Art. III doctrine that requires a litigant to have "standing" to invoke the power of a federal court is perhaps the most important of these doctrines. "In essence the question of standing is whether the litigant is entitled to have the court decide the merits of the dispute or of particular issues." *Warth.* Standing doctrine embraces several judicially self-imposed limits on the exercise of federal jurisdiction, such as the general prohibition on a litigant's raising another person's legal rights, the rule barring adjudication of generalized grievances more appropriately addressed in the representative branches, and the requirement that a plaintiff's complaint fall within the zone of interests protected by the law invoked. The requirement of standing, however, has a core component derived directly from the Constitution. A plaintiff must allege personal injury fairly traceable to the defendant's allegedly unlawful conduct and likely to be redressed by the requested relief.

Like the prudential component, the constitutional component of standing doctrine incorporates concepts concededly not susceptible of precise definition. The injury alleged must be, for example, "distinct and palpable," and not "abstract" or "conjectural" or "hypothetical," *Los Angeles v. Lyons,* [infra]. The injury must be "fairly" traceable to the challenged action, and relief from the injury must be "likely" to follow from a favorable decision. See *Simon v. Eastern Kentucky Welfare Rights Org.,* [infra]. (These terms cannot be defined so as to make application of the constitutional standing requirement a mechanical exercise.)

The absence of precise definitions, however, [hardly] leaves courts at sea in applying the law of standing. Like most legal notions, the standing concepts have gained considerable definition from developing case law. [More] important, the law of Art. III standing is built on a single basic idea—the idea of separation of powers. It is this fact which makes possible the gradual clarification of the law through judicial application. * * *

Respondents allege two injuries in their complaint to support their standing to bring this lawsuit. First, they say that they are harmed directly by the mere fact of Government financial aid to discriminatory private schools. Second, they say that the federal tax exemptions to racially discriminatory private schools in their communities impair their ability to have their public schools desegregated. [N]either suffices to support respondents' standing.

Respondents' first claim of injury [might] be a claim simply to have the Government avoid the violation of law alleged in respondents' complaint. Alternatively, it might be a claim of stigmatic injury, or denigration, suffered by all members of a racial group when the Government discriminates on the basis of race. Under neither interpretation is this claim of injury judicially cognizable.

This Court has repeatedly held that an asserted right to have the Government act in accordance with law is not sufficient, standing alone, to confer jurisdiction on a federal court. In *Schlesinger v. Reservists Committee to Stop the War*, 418 U.S. 208, 94 S.Ct. 2925, 41 L.Ed.2d 706 (1974), for example, the Court rejected a claim of citizen standing to challenge Armed Forces Reserve commissions held by Members of Congress as violating the Incompatibility Clause of Art. I, § 6, of the Constitution. As citizens, the Court held, plaintiffs alleged nothing but "the abstract injury in nonobservance of the Constitution...." More recently, in *Valley Forge*, we rejected a claim of standing to challenge a Government conveyance of property to a religious institution. Insofar as the plaintiffs relied simply on "their shared individuated right" to a Government that made no law respecting an establishment of religion, we held that plaintiffs had not alleged a judicially cognizable injury. * * *

Neither do they have standing to litigate their claims based on the stigmatizing injury often caused by racial discrimination. There can be no doubt that this sort of noneconomic injury is one of the most serious consequences of discriminatory government action and is sufficient in some circumstances to support standing. Our cases make clear, however, that such injury accords a basis for standing only to "those persons who are personally denied equal treatment" by the challenged discriminatory conduct. [If an] abstract stigmatic injury were cognizable, standing would extend nationwide to all members of the particular racial groups against which the Government was alleged to be discriminating by its grant of a tax exemption to a racially discriminatory school, regardless of the location of that school. [A] black person in Hawaii could challenge the grant of a tax exemption to a racially discriminatory school in Maine. Recognition of standing in such circumstances would transform the federal courts into "no more than a vehicle for the vindication of the value interests of concerned bystanders." *United States v. SCRAP*, [infra]. Constitutional limits on the role of the federal courts preclude such a transformation.

It is in their complaint's second claim of injury that respondents allege harm to a concrete, personal interest that can support standing in some circumstances. The injury they identify—their children's diminished ability to receive an education in a racially integrated school—is, beyond any doubt, not only judicially cognizable but, as shown by cases [since] *Brown v. Board of Education*, [p. 1085 supra,] one of the most serious injuries recognized in our legal system. Despite the constitutional importance of curing the injury alleged by respondents, however, the federal judiciary may not redress it unless standing requirements are met. In this case, respondents' second claim of injury cannot support standing because the injury alleged is not fairly traceable to the Government conduct respondents challenge as unlawful.[22]

---

22. Respondents' stigmatic injury, though not sufficient for standing in the abstract form in which their complaint asserts it, is judicially cognizable to the extent that respondents are personally subject to discriminatory treatment. See *Heckler v. Mathews*, [infra] [involving the denial of monetary benefits on an allegedly discriminatory basis]. The stigmatic injury

The illegal conduct challenged by respondents is the IRS's grant of tax exemptions to some racially discriminatory schools. The line of causation between that conduct and desegregation of respondents' schools is attenuated at best. From the perspective of the IRS, the injury to respondents is highly indirect and "results from the independent action of some third party not before the court." *Simon.* * * *

The diminished ability of respondents' children to receive a desegregated education would be fairly traceable to unlawful IRS grants of tax exemptions only if there were enough racially discriminatory private schools receiving tax exemptions in respondents' communities for withdrawal of those exemptions to make an appreciable difference in public school integration. Respondents have made no such allegation. It [is] entirely speculative, as respondents themselves conceded in the Court of Appeals, whether withdrawal of a tax exemption from any particular school would lead the school to change its policies. It is just as speculative whether any given parent of a child attending such a private school would decide to transfer the child to public school as a result of any changes in educational or financial policy made by the private school once it was threatened with loss of tax-exempt status. It is also pure speculation whether, in a particular community, a large enough number of the numerous relevant school officials and parents would reach decisions that collectively would have a significant impact on the racial composition of the public schools. * * *

The Court of Appeals relied for its contrary conclusion on *Gilmore v. City of Montgomery*, [p. 1353 supra] [and] *Norwood v. Harrison*, [p. 1353 supra]. [Neither], however, requires that we find standing in this lawsuit.

In *Gilmore*, the plaintiffs [alleged] that the city was violating [their] equal protection right by permitting racially discriminatory private schools and other groups to use the public parks. The Court recognized plaintiffs' standing to challenge this city policy insofar as the policy permitted the exclusive use of the parks by racially discriminatory private [schools]. Standing in *Gilmore* thus rested on an allegation of direct deprivation of a right to equal use of the parks. * * *

In *Norwood v. Harrison*, parents of public school children in Tunica County, Miss., filed a statewide class action challenging the State's provision of textbooks to students attending racially discriminatory private schools in the State. The Court held the State's practice unconstitutional because it breached "the State's acknowledged duty to establish a unitary school system." The Court did not expressly address the basis for the plaintiffs' standing.

In *Gilmore*, however, the Court identified the basis for standing in *Norwood*: "The plaintiffs in Norwood were parties to a school desegregation order and the relief they sought was directly related to the concrete injury they suffered." Through the school-desegregation decree, the plaintiffs had acquired a right to have the State "steer clear" of any perpetuation of the racially dual school system that it had once sponsored. The interest acquired was judicially cognizable

thus requires identification of some concrete interest with respect to which respondents are personally subject to discriminatory treatment. That interest must independently satisfy the causation requirement of standing doctrine.

[Here,] respondents identify only one interest that they allege is being discriminatorily impaired—their interest in desegregated public school education. Respondents' asserted stigmatic injury, therefore, is sufficient to support their standing in this litigation only if their school-desegregation injury independently meets the causation requirement of standing doctrine.

because it was a personal interest, created by law, in having the State refrain from taking specific actions. * * *

III. "The necessity that the plaintiff who seeks to invoke judicial power stand to profit in some personal interest remains an Art. III requirement." *Simon.* Respondents have not met this fundamental requirement. The judgment of the Court of Appeals is accordingly reversed, and the injunction issued by that court is vacated.

JUSTICE BRENNAN, dissenting.

[In] these cases, the respondents have alleged at least one type of injury that satisfies the constitutional requirement of "distinct and palpable injury."[3] In particular, they claim that the IRS's grant of tax-exempt status to racially discriminatory private schools directly injures their children's opportunity and ability to receive a desegregated education. * * *

The Court acknowledges that this alleged injury is sufficient to satisfy constitutional standards. [Moreover,] in light of the injuries they claim, the respondents have alleged a direct causal relationship between the Government action they challenge and the injury they suffer: [Common] sense alone would recognize that the elimination of tax-exempt status for racially discriminatory private schools would serve to lessen the impact that those institutions have in defeating efforts to desegregate the public schools.

The Court admits that "[t]he diminished ability of respondents' children to receive a desegregated education would be fairly traceable to unlawful IRS grants of tax exemptions [if] there were enough racially discriminatory private schools receiving tax exemptions in respondents' communities for withdrawal of those exemptions to make an appreciable difference in public school integration," but concludes that "[r]espondents have made no such allegation." With all due respect, the Court has either misread the complaint or is improperly requiring the respondents to prove their case on the merits in order to defeat a motion to dismiss. For example, the respondents specifically refer by name to at least 32 private schools that discriminate on the basis of race and yet continue to benefit illegally from tax-exempt status. Eighteen of those schools [are] located in the city of Memphis, Tenn., which has been the subject of several court orders to desegregate. * * *

More than one commentator has noted that the causation component of the Court's standing inquiry is no more than a poor disguise for the Court's view of the merits of the underlying claims. The Court today does nothing to avoid that criticism. * * *

JUSTICE STEVENS, with whom JUSTICE BLACKMUN joins, dissenting.

[In the] final analysis, the wrong respondents allege that the Government has committed is to subsidize the exodus of white children from schools that would otherwise be racially integrated. The critical question in these cases, therefore, is whether respondents have alleged that the Government has created that kind of subsidy.

[If] the granting of preferential tax treatment would "encourage" private segregated schools to conduct their "charitable" activities, it must follow that the withdrawal of the treatment would "discourage" them, and hence promote the

---

3. Because I conclude that the second injury alleged by the respondents is sufficient to satisfy constitutional requirements, I do not need to reach what the Court labels the "stigmatic injury." * * *

process of desegregation. [This] causation analysis is nothing more than a restatement of elementary economics: when something becomes more expensive, less of it will be purchased. [W]ithout tax-exempt status, private schools will either not be competitive in terms of cost, or have to change their admissions policies, hence reducing their competitiveness for parents seeking "a racially segregated alternative" to public schools, which is what respondents have alleged many white parents in desegregating school districts seek.

[Because] [c]onsiderations of tax policy, economics, and pure logic all confirm the conclusion that respondents' injury in fact is fairly traceable to the Government's allegedly wrongful conduct[,] [t]he Court [is] forced to introduce the concept of "separation of powers" into its analysis. [In doing so,] the Court could be saying that it will require a more direct causal connection when it is troubled by the separation of powers implications of the case before it. That approach confuses the standing doctrine with the justiciability of the issues that respondents seek to raise. The purpose of the standing inquiry is to measure the plaintiff's stake in the outcome, not whether a court has the authority to provide it with the outcome it seeks.

[As the Court has previously recognized,] the " 'fundamental aspect of standing' is that it focuses primarily on the *party* seeking to get his complaint before the federal court rather than 'on the issues he wishes to have adjudicated,' " *United States v. Richardson*, 418 U.S. 166, 174, 94 S.Ct. 2940, 2945, 41 L.Ed.2d 678, 686 (1974). [If] a plaintiff presents a nonjusticiable issue, or seeks relief that a court may not award, then its complaint should be dismissed for those reasons, and not because the plaintiff lacks a stake in obtaining that relief and hence has no standing. Imposing an undefined but clearly more rigorous standard for redressability for reasons unrelated to the causal nexus between the injury and the challenged conduct can only encourage undisciplined, ad hoc litigation.

[Alternatively], the Court could be saying that it will not treat as legally cognizable injuries that stem from an administrative decision concerning how enforcement resources will be allocated. This surely is an important point. Respondents do seek to restructure the IRS's mechanisms for enforcing the legal requirement that discriminatory institutions not receive tax-exempt status. Such restructuring would dramatically affect the way in which the IRS exercises its prosecutorial discretion. The Executive requires latitude to decide how best to enforce the law, and in general the Court may well be correct that the exercise of that discretion, especially in the tax context, is unchallengeable.

However, as the Court also recognizes, this principle does not apply when suit is brought "to enforce specific legal obligations whose violation works a direct harm." [Here,] respondents contend that the IRS is violating a specific constitutional limitation on its enforcement discretion. There is a solid basis for that contention. In *Norwood*, we wrote: "A State's constitutional obligation requires it to steer clear, not only of operating the old dual system of racially segregated schools, but also of giving significant aid to institutions that practice racial or other invidious discrimination."

Deciding whether the Treasury has violated a specific legal limitation on its enforcement discretion does not intrude upon the prerogatives of the Executive, for in so deciding we are merely saying "what the law is." * * *

In short, I would deal with the question of the legal limitations on the IRS's enforcement discretion on its merits, rather than by making the untenable assumption that the granting of preferential tax treatment to segregated schools does not make those schools more attractive to white students and hence does not inhibit the process of desegregation.[a]

Notes and Questions

1. *Origins of the doctrine.* The Court appears to have referred to "standing" on only eight occasions prior to 1965, with the earliest coming in *Stark v. Wickard*, 321 U.S. 288, 64 S.Ct. 559, 88 L.Ed. 733 (1944). Cass R. Sunstein, *What's Standing After Lujan? Of Citizen Suits, "Injuries," and Article III,* 91 Mich.L.Rev. 163, 169 (1992).[a] Prior to the modern age, the *typical* plaintiff in federal court may have suffered injury-in-fact, but the Court seems not to have regarded injury-in-fact as an absolute requirement of a judicially cognizable case or controversy under Article III.[b] What should be the relevance, if any, of this historical practice?

2. *Nature and purposes.* As Stevens, J., noted in *Allen*, the Court has frequently stated that standing doctrine addresses issues of parties—and focuses, in particular, on the nature and sufficiency of the litigants' asserted injury or interest in the litigation—rather than the fitness of the issues for judicial resolution or even the question whether constitutionally protected rights have been invaded. See, e.g., *Flast v. Cohen*, 392 U.S. 83, 95, 88 S.Ct. 1942, 1950, 20 L.Ed.2d 947, 958–59 (1968), p. 1424, infra.[c] What purposes are served by this distinctive focus on appropriate parties? Consider the following views:

(a) Judicial review is an anomalous and potentially precarious function in a predominantly democratic government, which should be permitted only where strictly necessary to stop concrete harms to identified individuals. See, e.g., *Valley Forge*, p. 1426 infra.

(b) Concretely adverse interests sharpen the issues for judicial resolution and enhance the likelihood of illuminating argument. See, e.g., *Baker v. Carr*, p. 34 supra.[d]

(c) Restricting judicial review to cases brought by concretely harmed individuals reflects "three interrelated policies of Article III: the smooth allocation of power among courts over time; the unfairness of holding later litigants to an adverse judgment in which they may not have been properly represented; and the importance of placing control over political processes in the hands of the people

---

a. Marshall, J., did not participate in the decision.

a. On the history of standing as a concept, see Steven L. Winter, *The Metaphor of Standing and the Problem of Self-Governance,* 40 Stan.L.Rev. 1371, 1418–25 (1988).

b. See, e.g., Winter, supra (arguing that, prior to the twentieth century, courts granted relief whenever a plaintiff asserted a right for which one of the forms of action afforded a remedy and that some of these forms, particularly the prerogative writs, permitted suit by persons lacking a distinctive personal stake in the dispute); Raoul Berger, *Standing to Sue in Public Actions: Is it a Constitutional Requirement?,* 78 Yale L.J. 816, 827 (1969) (asserting that when the Constitution was adopted, "the English practice in prohibition, certiorari, quo warranto, and informers' and relators' actions encouraged strangers to attack *unauthorized action*").

c. The Court has not been entirely consistent. Compare *Warth v. Seldin*, 422 U.S. 490, 500, 95 S.Ct. 2197, 2206, 45 L.Ed.2d 343, 355–56 (1975): the question of standing "is whether the constitutional or statutory provision on which the claim rests properly can be understood as granting persons in the plaintiff's position a right to judicial relief."

d. But cf. Louis L. Jaffe, *The Citizen as Litigant in Public Actions: The Non–Hohfeldian or Ideological Plaintiff,* 116 U.Pa.L.Rev. 1033, 1038 (1968): "[T]he very fact of [an 'ideological plaintiff'] investing money in a lawsuit from which one is to acquire no further monetary profit argues, to my mind, a quite exceptional kind of interest, and one peculiarly indicative of a desire to say all that can be said in the support of one's contention. From this I would conclude that, insofar as the argument for a traditional plaintiff runs in terms of the need for effective advocacy, the argument is not persuasive."

most closely involved." Lea Brilmayer, *The Jurisprudence of Article III: Perspectives on the "Case or Controversy" Requirement,* 93 Harv.L.Rev. 297, 302.[e]

3. *Standing and the separation of powers.* The concept of standing, and the concerns about the scope of judicial power that underlie it, have attained prominence as plaintiffs increasingly have sought to use the Constitution as a sword to establish affirmative rights against the government, rather than as a shield against invasion of traditionally recognized liberty and property interests.[f] As *Allen* emphasized, separation-of-powers considerations are obviously at stake when plaintiffs ask courts to grant judicial remedies against other branches of government.[g] But is standing doctrine, as formulated in *Allen* and elsewhere to focus on the plaintiff's personal stake in the controversy, a sensible response to those considerations? Might doctrines that focus on the nature of the issue sought to be adjudicated or the character of the relief requested permit a more straightforward assessment of the extent to which separation-of-powers concerns are implicated in particular cases?

4. *The doctrinal requirement of injury in fact.* The Court's insistence that standing minimally requires injury-in-fact has occasioned sharp disputes about what constitutes an "injury" in the constitutional sense.[h]

(a) *Non-economic injuries.* In principle, at least, the Court has regularly accepted the proposition that non-economic injuries can satisfy the constitutional requirement, provided that they are pleaded with sufficient specificity.

(i) SIERRA CLUB v. MORTON, 405 U.S. 727, 92 S.Ct. 1361, 31 L.Ed.2d 636 (1972), held that the Sierra Club lacked standing to sue to enjoin governmental approval of the construction of a ski resort in the Sequoia National Forest. The Court allowed that non-economic harm could satisfy the injury requirement, but insisted that "the party seeking review be himself among the injured": "Nowhere did the Club state that its members use [the area in question] for any purpose,[i] much less that they use it in any way that would be significantly affected by the proposed actions of the [defendants]."[j] Did denial of standing to the Sierra Club, whose capacity to serve as an effective advocate could not be doubted, serve any sensible purpose? On the other hand, wouldn't it have been easy enough for the club to allege injury to itself or its members?

(ii) UNITED STATES v. STUDENTS CHALLENGING REGULATORY AGENCY PROCEDURES (SCRAP), 412 U.S. 669, 93 S.Ct. 2405, 37 L.Ed.2d 254

e. For a contrary perspective, see Mark V. Tushnet, *The Sociology of Article III: A Response to Professor Brilmayer,* 93 Harv.L.Rev. 1698 (1980).

f. For an exploration of these issues by then-Judge Scalia, which foreshadows more recent doctrinal developments, see Antonin Scalia, *The Doctrine of Standing as an Essential Element of the Separation of Powers,* 17 Suffolk U.L.Rev. 881, 894 (1983).

g. For a more recent linkage, see *Lujan v. Defenders of Wildlife,* p. 1422 infra. Compare *Flast v. Cohen,* p. 1424 infra, which asserts that the question of standing "does not, by its own force, raise separation of powers problems related to improper judicial interference in areas committed to other branches of the Federal Government. Such problems arise, if at all, only from the substantive issues the individual seeks to have adjudicated."

h. On this question, see generally Gene R. Nichol, Jr., *Injury and the Disintegration of Article III,* 74 Calif.L.Rev. 1915 (1986).

i. The conditions under which an organization can sue to redress injuries to its members were summarized in *Hunt v. Washington State Apple Advertising Comm'n,* 432 U.S. 333, 97 S.Ct. 2434, 53 L.Ed.2d 383 (1977): "[A]n association has standing to bring suit on behalf of its members when: (a) its members would otherwise have standing to sue in their own right; (b) the interests it seeks to protect are germane to the organization's purpose; and (c) neither the claim asserted nor the relief requested requires the participation of individual members in the lawsuit."

j. Blackmun, J., joined by Brennan and Douglas, JJ., dissented.

(1973), upheld the standing of a group of law students to challenge the failure of the ICC to prepare an environmental impact statement before declining to suspend a surcharge on railroad freight rates. The theory of the suit was that the surcharge on rail rates would result in damage to the outdoor environment in the Washington, D.C., metropolitan area that the students used for recreational purposes: higher rail rates would increase the cost of recycled products and thus occasion "the need to use more natural resources to produce such goods, some of which resources might be taken from the Washington area, and resulting in more refuse that might be discarded in national parks in the Washington area." If so, the result would be an injury to the plaintiffs' recreational interests.[k]

(b) *Injury and the equal protection clause.* HECKLER v. MATHEWS, 465 U.S. 728, 104 S.Ct. 1387, 79 L.Ed.2d 646 (1984), held that appellee had standing to contend that a statute denied him social security benefits on the basis of gender, even though the statute provided that if it were declared invalid the class of beneficiaries would be narrowed rather than broadened (thus resulting in appellee's receiving no benefits in any event): "[T]he right to equal treatment guaranteed by the Constitution is not co-extensive with any substantive rights to the benefits denied the party discriminated against. [Rather,] discrimination itself [can] cause serious non-economic injuries to those persons who are personally denied equal treatment solely because of their membership in a disfavored group. Accordingly, [the] appropriate remedy is a *mandate* of equal treatment, a result that can be accomplished by withdrawal of benefits from the favored class as well as by extension of benefits to the excluded class."

What, exactly, was the injury suffered by the plaintiff in *Mathews*? Is the decision in that case consistent with the holding of *Allen* that the stigma suffered by the plaintiffs did not constitute cognizable injury?

5. *Standing and the merits.* Consider the argument of William A. Fletcher, *The Structure of Standing,* 98 Yale L.J. 221 (1988), that it is a systematic mistake to conceive the standing inquiry as focused on the concept of "injury in fact" and abstracted from the existence of underlying rights. According to Professor Fletcher, people should always have standing to sue for redress of violations of their rights, and the standing question should essentially be one of what rights, if any, people possess under particular constitutional and statutory provisions.[l] Under this approach, *Heckler* was rightly decided because the plaintiffs clearly asserted a right under the equal protection clause. With respect to *Allen,* the central question would become whether the plaintiffs had an enforceable right under applicable law to an injunction against the challenged conduct of officials in the Treasury Department. The answer to this question might of course depend on whether the defendants had caused the plaintiffs harm and whether relief would redress it—questions that the Court emphasized in *Allen.* But what, if anything, is gained by severing the question of standing—conceived as involving issues of injury, causation, and redressability—from the question of what judicially enforceable rights the Constitution confers on whom? However *Allen* is

---

k. Even if *SCRAP* remains good law on the issue of what constitutes a constitutionally cognizable injury, it seems doubtful that the pleading would any longer suffice to satisfy the causation and redressability requirements, discussed below. See *Lujan v. National Wildlife Federation,* 497 U.S. 871, 110 S.Ct. 3177, 111 L.Ed.2d 695 (1990) (noting that *SCRAP*'s "expansive expression of what would suffice" for standing "has never since been emulated by this Court").

l. For expression of similar views, see Cass R. Sunstein, *Standing and the Privatization of Public Law,* 88 Colum.L.Rev. 1432 (1988); Lee A. Albert, *Standing to Challenge Administrative Action: An Inadequate Surrogate for Claim for Relief,* 83 Yale L.J. 425 (1974); David P. Currie, *Misunderstanding Standing,* 1981 Sup.Ct.Rev. 41 (1981).

analyzed, doesn't *Heckler* lend support to the theory that standing questions are intimately bound up with questions about the nature of the *rights* conferred by particular constitutional and statutory provisions?

6. *The causation requirement.* (a) In WARTH v. SELDIN, 422 U.S. 490, 95 S.Ct. 2197, 45 L.Ed.2d 343 (1975), a variety of plaintiffs alleged that the town zoning ordinance in Penfield, N.Y., violated the Constitution and federal civil rights statutes. The Court held that none of the groups had standing. Among those whose claims were dismissed were low-income individuals who wished to live in Penfield and claimed that the town's zoning laws prevented construction of low-income housing in which they could afford to live. The Court, per POWELL, J., deemed it too uncertain that, "absent the [defendants'] restrictive zoning practices, there is a substantial probability that [plaintiffs] would have been able to purchase or lease in Penfield and that, if the court affords the relief requested, the asserted inability of [plaintiffs] will be removed."

(b) In SIMON v. EASTERN KENTUCKY WELFARE RIGHTS ORG., 426 U.S. 26, 96 S.Ct. 1917, 48 L.Ed.2d 450 (1976), a class action on behalf of all persons unable to afford hospital services, the Court, again per POWELL, J., held that plaintiffs lacked standing to challenge an IRS Revenue Ruling eliminating a requirement that non-profit hospitals provide some care for indigents in order to qualify for favorable tax treatment. The Court termed it "purely speculative" that "the denial of access to hospital services [from which the plaintiffs suffered] in fact results from the petitioners' new Ruling, or that a court-ordered return by petitioners to their previous policy would result in these respondents' receiving the hospital services they desire."

(c) Compare REGENTS OF THE UNIVERSITY OF CALIFORNIA v. BAKKE, p. 1133 supra, in which the Court upheld the standing of a white plaintiff to challenge a special admissions program for minority applicants to medical school. Writing on this point for a majority of five, Powell, J., rejected arguments that Bakke lacked standing because he had not shown that he would have been admitted but for the affirmative action program or that invalidation of the program would result in his admission. Bakke's injury, the Court held, consisted in his deprivation, on grounds of race, of the chance to compete for every place in the entering class.[m]

Does *Bakke* suggest that satisfaction of the causation requirement will frequently turn on how the alleged injury is characterized? Could the plaintiffs in *Warth, Simon,* and possibly *Allen* have established standing if they had only alleged denial of a constitutionally guaranteed chance or opportunity, rather than denial of a specific benefit? Consider Sunstein, note 1 supra, at 1464–69: "The central problem [is] how to characterize the relevant injury. [In *Simon,*] for example, the plaintiffs might have characterized their injury as an impairment of the opportunity to obtain medical services under a regime undistorted by unlawful tax incentives. In *Allen,* the plaintiffs themselves argued that their injury should be characterized as the deprivation of an opportunity to undergo desegregation in

---

m. *Northeastern Florida Chapter of the Associated General Contractors of America v. City of Jacksonville,* 508 U.S. 656, 113 S.Ct. 2297, 124 L.Ed.2d 586 (1993), per Thomas, J., pursued a similar analysis, holding that the challenger to an affirmative action set-aside program need not show that, but for the program, the challenger would have received a concrete benefit: "The 'injury in fact' in an equal protection case of this variety is the denial of

equal treatment resulting from the imposition of [a barrier that makes it more difficult for members of a group to obtain a benefit], not the ultimate inability to obtain the benefit." The Court distinguished *Warth* on the ground that the plaintiffs in that case based their claim to standing on the denial of concrete benefits, not exclusion from the opportunity to compete for a benefit (in *Warth,* the benefit of zoning approval) on an equal basis.

school systems unaffected by unlawful tax deductions. Thus recharacterized, the injuries are not speculative at all. [The] harm might be characterized broadly if the relevant source of law is designed to prohibit the injury thus characterized. A related route would be to ask straightforwardly whether Congress intended to confer on the plaintiff a right to bring suit. [Thus, if *Simon*] was rightly decided, it was because the tax statutes have been interpreted so as to deny standing, not because of a problem with causation; and if people now thought to be indirectly or incidentally harmed by regulatory action or inaction are to be denied standing, it is because the denial is a sensible reading of congressional purposes in enacting regulatory legislation." See also Abram Chayes, *Public Law Litigation and the Burger Court*, 96 Harv.L.Rev. 4, 18–19 (1982).

7. *Redressability.* In perhaps the majority of cases, the requirement that an injury be redressable can be viewed as an aspect of the causation requirement: if a defendant has caused injury, relief against the defendant will ordinarily remedy the injury. Occasionally, however, the redressability requirement exercises independent bite.

In *Los Angeles v. Lyons*, 461 U.S. 95, 103 S.Ct. 1660, 75 L.Ed.2d 675 (1983), for example, the plaintiff had been choked to unconsciousness by the Los Angeles police after being stopped for a traffic violation. Alleging that the department had a policy of applying life-threatening chokeholds unnecessarily, Lyons sued for injunctive relief. Standing could not be grounded on the threat of future injury, the Court held, because it was too speculative that Lyons himself would be subjected to a choke-hold again. And, although Lyons undoubtedly had suffered an injury in the past, that injury could not be redressed by an injunction against future police conduct.[n]

As *Lyons* explicitly recognized, the plaintiff undoubtedly had standing to seek *damages* relief for the injury caused him in the past. What purpose is served by treating eligibility for injunctive relief—which the redressability requirement precluded—as a component of standing or the Article III case or controversy requirement? Wouldn't Lyons's entitlement to an injunction have been better addressed within the familiar framework governing entitlement to equitable remedies? See Richard H. Fallon, Jr., *Of Justiciability, Remedies, and Public Law Litigation: Notes on the Jurisprudence of Lyons*, 59 N.Y.U.L.Rev. 1 (1984).

8. *Congressional authority to confer standing.* The Endangered Species Act requires that federal agencies consult with executive branch officials to ensure that any action funded by the agency is not likely to jeopardize endangered species and authorizes "any person" to sue to enjoin violations. LUJAN v. DEFENDERS OF WILDLIFE, 504 U.S. 555, 112 S.Ct. 2130, 119 L.Ed.2d 351 (1992), per SCALIA, J., held that the case-or-controversy requirement prevented a challenge by environmental groups to a federal administrative regulation exempting projects funded in foreign nations: "The question presented here is whether the public interest in proper administration of the laws (specifically, in agencies' observance of a particular, statutorily prescribed procedure) can be converted into an individual right by a statute that denominates it as such, and that permits all citizens (or, for that matter, a subclass of citizens who suffer no distinctive concrete harm) to sue. If the concrete injury requirement has the separation-of-powers significance we have always said, the answer must be obvious: To permit Congress to convert the undifferentiated public interest in executive officers' compliance with the law into an 'individual right' vindicable in the courts is to permit Congress to transfer

---

n. Marshall, J., joined by Brennan, Blackmun, and Stevens, JJ., dissented.

from the President to the courts the Chief Executive's most important constitutional duty, to 'take Care that the Laws be faithfully executed,' Art. II, § 3. * * *

"Nothing in this contradicts the principle that '[the] injury required by Art. III may exist solely by virtue of statutes creating legal rights, the invasion of which creates standing.' *Warth.* [Cases previously cited by the Court] as an illustration of that principle involved Congress's elevating to the status of legally cognizable injuries concrete, de facto injuries that were previously inadequate in law (namely, injury to an individual's personal interest in living in a racially integrated community, see *Trafficante* [v. *Metropolitan Life Ins. Co.,* 409 U.S. 205, 93 S.Ct. 364, 34 L.Ed.2d 415 (1972),] and injury to a company's interest in marketing its product free from competition. As we said in *Sierra Club,* '[Statutory] broadening [of] the categories of injury that may be alleged in support of standing is a different matter from abandoning the requirement that the party seeking review must himself have suffered an injury.' Whether or not the principle set forth in *Warth* can be extended beyond that distinction, it is clear that in suits against the government, at least, the concrete injury requirement must remain."

KENNEDY, J., joined by Souter, J., joined the opinion, adding: "Congress has the power to define injuries and articulate chains of causation that will give rise to a case or controversy where none existed before, and I do not read the Court's opinion to suggest a contrary view. See *Warth.* In exercising this power, however, Congress must at the very least identify the injury it seeks to vindicate and relate the injury to the class of persons entitled to bring suit. The citizen-suit provision of the Endangered Species Act does not meet these minimal requirements, because while the statute purports to confer a right on 'any person [to] enjoin [the] United States and any other governmental instrumentality or agency [who] is alleged to be in violation of any provision of this chapter,' it does not of its own force establish that there is an injury in 'any person' by virtue of any 'violation.' "

BLACKMUN, J., joined by O'Connor, J., dissented: "There may be factual circumstances in which a congressionally imposed procedural requirement is so insubstantially connected to the prevention of a substantive harm that it cannot be said to work any conceivable injury to an individual litigant. But, as a general matter, the courts owe substantial deference to Congress' substantive purpose in imposing a certain procedural requirement."

Stevens, J., dissented from the Court's reasoning on separate grounds.

Will the notion of a concrete or actual injury bear the weight that *Lujan* places on it? In what sense was denial of an equal opportunity to compete to enter the University of California an injury in *Bakke,* but the opportunity to purchase housing in an undistorted market not an injury in *Warth?* Why was "stigma" sufficient to ground standing in *Heckler v. Mathews,* but not in *Allen v. Wright?*

Consider Cass R. Sunstein, *What's Standing After Lujan? Of Citizen Suits, Injuries, and Article III,* 91 Mich.L.Rev. 163, 190 (1992): "[T]he real question is what harms *that people perceive as such* ought to be judicially cognizable. [W]hether there is a so-called nonjusticiable ideological interest, or instead a legally cognizable 'actionable injury,' is a product of legal conventions and nothing else." Is this argument persuasive? If so, should Congress be able to alter the prevailing legal conventions by legislation?

How would (and should) the Court resolve a hypothetical formulated by Professor Sunstein, supra, at 234: "Suppose [that] Congress attempts to create a citizen suit" by first legislating that "all Americans have [a] property right—a tenancy in common—[in] clean air anywhere in the country, or pristine areas, or the continued existence of endangered species anywhere in the United States or abroad. If this seems odd, we might note that Congress could surely create property rights in unowned land within the United States. [And] surely Congress' capacity to create property rights is not limited to land. If Congress thus creates property rights," can it then further prescribe that violation of those rights constitutes injury to all right-holders, and thereby authorize standing to sue by all citizens? *Lujan* appears to signal that it could not, but compare the opinion of Kennedy, J., joined by Souter, J., concurring.[a]

SECTION 2. TAXPAYER STANDING AND OTHER STATUS–BASED STANDING ISSUES

In FROTHINGHAM v. MELLON, 262 U.S. 447, 43 S.Ct. 597, 67 L.Ed. 1078 (1923), a federal taxpayer contended that a federal statute providing funds to states undertaking programs to reduce maternal and infant mortality exceeded Congress' power, and "that the effect of the appropriations complained of will be to increase the burden of future taxation and thereby take her property without due process of law." The Court, per SUTHERLAND, J., dismissed "for want of jurisdiction." A federal taxpayer's "interest in the moneys of the treasury [is] shared with millions of others, is comparatively minute and indeterminable, and the effect upon future taxation, of any payment out of the funds, so remote, fluctuating and uncertain, that no basis is afforded for an appeal to the preventive powers of a court of equity." To permit such suits might result in attacks on "every other appropriation act and statute whose administration requires the outlay of public money * * *. The bare suggestion of such a result, with its attendant inconveniences, goes far to sustain the conclusion which we have reached, that a suit of this character cannot be maintained." A person asking the Court to hold a federal act unconstitutional "must be able to show, not only that the statute is invalid, but that he has sustained or is immediately in danger of sustaining some direct injury as the result of its enforcement, and not merely that he suffers in some indefinite way in common with people generally." Here, the complaint "is merely that [federal officials] will execute an act of Congress asserted to be unconstitutional; and this we are asked to prevent. To do so would be, not to decide a judicial controversy, but to assume a position of authority over the governmental acts of another and coequal department, an authority which plainly we do not possess."

———

FLAST v. COHEN, 392 U.S. 83, 88 S.Ct. 1942, 20 L.Ed.2d 947 (1968), per WARREN, C.J., upheld the standing of federal taxpayers to challenge federal

a. For further critical discussion of *Lujan*, see Richard J. Pierce, Jr., *Lujan v. Defenders of Wildlife: Standing as a Judicially Imposed Limit on Legislative Power,* 42 Duke L.J. 1170, 1194–95 (1993); Gene R. Nichol, Jr., *Justice Scalia, Standing, and Public Law Litigation,* 42 Duke L.J. 1141 (1993). For more favorable commentary, see Marshall J. Breger, *Defend-* *ing Defenders: Remarks on Nichol and Pierce,* 42 Duke L.J. 1202 (1993); John G. Roberts, Jr., *Article III Limits on Statutory Standing,* 42 Duke L.J. 1219 (1993). See also Scott H. Bice, *Congress' Power to Confer Standing in the Federal Courts,* in Constitutional Government in America 291 (Collins ed., 1980).

expenditures for parochial schools under the religion clauses of the first amendment. The Court noted, at the outset, that standing doctrine blends "constitutional requirements and policy considerations" and implied that *Frothingham* rested largely on policy grounds. It framed the essence of the standing inquiry as distinct from the fitness of the issues presented for resolution on the merits: "[The] fundamental aspect of standing is that it focuses on the party seeking to get his complaint before a federal court and not on the issues he wishes to have adjudicated." But the Court then acknowledged that "in ruling on standing, it is both appropriate and necessary to look to the substantive issues [to] determine whether there is a logical nexus between the status asserted and the claim sought to be adjudicated [to] assure that [the litigant] is a proper and appropriate party to invoke federal judicial power [so as] to satisfy Article III requirements": "The nexus demanded of federal taxpayers has two aspects to it. First, the taxpayer must establish a logical link between that status and the type of legislative enactment attacked. * * * Secondly, the taxpayer must establish a nexus between that status and the precise nature of the constitutional infringement alleged."

"The taxpayer-appellants in this case have satisfied both nexuses * * *." With respect to the first, it sufficed that the "constitutional challenge is made to an exercise by Congress of its power under Art. I, § 8, to spend for the general welfare, and the challenged program involves a substantial expenditure of federal tax funds." With respect to the second, "appellants have alleged that the challenged expenditures violate the Establishment and Free Exercise Clauses of the First Amendment." In light of its historic purposes, the Establishment Clause "operates as a specific constitutional limitation upon the exercise by Congress of the taxing and spending power conferred by Art. I, § 8."

Frothingham was distinguishable. Although the "taxpayer in *Frothingham* attacked a federal spending program [and therefore] established the first nexus required," her general allegation that "Congress [had] exceeded the general powers delegated to it" failed to identify any specific limitation on spending that Congress had breached. The Court reserved the question whether "the Constitution contains other specific limitations" that would support standing by taxpayers to challenge federal expenditures.

HARLAN, J., dissenting, protested that the Court's dual nexus standard for taxpayer standing was "entirely unrelated" to the purportedly controlling standard of whether the plaintiff had the requisite personal stake to justify standing. "It is surely clear that a plaintiff's interest in the outcome of a suit in which he challenges the constitutionality of a federal expenditure is not made greater or smaller" by the nature of the program being attacked or the constitutional provision under which the attack is mounted. "[H]ow can it be said that Mrs. Frothingham's interests in her suit were, as a consequence of her choice of a constitutional claim, necessarily less intense than those, for example, of the present appellants?"

The plaintiff's claim did not rest on any distinctive individual stake in the outcome, but involved an assertion of standing to represent the public interest— shared equally by all citizens—in the observance of the establishment clause. "Individual litigants have standing to represent the public interest, despite their lack of economic or other personal interests, if [but only if] Congress has appropriately authorized such suits.[a] [Any] hazards to the proper allocation of

---

a. Harlan, J., relied on *Scripps-Howard Radio v. FCC,* 316 U.S. 4, 15, 62 S.Ct. 875, 882, 86 L.Ed. 1229 (1942), and *Associated Industries v. Ickes,* 134 F.2d 694 (2d Cir.1943).

authority among the three branches of the Government would be substantially diminished if public actions had been pertinently authorized by Congress and the President."

Notes and Questions

1. *The double nexus test.* Was Harlan, J., correct that *Flast*'s double nexus requirement provided a flimsy and artificial measure of the plaintiff's "personal stake" in the outcome of the litigation—at least insofar as the "personal stake" requirement is somehow linked to taxpayer status and the notion that the taxpayer has suffered a pocketbook injury?

2. *Flast and the public action.* Was Harlan, J., also correct that (i) the injury suffered by the plaintiffs in *Flast*, if any, was essentially indistinguishable from that suffered by all other citizens and, thus, (ii) the Court had effectively authorized "public actions" to vindicate the public interest in enforcement of the establishment clause?

What, if anything, is constitutionally troublesome about all citizens being able to sue to ensure governmental compliance with constitutional mandates? Would the problems be cured, as Harlan, J., suggested, by congressional authorization of such suits?[b]

If *Flast* did authorize public actions to challenge the constitutionality of federal spending under the establishment clause, note that the double nexus test, coupled with other express reservations in the opinion, left the Court the option of limiting citizen or taxpayer actions to suits under that provision only. Would it be fair to describe *Flast* as an *experiment* with public action lawsuits to enforce the Constitution?

Or is the concept of a "public action" possibly not a helpful one in this context? Consider the argument of Professor Fletcher, p. 1420 supra, at 271–72, that the question should not be whether citizens or taxpayers should generally have standing to sue to enforce the Constitution, but whether "the purposes of the particular clause at issue will be best served by permitting federal taxpayers to sue to enforce its obligations." On this analysis, could *Flast*, which was brought under the establishment clause, be persuasively distinguished from *Frothingham*, in which the plaintiff relied, *inter alia*, on the "general welfare" limitation on spending of article I, § 8, and on the due process clause?

VALLEY FORGE CHRISTIAN COLLEGE v. AMERICANS UNITED FOR SEPARATION OF CHURCH AND STATE, INC., 454 U.S. 464, 102 S.Ct. 752, 70

Scripps-Howard held that the Communications Act conferred standing on a radio station, as a "person aggrieved," to contest the FCC's grant of a license to an additional station: "The purpose of the Act was to protect the public interest in communications. [T]hese private litigants have standing [as] representatives of the public interest." Consider Louis L. Jaffe, *Standing to Secure Judicial Review: Public Actions*, 74 Harv.L.Rev. 1265, 1314 (1961): "It might be argued that whatever the purported rationale [of] *Scripps-Howard*, a decision upholding the justiciability of a suit brought by a

person of a very limited class which is in fact adversely affected is not a precedent for permitting actions by the unlimited class of citizen or taxpayer. But in *Associated Industries* Judge Frank, following what he believed to be the rationale of [*Scripps-Howard*], did apply it to a consumer, a member of a class which is coterminous with the entire human population [and] characterized the appellant as a 'private Attorney General.' "

b. For further discussion of congressionally authorized standing, see p. 1422 supra.

L.Ed.2d 700 (1982), per REHNQUIST, J., held that respondents lacked standing as taxpayers or citizens to challenge, as violative of the establishment clause, the giving of surplus federal property to a church college that trained students "for Christian services as either ministers or laymen": "While the [power of judicial review] is a formidable means of vindicating individual rights, when employed unwisely or unnecessarily it is also the ultimate threat to the continued effectiveness of the federal courts in performing that role. * * * Proper regard for the complex nature of our constitutional structure requires neither that the judicial branch shrink from a confrontation with the other two coequal branches of the Federal Government, nor that it hospitably accept for adjudication claims of constitutional violation by other branches of government where the claimant has not suffered cognizable injury. * * * Article III, which is every bit as important in its circumscription of the judicial power of the United States as in its granting of that power, is not merely a troublesome hurdle to be overcome if possible so as to reach the 'merits' of a lawsuit.

"[R]espondents fail the first prong of the [*Flast*] test for taxpayer standing [in] two respects. First, the source of their complaint is not a congressional action, but a decision by HEW to transfer a parcel of federal property. *Flast* limited taxpayer standing to challenges directed 'only [at] exercises of congressional power.' * * * Second, [the] property transfer [was] not an exercise of authority conferred by the Taxing and Spending Clause of Art. I, § 8. The authorizing legislation [was] an evident exercise of Congress' power under the Property Clause, Art. IV, § 3, cl. 2. * * *

"Any doubt that once might have existed concerning the rigor with which the *Flast* exception to the *Frothingham* principle ought to be applied should have been erased by this Court's recent decisions in *United States v. Richardson* and *Schlesinger v. Reservists Committee to Stop the War*. In *Richardson*, the plaintiff [was denied] standing as a federal taxpayer to argue that legislation which permitted the Central Intelligence Agency to withhold from the public detailed information about its expenditures violated the Accounts Clause of the Constitution.[18] [Plaintiffs] in [*Schlesinger* similarly lacked standing as federal taxpayers to argue] that the Incompatibility Clause of Art. I[19] prevented certain Members of Congress from holding commissions in the Armed Forces Reserve.

"[*Reservists* and *Richardson* cannot] be distinguished on the ground that the Incompatibility and Accounts Clauses are in some way less 'fundamental' than the Establishment Clause. Each establishes a norm of conduct which the Federal Government is bound to honor. [W]e know of no principled basis on which to create a hierarchy of constitutional values or a complementary 'sliding scale' of standing which might permit respondents to invoke the judicial power of the United States. 'The proposition that all constitutional provisions are enforceable by any citizen simply because citizens are the ultimate beneficiaries of those provisions has no boundaries.' *Reservists*.

"The complaint in this case shares a common deficiency with those in *Reservists* and *Richardson*. Although [the plaintiffs] claim that the Constitution has been violated, [they] fail to identify any personal injury suffered by the plaintiffs *as a consequence* of the alleged constitutional error, other than the psychological consequence presumably produced by observation of conduct with which one disagrees. That is not an injury sufficient to confer standing under

18. U.S. Const., Art. I, § 9, cl.7 ("[A]nd a regular Statement and Account of the Receipts and Expenditures of all public Money shall be published from time to time").

19. U.S. Const., Art. I, § 6, cl.2 ("[N]o Person holding any Office under the United States, shall be a Member of either House during his Continuance in Office").

Art. III, even though the disagreement is phrased in constitutional terms. It is evident that respondents are firmly committed to the constitutional principle of separation of church and State, but standing is not measured by the intensity of the litigant's interest or the fervor of his advocacy."

BRENNAN, J., joined by Marshall and Blackmun, JJ.,[a] dissented: "The Court makes a fundamental mistake when it determines that a plaintiff has failed to satisfy [the] 'injury-in-fact' test, or indeed any other test of 'standing,' without first determining whether the Constitution [defines] injury, and creates a cause of action for redress of that injury, in precisely the circumstance presented to the Court. * * *[5] [One] of the primary purposes of the Establishment Clause was to prevent the use of tax moneys for religious purposes. *The taxpayer was the direct and intended beneficiary of the prohibition on financial aid to religion.*"

As for the fact that HEW transferred the property, "to be sure, the First Amendment is phrased as a restriction on Congress' legislative authority. [But] it is difficult to conceive of an expenditure for which the last governmental actor, either implementing directly the legislative will, or acting within the scope of legislatively delegated authority, is not an Executive Branch official. The First Amendment binds the Government as a whole, regardless of which branch is at work in a particular instance.

"The Court's second purported distinction between this case and *Flast* is equally unavailing. [It] can make no constitutional difference [whether] the donation to the petitioner here was in the form of a cash grant to build a facility, see *Tilton v. Richardson,* [p. 986 supra], or in the nature of a gift of property including a facility already built. [Whether] undertaken pursuant to the Property Clause or the Spending Clause, the breach of the Establishment Clause, and the relationship of the taxpayer to that breach, is precisely the same."

Notes and Questions

1. *Significance of Valley Forge.* Is *Flast*'s significance now pretty much restricted to cases challenging congressional spending under the establishment clause?[a] Should it be?[b] Is it disturbing that there may be constitutional violations that no one has standing to challenge?

2. *Generalized grievances.* Although *Valley Forge* appears to deny that the plaintiffs had suffered any injury at all, several of the cases on which it relied placed weight on the notion that "generalized grievances" are not appropriate for judicial resolution, but should instead be remitted to the political process. How is the line to be drawn between "generalized grievances" that will not support standing and genuine "injuries" that, even if widely shared, will support standing? Compare, e.g., *SCRAP* ("standing is not to be denied simply because many people suffer the same injury"; otherwise, "the most injurious and widespread Government actions could be questioned by nobody"); *Public Citizen v. United States Dep't of Justice,* 491 U.S. 440, 449–50, 109 S.Ct. 2558, 2564–65, 105 L.Ed.2d

---

a. Stevens, J., dissented separately.

5. When the Constitution makes it clear that a particular person is to be protected from a particular form of government action, then that person has a "right" to be free of that action; when that right is infringed, then there is injury, and a personal stake, within the meaning of Art. III.

a. For a recent decision applying the *Flast* exception for taxpayer challenges under the

establishment clause to an exercise of Congress' power under the taxing and spending clause, see *Bowen v. Kendrick,* p. 986 supra.

b. For critical commentary, see Gene R. Nichol, Jr., *Standing on the Constitution: The Supreme Court and Valley Forge,* 61 N.C.L.Rev. 798 (1983).

377, 388–89 (1989) (upholding plaintiffs' standing to sue under a federal statute creating a right to receive information and rejecting the argument that because any other citizen could seek the same information, the case involved a mere generalized grievance).

Should the political process be trusted to deal fairly with grievances that are widely shared? Consider Scalia, p. 1419 supra, at 894–95: "[T]he law of standing roughly restricts courts to their traditional undemocratic role of protecting individuals and minorities against impositions of the majority, and excludes them from the even more undemocratic role of prescribing how the other two branches should function in order to serve the interest *of the majority itself.* [U]nless the plaintiff can show some respect in which he is harmed *more* than the rest of [us] he has not established any basis for concern that the majority is suppressing or ignoring the rights of a minority that wants protection, and thus has not established the prerequisite for judicial intervention."

How does this analytical approach apply to *Valley Forge*? Were the plaintiffs, in (then-Judge) Scalia's terms, members of a "minority" or a "majority"? Does it matter? Should it? Compare Cass R. Sunstein, *What's Standing After Lujan? Of Citizen Suits, Injuries, and Article III*, 91 Mich.L.Rev. 163, 219 (1992): "[S]ome majorities are so diffuse and ill-organized that they face systematic transaction costs barriers to the exercise of ongoing political influence [and their interests may] require judicial protection."

Consider again the suggestion of Fletcher, supra, that the crucial question is not whether a grievance is widely shared, but whether it stems from a violation of the plaintiff's constitutional rights. Within this framework, it should be no obstacle to standing that some constitutional rights—such as the rights to be free of race- and gender-based discrimination and governmental establishment of religion, for example—are widely shared. But might it also be the case that some constitutional provisions—such as possibly the "incompatibility clause" involved in *Reservists*—create no enforceable rights at all? On what basis might distinctions between constitutional provisions that do and do not create individual rights be drawn?

3. *Local and state taxpayer standing.* (a) In denying the standing of a federal taxpayer to challenge federal expenditures, *Frothingham* distinguished the case of municipal taxpayers: "The interest of a taxpayer of a municipality in the application of its moneys is direct and immediate and the remedy by injunction to prevent their misuse is not inappropriate."

(b) ASARCO INC. v. KADISH, 490 U.S. 605, 109 S.Ct. 2037, 104 L.Ed.2d 696 (1989), per KENNEDY, J., held that the exception from the *Frothingham* rule for municipal taxpayers does not apply to state taxpayers: "we have refused to confer standing upon a state taxpayer absent a showing of 'direct injury,' pecuniary or otherwise." BRENNAN, J., joined by White, Marshall and Blackmun, JJ., did not join this part of the Court's opinion.

(c) Although denying that state taxpayers possess standing to challenge state expenditures in federal court, *ASARCO* also adhered to the rule, pronounced in *Doremus*, that state courts are not bound by Article III standing requirements even when ruling on federal constitutional claims. What happens, however, when a plaintiff who would not have standing in federal court sues in state court and prevails on the merits? Does the defendant then have standing to seek review of the state judgment in the Supreme Court? *ASARCO*, 6–2, answered in the affirmative.

REHNQUIST, C.J., joined by Scalia, J., filed a partial dissent objecting to the disparity created by *ASARCO*: "although the *Doremus* case is good law for plaintiffs who lack standing but lost in the state court on the merits of their federal claim, it is not good law for such plaintiffs who prevailed on the merits of their federal question in the state courts." Consider Paul Freund in *Supreme Court & Supreme Law* 35 (E. Cahn ed. 1954): "I think it is a needed change to make standing to raise a federal constitutional question, itself a federal question, so that it will be decided uniformly throughout the country. I disagree with *Doremus* in so far as it lets the state judgment stand and merely declines review. [T]he Court should have [held that] the petition should stand dismissed in the state court and the decree vacated so that it would not be a precedent even in the state court."

Would acceptance of Professor Freund's proposal unjustifiably intrude on the autonomy of state courts by prohibiting them to render advisory opinions, for example? See William A. Fletcher, *The "Case or Controversy" Requirement in State Court Adjudication of Federal Questions*, 78 Calif.L.Rev. 263 (1990) (noting that no such problem would arise if state advisory opinions were denied precedential or res judicata effect). See generally Nicole A. Gordon & Douglas Gross, *Justiciability of Federal Claims in State Court*, 59 Notre Dame L.Rev. 1145 (1984); William P. Murphy, *Supreme Court Review of Abstract State Court Decisions on Federal Law: A Justiciability Analysis*, 25 St.L.U.L.J. 473 (1981).

5. *Standing of voters.* Numerous cases have upheld the standing of individual voters to claim deprivations of constitutional voting rights of various kinds. See, e.g., *Baker v. Carr*, p. 34 supra (alleging malapportionment in violation of one-person, one-vote requirement); *Rogers v. Lodge*, p. 1254 supra (involving race-based dilution of voting power); *Davis v. Bandemer*, p. 1255 supra (challenging political gerrymander). What, precisely, is the nature of the injury in such cases?[c] Why don't they involve mere "generalized grievances"?

Compare UNITED STATES v. HAYS, 515 U.S. ___, 115 S.Ct. 2431, 132 L.Ed.2d 635 (1995), per O'CONNOR, J., holding that persons living outside a voting district lack standing to challenge the legislation establishing the district as an unconstitutional racial gerrymander. The plaintiffs had not suffered the "representational harm" of having their representatives feel especially beholden to a racially defined constituency, nor been subjected personally to racially discriminatory treatment. Concurring separately, STEVENS, J., analyzed the standing question as largely inseparable from the merits and concluded that the plaintiffs lacked standing because they had failed to allege a constitutional violation.

---

c. See generally Pamela S. Karlan, *The Rights to Vote: Some Pessimism About Formalism*, 71 Tex.L.Rev. 1705 (1993) (distinguishing among the kinds of interests that potentially might be at stake in voting rights cases); Richard H. Pildes & Richard G. Niemi, *Expressive Harms, "Bizarre Districts," and Voting Rights: Evaluating Election–District Appearances After Shaw v. Reno*, 92 Mich. L.Rev. 483, 492–516 (1993).

Appendix A
THE JUSTICES OF THE
SUPREME COURT

Originally prepared by JOHN J. COUND

Professor of Law, University of Minnesota

The data which follow, summarizing the prior public careers of those individuals who have served on the Supreme Court of the United States, are not presented with any notion that they did presage or now explain their judicial performance or constitutional philosophy. The experience which the justices have at any one time brought to bear upon the issues before the Court, however, seem worthy of interest, and may serve as a consideration in assessing charges that the Court has in particular cases rendered "ivory tower" decisions, unaware or heedless of "the realities."

Two conclusions are manifest. First, the diversity of distinguished experience which the bench of the Court has at all times reflected, always among its members and frequently in a single justice, is startling. William Howard Taft is unique, but surely few Americans have lived lives of diversified public service so rich as John Jay, Levi Woodbury, Lucius Q.C. Lamar, Charles Evans Hughes and Fred M. Vinson. Second, a broad background in public service has not assured prominence upon the Court, nor has its absence precluded it. Gabriel Duvall, with prior executive, legislative and judicial experience, was forgotten in the first edition of the *Dictionary of American Biography*. Samuel F. Miller and Joseph P. Bradley, with no prior public offices, surely stand among the front rank of the justices. (The interested student will find stimulation in Frankfurter, *The Supreme Court in the Mirror of Justice*, 105 U.Pa.L.Rev. 781 (1957), which treats particularly of the relevance of prior judicial office).

In the data, the first dates in parentheses are those of birth and death; these are followed by the name of the appointing President, and the dates of service on the Court. The state in which the justice was residing when appointed and his political affiliation at that time are then given. In detailing prior careers, I have followed chronological order, with two exceptions: I have listed first that a justice was a signer of the Declaration of Independence or the Federal Constitution, and I have indicated state legislative experience only once for each justice. I have not distinguished between different bodies in the state legislature, and I have omitted service in the Continental Congresses. Private practice, except where deemed especially significant, and law teaching have been omitted, except where the justice was primarily engaged therein upon his appointment. (Blackmun, Burger, Douglas, Fortas, Holmes, Hughes, Kennedy, L.Q.C. Lamar, Lurton, McReynolds,

1431

Murphy, Roberts, W. Rutledge, Stevens, Stone and Van Devanter in addition to Taft and Frankfurter, had all taught before going on the Court; Story, Strong and Wilson taught while on the court or after leaving it). The activity in which a justice was engaged upon appointment has been italicized. Figures in parentheses indicate years of service in the position. In only a few cases, a justice's extra-Court or post-Court activity has been indicated, or some other note made. An asterisk designates the Chief Justices.

For detailed information on the men who have served as members of the Supreme Court, see L. Friedman & F. Israel, eds., *The Justices of the United States Supreme Court 1789–1969: Their Lives and Major Opinions* (Chelsea House, 1969), and the bibliographical references collected therein.

The accompanying Table of Justices on pages [3] and [4] has been planned so that the composition of the Court at any time can be readily ascertained.

(This material has been compiled from a great number of sources, but special acknowledgment must be made to the *Dictionary of American Biography* (Charles Scribner's Sons), the A.N. Marquis Company works, and Ewing, *The Judges of the Supreme Court, 1789–1937* (University of Minnesota Press, 1938).)

BALDWIN, HENRY (1780–1844; Jackson 1830–1844). Pa.Dem.—U.S., House of Representatives (5). *Private practice.*

BARBOUR, PHILIP P. (1783–1841; Jackson, 1836–1841). Va.Dem.—Va., Legislature (2). U.S., House of Representatives (14). Va., Judge, General Court (2); President, State Constitutional Convention, 1829–30, *U.S., Judge, District Court (5).*

BLACK, HUGO L. (1886–1971; F.D. Roosevelt, 1937–1971). Ala.Dem.— Captain, Field Artillery, World War I. Ala., Judge, Police Court (1); County Solicitor (2). *U.S., Senate (10).*

BLACKMUN, HARRY A. (1908–____; Nixon, 1970–1994). Minn.Rep.—Resident Counsel, Mayo Clinic, (10). *U.S., Judge, Court of Appeals (11).*

BLAIR, JOHN (1732–1800; Washington, 1789–1796). Va.Fed.—Signer, U.S. Constitution, 1787. Va., Legislature (9); Judge and Chief Justice, General Court (2), *Court of Appeals (9).* His opinion in *Commonwealth v. Caton,* 4 Call 5, 20 (Va.1782), is one of the earliest expressions of the doctrine of judicial review.

BLATCHFORD, SAMUEL (1820–1893; Arthur, 1882–1893). N.Y.Rep.—U.S., Judge, District Court (5); *Circuit Court (10).*

BRADLEY, JOSEPH P. (1803–1892; Grant, 1870–1892). N.J.Rep.—Actuary. *Private practice.*

BRANDEIS, LOUIS D. (1856–1941; Wilson, 1916–1939). Mass.Dem.—*Private practice.* Counsel, variously for the government, for industry, and "for the people", in numerous administrative and judicial proceedings, both state and federal.

BRENNAN, WILLIAM J. (1906–____; Eisenhower, 1956–1990). N.J.Dem.— U.S. Army, World War II. N.J., Judge, Superior Court (1); Appellate Division (2); *Supreme Court (4).*

BREWER, DAVID J. (1837–1910; B. Harrison, 1889–1910). Kans.Rep.— Kans., Judge, County Criminal and Probate Court (1), District Court (4); County Attorney (1); Judge, Supreme Court (14), *U.S., Judge, Circuit Court (5).*

BREYER, STEPHEN GERALD (1937–____; Clinton, 1994–____); Mass.Dem.: U.S., *Judge, Court of Appeals (13½).*

BROWN, HENRY, B. (1836–1913; B. Harrison, 1890–1906). Mich.Rep.— U.S., Assistant U.S. Attorney (5). Mich., Judge, Circuit Court (1). *U.S., Judge, District Court (15).*

The years listed (top and bottom of chart): 1789, 1790, 1791, 1793, 1795, 1796, 1798, 1799, 1801, 1804, 1806, 1807, 1811, 1823, 1826, 1829, 1830, 1835, 1836, 1837, 1841, 1845, 1846, 1851, 1853, 1858, 1862, 1863, 1864, 1865, 1867, 1870, 1872, 1874, 1877, 1880, 1881, 1882, 1888, 1889, 1890, 1892, 1893, 1894, 1895, 1898, 1902, 1903, 1906.

Columns of Justices (left to right):

- Jay; Rutledge, J.; Ellsworth; Marshall, J.; Taney; Chase, Salmon; Waite; Fuller; White, E.
- Rutledge, J.; Johnson, T.; Paterson; Livingston; Thompson; Nelson; Hunt; Blatchford; White, E.
- Cushing; Story; Woodbury; Curtis; Clifford; Gray; Holmes
- Wilson; Washington; Baldwin; Grier; Strong; Woods; Lamar, L.; Jackson, H.; Peckham
- Blair; Chase, Samuel; Duval; Barbour; Daniel; Miller; Brown; Moody
- Iredell; Moore; Johnson, W.; Wayne; Bradley; Shiras; Day
- Todd; Trimble; McLean; Swayne; Matthews; Brewer
- Catron; Harlan
- Field; McKinley; Campbell; Davis; McKenna

*Catron died in 1865, Wayne in 1867; their positions were abolished by Congress to prevent their being filled by President Johnson; a new position was created in 1869, which traditionally has been regarded as a re-creation of Wayne's seat.

Years (across top): 1909 1910 1912 1914 1916 1921 1922 1923 1925 1930 1932 1937 1938 1939 1940 1941 1943 1945 1946 1949 1953 1955 1956 1957 1958 1962 1965 1966 1967 1968 1969 1970 1972 1975 1981 1982 1983 1986 1987 1988 1989 1990

Column 1: White, E. — Taft — Hughes — Stone — Vinson — Warren — Burger — Rehnquist

Column 2: ** Van Devanter — Black — Powell — Kennedy

Column 3: Cardozo — Frankfurter — Goldberg / Fortas — Blackmun

Column 4: Lurton — McReynolds — Byrnes / Rutledge — Minton — Brennan — Souter

Column 5: Lamar, J. — Brandeis — Douglas — Stevens

Column 6: Butler — Murphy — Clark — Marshall, T.

Column 7: Hughes — Clarke — Sutherland — Reed — Whittaker — White, B.

Column 8: Pitney — Sanford — Roberts — Burton — Stewart — O'Connor

Column 9: Stone — ** Jackson, R. — Harlan — Rehnquist — ** Scalia

Years (repeated at bottom): 1909 1910 1912 1914 1916 1921 1922 1923 1925 1930 1932 1937 1938 1939 1940 1941 1943 1945 1946 1949 1953 1955 1956 1957 1958 1962 1965 1966 1967 1968 1969 1970 1972 1975 1981 1982 1983 1986 1987 1988 1989 1990

** Fuller died in 1910 and White was named Chief Justice. Hughes resigned in 1941, and Stone was named Chief Justice. Burger resigned in 1986 and Rehnquist was named Chief Justice.

*BURGER, WARREN E. (1907–1995; Nixon, 1969–1986). Va.Rep.—U.S., Assistant Attorney General, Civil Division (3), *Judge, Court of Appeals (13).*

BURTON, HAROLD H. (1888–1964; Truman, 1945–1958). Ohio Rep.— Capt., U.S.A., World War I. Ohio, Legislature (2). Mayor, Cleveland, O. (5). *U.S., Senate (4).*

BUTLER, PIERCE (1866–1939; Harding, 1922–1939). Minn.Dem.—Minn., County Attorney (4). *Private practice.*

BYRNES, JAMES F. (1879–1972; F.D. Roosevelt, 1941–1942). S.C.Dem.— S.C., Solicitor, Circuit Court (2). U.S., House of Representatives (14); *Senate (12).* Resigned from the Court to become U.S. Director of Economic Stabilization.

CAMPBELL, JOHN A. (1811–1889; Pierce, 1853–1861). Ala.Dem.—*Private practice.* After his resignation, he became Assistant Secretary of War, C.S.A.

CARDOZO, BENJAMIN N. (1870–1938; Hoover, 1932–1938). N.Y.Dem.— N.Y., Judge, Supreme Court (6 weeks); Associate Judge and *Chief Judge, Court of Appeals (18).*

CATRON, JOHN (1778–1865; Van Buren, 1837–1865). Tenn.Dem.—Tenn., Judge and Chief Justice, Supreme Court of Errors and Appeals (10). *Private practice.*

*CHASE, SALMON P. (1808–1873; Lincoln 1864–1873). Ohio Rep.—U.S., Senate (6). Ohio, Governor (4). *U.S., Secretary of the Treasury (3).*

CHASE, SAMUEL (1741–1811; Washington, 1796–1811). Md.Fed.—Signer, U.S., Declaration of Independence, 1776. Md., Legislature (20); Chief Judge, Court of Oyer and Terminer (2), *General Court (5).* Impeached and acquitted, 1804–05.

CLARK, TOM C. (1899–1977; Truman, 1949–1967). Tex.Dem.—U.S. Army, World War I. Tex., Civil District Attorney (5). U.S., Assistant Attorney General (2), *Attorney General (4).*

CLARKE, JOHN H. (1857–1945; Wilson, 1916–1922). Ohio Dem.—*U.S. Judge, District Court (2).*

CLIFFORD, NATHAN (1803–1881; Buchanan, 1858–1881). Me.Dem.—Me., Legislature (4); Attorney General (4). U.S., House of Representatives (4); Attorney General (2); Minister Plenipotentiary to Mexico, 1848. *Private practice.*

CURTIS, BENJAMIN R. (1809–1874; Fillmore, 1851–1857). Mass.Whig.— Mass., Legislature (1). *Private practice.*

CUSHING, WILLIAM (1732–1810; Washington, 1789–1810). Mass.Fed.— Mass., Judge, Superior Court (3); Justice and *Chief Justice, Supreme Judicial Court (14).*

DANIEL, PETER V. (1784–1860; Van Buren, 1841–1860). Va.Dem.—Va., Legislature (3); Member, Privy Council (23). *U.S., Judge, District Court (5).*

DAVIS, DAVID (1815–1886; Lincoln, 1862–1877). Ill.Rep.—Ill., Legislature (2); *Judge, Circuit Court (14).* His resignation to become U.S. Senator upset the agreed-upon composition of the Hayes-Tilden Electoral Commission.

DAY, WILLIAM R. (1849–1923; T. Roosevelt, 1903–1922). Ohio Rep.—Ohio, Judge, Court of Common Pleas (4). U.S., Assistant Secretary of State (1), Secretary of State (½); Chairman, U.S. Peace Commissioners, 1898; *Judge, Circuit Court of Appeals (4).*

DOUGLAS, WILLIAM O. (1898–1980; F.D. Roosevelt, 1939–1975). Conn. Dem.—Pvt., U.S. Army, World War I. *U.S., Chairman, Securities and Exchange Commission (3).* His was the longest tenure in the history of the Court.

DUVAL(L), GABRIEL (1752–1844; Madison, 1811–1935). Md.Rep.—Declined to serve as delegate, U.S. Constitutional Convention, 1787. Md., State Council (3). U.S., House of Representatives (2). Md., Judge, General Court (6). *U.S., Comptroller of the Treasury (9).*

*ELLSWORTH, OLIVER (1745–1807; Washington, 1796–1800). Conn. Fed.—Delegate, U.S. Constitutional Convention, 1787. Conn., Legislature (2); Member, Governor's Council (4); Judge, Superior Court (5). *U.S., Senate (7).*

FIELD, STEPHEN J. (1816–1899; Lincoln, 1863–1897). Calif.Dem.—*Calif., Justice, and Chief Justice, Supreme Court (6).*

FORTAS, ABE (1910–1982; L.B. Johnson, 1965–1969). Tenn.Dem.—U.S. Government attorney and consultant (A.A.A., S.E.C., P.W.A., Dep't of Interior (9); Undersecretary of Interior (4). *Private practice in Washington, D.C.* Nominated as Chief Justice; nomination withdrawn, 1968. Resigned.

FRANKFURTER, FELIX (1882–1965; F.D. Roosevelt, 1939–1962). Mass. Independent.—U.S., Assistant U.S. Attorney (4); Law Officer, War Department, Bureau of Insular Affairs (3); Assistant to Secretary of War (1). *Professor of Law (25).*

*FULLER, MELVILLE W. (1833–1910; Cleveland, 1888–1910). Ill.Dem.— Ill., Legislature (2). *Private practice.*

GINSBURG, RUTH BADER (1933–____; Clinton 1993–____); N.Y.Dem.; U.S., *Judge, Court of Appeals (13).*

GOLDBERG, ARTHUR J. (1908–____; Kennedy, 1962–1965). Ill.Dem.— Major, U.S.A., World War II. General Counsel, USW–AFL–CIO (13). *U.S., Secretary of Labor (1).* Resigned to become Ambassador to U.N.

GRAY, HORACE (1828–1902; Arthur, 1881–1902). Mass.Rep.—*Mass.,* Associate Justice and *Chief Justice, Supreme Judicial Court (18).*

GRIER, ROBERT O. (1794–1870; Polk, 1846–1870). Pa.Dem.—*Pa., Presiding Judge, District Court (13).*

HARLAN, JOHN M. (1833–1911; Hayes, 1877–1911). Ky.Rep.—Ky., Judge, County Court (1). Col., Union Army, 1861–63. Ky., Attorney General (4). U.S., Member, President's Louisiana Commission, 1877. *Private practice.* Grandfather of:

HARLAN, JOHN M. (1899–1971; Eisenhower, 1955–1971). N.Y.Rep.—Col., U.S.A.A.F., World War II. N.Y. Chief Counsel, State Crime Commission (2). *U.S., Judge, Court of Appeals (1).*

HOLMES, OLIVER W., JR. (1841–1935; T. Roosevelt, 1902–1932). Mass. Rep.—Lt. Col., Mass. Volunteers, Civil War. *Mass.,* Associate Justice, and *Chief Justice, Supreme Judicial Court (20).*

*HUGHES, CHARLES E. (1862–1948; Taft, 1910–1916, and Hoover, 1930–1941). N.Y.Rep.—N.Y., Counsel, legislative committees investigating gas and insurance industries, 1905–06. U.S., Special Assistant to Attorney General for Coal Investigation, 1906. *N.Y., Governor (3).* [Between appointments to the Supreme Court: Presidential Nominee, Republican Party, 1916. U.S., Secretary of State (4). *Member, Permanent Court of Arbitration, The Hague (4). Judge,*

Permanent Court of International Justice (2).] Chief Justice on second appointment.

HUNT, WARD (1810–1886; Grant, 1872–1882). N.Y.Rep.—N.Y., Legislature (2). Mayor of Utica, N.Y. (1). N.Y. Associate Judge, and Chief Judge, Court of Appeals (4); *Commissioner of Appeals (4).* He did not sit from 1879 to his retirement in 1882.

IREDELL, JAMES (1750–1799; Washington, 1790–1799). N.C.Fed.—Comptroller of Customs (6), Collector of Port (2), Edenton, N.C., N.C., Judge, Superior Court (½); Attorney General (2); Member, Council of State, 1787; *Reviser of Statutes (3).*

JACKSON, HOWELL E. (1832–1895; B. Harrison, 1893–1895). Tenn. Dem.—Tenn., Judge, Court of Arbitration (4); Legislature (1). U.S. Senate (5); *Judge, Circuit Court of Appeals (7).*

JACKSON, ROBERT H. (1892–1954; F.D. Roosevelt, 1941–1954). N.Y.Dem.—U.S., General Counsel, Bureau of Internal Revenue (2); Assistant Attorney General (2); Solicitor General (2); *Attorney General (1).*

*JAY, JOHN (1745–1829; Washington, 1789–1795). N.Y.Fed.—N.Y., Chief Justice, Supreme Court (2). U.S., Envoy to Spain (2); Commissioner, Treaty of Paris, 1782–83; Secretary for Foreign Affairs (6). Co-author, The Federalist.

JOHNSON, THOMAS (1732–1819; Washington, 1791–1793). Md.Fed.—Md., Brigadier-General, Militia (1); Legislature (5); Governor (2); *Chief Judge, General Court (1).*

JOHNSON, WILLIAM (1771–1834; Jefferson, 1804–1834). S.C.Rep.—S.C., Legislature (4); *Judge, Court of Common Pleas (6).*

KENNEDY, ANTHONY M. (1936–____); Reagan (1988–____); Calif.Rep.; U.S., *Judge, Court of Appeals* (11).

LAMAR, JOSEPH R. (1857–1916; Taft, 1910–1916). Ga.Dem.—Ga., Legislature (3); Commissioner to Codify Laws (3); Associate Justice, Supreme Court (4). *Private practice.*

LAMAR, LUCIUS Q.C. (1825–1893; Cleveland, 1888–1893). Miss.Dem.— Ga., Legislature (2). U.S., House of Representatives (4). Draftsman, Mississippi Ordinance of Secession, 1861. C.S.A., Lt. Col. (1); Commissioner to Russia (1); Judge-Advocate, III Corps. Army of No. Va. (1). U.S., House of Representatives (4); Senate (8); *Secretary of the Interior (3).*

LIVINGSTON, (HENRY) BROCKHOLST (1757–1823; Jefferson, 1806–1823). N.Y.Rep.—Lt. Col., Continental Army. *N.Y., Judge, Supreme Court (4).*

LURTON, HORACE H. (1844–1914; Taft, 1909–1914). Tenn.Dem.—Sgt. Major, C.S.A. Tenn., Chancellor (3); Associate Justice and Chief Justice, Supreme Court (7). *U.S., Judge, Circuit Court of Appeals (16).*

McKENNA, JOSEPH (1843–1926; McKinley, 1898–1925). Calif.Rep.—Calif., District Attorney (2); Legislature (2). U.S., House of Representatives (7); *Judge, Circuit Court of Appeals (5); Attorney General (1).*

McKINLEY, JOHN (1780–1852; Van Buren, 1837–1852). Ala.Dem.—Legislature (4). U.S., Senate (5); House of Representatives (2); *re-elected to Senate,* but appointed to Court before taking seat.

McLEAN, JOHN (1785–1861; Jackson, 1829–1861). Ohio Dem.—U.S., House of Representatives (4). Ohio, Judge, Supreme Court (6). U.S., Commissioner, General Land Office (1); *Postmaster-General (6).*

McREYNOLDS, JAMES C. (1862–1946; Wilson, 1914–1941). Tenn.Dem.— U.S., Assistant Attorney General (4); *Attorney General (1)*.

*MARSHALL, JOHN (1755–1835; J. Adams, 1801–1835). Va.Fed.—Va., Legislature (7); U.S., Envoy to France (1); House of Representatives (1); *Secretary of State (1)*.

MARSHALL, THURGOOD (1908–1993; L.B. Johnson, 1967–1991). N.Y.Dem.—Counsel, Legal Defense and Educational Fund, NAACP (21). U.S., Judge, Court of Appeals (4); *Solicitor General (2)*.

MATTHEWS, STANLEY (1824–1889; Garfield, 1881–1889). Ohio Rep.— Ohio, Judge, Court of Common Pleas (2); Legislature (3). U.S., District Attorney (3). Col., Ohio Volunteers. Ohio, Judge, Superior Court (2). Counsel before Hayes-Tilden Electoral Commission, 1877. U.S., Senate (2). *Private practice.* His first appointment to the Court by Hayes in 1881 was not acted upon by the Senate.

MILLER, SAMUEL F. (1816–1890; Lincoln, 1862–1890). Iowa Rep.—Physician. *Private practice.*

MINTON, SHERMAN (1890–1965; Truman, 1949–1956). Ind.Dem.—Capt., Inf., World War I. U.S., Senate (6); *Judge, Court of Appeals (8)*.

MOODY, WILLIAM H. (1853–1917; T. Roosevelt, 1906–1910). Mass.Rep.— U.S., District Attorney (5), House of Representatives (7); Secretary of the Navy (2); *Attorney General (2)*.

MOORE, ALFRED (1755–1810; J. Adams, 1799–1804). N.C.Fed.—N.C., Col. of Militia; Legislature (2); Attorney General (9). U.S. Commissioner, Treaty with Cherokee Nation (1); *N.C., Judge, Superior Court (1)*.

MURPHY, FRANK (1893–1949; F.D. Roosevelt, 1940–1949). Mich.Dem.— Capt., Inf., World War I. U.S., Assistant U.S. Attorney (1). Mich., Judge, Recorder's Court (7). Mayor, Detroit, Mich. (3). U.S., Governor-General, and High Commissioner, P.I. (3). Mich., Governor (2). *U.S., Attorney General (1)*.

NELSON, SAMUEL (1792–1873; Tyler, 1845–1872). N.Y.Dem.—N.Y., Judge, Circuit Court (8); Associate Justice, and *Chief Justice, Supreme Court (14)*.

O'CONNOR, SANDRA DAY (1930–____; Reagan, 1981–____. Ariz.Rep.— Ariz., Assistant Attorney General (4); Legislature (6). Ariz., Judge, Superior Court (4); *Court of Appeals (2)*.

PATERSON, WILLIAM (1745–1806; Washington, 1793–1806). N.J.Fed.— Signer, U.S. Constitution, 1787. N.J., Legislature (2); Attorney General (7). U.S., Senate (1). *N.J., Governor (3)*. Reviser of English Pre-Revolutionary Statutes in Force in N.J.

PECKHAM, RUFUS W. (1838–1909; Cleveland, 1895–1909). N.Y.Dem.— N.Y., District Attorney (1); Justice, Supreme Court (3); *Associate Judge, Court of Appeals (9)*.

PITNEY, MAHLON (1858–1924; Taft, 1912–1922). N.J.Rep.—U.S., House of Representatives (4). N.J., Legislature (2); Associate Justice, Supreme Court (7); Chancellor (4).

POWELL, LEWIS F. (1907–____; Nixon, 1972–1987). Va.Dem.—Col., U.S.A.A.F., World War II. *Private practice.*

REED, STANLEY F. (1884–1980; F.D. Roosevelt, 1938–1957). Ky.Dem.— Ky., Legislature (4). 1st Lt., U.S.A., World War I. U.S., General Counsel, Federal

Farm Board (3); General Counsel, Reconstruction Finance Corporation (3); *Solicitor General (3).*

REHNQUIST, WILLIAM H. (1924–____; Nixon, 1972–____). Ariz.Rep.— U.S.A.F., World War II. Law Clerk, Justice Jackson, 1952–53. *U.S., Assistant Attorney General (3).*

ROBERTS, OWEN J. (1875–1955; Hoover, 1930–1945). Pa.Rep.—Pa., Assistant District Attorney (3). U.S., Special Deputy Attorney General in Espionage Act Cases, World War I; Special Prosecutor, Oil Cases, 1924. *Private practice.*

*RUTLEDGE, JOHN (1739–1800; Washington, 1789–1791, and Washington, 1795). S.C.Fed.—Signer, U.S. Constitution, 1787. S.C., Legislature (18); Attorney General (1); President and Governor (6); *Chancellor (7).* [Between appointments to the Supreme Court: *S.C., Chief Justice, Court of Common Pleas and Sessions (4).*] He did not sit under his first appointment; he sat with a recess appointment as Chief Justice, but his regular appointment was rejected by the Senate.

RUTLEDGE, WILEY B. (1894–1949; F.D. Roosevelt, 1943–1949). Iowa Dem.—Mo., then Iowa, Member, National Conference of Commissioners on Uniform State Laws (10). *U.S., Judge, Court of Appeals (4).*

SANFORD, EDWARD T. (1865–1930; Harding, 1923–1930). Tenn.Rep.— U.S., Assistant Attorney General (1); *Judge, District Court (15).*

SCALIA, ANTONIN (1936–____); Reagan (1986–____); Va.Rep.—U.S., Assistant Attorney General (3); *Judge, Court of Appeals* (4).

SHIRAS, GEORGE (1832–1924; B. Harrison, 1892–1903). Pa.Rep. *Private practice.*

SOUTER, DAVID H. (1939–____); Bush (1990–____); N.H.Rep.; N.H., Deputy Attorney General (5); Attorney General (2); Associate Justice, Superior Court (5), Associate Justice, Supreme Court (7); U.S., *Judge, Court of Appeals* (5 mo.).

STEVENS, JOHN PAUL (1920–____; Ford, 1975–____). Ill.Independent.— U.S.N.R., World War II. Law Clerk, Justice Wiley Rutledge, 1947–48. *Judge, Court of Appeals (5).*

STEWART, POTTER (1915–1985; Eisenhower, 1958–1981). Ohio Rep.—Lt., U.S.N.R., World War II. *U.S., Judge, Court of Appeals (4).*

*STONE, HARLAN F. (1872–1946; Coolidge, later F.D. Roosevelt, 1925– 1946). N.Y.Rep.—*U.S., Attorney General (1).* Chief Justice, 1941–1946.

STORY, JOSEPH (1779–1845; Madison, 1811–1845). Mass.Rep.—Mass., Legislature (5). U.S., House of Representatives (2). *Private practice.*

STRONG, WILLIAM (1808–1895; Grant, 1870–1880). Pa.Rep.—U.S., House of Representatives (4). Pa., Justice, Supreme Court (11). *Private practice.*

SUTHERLAND, GEORGE (1862–1942; Harding, 1922–1938). Utah Rep.— Utah, Legislature (4). U.S., House of Representatives (2); Senate (12). *Private practice.*

SWAYNE, NOAH H. (1804–1884; Lincoln, 1862–1881). Ohio Rep.—Ohio, County Attorney (4); Legislature (2). U.S., District Attorney (9). *Private practice.*

*TAFT, WILLIAM H. (1857–1930; Harding, 1921–1930). Conn.Rep.—U.S., Collector of Internal Revenue (1). Ohio, Judge, Superior Court (3). U.S.,

Solicitor General (2); Judge, Circuit Court of Appeals (8); Governor-General, P.I. (3); Secretary of War (4); President (4). *Professor of Law.*

*TANEY, ROGER B. (1777–1864; Jackson, 1836–1864). Md.Dem.—Md., Legislature (7); Attorney General (2). U.S., Attorney General (2), Secretary of the Treasury (¾; rejected by the Senate). *Private practice.*

THOMAS, CLARENCE (1948–____; Bush 1991–____); Ga.Rep.; Mo., Assistant Attorney General (3); U.S., Chair, E.E.O.C. (8), *Judge, Court of Appeals (1½).*

THOMPSON, SMITH (1768–1843; Monroe, 1823–1843). N.Y.Rep.—N.Y., Legislature (2); Associate Justice, and Chief Justice, Supreme Court (16). *U.S., Secretary of the Navy (4). ·*

TODD, THOMAS (1765–1826; Jefferson, 1807–1826). Ky.Rep.—*Ky., Judge, and Chief Justice, Court of Appeals (6).*

TRIMBLE, ROBERT (1777–1828; J.Q. Adams, 1826–1828). Ky.Rep.—Ky., Legislature (2). Judge, Court of Appeals (2). U.S., District Attorney (4); *Judge, District Court (9).*

VAN DEVANTER, WILLIS (1859–1941; Taft, 1910–1937). Wyo.Rep.—Wyo., Legislature (2); Chief Justice, Supreme Court (1). U.S., Assistant Attorney General (Interior Department) (6); *Judge, Circuit Court of Appeals (7).*

*VINSON, FRED M. (1890–1953; Truman, 1946–1953). Ky.Dem.—Ky., Commonwealth Attorney (3). U.S., House of Representatives (14); Judge, Court of Appeals (5); Director, Office of Economic Stabilization (2); Federal Loan Administrator (1 mo.); Director, Office of War Mobilization and Reconversion (3 mo.); *Secretary of the Treasury (1).*

*WAITE, MORRISON R. (1816–1888; Grant, 1874–1888). Ohio Rep.—Ohio, Legislature (2). Counsel for United States, U.S.—Gr. Brit. Arbitration ("Alabama" Claims), 1871–72. *Private practice.*

*WARREN, EARL (1891–1974; Eisenhower, 1953–1969). Calif.Rep.—1st Lt., Inf., World War I. Deputy City Attorney (1); Deputy District Attorney (5); District Attorney (14); Attorney General (4); *Governor (10).*

WASHINGTON, BUSHROD (1762–1829; J. Adams, 1798–1829). Pa.Fed.—Va., Legislature (1). *Private practice.*

WAYNE, JAMES M. (1790–1867; Jackson, 1835–1867). Ga.Dem.—Ga., Officer, Hussars, War of 1812; Legislature (2). Mayor of Savannah, Ga. (2). Ga., Judge, Superior Court (5). *U.S., House of Representatives (6).*

WHITE, BYRON R. (1917–____; Kennedy, 1962–1993). Colo.Dem.—U.S.N.R., World War II. Law Clerk, Chief Justice Vinson, 1946–47. *U.S., Deputy Attorney General (1).*

*WHITE, EDWARD D. (1845–1921; Cleveland, later Taft, 1894–1921). La. Dem.—La., Legislature (4); Justice, Supreme Court (2). *U.S., Senate (3).* Chief Justice, 1910–1921.

WHITTAKER, CHARLES E. (1901–1973; Eisenhower, 1957–1962). Mo. Rep.—U.S., Judge, District Court (2); *Court of Appeals (1).*

WILSON, JAMES (1724–1798; Washington, 1789–1798). Pa.Fed.—Signer, U.S. Declaration of Independence, 1776, and U.S. Constitution, 1787. Although he was strongly interested in western-land development companies for several years prior to his appointment, his primary activity in the period immediately preceding his appointment was in obtaining ratification of the Federal and Pennsylvania Constitutions.

WOODBURY, LEVI (1789–1851; Polk, 1845–1851). N.H. Dem.—N.H., Associate Justice, Superior Court (6); Governor (2); Legislature (1). U.S., Senate (6); Secretary of the Navy (3); Secretary of the Treasury (7); *Senate (4).*

WOODS, WILLIAM B. (1824–1887; Hayes, 1880–1887). Ga.Rep.—Mayor, Newark, O. (1). Ohio, Legislature (4). Brevet Major General, U.S. Vol., Civil War. Ala., Chancellor (1). *U.S., Judge, Circuit Court (11).*

Appendix B
THE CONSTITUTION OF THE UNITED STATES

PREAMBLE

We the People of the United States, in Order to form a more perfect Union, establish Justice, insure domestic Tranquility, provide for the common defence, promote the general Welfare, and secure the Blessings of Liberty to ourselves and our Posterity, do ordain and establish this Constitution for the United States of America.

ARTICLE I

Section 1. All legislative Powers herein granted shall be vested in a Congress of the United States, which shall consist of a Senate and House of Representatives.

Section 2. [1] The House of Representatives shall be composed of Members chosen every second Year by the People of the several States, and the Electors in each State shall have the Qualifications requisite for Electors of the most numerous Branch of the State Legislature.

[2] No Person shall be a Representative who shall not have attained to the Age of twenty five Years, and been seven Years a Citizen of the United States, and who shall not, when elected, be an Inhabitant of that State in which he shall be chosen.

[3] Representatives and direct Taxes shall be apportioned among the several States which may be included within this Union, according to their respective Numbers, which shall be determined by adding to the whole Number of free Persons, including those bound to Service for a Term of Years, and excluding Indians not taxed, three fifths of all other Persons. The actual Enumeration shall be made within three Years after the first Meeting of the Congress of the United States, and within every subsequent Term of ten Years, in such Manner as they shall by Law direct. The Number of Representatives shall not exceed one for every thirty Thousand, but each State shall have at Least one Representative; and until such enumeration shall be made, the State of New Hampshire shall be entitled to chuse three, Massachusetts eight, Rhode Island and Providence Plantations one, Connecticut five, New York six, New Jersey four, Pennsylvania eight, Delaware one, Maryland six, Virginia ten, North Carolina five, South Carolina five, and Georgia three.

[4] When vacancies happen in the Representation from any State, the Executive Authority thereof shall issue Writs of Election to fill such Vacancies.

[5] The House of Representatives shall chuse their Speaker and other Officers; and shall have the sole Power of Impeachment.

Section 3. [1] The Senate of the United States shall be composed of two Senators from each State, chosen by the Legislature thereof, for six Years; and each Senator shall have one Vote.

[2] Immediately after they shall be assembled in Consequence of the first Election, they shall be divided as equally as may be into three Classes. The Seats of the Senators of the first Class shall be vacated at the Expiration of the Second Year, of the second Class at the Expiration of the fourth Year, and of the third Class at the Expiration of the sixth Year, so that one third may be chosen every second Year; and if Vacancies happen by Resignation, or otherwise, during the Recess of the Legislature of any State, the Executive thereof may make temporary Appointments until the next Meeting of the Legislature, which shall then fill such Vacancies.

[3] No Person shall be a Senator who shall not have attained to the Age of thirty Years, and been nine Years a Citizen of the United States, and who shall not, when elected, by an Inhabitant of that State for which he shall be chosen.

[4] The Vice President of the United States shall be President of the Senate, but shall have no Vote, unless they be equally divided.

[5] The Senate shall chuse their other Officers, and also a President pro tempore, in the Absence of the Vice President, or when he shall exercise the Office of President of the United States.

[6] The Senate shall have the sole Power to try all Impeachments. When sitting for that Purpose, they shall be on Oath or Affirmation. When the President of the United States is tried, the Chief Justice shall preside: And no Person shall be convicted without the Concurrence of two thirds of the Members present.

[7] Judgment in Cases of Impeachment shall not extend further than to removal from Office, and disqualification to hold and enjoy any Office of honor, Trust, or Profit under the United States: but the Party convicted shall nevertheless be liable and subject to Indictment, Trial, Judgment, and Punishment, according to Law.

Section 4. [1] The Times, Places and Manner of holding Elections for Senators and Representatives, shall be prescribed in each State by the Legislature thereof; but the Congress may at any time by Law make or alter such Regulations, except as to the Places of chusing Senators.

[2] The Congress shall assemble at least once in every Year, and such Meeting shall be on the first Monday in December, unless they shall by Law appoint a different Day.

Section 5. [1] Each House shall be the Judge of the Elections, Returns, and Qualifications of its own Members, and a Majority of each shall constitute a Quorum to do Business; but a smaller Number may adjourn from day to day, and may be authorized to compel the Attendance of absent Members, in such Manner, and under such Penalties as each House may provide.

[2] Each House may determine the Rules of its Proceedings, punish its Members for disorderly Behavior, and, with the Concurrence of two thirds, expel a Member.

[3] Each House shall keep a Journal of its Proceedings, and from time to time publish the same, excepting such Parts as may in their Judgment require

Secrecy; and the Yeas and Nays of the Members of either House on any question shall, at the Desire of one fifth of those Present, be entered on the Journal.

[4] Neither House, during the Session of Congress, shall without the Consent of the other, adjourn for more than three days, nor to any other Place than that in which the two Houses shall be sitting.

Section 6. [1] The Senators and Representatives shall receive a Compensation for their Services, to be ascertained by Law, and paid out of the Treasury of the United States. They shall in all Cases, except Treason, Felony and Breach of the Peace, be privileged from Arrest during their Attendance at the Session of their respective Houses, and in going to and returning from the same; and for any Speech or Debate in either House, they shall not be questioned in any other Place.

[2] No Senator or Representative shall, during the Time for which he was elected, be appointed to any civil Office under the Authority of the United States, which shall have been created, or the Emoluments whereof shall have been increased during such time; and no Person holding any Office under the United States, shall be a Member of either House during his Continuance in Office.

Section 7. [1] All Bills for raising Revenue shall originate in the House of Representatives; but the Senate may propose or concur with Amendments as on other Bills.

[2] Every Bill which shall have passed the House of Representatives and the Senate, shall, before it become a Law, be presented to the President of the United States; If he approve he shall sign it, but if not he shall return it, with his Objections to the House in which it shall have originated, who shall enter the Objections at large on their Journal, and proceed to reconsider it. If after such Reconsideration two thirds of that House shall agree to pass the Bill, it shall be sent together with the Objections, to the other House, by which it shall likewise be reconsidered, and if approved by two thirds of that House, it shall become a Law. But in all such Cases the Votes of both Houses shall be determined by yeas and Nays, and the Names of the Persons voting for and against the Bill shall be entered on the Journal of each House respectively. If any Bill shall not be returned by the President within ten Days (Sundays excepted) after it shall have been presented to him, the Same shall be a Law, in like Manner as if he had signed it, unless the Congress by their Adjournment prevent its Return in which Case it shall not be a Law.

[3] Every Order, Resolution, or Vote, to Which the Concurrence of the Senate and House of Representatives may be necessary (except on a question of Adjournment) shall be presented to the President of the United States; and before the Same shall take Effect, shall be approved by him, or being disapproved by him, shall be repassed by two thirds of the Senate and House of Representatives, according to the Rules and Limitations prescribed in the Case of a Bill.

Section 8. [1] The Congress shall have Power To lay and collect Taxes, Duties, Imposts and Excises, to pay the Debts and provide for the common Defence and general Welfare of the United States; but all Duties, Imposts and Excises shall be uniform throughout the United States;

[2] To borrow money on the credit of the United States;

[3] To regulate Commerce with foreign Nations, and among the several States, and with the Indian Tribes;

[4] To establish an uniform Rule of Naturalization, and uniform Laws on the subject of Bankruptcies throughout the United States;

[5]   To coin Money, regulate the Value thereof, and of foreign Coin, and fix the Standard of Weights and Measures;

[6]   To provide for the Punishment of counterfeiting the Securities and current Coin of the United States;

[7]   To Establish Post Offices and Post Roads;

[8]   To promote the Progress of Science and useful Arts, by securing for limited Times to Authors and Inventors the exclusive Right to their respective Writings and Discoveries;

[9]   To constitute Tribunals inferior to the supreme Court;

[10]   To define and punish Piracies and Felonies committed on the high Seas, and Offenses against the Law of Nations;

[11]   To declare War, grant Letters of Marque and Reprisal, and make Rules concerning Captures on Land and Water;

[12]   To raise and support Armies, but no Appropriation of Money to that Use shall be for a longer Term than two Years;

[13]   To provide and maintain a Navy;

[14]   To make Rules for the Government and Regulation of the land and naval Forces;

[15]   To provide for calling forth the Militia to execute the Laws of the Union, suppress Insurrections and repel Invasions;

[16]   To provide for organizing, arming, and disciplining, the Militia, and for governing such Part of them as may be employed in the Service of the United States, reserving to the States respectively, the Appointment of the Officers, and the Authority of training the Militia according to the discipline prescribed by Congress;

[17]   To exercise exclusive Legislation in all Cases whatsoever, over such District (not exceeding ten Miles square) as may, by Cession of particular States, and the Acceptance of Congress, become the Seat of the Government of the United States, and to exercise like Authority over all Places purchased by the Consent of the Legislature of the State in which the Same shall be, for the Erection of Forts, Magazines, Arsenals, dock-Yards, and other needful Buildings;—And

[18]   To make all Laws which shall be necessary and proper for carrying into Execution the foregoing Powers, and all other Powers vested by this Constitution in the Government of the United States, or in any Department or Officer thereof.

Section 9.   [1] The Migration or Importation of Such Persons as any of the States now existing shall think proper to admit, shall not be prohibited by the Congress prior to the Year one thousand eight hundred and eight, but a Tax or duty may be imposed on such Importation, not exceeding ten dollars for each Person.

[2]   The privilege of the Writ of Habeas Corpus shall not be suspended, unless when in Cases of Rebellion or Invasion the public Safety may require it.

[3]   No Bill of Attainder or ex post facto Law shall be passed.

[4]   No Capitation, or other direct, Tax shall be laid, unless in Proportion to the Census or Enumeration herein before directed to be taken.

[5]   No Tax or Duty shall be laid on Articles exported from any State.

[6]   No Preference shall be given by any Regulation of Commerce or Revenue to the Ports of one State over those of another: nor shall Vessels bound to, or from, one State be obliged to enter, clear, or pay Duties in another.

[7]   No money shall be drawn from the Treasury, but in Consequence of Appropriations made by Law; and a regular Statement and Account of the Receipts and Expenditures of all public Money shall be published from time to time.

[8]   No Title of Nobility shall be granted by the United States: And no Person holding any Office of Profit or Trust under them, shall, without the Consent of the Congress, accept of any present, Emolument, Office, or Title, of any kind whatever, from any King, Prince, or foreign State.

Section 10.   [1] No State shall enter into any Treaty, Alliance, or Confederation; grant Letters of Marque and Reprisal; coin Money; emit Bills of Credit; make any Thing but gold and silver Coin a Tender in Payment of Debts; pass any Bill of Attainder, ex post facto Law, or Law impairing the Obligation of Contracts, or grant any Title of Nobility.

[2]   No State shall, without the Consent of the Congress, lay any Imposts or Duties on Imports or Exports, except what may be absolutely necessary for executing it's inspection Laws: and the net Produce of all Duties and Imposts, laid by any State on Imports or Exports, shall be for the Use of the Treasury of the United States; and all such Laws shall be subject to the Revision and Controul of the Congress.

[3]   No State shall, without the Consent of Congress, lay any Duty of Tonnage, keep Troops, or Ships of War in time of Peace, enter into any Agreement or Compact with another State, or with a foreign Power, or engage in War, unless actually invaded, or in such imminent Danger as will not admit of delay.

ARTICLE II

Section 1.   [1] The executive Power shall be vested in a President of the United States of America. He shall hold his Office during the Term of four Years, and, together with the Vice President, chosen for the same Term, be elected, as follows:

[2]   Each State shall appoint, in such Manner as the Legislature thereof may direct, a Number of Electors, equal to the whole Number of Senators and Representatives to which the State may be entitled in the Congress; but no Senator or Representative, or Person holding an Office of Trust or Profit under the United States, shall be appointed an Elector.

[3]   The Electors shall meet in their respective States, and vote by Ballot for two Persons, of whom one at least shall not be an Inhabitant of the same State with themselves. And they shall make a List of all the Persons voted for, and of the Number of Votes for each; which List they shall sign and certify, and transmit sealed to the Seat of the Government of the United States, directed to the President of the Senate. The President of the Senate shall, in the Presence of the Senate and House of Representatives, open all the Certificates, and the Votes shall then be counted. The Person having the greatest Number of Votes shall be the President, if such Number be a Majority of the whole Number of Electors appointed; and if there be more than one who have such Majority, and have an equal Number of Votes, then the House of Representatives shall immediately chuse by Ballot one of them for President; and if no Person have a Majority, then from the five highest on the List the said House shall in like Manner chuse the

President. But in chusing the President, the Votes shall be taken by States the Representation from each State having one Vote; A quorum for this Purpose shall consist of a Member or Members from two thirds of the States, and a Majority of all the States shall be necessary to a Choice. In every Case, after the Choice of the President, the Person having the greater Number of Votes of the Electors shall be the Vice President. But if there should remain two or more who have equal Votes, the Senate shall chuse from them by Ballot the Vice President.

[4] The Congress may determine the Time of chusing the Electors, and the Day on which they shall give their Votes; which Day shall be the same throughout the United States.

[5] No person except a natural born Citizen, or a Citizen of the United States, at the time of the Adoption of this Constitution, shall be eligible to the Office of President; neither shall any Person be eligible to that Office who shall not have attained to the Age of thirty five Years, and been fourteen Years a Resident within the United States.

[6] In case of the removal of the President from Office, or of his Death, Resignation or Inability to discharge the Powers and Duties of the said Office, the Same shall devolve on the Vice President, and the Congress may by Law provide for the Case of Removal, Death, Resignation or Inability, both of the President and Vice President, declaring what Officer shall then act as President, and such Officer shall act accordingly, until the Disability be removed, or a President shall be elected.

[7] The President shall, at stated Times, receive for his Services, a Compensation, which shall neither be increased nor diminished during the Period for which he shall have been elected, and he shall not receive within that Period any other Emolument from the United States, or any of them.

[8] Before he enter on the Execution of his Office, he shall take the following Oath or Affirmation: "I do solemnly swear (or affirm) that I will faithfully execute the Office of President of the United States, and will to the best of my Ability, preserve, protect and defend the Constitution of the United States."

Section 2. [1] The President shall be Commander in Chief of the Army and Navy of the United States, and of the militia of the several States, when called into the actual Service of the United States; he may require the Opinion, in writing, of the principal Officer in each of the Executive Departments, upon any Subject relating to the Duties of their respective Offices, and he shall have Power to grant Reprieves and Pardons for Offenses against the United States, except in Cases of Impeachment.

[2] He shall have Power, by and with the Advice and Consent of the Senate to make Treaties, provided two thirds of the Senators present concur; and he shall nominate, and by and with the Advice and Consent of the Senate, shall appoint Ambassadors, other public Ministers and Consuls, Judges of the supreme Court, and all other Officers of the United States, whose Appointments are not herein otherwise provided for, and which shall be established by Law; but the Congress may by Law vest the Appointment of such inferior Officers, as they think proper, in the President alone, in the Courts of Law, or in the Heads of Departments.

[3] The President shall have Power to fill up all Vacancies that may happen during the Recess of the Senate, by granting Commissions which shall expire at the End of their next Session.

Section 3. He shall from time to time give to the Congress Information of the State of the Union, and recommend to their Consideration such Measures as he shall judge necessary and expedient; he may, on extraordinary Occasions, convene both Houses, or either of them, and in Case of Disagreement between them, with Respect to the Time of Adjournment, he may adjourn them to such Time as he shall think proper; he shall receive Ambassadors and other public Ministers; he shall take Care that the Laws be faithfully executed, and shall Commission all the Officers of the United States.

Section 4. The President, Vice President and all civil Officers of the United States, shall be removed from Office on Impeachment for, and Conviction of, Treason, Bribery, or other high Crimes and Misdemeanors.

ARTICLE III

Section 1. The judicial Power of the United States, shall be vested in one supreme Court, and in such inferior Courts as the Congress may from time to time ordain and establish. The Judges, both of the supreme and inferior Courts, shall hold their Offices during good Behaviour, and shall, at stated Times, receive for their Services a Compensation, which shall not be diminished during their Continuance in Office.

Section 2. [1] The judicial Power shall extend to all Cases, in Law and Equity, arising under this Constitution, the Laws of the United States, and Treaties made, or which shall be made, under their Authority;—to all Cases affecting Ambassadors, other public Ministers and Consuls;—to all Cases of admiralty and maritime Jurisdiction;—to Controversies to which the United States shall be a Party;—to Controversies between two or more States;—between a State and Citizens of another State;—between Citizens of different States;—between Citizens of the same State claiming Lands under the Grants of different States, and between a State, or the Citizens thereof, and foreign States, Citizens or Subjects.

[2] In all Cases affecting Ambassadors, other public Ministers and Consuls, and those in which a State shall be a Party, the supreme Court shall have original Jurisdiction. In all the other Cases before mentioned, the supreme Court shall have appellate Jurisdiction, both as to Law and Fact, with such Exceptions, and under such Regulations as the Congress shall make.

[3] The trial of all Crimes, except in Cases of Impeachment, shall be by Jury; and such Trial shall be held in the State where the said Crimes shall have been committed; but when not committed within any State, the Trial shall be at such Place or Places as the Congress may by Law have directed.

Section 3. [1] Treason against the United States, shall consist only in levying War against them, or, in adhering to their Enemies, giving them Aid and Comfort. No Person shall be convicted of Treason unless on the Testimony of two Witnesses to the same overt Act, or on Confession in open Court.

[2] The Congress shall have Power to declare the Punishment of Treason, but no Attainder of Treason shall work Corruption of Blood, or Forfeiture except during the Life of the Person attainted.

ARTICLE IV

Section 1. Full Faith and Credit shall be given in each State to the public Acts, Records, and judicial Proceedings of every other State. And the Congress may by general Laws prescribe the Manner in which such Acts, Records and Proceedings shall be proved, and the Effect thereof.

Section 2. [1] The Citizens of each State shall be entitled to all Privileges and Immunities of Citizens in the several States.

[2] A Person charged in any State with Treason, Felony, or other Crime, who shall flee from Justice, and be found in another State, shall on demand of the executive Authority of the State from which he fled, be delivered up, to be removed to the State having Jurisdiction of the Crime.

[3] No Person held to Service or Labour in one State, under the Laws thereof, escaping into another, shall, in Consequence of any Law or Regulation therein, be discharged from such Service or Labour, but shall be delivered up on Claim of the Party to whom such Service or Labour may be due.

Section 3. [1] New States may be admitted by the Congress into this Union; but no new State shall be formed or erected within the Jurisdiction of any other State; nor any State be formed by the Junction of two or more States, or Parts of States, without the Consent of the Legislatures of the States concerned as well as of the Congress.

[2] The Congress shall have Power to dispose of and make all needful Rules and Regulations respecting the Territory or other Property belonging to the United States; and nothing in this Constitution shall be so construed as to Prejudice any Claims of the United States, or of any particular State.

Section 4. The United States shall guarantee to every State in this Union a Republican Form of Government, and shall protect each of them against Invasion; and on Application of the Legislature, or of the Executive (when the Legislature cannot be convened) against domestic Violence.

ARTICLE V

The Congress, whenever two thirds of both Houses shall deem it necessary, shall propose Amendments to this Constitution, or, on the Application of the Legislatures of two thirds of the several States, shall call a Convention for proposing Amendments, which, in either Case, shall be valid to all Intents and Purposes, as part of this Constitution, when ratified by the Legislatures of three fourths of the several States, or by Conventions in three fourths thereof, as the one or the other Mode of Ratification may be proposed by the Congress; Provided that no Amendment which may be made prior to the Year One thousand eight hundred and eight shall in any Manner affect the first and fourth Clauses in the Ninth Section of the first Article; and that no State, without its Consent, shall be deprived of its equal Suffrage in the Senate.

ARTICLE VI

[1] All Debts contracted and Engagements entered into, before the Adoption of this Constitution shall be as valid against the United States under this Constitution, as under the Confederation.

[2] This Constitution, and the Laws of the United States which shall be made in Pursuance thereof; and all Treaties made, or which shall be made, under the Authority of the United States, shall be the supreme Law of the Land; and the Judges in every State shall be bound thereby, any Thing in the Constitution or Laws of any State to the Contrary notwithstanding.

[3] The Senators and Representatives before mentioned, and the Members of the several State Legislatures, and all executive and judicial Officers, both of

the United States and of the several States, shall be bound by Oath or Affirmation, to support this Constitution; but no religious Test shall ever be required as a Qualification to any Office or public Trust under the United States.

ARTICLE VII

The Ratification of the Conventions of nine States shall be sufficient for the Establishment of this Constitution between the States so ratifying the Same.

ARTICLES IN ADDITION TO, AND AMENDMENT OF, THE CONSTITUTION OF THE UNITED STATES OF AMERICA, PROPOSED BY CONGRESS, AND RATIFIED BY THE LEGISLATURES OF THE SEVERAL STATES PURSUANT TO THE FIFTH ARTICLE OF THE ORIGINAL CONSTITUTION.

AMENDMENT I [1791]

Congress shall make no law respecting an establishment of religion, or prohibiting the free exercise thereof; or abridging the freedom of speech, or of the press; or the right of the people peaceably to assemble, and to petition the Government for a redress of grievances.

AMENDMENT II [1791]

A well regulated Militia, being necessary to the security of a free State, the right of the people to keep and bear Arms, shall not be infringed.

AMENDMENT III [1791]

No Soldier shall, in time of peace be quartered in any house, without the consent of the Owner, nor in time of war, but in a manner to be prescribed by law.

AMENDMENT IV [1791]

The right of the people to be secure in their persons, houses, papers, and effects, against unreasonable searches and seizures, shall not be violated, and no Warrants shall issue, but upon probable cause, supported by Oath or affirmation and particularly describing the place to be searched, and the persons or things to be seized.

AMENDMENT V [1791]

No person shall be held to answer for a capital, or otherwise infamous crime, unless on a presentment or indictment of a Grand Jury, except in cases arising in the land or naval forces, or in the Militia, when in actual service in time of War or public danger; nor shall any person be subject for the same offence to be twice put in jeopardy of life or limb; nor shall be compelled in any criminal case to be a witness against himself, nor be deprived of life, liberty, or property, without due process of law; nor shall private property be taken for public use, without just compensation.

AMENDMENT VI [1791]

In all criminal prosecutions, the accused shall enjoy the right to a speedy and public trial, by an impartial jury of the State and district wherein the crime shall have been committed, which district shall have been previously ascertained by law, and to be informed of the nature and cause of the accusation; to be confronted with the witnesses against him; to have compulsory process for obtaining witnesses in his favor, and to have the Assistance of Counsel for his defence.

AMENDMENT VII [1791]

In Suits at common law, where the value in controversy shall exceed twenty dollars, the right of trial by jury shall be preserved, and no fact tried by jury, shall be otherwise re-examined in any Court of the United States, than according to the rules of the common law.

AMENDMENT VIII [1791]

Excessive bail shall not be required, nor excessive fines imposed, nor cruel and unusual punishments inflicted.

AMENDMENT IX [1791]

The enumeration in the Constitution, of certain rights, shall not be construed to deny or disparage others retained by the people.

AMENDMENT X [1791]

The powers not delegated to the United States by the Constitution, nor prohibited by it to the States, are reserved to the States respectively, or to the people.

AMENDMENT XI [1798]

The Judicial power of the United States shall not be construed to extend to any suit in law or equity, commenced or prosecuted against one of the United States by Citizens of another State, or by Citizens or Subjects of any Foreign State.

AMENDMENT XII [1804]

The Electors shall meet in their respective states and vote by ballot for President and Vice-President, one of whom, at least, shall not be an inhabitant of the same state with themselves; they shall name in their ballots the person voted for as President, and in distinct ballots the person voted for as Vice-President, and they shall make distinct lists of all persons voted for as President, and of all persons voted for as Vice-President, and of the number of votes for each, which lists they shall sign and certify, and transmit sealed to the seat of the government of the United States, directed to the President of the Senate;—The President of the Senate shall, in the presence of the Senate and House of Representatives, open all the certificates and the votes shall then be counted;—The person having the greatest number of votes for President, shall be the President, if such number be a majority of the whole number of Electors appointed; and if no person have such majority, then from the persons having the highest numbers not exceeding three on the list of those voted for as President, the House of Representatives shall choose immediately, by ballot, the President. But in choosing the President, the votes shall be taken by states, the representation from each state having one vote; a quorum for this purpose shall consist of a member or members from two-thirds of the states, and a majority of all the states shall be necessary to a choice. And if the House of Representatives shall not choose a President whenever the right of choice shall devolve upon them before the fourth day of March next following, then the Vice-President shall act as President, as in the case of the death or other constitutional disability of the President.—The person having the greatest number of votes as Vice-President, shall be the Vice-President, if such number be a majority of the whole number of Electors appointed, and if no person have a majority, then from the two highest numbers on the list, the Senate shall choose the Vice-President; a quorum for the purpose shall consist of two-thirds of the whole number of Senators, and a majority of the whole number shall be necessary to a choice. But no person constitutionally ineligible to the office of President shall be eligible to that of Vice-President of the United States.

AMENDMENT XIII [1865]

Section 1. Neither slavery nor involuntary servitude, except as a punishment for crime whereof the party shall have been duly convicted, shall exist within the United States, or any place subject to their jurisdiction.

Section 2. Congress shall have power to enforce this article by appropriate legislation.

AMENDMENT XIV [1868]

Section 1. All persons born or naturalized in the United States, and subject to the jurisdiction thereof, are citizens of the United States and of the State wherein they reside. No State shall make or enforce any law which shall abridge the privileges or immunities of citizens of the United States; nor shall any State deprive any person of life, liberty, or property, without due process of law; nor deny to any person within its jurisdiction the equal protection of the laws.

Section 2. Representatives shall be apportioned among the several States according to their respective numbers, counting the whole number of persons in each State, excluding Indians not taxed. But when the right to vote at any election for the choice of electors for President and Vice President of the United States, Representatives in Congress, the Executive and Judicial officers of a State, or the members of the Legislature thereof, is denied to any of the male inhabitants of such State, being twenty-one years of age, and citizens of the United States, or in any way abridged, except for participation in rebellion, or other crime, the basis of representation therein shall be reduced in the proportion which the number of such male citizens shall bear to the whole number of male citizens twenty-one years of age in such State.

Section 3. No person shall be a Senator or Representative in Congress, or elector of President and Vice President, or hold any office, civil or military, under the United States, or under any State, who having previously taken an oath, as a member of Congress, or as an officer of the United States, or as a member of any State legislature, or as an executive or judicial officer of any State, to support the Constitution of the United States, shall have engaged in insurrection or rebellion against the same, or given aid or comfort to the enemies thereof. But Congress may by a vote of two-thirds of each House, remove such disability.

Section 4. The validity of the public debt of the United States, authorized by law, including debts incurred for payment of pensions and bounties for services in suppressing insurrection or rebellion, shall not be questioned. But neither the United States nor any State shall assume or pay any debt or obligation incurred in aid of insurrection or rebellion against the United States, or any claim for the loss or emancipation of any slave; but all such debts, obligations and claims shall be held illegal and void.

Section 5. The Congress shall have power to enforce, by appropriate legislation, the provisions of this article.

AMENDMENT XV [1870]

Section 1. The right of citizens of the United States to vote shall not be denied or abridged by the United States or by any State on account of race, color, or previous condition of servitude.

Section 2. The Congress shall have power to enforce this article by appropriate legislation.

AMENDMENT XVI [1913]

The Congress shall have power to lay and collect taxes on incomes, from whatever source derived, without apportionment among the several States, and without regard to any census or enumeration.

AMENDMENT XVII [1913]

[1] The Senate of the United States shall be composed of two Senators from each State, elected by the people thereof, for six years; and each Senator shall have one vote. The electors in each State shall have the qualifications requisite for electors of the most numerous branch of the State legislatures.

[2] When vacancies happen in the representation of any State in the Senate, the executive authority of such State shall issue writs of election to fill such vacancies: *Provided,* That the legislature of any State may empower the executive thereof to make temporary appointments until the people fill the vacancies by election as the legislature may direct.

[3] This amendment shall not be so construed as to affect the election or term of any Senator chosen before it becomes valid as part of the Constitution.

AMENDMENT XVIII [1919]

Section 1. After one year from the ratification of this article the manufacture, sale, or transportation of intoxicating liquors within, the importation thereof into, or the exportation thereof from the United States and all territory subject to the jurisdiction thereof for beverage purposes is hereby prohibited.

Section 2. The Congress and the several States shall have concurrent power to enforce this article by appropriate legislation.

Section 3. This article shall be inoperative unless it shall have been ratified as an amendment to the Constitution by the legislatures of the several States, as provided in the Constitution, within seven years from the date of the submission hereof to the States by the Congress.

AMENDMENT XIX [1920]

[1] The right of citizens of the United States to vote shall not be denied or abridged by the United States or by any State on account of sex.

[2] Congress shall have power to enforce this article by appropriate legislation.

AMENDMENT XX [1933]

Section 1. The terms of the President and Vice President shall end at noon on the 20th day of January, and the terms of Senators and Representatives at noon on the 3d day of January, of the years in which such terms would have ended if this article had not been ratified; and the terms of their successors shall then begin.

Section 2. The Congress shall assemble at least once in every year, and such meeting shall begin at noon on the 3d day of January, unless they shall by law appoint a different day.

Section 3. If, at the time fixed for the beginning of the term of the President, the President elect shall have died, the Vice President elect shall become President. If the President shall not have been chosen before the time fixed for the beginning of his term, or if the President elect shall have failed to qualify, then the Vice President elect shall act as President until a President shall have qualified; and the Congress may by law provide for the case wherein neither a President elect nor a Vice President elect shall have qualified, declaring who shall then act as President, or the manner in which one who is to act shall be selected, and such person shall act accordingly until a President or Vice President shall have qualified.

Section 4. The Congress may by law provide for the case of the death of any of the persons from whom the House of Representatives may choose a President whenever the right of choice shall have devolved upon them, and for the case of the death of any of the persons from whom the Senate may choose a Vice President whenever the right of choice shall have devolved upon them.

Section 5. Sections 1 and 2 shall take effect on the 15th day of October following the ratification of this article.

Section 6. This article shall be inoperative unless it shall have been ratified as an amendment to the Constitution by the legislatures of three-fourths of the several States within seven years from the date of its submission.

Amendment XXI [1933]

Section 1. The eighteenth article of amendment to the Constitution of the United States is hereby repealed.

Section 2. The transportation or importation into any State, Territory, or possession of the United States for delivery or use therein of intoxicating liquors, in violation of the laws thereof, is hereby prohibited.

Section 3. This article shall be inoperative unless it shall have been ratified as an amendment to the Constitution by conventions in the several States, as provided in the Constitution, within seven years from the date of the submission hereof to the States by the Congress.

Amendment XXII [1951]

Section 1. No person shall be elected to the office of the President more than twice, and no person who has held the office of President, or acted as President, for more than two years of a term to which some other person was elected President shall be elected to the office of President more than once. But this Article shall not apply to any person holding the office of President when this Article was proposed by the Congress, and shall not prevent any person who may be holding the office of President, or acting as President, during the term within which this Article becomes operative from holding the office of President or acting as President during the remainder of such term.

Section 2. This article shall be inoperative unless it shall have been ratified as an amendment to the Constitution by the legislatures of three-fourths of the several States within seven years from the date of its submission to the States by the Congress.

Amendment XXIII [1961]

Section 1. The District constituting the seat of Government of the United States shall appoint in such manner as the Congress may direct:

A number of electors of President and Vice President equal to the whole number of Senators and Representatives in Congress to which the District would be entitled if it were a State, but in no event more than the least populous state; they shall be in addition to those appointed by the states, but they shall be considered, for the purposes of the election of President and Vice President, to be electors appointed by a state; and they shall meet in the District and perform such duties as provided by the twelfth article of amendment.

Section 2. The Congress shall have power to enforce this article by appropriate legislation.

Amendment XXIV [1964]

Section 1. The right of citizens of the United States to vote in any primary or other election for President or Vice President, for electors for President or Vice President, or for Senator or Representative in Congress, shall not be denied or abridged by the United States or any State by reason of failure to pay any poll tax or other tax.

Section 2. The Congress shall have power to enforce this article by appropriate legislation.

Amendment XXV [1967]

Section 1. In case of the removal of the President from office or of his death or resignation, the Vice President shall become President.

Section 2. Whenever there is a vacancy in the office of the Vice President, the President shall nominate a Vice President who shall take office upon confirmation by a majority vote of both Houses of Congress.

Section 3. Whenever the President transmits to the President pro tempore of the Senate and the Speaker of the House of Representatives his written declaration that he is unable to discharge the powers and duties of his office, and until he transmits to them a written declaration to the contrary, such powers and duties shall be discharged by the Vice President as Acting President.

Section 4. Whenever the Vice President and a majority of either the principal officers of the executive departments or of such other body as Congress may by law provide, transmit to the President pro tempore of the Senate and the Speaker of the House of Representatives their written declaration that the President is unable to discharge the powers and duties of his office, the Vice President shall immediately assume the powers and duties of the office as Acting President.

Thereafter, when the President transmits to the President pro tempore of the Senate and the Speaker of the House of Representatives his written declaration that no inability exists, he shall resume the powers and duties of his office unless the Vice President and a majority of either the principal officers of the executive department or of such other body as Congress may by law provide, transmit within four days to the President pro tempore of the Senate and the Speaker of the House of Representatives their written declaration that the President is unable to discharge the powers and duties of his office. Thereupon Congress shall decide the issue, assembling within forty-eight hours for that purpose if not in session. If the Congress, within twenty-one days after receipt of the latter written declaration, or, if Congress is not in session, within twenty-one days after

Congress is required to assemble, determines by two-thirds vote of both Houses that the President is unable to discharge the powers and duties of his office, the Vice President shall continue to discharge the same as Acting President; otherwise, the President shall resume the powers and duties of his office.

AMENDMENT XXVI [1971]

Section 1.   The right of citizens of the United States, who are eighteen years of age or older, to vote shall not be denied or abridged by the United States or by any State on account of age.

Section 2.   The Congress shall have power to enforce this article by appropriate legislation.

AMENDMENT XXVII [1992] *

No law, varying compensation for the services of Senators and Representatives, shall take effect, until an election of Representatives shall have intervened.

---

* On May 7, 1992, more than 200 years after it was first proposed by James Madison, the Twenty–Seventh Amendment was ratified by a 38th State (Michigan).   Although Congress set no time limit for ratification of this amendment, ten of the *other* amendments proposed at the same time (1789)—now known as the Bill of Rights—were ratified in a little more than two years.   After all this time, is the ratification of the Twenty–Seventh Amendment valid? Does it matter that many of the states that ratified the amendment did not exist at the time it was first proposed?